THE OXFORD HANDBOOK OF

ARCHAEOLOGY AND ANTHROPOLOGY OF HUNTER-GATHERERS

For more than a century, the study of hunting and gathering societies has been central to the development of both archaeology and anthropology as academic disciplines, and has also generated widespread public interest and debate. *The Oxford Handbook of the Archaeology and Anthropology of Hunter-Gatherers* provides a comprehensive review of hunter-gatherer studies to date, including critical engagements with older debates, new theoretical perspectives, and renewed obligations for greater engagement between researchers and indigenous communities. Chapters provide in-depth archaeological, historical, and anthropological case-studies, and examine far-reaching questions about human social relations, attitudes to technology, ecology, and management of resources and the environment, as well as issues of diet, health, and gender relations—all central topics in hunter-gatherer research, but also themes that have great relevance for modern global society and its future challenges.

The *Handbook* also provides a strategic vision for how the integration of new methods, approaches, and study regions can ensure that future research into the archaeology and anthropology of hunter-gatherers will continue to deliver penetrating insights into the factors that underlie all human diversity.

Vicki Cummings is Reader in Archaeology at the University of Central Lancashire.

Peter Jordan is Director of the Arctic Centre at the University of Groningen.

Marek Zvelebil[†] was Professor of European Prehistory at the University of Sheffield.

THE OXFORD HANDBOOK OF THE

ARCHAEOLOGY AND ANTHROPOLOGY OF HUNTER-GATHERERS

Edited by
VICKI CUMMINGS, PETER JORDAN, AND
MAREK ZVELEBIL

UNIVERSITY PRESS

UNIVERSITY PRESS

Great Clarendon Street, Oxford, OX2 6DP,
United Kingdom

Oxford University Press is a department of the University of Oxford.
It furthers the University's objective of excellence in research, scholarship,
and education by publishing worldwide. Oxford is a registered trade mark of
Oxford University Press in the UK and in certain other countries

© Oxford University Press 2014

The moral rights of the authors have been asserted

First published 2014
First published in paperback 2018

Impression: 1

All rights reserved. No part of this publication may be reproduced, stored in
a retrieval system, or transmitted, in any form or by any means, without the
prior permission in writing of Oxford University Press, or as expressly permitted
by law, by licence or under terms agreed with the appropriate reprographics
rights organization. Enquiries concerning reproduction outside the scope of the
above should be sent to the Rights Department, Oxford University Press, at the
address above

You must not circulate this work in any other form
and you must impose this same condition on any acquirer

Published in the United States of America by Oxford University Press
198 Madison Avenue, New York, NY 10016, United States of America

British Library Cataloguing in Publication Data

Data available

Library of Congress Cataloging in Publication Data

Data available

ISBN 978-0-19-955122-4 (Hbk.)
ISBN 978-0-19-883104-4 (Pbk.)

Printed and bound by
CPI Group (UK) Ltd, Croydon, CR0 4YY

Links to third party websites are provided by Oxford in good faith and
for information only. Oxford disclaims any responsibility for the materials
contained in any third party website referenced in this work.

This handbook is dedicated to Marek Zvelebil (1952–2011)

Acknowledgements

First and foremost, our thanks are to the contributors to this handbook. They have not only provided the content, but they have also been incredibly patient with us during the course of the production of this volume. Many chapter authors also agreed to assist us in the peer-review process, and we also drew extensively on the expertise of many other scholars in this process. We are extremely grateful to everyone who has helped in this way. Oxford University Press has provided guidance and assistance along the way and we would particularly like to thank Hilary O'Shea, Michael Dela Cruz, Jennifer Vafidis, and Jenny Wagstaff.

We would also like to acknowledge the support offered to us from our respective universities, friends, and academic colleagues. Vicki also received substantial support from the University of Central Lancashire, including a sabbatical, which has enabled her to work on this volume.

Finally, on behalf of the extended international family of hunter-gatherer scholars, we would like to dedicate this handbook to the memory of one of the world's leading specialists in this research field, Professor Marek Zvelebil (1952–2011)*.

Vicki Cummings and Peter Jordan
Preston and Groningen, November 2013

---

* This handbook was designed and produced by three editors: Vicki Cummings, Peter Jordan, and Marek Zvelebil. Marek played a major role in the early stages of planning the handbook's overall thematic structure and primary intellectual content, and also played an important role in contacting potential scholars to contribute. Numerous chapters also benefited from his insightful comments and editorial suggestions during the extended peer-review process. In finally bringing such an extensive publication project through to completion, we hope that he too would have been proud of the results of yet another major hunter-gatherer research initiative that he had been so closely involved in launching.

Contents

List of Figures   xv
List of Tables   xxiii
List of Contributors   xxv

Introduction   1
PETER JORDAN AND VICKI CUMMINGS

PART I THEORETICAL FRAMEWORKS

1. Analytical Frames of Reference in Hunter-Gatherer Research   33
   PETER JORDAN AND VICKI CUMMINGS

2. Defining Hunter-Gatherers: Enlightenment, Romantic, and Social Evolutionary Perspectives   43
   ALAN BARNARD

3. Historical Frames of Reference for 'Hunter-Gatherers'   55
   MARK PLUCIENNIK

4. Adaptive and Ecological Approaches to the Study of Hunter-Gatherers   69
   RAVEN GARVEY AND ROBERT L. BETTINGER

5. Historical and Humanist Perspectives on Hunter-Gatherers   92
   AUBREY CANNON

6. Hunter-Gatherer-Fishers, Ethnoarchaeology, and Analogical Reasoning   104
   PAUL J. LANE

7. Man the Hunter, Woman the Gatherer? The Impact of Gender Studies on Hunter-Gatherer Research (A Retrospective)   151
   KATHLEEN STERLING

PART II THE EARLIEST HUNTER-GATHERERS

8. The First Hunter-Gatherers   177
   JENNIE ROBINSON

9. The Neanderthals: Evolution, Palaeoecology, and Extinction   191
   JOÃO ZILHÃO

10. Modern Human Origins in Africa: A Review of the Fossil,
    Archaeological, and Genetic Perspectives on Early *Homo sapiens*   214
    KEVIN L. KUYKENDALL AND ISABELLE S. HEYERDAHL-KING

11. Upper Palaeolithic Hunter-Gatherers in Western Asia   252
    OFER BAR-YOSEF

12. The European Upper Palaeolithic   279
    PAUL PETTITT

13. The Palaeolithic of Northern Asia   310
    ANATOLY P. DEREVIANKO, SERGEI V. MARKIN, AND
    ANDREI V. TABAREV

14. *Homo sapiens* Societies: South Asia   328
    MICHAEL D. PETRAGLIA AND NICOLE BOIVIN

15. *Homo sapiens* Societies in Indonesia and South-Eastern Asia   346
    SUSAN O'CONNOR AND DAVID BULBECK

16. Hunter-Gatherers in Australia: Deep Histories of Continuity
    and Change   368
    IAIN DAVIDSON

17. Into the Americas: The Earliest Hunter-Gatherers in
    an Empty Continent   405
    MARCEL KORNFELD AND GUSTAVO G. POLITIS

PART III POST-GLACIAL COLONIZATIONS AND TRANSFORMATIONS

18. Hunter-Gatherers in the Post-Glacial World   437
    VICKI CUMMINGS

19. Post-Glacial Transformations Among Hunter-Gatherer
    Societies in the Mediterranean and Western Asia   456
    ANDREW M. T. MOORE

20. Post-Glacial Transformations in Africa ANDREW B. SMITH	479
21. Post-Glacial Transformations in South and South-East Asia RYAN RABETT AND SACHA JONES	492
22. Post-Pleistocene Transformations of Hunter-Gatherers in East Asia: The Jomon and Chulmun JUNKO HABU	507
23. Post-Glacial Transformations: Danubian Europe JIŘÍ SVOBODA	521
24. Transformations? The Mesolithic of North-West Europe GRAEME WARREN	537
25. The Resettlement of Northern Europe FELIX RIEDE	556

PART IV PREHISTORIC HUNTER-GATHERER INNOVATIONS

26. Prehistoric Hunter-Gatherer Innovations PETER JORDAN AND VICKI CUMMINGS	585
27. Stone Tool Technology STEVEN L. KUHN AND AMY E. CLARK	607
28. Art for the Living J. D. LEWIS-WILLIAMS	625
29. Social Complexity BRIAN HAYDEN	643
30. Ceramic Technology PETER HOMMEL	663
31. Coastal Adaptations C. R. WICKHAM-JONES	694
32. Mortuary Practices LIV NILSSON STUTZ	712
33. Plant Domestications DAVID R. HARRIS	729

34. Animal Domestications 749
    ALAN K. OUTRAM

PART V THE PERSISTENCE OF HUNTING AND GATHERING AMONGST FARMERS IN PREHISTORY AND BEYOND

35. Hunting and Gathering in a Farmers' World 767
    VICKI CUMMINGS

36. The Persistence of Hunting and Gathering: Neolithic Western Temperate and Central Europe 787
    DETLEF GRONENBORN

37. The Persistence of Hunting and Gathering Amongst Farmers in Prehistory in Neolithic North-West Europe 805
    D. C. M. RAEMAEKERS

38. The Continuity of Hunting and Gathering in the Neolithic and Beyond in Britain and Ireland 824
    VICKI CUMMINGS AND OLIVER J. T. HARRIS

39. Forager–Farmer Contacts in Northern Fennoscandia 838
    CHARLOTTE DAMM AND LARS FORSBERG

40. The Persistence of Hunting and Gathering Amongst Farmers in South-East Asia in Prehistory and Beyond 857
    HUW BARTON

41. The Emergence of Forager–Farmer Interaction in North America 881
    KATHERINE A. SPIELMANN

PART VI ETHNOHISTORY AND ANTHROPOLOGY OF 'MODERN' HUNTER-GATHERERS

42. The Ethnohistory and Anthropology of 'Modern' Hunter-Gatherers 903
    PETER JORDAN

43. Hunter-Gatherer Research Traditions in Southern Africa 918
    ROBERT K. HITCHCOCK

44. Central African Hunter-Gatherer Research Traditions 936
    BARRY S. HEWLETT AND JASON M. FANCHER

45. Regional Hunter-Gatherer Research Traditions: Australia 958
    Ian Keen

46. From Ethnohistory to Ethnogenesis: A Historiography of Hunter-Gatherer Cultural Anthropology in California and the Great Basin 973
    David Robinson

47. Exploring Hunter-Gatherer-Fisher Complexity on the Pacific Northwest Coast of North America 991
    Sean O'Neill

48. Regional Hunter-Gatherer Traditions in South-East Asia 1010
    Jana Fortier

49. Regional Hunter-Gatherer Research Traditions: South America 1031
    Gustavo G. Politis and Almudena Hernando

50. The Ethnohistory and Anthropology of 'Modern' Hunter-Gatherers: North Japan (Ainu) 1054
    Mark J. Hudson

51. Hunter-Gatherer Transformations in Northern Europe After 1500 AD 1071
    Jussi-Pekka Taavitsainen

PART VII FUTURE DIRECTIONS IN HUNTER-GATHERER RESEARCH

52. New Approaches in the Study of Hunter-Gatherers 1093
    Peter Jordan and Vicki Cummings

53. Future Directions in Hunter-Gatherer Research: Technology 1110
    Robert L. Kelly

54. Cultural Transmission Theory and Hunter-Gatherer Archaeology 1127
    Jelmer W. Eerkens, Robert L. Bettinger, and Peter J. Richerson

55. Archaeogenetics of Africa and of the African Hunter-Gatherers 1143
    Viktor Černý and Luísa Pereira

56. Landscapes of Mobility: The Flow of Place 1163
    Bruno David, Lara Lamb, and Jack Kaiwari

57. Personhood and Social Relations 1191
    Nyree Finlay

58. Materials, Biographies, Identities, Experiences: New Approaches
    to Materials in Hunter-Gatherer Studies 1204
    Hannah Cobb

59. Hunter-Gatherer Religion and Ritual 1221
    David S. Whitley

60. Hunter-Gatherer Gender and Identity 1243
    Robert Jarvenpa and Hetty Jo Brumbach

61. Hunter-Gatherer Diet, Subsistence, and Foodways 1266
    Rick Schulting

Index 1289

List of Figures

6.1	Yellen's (1977) ring model for Ju/'hoãnsi base camps combined with hut-based 'drop' and 'toss' zones	114
6.2	Schematic representations of an archetypal 'forager' settlement-subsistence system in (a) temporal and (b) synchronic perspective	117
6.3	Schematic representations of an archetypal 'collector' settlement-subsistence system in (a) temporal and (b) synchronic perspective	118
9.1	Top: Neanderthal craniofacial features (left) compared with a typical Modern Human. Bottom: Distinctive features of the Neanderthals' postcranial skeleton	194
9.2	Stone tools of the Neanderthal-associated Middle Palaeolithic. Left: sidescraper. Right: Levallois point with bitumen-covered base	197
9.3	Stone tools of the Neanderthal-associated early Upper Palaeolithic of Europe. Top left: Altmühlian foliate point (*Blattspitze*). Top right: two Châtelperron points. Bottom: Uluzzian backed microliths	198
9.4	Pierced and grooved pendants from the Châtelperronian levels of the Grotte du Renne (France): a–d. fox canines; e–f. reindeer phalanges; g–j. bovid incisors; k. red deer canine; l. fossil belemnite	202
10.1	Regions of the human skull and osteological terms used in the text to compare modern human anatomy to ancestral forms	218
10.2	Schematic of timeline for the major factors involved in MHO from behavioural (archaeology), morphological (fossils), and genetic evidence	234
11.1	Map of the region with a few of the major sites mentioned in the text	255
11.2	Winter and summer locations of hunter-gatherers in the Zagros and the Caucasus foothills. The model is based on Terminal Pleistocene occupations in western Georgia	268
11.3	Terminal Pleistocene Epi-Palaeolithic Early Natufian settlement pattern along a transect from the Mediterranean Sea to Lisan Lake in the Jordan Valley	268
13.1	A stone bracelet, a ring, bone bead-like elements, and needles from layer 11 of Denisova cave	313

13.2	Western and eastern Siberia: 1 – stone tools and wedge-shaped microcore from Ust'-Belaya site; 2 – composite tool from Chernoozerie-II site; 3 – Final Palaeolithic hunter in winter clothing with dart and atlatl, reconstruction; 4 – bone and antler grooved tools from Maininskaya site; 5 – clay figurine from Maininskaya site; 6 – pebble core from Kokorevo-I site	322
13.3	TransBaikal region and Yakutia: 1 – microblade cores and transversal burins, Ust'-Menza site; 2 – artefacts from Dyuktai cave; 3 – remains of light dwelling construction at Studenoe site; 4 – remains of 'polynary structure' at Ust'-Menza-3 site; 5 –Final Palaeolithic hunter in winter clothing, reconstruction; 6 – remains of dwelling at Ust-Timpton site	323
13.4	Russian Far East: 1 – stone knives from Suvorovo-III site; 2 – stone images of salmon fish from the Far-eastern Palaeolithic sites; 3–4 – microritual complexes with stones and bifacial point; 5 – Final Palaeolithic salmon-fisher, reconstruction; 6 – dwelling with the burial of a dog at Ushki-I site, level VI; 7 – double burial in dwelling at Ushki-I site, level VI	324
14.1	Indian subcontinent showing key localities mentioned in the text	329
14.2	Dispersal routes into the Indian subcontinent based on least cost analysis	331
14.3	Stone tool technology, Jwalapuram, Jurreru River Valley, India. (a) Middle Palaeolithic; (b) Microlithic	333
14.4	Map of Holocene archaeological sites in the Central Ganges plains	338
14.5	South Asian monsoon strength, human fossils, and key archaeological sites and industries	339
15.1	Map showing location of archaeological sites mentioned in the text	347
15.2	Niah cave entrance	351
15.3	Lene Hara cave, East Timor	355
15.4	Single piece *Trochus* shellfish hook from Lene Hara dated to the terminal Pleistocene	356
15.5	Graphs of uncalibrated radiocarbon dates and other chronometric dates between 10,000 and 40,000 years BP from South-East Asian cultural contexts	359
16.1	Temperature differences from modern over the last 140 thousand years	370
16.2	Geographic features of the Australian region referred to in the chapter	371
16.3	Distribution of vegetation zones at OIS 2 from Hope et al. (2004)	372
16.4	Chronological distribution for the arid zone of new sites and sites previously occupied by biogeographic region using the time intervals defined for this chapter	381

16.5	Chronological distribution for Queensland of new sites and sites previously occupied by geographic region using the time intervals defined for this chapter	382
16.6	Thylacine painting at Yeddonba, Mount Pilot, near Beechworth, Victoria	386
17.1	The Americas with selected early hunter-gatherer sites	407
17.2	Paisley cave V	409
17.3	Excavation of the Quebrada Santa Julia site in Chile	410
17.4	View of the entrance of the site Caverna da Pedra Pintada	410
17.5	Examples of early American projectile points	413
17.6	The Hell Gap site, Wyoming, under excavation in the 1960s	415
18.1	Oxygen isotope levels from ice cores (y-axis) reflect temperature changes from the late glacial into the post-glacial period	439
19.1	Selected Neolithic sites in Western Asia	460
19.2	Selected Mesolithic sites in the Mediterranean	464
19.3	Selected Neolithic sites in the Mediterranean	467
21.1	Locations of archaeological sites mentioned in the text	493
22.1	Map of sites in Japan and South Korea mentioned in the text, and regions of Japan	511
23.1	Lepenski Vir. Bases of elaborate trapezoidal houses and details of stone sculptures located inside	524
23.2	Example of a Mesolithic microregion: the Bohemian Switzerland National Park, showing the position of the Mesolithic rock shelters	526
23.3	Bezděz rock shelter, North Bohemia	527
23.4	Okrouhlík rock shelter on the confluence of the Kamenice and Bělá rivers	531
23.5	Fish cave, North Bohemia	532
24.1	Location of key regions discussed in the text	538
24.2	Changing sea levels since the late glacial had a profound influence on the north European landscape	539
25.1	The 20-year interval measure of climatic variance derived δO^{18} temperature proxy record of the GISP2 ice-core and its long-term trend	557
25.2	The mobility required to maintain viable bio-social networks amongst foragers (mating distance) has been investigated in ethnographic field studies, and, using different estimates of late glacial population densities, can be extrapolated for the late glacial	563
27.1	Geometric inserts for composite tools: (a) Klissoura cave, Greece, c.40,000 BP; (b) Sibudu cave, S. Africa, c.70,000 BP	610
27.2	Bifacial Acheulian hand axe (Göllü Dağ, Turkey)	612

27.3	Acheulian cleaver flake from prepared core (Kaletepe Dersi 3, Turkey)	613
27.4	Modern experimental Levallois core and flake	614
28.1	Engraved ochre from Blombos cave, South Africa	627
28.2	Aurignacian figurines from southern Germany	629
28.3	Magdalenian image from Niaux, France	629
28.4	Painted 'signs'	630
28.5	Magdalenian cave painting at Niaux, France	631
29.1	The presence/absence distribution of native copper on the Northwest Plateau of North America	647
29.2	The presence/absence distribution of tubular stone pipes on the Northwest Plateau of North America	648
29.3	The graph at the top displays Lorenz curves and corresponding Gini coefficients indicating the degree of departure of an ideal egalitarian distribution of housepit sizes at Keatley Creek and two other sites. The bottom graph shows the degree to which the number of housepits per site in the region departs from a hypothetical line of equality	652
30.1	(a) The 'Black Venus' found at the site of Dolni Vestonice, in the Pavlov Hills of the Czech Republic; (b) Terracotta human figure found at the Maïninskaya site, near Maïna on the Yenisei River in Siberia; (c) Line drawing of ceramic fragment from Tamar Hat near the Mediterranean coast of Algeria, interpreted (by some) as a fragment of a zoomorphic figurine	665
30.2	Vessel from the site of Gasya in the Russian Far East	667
30.3	Middle Jomon pottery vessel from the site of Ookubu, Honshu (Japan)	668
30.4	Fragment of decorated pottery from the site of San Jacinto I in northern Columbia	669
30.5	Sketch map showing the approximate distribution and chronology for the emergence of ceramics in hunter-gatherer societies across the world	677
34.1	Biometry pig (*Sus*) third molars from prehistoric Denmark from the Mesolithic to Iron Age	751
34.2	Diagram showing the position of the bit in a horse's mouth, and how it can cause wear on the second premolar and also irritate the bone of the jaw in front of the tooth row (diastema) causing further pathologies	754
34.3	Plots of the $\Delta^{13}C$ ($= \delta^{13}C_{18:0} - \delta^{13}C_{16:0}$) values for archaeological animal fat residues in Neolithic pottery from: (a) NW Anatolia, (b) Central Anatolia, (c) SE Europe/N Greece, (d) Eastern Anatolia and the Levant	755

34.4	A horse being milked in modern-day Kazakhstan. The milk is fermented into a mildly alcoholic drink called *koumiss*, which is sometimes also smoked to add further flavour	758
36.1	(a) The dispersal of farming across western Eurasia; (b) Genetic matrilineal distances between modern Western Eurasian populations and LBK samples; (c) The three streams of Neolithization with aDNA haplotypes superimposed	788
36.2	Lateralization of triangular points with extension of the pottery traditions of La Hoguette and Limburg and the Rhine-Maas-Schelde (RMS) complex	789
36.3	Schwanfeld, Ldkr. Würzburg, Bavaria. Plan of the site with findspots of radiolarites and microliths of Mesolithic tradition	793
36.4	Imports of northern Late Mesolithic artefacts on southern European Early Neolithic sites	795
37.1	Map of the study area	806
37.2	Spatial-temporal scheme for north-western Europe between Antwerp and Hamburg	807
37.3	Triangular diagram depicting the proportion of bone assemblages reduced to the categories wild, domestic, and pig	808
37.4	Stable isotope for human bones from Hardinxveld (De Bruin and Polderweg), Schipluiden, and Swifterbant compared to those from the Iron Gate sites Lepenski Vir, Vlasac, and Schela Cladovei, from Portugal and Denmark	813
37.5	Map of Swifterbant area. Indicated are the Neolithic IJssel river system and the river dunes series delimiting the Late Glacial river valley	815
37.6	Fish trap from Emmeloord	816
39.1	Fennoscandia with geographical features, regions, and place names mentioned in the text	839
39.2	Distribution of battle axes of the TRB and Corded Ware cultures in northern areas	844
39.3	Map of the dating of cereal pollen	845
40.1	Hunter-gatherers in South-East Asia	862
40.2	Oro using a woven circle of vine to indicate a brass gong	866
40.3	A bundle of rattan recently collected in the forest and ready for transport	867
40.4	Splitting and shaving forest rattan in preparation for making woven baskets	867
41.1	Locations of North American hunter-gatherer populations	883

41.2	Locations of the three case studies discussed in the text, Iroquois-Algonquian, Middle Missouri, and Plains–Pueblo	884
43.1	Map of southern Africa, showing the major San language groups	920
44.1	The general location of the largest groups of Congo Basin hunter-gatherers	937
47.1	Pacific Northwest Coast culture area	993
48.1	Location of referenced South-East Asian hunter-gatherer societies	1011
49.1	Map of southern South America showing the approximate location of the hunter-gatherers mentioned in the chapter	1032
49.2	Map of northern South America showing the approximate location of the hunter-gatherers mentioned in the chapter	1034
49.3	A Tehuelche camp	1036
49.4	A Hotï man entering his recently built hut. He is transporting most of the family belongings in his basket	1039
49.5	Nukak wet-season camp	1043
50.1	Area of historic Ainu settlement	1055
51.1	The annual routes of the seven families areas of Suenjil in the 1930s	1072
51.2	The spread of the Finnish settlement in Finnish Lapland	1078
51.3	The migrations of reindeer nomads in the Finnish territory	1083
51.4	Changing roles: tutkija muuttuu tutkittavaksi	1087
53.1	A selection of Ju/'hoansi technology	1113
53.2	A selection of Nuvugmiut technology	1114
53.3	Relationship between number of complex tools and Read's measure of risk: length of growing season times the number of residential moves per year	1117
54.1	Variation in means, as measured by CV, with latitude in three projectile point types in the North American Great Basin	1136
54.2	Variation over time in the thickness and amount of mica in pottery assemblages from radiocarbon-dated houses in southern Owens Valley	1137
55.1	Schematic formation of a haplogroup; the constituent haplotypes emerge in certain time and space	1144
55.2	African mtDNA phylogeny showing the root ~200 ka, the divergence of the Khoisan pool ~100 ka, and first non-African diversification some ~70 ka	1146
58.1	Price's schematic illustration to indicate characteristics of tree types as they cross-cut and are associated with different objects in the Scandinavian Mesolithic	1214

61.1	Middle Jomon site of Kowashimizu, Chiba Prefecture, Japan, with 260 pit-houses surrounding a central space containing more than 1,000 storage pits	1274
61.2	View over the prehistoric pit-house village of Keatley Creek, interior British Columbia, Canada	1274
61.3	Salmon drying racks being prepared for the main autumn runs along a tributary of the Fraser River north of Lillooet, British Columbia, Canada, June 1994	1275
61.4	The interior of the Whale House of the Gaanaxtedi Clan of Klukwan, Alaska, c.1895	1277
61.5	Bivariate plot of stable carbon and nitrogen isotope results on human bone collagen from the Late-Final Jomon site of Inariyama, Aichi Prefecture, Japan, with inset showing tooth ablation types	1278
61.6	Jomon 'biscuits' with impressed designs, from Ondashi, Yamagata Prefecture, Japan	1278

List of Tables

6.1	Spatial and ecological distribution of the more intensively studied, from an ethnoarchaeological perspective, hunter-gatherer-fisher societies	110
6.2	Main differences between dry and wet season Ju/'hoãnsi (!Kung) base camps	113
6.3	Foragers versus collectors	119
6.4	'Simple' and 'complex' hunter-gatherer-fishers compared	121
6.5	Classes of hunter-gatherer-fisher tools	124
6.6	Spatial distribution of female and male activities associated with moose hunting among Chipewyan hunter-fishers	132
10.1	A comparison of definitions of modern cranial morphology	220
10.2	Morphological and temporal groupings of African Pleistocene fossil hominids relevant to MHO	221
10.3	Fossil specimens, sites, and dates relevant to MHO in Africa	222
14.1	Key evidence for modern behavioural traits in South Asia	337
16.1	Subdivisions of marine oxygen isotope stages used in this chapter with dates	370
16.2	Numbers of sites (a) in each region by time period indicating numbers of 2,000-year gaps in sequence in a 5,000-year period; (b) in the form b/a	383
16.3	Numbers of sites (a) in each region by time period indicating numbers of 2,000-year gaps in sequence in a 5,000-year period; (b) in the form b/a	383
20.1	Timeline of important events in Africa	486
22.1	Approximate dates (calibrated BP) for the six Jomon and four Chulmun sub-periods	508
25.1	The demographic framework for the resettlement of northern Europe	559
25.2	The causes for migration found in the ethnography and ethnohistory of the Canadian Arctic	568
27.1	Estimated dates for appearance of significant production methods and artefact forms	609
30.1	A selection of radiocarbon dates for Late Pleistocene sites with hunter-gatherer pottery in Japan, China, Korea, and eastern Russia	670

30.2	A selection of radiocarbon dates from sites with early hunter-gatherer pottery across Siberia, European Russia, and Ukraine	671
30.3	A selection of radiocarbon dates from sites with early hunter-gatherer pottery across Fennoscandia and around the Baltic coast	672
30.4	A selection of radiocarbon dates from sites with early hunter-gatherer pottery across northern Africa	673
30.5	A selection of radiocarbon dates from sites with early hunter-gatherer pottery across South America and southern North America	674
30.6	A selection of radiocarbon dates from sites with early hunter-gatherer pottery across the Arctic and subarctic of eastern Asia and western North America	676
37.1	Overview of Late Mesolithic and Neolithic bone assemblages	811
37.2	Overview of Late Mesolithic and Neolithic wild plant food resources	817
40.1	Examples of the forest products collected by hunter-gatherers from the Malay Peninsula and Borneo for trade	863
43.1	Numbers of San and Khoekhoe in southern Africa, 2010	919
44.1	Major ethnolinguistic groups of Congo Basin hunter-gatherers	937
47.1	Some causal factors in the rise of complexity towards the 'Developed Northwest Coast Pattern'	1002
48.1	The most widely known common names of hunter-gatherer groups	1014
54.1	Content, context, and mode of information transmission	1130
54.2	Cognitive biases in CT	1131

List of Contributors

Alan Barnard is Professor of the Anthropology of Southern Africa at the University of Edinburgh.

Huw Barton is Senior Lecturer in Bioarchaeology, University of Leicester.

Ofer Bar-Yosef is George Grant MacCurdy and Janet G. B. MacCurdy Professor of Prehistoric Archaeology at Harvard University.

Robert L. Bettinger is Professor of Anthropology at University of California, Davis.

Nicole Boivin is Senior Research Fellow at the University of Oxford.

Hetty Jo Brumbach is Associate Curator of Anthropology at the University at Albany, SUNY and Research Associate at the New York State Museum.

David Bulbeck is Senior Research Associate at the Department of Archaeology and Natural History, Australian National University.

Aubrey Cannon is a Professor in the Department of Anthropology, McMaster University.

Viktor Černý is Researcher at the Institute of Archaeology in Prague, Academy of Science of the Czech Republic and Associate Professor in Anthropology at the Faculty of Sciences, Charles University in Prague.

Amy E. Clark is a doctoral candidate in Anthropology at the University of Arizona, Tucson.

Hannah Cobb is Technical Lecturer in Archaeology at the University of Manchester.

Vicki Cummings is Reader in Archaeology at the University of Central Lancashire.

Charlotte Damm is Professor of Archaeology, Department of Archaeology and Social Anthropology, University of Tromsø.

Bruno David is Co-Director of the Programme for Australian Indigenous Archaeology, Monash University.

Iain Davidson is Emeritus Professor of Archaeology at the University of New England.

Anatoly P. Derevianko is Director of the Institute of Archaeology and Ethnography, Novosibirsk.

Jelmer W. Eerkens is a Professor in the Department of Anthropology, University of California, Davis.

Jason M. Fancher is a recent graduate of Washington State University's doctoral program in Anthropology.

Nyree Finlay is a Senior Lecturer in Archaeology at the University of Glasgow.

Lars Forsberg is Professor of Archaeology in the Department of Archaeology, History, Cultural Studies and Religion, University of Bergen.

Jana Fortier is a Lecturer at the University of California, San Diego.

Raven Garvey is a doctoral candidate at the University of California, Davis.

Detlef Gronenborn is Research Curator at the Römisch-Germanisches Zentralmuseum and Adjunct Professor at the Johannes-Gutenberg-University, Mainz.

Junko Habu is Professor at the Department of Anthropology, University of California, Berkeley.

David R. Harris is Emeritus Professor of Human Environment at the Institute of Archaeology, University College London.

Oliver J. T. Harris is Lecturer in Archaeology at the University of Leicester.

Brian Hayden is Professor Emeritus at Simon Fraser University.

Almudena Hernando is a Professor at the Universidad Complutense de Madrid.

Barry S. Hewlett is Professor of Anthropology at Washington State University, Vancouver.

Isabelle S. Heyerdahl-King is a doctoral candidate and teaching assistant at the University of Sheffield.

Robert K. Hitchcock is Professor of Geography and an adjunct Professor of Anthropology at Michigan State University, East Lansing, Michigan.

Peter Hommel is a postdoctoral researcher at the Institute of Archaeology, University of Oxford.

Mark J. Hudson is Director of the Center for Sustainable Environments and Culture and Professor of Anthropology at Nishikyushu University (University of West Kyushu).

Robert Jarvenpa is Professor of Anthropology and former chair of the Department of Anthropology at the University at Albany, SUNY.

Sacha Jones is a Research Fellow at the McDonald Institute for Archaeological Research at the University of Cambridge.

Peter Jordan is Director of the Arctic Centre at the University of Groningen.

Jack Kaiwari is a leader of the Yoto'uki clan, Rumu tribe of the mid-Kikori River region of the Gulf Province, Papua New Guinea.

Ian Keen is a Visiting Fellow at the Australian National University.

Robert L. Kelly is Professor of Anthropology at the University of Wyoming.

Marcel Kornfeld is Professor of Anthropology at the University of Wyoming.

Steven L. Kuhn is Professor in the School of Anthropology at the University of Arizona, Tucson.

Kevin L. Kuykendall is Senior Lecturer in Palaeoanthropology at the University of Sheffield.

Lara Lamb is a Senior Lecturer in Anthropology, Monash University.

Paul J. Lane is Professor at the Department of Archaeology and Ancient History, Uppsala University, Sweden.

J. D. Lewis-Williams is Professor Emeritus of Cognitive Archaeology in the University of the Witwatersrand, Johannesburg.

Sergei V. Markin is Leading Research Fellow at the Institute of Archaeology and Ethnography, Novosibirsk.

Andrew M. T. Moore is Dean of Graduate Studies at Rochester Institute of Technology, New York.

Susan O'Connor is Professor and Head of the Department of Archaeology and Natural History, College of Asia and the Pacific, Australian National University.

Sean O'Neill is a doctoral candidate at the University of Aberdeen.

Alan K. Outram is Associate Professor of Archaeological Science at the University of Exeter.

Luísa Pereira is a researcher and group leader at IPATIMUP (Institute of Molecular Pathology and Immunology of the University of Porto) and Affiliated Professor at the Faculty of Medicine, University of Porto, Portugal.

Michael D. Petraglia is Senior Research Fellow and Co-Director of the Centre for Asian Art, Archaeology and Culture, University of Oxford.

Paul Pettitt is Professor of Archaeology at Durham University.

Mark Pluciennik is a university Fellow at the University of Leicester.

Gustavo G. Politis is a researcher in the Consejo Nacional de Investigaciones Científicas y Técnicas of Argentina (CONICET) and a Professor at the Universidad Nacional del Centro de la Provincia de Buenos Aires and at the Universidad Nacional de La Plata.

Ryan Rabett is a Research Fellow at the McDonald Institute for Archaeological Research at the University of Cambridge.

D. C. M. Raemaekers is Professor of Prehistoric and Protohistoric Archaeology at the University of Groningen.

Peter J. Richerson is a Distinguished Professor Emeritus at the University of California, Davis.

Felix Riede is Assistant Professor in Prehistoric Archaeology at the University of Aarhus in Denmark.

David Robinson is Senior Lecturer in Archaeology at the University of Central Lancashire.

Jennie Robinson is Undergraduate Programmes Director and Head of Year for Management at Leeds University Business School.

Rick Schulting is Lecturer in Scientific and Prehistoric Archaeology, University of Oxford.

Andrew B. Smith is Associate Professor Emeritus at the University of Cape Town.

Katherine A. Spielmann is Professor of Anthropology in the School of Human Evolution and Social Change at Arizona State University.

Kathleen Sterling is an Assistant Professor of Anthropology at Binghamton University (State University of New York).

Liv Nilsson Stutz is a Lecturer at the Department of Anthropology, Emory University.

Jiří Svoboda is Professor of Anthropology at the Masaryk University, Brno.

Jussi-Pekka Taavitsainen is Professor of Archaeology at the University of Turku.

Andrei V. Tabarev is Leading Research Fellow at the Institute of Archaeology and Ethnography, and a lecturer-professor in the Novosibirsk State University and Novosibirsk State Pedagogical University.

Graeme Warren is College Lecturer in the School of Archaeology, University College Dublin.

David S. Whitley is a principal at ASM Affiliates, Inc.

C. R. Wickham-Jones is Lecturer in Archaeology at the University of Aberdeen.

João Zilhão is Research Professor at Universitat de Barcelona.

Marek Zvelebil (1952–2011) was Professor of European Prehistory at the University of Sheffield.

INTRODUCTION

PETER JORDAN AND VICKI CUMMINGS

THE study of hunting and gathering populations remains a vibrant interdisciplinary research field situated at the intellectual heart of both archaeology and anthropology. Early considerations of hunting and gathering societies can be found among the work of eighteenth-century intellectuals, and a more detailed treatment of the foraging way of life was central to the founding and development of both archaeology and anthropology as closely related academic disciplines in the nineteenth century.

Over the past hundred years or so, hunter-gatherer research has undergone cumulative expansion and diversification, and has also weathered a range of internal and external critiques. Today, the study of hunter-gatherers remains as important as ever, but grappling with the immense and increasingly specialized research literature can be a daunting challenge. This handbook makes a detailed review of the field both timely and also a valuable exercise for researchers, scholars, teachers, and students. The topics, materials, and ongoing debates examined throughout this handbook demonstrate that interest in hunter-gatherers is alive and well, and that the research field is flourishing, with several important themes requiring future research.

WHY STUDY HUNTER-GATHERERS?

The investigation of hunter-gatherers is central to the disciplines of archaeology and anthropology, both of which attempt to document and explain the immense diversity in human cultures (Ames 2004, 364). Until around 12,000 years ago, virtually all humanity lived as foragers (Lee and Daly 1999, 1). Therefore, the hunter-gatherer lifestyle represents the conditions in which key periods of human evolution occurred prior to the emergence and subsequent spread of agro-pastoral farming in the Holocene (Barnard 2004, 1). While living as foragers humanity developed the definitive physical traits and mental capacities that are shared by all people to this day (e.g. Mithen 1996). Due to this important historical legacy, the study of hunting and gathering societies has come to serve as a testing ground for general theories about human evolution, as well as to speculate about the 'original' social, ideological, and political condition of all humanity.

The study of forager societies may also hold the key to some of the central questions about human social life, politics, and gender, as well as diet, nutrition, sustainable human–environment relations, and perhaps also 'long-term human futures' (Lee and Daly 1999, 1). For this reason, 'ideas observed, tested, or refined with the study of hunter-gatherers have been among the most important areas of anthropological research' (Hitchcock and Biesele 2000, 3).

EARLY RESEARCH ON HUNTER-GATHERER SOCIETIES

The communities who eventually became labelled as 'hunter-gatherers' saw increasing attention in European political and social thought from the sixteenth century onwards (Lee and Daly 1999, 7; see Barnard, Pluciennik, Part I). Speculations about these societies drew on the accounts of 'savages' that were being collected by European travellers and explorers in newly discovered areas of the globe, all of which made the subsequent intellectual treatment and classification of these diverse populations a highly contingent and subjective exercise (Pluciennik, Part I). However, the more formal intellectual development of hunter-gatherer studies closely parallels the disciplinary history of North American anthropology (covering all four sub-fields: cultural, physical, and linguistic anthropology, and also archaeology), and in Europe, the history of social anthropology (i.e. the ethnographic study of contemporary societies) and archaeology (the study of past societies through their surviving material remains).

With rapid nineteenth-century growth in European imperialism, colonial settlement, and increasing general knowledge about the 'exotic' peoples living in other parts of the world, as well as growing archaeological appreciation of the extended antiquity of humanity, contemporary thinkers tried to rationalize this new information, and attempted to find ways of classifying human cultural diversity into logical schema. Scholars also began to theorize about early human origins, as well as the later developments that had generated the contemporary conditions of cultural diversity: anthropology focused on the study of 'traditional' non-European societies; archaeology emerged as a discipline tasked with making sense of past societies. In the latter half of the nineteenth century, scholars began to erect complex social evolutionary schemes that mapped out different general stages in the progression of humanity towards higher levels of cultural, moral, and intellectual achievement. Specific stages such as *savagery*, *barbarism*, and *civilization* were defined by differences in economy, social forms, and technological attributes. Hunting societies were essential elements in these progressive evolutionary schema, because they were used to illustrate some of the lower sub-stages, thereby forming a base-line against which subsequent developments and achievements could be measured and contrasted (e.g. Morgan 1877). However, these ideas were closely associated with a unique perspective on the world that was developing among Western educated elites at this time (see Pluciennik, Part I).

More generally, many founding researchers in anthropology either undertook extended ethnographic fieldwork, or completed detailed analytical treatments of hunter-gatherer societies. Fieldworkers included Franz Boas (1966), who visited the Canadian Arctic (1888) and the Pacific Northwest Coast, followed by Kroeber's extensive research in California (Kroeber 1925), and Robert Lowie's work among the Crow Indians (Lowie 1935). Other important research traditions included Danish studies in Greenland and Arctic Canada, early ethnographic fieldwork in Australia (Keen, Part VI), and also major international projects, including the Jesup North Pacific Expedition (Lee and Daly 1999, 7–8).

Working in the late nineteenth and early twentieth centuries, Boas's experience of fieldwork led him to attack classical evolutionary schemes on both empirical and moral grounds—he argued they were inherently racist and based largely on armchair speculation, rather than direct and detailed knowledge gathered first hand through extended ethnographic field research with specific groups. In *Race, language and culture* (Boas 1911), he examined how these three attributes varied independently: some cultures could have a simple technology but a very complex world view; all languages were equally complex and suitable for abstract thought; and there was also important variations in cultural achievements within one and the same 'race'.

Boas went on to develop a contrasting perspective on human cultural diversity. In rejecting uniform patterns or discrete cultural stages, he argued that all local cultures are essentially unique formations, which needed to be understood on their own terms ('cultural relativism'), and that their traits and attributes were historically contingent constellations produced through highly specific cultural histories or via contacts and diffusion. As a result, these distinctive cultural patterns should always be studied on an individual case-by-case basis ('historical particularism'), and could never be lumped together into universal stages, as social evolutionary thinkers had suggested.

As the founder of American anthropology, Boas also argued for conducting extended ethnographic field research, generating a discipline with a distinctive emphasis on understanding the unique features of local cultures via sustained fieldwork (Lee and Daly 1999, 7). He also argued that ethnographic museum collections were better ordered according to tribes living in different geographical areas, rather than the kinds of typological categories or hypothetical evolutionary schemes that were influential, especially in late nineteenth-century Europe (Trigger 2006, 180–1). Later, Boasian thinking also fed into some of the first detailed ethnographic treatments of North American culture areas (e.g. Wissler 1917; and see Garvey and Bettinger, Part I, this volume).

A focus on hunter-gatherers can be identified in the work of other early European anthropologists. For example, in France early library-based research was conducted by Emile Durkheim, writing on Australian Aborigine religion in *The elementary forms of the religious life* (French = 1912; English version 1915 which is the one cited here), and Marcel Mauss (Mauss and Beauchat 1979 [1906]) on the seasonal life of the Eskimo. Two decades later, Claude Lévi-Strauss started with hunter-gatherers and fieldwork in Brazil, before looking at the origins of kinship and mythology (Lévi-Strauss 1969 [1949]). Important early work by British anthropologists included Malinowski on Australian Aborigines (1913) and Radcliffe-Brown (1922) among the Andaman Islanders. Radcliffe-Brown (1931) later produced a classic work on Australian Aborigine social organization and helped to establish a focus on studies of kinship as a definitive feature of British social anthropology.

Hunter-gatherer research was also central to the later intellectual growth of archaeology as it outgrew its early Antiquarian origins. With the main bulk of human evolutionary history spent as hunters and gatherers, those studying human origins and the earlier prehistoric past also came to focus on understanding early forager societies. In fact, the study of hunter-gatherers can be linked directly to the emergence of *prehistoric* archaeology. In Scandinavia, early treatments of long-term human cultural development had used general changes in material culture to define successive technological stages or eras, each reflecting discrete temporal segments (Thomson's three-age system of Stone, Bronze, and Iron: see Rowley-Conwy 2007). Meanwhile, studies in France and England began to focus on understanding the very earliest ages of mankind, which triggered an increasing interest in early hunting societies, and the realization that the Stone Age of Europe needed to be divided into the Old Stone Age (Palaeolithic) and New Stone Age (Neolithic: Trigger 2006, 121–38).

In the later nineteenth century, it is also possible to identify a growing mutual engagement between the archaeological and anthropological study of hunter-gatherers, a trend that persists through to the present. Early prehistorians started to draw on ethnographic parallels to speculate about the kinds of human existence that defined earlier stages of prehistory (Trigger 2006, 138–55). For example, Lubbock, in *Prehistoric times: as illustrated by ancient remains, and the manners and customs of modern savages* (Lubbock 1865) drew on general ethnographic sketches of modern tribal societies. He reasoned that, just as modern elephants provide information about the anatomy of extinct mammoths, so 'modern primitive societies' could shed some light on the behaviour of prehistoric humans. However, most of the ethnographic descriptions were used to draw only very general analogies between 'primitive' and 'prehistoric' peoples. Only in a few specific cases did Lubbock identify more specific parallels, for example, noting similarities in the tool-kits of the modern Inuit and the societies of the Upper Palaeolithic (Trigger 2006, 171–3).

This early archaeological use of ethnographic information also implicitly reflected contemporary social evolutionary thinking. Modern hunter-gatherers were assumed to have become trapped in an earlier mode of human existence, and as prehistoric archaeologists struggled to make sense of the artefacts they were finding, they looked to detailed ethnographic studies to provide relatively direct insights into what was assumed to be a distinctive general stage of human development. In this way, the study of hunter-gatherer ethnography formed a way for archaeologists to understand an earlier stage of prehistoric existence that almost all other humanity was assumed to have progressed away from. The increasing use of ethnography in archaeology continued with William Sollas (1911), who was the first to define 'hunter-gatherers' as a specific way of life in *Ancient hunters and their modern representatives*. Again, he used ethnographic descriptions of contemporary hunter-gatherer groups such as the modern Eskimo, who were argued to represent prehistoric Magdelanian people, and African Bushmen, who were used as parallels for Aurignacian hunters.

Thus, by the end of the nineteenth century, and into the early part of the twentieth century, it is possible to identify the emergence of the concept of 'hunter-gatherers' as representing a distinct kind of society, as well as several influential research traditions, including progressive social evolutionary thinking and the Boasian school of 'historical particularism'. Finally, it is possible to identify the increasing use of ethnographic parallels from modern hunter-gatherer societies to help understand and illustrate the archaeological record.

The Emergence of Modern Hunter-Gatherer Studies

In the early part of the twentieth century, and particularly in the 1930s, anthropological analysis of hunter-gatherers was starting to move towards two overarching themes: the structuring role of kinship in band societies, and the role of ecology and adaptation. The growing interest in kinship in hunter-gatherer 'band' societies was led by Radcliffe-Brown (1931), and helped to establish the distinctive functionalist focus of British social anthropology. Growing interest in exploring the role of ecology and adaptation emerged in North America. Boas's historical particularism still formed the mainstream of anthropological thinking, but there was growing interest in revisiting and updating some of the concepts surrounding cultural evolution, a trend closely associated with the Neo-evolutionary thinking of Leslie White and Julian Steward (Trigger 2006, 387).

White regarded himself as the intellectual heir of L. H. Morgan (Trigger 2006, 387) and engaged in an explicit rejection of Boasian historical particularism, offering instead the concept of 'general evolution'. However, White ignored the influence of the environment on culture, and focused instead on what he saw as main lines of cultural development (Trigger 2006, 388)—cultures were best regarded as elaborate thermo-dynamic systems that gained increasing control of energy flows, and functioned to make human life more secure and enduring. With reliance only on human muscle, energy capture by hunter-gatherers was rather limited, placing them at the lower end of this spectrum. In contrast, industrialists and urban civilizations had harnessed control of fossil fuels and were in the process of mastering nuclear power, placing them at higher levels of these general sequences of development.

In contrast, the new framework of 'cultural ecology' emerged through the fieldwork of Julian Steward in the Great Basin (see Garvey and Bettinger, Part I, and Robinson, Part VI). This research examined the distinctive social organization of hunter-gatherer bands (Steward 1936; 1938; and see 1955), but also sought general explanatory factors for these patterns by examining the historical dynamics of human–environment adaptations. Steward's key contribution to the study of hunter-gatherers was therefore to focus on what bands actually *did* for a living. This led to a more empirical and ecologically orientated approach to the study of cultural evolution, with historically contingent patterns of adaptation regarded as being crucial in determining potentially different lines of cultural development, as well as the general limits of variation in different cultural systems. Steward's cultural ecology went on to generate a contrasting *multilinear* approach to the study of cultural evolution (Trigger 2006, 389). Steward also argued that hunter-gatherer societies were ideal for this kind of approach because the details of these kinds of 'simpler cultures' are much more directly conditioned by the characteristics of the local environment than more complex ones. For example, the timing and characteristics of important food sources such as fish runs and game migrations would effectively determine the social organization and other habits of forager tribes exploiting those resources (Steward 1955).

Many now regard Steward as the 'founder of modern hunter-gatherer studies' (Lee and DeVore 1968, 5). His cultural ecology was particularly attractive to a new generation of anthropologists because it overcame the cautious Boasian paradigm by proposing a 'materialist' and natural science perspective on human behaviour, especially among 'simpler' band-scale societies (Schweitzer 2000, 35). Cultural ecology had a dramatic impact on American anthropology in the 1950s and 1960s. However, it was never a nomothetic approach, and sought initially to understand only the particular details of local cultural patterns on a case-by-case basis, rather than to derive general principles that could be applicable to any culture–environmental situation (Kelly 1995, 42–3; see Garvey and Bettinger, Part I).

Slightly later, Service (1962; 1966; 1975) blended the work of White and Steward in an attempt to reconcile the two, and used ethnographic data to illustrate highly general developmental sequences, for example, from bands and chiefdoms through to states. This generated renewed interest in understanding hunter-gatherers as quintessential examples of 'band-scale' societies, and also reinforced the importance of Radcliffe-Brown's (1931) model of patrilocal band organization in Australia, to which Steward had added other kinds of band. Service later went on to argue that the patrilocal band was typical for all hunter-gatherers in the present and also the past, though this generated heated debate (Lee and DeVore 1968, 7). More generally, these developments were positive because they focused attention on the extent to which potential regularities might actually unite different hunter-gatherer societies, encouraging further cross-cultural research into the general features of hunter-gatherer societies and their adaptive dynamics.

It is important to note, however, that the growing interest in hunter-gatherers and their functional ecological and social relations with local environments was not a development limited to North American anthropology. In Europe, there had been earlier interests in applying ecological-functionalist frameworks to the hunter-gatherer archaeological record, as illustrated by Grahame Clark's work on the Mesolithic hunter-gatherers of Britain and continental Europe (e.g. Clark 1954). Clark had been influenced by several antecedent developments, including new interest in exploring prehistoric cultures in their ecological settings, an approach that first emerged in Scandinavia. He was also exposed to the functionalist approaches of Malinowski and Radcliffe-Brown, and was developing an interest in exploring how people actually lived in the past; that is, a focus on the people, not just the details of their tools and artefacts.

This raised new questions about how and why specific items of material culture were produced and used. These different strands of thinking eventually coalesced into an archaeological approach that was not dissimilar to the cultural ecology developed by American anthropologists; that is, that culture is functional and enabled survival, and that all aspects of human culture are influenced to a greater or lesser extent by ecology, such that culture and environment are factors within a single system (Clark 1939). Clark also used ethnographic analogies, but in different ways to his predecessors, looking at specific tool assemblages and not entire cultures, as had hitherto been the practice.

On a more empirical level, Clark also undertook major fieldwork at the Mesolithic site of Star Carr just after the Second World War (1949–52), which set a new standard for the archaeological investigation of hunter-gatherer wetland sites and palaeoeconomic reconstruction. At this time, Hawkes (1954) was arguing that without written records to rely on, prehistoric archaeologists should concentrate on studying lower-level behavioural inferences, such as the details of economic activities and perhaps broader details of social relations, as these were the easiest to identify in the material record. Evidence pertaining to the spirituality, religion, and beliefs of prehistoric societies was likely to remain so ambiguous that attempts to understand these facets of prehistoric life were best regarded as exercises in controlled speculation (Hawkes's ladder of inference). This kind of thinking about what archaeological analysis could—and could not—reconstruct in the way of details about prehistoric societies and their behaviour tended to reinforce existing trends. Understanding prehistoric hunter-gatherers was therefore regarded as being an exercise in the reconstruction of palaeoeconomy; that is, past subsistence activities.

By the mid-twentieth century, there was also growing interest among American archaeologists in exploring evidence for adaptive human–environment relations, especially in relation to the continent's rich archaeological record of prehistoric hunter-gatherers. These ideas and interests eventually crystallized into the 'New Archaeology' paradigm led by Lewis Binford, who had been a student of Leslie White. Binford followed White (1959) in defining culture as man's 'extrasomatic means of adaptation'; that is, that culture serves primarily as a means of adapting to local environments (Binford 1962). These arguments led Binford to start to explore, isolate, and examine the functional dimensions of particular cultural systems.

If culture can be generally regarded as serving some kind of adaptive function, then the specific details of particular cultural systems can be regarded as human responses to the demands of local environments. Moreover, if the environment changes over time, then culture will also need to adjust. Although there may be additional changes in population, leading to demographic pressures, Binford argued that all culture change was ultimately rooted in ecological factors (Trigger 2006, 395–6). It was on the basis of these assumptions that he was led to argue that archaeology had a unique contribution to make—it could address the same kinds of research problems as Steward's cultural ecology, but importantly, could do so over much longer time-scales. This defined the goal of archaeology as the study of 'culture process' (Binford 1965).

These emerging interests in the study of long-term adaptation are often presented as a rather clean break with earlier scholarship, but addressing these new topics only became feasible after the development of radiocarbon dating methods. Prior to the 1950s, archaeologists had faced the primary problem of how best to date archaeological materials, and had used artefact-focused analysis methods such as seriation to reconstruct relative chronologies and broad culture historical sequences (Binford and Johnson 2002, viii; Lyman et al. 1997). With new methods to reconstruct absolute chronologies, archaeologists could shift their research goals towards understanding how adaptive pressures had generated cultural variability and change at different spatial and temporal scales. More generally, however, these renewed concerns with understanding prehistoric adaptation built on and directly complemented an earlier generation of functional-ecological research in both America and in Europe, e.g. in the work of Graham Clark, as noted above (Trigger 2006, 393).

New Archaeologists also emphasized that the reconstruction of culture change was best undertaken by analysing those aspects of behaviour that were most closely associated with adaptation, such as the details of economy and technology. This was a challenging endeavour, and so many early efforts sought to understand adaptation and change in smaller-scale societies, whose relationships with the environment were more direct and empirically measurable—these hunting and gathering cultures also formed a major part of the archaeological record, especially in North America. As with Steward's cultural ecology, Binford's parallel concerns with understanding long-term processes of adaptation ensured that hunter-gatherers remained in central focus. Moreover, this renewed interest in identifying and explaining cross-cultural regularities in hunter-gatherer technology, subsistence, and other behavioural attributes now united archaeologists and anthropologists around a common goal.

THE FOUNDING CONFERENCES: 'MAN THE HUNTER'

After the Second World War, anthropological research into hunter-gatherers had coalesced around the two primary themes of kinship and ecological relations, while archaeologists were also becoming increasingly interested in acquiring cross-cultural ethnographic data on forager societies in order to help them better understand the archaeological record. Ethnographic field research conducted within a cultural ecology framework was also generating large bodies of new empirical data on hunter-gatherer subsistence and social relationships, and this required critical synthesis in relation to some of the new theoretical concerns that emerged at the same time (Burch 1994, 2).

In the mid-1960s, a series of summary meetings was held to review progress on key issues. These included the *Conference on band organisation* in 1965, and the *Conference on cultural ecology* in 1966. However, the *Man the hunter* meeting in 1966 is now widely regarded as the consolidation of a new phase in hunter-gatherer studies (Lee and DeVore 1968). In the following decades, these foundational conferences 'had tremendous impact on the anthropological view of hunter-gatherers...and defined what was germane to know about them' (Binford 2001, 21).

The main goal of *Man the hunter* was to present new data and clarify conceptual issues; moreover, this endeavour had a strongly multi-disciplinary nature from the very outset (Lee and DeVore 1968, vii). The aim was to examine new ethnographic field data and look more closely at kinship, social dynamics, and ecological relations, in order to understand the long-term evolution of hunter-gatherer adaptations. In the end, the conference boasted a remarkably diverse array of speakers, including archaeologists, anthropologists, and demographers, whose theoretical approaches spanned ecological and structuralist schools. Papers examined ecology, social and territorial organization, marriage and kinship, demography and population ecology, as well as prehistoric archaeology and the use of ethnographic analogies. The conference title suggests only a narrow concern with 'man' and the dynamics of 'hunting', but female gender and the utilization of plant resources was an important secondary theme as it became clear that only in Arctic and subarctic regions did populations rely almost entirely on meat (Lee and DeVore 1968, 7). Analysis of gender roles in hunter-gatherer societies has been a central theme ever since (see Sterling, Part I; Jarvenpa and Brumbach, Part VII).

Discussions at *Man the hunter* were also flavoured by a touch of romanticism: many who attended wanted to understand the essential features of human existence, and were evidently drawn to the study of hunter-gatherers because it was thought that the 'human condition was likely to be more clearly drawn here than among other kinds of societies' (Lee and DeVore 1968, x).

Early Formulations of Hunter-Gatherers: 'Nomadic Style'

By the close of the meeting it was clear that the conference had 'raised more questions than it answered, [and] there seemed to be a widespread feeling among participants that a useful beginning had been made in understanding the hunters better' (Lee and DeVore 1968, 11). Nevertheless, Lee and DeVore in their introductory chapter also attempted some sense of synthesis, and made two basic assumptions about hunter-gatherers: 1. they live in small groups; 2. they move around a lot. In addition, it was argued—derived largely on materials gathered from southern Africa—that the hunter-gatherer economic system was based on several core features, including a home base or camp, a gendered division of labour, with males hunting and females gathering, and perhaps most importantly, a central pattern of sharing out the collected food resources. This, they argued, provides a kind of organizational base-line from which subsequent developments can be derived (Lee and DeVore 1968, 12). The behavioural implications of this basic hunter-gatherer economic system were simple but important:

1. If hunter-gatherers do move around a lot to get food, the amount of personal property has to be kept low, and this constraint on property ownership also keeps wealth differentials low, ensuring an egalitarian social order.
2. The nature of the food supply keeps hunter-gatherer groups small in size—normally under 50 persons—as larger concentrations rapidly exhaust local resources and cause members to disperse into smaller foraging units.
3. Hunter-gatherer groups do not maintain exclusive rights to resources: fluid and flexible situations are the norm due to the waxing and waning of inter-group obligations, and widespread visiting and guesting. This ensures reciprocal access to food resources, with this open-access system underpinned by inter-group marriage.
4. Production of food surpluses is not common. Everybody knows where food resources are located and so the environment itself is the store house. Also, each person can monitor the movement of others, so there is no fear that these resources will be secretly appropriated.
5. Frequent visiting prevents particular groups from becoming too attached to specific territories, and a lack of personal and collective property means that mobility is not impeded. Conflict is easily resolved by group fissioning and reformation into new social units.

Lee and DeVore argued that these patterns equated to 'nomadic style', and were best exemplified by the forager groups documented by anthropologists in southern Africa, who eventually came to serve as paradigmatic examples of hunter-gatherer band societies.

Man the hunter was also important on another level because it started to overturn lingering assumptions that all foragers were typically people clinging on the brink of starvation, with an inadequate and unreliable food supply forcing them to move around frequently to find scarce resources. The earlier consensus propagated by many nineteenth-century social evolutionary thinkers was that the hunting and gathering lifestyle was, by its very essence, dictated by the economics of scarcity.

These lingering assumptions were confronted by Marshall Sahlins, who outlined an alternative perspective on the ideology of foraging (Sahlins 1968; and see 1972). He presented limited ethnographic data from Africa and Australia that appeared to demonstrate that foragers actually work very few hours to meet their basic economic needs, which Sahlins interpreted as a reflection of deeper cultural confidence in being able to procure resources in even the most extreme environment (Lee and DeVore 1968, 6).

On the basis on these insights, Sahlins branded hunter-gatherers the 'original affluent society', but it is important to note that these reinterpretations of foraging societies emerged at the same time as a growing Western unease with the contemporary world. A sense of moral decay was reflected in growing concerns about the escalation of the Vietnam War, and in growing awareness of the environmental impacts of relentless industrialization (Kelly 1995, 15–16). In contrast, anthropologists found that foragers presented an alternative and perhaps more desirable way in which human societies could operate. Ethnographers were able to portray the forager lifestyle as one that consisted primarily of lounging about and socializing, rather than working long and hard just to secure a basic living. These hunter-gatherers did not have a less complex culture because they had no time; rather, the simplicity of their lives stemmed from a *zen* philosophy that, because they wanted little, they effectively had all they needed.

Sahlins's influential arguments added further detail to Lee and DeVore's initial formulations of 'nomadic style', and led to the creation of a generalized foraging model that combined deep environmental confidence, a lack of materialism, low population density, egalitarianism, lack of territoriality, minimum storage, and an easy flux in band composition (Kelly 1995, 14–15).

Debating Hunter-Gatherer Variability

The *Man the hunter* conference 'set the tone for discussion up through to the present time' (Binford 2001, 21), and crucially, stimulated further ethnographic fieldwork to collect the empirical data required to test and refine these early models. But even at the original conference there had been preliminary discussions about documented aspects of forager behaviour that did not equate with the predictions of 'nomadic style'. A good example is Suttles's (1968) chapter, which focused on the Pacific Northwest Coast (see O'Neill, Part VI). He started to speculate that many definitive features of 'nomadic style' would eventually break down due to the inevitable logistical challenges associated with managing variability in the kind of salmon-based fishing economy that characterized the region. According to his analysis, small nomadic bands would eventually be replaced by surplus-producing, and wealth-accumulating, groups who had developed the kinds of essential technological facilities that were required to bank up resources, providing a means of coping with seasonal vagaries in the salmon supply.

The key insight from Suttles's study is that if maintaining a secure food supply requires increasing territorial control of resources and associated mass-capture facilities, then the 'loose non-corporate nature of the small-scale society cannot be maintained' (Lee and

DeVore 1968, 12). Crucially, as earlier small-scale egalitarian bands start to be replaced by new forms of social and economic organization, this process opens out long-term developmental trajectories that could eventually lead to major transformations in social relations and technologies. In time, these could also establish the foundations for new kinds of political institution, such as clan organizations, governments, and even the state, all of which ultimately find their origins in the breakdown of nomadic style and the coeval shifts in the internal dynamics of hunter-gatherer societies (Lee and DeVore 1968, 12; and see Hayden, Part IV for a similar argument).

Early formulations of nomadic style had provided a useful starting point, but by the 1970s and earlier 1980s, however, it was becoming increasingly clear that variability extended well beyond these early attempts to summarize typical features of hunter-gatherer society. Researchers attempted to reclassify the forms, causes, and constraints of this diversity, and in the process, variability within as well as between hunter-gatherer groups was increasingly recognized (Kent 1996, 16).

Several early attempts at formulating higher-resolution taxonomic systems became particularly influential, including Woodburn's (1980; 1982) distinction between immediate return and delayed return hunter-gatherers. Additional contrasts were also drawn between 'simple' and 'complex' hunter-gatherer societies. Simple hunter-gatherers were best exemplified by nomadic style, which was argued to represent a broadly accurate portrayal of many African and some Australian groups. In contrast, many other hunter-gatherer societies exhibited a wide range of strikingly different attributes and behaviours. The societies of the Pacific Northwest Coast are generally deployed as the definitive ethnographic example of 'complex' hunter-gatherers: they exhibit high population densities, accumulate enormous material wealth, live in permanent settlements, and engage in competitive feasting to maintain entrenched social stratification (Arnold 1996; Hayden 1981; Price 1981; Price and Brown 1985; Testart 1982; Woodburn 1980; Yesner 1980; and see Zvelebil 1998, 7; also O'Neill, Part VI).

The distinction between simple and complex hunter-gatherers was initially regarded as an important conceptual breakthrough, and provided a useful way of thinking through some of the more extreme ethnographic contrasts in hunter-gatherer variability. More recently, this kind of binary thinking has been criticized for reducing the inherent flexibility and variability of forager behaviour, social structure, and ideology into rather simplistic oppositional categories such as simple/complex, immediate return/delayed return, mobile/sedentary. In archaeology, these typologies also became problematic because they went on to serve as rigid conceptual frameworks into which disparate evidence was often fitted, with interpretations often illustrated through reference to standard sets of ethnographic examples, such as the Kalahari San and Northwest Coast groups (Kelly 1995, 34; Schweitzer 2000, 45).

New Archaeology, Ethnoarchaeology, and Hunter-Gatherers

From Lubbock (1865), through to Sollas (1911) and Clark (1939), archaeologists studying prehistoric hunter-gatherers had made frequent use of ethnographic analogues to understand

and illustrate the lifeways of prehistoric hunter-gatherers. These parallels tended to be rather descriptive, and generally drew on social evolutionary frameworks in order to justify making links between societies living in such different time periods—if all foraging cultures formed a single uniform stage of human development, then ethnography could provide a rather direct entry route into understanding the hunting societies of the more distant past.

Renewed interest in the use of ethnographic analogy emerged within the New Archaeology of the 1960s and 1970s. With increasing interest in developing more robust and explicitly scientific approaches to the study of long-term culture change, archaeologists were seeking to identify general cross-cultural patterning in human behaviour. Anthropologists could generate this kind of insight through close scrutiny of ethnographic datasets, but archaeologists faced an additional challenge in that they had to study prehistoric objects, artefacts, and other material residues in order to indirectly infer these kinds of behaviours among past societies.

Archaeologists eventually realized that they could not understand the archaeological record in isolation, but needed to develop a series of low-level inferences about how different kinds of behaviour generated distinctive archaeological signatures ('Middle Range Theory'). Moreover, they could not rely on ethnographers to provide these insights, but needed to undertake their own field studies. These concerns eventually promoted the development of hunter-gatherer 'ethnoarchaeology', which saw archaeologists engaging in long-term fieldwork with living populations (see Lane, Part I; David and Kramer 2001). Seminal work included Binford's 1978 study of the Nunamiut in Alaska, Gould's work in Australia (Gould 1969), and John Yellen's 1977 study of the Kung (David and Kramer 2001; and see Lane, Part I for a full discussion of hunter-gatherer ethnoarchaeology).

As part of these wider methodological developments, the use of ethnographic parallels was also subjected to much closer scrutiny. In time, a more explicitly theorized treatment of ethnographic analogies became one of the core methodological achievements of New Archaeology and its processual offspring. In seeking to make more systematic use of existing ethnographic datasets—as well as to generate new findings through ethnoarchaeology—archaeologists went on to become both the greatest producers, and also the most eager and enthusiastic consumers, of information pertaining to hunter-gatherer behavioural and socio-political diversity (Ames 2004).

A good example of this kind of interdisciplinary research trend is Binford's influential forager-collector model, which is presented in 'Willow smoke and dogs' tails' (1980). As noted above, archaeologists had earlier assumed that all hunter-gatherers formed a single kind of society, and this justified the general use of modern ethnographic analogies in archaeological interpretations, irrespective of specific environmental settings, and fundamental differences in subsistence, mobility strategies, and other aspects of behaviour. This kind of logic enabled modern San forager groups from the Kalahari Desert to be readily used as rather direct analogues for a wide range of prehistoric hunter-gatherer societies.

Fresh from ethnoarchaeological fieldwork in Alaska (Binford 1978), Binford wanted to demonstrate that there were many hunting and gathering societies whose behavioural attributes were fundamentally different to those of the San, who were still being regarded as the paradigmatic examples of the nomadic style thought to typify all hunter-gatherers (Binford 1980). Having worked closely with the Nunamiut in Alaska, Binford wanted to highlight that there were potentially very different ways of positioning people relative to resources, and that these contrasting strategies (foraging versus collecting) tended to co-vary in a rather predictable way with both latitude and the seasonal availability of local resources. Establishing these broad distinctions in adaptive strategies provided a way of summarizing this recognized ethnographic variability in ways that could be useful to archaeologists seeking to make sense of prehistoric data. In fact, Binford went on to devote most of his career to 'accounting for patterns of variability in hunter-gatherer adaptation' (Trigger 2006, 394). In turn, his work made fundamental contributions to hunter-gatherer studies more generally, and also served to maintain the inherently interdisciplinary character of this endeavour.

In Britain, another version of New Archaeology was developing with the work of David Clarke (1968), which attempted to systematize the analysis of material culture traditions. Prior to this, the main concern had been development of artefact typologies, rather than reconstruction of human behaviour (Trigger 2006, 431). Clarke wanted to develop a fuller understanding of material culture, and a substantial part of his research involved quantitative analysis of the Western North American Indian (WNAI) datasets. The WNAI were argued by Clarke to constitute some of the most detailed hunter-gatherer ethnographic records in the world, and had been assembled under the direction of Alfred Kroeber, a student of Boas. They recorded the lifeways and cultural traditions of scores of different hunter-gatherers in the most minute detail, and provided Clarke with a factual basis for developing more resolutely anthropological (or behavioural) perspective on spatial distribution patterns in material culture, generating deeper, cross-cultural insights that would eventually have utility for archaeologists (Clarke 1968, 368–88).

REVISIONIST APPROACHES AND CULTURE-CONTACT

In the immediate post-*Man the hunter* era, the paradigmatic goal for modern hunter-gatherer studies was to reveal definitive socio-economic and cultural patterns, so that once these common attributes had been identified, higher-level generalizations could eventually be drawn from the confusion and 'noise' of particularistic ethnographic detail. Such systematic behavioural insights would also be useful for making archaeological inferences. In seeking cross-cultural regularities—rather than variations—between hunter-gatherer groups (Bird-David 1996), the general quest was to identify and understand archetypal forager societies. Eventually, hunter-gatherers from the Kalahari Desert of South Africa came to be understood as typical not just of all contemporary foragers, but also to personify the original human condition (Kelly 1995, 15).

Moreover, the cultural ecology framework developed by Julian Steward and used in many of these interpretations tended to implicitly replicate the nineteenth-century view that modern hunter-gatherers were largely timeless populations, at stable equilibrium with their respective environments, having had little motivation to change over the millennia (Kelly 1995, 47). The Kalahari San, for example, were widely assumed to constitute exemplars of an older form of human life, that prevailed everywhere on earth until pastoralism and agriculture began to expand some 12,000 years ago (Suzman 2004). Indeed, Suzman (2004) argues that the 1960s and 1970s was the last stage in 'lost world anthropology', when researchers still hoped to find the last remaining populations of these kinds of authentic hunter-gatherers.

However, those scholars who continued to advocate a strongly ecological approach to the study of human culture left themselves increasingly exposed to criticism from more mainstream anthropology. Beyond the sub-field of hunter-gatherer studies, there were renewed interests in the dynamics of culture-contact, and in acknowledging the enormous impacts that colonialism and imperialism had had on all indigenous cultures. Particularly problematic was the implicit choice within hunter-gatherer studies to portray modern forager groups as relatively pristine, isolated, and self-sufficient units, whose internal dynamics were stripped of both history, as well as the effects of participating in wider spheres of interaction (Kelly 1995, 47). These older assumptions were subjected to withering critique in the 1980s and early 1990s, which eventually called into question the very empirical and epistemological basis of modern hunter-gatherer studies (see, for example, Lee 1992).

Initially, this critique focused on ethnographic portrayals of forager groups in southern Africa, and went on to become known as the Kalahari Debate (see Hitchcock, Part VI). These groups had been presented as hunters and gatherers living under changing circumstances, but still exemplars of a long-standing kind of original human adaptation. This 'traditionalist' perspective was increasing challenged by 'revisionist' arguments, which took into account the complex history of the wider region. These alternative insights emphasized that all the Kalahari foraging groups had been in long-term culture-contact with surrounding farmers and pastoralists, and rather than epitomizing some kind of original human condition, were perhaps better understood as a kind of impoverished rural underclass, which had been pushed into marginal areas through the impacts of wider economic and political developments that had played out across the region, including the more recent effects of European colonialism (Wilmsen 1983; 1989).

While focusing on forager groups in Africa, the revisionist position in the Kalahari Debate had implications for all hunter-gatherer studies. If culture-contact had been a defining feature of *all* modern hunter-gatherer groups, then could they still be understood as a timeless, self-contained, and relatively distinctive kind of society, or were many aspects of their behaviour a product of more recent historical developments such as colonialism (Bender and Morris 1988; Kent 1992; Lee 1992; Solway and Lee 1990; Wilmsen and Denbow 1990)?

As debates intensified, it became increasingly clear that hunter-gatherers had also been in different kinds of culture-contact for many millennia, rather than a few decades or a couple of centuries. Spielman and Eder (1994), for example, review the immense literature on forager–farmer contacts amongst some of the 'classic' foraging societies, including the Kalahari San, the Efe of north-east Zaire, the Kenyan Okiek, as well as the Agta of the Phillipines and some South Asian groups, including the Hill Pandaram. Common dynamics in these relationships include the acquisition of carbohydrate-rich foods produced by farmers in exchange for forest products such as honey, resins, and medicinal plants, and for labour procured by foragers.

These insights cast further doubt on the assumption that any modern hunter-gatherer groups can be regarded as survivals of an older and relatively unchanged kind of human existence—all are products of complex local transformations, and so their present-day behaviours and attributes must be explained through reference to these wider processes. Headland and Reid (1989, 52) concluded that until the misconception of hunter-gatherers as primitive and isolated was corrected, 'our image of hunter-gatherer culture and ecology will remain incomplete and distorted'.

More generally, these debates about the role of history and culture-contact formed part of wider moves in anthropology to address the deep impacts of Western colonialism on societies that ethnographers had hitherto regarded as being exotic, timeless, and traditional (Asad 1991). In turn, however, revisionist portrayals of hunter-gatherers were critiqued for generating negative new stereotypes—foragers were presented as powerless colonial victims, or as a rural proletariat that was defined by a culture of poverty (Kelly 1995, 29).

Perhaps the major outcome of wider revisionist critique is that hunter-gatherer societies are now considered within their wider ecological and historical setting, rather than as direct analogies for the social organization and behaviour of ancient humans and early hominins (Ames 2004, 366). As the importance of culture-contact among hunter-gatherers became more widely acknowledged, anthropologists actually embraced this theme as a major new research direction focused on understanding the inherent flexibility and dynamism of foraging societies within particular historical and ecological settings (see chapters in Part VI). Paradoxically, these new anthropological insights into forager–farmer contacts, and the historical contingency of much hunter-gatherer behaviour became of increasing interest to archaeologists in the 1990s, as they sought new ways to understand potentially analogous encounters in prehistory, such as the transition to farming in Europe (see below and Part V).

Historical and Humanist Research Traditions

Anthropology of Hunter-Gatherers

Even directly after *Man the hunter*, many researchers were moving away from ecological and adaptive approaches, and were starting to explore other themes and topics (Lee and Daly 1999, 9). Hunter-gatherer studies had initially grown from a subsistence definition, and rest on the implicit assumption that populations that rely entirely on wild resources for their subsistence will have similar kinds of social organization and follow similar patterns of behaviour. Even with the development of broader hunter-gatherer typologies (see above), this generated a number of tensions within the wider anthropological endeavour, which in North America still traced its roots back to the work of Boas. For example, Kent (1996, 1) notes that 'while understanding *diversity* has been a hallmark of anthropological enquiries since the inception of the discipline hunter-gatherer (or forager) studies tend to stress *similarities*'. Kent also argued that these dominant theoretical orientations had emphasized economics, particularly subsistence, at the expense of other realms of culture (Kent 1996, 17; and see Barnard 2004; Schweitzer 2000, 46).

In response, some hunter-gatherer researchers increasingly employed historical frameworks and went on to examine the fate of foragers as they became encapsulated minorities within empires and nation states in both Africa and beyond. But even as the traditionalist/revisionist Kalahari Debate raged back and forth, neither side actually examined the Bushman's own perception of the world (Barnard 2004, 7). In response, Bird-David (1996, 302) argued that the diverse ways in which hunter-gatherers understand their worlds have long been overlooked and that 'more attention should be given to symbolic worlds and world views of these peoples'. In a series of seminal papers (1990; 1992; 1996) she explored forager relationships with the environment, arguing persuasively that what lies at the core of local concerns is not maximization of leisure time (cf. Sahlins 1968; 1972), but an aim to maintain good and caring relationships with others and with the environment (Bird-David 1990). This increasing concern with investigating hunter-gatherer 'world views' has led to renewed interest in engaging with older anthropological constructs such as shamanism and animism, as well as more general research in hunter-gatherer perceptions of the environment (e.g. Ingold 2000; Layton and Ucko 1999; Whitley 2000; 2001).

Ironically, much of this work on traditional world views tended to be rather ahistorical, highlighting 'traditional' bonds with the land, rather than the historical dynamics of culture-contact. Other research has actually bridged these different concerns, and highlights the enduring cosmological significance of foraging within a rapidly changing world. Many modern foragers continue to regard hunting and gathering as an expression of cultural identity and as means of fulfilling the kinds of moral obligations to ancestors and to the land that are implicit to a sense of belonging. These bonds provide the emotional and spiritual resources that underpin cultural resilience, although the challenges to indigenous cultures raised by encroaching settlement, deforestation, and other environmental impacts remain profound (see chapters in Part VI).

Archaeology of Hunter-Gatherers

These debates eventually fed through to archaeological research into prehistoric hunter-gatherers, and it is worth tracing some of these impacts here. Two new and interlocking streams of research can be identified: (a) 'complex' hunter-gatherers and (b) forager–farmer contacts.

In the 1980s, archaeologists started to (re-) 'discover' a range of traits and behaviours among ethnographically documented hunter-gatherers that did not fit with the early nomadic style model of Lee and DeVore (1968). As new typologies were formulated, 'complex' hunter-gathers were added to the range of potential social forms, with Northwest Coast groups serving as the definitive ethnographic examples (see O'Neill, Part VI). In European archaeology, the emergence of these new typologies coincided with the discovery of elaborate Mesolithic hunter-gatherer mortuary sites in the Baltic region, which seemed to point to the existence of similarly 'complex' hunter-gatherer societies in prehistory, especially in areas with rich aquatic ecosystems, which provided a resource base for relatively sedentary and socially stratified societies prior to the transition to farming (see Nilsson Stutz, Part IV).

Prior to this, it had been assumed that all prehistoric hunter-gatherers were mobile bands with an egalitarian social order who would inevitably be replaced by the expansion of agricultural societies with the onset of the Neolithic—this kind of scenario had been predicted by nineteenth-century social evolutionary thinking, and was still implicit in understandings of the Mesolithic–Neolithic transition. For the first time, archaeologists started to acknowledge the existence of well-established and economically viable hunter-fisher-gatherer populations along many of Europe's coastal regions and major waterways. Moreover, there were increasing indications that the expansion of the agricultural frontier had stalled for long periods—in some cases, for millennia—at the margins of these complex hunter-gatherer societies, for example, in northern Europe. Although agricultural expansion had ended for a time, it was also clear from the archaeological evidence that there was a lively network of interaction and exchange across these enduring forager–farmer frontiers.

At this point, insights from the Kalahari Debate (see above)—and about culture-contact more generally—became increasingly important, serving as ethnographic parallels for investigating the dynamic settings that characterized similar kinds of contact zones in prehistory (Trigger 2006, 440–1). It was argued, for example, that exchange of partners across these frontiers can eventually destabilize hunter-gatherer societies, but in earlier contact phases, these new encounters provided structured opportunities for foragers to select which attributes they chose to adopt or reject. What eventually emerged from these ethnographically informed archaeological debates was a greater appreciation of the agency of hunter-gatherers, and also the potential for economic intensification within wider hunter-gatherer adaptations, rather than the rapid replacement of foraging by farming (Zvelebil 1986; 2008; Zvelebil and Rowley-Conwy 1984; and see Fewster 2001 and Part V).

Foragers could also actively select which attributes they adopted from farmers, ranging from domesticates, through to prestige goods, new technologies, or even new ways of perceiving the world, all of which could also be adopted in different sequences—economic transformations did not necessarily precede ideological transformation (see below; e.g. Thomas 1988; and see Cummings, Part V). Over time, the Neolithic came to be understood as a long-term process of Neolithization, and the agency of local foragers also meant that it was not a uniform and monolithic phenomenon, but was characterized by enormous regional variability and historical contingency (Zvelebil 1998; 2005; also see Part V introduction by Cummings).

Post-Processual and Interpretive Archaeologies

As anthropologists began to move away from the core themes of *Man the hunter* and undertake more historically-oriented and humanistic studies of hunting and gathering, broadly similar intellectual shifts eventually started to take place among some British and Scandinavian archaeologists (see Cannon, Part I, this volume). Much of this new post-processual movement was a deliberate reaction to the unique intellectual history of New Archaeology and its processual descendants, which had drawn heavily on the Neo-evolutionary approaches of White and Steward—this had been especially pronounced in hunter-gatherer studies (see above). These adaptive and ecological approaches had never dominated in mainstream anthropology, and actually had been a rather minority viewpoint, just as they were adopted readily into archaeology, and even dominated the discipline for a time. Many archaeologists had adopted a commitment to seeking cross-cultural understanding of ecological and adaptive relationships between prehistoric hunter-gatherers and their environments, and also rigorous construction of analogies and development of Middle Range Theory (see Lane, Part I). At the core of this approach was the argument that behaviour and technology basically served an adaptive function, especially among small-scale societies like hunter-gatherers.

In contrast, post-processual archaeologists asserted that all material culture and social action were meaningfully constituted, and in seeking to counterbalance the earlier emphasis on adaptation and economic factors, became increasingly interested in exploring the higher rungs of Hawkes's ladder of inference, for example, in relation to ideology and world view (see above; Trigger 2006, 442–3). Also rejected was an emphasis on seeking cross-cultural regularities—much of this reflected the inevitable rediscovery of the long-standing anthropological concept of culture as a source of the cross-cultural idiosyncratic variation in human beliefs and behaviours (Trigger 2006, 444). As a result, post-processual archaeology championed relativistic and particularistic readings of the archaeological record, an approach that can be broadly traced back to the anthropology of Boas, and later to the new cultural anthropology of Clifford Geertz (1965; 1973; and see Clifford 1988; Turner 1967). Thus, the argument was that all cultures are unique and all sequences of change are historically contingent.

Emphasizing historical contingency and cultural relativism also fed into critiques of the ways in which New Archaeology had employed ethnographic analogies, at least in a rigorous scientific and uniformitarian sense that Binford had originally envisaged. In addition to the argument that all cultures need to be understood on their own terms, a further problem was that even the earliest ethnographic or historical records of indigenous cultures were produced long after sustained contact with European populations. These made it difficult to justify the drawing of analogies between modern and prehistoric hunter-gatherers, as the recent colonial histories of the latter had generated very different kinds of attributes and behaviours that would not have been present in earlier periods.

Paradoxically, even though post-processual archaeology rejected the attempt to use ethnoarchaeological research to build Middle Range Theory it still drew readily but often implicitly on ethnographic insights. These were often deployed in an illustrative and rather eclectic way (e.g. Tilley 1994), and only if they supported a desired interpretation or particular perspective, an approach that can lack analytical rigour and intellectual transparency. In the end, however, post-processual archaeology—like processual archaeology—went on to become a heavy consumer of anthropological theory, but in reacting to New Archaeology, opted to borrow from the cultural and idealist side of the anthropology spectrum, rather than from the materialist, adaptive, and functional side that Binford had advocated (Trigger 2006, 480–3).

More generally, however, the broader post-processual critique has been much more muted in hunter-gatherer archaeology than in the archaeology of later periods such as the Neolithic (see Cannon 2011; see also Cannon, Part I). In part, this may be due to the coarse-grained nature of much of the hunter-gatherer archaeological record, which often lends itself to reconstructing little more than artefact typologies and broader patterns in settlement and subsistence behaviour. In contrast, European Neolithic archaeologists have long been confronted by dramatic monumental architecture, which demands a wider range of interpretations. On other levels, the struggle to develop more resolutely social and symbolic insights into prehistoric foragers may reflect the deeper legacy of ecological and adaptive approaches, which have been absolutely central to the emergence of hunter-gatherer studies. It was also compounded by the early post-processual rejection of the ethnoarchaeology project on ideological and empirical grounds—additional field research among contemporary foraging populations could have generated new ways of thinking about the symbolic and social dimensions to hunter-gatherer landscapes and material culture, and there are now growing signs that this kind of broader research agenda is eventually starting to gather pace (see, for example, Lane, Part I; Jarvenpa and Brumbach, Part VII; David and Kramer 2001).

Current Challenges

Contemporary research into the archaeology and anthropology of hunters and gatherers has now become extremely diverse, though the specialist field appears to have remained distinctive and intellectually vibrant enough to have generated and accommodated many different approaches and a diversity of theoretical interests. These equip hunter-gatherer studies with the capacity to investigate, among other things, variability in technology and the use of habitats, gender roles and their relationship to diet, nutrition, health, and demography, as well as the use and spread of languages, local world views and cosmologies, the dynamics of social organization, and long-term responses to environmental change (Panter Brick et al. 2001b, 6–7).

Despite the apparent intellectual resilience of hunter-gatherer studies, several recent milestone reviews have raised major concerns, some even predicting the imminent demise of the field as a distinct arena of enquiry (e.g. Ames 2004, 371; Burch 1994, 454). First, one basic concern, especially for field anthropologists, is that opportunities to collect new ethnographic data are rapidly disappearing due to relentless assimilation and the wider transformations generated by the acceleration of globalization and associated environmental degradation. In contrast, this is not the case for the archaeology of hunter-gatherers, and much important research remains to be done, from building basic cultural and chronological sequences in many remoter regions, through to developing new research directions in some of the better-studied areas. And in more recent periods, much more research could be directed at analysis of colonial era archives to improve current understandings of hunter-gatherer ethnohistory, an opportunity highlighted by several chapters in Part VI.

Second, in the decades since *Man the hunter*, hunter-gatherer studies have become ever more interdisciplinary, but as specialization has increased, lines of communication between many different research areas have broken down (Panter-Brick et al. 2001a). Some certainly lament the increasing 'balkanization' of the subject into a series of distinct and highly focused branches, whose leading proponents rarely communicate with one another (Panter-Brick et al. 2001b, 1). This situation has left hunter-gatherer studies without a coherent paradigm (or even common assumptions) with which to explain behavioural variability, or to set common research priorities (Ames 2004, 370). At present there are certainly multiple, occasionally overlapping approaches, which range from strongly materialist to the strongest post-modernist approaches. Some scholars are particularly critical of a growing focus on generating particularistic histories; that is, research conducted without any overarching theory to bind it all together (Ames 2004, 371).

Third, some even go far as to argue that hunter-gatherer studies are based on an unfruitful concept in the first place, as revealed by the initial internal critiques of 'nomadic style', as well as external revisionist critiques such as the Kalahari Debate. At a deeper level, the very concept of a hunter-gatherer has also been recast as a unique, historically contingent, and now outdated reflection of earlier modes of Western intellectual thinking; many other approaches to understanding cultural diversity appear to offer more fruitful research directions and require greater exploration (see Pluciennik, Part I). Even if it is agreed that 'hunters and gatherers' *do* actually exist at some conceptual and empirical level, almost everything else about them is a matter for relentless contestation (Lee 1992). In exploring some of these debates, Kelly argues, however, that the term 'hunter-gatherer' remains a useful heuristic device and a good point of analytical departure (Kelly 1995, 34–5).

RESEARCH OUTLOOK

Looking across current research into the archaeology and anthropology of hunter-gatherers, several broad directions of current enquiry can be identified:

First, these include what might generally be termed 'purists', who tend to trace their intellectual inheritance back to the ecological and adaptive approaches of Julian Steward (1936; 1938; 1955), maintaining a rigorous commitment to a scientific, cross-cultural and comparative analysis of human behaviours. A good recent example is the work of Binford (2001), who combines analysis of ethnographic datasets from 390 groups of modern foragers with detailed information on environments (world climates, plants, animals) to develop global scale 'pattern recognition' in hunter-gatherer behavioural variability. Earlier forms of cultural ecology have now been replaced by a new generation of approaches, including human behavioural ecology, and genes-culture co-evolutionary theory (Durham 1991) or the 'dual inheritance theory' of Boyd and Richerson (1985; 2005), which examines the role of social learning and decision-making processes in the replication of cultural traditions (see Garvey and Bettinger, Part I). Advocates argue that together the different elements of this broad Neo-Darwinian perspective generate a coherent framework for integrating insights from optimal foraging theory, demography, health, nutritional status, technology, cultural diversification, territoriality, and mobility, but in ways that emphasize the capacity for human decision-making processes, the dynamics of social learning, and the specific costs and benefits of different lines of activity (Kelly 1995; Shennan 2002; 2004; 2009).

In archaeology, much research into hunter-gatherers, particularly in North America, tends to follow this kind of ecologically orientated and broadly Neo-Darwinian approach, but there are also important exceptions. When applied in ethnoarchaeological field studies, the approach tends to follow older concerns with generating robust models that are testable, and generalizable, e.g. via faunal studies (David and Kramer 2001, 116–37).

Second, it is possible to identify a more loosely defined group of researchers interested in exploring historically contingent, humanist, interpretive, or 'multi-vocalist' perspectives on hunter-gatherers (see Cannon, Part I, this volume). The concern here is exploring forager flexibility and diversity, the uniqueness of local cultures, as well as the significance, lived experience, identities, and personhoods caught up in the practices of hunting and gathering. These different anthropological approaches and research themes are not necessarily mutually exclusive, and divergent sets of insights can be creatively combined, as the goal is to create a more holistic understanding of different cultures (Kent 1996). In archaeology, a similar trend can be identified in the recent post-processual or interpretive streams of hunter-gatherer research, but development of these alternative approaches has tended to remain rather limited to date, and often characterizes scholarship in northern Europe. The more general goal is to assert the meaningful nature of material culture and the subjectivity of human experience and social action, rather than deploy more rigorous cross-cultural analogies to explain human behavioural responses to environmental constraints (Cunningham 2003).

More generally, the archaeological investigation of hunter-gatherers is now being revolutionized by new methodologies that enable the 'biographic' life-histories of individuals to be reconstructed in an unprecedented degree of detail, for example, in relation to scientific analysis of diet, health, activity patterns, and mobility (see Schulting, Part VII), but also in relation to interpretations of personhood, social identities, and the performance of mortuary rituals (see Nilsson Stutz, Part IV). These studies of individual life-histories across cemetery populations, regions, and periods transcend any simplistic distinction between the kinds of adaptive and symbolic perspectives noted above, and represent one arena where perhaps the most detailed and exciting hunter-gatherer archaeology remains to be done (see Jordan and Cummings, Part VII).

Finally, looking back over the past century-and-a-half, one further development of fundamental importance in hunter-gatherer studies—and in anthropology more generally—has also been a growing engagement between the societies being studied, and those conducting the research. If in the eighteenth and nineteenth centuries there was a massive gulf, with scholars objectifying hunters and treating them as objects of scrutiny, then by the start of Boasian field anthropology, the boundaries were starting to break down through the experiences of undertaking sustained fieldwork (Lee and Daly 1999, 7). These developments eventually promoted a general moral and ethical concern among anthropologists to make their research more meaningful and relevant to local peoples, as well as to include members of these communities into professional research activities. This greater engagement with indigenous peoples has not been a smooth or easy process, and demands balancing the roles of scholar as well as advocate, and also the need to liaise closely with members of local indigenous groups, a point emphasized by several chapters in Part VI (Lee and Daly 1999, 7).

The New Archaeology also fundamentally changed older perceptions of hunter-gatherers by emphasizing their cultural variability and long-term dynamism, albeit in terms of sophisticated adaptive responses to the local environment. Hitherto it had been assumed that since the nineteenth century many first nation populations in North America had changed little over time and were relatively backward and culturally static (Trigger 2006, 409). Importantly, greater global engagement between archaeologists and local indigenous communities is now becoming an essential component of all contemporary archaeological research and fieldwork.

In more recent periods then, the long-term trend in both anthropology and archaeology has been towards building better and more inclusive working relationships with indigenous peoples. The production of knowledge has increasingly become a two-way process. It is no longer possible to be a detached observer, and the role of field researcher has now become merged with the role of public communicator, and occasionally legal advocate. More generally, research into hunter-gatherer populations both past and present has been increasingly influenced by agendas set by local communities and interest groups. However, the practice of an ethically responsible scholarship remains challenging on many levels (Trigger 1996, 11–12; and see chapters in Part VI).

Why an Oxford Handbook of Hunter-Gatherers?

These different research streams have generated an enormous and ever-expanding interdisciplinary literature on hunter-gatherers. Even as 'hunter-gatherer studies' began to regard itself as a distinctive sub-discipline in the late 1960s, there has never been much consensus, and vibrant debate was an important trend from the outset (Lee and DeVore 1968). Grappling with the breadth and intellectual diversity of this scholarship has now become a daunting task, even for established researchers seeking to explore new themes, approaches, (pre)historic periods, and/or geographic regions.

After *Man the hunter* was published in 1968, scholars interested in the archaeology and anthropology of hunter-gatherers began to meet on a more regular basis at the CHAGS meetings (Conference on Hunting and Gathering Societies). These conferences served to provide a common forum for debate, ensuring that the field—as far as possible—maintained a sense of collective focus and identity, often around exploration of new themes and overarching debates (see Sterling, Chapter 7, this volume, for a summary; and Lee and Daly 1999, 10–11). Most of these meetings also generated critical syntheses in the form of books and edited volumes, as well as debates that were played out in different specialist journals. Together, these milestone meetings and associated publications can be used to chart the development and growing diversification of the field from the late 1960s onwards.

Over recent decades additional 'flagship' publications in hunter-gatherer research have included the Smithsonian Institution's multi-volume *Handbook of North American Indians*, which includes basic ethnographic and some archaeological and environmental information pertaining to a wide range of cultures, many of whom were traditionally hunter-gatherers. Similar series exist for other world regions. Lee and Daly's (1999) *Cambridge encyclopaedia of hunters and gatherers* provides short regional archaeological summaries and basic ethnographic descriptions of global hunter-gatherer populations, as well as short essays on general themes. Other important recently edited books have included Panter-Brick et al.'s *Hunter-gatherers: an interdisciplinary perspective* (2001a), and Barnard's *Hunter-gatherers in history, archaeology and anthropology* (2004); the field also now has its own online journal: *Before farming: the archaeology and anthropology of hunter-gatherers*.

More generally, however, the archaeologists studying prehistoric hunter-gatherers have tended to publish on more regionally focused periods and topics, though some major recent volumes include the regular proceedings of the Mesolithic in Europe conference (MESO) which is held every five years (Bonsall 1990; Larsson et al. 2000; McCartan et al. 2008). Large-scale international and interdisciplinary collaborative research projects such as the *Baikal Hokkaido Archaeology Project* are now starting to make important contributions to the literature on prehistoric hunter-gatherers, for example, Weber et al.'s *Prehistoric hunter-gatherers of the Baikal Region, Siberia* (2010). Other recent comparative archaeological studies include Eren's *Hunter-gatherer behavior: human response during the Younger Dryas* (2012), which explores how forager populations adapted behaviourally and technologically in the face of major climatic change. In addition, regional and specialist journals continue to publish a steady flow of papers on prehistoric hunter-gatherers and their adaptive dynamics, culture-contacts, and general lifeways.

On some levels, the growing intellectual diversity in hunter-gatherer studies is a sign of a healthy research field that is engaging with new themes and approaches, but it also courts the danger of intellectual fragmentation (Panter-Brick et al. 2001b, 1). After several years of delay, a new CHAGS meeting was held in Liverpool, UK, in June 2013, with its organizers promising to generate reflection on the current state of hunter-gatherer research in relation to the overarching theme of cultural resilience and vulnerability. Individual conference sessions spanned such diverse topics as population genetics of hunter-gatherers, analysis of craft traditions and social learning, through to the language of perception, and the study of forager ritual and dance. It is interesting that all these topics can still happily find a common intellectual 'home' under the banner of hunter-gatherer studies, which remain at the very heart of anthropological enquiry, and serving to illuminate and illustrate many of the basic theoretical problems and their practical solutions (Myers 2004, 175). And looking further ahead, the next CHAGS has already been scheduled for Vienna, Austria, in 2015. Despite these positive developments, it has been some time since there has been an attempt to publish an extended critical overview of hunter-gatherer studies, especially one that combines research into both the archaeology *and* anthropology of hunter-gatherers, and also integrates theoretical perspectives with regional and thematic case studies.

The *Oxford handbook on the archaeology and anthropology of hunter-gatherers* aims to fill this important gap in the current academic literature. It seeks to critically review past developments, but more importantly, to outline some of the most important new directions for future research. In order to meet these goals, the handbook's structure and content is aimed at three overlapping readerships: undergraduate and postgraduate students; early-career researchers requiring detailed introductions to central themes and long-standing debates; and established scholars seeking fresh perspectives and new directions for future research. Finally, it aims to provide a detailed resource for those with a more general interest in hunter-gatherer societies of the past and present.

Handbook: Summary of Contents

The handbook is organized into seven thematic parts, each containing chapters with more detailed case studies. Each part opens with an extended introductory essay, which situates the content of individual chapters within a general intellectual framework, and identifies emerging directions for future research and debate.

Part I establishes a general conceptual framework for the handbook. It undertakes a critical engagement with the underlying theoretical trends that have shaped and informed the development of hunter-gatherer research over recent centuries, and explores the main analytical frames of reference, including ecological and adaptive approaches, historical and particularistic perspectives, as well as key research methodologies such as ethnoarchaeology, and also cross-cutting themes such as hunter-gatherer gender relations.

Part II explores hunting and gathering as a distinctive way of life that formed the general behavioural context for early human evolution. In placing these developments within a long-term global context, it critically engages with evidence for foraging activities among Neanderthal and early modern human societies, and focuses on understanding local developments, extinctions, and transformations, as well as wider population dispersals within several key regions, including Africa, Europe, Asia, and Australia.

Part III investigates the accelerating global transformations that were affecting hunter-gatherer societies in Europe, Africa, and Asia in the terminal Pleistocene and earlier Holocene. It details the enormous climatic and biogeographic shifts that were taking place at this time, and tracks some of the human responses to the local and regional opportunities and constraints that this environmental change generated, including colonization of new regions and continents and the emergence of new kinds of subsistence strategies.

Part IV highlights the innovative characteristics of many prehistoric hunter-gatherer societies, and aims to overturn the lingering assumption that most pre-agricultural societies tended to lack an internal capacity for cultural change. Specifically, it investigates how earlier hunter-gatherers were caught up in the processes that led to humans becoming a fully technological species, highly reliant on the use of material culture, and capable of uniquely artistic expression. Other chapters explore how many of the innovations and cultural developments that tend to be associated with early farming societies actually emerged first in preceding hunter-gatherer societies. These include social complexity, the world's earliest pottery technologies, as well as initial steps towards plant and animal domestications. It was these latter two innovations that eventually generated the potential for full reliance on new agro-pastoral economies, albeit at the expense of earlier foraging traditions. Other chapters explore how hunter-gatherers were responsible for cumulative elaborations in mortuary behaviour, and also for new kinds of coastal adaptation that provided the setting for new forms of symbolic, social, and political elaboration.

Focus then shifts towards understanding the eventual fate—but also the remarkable cultural resilience and behavioural dynamism—of hunter-gatherer societies living in a world increasingly characterized by the relentless expansion of agro-pastoral farming, as well as the challenges and opportunities associated with coeval developments such as the rise of urbanism, nation states, and global empires. Part V explores how some of these earlier developments triggered the emergence of complex and historically contingent forager–farmer interactions in a range of dynamic frontier settings; it also explores how these changes led in some areas to the eventual demise and/or assimilation of older patterns of hunting and gathering, but in others to the rise of increasingly 'commercialized' foraging practices. In many world regions, the rise of exchange-orientated hunter-gatherer societies reflected opportunities for close interaction and balanced coexistence with adjacent farmers, pastoralists, and in more recent periods, with the commercial demands of states and empires.

Part VI builds on these themes, and explores some of the ethnographically documented forager societies of more recent historical periods. Chapters present detailed critical reviews of the ethnohistoric and anthropological understandings of 'modern' hunter-gatherers (after 1500 AD) in several key world regions, including 'classic' study regions like Australia and Africa, which have figured prominently in general discussions about hunter-gatherers and their cultural dynamics, as well as other groups or regions that are relatively new to these international debates. Rather than present general ethnographic descriptions of local populations (see, e.g. Lee and Daly 1999), chapters aim primarily to understand regional research traditions, examining why certain perspectives and approaches have tended to characterize discussion of specific hunter-gatherer societies, and also exploring the range of future work that remains to be done in many of these regions.

Part VII concludes the handbook by tracing out new avenues for the long-term development of hunter-gatherer research. Chapters in this part affirm the diversity and vibrancy in current hunter-gatherer research, methodologically, empirically, and theoretically. Together, authors contributing to this part outline a sense of long-range strategic vision for how the integration of new methods, approaches, and study regions can ensure that the field of hunter-gatherer research continues to generate penetrating insights into the factors underlying human cultural and behavioural diversity, and also how the academic study of hunter-gatherer populations and their archaeological and cultural heritage now increasingly involves active participation by, and engagement with, indigenous peoples and descendant communities right across the globe.

Conclusion

The study of hunter-gatherers has been central to the development of archaeology and anthropology, and has also had increasing relevance for indigenous peoples and 'descendant' communities. Whatever the inherent problems with defining hunter-gatherers, and despite the occasional doom-laden predictions that hunter-gatherer studies would eventually fragment due to intellectual diversification, or simply implode due to lack of new field data, the myriad regions, time periods, and general themes and topics considered throughout the handbook indicate that the research field remains alive and well. Much more important research and critical synthesis lies ahead, and this task will form an important challenge for future generations of archaeologists and anthropologists.

Older images of hunter-gatherers as being a timeless and essentially uniform category of society lacking capacity for development and innovation are now long gone, and the notion of 'hunter-gatherer' perhaps now best serves as a point of analytical departure into the analysis of a remarkably dynamic way of life that expresses a deep and enduring cultural significance, but one that also exhibits enormous diversity, flexibility, and resilience across time and space. Together then, all contributors to the handbook engage with far-reaching questions about the fundamental nature of human subsistence, spirituality, and social life. Their chapters investigate many of the common underpinnings of all human cultural diversity, including the topics of diet, health, and demography, as well as human understandings and perceptions of ecology, materiality, and landscape. All of these are overarching themes that continue to have a pressing contemporary relevance for global humanity.

References

Ames, K. M. 2004. Supposing hunter-gatherer variability. *American Antiquity* 69, 364–74.
Arnold, J. 1996. The archaeology of complex hunter-gatherers. *Journal of Archaeological Method and Theory* 3, 77–126.
Asad, T. 1991. Afterword: from the history of colonial anthropology to the anthropology of western hegemony. In G. W. Stocking, Jr. (ed.), *Colonial situations: essays on the contextualization of ethnographic knowledge*, 314–24. Madison: University of Wisconsin Press.
Barnard, A. 2004. Hunter-gatherers in history, archaeology and anthropology: introductory essay. In A. Barnard (ed.), *Hunter-gatherers in history, archaeology and anthropology*, 1–13. Oxford: Berg.
Bender, B. and Morris, B. 1988. Twenty years of history, evolution and social change in gatherer-hunter studies. In T. Ingold, D. Riches, and J. Woodburn (eds), *Hunters and gatherers: history, evolution and social change*, 1–14. Oxford: Berg.
Binford, L. 1962. Archaeology as anthropology. *American Antiquity* 28, 217–25.
Binford, L. 1965. Archaeological systematics and the study of culture progress. *American Antiquity* 31, 203–10.
Binford, L. 1978. *Nunamiut ethnoarchaeology*. New York: Academic Press.
Binford, L. 1980. Willow smoke and dogs' tails: hunter-gatherer settlement systems and archaeological site formation. *American Antiquity* 45, 4–20.

Binford, L. 2001. *Constructing frames of reference: an analytical method for archaeological theory building using ethnographic and environmental data sets.* Berkeley, CA: University of California Press.

Binford, L. and Johnson, A. 2002. Foreword. In B. Fitzhugh and J. Habu (eds), *Beyond foraging and collecting: evolutionary change in hunter-gatherer settlement systems,* vii–xiii. New York: Kluwer Plenum.

Bird-David, N. 1990. The giving environment: another perspective on the economic system of hunter gatherers. *Current Anthropology* 31, 183–96.

Bird-David, N. 1992. Beyond 'the original affluent society'. *Current Anthropology* 33, 25–47.

Bird-David, N. 1996. Hunter gatherer research and cultural diversity. In S. Kent (ed.), *Cultural diversity among twentieth-century foragers: an African perspective,* 297–304. Cambridge: Cambridge University Press.

Boas, F. 1911. *Race, language and culture.* New York: MacMillan.

Boas, F. 1966. *Kwakiutl ethnography,* ed. H. Codere. Chicago: University of Chicago Press.

Bonsall, C. (ed.) 1990. *The Mesolithic of Europe.* Edinburgh: John Donald.

Boyd, R. and Richerson, P. J. 1985. *Culture and the evolutionary process.* Chicago: University of Chicago Press.

Burch, E. 1994. The future of hunter gatherer research. In E. S. Burch and L. J. Ellana (eds), *Key issues in hunter-gatherer research,* 451–5. Oxford: Berg.

Cannon, A. (ed.) 2011. *Structured worlds: the archaeology of hunter gatherer thought and action.* London: Equinox.

Clark, J. G. D. 1939. *Archaeology and society.* London: Methuen.

Clark, J. G. D. 1954. *Excavations at Star Carr.* Cambridge: Cambridge University Press.

Clarke, D. L. 1968. *Analytical archaeology.* London: Meuthen.

Clifford, J. 1988. *The predicament of culture.* Cambridge, MA: Harvard University Press.

Cunningham, J. 2003. Transcending the 'obnoxious spectator': a case for processual pluralism in ethnoarchaeology. *Journal of Anthropological Archaeology* 22, 389–410.

David, N. and Kramer, C. 2001. *Ethnoarchaeology in action.* Cambridge: Cambridge University Press.

Durham, W. H. 1991. *Coevolution: genes, culture and human diversity.* Stanford, CA: Stanford University Press.

Durkheim, E. 1915 [1912]. *The Elementary Forms of the Religious Life.* London: George Allen & Unwin.

Eren, M. I. (ed.) 2012. *Hunter-gatherer behavior: human response during the Younger Dryas.* Walnut Creek, CA: Left Coast Press.

Fewster, K. J. 2001. Petso's field: ethnoarchaeology and agency. In K. J. Fewster and M. Zvelebil (eds), *Ethnoarchaeology and hunter-gatherers: pictures at an exhibition,* 81–90. Oxford: British Archaeological Reports International Series 995.

Geertz, C. 1965. The impact of the concept of culture on the concept of man. In J. R. Platt (ed.), *New views of man,* 93–118. Chicago: University of Chicago Press.

Geertz, C. 1973. *The interpretation of culture. Selected essays.* New York: Basic.

Gould, R. A. 1969. *Yiwara: foragers of the Australian desert.* London: Collins.

Hawkes, C. 1954. Archaeological theory and method: some suggestions from the Old World. *American Anthropologist* 56, 155–68.

Hayden, B. 1981. Research and development in the stone age: technological transitions among hunter/gatherers. *Current Anthropology* 2, 519–48.

Headland, T. N. and Reid, L. A. 1989. Hunter-gatherers and their neighbors from prehistory to the present. *Current Anthropology* 30, 43–66.

Hitchcock, R. K. and Biesele, M. 2000. Introduction. In P. P. Schweitzer, M. Biesele, and R. K. Hitchcock (eds), *Hunters and gatherers in the modern world: conflict, resistance, and self-determination*, 1–28. Oxford: Berghahn.

Ingold, T. 2000. *The perception of the environment: essays in livelihood, dwelling and skill*. London: Routledge.

Kelly, R. 1995. *The foraging spectrum: diversity in hunter-gatherer lifeways*. Washington, DC Smithsonian Institution.

Kent, S. 1992. The current forager controversy: real versus ideal views of hunter-gatherers. *Man* 27, 45–70.

Kent, S. (ed.) 1996. *Cultural diversity among twentieth century foragers*. Cambridge: Cambridge University Press.

Kroeber, A. L. 1925. *Handbook of the Indians of California*. Washington, DC: Bureau of American Ethnology Bulletin 78.

Larsson, L., Kindgren, H., Knutsson, K., Loeffler, D., and Akerlund, A. (eds) 2000. *Mesolithic on the move*. Oxford: Oxbow Books.

Layton, R. and Ucko, P (eds) 1999. *The archaeology and anthropology of landscape: shaping your landscape*. London: Routledge.

Lee, R. 1992. Art, science, or politics? The crisis in hunter-gatherer studies. *American Anthropologist* 94, 31–54.

Lee, R. and Daly, R. 1999. Foragers and others. In R. Lee and R. Daly (eds), *The Cambridge encyclopedia of hunters and gatherers*, 1–19. Cambridge: Cambridge University Press.

Lee, R. and DeVore, I. (eds) 1968. *Man the hunter*. Chicago: Aldine.

Lévi-Strauss, C. 1969 [1949]. *Les Structures élémentaires de la parenté*. Paris: de Gruyter [*The Elementary Structures of Kinship*, ed. Rodney Needham, trans. J. H. Bell, J. R. von Sturmer, and Rodney Needham, 1969].

Lowie, R. H. 1935. *The Crow Indians*. New York: Farrar & Rinehart.

Lubbock, J. 1865. *Pre-historic times: as illustrated by ancient remains, and the manners and customs of modern savages*. London: Williams & Norgate.

Lyman, R. L., O'Brien, M. J., and Dunnel, R. C. 1997. *The rise and fall of culture history*. London: Plenum Press.

McCartan, S. B., Schulting, R. J., Warren, G., and Woodman, P. C. (eds) 2008. *Mesolithic horizons*. Oxford: Oxbow Books.

Malinowski, B. 1913. *The family among the Australian Aborigines: a sociological study*. London: University of London Press.

Mauss, M. and Beauchat, H. 1979 [1906]. *Seasonal variations of the Eskimo*. London: Routledge & Kegan Paul.

Mithen, S. 1996. *Prehistory of the mind*. London: Thames and Hudson.

Morgan, L. H. 1963. [1877] *Ancient society*, ed. E. Leacock. New York: Meridian.

Myers, L. D. 2004. Subtle shifts and radical transformations in hunter-gatherer research in American anthropology: Julian Steward's contributions and achievements. In A. Barnard (ed.), *Hunter-gatherers in history, archaeology and anthropology*, 1–14. Oxford: Berg.

Panter-Brick, C., Layton, R. H., and Rowley-Conwy, P. (eds) 2001a. *Hunter-gatherers: an interdisciplinary perspective*. Cambridge: Cambridge University Press.

Panter-Brick, C., Layton, R. H., and Rowley-Conwy, P. 2001b. Lines of enquiry. In C. Panter-Brick, R. H. Layton, and P. Rowley-Conwy (eds), *Hunter-gatherers: an interdisciplinary perspective*, 1–11. Cambridge: Cambridge University Press.

Price, T. D. 1981. Complexity in 'non-complex' societies. In S. E. van der Leeuw (ed.), *Archaeological approaches to the study of complexity*, 55–99. Amsterdam: Universiteit van Amsterdam.

Price, T. D. and Brown, J. (eds) 1985. *Prehistoric hunter-gatherers: the emergence of cultural complexity*. Orlando, FL: Academic Press.

Radcliffe-Brown, A. R. 1922. *The Andaman islanders: a study in social anthropology*. Cambridge: Cambridge University Press.

Radcliffe-Brown, A. R. 1931. The social organisation of Australian tribes. *Oceania* 1, 34–63, 322–41, 426–56.

Richerson, P. J. and Boyd, R. 2005. *Not by genes alone: how culture transformed human evolution*. London and Berkeley, CA: University of California Press.

Rowley-Conwy, P. 2007. *From genesis to prehistory: the archaeological three age system and its contested reception in Denmark, Britain and Ireland*. Oxford: Oxford University Press.

Sahlins, M. 1968. Notes on the original affluent society. In R. Lee and I DeVore (eds), *Man the hunter*, 85–9. Chicago: Aldine.

Sahlins, M. 1972. *Stone age economics*. Chicago: Aldine-Atherton.

Schweitzer, P. 2000. Silence and other misunderstandings: Russian anthropology, western hunter-gatherer debates, and Siberian peoples. In P. P. Schweitzer, M. Biesele, and R. K. Hitchcock (eds), *Hunters and gatherers in the modern world: conflict, resistance and self-determination*, 29–54. New York: Berghahn.

Service, E. R. 1962. *Primitive social organization: an evolutionary perspective*. New York: Random House.

Service, E. R. 1966. *The hunters*. Englewood Cliffs, NJ: Prentice-Hall.

Service, E. R. 1975. *Origins of the state and civilisation*. New York: Norton.

Shennan, S. J. 2002. *Genes, memes and human history: Darwinian archaeology and cultural evolution*. London: Thames and Hudson.

Shennan, S. J. 2004. An evolutionary perspective on agency in archaeology. In A. Gardner (ed.), *Agency uncovered: archaeological perspectives on social agency, power, and being human*, 139–89. London: University College London Press.

Shennan, S. J. (ed.) 2009. *Pattern and process in cultural evolution*. Berkeley, CA: University of California Press.

Sollas, W. 1911. *Ancient hunters and their modern representatives*. London: MacMillan.

Solway, J. and Lee, R. 1990. Foragers, genuine or spurious? *Current Anthropology* 31, 109–45.

Spielman, K. A. and Eder, J. F. 1994. Hunters and farmers: then and now. *Annual Review of Anthropology* 23, 303–23.

Steward, J. H. 1936. The economic and social basis of primitive bands. In R. H. Lowie (ed.), *Essays on anthropology in honour of Alfred Louis Kroeber*, 311–50. Berkeley, CA: University of California Press.

Steward, J. H. 1938. *Basin-Plateau Aboriginal sociopolitical groups, bulletin*, 120. Washington, DC: Bureau of American Ethnology.

Steward, J. H. 1955. *Theory of culture change*. Urbana, IL: University of Illinois Press.

Suttles, W. 1968. Coping with abundance: subsistence on the Northwest Coast. In B. Lee and I. DeVore (eds), *Man the hunter*, 56–68. Chicago: Aldine.

Suzman, J. 2004. Hunting for histories: rethinking historicity in the western Kalahari. In A. Barnard (ed.), *Hunter-gatherers in history, archaeology and anthropology*, 201–16. Oxford: Berg.

Testart, A. 1982. The significance of food storage among hunter-gatherers: residence patterns, population densities, and social inequalities. *Current Anthropology* 23, 523–37.

Thomas, J. 1988. Neolithic explanations revisited: the Mesolithic–Neolithic transition in Britain and south Scandinavia. *Proceedings of the Prehistoric Society* 54, 59–66.

Tilley, C. 1994. *A phenomenology of landscape: places, paths, and monuments*. Oxford: Berg.

Trigger, B. 2006. *A history of archaeological thought* (2nd edition). Cambridge: Cambridge University Press.

Turner, V. 1967. *Forest of symbols: aspects of Ndembu ritual*. Ithaca, NY: Cornell University Press.

Weber, A., Katzenburg, M. A., and Schurr, T. (eds) 2010. *Prehistoric hunter-gatherers of the Baikal Region, Siberia*. Philadelphia, PA: University of Pennsylvania Press.

White, L. 1959. *The evolution of culture*. New York: McGraw-Hill.

Whitley, D. 2000. *The art of the shaman: rock art of California*. Salt Lake City: University of Utah Press.

Whitley, D. (ed.) 2001. *Handbook of rock art research*. Waltnut Creek, CA: AltaMira Press.

Wilmsen, E. N. 1983. The ecology of illusion: anthropological foraging in the Kalahari. *Reviews in Anthropology* 10, 9–20.

Wilmsen, E. N. 1989. *Land filled with flies: a political economy of the Kalahari*. Chicago: University of Chicago Press.

Wilmsen, E. and Denbow, J. 1990. Paradigmatic history of San-speaking peoples and current attempts at revision. *Current Anthropology* 31, 489–524.

Wissler C,. 1917. *The American Indian*. New York: Douglas C. McMurtrie.

Woodburn, J. 1980. Hunter gatherers today and reconstruction of the past. In A. Gellner (ed.), *Soviet and western anthropology*, 95–117. London: Duckworth.

Woodburn, J. 1982. Egalitarian societies. *Man* 17, 431–51.

Yellen, J. 1977. *Archaeological approaches to the present*. New York: Academic Press.

Yesner, D. R. 1980. Maritime hunter-gatherers: ecology and prehistory. *Current Anthropology* 21, 727–50.

Zvelebil, M. (ed.) 1986. *Hunters in transition: Mesolithic societies of temperate Eurasia and their transition to farming*. Cambridge: Cambridge University Press.

Zvelebil, M. 1998. What's in a name: the Mesolithic, the Neolithic and social change at the Mesolithic–Neolithic transition. In M. Edmonds and C. Richards (eds), *Understanding the Neolithic of northwest Europe*, 1–36. Glasgow: Cruithne Press.

Zvelebil, M. 2005. Homo habitus: agency, structure and the transformation of tradition in the constitution of the TRB foraging-farming communities in the North European plain (ca 4500–2000 BC). *Documenta Praehistorica* 32, 87–101.

Zvelebil, M. 2008 Innovating hunter-gatherers: the Mesolithic in the Baltic. In G. Bailey and P. Spikins (eds), *The Mesolithic in Europe*, 18–59. Cambridge: Cambridge University Press.

Zvelebil, M. and Rowley-Conwy, P. 1984. Transition to farming in northern Europe: a hunter gatherer perspective. *Norwegian Archaeological Review* 17, 104–28.

PART I
THEORETICAL FRAMEWORKS

CHAPTER 1

ANALYTICAL FRAMES OF REFERENCE IN HUNTER-GATHERER RESEARCH

PETER JORDAN AND VICKI CUMMINGS

THE study of hunting and gathering societies has a rich and extended intellectual history. This part of the handbook considers the origins of the term 'hunter-gatherer' and explores the rise of the subject as a distinct field of interdisciplinary enquiry. It also explores some of its main research trajectories and considers how these traditions have evolved and changed, and also how they continue to structure current academic enquiry.

The first two chapters look at the intellectual developments and wider cultural and historical contexts within which the concept of 'hunter-gatherers' as a distinct category of society first emerged (Barnard; Pluciennik). The next two chapters examine the main trajectories in current hunter-gatherer research, the first emphasizing the role of adaptation and ecology (Garvey and Bettinger), and a second, more recent critique of this approach, advocating a return to more particularistic analysis of contingent historical sequences, combined with a renewed emphasis on human perceptions and lived experiences (Cannon).

Archaeologists studying past hunter-gatherer societies have always made widespread use of ethnographic information about contemporary hunter-gatherers in order to inform their research and strengthen their interpretations, and have increasingly conducted their own ethnographic fieldwork, using various forms of 'analogic' reasoning to build the results into their archaeological explanations. The chapter by Lane provides a comprehensive critical review of the expansive hunter-gatherer 'ethnoarchaeological' literature, highlighting both its achievements and also scope for diversification of future research themes and better integration of results derived from different starting assumptions. Part I of the handbook is concluded by a retrospective review of the increasing role played by gender studies in hunter-gatherer research (Sterling and see Jarvenpa and Brumbach in Part VII). Together, these intellectual legacies, overarching research trajectories, and cross-cutting themes provide the remaining parts of the handbook with its main analytical frames of reference.

Foundational Concepts: Defining 'Hunter-Gatherers'

In its narrowest sense, the term 'hunter-gatherers' provides a simple means of classifying human cultural diversity according to economic and subsistence criteria. However, these concepts were only able to emerge and take hold within specific historical contexts. Barnard and Pluciennik both examine the intellectual—and also the wider social and political—developments that made the emergence of the term possible, but they do so from slightly different perspectives, and reach contrasting conclusions.

'Hunter-Gatherers' as an Enduring Definition

Barnard presents a more linear analysis, tracing the slow emergence of the concept of 'hunter-gatherers' over recent centuries, and pinpoints a point of intellectual crystallization within the eighteenth-century Scottish Enlightenment. Here, thinkers like Adam Smith were considering basic Enlightenment challenges such as the links between subsistence activities and forms of social life, and were starting to identify hunter-gatherers as being able to live in small-scale but viable societies, possessing fundamental differences to societies subsisting by pastoralism or agriculture. In this period, economics was starting to be regarded as the primary driving force of social interaction, and also the precipitator of evolution of human society into new forms of existence. In fact, it was this combination of subsistence categories to define cultural diversity, and the gradual emergence of social evolutionist thinking that enabled hunter-gatherer studies to emerge as a distinct discipline. In the nineteenth century, we start to see the concerted consolidation of 'unilinear' evolutionist thinking—the idea that all humanity had proceeded through the same series of highly generalized and distinct stages, perhaps best exemplified by L. H. Morgan's three-stage schema of evolution, defined by the stages of 'savagery', 'barbarism', and eventually 'civilization', each with three further sub-periods. Hunter-gatherers of the archaeological past and ethnographic present were, of course, allocated to the lower rungs of this evolutionary ladder. In the middle part of the twentieth century this was followed by the emergence of a new form of 'universal' evolutionism, in which scholars like V. G. Childe more broadly defined 'revolutionary' stages in global human development, for example, with the replacement of hunter-gatherers by an expanding tide of Neolithic farmers (1936; 1942; 1956; 1962).

A more fundamental shift in hunter-gatherer research took place with the work of Julian Steward (1955), who introduced the idea of 'multilinear' cultural evolution through his analysis of hunter-gatherer groups. Although Steward's approach built on, and consolidated, an older culture–area research tradition, he was responsible for moving anthropology away from the 'particularist' approach that had been developed by Franz Boas, and that saw each culture as being distinct (see below). In contrast, Steward argued that people are in large part defined by what they do for a living, and examined how societies use technology to adapt to specific environments, so that groups living in similar environments developed similar features, although their technology will be a product of history (see below).

Steward's ideas were enormously influential among a new generation of scholars, and by the 1960s had led directly to the dawn of hunter-gatherer studies, and also to its defining interest in questions of adaptation, ecology, and associated impacts on social life, culminating in the 1966 *Man the hunter* conference (Lee and DeVore 1968). Although Steward had set the scene for the rise of modern hunter-gatherer studies as a distinct sub-discipline, doubts were already creeping in about terminology and the variability and distinctiveness of hunter-gatherers from the outset. However, a basic concept of 'hunter-gatherers' survives, even though it has gone through a series of sustained critiques and re-evaluations. Barnard concludes that the notion of 'hunter-gatherers' is still needed in academic discourse, despite its inherent shortcomings and problems of definition.

'Hunter-Gatherers' as an Outdated Concept

In contrast, Pluciennik covers broadly similar ground, but develops a broader and more contextual analysis of the concept of hunter-gatherers, reaching contrasting conclusions about its future analytical utility. He grounds his discussion in the historical processes of colonialism and capitalism, and in emerging concerns in seventeenth-century Europe about property rights and the economy, all of which generated a series of 'othering' discourses of which hunter-gatherers were only one element. He therefore situates an early formulation of ideas about hunter-gatherers in the growing 'improvement' movements of the seventeenth century (i.e. somewhat earlier than Barnard), which was both antithetical to hunting and gathering societies, but also constructed them as both a distinct and a 'lower' kind of society. Along with Barnard, he concludes that these initial subsistence classifications also needed the critical injection of social evolutionary thinking to condense and simplify the overall schema, and to place hunter-gatherers as being the furthest from civilization, and also the earliest in absolute historical, stadial, and also evolutionary terms. In particular, these emerging ideas about hunter-gatherers were filled out and developed against a looming backdrop of colonialism; the notion of 'hunter-gatherers' also provided a useful point of contrast with European pinnacles of cultural achievement.

Pluciennik's analysis concludes that the notion of 'hunter-gatherers' is a rather crude, typological, and inherently value-laden means of classifying human cultural diversity from an external 'othering' perspective; he also explores comparative case studies from Greece, southern Asia, and China to demonstrate the term's historically contingent ancestry, but also to signal that there are many other productive ways of conceptualizing historical human difference and exploring cultural diversity. In this way, Pluciennik's research illustrates a central paradox in current hunter-gatherer research, namely that the term emerged from an earlier scientific passion for classification that was central in the Enlightenment, and that it was also a key 'base-line' element in the hierarchical schema that served to illustrate progressive social evolutionary thinking. The term has clearly outgrown most of these earlier definitions and associations, but the concept of 'hunter-gatherers' still has an enduring intellectual currency, whether as a point of analytical departure, as a useful shorthand for broad categorizations of different societies or as the general phases in long-term human history, or merely as a deeply outdated notion that nonetheless is worthy of study, if only as a focus of historiographic interest (as Pluciennik concludes).

Divergent Hunter-Gatherer Research Trajectories: Adaptive Behaviour and Social Action

'Adaptive' Approaches

The study of adaptation and human–environment relations has been central to hunter-gatherer studies since the pioneering work of Julian Steward, and the rise of New Archaeology. Garvey and Bettinger provide a detailed review of this rapidly evolving research tradition. They regard current hunter-gatherer studies as the direct intellectual descendant of earlier traditions in American anthropology, which emphasized systematic ethnographic fieldwork, and focused on identifying and documenting the enormous cultural diversity that was present among indigenous groups living in highly different environments, many of whom subsisted by hunting, fishing, and gathering.

Engaging with this cultural diversity made Franz Boas highly sceptical of the simple unilinear social evolutionary schema that were popular in Europe in the later nineteenth century, especially as these frameworks tended to homogenize all hunter-gatherers into a single stage of development. He also championed 'historical particularism' and argued that each culture was unique and should be studied on its own terms. However, ideas about the role of environment as a causal factor generating broad cultural patterns matured slowly into an eventual concern with rigorous analysis of adaptation. Clark Wissler and Alfred Kroeber worked after Boas, and began to note broad 'culture–area' patterns; like Boas, they also saw that North American hunter-gatherers were not homogeneous like progressive social evolutionists had predicted, but that there were important regional differences, and more importantly, that specific suites of cultural traits tended to coincide with the distributions of major food resources.

During the early twentieth century, Garvey and Bettinger traced a growing anthropological interest in culture–environment relations, although this tended to assume a kind of 'environmental possibilism', where the local ecology set various limits on local cultures but did not determine the specific patterns that emerged; however, they also noted that Kroeber and Lowie, who were leading proponents of cross-cultural studies, regarded environmental factors as being too complex to resolve at that specific time. It was in this tradition of research that Julian Steward became increasingly active, particularly through his ethnographic work among hunter-gatherers of the Great Basin. Steward argued that understanding cultural adaptations required systematic comparison of groups living in similar environments, and through his work with hunter-gatherer cultures, was able to conclude that human cultures were not a patchwork of accidents and connections, but that similar adaptations emerged in similar environments (Steward 1955), an approach that became known as 'cultural ecology'. This was not, as critics often asserted, an argument for environmental determinism—Steward made an important conceptual distinction between (a) the technologies that people use to adapt to a particular environment—these play a very important role in adaptations, and form the 'cultural core', but are historically contingent; and (b) the external environments to which people adapt. In this way, groups can potentially develop very different techno-environmental interactions, generating *multi*-linear patterns of evolution, rather than *uni*-linear patterns of progressive social evolution, which Steward strongly rejected.

Garvey and Bettinger illustrate how Steward's cultural ecology had a profound and lasting influence on hunter-gatherer studies. His work was read widely by a new generation of scholars, including Lewis Binford, architect of New Archaeology, and leading proponent of hunter-gatherer ethnoarchaeology (see Lane), who argued that archaeologists should engage themselves with the scientific analysis of long-term human adaptations, as material residues of these events and processes were more readily recoverable through excavation and analysis than other features of human activity, such as spirituality and belief. Steward's cultural ecology, and the associated research tradition of neofunctionalism, also inspired other anthropologists to undertake sustained fieldwork to study and record how diverse groups—many of whom were hunter-gatherers—were adapted to their environments. Much earlier debate about hunter-gatherers had proceeded without good field data, and from the 1960s researchers started to meet regularly to discuss ideas and compare field data about hunter-gatherers; the *Man the hunter* conference was one such meeting (Lee and DeVore 1968). This tried to bring together all known knowledge of hunter-gatherer lifeways, best summarized in the notion of 'nomadic style', but also marked a tipping point into a new and coordinated hunter-gatherer research programme that concerned itself with understanding culture–environment interactions among populations that subsisted by hunting and gathering. In this way, Steward's legacy also ensured the persistence of a strong and overarching adaptive focus in hunter-gatherer studies that endures to this day.

Garvey and Bettinger also trace how the field has evolved and changed over recent decades. The weakness of cultural ecology—and neofunctionalism—was that it tended to assume a group-level process of natural selection to account for observed cultural patterns, and did not focus on selection at the level of the individual. As a result, cultural ecology could only generate *post hoc* descriptive accounts, but could not really explain the causes of new adaptations, which had to be sought among variations in the behaviour of specific individuals. To study these processes, researchers adopted a range of new models, theory, and methods from biology, generating 'human behavioural ecology', which argues that human behaviour is individually motivated and subject to natural selection.

This research tradition has expanded and diversified to cover analysis of subsistence strategies, technology, and also social and reproductive dynamics among hunter-gatherer societies of the archaeological record and ethnographic present, either by systematic observation, measurement, and modelling of observed behaviours, or by extrapolating behavioural strategies from analysis of patterning in the archaeological record. Finally, Garvey and Bettinger bring their review right up to date by noting new developments in 'selectionist archaeology' and the application of 'dual-inheritance theory', both of which have some overlaps with human behavioural ecology, all of which generate testable hypotheses, and adopt a rigorous scientific approach to the study of human behavioural variability and change. Together, these different perspectives are united by more general attempts to study human cultural diversity through the application of Neo-Darwinian approaches, which in time—they argue—could form a single unifying framework for the wider social sciences. They conclude that the study of hunter-gatherer societies and their adaptations—both past and present—is absolutely central to the further development of this intellectually diverse and thriving research field.

'Interpretive' Approaches

Cannon identifies a contrasting and more 'interpretive' research direction. His chapter outlines a series of research agendas that in many ways follow on from Pluciennik's conclusion that there are more productive ways of studying human experience and cultural difference than the crude and categorical distinctions expressed in such terms as 'hunter-gatherer'. For both Cannon and Pluciennik then, the term 'hunter-gatherer' or 'hunter-gatherer archaeology' represents more of a useful point of interpretive departure into more localized studies of specific and contingent historical trajectories, as well as the cumulative human actions and the diverse lived experiences that these histories contain. For Cannon, the real aim is to write human histories that can be both particularist and comparative, and also as rich, unique, and 'multi-vocal' as any other world region or periods of economic history; the fact that they can be broadly labelled 'hunter-gatherer' histories is more of an incidental outcome than a central research concern with understanding a specific 'kind' of society, which is categorized according to rather simple subsistence criteria.

Cannon suggests that *three* key developments have opened the way for this more particularistic and interpretive hunter-gatherer research agenda. The first was the 1980s 'revisionist critique' in hunter-gatherer studies, which overturned any lingering assumptions that ethnographically documented hunter-gatherers were 'primitive', 'isolated', or 'pristine' survivals from earlier phases of human social or economic life; instead, local historical trajectories, long-term and widespread forager–farmer and forager–'other' contacts were highlighted, and the roles of hunter-gatherers were increasingly situated within wider regional and global socio-economic and political systems (Shott 1992; Schrire 1995). These anthropological developments were also linked with coeval developments in archaeology, which saw new interests in the dynamics of prehistoric forager–farmer contacts and the active roles played by hunter-gatherers in major transitions such as the dispersal of farming and new forms of material culture. The current consensus is now that all documented hunter-gatherer societies—of the prehistoric past or present—are the products of unique and dynamic histories, which often include external impacts, as well as internal developments.

The challenge then is how best to explore and describe these extended and highly contingent historical sequences, and Cannon identifies two further productive developments. One reflects the wider post-modern critique of academic objectivity and the validity of cross-cultural analyses in archaeology and anthropology. Incorporated into the initial post-processual archaeology critique and its maturation into a humanized 'interpretive' archaeology, they have generated new questions and theoretical perspectives into social identity and spirituality, how people think, perceive, and engage meaningfully with the world, and also highlight the roles of human agency and social practice and their contributions to historically contingent culture change. To date, however, application of this body of interpretive theory to hunter-gatherer case studies has been rather limited, and so Cannon highlights a third important development, which is the enormous and ongoing growth in basic empirical datasets in many areas of the world that often include extended phases of hunter-gatherer archaeology. These detailed sequences now provide rich and timely potential for applying many of the new questions and interpretive approaches that he has described.

Again, we see a potential paradox in the rejection of the term 'hunter-gatherers', with all its economic categorizations and unilinear social evolutionary associations, but also in the shift away from scientific analysis of foragers' adaptive behaviour (see Garvey and Bettinger), and towards development of Pluciennik's broader agenda of using the term as a useful point of departure into a more interpretive historical exploration of cultural diversity and human experience. Cannon, however, senses enormous opportunities here for the writing of new kinds of hunter-gatherer histories, which can be both particularistic and 'multi-vocal', as well as comparative and empirical.

Cross-Cutting Research Themes: Ethnoarchaeology, Analogic Reasoning, and Gender Studies

In the final chapters in this part, authors engage with two *cross-cutting* themes in hunter-gatherer research that have played central roles within the development of the field, and both of which increasingly transcend the 'adaptive' and 'interpretive' streams of research examined above.

Ethnoarchaeology

Archaeologists have always made widespread use of ethnographic parallels and insights in their research and interpretation of prehistoric hunter-gatherers, and as a result of this, the two disciplines have developed close working relationships. From the mid-twentieth century, archaeologists have done their own 'ethnoarchaeological' fieldwork in order to directly collect ethnographic datasets that are more suitable for their archaeological research questions (see David and Kramer 2001). Ethnoarchaeology is therefore the ethnographic field research conducted by trained archaeologists working with living communities. Many seminal ethnoarchaelogical studies have focused on contemporary hunter-gatherers, their lifeways, and economic behaviours, and have thereby made a major contribution to hunter-gatherer studies more generally.

Lane opens his chapter by considering the foundational framework for ethnoarchaeology—'analogical reasoning'. This approach is central to all archaeological interpretation, and ethnoarchaeology emerged as a means of strengthening the analogies that could be drawn between field observations made among living communities, and the inferences that could be made about non-observable behaviours in the past, and which are only preserved in the form of the archaeological record.

Ethnoarchaeology became a central tool in the New Archaeology research agenda, and was promoted as a means for developing low-level inferences ('Middle Range Theory') about specific patterns of ethnographically observable behaviour, and the likely material remains that would be generated; these insights, in turn, would facilitate a more precise understanding of the events and processes that had generated the archaeological record.

Given these strong links with New Archaeology, Lane notes that much subsequent work has continued to focus on rigorous documentation of behaviours combined with scientific analyses to test hypotheses and to model its adaptive values (see Garvey and Bettinger).

Contemporary hunter-gatherers were initially targeted as representing rather direct behavioural analogues for prehistoric foragers. For example, there has been a sustained focus on studying foragers living in African savannah habitats, and on activities such as carcass processing, hunting and scavenging, and associated site formation patterns; this has been motivated by the desire to build robust analogies between these contemporary groups and the occupation of similar habitats by Plio-Pleistocene hominins during earlier phases of human evolution, all of which strengthens correspondences between the ethnographic and archaeological settings. Similarly, ethnoarchaeological studies were conducted among hunter-gatherers by Binford (1978; 1983), but as an archaeologist, he was primarily interested in understanding Mousterian assemblages from European Middle Palaeolithic, and so chose to do ethnoarchaeological fieldwork among the Alaskan Nunamiut. These groups were also big game hunters and occupied similar environments to those of Palaeolithic Europe.

Lane provides a detailed review of central themes in the 'mainstream' hunter-ethnoarchaeological literature, including: site structure and formation processes; mobility strategies, sedentism, and seasonality; tool-kit diversity; butchery strategies, carcass processing, and the transport of faunal assemblages. Much of this work replicates the broadly 'adaptive' focus that was established by New Archaeology, but that has since diversified substantially. Despite this, much early ethnoarchaeological work was criticized by post-processual archaeologists for ignoring the fact that many aspects of material culture and social interaction are 'meaningfully constituted', and reflect contingent values and beliefs, and not just adaptive processes. As a result, the hunter-gatherer ethnoarchaeological literature is strongly biased towards 'adaptive' approaches, with only very few case studies focusing on material style and identity, mortuary behaviour, symbolic uses of space, and agency, spirituality, and belief more generally (all of which could be grouped under Cannon's broadly 'interpretive' research agenda).

Given the increasing theoretical diversity in hunter-gatherer studies, archaeologists working in different research traditions now tend to undertake ethnographic fieldwork and use ethnographic analogies in *two* broadly contrasting ways. While both start out with what are assumed to be 'universal' features of human existence, these are different: (a) some start with the assumption that culture serves as an extrasomatic means of adaptation ('adaptative' approaches); or else (b) they emphasize the symbolic constitution of human social action ('interpretive' approaches). In addition, archaeologists have also used a third kind of ethnographic analogy—direct historical analogies. These assume a direct cultural continuity between the prehistoric populations that generated a local archaeological record and the 'descendant' communities and their ethnographically documented behaviours that continue to exist in the same region (Cunningham 2003). Lane also emphasizes that all these forms of analogical reasoning can be combined and integrated, and that archaeological interpretations will be strengthened by using a multi-level analogic analysis.

Lane concludes that ethnoarchaeological research transcends archaeology and anthropology, and has substantially boosted the study of hunter-gatherers worldwide, making fundamental theoretical and empirical contributions to central debates about forager lifeways. In particular, the inherent emphasis on fine-grained documentation of behaviours and material residues has led directly to seminal publications and major breakthroughs in the analysis of variability in hunter-gatherers and their human–environment relations. Lane also points out that there is an urgent need for more 'interpretive' ethnoarchaeological work among hunter-gatherers, and that this will raise interesting challenges about how best to integrate divergent insights into adaptive behaviours and meaningful social action. Today, ethnoarchaeology remains a vibrant and exciting research tradition, one that has been situated at the very heart and soul of hunter-gatherer studies as they have evolved and diversified over recent decades; this important 'vanguard' role looks set to continue, as Jarvenpa and Brumbach highlight in their chapter in the concluding part of this handbook.

Gender Studies

In the final chapter of Part I, Sterling explores a further cross-cutting theme, and develops a retrospective exploration of the impact of gender studies on hunter-gatherer research. She starts by tracing initial reactions to the *Man the hunter* conference and volume (Lee and DeVore 1968), many of which fundamentally questioned the roles and perceptions of men and women in forager societies, as well as the contributions of hunting and also gathering to subsistence and community life more generally. By critically reviewing the development of gender-related themes and topics in the CHAGS (Conference on Hunting and Gathering Societies) conferences and its associated publications over a number of decades, she is able to chart the steady integration and consolidation of gender research among hunter-gatherer societies, but also note that this was achieved more quickly in ethnographic studies than in archaeology, where such research has lagged due to the interpretive challenges associated with working with archaeological data where direct behavioural observation is not possible but must be inferred. While Sterling's study places gender research among hunter-gatherers in a more historical context, the review is also complemented by Jarvenpa and Brumbach's chapter in Part VII, which explores the directions that new work on gender, identity, and the sexual division of labour is taking in current hunter-gatherer research. Clearly, gender-related research has undergone enormous development in hunter-gatherer studies and continues to form a vibrant research frontier, bringing together anthropology, ethnoarchaeology, and archaeology, and also transcending all the main research trajectories, including adaptive (Garvey and Bettinger) and interpretive approaches (Cannon).

Conclusion

This opening part of the handbook demonstrates that the concept of 'hunter-gatherers' has a complex, controversial, and highly contingent history. However, after seminal publications by Julian Steward in the 1950s, 'hunter-gatherer studies' eventually emerged as a distinct field of interdisciplinary enquiry in the 1960s, these developments closely allied on the one hand with the research agenda of the New Archaeology, and also linked more generally to attempts to lead anthropology away from an enduring Boasian concern with historical particularism and into more scientific and analytical directions. Since the 1966 *Man the hunter* conference (Lee and DeVore 1968), the field has weathered a series of 'internal' critiques, such as the 1970s/1980s debates about hunter-gatherer variability and social complexity, and also sustained external attacks such as the 1980s revisionist 'Kalaharai Debate' about the role of history, colonialism, and culture contact (and see Hitchcock). As a result, hunter-gatherer studies have developed into many divergent directions. The inherent problems with defining hunter-gatherers remain, but whether as a distinct kind of society, or as a point of analytical departure, the term remains in widespread academic usage.

The current diversity in current hunter-gatherer research is also reflected by an enormous breadth in intellectual orientation, although authors in Part I make it clear that a useful distinction can still be made between 'adaptive' and 'interpretive' approaches. While the former research stream might be argued to represent the direct intellectual descendants of Julian Steward, and of hunter-gatherer studies as originally conceived (i.e. as being a scientific and cross-cultural comparative project, including a focus on measurable aspects of human foraging behaviour and its scientific analysis and explanation), the latter consists of a more diverse set of 'interpretive' approaches, whose concern with the study of hunter-gatherer societies is more incidental than explicit, and which have a primary concern with exploring particularistic histories, lived experiences, and social action.

Whatever the specific theoretical orientation adopted, this part also highlights the richness and vibrancy of current hunter-gatherer studies, both in the study of the archaeological past, and in the study of contemporary societies who practise hunting and gathering. Although there have been numerous signs of the field fractioning and diverging—triggering prediction of its inherent demise—this handbook makes it clear that there remains an abiding interest in hunter-gatherers, and in a way of life that once defined all human existence prior to the rise of farming and urban life only a few millennia ago.

References

Binford, L. 1978. *Nunamiut ethnoarchaeology*. New York: Academic Press.
Binford, L. 1983. *In pursuit of the past*. London: Thames and Hudson.
Childe, V. G. 1936. *Man makes himself*. London: Watts.
Childe, V. G. 1942. *What happened in history*. Harmondsworth: Penguin Books.
Childe, V. G. 1956. The new stone age. In H. L. Shapiro (ed.), *Man, culture, and society*, 95–111. New York: Oxford University Press.
Childe, V. G. 1962. Old world prehistory: Neolithic. In S. Tax (ed.), *Anthropology today*, 152–68. Chicago, IL: University of Chicago Press.
Cunnningham, J. J. 2003. Transcending the 'obnoxious spectator': a case for processual pluralism in ethnoarchaeology. *Journal of Anthropological Archaeology* 22, 389–410.
David, N. and Kramer, C. 2001. *Ethnoarchaeology in action*. Cambridge: Cambridge University Press.
Lee, R. and DeVore, I. (eds) 1968. *Man the hunter*. Chicago: Aldine.
Schrire, C. 1995. *Digging through darkness: chronicles of an archaeologist*. Charlottesville: University of Virginia Press.
Shott, M. 1992. On recent trends in the anthropology of foragers: Kalahari revisionism and its archaeological implications. *Man* 27, 843–71.
Steward, J. 1955. *Theory of culture change: the methodology of multilinear evolution*. Urbana, IL: University of Illinois Press.

CHAPTER 2

DEFINING HUNTER-GATHERERS

Enlightenment, Romantic, and Social Evolutionary Perspectives

ALAN BARNARD

The concept of the 'hunter-gatherer' as we understand it today is a product of speculation, debate, and theory. These elements are almost as significant in the development of the concept as are the ethnographic observations and archaeological discoveries that inform them. In this chapter, I shall examine changing ideas of 'hunters', 'foragers', 'hunters-and-gatherers' or 'hunter-gatherers', and the interplay between theory and observation in their definition.

I shall try to show that the hunter-gatherer, whose broad, agreed definition is now widely understood across the social sciences and even among the general public, was actually quite slow to emerge. The hunter-gatherer we now recognize is simply a person whose community only hunts and gathers, or that hunts, gathers, and fishes, for all or nearly all of its subsistence. 'Pure' hunter-gatherers are generally meant to have no domesticated animals except the dog, and to grow no crops at all. Yet in the last few decades the search for such purity has waned, and the definition has widened slightly to include at least some peoples who may have slight and marginal subsistence from domestication, and who do some trading with their neighbours. In these recent decades, social aspects of the hunter-gatherer life have become a greater part of its defining characteristics. Such social aspects were first recognized in the Enlightenment, and the loosening of the definition in recent decades in a sense aims to capture such long-known (or long-speculated about) notions, while devaluing specific concerns with subsistence. Typically today, hunter-gatherers are thought to live in stable, sustainable, and usually egalitarian communities or societies, but surrounded by more powerful, non-hunter-gatherer neighbours with whom they may trade and interact in other ways. They do not necessarily share the social values (and social hierarchies) of these neighbours.

Such a concept of hunting-and-gathering society did not really exist before the Enlightenment. In pre-Enlightenment Europe the 'hunter-gatherer' was subsumed within a definition of human nature, where, at best, it characterized a largely hypothetical, pre-social existence known mainly to philosophers and those who read their works. It was not necessarily known to explorers or to the wider public. Classical, medieval, and

Renaissance thinkers in Europe had little interest in hunter-gatherer societies, since they defined society itself in terms of principles other than subsistence. 'Hunter-gatherer' is essentially a subsistence category. It is true, of course, that these points are debatable: Pluciennik (2002) sees the seventeenth rather than the eighteenth century as the point at which hunter-gatherers were 'invented'. Yet he also sees merit in the occasional references to hunter-gatherers in earlier times in Europe, in medieval Islamic writings, and in the 'cyclical' cosmologies of Chinese and Hindu thought (Pluciennik 2004; cf. Pluciennik, Part I, this volume). However, in my view the idea of the 'hunter-gatherer', and especially of 'hunting-and-gathering society', became truly meaningful only when Enlightenment philosophers turned their attention from political principles to economic principles as the defining features of societies. For Enlightenment romantics, for Romantic philosophers (and for their successors in anthropology and archaeology), the hunter-gatherer represented a primitive and often noble figure. For early evolutionists, the concept was largely insignificant, with thinkers either more interested in 'higher' stages of social evolution, or more concerned with the evolution of religion or other non-economic objects. Some simply concentrated on the development of tool technology rather than on the forms of society in which these tools were used. As we shall see, it was only among relatively late evolutionists that the idea of hunter-gatherers as a societal type once again really took hold. This late evolutionist understanding (from the 1930s and especially in the 1950s and 1960s) forms the basis of hunter-gatherer studies as we now understand the field.

Before Hunter-Gatherers

It is commonplace in the anthropological sciences to think of Thomas Hobbes as one of the first to imagine hunter-gatherers. While it may be true that his famous statement on 'the life of man, solitary, poore, nasty, brutish, and short' describes a condition in which there is 'no Culture of the Earth', nevertheless this is also 'a time of Warre, where every man is Enemy to every man' and in which there is 'no Society'—by which he meant what would now be called sociality (Hobbes 1996 [1651], 89). Hobbes, and others in his time, simply had no notion of a hunter-gatherer society, nor even of the possibility of a sociable and peaceable hunter-gatherer existence. In fact, every major seventeenth-century philosopher who came close to describing a hunter-gatherer existence failed to understand it as a social way of life.

At best, most seventeenth-century political philosophers were interested in an imagined state of nature, either reasonably successful in its own terms (for example, in the writings of Hugo Grotius or John Locke), or quite unsuccessful (in the work of Hobbes or Samuel Pufendorf). They did not see either the state of nature or a hunting-and-gathering way of life as a stage of economic development. Even seventeenth- and eighteenth-century ethnographic descriptions, such as those of peoples now known as 'Bushmen' or 'San', did not distinguish hunter-gatherers as truly different from their pastoralist neighbours (see, e.g. Kolb 1968 [1719]). The word 'Khoisan', implying a collective ethnic unit comprising both 'Khoi' or 'Khoe' herders and 'San' or 'Saan' hunter-gatherers, is of twentieth-century origin. Yet ironically, the concept it designates was in fact already present in early European depictions of 'Hottentots', in which 'Sonquas' (San) are described simply as a tribe of 'Hottentots' who have no cattle and who live in the woodlands, scrub, or desert by hunting wild animals (see Barnard 2007, 11–16).

Enlightenment Perspectives

The idea of the hunter-gatherer as one who lived in a small-scale but viable society, different from the societies of pastoralists and cultivators, appeared during the European Enlightenment of the late eighteenth century. It emerged through the work of Montesquieu and his followers, especially in Scotland, but it emerged quite slowly. The first European intellectuals to describe hunter-gatherers as such (or more precisely, as 'hunters') did so with an awareness of a relation between mode of subsistence and structure of society, although it was not in its earliest form quite the same as we imagine it today.

Montesquieu (1989 [1748], 290–2), who was among the very first to discuss the attributes of hunter-gatherer societies, saw hunter-gatherers as similar enough to pastoralists to see them as sharing attributes such as these: having 'mores' rather than 'laws', sharing a lack of land ownership, keeping a nomadic way of life, and possessing a 'weak' institution of marriage. The one attribute of hunter-gatherers he notes as truly different from that of herders is their inability to unite as groups. In Montesquieu's words (1989 [1748], 290), 'One difference between savage peoples and barbarian peoples is that the former are small scattered nations which... cannot unite, whereas barbarian nations are ordinarily small nations that can unite together. The former are usually hunting peoples; the latter, pastoral peoples.'

Also writing in the 1740s, Anne-Robert-Jacques Turgot was probably the first to argue for hunting-and-gathering society as a stage of human evolution. However, his relevant work (Turgot 1973 [1808]) was not published until the early nineteenth century and had very little direct influence. Be that as it may, Turgot's vision of hunter-gatherers was of a single forest-dwelling family emerging from the biblical Flood, and without land or possessions.

> Without provisions, and in the depths of forests, men could devote themselves to nothing but obtaining their subsistence. The fruits which the earth produces in the absence of agriculture are not enough; men had to resort to the hunting of animals, which, being limited in number and incapable in a given region of providing many men with food, have for this very reason accelerated the dispersion of peoples and their rapid diffusion.
>
> Families or small nations widely separated from one another, because each required a very large area to obtain its food: that was the state of hunters.
>
> (Turgot 1973 [1808], 65)

The most significant early figure with clear ideas on hunter-gatherers was perhaps Jean-Jacques Rousseau, a romantic and a primitivist at heart, who like his seventeenth-century predecessors sought to understand the nature of human existence by conjectures on what it must have been like before the 'social contract'. He grounded his thinking in the assumption that early humankind was primitive, propertyless, free, and individualistic. Rousseau (1973 [1755], 84–94) speculated at length on the development of tools, fishing techniques, fire, and so on, and consequent rise of language and interaction between what would later be called hunter-gatherer bands. Yet his 'state of hunters', like that of seventeenth-century thinkers, seems to have been intrinsically unstable. For Rousseau, a kind of Neolithic Revolution (through which to define in retrospect the previous stage) would closely follow. 'Metallurgy and agriculture were the two arts which produced this great revolution', he wrote. 'The poets tell us it was gold and silver, but, for the philosophers, it was iron and corn, which first civilized men, and ruined humanity' (Rousseau 1973 [1755], 92).

Nevertheless, the 'hunter-gatherer' as we understand this concept today was in fact far more an invention of the Scottish than one of the French Enlightenment (Barnard 2004). This is because the eighteenth-century Scottish intelligentsia, with their belief in economics as the driving force of social life and precipitator of evolution, spent much time in debate on the relationships between subsistence, property, and society. Most prominent among those Scots was Adam Smith, who spoke of the 'age of hunters' or of 'hunting', in contrast to the successive ages of shepherds (or of pasturage), of agriculture (or of farming), and of commerce. He speculated that there was little government in the age of hunters, but rather with relatively independent families living democratically in loose-knit communities. Such communities would be small:

> In the age of hunters it is impossible for a very great number to live together. As game is their only support they would soon exhaust all that was within their reach. Thirty or forty families would be the most that could live together, that is, about 140 or 150 persons. These might live by the chase in the country about them. They would also naturally form themselves into these villages, agreeing to live near together for their mutuall [sic] security.
>
> (Smith 1978 [1763], 213)

Even before Smith, Sir John Dalrymple created a theory of societal progress based on stages in the evolution of concepts of property. He writes: 'The first state of society is that of hunters and fishers; among such a people the idea of property will be confined to a few, and but a very few moveables; and subjects which are immovable, will be esteemed to be common' (Dalrymple 1758, 75). Around the same time, Lord Kames, a famous Scottish judge, asserted that hunting and fishing 'were the original occupations of man' (Kames 1758, 77), although his hunter-fishers failed to develop true society, which in his view came about only after barter progressed into commerce in a later, agricultural, stage. Lord Monboddo, Kames's great opponent both on legal matters and on their incipient anthropological ones, argued instead, that 'Man did not become carnivorous till he became a hunter, and he could not be a hunter till he had invented some kind of arms; and not even immediately after that; for the Orang Outangs, though they use sticks, do not hunt, but live upon the natural fruits of the earth' (Monboddo 1774, 225).

Among other Scots who wrote on the issue, many were concerned with the sequence of the means of subsistence; which came first—gathering, hunting, or fishing? Some speculated on the kind of society that existed in such early times. Most were interested in some aspect of property and the property relations among members of hunter-gatherer groups. For example, the great polymath Adam Ferguson (1966 [1767], 82) wrote: 'The food of to-morrow is yet wild in the forest, or hid in the lake; it cannot be appropriated before it is caught; and even then, . . . it accrues to the community, and is applied for immediate use, or becomes an accession to the stores of the public' (Ferguson 1966 [1767], 82). His interest lay in understanding the origins and what would later be called the evolution of human society, and his speculations more than those of most of his Scottish contemporaries were based on the ethnographic observations of travellers and probably also his awareness of differences between his own native Highland culture and the Lowland lifestyle he adopted when in Edinburgh.

Few of the Scots were interested directly in living hunter-gatherer peoples. An important exception, though, was William Robertson—a great scholar of comparative ethnography and long-serving Principal of Edinburgh University. In the second volume of his four-volume *History of America*, he discussed primitive food-gathering, nomadism, the stage of fishing (which, he believed, preceded hunting), and the hunting peoples of both North and South America. Drawing from a huge number of sources, in many languages, his 'history' went beyond the speculative style of his contemporaries and gave us the first comparative ethnographic treatment of hunter-gatherer societies. Indeed he also attempted to show the differences between hunter-gatherers and those around them. Along with Rousseau, William Robertson (e.g. 1809, 107) was one of the first commentators to note that hunting and gathering lifestyles were ones of freedom and leisure, and that they entailed less work than agriculture.

Back on the Continent, Immanuel Kant represented an interesting blend of positions. Drawing on Rousseau, Kant (1991 [1786], 229–31) also depicted both hunter-gatherers and herders as living in an 'age of leisure and peace' and agriculturalists as living in an 'age of labour and discord'. Like the Scots he saw an evolution from hunting to herding to agriculture, and he remarks on it being possibly a slow evolution though with the transition to herding nevertheless a 'major leap'. His views on the exact nature of a life based on digging roots and gathering fruits are ambiguous, but he seems to have seen pastoralism, in particular, as idyllic, with inequalities emerging along with 'sociability and civil security' in the age of agriculture.

Romantic Images and Successors to the Romantic Tradition

It is not easy to find images of the hunter-gatherer in Romantic philosophy. This is partly because the idea of subsistence and its relation to social life was so quintessentially an Enlightenment problem, just as it later was an evolutionist problem. The Romantics rejected the search for such rational correspondences, and classic figures in the Romantic Movement wrote virtually nothing at all on hunter-gatherers as a category.

Those on the boundary between the Enlightenment and the Romantic perspectives, like Rousseau or like Johann Gottfried Herder, expressed Enlightenment rather than Romantic ideals when they described this category. Herder drew heavily on the work of William Robertson in his descriptions of hunter-gatherer peoples. He comments on Native North Americans who live a hard life by collecting roots and seeds, and bats, grubs, and worms (Herder 1800 [1784–91], 168). His interest is hunter-gatherers replicated his interest in 'peoples' more broadly. Reacting against the universalistic tendencies of the Enlightenment (which would later reappear in evolutionism), Herder believed that each people or *Volk* possessed their own culture or *Kultur*. This became the guiding principle of first German and later the American anthropology of Franz Boas, which is derived from the German tradition.

Between 1799 and 1804, the Prussian baron Alexander von Humboldt travelled extensively in Central and South America. He spent part of that time, in 1800, travelling among hunter-gatherers in the Orinoco Basin of South America. Humboldt's (1849, 191–4) most interesting description is of a people he refers to as the Otomacs, who eat not only fish, tortoises, lizards, ants, tree gums, and ferns, but apparently also earth and clay. They do this in the wet season, when the river waters flood the land, and stack balls of clay, with no organic content at all, in their huts ready to bake lightly and eat.

Although Humboldt comments extensively on ethnographic matters, his ethnographic descriptions offer little clear idea of what he might have thought about 'hunter-gatherers' as a category. Nor do we find such a category in the writings of Romantic philosophers generally, since neither he nor his German-language contemporaries were much interested in hunter-gatherers as precursors to 'barbarian' or 'savage' ways of life. That would have to wait until the return of evolutionist ideas, first in Scandinavia and then in Britain, and then the emergence of *Kulturkreis* theory in Germany and Austria and its successor tradition of culture-area theory in American anthropology. In many respects these latter anthropological traditions are the successors to the Romantic school in philosophy, and in them we have the logical development both of Herder's comparative concern with the diversity of 'nations' or 'peoples' and Humboldt's style of ethnographic explanation.

Kulturkreis theory rested on the existence of 'culture circles', really strata of culture spread across the globe by waves of migration and diffusion. Father Wilhelm Schmidt's (1934) scheme, for example, was one of four such strata: the Primitive or *Urkultur*, the Primary culture circle, the Secondary, and the Tertiary. The Primitive culture circle contained four cultures, and all were hunter-gatherers. The Central Primitive was made up of exogamous, monogamous groups. The Southern Primitive was made up of exogamous groups and sex totems. The Arctic Primitive had an egalitarian social structure, again along with exogamous groups. The 'Boomerang Culture', which was believed to be the youngest and a transitional type, had a mixture of 'primitive' and matriarchal features. Each culture contained many peoples, widely distributed around the world. The Central Primitive Culture included Pygmies of South-East Asia, South Asia, and Africa. The Southern Primitive Culture included Kalahari Bushmen, Tasmanians and some other Australian Aborigines, and Ona and Yahgan of the southern tip of South America. The Northern Primitive Culture was similarly widespread across the Subarctic and Arctic, while 'Boomerang' culture included Australian Aborigines and some Asian and African hunter-gatherers. From Primitive hunting developed reindeer herding, the earliest form of pastoralism, and this marked the transition to the Primary culture circle.

In North America, the culture-area theorists developed a watered-down version of the perspective. They focused on the characteristics of specific regions rather than on global migrations. However, they also developed new ways of thinking about environmental influences, including global and hemisphere-wide climatic influences on flora and game distribution. Clark Wissler (e.g. 1923), in particular, worked on this problem, both at a theoretical level and in relation to specific large-scale migrations of hunter-gatherers and later subsistence types. He also sought to bring together archaeological and ethnological material. His efforts paved the way for Julian Steward's multi-linear evolutionism and cultural ecology, which as we shall see grew from within American anthropology, and indeed from an interest in culture areas of the Americas, in the decades that followed.

Ironically, North American anthropology in its professional, academic form, developed through the efforts of a number of scholars with ethnographic interest in hunter-gatherers.

Most prominent among these, by far, was the founder of the tradition, Franz Boas, who began his observations of Inuit culture in 1883, and his studies of Northwest Coast material culture in 1885, with fieldwork in the Northwest Coast from 1886. Yet it would require an evolutionist perspective to bring out hunter-gatherer studies as a sub-discipline. Almost from the start, Boas's (1896) anthropology was anti-evolutionist and particularist, and emphasized a concept of cultural diversity more reminiscent of Herder than of any tradition alive in Boas's time. Boas's anti-evolutionism took on special significance later in opposition to the racist ideology of Madison Grant (1916).

The Gradual Emergence of Evolutionist Visions

In its essence, the category hunter-gatherer entails more than an interest in subsistence: it is also an evolutionist concept. Even those evolutionists who are more interested in religion than in subsistence, or who de-emphasize economic structures in favour of kinship or political processes, recognize it as their own. Nevertheless, the idea of the hunter-gatherer did not emerge in its present form spontaneously with the development of evolutionary theory, but grew through concerns with the relationship between tool traditions and subsistence, and between subsistence and social organization.

Sir John Lubbock, in *Pre-historic times*, was the first to distinguish Palaeolithic and Neolithic. Lubbock wrote of these first two of his 'four great epochs' (the others being Bronze and Iron):

I. That of the Origin; when man shared the possession of Europe with the Mammoth, the Cave bear, the Wooly-haired rhinoceros, and other extinct animals. This we may call the 'Palaeolithic' period.
II. The later or polished Stone Age; a period characterised by beautiful weapons and instruments made of that or other kinds of stone... This we may call the 'Neolithic' period. (Lubbock 1892 [1865], 2)

What was missing, of course, was the recognition of a Mesolithic—a concept that was only to come into use in the early twentieth century, although it had been hinted at earlier. Its omission reflects the lack of concern, even by this, the greatest of nineteenth-century polymaths, for a notion of living or recent hunter-gatherers, as distinct from either the ape-men of Palaeolithic Europe or the builders of Neolithic monuments such as Stonehenge or Avebury. Lubbock's only mention of Bushmen in *Pre-historic times* was in reference to 'mental differences' (Lubbock 1892, 571). Similarly in *The origin of civilisation* (Lubbock 1874), which is based on a series of lectures he gave in 1868, there is no comment on hunting or gathering, and very little mention of any hunter-gatherer societies. The emphasis is on religion, and other topics include only art, kinship, moral character, language, and law—and not subsistence. The Mesolithic is still a concept undergoing revision, particularly with reference to the idea of hunting-and-gathering society as an adaptation coinciding chronologically with the Neolithic (see, e.g. Zvelebil 2009).

Meanwhile in Denmark, the idea of Stone, Bronze, and Iron ages was being developed. Christian Jürgensen Thomsen was the major early figure, writing in the 1830s, but it was Sven Nilsson (1868 [1862]) who reinterpreted these three ages as four subsistence strategies: savage (hunter-gatherer), herdsman, agriculturist, and civilized man. Anticipating the late twentieth-century ideas of James Woodburn (e.g. 1980), Nilsson (1868, lxiv–lxv) defined his 'savage' as a person with 'few other than material wants', and 'who acts only for the day which *is*, not for the day which is *coming*'. As in the Enlightenment, interests in the specifics of economic life led to working out the comparative and theoretical intricacies of relations between the different modes of subsistence. And as ever, until quite late in the history of anthropology, the theoretical underpinnings of hunter-gatherer studies preceded the collection of good ethnographic data. Exactly when data took over from theory is, of course, open to debate, but it was probably not until the 1960s that a definitive change towards the collection and interpretation of fresh empirical data occurred in hunter-gatherer studies.

Ironically, given the interest in hunter-gatherers among Marxist anthropologists in France and North America in the 1970s and 1980s, Karl Marx seems to have had virtually no understanding of 'hunter-gatherers' as a category. In 1857, he wrote: 'We may take it for granted that pastoralism, or more generally a migratory life, is the first form of maintaining existence, the tribe not settling in a fixed place but using up what it finds locally and then passing on' (Marx 1964, 68). Marx's notion of 'primitive communism' was more an agricultural one than a hunter-gatherer one, and the same is true of Lewis Henry Morgan's understandings of that concept, which is explored extensively in *Houses and house-life of the American Aborigines* (Morgan 2003 [1881], 42–131).

Lewis Henry Morgan carried out ethnographic fieldwork among the Iroquois, a farming-fishing-gathering-hunting people of northern New York and southern Ontario, and speculated on the evolution of social institutions. In his most influential work, *Ancient society* (Morgan 1877, 4–6), he argued that seven interconnected 'primary institutions' governed the evolution of society: subsistence, government, language, the family, religion, house life and architecture, and property. His scheme of evolution included three 'ethnical periods', savagery, barbarism, and civilization, and each of these was divided into three further sub-periods. Although his main interest was with the evolution of kinship structures and political organization, he devotes some attention too to subsistence (1877, 9–27). Within the savage state, Lower Savagery was marked by subsistence by fruits and nuts and by the development of language. In Middle Savagery, fishing became possible and fire was discovered. This is the stage Morgan believed was occupied by contemporary Australian Aborigines. Upper Savagery was marked by the invention of the bow and arrow, and it ended with the invention of pottery. Living hunter-gatherers were equated mainly with Upper Savagery, and only some with the Middle sub-period.

Morgan died in 1881. Evolutionism continued as the dominant paradigm in the UK, with Lubbock, John Ferguson McLennan, Sir Edward Burnett Tylor, and later Sir James Frazer as its leading advocates. In the US, with Morgan gone, theoretical interest waned but ethnography was boosted by government needs to expand westwards and through the efforts of a number of young men (and at least one woman), some in government service at the Bureau of American Ethnology. The most important of these was John Wesley Powell, an evolutionist and American champion of the ideas of Charles Darwin, who headed the Bureau from 1879 until his death in 1902.

Lubbock died in 1913. There was much discussion in the early twentieth century of the applicability of his model elsewhere in the world, particularly in southern Africa where both hunter-gatherer ethnography and theoretical archaeology were in ascendancy (see Barnard 2007; Deacon 1990). Lubbock's evolutionism, and everyone else's at the time, had been what Julian Steward (1955, 15–16) would later call 'unilinear'—all humankind passing through the same specific set of sequential stages. The new evolutionism that emerged in the early twentieth century was, in contrast, 'universal'—still sequential, but with broad stages only, such as 'savage' (hunter-gatherer), 'barbarian', 'civilization'. Chief among its protagonists was the Marxist, V. Gordon Childe (1935, 7–8), who followed Lubbock's idea of the 'Neolithic' stone tool tradition with the notion of a 'Neolithic Revolution'. For decades to come, the significance, or otherwise, of this 'revolutionary' change in subsistence would be debated.

In those following decades, the most significant development in hunter-gatherer studies was certainly the publication of Julian Steward's (1955) *Theory of culture change*. Fortuitously, early after the Second World War, Steward had run out of offprints of several of his pre-war articles, and a meeting with a publisher persuaded him that he should recast them as a book. In the revised work he developed his own tradition of 'multilinear' evolution in contrast to unilineal and universal. Steward's multilinear evolutionism added history to evolution, and in terms of hunter-gatherer studies came to examine the influence of environmental circumstances on social organization. Steward (1955, 122–50) argued for a distinction between 'patrilineal band' societies, such as Australian Aborigines, and 'composite band' societies, such as Canadian Subarctic First Nations. Elman Service (1962, 59–109) later refined the model by redefining 'patrilineal' as 'patrilocal', but either way the description did not do justice to the data.

What was of fundamental importance, very simply, is that Steward's and Service's books were widely read among the new generation of postgraduate students in North American anthropology departments. Many of the best of such students took an interest in, and did fieldwork among, hunter-gatherers. What came to define their interest, in spite of their evolutionism, was an optimistic belief in the egalitarianism, peacefulness, 'original affluence' (in the sense of limited wants, and therefore needs that are easily satisfied), and other good things about many hunter-gatherer societies (see e.g. Sahlins 1974). They gathered to exchange ideas, and also to compare data, especially in 1966 for what turned out to be one of the most significant conferences of the decade, if not in the history of the discipline of anthropology.

After Man the Hunter

The Man the Hunter conference, held in Chicago in 1966 (Lee and DeVore 1968), marked in many ways the culmination of hunter-gatherer studies. A new generation, many influenced by the recently published theoretical ideas of Julian Steward, brought empirical evidence to the table. Debates on band structures, kinship arrangements, demography, leisure time, prehistory, primitiveness, and so on, ensued. In some respects, Man the Hunter was part of the revolutionary zeitgeist that was present throughout the Western world, although it is perhaps easy to overestimate the coincidence of its publication in 1968 and the events of Paris and elsewhere that same year.

After Man the Hunter there was a lull in the proceedings. The next major hunter-gatherers conference was in fact in Paris, in 1978, organized by leading Marxist anthropologist Maurice Godelier and formally opened by Claude Lévi-Strauss. It was called the International Conference on Hunting-and-Gathering Societies, with no initial notion that a series now up to ten was being inaugurated. Further conferences were held in Quebec in 1980, then Bad Homberg (Germany) in 1983, London in 1984, Darwin (Australia) in 1988, Fairbanks in 1990, Moscow in 1993, Osaka in 1998, Edinburgh in 2002, and in Liverpool in 2013.

If doubt about the category had not crept in by 1978, it was to do so just two years later. At the Second International Conference on Hunting-and-Gathering Societies in Quebec, Bernard Arcand argued that the category 'hunter-gatherer society' is ill-conceived in that it identifies no single, specific kind of society. He was to reiterate this comment in print some years later (Arcand 1988), and to suggest there that the continued existence of the category is predicated on a need for it in Western discourse. With the emergence of Japanese hunter-gatherer studies, the fall of the Soviet Union, and subsequent international hunter-gatherers conferences in Moscow and Osaka, one may wish to add 'and in international academic discourse'. Russian and Japanese ethnographic studies of hunter-gatherers have long been prominent, and have peculiar histories. For example, in the Soviet Union of the 1920s A. N. Maksimov regarded some hunter-gatherers, such as Australian Aborigines, as more advanced than simple horticulturalists (see Artemova 2004, 79–81). In Japan, hunter-gatherer studies emerged from primatology and human–primate comparisons, as from the early 1970s researchers trained in primate studies began to examine human hunter-gatherer social life (see Ichikawa 2004, 105–7).

The interest shown by people of recent hunter-gatherer descent may make such comments superfluous, and certainly the agendas of political activists are quite different from those of romantics, evolutionists, and heritors of the Enlightenment. Whatever faults it possesses, the category has endured. It is now no longer defined as narrowly as in 1966, because since the 1980s at least, we all realized we were talking mainly about 'former' or 'recent' hunter-gatherer societies, or 'part-time' hunter-gatherers. Still, many of the attributes of 'hunting-and-gathering societies' do seem to remain after pure hunting and gathering is no longer viable (Barnard 2002). The characteristics identified by Bruce Winterhalder (2001) as typical of hunter-gatherers—underproduction and lack of accumulation, food sharing, egalitarianism, and a division of labour involving men hunting and women gathering—all seem intact.

If it is a category needed in Western or academic discourse, then many would say, 'So be it', for the category seems to maintain its strength as an object of debate. As in the Enlightenment, it continues to lie at the very foundation of Western understandings of what it means to be human—*even though* only a very tiny percentage (or perhaps *because* only a tiny percentage) of the world's population still live as hunters and gatherers.

References

Arcand, B. 1988. Il n'y a jamais eu de société de chasseurs-cueilleurs. *Anthropologie et Sociétés* 12, 39–58.

Artemova, O. Y. 2004. Hunter-gatherer studies in Russia and the Soviet Union. In A. Barnard (ed.), *Hunter-gatherers in history, archaeology and anthropology*, 77–88. Oxford: Berg.

Barnard, A. 2002. The foraging mode of thought. In H. Stewart, A. Barnard, and K. Omura (eds), *Self- and other images of hunter-gatherers* (Senri Ethnological Studies 60), 5–24. Osaka: National Museum of Ethnology.

Barnard, A. 2004. Hunting-and-gathering society: an eighteenth-century Scottish invention. In A. Barnard (ed.), *Hunter-gatherers in history, archaeology and anthropology*, 31–43. Oxford: Berg.

Barnard, A. 2007. *Anthropology and the Bushman*. Oxford: Berg.

Boas, F. 1896. Limitations of the comparative method of anthropology. *Science* 4, 901–8.

Childe, V. G. 1935. Changing methods and aims in prehistory: Presidential Address for 1935. *Proceedings of the Prehistoric Society* 1, 1–15.

Dalrymple, J. 1758. *Essay towards a general history of feudal property in Great Britain* (2nd edition). London: A. Millar.

Deacon, J. 1990. Weaving the fabric of Stone Age research in southern Africa. In P. Robertshaw (ed.), *A history of African archaeology*, 39–58. London: James Currey.

Ferguson, A. 1966 [1767]. *An essay on the history of civil society*. Edinburgh: Edinburgh University Press.

Grant, M. 1916. *The passing of the great race; or, the racial basis of European history*. New York: Charles Scribner's Sons.

Herder, J. G. 1800 [1784–91]. *Outlines of a philosophy of the history of man*, trans. T. Churchill. London: J. Johnson.

Hobbes, T. 1996 [1651]. *Leviathan*, ed. R. Tuck. Cambridge: Cambridge University Press.

Humboldt, A. von 1849. *Aspects of nature, in different lands and different climates*, Vol. I, trans. Mrs Sabine. London: Longman, Brown, Green, and Longmans.

Ichikawa, M. 2004. The Japanese tradition in central African hunter-gatherer studies, with comparative observations on the French and American traditions. In A. Barnard (ed.), *Hunter-gatherers in history, archaeology and anthropology*, 103–14. Oxford: Berg.

Kames, H. Home, Lord. 1758. *Historical law tracts*. Edinburgh: A. Kincaid and J. Bell.

Kant, I. 1991 [1786]. Conjectures on the beginning of human history. In *Kant: political writings* (2nd edition), ed. H. Reiss and trans. H. B. Nisbet, 221–34. Cambridge: Cambridge University Press.

Kolb, P. 1968 [1719]. *The present state of the Cape of Good Hope*, Vol. I. New York: Johnson Reprint Company.

Lee, R. B. and DeVore, I. (eds) 1968. *Man the hunter*. Chicago: Aldine.

Lubbock, J. 1874 [1870]. *The origin of civilisation and the primitive condition of man: mental and social condition of savages*. New York: D. Appleton and Company.

Lubbock, J. 1892 [1865]. *Pre-historic times, as illustrated by ancient remains and the manners and customs of modern savages* (5th edition). New York: D. Appleton and Company.

Marx, K. 1964. *Pre-capitalist economic formations*, trans. J. Cohen. London: Lawrence and Wishart.

Monboddo, J. Burnet, Lord. 1774. *Of the origin and progress of language*, Vol. I (2nd edition). Edinburgh: J. Balfour.

Montesquieu. 1989 [1748]. *The spirit of the laws*, trans. and ed. A. M. Cohler, B. C. Miller, and H. S. Stone. Cambridge: Cambridge University Press.

Morgan, L. H. 1877. *Ancient society, or researches in the lines of human progress from savagery through barbarism to civilization*. Chicago: Charles H. Kerr and Company.

Morgan, L. H. 2003 [1881]. *Houses and house-life of the American Aborigines*. Salt Lake City: University of Utah Press.

Nilsson, S. 1868 [1862]. *The prehistoric inhabitants of Scandinavia* (3rd edition), ed. J. Lubbock. London: Longmans, Green, and Co.

Pluciennik, M. 2002. The invention of hunter-gatherers in seventeenth-century Europe. *Archaeological Dialogues* 9, 98–150.

Pluciennik, M. 2004. The meaning of 'hunter-gatherer' modes of subsistence: a comparative historical perspective. In A. Barnard (ed.), *Hunter-gatherers in history, archaeology and anthropology*, 17–29. Oxford: Berg.

Robertson, W. 1809 [1777]. *The history of America*, Vol. 2. Alston, Cumberland: T. Walton and Co.

Rousseau, J.-J. 1973 [1755]. A discourse on the origin of inequality. In *The Social Contract and Discourses*, trans. G. D. H. Cole, 31–126. London: J. M. Dent and Sons.

Sahlins, M. 1974. *Stone Age economics*. London: Tavistock Publications.

Schmidt, W. 1934. Primitive man: a brief critical examination of the subject and a systematic statement based on demonstrated facts. In E. Eyre (ed.), *European civilization: its origin and development, Vol. I: Prehistoric man and earliest known societies*, 1–82. Oxford: Oxford University Press.

Service, E. R. 1962. *Primitive social organisation: an evolutionary perspective*. New York: Random House.

Smith, A. 1978 [lectures delivered 1762–3]. *Lectures on jurisprudence*, (ed. R. L. Meek, D. D. Raphael, and P. G. Stein. Oxford: Clarendon Press.

Steward, J. H. 1955. *Theory of culture change: the methodology of multilinear evolution*. Urbana: University of Illinois Press.

Turgot, A.-R.-J. 1973 [1808]. On universal history. In *Turgot on progress, sociology and economics*, trans. and ed. R. L. Meek, 61–118. Cambridge: Cambridge University Press.

Winterhalder, B. 2001. The behavioral ecology of hunter-gatherers. In C. Panter-Brick, R. H. Layton, and P. Rowley-Conwy (eds), *Hunter-gatherers: an interdisciplinary perspective*, 12–38. Cambridge: Cambridge University Press.

Wissler, C. 1923. *Man and culture*. New York: Thomas Y. Crowell.

Woodburn, J. 1980. Hunters and gatherers today and reconstruction of the past. In E. Gellner (ed.), *Soviet and Western anthropology*, 95–117. London: Duckworth.

Zvelebil, M. (ed.) 2009. *Hunters in transition: Mesolithic societies of temperate Eurasia and their transition to farming*. Cambridge: Cambridge University Press.

CHAPTER 3

HISTORICAL FRAMES OF REFERENCE FOR 'HUNTER-GATHERERS'

MARK PLUCIENNIK

INTRODUCTION

How might we consider ideas of 'hunter-gatherers' historically and historiographically? Certainly with caution, because the hyphenated version appears less than one hundred years ago. Before that there are very occasional references to 'hunters and gatherers', but arguably any recognizably anthropological sense of the term develops primarily in western Europe from the sixteenth and seventeenth centuries and crystallizes fully only in the eighteenth century (Barnard 1999; 2004; Barnard, Part I, this volume; Pluciennik 2002). Its categorial arrival is especially neatly encapsulated in European expressions of 'speculative histories'—social evolution—around 1750, such as Adam Smith's 'Age of Hunters'. Yet there have also been strong claims that the concept of 'hunter-gatherers' has been present for very much longer: in Europe at least since Classical Greece and Rome (e.g. Rudebeck 2000; Zvelebil 2002), but also recorded elsewhere such as in South Asia (e.g. Pandey 1989). This chapter therefore briefly examines the broader history of alterity, though focusing on the role of subsistence. This approach is taken because 'hunter-gatherers' are just one way in which cultural and societal concepts of difference set the frameworks for encounters with, perceptions and representations of, and relationships with people and indeed other beings.

Terminologically, the particular category we now call 'hunter-gatherers' came into meaningful existence only through initially Western anthropological understandings. Intellectually, the concept arose in Europe in relation to economic concerns, intimately connected with nascent capitalism, property rights, colonial practices and attitudes, and as part of the developing Enlightenment and scientific passion for classification. Strongly associated with social evolution, the term became increasingly rigidly defined until it perhaps reached its semantically most restricted point in the 1960s. Since then, and despite several attempts, in international academic discourse its meaning has tended to overflow its confines, until some have questioned whether the term has any utility at all.

Here I attempt to show that in understanding historical frameworks for 'hunter-gatherers' we have to be careful not to conflate contemporary anthropological or other projects with past meanings and values of cultural differences. I examine the case of ancient Greece and perception of 'barbarians', and briefly other literary traditions in India, China, and South-West Asia before returning to the anthropological project and its particular construction of the 'hunter-gatherer' as the exemplar of difference *and* similarity. The corollary is that we should be aware that our frameworks and conceptions are likewise to a large extent historical and contingent. It would surely be an anthropological conceit and failure to understand the importance of context to suggest that we had identified a universal category that others had simply not defined correctly. I shall argue that the various historical, cultural, and extra-disciplinary constructions that have been claimed to reference an understanding of alterity identical to the modern anthropological category are demonstrably not the same and should not be considered semantically or historically equivalent. Any perceived overlap is not simply a matter of preferred epistemological positioning, but goes to the heart of culturally sensitive historical practice. We need to distinguish between the desire to understand any history of 'hunter-gatherers' in our designated terms, and how various groups of people, actual or purported, may have been understood or conceptualized in other times and cultures.

Alterity

How should we conceptualize alterity or otherness? Philosophically and logically speaking, otherness is needed to circumscribe, differentiate, and experience the self, but there are potentially many processes and axes involved in such differentiation. Others may be literally or metaphorically described as 'beasts' or otherwise sub-, non- or differently-human, such as the five 'races' described by Linnaeus (for the Western tradition in the modern period alone see e.g. Hodgen 1964; Jahoda 1999; Pagden 1986). The boundary between 'us' and 'them' may even be seen as so far distant that it is not perceived as a question of cultural difference, but rather one of essential nature. Thus we may agree that 'alterity really has far more to do with the Self than with the Other' (Roberts 2007, 6). Historically and culturally, many may feel more comfortable having their senses of self, place, and consequent prejudices confirmed, than confronting novelty in the form of inevitably threatening others. Threatening, because alterity 'leaks'; there is the capacity to disrupt societally agreed norms and boundaries between self and other. Thus the other is provocative even when appropriated through forms of domination or objectification. For many societies and periods, the distant was the realm of the fabulous, the imagined, and the uncertain. In contrast, the anthropological project of the Enlightenment typically required a sense of human unity, even if within that there were judged to be degrees of ability and achievement. As an epitome of human difference in the past or present, the ethnographic category 'hunter-gatherers' became a primary receptacle for these archaeological and anthropological concerns. In some circumstances valorization of difference led to a fascination with the exotic, or even a kind of yearning or nostalgia for what never has been—the noble savage, eco-savages, spiritually whole savages, golden ages. In others, and notably in social evolutionary schemes, hunter-gatherers formed the origins and base-line of humanity and were contrasted to superior successors.

There are then both histories of alterity, and of what we now term 'hunter-gatherers' within those self-sensibilities. There are many versions of others including hunter-gatherers, just as there are historically different senses of self/selves, and their related cultural norms and values, with which to contrast and from which to measure actual, apparent, or imagined characteristics of others. Nor should we expect societies to be characterized by single, homogeneous, and exclusive *Weltanschauungen* (world views), although shared stereotypes of others—supposedly essential characteristics—do exist and are often highly influential. However, many of these can be treated as polar opposites *or* gradational; they can also be used in different combinations in various contexts.

If concepts of alterity are so variable, does it make sense to talk about 'typical' parameters of alterity, especially vis-à-vis hunter-gatherers? The most easily studied attitudes to others are those expressed from within literate societies which tend to be nucleated, urban, settled, and hierarchical, and in which (until recently) the bulk of the population laboured to produce cultivated food. Authors were typically male, necessarily literate, and part of an educational and social elite. But the sense of self (and hence other) could vary, as could the boundaries to normalcy: the antithesis to 'agriculture' was not necessarily the most important aspect of difference. These could include manners, movement, geographical location, language, skin colour or other physical characteristics, as well as 'lifestyle', religion, purity, foods, sexual mores or other cultural idiosyncrasies; or nearness to God, purported ancestors, particular animals or mythical beings.

Axes of Alterity

At starkest, hunter-gatherers have been treated as opposites within a binary logic. In those kinds of frameworks, descriptions of self are lists that enumerate the positive qualities of the group concerned: the other is then typified by the corresponding lack. For many societies throughout history agriculture was a highly visible source of food and consumer of labour. In both the United States and Germany as late as 1870, around 50 per cent of employment was in agriculture (Daly 1981, 12; Daunton 2007, 14). Until very recently, then, the general answer to the question: 'What do "we" do?' was: 'Work and farm'. But that does not mean that 'foraging' in the anthropological sense acts as the categorial antonym.

Most will be familiar with ideas of a Golden Age such as the Judaeo-Christian-Islamic 'Garden of Eden' or Paradise, located in the past or future; descriptions of Paradise lost or to be regained typically include the lack of agricultural labour. Some notion of 'gathering' in the sense of 'plucking fruit freely from trees' can certainly be found, but does not imply hunting-gathering as either a lifestyle or social form. This is so whether the sources were potentially aware of real 'foragers' or not: rather, they occur in the genres of theological or moral texts. Thus the Buddhist Uttarakuru can be glossed as 'a place where there was no need to work because food was available from all the trees', or along with the purest speech, most beautiful women and intense sexual pleasure, the 'milk trees eliminate the need for cultivating food' (Thapar 1971, 415). Warder (1961, 49) notes that some Buddhist texts describe a 'history' in which the earliest morally perfect societies were nourished by the earth which comprised a 'delicious edible substance'. Jain texts discuss pre-farming 'wish-fulfilling trees which granted people whatever they wished' (Paddaya 1995, 117). Sumerian and Babylonian texts similarly refer to labour-free existence (Albright 1965). Hesiod's *Works and Days*, perhaps from the eighth century BC, proposes that 'previously, the tribes of men used to live upon the earth entirely apart from evils, and without grievous toil' (90 [2006, 95]) and describes the first golden race who did not grow old but rather 'had all good things: the grain-giving field bore crops of its own accord' (109 [2006, 97]). Thus, while people who 'gather' and 'hunt' can always be found, a more nuanced view suggests that pointing to people who lack agriculture is not the same as finding hunter-gatherers.

Further, agriculture was not the main positive value to which other forms of behaviour were opposed or contrasted. It was only when some societies were beginning to move away from total reliance upon agriculture towards manufacturing and commerce, and in trying to understand *that* distinction within a global and colonial world, that the *economic* invention of hunter-gatherers made rational sense (cf. Barnard 2004, 31–2). In other contexts it was typically through combinations of other characteristics, perhaps reflecting a more restricted set of cultural encounters, that contrasting distinctions were made. These axes of difference were often described in terms of geographical distance. Descriptions were typically mixtures of environmental and cultural strangeness. They incorporated aspects of others derived from realms of encounter, hearsay, theology, cosmography, and imagination or invention.

Greeks and Barbarians

Cartledge (2002, 11) suggests that:

> [F]or the Classical Greeks the Greek-barbarian polarity was but one instance of the ideological habit of polarization that was a hallmark of their mentality and culture...Thus whereas Greeks were ideally seen as not-barbarians, barbarians were equally envisaged as being precisely what Greeks were not.

But this polarization itself has a historical trajectory. Who were these 'Greek' selves? Archaic period identity may rather have been considered as aggregative. Only when the Persians were identified as a singular threat did a particular consolidated notion of Greekness come into focus, and with it the possibility of a rather more oppositional view of what constituted a barbarian. Thus one mechanism by which difference can be mobilized is perception of an 'enemy', a presented and unavoidable other. Prior to that, argues J. Hall, ancient 'Greek' identity was rather based 'on similarity with peer groups' who invoked 'common descent from Hellen', but this 'cumulative aggregation of identity was enacted in the absence of any clear, determinate boundary between Greek and non-Greek' (E. Hall 1989; J. Hall 1997, 47). Unlike modern colonial expansion, Malkin (2001, 14) suggests that 'the non-Greek world one reached, explored, and colonized probably seemed not so much "absolutely other" as more of "the same"'. However, by the fifth and fourth centuries BC attitudes had hardened, and perhaps stereotypes were more easily available. Within this world one can clearly find examples of 'barbarians' such as those speaking the 'wrong' language—of whom the fact that they do not practise agriculture is also a noteworthy fact; but to treat that as proof that hunter-gatherers have always been a salient and available category is to miss the historical subtleties of the construction of difference. In many surviving texts, it is rather the mobility of, say, the

Scythians that is the unsettling feature. Insofar as antitheses were operative, Coleman (1997, 202) points out that in fifth-century Athens male ideals were: wisdom, manliness, courage, discipline/restraint, and justice. Thus 'barbarians were pictured as stupid, cowardly, cruel, unrestrained, and lawless'.

It is instructive to consider the descriptions of barbarians in Book Four of Herodotus's *History*. These include named 'tribes' including the Scythians, though one should note that for Herodotus there were many different 'Scythians', as well as the fantastic. Hartog (1988, especially 193–206), observes that the primary trope for Scythians and other distant peoples is that of the nomad. Lack of agriculture (here, 'ploughing and sowing': the contrast is rather with pastoralists) *is* important, but it is the alleged fact that Scythians do not eat bread, for example, that is the curious fact and an inversion from the norm. This dietary peculiarity is similarly the most barbarous fact about the Mossynoeci, on the Black Sea coast, for Xenophon (Cartledge 2002, 59). In fact, in Herodotus we can find the Callipedae and the Alazonians who 'resemble the Scythians in their usages, but sow and eat corn, also onions, garlic, lentils, and millet'; nearby we have 'Scythian cultivators' and 'Scythian husbandmen'; there are the Thyssagetae and Iyrcae, who are said to live by hunting but have dogs and horses; the bald-headed Argippaeans who 'have but few sheep'; plus cannibals and various other tribes, some named, many fantastic, of whom Herodotus admits he has scant knowledge or does not believe the tales told. Which of these should we equate to hunter-gatherers? Also present in Herodotus are the climatic extremes mirrored in fantastic behaviour or physiognomy: *topoi* that are repeated in medieval Islamic, Renaissance, and Enlightenment thought too.

For Aristotle, explicitly surveying different ways of life in his *Politics*:

> The laziest are shepherds, who lead an idle life, and get their subsistence without trouble from tame animals; their flocks having to wander from place to place in search of pasture, they are compelled to follow them, cultivating a sort of living farm. Others support themselves by hunting, which is of different kinds. Some, for example, are brigands, others...are fishermen, and others live by the pursuit of birds or wild beasts. The greater number obtain a living from the cultivated fruits of the soil. Such are the modes of subsistence which prevail among those...whose food is not acquired by exchange and retail trade—there is the shepherd, the husbandman, the brigand, the fisherman, the hunter. Some gain a comfortable maintenance out of two employments, eking out the deficiencies of one of them by another: thus the life of a shepherd may be combined with that of a brigand, the life of a farmer with that of a hunter.

We should treat these examples from ancient Greece neither as incomplete ethnographies nor an inchoate desire to categorize hunter-gatherers as a type apart. There were many ways people could and can be different: what largely matters here is the contrast with the Self.

Barbarians and Tribals

What about areas where the existence of hunter-gatherers in a modern anthropological sense can be assumed? In southern Asia too a variety of axes of differentiation can be found. Thapar (1971, 408) suggests that the earliest recognizable distinctions occurred on grounds of language and physiognomy but 'admitted to many nuances' including political and ritual status as well as economic power. By the early centuries AD, she notes how the term 'mleccha'—translated as 'barbarian'—is linked to language, speech, and food, such as those who ate wheat rather than rice (Meserve 1982, 67; Thapar 1971, 410). Along with derogatory or simply abusive terms for others—black-skinned, snub-nosed, treacherous, like demons—an important related aspect was (im)purity: the correct language had to be used for the proper performance of certain rites, for example. Thapar also notes that what constituted the other varied with geographical direction (e.g. placed to the north or south), location (urban, rural, mountain, forest), religion, occupation, birth, etc. This was complicated historically by the growth of caste-based societies (including mixed castes) and the variety of religious practices. Tribes—understood as including the category of hunter-gatherers, but also swidden cultivators and pastoralist and gathering groups—could be included in the ranks of the *mlecchas*; we could also note that 'hunter' was an 'unclean' occupation (Thapar 1971, 413–14, 416). Both prior to and during colonial rule and subsequently, terms such as 'forest-dwellers', 'hillmen', and 'tribals' were used, but none of these are exact synonyms for 'hunter-gatherers' (Pluciennik 2004, 21–3).

There were in fact excellent possibilities for empirical knowledge of foragers in southern Asia, but these particular 'forest-dwellers' were typically encountered in different ways within the complex socio-economic and religious landscapes of the Indian subcontinent (and elsewhere), and integrated in trade networks for forest products for example (Morrison and Junker 2002). Shifting agriculture, foraging, and pastoralism rather formed a dynamic spectrum of rural–mountain–forest activities along with trade and indeed banditry, for example, producing complex socio-economic histories.

This fluid nexus, especially apparent among the landless poor and those marginalized within village or even urban society, perhaps led to a more amorphous notion of '*mleccha*' in which 'foraging' per se was not a particular focus (cf. Savyasaachi 2001, 80). Although later some foragers were distinguished because they were seen to encapsulate a more individualistic, unhierarchical world beyond the urban (Omvedt 1980), Thapar (1971, 436) argues that in general there is a distinctive Indian concept of the other. While there were specified cultural differences, 'the separateness was seen not so much in terms of what the barbarians did as in the fact that they did not observe the norms of ritual purity and were to that extent polluted'.

Rather than oppositional understandings of self and other, Halbfass (1988, 172) argues that the complex hierarchies present within Hindu thought lend themselves more to the idea of concentric circles of differences from a ritually pure centre. Thus, despite the difficulties of summarizing the huge variety of historical, geographical, and cultural contexts for written traditions over millennia, and undoubted encounters with what we would now call 'hunter-gatherers', this economic categorization does not appear to have played a large part in the construction of alterity within southern Asia. It might be considered an intellectual violence to abstract and impose a concept of 'hunter-gatherer' here too.

Chinese historiography presents a further contrast. As in many traditions, 'golden ages' can be found in Confucian and Taoist as well as later Buddhist writings (Bodde 1981), but the cosmological related to the cardinal directions can also be found in relatively early texts, with north, south, east, and west 'barbarians' surrounding the middle country, China, with its connotations of 'good balance, centralization [and] government' (Ecsedy 1974, 333–4). Lattimore (1951, 455) proposes that there is no generic Chinese equivalent of the Greek *barbaroi*, though there are 'a few names' that classify people as 'shepherds' or 'jungle people'; but see Wilkinson (2000, 710–11).

Agriculture and the idea of agriculture, compared to the 'wastelands' inhabited by the other peoples, was though a clear and valorized component of Han dynasty thought, for example, during the second century BC to second century AD. The politically and indeed violently physically encountered other at that time appears to be mainly the Xiongnu, nomadic steppe peoples of Mongolia, to whom various epithets could be attached beyond their wandering habits: idleness, treachery, cruelty. Their land to the north was cold, barren, and inhospitable compared to the 'harmony' of the Middle Kingdom (Meserve 1982, 51–61). E. Hall (1989, 60-2) argues that it is at this time and in an analogous way to the Greek–Persian distinction that a Chinese concept of what constitutes otherness crystallizes, when a 'common enemy' and also a sense of a unified central culture is in place. The contrast here is between 'the "inner" Chinese agriculturalists and the "outer" barbarians, nomadic, and pastoral peoples'. Citing Müller (1980), she refers to the *Records of the Grand Historian* or *Shiji* dating to around 100 BC, and including the 'Treatise on the Xiongnu', in which 'their customs and character are transparently conceived as the reverse of Han ideals... The Chinese prided themselves on their building skills and their well-run farms; the [Xiongnu] are therefore nomads who know nothing of walled cities and agriculture', despise their old people, and are illiterate and cowardly.

The examples above suggest that any concept directly and consistently equivalent to that of hunter-gatherers is surprisingly difficult to find in the past. The construction of difference depends upon available intellectual and cultural resources, as well as authorial and rhetorical intent. One could adduce other historical examples: medieval Islamic scholars (most notably the great Arab historian Ibn Khaldun: see e.g. Pluciennik 2004, 25–7) often displayed ambivalence towards other ways of life, but the major contrast was between settled urban existence and rural peasants and pastoralists. Agriculture or its lack is not an important *topos*, although eating uncooked food sometimes is. Al-Azmeh (1992, 7) points to three major indices of barbarity: 'filth, the inverse of refinement and urbanity', 'profligate sexuality and the lack of jealousy', and incorrect or lack of funerary rites. If desert-dwellers could be characterized as 'savage', they were also valorized as 'hard' compared with the eventually enervating effects of the city. There was also a strong environmental component to Arabic geographies (at least partly influenced by earlier Greek writers), and the cold of the north in the seventh clime, just like the extreme heat of the African south, produced mental dullness and animal-like behaviour that compared unfavourably with the preferred zone in which the Arabic world was centred (Al-Azmeh 1992; Meserve 1982, 67–75).

The Precursors to Hunter-Gatherers

If one accepts that the contemporary anthropological category of 'hunter-gatherer' is a relatively recent construction, then we might expect that there were often instrumental purposes to its establishment and definitions; that the connotations drew upon contemporary mores, values, and concerns; and that the category itself has a history. By far the most influential framework for its categorial development was that of social evolution, and especially as understood within the modern colonial project (Meek 1971; 1976; Pluciennik 2005). But it is also worth examining the factors leading up to its establishment, the surrounding cultural resources, and how these were used in various contexts.

One useful place to start is to consider how peasants and other others could be a complete mixture of characteristics and traits, fantasy, constructed, semi-invented, described, encountered, recorded, and varying according to the needs and perceptions of the author or audience, in what Freedman (1999, 301) calls the 'panoply of othering discourses' present within medieval European thought. There were 'several major axes of pejorative discourse' including ridiculous, dangerous, the lowly but useful, or base and useless, human, semi-human or bestial, avaricious, and savage (Freedman 1999, 136).

Just as later for hunter-gatherers and 'natives' generally, the terms 'lazy' and 'indolent' were commonly used to condemn; such groups could also be described as servile, hard-working, and industrious if treated in the manner of pack animals. There was a crossover of vocabulary (and imagery) among despised groups such as 'Saracens, Jews, or lepers' and peasants (Freedman 1999, 137). On the extremes were the 'denizens of the woods [who] are misshapen, large, hirsute, bestial, and frightening...the forest is the site of the strange, the savage' (Freedman 1999, 141)—the etymology of 'savage' with its roots in *sylvaticus* is itself revealing of patterns of thought and continuity.

Mellinkoff (1993, LI–LII, 231) demonstrates the visual repertoire available within European late medieval art to signal the other: through costume, physical features and gestures, including the idea of lewd exposure by peasants (cf. 'naked savages'), and association with taboo activities, events or materials: blood, death, money, impurity, uncleanness, or immorality. Even though unstable and contextual, there were clearly ideas of the (European) Self and acceptable bounds to normalcy, which others could variously transgress.

What were the ideals of the Self? Within the dominant male and elite gaze, there are examples such as the highly influential *Book of the Courtier* by Castiglione, first published in 1527 and widely translated during the sixteenth century. The emphasis here is on birth, manners, and education: coming from 'good stock'; knowledge of correct manners and behaviour, and possession of physical and other skills. One's duty is especially 'to be skilfull in all kynd of marciall feates...whiche is his cheef profession'. Similar contours are drawn by, for example, Henry Peacham, whose 1622 *The Compleat Gentleman* is mostly about being well educated (e.g. in geometry, poetry, 'musicke', and drawing) as well as 'warre'.

The importance of this for understanding the meaning of terms such as 'hunter' in the early modern world is that as there were increasing encounters with non-European peoples, these vocabularies of self and otherness became further entangled with first-hand descriptions. These included biblical and Classical authorities, economic, political, and moral discourses, and both colonial and non-colonial experiences—of the allegedly 'feckless poor' and of vagrancy at 'home', for example. There were many literary and pictorial genres, each using appropriate tropes and language, ranging from travel and accounts of missionary endeavours to later novels, ethnographies, and bureaucratic descriptions. Especially important from the seventeenth century onwards were discourses on 'political philosophy', and treatises speculating on how rights to property and ideas of good government arose.

English portrayals of the Irish epitomize these cross-fertilizations. Canny (1998, 191) shows how attitudes towards 'natives' from 'settlers' were mutually informed and justified by, and imitative of, actual or reported experiences in Ireland and the New World. The English often cited Spanish examples, or transferred understandings from Irish experiences to the New World or vice versa. But they also drew on other sources. In the travel literature that was read by sixteenth-century Englishmen, nomadic people were considered to be at the opposite pole of civilization from themselves. Boemus, for example (in his 1611 *Manners, lawes and customes of all nations*...) found the Scythians to be the most barbarous people in the world because they 'neither possessed any grounds, nor had any seats or houses to dwell in, but wandered through wilderness and desert places driving their flocks and heardes of beasts before them'. This argument was similarly used as a way to justify dispossession by devaluing Irish transhumance practices, or those of people in North America, where people could be described as 'ranging' over the land rather than inhabiting it (Purchas 1906 [1625] 231). Only proper use of land could give title, but what constituted 'proper' in effect meant farming—and permanent settlement—in the accepted European manner (Elliott 1998; Pagden 1998). This settlement tactic was used to exclude hunter-gatherers, and did so, notably in parts of northern America. But many others were 'farmers' by our contemporary reckoning. There were various other factors to take into account. As Brother Franciscus de Victoria expressed it in 1537 (de Victoria 2005), as part of the Spanish debates over lawful dominion of the new lands, the 'Indians':

> have no proper laws nor magistrates, and are not even capable of controlling their family affairs; they are without any literature or arts, not only the liberal arts, but the mechanical arts also; they have no careful ['proper'] agriculture and no artisans; and they lack many other conveniences, yea necessaries, of human life. It might, therefore, be maintained that in their own interests the sovereigns of Spain might undertake the administration of their country...

From the point of view of the settler or exploiter, as one needed to 'remove' people one could brand them as primitive, not really there (the 'law' of *terra nullius*), not really human (e.g. without souls or grace), not really occupying the land properly—without fences or enclosure, for example—or according to God's law. Alleged lack of agriculture could become part of the colonial armoury whether those it was aimed at were hunter-gatherers or not, but it was by no means essential nor even particularly prominent.

The Invention of Hunter-Gatherers

What then changed towards the middle of the eighteenth century and enabled hunter-gatherers (or at least 'hunters') to appear as an anthropological category? The kind of confrontation produced especially by the New World encouraged better definition of the European Self. Thus, for example, Woolf (1992, 89) argues that by the end of the eighteenth century 'writers and intellectuals had arrived at a definition of what characterized all Europe, beyond its differences, by contrast with the "other", non-European societies'. He suggests that such definitions of Europe rested on 'three particular qualities: economic activity, sociability, and public governance' (Woolf 1992, 92). McGrane (1989) proposes that the non-European other was viewed primarily first through the lens of Christianity; then through the Enlightenment trope of ignorance/knowledge; in the nineteenth century in relation to time (cf. Fabian 1983, see also Fabian 2006); and finally, within the twentieth century, cultural difference.

There were many complexities and currents that contributed to the definition of self and other, and eventually hunter-gatherers. While Barnard (2004) persuasively argues that it is in later eighteenth-century Scotland that the explicit notion of hunter-gatherer society arises, many of the roots can be seen earlier (Pluciennik 2002; 2005, 19–31).

Colonial settlement and concomitant dispossession went hand in hand with developments in ideas of property rights from at least the seventeenth century onwards. Permanent occupation, the input of labour, and productive use gave 'rights' to settle and own within a nascent capitalist system of appropriation. There was an increasing sense of a moral duty and religious obligation to enclose, improve, and cultivate the soil. All this militated against but also served to construct those whom we now term 'hunter-gatherers'.

Crucially, along with the notion of improvement went that of overall and historical progress, which resonated with influential and successful members of the intelligentsia at this time. Ideas of individual salvation, of materialism, of the moral worth of labour and improvement which could also be applied to nations, encounters with those perceived as technologically less skilled and culturally inferior, and the decline in the authority of both the Bible and the ancients all played a part, as did the Enlightenment penchant for the application of Reason and the classification and ordering of things. In speculative histories and anthropologically, hunter-gatherers were at the beginning, the bottom, the lowest. Just as 'race' needed the systematic biological classification of the Enlightenment to come into focus and give it more condensed agency in the form of racism (cf. Muldoon 2000), so the concept of non-agricultural hunter-gatherers needed the framework of social evolution to condense and simplify—by categorizing and defining—this 'type' of society.

The Cultivation of Difference

By the later eighteenth century the idea of the 'gentleman famer' was also present—exactly the kind of people who were reading and writing about the new sciences of economy, and agricultural improvement, and speculative histories of property law. Lord Kames, who wrote a speculative history of man in 1774, two years later produced *The Gentleman Farmer. Being an Attempt to improve Agriculture, By subjecting it to the Test of Rational Principles*. The anthropological idea of 'hunters' was gradually filled out, mostly under circumstances, or against a background of colonialism, expropriation, genocide (intentional or not), and in large part in opposition to an image of what people *should* be like as they progressed towards the European pinnacle.

But vocabulary was also fluid—there were many ways of being pejorative: 'red' or 'black', 'hairy', with small genitalia and lacking sexual ardour (as the inhabitants of the New World generally were characterized by the Comte de Buffon), unable to speak properly, pagan, heretics, devil worshippers, without souls, incapable of receiving God's grace, childlike, wild, unmannered, naked, bestial, irrational, immodest, immoral, unsettled, lazy, forest dwellers, the 'natural slaves' proposed by Aristotle. Another famous typology—'savage', 'barbarian', 'civilized'—could sometimes be equated to that of hunter-gatherer, pastoralist, farmer. Such terms of simplification could only come into proper focus with the invention of a system and stereotype; and for various reasons the economy (or rather, subsistence) became the defining characteristic.

Once accepted, the framework of social evolution had a grossly disproportionate effect on those assigned to the hunter-gatherer stage and type. It was the earliest in absolute historical, stadial, and evolutionary terms; the most primitive; the furthest away from civilized us. Hunter-gatherers were assigned geographical as well as temporal and cultural distance (Gamble 1992). Theirs were the societies which needed the most 'translation' and representation by ethnographers to make them comprehensible and to bring them into 'our' time (Fabian 1983; 2006). A substantial part of their later anthropological career is neatly encapsulated in works of G. P. Murdock. In 1934, shortly after the invention of hyphenated 'hunter-gatherers' he wrote about them in his book *Our Primitive Contemporaries* (Murdock 1934). In 1966 offering an overview at the Man the Hunter conference, he excluded the rather too complex Pacific coast groups as being outside the acceptable range of hunter-gatherer groups (Murdock 1968, 13).

In the same volume, of course, Lee and DeVore (1968, 11)—tongue-in-cheek or not— famously characterized hunter-gatherers as 'living in small groups' and 'moving around a lot'. This was perhaps the point at which the eighteenth-century project to define people by their 'economies' reached its culmination. Since then anthropologists and archaeologists have been back-pedalling and offering alternative, less restrictive, somehow *kinder* and certainly more culturalist definitions. Bender (1978) drew attention to the gendered ordering and proposed 'gatherer-hunter'; Bird-David (1994) offered public sociality; Lee and Daly (1999, 3) preferred to talk about typical 'areas of convergence' rather than checklists of traits. Some even wondered whether there was merit in discarding the category entirely (Barnard 1983, 193). Kusimba (2005, 354) notes that attempts to apply a universal definition tend to set up a 'circularity of interpretation' in which the 'nature of the society in question is assumed from the start'. A more productive way, she suggests, is to realize that 'hunting and gathering is an activity [*sic*] that is part of a variety of different economies both past and present', though she continues to treat the activities as essentially conjoined. But there is nothing sacred about the terms, nor its hyphenated history. Whether we find the rubric 'hunter-gatherer' and its connotations useful or even essential will depend on what kinds of questions engage us. If we are interested in historical human differences and cultural diversity, then the crude subsistence division suggested by 'hunter-gatherer' is probably of limited value though certainly of historiographic interest. Thinking about alternative boundaries of alterity may be useful places from which to start.

REFERENCES

Al-Azmeh, A. 1992. Barbarians in Arab eyes. *Past and Present* 134, 3–18.
Albright, W. 1965. Primitivism in ancient western Asia (Mesopotamia and Israel). In A. Lovejoy and G. Boas (eds), *Primitivism and related ideas in antiquity*, 421–32. New York: Octagon Books.
Aristotle. *Politics*, trans. Benjamin Jowett. The Internet Classics Archive: http://classics.mit.edu/Aristotle/politics.html.
Barnard, A. 1983. Contemporary hunter-gatherers: current theoretical issues in ecology and social organization. *Annual Review of Anthropology* 12, 193–214.
Barnard, A. 1999. Images of hunters and gatherers in European social thought. In R. Lee and R. Daly (eds), *The Cambridge encyclopedia of hunters and gatherers*, 375–83. Cambridge: Cambridge University Press.
Barnard, A. 2004. Hunting-and-gathering society: an eighteenth-century Scottish invention. In A. Barnard (ed.), *Hunter-gatherers in history, archaeology and anthropology*, 31–43. Oxford: Berg.
Bender, B. 1978. Gatherer-hunter to farmer: a social perspective. *World Archaeology* 10, 204–22.
Bird-David, N. 1994. Sociality and immediacy: or, past and present conversations on bands. *Man* NS, 29, 583–603.

Bodde, D. 1981. Harmony and conflict in Chinese philosophy. In C. Le Blanc and D. Borei (eds), *Essays on Chinese civilization*, 237–98. Princeton: Princeton University Press.

Boemus, J. 1611. *Manners, lawes and customes of all nations*. London: G. Eld.

Canny, N. 1998. The ideology of English colonization: from Ireland to America. In D. Armitage (ed.), *Theories of empire, 1450–1800*, 179–202. Aldershot: Ashgate.

Cartledge, P. 2002. *The Greeks: a portrait of self and others* (2nd edition). Oxford: Oxford University Press.

Coleman, J. 1997. Ancient Greek ethnocentrism. In J. Coleman and C. Walz (eds), *Greeks and barbarians*, 175–220. Bethesda, MD: CDL Press.

Daly, P. 1981. Agricultural employment: has the decline ended? *Monthly Labor Review* 104, November, 11.

Daunton, M. 2007. *Wealth and welfare: an economic and social history of Britain, 1851–1951*. Oxford: Oxford University Press.

Ecsedy, H. 1974. Cultivators and barbarians in ancient China. *Acta Orientalia Hungarica* 28, 327–49.

Elliott, J. 1998. The seizure of overseas territories by the European powers. In D. Armitage (ed.), *Theories of empire, 1450–1800*, 139–57. Aldershot: Ashgate.

Fabian, J. 1983. *Time and the other: how anthropology makes its object*. New York: Columbia University Press.

Fabian, J. 2006. The other revisited: critical afterthoughts. *Anthropological Theory* 6, 139–52.

Freedman, P. 1999. *Images of the medieval peasant*. Stanford: Stanford University Press.

Gamble, C. 1992. Uttermost ends of the earth. *Antiquity* 66, 710–20.

Halbfass, W. 1988. *India and Europe: an essay in understanding*. Albany, NY: SUNY Press.

Hall, E. 1989. *Inventing the barbarian*. Oxford: Clarendon Press.

Hall, J. 1997. *Ethnic identity in Greek antiquity*. Cambridge: Cambridge University Press.

Hartog, F. 1988. *The Mirror of Herodotus: the representation of the Other in the writing of history*, trans. J. Lloyd. Berkeley: University of California Press.

Hesiod. 2006. *Theogony; works and days; Testimonia*, ed. and trans. Glenn Most (Loeb Classical Library 57). Cambridge, MA: Harvard University Press.

Hodgen, M. 1964. *Early anthropology in the sixteenth and seventeenth centuries*. Philadelphia: University of Pennsylvania Press.

Jahoda, G. 1999. *Images of savages: ancient roots of prejudice in Western culture*. London: Routledge.

Kames, H. 1776. *The Gentleman Farmer. Being an Attempt to improve Agriculture, By subjecting it to the Test of Rational Principles*. Edinburgh and London: W. Creech and T. Cadell.

Kusimba, S. 2005. What is a hunter-gatherer? Variation in the archaeological record of eastern and southern Africa. *Journal of Archaeological Research* 13, 337–66.

Lattimore, O. 1951. *Inner Asian frontiers of China* (2nd edition). New York: Capitol Publishing/American Geographical Society.

Lee, R. and Daly, R. 1999. Introduction: foragers and others. In R. Lee and R. Daly (eds), *The Cambridge encyclopedia of hunters and gatherers*, 1–19. Cambridge: Cambridge University Press.

Lee, R. and DeVore, I. 1968. Problems in the study of hunters and gatherers. In R. Lee and I. DeVore (eds), *Man the hunter*, 3–12. Chicago: Aldine.

McGrane, B. 1989. *Beyond anthropology: society and the other*. New York: Columbia University Press.

Malkin, I. 2001. Introduction. In I. Malkin (ed.), *Ancient perceptions of Greek ethnicity*, 1–28. Cambridge, MA: Harvard University Press.

Meek, R. 1971. Smith, Turgot, and the 'four stages' theory. *History of Political Economy* 3, 9–27.
Meek, R. 1976. *Social science and the ignoble savage*. Cambridge: Cambridge University Press.
Mellinkoff, R. 1993. *Outcasts: signs of otherness in northern European art of the late middle ages (Volume One: Text)*. Berkeley: University of California Press.
Meserve, R. 1982. The inhospitable land of the barbarians. *Journal of Asian History* 16, 51–89.
Morrison, K. and Junker, L. (eds) 2002. *Forager-traders in South and Southeast Asia*. Cambridge: Cambridge University Press.
Muldoon, J. 2000. Race or culture: medieval notions of difference. In B. Lang (ed.), *Race and racism in theory and in practice*, 79–98. Lanham, MD: Rowman & Littlefield.
Müller, C. C. 1980 Herausbildung der Gegensätze: Chinesen und Barbaren in der frühen Zeit. In W. Bauer (ed.), *China und die Fremden. 3000 Jahre Auseinandersetzung in Krieg und Frieden*, 43–76. München: C. H. Beck.
Murdock, G. P. 1934. *Our Primitive Contemporaries*. New York: Macmillan.
Murdock, G. P. 1968. The current status of the world's hunting and gathering peoples. In R. Lee and I. DeVore (eds), *Man the hunter*, 13–20. Chicago: Aldine.
Omvedt, G. 1980. Adivasis, culture and modes of production in India. *Bulletin of Concerned Asian Scholars* 12, 15–22.
Paddaya, K. 1995. Theoretical perspectives in Indian archaeology. In P. Ucko (ed.), *Theory in archaeology: a world perspective*, 110–49. London: Routledge.
Pagden, A. 1986. *The fall of natural man: the American Indian and the origins of comparative ethnology*. Cambridge: Cambridge University Press.
Pagden, A. 1998. Dispossessing the barbarian: the language of Spanish Thomism and the debate over the property rights of the American Indians. In D. Armitage (ed.), *Theories of empire, 1450–1800*, 159–78. Aldershot: Ashgate.
Pandey, D. 1989. An 11th century literary reference to prehistoric times in India. In R. Layton (ed.), *Who needs the past? Indigenous values and archaeology*, 57–8. London: Unwin Hyman.
Peacham, H. 1622. *The compleat gentleman*. London: Francis Constable.
Pluciennik, M. 2002. The invention of hunter-gatherers in seventeenth-century Europe. *Archaeological Dialogues* 9, 98–150.
Pluciennik, M. 2004. The meaning of 'hunter-gatherers' and modes of subsistence: a comparative historical perspective. In A. Barnard (ed.), *Hunter-gatherers in history, archaeology and anthropology*, 17–29. Oxford: Berg.
Pluciennik, M. 2005. *Social evolution*. London: Duckworth.
Purchas, S. 1906 [1625]. *Hakluytus Posthumus, or, Purchas his pilgrimes, contayning a history of the world in sea voyages and lande travells by Englishmen and others*. Glasgow: James MacLehose and Sons.
Roberts, K. 2007. *Alterity and narrative: stories and the negotiation of Western identities*. Albany, NY: SUNY Press.
Rudebeck, E. 2000. *Tilling nature, harvesting culture: exploring images of the human being in the transition to agriculture*. Stockholm: Almqvist and Wiksell International.
Savyasaachi. 2001. Forest dwellers and tribals in India. In S. Visvanathan (ed.), *Structure and transformation: theory and society in India*, 71–95. Oxford: Oxford University Press.
Thapar, R. 1971. The image of the barbarian in early India. *Comparative Studies in Society and History* 13, 420–32.
de Victoria, F. 2005 [1537]. *De Indis recenter inventis, relectio prior*, trans. John Pawley Bate Available from http://www.constitution.org/victoria/victoria_4.htm.
Warder, A. 1961. The Pali Cvanon and its commentaries as an historical record. In C. Philips (ed.), *Historians of India, Pakistan and Ceylon*, 44–56. Oxford: Oxford University Press.

Wilkinson, E. 2000. *Chinese history: a manual* (2nd edition). Cambridge, MA: Harvard University Asia Center.

Woolf, S. 1992. The construction of a European world-view in the Revolutionary-Napoleonic years. *Past and Present* 137, 72–101.

Zvelebil, M. 2002. Comment on Mark Pluciennik. *Archaeological Dialogues* 9, 123–9.

CHAPTER 4

ADAPTIVE AND ECOLOGICAL APPROACHES TO THE STUDY OF HUNTER-GATHERERS

RAVEN GARVEY AND ROBERT L. BETTINGER

Introduction

HUNTER-GATHERERS are fundamental to the modern understanding of human adaptation. Indeed, a cohesive theory of human evolution and adaptation is scarcely conceivable without the information that their study has provided. Hunter-gatherers and their cultural adaptations have been alternately denigrated as simplistic in the extreme and celebrated as elegant responses to complex ecological problems. This disciplinary waffling is due both to social and political currents that influence the popular perception of hunter-gatherers, and to changing approaches to evolution and adaptation more generally, which are of course also influenced by social circumstances (Giere 1988; Kuhn 1962), as outlined in several notable works (e.g. Barnard 2000; Bettinger 1991; Bohannan and Glazer 1988; Harris 1968; 1998; Hodder 1983; 2002; Kelly 1995; McGee and Warms 2000; Willey and Sabloff 1980). Here, we are less interested in the influences than their consequences and in reviewing a broad range of approaches to the ecology and adaptations of hunter-gatherers, from the Enlightenment to the present.

While it developed quite separately from Darwinian evolutionary theory, anthropology arose as a means of answering many of the same questions, and many anthropologists have sought to explain the human condition in evolutionary terms, frequently borrowing methods from the biological sciences. It has always been clear, at the same time, that culture prevents mindless ecological interpretation of human behaviour using models developed for much simpler organisms, and the history of anthropology is, in essence, a history of wrangling over the degree to which culture sets us apart from the rest of the animal kingdom. Changing opinions on this matter are closely reflected in different anthropological approaches to hunter-gatherer ecology, hunter-gatherers being viewed as more easily dealt with and more intimately intertwined with the natural world than more complex societies (Bettinger 1991).

Differing approaches to hunter-gatherer adaptations and ecology reflect changing opinions in two arenas: scale of adaptation and force of environment. Decisions about scale—whether individual attributes or general behavioural propensities are more adaptively important—profoundly affect the mode of inquiry, producing distinct methodologies, each with strengths and shortcomings. Studies of larger scale (e.g. of whole cultural systems) are frequently historical accounts of individual groups, their adaptation to a particular environment and changes in that environment over time. Conversely, smaller-scale studies (e.g. of specific behaviours) are more given to cross-cultural, statistical comparison and law-like generalization, usually without reference to individual cultures. Balancing these alternative treatments of adaptation has been likened to 'sailing a perilous course between a pseudo-explanatory reductionist atomism and stultifying non-explanatory holism' (Mayr 1983, 329).

The influence of environment, too, has been variably interpreted; it is of little significance to some and of overwhelming importance to others. The role of culture, the premier human adaptation, is similarly contested, a product of natural selection on the one hand, insulation against selection on the other. In short, the intersection of culture with the environment remains a subject of considerable disagreement between the various strands of ecological and evolutionary explanation of human behaviour. To place modern understandings of cultural evolution and, specifically, hunter-gatherer adaptations and ecology, in a broader context, we trace the history of philosophical approaches to these issues, offering a critical review, from natural theology to neurobiology.

Speculation and Description: Adaptation Before Ecology (1600–1930)

That organisms are physically and behaviourally adapted to their environments has intrigued both lay and specialist audiences for millennia (Bettinger 1991; Burrow 1966). Seeking rational, experiential evidence of divinity, adherents to natural theology were among the first to undertake systematic studies of these adaptations, which they regarded as proof of divine creation (Paley 2006 [1802]). This theological world view neither requires nor provides explanation of adaptive change and, prior to the late eighteenth century, there was no sense that the earth was old enough or had changed enough to require it. Environment was the unchanging scenery to which organisms were divinely and forever suited.

Charles Darwin (e.g. 1859; 1871), of course, rejected this static view, owing in part to his reading of James Hutton and Charles Lyell (1990 [1830–3]), who argued that the world was very old and constantly changing, and Thomas Malthus (1803), who argued that populations tended to grow until limited by available resources, meaning those resources would always be in short supply. An old earth, teeming with individuals in constant competition for scarce resources, gave context to Darwin's meticulous biological fieldwork and ultimately led him to the theory of natural selection: favourable, heritable traits become more prevalent in successive generations; populations of individuals adapt (Darwin 1859; Maynard Smith 1958).

The tenets of Darwinian evolution thrust environmental agency to the fore and, because environments change, adaptation must be treated as an ongoing process rather than a static condition (Kelly 1995).

Darwin's (1859) allusion to human evolution in the final pages of *On the origin of species* sparked a crusade to classify the world's populations into a developmental scheme (Schutkowski 2006). Biological anthropologists, grappling with 'man's place' in nature, enumerated the physical differences observed among these populations and sought to identify environmental factors that might account for what they took to be the hierarchical 'races of man' (Huxley 1863; Rodman 1994). Early social anthropologists were similarly preoccupied with development in relation to the Enlightenment notion of progress. Herbert Spencer, the English philosopher and social theorist, was singularly influential in arguing for human progress through a hierarchy of cultural stages, selection being one of the major forces responsible for the perceived superiority of industrialized nations (Bettinger 1991; Kelly 1995; Spencer 1868). On this view, known as progressive social evolutionary theory (PSET), hunter-gatherer 'primitives' were developmentally retarded, wholly at the whim of nature, struggling to wrest a living from the land, and ultimately doomed to extinction at the hands of groups more advanced (Bettinger 1991; Kelly 1995; Powell 1888). This made the world's hunter-gatherers all of a kind, their primitive stage of development eclipsing all but the most outstanding differences in technology and environment. When addressed at all, differences were attributed to contact with civilized neighbours (i.e. diffusion) or ill-defined peculiarities of environment; primitives simply lacked the mental faculties to adapt on their own (Kelly 1995; Morgan 1877). More evolutionarily advanced, 'civilized' folk had technology that liberated them from the uncertainties of daily food procurement, i.e. from the environment, and freed time for intellectual pursuits that were both the cause and consequence of their superiority (Bettinger 1991; Kelly 1995).

While framed in evolutionary terms, PSET differed markedly from Darwinian evolutionary theory. In particular, PSET made little room for the concept of adaption, cultures being inevitably transformed by selection, the environment serving only to hasten or slow the process to suit a particular interpretation; a harsh environment could be an obstacle that a 'primitive' group failed to overcome (Kelly 1995) or a challenge that fostered civilization's ingenuity (Chinard 1947).

Although a truly modern approach to ecological adaptation was still decades off, by the turn of the twentieth century American anthropologists were taking a keener interest in the environment and its influence on culture. This is almost certainly due to circumstances peculiar to the New World. American anthropology was just beginning to form as a discipline when settlers first began pushing west into the American frontier, experiencing new, often harsh, environments. Frontier reports of encounters with living hunter-gatherers who had successfully surmounted environmental obstacles that settlers were struggling mightily to overcome made American anthropologists sensitive to the problems of environment and adaptation and kindled what would prove to be a lasting interest in hunter-gatherers (Bettinger 1991; Kelly 1995). The absence of these same circumstances in the Old World delayed the development there of anthropological interest in hunter-gatherer adaptations.

Historical particularism, the first school of American anthropological thought, reflected these sentiments in its attention to environment and its explicit recognition that hunter-gatherers, however simple, were ecologically savvy. The father of historical particularism, and of American anthropology itself, Franz Boas, was sympathetic to Darwinian evolution, and indeed had conducted a surprisingly sophisticated study of human phenotypic plasticity, concluding that environment had a significant effect on adaptation (Boas 1910; 1912; cf. Sparks and Jantz 2002). On the other hand, Boas staunchly opposed PSET's unilineal view of evolution and argued that cultural similarities need not indicate parallel evolutionary development (Boas 1920; Harris 1968; Kelly 1995; McGee and Warms 2000). Boas advocated detailed field studies and appreciation of every culture on its own terms, in light of its own history and environment. As part of this agenda, Boas oversaw scores of students' fieldwork in the US and abroad (e.g. Garfield 1931; Mead 1961 [1928]; Radin 1923) and directed the ambitious Jesup North Pacific Expedition, which resulted in many important ethnographies on the peoples of Siberia and Alaska (Boas 1898; Bogoras 1910; Jochelson 1908; 1926; Teit 1906). Field research was key, Boas argued, and armchair generalizations would only perpetuate the wrongheaded notion of step-wise social progression.

Despite Boas's resistance to the comparative method and universal laws of human behaviour, his intellectual progeny, Clark Wissler and Alfred Kroeber in particular, were intrigued by broad cultural patterns they observed across whole regions of the US, which they argued were more than historical happenstance. Among other things, these regional commonalities established that, in North America at least, hunter-gatherers were not homogeneous, as progressive social evolutionists had argued. Instead, they expressed a wide range of cultural manifestations (e.g. Inuit vs. Shoshone vs. Northwest Coast) that seemed more a function of environment than developmental trajectory (Bettinger 1991). Ethnographic and archaeological distributions seemed to indicate suites of cultural traits coinciding with major food resources, which were interpreted as cultural adaptations to the geographic centre of a resource's range (Kelly 1995; Wissler 1926). These 'culture areas', defined according to human–resource relationships, reflect an incipient science of ecology that was taking shape in the first decades of the twentieth century. Kroeber (1939) did much to develop and publicize these patterns but cautioned that individual traits frequently and unpredictably cross-cut culture areas, obfuscating any simple relationship between culture and environment.

It is clear that, between Darwin's *Origin* in 1859 and the incorporation of a formal ecological perspective around 1930, anthropology understood that the environment had an important role in shaping culture. From the mid-nineteenth to the turn of the twentieth century, speculative descriptions of cultural evolution were predicated on the notion (often implicit) that the environment was an obstacle to overcome, an impediment to progress, and a swift punisher of those who failed to keep up. Hunter-gatherers were thus closely aligned with nature, scarcely different from the rest of the animal kingdom and in the precarious position of having to adopt more sophisticated neighbours' technologies (rather than adapt) or face extinction (Bettinger 1991). In the first decades of the twentieth century, Boas and his students were rather more explicit in their treatment of the environment, subscribing to what is termed 'environmental possibilism': environment poses limits, determining what is not possible, but not the form culture will take among the realm of remaining possibilities (Forde 1934; Kroeber 1939). For the possibilists, then, observed cultural traits had little to do with adaptation. Yet, the same detailed field methods and knowledge of environment that guided environmental possibilists produced a fundamentally different ecological approach in which environment was not merely limiting, but creative and enabling—producing adaptations—as Darwin had proposed nearly a century earlier (Gould 1982).

The Advent of an Ecological Approach to Hunter-Gatherers: Cultural Ecology and Neofunctionalism

Julian Steward believed that while the natural environment limits the range and trajectory of cultural adaptations, technology was a powerful, enabling counterbalance (Barnard 2000; Steward 1955). As the product of a particular history, technology was key to resource extraction, determining the amount of energy potentially available. Technology and all behaviours shaped by the use of technology in a particular environment, most importantly subsistence behaviour, define the 'culture core'. Steward considered it the goal of anthropology to study the course of cultural evolution in relation to the interaction between culture core and environment (Barnard 2000; Bohannan and Glazer 1988; McGee and Warms 2000; Orlove 1980; Steward 1955).

Steward believed that understanding cultural adaptation required comparison of groups living in similar environments (McGee and Warms 2000, 226). While his Berkeley professors Kroeber and Lowie were culture area proponents, thus more willing to entertain cross-cultural studies than their mentor, Boas, they had stopped well short of exploring causal links between culture and environment, believing them too complicated to resolve at the time (Kelly 1995; Kroeber 1939). Unwilling to accept that human culture was a purely historical patchwork of accidents and connections, Steward looked cross-culturally and found recurrent cultural adaptations in similar environments, which he concluded represented general ecological adaptations (Bohannan and Glazer 1988; McGee and Warms 2000; Orlove 1980; Steward 1955).

Like the Boasians, Steward began with specific cultural behaviours in specific local environments. His most extensive archaeological and ethnographic fieldwork was in the Great Basin, where sparse, unpredictable resources and simple technology kept human population thinly spread and annually mobile, preventing the development of large, land-holding groups. The culture–environment interactions that Steward observed in the Great Basin inspired his clearest synthesis of cultural ecology in relation to what he termed the family band—small, nuclear family-centred groups that were ideally suited to small, constantly shifting resource patches. While of roughly the same size, Great Basin family bands differed fundamentally from the more familiar hunter-gatherer form of organization known as the patrilineal band, whose core components (patrilocal post-marital residence and descent, band exogamy, and communal land ownership) Steward (1936) had earlier identified as functional adaptations to a combination of environmental factors different from those of the Great Basin. He had argued that patrilineal bands arise when pedestrian hunter-gatherers armed with simple technologies occupy environments where scattered, non-migratory game constitute a major part of the diet (Steward 1936; 1955). Just as Great Basin Shoshone represented the prototypical family band, hunter-gatherers in southern Africa, the Philippines, and Australia represented Steward's patrilineal band, their widespread distribution attesting that the core elements of this type of organization recurred regularly under similar environmental conditions (Steward 1955; Bohannan and Glazer 1988). Deviations from the basic configuration were explained as the effects of diffusion or unique local circumstances.

Cultural ecology was like historical particularism in its holism but not in its recognition of general principles of cultural evolution. Cultural ecologists deduced holistic 'culture types' from recurrent constellations of (atomistic) adaptive traits (Steward 1955); historical particularists eschewed evolutionary principles, viewing adaptation as a purely historical process of settling-in to one's environment. Still, while cultural ecologists shared an interest in evolution via technology and energy capture with contemporary thinkers such as Leslie White (1959), their aims and approaches were worlds apart. White believed that all cultures evolved through the same broad, inevitable stages, much as Morgan (1877) and Tylor (1871) had. That Steward and the cultural ecologists took a far more empirical and particularistic tack makes their approach better suited to studies of hunter-gatherer adaptations.

Cultural ecology's dissatisfaction with structural description and interest in functional adaptation parallels the conceptual dissatisfactions that led to evolutionary biology's New Synthesis, also during the 1930s, when Darwinian principles of evolution were combined with Mendelian genetics (Gould 1982). In biological anthropology this meant a shift from assessing 'man's place' in nature on the basis of similarities in form and structure, to taxonomies based on adaptive function. Washburn (1951, 144) wrote of the New Synthesis: 'population genetics presents the anthropologist with a clearly formulated, experimentally verified, conceptual scheme.' While not responding directly to these developments, Steward recognized the same potential in relation to ecological studies of culture, marking a shifting point from anthropological studies that used the language of evolution to studies that used Darwinian principles, however clumsily at first.

Cultural ecology was alternately criticized as environmental determinism and watered-down progressive social evolution. Steward anticipated the determinism charge. On his view, technology is a product of history (cultural history), not of environment. The environmental determinist agrees with Steward that behaviour is determined by the action of a given technology in a given environment, but goes on to argue that technology itself is primarily shaped by environment, which leaves no room for culture. This is why Steward argued that environment and technology had to be treated as independent 'givens' (Bettinger 1991; Steward 1955; 1968). Critics, of course, noted that technology was quite clearly shaped by environment. Indeed, cultural ecologists themselves tended to interpret technology not as historical accidents but as adaptive responses to environment. In the final analysis, though, Steward was right to keep technology and environment separate. We know, for example, that the Great Basin Shoshone adjusted their technology to fit local variations in environment, using finer-meshed nets for small fish, larger-meshed nets for rabbits. This variation is clearly a response to environment, made possible by a technology that permits a wide range of mesh sizes. In that sense, small-meshed nets were in the technological repertoire of the Death Valley Shoshone, even though they never brought them into play, lacking any reason for doing so, unlike the Shoshone of Elko, whose environment offered greater opportunities for fishing. When they first moved into their fish-rich environment, the Shoshone of Elko did not 'invent' small-meshed fishing nets, but merely applied that capability, which they had always had, as would have the Death Valley Shoshone had the opportunity arisen. What no Great Basin group had in its aboriginal technological repertoire was a mode of transportation that would have permitted them to move faster, over longer distances and in this way more effectively respond to shifting resource distributions. This changed with the introduction of the horse in the northern and eastern Great Basin, which produced major changes in diet and allowed social groups to grow much larger than the pre-contact family band. So Steward's point was not that technology had no relationship to environment, but rather that every culture is limited by its technology and that those limits are not imposed by the environment but by the nature of the technology itself. Insofar as limits are concerned, technology is indeed independent of environment.

More troubling was that in emphasizing technology, cultural ecology produced a long view of cultural evolution not too different from progressive social evolutionary theory. Although Steward rejected unilineal evolution, insisting that all cultural manifestations (not merely those of hunter-gatherers) are strongly influenced by techno-environmental interactions, cultural ecology seemed to imply that as technology improved, these interactions become less influential (Orlove 1980)—precisely as progressive social evolutionary theorists had argued.

These problems aside, cultural ecology had a profound and lasting influence on anthropology. Nearly all subsequent approaches to the study of culture—and especially to the study of hunter-gatherers—drew heavily on some form of culture ecological interpretation of adaptation. This influence is perhaps most pronounced in neofunctionalism, which carried cultural ecological interpretation to an extreme in arguing that even seemingly dysfunctional cultural behaviours could be interpreted as adaptive responses to the 'quality, quantity and distribution of resources' (Orlove 1980, 237). Coupled with the biological view that individual behaviour needed to be understood in terms of its population-level consequences, this led neofunctionalists to interpret culture as an adaptation that functioned to maintain group homeostasis. Thus, all components of culture—all observable cultural traits—must also be adaptive. Starting from this premise, neofunctionalists quickly gravitated to cultural oddities and the ways in which they met cultural needs and contributed to group survival (Bettinger 1991).

Neofunctionalist treatments of 'ethnographic riddles' made for captivating reading and resulted in many detailed treatments of ecological relationships (Orlove 1980, 243). Rappaport's (1968) work on ritual in New Guinea, Piddocke's (1969) explanation of the Kwakiutl potlatch, and Freeman's (1971) assessment of infanticide among the Netsilik Eskimo, for example, make functional 'sense' of behaviours that many Westerners find puzzling or disturbing. Warfare, excessive feasting, and infanticide are not merely rational, they turn out to be requisite for survival, maintaining population below local carrying capacity or redistributing essential resources. Interest in the regulating function of cultural behaviour reflected the neofunctionalist view that populations are the units of selection and that cultural 'systems should tend towards homeostatic equilibrium, with populations at or close to carrying capacity; population growth above these limits induces change' (Dow 1976; Orlove 1980, 242; Rappaport 1971a; 1971b).

Neofunctional accounts were roundly criticized in anthropology and biology alike because they rested on group rather than individual selection, consistently failed to demonstrate empirical links between purportedly functional behaviours and the need they were said to fill, and focused on the consequences rather than causes of adaptation (Bettinger 1991; Gould and Lewontin 1979; Levins and Lewontin 1985; Williams 1966).

The group selection criticism was particularly problematic. From the start, anthropological theory took whole groups or cultures as the units of analysis and explanation. This separated anthropological from biological theory until the early 1960s, when Wynne-Edwards (1962) argued that much animal behaviour increased the fitness of groups rather than individuals, which ran counter to the methodological individualism at the heart of New

Synthetic evolutionary theory. Evolutionary biologists quickly dispatched group selection, however, demonstrating mathematically and conceptually that group selection should be exceedingly rare in nature (Price 1970; 1972; Williams 1966; Wilson 2005). Neofunctionalist explanations of culture were rejected on similar grounds. Experimental evidence (Koeslag 1997; 2003; Soltis et al. 1995) and reworking of fundamental mathematical models including Hamilton's Rule (Bourke and Franks 1995; Trivers and Hare 1976; Wilson 2005) now suggest that group selection is likely an important evolutionary force, but this is not enough to save neofunctionalism, which suffers more fundamental flaws.

Neofunctionalists usually failed to establish causal links between behaviours of interest and the needs they are supposed to fill. For example, Piddocke (1969) argues that the seemingly extravagant and wasteful feasting that attended the Kwakiutl potlatch conceals an ingenious system for redistributing the boom and bust resources of the Northwest Coast of North America. The potlatch might have redistributed resources, but Piddocke fails to show that it actually did, that the Kwakiutl system could not survive without some level of redistribution, or that this was not accomplished by other Kwakiutl behaviours (e.g. trade, temporary resettlement, etc.: Hempel 1959; Orans 1975). Assuming a need has been correctly identified in the first place (Levins and Lewontin 1985), neofunctionalism faces the more fundamental problem of demonstrating how the trait said to satisfy that need came into being, i.e. does this or that need trigger behaviours to satisfy it (Bettinger 1991)?

Functional arguments are not inherently bad—indeed the study of adaptation is inherently functional. The view of such studies, however, has long since moved beyond static analysis of cultural oddities to work on larger adaptive systems and the more dynamic processes of adaptation and cultural change.

The New Archaeology

In the early 1960s, a crop of young US scholars became convinced, and in turn convinced many of their peers, that archaeology lacked the conceptual tools needed to tackle the problem of human adaptation and that a major overhaul of both theory and method was long overdue. These 'new' archaeologists were particularly interested in human–environment interactions, which had been pushed into public consciousness with the publication of works such as Rachel Carson's *Silent Spring* (1962) and Paul Ehrlich's *Population Bomb* (1968). The recognition in anthropology that industry and scientific 'progress' had a serious environmental downside promoted an increasingly neo-Malthusian view that sustainable adaptations always limited growth to levels below carrying capacity and that hunter-gatherers alone had managed this simple solution to responsible living (e.g. Lee and DeVore 1968). Understanding hunter-gatherer relationships with the earth and its resources—and whatever caused the rest of us to turn away from such an idyllic lifestyle—was intellectually stimulating and seemed socially relevant. Paradoxically, while science and scientists were no longer infallible or beyond reproach, there was a conscious effort to make the social sciences more scientific, specifically more like the biological sciences (Bettinger 1991; Orlove 1980). A scientific approach was the key plank in Lewis Binford's (1962) platform for a revolution in archaeology, that only by testing explicit hypotheses about specific adaptations to specific environments could archaeologists understand the general laws, mechanisms, and processes of culture change.

This 'New Archaeology', or processualism, drew on Steward's cultural ecology and biological evolutionary theory (Binford 1962; 1965; Binford and Binford 1968; Trigger 1989). Cultural ecology provided a basic framework for interpreting culture–environment interactions, biology provided the terminology and conceptual models of adaptation and selection, culture being viewed as an 'extrasomatic means of adaptation' (White 1959, 8). Perhaps the most important borrowing was of the ecosystems concept, which replaced the longstanding view that kept humans and nature separate with the view that humans are an integral part of environmental systems. Culture was the adaptive mechanism by which humans maintained themselves within limits imposed by carrying capacity, ensuring environmental homeostasis within a broader ecosystem (Boserup 1965; Birdsell 1968; Frisancho and Schechter 1997; Harner 1970; Kelly 1995; Laughlin and Brady 1978; Lee and DeVore 1968; Orlove 1980). That is, systems 'seek' to maintain equilibrium in the face of change generated by sources both internal (e.g. innovation or invention) and external (e.g. the environment), resulting in adaptation (Clarke 1968). Adaptive processes were explored in cases where change was highly visible in the archaeological record, such as tipping points from one mode of subsistence to another, e.g. from hunting and gathering to agriculture. Study of the feedback interactions between the various natural and cultural systems at work in these situations led to an understanding of fundamental adaptive processes, which could then be applied more generally to less dramatic cases of cultural change.

Archaeologists eventually realized that translating the various fragmentary components of the archaeological record into reliable interpretations of human behaviour would require a family of more modest conceptual tools that dealt with the processes that go into the formation of archaeological sites. The processes that shape living ecosystems can be directly observed; archaeologists, however, must make inferences about these processes by observing the archaeological remains of long-dead systems, frequently using 'middle range' models and analogues developed through ethnoarchaeological studies of living hunter-gatherers and controlled scientific observation and experimentation (Binford 1977; 1978a; 1978b; 1980; Lee and DeVore 1968; Merton 1968). Many middle range approaches—including Binford's butchering strategy (Binford 1978b) and forager-collector models (Binford 1980), Vita-Finzi and Higgs's (1970) site catchment analyses, and Lee's work on calorific input-output among the !Kung (e.g. Lee 1969)—are firmly grounded in economic efficiency, which concept is also fundamental to human behavioural ecology. (For an extended discussion of Binford's (1978b) butchering strategy model's resemblance to optimal foraging theory, see Bettinger 1991, 107–10.) Middle Range Theory, as applied by New Archaeologists, may have anticipated human behavioural ecology's platform, but anthropologists' first assessments of economic efficiency were at the group level. The New Archaeology aimed to understand cultural systems holistically, but middle range necessity required reducing systems to their constituent parts, exploring their adaptations in turn. However, while Middle Range Theory helps to explain the functional connection between these parts, it is silent on how they came to be connected, i.e. what caused the adaptation or how the process leading to it should be modelled (e.g. Binford 1968). Adaptations were usually portrayed as rational, the sort of thing a group of well-informed individuals would collectively agree was a prudent course of action in the presence of a consciously perceived adaptive challenge—but no one thought anything like this actually occurred. Instead, processualists were content to describe the functional benefits of cultural change entailing new technologies or behaviours, leaving the mechanisms of change for others to sort out (Bettinger 1991).

As detailed by Abbott et al. (1996), Parry and Kelly (1987) provide a useful example in their analysis of the technological shift from formal to expedient cores in North America. Parry and Kelly (1987) show that as North American hunter-gatherers became less residentially mobile, they shifted from bifacial to generalized cores. Bifacial cores are more costly to produce but generate more cutting edge per unit weight, which suited the earlier, more highly mobile Palaeoindian lifestyle (Abbott et al. 1996; Kelly 1988; Parry and Kelly 1987; cf. Bamforth 2002a; Carper 2005). As mobility diminished, weight-to-cutting-edge ratio became less critical and the more costly bifacial cores increasingly fell out of use. Thus, generalized core technology is an adaptation; technology had magically adjusted to the new condition of sedentism, just as if there had been a group-level evaluation and decision about the costs and benefits of bifacial and generalized cores. In the presence of sedentism, a generalized core and flake technology may be adaptive—or may even be an adaptation. As with Piddocke and the potlatch, however, Parry and Kelly do not demonstrate this empirically, nor do they explain how the shift actually came about, merely that it did and that the result was functional. The flaw of processualism, then, was its failure to define evolutionary forces in enough detail to model the processes through which they acted.

Neo-Darwinian Approaches

As noted above, anthropology developed separately from Darwinian evolution and essayed quite different evolutionary explanations of culture and cultural change. The New Archaeology aspired to but did not fundamentally change this, being more philosophical, idealist, and transformational than empirical, materialist, or evolutionary (Dunnell 1980). In fact, it is only in the last three decades that anthropologists have formally applied Neo-Darwinian principles to the study of hunter-gatherers. There are at least three such approaches—human behavioural ecology, selectionist archaeology, and dual inheritance theory, which while differing in their approach to adaptation and ecology are not mutually exclusive and in many ways are complementary.

Human Behavioural Ecology

Human behavioural ecologists study the ecological relationships that shape human cultural and biological adaptations (Winterhalder and Smith 1992). This was already a topic of considerable anthropological interest when human behavioural ecology (HBE) emerged out of sociobiology in the late 1970s, but with an important difference in selective scale (Laland and Brown 2002). Behavioural ecologists wanted nothing to do with group selection, asserting instead that human behaviour is individually motivated; individuals behave in ways that maximize their own reproductive success in light of current ecological circumstances. Natural selection is said to account for this propensity (Borgerhoff Mulder 1991; Smith 1983). Behaviours change with conditions, the goal of fitness maximizing remaining constant.

Human behavioural ecologists quickly gravitated to optimal foraging theory as a source of ready-made models (e.g. Charnov 1976; MacArthur and Pianka 1966; Smith 1983; Stephens and Krebs 1986), and to hunter-gatherers and other simple social formations where the food quest bulked large, as logical subject matters for their application (Stephens and Krebs 1986). Optimal foraging models attracted archaeological interest because the archaeological record is frequently rich in subsistence remains, and foraging models make clear predictions about subsistence change in response to environmental variations. Using probabilistic, cost-benefit decision models and environmental data, researchers could model foraging goals, currencies, constraints, and decision-making criteria. Empirical data could be compared to model predictions to determine whether foragers were maximizing their rate of calorific return, which became the standard proxy measure for fitness (Stephens and Krebs 1986; Winterhalder and Smith 1992). In this way, human behavioural ecologists could sidestep many of the culturally motivated explanations of human behaviour that had stymied their disciplinary forebears; consciously or unconsciously, individuals seek to maximize their fitness.

Human behavioural ecologists have since broadened foraging theory by adding new model parameters or collecting new kinds of behavioural or environmental data, permitting consideration of factors initially ignored. For example, early tests, including studies of the Aché of Paraguay (Hawkes et al. 1982; Hill and Hawkes 1983), showed that living hunter-gatherers do not always maximize their rate of calorific return (Bettinger 1991; Hildebrandt and McGuire 2002; Kaplan and Hill 1992). Hill and Hawkes (1983) report that Aché men who have the most offspring often forage sub-optimally, spending more time hunting than they should, sometimes ignoring items in the 'optimal set' (Bamforth 2002b; Hill and Hawkes 1983; see Stephens and Krebs (1986) for a detailed description of optimal foraging models). In response, HBE broadened its theory to include myriad alternative fitness goals and currencies, including mating opportunities and prestige (Hawkes 1990; 1991; McGuire and Hildebrandt 2005), and beyond this to include non-foraging behaviours such as tool and tool stone use (Bettinger et al. 2006; Garvey 2008; 2013; Ugan et al. 2003), general life history studies (Charnov 1993; Kaplan et al. 2003), menopause (Hawkes et al. 1998; 2000; Hill and Hurtado 1991), group size (Smith 1985), birth-spacing (Blurton Jones 1986; 1987; 1997), family size (Borgerhoff Mulder 2000), polyandry (Crook and Crook 1988; Smith 1998) and the demographic transition (Borgerhoff Mulder 1998). These diverse inquiries all share the assumption that natural selection predisposed humans to behave optimally in response to environmental changes and challenges.

The increasing HBE interest in showing that outwardly 'sub-optimal' behaviours are in fact rational and fitness-enhancing is reminiscent of the earlier neofunctionalist agenda, but neofunctionalism and HBE are worlds apart. HBE generates empirically testable mathematical models, not ad hoc descriptions or 'just so' stories as some have suggested (Lyman and O'Brien 1998). Less easily dismissed is the criticism of evolutionary psychologists that HBE does not distinguish exaptations from adaptations (Symons 1987; Cosmides and Tooby 1987); exaptations happen to be beneficial for survival but were not selected in relation to that benefit, in contrast to adaptations, which were (Gould and Vrba 1982; Laland and Brown 2002). Symons (1987) argues that behavioural adaptation is the result of selective forces that act on the cognitive architecture that guides behaviour, not on the behaviours themselves. Accordingly, behaviours that promote fitness today may not have been shaped by the conditions of today, meaning that an observed correlation between a behaviour and reproductive success does not prove a causal connection (Laland and Brown 2002; Symons 1987). Human behavioural ecologists counter that, unlike cognitive architecture, behaviour can be directly observed, mathematically modelled, and, because it appears to be adaptive, anthropologists stand to learn a lot about human adaptability through its study (Borgerhoff Mulder et al. 1997; Grafen 1984; Laland and Brown 2002).

The evolutionary psychology criticism of HBE echoes the evolutionary biological criticism of adaptationist explanation (e.g. Williams 1966). In a pithy critique, Gould and Lewontin (1979) argue that the adaptationist propensity to recursively model a single adaptive explanation (predict > test > modify predictions > test > modify predictions,... etc.) precludes alternative evolutionary explanations. They further argue that adaptive explanation reduces an organism to a cobbled-together sum of its optimal parts (Gould and Lewontin 1979, 585). Human behavioural ecologists counter that adjusting model parameters when observations fail to meet initial expectations is what good scientists do and that critics have never offered a workable alternative. It is better to have a robust, albeit potentially flawed, method than none at all (Resnik 1997, 43). Nor does HBE apologize for its reductionist methodology; it is designed to reduce the unnumbered complexities of reality to a tractable number of abstractions (Friedman 1953, 36; Winterhalder and Smith 1992).

To illustrate the HBE approach, we return to the North American technological shift from bifacial to generalized cores. Parry and Kelly viewed this as a cost-benefit problem, explaining that, 'the choice of expedient over formal core technology involves a trade-off between the cost of transporting tools and raw materials... and the costs of manufacturing and using tools' (Parry and Kelly 1987, 299). HBE makes the same assumptions somewhat more formally, i.e. that the combination of behavioural plasticity and fitness optimizing should produce lithic technologies that maximize benefit relative to cost. In HBE, however, natural selection shapes the fitness behaviour of individuals (not cultures), which is simpler to model. Such a model might incorporate experimental data on the costs of manufacture and raw-material procurement, opportunity costs of production and transport, and tool use times (Beck et al. 2002; Bettinger et al. 2006; Garvey 2008; 2013; Ugan et al. 2003) leading to predictions about preferences for lithic technology at differing degrees of sedentism.

Individuals are archaeologically elusive, of course (Bamforth 2002b), but the archaeological record captures the distribution of individual behaviours, which should centre on alternatives optimal for individuals. A more difficult problem for archaeological application of HBE is whether it requires a level of environmental reconstruction beyond our present means. Optimal diet breadth, for example, can only be modelled reliably if the abundance and handling times of available resources are known (Bettinger 1991; Smith 1983). The extent of this problem and possible solutions are widely debated.

Environment also is the root of another, quite different, criticism that because a good deal of HBE research tracks behaviour in relation to environmental change, it is really just a dressed up version of environmental determinism. However, while much HBE is concerned with environmental explanation, there are many other avenues of application, as the core-to-flake example above shows. Further, Julian Steward's argument that behaviour is as much a function of technology as environment, applies in full to HBE. In the diet breadth model, for example, resources are ranked by rate of return on handling time, which is strongly affected by technology (Broughton and O'Connell 1999, 156; Hawkes and O'Connell 1992, 63–4; cf. Lyman and O'Brien 1998). In short, that technology is a product of culture and culture history prevents characterizing HBE as environmental determinism.

Selectionist Archaeology

Like HBE, selectionist archaeology is less concerned with culture than with selective pressures and their product (Shennan 2008). Dunnell (1978; 1980), for example, argues that if culture is an 'extrasomatic means of adaptation' (White 1959, 8), the archaeological record represents the fossilized remains of human behavioural phenotypes. The New Archaeology had made similar claims, but Dunnell argued that New Archaeologists had followed an essentially non-Darwinian tack in their preoccupation with culture systems modelled as though they were living organisms (Dunnell 1980; see also Bettinger 1991). For Dunnell (1980; 1982; 1989) and a growing group of selectionists (e.g. Neff 1993; Neiman 1995; O'Brien 1996a; 1996b; Rindos 1980; Shennan 2002), evolutionary principles can and should be applied literally, rather than metaphorically, to the archaeological record. Archaeologists should focus on things that can be directly observed and measured. Human behaviour and hunter-gatherer societies do not figure prominently in this programme. The archaeological record is said to be better suited to establishing artefact lineages, determining rates of technological change, and understanding selective forces, than it is to reconstructing complex and elusive dynamic behaviours (Lyman and O'Brien 1998). That selectionist archaeology rejects behavioural explanation is surprising given how well the approach lends itself to studies of dual inheritance, which focus almost exclusively on behaviour, often referencing hunter-gatherer societies for insights (see below).

Early selectionist work argued for a 'fundamental dichotomy' between style and function (Dunnell 1978; 1980; O'Brien and Holland 1992). Functional attributes affect 'fitness', which is reflected in strongly patterned temporospatial distributions (Dunnell 1980; Maschner and Mithen 1996). Some selectionists go so far as to equate the differential persistence of artefact variants with the biological fitness of their makers (Leonard and Jones 1987); individuals who produce and use artefacts that make them better adapted to an environment live longer and produce more offspring, ensuring the persistence of the artefacts that made that possible. Neff warns, however, that while culture clearly affects survival and reproduction, there is no reason to think that the 'contemporary design of a cultural trait is necessarily the result of past effects on biological success' (Neff 2000, 427). This, of course, is precisely the criticism Hempel (1959) levelled against functionalist explanation.

Stylistic attributes, on the other hand, are said to be selectively neutral and thus vary randomly in frequency through time. Critics of selectionist archaeology, however, question the style–function distinction, arguing that 'any attempt to create a rigid boundary between style and function will fail' (Bettinger et al. 1996, 133), and that style can be functional in ways that are key to cultural evolution (Boyd and Richerson 1987; Richerson and Boyd 2005).

Of late, selectionists have become increasingly interested in interpreting the archaeological record in terms of transmission. Selectionists argue that, as extensions of the human phenotype, artefacts can be organized and analysed using the phylogenetic methods of evolutionary biology. Phylogenies and clade-diversity diagrams are used to determine evolutionary relationships between artefacts believed to share a common ancestry (e.g. Jordan and Shennan 2003; Lipo et al. 1997; O'Brien and Lyman 2003; Neiman 1995; O'Brien et al. 2001; Tehrani and Collard 2002), and are akin to artefact frequency seriations, popular during the first decades of the twentieth century (e.g. Ford 1949; Rouse 1939). Whether cultural phylogeny is susceptible to analysis using the methods of genetics is problematic, however (Eerkens et al. 2005); genetic transmission is always vertical, parent to offspring; much cultural transmission is horizontal between otherwise unrelated age mates as Kroeber (1963) long ago emphasized.

With reference to our North American lithic example, the archaeological selectionist (as represented in this case specifically by Abbott et al. 1996) sees core and flake technologies as competing cultural variants rather than adaptations, i.e. variants whose presence is the result of selection, which the selectionist requires be demonstrated rather than assumed, eliminating other evolutionary possibilities (mutation, drift, and sorting). Abbott and colleagues (1996) argue that the wide geographical distribution and unidirectional shift from formal to informal cores make it possible that selection favours informal cores as groups become more sedentary, but reject the Parry and Kelly (1987) argument that sedentism produced this adaptation, arguing that the presence of one behaviour (e.g. sedentism) cannot provide an evolutionary explanation for another (e.g. informal core technology). Instead, they argue that the widespread functional connection between flake technology and sedentism is a product of indirect selection or sorting. In their account, informal core technology and sedentism are functionally linked by-products of the shift from hunting and gathering to maize agriculture (Abbott et al. 1996), a highly successful adaptation to population pressure that spread widely across much of North America.

Dual Inheritance Theory (DIT)

Dual inheritance theorists look to hunter-gatherers and other simple societies to understand how cultural information changes as it is passed from person to person. They argue that while important human behaviours are the result of natural selection acting on genes, many more are acquired by cultural transmission. That is, genetic and cultural evolution interact to produce human behaviours, but cultural information is transmitted in ways that genetic information is not and thus requires a different set of interpretive tools (Bettinger et al. 1996). DIT recognizes at least four distinctive modes of cultural transmission (guided variation, and directly biased, conformist, and indirectly biased transmission). Each one entails more than simple copying, which alone carries no fitness advantage for reasons that are easy to understand. Copying saves on learning costs, but a population in which everyone copies and no one learns cannot respond to environmental change. Environmental change will thus favour learning, the frequency of which will increase until the cost of learning and the cost of copying (i.e. copying an individual with the wrong behaviour, e.g. one out of tune with the current environment) are the same—meaning that individuals who copy enjoy no selective advantage over individuals who learn, so copying confers no population level selective advantage.

Dual inheritance theory holds that the human ability to shift behaviour to optimize fitness and capacity for cultural transmission both evolved through natural selection (Ames 1996, 113). In DIT, cultural evolution is driven by natural selection acting on behavioural variation generated by individual and social learning (Bettinger et al. 1996, 134; Boyd and Richerson 1985; Campbell 1965). While accepting Neo-Darwinian methodological individualism in common with SA and HBE, i.e. that individual decisions and learning behaviour are major drivers of cultural evolution (Ames 1996; Boyd and Richerson 1985; Durham 1991; Richerson and Boyd 2005), DIT argues that important processes act at the group level and that group level phenomena (e.g. cultural transmission) strongly influence individual behaviours in ways that result in group selection (Soltis et al. 1995; Wilson and Sober 1994).

DIT concentrates more on the processes of cultural transmission than HBE and SA without ignoring trait-centred studies. For example, Eerkens and Lipo (2005) use computer simulation to obtain base-line values of variation generated as the result of copying error. They compare these values to measurements on projectile points from eastern California to gauge the degree and thus the source of archaeological variation. These and other methods offer archaeologists a means of discerning whether patterns observed in the archaeological record are 'culturally or behaviourally significant or whether they are simply due to drift-like processes' (Eerkens and Lipo 2005, 330). Eerkens et al. (2005) perform a similar modelling exercise to simulate guided variation, conformist transmission, and indirect bias. This type of modelling generates testable hypotheses of the archaeological signatures of different transmission systems (Bettinger and Eerkens 1999).

Returning to our North American lithic example for the final time, a DIT approach might begin with a trait-centred analysis of the formal–informal core transition, mapping temporospatial distributions of each core type. These data could then be compared to computer simulations of patterns generated by different transmission models, with the goal of understanding the cause of the technological shift rather than to interpret its functional outcome. Importantly, while DIT would surely weigh the selective advantages of formal and informal cores in relation to settlement mobility, it would give equal weight to the social learning mechanisms that might have persuaded individuals to choose one form over the other. The approach admits the possibility that learning biases could have caused a shift to informal cores even had they been poorly suited to the sedentary lifestyle.

Perhaps the most distinctive feature of the DIT programme is this implication that circumstances will sometimes favour cultural behaviours that are truly maladaptive. In this, it is distinct from virtually every other approach to human adaptation, which have always strived to show that all cultural behaviours, however foolish and maladaptive they may outwardly seem, are rational and adaptive when closely inspected. In contrast, dual inheritance theorists seek to understand how deleterious traits spread and why they persist even in the face of decreased fitness (Richerson and Boyd 2005; Henrich 2004).

There is a growing sense that dual inheritance theory has the potential to unite (perhaps more correctly reunite) all of the social sciences under a single explanatory framework (Gintis 2006; Laland and Brown 2002; Mesoudi et al. 2006). Importantly, the approach does not appear to lose explanatory power in the breadth of its application. DIT deals in mathematical models that permit considerable latitude for explorations at different temporal and spatial scales, making it possible to connect individual behaviours with population outcomes (Mesoudi et al. 2006). Anthropological applications have been few and archaeological applications fairly simple (i.e. distinguishing types of transmission), but this is sure to improve as continuing psychological and neurobiological studies of transmission and learning enrich our understanding and permit construction of better models.

Conclusions

Since Darwin's (1859) early writings on evolution by natural selection, and especially since the New Synthesis of the 1930s, evolutionary scientists have accepted the importance of adaptation. More elegantly put, if selection leads to 'continuous incorporation of favourable variation into altered forms, then evolutionary change must be fundamentally adaptive' (Gould 1982, 381). Paradigm shifts in anthropology have turned mainly on the issue of adaptive scale and the degree to which humans are subject to natural selection. The emerging reality is that adaptation occurs at multiple levels (e.g. broad behavioural propensities, subsistence systems, individual artefacts), and there is much important work left to do in synthesizing the work that has been done at different levels, i.e. reconciling micro- and macro-evolutionary agendas. There is also the question of the underlying goal of anthropology as a discipline. Evolutionary anthropological research was for a long time descriptive, focusing on the static products of evolutionary forces and almost exclusively on aspects of culture that appear to be functional adaptations (Bettinger et al. 1996). Anthropologists have more recently shown greater interest in the dynamic causes of cultural change and, in some cases, aspects of culture that are maladaptive. In all cases, however, the trend is towards prediction and a far more robust treatment of human behaviour than simple ad hoc description (Broughton and O'Connell 1999, 154).

How much humans are subject to natural selection has been debated since at least the Enlightenment, reflecting a deep philosophical preoccupation with the problem of human free will. Hunter-gatherers have always been at the heart of this debate because they have always been taken to represent unmarred, uncomplicated examples of humankind interacting with nature, thus offering a base-line measure of human free will. Anthropologists have sought to understand how much culture insulates humans against environmental pressures by comparing modern industrial nations with their polar opposites: hunter-gatherers. Social theories most closely aligned with evolutionary biology (e.g. sociobiology and HBE) have been criticized for implying that humans are little different from the rest of the animal kingdom, driven only by the 'instinct' to behave rationally given the demands of environment. While purely historical explanations of culture and cultural change (e.g. Sahlins 1978) are far less deterministic, they have proven wholly unsatisfying to human evolutionists. It would seem there is a middle ground emerging in Neo-Darwinian models of human behaviour that place less emphasis on the physical than the social environment, which has increasingly moved to the fore. There is a growing recognition in human behavioural ecology, selectionist archaeology, and dual inheritance research that a truly modern theory of adaptation must incorporate modes of social learning and transmission as well as modes of subsistence, and recognize the importance of social variables (e.g. prestige) alongside environmental ones (e.g. ungulate density). This new understanding of adaptation will no doubt take shape around the hunter-gatherers of the archaeological past and ethnographic present.

References

Abbott, A., Leonard, R., and Jones, G. 1996. Explaining the change from biface to flake technology. In H. Maschner (ed.), *Darwinian archaeologies*, 33–42. New York: Plenum Press.

Ames, K. 1996. Archaeology, style, and the theory of coevolution. In H. Maschner (ed.), *Darwinian archaeologies*, 109–31. New York: Plenum Press.

Bamforth, D. 2002a. High-tech foragers? Folsom and later Paleoindian technology on the Great Plains. *Journal of World Prehistory* 16, 55–98.

Bamforth, D. 2002b. Evidence and metaphor in evolutionary archaeology. *American Antiquity* 67, 435–52.

Barnard, A. 2000. *History and theory in anthropology*. Cambridge: Cambridge University Press.

Beck, C., Taylor, A., Jones, G. T., Fadem, C., Cook, C., and Millward, S. 2002. Rocks are heavy: transport costs and paleoarchaic quarry behavior in the Great Basin. *Journal of Anthropological Archaeology* 21, 481–507.

Bettinger, R. 1991. *Hunter-gatherers: archaeological and evolutionary theory*. New York: Plenum Press.

Bettinger, R., Boyd, R., and Richerson, P. 1996. Style, function, and cultural evolutionary processes. In H. Maschner (ed.), *Darwinian archaeologies*, 133–64. New York: Plenum Press.

Bettinger, R. and Eerkens, J. 1999. Point typologies, cultural transmission, and the spread of bow-and-arrow technology in the prehistoric Great Basin. *American Antiquity* 64, 231–42.

Bettinger, R., Winterhalder, B., and McElreath, R. 2006. A simple model of technological intensification. *Journal of Archaeological Science* 33, 538–45.

Binford, L. 1962. Archaeology as anthropology. *American Antiquity* 28, 217–25.

Binford, L. 1965. Archaeological systematics and the study of culture process. In M. Leone (ed.), *Contemporary archaeology*, 125–32. Carbondale: Southern Illinois University Press.

Binford, L. 1968. Post-Pleistocene adaptations. In S. Binford and L. Binford (eds), *New perspectives in archaeology*, 313–41. Chicago: Aldine.

Binford, L. 1977. Forty-seven trips: a case study in the character of archaeological formation processes. In R. Wright (ed.), *Stone tools as cultural markers: change, evolution, and complexity*, 24–36. Canberra: Australian Institute of Aboriginal Studies.

Binford, L. 1978a. Dimensional analysis of behavioral and site structure: learning from an Eskimo hunting stand. *American Antiquity* 43, 330–61.

Binford, L. 1978b. *Nunamuit ethnoarchaeology*. New York: Academic Press.

Binford, L. 1980. Willow smoke and dogs' tails: hunter-gatherer settlement systems and archaeological site formation. *American Antiquity* 45, 4–20.

Binford, S. and Binford, L. 1968. *New perspectives in archaeology*. Chicago: Aldine.

Birdsell, J. 1968. Some predictions for the Pleistocene based on equilibrium systems for recent hunter-gatherers. In R. Lee and I. DeVore (eds), *Man the hunter*, 229–40. Chicago: Aldine.

Blurton Jones, N. 1986. Bushman birth spacing: a test for optimal inter-birth intervals. *Ethology and Sociobiology* 7, 91–105.

Blurton Jones, N. 1987. Bushman birth spacing: direct tests of some simple predictions. *Ethology and Sociobiology* 8, 183–204.

Blurton Jones, N. 1997. Too good to be true? Is there really a trade-off between number and care of offspring in human reproduction? In L. Betzig (ed.), *Human nature: a critical reader*, 83–6. Oxford: Oxford University Press.

Boas, F. 1898. The mythology of the Bella Coola Indians. In F. Boas (ed.), *Publications of the Jesup North Pacific Expedition*, volume 1, part 2. New York: American Museum of Natural History.

Boas, F. 1910. *Report presented to the 61st Congress on changes in bodily form of descendants of immigrants*. Washington, DC: Government Printing Office.

Boas, F. 1912. Changes in the bodily form of descendants of immigrants. *American Anthropologist, New Series* 14, 530–62.

Boas, F. 1920. The methods of ethnology. *American Anthropologist* 22, 311–22.

Bogoras, W. 1910. The Chukchee. In F. Boas (ed.), *Publications of the Jesup North Pacific Expedition*, volume 7. New York: American Museum of Natural History.

Bohannan, P. and Glazer, M. 1988. *High points in anthropology*. New York: McGraw-Hill.

Borgerhoff Mulder, M. 1991. Human behavioural ecology. In J. Krebs and N. Davies (eds), *Behavioral ecology: an evolutionary approach*, 69–98. Oxford: Blackwell Scientific.

Borgerhoff Mulder, M. 1998. Demographic transition: are we any closer to an evolutionary explanation? *Trends in Ecology and Evolution* 13, 266–70.

Borgerhoff Mulder, M. 2000. Optimizing offspring: the quantity-quality tradeoff in agropastoral Kipsigis. *Evolution and Human Behavior* 21, 391–410.

Borgerhoff Mulder, M., Thornhill, N., Voland, E., and Richerson, P. 1997. The place of behavioral ecological anthropology in evolutionary social science. In P. Weingart, S. Mitchell, P. Richerson, and S. Massen (eds), *Human by nature: between biology and the social sciences*, 253–82. New York: Lawrence Erlbaum.

Boserup, E. 1965. *The conditions of agricultural growth*. Chicago: Aldine.

Bourke, A. and Franks, N. 1995. *Social evolution in ants*. Princeton: Princeton University Press.

Boyd, R. and Richerson, P. 1985. *Culture and the evolutionary process*. Chicago: University of Chicago Press.

Boyd, R. and Richerson, P. 1987. The evolution of ethnic markers. *Cultural Anthropology* 2, 65–79.

Broughton, J. and O'Connell, J. 1999. On evolutionary ecology, selectionist archaeology, and behavioral archaeology. *American Antiquity* 64, 153–214.

Burrow, J. 1966. *Evolution and society: a study in Victorian social theory*. Cambridge: Cambridge University Press.

Campbell, D. 1965. Variation and selective retention in sociocultural evolution. In H. Barringer, G. Blanksten, and R. Mack (eds), *Social change in developing areas: a reinterpretation of evolutionary theory*, 19–49. Cambridge, MA: Schenkman.

Carper, R. 2005. On the use of symmetry to assess biface production goals. *Lithic Technology* 30, 127–44.

Carson, R. 1962. Silent spring. *New Yorker*, 16, 23, and 30 June.

Charnov, E. 1976. Optimal foraging: the marginal value theorem. *Theoretical Population Biology* 9, 129–36.

Charnov, E. 1993. *Life history invariants: some explorations of symmetry in evolutionary ecology*. Oxford: Oxford University Press.

Chinard, G. 1947. Eighteenth century theories on America as a human habitat. *Proceedings of the American Philosophical Society* 91, 27–57.

Clarke, D. 1968. *Analytical archaeology*. London: Methuen.

Cosmides, L. and Tooby, J. 1987. From evolution to behavior: evolutionary psychology as the missing link. In J. Dupré (ed.), *The latest on the best: essays on evolution and optimality*. Cambridge, MA: MIT Press.

Crook, J. and Crook, S. 1988. Tibetan polyandry: problems of adaptation and fitness. In L. Betzig, M. Borgerhoff Mulder, and P. Turke (eds), *Human reproductive behavior*, 97–114. Cambridge: Cambridge University Press.

Darwin, C. 1859. *On the origin of species by means of natural selection, or the preservation of favoured races in the struggle for life*. London: John Murray.

Darwin, C. 1871. *The descent of man, and selection in relation to sex*. London: John Murray.

Dow, J. 1976. Systems models of cultural ecology. *Social Science Information* 15, 953–76.

Dunnell, R. 1978. Style and function: a fundamental dichotomy. *American Antiquity* 43, 192–202.

Dunnell, R. 1980. Evolutionary theory and archaeology. In M. Schiffer (ed.), *Advances in archaeological method and theory: selections for students*, 35–99. New York: Academic Press.

Dunnell, R. 1982. Science, social science, common sense. *Journal of Anthropological Research* 38, 1–25.

Dunnell, R. 1989. Aspects of the application of evolutionary theory in archaeology. In C. Lamberg-Karlovsky (ed.), *Archaeological thought in America*, 35–49. Cambridge: Cambridge University Press.

Durham, W. 1991. *Coevolution: genes, culture, and human diversity*. Stanford: Stanford University Press.

Eerkens, J., Bettinger, R., and McElreath, R. 2005. Cultural transmission, phylogenetics, and the archaeological record. In C. Lipo, M. O'Brien, M. Collard, and S. Shennan (eds), *Mapping our ancestors: phylogenetic methods in anthropology and prehistory*, 169–83. Somerset, NJ: Transaction Publishers.

Eerkens, J. and Lipo, C. 2005. Cultural transmission, copying errors, and the generation of variation in material culture and the archaeological record. *Journal of Anthropological Archaeology* 224, 316–34.

Ehrlich, P. 1968. *The population bomb*. Cutchogue, NY: Buccaneer Books.

Ford, J. 1949. Cultural dating of prehistoric sites in the Virú Valley, Peru. *American Museum of Natural History, Anthropological Papers* 43 (Part 1).

Forde, C. D. 1934. *Habitat, economy, and society*. New York: Harcourt, Brace, and Company.

Freeman, M. 1971. A social and ecologic analysis of systematic female infanticide among the Netsilik Eskimo. *American Anthropologist* 73, 1011–78.

Friedman, M. 1953. *Essays in positive economics*. Chicago: University of Chicago Press.

Frisancho, A. and Schechter, D. 1997. Adaptation. In F. Spencer (ed.), *History of physical anthropology: an encyclopedia*, 6–12. New York: Garland Publishing.

Garfield, V. 1931. Change in the marriage customs of the Tsimshian. MA thesis, University of Washington, Seattle.

Garvey, R. 2008. A behavioral ecological approach to a proposed middle Holocene occupational gap. *Before Farming* 2008/2, article 2.

Garvey, R. 2013. A model of lithic raw material procurement. In N. Goodale and W. Andrefsky, Jr. (eds), *Lithic technological systems and evolutionary theory* (in press). New York: Cambridge University Press.

Giere, R. 1988. *Explaining science: a cognitive approach*. Chicago: University of Chicago Press.

Gintis, H. 2006. A framework for the integration of the behavioral sciences. *Behavioral and Brain Sciences* 30, 1–61.

Gould, S. 1982. Darwinism and the expansion of evolutionary theory. *Science* 216, 380–7.

Gould, S. and Lewontin, R. E. 1979. The spandrels of San Marco and the Panglossian paradigm: a critique of the adaptationist programme. *Proceedings of the Royal Society of London, Series B, Biological Sciences* 205, 581–98.

Gould, S. and Vrba, E. 1982. Exaptation—a missing term in the science of form. *Paleobiology* 8, 4–15.

Grafen, A. 1984. Natural selection, kin selection and group selection. In J. Krebs and N. Davies (eds), *Behavioural ecology: an evolutionary approach*, 62–84. Oxford: Blackwell Scientific.

Harner, M. 1970. Population pressure and the social evolution of agriculturalists. *Southwest Journal of Anthropology* 26, 67–86.

Harris, M. 1968. *The rise of anthropological theory: a history of theories of culture*. New York: Thomas Y. Crowell Company.

Harris, M. 1998. *Theories of culture in postmodern times*. Walnut Creek, CA: AltaMira Press.

Hawkes, K. 1990. Why do men hunt? Some benefits for risky strategies. In E. Cashdan (ed.), *Risk and uncertainty in tribal and peasant economies*, 145–66. Boulder: Westview Press.

Hawkes, K. 1991. Showing off: tests of an hypothesis about men's foraging goals. *Ethology and Sociobiology* 12, 29–54.

Hawkes, K., Hill, K., and O'Connell, J. 1982. Why hunters gather: optimal foraging and the Aché of Eastern Paraguay. *American Ethnologist* 9, 379–98.

Hawkes, K. and O'Connell, J. 1992. On optimal foraging models and subsistence transitions. *Current Anthropology* 33, 63–6.

Hawkes, K., O'Connell, J., Blurton Jones, N., Alvarez, H., and Charnov, E. 1998. Grandmothering, menopause, and the evolution of human life histories. *Proceedings of the National Academy of Sciences* 95, 1336–9.

Hawkes, K., O'Connell, J., Blurton Jones, N., Alvarez, H., and Charnov, E. 2000. The grandmother hypothesis and human evolution. In L. Cronk, N. Chagnon, and W. Irons (eds), *Adaptation and human behavior: an anthropological perspective*, 237–60. New York: Aldine de Gruyter.

Hempel, C. 1959. The logic of functional analysis. In L. Gross (ed.), *Symposium of sociological theory*. New York: Harper & Row.

Henrich, J. 2004. Demography and cultural evolution: why adaptive cultural processes produced maladaptive losses in Tasmania. *American Antiquity* 69, 197–214.

Hildebrandt, W. and McGuire, K. 2002. The ascendance of hunting during the California middle Archaic: an evolutionary perspective. *American Antiquity* 67, 231–56.

Hill, K. and Hawkes, K. 1983. Neotropical hunting among the Aché of Eastern Paraguay. In R. Hames and W. Vickers (eds), *Adaptations of native Amazonians*, 139–88. New York: Academic Press.

Hill, K. and Hurtado, A. 1991. The evolution of premature reproductive senescence and menopause in human females. *Human Nature* 2, 313–50.

Hodder, I. 1983. *The present past: an introduction to anthropology for archaeologists*. London: Batsford.

Hodder, I. 2002. *Archaeological theory today*. Malden, MA: Blackwell Publishers.

Huxley, T. 1863. *Evidence as to man's place in nature*. London: Williams and Norgate.

Jochelson, W. 1908. The Koryaks. In F. Boas (ed.), *Publications of the Jesup North Pacific Expedition*, volume 6. New York: American Museum of Natural History.

Jochelson, W. 1926. The Yukaghir and Yukaghirized Tungus. In F. Boas (ed.), *Publications of the Jesup North Pacific Expedition*, volume 9, 343–469. New York: American Museum of Natural History.

Jordan, P. and Shennan, S. 2003. Cultural transmission, language, and basketry traditions amongst the California Indians. *Journal of Anthropological Archaeology* 22, 43–74.

Kaplan, H. and Hill, K. 1992. The evolutionary ecology of food acquisition. In E. Smith and B. Winterhalder (eds), *Evolutionary ecology and human behavior*, 167–201. Chicago: Aldine.

Kaplan, H., Lancaster, J., and Robson, A. 2003. Embodied capital and the evolutionary economics of the human lifespan. *Population and Development Review* 29, Supplement, 152–82.

Kelly, R. 1988. The three sides of a biface. *American Antiquity* 53, 717–34.

Kelly, R. 1995. *The foraging spectrum: diversity in hunter-gatherer lifeways*. Washington, DC: Smithsonian Institution.

Koeslag, J. 1997. Sex, the prisoner's dilemma game, and the evolutionary inevitability of cooperation. *Journal of Theoretical Biology* 189, 53–61.

Koeslag, J. 2003. Evolution of cooperation: cooperation defeats defection in the cornfield model. *Journal of Theoretical Biology* 224, 399–410.

Kroeber, A. 1939. *Cultural and natural areas of native North America*. Berkeley: University of California Press.

Kroeber, A. 1963. *Anthropology: culture patterns and processes*. New York: Harbinger.
Kuhn, T. 1962. *The structure of scientific revolutions*. Chicago: University of Chicago Press.
Laland, K. and Brown, G. 2002. *Sense and nonsense: evolutionary perspectives on human behavior*. Oxford: Oxford University Press.
Laughlin Jr., C. and Brady, I. (eds) 1978. *Extinction and survival in human populations*. New York: Columbia University Press.
Lee, R. 1969. !Kung Bushman subsistence: an input-output analysis. In D. Damas (ed.), *Contributions to anthropology: ecological essays*, 73–94. Ottowa: National Museums of Canada Bulletin 230.
Lee, R. and DeVore, I. 1968. *Man the hunter*. Chicago: Aldine.
Leonard, R. D. and Jones, G. T. 1987. Elements of an inclusive evolutionary model for archaeology. *Journal of Anthropological Archaeology* 6, 199–219.
Levins, R. and Lewontin, R. 1985. *The dialectical biologist*. Cambridge, MA: Harvard University Press.
Lipo, C., Madsen, M., Dunnell, R., and Hunt, T. 1997. Population structure, cultural transmission, and frequency seriation. *Journal of Anthropological Archaeology* 16, 301–33.
Lyell, C. 1990 [1830–3]. *Principles of geology*. Chicago: University of Chicago Press.
Lyman, R. L. and O'Brien, M. 1998. The goals of evolutionary archaeology: history and explanation. *Current Anthropology* 39, 615–52.
MacArthur, R. and Pianka, E. 1966. On optimal use of a patchy environment. *American Naturalist* 100, 603–9.
McGee, R. J. and Warms, R. 2000. *Anthropological theory: an introductory history*. Boston: McGraw-Hill.
McGuire, K. and Hildebrandt, W. 2005. Re-thinking Great Basin foragers: prestige hunting and costly signaling during the middle Archaic period. *American Antiquity* 70, 695–712.
Malthus, T. 1803. *An essay on the principle of population*. London: Johnson.
Maschner, H. and Mithen, S. 1996. Darwinian archaeologies: an introductory essay. In H. Maschner (ed.), *Darwinian archaeologies*, 3–14. New York: Plenum Press.
Maynard Smith, J. 1958. *The theory of evolution*. London: Penguin Books.
Mayr, E. 1983. How to carry out the adaptationist program? *American Naturalist* 121, 324–34.
Mead, M. 1961 [1928]. *Coming of age in Samoa: a psychological study of primitive youth for western civilization*. New York: William Morrow.
Merton, R. 1968. *Social theory and social structure*. New York: Free Press.
Mesoudi, A., Whiten, A., and Laland, K. 2006. Towards a unified science of cultural evolution. *Behavioral and Brain Sciences* 29, 329–83.
Morgan, L. 1877. *Ancient society*. New York: World Publishing.
Neff, H. 1993. Theory, sampling, and analytical techniques in the archaeological study of prehistoric ceramics. *American Antiquity* 58, 23–44.
Neff, H. 2000. On evolutionary ecology and evolutionary archaeology: some common ground? *Current Anthropology* 41, 427–9.
Neiman, F. 1995. Stylistic variation in evolutionary perspective: inferences from decorative diversity and interassemblage distance in Illinois Woodland ceramic assemblages. *American Antiquity* 60, 7–36.
O'Brien, M. 1996a. The historical development of an evolutionary archaeology: a selectionist approach. In H. Maschner (ed.), *Darwinian archaeologies*, 17–32. New York: Plenum Press.
O'Brien, M. 1996b. Evolutionary archaeology: an introduction. In M. O'Brien (ed.), *Evolutionary archaeology: theory and application*, 1–15. Salt Lake City: University of Utah Press.

O'Brien, M., Darwent, J., and Lyman, R. L. 2001. Cladistics is useful for reconstructing archaeological phylogienies: Palaeoindian points from the Southeastern United States. *Journal of Archaeological Science* 28, 1115–36.

O'Brien, M. and Holland, T. 1992. The role of adaptation in archaeological explanation. *American Antiquity* 57, 36–59.

O'Brien, M. and Lyman, R. L. 2003. *Cladistics and archaeology*. Salt Lake City: University of Utah Press.

Orans, M. 1975. Domesticating the functional dragon: an analysis of Piddocke's potlatch. *American Anthropologist* 77, 312–28.

Orlove, B. 1980. Ecological anthropology. *Annual Review of Anthropology* 9, 235–73.

Paley, W. 2006 [1802]. *Natural theology; or, evidences of the existence and attributes of the deity*, ed. M. Eddy and D. Knight. New York: Oxford University Press.

Parry, W. and Kelly, R. 1987. Expedient core technology and sedentism. In J. Johnson and C. Morrow (eds), *The organization of core technology*, 285–304. Boulder, CO: Westview Press.

Piddocke, S. 1969. The potlatch system of the southern Kwakiutl: a new perspective. In A. Vayda (ed.), *Environment and cultural behavior*, 130–56. Garden City, NJ: Natural History Press.

Powell, J. 1888. Competition as a factor in human evolution. *American Anthropologist* 1, 297–323.

Price, G. 1970. Selection and covariance. *Nature* 227, 520–1.

Price, G. 1972. Fisher's 'fundamental theorem' made clear. *Annals of Human Genetics* 36, 129–40.

Radin, P. 1923. The Winnebago Tribe. In *Thirty-seventh Annual Report of the United States Bureau of American Ethnology*, 35–550. Washington, DC: Smithsonian Institution.

Rappaport, R. 1968. *Pigs for the ancestors: ritual in the ecology of a New Guinea people*. New Haven: Yale University Press.

Rappaport, R. 1971a. Ritual, sanctity, and cybernetics. *American Anthropologist* 73, 59–76.

Rappaport, R. 1971b. The sacred in human evolution. *Annual Review of Ecological Systems* 2, 23–44.

Resnik, D. 1997. Adaptationism: hypothesis or heuristic? *Biology and Philosophy* 12, 39–50.

Richerson, P. and Boyd, R. 2005. *Not by genes alone: how culture transformed human evolution*. Chicago: University of Chicago Press.

Rindos, D. 1980. Symbiosis, instability, and the origins and spread of agriculture: a new model. *Current Anthropology* 21, 751–72.

Rodman, P. 1994. The human origins program and evolutionary ecology in anthropology today. *Evolutionary Anthropology* 2, 215–24.

Rouse, I. 1939. Prehistory in Haiti, a study in method. *Publications in Anthropology* 21. New Haven: Yale University.

Sahlins, M. 1978. *Culture and practical reason*. Chicago: University of Chicago Press.

Schutkowski, H. 2006. *Human ecology: biocultural adaptation in human communities*. Berlin: Springer.

Shennan, S. 2002. *Genes, memes and human history*. London: Thames and Hudson.

Shennan, S. 2008. Evolution in archaeology. *Annual Review of Anthropology* 37, 75–91.

Smith, E. 1983. Anthropological applications of optimal foraging theory: a critical review. *Current Anthropology* 24, 625–51.

Smith, E. 1985. Inuit foraging groups: some simple models incorporating conflicts of interest, relatedness and central-place sharing. *Ethology and Sociobiology* 6, 27–47.

Smith, E. 1998. Is Tibetan polyandry adaptive? Methodological and metatheoretical analyses. *Human Nature* 9, 225–61.

Soltis, J., Boyd, R., and Richerson, P. 1995. Can group-functional behaviors evolve by cultural group selection? An empirical test. *Current Anthropology* 63, 473–94.

Sparks, C. and Jantz, R. 2002. A reassessment of human cranial plasticity: Boas revisited. *Proceedings of the National Academy of Sciences* 99, 14636–9.
Spencer, H. 1868. Progress: its law and cause. *In Essays* 1, 1–60. London: Williams and Norgate.
Stephens, D. and Krebs, J. 1986. *Foraging theory*. Princeton: Princeton University Press.
Steward, J. 1936. The economic and social basis of primitive bands. In R. Lowie (ed.), *Essays in honor of A. L. Kroeber*, 331–50. Berkeley: University of California Press.
Steward, J. 1955. *Theory of culture change: the methodology of multilinear evolution*. Urbana: University of Illinois Press.
Steward, J. 1968. The concept and method of cultural ecology. In D. Sills (ed.), *International encyclopedia of the social sciences*, 337–44. New York: Macmillan.
Symons, D. 1987. If we're all Darwinians, what's the fuss about? In C. Crawford, M. Smith, and D. Krebs (eds), *Sociobiology and psychology*, 121–46. Hillsdale, NJ: Erlbaum.
Tehrani, J. and Collard, M. 2002. Investigating cultural evolution through biological phylogenetic analyses of Turkmen textiles. *Journal of Anthropological Archaeology* 21, 443–63.
Teit, J. 1906. The Lilloot Indians. In *Publications of the Jesup North Pacific Expedition*, volume 2, part 5. New York: American Museum of Natural History.
Trigger, B. 1989. *A history of archaeological thought*. New York: Cambridge University Press.
Trivers, R. and Hare, H. 1976. Haplodiploidy and the evolution of the social insects. *Science* 179, 90–2.
Tylor, E. 1871. *Primitive culture: researches into the development of mythology, philosophy, religion, language, art, and custom*. London: J. Murray.
Ugan, A., Bright, J., and Rogers, A. 2003. When is technology worth the trouble? *Journal of Archaeological Science* 30, 1315–29.
Vita-Finzi, C. and Higgs, E. 1970. Prehistoric economy in the Mount Carmel area of Palestine: site catchment analysis. *Proceedings of the Prehistoric Society* 36, 1–37.
Washburn, S. 1951. The new physical anthropology. *Transactions of the New York Academy of Sciences*, Series II 13, 298–304.
White, L. 1959. *The evolution of culture*. New York: McGraw-Hill.
Willey, G. and Sabloff, J. 1980. *A history of American archaeology*. New York: Freeman.
Williams, G. 1966. *Adaptation and natural selection: a critique of some current evolutionary thought*. Princeton: Princeton University Press.
Wilson, D. and Sober, E. 1994. Reintroducing group selection to the human behavioral sciences. *Behavioral and Brain Sciences* 17, 585–654.
Wilson, E. 2005. Kin selection as the key to altruism: its rise and fall. *Social Research* 72, 159–66.
Winterhalder, B. and Smith, E. 1992. Evolutionary ecology and the social sciences. In E. Smith and B. Winterhalder (eds), *Evolutionary ecology and human behavior*, 3–23. New York: Aldine de Gruyter.
Wissler, C. 1926. *The relation of nature to man in aboriginal America*. New York: Oxford University Press.
Wynne-Edwards, V. 1962. *Animal dispersion in relation to social behavior*. London: Oliver and Boyd.

CHAPTER 5

HISTORICAL AND HUMANIST PERSPECTIVES ON HUNTER-GATHERERS

AUBREY CANNON

Introduction

A growing alternative to prevailing ecological/evolutionary approaches to hunter-gatherer research emerged in the context of three late twentieth-century developments in anthropology and archaeology. One was the revisionist perspective on contemporary hunter-gatherers, which explicitly acknowledged their histories and long-term interactions with neighbouring farmers and stratified regional socio-political systems. The resulting debate and consensus on the historical specificity of all hunter-gatherers irrevocably expunged the notion of primitive society (Shott 1992) and any efforts to construct a common evolutionary base-line from ethnographic observations. The second major development, which has only slowly penetrated the domain of hunter-gatherer research, especially in archaeology, is the post-modernist critique of Western-based academic assumptions, including notions of objectivity and the validity of comparative analysis. With recognition of alternative perspectives and a critically reflective view of commonly used concepts such as efficiency, social status, prestige, landscape, and cosmology, anthropologists and archaeologists are increasingly free and able to recognize differences among past and present hunter-gatherers and on this basis are able to seek evidence for alternative ways of being and acting in the world. Combined with theoretical influences drawn from practice theory in its various forms, the result has been a growing theoretical and methodological capacity to study specific long-term hunter-gatherer histories. Finally, with the ever-increasing volume of available archaeological data, the means are in place to write histories of hunting and gathering peoples, which parallel in almost every way the histories of all peoples in all times.

Revisionism

Michael Shott (1992) provides a comprehensive and insightful review of the so-called revisionist debate in the ethnology of hunter-gatherers, which focused most intently on the ethnographies of the Kalahari and efforts to see these groups and their ways of life as exemplary of a basic form of human adaptation. In part this was enabled through emphasis on their apparent isolation, in contrast to other extant hunter-gatherers that were more obviously incorporated into and extensively influenced by world economic and political systems.

The revisionist critique began with the charge that this view of relative isolation was unfounded and that much of what was observed among such groups in the mid-to-late twentieth century was the result of a specific historical trajectory of interaction with local farming populations and European colonial powers (Schrire 1980). The sometimes acrimonious debate that ensued (e.g. Solway and Lee 1990; Wilmsen and Denbow 1990) often turned on minor points of fact, terminology, and emphasis, but in the end the prevailing perspective had undeniably shifted away from a view of hunter-gatherers as isolated from historical developments and in any way representative of pristine and simple foragers. In its place was universal acknowledgement that extant hunter-gatherers were the products of unique and dynamic historical trajectories, involving colonial influences and internal developments. Further, there was explicit acknowledgement of the role of contemporary social values and priorities in hunter-gatherer ethnography as much as in any other form of knowledge. Hunter-gatherers as a societal type came into question (Barnard 2004; Myers 1988; Pluciennik 2004) and hunter-gatherer ethnology, as the broadly comparative, generalizing study of recent and contemporary culture groups, is much less prominent as a distinct area of study in the early twenty-first century.

With its basic lessons learned and thoroughly incorporated into contemporary academic discourse, interest in the revisionist debate has also largely receded, though one active exception has been a vigorous though less-extensive debate about the concept of shamanism and its use to describe a broad pattern of ancient and more recent ritual practices and associated beliefs from around the world. On one side are researchers who draw parallels between ethnographically recorded practices and visual depictions, mainly in rock art, and similar depictions in archaeological contexts, which are used to infer similar shamanistic practices and associated beliefs. A common assumption is that these similarities derive from a baseline of religious experience and practices among hunter-gatherers, which has existed in one form or another since the Late Palaeolithic and has persisted into the recent past among hunter-gatherers around the world (Lewis-Williams 2006; Pearson 2002). At the other end of the spectrum are those who assert that use of the term 'shamanism' to describe the practices and beliefs of peoples outside of eastern Siberia, where the term was originally applied, constitutes an ahistorical and primitivist perspective that would deny the unique historical developments and cultural perceptions of ancient and more recent hunter-gatherers (Kehoe 2000). Other views contend that while many cosmological beliefs are highly persistent and durable, extending into prehistory, the specific practices and roles of shamans are historically contingent and variable (McCall 2007).

The shamanism debate shows the difficulty that archaeologists still have in reconciling an understanding that all ancient and contemporary hunter-gatherers are products of long, unique, and complex histories, often involving major disruptions and change, with the clear and striking parallels that seem to exist between ancient and contemporary practices. Do apparent similarities among practices and beliefs, of whatever degree, indicate common cultural patterns or are they only superficially similar and in reality far more variable in their contexts and meanings? The answer with respect to shamanism may come from better understanding of specific histories of cultural transmission and reinvention coupled with neuropsychological understanding of common ways in which the human brain organizes experience and desire into cosmology and practice. But no matter what the answer is with respect to this particular issue, the pervasive influence of revisionism is apparent in the care that all sides take to emphasize the historical trajectories of recent and contemporary hunter-gatherers and the uniqueness of their cultural perspectives as products of those histories.

The main implication of the revisionist debate is the elimination of a capacity for unreflective categorical comparison of cultures on the basis of a suite of characteristics thought to accompany an economic base in hunting, fishing, and gathering. In its wake there is far more critical awareness of the specificity and complexity of hunter-gatherer characteristics and circumstances past and present. Far from leaving investigators floundering in a sea of unrelated and incomparable observations, the effect of this awareness has been to open new possibilities for research, and even comparison, albeit with an emphasis on difference as much as assumed or inferred similarity.

Post-Modernism

While the post-modernist critique in ethnology was so effective as to undermine the very notion of hunter-gatherers as a Western construct of questionable analytical value (Myers 1988, 274–6), it is only very recently, and largely in the context of European Mesolithic studies, that post-modernist perspectives have begun to influence the ways archaeologists approach the evidence, behaviours, and histories of ancient hunter-gatherers (e.g. papers in Milner and Woodman 2005). Long after the substantial influence of post-modernism on the archaeology of the European Neolithic and Bronze Age and post-processual archaeology more generally, there has been a recent growth of interest in the application of similar perspectives in Mesolithic studies. A small but increasing number of archaeologists are endeavouring to understand the world as seen and experienced in the past, echoing earlier articulation of a 'humanistic' approach to the study of hunter-gatherers, which sought to explain patterns of behaviour in relation to the motivations and values of the participants (Riches 1982). Although widely varying, most of these studies seek new ways of appreciating differences in perspectives between past hunter-gatherers and contemporary Western researchers and among past hunter-gatherers across time and space. Among other strategies, researchers take an explicitly phenomenological approach (Cobb 2009; Fuglestvedt 2011), employ queer theory (Cobb 2005), or adopt deliberately naïve perspective (Nilsson 2003) to force an appreciation of difference in the ways that past hunter-gatherers perceived themselves and their environments and to try to understand the perceptions, values, and motivations that guided their actions.

Adoption of post-modernism's critically reflective stance is typically used to disrupt conventional thinking (see Strassburg 2003) and to open new possibilities for the interpretation and explanation of the diverse histories represented in the available empirical evidence. Critiques of economically defined site types and the concept of the seasonal round (e.g. Conneller 2005; Milner 2005), for example, open the possibility of exploring historical and contingent alternatives to typological descriptions of site use and movement through the landscape. The emphasis is on variability, in place of an ahistorical functionalist system. Similar criticism of the concept of social complexity is said to create space for alternative narrative engagements (Warren 2005), and an increasingly rich empirical record is showing many different patterns and historical trajectories for what might be termed social complexity among hunters and gatherers (Sassaman 2004). Reference to acculturation to describe the outcome of interaction between farmers and foragers is similarly criticized for its use as an unproblematic and universal description and explanation of social change (Borić 2005), with the aim of constructing more complex and nuanced narratives in its place.

Beyond concern with the redefinition of larger-scale historical patterns and processes and examination of variability within these, archaeologists are also seeking more subtle appreciation of differences in meaning and perception in hunter-gatherer behaviour. In the process they question the universality of Western-based priorities. The result is a proliferation of studies that emphasize cultural, historical, and situational experience and meaning. A focus on seasonal mobility, for example, considers what it meant in relation to social interaction, identity, and history (Milne 2011; Oetelaar and Oetelaar 2011; Wickham-Jones 2005). Ecological studies consider the effects of actions or events that change environments and perceptions of place, which in turn affect their subsequent use (Funk 2004; Ingold 2000, 192; Nilsson 2003; Zvelebil 2003). The individual experience of learning and enacting relationships among people, places, materials, and animals is recognized as the basis for creating patterns, but also for having the potential for variation and change through individual differences in perception and action (S. Price 2009).

Archaeologists also seek new insight into alternative sensory perceptions and their effects on world view and action. Simulation of light levels within ancient Arctic dwellings (Dawson et al. 2007), for example, suggests less reliance on vision as the dominant sense in craft production and more reliance on the sense of touch in intricate tasks such as sewing. The soundscape associated with flint-knapping is cited as intrinsic to the cultural perception and meaning of place (Mills and Pannett 2009), and the sensory and emotional experience of mortuary ritual is viewed as an essential basis for understanding its meaning (Hofmann 2005, 202–4). All of these types of study stress subtle and sometimes not so subtle differences among cultures and events, between places and within places over time, and among individuals at any given time. These are the variations that are recognized as constituting patterning and history.

More broadly, attention is focused on notions of world view, symbolism, and cosmology as the larger frameworks that guided past behaviour and perception (Aldenderfer 2002; Cannon 2002; Cummings 2003; Nilsson 2003; Riches 1982; Zvelebil 2003; 2008). Although meant to capture something of the fundamental underlying structure of cultural meaning, perception, and motivation, broad characterizations of world view are generally insufficient in themselves to explain particular patterns of behaviour. There is also a long-recognized danger of tautology in using evidence of patterned activity to discern the meanings and purposes that in turn are used to explain the activity (Riches 1982, 6). Conceptions of hunter-gatherer world view are most effective as explanations when they are contextually constructed on the basis of wide-ranging observation of consistencies among multiple situations and historical trajectories evident within an abundance of independent empirical evidence (e.g. Cannon 2011; Fuglestvedt 2011).

With emphasis on contextual relationships, meaning, interpretation, and multi-vocality, post-modernist hunter-gatherer archaeology is much more in line with other post-modern or post-processual archaeologies (Hodder 1999, 12). Observations of contextual relationships among traces and landscapes are used to reveal patterns and differences in ways of perceiving and being part of the material world. Stress is placed on the structure of connections among all aspects of cultural practice and perception, an approach long recognized as opposed to more materialist and deterministic explanations of hunter-gatherer cultural forms (Douglas 1972, 513–14). Interestingly, it is the contextual perception of elements in relation to one another that has been shown in recent experimental studies to distinguish various Asian cultural perceptions from the tendency to view elements in isolation or in relation to formal categories, which is more typical of Western perception and thinking (Nisbett and Masuda 2003). Archaeology, as a Western-based discipline, may simply be unlearning a peculiarly atypical cultural mode of thinking in applying contextual analysis of hunter-gatherers in place of studies that focus on isolated elements such as technology, subsistence, or ritual. Anthropologists and archaeologists are also gaining new insight into hunter-gatherer perceptions and motivations by making efforts to incorporate indigenous perspectives in research, for example through the study of oral histories and traditions or in the emerging practice of indigenous archaeology (Cruikshank 2005; Damm 2005; Fredericksen 2002; Yellowhorn 2006).

Although intriguing and often provocative, to date most post-modernist critiques of hunter-gatherer archaeology have not developed beyond the conceptualization stage, and typically take the form of shorter studies that draw attention to the inadequacies of modernist approaches and the potential for a more critically self-reflective hunter-gatherer archaeology. In almost every case the challenge to traditional concepts is theoretically driven, with the common purpose to emphasize diversity and historical specificity among past cultures. Some deconstructionist efforts are less well developed and less fully articulated than others, and at their worst have been described as nihilistic for failing to acknowledge any observational basis for discriminating among alternative interpretations (Zvelebil 2009, lii–liii). Although none as yet has risen fully to its own challenge to develop alternative interpretations of the available evidence, all at least have the capacity to stimulate alternative approaches to analysis and explanation.

The particular value of studies that incorporate contextual analyses of world view and history is that they emphasize empirical variability (e.g. Spikins 2008; Zvelebil 2008), which is more often minimized in positivist approaches that seek instead to obtain a better fit with broadly defined categories and processes. The result is widespread recognition of the complexity of variations and interactions among hunter-gatherers and their neighbours over the course of time, evident in the use of metaphors such as mosaic, tapestry, web, and constellation (Borić 2005; Pluciennik 2008; Spikins 2008; Zvelebil 2003) to describe cultural patterns and relationships.

Beyond creation of more realistic and theoretically sophisticated constructions of the past, the greater value derived from this emphasis on diversity is in forcing new appreciation for forms of evidence that otherwise might have been categorized or ignored. The detail of the empirical record has the potential to allow for conceptualization of systems of meaning that in turn provide a means for understanding cultural differences and unique patterns of historical development. Appreciation of complexity and variability among archaeologically observed hunter-gatherers also highlights the conceptual poverty of explanations that stress cross-cultural processes of environmental adaptation or social aggrandizement, which depend on only a narrow range of empirical observation. In their place are increasingly detailed studies that use virtually all forms of available evidence to construct the contingent circumstances and events of hunter-gatherer history.

Historical Perspectives

With the necessary theoretical and methodological tools in place and the availability of an increasingly rich empirical record, archaeologists can begin to construct long-term histories of hunter-gatherers. A particular focus of these histories, which was highlighted by the revisionist perspective in ethnology, is the interaction between foraging peoples and neighbouring farmers and European colonial powers (e.g. Schrire 1995). Long-standing patterns of interaction and trade between foragers and farmers that pre-date incorporation into broader world economic and political systems have also been extensively documented (Junker 2002; Spielmann and Eder 1994). Given the contemporary importance of these issues and the long-standing archaeological focus on the 'origins of agriculture', it is not surprising that many hunter-gatherer histories centre on interactions with farmers or transitions towards becoming farmers. The proliferation of detailed studies on this topic is emphasizing the diversity of circumstances and outcomes of forager–farmer interaction.

With the increasing abundance of data, histories of forager–farmer interaction are being written in very specific detail for different localities in the world. This is particularly evident in Europe, where archaeological histories run the gamut of possible outcomes. In central and north-western Europe, for example, a case has been made for hostility and conflict between migrating farmers and indigenous foraging populations, leading to the rapid displacement of the latter (Keeley 1997). In contrast, there is evidence for long-term coexistence of farmers and foragers within a few kilometres of one another on the European Plain in Poland (Zvelebil 2008, 55). Foragers in various parts of northern and north-eastern Europe are variously seen as engaged in exchange-based, patron–client relationships with farmers, partially borrowing and incorporating farmer lifeways, or resisting such lifeways by rejecting farming symbolically and in practice (Zvelebil 2008, 54–7). Criticism of assimilation and acculturation models in south-eastern Europe, because of their tendency to reinforce artificial categorization of cultures, has led to recognition of greater fluidity in individual and collective identity and the hybrid nature of cultures. This perspective and accumulating evidence suggests a level of variability in Mesolithic–Neolithic transformations 'that surpasses any of the archaeological or ethnographic models currently available' (Borić 2005, 100).

Rich, detailed evidence is also allowing for a range of specific histories that emphasize broader themes outside of developments associated with the advent of agriculture. Examination of Archaic period cultures in south-eastern North America, for example, has shown centuries of changing relationships between groups, shifting between periods of exchange and coexistence and periods of separation and resistance to avoid domination and threats to egalitarian ideals (Sassaman 2000; 2001). Also in the American south-east, the histories of monument construction associated with the Archaic Poverty Point site and culture have been used to weave together a historical understanding of multi-scalar local and inter-regional interaction based on migration, shifting alliances, and community formation (Sassaman 2005).

In north-western North America fine-scaled stratigraphic analysis, extensive dating of deposits, and multifaceted analysis of faunal, floral, and artefactual remains have provided a basis for a detailed history of emerging social differentiation among Plateau hunter-gatherers at the Keatley Creek site. The results suggest rapid changes in household structure and status differentiation dependent on contingencies of climate change and demography and the exercise of agency in choosing affiliation with household groups (Prentiss et al. 2007). On the central Northwest Coast, an accumulating variety of multi-site data provides a detailed picture of regional settlement expansion and economic intensification, triggered by contingent climatic events affecting staple food supplies but structured by histories and cosmologies that maintained and sustained long-standing patterns of resource use and settlement (Cannon 1998; 2002; 2011).

All of these examples of hunter-gatherer history have a few basic characteristics in common. Each emphasizes the important role of contingent circumstances and events, and also the structures of history and culture that shape perceptions and responses to circumstances and events. They further stress the role of individual and collective agency in determining courses of action consistent with patterns of perception and motivation. All such studies depend heavily on a rich and detailed empirical base, which is critical for defining the forms and roles of structures, contingencies, and agency (Aldenderfer 2002; Hodder 1999; Sassaman 2000; 2004). The productive capacity of historical perspectives is realized through their use of the broadest possible range of existing empirical evidence and their demand for new forms of evidence to create and to evaluate alternative understandings and explanations of events and developments and their interrelationships. This extends to intensive dating programmes, detailed stratigraphic analyses, traditional and non-traditional analyses of technologies, innovative uses of faunal and floral evidence, and the incorporation of human osteological, aDNA, and isotopic analysis.

Despite concerns that the historical turn in hunter-gatherer ethnology and subsequently archaeology would lead to a shift to particularism and away from more general comparative analysis and interpretation, this has not happened in practice. Instead, particular histories are cited as examples of more general processes, including responses to change (Myers 1988), resistance to domination (Sassaman 2000), the emergence of social differentiation (Prentiss et al. 2007), and maintenance of sustainable living standards (Cannon 2011). The meaning and value of these histories comes from their comparison to other cultures in other times and places as well as their relevance to contemporary social, cultural, and political concerns. As with all histories, there will always be room for new interpretations, depending on the assembly or analysis of empirical evidence and applications of the novel perspectives of researchers and the times in which they live.

As document-based studies have shown, many different histories can be generated from the same empirical evidence. With respect to hunter-gatherers, there are as yet few examples of detailed long-term archaeological histories and fewer still of alternative interpretations of those histories, but the example of Ofnet, the site of a Late Mesolithic skull cache in Bavaria, provides an illustration of the multiple readings possible from the same observations. For some, the pit filled with skulls, many bearing the marks of physical trauma, is unequivocal evidence of a massacre (Frayer 1997). For others, who view the site and its evidence far more critically, Ofnet is full of ambiguity and possibilities for interpretation, which can only be realized if focus shifts from contemporary concerns to the role of the site within the lives of people in the past (Hofmann 2005). Although not fully developed in this case, the articulation of alternative interpretations, such as ritual efforts to isolate and control various forms of 'bad death', including death by violence and possibly disease or other circumstances, opens a basis for re-examination of the evidence in this case and for broader comparison with burial evidence from other contexts.

Given the empirical detail they require and the open possibility for re-interpretation that will likely always remain, it is fair to consider the ultimate value in constructing long-term hunter-gatherer histories. At some banal level it could be said that the histories of all peoples and times are equally deserving of contemporary and future knowledge regardless of their contribution or relevance to the needs of the present. At the other extreme would be reference to the practical political value in historicizing hunter-gatherer interactions with the landscape and its resources, for example in support of land claims or a role for traditional resource management (Butler 2006), though, arguably, millennia-long histories should not be required for such purposes. The ultimate value of hunter-gatherer histories will more likely play out over time in relation to the insights they provide concerning common characteristics of humanity and as illustrations of common themes in human history, e.g. social domination and resistance, economic and environmental sustainability, growth and maintenance of social and political interrelationships, or the role of cosmology and values, especially in the context of dramatic social or economic change (Myers 1988). Some value will come from the performances and entertainment inherent in all history (Dening 1996), which is always more interesting and detailed when empirically based than is possible from mere imaginations of the past.

Archaeology will continue to ascertain and write hunter-gatherer histories of interest and value, contingent only on the archaeological imagination and the limits of evidence and methods for deriving new empirical observations. The greater challenge will be to preserve the capacity for creating new histories through site preservation and the archiving of documentation and collections from past excavations. These will provide the last opportunities for writing new histories into the future.

Discussion

Although hunter-gatherer archaeology is more often motivated by opportunities to apply optimization models or the quest for signs of economic intensification, emergent social complexity and other 'firsts' in some imagined collective human historical trajectory, more and more the trend is towards documenting and explaining local and regional histories (T. Price 2009; Sassaman 2010; Sassaman and Holly 2011). Typically these are constructed for their own sake, but they are also often cast in a broadly comparative perspective that may include other hunter-gatherers or human cultures of various kinds in different times and places. Historical explanations for developments among hunting and gathering cultures draw upon the same types of culturally specific structures of thought and behaviour, choices and actions, or agency, and contingent circumstances and events that are used to explain history in any context. They are framed, as all history must be, in relation to everyday lives of unique times, places, and peoples in the past.

The historicist perspective in hunter-gatherer studies must maintain a productive balance between the theoretical and the empirical, and will constantly confront the issue of having to define its relevance even as histories continue to be constructed on the basis of a richer and ever more detailed empirical record. Broader theoretical challenges will no doubt continue, though the trend towards more historical approaches has very strong momentum (e.g. Sassaman 2010; Sassaman and Holly 2011). Nevertheless, concern has been voiced that a focus on history in hunter-gatherer studies undermines efforts to achieve a true comparative science of foraging cultures past and present (e.g. Binford 2001, 30). Others have expressed apprehension that post-revisionist anthropology and archaeology risk becoming simply the latest example in the posited long-term oscillation between particularist and generalist approaches (Shott 1992). In fact, it has long been recognized that humanist approaches rely on larger frameworks of comparative research (Myers 1988, 276). The histories of hunters and gatherers that archaeologists write now and into the future will still be broadly comparative studies of the processes of culture and history (Sassaman 2000, 164), even as they highlight the unique actions, circumstances, and historical trajectories of individuals and groups in the past.

REFERENCES

Aldenderfer, M. 2002. Explaining changes in settlement dynamics across transformations of modes of production: from hunting to herding in the south-central Andes. In B. Fitzhugh and J. Habu (eds), *Beyond foraging and collecting: evolutionary change in hunter-gatherer settlement systems*, 387–412. New York: Kluwer Academic/Plenum Press.

Barnard, A. 2004. Hunting-and-gathering society: an eighteenth-century Scottish invention. In A. Barnard (ed.), *Hunter-gatherers in history, archaeology and anthropology*, 31–43. Oxford: Berg.

Binford, L. 2001. *Constructing frames of reference: an analytical method for archaeological theory building using hunter-gatherer and environmental data sets*. Berkeley: University of California Press.

Borić, D. 2005. Fuzzy horizons of change: orientalism and the frontier model of the Meso-Neolithic transition. In N. Milner and P. Woodman (eds), *Mesolithic studies at the beginning of the 21st century*, 81–105. Oxford: Oxbow.

Butler, C. 2006. Historicizing indigenous knowledge: practical and political issues. In C. Menzies (ed.), *Traditional ecological knowledge and natural resource management*, 107–26. Lincoln: University of Nebraska Press.

Cannon, A. 1998. Contingency and agency in the growth of Northwest Coast maritime economies. *Arctic Anthropology* 35, 57–67.

Cannon, A. 2002. Sacred power and seasonal settlement on the central Northwest Coast. In B. Fitzhugh and J. Habu (eds), *Beyond foraging and collecting: evolutionary change in hunter-gatherer settlement systems*, 311–38. New York: Kluwer Academic/Plenum Press.

Cannon, A. 2011. Cosmology and everyday perception in Northwest Coast production, reproduction and settlement. In A. Cannon (ed.), *Structured worlds: the archaeology of hunter-gatherer thought and action*, 54–68. London: Equinox.

Cobb, H. 2005. Straight down the line? A queer consideration of hunter-gatherer studies in north-west Europe. *World Archaeology* 37, 630–6.

Cobb, H. 2009. Being-in-the-(Mesolithic) world: place, substance and person in the Mesolithic of western Scotland. In S. McCartan, R. Schulting, G. Warren, and P. Woodman (eds), *Mesolithic horizons*, 368–72. Oxford: Oxbow.

Conneller, C. 2005. Moving beyond sites: Mesolithic technology in the landscape. In N. Milner and P. Woodman (eds), *Mesolithic studies at the beginning of the 21st century*, 42–55. Oxford: Oxbow.

Cruikshank, J. 2005. *Do glaciers listen? Local knowledge, colonial encounters, and social imagination*. Vancouver: UBC Press.

Cummings, V. 2003. The origins of monumentality? Mesolithic world-views of the landscape in western Britain. In L. Larson, H. Kindgren, K. Knutsson, D. Loeffler, and A. Åkerlund (eds), *Mesolithic on the move: proceedings of the sixth international conference on the Mesolithic in Europe*, 74–81. Oxford: Oxbow.

Damm, C. 2005. Archaeology, ethno-history and oral traditions: approaches to the indigenous past. *Norwegian Archaeological Review* 38, 73–87.

Dawson, P., Levy, R., Gardner, D., and Walls, M. 2007. Simulating the behaviour of light inside Arctic dwellings: implications for assessing the role of vision in task performance. *World Archaeology* 39, 17–35.

Dening, G. 1996. *Performances*. Chicago: University of Chicago Press.

Douglas, M. 1972. Symbolic orders in the use of domestic space. In P. Ucko, R. Tringham, and G. Dimbleby (eds), *Man, settlement and urbanism*, 513–21. London: Duckworth.

Frayer, D. 1997. Ofnet: evidence for a Mesolithic massacre. In D. Martin and D. Frayer (eds), *Troubled times: violence and warfare in the past*, 181–216. Amsterdam: Gordon and Breach.

Fredericksen, C. 2002. Caring for history: Tiwi and archaeological narratives of Fort Dundas/Punata, Melville Island, Australia. *World Archaeology* 34, 288–302.

Fuglestvedt, I. 2011. Humans, material culture and landscape: outline to an understanding of developments in worldviews on the Scandinavian Peninsula, c.10000–4500 BP. In A. Cannon (ed.), *Structured worlds: the archaeology of hunter-gatherer thought and action*, 32–53. London: Equinox.

Funk, C. 2004. Optimal foraging theory and cognitive archaeology: Cup'ik cultural perception in southwestern Alaska. In G. Crothers (ed.), *Hunters and gatherers in theory and archaeology*, 279–98. Carbondale, IL: Center for Archaeological Investigations.

Hodder, I. 1999. *The archaeological process: an introduction*. Oxford: Blackwell.

Hofmann, D. 2005. The emotional Mesolithic: past and present ambiguities of Ofnet cave. In N. Milner and P. Woodman (eds), *Mesolithic studies at the beginning of the 21st century*, 194–211. Oxford: Oxbow.

Ingold, T. 2000. *The perception of the environment: essays in livelihood, dwelling and skill*. London: Routledge.

Junker, L. 2002. Long-term change and short-term shifting in the economy of Philippine forager-traders. In B. Fitzhugh and J. Habu (eds), *Beyond foraging and collecting: evolutionary change in hunter-gatherer settlement systems*, 339–86. New York: Kluwer Academic/Plenum Press.

Keeley, L. 1997. Frontier warfare in the early Neolithic. In D. Martin and D. Frayer (eds), *Troubled times: violence and warfare in the past*, 303–19. Amsterdam: Gordon and Breach.

Kehoe, A. 2000. *Shamans and religion: an anthropological exploration in critical thinking*. Prospect Heights, IL: Waveland Press.

Lewis-Williams, D. 2006. Building bridges to the deep human past: consciousness, religion and art. In F. LeRon Shults (ed.), *The evolution of rationality: interdisciplinary essays in honor of J. Wentzel van Huyssteen*, 149–66. Grand Rapids, MI: William B. Eerdmans Publishing.

McCall, G. 2007. Add shamans and stir? A critical review of the shamanism model of forager rock art production. *Journal of Anthropological Archaeology* 26, 224–33.

Mills, S. and Pannett, A. 2009. Sound like sociality: new research on lithic contexts in Mesolithic Caithness. In S. McCartan, R. Schulting, G. Warren, and P. Woodman (eds), *Mesolithic horizons*, vol. 2, 717–21. Oxford: Oxbow.

Milne, S. 2011. Landscape learning and lithic technology: seasonal mobility, enculturation and tool apprenticeship among the early Palaeo-Eskimos. In A. Cannon (ed.), *Structured worlds: the archaeology of hunter-gatherer thought and action*, 95–115. London: Equinox.

Milner, N. 2005. Seasonal consumption practices in the Mesolithic: economic, environmental, social or ritual? In N. Milner and P. Woodman (eds), *Mesolithic studies at the beginning of the 21st century*, 56–68. Oxford: Oxbow.

Milner, N. and Woodman, P. (eds) 2005. *Mesolithic studies at the beginning of the 21st century*. Oxford: Oxbow.

Myers, F. 1988. Critical trends in the study of hunter-gatherers. *Annual Review of Anthropology* 17, 261–82.

Nilsson, B. 2003. Sorbus aucuparia or extremely red rowan-berries? Some naïve reflections of archaeology, palaeo-ecology and the non-scientific dimensions of scientific landscape. In L. Larson, H. Kindgren, K. Knutsson, D. Loeffler, and A. Åkerlund (eds), *Mesolithic on the move: proceedings of the sixth international conference on the Mesolithic in Europe*, 145–8. Oxford: Oxbow.

Nisbett, R. and Masuda, T. 2003. Culture and point of view. *Proceedings of the National Academy of Sciences* 100, 11163–70.

Oetelaar, G. and Oetelaar, D. 2011. The structured world of the *Niitsitapi*: the landscape as historical archive among hunter-gatherers of the northern Plains. In A. Cannon (ed.), *Structured worlds: the archaeology of hunter-gatherer thought and action*, 69–94. London: Equinox.

Pearson, J. 2002. *Shamanism and the ancient mind: a cognitive approach to archaeology*. Walnut Creek, CA: AltaMira Press.

Pluciennik, M. 2004. The meaning of 'hunter-gatherers' and modes of subsistence: a comparative historical perspective. In A. Barnard (ed.), *Hunter-gatherers in history, archaeology and anthropology*, 17–29. Oxford: Berg.

Pluciennik, M. 2008. The coastal Mesolithic of the European Mediterranean. In G. Bailey and P. Spikins (eds), *Mesolithic Europe*, 328–56. Cambridge: Cambridge University Press.

Prentiss, A., Lyons, N., Harris, L., Burns, M., and Godin, T. 2007. The emergence of status inequality in intermediate scale societies: a demographic and socio-economic history of the Keatley Creek site, British Columbia. *Journal of Anthropological Archaeology* 26, 299–327.

Price, S. 2009. Wood and wild animals: towards an understanding of a Mesolithic world. In S. McCartan, R. Schulting, G. Warren, and P. Woodman (eds), *Mesolithic horizons*, 683–9. Oxford: Oxbow.

Price, T. 2009. The way forward. In S. McCartan, R. Schulting, G. Warren, and P. Woodman (eds), *Mesolithic horizons*, xxxiii–xxxv. Oxford: Oxbow.

Riches, D. 1982. *Northern nomadic hunter-gatherers*. London: Academic Press.

Sassaman, K. 2000. Agents of change in hunter-gatherer technology. In M. Dobres and J. Robb (eds), *Agency in archaeology*, 148–68. London: Routledge.

Sassaman, K. 2001. Hunter-gatherers and traditions of resistance. In T. Pauketat (ed.), *The archaeology of tradition: agency and history before and after Columbus*, 218–36. Gainesville: University Press of Florida.

Sassaman, K. 2004. Complex hunter-gatherers in evolution and history: a North American perspective. *Journal of Archaeological Research* 12, 227–80.

Sassaman, K. 2005. Poverty Point as structure, event, process. *Journal of Archaeological Method and Theory* 12, 335–64.

Sassaman, K. 2010. *The Eastern Archaic historicized*. Lanham, MD: AltaMira Press.

Sassaman, K. and Holly, D. (eds) 2011. *Hunter-gatherer archaeology as historical process*. Tucson: University of Arizona Press.

Schrire, C. 1980. An inquiry into the evolutionary status and apparent identity of San hunter-gatherers. *Human Ecology* 8, 9–32.

Schrire, C. 1995. *Digging through darkness: chronicles of an archaeologist*. Charlottesville: University of Virginia Press.

Shott, M. 1992. On recent trends in the anthropology of foragers: Kalahari revisionism and its archaeological implications. *Man* 27, 843–71.

Solway, J. and Lee, R. 1990. Foragers, genuine or spurious? Situating the Kalahari San in history. *Current Anthropology* 31, 109–46.

Spielmann, K. and Eder, J. 1994. Hunters and farmers: then and now. *Annual Review of Anthropology* 23, 303–23.

Spikins, P. 2008. Mesolithic Europe: glimpses of another world. In G. Bailey and P. Spikins (eds), *Mesolithic Europe*, 1–17. Cambridge: Cambridge University Press.

Strassburg, J. 2003. Rituals at the Meso 2000 conference and the Mesolithic-Neolithic terminological breakdown. In L. Larson, H. Kindgren, K. Knutsson, D. Loeffler, and A. Åkerlund (eds), *Mesolithic on the move: proceedings of the sixth international conference on the Mesolithic in Europe*, 542–6. Oxford: Oxbow.

Warren, G. 2005. Complex arguments... In N. Milner and P. Woodman (eds), *Mesolithic studies at the beginning of the 21st century*, 69–80. Oxford: Oxbow.

Wickham-Jones, C. 2005. Summer walkers? Mobility and the Mesolithic. In N. Milner and P. Woodman (eds), *Mesolithic studies at the beginning of the 21st century*, 30–41. Oxford: Oxbow.

Wilmsen, E. and Denbow, J. 1990. Paradigmatic history of San-speaking peoples and current attempts at revision. *Current Anthropology* 31, 489–524.

Yellowhorn, E. 2006. The awakening of internalist archaeology in the aboriginal world. In R. Williamson and M. Bisson (eds), *The archaeology of Bruce Trigger: theoretical empiricism*, 194–209. Montreal-Kingston: McGill-Queens University Press.

Zvelebil, M. 2003. Enculturation of Mesolithic landscapes. In L. Larson, H. Kindgren, K. Knutsson, D. Loeffler, and A. Åkerlund (eds), *Mesolithic on the move: proceedings of the sixth international conference on the Mesolithic in Europe*, 65–73. Oxford: Oxbow.

Zvelebil, M. 2008. Innovating hunter-gatherers: the Mesolithic in the Baltic. In G. Bailey and P. Spikins (eds), *Mesolithic Europe*, 18–59. Cambridge: Cambridge University Press.

Zvelebil, M. 2009. The Mesolithic and the 21st century. In S. McCartan, R. Schulting, G. Warren, and P. Woodman (eds), *Mesolithic horizons*, xlvii–lviii. Oxford: Oxbow.

CHAPTER 6

HUNTER-GATHERER-FISHERS, ETHNOARCHAEOLOGY, AND ANALOGICAL REASONING

PAUL J. LANE

Introduction

HUNTING and gathering was the only mode of subsistence among human and proto-human populations until c.10–12,000 years ago, and remained a significant subsistence strategy in many parts of the world until the last c.500 years. Even to this day groups of hunter-gatherers can be found in approximately 40 different countries around the world (Lee and Daly 2002). Given this temporal depth, it is unsurprising that throughout the history of the discipline archaeologists have drawn extensively on ethnographic and anthropological accounts of living hunting-gathering-fishing (hereafter HGF) societies to aid their interpretation of archaeological traces of such societies. In addition, for over 40 years at least, archaeologists have been conducting their own *ethnoarchaeological* research among a sample of these with specific archaeological questions in mind. This chapter reviews the use of ethnographic analogies to interpret the archaeological signatures of HGF societies and behaviour, and the pattern and nature of ethnoarchaeological research among them.

Ethnoarchaeology can be defined as the study of contemporary societies, their material culture and the material consequences of their behaviour for the purposes of formulating and strengthening analogies for use in the interpretation of archaeological evidence. It is best regarded as one of several research strategies that archaeologists can employ to enhance 'understanding of the relationships of material culture to culture as a whole, both in the living context and as it enters the archaeological record, and to exploiting such understandings in order to inform archaeological concepts and to improve interpretation' (David and Kramer 2001, 2). There has been a long history of using ethnographic data and comparisons in archaeology, and their incorporation into archaeological interpretation was fundamental to the establishment of archaeology as an academic discipline in that it laid the basis for analogical reasoning (Orme 1973).

However, a particular defining attribute of ethnoarchaeology, which distinguishes it from the more general and widespread use of ethnographic precedents and parallels, is that it entails an element of field research by trained archaeologists among living communities. While field methods vary on a case-by-case basis, ethnoarchaeological studies typically involve the use of standard techniques of archaeological recording and materials analysis in conjunction with anthropological methods of participant observation, informal and formal interviews, and sometimes questionnaires (for fuller discussion see David and Kramer 2001, 63–90; for further discussion of ethical issues and responsibilities see Fewster 2001a). The value of ethnographic information in archaeological reasoning, whether collected by trained archaeologists as part of an ethnoarchaeological project or by others—such as ethnologists and anthropologists—also depends on the quality of the analogies that are drawn, and strengthening analogies must be regarded as a continuous interpretive challenge.

Analogical Reasoning

Ethnographic Analogies

The use of analogy is a form of inductive reasoning and remains a cornerstone of archaeological interpretation (Shelley 1999; Wylie 1985). Analogy involves the comparison of different things, settings, or practices that share certain properties so as to infer or imply other non-observable commonalities. In drawing analogies, archaeologists necessarily rely on the uniformitarian principle that it is possible to extrapolate information about past events and processes (which by definition are not observable) from observations made in the present, although there is considerable variation in the nature of the specific uniformitarian assumptions employed (Cameron 1993; Gould 1965).

At its most basic, analogical reasoning relies on the principle that if two objects, events, or situations share a number of observable similarities they are likely to share other, less observable similarities as well. Thus, for example, J. G. D. Clark suggested that the presence of flint scrapers at the early Mesolithic site of Star Carr in North Yorkshire, England, indicated that skin-working was carried out at the site, and hence, on the basis of 'analogy with the hunting peoples of North America and Greenland' among whom women are usually responsible for preparing skins, women as well as men must have been present at Star Carr (Clark 1954, 10–11). As Wylie (1985, 71, 83, 100–4), among others, has pointed out, this is a relatively simple formal analogy, the main basis for the comparison being shared similarities in subsistence practices and perhaps prevailing environmental conditions. It could be strengthened by increasing the number of documentable similarities between the material recovered from Star Carr and the available information about northern hunter-gatherer societies. However, while a greater number of observable commonalities between the 'subject' (i.e. archaeological) and 'source' (i.e. ethnographic) sides of an analogy can increase the likelihood that they also have other non-observable factors in common, and hence strengthen the analogy, this is not always the case. This is for the simple reason that the shared similarities may not be of relevance to the presence or absence of the other, inferred commonalities (Salmon 1982; Wylie 1985).

In the Star Carr case, for example, Clark's analogy would have been strengthened if he had provided independent support for his inference that scrapers were indeed used for hide working, other material remains indicated hide working had taken place, and/or that women were present at the site, and, most critically, there is a causal and invariable association between a particular task and the gender of those who perform it. Subsequent research has strengthened some aspects of this analogy. For instance, microwear analyses of a sample of formal tools, including scrapers, have provided independent evidence that although scrapers were also used for working other materials including wood and antler at least some were used, as surmised by Clark, for hide working (Dumont 1983). These also had more rounded edges than those used to work other materials, and so are potentially morphologically distinguishable. Nonetheless, as debate about Clark's varied interpretations of Star Carr has highlighted (see Lane and Schadla-Hall 2004), there remains considerable uncertainty as to the social composition of the site's occupants at different stages during its history.

The major challenges in the use of analogy, therefore, are establishing how reliable and how suitable a particular comparison is between the ethnographic (source) and archaeological (subject) sides of the comparison (see Shelley 1999; Stahl 1993; Wylie 1988). One strategy much favoured by processualist archaeologists for achieving this is through cross-cultural analysis of ethnographic data (McNett 1979). The basic premise of this approach is that if a certain correlation can be shown to exist between a particular behaviour or social practice and its material consequences among, say, all documented HGFs then this is likely to be a defining, universal feature of hunter-gatherer societies across space and time.

An example of this is Shott's (1986) analysis of the relationships between technological organization and settlement mobility among foragers. The danger of the approach is that it can mean archaeologists interpret their data solely in terms of the ethnographically documented range of human behaviour, and omit to consider that other forms may have existed in the past for which there are no modern analogues. Wobst (1978) famously described this as the 'tyranny of the ethnographic record'. Conversely, the approach can be used effectively to critique commonplace assumptions about different categories of human societies, as for example in Marlowe's (2004) study in which he found that contrary to the dominant view, post-marital residence among the majority of ethnographically documented foragers is *not* virilocal, or Kelly's (1995) wide-ranging review which remains a rich seam of information about the diversity of hunter-gatherer lifeways and social organization.

An alternative strategy has been to impose certain boundary conditions on the ethnographic side of the analogy. It is often held, for example, that analogies are stronger if historical continuities can be shown between the archaeological 'subject' and ethnographic 'source' sides of the comparison. Equally, as was seemingly implicit in Clark's selection of ethnographic parallels, it is common for archaeologists to restrict the 'source' side of their analogies to 'societies occupying comparable environments pursuing similar subsistence strategies' to those evidenced in the archaeological 'subject' side of their study (Stahl 1993, 244).

Gould's (1978; 1980) proposition that archaeologists should develop arguments by *anomaly* rather than analogy is a more sophisticated version of this. Briefly, the key notion behind this suggestion is that since environments and ecologies constrain much human behaviour, particularly in pre-industrial societies, detailed documentation of these variables can generate a series of predictive consequences—along the lines 'given these ecological parameters and this level of technological capability, then we would expect humans in the past to have behaved in the following ways and leave the following types of archaeological signature'. Where the archaeological record suggests that a past society did not behave as might be expected given these ecological and technological constraints, in Gould's terms such behaviour could be called 'anomalous' and provide particular insights into the specifics of that society's cultural practices (see especially Gould 1980, 29–47).

While certainly illuminating aspects of the adaptive strategies of Western Desert Aborigines and changes in these over time, Gould's model of 'argument by anomaly' has been criticized on a number of fronts. In particular, as Stahl (1993, 244) makes clear, an inherent danger of imposing the ecological conditions is that they implicitly introduce notions of unilinear evolution by suggesting that analogies are stronger when comparing societies at 'comparable stages of evolutionary development'. Moreover, as subsequent debate highlighted (Binford 1985; Gould 1985; Gould and Watson 1982; Wylie 1982), the kind of inferential argument that Gould suggested archaeologists adopt was no less reliant on the use of analogical reasoning than those he had set out to critique (see especially Wylie 1982). Far more critical, as Wylie (1985; 1988) discusses, is demonstrating the relevance of the observed similarities through a combination of explicit testing of hypotheses concerning causal relationships between human behaviour and material culture patterning, and expansion of our knowledge of the operation of causal processes in different ethnographic contexts.

Middle Range Theory

One area where ethnoarchaeological research has made significant contributions to the goal of strengthening the use of ethnographic analogies has been in the development of 'Middle Range Theory' (hereafter MRT). This term is closely associated with the ethnoarchaeological work of Lewis Binford, who contrasted it with more general or 'explanatory' theory. Specifically, MRT is concerned with how archaeologists 'get from contemporary facts to statements about the past' and in particular how they 'convert...observationally static facts of the archaeological record to statements of dynamics' about past human behaviour (Binford 1977, 6). To do this, Binford argues, archaeologists need to identify invariant aspects of human behaviour that correlate with particular material patterning, whether this patterning is exhibited at a landscape scale of analysis (e.g. Binford 1980; 1982), that of the 'site' or structure (e.g. Binford 1978a; 1978b), or at the level of the artefact or ecofact (e.g. Binford 1981).

Since human behaviour is shaped and influenced by cultural beliefs and practices, which are highly variable across space and time and are therefore unreliable sources of uniformitarian principles, Binford's strategy has been to focus on certain universals, such as human bodily mechanics and animal anatomies, and how these shape material culture patterning through different energy transfers (see especially Binford 1981, 26–9; Binford 1983, 61–76). Moreover, since the relationships between the dynamics of behaviour and the static record of material culture patterning are only observable in the present, ethnoarchaeology and other forms of 'actualistic' research (such as experimental archaeology) are essential components of theory building within the discipline.

From the mid-1980s, MRT was subject to considerable criticism and critique (Tschauner 1996), particularly from post-processual archaeologists. The latter argued that all forms of human behaviour are meaningfully constituted and, as such, in order to be understandable must be studied in terms of the cultural and historical contexts in which they occur. Preferring the terms 'action' or 'practice', and latterly 'agency', rather than 'behaviour', post-processualists hold that even a seemingly simple task such as tossing a bone is mediated by belief and custom, and potentially also has underlying symbolic significance as well as a practical utility. A classic example of this, albeit not conducted among HGFs, is Hodder's study of bone discard among Mesakin and Moro Nuba in central Sudan (Hodder 1982, 155–61).

A further tenet of post-processualist archaeology is that material culture does not merely reflect aspects of identity, social organization, or human behaviour more generally, but also plays an active part in the creation and recreation of social practice. Ethnoarchaeological studies of such concepts with reference to HGFs have been limited (see below), but in common with similar studies among food-producing and urban societies, these have tended to place particular emphasis on the 'meaning of things', exploring the cultural basis for different material expressions of collective and individual identity, and the historical contingencies of individual and group practice. Post-processualists typically also express a corresponding scepticism towards the possible existence of causal, law-like relationships between material culture patterning and human behaviour.

Despite these contrasting emphases, as Cunningham (2003, 396–400) argues, the processualist and post-processualist schools both posit the existence of 'core universals'—such as the post-processualist claim that all human behaviour is meaningfully constituted, or the processualist position that culture is humanity's 'extrasomatic means of adaptation' that emanates from responses to ecological processes. Ethnographic analogies developed as part of MRT similarly rely on 'core universals'—such as those of animal anatomies, human bodily mechanics, or human neuropsychological experiences while in a state of altered consciousness—but these are of a lower order in that they are used to establish causal relationships between *specific* categories of behaviour and forms of material culture patterning.

Cunningham (2003, 400–2) contrasts these kinds of comparative analogical arguments with a fourth approach, which he terms 'historical analogy'. This is an elaboration of the 'direct historical approach' developed in North American archaeology during the early part of the twentieth century (Lyman and O'Brien 2001), and refers to the forms of analogical inference where direct, historical continuity between the ethnographic source of the analogy and the archaeological subject of analysis can be demonstrated. However, although the use of historical analogies is not reliant on the assertion of any 'core universal', and thus is more sensitive to identifying contextual variations, as Stahl (2001, 19–40) has discussed at length, without careful scrutiny of both the source and subject sides the approach is as prone to 'affirming the consequent' as any of the other forms of analogical reasoning used in archaeology.

Furthermore, there is no reason why these different strategies cannot be combined so as to produce even more robust analogies, as Wylie's discussions of the nature of analogy make clear. A good example of this is Lewis-Williams's development of a new approach to the interpretation of southern African rock art (Lewis-Williams 1981; 2002), which became glossed for a while in the literature as the 'trance hypothesis'. The core thesis of Lewis-Williams's argument has been that hunter-gatherer rock art in the region was primarily associated with a range of shamanistic beliefs, rituals, and experiences. His model thus challenged older, more naturalistic readings of the art, and he and his associates have often argued convincingly that instead of being depictions of the way of life of Later Stone Age foragers, the art comprises diverse representations of the different experiences of trance, coupled with those of encounters with the spirit world during trance, the diverse symbols of supernatural potency, and images of trance dances.

The significant point here is that although southern Africa's modern hunter-gatherer San populations no longer produce rock art, Lewis-Williams was able to develop robust analogies through a series of related bridging arguments. These included the evidence that can be drawn from the rich documentary record compiled in the nineteenth century of San shamanistic practices and their experiences during trance; modern ethnographic studies of shamanism and trance dances among contemporary San; and archaeological and historical sources that demonstrate cultural continuity between modern San and the Later Stone Age producers of the art. He also linked information from these sources with evidence from neuropsychological research on more general experiences of altered states of consciousness (of which trance is one category), and noted a remarkable correspondence between these 'core universals', the imagery and composition of the rock art, and San accounts of trance and their interpretation of the meaning of these experiences. By drawing on these diverse lines of evidence and showing the relevance of the correspondences between the 'source' and 'subject' sides of the analogy, a robust argument could be developed (see Lewis-Williams 1991). Even so, as subsequent debate on his apparent neglect of the gendered dimensions of this rock art (e.g. Solomon 1992; 2006) and of its temporality (e.g. Yates et al. 1994) has shown, however strong an ethnographic analogy is it can never provide a comprehensive model of the past and alternative interpretations must always be considered and actively sought.

Hunter-Gatherer-Fisher Ethnoarchaeology

Research Patterns

The pattern of ethnoarchaeological research among contemporary hunter-gatherer communities has been very uneven and heavily biased towards a limited number of societies that live in tropical, sub-tropical, and arctic environments (Table 6.1). In most cases, these HGFs were selected for study with specific, broader anthropological research questions in mind (see below). Unfortunately, archaeological use of the interpretive insights gained from such studies often neglects the selective nature of this ethnoarchaeological research with the result that the analogies are often used far too uncritically and without due consideration of relevance on both the source and subject sides.

As Table 6.1 suggests, the most intensively studied African HGFs are the northern Kalahari Ju/'hoãnsi (also known as the !Kung, or !Kung San) and other Kalahari Khoisan groups, various Pygmy (Efe, Bofi, and Aka) societies, and the Hadzabe (or Hadza) of northern Tanzania. In Australia, Western Desert and Central Australian Aborigines, notably the Ngatatjara, Pintupi, and Alywarra, have received most attention. In Arctic North America, the Alaskan Nunamiut are best known from an ethnoarchaeological perspective, although there has been a fair degree of research among other Inuit and also Northern Dene (Athapaskan) communities. Some hunter-fisher societies of Western Siberia, notably the Khanty, have become the

Table 6.1 Spatial and ecological distribution of the more intensively studied, from an ethnoarchaeological perspective, hunter–gatherer–fisher societies

	Desert/dry savannah	Sub-humid savannah	Rainforest
Low latitude HGFs			
Africa	G/wi, Ju/'hoãnsi, Kua, !Xo	Hadzabe	Aka, Bofi, Efe
South America			Aché, Awá, Hiwi, Nukak
Australia	Alywarra, Ngatatjara, Pintupi		
	Arctic tundra	Subarctic maritime	Subarctic boreal forest and taiga
High latitude HGFs			
North America	Nunamiut and other Inuit	Yup'ik	Algonquian, Northern Dene (Athapaskan), Ingalik
Asia			Khanty

focus of research in recent decades. There is also a growing trend of research among various South American forager societies including the Aché, Awá, Hiwi, and Nukak.

This is by no means a comprehensive list, and in some respects the less well-known studies, which tend not to be so concerned with grand anthropological theorizing, are of greater value for understanding the hunter-gatherer archaeological record of the areas in which they were conducted. This is particularly true, for example, of the various studies of upland groups in central Kenya such as the Okiek (Marshall 1994; 2001) and Mukogodo (Mutundu 1999), the many and diverse hunter-gatherer groups of northern and central India (e.g. Nagar 2008), and the Ainu and related hunter-gatherers of northern Japan (e.g. Kosugi 1997; Sato 2009). Cooper's (1994) research on the Onge, a group of Andaman Islanders, provides valuable insights into the activities of coastal dwelling hunter-gatherer-fishers and shellfish collectors of broad disciplinary relevance. Similarly, Pookajorn's (1985) study of Mlabrai forest hunters of northern Thailand was one of the first to examine the use of caves, for which there is extensive evidence in the global archaeological record, from an ethnoarchaeological perspective. Moreover, his observation that Mlabrai utilize caves 'only in periods of very heavy rain and wind storms' (Pookajorn 1985, 219) certainly runs counter to widespread archaeological assumptions about the importance of caves and rock shelters as home bases, a point also made by Nicholson and Cane (1991, 273) on the basis of their research among Western Desert Australian Aborigines.

Research Biases

The uneven distribution and somewhat selective nature of ethnoarchaeological research among contemporary HGFs has no doubt been influenced by circumstance and opportunity. However, the choice of study area by a particular scholar, inevitably, is also informed by their research interests within the broader discipline which in turn shapes which topics are investigated and how the results are presented. For example, the vast majority of the ethnoarchaeological and closely related anthropological studies conducted among the Hadzabe have focused on issues relating to the processing and discard of animal carcasses (Bunn et al. 1988; O'Connell et al. 1990; 1992; Lupo 1994; 2001; 2006; Lupo and O'Connell 2002); hunting and scavenging practices (Bunn 2001; O'Connell et al. 1988); the spatial structure of base camps (O'Connell et al. 1991); and associated aspects of site formation (Lupo 1995; Mallol et al. 2007).

The reasons behind this particular focus lie partly in the fact that Hadzabe occupy and utilize a savannah habitat that is broadly comparable to the one occupied by Plio-Pleistocene hominins as reconstructed for the fossil-rich areas around Lake Turkana (Kenya) and Olduvai Gorge (Tanzania). Hadzabe typically obtain meat by hunting with bows and poisoned arrows, using a combination of encounter and intercept strategies, and process and discard parts of the carcasses at the kill sites before transporting the remaining portions to their home bases. Unusually, compared with many other modern HGFs in the tropics, Hadzabe tend to focus almost exclusively on medium- and large-sized game species (especially giraffe, zebra, impala, and warthog), with smaller animals only rarely being taken. Like the environment they inhabit, the range of taxa exploited is closely similar to that represented on Plio-Pleistocene sites in the region. Hadzabe also regularly scavenge large animals killed by other predators, another activity thought to have been important for Plio-Pleistocene hominins (O'Connell et al. 1988). Because of such general similarities, understanding the processes that affect the composition and patterning of discarded body parts at kill sites and home bases, and hence the formation of the archaeological record of such activities, has the potential to inform debates concerning whether early hominins obtained their meat intake by hunting or scavenging, or a combination of these, and whether they had home bases that were provisioned from various resource extraction areas such as kill sites.

In other words, there are a number of source and subject side correspondences between Hadzabe practices and habitat and the Plio-Pleistocene fossil record that suggest the potential for developing analytically robust analogies through ethnoarchaeological research, so as to further aid interpretation of Plio-Pleistocene sites. Cumulatively these studies have provided a sustained critique of older models of the importance of big game hunting to hominid evolution. However, the focus on these issues may have deflected attention away from equally important topics. For instance, the relative importance of plant food to diets, and hence the significance of gathering, is still a largely neglected topic within Plio-Pleistocene research, but it is central to an understanding of HGF behaviour more generally, and very probably also that of early hominins. Equally, scant consideration is given in these studies to the historical trajectory of the Hadzabe and the possibility raised by Woodburn (1980) that at some time in the past their hunting and gathering strategy might have been quite different from the one they follow now. That said, there are important exceptions, notably Vincent's (1985) pioneering work on Hadzabe plant-gathering practices (see also Marlowe and Berbesque 2009) and ongoing research by Mabulla (2003; 2007) linking Hadzabe patterns of mobility and landscape use and their material signatures to the later Pleistocene and Holocene archaeological record of the Lake Eyasi basin.

In a similar vein, Binford's studies among the Nunamiut, as he makes abundantly clear in his more synthetic publications (e.g. Binford 1983), were deeply informed by his earlier interest in the causes of assemblage variability in Mousterian archaeological horizons (e.g. Binford 1973), and by subsequent arguments concerning the significance of hunting, home bases, and food sharing as drivers of hominid evolution (Binford 1981; also see e.g. Binford 1984 versus Isaac 1978; and Binford 1988 versus Bunn and Kroll 1988). Given this, his choice of the Nunamiut over other HGFs is logical, since the Nunamiut, like their Middle Palaeolithic counterparts are big game hunters and occupy an environment broadly similar to that which prevailed during the Middle Palaeolithic in Western Europe. Had his interests lain with the Upper Palaeolithic, given the ample evidence for a marked increase in exchange during the Aurignacian (Gamble 1999, 360–1), this might have taken him to conduct research among Ju/'hoãnsi (or other Kalahari San) in view of their well-documented gift exchange systems (see below) or perhaps Central Australia (Feblot-Augustins and Perlès 1992; Gould 1980).

While this latter point is pure speculation, it is important that all ethnoarchaeological studies are read critically, and the influence of broader research goals on the pattern of ethnoarchaeological research is always kept in mind when using the results of such studies. This is especially important since not all researchers are as explicit as Binford and O'Connell and colleagues have been as to their ultimate objectives (see also Griffin and Solheim 1990, 153–7 for similar points concerning research among the Agta in the Philippines).

The following sections offer a summary of the more intensively researched themes. The range of topics investigated is broad, however, and many other equally important themes could be discussed, such as the utilization of marine resources (e.g. Bird and Bliege Bird 2000; Bird et al. 2002), interactions with neighbouring farming and herding populations (e.g. Hayden 2003; Ikeya and Nakai 2009), and processes of sedentism, plant domestication, and subsistence change (e.g. Hitchcock 1987; Kent and Vierich 1989; Marshall 2001).

Key Themes in Hunter-Gatherer-Fisher Ethnoarchaeology

Site Structure and Formation Processes

A primary objective of archaeological interpretation is understanding the significance of observable variability in the formal, spatial, and chronological characteristics of archaeological phenomena, ranging in scale from the individual object through that of the 'site' to entire landscapes. Much ethnoarchaeological research among HGFs has been directed towards this goal, with particular emphasis on determining how the spatial patterning observable on HGF sites is generated. Among the diverse range of issues considered from this perspective, studies of variations in butchery practices and carcass disposal; types of discard around hearths and in structures; differences between residential sites/base camps and special activity sites (i.e. kill sites, hunting stands, special-purpose camps, etc.); the social composition of settlements and activity areas; season of site occupation; and degrees of mobility, have dominated.

Yellen's 'Ring Model'

One of the pioneering studies of this kind was Yellen's (1977a) investigation of Ju/'hoãnsi site structure, discard practices, and settlement systems in northern Botswana. During their annual round of activities, Ju/'hoãnsi create and utilize a variety of different types of site, only some of which are residential. The latter are divided into dry- and wet-season camps, which differ in several respects (Table 6.2). Despite these general differences, however, dry- and wet-season camps are quite similar, especially in terms of their internal organization, which typically comprises three concentric zones of activity. At the centre is an area of communal space, used for such activities as sharing meat, trance dancing, and other rituals, which is generally devoid of any discarded materials. Family shelters, consisting of a light brushwood frame with grass covering, are arranged around this space in an arc or a rough circle. These are used simply for sleeping, as a source of shade, and for storing personal belongings. The entrances to the shelters all face inwards to the camp centre. Each has a hearth, used for both cooking and warmth, located outside the entrance. These form the main focus for food processing, cooking, tool and ornament manufacturing and repair, and socializing. As a consequence, it is here that the highest densities and greatest diversity of discarded material occur. The areas behind the houses are utilized for various types of special activities, particularly those related to certain 'unpleasant' tasks such as roasting animal heads, hide preparation and defecation, but also quiver making (Yellen 1977a, 85–125). Based on these observations, most base camps appear to have a characteristic 'archaeological signature', which Yellen termed the 'ring model', that could be used to differentiate base camps from other types of HGF sites (e.g. kill sites, work camps, and special-use sites) in the archaeological record (Figure 6.1).

Parallel studies made among the Kua, another San group who occupy part of the Central Kalahari (Bartram et al. 1991), found similar structuring of activity into different zones, although their base camps tend to have a linear rather than a circular structure. Additionally, each Kua household group usually has its own windbreak, used mostly for daytime activities and for shade, as well as a house used for sleeping and storage. Both types of structure generally have a hearth, and discarded debris tends to accumulate on the opposite sides to the

Table 6.2 Main differences between dry and wet season Ju/'hoãnsi (!Kung) base camps (based on Yellen 1977a, 64–80)

Dry season	Wet season
Comparatively large, several structures	Relatively small, only a few structures
Occupied for relatively long periods (up to c.6 months)	Occupied for short periods, often only a few days
Better-constructed dwellings	Rather flimsily constructed dwellings
Diverse material culture assemblages representative of a wide range of activities	Limited range of activities performed, and correspondingly low diversity of material culture inventories
Relatively high density of discarded materials, especially secondary refuse	Low overall densities of discarded material, and higher proportion of primary refuse
Concentrated around limited number of permanent waterholes	Widely distributed across Ju/'hoãnsi territory

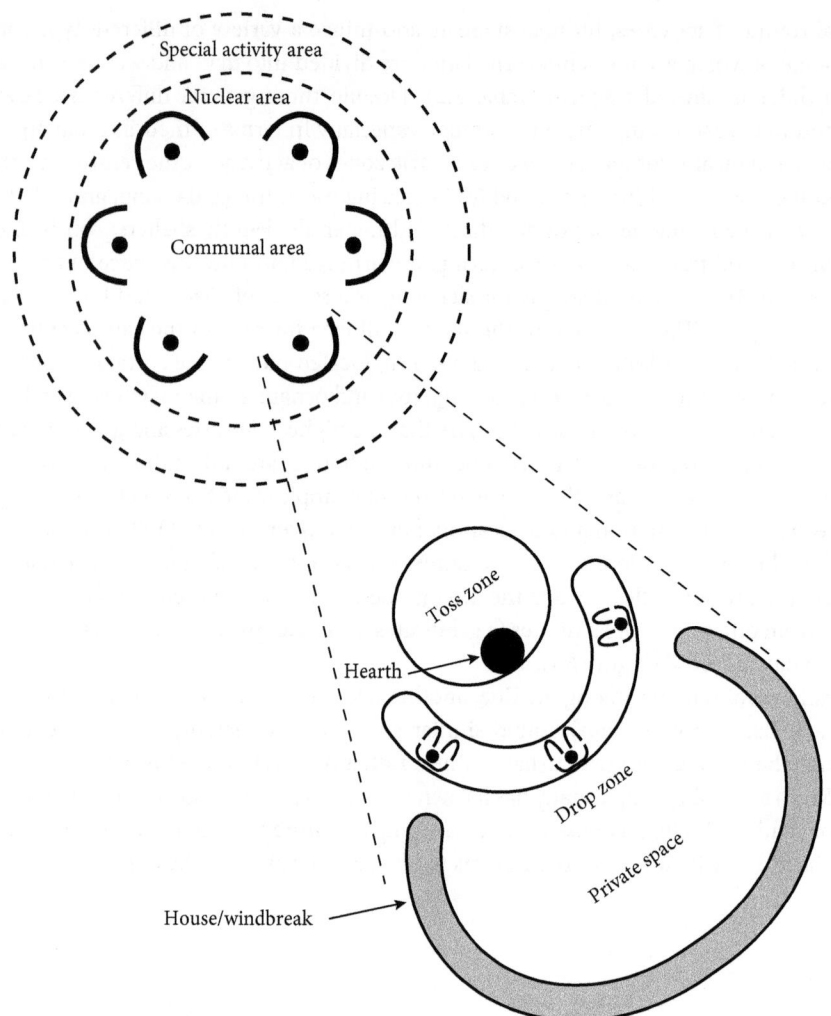

FIGURE 6.1 Yellen's (1977a) ring model for Ju/'hoãnsi base camps combined with hut-based 'drop' and 'toss' zones, as suggested by Whitelaw (1994), following Binford (1978b; 1983).

one where people normally sit, with artefact-free zones inside the windbreaks and sleeping shelters (Bartram et al. 1991, 104–31).

Binford's 'Toss' and 'Drop' Zones

Investigation of the regularities in the patterning of discarded material around internal and external hearths, sleeping areas, and other on-site facilities at different types of HGF sites also formed a major component of Binford's research among the Nunamiut (1978a; 1983, 144–60). He found, for example, that two distinct zones of discarded material tend to be created around open hearths—a 'drop zone', generally composed of small waste items that accumulate where people are seated, and a 'toss zone', either behind or in front of the seating area, which typically comprise larger items deliberately thrown away from the seating area. As a result, even after limited use two concentric semicircles of size-sorted debris are created (Figure 6.1).

This patterning is complicated by other factors, however. For example, cleaning up living space (often referred to as 'site maintenance activities') can result in debris from the toss zone being moved to secondary discard areas, such as rubbish dumps or refuse pits, and hence some loss of the spatial resolution and size-related distinctiveness of the assemblages in each 'zone'. As one might expect, Binford found that this happened more frequently on base camps than at hunting stands, principally because the latter are occupied for far less time than the former. Similarly, Binford found that 'toss zones' were absent from around internal hearths, principally because Nunamiut were disinclined to discard larger, more obtrusive material in the vicinity of their sleeping space and tended to tidy up those pieces that were discarded. More critically, Binford has argued that the distinctive patterning he found at Nunamiut sites is characteristic of open hearths more generally because of the constraints imposed by the mechanics of the human body when in a seated position—which effectively physically limit how far objects can be thrown from a seated position, and his model has been widely used to interpret spatial patterning on archaeological HGF sites that range widely in date and cultural affiliation.

Mobility, Foragers, and Collectors

Studies such as those by Yellen and Binford drew archaeological attention to the structured nature of HGF activities and the diverse range of activities and processes that generate and modify such patterning. See, for example, O'Connell's (1987) comparison of Australian Alywara site structure with those of the Nunamiut and Ju/'hoãnsi, and his proposition that the degree of reliance on food storage, seasonal weather patterns, duration of site occupation, and household population size may all be determining factors. Another model closely associated with Binford's ethnoarchaeological and comparative work extends this consideration of the structured patterning of HGF activities beyond the level of the site to settlement systems and the wider landscape. This is the distinction drawn between 'foragers' and 'collectors'. Although other models that bear some similarity have been proposed (e.g. Woodburn's (1980; 1982) concepts of 'immediate-' and 'delayed-return' systems; Testart's (1982) food storage model, Price and Brown's (1985) distinction between simple (or generalized) and complex foragers; and Bettinger's (1999) distinctions between 'travellers' and 'processors'), Binford's formulation of the forager/collector continuum (and subsequent refinements of this, e.g. Brumbach and Jarvenpa 1997; Savelle 1987) has been the most influential among archaeologists and has been widely used.

Specifically, Binford (1980) argued that a basic distinction can be made between different HGF subsistence and settlement systems according to the relative emphasis that is placed on 'residential mobility' as against 'logistical mobility'. He defines 'residential mobility' as the movement of the entire membership of a residential settlement from one location to another (Binford 1980, 5–7), contrasting this with the various kinds of temporary movement made by either individuals or small task groups away from and back to the main residential site, which he terms 'logistical mobility' (Binford 1980, 10–12). These different mobility strategies (often expressed as 'circulating' and 'radiating' mobility, respectively) have different spatial characteristics (Foragers: Figure 6.2, Collectors: Figure 6.3) and consequently may potentially leave rather different material 'signatures' in the archaeological record (Table 6.3).

Binford (1980, 12) emphasized that in their ideal form, these represent the extremes of what in reality is a continuum between relatively 'simple' and more 'complex' settlement systems. Consequently, when viewed from a global, cross-cultural perspective, different HGF populations exhibit considerable variation with respect to these two types of mobility. At one extreme are those societies characterized by high annual residential mobility and low logistical mobility. Binford termed these kinds of society 'foragers', and recent contemporary examples include the G/wi (Botswana), Agta (Philippines), Aché (Paraguay), and various Western Desert Australian Aborigines. At the other extreme are those societies characterized by low annual residential mobility and high logistical mobility, which Binford referred to as 'collectors'. Modern examples include the Nunamiut and other high-latitude Inuit HGFs (e.g. Boismier 1991), and several historically documented Great Basin societies in North America and maritime hunter-gatherers, including the Chumash of Southern California (Arnold 1995) among others.

Criticisms and Modifications of the Forager/Collector Model

Following publication of Binford's initial formulation of the core differences between 'foragers' and 'collectors', various scholars have suggested further differences, proposed modifications to the scheme, and made several criticisms as more comparative archaeological and ethnoarchaeological studies have been assembled. Wiessner (1982), for example, criticized Binford for ignoring the various social mechanisms such as gift exchange, that HGFs can deploy to reduce risk, citing the Ju/'hoãnsi *hxaro* system of down-the-line-exchange that allows individual Ju/'hoãn to access the resource areas of their exchange partners during times of scarcity or need. Foraging systems also tend to occur in low-latitude areas, and are associated with environments where resources are typically evenly distributed throughout the year. Conversely, environments where resources are typically concentrated and/or only seasonally available, such as those found in higher latitudes, are more appropriately exploited following a collector logistical strategy (Table 6.4; Kelly 1983; 1995, 120–2). From this observation, Kelly surmised that as overall food density increases, so also does the frequency of annual residential moves.

Sedentism

Sedentism inevitably involves a reduction in mobility, and can therefore have a number of consequences for the organization of space within settlements and the range of site types that exist within the overall settlement system. Greater residential stability is often correlated with changes in the ratio of primary to secondary refuse within a site; an increase in the range of storage facilities; changes in the average spacing of houses from one another; increased evidence for the physical demarcation of residential space; and a general increase in the complexity of within-site spatial patterning (for Kalahari examples, see Hitchcock 1987; Kent 1991; 1995).

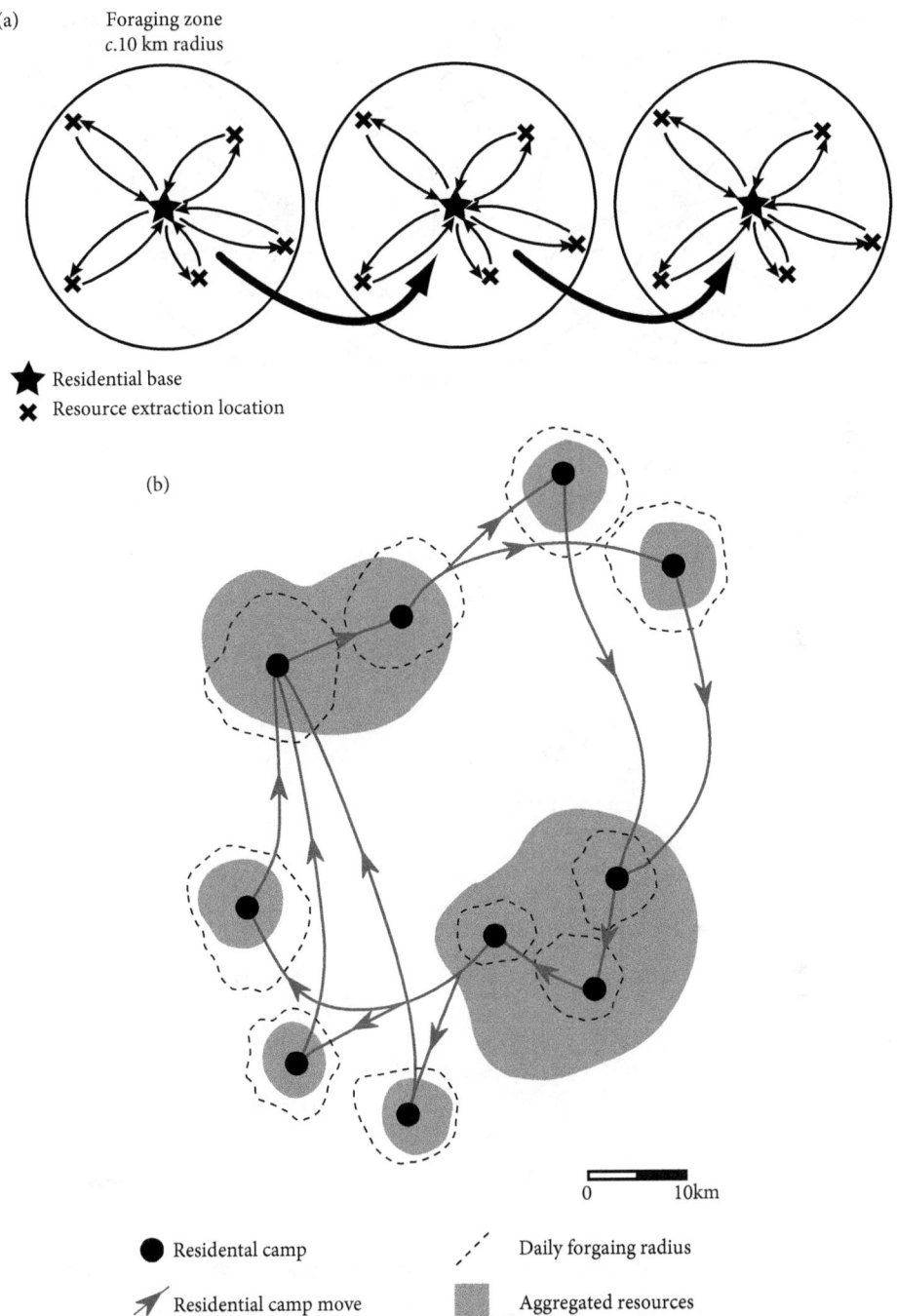

FIGURE 6.2 Schematic representations of an archetypal 'forager' settlement-subsistence system in (a) temporal (after Habu 2004, 8, fig. 1.3, and Savelle 1987, 46, fig. 14) and (b) synchronic (after Savelle 1987, 4, fig. 1) perspective.

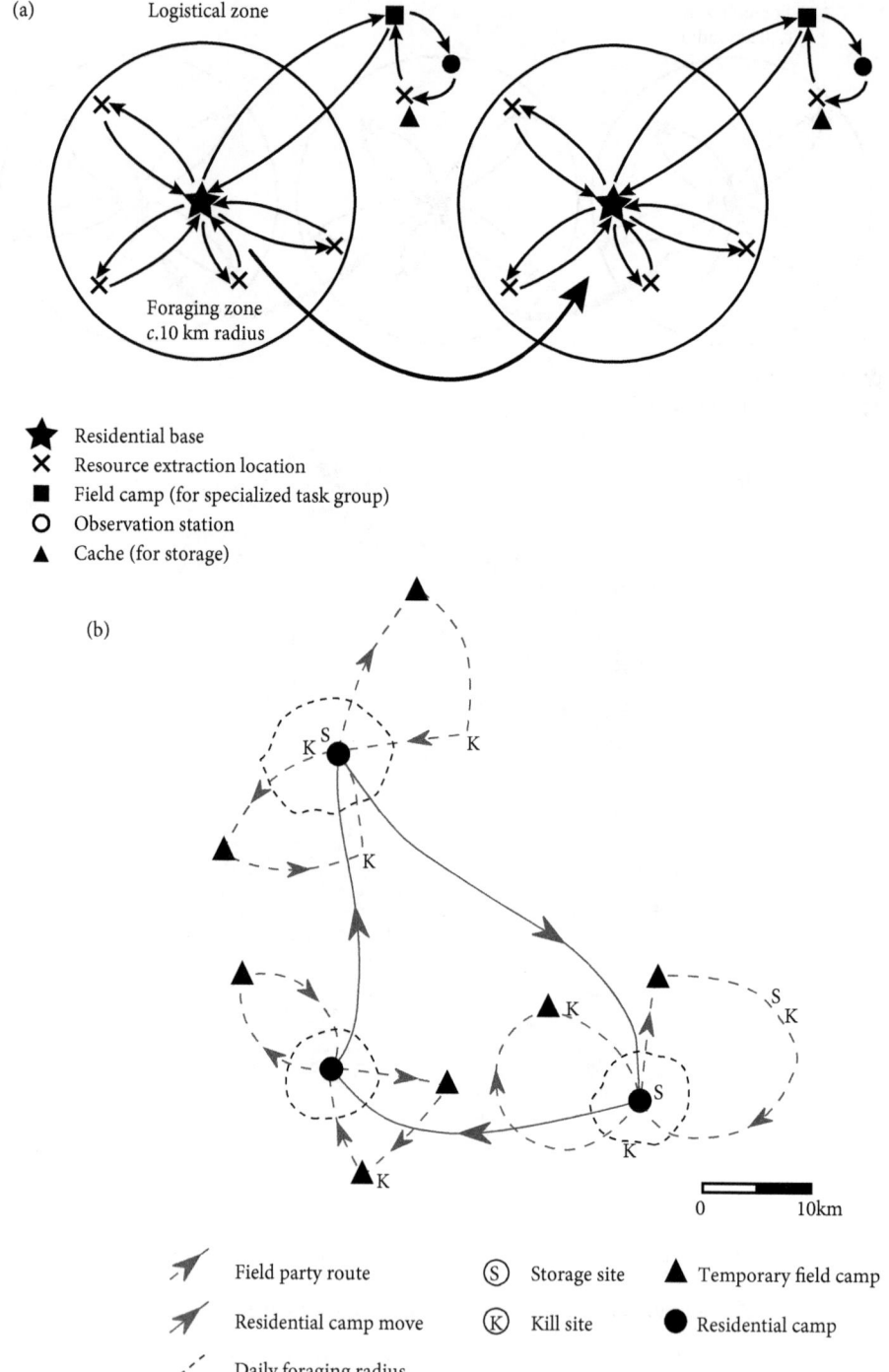

FIGURE 6.3 Schematic representations of an archetypal 'collector' settlement-subsistence system in (a) temporal (after Habu 2004, 10, fig. 1.5, and Savelle 1987, 46, fig. 14) and (b) synchronic (after Savelle 1987, 5, fig. 2) perspective.

Table 6.3 Foragers versus collectors

	Foragers		Collectors
Resource procurement	Generalized, opportunistic, encounter strategy	On a day-to-day basis Immediate return. Low-bulk extraction	Specialized resource procurement, radiating mobility. Delayed return
Foraging radius	Mostly restricted to 2-hour catchment		Wide-ranging, special purpose trips often travel several days' distance
Storage	Relatively rare	Limited evidence or lacking	Common. Caches and other forms—low visibility, few artefacts
Site types	Residential bases—frequently relocated, low energy expenditure on dwellings and related features	Processing, manufacturing, maintenance, wide range of tool types, relatively coarse-grained, potentially structured, hearths	Residential bases—longer residential stays, high energy expenditure on dwellings and related features. Processing, maintenance, high-to-medium visibility, diverse and structured tool types, potentially structured, hearths
	Foraging locations—task specific, e.g. kill/butchery sites; plant extraction/collection	Extractive, frequent but low visibility, aggregate assemblages, often expedient, possible cooking hearths	Field camps—often seasonal, short term. Processing, manufacturing, maintenance—medium-to-low visibility, often specialized tool-kits, possible cooking hearths
	Overnight camps	Rare, low visibility, fine-grained assemblages, possible hearths	Stations—hunting blinds, observation posts, ambush sites, etc. Information gathering, maintenance, some manufacturing—medium-to-low visibility, varied tool-kits, structured, possible hearths
Settlement strategy	High residential mobility, low logistical mobility	Base camps moved repeatedly over the course of a year, small residential groups. 'Mapping onto' different, seasonally available resources	Low residential mobility, high logistical mobility. Large, semi-permanent residential groups near caching localities. Highly structured resource procurement, with bases forming a 'hub'

(*Continued*)

Table 6.3 Continued

	Foragers		Collectors	
Butchery strategies	Kill sites/butchery locations	Limited culling of low-utility parts; partly dependent on size of prey	**Butchery strategies** Kill sites/butchery locations	Filleting, removal of low-utility parts; systematic carcass processing
	Residential bases	Secondary and tertiary butchery	Residential bases	Secondary and tertiary butchery, drying, storage, mass processing
	Residential base assemblages	Characterized by mix of low-, medium-, and high-utility anatomical parts; combination of primary and secondary discard	Residential base assemblages	Characterized by medium- and high-utility anatomical parts; cracked and fractured bones; mostly secondary discard
Technological characteristics	Mostly expedient Multifunctional	Generalized, maintainable tool-kits, potentially smaller tools	**Technological characteristics** Mostly curated Single purpose	Specialized, reliable tool-kits, potentially larger/more complex tools
Raw-material procurement strategies	Embedded		**Raw-material procurement strategies** Direct procurement	
Exchange systems	Generalized reciprocity	Long-distance, down-the-line exchange common	**Exchange systems** Gift exchange, socially targeted reciprocity	Competitive ritual feasting, prestige goods

Based on Binford 1978a; 1978b; 1979; 1980; 1982; David and Kramer 2001, 235, table 8.2; Kelly 1995; Savelle 1987.

Table 6.4 'Simple' and 'complex' hunter-gatherer-fishers compared

Variable	Simple	Complex
Environment	Unpredictable or variable	Highly predictable or less variable
Diet	Terrestrial game	Marine or plant foods
Settlement size	Small	Large
Residential mobility	Medium to high	Low to none
Demography	Low population density relative to food	High population density relative to food resources
Food storage	Little to no dependence	Medium to high dependence
Social organization	No corporate groups	Corporate descent groups (lineages)
Political organization	Egalitarian	Hierarchical; classes based on wealth or descent
Occupational specialization	Only for older persons	Common
Territoriality	Social-boundary defence	Perimeter defence
Warfare	Rare	Common
Slavery	Absent	Frequent
Ethic of competition	Not tolerated	Encouraged
Resource ownership	Diffuse	Tightly controlled
Exchange	Generalized reciprocity	Wealth objects, competitive feasts

Source: Kelly 1995, 294, table 8.1.

Not all of these changes necessarily occur, however, even among neighbouring communities. For instance, Hitchcock found that recently sedentary Nata River Basarwa in Botswana tended to separate camp space into age- and gender-specific activity areas (and on occasion, also by status), whereas the residential space of recently sedentary Kua remained undifferentiated and similar to the pattern among mobile Kua and Tyua communities in the same area. This, he suggests, was largely because their decreased residential mobility was offset by increased logistical mobility and the consequent performance of a range of activities away from their residential camps (Hitchcock 1987, 411–12). Another factor which may be important is site size. For instance, at Kutse in central Botswana, Kent (1995) noted that among a newly sedentary generation of G/wi, G//ana, and Kua speakers, individual houses were initially spaced close together. Within a few years, however, the area of the settlement had expanded dramatically, with only a moderate increase in the size of the population. Kent attributed this change to the increased amount of social friction between different residents, which, in turn, she attributes to the disruption caused by sedentism to the pre-existing pattern of exchange partnerships.

Food Storage

Food storage is another strategy that allows collectors to offset the shortfalls that might be created when critical resources are unevenly distributed either seasonally or spatially. Conversely, in a foraging system when a resource has been depleted foragers need only relocate their residential base to another resource patch—a strategy often referred to as 'mapping onto' resources. The development of food storage coupled with increased sedentism may encourage more intensive use of plants and animals and deliberate manipulation of their reproductive cycles, leading ultimately to domestication. Related to this is the argument that by limiting seasonal mobility, the conditions and opportunities are created that allow an increase in population, the accumulation of private property, and social differentiation (Testart 1982; Woodburn 1982).

Seasonal Availability of Resources

Equally, the distribution of critical resources (such as surface water in the Kalahari and its seasonal variability) can have a determinate influence on mobility patterns in environments where other resources are homogeneously distributed. Thus, for instance, as discussed above, Ju/'hoãnsi spend relatively long periods during the dry season camped beside the few permanent water-bearing pans in their landscape, giving rise to a pattern Kent referred to as 'tethered' mobility (Kent 1992a). Fisher and Strickland (1989) make a similar point with reference to Efe Pygmies, for whom the villages and gardens of neighbouring Lese constitute fixed nodes in their annual settlement round as they can obtain important resources from these farming communities (notably cultivated foods, but also material goods such as clothing and metal implements) in exchange for forest products including honey. Fisher and Stickland term this 'constrained mobility'. Another equally important variable recorded by Kent (1992a; Kent and Vierich 1989) concerns 'anticipated mobility', in other words the length of time a group expects to stay at a location, which she found among various Kalahari groups influenced their decisions concerning how much time and energy they invested in constructing shelters, storage facilities and site maintenance activities, far more than the actual length of time spent at a site.

In arctic and subarctic environments, where gathered plant resources make only a minimal contribution to dietary intake, the migratory patterns of large game and/or seasonal availability of certain key resources (such as salmon) may similarly 'tether' communities to particular places and mobility regimes. In the subarctic, boreal forests of northern Canada, for example, the seasonal mobility patterns of Chipewyan and some other Northern Dene hunter-fishers was typically tripartite in structure. At the height of the summer, band members were concentrated in large, tented settlements close to seasonally available fish. By the late nineteenth century, Chipewyan were also stationing their summer camps close to European trading posts, where furs could be exchanged. As well as such commercial activity, the summer period was also a time for intra-community socializing and renewal of distant kinship bonds. As autumn drew closer, these groups would break up into smaller canoe parties that would disperse to the major wintering grounds. Here, 'winter staging communities' would be established. Although smaller, more compact, and with reduced populations compared to the summer settlements, the log cabins and log-tent dwellings at these camps were more durable (and hence potentially more visible, archaeologically) than the summer tents, and were associated with more ancillary structures including dog kennels, drying racks, and privies. Over the winter months, hunting and fishing parties would periodically leave the camp for short-term, ephemeral hunting camps and primary processing sites, returning later with their prey and fish catches for processing (Jarvenpa and Brumbach 1988, 601–3).

As such, the tripartite system fits well in the 'collector' category of Binford's model, and the debris generated from on-site activities at winter staging encampments typically reflects a range of general maintenance, tool making, and processing activities. However, as discussed by Brumbach and Jarvenpa (1997; Jarvenpa and Brumbach 1988), the structure of the Chipewyan settlement system (and by implication those of other HGFs) is contingent on other factors, including historical and individual circumstances; relationships with neighbouring non-HGF communities; and the gendered division of labour. Thus, while Chipewyan settlement strategies have moved increasingly towards a more centrally based, logistical, 'collecting' model, such a simple characterization obscures an increased gendered division of labour (see below), and reduces 'hunting' to an activity centred on the dispatch of prey rather than treating it as a socialized sequence of activity from procurement to consumption and discard via various processing activities. As their data indicate, when examined in more detail it is apparent these different activities require greater or lesser degrees of logistical organization, and this balance can change over time as external factors change. In this particular case, for instance, they note that as part of the population became more sedentary, another portion (men) needed to 'become increasingly mobile and logistically organized' (Brumbach and Jarvenpa 1997, 434).

Summary

Given all this variation, while there is broad scholarly consensus that Binford's model has considerable heuristic value, most now agree that the majority of HGF societies probably fall somewhere between the two extremes (Bettinger 1987; Chatters 1987), such that their subsistence-settlement systems exhibit elements of both a foraging and collection mode of resource procurement. This is well borne out by two recent ethnoarchaeological studies among South American 'foragers' (Greaves 2006; Politis 2006), both of which indicate that multiple types of mobility occur within HGF societies, a point also noted over 80 years ago by Thomson (1939) with reference to the strategies pursued by the Wikmunkan of Cape York Peninsula, Australia. In view of this, the interpretation of the causes of spatial patterning in the archaeological record becomes all the more complicated and probably no single ethnographic analogy will ever suffice.

Hunter-Gatherer-Fishers and Tool-kit Diversity

In addition to other critiques of the forager/collector model, it has also been noted that the degree to which an HGF society pursues logistical mobility or residential mobility can have implications for their technological organization, such that forager tool use is more likely to be 'expedient' (i.e. made on the spot for the purpose in hand), whereas collectors are more likely to retain (or 'curate') tools for future use (Bettinger 1991, 66–70). Also, because they are more mobile, foragers might be more likely to make smaller, multifunctional tools (Shott 1986, 20). Bleed (1986), however, has argued that the key issues relate less to portability and more to 'maintainability' and 'reliability', leading him to propose that foragers place greater emphasis on having generalized but maintainable tool-kits, whereas collectors have greater need for specialized but reliable tools.

Table 6.5 Classes of hunter-gatherer-fisher tools

Instruments—e.g. digging sticks, baskets, net bags; scrapers, knives; bow-drills; bone needles; grinding stones (employed mostly for procuring and transporting immobile resources—such as tubers, fruits, other edible plants; processing plant and animal resources; or manufacturing)

Weapons—e.g. arrows, spears, clubs, throwing sticks, nets, fish hooks (employed mostly for procuring mobile resources—i.e. wild terrestrial and aquatic species of game)

Tended facilities—e.g. hunting blinds, fish weirs; hearths (employed to catch mobile prey, but require humans to be present; or for processing resources)

Untended facilities—e.g. snares, pit (or dead-fall) traps; meat safes; storage pits/caches (employed to catch mobile prey regardless of whether humans are present or not; or for storage)

Source: Based on Torrence 1983 and Orme 1981.

The diversity of tool-kits and the complexity of individual tools may also be loosely related to whether a forager or collector strategy is pursued. For instance, Torrence (1983; 2001) has argued that cross-culturally, HGF tools can be categorized into four classes (Table 6.5). She also notes that, typically, low-latitude forager tool assemblages are dominated by 'instruments', while the diversity of tool-kits and the complexity of individual tools (measured in terms of the number of constituent parts) increases with latitude, and hence are more commonly associated with collectors. The reason for these differences, Torrence argues, relates to the degree of risk involved in subsistence strategies, by which is meant relative levels of predictability or uncertainty of food supply, with levels of risk increasing with latitude because of greater seasonality in resource availability (Torrence 1989).

Time-stress and risk may also influence the scheduling of activities such as raw material procurement, and tool manufacturing and maintenance (Torrence 1989). Additionally, Binford (1979) has suggested that there are two broad differences between the ways in which the task of obtaining raw material for tools is scheduled relative to other activities. Specifically, in some instances HGFs make special trips to obtain raw materials—this Binford terms 'direct procurement'. Under other circumstances, raw-material acquisition takes place during daily food-getting activities and related mobility, a system Binford refers to as 'embedded procurement'. However, as Bamforth (2006, 521) notes:

> it may not be particularly useful to search for archaeological signatures of embedded or direct procurement among mobile hunters and gatherers [since] in essence...procurement among such groups is probably embedded in an overall seasonal round of movements and procurement of large amounts of material is probably direct in the sense that it requires a trip to a source and expenditure of effort...while at that source.

Butchery Practices and Faunal Distributions

Some of the most profound contributions of ethnoarchaeological research over the last four decades relate to the development of greater understanding of the multiple causes of variation in the composition, condition, and spatial patterning of faunal assemblages on archaeological sites, especially those occupied by HGFs (Gifford-Gonzalez 1989; 1991). The main themes to have been investigated are prey-animal butchery, processing, carcass transport, and marrow extraction (Bartram et al. 1991; Binford 1981; Bunn 1993; Bunn et al. 1988; Enloe 1983; Fisher 1993; Gould 1996; Jarvenpa and Brumbach 1983; Lupo 1994; 2001; 2006; Lupo and O'Connell 2002; O'Connell et al. 1988; O'Connell and Marshall 1989). Other topics that have received attention include cooking procedures (Kent 1993; Lupo 1995), sharing and body part distribution (Binford 1984; Enloe 2003; Hawkes et al. 2001; Kelly et al. 2005; Kent 1993; Marshall 1994; Yellen 1977b; 1991b), and the resultant spatial patterning and composition of faunal assemblages at different categories of site and points within the landscape (Binford 1982; O'Connell et al. 1988; 1992; Yellen 1991a).

Parallel studies of the effects of various taphonomic processes, from the trampling effects of human foot traffic or the scavenging impacts of dogs and carnivores to the sorting of material by fluvial and other geomorphological processes (see Lyman 1987; 1994 and references therein), have also often been undertaken in tandem with more strictly ethnoarchaeological ones (e.g. Hudson 1993; Lupo 1995). As with other aspects of HGF systems and practices, early work by Binford (1978a; 1981) among the Nunamiut has been particularly influential, although the insights these offered have been expanded and in some cases critiqued by more recent research among a wider range of HGF communities.

Inter- and Intra-Site Variations in Faunal Assemblages

Binford's primary concerns were with explaining variations in inter- and intra-site patterning and composition of faunal assemblages, and with bone taphonomy. Influenced by his interests in HGF mobility and settlement systems (Binford 1980; 1982), his work tracks the movement of animal carcasses from kill sites to butchery locations and residential settlements, documenting how carcasses were dismembered and where different bones eventually entered the archaeological record of Nunamiut activity in the Anaktuvuk Pass area of northern Alaska. Caribou are a key resource and seasonally abundant during the spring, when they migrate from their winter grazing areas across Nunamiut territory to open tundra to the north-east. Nunamiut establish temporary hunting camps and hunting stands along these migration routes from which they track caribou movements and hunt their prey (Binford 1978b).

Once killed, the caribou are typically dragged to a nearby butchering area. These are special-purpose sites and have their own distinctive archaeological signature, the spatial organization of which is conditioned as much by the physical anatomy of the caribou as by the range of activities performed there. Specifically, 'in order to remove the skin from a caribou and prepare the joints of meat, the animal is laid down in a clear area and a man works around it', with the result that a relatively clear 'circle is created, with the waste products deposited on the periphery away from the area where the butchery took place' (Binford 1983, 124, see also figs 59–61, 122–3, and 169–70).

Decisions concerning processing at kill sites and transportation back to camp are also influenced by concerns to maximize nutritional returns relative to the economic utility of different anatomical parts and the costs of transporting and processing them. Thus, as part of his studies among Nunamiut, Binford (1981) sought to quantify the food utility of different body parts, focusing on caribou and sheep in particular. His modified general utility index (MGUI) has been widely used and is an attempt to document the degree to which different body parts render different amounts of meat, marrow, and bone grease, and so have different food utility to Nunamiut. He further argued that these differences have a determining effect on how carcasses and bones are processed, although these strategies can vary according location, season, health of the animal, hunting group size, taxonomic identity, and other factors (Lupo 2006; Lupo and Schmitt 2005).

Carcass Processing, Marrow Extraction, and Sharing

One topic that has been discussed extensively concerns marrow extraction. In terms of Binford's 'foragers' and 'collectors' model, the former might be expected to minimally process carcasses at kill sites, disarticulating them only so as to facilitate transport back to their home base for redistribution among other group members for further processing, cooking, and immediate consumption, as for instance is the case among Alyawara Aborigines of central Australia (O'Connell and Marshall 1989), and the Kua of Botswana (Bartram et al. 1991). Collectors, on the other hand, would be expected to fillet meat and remove it for drying and subsequent storage. They might also be expected to mass process bones for marrow extraction for bulk storage (Enloe 1983, 84), as documented among Nunamiut. Enloe suggests these different strategies could well have distinct archaeological signatures, both in terms of the spatial distribution of cracked and fractured bones (in dumps where mass processed, and more widely dispersed around dwellings and shelters in immediate return situations), and in the morphological characteristics of the processed bones (see also Binford 1984, 157–8).

There are, however, a number of contrary examples that caution against making any universal correlations between, for instance, 'foragers' and 'collectors'. For example, the Hadzabe, who practise an immediate-return foraging mobility strategy, typically remove the limb bones from medium- and large-size species (roughly between impala and wildebeest/zebra) at kill sites, transporting other parts back to their base camp (O'Connell et al. 1988; 1990). Okiek, on the other hand, who are delayed-return hunter-gatherers and occupy a highly productive environment, although they disarticulate their prey at kill sites will typically transport all of the skeletal parts (of all size ranges of prey) back to their settlements (Marshall 1994).

Sharing further complicates the patterning of faunal remains in the archaeological record. Sharing has long been regarded as one of the most significant defining characteristics of HGF behaviour central to the regulation of access to food, material goods, territories, and other resources, and hence its recognition in the archaeological record has been given considerable analytical significance. One of the earliest studies of faunal assemblages to indicate some of the issues involved was that by Yellen (1977b; 1991a; 1991b), who noted that among Ju/'hoãnsi smaller prey (such as porcupine) tended not to be shared. Conversely, the different body parts of a larger animal, such as a kudu or gemsbok, could be exchanged several times before being processed or consumed as individuals attempted to meet pre-existing social obligations. The resultant distribution of bones from different-sized prey partly reflected this, with the bones from larger prey being more widely dispersed across camps whereas those from smaller prey tended to cluster around individual shelters. Post-depositional processes may well obscure such patterning, however, and other approaches including refitting studies and assemblage diversity indices may provide more robust ways of identifying sharing in archaeological contexts (see Enloe 2003).

The possibility that the intensity of bone fracture related to marrow extraction might be directly correlated with levels of food stress or inversely with hunting success has also been raised. For instance, Ngatatjara Aborigines, who live in a very arid and resource-poor part of northern Australia, typically process bones to such an extent that very few taxonomically identifiable fragments survive (Gould 1996). Evidence from other modern HGFs lends some support to this hypothesis. Nunamiut elders, for example, recounted to Binford that during 'good years', when resources were abundant and encounter rates with high-yield prey were frequent, marrow extraction from low-yield bones was much rarer than during 'bad years', when they had less hunting success (Binford 1978a). However, additional ethnoarchaeological studies have indicated that diverse factors may complicate matters, not least the social pressures placed on sharing the product of a hunt and cultural rules concerning the distribution of different body parts (Jarvenpa and Brumbach 1983), and decisions about transport costs, health of the animal, composition of the hunting party, and so forth (Lupo 2006). Taphonomic factors also need to be kept in mind. For example, middle shafts of long bones from all size classes of animal are denser than other parts but contain less grease—making them more likely to survive in the archaeological record (Lyman 1994), thereby potentially skewing assessments of utility and intensity of processing.

Butchery Practices and Cut Marks

Studies such as those conducted by Binford (1981; 1988) among Nunamiut and Lupo (1994; 1995) and others among Hadzabe (Bunn et al. 1988; Lupo and O'Connell 2002) have highlighted that there is often some regularity in the anatomical patterning and morphological characteristics of cut marks produced during different stages of carcass butchery. Such regularities might allow archaeologists to differentiate between skinning, dismembering, and defleshing, and perhaps also between the use of stone as opposed to metal tools (e.g. Lupo 1995).

Although greater butchering intensity is likely to produce more cut marks, Bunn (2001) has argued that no simple relationship exists between the amount of flesh removed and the frequency of cut marks. His study of Hadzabe butchery suggests that, instead, the strength of muscle attachments has a greater determining effect on the number of cut marks on a particular bone. The manner in which bones are broken, fracture patterns and the distribution of cut marks and other surface modifications are also influenced by cooking practices, particularly whether roasting or pot-boiling is employed. For instance, irregular transverse fractures are a common characteristic of long bones that have been chopped up for boiling in pots (Gifford-Gonzalez 1989), while the distribution of cut marks and fractures can be used for some body parts to determine whether meat was roasted on or off the bone (Koon et al. 2010, 63).

Faunal Assemblages and Optimal Foraging

Some recent ethnoarchaeological studies of faunal material have also been influenced by certain precepts of Optimal Foraging Theory (see Bettinger 1991; Kelly 1995), notably those concerning the prey choices made by HGFs (e.g. Bird et al. 2009; Hawkes et al. 1982; Hill 1988; Lupo and Schmitt 2002; 2005) In essence, this model predicts that if HGF decisions are made optimally, then the decision to try to capture a prey animal (or gather plant resources) on encounter will involve an assessment of whether the energy returns from successful capture will outweigh the energy expended in the hunt (or collection) and subsequent transport and processing. Thus in the case of animal resources, according to the model, efforts will always be made to capture the highest-ranked prey on encounter. However, as the likely on-encounter return declines so the decision whether to pursue or not is mediated by assessment of whether 'the expected return from searching for and handling all resources of higher rank' (Bird and O'Connell 2006, 147) offers a better option.

The critical significance of this observation is that, under conditions of optimal foraging behaviour, whether plant and animal resources are included in diets is more a function of the degree of availability of higher-ranked resources than due simply to variations in abundance or rate of encounter. By the same token, it needs to be recognized that HGFs, like any other human society, are social beings and that their decisions are always as informed by cultural concerns as by ecological imperatives or matters governing energy expenditure and returns. An excellent example of this is provided by Lupo and Schmitt's (2005) work, where they note that despite being most successful using snares to capture small game such as duiker, Aka and Bofi hunters in the Central African Republic rely more heavily on net hunting, which is more 'inefficient' in terms of calorific yields. Their preference for net hunting over snares is due to the social benefits that can accrue to hunters from participation in this more public form of hunting, which outweigh other concerns (cf. also Hawkes et al. 2001 on hunting strategies among Hadzabe men).

Alternative and Emergent Approaches

Studies of site formation processes, HGF settlement systems, the spatial organization of campsites, hunting behaviour, and butchery practices have tended to dominate ethnoarchaeological research among HGFs, particularly where the ultimate goal of such research has been to develop robust analogies for interpreting Plio-Pleistocene and early Pleistocene sites and assemblages. Much less attention has been given to the investigation of what might be termed more 'social' or 'cultural' aspects of HGF behaviour and societies (although, as noted above, this is a false distinction, since all elements of HGF behaviour are social). There were some notable exceptions to this even during the heyday of processualist approaches, and increasingly more research is being conducted on such topics. This section reviews some of the more prominent trends and debates.

Material Style and Identity

There have been relatively few ethnoarchaeological studies of the stylistic attributes of HGF material culture, or of their symbolic systems and material expressions of identity (Jordan 2003, 10). This contrasts with ethnoarchaeological research on farming, herding, and urban societies, and is a gap that future researchers should try to fill. Of the few studies that have been undertaken, however, several have been quite influential in the wider discipline. For instance, it is now widely recognized that overt, stylistic material culture boundaries correlate directly with social boundaries *only* under certain, highly specific circumstances.

Wiessner's (1983) study of the formal variations of arrowheads between different San groups in Botswana was one of the first ethnoarchaeological studies to propose this, through an examination of the proposition that formal variation in material culture conveys information about personal and social identity.

Whereas Wiessner found that this was indeed the case, she noted that artefact style communicated information about both individual identity—which she characterized as 'assertive style'—and group identity or 'emblemic style'. Thus, for instance, she found that Ju/'hoãnsi (!Kung) projectile points differed from those made by !Xo and G/wi, and that members of each group could differentiate their arrows from those of others, suggesting that these items of material culture were recognized as emblems of the different socio-linguistic groups. However, informants from all three groups were typically unable to identify which linguistic groups had made the arrows they recognized as 'different'. Moreover, 'no single attribute carried information about linguistic group affiliation' (Wiessner 1983, 270). Among Ju/'hoãnsi the critical variable was size, whereas for G/wi and !Xo tip and body shape were more significant. As Wiessner observed, the study suggests that different artefact attributes can convey different types of meanings within any group, and that the significance and meaning content of a particular attribute can vary between groups. This has obvious ramifications for the way in which archaeologists seek to define the boundaries of social groups from the spatial patterning of artefact styles.

Subsequently, Wiessner's study was criticized by Sackett (1985), who questioned whether her data truly indicated that San groups were consciously producing projectile points that differed from those of other groups, not least because the great distances that separate the groups mean that a member of one community may never see an arrowhead made by one of the other groups. Sackett suggested, instead, that formal differences in material culture commonly arise as a result of habit, by which is meant the taken-for-granted ways of doing and making things that one can find in any small community. Sackett (1986) termed this category of stylistic difference 'isochrestic variation', and contrasted it with more purposive forms of variation that are specifically intended to convey particular messages.

Technical Choices and *Chaînes Opératoires*

The concept that much formal and stylistic difference in artefacts derives from habit has been developed in more recent years from the perspective of the anthropology of technology associated with the work of various French anthropologists, notably Mauss (1934), Leroi-Gourhan (1964; 1965), and Lemmonier (1986). Taken together, key features of these approaches are that all humanly produced 'objects' have a life history and that these can be reconstructed through a study of the sequence of activities involved in the creation, use, and subsequent disposal of the 'object'. Individual activity sequences are often referred to as the *chaîne opératoire* (or operational procedures) of a particular technological practice (also sometimes rendered as a 'technical' or 'behavioural chain').

An additional critical feature of the *chaînes opératoires* approach, which can be traced back to Mauss's concerns, is that each stage in a sequence involves the interaction between a restricted range of bodily techniques and a particular material or set of materials. Much like riding a bicycle, once these techniques are learned they are in a sense 'remembered' in the body (sometimes known as 'incorporated memory') and only find expression when the task is performed again—and like riding a bicycle, the performance of these bodily techniques is largely subconscious. The resultant material forms associated with a particular *chaîne opératoire* are hence an expression of a habituated practice—ways of acting in and on the world—shared by a particular social group. Documenting the degree of uniqueness of the *chaîne opératoire* of a particular technology and its spatial and temporal distribution is thus becoming a powerful tool for reconstructing past social identities.

While the *chaîne opératoire* approach has been widely adopted within archaeological studies of HGF artefact assemblages (especially in lithics analysis where its application builds on older traditions of refitting and the study of reduction sequences), and also now with reference to entire landscapes, there have been very few ethnoarchaeological studies conducted from this perspective among modern foragers.

A notable exception is Wingfield's (2003) study of ostrich eggshell (OES) bead manufacture among San communities in north-western Botswana. As part of this, he compared the stages of manufacture and the different materials, tools, and techniques used by two different San groups in their manufacture of OES beads. Both primarily produce OES beads nowadays for sale to craft cooperatives and the wider tourist industry. One group, based in the settlement of D'kar, were more urbanized, sedentary, and less reliant on wild products for their subsistence than members of the other group who reside in more remote areas of the Kalahari. The *chaîne opératoire* used by both groups was virtually identical in terms of the bodily techniques employed and stages of the manufacturing process, and no formal differences in the OES beads were observable. However, as might be expected, those residing in remoter parts of the Kalahari typically used a range of wild products as tools and processing materials, whereas those in D'kar relied more on manufactured, and often shop-bought, materials.

Two more generic points can be drawn from the study. First, although operating in different 'resource landscapes' the overall form of the finished artefact and the *chaîne opératoire* involved in the manufacturing process were virtually indistinguishable. However, this apparent conservatism in both form and technique actually masks a significant level of technological opportunism and response to changing circumstances. As he notes elsewhere (Wingfield 2005, 127), OES bead manufacture has a long history in the region (Mitchell 2003) spanning upwards of 30,000 years, yet in light of this ethnoarchaeological work the apparent continuity of these 'techniques of the body' quite possibly obscures 'a whole range of discontinuities in people's relationships with their environments'.

Gender

The importance of gendered identities and their potential archaeological manifestations are further aspects of HGF social practice examined in recent years by ethnoarchaeologists. Most early anthropological research was highly androcentric, either ignoring completely the activities of women in HGF societies, diminishing the contributions of women's labour and/or technological skills or assuming, even in the face of evidence for a strong egalitarian ethos, that women's roles were subordinate to those of men, especially hunters. This has since changed largely as a result of a wider feminist critique of anthropology (e.g. Conkey and Spector 1984; Slocum 1975; Tanner 1981) and empirical studies of the social and economic contributions of women, especially in terms of gathering (e.g. Dahlberg 1981) and their involvement in hunting (e.g. Jarvenpa and Brumbach 1995; Estioko-Griffin and Griffin 1981; Kent 1996), and with reference to craft activities, such as hide-working (Frink and Weedman 2005).

A direct consequence of these trends is that much greater attention is now typically given in ethnoarchaeological studies of HGFs to evidence for the sexual division of labour (e.g. Jarvenpa and Brumbach 2006a), the possible differentiation of tool-kits used by men and women (e.g. Frink et al. 2003), the division of dwelling and settlement space according to gendered task-scapes (e.g. Whitelaw 1994), and possible biological, demographic, and/or social variations between women and men (e.g. Hilton and Greaves 2008). Identification of the gendered association of artefacts and physical spaces in archaeological contexts, nonetheless, remains problematic owing to the inherent indeterminacy of archaeological data. Despite this, awareness of the possibility that gender differences, and sexual relations and orientations (see Cobb 2005) may have contributed to the structuring of archaeological records in different contexts has encouraged archaeologists to address the interpretation of HGF sites in a more critical fashion. In particular, there is now greater awareness that women and children, and not just men, could have contributed to their formation (e.g. Kent 1998; Politis 2005; Wadley 1997), and that these contributions may not have been analogous to gendered divisions of labour recorded among modern foragers (Kuhn and Stiner 2006).

Recent ethnoarchaeological studies and cross-cultural surveys highlight the interpretive impact of these developments and some of the challenges that remain (see Jarvenpa and Brumbach's 'Hunter-Gatherer Gender and Identity'). For instance, in their study of the routine practices of Chipewyan women in northern Saskatchwen, Canada, Jarvenpa and Brumbach (1995) found that they were actively engaged in tool use and manufacture (contrary to the implicit assumption of the 'man the toolmaker' myth), and there was considerable overlap in expertise and practice between men and women despite the persistence of an ostensible gendered division of labour. More critically, they found that women often butchered large animals (again contrary to a common, androcentric assumption in archaeology) and were responsible for maintaining various food storage facilities and processing technologies that were essential for group survival during the winter months (Table 6.6). All of these activities are as much about 'hunting' as the actual dispatch of animals (Brumbach and Jarvenpa 1997, 417–18), especially if 'hunting' is understood as a set of connected, social activities that extend to, and include, the relations between humans and their prey. Moreover, as they note elsewhere, the fact that women usually do not actually dispatch animals is not due to any innate inability but simply that they are 'too busy converting carcasses into vital subsistence products' and managing their other commitments (such as those associated with child-minding and rearing) to have time to engage in hunting (Brumbach and Jarvenpa 2007, 191).

Frink's (2009) research among Yup'ik communities in western coastal Alaska, who rely on fishing and hunting for their subsistence base, similarly highlights the fundamental contribution that women make to the processing of food and the levels of skill required. His study also underlines the importance of experience and the long apprenticeship required to become truly competent in what superficially can appear to be quite 'simple' tasks. This not only serves as a critique of common assumptions in the archaeological literature about women's technologies and associated tasks relative to those of men, but also indicates that age may be an equally important dimension of social variability in HGF groups, just as it is in other societies.

Table 6.6 Spatial distribution of female and male activities associated with moose hunting among Chipewyan hunter-fishers

	Kill sites		Hunting camp		Village site	
	Bush centred	Village centred	Bush centred	Village centred	Bush centred	Village centred
Female activity and materials	Assist men	Absent	Fine butchering; dry meat and grease making; initial meat sharing and consumption	Absent	Hide and pemmican making; final meat distribution, storage, and consumption	Fine butchering; dry meat, grease, and pemmican making; hide making; meat distribution, storage, and consumption
Male activity and materials	Dispatch animals; rough butchering	Dispatch animals; rough butchering	Assist women	Initial meat consumption	Assist women	Assist women

Source: Brumbach and Jarvenpa 1997, 431, table 2.

Cross-cultural comparisons between circumpolar hunters, forager-herders, and hunter-fishers (Chipewyan, Khanty, Sámi, and Iñupiaq) have helped to draw out further points of more general relevance (Jarvenpa and Brumbach 2006b; 2009). Specifically, in daily practice normative models of gender roles are often abandoned, and routine tasks of hunting, processing, and distributing food can be performed by groups of very variable social composition. Nevertheless, some regularities in terms of the composition and spatial location of the tool-kits associated with women, compared with those associated with men or used jointly by both genders, are evident in all of these societies. Thus, for example, 'women's gear' is often more commonly found in localities that tend to have high archaeological visibility, such as settlements and high-intensity processing areas. Also, as prey size increases, the tasks of butchering, processing, storing, and distributing food tend to fall to women rather than men at least in these particular societies. As Jarvenpa and Brumbach (2009) note, many of these categories of residue have typically been assumed to have been generated by men, whereas these ethnoarchaeological observations undermine such assumptions and indicate a need to reassess many of the time-honoured approaches to identity in HGF archaeology.

Agency, Belief, and Spirituality

The interpretation of archaeological signatures is further 'complicated' (itself a feminist concept) once issues of individual agency and historical contingencies are taken into account. Fewster's (2001b) research among mixed San (Basarwa) communities living in and around the town of Serowe, central Botswana, is one of the most explicit efforts to develop ethnographic analogies at the level of agency. Her work focused on the relationships between foragers (San/Basarwa) and neighbouring agro-pastoralists (Bamangwato) and their material culture repertoires. She used as her theoretical frame the dualism of structure and agency that is at the heart of Giddens's (1984) concept of structuration, which posits that these act recursively on each other such that each is both the outcome and medium of the other.

The study is interesting partly because it provides rich insights into the specificity of forager–farmer interactions along with 'ethnographic spoilers' (Yellen 1977a, 8) concerning the material manifestation of these. For example, although the Basarwa settlement contained several cattle pens and evidence for the manufacture of various wooden agricultural and food-processing tools, the majority of the population neither farmed nor had their own cattle. Instead, owing to a long history of subordination by neighbouring agro-pastoral Tswana communities these San, like many others elsewhere in Botswana, worked as cattle herders for Bamangwato families and obtained some income by selling wooden items such as pestles and mortars to them, but rarely used such objects or consumed domestic livestock. The material repertoire of their settlement was thus not a direct reflection of their preferred subsistence strategy, which remained foraging insofar as it was possible for them to pursue this. Even more significantly, during her research Fewster encountered one individual who had made a conscious decision to adopt farming. As her account of this particular event and the agents involved shows, his behaviour, which might typically be dismissed as 'unrepresentative', in fact characterizes far better than higher level theories of human evolution the 'messiness' of daily life, and is illustrative of how humans have always had the capacity to routinely renegotiate the structural rules that govern their lives (Fewster 2006, 85). Although, as the detailed Chipewyan life histories collected by Jarvenpa and Brumbach (1988, 607–11) illustrate, decisions to do so may have unforeseen and unfortunate consequences.

In his study of Siberian Khanty hunter-fishers, Jordan (2001; 2003; 2004) has employed similar ideas, arguing in particular that two scales of agency need to be acknowledged—that of the individual, and the 'group agency' of particular communities. He argues further that these different scales need to be examined from both a socio-ecological perspective—with a focus on the adaptive fit of different strategies—and from practice-based perspectives that examine the specificity of individual and group choices, their historical and cultural contingency, and their meaning for the actors involved. As an example of this, we might consider the seasonal mobility pattern of the Khanty and how this structures their encounters with and uses of different landscape resources. This behaviour can be understood in terms of its adaptive suitability to the environment, and measured, for instance, in terms of energy efficiency, calorific returns, and responsiveness to environmental stress. Yet, for Khanty communities, their landscapes are understood in different terms, and are conceived as being 'inhabited by living persons, different generations of divine beings and the human dead, whose presence in key locations informs patterns of human territoriality and long-term resource procurement' with the result that inhabiting this landscape is a constant 'complex choreography of movement [and] a stream of social interactions with the materiality of the world' (Jordan 2004, 116–17).

Since their perceptions of landscape inform daily, seasonal, and historical practice, then it follows that Khanty beliefs about the nature of the universe also shape and inform the material manifestations of these and their inscription on the landscape. Khanty constructs of the animal kingdom and particularly their prey is just one of many examples that Jordan provides which have implications for archaeological interpretation and theory building (2001; 2003). Thus, for instance, Khanty consider that successful hunting of elk, their main meat and fat source typically hunted during the winter months, 'is as much about the inclination of the animal as the skill of the hunter' (Jordan 2003, 106), and that the elk is under the protection of a spirit master. Out of respect for the spirit master and the elk, various rites are performed at kill sites and certain body parts including the elk's skull, because they are regarded as 'clean', need to be protected from potentially polluting forces such as dogs. For this reason, although the practice is less common now, older generations often placed 'the smashed bones and skulls of all the elk they had killed' in special-purpose middens, one for each household, in the forest behind their settlements (Jordan 2003, 107). Taboos and beliefs such as these are thus as influential on the formation of archaeological traces of practice as seemingly more 'adaptive' aspects of HGF settlement systems, and as Jordan (2004, 118) notes elsewhere, 'artefacts deposited at sites store up, as residues of communication, the symbolism that the place, image or artefact has carried on the wider seasonal round'.

The Histories and Intimacies of Things

In an early study of beadwork worn by different Kalahari San groups (G/wi, Ju/'hoãnsi, !Xo, and Nharo), Wiessner (1984) further explored the use of material culture style in the construction and negotiation of personal identity. She noted, in particular, that glass-beaded headbands (normally, but not exclusively, worn by women) are highly personal items associated with a sense of well-being that are worn, as her informants put it, 'when one's heart soars' (Wiessner 1984, 200). The effort women invested in making headbands and the degree of complexity of the designs varied, although all of the groups Wiessner studied shared a basic design repertoire, despite language differences and the vast distances between them. Overall, headbands that had more intricate or complex designs, and so had required more energy invested in their manufacture, are regarded as 'more beautiful' and are preferentially selected by women as a way of projecting positive images of themselves to others (Wiessner 1984, 207–8). Like many other items, headbands are redistributed within reciprocal, obligatory gift exchange networks known as *hxaro* (on the dangers of extending the Ju/'hoãnsi model to other contexts, see Mitchell 2003).

As well as directing some exchanges towards those for whom they feel socially responsible, Kalahari San also actively use these networks to maintain reciprocal relations that they judge may be to their future advantage. The exchange of 'beautiful' beaded headbands helps to sustain these by illustrating to exchange partners that they are valued and worthy of such gifts (Mitchell 2003), hence in these contexts it is the assertive significance of beaded headbands that is emphasized rather than their potential use in a more emblematic fashion. Wiessner's studies also highlight, in common with similar research among farming and herding populations (Hodder 1982), that there are no universal criteria that can be used to differentiate between the emblemic and assertive aspects of artefact formal variation, and that interpreting the meaning of different attributes requires an understanding of the historical contexts of their use, production, and circulation.

A more fundamental alternative understanding of HGF material culture has been proposed recently by González-Ruibal and colleagues (2011). Like Wiessner's pioneering work, this is also based on the study of arrows, although in this case those made by the Awá, a small community that lives in the Brazilian part of the Amazon rainforest. Their study documents the manufacture, use, and deposition of arrows, providing details of the *chaîne opératoire* involved, the technical choices this entails and the social significance given to arrow use and manufacturing. Like San arrowheads and OES beads, Awá arrows carry a symbolic load and have particular cultural associations and values, although unlike the San case they are rarely exchanged. Arrows also have particular diacritical marks that allow identification of each individual maker.

Where González-Ruibal and colleagues move the theoretical debate forward, however, lies not in these specifics but in their challenge to long-held assumptions about material culture widely shared by 'processualist' and 'post-processualist' archaeologists alike. Specifically, the authors argue that despite all of the insights gained from the recent focus on artefact biographies and their mediating role in the construction of identities stimulated by the post-processualist debate in archaeology, the majority of these studies rely on an 'objectification approach' to material culture that maintains a 'duality between people and things' in a manner similar to older processualist models (González-Ruibal et al. 2011, 2). Both give primacy to human agents and human consciousness in the making and shaping of the material world, even though both accept that 'natural' processes and events also impinge on human action and thought, and can impose constraints on these. In contrast, González-Ruibal and colleagues argue for a more ontologically informed understanding of the 'intimacy of things' that abandons categorical distinctions between 'subject' and 'object', 'humans' and 'things', 'nature' and 'culture'. While they reach these conclusions in part through a reading of Bourdieu's (1977) notion of *doxa*—the 'taken-for-granted' aspect of all human actions—and current theoretical literature on Actor Network Theory (Latour 2005) and related material, the fundamental significance of bows and arrows in the constitution of selfhood among Awá was even more revelatory.

Contrary to all models of balancing energy use against returns, Awá invest inordinate amounts of time and effort in the manufacturing of arrows. They take many more arrows with them on hunting trips than they ever need—often causing damage to their flights by doing so, thereby reducing their efficiency. Once fired, Awá gather up as many as can be recovered from the forest, including broken ones, returning them to their camps but rarely repairing any damage. Even those who hunt with shotguns still carry arrows at other times and are careful not to abandon the technology, making sure the next generation is properly instructed in arrow manufacture and use. Bundles of arrows are stored in the rafters of their houses, and, away from the context of the hunt, Awá (including women and children) are often to be seen carrying, handling, and working with arrows. Most importantly, while arrows have multiple symbolic associations that stem from cultural practices and beliefs, arrows do not serve as 'images' or 'representations' since such concepts 'imply a mediated relation with things and a metaphorical construction of reality' (González-Ruibal et al. 2011, 12). Instead, for Awá, arrows are not 'a displacement of self, but an intimate part of the self', such that the relationship between 'the constitution of things and selves [goes] hand in hand' (González-Ruibal et al. 2011, 12). As González-Ruibal and colleagues observe, such a relationship between people and their material world, as Awá understand it, and contrary to the tenets of much previous ethnoarchaeology and in a manner that resonates with Jordan's

(2003) account of Khanty understanding of the nature of the universe, is *not* analogical but ontological (Jordan 2003).

It is worth drawing attention here to the suggestion, as discussed for instance by Gamble (1999, 365), that the development of a perspective that sees objects as capable of having representational and metaphorical significance, rather than simply being treated as 'adjuncts to persons, meaningful only when attached in acquisition, manufacture or use and linked in action by rhythms', was a distinct feature of the transition to modern human behaviour. Gamble argues that as a consequence of this conceptual shift, for the first time, objects 'became personified' capable of representing 'either that person or the existence of an extended network *in absentia*' (Gamble 1999, 365). The recent research by González-Ruibal and colleagues, however, reminds us that while this may have been the case, this did not result in the abandonment of animist—by which is meant an ontology that accords purposive and active agency to non-human beings and things (Brown and Walker 2008, 297–8)—conceptions of the world. Clearly, the interplay between metaphorical and ontological conceptions of material things among HGFs is an area that would benefit from further research.

Integrating Ethnoarchaeology, History, and Archaeology

As studies such as those outlined above highlight, HGF societies are by no means inherently conservative or resistant to change, and the integration of ethnohistorical and archaeological data into ethnoarchaeological studies offers considerable analytical potential. Unfortunately, for a long time ethnoarchaeologists, in their desire to develop robust analogies with which to interpret the material remains of humanity's oldest and longest-lasting mode of subsistence (and associated technologies, social system, and belief structures), often downplayed the role of history in the shaping of the HGF societies they studied. Yet no contemporary HGF can be regarded as completely isolated or untouched by the activities of non-HGF societies. In some cases, such as the Amazonian rainforest, such contact is relatively recent, but in others, as has been forcefully argued with reference to many Kalahari hunter-gatherers (see Barnard 2006; Kent 1992b; Reid 2005, and references therein), such contact in one form or another has extended over centuries and even millennia. This basic fact presents ethnoarchaeologists, and archaeologists more generally, with methodological, theoretical, and ethical challenges, that are only now being fully addressed.

Specifically, in marked contrast to earlier phases of research, scholars engaged currently in ethnoarchaeological research acknowledge that surviving forager groups cannot be regarded as if they are 'living fossils' of a 'prehistoric past'. Many researchers now summarize the recent history of interaction between these communities and some of their agricultural and/or pastoral neighbours, and some even document the steady increase in the role of the colonial and post-colonial state in the lives and livelihoods of these HGF populations, as well as the activities of church missions, development NGOs, and the tourism industry (e.g. Lee 2006; Woodburn 1997). Nevertheless, it is still the case that comparatively few ethnoarchaeological studies (cf., however, Brumbach and Jarvenpa 1989 and their other publications on

Northern Dene) provide any insights into HGF history or ethnogenesis, and provide only minimal information concerning the recent archaeology of the region where they live. This is rather paradoxical since the wealth of data collected concerning how traces of different activities performed by forager and HGF groups are manifest in the landscape surely have greatest potential for informing our understanding of the formation of the *recent* archaeological record of the same region, rather than that of the very distant Plio-Pleistocene past. It could also be regarded as ethically irresponsible, since over at least the last century there have been many incursions into HGF territories by other groups, some of whom are increasingly hostile to the continued presence of HGFs (e.g. Good 1999).

A further compelling case for integrating historical perspectives into ethnoarchaeological research is provided by the work of projects such as the joint Spanish and Argentinian study along the north shore of the Beagle Channel, Tierra del Fuego, that began in the mid-1980s (Vila et al. 2007). Among other elements, this has involved a critical analysis of all the existing written and graphic ethnographic sources spanning several centuries of documentation by outside observers; detailed study of European museum collections of Fuegian ethnographic material; and targeted archaeological excavation of sites spanning the time periods covered by these sources. As Estévez (2009, 140) notes in a review of the results of this work, the different ethnographic 'snapshots' of Fuegian communities provided by this long-term record portray very different kinds of forager society at different moments in time. While some of these differences may be attributable to changing paradigms of ethnographic research and observation, the records also indicate that Fuegian HGFs were dynamic, flexible, and capable of changing very quickly. Thus, while the project hoped to draw on the ethnographic sources to interpret the archaeological record of this section of Tierra del Fuego, as the project progressed it became apparent that a reliance on ethnographic analogies was typically 'suitable only in the initial stage of suggesting hypotheses because the ethnographic record is biased (socially and historically) and subjective' (Estévez 2009). It is critical, therefore, that archaeologists wanting to develop ethnographic analogies must ask themselves the question 'which kind of source, from when, and collected by whom, should be used in an analogy?' (Estévez 2009); and ethnoarchaeologists need to pay greater heed than before to how historical events and processes have shaped the societies they study (Stahl 1993).

Longitudinal studies, such as Wiessner's (2002) research on Ju/'hoãnsi, spanning 34 years, are also extremely informative—in this particular case highlighting that HGFs are perfectly capable of generating surpluses (contrary to some common archaeological assumptions), both in tangible form from hunting large game and in an intangible manner in the form of skills in trance healing. In the Ju/'hoãnsi case, both of these surpluses are routinely distributed, and a similar emphasis on resource redistribution is common among a wide range of HGF societies. Her data also indicate that even with respect to hunting, objectives other than simply meeting provisioning needs can motivate hunters including attracting mates, reciprocity, nepotism, and achieving long-term political goals, and that the importance of these can vary over the lifespan of an individual. Aside from the evolutionary implications of the data presented, it is clear also that all of these competing motivations could have an effect on a wide range of material features of Ju/'hoãnsi life, from the circulation of different arrows and other portable material signals of identity to camp size, duration of occupation, and patterns of meat distribution, reinforcing the point made throughout this chapter that considerations of issues of agency, belief, and history are as important to understanding the structure and content of archaeological records as studies of mobility, discard patterns, or the mechanics of animal butchery.

SUMMARY AND CONCLUSION

Formal ethnoarchaeological research conducted over the past 40-plus years has greatly improved understanding of the diversity of modern HGF societies and the material manifestations of their organization, practices, and beliefs, and is likely to continue to do so. Collectively, these data have significantly improved the interpretation of archaeological records of past HGF societies. Many archaeologists, and not just those whose interests lie in HGF research, routinely draw on the insights from this work. As ethnoarchaeological research among such societies has progressed, so awareness of the challenges of developing and using ethnographic analogies in the archaeological interpretive process has increased and, overall, rather more cautious uses of analogy with more overtly stated boundary conditions have emerged.

In the first few decades of research, emphasis was placed on the investigation of site formation processes, butchery practices, disposal of faunal remains, mobility strategies, and the organization of subsistence technologies. While the range of themes now studied has broadened to include, among others, stylistic variation in artefacts, material expressions of identity, the gendered division of labour, and issues of agency and belief, the earlier research themes and questions are still major concerns. From a paradigmatic perspective, naturalist approaches (i.e. those modelled after the natural sciences, David and Kramer 2001, 37–41) still dominate, with emphasis placed on the development of middle-range theories, the formulation and testing of hypotheses concerning HGF behaviour and its material expressions, and interpretation of material records of human activity from the perspective of evolutionary ecology.

It is important to recognize the enormous contributions such studies have made to scholarly understanding of the complexity of HGF societies and behaviour, and that such studies continue to have validity. Ethnoarchaeological research of this kind, for instance, played a critical role in demonstrating that HGFs living in the tropics face very different resource stresses from those occupying high latitudes, and hence tend to develop different technological and social responses (Hayden 1981). Equally, understanding of the diverse range of factors that influence the spatial patterning of artefactual, faunal, and structural remains typically found on archaeological sites associated with HGFs would be greatly impoverished if it were not for such ethnoarchaeological research. It is also important to recognize that, even though no modern HGF community can or should be likened precisely to those of 'prehistory', the practices of some, such as the Hadzabe, *do* result in patterning which, of all modern analogues, most closely resembles that produced by our common hominin ancestors in the Plio-Pleistocene, particularly at the FLK Zinj site in Olduvai Gorge Bed I, Tanzania (Domínguez-Rodrigo 2002). In an imperfect world, such analogies are sometimes the best available—although in many cases their proponents could do more to highlight their limitations rather than just their applications.

Notwithstanding these points, it is regrettable that far fewer ethnoarchaeological studies have been conducted among HGFs from an explicitly anti-naturalist perspective (cf.

González-Ruibal et al. 2011). Equally, current understanding of, for example, the symbolic dimensions of settlement space, mortuary practices and artefacts; the meaning of stylistic forms and their role as markers of social change; material expressions and constructions of identity; power relations; and perceptions of landscape, all remain poorly investigated among modern HGFs, let alone such communities in the past. Fortunately, this situation is changing as new approaches to the ethnoarchaeological study of HGFs influenced by theories of practice have emerged in recent decades and have brought to the fore many key issues concerning the importance of gender, identity, individual agency, and historical contingencies. Such studies have been less concerned to produce similitudes of behaviour that can be 'mapped onto' particular material patterns, and instead have turned to the exploration of 'the perennial *frisson*' between structure, agency, and the material world (Fewster 2006, 85) with emphasis being given to understanding materiality and the embodiment of practice.

Precisely how these contrasting approaches can be reconciled remains unclear, although Jordan's (2003, 2–23) schema concerning ways to examine different scales of individual and group agency from both socio-ecological and more practice- and semiotic-oriented perspectives offers one possibility. A further trend that is likely to become increasingly important in the coming decades is the closer integration of historical perspectives and evidence from the regional archaeological record into ethnoarchaeological studies, such as in the manner already being followed by some research teams (e.g. Brumbach and Jarvenpa 1989; 1997; Vila et al. 2007). Equally, it is likely that members of surviving HGF communities themselves will be drawn into the research process as active researchers and not just as the subjects of this research, as wider disciplinary ethical concerns and efforts to promote indigenous and cosmopolitan archaeologies become more prominent.

In terms of priorities for future research, four themes stand out. The first is widening and deepening the geographical scope of ethnoarchaeological studies among contemporary HGFs. While many different HGFs have been the focus of some ethnoarchaeological research, it is also the case that only a few have been the focus of sustained research. Additional research among less well-studied communities, in a more diverse range of ecological settings and with a wider range of relationships with their non-HGF neighbours, has the potential to be particularly beneficial. Second, and following from this (and again acknowledging that there have been some prior studies of this kind), more research could be undertaken precisely on the diverse range of relationships between HGFs and non-HGFs. This is for two reasons. On the one hand, as the survival of HGF subsistence strategies testifies, in every part of the world long after the initial transition to agriculture HGFs were in contact with farming, herding, and subsequently urban populations. Such relations were diverse, and ranged from outright hostility or minimizing contact to more intertwined interaction. Understanding such interactions in the present and recent past in greater depth could greatly enhance current interpretations of similar situations earlier in human history.

Another reason why ethnoarchaeological research on this topic should be prioritized is that it clearly touches on the recent history of the HGF communities themselves, and so has the potential to illustrate that ethnoarchaeological research has relevance for those same communities and not just the scholarly community. The third priority area for research, namely detailed critical study of museum collections of ethnographic and historic HGF material culture in light of the history of the groups that produced them, would further contribute to such goals. This has been ably demonstrated by a few previous studies (e.g.

Allen 2011; Weniger 1992), especially where such work is coupled (as in the ongoing work on Fuegian communities) with archaeological research into the recent past of these societies.

The fourth priority, developing truly collaborative projects with HGF communities, similarly follows logically from the previous ones. From my own perspective, I consider that it is precisely in such collaborative ventures which give equal weight to naturalist and ontological understandings of patterning, temporality, being, and dwelling in hunter-gatherer-fisher worlds that the future of ethnoarchaeological research among such societies lies. Without giving due recognition to alternative ways of seeing and being in the world, ethnoarchaeology is not only in danger of reducing the complexity of contemporary HGF societies to rather sterile metrics of energy expenditure and the material residues of their actions in the world, but could also end up missing the point of conducting research among living communities. The latter must surely be to understand the contours of human differences and commonalities. Hunter-gatherer-fisher societies around the globe have welcomed ethnoarchaeologists into their worlds. Perhaps the time has come for the archaeological community to extend a welcome to our world to these same societies in a manner that places their constructs of the natural, human, and spiritual worlds on an equal intellectual footing to our own Western rationalist philosophies, albeit with all due recognition of the anti-modernist perils that such strategies can entail.

Acknowledgements

I would like to thank the editors for their insightful comments on earlier drafts and extraordinary patience while I was writing this chapter. Thanks are also due to two anonymous reviewers, Peter Mitchell, Alfredo González-Ruibal and Terry O'Connor for their helpful comments on particular sections. All remaining mistakes are my own.

References

Allen, H. 2011. Thompson's spears: innovation and change in eastern Arnhem land projectile technology. In Y. Musharbash and M. Barber (eds), *Ethnography and the production of anthropological knowledge: essays in honour of Nicolas Peterson*, 69–88. Canberra: ANU E Press.
Arnold, J. E. 1995. Transportation innovation and social complexity among maritime hunter-gatherer societies. *American Anthropologist* 97, 733–47.
Bamforth, D. B. 2006. The Windy Ridge quartzite quarry: hunter-gatherer mining and hunter-gatherer land use on the North American Continental Divide. *World Archaeology* 38, 511–27.
Barnard, A. 2006. Kalahari revisionism, Vienna and the 'indigenous peoples' debate. *Social Anthropology* 14, 1–16.
Bartram, L. E., Kroll, E. M., and Bunn, H. T. 1991. Variability in camp structure and bone food refuse patterning at Kua San hunter-gatherer camps. In E. M. Knoll and T. D. Price (eds), *The Interpretation of Archaeological Spatial Patterning*, 77–148. New York: Plenum Press.
Bettinger, R. L. 1987. Archaeological approaches to hunter-gatherers. *Annual Review of Anthropology* 16, 121–42.

Bettinger, R. L. 1991. *Hunter-gatherers: archaeological and evolutionary theory.* London: Plenum Press.

Bettinger, R. L. 1999. From traveler to processor: regional trajectories of hunter-gatherer sedentism in the Inyo-Mono region, California. In B. R. Billman and G. M. Feinman (eds), *Settlement Pattern Studies in the Americas: Fifty Years Since Viru*, 39–55. Washington, DC: Smithsonian Institution.

Binford, L. R. 1973. Interassemblage variability—the Mousterian and the 'functional' argument. In C. Renfrew (ed.), *The explanation of culture change: models in prehistory*, 227–54. London: Duckworth.

Binford, L. R. 1977. General introduction. In L. R. Binford (ed.), *For theory building in archaeology: essays on faunal remains, aquatic resources, spatial analysis, and systemic modelling*, 1–10. London: Academic Press.

Binford, L. R. 1978a. *Nunamiut ethnoarchaeology.* London: Academic Press.

Binford, L. R. 1978b. Dimensional analysis of behavior and site structure: learning from an Eskimo hunting stand. *American Antiquity* 43, 330–61.

Binford, L. R. 1979. Organisation and formation processes: looking at curated technologies. *Journal of Anthropological Research* 35, 255–73.

Binford, L. R. 1980. Willow smoke and dogs' tails: hunter-gatherer settlement systems and archaeological site formation. *American Antiquity* 45, 4–20.

Binford, L. R. 1981. *Bones: ancient men and modern myths.* London: Academic Press.

Binford, L. R. 1982. The archaeology of place. *Journal of Anthropological Archaeology* 1, 5–31.

Binford, L. R. 1983. *In pursuit of the past: decoding the archaeological record.* London: Thames and Hudson.

Binford, L. R. 1984. Butchering, sharing, and the archaeological record. *Journal of Anthropological Archaeology* 3, 235–57.

Binford, L. R. 1985. 'Brand X' versus the recommended product. *American Antiquity* 50, 580–90.

Binford, L. R. 1988. Fact and fiction about the Zinjanthropus floor: data, arguments, and interpretations. *Current Anthropology* 29, 123–35.

Bird, D. W. and Bliege Bird, R. 2000. The ethnoarchaeology of juvenile foraging: shellfishing strategies among Meriam children. *Journal of Anthropological Archaeology* 19, 461–76.

Bird, D. W., Bliege Bird, R., and Codding, B. F. 2009. In pursuit of mobile prey: Martu hunting strategies and archaeofaunal interpretation. *American Antiquity* 74, 3–29.

Bird, D. W. and O'Connell, J. F. 2006. Behavioral ecology and archaeology. *Journal of Archaeological Research* 14, 143–88.

Bird, D. W., Richardson, J. L., Veth, P. M., and Barham, A. J. 2002. Explaining shellfish variability in middens on the Meriam Islands, Torres Strait, Australia. *Journal of Archaeological Science* 29, 457–69.

Bleed, P. 1986. The optimal design of hunting weapons: maintainability or reliability. *American Antiquity* 51, 737–47.

Boismier, W. A. 1991. Site formation among subarctic peoples: an ethnohistorical approach. In C. S. Gamble and W. A. Boismier (eds), *Ethnoarchaeological approaches to mobile campsites: hunter-gatherer and pastoralist case studies*, 189–214. Ann Arbor: International Monographs in Prehistory, Ethnoarchaeological Series, Vol. 1.

Bourdieu, P. 1977. *Outline of a theory of practice*, trans. R. Nice. Cambridge: Cambridge University Press.

Brown, L. A. and Walker, W. H. 2008. Prologue: archaeology, animism and non-human agents. *Journal of Archaeological Method and Theory* 15, 297–9.

Brumbach, H. J. and Jarvenpa, R. 1989. *Ethnoarchaeological and cultural frontiers: Athapaskan, Algonquian and European adaptations in the central subarctic*. New York: Peter Lang.

Brumbach, H. J. and Jarvenpa, R. 1997. Ethnoarchaeology of subsistence space and gender: a subarctic Dene case. *American Antiquity* 62, 414–36.

Brumbach, H. J. and Jarvenpa, R. 2007. Gender dynamics in hunter-gatherer society: archaeological methods and perspectives. In S. M. Nelson (ed.), *Identity and subsistence: gender strategies for archaeology*, 169–201. Walnut Creek, CA: AltaMira Press.

Bunn, H. T. 1993. Bone assemblages at base camps: a further consideration of carcass transport and bone destruction by the Hadza. In J. Hudson (ed.), *From bones to behavior: ethnoarchaeological and experimental contributions to the interpretation of faunal remains*, 156–68. Carbondale: Southern Illinois University, Center for Archaeological Investigations Occasional Paper 21.

Bunn, H. T. 2001. Hunting, power scavenging, and butchering by Hadza foragers and by Plio-Pleistocene Homo. In C. Stanford and H. T. Bunn (eds), *Meat-eating and human evolution*, 199–218. Oxford: Oxford University Press.

Bunn, H., Bartram, L. and Kroll, E. 1988. Variability in bone assemblage formation from Hadza hunting, scavenging and carcass processing. *Journal of Anthropological Archaeology* 7, 412–57.

Bunn, H. T. and Kroll, E. 1988. Reply to L. R. Binford: fact and fiction about the Zinjanthropus floor: data, arguments, and interpretations. *Current Anthropology* 29, 135–49.

Cameron, D. W. 1993. Uniformitarianism and prehistoric archaeology. *Australian Archaeology* 36, 42–9.

Chatters, J. G. 1987. Hunter-gatherer adaptations and assemblage structure. *Journal of Anthropological Archaeology* 6, 336–75.

Clark, J. G. D. 1954. *Excavations at Star Carr*. Cambridge: Cambridge University Press.

Cobb, H. 2005. Straight down the line? A queer consideration of hunter-gatherer studies in north-west Europe. *World Archaeology* 73, 630–6.

Conkey, M. W. and Spector, J. D. 1984. Archaeology and the study of gender. *Advances in Archaeological Method and Theory* 7, 1–39.

Cooper, Z. 1994. Abandoned Onge encampments and their relevance in understanding the archaeological record in the Andaman islands. In B. Allchin (ed.), *Living traditions: studies in the ethnoarchaeology of south Asia*, 235–63. New Delhi: Oxford University Press and IBH Publishing Co.

Cunningham, J. J. 2003. Transcending the 'obnoxious spectator': a case for processual pluralism in ethnoarchaeology. *Journal of Anthropological Archaeology* 22, 389–410.

Dahlberg, F. (ed.) 1981. *Woman the gatherer*. New Haven: Yale University Press.

David, N. and Kramer, C. 2001. *Ethnoarchaeology in action*. Cambridge: Cambridge University Press.

Domínguez-Rodrigo, M. 2002. Hunting and scavenging by early humans: the state of the debate. *Journal of World Prehistory* 16, 1–54.

Dumont, J. V. 1983. An interim report of the Star Carr microwear study. *Oxford Journal of Archaeology* 2, 127–45.

Enloe, J. G. 1983. Ethnoarchaeology of marrow cracking: implications for the recognition of prehistoric subsistence organisation. In J. Hudson (ed.), *From bones to behavior: ethnoarchaeological and experimental contributions to the interpretation of faunal remains*, 82–97. Carbondale: Southern Illinois University, Center for Archaeological Investigations Occasional Paper 21.

Enloe, J. G. 2003. Food sharing past and present: archaeological evidence for economic and social interactions. *Before Farming* 1, 1–23.

Estévez, J. 2009. Ethnoarchaeology in the uttermost part of the Earth. *Arctic Anthropology* 46, 132–43.

Estioko-Griffin, A. and Griffin, P. B. 1981. Woman the hunter: the Agta. In F. Dahlberg (ed.), *Woman the gatherer*, 121–51. New Haven: Yale University Press.

Feblot-Augustins, J. and Perlès, C. 1992. Perspectives ethnoarchéologiques sur les échanges à longue distance. In F. Audouze (ed.), *Ethnoarchéologie: justification, problèmes, limites, XIIe recontres internationales d'archéologie et d'histoire d'Antibes*, 195–209. Juan-les-Pins: APDCA.

Fewster, K. 2001a. The responsibilities of ethnoarchaeologists. In M. Pluciennik (ed.), *The responsibilities of archaeologists*, 65–73. Oxford: BAR International Series 981.

Fewster, K. 2001b. Petso's field: ethnoarchaeology and agency. In K. J. Fewster and M. Zvelebil (eds), *Ethnoarchaeology and hunter-gatherers: pictures at an exhibition*, 81–9. Oxford: BAR International Series 955.

Fewster, K. 2006. The potential of analogy in post-processual archaeologies: a case study from Basimane ward, Serowe, Botswana. *Journal of the Royal Anthropological Institute* 12, 61–87.

Fisher, J. W. Jr. 1993. Foragers and farmers: material expressions of interaction at elephant processing sites in the Ituri Forest, Zaire. In J. Hudson (ed.), *From bones to behavior: ethnoarchaeological and experimental contributions to the interpretation of faunal remains*, 247–62. Carbondale: Southern Illinois University, Center for Archaeological Investigations Occasional Paper 21.

Fisher, J. W. Jr. and Strickland, H. C. 1989. Ethnoarchaeology among the Efe Pygmies, Zaire: spatial organisation of campsites. *American Journal of Physical Anthropology* 78, 473–84.

Frink, L. 2009. The identity division of labor in Native Alaska. *American Anthropologist* 111, 21–9.

Frink, L., Hoffman, B. W., and Shaw, R. D. 2003. Ulu knife use in Western Alaska: a comparative ethnoarchaeological study. *Current Anthropology* 44, 116–22.

Frink, L. and Weedman, K. (eds) 2005. *Gender and hide production*. Walnut Creek, CA: AltaMira Press.

Gamble, C. S. 1999. *The palaeolithic societies of Europe*. Cambridge: Cambridge University Press.

Giddens, A. 1984. *The constitution of society: outline of a theory of structuration*. Cambridge: Polity Press.

Gifford-Gonzalez, D. P. 1989. Ethnographic analogues for interpreting modified bones: some cases from east Africa. In R. Bonnischen, and M. H. Sorg (eds), *Bone modification*, 179–246. Orono, ME: University of Maine—Peopling of the Americas Publications.

Gifford-Gonzalez, D. P. 1991. Bones are not enough: analogues, knowledge, and interpretive strategies in zooarchaeology. *Journal of Anthropological Archaeology* 10, 215–54.

González-Ruibal, A., Hernando, A., and Politis, G. 2011. Ontology of the self and material culture: arrow-making among the Awá hunter-gatherers (Brazil). *Journal of Anthropological Archaeology* 30, 1–16.

Good, K. 1999. The state and extreme poverty in Botswana: the San and destitutes. *Journal of Modern African Studies* 37, 185–205.

Gould, R. A. 1978. The anthropology of human residues. *American Anthropologist* 80, 815–35.

Gould, R. A. 1980. *Living archaeology*. Cambridge: Cambridge University Press.

Gould, R. A. 1985. The empiricist strikes back: reply to Binford. *American Antiquity* 50, 638–44.

Gould, R. A. 1996. Faunal reduction at Puntutjarpa Rockshelter, Warburten Ranges, Western Australia. *Archaeology of Oceania* 31, 72–86.

Gould, R. A. and Watson, P. J. 1982. A dialogue on the meaning and use of analogy in ethnoarchaeological reasoning. *Journal of Anthropological Archaeology* 1, 344–81.

Gould, S. J. 1965. Is uniformitarianism necessary? *American Journal of Science* 263, 223–8.

Greaves, R. D. 2006. Forager landscape use and residential organisation. In F. Seller, R. Greaves, and P.-L. Yu (eds), *Archaeology and ethnoarchaeology of mobility*, 127–52. Gainesville: University Press of Florida.

Griffin, P. B. and Solheim II, W. G. 1990. Ethnoarchaeological research in Asia. *Asian Perspectives* 28, 145–62.

Habu, J. 2004. *Ancient Jomon of Japan*. Cambridge: Cambridge University Press.

Hawkes, K., Hill, K., and O'Connell, J. F. 1982. Why hunters gather: optimal foraging and the Ache of Eastern Paraguay. *American Ethnologist* 9, 379–98.

Hawkes, K., O'Connell, J. F., and Blurton Jones, N. 2001. Hadza meat sharing. *Evolution and Human Behavior* 22, 113–42.

Hayden, B. 1981. Subsistence and ecological adaptations of modern hunter-gatherers. In R. S. O. Harding and G. Teleki (eds), *Omnivorous primates: gathering and hunting in human evolution*, 344–421. New York: Columbia University Press.

Hayden, B. 2003. Were luxury foods the first domesticates? Ethnoarchaeological perspectives from Southeast Asia. *World Archaeology* 34, 458–69.

Hill, K. 1988. Foraging decisions among Ache hunter-gatherers: new data and implications for optimal foraging models. *Ethology and Sociobiology* 8, 1–36.

Hilton, C. E. and Greaves, R. D. 2008. Seasonality and sex differences in travel distance and resource transport in Venezuelan foragers. *Current Anthropology* 49, 144–53.

Hitchcock, R. 1987. Sedentism and site structure: organisational changes in Kalahari Basarwa residential locations. In S. Kent (ed.), *Method and theory for activity area research*, 374–423. New York: Columbia University Press.

Hodder, I. R. 1982. *Symbols in action: ethnoarchaeological studies of material culture*. Cambridge: Cambridge University Press.

Hudson, J. 1993. The impacts of domestic dogs on bone at forager camps. In J. Hudson (ed.), *From bones to behavior: ethnoarchaeological and experimental contributions to the interpretation of faunal remains*, 301–23. Carbondale: Southern Illinois University, Center for Archaeological Investigations.

Ikeya, K. and Nakai, S. 2009. Historical and contemporary relations between Mlabri and Hmong in Northern Thailand. In K. Ikeya, H. Ogawa, and P. Mitchell (eds), *Interactions between hunter-gatherers and farmers: from prehistory to present*, 247–61. Osaka: National Museum of Ethnology.

Isaac, G. L. 1978. Food sharing and human evolution: archaeological evidence from the Plio-Pleistocene of East Africa. *Journal of Anthropological Research* 34, 311–25.

Jarvenpa, R. and Brumbach, H. J. 1983. Ethnoarchaeological perspectives on an Athapaskan moose kill. *Arctic* 36, 174–84.

Jarvenpa, R. and Brumbach, H. J. 1988. Socio-spatial organisation and decision-making processes: observations among the Chipewyan. *American Anthropologist* 90, 598–618.

Jarvenpa, R. and Brumbach, H. J. 1995. Ethnoarchaeology and gender: Chipewyan women as hunters. *Research in Economic Anthropology* 16, 39–82.

Jarvenpa, R. and Brumbach, H. J. 2006a. Revisiting the sexual division of labor: thoughts on ethnoarchaeology and gender. *Archeological Papers of the American Anthropological Association* 16, 97–107.

Jarvenpa, R. and Brumbach, H. J. 2006b. Chipewyan hunters: a task differentiation analysis. In R. Jarvenpa and H. J. Brumbach (eds), *Circumpolar lives and livelihood: a comparative ethnoarchaeology of gender and subsistence*, 54–78. Lincoln: University of Nebraska Press.

Jarvenpa, R. and Brumbach, H. J. 2009. Fun with Dick and Jane: ethnoarchaeology, circumpolar toolkits, and gender 'inequality'. *Ethnoarchaeology* 1, 57–78.

Jordan, P. 2001. Ideology, material culture and Khanty ritual landscapes in Western Siberia. In K. J. Fewster and M. Zvelebil (eds), *Ethnoarchaeology and hunter-gatherers: pictures at an exhibition*, 25–42. Oxford: BAR International Series 955.

Jordan, P. 2003. *Material culture and sacred landscape: the anthropology of the Siberian Khanty*. Walnut Creek, CA: AltaMira Press.

Jordan, P. 2004. Examining the role of agency in hunter-gatherer cultural transmission. In A. Gardner (ed.), *Agency uncovered: archaeological perspectives on social agency, power and being human*, 107–34. London: UCL Press.

Kelly, R. L. 1983. Hunter-gatherer mobility strategies. *Journal of Anthropological Research* 39, 277–306.

Kelly, R. L. 1995. *The foraging spectrum: diversity in hunter-gatherer lifeways*. Washington, DC: Smithsonian Institution.

Kelly, R. L., Poyer, L., and Tucker, B. 2005. An ethnoarchaeological study of mobility, architectural investment, and food sharing along Madagascar's Mikea. *American Anthropologist* 107, 403–16.

Kent, S. 1991. The relationship between mobility strategies and site structure. In E. M. Kroll and T. D. Price (eds), *The interpretation of archaeological spatial patterning*, 33–59. New York: Plenum Press.

Kent, S. 1992a. Studying variability in the archaeological record: an ethnoarchaeological model for distinguishing mobility patterns. *American Antiquity* 57, 635–60.

Kent, S. 1992b. The current forager controversy: real versus ideal views of hunter-gatherers. *Man* NS 27, 45–70.

Kent, S. 1993. Variability in faunal assemblages: the influence of hunting skill, sharing, dogs and mode of cooking on faunal remains at a sedentary Kalahari community. *Journal of Anthropological Archaeology* 12, 323–85.

Kent, S. 1995. Does sedentarization promote gender inequality? A case study from the Kalahari. *Journal of the Royal Anthropological Institute* 1, 513–36.

Kent, S. 1996. Hunting variability at a recently sedentary Kalahari village. In S. Kent (ed.), *Cultural diversity among twentieth-century foragers: an African perspective*, 125–56. Cambridge: Cambridge University Press.

Kent, S. 1998. Invisible gender—invisible foragers: southern African hunter-gatherer spatial patterning and the archaeological record. In S. Kent (ed.), *Gender in African prehistory*, 39–67. Walnut Creek, CA: AltaMira Press.

Kent, S. and Vierich, H. 1989. The myth of ecological determinism: anticipated mobility and site spatial organisation. In S. Kent (ed.), *Farmers as hunters: the implications of sedentism*, 96–130. Cambridge: Cambridge University Press.

Koon, H. E. C., O'Connor, T. P., and Collins, M. J. 2010. Sorting the butchered from the boiled. *Journal of Archaeological Science* 37, 62–9.

Kosugi, Y. 1997. Ethnographic reconstruction from the material culture of the Kuril Ainu. *Bulletin of the National Museum of Ethnology* 21, 391–502.

Kuhn, S. L. and Stiner, M. C. 2006. What's a mother to do? The division of labor among Neanderthals and modern humans in Eurasia. *Current Anthropology* 47, 953–80.

Lane, P. J. and Schadla-Hall, R. T. 2004. The many ages of Star Carr: do 'cites' make the 'site'? In A. Barnard (ed.), *Hunter-gatherers in history, archaeology and anthropology*, 145–61. Oxford: Berg.

Latour, B. 2005. *Reassembling the social: an introduction to actor-network-theory*. Oxford: Oxford University Press.

Lee, R. B. 2006. Commonalities and diversities in contemporary hunter-gatherers: from settlement archaeology to development ethnography. *Archeological Papers of the American Anthropological Association* 16, 157–69.

Lee, R. B. and Daly, R. 2002. Introduction: foragers and others. In R. B. Lee and R. Daly (eds), *The Cambridge encyclopedia of hunters and gatherers*, 10–28. Cambridge: Cambridge University Press.

Lemmonier, P. 1986. The study of material culture today: towards an anthropology of technology. *Journal of Anthropological Archaeology* 5, 147–86.

Leroi-Gourhan, A. 1964. *Le geste et la parole, I: technique et tangage*. Paris: Albin Martin.

Leroi-Gourhan, A. 1965. *Le geste et la parole, II: la mémoire et les rythmes*. Paris: Albin Martin.

Lewis-Williams, J. D. 1981. *Believing and seeing: symbolic meanings in southern San rock paintings*. London: Academic Press.

Lewis-Williams, J. D. 1991. Wrestling with analogy: a methodological dilemma in Upper Palaeolithic art research. *Proceedings of the Prehistoric Society* 57, 149–62.

Lewis-Williams, J. D. 2002. *A cosmos in stone: interpreting religion and society through rock art*. Walnut Creek, CA: AltaMira Press.

Lupo, K. D. 1994. Butchering marks and carcass acquisition strategies: distinguishing hunting from scavenging in archaeological contexts. *Journal of Archaeological Science* 21, 827–37.

Lupo, K. D. 1995. Hadza bone assemblages and hyena attrition: an ethnographic example of the influence of cooking and mode of discard on the intensity of scavenger ravaging. *Journal of Anthropological Archaeology* 14, 288–314.

Lupo, K. D. 2001. Archaeological skeletal part profiles and differential transport: an ethnoarchaeological example from Hadza bone assemblages. *Journal of Anthropological Archaeology* 20, 361–78.

Lupo, K. D. 2006. What explains the carcass field processing and transport decisions of contemporary hunter-gatherers? Measures of economic anatomy and zooarchaeological skeletal part representation. *Journal of Archaeological Method and Theory* 13, 19–66.

Lupo, K. D. and O'Connell, J. F. 2002. Cut and tooth mark distributions on large animal bones: ethnoarchaeological data from the Hadza and their implications for current ideas about early human carnivory. *Journal of Archaeological Science* 29, 85–109.

Lupo, K. D. and Schmitt, D. 2002. Upper Paleolithic net-hunting, small prey exploitation, and women's work effort: a view from the ethnographic and ethnoarchaeological record of the Congo Basin. *Journal of Archaeological Method and Theory* 9, 147–79.

Lupo, K. D. and Schmitt, D. 2005. Small prey hunting technology and zooarchaeological measures of taxonomic diversity and abundance: ethnoarchaeological evidence from Central African Forest foragers. *Journal of Anthropological Archaeology* 24, 335–53.

Lyman, R. L. 1987. Archaeofaunas and butchery studies: a taphonomic perspective. *Advances in Archaeological Method and Theory* 10, 249–337.

Lyman, R. L. 1994. *Vertebrate taphonomy*. Cambridge: Cambridge University Press.

Lyman, R. L. and O'Brien, M. J. 2001. The direct historical approach, analogical reasoning, and theory in Americanist archaeology. *Journal of Archaeological Method and Theory* 8, 303–42.

Mabulla, A. 2003. Archaeological implications of Hadzabe forager land use in the Eyasi Basin, Tanzania. In C. M. Kusimba and S. B. Kusimba (eds), *East African archaeology: foragers, potters, smiths and traders*, 33–58. Philadelphia: University of Pennsylvania Museum of Archaeology and Anthropology.

Mabulla, A. 2007. Hunting and foraging in the Eyasi Basin, northern Tanzania: past, present and future prospects. *African Archaeological Review* 24, 15–33.

McNett, Jr. C. W. 1979. The cross-cultural method in archaeology. *Advances in Archaeological Method and Theory* 2, 39–76.

Mallol, C., Marlowe, F. W., Wood, B. M., and Porter, C. C. 2007. Earth, wind, and fire: ethnoarchaeological signals of Hadza fires. *Journal of Archaeological Science* 34, 2035–52.

Marlowe, F. W. 2004. Marital residence among foragers. *Current Anthropology* 45, 277–84.

Marlowe, F. W. and Berbesque, J. C. 2009. Tubers as fallback foods and their impact on Hadza hunter-gatherers. *American Journal of Physical Anthropology* 140, 751–8.

Marshall, F. 1994. Food sharing and body part representation in Okiek faunal assemblages. *Journal of Archaeological Science* 21, 65–77.

Marshall, F. B. 2001. Agriculture and use of wild and weedy greens by the Piik ap Oom Okiek of Kenya. *Economic Botany* 55, 32–46.

Mauss, M. 1934. Les techniques du corps. *Journal de Psychologie* 32, 271–93.

Mitchell, P. 2003. Anyone for *hxaro*? Thoughts on the theory and practice of exchange in southern African Later Stone Age. In P. Mitchell, A. Haour, and J. Hobart (eds), *Researching Africa's past: new contributions from British archaeologists*, 35–43. Oxford: Oxbow.

Mutundu, K. K. 1999. *Ethnohistoric archaeology of the Mukogodo in north central Kenya*. Oxford: BAR International Series 775.

Nagar, M. 2008. *Hunter-gatherers in north and central India: an ethnoarchaeological study*. Oxford: BAR International Series 1749.

Nicholson, A. and Cane, S. 1991. Desert camps: analysis of Australian Aboriginal proto-historic campsites. In C. S. Gamble and W. A. Boismier (eds), *Ethnoarchaeological approaches to mobile campsites: hunter-gatherer and pastoralist case studies*, 263–354. Ann Arbor: International Monographs in Prehistory, Ethnoarchaeological Series, Vol. 1.

O'Connell, J. F. 1987. Alyawara site structure and its archaeological implications. *American Antiquity* 52, 74–108.

O'Connell, J. F., Hawkes, K., and Blurton Jones, N. 1988. Hadza hunting, butchering, and bone transport and their archaeological implications. *Journal of Anthropological Research* 44, 113–62.

O'Connell, J. F., Hawkes, K., and Blurton Jones, N. 1990. Reanalysis of large mammal body part transport among the Hadza. *Journal of Archaeological Science* 17, 301–16.

O'Connell, J. F., Hawkes, K., and Blurton Jones, N. 1991 Distribution of refuse-producing activities at Hadza residential base camps: implications for analyses of archaeological site structure. In E. M. Kroll and T. D. Price (eds), *The interpretation of archaeological spatial patterning*, 61–76. New York: Plenum Press.

O'Connell, J. F., Hawkes, K., and Blurton Jones, N. 1992. Patterns in the distribution, site structure and assemblage composition of Hadza kill-butchering sites. *Journal of Archaeological Science* 19, 319–45.

O'Connell, J. F. and Marshall, B. 1989. Analysis of kangaroo body part transport among the Alyawara of central Australia. *Journal of Archaeological Science* 16, 393–405.

Orme, B. 1973. Archaeology and ethnography. In C. Renfrew (ed.), *The explanation of culture change: models in prehistory*, 481–91. London: Duckworth.

Orme, B. 1981. *Anthropology for archaeologists: an introduction*. London: Duckworth.

Politis, G. G. 2005. Children's activity in the production of the archaeological record of hunter-gatherers: an ethnoarchaeological approach. *Global Archaeological Theory* 2, 121–43.

Politis, G. G. 2006. The different dimensions of mobility among the Nukak foragers of the Colombian Amazon. In F. Seller, R. Greaves, and P.-L. Yu (eds), *Archaeology and ethnoarchaeology of mobility*, 23–43. Gainesville: University Press of Florida.

Pookajorn, S. 1985. Ethnoarchaeology with the Phi Tong Luang (Mlabrai): forest hunters of northern Thailand. *World Archaeology* 17, 206–21.

Price, T. D. and Brown, J. A. 1985. Aspects of hunter-gatherer complexity. In T. D. Price and J. A. Brown (eds), *Prehistoric hunter-gatherers: the emergence of cultural complexity*, 3–20. New York: Academic Press.

Reid, A. 2005. Interaction, marginalization, and the archaeology of the Kalahari. In A. B. Stahl (ed.), *African archaeology: a critical introduction*, 353–77. Oxford: Blackwell.

Sackett, J. R. 1985. Style and ethnicity in the Kalahari: a reply to Wiessner. *American Antiquity* 50, 154–9.

Sackett, J. R. 1986. Isochrestism and style: a clarification. *Journal of Anthropological Archaeology* 5, 266–77.

Salmon, M. H. 1982. *Philosophy and archaeology*. London: Academic Press.

Sato, H. 2009. Ethnoarchaeology of trap hunting among the Matagi and the Udehe, traditional hunting peoples living around the Sea of Japan. In S. Sasaki (ed.), *Human–nature relations and the historical backgrounds of the hunter-gatherer cultures in northeast Asian forests (Russian Far East and Northeast Japan)*, 25–46. Osaka: National Museum of Ethnology.

Savelle, J. M. 1987. *Collectors and foragers: subsistence-settlement system change in the central Canadian Arctic, AD 1000–1960*. Oxford: BAR International Series 358.

Shelley, C. 1999. Multiple analogies in archaeology. *Philosophy of Science* 66, 579–605.

Shott, M. 1986. Technological organisation and settlement mobility: an ethnographic examination. *Journal of Anthropological Research* 42, 15–52.

Slocum, S. 1975. Woman the gatherer: male bias in anthropology. In R. R. Reiter (ed.), *Toward an anthropology of women*, 36–50. New York: Monthly Review Press.

Solomon, A. 1992. Gender, representation and power in San ethnography and rock art. *Journal of Anthropological Archaeology* 11, 291–329.

Solomon, A. 2006. Roots and revolutions: a critical overview of early and late San rock art research. *Afrique and Histoire* 2, 77–110.

Stahl, A. B. 1993. Concepts of time and approaches to analogical reasoning in historical perspective. *American Antiquity* 58, 235–60.

Stahl, A. B. 2001. *Making history in Banda: anthropological visions of Africa's past*. Cambridge: Cambridge University Press.

Tanner, N. M. 1981. *On becoming human*. Cambridge: Cambridge University Press.

Testart, A. 1982. The significance of food storage among hunter-gatherers: residence patterns, population densities and social inequalities. *Current Anthropology* 23, 523–37.

Thomson, D. F. 1939. The seasonal factor in human culture, illustrated from the life of a contemporary nomadic group. *Proceedings of the Prehistoric Society* 5, 209–21.

Torrence, R. 1983. Time budgeting and hunter-gatherer technology. In G. N. Bailey (ed.), *Hunter-gatherer economy in prehistory*, 11–22. Cambridge: Cambridge University Press.

Torrence, R. 1989. *Time, energy and stone tools*. Cambridge: Cambridge University Press.

Torrence, R. 2001. Hunter-gatherer technology viewed at different scales. In C. Panter-Brick, R. Layton, and P. Rowley-Conwy (eds), *Hunter-gatherers: an interdisciplinary perspective*, 73–98. Cambridge: Cambridge University Press.

Tschauner, H. 1996. Middle-range theory, behavioural archaeology, and postempiricist philosophy of science in archaeology. *Journal of Archaeological Method and Theory* 3, 1–30.

Vila, A., Mameli, L., Terradas, X., Estévez, J., Moreno, F., Verdún, E., Briz, I., Zurro, D., Clemente, I., and Barceló, J. A. 2007. Investigaciones etnoarqueológicas en Tierra del Fuego

(1986–2006): reflexiones para la Arqueología prehistórica europea. *Trabajos de Prehistoria* 64, 37–53.

Vincent, A. S. 1985. Plant foods in savannah environments: a preliminary report of tubers eaten by the Hadza of northern Tanzania. *World Archaeology* 17, 131–47.

Wadley, L. 1997. Where have all the dead men gone? Stone Age burial practices in South Africa. In L. Wadley (ed.), *Our gendered past: archaeological studies of gender in southern Africa*, 107–33. Johannesburg: Witwatersrand University Press.

Weniger, G. C. 1992. Function and form: an ethnoarchaeological analysis of barbed points from northern hunter-gatherers. In F. Audouze (ed.), *Ethnoarchéologie: justification, problèmes, limites, XIIe recontres internationales d'archéologie et d'histoire d'Antibes*, 257–68. Juan-les-Pins: APDCA.

Whitelaw, T. M. 1994. Order without architecture: functional, social and symbolic dimensions in hunter-gatherer settlement organisation. In M. Parker Pearson and C. Richards (eds), *Architecture and order: approaches to social space*, 217–43. London: Routledge.

Wiessner, P. 1982. Beyond willow smoke and dogs' tails: a comment on Binford's analysis of hunter-gatherer settlement systems. *American Antiquity* 47, 171–8.

Wiessner, P. 1983. Style and social information in Kalahari San projectile points. *American Antiquity* 48, 253–76.

Wiessner, P. 1984. Reconsidering the behavioral basis for style: a case study among the Kalahari San. *Journal of Anthropological Archaeology* 3, 190–234.

Wiessner, P. 2002. Hunting, healing, and *hxaro* exchange: a long-term perspective on !Kung (Ju/'hoansi) large-game hunting. *Evolution and Human Behavior* 23, 407–36.

Wingfield, C. 2003. Ostrich eggshell beads and the environment, past and present. In P. Mitchell, A. Haour, and J. Hobart (eds), *Researching Africa's past: new contributions from British archaeologists*, 54–68. Oxford: Oxbow.

Wingfield, C. 2005. Historical time versus the imagination of antiquity: critical perspectives from the Kalahari. In W. James and D. Mills (eds), *The qualities of time: anthropological approaches*, 119–35. Oxford: Berg.

Wobst, M. H. 1978. The archaeo-ethnology of hunter-gatherers or the tyranny of the ethnographic record in archaeology. *American Antiquity* 43, 303–9.

Woodburn, J. 1980. Hunters and gatherers today and reconstruction of the past. In E. Gellner (ed.), *Soviet and western anthropology*, 95–117. London: Duckworth.

Woodburn, J. 1982 Egalitarian societies. *Man* 17, 431–51.

Woodburn, J. 1997. Indigenous discrimination: the ideological basis for local discrimination against hunter-gatherer minorities in sub-Saharan Africa. *Ethnic and Racial Studies* 20, 345–61.

Wylie, A. 1982. An analogy by any other name is just as analogical: a commentary on the Gould–Watson dialogue. *Journal of Anthropological Archaeology* 1, 382–401.

Wylie, A. 1985. The reaction against analogy. *Advances in Archaeological Method and Theory* 8, 63–111.

Wylie, A. 1988. 'Simple' analogy and the role of relevance assumptions: implications of archaeological practice. *International Studies in the Philosophy of Science* 2, 134–50.

Yates, R. J., Manhire, A., and Parkington, J. E. 1994. Rock painting and history in the south-western Cape. In T. A. Dowson and J. D. Lewis-Williams (eds), *Contested images: diversity in southern African rock art research*, 315–29. Johannesburg: Witwatersrand University Press.

Yellen, J. E. 1977a. *Archaeological approaches to the present*. New York: Academic Press.

Yellen, J. E. 1977b. Cultural patterning in faunal remains: evidence from the !Kung Bushmen. In D. Ingersoll, J. E. Yellen, and W. MacDonald (eds), *Experimental archaeology*, 271–331. New York: Columbia University Press.

Yellen, J. E. 1991a. Small mammals: !Kung utilization and the production of faunal assemblages. *Journal of Anthropological Archaeology* 10, 1–26.

Yellen, J. E. 1991b. Small mammals: post-discard patterning of !Kung San faunal remains. *Journal of Anthropological Archaeology* 10, 152–92.

CHAPTER 7

MAN THE HUNTER, WOMAN THE GATHERER? THE IMPACT OF GENDER STUDIES ON HUNTER-GATHERER RESEARCH (A RETROSPECTIVE)

KATHLEEN STERLING

INTRODUCTION

GENDER is an unusual category, in that whether it is dealt with directly or not dealt with at all, it appears to be one of the few universals of modern human culture. Brumbach and Jarvenpa write '...[gender] may be the oldest and most fundamental distinction shaping human experience' (Brumbach and Jarvenpa 2006, 503). If this is indeed the case, every anthropological study should address gender in a substantial way. The narratives of hunter-gatherers are a fundamental part of the narrative we have constructed of humanity, and this story has long held that women are not the innovators or drivers of progress, but bit players. This remains the popular notion, but it has changed within academia, with increasing attention paid to women's lives and activities and to the cultural construction of gender throughout time and space. This is particularly true in studies of living populations, and in archaeology where historic information is available through visual representations of sexed individuals or a significant sample of skeletal remains. Outside these situations, gender analysis requires more creativity, and many researchers have risen to the challenge. However, given the relatively low number of living hunter-gatherer societies and the comparatively small amount of material culture they leave behind, has there been as much development of gender studies within hunter-gatherer studies? It would be impossible to survey all of anthropology, but a focus on one area—the Conferences on Hunting and Gathering Studies (CHAGS)—may be a good vector to see how gender studies may or may not have made inroads into the various sub-fields of anthropology concerned with hunter-gatherer groups.

Gender Studies

Gender and feminist studies have certainly had an impact on hunter-gatherer studies, but what has the extent of that impact been? First, it would be useful to describe the goals of the practitioners of gender studies. This is not easy to do: no one person's ideas or standpoints can be taken as representative of the whole, or even of a large group of people. Any statement about the goals of gender studies would necessarily leave out points that some practitioners would consider essential. The simplest, most inclusive statement I can come up with to define gender studies for the purposes of this discussion is this: gender studies takes gender as a central part of people's identities and practices, and it thus is visible and important at all scales of culture, from the individual to larger society. No broad cultural study can thus be complete without consideration of gender. My own position is that gender should be a normal, but not normativized aspect of cultural analysis, and should be integrated rather than considered separately. This is not to say that gender should not be the *focus* of certain studies, but that gender should not *always* or nearly always be considered as a separate issue within broader analysis.

One of the most enduring debates about gender is between supporters of the view that gender roles are natural, and those who see gender as cultural. This is a somewhat simplistic picture, since few people believe that the contributions of nature versus nurture in human behaviour fall 100 per cent on one side or the other. However, gender is often conflated with sex, and differences are thus framed as natural and important in ways that other differences such as race are not. There are indeed important sex-based differences, but normative ideas of gender go far beyond these differences. The reason this matters to hunter-gatherer studies is that hunter-gatherers are seen as 'natural' people (Sterling 2011), and therefore their gender systems should reflect something that is natural about all people. This is problematic for a number of reasons. For one, there is a great deal of diversity in all aspects of hunting and gathering peoples past and present. This diversity is lost when we assume that they behave in ways that are natural, and for gender studies, what is seen as 'natural' is more likely to be what we see in our own lives. In addition, there are so few hunting and gathering groups living today, and gender was not an important category of analysis to ethnographers before the second wave of feminism began to influence anthropology. Lastly, it is very difficult to analyse gender in past groups. Early ethnographies are difficult enough (see Galloway 1992 about analysing early ethnographers), but archaeological analyses of past groups have their obvious limitations. The result is often circular, where we assume certain (modern, Western) things about gendered behaviours among hunter-gatherers because those behaviours are natural, and we then confirm the naturalness of these behaviours by finding them among hunting and gathering groups, past and present.

Whitehouse (2006) points out that much of the writing on gender in European prehistory has been in English, even when the author's first language is not English. It would not be surprising if this were the case in other parts of the world and during different time periods as well. This not only reflects the largest audience for this type of scholarship; it may also reflect something about gender in the Anglophone world. If addressing gender results in replicating Anglo-American men, women, and children in other times and places, nothing is added to our understanding of hunter-gatherer lives. The key thing to remember about gender is that it is not only about adult women, it is not always binary, and while it may exist everywhere, its manifestation is not universal.

The field of 'hunter-gatherer studies' is also not easily defined. It straddles a number of fields, primarily those that are included in the Anglo-American idea of anthropology as a discipline that includes several sub-fields. It would be impossible to investigate all of the publications that could be considered part of hunter-gatherer studies. Instead of making this attempt, I focus on the volume *Man the hunter*, on a few key publications that came as immediate reactions to this volume, and on the publications resulting from the Conferences on Hunting and Gathering Societies (CHAGS), inspired by the 'Man the Hunter' conference. The participants at these conferences include people who have identified themselves as practitioners of hunter-gatherer studies, although the conferences and the resulting publications should also not be seen as exhaustive. Because there is no one central organization in charge of CHAGS, the early programmes are not published, nor is there always a good-sized body of materials that can be identified as research resulting from these conferences. The more recent CHAGS consistently have edited volumes that are identified as resulting from the conferences. Although I have made every attempt to track down the publications from these conferences, there are certainly gaps.

Man the Hunter and Reaction

The 'Man the Hunter' conference and subsequent volume marks a good place to begin, as it marks the beginning of hunter-gatherer studies as a discrete area of study that encompasses the sub-fields of anthropology. One of the key premises of *Man the hunter* was that since over 99 per cent of human history has been spent hunting and gathering, it was essential to document this way of life as fully as possible before the last of the cultures disappear. Implicit in this premise is the idea that there are enough commonalities between these cultures beyond broader subsistence practices.

The conference occurred during the rise of second-wave feminism in the West, a movement that was primarily political and had not yet had a major impact on academia. Though the title 'Man the Hunter' was meant to be pithy and not to focus on men and only on hunting, this title demonstrated the biases of anthropology at the time: that men's activities were the most important and illustrative of a culture, and that hunting is the most important subsistence activity of these societies. The fact that a diversity of subsistence practices and other cultural practices was essentially summed up in a single word—'hunting'—that everyone understands shows the extent to which this was and is entrenched in anthropological practice. The editors explain that 'man' refers to all humans and 'hunter' is shorthand for hunting and gathering (Lee and DeVore 1968b), though throughout the volume there is very little consideration of humans who are not men, and little value given to gathering. A good example of this can be found in the second discussion section. There is a sub-section entitled 'Hunting vs. gathering as factors in subsistence', which addresses calories, technology, and ecology, and the only person to address any social factors in gathering was Lorna Marshall, who hypothesized why !Kung women do not gather more vegetable foods than they do (Lee and DeVore 1968a, 94). A quick glance at the list of participants shows that, as was the case across academia at the time, the vast majority of the participants were men. Knowledge production in anthropology, as in other fields, is socially situated. A broader range of research questions is posed when there is a broader range of researchers (Harding 1987; Longino 1990). In the discussion section that compared hunting and gathering, the only person who did not ignore the *people* engaged in these tasks was the sole woman who was participating. While it is incorrect to associate gender studies only with female researchers, the study of gender only became a priority in anthropology when female researchers entered the field in greater numbers and started studying women.

The normative approach to men's and women's roles in hunter-gatherer groups is evident throughout the volume. In Lee and DeVore's brief discussion in the introduction to the volume of the patrilocal band, which Service once proposed was the basic form for all past hunter-gatherer bands (Service 1962, 1), with other forms of band organization seen as 'artefacts of recent acculturation and breakdown' (Lee and DeVore 1968a, 7), it would be obvious to the gender-sensitive researcher today that this description of the patrilocal band was a result of writing current Western ideas of what is natural into the past. For Lee and DeVore, the lack of universality of the patrilocal band is an error outweighed by Service's highlighting the effects of contact with hunter-gatherer groups.

One section, 'Marriage and models in Australia', seems a natural place to discuss men, women, and children as social beings, though there is often a lack of recognizable people. L. R. Hiatt's chapter 'Gidjingali marriage arrangements', has a list of rules which is illustrated in various kinship charts, and a lengthy critique of Lévi-Strauss. No practices associated with marriage are described, and while Hiatt mentions in a footnote that there are sometimes conflicts between women and their families in marriage arrangements, he declines to discuss these situations (Hiatt 1968). Meggitt discusses the origins of 'marriage classes' and what this means for the potential availability of mates across Australia (Meggitt 1968), and Yengoyan adds the factors of environment and resource availability (Yengoyan 1968). Despite the title of his chapter, Rose gives little attention to initiation, and his interest is not in what goes on during male initiation, but what it means for marriageability (Rose 1968). The discussion at the end of this section focuses on models, statistics, and Lévi-Strauss.

In a great many contributions throughout the volume the authors do not use any words that make you think of actual people. The use of 'men' and 'women' is rare, but typically *sensu stricto*, unlike in the title of the volume. *Man the hunter* was not particularly misogynist; men's activities were privileged, but people seem to be little more than cogs in an ecological machine. It is clear that the concept of gender was all but unknown to the participants, and in general, the social lives of hunter-gatherers were not addressed in this volume.

Woman the Gatherer

The title *Man the hunter* at this historical moment sparked reactions. This conference and volume was not the first major anthropological work to present an unbalanced picture of humans, but it appeared at the same time as women's representation increased in anthropology and as political feminism was very visible. A few articles appeared shortly after *Man the hunter* that directly addressed the lack of women, though few of these articles challenged normative gender roles. In her 1974 article 'Woman the gatherer', Betty Hiatt uses the Lee and DeVore shorthand of 'hunting' to mean 'hunting, gathering, and fishing'. She accepts a natural, biological link between women and family that does not exist between men and family, which leads to separate sex-linked roles. Her emphasis is on the point that gathering activities are more reliable means to get food, so that in places where vegetable foods are widely available, women's economic activity is more important to the diets of hunter-gatherers. She does not question the idea that women's childbearing and child-rearing make them unsuited to hunting in the strictest sense of the word. Her definition of hunting is sometimes expansive, however, as she notes that '[i]n Tasmania, in historic times, women gathered shellfish, vegetables, small animals and seals' (Hiatt 1974, 7). While many authors' definitions of gathering will include shellfish because they do not move, and sometimes small animals for varying reasons, seals are not typically considered a gathered resource. Despite shifting the focus from 'Man the Hunter', Hiatt's article does not represent an early study of gender among hunter-gatherers.

Sally (Linton) Slocum's article 'Woman the gatherer', published in *Women in perspective: a guide for cross-cultural studies* and *Toward an anthropology of women*, and based on an earlier conference paper, addressed the androcentric bias of 'man-the-hunter'-focused models of human evolution by turning them on their heads. Beyond merely pointing out male bias, she rewrites the then-common narrative of human evolution as driven by men's hunting activities as instead driven by women's gathering activities. She presents this tongue-in-cheek alternative not as a better story, but as an equally plausible one that points out the inadequacies of any model of the human past that leaves out more than half of humanity (Slocum 1977).

At about the same time (1974), the faculty at Colorado Women's College proposed a course on contemporary hunter-gatherers. After considering calling the course 'Man the Hunter', Sally Geis, the chair at the time, suggested thinking about what women did while men hunted. A review of the literature found very few publications that addressed this directly. Frances Dahlberg edited a volume called *Woman the gatherer*, consisting of six papers that were inspired by the course, by *Man the hunter*, by Slocum's 'Woman the gatherer', and by other feminist-inspired anthropology of the late 1970s. This volume is in the same spirit as most feminist anthropology of this time: the papers point out androcentric bias in studies of human evolution, primatology, and contemporary hunter-gatherer studies, and they look for the missing females in these fields. The focus is on women's contributions to society, and the conception of women is still fairly essentialized, even as Dahlberg points out that contemporary concepts of the sexes cannot be applied to the past (Dahlberg 1981). Like much of the scholarship of this period that addresses sex roles and focuses on women's contributions, this volume contains no papers that investigate *gender* as we now conceive of it. This is still very much the corrective phase of feminist anthropology, pointing out androcentric bias and seeking the 'missing women'.

Tanner and Zihlman also wrote a paper in the corrective mode, placing gathering of plant foods at the centre of hominin evolution, extending Slocum's argument. Their premise, following Washburn and Lancaster, is that subsistence patterns were interrelated with social patterns. Thus, starting from the premise that hunting evolved first and drove human evolution leads to very different conclusions about *Australopithecus* than Tanner and Zihlman's premise, that gathering evolved first. Tanner and Zihlman looked at early hominid dentition, faunal remains, ethnographic data, and chimpanzee behaviour to conclude that gathered plant foods were the primary source of nutrition for early hominins, and they discuss what types of simple, mostly perishable tools may have aided Australopithecines in gathering. Certain assumptions about male and female behaviour are taken as natural, such as that males would not care for young. They end their paper with a warning against looking at contemporary societies, particularly Western societies, to understand what is natural for humans (Tanner and Zihlman 1976).

Feminist Inspiration

The late 1970s marks the beginning of feminist anthropology. Women's political movements in the West were strong, and many women looked to anthropology seeking the origins of women's lower status (Reiter 1975a). However, the anthropological literature could not provide answers. Women's tasks were considered inaccessible in the archaeological/palaeoanthropological record or to male ethnographers, and their roles were considered connected to their reproductive capacities (or limitations). An increasing number of publications focused on not only critiquing male bias in anthropology, but developing research on women and female primates. It is in these publications, such as *Toward an anthropology of women* (Reiter 1975b) that questions of *gender*, although only women's gender, are first investigated. Archaeology, notably, was much later than the other sub-fields of anthropology in developing feminist approaches and theorizing about gender (Conkey and Spector 1984).

In a paper that was originally presented at both the American Anthropological Association meetings in 1975 and CHAGS in 1978, Collier and Rosaldo (1981) investigated gender through societal structures, and particularly among hunter-gatherers and gardeners. Comparing such groups from all over the world, they write 'themes of motherhood and sexual reproduction are far less central to such peoples' conceptions of "woman" than we had assumed' (Collier and Rosalso 1981, 276). They also note '... Man the Hunter, which we thought to be *our* myth, turned out to characterize *their* conception of maleness' (Collier and Rosalso 1981, 275). In other words, while we tend to focus on women when we think of gender, in these cases, it is the construction of men's identities that was emphasized in the societies Collier and Rosaldo looked at. Also, where we tend to juxtapose binaries, they found no particular opposite or complementary role to 'Man the Hunter', nor were 'men' associated with 'culture' and 'women' with 'nature', nor any of the other structuralist categories commonly used at the time. They noted that hunter-gatherers have been used as models of what is natural for human behaviour, and that feminists have hoped to find evidence for a natural egalitarianism, while others find the universality of male dominance. Their approach to inequality among these groups was to look at ritualized ideas and behaviours, their place in everyday social relations, and how this leads to differences in status. Collier and Rosaldo found that marriage was the best entry point for the analysis of gender in non-class societies. Marriage was connected to social relations throughout the group, food sharing, autonomy or lack thereof, and politics—obligations. They find that with a few exceptions, women gain new duties and lose status and personal freedom, while men see very little change in their duties and they gain greater social status upon marriage. Men's greater need for marriage leads to developing ways to reduce this power that women might otherwise have or the conflicts that might arise. This need of marriage is to have someone to provide them and their families with food, since the food they hunt is shared among the group; this provider is also the means by which men become adults. Marriage makes men independent, though obliged to in-laws, but provides fewer benefits to women (Collier and Rosalso 1981).

'Archaeology and the study of gender' (Conkey and Spector 1984) was a groundbreaking paper in archaeology, and marks the beginning of serious consideration of gender in archaeological scholarship. Conkey and Spector note that the literature is 'permeated with assumptions, assertions, and purported statements of "fact" about gender' (Conkey and Spector 1984, 2), although gender was not considered a topic of analysis. While there were a few publications that preceded Conkey and Spector, this article is probably the earliest attempt by archaeologists, one of whom specializes in prehistoric hunter-gatherers, to think seriously about gender in archaeologically known groups.

Conferences on Hunting and Gathering Societies (CHAGS)

CHAGS I and II

The first CHAGS was held in 1978 in Paris, to commemorate the tenth anniversary of *Man the hunter*. Another conference followed in Quebec in 1980, and this conference involved scholars from hunter-gatherer groups. These conferences were open to anyone who could get to them (Lee and Daly 2004). There is no central administration of CHAGS; nonetheless, conferences were held around the world except in Africa every two to five years until 2002, and with the exception of the Quebec conference, edited volumes are available.

Eleanor Leacock and Richard Lee edited *Politics and history in band societies* shortly after the first CHAGS (Leacock and Lee 1982b). Given the title of the volume and Leacock's renown as a feminist anthropologist, we can expect that gender should appear in at least some of the contributions. In their introduction, Leacock and Lee mention relations between the sexes and the concept of 'human nature' in the very first pages, then praise *Man the hunter* while noting that the title 'Woman the Gatherer' would have been equally accurate (Leacock and Lee 1982a, 2–3).

The volume is divided into three parts. In the first part, 'Dynamics of egalitarian foraging societies', a few authors address differences between men, women, and children. While most chapters have no explicit discussion of gender, the authors do use inclusive pronouns, which is a departure from earlier anthropological writing and evidence that the authors were aware of the feminist critiques of anthropology. The contributions also point out the complications and the outliers rather than trying to shoehorn them into their hypotheses. This may be in part due to the fact that all of the authors are writing about living or recent groups, not archaeological ones. The feminist critique of anthropology had not reached archaeology at this point, and the post-processual critique was just beginning. It is unlikely that at this point an archaeologist would have participated in a volume titled *Politics and history in band societies*.

Lee's contribution, 'Politics, sexual and non-sexual, in an egalitarian society', makes clear through the title that gender will not disappear. Lee looks at the degree of equality between !Kung men and women, how they reconcile leadership with egalitarianism, and connections between economics and politics. He creates a complicated picture of the people he knew, where rules seem to be suggestions rather than constraints. There is still no analysis of gender, however. While the men and women he presents are individuals, Lee still presents limited ways of being men and women (Lee 1982). In another contribution, Hamilton critiques the ways in which Western researchers have considered Aboriginal connections to land and divisions between economic and ritual life. Her conclusion is that patrilineality and patrilocality is not the norm it has been assumed to be, though again, gender is not an explicit area of analysis (Hamilton 1982). Turnbull's chapter, 'The ritualization of potential conflict between the sexes among the Mbuti', looks at ways in which adults defuse possible violence and how children imitate and elaborate on the conflict they witness. Sexuality plays a prominent role, and this sexuality is not necessarily reproductive or indeed heterosexual. Turnbull also addresses the ways in which children learn to behave as adults through observation and instruction, which is gendered. By looking at how identity is transformed through life and what men and women can, may, and may not do, Turnbull's contribution addresses gender in a similar way as researchers do today, even if he does not use the word 'gender' (Turnbull 1982).

In the other two parts, 'Forager–farmer relations' and 'Contemporary political struggles', gender is not a major component of the analysis, although it is not ignored. Many of the chapters in these sections describe a wide variety of aspects of identity and interactions between people, including gender, race, ethnicity, class, and how they relate to different groups' impact on one another. In short pieces, there is little room to analyse all of these aspects, and though some aspects get little attention, they are still included. The exception is Leacock's chapter, 'Relations of production in band society', the only contribution that actually uses the word 'gender'. Leacock discusses a number of cases in which relations between men and women changed quickly and drastically upon contact with Europeans (Leacock 1982). The focus on the fluidity of roles and interactions, the fact that these things can change with time and circumstance, is what separates 'gender' from 'sex'.

CHAGS III

CHAGS III was held in Bad Homberg, Germany, in 1983 as a small gathering of invited scholars. This conference was centred on the theme of sociology and land use among hunter-gatherers. The resulting volume is *Past and present in hunter-gatherer studies*, edited by Carmel Schrire (1984a). Six of the chapters in the book are from conference participants, and three were invited to contribute after. At this point in hunter-gatherer studies it seems unlikely that anyone could ignore women, even if gender is not yet being widely problematized. Nevertheless, Schrire and others often use 'men' to mean 'people'; but Schrire addresses the stereotypes of hunter-gatherer life and the harm they do, and many of these stereotypes are of women's and girls' value (Schrire 1984b). Jones specifically writes about the tools men and women use for subsistence activities (Jones 1984), and Gordon makes mention of violent interactions between the !Kung and others, often following 'interfering with Bushmen women' (Gordon 1984, 203). Lewis-Williams discusses sexual division of labour among the San, particularly among medicine people, though he also notes that men's and women's work is cooperative in both symbolic and daily labour (Lewis-Williams 1984). Griffin writes about the Agta of the Philippines, a group that is well known for women's hunting. Griffin describes the similarities and differences between men's and women's hunting, and describes the environment and technologies used, but avoids discussion of the fact that women regularly hunt in this group (Griffin 1984). It seems like a missed opportunity to analyse why this group behaves in a way that seems to be unique among living hunter-gatherers. In the other contributions, gender is not explicitly addressed, but these are not necessarily androcentric chapters either. Many of the authors take a critical approach to hunter-gatherer studies, which hints at a 'climate' that would allow for the analysis of gender, even if that does not happen here. One difference between this volume and the one edited by Leacock and Lee is that Schrire's volume mixes different sub-fields of anthropology, just before archaeology begins to engage with gender following Conkey and Spector's groundbreaking article.

CHAGS IV

CHAGS IV was held in London in 1986, and was again open to all who wished to and could afford to participate (Lee and Daly 2004). The resulting volumes, *Hunters and gatherers, volume I: history, evolution and social change* (Ingold et al. 1988a) and *Hunters and gatherers, volume II: property, power and ideology* (Ingold et al. 1988b) are a selection of the seventy-four papers presented at the conference (Ingold 1988). The titles indicate a high degree of critical and political engagement, some of which extends to gender studies. Volume I primarily focuses on histories of hunter-gatherer groups. These histories are heavily descriptive rather than analytical, filling in details of peoples who are often seen as timeless. Marriage is occasionally described, and in most papers adult men and women are the key actors, with the very young and very old playing smaller roles. A few chapters explicitly address gender: Gardner has a section in his contribution about gender relations and husband–wife relations. In particular, Paliyan have quite different ideas of proper behaviour for women than the Tamils with whom they interact, and they are subject to pressures to change (Gardner 1988). This section is separate from other sections in the paper that address marriage and remarriage. Sandbukt's chapter contains the word 'gender' in the title. About half the chapter discusses what females and children must avoid, and how males have power over their lives and labour. These strict rules exist more as ideology than practice, and the reality of people's lives is quite variable (Sandbukt 1988). In the end, a pattern emerges. Like previous edited volumes resulting from CHAGS, the researchers working with living or recent hunter-gatherers are the most likely to address gender. This volume is focused on history, and the deeper in time the author investigates, the less likely he or she is to consider gender, though the language typically remains inclusive. The exception is the palaeoanthropological article, which uses 'man' to refer to people except when discussing sexual dimorphism (Foley 1988). While feminism and gender studies in anthropology were no longer restricted to socio-cultural anthropology at the time of this conference, it remained difficult for researchers to address gender in the deep past. The second volume follows the same pattern. The section called 'Equality and domination' (Sharp 1988) is primarily composed of ethnographic accounts, and these articles pay attention to gender. One chapter has the word 'gender' in the title (Cooper 1990)—again an ethnographic account. Many of the chapters touch on gender, even if only briefly, but all of the contributions are ethnographic.

CHAGS V

CHAGS V, held in Darwin, Australia, in 1988 addressed development, cultural identity and political processes, changing social and economic inequality in the present, and the place of hunters and gatherers in Western thought and anthropology, and the volume that collects the papers on prehistoric demography (Keen and Yamada 2001a, 1) addresses demography in the most narrow sense, almost to the exclusion of the other themes of the conference. There are only the briefest mentions of fertility and birth spacing (Shnirelman 2001) and marriage. Only one paper mentions men's and women's economic roles (Burch and Ellanna 1994b), though without any analysis. All of the studies in this volume employ either the direct historical approach or ethnographic analogy for archaeological data, or they are ethnographic studies themselves. This makes the lack of discussion of gender in demographic processes all the more curious, and this is a dramatic departure from earlier CHAGS publications.

The other volume published from this conference comes from a session called 'Emergent social and economic inequalities among contemporary hunters and gatherers', and was published in a volume called *Emergent inequalities in Aboriginal Australia*. There is a good deal of variation in how the authors address or ignore gender. Keen writes that women's lack of power is due to patrilocality, but that this is something that changes as women age. However, various societal structures maintain women's inferior position in governance, limiting their power to their own reproduction and certain domestic affairs. In Kolig's contribution, he deliberately avoids extensive discussion of gender, which he sees as tangential to his discussion of power, and as concerning only women: '... one would have to say, that women if they are to be exchanged between clans, as seems to have traditionally been the case, cannot have the same powers as those who control the exchange. However, I do not wish to enter into a detailed debate on the traditional or post-contact gender situation with regard to power. Doing so would lead us too far from our main theme' (Kolig 1989, 64). Burbank and Chisholm discuss changes in family structure that have implications for gender relations and maternal and child health. They note that 'the emergence of greater socio-sexual equality between older and younger south-east Arnhem Land men has, paradoxically, contributed to the emergence of a new inequality between older and younger women, or married and unmarried women and their children' (Burbank and Chisholm 1989, 85). Julie Finlayson looks at the effects of the disproportionate Aboriginal reliance on welfare as compared to European-descended populations and how government policies relating to who gets paid what has led to changes in gender relations. This has happened because unemployed men move to the domestic sphere, which has not traditionally been their place, while women receiving cash benefits are less economically dependent on men and simultaneously have more claims made upon them by men through the appropriation of their payments and their labour. Overall, this volume has a great diversity of authors' opinions on the importance of gender when looking at inequality, though most give at least some attention to the subject.

CHAGS VI

CHAGS VI, held in Fairbanks, Alaska, in 1990 resulted in the edited volume *Key issues in hunter-gatherer research* (Burch and Ellanna 1994a). This was the first CHAGS held after the fall of the Soviet Union, and thus was the first with a considerable contingent from Russia. As the title suggests, key issues are identified and addressed. The very first of these issues is gender, marking the first appearance of gender as a separate, important section within a CHAGS publication. Two chapters and an editorial comprise this section; most sections comprise two or three chapters and an editorial, indicating that this subject was given equal weight with others, though some sections contain more or fewer papers. The editors point out two areas they do not include in this volume: revisionism and optimal foraging theory. They explain that these debates are very active and resulting in many publications, and so there is little reason for them to devote space to these issues. The implication is that the editors view the subjects they *did* include as important, but understudied. The brief editorial introducing the gender section illustrates some interesting issues in thinking about gender among hunter-gatherers. The editors decry the historical emphasis on hunting to the detriment of gathering, and point out a number of publications that demonstrate the importance in caloric terms of women's gathering activities. Immediately after that, the authors point out cases of women hunting and fishing, with men's gathering activities relegated to a parenthetical comment, in a way that continues to valorize hunting as the more prestigious activity. They do, however, make an essential point at the end of the editorial: '…gender issues are only analytically distinct from many other issues. One cannot really make sense of the division of labour along gender lines in a given society without reference to the allocation of power and responsibility, ritual, symbolism, communication, and emotional expression. The straightforward focus of many early gender studies on the amount of time males and females spent in different activities is no longer sufficient' (Burch and Ellana 1994b, 13). They emphasize the necessity of integrating gender into wider analysis, even if their conception of gender is presented in terms of differences between adult women's and men's lives.

The two research articles in this section are ethnographic. The articles focus on very different people who live gender in different ways, but what they have in common is that both describe the ideology of gender and the ways in which daily practice coincides with, conflicts with, and reinforces these ideologies. Women's exercise of power is also key here, and the two articles illustrate very different kinds of power for women. Both chapters focus on the interactions between adult men and women, though Sharp's chapter includes some Chipewyan opinion of children and the elderly, who are seen as dependants, and the ways in which women are often equated with these groups. Sharp also situates his theoretical approach within the broader issues of gender and politics in North American cultures (Sharp 1994).

Outside the gender section of this volume, the papers achieve variable success in integrating gender into their analyses. Gender is rarely seen at an intersection with other issues such as territory, place, or government intervention. Women are not ignored, but by this point the study of gender has progressed well beyond merely including women. Again, archaeological research has less discussion of gender, even though there are cases in which multiple burials are available (e.g. Andrews 1994; Yesner 1994) and this is one of the areas of archaeology where gender is typically seen as being more 'accessible'. Another contribution (Jones et al. 1994), a comparison of ethnographies that focuses on children's food production work and the reproductive advantages this work can bring to their mothers, discusses men, women, boys, and girls, but still manages largely to avoid discussing gender. Gender reappears in the section on culture contact, most notably in Mearns's (1994) chapter about Aboriginal women's responsibilities to continue traditions in a changing world. Mearns discusses change and continuity in the Dreaming in the Northern Territory in Australia, with particular attention to the ways in which interaction with Australian authorities led to threats to women's sacred sites in the interests of protecting men's ritual business. Women had to negotiate both the gender norms of their culture with those of the state (Schweitzer et al. 2000). Overall, gender gets more attention in this volume than in previous CHAGS publications, though that attention is primarily ethnographic.

The volume ends with a section addressing future directions for hunter-gatherer research. There is some attention to *topics* of future research, but most attention is given to *how* that research may be conducted. The future of modern hunter-gatherers and their descendants is in question. In terms of the topics suggested, they are primarily present-oriented—relations between hunter-gatherers and states, land and resource use, and social relations. Neither archaeological, historical, linguistic, nor biomedical approaches are suggested by the contributors here. These proscriptions will certainly allow for analysis of gender, though in limited aspects of hunter-gatherer studies.

CHAGS VII

CHAGS VII was held in Moscow in 1993. *Hunters and gatherers in the modern world* resulted, though the editors of this volume make no mention of any other publications that may have resulted, for example from their Russian colleagues who convened the conference, or presenters who did not address the situation of modern hunter-gatherer peoples. The dominant theme of the volume is struggle. That struggle is manifested and revealed in different ways, but there is an air of doom here. The other notable commonality is a sense of excitement at engagement with Russian anthropologists and their (mostly) Siberian case studies.

There are five sections of the volume, one of which is called 'Gender and representation'. Although the other sections address areas in which gender could potentially be analysed, the attention to gender outside the section specifically designated for it is often quite minimal, if present. The chapter about interpersonal violence (Goulet 2000), often under the influence of alcohol, gives the impression that women do not get drunk and involved in violence as often as men, though this is not expressly stated. The focus is on men, and women and children appear on the side. The author could have taken the opportunity to investigate men's gender, an approach we have not yet seen through the CHAGS publications. Chindina (2000) identifies potentially interesting ethnic differences between men's and women's graves in Bronze Age cemeteries in south-western Siberia, though there is no further analysis. Batianova discusses ritual violence in two groups in Siberia. Most of what she discusses is murder and suicide (often achieved by asking someone to kill him or her), though she also touches on infanticide and euthanasia. Most of this violence is deadly violence, or potentially so. The last part of her chapter addresses violence against women, including abduction for marriage, intense games between the sexes, and rape (although Batianova does not use this word). All of these forms of violence arise in predictable situations and the reactions are also predictable (Batianova 2000). Kim writes about Sel'kup world view, where gender plays a role in some aspects. She discusses the idea of male souls, how deficiency in the 'male source' is thought to result in defective people or women, and the connection to certain animals (Kim 2000).

The section on gender and representation has five articles, about the same number as the other sections. In 'Gender role transformation among Australian Aborigines', Tonkinson

(2000) begins not by describing the changes in gender roles, but in anthropology's ideas about these roles among Australian Aborigines. He next moves to the problem of reconstructing gender roles before European contact while relying on oral histories and colonial accounts that ignored women as unimportant; but more importantly, the ways in which Westerners typically think about gender roles as connected to structures of dominance obscures features such as complementarity. A major problem for anthropologists is how to account for what appears to be high degrees of female autonomy coexisting with high levels of inequality between the sexes that heavily favours men. Tonkinson also points out that most scholars interested in gender in Aboriginal society have been women, though the conclusions they have drawn have been quite different, including relative equality, complete male domination, and separate spheres. There are also intersections that relate to power, such as age and context. These and other factors are important both before and after European contact, though the results are quite different. Post-contact, Aboriginal women were more likely to adopt European lifestyles than men, perhaps because women found a wider range of possibilities while men found more restrictions. Women often acted as intermediaries between Europeans and other Aborigines, giving them a level of power that did not exist before. Women were not just given power by Europeans; they argued for it, at times in ways that could be considered deceptive. Tonkinson primarily discusses changes in women's roles, but he also addresses changes for men. It was still rare at this point to think about the fact that men have gender too, and Tonkinson's chapter is wonderfully complex.

Federova writes about women's tasks in Mansi society, particularly in subsistence activities. While she does note that these roles can vary from family to family, this is more about the presence or absence of men than any tension between ideology and practice. Federova's chapter is more like some of the early works that resulted from the feminist critique of anthropology, describing women's and to a lesser extent children's lives, but not analysing gender (Fedorova 2000). Staniukovich looks at oral literature, in particular an epic about a female peacemaker. It is a story that has been described by Western publishers as a piece of entertainment that was not part of traditional belief systems, but Staniukovich finds this to be untrue. She finds that as a general rule, women's epics emphasize peace and men's epics emphasize violence and vengeance. However, these epics are often complementary, telling two sides of the same story that often end with peace prevailing (Staniukovich 2000).

Not all of the papers in 'Gender and representation' address gender, and not all of the papers on gender presented at the conference are included in this volume. One of the published contributions addresses the ideology and power of naming, as done by Bushmen and by Europeans (naming Bushmen: Widlok 2000). Another looks at government and foreign NGO attempts to move the Baka to a sedentary life (Hewlett 2000). These are very interesting articles, but it means that there are in fact only two articles that focus on gender in the volume, while a quick glance at the table of contents gives the impression that gender occupies roughly equal space with other concerns. Among the unpublished papers for which I was only able to find titles were presentations called 'Is self-determination a gendered concept?', presented by Diane Bell, 'Women's life histories from northern Canada: explaining new changes with old stories', presented by Julie Cruikshank, 'The choice of widowhood among Walpiri women', presented by Françoise Dussart, 'Redefining place: Aboriginal women and change', presented by Mary Edmunds, and 'Land-use rights of Ojibwa-Cree women', presented by Krystyna Sieciechowicz. These papers were part of a session called 'Gender in hunter-gatherer societies in a changing and contemporary world', of which only

Mearns's contribution was published. There was another gender symposium, 'Economic, political and ideological dimensions of gender', for which I was unable to find a list of participants or titles (University of Alaska Fairbanks 1990).

CHAGS VIII

CHAGS VIII, held in Osaka, Japan, in 1998 had one of the twenty-one sessions devoted to gender. Papers from this session, titled 'Gender and the dynamics of culture', were published together with sessions titled 'Ethnicity, church and state' and 'Identity, transformation and performance' in a volume titled *Identity and gender in hunting and gathering societies* (Keen and Yamada 2001b). The volume is divided into two parts: Part I, 'Changing identity in post-foraging societies', combines the papers from 'Ethnicity, church and state' and 'Identity, transformation and performance'; Part II is 'Gender and the dynamics of culture'. In their general introduction, Keen and Yamada note that '[w]hile the two parts are discrete, there are connecting themes... Part I focuses on questions of identity in the context of relations with the state and the wider society, including the effects of assimilationist policies, symbols of identity, indigenous and anthropological constructions of identity' (Yamada 2001, 238).

One of the lessons of gender studies is that gender is an integral part of culture, and particularly of identity. Yet the authors in Part I choose not to address gender, despite several obvious openings. In the section of Part I called 'Performance, symbols and narrative styles' Hiwasaki points to the fact that the concept of identity as performance comes from Judith Butler (Hiwasaki 2001), who was writing specifically about gender. Only Shnirelman, in his paper about Tlingit acculturation, touches on the subject of gender, and he does this outside of a section dedicated to marriage and adoption (which, strangely, does not discuss gender at all). He does not attempt any in-depth analysis, simply noting that certain roles have changed in recent years, with women taking on teaching and craft production that was traditionally the realm of men (Shnirelman 2001).

The title of Inoue's article begins 'Hunting as a symbol of cultural tradition', and the very first sentence starts 'This chapter focuses on the cultural aspects of hunting, trapping, fishing and gathering activities...' (Inoue 2001, 89), which repeats the now quite old elision used in *Man the hunter* to refer to a range of subsistence activities. Hunting is indeed the focus here, although there is mention of traditional craftwork, particularly traditional clothing, as well as food-sharing. The perception of these practices among the Gwich'in is contrasted with Western practices, but there is no discussion of gender despite the fact that this is one of the areas in which gender typically gets attention in hunter-gatherer studies.

In Part II, the section specifically devoted to gender, it is not always clear that the papers address their topics through the lens of gender studies. In one case, for example, it seems that a paper was part of this session and this part of the volume because it addresses marriage, reproduction, and extra-marital sex. Imamura's paper discusses relations between men, women, and children, but it is focused on heterosexual relationships in and around marriage, and the word 'sex' could accurately have been used in place of 'gender' (Imamura 2001). In contrast, Quraishy's contribution addresses evolving gender relations and increasing inequality between men and women as the Alu Kurumba foragers moved from hunting and gathering to broader subsistence strategies that included earlier strategies as well as agriculture and wage labour. Considering different examples of gendered division of labour, Quraishy concludes that market economies lead to high levels of inequality. Even when the division of labour is strict and the work done by one sex is valued more than that done by the other (typically, men's hunting being most highly valued), inequality remains low (Quraishy 2001). Venkateswar also looks at gender among hunter-gatherer groups in India, addressing the effects of colonialism, first by the British, then by India. She studies two groups and, refreshingly, she addresses her own gender and ethnic presentation, and what it means for her relationships with the people she interviews. For one group, the Onge, Venkateswar describes how women are actively resisting deliberate efforts by the Indian state, often with the complicity of Onge men, to subordinate women as part of a campaign of acculturation. She is made very aware of her outsider status by the women, when she expected to find greater cooperation due to their shared gender. Among the Andamanese, the same gender and ethnic presentation provokes a much more sympathetic response than Venkateswar received among the Onge. In this case, being an outsider means that she will not judge their behaviour the way other Indian women might. Venkateswar presents a very complicated picture of gender relations that explicitly draws on a broad range of feminist anthropological approaches (Venkateswar 2001, 28). Fedorova addresses etiquette among the Mansi, a Siberian ethnic group. The rules of etiquette for women mostly concern married women of childbearing age; and most women are basically autonomous and have been historically, in terms of providing for themselves and their children. In this case, women's gender evolves with age, with prepubescent girls and older women able to do certain things that other women may not. Many of the taboos related to women were rarely observed during the Soviet period, especially in more densely-populated areas. Federova describes the etiquette that women must obey, but there is no analysis of it, little discussion of how culture-contact impacted on these taboos, and there is practically no mention of men's gendered behaviour (Fedorova 2001).

Lastly, Yamada opens her discussion of gender among the Ainu with a brief discussion of the critique of the assumption of the universality of the gendered division of labour, pointing out that the idea of binary gender roles cannot even be supported by the supposed binary existence of sex. Yet, despite her critique of the modern industrialized anthropologist's view of gender, it appears that the Ainu express their ideas about gender in ways that sound very familiar. Male deities hunt and build, female deities embroider and serve food. Yamada weaves her discussion of gender into a broader discussion of Ainu cultural-revitalization movements, in terms of reclaiming and transmitting traditional language and rituals. Yamada has put gender squarely where it belongs—as an inseparable part of daily life, practised, interpreted, and observed in every aspect of behaviour. She also notes that women have expressed more interest and pride in their Ainu identity, while men have been more content to identify themselves as Japanese. Older women have been the repositories of much of the knowledge about Ainu culture, and it has increased their importance as younger women in particular want to learn about Ainu culture. The traditional gender roles of the Ainu give women greater power and autonomy, yet they take nothing from men (Yamada 2001).

Very few of the other publications from CHAGS VIII address gender. Anderson and Ikeya's volume (2001), *Parks, property, and power: managing hunting practice and identity within state policy regimes,* has very little mention of women and children and no analysis of gender, which is unsurprising since the primary subjects are hunting and mining, activities not typically associated with women and children. It bears repeating that gender is not only about women, but it seems to be the case that when women are not a primary subject gender is more easily ignored. *Social economy of modern hunter-gatherers* focuses mostly on hunting and meat-sharing, although vegetable foods are mentioned, so women's tasks in preparation of tools and processing of animals is a frequently discussed subject, but there is little analysis of gender beyond comparing tasks (Wenzel et al. 2000). The volume titled *Self- and other-images of hunter-gatherers* has a few articles that address gender. Most have just brief mention of gender, but Kaare's (2002) contribution goes extensively into the subject. Kaare writes, 'Akie metaphors of kinship and gender are key to our understanding of the broader context of their understanding of their cosmology and central ideas about fertility, social (re)production, procreation and the continuity of meaningful life' (Kaare 2002, 28). Kaare describes how the Akie believe gender roles and subsistence activities were chosen in the past and their importance to daily life and interaction with their neighbours. Symbolism is everywhere in the world, and everyday objects have meaning connected to gender and kinship. This is the only paper outside of the gender session/volume that takes gender as a central part of its analysis.

The session convened by Habu et al. was held in Aomori, the location of the Jomon site Sannai Muryama, before the main sessions in Osaka (Habu 2003). The rare mention of gender is found in Hudson's paper discussing fetishism of foragers, where he notes that women played an important role in the 'let's all meet at Sannai Muryama' event, but that he does not have the space to go into the rather important aspects of gender, which he recognizes as needing a 'sophisticated' analysis. He does write a bit about women and matriarchical versus patriarchical societies, and that the importance of women in these events is not 'an extreme feminism', but a way to link to a past that is imagined as being matriarchal. However, this article is not about hunter-gatherers but about how modern Japanese feel about them (Hudson 2003).

CHAGS IX

CHAGS IX was the last CHAGS (so far), held in Edinburgh in 2002. One session, 'Hunting and gathering as a theme in the history of anthropology', resulted in the volume *Hunter-gatherers in history, archaeology and anthropology* (Barnard 2004b). The articles in this book mostly look at the study of hunter-gatherers; some authors look at the histories of the study of hunter-gatherers in general (e.g. Barnard 2004a; Pluciennik 2004; Yengoyan 2004); others describe the histories of research by scholars of different nationalities (e.g. Artemova 2004; Ichikawa 2004; Ingold 2004; Schweitzer 2004); and reinterpreting hunter-gatherer archaeology, anthropology, and history of the hunter-gatherer studies (e.g. Lane and Schadla-Hall 2004; Myers 2004). There is, however, almost no discussion of gender, although the gender of practitioners and the use of theories of gender have both been important to the evolution of hunter-gatherer studies.

The other volume published from this conference was Hewlett and Lamb's (2005b) *Hunter-gatherer childhoods: evolutionary, developmental and cultural perspectives*. Most, but not all of the participants were young scholars themselves. Given the main title, one might expect that gender would be an integral part of many, if not all, of the papers. In fact, the subtitle is more telling. All of the papers use ethnographic data; evolutionary approaches are the most common and focus on how adults and children 'try to enhance their reproductive fitness (i.e. adaptation) in particular social, ecological, and demographic settings' (Hewlett and Lamb 2005a, 11). All of the papers use developmental approaches as well, which the editors describe as analysis that is age-specific, and cultural approaches emphasize children's points of view. This is the volume that brings together more biological anthropologists than all of the previous CHAGS publications, and it happens to be the one that is least concerned with issues of gender. The editors rightly observe that childhood has been an ignored aspect of hunter-gatherer studies (Hewlett and Lamb 2005a), much as gender was. Every author talks specifically about mothers, fathers, children, sex, etc., but in a way that implies that various practices exist primarily because they are adaptive. Those who take 'culturalist' approaches are the exception. Bird-David suggests several reasons why the history of hunter-gatherer studies would make scholars uneasy studying children. She also notes that childhood is not a clearly defined state, but juxtaposes 'child' and 'adult'. Children are considered as a single category, but when they become adults they are men and women (Bird-David 2005). Bonnie Hewlett looks at expressions of grief among older children, and finds that among other factors, there are gendered aspects to that expression. Ngandu men are not supposed to cry—only women and children may—although men insisted that their grief was equal to women's. For a male child to remain stoical is to appear more like a man. This is not at all the case for the Aka, though prolonged crying is discouraged as it may cause sickness. Hewlett also investigated how many deaths the children remembered, and found that they remembered more male deaths than female deaths, and male deaths caused more grief (B. L. Hewlett 2005). Kamei looks at Baka children's play, noting that the gendered division of labour observed among adults is reflected in some of the games that children play, although there are a lot of activities in which both boys and girls participate equally (Kamei 2005). Given that childhood is a time of socialization and not just physical and mental development, it must be a time during which children learn to be adults of a certain gender. I find it puzzling that so many of the issues surrounding childhood, such as learning and socialization, sex, marriage, family life, etc. are gendered experiences, yet there is very little attention to this aspect of gender in this volume with the exception of Kamei's work.

Conclusions

Looking at the publications from CHAGS, there can be no doubt that gender studies has had an impact on hunter-gatherer studies, but that impact has been uneven. In socio-cultural anthropology, the feminist critique began at about the same time as the publication of *Man the hunter*, and the reaction was swift and cutting. Since the publication of *Man the hunter*, there has been an increase in scholarly attention to gender in hunter-gatherer studies, particularly in ethnographic work, and this increase happened early and quickly. Other subfields of anthropology were much slower to address gender, and there still appears to be a lot of ground to be made up. It may be the case that archaeologists and biological anthropologists who study gender among hunter-gatherers are not the same scholars who participate in CHAGS, but there is no evidence for this, nor any clear reason why this would be so. Since the last CHAGS was held in 2002, no doubt we would see an increase across sub-fields of attention to gender were another conference held today. Beyond the CHAGS publications, archaeologists have published a number of works addressing gender and hunter-gatherer groups, some of which are book-length, such as Owen's (2005) *Distorting the past*, which combines ethnographic and archaeological evidence of the late Upper Palaeolithic in Germany, and Adovasio, Soffer, and Page's (2007) *The invisible sex*, which addresses women in both Old World and North American early prehistory. As the dates of these publications indicate, hunter-gatherer archaeology has lagged in terms of addressing gender, but these and other publications indicate that rapid progress is being made, progress that will probably continue.

If hunter-gatherer studies continue to change in similar ways to the rest of anthropology, in the future we should expect to see increasing attention to men's (e.g. Mansur and Piqué 2007) and children's genders, third (or fourth, fifth, etc.) genders, sexuality, the use of queer theories (e.g. Cobb 2005), and intersectionalities between gender studies and other areas of social theory. Theories of agency and attention to the body (e.g. Sneider 2012) as a unit of analysis also have great potential to contribute to the study of gender among hunter-gatherers. Ethnoarchaeological studies, such as Jarvenpa and Brumbach's (2006) *Circumpolar lives and livelihood,* are another example of a direction in which future archaeological contributions may go. Gender may continue to be treated in separate sections of publications, or even in separate books, but hunter-gatherer studies, like the rest of anthropology, have reached a point where it is increasingly difficult to ignore gender. Since we still have difficulty separating hunter-gatherer cultures from an idea of 'natural' humans, the study of gender and related topics in hunter-gatherer groups will have an impact that reaches well beyond these groups.

Acknowledgements

I would like to thank the editors for inviting me to contribute to this volume, and Meg Conkey and an anonymous reviewer for suggestions. Any mistakes remain mine.

References

Adovasio, J. M., Soffer, O., and Page, J. 2007. *The invisible sex: uncovering the true roles of women in prehistory*. Washington, DC: Smithsonian Institution.

Anderson, D. G. and Ikeya, K. 2001. *Parks, property, and power: managing hunting practice and identity within state policy regimes: papers presented at the Eighth International Conference on Hunting and Gathering Societies (CHAGS 8), National Museum of Ethnology, Osaka, October 1998*. Osaka: National Museum of Ethnology.

Andrews, E. F. 1994. Territoriality and land use among the *Akulmiut* of Western Alaska. In E. S. Burch and L. J. Ellanna (eds), *Key issues in hunter-gatherer research*, 65–93. Oxford: Berg.

Artemova, O. Y. 2004. Hunter-gatherer studies in Russia and the Soviet Union. In A. Barnard (ed.), *Hunter-gatherers in history, archaeology and anthropology*, 77–88. Oxford: Berg.

Barnard, A. 2004a. Hunter-gatherers in history, archaeology and anthropology: introductory essay. In A. Barnard (ed.), *Hunter-gatherers in history, archaeology and anthropology*, 1–13. Oxford: Berg.

Barnard, A. (ed.) 2004b. *Hunter-gatherers in history, archaeology and anthropology*. Oxford: Berg.
Batianova, E. P. 2000. Ritual violence in Northeastern Siberia. In P. P. Schweitzer, M. Biesele, and R. K. Hitchcock (eds), *Hunters and gatherers in the modern world: conflict, resistance, and self-determination*, 150–63. New York: Berghahn.
Bird-David, N. 2005. Studying children in 'hunter-gatherer societies'. In B. S. Hewlett and M. E. Lamb (eds), *Hunter-gatherer childhoods: evolutionary, developmental, and cultural perspectives*, 92–101. Hawthorne: Aldine de Gruyter.
Brumbach, H. J. and Jarvenpa, R. 2006. Gender dynamics in hunter-gatherer society: archaeological methods and perspectives. In S. M. Nelson (ed.), *Handbook of gender in archaeology*, 503–35. Lanham, MD: AltaMira Press.
Burbank, V. K. and Chisholm, J. S. 1989. Old and new inequalities in a southeast Arnhem Land community: polygyny, marriage age, and birth spacing. In J. C. Altman (ed.), *Emergent inequalities in Aboriginal Australia*, 85–93. Sydney: University of Sydney.
Burch, E. S. and Ellanna, L. J. (eds) 1994a. *Key issues in hunter-gatherer research*. Oxford: Berg.
Burch, E. S. and Ellanna, L. J. 1994b. Editorial. In E. S. Burch and L. J. Ellanna (eds), *Key issues in hunter-gatherer research*, 11–13. Oxford: Berg.
Chindina, L. A. 2000. Warfare among the hunters and fishermen of western Siberia. In P. P. Schweitzer, M. Biesele, and R. K. Hitchcock (eds), *Hunters and gatherers in the modern world: conflict, resistance, and self-determination*, 77–93. New York: Berghahn.
Cobb, H. 2005 Straight down the line? A queer consideration of hunter-gatherer studies in north-west Europe. *World Archaeology* 37, 630–6.
Collier, J. and Rosalso, M. 1981. Politics and gender in simple societies. In S. Ortner and H. Whitehead (eds), *Sexual meanings: the cultural construction of gender and sexuality*, 275–329. Cambridge: Cambridge University Press.
Conkey, M. W. and Spector, J. D. 1984. Archaeology and the study of gender. *Advances in archaeological method and theory* 7, 1–32.
Cooper, Z. 1990. The end of 'Bibipoiye' (dog not) days in the Andamans. In B. Meehan and N. White (eds), *Hunter-gatherer demography: past and present*, 117–25. Sydney: University of Sydney.
Dahlberg, F. (ed.) 1981. *Woman the gatherer*. New Haven: Yale University Press.
Fedorova, E. G. 2000. The role of women in Mansi Society. In P. P. Schweitzer, M. Biesele, and R. K. Hitchcock (eds), *Hunters and gatherers in the modern world: conflict, resistance, and self-determination*, 391–8. New York: Berghahn.
Fedorova, E. G. 2001. Mansi female culture: rules of behaviour. In I. Keen and T. Yamada (eds), *Identity and gender in hunting and gathering societies*, 227–35. Osaka: National Museum of Ethnology.
Foley, R. 1988. Hominids, humans and hunter-gatherers: an evolutionary perspective. In T. Ingold, D. Riches, and J. Woodburn (eds), *Hunters and gatherers, volume I: history, evolution and social change*, 207–21. Oxford: Berg.
Galloway, P. 1992. The unexamined habitus: direct historical analogy and the archaeology of the text. In J.-C. Gardin and C. Peebles (eds), *Representations in archaeology*, 178–95. Bloomington: Indiana University Press.
Gardner, P. M. 1988. Pressures for Tamil propriety in Paliyan social organization. In T. Ingold, D. Riches, and J. Woodburn (eds), *Hunters and gatherers, volume I: history, evolution and social change*, 91–106. Oxford: Berg.
Gordon, R. J. 1984. The !Kung in the Kalahari exchange: an ethnohistorical perspective. In C. Schrire (ed.), *Past and present in hunter gatherer studies*, 195–244. Orlando: Academic Press.

Goulet, J.-G. 2000. Visions of conflict, conflicts of vision among contemporary Dene Tha. In P. P. Schweitzer, M. Biesele, and R. K. Hitchcock (eds), *Hunters and gatherers in the modern world: conflict, resistance, and self-determination*, 55–76. New York: Berghahn.

Griffin, P. B. 1984. Forager resource and land use in the humid tropics; the Agta of Northeastern Luzon, the Philippines. In C. Schrire (ed.), *Past and present in hunter gatherer studies*, 195–121. Orlando: Academic Press.

Habu, J. (ed.) 2003. *Hunter-gatherers of the North Pacific rim: papers presented at the eighth International Conference on Hunting and Gathering Societies (CHAGS 8), Aomori and Osaka, October 1998*. Osaka: National Museum of Ethnology.

Hamilton, A. 1982. Descended from father, belonging to country. In E. Leacock and R. B. Lee (eds), *Politics and history in band societies*, 85–108. Cambridge: Cambridge University Press.

Harding, S. (ed.) 1987. *Feminism and methodology: social science issues*. Bloomington: Indiana University Press.

Hewlett, B. L. 2005. Vulnerable lives: the experience of death and loss among the Aka and Ngandu adolescents of the Central African Republic. In B. S. Hewlett and M. E. Lamb (eds), *Hunter-gatherer childhoods: evolutionary, developmental, and cultural perspectives*, 322–42. Hawthorne: Aldine de Gruyter.

Hewlett, B. S. 2000. Central African government's and international NGO's perceptions of Baka Pygmy development. In P. P. Schweitzer, M. Biesele, and R. K. Hitchcock (eds), *Hunters and gatherers in the modern world: conflict, resistance, and self-determination*, 380–90. New York: Berghahn.

Hewlett, B. S. and Lamb, M. E. 2005a. Emerging issues in the study of hunter-gatherer children. In B. S. Hewlett and M. E. Lamb (eds), *Hunter-gatherer childhoods: evolutionary, developmental, and cultural perspectives*, 3–18. Hawthorne: Aldine de Gruyter.

Hewlett, B. S. and Lamb, M. E. (eds) 2005b. *Hunter-gatherer childhoods: evolutionary, developmental, and cultural perspectives*. Hawthorne: Aldine de Gruyter.

Hiatt, B. 1974. Woman the gatherer. In F. Gale (ed.), *Woman's role in Aboriginal society*, 2–16. Canberra: Australian Institute of Aboriginal Studies.

Hiatt, L. R. 1968. Gidjingali marriage arrangements. In R. B. Lee and I. DeVore (eds), *Man the hunter*, 165–75. Chicago: Aldine.

Hiwasaki, L. 2001. Presenting unity, performing diversity: identity negotiations in Stó:Lo territory. In I. Keen and T. Yamada (eds), *Identity and gender in hunting and gathering societies*, 69–87. Osaka: National Museum of Ethnology.

Hudson, M. J. 2003. Foragers as fetish in modern Japan. In J. Habu, J. M. Savelle, S. Koyama, and H. Hongo (eds), *Hunter-gatherers of the North Pacific rim: papers presented at the eighth International Conference on Hunting and Gathering Societies (CHAGS 8), Aomori and Osaka, October 1998*, 263–74. Osaka: National Museum of Ethnology.

Ichikawa, M. 2004. The Japanese tradition in central African hunter-gatherer studies, with comparative observations on the French and American traditions. In A. Barnard (ed.), *Hunter-gatherers in history, archaeology and anthropology*, 103–14. Oxford: Berg.

Imamura, K. 2001. The folk-interpretation of human reproduction among the |Gui and ||Gana and its implications for father–child relations. In I. Keen and T. Yamada (eds), *Identity and gender in hunting and gathering societies*, 185–94. Osaka: National Museum of Ethnology.

Ingold, T. 1988. Preface. In T. Ingold, D. Riches, and J. Woodburn (eds), *Hunters and gatherers, volume I: history, evolution and social change*, 1–3. Oxford: Berg.

Ingold, T. 2004. On the social relations of the hunter-gatherer band. In R. B. Lee and R. Daly (eds), *The Cambridge encyclopedia of hunters and gatherers*, 399–410. Cambridge: Cambridge University Press.

Ingold, T., Riches, D., and Woodburn, J. (eds) 1988a. *Hunters and gatherers, volume I: history, evolution and social change.* Oxford: Berg.

Ingold, T., Riches, D., and Woodburn, J. (eds) 1988b. *Hunters and gatherers, volume II: property, power and ideology.* Oxford: Berg.

Inoue, T. 2001. Hunting as a symbol of cultural tradition: the cultural meaning of subsistence activities in Gwich'in Athabascan society of northern Alaska. In I. Keen and T. Yamada (eds), *Identity and gender in hunting and gathering societies*, 89–102. Osaka: National Museum of Ethnology.

Jarvenpa, R. and Brumbach, H. J. (eds) 2006. *Circumpolar lives and livelihood.* Lincoln: University of Nebraska Press.

Jones, N. B., Hawkes, K., and Draper, P. 1994. Differences between Hadza and !Kung children's work: affluence or practical reason? In E. S. Burch and L. J. Ellanna (eds), *Key issues in hunter-gatherer research*, 189–215. Oxford: Berg.

Jones, R. 1984. Hunters and history: a case study from western Tasmania. In C. Schrire (ed.), *Past and present in hunter gatherer studies*, 27–65. Orlando: Academic Press.

Kaare, B. 2002. Cosmology, belonging and construction of community identity: the politics of being hunter-gatherers among the Akie-Dorobo of Tanzania. In H. Stewart, A. Barnard, and K. Omura (eds), *Self- and other-images of hunter-gatherers: papers presented at the Eighth International Conference on Hunting and Gathering Societies (CHAGS 8)*, 25–46. Osaka: National Museum of Ethnology.

Kamei, N. 2005 Play among Baka children in Cameroon. In B. S. Hewlett and M. E. Lamb (eds), *Hunter-gatherer childhoods: evolutionary, developmental, and cultural perspectives*, 343–59. Hawthorne: Aldine de Gruyter.

Keen, I. and Yamada, T. 2001a. General introduction. In I. Keen and T. Yamada (eds), *Identity and gender in hunting and gathering societies*, 1–2. Osaka: National Museum of Ethnology.

Keen, I. and Yamada, T. (eds) 2001b. *Identity and gender in hunting and gathering societies.* Osaka: National Museum of Ethnology.

Kim, A. A. 2000. Sel'kup knowledge of religion. In P. P. Schweitzer, M. Biesele, and R. K. Hitchcock (eds), *Hunters and gatherers in the modern world: conflict, resistance, and self-determination*, 460–74. New York: Berghahn.

Kolig, E. 1989. The powers that be and those who aspire to them. In J. C. Altman (ed.), *Emergent inequalities in Aboriginal Australia*, 43–65. Sydney: University of Sydney.

Lane, P. J. and Schadla-Hall, R. T. 2004. The many ages of Star Carr: do 'cites' make the 'site'? In A. Barnard (ed.), *Hunter-gatherers in history, archaeology and anthropology*, 145–61. Oxford: Berg.

Leacock, E. 1982. Relations of production in band society. In E. Leacock and R. B. Lee (eds), *Politics and history in band societies*, 159–70. Cambridge: Cambridge University Press.

Leacock, E. and Lee, R. B. 1982a. Introduction. In E. Leacock and R. B. Lee (eds), *Politics and history in band societies*, 1–20. Cambridge: Cambridge University Press.

Leacock, E. and Lee, R. B. (eds) 1982b. *Politics and history in band societies.* Cambridge: Cambridge University Press.

Lee, R. B. 1982. Politics, sexual and non-sexual, in an egalitarian society. In E. Leacock and R. B. Lee (eds), *Politics and history in band societies*, 37–59. Cambridge: Cambridge University Press.

Lee, R. B. and Daly, R. 2004. Introduction. In R. B. Lee and R. Daly (eds), *The Cambridge encyclopedia of hunters and gatherers*, 1–19. Cambridge: Cambridge University Press.

Lee, R. B. and DeVore, I. (eds) 1968a. *Man the hunter.* Chicago: Aldine.

Lee, R. B. and DeVore, I. 1968b. Problems in the study of hunters and gatherers. In R. B. Lee and I. DeVore (eds), *Man the hunter*, 3–12. Chicago: Aldine.

Lewis-Williams, D. 1984. Ideological continuities in prehistoric southern Africa: the evidence of rock art. In C. Schrire (ed.), *Past and present in hunter gatherer studies*, 225–52. Orlando: Academic Press.

Longino, H. E. 1990. *Science as social knowledge: values and objectivity in scientific inquiry*. Princeton: Princeton University Press.

Mansur, M. E. and R. Piqué. 2007 An ethnoarchaeological approach to the Selknam ceremony of Hain: a discussion of the impact of ritual on social organisation in hunter-gatherer societies. In K. Hardy (ed.), *Archaeological invisibility and forgotten knowledge*, 180–91. BAR International Series, vol. 2183. Oxford: Archaeopress.

Mearns, L. 1994. To continue the Dreaming: Aboriginal women's traditional responsibilities in a transformed world. In E. S. Burch and L. J. Ellanna (eds), *Key issues in hunter-gatherer research*, 263–87. Oxford: Berg.

Meggitt, M. J. 1968. 'Marriage classes' and demography in central Australia. In R. B. Lee and I. DeVore (eds), *Man the hunter*, 176–84. Chicago: Aldine.

Myers, L. D. 2004. Subtle shifts and radical transformations in hunter-gatherer research in American anthropology: Julian Steward's contributions and achievements. In A. Barnard (ed.), *Hunter-gatherers in history, archaeology and anthropology*, 175–86. Oxford: Berg.

Owen, L. R. 2005. *Distorting the past: gender and the division of labor in the European Upper Paleolithic*. Tübingen: Kerns Verlag.

Pluciennik, M. 2004. The meaning of 'hunter-gatherers' and modes of subsistence: a comparative historical perspective. In A. Barnard (ed.), *Hunter-gatherers in history, archaeology and anthropology*, 17–29. Oxford: Berg.

Quraishy, Z. B. 2001. Gender politics in the socio-economic organisation of contemporary foragers: a case study from India. In I. Keen and T. Yamada (eds), *Identity and gender in hunting and gathering societies*, 195–205. Osaka: National Museum of Ethnology.

Reiter, R. R. 1975a. Introduction. In R. R. Reiter (ed.), *Toward an anthropology of women*, 11–19. New York: Monthly Review Press.

Reiter, R. R. (ed.) 1975b. *Toward an anthropology of women*. New York: Monthly Review Press.

Rose, F. G. G. 1968. Australian marriage, land-owning groups, and initiations. In R. B. Lee and I. DeVore (eds), *Man the hunter*, 200–8. Chicago: Aldine.

Sandbukt, Ø. 1988. Tributary tradition and relations of affinity and gender among the Sumatran Kubu. In T. Ingold, D. Riches, and J. Woodburn (eds), *Hunters and gatherers, volume I: history, evolution and social change*, 107–16. Oxford: Berg.

Schrire, C. (ed.) 1984a. *Past and present in hunter gatherer studies*. Orlando: Academic Press.

Schrire, C. 1984b. Wild surmises on savage thoughts. In C. Schrire (ed.), *Past and present in hunter gatherer studies*, 1–25. Orlando: Academic Press.

Schweitzer, P. P. 2004. No escape from being theoretically important: hunter-gatherers in German-language debates of the late nineteenth and early twentieth centuries. In A. Barnard (ed.), *Hunter-gatherers in history, archaeology and anthropology*, 69–76. Oxford: Berg.

Schweitzer, P. P., Biesele, M., and Hitchcock, R. K. (eds) 2000. *Hunters and gatherers in the modern world: conflict, resistance, and self-determination*. New York: Berghahn.

Service, E. 1962. *Primitive social organisation: an evolutionary perspective*. New York: Random House.

Sharp, H. S. 1988. Dry meat and gender: the absence of Chipewyan ritual for the regulation of hunting and animal numbers. In T. Ingold, D. Riches, and J. Woodburn (eds), *Hunters and gatherers, volume I: history, evolution and social change*, 183–91. Oxford: Berg.

Sharp, H. S. 1994. The power of weakness. In E. S. Burch and L. J. Ellanna (eds), *Key issues in hunter-gatherer research*, 35–58. Oxford: Berg.

Shnirelman, V. A. 2001. Ethnicity in the making. In I. Keen and T. Yamada (eds), *Identity and gender in hunting and gathering societies*, 53–65. Osaka: National Museum of Ethnology.

Slocum, S. 1977. Woman the gatherer: male bias in anthropology. In R. R. Rapp (ed.), *Toward an anthropology of women*, 36–50. New York: Monthly Review Press.

Sneider, L. 2012 Gender, literacy, and sovereignty in Winnemucca's 'Life among the Piutes'. *American Indian Quarterly* 36, 257–87.

Staniukovich, M. V. 2000. Peacemaking ideology in a headhunting society. In P. P. Schweitzer, M. Biesele, and R. K. Hitchcock (eds), *Hunters and gatherers in the modern world: conflict, resistance, and self-determination*, 399–409. New York: Berghahn.

Sterling, K. 2011. Inventing human nature. In R. Bernbeck and R. H. McGuire (eds), *Ideologies in archaeology*, 175–93. Tucson: University of Arizona Press.

Tanner, N. and Zihlman, A. 1976. Women in evolution. Part I: innovation and selection in human origins. *Signs* 1, 585–608.

Tonkinson, R. 2000. Gender role transformation among Australian Aborigines. In P. P. Schweitzer, M. Biesele, and R. K. Hitchcock (eds), *Hunters and gatherers in the modern world: conflict, resistance, and self-determination*, 343–60. New York: Berghahn.

Turnbull, C. M. 1982. The ritualization of potential conflict between the sexes among the Mbuti. In E. Leacock and R. B. Lee (eds), *Politics and history in band societies*, 133–55. Cambridge: Cambridge University Press.

University of Alaska Fairbanks. 1990. *Pre-circulated papers and abstracts, Sixth International Conference on Hunting and Gathering Societies. CHAGS 6, Hunting and gathering societies: changing peoples, changing theories, Fairbanks, Alaska, 1990*. Dept. of Anthropology, University of Alaska, Fairbanks.

Venkateswar, S. 2001. Gender/power: a view from the 'outside'. In I. Keen and T. Yamada (eds), *Identity and gender in hunting and gathering societies*, 207–26. Osaka: National Museum of Ethnology.

Wenzel, G. W., Hovelsbud-Broda, G., and Kishigami, N. (eds) 2000. *Social economy of modern hunter-gatherers*. Hokkaido: Senri Ethnological Series.

Whitehouse, R. 2006. Gender archaeology in Europe. In S. M. Nelson (ed.), *Handbook of gender in archaeology*, 733–83. Lanham, MD: AltaMira Press.

Widlok, T. 2000. Hai//Om naming practices. In P. P. Schweitzer, M. Biesele, and R. K. Hitchcock (eds), *Hunters and gatherers in the modern world: conflict, resistance, and self-determination*, 361–79. New York: Berghahn.

Yamada, T. 2001. Gender and cultural revitalization movements among the Ainu. In I. Keen and T. Yamada (eds), *Identity and gender in hunting and gathering societies*, 237–57. Osaka: National Museum of Ethnology.

Yengoyan, A. 1968. Demographic and ecological influences on Aboriginal Australian marriage sections. In R. B. Lee and I. DeVore (eds), *Man the hunter*, 185–99. Chicago: Aldine.

Yengoyan, A. 2004. Anthropological history and the study of hunters and gatherers: cultural and non-cultural. In A. Barnard (ed.), *Hunter-gatherers in history, archaeology and anthropology*, 57–66. Oxford: Berg.

Yesner, D. R. 1994. Seasonality and resource 'stress' among hunter-gatherers: archaeological signatures. In E. S. Burch and L. J. Ellanna (eds), *Key issues in hunter-gatherer research*, 151–67. Oxford: Berg.

PART II

THE EARLIEST HUNTER-GATHERERS

CHAPTER 8

THE FIRST HUNTER-GATHERERS

JENNIE ROBINSON

IF there is one thing that palaeoanthropologists understand, it is the continuum between species, genera, and all forms of life. Human beings are defined by their relationships with (and divergence from) other primates, living and historical, and primates by their relationship with other mammals, and so on. Therefore, when considering who are hunter-gatherers and then who are the first of these hunter-gatherers, palaeoanthropologists are one of the few types of archaeologist whose job is *not* to think immediately of *Homo sapiens* communities, but of creatures who are positively not *Homo sapiens*. It is tempting to think of hunter-gatherer behaviour as the first version of human food-getting strategy: that 'the first hunter-gatherers' is the same as 'the first eaters'. If this were true then, given the unbroken continuum of the evolution of humans from primate ancestors, it would be impossible to identify the first creature to get its own food: any species that you picked out as a possible 'first' would itself have an ancestor. Moreover, once we get back further than hominins, archaeologists and anthropologists tend to lose interest.

However, we do not need to stretch our brains back to the primordial soup. The first hunter-gatherers are *not* the same as the first eaters. For one thing, it appears reasonably certain that the earliest hominins were vegetarians, with hunting coming on board much later, having gone through a stage of scavenging before hunting. We might characterize the development of human subsistence as: gathering, then scavenger-gathering, then hunter-scavenger-gathering with scavenging probably reducing in importance as hunting increased. Having said that, whether you then characterize very early vegetarian ancestors as 'gatherers' depends very much on the definition you use. Does 'gatherer' equal 'plant eater' (and thus include a huge range of living herbivores, frugivores, and folivores—or prey, as they are otherwise known)? Or does it imply a certain level of sociology: division of labour, planning, mapping, or sharing? How would these aspects be evidenced in the fossil record? More pragmatically, is there a physical and cognitive difference between gathering (collecting, carrying, hoarding, delayed consumption) and simply grazing as you go? If so, we exclude most non-human animals—and quite a few hominins—who eat plants from the term 'gatherer', yet it would be difficult to exclude carnivores such as raptors and cats from the term 'hunter'. A question about who the first hunter was would surely involve an animal predator. And, humans are not the only omnivore: a significant minority of living non-human animals, including our closest relative the chimpanzee, our best friend the dog, and our usual taphonomic body double, the pig, are also omnivores.

Disentangling the non-human animals from those human ancestors is difficult simply because subsistence behaviour is a fundamentally natural, animalistic behaviour. Hunter-gathererism might be considered a human behaviour now, but it is not unique. It did not appear at the same time as hominins appeared, it did not appear as a package deal, and however culturally complex it might be today, it is derived from the need to eat, which is common to all life. This chapter goes on to examine the emergence of the component parts of hunting and gathering as a human behaviour, having noted its relationship to the subsistence behaviours of other animals.

This semantic nit-picking might be annoying, but it is necessary if we are to answer any questions regarding 'firsts' in human behaviour. If hunting and gathering is defined in terms of a modern human behaviour then this can only extend to *Homo sapiens*, and this chapter should be written about the first examples of this species, occurring in Africa at sites like Omo (Butzer 1969; McDougall et al. 2005), Blombos Cave (Grine et al. 2000, Jacobs et al. 2006), Herto (White et al. 2003), and Klasies River Mouth (Churchill et al. 1996; Rightmire and Deacon 1991; 2001) around 200–100 kya (thousand years ago), and in the Upper Palaeolithic of Europe from 40 kya (Lartet 1868; Trinkaus et al. 2003; Wild et al. 2005). There is even disagreement over which fossil should be called the earliest example of *Homo sapiens*, because it is not clear how far we should allow anatomical variation to be tolerated within one species. Modern humans are extremely uniform in their appearance and genetic codes, but there may have been more variability in the deep past, as there is more variability in other modern animal species.

If we are extending our interest in the history of human behaviour to ancestral hominins then we can certainly talk about the food-getting behaviour of Neanderthals. As the most recent non-sapiens hominin, we have a relative wealth of archaeological record from them, and it seems certain that they were collecting, storing, and cooking plant foods (Henry et al. 2011) as well as hunting and butchering large game (Richards and Trinkaus 2009).

We have enough evidence to at least debate the subsistence strategy of *Homo erectus* and possibly some transitional *Homo*, and to a certain extent of *Australopithecus* and *Paranthropus*. Evidence for the diets of these hominins exists archaeologically (as stuff, primarily stone tools and animal bone debris), chemically (the analysis of isotopic signatures in tooth enamel and bone), and anatomically (as skeletal form indicating function, and microscopically, as wear patterns on teeth). In some cases there is evidence for butchery sites, 'home-base' sites where food was brought for eating and sharing, and fire and/or cooking traces on animal bones. However, our evidence is always sparse even compared to the evidential luxuries available to archaeologies of later, much shorter periods, let alone in proportion to the time period covered. This makes this chapter largely a biological or subsistence one: readers should note that there is little scope for discussing how subsistence was culturally regarded by early hominins.

Who, When, and Where? A Potted Guide

Some context of when and who we are talking about is necessary, but this chapter is not intended to be a thorough guide to the many species that populate our lineage prior to *Homo sapiens*. Not only would this information fill whole books (great examples of which are Aiello and Dean (2002), Bilsborough (1992), and Foley and Lewin (2003)), but any account would be out of date by the time you read this. New discoveries are being announced all the time, scholars differ in how many species they accept as biological likelihoods, and, with such a tiny assemblage, a small amount of new information can change the whole picture.

Instead, this part offers a rough guide to hominins, *sensu* Wood and Lonergan (2008), who offer a superb guide to the names and types of hominins currently known, as well as an explanation of why there is disagreement about the number of species, and which is strongly recommended to the reader. They talk of grades of hominins; groups of species grouped together by major characteristics, which is easier (and shorter) than trying to list every species.

The earliest grade defined by Wood and Lonergan (2008) is that of possible or probable hominins, which includes two genera that are doubtful, and one which is a likely candidate for hominin-ship. The fragmentary nature of the evidence and similarity of appearance of other primate groups means that, at the time of writing, some fossils cannot be established as those of upright walking hominins. The broad dates for the very early, unlikely candidates is 5.7–7 mya (million years ago), while the probable candidate, genus *Ardipithecus*, dates to 5.8–4.3 mya. These fossils are all from East Africa: Chad, Kenya, and Ethiopia.

The second grade is archaic hominins, and this includes well-known as well as newly recognized species of the genus *Australopithecus* (referred to in lay terms as australopithecines), a genus defined by Dart (1925), plus the one known member of a recently established additional genus, *Kenyanthropus* (Leakey et al. 2001). This group dates 4.5–2.4 mya and represents creatures that were definitely bipedal but with relatively small bodies and brains. Some members show signs of remaining comfortable in tree environments as well as being bipeds on the ground. In this grade, *Australopithecus* is known from both South African and East African locales whilst the aptly named *Kenyanthropus* is currently known only from Kenya.

The third grade, megadont archaic hominins, includes those species who exhibit significant specialization in their dentition and masticatory anatomy (and presumably in their diets, of which more below). These species were initially categorized as *Australopithecus*, but most workers now use a different genus name, *Paranthropus*, to distinguish them, although most people agree that *Paranthropus* is likely to be ancestrally derived from *Australopithecus*. These hominins had bodies and brains almost as small as the previous group, but bigger faces and teeth, and date 2.5–1.4 mya. Again, species from both East and South African locales are recognized.

Australopithecus, *Paranthropus*, and *Kenyanthropus* are genus names, on an equivalent level with *Homo*. The beginnings of *Homo* are characterized by Wood and Lonergan (2008) first as transitional hominins, a grade containing long-established but scantily evidenced species from East Africa that may or may not be reclassified when more evidence is uncovered, dating around 2.4–1.6 mya. Following the transitional homins are pre-modern *Homo*, a large grade containing the famous faces of our more recent ancestry, some thoroughly well known and established such as *Homo erectus* and *Homo neanderthalensis*, and other newer ones such as *Homo floresiensis*. The timeline here is 1.9 mya to 28 kya. This grade is first seen in East Africa (*H. ergaster*: there are some South African fossils assigned to early *Homo* but not currently classifiable beyond that), then develops into *H. erectus* which later moves into Asia and Europe, giving rise to the Neanderthals in Europe (and some transitional forms) but keeping the classic *H. erectus* form in the Far East. Finally—for now—comes the grade 'anatomically modern humans', which contains only one species, *Homo sapiens* (*sensu stricto*) from about 200 kya onwards.

Note that the time zones overlap for most grades, and that these broad dates are judged on the fossil finds that we have. Since it is unlikely that our fossil collections contain the very first and very last member of any species or genus, we can assume that each time zone is a minimum, and the overlap was probably more extensive. The fact that for the majority of hominin history it has been the norm for several species and/or genera to be sharing resources and landscape, including *Homo sapiens* for the majority of its tenure, is at odds with our experience of the world, but of course has strong implications for the evolution of diet and subsistence strategy.

The sections below outline the evidence, circumstantial (i.e. anatomical) and direct (chemical or archaeological), for the development of the various components of the human diet. Each section is formatted in accordance with the history of investigation: for earlier hominins, anatomy first and direct evidence later, as the latter relies heavily on recent scientific techniques. For *Homo*, archaeological investigations came first, largely because there just is more archaeology available for them, and anatomical modelling came later.

Plant-Based Subsistence: Archaic Hominins (5.8–1.4 mya)

Circumstantial Evidence: Form Indicates Function

Information about the diet of very early hominins is based on fragmentary skeletal evidence which has been examined on the basis that form indicates function. Where the function is not obvious, analogies are drawn from closely related living animals, or from animals with analogous diets (e.g. Constantino et al. 2011) where we can see what something is for. It is a case of examining the fossil remains of hominin teeth and bodies and reverse-engineering their diets and behaviours from the physical adaptations made to them. As we are dealing with biological function there is little concern in the literature with the philosophical rightness of using this kind of analogy. It is well understood that analogy generates assumptions, not facts, which are often broader than we would like—but, for some small scraps of hominins, that is all we can get.

For example, when *Ardipithecus* was first announced in 1994, its thin tooth enamel (thin compared to that of *Australopithecus*) was cited as evidence for fruit adaptation. Chimpanzees (*Pan troglodytes*) have especially thin enamel on the occlusal (biting) surface of their incisors which is considered an adaptation to a heavy reliance on ripe fruits (Suwa et al. 2009), and so the same was applied to *Ardipithecus*. However, the more recent publications have argued that the enamel on *Ardipthecus* teeth is not as thin as in chimps, just thinner than in *Australopithecus*, so is not necessarily indicative of reliance on ripe fruit (or sharing special traits with *Pan*), but of generalized woodland plant eating (Suwa et al. 2009; White et al. 1994), reminding us to avoid relying too heavily on analogy.

Another example of form indicating function is in one of the best-established *Australopithecus* species, *Au. afarensis*. This hominin dates between 3 and 2 million years, and includes the famous specimen 'Lucy' or AL-288-1 (Johanson and Maitland 1981), a 40 per cent complete skeleton. This hominin's teeth are indicative of generalized vegetarianism (Bilsborough 1992), with neither molars nor incisors dominating. Coupled with recent evidence that the East African landscape in which it lived was more heavily forested than originally thought, it is likely that this species was a fruit and plant eater, taking advantage of all and any plant foodstuffs without specialization. *Au. afarensis* was a biped but was probably also comfortable climbing trees, with mobile shoulder joints and long, curved fingers. A life spent in forested environments would be consistent with a vegetarian diet emphasizing fruit, and chimes well with research on possible home-base sites (see below). In contrast, the paranthropines (the megadont grade) show strong specialization in their reduced anterior dentition and expanded, powerful molars—indeed, the first specimen of the East African megadonts was nicknamed 'Nutcracker Man' (Leakey 1959; Lee-Thorp 2011). This level of dental specialization indicates a dietary specialization, unlike the generalized *Au. afarensis*, and investigations into this specialization have resulted in lines of direct evidence.

Direct Evidence for Plant-Based Foods

Megadont archaic hominins, or paranthropines if one prefers, are the robust-faced group comprised of the species *P. robustus* from South Africa, and *P. boisei* and (much earlier and probably ancestral) *P. aethiopicus* from East Africa. These hominins exhibit a markedly specialized dentition of large square molars of the crushing-grinding type seen in herbivorous chewers like sheep and horses, with very small, flat incisors. The enamel on their teeth was very thick, in contrast to *Ardipithecus*. Combined with this are faces that are wide and flat, small braincases, flared cheekbones accommodating very large chewing muscles, and in some cases (probably males, according to living ape analogies) a sagittal crest. The whole skull is heavy, buttressed, flattened, and strong, which looks very aggressive but probably indicates reinforcement against powerful chewing rather than fast sharp snapping of jaws. As noted above, this anatomy was initially taken to indicate the need for powerful crushing of hard-cased food items such as nuts or seeds.

Although this seems a simple case of form indicating function (Rak 1983), recent attempts to determine the hardness of the food items eaten by these creatures from scratches and striations on their teeth demonstrate how advances in scientific technique can overturn these assumptions. Using high-resolution microwear analysis, Ungar et al. (2008) showed that in seven *P. boisei* specimens there was no evidence, from tooth wear at least, that the individual had eaten anything especially hard in the few days prior to death. These authors posited that paranthropines had the ability to eat rock-hard seeds and tough plants when necessary, but that it was an emergency fallback ability rather than a usual choice. This is an example of Liem's paradox, which states that very derived (specialized) adaptations do not necessarily indicate the preferred day-to-day habits of a creature, but its last resorts (Liem 1990). Therefore paranthropines may have been eating a much softer diet than has been traditionally considered, while preserving the ability to eat very hard foods in times of crisis. A special edition of *American Journal of Physical Anthropology* (2009) devoted to fallback foods and their importance in primate and hominin evolution highlights the increasing interest in this topic as a key force in evolutionary change.

Isotopic analysis by Sponheimer and Lee-Thorp (2006) on *P. robustus* specimens supports the idea that paranthropines were not limited to crunching tough food items, or perhaps not crunching them at all. This study indicated that the diet of these hominins was more variable than had been previously thought. The isotopic evidence from this study indicated a high level of grasses or sedges in the diet, but the authors also noted that this could have occurred not only by *P. robustus* eating grasses, but also from *P. robustus* preying on animals that ate grasses, although there is no other evidence for meat eating at this time.

This study was superseded (Cerling et al. 2011) by further investigations into the carbon isotope ratios of both *P. robustus* and *P. boisei*. Here, dental enamel samples of both species were analysed, and revealed that *P. boisei* was eating a diet almost entirely composed of C3 plant stuffs (grasses and sedges) with little input from C4 plants (nuts, seeds, berries, fruits), and moreover, that the very high levels of C3 could only come from a diet directly reliant on eating grasses—eating animals that ate grasses could not produce high enough levels. This means that the species formerly known as 'Nutcracker Man' should really be nicknamed 'Grass-grazer Man'! In contrast, *P. robustus* showed a more varied diet including C3 and C4 foods.

Of interest here is the fact that the facial and dental anatomy of the two species is very similar, but they occupy different territories (*P. boisei* known from East Africa, *P. robustus* from South Africa). If we take the assumption that form indicates function then these two similar forms should be eating a similar diet, but evidently the East African group went down the route of a dietary specialism to the exclusion of other foods whilst the South African group retained a generalized vegetarian diet common to many primates in similar environments. Here we can see that whilst form = function works broadly (we can see that neither of these two were snapping carnivores) it should not be assumed that it works down to the detail of being able to distinguish between two different, equally viable, African vegetarian diets.

The Invention of Meat Eating: Pre-Modern *Homo* (1.9 mya–28 kya)

In hindsight, it seems that the inception of meat eating amongst hominins ought to be a big fanfare, a marked leap in human evolution. After all, most other animals are strongly specialized to either carnivory or herbivory, and changing from the primate norm of vegetarian food to a mixed diet, and the behavioural changes that must go alongside, could rightly be described as a big deal. In terms of the bodily changes that seem to go with meat eating (see below), changes are quite impressive, but of course we are viewing the effect in a very few fossilized individuals. The archaeological record shows changes coming in slowly, with meat eating creeping in as an extension of gathering behaviour at first.

Direct Evidence for Animal-Based Foods: Small Animal Protein

The classic archaic hominins, then, have been characterized as devoted vegetarians of various types. It is tempting to link the appearance of animal protein in the diet with the appearance of *Homo* as either a cause or a symptom. However, this is not strictly true: there is direct evidence that *Au. africanus* was eating at least a little animal protein and, given the immense time depth and archaeological paucity of this period, we might assume that which we have evidence for is only a small part of hominins' repertoire.

Au. africanus is the South African australopithecine (2.8 mya), a small-brained, small-statured biped who was probably prey more often than predator (Brain 1981). This species has slightly smaller front teeth than *Au. afarensis*, but there is nothing particularly indicative or specialized about its dentition and it was assumed to be a general vegetarian primate whose diet was governed by what was available in its dry, grassy Transvaal landscape. However, modern investigations have shown that long thin slivers of animal bone found on *Au. africanus* sites bear the microscopic marks of termite bites (Backwell and d'Errico 2001). This might be a mystery if it were not for the analogy of chimps: the Gombe chimpanzee group were famously witnessed 'fishing' for termites by probing specially prepared long slim sticks into termite mounds, causing the termites to clamp their jaws onto the stick, and then pulling out the stick and eating the termites (Goodall 1986). From this analogy it seems perfectly likely that *Au. africanus* was at least partially insectivorous, was deliberately modifying items in order to get termites, and was probably learning and passing on this behaviour through observation of each other. The fact that *Au. africanus* was ingesting termite protein has been corroborated by studies of stable isotope in the tooth enamel which shows that animal protein contributed a portion of their diet (Lee-Thorp and Sponheimer 2006). *Au. africanus* is, then, the first hominin for whom we have evidence that animal protein was being eaten. Whether fishing for termites counts as hunting, or fishing, or gathering remains debatable.

Large Animal Protein

During the 1980s the idea that scavenging, not hunting, had been the first mode of meat eating in human ancestors became popular, although it had first been voiced by Leakey in 1967 (Blumenschine 1987). Cut marks on bones at Olduvai Gorge and Koobi Fora (Bunn 1981; Potts and Shipman 1981) were matched with Acheulian hand axes: symmetrical, uniform, teardrop-shaped tools flaked on both sides, sharp and heavy, probably for hand-held work such as butchering and smashing, rather than throwing. These hand axes are strongly associated with *H. erectus*, meaning that this hominin was pronounced to be eating meat taken from carcasses after a carnivore had eaten from it. However, it is hard to say that *H. erectus* is the first and only toolmaker or butcher: at Olduvai it is unclear whether *P. boisei*, *H. habilis*, or *H. erectus* is the maker of the Oldowan industry, and there is association at Olduvai of *P. boisei* fossils with animal bones.

An important example here is the hippopotamus butchery site at Koobi Fora, documented by Glynn Isaac (1978a) which shows that more than diet can be inferred from this type of archaeology. Here, Isaac demonstrated that 119 stone flakes associated with a hippo carcass (presumed to have died naturally) were transported from at least three kilometres away and knapped at the site (Isaac 1978a). The transport of materials in this manner is perhaps the first archaeological evidence of this extent of planning depth in relation to food.

Isaac (1971; 1978a; 1978b) developed models of landscape use by hominins who were transporting food and stone around the landscape: to butchery sites, and to notional home-base sites: specified areas where hominins returned repeatedly, bringing food back either to share and/or to defend it from other predators, in the case of meat. These sites were typically around streams and so would have had vegetation and perhaps shady trees. This has implications for our concept of plant-food gathering (as opposed to grazing) as well as meat eating: Isaac postulated that carrying food, saving it for later, bringing it back to a home, to a group, was a meaningful development that marked out hominin behaviour as different from other animals. He envisioned dragging carcasses back, but also discussed the issue of carrying plant foods such as berries and shoots in two hands, and suggested that non-fossilizing items such as a simple tray of bark could have been used to make this possible. He further suggested that the division of labour originated here, with females too encumbered with young to range far from the home-base (but able to carry a bark tray) and males transporting meat from the wider landscape back to the home-base to provision females and young. Notably, Isaac did not pinpoint the origin of meat eating, home-basing, or provisioning to any specific hominin, but the temporal range of his sites made *P. boisei* and *H. erectus* likely candidates.

Isaac's work was reviewed by Rose and Marshall (1996), whose research in primatology was brought to bear on the issues Isaac had suggested were unique to humans. Their paper combined several fields of research and is worth seeking out for the bibliography alone. They refuted the division of labour idea and of defensible homesteads, but supported the idea of home-base sites generally. They agreed that transport of resources and delayed consumption were only seen amongst humans. Amongst both positive and negative respondents were Fruth and McGrew, who suggested that the assemblages of stone and bones on the ground near watercourses were not evidence of hominins living on the ground under trees, but perhaps building platforms in the trees, as chimps do, as this would form a much better protection against most carnivores if meat was indeed being brought back to the home-base. In this scenario, the archaeological debris would have dropped onto the ground as the platform disintegrated, not been originally laid there. Fruth and McGrew also provided examples of bonobos transporting fruit for several hundred metres by walking either bipedally or tripedally to free one or more front limbs for carrying, and outlined more extensive examples of food sharing in chimps, but agreed that delayed consumption had no parallel in the non-human world (Fruth and McGrew 1996). Other respondents included Bunn, who noted that local plant resources would rapidly become depleted in any scenario where hominins were staying close to one spot.

Circumstantial Evidence: Anatomy and Dentition

The advent of meat eating is supported by changes in the hominin skeleton around the time of Isaac's butchery sites and the appearance of the Acheulian. In many ways *H. ergaster*, the early African version of *Homo erectus* dating from 1.9 mya, and *H. erectus* from 1.6 mya, mark a new era: the first time we have a well-established, predictable anatomy, strongly associated with a stone-tool industry which is uniform and symmetrical in manufacture, and with a much larger brain than has been seen before.

The anatomy of *H. ergaster/erectus* supports the advent of meat eating in several ways and is best explained by Aiello and Wheeler's 'expensive tissue hypothesis' (1995, and reviewed and revised in Isler and van Schaik, 2009; Barrickman and Lin 2010; and Ruxton and

Wilkinson 2011). This theory draws on: the large increase in brain size compared to earlier hominins; changes in body height and build; the taller, flatter, more slender and human-like torso shape; and dentition. Readers should note that the two species are somewhat conflated in this hypothesis: the real brain increase is seen in *H. erectus* not in *H. ergaster*, but what we know of the postcranial (neck down) anatomy of these two species is mostly down to the almost complete skeleton of a young male, WT-15000, from Nariokotome (Walker and Leakey 1993), described on its discovery as *H. erectus* (Brown et al. 1985) but following development of our understanding of these species, now classified as *H. ergaster* (Wood and Lonergan 2008).

Homo erectus had a brain of 900–1,000 cm^3, much bigger than australopithecines and paranthropines (500–600 cm^3), transitional early *Homo* (500–775 cm^3) and *H. ergaster* at 760 cm^3, although not as large as ours (around 1,450 cm^3). The brain is a highly expensive organ to maintain in terms of energy consumed for its size, so larger brained creatures need to consume more calories than small brained ones. If a species has a larger brain than its ancestors, it must be getting more calories: either there are increased calories in the diet, or some other organ is reducing to free up extra calories for the brain. Aiello and Wheeler argued that in *H. erectus* we see both.

The ribcage shape of *H. ergaster* in WT-15000 provides evidence for the reduction of another organ to pay for the expansion of the brain. In earlier hominins such as *Au. afarensis* (see AL-288) and in modern apes, the ribcage is narrow at the shoulder but splayed out wide at the base, making a cone shape that results in the familiar pot-bellied torso shape of the non-human great apes. The narrow top facilitates shoulder and arm flexibility for tree swinging while the wide base houses a very long gut. This long gut is necessary because these animals (and by extension, hominins, which share the pot-belly ribcage shape such as *Au. afarensis*) eat material that takes a long time to process: heavy vegetation, fruit rinds, and waxy leaves that would be indigestible to modern humans with their short gut. Only by spending a long time inside the gut being processed can these plant materials be broken down into a form that can be absorbed as animal energy. What is more, the amount of calories yielded by a waxy leaf, once you have accounted for the calories expended in the long processing of it, are quite low. In a modern human, though, that leaf would be out the other end virtually intact before it had a chance to start breaking down, thus yielding no calories to the human, and costing a few in pushing it along.

Modern humans have a flat, rectangular ribcage and abdominal region, housing a shorter gut, which can be seen in those people without excess fat. In *H. ergaster* we see something halfway—the ribcage shape is not as flat and square as ours, but it is less cone shaped than that of earlier hominins, resembling a bell (Aiello and Wheeler 1995). So we can deduce that *H. ergaster*'s gut was shorter than that of its predecessors but not as short as ours. This means that the gut tissue itself, which is metabolically the second most expensive after the brain, would be reduced, freeing up extra calories for use by the brain. But what about the loss of gut length? Would this not mean a loss of calories from less processing, thus outweighing any calorific increase gained by reducing the gut length? Yes, it would—if *H. ergaster* was eating the same diet as the longer-gutted archaic hominins, this would mean a net reduction in calorific yield, not the net increase required for a bigger brain. The only way for a large brain as seen in *H. ergaster* and then the increase in brain size we see in *H. erectus* to combine a brain increase with small gut is to consume a diet that yields more calories in a shorter processing time: i.e. that is more easily and quickly digestible.

Animal muscle, or meat, is a food that fits the bill. Hominins are already made of meat and their bodies require animal energy to run. Transforming animal muscle into animal energy is a lot less hassle than transforming leaves and shoots into animal energy. Meat contains a lot more calories than vegetable matter because it is already a concentrated form of animal energy, plus, less of our own processing energy is used to digest it. (This is an oversimplification of course; meat requires extra biochemical kit to process it, and this must have evolved alongside behaviour. For example, Pfefferle et al. (2011) showed that human brains have more phosphocreatine circuit proteins—for getting energy out of meat—than do chimps, meaning that our brains can leach more energy out of the same piece of meat than chimps' brains can, although skeletal muscle gets the same amount in both species. This is a genetically embedded specialism of our brains, which indicates selection for meat eating specifically related to the brain's energy requirements.)

Other elements of the anatomy and archaeology of *H. ergaster* and *H. erectus* support the idea that they were adapted to eating meat. The dentition has molars and incisors in similar proportion to each other, in terms of size, as they are in modern humans, reflecting a more omnivorous diet (of course, these hominins would still have eaten a large proportion of vegetable matter in addition to meat, just as humans do today to varying degrees). The teeth are still larger overall than those of later *H. sapiens* but significantly smaller than australopithecines, and essentially, the human shape and format of the teeth, set in a parabolic (horseshoe shaped) arc, rather than a long rectangular palate as in archaic hominins and other apes, is recognizable in *H. ergaster* and *H. erectus*.

A well-known individual that may be evidence of the personal consequences of meat eating is the partial female skeleton KNM-ER 1808. This specimen's femur shows thickened cortical bone consistent with Vitamin A poisoning (Walker et al. 1982). This condition, which leads to a slow and painful death, arises from eating carnivore liver, which is far too high in this vitamin to be consumed by humans (every schoolchild knows that polar bear liver is poisonous, but so is the liver of other carnivores including lion and leopard). KNM-ER 1808 lived for several weeks after consuming an overdose of Vitamin A (long enough for it to modify her bones before death) in a debilitated state, possibly indicating that she was to some extent cared for by other members of her group, although this must remain speculative. It seems that in the earliest stages of meat eating, hominins had not, quite understandably, established sufficient knowledge of what kinds of meat were not all right to eat.

Although there is no evidence directly to suggest whether the unfortunate 1808 ate from livers that had been scavenged or hunted, it is unlikely that hominins would go out to hunt lions. Therefore the balance of likelihood is that this liver was from an animal that had died by other means and *H. ergaster* or *H. erectus* had made use of the carcass. (However, while lions, as group hunters, are a very unlikely target, Tunnell (1996) reports an instance of a mob of baboons attacking a leopard—so perhaps it is not an impossible idea to suggest a carnivore may occasionally have been killed by a group of hominins.)

The origins of deliberate, organized hunting remain archaeologically unknown. *H. erectus* was the first species to move outside of Africa, populating south-east Europe, where it evolved into a series of transitional forms, one of which presumably became the Neanderthals, and China and Indonesia, where it established itself as *H. erectus*. (Again this is a very simplified account of a hotly debated issue.) The Neanderthals are demonstrably big-game hunters, but these are the first hominins for whom that can be said. It is entirely likely that earlier *Homo* meat eaters, scavenging large game and collecting small animals, would have hunted larger animals opportunely, becoming more adept and confident over time, but this sadly must remain speculation.

The Uniqueness of Human Hunter-Gathering

The Other Hunter-Gatherers

Finally, a bold statement was made above that human hunter-gathering is not unique. A reviewer of this chapter asked that the aspects that separate humans from other animals be stressed, but it turns out to be hard to find such aspects for most of the history of hominins. Although the level of technological achievement and organized big-game hunting of the Neanderthals and later humans certainly differs from any other primate's strategy, these come in relatively late, and for the majority of the timeline of hominins, our ancestors were behaving in a fairly generalized primate fashion. Even when meat eating creeps in, it is through behaviours that have either identical (termite fishing) or strongly correlative counterparts in chimpanzee life.

Although, as noted, humans are certainly not unique in being omnivores, we cannot really term pigs or dogs hunter-gatherers: both are foragers and opportunists for the most part. However, chimpanzees may quite genuinely be termed hunter-gatherers. Isaac (1978a) highlighted the example of chimps, but claimed that taking food back to a recognized home-base to eat later, and sharing, were two behaviours that marked a difference between chimps and early *Homo*. However, since then several studies have observed chimps behaving in ways that undermine some of Isaac's tenets of humanness. Chimps cooperate in running down prey and have a pecking order in terms of sharing the meat from the kill, including a preference for certain parts of the prey (Boesch and Boesch 1989). Meat may be used socially as a manipulation/reward: some workers have claimed that female chimps swap sex for meat from males (Gilby 2006; Gomes and Boesch 2009). Chimps also have a complex gathering and sharing behaviour when it comes to plant foods (Bethell et al. 2000; Slocombe and Newton-Fisher 2005). Chimps not only modify twigs to fish for termites (Goodall 1986) but have a wide range of tool-using behaviours that vary in the number and degree of their expression from group to group—i.e. there are differences in material culture signatures between groups (McGrew 1977; Whiten et al. 1999). At the time of writing, the storing of food for lean times, and food processing (cooking, combining, drying) appear the only parts of human subsistence behaviour that chimps do not do. However, there are animal homologues—plenty of other animals such as pikas and ground squirrels gather and store dry food for winter either in caches they return to (pikas) or burrows they live in (squirrels) (Hickman and Roberts 1995), while others such as bears stockpile calories as body fat; Japanese snow macaques learned to wash potatoes in saltwater to season the flavour, which may tenuously count as food preparation (Kawamura 1959; Kawai 1965); and the history of this area of research shows that the surest way to ensure that chimps are spotted doing something is to publish a paper claiming that they do not do it.

Given that chimpanzees in the wild spontaneously exhibit these behaviours it is difficult to claim that hunter-gatherer behaviour belongs only to humans, or that it defines humans.

Chimps are modern living animals so they are not, of course, ancestral to us or 'the first hunter-gatherers'—indeed, what we really lack is any archaeological or fossil record for chimpanzees: it would be very interesting to know whether it was *Homo* or *Pan* who were first with various aspects of hunter-gathering. It seems likely that the two strategies developed independently, one as a savannah-based strategy and the other (the *Pan* version) as an arboreal strategy, and this may in fact be the difference between the two.

In sum, this chapter has reviewed what we know of hunter-gathering, or its antecedents, in our ancestors and in our close relatives. These ancestors date from at least five million years ago and we have seen how meat eating develops in later stages from a default setting of primate vegetarianism and how the dentition, anatomy, and archaeology of hominins demonstrate this.

REFERENCES

Aiello, C. and Wheeler, P. 1995. The expensive tissue hypothesis: the brain and the digestive system in human and primate evolution. *Current Anthropology* 36, 199–221.

Aiello, L. and Dean, C. 2002. *An introduction to human evolutionary anatomy*. London: Academic Press.

Backwell, L. R. and d'Errico, F. 2001. Evidence of termite foraging by Swartkrans early hominins. *Proceedings of the National Academy of Sciences USA* 98, 1358–63.

Barrickman, N. L. and Lin, M. J. 2010. Encephalization, expensive tissues, and energetics: an examination of the relative costs of brain size in strepsirrhines. *American Journal of Physical Anthropology* 143, 579–90.

Bethell, E., Whiten, A., Muhumaza, G., and Kakura, J. 2000 Active plant food division and sharing by wild chimpanzees. *Primate Report* 56, 67–70.

Bilsborough, A. 1992. *Human evolution*. Edinburgh: Blackie Academic and Professional (Chapman Hall).

Blumenschine, R. J. 1987. Characteristics of an early hominin scavenging niche. *Current Anthropology* 28, 383–404.

Boesch, C. and Boesch, H. 1989. Hunting behavior of wild chimpanzees in the Tai National Park. *American Journal of Physical Anthropology* 78, 547–73.

Brain, C. K. 1981. *The hunters or the hunted? An introduction to African cave taphonomy*. Chicago: University of Chicago Press.

Brown, F., Harris, J., Leakey, R., and Walker, A. 1985. Early *Homo erectus* skeleton from west Lake Turkana, Kenya. *Nature* 316, 788–92.

Bunn, H. T. 1981. Archaeological evidence for meat eating by Plio-Pleistocene hominins from Koobi Fora and Olduvai Gorge. *Nature* 291, 574–7.

Butzer, K. W. 1969. Early *Homo sapiens* remains from the Omo River region of south-west Ethiopia: geological interpretation of two Pleistocene hominin sites in the Lower Omo Basin. *Nature* 222, 1133.

Cerling, T. E., Mbua, E., Kirera, F. M., Manthi, F. K., Grine, F. E., Leakey, M. G., Sponheimer, M., and Uno, K. T. 2011. Diet of *Paranthropus boisei* in the early Pleistocene of East Africa. *Proceedings of the National Academy of Sciences USA* 108, 9337–41.

Churchill, S. E., Pearson, O. M., Grine, F. E., Trinkaus, E., and Holliday, T. W. 1996. Morphological affinities of the proximal ulna from Klasies River main site: archaic or modern? *Journal of Human Evolution* 31, 213–37.

Constantino, P. J., Lee, J. J.-W., Morris, D., Lucas, P. W., Hartstone-Rose, A., Lee, W.-K., Dominy, N. J., Cunningham, A., Wagner M., and Lawn B. R. 2011. Adaptation to hard-object feeding in sea otters and hominins. *Journal of Human Evolution* 61, 89–96.

Dart, R. A. 1925. *Australopithecus africanus:* the man-ape of South Africa. *Nature* 115, 195–9.

Foley, R. and Lewin, R. 2003. *Principles of human evolution.* London: Wiley-Blackwell.

Fruth, B. and McGrew, W. C. 1996. Reply to Rose and Marshall, meat eating, hominid sociality, and home bases revisited. *Current Anthropology* 37, 307–38.

Gilby, I. C. 2006. Meat sharing among the Gombe chimpanzees: harassment and reciprocal exchange. *Animal Behaviour* 71, 953–63.

Gomes, C. M. and Boesch, C. 2009. Wild chimpanzees exchange meat for sex on a long-term basis. *PLoS ONE* 4, e5116.

Goodall, J. 1986. *The chimpanzees of Gombe: patterns of behaviour.* Cambridge, MA: Harvard University Press.

Grine, G. E., Henshilwood, C. S., and Sealy, J. C. 2000. Human remains from Blombos Cave, South Africa (1997–1998 excavations). *Journal of Human Evolution* 38, 755–65.

Henry, A. G., Brooks, A. S., and Piperno, D. R. 2011. Microfossils in calculus demonstrate consumption of plants and cooked foods in Neanderthal diets (Shanidar III, Iraq; Spy I and II, Belgium). *Proceedings of the National Academy of Sciences USA* 108, 486–91.

Hickman, C. P. and Roberts, L. S. 1995. *Animal diversity.* Dubuque, IA: Brown Communications.

Isaac, G. 1971. The diet of early man: aspects of archaeological evidence from lower and middle Pleistocene sites in Africa. *World Archaeology* 2, 278–99.

Isaac, G. 1978a. The food sharing behaviour of protohuman hominids. *Scientific American* 238 (4), 90–108.

Isaac, G. 1978b. Food sharing and human evolution: archaeological evidence from the PlioPleistocene of East Africa. *Journal of Anthropological Research* 34, 311–25.

Isler, K. and van Schaik, C. P. 2009. The expensive brain: a framework for explaining evolutionary changes in brain size. *Journal of Human Evolution* 57, 392–400.

Jacobs, Z., Duller, G. A. T., Wintle, A. G., and Henshilwood, C. S. 2006. Extending the chronology of deposits at Blombos Cave, South Africa, back to 140 ka using optical dating of single and multiple grains of quartz. *Journal of Human Evolution* 51, 255–73.

Johanson, D. C. and Maitland, A. E. 1981. *Lucy: the beginning of humankind.* St Albans: Granada.

Kawai, M. 1965. Newly acquired precultural behavior of the natural troop of Japanese monkeys on Koshima islet. *Primates* 6, 1–30.

Kawamura, S. 1959. The process of sub-culture propagation among Japanese macaques. *Primates* 2, 43–60.

Lartet, L. 1868. Une sépulture des troglodytes du Périgord (crânes des Eyzies). *Bulletins de la Société d'anthropologie de Paris* 3.

Leakey, L. 1959. A new fossil skull from Olduvai. *Nature* 184, 4685.

Leakey, M. G., Spoor, F., Brown, F., Gathogo, P. N., Kiarie, C., and Leakey, L. N. 2001. New hominin genus from eastern Africa shows diverse middle Pliocene lineages. *Nature* 410, 433–40.

Lee-Thorp, J. A. 2011. The demise of Nutcracker Man. *Proceedings of the National Academy of Sciences USA* 108, 9319–20.

Lee-Thorp, J. A. and Sponheimer, M. 2006. Biogeochemical approaches to investigating hominin diets. *Yearbook of Physical Anthropology* 49, 131–48.

Liem, K. F. 1990. Aquatic versus terrestrial feeding modes: possible impacts on the trophic ecology of vertebrates. *Animal Zoology* 30, 209–21.

McDougall, I., Brown, F. H., and Fleagle, J. G. 2005. Stratigraphic placement and age of modern humans from Kibish, Ethiopia. *Nature* 433, 733–6.

McGrew, W. C. 1977. Socialisation and object manipulation of wild chimpanzees. In S. Chevalier-Skolnikoff and F. E. Poirier (eds), *Primate biosocial development: biological, social and ecological determinants*, 261–88. New York: Garland.

Pfefferle, A. D., Warner, L. R., Wang, C. W., Nielsen, W. J., Babbitt, C. C., Fedrigo O., and Wray, G. A. 2011. Comparative expression analysis of the phosphocreatine circuit in extant primates: implications for human brain expansion. *Journal of Human Evolution* 60, 205–12.

Potts, R. and Shipman, P. 1981. Cutmarks made by stone tools on bones from Olduvai Gorge, Tanzania. *Nature* 291, 577–80.

Rak, Y. 1983. *The Australopithecine face*. New York: Academic Press.

Richards, M. and Trinkaus, E. 2009. Isotopic evidence for the diets of European Neanderthals and early modern humans. *Proceedings of the National Academy of Sciences USA* 106, 16034–9.

Rightmire, P. and Deacon, H. 1991. Comparative studies of Late Pleistocene human remains from Klasies River mouth, South Africa. *Journal of Human Evolution* 20, 131–56.

Rightmire, P. and Deacon, H. 2001. New human teeth from Middle Stone Age deposits at Klasies River, South Africa. *Journal of Human Evolution* 41, 535–44.

Rose, L. M. and Marshall, F. 1996. Meat eating, hominid sociality, and home bases revisited. *Current Anthropology* 37, 307–38.

Ruxton, G. D. and Wilkinson, D. M. 2011. Thermoregulation and endurance running in extinct hominins: Wheeler's models revisited. *Journal of Human Evolution* 61, 169–75.

Slocombe, K. and Newton-Fisher, N. E. 2005. Fruit sharing between wild adult chimpanzees (*Pan troglodytes schweinfurthii*): a socially significant event? *American Journal of Primatology* 65, 385–91.

Sponheimer, M. and Lee-Thorp, J. A. 2006. Enamel diagenesis at South African australopith sites: implications for paleoecological reconstruction with trace elements. *Geochimica et Cosmochimica Acta* 70, 1644–54.

Suwa, G., Asfaw, B., Kono, R. T., Kubo, D., Lovejoy, C. O., and White, T. D. 2009. The *Ardipithecus ramidus* skull and its implications for hominin origins. *Science* 326, 68, 68e1–e7.

Trinkaus, E., Moldovan, O., Milota, S., Bîlgăr, A., Sarcina, L., Athreya, S., Bailey, S., Rodrigo, R., Mircea, G., Higham, T., Ramsey, C., and van der Plicht, J. 2003. An early modern human from the Peştera cu Oase, Romania. *Proceedings of the National Academy of Sciences USA* 100, 11231–6.

Tunnell, G. 1996. Reply to Rose and Marshall. *Current Anthropology* 37, 307–38.

Ungar, P. S., Grine, F. E., and Teaford, M. F. 2008. Dental microwear and diet of the Plio-Pleistocene hominin *Paranthropus boisei*. *PLoS ONE* 3, e2044.

Walker, A. and Leakey, R. (eds) 1993. *The Nariokotome Homo erectus skeleton*. New York: Springer.

Walker, A., Zimmerman, M. R., and Leakey, R. E. F. 1982. A possible case of hypervitaminosis A in *Homo erectus*. *Nature* 296, 248–50.

White, T. D., Asfaw, B., DeGusta, D., Gilbert, H., Richards, G. D., and Suwa, G. 2003. Pleistocene *Homo sapiens* from Middle Awash, Ethiopia. *Nature* 423, 742–7.

White, T. D, Suwa, G., and Asfaw, B. 1994. *Australopithecus ramidus*, a new species of early hominin from Aramis, Ethiopia. *Nature* 371, 306–12.

Whiten, A., Goodall, J., McGrew, W. C., Nishida, T., Reynolds, V., Sugiyama, Y., Tutin, C. E. G., Wrangham, R. W., and Boesch, C. 1999. Cultures in chimpanzees. *Nature* 399, 682–5.

Wild, E. M., Teschler-Nicola, M., Kutschera, W., Steier, P., Trinkaus, E., and Wanek, W. 2005. Direct dating of early Upper Palaeolithic human remains from Mladeč. *Nature* 435, 332–5.

Wood, B. and Lonergan, N. 2008. The hominin fossil record: taxa, grades and clades. *Journal of Anatomy* 212, 354–76.

CHAPTER 9

THE NEANDERTHALS
Evolution, Palaeoecology, and Extinction

JOÃO ZILHÃO

History

The first Neanderthal fossils ever found were a child skull from the cave site of Engis, Belgium (in 1829–30; Toussaint et al. 2001), and a partial adult skull from Forbes' Quarry, Gibraltar (in 1848; Stringer 2000). However, the significance of these finds went unrecognized until after the August 1856 discovery of human remains in the Neander valley, near Düsseldorf, Germany (Schmitz 2006; Schmitz and Thissen 2002). A local scholar, Johann Carl Fuhlrott, recovered the bones from the workmen who had dug them out of a cave destroyed by limestone quarrying, the Kleine Feldhofer Grotte (Fuhlrott 1859), triggering a controversy that, in many respects, remains unresolved (Trinkaus and Shipman 1994; Wolpoff 2009).

Hermann Schaaffhausen, the eminent Bonn academic who reported on the discovery had no doubts: 'the extraordinary shape of the skull is due to a natural configuration unknown even among today's most barbarian races' (Schaaffhausen 1858). In other words, this was an extinct human. Others disagreed. For instance, August Mayer, a colleague from Schaaffhausen's own university, argued that 'the flexure [of the femora] is not normal, and is observable, like the inward flexure of the tuberosities of the ischial bones, in those who have been riders from their youth up', while the salient supraorbital arch might simply be a consequence of rickets, which is also known to cause deformation of the limb members. In other words, albeit pathological, the skeleton belonged to an extant human, probably a Mongol Cossack of the Russian army that, in 1814, cut across Germany to attack France—hurt, he would have taken refuge in the cave where he eventually died (Mayer 1864).

As Darwinian evolution gained ground among nineteenth-century natural scientists, the Neander valley individual became widely accepted as a fossil human, one that the anatomist

William King (1864) first proposed to classify as a separate species, *Homo neanderthalensis*, on the following terms:

> The distinctive faculties of Man are visibly expressed in his elevated cranial dome—a feature which, though much debased in certain savage races, essentially characterises the human species. But, considering that the Neanderthal skull is eminently simial, both in its general and particular characters, I feel myself constrained to believe that the thoughts and desires which once dwelt within it never soared beyond those of a brute. The Andamaner, it is indisputable, possesses but the dimmest conceptions of the existence of the Creator of the Universe: his ideas on this subject, and on his own moral obligations, place him very little above animals of marked sagacity; nevertheless, viewed in connection with the strictly human conformation of his cranium, they are such as to specifically identify him with *Homo sapiens*. Psychical endowments of a lower grade than those characterising the Andamaner cannot be conceived to exist: they stand next to brute benightedness. . . . Applying the above argument to the Neanderthal skull, and considering...that it more closely conforms to the brain-case of the Chimpanzee...there seems no reason to believe otherwise than that similar darkness characterised the being to which the fossil belonged.

In a footnote to his paper, King noted that the distinction should in fact be set at the generic, not the specific level, and this notion of the fundamental separateness of the Neanderthals, in morphology as much as in cognition and behaviour, set the background for an enduring public perception, especially in English-speaking countries, where the word became a dictionary-recognized synonym for 'brutish primitive'. The French anatomist Marcelin Boule's (1913) description of the complete skeleton discovered in 1908 at La Chapelle-aux-Saints, which he reconstructed as belonging to an ape-like, hunchback creature with a stooping, imperfectly bipedal gait, lent further support to this perception. Ironically, this reconstruction, misguided primarily by faulty views of functional anatomy, also suffered from an error symmetrical to Mayer's: mistaking for the normal condition the arthritic deformations of the skeleton of an elderly individual (Straus and Cave 1957; Trinkaus 1985).

Mayer's position hailed from a rejection of evolution, but views of the Neanderthal as human (albeit as variant instead of deviant) were again proposed from within natural science as the Neo-Darwinian synthesis came together. A study of the articulated skeletons excavated in 1930s Palestine from the Mount Carmel cave sites of Tabun (Neanderthal) and Skhul (Modern) concluded that 'we encountered so many characters which linked Skhul to the Tabun type that we were ultimately obliged to presume that we had before us the remains of a single people' (McCown and Keith 1939). From the variation observed in these fossils, one of the fathers of the synthesis, Theodosius Dobzhansky, then made a ponderous inference: since the distinction between Neanderthals and Moderns 'was doubtless a resultant of numerous interacting genes', and 'two types differing in a system of genes cannot crystallize out of a mixed population without the interbreeding of these types being prevented by a spatial separation', it followed that 'these types . . . formed earlier in different geographical regions' and that 'the Mount Carmel population arose . . . as the result of hybridization of a Neandertaloid and a modern type'. In conclusion, 'the Neanderthal and the modern types were not isolated reproductively, and, hence, were races of the same species rather than distinct species' (Dobzhansky 1944).

This race or sub-species view became dominant until the late 1980s, when the genetics of extant humans was brought to bear on issues of ancestry and the post-war orthodoxy was challenged by the 'mitochondrial Eve' hypothesis (Cann et al. 1987). At that time, most authors (but not all; cf. Arensburg and Belfer-Cohen 1998) had come to recognize that, *contra* McCown and Keith, the Tabun and Skhul fossils belonged to populations distinct in both chronology and morphology (Howell 1998), while new palaeontological and dating evidence showed that anatomical modernity appeared earlier in Africa than in Europe (Bräuer 1984; Stringer et al. 1984; Valladas et al. 1988). A powerful case was thus made for extant humans worldwide to descend entirely from a small East African population that underwent a speciation event some 150,000 years ago. Its subsequent expansion, 'Within-Africa' first, and then, sometime after 50,000 years ago, 'Out-of-Africa' too, would have resulted in the replacement of coeval archaic populations; consequently, extinction without descent would have been the evolutionary fate of the Eurasian Neanderthals (Klein 2003).

This debate remains unresolved, largely because it is not simply one about the accumulating empirical evidence—it remains strongly influenced by a research history that conditions proposition testing. For instance, where the issue of hybridization is concerned, if you work under Neanderthals-as-sub-species assumptions then rejection of the null hypothesis consists in showing that interbreeding did not occur or was at best exceptional; but, if you take the Neanderthals to have been a separate species, then you will require demonstration that interbreeding was the rule before accepting that your position has been falsified. For consumers of the information, proper awareness of the last 150 years of Neanderthal history is therefore a necessary prerequisite to fully understand the interpretations of the archaeological, palaeontological, and genetic evidence used to reconstruct the first 150,000. Conversely, for the producers of that information, the deep paradigmatic foundation of current debates means that assumptions should be made explicit and transparent. In compliance with this obligation, let it be known that the present essay is written from the *Homo sapiens neanderthalensis* or sub-species perspective.

Biology

Although details of taxonomic definition and individual classification of the fossils involved remain to be clarified, there is overall agreement that the Neanderthal and Modern lineages began to diverge about half a million years ago. For the European variant, the split resulted in the fixation of a number of characteristics that are best seen in the so-called 'classical' Neanderthals of the period between 120,000 and 35,000 years ago, at a time when their distribution extended from Portugal to Uzbekistan and from Germany to Israel. However, many of these characteristics can be traced back to fossils of the ancestral *Homo heidelbergensis* type, namely the Sima de los Huesos (Atapuerca, Spain) and Tautavel (France) samples, or the isolated skulls from Swanscombe (England) and Petralona (Greece), which all date to >200,000 years ago (Hublin 1998).

In the head, Neanderthals—whose braincase was on average, at ~1500 cm^3, somewhat larger than that of extant humans—were principally characterized by the combination of an occipital bun with a low forehead, a projecting face, a chinless mandible, and an overall globular shape (when viewed from behind: Figure 9.1). In the body—and as should be expected, given the predominantly glacial climates under which they evolved—Neanderthals featured proportions typical of today's subarctic populations, with long trunks and short limbs, particularly where the distal parts (arm and shin) are concerned; in contrast, Pleistocene

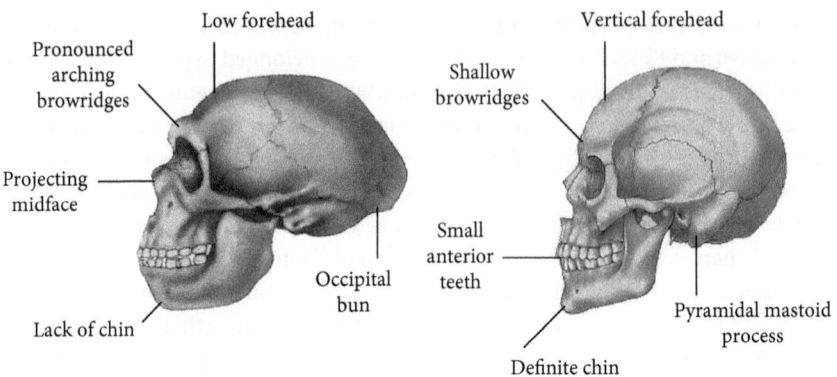

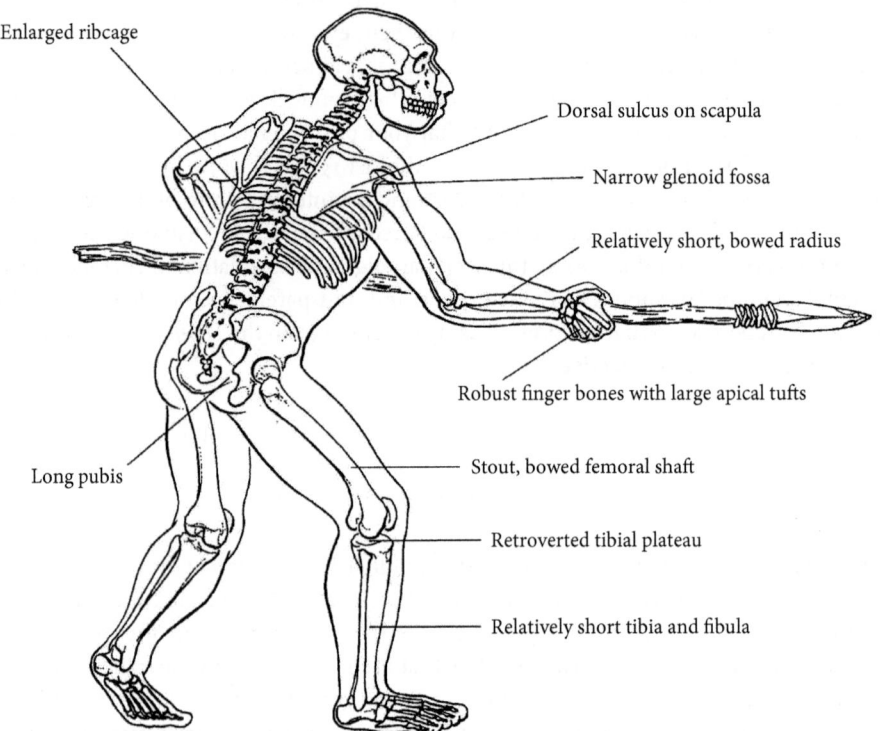

FIGURE 9.1 Top: Neanderthal craniofacial features (left) compared with a typical Modern Human. Bottom: Distinctive features of the Neanderthals' postcranial skeleton (after Churchill 1998).

African humans featured slenderer, linear bodies with long limbs, a pattern that goes back in time to the *Homo erectus* people of 1.5 million years ago and reflects their tropical eco-geography. Other distinctive postcranial features of the Neanderthals, such as the shape of the pelvis and the enlarged ribcage, may be indirect reflections of the body proportions, but some (in the bones of legs, arms, and fingers) relate to their very robust musculature (Churchill 1998; Holliday 1997; Trinkaus and Howells 1979).

Many of the classical Neanderthals' distinctive cranial features are adaptively neutral and can be observed in the skeletons of very young individuals, which implies a genetic basis. Their emergence is thus best explained through isolation by distance, but selection must also have been at work in the production of some of the differences that separate them from earlier representatives of the lineage. For instance, although their big noses and projecting mid-faces are often portrayed as emblematic, the length of Neanderthal faces was in fact significantly reduced by comparison with earlier African, Asian, and European fossils; the marked contrast with early modern and extant humans results from the fact that facial reduction was even more pronounced in the African lineage and continued through the later Pleistocene and the Holocene (Trinkaus 2003). This parallel, albeit geographically unevenly expressed, trend suggests a common underlying cause, possibly the overall reduction in tooth size—with attendant repercussions for the facial and mandibular skeleton and in response to cultural developments, namely the increased consumption of cooked food and the use of manufactured tools for tasks previously carried out with recourse to mandibular-maxillary force (Weaver 2009).

Support for an isolation-by-distance model comes from the growing body of palaeogenetic data concerning the mtDNA of Neanderthals, which features a pattern of nucleotide substitutions unknown among extant humans (Krings et al. 1997; 2000; Serre et al. 2004). This evidence is consistent with the palaeontological evidence for the timing of the Neanderthal/Modern split (half a million years ago), but is otherwise of limited phylogenetic value because contamination and preservation issues have so far prevented the production of reliable results for any other group of fossil humans, including those for which the comparison would be most enlightening—African and Near Eastern early Moderns and Upper Palaeolithic Europeans (Cooper et al. 2004). As a result, it remains possible that the Neanderthal mtDNA pattern is simply archaic rather than specifically Neanderthal, i.e. that it corresponds to one among many other now extinct haplotypes, and one whose past distribution was not necessarily confined to the geographical and taxonomic boundaries indicated by the data currently available.

Moreover, the amount of mtDNA difference between Neanderthals and extant humans is significantly lower than that which can be found even within a single band of our closest living relatives, the chimpanzees (Gagneux et al. 1999). This fact suggests that the palaeogenetics of the last 100,000 years of human evolution is influenced by population size, structure, and history more than by taxonomy. And, indeed, Briggs et al.'s (2009) study of the total mtDNA genome of six Neanderthal individuals found that their diversity was approximately one-third of that in extant humans, which, together with evidence derived from mtDNA protein evolution, they take to suggest a smaller long-term effective population size. In a study of the hypervariable region I of the mtDNA of 12 individuals, Fabre et al. (2009) concluded, in turn, that some level of population structure is subsumed in that apparent genetic homogeneity—in agreement with some palaeontological evidence, these authors found that, genetically, Neanderthals can be divided into at least three groups, one in western Europe, a second in the Mediterranean area, and a third in western Asia.

Technology and Subsistence

Under the influence of the paradigmatic view that biological species must differ in behaviour as much as in morphology, numerous attempts have been made to define species-specific

Neanderthal and Modern Human cultures (e.g. Henshilwood and Marean 2003). However, no such definition exists that does not end up with some Moderns being behaviourally 'Neanderthal' and some Neanderthals being behaviourally 'Modern' (Speth 2004; Zilhão 2001; 2006a). More importantly, such a line of reasoning overlooks the heterogeneity of Neanderthal lifeways across time and space—the geographical structuration of Neanderthal populations increasingly apparent in aspects of their genetics and skeletal anatomy is in fact a well-known feature of their ecological and cultural adaptations. In short, there is no such thing as 'Neanderthal behaviour'.

From the point of view of lithic technology, Neanderthal cultures had a common basis in the use of the Levallois method, which they shared with coeval Modern cultures of Africa and the Near East. This method enables the extraction of blanks (flakes, points, and blades) whose shape is predetermined by a careful preparation of the core. This technique was invented some 250,000 years ago and in an Acheulian context, its advantage consisting in the better control over and more efficient exploitation of good quality lithic raw materials that it allows; however, simpler (e.g. the discoidal method) and expedient techniques continued to be used alongside, especially when dealing with lesser grade rocks. Eventually (in most regions, no later than ~100,000 years ago), hand axes and cleavers were all but abandoned, and stone-tool assemblages became entirely made on flake blanks obtained with such techniques. In terms of archaeological periodization, the crossing of this threshold defines the beginning of the Middle Palaeolithic, which, in Neanderthal Eurasia, goes under the name of 'Mousterian'.

Most blanks obtained by the Levallois and related methods were used with no secondary modification ('retouch') of the edges. However, retouched tools were sometimes produced in considerable amounts, with use-wear analysis showing that a certain measure of correlation exists between typology and function at major group level (Figure 9.2): sidescrapers and knives, mostly used in meat processing and hide working tasks; notches and denticulates, primarily wood working tools; and points, for which breakage evidence suggests use as tips of wooden spears, further indicated by the identification of mastic residues in a number of them (Boëda et al. 1999; 2009; Koller et al. 2001; Mellars 1996). The variation in the frequency of the different types of sidescrapers or in the proportions of sidescrapers, points, and denticulates represented in any given assemblage has led to recognition of different Mousterian facies (e.g. the Typical-, Ferrassie-, or Quina-types), variously interpreted as indicative of cultural preferences (and thereby as definitional of long-lasting ethnic entities) or site function (and thereby as definitional of settlement-subsistence systems) (Binford 1973; Bordes 1968). In fact, this variation seems to be primarily related to raw-material economy, with retouched tools in general, and sidescrapers in particular, increasing in numbers as a function of distance to sources and the need to recycle the dull edges of used blanks (Dibble 1995; Geneste 1989).

Around 50,000 years ago, however, marked regional patterns become apparent in the material culture of Neanderthals. From French Burgundy in the west to the Ukraine in the east, this period sees the rise of the Micoquian, characterized by different types of retouched tools that are functionally equivalent to the sidescrapers, knives, and points of the Mousterian but made not on raw flaked blanks but on bifacially shaped ones, a method that allows for more prolonged utilization and reflects raw-material economization (Bosinski 1967; Uthmeier 2004). Eventually, the Micoquian generated the fully Upper Palaeolithic cultures of the last Neanderthals of northern and central Europe, which

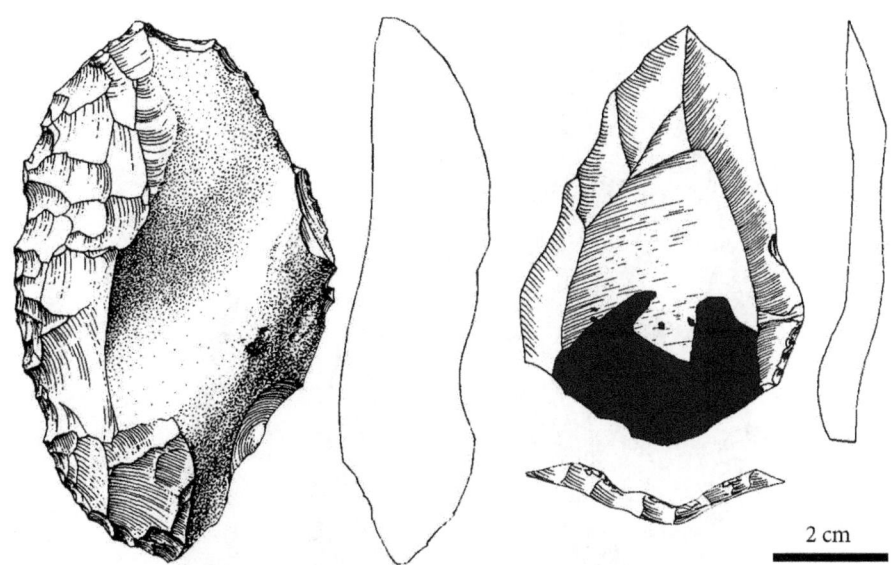

FIGURE 9.2 Stone tools of the Neanderthal-associated Middle Palaeolithic. Left: sidescraper (from level XIV of the Grotte du Renne, France, after Girard 1980). Right: Levallois point with bitumen-covered base (from layer IV-3 of Umm-el-Tlel, Syria, after Boëda et al. 2009).

associated the volumetric reduction of so-called prismatic cores (aimed at the extraction of laminary blanks transformed by retouch into endscrapers and knives) with the production of bifacially shaped leaf-points: the Altmühlian of Germany, and the Szeletian of Moravia, Hungary, and southern Poland (Hopkinson 2004; Kozłowski 1988; Otte 1990; Richter 2000; Zilhão 2009) (Figure 9.3). These cultures are contemporaneous with the Uluzzian of Italy and Greece, defined by crescent-shaped microliths, and the Châtelperronian of France and northern Spain, defined by its curved-backed Châtelperron points. In southern and western Iberia, however, this indigenous Middle-to-Upper Palaeolithic transition did not occur, and Neanderthals continued to manufacture Mousterian stone tool-kits until the very end of their evolutionary trajectory (Zilhão 2006a; 2006b; 2007; Zilhão and d'Errico 1999).

Stone tools, and inferences derived from them, provide the bulk of the evidence concerning the technology used by Neanderthals to obtain and process subsistence resources. Exceptional finds, such as the Schöningen wooden spears (Thieme 1997), illuminate the nature of the hunting weaponry used in Europe some 400,000 years ago. Whether these particular examples were for thrusting or throwing remains a matter of debate, but in either case they imply close-quarter interaction between the hunters and their prey, perhaps explaining the frequent occurrence of healed bone fractures in Neanderthal skeletons (Berger and Trinkaus 1995). The earliest evidence for the use of lighter projectiles post-dates ~50,000 years ago, and comes from the weight and tip geometry of the Châtelperron points, which fall in the range of ethnographic dart-tips and are consistent with the possibility that spear-throwers were already in use at this time (Shea 2006). However, the earliest currently known examples of such arm-extending machinery (spear-thrower hooks made of reindeer antler) are of later Upper Palaeolithic age (Solutrean or Magdalenian: Cattelain 1989),

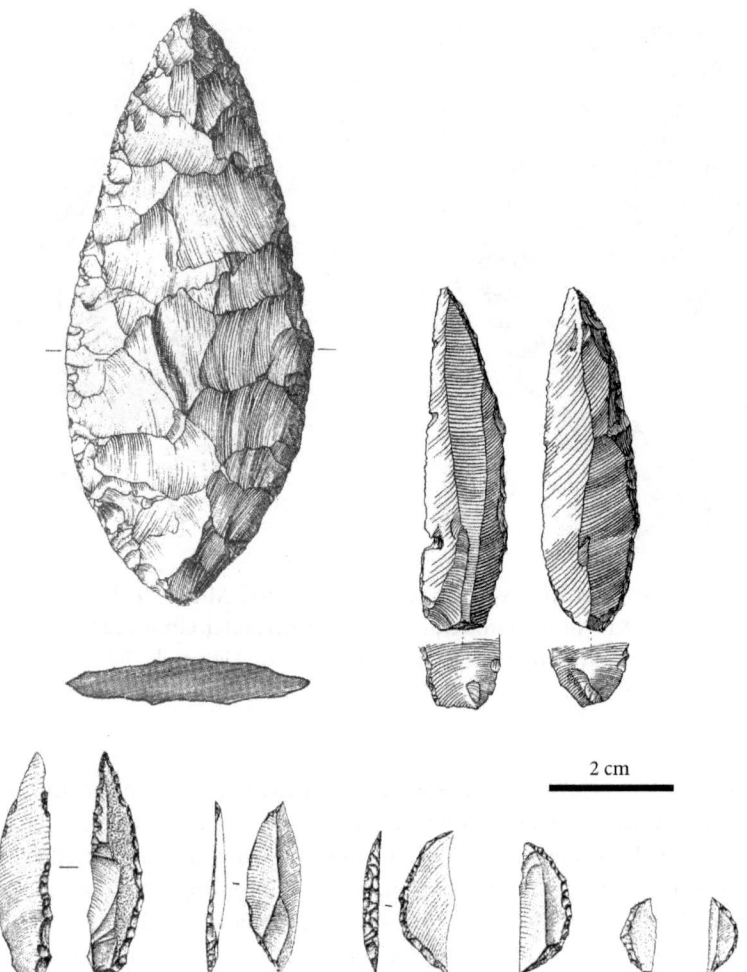

FIGURE 9.3 Stone tools of the Neanderthal-associated early Upper Palaeolithic of Europe. Top left: Altmühlian foliate point (*Blattspitze*) (from Horizon 2 of the Ilsenhöhle, Ranis, Germany, after Hülle 1977). Top right: two Châtelperron points (from the Grotte des Fées at Châtelperron, after Lacaille 1947). Bottom: Uluzzian backed microliths (from level EI-II of Grotta del Cavallo, Italy, after Palma di Cesnola 1993).

and no unambiguous biological evidence of their habitual use (in terms of scapula and humerus morphology) has so far been found among either early Moderns or Neanderthals (Trinkaus 2008).

The faunal remains associated with these stone tools show that, from western Europe to the Near East, Middle Palaeolithic sites yield spectra of large-animal prey evidencing species compositions and patterns of carcass exploitation similar to those of the later, Modern-Human-related Upper Palaeolithic (Marean and Kim 1998; Speth and Tchernov 2001). This evidence has led to the abandonment of a view of Neanderthal subsistence that became widespread at the height of the popularity of the Eve hypothesis: that, because they lacked the ability to pursue and kill big game or were less effective at such tasks than early Moderns, Neanderthals would have acquired their meat mostly from scavenging, not hunting (e.g. Binford 1983; 1989; Stiner and Kuhn 1992). In fact, Neanderthals produced 'specialized' mass hunting sites of reindeer, horse, aurochs, or bison—such as Mauran and La Borde, in southern France, or Salzgitter-Lebenstedt, in northern Germany (Brugal and Jaubert 1996; Gaudzinski and Roebroeks 2000)—recognizable as such on the basis of the same criteria applied to their Modern Human-associated counterparts. When anthropically accumulated late Middle and early Upper Palaeolithic faunal assemblages of Europe are compared, the variation observed is inter-regional and primarily explained by the presence/absence, seasonal availability, and behaviour of the prey animals, not the taxonomy of their human predators (Grayson and Delpech 2002).

This recognition has led to reversals of the argument, namely the notion that the Neanderthals' focus on large-mammal hunting would have been extreme, explaining why they were eventually outcompeted by Modern Humans with greater behavioural flexibility and a broader subsistence base (O'Connell 2006). Coupled with the archaeological evidence on subsistence, data from stable isotope analysis of the bones of the Neanderthals themselves do suggest that, across their northernmost range, they were top-level carnivores that obtained most of their dietary protein from large herbivores (Richards and Trinkaus 2009). Elsewhere, however, a more nuanced picture is apparent. In the Levant, for instance, Neanderthal foraging can only be described as broad-spectrum, as it included the regular exploitation of small animals (namely, tortoise) and plant foods (namely, grass seeds, legumes, acorns, and pistachio nuts), the latter documented by phytoliths and macrobotanical remains from a number of sites (Henry 2003; Lev et al. 2005; Madella et al. 2002). And, in areas of the Iberian Peninsula where, due to tectonics or the steepness of the continental platform, the band of littoral territory lost to post-glacial submersion by the rising sea level is rather narrow, shell-midden accumulations can be observed at Neanderthal sites where they differ from those of the regional Upper Palaeolithic and Mesolithic only in their distinctive stone-tool component (Antunes 2000; Montes 1988; Ramos et al. 2005). In fact, such an exploitation of aquatic resources by Iberian Neanderthals was in no way restricted to the gathering of oysters, cockles, mussels, limpets, and topshells: seals were also taken (Stringer et al. 2008), while there is unambiguous evidence for the hunting and consumption of migratory ducks from at least 120,000 years ago (Blasco and Fernández-Peris 2009). In short, ethnographically documented hunter-gatherers are the proper analogues for the subsistence behaviour of Neanderthals as much as for that of coeval Middle and later Upper Palaeolithic Modern Human societies.

Social Organization and Symbolism

Much as with subsistence, Neanderthal species-specific modes of social organization have also been proposed. Across the different levels of Combe-Grenal, one of the major Mousterian rock shelters of south-western France, Binford (1992) observed a repeated spatial patterning of stone tools and animal body parts. From this, he inferred that the central parts of the site corresponded to female activity areas while the peripheral ones corresponded to areas where male-associated tasks were carried out. In the central areas, females extracted the bone marrow contained in the long bones and the brains and tongues contained in the skulls, and processed plant foods; in the peripheral areas, males conducted the heavy-duty butchery of scavenged carcasses or parts thereof. Climbing the ladder of inference one step up, this spatial segregation was then suggested to reflect a society organized around closely integrated groups of females and dependent children that 'nested' more or less year-round at such sites as Combe-Grenal, to which males, who otherwise formed separate foraging units based elsewhere in the region, would pay regular visits, namely for mating purposes.

Soffer (1994), instead, suggested that the Neanderthal problem resided not in too much division of labour, as envisioned by Binford, but rather in too little of it. For her, the 'division of labour, sharing, and biparental provisioning of the young', the 'interdependent family', and the 'equally unique human constructs of kinship and descent' were the solution brought by Modern Humans to solve the environmental problems encountered while dispersing into Eurasia; these social features would underpin the competitive advantage held over indigenous Neanderthals, ultimately explaining why one group prevailed and the other disappeared. Following up on these suggestions, Kuhn and Stiner (2006) argued that the lack of the age- and gender-based division of labour characteristic of recent foragers implied that, among Neanderthals, females and juveniles were active participants in the hunting of large terrestrial game. This participation placed them at significant risk (even if it was restricted to game beating and driving) and dampened their demographic potential, especially in the face of competition from Moderns.

A key point in Kuhn and Stiner's argument is that nowhere in the Neanderthal record would we see evidence that females had taken on the role of technology specialists, contrary to what should be expected from the fact that Neanderthals inhabited the kinds of cold-temperate or subarctic environments where such a specialization is universally documented in the ethnographic record. Those authors' testable proposition is that the types of artefacts used to make tailored, weather-resistant clothing and well-insulated artificial shelters that could indicate such a gendered technological specialization (for instance, needles and awls made of bone, antler, or ivory) only become common in the Upper Palaeolithic. While this is undoubtedly true, it is no less true that their earliest occurrence in significant numbers is in one Upper Palaeolithic context that is unambiguously associated with the Neanderthals—the Châtelperronian of France. At the key site of the Grotte du Renne (Arcy-sur-Cure), functional analysis and experimental replication showed that the 50 Châtelperronian awls recovered therein had been subjected to an intensive use (a minimum of 20,000 perforations on 2.5 mm-thick leather), with many, given their fineness, having probably been used on less resistant materials, such as furs, bird hides, or intestines (d'Errico et al. 2003). Tailoring and shoemaking are also intimated by results from the analysis of the residue found on a flint flake from the German site of Neumark-Nord, dated to >100,000 years ago, which showed it to be an extract of oak bark macerated in water, of a kind used until recent historical times in the tanning of hides for the manufacture of waterproof clothing and shoe wear (Meller 2003).

This should come as no surprise. Good quality artificial insulation was a prerequisite for survival in the cold Ice Age winters of northern and central Europe. Thermoregulatory models (Aiello and Wheeler 2003) show that the lowest external temperature Neanderthals would have been able to support if dressed in a modern business suit was −24°C. In the absence of even such a basic level of clothing, only a thickness of body fat below the skin in excess of 3 cm could have provided equivalent protection. The weight of such fat, however, would be of some 50 kg, an amount that would leave the average 80 kg male Neanderthal very little left for muscle, bone, and other tissue. Moreover, the palaeoclimatic data show that Neanderthals settled central Europe at times when, considering the wind-chill effect, average winter temperatures were between −20 and −30°C (Van Andel and Davies 2003). The implication is clear: Neanderthal groups living in such environments must have had not only good quality clothing but also all the other gear (for habitation, transportation, or travel) without which survival would have been impossible. Even if preservation issues dictate that direct archaeological evidence is rarely present, the palaeoecology of northern Neanderthals implies levels of technology and social division of labour akin to those of ethnographically documented hunter-gatherers inhabiting regions with similar environmental constraints. In fact, much the same can be said for the short intervals of the last 250,000 years during which climate was much like that of the present time, given the low winter temperatures reached even under such milder climatic conditions in the regions of northern Germany where Neanderthal interglacial settlement is documented (Sørensen 2009).

Another characteristic of subarctic peoples is the extensive nature of their raw-material procurement and exchange networks, and in this regard the evidence from late Neanderthal societies is consistent with the gender-specialization patterns seen at the Grotte du Renne. For instance, based on ethnographically derived criteria, three of the four instances of raw-material displacements in excess of 300 km recorded in the Szeletian correspond to a down-the-line mode of exchange (Féblot-Augustins 2008). These finds underpin the existence of extended social networks and, by contrast with the much more restricted provenance of lithic raw materials documented in western Europe, further document a level of variability in technology, settlement, and group organization that is inconsistent with the notion of a stereotyped, species-specific 'Neanderthal behaviour'.

Evidence for the use of personal ornaments (Zilhão 2007) comes mostly from the Châtelperronian of France: the Saint-Césaire burial contained several *Dentalium* beads, the Quinçay rock shelter yielded six perforated canines (of wolf, fox, and red deer), and a minimum of 34 pendants made of tooth, bone, mammoth ivory, and fossil shell were recovered in levels VIII–X of the Grotte du Renne (Figure 9.4). On the basis of dating results, a minor portion of which are too young for the Châtelperronian contexts whence the samples came, it has been suggested that these Grotte du Renne ornaments could be intrusive from overlying, Modern Human-associated Upper Palaeolithic levels (Higham et al. 2010). However, this interpretation is at odds with the overall pattern of stratigraphic integrity revealed by the distribution of the associated pigments and pigment-processing tools and of the key stone tool types, and the poor preservation of collagen at the site is the parsimonious explanation for the dating anomalies (Caron et al. 2011). *Dentalium* tubes also occur in the Uluzzian (namely at the site of Klisoura 1, in Greece, whence two dozen are reported), and a scatter of finds, isolated or in smaller numbers, has been made in Altmühlian and coeval contexts excavated in the late nineteenth and early/mid twentieth centuries.

These finds date to between 40,000 and 45,000 years ago, but even older ornamental material—perforated, ochre-painted *Glycymeris insubrica* and *Acanthocardia tuberculata* shells—comes from the ~50,000-year-old Mousterian level II of Cueva de los Aviones (Murcia, Spain). At this site, the perforated shells were associated with red and yellow pigments, including a concentration of prisms, granules, and powder of pure natrojarosite, probably the contents of a small purse made of perishable material; this yellow iron mineral

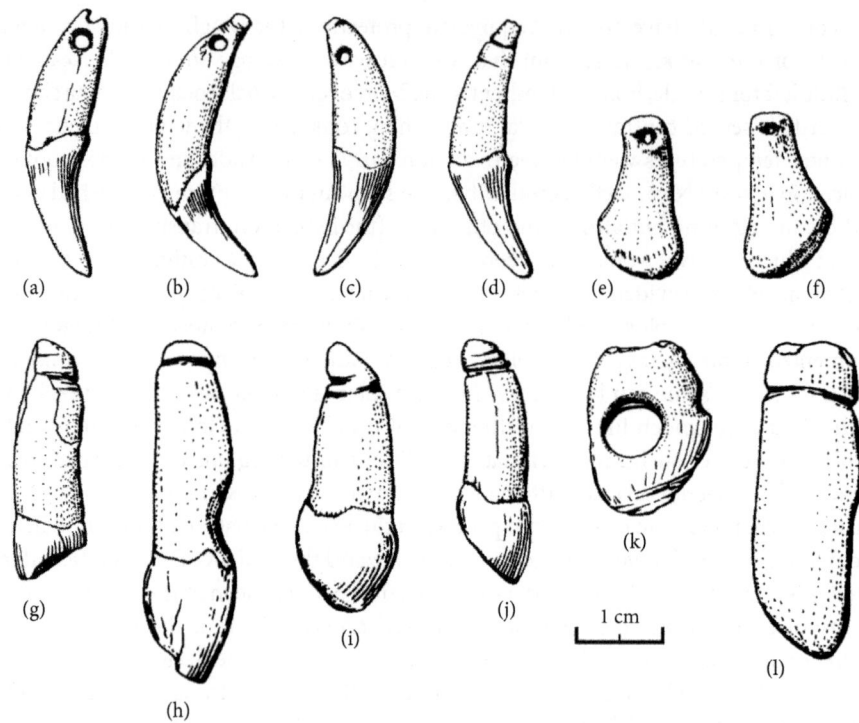

FIGURE 9.4 Pierced and grooved pendants from the Châtelperronian levels of the Grotte du Renne (France): a–d. fox canines; e–f. reindeer phalanges; g–j. bovid incisors; k. red deer canine; l. fossil belemnite (after Zilhão and d'Errico 1999, modified).

was used in Ancient Egypt for cosmetics or paint (namely, for the rendition of the female skin) (Zilhão et al. 2010). Neanderthal body painting, in this case using black, is also intimated by the use-wear apparent in crayon-shaped pieces found among the hundreds of manganese dioxide fragments recovered in the Mousterian levels of the south-western French cave site of Pech de l'Azé I, dated to >43,000 years ago (Soressi and d'Errico 2007). And a very persuasive case for the ornamental use of the wing feathers of large birds of prey (hawks, vulture, lammergeier) has been made on the basis of cut-marks and skeletal representation patterns in the avifauna from the ~44,000-year-old Mousterian levels of the Fumane rock shelter in northern Italy (Peresani et al. 2011).

Although claims for Mousterian figurative art (Marquet and Lorblanchet 2003) and musical instruments (Turk et al. 2006) remain controversial or unsupported (d'Errico et al. 1998; Pettitt 2003), the evidence for body painting and use of personal ornaments sufficiently demonstrates that Neanderthals possessed cognitive capabilities identical to those of Modern Humans and evolved symbolically organized cultures in Europe at about the same time as evidence to that effect first appeared in Africa (McBrearty and Brooks 2000). That much is supported by the practice of ritual burial, the earliest examples of which being the articulated skeletons from Tabun (Neanderthal), Skhul, and Qafzeh (both Modern), in Israel, dated to between 100,000 and 130,000 years ago (Grün et al. 2005). In Europe, the practice is best illustrated by the cemetery excavated in level CD of the La Ferrassie rock shelter in France. Dated to between 60,000 and 75,000 years ago on the basis of the typology of the stone-tool assemblage recovered therein, this level featured several contiguous burial pits containing the remains of seven individuals of different age classes—foetuses, infants, children, and adults. Grave offerings were found in two of these burials: a bone decorated with four sets of parallel incisions was associated with individual number 1, an adult male; and three flint tools (a point and two very large sidescrapers) had been deposited over the body of individual number 6, a 3- to 5-year-old child whose burial pit was covered by a large rock slab decorated with cup-holes on its down facing side (Peyrony 1934). Patterned, abstract markings (sets of notches or V-shaped motifs, with residues of red pigment being preserved on the bottom of the notches of the two most intensively decorated objects) are also apparent in nine of the Châtelperronian awls from the Grotte du Renne (d'Errico et al. 2003).

Many of these developments are restricted to the later part of the Neanderthals' history, and popular explanations for this chronological pattern have been that they reflected acculturation by, or 'imitation without understanding' of Modern Humans encroaching into Neanderthal territory (Hublin 2000; Stringer and Gamble 1993). However, improvements in dating and in the understanding of the site formation processes involved in the few instances of putative interstratification between Neanderthal- and Modern-associated cultures have since removed the empirical basis of such speculations—it is now clear that the emergence of the Châtelperronian and coeval Neanderthal archaeological entities with symbolic artefacts pre-dates by several millennia the earliest anatomical evidence for Modern Humans in Europe (Zilhão 2006a; 2007; Zilhão et al. 2006; 2008). The implication is that Neanderthal cognition and culture were fully symbolic, as is now widely acknowledged, even by former proponents of alternative views (d'Errico and Stringer 2011).

Shennan (2001) and Powell et al. (2009) have shown that a relationship exists between innovation and demography. When population increases, the probability that innovative behaviours will be retained increases too, and especially so if such growth is associated with the establishment and maintenance of long-distance contact, because that enlarges the population on a scale proportional to the square of the distance radius. Although developed for the African case, their models explain equally well the emergence of 'behavioural modernity' among late European Neanderthals, and in fact the population growth that such models imply is consistent with several features of the archaeological record. With the end, around 60,000 years ago, of a period of ten to fifteen millennia of very cold and arid conditions, both the British and Fenno-Scandinavian ice caps and the tundra belts around them retreated markedly, making the northern European plains available for settlement. And, indeed, Mousterian and Neanderthal-associated early Upper Palaeolithic sites are recorded between 60,000 and 40,000 years ago as far north as the 53rd parallel, namely at the sites of Lichtenberg, Lower Saxony (Germany), and Creswell Crags, Derbyshire (England) (Jacobi 1990; Veil et al. 1994).

As documented in the ethnographic record, body ornaments play the role of conveyors of the social identity of persons (Wobst 1977), a need that can only emerge when demographic thresholds are crossed that imply a strong probability of encounter with strangers or people infrequently met. Even under such low population densities as are characteristic of hunter-gatherer groups, such encounters would have been a common experience in the lifetime of individuals involved in networks of raw-material circulation with radii in excess of 300 km, such as those documented for the Szeletian of central Europe. Thus, the notion that the northward expansion of the human range implied by the location of settlement sites was accompanied by a growth in both absolute and relative population numbers is consistent with the evidence for personal ornamentation and long-distance exchange of raw materials. As with subsistence, the implication of these observations is that ethnographically documented hunter-gatherers are the proper analogy with which to approach the division of labour and the social organization—at family, band, and mating-network level—of at least the 'classical' Neanderthals of the last 100,000 years.

Extinction

The combination of mtDNA polymorphisms typically found in Neanderthal fossils does not exist among extant humans (Cooper et al. 2004; Krings et al. 1997; 2000). Moreover, even if individual features of the Neanderthals' distinctive cranio-facial anatomy can still be observed today, the complete, integrated package of such features ceases to exist in the palaeontological record after 35,000 years ago. For the last two decades of the twentieth century, these observations provided strong support for the twin notions that (a) Neanderthals were indeed a different species and (b) their disappearance was a process of extinction without descent.

However, uniparentally transmitted genetic systems such as mtDNA can disappear simply as a result of chance or drift, and the extinction of a particular such lineage by no means implies that its bearers did not contribute genetically to subsequent populations (and all the more so in the case of mtDNA, which comprises only 0.0006 per cent of the total human genome). In fact, the history of Modern Human dispersals reconstructed from the mtDNA of extant people (Forster 2004) dates the immigration of the bearers of the oldest European variants (haplotypes H, I, and U) to about 30,000 years ago. Since, as documented by the fossils recovered at the Romanian cave site of Oase (Rougier et al. 2007; Trinkaus et al. 2003; Zilhão et al. 2007), Moderns are documented in Europe since about 40,000 years ago, it follows that the mtDNA haplotypes of the first Modern Europeans are as extinct as those of the Neanderthals; but it does not follow that such early European Moderns belonged to a different species, nor that such a different species became extinct without descent. By the same token, no such inferences can be made for the Neanderthals on the basis of their mtDNA.

On the other hand, studies of species interfertility versus time of divergence show that, among the many lineages of mammals for which fossil or molecular data are available, 1.4 million years is the minimum amount of time necessary for reproductive separation to emerge between two lineages splitting, and then evolving in isolation, from a recent common ancestor (Holliday 2006). This minimum was observed among different species of gazelles. Among humans, however, the interval between generations is at least four times longer. The implication is that, by mammal standards, one should not expect reproductive isolation to exist among any two contemporary human lineages separated by less than 5 million years of divergence—ten times the duration of the interval that, on the basis of both palaeontological and molecular arguments, separates the time of Neanderthal/Modern split from the time of Neanderthal/Modern contact.

Palaeontological evidence to the effect that Neanderthals did contribute to subsequent populations began to surface around the turn of the last century, as a result of new fossil finds and the study of hitherto undescribed ones. The 4.5-year-old child buried 30,000 years ago at the Lagar Velho rock shelter in Portugal featured a mosaic of genetically inherited characteristics that, for the most part, were Modern (such as a clear, prominent chin and a high cranial vault), but with some reminiscent or even distinctive of the Neanderthals and other archaic Eurasian populations (such as the robusticity of the leg bones, the arctic, cold-adapted body proportions, and several minor features in cranium, mandible, and dentition: Bayle et al. 2010; Duarte et al. 1999; Zilhão and Trinkaus 2002). Similar observations have since been made for every sufficiently complete early Modern European fossil dated to within five millennia of the time of contact, namely the Mladeč sample and the Romanian skulls from Cioclovina and Muierii (Teschler-Nicola 2006; Trinkaus 2007; Wolpoff 2009). These findings were not uncontroversial; other palaeontologists maintained the opinion that the features in question did not suffice to dilute the overall morphological contrast between the two fossil types, and that explanations other than admixture at the time of contact (e.g. convergence, or the persistence of ancestral traits) could conceivably explain them (Tattersall and Schwartz 1999; 2008).

The successful sequencing of a draft of the Neanderthals' nuclear genome—based on DNA extracted from three fossils from the Croatian cave site of Vindija (Green et al. 2010)—has gone a long way to settling this debate. The comparison with present-day humans showed that as much as 1–4 per cent of our genes are inherited from the Neanderthals, and significantly more so among Eurasians than among Africans. The fact that no difference could be found in this regard between a Papuan and a Frenchman has been taken to indicate that the interbreeding event(s) occurred some 50,000 years ago in the Near East, whence stem populations of Moderns carrying Neanderthal genes would have spread to become the ancestors of all extant Eurasians. As pointed out by Green et al., however, this observation neither implies that interbreeding was rare and localized nor does it counter the palaeontological and archaeological evidence that it occurred in Europe too. This is due to the fact that any evidence of a European-specific gene-flow from the Neanderthals is likely to be masked by the effects of subsequent immigrations, namely those that occurred some 30,000 years later in connection with the spread of agriculture from the Near East (Haak et al. 2010).

A scenario of assimilation (Smith et al. 2005) is also supported by the archaeological evidence (Zilhão 2007). The Protoaurignacian is an archaeological culture that is dated in western, central, and southern Europe to the same time interval as the Oase fossils and, as such, is the first cultural entity that can reliably be related to European early Moderns. The composition of Protoaurignacian assemblages of personal ornaments, however, suggests a dual ancestry. For the most part, they are made of the small marine shell beads of diverse taxonomy and similar basket-shaped morphology found at an earlier time among Modern cultures of the Near East and Africa, where they go back to >70,000 years ago (Bouzouggar et al. 2007; d'Errico et al. 2009; Henshilwood et al. 2004; Vanhaeren et al. 2006). But they also include pierced animal teeth, namely of red deer and fox, a type of personal ornament that, although completely unknown in Africa and the Near East prior to the time of contact with Neanderthals in Europe, is characteristic of the Neanderthal-associated Châtelperronian.

The pending issue is why, in an admixture scenario, the configuration that prevailed was the African one. Demography is a possible explanation (Relethford 2003). During the Ice Ages, most of Eurasia was uninhabitable, and the carrying capacity of the settled periglacial areas was significantly lower than in the tropics, which means that between 100,000 and 40,000 years ago a large majority of all the planet's human beings lived in Africa;

consequently, numbers alone predict that any expansion of African peoples into Eurasia would result in the eventual swamping of the aboriginal ones, namely the Neanderthals. Another possibility is selection (Eswaran 2002; Eswaran et al. 2005; Garrigan and Kingan 2007; Hawks et al. 2007; Weaver and Roseman 2005). If the bearers of the African genome held some advantage, for instance in fertility (either as a result of more gracile morphology that facilitated childbirth, or as a result of simply being African, i.e. of human fertility being naturally higher in tropical than in subarctic environments), their anatomical *Gestalt* would prevail very rapidly, in no more than a few millennia, even if the number of people involved in the initial dispersals into Eurasia was small and admixture levels were high.

The combined weight of the palaeontological, archaeological, and genetic records promises finally to solve the riddle of Neanderthal extinction. On current evidence, the answer seems to be as complex as the problem. Yes, Neanderthals became extinct, but no, not without descent. If they contributed genetically and culturally to Eurasian populations of the post-contact period, then they belong in the ancestry of extant humans. And if they interbred with Modern Humans of African origin to the significant extent indicated by the genomic data, then they fully belong in the human species. To go back to the terms of King's definition, current evidence would therefore seem to indicate that the range of human biological, cognitive, and cultural variation encompasses the Neanderthal as much as the Andamanese islander or the Victorian gentleman.

REFERENCES

Aiello, L. and Wheeler, P. 2003. Neandertal thermoregulation and the glacial climate. In T. H. van Andel and W. Davies (eds), *Neanderthals and modern humans in the European landscape during the last glaciation*, 147–66. Cambridge: McDonald Institute for Archaeological Research.

Antunes, M. T. (ed.) 2000. *Últimos Neandertais em Portugal: evidência, odontológica e outra*. Lisbon: Academia das Ciências.

Arensburg, B. and Belfer-Cohen, A. 1998. Sapiens and Neandertals: rethinking the Levantine Middle Paleolithic hominids. In T. Akazawa, K. Aoki, and O. Bar-Yosef (eds), *Neandertals and modern humans in Western Asia*, 311–22. New York: Plenum Press.

Bayle, P., Macchiarelli, R., Trinkaus, E., Duarte, D., Mazurier, A., and Zilhão, J. 2010. Dental maturational sequence and dental tissue proportions in the early Upper Paleolithic child from Abrigo do Lagar Velho, Portugal. *Proceedings of the National Academy of Sciences USA* 107, 1338–42.

Berger, T. D. and Trinkaus, E. 1995. Patterns of trauma among the Neandertals. *Journal of Archaeological Science* 22, 841–52.

Binford, L. 1973. Interassemblage variability: the Mousterian and the 'functional' argument. In C. Renfrew (ed.), *The explanation of culture change: models in prehistory*, 227–54. London: Duckworth.

Binford, L. 1983. *In pursuit of the past*. London: Thames and Hudson.

Binford, L. 1989. Isolating the transition to cultural adaptations: an organizational approach. In E. Trinkaus (ed.), *The emergence of modern humans: biocultural adaptations in the Later Pleistocene*, 18–41. Cambridge: Cambridge University Press.

Binford, L. 1992. Hard evidence. *Discover* February, 44–51.

Blasco, R. and Fernández-Peris, J. 2009. Middle Pleistocene bird consumption at Level XI of Bolomor Cave (Valencia, Spain). *Journal of Archaeological Science* 36, 2213–23.

Böeda, E., Bonilauri, S., Connan, J., Jarvie, D., Mercier, N., Tobey, M., Valladas, H., and Al Sakhel, H. 2009. New evidence for significant use of bitumen in Middle Palaeolithic technical systems at Umm El Tlel (Syria) around 70,000 BP. *Paléorient* 34, 67–83.

Böeda, E., Geneste, J.-M., Griggo, C., Mercier, N., Muhesen, S., Reyss, J.-L., Taha, A., and Valladas, H. 1999. A Levallois point embedded in the vertebra of a wild ass (*Equus africanus*): hafting, projectiles and Mousterian hunting weapons. *Antiquity* 73, 394–402.

Bordes, F. 1968. *Le Paléolithique dans le monde*. Paris: Hachette.

Bosinski, G. 1967. *Die mittelpaläolithischen Funde im westlichen Mitteleuropa*. Cologne/Vienna: Fundamenta A/4.

Boule, M. 1913. *L'homme fossile de La Chapelle-aux-Saints*. Paris: Masson.

Bouzouggar, A., Barton, N., Vanhaeren, M., d'Errico, F., Collcutt, S., Higham, T., Hodge, E., Parfitt, S., Rhodes, E., Schwenninger, J.-L., Stringer, C., Turner, E., Ward, S., Moutmir, A., and Stambouli, A. 2007. 82,000-year-old shell beads from North Africa and implications for the origins of modern human behavior. *Proceedings of the National Academy of Sciences USA* 104, 9964–9.

Bräuer, G. 1984. A craniological approach to the origin of anatomically modern *Homo sapiens* in Africa and implications for the appearance of modern Europeans. In F. Smith and F. Spencer (eds), *The origins of modern humans: a world survey of the fossil evidence*, 327–410. New York: Alan R. Liss.

Briggs, A. W., Good, J. M., Green, R. E., Krause, J., Maricic, T., Stenzel, U., Lalueza-Fox, C., Rudan, P., Brajkovic, D., Kucan, Ž., Gusic, I., Schmitz, R., Doronichev, V. B., Golovanova, L. V., Rasilla, M., Fortea, J., Rosas, A., and Pääbo, S. 2009. Targeted retrieval and analysis of five Neandertal mtDNA genomes. *Science* 325, 318–21.

Brugal, J. P. and Jaubert, J. 1996. Stratégie d'exploitation et mode de vie des populations du Paléolithique moyen: exemples des sites du sud de la France. In Société Préhistorique Française (ed.), *La vie préhistorique*, 148–55. Paris: Faton.

Cann, R. L., Stoneking, M., and Wilson, A. C. 1987. Mitochondrial DNA and human evolution. *Nature* 325, 31–6.

Caron, F., d'Errico, F., Del Moral, P., Santos, F., and Zilhão, J. 2011. The reality of Neandertal symbolic behavior at the Grotte du Renne, Arcy-sur-Cure. *PLoS ONE* 6, e21545 (doi:10.1371/journal.pone.0021545).

Cattelain, P. 1989. Un crochet de propulseur solutréen de la grotte de Combe-Saunière 1 (Dordogne). *Bulletin de la Société Préhistorique Française* 86, 213–16.

Churchill, S. E. 1998. Cold adaptation, heterochrony, and Neandertals. *Evolutionary Anthropology* 7, 46–61.

Cooper, A., Drummond, A. J., and Willerslev, E. 2004. Ancient DNA: would the real Neandertal please stand up? *Current Biology* 14, R431–3.

d'Errico, F., Julien, M., Liolios, D., Vanhaeren, M., and Baffier, D. 2003. Many awls in our argument: bone tool manufacture and use in the Châtelperronian and Aurignacian levels of the Grotte du Renne at Arcy-sur-Cure. In J. Zilhão and F. d'Errico (eds), *The chronology of the Aurignacian and of the transitional technocomplexes: dating, stratigraphies, cultural implications*, 247–70. Lisbon: Instituto Português de Arqueologia.

d'Errico, F. and Stringer, C. B. 2011. Evolution, revolution or saltation scenario for the emergence of modern cultures? *Philosophical Transactions of the Royal Society B* 366, 1060–9.

d'Errico, F., Vanhaeren, M., Barton, N., Bouzouggar, A., Mienis, H., Richter, D., Hublin, J.-J., McPherron, S. P., and Lozouet, P. 2009. Additional evidence on the use of personal ornaments in the Middle Paleolithic of North Africa. *Proceedings of the National Academy of Sciences USA* 106, 16051–6.

d'Errico, F., Villa, P., Pinto, A., and Ruiz, R. 1998. A Middle Palaeolithic origin of music? Using cave-bear bone accumulations to assess the Divje Babe I bone 'flute'. *Antiquity* 72, 65–79.

Dibble, H. 1995. Middle Paleolithic scraper reduction: background, clarification, and review of the evidence to date. *Journal of Archaeological Method and Theory* 2, 299–368.

Dobzhansky, T. H. 1944. On species and races of living and fossil man. *American Journal of Physical Anthropology* 2, 251–65.

Duarte, C., Maurício, J., Pettitt, P. B., Souto, P., Trinkaus, E., van der Plicht, H., and Zilhão, J. 1999. The Early Upper Paleolithic human skeleton from the Abrigo do Lagar Velho (Portugal) and modern human emergence in Iberia. *Proceedings of the National Academy of Sciences USA* 96, 7604–9.

Eswaran, V. 2002. A diffusion wave out of Africa: the mechanism of the modern human revolution? *Current Anthropology* 43, 749–74.

Eswaran, V., Harpending, H., and Rogers, A. R. 2005. Genomics refutes an exclusively African origin of humans. *Journal of Human Evolution* 49, 1–18.

Fabre, V., Condemi, S., and Degioanni, A. 2009. Genetic evidence of geographical groups among Neanderthals. *PLoS ONE* 4, e5151.

Féblot-Augustins, J. 2008. Paleolithic raw material provenance studies. In D. M. Pearsall (ed.), *Encyclopedia of archaeology*, vol. 2, 1187–98. New York: Elsevier.

Forster, P. 2004. Ice Ages and the mitochondrial DNA chronology of human dispersals: a review. *Philosophical Transactions of the Royal Society London B* 359, 255–64.

Fuhlrott, J. C. 1859. Menschliche Ueberreste aus einer Felsengrotte des Düsselthals. Ein Beitrag zur Frage über die Existenz fossiler Mensche. *Verhandlungen des naturhistorischen Vereines der preussischen Rheinlande und Westphalens* 16, 131–53.

Gagneux, P., Wills, C., Gerloff, U., Tautz, D., Morin, P. A., Boesch, C., Fruth, B., Hohmann, G., Ryder, O. A., and Woodruff, D. S. 1999. Mitochondrial sequences show diverse evolutionary histories of African hominoids. *Proceedings of the National Academy of Sciences USA* 96, 5077–82.

Garrigan, D. and Kingan, S. B. 2007. Archaic human admixture: a view from the genome. *Current Anthropology* 48, 895–902.

Gaudzinski, S. and Roebroeks, W. 2000. Adults only: reindeer hunting at the Middle Palaeolithic site Salzgitter-Lebenstedt, northern Germany. *Journal of Human Evolution* 38, 497–521.

Geneste, J.-M. 1989. Économie des ressources lithiques dans le Moustérien du sud-ouest de la France. In M. Otte (ed.), *L'Homme de Néandertal. Vol. 6. La subsistance*, 75–97. Liège: Service de Préhistoire de l'Université de Liège.

Girard, C. 1980. Les industries moustériennes de la grotte du Renne à Arcy-sur-Cure. *Gallia Préhistoire* 23, 1–36.

Grayson, D. K. and Delpech, F. 2002. Specialized early Upper Palaeolithic hunters in southwestern France? *Journal of Archaeological Science* 29, 1439–49.

Green, R. E., Krause, J., Briggs, A. W., Maricic, T., Stenzel, U., Kircher, M., Patterson, N., Li, H., Zhai, W., Fritz, M. H.-Y., Hansen, N. F., Durand, E. Y., Malaspinas, A.-S., Jensen, J., Marques-Bonet, T., Alkan, C., Prüfer, K., Meyer, M., Burbano, H. A., Good, J. M., Schultz, R., Aximu-Petri, A., Butthof, A., Höber, B., Höffner, B., Siegemund, M., Weihmann, A., Nusbaum, C., Lander, E. S., Russ, C., Novod, N., Affourtit, J., Egholm, M., Verna, C., Rudan, P., Brajkovic, D., Kucan, Ž., Gušic, I., Doronichev, V. B., Golovanova, L. V., Lalueza-Fox, C., de la Rasilla, M., Fortea, J., Rosas, A., Schmitz, R. W., Johnson, P. L. F., Eichler, E. E., Falush, D., Birney, E., Mullikin, J. C., Slatkin, M., Nielsen, R., Kelso, J., Lachmann, M., Reich, D., and Pääbo, S. 2010. A draft sequence of the Neandertal genome. *Science* 328, 710–22.

Grün, R., Stringer, C., McDermott, F., Nathan, R., Porat, N., Robertson, S., Taylor, L., Mortimer, G., Eggins, S., and McCulloch, M. 2005. U-series and ESR analyses of bones and teeth relating to the human burials from Skhul. *Journal of Human Evolution* 49, 316–34.

Haak, W., Balanovsky, O., Sanchez, J. J., Koshel, S., Zaporozhchenko, V., Adler, C. J., Der Sarkissian, C. S. I., Brandt, G., Schwarz, C., Nicklisch, N., Dresely, V., Fritsch, B., Balanovska, E., Villems, R., Meller, H., Alt, K. W., and Cooper, A. 2010. Ancient DNA from European early Neolithic farmers reveals their Near Eastern affinities. *PLoS Biology* 8, e1000536.

Hawks, J., Wang, E. T., Cochran, G. M., Harpending, H. C., and Moyzis, R. K. 2007. Recent acceleration of human adaptive evolution. *Proceedings of the National Academy of Sciences USA* 104, 20753–8.

Henry, D. O. (ed.) 2003. *Neanderthals in the Levant: behavioral organization and the beginnings of human modernity*. London: Continuum.

Henshilwood, C., d'Errico, F., Vanhaeren, M., van Niekerk, K., and Jacobs, Z. 2004. Middle Stone Age shell beads from South Africa. *Science* 304, 404.

Henshilwood, C. and Marean, C. 2003. The origin of modern human behavior: critique of the models and their test implications. *Current Anthropology* 44, 627–51.

Higham, T. F. G., Jacobi, R. M., Julien, M., David, F., Basell, L., Wood, R., Davies, W., and Bronk Ramsey, C. 2010. Chronology of the Grotte du Renne (France) and implications for the context of ornaments and human remains within the Châtelperronian. *Proceedings of the National Academy of Sciences USA* 107, 20234–9.

Holliday, T. W. 1997. Body proportions in Late Pleistocene Europe and modern human origins. *Journal of Human Evolution* 32, 423–47.

Holliday, T. W. 2006. Neanderthals and modern humans: an example of a mammalian syngameon? In K. Harvati and T. Harrison (eds), *Neanderthals revisited: new approaches and perspectives*, 289–306. New York: Springer.

Hopkinson, T. 2004. Leaf points, landscapes and environment change in the European Late Middle Palaeolithic. In N. J. Conard (ed.), *Settlement dynamics of the Middle Paleolithic and Middle Stone Age, Volume II*, 227–58. Tübingen: Kerns.

Howell, F. C. 1998. Evolutionary implications of altered perspectives on hominine demes and populations in the Later Pleistocene of Western Eurasia. In T. Akazawa, K. Aoki, and O. Bar-Yosef (eds), *Neandertals and modern humans in Western Asia*, 5–27. New York: Plenum Press.

Hublin, J.-J. 1998. Climatic changes, paleogeography, and the evolution of the Neandertals. In T. Akazawa, K. Aoki, and O. Bar-Yosef (eds), *Neandertals and modern humans in Western Asia*, 295–310. New York: Plenum Press.

Hublin, J.-J. 2000. Modern-nonmodern hominid interactions: a Mediterranean perspective. In O. Bar-Yosef and D. Pilbeam (eds), *The geography of Neandertals and modern humans in Europe and the Greater Mediterranean*, 157–82. Cambridge, MA: Peabody Museum.

Hülle, W. M. 1977. *Die Ilsenhöhle unter Burg Ranis/Thüringen. Eine paläolitische Jägerstation*. Stuttgart: Gustav Fischer.

Jacobi, R. 1990. Leaf-points and the British early Upper Palaeolithic. In J. Kozłowski (ed.), *Feuilles de pierre: les industries à pointes foliacées du Paléolithique supérieur européen. Actes du Colloque de Cracovie 1989*, 271–89. Liège: Université de Liège.

King, W. 1864. The reputed fossil man of the Neanderthal. *Quarterly Journal of Science* 1, 88–97.

Klein, R. G. 2003. Whither the Neanderthals? *Science* 299, 1525–7.

Koller, J., Baumer, U., and Mania, D. 2001. High-tech in the middle Palaeolithic: Neandertal-manufactured pitch identified. *European Journal of Archaeology* 4, 385–97.

Kozłowski, J. 1988. The transition from the Middle to the Early Upper Paleolithic in central Europe and the Balkans. In J. F. Hoffecker and C. A. Wolf (eds), *The Early Upper Paleolithic; evidence from Europe and the Near East*, 193–235. Oxford: British Archaeological Reports.

Krings, M., Capelli, C., Tschentscher, F., Geisert, H., Meyer, S., von Haeseler, A., Grossschmidt, K., Possnert, G., Paunovic, M., and Pääbo, S. 2000. A view of Neandertal genetic diversity. *Nature Genetics* 26, 144–6.

Krings, M., Stone, A., Schmitz, R. W., Krainitzki, H., Stoneking, M., and Pääbo, S. 1997. Neandertal DNA sequences and the origin of modern humans. *Cell* 90, 19–30.

Kuhn, S. and Stiner, M. 2006. What's a mother to do? The division of labor among Neandertals and Modern Humans in Eurasia. *Current Anthropology* 47, 953–80.

Lacaille, A. D. 1947. Châtelperron: a new survey of its Palaeolithic industry. *Archaeologia* 92, 95–119.

Lev, E., Kislev, M.,E., and Bar-Yosef, O. 2005. Mousterian vegetal food in Kebara Cave, Mt. Carmel. *Journal of Archaeological Science* 32, 475–84.

McBrearty, S. and Brooks, A. 2000. The revolution that wasn't: a new interpretation of the origin of modern human behavior. *Journal of Human Evolution* 39, 453–563.

McCown, T. D. and Keith, A. 1939. *The Stone Age of Mount Carmel. Vol. 2. The fossil human remains from the Levalloiso-Mousterian*. Oxford: Clarendon Press.

Madella, M., Jones, M. K., Goldberg, P., Goren, Y., and Hovers, E. 2002. The exploitation of plant resources by Neanderthals in Amud Cave (Israel): the evidence from phytolith studies. *Journal of Archaeological Science* 29, 703–19.

Marean, C. and Kim, S. Y. 1998. Mousterian large-mammal remains from Kobeh Cave: behavioral implications for Neanderthals and early modern humans. *Current Anthropology* 39 Supplement, S79–S113.

Marquet, J.-C. and Lorblanchet, M. 2003. A Neanderthal face? The proto-figurine from La Roche-Cotard, Langeais (Indre-et-Loire, France). *Antiquity* 77, 661–70.

Mayer, A. 1864. Ueber die fossilen Ueberreste eines menschlichen Schädels und Skeletes in einer Felsenhöhle des Düssel- oder Neander- Thales. *Archiv für Anatomie, Physiologie und Wissenschaftliche Medicin* 30, 1–26.

Mellars, P. A. 1996. *The Neanderthal legacy*. Princeton: Princeton University Press.

Meller, H. 2003. *Geisteskraft. Alt- und Mittelpaläolithikum*. Halle: Landesmuseum für Vorgeschichte.

Montes, R. 1988. Restos malacológicos y paleontológicos del Musteriense en la costa de Murcia (Sureste de España). *Anales de Prehistoria y Arqueología de la Universidad de Murcia* 4, 27–31.

O'Connell, J. F. 2006. How did modern humans displace Neanderthals? Insights from hunter-gatherer ethnography and archaeology. In N. J. Conard (ed.), *When Neanderthals and modern humans met*, 43–64. Tübingen: Kerns Verlag.

Otte, M. 1990. Les industries à pointes foliacées du nord-ouest européen. In J. Kozłowski (ed.), *Feuilles de pierre: les industries à pointes foliacées du Paléolithique supérieur européen. Actes du Colloque de Cracovie 1989*, 247–69. Liège: Université de Liège.

Palma di Cesnola, A. 1993. *Il Paleolitico superiore in Italia*. Florence: Garlatti e Razzai.

Peresani, M., Fiore, I., Gala, M., Romandini, M., and Tagliacozzo, A. 2011. Late Neandertals and the intentional removal of feathers as evidenced from bird bone taphonomy at Fumane Cave 44 ky B.P., Italy. *Proceedings of the National Academy of Sciences USA* 108, 3888–93.

Pettitt, P. B. 2003. Is this the infancy of art? Or the art of an infant? A possible Neanderthal face from La Roche-Cotard, France. *Before Farming* 11, 1–3.

Peyrony, D. 1934. La Ferrassie. Moustérien—Périgordien—Aurignacien. *Préhistoire* 3, 1–92.

Powell, A., Shennan, S., and Thomas, M. G. 2009. Late Pleistocene demography and the appearance of modern human behavior. *Science* 324, 1298–1301.

Ramos, J., Aguilera, R., Cortés, M., and Bañares, M. M. 2005. El parque arqueológico de La Araña: una vía para el estudio, la conservación y la puesta en valor de yacimientos paleolíticos. In M. Santonja, A. Pérez-González, and M. Machado (eds), *Geoarqueología y patrimonio en la Península Ibérica y el entorno mediterráneo*, 625–38. Almazán: ADEMA.

Relethford, J. 2003. *Reflections of our past*. Boulder: Westview.

Richards, M. P. and Trinkaus, E. 2009. Isotopic evidence for the diets of European Neanderthals and early modern humans. *Proceedings of the National Academy of Sciences USA* 106, 16034–9.

Richter, J. 2000. Social memory among late Neanderthals. In J. Örschiedt and G. Weniger (eds), *Neanderthals and modern humans—discussing the transition, central and eastern Europe from 50.000–30.000 B.P.*, 123–32. Mettmann: Neandertal Museum.

Rougier, H., Milota, Ş., Rodrigo, R., Gherase, M., Sarcină, L., Moldovan, O., Zilhão, J., Constantin, S., Franciscus, R. G., Zollikofer, C. P. E., Ponce de León, M., and Trinkaus, E. 2007. Peştera cu Oase 2 and the cranial morphology of early modern Europeans. *Proceedings of the National Academy of Sciences USA* 104, 1165–70.

Schaaffhausen, H. 1858. Zur Kenntnis der ältesten Rassenschädel. *Archiv für Anatomie, Physiologie und Wissenschaftliche Medizin* 24, 453–78.

Schmitz, R. W. 2006. *Neanderthal 1856–2006*. Mainz: Philipp von Zabern.

Schmitz, R. W. and Thissen, J. 2002. *Die Geschichte geht weiter*. Heidelberg: Spektrum.

Serre, D., Langaney, A., Chech, M., Teschler-Nicola, M., Paunović, M., Mennecier, Ph., Hofreiter, M., Possnert, G., and Pääbo, S. 2004. No evidence of Neandertal mtDNA contribution to early modern humans. *PLoS Biology* 2, 313–17.

Shea, J. J. 2006. The origins of lithic projectile point technology: evidence from Africa, the Levant, and Europe. *Journal of Archaeological Science* 33, 823–46.

Shennan, S. 2001. Demography and cultural innovation: a model and its implications for the emergence of modern human culture. *Cambridge Archaeological Journal* 11, 5–16.

Smith, F. H., Janković, I., and Karavanić, I. 2005. The assimilation model, modern human origins in Europe, and the extinction of Neandertals. *Quaternary International* 137, 7–19.

Soffer, O. 1994. Ancestral life ways in Eurasia: the Middle and Upper Paleolithic records. In M. H. Nitecki and D. V. Nitecki (eds), *Origins of anatomically modern humans*, 101–19. New York: Plenum Press.

Sørensen, B. 2009. Energy use by Eem Neanderthals. *Journal of Archaeological Science* 36, 2201–5.

Soressi, M. and d'Errico, F. 2007. Pigments, gravures, parures: les comportements symboliques controversés des Néandertaliens. In B. Vandermeersch and B. Maureille (eds), *Les Néandertaliens: biologie et cultures*, 297–309. Paris: Éditions du CTHS.

Speth, J. D. 2004. News flash: negative evidence convicts Neanderthals of gross mental incompetence. *World Archaeology* 36, 519–26.

Speth, J. D. and Tchernov, E. 2001. Neanderthal hunting and meat-processing in the Near East: evidence from Kebara Cave (Israel). In C. B. Stanford and H. T. Bunn (eds), *Meat eating and human evolution*, 52–72. Oxford: Oxford University Press.

Stiner, M. C. and Kuhn, S. L. 1992. Subsistence, technology and adaptive variation in Middle Paleolithic Italy. *American Anthropologist* 94, 306–39.

Straus, W. L. Jr. and Cave, A. J. E. 1957. Pathology and the posture of Neanderthal man. *Quarterly Review of Biology* 32, 348–63.

Stringer, C. 2000. Gibraltar and the Neanderthals 1848–1998. In C. Stringer, R. N. E. Barton, and C. Finlayson (eds), *Neanderthals on the edge: 150th anniversary conference of the Forbes' Quarry discovery, Gibraltar*, 133–7. Oxford: Oxbow.

Stringer, C., Finlayson, J. C., Barton, R. N. E., Fernández-Jalvo, Y., Caceres, I., Sabin, R. C., Rhodes, E. J., Currant, A. P., Rodríguez-Vidal, J., Giles-Pacheco, F., and Riquelme-Cantal, J. A. 2008. Neanderthal exploitation of marine mammals in Gibraltar. *Proceedings of the National Academy of Sciences USA* 105, 14319–24.

Stringer, C. and Gamble, C. 1993. *In search of the Neanderthals*. London: Thames and Hudson.

Stringer, C., Hublin, J.-J., and Vandermeersch, B. 1984. The origin of anatomically modern humans in Western Europe. In F. Smith and F. Spencer (eds), *The origins of modern humans: a world survey of the fossil evidence*, 51–135. New York: Alan R. Liss.

Tattersall, I. and Schwartz, J. H. 1999. Hominids and hybrids: the place of Neanderthals in human evolution. *Proceedings of the National Academy of Sciences USA* 96, 7117–19.

Tattersall, I. and Schwartz, J. H. 2008. The morphological distinctiveness of *Homo sapiens* and its recognition in the fossil record: clarifying the problem. *Evolutionary Anthropology* 17, 49–54.

Teschler-Nicola, M. (ed.) 2006. *Early modern humans at the Moravian Gate: the Mladeč caves and their remains*. Vienna: Springer.

Thieme, H. 1997. Lower Palaeolithic hunting spears from Germany. *Nature* 385, 807–10.

Toussaint, M., Pirson, S., and Bocherens, H. 2001. Neandertals from Belgium. *Anthropologica et Praehistorica* 112, 21–38.

Trinkaus, E. 1985. Pathology and the posture of the La Chapelle-aux-Saints Neandertal. *American Journal of Physical Anthropology* 67, 19–41.

Trinkaus, E. 2003. Neandertal faces were not long; modern human faces are short. *Proceedings of the National Academy of Sciences USA* 100, 8142–5.

Trinkaus, E. 2007. European early modern humans and the fate of the Neandertals. *Proceedings of the National Academy of Sciences USA* 104, 7367–72.

Trinkaus, E. 2008. Behavioral implications of the Muierii 1 early modern human scapula. *Annuaire Roumain d'Anthropologie* 45, 27–41.

Trinkaus, E. and Howells, W. W. 1979. The Neanderthals. *Scientific American* 241, 118–33.

Trinkaus, E., Moldovan, O., Milota, Ş., Bîlgăr, A., Sarcina, L., Athreya, S., Bailey, S. E., Rodrigo, R., Mircea, G., Higham, T., Bronk Ramsey, C. H., and van der Plicht, J. 2003. An early modern human from the Peştera cu Oase, Romania. *Proceedings of the National Academy of Sciences USA* 100, 11231–6.

Trinkaus, E. and Shipman, P. 1994. *The Neandertals: of skeletons, scientists, and scandal*. New York: Vintage.

Turk, I., Blackwell, B. A. B., Turk, J., and Pflaum, M. 2006. Résultats de l'analyse tomographique informatisée de la plus ancienne flûte découverte à Divje babé I (Slovénie) et sa position chronologique dans le contexte des changements paléoclimatiques et paléoenvironnementaux au cours du dernier glaciaire. *L'anthropologie* 110, 293–317.

Uthmeier, Th. 2004. *Micoquien, Aurignacien und Gravettien in Bayern. Eine regionale Studie zum Übergang vom Mittel- zum Jungpaläolithikum*. Bonn: Rudolf Habelt.

Valladas, H., Reyss, J. L., Joron, J. L., Valladas, G., Bar-Yosef, O., and Vandermeersch, B. 1988. Thermoluminescence dating of Mousterian 'Proto-Cro-Magnon' remains from Israel. *Nature* 331, 614–16.

Van Andel, T. H. and Davies, W. (eds) 2003. *Neanderthals and modern humans in the European landscape during the last glaciation*. Cambridge: McDonald Institute for Archaeological Research.

Vanhaeren, M., d'Errico, F., Stringer, C., James, S. L., Todd, J. A., and Mienis, H. K. 2006. Middle Paleolithic shell beads in Israel and Algeria. *Science* 312, 1785–7.

Veil, S., Breest, K., Höfle, H.-C., Meyer, H.-H., Plisson, H., Urban-Küttel, B., Wagner, G. A., and Zöller, L. 1994. Ein mittelpaläolithischer Fundplatz aus der Weichsel-Kaltzeit bei

Lichtenberg, Lkr. Lüchow-Dannenberg. Zwischenbericht über die archäologischen und geowissenschaftlichen Untersuchungen 1987–1992. *Germania* 72, 1–66.

Weaver, T. D. 2009. The meaning of Neandertal skeletal morphology. *Proceedings of the National Academy of Sciences USA* 106, 16028–33.

Weaver, T. D. and Roseman, C. C. 2005. Ancient DNA, late Neandertal survival, and modern-human–Neandertal genetic admixture. *Current Anthropology* 46, 677–83.

Wobst, M. 1977. Stylistic behavior and information exchange. In C. E. Cleland (ed.), *Papers for the director: research essays in honor of James B. Griffin*, 317–42. Ann Arbor: Museum of Anthropology of the University of Michigan.

Wolpoff, M. 2009. How Neandertals inform human variation. *American Journal of Physical Anthropology* 139, 91–102.

Zilhão, J. 2001. *Anatomically archaic, behaviorally modern: the last Neanderthals and their destiny*. Amsterdam: Stichting Nederlands Museum voor Anthropologie en Praehistoriae.

Zilhão, J. 2006a. Neandertals and moderns mixed, and it matters. *Evolutionary Anthropology* 15, 183–95.

Zilhão, J. 2006b. Chronostratigraphy of the Middle-to-Upper Paleolithic transition in the Iberian Peninsula. *Pyrenae* 37, 7–84.

Zilhão, J. 2007. The emergence of ornaments and art: an archaeological perspective on the origins of behavioural 'modernity'. *Journal of Archaeological Research* 15, 1–54.

Zilhão, J. 2009. Szeletian, not Aurignacian: a review of the chronology and cultural associations of the Vindija G1 Neandertals. In M. Camps and P. Chauhan (eds), *A sourcebook of Paleolithic transitions*, 407–26. New York: Springer.

Zilhão, J., Angelucci, D., Badal-García, E., d'Errico, F., Daniel, F., Dayet, L., Douka, K., Higham, T. F. G., Martínez-Sánchez, M. J., Montes-Bernárdez, R., Murcia-Mascarós, S., Pérez-Sirvent, C., Roldán-García, C., Vanhaeren, M., Villaverde, V., Wood, R., and Zapata, J. 2010. Symbolic use of marine shells and mineral pigments by Iberian Neandertals. *Proceedings of the National Academy of Sciences USA* 107, 1023–8.

Zilhão, J. and d'Errico, F. 1999. The chronology and taphonomy of the earliest Aurignacian and its implications for the understanding of Neanderthal extinction. *Journal of World Prehistory* 13, 1–68.

Zilhão, J., d'Errico, F., Bordes, J.-G., Lenoble, A., Texier, J.-P., and Rigaud, J.-Ph. 2006. Analysis of Aurignacian interstratification at the Châtelperronian-type site and implications for the behavioral modernity of Neandertals. *Proceedings of the National Academy of Sciences USA* 103, 12643–8.

Zilhão, J., d'Errico, F., Bordes, J.-G., Lenoble, A., Texier, J.-P., and Rigaud, J.-Ph. 2008. Grotte des Fées (Châtelperron): history of research, stratigraphy, dating, and archaeology of the Châtelperronian type-site. *Paleoanthropology* 2008, 1–42.

Zilhão, J. and Trinkaus, E. (eds) 2002. *Portrait of the artist as a child: the Gravettian human skeleton from the Abrigo do Lagar Velho and its archaeological context*. Lisbon: Instituto Português de Arqueologia.

Zilhão, J., Trinkaus, E., Constantin, S., Milota, Ş., Gherase, M., Sarcina, L., Danciu, A., Rougier, H., Quilès, J., and Rodrigo, R. 2007. The Peştera cu Oase people, Europe's earliest modern humans. In P. Mellars, K. Boyle, O. Bar-Yosef, and C. Stringer (eds), *Rethinking the human revolution*, 249–62. Cambridge: McDonald Institute for Archaeological Research.

CHAPTER 10

MODERN HUMAN ORIGINS IN AFRICA
A Review of the Fossil, Archaeological, and Genetic Perspectives on Early Homo sapiens

KEVIN L. KUYKENDALL AND ISABELLE S. HEYERDAHL-KING

IT is now a widely supported view in palaeoanthropology that modern human origins (MHO) is dated to about 200,000 BP in Africa (Relethford 2008; Trinkaus 2005; but see Wolpoff et al. 2000). The debate about the geographic and evolutionary origins of *Homo sapiens* has for several decades been polarized by the well-known 'Replacement' and 'Continuity' models (Relethford 1999; Smith and Harrold 1997; Stringer 2001; Wolpoff et al. 2000), but the impact of mitochondrial DNA (mtDNA) research since the ground-breaking study by Cann et al. (1987) has given widespread support to the Replacement model, and firmly established the chronological and geographic framework for MHO at approximately 200,000 BP somewhere on the African continent.

The Replacement model of modern human origins (e.g. Aiello 1993; Klein 2008; Mellars 2006b; Stringer 2001) states that *Homo sapiens* evolved relatively recently in Africa at about 200,000 BP, probably in a small isolated population, and subsequently spread via migration throughout Africa and to Asia, Europe, and other regions. As these early modern human populations dispersed, gene flow with other populations (by definition comprising other species, such as *Homo neanderthalensis*) was very limited if it happened at all—the African speciation event resulted in a biologically and behaviourally distinct new species.

In contrast, the Continuity model (e.g. Aiello 1993; Frayer et al. 1994; Relethford 1999; Smith et al. 1989; Wolpoff et al. 2000) states that modern humans evolved as a result of a long-term and geographically widespread process throughout Africa, Europe, and Asia following the initial dispersal of *Homo erectus* populations out of Africa approximately 2 mya. Over this time period, persistent but low levels of gene flow among transient populations migrating within and between regions (a process termed 'reticulation', involving hybridization between closely related populations or even species over time) prevented any distinct speciation event(s), and modern human populations in all regions demonstrate variability due to genetic drift and local geographic adaptation resulting from this long-term evolutionary process.

Genetic, archaeological, and fossil evidence has established the timing of later modern human dispersals out of Africa and into India, Australia, and Europe between roughly 65,000 and 40,000 BP and later (Endicott et al. 2009; Mellars 2006a; 2006b; Oppenheimer 2009). Variations on the Replacement scenario such as the 'Out of Africa' and 'Recent African Origins' models (hereafter all included in the term 'Replacement') were developed incorporating genetic, archaeological, and fossil interpretations about the dispersal and spread of modern humans from a relatively recent and localized African origin event (Klein 2008; Stringer 2001). We do not address the issues of these debates in detail, as we focus on the African evidence for MHO in the period preceding the major dispersals out of Africa.

Research in east and north Africa over the past decade involving the recovery of new fossils, and the re-dating of existing hominid fossil sites (Clark et al. 2003; McDougall et al. 2005; Smith et al. 2007; White et al. 2003) has established that some key features of modern morphology appear earliest in fossils dated to between 195,000 and 155,000 BP in these regions, affirming Africa's place geographically in agreement with the genetic framework for MHO. Paradoxically, all such fossils demonstrate a morphological pattern placing them outside the observed range of variation in extant *H. sapiens* populations, but it is generally agreed that they represent the most recent ancestral populations of modern humans. The taxonomic relationship of these fossils to later populations of *H. sapiens* worldwide remains uncertain, and there are various models of subsequent modern human dispersals (Dennell and Roebroeks 2005; Klein 1999; 2008; Walter et al. 2000), differing in the timing, route, and frequency of population dispersal from, as well as into Africa. Other models featuring assimilation with populations established in other regions have also discussed the timing and effect of early modern human dispersals (Smith et al. 1989; 2005), and variants of these models have also been presented (reviewed by Aiello 1993).

Over approximately the past two decades, genetic research involving both modern and ancient mtDNA has consistently been presented in support of the Replacement model over Continuity (Cann 1988; Krings et al. 1997; 1999; Pääbo 1999; Pääbo et al. 2004; Stoneking 1993; 2008; but see Jorde et al. 1995; Relethford 1998; 2001; Templeton 1993; 2002), effectively de-emphasizing the significance of any potential gene flow in the Replacement scenario for MHO. Such analyses have not documented any evidence of overlap in mtDNA sequence variation between *H. neanderthalensis* (the Neanderthals) and modern human samples, but different statistical models all conclude that some degree of admixture cannot be ruled out (Currat and Excoffier 2004; Nordberg 1998; Serre et al. 2004). In contrast, recent reports of the successful sequencing of the modern human and Neanderthal genomes present strong evidence from genomic DNA comparisons that admixture did in fact take place between some populations of early *H. sapiens* and those of contemporary 'non-modern' species such as the Neanderthals (Green et al. 2010) and the 'Denisovans' from southern Siberia (Krause et al. 2010). Other research with genomic data also provides evidence of ancient admixture (Plagnol and Wall 2006), though the extent and evolutionary significance of any such population interaction is likely to remain a subject of debate. Thus, aspects of both Continuity and Replacement models may be relevant to understanding MHO and population dispersal on a regional and a global scale—an idea informally termed 'leaky replacement' by Pääbo (Gibbons 2011). If substantiated, this would indicate that the morphological and taxonomic distinctions that palaeoanthropologists attribute to Middle and Upper Pleistocene hominid fossils were not so apparent to the hominids themselves when they were alive.

The Upper Palaeolithic archaeological record of Europe has been used to argue for a 'behavioural revolution' associated with a sudden advance in the cognitive capacities of modern humans after 40,000 BP, involving technological innovations similar to some modern hunter-gatherer groups, and the acquisition of symbolic behaviour (Bar-Yosef 2002; Klein 2008; Mellars 2005). A contrasting interpretation of the Middle Stone Age (MSA) archaeological record in sub-Saharan Africa recognizes the long-term gradual acquisition of modern behavioural capabilities between approximately 300,000 and 60,000 BP (McBrearty 2007; McBrearty and Brooks 2000), including the changes in stone-tool technology marking the beginning of the MSA, and the presence of red ochre. It is now well established that the African MSA archaeological record includes material remains indicative of some modern behaviours which are twice as old (80,000–70,000 BP), if not older, than those in Europe (*c.*40,000 BP). There is a lack of consensus over the definition and recognition of behavioural modernity (Bar-Yosef 2007; Henshilwood et al. 2002; McBrearty 2007; McBrearty and Brooks 2000; Mellars 2005; Renfrew 2008), and interpretations of the archaeological evidence remain controversial (d'Errico and Stringer 2011).

One implication of this recent palaeontological and archaeological research is that the earliest specimens recognized on morphological grounds as modern humans appeared as much as 100,000 years before behavioural modernity became widespread (McBrearty 2007; Thackeray 1992). In addition, current evidence indicates that modern human populations did not disperse widely from the African continent until even later at approximately 60,000–50,000 BP (Mellars 2006b; Oppenheimer 2009), suggesting that early *H. sapiens* populations were not behaviourally modern (Klein 2008). Renfrew (2008) refers to this disparity between our biological and behavioural evolution as the 'sapient paradox'.

While some prominent views focus on a single local event such as a genetic mutation (Klein 2008) or a dietary shift (Crawford et al. 1999) that gave rise to a new cognitive capacity, the available dates and the geographic distribution of both the earliest putatively morphologically modern fossils and behaviourally modern archaeology suggest that different hominid populations at different times and places demonstrate different aspects of modernity. Thus, in contrast to conventional Replacement and Revolution models, MHO has more recently been presented as a mosaic and discontinuous process (d'Errico and Stringer 2011; Stringer 2011b).

The three lines of available evidence—fossil morphology, archaeology, and genetics—contribute conceptually different kinds of information concerning the evolution of modernity in humans. Palaeoanthropology has yet to construct a coherent synthesis relating to MHO, particularly in light of recent evidence that contradicts the prevalent interpretations of the past few decades. The terms 'modernity', 'modern humans', and '*Homo sapiens*' may not be synonymous in this scientific palaeoanthropological discourse, even though they all refer to living human populations.

This chapter will review the available evidence from the fossil and archaeological records of Africa between roughly 300,000 and 40,000 BP and consider the evolutionary pattern of morphological and behavioural modernity. The long-standing temporal and geographic framework provided by mtDNA research in the 1980s will be evaluated against recent studies of ancient DNA, archaeological evidence, palaeontology, and models of early *H. sapiens* origin and dispersal in Africa.

The Fossil Record and Modern Human Morphology

The species *Homo sapiens* was first classified by Linnaeus in 1758, and is unique in having no designated type specimen or formal taxonomic description (Tattersall and Schwartz 2008; Wood and Richmond 2000). Any palaeontological assessment of the evolutionary origin of *H. sapiens* (i.e. of morphological modernity) requires agreement over the relevant anatomical criteria that define the species. While several definitions have been proposed, the widespread use of ambiguous prefixes such as 'archaic', 'early', and 'anatomically modern' to the taxon *H. sapiens* reflects the lack of consensus over a definition, and the difficulties encountered in applying one equally to extant and to fossil samples. It has also proved difficult to find the objective language required to describe and compare the fossil assemblages constituting an evolving lineage without the implication of deterministic or typological undertones about species, and of the inevitability of our own evolutionary 'progress'.

The description and analysis of early African fossils of *H. sapiens* is based primarily on cranial remains, which constitute the majority of the fossil record for the period under discussion. The available postcranial fossils are isolated and fragmentary, but suggest that modern human postcranial morphology evolved in African hominids between 600,000 and 125,000 BP (Pearson 2008). Perhaps due to a reduction in habitual load levels, this is followed by a gradual reduction in postcranial robusticity during the Late Pleistocene (Trinkaus 1997). Thus, the postcranial skeleton demonstrates a mosaic pattern of robusticity, but the evolution of the modern postcranial skeleton appears to pre-date that of the cranium.

Most descriptions of modern human cranial morphology (see Figure 10.1) concentrate on four regions of the skull (Stanford et al. 2009; Stringer 2001; Trinkaus 2005):

- a large and rounded cranial vault with a more vertical frontal bone, expanded or 'bossed' parietals, and a rounded and more gracile occipital region. Cranial capacity approximates an estimated species mean of 1350 cc;
- the supraorbital region is generally more gracile, and is characterized by superciliary arches which are divided in the midline, rather than a pronounced supraorbital torus;
- the facial skeleton is less prognathic with smaller width and height dimensions, associated with reduced size of the dentition; and
- the mandible is reduced in size (again associated with reduced dentition), but presents a distinct bony chin.

However, all of these features are variably expressed among both living representatives and fossil specimens putatively recognized as *H. sapiens*.

Despite a long-standing emphasis on modern human cognitive evolution (Dunbar 2003; Mithen 1995), cranial capacity itself is not a particularly useful trait in determining morphological modernity, though it probably has had a developmental effect on structural relationships between regions of the skull (Lieberman et al. 2002). Neanderthals and at least some specimens of *Homo heidelbergensis* had cranial capacities within the extant human range (Aiello and Dunbar 1993; Klein 2009; Wood and Collard 1999) making a human-sized brain a primitive trait in this context, and brain size itself is not a focus of MHO models.

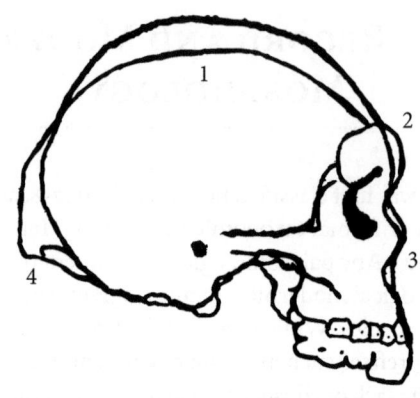

	Region cranium	Key terms	Description of variation
1	Cranial vault – top of skull	Frontal bone – forehead Parietal bones – top and upper part of the side of skull	Overall shape from high and rounded with near-vertical frontal to long and low in lateral view with receding frontal
2	Supraorbital area or 'brow ridge'	Torus – a pronounced ridge of bone. Continuous over both orbits when supraorbital. Sulcus – a groove or furrow Superciliary arch – variable ridge of bone over individual orbits	From complete absence of bony ridge through moderate and marked superciliary arches to a continuous torus which when markedly expressed is accompanied superiorly by a sulcus
3	Face	Prognathic - protruding in lateral view Orthognathic - vertical and 'tucked under' in lateral view	From fully orthognathic through varying degrees of prognathism in the middle and lower part of the face
4	Occipital area – back of skull	Torus – a pronounced ridge of bone. Horizontal in the occipital area	From smooth and rounded through varying degrees of expression of a bony ridge, culminating in a 'beak-like' torus in lateral view

FIGURE 10.1 Regions of the human skull and osteological terms used in the text to compare modern human anatomy to ancestral forms.

Instead, some models invoke genetic, dietary, and other factors thought to produce internal reorganization of an already-large brain, or to favour selection for advanced cognitive functions thus made possible (Aiello and Dunbar 1993; Erren and Erren 2004; Finlay et al. 2001; Klein 2008; Mithen 1995).

Table 10.1 compares three published definitions of modern *H. sapiens* cranial morphology, and reflects the criteria used in assessing Middle and Upper Palaeolithic hominid fossils in Europe, Africa, and Asia. These definitions variably comprise the gross cranial anatomical (non-metric) traits which differ from those of earlier species of *Homo* in the four general regions of the cranium described above. The first is a summary taken from a standard palaeoanthropology textbook (Stanford et al. 2009). Klein (2009, 622) provides more detail in a 'reasonable working description of modern humans', and Tattersall and Schwartz (2008) propose a list of specific cranial osteological traits for the temporal bone, mandible, supraorbital region, and vault. By any such definition, the traits proposed to describe modern human morphology vary extensively in both extant human crania and the relevant fossils, and do not successfully classify all extant specimens observed. Tattersall and Schwartz (2008) reported that not all specimens in their extant reference sample displayed all traits described, and in their widely cited definition of 'anatomically modern humans', Day and Stringer (1982) noted that an individual skull was required to demonstrate only 75 per cent of the criteria defined. Additional studies (reviewed by Pearson 2008) have utilized multivariate techniques to explore patterns of variation among fossil and modern crania, but morphological definitions are unable to classify all modern human crania correctly (Wolpoff 1986; Wolpoff and Caspari 1996), or even to delineate a distinct morphological boundary between *H. sapiens* and ancestral species (Krantz 1980; Wood and Richmond 2000). The morphological definition of our species remains arbitrary and controversial.

A brief summary of the hominid fossil record illustrates the challenges in applying a morphological definition to identify the earliest modern humans. Coalescence dates from mtDNA research (Cann et al. 1987; Pääbo 1999) provide the most widely accepted chronological framework for MHO (but see discussion), which places the common ancestor of all extant human populations at approximately 200 000 BP. Thus, Table 10.2 presents a comparison of three temporal groups of hominid fossil crania (similar to such groups discussed by Brauer 2008 and Trinkaus 2005), and the morphological criteria used to evaluate the appearance of modern *H. sapiens* after 200,000 BP. Hominid fossils dated older than 200,000 BP are generally characterized by primitive or ancestral features, and are not classified as *H. sapiens* (Group 3 in Table 10.2). The hominid fossils dated younger than 200,000 BP can be arranged into two fairly distinct but overlapping morphological groups, each also distinct from earlier fossil taxa (Groups 2 and 1 in Table 10.2). While both groups after 200,000 BP have been referred to in the literature as *H. sapiens*, the earlier (Group 2) is distinguished from extant human populations by retained primitive features and robusticity, and a variable mosaic morphological pattern. Table 10.3 lists hominid fossils included in these three groups, including some brief contextual information about each.

Group 3—Pre-200, 000 BP

Prior to 200,000 BP fossil crania exhibiting ancestral morphology (see Table 10.2) are commonly attributed to *H. heidelbergensis* (Schoetensack 1908); some researchers refer part

Table 10.1 A comparison of definitions of modern cranial morphology

Cranial trait or region	Stanford et al. (2009)	Klein (2009)	Tattersall and Schwartz (2008)
vault/general characteristic	• large endocranial capacity— average 1350 cc • limited development of occipital torus	• endocranial capacity greater than 1350 cc • relatively high and parallel sided with some parietal bossing • rounded occipital lacking transverse torus	• fully segmented cranial sutures with some segments deeply interdigitated • narrow, high occipital plane of the occipital bone
supraorbital area of frontal	• limited development of brow ridges	• continuous bar rarely present • bipartite variably bulging superciliary arches	• bipartite supraorbital area with continuous medial segment and more or less swollen glabella undercut by a distinct lateral plate
facial skeleton	• small face • canine fossa	• relatively flat and tucked in • canine fossa below each orbit	
temporal bone	• prominent mastoid process		• extension of the vaginal process to the lateral margin of the ectotympanic tube • approximation of the vaginal process to the mastoid process • extreme lateral placement of the styloid process at the base of which the stylomastoid foramen lies posteromedially • retention into adulthood of a discernible arcuate eminence on the internal superior face of the petrosal
mandible	• small teeth and jaw • chin	• distinct chin (mostly) • no retromolar space	• symphyseal region of the mandible thicker from inside to outside than the corpora on either side when viewed inferiorly • inverted-T-shaped chin with a central vertical keel bounded by lateral depressions and a horizontal inferior bar running between more or less well defined tubercles laterally

Table 10.2 Morphological and temporal groupings of African Pleistocene fossil hominids relevant to MHO

Cranial trait or region	Group 3 < 200,000 BP	Group 2 200,000–40,000 BP	Group 1 <40,000 BP
endocranial capacity (cc)	• Between 1000 and 1300	• between 1150 and 1580	• greater than 1350
vault shape	• long and low • receding frontal • euryon low on the temporal • strongly expressed occipital torus	• intermediate • higher frontal angle • euryon variably higher or lower on parietals • occipital torus reduced or not present	• high and rounded • more vertical frontal • euryon high on the parietals • minimal/absence of occipital torus
supraorbital area of frontal	• strongly expressed supraorbital torus	• supraorbital torus varying in depth and continuity	• greatly reduced supraorbital area • superciliary arches divided in the midline
facial skeleton	• long and broad with mid- and lower facial prognathism • robust dentition	• smaller face, generally mesognathic • some reduction in the dentition	• small orthognathic face 'tucked under' neurocranium as a result of reduced dentition
mandible	• receding mandibular symphysis (absence of bony chin)	• vertical or projecting symphysis (bony chin)	• presence of projecting symphysis (bony chin)

Note: MHO (adapted from Klein 2009).

Table 10.3 Fossil specimens, sites, and dates relevant to MHO in Africa

Specimen	Skeletal elements	Site	Country	Group	Discovery date	Age (thousands of years BP)	References
Bodo	C	Bodo	Ethiopia	3	1976	600	Clark et al. 1994; Rightmire 1996
Florisbad	C	Florisbad	South Africa	3	1932	260	Grün et al. 1996; Dreyer 1935
Kabwe	C	Broken Hill	Zambia	3	1921	>125	Grine and Klein 1993; Woodward 1921
Omo 1	C	Omo River	Ethiopia	2	1967	195	Fleagle et al. 2008; Day and Stringer 1991
Omo 2	(C)	Omo River	Ethiopia	2	1967	195	McDougall et al. 2005; Day and Stringer 1991
Irhoud 1	C	Jebel Irhoud	Morocco	2	1962	190–130	Grün and Stringer 1991; Ennouchi 1962
Irhoud 2	(C)	Jebel Irhoud	Morocco	2	1968	190–130	Grün and Stringer 1991; Ennouchi 1968
Herto	C	Herto, Middle Awash	Ethiopia	2	1997	160	Clark et al. 2003; White et al. 2003
EH06 Eyasi F	F	Lake Eyasi	Tanzania	2	1935	132	Domínguez-Rodrigo et al. 2008
Singa	C	Singa	Sudan	2	1924	133	McDermott et al. 1996; Woodward 1938
LH18 Ngaloba	C	Laetoli, Ngaloba	Tanzania	2	1974	129–108	Manega 1995; Magori and Day 1983
Mumba Cave	D	Mumba Cave	Tanzania	2	1935	130–110	Bräuer and Mehlman 1988
Klasies River	F	Klasies River Mouth	South Africa	2	1967	125–75	Rightmire and Deacon 1991
Dar es Soltan 5	(C)	Rabat-Temara	Morocco	2	1975	110–80	Nespoulet et al. 2008; Hublin 1992
Qafzeh VI	C	Jebel Qafzeh	Israel Palestine	2	1934	100–90	Schwarcz et al. 1988; Vallois and Vandermeersch 1972

Site		Location		Year	Age	Reference
Qafzeh IX	C	Jebel Qafzeh	Israel Palestine	2	1969	100–90	Schwarcz et al. 1988
							Vallois and Vandermeersch 1972
Skhul V	C	Skhul es Mugharat	Israel Palestine	2	1934	119	Grün et al. 2005
							Garrod et al. 1937
Bouri	F	Bouri, Middle Awash	Ethiopia	2	1993	105–80	Yellen et al. 2005
							Haile-Selassie et al. 2004
Aduma	F	Aduma, Middle Awash	Ethiopia	2	1994–96	105–70	Yellen et al. 2005
							Clark et al. 1994
Blombos	D	Blombos Cave	South Africa	2	1993–98	70	Henshilwood et al. 2001
							Grine et al. 2000
De Kelders I	D	Die Kelders	South Africa	?	1992–93	80–60	Avery et al. 1997
Taramsa Hill	J	Taramsa Hill	Egypt	2	1994	80–50	Vermeersch et al. 1998
Hofmeyr	C	Hofmeyr	South Africa	1	1952	36	Grine et al. 2007
Border Cave	F	Border Cave	South Africa	1	1940	105	Rightmire et al. 1979
Hoedjiespunt I	D	Hoedjiespunt I	South Africa	2	1993–96	>74	Berger and Parkington 1995
							Stynder et al. 2001
Equus Cave	D	Equus Cave	South Africa	2	–	93–44	Grine and Klein 1985
Sea Harvest	D	Sea Harvest	South Africa	2	–	–	Grine and Klein 1993
Pinnacle Point	D	Pinnacle Point	South Africa	2	2000	164	Marean 2010
Mugharat el-Aliya	D	Mugharat el-Aliya	Morocco	1	1939	>27	Wrinn and Rink 2003
Contrebandiers	F/D	Rabat-Temara	Morocco	2	1975	110–108	Hublin 1992
							Nespoulet et al. 2008
el Harhoura	F/D	Rabat-Temara	Morocco	1	1977	41–25	Hublin 1992
							Nespoulet et al. 2008
							Hublin 1992
Porc-Epic	D	Dire Dawa	Ethiopia	2	1933	77–61	Clark et al. 1984
Nazlet Khater	J	Nazlet Khater 2	Egypt	1	1980	33	Vermeersch et al. 1984
							Pinhasi and Semal 2000

or all of the African fossils in this group to either *Homo rhodesiensis* (Rightmire 2008; Woodward 1921) or *Homo helmei* (Dreyer 1935; Foley and Lahr 1997). *H. heidelbergensis* has been a controversial taxon (Harvati 2007; Rightmire 1998) historically referred to informally as 'archaic *Homo sapiens*' and used as a 'catch-all' group to which specimens were attributed by default if they could not be classified as *H. erectus*, Neanderthal, or *H. sapiens*. This group of fossils arguably extends back to at least 600,000 BP (Rightmire 1998; Stringer 1985), and includes the following key African specimens:

- the Bodo cranium from Ethiopia which has been dated to 600,000 BP (Clark et al. 1994; Rightmire 1996);
- the Kabwe cranium (Woodward 1921) from Zambia, which has been dated to between 600,000 and 400,000 BP by faunal association (Klein 1973), although a later Middle Pleistocene age has also been suggested (Barham et al. 2002; Stringer 2011a);
- the Florisbad cranium (Dreyer 1935) from South Africa which has been dated to approximately 260,000 BP (Grün et al. 1996).

In addition to these, there are a number of European fossils including the Mauer mandible (Schoetensack 1908) and the Petralona cranium (Stringer et al. 1979; 1983) currently assigned to *H. heidelbergensis* (Mounier et al. 2009; Rightmire 1988). Both the European and African cranial remains exemplify the typical morphology for this group (Harvati 2007; Rightmire 1998):

- very robust construction throughout
- cranial capacity between 1100 and 1300 cc
- location of greatest cranial breadth low on the temporal bone
- a long, low vault with sloping frontal and pronounced occipital torus
- strong expression of the supraorbital torus
- large, widely spaced quadrangular orbits
- a large, wide, and prognathic face
- a large nasal aperture
- large teeth and a robust mandible with no bony chin (i.e. the mandible is vertical or receding in the midline profile and lacks a central bony protuberance)

These traits are variably expressed in different *H. heidelbergensis* specimens, and individuals may demonstrate some aspects of a more modern morphological pattern, such as a rounded occipital region or reduced facial prognathism (Harvati 2007; Rightmire 2008). Thus, the overall pattern is a mosaic of primitive features found in earlier hominid taxa, with large faces, cranial shape, and overall robusticity distinguishing them from *H. sapiens*.

Group 2—200,000 to 40, 000 BP

Based on the genetic framework, and the Upper Palaeolithic record in Europe, the period between 200,000 and 40,000 BP is that in which we should expect to recover the earliest *H. sapiens* fossils in Africa. The existing hominid fossil assemblage from this period demonstrates a composite or mosaic morphological pattern including both ancestral and modern traits. There is considerable inter- and intra-population variation, which is exemplified by remains from Omo Kibish (Day and Stringer 1982; 1991) and Herto (White et al. 2003) in Ethiopia, from Jebel Irhoud in Morocco (Ennouchi 1962; 1968), and from the Levantine sites of Jebel Qafzeh (Vallois and Vandermeersch 1972; Vandermeersch 1969), and Skhul (Garrod et al. 1937) in Israel. These sites have yielded assemblages of individual crania displaying characteristically variable morphology such as a rounded or angled occipital region, a weak or moderate supraorbital torus, and a large and/or projecting facial skeleton in combination with traits associated with modern morphology such as a bony chin. Even at sites with largely fragmentary remains, such as Klasies River in South Africa (Rightmire and Deacon 1991), this variable mosaic pattern is demonstrated among the individuals represented. Fragmentary material from additional sites in this time period which is not easily diagnosable (e.g. isolated teeth) is also included for this group in Table 10.3.

Omo. The oldest specimens in Group 2 are the remains from the Kibish Formation in the Omo Valley of Ethiopia. Two crania designated Omo 1 and 2 and a small amount of postcranial material are associated with the same stratigraphic unit (Member 1) (Butzer 1969). Originally dated to about 130,000 BP (Butzer 1969), new radiometric dates assign an age of approximately 196,000 BP to Member 1 (Fleagle et al. 2008), making the Omo fossils the earliest putative representatives of *H. sapiens*. Despite their similar depositional context, the observable morphological differences between the Omo 1 and 2 crania have led some to classify them differently (Stringer 1989; Trinkaus 2005), though Rightmire (1976) considered them to be closely related.

Omo 1, a highly fragmented cranium and mandible, has been reconstructed to reveal a large robust vault with expanded parietals, a rounded shape, and the absence of an occipital torus. The large and robust mandible has a bony chin. Significantly, this is the earliest fossil individual to display traits regarded as autapomorphies of *H. sapiens*, and the new dating sits conveniently within the 200,000 BP framework for MHO. In combination with these morphologically modern traits, Omo 1 is notably robust, demonstrating a moderately developed supraorbital region, a large and long face with a wide interorbital pillar and nasal aperture (Day and Stringer 1982; 1991). Omo 2 is a relatively complete cranial vault with partial basicranium demonstrating long and low morphology with a sloping frontal and prominent occipital torus. It lacks the supraorbital region, face, and mandible (Day and Stringer 1982; 1991), but is markedly more robust and primitive in appearance compared to Omo 1, and it has been classified as *H. heidelbergensis* or 'archaic *H. sapiens*' (Trinkaus 2005).

The Levant. Climatically and geographically, the Levant has been regarded as an extension of the African continent, and is one of the likely dispersal routes out of Africa (Lahr and Foley 1998). Hominid fossils representing penecontemporaneous Levantine populations of Mugharet es-Skhul and Jebel Qafzeh in Israel also display the mosaic morphology described. Mugharet es-Skhul is dated to approximately 120,000 BP (Grün et al. 2005) and has produced ten individuals including a number of nearly complete skeletons. Though somewhat damaged, Skhul V is the best preserved and most commonly described skull from the site. This specimen has a short and rounded vault with no occipital torus. The face is large and moderately prognathic, and the supraorbital torus is both continuous and accompanied by a sulcus (Garrod et al. 1937—a trait more commonly associated with earlier hominids such as *H. erectus*. The Skhul V mandible is large and robust, described by Garrod et al. (1937, 201) as having a 'mandibular area greater than that of the Heidelberg [Mauer] jaw'. The mandible also has a prominent bony chin, again demonstrating a mosaic combination of primitive and derived features.

Remains from the site of Jebel Qafzeh, dated to around 92,000 BP (Schwarcz et al. 1988) comprise two complete immature skeletons and the remains of ten other individuals including two fragmented but largely complete adult crania. Qafzeh VI is a large and robust cranium with a long but rounded vault that lacks an occipital torus. There is a moderately expressed supraorbital torus above a large but orthognathic (i.e. vertical in profile) face with large orbits and a wide nasal cavity (Vandermeersch 1969; Vallois and Vandermeersch 1972). Qafzeh IX demonstrates a short vault with a rounded occipital region, and a comparatively reduced supraorbital torus. There is a moderate degree of lower facial prognathism and the mandible has a prominent bony chin.

Remains from the Omo valley and the Levantine sites exemplify the mosaic morphology of the Group 2 specimens. A number of other African sites have yielded one or more individuals with similarly mosaic cranial morphology (see Table 10.3). These include Jebel Irhoud from Morocco (Ennouchi 1962; 1968), dated to between 190,000 and 130,000 BP (Grün and Stringer 1991); Herto from Ethiopia (White et al. 2003), dated to 160,000 BP (Clark et al. 2003); cranial fragments from Bouri in Ethiopia (Haile-Selassie et al. 2004), dated to between 110,000 and 80,000 BP (Yellen et al. 2005); the pathological Singa cranium (Spoor et al. 1998; Woodward 1938) from the Sudan, dated to around 130,000 BP (McDermott et al. 1996); the LH 18 (Ngaloba) cranium from Laetoli, Tanzania (Magori and Day 1983), dated to between 129,000 and 108,000 BP (Manega 1995); and the Klasies River and Border Cave assemblages from South Africa, dated between approximately 125,000 and 100,000 BP (Rightmire et al. 1979; Rightmire and Deacon 1991).

The interpretation of the Herto cranium BOU-VP-16/1 clearly demonstrates the difficulty presented by the mosaic and variable morphology of this group of fossils. Compared to earlier fossils, this specimen demonstrates a remarkable similarity to extant *H. sapiens* crania, but it is characterized by very robust features and is metrically large relative to the modern comparative sample in most assessments reported by White et al. (2003). Thus, the Herto fossils were characterized as 'on the verge of anatomical modernity but not yet fully modern' (White et al. 2003, 745), and attributed to new sub-species *H. sapiens idaltu*.

The specimens we have designated as Group 2 hominids represent populations of our immediate ancestors in Africa, but the mosaic morphological pattern described sets them apart from extant populations of *H. sapiens*. The taxonomic status of these fossils remains uncertain even though the common use of such terms as 'essentially modern' (Mellars 2005; 2006b) suggests a general consensus regarding their overall similarity to later *H. sapiens* populations, and reflects a difficulty in reconciling the continuous evolutionary process with the generally typological practice of taxonomy.

Group 1—After 40, 000 BP

It is not until after 40,000 BP that the fossil record in Africa and other regions of the Old World first yields individuals who more consistently display the defining traits of extant *H. sapiens*. These late Upper Pleistocene humans bear a greater resemblance to more recent and extant humans than any previous populations, and we refer to them as Group 1. There have been a few proposed earlier examples, such as one of the Klasies River specimens in South Africa, dated to 125,000–75,000 BP (Rightmire and Deacon 1991). This fragmentary frontal bone presents a gracile and modern-looking supraorbital region with superciliary arches rather than a prominent supraorbital torus. However, the specimen may not be adult, and other fossils from the Klasies River assemblage also demonstrate more robust morphology as described for Group 2.

In Table 10.3, Group 1 or modern *H. sapiens* demonstrates the following morphological features (Klein 2009; Schwartz and Tattersall 2000; Tattersall and Schwartz 2008; Trinkaus 2005):

- a generally more gracile construction
- an average cranial capacity of approximately 1350 cc
- location of greatest breadth high on the cranial walls, which are nearly vertical with some bossing
- a high and shorter vault that is rounded in the occipital region with a steeply rising frontal
- more circular orbits with a narrow interorbital pillar and superciliary arches rather than a supraorbital torus
- a relatively small orthognathic face and a reduced nasal aperture
- reduced size of the dentition
- a more gracile mandible with a pronounced chin including a midline bony protuberance

Modern human morphological traits do not occur simultaneously in the fossil record, and the morphological boundary between Group 2 and Group 1 is not clearly defined. Earlier Group 1 specimens demonstrating modern morphology remain noticeably more robust than most later populations, or extant humans. These specimens include the Hofmeyr cranium from South Africa, dated to 36,000 BP (Grine et al. 2007); the Peștera cu Oase remains from Romania (Trinkaus et al. 2003), dated to 34,000–32,000 BP (Rougier et al. 2007); and the Cro-Magnon (Broca 1868) remains from France (Vallois and Billy 1965), dated to 28,000 BP (Henri-Gambier 2002). Table 10.3 lists other fossils from this time period in southern Africa and elsewhere, but many of these specimens are fragmentary or consist of isolated teeth and thus do not provide as much useful information about cranial morphology and its variation.

Other regions such as Australasia document fossils of early modern populations that may have dispersed from Africa at or after 50,000 BP (Bowler et al. 2003). The Lake Mungo remains from New South Wales, Australia, dated to about 40,000 BP (Bowler et al. 2003), pre-date the earliest modern European remains by a few thousand years, and demonstrate a generally more gracile morphological pattern (Bowler et al. 1970). The more robust but later Kow Swamp remains, also from New South Wales and dated to 15,000 BP (Stone and Cupper 2003) display some of the presumably primitive characters described above in our Group 2 (Thorne 1971). Even within the more recent period, some fossils demonstrate a mosaic morphology combining presumed modern and ancestral features.

As mentioned above, the various proposed definitions of modern human morphology do not clearly apply to either all recent (extant) or extinct populations of *H. sapiens* (Wolpoff 1986; Wolpoff and Caspari 1996). Two illustrative examples of such extant populations are the late Holocene (i.e. 3000 BP to historical times) Patagonian and Tierra del Fuegan populations (Bernal et al. 2006), and many living aboriginal Australians (Curnoe 2011). Individuals from both populations commonly demonstrate generally robust cranial morphology in combination with other traits generally regarded as primitive. These include a longer, lower overall cranial shape and a moderately expressed supraorbital torus. In some aboriginal populations this robusticity falls at the extremes of variation in extant *H. sapiens* (Curnoe 2011). These individuals do not fulfil the morphological definitions described above, but there is no argument about whether these humans should be classified as modern. The heterogeneous distribution of 'modern traits' (i.e. polymorphism) in both extant and extinct populations has been explained through an evolutionary process underlying MHO that involved population expansion with interbreeding (Templeton 2002).

Despite extensive discussion over many decades in the literature, there is not yet a clear consensus on a practical definition of morphological modernity incorporating both fossil and living samples. As Cartmill (2001, 104) has commented, '…the phrase "anatomically modern" has no clear or established meaning—but [is] simply a scientific-sounding way of evading the fact that there is no agreement on the list and distribution of the defining autapomorphies of the human species'.

Archaeology of Modern Behaviour

Notions of modernity in palaeoanthropology are based on the general interpretation that some extinct hominid populations were 'more like us' in comparison to populations of other hominid species such as Neanderthals and *H. heidelbergensis* (Howells 1959; Ingold 1995). While a morphological trait list arguably has some utility in determining which fossils essentially look like us, an archaeological trait list is more problematic given that most modern humans no longer fashion stone tools or subsist through a hunting and gathering lifestyle. What is modern behaviour and how is it represented archaeologically? In both the Replacement and Continuity models of MHO, the African palaeoanthropological and archaeological record in some way represents our direct ancestry. The challenge is in the identification of the essential components of behavioural modernity that distinguish early *H. sapiens* populations from those ancestral, as well as from other contemporary hominid populations (e.g. Neanderthals) that may demonstrate similar behavioural capabilities (d'Errico and Stringer 2011).

Historically, the Upper Palaeolithic (especially of Europe and the Levant) has provided the archaeological standard for identifying the earliest material occurrences of modern human behaviour, and most discussions have taken place in the context of Neanderthal–*H. sapiens* population interactions during the Upper Palaeolithic (e.g. Clark and Lindly 1989; Harrold 1989; Mellars 2004). The signatures or innovations characterizing modern human behavioural capacity in the Upper Palaeolithic archaeological record relate to increased technological complexity, diversity in subsistence behaviour comparable to modern hunter-gatherer economies, advanced cognitive capacity and symbolic expression, and include (Bar-Yosef 2002; Klein 2008; McBrearty and Brooks 2000; Mellars 2005; Willoughby 2007):

- increased diversity and standardization of stone artefact types
- increased use of blade technology, including compound tools
- widespread use of worked bone and other organic materials for tools
- appearance of personal ornaments in perforated shells, teeth, and beads

- evidence of long-distance distribution and exchange networks (e.g. for ochre, lithic materials, shell)
- exploitation of aquatic and other subsistence resources requiring specialized technology or knowledge (e.g. seasonal behaviour), generally equivalent to that of modern hunter-gatherer populations
- spatially structured occupation sites
- evidence for ceremony and ritual in art and burial

Definitions, discussions, and debates about these signatures of behavioural modernity are abundant (e.g. Bar-Yosef 2002; Henshilwood et al. 2002; Ingold 1995; Klein 2008; McBrearty 2007; McBrearty and Brooks 2000; Shea 2011; Wadley 2001; Willoughby 2007), and attempt to synthesize historical interpretations, limitations of dating techniques, and questions about taphonomic and archaeological context. In any interpretation, the earliest archaeological indicators of modernity begin to appear gradually in Africa from as early as 250,000–300,000 BP, coinciding generally with the MSA period (Barham 2002; McBrearty and Brooks 2000; Wadley 2001) and pre-dating the earliest appearance of putatively modern morphology. In contrast, the complete repertoire of 'modern behaviour' as represented by the European Upper Palaeolithic after about 40,000 BP, appears long after the appearance of modern morphological features in Africa.

African field research over the past two decades has revealed a number of MSA sites and artefact assemblages which document evidence for differing combinations of the signature modern behaviours as early as 140,000–60,000 BP (Henshilwood et al. 2001; McBrearty and Brooks 2000; Texier et al. 2010; Wadley 2001; Willoughby 2007), on the order of twice as old as the European Upper Palaeolithic or the African Later Stone Age (LSA). These early occurrences of modern behavioural signatures in the African MSA led to an intense debate about the definition and evolution of 'modernity' and of the notion of an Upper Palaeolithic behavioural revolution, stimulated largely by McBrearty and Brooks's (2000) extensive review. Many subsequent discussions have considered the theoretical framework required for interpreting African archaeology independently of the European Upper Palaeolithic traditions (Barham 2002; d'Errico 2003; Henshilwood et al. 2001; 2002; McBrearty and Brooks 2000; Marean 2010; Mellars 2005; Shea 2011; Wadley 2001).

As originally defined (Goodwin and Van Riet Lowe 1929), the Earlier, Middle, and Later Stone Age sequence was a (primarily southern) African equivalent to the European Palaeolithic; the MSA was thought to be broadly comparable to the Middle Palaeolithic, including the Mousterian (Bordes 1968; Deacon and Deacon 1999; Klein 1999). Technologically, MSA lithic assemblages are distinguished from the earlier Acheulian assemblages by the scarcity or absence of large bifacial core tools such as hand axes and cleavers and by the prevalence of a variety of retouched flake, point, and blade tools produced using a prepared core technique (Clark 1988; Deacon and Deacon 1999). Such flake-dominated lithic assemblages are widespread and variable throughout Africa and Eurasia following the Acheulian, and include Mousterian assemblages as well as the diversity of MSA industries throughout Africa (Foley and Lahr 1997). In addition, elements previously associated with the Upper Palaeolithic have been reported in an MSA context, including blade and bone tools, barbed points, ochre pigment, and items of personal adornment such as beads (Wadley 2001). For some researchers, the presence of these elements is an indication of increased technological complexity, subsistence diversity, and symbolic expression, signifying the advanced cognitive capacity of the hominids producing them (Barham 2002; Deacon and Deacon 1999; McBrearty and Brooks 2000; Willoughby 1993).

MSA sites span the period from approximately 280,000–30,000 BP (Jacobs et al. 2008) between the Acheulian and the Later Stone Age, though the exact chronological range has been difficult to define (McBrearty 2007; Wadley 2005). MSA artefact assemblages are generally characterized as a flake-based technology in contrast to the preceding core-based Acheulian, and different regional industries have been named within the MSA on the basis of technical or stylistic variation from sites throughout Africa (Ambrose 2001; Clark 1988; Wurz 2002). This variation in the MSA is significant in contrast to the long-term stability of the Acheulian artefact assemblages (Ambrose 2001; Foley and Lahr 1997). The different MSA industries have generally been named after sites where they were first described, and are defined on the basis of regionally variable tool types such as the backed blades of South Africa's Howiesons Poort (Deacon 1992; Goodwin and Van Riet Lowe 1929; Thackeray 1992), the microlith-based Aduma Industry of the Awash Valley, Ethiopia (Yellen et al. 2005), and the tanged points of the Aterian in north Africa (Bouzouggar et al. 2007; d'Errico et al. 2009; Hublin 1992). Because at least some such industries demonstrate temporal patterns in occurrence (i.e. they are chronologically restricted or transient in stratigraphic sections), these apparently arbitrarily standardized technological and stylistic patterns have been interpreted to represent the presence of different cultural traditions (Singer and Wymer 1982), or widespread social networks (Barham 2002), as observed in later Upper Palaeolithic and Later Stone Age assemblages. The Aterian of north-west Africa has for some time been associated with sites dated in the range 40,000–20,000 BP, or with an older sequence between 90,000 and 60,000 BP (Cremaschi et al. 1998; Wrinn and Rink 2003) but an earlier date of 145,000 BP has recently been published for the Aterian in Morocco (Richter et al. 2010), suggesting that this industry—and whatever it indicates about modern behaviour—has a much longer presence in the archaeological record of north-west Africa.

Certain technological features of MSA assemblages are reported to reflect the capacity for modern cognitive ability. Worked bone tools and points dating to approximately 70,000 BP or older have been reported at sites such as Blombos Cave, South Africa (Henshilwood et al. 2001), and Katanda in the Congo (Yellen et al. 1995). Recently, it has been shown that silcrete raw materials excavated at Pinnacle Point, South Africa, in stratigraphic contexts starting about 71,000 BP had been heat-treated to improve flaking quality for the production of Still Bay and Howiesons Poort tools (Brown et al. 2009).

The technological features of different named MSA industries relate functionally to the use of hafted points for hand-held tools and thrusting spears, and to the production of composite tools utilizing multiple hafted flakes, representing a significant technological and cognitive change compared to the large hand-held bifaces of the Acheulian (Barham 2002; Deacon 1992). The behavioural implication is that such tools require a more complex cognitive process of planning and foresight in core reduction and tool assembly (e.g. flake production, shaft preparation, hafting with mastic) (Lombard 2005; Wadley et al. 2009), and which may be performed at different places and times (Ambrose 2001; Willoughby 2007). Generally, these technological innovations indicate the capacity to exploit more diverse food items, at least in some areas including fishing and other aquatic resources (Marean 2010), reflecting the presence of a well-developed hunter-gatherer subsistence strategy comparable to that of modern groups.

Perhaps the most intriguing evidence for modern cognitive behaviours in the MSA comes from artefacts that indicate a capacity for aesthetic symbolic expression rather than functional innovation. The earliest proposed archaeological evidence for modern symbolic behaviour includes the occurrence of large numbers of pigment chunks (ochre) at Twin Rivers in Zambia (400,000–170,000 BP) and Lake Baringo in Kenya (300,000–285,000 BP) (Barham 2004; Marean et al. 2007). While ochre may have been used for some functional purposes such as hafting mastic (Lombard 2005) or hide preparation (Watts 2002) some of the pigment artefacts show signs of wear and shaping suggesting that they were used as 'crayons' to apply colour to surfaces and possibly skin—suggesting use as decoration or adornment. Pigment chunks are 'virtually ubiquitous' in the southern African record after approximately 160,000 BP (Henshilwood et al. 2009, 29) and have been recovered from key sites such as Blombos, Pinnacle Point, Klasies River, and Rose Cottage Cave (Henshilwood et al. 2009; Marean et al. 2007; Watts 2002). That these materials represent symbolic and not solely functional behaviours is inferred from the predominance (as much as 90 per cent) of red ochre over other colours, which is known from ethnographic studies to have a widespread association with ritual practice (Barham 2004; Watts 2002). The high value of this resource is suggested by its distribution with respect to the archaeological occurrences; the known geological sources of red ochre may range as much as 50 kilometres from different sites (Henshilwood et al. 2009), and more than twice that distance at Border Cave (Watts 2002).

Perhaps the most compelling evidence for the symbolic use of ochre is from Blombos Cave in South Africa, where an assemblage of inscribed ochre chunks has been dated to about 77,000 BP (Henshilwood et al. 2002; 2009). These incised patterns may be a form of representational or symbolic information, though some have suggested that they may have been produced to score the surface prior to rubbing or grinding in a functional, not symbolic context (Klein 2008).

The site of Blombos Cave has also produced a sample of 41 *Nassarius* marine gastropod shells with perforations and use wear suggesting that they were suspended for use as beads in personal adornment (Henshilwood et al. 2004). A similar assemblage from the site of Grotte des Pigeons in Morocco is dated even earlier at approximately 82,000 BP (Bouzouggar et al. 2007), and a small number of similar shells possibly dating as early as 135,000–100,000 BP have been reported from Mugharet-es-Skhul in Israel and Oued Djebbana in Algeria (Vanhaeren et al. 2006).

As with the chunks of ochre, some of these shells appear to have been transported over distances between 20 and 190 kilometres from the nearest coastal sources (Bouzouggar et al. 2007; Vanhaeren et al. 2006), indicating selection and preference of valued objects, as well as the possibility of long-distance trade networks.

Recently, a sample of 270 fragments of engraved ostrich eggshell has been reported from Diepkloof Rock Shelter in South Africa's Western Cape, in association with a Howiesons Poort MSA tool assemblage dated to 60,000 BP (Texier et al. 2010). While the eggshells themselves were objects used in a functional context as containers, these engraved eggshell fragments present a range of geometric motifs suggesting the adherence to stylistic rules and the symbolic expression of group identity which are associated with modern cognitive and symbolic behavioural capacity.

While no single African site or region has produced the full list of artefacts used to define modern human behaviour as it appears in the European Upper Palaeolithic after 40,000 BP, the African archaeological record as a whole demonstrates that populations of hominids between 140,000 and 70,000 BP were engaging in cognitive behaviours that, according to the definition given above, are considered to be functionally or symbolically 'modern'. Taken together, the significance of these technological features is that they demonstrate the capacity of hominids in the MSA to distinguish between different choices of raw materials for making tools, and to innovate and socially transmit a complex process of raw material preparation and tool manufacture resulting in a stylistically or technically standardized functional product such as a composite tool. These cases indicate the existence of a degree of intentional standardization and repetition of a pattern of procurement, process, and production of the artefacts has been interpreted in the context of socially constructed standards of behaviour, or as statements of cultural identity (Barham et al. 2002; Henshilwood et al. 2009).

The fact that the complete package of modernity as represented by the European Upper Palaeolithic is not evident in the African archaeological record may be an indication of the pattern and process of evolution and behavioural adaptation. Recent archaeological evidence from European Middle Palaeolithic sites suggests that Neanderthals were capable of some 'modern' behaviours (d'Errico 2003; d'Errico et al. 1998), adding a further dimension to the controversial definition of 'modern humans'. Future research may document even earlier evidence for other 'modern behaviours' in Africa or elsewhere. As with the determination of modern human morphology, the boundary between 'almost modern' and 'modern' is to some degree arbitrary, and it is thus difficult to find consensus regarding the archaeological interpretation of MHO.

Discussion

In our review of the palaeoanthropological models for MHO in Africa, we have recognized a temporal and geographic framework that has predominated since the 1980s, and which was advanced to a large extent by interpretations of mtDNA variation among modern human populations (Garrigan and Hammer 2006; Klein 2008; Stringer 1994; Templeton 2007). In the most basic form, this framework calls for a single origin of modern humans at about 200,000 BP in Africa as proposed in the Replacement model and its variants (Klein 2008; Stringer 2001). Over roughly the past two decades, the available fossil record has been widely regarded to be compatible with this framework (but see Frayer et al. 1994; Smith et al. 1989; Wolpoff et al. 2000), and popular interpretations of the fossil and archaeological record supported some version of the Replacement model over Continuity in light of the genetic evidence (Aiello 1993; Lahr and Foley 1998). However, the most recent new fossil, archaeological, and genetic evidence concerning MHO suggests that this widely popularized framework is too simplistic, and does not capture the complexity of the evolutionary processes involved in MHO (Stringer 2011b; Templeton 2005). At the core of this discussion is whether the 200,000 BP date associated with the genetic ancestor has any objective relevance to the available fossil and archaeological evidence for MHO.

We have reviewed the African hominid fossil record between 195,000 and 165,000 BP, which is characterized by a morphological pattern resembling that of extant human populations, but to widely varying degrees. At the same time, it has been demonstrated that the mosaic morphological pattern characterizing this hominid fossil assemblage is distinct from that of either earlier (*H. heidelbergensis*) or later (extant *H. sapiens*) hominids. The fact that these fossils are commonly described as 'near', 'early', or 'archaic' modern humans (Bräuer 2008; Klein 2008; Stringer 2001; Trinkaus 2005) is a reflection of the difficulty in classifying the mosaic morphological pattern described, and their taxonomic affiliation remains controversial (Foley 2001; Wood and Richmond 2000). While there is currently little debate that these fossils represent ancestral human populations on our direct evolutionary lineage, the resolution of their taxonomic status as either early representatives of *H. sapiens* or as a separate species is ultimately necessary.

The African archaeological record similarly documents a mosaic and gradual proliferation of different components of the modern behavioural repertoire from as early as 300,000 BP in Africa, and certainly by 80,000–70,000 BP—in either case, much earlier than that of the European Upper Palaeolithic archaeological record after 40,000 BP which forms the basis of the Revolution model. However, the African archaeological record has not yet produced evidence of the full suite of modern behavioural features such as parietal or mobiliary artwork during this period (e.g. such as that from the European Upper Palaeolithic caves at Chauvet-Pont-d'Arc and Altamira (Chauvet et al. 1995; Clottes et al. 1995; Valladas et al. 1992)); the earliest occurrences for these and other features are from sites outside of Africa (Conard 2010). The interpretation of modernity is further complicated by recent archaeological evidence that other hominid species (Neanderthals) demonstrate some modern behavioural capabilities (d'Errico 2003; d'Errico et al. 1998). In this context, it is necessary to resolve whether the African MSA archaeological record documents the origins of 'fully modern' human behaviour.

At present, the available genetic, fossil, and archaeological evidence suggests that MHO was the result of an evolutionary process that was mosaic, accumulative, and dispersed both geographically and temporally. Any current interpretation of modern human origins is faced with explaining the origin of the species *H. sapiens* and that of modern behaviour as interdependent evolutionary phenomena, but phenomena which paradoxically were separated temporally by as much as 100 ky. In order to more effectively evaluate this interpretation, an improved synthesis of the diverse evidence available is needed.

Genes, Fossils, and Archaeology

Our knowledge of MHO comes from three physically and conceptually different sources of information: the hominid fossil record, material remnants of hominid behaviour, and extant and ancient human genetic variation. These provide disparate perspectives on our evolutionary history, and their successful integration remains a challenge to palaeoanthropology (see Figure 10.2). Evolutionary models may emphasize the apparent correspondence between results from these different sources of information, such as similarity between the mtDNA coalescence date of 200,000 BP and the dating of the earliest putative modern hominid fossils (see above), or the significance of FOX-P2 gene mutations on articulate speech in the context of evolutionary models for the origin of symbolic language (Enard et al. 2002; Krause et al. 2007). However, these connections overlook the inherent complexity of our species' evolutionary history, as well as some of the methodological challenges in synthesizing information gained from these different sources.

The 200,000 BP genetic framework is often presented and discussed as if the mtDNA most recent common ancestor (MRCA) corresponds to an identifiable ancestor (e.g.

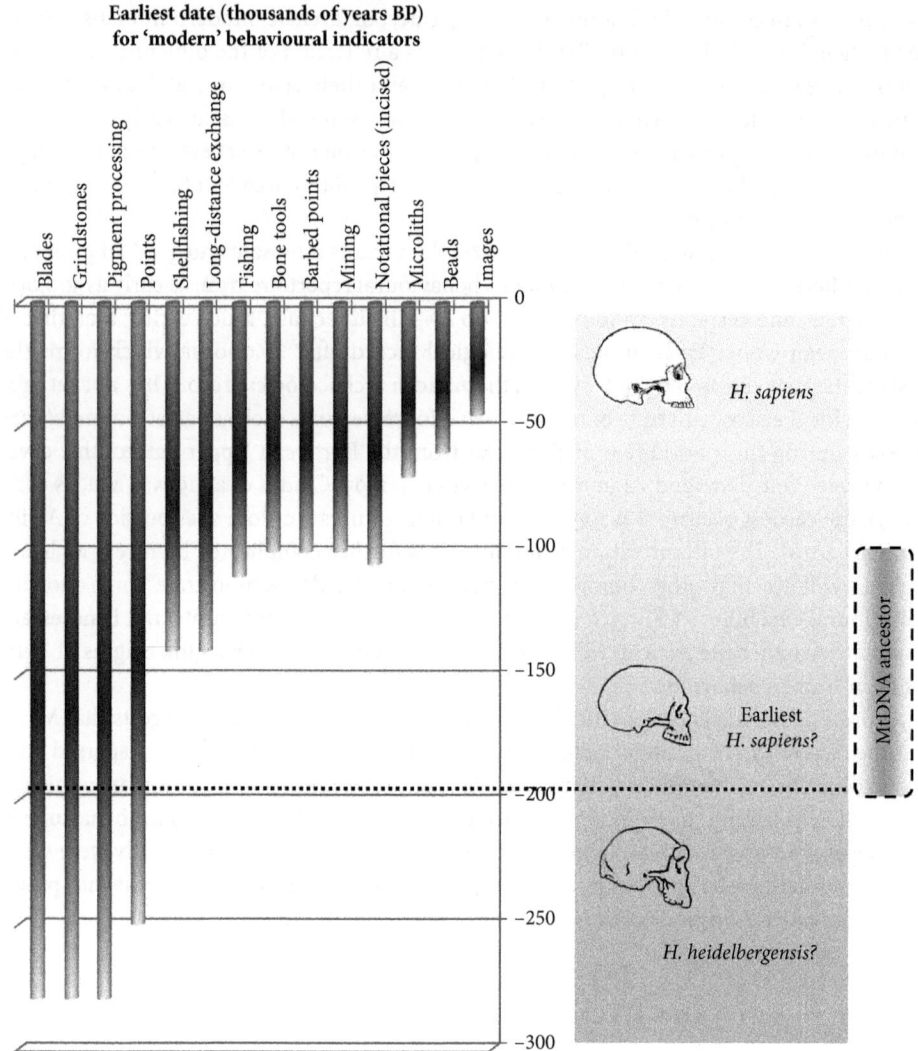

FIGURE 10.2 Schematic of timeline for the major factors involved in MHO from behavioural (archaeology), morphological (fossils), and genetic evidence (adapted from McBrearty and Brooks 2000; d'Errico 2003).

a species), and the date is discussed as if it were similar in nature to the geological dates associated with hominid fossils. In reality, there are a number of long-standing criticisms of methodological issues central to the molecular-clock model (see below) that challenge the simplicity and accuracy of this dating framework (e.g. Ayala 1995; Endicott et al. 2009; Excoffier 2002; Garrigan and Hammer 2006; Harpending and Rogers 2000; Relethford 1999; 2008; Templeton 1993; 2005). The relationship of molecular-clock dates to the fossil record is controversial, and is the subject of an ongoing debate throughout evolutionary biology (Donoghue and Benton 2007; Ho and Larson 2006; Pulquério and Nichols 2007; Steiper and Young 2006).

While the molecular clock is a widely used and valuable tool, the resulting dates for particular MRCAs often conflict with dates from palaeontological and archaeological sources, as well as with other molecular-clock calculations (Donoghue and Benton 2007; Endicott et al. 2009; Ho and Larson 2006). Published molecular-clock date estimates for the human mtDNA ancestor actually range from younger than 100,000 BP to considerably older than 200,000 BP (Cann et al. 1987; Hasegawa et al. 1993; Ho 2005; Horai et al. 1995; Ingman et al. 2000; Templeton 1993; 2005; Vigilant et al. 1989; 1991). The differences in published dates result from methodological variation with respect to different essential clock components. These include the calibration of the molecular clock from the estimated date of chimpanzee–human divergence, which may range from 4 to 8 Ma or more (Bradley 2008; Endicott et al. 2010; Templeton 1993), and the use of different mutation and/or substitution-rate models, some of which now account for the effect of purifying selection and other factors (Ho 2005; Soares et al. 2009; Templeton 1993; 2005). Endicott et al. (2009) examined the analyses underlying the established mitochondrial time-scale for human evolution and dispersal compared to palaeontological and archaeological evidence, concluding that uncertain calibration dates and rate heterogeneity depreciate our confidence in the molecular time-scale of human evolution.

From a statistical perspective, the 95 per cent confidence limits associated with molecular coalescence-date estimates are very wide, in the order of hundreds of thousands of years (Ruvolo 1996). Templeton (1993) concluded that the mitochondrial ancestor could have lived at any time between 102,000 and 554,000 BP if the molecular clock ran perfectly (i.e. randomly), and even older if it did not. Thus, the statistically meaningful estimate for the date of the mitochondrial MRCA actually spans a time period roughly equivalent to that between the fossils from Bodo and Border Cave, which are clearly different species (see Table 10.3).

A more conceptual challenge to synthesizing the fossil and genetic data relates to the nature of a molecular MRCA compared to a recognized fossil species. In population genetics, coalescence theory (Ayala 1995; Rosenberg and Nordborg 2002; Templeton 2007) predicts that all extant gene variants can be traced back in time to a single common ancestral gene (or MRCA), and the coalescence date represents the time estimated by the molecular clock to account for the observed genetic variation. Thus, the pervasive 200,000 BP chronological marker for MHO represents the coalescence date for the sampled mtDNA variation observed in living humans.

The mtDNA common ancestor identified in coalescence theory is an ancestor only for a particular gene lineage. Rather than identifying a unitary ancestor as we would identify in the fossil record, each gene lineage coalesces via a different path to common ancestry, a different coalescent time, and a different geographic place of origin (Ayala 1995; Weiss 2010). Many geneticists have emphasized that the 'mitochondrial ancestor' relates only to a particular gene lineage (Cann 1988; Jorde et al. 1998; Stoneking 2008; Templeton 1993), but the erroneous notion of 'mitochondrial Eve' as an individual ancestral female, or even as representing a specific ancestral modern human population achieved prominence as a highly perpetuated metaphor for MHO, even 'among some biologists who ought to know better' (Stoneking 2008, S49).

The broad implication of these issues is that gene lineages or gene trees and their coalescent times do not correspond precisely to species or phylogenetic trees and their associated geological dates. Gene trees are not species trees (Nichols 2001), and gene divergence is expected to precede population or morphological divergence (Endicott et al. 2009; Ingman and Gyllensten 2001; Stoneking 1993). Thus, the mtDNA ancestor was not necessarily morphologically or behaviourally a modern human (Cann et al. 1987; Stoneking 2008), and cannot manifestly be associated with any recognized ancestral fossil species or specimens.

The successful integration of information from these three conceptually different sources of data without allowing one to override the others (Templeton 2005) remains problematic. The uncertainties about the mtDNA coalescent date do have consequences for our palaeontological and archaeological interpretations about the evolution of human modernity. This has taxonomic implications for those critical fossils dated to the range between 100,000 and 200,000 BP: we cannot confidently determine whether they pre-date, or post-date the genetic divergence of mtDNA lineages—in other words, whether they lived at the time of the earliest genetically modern humans, or at the time of our ancestral genetic lineage.

Homo sapiens and Modern Humans

From a palaeontological perspective, one of the key issues is the definition and recognition of *H. sapiens*, especially in the taxonomic interpretation of key fossils after about 200,000 BP. As with any other biological species (Mayr and Ashlock 1991), the taxonomic definition of *H. sapiens* can incorporate a diversity of potential traits, and types of traits, to provide a variety of biological and behavioural information. While taxonomic assessments of fossil specimens necessarily rely heavily on skeletal morphology, inferences about some aspects of behaviour are often included (Leakey et al. 1964), and some morphological traits such as bipedalism or an increased brain size have at times been given extra weight in evaluating hominid taxonomy due to their behavioural implications (Mayr 1963). Recent advances in ancient DNA analysis have raised the possibility of reconstructing phenotypes from genetic analysis of fossils (Bradley 2008; Lalueza-Fox et al. 2007), and even of identifying new species on genetic evidence alone (Reich et al. 2010). The diversity of traits that can now be incorporated, and the varied potential interpretations of their adaptive or evolutionary significance, contribute to the challenges in classifying early human fossils.

It would once have been a reasonable expectation that the earliest fossils classified as *H. sapiens* would be roughly contemporaneous with the earliest archaeological evidence for modern behaviour (i.e. LSA or Upper Palaeolithic technology), particularly in the context of the Replacement model and its assumptions. But, since the 1980s, the recovery of new archaeological sites and fossils and the improvement of geological dating techniques have made it increasingly clear that fossils demonstrating some key features of *H. sapiens* morphology are associated with MSA (not LSA) tool-kits in Africa (Smith and Harrold 1997; Thackeray 1992). By most accounts, such human populations cannot be described as behaviourally modern (Ambrose and Lorenz 1990; Klein 2000), even though they are generally affiliated with *H. sapiens*. As Stringer (2001, 568) commented, this group of fossils 'probably belong to *H. sapiens* cladistically, but do not necessarily represent "modern" humans'.

From some perspectives, this may be a startling conclusion. As with any species, the evolutionary origin of *H. sapiens* encompasses the whole organism, and as Trinkaus (1989, 5) observed, 'it is only logical to expect that these palaeontologically and archaeologically documented changes are but different reflections of the same evolving behavioural/adaptive system'. In contrast to the above interpretations, we logically expect any specimen classified in the species *Homo sapiens* to be both biologically and behaviourally 'like us' (Ingold 1995).

The debate over the traits establishing behavioural modernity is at least as contentious as that over morphology. The central issue is whether behavioural modernity evolved rapidly and coincided with the dispersals of *H. sapiens* from Africa after roughly 40,000 BP as proposed in the Revolution model (Bar-Yosef 2002; Mellars 2005), or whether aspects of behavioural modernity evolved more gradually in a mosaic fashion over a period of 100 ky or more during the African MSA (d'Errico and Stringer 2011; McBrearty 2007; McBrearty and Brooks 2000). Historically, the Revolution model developed at a time when the Upper Palaeolithic in Europe was interpreted as the first expression of modern human behaviour (McBrearty 2007), and when the modern human origins debate was largely focused on the relationship between early *H. sapiens* and Neanderthals in Europe. While proponents of the Revolution model still focus on the European Upper Palaeolithic and the 'impossible coincidence' that both Neanderthal and *H. sapiens* populations could have independently evolved such behaviours at the same time (Mellars 2005), it is also acknowledged that the African MSA presents evidence reflecting a capacity for some behaviours once thought to be exclusive components of the Upper Palaeolithic repertoire. Opponents of the Revolution model have stated that the European Upper Palaeolithic bears no relevance in explaining how the different components of modern behaviour (sophisticated behaviour, advanced cognition, spoken language, etc.) originated in Africa at earlier periods (McBrearty 2007).

In the midst of such conflicting viewpoints, the fundamental issue is whether modernity is only reflected in the complete suite of behavioural and cognitive capabilities that appear to have a sudden origin in the symbolic artistic renderings of the Upper Palaeolithic in Europe. From the perspective of the African archaeological record, the various behavioural components relating to MSA technological capability, hunter-gatherer subsistence strategies, long-distance resource networks, and different forms of symbolic expression appeared more gradually, but reflect the fundamental behavioural capacities that define human modernity. Is modernity the complete (Upper Palaeolithic) package, or some essential capacity that may vary from site to site, and through time?

A philosophical debate concerning the relationship between species definitions and species concepts has a long history in evolutionary biology (Blackman 1995; De Queiroz 2007; Hey 2001), and some consideration of these perspectives may be illuminating to better understand the paradox that the earliest *H. sapiens* populations cannot be characterized as 'modern humans'. In particular, the taxonomic definitions of *H. sapiens* (i.e. lists of behavioural and morphological traits) may not be congruent with species concepts (either expressed or implicit) reflected in evolutionary models for modern human origins. Different species concepts have been considered in discussions of the evolutionary relationship between *H. sapiens* and *H. erectus* (Rightmire 1984) or Neanderthals (Holliday 2006; Tattersall and Schwartz 2008), but there appears to be less attention to this issue as it applies to early *H. sapiens*.

For example, Replacement scenarios generally emphasize modern human uniqueness (Klein 2000; 2008; Tattersall 2009; 2010), and minimize the role of gene flow during dispersals out of Africa (Cann et al. 1987; Stoneking 2008). It is hypothesized that human uniqueness originated in a rapid adaptive change brought about by genetic, environmental, or demographic factors resulting in higher cognitive processing and the acquisition of symbolic language to endow the descendant populations with a competitive advantage

(Klein 2008; Mellars 2006b). In this reconstruction, the requisites of Mayr's Biological Species Concept (BSC) are implicit in the role of reproductive isolation (De Queiroz 2005; Mayr 1996), and the sudden appearance of cognitive traits invokes a punctuated mode of speciation. Generally, these features are compatible with genetic analyses suggesting the occurrence of a population bottleneck that by some accounts corresponds with expansions out of Africa and the archaeological presence of modern tool technology (Amos and Hoffman 2010; Harpending et al. 1998; Ingman et al. 2000; Jorde et al. 1998). However, differences in ancient population size and genetic drift may also explain extant genetic variation (Relethford and Harpending 1995), and the timing is problematic between various proposed population bottlenecks, migration events, early *H. sapiens* fossils, and relevant features of the archaeological record (Endicott et al. 2009; Hawks et al. 2000). To add further challenges, recent ancient DNA studies (mentioned above) indicate that early modern human populations and their contemporaries actually did interbreed (Green et al. 2010; Krause et al. 2010; Reich et al. 2010); biologically and behaviourally they were not so unique. Ultimately, this hypothetical adaptive scenario invokes complex features to identify modern human origins which have no tangible evolutionary association with the morphological traits used to identify putative *H. sapiens* fossils at or after 200,000 BP, and which leave no explicit trace in the fossil or archaeological record until after 50,000–40,000 BP.

From a different perspective, at least some of the populations represented in the fossil record, such as the Group 2 hominids discussed above, are placed directly on the ancestral lineage for modern human populations. There are a number of alternative species concepts (to the BSC), including Simpson's (1961) Evolutionary Species Concept, that recognize the temporal dimension of lineages to be fundamental to understanding and recognizing species (De Queiroz 2007; Holliday 2003; Simpson 1961; Wilson 1995). The Evolutionary Species Concept recognizes ancestral-descendant populations (lineages), and distinct morphological clusters on a common lineage can be recognized taxonomically. In this case, the evolving human lineage (and the definition of our species) would incorporate morphological and behavioural change between earlier and later populations, and this concept may provide a more useful basis for interpretation of the observed fossil and archaeological record. To some degree, proposed taxa such as *H. helmei* (Foley and Lahr 1997) and *H. sapiens idaltu* (White et al. 2003) could be compatible with a lineage concept, but the fossil record in this time period is sparse, and the proposed taxonomic and phylogenetic relationship of either taxon to presumed early *H. sapiens* fossil specimens, or to each other, remains controversial.

There has already been much debate about species concepts (Blackman 1995; Chandler and Gromko 1989; Hey 2006; Kimbel and Martin 1993; Lee and Wolsan 2002; Mallet 2010; Mayr 1996) and further attempts to achieve some insight into the definition and recognition of early *H. sapiens* and MHO are likely to be frustrating given the diverse genetic, palaeontological, and archaeological evidence now available. Ultimately, it is necessary to clarify the taxonomic status of the Group 2 hominid fossils in order to successfully incorporate such diverse perspectives concerning the role of various evolutionary processes and the timing of different events underlying the origin of modern humans. As Tattersall and Schwartz (2008, 54) concluded, '...we will never properly understand hominid diversity in the late Middle Pleistocene and the Late Pleistocene or, indeed, the details of the emergence of our own species, until the identities of these fossils and the affinities of the taxa to which they belong have been established...'

While it seems logically obvious to define our own species in the context of extant human populations, it becomes increasingly difficult to reconcile a morphological definition of extant *H. sapiens* with the fossil or archaeological record as we approach the point of earliest origins. In addition, there is a philosophical dilemma in our inability to reconcile the distinction between the taxonomic unit designated as *H. sapiens* and the behavioural and cognitive entity we identify with as modern humans.

Summary and Conclusion

We have presented a review of the evidence for MHO in Africa drawing on the fossil record, archaeology, and genetic research relevant to the time period between approximately 200,000 and 40,000 BP. On the basis of the popular 200,000 BP coalescent date from mtDNA research in modern human populations, we have reviewed three morphological and temporal groups of hominid fossil specimens which are relevant to MHO, and which constitute an evolving lineage characterized by a mosaic morphological pattern documenting the gradual evolution of modern human traits.

The archaeological record similarly documents a gradual and mosaic evolutionary process for modern behaviour, beginning as early as 300,000 BP with the appearance of MSA tool technology and culminating at approximately 70,000–80,000 BP with composite tool preparation, long-distance transport networks, symbolic decoration, and other features not documented outside of Africa until after 40,000 BP.

In our view, a critical evaluation of this evidence no longer supports either a sudden Replacement scenario, or a behavioural revolution to explain the origin of modern human populations. The commonly presented 200,000 BP genetic framework for MHO has not yet resolved a number of significant theoretical and analytical challenges, and raises important questions concerning the nature of the underlying evolutionary processes and the resultant timing of genetic, morphological, and behavioural modernity. The 200,000 BP date estimate does not correspond with any conspicuous single event in our morphological or behavioural evolutionary history, but conceivably marks the initial divergence in a long- term, gradual, and mosaic process that resulted in our origins.

In attempting to incorporate the evidence from such diverse sources, we have undoubtedly left out much relevant information. Nevertheless, it seems apparent from our review that modern human origins involved a much more complex evolutionary process than that presented by current models. These diverse components (genetics, morphology, behaviour) are certainly interrelated, but the achievement of a coherent synthesis of MHO, and of a definition of modernity, is challenged by the observed independent patterns and processes involved in each. The definition of modernity, and of modern *H. sapiens*, must integrate the complexity of these different perspectives without allowing any single source of evidence to predominate. In the end, we should interpret the evidence to refine not only our understanding of our evolutionary history, but also our definition of ourselves as a species.

References

Aiello, L. C. 1993. The fossil evidence for modern human origins in Africa: a revised view. *American Anthropologist* 95, 73–96.

Aiello, L. C. and Dunbar, R. 1993. Neocortex size, group size, and the evolution of language. *Current Anthropology* 34, 184–93.

Ambrose, S. H. 2001. Paleolithic technology and human evolution. *Science* 291, 1748–53.

Ambrose, S. H. and Lorenz, G. K. 1990. Social and ecological models for the Middle Stone Age in southern Africa. In P. Mellars (ed.), *The emergence of modern humans: an archaeological perspective*, 3–33. Edinburgh: Edinburgh University Press.

Amos, W. and Hoffman, J. I. 2010. Evidence that two main bottleneck events shaped modern human genetic diversity. *Proceedings of the Royal Society B: Biological Sciences* 277, 131–7.

Avery, G., Cruz-Uribe, K., Goldberg, P., Grine, F.E., Klein, R. G., Lenardi, M. J., Marean, C. W., Rink, W. J., Schwarcz, H. P., Thackeray, A. I., and Wilson, M. L. 1997. The 1992–1993 excavations at the Die Kelders Middle and Later Stone Age cave site, South Africa. *Journal of Field Archaeology* 24, 263–91.

Ayala, F. J. 1995. The myth of Eve: molecular biology and human origins. *Science* 270, 1930–6.

Barham, L. 2002. Backed tools in Middle Pleistocene central Africa and their evolutionary significance. *Journal of Human Evolution* 43, 585–603.

Barham, L. 2004. Art in human evolution. In G. Berghaus (ed.), *New perspectives on prehistoric art*, 105–30. Westport: Praeger.

Barham, L., Pinto Llona, A., and Stringer, C. 2002. Bone tools from Broken Hill (Kabwe) cave, Zambia, and their evolutionary significance. *Before Farming* 2, 1–12.

Bar-Yosef, O. 2002. The Upper Paleolithic revolution. *Annual Review of Anthropology* 31, 363–93.

Bar-Yosef, O. 2007. The archaeological framework of the Upper Paleolithic revolution. *Diogenes* 54, 3–18.

Berger, L. R. and Parkington, J. E. 1995. Brief communication: a new Pleistocene hominid-bearing locality at Hoedjiespunt, South Africa. *American Journal of Physical Anthropology* 98, 601–9.

Bernal, V., Perez, S. I. and Gonzalez, P. N. 2006. Variation and causal factors of craniofacial robusticity in Patagonian hunter-gatherers from the late Holocene. *American Journal of Human Biology* 18, 748–65.

Blackman, R. 1995. What's in a name? Species concepts and realities. *Bulletin of Entomological Research* 85, 1–4.

Bordes, F. 1968. *The Old Stone Age*. New York: McGraw-Hill.

Bouzouggar, A., Barton, N., Vanhaeren, M., d'Errico, F., Collcutt, S., Higham, T., Hodge, E., Parfitt, S., Rhodes, E., Schwenninger, J.-L., Stringer, C., Turner, E., Ward, S., Moutmir, A., and Stambouli, A. 2007. 82,000-year-old shell beads from North Africa and implications for the origins of modern human behavior. *Proceedings of the National Academy of Sciences USA* 104, 9964–9.

Bowler, J. M., Johnston, H., Olley, J. M., Prescott, J. R., Roberts, R. G., Shawcross, W., and Spooner, N. A. 2003. New ages for human occupation and climatic change at Lake Mungo, Australia. *Nature* 421, 837–40.

Bowler, J. M., Jones, R., Allen, H., and Thorne, A. G. 1970. Pleistocene human remains from Australia: a living site and human cremation from Lake Mungo, Western New South Wales. *World Archaeology* 2, 39–60.

Bradley, B. J. 2008. Reconstructing phylogenies and phenotypes: a molecular view of human evolution. *Journal of Anatomy* 212, 337–53.

Bräuer, G. 2008. The origin of modern anatomy: by speciation or intraspecific evolution? *Evolutionary Anthropology: Issues, News, and Reviews* 17, 22–37.

Bräuer, G. and Mehlman, M. J. 1988. Hominid molars from a middle stone age level at the Mumba Rock Shelter, Tanzania. *American Journal of Physical Anthropology* 75, 69–76.

Broca, P. 1868. Sur les crânes et ossements des Eyzies. *Bulletins de la Société d'anthropologie de Paris*, 3, 350–92.

Brown, K. S., Marean, C. W., Herries, A. I. R., Jacobs, Z., Tribolo, C., Braun, D., Roberts, D. L., Meyer, M. C., and Bernatchez, J. 2009. Fire as an engineering tool of early modern humans. *Science* 325, 859–62.

Butzer, K. W. 1969. Geological interpretations of two Pleistocene hominid sites in the Lower Omo Basin. *Nature* 222, 1133–5.

Cann, R. L. 1988. DNA and human origins. *Annual Review of Anthropology* 17, 127–43.

Cann, R. L., Stoneking, M., and Wilson, A. C. 1987. Mitochondrial DNA and human evolution. *Nature* 325, 31–6.

Cartmill, M. 2001. Taxonomic revolutions and the animal–human boundary. In R. Corbey and W. Roebroeks (eds), *Studying human origins: disciplinary history and epistemology*, 97–106. Amsterdam: Amsterdam University Press.

Chandler, C. and Gromko, M. 1989. On the relationship between species concepts and speciation processes. *Systematic Biology* 38, 116–25.

Chauvet, J.-M., Brunel Deschamps, E., and Hillaire, C. 1995. *La grotte Chauvet à Vallon-Pont-d'Arc*. Paris: Seuil.

Clark, G. and Lindly, J. M. 1989. Modern human origins in the Levant and Western Asia: the fossil and archeological evidence. *American Anthropologist* 91, 962–85.

Clark, J. D. 1988. The Middle Stone Age of East Africa and the beginnings of regional identity. *Journal of World Prehistory* 2, 235–305.

Clark, J. D., Beyene, Y., WoldeGabriel, G., Hart, W. K., Renne, P. R., Gilbert, H., Defleur, A., Suwa, G., Katoh, S., Ludwig, K. R., Boisserie, J.-R., Asfaw, B., and White, T. D. 2003. Stratigraphic, chronological and behavioural contexts of Pleistocene *Homo sapiens* from Middle Awash, Ethiopia. *Nature* 423, 74–2.

Clark, J. D., de Heinzelin, J., Schick, K., Hart, W., White, T., WoldeGabriel, G., Walter, R., Suwa, G., Asfaw, B., and Vrba, E. 1994. African *Homo erectus*: old radiometric ages and young Oldowan assemblages in the Middle Awash Valley, Ethiopia. *Science* 264, 1907–10.

Clark, J. D., Williamson, K. D., Michels, J. W., and Marean, C. 1984. A Middle Stone Age occupation at Porc-Epic Cave, Dire Dawa (east-central Ethiopia). *African Archaeological Review* 2, 37–71.

Clottes, J., Chauvet, J.-M., Brunel-Deschamps, E., Hillaire, C., Daugas, J.-P., Arnold, M., Cachier, H., Evin, J., Fortin, P., Oberlin, C., Tisnerat, N., and Valladas, H. 1995. Les peintures paléolithiques de la Grotte Chauvet-Pont d'Arc, à Vallon-Pont-d'Arc (Ardèche, France): datations directes et indirectes par la méthode du radiocarbone. *Comptes rendus de l'Académie des sciences. Série 2. Sciences de la terre et des planètes* 320, 1133–40.

Conard, N. 2010. Cultural modernity: consensus or conundrum? *Proceedings of the National Academy of Sciences USA* 107, 7621–2.

Crawford, M., Bloom, M., Broadhurst, C., Schmidt, W., Cunnane, S., Galli, C., Gehbremeskel, K., Linseisen, F., Lloyd-Smith, J., and Parkington, J. 1999. Evidence for the unique function of docosahexaenoic acid during the evolution of the modern hominid brain. *Lipids* 34, S39–S47.

Cremaschi, M., Lernia, S. D., Garcea, E. A. A., and Afuda, U. 1998. Some insights on the Aterian in the Libyan Sahara: chronology, environment, and archaeology. *African Archaeological Review* 15, 261–86.

Curnoe, D. 2011. A 150-year conundrum: cranial robusticity and its bearing on the origin of Aboriginal Australians. *International Journal of Evolutionary Biology* 2011, 1–18.

Currat, M. and Excoffier, L. 2004. Modern humans did not admix with Neanderthals during their range expansion into Europe. *PLoS Biology* 2, 2264–74.

Day, M. H. and Stringer, C. 1982. A reconstruction of the Omo Kibish remains and the erectus–sapiens transition. In D. Lumley and D. Lumley (eds), *L'homo erectus et la place de l'homme de Tautavel parmi les hominides fossiles. Premier Congrès Internationale de Paléontologie Humaine*, 814–46. Nice: CNRS.

Day, M. H. and Stringer, C. 1991. Les restes craniens d'Omo-Kibish et leur classification a l'interieur du genre Homo. *L'Anthropologie* 95, 573–94.

Deacon, H. J. 1992. Southern Africa and modern human origins. *Philosophical Transactions of the Royal Society of London* 337, 177–83.

Deacon, H. J. and Deacon, J. 1999. *Human beginnings in South Africa: uncovering the secrets of the Stone Age*. Cape Town: David Philip.

Dennell, R. and Roebroeks, W. 2005. An Asian perspective on early human dispersal from Africa. *Nature* 438, 1099–104.

De Queiroz, K. 2005. Ernst Mayr and the modern concept of species. *Proceedings of the National Academy of Sciences USA* 102 Supplement 1, 6600–7.

De Queiroz, K. 2007. Species concepts and species delimitation. *Systematic Biology* 56, 879–86.

d'Errico, F. 2003. The invisible frontier: a multiple species model for the origin of behavioral modernity. *Evolutionary Anthropology: Issues, News, and Reviews* 12, 188–202.

d'Errico, F. and Stringer, C. B. 2011. Evolution, revolution or saltation scenario for the emergence of modern cultures? *Philosophical Transactions of the Royal Society of London B: Biological Sciences* 366, 1060–9.

d'Errico, F., Vanhaeren, M., Barton, N., Bouzouggar, A., Mienis, H., Richter, D., Hublin, J. J., McPherron, S. P., and Lozouet, P. 2009. Additional evidence on the use of personal ornaments in the Middle Paleolithic of North Africa. *Proceedings of the National Academy of Sciences USA* 106, 16051–6.

d'Errico, F., Zilhao, J., Julien, M., Baffier, D., and Pelegrin, J. 1998. Neanderthal acculturation in Western Europe? A critical review of the evidence and its interpretation. *Current Anthropology* 39, S1–S44.

Domínguez-Rodrigo, M., Mabulla, A., Luque, L., Thompson, J., Rink, J., Bushozi, P., Díez-Martin, F., and Alcala, F. 2008. A new archaic *Homo sapiens* fossil from Lake Eyasi, Tanzania. *Journal of Human Evolution* 54, 899–903.

Donoghue, P. C. J. and Benton, M. J. 2007. Rocks and clocks: calibrating the Tree of Life using fossils and molecules. *Trends in Ecology & Evolution* 22, 424–31.

Dreyer, T. F. 1935. A human skull from Florisbad. *Proceedings of the Academy of Sciences of Amsterdam* 38, 119–28.

Dunbar, R. 2003. The social brain: mind, language, and society in evolutionary perspective. *Annual Review of Anthropology* 32, 163–81.

Enard, W., Przeworski, M., Fisher, S. E., Lai, C. S. L., Wiebe, V., Kitano, T., Monaco, A. P., and Pääbo, S. 2002. Molecular evolution of FOXP2, a gene involved in speech and language. *Nature* 418, 869–72.

Endicott, P., Ho, S. Y. W., Metspalu, M., and Stringer, C. 2009. Evaluating the mitochondrial timescale of human evolution. *Trends in Ecology & Evolution* 24, 515–21.

Endicott, P., Ho, S. Y. W., and Stringer, C. 2010. Using genetic evidence to evaluate four palaeoanthropological hypotheses for the timing of Neanderthal and modern human origins. *Journal of Human Evolution* 59, 87–95.

Ennouchi, E. 1962. Un crâne d'Homme ancient au Jebel Irhoud (Maroc). *Comptes Rendus de L'Académie des Sciences, Paris* 256, 4330–2.

Ennouchi, E. 1968. Le deuxième crâne de l'Homme d'Irhoud. *Annals de Paléontologie (Vertebres)* 54, 117–28.

Erren, T. C. and Erren, M. 2004. Can fat explain the human brain's big bang evolution? Horrobin's leads for comparative and functional genomics. *Prostaglandins, Leikotrienes and Essential Fatty Acids* 70, 345–7.

Excoffier, L. 2002. Human demographic history: refining the recent African origin model. *Current Opinion in Genetics & Development* 12, 675–82.

Finlay, B., Darlington, R., and Nicastro, N. 2001. Developmental structure in brain evolution. *Behavioural and Brain Sciences* 24, 263–308.

Fleagle, J. G., Assefa, Z., Brown, F. H., and Shea, J. J. 2008. Paleoanthropology of the Kibish Formation, southern Ethiopia: introduction. *Journal of Human Evolution* 55, 360–5.

Foley, R. 2001. In the shadow of the modern synthesis? Alternative perspectives on the last fifty years of paleoanthropology. *Evolutionary Anthropology: Issues, News, and Reviews* 10, 5–14.

Foley, R. and Lahr, M. M. 1997. Mode 3 technologies and the evolution of modern humans. *Cambridge Archaeological Journal* 7, 3–36.

Frayer, D. W., Wolpoff, M. H., Thorne, A. G., Smith, F. H., and Pope, G. G. 1994. Getting it straight. *American Anthropologist* 96, 424–38.

Garrigan, D. and Hammer, M. F. 2006. Reconstructing human origins in the genomic era. *Nature Reviews Genetics* 7, 669–80.

Garrod, D., Bate, D., McCown, T., and Keith, A. 1937. *The Stone Age of Mount Carmel: excavations at Wady el-Mughara*. Oxford: Clarendon Press.

Gibbons, A. 2011. Modern human origins, *Nature* 372, 392–4.

Goodwin, A. J. H. and Van Riet Lowe, C. 1929. The Stone Age cultures of South Africa. *Annals of the South African Museum* 27, 1–289.

Green, R. E., Krause, J., Briggs, A. W., Maricic, T., Stenzel, U., Kircher, M., Patterson, N., Li, H., Zhai, W., Fritz, M. H. Y., Hansen, N. F., Durand, E. Y., Malaspinas, A. S., Jensen, J. D., Marques-Bonet, T., Alkan, C., Prufer, K., Meyer, M., Burbano, H. A., Good, J. M., Schultz, R., Aximu-Petri, A., Butthof, A., Hober, B., Hoffner, B., Siegemund, M., Weihmann, A., Nusbaum, C., Lander, E. S., Russ, C., Novod, N., Affourtit, J., Egholm, M., Verna, C., Rudan, P., Brajkovic, D., Kucan, Z., Gusic, I., Doronichev, V. B., Golovanova, L. V., Lalueza-Fox, C., de la Rasilla, M., Fortea, J., Rosas, A., Schmitz, R. W., Johnson, P. L. F., Eichler, E. E., Falush, D., Birney, E., Mullikin, J. C., Slatkin, M., Nielsen, R., Kelso, J., Lachmann, M., Reich, D., and Pääbo, S. 2010. A draft sequence of the Neandertal genome. *Science* 328, 710–22.

Grine, F. E., Bailey, R. M., Harvati, K., Nathan, R. P., Morris, A. G., Henderson, G. M., Ribot, I., and Pike, W. G. 2007. Late Pleistocene human skull from Hofmeyr, South Africa, and modern human origins. *Science* 315, 226–9.

Grine, F. E., Henshilwood, C. S., and Sealy, J. C. 2000. Human remains from Blombos Cave, South Africa: 1997–1998 excavations. *Journal of Human Evolution* 38, 755–65.

Grine, F. E. and Klein, R. G. 1985. Pleistocene and Holocene human remains from Equus Cave, South Africa. *Anthropology* 8, 55–98.

Grine, F. E. and Klein, R. G. 1993. Late Pleistocene human remains from the Sea Harvest Site, Saldanha Bay, South Africa. *South African Journal of Science* 89, 145–52.

Grün, R., Brink, J. S., Spooner, N. A., Taylor, L., Stringer, C., Franciscus, R. G., and Murray, S. A. 1996. Direct dating of the Florisbad hominid. *Nature* 382, 500–1.

Grün, R. and Stringer, C. B. 1991. Electron spin resonance dating and the evolution of modern humans. *Archaeometry* 33, 153–99.

Grün, R., Stringer, C., McDermott, F., Nathan, R., Porat, N., Robertson, S., Taylor, L., Mortimer, G., Eggins, S., and McCulloch, M. 2005. U-series and ESR analyses of bones and teeth relating to the human burials from Skhul. *Journal of Human Evolution* 49, 316–34.

Haile-Selassie, Y., Asfaw, B., and White, T. D. 2004. Hominid cranial remains from Upper Pleistocene deposits at Aduma, Middle Awash, Ethiopia. *American Journal of Physical Anthropology* 123, 1–10.

Harpending, H., Batzer, M. A., Gurven, M., Jorde, L. B., Rogers, A., and Sherry, S. T. 1998. Genetic traces of ancient demography. *Proceedings of the National Academy of Sciences USA* 95, 1961–7.

Harpending, H. and Rogers, A. 2000. Genetic perspectives on human origins and differentiation. *Annual Review of Genomics and Human Genetics* 1, 361–85.

Harrold, F. B. 1989. Mousterian, Chatelperronian and Early Aurgnacian in Western Europe: continuity or discontinuity? In P. Mellars and C. Stringer (eds), *The human revolution: behavioural and biological perspectives on the origins of modern humans*, 714–42. Edinburgh: Edinburgh University Press.

Harvati, K. 2007. 100 years of *Homo heidelbergensis*—life and times of a controversial taxon. *Mitteilungen der Gesellschaft für Urgeschichte* 16, 85–94.

Hasegawa, M., Di Rienzo, A., Kocher, T. D., and Wilson, A. C. 1993. Toward a more accurate time scale for the human mitochondrial DNA tree. *Journal of Molecular Evolution* 37, 347–54.

Hawks, J., Hunley, K., Lee, S., and Wolpoff, M. 2000. Population bottlenecks and Pleistocene human evolution. *Molecular Biology and Evolution* 17, 2–22.

Henri-Gambier, D. 2002. Les fossiles de Cro-Magnon (Les Eyzies-de-Tayac, Dordogne): nouvelles données sur leur position chronologique et leur attribution culturelle. *Bulletin et Mémoires de la Société d'Anthropologie de Paris* 14, 89–112.

Henshilwood, C. S., d'Errico, F., Marean, C. W., Milo, R. G., and Yates, R. 2001. An early bone tool industry from the Middle Stone Age at Blombos Cave, South Africa: implications for the origins of modern human behaviour, symbolism and language. *Journal of Human Evolution* 41, 631–78.

Henshilwood, C. S., d'Errico, F., Vanhaeren, M., van Niekerk, K., and Jacobs, Z. 2004. Middle Stone Age shell beads from South Africa. *Science* 304, 404.

Henshilwood, C. S., d'Errico, F., and Watts, I. 2009. Engraved ochres from the Middle Stone Age levels at Blombos Cave, South Africa. *Journal of Human Evolution* 57, 27–47.

Henshilwood, C. S., d'Errico, F., Yates, R., Jacobs, Z., Tribolo, C., Duller, G. A. T., Mercier, N., Sealy, J. C., Valladas, H., Watts, I., and Wintle, A. G. 2002. Emergence of modern human behavior: Middle Stone Age engravings from South Africa. *Science* 295, 1278–80.

Hey, J. 2001. The mind of the species problem. *Trends in Ecology & Evolution* 16, 326–9.

Hey, J. 2006. On the failure of modern species concepts. *Trends in Ecology & Evolution* 21, 447–50.

Ho, S. Y. W. 2005. Time dependency of molecular rate estimates and systematic overestimation of recent divergence times. *Molecular Biology and Evolution* 22, 1561–8.

Ho, S. Y. W. and Larson, G. 2006. Molecular clocks: when times are a-changin'. *Trends in Genetics* 22, 79–83.

Holliday, T. 2003. Species concepts, reticulation, and human evolution. *Current Anthropology* 44, 653–73.

Holliday, T. 2006. Neanderthals and modern humans: an example of a mammalian syngameon? In J.-J. Hublin, K. Harvati, and T. Harrison (eds), *Neanderthals revisited: new approaches and perspectives*, 281–97. Dordrect: Springer.

Horai, S., Hayasaka, K., Kondo, R., Tsugane, K., and Takahata, N. 1995. Recent African origin of modern humans revealed by complete sequences of hominoid mitochondrial DNAs. *Proceedings of the National Academy of Sciences USA* 92, 532–6.

Howells, W. W. 1959. *Mankind in the making: the story of human evolution.* New York: Doubleday & Company.

Hublin, J. J. 1992. Recent human evolution in northwestern Africa. *Philosophical Transactions of the Royal Society of London B: Biological Sciences* 337, 185–91.

Ingman, M. and Gyllensten, U. 2001. Analysis of the complete human mtDNA genome: methodology and inferences for human evolution. *Journal of Heredity* 92, 454–61.

Ingman, M., Kaessmann, H., Pääbo, S., and Gyllensten, U. 2000. Mitochondrial genome variation and the origin of modern humans. *Nature* 408, 708–13.

Ingold, T. 1995. 'People like us': the concept of the anatomically modern human. *Cultural Dynamics* 7, 187–214.

Jacobs, Z., Roberts, R. G., Galbraith, R. F., Deacon, H. J., Grün, R., Mackay, A., Mitchell, P., Vogelsang, R., and Wadley, L. 2008. Ages for the Middle Stone Age of southern Africa: implications for human behavior and dispersal. *Science* 322, 733–5.

Jorde, L. B., Bamshad, M., and Rogers, A. R. 1998. Using mitochondrial and nuclear DNA markers to reconstruct human evolution. *BioEssay* 20, 126–36.

Jorde, L. B., Bamshad, M. J., Watkins, W., Zenger, R., Fraley, A. E., Krakowiak, P. A., Carpenter, K. D., Soodyall, H., Jenkins, T., and Rogers, A. R. 1995. Origins and affinities of modern humans: a comparison of mitochondrial and nuclear genetic data. *American Journal of Human Genetics* 57, 523–38.

Kimbel, W. and Martin, L. 1993. *Species, species concepts, and primate evolution.* New York: Plenum Press.

Klein, R. G. 1973. Geological antiquity of Rhodesian Man. *Nature* 244, 311–12.

Klein, R. G. 1999. *The human career: human biological and cultural origins.* Chicago: University of Chicago Press.

Klein, R. G. 2000. Archeology and the evolution of human behavior. *Evolutionary Anthropology: Issues, News, and Reviews* 9, 17–36.

Klein, R. G. 2008. Out of Africa and the evolution of human behavior. *Evolutionary Anthropology: Issues, News, and Reviews* 17, 267–81.

Klein, R. G. 2009. *The human career: human biological and cultural origins.* Chicago: University of Chicago Press.

Krantz, G. 1980. Sapienization and speech [and comments and reply]. *Current Anthropology* 21, 773–92.

Krause, J., Fu, Q., Good, J. M., Viola, B., Shunkov, M. V., Derevianko, A. P., and Pääbo, S. 2010. The complete mitochondrial DNA genome of an unknown hominin from southern Siberia. *Nature* 464, 894–7.

Krause, J., Lalueza-Fox, C., Orlando, L., Enard, W., Green, R. E., Burbano, H. A., Hublin, J.-J., Hänni, C., Fortea, J., de la Rasilla, M., Bertranpetit, J., Rosas, A., and Pääbo, S. 2007. The derived FOXP2 variant of modern humans was shared with Neandertals. *Current Biology* 17, 1908–12.

Krings, M., Geisert, H., Schmitz, R. W., Krainitzki, H., and Pääbo, S. 1999. DNA sequence of mitochondrial hypervariable Region II from the Neandertal type specimen. *Proceedings of the National Academy of Sciences USA* 96, 5581–5.

Krings, M., Stone, A., Schimitz, R. W., Krainitzki, H., Stoneking, M., and Pääbo, S. 1997. Neandertal DNA sequences and the origin of modern humans. *Cell* 90, 19–30.

Lahr, M. M. and Foley, R. A. 1998. Towards a theory of modern human origins: geography, demography, and diversity in recent human evolution. *Yearbook of Physical Anthropology* 41, 137–78.

Lalueza-Fox, C., Rompler, H., Caramelli, D., Staubert, C., Catalano, G., Hughes, D., Rohland, N., Pilli, E., Longo, L., Condemi, S., de la Rasilla, M., Fortea, J., Rosas, A., Stoneking, M., Schoneberg, T., Bertranpetit, J., and Hofreiter, M. 2007. A Melanocortin 1 receptor allele suggests varying pigmentation among Neanderthals. *Science* 318, 1453–5.

Leakey, L., Tobias, P. V., and Napier, J. 1964. A new species of the genus Homo from Olduvai Gorge. *Nature* 202, 7–9.

Lee, M. and Wolsan, M. 2002. Integration, individuality and species concepts. *Biology and Philosophy* 17, 651–60.

Lieberman, D. E., McBratney, B. M., and Krovitz, G. 2002. The evolution and development of cranial form in *Homo sapiens*. *Proceedings of the National Academy of Sciences USA* 99, 1134–9.

Lombard, M. 2005. Evidence of hunting and hafting during the Middle Stone Age at Sibidu Cave, KwaZulu-Natal, South Africa: a multianalytical approach. *Journal of Human Evolution* 48, 279–300.

McBrearty, S. 2007. Down with the revolution. In P. Mellars, K. Boyle, O. Bar-Yosef, and C. Stringer (eds), *Rethinking the human revolution*, 133–51. Cambridge: MacDonald Institute for Archaeological Research.

McBrearty, S. and Brooks, A. S. 2000. The revolution that wasn't: a new interpretation of the origin of modern human behavior. *Journal of Human Evolution* 39, 453–563.

McDermott, F., Stringer, C., Grün, R., Williams, C. T., Din, V. K., and Hawkesworth, C. J. 1996. New Late-Pleistocene uranium-thorium and ESR dates for the Singa hominid (Sudan). *Journal of Human Evolution* 31, 507–16.

McDougall, I., Brown, F., and Fleagle, J. G. 2005. Stratigraphic placement and age of modern humans from Kibish, Ethiopia. *Nature* 433, 733–6.

Magori, C. C. and Day, M. H. 1983. Laetoli Hominid 18: an early *Homo sapiens* skull. *Journal of Human Evolution* 12, 747–53.

Mallet, J. 2010. Group selection and the development of the biological species concept. *Philosophical Transactions of the Royal Society B: Biological Sciences* 365, 1853–63.

Manega, P. 1995. *New geochronological results from the Ndutu, Niasiusiu and Ngaloba beds at Olduvai and Laetoli in northern Tanzania: their significance for the evolution of modern humans (Abstract).* Bellagio Conference, Italy.

Marean, C. W. 2010. Pinnacle Point Cave 13B (Western Cape Province, South Africa) in context: the Cape Floral kingdom, shellfish, and modern human origins. *Journal of Human Evolution* 59, 425–43.

Marean, C. W., Bar-Matthews, M., Bernatchez, J., Fisher, E., Goldberg, P., Herries, A. I. R., Jacobs, Z., Jerardino, A., Karkanas, P., Minichillo, T., Nilssen, P. J., Thompson, E., Watts, I., and Williams, H. M. 2007. Early human use of marine resources and pigment in South Africa during the Middle Pleistocene. *Nature* 449, 905–8.

Mayr, E. 1963. The taxonomic evaluation of fossil hominids. In S. Washburn (ed.), *Classification and human evolution*, 332–46. Chicago: Aldine.

Mayr, E. 1996. What is a species, and what is not? *Philosophy of Science* 63, 262–77.

Mayr, E. and Ashlock, P. D. 1991. *Principles of systematic zoology* (2nd edition). New York: McGraw-Hill.

Mellars, P. 2004. Neanderthals and the modern human colonization of Europe. *Nature* 432, 461–5.

Mellars, P. 2005. The impossible coincidence: a single-species model for the origins of modern human behavior in Europe. *Evolutionary Anthropology: Issues, News, and Reviews* 14, 12–27.

Mellars, P. 2006a. Archeology and the dispersal of modern humans in Europe: deconstructing the 'Aurignacian'. *Evolutionary Anthropology: Issues, News, and Reviews* 15, 167–82.

Mellars, P. 2006b. Why did modern human populations disperse from Africa ca. 60,000 years ago? A new model. *Proceedings of the National Academy of Sciences USA* 103, 9381–6.

Mithen, S. 1995. Palaeolithic archaeology and the evolution of mind. *Journal of Archaeological Research* 3, 305–32.

Mounier, A., Marchal, F., and Condemi, S. 2009. Is *Homo heidelbergensis* a distinct species? New insight on the Mauer mandible. *Journal of Human Evolution* 56, 219–46.

Nespoulet, R., Debenath, A., El Hajraoui, A., Michel, P., Campmas, E., Oujaa, A., Ben-Ncer, A., Lacombe, J.-P., Amani, F., Stoetzeli, E., and Oudad, L. 2008. Le contexte archéologique des restes humains atériens de la région de Rabat-Témara (Maroc): apport des fouilles des grottes d'el Mnasra et d'el Harhoura 2. *Actes RQM4, Oujda* 356–75.

Nichols, R. 2001. Gene trees and species trees are not the same. *Trends in Ecology and Evolution* 16, 358–64.

Nordberg, M. 1998. On the probability of Neanderthal ancestry. *American Journal of Human Genetics* 63, 1237–40.

Oppenheimer, S. 2009. The great arc of dispersal of modern humans: Africa to Australia. *Quaternary International* 202, 2–13.

Pääbo, S. 1999. Human evolution. *Trends in Genetics* 15, M13–M16.

Pääbo, S., Poinar, H., Serre, D., Jaenicke-Despres, V., Hebler, J., Rohland, N., Kuch, M., Krause, J., Vigilant, L., and Hofreiter, M. 2004. Genetic analyses from ancient DNA. *Annual Review of Genetics* 38, 645–79.

Pearson, O. M. 2008. Statistical and biological definitions of 'anatomically modern' humans: suggestions for a unified approach to modern morphology. *Evolutionary Anthropology: Issues, News, and Reviews* 17, 38–48.

Pinhasi, R. and Semal, P. 2000. The position of the Nazlet Khater specimen among prehistoric and modern African and Levantine populations. *Journal of Human Evolution* 39, 269–88.

Plagnol, V. and Wall, J. 2006. Possible ancestral structure in human populations. *PLoS Genetics* 2, 972–9.

Pulquério, M. J. F. and Nichols, R. A. 2007. Dates from the molecular clock: how wrong can we be? *Trends in Ecology and Evolution* 22, 180–4.

Reich, D., Green, R. E., Kircher, M., Krause, J., Patterson, N., Durand, E. Y., Viola, B., Briggs, A. W., Stenzel, U., Johnson, P. L. F., Maricic, T., Good, J.M., Marques-Bonet, T., Alkan, C., Fu, Q., Mallick, S., Li, H., Meyer, M., Eichler, E. E., Stoneking, M., Richards, M., Talamo, S., Shunkov, M. V., Derevianko, A. P., Hublin, J.-J., Kelso, J., Slatkin, M., and Pääbo, S. 2010. Genetic history of an archaic hominin group from Denisova Cave in Siberia. *Nature* 468, 1053–60.

Relethford, J. H. 1998. Genetics of modern human origins and diversity. *Annual Review of Anthropology* 27, 1–23.

Relethford, J. H. 1999. Models, predictions, and the fossil record of modern human origins. *Evolutionary Anthropology: Issues, News, and Reviews* 8, 7–10.

Relethford, J. H. 2001. Ancient DNA and the origin of modern humans. *Proceedings of the National Academy of Sciences USA* 98, 390–1.

Relethford, J. H. 2008. Genetic evidence and the modern human origins debate. *Heredity* 100, 555–63.

Relethford, J. H. and Harpending, H. C. 1995. Ancient differences in population size can mimic a recent African origin of modern humans. *Current Anthropology* 36, 667–74.

Renfrew, C. 2008. Neuroscience, evolution and the sapient paradox: the factuality of value and of the sacred. *Philosophical Transactions of the Royal Society of London B: Biological Sciences* 363, 2041–7.

Richter, D., Moser, J., Nami, M., Eiwanger, J., and Mikdad, A. 2010. New chronometric data from Ifri n'Ammar (Morocco) and the chronostratigraphy of the Middle Palaeolithic in the Western Maghreb. *Journal of Human Evolution* 59, 672–9.

Rightmire, G. P. 1976. Relationships of Middle and Upper Pleistocene hominids from sub-Saharan Africa. *Nature* 260, 238–40.

Rightmire, G. P. 1984. Homo sapiens in sub-Saharan Africa. In F. Smith and F. Spencer (eds), *The origins of modern humans: a world survey of the fossil evidence*, 295–325. New York: Alan R. Liss.

Rightmire, G. P. 1988. Homo erectus and later Middle Pleistocene humans. *Annual Review of Anthropology* 17, 239–59.

Rightmire, G. P. 1996. The human cranium from Bodo, Ethiopia: evidence for speciation in the Middle Pleistocene? *Journal of Human Evolution* 31, 21–38.

Rightmire, G. P. 1998. Human evolution in the Middle Pleistocene: the role of *Homo heidelbergensis*. *Evolutionary Anthropology: Issues, News, and Reviews* 6, 218–27.

Rightmire, G. P. 2008. Homo in the Middle Pleistocene: hypodigms, variation, and species recognition. *Evolutionary Anthropology: Issues, News, and Reviews* 17, 8–21.

Rightmire, G. P., Beaumont, P. B., Bilsborough, A., Butzer, K., Davies, O., Gilead, I. J., Groves, C. P., Howells, W. W., Irsigler, F. J., Luchterhand, K., Merrick, H. V., Rolland, N., Thurzo, M., Wilson, S. R. and, Wymer, J. J. 1979. Implications of border cave skeletal remains for Later Pleistocene human evolution [and comments and reply]. *Current Anthropology* 20, 23–35.

Rightmire, G. P. and Deacon, H. J. 1991. Comparative studies of Late Pleistocene human remains from Klasies River Mouth, South Africa. *Journal of Human Evolution* 20, 131–56.

Rosenberg, N. A. and Nordborg, M. 2002. Genealogical trees, coalescent theory and the analysis of genetic polymorphisms. *Nature Reviews Genetics* 3, 380–90.

Rougier, H., Milota, Ş., Rodrigo, R., Gherase, M., Sarcină, L., Moldovan, O., Zilhão, J., Constantin, S., Franciscus, R. G., Zollikofer, C. P. E., Ponce de León, M., and Trinkaus, E. 2007. Peştera cu Oase 2 and the cranial morphology of early modern Europeans. *Proceedings of the National Academy of Sciences USA* 104, 1165–70.

Ruvolo, M. 1996. A new approach to studying modern human origins: hypothesis testing with coalescence time distributions. *Molecular Phylogenetics and Evolution* 5, 202–19.

Schoetensack, O. 1908. Der Unterkiefer des *Homo heidelbergensis* aus den Sanden von Mauer bei Heidelberg. Ein Beitrag zur Paläontologie des Menschen. *Molecular and General Genetics* 1, 408–10.

Schwarcz, H. P., Grün, R., Vandermeersch, B., Bar-Yosef, O., Valladas, H., and Tchernov, E. 1988. ESR dates for the hominid burial site of Qafzeh in Israel. *Journal of Human Evolution* 17, 733–7.

Schwartz, J. H. and Tattersall, I. 2000. The human chin revisited: what is it and who has it? *Journal of Human Evolution* 38, 367–409.

Serre, D., Langaney, A., Chech, M., Teschler-Nicola, M., Paunovic, M., Mennecier, P., Hofreiter, M., Possnert, G., and Pääbo, S. 2004. No evidence of Neandertal mtDNA contribution to early modern humans. *PLoS Biology* 2, E57.

Shea, J. J. 2011. Homo sapiens is as Homo sapiens was. *Current Anthropology* 52, 1–35.

Simpson, G. 1961. *Principles of animal taxonomy*. New York: Columbia University Press.

Singer, R. and Wymer, J. 1982. *The Middle Stone Age at Klasies River Mouth in South Africa*. Chicago: University of Chicago Press.

Smith, F. H., Falsetti, A. B., and Donnelly, S. M. 1989. Modern human origins. *Year Book of Physical Anthropology* 32, 35–68.

Smith, F. H., Jankovic, I., and Karavanic, I. 2005. The assimilation model, modern human origins in Europe, and the extinction of Neandertals. *Quaternary International* 137, 7–19.

Smith, S. L. and Harrold, F. B. 1997. A paradigm's worth of difference? Understanding the impasse over modern human origins. *American Journal of Physical Anthropology* 104, 113–38.

Smith, T. M., Tafforeau, P., Reid, D. J., Grün, R., Eggins, S., Boutakiout, M., and Hublin, J.-J. 2007. Earliest evidence of modern human life history in North African early *Homo sapiens*. *Proceedings of the National Academy of Sciences USA* 104, 6128–33.

Soares, P., Ermini, L., Thomson, N., Mormina, M., Rito, T., Röhl, A., Salas, A., Oppenheimer, S., Macaulay, V., and Richards, M. B. 2009. Correcting for purifying selection: an improved human mitochondrial molecular clock. *American Journal of Human Genetics* 84, 740–59.

Spoor, F., Stringer, C., and Zonneveld, F. 1998. Rare temporal bone pathology of the Singa calvaria from Sudan. *American Journal of Physical Anthropology* 107, 41–50.

Stanford, C., Allen, J., and Anton, S. 2009. *Biological anthropology: the natural history of humankind*. Harlow: Pearson/Prentice Hall.

Steiper, M. E. and Young, N. M. 2006. Primate molecular divergence dates. *Molecular Phylogenetics and Evolution* 41, 384–94.

Stone, T. and Cupper, M. L. 2003. Last Glacial Maximum ages for robust humans at Kow Swamp, southern Australia. *Journal of Human Evolution* 45, 99–111.

Stoneking, M. 1993. DNA and recent human evolution. *Evolutionary Anthropology: Issues, News, and Reviews* 2, 60–73.

Stoneking, M. 2008. Human origins: the molecular perspective. *EMBO Reports* 9, 546–50.

Stringer, C. 1983. Some further notes on 190he morphology and dating of the Petralona hominid. *Journal of Human Evolution* 12, 731–42.

Stringer, C. 1985. Middle Pleistocene hominid variability and the origin of late Pleistocene humans. In E. Delson (ed.), *Ancestors: the hard evidence*, 289–95. New York: Liss.

Stringer, C. 1989. Documenting the origin of modern humans. In E. Trinkaus (ed.), *The emergence of modern humans: biocultural adaptations in the later Pleistocene*, 67–96. Cambridge: Cambridge University Press.

Stringer, C. 1994. Out of Africa—a personal history. In M. Nitecki and D. Nitecki (eds), *Origins of anatomically modern humans*, 149–72. New York: Plenum Press.

Stringer, C. 2001. Modern human origins: progress and prospects. *Philosophical Transactions of the Royal Society of London B: Biological Sciences* 357, 563–79.

Stringer, C. 2011a. The chronological and evolutionary position of the Broken Hill cranium (abstract). *American Journal of Physical Anthropology* 144 (Supplement 52), 287.

Stringer, C. 2011b. *The origin of our species*. London: Penguin.

Stringer, C. B., Howell, F. C., and Melentis, J. K. 1979. The significance of the fossil hominid skull from Petralona, Greece. *Journal of Archaeological Science* 6, 235–53.

Stynder, D. D., Moggi-Cecchi, J., Berger, L. R., and Parkington, J. E. 2001. Human mandibular incisors from the late Middle Pleistocene locality of Hoedjiespunt 1, South Africa. *Journal of Human Evolution* 41, 369–83.

Tattersall, I. 2009. Becoming modern *Homo sapiens*. *Evolution: Education and Outreach* 2, 584–9.

Tattersall, I. 2010. The rise of modern humans. *Evolution: Education and Outreach* 3, 399–402.

Tattersall, I. and Schwartz, J. H. 2008. The morphological distinctiveness of *Homo sapiens* and its recognition in the fossil record: clarifying the problem. *Evolutionary Anthropology: Issues, News, and Reviews* 17, 49–54.

Templeton, A. R. 1993. The 'Eve' hypothesis: a genetic critique and reanalysis. *American Anthropologist* 95, 51–72.
Templeton, A. R. 2002. Out of Africa again and again. *Nature* 416, 45–51.
Templeton, A. R. 2005. Haplotype trees and modern human origins. *American Journal of Physical Anthropology* 128, 33–59.
Templeton, A. R. 2007. Genetics and recent human evolution. *Evolution*, 61, 1507–19.
Texier, P. J., Porraz, G., Parkington, J., Rigaud, J. P., Poggenpoel, C., Miller, C., Tribolo, C., Cartwright, C., Coudenneau, A., Klein, R., Steele, T., and Verna, C. 2010. From the cover: a Howiesons Poort tradition of engraving ostrich eggshell containers dated to 60,000 years ago at Diepkloof Rock Shelter, South Africa. *Proceedings of the National Academy of Sciences USA* 107, 6180–85.
Thackeray, A. I. 1992. The Middle Stone Age south of the Limpopo River. *Journal of World Prehistory* 6, 385–440.
Thorne, A. G. 1971. Mungo and Kow Swamp: morphological variation in Pleistocene Australians. *Mankind* 8, 85–9.
Trinkaus, E. 1989. Issues concerning human emergence in the later Pleistocene. In E. Trinkaus (ed.), *The emergence of modern humans: biocultural adaptations in the later Pleistocene*, 1–17. Cambridge: Cambridge University Press.
Trinkaus, E. 1997. Appendicular robusticity and the paleobiology of modern human emergence. *Proceedings of the National Academy of Sciences USA* 94, 13367–73.
Trinkaus, E. 2005. Early modern humans. *Annual Review of Anthropology* 34, 207–30.
Trinkaus, E., Moldovan, O., Milota, Ş., Bîlgăr, A., Sarcina, L., Athreya, S., Bailey, S. E., Rodrigo, R., Mircea, G., Higham, T., Ramsey, C. B., and van der Plicht, J. 2003. An early modern human from the Pestera cu Oase, Romania. *Proceedings of the National Academy of Sciences USA* 100, 11231–6.
Valladas, H., Cachier, H., Maurice, P., de Quirost, F. B., Clottes, J., Valdes, V. C., Uzquiano, P., and Arnold, M. 1992. Direct radiocarbon dates for prehistoric paintings at the Altamira, El Castillo and Niaux caves. *Nature* 357, 68–70.
Vallois, H. V. and Billy, G. 1965. Nouvelles recherches sur les hommes fossiles de l'Abri de Cro-Magnon. *L'Anthropologie* 69, 47–54, 75–82.
Vallois, H. V. and Vandermeersch, B. 1972. Le crâne Moustérien de Qafzeh (Homme VI): étude anthropologique. *L'Anthropologie* 76, 71–96.
Vandermeersch, B. 1969. Les nouveaux squelettes moustériens découverts à Qafzeh (Israel) et leur signification. *Comptes Rendus de l'Académie des Sciences de Paris* 268, 2562–5.
Vanhaeren, M., d'Errico, F., Stringer, C., James, S. L., Todd, J. A., and Mienis, H. 2006. Middle Paleolithic shell beads in Israel and Algeria. *Science* 312, 1785–8.
Vermeersch, P. M., Gijselings, G., and Paulissen, E. 1984. Discovery of the Nazlet Khater man, Upper Egypt. *Journal of Human Evolution* 13, 281–6.
Vermeersch, P. M., Paulissen, E., Stoke, S., Charlier, C., van Peer, P., Stringer, C., and Lindsay, W. 1998. A Middle Palaeolithic burial of a modern human at Taramsa Hill. Egypt. *Antiquity* 72, 475–82.
Vigilant, L., Pennington, R., Harpending, H., Kocher, T. D., and Wilson, A. C. 1989. Mitochondrial DNA sequences in single hairs from a southern African population. *Proceedings of the National Academy of Sciences USA* 86, 9350–4.
Vigilant, L., Stoneking, M., Harpending, H., Hawkes, K., and Wilson, A. C. 1991. African populations and the evolution of human mitochondrial DNA. *Science* 253, 1503–7.
Wadley, L. 2001. What is cultural modernity? A general view and a South African perspective from Rose Cottage Cave. *Cambridge Archaeological Journal* 11, 201–21.

Wadley, L. 2005. A typological study of the final Middle Stone Age stone tools from Sibudu Cave, KwaZulu-Natal. *South African Archaeological Bulletin* 60, 51–63.

Wadley, L., Hodgskiss, T., and Grant, M. 2009. From the cover: implications for complex cognition from the hafting of tools with compound adhesives in the Middle Stone Age, South Africa. *Proceedings of the National Academy of Sciences USA* 106, 9590–94.

Walter, R. C., Buffler, R. T., Bruggemann, J. H., Guillaume, M. M., Berhe, S. M., Negassi, B., Libsekal, Y., Cheng, H., Edwards, R. L., von Cosel, R., Néraudeau, D., and Gagnon, M. 2000. Early human occupation of the Red Sea coast of Eritrea during the last interglacial. *Nature* 405, 65–9.

Watts, I. 2002. Ochre in the Middle Stone Age of southern Africa: ritualised display or hide preservative? *South African Archaeological Bulletin* 57, 1.

Weiss, K. 2010. Seeing the forest through the gene-trees: what is the pattern in the human genome and what does it mean? *Evolutionary Anthropology: Issues, News, and Reviews* 19, 210–21.

White, T. D., Asfaw, B., DeGusta, D., Gilbert, H., Richards, G. D., Suwa, G., and Howell, F. C. 2003. Pleistocene *Homo sapiens* from Middle Awash, Ethiopia. *Nature* 423, 742–7.

Willoughby, P. R. 1993. The Middle Stone Age in East Africa and modern human origins. *The African Archaeological Review* 11, 3–20.

Willoughby, P. R. 2007. *The evolution of modern humans in Africa: a comprehensive guide.* Plymouth: AltaMira Press.

Wilson, B. 1995. A (not-so-radical) solution to the species problem. *Biology and Philosophy* 10, 339–56.

Wolpoff, M. H. 1986. Describing anatomically modern *Homo sapiens*: a distinction without a definable difference. In V. V. Novotny and A. Mizerova (eds), *Fossil man: new facts, new ideas. Papers in honour of Jan Jelinek's life anniversary Anthropos (Brno)*, 23, 41–53.

Wolpoff, M. H. and Caspari, R. 1996. The modernity mess. *Journal of Human Evolution* 30, 167–72.

Wolpoff, M. H., Hawks, J., and Caspari, R. 2000. Multiregional, not multiple origins. *American Journal of Physical Anthropology* 112, 129–36.

Wood, B. and Collard, M. 1999. The human genus. *Science* 284, 65–71.

Wood, B. and Richmond, B. G. 2000. Human evolution: taxonomy and paleobiology. *Journal of Anatomy* 197, 19–60.

Woodward, A. 1921. A new man from Rhodesia, S. Africa. *Nature* 108, 371–2.

Woodward, A. 1938. A fossil skull of an ancestral bushman from the Anglo-Egyptian Sudan. *Antiquity* 12, 190–5.

Wrinn, P. and Rink, W. J. 2003. ESR dating of tooth enamel from Aterian levels at Mugharet el 'Aliya (Tangier, Morocco). *Journal of Archaeological Science* 30, 123–33.

Wurz, S. 2002. Variability in the Middle Stone Age lithic sequence, 115,000–60,000 years ago at Klasies River, South Africa. *Journal of Archaeological Science* 29, 1001–15.

Yellen, J., Brooks, A. S., Cornelissen, E., Mehlman, M. J., and Stewart, K. 1995. A Middle Stone Age worked bone industry from Katanda, Upper Semliki Valley, Zaire. *Science* 268, 553–6.

Yellen, J., Brooks, A. S., Helgren, D., Tappen, M., Ambrose, S., Bonnefille, R., Feathers, J., Goodfriend, G., Ludwig, K., Renne, P. R., and Stewart, K. 2005. The archaeology of Aduma Middle Stone Age sites in the Awash Valley, Ethiopia. *Palaeoanthropology* 10, 25–100.

CHAPTER 11

UPPER PALAEOLITHIC HUNTER-GATHERERS IN WESTERN ASIA

OFER BAR-YOSEF

The history of prehistoric research in western Asia is probably as complex as in other regions where representatives of different schools of archaeology who conducted fieldwork published their results in more than one language. In retrospect the number of foreign and local scholars who were and are involved in exposing the region discussed that is often referred to as the Near East, or Middle East, is larger than in any other region of the globe due to the historical attraction of the Holy Land since the early nineteenth century. Not surprisingly the impact of the early achievements of European prehistoric research has had a major influence on the research of this region. Therefore, following a brief summary of the geographical features of western Asia and their mosaic ecological nature, I will discuss, for the benefit of the uninitiated, the conundrum of archaeological cultural terminology used today in the sub-regions of the Near East. This will be followed by a review of the cultural sequence of the Levant, the best-studied area with its Late Pleistocene floral and faunal associations. The two other areas, the Zagros and the Caucasus, are much less known and each section will include both the cultural sequence and the dietary remains. The last section will attempt to reconstruct patterns of seasonal movements of past hunter-gatherers. The reader should note that throughout these pages calibrated BP dates are used, calculated by employing the Calpal software.

Geographic Background and Past Climate

What distinguishes the geographical features of western Asia is their nature—a mosaic of landscapes, except for the desertic Arabian Peninsula and a large portion of the Iranian plateau. The topographic variability created by mountains, alluvial valleys and plains, coastal areas of the Mediterranean, Black Sea, Caspian Sea, and the Persian Gulf, has almost no comparison in most of Eurasia and Africa. In short, this region provided to Pleistocene hunter-gatherers an array of different environments with variable food resources, often within short distances of a few or dozens of kilometres. Hence, the climatic and vegetational variability facilitated the coexistence of a mixture of Palaearctic (European), oriental (Asian), and tropical (African) plants and animals.

In examining the region in detail additional features emerge. The coastal plains are often narrow in comparison to those of other continents. The Anatolian plateau is bounded by the Pontic mountains in the north and the Taurus mountains in the south, each range being about 1,500 km long. Both mountain chains join the 1,800 km long Zagros ranges and its intermontane valleys, which, together with the Lesser and Higher Caucasus mountains, create a deeply dissected landmass. East of the Zagros the Iranian plateau is bordered by the Elburz and Kopet Dagh mountains in the north, and the Khurasan and Baluchistan mountains in the east. The immense Mesopotamia plain slopes from the foothills of the Zagros and Taurus into the Persian Gulf and is crossed by the Euphrates and the Tigris rivers with copious tributaries of the latter, descending from the Zagros mountains. Their main flow follows the spring melting of the snow that every winter covers the tops of these mountain ranges. West of the Mespotamian naturally watered plain, the Syro-Arabian desert stretches south-east into the Arabian Peninsula, being the easternmost portion of the Saharan belt.

The Mediterranean Levant is generally identified by archaeologists as a special area within western Asia. It stretches along the eastern Mediterranean shoreline, and is about 1,300 km long and 150–350 km wide. Topographically, it includes the coastal mountain range (overall lower than the Taurus), the Dead Sea System or the Rift of the Orontes-Jordan Valleys, inland mountain ranges, and the eastward-sloping plateau, which is dissected by many wadis flowing into the Syro-Arabian desert.

During the Upper Palaeolithic the climate of western Asia was dominated by cool, rainy winters and hot, dry summers as recorded in the available speleothems (Bar-Matthews and Ayalon 2003). Winter temperatures were milder in the coastal plains and more severe inland or at higher elevations. Annual rainfall was affected by the distance from the sea, local altitude, and the routes of the Atlantic storm tracked through the Mediterranean basin or northern Europe. The region of the Caucasus was affected by the Black Sea and the ephemeral summer rains played a major role in preserving an older Pleistocene Euxinian and sub-Euxinian mesic deciduous mixed forest along its southern and western shores. The entire area between the Higher and Lesser Caucasus slopes eastward towards the Caspian Sea, and is gradually drier than the western end (Zohary 1973). The central Anatolian and Iranian plateaus, the Syro-Arabian desert, and Mesopotamia were in general the drier subregions, while in the Mediterranean Levant, rainfall decreased in a north–south direction from the Taurus mountains to the tip of the Sinai Peninsula. That zone is characterized by Mediterranean vegetation consisting of woodlands or open parklands on and along the coastal ranges. In contrast, western Anatolia is covered with broad-leafed and needle-leafed trees and shrubs resistant to cold, while cold-adapted deciduous broad-leaved woodland characterizes the eastern mountains and large areas of the Zagros. Dwarf shrubland and steppic vegetation (Irano-Turanian) dominate the eastern Anatolian plateau and form a wide arching belt south of the northern Levantine, Taurus, and northern Zagros hilly ranges. Further south, open xenomorphic dwarf shrubland and desert plant associations (Saharo-Arabian) cover areas that have an annual precipitation of less than 300–400 mm.

The current complex climatic system of western Asia makes it difficult to reconstruct the patterns of past climates without a large number of independent sources such as speleothems as well as marine and pollen cores. Presently, large annual fluctuations in rainfall characterize the precipitation of the region with storm tracks following various paths. Clouds that carry humidity along the Mediterranean Sea and move in a more arid, southerly direction are richer in 18O relatively to 16O, but the reverse characterize the northern rainfall storms. Late Pleistocene cyclones that descended through Europe and turned east left most of the southern Levant dry (e.g. Enzel et al. 2008). Isotope studies of speleothems in Israel, chemical analyses, and dating of the palaeo-lake Lisan in the Jordan Valley have demonstrated that the rainfall distribution was similar to that of today although at certain times the amount of precipitation was higher than the currently known averages (e.g. Bar-Matthews et al. 2002; Bar-Matthews and Ayalon 2003; Robinson et al. 2006). In sum, rather than palaeo-temperature fluctuations, decadal and centennial variability of annual precipitation was responsible for the expansion and contraction of vegetation belts as recorded in the marine palynological sequences, in a few lakes, and lake levels. Therefore, we can assume that the Upper Pleistocene palaeo-climate of western Asia was different to today's climate (e.g. Enzel et al. 2008). Climatic changes caused landscape modifications that resulted in spatial shifts of plant and faunal associations generally in the order of 10–50 km. Thus, the main faunal associations of western Asia remained Eurasiatic and their relative stability through time facilitates our discussion of hunting strategies (e.g. Bar-Oz 2004; Firouz 2005; Harrison and Bates 1991; Yom-Tov and Tchernov 1988). However, the main stumbling block for reaching a balanced view of human dietary intakes from these environments is due to the paucity of plant remains in the excavations in spite of increased use of flotation techniques during the last three decades. I will therefore employ the results of the Ohalo II excavations (Nadel et al. 2004) and a few isolated finds to discuss the vegetal diets.

In retrospect, periods of improved environmental conditions enhanced habitat expansions of plant and animal resources but more importantly made them predictable and reliable. Accessibility of the latter to humans depended on technological capacities and social organization. Under favourable conditions and efficient organization, the hunter-gatherer population increased, which led to the expansion of their territories, a phenomenon well recorded during the post-LGM time (e.g. Bar-Yosef 2002; Bar-Yosef and Belfer-Cohen 2010; Bar-Yosef and Killebrew 1984; Goring-Morris 1995; 2002; 2009; Maher 2007a; 2007b; Richter et al. 2010). Decreased precipitation, when accompanied by a drop in the annual average of temperatures, resulted in worsening conditions affecting steppe areas (e.g. the Levant, Iranian, and Anatolian plateaux), as well as mountainous regions such as the Taurus and the Zagros. Foragers inhabiting the affected landscapes had to accommodate their mobility patterns, exploitation strategies, and population size in order to survive under the new climatic regime even if it lasted no more than a millennium. Such tough times would be expressed archaeologically in stratigraphic breaks and the missing of discarded material culture components that would have otherwise been present in the sites. The overall picture was different among camps located within forested or open woodland landscapes. Continued or repeated occupation is expressed in the rapidly accumulated remains that may indicate not only successful survival but also a certain degree of semi-sedentism. Staying put in a particular location was triggered by the need to defend a territory or symbolically declare its ownership. Semi-sedentism can be recognized through the annual accumulation of discarded faunal and carbonized plant remains.

CULTURAL TERMINOLOGY

Before delving into the discussion of foragers' lifeways during the Late Pleistocene, we need to briefly discuss terminological issues for the benefit of readers who are not necessarily familiar with the history of investigations of this region. The terms imposed by the British, French, and German scholars in the 1930s were derived from the European sequence. Hence stone tools were classified as Palaeolithic, subdivided into Lower, Middle and Upper Palaeolithic, Mesolithic, and Neolithic. The realization that Mesolithic designates the post-Pleistocene microlithic industries led to the adoption in western Asia of the North African term 'Epi-Palaeolithic'. Hence, the current subdivision of the Upper Palaeolithic incorporates the 'Upper Palaeolithic' (c.49,000/48,000–24,000/22,000 cal BP) and 'Epi-Palaeolithic' (subdivided into Early, Middle, and Late from c.24,000/22,000–11,500 cal BP; see Bar-Yosef and Belfer-Cohen 2010). This is followed by the Neolithic. At the same time the cultural terms in the Levant (the best-studied area within western Asia) employed the combined approach of D. Garrod, R. Nueville, D. Clark, and F. Bordes (followed by later researchers) and resulted in a series of cultural names such as Emiran, Early Ahmarian, Levantine Aurignacian, Late Ahmarian, Mazraqan, Kebaran, Geometric Kebaran, Natufian, etc.

The Taurus, Zagros, and the southern Caucasus are larger but less researched and not as well dated as the Levant, and therefore only brief comments are provided here concerning the two latter regions (Figure 11.1). In the Zagros area several excavated caves produced

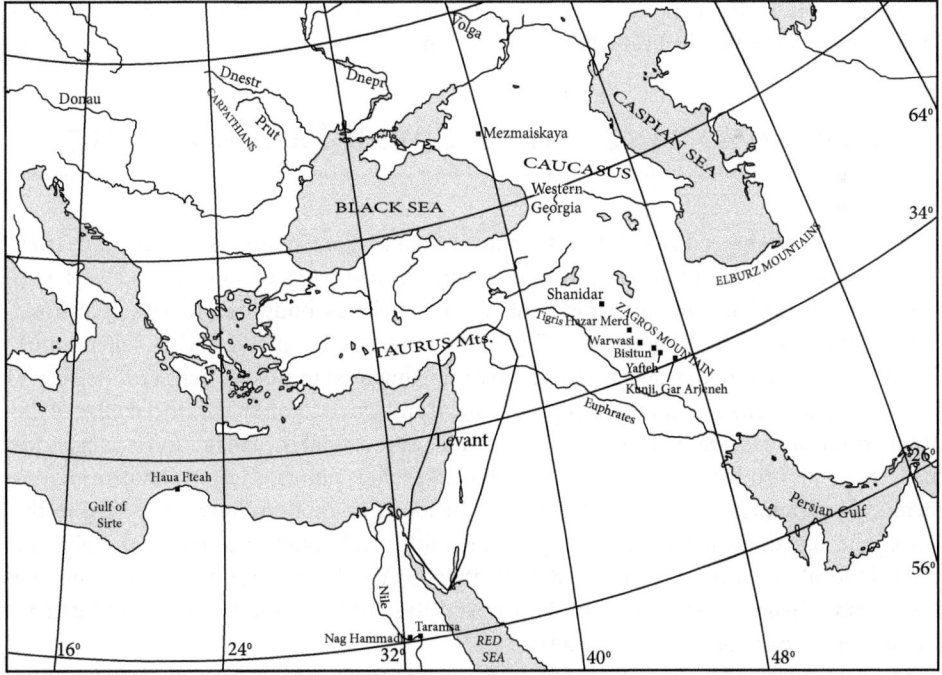

FIGURE 11.1 Map of the region with a few of the major sites mentioned in the text.

lithic industries including the earliest Upper Palaeolithic that was called Baradostian (Solecki 1963). More recently it was also referred to as 'Zagros Aurignacian' (Olszewski 1993; Olszewski and Dibble 2006; Otte and Kozlowski 2004) and seen as the origin of this culture that is better known from western Europe. The Zagros 'Aurignacian' is not similar to the Levantine Aurignacian as it does not contain typical Aurignacian bone and antler objects and has no nosed scrapers on thick flat flakes. The presence of various types of carinated cores does not differ from what is known in the Caucasus area as an industry of 'carinated cores' (see below). The later Zagros assemblages are of microlithic nature, labelled as Zarzian (e.g. Wahida 1999) and contain geometrics in the final phase.

In the Caucasus, where European terminology is still prevalent, the terms Upper Palaeolithic and Mesolithic are in use (Lubin 1989; Meshveliani et al. 2004; 2007). The earliest Upper Palaeolithic dates to $c.38,000$–$36,000$ cal BP and the Mesolithic, coeval with the Younger Dryas, and dates to 12,800–11,200 cal BP (for details see below). The process of classification, often based on the detailed studies of a relatively large number of sites and assemblages, takes into account the geographic-ecological location of the lithic and bone and antler assemblages. During the last four decades the principle of defining 'cultures' and/or 'industries' remained the same as traditionally employed in Palaeolithic research, namely that the common morphotypes of stone tools as well as the recorded operational sequence (*chaîne opératoire* sometimes referred to as the 'reduction sequence') are seen as the particular attributes that justify giving an industry its unique name. Additional aspects such as bone tools, body decorations, imagery, palaeo-economy (based on animal bone analysis and on rarely preserved carbonized plant remains) are currently also included in the definition of a social entity. It should be stressed that the chronological and stratigraphic sequence, employed here for the purpose of discussing the known and unknown about Upper Palaeolithic foragers in western Asia, relies mainly on the investigations conducted in the southern Levant, the best-studied sub-region.

The Levantine Early Upper Palaeolithic

The onset of the Upper Palaeolithic is demonstrated by the techno-typological shift from previously Mousterian industries, in manufacturing new types of stone tools and somewhat later marked by the appearance of marine shells as body decorations (Bar-Yosef 2000; Kuhn et al. 2001; Meignen and Bar-Yosef 2002; Bar-Yosef and Belfer-Cohen 2010). The technical and typological transition is best documented in Boker Tachtit in the Negev, Ksar Akil in the Lebanese mountains (Marks 1993) and Üçağızlı on the northern edge of the Mediterranean coast (Kuhn et al. 2009). Uni- and bidirectional core reduction strategies for blade removals produced a few reversed (Y-type) Levallois points. Faceted platforms reflect technical continuity, and in accordance with the idea that modern humans arrived in the Levant through the Nile Valley, the origin of their lithic technology is sought in the 'Nubian' cores, in localities such as Taramsa (Bar-Yosef 2000; Van Peer 2004). Based on calibrated dates from Kebara cave the IUP (Initial Upper Palaeolithic) in the Levant should date to $c.50,000/49,000$–$47,000/46,000$ cal BP.

The particular industries from this phase were originally grouped under the term 'Transitional Industries' (assuming that there is a cultural continuity) or Emiran, although the preferred term today is Initial Upper Palaeolithic (IUP). Among the retouched pieces, the Emireh point, known for its basal bifacial shaping, is common only in the central and southern Levant (Copeland 2000). From the central and northern Levant, blades and flakes with transverse removal at the tip, known as 'chamfered pieces' or *chanfriens* in French, occurred in Ksar Akil, Abri Antelias, Abu Halka, Üçağızlı, and Canal caves (Kuhn et al. 2009). Additional IUP assemblages were uncovered in the El-Kowm basin (Figure 11.1). None of the excavated sites, whether caves or open-air localities, produced information about group size and social activities such as mortuary practices. In the features such as hearths and evidence for ash removal, the main finds are lithic assemblages, animal bones. In Ksar Akil and Üçağızlı, several contexts contained marine shells that were used as beads. Their presence, in addition to the increasing production of blades, is considered as a cultural marker of the Upper Palaeolithic revolution.

Similar IUP assemblages are not known from the Zagros mountains and the Caucasus region that were occupied later by new groups of people. The absence of the IUP contexts from the Taurus and the Anatolian plateau could be due to paucity of research.

The next cultural phase in the Levant is characterized by the blade-dominated assemblages of the Early Ahmarian industry that dates to c.46,000/45,000–38,000/36,000 cal BP. Most of the recorded assemblages are from the Mediterranean and the steppic belts (e.g. Ksar Akil, Kebara), or areas forested in the past such as Wadi Hassa in Jordan (Tor Sadaf) and the Negev Highlands. None of these sites produced more information than the presence of several hearths in certain levels. The same observations hold for both caves and open-air sites. Estimating from surface areas the size of the social groups does not indicate the cohabitation of a band of foragers. The only unique find was the burial of 'Egbert' a modern human, attributed to layer 17 in Ksar Akil. Unfortuantely not much is known about this burial and the fossil itself disappeared, but a good cast was preserved (Bergman and Stringer 1989).

The Upper Palaeolithic sequence of the Levant was interrupted by the appearance of the Aurignacian (c.36,000/34,000–31,000/29,000 cal BP), originally labelled as Levantine Aurignacian although the assemblages are very similar to the European ones (e.g. Belfer-Cohen and Bar-Yosef 1999; Bar-Yosef and Zilhao 2006; Belfer-Cohen and Goring-Morris 2007). In addition to the classical Aurignacian elements such as nosed, carinated scrapers and Dufour bladelets, the assemblages contain the el-Wad point that resembles the Font Yves point in France and the Krems point in central Europe. Other striking similarities between the European Aurignacian and the Levantine contexts include body decorations such as pendants from deer teeth, and a proliferation of bone and antler tools, including split base points. A limestone slab with an incised 'horse' from Hayonim cave adds to the artistic aspects of this culture (Marshack 1997).

The Levantine Aurignacian is geographically limited to the coastal and inland ranges of the northern and central Levant. As mentioned above, several Zagros assemblages originally referred to as Baradostian bear superficial resemblance to the Aurignacian (Olszewski and Dibble 2006; Otte and Kozlowski 2007). They are similar to the assemblages in the Caucasus, so the composition of the assemblages does not fall within the European or the Levantine Aurignacian. The Aurignacian expansion eastward from its 'core area' in western Europe (Kozlowski 1992) possibly reached Afghanistan (Davis 2004). The Late Ahmarian (c.34,000–24,000/23,000 cal BP) was in part contemporary with the Aurignacian. Its main distribution is in numerous open-air sites in the semi-arid areas of Sinai, the Negev, and southern Jordan, areas that were avoided by the Aurignacian invading groups or those who could not displace the locals. The bearers of the Late Ahmarian took back their living territories and are therefore found in a few caves located within the Mediterranean open forests such as Qafzeh cave (Bar-Yosef and Belfer-Cohen 2005). From this site two fossil skulls were found and attributed to the Upper Palaeolithic context. Unfortunately they could not be dated directly.

The Late Ahmarian assemblages are characterized by the production of blades and numerous bladelets commonly with lipped and punctiform platforms. Several assemblages, apparently the earlier ones in this entity, include the el-Wad points. These are blades and bladelets with tips shaped often by semi-abrupt and fine retouch, and sometimes they bear additional retouch along one or two edges. An experimental study demonstrated that these could have served as projectile points (Bergman 1981).

The sites of the Late Ahmarian are not richer in many other finds than the earlier times. In caves or open-air sites, the preserved features are the hearths, thus providing similar observations about the occupations of their earlier predecessors. The only site that demonstrates the continuous accumulation of Upper Palaeolithic humans is Ksar 'Akil. However, whether it served as a location for meetings of bands or simply its local conditions allowed semi-sedentism is yet unknown, but it definitely had a special place among all excavated sites that are dated to the Upper Palaeolithic.

The emergence of microlithic forms or small and narrow bladelets characterized the so-called Mazraqan and either precedes what is often labelled as the Epi-Palaeolithic of the Levant or forms its earlier techno-typological phase (Belfer-Cohen and Goring-Morris 2003; Goring-Morris and Belfer Cohen 2003; Goring-Morris 1995). It seems that during this period, prior to the LGM, the steppic zone received a higher amount of annual rainfall (Bar-Matthews and Ayalon 2003) and became the 'homeland' of many groups of foragers, often camping next to water sources such as lakes, temporary ponds, and springs in oases. The development of the microlithic form may indicate the improvement of the projectiles of their Late Ahmarian ancestors, and ensured their survival in the drier areas.

The Levantine Epi-Palaeolithic—Cultural Entities

The history of research, prior to the intensive practice of radiocarbon dating, resulted in splitting the entire Upper Palaeolithic into two time segments. The later one—the Epi-Palaeolithic lasted from the LGM to the onset of the Holocene (c.24,000/22,000–11,700/11,500 cal BP. This sequence is currently better dated than the earlier part of the Upper Palaeolithic although no agreement could be reached concerning the cultural terminology. Often archaeologists refer to terms such as Early Epi-Palaeolithic (e.g. Nebekian, Kebaran), Middle Epi-Palaeolithic (e.g. Nizzanan, Qalhan, Geometric Kebaran), and Late Epi-Palaeolithic (Natufian, Mushabian, and Ramonian). Additional names are available in the literature but I chose to lump assemblages under a few terms. Interestingly, east of the Jordan Rift Valley there is a greater typological variability among the microliths that characterize the different assemblages and are the basis for the cultural definitions. The two sub-regions of the southern Levant were separated by the Lisan Lake, the forerunner of the Dead Sea, at least until the end of the LGM. Effectively the Jordan Valley (from the Hula to the Dead Sea) and the Arava Valley (that stretches from the Dead Sea to the Gulf of Aqaba/Eilat) mark a permeable cultural boundary.

The exposure of Ohalo II that dates to 23,000/21,000 cal BP (Nadel 2003; Nadel et al. 2004 and references therein) produced a camp on the western shore of Lake Kinneret comprising a series of brush huts. Material culture incorporated rich lithic industry, bone tools, and a grinding stone for food preparation (see below). A wealth of plant remains demonstrate gathering from the level of the valley to the top of the hills above (see below). It seems that the cluster of those oval habitations was occupied sometimes seasonally and sometimes annually as reflected in the times of plant gathering. Hunting was carried out as well as some fishing. One supine burial between the huts was uncovered. This is the best-documented camp of foragers exposed in south-west Asia.

A somewhat similar camp was established on the east side of Lake Kinneret but only a couple of habitations, dug into the deep calcareous sandy deposit, were exposed, and a third one was only tested. The cultural material is chronological spread from the Kebaran to the Geometric Kebaran. Basalt mortars and pestles were found and a rich assemblage of animal bones, but no plant remains were preserved. A burial of a woman was uncovered under the lower floor of the hut numbered as Ein Gev I (Arensburg and Bar-Yosef 1973).

That human burials were made on site is also indicated by the burial in Neve David, a Geomeric Kebaran site at the foot of Mt Carmel, covered by several broken mortars (Kaufman and Ronen 1987). Indeed, the identified social-cultural entities since the early Epi-Palaeolithic in the Levant present an increasing complexity of settlement systems, spatial patterns of site distribution, core reduction variability in making flint stone tools, use of mortars, hints for a stable social organization, and artistic representations. All of these traits culminate during the Natufian culture. (e.g. Bar-Yosef 2002; Bar-Yosef and Valla 1991; Belfer-Cohen and Bar-Yosef 2000; Byrd 2005; Garrard 1982; 1998; Goring-Morris 1995; 2009; Henry 1989; Valla 2000; 2004; Valla et al. 2007; Wright and Garrard 2003).

The Natufian culture is subdivided to Early, Late, and Final Natufian. The Early Natufian culture (c.14,500–13,500 cal BP) flourished during the Bølling-Allerød times. It is characterized by semi-sedentary or sedentary hamlets or villages as shown by the presence of commensals such as mice and house sparrows (Auffrey et al. 1989). The domestic dwellings were rounded pit-houses, with a flimsy upper structure made of branches and straw. The only public building uncovered in Eyana (Ain Mallaha) was a 'kiva'-type underground semicircular, subterranean building, about 9 m in diameter, with a roof supported by wooden poles (Valla 1988). Two superimposed floors produced numerous non-domestic objects, such as a large number of polished pebbles, a tortoise shell, a partial human skull, bone objects, and a wealth of faunal remains and lithics. Natufian sites contain rich lithic assemblages, bones, and ground-stone objects, mainly mortars and pestles, 'stone pipes', and grooved elements. The latter are often 'shaft straighteners' possibly reflecting the use of bows and arrows that is currently supported by edge damage on the common lunates (Yaroshevich et al. 2010). Whetstones served for shaping bone objects. Sickles with glossed blades indicate the harvesting of cereals and straw for building purposes.

On-site cemeteries are found where the dead were either in supine or flexed positions, or sometimes laid to rest in collective graves. A significant preponderance of the skeletons at that time wore body decorations made of *Dentalium* sp. shells, bone beads, and pendants (D. E. Bar-Yosef 1989; 1991).

The Natufian culture provided the earliest prehistoric animal figurines in the Levant (shaped from bones and limestone), and rare human images, as well as a series of incised slabs displaying various patterns (e.g. Belfer-Cohen and Bar-Yosef 2009). The Younger Dryas, as mentioned above, had its major impact on Final Natufian society in the southern Levant. Under fluctuating environmental conditions, the decreasing reliability and predictability of plant and animal resources presented two options. The first was to increase mobility and the second to settle down where resources were predictable, near perennial streams or springs, in order to defend their food supplies. This option was favoured in the northern Levant where Mureybet and Abu Hureyra exposed, although partially, important Late/Final Natufian occupations.

The Final Natufian groups, who adopted a more mobile settlement pattern, rarely buried their dead with their adornments, and increased their consumption of low-ranked resources such as juvenile gazelles, bone grease, and fast-moving small game like hare and the gathering of tortoises (Munro 2004a; 2004b; 2004c). Certain groups in areas where precipitation allowed continued habitation (e.g. Mt Carmel, Hula Valley), or along the banks of the Euphrates, demonstrate the first signs of cultivation, generally referred to as 'low level food production'. A clear indication of the change in subsistence is reflected in the first appearance of green beads, apparently marking the onset of cultivation. None of these processes can be understood without taking into account ethnographic and historical records concerning adaptations of foragers to environments where resources and their spatial distribution are determined by similar climate (cold and rainy winters and dry summers) and geographic physical features. One may try to understand/evaluate the survival strategies of south-western Asian foragers by taking into account past ecological conditions, densities of foragers per kilometre squared, viable group size (tribes *sensu* Birdsell 1970; 1976; 1985), the nature of seasonal movements, and the minimal territorial requirements within the geographic mosaic of this vast region.

Upper and Epi-Palaeolithic Levantine Diets—Plants

Reports on the Upper Palaeolithic including the Epi-Palaeolithic faunas are mostly available from the Levant with much less information from the Taurus, Zagros, and the Caucasus sites (see below). We should remember the biased impression that hunting produced the essential portion of foragers' diet in the region. This is due to the generally good preservation of animal bones and the paucity of plant remains. Indeed, when the information on low to mid-latitude hunter-gatherers is taken into account, the role of vegetal diets becomes clear and the bias against plants in the archaeological record is irritating.

For example, papers in *Man the hunter* (Lee and DeVore 1968) and in Kelly's volume (1995) indicate that foragers (tropical, sub-tropical, and Mediterranean) consumed more vegetal food than meat and/or fish until the Holocene. The best example is the site of Ohalo II, on the shores of Lake Kinneret (Sea of Galilee) that dates to c.21,000–19,000 years ago

(Nadel et al. 2004), where carbonized assemblages of some 90,000 remains of over 100 species were recovered. Those include wild cereals such as emmer wheat, barley, oat, as well as pea, lentil, vetch, almond, fig, grape, and olive. The full list of plant remains represents three habitats—a saline marsh, lakeshore, and a Mediterranean park forest on the slopes of the Jordan Valley (Kislev et al. 1992; Nadel et al. 2004; Weiss et al. 2008; Zohary et al. 2012).

An additional line of evidence for plant food processing is the presence of grinding objects (Belfer-Cohen and Hovers 2005; Wright 1994; 2000) and later mortars and pestles, but their function is poorly understood. Among the earliest ones is the large grinding slab found in Ohalo II with fossil starch remains that indicate its function (Piperno et al. 2004). A smaller somewhat earlier Upper Palaeolithic grinding slab with a hand stone covered with red ochre probably indicates the last use of these objects at Qafzeh cave (Ronen and Vandermeersch 1972; Bar-Yosef and Belfer-Cohen 2005). In addition, a basalt block with a cup-hole was uncovered in Nahal Ein Gev I, a site characterized by the Atlitain industry (Belfer-Cohen et al. 2004). These sites fall within the range of 29,000–19,000 cal BP and thus extend back in time the appearance of grinding tools as part of the prehistoric cultural tool-kit.

The first deep mortars with pestles appear mainly in Kebaran and Geometric Kebaran sites such as Ein Gev I, Neve David, and other sites (Bar-Yosef and Belfer-Cohen 1989) and mark a change in food preparation not well understood. This tool type is common in all Natufian occupations with the additional deep mortars, sometimes known as 'stone pipes' due to their use in burial contexts, possibly as 'tomb stones'. Rich Late Natufian plant assemblages were recovered at two sites in the Euphrates Valley, namely Abu Hureyra I (Hillman 2000) and Mureybet I (van Zeist and Bakker-Herres 1986; Willcox et al. 2009). Their contents resemble the assemblage from Ohallo II, possibly with the indication for cultivation (Hillman et al. 2001). Additionally, a very important but as yet unpublished assemblage was recovered at Dederiyeh cave, some 50 km west of these villages.

All of these plant collections reflect a wide range of gathering seeds, leaves, and fruits including wild cereals, legumes, acorns, pistachio nuts, and more. Special attention was given to cereals during the Late Natufian that indicates the first efforts in cultivation aimed at providing staple food for larger communities in the northern Levant or even the first trials of plant cultivation (Bar-Yosef Mayer and Porat 2008; Willcox et al. 2009).

Upper and Epi-Palaeolithic Levantine Diets—Fauna

Before we delve into the faunal records it is important to note that most of the mammals in the Levant are Asian and Palaeoarctic and not of African origin (e.g. Tchernov 1992; 1997). The main faunal exchanges between Africa and Eurasia occurred during the Miocene and Pliocene and dwindled during the Lower Pleistocene (Bar-Yosef and Belmaker 2011). There is no evidence for faunal exchanges during the Upper Pleistocene with North Africa (contra Tchernov 1992). Differences in the recorded archaeological faunal assemblages were the result of species availability in the immediate catchment area of each site at a given time.

The stratified assemblages of faunal collections display specific ecological and topographic settings (e.g. Bar-Oz 2004; Davis 1982; Garrard 1982; 1998; Garrod and Bate 1937; Hooijer 1961; Kuhn et al. 2009; Munro 2004a; 2004b; 2004c; Munro and Bar-Oz 2005; Rabinovich 2003 and references therein; Stiner 2002; 2005; Tchernov 1997). Assemblages originate from the excavations in the 1930s and the reports are not detailed enough for the requirements of modern archaeozoological questions. During the entire Last Glacial cycle the most common species in the Levant were spatially distributed according to the local topographic and vegetational zones. Thus, hunting targets represent the availability of large and medium-size game in each area within the sub-region with minor shifts from north to south and west to east. The Mediterranean vegetational belt of oak and terebinth forests accommodated three species of deer (fallow deer, red deer, and roe deer), wild boar, cattle, and gazelle (mainly in the south). Bezoar goats were present in the forested highlands of the Lebanese mountains and the Taurus, where foothill habitats were shared with wild sheep. The latter are not known south of this sub-region. Open parklands were generally east of the highlands and the natural environment of mountain and Persian gazelles, wild boar, ibex (mainly in cliff or rocky landscapes), onager, and wild ass. In the northern Levant wild cattle roamed along the ecotone of the Mediterranean forest and the open parkland and were more common than in the southern Levant. The semi-arid belt was occupied mainly by Persian gazelle and onager, and in the highlands (e.g. southern Jordan) there were bezoar goat and ibex. Ibex and gazelles were also common in the Negev and Sinai. Bones of fox, hare, and tortoise are found in almost every site. The presence of foxes may represent their attraction to human rubbish while their hunting may have been for their canine teeth and pelts. The hare and the tortoise indicate different hunting and gathering techniques (Stiner et al. 2000).

When examining the assemblages on a site-by-site basis we recognize the specific environmental differences that also provide some vegetational information concerning hunting territories that in the Levant had a relatively small radius (10–20 km). This is exemplified by a few samples gathered from the literature. Üçağızlı is the northernmost cave along the Eastern Mediterranean seaboard which provided well-dated IUP and EUP assemblages. The most abundant species as the source of meat and other products are fallow deer, bezoar goat, and roe deer (Kuhn et al. 2009). In addition wild boar, red deer, and aurochs or wild cattle were present. Mortality patterns reflect all ages, indicating non-selective hunting to prime adult biased age profile as seen in other Upper Palaeolithic sites (Stiner 2005). Both the macrovertebrates and the microvertebrates document the same general environment of cliff and rocky habitat, and forested surroundings.

A similar composition was discovered in Ksar Akil, a rock shelter that enjoys the topographic conditions of a narrow valley with higher mountains around, close to the relatively narrow coastal plain (Hooijer 1961). Most of the Upper Palaeolithic layers, 18 m thick, demonstrate the dominance of fallow deer, roe deer, and bezoar goats with minimal representation of gazelle and wild cattle. Further south, Kebara cave, like el-Wad and Sefunim caves, presents high frequencies of mountain gazelle and fallow deer together with roe deer, wild cattle, and rare hartebeest (*Alcelaphus*) (Speth and Clark 2006). In the mid-hilly area between Mt Carmel and the eastern slopes of the mountains towards the Jordan Valley, the Upper Palaeolithic layers at Qafzeh cave produced the bones of mountain gazelle, red deer, roe deer, and fallow deer. The microvertebrates are better indicators of the proximity of the site to the drier environment of the Jordan Valley that was covered by the brackish–salty Lisan Lake.

Closer to Lake Kinneret, Emireh cave exhibits the same combination of mammals with fallow deer, gazelle, bezoar goat, cattle, and equids mostly hunted in the hilly area west of the site. On the east side of the lake, and at the foot of the Golan Heights, the open parkland and forested plateau provided both red deer and gazelle (Nahal Ein Gev I, c.27,000/25,000 cal BP) and the same species with wild boar, wild cattle, red deer, and bezoar goat were recovered in Ohalo II on the west side. Even further south in the Jordan Valley the Wadi Fazael sites contained the bones of fallow deer and gazelle.

In the Judaean Desert, an area in the 'shadow of the rains', at el-Quseir and Mazraq en-Naj the same species were hunted including wild boar and ibex, and so is the case of Erq el Ahmar rock shelter that lies closer to the watershed of the hills (Rabinovich 2003). Thus, the Late Pleistocene climate was wetter than today and most hilly areas were covered by Mediterranean dense and open forests. The climate change, as reflected in the rapidly decreasing levels of Lake Lisan, is marked towards the end of the LGM (Bookman et al. 2006).

Differences in mammalian associations are expressed in sites located in the steppic, semi-arid belt, often in oases or next to temporary ponds. In the Syro-Arabian desert and the eastern reaches of the Transjordanian plateau sites contain bones of gazelle, wild camel, wild ass, onager, and ibex, in areas with more cliffs and rocks (Palmyra oasis, Wadi Jilat, Wadi Hasa, Ras en-Naqeb, etc.). Finally, it should be noted that only a minimal presence of carnivores such as hyena and leopards was recorded in Upper Palaeolithic caves and open-air camps. There is no evidence for intensive occupations of hyenas in any particular cave. Apparently, the human presence in the region seems to have been dominant during the Upper Pleistocene.

During the Epi-Palaeolithic period that is better known from the southern Levant we have a wealth of information about the hunting habits of various social entities (e.g. Kebaran, Geometric Kebaran, and others) and in particular from a number of Natufian sites due to intensive and extensive field and laboratory research as well as the study of gazelle behaviour. During the early and middle Epi-Palaeolithic the trend was hunting the locally available game with an emphasis on prime adults. Hence in forested and parkland landscapes mountain gazelle dominated the fallow deer often in rations of 2:1 or 3:1 (Bar-Oz 2004). In semi-arid areas, mountain and Persian gazelles (the migratory creatures common in the Transjordan and Syro-Arabian desert) were the dominant species with a minimal representation of onagers and ibex. As temperatures continued to rise during the Terminal Pleistocene, in many areas gazelles became the dominant game while other species dwindled. Collections from the time of the Natufian culture (c.14,500–11,500 cal BP) demonstrate a tendency for intensification expressed in the hunt of juveniles, increasing index of small game (high energy for less calories in capturing hare, partridge, and tortoise), and greater bone fragmentation resulting from marrow and grease extraction. During the Late Natufian there is a tendency to return to an earlier mode of exploitation of prime adults, a manner that correlates with the archaeological evidence for higher mobility of these groups in the southern Levant probably caused by the Younger Dryas (Munro 2009).

A somewhat different pattern is evidenced at Mt Carmel sites such as in el-Wad cave and terrace where the increase in gazelle hunting is interpreted as the choice and preference of local hunters and not determined by climatic conditions such as the Younger Dryas (Bar-Oz et al. 2004; Lev-Ydun and Weinstein-Evron 2005). This apparent contradiction emerges from the poor chronological resolution of the entire Natufian period and the fragmentary evidence for the role that the Younger Dryas, a world phenomenon, played in the southern Levant.

In the context of Natufian culture, one should note the presence of domesticated dogs that were uncovered in graves in Eynan (Ain Mallaha) and the Terrace of Hayonim cave as well as in el Wad (Davis and Valla 1978; Garrod and Bate 1937; Tchernov and Valla 1997). The role played by dogs is yet unknown although it is often assumed that they assisted in hunting. However, additional remains from later contexts are either not found or not reported. Perhaps the adoption of dogs was an aspect of the social mechanism aimed at security (both ritualistic and defensive) of the house agglomerations that characterize the Early Natufian settlements.

An additional aspect of Levantine diets was the practice of freshwater fishing as recorded in Ohalo II, although the amount of larger fish is rather small (Nadel et al. 2004) and the high frequencies of small fish represent the natural death assemblage on Lake Kinnert beach (Zohar and Belmaker 2003). Marine fishing probably began during the Early Natufian, with the gathering of littoral fish (Bar-Yosef Mayer and Zohar 2010). Waterfowl seem to have been a dietary source at Ohalo II (Simmons 2004) and migratory birds are found both along the Jordan Valley and the coastal plain (Tchernov 1962). The presence of raptor bones such as vultures may represent symbolic needs as in the case of the Aurignacian layer at Hayonim cave (Tchernov 1997) or a similar discovery at Shanidar cave (Solecki and McGovern 1980).

The first marked changes in the faunal spectra occurred when pigs, cattle, goat, and sheep were corralled and eventually domesticated, a process that began in the closing millennium of the Pleistocene and increased during the first millennia of the Holocene, heralding, with the cultivation of selected plants, the onset of the Neolithic.

Hunters in the Zagros

Most cave sites in the Zagros are located in inter-montane valleys and were excavated at different times. The largest is Shanidar cave known for its several Neanderthal burials and rich lithic collections, and top Late Pleistocene–Early Holocene deposits (Solecki 1963; Solecki and Solecki 1993). Other caves such as Zarzi, Warwasi, Warkaini, Yafteh and Eshkaft-e Gavi, and Qaleh-bozi (Isfahan) that are situated on the Iranian plateau produced some Upper Palaeolithic assemblages (Hole and Flannery 1967; Otte et al. 2007; Wahida 1999). In a recent analysis Bordes and Shidrag (2005) identified an older industry of straight blades and bladelets detached from prismatic cores, with Arjeneh points that resemble the Levantine el Wad points. The later phase of the Upper Palaeolithic features carinated cores including the lateral version and twisted retouched bladelets. Originally this industry was named Baradostian and dated to $c.40{,}000$–$28{,}000$ cal BP. Several scholars considered it as the origins of the entire Eurasian 'Aurignacian' cultural entity (Olszewski and Dibble 1994; Otte et al. 2007). However, as mentioned above, this cultural attribution is contested, as are the radiocarbon dates in relationship to the stratigraphy and the studied lithic assemblages. The most parsimonious solution for the onset of the Upper Palaeolithic would place it at $c.40{,}000/38{,}000$ cal BP, and thus the reported carinated cores could have been an earlier practice of this technique. Further information from the field is needed in order to possibly tie it to later expressions in the Caucasus region.

The Zarzian entity corresponds broadly to the entire Epi-Palaeolithic and dates from the LGM to the beginning of the Holocene (Garrod 1930; Olszewski 1993; Wahida 1999). This microlithic industry has a tendency for increasing frequencies of geometric microliths as well as the appearance of grinding stones and a few axes in its later phase. In the Alburz region adjacent to the Caspian Sea, research follows early pioneering investigations (Chevrier et al. 2006; McBurney 1968) and short reports of the lithic assemblages indicate affinities with the late Upper Palaeolithic as demonstrated by bladelet cores, retouched bladelets, and simple endscrapers.

Only a few detailed faunal studies of the above sites have been published and in general wild sheep, goats, and red deer were the main hunted ungulates, together with low frequencies of gazelle, wild boar, and cattle (Hole and Flannery 1967). Fish remains were found in Yafteh cave together with an emphasis on sheep, with small numbers of gazelle and cervids and only a few wild boar (Otte et al. 2007).

Hunter-Gatherers in the Caucasus

The Upper Palaeolithic sequence of the southern hills of the Caucasus mountains has benefited from new field projects conducted in Ortvale Klde, Dzudzuana, and Kotias Klde caves that together provided some 150 radiocarbon dates for Late Mousterian, Upper Palaeolithic as well as Mesolithic assemblages that together with previously excavated sites facilitate the formation of cultural sequences and regional variants (e.g. Adler et al. 2006a, 2006b; 2008; Bar-Yosef et al. 2011; Meshveliani et al. 2004; 2007). A major achievement of these joint efforts is demonstrating that contrary to former claims, there is no cultural transition from the Late Mousterian to Early Upper Palaeolithic. The past proposal was based on mixing two layers at the stratigraphic contact between the Late Mousterian and early Upper Palaeolithic.

The earliest Upper Palaeolithic contexts recorded at Ortvale Klde and Dzudzuana date to $c.38,200-36,800$ cal BP and are roughly contemporary with the similar lithic industry reported from Mezmaiskaya cave on the northern slopes of the Caucasus (Adler et al. 2006b; Golovanova et al. 2006). The industry known from Dzudzuana Unit D and Ortvale Klde layer 4 is dominated by backed and retouched blades and bladelets, endscrapers, and a few bone tools. An important discovery was the microscopic evidence for the use of wild flax fibres found also in Units C and B (Kvavadze et al. 2009). Research also identified spores of the fungus *Chaetomium*, which commonly grows on clothes and textiles and destroys them. In addition, tur (*Capra caucasica*) wool, spun and dyed in grey and green, adds to the often missing material culture. The apparent contemporaneity of the three sites, separated geographically by the Caucasus ridges, may indicate that the assemblages represent the same social entity of local foragers who mark the dispersal of Modern Humans. Hence, the newcomers crossed the physiographic boundary of the Caucasus mountains relatively fast.

Following a stratigraphic-cultural break, Unit C at Dzudzuana (27,000–24,000 cal BP) is characterized by a reduction sequence based on carinated cores. Although such forms do occur in Aurignacian contexts, the Georgian assemblages do not resemble the Aurignacian tradition of western Europe. The industry of Unit C, rich in microlithic forms, contain bone and antler tools, mostly awls and points and a few pendants made from teeth or stones. The main gap that is coeval with the LGM between this site and others should be filled by contexts excavated in the western lowlands that border the Black Sea. However, these are mostly undated.

The Unit B assemblage is rich in blades and bladelets detached from bipolar cores, many retouched on anvil (backing shaped by bipolar retouch) creating the well-known type of microgravette. This Epi-Gravettian assemblage dates to c.16,500–13,200 cal BP but could have first appeared in other sites at an earlier time.

Additional typological variability characterizes the post-LGM conditions mostly in caves located between Dzudzuana and the Black Sea coast. Among these one may notice the curved backed bladelets, small shouldered points (dated to c.17,900–17,600 cal BP; Korkia 1998), and assemblages with microgravettes with large numbers of geometric microliths such as triangles and lunates.

Recent excavations at Kotias Klde, situated on the plateau above the Kvirila River at 720 m above sea level (Meshveliani et al. 2007) established the dates for a Mesolithic industry rich in scalene and isoscale triangles, as 12,800–11,200 cal BP, indicating its contemporaneity with the Younger Dryas. A similar assemblage was uncovered in Darkveti rock shelter at the level of the river, 420 m above sea level. The faunal spectra of these cultural sequences change, apparently due to the prevailing environmental conditions affected by Late Pleistocene climatic fluctuations. The lack of plant remains from the excavated sites forces us to rely on the faunal assemblages for reconstruction of past diets as well as patterns of seasonal exploitation. However, microscopic remains discovered, such as wild flax fibres, indicate that gathering leaves, fruits (such as nuts), and seeds was practised at the time.

During the Late Mousterian the tur (*Capra caucasica*) was the main game, as shown by the abundance of its bones in several layers (7–5) at Ortvale Klde. It was also common in layer 4 that dates to the early Upper Palaeolithic (Adler and Tushabramashvili 2004; Adler et al. 2006b). Given the location of the site along a migratory route of tur herds (e.g. Adler et al. 2006a), late autumn or early spring are seen as the hunting seasons. Similar observations were made concerning Unit D in Dzudzuana although the sample is small.

Units C and B in Dzudzuana and Unit C in Kotias Klde share the common hunting of aurochs, steppe bison, some tur and equids, mostly of prime adults. The shift in the faunal composition may indicate the warmer spells within the cold period of MIS3.

A major change is gleaned from layer B (Mesolithic) that dates to the Younger Dryas. Brown bears and large wild boars were hunted during the summer (Bar-Oz et al. 2009; Meshveliani et al. 2007) possibly for the pelts and meat.

Discussion and Conclusions—Eclectic View of Settlement Patterns Across South-West Asia

Seasonal moves are considered the essence of annual settlement pattern of foragers (e.g. Binford 1980; Kelly 1995). Beyond ethnographic information and indirect and direct analogies, archaeological testing is the only way to uncover past group behaviours. It is superfluous to mention that location and accessibility of food resources, more than other needs of the social unit, determine the moves whether residential, logistical, or a combination of both. Rarely, if ever, do models that explain the optimal strategies practised by hunter-gatherers take into account issues of territoriality and disputes between groups or tribes.

Pleistocene zooarchaeology serves, in this region, in view of the paucity of plant remains, as the main source concerning the majority of sites. Today, the main progress in this field allows one to reconstruct the environment, hunting techniques, population spread over the landscape, season of site occupation, and the amount of intensive use of animal tissues such as marrow. One aspect that has been neglected is the need to find out whether several contexts that were uncovered in sites of later periods provide evidence for feasting. With a recently published Late Natufian example (Munro and Grosman 2010), and several Neolithic cases (e.g. Twiss 2008 and references therein), it is time to search for similar evidence among earlier Palaeolithic occupations.

Additional specific behaviours such as 'rite of passage' among Palaeolithic hunters are rare, although a more recent example for possible interpretation of hunting brown bear and wild boar as resulting from 'rite of passage' during the Mesolithic at Kotias Klde (western Georgia) is mentioned. Indeed, the specific collection of brown bear bones together with wild boar, red deer, and roe deer in Kotais Klde is interpreted as reflecting two activities. The deer were hunted for their meat, marrow, and pelts, while the hunting of the brown bears and wild boar in the open may indicate an encounter and not intercept hunt, and thus could have signified the practice of a special ritual, similar to other prehistoric expressions involving bears (e.g. cave art) and ethnographic examples (Bar-Oz et al. 2009). As Mesolithic hunters had additional needs beyond obtaining the fur, claws, fingers, and teeth of bears, one may consider the possible demands for a 'rite of passage' for younger hunters.

The search for prehistoric seasonality of past foragers in different eco-zones at various times is a common subject that also informs us about the use of landscapes. Moving away from the individual site catchment analysis to a presumed exploited territory (Bailey and Davidson 1983; Higgs and Vita Finzi 1970), several models are proposed (Figure 11.2 and Figure 11.3).

Among the three parallel vegetation belts of the Levant that stretch from the Taurus foothills through the Sinai Peninsula the richest in plant and animal resources is the Mediterranean forest and its ecotone with the open Irano-Turanian parkland. It is also where resources are predictable and climatic changes had only minor impacts. Thus relatively small territories could be reconstructed and in an earlier study we estimated population densities of up to $c.1$ person per square kilometre (Bar-Yosef and Belfer-Cohen 1989).

The topographically higher mountains along part of the coastal range, namely the Lebanese mountains, as well as a few higher areas on the east side of the Rift Valley, would probably accommodate fewer foragers. Predicted seasonality suggests that summer time was spent in the hilly, mountain areas and winter in the lowlands and the coastal plain (Figure 11.2). The relatively short distances for the exploitation of both plants and animals (20–50 km) were determined by the distribution of water sources, edible plant species (mostly in the open oak forest and its margins), and the available game. Flint resources were also available everywhere within this region where Turonian, Cenomanian, Senonian, and Eocene good-quality flint nodules were available. The identification of seasonality is often gathered from the plants (if preserved) and animal bones. Higher frequencies of young deer or gazelles indicate spring–summer occupations though prime adult individuals were

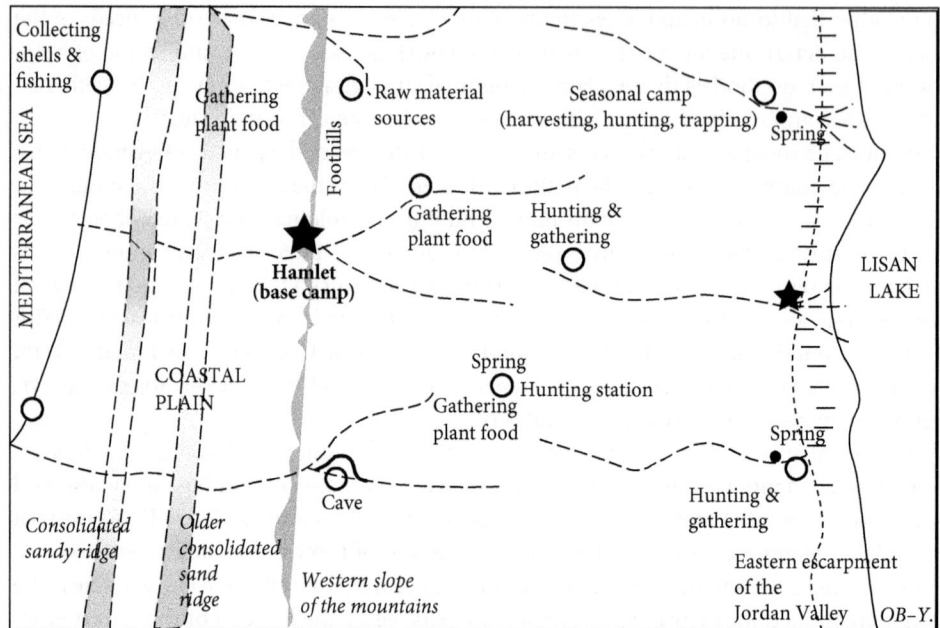

FIGURE 11.2 Winter and summer locations of hunter-gatherers in the Zagros and the Caucasus foothills. The model is based on Terminal Pleistocene occupations in western Georgia (for details see the text).

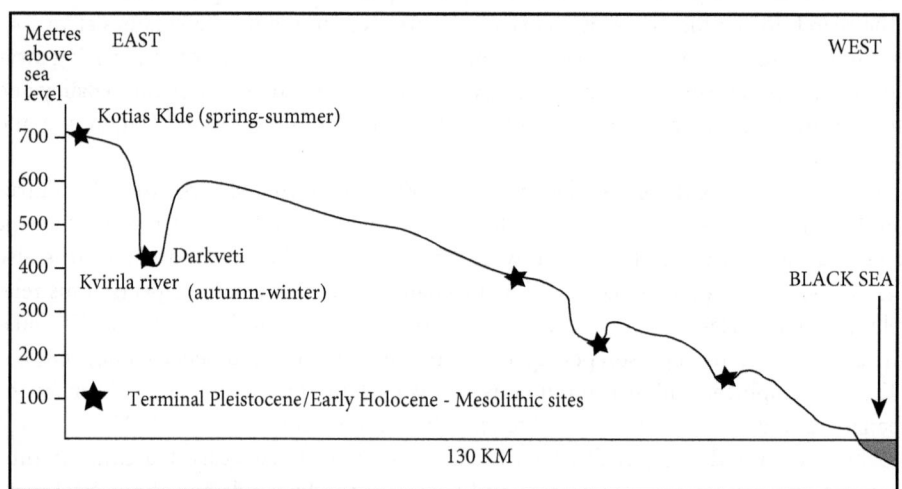

FIGURE 11.3 Terminal Pleistocene Epi-Palaeolithic Early Natufian settlement pattern along a transect from the Mediterranean Sea to Lisan Lake in the Jordan Valley. The disappearance of the Lisan Lake opened larger areas as habitats for gazelles and other mammals, birds, and reptiles.

preferred. Unfortunately, migratory birds cannot provide seasonal information due to the midway location of the Levant between Europe and Africa. Hence, migratory birds could have been hunted or trapped during both autumn and spring.

The collection of edible plant species in Ohalo II, mentioned above, represents gathering around the site as well as according to the altitude of the slopes of eastern Galilee. Although the site dates to the LGM, its potential as a semi-sedentary location may remind us of the rich Kebaran and Geometric Kebaran sites along the coastal plain from Mt Carmel to the northern Negev. The difference between them is that Ohallo II was occupied for a relatively short time as shown by the stratigraphy of the huts (Tsatskin and Nadel 2003). Somewhat similar information is provided by the sites of Ein Gev I–III (three huts with 1–1.5 m deposits rich in animal bones but no plant remains due to the sandy sediments). The coastal plain sites such as Neve David, Nahal Hadera V, Hefsibah, Soreq sites, Ashdod 8, and others, produced evidence for repeated occupations (probably during wintertime) that resulted in extremely rich lithic assemblages. In several cases the calculated contents of the original accumulation is up to $c.1$ million pieces.

Similar richness is reported from sites such as Jilat and Kharaneh IV on the Jordanian plateau, in proximity to the Azraq basin, where temporary lakes and ponds already attracted both animal and humans by the end of the Late Glacial Maximum (Garrard et al. 1988; Garrard 1988; $c.24,000/22,000-19,000/18,000$ cal BP). The amount of lithics in these sites outstrips many of their contemporaneous ones located on the Mediterranean coast, and may also hint at periods of semi-sedentism, although the best evidence is the presence of commonsals (e.g. Tchernov 1991a; 1991b). However, the environment began to deteriorate during the Bølling-Allerød but in particular during the Younger Dryas. This forced local populations in affected areas or sub-regions to adopt a regime of high mobility that lasted through into the Neolithic (Garrad et al. 1988; Bar-Yosef and Belfer-Cohen 1991).

Due to their topographic features, the Zagros and the Caucasus regions offered modes of exploitation according to the differences between inter-montane valley floors and higher altitudes. Local faunas dominated by tur, bezoar goats, sheep, steppe bison, and aurochs allowed procurement from low areas to the highlands within each valley (Figure 11.2). As the best record currently available is from the Caucasus, the following comments refer to that region.

The Caucasus lies further north and thus was more seriously affected by the climatic fluctuations during the Upper Palaeolithic. One may expect that optimal movements of small bands took place along river valleys and their tributaries and would mark the seasonal shifts between summer and winter camps. Harsher winters encouraged occupations in rock shelters and caves in either the main or side valleys, where mammals such as migratory tur herds, bison, aurochs, and various species of deer were available. Milder winters would make the pursuit of game in higher altitudes feasible, for example the following of tur herds either on their way to upland meadows or down to the river valleys. The interpretation of the Late Mousterain and early Upper Palaeolithic deposits is more complicated. Based on the dominance of tur bones in the deposits of Ortvale Klde (including the early Upper Palaeolithic) and the presence of prime adults and juveniles (about 2:1; Bar-Oz and Adler 2005) it was suggested that the main hunting technique was via intercept or ambush and not through direct encounter, and that it lasted from autumn to early spring. Given that the meat of male adults in the autumn, especially during the rut period, is generally lean (Speth and Spielmann 1983) it is often less desired by foragers. Although the current interpretation is based on the demographic structure and migratory seasonal routes of the tur herds and the strategic location of Ortvale Klde, it seems that hunting from spring to autumn is also a viable option. The topographic locations of contemporary Mesolithic (YD age) occupations vary between rock shelters in the river valleys, caves in the uplands (such as Kotai Klde; Meshveliani et al. 2007), and open-air sites (Figure 11.2). The dominance of prime adult steppe bison, aurochs, and deer in both Dzudzuana Units C and B (before and after the LGM) and in Kotias Klde Unit B, indicates hunting during the summer. This means that the altitudes of 600–800 m above sea level could have been occupied in the summer and it is suggested that they were exploited during warmer spells within post-LGM conditions and even the YD.

In sum, the review of Upper Palaeolithic hunting and gathering in western Asia clearly demonstrates that the animal bone assemblages represent the available game in the area where each site is located. There is very little evidence for preferred certain mammals as the main target, as suggested for example for the Natufian sites in Mt Carmel. Details concerning the eventual consumption of microvertebrates are missing due to incomplete faunal reports or lack of attention to the exploitation of what we may call 'famine food'. Additional limitations on reconstructing past diets are due to bad preservation, small amounts of plant remains, minimal research of phytoliths, and none concerning starch analysis If we take the case of Ohalo II as representing what is not retrieved from sites, we may conclude that the plant diets were variable and rich depending on the area where the sites are located. Full-scale gathering was most probably practised prior to the Upper Palaeolithic. Gathering and collecting were affected by seasonal availability, and were often conducted around the occupied site, within a radius of 5–10 km (Figure 11.3). Similarly, hunting and trapping exploited the local resources within the territory of each group. However, inter-group relationships across particular territories were possibly important for securing the biological viability of the tribe, but little is known about such concerns before the Neolithic period.

REFERENCES

Adler, D. S. and Tushabramishvili, N. 2004. Middle Palaeolithic patterns of settlement and subsistence in the southern Caucasus. In N. Conard (ed.), *Middle Palaeolithic settlement dynamics*, 91–132. Tübingen: Kerns Verlag.

Adler, D. S., Bar-Oz, G., Belfer-Cohen, A., and Bar-Yosef, O. 2006a. Ahead of the game: Middle and Upper Palaeolithic hunting behaviors in the southern Caucasus. *Current Anthropology* 47, 89–118.

Adler, D. S., Belfer-Cohen, A., and Bar-Yosef. O. 2006b. Between a rock and a hard place: Neanderthal–modern human interactions in the southern Caucasus. In N. Conard (ed.), *When Neanderthals and modern humans met*, 165–88. Tübingen: Kerns Verlag.

Adler, D. S., Bar-Yosef, O., Belfer-Cohen, A., Tushabramishvili, N., Boaretto, E., Mercier, N., Valladas, H., and Rink. W. J. 2008. Dating the demise: Neandertal extinction and the establishment of modern humans in the southern Caucasus. *Journal of Human Evolution* 55, 817–33.

Arensburg, B. and Bar-Yosef, O. 1973. Human remains from Ein Gev I, Jordan Valley, Israel. *Paléorient* 1, 201–6.

Auffrey, J. C., Tchernov, E., and Nevo, E. 1989. Origine de commensalisme de la souris domestique (Mus musculus domesticus) vis-à-vis l'homme. *Comptes Rendues de l'Académie des Sciences Paris 307 (Serie III)*, 517–22.

Bailey, G. N. and Davidson, I. 1983. Site exploitation of territories and topography: two case studies from Palaeolithic Spain. *Journal of Archaeological Science* 10, 87–116.

Bar-Matthews, M. and Ayalon, A. 2003. Climatic conditions in the Eastern Mediterranean during the Last Glacial (60–10 ky) and their relations to the Upper Palaeolithic in the Levant as inferred from oxygen and carbon isotope systematics of cave deposits. In A. N. Goring-Morris and A. Belfer-Cohen (eds), *More than meets the eye: studies on Upper Palaeolithic diversity in the Near East*, 13–18. Oxford: Oxbow.

Bar-Matthews, M., Ayalon, A., Gilmour, M., Matthews, A., and Hawkesworth, C. 2002. Sea-land oxygen isotopic relationships from planktonic foraminifera and speleothems in the Eastern Mediterranean region and their implication for paleorainfall during interglacial intervals. *Geochimica et Coxmochimica Acta* 66, 1–19.

Bar-Oz, G. 2004. *Epipalaeolithic subsistence strategies in the Levant: a zooarchaeological perspective*. Boston: Brill.

Bar-Oz, G. and Adler, D. S. 2005. Taphonomic history of the Middle and Upper Palaeolithic faunal assemblage from Ortvale Klde. *Georgian Republic Journal of Taphonomy* 3, 185–211.

Bar-Oz, G., Belfer-Cohen, A., Meshveliani, T., Jakeli, N., Matskevich, Z., and Bar-Yosef, O. 2009. Bear in mind: bear hunting in the Mesolithic of the southern Caucasus. *Archaeology, Ethnology and Anthropology of Eurasia* 37, 15–24.

Bar-Oz, G., Dayan, T., Kaufman, D., and Weinstein-Evron, M. 2004. The Natufian economy at el-Wad Terrace with special reference to gazelle exploitation patterns. *Journal of Archaeological Science* 31, 217–31.

Bar-Yosef, D. E. 1989. Late Paleolithic and Neolithic marine shells in the southern Levant as cultural markers. In C. F. Hayes (ed.), *Shell bead conference*, 169–74. Rochester, NY: Rochester Museum and Science Center.

Bar-Yosef, D. E. 1991. Changes in the selection of marine shells from the Natufian to the Neolithic. In O. Bar-Yosef and F. R. Valla (eds), *The Natufian culture in the Levant*, 629–36. Ann Arbor: International Monographs in Prehistory.

Bar-Yosef, O. 2000. Late Middle and early Upper Palaeolithic in western Asia. In O. Bar-Yosef and D. Pilbeam (eds), *The geography of Neandertals and modern humans in Europe and the Greater Mediterranean*, 130–56. Cambridge: American School of Prehistoric Research, Peabody Museum.

Bar-Yosef, O. 2002. Natufian: a complex society of foragers. In B. Fitzhugh and J. Habu (eds), *Beyond foraging and collecting*, 91–149. New-York: Kluwer Academic/Plenum Press.

Bar-Yosef, O. and Belfer-Cohen, A. 1989. The origins of sedentism and farming communities in the Levant. *Journal of World Prehistory* 3, 447–98.

Bar-Yosef, O. and Belfer-Cohen, A. 1991. From sedentary hunter-gatherers to territorial farmers. In S. A. Gregg (ed.), *Between bands and states*, 181–202. Carbondale, IL: Center for Archaeological Investigations.

Bar-Yosef, O. and Belfer-Cohen, A. 2005. The Qafzeh Upper Palaeolithic assemblages: 70 years later. *Eurasian Prehistory* 2, 145–80.

Bar-Yosef, O. and Belfer-Cohen, A. 2010. The Levantine Upper and Epi-Palaeolithic. In E. Garcea (ed.), *South-eastern Mediterranean peoples between 130,000 and 10,000 years*, 144–67. Oxford: Oxbow.

Bar-Yosef, O., Belfer-Cohen, A., Meshveliani, Z. T., Jakeli, N., Bar-Oz, G., Boaretto, E., Goldberg, P., Kvavadze, E., and Matskevich, 2011. Dzudzuana: an Upper Paleolithic cave site in the Caucasus foothills (Georgia). *Antiquity* 85, 331–49.

Bar-Yosef, O. and Belmaker, M. 2011. Early and Middle Pleistocene faunal and hominind dispersals though southwestern Asia. *Quaternary Science Reviews* 30, 1318–37.

Bar-Yosef, O. and Killbrew, A. 1984. Wadi Sayakh—a geometric Kebaran site in southern Sinai. *Paléorient* 10, 95–102.

Bar-Yosef, O. and Valla, F. (eds) 1991. *The Natufian culture in the Levant*. Ann Arbor: International Monographs in Prehistory.

Bar-Yosef, O. and Zilhao, J. (eds) 2006. *Towards the definition of the Aurignacian*. Lisbon: IPA.

Bar-Yosef Mayer, D. E. and Porat, N. 2008. Green stone beads at the dawn of agriculture. *Proceedings of the National Academy of Sciences USA* 105, 8548–51.

Bar-Yosef Mayer, D. E. and Zohar, I. 2010. The role of aquatic resources in the Natufian culture. *Eurasian Prehistory* 7, 31–45.

Belfer-Cohen, A. and Bar-Yosef, O. 1999. The Levantine Aurignacian: 60 years of research. In W. Davies and R. Charles (eds), *Dorothy Garrod and the progress of the Palaeolithic: studies in the prehistoric archaeology of the Near East and Europe*, 118–34. Oxford: Oxbow.

Belfer-Cohen, A. and Bar-Yosef, O. 2000. Early sedentism in the Near East: a bumpy ride to village life. In I. Kuijt (ed.), *Life in Neolithic farming communities: social organisation, identity and differentiation*, 19–37. New York: Kluwer Academic/Plenum Press.

Belfer-Cohen, A. and Bar-Yosef, O. 2009. First things first: abstract and figurative artistic expressions in the Levant. In P. G. Bahn (ed.), *An inquiring mind: studies in honor of Alexander Marshack*, 25–37. Oxford: Oxbow.

Belfer-Cohen, A., Davidzon, A., Goring-Morris, A. N., Lieberman, D. and Spears, M. 2004. Nahal Ein Gev I: a late Upper Palaeolithic site by the Sea of Galilee, Israel. *Paléorient* 30, 25–46.

Belfer-Cohen, A. and Goring-Morris, A. N. 2003. Current issues in Levantine Upper Palaeolithic research. In A. N. Goring-Morris and A. Belfer-Cohen (eds), *More than meets the eye: studies on Upper Palaeolithic diversity in the Near East*, 1–12. Oxford: Oxbow.

Belfer-Cohen, A. and Goring-Morris, A. N. 2007. From the beginning: Levantine Upper Palaeolithic cultural continuity. In P. Mellars, K. Boyle, O. Bar-Yosef, and C. B. Stringer (eds), *Rethinking the human revolution*, 199–206. Cambridge: McDonald Institute for Archaeological Research University.

Belfer-Cohen, A. and Hovers, E. 2005. The ground stone assemblages of the Natufian and Neolithic societies in the Levant—a brief review. *Journal of the Israel Prehistoric Society* 35, 299–308.

Bergman, C. A. 1981. Point types in the Upper Palaeolithic sequence at Ksar Akil, Lebanon. In J. Cauvin and P. Sanlaville (eds), *Préhistoire du Levant*, 319–30. Paris: CNRS.

Bergman, C. A. and Stringer, C. B. 1989. Fifty years after: Egbert, an early Upper Palaeolithic juvenile from Ksar Akil, Lebanon. *Paléorient* 15, 99–112.

Binford, L. R. 1980. Willow smoke and dogs' tails: hunter-gatherer settlement systems and archaeological site formation. *American Antiquity* 45, 4–20.

Birdsell, J. B. 1970. Local group composition among the Australian Aborigines: a critique of the evidence from fieldwork conducted since 1930. *Current Anthropology* 11, 115–42.

Birdsell, J. B. 1976. Realities and transformations: the tribes of the Western Desert of Australia. In N. Peterson (ed.), *Tribes and boundaries in Australia*, 95–120. Canberra: Australian Institute of Aboriginal Studies.

Birdsell, J. B. 1985. Biological dimensions of small, human founding populations. In B. R. Finney and E. M. Jones (eds), *Interstellar migration and the human experience*, 110–19. Berkeley: University of California Press.

Bookman, R., Bartov, Y., Enzel, Y., and Stein, M. 2006. Quaternary lake levels in the Dead Sea basin: two centuries of research. In Y. Enzel, A. Agnon, and M. Stein (eds), *New frontiers in Dead Sea palaeoenvironmental research*, 155–70. Boulder: Geological Society of America.

Bordes, J.-G. and Shidrag, S. 2005. Le Paléolithique supérieur du Zagros: sites de la région de Kermanshah et de Khorramabad (Yafteh). In J. Jaubert and F. Biglari (eds), *Le Paléolithique d'Iran*, 115–36. Bordeaux: Mission Archaéologique Française en Iran.

Byrd, B. F. 2005. Reassessing the emergence of village life in the Near East. *Journal of Archaeological Research* 13, 231–90.

Chevrier, B., Berillon, G., Asgari Khaneghah, A., Antoine, P., Bahain, J.-J., and Zeitoun, V. 2006. Moghanak, Otchounak, Garm Roud 2: nouveaux assemblages paléolithiques dans le nord de l'Iran. Premières caractérisations typo-technologiques et attributions chrono-culturelles. *Paléorient* 32, 59–79.

Copeland, L. 2000. Forty-six Emireh points from the Lebanon in the context of the Middle to Upper Palaeolithic transition in the Levant. *Paléorient* 26, 73–92.

Davis, R. S. 2004. Kara Kamar in northern Afghanistan: Aurignacian, Aurignacoid, or just plain Upper Palaeolithic? In A. P. Derevianko and T. I. Nokhrina (eds), *Archaeology and palaeoarchaeology and palaeoecology of Eurasia. Papers in honor of Vadim Ranov*, 210–17. Novosibirsk: Institute of Archaeology and Ethnography SB RAS Press.

Davis, S. J. M. 1982. Climatic change and the advent of domestication of ruminant artiodactyls in the late Pleistocene-Holocene period in the Israel region. *Paléorient* 8, 5–16.

Davis, S. J. M. and Valla, F. 1978. Evidence for domestication of the dog 12,000 years ago in the Natufian of Israel. *Nature* 276, 608–10.

Enzel, Y., Amit, R., Dayan, U., Crouvi, O., Kahana, R., Ziv, B., and Sharon, D. 2008. The climatic and physiographic controls of the eastern Mediterranean over the late Pleistocene climates in the southern Levant and its neighboring deserts. *Global and Planetary Change* 60, 165–92.

Firouz, E. 2005. *The complete fauna of Iran*. London: I. B. Tauris.

Garrard, A. N. 1982. The environmental implications of a re-analysis of the large mammal fauna from Wadi el-Mughara caves, Palestine. In J. T. Bintliff and W. Van Zeist (eds), *Palaeoclimates, palaeoenvironments and human communities in the Eastern Mediterranean region in later prehistory*, 165–87. Oxford: BAR International Series 133.

Garrard, A. N. 1998. Environment and cultural adaptations in the Azraq Basin: 24,000–7,000 BP. In D. O. Henry (ed.), *The prehistoric archaeology of Jordan*, 139–50. Oxford: Archaeopress.

Garrard, A. N., Betts, A., Byrd, B., Colledge, S., and Hunt, C. 1988. Summary of palaeoenvironmental and prehistoric investigations in the Azraq Basin. In A. N. Garrard and H. G. Gebel (eds), *The prehistory of Jordan*, 311–37. Oxford: BAR International Series 396.

Garrod, D. A. E. 1930. The Palaeolithic of southern Kurdistan. *Bulletin of the American School of Prehistoric Research* 6, 13–43.

Garrod, D. A. E. and Bate, D. M. A. 1937. *The Stone Age of Mt. Carmel: excavations at the Wadi-Mughara*, Vol. 1. Oxford: Clarendon Press.

Golovanova, L. V., Cleghorn, N. E., Doronichev, V. B., Hoffecker, J. F., Burr, G. S., and Sulergizkiy, L. D. 2006. The early Upper Palaeolithic in the northern Caucasus: new data from Mezmaiskaya cave 1997 excavation. *Eurasian Prehistory* 4, 43–78.

Goring-Morris, A. N. 1995. Complex hunter-gatherers at the end of the Palaeolithic (20,000–10,000 BP). In T. E. Levy (ed.), *The archaeology of society in the Holy Land*, 141–68. London: Leicester University Press.

Goring-Morris, A. N. 2002. EpiPalaeolithic. Upper Palaeolithic, Kebaran, Geometric Kebaran. In P. N. Peregrine and M. Ember (eds), *Encyclopedia of prehistory, volume 8: South and Southwest Asia*, 122–6. New York: Kluwer Academic/Plenum Press.

Goring-Morris, A. N. 2009. Two Kebaran occupations near Nahal Soreq: a reconstruction of group ranges in the early Epipalaeolithic of the Israeli littoral. *Eurasian Prehistory* 6, 75–93.

Goring-Morris, A. N. and Belfer-Cohen, A. (eds) 2003. *More than meets the eye: studies on Upper Palaeolithic diversity in the Near East*. Oxford: Oxbow.

Goring-Morris, N. and Kolska Horwitz, L. 2007. Funerals and feasts during the Pre-Pottery Neolithic B of the Near East. *Antiquity* 81, 902–19.

Harrison, D. L. and Bates, P. J. J. 1991. *The mammals of Arabia*. Sevenoaks: Harrison Zoological Museum.

Henry, D. O. 1989. *From foraging to agriculture: the Levant at the end of the Ice Age*. Philadelphia: University of Pennsylvania Press.

Higgs, E. S. and Vita-Finzi, C. 1972. Prehistoric economies: a territorial approach. In E. S. Higgs (ed.), *Papers in economic prehistory*, 27–36. Cambridge: Cambridge University Press.

Hillman, G. C. 2000. Abu Hureyra 1: the Epipalaeolithic. In A. M. T. Moore, G. C. Hillman, and A. J. Legge (eds), *Village on the Euphrates: from foraging to farming at Abu Hureyra*, 327–99. Oxford: Oxford University Press.

Hillman, G. C., Hedges, C. R., Moore, A., Colledge, S., and Pettitt, P. 2001. New evidence of Late Glacial cereal cultivation at Abu Hureyra on the Euphrates. *Holocene* 11, 383–93.

Hooijer, D. 1961. The fossil vertebrates of Ksar Akil, a Palaeolithic rockshelter in Lebanon. *Zoologische Verhandelingen* 49, 4–65.

Hole, F. and Flannery, K. 1967. The prehistory of southwestern Iran: a preliminary report. *Proceedings of the Prehistoric Society* 33, 151–206.

Kaufman, D. and Ronen, A. 1987. La sepulture Kebarienne Geometrique de Neveh David, Haifa, Israel. *L'Anthropologie* 91, 335–42.

Kelly, R. L. 1995. *The foraging spectrum: diversity in hunter-gatherers lifeways*. Washington, DC: Smithsonian Institution.

Kislev, M. E., Nadel, D., and Carmi, I. 1992. Epipalaeolithic (19,000 BP) cereal and fruit diet at Ohalo II, Sea of Galilee, Israel. *Review of Palaeobotany and Palynology* 73, 161–6.

Korkia, L. D. 1998. *Upper Palaeolithic culture of the north-eastern Black Sea littoral of Georgia*. Tblisi: Metsniereba (in Georgian with Russian summary).

Kozlowski, J. K. 1992. The Balkans in the Middle and Upper Palaeolithic: the gate to Europe or a cul de sac? *Proceedings of the Prehistoric Society* 58, 1–20.

Kuhn, S. L., Stiner, M. C., Güleç, E., Özer, I., Yılmaz, H., Baykara, I., Açıkkol, A., Goldberg, P., Martínez Molina, K., Ünay, E., and Suata-Alpaslan, F. 2009. The early Upper Palaeolithic occupations at Uçağızlı Cave (Hatay, Turkey). *Journal of Human Evolution* 56, 87–113.

Kvavadze, E., Bar-Yosef, O., Belfer-Cohen, A., Boaretto, E., Jakeli, N., Matskevich, Z., and Meshveliani, T. 2009. 30,000 years old wild flax fiber: testimony for fabricating prehistoric linen. *Science* 325, 1359.

Lee, R. B. and DeVore, I. (eds) 1968. *Man the hunter*. Chicago: Aldine.

Lev-Yadun, S. and Weinstein-Evron, M. 2005. Modeling the influence of wood use by the Natufians of El-wad in the forest of Mount Carmel. *Journal of the Israel Prehistoric Society* 35, 285–98.

Lubin, V. P. 1989. The Palaeolithic of the Caucasus. In P. I. Boriskovski (ed.), *The Palaeolithic of the Caucasus and Northern Asia*, 9–142. Moscow: Institute of Archaeology.

McBurney, C. B. M. 1968. The cave of Ali Tappeh. *Proceedings of the Prehistoric Society* 34, 385–413.

Maher, L. A. 2007a. Excavations at the Geometric Kebaran site of 'Uyun al-Hammam, al-Kura district, Jordan. *Annual of the Department of Antiquities of Jordan* 51, 263–72.

Maher, L. A. 2007b. Microliths and mortuary practices: new perspectives on the epipalaeolithic in northern and eastern Jordan. In T. E Levy, P. Daviau, R. W. Younker, and M. Shaer (eds), *Crossing Jordan: North American contributions to the archaeology of Jordan*, 195–202. London: Equinox.

Marks, A. E. 1993. The early Upper Palaeolithic: the view from the Levant. In H. Knecht, A. Pike-Tay, and R. White (eds), *Before Lascaux: the complete record of the early Upper Palaeolithic*, 5–22. Boca Raton: CRC Press.

Marshack, A. 1997. Palaeolithic image making and symboling in Europe and the Middle East: a comparative review. In M. Conkey, O. Soffer, D. Stratmann, and N. G. Jablonski (eds), *Beyond art: Pleistocene image and symbol*, 53–91. San Francisco: Memoirs of California Academy of Sciences.

Meignen, L. and Bar-Yosef, O. 2002. The lithic industries of the Middle and Upper Paleolithic of the Levant: continuity or break? *Archaeology, Ethnology and Anthropology of Eurasia* 3, 12–21.

Meshveliani, T., Bar-Oz, G., Bar-Yosef, O., Belfer-Cohen, A., Boaretto, E., Jakeli, N., Koridze, I., and Matskevich, Z. 2007. Mesolithic hunters at Kotias Klde, western Georgia: preliminary results. *Paléorient* 33, 47–58.

Meshveliani, T., Bar-Yosef, O., and Belfer-Cohen, A. 2004. The Upper Palaeolithic of western Georgia. In P. J. Brantigham, S. L. Kuhn, and K. W. Kerry (eds), *The early Upper Palaeolithic beyond Western Europe*, 129–43. Berkeley: University of California Press.

Munro, N. D. 2004a. Zooarchaeological measures of hunting pressure and occupation intensity in the Natufian. *Current Anthropology* 45 (Supplement), S5–S33.

Munro, N. D. 2004b. Small game and the transition to agriculture in the southern Levant. In C. Delage (ed.), *The last hunter-gatherer societies in the Near East*, 169–88. Oxford: BAR International Series.

Munro, N. D. 2004c. Small game indicators of human foraging efficiency and early herd management at the transition to agriculture in south-west Asia. In J.-P. Brugal and J. Desse (eds), *Petits Animaux et sociétés humaines du complément alimentaire aux ressources utilitaires*, 515–31. Antibes: APDCA.

Munro, N. D. 2009. Epipalaeolithic subsistence intensification in the southern Levant: the faunal evidence. In J. J. Hublin and M. Richards (eds), *The evolution of hominin diets*, 141–55. London: Springer.

Munro, N. D. and Bar-Oz, G. 2005. Gazelle bone fat processing in the Levantine Epipalaeolithic. *Journal of Archaeological Science* 32, 223–39.

Munro, N. D. and Grosman, L. 2010. Early evidence (ca. 12,000 BP) for feasting at a burial cave in Israel. *Proceedings of the National Academy of Sciences USA* 107, 15362–6.

Nadel, D. 2003. The Ohalo II flint assemblage and the beginning of the Epipalaeolithic in the Jordan Valley. In A. Belfer-Cohen and A. N. Goring-Morris (eds), *More than meets the eye: studies on Upper Palaeolithic diversity in the Near East*, 216–29. Oxford: Oxbow.

Nadel, D., Weiss, E., Simchoni, O., Tsatskin, A., Danin, A., and Kislev, M. 2004. Stone Age hut in Israel yields world's oldest evidence of bedding. *Proceedings of the National Academy of Sciences USA* 101, 6821–6.

Olszewski, D. I. 1993. The Zarzian occupation at Warwasi rockshelter, Iran. In D. I. Olszewski and H. L. Dibble (eds), *The Paleolithic prehistory of the Zagros-Taurus*, 207–36. Philadelphia: The University Museum, University of Pennsylvania.

Olszewski, D. I. and Dibble, H. L. 1994. The Zagros Aurignacian. *Current Anthropology* 35, 68–75.

Olszewski, D. I. and Dibble, H. L. 2006. To be or not to be Aurignacian: the Zagros Upper Palaeolithic. In O. Bar-Yosef and J. Zilhao (eds), *Towards a definition of the Aurignacian*, 355–73. Lisbon: American School of Prehistoric Research and Instituto Português de Arqueologia.

Otte, M., Biglari, F., Flas, D., Shidrang, S., and Zwyns, N. 2007. The Aurignacian in the Zagros region: new research at Yafreh cave, Lorestan, Iran. *Antiquity* 81, 82–96.

Otte, M. and Kozlowski, J. K. 2004. The significance of the Baradostian in the origin of the Upper Palaeolithic of Eurasia. *L'anthropologie* 108, 395–406.

Otte, M. and Kozlowski, J. K. 2007. *L'Aurignacien du Zagros*. Liège: ERAUL 118.

Piperno, D. R., Weiss, E., Holst, I., and Nadel, D. 2004. Processing of wild cereal grains in the Upper Palaeolithic revealed by starch grain analysis. *Nature* 430, 670–3.

Rabinovich, R. 2003. The Levantine Upper Palaeolithic faunal record. In A. N. Goring-Morris and A. Belfer-Cohen (eds), *More than meets the eye: studies on Upper Palaeolithic diversity in the Near East*, 33–48. Oxford: Oxbow.

Ranov, V. 1995. The Levallois paradox. In H. Dibble and O. Bar-Yosef (eds), *The definition and interpretation of Levallois technology*, 69–78. Madison: Prehistory Press.

Richter, T., Stock, J. T., Maher, L., and Hebron, C. 2010. An early Epi-Palaeolithic sitting burial from Azraq Oasis, Jordan. *Antiquity* 84, 321–34.

Robinson, S. A., Black, S., Sellwood, B. W., and Valdes, P. J. 2006. A review of palaeoclimates and paleoenvironments in the Levant and Eastern Mediterranean from 25,000 and 5000 years BP: setting the environmental background for the evolution of human civilisation. *Quaternary Science Reviews* 25, 1517–42.

Ronen, A. and Vandermeersch, B. 1972. The Upper Paleolithic sequence in the cave of Qafza (Israel). *Quaternaria* 16, 189–202.

Rossignol-Strick, M. 1995. Sea-land correlation of pollen records in the eastern Mediterranean for the glacial-interglacial transition: biostratigraphy versus radiometric time-scale. *Quaternary Science Reviews* 14, 893–915.

Simmons, T. 2004. 'A feather for each wind that blows': utilizing avifauna in assessing changing patterns in paleoecology and subsistence at Jordan Valley archaeological sites. In N. Goren-Inbar and J. D. Speth (eds), *Human paleoecology in the Levantine Corridor*, 191–206. Oxford: Oxbow.

Solecki, R. L. and McGovern, T. H. 1980. Predatory birds and prehistoric man. In S. Diamond (ed.), *Theory and practice: essays presented to Gene Weltfish*, 79–95. The Hague: Mouton Publishers.

Solecki, R. S. 1963. Prehistory in Shanidar Valley, Northern Iraq. *Science* 139, 179–93.

Solecki, R. S. and Solecki, R. L. 1993. The pointed tools from the Mousterian occupations of Shanidar cave, Northern Iraq. In D. I. Olszewski and H. L. Dibble (eds), *The Paleolithic prehistory of the Zagros-Taurus*, 119–46. Philadelphia: The University Museum, University of Pennsylvania.

Speth, J. D. and Clark, J. L. 2006. Hunting and overhunting in the Levantine late Middle Palaeolithic. *Before Farming* 3, 1–42.

Speth, J. D. and Spielmann, K. A. 1983. Energy source, protein metabolism, and hunter-gatherer subsistence strategies. *Journal of Anthropological Archaeology* 2, 1–31.

Stiner, M. C. (ed.) 2005. *The faunas of Hayonim Cave, Israel: a 200,000-year record of Palaeolithic diet, demography and society*. Cambridge, MA: Peabody Museum, Harvard University.

Stiner, M. C., Munro, N. D., and Surovell, T. A. 2000. The tortoise and the hare: small game use, the Broad Spectrum Revolution, and Palaeolithic demography. *Current Anthropology* 41, 39–73.

Tchernov, E. 1962. Palaeolithic avifauna in Palestine. *Bulletin of the Research Council of Israel* 11, 95–131.

Tchernov, E. 1991a. Biological evidence for human sedentism in southwest Asia during the Natufian. In O. Bar-Yosef and F. R. Valla (eds), *The Natufian culture in the Levant*, 315–40. Ann Arbor: International Monographs in Prehistory.

Tchernov, E. 1991b. On mice and men: biological markers for long-term sedentism: a reply. *Paléorient* 17, 153–60.

Tchernov, E. 1992. The Afro-Arabian component in the Levantine mammalian fauna—a short biogeographical review. *Israel Journal of Zoology* 38, 155–92.

Tchernov, E. 1997. Are late Pleistocene environmental factors, faunal changes and cultural transformations causally connected? The case of the southern Levant. *Paléorient* 23, 209–28.

Tchernov, E. and Valla, F. R. 1997. Two new dogs, and other Natufian dogs, from the southern Levant. *Journal of Archaeological Science* 24, 65–95.

Tsatskin, A. and Nadel, D. 2003. Formation processes at the Ohalo II submerged prehistoric campsite, Israel, inferred from soil micromorphology and magnetic susceptibility studies. *Geoarchaeology* 18, 409–32.

Twiss, K. C. 2008. Transformations in an early agricultural society: feasting in the southern Levantine Pre-Pottery Neolithic. *Journal of Anthropological Archaeology* 27, 418–42.

Valla, F. R. 1988. Aspect du sol de l'abri 131 de Mallaha (Eynan). *Paléorient* 15, 283–96.

Valla, F. R. 2000. La sedentarisation au Proche orient: la Culture Natoufienne. In J. Guilane (ed.), *Premiers paysans du monde: naissance des agricultures*, 13–29. Paris: Éditions Errance.

Valla, F. R. 2004. Natufian behavior in the Hula Basin: the quesiton of territoriality. In N. Goren-Inbar and J. D. Speth (eds), *Human paleoecology in the Levantine Corridor*, 207–20. Oxford: Oxbow.

Valla, F. R., Khalaily, H., Valladas, H., Kaltnecker, E., Bocquentin, F., Cabellos, T., Mayer, D. A. B.-Y., Le Dosseur, G., Regev, L., Chu, V., Weiner, S., Boaretto, E., Samuelian, N., Valentin, B., Delerue, S., Poupeau, G., Bridault, A., Rabinovich, R., Simmons, T., Zohar, I., Ashkenazi, S., Huertas, A. D., Spiro, B., Mienis, H. K., Rosen, A. M., Porat, N., and Belfer-Cohen, A. 2007. Les fouilles de Ain Mallaha (Eynan) de 2003 à 2005: quatrième rapport préliminaire. *Journal of the Israel Prehistoric Society* 37, 135–383.

Van Peer, P. 2004. Did Middle Stone Age moderns of sub-Saharan African descent trigger an Upper Palaeolithic revolution in the Lower Nile Valley? *Anthropologie, International Journal of the Science of Man* 42, 215–26.

van Zeist, W. and Bakker-Herres, J. A. H. 1986. Archaeobotanical studies in the Levant. III: Late Paleolithic Mureybet. *Palaeohistoria* 26, 171–99.

Wahida, G. A. 1999. The Zarzian industry of the Zagros mountains. In W. Davies and R. Charles (eds), *Dorothy Garrod and the progress of the Palaeolithic*, 181–208. Oxford: Oxbow.

Weiss, E., Kislev, M. E., Simchoni, O., Nadel, D., and Tschauner, H. 2008. Plant-food preparation area on an Upper Paleolithic brush hut floor at Ohalo II, Israel. *Journal of Archaeological Science* 35, 2400–14.

Willcox, G. 2008. Les nouvelles données archéobotaniques de Mureybet et la néolithisation du Moyen Euphrate. In J. J. Ibanez (ed.), *Le site néolithique de Tell Mureybet (Syrie du Nord). En hommage à Jacques Cauvin*, 103–14. Oxford: BAR International Series 1843.

Willcox, G., Buxo, R., and Herveux, L. 2009. Late Pleistocene and early Holocene climate and the beginnings of cultivation in northern Syria. *The Holocene* 19, 151–8.

Wright, K. I. 1994. Ground-stone tools and hunter-gatherer subsistence in southwest Asia: implications of the transition to farming. *American Antiquity* 59, 238–63.

Wright, K. I. 2000. The social origins of cooking and dining in early villages of western Asia. *Proceedings of the Prehistoric Society* 66, 89–121.

Wright, K. I. and Garrard, A. 2003. Social identities and the expansion of stone bead-making in Neolithic Western Asia: new evidence from Jordan. *Antiquity* 296, 267–84.

Yaroshevich, A., Daufman, D., Nuzhnyy, D., Bar-Yosef, O., and Weinsein-Evron, M. 2010. Design and performance of microlith implemented projectiles during the middle and the late EpiPalaeolithic of the Levant: experimental and archaeological evidence. *Journal of Archaeological Science* 37, 368–88.

Yom-Tov, Y. and Tchernov, E. (eds) 1988. *The zoogeography of Israel*. Dordrecht: Springer.

Zohar, I. and Belmaker, M. 2003. Size does matter: methodological comments on sieve size and species richness in fishbone assemblages. *Journal of Archaeological Science* 32, 1–7.

Zohary, D., Hopf, M., and Weiss, E. 2012. *Domestication of plants in the old world: the origin and spread of cultivated plants in southwest Asia, Europe and the Mediterranean Basin*. Oxford: Oxford University Press.

Zohary, M. 1973. *Geobotanical foundations of the Middle East*. Vols. I and II. Stuttgart: Gustav Fischer Verlag.

CHAPTER 12

THE EUROPEAN UPPER PALAEOLITHIC

PAUL PETTITT

THE term Upper Palaeolithic derives from excavations in western Europe—particularly south-west France—from the 1860s. The uppermost Pleistocene deposits of caves and rock shelters of the Dordogne and neighbouring departments provided a sequence of typologically distinct lithic and organic assemblages eponymously named after French sites, notably the Aurignacian (after Aurignac), Gravettian (La Gravette), Solutrean (Solutré), Magdalenian (La Madeleine), and Azilian (Mas d'Azil) for much of the period between ~35,000 and 10,000 (uncal) BP. These were soon associated with an intrusive appearance of *Homo sapiens*, who replaced the last European archaics, the Neanderthals (Sackett 1991). Today, however, it is recognized that this small corner of the vast Eurasian landmass is not representative of the biological and behavioural processes that can be observed across Eurasia in the last 40,000 years of the Upper Pleistocene which represent the gradual dispersal of our own species from its presumed origins in Africa (Bar-Yosef 2002; Brantingham et al. 2004). As more sites have been excavated with modern techniques, particularly in eastern and Mediterranean Europe, a picture has emerged of the complex development of aspects of Upper Palaeolithic material culture from at least 40,000 BP: of assemblage change that, while broadly similar at the European scale, bears distinct regional character; of significant assemblage change every 10,000 years or so, enough to warrant several major subdivisions of the European Upper Palaeolithic; and the complex, cumulative emergence of the traditional 'package' of new innovations, including systematic blade and bladelet technology on prismatic cores, high-degrees of typological (morphometric) standardization of tools, long-distance movement of raw materials, creation of tools on bone, antler, and ivory, personal ornamentation of shell, stone, bone, and ivory, figurative and non-figurative art, burial and other mortuary activity, and the complex, seasonally-scheduled use of resource landscapes (e.g. Bar-Yosef 2002; Mellars and Stringer 1989; Straus 2005). Ultimately, these came to be associated with the 'human revolution'—a dramatic behavioural change underpinned by the cognitive evolution which defines our species (see discussion in d'Errico 2003; Mellars 1990; 2004; Mellars and Stringer 1989).

Today, it is recognized that the characteristics of the period emerged not in one 'event' that subsequently spread as a package, but piecemeal over several tens of thousands of years (Straus 2005). Rather than representing the hallmark of cognitively 'modern' behaviour (Henshilwood and Marean 2003), the European Upper Palaeolithic is now viewed as a complex, evolving adaptation of *Homo sapiens* to the often demanding environments of the first northern latitudes into which they dispersed. In addition, some characteristics which became common elements of the Upper Palaeolithic have been found in uncontaminated Late Middle Palaeolithic contexts, suggesting that to an extent at least some Neanderthals had evolved aspects of 'modern' behaviour independent of dispersing moderns (d'Errico 2003; Zilhão 2007). This aside, to generalize about *the* Upper Palaeolithic would be significantly misleading: many (or more) differences separate the period after ~20,000 BP and that before ~30,000 BP than do the Upper Palaeolithic from the preceding Middle Palaeolithic, and this does not seem to relate to poor sampling in the earlier range but to real behavioural differences. The European Upper Palaeolithic, after all, encompassed some 30,000 years and spanned thousands of kilometres, and must be viewed against the context of dramatically unstable climates which were often severe and thus posed significant adaptive pressures. From the point of view of hunter-gatherers, however, the period documents the emergence of the hunter-fisher-gatherer adaptations recognizable in the ethnographic present from pre-modern hunter-gatherer systems of *Homo sapiens*. The modern adaptation had certainly come about across much of Europe by ~20,000 BP, although it is unclear as to whether preceding Upper Palaeolithic adaptations were similarly 'modern' and that this can be held to define the entire Upper Palaeolithic, or whether populations before 20,000 BP or 30,000 BP were in some respects pre-modern (Kuhn and Stiner 2001). Heuristically, it makes sense to divide the period into five broad phases—the Initial (IUP), Early (EUP), Mid (MUP), Late (LUP), and Terminal Upper Palaeolithic (TUP), although it should be noted that any scheme such as this will mask considerable variation in space and time, as well as similarities and ruptures that both link and divide these subdivisions.

The geographical and chronological edges of the European Upper Palaeolithic are blurred. At least some IUP assemblages may have been made by archaic humans (i.e. *Homo neanderthalensis*), and from an economic and artistic perspective some TUP assemblages have more in common with succeeding Mesolithic adaptations of the Holocene. At no point in time must one assume that Upper Palaeolithic populations were essentially continuous across the European landmass; assessing the archaeological record in chronological context in association with demographic modelling suggests that Upper Palaeolithic populations were remarkably small—as one would expect for hunter-gatherers in northern tundra environments—and that their distribution and success altered considerably in response to climatic change and the concomitant fortunes of the herbivorous prey on which they were largely dependent (Bocquet-Appel and Demars 2000; Van Andel and Davies 2003). From time to time cultural 'hotspots' become visible, such as the precocious floruit of portable art in the EUP of south-western Germany, the great Pavlovian/Willendorfian and Kostenki/Avdeevo groups of the central and eastern European MUP, and the Magdalenian of the central and western European LUP. Relatively intensive excavation in many regions over the last century or more probably indicates that these groupings are real, and represented some of the most civilized places on Earth at the time, although large areas of Europe—for example, much of the Balkans—are still relatively poorly researched.

Today, the European Upper Palaeolithic is recognized as being widespread, dynamic, complex, and continuously innovative. The latter may indeed separate it from the preceding

Middle Palaeolithic. Many of the defining elements of 'civilization' archaeologists recognize appeared or were elaborated in the Upper Palaeolithic, such as long-distance exchange, art and symbolism, burial, semi-sedentism, storage, and intensive relationships with wild resources. Despite this, general accounts remain biased towards a small set of 'iconic' sites and objects typically from France (e.g. Mellars 2001). Regions such as this reflect *refugia*—regions where hunter-gatherer populations were able to stay put even in severely cold stadials and in which, therefore, the archaeological record is relatively rich; the archaeology of peripheral regions to the north and south of these, however, remind us of the constant remodelling of human distribution and reveal humans at the edges of their adaptive abilities.

Chronology and Environments, Populations, and Dispersals

Fossils of *Homo sapiens* are present in eastern and central Europe ~36–35,000 BP, e.g. in Spitsynskayan and Gorodzovskayan sites in Russia (Chabai 2003), Peștera cu Oase, Romania (Rougier et al. 2007; Trinkaus et al. 2003), and Mladeč, Czech Republic (Svoboda 2003), and indicate that in these regions at least the IUP was their creation. Although fossil associations with the succeeding EUP are equally rare (Churchill and Smith 2000), there is general agreement that this is solely the work of *Homo sapiens,* as the few associations that exist—for example at Brassempouy, France—are of this taxon, even if direct dating of the eponymous Cro-Magnon remains demonstrated that they are of MUP antiquity—even if the term is still used as an informal label for Pleistocene European *Homo sapiens* (Henry-Gambier 2002; Henry-Gambier et al. 2004). Thus, a parsimonious interpretation sees the IUP/EUP as the signature of the earliest members of our own species dispersing through Europe. It is now agreed that this major European dispersal of *Homo sapiens* occurred broadly between ~40,000 and ~30,000 BP (Bar-Yosef 2002; Mellars 2006), and that these new populations were at least in part behaviourally 'modern'. Details of the pattern of dispersal are unclear, although there is general agreement that it targeted specific regions and moved along specific paths, rather than being a generalized 'wave-of-advance' (Davies 2001), and the prevalence of the IUP in the Mediterranean and along the Danube suggests the primacy of these dispersal routes. More broadly, the appearance of modern humans in southern Siberia by ~40 ka BP (Goebel and Aksenov 1995) reveals that the initial dispersal into Europe was part of a much wider-range expansion of our species.

It is unclear whether or not these initial European *Homo sapiens* populations were contemporary in some regions with Neanderthals and, if so, whether and how they interacted; nor is it clear whether some Neanderthal communities had adopted elements of Upper Palaeolithic behaviour independently or through contact. Much debate in the 1990s centred upon the issue of contemporaneity, notably in south-west France, where supposed interstratifications of Châtelperronian (Neanderthal) and Aurignacian (modern human) material were taken to support this (Gravina et al. 2005; Mellars 1999). Now, however, these have been shown to result from taphonomic mixing at the two sites of concern (Bordes 2003; Zilhão and d'Errico 2003; Zilhão et al. 2006) and ambitious dating projects have shown that in general assemblages thought to be of Neanderthal manufacture are systematically older than those indicative of *Homo sapiens* (Jöris and Street 2008; Zilhão and d'Errico 1999; cf. an unconvincing Benazzi et al. 2011). Space precludes consideration of these major issues here; the literature is vast, yet the data relatively poor; chronological imprecision, lack of diagnostic human fossils and resulting ambiguity about what human species IUP technocomplexes represent, and an uneven distribution of well-excavated sites are major concerns. Suffice it to say that a consensus seems to be emerging that (a) Neanderthals had adopted some elements of 'Upper Palaeolithic' behaviour, such as the use of pigments, feathers, hafting mastics, carving of bone into points; and (b) that in most—if not all—areas of Europe they had become extinct before the arrival of *Homo sapiens* (Jöris and Street 2008; d'Errico 2003; Zilhão and d'Errico 1999). Thus from a human point of view *Homo sapiens* seems to have dispersed into virgin territory.

Greenland ice cores reveal considerable climatic instability during Marine Isotope Stages 3 (~61–25,000 BP) and 2 (~25–10,000 BP), with the severe conditions of the Last Glacial Maximum (henceforth LGM) centred around ~20,000 BP as a major structuring feature (e.g. Svensson et al. 2008). At least nine relatively warm interstadial periods of 500–3,000 years' duration are recognized in the Greenland cores, interspersed with cool or cold stadials. During the former mean temperatures could reach within one degree of the present; during the latter snow could be on the ground throughout much of Europe for 6–9 months of the year. The prevailing environments between 45° and 55° latitude were open tundra, with boreal woodland established during some of the longer interstadials and with more dominance in the southern European peninsulas between 40° to 45° latitude (papers in Van Andel and Davies 2003). This supported a rich 'mammoth steppe' community in which vital nutritional resources were generally available on the hoof, in the form of gregarious herbivores, notably reindeer, horse, mammoth, woolly rhinoceros, bison, extinct wild cattle (aurochsen), and in montane areas ibex and chamois. Small terrestrial herbivores were also exploited for food, and fur-bearers for clothing; fish was being systematically exploited by ~30,000 BP and probably earlier, and carbonized remains of plant foods show that this supplemented the hunted and trapped foodstuffs when available.

The estimation of population sizes is difficult, especially for a continent larger than present (due to the continental shelves exposed by lowered sea levels), although the modelling of metapopulations based on modern data on hunter-gatherer population densities in similar environments and counts of archaeological sites per geographic region reveal that the European population was exceptionally low, with perhaps 2,000 to 30,000 individuals across the continent during the EUP and MUP rising to no more than 70,000 for the LUP (Bocquet-Appel and Demars 2005). To put this in perspective, at maximum this would be the population of seven small Roman towns, scattered across the entire continent. The archaeological record suggests that distribution was strongly regionalized, with populational centres focused on dense resource clusters and ecotonal areas where uplands met river valleys. These were separated by empty gaps, and a diachronic picture of shifting human distribution in response to the unstable climate, regional extinctions, and major population displacements is the rule for the duration of the period.

Biogeographically, one can divide Europe into several regions latitudinally (based on a shorter growing season the further north one goes) and longitudinally (based on proximity to or distance from the ameliorating effects of the Atlantic Ocean); Gamble (1986) employed a scheme of nine regions, the population histories of which were often dissimilar. This is no surprise; some southern regions acted as refugia, notably northern Iberia and southern France, the Italian peninsula, and the Russian Plain; by contrast others received temporary dispersals from such sources only when climate allowed, such as the Northern European Plain. Vast areas were abandoned during the severe conditions of the LGM when populations survived only in the refugia of southern Europe (papers in Banks et al. 2008; Soffer and Gamble 1990). Only in the last two thousand years of the Pleistocene did Upper Palaeolithic groups disperse to southern Scandinavia for the first time (Eriksen 1996; Schild 1996).

The Initial Upper Palaeolithic (IUP) ~50–35,000 BP: New Behaviours in Unclear Contexts

Elements of the 'classic' Upper Palaeolithic, notably shell ornaments and blade technology, had appeared in the Near East by ~50,000 BP and Africa much earlier (Kuhn 2003). In this time period prismatic blade technology—a hallmark of the Upper Palaeolithic—occurs alongside Middle Palaeolithic Levallois technology at sites such as Bocher Tachtit and El Wad (Israel) and Ksar Akil (Lebanon). It is unclear, however, whether IUP populations of the Near East formed the appropriate area of origin for the presumed dispersal of *Homo sapiens* into Europe: the IUP appears relatively early at other locations at the gates of Europe such as around the Black Sea (Bar-Yosef 2000; Kozlowski 1998) and a simple northwards and westwards dispersal along the Mediterranean and Danube corridors (e.g. Mellars 1992; 2006) may not have been the only entry route into the continent. That said, early examples of technologically mixed assemblages with Levallois and prismatic blade elements have been identified at Temnata and Bacho Kiro caves in Bulgaria (Kozlowski 2000), and in the Bohunician of the Czech Republic (Svoboda 2003), and although fossil associations are lacking for these it seems sensible to assume that they represent early dispersals of Modern Human hunter-gatherers into Europe via the Balkans. Formally speaking, the Bohunician— assemblages similar to which have been found in Russia—appears to be the earliest Upper Palaeolithic technocomplex in Europe, probably relating to the sustained warm interglacial of GI12 with radiocarbon dates ~41,000 BP (Hoffecker 2011; Svoboda 2003). Assemblages of this period are generally small and poorly understood, such as those of cultural layers 1 and 2 at Willendorf, Austria (Haesaerts and Teyssandier 2003), but nevertheless demonstrate that new technologies—and probably new populations—were established as far as Iberia and southern France and central Europe as far north as southern Germany by ~38,000 BP. At Geissenklösterle cave in the Swabian Alb carinated and nosed endscrapers and burins were produced on blades from unidirectional cores, and mammoth ivory working was established; activity was organized around a hearth, and a diverse number of perforated fox canine, mammoth ivory, and fish vertebrae beads attest to the use of systems of personal ornamentation (Bolus 2003).

The Upper Palaeolithic chronocultural sequence established in western Europe from the mid-nineteenth century onwards is insufficient to explain the complex patterning of IUP Europe between ~45–35,000 BP (Kozlowski and Otte 2000). Several regional technocomplexes are visible, some of which are broadly contemporary, reflecting considerable variation on technological themes including examples of Upper Palaeolithic lithic technology and organic objects in the context of a Middle Palaeolithic substrate. These have often been referred to by the misleading title 'transitional assemblages', implying that they are technologically transitional between the Middle and Upper Palaeolithic, but not meaning to imply that they represent continuity between the two. Several of these are generally thought to have been made by late Neanderthals on the basis of their Middle Palaeolithic technology and despite an almost total lack of convincing fossil associations, although this is debatable (cf. Benazzi et al. 2011): the Eastern Szeletian of the Crimea and northern Caucasus is a mix of bifacial and discoidal technologies with few blades (Chabai 2003); on the Northern European Plain Lincombian-Ranisian-Jerzmanowician (LRJ) assemblages are dominated by leaf-shaped points; the Châtelperronian of southern France and the northern and western Iberian littoral are dominated by curved-backed points/knives and much debate has revolved around the presence of items of worked bone and personal ornamentation in the rich site of the Grotte du Renne at Arcy-sur-Cure, France, although considerable debate exists as to the integrity of the site (Caron et al. 2011; cf. Higham et al. 2010); the Uluzzian of Italy is dominated by crescent-backed pieces; and the Szeletian of Hungary, Slovakia, and Moravia is dominated by leaf-points (Djindjian et al. 2003).

These technocomplexes aside—and it may turn out that some of these were actually of *Homo sapiens* creation—IUP technocomplexes such as the Bachokirian, Bohunician, and Protoaurignacian probably represent small-scale dispersals of *Homo sapiens* during the relatively warm interstadials such as GI9 and 10, although it is difficult to demonstrate this exactly due to the imprecision of radiocarbon dating in the period (Higham 2011). Considerable assemblage variability is recognizable in the eastern European IUP (Chabai 2003; Hoffecker 2011; Sinitsyn 2003). Fossil associations reveal that the Spitsynskayan and Gorodzovskayan, known in particular from the Kostenki localities on the Don, were associated with *Homo sapiens* in the region from at least ~36,000 BP, and it is noticeable that in addition to blade and bladelet technology these include rich inventories of organic tools, personal ornamentation, and, in the latter case, burial, and these are clearly intrusive to the region with no connection to preceding assemblages of Neanderthal manufacture (Chabai 2003; Hoffecker 2011; Sinitsyn 2003).

The Protoaurignacian is fairly well represented in Mediterranean Europe from Iberia to Italy and in the Balkans (Kozlowski and Otte 2000; Onoratini 2004), a distribution that some have seen as representing an initial east–west dispersal of *Homo sapiens* in Europe (Mellars 2006). Like Spitsynian assemblages of the Kostenki-Borshchevo sites it has been found stratified underneath the Campanian Ignimbrite tephra at several sites including Castelcivita cave in southern Italy, indicating that it was established in the region prior to the age of the eruption ~37,000 BP (Fedele et al. 2008; Hoffecker 2011: the age of the eruption has been established at ~40,000 (cal) BP by Ar-Ar and other dating methods. Radiocarbon measurements for the tephra are relatively inaccurate and the measurement of ~37,000 (uncal) BP is relatively imprecise). It is poorly understood, and one should not assume that it was evenly distributed in the region; it probably represents small-scale, targeted dispersals to resource-rich areas. Neither does it follow that wherever it appeared it developed into the Classic Aurignacian; in south-east France, for example, the latter is virtually absent (Floss 2003).

IUP lithic assemblages saw the introduction of prismatic blade technology and the production of endscrapers and burins on blades. In addition to this, the production of bladelets from carefully controlled cores and their retouch into regionally distinct typological forms such as Dufour and Font Yves bladelets of southern France is a noticeable element in western Europe (Mellars 2006). Early blade industries at several sites in the Kostenki-Borschchevo area on the Don River, Russia, are at present difficult to define, although suggest that diversity had already been established (Valoch 2007a). Personal ornamentation in the form of perforated marine shells of restricted taxa have been found in the Bachokirian and Protoaurignacian, e.g. at Fumane and Riparo Mochi in Italy and La Lalouza in France, all in the Mediterranean (Kuhn and Stiner 1998; Taborin 1993).

The Early Upper Palaeolithic (EUP) ~35/32–29,000 bp: Growing Behavioural Complexity

Various endscrapers on blades, particularly carinated and nosed forms, and burins are defining characteristics of the Protoaurignacian. After ~35,000 BP, alongside retouched bladelets and a number of tool forms of antler, bone, and ivory, including armatures (*sagaies*), points, awls, personal ornamentation, and items bearing enigmatic engravings, they become characteristic of the Classic Aurignacian or *Aurignacien Evolué*. From this time, at least in mid-latitude Europe, sites are more numerous, tend to be larger, and contain wider varieties of artefacts, including art. The Classic Aurignacian is strongly associated with the first evidence for the dispersal of *Homo sapiens* into northern Europe (Zilhão and d'Errico 2003); after ~32,000 BP assemblages are found in northern France, Belgium, and, in very small numbers, Britain (Jacobi and Pettitt 2000), and their number increases suggesting a denser population (Van Andel et al. 2003). It appears around this time at Willendorf, Austria, one of the best dated sequences of the period (Haesaerts and Teyssandier 2003).

Attempts to isolate a particular geographical region where the Aurignacian originated are unconvincing, at least due to the imprecision of dating methods (Verpoorte 2005), although the Bachokirian of Bulgaria certainly approaches Aurignacian typological forms (Kozlowski and Otte 2000). In south-west Germany, the Classic Aurignacian dates to ~35,000 BP (Terberger and Street 2003), although claims have been made—unconvincingly—for an earlier appearance (and perhaps origin) in the region (e.g. Conard et al. 2003; cf. Zilhão and d'Errico 2003). From this time it is also present in northern Spain and south-west France (Zilhão and d'Errico 1999), which either indicates a rapid dispersal (perhaps from east to west) or a multi-regional origin out of the preceding Protoaurignacian. In some areas the Aurignacian apparently did not appear or was remarkably rare, as in south-east France (Combier 1990).

In Russia, a sequence of IUP industries is recognizable from the Streletskayan and Spitsynskayan ~36,000 BP; the Gorodzovskayan from ~32,000 BP, and the Aurignacian from ~29,000 BP, the latter presumably reflecting a late eastwards dispersal of the technocomplex. Remains of *Homo sapiens* have been found with the Spitsynskayan,

Gorodzovskayan, and Aurignacian of Russia and Ukraine (Chabai 2003). Although there are broad similarities between the Aurignacian of eastern Europe and that further west—the presence of Mladeč-type points, Dufour bladelets, and carinated endscrapers for example—differences are noticeable and presumably reflect separate dispersal events (Hoffecker 2011). Well-made and highly-standardized bifacially-thinned triangular artefacts are characteristic of the Streletskayan in an otherwise Middle Palaeolithic technology, which may suggest local innovation (Bradley et al. 1995). The Gorodzovskayan includes blade technology, a rich variety of bone and mammoth ivory tools (some of which bear engraved decoration), personal ornamentation, and two burials at Kostenki 14 and 15 (Chabai 2003). At Kostenki the Aurignacian seems to replace this, with contrasting lithic assemblages dominated by Dufour bladelets; it seems to have appeared earlier in Crimea, however (Chabai 2003).

A particular feature of the EUP are variously retouched bladelets which vary chronologically, e.g. those of Paglicci, Italy (Palma di Cesnola 2006). Some forms indentified as 'burins'—for which one might expect function as chisel edge or as a core—clearly functioned as weapon tips; birch pitch has been identified on carinated 'burins' from Les Vachons, France, for example (Dinnis et al. 2009). As with lithic armatures, chronological patterning is evident in *sagaies*, with massive-based forms appearing early and split-based forms a little later (Bolus and Conard 2006). The elaboration of organic and lithic weapon tips allowed from this period a degree of complementarity: while lithic tips are more lethal, they are prone to breaking; by contrast, while antler points are less likely to kill immediately, they are far less likely to break. Decisions were clearly being made about whether weapons should be reliable (in situations when they could not be repaired immediately) or lethal (where replacement tips could be applied: Knecht 1997). Further organization of raw-material economies is indicated by raw-materials transfers of over 160 km in western Europe and 300 km in central Europe (Féblot-Augustins 1997).

At face value EUP archaeology does not suggest that behaviour was 'fully modern': unambiguous evidence of dwelling structures, burials, and cave art is totally lacking, and it is debatable whether hunting strategies were more similar to those of the preceding Middle Palaeolithic than to the succeeding Mid Upper Palaeolithic. A number of sites such as the Abri Pataud, France, reveal that activities were organized around hearths (Movius 1966), and at Klissoura, Greece, these were lined with fired clay ~32,000 BP, which suggests a degree of planning in the organization of space (Pawlikowski et al. 2000).

Some faunal assemblages are dominated by single species, although many are more mixed, suggestive of opportunistic hunting strategies like their Neanderthal predecessors (Grayson and Delpech 2002). Reindeer were clearly an important resource in south-west France (Bordes 2003), and in the Swabian Jura reindeer and horse were hunted and mammoth were procured in low numbers, although whether this was through hunting or scavenging is unclear (Niven 2003). In eastern Europe kill and butchery sites are better represented and attest the dominance of these three taxa (Hoffecker 2011). In addition to these, small animals such as birds, tortoises, hares, and in coastal areas shellfish, were important dietary elements, indicating a growth in dietary breadth (Stiner et al. 1999).

Although elements of personal ornamentation are present in the IUP, their number increases significantly in the EUP, suggesting that exchange networks were widespread and integral to Aurignacian settlement strategies. Of a wide range of choices specific shell taxa were selected for suspension, and these varied geographically, suggesting that ethnolingustic diversity had already emerged by ~32,000 BP (Vanhaeren and d'Errico 2006). The production of personal ornamentation was highly organized; rock shelters in the Castelmerle Valley, Dordogne, reveal the production of beads of mammoth ivory, pendants of shells imported from the Atlantic over 200 km to the west, and copies of those shells on mammoth ivory probably obtained from over 200 km to the north-east (White 1989).

From ~33,000 BP portable and rock art appears in several Aurignacian regions. Several caves of the Ach Valley in the Swabian Alb have produced examples of carving in mammoth ivory, small objects representing carnivores, herbivores, including mammoths, water birds, and examples of 'lion men', with human(oid) bodies and lions' heads (Conard 2003; Conard and Floss 2001; Hahn 1993). One, on the tip of a mammoth tusk from Hohlenstein Stadel, displays a subtle mixing of lion and human traits: the shape of its upper arms, for example, resembles the rear legs of a lion (Schmid et al. 1989). Clearly, a sophisticated mythology and symbolism had emerged by this time. The first unambiguous human representations are also found in the region; these take the form of a small ivory bas-relief carving of a human figure in frontal perspective from the Geissenklösterle cave (Hahn 1982) and a two-dimensional outline figure of a similarly frontal perspective, human sculpted from schist from the Galgenberg Hill at Stratzing, Austria (Hahn 1993). The recent discovery of a three-dimensional sculpture of a female 'venus' from the lower Aurignacian of Hohle Fels Cave suggests that this tradition originated in the Classic Aurignacian, despite its floruit in the Mid Upper Palaeolithic (Conard 2009). Some objects engraved with grouped lines, dots, and crescents may be artificial memory systems, such as a bone plaque from the Abri Blanchard in the Castlemerle Valley, which has been seen by some as a lunar calendar (Marshack 1972), a view which has been questioned by others (d'Errico et al. 2003). The Geissenklösterle cave also yielded three flutes, including one of mammoth ivory and another on the radius of a swan (Conard et al. 2004; Hahn and Münzel 1995). Some 20 are known for the Upper Palaeolithic in general, and equally early examples are known from Isturitz in the French Pyrenees which, despite the name, appear to have been reed- or trumpet-sounded and far more sophisticated technically than simple 'penny whistles' (d'Errico et al. 2003).

Rock art appeared in the Aurignacian, and, with the possible exception of the spectacular deep cave paintings of the Grotte Chauvet, Ardeche (Clottes 2003), takes the form of technically simple outline paintings and engravings on the walls and ceilings of rock shelters as well as large stone blocks scattered around these occupation sites. Establishing the age of the Chauvet art—which contains several scenes of herbivores and carnivores depicted with concern for perspective and with considerable attention to detail, is critical; if it truly is of Aurignacian age then deep cave art emerged suddenly in this period fully developed technically. Some, however, believe it is LUP in age, and that an Aurignacian attribution has not been demonstrated (Pettitt et al. 2009). The rock art of unambiguous Aurignacian age includes engravings of herbivores and 'vulvae' (female pubic triangles) in a group of rock shelters in and off the Vézère Valley, Dordogne, and simple paintings on several rock fragments from the Fumane cave, north-east Italy (Broglio et al. 2006; Delluc and Delluc 1991). It may be no coincidence that the latter includes simple human figures in frontal perspective. It must be said that art in general is relatively rare in EUP contexts and was perhaps not fully developed across the entire European range of *Homo sapiens*.

The Mid Upper Palaeolithic (MUP): Subarctic Adaptations and Regional Variations on Wider Themes

The Aurignacian had come to an end everywhere by ~28,000 BP. From this time climate was deteriorating towards the severe conditions of the Last Glacial Maximum. It is testimony to the adaptive strengths of Mid Upper Palaeolithic hunter-gatherers that they were able to adapt to such conditions *in situ*, probably the first example of humans staying put in conditions which were effectively subarctic in mid-latitude Europe (Robroeks et al. 2000). What emerged was several regional variants on a Europe-wide technocomplex for which the general term 'Gravettian' derives from a relatively peripheral western expression of the group (Rigaud 2000). The origins of the Gravettian *sensu lato* are obscure, and possibly occurred in the late Aurignacian of western Europe or the backed assemblages of EUP eastern Europe.

MUP lithic assemblages were blade-based and dominated by tanged and shouldered points, the latter especially characteristic of the east. In the west, backed blades (Gravette Points) and small microgravettes additionally functioned as projectiles, although it is unclear whether they belonged to arrows or javelins (Cattelain 1997; Soriano 1998). Considerable change in lithic inventories is observable in the French Gravettian (Périgordian) and to a lesser extent the Italian, and it has been possible to determine chronological phases on the basis of dominant points (Gravette and Font Robert), burins, and truncated pieces (David 1985; Mussi 2001; Roebroeks et al. 2000 and references therein), and broader phases are recognizable on the basis of lithic points in the eastern Balkans and more widely in eastern Europe (Otte 1985; Tsonev 1997). Such changes probably represent population movements and demographic ruptures, for example with the intrusion of the 'Noaillian' into the south-west French Gravettian ~27,000 BP and the wholesale relocation of the Pavlovian to the Russian Plain ~25,000 BP (David 1985; Soffer 1985). On a continental scale, movements are reflected in the overall distribution of radiocarbon-dated sites (Pettitt 2000).

Raw-material transfers reveal relatively restricted mobility, as is not surprising for such cold conditions, although distances of up to 160 km have been noted, e.g. in Switzerland and southern Germany (Féblot-Augustins 1997; Scheer 1993). Conical sectioned *sagaies* are common throughout the Gravettian (Kozlowski 1986) and the alternation between the dominance of lithic and organic armatures defines part of the chronological patterning observed in the period (Pike-Tay and Bricker 1993). In the organic realm, bone and ivory spatulae, polishers, chisels, and perforated *bâtons* of reindeer antler are common in central and eastern Europe, and amber seems to have gained importance as an exchangeable material (Kozlowski 1986; Soffer 1985).

As with the EUP, MUP settlement comprised core areas in mid latitudes where mammalian resources were most diverse, from Iberia in the west to south-west Siberia in the east (Guthrie and van Kolfschoten 2000; Pavlov and Indrelid 2000), and more temporary occupation of the peripheries to the north, such as Belgium and Britain (Jacobi et al. 2010; Roebroeks 2000). In the centres, notably the Pavlovian/Willendorfian of Moravia/Austria/Slovakia and the Kostenki/Avdeevo of Ukraine/Russia, settlement was remarkably long-term (Valoch 2007a). Similarities are found between the cores and areas to the south, such as the Balkans, which probably represent population movements into southern refugia (Kozlowski 2005).

MUP sites vary in size from small hunting camps to large semi-sedentary settlements and, where present, caves were still utilized. In contrast to the EUP, dwelling structures are known across Europe, and take the form of simple-footed tents with post holes, more elaborately constructed tents with stone weights, and in central and eastern Europe semi-subterranean forms often using elaborate mammoth-bone architecture (Kozlowski 1986). A degree of regionalization is observable in the form of small structures (Otte 1981). Storage pits are a common characteristic on MUP sites of the Russian Plain, and clearly formed critical elements of a semi-sedentary settlement system. It remains unclear, however, whether this was practised routinely further west (Soffer 1989).

Mammoth, reindeer, horse, wolf, hare, and fox were important resources for food and raw materials in the Pavlovian (Kozlowski 1986; Nývltová-Fišáková 2000), and woolly rhino and bison supplemented these more widely (Guthrie and van Kolfschoten 2000); bison, reindeer, and horse were important resources on the Russian steppe (Borziyak 1993; Leonova 1994). At Kraków Spadzista Street, Poland, at least 86 individual mammoths are represented. Bones from several mammoths formed superstructures of dwelling structures at the site (Wojtal and Sobczyk 2005). A rise in the use of smaller, trapped animals is evident also; stable isotope analysis of human bones from Mid Upper Palaeolithic contexts from the United Kingdom to Sungir' indicate that up to 50 per cent of dietary protein was obtained from river fish (Richards et al. 2001).

In Moravia/Slovakia/Austria the rich Pavlovian/Willendorfian technocomplex ~28–25,000 BP represents an early expression of semi-sedentary settlement on large river-bank camps with considerable investment of effort into architecture and a rich material culture. At major sites such as Dolní Věstonice, Pavlov, and Milovice on the Dyje River, Moravia, camps were occupied for many months at a time, heavy winter structures were reused, pits and post holes are indicative of below- and above-ground storage, and tool-kits utilized exotic flints, bone, and ivory (Oliva 2005; Svoboda et al. 2000). Fired fragments of loess from these sites preserve traces of textiles, matting, and basketry, produced with various methods that indicate that textile production had already arrived at a high level of sophistication (Soffer et al. 2000), even if the specific nature of matting, netting, and clothing is debatable (Valoch 2007b).

An equally rich technocomplex developed ~25,000 BP on the Dnestr, Dnepr, and Don rivers in Ukraine and Russia, termed the Kostenki-Avdeevo group (Grigor'ev 1993; Hoffecker 2002), is in many respects similar to the Pavlovian/Willendorfian, and probably derived from it given that at this time Moravia seems to have been deserted (Svoboda et al. 1996). At Kostenki I, semi-subterranean dwelling structures were excavated in a large oval shape around a line of nine centrally located open-air hearths, the whole site riddled with storage pits and smaller stake holes presumably indicative of drying racks and above-ground storage (Grigor'ev 1993). The dwellings seem to have been roofed with mammoth tusk and possessed several chambers and associated storage pits. As with the Pavlovian/Willendorfian, bone, antler, and ivory objects are abundant, and include beads, pendants, spatulae, points, and female humanoid 'venuses', the latter often being recovered from pits (Grigor'ev 1993; Gvozdover 1995).

Compared to the EUP, the MUP saw a veritable explosion of portable and rock art, probably because it played an important role in the survival strategies of the severe conditions of the period (Gamble 1982). Sculpture in the round on soft stones, bone, and ivory is found across the region; engraved decoration was used to cover many organic implements, and in western Europe art appears on the walls of deep caves. An artistic focus on the human body is noticeable in the wide distribution of human female figurines across Europe and hand stencils in French and Spanish cave art. Most noticeable are the 'venus figurines', small, three-dimensional carvings of female humanoids on mammoth ivory and soft stone which typically emphasize breasts, hips, bellies, and buttocks at the expense of detail on the heads and limbs. These are found widely across mid-latitude Europe from France to Russia; they share general traits, although they vary regionally in form, suggesting that regional groups placed their own interpretation on whatever wider cosmological theme they reflect (Delporte 1993a; Gamble 1982; Iakovleva 2005; Leroi-Gourhan 1968; Mussi et al. 2000; Svoboda 2008). Where context is known, they are often tucked away in caves in western Europe and deposited in pits in central and eastern Europe, one of a number of similarities they share with burials of the period, with which they may be cosmologically linked (Pettitt 2006). These often bear details of clothing, including headdresses, personal ornamentation, and banded items that may be ritual in nature (Soffer et al. 2000). Many are broken, particularly in the Pavlovian, which may relate to ritual use, although others, such as the 'Black Venus' of Dolní Věstonice, are highly worn, suggesting long use-lives. This latter 'venus' is made of fired loess, human and animal figurines of which are common in the Pavlovian/Willendorfian and represent the earliest known ceramic technology (Vandiver et al. 1989). Thermal fracturing is evident on such figurines found in the 'Wizard's Hut', a lean-to dwelling structure on the periphery of the Dolní Věstonice I settlement. This was caused by firing in a simple kiln when wet, or by immersion in water when still hot, probably for ritual purposes.

Unless some of the Grotte Chauvet art is genuinely EUP, it seems that art in deep caves appeared in the MUP. Highly naturalistic outline paintings and engravings of herbivores, such as those in 'silhouette' style in the Grotte Mayenne-Sciences in northern France and in the Grotte Cosquer near Marseilles, and complex paintings such as the panel of 'dappled horses' at Pech Merle, Lot, demonstrate considerable observational skills and technical execution (Clottes and Courtin 1996; Lorblanchet 1995; Picard 1997; Pigeaud 2002). A concern with the interplay between light, shadow, the topography of the cave surfaces, and the art itself is a common trait from the MUP onwards (Groenen 1997). Negative hand stencils and positive prints are known from several dozen caves, usually in small number, although >200 are known from Gargas in the French Pyrenees and Maltraveso, Spain (Ripoll López et al. 1999; Sahly 1966). The attenuation of fingers on a number of these suggests that they formed part of an elaborate symbolic system, and in Les Garennes cave, Charente, human remains were apparently placed underneath a hand stencil (Henry-Gambier et al. 2007), surely suggestive of wider significance.

Over 50 burials are known from MUP in central and eastern Europe, many of which derive from sites where the practice was relatively common (Pettitt 2011; Zilhão and Trinkaus 2002). These are absent in France, where remains were tucked away in caves such as at least five in Cussac cave, Dordogne (Aujoulat et al. 2001). At least two of these were emplaced in bear hibernation 'wallows', and may indicate the beginnings of hunter-gatherers' long-term cosmological association with bears, for which evidence is more common in the LUP (Germonpré and Hämäläinen 2007). The burials are usually young males, although females occur in association with other males in double and two triple burials from Barma Grande,

Liguria, and Dolní Věstonice. Burials were emplaced in shallow graves, and are usually associated with ochre, remains of herbivores, and often elaborate personal ornamentation and other items of mammoth ivory. The spectacular burials from Sungir', Russia at ~28,000 BP are usually considered to be part of the corpus of MUP burials, although culturally they belong to the latest phase of the EUP Streletskayan (Anikovich 2005). Given the bias towards males, the odd circumstances of the double and triple burials, and high levels of pathologies noted on the dead, one should, perhaps, view these as ritual containments rather than burials in the modern sense (Pettitt 2011).

The Late Upper Palaeolithic (LUP): Emergence of the 'Modern' Hunter-Gatherer Adaptation

The effects of the LGM on later Mid Upper Palaeolithic groups was profound: the Gravettian had disappeared from east to west by 20,000 BP and where groups persisted in mid-latitude and southern refugia such as Iberia and south-west France, the Carpathian Basin, the Italian and Balkan peninsulas, and the Russian Plain, raw-material transfers emphasize local sources (Soffer and Gamble 1990; Svoboda and Novák 2004). A degree of similarity is observable between mid-latitude assemblages such as the Hungarian Sagvarian, the Austrian Grubgrabian, and the Badegoulian of central Germany to southern France (Svoboda and Novák 2004; Terberger and Street 2003), whereas the Epigravettian persisted further to the south, notably around the Adriatic, e.g. Italy, Slovenia, Croatia, and Greece, as well as further to the east from Romania to the Don and Dnestr rivers. One particularly regional development is the Solutrean of Iberia and southern France. It may be divided into early (~21–20,000 BP) and late (~20–19,000 BP) stages, the former restricted to an area of presumed origin from eastern Spain to south-east France, the latter extended across much of the Iberian Peninsula and to the Paris Basin in the north (Djindjian et al. 1999). Even in such a relatively short period, the cultural stratigraphy of the Solutrean is complicated, and may reflect origins of the early Solutrean in the Gravettian assemblages of mid-latitude Europe and origins of the later Solutrean ultimately through contact between North Africa and Iberia (Otte and Noiret 2002).

Lithic technology reached its apogee during the Solutrean, with bifacially worked leaf-points and shouldered points appearing and evidence of the use of heat treatment to improve the flaking qualities of flint. In the Ambrosio cave, Spain, for example, small hearths ancillary to main hearths were used to bake flint prior to knapping (Ripoll López and Muñoz Ibánez 2002). Raw-material movements suggest relatively local land use as with the MUP, such as at the reference site for the Solutrean, Laugerie-Haute, Dordogne (Demars 1995). Further development occurred in the organic realm: eyed needles appeared, and the spear-thrower (propulseur, Atl-Atl) is clearly represented by plain crook ends carved from antler (Cattelain 1987; 1997). Portable art is relatively rare during the LGM, although cave and rock-shelter art is known in Spain and France. A degree of continuity with the MUP is noticeable, with similar outline animals (Combier et al. 1959), also the large sculpted rock-shelter wall of the Roc de Sers, Charente, which was clearly planned as a 13 metre-long diorama of horse, ibex, and humans reveals that low- and high-relief sculpture was now an important artistic form (Tymula 2002).

The regional technocomplexes of the LGM were probably relatively brief, and may be seen as punctuated phenomena similar to the lithic phases that subdivide MUP and subsequent LUP technocomplexes, although they do appear to have been relatively distinctive and presumably evidence of population movements. Following the LGM the European LUP can be broadly divided into three broad geographical areas: the Epigravettian of Mediterranean regions from Iberia through Italy and the Balkans to Anatolia; the Magdalenian and associated peripheral groups of mid-latitude western and central Europe; and the Mezinian and associated groups in eastern Europe (Kozlowski 2005; Mussi 2001; Pidoplichko 1998; Sacchi 2003). The Epigravettian persisted east of the Carpathians in several regional variants centred on the major Ukrainian and Russian rivers, notably the Molodovan (Prut and Dnestr), Zamiatnine (Don), and Pushkarian (Desna), which employed tools similar to those of the preceding Eastern Gravettian (Hoffecker 2002). Eyed needles are common on most sites of the period (e.g. Mezin, Mezhirich) and fur-bearers were trapped.

Dwelling structures employing large numbers of mammoth bones increase in number, with some sites such as Dobranichevka and Yudonovo yielding several examples (Pidoplichko 1998). These are variable in size, and seem to reflect lighter summer structures and heavier-duty winter dwellings, and the tradition persisted until at least ~15,000 BP. Analysis of the stratification of pit fills suggests that these sites were repeatedly revisited and used for several months at a time, and pits were reused for storage and, later, refuse disposal (Soffer et al. 1997).

After the LGM the archaeological record is more abundant, more widespread, and contains some of the most spectacular archaeology of the period. Over several thousand years human groups recovered from the LGM, increased in number, intensified their relationship with critical resources, and re-expanded out of their southern refugia, recolonizing the Northern European Plain. In France, the Solutrean was replaced by the Badegoulian, possibly an intrusion from the east. Small, square-planned tents are implied by the distribution of stones used for paving in the Badegoulian level of Plateau Parrain in northern France (Gaussen 1980). The Magdalenian spanned the period ~17–11,000 BP and was at its height distributed from Iberia and France through Italy, Switzerland, Czech Republic, Belgium, The Netherlands to Poland, with late, related groups sporadically appearing in the United Kingdom (papers in Rigaud 1989; Sacchi 2003). Blade technology reached its apogee during the period, and although lithic inventories are relatively homogeneous—dominated by endscrapers and burins—organic armatures underwent considerable evolution. Raw-material movements of 700 km have been recorded, e.g. between Germany and Poland (Féblot-Augustins 1997). A broad range of herbivores continued to be exploited, although reindeer and horse were particularly valued across mid-latitude Europe, red deer in Iberia, and ibex and chamois in montane areas. Horses could be exploited in specialized ways, e.g. in the Late Magdalenian of the Paris Basin, or unspecialized, e.g. Germany (Gaudzinski and Street 2003; Turner 2003). In the Magdalenian levels of Solutré, Burgundy, horses were intercepted against a cliff face, and high numbers of bison and reindeer supplemented them (Turner 2002). By ~14,000 BP the wolf had been domesticated across Europe, possibly through symbiotic use in hunting and for traction (Sacchi 2003).

The Magdalenian probably originated in the Badegoulian of Iberia and south-west France, spreading from there as the climate ameliorated (Djindjian et al. 1999). Sites are remarkably variable in size and reflect small hunting stands <100 m² up to semi-sedentary camps >750 m², although most were focused on fords where reindeer could be intercepted, such as in the Périgord (White 1987). A number of caves and rock shelters were the focus of seasonal aggregations—such as La Madeleine and Laugerie-Haute, Dordogne, and art tends to be abundant in such sites, from the deep caves like Altamira, sculpted rock-shelter walls such as L'Angles-sur-L'Anglin, and rich inventories of portable art. Such sites have provided long sequences which have been linked to provide reliable cultural sequences for the period. As a result the Magdalenian may be divided into Early (~17–15,000 BP), Middle (~15,000–13,500 BP), and Late (~13,500–12,000 BP) phases, within which one can recognize distinct cultural traits in all archaeological materials. In the organic realm *sagaies* vary in form and were often engraved with non-figurative signs, and hafting sleeves (*navettes*) are but one example of a chronologically restricted form, in this case of the Middle Magdalenian. Uniserial and biserial barbed harpoons appeared during the Middle and Late Magdalenian respectively. Dwelling structures are well known from the period, and by the Late Magdalenian remarkably uniform trapeziform tents are known from the Paris Basin and Germany, suggesting uniform templates for these mobile structures (Jöris and Terberger 2001).

Single inhumations continued, and are often richly adorned, such as the infant from La Madeleine (Vanhaeren and d'Errico 2001). These are rare, however, and as with those of the MUP probably should not be considered 'normal'. A concern with defleshing and fragmentation of the body, including the production of skull cups is noticeable (Pettitt 2011 and references therein). The greater majority of decorated caves belong to the Magdalenian. Approaching 400 sites with parietal art are known, mostly in France and Spain but with several in the United Kingdom, Germany, Italy, Sicily, and the Urals (Bahn and Vertut 1997; Bicho et al. 2007; Clottes 2001). These are mainly caves, although in Iberia include several areas of open-air art, such as Portugal's Côa Valley (Baptista and Fernandes 2007), which display similar concerns with context and space as seen in the deep caves (Balbín Behrmann and Alcolea Gonzalez 1999). Aggregation sites such as Altamira attracted much artistic activity, probably embedded in the attachment rituals that groups performed during these meetings (Conkey 1980; Gamble 1999).

Cave art often displays considerable attention to placement, light/shadow, preparation of the surface, planning, volume, detail, perspective, and movement (Azéma 2009; Vialou 2001). In well-studied systems such as the Volp caves in Ariège (Trois Frères, Enlene, and le Tuc d'Audoubert) the art clearly formed part of wider use of the caves, of which the creation of space and deposition of portable art was also important (Bégouën and Clottes 1991). In the La Garma cave, Cantabria, remarkable preservation of Middle Magdalenian archaeology on the cave's floor has revealed small enclosures of stone and stalagmite blocks associated with parietal art (Arias 1999; Ontañón 2003).

Magdalenian figurative art is overwhelmingly dominated by the depiction of herbivores, typically cervids, equids, and bovids, either singularly or in groups, although without any landscape context. Over 100 human depictions are known from French and Spanish caves (Corchón Rodríguez 1998; Delluc and Delluc 2009). In France, males always occur singularly, yet were placed in central positions. Human figurines are almost always part-animal, such as the antlered 'sorcerors' (e.g. Gabbillou) and javelined 'wounded men' (e.g. Cougnac) and 'killed men' (e.g. Cosquer) of southern France (Rousseau 1996). The first true portraits are engraved on stone plaquettes from La Marche, France (Pales and Tassin de Saint-Péreuse 1976). Non-figurative 'signs' occur from the Early Magdalenian onwards; these take various forms, such as lines of dots, tectiforms (hut shapes), and claviforms (club shapes), and may occur in isolation or in association with figurative art, in which case they may be communicating information about the depicted animal. A great degree of graphic mutability between depictions of animals, humans, and signs, and an overall tendency towards stylization of the animal and human form is evident (Lorblanchet 1989). Leroi-Gourhan (1968) grouped Upper Palaeolithic art into four great 'styles', the third of which corresponds to the Solutrean/Early Magdalenian and in which style and colour were perfected, and the fourth to the Middle and Late Magdalenian and in which true naturalism and perspective appeared. Chauvet, if Magdalenian, would be an exemplar of this, although it is conceivable that it is EUP in age, as discussed above. Non-figurative signs certainly became more common and formalized during the Middle and Late Magdalenian (Conkey 1985).

The art of Lascaux, one of the most spectacular decorated 'sanctuaries', dates to ~18,000 BP and is culturally either Solutrean, Badegoulian, or Early Magdalenian (Aujoulat 2005). Over 2,000 paintings and engravings have been recognized in the relatively small cave, and the painted scenes in its major chambers such as the Hall of the Bulls and Lateral Passage display a sophisticated understanding of the pelage of aurochs, deer, and horse, and seem to represent a rutting calendar among other themes. The Middle Magdalenian may be regarded as its classic expression, however, and many iconic examples of western European art belong to this phase (which actually includes the Cantabrian Lower Magdalenian). The spectacular bison, does, horses, and signs painted on the ceiling of the Polychrome Chamber at Altamira—actually only a small percentage of over 2,000 paintings and engravings in the cave—date to ~15–16,000 BP and were probably created by the same talented artist (Beltran 1999; Bernaldo de Quiros 1991). Portable art reached a floruit in the period, especially in the circum-Pyrenean region, and includes iconic categories such as stone plaquettes engraved and painted with animal outlines (Sieveking 1987), circular bone *rondelles* bearing engraved animals, which were probably attached to clothing, *baguettes demi ronde—sagaies* formed by two half-circular sectioned rods of reindeer antler—which bear deeply incised curvilinear decoration (Sacchi 2003), engraved doe heads on bones and cave walls, sculpted antler propulseur crooks including the 'faun and bird' theme, and bone *contours découpé*—outlines of horse, deer, chamois, and ibex heads cut from bone, often hyoids. *Bâtons percés* of reindeer antler, pierced with a wide hole at the palmar point of the antler, although appearing in the EUP, became numerous across Europe in the LUP, and often bear engraved figurative decoration. The use of these enigmatic items remains unclear; early interpretations invoked a ritual function (thus the term *bâtons du commandement*), although modern perspectives invoke physical functions from line-plays for fishing, strap-fasteners for tents or sleighs, and as props for textile production (Averbouh 2010; Rigaud 2001). From this time bone and antler objects came to bear complex codes of information in the form of complex groupings of incised lines (d'Errico et al. 2003). The wider acculturation of the landscape is evident in contrasts between Middle Magdalenian sites: rich sets of engraved bone and antler items were recovered from La Vache cave (Ariège), in which parietal art was rare; by contrast, spectacular parietal paintings were left deep in Niaux cave across the Vicdessos valley, in which occupation does not seem to have been as intense (Delporte 1993b). By the Late Magdalenian a high degree of stylization is noticeable, with Gönnersdorf-style human females particularly widespread, both engraved onto stone plaques (e.g. at Gönnersdorf) and cave walls (in France and Spain) and carved out of ivory and bone (e.g. Andernach and Oelknitz, Germany) (Bosinski et al. 2001; Marshack 1991). In addition to these, a continuation of 'vulvae' from the EUP and the widespread depiction of animal heads and bodies lacking heads is evidence of a concern with the fragmentation of the body (Pettitt 2011).

In Mediterranean Europe from Italy to Greece, the Epigravettian represents a LUP persistence of Gravettian themes, and in southern France and Italy can be divided into early ~20–16,000 BP) and late (16–12,000 BP) phases (Djindjian et al. 1999). Backed blades and bladelets, the latter including 'microgravettes' and regionally distinct points including shouldered forms characterize the period. East of the Carpathians the situation becomes more complex, and Epigravettian assemblages give way to regional groups derived from the Eastern European Gravettian. In Ukraine, elaborate mammoth bone dwelling structures continue in the eastern equivalent of the Magdalenian, the Mezinian, which at Mezin itself dates to ~15,000 BP (Pidoplichko 1998), and to a regional variant, the Eliseevichian, on the Desna. Analysis of dwelling structures, pit distribution and reuse at Mezhirich, Ukraine, suggests a degree of year-round settlement (Soffer et al. 1997), which probably characterizes most major sites. Horse, reindeer, and bison were important hunted resources, and were clearly scheduled by season (Borziyak 1993). At Amvrosievka, Ukraine, for example, bison were hunted in spring and summer (Krotova and Belan 1993). Sites of these groups, like the earlier Kostenki-Avdeevo groups from which they derived, are rich in objects of bone, antler, and ivory, including points, spatulae, flat pendants and armlets, and unmodified bones engraved with meticulous and complex chevron and lozenge decoration. In the broad category of portable art one can include highly stylized figurines similar in principle to those of the Late Magdalenian (Klein 1973; Marshack 1991).

TERMINAL UPPER PALAEOLITHIC ADAPTATIONS

The last ~3,000 years of the Pleistocene saw unstable climatic conditions, alternating between a 2,000-year-long interstadial, separated into two halves (the Meiendorf and Allerød) by a short stadial (the Older Dryas), and a final 800-year-long stadial (the Younger Dryas). In many respects the amelioration represented by the Lateglacial Interstadial ~13–11,000 BP and establishment of boreal woodland over much of Europe in its latter half may be seen as a 'false start' to the Holocene warming and concomitant development of 'Mesolithic' hunter-gatherer adaptations. It is in this period that many of the characteristics of the LUP such as cave art and rich portable art disappear, replaced by lithic and organic inventories and art forms which now hark forward to the Mesolithic.

In Spain, Portugal, and southern France eastwards to the Upper Danube, the Late Magdalenian evolved into the Azilian after ~12,000 BP (Straus 1996). This was in most regions associated with red deer, roe deer, and boar, mixed woodland species that largely replaced reindeer and horse as the grasslands were broken up by boreal forest. Several multi-stratified sites document the evolution of the Azilian from the Late Magdalenian, such as La Madeleine itself. Burins and organic armatures such as *sagaies* decreased in number, replaced by a growing geometric microlithic element that foreshadowed the Mesolithic. The harpoons that survive took on more 'organic' shapes and often bear hatched and geometric decoration (Fernández-Tresguerres 1990). In Iberia, a pattern of broad-spectrum resource use established during the LUP intensified further, and estuarine and marine resources supplemented riverine (Fernández-Tresguerres 1990). Rich inventories of cave and portable art disappeared, although rare examples of engraved animal outlines on plaquettes and on cave walls do exist, usually filled with hatched lines. Non-figuratively engraved and painted pebbles are a characteristic of the Azilian, microscopic analyses of which indicate that they were often created at the same time, i.e. as an overall decorative scheme (d'Errico 1988; 1994).

In the Mediterranean region the Late Epigravettian persisted to the end of the Pleistocene (Kozlowski 2005) and in Italy blurred into the Early Mesolithic (Mussi 2001). Similar species to the Azilian were exploited, with the addition of ibex in northern Italy. Portable art is relatively well represented in Italy, with zoomorphic, anthropomorphic, and geometric themes clearly inherited from the preceding Magdalenian, and a late tradition of inhumations clearly reflects earlier MUP traditions but also includes the cave 'cemetery' of Arene Candide, Liguria, in which stones were used to mark graves and a degree of organization is apparent ~10,000 BP (Cardini 1980; Formicola et al. 2005). At Villabruna rock shelter in the Veneto a single inhumation was placed in a stone-lined grave. Stones covering it bore painted designs in ochre (Broglio 1995).

The recolonization of northern Europe had occurred by the Meindorf, in the form of Late Magdalenian groups who had re-established reindeer hunting in the Paris Basin, horse hunting in the Belgian Ardennes, and the hunting of both species in the Rhineland and Thuringian Basin by the early part of the interstadial (Housley et al. 1997). Several late Magdalenian sites on the banks of the Seine have been remarkably preserved due to seasonal overbank floods, and reveal activities around and away from hearths on kill/butchery sites such as Verberie and camp sites such as Pincevent (Leroi-Gourhan and Brézillon 1972). Spatial patterning at the latter indicates several tent structures (Bodu 2010; Enloe and Audouze 2010). The Paris Basin sites take the form of kill/butchery locations such as Verberie, or more general purpose camp sites such as Pincevent. Refitting lithics between the Swiss Late Magdalenian sites of Champréveyres and Monruz, both on the edge of Lake Neuchatel, show how groups relocated camps over short distances (Cattin 2010). Late Magdalenian groups recolonized Britain at the start of the Interstadial (Jacobi and Higham 2009), although in a variant form, the Creswellian, which is also found in the Netherlands and Belgium (Jacobi 1991). This is perhaps not surprising, as a degree of regionality is observable in northern Europe at this time, with the Polish Late Magdalenian, for example, forming a specific group (Połtowicz 2006).

Gradually, shouldered points entered Late Magdalenian assemblages in the north and by ~12,500 BP define the Hamburgian from Poland in the East to Belgium in the west and brief appearances in the United Kingdom and Denmark (Fischer 1991; Grimm and Weber 2008), and reindeer continued to be a major resource. Following this the curved-backed point tradition spread across western Europe during the Allerød. This seems to have originated in southern France during the first half of the Lateglacial Interstadial, first in association with reindeer, and spread northwards in the wake of the disappearance of this species as forests spread with new resources such as red deer and elk (Thévenin 1997). North of the Loire, Azilian points (*bipointes*) gave way to *monopointes/federmesser* (penknife points), which may be seen as weapon forms specifically adapted to the Northern European Plain (Schwabedissen 1954). At Le Closeau at Rueil-Malmaison in the Paris Basin, horse, red deer, and wild boar were exploited just before the Allerød (Bodu 1998). Following the Allerød the cold conditions of the Younger Dryas saw the return of open conditions and the establishment of the Ahrensburgian from the Belgian Ardennes to east of the Oder river and brief offshoots in the United Kingdom (Arts 1988; Brinch Petersen 2009). It is possible that the Ahrensburgian originated in the tanged-point Bromme (Brommian) of southern Scandinavia; the two were certainly intimately related, although this is a debatable point (cf. Kobusiewicz 2002 and Brinch Petersen 2009). Towards the end of the Pleistocene at Stellmoor, Schleswig-Holstein, reindeer were intercepted in a valley and shot with arrows as they entered water, the waterlogged sediments preserving a number of wooden arrowshafts (Bratlund 1991; Rust 1943). This is the earliest demonstrable evidence of the bow, although its use may stretch further back into the Upper Palaeolithic (Cattelain 1997).

The decline in archaeological visibility of art during the TUP reflects the loss of the great traditions of rock/cave art and, presumably, the rise in availability of perishable materials (wood, bark) on which to create art. Carved figurines of amber from *federmessergruppen* contexts reveal the origins of a tradition that persisted through the Mesolithic, and the few other examples of art in the north reveal the persistence of geometric and hatched infilling of animal outlines. Stones painted with red ochre, and engraved geometric decoration seem to have been widespread: they are known, for example, from the Italian Epigravettian as late as the Allerød (Dalmeri et al. 2006; Leonardi 1976) and in Ukraine down to the same period (Gorelik 2005).

References

Anikovich, M. V. 2005. Sungir in cultural context and its relevance for modern human origins. *Archaeology, Ethnology & Anthropology of Eurasia* 2, 37–47.

Arias, P. 1999. La Garma (Kantabrien/Spanien). Eiszeitliche wandkundst und wohnplätze in einer verschlossenen höhle. *Jahrbuch des Römisch-Germanischen Zentralmuseum Mainz* 46, 3–20.

Arts, N. 1988. A survey of Final Palaeolithic archaeology in the southern Netherlands. In M. Otte (ed.), *De la Loire de l'Oder: les civilisations du Paléolithique Final dans le Nord-Ouest Européen*, 287–356. Oxford: British Archaeological Reports International Series 444.

Aujoulat, N. 2005. *The splendour of Lascaux*. London: Thames and Hudson.

Aujoulat, N., Geneste, J.-M., Archambeau, C., Delluc, M., Duday, H., and Gambier, D. 2001. La Grotte ornée de Cussac (Dordogne) observations liminaires. *Paléo* 13, 9–18.

Averbouh, A. 2010. Utilisation et transformation des matières osseuses au Buisson Campin (Verberie, Oise). In E. Zubrow, F. Audouze, and J. G. Enloe (eds), *The Magdalenian household: unravelling domesticity*, 76–90. Albany: State University of New York Press.

Azéma, M. 2009. *L'art des cavernes en action*. Paris: Éditions Errance (2 volumes).

Bahn, P. and Vertut, J. 1997. *Journey through the Ice Age*. London: Weidenfeld & Nicolson.

Balbín Behrmann, R. de and Alcolea Gonzalez, J. J. 1999. Vie quotidienne et vie religieuse: les sanctuaries dans l'art Paléolithique. *L'Anthropologie* 103, 23–49.

Banks, W. E., d'Errico, F., Townsend Peterson, A., Vanhaeren, M., Kegeyama, M., Sepulchre, P., Ramstein, G., Jost, A., and Lunt, D. 2008. Human ecological niches and ranges during the LGM in Europe derived from an application of eco-cultural modelling. *Journal of Archaeological Science* 35, 481–91.

Baptista, A. and Fernandes, A. 2007. Rock art and the Côa Valley Archaeological Park: a case study in the preservation of Portugal's prehistoric parietal art. In P. B. Pettitt, P. Bahn, and

S. Ripoll (eds), *Creswell Palaeolithic cave art in European context*, 263–79. Oxford: Oxford University Press.

Bar-Yosef, O. 2000. The Middle and early Upper Palaeolithic in southwest Asia and neighbouring regions. In O. Bar-Yosef and D. Pilbeam (eds), *The geography of Neanderthals and modern humans in Europe and the Greater Mediterranean*, 127–56. Cambridge, MA: Peabody Museum Bulletin 8.

Bar-Yosef, O. 2002. The Upper Paleolithic revolution. *Annual Review of Anthropology* 31, 363–93.

Bégouën, R. and Clottes, J. 1991. Portable and wall art in the Volp caves, Montesquieu-Avantès (Ariège). *Proceedings of the Prehistoric Society* 57, 65–79.

Beltran, A. 1999. *The cave of Altamira*. New York: Abrams.

Benazzi, S., Douka, K., Fournai, C., Bauer, C. C., Kullmer, O., Svoboda, J., Pap, I., Mallegni, F., Bayle, P., Coquerelle, M., Condemi, S., Ronchitelli, A., Harvati, K., and Weber, G. W. 2011. Early dispersal of modern humans in Europe and implications for Neanderthal behaviour. *Nature* 479, 525–8.

Bernaldo de Quiros, F. 1991. Reflections on the art of the cave of Altamira. *Proceedings of the Prehistoric Society* 57, 81–90.

Bicho, N., Carvalho, A. F., González-Sainz, C., Sanchidrián, J. L., Villaverde, V., and Straus, L. G. 2007. The Upper Paleolithic rock art of Iberia. *Journal of Archaeological Method and Theory* 14, 81–151.

Bocquet-Appel, J.-R. and Demars, P.-Y. 2000. Population kinetics in the Upper Palaeolithic in Western Europe. *Journal of Archaeological Science* 27, 551–70.

Bocquet-Appel, J.-R. and Demars, P.-Y. 2005. Estimates of Upper Palaeolithic metapopulation size in Europe from archaeological data. *Journal of Archaeological Science* 32, 1656–68.

Bodu, P. 1998. Magdalenians-Early Azilians in the centre of the Paris Basin: a filiation? The example of Le Closeau (Rueil-Malmaison, France). In S. Milliken (ed.), *The organisation of lithic technology in Late Glacial and Early Postglacial Europe*, 131–47. Oxford: British Archaeological Reports International Series 700.

Bodu, P. 2010. Espaces et habitats au Tardiglaciaire dans le Bassin Parisien: une illustration avec les Gisements Magdalenian de Pincevent et Azilien du Closeau. In E. Zubrow, F. Audouze, and J. G. Enloe (eds), *The Magdalenian household: unravelling domesticity*, 176–97. Albany: State University of New York Press.

Bolus, M. 2003. The cultural context of the Aurignacian of the Swabian Jura. In J. Zilhão and F. d'Errico (eds), *The chronology of the Aurignacian and of the transitional technocomplexes: dating, stratigraphies, cultural implications*, 153–63. Lisbon: Trabalhos de Arqueologia 33.

Bolus, M. and Conard, N. J. 2006. Sur zeitstellung von geschossspitzen aus organischen materialen im Späten Mittelpaläolithikum und Aurignacien. *Archäologisches Korrespondenzblatt* 36, 1–15.

Bordes, J.-G. 2003. Lithic taphonomy of the Châtelperronian/Aurignacian interstratifications in Roc de Combe and le Piage (Lot, France). In J. Zilhão and F. d'Errico (eds), *The chronology of the Aurignacian and of the transitional technocomplexes: dating, stratigraphies, cultural implications*, 223–44. Lisbon: Trabalhos de Arqueologia 33.

Borziyak, I. A. 1993. Subsistence practices of Late Paleolithic groups along the Dnestr River and its tributaries. In O. Soffer and N. D. Praslov (eds), *From Kostenki to Clovis: Upper Paleolithic-Paleo-Indian adaptations*, 67–84. New York: Plenum Press.

Bosinski, G., d'Errico, F., and Schiller, P. 2001. *Die gravierten frauendarstellungen von Gönnersdorf*. Stuttgart: Franz Steiner Verlag.

Bradley, B. A., Anikovich, M., and Giria, E. 1995. Early Upper Palaeolithic in the Russian Plain: Streletskayan flaked stone artefacts and technology. *Antiquity* 69, 989–98.

Brantingham, P. J., Kuhn, S. L., and Kerry, K. W. (eds) 2004. *The early Upper Palaeolithic beyond Western Europe.* Berkeley: University of California.

Bratlund, B. 1991. A study of hunting lesions containing flint fragments on reindeer bones at Stellmoor, Schleswig-Holstein, Germany. In N. Barton, A. J. Roberts, and D. A. Roe (eds), *The Late Glacial in north-west Europe,* 193–207. London: CBA Research Report 77.

Brinch Petersen, E. 2009. The human settlement of southern Scandinavia 12 500–8700 cal BC. In M. Street, N. Barton, and T. Terberger (eds), *Humans, environment and chronology of the Late Glacial of the North European plain,* 89–129. Mainz: Verlag des Römisch-Germanischen Zentralmuseums.

Broglio, A. 1995. Les sépultures Épigravettiens de la Vénétie (Abri Tagilente et Abri Villabruna). In M. Otte (ed.), *Nature et culture,* 647–69. Liège: ERAUL 68.

Broglio, A., de Stefani, M., Guiroli, F., and Peresani, M. 2006. The Aurignacian paintings of the Fumane cave (Lessini mountains, Venetian Prealps): the territory, the site, Aurignacian frequentation. *International Newsletter on Rock Art* 44, 1–8.

Cardini, L. 1980. La Necropoli Mesolitica delle Arene Candide (Liguria). *Memorie dell'Instituto Italiano di Paleontologia Umana* 3, 9–31.

Caron, F., d'Errico, F., Del Moral, P., Santos, F., and Zilhão, J. 2011. The reality of Neanderthal symbolic behavior at the Grotte du Renne, Arcy-sur-Cure, France. *PLoS ONE* 6, 1–11.

Cattelain, P. 1987. Un crochet de propulseurs solutréen de la Grotte de Combe-Sauniere 1 (Dordogne). *Bulletin de la Société Préhistorique Française* 86, 213–16.

Cattelain, P. 1997. Hunting during the Upper Palaeolithic: bow, spearthrower, or both? In H. Knecht (ed.), *Projectile technology,* 213–40. New York: Plenum Press.

Cattin, M.-I. 2010. Comparing social organisations of the Magdalenian hunter-gatherers. In E. Zubrow, F. Audouze, and J. G. Enloe (eds), *The Magdalenian household: unravelling domesticity,* 213–21. Albany: State University of New York Press.

Chabai, V. P. 2003. The chronological and industrial variability of the Middle to Upper Paleolithic transition in Eastern Europe. In J. Zilhão and F. d'Errico (eds), *The chronology of the Aurignacian and of the transitional technocomplexes: dating, stratigraphies, cultural implications,* 71–86. Lisbon: Trabalhos de Arqueologia 33.

Churchill, S. E. and Smith, F. H. 2000. Makers of the Early Aurignacian of Europe. *Yearbook of Physical Anthropology* 43, 61–115.

Clottes, J. 2001. Paleolithic Europe. In D. Whitley (ed.), *Handbook of rock art research,* 459–81. New York: AltaMira Press.

Clottes, J. 2003. *Return to Chauvet cave: excavating the birthplace of art.* London: Thames and Hudson.

Clottes, J. and Courtin, J. 1996. *The cave beneath the sea: Palaeolithic images at Cosquer.* New York: Abrams.

Combier, J. 1990. De la fin du Moustérien au Paléolithique Supérieur: le données de la region Rhodannniene. *Mémoires de la Musée d'Isle de France* 3, 267–77.

Combier, J., Drouot, E., and Huchard, P. 1959. Les Grottes Solutréennes à gravures parietals du Canyon inférieur de l'Ardèche. *Mémoires de la Société Préhistorique Française* 5, 61–117.

Conard, N. J. 2003. Palaeolithic ivory sculptures from southwestern Germany and the origins of figurative art. *Nature* 426, 830–2.

Conard, N. J. 2009. A female figurine from the basal Aurignacian of Hohle Fels cave in southwestern Germany. *Nature* 459, 248–52.

Conard, N. J., Dippon, G., and Goldberg, P. 2003. Chronostratigraphy and archaeological context of the Aurignacian deposits of Geissenklösterle. In J. Zilhão and F. d'Errico (eds), *The chronology of the Aurignacian and of the transitional technocomplexes: dating, stratigraphies, cultural implications*, 165–76. Lisbon: Trabalhos de Arqueologia 33.

Conard, N. J. and Floss, H. 2001. Une statuette en ivoire de 30,000 BP trouvée au Hohle Fels près de Schelkingen (Baden-Wurttemberg, Allemagne). *Paléo* 13, 241–4.

Conard, N. J., Malina, M., Münzel, S. C., and Seeberger, F. 2004. Eine mammutelfenbeinflöte aus dem Aurignacien des Geissenklösterle. *Archäologisches Korrespondenzblatt* 34, 447–62.

Conkey, M. W. 1980. The identification of prehistoric hunter-gatherer aggregation sites: the case of Altamira. *Current Anthropology* 21, 609–21.

Conkey, M. W. 1985. Ritual communication, social elaboration, and the variable trajectories of Paleolithic material culture. In T. D. Price and J. A. Brown (eds), *Prehistoric hunter-gatherers*, 299–323. New York: Academic Press.

Corchón Rodríguez, M. S. 1998. Nuevas representaciones de antropomorfos en el Magdaleniense Medio Cantábrico. *Zephyrus* 51, 35–60.

Dalmeri, G., Bassetti, M., Cusinato, A., Kompatscher, M. H., and Kompatscher, K. 2006. Le site Épigravettien de l'Abri Dalmeri: aspects artistiques à fin du Paléolithique Supérieur en Italie du Nord. *L'Anthropologie* 110, 510–29.

David, N. 1985. *Excavation of the Abri Pataud, Les Eyzies (Dordogne): the Noaillian (Level 4) assemblages and the Noaillian culture in Western Europe*. Harvard: American School of Prehistoric Research Research Bulletin 37.

Davies, W. 2001. A very model of a modern human industry: new perspectives of the origins and spread of the Aurignacian in Europe. *Proceedings of the Prehistoric Society* 67, 195–217.

Delluc, B. and Delluc, G. 1991. L'art pariétal archaïque en Aquitaine. Gallia Préhistoire XXVIII supplément. Paris: CNRS.

Delluc, B. and Delluc, G. 2009. Art Paléolithique en Périgord: les representations humaines pariétales. *L'Anthropologie* 113, 629–61.

Delporte, H. 1993a. Gravettian female figurines: a regional survey. In H. Knecht, A. Pike-Tay, and R. White (eds), *Before Lascaux: the complex record of the early Upper Palaeolithic*, 243–57. Boca Raton: CRC Press.

Delporte, H. 1993b. L'art mobilier de la Grotte de La Vache: premier essai de vue générale. *Bulletin de la Société Préhistorique Française* 90, 131–6.

Demars, P.-Y. 1995. Le Solutréen de Laugerie-Haute (Dordogne). *Gallia Préhistoire* 37, 1–53.

d'Errico, F. 1988. Lecture technologique de l'art mobilier gravé: nouvelles méthods et premiers résultats sur les galets gravés de Rochedane. *L'Anthropologie* 92, 101–22.

d'Errico, F. 1994. *L'art gravé Azilien: de la technique à la signification*. XXXIst Supplement to Gallia Préhistoire. Paris: CNRS. (NB: this is in French, but there is a useful English abstract and numerous figures are intelligible.)

d'Errico, F. 2003. The invisible frontier: a multiple species model for the origin of behavioural modernity. *Evolutionary Anthropology* 12, 188–202.

d'Errico, F., Henshilwood, C., Lawson, G., Vanhaeren, M., Tillier, A.-M., Soressi, M., Bresson, F., Maureille, B., Nowell, A., Lakarra, J., Backwell, L., and Julien, M. 2003. Archaeological evidence for the emergence of language, symbolism, and music—an alternative multidisciplinary perspective. *Journal of World Prehistory* 17, 1–70.

Dinnis, R., Pawlik, A., and Gaillard, C. 2009. Bladelet cores as weapon tips? Hafting residue identification and micro-wear analysis of three carinated burins from the late Aurignacian of Les Vachons, France. *Journal of Archaeological Science* 36, 1922–34.

Djindjian, F., Kozlowski, J. K., and Bazile, F. 2003. Europe during the Early Upper Paleolithic (40,000–30,000 BP): a synthesis. In J. Zilhão and F. d'Errico (eds), *The chronology of the*

Aurignacian and of the transitional technocomplexes: dating, stratigraphies, cultural implications, 29–47. Lisbon: Trabalhos de Arqueologia 33.

Djindjian, F., Kozlowski, J. K., and Otte, M. 1999. *Le Paléolithique Supérieur en Europe*. Paris: Armand Collin.

Enloe, J. G. and Audouze, F. 2010. The Magdalenian site of Verberie (Le Buisson Campin): an overview. In E. Zubrow, F. Audouze, and J. G. Enloe (eds), *The Magdalenian household: unravelling domesticity*, 15–21. Albany: State University of New York Press.

Eriksen, B. V. 1996. Resource exploitation, subsistence strategies, and adaptiveness in Late Pleistocene-Early Holocene Northwest Europe. In L. G. Straus, B. V. Eriksen, L. M. Erlandson, and D. E. Yesner (eds), *Humans at the end of the Ice Age: the archaeology of the Pleistocene-Holocene transition*, 101–28. New York: Plenum Press.

Féblot-Augustins, J. 1997. *La circulation des matières premières au Paléolithique*. Liège: Etudes et Recherches Archéologiques de l'Université de Liège 75.

Fedele, F. G., Giacco, B., and Hajdas, I. 2008. Timescales and cultural process at 40,000 BP in the light of the Campanian Ignimbrite eruption, Western Eurasia. *Journal of Human Evolution* 55, 834–57.

Fernández-Tresguerres, J. A. 1990. Arpones decorados Azilienses. *Zephyrus* 43, 47–51.

Fischer, A. 1991. Pioneers in deglaciated landscapes: the expansion and adaptation of Late Palaeolithic societies in southern Scandinavia. In N. Barton, A. J. Roberts, and D. A. Roe (eds), *The Late Glacial in north-west Europe*, 100–21. London: CBA Research Report 77.

Floss, H. 2003. Did they meet or not? Observations on Châtelperronian and Aurignacian settlement patterns in eastern France. In J. Zilhão and F. d'Errico (eds), *The chronology of the Aurignacian and of the transitional technocomplexes: dating, stratigraphies, cultural implications*, 273–87. Lisbon: Trabalhos de Arqueologia 33.

Formicola, V., Pettitt, P. B., Maggi, R., and Hedges, R. E. M. 2005. Tempo and mode of formation of the late Epigravettian necropolis of Arene Candide, Italy: evidence from the direct radiocarbon dates of the skeletons. *Journal of Archaeological Science* 32, 1598–602.

Gamble, C. S. 1982. Interaction and alliance in Palaeolithic society. *Man* 17, 92–107.

Gamble, C. S. 1986. *The Palaeolithic settlement of Europe*. Cambridge: Cambridge University Press.

Gamble, C. S. 1999. *The Palaeolithic societies of Europe*. Cambridge: Cambridge University Press.

Gaudzinski, S. and Street, M. 2003. Reconsidering hunting specialisation in the German Magdalenian faunal record. In S. Costamagno and V. Laroulandie (eds), *Mode de vie au Magdalénien: apports de l'archéozoologie*, 11–21. Oxford: British Archaeological Reports International Series 1144.

Gaussen, J. 1980. *Le Paléolithique Supérieur de plein air en Périgord: secteur Mussidan-Saint-Astier, moyenne vallée d'Isle*. Paris: XIVe Supplément à Gallia Préhistoire.

Germonpré, M. and Hämäläinen, R. 2007. Fossil bear bones in the Belgian Upper Paleolithic: the possibility of a proto bear-ceremonialism. *Arctic Anthropology* 44, 1–30.

Goebel, T. and Aksenov, M. 1995. Accelerator radiocarbon dating of the Initial Upper Palaeolithic in southeast Siberia. *Antiquity* 69, 349–57.

Gorelik, A. 2005. On the characteristics of the Final Palaeolithic mobiliary art of the south-eastern Ukraine. *Archäologisches Korrespondenzblatt* 35, 283–97.

Gravina, B., Mellars, P. A., and Bronk Ramsey, C. 2005. Radiocarbon dating of interstratified Neanderthal and early modern human occupations at the Châtelperronian type-site. *Nature* 438, 51–6.

Grayson, D. K. and Delpech, F. 2002. Specialized early Upper Palaeolithic hunters in southwestern France? *Journal of Archaeological Science* 29, 1439–49.

Grigor'ev, G. P. 1993. The Kostenki-Avdeevo archaeological culture and the Willendorf-Pavlov-Kostenki-Avdeevo cultural unity. In O. Soffer and N. D. Praslov (eds), *From Kostenki to Clovis: Upper Paleolithic-Paleo-Indian adaptations*, 51–65. New York: Plenum Press.

Grimm, S. B. and Weber, M.-J. 2008. The chronological framework of the Hamburgian in the light of old and new 14C dates. *Quartär* 55, 17–40.

Groenen, M. 1997. *Ombre et lumière dans l'art des grottes*. Brussels: Université Libre de Bruxelles.

Guthrie, D. and van Kolfschoten, T. 2000. Neither warm and moist, nor cold and arid: the ecology of the Mid Upper Palaeolithic. In W. Roebroeks, M. Mussi, J. Svoboda, and K. Fennema (eds), *Hunters of the golden age: the Mid Upper Palaeolithic of Eurasia 30,000–20,000 BP*, 13–20. Leiden: University of Leiden.

Gvozdover, M. 1995. *Art of the mammoth hunters: the finds from Avdeevo*. Oxford: Oxbow.

Haesaerts, P. and Teyssandier, N. 2003. The early Upper Palaeolithic occupations of Willendorf II (Lower Austria): a contribution to the chronostratigraphic and cultural context of the beginning of the Upper Palaeolithic in central Europe. In J. Zilhão and F. d'Errico (eds), *The chronology of the Aurignacian and of the transitional technocomplexes: dating, stratigraphies, cultural implications*, 133–51. Lisbon: Trabalhos de Arqueologia 33.

Hahn, J. 1982. Demi-relief aurignacien en ivoire de la Grotte Geissenklösterle, près d'Ulm (Allemagne Féderale). *Bulletin de la Société Préhistorique Française* 79, 73–7.

Hahn, J. 1993. Aurignacian art in central Europe. In H. Knecht, A. Pike-Tay, and R. White (eds), *Before Lascaux: the complex record of the early Upper Palaeolithic*, 229–41. Boca Raton: CRC Press.

Hahn, J. and Münzel, S. 1995. Knochenflöten aus dem Aurignacien des Geissenklösterle bei Blaubeuren, Alb-Donau-Kreis. *Fundberichte aus Baden-Württemberg* 20, 1–12.

Henry-Gambier, D. 2002 Les fouilles de Cro-Magnon (Les-Eyzies-de-Tayac, Dordogne): nouvelles données sur leur position chronologique et leur attribution culturelle. *Paléo* 14, 201–4.

Henry-Gambier, D., Beauval, C., Airvaux, J., Aujoulat, N., Baratin, J. F., and Buisson-Catil, J. 2007. New hominid remains associated with Gravettian parietal art (Les Garennes, Vilhonneur, France). *Journal of Human Evolution* 53, 747–50.

Henry-Gambier, D., Maureille, B., and White, R. 2004. Vestiges humains des niveaux de l'Aurignacien Ancien du site du Brassempouy (Landes). *Bulletins et Mémoirs de la Société d'Anthropologie de Paris* 16, 49–87.

Henshilwood, C. and Marean, C. 2003. The origin of modern human behaviour: critique of the models and their test implications. *Current Anthropology* 44, 627–51.

Higham, T. F. G. 2011. European Middle and Upper Palaeolithic radiocarbon dates are often older than they look: problems with previous dates and some remedies. *Antiquity* 55, 235–49.

Higham, T. F. G., Jacobi R., Julien, M., David, F., Basell, L., Wood, R., Davies, W., and Bronk Ramsey, C. 2010. Chronology of the Grotte du Renne (France) and implications for the context of ornaments and human remains within the Châtelperronian. *Proceedings of the National Academy of Sciences USA* 107, 20234–9.

Hoffecker, J. F. 2002. *Desolate landscapes: Ice-Age settlement in eastern Europe*. New Brunswick: Rutgers University Press.

Hoffecker, J. F. 2011. The Early Upper Paleolithic of eastern Europe reconsidered. *Evolutionary Anthropology* 20, 24–39.

Housley, R. A., Gamble, C. S., Street, M., and Pettit, P. B. 1997. Radiocarbon evidence for the Lateglacial human recolonisation of northern Europe. *Proceedings of the Prehistoric Society* 63, 25–54.

Iakovleva, L. 2000. The Gravettian art of eastern Europe as exemplified in the figurative art of Kostenki I. In W. Roebroeks, M. Mussi, J. Svoboda, and K. Fennema (eds), *Hunters of the golden age: the Mid Upper Palaeolithic of Eurasia 30,000–20,000 BP*, 125–33. Leiden: University of Leiden. (NB: cast your eyes over the paper by Vasil'ev in the same volume for examples of Siberian Mid Upper Palaeolithic art.)

Jacobi, R. M. 1991. The Creswellian, Creswell and Cheddar. In N. Barton, A. J. Roberts, and D. A. Roe (eds), *The Late Glacial in north west Europe: human adaptation and environmental change at the end of the Pleistocene*, 128–40. London: Council for British Archaeology Research Report 77.

Jacobi, R. M. and Higham, T. F. G. 2009. The early Lateglacial re-colonisation of Britain: new radiocarbon evidence from Gough's cave, southwest England. *Quaternary Science Reviews* 28, 1895–913.

Jacobi, R. M., Higham, T. F. G., Haesaerts, P., Jadin, I., and Basell, L. S. 2010. Radiocarbon chronology for the early Gravettian of northern Europe: new AMS determinations for Maisières-Canal, Belgium. *Antiquity* 84, 26–40.

Jacobi, R. M. and Pettitt, P. B. 2000. An Aurignacian point from Uphill Quarry, Somerset, and the colonisation of Britain by *Homo sapiens sapiens*. *Antiquity* 74, 513–18.

Jöris, O. and Street, M. 2008. At the end of the ^{14}C time scale—the Middle to Upper Palaeolithic record of western Eurasia. *Journal of Human Evolution* 55, 782–802.

Jöris, O. and Terberger, T. 2001. Zur rekonstruktion eines zeltes mit trapezförmigem grundriss am Magdalénien-fundplatz Gönnersdorf/Mittelrhein. Eine 'Quadratur des Kreises'? *Archäologisches Korrespondenzblatt* 31, 163–72.

Klein, R. G. 1973. *Ice Age hunters of the Ukraine*. Chicago: University of Chicago Press..

Knecht, H. 1997. Projectile points of bone, antler and stone. In H. Knecht (ed.), *Projectile technology*, 191–212. New York: Plenum Press.

Kobusiewicz, M. 2002. Ahrensburgian and Swiderian: two different modes of adaptation? In B. Eriksen and B. Bratlund (eds), *Recent studies in the Final Palaeolithic of the European Plain. Proceedings of a UISPP Symposium, Stockholm, 14–17 October 1999*, 117–22. Aarhus: Aarhus University Press.

Kozlowski, J. K. 1986. The Gravettian in central and eastern Europe. *Advances in World Archaeology* 5, 131–200.

Kozlowski, J. K. 1998. The Middle and the early Upper Palaeolithic around the Black Sea. In T. Akazawa, K. Aoki, and O. Bar-Yosef (eds), *Neanderthals and modern humans in Western Asia*, 461–82. New York: Plenum Press..

Kozlowski, J. K. 2000. The problem of cultural continuity between the Middle and Upper Palaeolithic in central and eastern Europe. In O. Bar-Yosef and D. Pilbeam (eds), *The geography of Neanderthals and modern humans in Europe and in the Greater Mediterranean*, 77–105. Cambridge, MA: Harvard University Peabody Museum Bulletin 8.

Kozlowski, J. K. 2005. Paléolithique Supérieur et Mésolithique en Méditerranée: cadre culturel. *L'Anthropologie* 109, 520–40.

Kozlowski, J. K. and Otte, M. 2000. La formation de l'Aurignacien en Europe. *L'Anthropologie* 104, 3–15.

Krotova, A. A. and Belan, N. G. 1993. Amvrosievka: a unique Upper Paleolithic site in eastern Europe. In O. Soffer and N. D. Praslov (eds), *From Kostenki to Clovis: Upper Paleolithic-Paleo-Indian adaptations*, 125–42. New York: Plenum Press.

Kuhn, S. L. 2003. In what sense is the Levantine Initial Upper Palaeolithic a 'transitional' industry? In J. Zilhão and F. d'Errico (eds), *The chronology of the Aurignacian and of the transitional technocomplexes: dating, stratigraphies, cultural implications*, 61–9. Lisbon: Trabalhos de Arqueologia 33.

Kuhn, S. L. and Stiner, M. C. 1998. The earliest Aurignacian of Riparo Mochi (Liguria, Italy). *Current Anthropology* 39, S175–89.

Kuhn, S. L. and Stiner, M. C. 2001. The antiquity of hunter-gatherers. In C. Panter-Brick, R. Layton, and P. Rowley-Conwy (eds), *Hunter-gatherers: an interdisciplinary perspective*, 99–142. Cambridge: Cambridge University Press.

Leonardi, P. 1976. Gravures zoomorphes, géometriques et linéaires épigravettiennes du Riparo Tagliente dans les Monts Lessini près de Vérone (Italie). *Congrès Préhistoire de France, XXe Session, Provence 1974*, 343–52.

Leonova, N. B. 1994. The Upper Paleolithic of the Russian Steppe zone. *Journal of World Prehistory* 8, 169–209.

Leroi-Gourhan, A. 1968. *The art of prehistoric man in Western Europe*. London: Thames and Hudson.

Leroi-Gourhan, A. and Brézillon, M. 1972. *Fouilles de Pincevent: essai d'analyse ethnographique d'un habitat Magdalénien (La Section 36)*. Paris: VIIe Supplément à Gallia Préhistoire/Etudes de CNRS.

Lorblanchet, M. 1989. From man to animal to sign in Palaeolithic art. In H. Morphy (ed.), *Animals into art*, 110–43. London: Hyman.

Lorblanchet, M. 1995. *Les grottes ornées de la préhistoire: nouveaux regards*. Paris: Éditions Errance.

Marshack, A. 1972. *The roots of civilisation*. New York: McGraw-Hill.

Marshack, A. 1991. The female image: a 'time-factored' symbol. A study in style and aspects of image use in the Upper Palaeolithic. *Proceedings of the Prehistoric Society* 57, 17–31.

Mellars, P. A. (ed.) 1990. *The emergence of modern humans: an archaeological perspective*. Edinburgh: Edinburgh University Press.

Mellars, P. A. 1992. Archaeology and the population-dispersal hypothesis of modern human origins in Europe. *Philosophical Transactions of the Royal Society of London Series B* 337, 225–34.

Mellars, P. A. 1999. The Neanderthal problem continued. *Current Anthropology* 40, 341–50.

Mellars, P. A. 2001. The Upper Palaeolithic revolution. In B. Cunliffe (ed.), *The Oxford illustrated prehistory of Europe*, 42–78. Oxford: Oxford University Press.

Mellars, P. A. 2004. Neanderthals and the modern human colonization of Europe. *Nature* 432, 461–5.

Mellars, P. A. 2006. Archeology and the dispersal of modern humans in Europe: deconstructing the 'Aurignacian'. *Evolutionary Anthropology* 15, 167–82.

Mellars, P. A. and Stringer, C. B. 1989. *The human revolution: behavioural and biological perspectives on the origin of modern humans*. Edinburgh: Edinburgh University Press.

Movius, H. L. Jr. 1966. The hearths of the Upper Perigordian and Aurignacian horizons at the Abri Pataud, Les Eyzies (Dordogne), and their possible significance. *American Anthropologist* 68, 296–325.

Mussi, M. 2001. *Earliest Italy: an overview of the Italian Paleolithic and Mesolithic*. New York: Kluwer Academic /Plenum Press.

Mussi, M., Cinq-Mars, J., and Bolduc, P. 2000. Echoes from the Mammoth Steppe: the case of the Balzi Rossi. In W. Roebroeks, M. Mussi, J. Svoboda, and K. Fennema (eds), *Hunters of the golden age: the Mid Upper Palaeolithic of Eurasia 30,000–20,000 BP*, 105–24. Leiden: University of Leiden.

Niven, L. 2003. Patterns of subsistence and settlement during the Aurignacian of the Swabian Jura, Germany. In J. Zilhão and F. d'Errico (eds), *The chronology of the Aurignacian and of the transitional technocomplexes: dating, stratigraphies, cultural implications*, 199–211. Lisbon: Trabalhos de Arqueologia 33.

Nývltová-Fišáková, M. 2000. Menu of the Gravettian people from southern Moravia. *Acta Universitatis Carolinae Medica* 41, 37–40.

Oliva, M. 2005. *Palaeolithic and Mesolithic Moravia*. Brno: Moravian Museum.
Onoratini, G. 2004. Le Protoaurignacien: première culture de l'homme modern de Provence et Ligurie. *L'Anthropologie* 108, 239–49.
Ontañón, R. 2003. Sols et structures d'habitat du Paléolithique supérieur, nouvelles données depuis les Cantabres: la Galerie Inférieur de La Garma. *L'Anthropologie* 107, 333–63.
Otte, M. 1981. *Le Gravettien en Europe Central*. Bruges: De Tempel.
Otte, M. 1985. Le Gravettien en Europe. *L'Anthropologie* 89, 479–503.
Otte, M. and Noiret, P. 2002. Origine du Solutréen: le rôle de l'Espagne. *Zephyrus* 55, 77–83.
Pales, L. and Tassin de Saint-Péreuse, M. 1976. *Les Gravures de La Marche: II. Les humaines*. Paris: Ophrys.
Palma di Cesnola, A. 2006. L'Aurignacien et le Gravettien Ancien de la Grotte Paglicci au Mont Gargano. *L'Anthropologie* 110, 355–70.
Pavlov, P. and Indrelid, S. 2000. Human occupation in northeastern Europe during the period 35,000–18,000 BP. In W. Roebroeks, M. Mussi, J. Svoboda, and K. Fennema (eds), *Hunters of the golden age: the Mid Upper Palaeolithic of Eurasia 30,000–20,000 BP*, 165–72. Leiden: University of Leiden.
Pawlikowski, M., Koumouzelis, M., Ginter, B., and Kozlowski, J. K. 2000. Emerging ceramic technology in structured Aurignacian hearths at Klissoura Cave 1 in Greece. *Archaeology, Ethnology and Anthropology of Eurasia* 4, 19–29.
Pettitt, P. B. 2000. Chronology of the Mid Upper Palaeolithic: the radiocarbon evidence. In W. Roebroeks, M. Mussi, J. Svoboda, and K. Fennema (eds), *Hunters of the golden age: the Mid Upper Palaeolithic of Eurasia 30,000–20,000 BP*, 21–30. Leiden: University of Leiden.
Pettitt, P. B. 2006. The living dead and the dead living: burials, figurines and social performance in the European Mid Upper Palaeolithic. In C. Knüsel and R. Gowland (eds), *The social archaeology of funerary remains*, 292–308. Oxford: Oxbow.
Pettitt, P. B. 2011. *The Palaeolithic origins of human burial*. London: Routledge.
Pettitt, P. B., Bahn, P., and Züchner, C. 2009. The Chauvet conundrum: are claims for the 'birthplace of art' premature? In P. Bahn (ed.), *An enquiring mind: studies in honor of Alexander Marshack*, 239–62. Oxford: Oxbow and Cambridge, MA: American School of Prehistoric Research Monograph Series.
Picard, J. 1997. Le cheval pommel de Pech-Merle. *Bulletin de la Société Préhistorique Française* 94, 471–81.
Pidoplichko, I. G. 1998. *Upper Palaeolithic dwellings of mammoth bones in the Ukraine*. Oxford: British Archaeological Reports International Series 712.
Pigeaud, R. 2002. La Grotte ornée Mayenne-Sciences (Thorigné-en-Charnie, Mayenne): grotte-limite aux marges du monde anté-magdalénien. *L'Anthropologie* 106, 445–89.
Pike-Tay, A. and Bricker, H. 1993. Hunting in the Gravettian: an examination of evidence from southwestern France. In G. Larsen Peterkin, H. Bricker, and P. A. Mellars (eds.), *Hunting and animal exploitation in the later Paleolithic and Mesolithic of Eurasia*, 127–43. Archaeological Papers of the American Anthropological Association 4.
Połtowicz, M. 2006. The eastern borders of the Magdalenian culture range. *Analecta Archaeologica Ressoviensia* 1, 11–28.
Richards, M. P., Pettitt, P. B., Stiner, M., and Trinkaus, E. 2001. Stable isotope evidence for increasing dietary breadth in the European mid-Upper Palaeolithic. *Proceedings of the National Academy of Sciences USA* 98, 6528–32.
Rigaud, A. 2001. Les bâtons percés: décors énigmatiques et fontion possible. *Gallia Préhistoire* 43, 101–51.

Rigaud, J.-Ph. (ed.) 1989. *Le Magdalenien en Europe*. Liège: Etudes et Recherches Archéologiques de l'Université de Liège 38.

Rigaud, J.-Ph. 2000. Human adaptation to the climatic deterioration of the Last Pleniglacial in southwestern France (30,000 to 20,000 BP). In W. Roebroeks, M. Mussi, J. Svoboda, and K. Fennema (eds), *Hunters of the golden age: the Mid Upper Palaeolithic of Eurasia 30,000–20,000 BP*, 325–36. Leiden: University of Leiden.

Ripoll López, S. and Muñoz Ibánez, F. 2002. *Economía, sociedad e ideología de los cazadores-recolectores*. Madrid: Universidad Nacional de Educación a Distancia.

Ripoll López, S., Ripoll Perelló, E., Collado Giraldo, H., Mas Cornellá, M., and Jordá Pardo, J. F. 1999. Maltravieso: el santuario extremeño de las manos. *Trabajos de Preistoria* 56, 59–84.

Roebroeks, W. 2000. A marginal matter: the human occupation of northwestern Europe—30,000 to 20,000 BP. In W. Roebroeks, M. Mussi, J. Svoboda, and K. Fennema (eds), *Hunters of the golden age: the Mid Upper Palaeolithic of Eurasia 30,000–20,000 BP*, 299–312. Leiden: University of Leiden.

Roebroeks, W., Mussi, M., Svoboda, J., and Fennema, K. (eds) 2000. *Hunters of the golden age: the Mid Upper Palaeolithic of Eurasia 30,000–20,000 BP*. Leiden: University of Leiden.

Rougier, H., Milota, Ş., Rodrigo, R., Gherase, M., Sarcină, L., Moldovan, O., Zilhão, J., Constantin, S., Franciscus, R. G., Zollikoffer, C. P. E., Ponce de León, M., and Trinkaus, E. 2007. Peştera cu Oase 2 and the cranial morphology of early modern Europeans. *Proceedings of the National Academy of Sciences USA* 104, 1165–70.

Rousseau, M. 1996. Dans l'art Paléolithique: 'l'homme tué' de la Grotte Cosquer et d'ailleurs, les hommes blessés. *Bulletin de la Société Préhistorique Française* 93, 204–7.

Rust, A. 1943. *Die Alt- und Mittelsteinzeitlichen funde von Stellmoor*. Neumünster: Wachholz.

Sacchi, D. 2003. *Le Magdalénien: apogée de l'art Quaternaire*. Paris: Maison des Roches.

Sackett, J. R. 1991. Straight archaeology French style: the phylogenetic paradigm in historic perspective. In G. A. Clark (ed.), *Perspectives on the past: theoretical biases in Mediterranean hunter-gatherer research*, 109–39. Philadelphia: University of Pennsylvania Press.

Sahly, A. 1966. *Les mains mutilées dans l'art préhistorique*. Toulouse: Privat.

Scheer, A. 1993. The organisation of lithic resource use during the Gravettian in Germany. In H. Knecht, A. Pike-Tay, and R. White (eds), *Before Lascaux: the complex record of the early Upper Palaeolithic*, 193–210. Boca Raton: CRC Press.

Schild, R. 1996. The North European Plain and eastern Sub-Balticum between 12,700 and 8000 BP. In L. Straus, B. V. Eriksen, L. M. Erlandson, and D. R. Yesner (eds), *Humans at the end of the Ice Age: the archaeology of the Pleistocene–Holocene transition*, 129–57. New York: Plenum Press..

Schmid, E., Hahn, J., and Wolf, U. 1989. Die altsteinzeitliche Elfenbeinstatuette aus der Höhle Stadel im Hohlenstein bei Asselfingen, Alb-Donau-Kreis. *Fundberichte aus Baden-Württemberg* 14, 33–118.

Schwabedissen, H. 1954. *Die Federmesser-Gruppen des nordwesterneuropäischen Flachlandes*. Neumünster: Wachholtz Verlag.

Sieveking, A. 1987. *Engraved Magadalenian plaquettes: a regional and stylistic analysis of stone, bone and antler plaquettes from Upper Palaeolithic sites in France and Cantabric Spain*. Oxford: British Archaeological Reports (International Series) 369.

Sinitsyn, A. A. 2003. The most ancient sites of Kostenki in the context of the Initial Upper Paleolithic of northern Eurasia. In J. Zilhão and F. d'Errico (eds), *The chronology of the Aurignacian and of the transitional technocomplexes: dating, stratigraphies, cultural implications*, 89–107. Lisbon: Trabalhos de Arqueologia 33.

Soffer, O. 1985. *The Upper Palaeolithic of the Russian Plain*. San Diego: Academic Press.

Soffer, O. 1989. Storage, sedentism and the Eurasian Palaeolithic record. *Antiquity* 63, 719–32.

Soffer, O., Adovasio, J. M., and Hyland, D. C. 2000. The 'Venus Figurines': textiles, basketry, gender and status in the Upper Palaeolithic. *Current Anthropology* 41, 511–37.

Soffer, O., Adovasio, J. M., Kornietz, N. L., Velichko, A. A., Gribchenko, Y. N., Lenz, B. R., and Suntsov, V. Y. 1997. Cultural stratigraphy at Mezhirich, an Upper Palaeolithic site in Ukraine with multiple occupations. *Antiquity* 71, 48–62.

Soffer, O. and Gamble, C. (eds) 1990. *The world at 18,000 BP. Volume 1. High latitudes.* London: Unwin Hyman.

Soriano, S. 1998. Les microgravettes du Périgordien de Rabier à Lanquais (Dordogne). *Gallia Préhistoire* 40, 75–94.

Stiner, M. C., Munro, N. D., Surovell, T. A., Tchernov, E., and Bar-Yosef, O. 1999. Paleolithic population growth pulses evidenced by small animal exploitation. *Science* 283, 190–4.

Straus, L. G. 1996. The archaeology of the Pleistocene–Holocene transition in southwest Europe. In L. G. Straus, B. Eriksen, J. M. Erlandson, and D. R. Yesner (eds), *Humans at the end of the Ice Age: the archaeology of the Pleistocene–Holocene transition*, 83–99. New York: Plenum Press.

Straus, L. G. 2005. The Upper Palaeolithic of Europe: an overview. *Evolutionary Anthropology* 4, 4–16.

Svensson, A., Andersen, K. K., Bigler, M., Clausen, H. B., Dahl-Jensen, D., Davies, S. M., Johnsen, S., Muscheler, R., Parrenin, F., Rasmussen, S. O., Rothlisberger, R., Seierstad, I., Steffensen, J. P., and Vinther, B. M. 2008. A 60,000 year Greenland stratigraphic ice core chronology. *Climate of the Past* 4, 47–57.

Svoboda, J. 2003. The Bohunician and the Aurignacian. In J. Zilhão and F. d'Errico (eds), *The chronology of the Aurignacian and of the transitional technocomplexes: dating, stratigraphies, cultural implications*, 123–31. Lisbon: Trabalhos de Arqueologia 33.

Svoboda, J. 2008. Upper Palaeolithic female figurines of Northern Eurasia. In J. Svoboda (ed.), *Petřkovice: on shouldered points and female figurines*, 193–223. Brno: Dolní Věstonice Studies 15.

Svoboda, J., Klima, B., Jarošova, L., and Škrdla, P. 2000. The Gravettian in Moravia: climate, behaviour and technological complexity. In W. Roebroeks, M. Mussi, J. Svoboda, and K. Fennema (eds), *Hunters of the golden age: the Mid Upper Palaeolithic of Eurasia 30,000–20,000 BP*, 197–217. Leiden: University of Leiden.

Svoboda, J., Ložek, V. and Vlček, E. 1996. *Hunters between east and west. The Paleolithic of Moravia.* New York: Plenum Press.

Svoboda, J. and Novák, M. 2004. Eastern central Europe after the Upper Pleniglacial: changing points of observation. *Archäologisches Korrespondenzblatt* 34, 463–77.

Taborin, Y. 1993. Shells of the French Aurignacian and Perigordian. In H. Knecht, A. Pike-Tay, and R. White (eds), *Before Lascaux: the complex record of the early Upper Palaeolithic*, 211–27. Boca Raton: CRC Press.

Terberger, T. and Street, M. 2003. New evidence for the chronology of the Aurignacian and the question of Pleniglacial settlement in western central Europe. In J. Zilhão and F. d'Errico (eds), *The chronology of the Aurignacian and of the transitional technocomplexes: dating, stratigraphies, cultural implications*, 213–21. Lisbon: Trabalhos de Arqueologia 33.

Thévenin, A. 1997. L'Azilien et les cultures à pointes à dos courbe: esquisse géographique et chronologique. *Bulletin de la Société Préhistorique Française* 94, 393–411.

Trinkaus, E., Moldovan, O., Milota, Ş., Bîlgăr, A., Sarcina, L., Athreya, S., Bailey, S. E., Rodrigo, R., Mircea, G., Higham, T., Bronk Ramsey, C., and van der Plicht, J. 2003. An early modern human from the Peștera cu Oase, Romania. *Proceedings of the National Academy of Sciences USA* 100, 11231–6.

Tsonev, T. 1997. Origin and evolution of the Gravettian culture in the eastern Balkans. *Archaeologica Bulgarica* 1, 1–4.

Turner, E. 2002. *Solutré: an archaeozoological analysis of the Magdalenian horizon.* Mainz: Römisch-Germanischen Zentralmuseums Monograph 46.

Turner, E. 2003. Horse hunting and the utilisation of horse carcasses during the Magdalenian in Europe. In S. Costamagno and V. Laroulandie (eds), *Mode de vie au Magdalénien: apports de l'Archéozoologie*, 47–64. Oxford: British Archaeological Reports International Series 1144.

Tymula, S. 2002. *L'art Solutréen du Roc de Sers (Charente)*. Paris: Éditions de la Maison des Sciences de l'Homme.

Valoch, K. 2007a. Kostěnki na Donu, mimořadný doklad stability osídlení maladém Paleolitu. *Acta Museum Moraviae Scientiae Sociales* 92, 53–70.

Valoch, K. 2007b. Textile in the Upper Palaeolithic? Some notes on the matter. *Archeologické Rozhledy* 59, 143–54.

Van Andel, T. H. and Davies, W. D., (eds) 2003. *Neanderthals and modern humans in the European landscape of the last glaciation—archaeological results of the Stage 3 Project.* Cambridge: McDonald Institute for Archaeological Research.

Van Andel, T. H., Davies, W. D. and Weninger, B. 2003. The human presence in Europe during the Last Glacial period I: human migrations and the changing climate. In T. H. Van Andel and W. D. Davies (eds), *Neanderthals and modern humans in the European landscape of the last glaciation—archaeological results of the Stage 3 Project*, 31–56. Cambridge: McDonald Institute for Archaeological Research.

Vandiver, P. B., Soffer, O., Klima, B., and Svoboda, J. 1989. The origins of ceramic technology at Dolní Věstonice, Czechoslovakia. *Science* 246, 1002–8.

Vanhaeren, M. and d'Errico, F. 2001. La parure de l'enfant de La Madeleine (fouille Peyrony): un nouveau regard sur l'enfance au Paléolithique Supérieur. *Paléo* 13, 201–40.

Vanhaeren, M. and d'Errico, F. 2006. Aurignacian ethno-linguistic geography of Europe revealed by personal ornaments. *Journal of Archaeological Science* 33, 1105–11.

Verpoorte, A. 2005. The first modern humans in Europe? A closer look at the dating evidence from the Swabian Jura (Germany). *Antiquity* 79, 269–79.

Vialou, D. 2001. Architecture de l'art pariétal Paléolithique. In M. Lejeune (ed.), *L'art pariétal Paléolithique dans son contexte naturel*, 7–14. Liège: ERAUL 107.

White, R. 1987. Glimpses of long-term shifts in Late Paleolithic land use in the Périgord. In O. Soffer (ed.), *The Pleistocene Old World: regional perspectives*, 263–75. New York: Plenum Press.

White, R. 1989. Production complexity and standardisation in Early Aurignacian bead and pendant manufacture: evolutionary implications. In P. Mellars and C. Stringer (eds), *The human revolution*, 366–90. Edinburgh: Edinburgh University Press.

Wojtal, P. and Sobczyk, K. 2005. Man and woolly mammoth at the Kraków Spadzista Street (B)—taphonomy of the site. *Journal of Archaeological Science* 32, 193–206.

Zilhão, J. 2007. The emergence of ornaments and art: an archaeological perspective on the origins of 'behavioural modernity'. *Journal of Archaeological Research* 15, 1–54.

Zilhão, J. and d'Errico, F. 1999. The chronology and taphonomy of the earliest Aurignacian and its implications for the understanding of Neanderthal extinction. *Journal of World Prehistory* 13, 1–68.

Zilhão, J. and d'Errico, F. 2003. The chronology of the Aurignacian and Transitional technocomplexes: where do we stand? In J. Zilhão and F. d'Errico (eds), *The chronology of the Aurignacian and of the transitional technocomplexes: dating, stratigraphies, cultural implications*, 313–49. Lisbon: Trabalhos de Arqueologia 33.

Zilhão, J., d'Errico, F., Bordes, J.-G., Lenoble, A. and Texier, J.-P. 2006. Analysis of Aurignacian interstratifications at the Châtelperronian type-site and implications for the behavioural modernity of Neanderthals. *Proceedings of the National Academy of Sciences (USA)* 103, 12643–8.

Zilhão, J. and Trinkaus, E. 2002. Social implications. In J. Zilhão and E. Trinkaus (eds.), *Portrait of the artist as a child: the Gravettian human skeleton from the Abrigo do Lagar Velho and its archaeological context*, 519–41. Lisbon: Trabalhos de Arqueologia 22.

CHAPTER 13

THE PALAEOLITHIC OF NORTHERN ASIA

ANATOLY P. DEREVIANKO, SERGEI V. MARKIN, AND ANDREI V. TABAREV

The periodization of the Old Stone Age in northern and central Asia (Mongolia) starts with the Lower Palaeolithic. The comparison of the oldest sites in the region points to the variability of the Lower Palaeolithic culture, possibly caused by the expansion waves of the oldest *Homo erectus* human populations into this part of Eurasia, which took place at various time periods. The first 'out of Africa' migration of the oldest hominids, which took place between 2 and 1.8 million years ago, resulted in occurrences of the Oldowan-type pebble industries in Eurasia. In northern Asia they are represented by the sites of Ulalinka, Karama, the minimal age of which is 800,000–600,000 BP, and by the Mongolian archaic pebble-tool complexes of Narijn-Gol 17. Spatial and temporal reconstructions of ancient migrations include another wave of ancient hominid relocations into Eurasia, this time from the Near East, already in the late *erectus* stage. The start of such movement refers to the time period between 450,000 and 350,000 BP, and this movement resulted in mechanical relocation and the subsequent spread of the late Acheulian or of the Acheulian-Mousterian industry with the Levallois technology and with bifacial tools.

In Siberia the evidence for relocation of carriers of such culture is based on the materials from the basal layers of the Denisova cave in Altai, from the destroyed Torgalyk site in Tuva (bifaces), and from Mongolia (technocomplexes from the lower levels of the Tsagan Agui cave and destroyed localities of Yarkh, Gobi Bottom, Khatan-Khairan-Uul 14, and complexes from Flint Valley) (Derevianko 2005a).

The next Palaeolithic stage of the region is represented by the Middle Palaeolithic sites, concentrated in northern Asia, primarily in Altai and its adjacent regions of southern Siberia–Kuznetski Alatau, Tuva, and, possibly, the Angara region. In Mongolia the Middle Palaeolithic sites are concentrated in Mongolian and Gobi Altai and on the northern shores of the Lakes Valley. The next Palaeolithic stage in Siberia and Mongolia is represented by various phases of formation and development of the Upper Palaeolithic culture. The discovery and study of the sites, the age of which is between 50,000 and 30,000 BP, in Altai, Yenissei Siberia, in the Angara region, in the western and eastern Baikal region, and various parts of Mongolian and Gobi Altai, make it possible to describe northern and central Asia as one of the regions where Upper Palaeolithic culture originated.

The Upper Palaeolithic is represented by several stages including the early Upper Palaeolithic, the Upper Palaeolithic itself (before, during, and right after the Late Glacial Maximum), and the Final Palaeolithic, which in most parts of Siberia is dated between 15,000 and 11,000 BP. Technologically, it demonstrates a variety of techniques with prismatic blades, flakes, and microblades. The last technique (microblade) appeared in the very early stage of the Upper Palaeolithic in Altai (as a modification of percussion) and spread over the whole of north-east Asia after the LGM (being based on pressure).

Middle Palaeolithic Sites and Materials

Altai is a region with a particularly high concentration of the Middle Palaeolithic sites in northern Asia (Derevianko and Markin 1992; Derevianko and Shunkov 2002; Shunkov 1990). The initial formation stage of the industries, developing in the direction of the Mousterian features, according to the materials from the Denisova cave (layers 22, 21) and Ust-Karakol 1 site (layer 19), refers to the second half of the Neo-Pleistocene in the interval between 282,000 and 133,000 BP. The materials from most cave and open sites (Denisova cave, Ust-Karakol 1, Strashaya with multiple layers, which form the middle part of the section, Okladnikova cave, Ust-Kanskaya cave, Tymechin 1, 2, lower layers of the Kara-Bom) refer to the time period between 100,000 and 44,800 BP. Finally, the latest (the upper layer of Okladnikova cave) Middle Palaeolithic complexes of the region refer, according to the radiocarbon dating, to the age of 33,500 BP.

In spite of the blank percentage fluctuations (blades, flakes, Levallois spalls) and tool varieties, which by themselves can serve as a basis for the definition of technical varieties (Derevianko and Shunkov 2004), we must point to definite uniformity of the material culture of the Middle Palaeolithic in Altai, the elements of which are represented at most sites. Natural factors, the economic specialization of the population, accessibility and quality of raw materials, variable types of settlement sites—all have served as determining factors in the formation of industries. Technocomplexes of the two multi-layered caves, Okladnikova and Chagyrskaya caves, stand out in the series of Middle Palaeolithic sites in Altai (Derevianko and Markin 1992; Derevianko et al. 2008). The specific feature of the industries is the domination of radial splitting. This strategy resulted in the mass production of spalls with the divergence of flaking and symmetrical axes. Among the secondary treatment techniques, the most vivid was the retouch technique, the application of which led to the formation of backed and working elements (retouch, various types of encouches). Scrapers and déjeté-type tools dominate the tool set. The majority of scrapers belong to single-side and transversal forms; there are fewer double parallel and convergent scrapers; there are single occurrences of scrapers with retouch along the perimeter, thinned-backed scrapers, *Quina*-type scrapers, ventrally and alternatively retouched scrapers. There are scraper-knives with natural and retouched backs. The déjeté-tools could be divided into various double and triple varieties; they can be differentiated according to the number of working edges, their orientation, shape, secondary treatment techniques, and angles between the working edges.

In the Yenissei basin, in addition to the destroyed Middle Palaeolithic objects (Kamenny Log II-B complex), the Dvuglazka grotto (layers 7–5) is known, the inventory of which consists of radial and parallel cores, Levallois points, scrapers on thick flakes, and notched-denticulate tools on irregular blades (Abramova 1985; Archeologiya 1992). On the slopes of the Sagly River and on the surface of the Tannu-Ola ridge, in Tuva, the Middle Palaeolithic artefact sets were collected. They include flat parallel cores, Levallois spalls, scrapers, endscrapers, encouches, and beak-like tools.

The Sites and Materials of the Early Upper Palaeolithic

The earliest manifestation of the Upper Palaeolithic culture in Altai is documented in the materials of layers 7, 8, and 11 of the Denisova cave. The radiocarbon date of layer 11, which refers to the isotope stage 3, is 48,650 ± 2380 years BP. The stone artefacts of the site demonstrate the use of parallel, and in fewer cases radial and Levallois flaking techniques. Evidence of microblade technology is also present. In the tool set, artefacts of the Middle and Upper Palaeolithic typologies are equally represented. The Middle Palaeolithic tools are represented by scrapers, Levallois points, and beak-like and notched-denticulate tools. The other part of the tool set consists of endscrapers, burins, borers, and retouched blades. Typical assemblages consist of leaf-like bifaces and backed bladelets, which refer to the micro-implement varieties. Bone implements include oval and flat needles with holes, points, and perforators, manufactured from large fragments of long bones. A rich selection of decorations includes pendants made of animal teeth, bead-like elements made of hollow long animal bones, and various bone rings, ornamented by parallel ring cuts. Beads made of ostrich shells have also been found. Also recovered are perforated decorations made of stone and shells. Unique artefacts include a stone bracelet made by applying polishing, filing, and boring techniques and a large stone ring made out of white coarse-grained marble (Figure 13.1). Similar artefact sets found in Altai, characterized by signs of evolved micro-prismatic flaking and Aurignacian tool types, originate from the multi-layered sections of Anui 3 (layers 11, 12) and Ushlep 6 (layer 8 is dated at 42,000 BP) (Derevianko and Shunkov 2004; Baryshnikov et al. 2005).

Another group of early Upper Palaeolithic Altai sites demonstrates clearly defined blade industries, which have no signs of Aurignacian elements in the tool sets (Derevianko et al. 1998; 2000). First of all, there are sites Kara-Bom (six occupation levels, dated between 43,300 ± 1600 and 30,990 ± 460 years BP) and Kara-Tenesh (four measurement results between 42,165 ± 4170 and 26,875 ± 625 years BP). These sites are included in the series of rare European-Mediterranean objects (Bohunice, Boker Taktik, Nazlet Khater 4), which refer to the first half of the isotope stage 3, extending from the pleniglacial 1 to the end of the Hengelo interstadial, the technocomplexes of which are based on the development of the Levallois blade technologies. Among the Kara-Bom materials there are objects of symbolic activity—pendants made out of bones and animal teeth and also traces of mineral colouring agents (Derevianko and Rybin 2003). Ochre traces have been also found in Maloyalomanskaya cave which are older than 33,500 BP (Derevianko 2001).

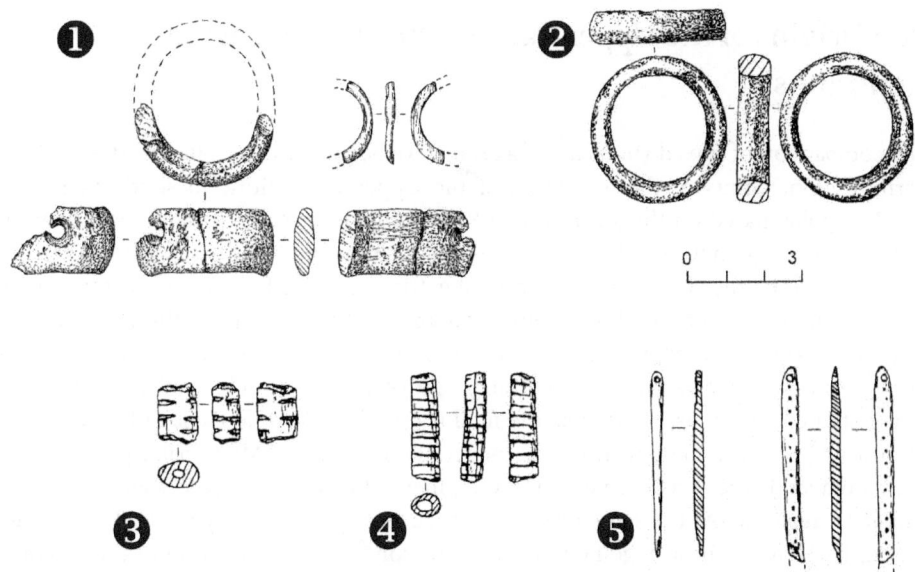

FIGURE 13.1 A stone bracelet, a ring, bone bead-like elements, and needles from layer 11 of Denisova cave. Layer 11 refers to the initial stage of the Upper Palaeolithic in Northern Asia.

Early Upper Palaeolithic sites have been discovered in other regions of southern Siberia. To the east of Altai, in the inner regions of the Kuznetskaya hollow, the Mokhovo 2 site is known, the materials of which have been dated at 30,330 ± 445 years BP. At this site cores with separate platforms and radial cores, well-defined oval bi-convex bifaces with thinned bases, scrapers, scraper-knives, and endscrapers on flakes have been discovered (Derevianko and Markin 1998). In Transbaikalia the beginning of the Upper Palaeolithic is reflected in the materials of the Makarovo 4 site, the age of which, according to radiocarbon dating, is older than 39,000–38,000 BP. The techno-morphological characteristic of the site is described by the combination of the Mousterian-Levallois and proto-prismatic techniques of stone flaking. Parallel flat flaking is common and is directed at serial manufacturing of blades. The common tools in this case are scrapers, thinned base points, endscrapers on the elongated spalls, transversal burins, retouched blades, knives on blades, and isolated cases of points and choppers (Aksenov 1987).

The northernmost site in the Angara basin is a multi-layered Ust-Kova site, the lower layer of which is characterized by the following dates: 30,100 ± 1500 and over 32,000 years BP. The complex of tools includes Levallois flakes, large flakes, scrapers, and chopping and other tools. A representative group of sites is known in western and eastern Transbaikalia: Podzvonkaya site, which is dated at 43,900 ± 960 years BP, Kamenka, dated in the A complex at 40,500 ± 3800 BP, Varvarina Gora (layer 3 with dates 30,600 ± 500 and 34,900 ± 780 years BP), and Tolbaga (layer 4 with dates 27,210 ± 300 and 34,800 ± 2100 years BP). Cores of the parallel flaking strategy and blades are widely represented in the industries of the sites (Konstantinov 1994; Lbova 2000; 2002; Tashak 2002).

The Origins of the Upper Palaeolithic in Northern and Central Asia

The comparison of mixed (in terms of age) materials, referring to different stages of the periodization, points to the formation of the Upper Palaeolithic in southern Siberia and Mongolia, based on the local Middle Palaeolithic industry. The main technological feature of the regional early Upper Palaeolithic technocomplexes is seen in the general trend of flaking procedures being directed at getting elongated blanks; at the same time, the combination of the Levallois-Mousterian and of the Upper Palaeolithic features in technology and typology and also the repetition of a series of features model a transition to the new epoch as a linear evolutionary process. The role of blade flaking increases in the studied region as far back as the final stage of the Middle Palaeolithic (60,000–50,000 BP), which is best seen on the materials from Altai (Mousterian layers of the Kara-Bom site). The consequences of development of blade flaking are seen in the early Upper Palaeolithic. At the same time, the heterogeneity of the early Upper Palaeolithic is seen in Altai and in Mongolia. One of the reasons for the separation of the original, or in other words, ancestral industry could have been the formation of various forms of human adaptation to the changes in climatic conditions, which are most obvious in the mountainous regions. The culture of Altai, in the chronological range between 50,000 and 40,000 BP, demonstrates two contemporaneous lines of development, or traditions based on a single Middle Palaeolithic tradition (Derevianko 2001; 2007). The first tradition (corresponding to horizons of the Denisova cave and of Ust-Karakol 1 site) with Aurignacian features, named the Ust-Karakol tradition, is characterized by the presence of blade and microblade technologies and of special microtools. Among the artefacts with Aurignacian features are endscrapers of high forms (Ust-Karakol), backed bladelets (level 11 at Denisova cave), and bone industry (pendants with grooves, needles and awls with geometric decoration).

Another tradition called the Kara-Bom tradition (corresponding to horizons of the Kara-Bom and Kara-Tenesh sites) also points to progress in the flaking technology, whereby the thickness of the blanks decreases and the elongation of the blanks increases; however, the formation of Aurignacian features does not take place. The technological analysis of industries of various types, in which not so much the morphologies of cores and blanks, but the operational sequences are recognized, in which these cores and blanks are included, also points to significant cultural differentiation of the early Upper Palaeolithic culture in the study region. An unexpectedly old age of the Ust-Karakol variation of the culture has been determined for layer 11 of the Denisova cave, the date value of which, obtained by applying the mass-spectrometry method, turned out to be a little less than 50,000 BP. It is quite amazing that such an old culture includes rich selections of bone decorations and along with the Mousterian artefacts contains signs of fully developed and not merely incipient microflaking. Not long ago it was believed that this treatment of raw material, which was considered to be a late stage in the evolutionary process, was characteristic of the culture of the second half of the Upper Palaeolithic, and not of the earlier time period. It is noteworthy that the culture of the Kara-Bom tradition also contains the non-utilitarian objects of human activity, which include decoration and figurative expressions. Thus, Altai, as an integral part of northern Asia, and Mongolia, as a part of central Asia, demonstrate at the early stages of the Upper Palaeolithic a binary-organized system, in which several cultural variants coexisted.

It is recognized that anatomically modern humans (*Homo sapiens*) were the carriers of Upper Palaeolithic culture. If compared to the previous *Homo* representatives, modern humans went through fundamental changes in social behaviour norms, ways of thinking, and social organization. There are several hypotheses about the origin of modern anthropological humans. Some researchers say that *Homo sapiens* originated in Africa about 200,000–100,000 BP and in the process of dissemination around the planet replaced the archaic human forms. According to the opinion of other scientists, archaic local forms turned into our sub-species independently from each other. Quite a few arguments in favour of the polycentric hypothesis of *Homo sapiens* origin and of its culture are given in the analysis of the materials from eastern Eurasia. The regional factor of *Homo sapiens* origin manifested itself in eastern and south-eastern Asia, where *Homo erectus* and similar human forms were developing a culture different from the cultures of the rest of Eurasia. The transition to the Upper Palaeolithic and its early stages had certain characteristic features, indicating that there was no migration flow capable of replacing the autochthonous cultures and the aboriginal population (Derevianko 2005b).

Post-Glacial Colonization and Transformations: Northern Asia

In the late glacial and post-glacial periods (17,000–10,800 BP), the vast territories of northern Eurasia (which in various sources are identified by the term 'Siberia') became an area of dynamic development for unique archaeological cultures. The characteristics of these cultures were, on the one hand, determined by the adaptation to the changing natural-climatic conditions and, on the other hand, by the technological base, developed during the LGM. According to the chronological pattern of the post-glacial period in Siberia, the second part of the Sartan glaciation was marked by the cooling wave (N'japan stage) in the interval between 15,000 and 13,000 BP. Later two climatic oscillations were defined as the Kokorev (13,000–12,000 BP) and the Taimyr (11,800–11,500 BP) interstadials, the Siberian analogues of Belling and Allerød. Between them there could have been a short-term cooling wave. Finally, the final Neo-Pleistocene is marked by the traces of drastic, short-term (11,500–10,500 BP) cooling, the Norilsk stage, which is similar to the Younger Dryas (Kind 1974).

In geographic terms, scientists usually talk about several large regions, the size and borders of which are connected with the basins of major rivers, mountain ranges and foothills, ocean proximity, or island conditions. Such regions are western Siberia (Ob River basin), eastern Siberia (Yenisei River basin), Altai, the Baikal region, Transbaikalia, Yakutia (the basins of Lena, Aldan, and Olekma rivers), the Amur region (Amur River basin), Primorye, Sakhalin Island, and the far north-east (Okhotsk region, Kamchatka and Chukchi peninsulas).

The environmental conditions of the Sartan in the Altai, if compared to the Karginian, are characterized by a worsening of the climate. In the period of the first half of the glaciation, based on the site cross-sections (of the Denisova, Kaminnaya, and Ust-Karakol I caves) of north-western Altai, the cold and dry conditions returned, contributing to the degradation of forest vegetation and the expansion of the nival and steppe biocenosis areas. Starting from 14,000 BP, this part of Altai was characterized by the distribution and subsequent migration of the interstadial steppes, periglacial forest-steppes and steppes, and later steppes and forest-steppes and periglacial mountainous forest landscapes.

A significant number of archaeological sites, many of which are characterized by the representative series of radiocarbon dates, attributed primarily to the upper and middle Yenissei River basins, suggest intensive peopling of this part of Siberia at the end of the Upper Palaeolithic. In this area, open type sites have been found, many of which are multi-layered sites. In addition a few caves have been found (Yeleneva). Sites of this region have been found in the deposits of low terraces, situated above the flood plain, and also at the higher levels, indicating that humans managed to explore various terrain types.

A significant site concentration was discovered in the prongs of the eastern Sayan Mountains. These localities are attributed to the deposits covering high cliff remnants (Karaulnyj Byk) and also slope (Afontova Gora I–IV) and alluvial (Listvenka) strata up to 40 m thick, alluvial sands, and loamy sands of lower terraces 10–12 m (resettlement location, Bolshaya Slizneva). The environment in which people lived during the Sartan in this part of the Yenissei River basin is characterized by the development of the periglacial cold landscapes (Shalunin Byk) or treeless areas with isolated patches of forest vegetation (Afontova Gora II), which gradually changed into forest-steppe landscapes (Bolshaya Slizneva). The Listvenka site was located in a zone of dark coniferous forests and meadow-valley steppes. Later this area was characterized by the development of forest-steppes, and finally of areas with no forest vegetation.

Another group of sites is located in the valley of the Upper Yenissei, at the junction of the Koibal steppe and the West Sayan mountains. A series of sites are attributed to the alluvial sands and loamy sands (Ui II, Golubaya I) and slope deposits (Kantegir II) of the terrace. Looking at the cross-sections of the Ui II site, one can conclude that in the period between 16,000 and 11,000 BP forest vegetation was developing, which was later replaced by a steppe-type environment. The particular feature of the multi-layered Maininskaya site is that it is located at two different elevation levels. The western part of the object with layers of 12,100–11,700 BP is located at the terrace, which is 25–27 m high. This was the time of the spread of forest vegetation. The eastern part of the site, with layers of 15,500–12,300 BP, is connected with 16–18 m high terrace and corresponds to the period of cold climatic conditions which facilitated the development of the forest-steppe, forest, and open steppe landscapes.

On the territory of Yakutia and Transbaikalia, the majority of the final Palaeolithic sites are situated in the developed river valleys on the alluvial terraces and in the Russian Far East (Primorye and the Amur region) generally in the delluvial thin-surface loamy soils. In the latter case, it is difficult to make a detailed distinction between the proper Pleistocene and early Holocene deposits. In addition, it is fairly difficult to give them a proper geographical characteristic. The palaeoclimatic data, which point to the significant difference between temperature conditions in the winter and summer months, regional particulars, and changes in the species composition within the year, and also variable landscape (mountainous, forest-steppe, forest-tundra, taiga, shore, etc.) predetermined development of various economic models. Hunting in combination with various types of gathering and fishing practices (river and lake fishing) played a leading role in the continental parts of Siberia during the final Palaeolithic.

Technologies Used by Hunter-Gatherers and Fishers

The archaeological materials found at sites in Siberia and the Russian Far East provide detailed information about the development of tool manufacturing technologies (primarily lithic tools) of the final Palaeolithic (17,000–11,000 BP). They are represented by a flexible and effective *chaîne opératoire* and unique design techniques of variable tools, which corresponded to the new specific features of the hunting-gathering-fishing economy.

The materials of the final stage of the Altai Palaeolithic, regardless of the area in which they were discovered, demonstrate significant similarity. They are all characterized by the coexistence of the Upper Palaeolithic and Archaic elements. The reduction technology at all sites is based on parallel and prismatic stone reduction, including narrow-faced and wedge-like cores. Various scrapers dominate among the tools, sometimes with partial bifacial treatment (Srostki, Urozhainaya). Equally expressive are the scrapers made on flakes and blades. Angle borers have also been found (Srostki); sometimes they have protuberances (Maima) or thinned needle-like points (Ust-Kuyum), Châtelperron-type knives (Srostki), burins, pointed tools, chisel-like tools, points, nosed tools, denticular-notched tools, rare bifaces (Denisova, Kaminnaya, Karaturuk), and stemmed tools. At several sites (Ust-Sema, Ust-Kuyum) pebble tools were found. On the sites of north-western (Denisova, Kaminnaya, Iskra) and north-eastern (Ushlep 2–6) Altai blades and truncated backed bladelets were found. At several sites bone artefacts were discovered: needles (Denisova, Kaminnaya), points (Tytkesken 3), cylindrical beads (*proniski*) made of tubular bird bones, rings made of ostrich eggshells (Denisova), and pendants made of perforated animal teeth (Denisova, Kaminnaya, Iskra). Near the village of Pobeda on the Chumysh River, specimens of tools made of bison bones were found, which included a dagger, slotted spear points, and harpoons.

The majority of the Yenissei sites are classified as main stationary sites with a complete cycle of stone treatment, with raw materials (quartzite, microquartzite, etc.) coming from the shore pebble accumulations close to the habitation sties (Vasil'ev et al. 2005). In some cases, it is possible to determine the seasonality of site organization. This way, the faunal data analysis from several sites (Bolshaya Slizneva, the eastern part of Maininskaya site) points to their occupation in the spring–autumn period (Vasil'ev 1996). The North-Minusinsk Depression and the western Sayan sites demonstrate functional specialization of various habitation locations. These can be areas of workshop sites (Maininskaya), semi-functional workshop sites, individual stone reduction workshops, debris disposal areas (Kokorevo I), and specialized accumulations of tools (Kokorevo II). Appearing as rare objects of the Yenissei Palaeolithic are the hunting camps (Nizhni Idzhir I) and the workshops (layer 8 of the Ui II site) for selecting and testing raw materials. In the area of Koibal steppe a cache called Sosnovoye Ozero (Pine Lake) is known, located in the artificially dug out pit, covered by a sandstone slab: eight points made of antler material, ten stone objects, and five fragments of horse bones—blanks for tool production.

The stone tools found at the Yenissei sites reflect two culture varieties, the difference between which is reflected primarily in the differences in the stone-splitting techniques and in the percentage of tools of various categories (Abramova 1979a; 1979b). Amorphous cores and microcores of various types are represented in the Afontov variety (Afontova Gora II, Kokorevo II, III, Tashtyk I, II, Maininskaya, Kantegir). Flakes served as primary blank types. Common artefacts are numerous scrapers, chisel-like tools, scrapers on flakes, borers, and choppers. Burins, points, retouched microblades, and tools made of the latter are not so common. The Kokorevo variety of the culture (Kokorevo I, Novoselovo VI, VII) is characterized by the presence of large cores for blades and wedge-like nuclei. Blade blanks were primarily used for tool manufacturing. Most of the tools are blade-based. These are scrapers, points, burins, endscrapers, and choppers. Wedge-like tools and borers are rare artefacts. In the strata of the multi-layered isolated sites (Listvenka) in the industries of various layers, both culture versions are represented. The blade industry of the Goluboi I site, dated at 12,000–13,000 BP, is unusual if compared to the sites of Yenissei Final Palaeolithic and contains small cores, narrow-faced microcores, retouched blades, scrapers on blades, backed blades, micropoints, and borers.

In the Russian Far East (Primorye, Amur region, Sakhalin Island), in Transbaikalia and Yakutia, the microblade technique dominated among the reduction systems, which consisted of applying pressure flaking in the manufacturing of standard microblades based on uniquely shaped wedge-like cores (Derevianko and Tabarev 2006; Kuzmin et al. 2007; Vasil'ev 2001). Bifaces, unifaces, blades, and large flakes are used as core blanks. Using small portative devices made of wood, antler, or bone allowed hunters to retain high mobility and to minimize the process of rejuvenating the composite tools (points, knifes), and also to minimize the number of trips to the raw material sources (Tabarev 1997). In a significant part of the region (eastern Siberia, Transbaikalia, Yakutia, and Amur region), the microblade technique survived during the whole of the final Pleistocene and transformed in the early Holocene into a yet more effective microprismatic technique.

The blade technique continued to coexist along with the microblade technique in the regions with quality raw-material sources (Transbaikalia, Yakutia, Primorye). This is based on the use of large sub-prismatic cores, with direct or indirect percussion (Tabarev 1994). Various bifacial forms are found and among them an increasingly important role was played by the projectile points (spear-points, javelins, arrows) and knives. A wide range of treatment tools has been found: burins, gravers, scrapers, drills, borers, small saws, etc. Among the burins, the so-called 'transversal' (diagonal) forms have been identified, having one or several negatives of burin spalls, which are twisted (directed from the dorsal to the ventral part of the tool). Particular attention should be paid to the development of wood-treatment tools: axes, adzes, gouges, and chisels, which could have been actively used not only for construction purposes, but also in making hunting traps, stream dams, etc. By the final Palaeolithic partial polishing of blade parts of tools was used in order to enhance their effectiveness.

In spite of the poor preservation of organic matter in many regions of Siberia and, particularly, of the Russian Far East, the archaeological materials definitely point to the existence of various bone, antler, tusk, fibre, skin, and shell treatment technologies, used for the production of tools (needles, awls, points) and also for various other economic purposes (containers, grass mats, and clothes).

Dwelling Structures and Settlement Patterns

The seasonal nature of the human economic activity and of the mobile/settled ways of life in the final Pleistocene is reflected in the traces of dwelling structures, which people used for living and for various economic activities. The majority of the Altai sites are settlement sites with a full cycle of stone treatment, based on the use of raw materials (siltstone, sandstone, hornstone, jasper-like material, quartzite, etc.) procured in the immediate vicinity from the habitation areas on the channel pebble beaches. The stone industry structure at a series of sites (Torgun, Urozhainaya) is reminiscent of workshop sites. At the Bigdon location, 'stationary' nuclei in the form of massive petrosilex and striate flint with numerous spall traces have been found. At some sites of north-eastern and central Altai and its northern foothills, artificial structures of various purposes have been found. Primarily, these are the surfaces (Ushlep 3, 5) or slightly deepened hearths (Dmitrievka, Nakhalovka I, Tochka II, Tytkesken 3, Maima) around which artefacts can be sometimes concentrated (Srostki). Another type of fireplace is represented by the structures (Maima, Ust-Kuyum) with a semicircular fencing made of flat pebbles. At the Ust-Kuyum site, there are possibly remains of the surface dwelling, with a diameter reaching six metres and also with pole holes and places for primary stone treatment with anvils and reduction products present. Another type of structure is characterized by the boulder and pebble accumulations in the form of fences of an unknown purpose with a diameter of up to one metre (Maima, Ushlep 3, 5).

A significant number of dwelling remains dated 17,000–11,500 BP are known at the archaeological sites of Transbaikalia (Studenoye-1-2, Ust-Menza-1-4, Kosaya Shivera) (Konstantinov 1994). All of them are represented by the surface skeleton structures of the shelter or tent of skins with stone fencing (40–70 cm in length) along the perimeter. The area of such dwellings varies from 5.5 to 50 square metres. The so-called 'polinary' structures have been identified. These are elongated dwellings (from 8 to 14 m in length, with width of about 3 m) with individual sections and dividing canopies. In the elongated dwellings, unlike the round structures, about three to four fireplaces were present, indicating cohabitation of several families and groups, similar to the long houses of the North American Iroquois.

On Sakhalin Island, at the Ogonki-V site, in accordance with the archaeological material concentration and traces of fireplace spots, parameters of two rounded-in-plan dwellings with surface areas around 50 and 60 square metres respectively, were reconstructed. According to the opinion of the leader of the excavations, the absence of working areas and hearths in the inter-dwelling space can indicate that the structures were used in the cold autumn–winter seasons in the timeframe between 19,000 and 16,000 BP (Vasilevski 2003).

Over a period of several years, the Russian scientist N. N. Dikov conducted research on the shores of Ushki Lake on the Kamchatka Peninsula. He studied multi-layered sites with traces of numerous dwelling structures of various types and sizes. The most ancient ones (14,000–13,000 BP), according to the author's opinion, are the large surface one- or two-chamber structures with an area of up to 100 square metres with one to three fireplaces. In the next period (between 12,000 and 10,500 BP), yet larger surface structures were added to them, having a floor area of up to 140 square metres and small tents with areas of 8 to

16 square metres. A special type is represented by mushroom-shaped dwellings (in plan), which cut 0.3–0.5 m into the ground with an area of up to 48 square metres. Up to 100–150 people could have been living in such a village during the hunting season (Dikov 1993).

The Anthropological Materials, Burial Practices, Rituals, Art Forms, and Social Relations among Northern Asian Hunter-Gatherers of the Final Palaeolithic

At the present time, the quantity of anthropological material known to archaeologists dated to between 17,000 and 11,000 BP remains quite insignificant; therefore the picture of ethnic dynamics and burial practices of the populations of Siberia and of the Russian Far East is very sketchy in its nature.

Rare anthropological finds of *Homo sapiens* were found on several sites of the Yenissei River. Thus, in layer 12 of Listvenki, a jaw of a child was found dated 13,470 ± 285 years BP, and at the site of Novoselovo VI a lower jaw of a young woman was found with a radiocarbon age of 11,600 ± 500 years BP.

However, there are also reasons to speak about complex mortuary rites and about the rich inventory which accompanied the buried people. For example, in layer VII at the Ushki-I site a round pit 0.7 m deep was excavated, richly decorated with red ochre. In spite of poor preservation of the anthropological material, numerous soft-stone beads were found in the burial place (881 pieces), as well as chalcedony gravers and stone points. At the same time, in layer VI several burial complexes were also found. The first one was the burial of a dog (dwelling 2), which was accompanied by a red ochre spot, an obsidian knife, a scraper, and a grindstone. The second burial complex was the burial of two small children in dwelling 3 in a specially prepared burial pit, which is approximately 20 cm deep. Children were placed in a cramped position on a special 'bedding' made of the incisor teeth of lemmings with various burial inventory objects (stone tools, cores, knife-like blades, polishing blocks, pendants made of perforated milk teeth). A more typical burial of several children was found in dwelling 10. In this burial ochre traces, lithic tool-kits (points, cores, scrapers), and decorations (amber pendant, animal figures made of stone by retouch, small shafts made of walrus tusk, etc.) were identified (Dikov 1993).

Clear evidence of ceremonial practices is demonstrated in the so-called microritual complexes, which have been found at several sites of the Russian Far East (Ustinovka-IV, Bogopol-IV, Suvorovo-IV). They are fixated in the form of vertically set stones in combination with points, microcores, and hearth remains, located in the central or most elevated parts of the sites. Their semantic meaning most likely corresponds to the solar symbols and their functional meaning is related to the territorial markers, which define the most comfortable locations for hunting and fishing (Tabarev 2006).

In spite of the fact that in the territory of Siberia and the Russian Far East no examples of cave art and monumental forms similar to the Magdalenian art of western Europe have been found, the visual arts of the inhabitants of the region can by no means be called poor or limited. One can say that a distinctive feature of the Siberian–Far Eastern final Palaeolithic art is reflected in a wide variety of small (mobile) forms (figurines, pendants, beads) manufactured out of various materials: stone, obsidian, amber, antler, bone, teeth, and also pebbles and engraved small blocks. In layer 5 of the Maininskaya site the most distinctive art form of the Yenissei Palaeolithic has been found: an anthropomorphic clay statuette of undetermined gender, the only one found in the territory of northern Asia. Quite interesting in terms of art type are the miniature plastic art forms made of flint: figurines of animals and birds, manufactured by applying the retouch technique, which served as personal and family amulets. Among them the most noticeable one is the set of salmon (Primorye, Amur region, Sakhalin Island), bear (Amur region, Primorye), and swimming bird (Amur region, Primorye) expressions. On the floor of dwelling 5 at the Ushki-1 site (Kamchatka Peninsula) a fish expression moulded out of red ochre has been found, which is the oldest geogliph known in the territory of northern Asia (Dikov 1993, 23).

The parameters of settlements and temporary sites, the dimensions and the number of the dwelling structures all point to the fact that local groups, which consisted of families, could have comprised from 30–40 to 100–150 people. This was an optimal number for the mobile hunter-gatherers, who were engaged in hunting and fishing activities. Depending on the season, these activities could have required either extreme energy concentration from the group, or division of labour and exploitation of the biological resources complex.

In most areas of the Altai, eastern Siberia, Transbaikalia, and Yakutia, the primary economy in the final Palaeolithic was based on hunting and river fishing, which required a fairly high level of mobility of small hunting groups on the tracks of seasonal habitation and relocation of animals.

In the regions of today's Russian Far East (Amur region, Primorye, Sakhalin Island, Kamchatka), the final Palaeolithic was characterized by the growth of spawning mass, which predetermined formation of a special type of economy: intensive seasonal salmon fishing. According to the ethnographic data, fish procurement requires collective effort, systematic organization and division of labour, occupation of the most convenient river locations by groups of fishermen, and even the acquisition of these river parts by certain families and kin.

It was the variety and richness of the biological resources and also an extremely high level of technological advancement that allow us to think that the social system of the Siberian and the Russian Far Eastern populations during the final Palaeolithic corresponds to the parameters of the so-called 'trans-egalitarian society' (Owens and Hayden 1997). In the frameworks of such societies, function mechanisms are in place for striving towards a certain status or certain prestige levels by individuals, families, groups and kin, and a tribal elite is formed, with the ritual-ceremonial practices dynamically developing.

Various archaeological factors speak in favour of this model. Firstly, this model is supported by child burials with mortuary objects, and also evidence for initiation (pendants made of milk teeth and microritual complexes). Secondly, there is the development of prestigious technologies—elegantly made stone and bone tools, mobile art objects, caches consisting of lithic material and blanks. Thirdly, there is evidence of importing exotic raw material from the adjoining regions. For example, obsidian was delivered to the shore valleys of Primorye from the continental parts of Korea (around 350 km), and to the territory of Sakhalin Island from the neighbouring island of Hokkaido (Gillam and Tabarev 2004; Kuzmin 2005, 173; Tabarev 2001).

Conclusions

The research and comparisons of the Middle Palaeolithic and early Upper Palaeolithic sites in northern Asia and Mongolia, dated by the methods of absolute dating at 30,000 and over BP, have demonstrated that the north-eastern part of Eurasia is one of the regions where the Upper Palaeolithic culture originated by way of transformation from the local

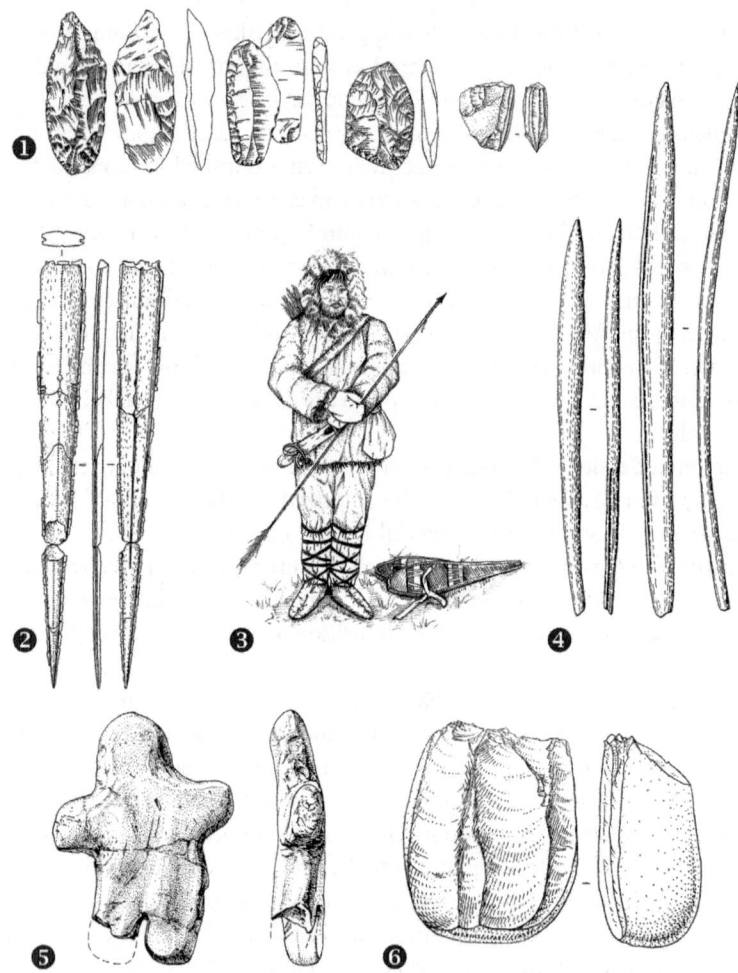

FIGURE 13.2 Western and eastern Siberia. 1 – stone tools and wedge-shaped microcore from Ust'–Belaya site; 2 – composite tool from Chernoozerie–II site; 3 – Final Palaeolithic hunter in winter clothing with dart and atlatl, reconstruction; 4 – bone and antler grooved tools from Maininskaya site (from Vasil'ev 1996, 99); 5 – clay figurine from Maininskaya site; 6 – pebble core from Kokorevo–I site.

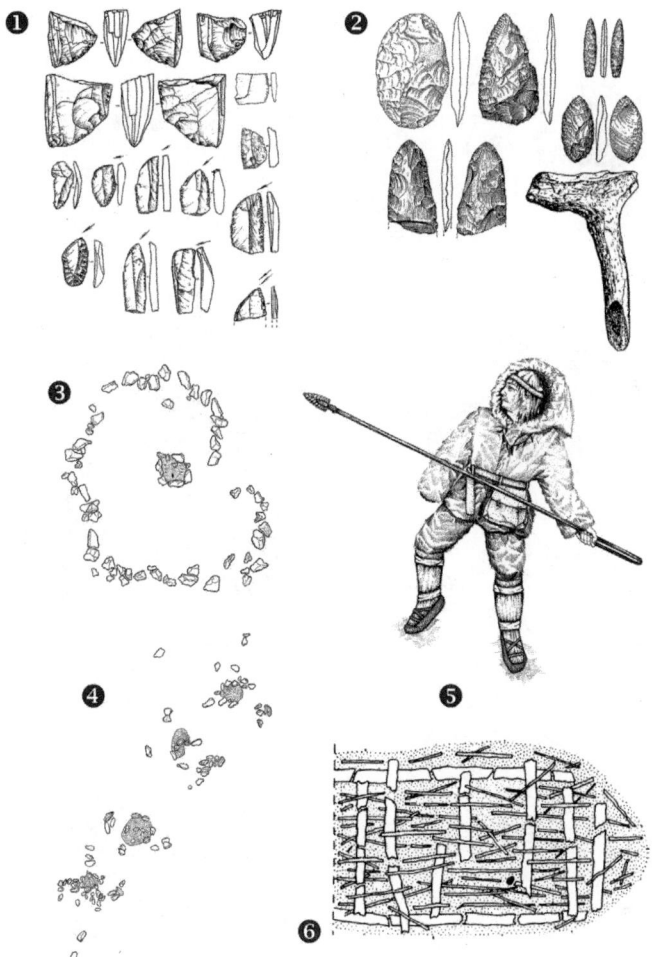

FIGURE 13.3 TransBaikal region and Yakutia. 1 – microblade cores and transversal burins, Ust'–Menza site (from Konstantinov 1994, plate 69); 2 – artefacts from Dyuktai cave; 3 – remains of light dwelling construction at Studenoe site (from Konstantinov 1994, plate 29); 4 – remains of 'polynary structure' at Ust'–Menza-3 site (from Konstantinov 1994, plate 34); 5 – Final Palaeolithic hunter in winter clothing, reconstruction; 6 – remains of dwelling at Ust–Timpton site.

Middle Palaeolithic culture. The chronology of the final Middle Palaeolithic (Okladnikova cave) and early Upper Palaeolithic (Denisova cave, Kara-Bom site) sites in Altai in the interval between 50,000 and 40,000 BP allows the possibility of lengthy coexistence of the late Mousterian industries and industries reflecting the process of formation of the Upper Palaeolithic culture, which indicates that the transition from one epoch to another took a relatively long time.

Altai, as an integral part of northern Asia, and Mongolia, as a part of central Asia, demonstrate that the early stages of the Upper Palaeolithic had a binary system, in which different

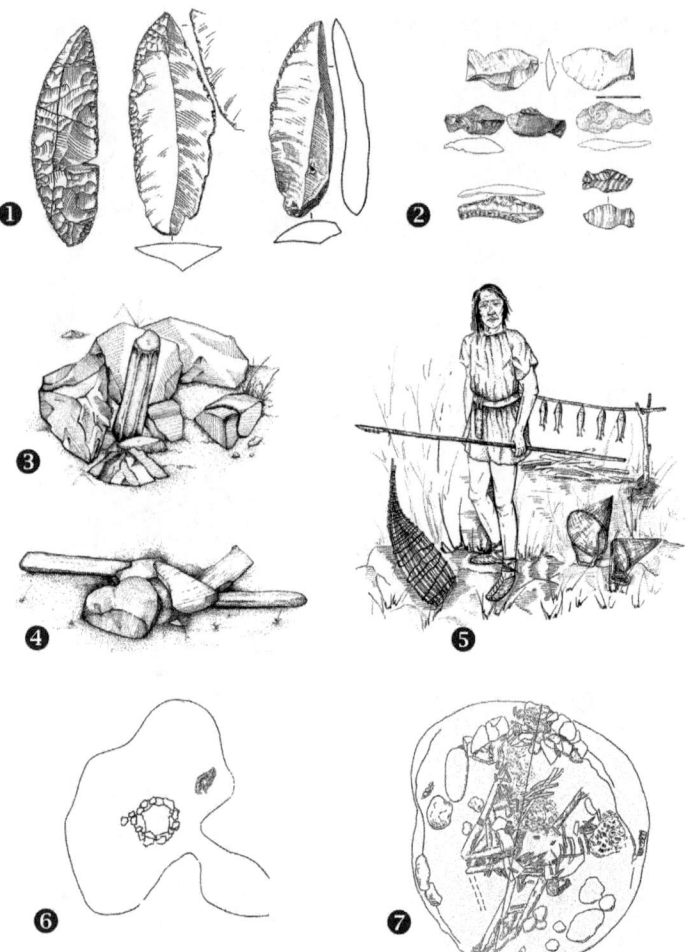

FIGURE 13.4 Russian Far East. 1 – stone knives from Suvorovo–III site (by Derevianko and Tabarev 2006, 46); 2 – stone images of salmon fish from the Far-eastern Palaeolithic sites (by Tabarev 2006, 117); 3–4 – microritual complexes with stones and bifacial point (by Tabarev 2006, 118): 5 – Final Palaeolithic salmon–fisher, reconstruction; 6 – dwelling with the burial of a dog at Ushki–I site, level VI (by Dikov 1993, 27); 7 – double burial in dwelling at Ushki–I site, level VI (by Dikov 1993, 28).

cultural variants coexisted. In the other regions of northern Asia (Kuznetsky Alatau, the valley of the middle reaches of the Angara River, Baikal region, Transbaikalia), where the early Upper Palaeolithic developed, large blade industries of a single tradition have so far been documented.

The epoch of the late glacial and post-glacial periods (17,000–10,800 BP), which was characterized by a general warming in climate and the formation of new landscapes, dictated to humans of the final Palaeolithic in northern Asia new conditions of existence and stimulated new ways of adaptation. The whole territory of northern Asia was finally inhabited by humans, and in spite of the significant fluctuations in the climate, we can definitely state that from that time on, only positive dynamics of population size have been observed.

On the wide territories of northern Asia in the final Palaeolithic, a series of flexible hunting, gathering, and fishing strategies were formed and developed (Figures 11.2–11.4). These strategies were directed at the exploitation of both specific (hoofed animals, swimming birds, rodents, salmon) and also complex types of bioresource. There are reasons to believe that in the taiga and coastal zones these strategies continued to play an important role during all of the following millennia, right up to the beginning of active exploration of the region by the settlers from the European region at the end of the nineteenth to the beginning of the twentieth century.

References

Abramova, Z. A. 1979a. *Paleolit Yenisseya. Afontovskaya cultura*. Novosibirsk: Nauka.
Abramova, Z. A. 1979b. *Paleolit Yenisseya. Kokorevskaya cultura*. Novosibirsk: Nauka.
Abramova, Z. A. 1985. Mustierski grot v Khakasii. *Kratkie soobsheniya instituta arkheologii*, vyp 181, 8–12.
Aksenov, M. P. 1987. Inventarny kompleks Makarovo IV. In *Problemy antropologii i arkheologii kamennogo veka Evrasia*, 23–25. Irkutsk: Irkutski gosudarstvenny universitet.
Arkheologiya, geologiya i paleogeografiya paleoliticheskikh pamjatnikov yuga Srednei Sibiri (Severo-minusinskaya vpadina, Kuznetski Alatau i Vostochnyi Sayan) 1992. Karsnoyarsk: Istitut Arkheologii i Etnografii SO RAN.
Baryshnikov, G. Y., Kungurov, A. L., Markin, M. M., and Semibratov, V. P. 2005. *Paleolit Gornoi Shorii*. Barnaul: Izd-vo Altayskogo Universiteta.
Derevianko, A. P. 2001. The Middle to Upper Palaeolithic transition in the Altai. *Archaeology, Ethnology and Anthropology of Eurasia* 3, 70–103.
Derevianko, A. P. 2005a. The earliest human migrations in Eurasia and the origin of the Upper Palaeolithic. *Archaeology, Ethnology and Anthropology of Eurasia* 2, 22–36.
Derevianko, A. P. 2005b. Formation of blade industries in eastern Asia. *Archaeology, Ethnology and Anthropology of Eurasia* 4, 2–29.
Derevianko, A. P. 2007. *K probleme obitaniya neandertalzev v Zentralnoy Azii i Sibiri*. Novosibirsk: Izd-vo IAET SO RAN.
Derevianko, A. P. and Markin, S. V. 1992. *Mustie Gornogo Altaya (po materialam peshery im. Okladnikova)*. Novosibirsk: Nauka.
Derevianko, A. P. and Markin, S. V. 1998. Paleolit severo-zapada Altae-Sayan. *Rossiyskaya arkheologiya* 4, 17–34.
Derevianko, A. P., Markin, S. V. and Zykin V. S. 2008. Peshera Chagyrskaya—novaya stoyanka srednego paleolita na Altaye. *Problemy arkheologii, etnografii, antropologii Sibiri i sopredelnykh territorii* 14, 52–55.
Derevianko, A. P., Petrin, V. T., Nikolayev, S. V., Dergacheva, M. I., Fedeneva, I. N., Krivoshapkin, A. I., and Chevalkov, L. M. 1998. Stoyanka Kara-Tenesh—pamyatnik nachalnoi pory pozdnego paleolita. In *Problemy paleoekologii, geologii i arkheologii paleolita Altaya*, 205–38. Novosibirsk: Izd-vo In-ta Arkheologii i Etnografii SO RAN.
Derevianko, A. P., Petrin, V. T. and Rybin, E. P. 2000. The Kara-Bom site and the characteristics of the Middle-Upper Palaeolithic transition in Altai. *Archaeology, Ethnology and Anthropology of Eurasia* 2, 33–52.

Derevianko, A. P. and Rybin, E. P. 2003. The earliest representation of symbolic behavior by Palaeolithic humans in the Altai mountains. *Archaeology, Ethnology and Anthropology of Eurasia* 3, 27–50.

Derevianko, A. P. and Shunkov, M. V. 2002. Middle Palaeolithic industries with foliate bifaces in Gorny Altai. *Archaeology, Ethnology and Anthropology of Eurasia* 1, 16–41.

Derevianko, A. P. and Shunkov, M. V. 2004. Formation of the Upper Palaeolithic traditions in the Altai. *Archaeology, Ethnology and Anthropology of Eurasia* 3, 12–40.

Derevianko, A. P. and Tabarev, A. V. 2006. Palaeolithic of the Primorye (Maritime) Province. In S. Nelson (ed.), *Archaeology of the Russian Far East: essays in Stone Age prehistory*, 41–54. Oxford: BAR International Series 1540.

Dikov, N. N. 1993. *Palaeolithic of Kamchatka and Chukotka in connection with the problem of initial peopling of America*. Magadan: Nauka.

Gillam, J. C. and Tabarev, A. V. 2004. On the path of Upper-Palaeolithic obsidians in the Russian Far East. *Current Research in the Pleistocene* 21, 3–6.

Kind, N. V. 1974. *Geokhronologiya pozdnego antropogena po izotopnym dannym*. Moscow: Nauka.

Konstantinov, M. V. 1994. *Kamenny vek vostochnoi chasti regiona Baikalskoi Azii*. Chita: Chitinski Pedagogicheski Institut.

Kuzmin, Y. V. 2005. *Geochronology and palaeoenvironment in Late Palaeolithic and Neolithic of temperate East Asia*. Vladivostok: Pacific Institute of Geography.

Kuzmin, Y. V., Keates, S. G. and Shen, C. (eds) 2007. *Origin and spread of microblade technology in northern Asia and North America*. Burnaby: Simon Fraser University Archaeology Press.

Lbova, L. V. 2000. *Paleolit severnoi zony Zapadnogo Zabaikalya*. Ulan-Ude: Izd-vo BNZ SO RAN.

Lbova, L. V. 2002. The transition from the Middle to Upper Palaeolithic in western Transbaykalia. *Archaeology, Ethnology and Anthropology of Eurasia* 1, 59–75.

Owens, D. and Hayden, B. 1997. Prehistoric rites of passage: a comparative study of transegalitarian hunter-gatherers. *Journal of Anthropological Archaeology* 16, 121–61.

Shunkov, M. V. 1990. *Mustierskie pamiatniki mezhgornykh kotlovin Zentralnogo Altaya*. Novosibirsk: Nauka.

Tabarev, A. V. 1994. The Ustinovka culture in the Stone Age of the Russian Far East: 40 years of discoveries. *Lithic Technology* 19, 21–34.

Tabarev, A. V. 1997. Palaeolithic wedge-shaped microcores and experiments with pocket devices. *Lithic Technology* 22, 139–49.

Tabarev, A. V. 2001. Russian Far East in the Final Palaeolithic: peopling, migrations, maritime, and riverine adaptation. In J. Gillespie, S. Tupakka, and C. de Mille (eds), *On being first: proceedings of the 31st Annual Chacmool Conference*, 511–26. Calgary: The Archaeological Association of the University of Calgary.

Tabarev, A. V. 2006. People of salmon: technology, art and ritual of the Stone Age cultures, Russia Far East. *Archaeological Education of the Japanese Fundamental Culture in East Asia, 21 COE Program Archaeology Series* 7, 111–124.

Tashak, V. I. 2002. Podzvonkaya: paleoliticheskiye materialy nizhnego kompleksa (Respublika Buryatiya). In *Arkheologiya i kulturnaya antropologiya Dalnego Vostoka i Zentralnoi Azii, Institut istorii, arkheologii i etnografii narodov Dalnego Vostoka*, 25–33. Vladivostok: DVO RAN.

Vasil'ev, S. A. 1996. *Pozdni paleolit Verkhnego Yenisseya (po materialam mnogosloinykh stoyanok raiona Mainy)*. St Petersburg: Zentr 'Peterburgskoye vostokovedeniye'.

Vasil'ev, S. A. 2001. The Final Palaeolithic in northern Asia: lithic assemblage diversity and explanatory models. *Arctic Anthropology* 38, 3–30.

Vasil'ev, S. A., Abramova, Z. A., Grigoreva, G. V., Lisicyn, S. N., and Sinicyn, G. V. 2005. *Pozdni paleolit Severnoi Evrazii: paleoekologiya i struktura poseleniy*. St Petersburg: Trudy Instituta Istorii Materialnoi Kultury RAN, t. 19.

Vasilevski, A. A. 2003. Periodization of the Upper Palaeolithic of Sakhalin and Hokkaido in the light of research conducted at the Ogonki-5 site. *Archaeology, Ethnology and Anthropology of Eurasia* 3, 51–69.

CHAPTER 14

HOMO SAPIENS SOCIETIES
South Asia

MICHAEL D. PETRAGLIA AND NICOLE BOIVIN

ONE in five people in the world today, or 1.5 billion people, inhabit South Asia. A remarkable range and diversity of cultures are found in the region, and no less than 850 languages and language dialects are spoken in the subcontinent. The inhabited spaces range from densely packed urban centres to isolated rural villages. Ethnographers and sociologists have documented the rich tapestry of cultural groups in South Asia, including study of village agriculturalists (Marriott 1955; Srinivas 1998), pastoral nomads (Leshnik and Sontheimer 1975), fishing communities (Reeves 2002), and foraging populations (Fortier 2009; Fürer-Haimendorf 1985; Morrison and Junker 2002).

The wide range of cultures in South Asia presents interdisciplinary researchers with an opportunity to examine the origin and evolution of societal formation and interconnections (Petraglia and Allchin 2007). Geneticists have examined a range of evolutionary and historical questions about South Asian populations, including the evaluation of human colonization (e.g. Kivisild et al. 2003), demic diffusions (e.g. Sahoo et al. 2006), demographic increases (e.g. Atkinson et al. 2008; Petraglia et al. 2009a), and caste relations (e.g. Watkins et al. 2008; Reich et al. 2009). Archaeologists have likewise examined a range of evolutionary, historical, and behavioural questions, including analysis of early human behaviours in the Acheulian (e.g. Petraglia 2006), economic and symbolic features of Neolithic society (e.g. Allchin 1963; Boivin et al. 2008; Fuller 2006; Fuller et al. 2007), the rise, spread, and collapse of the Indus civilization (e.g. Kenoyer 1998; Possehl 2002), and the development of historic empires and states (e.g. Sinopoli 2005; Sinopoli and Morrison 2007). Biological anthropologists have examined the population affinities of Early Holocene foragers (e.g. Lukacs 2007), the physical anthropology of proto-historic populations (e.g. Kennedy 2000; Walimbe 2007), and the cranial diversity of South Asian populations relative to other regions (e.g. Stock et al. 2007).

The aim of this chapter is to outline how the contemporary societal diversity in South Asia, especially that of foraging populations, developed in prehistory. Emphasis here is placed on archaeological findings from Middle and Late Palaeolithic contexts of the Late Pleistocene, and Mesolithic sites of the Holocene (Figure 14.1). We highlight some of the main archaeological evidence from these periods, summarizing what is currently known about human colonization of the subcontinent in the Late Pleistocene; dispersal routes taken during human expansion; the relationship between climate change, geography, and demography; and the evolution of modern human behaviour.

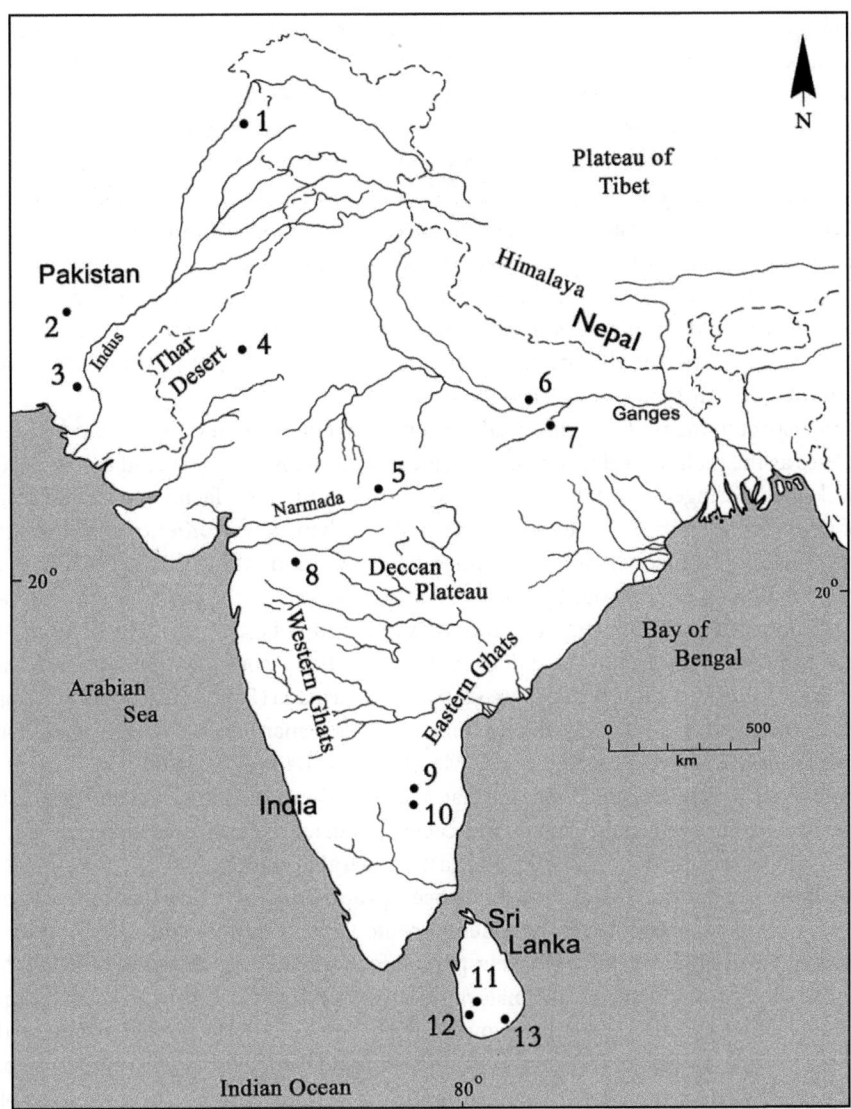

FIGURE 14.1 Indian subcontinent showing key localities mentioned in the text. 1. Site 55; 2. Mehrgargh; 3. Sindh (Ongar); 4. Didwana (16R Dune); 5. Bhimbetka; 6. Ganges sites; 7. Middle Son River (Patpara, Bagor I); 8. Patne; 9. Kurnool; 10. Jurreru River Valley (Jwalapuram 3, 9); 11. Batadomba Lena cave; 12. Fa Hien cave; 13. Site 49; Site 50.

Dispersals Out of Africa

The Indian subcontinent has been depicted as a transit zone in Out of Africa dispersal models (Kingdon 1993; Lahr and Foley 1994), a view that gained considerable support from genetic studies of human populations in the Andaman islands and elsewhere (e.g. Endicott et al. 2003; Thangaraj et al. 2005). Though mitochondrial DNA (mtDNA) coalescence ages vary widely (Endicott et al. 2009), most studies indicate that South Asian lineages (specifically U2i, M2, and R5) colonized the region by 70,000–50,000 years ago (Kivisild et al. 2000; Metspalu et al. 2004). Some mutation clock estimates continue to place modern humans in South Asia by 70,000 years ago (Soares et al. 2009) and perhaps before this lower age limit (Oppenheimer 2008). There is the possibility that L-haplogroup lineages dispersed from Arabia to India by 85,000–80,000 years ago, although there is no trace of this movement in the modern gene pool (Cabrera et al. 2009). Unfortunately, the fossil record does not help to determine the arrival date of modern human populations into South Asia. The oldest skeletal remains of *H. sapiens* date to c.31,000 years ago in the Fa Hien cave of Sri Lanka (Deraniyagala 1992) and c.20,000 years ago in the Jwalapuram Locality 9 rock shelter in India (Clarkson et al. 2009). Poor preservation of fossils continues to present significant challenges for identifying the species responsible for stone tool production in the period between c.85,000 and 30,000 years ago.

With respect to the routes of dispersal, a majority of current Out of Africa models depict coastlines as the main corridor for the movement of humans as they spread eastwards (e.g. Bulbeck 2007; Stringer 2000). In this view, coastlines would have facilitated a rapid dispersal of populations from Africa to South-East Asia, perhaps of the order of a few thousand years (Macaulay et al. 2005). Study of topographic conditions along the Indian Ocean rim indicates that populations would probably have travelled along the coasts as they migrated into the subcontinent (Field and Lahr 2005). Examination of the topography of South Asia indicates that once present on the Indian coast, populations would have rapidly penetrated the interior, utilizing major river valleys, such as the Narmada (Field et al. 2007; Figure 14.2). However, despite searches along the present-day littoral margins, only a few near coastal and estuarine sites have been identified (Marathe 1981; Rath et al. 1997) and none of the identified localities provide evidence for marine adaptation. Of course, there is the possibility that some archaeological sites and landscapes are currently inundated along the shallow coastal shelf, especially on the western and eastern margins of India.

An alternative to the coastal model has been proposed, suggesting that human populations would have found a transcontinental route to be a more favourable corridor for expansion (Korisettar 2007). In this view, populations spreading from the west would have expanded along corridors in the Himalayan passes, eventually reaching interior basins of the peninsula. The peninsular basins would have been attractive to human groups as they provided reliable sources of fresh water (in the form of lakes, streams, and springs), abundant raw materials for stone tool manufacture, and a high concentration of animal and plant resources. Occupation in the basins may be expected to have been especially attractive during periods of heightened aridity, when other marginal landscapes became increasingly inhospitable. Archaeological evidence provides considerable support for the terrestrial route given the abundance of Late Pleistocene sites in these favourable settings (e.g. see Pappu and Deo 1994; Sharma and Clark 1983), although the precise corridors of human movements remain unknown.

Debate has ensued concerning the timing of human dispersals and their archaeological associations. In a summation of the genetic and archaeological evidence from Africa to Australia, Mellars (2006) claimed that the southern dispersal route was firmly established at 60,000 years ago, the event marked by crescentic blade and microblade industries and symbolic traits associated with modern human behaviour. Mellars linked crescentic tool forms in Sri Lanka and India to African industries, such as Howieson's Poort, and further he observed similarities in engraved pieces found at Blombos (South Africa) with those of

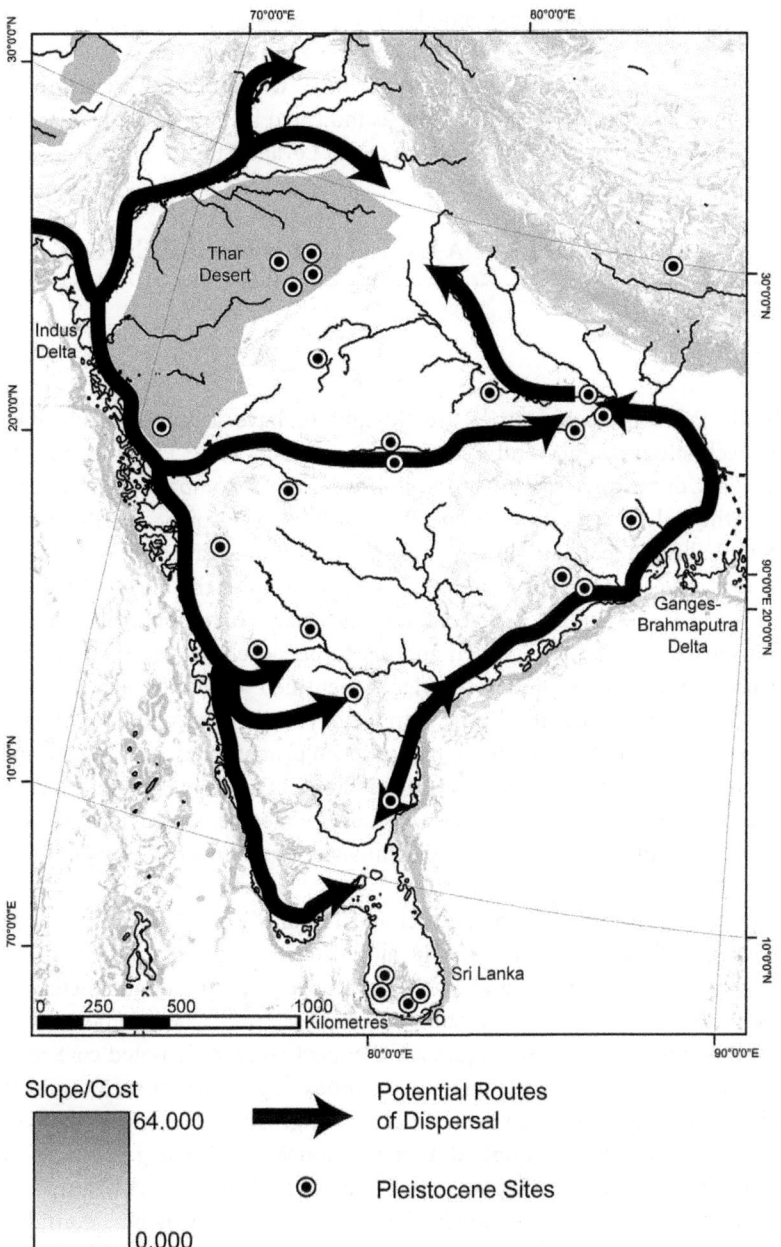

FIGURE 14.2 Dispersal routes into the Indian subcontinent based on least cost analysis (after Field et al. 2007). Populations would have expanded along coastlines and into the interior along river valleys.

Patne in India. To Mellars, this strongly indicated a direct connection between early human colonists in Asia and their ancestors in Africa. However, the links drawn by Mellars between African technologies and formally similar, but chronologically much later, South Asian technologies make this argument problematic. In contrast, as will be discussed further below, Petraglia and team have contended that the movement of *Homo sapiens* to South Asia was likely accompanied by a Middle Palaeolithic technology (James and Petraglia 2005; Petraglia et al. 2007; 2010; Boivin et al. 2013). In this view, if movements occurred between 70,000 and 50,000 years ago (if not before), as indicated by genetic coalescence ages, the dispersal would have been accompanied by flake and Levallois technologies.

The Middle Palaeolithic Record

Technology

Early Middle Palaeolithic industries are thought to have arisen gradually from Late Acheulian technology (James and Petraglia 2009; Misra 1989; Petraglia 2006). In the Late Acheulian, diminutive hand axes and cleavers are accompanied by prepared core technology, the hallmark of the Middle Palaeolithic. At Patpara and Bamburi, in the Middle Son Valley, Acheulian sites with hand axes and cleavers have been dated to 140,000–130,000 years ago (Petraglia et al. 2012), indicating the late survival of archaic hominins. The Late Acheulian archaeological sites may correspond with the Narmada hominin (Cameron et al. 2004), which appears to be closely related to *Homo heidelbergensis* (Athreya 2007). The oldest assemblages identified as Middle Palaeolithic date to c.126,000–108,000 years ago in the 16R Dune (Achyuthan et al. 2007), although little is known about this assemblage because it has not been properly described. It is also unclear who made the Middle Palaeolithic artefacts from the 16R Dune. The possibilities are that an unknown archaic hominin produced them, or that *Homo sapiens* were responsible for their manufacture, perhaps corresponding with human occupation in the Levant at this time (Petraglia et al. 2010).

Although no formal count has yet been conducted of Middle Palaeolithic sites, archaeologists have identified many hundreds of localities across the subcontinent as documented in monographs, theses, and journal articles. Characteristic core reduction methods include plain flake, discoidal, Levallois, and blade techniques (James 2007; James and Petraglia 2005). Levallois and discoidal techniques are the most commonly noted core preparation techniques, but unprepared and cylindrical methods (e.g. Jayaswal 1978) and blade and flake-blade components have also been described (e.g. James 2007; Misra 1985). Middle Palaeolithic tools are typically informal, though retouched flakes (e.g. scrapers, notches), burins, and points are present (Pappu 2001; Petraglia et al. 2007; 2012; Figure 14.3a). The Soan, sometimes argued to be an earlier Pleistocene technology, is now considered Late Pleistocene in age (Chauhan 2007; Lycett 2007).

Middle Palaeolithic assemblages show geographic variation in the frequency of core reduction methods and tool types (James 2007; 2011). Regular flake cores and discoidal techniques have wide distribution across India, and blade assemblages seem to be more common in northern regions. Mousterian and Levallois cores in Pakistan stand out from many sites in peninsular India. Levallois flake- and blade-core industries, found at sites such as Ongar, in Sindh, Pakistan, are rather distinctive (Biagi 2006). Here, classic Levallois cores are accompanied by a variety of retouched tool types such as scrapers and points, perhaps corresponding with Neanderthal occupation.

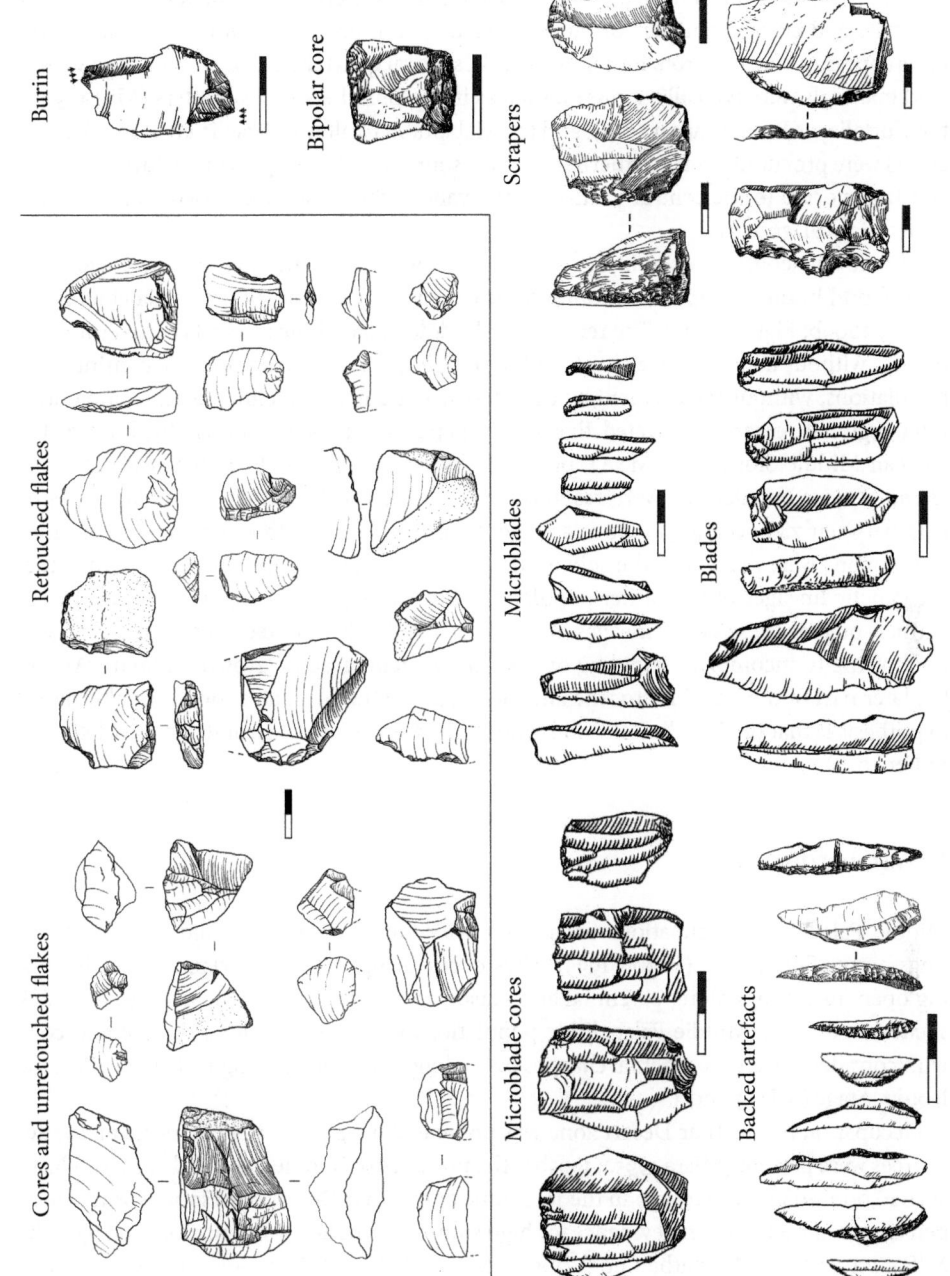

FIGURE 14.3 Stone tool technology, Jwalapuram, Jurreru River Valley, India. (a) Middle Palaeolithic; (b) Microlithic (after Petraglia et al. 2009a, figure 4).

Middle Palaeolithic industries were made from a variety of raw materials, especially quartzite and chert. Transport distances have not been properly examined, though most tools appear to be made from local raw materials. Local quartzite cobble sources and weathered materials were typically accessed, such as in the Bhimbetka rock shelters (Misra 1985), the Kortallayar Basin (Pappu 2001), and the Malaprabha Valley (Petraglia et al. 2003). Local cherts were procured from weathering bedrock sources in the margins of the Jurreru Valley, and transported to the central portion of the valley, where they were used and discarded (Petraglia et al. 2009b).

Middle Palaeolithic assemblages from between 78,000 and 38,000 years ago have been found in the Jwalapuram localities of the Jurreru River Valley (Petraglia et al. 2007; 2009a; 2009b; Figure 14.3a). The recovery of Middle Palaeolithic artefacts across this time period, without major changes in stone tool typology or industries, implies continuity of populations, without replacement by outsiders using different technologies. Comparative inter-regional research indicated that the Jwalapuram cores are similar to those of the African Middle Stone Age (MSA), produced by *Homo sapiens* (Petraglia et al. 2007). If *Homo sapiens* populations were responsible for Middle Palaeolithic assemblages occurring between 78,000 and 38,000 years ago, then it is possible that populations of modern humans were present in the subcontinent earlier than realized. This could imply that the genetic lineages of the earlier populations (i.e. those prior to 70,000 years ago) went extinct, or that these early lineages are currently difficult to detect in the modern gene pool owing to incomplete sampling or substantive demographic growth in South Asia in the later part of the Late Pleistocene and Holocene (Petraglia et al. 2009a). An alternative hypothesis is that the Middle Palaeolithic tool-kits were made by Neanderthals (Mellars in Balter 2010).

Environments

Middle Palaeolithic occupations occur in a wide range of physical and ecological settings across South Asia (Pappu 1995). Sites occur in upland and lowland zones, including open-air settings along perennial and seasonal streams, inter-dunal settings, and rock shelters and caves. Middle Palaeolithic populations were clearly able to survive and cope with considerable environmental changes over a long time period, ranging between Marine Isotope Stage (MIS) 5 and 3.

Occupation in the Thar Desert zone was possible during periods when perennial water sources were present (Misra 1995a; 1995b). The presence of Middle Palaeolithic assemblages at $c.126,000–108,000$ years ago in the 16R Dune of the Thar Desert corresponds with a high percentage of C_4 plants and evidence for high summer rains and a strong monsoon with the MIS 5 interglacial (Achyuthan et al. 2007). Middle Palaeolithic populations were present in peninsular India during MIS 5a, when rivers and wetlands and wooded grasslands were present along the Jurreru River Valley floodplain (Petraglia et al. 2007; 2009b). Even during the most severe climatic intervals in the Late Pleistocene, South Asia probably contained a mosaic of ecological settings, including woodlands, grasslands, tropical forests, and deserts, thereby allowing populations to survive and adapt to changing conditions (Petraglia et al. 2009a; 2010; Boivin et al. 2013). However, there is no evidence for Middle Palaeolithic occupations in the Thar Desert in MIS 4, suggesting that foragers may not have been able to cope with arid and hyper-arid conditions, especially if fresh drinking water was not available (Deotare et al. 2004; Misra 2001).

One particularly notable event that corresponds with Middle Palaeolithic occupation in the subcontinent is the Toba volcanic super-eruption of 74,000 years ago. This tremendous volcanic eruption is suggested to have been a catalyst behind global climatic cooling, environmental deterioration, and a genetic bottleneck in human populations (Ambrose 1998). Volcanic ash is found across South Asia (Jones 2007; Westgate et al. 1998), associated with Middle Palaeolithic assemblages in the Middle Son Valley in northern India (Jones and Pal 2009) and in southern India along the Jurreru River Valley (Petraglia et al. 2007). The ash would have had deleterious effects on local ecological settings, clogging small rivers and polluting fresh drinking water (Jones 2010; Petraglia et al. 2009b). It is conceivable that some areas may have experienced more harmful ecological effects, perhaps leading to population contractions and displacements (Jones 2007; 2010). However, the similarity of Middle Palaeolithic tool-kits across the Toba isochron suggests that Middle Palaeolithic populations continued to survive well after the eruption (Petraglia et al. 2007), living in places until MIS 3.

The Late Palaeolithic and Mesolithic Record

Blade cores have been associated with an Upper Palaeolithic industry, and typically subdivided into flake-blade, blade-based, and blade and burin categories (Murty 1979). Sites of the so-called Upper Palaeolithic industry are not as common as Middle Palaeolithic sites and their assemblages appear to be variable in terms of core reduction methods and tool types, though there is a general increase in the production of burins and backed tools at some sites (Murty 1979; Paddayya 1984). Holocene microlithic industries are usually referred to as Mesolithic, with the assumption that such industries represent a technological transition from the late Upper Palaeolithic (Misra 2001). Such characterizations are questionable owing to the recognition of the significant age depth of microlithic industries across South Asia (Petraglia et al. 2009a). Currently, there is uncertainty as to whether there is contemporaneity between flake- and blade-based technology and microlithic industries in South Asia, hence a Late Palaeolithic label has been proposed to characterize the wide diversity of technologies from about 45,000 to 10,000 years ago (James and Petraglia 2005).

Microlithic industries in India and Sri Lanka are now known in Late Pleistocene and Holocene contexts, without doubt corresponding with modern human occupation (Petraglia et al. 2009a). Calibrated radiocarbon ages place microlithic industries at $c.$35,000 years ago at the Jwalapuram Locality 9 rock shelter in southern India (Clarkson et al. 2009) (Figure 14.3b) and perhaps slightly earlier at the Batadomba Lena cave in Sri Lanka (Deraniyagala 1992). Though microblades unite these small tool industries, the assemblages should not be viewed as technologically homogeneous, as substantive changes in core technology may be documented (Clarkson et al. 2009).

Microlithic industries appear to arise at about the same time when significant population increases are documented by mtDNA analysis (Atkinson et al. 2008). A demographic increase from about 35,000–28,000 years ago (Kivisild et al. 1999) corresponds with a period of climatic deterioration and habitat fragmentation (Petraglia et al. 2009a). Microlithic innovations arise at about this time, suggesting that populations developed more sophisticated hunting technologies in the face of environmental and demographic pressures.

Traits considered to be part of the modern human behavioural package are relatively late and sparse in Late Palaeolithic contexts (Table 14.1; James 2007; James and Petraglia 2005; Petraglia 2007). The archaeological record shows no rapid or sudden appearance of a modern behavioural package that can be considered to signal a 'human revolution' equivalent to the Aurignacian in Europe, nor does it indicate the spread of an Upper Palaeolithic package between 50,000 and 40,000 years ago. Though ochre utilization may stretch back as far as the Acheulian (Bednarik 1990), the clearest signs for complex behaviours begin $c.45,000$ years ago with the construction of structures and the manufacture of symbolic items. At $c.35,000$–30,000 years ago novel technologies are introduced, including the manufacture of bone tools and geometric microliths (Clarkson et al. 2009; Deraniyagala 1992). The gradual and patchy assembly of modern traits in South Asia (James and Petraglia 2005) is a feature that is found in other regions, such as in Australia, where symbolism develops slowly and sporadically (Brumm and Moore 2005). Despite the fact that Late Pleistocene symbolic evidence is spatially and temporally sparse, populations were clearly capable of explicit symbolic behaviours, showing adaptations that were as advanced as modern foraging populations (James 2007).

The distinction between microlithic-using cultures of the Late Pleistocene are not yet easily distinguished from similar Mesolithic assemblages in the Holocene. Nevertheless, it is clear that microlithic industries continue to be used late into the Holocene, and in association with increased societal diversity and complexity (Misra 2001). At about 8,000 years ago there is evidence for increased sedentism of foraging populations along oxbow lakes of the Ganges (Chattopadhyaya 1996). Populations appear to have expanded into new and previously unoccupied or lightly occupied areas, including coasts and deserts. Shell middens in Sri Lanka appear to extend back to the mid-Holocene at least. Recent evidence from northern India indicates that foragers may have been locally exploiting wild rice by 9,000 years ago, perhaps eventually leading to domestication (Fuller 2007). Such foraging lifestyles continue through to the modern period in South Asia, with foragers participating in increasingly complex and diverse webs of interaction and trade across the subcontinent (Morrison and Junker 2002). Foragers sometimes adopted elements of adjacent domesticate-oriented economies, but also appear to have retained distinctive identities.

The pattern of increased population growth in the terminal Pleistocene and the Holocene resulted in experiments in economic lifeways, diversified patterns of land use, and intensified exploitation of animal and plant resources in the subcontinent. The large number of Mesolithic sites in the Holocene has led archaeologists to infer that there was a marked population growth in South Asia at this time (Misra 2001), a thesis supported by genetic data (Petraglia et al. 2009a). The increased food supply available in the Mesolithic is thought to have led to a reduction in mobility in some cases, as reflected in the large size of many sites, evidence for huts and communal hearths, the substantial appearance of habitation deposits, and the presence of cemeteries, particularly in the Ganges Valley (Chattopadhyaya 1996; Figure 14.4). More sedentary lifestyles are also associated with the emergence of agriculture, which at the site of Mehrgarh in Baluchistan dates as early as 8,000 years ago (Jarrige et al. 2006). Elsewhere in South Asia, Neolithic lifeways generally

Table 14.1 Key evidence for modern behavioural traits in South Asia

Period	Locality	Evidence	Source
Middle Palaeolithic	Bhimbetka rock shelter	Stone arrangements interpreted as structures^	Misra 1989
	Jwalapuram Locality 3	Ochre piece between 78,000 and 74,000 years ago associated with lithic artefacts	Petraglia et al. 2007
Late Palaeolithic	Site 55	Stone-lined pit and low wall, dated to 45,000 years ago	Dennell et al. 1992
	Kurnool caves	Bone tools from Upper Palaeolithic horizons	Murty and Reddy 1975; Thimma Reddy 1977*
	Multiple sites	Ostrich eggshell fragments (unmodified) from Late Pleistocene contexts in India	Kumar et al. 1988; 1990
	Patne	Two ostrich eggshell beads, one geometrically incised fragment of ostrich eggshell, from Upper Palaeolithic levels, dated to 25,000 years ago	Sali 1989
	Lohanda Nala	19,000–26,000 years ago, bone harpoon+	Misra 1977; Bednarik 2003
	Bhimbetka rock shelter	Human burial with two ostrich eggshell beads	Bednarik 2003
	Baghor I	Sandstone platform and rock pattern in Late Palaeolithic	Kenoyer et al. 1983
	Jwalapuram Locality 9 rock shelter	Beads, harpoon in Late Pleistocene microlithic levels	Clarkson et al. 2009
	Chandresal, Kota	Ostrich eggshell beads and fragments, one engraved; c.39,000–36,000 years ago, on eggshell	Kumar et al. 1988
	Nagda, Ujjain, Ramnagar, Mandasor	One ostrich eggshell disc at Nagda; five engraved eggshell frags at Ramnagar EUP Level >31,000 years ago	Kumar et al. 1988; Bednarik 1992
	Batadomba-lena	Bone points, ostrich eggshell beads, 28,500 years ago	Deraniyagala 1992
	Site 49 and 50 Khaparkheda	Bone points at 28,000 years ago Ostrich eggshell bead manufacturing site	Deraniyagala 1992 Mishra et al. 2004

^ James and Petraglia 2005 note these as controversial.
* Called into question by Petraglia 1995;
+ Misinterpreted as mother goddess figurine by Misra 1977.

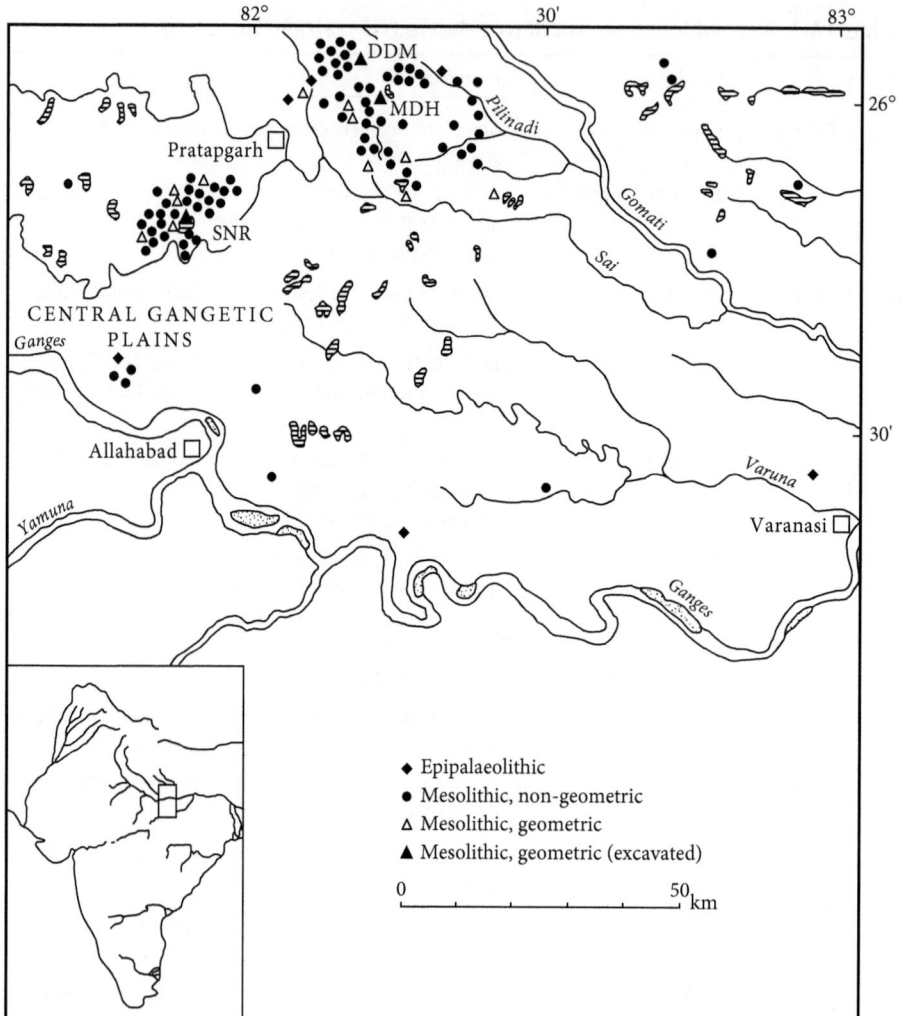

FIGURE 14.4 Map of Holocene archaeological sites in the Central Ganges plains (after Chattopadhyaya 1996).

emerged later, and according to different pathways, involving varying degrees and sources of external influence, and various processes of demographic change. Forager lifestyles nonetheless continued in many regions, with hunter-gatherers often playing key economic roles alongside emerging protohistoric and historic states. It has been pointed out that far from being primitive 'fossils', South Asian hunter-gatherers in the historic period and up until recent times can more appropriately be understood as specialized productive units similar to caste groups—Fox's so-called 'professional primitives' (Fox 1969; see also Morrison 2007).

CONCLUSION

South Asia is the most densely populated region of the world today, and includes a diverse array of cultural and linguistic groups. The region has an abundance of Pleistocene and Holocene archaeological sites ranging over the last 130,000 years, providing palaeoanthropologists and evolutionary anthropologists the opportunity to examine changes in environments and demography through time (Figure 14.5). Archaic hominins using Acheulian technology appear to survive to at least 140,000–130,000 years ago. Genetic coalescence ages place *Homo sapiens* in the subcontinent between 70,000 and 50,000 years ago, apparently corresponding with the Middle Palaeolithic. Population geneticists and archaeologists have demonstrated that the subcontinent was one of the most populated places on Earth in the Late Pleistocene, indicating that foragers in South Asia were quite successful in their adaptations to variable and changing environments. Microlithic innovations, and better hunting weaponry, may have provided hunter-gatherers with adaptive advantages in the face of population increase and the filling of favourable habitats. Cultural diversity is evident from the Palaeolithic and into the historic era, providing opportunities for archaeologists to examine how hunter-gatherer groups evolved and diversified and how they coexisted alongside state-level societies. Though the archaeological sites of South Asia are numerous and well preserved, its Palaeolithic record has not been as well examined as those in other parts of the world. Given South Asia's critical geographic location, this has resulted in strong biases in models about the evolution and dispersal of human populations. In light of India's rapid economic development, and the associated alteration and destruction of the region's archaeological sites, the time is ripe for focused study of the subcontinent's early

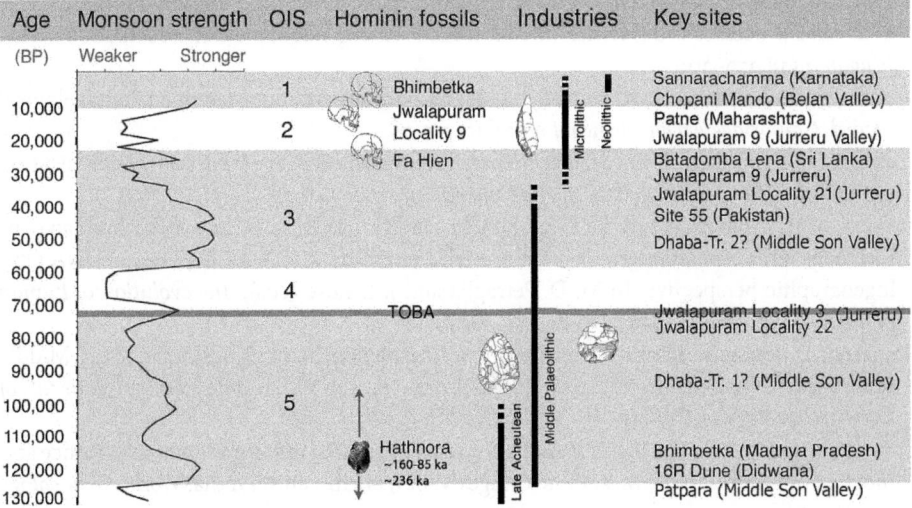

FIGURE 14.5 South Asian monsoon strength, human fossils, and key archaeological sites and industries (after Petraglia et al. 2012).

hunter-gatherers, their adaptations to and manipulation of the environment, and their distinctive regional trajectories.

References

Achyuthan, H., Quade, J., Roe, L., and Placzek, C. 2007. Stable isotopic composition of pedogenic carbonates from the eastern margin of the Thar Desert, Rajasthan, India. *Quaternary International* 162–3, 50–60.

Allchin, R. 1963. *Neolithic cattle-keepers of South India*. Cambridge: Cambridge University Press.

Ambrose, S. H. 1998. Late Pleistocene human population bottlenecks, volcanic winter and differentiation in modern humans. *Journal of Human Evolution* 34, 623–51.

Athreya, S. 2007. Was *Homo heidelbergensis* in South Asia? A test using the Narmada fossil from central India. In M. D. Petraglia and B. Allchin (eds), *The evolution and history of human populations in South Asia*, 137–70. Dordrecht: Springer.

Atkinson, Q. D., Gray, R. D., and Drummond, A. J. 2008. mtDNA variation predicts population size in humans and reveals a major southern Asian chapter in human prehistory. *Molecular Biology Evolution* 25, 468–74.

Balter, M. 2010. Of two minds about Toba's impact. *Science* 327, 1187–8.

Bednarik, R. 1990. An Acheulian haematite pebble with striations. *Rock Art Research* 7, 75.

Bednarik, R. 1992. Palaeoart and archaeological myths. *Cambridge Archaeological Journal* 2, 27–43.

Bednarik, R. 2003. The earliest evidence of palaeoart. *Rock Art Research* 20, 89–135.

Biagi, P. 2006. The Levalloisian assemblages of Sindh (Pakistan) and their importance in the Middle Palaeolithic of the Indian subcontinent. *Archaeology of Early Northeastern Africa, Studies in African Archaeology* 9, 1005–17.

Boivin, N., Fuller, D. Q., Dennell, R., Allaby, R., and Petraglia, M. D. 2013. Human dispersal across diverse environments of Asia during the Upper Pleistocene. *Quaternary International*, http://dx.doi.org/10.1016/j.quaint.2013.01.008

Boivin, N., Fuller, D., Korisettar, R. and Petraglia, M. 2008. First farmers in south India: the role of internal processes and external influences in the emergence of the earliest settled societies. *Pragdhara* 18, 179–200.

Brumm, A. and Moore, M. W. 2005. Symbolic revolutions and the Australian archaeological record. *Cambridge Archaeological Journal* 15, 157–75.

Bulbeck, D. 2007. Where river meets sea: a parsimonious model for *Homo sapiens* colonization of the Indian Ocean rim and Sahul. *Current Anthropology* 48, 315–21.

Cabrera, V. M., Abu-Amero, K. K., Larruga, J. M., and González, A. M. 2009. The Arabian peninsula: gate for human migrations out of Africa or cul-de-sac? A mitochondrial DNA phylogeographic perspective. In M. D. Petraglia and J. I. Rose (eds), *The evolution of human populations in Arabia*, 79–87. Dordrecht: Springer.

Cameron, D., Patnaik, R. and Sahni, A. 2004. The phylogenetic significance of the Middle Pleistocene Narmada hominin cranium from central India. *International Journal of Osteoarchaeology* 14, 419–47.

Chattopadhyaya, U. C. 1996. Settlement pattern and the spatial organization of subsistence and mortuary practices in the Mesolithic Ganges Valley, north-central India. *World Archaeology* 27, 461–76.

Chauhan, P. R. 2007. Soanian cores and core-tools from Toka, northern India: towards a new typo-technological organization. *Journal of Anthropological Archaeology* 26, 412–41.

Clarkson, C., Petraglia, M., Korisettar, R., Haslam, M., Boivin, N., Crowther, A., Ditchfield, P., Fullar, D., Miracle, P., Harris, C., Connell, K., James, H., and Koshy, J. 2009. The oldest and longest enduring microlithic sequence in India: 35000 years of modern human occupation and change at the Jwalapuram Locality 9 rockshelter. *Antiquity* 83, 326–48.

Dennell, R., Rendell, H., Halim, M., and Moth, E. 1992. A 45,000-year-old open-air Paleolithic site at Riwat, northern Pakistan. *Journal of Field Archaeology* 19, 17–33.

Deotare, B., Kajale, M., Rajaguru, S., and Basavaiah, N. 2004. Late Quaternary geomorphology, palynology, and magnetic susceptibility of playas in western margin of the Indian Thar Desert. *Indian Geophysical Union* 8, 15–25.

Deraniyagala, S. U. 1992. *The prehistory of Sri Lanka*. Colombo: Archaeological Survey Department.

Endicott, P., Ho, S. Y. W., Metspalu, M., and Stringer, C. 2009. Evaluating the mitochondrial timescale of human evolution. *Trends in Ecology and Evolution* 24, 515–21.

Endicott, P., Thomas, M., Gilbert, P., Stringer, C., Lalueza-Fox, C., Willer Siev, G., Hansen, A., and Cooper, A. 2003. The genetic origins of the Andaman Islanders. *American Journal of Human Genetics* 72, 178–84.

Field, J. S. and Lahr, M. M. 2005. Assessment of the southern dispersal: GIS-based analyses of potential routes at Oxygen Isotopic Stage 4. *Journal of World Prehistory* 19, 1–45.

Field, J. S., Petraglia, M. D., and Lahr, M. M. 2007. The southern dispersal hypothesis and the South Asian archaeological record: examination of dispersal routes through GIS analysis. *Journal of Anthropological Archaeology* 26, 88–108.

Fortier, J. 2009. The ethnography of South Asian foragers. *Annual Reviews of Anthropology* 38, 99–114.

Fox, R. G. 1969. 'Professional primitives': hunters and gatherers of nuclear South Asia. *Man in India* 49, 139–60.

Fuller, D. 2006. Agricultural origins and frontiers in South Asia: a working synthesis. *Journal of World Prehistory* 20, 1–86.

Fuller, D. 2007. Non-human genetics, agricultural origins and historical linguistics in South Asia. In M. D. Petraglia and B. Allchin (eds), *The evolution and history of human populations in South Asia*, 393–443. Dordrecht: Springer.

Fuller, D. Q., Boivin, N., and Korisettar, R. 2007. Dating the Neolithic of South India: new radiometric evidence for key economic, social, and ritual transformations. *Antiquity* 81, 755–78.

Fürer-Haimendorf, C. von. 1985. *Tribal populations and cultures of the Indian subcontinent*. Leiden: E. J. Brill.

James, H. V. A. 2007. The emergence of modern human behavior in South Asia: a review of the current evidence and discussion of its possible implications. In M. D. Petraglia and B. Allchin (eds), *The evolution and history of human populations in South Asia*, 201–27. Dordrecht: Springer.

James, H. V. A. 2011. Becoming human: the emergence of modern human behaviour in South Asia. PhD dissertation, University of Cambridge, Cambridge, UK.

James, H. and Petraglia, M. D. 2005. Modern human origins and the evolution of behavior in the later Pleistocene record of South Asia. *Current Anthropology* 46, S3–S27.

James, H. and Petraglia, M. D. 2009. The Lower to Middle Paleolithic transition in South Asia and its implications for hominin cognition and dispersals. In M. Camps and P. Chauhan (eds), *Sourcebook of Paleolithic transitions*, 255–64. New York: Springer.

Jarrige, J.-F., Jarrige, C., and Quivron, G. 2006. Mehrgarh Neolithic: the updated sequence. In C. Jarrige and V. Lefevre (eds), *South Asian Archaeology 2001*, 129–42. Paris: ADPF Éditions Recherche sur les Civilisations.

Jayaswal, V. 1978. *Palaeohistory of India: a study of the prepared core technique.* Delhi: Agam Kala Prakashan.

Jones, S. C. 2007. The Toba supervolcanic eruption: tephra-fall deposits in India and palaeoanthropological implications. In M. D. Petraglia and B. Allchin (eds), *The evolution and history of human populations in South Asia*, 173–200. Dordrecht: Springer.

Jones, S. C. 2010. Palaeoenvironmental response to the 74 ka Toba ash-fall in the Jurreru and Middle Son valleys in southern and north-central India. *Quaternary Research* 73, 336–50.

Jones, S. C. and Pal, J. N. 2009. The Palaeolithic of the Middle Son valley, north-central India: changes in hominin lithic technology and behaviour during the Upper Pleistocene. *Journal of Anthropological Archaeology* 28, 323–41.

Kennedy, K. 2000. *God-apes and fossil men: palaeoanthropology of South Asia.* Ann Arbor: University of Michigan Press.

Kenoyer, J. M., 1998. *Ancient cities of the Indus Valley civilization.* Karachi: Oxford University Press and American Institute of Pakistan Studies.

Kenoyer, J. M, Clark, J., Pal, J. N., and Sharma, G. 1983. An Upper Palaeolithic shrine in India? *Antiquity* 57, 88–94.

Kingdon, J. 1993. *Self-made man: human evolution from Eden to extinction.* New York: John Wiley.

Kivisild, T., Kaldma, K., Metspalu, M., Parik, J., Papiha, S., and Villems, R. 1999. The place of the Indian mtDNA variants in the global network of maternal lineages and the peopling of the Old World. In R. Deka and S. Papiha (eds), *Genomic diversity*, 135–52. New York: Plenum Press.

Kivisild, T., Papiha, S., Rootsi, S., Parik, J., Kaldma, K., Reidla, M., Laos, S., Metspalu, M., Pielberg, G., Adojaan, M., Metspalu, E., Mastana, S., Wang, Y., Gölge, M., Demirtas, H., Schnakenberg, E., De Stefano, G., Geberhiwot, T., Claustres, M., and Villems, R. 2000. An Indian ancestry: a key for understanding human diversity in Europe and beyond. In C. Renfrew and K. Boyle (eds), *Archaeogenetics: DNA and the population prehistory of Europe*, 267–75. Cambridge: McDonald Institute for Archaeological Research.

Kivisild, T., Rootsi, S., Metspalu, M., Mastana, S., Kaldma, K., Parik, J., Metspalu, E., Adojaan, M., Tolk, H., Stepanov, V., Gölgi, M., Usanga, E., Papiha, S., Cinnioğlu, C., King, R., Cavalli Sforza, L., Underhill, P., and Villems, R. 2003. The genetic heritage of the earliest settlers persists both in Indian tribal and caste populations. *American Journal of Human Genetics* 72, 313–32.

Korisettar, R. 2007. Toward developing a basin model for Paleolithic settlement of the Indian subcontinent: geodynamics, monsoon dynamics, habitat diversity and dispersal routes. In M. D. Petraglia and B. Allchin (eds), *The evolution and history of human populations in South Asia*, 69–96. Dordrecht: Springer.

Kumar, G., Narvare, G., and Pancholi, R. K. 1988. Engraved ostrich eggshell objects: new evidence of Upper Palaeolithic art in India. *Rock Art Research* 5, 43–53.

Kumar, G., Sahni, A., Pancholi, R. K., and Navare, G. 1990. Archaeological discoveries and a study of Late Pleistocene ostrich egg shells and egg shell objects in India. *Man and Environment* 15, 29–40.

Lahr, M. M. and Foley, R. 1994. Multiple dispersals and modern human origins. *Evolutionary Anthropology* 3, 48–60.

Leshnik, L. and Sontheimer, G. D. (eds) 1975. *Pastoralists and nomads in South Asia.* Weisbaden: Otto Harra.

Lukacs, J. 2007. Interpreting biological diversity in South Asian prehistory: early Holocene population affinities and subsistence adaptations. In M. D. Petraglia and B. Allchin (eds), *The evolution and history of human populations in South Asia*, 271–96. Dordrecht: Springer.

Lycett, S. J. 2007. Is the Soanian techno-complex a Mode 1 or Mode 3 phenomenon? A morphometric assessment. *Journal of Archaeological Science* 34, 1434–40.

Macaulay, V., Hill, C., Achilli, A., Rengo, C., Clarke, D., Meehan, W., Blackburn, J., Semino, O., Scozzari, R., Cruciani, F., Taha, A., Shaari, N. K., Raja, J. M., Ismail, P., Zainuddin, X., Goodwin, W., Bulbeck, D., Bandelt, H. J., Oppenheimer, S., Torroni, A., and Richards, M. 2005. Single, rapid coastal settlement of Asia revealed by analysis of complete mitochondrial genomes. *Science* 308, 1034–6.

Marathe, A. R. 1981. *Geoarchaeology of the Hiran Valley, Saurashtra, India*. Poona: Deccan College Postgraduate and Research Institute.

Marriott, M. (ed.) 1955. *Village India: studies in the little community*. Chicago: University of Chicago Press.

Mellars, P. 2006. Going East: new genetic and archaeological perspectives on the modern human colonization of Eurasia. *Science* 313, 796–800.

Metspalu, M., Kivisild, T., Metspalu, E., Parik, J., Hudjashov, G., Kaldma, K., Serk, P., Karmin, M., Behar, D., Thomas, M., Gilbert, P., Endicott, P., Mastana, S., Papiha, S., Skorecki, K., Torroni, A., and Villems, R. 2004. Most of the extant mtDNA boundaries in South and Southwest Asia were likely shaped during the initial settlement of Eurasia by anatomically modern humans. *BMC Genetics* 5, 26.

Mishra, S., Ota, S. B., and Naik, S. 2004. Late Pleistocene ostrich egg shell bead manufacture at Khaparkhera, District Dhar, Madhya Pradesh. In *Abstracts of Academic Symposia, Rock Art Society of India, International Rock Art Congress, Agra, 28 November to 2 December 2004*, 22.

Misra, V. D. 1977. *Some aspects of Indian archaeology*. Allahabad: Prabhat Prakashan.

Misra, V. N. 1985. The Acheulean succession at Bhimbetka, Central India. In V. N. Misra and P. Bellwood (eds), *Recent advances in Indo-Pacific prehistory*, 35–47. New Delhi: Oxford IBH.

Misra, V. N. 1989. Stone Age India: an ecological perspective. *Man and Environment* 14, 17–64.

Misra, V. N. 1995a. Geoarchaeology of the Thar Desert, North West India. In S. Wadia, R. Korisettar, and V. S. Kale (eds), *Quaternary environments and geoarchaeology of India*, 210–30. Bangalore: Geological Society of India.

Misra, V. N. 1995b. The evolution of environment and culture in the Rajasthan desert during the Late Quaternary. In E. Johnson (ed.), *Ancient peoples and landscapes*, 77–103. Lubbock, TX: Texas Tech University Press.

Misra, V. N. 2001. Prehistoric human colonization of India. *Journal of Bioscience* 26, 491–531.

Morrison, K. 2007. Foragers and forager-traders in South Asian worlds: some thoughts from the last 10,000 years. In M. D. Petraglia and B. Allchin (eds), *The evolution and history of human populations in South Asia*, 321–39. Dordrecht: Springer.

Morrison, K. and Junker, L. (eds) 2002. *Forager-traders in South and Southeast Asia*. Cambridge: Cambridge University Press.

Murty, M. L. K. 1979. Recent research on the Upper Palaeolithic phase in India. *Journal of Field Archaeology* 6, 301–20.

Murty, M. L. K. and Reddy, K. T. 1975. The significance of lithic finds in the cave areas of Kurnool, India. *Asian Perspectives* 18, 214–26.

Oppenheimer, S. 2008. The great arc of dispersal of modern humans: Africa to Australia. *Quaternary International* 202, 2–13.

Paddayya, K. 1984. India. In O. Bar-Yosef (ed.), *Neue Forschungen Zur-Altsteinzeit*, 345–403. Munich: Verlag C. H. Beck.

Pappu, R. S. 1995. The contribution of the earth sciences to the development of Indian archaeology. In S. Wadia, R. Korisettar, and V. S. Kale (eds), *Quaternary environments and geoarchaeology of India*. Bangalore: Geological Society of India, 414–35.

Pappu, R. S. and Deo, S. J. 1994. *Man-land relationships during Palaeolithic times in the Kaladgi Basin, Karnataka*. Pune: Deccan College.

Pappu, S. 2001. Middle Palaeolithic stone tool technology in the Kortallayar Basin, South India. *Antiquity* 75, 107–17.

Patnaik, R., Chauhan, P. R., Rao, M. R., Blackwell, B. A. B., Skinner, A. R., Sahni, A., Chauhan, M. S., and Khan, H. S. 2009. New geochronological, paleoclimatological, and archaeological data from the Narmada Valley hominin locality, central India. *Journal of Human Evolution* 56, 114–33.

Petraglia, M., Clarkson, C., Boivin, N., Haslam, M., Korisettar, R., Chaubey, G., Ditchfield, P., Fuller, D., James, H., Jones, S., Kivisild, T., Koshy, J., Lahr, M. M., Metspalu, M., Roberts, R., and Arnold, L. 2009a. Population increase and environmental deterioration correspond with microlithic innovations in South Asia c.35,000 years ago. *Proceedings of the National Academy of Sciences USA* 106, 12261–6.

Petraglia, M., Korisettar, R., Kasturi Bai, M., Boivin, N., Janardhana, B., Clarkson, C., Cunningham, K., Ditchfield, P., Fuller, D., Hampson, J., Haslam, M., Jones, S., Koshy, J., Miracle, P., Oppenheimer, C., Roberts, R., and White, K. 2009b. Human occupation, adaptation and behavioral change in the Pleistocene and Holocene of South India: recent investigations in the Kurnool District, Andhra Pradesh. *Journal of Eurasian Prehistory* 6, 19–166.

Petraglia, M. D. 1995. Pursuing site formation research in India. In S. Wadia, R. Korisettar, and V. S. Kale (eds), *Quaternary environments and geoarchaeology of India*, 446–65. Bangalore: Geological Society of India.

Petraglia, M. D. 2006. The Indian Acheulean in global perspective. In N. Goren-Inbar and G. Sharon (eds), *Axe age: Acheulian tool-making from quarry to discard*, 389–414. London: Equinox Publishing.

Petraglia, M. D. 2007. Mind the gap: factoring the Arabian peninsula and the Indian subcontinent into Out of Africa models. In P. Mellars, K. Boyle, O. Bar-Yosef, and C. Stringer (eds), *Rethinking the human revolution*, 383–94. Cambridge: McDonald Institute for Archaeological Research.

Petraglia, M. D. and Allchin, B. (eds) 2007. *The evolution and history of human populations in South Asia*. Dordrecht: Springer.

Petraglia, M. D., Ditchfield, P., Jones, S., Korisettar, R., and Pal, J. N. 2012. The Toba volcanic super-eruption, environmental change, and hominin occupation history in India over the last 140,000 years. *Quaternary International* 258, 119–34.

Petraglia, M. D., Haslam, M., Fuller, D. Q., and Boivin, N. 2010. Out of Africa: new hypotheses and evidence for the dispersal of *Homo sapiens* along the Indian Ocean rim. *Annals of Human Biology* 37, 288–311.

Petraglia, M. D., Korisettar, R., Boivin, N., Clarkson, C., Ditchfield, P., Jones, S., Koshy, J., Lahr, M. M., Oppenheimer, C., Pyle, D., Roberts, R., Schwenninger, J.-L., Arnold, L., and White, K. 2007. Middle Paleolithic assemblages from the Indian subcontinent before and after the Toba super-eruption. *Science* 317, 114–16.

Petraglia, M. D., Schuldenrein, J., and Korisettar, R. 2003. Landscapes, activity, and the Acheulean to Middle Paleolithic transition in the Kaladgi Basin, India. *Eurasian Prehistory* 1, 3–24.

Possehl, G. 2002 *The Indus civilization: a contemporary perspective*. Walnut Creek, CA: AltaMira Press.

Rath, A., Thimma Reddy, K., and Vijaya Prakash, P. 1997. Middle Palaeolithic assemblage from Ramayogi Agraharam in the red sediments in the Visakhapatnam coast. *Man and Environment* 22, 31–8.

Reeves, P. 2002. Regional diversity in South Asian inland fisheries: colonial Bengal and Uttar Pradesh compared. *South Asia: Journal of South Asian Studies* 25, 121–35.

Reich, D., Thangaraj, K., Patterson, N., Price, A. L., and Singh, L. 2009. Reconstructing Indian population history. *Nature* 461, 489–94.

Sahoo, S., Singh, A., Himabindu, G., Banerjee, J., Sitalaximi, T., Gaikwad, S., Trivedi, R., Endicott, P., Kivisild, T., Metspalu, M., Villems, R., and Kashyap, V. K. 2006. A prehistory of Indian Y chromosomes: evaluating demic diffusion scenarios. *Proceedings of the National Academy of Sciences USA* 103, 843–8.

Sali, S. A. 1989. *The Upper Palaeolithic and Mesolithic cultures of Maharashtra*. Pune: Deccan College Post-Graduate and Research Institute.

Sharma, G. R. and Clark, J. D. 1983. *Palaeoenvironments and prehistory in the Middle Son Valley*. Allahabad: Abinash Prakashan.

Sinopoli, C. 2005. *The political economy of craft production: crafting empire in South India, c.1350–1650*. Cambridge: Cambridge University Press.

Sinopoli, C. and Morrison, K. 2007. *The Vijayanagara metropolitan survey: volume 1*. Ann Arbor: Anthropological Papers of the Museum of Anthropology, University of Michigan.

Soares, P., Ermini, L., Thomson, N., Mormina, M., Rito, T., Rohl, A., Salas, A., Oppenheimer, S., Macaulay, V., and Richards, M. B. 2009. Correcting for purifying selection: an improved human mitochondrial molecular clock. *American Journal of Human Genetics* 84, 1–20.

Srinivas, M. N. 1998. *Village, caste, gender and method: essays in Indian social anthropology*. Delhi: Oxford University Press.

Stock, J. T., Lahr, M. M., and Kulatilake, S. 2007. Cranial diversity in South Asia relative to modern human dispersals and global patterns of human variation. In M. D. Petraglia and B. Allchin (eds), *The evolution and history of human populations in South Asia*, 245–68. Dordrecht: Springer.

Stringer, C. 2000. Coasting out of Africa. *Nature* 405, 24–7.

Thangaraj, K., Chaubey, G., Kivisild, T., Reddy, A. G., Kumar Singh, V., Rasalkar, A. A., and Singh, L. 2005. Reconstructing the origin of Andaman Islanders. *Science* 308, 996.

Thimma Reddy, K. 1977. Billasurgam: an Upper Palaeolithic cave site in South India. *Asian Perspectives* 20, 206–27.

Walimbe, S. R. 2007. Population movements in the Indian subcontinent during the protohistoric period: physical anthropological assessment. In M. D. Petraglia and B. Allchin (eds), *The evolution and history of human populations in South Asia*, 297–319. Dordrecht: Springer.

Watkins, W. S., Thara, R., Mowry, B. J., Zhang, Y., Witherspoon, D. J., Tolpinrud, W., Bamshad, M. J., Tirupati, S., Padmavati, R., Smith, H., Nancarrow, D., Filippich, C., and Jorde, L. B. 2008. Genetic variation in South Indian castes: evidence from Y-chromosome, mitochondrial, and autosomal polymorphisms. *BMC Genetics* 9, 86.

Westgate, J., Shane, R., Pearce, N., Perkins, W., Korisettar, R., Chesner, C., Williams, M., and Acharyya, S. 1998. All Toba tephra occurrences across peninsular India belong to the 75,000 yr BP eruption. *Quaternary Research* 50, 107–12.

Williams, M. A. J. and Clarke, M. F. 1995. Quaternary geology and prehistoric environments in the Son and Belan Valleys, North Central India. In S. Wadia, R. Korisettar, and V. S. Kale (eds), *Quaternary environments and geoarchaeology of India*, 282–309. Bangalore: Geological Society of India.

CHAPTER 15

HOMO SAPIENS SOCIETIES IN INDONESIA AND SOUTH-EASTERN ASIA

SUSAN O'CONNOR AND DAVID BULBECK

This chapter describes the archaeology of island and mainland South-East Asia during the Late Pleistocene period between approximately 70,000 and 10,000 years BP. The start of this period corresponds to when *Homo sapiens* reached South-East Asia following their rapid dispersal from their African homeland along the northern rim of the Indian Ocean. Between 30,000 and 15,000 BP, and to a lesser extent at other times during the Late Pleistocene, sea levels across South-East Asia were much lower than at present and the climate was generally cooler and drier. The continental shelf between Borneo and the islands to the west of Lombok was exposed as low-lying land, creating the subcontinent of Sunda which, to its north, further connected to present-day Thailand. During the period of lowest sea levels, referred to as the Last Glacial Maximum (LGM), Sunda further included Palawan as a peninsula. However, the Philippine islands east of Palawan, as well as Sulawesi and the triangular belt of islands between Lombok, Halmahera, and Timor—collectively, a region known as Wallacea—remained an island world throughout the period covered here (Figure 15.1).

It is uncertain exactly when *Homo sapiens* entered South-East Asia. Some recent estimates from human mitochondrial DNA research range between 40,000 and 74,000 BP, with a median estimate of around 55,000 years ago (Soares et al. 2009). Whether there is a relationship with the cataclysmic eruption of the Toba volcano, which occurred 74,000 years ago BP in present-day north Sumatra, is unclear. If early *Homo sapiens* were already present in South-East Asia at the time, they may have suffered widespread depopulation, and the mitochondrial DNA dates would accordingly reflect the subsequent proliferation of the small set of surviving lineages. Alternatively, the Indian and Sunda subcontinents may have then been occupied by archaic hominins, but they were effectively obliterated by the fallout from the Toba eruption, thus paving the way for *Homo sapiens*' entry. A crucial site in this context is Kota Tampan, in the Malay Peninsula, where the Toba ash sealed the occupants' living floors (Figure 15.1). As discussed below, the Kota Tampan stone artefacts are too generically similar to those from later Malay Peninsula sites to be confident in assigning

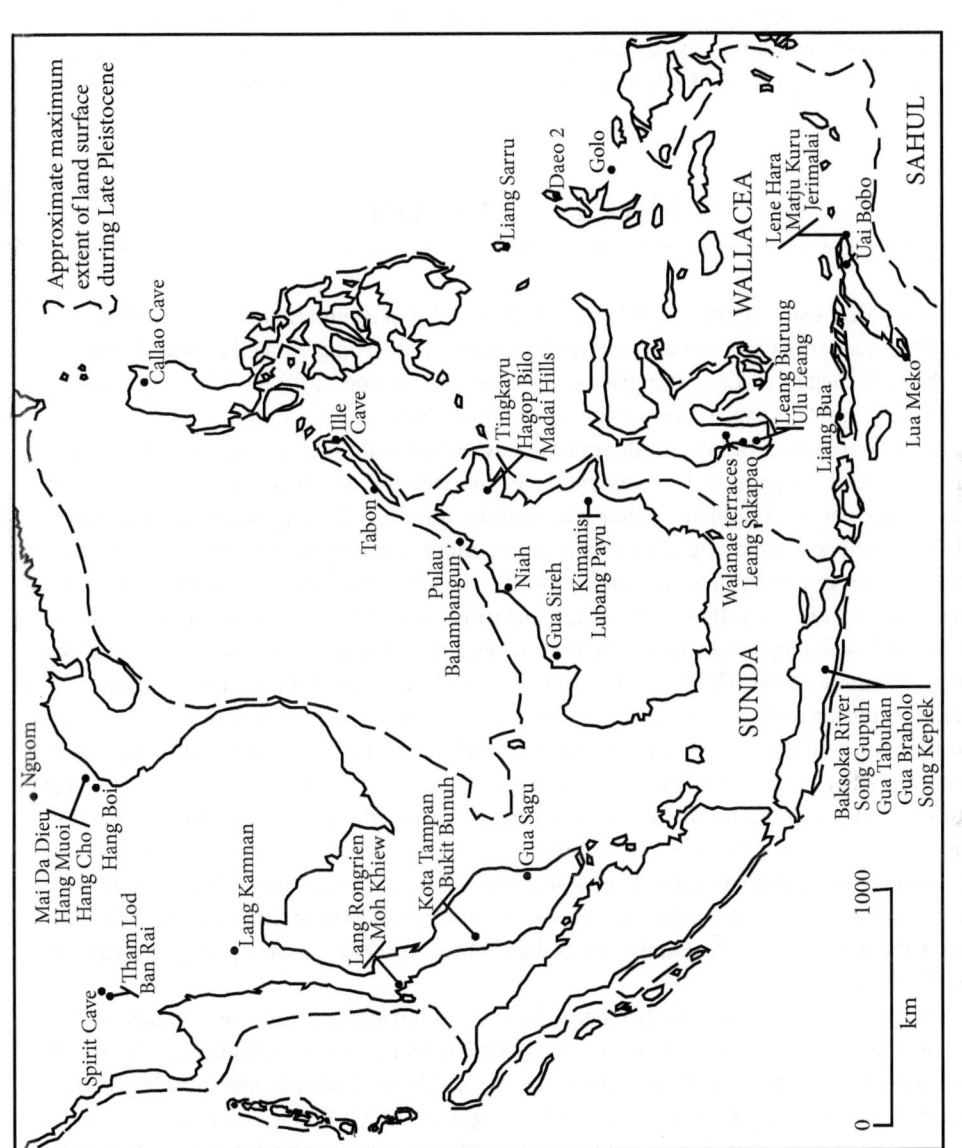

FIGURE 15.1 Map showing location of archaeological sites mentioned in the text.

the former and the latter to different species of *Homo*. On the other hand, the claimed survival of the very archaic hominin *Homo floresiensis* in hinterland Flores until the late Pleistocene, associated with a stone artefact industry broadly similar to those attributed to early *Homo sapiens* in Sunda, casts doubt on the use of stone tool technology as a means of distinguishing between species of *Homo* (contra Foley 1987 and Foley and Lahr 1997). Although archaeologists can be confident that *Homo sapiens* had dispersed farther east to Australia and New Guinea by 50,000–55,000 years ago (Hiscock 2008, 44), this would leave unanswered the question of whether or not Kota Tampan also marks the presence of *Homo sapiens*.

Malay Peninsula

Late Pleistocene sites in the Malay Peninsula include Bukit Bunuh (dated by optically stimulated luminescence to 39,000 BP), and the basal deposit with uncalibrated radiocarbon dates in the rock shelters of Lang Rongrien (27,000 to over 40,000 BP), Moh Khiew (26,000 BP and older), and Gua Sagu (15,000 BP at its base) in addition to Kota Tampan.

Kota Tampan and Bukit Bunuh are both ancient lakeside sites where water-worn pebbles had been knapped to leave assemblages numerically dominated by primary flakes. The cobbles at Kota Tampan either had shallow unifacial flaking, including one example with traces of grinding along its edge, or more invasive flaking, resulting in cores with one or more distinct striking platforms. Bukit Bunuh has produced some cores (namely, nodules with distinct striking platforms) as well as a predominance of cobbles with shallow flaking, many flaked on both faces, including hand axe-like forms (Bulbeck 2003; Mokhtar 2006). The small assemblage from basal Lang Rongrien is dominated by flakes including a range of utilized and/or retouched flakes and also contains some cores. Similar cores, along with unifacially flaked cobbles, and numerous flakes lacking documented evidence for utilization or retouch, have been described for the basal assemblage at Moh Khiew. Moh Khiew also has a terminal Pleistocene assemblage that differs from the basal assemblage through the addition of bifacially flaked cobbles and demonstrably utilized flakes (Anderson 1990; Pookajorn 1996). Finally, the basal Gua Sagu assemblage consists only of bifacially flaked cobbles and primary flakes (Zuraina et al. 1998a), making it the oldest Malay Peninsula assemblage whose absence of cores gives it an entirely Hoabinhian status.

There is a lack of evidence for habitation between 15,000 and 25,000 BP, which suggests that during the LGM the population, with its focus on coastal and lowland resources, relocated to places now under the sea (Bulbeck 2003). The pre-LGM faunal assemblages include primates, squirrels, bamboo rat, porcupine, pig, and barking deer at Moh Khiew, and canid, bovid, elephant, sambar deer, Eld's deer, marine/estuarine fish, and tortoise remains at Lang Rongrien. The differences between these two sites suggest regular occupation at Moh Khiew in contrast to Lang Rongrien's intermittent occupation by foragers practising a seasonal round that involved transhumance between the interior and the coast (Mudar and Anderson 2007). Terminal Pleistocene faunal remains include gibbon, monkeys, squirrels, porcupines, murids, pigs, deer, bovids, sun bear, fish, and freshwater shellfish at Moh Khiew (Pookajorn 1996), and tiger and bamboo rat at basal Gua Sagu (Zuraina et al. 1998a). Between c.40,000 and 10,000 BP, and especially during the LGM, the pronouncedly seasonal rainfall created a savannah-woodland mosaic across the peninsula hinterland, in contrast to the Holocene rainforests (Mudar and Anderson 2007).

Central Thailand

Hunter-foragers were still utilizing the highlands of central Thailand during the drier conditions of the LGM and terminal Pleistocene. The large riverside cave Tham Lod near Mae Hong Son has an occupation sequence extending from 34,000 BP (39,960 cal BP) to 12,000 BP (Marwick 2008a). It was not available for occupation before this date as it formed part of the ancient stream bed. Climatic reconstructions based on isotope analysis of the freshwater bivalves in Tham Lod indicate that the terminal Pleistocene climate was both drier and more variable than the Holocene, supporting dry open woodland.

Whereas the basal assemblages from sites of similar antiquity such as Lang Rongrien and Lang Kamnan indicate low-intensity episodic use, Tham Lod has a continuous sequence (Marwick 2008b). The stone artefact assemblage is comprised mostly of unretouched quartzite and sandstone flakes, flaked pieces and amorphous cores (Marwick 2008b). The faunal assemblage includes riverine resources such as freshwater bivalves and an array of mammal species. Wattanapituksakul (2006) identified 31 taxa; mostly Cervidae, *Sus scrofa* (pig), Bovinae, and Pecora. Unexpected inclusions are the bear, *Ursus tibetanus*, Rhinocerotidae, and *Naemorhaedus*. The faunal sequence from Tham Lod is difficult to interpret as the mammals derive from diverse habitats. For example, while the habitat of *U. tibetanus* and *Naemorhaedus* is open montane forest, the Rhinocerotidae are associated with dense wet forest and swamp. The representation of all three throughout the Pleistocene and Holocene levels is, in the face of significant climatic change, suggestive of mobile hunter foragers utilizing a wide range of environments (Marwick 2008b, 161–2).

Tham Lod appears to have been abandoned at the beginning of the Holocene as the nearby upland rock-shelter site of Ban Rai, dating from 10,600 BP to 7200 BP, was first occupied. As at Tham Lod, the Ban Rai assemblage is dominated by flakes, but the cores have Hoabinhian affinities and may have functioned as core tools. Ban Rai is typical of other mainland sites such as Spirit cave and Tham Phaa Chan (Steep Cliff cave) in being initially occupied at the Pleistocene–Holocene transition and in terms of the emphasis on Hoabinhian cobble tools and flakes. Subsistence evidence at Ban Rai includes freshwater molluscs and mammalian faunal remains such as *Cervus* spp. and *Sus scrofa*; however, the poor condition of the bone assemblage limited its analytical utility.

Marwick (2008a) sees the occupation histories of the two sites as reflecting changes in mobility that relate at least in part to changing climate. During the LGM when fresh water was in short supply and vegetation was more open, the riverine location of Tham Lod afforded a good residential locus. During the wetter Holocene, vegetation near the river would have been dense closed forest, and the more open hilltop locations such as surround Ban Rai would have provided better access to montane communities, but distance to fresh water and stone raw-material sources may have promoted mobility.

No evidence of vegetable food processing has been recovered from these sites but the nearby site of Spirit cave contains an extensive range of plant remains as well as fauna.

Faunal remains include sambar deer, pig, bamboo rat, porcupine, macaque, gibbon, langur, slow loris, banded civet cat, marten, flying squirrel, otter, crabs, and fish (Higham 1977).

Microscopic studies of use-wear and polish on Hoabinhian cobble tools have been attempted but have had limited success owing to the coarse nature of the raw materials used to make the tools. Such studies suggest that the flaked cobbles were used for working wood and bone rather than soft materials such as meat or vegetable matter (Bannanurag 1988).

North Vietnam

In lowland North Vietnam, the earliest radiocarbon dates for well-described habitation remains are of LGM antiquity: 16,000–18,000 BP at Xom Trai, 18,000–23,000 BP at Nguom rock shelter, 18,000–21,000 BP at Hang Muoi rock shelter, and back to 20,000 BP at Hang Cho cave and Mai Da Dieu (uncalibrated dates). A sondage at Hang Cho recovered charcoal in a calcareous concretion dated to 30,000 BP, while at Nguom a small assemblage of retouched and other stone flakes in the basal deposit is estimated to date to 40,000 BP (Nguyen 2008; Tong 2007; Van Tan 1997; Yi et al. 2008).

Van Tan (1997, 37–8) has distinguished these earliest flake-based assemblages with the term Nguomian, and Vietnamese archaeologists routinely describe the LGM-related assemblages as Sonvian. Sonvian is distinguished from the later Hoabinhian assemblages by dint of peripheral flaking of the worked cobbles, rather than a tendency to flake across all of one or both faces of the cobbles (Bellwood 1992). An alternative interpretation would posit the same technology, focused on cobble flaking, from the LGM through to the early Holocene, associated with the production of smaller flakes through time as the cobbles were flaked across a larger area before being discarded (Yi et al. 2008).

Plant remains from LGM contexts are dominated by nutshell fragments assigned to the *Juglans* (walnut) genus, in contrast to the *Canarium* nut, *Quercus,* and *Castanopsis* identifications from terminal Pleistocene deposits. The changeover reflects an estimated temperature decrease of 5–7 degrees, but high rainfall throughout, as the evergreen *Juglans* forest of the LGM gave way to *Quercus/Castanopsis* forest by the terminal Pleistocene (Nguyen 2008).

Medium-sized to large mammals are well represented in the LGM levels, and include deer, pig, cattle, wolves, cats, porcupines, macaques, and the locally extinct orang-utan (Bellwood 1992; Yi et al. 2008). A similar range of mammals, minus the orang-utan but including small carnivores and squirrel, is described for the terminal Pleistocene site of Hang Boi (Rabett et al. 2009). Land snails and small riverine animals such as tortoise, fish, and freshwater shellfish and crabs are in evidence from the LGM onwards (Rabett et al. 2009; Yi et al. 2008) and point to a broad-spectrum diet, in what would appear to have been one of the most intensively inhabited areas of Late Pleistocene South-East Asia.

Java

In Java the Pacitanian stone bifaces, choppers, and flakes from the Baksoka River terraces are linked to Late Pleistocene *Homo sapiens* by some archaeologists, but other archaeologists associate them with Middle Pleistocene *Homo erectus* (Keates 2004; Simanjuntak 2004). In contrast, the Tabuhan period remains from the Gunung Sewu rock shelters (Sémah et al. 2003) are universally assigned to Late Pleistocene *Homo sapiens*. Song Gupuh has stone artefacts dating from approximately 50,000 BP but these were sparsely deposited, and probably manufactured outside of the site until 12,000 BP (Morwood et al. 2008). Discrete habitation layers date back to around 45,000 BP at Gua Tabuhan, while the earliest habitation at Gua Braholo and Song Keplek, based on radiocarbon determinations, is *c*.33,000 and 24,000 BP respectively (Simanjuntak 2004).

At all of these three sites, the stone artefacts—which consist of poorly described flakes of local chert—are sparse in layers older than 12,000 BP. At all four Gunung Sewu sites, the oldest faunal fragments are predominantly from large ungulates such as deer, pigs, and bovids (Mahareni 2002; Morwood et al. 2008; Sémah et al. 2003). A wider range of mammals, including species that would be better adapted to forested conditions, is present in deposits that post-date the LGM. These include bears, elephants, rhinoceros, tapir, monkeys, viverrids, and squirrels, in addition to the still common deer, pigs, and bovids. After 12,000 years ago, which marks the start of the Keplek period, the entire signature of human occupation at Gunung Sewu changes, with evidence of intensive habitation, occasional burials, *in situ* stone working, the production of bone points, and hunting activities focused on monkeys and other rainforest animals (Morwood et al. 2008; Simanjuntak 2004).

Borneo

The Niah caves of Borneo were first used by foragers about 45,000 years ago, a time when the sea was about 30 km distant and when the landscape around the cave complex was

FIGURE 15.2 Niah cave entrance (photo courtesy Graeme Barker).

considerably more varied than the equatorial rainforest that surrounds it today (Barker 2005, 106) (Figure 15.2).

The Pleistocene foragers pursued varied subsistence strategies exploiting the forests, a range of freshwater environments, and later the establishing coastal estuaries for mammals, birds, fish, shellfish, and plant resources (Barker et al. 2007). Pig seems to have been the favoured prey species (*Sus barbatus*), but a wide range of animals including several primate taxa, langurs, macaques, porcupine, monitor lizard and smaller lizards, snakes, birds, and bats feature in the faunal assemblage as well as molluscs and fish (Barker et al. 2007).

Niah continued to be used during the LGM when lower temperatures and a downward migration of the montane forest are indicated by the presence of the lesser gymnure (*Hylomys suillus*) and the ferret badger (*Helictis orientalis*), species that are today restricted to the highlands of Mount Kinabalu (Cranbrook 2000, 78). The capture technology associated with the vast array of species is complex and shows marked variation over time. For example, the Niah fish assemblage includes large individuals from freshwater streams and estuaries, suggesting the use of nets or spears in their capture (Barker et al. 2007). Niah also has one of the largest collections of bone tools in the region with over 146 items. They occur from the earliest excavation layers where they appear to have fulfilled many functions, but only become abundant between 11,000 BP and 4000 BP. The increased emphasis on bone technology at this time has been suggested to relate to coastal exploitation strategies as mangrove environments were established following Holocene sea level rise (Rabett 2005). Some terminal Pleistocene examples of bone bi-points and worked stingray spines still have mastic and fibrous binding adhering to the shafts demonstrating how they were hafted into composite tools. The position of the binding and the type of point suggest that they functioned as fishing leisters and possibly even as projectile tips for arrows used with a bow (Barton et al. 2009).

Niah is also unique in preserving evidence of Pleistocene plant exploitation and includes fragments of fruits, nuts, and parenchyma (Paz 2005) as well as microscopic starch grains (Barton 2005). 'The data indicate the collection, processing in the cave, and presumably consumption of rainforest tuberous plants such as aroids, taro, yam, and sago palm' (Barker 2005, 97). Interestingly, many of the tubers required extensive multistage processing to render them safely edible, demonstrating that these early foragers possessed a high degree of knowledge about these plants. The stone artefact technology from Niah is poorly reported. The lower industry is apparently a collection of amorphous 'chunks and chips, without coherent core forms and with few conchoidal flakes' made on coarse-grained raw materials (Bellwood 1997, 173). Cobble tools are found, but not in the oldest levels, and some of the cobble tools are edge ground. While the exact dating of these is not known they are apparently found in terminal Pleistocene and early Holocene contexts (Bellwood 1997, 173; Zuraina 1982).

Borneo has a number of other sites with evidence of Late Pleistocene habitation. In Sabah (north-east Borneo), geomorphological research at Tingkayu demonstrates the existence of a lake between 28,000 and 17,000 BP. Stone artefacts, which include thin, pointed tools flaked across both faces, have been recovered from two sites at the rim of the former lake. The rock shelter of Hagop Bilo, within the area covered by Lake Tingkayu, was occupied as of 17,000 BP by foragers whose lithics included elongated ('blade-like') flakes until 12,000 BP (Bellwood 1988).

Pulau Balambangun (today an island, formerly connected to mainland Sabah) was occupied between 17,000 BP and the early Holocene by foragers who exploited marine, mangrove, and freshwater resources (Zuraina et al. 1998b), while the rock shelters of Sabah's Madai

Hills reveal an undifferentiated 'core-flake' assemblage dating back to the Pleistocene/Holocene junction (Bellwood 1988).

The stone artefacts from Kimanis and Lubang Payu, in East Kalimantan due south of Sabah, are also classified with the functionally versatile 'core-flake' tradition. Despite lying inland, these sites contain small amounts of marine shell, including cowry ornaments dating between the terminal Pleistocene and mid-Holocene, and shell scrapers dating back to the early Holocene (Arifin 2004).

Philippine and Talaud Islands

In the Philippines, the oldest evidence for a human presence comes from Callao cave in Luzon and Tabon cave in Palawan. Callao was briefly occupied at 26,000 BP, and also at the much earlier time of 67,000 BP, as registered by an assemblage of human-modified bone, which includes pig, deer, and rodents, and a human toe bone (Mijares et al. 2010; Piper and Mijares 2008). Early occupation at Tabon is dated to between 47,000 and 17,000 BP, based on the age of fragmentary *Homo sapiens* fossils recovered with the habitation debris (Détroit et al. 2004). Although Palawan was connected to Borneo at times of lowest sea levels, and indeed supported a tiger population around 12,000 years ago (Piper et al. 2008), the early presence of humans in Luzon is indubitable evidence of their ability to undertake sea crossings by 67,000 BP.

The 26,000-year-old stone artefacts from Callao cave include blade-like flakes similar to those from Hagop Bilo (Mijares 2008). A comparable lithic technology dates back to a similar age at the rock shelter of Liang Sarru, in the Talaud Islands, which lie between Mindanao and North Sulawesi (Tanudirjo 2001). The first phase of occupation, dated between 30,000 and 28,000 BP, was followed by the site's most intensive use between 21,000 and 17,000 BP during the LGM, and a third phase between approximately 10,000 and 7000 BP. The colonization (and possible recolonization) of the Talaud Islands attests to early maritime seafaring, with a reach extending even to the smallest and most remote islands of Wallacea. The faunal refuse in all phases essentially consists of marine shellfish, dominated by the families Neritidae, Turbinidae, and Trochidae (Soegondho 2006). In contrast to the blade-like flakes at Liang Sarru and Callao cave's Pleistocene layers, the Tabon lithic technology reflects a less-structured method of core reduction that is dominant in Philippine sites, generally, until at least the mid-Holocene (Patole-Edoumba 2009).

South-west Sulawesi

On Sulawesi island, current evidence on Pleistocene archaeology is restricted to the south-west peninsula. Keates (2004) describes the stone artefacts from the Walanae terraces as typologically similar to Java's Pacitanian forms, and suggests an association with *Homo sapiens* (loosely dated to the earlier part of the Late Pleistocene), but reliable chronometric evidence is unavailable. The earliest chronometric dates, from two rock shelters in karsts that abut the coastal plain, suggest habitation between *c.*30,000 and 20,000 BP.

Leang Sakapao 1 yielded some marine shell at its base dated to 25,390 ± ?310 BP (Bulbeck et al. 2004), which would calibrate to between c.30,000 and 29,000 BP. Above the marine shell, sealed by a thin travertine layer, 704 stone artefacts, some faunal fragments including pig, and freshwater shell dated to between c.31,000 and 25,000 BP—overestimates, given the dissolution of ancient calcium carbonate in the local karstic stream—were excavated (Bulbeck et al. 2004).

Leang Burung 2 similarly revealed a pronounced difference between its basal deposit of yellow-brown clay and the overlying deposit with freshwater shell. The basal deposit produced only 49 stone artefacts, but it also had 158 faunal fragments of which 46 per cent (excluding ambiguous identifications) were identified as belonging to three primary forest ungulates: the pig-deer or babirusa, and the two species of *Anoa* pygmy water-buffalo. The overlying deposit on the other hand produced over 5,400 stone artefacts and dates on freshwater shell between 31,000 and 20,000 BP, but only 311 faunal fragments. Of these, merely 4.6 per cent (excluding ambiguous identifications) were babirusa or *Anoa*, contrasting with a greater take of the local *Sus celebensis* boar which is a specialist of secondary forest and other relatively open habitats (Glover 1981; Simons and Bulbeck 2004).

Thus, habitation continued at both sites during a period when the sea level dropped rapidly, but the change in faunal composition points to more arid conditions (O'Connor and Aplin 2007). Both sites were evidently abandoned by the height of the LGM, permanently (Leang Sakapao 1) or until around 1,000 years ago (Leang Burung 2).

Similarities between Leang Sakapao 1 and Leang Burung 2 (post-30,000 BP) include flakes with gloss from cutting siliceous vegetation, other utilized/retouched flakes, and the predominance of freshwater shell in the faunal material. Both sites also have evidence for art: pieces of ochre, three of them with signs of abrasion, at Leang Burung 2; hand stencils at both sites; and paintings of pigs at Leang Sakapao 1 (contrasting with the absence of zoomorphs from the numerous rock shelters with Holocene occupation and parietal art in the immediate vicinity—Sumantri 1996).

The differences between the two sites can be attributed to the elevated position and poor accessibility of Leang Sakapao 1 compared with the valley-floor entrance to Leang Burung 2. The latter site contains more abundant habitation refuse and a wider range of flakes including claimed Levallois points, a retouched point, and retouched scrapers. Neither site, however, has yielded the blunted-backed microliths, polished bone points, and hollow-based arrowheads that characterize Holocene Toalean assemblages in south-west Sulawesi (Bulbeck et al. 2004; Glover 1976; 1981).

Nusa Tenggara

The northern Moluccan islands comprising Halmahera, Morotai, Bacan, Obi, and other small satellite islands occupy an important geographical position between Sulawesi, the southern Philippines, and New Guinea (Bellwood et al. 1998). Earliest occupation here from Golo cave on Gebe Island dates to c.31,000 BP (Bellwood et al. 1998, 249), and from Daeo 2 and other sites on Halmahera there is a continuous sequence covering the last 15,000 years. The Moluccan islands are clearly within the natural range of a variety of important food plants, including sago, and the region has even been implicated in the domestication of

FIGURE 15.3 Lene Hara cave, East Timor.

some of these plants as part of a putative New Guinea centre of plant domestication (Yen 1995). Although direct evidence of plant exploitation is not preserved, pitted stones were recovered from the early Holocene levels in the Moluccan sites Tanjung Pinang in southern Morotai and Um Kapat Papo on Gebe, and were identified by local people as used for processing kenari nuts (genus *Canarium*) (Bellwood et al. 1998, 242, 247). Other economic evidence relating the Moluccan region to Melanesia is found in the faunal record. A species of wallaby *Dorcopsis muelleri* occurs in the early Holocene levels of Golo cave on Gebe Island, and was probably brought in from Misool, which was part of mainland Sahul before 10,500 BP. The same wallaby is also found in preceramic levels dating to between 5000 and 3400 BP at Gua Siti Nafisah at Nusliko on southern Halmahera (Flannery et al. 1998).

Nusa Tenggara has amongst the oldest evidence for modern human presence in Wallacea, with the newly discovered site of Jerimalai shelter in East Timor dating back to c.42,000 cal BP (38,255 ± ?596 BP Wk-17831) (O'Connor 2007). Other caves and shelters, also on the north coast of East Timor, have produced Pleistocene dates of between 42,000 cal BP (Lene Hara; Figure 15.3) and 35,000 cal BP (Matja Kuru 2) (O'Connor et al. 2002; 2010b). The stone artefact assemblages mirror those at Jerimalai, in being comprised of small cores, flakes, and retouched flakes and in containing no repetitively produced or specialized forms (types).

Forager subsistence in the coastal sites of East Timor was heavily reliant on marine resources including marine turtle *Chelonia mydas*, fish, shellfish, crabs, and urchins. The presence of tuna and other pelagic species from the earliest occupation levels indicates that open-water fishing was an early adaptation requiring a high degree of planning and complex technology (O'Connor et al. 2011). O'Connor et al. (2011) suggested that angling or

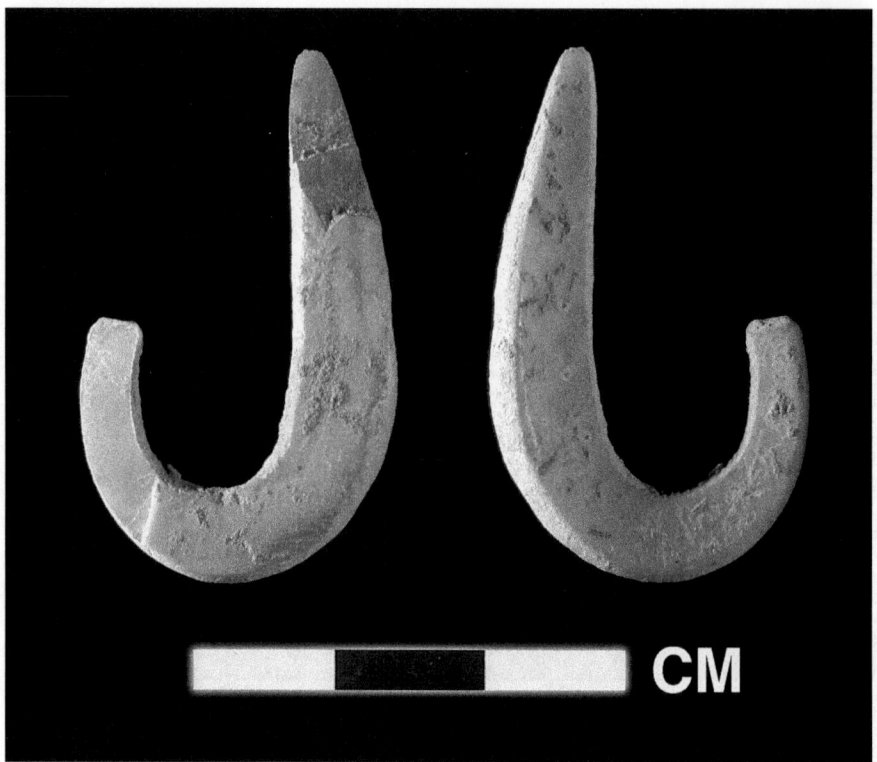

FIGURE 15.4 Single-piece *Trochus* shellfish hook from Lene Hara dated to the terminal Pleistocene.

netting equipment and the use of boats would likely have been deployed to catch the pelagic species, a view supported by the rare find of a partial fish hook in Jerimalai in a level dated between 23,000 BP and 16,000 cal BP, and a complete single-piece fish hook from Lene Hara directly dated to the terminal Pleistocene (9741 ± ?60 NZA1700, calibrated range 10,205 to 11,128, 2 sigma) (O'Connor et al. 2011; O'Connor and Veth 2005) (Figure 15.4). Marine shellfish are predominantly rocky platform taxa such as *Nerita* spp., *Strombus* spp., *Trochus* spp., *Turbo* sp., and chiton. While such an early focus on marine resources may seem unusual, the north coast of Timor drops steeply to the continental shelf, and during the time span of human occupation coastal resources would always have been accessible, even during the LGM when sea level was 120 m lower than present.

Added to this is the fact that the non-marine fauna available to the first foragers in the smaller islands of Wallacea was in general extremely limited (O'Connor and Aplin 2007). Only murids, lizards, snakes, and bats have been found in the Timor faunas. The Timor murids included multiple genera of very large endemic rats, the largest approximately the size of a big cat (5 kg). In the inland cave sites such as Uai Bobo 1 and 2, first occupied about 13,000 years ago, these large rodents seem to have comprised the mainstay of the diet in the preceramic levels (Glover 1986). All of the large murids are now extinct, disappearing probably in the past few thousand years (O'Connor and Aplin 2007). On the other hand, pigmy *Stegodon*, a giant extinct land turtle *Geochelone atlas*, and a Komodo dragon-sized monitor have been recovered from Pleistocene-aged deposits in Flores and West Timor (O'Connor and Aplin 2007). In Flores these are clearly associated with a pre-modern hominin (Morwood et al. 2005). Currently there is no published evidence that these extinct taxa ever coexisted with hominins in Timor, although Morwood (pers. comm.) recently reported stone artefacts associated with Stegodon remains in West Timor deposits and has suggested that modern humans caused the extinction of these species very rapidly following their arrival in the island. This issue needs further investigation, but if this proves to be the case it will require a revision of our thinking on early modern human hunting adaptations in Wallacea.

The stone tool assemblages from the East Timor sites show no indication of technological specialization and very little change over the 40,000-year span of occupation, being predominantly small flakes, cores, and small numbers of retouched flakes made on chert. A variety of bone points are found in the forager levels at Lene Hara and Jerimalai, but their function is presently unclear. A rich array of shell artefacts also occur. These include retouched operculums of large *Turbo* sp. shells presumed to have functioned as scrapers, and a variety of decorative items including drilled shell discs and shaped pendants. Shell beads from Matja Kuru 2 have been directly dated to the early Holocene *c.*9200 BP (O'Connor 2010, 228).

Painted rock art adorns the walls of some of the East Timor caves. Most of the surviving painted art is probably late Holocene in age. However, U-series dating of layered ochre pigment encrusted in limestone wall fragments indicates that painting has been ongoing over the past 30,000 years (Aubert et al. 2007; O'Connor 2003), and one of a series of engraved faces at Lene Hara has been recently dated by the same technique to between 13,000 and 11,000 years old (O'Connor et al. 2010a).

Surrounding islands have surprisingly produced no evidence of occupation by *Homo sapiens* as early as East Timor's. Flores, to the west of Timor, appears not to have been occupied by modern humans before the terminal Pleistocene (Morwood et al. 2005). Lua Meko, a cave site on Roti (the small island to the west of Timor) has a basal date of 24,000 BP associated with very low numbers of stone artefacts and sparse marine shellfish (Mahirta 2003, 99). This patterning may however be more apparent than real and result from limited sampling of cave and open site deposits on the different islands (O'Connor et al. 2010b).

Discussion and Conclusions

Modern Humans' Colonization of South-East Asia

There are tantalizing indications that modern humans had colonized South-East Asia before 50,000 years ago, especially at Kota Tampan, the only known site in the region covered by ash from the Toba super-volcano explosion, and Callao cave in Wallacea. We would certainly expect a presence of modern humans in South-East Asia by 50,000 years ago, which is a conservative estimate for their appearance in Australia (Hiscock 2008, 44; O'Connor 2007). Chronometric evidence for Australia's earliest habitation has been achieved by the use of techniques that break the radiocarbon barrier, such as optically stimulated luminescence and electron-spin resonance (Roberts et al. 2005), and the application of these techniques in South-East Asia is still in its infancy. Certainly by 40,000–45,000 years ago, an antiquity within the reach of radiocarbon dating, evidence for habitation appears at locations as widely dispersed as the Malay Peninsula, Sarawak, and East Timor, and by 35,000 cal years ago modern humans were colonizing islands as small and remote as the Talauds in the Molucca Sea.

Can South-East Asian archaeology provide an insight into how modern humans reached the Pleistocene continent of Sahul that stretched from New Guinea in the north to Tasmania in the south? A southern route into Sahul through the Lesser Sundas has often been advocated as the most parsimonious due to minimum distances between island hops and greatest intervisibility between islands. Early migration along this route is supported by the date of 42,000 cal BP for settlement in East Timor (O'Connor 2007). Some authors have favoured a northern route through Borneo, Sulawesi, and then into the northern Moluccan islands and the Bird's Head of Papua (e.g. Allen and O'Connell 2008) but excavations in the northern Moluccas have not yet produced evidence of settlement earlier than $c.32,000$ years ago (Bellwood et al. 1998).

However, there are two main problems with attempting to trace the route to Sahul through South-East Asia's Pleistocene archaeology: finding and dating any sites involved in this colonization thrust; and determining whether sites of relevant antiquity represent migration towards Sahul rather than colonization within the confines of South-East Asia.

An unwarranted perspective on South-East Asia as merely a gateway to archaeologically more important regions has also led to underutilization of Heaney's (1991) concept of a 'savannah corridor'. In our view the emphasis should lie more on viewing savannah (actually, savannah-forest mosaic) as an optimal habitat for hinterland human occupation than as a path of least resistance for humans fleeing South-East Asia. All of the sites in our review with lengthy sequences of Pleistocene habitation testify to human-friendly habitats varying from the temperate forests of North Vietnam to the mixed forests of Niah and the savannah-forest mosaics of the Malay Peninsula, South Sulawesi, and East Timor (see also Bird et al. 2005).

The equatorial and monsoonal forests that have cloaked Holocene South-East Asia required additional adaptations which first come into archaeological visibility with the terminal Pleistocene. In fact, the archaeological evidence suggests that aridity rather than relentless forest may have been the main deterrent to human occupation in many parts of South-East Asia during the height of the LGM. Local aridity appears to have been involved in the scanty habitation of the south-west Sulawesi karsts, the southern Malay Peninsula, and East Timor between $c.22,000$ and 15,000 years ago. During that period, the great majority of chronometric dates (see Figure 15.5) come from sites in Borneo (which may then have been particularly favourable to human occupation) and lowland North Vietnam (which was cool but well-forested at the time).

According to the theory of an African homeland for modern humans and their dispersal along the northern rim of the Indian Ocean (Oppenheimer 2003), early modern humans would have been adapted to relatively open vegetation and coastal habitats, as demonstrated here for South-East Asia. Most South-East Asian sites along the Pleistocene coastline would of course now be submerged, but as noted in our review, evidence for the exploitation of marine resources is not uncommon at Pleistocene sites. A maritime voyaging capacity would have been a prerequisite for the colonization of Wallacea.

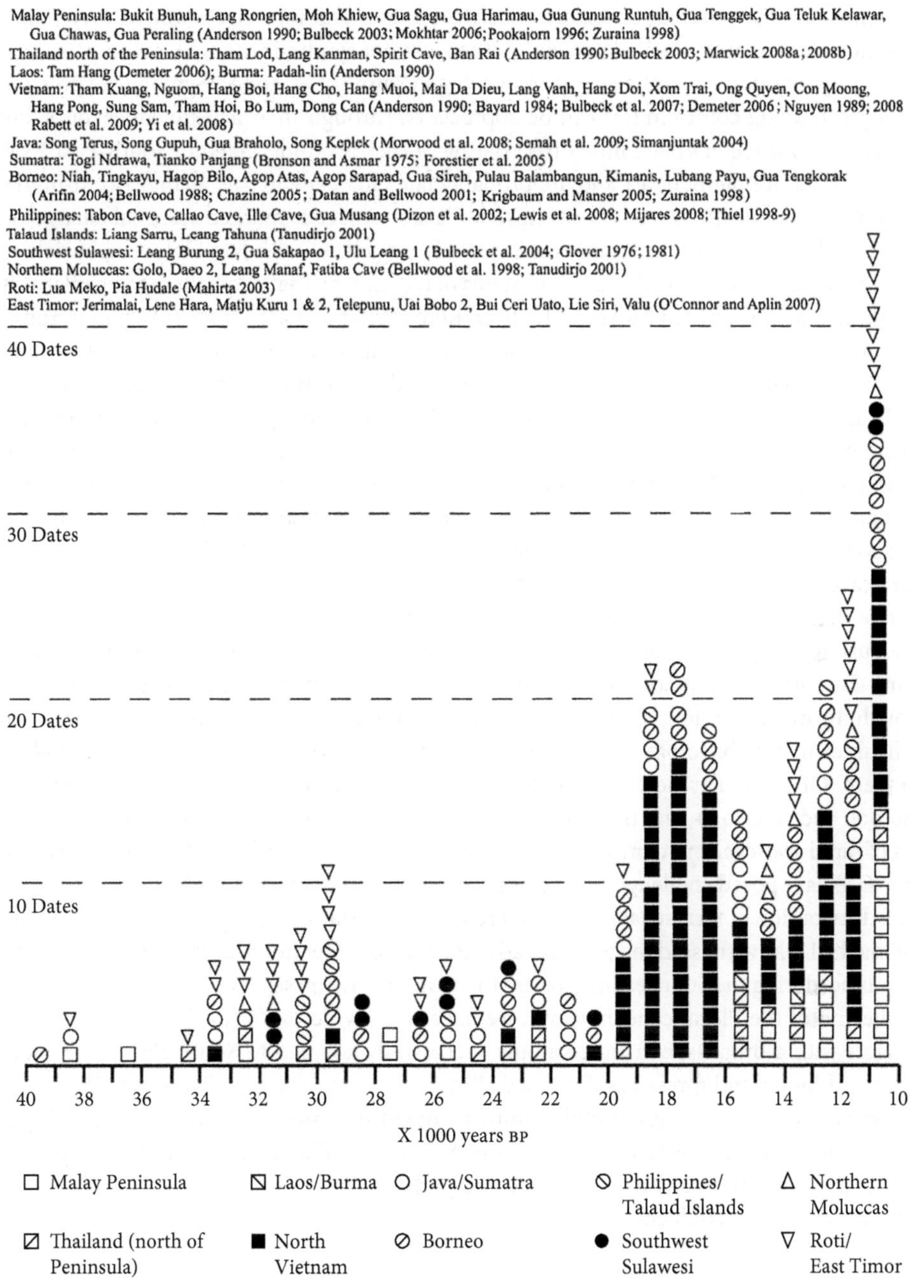

Malay Peninsula: Bukit Bunuh, Lang Rongrien, Moh Khiew, Gua Sagu, Gua Harimau, Gua Gunung Runtuh, Gua Tenggek, Gua Teluk Kelawar, Gua Chawas, Gua Peraling (Anderson 1990; Bulbeck 2003; Mokhtar 2006; Pookajorn 1996; Zuraina 1998)
Thailand north of the Peninsula: Tham Lod, Lang Kanman, Spirit Cave, Ban Rai (Anderson 1990; Bulbeck 2003; Marwick 2008a; 2008b)
Laos: Tam Hang (Demeter 2006); Burma: Padah-lin (Anderson 1990)
Vietnam: Tham Kuang, Nguom, Hang Boi, Hang Cho, Hang Muoi, Mai Da Dieu, Lang Vanh, Hang Doi, Xom Trai, Ong Quyen, Con Moong, Hang Pong, Sung Sam, Tham Hoi, Bo Lum, Dong Can (Anderson 1990; Bayard 1984; Bulbeck et al. 2007; Demeter 2006; Nguyen 1989; 2008 Rabett et al. 2009; Yi et al. 2008)
Java: Song Terus, Song Gupuh, Gua Braholo, Song Keplek (Morwood et al. 2008; Semah et al. 2009; Simanjuntak 2004)
Sumatra: Togi Ndrawa, Tianko Panjang (Bronson and Asmar 1975; Forestier et al. 2005)
Borneo: Niah, Tingkayu, Hagop Bilo, Agop Atas, Agop Sarapad, Gua Sireh, Pulau Balambangun, Kimanis, Lubang Payu, Gua Tengkorak (Arifin 2004; Bellwood 1988; Chazine 2005; Datan and Bellwood 2001; Krigbaum and Manser 2005; Zuraina 1998)
Philippines: Tabon Cave, Callao Cave, Ille Cave, Gua Musang (Dizon et al. 2002; Lewis et al. 2008; Mijares 2008; Thiel 1998-9)
Talaud Islands: Liang Sarru, Leang Tahuna (Tanudirjo 2001)
Southwest Sulawesi: Leang Burung 2, Gua Sakapao 1, Ulu Leang 1 (Bulbeck et al. 2004; Glover 1976; 1981)
Northern Moluccas: Golo, Daeo 2, Leang Manaf, Fatiba Cave (Bellwood et al. 1998; Tanudirjo 2001)
Roti: Lua Meko, Pia Hudale (Mahirta 2003)
East Timor: Jerimalai, Lene Hara, Matju Kuru 1 & 2, Telepunu, Uai Bobo 2, Bui Ceri Uato, Lie Siri, Valu (O'Connor and Aplin 2007)
40 Dates
30 Dates
20 Dates
10 Dates
40
38
36
34
32
30
28
26
24
22
20
18
16
14
12
10
X 1000 years BP
Malay Peninsula
Laos/Burma
Java/Sumatra
Philippines/ Talaud Islands
Northern Moluccas
Thailand (north of Peninsula)
North Vietnam
Borneo
Southwest Sulawesi
Roti/ East Timor

FIGURE 15.5 Graphs of uncalibrated radiocarbon dates and other chronometric dates between 10,000 and 40,000 years BP from South-East Asian cultural contexts.

Archaeologists widely agree that the success of modern humans in colonizing every landmass north of Antarctica relied on a unique capacity for symbolic thought, as is particularly well documented in Australia's early archaeology (Balme et al. 2009). Symbolic expression amongst foraging communities can be appreciated through their artistic endeavours, but unfortunately there has been little direct dating of rock art undertaken in South-East Asia. Most art sites are pigment art and are probably late Holocene in age, as they occur on the walls of very active limestone caves whose walls are subject to marked seasonal changes in moisture. In some cases, the images are spatially associated with late Holocene burials or contain motifs of introduced animals or items of technology that allow them to be relatively dated, such as the painted horses in Ile Kere Kere shelter in East Timor (O'Connor 2003). However, there are indications of a much older rock art tradition in the region. A systematic rock art dating programme undertaken in south-eastern Borneo produced a range of Th/U and 14C ages with a minimum age of c.9800 BP (Plagnes et al. 2003). This art, featuring predominantly hand and arm stencils with decorative infill, may signal clan affiliations or even represent tattooing (Chazine 2005). Ochre at Leang Burung 2 and the painted rock art at Leang Sakapao 1 point to artistic traditions in Sulawesi in the order of 30,000 to 20,000 years ago. Recent work on red pigment interlayered between calcite skins from Lene Hara cave in East Timor suggests that the practice of painting on walls extends back to the first modern human occupation at least 30,000 years ago (Aubert et al. 2007).

Figure 15.5 shows an overall pattern of an increasing number of chronometric dates for South-East Asia from 40,000 to 10,000 years ago. Such a pattern may reflect population growth during the period, although at least part of the explanation would be the increased difficulties that archaeology faces in locating and dating archaeological remains the older they are. Of particular note may be the apparent dips in the number of dates between c.30,000 and 20,000 BP, and then between c.16,000 and 14,000 BP. Both intervals were periods of rapid sea-level and climate change leading into and out of the height of the LGM, and appear to have posed challenges to South-East Asia's inhabitants in adapting to the reconfigured distribution of terrestrial and coastal resources. Certainly, the period immediately following the LGM witnessed the widespread dispersal of populations based in Borneo and the islands bordering the Sulu Sea in response to the rapidly rising sea levels (Soares et al. 2008). By the end of the Pleistocene, however, we have clear evidence for healthy populations of foragers with a broad-spectrum economy successfully adapted to South-East Asia's mangrove and hinterland forests, as discussed above and emphasized by Figure 15.5. Moreover, the transfer of economically useful mammals, noted in easternmost Wallacea, continued with the introduction of *Sus celebensis* from Sulawesi to Flores in the early Holocene—a species that was minimally a commensal, and perhaps domesticated in parts of south-west Sulawesi at the time (Bulbeck 2008).

Lithic Technologies

As noted by Bellwood (1992; 1997) and other commentators, stone artefact assemblages in South-East Asia have traditionally been broadly divided between cobble-based assemblages, where the size and shape of the flaked river cobble are largely retained even at the end of the flaking process, and core-flake assemblages, where the dedicated production of single or, more typically, multiple striking platforms results in cores of very different size and shape from the original nodules procured for knapping. The differences between these two technological pathways are particularly clear for the Holocene when they respectively correspond to the Hoabinhian of northern Sumatra/mainland South-East Asia on the one hand, and the 'flake-blade' assemblages of island South-East Asia (excluding northern Sumatra) on the other hand. The distinction is, however, blurred during the Pleistocene as indicated by the core-flake assemblage from basal Lang Rongrien, the early flake-dominated technologies of Vietnam, Niah's cobble axes, and the Tingkayu assemblage with its finely shaped bifaces. Flake-blade assemblages tend to be found in places with more abundant and/or finer chert, and Hoabinhian assemblages where coarser stone (e.g. quartzite or volcanic) is the only material available, but the association is far from perfect. The core-flake-blade technology appears to have had the versatility to continue unabated into the Holocene, despite the trend to warmer wetter conditions, with marked change restricted to certain local specializations such as the Toalean of south-west Sulawesi (Bellwood 1997).

The Hoabinhian on the other hand may well represent an adaptation to forest expansion, in such aspects as the use of flaked pebbles for woodworking and forest clearance (Anderson 1990; Bannanurag 1988). In this respect the appearance of ground edges on cobble tools reaching back to the LGM at Xom Trai (Nguyen 1989) and Niah, and present in the Malay Peninsula during the Holocene (Anderson 1990; Bulbeck 2003), may be viewed as a technique for rejuvenating or extending the use-life of these timber-working tools. Grinding of the edges of cobble tools has been used to define a terminal Pleistocene to early Holocene variant of the Hoabinhian, labelled the Bacsonian, in North Vietnam. The Bacsonian is also associated with South-East Asia's oldest pottery and, possibly, incipient plant cultivation (Nguyen et al. 2004).

Several important points seem to emerge from this brief review of lithic technology in South-East Asia. Firstly, previous characterizations of South-East Asian industries as illustrating a unidirectional progression from earliest flake-based assemblages through to Holocene cobble-based Hoabinhian assemblages, reflecting a shift from Pleistocene hunters to Holocene forest clearers, is a gross oversimplification. Secondly, the long-term persistence of relatively simple reduction pathways in this region probably tells us about early moderns' need for versatile tool-kits. Where they survive in the archaeological record, tools made of organic materials and subsistence remains demonstrate the use of sophisticated composite tools, plant exploitation strategies, and capture technologies for game and fish. All attest to the remarkable adaptations that early moderns made to a diversity of environments ranging from dense rainforest to dry depauperate limestone coastlines. In the future, changes in stone tools will no doubt tell us more about behavioural variation in South-East Asia, but this will require the application of different conceptual and analytical frameworks to the assemblages than have hitherto been applied (e.g. Marwick 2007; 2008c).

The Late Pleistocene Legacy in Holocene South-East Asia

South-East Asia is well documented as a region where forest-based foragers, maritime foragers, and agricultural communities have lived in a complementary relationship from at least the mid-Holocene into ethnographic times. The plants and animals tended by agricultural communities have included taxa introduced to the region from the New Guinea region as well as China, but also local domesticates, especially root and tree crops (Barker

2006; Bellwood 1992; 1997). Of particular relevance, complex and varied management practices of tree and root crops, if not cultivation, were clearly occurring early in the Holocene (Donohue and Denham 2010).

In view of the intimate knowledge of the forest implied by the plant remains from sites such as Niah and Spirit cave, it is likely that yams, taro, sago, and some fruit trees may have been actively managed rather than just exploited in their wild form, indeed by people with a similar lifestyle to groups recorded ethnographically as South-East Asian forest foragers (Barker 2006). The persistence of foragers till ethnographic times is perhaps a useful template for thinking about the past as it reflects the versatility and resilience of populations able to efficiently exploit the enormous variety of plants and maritime resources across South-East Asia.

References

Allen, J. and O'Connell, J. 2008. Getting from Sunda to Sahul. In G. Clark, F. Leach, and S. O'Connor (eds), *Islands of inquiry, colonisation, seafaring and the archaeology of maritime landscapes*. Terra Australis 29, 31–46. Canberra: ANU E-Press.

Anderson, D. D. 1990. *Lang Rongrien rockshelter: a Pleistocene-early Holocene archaeological site from Krabi, southwestern Thailand*. Philadelphia: University of Pennsylvania Museum.

Arifin, K. 2004. Early human occupation of the East Kalimantan rainforest (the Upper Birang River region, Berau). PhD thesis. Australian National University.

Aubert, M., O'Connor, S., McCulloch, M., Mortimer, G., Watchman A., and Richer-Lalèche, M. 2007. Uranium-series dating rock art in East Timor. *Journal of Archaeological Science* 34, 991–6.

Balme, J., Davidson, I., McDonald, J., Stern, N., and Veth, P. 2009. Symbolic behaviour and the peopling of the southern arc route to Australia. *Quaternary International* 202, 59–68.

Bannanurag, R. 1988. Evidence for ancient woodworking: a microwear study of Hoabinhian tools. In B. Bronson and P. Charoenwongsa (eds), *Prehistoric studies: the stone and metal ages in Thailand*, 61–79. Bangkok. Thai Antiquity Working Group.

Barker, G. 2005. The archaeology of foraging and farming at Niah cave, Sarawak. In G. Barker and D. Gilbertson (eds), *The human use of caves in peninsula and island Southeast Asia*. Special Issue *Asian Perspectives* 44, 90–106.

Barker, G. 2006. *The agricultural revolution in prehistory: why did foragers become farmers?* Oxford: Oxford University Press.

Barker, G., Barton, H., Bird, M., Daly, P., Datan, I., Dykes, A., Farr, L., Gilbertson, D., Harrisson, B., and Hunt, C. 2007. The 'human revolution' in lowland tropical Southeast Asia: the antiquity and behaviour of anatomically modern humans at Niah cave (Sarawak, Borneo). *Journal of Human Evolution* 52, 243–61.

Barker, G., Reynolds, T., and Gilbertson, D. 2005. The human use of caves in peninsula and island South East Asia: research themes. In G. Barker and D. Gilbertson (eds), *The human use of caves in peninsula and island Southeast Asia*. Special Issue *Asian Perspectives* 44, 1–15.

Barton, H. 2005. The case for rainforest foragers: the starch record at Niah cave, Sarawak. In G. Barker and D. Gilbertson (eds), *The human use of caves in peninsula and island southeast Asia*. Special Issue *Asian Perspectives* 44, 56–72.

Barton, H., Piper, P. J., Rabett, R., and Reeds, I. 2009. Composite hunting technologies from the terminal Pleistocene and early Holocene, Niah cave, Borneo. *Journal of Archaeological Science* 36, 1708–14.

Bayard, D. T. 1984. A checklist of Vietnamese radiocarbon dates. *Southeast Asian Archaeology at the XV Pacific Science Congress.* Otago University Studies in Prehistoric Anthropology 16, 161–8.

Bellwood, P. (ed.) 1988. *Archaeological research in south-eastern Sabah.* Sabah: Sabah Museum Monograph 2.

Bellwood, P. 1992. Southeast Asia before history. In N. Tarling (ed.), *The Cambridge history of Southeast Asia, volume 1: from early times to c.1800,* 51–136. Cambridge: Cambridge University Press.

Bellwood, P. 1997. *Prehistory of the Indo-Malaysian archipelago.* Honolulu: University of Hawaii Press.

Bellwood, P., Nitihaminoto, G., Irwin, G., Gunadi, Waluyo, A., and Tanudirjo, D. 1998. 35,000 years of prehistory in the northern Moluccas. In G.-J. Bartstra (ed.), *Bird's head approaches: Irian Jaya studies, a programme for interdisciplinary research.* Modern Quaternary Studies in Southeast Asia 15, 233–75. Leiden: A. A. Balkema.

Bird, M., Taylor, I. D., and Hunt, C. 2005. Palaeoenvironments of insular Southeast Asia during the Last Glacial period: a savanna corridor in Sundaland? *Quaternary Science Reviews* 24, 2228–42.

Bronson, B. and Asmer, T. 1975. Prehistoric investigations at Tianko Panjang cave, Sumatra. *Asian Perspectives* 18, 128–45.

Bulbeck, D. 2008. An integrated perspective on the Austronesian diaspora: the switch from cereal agriculture to maritime foraging in the colonisation of island Southeast Asia. *Australian Archaeology* 67, 31–51.

Bulbeck, D., Hiscock, P., and Sumantri, I. 2004. Leang Sakapao 1, a second dated Pleistocene site from South Sulawesi, Indonesia. In S. G. Keates and J. M. Pasveer (eds), *Quaternary research in Indonesia.* Modern Quaternary Research in Southeast Asia 18, 118–28. London: Taylor & Francis.

Bulbeck, D., Oxenham, M., Nguyen Lan Cuong, and Nguyen Kim Thu. 2007. Implications of the terminal Pleistocene skull from Hang Muoi, North Vietnam. *Vietnam Archaeology* 2, 42–52.

Bulbeck, F. D. 2003. Hunter-gatherer occupation of the Malay Peninsula from the Ice Age to the Iron Age. In J. Mercader (ed.), *The archaeology of tropical rain forests,* 119–60. New Brunswick: Rutgers University Press.

Chazine, J.-M. 2005. Rock art, burials, and habitations: caves in East Kalimantan. In G. Barker and D. Gilbertson (eds), *The human use of caves in peninsula and island Southeast Asia.* Special Issue *Asian Perspectives* 44, 219–30.

Cranbrook, Earl of. 2000. Northern Borneo environments of the past 40,000 years: archaeozoological evidence. *Sarawak Museum Journal* 55 (new series 76), 61–109.

Datan, I. and Bellwood, P. 1991. Recent research at Gua Sireh (Serian) and Lubang Angin (Gunung Mulu National Park), Sarawak, Malaysia. *Bulletin of the Indo-Pacific Prehistory Association* 11, 386–405.

Demeter, F. 2006. New perspectives on the peopling of Southeast and East Asia during the late upper Pleistocene. In M. Oxenham and N. Tayles (eds), *Bioarchaeology of Southeast Asia,* 112–32. Cambridge: Cambridge University Press.

Détroit, F., Dizon, E., Falguères, C., Hameau, S., Ronquillo W., and Sémah F. 2004. Upper Pleistocene *Homo sapiens* from Tabon cave (Palawan, the Philippines): description and dating of new discoveries. *Comptes rendus Palevol* 3, 705–12.

Donohue, M. and Denham, T. 2010. Farming and language in island Southeast Asia: reframing Austronesian history. *Current Anthropology* 51, 223–56.

Flannery, T. F., Bellwood, P., White, J. P., Ennis, T., Irwin, G., Schubert K., and Balasubramaniam, S. 1998. Mammals from Holocene archaeological deposits on Gebe and Morotai Islands, northern Moluccas, Indonesia. *Australian Mammalogy* 20, 391–400.

Foley, R. 1987. Hominid species and stone-tool assemblages: how are they related? *Antiquity* 61, 380–92.

Foley, R. and Lahr, M. M. 1997. Mode 3 technologies and the evolution of modern humans. *Cambridge Archaeological Journal* 7, 3–36.

Forestier, H., Simanjuntak, T., Guillaud, D., Driwantoro, D., Wiradnyana, K., Siregar, D., Due Awe, R., and Budiman. 2005. Le site de Tögi Ndrawa, île de Nias, Sumatra nord: les premières traces d'une occupation hoabinhienne en grotte en Indonésie. *Comptes rendus Palevol* 4, 727–33.

Glover, I. C. 1976. Ulu Leang cave, Maros: a preliminary sequence of post-Pleistocene cultural development in South Sulawesi. *Archipel* 11, 113–54.

Glover, I. C. 1981. Leang Burung 2: an Upper Palaeolithic rockshelter in South Sulawesi, Indonesia. *Modern Quaternary Research in Southeast Asia* 6, 1–38.

Glover, I. C. 1986. *Archaeology in eastern Timor, 1966–67*. Terra Australia 11. Canberra: The Australian National University.

Heaney, L. R. 1991. A synopsis of climatic and vegetational change in Southeast Asia. *Climatic Change* 19, 53–61.

Higham, C. 1977. Economic change in prehistoric Thailand. In C. A. Reed (ed.), *Origins of agriculture*, 385–412. The Hague: Mouton.

Hiscock, P. 2008. *Archaeology of ancient Australia*. London and New York: Taylor & Francis.

Keates, S. G. 2004. Notes on the Palaeolithic finds from the Walanae valley, southwest Sulawesi, in the context of the Late Pleistocene of island Southeast Asia. In S. G. Keates and J. M. Pasveer (eds), *Quaternary research in Indonesia*. Modern Quaternary Research in Southeast Asia 18, 95–109. London: Taylor & Francis.

Krigbaum, J. and Manser, J. 2005. The West Mouth burial series from Niah cave: past and present. In Zuraina Majid (ed.), *The Perak Man and other prehistoric human skeletons from Malaysia*, 175–206. Penang: Centre for Archaeological Research Malaysia.

Lewis, H., Paz, V., Lara, M., Barton, H., Piper, P., Ochoa, J., Vitales, T., Carlos, A. J., Higham, T., Neri, L., Hernandez, V., Stevenson, J., Robles, E. C., Ragrario, A., Padillo, R., Solheim II, W., and Ronquillo, W. 2008. Terminal Pleistocene to mid-Holocene occupation and an early cremation at Ille Cave, Palawan, Philippines. *Antiquity* 82, 318–35.

Mahareni, E. 2002. Late Pleistocene vertebrates in Gunung Sewu. In T. Simanjuntak (ed.), *Gunung Sewu in prehistoric times*, 133–47. Yogyakarta: Gadjah Mada University.

Mahirta. 2003. Human occupation on Roti and Sawu Islands, Nusa Tenggara Timur. PhD thesis. Department of Archaeology and Anthropology, Australian National University.

Marwick, B. 2007. Approaches to stone artefact archaeology in Thailand: an historical review. *Silpakorn University International Journal* 7, 49–88.

Marwick, B. 2008a. Stone artefacts and recent research in the archaeology of mainland Southeast Asian hunter-gatherers. *Before Farming* 2008/4, http://www.waspress.co.uk/journals/beforefarming/journal_20084/abstracts/index.php.

Marwick, B. 2008b. Stone artefacts and human ecology at two rockshelters in northwest Thailand. PhD thesis. Australian National University.

Marwick, B. 2008c. Beyond typologies: the reduction thesis and its implications for lithic assemblages in Southeast Asia. *Bulletin of the Indo-Pacific Prehistory Association* 28, 108–16.

Mijares, A. S. B. 2008. The Late Pleistocene to early Holocene foragers of northern Luzon. *Bulletin of the Indo-Pacific Prehistory Association* 28, 99–107.

Mijares, A. S., Détroit, F., Piper, P., Grün, R., Bellwood, P., Aubert, M., Champion, G., Cuevas, N., De Leon, A., and Dizon, E. 2010. New evidence for a 67,000-year-old human presence at Callao cave, Luzon, Philippines. *Journal of Human Evolution* 59, 123–32.

Mokhtar, S. 2006. Bukit Bunuh, Lenggong, Malaysia: new evidence of Late Pleistocene culture in Malaysia and Southeast Asia. In E. A. Bacus, I. C. Glover, and V. Pigott (eds), *Uncovering Southeast Asia's past*, 60–4. Singapore: National University of Singapore Press.

Morwood, M. J., Brown, P., Jatmiko Sutikna, T., Saptomo, E. W., Westaway, K. E., Due, R. A., Roberts, R. G., Maeda, T., Wasisto, S., and Djubiantono, T. 2005. Further evidence for small-bodied hominins from the late Pleistocene of Flores, Indonesia. *Nature* 437, 1012–17.

Morwood, M. J., Sutikna, T., Saptomo, E. W., Westaway, K. E., Jatmiko, Awe Due, R., Moore, M. W., Yuniawati, D. Y., Hadi, P., Zhao, J.-X., Turney, C. S. M., Fifield, K., Allen, H., and Soejono, R. P. 2008. Climate, people and faunal succession on Java, Indonesia: evidence from Song Gupuh. *Journal of Archaeological Science* 35, 1776–89.

Mudar, K. and Anderson, D. 2007. New evidence for Southeast Asian Pleistocene foraging economies: faunal remains from the early levels of Lang Rongrien rockshelter, Krabi, Thailand. *Asian Perspectives* 46, 298–335.

Nguyen K. S., Pham Minh Huyen, and Tong Trung Tin. 2004. Northern Vietnam from the Neolithic to the Han period. In I. Glover and P. Bellwood (eds), *Southeast Asia: from prehistory to history*, 177–208. London: Routledge.

Nguyen, V. 2008. Hoabinhian macrobotanical remains from archaeological sites in Vietnam: indicators of climate changes from the Late Pleistocene to early Holocene. *Bulletin of the Indo-Pacific Prehistory Association* 28, 80–3.

Nguyen, V. V. 1989. *Die Radiocarbon-Chronologie für die Ur- und Fruhgeschichte in Nord Vietnam*. DPhil thesis. Berlin: Akademie der Wissenschaften.

O'Connor, S. 2003. Report of nine new painted rock art sites in East Timor in the context of the western Pacific region. *Asian Perspectives* 42, 96–128.

O'Connor, S. 2007. New evidence from East Timor contributes to our understanding of earliest modern human colonization east of the Sunda Shelf. *Antiquity* 81, 523–35.

O'Connor, S. 2010. Continuity in shell artefact production in Holocene East Timor. In B. Bellina-Pryce, L. Bacus, O. Pryce, and J. Wisseman Christie (eds), *50 years of prehistoric and historical archaeology in continental and insular Southeast Asia: essays in honour of Ian Glover*, 218–33. Bangkok: Rivers Books.

O'Connor, S. and Aplin, K. 2007. A matter of balance: an overview of Pleistocene occupation history and the impact of the Last Glacial phase in East Timor and the Aru Islands, eastern Indonesia. *Archaeology in Oceania* 42, 82–90.

O'Connor, S., Aplin, K., St. Pierre, E., and Feng, X. 2010a. Faces of the ancestors revealed: discovery and dating of Pleistocene-aged petroglyphs in Lene Hara cave, East Timor. *Antiquity* 84, 649–65.

O'Connor, S., Barham, A., Spriggs, M., Veth, P., Aplin, K., and St. Pierre, E. 2010b. Cave archaeology and sampling issues in the tropics: a case study from Lene Hara cave, a 42,000 year old occupation site in East Timor, island Southeast Asia. *Australian Archaeology* 71, 29–40.

O'Connor, S., Ono, R., and Clarkson, C. 2011. Pelagic fishing at 42,000 BP and the maritime skills of modern humans. *Science* 334, 1117–21.

O'Connor, S., Spriggs, M., and Veth, P. 2002. Excavation at Lene Hara cave establishes occupation in East Timor at least 30,000–35,000 years ago. *Antiquity* 76, 45–50.

O'Connor, S. and Veth, P. 2005. Early Holocene shell fish hooks from Lene Hara cave, East Timor establish complex fishing technology was in use in island Southeast Asia five thousand years before Austronesian settlement. *Antiquity* 79, 249–56.

Oppenheimer, S. 2003. *Out of Eden: the peopling of the world*. London: Constable and Robinson.

Patole-Edoumba, E. 2009. A typo-technological definition of Tabonian industries. *Bulletin of the Indo-Pacific Prehistory Association* 29, 21–5.

Paz, V. 2005. Rock shelters, caves, and archaeobotony in Island Southeast Asia. In G. Barker and D. Gilbertson (eds), *The human use of caves in peninsular and island Southeast Asia*. Special issue, *Asian Perspectives* 44, 107–18.

Piper, P. J. and Mijares, A. S. B. 2008. *A preliminary report on a Late Pleistocene animal bone assemblage from Callao Cave, Peñablanca, Northern Luzon, Philippines*. Manila: Archaeological Studies Programme, University of the Philippines and the Archaeological Museum of the Philippines.

Piper, P. J., Ochoa, J., Lewis, H., Paz, V., and Ronquillo, W. P. 2008. The first evidence for the past presence of the tiger *Panthera tigris* (L.) on the island of Palawan, Philippines: extinction of an island population. *Palaeogeography, Palaeoclimatology, Palaeoecology* 264, 123–7.

Plagnes, V., Causse, C., Fontugnew, M., Valladas, H., Chazine, J.-M., and Fage, L.-H. 2003. Cross dating (Th/U-14C) of calcite covering prehistoric paintings in Borneo. *Quaternary Research* 60, 172–9.

Pookajorn, S. 1996. Human activities and environmental changes during the Late Pleistocene to middle Holocene in southern Thailand and Southeast Asia. In L. G. Straus, B. V. Eriksen, J. M. Erlandson, and D. R. Yesner (eds), *Humans at the end of the Ice Age: the archaeology of the Pleistocene-Holocene transition*, 201–13. New York: Plenum Press.

Rabett, R. J. 2005. The early exploitation of Southeast Asian mangroves: bone technology from caves and open sites. *Asian Perspectives* 44, 154–79.

Rabett, R., Barker, G., Hunt, C. O., Naruse, T., Piper, P., Raddatz, E., Reynolds, T., Nguyen Van Son, Stimpson, C., Szabó, K., Nguyen Cao Tan, and Wilson, J. 2009. The Tràng An project: late-to-post-Pleistocene settlement of the lower Song Hong valley, North Vietnam. *Journal of the Royal Asiatic Society* 19, 83–109.

Roberts, G. R., Morwood, M. J., and Westaway, K. E. 2005. Illuminating Southeast Asian prehistory: new archaeological and paleoanthropological frontiers for luminescence dating. *Asian Perspectives* 44, 293–319.

Sémah, F., Sémah, A.-M., and Simanjuntak, T. 2003. More than a million years of human occupation in insular Southeast Asia. In J. Mercader (ed.), *Under the canopy: the archaeology of tropical rain forests*, 162–90. New Brunswick: Rutgers University Press.

Simanjuntak, T. 2004. New insight on the prehistoric chronology of Gunung Sewu, Java, Indonesia. In S. G. Keates and J. M. Pasveer (eds), *Quaternary research in Indonesia*. Modern Quaternary Research in Southeast Asia 18, 9–30. London: Taylor & Francis.

Simons, A. and Bulbeck, D. 2004. Late Quaternary faunal successions in South Sulawesi, Indonesia. In S. G. Keates and J. M. Pasveer (eds), *Quaternary research in Indonesia*. Modern Quaternary Research in Southeast Asia, 18 167–89. London: Taylor & Francis.

Soares, P., Ermini, L., Thomson, N., Mormina, M., Rito, T., Röhl, A., Salas, A., Oppenheimer, S., Macaulay, V., and Richards, M. B. 2009. Correcting for purifying selection: an improved human mitochondrial molecular clock. *American Journal of Human Genetics* 84, 1–20.

Soares, P., Trejaut, J. A., Loo, J.-H., Hill, C., Mormina, M., Lee, C.-L., Chen, Y.-M., Hudjashov, G., Forster, P., Macaulay, V., Bulbeck, D., Oppenheimer, S., Li, M., and Richards, M. B. 2008. Climate change and post-glacial human dispersals in Southeast Asia. *Molecular Biology and Evolution* 25, 1209–18.

Soegondho, S. 2006. Prehistoric research in the northern part of Sulawesi with special reference to Liang Sarru. In T. Simanjuntak, M. Hisyam, B. Prasetyo, and Titi Surti Nastiti (eds),

Archaeology: Indonesian perspective—R.P. Soejono's Festschrift, 232–46. Jakarta: International Institute of Sciences.

Sumantri, I. 1996. Pola Pemukiman Gua-Gua Prasejarah di Biraeng Pangkep, Sulawesi Selatan. Unpublished Sarjana thesis. Jakarta: University of Indonesia, Department of Archaeology.

Tanudirjo, D. 2001. Islands in between: prehistory of the northeastern Indonesian archipelago. PhD thesis. Australian National University.

Thiel, B. 1990. Excavations at Musang cave, northeast Luzon, Philippines. *Asian Perspectives* 28, 61–81.

Tong, T. T. 2007. Twentieth-century achievements in the archaeology of Vietnam. *Vietnam Archaeology* 2, 5–21.

Van Tan, H. 1997. The Hoabinhian and before. *Bulletin of the Indo-Pacific Prehistory Association* 16, 35–41.

Wattanapituksakul, S. 2006. Late Pleistocene mammal teeth from Tham Lod rockshelter, Amphoe Pang Mapha, Changwat Mae Hong Son. MA thesis. Department of Geology. Bangkok, Chulalongkorn University.

Yen, D. E. 1995. The development of Sahul agriculture with Australia as bystander. *Antiquity* 69, 831–47.

Yi, S., Lee, J.-J., Kim, S., Yoo, Y., and Kim, D. 2008. New data on the Hoabinhian: investigations at Hang Cho cave, northern Vietnam. *Bulletin of the Indo-Pacific Prehistory Association* 28, 73–9.

Zuraina, M. 1982. The West Mouth, Niah, in the prehistory of Southeast Asia. *Sarawak Museum Journal* 31 Special Issue 2, 1–200.

Zuraina, M. 1998. Radiocarbon dates and culture sequence in the Lenggong Valley and beyond. *Malaysia Museums Journal* 34, 241–9.

Zuraina, M., Ang Bee Huat, and Ignatius, J. 1998a. Late Pleistocene-Holocene sites in Pahang: excavations of Gua Sagu and Gua Tenggek. *Malaysia Museums Journal* 34, 65–115.

Zuraina, M., Ignatius, J., Tjia, H. D., and Koon, P. 1998b. Some interesting late Pleistocene–early Holocene finds from excavations in Balambangan Island, Sabah, Malaysia. *Sabah Society Journal* 15, 29–40.

CHAPTER 16

HUNTER-GATHERERS IN AUSTRALIA

Deep Histories of Continuity and Change

IAIN DAVIDSON

The first people came to Australia and its adjacent islands some time before 45,000 years ago as a result of several voyages from island to island across the sea, at a time when Australia and the island of New Guinea were joined on a single large continent that has come to be called Sahul. This continent stretched from tropical New Guinea in the north to cool Tasmania below latitude 40°S. Changes in temperature and sea level that were experienced during the time of people on this continent were as great as any experienced by modern humans, yet the first people moved quickly into all environments of the region and diversified there.

The theme of the chapter is that the archaeological evidence should be interpreted in terms of the way in which that diversity was created. Discussion of evidence derived from ethnographic accounts of present day or recent people is necessary to show the extent of diversity and to show what was the end point of the process of emergence of variation. In addition, because there were no major breaks in the archaeological sequence as there were elsewhere in the world, it is not meaningful to make distinctions such as are made elsewhere in the world between Palaeolithic and other archaeology, and the chapter refers to the whole period of human presence in Sahul before Europeans arrived.

Australia and its adjacent islands were first colonized by relatively small numbers of people in watercraft. They presumably spoke one, or at most a few, languages and there was little variation at the time of their arrival. At the time Europeans arrived to describe (and disrupt) their descendants, there were more than 1,350 languages in the region and much variation in social and material culture. The central issue is how that diversity emerged from those small beginnings. Remarkably, agriculture emerged in New Guinea at a time when it was still joined to the rest of Sahul, but neither the ideas nor the species ever spread to Australia. So the task of understanding the generation of diversity in Australia and its adjacent islands includes understanding how the hunter-gatherers of Australia became resilient to the opportunities that may have been presented by contact with agriculturalists. The story is one of adaptation first to the variety of environments that the first colonists found on arrival, then to changing environmental conditions, and at the same time to the social and cultural differences that emerged among the diversifying peoples of the region.

All of the people who have lived in Australia and New Guinea have been fully modern in their anatomy (Brown 1997). According to skeletal evidence, modern humans emerged in Africa perhaps 200,000 years ago (McDougall et al. 2005; White et al. 2003). Genetic evidence converges on similar dates (Atkinson et al. 2009) but also suggests that the major expansion of modern humans out of Africa occurred 50,000–70,000 years ago (Atkinson et al. 2008). People reached Australia some time before 45,000 years ago (O'Connell and Allen 2004; 2007).

The earliest evidence for modern human skeletal form outside Africa dates to around 100,000 years ago and was found only 300 km into south-west Asia at the sites of Qafzeh and Skhul (Vandermeersch 1981). These modern people were accompanied by Mousterian stone industries more commonly associated with Neanderthals (Hovers 2009) as well as by ochre, beads, and other objects usually associated only with modern human behaviour (Bar-Yosef Mayer et al. 2009; Hovers et al. 2003; Vandermeersch 1966). The evidence from other sites in the region (e.g. Kebara: Bar-Yosef and Vandermeersch 1991; Bar Yosef et al. 1996) seems to suggest that people with modern skeletal form did not continue to live in the region, but reappeared there after 45,000 years ago as part of the emergence of modern humans from Africa indicated by the genetics.

A recent study suggests that the early Australian skeletal evidence can be related most closely to the early modern humans from South-West Asia (Schillaci 2008), showing the need for more research in South and South-East Asia in the inland as well as the coastal routes between South-West Asia and Australia. It also raises unanswered questions about the implications of the longer time frame that results from recognizing the Skhul/Qafzeh people as ancestral to modern human populations elsewhere. For example, the fact that stone industries normally associated with Neanderthals may be accompanied by materials normally associated only with modern humans means that the appearance of modern humans in many regions may not be identifiable from the stone industries alone—modern humans may have been associated with Mousterian stone industries. Nevertheless, the key issues for the arrival of people in Australia relate to the environmental conditions from just prior to 45,000 years ago.

THE ENVIRONMENTAL CONDITIONS OF THE LAST 45,000 YEARS

The general pattern of climate change has been well studied for northern and southern hemispheres through the analysis of the chemical composition of the ice preserved in Greenland and Antarctica, respectively, particularly the oxygen isotopes (Bender et al. 1994). The general pattern is shown in Figure 16.1 drawn using the online data from the Vostok core in Antarctica (Petit et al. 1999), and indicating the marine oxygen isotope stages (OIS) as names for major climatic fluctuations. These OIS stages will form the fundamental chronological framework for this chapter (Table 16.1). One of the main impacts of these climatic changes was a series of changes in sea level, which, with local variations, was generally more than 70 m lower than present levels for all of the period between 75,000 and 15,000 years ago (OIS 4–2) (Cutler et al. 2003).

The lowered sea levels of OIS 4–2 not only created the continents of Sunda and Sahul, but within Sahul the dominant feature for the first colonists was the Arafura Plain (see Figure

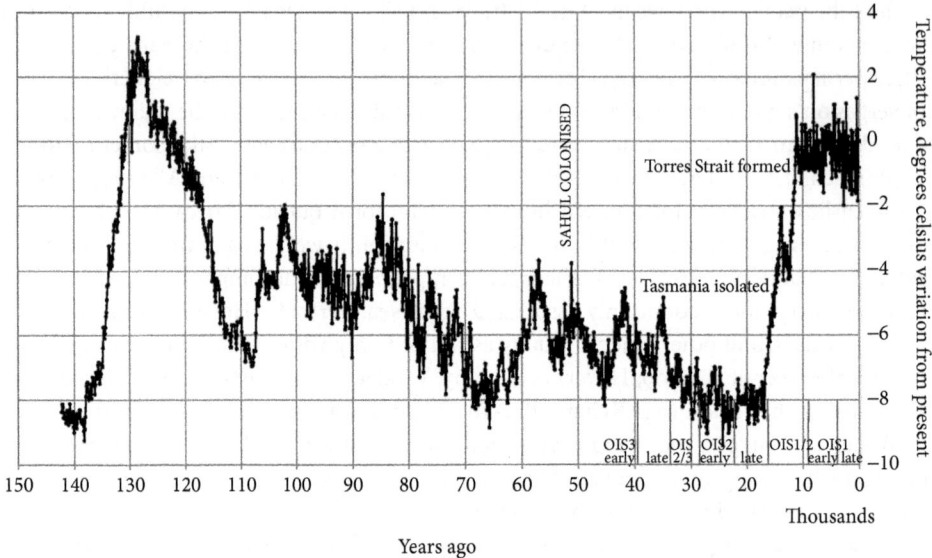

FIGURE 16.1 Temperature differences from modern over the last 140 thousand years. The small numbers at the bottom of the graph are the numbered oxygen isotope stages.

Table 16.1 Subdivisions of marine oxygen isotope stages used in this chapter with dates. (See caption to Figure 16.4 for derivation.)

OIS stage name used here	Start date (thousand years ago)	End date (thousand years ago)
OIS 1 late	5.1	0
OIS 1 early	10.8	5.1
OIS 1/2	17.85	10.8
OIS 2 late	23.35	17.85
OIS 2 early	29.45	23.35
OIS 2/3	34.8	29.45
OIS 3 late	40.5	34.8
OIS 3 early		40.5

16.2 for geographic features of Sahul) connecting northern Australia with New Guinea (Chivas et al. 2001). This plain was dominated by Lake Carpentaria, 500 km long, 250 km wide and 15 m deep (Jones and Torgersen 1988), which had substantial periods of freshwater particularly from 17,500 to 14,000 years ago (Reeves et al. 2007). Likewise Tasmania was joined to the mainland by a Bassian Plain with a rather smaller Lake Bass. People crossed the Bassian Plain almost as soon as it opened up (Lambeck and Chappell 2001). Tasmania remained joined to the mainland until about 14,000 years ago but, in the north, it was not until after 9,000 years ago that sea level rose sufficiently to form Torres Strait and separate

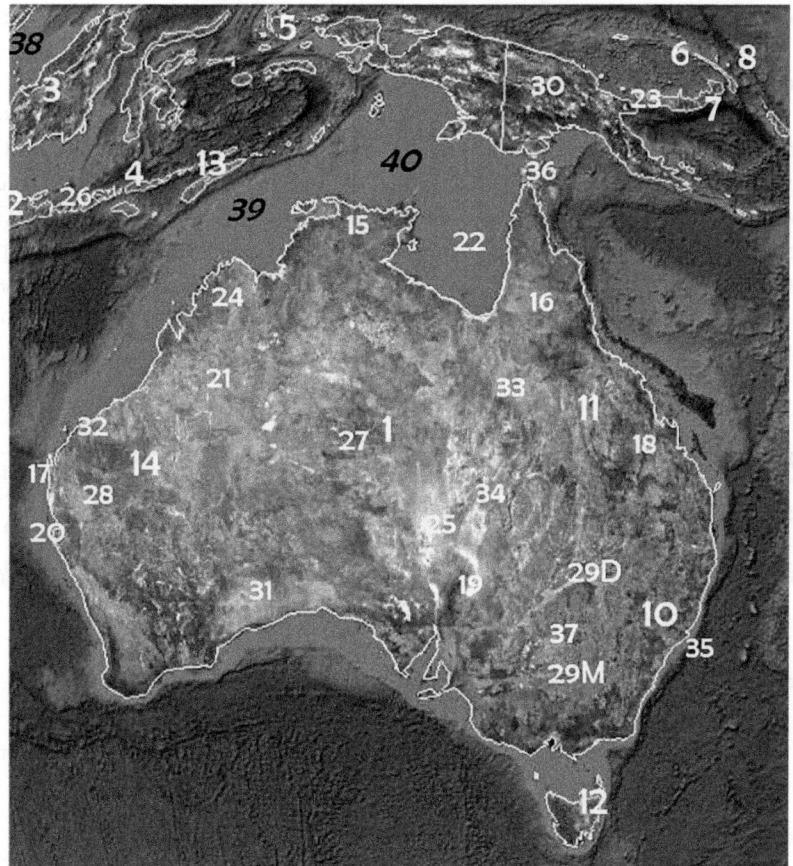

FIGURE 16.2 Geographic features of the Australian region referred to in the chapter. Major geographic locations (large white numbers): 1. Australia; 2. Bali; 3. Borneo; 4. Flores; 5. Gebe; 6. Island Melanesia; 7. New Britain; 8. New Guinea; 9. New Ireland; 10. New South Wales; 11. Queensland; 12. Tasmania; 13. Timor; 14. Western Australia. Lesser geographic locations (small white numbers): 15. Arnhem Land; 16. Cape York Peninsula; 17. Carnarvon; 18. Central Queensland Highlands; 19. Flinders Lofty Block; 20. Geraldton; 21. Great Sandy Desert; 22. Gulf of Carpentaria; 23. Huon Peninsula; 24. Kimberley; 25. Lake Eyre; 26. Lesser Sundas; 27. McDonnell Ranges; 28. Murchison; 29. Murray Darling basin (29M River Murray, 29D River Darling); 30. New Guinea Highlands; 31. Nullarbor Plain; 32. Pilbara; 33. Selwyn Ranges; 34. Simpson-Strezlecki; 35. Sydney; 36. Torres Strait; 37. Willandra Lakes. Geographic names for Pleistocene entities (large black italics): 38. Arafura Plain; 39. Sahul; 40. Sunda.

Australia from New Guinea (Yokoyama et al. 2001). The conditions that applied when Sahul was first colonized had applied many times in the past since the arrival of *Homo erectus* in Sunda, without any indication of colonization, suggesting that the stimulus for colonization was not environmental, but more probably behavioural.

In addition there were changes in temperature, precipitation, and atmospheric circulation (Turney et al. 2006; Williams et al. 2009), and in vegetation (Hope et al. 2004). It seems likely that the Arafura Plain supported savannah grassland, a preferred habitat for the colonizing humans who could follow it through Sunda to Sahul (Bird et al. 2005; Hope et al. 2004) and could have had relatively easy passage as far as western New South Wales (NSW) (Figure 16.3). To the south was steppic vegetation as far as Tasmania which, like the east coast of Australia, also had reduced areas of cool temperate rainforests. During the Last Glacial Maximum (OIS 2), there were small glaciated areas in Tasmania and the Snowy Mountains (Barrows et al. 2002) and expansions of those that are still extant in the New Guinea Highlands (Allison and Peterson 1989). The cool temperatures of OIS 3–2 were accompanied by expansion of the arid zone through reduction of precipitation, but in some situations, such as Lake Mungo and other now-dry lakes of the Murray Darling region, reduced evaporation

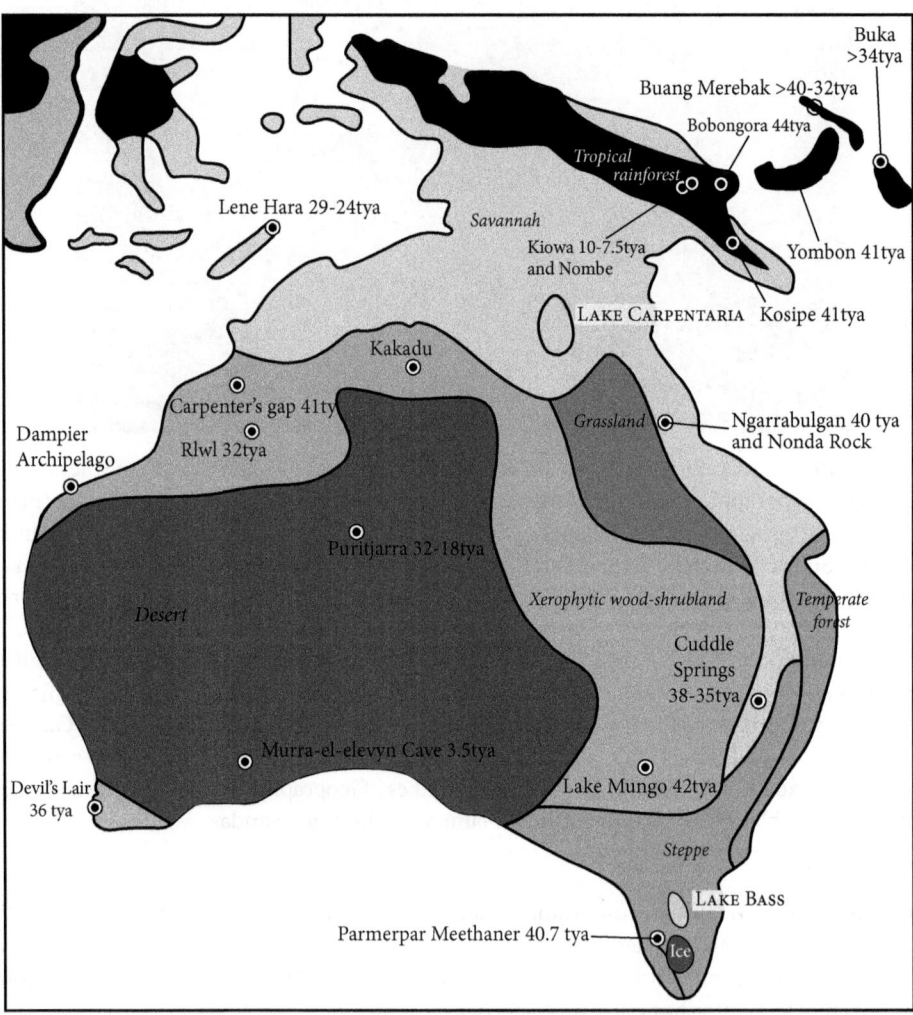

FIGURE 16.3 Distribution of vegetation zones at OIS 2 from Hope et al. (2004). Also shown are sites and dates mentioned in the text.

and the particularities of hydrological conditions meant that the lakes were often full (e.g. Bowler 1998).

There was an early view that the evidence from Lake Mungo could be interpreted to suggest that 'the distinctive Australian economy was already in train and that the major adaptations to the continent had been made' by 30,000 years ago (Jones 1975). This might imply great continuity, except that in a consistently changing environment the implied versatility of this behaviour was much more complex than was envisaged at the time (Davidson 1999b). In many parts of Australia there is abundant evidence not only for substantial environmental change in response to climate change, but also of landscape changes that are not necessarily driven by patterns of past climate variation (e.g. Butzer and Helgren 2005; Pickup 1991). Rather, environments changed in response to the interaction of extreme weather events on one hand, and, on the other, Aboriginal land use and burning.

At the intermediate scale, there has also been a pattern of climate change and corresponding environmental change due to variations in frequency of 2–8-year El Niño-Southern Oscillation (ENSO) events on a millennial time-scale throughout the Holocene (Moy et al. 2002) and possibly longer. Despite the appearance of periodicity and without the extensive documentation of modern climatology, the dominant effect for humans living on the land was one of unpredictability. Sedimentary sequences in central Australia provide evidence of 'superflood' events such as those at 520, 680, and 790 calibrated radiocarbon years ago (Pickup 1991). The 680-year-old event coincided with stream channels in one part of the region that were 3–6 km wide. It is difficult to understand how people could have coped with events of such severity and such unpredictability, both in terms of the direct effects when shelter was minimal, and of the impact of such events on resource availability. It seems likely that it was such extreme, unpredictable events that were responsible for local extinctions rather than longer-term variations in climate and environment (Davidson 1990). There is some evidence that extreme environmental events led, in some situations, to long periods of abandonment of regions (e.g. Allen et al. 2008). Under this model we might expect that there was more risk for people as the climate changed relatively rapidly during the transitions OIS3/2 and OIS2/1 or similar high-gradient episodes.

Variation at Contact

Genetic Evidence

Recent mtDNA studies suggest that several genetic lineages emerged in Africa after 150,000 years ago and the geneticists have named these L1, L2, and L3 (Chen et al. 1995; Watson et al. 1997). Members of the L2 and L3 genetic lineages appear to have been involved in successful migration out of Africa between 85,000 and 55,000 years ago (Forster and Matsumura 2005; Macaulay et al. 2005; Oppenheimer 2004). Oppenheimer (2004) argued that the first colonists out of Africa crossed the narrow strait between Ethiopia and Yemen, the Bab-el-Mandeb, and followed the coast rapidly (Macaulay et al. 2005) to Australia, but there is currently a poverty of evidence for that argument from archaeology, although recent evidence from Arabia demonstrates that there is more to be found

(Armitage et al. 2011). The small amount of evidence of modern people who made their way to Australia can be traced (Balme et al. 2009) from the Bab-el-Mandeb to the eastern shores of Sunda, the continent that formed at low sea level from the islands of South-East Asia. It is premature to assess the significance of the finding that modern New Guineans shared some of their genes with Neanderthals just as modern people did elsewhere (Green et al. 2010), and still more uncertain what should be made of the fact that they shared some genes with the finger bone from Denisova in Siberia (Reich et al. 2010; see also Davidson 2013).

Mitochondrial and Y chromosome DNA studies of Andamanese imply separation dates of ~65,000 years ago (Thangaraj et al. 2005) and mitochondrial DNA studies suggest dates ~60,000 years ago for Malaysian Orang Asli (Macaulay et al. 2005). All of these populations are from regions affected by the eruption of Mt Toba, in Sumatra 74,000 years ago (Ambrose 2003), and coalescence dates are after that proposed 'bottleneck' event.

Studies of mtDNA suggest that movement into island Melanesia was delayed by up to 10,000 years after the first occupation of New Guinea with evidence that the colonists north and east of New Guinea were always separate from the colonists of southern Sahul (Friedlaender et al. 2005). Further, the haplotypes found in northern island Melanesia may be representative of the earliest haplotypes in the Sahul region (Merriwether et al. 2005). We cannot tell whether the implied split between northern and southern populations of Sahul occurred before or after landfall. Separate studies of mtDNA (van Holst Pellekaan et al. 2006) and of mtDNA and Y chromosome (Hudjashov et al. 2007) show consistently that variations within the region of Sahul have deep roots going back to the first colonization of the continent at 40,000–50,000 years ago. Taken together this evidence allows the possibility of separate colonizations to the north and south of Sahul, a possibility explored by van Holst Pellekaan (van Holst Pellekaan 2013).

Languages at Contact

When the first Europeans arrived to settle Australia in 1788, they brought with them the Guugu-Yimidhirr vocabulary collected by Cook in north Queensland 18 years before and 2,000 km to the north. They found that it did not help them communicate with people of the Sydney region who spoke the Iyora variant of the Daruk language (Attenbrow 2003, 30–6; Wilkins and Nash 2008). A subsequent expedition set off inland, with Iyora guides, to reach the Hawkesbury River near modern Windsor, a distance that is a daily commute for some people today. The Iyora people were able to speak with the inland Darkinyung people that they encountered, but they recognized that the language was different (Wilkins and Nash 2008). It subsequently emerged that there were over 250 languages in Australia and another 1,100 in New Guinea.

The Pama-Nyungan (PN) languages of Australia (Blake 1988; Evans 1988) occupied about 80 per cent of the country and the remainder, the non-PN languages, were in the ecologically rich north and north-west of the continent (Evans 2005). There is much argument about how this came about. There are two principal views (Bowern 2010): the consensus view is that PN expanded late in Australian prehistory (in the middle of OIS 1), probably from its area of current greatest diversity in the south-west of the Gulf of Carpentaria; and the other view is that PN languages represent the residual of the earliest languages of the continent (e.g. Dixon 1997). The second view seems unlikely to be sustained because it would require that Australian languages could not be analysed historically in the way other languages can, when other ways of viewing the evidence suggest they can (Evans 2005; see also McConvell and Bowern 2011.. A third view (Clendon 2006), also without much support from linguists (see comments published with Clendon's paper), is a variant of the second, but sees an expansion into the arid zone from south-east Australia after the end of OIS 2. Studies of the words for social (McConvell 1996), botanical (Nash 1997), and technological (Evans and Jones 1997; McConvell and Smith 2003) features, as well as a broader set of cognates (O'Grady and Fitzgerald 1997) have shown that many aspects of the patterning of behaviour across Australia can be reconstructed from the comparative analysis of these PN languages. Several analyses attempt to link PN expansion to elements of the archaeology, mostly the apparent changes of the last 5,000 years (Evans and McConvell 1998), though these changes are less coherent than they once seemed (Davidson 2000; Hiscock 2008). Clendon (2006) makes the important point that the history of physical connection between northern Australia and southern New Guinea means that it should be possible to find cultural connections that derive from a shared history on land that is now beneath the sea, but the current attempts from linguistics do not seem to have been successful (Bowern 2006; Evans 2006). Languages of the islands of East Torres Strait are Papuan, while those of West Torres Strait are Pama-Nyungan (Hunter et al. 2011).

The dynamic nature of the linguistics of any particular region within Australia is revealed by the numerous examples where place names include words that do not belong in the language currently spoken in that region (e.g. Baker 2002; Sutton 2002). The curiosity of such anomalies is that they cannot simply represent abandonment of regions by speakers of earlier languages, since the names can only be carried on by speakers who know the names of the places. Considerable complexity is implied about the impact of population movements on language distributions.

The languages of New Guinea are much more complex with at least 20 major language groupings that often appear unrelated to each other. One group, the more than 400 Trans New Guinea (TNG) languages, can probably be traced back more than 10,000 years to the Pleistocene (Pawley 2005) and may be associated with the emergence of agriculture in the Highlands (Pawley 2007). The more recent Austronesian languages (Pawley and Ross 1993) resulted from migration of people from the north bringing with them pottery, pigs, chickens, and possibly dogs, as well as other cultural features visible and invisible in the archaeological record (Shennan and Collard 2005; Spriggs 2007). In addition there are several languages that belong to neither group, some of which may also have more ancient roots (M. Ross 2005).

Recent multivariate analysis of structural features of the languages of Sahul and adjacent islands promises to open up new areas of understanding of regional histories (Reesink et al. 2009). This analysis seems to confirm the separation between PN and non-PN languages within Australia, and to show links between languages of west New Guinea and those of eastern Indonesia. There is a clear separation between the older languages of New Guinea and those of Australia on the one hand and those associated with the arrival of the Austronesians about 3,500 years ago on the other (Gray et al. 2009). There are some Austronesian influences among the languages of Torres Strait (David et al. 2004) but when these reach into areas of mainland Australia they seem to be borrowings within the last few centuries from the Macassans (Walker and Zorc 1981). Whatever the contacts between Austronesians and Australians, the Australian hunter-gatherers do not seem to have been overwhelmed by the advantages that we may think the agriculturalists had to offer.

Material Culture

In addition to the abundant evidence from the time of contact for the diversity of languages in Sahul, there is also documentation, albeit less complete, of variation in many other social and material ways. For Australia alone, these include spear throwers (atlatls in some parts of the world, *woomera* in some parts of Australia) (Davidson 1930), netting and basketry (Davidson 1933), spears (Davidson 1934), watercraft (Davidson 1935), boomerangs (Davidson 1936a; McAdam 2001), rock art (Davidson 1936b), other features of decorative art (Davidson 1937), footwear (Davidson 1947), and practices in the disposal of the dead (Davidson 1948), as well as body decoration (Brady 2005; Gorman 2008), and beads and pendants (McAdam 2008). For a summary see Satterthwaite and Arthur (2005). In each of these cases, there were variations across the continent that can be considered as stylistic and hence, at one level, symbolic. Comparisons with and within New Guinea would simply emphasize this point. It is one of the functions of the analysis of the long history of people on Sahul to show how such diversity could have emerged from presumably less-variable origins.

Ritual and Social Organization

Despite the record by non-indigenous people of some commonalities across Australia in the importance of kinship, the importance of ancestors, use of totems, and the role of gender in production and distribution of food, there were also variations in the social organization across the continent. These can be seen particularly, but not only, in the details of kin classification and its role in structuring marriage rules, degrees of polygyny, ideological relations with land and nature, and the symbolic sources of power (e.g. Keen 2004). In addition, there were variations in rituals associated with initiation (e.g. genital modification such as circumcision and subincision, Tindale 1974) which seem to have been changing in their spatial distributions at the time of European disruption. It is inescapable that these variations were structured symbolically.

The symbolic and spiritual life of different Aboriginal groups was dominated in most cases by the belief system that came to be known as 'the Dreaming.' This was probably not such a unitary phenomenon across Australia because 'subtle (and probably important) variations occurred in different regions' (Stanner 1979 (1962), 115) among those beliefs (see also Wolfe 1991). Detailed accounts of the material consequences of the ritual, mythology, and ancestral connections between places are surprisingly scarce, but there are some accounts that credibly link these with rock engravings in north-west Western Australia (e.g. Palmer 1977). One argument suggested that the forms of images, and associated symbolism and beliefs, can be traced back to the Pleistocene (Taçon et al. 1996), but the argument is flawed (Davidson 1999a). A more comprehensive assessment suggests that it may not be possible to trace the ritual system back more than two millennia (David 2002), though ritual itself is certainly older, and, particularly in the region where the Dreaming was first defined by non-Aboriginal scholars, used many of the same images as those rituals later associated with it (Ross and Davidson 2006). What seems most likely then is that the uncertainty of the timing of the emergence of such beliefs derives in part from the nature of the belief system itself. This posits that the facts of the Dreaming are not created when something is added to the system, but that previously existing unknown truths are successively revealed (e.g. Tonkinson 1974, 84–6). In northern Australia there is some evidence that population changes in response to environmental change led to new inhabitants of the region producing mythological accounts, probably as recently as 600 years ago, of the material remains (mounds) of earlier shellfish exploitation (Hiscock and Faulkner 2006). These were not unchanging people in an unchanging environment, but people who maintained a belief that they were unchanging whatever their environment.

The relationships between art and the beliefs are complex and cannot be understood simply from rock (and other) art images (or sites) themselves, even when talking to people embedded in the belief system (Merlan 1989; Morphy 1991). A consequence of this is that, even in a situation where people can talk about the various meanings of non-iconic signs (Munn 1973), the system can adapt to new meanings as appropriate. It is impossible to infer the original meanings or associated beliefs from images that were made long before the memory embedded in oral histories. In many respects, this is the key to continuity and change among Australian hunter-gatherers—the system is structured to appear unchanging so that changes can be easily incorporated. It is, therefore, the archaeological record that records change most faithfully, but, as with the Dreaming, it is not a constant. It can only acquire relevance to Aboriginal people whose past it represents through successive revelation (see a similar argument in Davidson 2010a).

INITIAL COLONIZATION

Where and When

Pope and Terrell (2008) estimated that the rate of colonization by modern humans leaving Africa was in the order of 1 km per year for the Asia Pacific region, more than twice the rate estimated for the colonization of Europe by modern humans (Mellars 2006) despite the fact that part of that process involved moving into new habitats far more unfamiliar than those encountered in passing from Africa to Asia to Europe. At that rate it would have taken only four to five thousand years to get to Tasmania after first landfall on Sahul.

With the Americas, Australia was one of the last two great continental landmasses colonized by humans (see comparison in Davidson 2013). The presence of people on Sahul is reliably dated to more than 45,000 years ago, before the Last Glacial Maximum (OIS 2) (O'Connell and Allen 2004; Summerhayes et al. 2010), but people did not reach the Americas until after OIS 2, perhaps 15,000 years ago (Goebel et al. 2008). Biological anthropology shows patterns of variation in both the skeletal evidence from the past (Brown 1997) and among recent populations (Birdsell 1967), though the interpretation of this evidence has been controversial (Lindsell 2001).

The first colonists came from outside, from Sunda, and there is increasing archaeological and environmental evidence from that landmass and the islands in the seas that separated it from Sahul. To the north, modern humans reached the north coast of Borneo by 45,000 years ago (Higham et al. 2009), with a variety of behaviours that enabled them to thrive on the edge of the tropical rainforests (Barker et al. 2007). By 32,000 years ago their behaviours included collecting large shells from the sub-tidal zone and making tools from them (Szabo et al. 2007).

To the south, the recently discovered *Homo floresiensis*, a species distantly related to humans, survived, on present dating, on Flores long after the dates for colonization of Australia (Morwood et al. 2004). It is possible that these Indonesian islands, the Lesser Sundas, were only colonized by modern humans coming later from the east (Balme et al. 2009). In support of this argument, genetic studies in Bali show a very weak signal of pre-agricultural populations (Karafet et al. 2005) that had coalescence ages of 8,200 years ago or 12,700 years ago, more likely involving colonization from further east in Indonesia or from Melanesia. This evidence is consistent with the view that modern humans colonized the Lesser Sundas from what is now Australia or Melanesia (Davidson 2007b).

Repeated sea crossings were necessary for people to get to Sahul (Birdsell 1977; Irwin 1992), and then to reach New Britain, New Ireland, and Buka off the north-east of the continent (Allen and Gosden 1991), consistent with the use of boats for deep-sea fishing (Balme 1995; O'Connor 2007a). This fact has been a key element in the demonstration that the first colonization of Australia is one of the clearest examples of the appearance of modern cognition (Davidson 2010b; Davidson and Noble 1992), particularly as a result of those capacities that were promoted by language and the use of symbols in communication. It has been suggested that there is not much archaeological evidence of symbol use early in Australian colonization (Brumm and Moore 2005), but the proportion of sites is actually highest in the earliest periods (Balme et al. 2009; Davidson 2007a) and the extent of the evidence is underestimated because of the difficulty of incorporating rock art into such syntheses (Veth et al. 2011). Another view is that it is difficult to find the whole 'package' of modern human behaviour in early Australian sites (Habgood and Franklin 2008), but others disagree (Stern 2009), and the view ignores the distinctive feature that modern human behaviour is flexible: there is patterning, but the nature of that patterning cannot be predicted for any given situation (Davidson 2010b). The most important feature of the 'package' of modern human behaviour is that there is no package. Symbolic communication and thought, and the flexibility to cope rapidly with novel environments, were part of the repertoire of the first colonists of Australia (Balme et al. 2009; Veth et al. 2011).

Where Did They Get to First?

What was the process of colonization within Sahul? It was previously suggested that the earliest sites in Australia tended to be concentrated in zones of greatest biogeographic diversity which acted as refuges during harsh climatic episodes (Veth 1989). This would suggest that the first colonists were opportunistic generalists. More recent work has tended to emphasize that after following the savannah to Sahul (Bird et al. 2005; Hope et al. 2004) people occupied all of its environments, other than grassland, relatively quickly (Balme et al. 2009). They were in the savannah at Ngarrabulgan in Cape York by 40,000 years ago (David et al. 1997); in tropical rainforests at Bobongora on the Huon Peninsula of the north coast of New Guinea by 44,000 years ago (O'Connell and Allen 2004) and Yombon on the island of New Britain by 40,700 years ago (Pavlides and Gosden 1994); in the wood and shrublands between the savannah and the arid zones at Carpenter's Gap (O'Connor and Fankhauser 2001) and Riwi (Balme 2000) in the southern Kimberley by 43,000 years ago; at Lake Mungo in the Willandra Lakes of NSW by 42,000 years ago (Olley et al. 2006); in the arid zone at Puritjarra by 35,000 years ago (Smith et al. 2001); in the savannah (or tall open woodland) of south-west Western Australia at Devil's Lair by 45,000 years ago (O'Connell and Allen 2004); and in the steppe environments of Tasmania at Parmerpar Meethaner by 40,700 years ago (Cosgrove 1995) very soon after the formation of the land bridge to the mainland (Lambeck and Chappell 2001).

In the process of expansion into different environments, one of the strategies was to use symbolic marking of places through rock art signalling identity beyond the group, and symbolic marking of persons using beads and possibly body decoration signalling identity within the group (Veth et al. 2011). Beads were present in some areas of Australia (Balme and Morse 2006) but also at Buang Merebak on New Ireland in island Melanesia by 32,000 years ago (Leavesley 2007). Most importantly, even at the early stages of such symbolic use, there seems to have been regional differentiation of style, at least between the Australian regions of Kimberley (Walsh 2000), Arnhem Land (Chaloupka 1993; Chippindale and Taçon 1998) and Cape York (Cole and Watchman 2005), and probably also the Pilbara (Lorblanchet 1992; Mulvaney 2013). The dating of rock art is subject to scepticism and uncertainty, but to ignore it for this reason, when it is clear that symbolic structuring of relations has been fundamental in all aspects of life in Australia, may be to make a greater error. Rock art has also been directly dated at Lene Hara in Timor to 29,000 years ago (Aubert et al. 2007).

Although there is no case for the crossing of Bass Strait after it was formed by the rising sea, there are archaeological indications of marine crossings elsewhere; people used watercraft to take marsupials east to New Ireland (Marshall and Allen 1991; White et al. 1991) by 9,000 years ago, and possibly west to Timor (O'Connor 2006). They must have also been used to move the dingo south into Australia where it seems to have remained genetically isolated until the arrival of Europeans (Savolainen et al. 2004), though the genetic coalescence ages are older than the archaeological estimate of 4,000 years ago (McNiven and Hitchcock 2004). But the Austronesians in their voyages in the western Pacific to New Guinea (from 3,500 or more years ago) and on into Melanesia did not sail south to settle Australia (Bellwood 2005; Gray et al. 2009), and pigs do not seem to have been moved across Torres Strait from New Guinea to Australia (for the genetic history of pigs, see Larson et al. 2005; 2007). This suggests that the barrier at Torres Strait was not principally ecological but social.

HISTORIES OF CONTINUITY AND CHANGE IN THE ARCHAEOLOGICAL RECORD

A Question of Numbers

The demographic pattern of colonization remains enigmatic given that initial population must have been small, though not too small or it would not have survived (McArthur 1976). A recent exploration of the population implications of genetic data suggests that population in Australia grew rapidly before 48,000 years ago and less rapidly after 40,000 years ago, while in New Guinea the rate of growth was much slower, beginning after 39,000 years ago and levelling off about 30,000 years ago (Atkinson et al. 2008). The population at contact with Europeans may have been quite small, around a million people in Australia (White and Mulvaney 1987), but it is difficult to estimate because of the depredations of smallpox shortly after European settlement (Campbell 2002).

One view is that the stochastic variation of environmental conditions may have had local impacts with global effects (Davidson 1990). This issue has been discussed for the arid zone (now expanded to the whole of Australia, with some contentious claims about the size of initial population: see Williams 2013) using the cumulative probabilities derived from calibration of all radiocarbon dates (Smith et al. 2008). This analysis suggested that there were peaks in inferred population densities of the arid zone at 19,000 years ago, 15,000 years ago, 10,500 years ago, 8,000 years ago, 4,500 years ago, and 1,500 years ago, with variations in particular regions, often depending on local hydrological contexts. The methodology can be criticized because it tends to underestimate taphonomic bias (Marwick 2009; O'Connor et al. 1999; Surovell and Brantingham 2007), and it is susceptible to other bias through the differential attention to the needs of absolute dating by excavators of particular sites (Straus 2005). It also tends both to give the appearance that there are many more data than there really are and to smooth over discontinuities in dating because of the inclusion of the most improbable ranges of dating uncertainty.

Another approach is to concentrate on the numbers of dated sites for the available databases from the arid zone (Smith et al. 2008) and Queensland (Ulm and Reid 2000) (This argument has not been updated to take into account the publication of a more complete database by Williams 2013.) A third database, for the top end of the Northern Territory, does not include dates from the Pleistocene (Brockwell et al. 2009). Figures 16.4 and 16.5 show the numbers of sites with dates within each 5,000-year block of OIS 3–1 for biogeographic regions in the arid zone and for regions in Queensland (for sources see the figure captions). If nothing else, these data demonstrate just how thin the archaeological record is generally for the Pleistocene. Among the arid zone data there are two exceptions which make it likely that the poverty of sites is not a good reflection of Pleistocene human behaviour in Australia: the Murray-Darling bioregion and the inland Pilbara. The first of these has been the subject of intensive research work since the discovery of the earliest human burials, including a cremation, in the 1960s and 1970s (Bowler et al. 1970; Bowler and Thorne 1976) and site numbers may be exaggerated by the surface exposure of small-scale activities (Allen et al. 2008). The second is the location of some of the most intensive archaeological activity in Australia, primarily in caves and rock shelters, as a result, principally, of iron ore mining and the associated Environmental Impact Assessment (see e.g. Brown 1987; Marwick 2002; Morse 2009). For Queensland, the only region with a rich spectrum of sites is the Cape York Peninsula, which has also been the focus of several intensive research programmes (e.g. David and Lourandos 1999; Morwood and Hobbs 1995). Careful analysis of the Nonda Rock dated sediments shows that there were episodes of minimal sediment deposition, particularly in OIS 2 late and 2/3, and others of very rapid deposition, particularly in OIS 2 early, within the one sequence (David et al. 2007), so that the uncritical use of age-depth curves will not enhance our understanding of the chronology represented by the dates themselves.

These small samples mean that it is difficult to interpret the patterns of gaps in the dates when they occur (Tables 16.2 and 16.3). For the Cape York Peninsula, however, for both stages of OIS 2 and for OIS 1/2 on our chronology, there were more sites with long gaps in the sequence than there were occupied sites (though in two of the major research projects there was much emphasis on the use of age-depth curves, so there may have been less emphasis

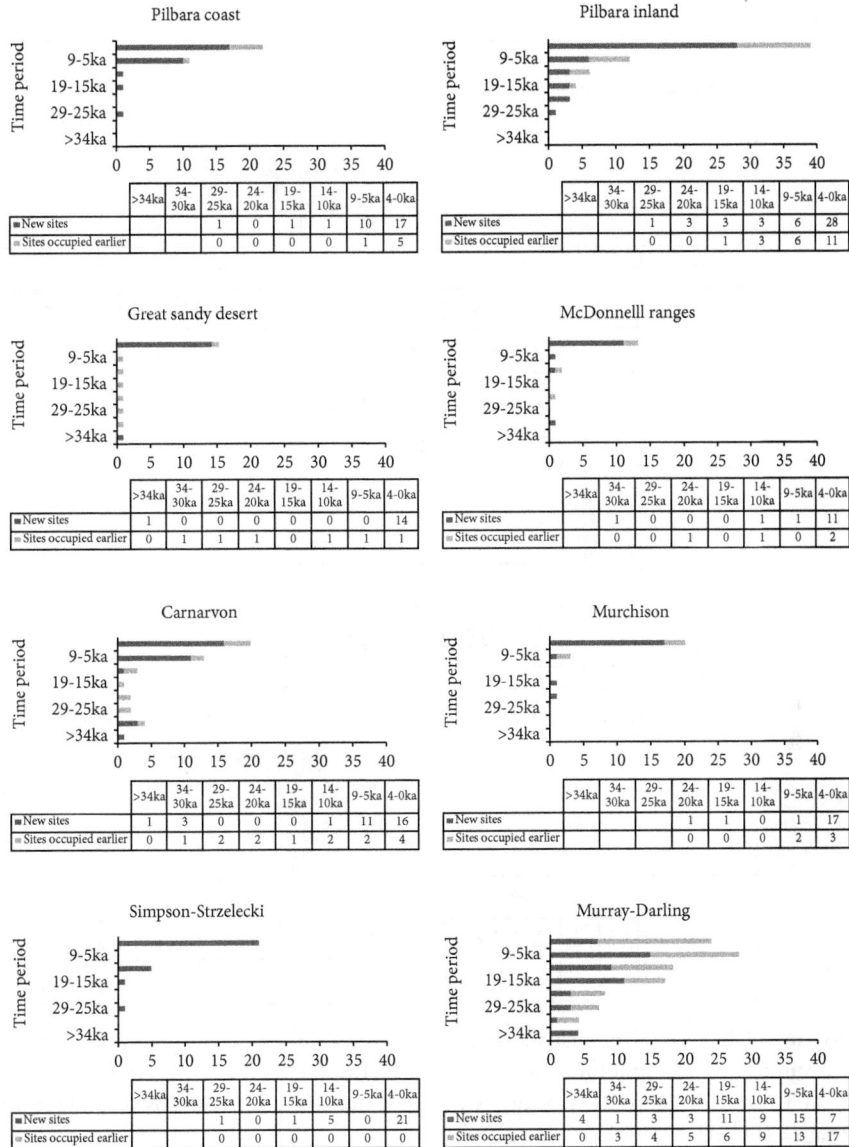

FIGURE 16.4 Chronological distribution for the arid zone of new sites and sites previously occupied by biogeographic region using the time intervals defined for this chapter. Data from Smith et al. 2008 (http://palaeoworks.anu.edu.au/databases.html). The method used here was to sort the database using the uncalibrated dates into 5,000-year groups. The dates for the boundaries between groups were then estimated using the CalPal 2005 data as 5,100 years ago, 10,800 years ago, 17,850 years ago, 23,350 years ago, 29,450 years ago, 34,800 years ago, 40,500 years ago. These groups, then, might correspond to OIS 1 late, 1 early, 1/2, 2 late (corresponding to the period of maximum ice advance of Australian glaciers, Barrows et al. 2002), 2 early, 2/3, 3 late, and 3 early (although OIS 3 lasted much longer than implied by this chronology) as indicated in Figure 16.1. Gaps in date sequences were recognized when there were two successive thousand-year periods undated within a 5,000-year block at a site. It was possible for there to be more gaps than sites if some sites with long sequences of dates nevertheless had no dates during a 5,000-year block.

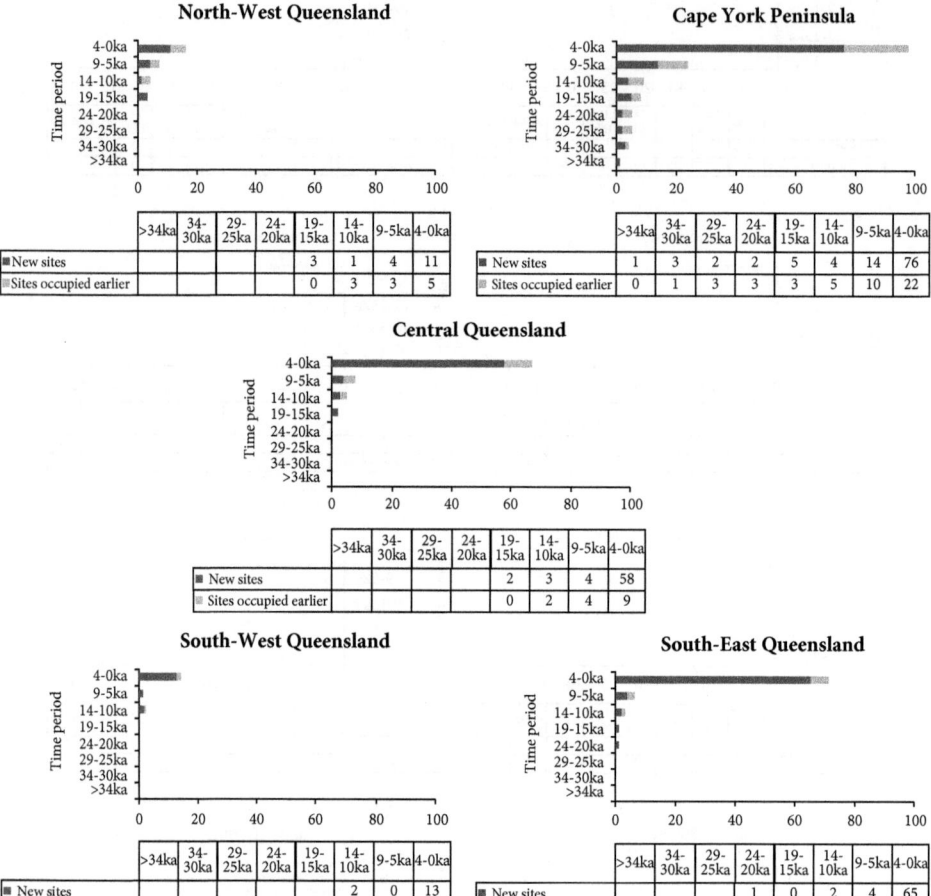

FIGURE 16.5 Chronological distribution for Queensland of new sites and sites previously occupied by geographic region using the time intervals defined for this chapter. Data from Ulm and Reid 2000 with additions (http://www.atsis.uq.edu.au/index.html?page=41664).

Table 16.2 Numbers of sites (a) in each region by time period indicating numbers of 2,000-year gaps in sequence in a 5,000-year period; (b) in the form b/a. So in the cell on the top left, there were 23 dated sites (a) in the Pilbara Coastal region and one 2,000 year gap in the sequence (b). Highlighted periods are for cases where there are more gaps than sites, indicating substantial abandonment of the region. Arid zone data sources as for Figure 16.4.

	OIS 1 late	OIS 1 early	OIS 1/2	OIS 2 late	OIS 2 early	OIS 2/3	OIS 3 late
Pilbara Coastal	1/23	0/11	0/1			0/1	
Pilbara Inland	5/39	10/12	5/6	**4/4**	1/3	0/1	
Great Sandy Desert	0/15	0/1	0/1	1/1	1/1	0/1	0/1
Carnarvon	3/20	4/13	**4/3**	**4/1**	**4/2**	**4/2**	**4/4**
Gascoyne		1/1	1/1	1/1	1/1		
Murchison	2/20	2/3	1/1	1/0			
Geraldton Sands		1/1	1/0	1/1	0/1	1/1	
Central Ranges	1	1/1					
MacDonnell Ranges	2/13	**2/1**	½	1/0	1/1	1/0	0/1
Channel Country			1/1				
Simpson-Strzelecki Dunefields	1/22	1/0					
Flinders Lofty Block		1/1	1/1				
Murray Darling	9/24	13/28	9/18	6/17	5/8	5/7	1/4

Table 16.3 Numbers of sites (a) in each region by time period indicating numbers of 2,000-year gaps in sequence in a 5,000-year period; (b) in the form b/a. Highlighted periods are for cases where there are more gaps than sites, indicating substantial abandonment of the region. Queensland data sources as for Figure 16.4.

	OIS 1 late	OIS 1 early	OIS 1/2	OIS 2 late	OIS 2 early	OIS 2/3	OIS 3 late
North-west Queensland	3/14	3/7	3/4	1/3			
Cape York Peninsula	10/98	19/24	**11/9**	**10/8**	5/5	3/5	0/4
Central Queensland	7/67	6/8	1/5	1/2			
South-west Queensland	1/14	0/1	½				
South-east Queensland	6/71	3/6	0/3	0/1	0/1		

on dating complete sequences (David and Chant 1995; Morwood and Hobbs 1995). The same phenomenon is seen over the same time range in the Carnarvon region of Western Australia, but it began earlier. In the small numbers of sites in the MacDonnell Ranges, there is a slight indication of this effect in the early Holocene/OIS 1 early. In the Murray-Darling, however, there is much more continuity of occupation, represented also in the relative numbers of occupied sites that had been used earlier.

A more detailed analysis of the Holocene (OIS 1) radiocarbon dates from the Top End of the Northern Territory shows that the numbers of dates reflect differential preservation of sites as well as behavioural changes and environmental changes (Brockwell et al. 2009). Similar arguments apply to most situations where there has been detailed assessment of the local and regional conditions, and the site formation and taphonomic factors (e.g. Attenbrow 2004).

Another set of data that has been used as a proxy for numbers of people is the relative abundance of stone artefacts. In the north in the Kimberley (e.g. Carpenter Gap 1, see O'Connor 2007b), in Arnhem Land (Jones and Johnson 1985), and in Cape York (David and Chant 1995; Morwood and Hobbs 1995), frequencies of stone artefacts varied markedly, and not in step either with climate change or with each other. In each case the variation may be between excavation trenches, between sites within a region, or among sites between regions. In the most exhaustive analysis, of Puritjarra in central Australia (Smith 2006), the estimated numbers of artefacts varied from 0.5 to 5.7 a year throughout the Pleistocene. But one man alone in the arid zone might have used 23 adze flakes during a year (Gould 1980, 128–30). Under these circumstances, it is not clear how such small numbers of archaeological artefacts relate to the use and periodic abandonment of a particular region, but it is clear that continuity of occupation was not the dominant theme in any of these regions, despite methods of analysing data that work towards finding continuity.

Numbers of artefacts were part of the initial argument that there had been a late Holocene intensification of site usage in New South Wales (Hughes and Lampert 1982), though the argument was criticized even before it was published because there are many factors that influence the number of artefacts in sites (Hiscock 1981). This argument then formed part of a broader claim that there was a widespread pattern of intensification of social relations in the mid to late Holocene in Australia (David and Lourandos 1999; Lourandos 1983; 1997), which was questioned early in its existence (Beaton 1983; Bird and Frankel 1991). More recent work has shown that the picture is much more complex locally, regionally, and globally within Australia (Attenbrow 2004, esp. 199–201). One of the reasons for the emphasis on intensification was a quest to understand the behaviour of Australians in terms that are more like ethnographic descriptions, and to account for the relations between Australia and New Guinea, that could be claimed to derive from being studied in different scholarly traditions (Lourandos 2008).

Measuring Impacts

Megafauna

Shortly after the appearance of humans in Australia, several large mammals and birds disappeared (Miller et al. 2005). There is ongoing controversy about the role of humans in this faunal change (Field et al. 2008) and about whether it resulted from processes similar to those on other continents (Grayson and Meltzer 2003; Roberts et al. 2001; a recent paper by Wroe et al. (2013) emphasizes the likely role of climatic and environmental change in extinction). It has been estimated that at least 45 species had become extinct in the 100,000 years before the arrival of humans, and only 13 in the following 10 millennia (Field et al. 2008)—a substantial increase in rate. The absence of good evidence for predation makes it difficult to assign a defining role to people, despite the increased rate of extinction. An argument that the final extinctions were the result of massive burning of the Australian environment, caused by people, seems to lack good evidence (which has long been known to be difficult to interpret, see Clark 1983) from regions in which extinctions took place (Lynch et al. 2007; Wroe and Field 2006). After exhausting critique, the evidence now seems to be robust that megafauna survived to coexist with people in some regions, until 36,000 years ago at Cuddie Springs, and somewhat later at Nombe in New Guinea (Field et al. 2008; Gillieson and Mountain 1983). The paradox of the argument is that part of the case that humans caused the extinction is that the extinction was so rapid that there are no sites where humans and megafauna coexisted, while the site with the best evidence that large animals survived for several millennia after human arrival, and where the two may have interacted, is not used to blame humans.

A different situation may apply for the marsupial carnivores, *Thylacoleo carnifex* (the marsupial lion) and *Thylacinus cynocephalus* (the Tasmanian tiger), as their prey were probably smaller than them and are not argued to have been affected by the environmental factors that may have destroyed megafauna. The first, *Thylacoleo*, was extinct all over Australia at the time Europeans arrived, and it is not clear exactly when it disappeared. It has been suggested that there is at least one painted image of this animal in the Kimberley (Akerman and Willing 2009), though, as with other claims for representations of extinct fauna, it is difficult to be certain what an extinct animal looked like when only skeletal remains are known. The latest date for *Thylacoleo* in a recent analysis would be 42,000 years ago (Roberts et al. 2001) though the bones were probably not *in situ* (Dortch 1984). If this was the latest date for the species and the image is correctly identified, then it is one of the earliest representations in the world.

Thylacinus survived later in Tasmania and became extinct, in Hobart Zoo, on 7 September 1936. Representations of this animal have been found in Kakadu (Chaloupka 1993), the Dampier Archipelago (Mulvaney 2009), and in south-eastern Australia (e.g. Figure 16.6). There is archaeological evidence of the animal in Kiowa in the New Guinea highlands at between 10,000 years ago and 7,500 years ago (Bulmer 1975), and the latest date in mainland Australia is about 3,500 years ago at Murra-el-elevyn cave on the Nullarbor Plain (Partridge 1967).

The latest dates suggested that the extinction of the thylacines may have been a result of competitive exclusion by the dingo (Archer 1974) with the now generally accepted dates, just before 3,000 years ago, for the arrival of the dingo from East or South-East Asia (McNiven and Hitchcock 2004; Savolainen et al. 2004). Dates are slightly earlier in New Guinea.

Fire

Fire is a natural part of the Australian environment, and some plants depend on it for propagation. In many parts of Australia, Aboriginal people used fire, sometimes referred to as 'firestick farming' (Jones 1969), in a mosaic pattern to 'clean up the country', as an aid in hunting, and to promote the growth of food plants that respond to burning (Latz 1995).

FIGURE 16.6 Thylacine painting at Yeddonba, Mount Pilot, near Beechworth Victoria (photo: Iain Davidson enhanced with DStretch (http://www.dstretch.com/).

When and where the practice occurred in the past has been a matter of controversy (Head 1994), particularly because of over-interpretation of some pollen cores. It was, nevertheless, one of many techniques by which Aboriginal people in the recent past managed, and modified, the food resources of their environments (Head 2000).

Subtle analysis of the evidence for Aboriginal burning in the past shows that the impacts were complex and different from one region to another and one time to another (Head 1996). There seems to be a signal that the impact of fire on vegetation increased as early as human colonization in northern Australia (Turney et al. 2001; Mooney et al.) and fire was also part of the early human occupation of the New Guinea Highlands by 40,700 years ago at Kosipe, both as hearths at the site and putatively in clearing vegetation (Fairbairn et al. 2006).

Measuring Responses

People living in Australia have always experienced dynamic environments, but they also seem to have been agents of change such that it may no longer be appropriate to isolate humans analytically from the ecosystems of which they have always been parts (Head 2008). This subtlety is probably the best way to see the joint history of humans and megafaunal species. For other species the story is equally complex. We cannot know about interactions with marine species for times when the cold climate during OIS 3 and OIS 2 led to sea levels much lower than at present (see Nicholson and Cane 1994), but there was exploitation of shellfish and creation of shell mounds near present shores initiating between 7,000 years ago and 4,000 years ago in different regions (Beaton 1985; Brockwell et al. 2009). In some regions (e.g. the coastal Pilbara) there was substantial change in dominant shellfish species as the coastal environment changed from mangroves suitable for *Terebralia palustris* to sand and mudflats more suitable for *Anadara granosa* (Bradshaw 1995). But there is also an argument that in some regions, and at different dates between 5,250 years ago and 3,000 years ago, preference was given to the rapidly reproducing *Anadara* because it could be a sufficiently reliable food source to supply ceremonial gatherings (Clune and Harrison 2009; Harrison 2009; Meehan 1982; Morrison 2003). Such arguments are part of a broader set of claims about social organization in OIS 1 late which emphasize that choices about resource use were not determined by the environment so much as by the needs for social interaction. The argument suggests that such interactions could be sustained by particular patterns of resource use.

Archaeological evidence has accumulated in Australia for the use of tubers and seeds by 30,000 years ago, and tree fruits in OIS 1 early, and for starchy residues on stone tools from various periods (Denham et al. 2009). But the evidence is so sparse that it would be adventurous to speculate about the social context of plant use at this stage. Some of the earlier arguments, such as those suggesting cycad manipulation to produce food for ceremony (Beaton 1982), seem to have been over-extended (Asmussen 2009). We are a long way from identifying signs of the complex social organization of subsistence (such as ritually defined restrictions on use and the timing of use of particular species) known to have operated in the Cape York Peninsula, and which may have been part of the reason why agricultural ideas have been difficult to transplant either from New Guinea or from Europe (Chase 1989). Examination of the various relationships and patterns of food production in Torres Strait suggest that the situation is indeed one of resilience in the face of incoming influences (McNiven and Hitchcock 2004). One factor involved may have been the ethnographically documented philosophy of demand sharing, which tended to militate against accumulation of goods, but not perhaps of ritual knowledge (Peterson 1997), though there is no evidence of its antiquity.

In New Guinea, however, where there are currently complex agricultural systems, direct signs of soil cultivation (Denham and Haberle 2008; Mooney et al 2011) and phytoliths of banana and taro and starch of taro just after 7,000 years ago (Denham et al. 2003) have been taken as signs of the beginning of agriculture. In reality, there is little evidence for difference between Australia and New Guinea subsistence practices until OIS 1 early (Denham et al. 2009). The nature of social complexity in New Guinea at the time of contact, often involving institutionalized inequality (e.g. Wiessner 2002), was quite different from the complexity of relative egalitarianism in Australia (e.g. Gould 1982).

For the exploitation of animals (other than megafauna), one detailed study suggests that in south-west Tasmania there was long-term (from OIS 3 until at least OIS 1/2) deliberate targeting of prey species (Bennett's wallabies), which involved people moving between patches as returns declined, thereby ensuring the rejuvenation of the prey (Cosgrove and Allen 2001). Sharing of the products of the hunt was surrounded, ethnohistorically, by ritual considerations including the attribution of rights to a kill according to the original owner of a spear (Peterson 1997). The challenge for archaeology is to find how and when this sharing and those rights can be recognized through material culture. There may be some indication of marking spear ownership in the variation in spear armatures shown in rock art in the Kimberley (Walsh and Morwood 1999). Other evidence may come from the emergence of bifacial stone spear-point technology in the north during OIS 1 (Clarkson 2007) and the proliferation of backed artefacts, possibly as armatures for spears, at about the same time in the remainder of Australia (Hiscock 2008, chapter 8). One suggestion has been that such artefacts proliferated in order to guard against risks of hunting failure through more reliable or maintainable technology (Hiscock 1994). On the other hand, it may be an indication of the marking of spears for the complex ritual conditions and that ritual not technology mitigated risk through sharing.

The other great institution for mitigation of risk was the practice of ceremony (Strehlow 1970; Yengoyan 1968) which brought people together to share in food abundances, ensuring the sharing of rights and rites, and facilitating the broadening of social connections. The singing of songs that linked places in the landscape over long distances also ensured the connection to other people who shared the mythology (Davidson et al. 2004; Minc 1986). In this way the ritual links between groups can give the appearance that the whole of Australia (except Tasmania) was connected (Sutton 1990), although in fact different ecological conditions could lead to demographic packing in particularly favourable circumstances (Pardoe 1995).

REGIONALIZATION OF SYMBOLIC COMMUNICATION

Several studies of rock art have emphasized the intensified regionalization of style during OIS 1 late (e.g. Cole and David 1990; David and Chant 1995; Flood 2004; Ridges 2006; Ross 2013; Taçon 1993; Walsh 2000). In each of the main regions, there was not only a distinctive art style of the recent past, but a sequence of changes in art style through time. In this way, symbolic connection with other people and with the landscape was a common, but not unchanging, theme for much of the time of human occupation of Australia. In each of the major rock art regions, Kimberley (Roberts 2000; Roberts et al. 1997; Walsh 2000), Kakadu (Chaloupka 1993; Chippindale and Taçon 1998), and more than one region of the Cape York Peninsula (Cole and Watchman 2005; Watchman 1993; 2001) there is a sequence of styles that may begin early and end late. Sequences have also been produced for the Pilbara (Mulvaney 2011; 2013), the Central Queensland Highlands (Morwood 1980), and Central Australia (J. Ross 2005). The dynamics of change between one style and another are poorly understood.

Elsewhere, such as the Victoria River Downs in the Northern Territory (David et al. 1994; Watchman et al. 2000) or the Selwyn Ranges in north-west Queensland (Davidson et al. 2005; Ridges et al. 2000), there appear to be art traditions that date only from the late Holocene, perhaps with little variation through time. Analysis of ochres in the paints from the Selwyn Ranges shows that ochres were traded into a region where there were other ochre quarries that were used for paints locally, strongly suggesting that the exchange of materials was for social rather than utilitarian reasons (Davidson et al. 2005). Analysis of the spatial associations of design elements in the Selwyn imagery shows different patterns for different image classes (Ridges 2006), suggesting that the art was involved in promoting social cohesion within the group and in expressing external links with other groups (Davidson et al. 2005). Thus the art may well have been part of the whole network of social relations that connected the Gulf of Carpentaria to Lake Eyre (Davidson et al. 2004; McBryde 1987; Mulvaney 1976).

It seems likely that the increased numbers of sites (despite local reductions) may reflect the greater capacity for survival in a hazardous environment through the social linkages embodied in the songlines associated with the various manifestations of the Dreaming and reflected in the expansion of regional rock-art traditions (e.g. Taçon 2008). How this relates in turn to the symbolic construction of environments in New Guinea that permitted the emergence of agriculture is beyond the scope of this chapter.

Conclusion

The Sahul story shows that the first people arrived by watercraft in small numbers some time before 45,000 years ago during OIS 3. They colonized all environments relatively rapidly, showing sufficient flexibility to adapt to arid environments at one extreme, and rainforest margins at the other. They survived climatic changes as the environmental zones fluctuated and systematic and stochastic conditions created long- and short-term variations, but it is probable that local groups became extinct from time to time.

Despite their small numbers at initial colonization, substantial diversity emerged by the time of European colonization, in a variety of stylistic or symbolic ways, but most markedly in language, particularly in what is now New Guinea. The archaeological evidence suggests that rock art shows some signs of an early symbolic differentiation of populations, which seems to have become very marked at or just before European settlement. But in almost all cases, rock art shows change through time in content and style suggesting that the symbolic associations were never static. There are some hints that symbolic marking was used differently in New Guinea, with less emphasis on the persisting marking of places, and more on the marking of people and of items made from perishable materials. One argument would suggest that these different ways of using symbolism to structure people's lives reflects the fundamental ideological differences between the fisher-gatherer-hunter way of life in Australia and the forager behaviour that led to the emergence of agriculture in parts of New Guinea (see the related argument for other regions in Davidson 2012).

In these ways, the initial fisher-gatherer-hunter populations of Sahul both changed and differentiated after colonization, in response to, as well as independently of, the changing environmental circumstances. As with other people adapting to climatic changes around the world, these were a changing people in a changing environment, capable of both adjustment and resilience despite the fact that there are now such contrasts between the agriculturalists in New Guinea and the fisher-gatherer-hunters in Australia.

Acknowledgements

Much of the research for the chapter was undertaken while I was Visiting Professor of Australian Studies at Harvard University (2008–9) and it was completed in 2010. Only minor amendments have been made since. I am very grateful for the improvements I was able to make after helpful comments by Helen Arthurson, Jane Balme, Claire Bowern, Nick Evans, Ian Lilley, Mark Moore, Andrew Pawley, and Peter White. The responsibility for everything else is mine.

References

Akerman, K. and Willing, T. 2009. An ancient rock painting of a marsupial lion, *Thylacoleo carnifex*, from the Kimberley, Western Australia. *Antiquity* 83. Online at http://www.antiquity.ac.uk/projgall/akerman319/.

Allen, H., Holdaway, S., Fanning, P., and Littleton, J. 2008. Footprints in the sand: appraising the archaeology of the Willandra Lakes, western New South Wales, Australia. *Antiquity* 82, 11–24.

Allen, J. and Gosden, C. (ed.) 1991. *Report of the Lapita Homeland Project*. Canberra: Australian National University.

Allison, I. and Peterson, J. A. 1989. Irian Jaya. In R. S. Williams and J. G. Ferrigno (eds) *Satellite image atlas of glaciers of the world H1–H20*. Online at http://pubs.usgs.gov/pp/p1386h/indonesia/indonesia.html. Accessed 27 March 2013. USGS Prof. Paper 1386-H.

Ambrose, S. H. 2003. Did the super-eruption of Toba cause a human population bottleneck? Reply to Gathorne-Hardy and Harcourt-Smith. *Journal of Human Evolution* 45, 231–7.

Archer, M. 1974. New information about the Quaternary distribution of the thylacine (Marsupialia, Thylacinidae) in Australia. *Journal of the Royal Society of Western Australia* 57, 43–50.

Armitage, S. J., Jasim, S. A., Marks, A. E., Parker, A. G., Usik, V. I., and Uerpmann, H.-P. 2011. The southern route 'Out of Africa': evidence for an early expansion of Modern Humans into Arabia. *Science* 331, 453–6.

Asmussen, B. 2009. Another burning question: hunter-gatherer exploitation of Macrozamia spp. *Archaeology in Oceania* 44, 142–9.

Atkinson, Q. D., Gray, R. D., and Drummond, A. J. 2008. mtDNA variation predicts population size in humans and reveals a major southern Asian chapter in human prehistory. *Molecular Biology and Evolution* 25, 468–74.

Atkinson, Q. D., Gray, R. D., and Drummond, A. J. 2009. Bayesian coalescent inference of major human mitochondrial DNA haplogroup expansions in Africa. *Proceedings of the Royal Society B: Biological Sciences* 276, 367–73.

Attenbrow, V. 2003. *Sydney's Aboriginal past*. Sydney: UNSW Press.

Attenbrow, V. 2004. *What's changing: population size or land-use pattern? The archaeology of Upper Mangrove Creek, Sydney Basin*. Canberra: Pandanus Books, Australian National University. http://epress.anu.edu.au/ta21_citation.html. Accessed 27 March 2013.

Aubert, M., O'Connor, S., McCulloch, M., Mortimer, G., Watchman, A., and Richer-LaFleche, M. 2007. Uranium-series dating rock art in East Timor. *Journal of Archaeological Science* 34, 991–6.

Baker, B. 2002. 'I'm going to Where-her-brisket-is': placenames in the Roper. In L. Hercus, F. Hodges, and J. Simpson (eds), *The land is a map: placenames of Indigenous origin in Australia*, 103–29. Canberra: Pandanus Books in association with Pacific Linguistics.

Balme, J. 1995. 30,000 years of fishery in western New South Wales. *Archaeology in Oceania* 30, 1–21.

Balme, J. 2000. Excavations revealing 40,000 years of occupation at Mimbi caves in south central Kimberley of Western Australia. *Australian Archaeology* 51, 1–5.

Balme, J., Davidson, I., McDonald, J., Stern, N., and Veth, P. 2009. Symbolic behaviour and the peopling of the southern arc route to Australia. *Quaternary International* 202, 59–68.

Balme, J. and Morse, K. 2006. Shell beads and social behaviour in Pleistocene Australia. *Antiquity* 80, 799–811.

Bar-Yosef, O., Arnold, M., Mercier, N., Belfercohen, A., Goldberg, P., Housley, R., Laville, H., Meignen, L., Vogel, J. C., and Vandermeersch, B. 1996. The dating of the Upper Paleolithic layers in Kebara cave, Mt Carmel. *Journal of Archaeological Science* 23, 297–306.

Bar-Yosef, O. and Vandermeersch, B. (eds) 1991. *Le Squelette Moustérien de Kébara 2*. Paris: Éditions du Centre National de la Recherche Scientifique.

Bar-Yosef Mayer, D. E., Vandermeersch, B., and Bar-Yosef, O. 2009. Shells and ochre in Middle Paleolithic Qafzeh cave, Israel: indications for modern behavior. *Journal of Human Evolution* 56, 307–14.

Barker, G., Barton, H., Bird, M., Daly, P., Datan, I., Dykes, A., Farr, L., Gilbertson, D., Harrisson, B., Hunt, C., Higham, T., Kealhofer, L., Krigbaum, J., Lewis, H., McLaren, S., Paz, V., Pike, A., Piper, P., Pyatt, B., Rabett, R., Reynolds, T., Rose, J., Rushworth, G., Stephens, M., Stringer, C., Thompson, J., and Turney, C. 2007. The 'human revolution' in lowland tropical Southeast Asia: the antiquity and behavior of anatomically modern humans at Niah cave (Sarawak, Borneo). *Journal of Human Evolution* 52, 243–61.

Barrows, T. T., Stone, J. O., Fifield, L. K., and Cresswell, R. G. 2002. The timing of the Last Glacial Maximum in Australia. *Quaternary Science Reviews* 21, 159–73.

Beaton, J. M. 1982. Fire and water: aspects of Australian Aboriginal management of cycads. *Archaeology in Oceania* 17, 51–8.

Beaton, J. M 1983. Does intensification account for changes in the Australian Holocene archaeological record? *Archaeology in Oceania* 18, 94–7.

Beaton, J. M 1985. Evidence for a coastal occupation time-lag at Princess Charlotte Bay (North Queensland) and implications for coastal colonization and population growth theories for Aboriginal Australia. *Archaeology in Oceania* 20, 1–20.

Bellwood, P. 2005. *First farmers: the origins of agricultural societies*. Oxford: Blackwell.

Bender, M., Sowers, T., Dickson, M.-L., Orchardo, J., Grootes, P., Mayewski, P. A., and Meese, D. A. 1994. Climatic correlations between Greenland and Antarctica during the past 100,000 years. *Nature* 372, 663–6.

Bird, C. F. M. and Frankel, D. 1991. Problems in constructing a prehistoric regional sequence: Holocene south-east Australia. *World Archaeology* 23, 179–92.

Bird, M., Taylor, I. D., and Hunt, C. 2005. Palaeoenvironments of insular Southeast Asia during the Last Glacial period: a savanna corridor in Sundaland? *Quaternary Science Reviews* 24, 2228–42.

Birdsell, J. B. 1967. Preliminary data on the trihybrid origin of the Australian Aborigines. *Archaeology and Physical Anthropology in Oceania* 2, 100–55.

Birdsell, J. 1977. The recalibration of a paradigm for the first peopling of Greater Australia. In J. Allen, J. Golson, and R. Jones (eds), *Sunda and Sahul*, 113–67. London: Academic Press.

Blake, B. J. 1988. Redefining Pama-Nyungan: towards a prehistory of Australian languages. *Aboriginal Linguistics* 1, 1–90.

Bowern, C. 2006. Comment on Clendon 2006. *Current Anthropology* 47, 51–2.

Bowern, C. 2010. Historical linguistics in Australia: trees, networks and their implications. *Philosophical Transactions of the Royal Society of London Series B: Biological Sciences*, 365, 3845–54.

Bowler, J. M. 1998. Willandra Lakes revisited: environmental framework for human occupation. *Archaeology in Oceania* 33, 120–55.

Bowler, J. M., Jones, R., Allen, H., and Thorne, A. G. 1970. Pleistocene human remains from Australia: a living site and human cremation from Lake Mungo, western New South Wales. *World Archaeology* 2, 39–60.

Bowler, J. M. and Thorne, A. 1976. Human remains from Lake Mungo: discovery and excavation of Lake Mungo III. In R. L. Kirk and A. G. Thorne (eds), *The origin of the Australians*, 127–38. Canberra: Australian Institute of Aboriginal Studies.

Bradshaw, E. 1995. Dates from archaeological excavations on the Pilbara coastline and island of the Dampier Archipelago, Western Australia. *Australian Archaeology* 41, 37–8.

Brady, D. 2005. Australian Aboriginal body scarification and drainage basins. Unpublished Honours thesis, School of Human and Environmental Studies, University of New England.

Brockwell, S., Faulkner, P., Bourke, P., Clarke, A., Crassweller, C., Guse, D., Meehan, B., and Sim, R. 2009. Radiocarbon dates from the top end: a cultural chronology for the Northern Territory coastal plains. *Australian Aboriginal Studies* 1, 54–76.

Brown, P. 1997. Australian palaeoanthropology. In F. Spencer (ed.), *History of physical anthropology: an encyclopedia*, 2 volumes, 138–45. New York: Garland.

Brown, S. 1987. *Towards a prehistory of the Hamersley Plateau, North West Australia*. Canberra: Australian National University.

Brumm, A. and Moore, M. W. 2005. Symbolic revolutions and the Australian archaeological record. *Cambridge Archaeological Journal* 15, 157–75.

Bulmer, S. 1975. Settlement and economy in prehistoric Papua New Guinea: a review of the archeological evidence. *Journal de la Société des océanistes* 31, 7–75.

Butzer, K. W. and Helgren, D. M. 2005. Livestock, land cover, and environmental history: the tablelands of New South Wales, Australia, 1820–1920. *Annals of the Association of American Geographers* 95, 80–111.

Campbell, J. 2002. *Invisible invaders: smallpox and other diseases in Aboriginal Australia, 1780–1880*. Melbourne: Melbourne University Press.

Chaloupka, G. 1993. *Journey in time: the world's longest continuing art tradition. The 50,000-year story of the Australian Aboriginal rock art of Arnhem Land*. Chatswood, Australia: Reed.

Chase, A. K. 1989. Domestication and domiculture in northern Australia: a social perspective. In D. R. Harris and G. C. Hillman (eds), *Foraging and farming: the evolution of plant exploitation*, 42–54. London: Unwin Hyman.

Chen, Y. S., Torroni, A., Excoffier, L., Santachiara-Benerecetti, A. S., and Wallace, D. C. 1995. Analysis of mtDNA variation in African populations reveals the most ancient of all human continent-specific haplogroups. *American Journal of Human Genetics* 57, 133–49.

Chippindale, C. and Taçon, P. S. C. 1998. The many ways of dating Arnhem Land rock-art, north Australia. In C. Chippindale and P. S. C. Taçon (eds), *The archaeology of rock-art*, 90–111. Cambridge: Cambridge University Press.

Chivas, A. R., García, A., van der Kaars, S., Couapel, M. J. J., Holt, S., Reeves, J. M., Wheeler, D. J., Switzer, A. D., Murray-Wallace, C. V., Banerjee, D., Price, D. M., Wang, S. X., Pearson, G., Edgar, N. T., Beaufort, L., De Deckker, P., Lawson, E., and Cecil, C. B. 2001. Sea-level and environmental changes since the last interglacial in the Gulf of Carpentaria, Australia: an overview. *Quaternary International* 83–5, 19–46.

Clark, R. L. 1983. Pollen and charcoal evidence for the effects of Aboriginal burning on the vegetation of Australia. *Archaeology in Oceania* 18, 32–7.

Clarkson, C. 2007. *Lithics in the land of the Lightning Brothers: the archaeology of Wardaman country*. Canberrra: Australian National University.

Clendon, M. 2006. Reassessing Australia's linguistic prehistory. *Current Anthropology* 47, 39–61.

Clune, G. and Harrison, R. 2009. Coastal shell middens of the Abydos coastal plain, Western Australia. *Archaeology in Oceania* 44, 70–80.

Cole, N. and David, B. 1990. Rock art and inter-regional interaction in northeastern Australian prehistory. *Antiquity* 64, 788–806.

Cole, N. and Watchman, A. 2005. AMS dating of rock art in the Laura region, Cape York Peninsula, Australia: protocols and results of recent research. *Antiquity* 79, 661–78.

Cosgrove, R. 1995. Late Pleistocene behavioural variation and time trends: the case from Tasmania. *Archaeology in Oceania* 30, 83–104.

Cosgrove, R. and Allen, J. 2001. Prey choice and hunting strategies in the Late Pleistocene: evidence from southwest Tasmania. In A. Anderson, I. Lilley, and S. O'Connor (eds), *Histories of old ages: essays in honour of Rhys Jones*, 397–429. Canberra, ACT: Pandanus Books.

Cutler, K. B., Edwards, R. L., Taylor, F. W., Cheng, H., Adkins, J., Gallup, C. D., Cutler, P. M., Burr, G. S., and Bloom, A. L. 2003. Rapid sea level fall and deep-ocean temperature change since the last interglacial period. *Earth and Planetary Science Letters* 206, 253–71.

David, B. 2002. *Landscapes, rock-art and the Dreaming: an archaeology of preunderstanding*. London: Leicester University Press.

David, B. and Chant, D. 1995. Rock art and regionalisation in North Queensland prehistory. *Memoirs of the Queensland Museum* 37, 357–528.

David, B. and Lourandos, H. 1999. Landscape as mind: land use, cultural space and change in north Queensland prehistory. *Quaternary International* 59, 107–23.

David, B., McNiven, I. J., Attenbrow, V., Flood, J., and Collins, J. 1994. Of Lightning Brothers and white cockatoos: dating the antiquity of signifying systems in the Northern Territory, Australia. *Antiquity* 68, 241–51.

David, B., McNiven, I., Mitchell, R., Orr, M., Haberle, S., Brady, L., and Crouch, J. 2004. Badu 15 and the Papuan-Austronesian settlement of Torres Strait. *Archaeology in Oceania* 39, 65–79.

David, B., Roberts, R. G., Magee, J., Mialanes, J., Turney, C., Bird, M., White, C., Fifield, L. K., and Tibby, J. 2007. Sediment mixing at Nonda Rock: investigations of stratigraphic integrity at an early archaeological site in northern Australia and implications for the human colonisation of the continent. *Journal of Quaternary Science* 22, 449–79.

David, B., Roberts, R., Tuniz, C., Jones, R., and Head, J. 1997. New optical and radiocarbon dates from Ngarrabuligan cave, a Pleistocene archaeological site in Australia: implications for the comparability of time clocks and for the human colonization of Australia. *Antiquity* 71, 183–7.

Davidson, D. S. 1930. Australian spear-thrower traits and their derivation. *Journal of the Polynesian Society* 43, 41–72.

Davidson, D. S. 1933. Australian netting and basketry techniques. *Journal of the Polynesian Society* 42, 257–99.

Davidson, D. S. 1934. Australian spear traits and their derivations. *Journal of the Polynesian Society* 43, 41–72, 143–62.

Davidson, D. S. 1935. Chronology of Australian watercraft. *Journal of Physical Science* 44, 1–63.

Davidson, D. S. 1936a. Australian throwing-sticks, throwing-clubs, and boomerangs. *American Anthropologist* 38, 76–100.

Davidson, D. S. 1936b. Aboriginal Australian and Tasmanian rock carvings and paintings. *American Philosophical Society Memoirs* 5, 1–151.

Davidson, D. S. 1937. A preliminary consideration of Aboriginal Australian decorative art. *American Philosophical Society Memoirs* 9, 1–147.

Davidson, D. S. 1947. Footwear of the Australian Aborigines: environmental vs cultural determinism. *Southwestern Journal of Anthropology* 3, 114–23.

Davidson, D. S. 1948. Disposal of the dead in Western Australia. *Proceedings of the American Philosophical Society* 93, 71–97.

Davidson, I. 1990. Prehistoric Australian demography. In B. Meehan and N. White (eds), *Hunter-gatherer demography: past and present*, 41–58. Sydney: Oceania Monographs.

Davidson, I. 1999a. Symbols by nature: animal frequencies in the Upper Palaeolithic of western Europe and the nature of symbolic representation. *Archaeology in Oceania* 34, 121–31.

Davidson, I. 1999b. The game of the name: continuity and discontinuity in language origins. In B. J. King (ed.), *The origins of language: what nonhuman primates can tell us*, 229–68. Santa Fe, NM: School of American Research.

Davidson, I. 2000. Review of McConvell, P. and N. Evans (eds) 1997. *Archaeology and linguistics: Aboriginal Australia in global perspective*. Oxford University Press, Melbourne. *Archaeology in Oceania* 35, 54–6.

Davidson, I. 2007a. Tasmanian Aborigines and the origins of language. In J. Mulvaney and H. Tyndale-Biscoe (eds), *Rediscovering Recherche Bay*, 69–85. Canberra: Academy of the Social Sciences in Australia.

Davidson, I. 2007b. 'As large as you need and as small as you can': implications of the brain size of Homo *floresiensis*. In A. Schalley and D. Khlentzos (eds), *Mental states: evolution, function, nature*, 35–42. Amsterdam: John Benjamins.

Davidson, I. 2009. Book review of Hiscock, P. 2008. *Archaeology of Ancient Australia*. *Journal of Field Archaeology* 34, 215–18.

Davidson, I. 2010a. Australian archaeology as a historical science. *Journal of Australian Studies* 34, 377–98.

Davidson, I. 2010b. The colonization of Australia and its adjacent islands and the evolution of modern cognition. *Current Anthropology* 51, 177–89.

Davidson, I. 2012. Symbolism and becoming a hunter-gatherer. L'art pléistocène dans le monde / Pleistocene art of the world / Arte pleistoceno en el mundo, Actes du Congrès IFRAO, Tarascon-sur-Ariège, septembre 2010, Symposium « Signes, symboles, mythes et idéologie… ». N° spécial de Préhistoire, Art et Sociétés, Bulletin de la Société Préhistorique Ariège-Pyrénées, *LXV–LXVI*, Book: pp. 292–3, CD: pp. 1689–1705.

Davidson, I. (2013). Peopling the last new worlds: the first colonisation of Sahul and the Americas. *Quaternary International*, 285, 1–29. doi: http://dx.doi.org/10.1016/j.quaint.2012.09.023.

Davidson, I., Cook, N. D. J., Fischer, M., Ridges, M., Ross, J., and Sutton, S. A. 2005. Archaeology in another country: exchange and symbols in North West Central Queensland. In I. Macfarlane, M.-J. Mountain, and R. Paton (eds), *Many exchanges: archaeology, history, community and the work of Isabel McBryde*, 101–28. Canberra: Aboriginal History Inc.

Davidson, I. and Noble, W. 1992. Why the first colonisation of the Australian region is the earliest evidence of modern human behaviour. *Archaeology in Oceania* 27, 135–42.

Davidson, I., Tarragó, I., and Sullivan, T. 2004. Market forces. In V. Donovan and C. Wall (eds), *Making connections: a journey along Central Australian Aboriginal trading routes*, 12–23. Brisbane: Arts Queensland.

Denham, T., Fullagar, R., and Head, L. 2009. Plant exploitation on Sahul: from colonisation to the emergence of regional specialisation during the Holocene. *Quaternary International* 202, 29–40.

Denham, T. and Haberle, S. 2008. Agricultural emergence and transformation in the Upper Wahgi valley, Papua New Guinea, during the Holocene: theory, method and practice. *The Holocene* 18, 481–96.

Denham, T. P., Haberle, S. G., Lentfer, C., Fullagar, R., Field, J., Therin, M., Porch, N., and Winsborough, B. 2003. Origins of agriculture at Kuk Swamp in the Highlands of New Guinea. *Science* 301, 189–93.

Dixon, R. M. W. 1997. *The rise and fall of languages*. Cambridge: Cambridge University Press.

Dortch, C. 1984. *Devil's Lair: a study in prehistory*. Perth: Western Australian Museum.

Evans, N. 1988. Arguments for Pama-Nyungan as a genetic subgroup, with particular reference to initial laminalization. *Aboriginal Linguistics* 1, 90–110.
Evans, N. 2005. Australian languages reconsidered: a review of Dixon (2002). *Oceanic Linguistics* 44, 242–86.
Evans, N. 2006. Comment on Clendon 2006. *Current Anthropology* 47, 53.
Evans, N. and Jones, R. 1997. The cradle of the Pama-Nyungans: archaeological and linguistic speculations. In P. McConvell and N. Evans (eds), *Archaeology and linguistics: Aboriginal Australia in global perspective*, 385–417. Melbourne: Oxford University Press.
Evans, N. and McConvell, P. 1998. The enigma of Pama-Nyungan expansion in Australia. In R. Blench and M. Spriggs (eds), *Archaeology and language II: correlating archaeological and linguistic hypotheses*, 174–92. London: Routledge.
Fairbairn, A., Hope, G. S., and Summerhayes, G. R. 2006. Pleistocene occupation of New Guinea's highland and subalpine environments. *World Archaeology* 38, 371–86.
Field, J., Fillios, M., and Wroe, S. 2008. Chronological overlap between humans and megafauna in Sahul (Pleistocene Australia-New Guinea): a review of the evidence. *Earth-Science Reviews* 89, 97–115.
Flood, J. 2004. Linkage between rock-art and landscape in Aboriginal Australia. In C. Chippindale and G. Nash (eds), *The figured landscapes of rock-art: looking at pictures in place*, 182–200. Cambridge: Cambridge University Press.
Forster, P. and Matsumura, S. 2005. Did early humans go North or South? *Science* 308, 965–6.
Friedlaender, J., Schurr, T., Gentz, F., Koki, G., Friedlaender, F., Horvat, G., Babb, P., Cerchio, S., Kaestle, F., Schanfield, M., Deka, R., Yanagihara, R., and Merriwether, D. A. 2005. Expanding southwest Pacific mitochondrial haplogroups P and Q. *Molecular Biology and Evolution* 22, 1506–17.
Gillieson, D. and Mountain, M.-J. 1983. Environmental history of Nombe rockshelter, Papua New Guinea highlands. *Archaeology in Oceania* 18, 45–53.
Goebel, T., Waters, M. R., and O'Rourke, D. H. 2008. The Late Pleistocene dispersal of modern humans in the Americas. *Science* 319, 1497–502.
Gorman, A. 2008. The primitive body and colonial administration: Henry Ling Roth's approach to body modification. In R. McDougall and I. Davidson (eds), *The Roth family, anthropology and colonial administration*, 93–103. Walnut Creek, CA: Left Coast Press.
Gould, R. A. 1980. *Living archaeology*. Cambridge: Cambridge University Press.
Gould, R. A. 1982. To have and have not: the ecology of sharing among hunter-gatherers. In N. M. Williams and E. S. Hunn (eds), *Resource managers: North American and Australian hunter-gatherers*, 69–91. Washington, DC: American Association for the Advancement of Science.
Gray, R. D., Drummond, A. J., and Greenhill, S. J. 2009. Language phylogenies reveal expansion pulses and pauses in Pacific settlement. *Science* 323, 479–83.
Grayson, D. K. and Meltzer, D. J. 2003. A requiem for North American overkill. *Journal of Archaeological Science* 30, 585–93.
Green, R. E., Krause, J., Briggs, A. W., Maricic, T., Stenzel, U., Kircher, M., Patterson, N., Li, H., Zhai, W., Fritz, M. H.-Y., Hansen, N. F., Durand, E. Y., Malaspinas, A.-S., Jensen, J. D., Marques-Bonet, T., Alkan, C., Prufer, K., Meyer, M., Burbano, H. A., Good, J. M., Schultz, R., Aximu-Petri, A., Butthof, A., Hober, B., Hoffner, B., Siegemund, M., Weihmann, A., Nusbaum, C., Lander, E. S., Russ, C., Novod, N., Affourtit, J., Egholm, M., Verna, C., Rudan, P., Brajkovic, D., Kucan, Z., Gusic, I., Doronichev, V. B., Golovanova, L. V., Lalueza-Fox, C., de la Rasilla, M., Fortea, J., Rosas, A., Schmitz, R. W., Johnson, P. L. F., Eichler, E. E., Falush,

D., Birney, E., Mullikin, J. C., Slatkin, M., Nielsen, R., Kelso, J., Lachmann, M., Reich, D., and Pääbo, S. 2010. A draft sequence of the Neandertal genome. *Science* 328, 710–22.

Habgood, P. J. and Franklin, N. R. 2008. The revolution that didn't arrive: a review of Pleistocene Sahul. *Journal of Human Evolution* 55, 187–222.

Harrison, R. 2009. The archaeology of the Port Hedland coastal plain and implications for understanding the prehistory of shell mounds and middens in northwestern Australia. *Archaeology in Oceania* 44 Supplement, 81–98.

Head, L. 1994. Landscapes socialised by fire: post-contact changes in Aboriginal fire use in northern Australia, and implications for prehistory. *Archaeology in Oceania* 29, 172–81.

Head, L. 1996. Rethinking the prehistory of hunter-gatherers, fire and vegetation change in northern Australia. *The Holocene* 6, 481–7.

Head, L. 2000. *Second nature: the history and implications of Australia as an Aboriginal landscape*. Syracuse: Syracuse University Press.

Head, L. 2008. Is the concept of human impacts past its use-by date? *The Holocene* 18, 373.

Higham, T., Barton, H., Turney, C., Barker, G., Ramsey, C., and Brock, F. 2009. Radiocarbon dating of charcoal from tropical sequences: results from the Niah Great Cave, Sarawak, and their broader implications. *Journal of Quaternary Science* 24, 189–97.

Hiscock, P. 1981. Comments on the use of chipped stone artefacts as a measure of 'intensity of site usage'. *Australian Archaeology* 13, 30–4.

Hiscock, P. 1994. Technological responses to risk in Holocene Australia. *Journal of World Prehistory* 8, 267–92.

Hiscock, P. 2008. *Archaeology of ancient Australia*. London: Routledge.

Hiscock, P. and Faulkner, P. 2006. Dating the Dreaming? Creation of myths and rituals for mounds along the Northern Australian coastline. *Cambridge Archaeological Journal* 16, 209–22.

Hope, G., Kershaw, A. P., van der Kaars, S., Xiangjun, S., Liew, P.-M., Heusser, L. E., Takahara, H., McGlone, M., Miyoshi, N., and Moss, P. T. 2004. History of vegetation and habitat change in the Austral-Asian region. *Quaternary International* 118–19, 103–26.

Hovers, E. 2009. *The lithic assemblages of Qafzeh cave*. New York: Oxford University Press.

Hovers, E., Ilani, S., Bar-Yosef, O., and Vandermeersch, B. 2003. An early case of color symbolism: ochre use by modern humans in Qafzeh cave with CA comment. *Current Anthropology* 44, 491.

Hudjashov, G., Kivisild, T., Underhill, P. A., Endicott, P., Sanchez, J. J., Lin, A. A., Shen, P., Oefner, P., Renfrew, C., Villems, R., and Forster, P. 2007. Revealing the prehistoric settlement of Australia by Y chromosome and mtDNA analysis. *Proceedings of the National Academy of Sciences USA* 104, 8726–30.

Hughes, P. J. and Lampert, R. J. 1982. Prehistoric population change in southern coastal New South Wales. In S. Bowdler (ed.), *Coastal archaeology in eastern Australia*, 16–28. Canberra: Australian National University.

Hunter, J., Bowern, C., and Round, E. 2011. Reappraising the effects of language contact in the Torres Strait. *Journal of Language Contact* 4, 1–35.

Irwin, G. 1992. *The prehistoric exploration and colonisation of the Pacific*. Cambridge: Cambridge University Press.

Jones, M. R. and Torgersen, T. 1988. Late Quaternary evolution of Lake Carpentaria on the Australia-New Guinea continental shelf. *Australian Journal of Earth Sciences* 35, 313–24.

Jones, R. 1969. Firestick farming. *Australian Natural History* 16, 224–8.

Jones, R. 1975. The Neolithic, Palaeolithic and the hunting gardeners: man and land in the Antipodes. In R. P. Suggate and M. M. Cresswell (eds), *Quaternary Studies*, 21–34. Wellington: Royal Society of New Zealand.

Jones, R. and Johnson, I. 1985. Deaf Adder Gorge: Lindner Site, Nauwalabila I. In R. Jones (ed.), *Archaeological Research in Kakadu National Park*, 165–227. Canberra: Australian National Parks and Wildlife Service.

Karafet, T. M., Lansing, J. S., Redd, A. J., Reznikova, S., Watkins, J. C., Surata, S. P., Arthawiguna, W. A., Mayer, L., Bamshad, M., Jorde, L. B., and Hammer, M. F. 2005 Balinese Y-chromosome perspective on the peopling of Indonesia: genetic contributions from pre-neolithic hunter-gatherers, Austronesian farmers, and Indian traders. *Human Biology* 77, 93–114.

Keen, I. 2004. *Aboriginal economy and society: Australia at the threshold of colonisation*. Melbourne: Oxford University Press.

Lambeck, K. and Chappell, J. 2001. Sea level change through the Last Glacial cycle. *Science* 292, 679–86.

Larson, G., Cucchi, T., Fujita, M., Matisoo-Smith, E., Robins, J., Anderson, A., Rolett, B., Spriggs, M., Dolman, G., Kim, T.-H., Thuy, N. T. D., Randi, E., Doherty, M., Due, R. A., Bollt, R., Djubiantono, T., Griffin, B., Intoh, M., Keane, E., Kirch, P., Li, K.-T., Morwood, M., Pedriña, L. M., Piper, P. J., Rabett, R. J., Shooter, P., Van den Bergh, G., West, E., Wickler, S., Yuan, J., Cooper, A., and Dobney, K. 2007. Phylogeny and ancient DNA of *Sus* provides insights into Neolithic expansion in Island Southeast Asia and Oceania. *Proceedings of the National Academy of Sciences USA* 104, 4834–9.

Larson, G., Dobney, K., Albarella, U., Fang, M., Matisoo-Smith, E., Robins, J., Lowden, S., Finlayson, H., Brand, T., Willerslev, E., Rowley-Conwy, P., Andersson, L., and Cooper, A. 2005. Worldwide phylogeography of wild boar reveals multiple centers of pig domestication. *Science* 307, 1618–21.

Latz, P. 1995. *Bushfires and bushtucker*. Alice Springs: Institute of Aboriginal Development.

Leavesley, M. G. 2007. A shark-tooth ornament from Pleistocene Sahul. *Antiquity* 81, 308–15.

Lindsell, P. 2001. Bergmann, Allen and Birdsell: patterns of ecogeographic adaptation in Aboriginal Australians. PhD thesis, Department of Archaeology and Palaeoanthropology, University of New England.

Lorblanchet, M. 1992. The rock engravings of Gum Tree Valley and Skew Valley, Dampier, Western Australia: chronology and functions of the sites. In J. McDonald and I. P. Haskovec (eds), *State of the art: regional rock art studies in Australia and Melanesia*, 39–59. Melbourne: Australian Rock Art Research Association.

Lourandos, H. 1983. Intensification: a late Pleistocene-Holocene archaeological sequence from southwestern Victoria. *Archaeology in Oceania* 18, 81–94.

Lourandos, H. 1997. *Continent of hunter-gatherers: new perspectives in Australian prehistory*. Cambridge: Cambridge University Press.

Lourandos, H. 2008. Constructing 'hunter-gatherers', constructing 'prehistory'. *Australian Archaeology* 67, 69–78.

Lynch, A. H., Beringer, J., Kershaw, P., Marshall, A., Mooney, S., Tapper, N., Turney, C., and Van Der Kaars, S. 2007. Using the paleorecord to evaluate climate and fire interactions in Australia. *Annual Review of Earth and Planetary Sciences* 35, 215–39.

McAdam, L. E. S. 2001. Boomerangs and drainage basins: variation in Aboriginal material culture in the region between Lake Eyre and the Gulf of Carpentaria. Honours thesis, Department of Archaeology and Palaeoanthropology, University of New England.

McAdam, L. E. S. 2008. Beads across Australia: an ethnographic and archaeological view of the patterning of Aboriginal ornaments. PhD thesis, Department of Archaeology and Palaeoanthropology, University of New England.

McArthur, N. 1976. Computer simulations of small populations. *Australian Archaeology* 4, 53–7.

Macaulay, V., Hill, C., Achilli, A., Rengo, C., Clarke, D., Meehan, W., Blackburn, J., Semino, O., Scozzari, R., Cruciani, F., Taha, A., Shaari, N. K., Raja, J. M., Ismail, P., Zainuddin, Z., Goodwin, W., Bulbeck, D., Bandelt, H.-J., Oppenheimer, S., Torroni, A., and Richards, M. 2005. Single, rapid coastal settlement of Asia revealed by analysis of complete mitochondrial genomes. *Science* 308, 1034–6.

McBryde, I. 1987. Goods from another country: exchange networks and the people of the Lake Eyre basin. In D. J. Mulvaney and J. P. White (eds), *Australians to 1788*, 252–73. Sydney: Fairfax, Syme and Weldon.

McConvell, P. 1996. Backtracking to Babel: the chronology of the Pama-Nyungan expansion in Australia. *Archaeology in Oceania* 31, 125–44.

McConvell, P. and Bowern, C. 2011. The prehistory and internal relationships of Australian languages. *Language and Linguistics Compass* 5, 19–32.

McConvell, P. and Smith, M. A. 2003. Millers and mullers: the archaeolinguistic stratigraphy of technological change in Holocene Australia. In H. Andersen (ed.), *Language contacts in prehistory: studies in stratigraphy*, 177–200. Amsterdam: John Benjamins.

McDougall, I., Brown, F. H., and Fleagle, J. G. 2005. Stratigraphic placement and the age of modern humans from Kibbish, Ethiopia. *Nature* 433, 733–6.

McNiven, I. and Hitchcock, G. 2004. Torres Strait Islander marine subsistence specialisation and terrestrial animal translocation. *Memoirs of the Queensland Museum.* Cultural Heritage Series 3, 105–62.

Marshall, B. and Allen, J. 1991. Excavations at Panakiwuk cave, New Ireland. In J. Allen and C. Gosden (eds), *Report of the Lapita Homeland Project*, 59–91. Canberra: Australian National University.

Marwick, B. 2002. Milly's Cave: evidence for human occupation of the Inland Pilbara during the Last Glacial Maximum. In S. Ulm, C. Westcott, J. Reid, A. Ross, I. Lilley, J. Prangnell, and L. Kirkwood (eds), *Barriers, borders, boundaries. Proceedings of the 2001 Australian Archaeological Association Annual Conference*, 21–33. Brisbane: Anthropology Museum, University of Queensland.

Marwick, B. 2009. Change or decay? An interpretation of late Holocene archaeological evidence from the Hamersley Plateau, Western Australia. *Archaeology in Oceania* 44 Supplement, 16–22.

Meehan, B. 1982. *Shell bed to shell midden*. Canberra: Australian Institute of Aboriginal Studies.

Mellars, P. 2006. A new radiocarbon revolution and the dispersal of modern humans in Eurasia. *Nature* 439, 931–5.

Merlan, F. 1989. The interpretive framework of Wardaman rock art: a preliminary report. *Australian Aboriginal Studies* 1989/2, 14–24.

Merriwether, D. A., Hodgson, J. A., Friedlaender, F. R., Allaby, R., Cerchio, S., Koki, G., and Friedlaender, J. S. 2005. Ancient mitochondrial M haplogroups identified in the Southwest Pacific. *Proceedings of the National Academy of Sciences USA* 102, 13034–9.

Miller, G. H., Fogel, M. L., Magee, J. W., Gagan, M. K., Clarke, S. J., and Johnson, B. J. 2005. Ecosystem collapse in Pleistocene Australia and a human role in megafaunal extinction. *Science* 309, 287–90.

Minc, L. D. 1986. Scarcity and survival: the role of oral tradition in mediating subsistence crises. *Journal of Anthropological Archaeology* 5, 39–113.

Mooney, S. D., Harrison, S. P., Bartlein, P. J., Daniau, A. L., Stevenson, J., Brownlie, K. C. et al. 2011. Late Quaternary fire regimes of Australasia. *Quaternary Science Reviews* 30, 28–46.

Morphy, H. 1991. *Ancestral connections: art and an Aboriginal system of knowledge*. Chicago: University of Chicago Press.

Morrison, M. 2003. Old boundaries and new horizons: the Weipa shell mounds reconsidered. *Archaeology in Oceania* 38, 1–8.

Morse, K. 2009. Emerging from the abyss: archaeology in the Pilbara region of Western Australia. *Archaeology in Oceania* 44 Supplement, 1–5.

Morwood, M. J. 1980. Time, space and prehistoric art: a principal components analysis. *Archaeology and Physical Anthropology in Oceania* 15, 98–109.

Morwood, M. J. and Hobbs, D. R. (eds) 1995. *Quinkan prehistory: the archaeology of Aboriginal art in S.E. Cape York Peninsula, Australia*. St. Lucia: Anthropology Museum, University of Queensland.

Morwood, M., Soejono, R. P., Roberts, R. G., Sutikna, T., Turney, C. S., Westaway, K. E., Rink, W. J., Zhao, J. X., van den Bergh, G. D., Due, R. A., Hobbs, D. R., Moore, M. W., Bird, M. I., and Fifield, L. K. 2004. Archaeology and age of a new hominin from Flores in eastern Indonesia. *Nature* 431, 1043–4.

Moy, C. M., Seltzer, G. O., Rodbell, D. T., and Anderson, D. M. 2002. Variability of El Niño/Southern oscillation activity at millennial timescales during the Holocene epoch. *Nature* 420, 162–5.

Mulvaney, D. J. 1976. 'The chain of connection': the material evidence. In N. Peterson (ed.), *Tribes and boundaries in Australia*, 72–94. Canberra: Australian Institute of Aboriginal Studies.

Mulvaney, K. 2009. Dating the Dreaming: extinct fauna in the petroglyphs of the Pilbara region, Western Australia. *Archaeology in Oceania* 44 Supplement, 40–8.

Mulvaney, K. 2013. Iconic imagery: Pleistocene rock art development across northern Australia. *Quaternary International* 285, 99–110.

Mulvaney, K. J. 2011. Murujuga Marni—Dampier Petroglyphs: shadows in the landscape, echoes across time. PhD thesis, School of Humanities, University of New England.

Munn, N. 1973. *Walbiri iconography: graphic representation and cultural symbolism in a Central Australian society*. Ithaca, NY: Cornell University Press.

Nash, D. 1997. Comparative flora terminology of the central Northern Territory. In P. McConvell and N. Evans (eds), *Archaeology and linguistics: Aboriginal Australia in global perspective.*, 187–206. Melbourne: Oxford University Press.

Nicholson, A. and Cane, S. 1994. Pre-European coastal settlement and use of the sea. *Australian Archaeology* 39, 108–17.

O'Connell, J. F. and Allen, J. 2004. Dating the colonization of Sahul (Pleistocene Australia-New Guinea): a review of recent research. *Journal of Archaeological Science* 31, 835–53.

O'Connell, J. F. and Allen, J. 2007. Pre-LGM Sahul (Pleistocene Australia-New Guinea) and the archaeology of early modern humans. In P. Mellars, K. Boyle, O. Bar-Yosef, and C. Stringer (eds), *Rethinking the human revolution: new behavioural and biological perspectives on the origins and dispersal of modern humans*, 395–410. Cambridge: McDonald Institute for Archaeological Research.

O'Connor, S. 2006. Unpacking the island Southeast Asian Neolithic cultural package, and finding local complexity. In E. A. Bacus, I. C. Glover, and V. C. Pigott (eds), *Uncovering Southeast Asia's past*, 74–87. Singapore: Singapore National University Press.

O'Connor, S. 2007a. New evidence from East Timor contributes to our understanding of earliest modern human colonisation east of the Sunda Shelf. *Antiquity* 81, 523–35.

O'Connor, S. 2007b. Revisiting the past: changing interpretations of settlement, subsistence, and demography. In M. Donaldson and K. Kenneally (eds), *Rock art of the Kimberley*, 57–79. Perth: The Kimberley Society.

O'Connor, S. and Fankhauser, B. 2001. Art at 40,000 BP? One step closer: an ochre covered rock from Carpenter's Gap Shelter 1, Kimberley region, Western Australia. In A. Anderson, I. Lilley and S. O'Connor (eds), *Histories of old ages: essays in honour of Rhys Jones*, 287–300. Canberra, Australia: Pandanus Books, Australian National University.

O'Connor, S., Veth, P., and Barham, A. 1999. Cultural versus natural explanations for lacunae in Aboriginal occupation deposits in northern Australia. *Quaternary International* 59, 61–70.

O'Grady, G. and Fitzgerald, S. 1997. Cognate search in the Pama-Nyungan language family. In P. McConvell and N. Evans (eds), *Archaeology and linguistics: Aboriginal Australia in global perspective*, 341–55. Melbourne: Oxford University Press.

Olley, J. M., Roberts, R. G., Yoshida, H., and Bowler, J. M. 2006. Single-grain optical dating of grave-infill associated with human burials at Lake Mungo, Australia. *Quaternary Science Reviews* 25, 2469–74.

Oppenheimer, S. 2004. *Out of Eden: the peopling of the world*. London: Robinson.

Palmer, K. 1977. Myth, ritual and rock art. *Archaeology and Physical Anthropology in Oceania* 12, 38–50.

Pardoe, C. 1995. Riverine, biological and cultural evolution in southeastern Australia. *Antiquity* 69, 696–713.

Partridge, J. 1967. A 3,300 year old Thylacine (Marsupialia: Thylacinidae) from the Nullarbor Plain, Western Australia. *Journal of the Royal Society of Western Australia* 50, 57–9.

Pavlides, C. and Gosden, C. 1994. 35,000-year-old sites in the rainforests of West New Britain, Papua New Guinea. *Antiquity* 68, 604–10.

Pawley, A. 2005. The chequered career of the Trans New Guinea phylum: recent historical research and its implications. In A. Pawley, R. Attenborough, J. Golson, and R. Hide (eds), *Papuan pasts: investigations into the cultural, linguistic and biological history of the Papuan speaking peoples*, 67–108. Canberra: Pacific Linguistics, Australian National University.

Pawley, A. 2007. Recent research on the historical relationships of the Papual languages, or, what does linguistics say about the prehistory of Melanesia. In J. S. Friedlaender (ed.), *Genes, language, and culture history in the Southwest Pacific*, 36–58. Oxford: Oxford University Press.

Pawley, A. and Ross, M. 1993. Austronesian historical linguistics and culture history. *Annual Review of Anthropology* 22, 425–59.

Peterson, N. 1997. Demand sharing: sociobiology and the pressure for generosity among foragers? In F. Merlan, J. Morton, and A. Rumsey (eds), *Scholar and sceptic: Australian Aboriginal studies in honour of L.R. Hiatt*, 171–90, 279–83. Canberra: Aboriginal Studies Press.

Petit, J. R., Jouzel, J., Raynaud, D., Barkov, N. I., Barnola, J.-M., Basile, I., Bender, M., Chappellaz, J., Davis, M., Delayque, G., Delmotte, M., Kotlyakov, V. M., Legrand, M., Lipenkov, V. Y., Lorius, C., Pépin, L., Ritz, C., Saltzman, E., and Stievenard, M. 1999. Climate and atmospheric history of the past 420,000 years from the Vostok ice core, Antarctica. *Nature* 399, 429–36.

Pickup, G. 1991. Event frequency and landscape stability on the floodplain systems of arid Central Australia. *Quaternary Science Reviews* 10, 463–72.

Pope, K. O. and Terrell, J. E. 2008. Environmental setting of human migrations in the circum-Pacific region. *Journal of Biogeography* 35, 1–21.

Reesink, G., Singer, R., and Dunn, M. 2009. Explaining the linguistic diversity of Sahul using population models. *PLoS Biology* 7, e1000241.

Reeves, J. M., Chivas, A. R., Garcia, A., and De Deckker, P. 2007. Palaeoenvironmental change in the Gulf of Carpentaria (Australia) since the last interglacial based on Ostracoda. *Palaeogeography, Palaeoclimatology, Palaeoecology* 246, 163–87.

Reich, D., Green, R. E., Kircher, M., Krause, J., Patterson, N., Durand, E. Y., Viola, B., Briggs, A. W., Stenzel, U., Johnson, P. L. F., Maricic, T., Good, J. M., Marques-Bonet, T., Alkan, C., Fu, Q., Mallick, S., Li, H., Meyer, M., Eichler, E. E., Stoneking, M., Richards, M., Talamo, S., Shunkov, M. V., Derevianko, A. P., Hublin, J.-J., Kelso, J., Slatkin, M., and Pääbo, S. 2010. Genetic history of an archaic hominin group from Denisova cave in Siberia. *Nature* 468, 1053–60.

Ridges, M. 2006. Scale and its effects on understanding regional behavioural systems: an Australian case study. In G. Lock and B. L. Molyneaux (eds), *Confronting scale in archaeology*, 145–61. New York: Springer.

Ridges, M., Davidson, I., and Tucker, D. 2000. The organic environment of paintings on rock. In G. K. Ward and C. Tuniz (eds), *Advances in dating Australian rock-markings. Papers from the first Australian rock-picture dating workshop*, 61–70. Melbourne: Australian Rock Art Association.

Roberts, R. G. 2000. Luminescence dating of Kimberley rock art. In G. L. Walsh (ed.), *Bradshaw art of the Kimberley*, 46–9. Toowong, Queensland: Takarakka Nowan Kas Publications.

Roberts, R. G., Flannery, T. F., Ayliffe, L. K., Yoshida, H., Olley, J. M., Prideaux, G. J., Laslett, G. M., Baynes, A., Smith, M. A., Jones, R., and Smith, B. L. 2001. New ages for the last Australian megafauna: continent-wide extinction about 46,000 years ago. *Science* 292, 1888–92.

Roberts, R. G., Walsh, G., Murray, A., Olley, J., Jones, R., Morwood, M., Tuniz, C., Lawson, E., Macphail, M., Bowdery, D., and Naumann, I. 1997. Luminescence dating of rock art and past environments using mud-wasp nests in northern Australia. *Nature* 387, 696–9.

Ross, J. 2005. Rock art of the red centre. In M. A. Smith and P. Hesse (eds), *23°S. Archaeology and environmental history of the Southern Deserts*, 217–30. Canberra, ACT: National Museum of Australia Press.

Ross, J. 2013. A continent of nations: the emergence of new regionally distinct rock art styles across Australia. *Quaternary International* 285, 161–71.

Ross, J. and Davidson, I. 2006. Rock art and ritual: an archaeological analysis of rock art in arid Central Australia. *Journal of Archaeological Method and Theory* 13, 305–41.

Ross, M. 2005. Pronouns as a preliminary diagnostic for grouping Papuan languages. In A. Pawley, R. Attenborough, J. Golson, and R. Hide (eds), *Papuan pasts: investigations into the cultural, linguistic and biological history of the Papuan speaking peoples*, 15–65. Canberra: Pacific Linguistics, Australian National University.

Satterthwaite, L. and Arthur, B. 2005. Technology and material culture. In B. Arthur and F. Morphy (eds), *Macquarie atlas of Indigenous Australia*, 48–65. North Ryde, NSW: Macquarie University.

Savolainen, P., Leitner, T., Wilton, A. N., Matisoo-Smith, E., and Lundeberg, J. 2004. A detailed picture of the origin of the Australian dingo, obtained from the study of mitochondrial DNA. *Proceedings of the National Academy of Sciences USA* 101, 12387–90.

Schillaci, M. A. 2008. Human cranial diversity and evidence for an ancient lineage of modern humans. *Journal of Human Evolution* 54, 814–26.

Shennan, S. and Collard, M. 2005. Investigating processes of cultural evolution on the north coast of New Guinea with multivariate and cladistic analyses. In R. Mace, C. J. Holden, and

S. Shennan (eds), *The evolution of cultural diversity: a phylogenetic approach*, 133–64. Walnut Creek, CA: Left Coast Press.

Smith, M. A. 2006. Characterising Late Pleistocene and Holocene stone artefact assemblages from Puritjarra rock shelter: a long sequence from the Australian desert. *Records of the Australian Museum* 58, 371–410.

Smith, M. A., Bird, M. I., Turney, C. S., Fifield, L. K., Santos, G. M., Hausladen, P. A., and Di Tada, M. L. 2001. New ABOX AMS-14C ages remove dating anomalies at Puritjarra rock shelter. *Australian Archaeology* 53, 45–7.

Smith, M. A., Williams, A. N., Turney, C. S. M., and Cupper, M. L. 2008. Human–environment interactions in Australian drylands: exploratory time-series analysis of archaeological records. *The Holocene* 18, 389.

Spriggs, M. 2007. The Neolithic and Austronesian expansion within Island Southeast Asia and into the Pacific. In S. Chiu and C. Sand (eds), *From Southeast Asia to the Pacific: archaeological perspectives on the Austronesian expansion and the Lapita cultural complex*, 104–40 Taipei: Academia Sinica.

Stanner, W. E. H. 1979 (1962). Religion, totemism and symbolism. In W. E. H. Stanner (ed.), *White man got no Dreaming: essays 1938–1973*, 106–43. Canberra: Australian National University Press.

Stern, N. 2009. The archaeological signature of behavioural modernity: a perspective from the southern periphery of the modern human range. In J. J. Shea and D. E. Lieberman (eds), *Transitions in Prehistory: essays in honor of Ofer Bar-Yosef*, 258–88. Oxford: Oxbow.

Straus, L. 2005. Comment on Gamble et al. *Cambridge Archaeological Journal* 15, 211–12.

Strehlow, T. G. H. 1970. Geography and the totemic landscape in Central Australia. In R. M. Berndt (ed.), *Australian Aboriginal anthropology*, 92–140. Perth: University of Western Australia Press.

Summerhayes, G. R., Leavesley, M., Fairbairn, A., Mandui, H., Field, J., Ford, A. and Fullagar, R. (2010). Human adaptation and plant use in Highland New Guinea 49,000 to 44,000 years ago. *Science* 330, 78–81.

Surovell, T. A. and Brantingham, P. J. 2007. A note on the use of temporal frequency distributions in studies of prehistoric demography. *Journal of Archaeological Science* 34, 1868–77.

Sutton, P. 1990. The pulsating heart: large scale cultural and demographic processes in Aboriginal Australia. In B. Meehan and N. White (eds), *Hunter-gatherer demography: past and present*, 71–80. Sydney: Oceania.

Sutton, P. 2002. On the translatability of placenames in the Wik region, Cape York Peninsula. In L. Hercus, F. Hodges, and J. Simpson (eds), *The land is a map: placenames of Indigenous origin in Australia*, 75–86. Canberra: Pandanus/Pacific Linguistics.

Szabo, K., Brumm, A., and Bellwood, P. 2007. Shell artefact production at 32,000–28,000 BP in island Southeast Asia: thinking across media? *Current Anthropology* 48, 701–23.

Taçon, P. S. C. 1993. Regionalism in the recent rock art of western Arnhem Land, Northern Territory. *Archaeology in Oceania* 28, 112–20.

Taçon, P. S. C. 2008. Rainbow colour and power among the Waanyi of Northwest Queensland. *Cambridge Archaeological Journal* 18, 163–76.

Taçon, P. S. C., Wilson, M., and Chippindale, C. 1996. Birth of the Rainbow Serpent in Arnhem Land rock art and oral history. *Archaeology in Oceania* 31, 103–24.

Thangaraj, K., Chaubey, G., Kivisild, T., Reddy, A. G., Singh, V. K., Rasalkar, A. A., and Singh, L. 2005. Reconstructing the origin of Andaman Islanders. *Science* 308, 996.

Tindale, N. 1974. *Aboriginal tribes of Australia: their terrain, environmental controls, distribution, limits, and proper names*. Canberra: Australian National University Press.

Tonkinson, R. 1974. *The Jigalong Mob: Aboriginal victors of the desert crusade*. Menlo Park, CA: Cummings.
Turney, C. S. M., Haberle, S., Fink, D., Kershaw, A. P., Barbetti, M., Barrows, T. T., Black, M., Cohen, T. J., Corrège, T., Hesse, P. P., Hua, Q., Johnston, R., Morgan, V., Moss, P., Nanson, G., Ommen, T. V., Rule, S., Williams, N. J., Zhao, J. X., D'Costa, D., Feng, Y. X., Gagan, M., Mooney, S., and Xia, Q. 2006. Integration of ice-core, marine and terrestrial records for the Australian Last Glacial Maximum and Termination: a contribution from the OZ INTIMATE group. *Journal of Quaternary Science* 21, 751–61.
Turney, C. S. M., Kershaw, A. P., Moss, P., Bird, M. I., Fifield, L. K., Cresswell, R. G., Santos, G. M., Tada, M. L. D., Hausladen, P. A., and Zhou, Y. 2001. Redating the onset of burning at Lynch's Crater (North Queensland): implications for human settlement in Australia. *Journal of Quaternary Science* 16, 767–71.
Ulm, S. and Reid, J. 2000. Index of dates from archaeological sites in Queensland. *Queensland Archaeological Research* 12, 1–129.
van Holst Pellekaan, S. 2013. Genetic evidence for the colonization of Australia. *Quaternary International* 285, 44–56.
van Holst Pellekaan, S. M., Ingman, M., Roberts-Thomson, J., and Harding, R. M. 2006. Mitochondrial genomics identifies major haplogroups in Aboriginal Australians. *American Journal of Physical Anthropology* 131, 282–94.
Vandermeersch, B. 1966. Découverte d'un objet en ocre avec traces d'utilisation dans le Moustérien de Qafzeh (Israël). *Bulletin de la Société Préhistorique Française* 66, 157–8.
Vandermeersch, B. 1981. *Les hommes fossiles de Qafzeh (Israël)*. Paris: CNRS.
Veth, P. M. 1989. Islands in the interior: a model for the colonisation of Australia's arid zone. *Archaeology in Oceania* 24, 81–92.
Veth, P., Stern, N., McDonald, J., Balme, J., and Davidson, I. 2011. The role of information exchange in the colonisation of Sahul. In R. Whallon, W. A. Lovis, and R. K. Hitchcock (eds), *Information and its role in hunter-gatherer bands*, 203–20. Los Angeles: Cotsen Institute of Archaeology Press.
Walker, A. and Zorc, R. D. 1981. Austronesian loan words in Yolngu-matha of Northeast Arnhem Land. *Aboriginal History* 5, 109–34.
Walsh, G. L. 2000. *Bradshaw art of the Kimberley*. Toowong, Queensland: Takarakka Nowan Kas Publications.
Walsh, G. L. and Morwood, M. J. 1999. Spear and spearthrower evolution in the Kimberley region, N.W. Australia: evidence from rock art. *Archaeology in Oceania* 34, 45–58.
Watchman, A. 1993. Evidence of a 25,000-year-old pictograph in Northern Australia. *Geoarchaeology* 8, 465–73.
Watchman, A. 2001. Wargata Mina to Gunbilmurrung: the direct dating of Australian rock art. In A. Anderson, I. Lilley, and S. O'Connor (eds), *Histories of old ages: essays in Honour of Rhys Jones*, 313–25. Canberra: Pandanus Books.
Watchman, A. L., David, B., McNiven, I. J., and Flood, J. M. 2000. Micro-archaeology of engraved and painted rock surface crusts at Yiwarlarlay (the Lightning Brothers site), Northern Territory, Australia. *Journal of Archaeological Science* 27, 315–25.
Watson, E., Forster, P., Richards, M., and Bandelt, H. J. 1997. Mitochondrial footprints of human expansions in Africa. *American Journal of Human Genetics* 61, 691–704.
White, J. P., Flannery, T. F., O'Brien, R., Hancock, R. V., and Pavlish, L. 1991. The Balof shelters, New Ireland. In J. Allen and C. Gosden (eds), *Report of the Lapita Homeland Project*, 46–58. Canberra: Australian National University.
White, J. P. and Mulvaney, D. J. 1987. How many people? In D. J. Mulvaney and J. P. White (eds), *Australians to 1788*, 115–17. Broadway, NSW: Fairfax, Syme and Weldon.

White, T. D., Asfaw, B., DeGusta, D., Gilbert, H., Richards, G. D., Suwa, G., and Howell, F. C. 2003. Pleistocene *Homo sapiens* from Middle Awash, Ethiopia. *Nature* 423, 742–7.

Wiessner, P. 2002. The vines of complexity: egalitarian structures and the institutionalization of inequality among the Enga. *Current Anthropology* 43, 233–69.

Wilkins, D. P. and Nash, D. 2008. The European 'discovery' of a multilingual Australia: the linguistic and ethnographic successes of a failed expedition. In W. B. McGregor (ed.), *Encountering Aboriginal languages: studies in the history of Australian linguistics*, 485–507. Canberra: Australian National University.

Williams, A. N. 2013. A new population curve for prehistoric Australia. *Proceedings of the Royal Society B: Biological Sciences* 280. doi: 10.1098/rspb.2013.0486.

Williams, M., Cook, E., van der Kaars, S., Barrows, T., Shulmeister, J., and Kershaw, P. 2009. Glacial and deglacial climatic patterns in Australia and surrounding regions from 35,000 to 10,000 years ago reconstructed from terrestrial and near-shore proxy data. *Quaternary Science Reviews* 28, 2398–419.

Wolfe, P. 1991. On being woken up: the Dreamtime in anthropology and in Australian settler culture. *Comparative Studies in Society and History* 33, 197–224.

Wroe, S. and Field, J. 2006. A review of the evidence for a human role in the extinction of Australian megafauna and an alternative explanation. *Quaternary Science Reviews* 25, 2692–703.

Wroe, S., Field, J. H., Archer, M., Grayson, D. K., Price, G. J., Louys, J., Tyler, F. J., Webb, G. E., Davidson, I., and Mooney, S. D. (2013). Climate change frames debate over the extinction of megafauna in Sahul (Pleistocene Australia-New Guinea). *Proceedings of the National Academy of Sciences.* doi: 10.1073/pnas.1302698110.

Yengoyan, A. P. 1968. Demographic and ecological influences on Aboriginal marriage sections. In R. B. Lee and I. DeVore (eds), *Man the hunter*, 185–99. Chicago: Aldine.

Yokoyama, Y., Purcell, A., Lambeck, K., and Johnston, P. 2001. Shore-line reconstruction around Australia during the Last Glacial Maximum and Late Glacial Stage. *Quaternary International* 83–5, 9–18.

CHAPTER 17

INTO THE AMERICAS
The Earliest Hunter-Gatherers in an Empty Continent

MARCEL KORNFELD AND GUSTAVO G. POLITIS

THE foremost question about early American prehistory is when were the continents occupied? A related question is who were the first hunter-gatherers onto the continents and where did they come from? Finally, a question about the peopling process: how and why did the peopling take place? Hunter-gatherer behaviour and mobility are critical components in answering these questions, particularly the last question concerning process. The gender and ideology of the first Americans are also important but form a relatively minor component of the current debates. To learn when the continents were occupied archaeological research is most useful, but bioarchaeological, genetic, and linguistic data buttress our answers and sometimes drive the search for new data. The origin of the first people onto the continents relies on archaeological data such as artefact styles, types, manufacturing techniques, and faunal association. In addition, global linguistic similarities provide clues to this question as does genetic evidence from DNA and skeletal variability. How and why the Americas were populated depends on large-scale comparisons of archaeological assemblages to infer mobility strategies and the changes in these strategies, as well as modelling cultural (demographic, social, and ideological) processes of low-density human populations.

To the best of our present knowledge the first hominids into the western hemisphere were fully modern humans (*Homo sapiens sapiens*) with fully developed cultural behaviours. Whether the behaviours were within the range of ethnographically described hunter-gatherers or represent all or some behaviours not within the known range is an open debate. Suffice it to say that at least some behaviours are argued to be unique to the groups under specific conditions of people-less or newly peopled continent (Hofman 1994; Kelly and Todd 1988; Rockman and Steele 2003). Also controversial is the timing of their arrival. Except for saying that it was at the end of the Pleistocene, and almost certainly after the Last Glacial Maximum (cf. Madsen 2004), the evidence for a pre-11,000 BP (called pre-Clovis in North America) is scarce (Adovasio and Page 2002; Dillehay 2009; Jenkins 2007; Meltzer 2001; Steele and Politis 2009) and controversial (Borrero 1995; Fiedel 1999; Haynes 2002; Lynch 2001). The controversy lies partially in the lack of a unifying cultural expression in the pre-11,000 BP evidence (12,900 calendar years ago[1]). At present every site and most of human arts appear unique with respect to other temporally related sites as well as possible predecessors or successors. Should this be expected of hunter-gatherers under conditions of extremely low population density, and just how low can the population density be for reproduction (socio-cultural and biological) to continue? Although who, how, and when the Americas were occupied is a topic on which more ink has been spilled than most others, it is unlikely to be resolved soon. Consequently, we briefly review the pre-11,000 BP evidence, and then focus our attention on the lifeways of the earliest foragers, Palaeoindians (Clovis, Folsom, and later complexes in North American and their contemporary counterparts: Fishtails projectile points, El Jobo, Paiján, and others in South America).

Pre-11,000 BP and Peopling Models

Since the establishment of fluted point horizon as a Late Pleistocene human occupation of the Americas and Clovis pre-dating Folsom (Bird 1938; Figgins 1927; Sellards 1952), the possibility of earlier occupations has been entertained. The recent review of Clovis radiocarbon dates (Waters and Stafford 2007) had slightly rejuvenated (by about 400 years) the appearance of this horizon and set this base-line to about 11,000 BP (cf. Haynes et al. 2007). The sites claiming pre-Clovis (pre-11,000 BP) occupation are especially scrutinized by the scientific community, and many have been discredited as providing such evidence on the basis of problematic dating, context (stratigraphy), or artefactual authenticity (Fiedel 1999; Meltzer 1993). The sites mentioned below are some of the current contenders in this debate and are representative of other similar sites.

The current scenario consists of three main competing archaeological models for understanding the early population of America south of the Late Pleistocene ice sheet. The first considers Clovis (about 11,000 BP) as representing the first wave of people entering the continent and expanding south very quickly (Buchanan and Hamilton 2009; Fiedel 2002; Haynes 1992; Martin 1967). The second proposes an early entry (between about 13,000 and 20,000 BP or 15,900 and 23,900 calendar years ago respectively) and a slower rate of expansion (Correal et al. 2005; Dillehay 2009; Fagundes et al. 2008; Lavallée 2003; Miotti 2006). Both models consider that the area of entry was Beringia, but while the first one favours an entry crossing the Ice-Free Corridor (Figure 17.1), the second proposes a littoral migration following the north-western coast of North America (Erlandson 2002; Fladmark 1979; Gruhn 1997). The exception is the recent revival of the Atlantic route by means of watercraft, following the border of the Last Glacial Maximum sea ice (Bradley and Stanford 2004; Greenman 1963; Stanford and Bradley 2006; cf. Goebel 2004; cf. Hamilton and Goebel 1999; cf. Straus et al. 2005). For these authors, people would derive from the Franco Cantabrian Solutrean industries of Europe. A third model proposes that humans entered the Americas before the Last Glacial Maximum (LGM), which means before about 20,000 years ago (23,900 calendar years ago). This model is based on sites such as Pedra Furada (dated between about 50,000 and 6000 BP—54,400 and 6,800 calendar years ago, Parenti 2001, and based on TL dates to more than 100,000 years ago, Valladas et al. 2003) and incorporates the recent findings of Santa Elina in Matto Grosso do Sul, Brazil (14C dated at 22,500 BP or 27,200 calendar years ago and by uranium-thorium to between about 25,000 and 27,000 years ago, Vilhena Vialou

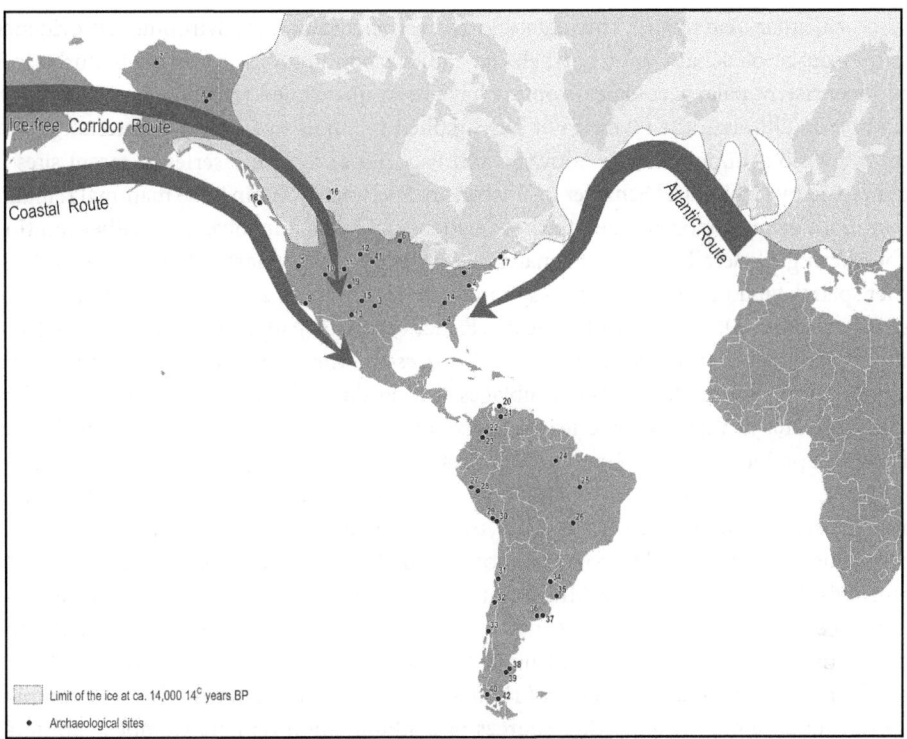

FIGURE 17.1 The Americas with selected early hunter-gatherer sites. In North America: 1–6 pre-11,000 BP, 7–19 fluted point or contemporary (1 Meadowcroft, 2 Cactus Hill, 3 Gault, 4 Page/Ladson, 5 Paisley caves, 6 Schaefer/Hebior, 7 Mesa, 8 Nenana (Swan Point, Broken Mammoth), 9 Arlington Springs/Daisy cave, 10 Sunshine, 11 Fenn, 12 Colby, 13 San Pedro Valley (Murray Springs, Lehner), 14 Adams, 15 Blackwater Draw, 16 Wally's Beach, 17 Debert, 18 On-Your-Knees, 19 Folsom). In South America: 20 Taima-Taima, 21 El Vano, 22 El Abra, Tequendama, Tibitó, 23 Pubenza, 24 Pedra Pintada, 25 Pedra Furada, 26 Santa Elina, 27 Paijan, 28 Guitarrero cave, 29 Qda. Jaguar, 30 Qda. de los Burros, 31 Qda. Sta. Julia, 32 Tagua-Tagua, 33 Monte Verde, 34 Pay Paso, 35 Co. de los Burros, 36 Arroyo Seco 2, 37 Cueva Tixi, Co. la China, Co. El Sombrero, 38 Co. Tres Tetas, Cueva Casa del Minero, 39 Piedra Museo, 40 Cueva del Medio, 41 Hell Gap, 42 Fell and Pali Aike caves.

2005). Among these three models, the first two are the most widely accepted by American archaeologists, while the other is usually rejected. The third model is mostly supported by Brazilian and French archaeologists (e.g. Guidón and Delibrias 1986; Guidón et al. 1994; Parenti 2001; Vilhena Vialou 2005). Moreover, the proposed age of the beginning of the human occupation in the third model does not fit with the most accepted models of *Homo sapiens* dispersal.

In support of the second model and perhaps the longest-running contender for a pre-Clovis site in North America is Meadowcroft shelter in Pennsylvania (Adovasio et al. 1978). The deeply stratified shelter contains unquestionable human artefacts in stratigraphic context to a depth of 2.5 m. The radiocarbon date of the deepest cultural layer is 14,500 BP

(17,600 calendar years ago). This date and the associated palaeoenvironmental evidence are the source of debate. In a nutshell the radiocarbon analysis, potential bioturbation, and inconsistent palaeoecological context have been questioned (Haynes 1991; Kelly 1987; Mead 1980), although the investigator has supplied rebuttals to all of the contested points (e.g. Adovasio et al. 1990; 1998; Adovasio and Page 2002). Another series of recent sites is exemplified by Hebior and Schaefer in Wisconsin. Such sites contain large mammal remains (mammoth or mastodon) argued to show evidence of human involvement, either hunting or butchering. Generally artefactual material is absent (except Schaefer; Joyce 2008) and it is either spatial, taphonomic, or assemblage analysis (Holen 2006; 2008; Holen and May 2002; Johnson 1991; 2008), or the season of death (Fisher 1987) that pattern in a way expected from cultural activities rather than other natural processes. These sites follow a long-standing tradition of identifying lithicless assemblages as a product of cultural behaviour (Stanford and Graham 1985). Yet another series of sites contain lithic assemblages below a well-defined Clovis occupation. As at the Gault site in Texas, the relationship of this lower occupation to Clovis is unclear (Collins 2008; Goodyear 1999; McAvoy and McAvoy 1997; Waters et al. 2011). In particular how much earlier is the lower occupation and could it be an earlier Clovis layer or just bioturbation (Morrow et al. 2012)? Finally, one of the most recent additions to pre-Clovis claim is Paisley Five Mile Point caves (Figure 17.2; Jenkins 2007). The site has yielded a series of human coprolites dating to 12,300 BP (14,400 calendar years ago). The investigative team has gone to great lengths to demonstrate that the results are not affected by modern or ancient contamination (Thomas et al. 2008), but doubts related to complex rock-shelter stratigraphy and other sources of contamination remain. Complex stratigraphy and post-depositional turbative processes plague other sites as well (Cinq-Mars 1979). Of particular interest are a series of early sites in Florida, perhaps best exemplified by Page/Ladson (Dunbar 2006). A few bone and chipped stone artefacts have been found in deeply buried, stratified, and apparently well-dated Pleistocene sequence in a sinkhole, with the artefacts pre-dating 11,000 BP. Although reported, the evidence from these sites is minuscule, with a total of 11 specimens (two bone and nine chipped stone), which by itself requires a full critical assessment.

In South America, supporting the second model are several pre-11,000 BP (12,900 calendar years ago) sites in different stages of investigation, analysis, and publication. It seems that Monte Verde (Dillehay 1997) has passed most of the tests and, although few critics still persist (Fiedel 1999; Haynes 1999), the great majority of archaeologists accepted the human origin of Monte Verde II, dating to approximately 12,500 BP (14,800 calendar years ago; Meltzer et al. 1997).

Another site dated older than 11,000 BP (12,900 calendar years ago) is Arroyo Seco 2, a multi-component open-air locality in the Argentinian Pampas (Fidalgo et al. 1986; Gutiérrez 2004; Politis and Beukens 1991; Politis et al. in press). The early component includes a lithic industry mostly composed of unifacial, marginally retouched quartzite artefacts stratigraphically associated with bone remains of extant and extinct megamammals (*Megatherium americanum*, *Equus neogeus*, *Toxodon* sp., *Glossotherium*, and *Paleolama*; Gutiérrez 2004; Salemme in press). This megafaunal assemblage contains at least three different dates of death for the animals sampled: *Megatherium*, about 12,150 BP (14,200 calendar years ago); *Toxodon*, about 11,750 BP (13,600 calendar years ago); *Equus*, about 11,200 BP (13,100 calendar years ago) (see Steele and Politis 2009). Based on several lines of evidence the researchers consider that the *Megatherium* and *Equus* remains provide evidence

FIGURE 17.2 Paisley cave V (photo courtesy of Dennis Jenkins).

of human activity (Gutiérrez 2004; Politis et al. in press). These show the first human occupation of the site, at about 12,150 BP (14,200 calendar years ago).

Other South American sites, with no diagnostic projectile points, have multiple 14C measurements that appear to be quite consistent, are in good context, and have para-Clovis ages. Two of these sites are Quebrada Santa Julia and Caverna da Pedra Pintada (Figure 17.3 and Figure 17.4). The Quebrada Santa Julia site is in the semi-arid Andean Pacific region of Chile where a recently dated layer yielded a date of 11,024 ± 47 BP (12,900 calendar years ago; Jackson et al. 2007). At the Caverna da Pedra Pintada site, located in Brazilian Amazonia, the Initial A stratum has a basal cultural layer date of 11,077 ± 106 BP (13,000 calendar years ago; Roosevelt et al. 1996). In southern Patagonia an additional key site is Cueva Casa del Minero (10,983 ± 39 BP or 12,900 calendar years ago; Paunero 2003). In the Sierras Centrales in Argentina, at the site El Alto3, there is a date of 11,010 ± 80 BP (12,900 calendar years ago) that needs to be confirmed with more dates (Rivero and Beberian 2006). Sites with similar chronology also occur in other parts of Brazil (Dias 2004; Kipnis 1998). Finally, it is important to note that in South America there is not a Clovis/Folsom counterpart (a unified

FIGURE 17.3 Excavation of the Quebrada Santa Julia site in Chile (photo courtesy of Donald Jackson and César Méndez).

FIGURE 17.4 View of the entrance of the site Caverna da Pedra Pintada (photo courtesy of Anne Roosevelt).

technological entity recurrently associated with the same fauna in a similar set of settings). The closest would be the fishtail projectile points in the Southern Cone, but these points are spatially more restricted and were found in different contexts and associations (see below).

The First Americans from Interdisciplinary Perspective

While the above sites bear on the question of when the Americas were first occupied, who the first Americans were engages several sister disciplines, in particular bioanthropology and linguistics. Craneometric studies demonstrate that in the Americas (particularly in South America) early skulls (i.e. Late Pleistocene-Early Holocene samples) are characterized by a long and narrow cranial vault (dolicocephalic morphology), while more recent populations exhibit a short and wider cranial vault, that is, a brachycephalic morphology (Neves and Pucciarelli 1991; Powell and Neves 1999). Two different hypotheses have been proposed to explain this difference in cranial morphology. On the one hand it has been suggested that these differences could result mainly from random (genetic drift) as well as non-random (directional selection and phenotypic plasticity) factors (Perez and Monteiro 2009; Powell and Neves 1999). On the other hand, it has been explained by the *two main biological components* hypothesis. This hypothesis points out that the morphological diversity of American groups resulted from two successive migrations that generated two morphological components: the first one (called Palaeoamericans) with a long and narrow cranial vault was derived from Pleistocene South Asian groups and the second one (called Amerindian) with a short and wide cranial vault, which migrated from north-east Asia to the Americas during the early Holocene (about 8000 BP) (Neves and Pucciarelli 1991; Pucciarelli et al. 2008).

Teeth and skeletal morphology link the earliest American populations to East and Central Asia, as well as to Australoid populations of the Pacific (Brace et al. 2004; Neves and Pucciarelli 1991; Neves et al. 1998; Powell and Steele 1992; Turner 1983; 2002). Perhaps best represented in East Asia by the modern Ainu, ancient Australoid populations likely gave rise to the first Americans, the modern Ainu, as well as some modern central Asian populations.

Like the osteological evidence, DNA provides similar results. Employing a variety of genetic methods, among them mtDNA, Y chromosome diversity, X chromosome, a variety of identified haplogroups (namely A–D), and specific alleles, all results point to the Central-East Asian origins (specifically the Altai-Baikal region of Siberia) of Native Americans (e.g. Merriwether 2002; Schurr 2004a; 2004b; Schurr and Wallace 1999). The relationship of these populations to the Japanese archipelago is also of interest. Based on the D1 haplogroup, Adachi and colleagues (2009) have linked early Jomon skeletons from the Funadomari site in Hokkaido Island to both the Ainu and Native Americans. They suggest that D1 was brought to Japan by the 'progenitors of the microblade and Mikoshiba cultures during the last "glacial period"' (Adachi et al. 2009, 263). The similarity of Mikoshiba, the Russian Far East mainland Osipovka (Gerasimov 1928), and Clovis technology has been noted (Kornfeld and Tabarev 2009), providing another line of evidence in the appropriate age range as possible proto-Clovis technology. However, the question remains regarding the timing of the genetic split (or the most recent common ancestor, MRCA) and the number of migrations. Early genetic studies integrated well with physical and linguistic evidence (see below) and argue for multiple migrations (e.g. Eshleman et al. 2003; Schurr 2004a); however, more recent results favour one migration (Fagundes et al. 2008), one migration followed by recurrent gene flow (e.g. Bourgeois et al. 2009; Wang et al. 2007), or two migrations (e.g. Perego et al. 2009). The arguments for these different scenarios centre on the nature of genetic diversity, mutation rates, the founder effect, genetic drift, and the effects of population bottlenecks. Most skeletal and genetic evidence is consistent with a number of peopling scenarios.

The timing of the genetic split, i.e. of the MRCA, is equally affected by arguments about the founder effect, mutation rates, genetic drift, and bottlenecks. Whereas earlier models suggested up to 45,000 calendar years for the founding haplogroups (e.g. Bonatto and Salzano 1997; Brown et al. 1998; Forster et al. 1996; Stone and Stoneking 1998), others have suggested that these estimates date the MRCA, the origin of the haplogroups, not the migration into the Americas and have adjusted the migration more in line with the archaeological evidence 12,000–14,000 calendar years ago (Shields et al. 1993; Ward et al. 1991). This coincides with very recent results based on nine-repeat allele that is consistent with a single migration estimated at 12,800 calendar years ago (approximately 11,800 BP; Schroeder et al. 2009).

Compared to geneticists, linguists have been less prolific in contributing to the debate on the first Americans. Nevertheless, historical linguistics provides appropriate results, although the age of the peopling of the Americas may be stretching its methods. The original historical linguistic approach to the peopling of the Americas by Greenberg (1987) defined three language families in the Americas: Amerind, Na-Dene, and Eskimo-Aleut. This corresponded relatively well with results from physical anthropology and the timing provided by archaeology (Greenberg et al. 1986), but appears no longer acceptable to the historical linguists (Hill 2004). Greenberg's method of mass comparison contains potential flaws both in its construction and in his application (Hill 2004). Nichols (1990; 1998; 2002) has more recently proposed four language groups, and thus four migrations into the Americas based on language analysis. Her method is dependent on reasonably well-accepted population markers, i.e. certain shared linguistic features that indicate a genetic relationship or common ancestry (Nichols 1992). Her analysis suggests possible language divergence of the first people as long as 35,000 calendar years ago.

The question in both the Nichols and Greenberg models relates to the expected rates of language change. According to Hill (2004) historical linguistics is plagued by punctualist or uniformitarian assumptions, i.e. how much of language change is determined by uniform rates of change that can be used as constants to calculate time from divergence and how much by socio-cultural and natural context. Clearly both are at play and the Last Glacial Maximum, the Younger Dryas, and the human response to these climatic events may be a major punctuating event (or series of events) that would make any estimates difficult or impossible. Hill (2004) suggests that 8,000 years may be the limit of reliable historical linguistics and thus not in the age range relevant to the question of when the Americas were occupied.

Clovis Foragers and Their Contemporaries

Based on a number of recognized sites, a population explosion occurs just before 11,000 BP (12,900 calendar years ago) in both North and South America. This explosion is

FIGURE 17.5 Examples of early American projectile points. Gainey point courtesy of Julie Morrow. Fishtail projectile points courtesy of Nora Flegenheimer.

accompanied by cultural cohesion, with the fluted projectile point horizon (Figure 17.5); however, this is much more noticeable in North America than in South America. Clovis sites in North America (Anderson and Faught 1998; 2000) are ubiquitous relative to anything earlier (Gainey in the northern Midwest is assumed to be Clovis). Many Clovis sites have been excavated, are well dated (e.g. Waters and Stafford 2007; cf. Haynes 1992; cf. Haynes et al. 2007), and published, but Clovis technology has only recently been fully summarized (Bradley et al. 2010). There are, however, serious questions about whether coeval complexes to Clovis exist in, for example, the Great Basin and the Northwest Plateau. Beck and Jones (2009; see also Bryan 1991) argue on the basis of Sunshine Locality and other Great Basin sites, that some of the Great Basin stemmed varieties of projectile points are coeval with Clovis.

Clovis sites have been typified as mammoth or megafaunal bone beds (e.g. Bilgery 1935; Frison and Todd 1986; Haury 1953; Haury et al. 1959; Hester 1972; Leonhardy 1966), but recently bison bone beds (Bement 2003; Haynes and Huckell 2007) and sites with diverse fauna have been added (e.g. Cannon and Meltzer 2004; Collins 2008; Ferring 2001). Also important are non-bone bed sites representing camps (e.g. Dincauze 1993; Frison 1982; Weber and Agogino 1997), aggregations (Robinson et al. 2009), raw-material procurement sites (Collins 2008; Gardner 1974; Goodyear 1989; Sanders 1990), blade caches (Collins 1999; Kilby 2008), burials (Lahren and Bonnichsen 1974), biface and blade caches (Frison and Bradley 1999; Kilby 2008; Mehringer 1988), and various types of rituals (Deller et al. 2009; Gillespie 2007). These clearly show that Clovis represents a dynamic and complex cultural system with regional specialization and adaptation rather than a monolithic continental cultural entity. Regardless of the regional differences in adaptive strategies and projectile point styles (Morrow and Morrow 1999a; 1999b) and considerable variation in the frequency of fluted artefacts in assemblages, fluting makes an abrupt appearance across the two continents around 11,000 BP (12,900 calendar years ago). However, in South America fluting is rare and there are strong technological differences in the reductions sequence between Clovis/Folsom and the fishtail projectile points (see Nami 1997; 2003). Other contemporaneous South American projectile points do not have any kind of fluting.

The traditional peopling of the Americas model (the first model), partially fuelled by discoveries of association of megafauna and human artefacts, sees groups with Clovis (or proto-Clovis) technology entering the Americas and quickly sweeping through the continents focusing their subsistence on hunting megafauna (Haynes 2002; Martin 1984). The model simultaneously explains the speed of peopling and extinction of the megafauna, but the model has been criticized and some would say disposed (Grayson and Meltzer 2002; 2003; see also Fiedel 2007). One issue that haunts Palaeoindian studies is the focus of Palaeoindian subsistence strategies (e.g. Byers and Ugan 2005; Cannon and Meltzer 2004; Collins and Bousman 1995; Kornfeld 1988; 2007; Kornfeld and Larson 2008; Meltzer and Smith 1988). This is perhaps the most contentious debate of early North American prehistory. Expectations of hunter-gatherer subsistence from ethnographic studies, ecology (Curran 1987; Surovell and Waguespack 2009), and taphonomy are major components of these debates. Although broad diet breadth is generally undeniable for the first foragers of the Americas, as a variety of animal species and some edible plant remains have been recovered from the earliest sites (e.g. Collins 2008; Dillehay 1997; Ferring 2001; Kooyman et al. 2006; McNett 1985; Roosevelt et al. 1996; Waters et al. 2011), specialized sites (bone beds and animal kills) still dominate the literature, but it is less clear whether they dominate the archeological record (Kornfeld 2007; Kornfeld and Larson 2008; Lepper 1999). One site of interest in this regard is Wally's Beach in Alberta, Canada, where the osteological remains contain a wide range of species that include horse, muskox, caribou, and many more (Kooyman et al. 2001), while an even wider range of species is noted in blood protein analysis of Clovis projectile points from the same site (Kooyman et al. 2006). Wally's Beach is of interest because of the diverse fauna that supports broad-spectrum early hunter-gatherer subsistence scenarios, a fauna not commonly associated with early Palaeoindians (horse, muskox, and others), and its location in the Alberta Corridor suggesting the traditional Alaska to North American Plains entry route for the earliest Americans. Wally's Beach as well as other studies of Plains Palaeoindian faunal assemblages (Hill 2007; Johnson 1977) are showing geographic and seasonal variation in subsistence strategies and specialization focus of early hunter-gatherers, leading to a conclusion that neither the earliest nor later Palaeoindians can be characterized monolithically.

Early Foragers of North America

Following Clovis in North America are Goshen and Folsom in the west, but in the south-east Clovis is followed by Cumberland and in the Midwest by the Barnes complex. Although the cultural succession is not well documented stratigraphically anywhere with the possible exception of the Plains, radiocarbon dates and spatial occurrences with respect to continental glaciers are suggestive (Lepper 1999). In the west, Goshen has been found stratigraphically below Folsom at the Hell Gap and Jimmy Pitts sites (Figure 17.6; Irwin-Williams et al. 1973; Larson et al. 2009; Sellet et al. 2009). Too little is yet known about

FIGURE 17.6 The Hell Gap site, Wyoming, under excavation in the 1960s.

Goshen except that the sites include several bison kills (Frison 1996; Kornfeld et al. 1999) as well as camps (Larson et al. 2009; Sellet et al. 2009). Thousands of Folsom sites are known, potentially because of distinctive fluting manufacturing technology (Clark and Collins 2003). Not only can the fluting be differentiated from Clovis, but several stages can easily be identified (Frison and Bradley 1980). This has resulted in numerous cutting-edge studies of Folsom technology and site distributions. For example, Judge's (1973) goal was to demonstrate Palaeoindian hunting strategies with data consisting largely of projectile points and he showed that hunting blinds and other hunting sites were spatially associated with playas in the Middle Rio Grande Valley of New Mexico, where bison would be expected to congregate. Amick (1996), Hofman (1991; 1992; 1999), Ingbar (1992), and others have focused on projectile points to understand Folsom technological organization, including long-distance movement of raw material and its implications for early Palaeoindian high-mobility strategies. Not all Folsom sites, however, show long-distance material transport (Frison and Bradley 1980; Ingbar 1992; Kornfeld 2003; Root et al. 1999), so the high mobility may be geographically, seasonally, or otherwise constrained. Such cutting-edge research deriving broad interpretive potential from projectile points has also increased our understanding of post-Folsom Palaeoindian hunter-gatherers (Jones et al. 2003; Lepper 1999; Pitblado 2003).

Although the Folsom site plays a crucial role in Palaeoindian studies, it was not fully reported until 2006 (Meltzer 2006). The Folsom site is a bison kill and processing location, like others of the same age (Bement and Carter 1999; Jodry 1999). However, Folsom camps are well known and the nature of the Lindenmeier camp has been a point of debate. While Wilmsen and Roberts (1978) suggest that it represents a macroband aggregation, Hofman (1994) questions whether such sites must be a part of the settlement strategy. Structures at Folsom localities represent some of the earliest American domiciles, suggesting a means of protection from harsh weather as well as at least some reduction in residential mobility (e.g. Irwin-Williams et al. 1973; Stiger 2006; Surovell and Waguespack 2007). Folsom workshops occur near quarry locations, sometimes associated with camps (e.g. Frison and Bradley 1980; Surovell et al. 2005), and Folsom blade caches have been reported (Schneider 1982; Tunnell 1978). Much of the Folsom literature fixates on the fluting (e.g. Clark and Collins 2003) because it is rather intricate, variable, and expensive (Winfrey 1990), does not serve any obvious purpose (cf. Ahler and Geib 2000), but its ritual significance has been mentioned frequently (Frison and Bradley 1980; Kornfeld 2006). Compared to Clovis or post-Folsom localities, the Folsom sites appear ubiquitous, occurring in much larger numbers than expected (Kornfeld 2003; Kornfeld and Frison 2000), placing in doubt the meteor impact hypothesis for the end of the Clovis (Firestone et al. 2006; Kennett and West 2008; cf. Holliday and Meltzer 2010).

Just as abruptly as fluting was invented over the two continents, the phenomenon ends in less than 1,500 years or generally before 10,000 BP (11,500 calendar years ago; the Dalton complex notwithstanding; the temporal range of fluted Dalton is not yet completely understood, Kay 2003). Some have postulated a logical link between fluting and peopling (e.g. Gillespie 2007; Kornfeld et al. 2001), but this remains a hypothesis. The next series of cultural complexes in the North American west is still related to Pleistocene fauna (*Bison antiquus*) and thus according to definition by Wormington (1957) Palaeoindian. In the east, the sites following 10,000 BP are generally considered Archaic. Much of what we know about late Palaeoindian foragers is again from Plains bison bone beds, representing either kill or butchery locations, but the story is slowly changing (Walker 2007). In the history of Palaeoindian studies, these sites were the first excavated and reported (e.g. Barbaur and Schultz 1932; Howard 1935; Howard et al. 1941; Jepsen 1953; Roberts 1942; Schultz 1943; Sellards 1938; Sellards et al. 1947). However, from her work at the Lubbock Lake as well as other zooarchaeological analysis, Johnson (e.g. 1977; Johnson and Holiday 2004) long ago noted that other animals are present even at these sites. The restudy of the collections from bison bone beds is yielding significant new information about the variability in Palaeoindian meat procurement strategies (e.g. Hill 2007; Hill 2008; Todd et al. 1990), a strategy that includes insurance caching since Clovis times (e.g. Frison and Stanford 1982; Frison and Todd 1986).

With big-game still dominating in most subsistence scenarios of early hunter-gatherers, men's roles in these early societies are emphasized. This is, however, beginning to change (e.g. Chilton 2004). Some have argued that plants and small animals, thought to be more in purview of women's labour, play a more significant role in Palaeoindian subsistence (e.g. Dillehay 2000; Hudecek-Cuffe 1998; Kornfeld 2007; Kornfeld and Larson 2008), while others see women's hands in the perishable artefacts that rarely survive the ravages of time (Adovasio et al. 2001). Gero (1995; see also Kornfeld 2007; and others) has argued for a perishability factor as responsible for diminishing the visibility of women, but Waguespack (2005) points out that this unfairly ties women to perishable artefacts that might have been manufactured by multiple genders. Waguespack views early hunter-gatherers traditionally as heavily big-game oriented, but suggests that women play crucial roles in the economy of such societies, taking on nearly 100 per cent of all other life-sustaining tasks. Others have argued that perhaps women's roles in hunting are underemphasized because hunting itself needs re-evaluating. That is, hunting should be viewed as a process that begins with monitoring game, planning, constructing entrapment or other facilities, driving animals, killing, skinning, butchering, and perhaps ending with distribution of meat and feasting (Kornfeld

2003; Kornfeld and Francis 1991). Women's roles in such a process are much more clearly defined.

EARLY FORAGERS OF SOUTH AMERICA

The scenario in South America is quite different from that in North America. However, as in the North, the pre-11,000 BP (12,900 calendar years ago) sites are very different from each other and do not form a clear pattern. They probably represent an early stage of occupation of the region, but the information is so spread apart that it is extremely difficult to connect them and see common traits. What seems to be clear is that shortly after 11,000 BP (12,900 calendar years ago) most of the main regions in South America shows strong human signals and at this time some regional trends can be seen. The most significant is the fishtail projectile point (FTPP) 'horizon' (Figure 17.5), which is based on a particular type of stemmed projectile point with rounded shoulders and an expanding stem termination (Bird 1969, 56–7; Nami 1997; Politis 1991). This type of point is distributed throughout the Southern Cone, roughly between the 25° and 50° south latitudes and has been found in different settings including multicomponent cave and rock-shelter sites, such as the first sites where these points were defined, Fell and Pali Aike (Bird 1988), Cueva del Medio (Nami and Nakamura 1995), Cueva Tixi (Mazzanti and Quintana 2001), Cerro La China (Flegenheimer and Zárate 1997), and Cerro El Sombrero Alero 1 (Flegenheimer 2003); open-air sites on hilltops, such as Cerro El Sombrero (Flegenheimer 2003), Cerro Amigo Oeste (Miotti et al. 2010), and Cerro los Burros (Meneghin 2005; Nami 2007); borders of ancient lagoons, rivers, or creeks (Tagua-Tagua, Nuñez et al. 1994; Paso Otero 5, Martínez 2006; Estancia La Suiza, Laguens et al. 2007), and others. Among these sites, Cerro El Sombrero Cima is most interesting because of the sheer number of fishtail points (more than a hundred), with both complete and fragmentary pieces (usually stems) recovered. Most of the complete FTPPs were very small and poorly made. The entire hilltop was interpreted as a gearing-up location, where people were producing and replacing points in the haft (Flegenheimer 2003), and where sub-adults played and learned technological skills (Politis 1998). The recently discovered site of Cerro Amigo Oeste in Northern Patagonia, where more than a hundred complete and fragmented FTPPs were found on the hilltop, suggests a similar situation to Cerro El Sombrero (Miotti et al. 2010).

Some FTPPs have been found in northern South America as isolated surface finds (e.g. Jaimes 1999). The most notable case is El Inga in highland Ecuador, where FTPPs were found on the surface along with a variety of other projectile point types (Mayer-Oakes 1986). Chronology and association between the different types of points at El Inga is not clear (Mayer-Oakes 1986; Nami 2002), thus it is difficult to evaluate whether the FTTPs are chronologically and culturally related with their Southern Cone counterparts, or whether they belong to an independent tradition (Borrero 1983).

With a few exceptions, the chronological span of FTPPs is restricted to between 10,800 and 10,200 BP (12,800 and 11,900 calendar years ago). The dates older than 11,000 BP occur as outliers (in Cueva del Medio for example, see discussion in Nami and Nakamura 1995) or the association with FTPP is not yet properly published (e.g. the date of 11,690 BP, i.e. 13,900 calendar years ago, from Cerro Los Burros, Meneghin 2006). The one early Holocene date of 8060 BP (8,900 calendar years ago) from Cerro El Sombrero Abrigo 1 (Flegenheimer and Zárate 1997) can also be considered an outlier. In Pampa and Patagonia these points do not seems to co-occur with other projectile point types and it is not yet clear which types follow. Only in Uruguay the FTPPs seem to be coeval with other defined models of stemmed projectile points: the K87, dated between about 10,400 and 9700 BP (Suárez 2009). While for some archaeologists the FTPP is a derivation of Clovis and Folsom (Fiedel 2002; Morrow and Morrow 1999a), for others the FTPP is the result of an independent regional technological tradition (Borrero 1983; Bryan and Gruhn 2003; Miotti 2003; Nami 1997; Politis 1991).

The FTPPs are usually associated with extinct mega-mammals, suggesting that they were the tools used to kill these animals. Two species of mega-mammals frequently associated with FTPPs are the American horse (*Equus* and *Hippidion*) and ground sloth (*Mylodon*, but see Borrero and Martin 2012). However, other extinct mammals occasionally associated with FTPPs are mastodon (*Stegomastodon*) in the central valley of Chile and *Eutatus* in the Tandilia mountain range of Argentina. And at Patagonian sites, the modern guanaco (*Lama guanicoe*) is found with FTPP, indicating that it too was a preferred prey.

The other possible early technological tradition in South America is defined by the El Jobo projectile points (Figure 17.5). The selanceolate, unstemmed projectile points are usually found in surface assemblages in north-western Venezuela. However, two similar points were found in Monte Verde, suggesting a long distance connection. Nevertheless, a similar but independent technological process could explain these kinds of isolated similarities, thousands of kilometres apart.

In the arid lands of Venezuela, El Jobo points occur at Taima-Taima (Ochsenius et al. 1979) associated with mastodon and dated between about 12,400 and 12,600 BP (14,600–15,000 calendar years ago). However, these dates, processed in the 1970s, have not been replicated with modern techniques and should be interpreted with caution. At another site, Los Vanos (Jaimes 1999), broken El Jobo points were found associated with giant ground sloth (*Eremotherium*) and dated to 10,710 BP (12,700 calendar years ago).

To the west, the sites in the Savanna de Bogotá, El Abra, and Tequendama caves and the open-air site Tibitó show the 'abriense' and 'tequendamiense' technological tradition (Ardila and Politis 1989; Correal and Van del Hammen 1977) and none of them contain projectile points or other diagnostic artefacts. While the Late Pleistocene sequences in the cave sites indicate the exploitation of medium- and small-size fauna (such as deer and rodents) in Tibitó, there is a good association with mastodon and American horse (Correal 1981). Among these sites, two have early dates: Tibitó 11,740 ± 110 BP (13,600 calendar years ago) and El Abra 10,720 ± 400 and 12,400 ± 160 BP (12,400 and 14,600 calendar years ago respectively; Gnecco and Aceituno 2004).

In northern South America a variety of supposedly Late Pleistocene projectile point types are found in different surface settings. These include FTPP, Paiján, Broad Stem, and even Clovis-like in the Paraguaná Peninsula (e.g. Ardila and Politis 1989; Jaimes 1999). For Gnecco and Aceituno (2004, 160) the proliferation of point types indicates a slow process of human dispersal into the region which results in such a 'speciation' of material culture. In the Rio Magdalena Valley a distinctive, triangular projectile point type with a narrow stem (locally called Restrepo, see López 2004) contributes to this morphological and technological variability. In several sites dated at about 10,400 BP (12,200 calendar years ago), Lopez (2004) also recovered faunal remains, such as bone of manatee, turtles, caiman, and a variety of fish, all indicating a strong, at least seasonal adaptation to riverine environments.

In western South America, both in the Andes and along the coast, new discoveries are indicating occupation by at least 11,000 BP (Aldenderfer 2008; Dillehay et al. 2003; Lavallée 2003; Sandweiss 2008). The history of occupations of Guitarrero cave, Pachamachay, Puente, Telarmachay, and Asana, all in the Peruvian Andes, shows the early peopling of high-elevation as starting between 11,000 and 9500 BP (Aldenderfer 2008). On the coast, Chauchat (1992) has shown that at about 12,000 years ago the Paiján sites in northern Peru represent an inland adaptation with seashore contacts. The multi-component site of the Quebrada Jaguay in southern Peru indicates a domestic centre for fishermen who targeted corvine or sea bass family and wedge clams during the Jaguay Phase (about 13,000 to 11,400 calendar years ago) (Sandweiss et al. 1998). These sites, along with others such as the Quebrada Tacahuay and Quebrada de los Burros, indicate a Late Pleistocene use of the marine resources. However, the known sites contain few finished artefacts and no human skeletons to compare for cultural relationships (Sandweiss 2008).

The South American Late Pleistocene sites do not show the classic North American big-game hunting model. Although mega-mammals, mostly mastodon, giant ground sloth, ground sloth, and *Equus* are present in a number of sites (e.g. Arroyo Seco 2, Cueva del Medio, Tibitó, Tagua-Tagua, El Vano, Taima-Taima, Piedra Museo, Tres Arroyos, and Paso Otero 5), these are always represented by low numbers of individuals compared with their North American counterparts. Moreover it is not clear which species have been hunted, scavenged, or are in the sites due to natural processes. In addition, many other sites show a subsistence based on aquatic resources (QJ-280, Quebrada Tacahuay), riverine resources (e.g. La Palestina, San Juan de Bedout, Nare), hunting of small and medium-size terrestrial mammals (such as at Tequendama, El Abra, and Pedra Pintada), and there is increasing evidence of plant exploitation and possible manipulation (Dillehay 1997; Piperno and Stother 2003). Although all of this differs from the classic North American big-game hunting model, it is not significantly different from recent reinterpretations of early North American foragers (e.g. Byers and Ugan 2005; Collins and Bousman 1995; Hill 2007; Kornfeld and Larson 2008). Moreover, the model that proposed the sudden extinction of big game at the end of the Pleistocene does not fit with the South American data. Several sites in the Pampas show that some Pleistocene genera including the giant ground sloth and some glyptodonts such as *Doedicurus*, *Neosclerocalyptus*, and giant armadillos like *Eutatus* survived into the early Holocene (Gutiérrez and Martínez 2008; Politis and Messineo 2008).

Conclusion

The answer to the first question (when were the Americas first occupied by hunter-gatherers?) is still unresolved. However, there is significant evidence of people on the continent prior to 11,000 BP (12,900 calendar years ago), evidence that diminishes precipitously by 12,500 BP (14,800 calendar years ago). How long prior to this people were in the Americas is difficult to say, except that it was likely following the Last Glacial Maximum. On the other hand, it is quite apparent that by the same time hunter-gatherers were in South as well as North America. Consequently, their prior arrival at point or points of entry, all of which are to the north, must precede by thousands of years.

There is significantly more agreement on the question of where the first hunter-gatherers arrived from. With the exception of a few researchers favouring the Franco-Cantabrian region of Europe, virtually all evidence points to *Homo sapiens sapiens* expanding through and then out of Asia and into the Americas. Linguistic as well as biological evidence corroborates on East or Central Asian origin of the first Americans, with some suggesting a South Asian origin.

The question of how and why the peopling occurred is still unresolved and probably irresolvable without a firm commitment as to when the event(s) occurred. Nevertheless, once on the continent, hunter-gatherers settled in and adopted a wide variety of subsistence, settlement, and technological strategies. Subsistence included the hunting of mega-mammals, the exploitation of aquatic and riverine resources, and the gathering of plant products complemented with the procurement of medium- and small-sized mammals. Residential mobility likely also ranged between relatively high and low strategies, perhaps approaching permanent settlement, depending on the season and regional resource structure. Technology likewise ranged from some North American Palaeoindian biface-focused groups to others with a low emphasis on biface production and little standardization.

Finally, it is important to mention that the occupation of the Americas was only possible due to the great exploratory curiosity and high adaptive flexibility of the first hunter-gatherers who entered the continent at the end of the Pleistocene. Thanks to these characteristics they populated the whole continent in a few millennia and they became well adapted to the many different environments they encountered.

Note

1. Where possible, dates are reported as uncorrected radiocarbon years before the present (BP) as well as best estimate (CalPal calibration: http://www.calpal-online.de/) calendar years ago. The latter is necessary for comparative purposes with non-radiocarbon (TL, uranium-thorium) dates and dates used in publications of related fields (linguistics, genomics; e.g. years since the last common ancestor means calendar years ago or years ago).

References

Adachi, N., Shinoda K., Umetsu K., and Matsumura K. 2009. Mitochondrial DNA analysis of Jomon skeletons from the Funadomari Site, Hokkaido, and its implications for the origin of Native American. *American Journal of Physical Anthropology* 138, 255–65.

Adovasio, J. M., Donahue, J., Pedler, D. R., and Stuckenrath R. 1998. Two decades of debate on Meadowcroft rockshelter. *North American Archaeologist* 19, 317–41.

Adovasio, J. M., Donahue, J., and Stuckenrath, R. 1990. The Meadowcroft rockshelter radiocarbon chronology 1975–1990. *American Antiquity* 55, 348–54.

Adovasio, J. M., Gunn, J. D., Donahue, J., Stuckenrath, R., Guilday, J., and Lord, K. 1978. Meadowcroft rockshelter. In A. L. Bryan (ed.), *Early man in America*, 140–80. Edmonton: University of Alberta.

Adovasio, J. M., Hyland, D. C., and Soffer, O. 2001. Perishable technology and early human populations in the New World. In J. Gillespie, S. Tupakka, and C. de Millie (eds), *On being first: cultural consequences of first peopling*, 201–22. Calgary: University of Calgary.

Adovasio, J. M. and Page, J. 2002. *The first Americans: in pursuit of archaeology's greatest mystery*. New York: Random House.
Ahler, S. A. and Geib, P. R. 2000. Why flute? Folsom point design and adaptation. *Journal of Archaeological Science* 27, 799–820.
Aldenderfer, M. 1999. The Pleistocene/Holocene transition in Perú and its effects upon human use of the landscape. *Quaternary International* 53/54, 11–19.
Aldenderfer, M. 2008. High elevation foraging societies. In H. Silverman and W. Isbell (eds), *Handbook of South American archaeology*, 131–44. Dordrecht: Springer.
Amick, D. S. 1996. Regional patterns of Folsom mobility and land use in the American Southwest. *World Archaeology* 27, 411–26.
Anderson, D. G. and Faught, M. K. 1998. The distribution of fluted Paleoindian: projectile points: update 1998. *Archaeology of Eastern North America* 26, 163–87.
Anderson, D. G. and Faught, M. K. 2000. Paleoindian artifact distributions: evidence and implications. *Antiquity* 74, 507–13.
Ardila, G. and Politis, G. 1989. Nuevos datos para un viejo problema: investigación y discusión en torno al poblamiento de América del Sur. *Revista del Museo del Oro* 23, 3–45.
Barbaur, E. H. and Schultz, C. B. 1932. *The Scottsbluff Bison Quarry and its artifacts*. Lincoln: Nebraska State Museum.
Beck, C. and Jones, G. T. 2009. *The archaeology of the eastern Nevada Paleoarchiac: part I, the Sunshine Locality*. Salt Lake City: University of Utah Press.
Bement, L. 2003. Field work at the Jake Bluff and certain sites. *Oklahoma Archaeological Survey Newsletter* 22, 1–2.
Bement, L. C. and Carter, B. J. 1999. *Bison hunting at Cooper Site: where lightning bolts drew thundering herds*. Norman: University of Oklahoma Press.
Bilgery, C. 1935. *Evidence of Pleistocene man in Denver Basin: a preliminary report*. Denver, CO: Manuscript on file at the Office of the State Archaeologist.
Bird, J. 1938. Antiquity and migration of early inhabitants of Patagonia. *Geographical Review* 28, 250–75.
Bird, J. 1969. A comparison of South Chilean and Ecuadorean 'fishtail' projectile points. *The Kriger Anthropological Society Papers* 40, 52–71.
Bird, J. 1988. *Travels and archaeology in South Chile*. Iowa City: University of Iowa Press.
Bonatto, S. L. and Salzano, F. M. 1997. A single and early migration for the peopling of the Americas supported by mitochondrial DNA sequence data. *Proceedings of the National Academy of Sciences USA* 94, 1866–71.
Borrero, L. 1983. Distribuciónes discontínuas depuntas de proyectil en Sudamérica. Vancouver, Canada: Paper presented at the 11th International Congress of Anthropological and Ethnological Sciences.
Borrero, L. 1995. Human and natural agency: some comments on Pedra Furada. *Antiquity* 69, 602–3.
Borrero, L. and Martin, F. 2012. Ground sloths and humans in southern Fuego-Patagonia: taphonomy and archaeology. *World Archaeology* 44, 102–17.
Bourgeois, S., Yotova, V., Wang, S., Bourtoumieu, S., Moreau, C. Michalski, R., Moisan, J.-P., Hill, K., Hurtado, A. M., Ruiz-Linares, A., and Labuda, D. 2009. X-chromosome lineages and the settlement of the Americas. *American Journal of Physical Anthropology*. Published on line.
Brace, C. L., Nelson, A. R., and Qifeng, P. 2004. Peopling of the New World: a comparative craniofacial view. In C. M. Barton, G. A. Clark, D. R. Yesner, and G. A. Pearson (eds), *The settlement of the American continents*, 28–38. Tucson: University of Arizona Press.

Bradley, B. A., Collins, M. B., and Hemmings, A. 2010. *Clovis technology*. Ann Arbor: International Monographs in Prehistory.

Bradley B. A. and Stanford, D. J. 2004. The North Atlantic ice-edge corridor: a possible Palaeolithic route to the New World. *World Archaeology* 36, 459–578.

Brown, M. D., Hosseini, S. H., Torroni, A., Bandelt, H. J., Allen, J. C., Schurr, T. G., Scozzari, R., Cruciani, F., and Wallace, D. C. 1998. mtDNA Haplogroup X: an ancient link between Europe/Western Asia and North America? *American Journal of Human Genetics* 63, 1852–61.

Bryan, A. L. 1991. The fluted point tradition in the Americas—one of several adaptations to late Pleistocene American environments. In R. Bonnichsen and K. L. Turnmire (eds), *Clovis: origins and adaptations*, 15–33. Corvallis: Oregon State University, Center for the Study of the First Americans.

Bryan, A. L. and Gruhn, R. 2003. Some difficulties in modeling the original peopling of the Americas. *Quaternary International* 109–10, 175–9.

Buchanan, B. and Hamilton, M. 2009. A formal test of the origin of variation in North American early Paleoindian projectile points. *American Antiquity* 74, 279–98.

Byers, D. A. and Ugan, A. 2005. Should we expect large game specialization in the late Pleistocene? An optimal foraging perspective on Early Paleoindian prey choice. *Journal of Archaeological Science* 32, 1624–40.

Cannon, M. D. and Meltzer, D. J. 2004. Paleoindian foraging: examining the faunal evidence for large mammal specialization and regional variability in prey choice. *Quaternary Science Reviews* 23, 1955–87.

Chauchat, C. 1992. *Prehistoire de la Côte Nord du Perou: le Paijanien du Cupisnique*. Paris: CNRS.

Chilton, E. S. 2004. Beyond 'big': gender, age, and subsistence diversity in Paleoindian societies. In C. M. Barton, G. A. Clark, D. R. Yesner, and G. A. Pearson (eds), *The settlement of the American continents*, 162–72. Tucson: University of Arizona Press.

Cinq-Mars, J. 1979. Bluefish Cave I: a late Pleistocene eastern beringian cave deposit in the northern Yukon. *Canadian Journal of Archaeology* 3, 1–32.

Clark, J. E. and Collins, M. B. (eds) 2003. *Folsom technology and lifeways*. Tulsa: Department of Anthropology, University of Tulsa, Oklahoma.

Collins, M. B. 1999. *Clovis blade technology*. Austin: University of Texas Press.

Collins, M. B. 2008. Update on the Gault Site Texas. Austin, Texas. Paper presented at the Paleoamerican Origins Workshop, 14–16 February.

Collins, M. B. and Bousman, B. (organizers) 1995. Rethinking Paleoindian subsistence on the southern Plains. Minneapolis, Minnesota: Symposium organized for the 60th Annual Meeting of the Society for American Archaeology.

Correal Urrego, G. 1981. *Evidencias culturales y megafauna pleistocénica en Colombia*. Bogotá: Fundación de Investigaciones Arqueológicas Nacionales, Banco de la República.

Correal Urrego, G., Gutiérrez Olano, J., Calderón, K., and Villada Cardozo, D. 2005. Evidencias arqueológicas y megafauna extinta en un salado del tardiglacial superior. *Boletín de Arqueología* 20, 1–58.

Correal Urrego, G. and Van der Hammen, T. 1977. *Investigaciones arqueológicas en los Abrigos Rocosos del Tequendama*. Bogotá: Biblioteca Banco Popular.

Curran, M. L. 1987. The spatial organization of Paleoindian populations in the late Pleistocene of the Northeast. PhD thesis. Ann Arbor, Michigan, University of Massachusetts.

Deller, B. D., Ellis, C. J., and Keron, J. R. 2009. Understanding cache variability: a deliberately burned early Paleoindian tool assemblage from the Crowfield site, southwestern Ontario, Canada. *American Antiquity* 74, 371–97.

Dias, A. S. 2004. Diversificar para poblar: el contexto arqueológico brasileño en la transición Pleistoceno-Holoceno. *Complutum* 15, 249–63.

Dillehay, T. D. 1997. *Monte Verde: a late Pleistocene settlement of southern Chile*. Washington, DC: Smithsonian Institution.

Dillehay, T. D. 2000. *The settlement of the Americas: a New Prehistory*. New York: Basic Books.

Dillehay, T. D. 2009. Probing deeper into the first American studies. *Proceedings of the National Academy of Sciences USA* 106, 971–8.

Dillehay, T., Rossen, J., Maggard, G., Stackelbelck, K., and Netherly, P. 2003. Localization and possible social aggregation in the Late Pleistocene and Early Holocene in the north coast of Perú. *Quaternary International* 109–10, 3–11.

Dincauze, D. F. 1993. Fluted points in the eastern forests. In O. Soffer and N. D. Praslov (eds), *From Kostenki to Clovis: problems in late Paleolithic adaptations*, 279–92. New York: Plenum Press.

Dunbar, J. S. 2006. Paleoindian archaeology. In S. D. Webb (ed.), *The first Floridians and last Mastodons*, 403–34. Dordrecht: Springer.

Erlandson, J. M. 2002. Anatomically modern humans, maritime adaptations, and the peopling of the New World. In N. Jablonski (ed.), *The first Americans: the Pleistocene colonization of the New World*, 59–92. San Francisco: Memoirs of the California Academy of Sciences.

Eshleman, J. A., Malhi, R. S., and Smith, D.G. 2003. Mitochondrial DNA studies of Native Americans: conceptions and misconceptions of the population prehistory of the Americas. *Evolutionary Anthropology* 12, 7–18.

Fagundes, N., Kanitz, R., Eckert, R., Valls, A. C., Bogo, M., Salzano, F., Smith, D. G., Silva, W. A. Jr, Zago, M. A., Ribeiro-dos-Santos, A. K., Santos, K. S. B., Petzl-Erler, M. L., and Bonatto, S. 2008. Mitochondrial population genomics support a single pre-Clovis origin with a coastal route for the peopling of the Americas. *American Journal of Human Genetics* 82, 583–92.

Ferring, C. R. (ed.) 2001. *The archeology and paleoecology of the Aubrey Clovis Site (41DN479) Denton County, Texas*. University of Texas, Denton: Center for Environmental Archaeology.

Fidalgo, F., Guzmán, L. M., Politis, G., Tonni, E., and Salemme, M. 1986. Investigaciones arqueológicas en el sitio 2 de Arroyo Seco (Partido de Tres Arroyos, Provincia de Buenos Aires, República Argentina). In A. Bryan (ed.), *New evidence for the peopling of America*, 221–70. Orono, ME: Center for the Study of Early Man.

Fiedel, S. J. 1999. Artifact provenience at Monte Verde: confusion and contradictions. *Scientific American Discovering Archaeology* 1, 1–12.

Fiedel, S. J. 2002. Initial human colonization of the Americas: an overview of the issues and the evidence. *Radiocarbon* 44, 407–36.

Fiedel, S. J. 2007. Quacks in the ice: waterfowl, Paleoindians and the discovery of America. In R. B. Walker and B. N. Driskell (eds), *Foragers of the terminal Pleistocene in North America*, 1–14. Lincoln: University of Nebraska Press.

Figgins, J. D. 1927. The antiquity of man in America. *Natural History* 27, 229–39.

Firestone, R., West, A., and Warwick-Smith, S. 2006. *The cycle of cosmic catastrophes: how a stone-age comet changed the course of world culture*. Rochester, VT: Bear and Company.

Fisher, D. C. 1987. Mastodon procurement by Paleoindians of the Great Lakes region: hunting or scavenging? In M. H. Nitecki and D. V. Nitecki (eds), *The evolution of human hunting*, 309–21. New York: Plenum Press.

Fladmark, K. 1979. Routes: alternate migration corridors for early man in North America. *American Antiquity* 44, 55–69.

Flegenheimer, N. 2003. Cerro El Sombrero: a locality with a view. In L. Miotti, M. Salemme, and N. Flegenheimer (eds), *Where the south winds blow: ancient evidence of Paleo South Americans*, 51–6. College Station: Center for the Study of the First Americans, Texas A&M University.

Flegenheimer, N. and Zárate, M. 1997. Considerations on radiocarbon and calibrated dates from Cerro La China and Cerro El Sombrero, Argentina. *Current Research in the Pleistocene* 14, 27–8.

Forster, P., Harding, R., Torroni, A., and Bandelt, H. J. 1996. Origin and evolution of Native American mtDNA variation: a reappraisal. *American Journal of Human Genetics* 59, 935–45.

Frison, G. C. 1982. The Sheaman site: a Clovis component. In G. C. Frison and D. J. Stanford (eds), *The Agate Basin site*, 143–57. New York: Academic Press.

Frison, G. C. (ed.) 1996. *The Mill Iron site*. Albuquerque: University of New Mexico Press.

Frison, G. C. and Bradley, B. 1980. *Folsom tools and technology of the Hanson site, Wyoming*. Albuquerque: University of New Mexico Press.

Frison, G. C. and Bradley, B. 1999. *The Fenn cache, Clovis weapons and tools*. Santa Fe: One Horse Land and Cattle Company.

Frison, G. C. and Stanford, J. 1982. Agate Basin components. In G. C. Frison and D. J. Stanford (eds), *The Agate Basin site*, 76–135. New York: Academic Press.

Frison, G. C. and Todd, L. C. 1986. *The Colby mammoth site*. Albuquerque: University of New Mexico Press.

Gardner, W. M. 1974. *The flint run Paleoindian complex: a preliminary report 1971–1973 season*. Washington, DC: Catholic University of America, Occasional Paper No. 1, Archaeology Laboratory.

Gerasimov, M. M. 1928. New sites of the stone period man near Khabarovsk. *News of the East Siberian Department of the Russian State Geographical Society* 53, 141 (in Russian).

Gero, J. 1995. Railroading epistemology: Paleoindians and women. In I. Hodder, M. Shanks, A. Alexandri, V. Buchli, J. Carman, J. Last, and G. Lucas (eds), *Interpreting archaeology*, 175–80. New York: Routledge.

Gillespie, J. D. 2007. Enculturing an unknown world: caches and Clovis landscape ideology. *Canadian Journal of Archaeology* 31, 171–89.

Gnecco, C. and Aceituno, J. 2004. Poblamiento temprano y espacios antropogénicos en el norte de Suramérica. *Complutum* 15, 151–64.

Goebel, T. 2004. The search for a Clovis progenitor in sub-arctic Siberia. In D. B. Madsen (ed.), *Entering America: Northeast Asia and Beringia before the Last Glacial Maximum*, 311–56. Salt Lake City: University of Utah Press.

Goodyear, A. C. 1989. A hypothesis for the use of cryptocrystalline raw material among Paleoindian groups of North America. In C. J. Ellis and J. C. Lothrop (eds), *Eastern Paleoindian lithic resource use*, 1–9. Boulder Westview Press.

Goodyear, A. C. 1999. Results of the 1999 Allandale Paleoindian Expedition. *Legacy* 4, 8–13.

Grayson, D. K. and Meltzer, D. J. 2002. Clovis hunting and large mammal extinction: a critical review of the evidence. *Journal of World Prehistory* 16, 313–59.

Grayson, D. K. and Meltzer, D. J. 2003. A requiem for North American overkill. *Journal of Archaeological Science* 30, 585–93.

Greenberg, J. H. 1987. *Language in the Americas*. Stanford, CA: Stanford University Press.

Greenberg, J. H., Turner, C. G., and Zegura, S. L. 1986. The settlement of the Americas: a comparison of the linguistic, dental, and genetic evidence. *Current Anthropology* 27, 477–88.

Greenman, E. 1963. The Upper Palaeolithic and the New World. *Current Anthropology* 4, 41–91.

Gruhn, R. 1997. Language classification and models of the peopling of the Americas. In P. McConvell and N. Evans (eds), *Archeology and linguistics: Aboriginal Australia in global perspective*, 99–110. Melbourne: Oxford University Press.

Guidon, N. and Delibrias, G. 1986. Carbon-14 dates point to man in the Americas 32,000 years ago. *Nature* 321, 769–71.

Guidon, N., Parenti, F., da Luz, M. F., Guérin, C., and Faure, M. 1994. Le plus ancient peuplement de l'Amérique: le Paleolithique du Nordeste brésilien. *Bulletin de la Société préhistorique française* 91, 246–50.

Gutiérrez, M. 2004. Análisis tafonómicos en el área Interserrana (Provincia de Buenos Aires). PhD thesis. Universidad Nacional de La Plata, Argentina.

Gutiérrez, M. and Martínez, G. 2008. Trends in the faunal human exploitation during the late Pleistocene and early Holocene in the Pampean region (Argentina). *Quaternary International* 191, 53–68.

Hamilton, T. D. and Goebel, T. 1999. Late Pleistocene peopling of Alaska. In R. Bonnichsen and K. L. Turnmire (eds), *Ice age peoples of North America* 156–99. Corvallis: University of Oregon Press.

Haury, E. W. 1953. Artifacts with mammoth remains, Naco, Arizona. *American Antiquity* 19, 1–14.

Haury, E. W., Sayles, E. B., and Wasley, W. W. 1959. The Lehner mammoth site, southeastern Arizona. *American Antiquity* 25, 2–30.

Haynes, C. V., Jr. 1991. More on Meadowcroft radiocarbon chronology. *Review of Archaeology* 12, 8–14.

Haynes, C. V., Jr. 1992. Contributions of radiocarbon dating to the geochronology of the peopling of the New World. In R. E. Taylor, A. Long, and R. S. Kra (eds), *Radiocarbon after four decades*, 355–74. New York: Springer-Verlag.

Haynes, C. V., Jr. 1999. Monte Verde and the pre-Clovis situation in America. *Scientific American Discovering Archaeology*, Special Report: Monte Verde Revisited. November/December, 17–19.

Haynes, C. V., Jr. and Huckell, B. B. (eds) 2007. *Murray Springs*. Tucson: Anthropological Papers of the University of Arizona Press No. 71.

Haynes, G. 2002. *The early settlement of North America*. Cambridge: Cambridge University Press.

Haynes, G., Anderson, D. G., Ferring, C. R., Fiedel, S. J., Grayson, D. K., Haynes, C. V., Jr., Holliday, V. T., Huckell, B. B., Kornfeld, M., Meltzer, D. J., Morrow, J., Surovell, T., Waguespack, N. M., Wigand, P., and Yohe, R. M., II. 2007. Comment on 'redefining the age of Clovis: implications for the peopling of the Americas.' *Science* 317, 320b.

Hester, J. J. (ed.) 1972. *Blackwater Locality No. 1: a stratified early man site in eastern New Mexico*. Ranchos de Taos, New Mexico: Fort Burgwin Research Center.

Hill, J. H. 2004. Evaluating historical linguistics for ancient human communities in the Americas. In C. M. Barton, G. A. Clark, D. R. Yesner, and G. A. Pearson (eds), *The settlement of the American continent*, 39–47. Tucson: University of Arizona Press.

Hill, M. E. 2007. A movable feast: variation in faunal resource use among centrals and western North American Paleoindian sites. *American Antiquity* 72, 417–38.

Hill, M. G. 2008. *Paleoindian subsistence dynamics on the northwestern Great Plains*. Oxford: British Archaeological Reports International Series 1756.

Hofman, J. L. 1991. Folsom land use: projectile point variability as a key to mobility. In A. Montet-White and S. Holen (eds), *Raw material economies among prehistoric hunter gatherers*, 335–55. Lawrence: University of Kansas Publications in Anthropology 19.

Hofman, J. L. 1992. Recognition and interpretation of Folsom technological variability on the southern Plains. In D. J. Stanford and J. Day (eds), *Ice Age hunters of the Rockies*, 193–224. Niwot: University of Colorado Press.

Hofman, J. L. 1994. Paleoindian aggregations on the Great Plains. *Journal of Anthropological Archaeology* 13, 341–70.

Hofman, J. L. 1999. Folsom fragments, site types, and assemblage formation. In D. S. Amick (ed.), *Folsom lithic technology*, 122–43. Ann Arbor: International Monographs in Prehistory.

Holen, S. R. 2006. Taphonomy of two Last Glacial Maximum mammoth sites in the central Great Plains of North America: a preliminary report on La Sena and Lovewell. *Quaternary International* 142–3, 30–43.

Holen, S. R. 2008. La Sena, Nebraska and Lovewell, Kansas sites, 18,000 C14 years BP. Paper presented at Paleoamerican Origins Workshop, Texas Archaeological Research Laboratory, Austin, Texas.

Holen, S. R. and May, D. W. 2002. The La Sena and Shaffer mammoth sites: history of investigations 1987–1998. In D. C. Roper (ed.), *Medicine Creek*. Tuscaloosa: University of Alabama Press.

Holliday, V. T. and Meltzer, D. J. 2010. The 12.9 ka ET impact hypothesis and North American Paleoindians. *Current Anthropology* 51, 575–607.

Howard, E. B. 1935. Evidence of early man in North America. *The Museum Journal* 24, 2–3.

Howard, E. B., Satterwaite, L., Jr., and Bache, C. 1941. Preliminary report on a buried Yuma site in Wyoming. *American Antiquity* 7, 70–4.

Hudecek-Cuffe, C. 1998. *Engendering Northern Plains Paleoindian archaeology*. Oxford: BAR International Series S699.

Ingbar, E. I. 1992. The Hanson site and Folsom on the Northwestern Plains. In D. J. Stanford and J. S. Day (eds), *Ice Age hunters of the Rockies*, 169–92. Niwot, CO: Denver Museum of Natural History and University of Colorado Press.

Irwin-Williams, C., Irwin, H. T., Agogino, G., and Haynes, C. V. 1973. Hell Gap: Paleo-Indian occupation on the High Plains. *Plains Anthropologist* 18, 40–53.

Jackson, D., Méndez, C., Seguel, R., Maldonado, A., and Vargas, G. 2007. Initial occupation of the Pacific coast of Chile during late Pleistocene times. *Current Anthropology* 48, 725–31.

Jaimes, A. 1999. Nuevas evidencias de cazadores-recolectores y aproximación al entendimiento al uso del espacio geográfico en el occidente de Venezuela: sus implicaciones en el contexto suramericano. *Arqueología del Area Intermedia* 1, 83–120.

Jenkins, D. L. 2007. Distribution and dating of cultural and paleontological remains at Paisley Five Mile Point caves in Northern Great Basin: an early assessment. In K. E. Graf and D. N. Schmitt (eds), *Paleoindian or Paleoarchaic: Great Basin human ecology at the Pleistocene-Holocene transition*, 57–81. Salt Lake City: University of Utah Press.

Jepsen, G. L. 1953. Ancient buffalo hunters of northwestern Wyoming. *Southwestern Lore* 19, 19–25.

Jodry, M. A. 1999. *Folsom technological organization and socioeconomic strategies*. PhD thesis. American University, Washington, DC.

Johnson, E. 1977. Animal food resources of Paleoindians. In E. Johnson (ed.), *Paleoindian lifeways*, 65–77. Lubbock, TX: The Museum Journal XVII, Western Texas Museum Association.

Johnson, E. 1991. Late Pleistocene cultural occupation on the southern Plains. In R. Bonnichsen and K. L. Turnmire (eds), *Clovis origins and adaptations*, 215–36. Corvallis: Oregon State University, Center for the Study of the First Americans.

Johnson, E. 2008. Hebior and Mud Lake sites, Wisconsin 12,500-13,500 14C yr BP. Paper presented at the Paleoamerican Origins Workshop, Texas Archaeological Research Laboratory. 14–16 February, Austin, Texas.

Johnson, E. and Holliday, V. T. 2004. Archaeology and Late Quaternary environments of the southern High Plains. In T. K. Pertulla (ed.), *Prehistory of Texas*, 283–95. College Station: Texas A&M University Press.

Jones, G. T., Beck, C., Jones, E. E., and Hughes, R. E. 2003. Lithic source use and paleoarchaic foraging territories in the Great Basin. *American Antiquity* 68, 5–38.

Joyce, D. 2008. Schaefer site, Wisconsin. Austin, Texas. Paper presented at the Paleoamerican Origins Workshop, Texas Archaeological Research Laboratory, 14–16 February.

Judge, J. J. 1973. *Paleoindian occupation of the Central Rio Grande Valley in New Mexico*. Albuquerque: University of New Mexico Press.

Kay, M. 2003. New radiocarbon dates for Dalton at Rodgers Shelter, Missouri. Paper presented at the 61st Plains Anthropological conference, Fayetteville, Arkansas, 22–25 October.

Kelly, R. L. 1987. A comment on the pre-Clovis deposits at Meadowcroft rockshelter. *Quaternary Research* 27, 332–4.

Kelly, R. L. and Todd, L. C. 1988. Coming into the country: early Paleoindian hunting and mobility. *American Antiquity* 53, 231–44.

Kennett, J. P. and West, A. 2008. Biostratigraphic evidence supports Paleoindian population disruption at ~12.9 ka. *Proceedings of the National Academy of Sciences USA* 105, E110.

Kilby, D. J. 2008. *An investigation of Clovis caches: content, function, and technological organization*. PhD thesis. Department of Anthropology, University of New Mexico, Albuquerque.

Kipnis, R. 1998. Early hunter-gatherers in the Americas: perspectives from central Brazil. *Antiquity* 72, 581–92.

Kooyman, B., Hills, L. V., McNeil, P., and Tolman, S. 2006. Late Pleistocene horse hunting at the Wally's Beach site (DhPg-8), Canada. *American Antiquity* 71, 101–21.

Kooyman, B., Newman, M. E., Cluney, C., Lobb, M., Tolman, S., McNeil, P., and Hills, L. V. 2001. Identification of horse exploitation by Clovis hunters based on protein analysis. *American Antiquity* 66, 686–91.

Kornfeld, M. 1988. The Rocky Foolsm site: a small Folsom assemblage from the Northwestern Plains. *North American Archaeologist* 9, 197–222.

Kornfeld, M. 2003. *Pull of the hills, landscape archaeology and Great Plains foraging economy*. Oxford: BAR International Series 1106.

Kornfeld, M. 2006. Paleoindian social strategies and the socio-techno-ideology of fluting. In S. Purin (ed.), *Préhistoire de l'Amérique/American Prehistory*, 71–7. Oxford: BAR International Series S1524.

Kornfeld, M. 2007. Are Paleoindians of the Great Plains and the Rocky Mountains subsistence specialists? In R. B. Walker and B. N. Driskell (eds), *Foragers of the Terminal Pleistocene in North America*, 32–58. Lincoln: University of Nebraska Press.

Kornfeld, M. and Francis, J. E. 1991. A preliminary historical outline of Northwestern High Plains gender systems. In D. Walde and Noreen D. Willows (eds), *Gender in archeology*, 444–51. Alberta: University of Calgary.

Kornfeld, M. and Frison, G. C. 2000. Paleoindian occupation of the high country: the case of the Middle Park of Colorado. *Plains Anthropologist* 47, 129–53.

Kornfeld, M., Frison, G. C., Larson, M. L., Miller, J. C., and Saysette, J. 1999. Paleoindian Bison procurement and paleoenvironments in the Middle Park of Colorado. *Geoarchaeology* 14, 655–74.

Kornfeld, M., Harkin, M., and Durr, J. 2001. Landscapes and peopling of the Americas. In J. C. Gillespie, S. Tupakka, and C. de Mille (eds), *On being first: presenting the first peoples in the Americas*, 149–62. Calgary: The Archeological Association of the University of Calgary.

Kornfeld, M. and Larson, M. L. 2008. Bonebeds and other myths: Paleoindian to Archaic transition on the North American Great Plains and Rocky Mountains. *Quaternary International* 191, 18–33.

Kornfeld, M. and Tabarev, A. 2009. The French connection? Or is it? *Current Research in the Pleistocene* 26, 78–81.

Laguens, A., Pautassi, E. A., Sario, G. M. and Cattáneo, R. 2007. ELS1, a Fishtail Projectile-Point site from Central Argentina. *Current Research in the Pleistocene* 24, 55–7.

Lahren, L. A. and Bonnichsen, R. 1974. Bone foreshafts from a Clovis burial in southwestern Montana. *Science* 186, 147–50.

Larson, M. L., Kornfeld, M., and Frison, G. C. (eds) 2009. *Hell Gap: a stratified Paleoindian campsite at the edge of the Rockies*. Salt Lake City: University of Utah Press.

Lavallée, D. 2000. *The first South Americans*. Salt Lake City: University of Utah Press.

Lavallée, D. 2003. The first peopling of the South Pacific American coast during the Pleistocene/Holocene transition—a case study: the prehistoric campsite. In L. Miotti, M. Salemme, and N. Flegenheimer (eds), *Where the south winds blow: ancient evidence of Paleo South Americans*, 17–20. College Station: Texas A&M University, Center for the Study of the First Americans.

Leonhardy, F. 1966. *Domebo: a Paleo-Indian mammoth kill in the prairie-plains*. Lawton, OK: Contribution No. 1, Museum of the Great Plains.

Lepper, B. T. 1999. Pleistocene peoples of midcontinental North America. In R. Bonnichsen and K. L. Turnmire (eds), *Ice Age peoples of North America*, 362–94. Corvallis: Oregon State University Press.

López, C. 2004. Landscape development and the evidence for early human occupation in the inter-Andeantropical lowlands of the Magdalena River, Colombia. PhD thesis. Temple University, Philadelphia, Pennsylvania.

Lynch, T. 2001. On the road again...reflections on Monte Verde. *Review of Archaeology* 22, 39–43.

McAvoy, J. M. and McAvoy, L. D. 1997. *Archaeological investigations of Site 44SX202, Cactus Hill, Sussex County, Virginia*. Richmond: Research Report No. 8, Virginia Department of Historic Resources.

McNett, C. W., Jr. (ed.) 1985. *Shawnee Minisink: a stratified Paleoindian-Archaic site in the Upper Delaware Valley of Pennsylvania*. Orlando: Academic Press.

Madsen, D. B. (ed.) 2004. *Entering America: Northeast Asia and Beringea before the Last Glacial Maximum*. Salt Lake City: University of Utah Press.

Martin, P. S. 1967. Prehistoric overkill. In P. S. Martin and H. E. Wright, Jr. (eds), *Pleistocene extinctions: the search for a cause*, 75–120. New Haven: Yale University Press.

Martin, P. S. 1984. Prehistoric overkill: the global model. In P. S. Martin and R. G. Klein (eds), *Quaternary extinctions*, 354–403. Tucson: University of Arizona Press.

Martínez, G. A. 2006. Arqueología del curso medio del río Quequén Grande: estado actual y aportes a la arqueología de la región pampeana. *Relaciones* 31, 249–76.

Mayer-Oakes, W. 1986. El Inga: a Paleoindian site in the Sierra of northern Ecuador. *Transactions of the American Philosophical Society* 76, 235.

Mazzanti, D. and Quintana, C. (eds) 2001. *Cueva Tixi: cazadores y recolectores de las sierras de Tandilia Oriental. 1 Geología, Paleontología y Zooarqueología*. Universidad Nacional de Mar del Plata, Argentina: Publicación especial 1.

Mead, J. I. 1980. Is It really that old? A comment about the Meadowcroft 'overview'. *American Antiquity* 45, 579–82.

Mehringer, P. J., Jr. 1988. Clovis cache found: weapons of ancient Americans. *National Geographic* 174, 500–3.

Meltzer, D. J. 1993. *Search for the first Americans*. Montreal: St. Remy Press.

Meltzer, D. J. 2001. Why we still don't know when the first people came to North America. In J. Gillespie, S. Tupakka, and C. De Mille (eds), *On being first: cultural innovation and environmental consequences of the first peopling*, 1–25. Calgary: Archaeological Association of the University of Calgary.

Meltzer, D. J. 2006. *Folsom*. Berkeley: University of California Press.

Meltzer, D. J., Grayson, D., Ardila, G., Barker, A. W., Dincauze, D., Haynes, C. V., Jr., Mena, F., Nuñez, L., and Stanford, D. J. 1997. On the Pleistocene antiquity of Monte Verde, southern Chile. *American Antiquity* 62, 659–63.

Meltzer, D. J. and Smith, B. D. 1988. Paleoindian and Early Archaic subsistence strategies in eastern North America. In S. Neusius (ed.), *Foraging, collecting, and harvesting: archaic period subsistence and settlement in the eastern woodlands*, 3–31. Carbondale, IL: Center for Archaeological Investigations, Southern Illinois University.

Meneghin, U. 2005. Yacimientos arqueológicos tempranos del Uruguay. *Orígenes* 3, 1–23.

Meneghin, U. 2006. Un nuevo resgistro radiocarbónico (c-14) en el yacimiento Urupez II, Maldonado, Uruguay. *Orígenes* 5, 1–18.

Merriwether, D. A. 2002. A mitochondrial perspective on the peopling of the New World. In N. G. Jablonski (ed.), *The first Americans: the Pleistocene colonization of the New World*, 295–310. San Francisco: Memoirs of the California Academy of Sciences 27.

Miotti, L. 2003. Patagonia: a paradox for building images of the first Americans during the Pleistocene/Holocene Transition. *Quaternary International* 109–10, 147–73.

Miotti, L. 2006. La fachada atlántica, como puerta de ingreso alternativa de la colonización humana de América del Sur durante la transición Pleistoceno/Holoceno. In J. C. Jiménez López (ed.), *2do. Simposio Internacional del Hombre Temprano en América*, 56–188. Mexico: INAPL.

Miotti, L., Hermo D., and Terranova, E. 2010 Fishtail points: first evidence of Late Pleistocenic hunter-gatherers in Somuncurá plateau (Rio Negro province, Argentina). *Current Research in the Pleistocene* 27, 22–4.

Morrow, J. E., Fiedel, S. J., Kornfeld, M., Johnson, D. L., Rutledge, M., and Wood, W. R. 2012. Pre-Clovis in Texas: a critical assessment of the Buttermilk Creek Complex. *Journal of Archaeological Science* 39, 3677–82.

Morrow, J. E. and Morrow, T. A. 1999a. Geographic variation in fluted projectile points: a hemispheric perspective. *American Antiquity* 64, 215–31.

Morrow, T. A. and Morrow, J. E. 1999b. On the fringe: Folsom points and performs in Iowa. In D. S. Amick (ed.), *Folsom lithic technology*, 65–81. Ann Arbor: International Monographs in Prehistory.

Nami, H. 1997. Investigaciones actualísticas para discutir aspectos técnicos de los cazadores-recolectores del tardiglacial: el problema Clovis-Cueva Fell. *Anales del Instituto de la Patagonia. Serie Ciencias Humanas* 25, 151–86.

Nami, H. 2002. An AMS 14C date from the Late-Pleistocene deposit in the Ilaló region, Eduador: implications for the highland Paleoindian occupation. *Current Research in the Pleistocene* 19, 70–2.

Nami, H. 2003. Experimentos para explorar la secuencia de reducción Fell de la Patagonia Austral. *Magallania* 31, 107–38.

Nami, H. 2007. Research in the Middle Negro River Basin (Uruguay) and the Paleoindian occupation of the Southern Cone. *Current Anthropology* 48, 164–74.

Nami, H. and Nakamura, T. 1995. Cronología radiocarbónica con AMS sobre muestras de hueso procedentes del sitio Cueva del Medio. *Anales del Instituto de la Patagonia* 23, 125–33.

Neves, W. A., Powell, J. F., Prous, A., and Pucciarelli, H. M. 1998. Lapa Vermelha IV, Hominid 1: morphological affinities of the earliest known American. *American Journal of Physical Anthropology* 26, 169.

Neves, W. A. and Pucciarelli, H. M. 1991. Morphological affinities of the first Americans: an exploratory analysis based on early South American human remains. *Journal of Human Evolution* 21, 261–73.

Nichols, J. 1990. Linguistic diversity and the first settlement of the New World. *Language* 66, 475–521.
Nichols, J. 1992. *Linguistic diversity in space and time*. Chicago: University of Chicago Press.
Nichols, J. 1998. *The first four discoveries of America: linguistic evidence*. Paper presented at the 1998 Annual Meeting of the American Association for the Advancement of Science, Philadelphia, PA.
Nichols, J. 2002. The first American languages. In N. G. Jablonski (ed.), *The first Americans: the Pleistocene colonization of the New World*, 273–94. San Francisco: Memoirs of the California Academy of Sciences 27.
Nuñez, L., Varela, J., Casamiquela, R., Schiappacasse, V., Niemeyer, H., and Villagrán, C. 1994. Cuenca de Tagua-Tagua en Chile: el ambiente del Pleistoceno y ocupaciones humanas. *Revista Chilena de Historia Natural* 67, 503–19.
Ochsenius, C. and Gruhn, R. 1979. *Taima-Taima: a Late Pleistocene Paleoindian hill site in northernmost South America*. Universidad Francisco de Miranda, Coro: Programa CIPICS, Monografías Científicas.
Parenti, F. 2001. *Le Gisement Quaternaire de Pedra Furada (Piaui, Brasil): stratigraphie, chronologie, évolution culturelle*. Paris: Éditions Recherche sur les Civilisations.
Paunero, R. 2003. The presence of a Pleistocene colonizing culture in La Maria archaeological locality: Casa del Minero 1. In L. Miotti, M. Salemme, and N. Flegenheimer (eds), *Where the south winds blow: ancient evidence of Paleo South Americans*, 127–32. College Station: Texas A&M University, Center for the Study of the First Americans.
Perego, U. A., Achilli, A., Angerhoffer, N., Accetturo, M., Pala, M., Olivieri, H., Kashani, B. H., Ritchie, K. H., Scozzari, R., Kong, Q. P., Myres, N. M., Salas, A., Semino, O., Bandelt, H. J., Woodward, S. R., and Torroni, A. 2009. Distinctive Paleo-Indian migration routes from Beringia marked by two rare mtDNA haplogroups. *Current Biology* 19, 1–8.
Perez, S. I. and Monteiro, L. R. 2009. Non-random factors in modern human morphological diversification: a study of variation in southern South American populations. *Evolution* 69, 978–93.
Piperno, D. and Stother, K. 2003. Phytolith evidence for Early Holocene *Cucurbita* domestication in southwest Ecuador. *Science* 299, 1054–7.
Pitblado, B. L. 2003. *Late Paleoindian occupation of the southern Rocky Mountains*. Boulder: University of Colorado Press.
Politis, G. G. 1991. Fishtail projectile points in the southern cone of South America: an overview. In R. Bonnichsen and K. L. Turnmire (eds), *Clovis origins and adaptations*, 287–301. Oregon State University, Corvallis: Center for the Study of the First Americans.
Politis, G. G. 1998. Arqueología de la infancia: una perspective etnoarqueológica. *Trabajos de Prehistoria* 55, 5–20.
Politis, G. G. and Beukens, R. 1991. Cronología de la ocupación humana de la región Pampeana. *Actas del X Congreso Nacional de Arqueología Argentina*. Tomo 2. Catamarca.
Politis, G. G., Gutiérrez, M., and Scabuzzo, C. (eds) In press. *Estado actual de las investigaciones en el sitio Arroyo Seco 2 (Partido de Tres Arroyos, Provincia de Buenos Aires, Argentina)*. Universidad del Centro de la Provincia de Buenos Aires, Olavarría, Argentina: Serie Monográfica INCUAPA 5.
Politis, G. G. and Messineo P. 2008. The Campo Laborde site: new evidence of the Holocene survival of Pleistocene megamammals in the Argentine pampas. *Quaternary International* 191, 94–114.
Politis, G. G., Scabuzzo, C., and Tykot, R. 2009. An approach to prehispanic diets in the pampas during early/middle Holocene. *International Journal of Osteoarchaeology* 19, 208–66.

Powell, J. F. and Neves W. A. 1999. Craniofacial morphology of the first Americans: pattern and process of the peopling of the New World. *Yearbook of Physical Anthropology* 42, 153–88.

Powell, J. F. and Steele, D. G. 1992. A multivariate craniometric analysis of North American Paleoindian remains. *Current Research in the Pleistocene* 9, 59–62.

Pucciarelli, H., Neves, W. A. González-José, R, Sardi M. L., and Ramirez-Rozzi, F. 2008. East-west cranial differentiation in pre-Columbian populations from North and Central America. *Journal of Human Evolution* 54, 296–308.

Rivero, D. and Berberián, E. 2006. El poblamiento inicial de las Sierras Centrales de Argentina: las evidencias arqueológicas tempranas. *Cazadores-recolectores del Cono Sur* 1, 127–38.

Roberts, F. H. H. 1942. Archeological and geological investigations in the San Jon District, eastern New Mexico. *Smithsonian Miscellaneous Collections* 103, 1–30.

Robinson, B. S., Ort, J. C., Eldridge, W. E., Burke, A. L., and Pelletier, B. G. 2009. Paleoindian aggregation and social context at Bull Brook. *American Antiquity* 74, 423–47.

Rockman, M. and Steele, J. (eds) 2003. *Colonization of unfamiliar landscapes*. London: Routledge.

Roosevelt, A. C., Costa, M. L., Machado, C. L., Michab, M., Mercier, N., Valladas, H., Feathers, J., Barnett, W., Silveira, M. I., Henderson, A., Sliva, J., Chernoff, B., Reese, D. S., Holman, J. A., Toth, N., and Schick, K. 1996. Paleoindian cave dwellers in the Amazon: the peopling of the Americas, *Science* 272, 373–84.

Root, M. J., William, J. D., Kay, M., and Shifrin, L. K. 1999. Folsom ultrathin biface and radial break tools in the Knife River flint quarry area. In A. S. Amick (ed.), *Folsom lithic technology*, 144–68. Ann Arbor International Monographs in Prehistory.

Salemme, M. In press. La fauna del sitio Arroyos Seco 2. In G. Politis, M. Gutiérrez, and C. Scabuzzo (eds), *Estado actual de las investigaciones en el sitio Arroyo Seco 2 (Partido de Tres Arroyos, Provincia de Buenos Aires, Argentina)*. Universidad del Centro de la Provincia de Buenos Aires, Olavarría, Argentina: Serie Monográfica INCUAPA 5.

Sanders, T. N. 1990. *Adams: the manufacturing of flaked stone tools at a Paleoindian site in Western Kentucky*. Buffalo, NY: Persimmon Press.

Sandweiss, D. H. 2008. Early fishing societies in western South America. In H. Silverman and W. Isbell (eds), *Handbook of South American archaeology*, 145–56. Paris: Springer.

Sandweiss, D. H., McInnis, H., Burger, R. L., Cano, A., Ojeda, B., Paredes, R., Sandweiss, M., and Glascock, M. D. 1998. Quebrada Jaguay: early South American maritime adaptations. *Science* 281, 1830–2.

Schneider, F. 1982. The Pelland and Moe site blades: Paleo-Indian culture history in the upper Midwest. *Plains Anthropologist* 27, 125–35.

Schroeder, K. B., Jakobsson, M., Crawford, M. H., Schurr, T. G., Boca, S. M., Conrad, D. F., Tito, R. Y., Osipova, L. P., Tarskaia, L. A., Zhadanov, S. I., Wall, J. D., Pritchard, J. K., Malhi, R. S., Smith, D. G., and Rosenberg, N. A. 2009. Haplotypic background of a private allele at high frequency in the Americas. *Molecular Biology Evolution* 26, 995–1016.

Schultz, C. B. 1943. Some artifact sites of early man in the Great Plains and adjacent areas. *American Antiquity* 8, 242–9.

Schurr, T. G. 2004a. Molecular genetic diversity in Siberians and Native Americans suggests an early colonization of the New World. In D. B. Madsen (ed.), *Entering America: Northeast Asia and Beringia before the Last Glacial Maximum*, 187–238. Salt Lake City: University of Utah Press.

Schurr, T. G. 2004b. An anthropological genetic view of peopling of the New World. In C. M. Barton, G. A. Clark, D. R. Yesner, and G. A. Pearson (eds), *The settlement of the American continents*, 11–27. Tucson: University of Arizona Press.

Schurr, T. G. and Wallace, D. C. 1999. mtDNA variation in Native Americans and Siberians and its implications for the peopling of the New World. In R. Bonnichsen (ed.), *Who were the first Americans? Proceedings of the 58th Annual Biology Colloquium, Oregon State University*, 41–77. Corvallis: Oregon State University, Center for the Study of the First Americans.

Sellards, E. H. 1938. Artifacts associated with fossil elephant. *Bulletin of the Geological Society of America* 49, 999–1010.

Sellards, E. H. 1952. *Early man in America*. New York: Greenwood Press.

Sellards, E. H., Evans, G. L., and Meade, G. E. 1947. Fossil bison and associated artifacts from Plainview, Texas, with description of artifacts by Alex d. Krieger. *Bulletin of the Geological Society of America* 58, 927–54.

Sellet, F., Donohue, J., and Hill, M. G. 2009. The Jim Pitts site: a stratified Paleoindian site in the Black Hills of South Dakota. *American Antiquity* 74, 735–58.

Shields, G. F., Schmiechen, A. M., Frazier, B. L., Redd, A., Voevoda, M. I., Reed, J. K., and Ward, R. H. 1993. mtDNA sequences suggest a recent evolutionary divergence for Beringian and northern North American populations. *American Journal of Human Genetics* 53, 549–62.

Stanford, D. J. and Bradley, B. A. 2006. The Solutrean-Clovis connection: reply to Straus, Meltzer, and Goebel. *World Archaeology* 38, 704–14.

Stanford, D. J. and Graham, R. 1985. Archaeological investigations of the Selby and Dutton mammoth kill sites, Yuma County, Colorado. *National Geographic Society Research Report* 19, 519–41.

Steele, J. and Politis, G. G. 2009. AMS 14C dating of early human occupation of South America. *Journal of Archaeological Science* 36, 419–29.

Stiger, M. 2006. A Folsom structure in the Colorado mountains. *American Antiquity* 71, 321–51.

Stone, A. C. and Stoneking, M. 1998. mtDNA analysis of a prehistoric Oneota population: implications for the peopling of the New World. *American Journal of Human Genetics* 62, 1153–70.

Straus, L. G., Meltzer, D. J., and Goebel, T. 2005. Ice Age Atlantis? Exploring the Solutrean-Clovis 'connection'. *World Archaeology* 37, 507–53.

Suárez, R. 2009. Arqueología durante la transición Pleistoceno-Holoceno: componentes paleoindios, organización de la tecnología lítica y movilidad de los primeros americanos en Uruguay. PhD thesis. Universidad Nacional de La Plata, Argentina.

Surovell, T. A. and Waguespack, N. M. 2007. Folsom hearth-centered use of space at Barger Gulch, Locality B. In R. H. Brunswig and B. L. Pitblado (eds), *Frontiers in Colorado Paleoindian archaeology*, 219–59. Boulder: University of Colorado Press.

Surovell, T. A. and Waguespack, N. M. 2009. Human prey choice in the Late Pleistocene and its relation to megafaunal extinction. In G. Haynes (ed.), *American megafaunal extinctions at the end of the Pleistocene*, 77–105. New York: Springer.

Surovell, T. A., Waguespack, N. M., Mayer, J. H., Kornfeld, M., and Frison, G. C. 2005. Shallow site archaeology: artifact dispersal, stratigraphy, and radiocarbon dating at Barger Gulch, Locality B. *Geoarchaeology* 20, 627–50.

Thomas, M., Gilbert, P., Jenkins, D. L., Gotherstrom, A., Naveran, N., Sanchez, J. J., Hofreiter, M., Thomsen, P. F., Binladen, J., Highram, T. F. G., Yohee, R. M. II, Parr, R., Cummings, L. S., and Willerslev, E. 2008. DNA from pre-Clovis human coprolites in Oregon, North America. *Science Express*. www.Science Express.ogr/3 April.

Todd, L. C., Hofman, J. L., and Schultz, C. B. 1990. Seasonality of the Scottsbluff and Lipscomb bison bonebeds: implications for modeling Paleoindian subsistence. *American Antiquity* 55, 813–27.

Tunnell, C. 1978. *The Gibson lithic cache from West Texas*. Austin: Texas Historical Commission, Office of the State Archaeologist.

Turner, C. G., II. 1983. Dental evidence for peopling of the Americas. In R. Shutler (ed.), *Early man in the New World*, 147–57. Beverly Hills, CA: Sage.

Turner, C. G., II. 2002. Teeth, needles, dogs, and Siberia: bioarchaeological evidence for the colonization of the New World. In N. G. Jablonski (ed.), *The First Americans: the Pleistocene colonization of the New World*, 123–58. San Francisco: Memoirs of the California Academy of Sciences.

Valladas, H., Mercier, N., Michab, M., Reyss, J. L., Joron, J. L., and Guidon, N. 2003. TL age-estimates of burnt quartz pebbles from the Toca do Boqueirão da Pedra Furada (Piauí, Northeastern Brazil). *Fundamhentos* 3, 42–56.

Vilhena Vialou, A. 2005. *Pré-história do Mato Grosso. Voumen 1. Santa Elina*. São Paulo: Ed. USP.

Waguespack, N. M. 2005. The organization of male and female labor in foraging societies: implications for early Paleoindian archaeology. *American Anthropologist* 107, 666–76.

Walker, R. 2007. Hunting in the Late Paleoindian period: faunal remains from Dust cave, Alabama. In R. B. Walker and B. N. Driskell (eds), *Foragers of the Terminal Pleistocene in North America*, 99–115. Lincoln: University of Nebraska Press.

Wang, S., Lewis, C. M., and Jakobsson, M. 2007. Genetic variation and population structure in Native Americans. *Public Library of Sciences Genetics* (http://www.plosgenetics.org/home.action) 3, e185.

Ward, R. H., Frazier, B. L., Dew-Jager, K., and Pääbo, S. 1991. Extensive mitochondrial diversity within a single Amerindian tribe. *Proceedings of the National Academy of Sciences USA* 88, 8720–4.

Waters, M. R., Forman, S. L., Jennings, T. A., Nordt, L. C., Driese, S. G., Feinburg, J. M., Keene, J. L., Halligan, J., Lindquist, A., Pierson, J., Hallmark, C. T., Collins, M. B., and Wiederhold, J. E. 2011. The Buttermilk Creek complex and the origins of Clovis at the Debra L. Friedkin site, Texas. *Science* 331, 1599–603.

Waters, M. R. and Stafford, T. W., Jr. 2007. Redefining the age of Clovis: implications for the peopling of the Americas. *Science* 315, 1122–6.

Weber, R. H. and Agogino, G. A. 1997. Mockingbird Gap Paleoindian site: excavations in 1967. In M. S. Duran and D. T. Kirkpatrick (eds), *Layers of time: papers in honor of Robert H. Weber*, 123–7. Albuquerque: The Archaeological Society of New Mexico 23.

Wilmsen, E. N. and Roberts, F. H. H., Jr. 1978. *Lindenmeier, 1934–1974*. Washington: Smithsonian Contributions to Anthropology.

Winfrey, J. 1990 An event tree analysis of Folsom point failure. *Plains Anthropologist* 35, 263–72.

Wormington, H. M. 1957. *Ancient man in North America*. Denver, CO: Denver Museum of Natural History, Popular Series No. 4.

PART III

POST-GLACIAL COLONIZATIONS AND TRANSFORMATIONS

CHAPTER 18

HUNTER-GATHERERS IN THE POST-GLACIAL WORLD

VICKI CUMMINGS

INTRODUCTION AND AIMS

THIS part of the handbook examines some of the major transformations affecting hunting and gathering societies during the opening phases of the current post-glacial period, the Holocene. After a series of climatic fluctuations at the end of the Pleistocene, the start of the Holocene is defined by the appearance of substantially warmer and more stable global temperatures. These changes triggered rapid environmental adjustments across the planet, including major sea-level rises, extensive flooding of coastal lowlands, deglaciation of extensive areas, especially in higher latitudes, coupled with major shifts in the distribution of various plant and animal species. Viewed in these terms, the post-glacial period is defined by the onset of major climatic and environmental change and human responses to that.

At this juncture, hunter-gatherer communities were living across a wide range of different world regions, and would have been forced to adjust to the challenges and opportunities generated by the new and often unfamiliar conditions. This should make research into the hunter-gatherer societies of this time period particularly interesting. However, for a number of reasons, the archaeology of this period has a rather unusual research history, but one that is now showing signs of major expansion and diversification as a number of central new research questions emerge.

In many parts of the Old World the archaeology of the post-glacial period has been defined as the 'Mesolithic'—the Middle Stone Age—and has been presented as a rather quiet backwater or lull in longer-term human history. One older, overarching theme in Mesolithic studies is the tracing of a series of rather basic human adjustments to the new environmental conditions, either by the development of new microlithic stone tool technologies across large areas, the emergence of broader-based subsistence strategies, or the colonization of new areas freed from the ice. These developments have been presented as a major disjuncture from what happened before (the Palaeolithic) and what would follow (the Neolithic, which saw the first sustained use of domesticates). Many older accounts suggest that after these initial changes, local Mesolithic hunter-gatherer populations reached a cultural ceiling, after which there was only limited development and innovation. As such, the Mesolithic has come to be presented as a rather uneventful and largely self-contained period, one that forms an awkward bridge between the dramatic rock art and elaborate material culture of Ice Age big game hunting societies of the preceding Upper Palaeolithic and the onset of farming societies in the succeeding Neolithic, with the coeval explosion in evidence for increased symbolic expression and monumentality.

Viewed in more global terms, this portrayal of the cultural adjustments taking place among hunter-gatherer societies at the end of the Pleistocene and into the Holocene is rather simplistic. This part of the handbook aims to redress this balance by examining some of the fundamentally important developments taking place in the post-glacial period across a broadly representative series of world regions. In tracing out the sequence of developments and adjustments taking place in these areas, several key themes become clear. First, there was often major continuity across the Palaeolithic–Mesolithic transition as populations adjusted to new conditions with older stocks of knowledge and cultural traditions, rather than a sudden rupture. Second, the Mesolithic period itself is marked by major regional diversity and also long-term cultural dynamism among local hunter-gatherer groups. For example, it is possible to ascertain great internal variability among the different communities occupying landscapes affected by changing environmental conditions. Some groups were certainly relatively small and mobile, leaving only ephemeral remains, but other cultural patterns also appear. For example, there were phases of marked cultural fluorescence in many areas, especially in rich aquatic ecosystems that formed the focus of new kinds of more permanent settlement and intensified cultural and economic activity. However, these developments did not necessarily occur in a linear sequence—in some areas, relatively settled and socially complex hunter-gatherers were later replaced by the return of lower population densities and more mobile bands.

It is now clear that the Mesolithic—broadly defined—is far from being a kind of cultural interlude, but is in fact a highly dynamic period with its own unique coherence, which sets it apart from other historical phenomena (Zvelebil 1998, 24). Other important technologies such as pottery, which had been invented by hunter-gatherers in the Upper Palaeolithic, also saw widespread uptake among hunter-gatherers in this early post-glacial period (see Hommel, this volume; Jordan and Zvelebil 2009). Of equal importance were the series of major economic and cultural changes already underway in several key regions, for example, in the rise of domesticated farming economies in the Near East at the end of the Pleistocene, a pattern of domestication led by hunter-gatherers that was mirrored in other regions of the globe at different times (see Harris; Outram, this volume).

This introductory chapter begins by discussing the general environmental changes that define the start of the Holocene across the world, and which form the framework by which this period has been generally understood. It then reviews some of the main traditions of archaeological research and interpretation into the Mesolithic, tracing how these concepts have been used to define the period and present depictions of its hunter-gatherers. These patterns of environmental change, coupled with the general review of archaeological approaches and interpretations, provide a general framework for reviewing the content of each of the chapters. These are organized into two groups. The first group focuses on developments taking place in temperate, lower-latitude regions, such as Africa, Asia, and the Mediterranean (Moore; Smith; Rabett and Jones; Habu, this volume). Here, the post-glacial period equated to warmer conditions and major ecological change. The second group focuses on more northerly regions of Europe, which were at this time emerging from much colder conditions, and also witnessed major changes (Svoboda; Warren; Riede, this volume).

The final discussion aims to recast this period as a major area for future research into hunter-gatherers. Thus, the primary goal of Part III is to examine the intersections of all these changes in environmental conditions, subsistence strategies, and social life as they are played out in the archaeological sequences drawn from different world regions. These recast the post-glacial period as a time of both major cultural continuity and also fundamental change, and serve to highlight the inherent variability and dynamism of prehistoric hunter-gatherer societies, an intriguing historical phenomenon, which archaeologists are just starting to acknowledge and address, drawing on a raft of new methods and approaches.

GLOBAL ENVIRONMENTAL CHANGES IN THE POST-GLACIAL PERIOD

The global climate has always been changing, and long-term human evolution has taken place in the context of frequent environmental fluctuations, with conditions frequently alternating between warmer and colder periods. Specific patterns of climate change across the world have been thoroughly explored through the analysis of a range of different types of evidence from terrestrial and aquatic organisms (Birks and Ammann 1999) through to the chemical composition of the ice preserved in Antarctica and Greenland (Bender et al. 1994). From a range of evidence, it is possible to identify the onset of significant changes in environmental conditions at the end of the glacial period (the Pleistocene) and into the post-glacial (the Holocene). Beginning around 11,500 BP, the Holocene is the present geological epoch and it is a unique phase of sustained climatic stability, marked by high sea levels and warmer conditions. In contrast, the end of the Pleistocene was marked by a series of sudden climatic fluctuations prior to the full onset of the Holocene (Figure 18.1).

At about 25,000 years ago there were full glacial conditions (the Late Glacial Maximum: LGM), which lasted until about 18,000 years ago. One of the key components

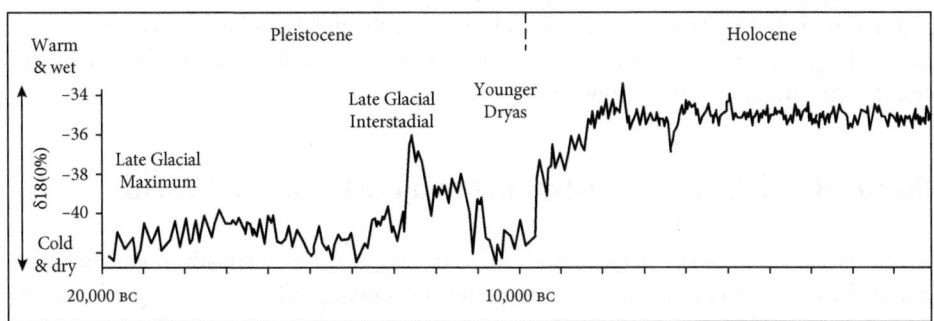

FIGURE 18.1 Oxygen isotope levels from ice cores (y-axis) reflect temperature changes from the late glacial into the post-glacial period (after Scarre 2013).

of the LGM was that thick ice sheets extended down from the Arctic, covering northern Eurasia and much of the northern part of North America, with smaller regional ice sheets located in other mountainous regions. As a result, temperatures on land were as much as 20°C lower than they are today (Roberts 1998, 62). A consequence of the fact that much of the world's water was frozen in the ice caps also meant that sea levels were significantly lower than today—as much as 100 m lower than present levels. Vegetation was also affected by glacial conditions: most of Europe was devoid of forest, there were significant reductions in tropical rainforests and in the tropics, vegetation was forced into lower altitudes (Roberts 1998, 66). The LGM was also relatively arid, with both cold and hot deserts expanding beyond their present locations (Scarre 2013, 179).

Towards the end of the Pleistocene, there were a series of shorter warm and cold periods prior to the onset of the full post-glacial. This included the Bølling-Allerød interstadial, which saw generally warmer conditions: at the height of this warmer phase the polar front was as high as Iceland (Roberts 1998, 70). However, these warmer conditions halted around 13,000 years ago with the sudden onset of the Younger Dryas, with a short, but extensive return to colder conditions. At its most extreme, the polar front reached as far south as Iberia during this brief cold period (Roberts 1998, 70). The Younger Dryas ended abruptly around 11,500 BP (Alley et al. 1993) with the full onset of warmer post-glacial conditions, which have remained relatively stable to the present day.

The effects of these periods of warming and cooling, and eventually the climatic stabilization that marked the onset of the Holocene, varied from region to region. The biggest changes in tropical and sub-tropical belts were to sea levels, which rose due to the melting ice sheets to the north. This caused the inundation of coastal areas and the loss of land, as well as the restructuring of major river systems. In contrast, higher latitudes were marked by extensive deglaciation, the replacement of polar deserts by tundra, followed by the spread of shrubs and pioneer forests and, eventually, deciduous woodland. Indeed, the climate was favourable enough during the onset of the Holocene that boreal woodland was found further north than its current geographic limit (Foley et al. 1994). Changes in vegetation also affected fauna: the megafauna that characterized the Upper Palaeolithic died out, and there was a northern movement of mammals that favoured open landscapes, including reindeer (caribou). The spread of deciduous woodland into the north was concomitant with the dispersal of mammals including deer, wild pig, and aurochs. Warming seas and oceans also led to increasingly rich coastal ecosystems, albeit ones subject to flooding and inundation through rising seas. Some parts of temperate Europe, for example, saw the loss of enormous landmasses, including Doggerland in what is now the North Sea. Other effects included the slow infilling of lakes, isostatic lift (the rebound of land due to the removal of the weight of ice), and the initiation of peat growth in some areas.

Hunter-Gatherers: Adjustments to a Post-Glacial World

By the onset of the post-glacial period, most of the world was already populated with well-established hunter-gatherer communities occupying different ecological niches. Modern humans *(Homo sapiens)* had already moved out of Africa in the Pleistocene and spread to virtually all parts of the globe. For example, Eurasia, apart from the most northern extremes, was inhabited by modern humans at various points: South Asia was occupied somewhere between 70 and 50,000 years ago (see Petraglia and Boivin, this volume), and South-East Asia and Indonesia were occupied around 50,000 years ago (see O'Connor and Bulbeck, this volume). Australia had been inhabited by people more than 45,000 years ago (see Davidson, this volume). Much of central and southern Europe had been inhabited from about 35,000 years ago (see Pettitt, this volume) and both North and South America were definitely occupied by people at the end of the Pleistocene, possibly even earlier (see Kornfeld and Politis, this volume).

In the following centuries and millennia these people faced major challenges as these broader environmental changes in the post-glacial period took effect and forced them to adjust to changing conditions. In part, and alongside another species, this required adjustments to how and where people made a living, but as a uniquely cultural species, there were also social, cultural, and technological adjustments. Major changes are documented in the forms of new lithic traditions and new forms of material culture utilized, including the dispersals of pottery among many groups across large areas; there also seem to have been major shifts in social organization, settlement, and subsistence. These developments are presented in detail in the chapters in this part of the handbook. However, in order to understand these developments it is important to place current knowledge against a background of broader research traditions, which this chapter now moves on to explore in more detail.

Traditions of Archaeological Research into the Mesolithic and the Post-Glacial Period

So how have archaeologists made sense of the post-glacial period? The way in which post-glacial cultures have been researched and understood by scholars in the past has framed the study of people living at this time. This is partly to do with older notions of characterizing humans, but also relates to how scholars have classified the post-glacial period, which in Europe has been tied to defining the challenges of defining the 'Mesolithic' (Zvelebil 1998). In the nineteenth century, archaeologists were clearly able to identify major differences between the material remains of Palaeolithic and Neolithic periods (Rowley-Conwy 2007). It was in the latter part of the nineteenth century that Lubbock suggested the Stone Age should be divided into the Old Stone Age (Palaeolithic) and New Stone Age (Neolithic), a sequence he suggested not only for Europe but also, tentatively, for parts of Africa and Asia (Lubbock 1865). By this point, archaeologists had found Palaeolithic stone tools associated with extinct Ice Age animals such as mammoths, who clearly had lived in a different geological period (Lyell's Pleistocene). This geological period was also characterized by a different environment, one defined by Ice Ages. In contrast, the Neolithic period was more recent, particularly associated at this point with polished stone tools, but also domesticated cattle (Rowley-Conwy 1996, 942; Zvelebil 1998, 2). It was Hodder Westropp in 1872 who first invented the controversial phrase the Mesolithic (Middle Stone Age) to describe the lithic assemblages that he claimed came from an intervening period between the Palaeolithic and Neolithic (Rowley-Conwy 2006). However, there was resistance to this, and debate on whether an intermediate phase was even necessary.

By the end of the nineteenth century, archaeologists were trying to make sense of the archaeological record by looking at modern living populations in order to understand the past (ethnology). A crucial component of this mode of thought was the idea that people evolved, both socially and physically, from 'primitive savages' through to civilization. Inspired by Darwinian evolution, it was suggested that humans evolved through a series of unilinear stages (see Pluciennik, this volume): at one end was the most basic of peoples—hunter-gatherers—while modern Western civilization saw itself as the most evolved (Trigger 2006, 171–7). Increasingly, archaeologists began to conceive of a major disjuncture between the Palaeolithic and Neolithic, the former being associated with hunter-gatherers, and the latter associated with agriculture. The Mesolithic, although still a highly contentious period at this point, was also placed firmly on the hunting and gathering side, essentially the 'wrong' side of civilization (see also Spikins 2008, 4).

The term 'Mesolithic' was not widely adopted until a few decades into the twentieth century, and even then, only by archaeologists studying particular areas (predominantly Europe). In the Near East, there was no need for a chronologically distinctive period, as people started the domestication process at the end of the Pleistocene. Here, then, the chronological sequence was the Palaeolithic, followed by the Epi-Palaeolithic (defined as the period of hunting and fishing with the harvesting of cereals) and then the Neolithic (agriculture). In other areas, archaeologists chose to describe this awkward intervening period as the proto-Neolithic or simply the Middle Stone Age (Spikins 2008, 4; Zvelebil 1998, 2). In other areas, other phrases were used to describe the cultural developments in the important transitional period between the Pleistocene and the Holocene (see chapters by Davidson; Politis and Kornfeld). So even from its earliest inception no one could quite agree precisely what the Mesolithic represented, whether or not it was a distinctive chronological period or whether it could be defined by a coherent set of traits.

One problem in attempts to understand the Mesolithic was that there had been very few archaeological investigations of the post-glacial period in the nineteenth and early twentieth centuries. This was because scholars focused primarily on either the preceding Palaeolithic period, or subsequent Neolithic period, with their distinctive stone tools sets (Bahn 1996, chapter 5). One exception was in Scandinavia, where the excellent preservation of Holocene archaeology in the form of shell middens meant that remains were investigated from an early stage, for example with the work of Worsaae in Denmark, who explored middens in the mid-nineteenth century (Trigger 2006, 80–2). This began a long tradition of work on the Scandinavian Mesolithic, which remains one of the most intensively studied regions of Europe in this period (see, for example, Larsson et al. 2003).

By the time Gordon Childe started writing his culture-historical archaeology in the early part of the twentieth century, Mesolithic studies in Europe were still under-developed in comparison with other prehistoric periods. Childe (1942) did eventually see the need for an intervening period between the Palaeolithic and Neolithic (Zvelebil 1998, 2), but in many areas the evidence was still poorly understood, primarily defined not by what it had, but by what it lacked: the sophisticated rock art and lithic technologies of the Palaeolithic, and the agriculture and pottery of the Neolithic.

A new phase of research into the European Mesolithic was initiated by Grahame Clark, who made a significant advance in Mesolithic studies by drawing on broader ecological approaches and discussing hunter-gatherer technological adaptions to the environment (Trigger 2006, 353–60). Clarke supported the notion that the Mesolithic was a culturally distinctive period of prehistory, and explored economic adaptations in order to try to understand social and cultural organization. Clark's work at the Mesolithic site of Star Carr was also significant, marking the start of a more concerted effort to investigate Mesolithic sites in this part of Europe (Clark 1954). With the development of the New Archaeology from the 1960s onwards, the processual interest in the role of environment in human culture further galvanized this ecological focus of the Mesolithic. The role of the environment and ecological adaptation saw intensive research (e.g. Evans 1975), and the palaeo-economic work at Cambridge in the 1970s was of particular importance and broader influence (see Higgs 1975).

At this point, work concentrated on understanding how people made a living from particular environmental situations, and this was achieved through quantifying assemblages (particularly animal bones), investigating seasonality, ascertaining how much time and energy was required to obtain food, and the calorific value of foodstuffs (Milner 2006, 71). It became clear that Mesolithic hunter-gatherers were exploiting a distinctive, and extremely rich, environmental niche. In addition to this, studies of lithic styles demonstrated that the Mesolithic was technologically different from both the preceding Palaeolithic and subsequent Neolithic (e.g. Woodman 1978; Wymer 1977). Thus Mesolithic research began to have a distinctive character, which emphasized the process of environmental adaptations by hunter-gatherers living in the rich environments of the early Holocene. This view of the Mesolithic was consistent with the anthropological view of hunter-gatherers as portrayed in *Man the hunter* as well-adapted to particular environmental circumstances. Grahame Clark's site of Star Carr came to be seen as representative of the Mesolithic as a whole at this time: small-scale, mobile hunter-gatherer bands settled into optimally exploited environments.

The combination of an increased interest in the Mesolithic period, the focus on how hunter-gatherers had adapted to the new environmental setting of the post-glacial period, and the sense that the Mesolithic was culturally distinctive led to a major shift in thinking in the 1980s. At this point, there was increased emphasis on the idea that Mesolithic communities were not only ecologically and technologically distinctive, but also culturally variable. For example, not all Mesolithic people were small-scale, mobile hunter-gatherers; it was argued that the Mesolithic, particularly of northern Europe, saw the first evidence for complex hunter-gatherer groups. This suggestion worked particularly well for southern Scandinavia, but soon came to dominate discussions of other parts of the world (e.g. Price 1985; Rowley-Conwy 1983; Rowley-Conwy and Zvelebil 1989; Zvelebil 1986; Zvelebil and Rowley-Conwy 1986). This idea was further supported by the excavations of substantial Mesolithic cemeteries such as at Skateholm in Sweden (Larsson 1984; 1988). The findings at Skateholm were not unique, but consistent with other Mesolithic cemeteries in Europe, such as Lepenski Vir in the Iron Gates of the Danube, Olenii Ostrov, northern Russia, and Teviéc and Hoëdic in Brittany, all of which were drawn into discussions at this time. Ethnographic parallels were deployed, particularly with the Northwest Coast, and issues such as storage, population density, and social ranking were discussed (Spikins 2008, 4). Continued palaeo-environmental work identified hunter-gatherer manipulations of the environment, including deliberate burning (e.g. Edwards 1990).

In the late 1980s and 1990s new perspectives on the Mesolithic emerged. The growth of interpretive (post-processual) archaeology which, until this point, had looked mainly at the Neolithic, expanded its focus to include discussions of hunter-gatherers in the post-glacial period, primarily in north-west Europe. Interpretive archaeology critiqued the ecological and adaptive approaches of processual archaeology, citing environmental determinism as one of the main problems of investigating the Mesolithic from an ecological viewpoint. Instead, focus was placed on Mesolithic people as active social agents, making choices about how to adapt to the post-glacial world, not just in terms of economy but also socially and culturally. Four key areas have been explored as part of the interpretive investigation of the Mesolithic. First, there was a growth in interest in the landscape inspired by phenomenological approaches (Tilley 1994) and work on perceptions of the environment (Ingold 2000). The landscape focus switched from looking at palaeo-economic site catchment analysis towards human experience. An important component of this approach was the use of ethnographic analogies with extant hunter-gatherer groups in order to explore the potential significance of landscape in terms of myths and belief systems (Cummings 2000; Zvelebil 2000), but also everyday space and place (McFadyen 2006). Second, there was an increased interest in Mesolithic belief systems and world views (Zvelebil and Fewster 2001). This related not only to perceptions of the landscape, but also explored human–animal relations (Conneller 2004) and the detailed exploration of Mesolithic cemeteries, particularly in Scandinavia (Nilsson Stutz). This has drawn on ethnographic accounts of both animism and shamanism (Zvelebil 2008, 48–52). The third theme explored in depth by interpretive archaeologists was that of identity. Again, drawing on ethnographic explorations of personhood (Fowler 2004), different possible constructions of person have been explored in Mesolithic Europe (Cobb 2007; Finlay, this volume). This approach has also drawn on growing investigations of gender in relation to the Mesolithic (e.g. Finlay 2006). Finally, there has been a renewed interest in technology, not just as an adaptation to environmental circumstances but as a social process. This approach is part of a wider interest in materiality (McFadyen 2006), and explores the life history of objects as they are made (the *chaîne opératoire*), used, and discarded (cf. Gosden and Marshall 1999). Scholars have been able to investigate the authorship of Mesolithic tools (Finlay 2000) and the deposition of specific sets of materials in particular places in the landscape (Warren 2006).

The current state of Mesolithic studies is that the Mesolithic is now seen as a unique and distinctive period in its own right, with its own internal dynamics (Spikins 2008; Zvelebil 2008). It is not a chronological stop gap, nor a simple story of environmental adaptation. Emphasis is now placed on addressing variability with an attempt to understand local adaptations, but also to reconstruct specific traditions and practices, mortuary rituals, and concepts of materiality and personhood (see Bailey and Spikins 2008; Conneller and Warren 2006). Overall then, in some world regions such as north-west Europe the last three decades have seen major intellectual shifts in the way that the Mesolithic has been researched and understood, though these developments have been limited for the most part to a few regions marked by long-term research histories with more detailed archaeological sequences.

Prehistoric Hunter-Gatherers of the Late Pleistocene and Early Holocene

Reflecting the environmental changes in the Holocene, the chapters in this part of the handbook are organized into two groups: those that present case studies of hunter-gatherers inhabiting tropical and relatively temperate zones in the late Pleistocene/early Holocene, and those that examine changes taking place in more northerly regions, specifically in Europe, which reflect the dense concentration of research effort directed there. These chapters approach the archaeology of the post-glacial period in these different world regions from a range of different research perspectives, as outlined above, illustrating unique sequences of hunter-gatherer culture change, while also highlighting how and why these patterns of change have been researched and understood, and where new research might proceed.

Hunter-Gatherer Culture Change in Western Asia and the Mediterranean

In the first chapter in this part, Moore discusses the post-glacial sequence in western Asia and around the Mediterranean. This case study is important because it illustrates the fact that we cannot employ the term 'Mesolithic' to describe all post-glacial developments across the world. This is because in western Asia, which remained temperate even during the LGM, the transition towards an agricultural way of life was already underway at the end of the late glacial. Here, hunter-gatherers had started to domesticate both plants and animals (the period known as the Epi-Palaeolithic). Therefore, in this area, we are dealing with cultural sequences where there were long processes of significant economic, social, and cultural change before the end of the Pleistocene. These societies would eventually become full agro-pastoral settled farming communities, which defined a new and fully 'Neolithic' way of life (and see introduction to Part V).

In his chapter, Moore highlights the fact that western Asia provided an extraordinarily rich environmental niche, which saw legume, cereal, and caprine domestication, followed by the taming of cattle and pigs. Moore suggests that it was the combination of new environmental conditions together with new social opportunities provided by larger and more permanent settlements that was the driving force behind these initial domestications (see also Harris; Hayden, this volume). Thus, in this narrative it is clear that it was the hunting and gathering peoples who innovated change in this area. By the start of the post-glacial in western Asia, domesticated plants and animals are found in association with the construction of sedentary villages, monumental architecture, complex burial rites, and lavish sets of material culture. This is the 'Neolithic'—in the earliest phase, this was aceramic (the Pre-Pottery Neolithic A and B) and later on, with pottery (the Neolithic). By the second phase of the Neolithic in western Asia settlements grew, including well-documented examples such as Çatal Hüyük.

In contrast, Moore notes that the shores of the Mediterranean did not see these developments and these areas were sparsely populated by hunter-gatherers in the post-glacial period. In the Aegean and Greece, Mesolithic hunter-gatherer sites are found primarily on the coast and seem to be indicative of mobile groups utilizing both terrestrial and marine resources. Within this area, the Franchthi cave has been thoroughly investigated and includes both occupation debris and burials. The central and western Mediterranean sequence shares many similarities with that of Greece. Occupation sites suggest sparsely populated landscapes, and highly mobile hunter-gatherers using both terrestrial and marine resources. The major difference with this area, however, is that inland sites are documented in the central and western Mediterranean, some at quite high altitudes, suggesting the slightly different resource exploitation of this area. Just as at the Franchthi cave, cave sites in this area also have long sequences of occupation, and some elaborate material culture is also recorded.

In Greece, hunting and gathering ceased with the arrival of the Neolithic from western Asia. This does seem to suggest a simple transition from the Mesolithic to the Neolithic, from hunter-gatherer to farmer as originally envisaged by scholars investigating this period (see Part V). However, in the central and western Mediterranean there is a thousand-year hiatus between hunter-gatherer occupation and the arrival of the first farmers, which Moore suggests is indicative of a severe decline in Mesolithic populations. This indicates a much more complex narrative than Mesolithic people being replaced by, or subsumed into, incoming Neolithic populations. Indeed, it highlights regional differences in the successes of hunting and gathering populations in the post-glacial world. It is quite clear, then, that there were not identical patterns of adaptation to the changing conditions of the post-glacial period. Furthermore, there is clear evidence for important internal dynamics in this period, as highlighted in the central and western Mediterranean sequence. Fruitful avenues of future research can focus on specific traditions of practices that emphasize local variability across this area.

Early Holocene Developments in Africa

Like other parts of the globe, post-glacial Africa saw substantial environmental change: rising sea levels, warmer and wetter conditions, and changing flora and fauna. All of these had considerable impacts on the people living there. What is important with the African sequences is that they highlight the variety of ways in which people adapted to these changing conditions. Smith outlines these changes in different regions. In northern Africa, the 'Khartoum Mesolithic' is found in the early post-glacial, represented in the archaeological record by the use of ceramics and a microlithic industry, and sites were associated with lakes and rivers. Smith suggests that these hunter-gatherers were reliant on both fish and wild sheep and also pots for seed processing. There are also some early examples of domesticated cattle in this sequence, probably from the Levant which, combined with the evidence for the extensive utilization of wild sheep, may point to hunter-gatherers experimenting with animal husbandry, resulting in a localized domestication event (also see Outram, this volume). It is clear that this sequence sees new relations with plants and animals, and people experimenting with both ceramic technology and local animal domestication. It is also interesting that these hunter-gatherers appear to have been subsequently replaced by the expansion of herders around the Mediterranean, although there was possibly some overlap between the extant, predominantly foraging, populations and the incoming herders. This highlights the fact that these populations did not exist in isolation, but were tied into broader regional and historical transformations. It would be fruitful to explore in more detail the role that the extant hunting and gathering population played as herders expanded into this region.

The sequence in southern Africa has been studied extensively, both archaeologically and in relation to rock art. Microlithic industries are found widely in the post-glacial period of southern Africa and there is evidence that people increasingly hunted solitary browsers and pigs. Smith notes that the way of life which commenced in the post-glacial continued until around 2,000 years ago, when domesticated animals and pottery were first introduced from the north. In this sequence, then, there was the long-term success of hunting and gathering lifeways and it makes an important contrast with archaeological sequences in North Africa, where there was an earlier shift to agriculture. Clearly, in this environmental context agriculture was not as easily adopted as it was to the north, but future research could examine other reasons—social, political, or economic—for the slower adoption of agriculture in this region. The foragers of southern Africa are also considered important for understanding historically documented hunter-gatherers in this area, where there is a long-standing debate on the continuity of various foraging populations, as well as the impact on incoming herders (see Hitchcock, Part VI).

Post-Glacial Hunter-Gatherers in South and South-East Asia

Rabett and Jones consider the evidence from the post-glacial period from both South and South-East Asia. There are some important contrasts between these two broader sequences, which illustrates not only the different ways people dealt with the changing environment in the post-glacial world, but also the unique internal social processes underway at this time. In some parts of South Asia, the Holocene sequence is poorly understood, but where it is known, sites are found in a range of habitats, suggesting a fairly large and dispersed hunting and gathering population within these landscapes. In contrast to the European Mesolithic, Rabett and Jones detail how there was no cultural transition from the Upper Palaeolithic to the Mesolithic, and no shift to microlithic technologies, which is found in many other areas of the world at this time. What does define the onset of the Holocene is the increasing amount of representational art, especially rock art. Some cemeteries are also known from this area, associated with settlement, and are suggestive of increased social complexity and territoriality. While technologically there was considerable continuity with what came before, culturally there seems to be some evidence for increased complexity within the Mesolithic. This points to a sequence where there were significant changes, driven not just by external environmental change, but also by important internal mechanisms, and these need to be studied in their own terms. It is only later in the Holocene that the eventual arrival of agriculture in this region is seen.

In South-East Asia, the start of the Holocene saw a continued emphasis on hunting and gathering the same species as in the Pleistocene, even though there were changing environmental conditions. Thus, in this area there is clear evidence for the continuity of practice. Moreover, marine resources had been important in South-East Asia since the arrival of the first modern humans from Africa, but there are post-glacial sites where the abundantly available marine resources were not utilized. Bone tool use did seem to increase in some areas, however, which may have coincided with the increased use of marine foods in these areas only. This demonstrates people's differing responses to changing environmental opportunities, and that environmental upheaval did not necessarily result in economic change. Thus, in this sequence it is possible to identify quite complex local patterns of adaptation and different technological and ecological groups. Rabett and Jones argue that the post-glacial period saw people both sticking to older ways of life and adapting to new changes in South-East Asia. The social and cultural implications of this could be explored in more detail in the future.

Late Pleistocene and Early Holocene Hunter-Gatherers of Korea and Japan

Habu discusses the post-glacial sequences in East Asia, discussing both the Jomon culture of the Japanese archipelago and the Chulmun culture of the Korean peninsula. These are some of the longest hunter-gatherer archaeological sequences in the world. However, these sequences also highlight some of the challenges of making sense of long-term hunter-gatherer archaeological sequences. They also challenge our notions of defining post-glacial hunter-gatherer society. The Jomon and Chulmun were both complex and sedentary hunter-gatherers, who were involved in the sophisticated management of wild plant resources. They had artistic ceramics and elaborate material culture. However, instead of being 'on the way' to becoming agriculturalists, as has been suggested for similar groups elsewhere (see above), these groups were very late in adopting agro-pastoralism. The Jomon period eventually ended with the arrival of rice agriculture around 2500 BP: this is the same as the Chulmun, arriving sometime in the second millennium BC.

The Jomon sequence is also interesting for hunter-gatherer studies more broadly because it does not show a steady increase in complexity and sedentism. Instead, Habu points to major reconfigurations in the middle Jomon period, with a return to more mobile bands after a period of social collapse. Indeed, three major periods of upheaval can be identified in the hunter-gatherer post-glacial sequence, dating to 11,000, 7000, and 4000 BP. These changes seem to be related to changing subsistence strategies, including specialization and the intensified use of specific wild resources. At certain points, there is evidence of the over-specialization of resources, which led to the collapse of socio-economic systems. This may well have happened at a number of points in prehistory, and also more recently as well. It highlights the importance of identifying internal changes in specific regional hunter-gatherer sequences and is an exciting avenue for future research in all world regions. This research is important because it highlights that the post-glacial period in East Asia was a period of growing population associated with the intensification of particular resource use. However, this was not a continuous development as there is now growing evidence for sudden cultural adjustments or perhaps even collapses. This sequence also shows that there was not a slow and steady period of increasing cultural elaboration and complexity, with an inevitable social evolutionary outcome, but a much more dynamic and complex sequence. These were multi-various societies with considerable variation over both space and time.

Mesolithic Europe

In the final three chapters this part of the handbook, the authors consider the post-glacial sequences of central and northern Europe. In the chapter on the post-glacial of Danubian Europe, Svoboda investigates the areas around the Danube River, the major river course in south-east Europe running from southern Germany to the Black Sea. This area was already the focus of occupation in the preceding Upper Palaeolithic (also see Pettitt, Part II), but Svoboda argues that this area became more peripheral to broader developments in the Mesolithic period. Svoboda argues that where there are Mesolithic settlements in the

Danubian area they are found in distinct regional clusters and are relatively small in size, especially when compared with many of the large north European sites. Likewise, lithics were primarily procured from localized resources, which again forms a notable contrast with preceding far-reaching exchange networks from the Upper Palaeolithic. Occupation took place on a range of sites, including at open-air sites, in caves, and in rock shelters, and there is good evidence for the utilization of a range of resources, including both aquatic foods, such as salmon, and terrestrial foods, showing the diversification of the economy at this time.

Danubian Europe also contains the well-documented but unique settlement site of Lepenski Vir, located in the Danube Gorges in modern-day Serbia, comprising trapezoidal structures with stone-lined hearths and red-plastered floors. These structures are also associated with burials and stone-carved fish sculptures, although there is the suggestion that these were later in date. Further sites have been identified along this 100 km of river after extensive investigations from the 1960s onwards (Whittle 1996, 25). This sequence is also well known for the burials found on the shores of the Danube in the Iron Gates, and includes sites at Vlasac, Schela Clodovei, and Lepenski Vir itself. However, Svoboda argues that much of the rest of the wider area may well have been only sparsely populated. Right at the end of the Mesolithic, the area saw the arrival of new peoples from the south-east, marking the start the Neolithic from about 6000 BC. This sequence, then, clearly illustrates the contingent nature of the Mesolithic in this area. There is evidence for both sparsely occupied areas and densely inhabited and socially complex micro-regions. It is also important to note that the group of sites around Lepenski Vir has been portrayed in the literature as one of the areas where 'complex' hunter-gatherers evolved in the post-glacial period, and that these people were well on their way to 'settling down' (Hodder 1990, 31).

Warren's chapter on the Mesolithic of north-west Europe argues that while the European Mesolithic has been exemplified by the presence of 'complex' hunter-gatherers (see above), the peoples within this area were actually very variable. Warren notes that the post-glacial of north-west Europe should be understood in terms of a variety of changes, which affected all aspects of life: he highlights in particular the massive environmental and climatic changes underway at this time. However, there were also considerable continuities with preceding periods, which should not be ignored. The outcome of this mix of continuity and change was multiple traditions, possibly originating from multiple populations. Warren notes that there is evidence for broad cultural groupings across north-west Europe in the early Mesolithic. By the later Mesolithic, however, smaller-scale territories can also be identified, although people were still involved in extensive trade networks. He suggests that there are subtle hints in the archaeological record for changes across broad areas of north-west Europe around about 7000 BC, which may have been the impact of climatic changes and even more catastrophic events. As with Habu, then, Warren is arguing that there was an ongoing series of social and cultural shifts throughout the Mesolithic, not just at the onset of the post-glacial period. This is a theme that could be explored in more depth in the future.

Warren then goes on to discuss the Ertebølle of southern Scandinavia, who have been presented by scholars as the archetypal 'complex' hunter-gatherer society of Mesolithic Europe. This group is notable for its broad-spectrum economy (including intensive use of marine resources), its early use of distinctive ceramics, the use of prestige material culture, and cemeteries. In the past, the Ertebølle have been presented as the culmination of generalized trends observed elsewhere in the European Mesolithic, and exemplars of complex hunter-gatherers at the end of the evolutionary path from simple to complex, who ultimately took up farming. Warren critiques this approach, arguing that the Ertebølle were one of a number of groups for whom complexity (in the ethnographic sense) came and went as they organized and reorganized themselves over time. It was not, therefore, the inevitable outcome of a long period of social, economic, and political evolution, but simply one possible outcome from many, and one that was flexible and optional. Likewise, other sequences in the European Mesolithic should not be simply compared to the Ertebølle sequence and (inevitably) found to be lacking in one or more components. Instead, Warren argues that each group should be understood in its own terms. Specifically, following on from Zvelebil (2009), he argues that the Mesolithic is actually a multitude of historical processes, all of which led to different end-points. He suggests that using the insights from interpretive archaeology and also initiating new research programmes should enable scholars to identify regional variability and the localized nature of specific cultural processes. In the last chapter in this part, Riede discusses the resettlement of northern Europe in the late glacial and post-glacial periods. The resettlement of previously uninhabited parts of Europe was enabled by the dramatic environmental and geological changes at the end of the glacial period. Riede illustrates how these processes can be studied not just through the now very detailed environmental data for this period, but also the archaeological evidence (especially in the form of lithics and technocomplexes), population modelling, and radiocarbon sequences from various key areas. Using this approach, Riede demonstrates that the resettlement process was not as straightforward as it had been assumed: it did not involve a simple 'wave of advance' where people gradually moved northwards. Instead, there were bursts of activity where people moved northwards, but these were frequently curtailed by a deterioration of environmental conditions, or at 12,900 BP by the eruption of the Laacher See volcano in Germany. In the British sequence for the late glacial period, for example, populations seem to have at some points been in contact with continental populations, while at other times they were isolated. Likewise, the populations newly expanded into southern Scandinavia found themselves isolated from other groups after the Laacher See eruption. Since there is good evidence for widespread trade networks between populations at this time, this enforced isolation may not have been desirable for the populations involved.

Using this regionally specific approach, Riede concludes that there were two main types of population expansion patterns in the late glacial period. The first saw hunter-gatherers moving into topographically diverse regions in northern Europe: these groups utilized a mixed hunting and gathering economy with reduced resource specialization. The second expansion was of specialized hunter-gatherers: these groups followed reindeer herds. These reindeer specialists may also have been able to acquire exotic and prestige resources such as amber and furs, which they then traded in much wider exchange networks. By the start of the Holocene, the northwards expansion continued as far as Fennoscandia, and reindeer utilization was increasingly accompanied by marine adaptations (and see Wickham Jones, this volume). Tool-kits were correspondingly expanded and complex patterns of trade and exchange were re-established. It is possible to argue that, while initially hunter-gatherers were exploiting specific environmental niches that had become available to them, in the long term, specific resource exploitation choices would have had enormous implications for the types of society that could exist (also see Hayden, this volume). Once again, this demonstrates the importance of exploring historically contingent histories of the Mesolithic, which would have had multiple outcomes.

Discussion and Future Research Directions

In earlier accounts, the post-glacial period, or Mesolithic as defined in many parts of Africa and Eurasia, has often been presented simply as a chronological juncture, the period between the Palaeolithic and the Neolithic. The Mesolithic has also been seen as a period when hunter-gatherers were in the process of adapting to new post-glacial environmental conditions. While accounts of this period have had an internal coherence, one result of this research trajectory has been that Holocene hunter-gatherers have been portrayed as rather homogeneous. It is obvious that the enormous environmental changes taking place at the end of the Pleistocene and into the early Holocene affected hunter-gatherer groups living in many different world regions. However, more recent scholarship has shown that these processes were more contingent and variable than had previously been thought. Diversity, not homogeneity, is key in the study of this period. While the chapters in this part of the handbook do not cover every part of the globe, they do give a sense of the more localized patterns of behaviour that were played out throughout the world in the post-glacial period. Very briefly, key elements of these broader patterns are now highlighted.

First, the post-glacial period can be understood as a period of both continuity and change. There are some examples of abrupt change at the start of the post-glacial, relating not only to the changing environmental conditions but also to the types of societies that were emerging at this time. This includes the emergence of 'complex' societies, but there was a range of other social configurations in the post-glacial period. Other changes can be seen in sequences across the globe, including changing technologies (stone, bone, and ceramic), resource utilization, and ritual practices. However, massive environmental changes did not always result in change. The chapters in this part demonstrate the importance of continuity in some areas, particularly relating to trade, exchange, mobility, and social organization. Traditions of practice, particularly social networks, seem to have continued unbroken from the Upper Palaeolithic into the Mesolithic in some areas.

Second, changing environmental conditions clearly had an enormous impact on the ways in which people could make a living. This varied across the globe, but there were substantial shifts in the types of flora and fauna available to people. Furthermore, ecosystems shifted and moved, landmasses disappeared as the sea levels rose, and new foods became available. However, there was a diverse range of responses to these changes. Some hunter-gatherer economies were in flux before the start of the Holocene, and involved the intensification of particular resources. In some cases, these intensifications eventually led to domestication and farming, yet others led to different types of hunting and gathering societies, such as the 'complex' Ertebølle of southern Scandinavia, or the Jomon of Japan. In other cases, there were no changes at all to hunter-gatherer economies. This demonstrates that people chose precisely how to respond to changing environmental conditions. There were certainly challenges for people dealing with a world in flux, but also opportunities—not just economic ones. Quite clearly, new environmental opportunities enabled people with resources to go on and pursue intense social, political, and ritual lives (also see Hayden, this volume).

Third, the post-glacial period saw considerable change and flux over time and there was quite clearly regional variation. Some parts of Europe, for example, were densely occupied in the Mesolithic, while it appears that other parts were virtually empty. Moreover, this was not consistent over time: some areas saw peaks and troughs of population, being inhabited at some points, devoid of people at others. Likewise, the social organization of groups was also liable to change. There is evidence for both 'simple' and 'complex' groups (in the ethnographic sense), but societies did not evolve from one to other in a linear progressive sequence. Instead, there is substantial evidence for internal dynamism, which saw groups regularly switching from one to the other and back again. The example of the Jomon of Japan suggests a dynamic and complex sequence of regular growth and collapse, and associated concentrations of population.

Thus, it is clear that the post-glacial is neither a period simply of environmental change nor a homogeneous, self-contained entity, but an important time when there was a whole series of historically contingent and dynamic processes underway. The authors of the chapters in this part of the handbook have highlighted current research into the post-glacial period as well as key areas for future research. Here the three areas that will see further exploration as the study of the post-glacial period expands are summarized.

1. Better information on local environmental variability is required. The diverse environmental conditions that occurred during the post-glacial period have been discussed. However, it is important to do further work on more localized sequences of environmental change. It is quite clear that post-glacial environmental changes manifested themselves quite differently in different parts of the globe—and these small differences were important to local populations. Understanding changing conditions over time in particular areas will enable scholars to understand the range of challenges people were presented with at this time and local responses to these.
2. A better sense of cultural variability across time and space is needed. Internal dynamism and variability in particular sequences has already been highlighted, showing localized outcomes for people in the post-glacial period. There was a range of social opportunities within the new environments of the post-glacial (see Hayden, this volume), which individuals, or entire groups, could use to their advantage, and with some sequences complex groups emerged. Yet this did not happen in many areas. We now need to try to understand regional sequences in their own terms, anticipating cultural variability. In many areas, this will require sustained archaeological programmes of research so that we have the necessary data to investigate this.
3. New data on their own are not enough. New ways of thinking about these detailed cultural and environmental sequences are also required. In order to understand the internal socio-political dynamics of these various post-glacial societies we need to integrate approaches from both processual and interpretive schools. By combining considerations of engagements with landscape, cosmology, identity, and technology, as well as environmental adaptations, we can explore the multitude of ways that hunter-gatherers existed in the post-glacial.

These, then, are the challenges—and opportunities—facing post-glacial studies in the twenty-first century: understanding the complex mix of changing environmental conditions, localized sequences, and individual cultural choices about how best to live in the post-glacial world.

Conclusion

This part highlights some of the challenges and opportunities involved in studying prehistoric hunter-gatherers in the post-glacial period. As outlined above, the post-glacial has clearly, and for a variety of reasons, been a problematic period for archaeologists to define and make sense of in the past. This is, in part, because of an enduring preoccupation in periods either side of the post-glacial, but also because of the enduring legacy of specific modes of thinking, which continue to pervade hunter-gatherer research. The basic challenge now is to move beyond the simpler and older chronological, technological, and socio-economic definitions of this period. While the range of chapters in this part do not cover every area of the globe, they do demonstrate how regional sequences are now understood in their own terms, and not just parts of broader accounts. All the chapters in this part make it clear this is an important period of ongoing change, driven in part by the environment and resulting in a range of technological, social, and economic responses. Critically, there is increasingly the sense of the more localized patterns of change being played out throughout the world. Many future research questions remain, so that this major phase of human cultural adjustment now forms one of the most exciting and important research fields in hunter-gatherer studies.

Acknowledgements

I am very grateful to Peter Jordan for offering useful comments on earlier drafts of this chapter.

References

Alley, R., Meese, C., Shuman, C., Gow, A., Taylor, K., Grotes, P., White, J., Ram, M., Waddington, E., Mayewski, P., and Zielinski, G. 1993. Abrupt increase in Greenland snow accumulation at the end of the Younger Dryas event. *Nature* 362, 527.

Bahn, P. 1996. *Cambridge illustrated history of archaeology*. Cambridge: Cambridge University Press.

Bailey, G. and Spikins, P. (eds) 2008. *Mesolithic Europe*. Cambridge: Cambridge University Press.

Bender, M., Sowers, T., Dickson, M.-L., Orchardo, J., Grootes, P., Mayewski, P. A., and Meese, D. A. 1994. Climatic correlations between Greenland and Antarctica during the past 100,000 years. *Nature* 372, 663–6.

Birks, H. and Ammann, B. 1999. Two terrestrial records of rapid climatic change during the glacial–Holocene transition (14,000–9,000 calendar years BP) from Europe. *Proceedings of the National Academy of Sciences USA* 97, 1390–4.

Childe, V. G. 1942. *What happened in history*. London: Penguin.
Clark, J. G. D. 1954. *Excavations at Star Carr*. Cambridge: Cambridge University Press.
Cobb, H. 2007. Mutable materials and the production of persons: reconfiguring understandings of identity in the Mesolithic of the northern Irish Sea basin. *Journal of Iberian Archaeology* 9/10, 123–36.
Conneller, C. 2004. Becoming deer: corporeal transformations at Star Carr. *Archaeological Dialogues* 11, 37–56.
Conneller, C. and Warren, G. (eds) 2006. *Mesolithic Britain and Ireland: new approaches*. Stroud: Tempus.
Cummings, V. 2000. The origins of monumentality? Mesolithic world-views of the landscape in western Britain. In L. Larsson, H. Kindgren, K. Knutsson, D. Loeffler, and A. Åkerlund (eds), *Mesolithic on the move*, 74–81. Oxford: Oxbow Books.
Edwards, K. 1990. Fire and Scottish Mesolithic: evidence from microscopic charcoal. In P. Vermeersch and P. van Peer (eds), *Contributions to the Mesolithic in Europe*, 71–9. Leuven: Leuven University Press.
Evans, J. G. 1975. *The environment of early man in the British Isles*. London: Book Club.
Finlay, N. 2000. Microliths and multiple authorship. In L. Larsson, H. Kindgren, K. Knutsson, D. Loeffler, and A. Åkerlund (eds), *Mesolithic on the move*, 169–76. Oxford: Oxbow Books.
Finlay, N. 2006. Gender and personhood. In C. Conneller and G. Warren (eds), *Mesolithic Britain and Ireland: new approaches*, 35–60. Stroud: Tempus.
Foley, J., Kutzbach, J., Coe, M., and Levis, S. 1994. Feedbacks between climate and boreal forests during the Holocene epoch. *Nature* 371, 52–4.
Fowler, C. 2004. *The archaeology of personhood*. London: Routledge.
Gosden, C. and Marshall, Y. 1999. The cultural biography of objects. *World Archaeology* 31, 169–78.
Higgs, E. (ed.) 1975. *Palaeoeconomy*. Cambridge: Cambridge University Press.
Hodder, I. 1990. *The domestication of Europe*. Oxford: Blackwell.
Ingold, T. 2000. *The perception of the environment: essays on livelihood, dwelling and skill*. London: Routledge.
Jordan, P. and Zvelebil, M. (eds) 2009. *Ceramics before farming: the dispersal of pottery among prehistoric Eurasian hunter-gatherers*. Walnut Creek, CA: Left Coast Press.
Larsson, L. 1984. *The Skateholm project: a late Mesolithic settlement and cemetery complex at a southern Swedish bay*. Lund: Lund University.
Larsson, L. 1988. *The Skateholm project I: Man and the environment*. Lund: Almqivst and Wiksell.
Larsson, L., Kindgren, H., Knutsson, K., Leoffler D., and Åkerlund A. (eds) 2000. *Mesolithic on the move: papers presented at the Sixth International Conference on the Mesolithic in Europe, Stockholm 2000*. Oxford: Oxbow Books.
Lubbock, J. 1865. *Pre-historic times*. London: Williams and Norgate.
McFadyen, L. 2006. Landscape. In C. Conneller and G. Warren (eds), *Mesolithic Britain and Ireland: new approaches*, 121–38. Stroud: Tempus.
Milner, N. 2006. Subsistence. In C. Conneller and G. Warren (eds), *Mesolithic Britain and Ireland: new approaches*, 61–82. Stroud: Tempus.
Price, T. 1985. Affluent foragers of Mesolithic southern Scandinavia. In T. Price and J. Brown (eds), *Prehistoric hunter-gatherers: the emergence of cultural complexity*, 341–63. Orlando: Academic Press.
Roberts, N. 1998. *The Holocene: an environmental history*. Oxford: Blackwell.

Rowley-Conwy, P. 1983. Sedentary hunters, the Ertebølle example. In G. Bailey (ed.), *Hunter-gatherer economy: a European perspective*, 111–26. Cambridge: Cambridge University Press.

Rowley-Conwy, P. 2006. Why didn't Westropp's 'Mesolithic' catch on in 1872? *Antiquity* 70, 940–4.

Rowley-Conwy, P. 2007. *From genesis to prehistory: the archaeological three age system and its contested reception in Denmark, Britain and Ireland.* Oxford: Oxford University Press.

Rowley-Conwy, P. and Zvelebil, M. 1989. Saving it for later: storage by prehistoric hunter-gatherers in Europe. In P. Halstead and J. O'Shea (eds), *Bad year economics*, 40–56. Cambridge: Cambridge University Press.

Scarre, C. 2013. The world transformed: from foragers and farmers to states and empires. In C. Scarre (ed.), *The human past*, 176–99. London: Thames and Hudson.

Spikins, P. 2008. Mesolithic Europe: glimpses of another world. In G. Bailey and P. Spikins (eds), *Mesolithic Europe*, 1–17. Cambridge: Cambridge University Press.

Tilley, C. 1994. *A phenomenology of landscape.* Oxford: Berg.

Trigger, B. 2006. *History of archaeological thought.* Cambridge: Cambridge University Press.

Warren, G. 2006. Technology. In C. Conneller and G. Warren (eds), *Mesolithic Britain and Ireland: new approaches*, 13–34. Stroud: Tempus.

Whittle, A. 1996. *Europe in the Neolithic: the creation of new worlds.* Cambridge: Cambridge University Press.

Woodman, P. 1978. *The Mesolithic in Ireland.* Oxford: BAR.

Wymer, J. 1977. *Gazetteer of Mesolithic sites in England and Wales.* London: Council for British Archaeology.

Zvelebil, M. (ed.) 1986. *Hunters in transition.* Cambridge: Cambridge University Press.

Zvelebil, M. 1998. What's in a name: the Mesolithic, the Neolithic and social change at the Mesolithic-Neolithic transition. In M. Edmonds and C. Richards (eds), *Understanding the Neolithic of North-western Europe*, 1–36. Glasgow: Cruithne Press.

Zvelebil, M. 2000. Enculturation of Mesolithic landscapes. In L. Larsson, H. Kindgren, K. Knutsson, D. Loeffler, and A. Åkerlund (eds), *Mesolithic on the move*, 65–73. Oxford: Oxbow Books.

Zvelebil, M. 2008. Innovating hunter-gatherers: the Mesolithic in the Baltic. In G. Bailey and P. Spikins (eds), *Mesolithic Europe*, 18–59. Cambridge: Cambridge University Press.

Zvelebil, M. 2009. The Mesolithic and the 21st century. In S. McCartan, R. J. Schulting, G. M. Warren, and P. C. Woodman (eds), *Mesolithic horizons: papers presented at the seventh international conference on the Mesolithic in Europe, Belfast 2005*, xlvii–lviii. Oxford: Oxbow Books.

Zvelebil, M. and Fewster, K. 2001. Pictures at an exhibition: ethnoarchaeology and hunter-gatherers. In K. Fewster and M. Zvelebil (eds), *Ethnoarchaeology and hunter-gatherers: pictures at an exhibition*, 143–57. Oxford: BAR.

Zvelebil, M. and Rowley-Conwy, P. 1986. Foragers and farmers in Atlantic Europe. In M. Zvelebil (ed.), *Hunters in transition*, 67–93. Cambridge: Cambridge University Press.

CHAPTER 19

POST-GLACIAL TRANSFORMATIONS AMONG HUNTER-GATHERER SOCIETIES IN THE MEDITERRANEAN AND WESTERN ASIA

ANDREW M. T. MOORE

Setting the Scene

At the beginning of the Holocene 11,500 years ago the shores of the Mediterranean Sea, their hinterlands, and several of the islands were thinly peopled with hunter-gatherers. These hunter-gatherer societies were to persist for two to three thousand years, depending on location, when they were succeeded by settlements of farmers whose ultimate origins lay in western Asia. The onset of the Holocene coincided approximately with the transition from the final phases of the Palaeolithic to the Mesolithic around much of the Mediterranean. At the extreme eastern end of the Mediterranean, however, the transition to farming had already taken place towards the end of the preceding late glacial. This chapter first describes the environmental setting of the region and the changes that took place during the early millennia of the Holocene, next it discusses the development of farming in western Asia, then it outlines the nature of the Mesolithic hunter-gatherer societies of the Mediterranean basin, and finally it considers the spread of farming through the Mediterranean and its consequences.

The coastline of the Mediterranean is unusually irregular and very long. The main axis of this tidal basin lies west to east. Immediately inland from the coast are steep ranges of mountains which for long stretches fall directly into the sea. In a few places only, for example at the head of the Adriatic and near the deltas of the Rhône and the Nile, does the land slope gently up from the coast. Offshore, there are many islands. Some of them like Sardinia, Sicily, and Cyprus are very large and most are readily visible from the mainland. A few were inhabited, at least intermittently, far back in the Palaeolithic, but many were permanently colonized only during the Holocene.

This distinctive geography has imposed certain constraints on human settlement. The mountains have inhibited communication on foot along the shoreline and also inland. Consequently, until modern times, most communication was by sea following the coast. The main variations in environment around the Mediterranean occur vertically up the slopes of the mountains over relatively short horizontal distances. Thus, hunter-gatherers and, later, herders with their flocks often moved up and down the mountains seasonally to obtain food and to seek pasture.

The climate of the Mediterranean today is characterized by mild, wet winters and hot, dry summers, with quite brief springs and autumns. This distinctive regime has been maintained since the mid Holocene but, during the period we are considering, it was not yet completely in place. Consequently, the vegetation at the beginning of the Holocene was significantly different from today. Importantly, too, although sea levels had risen substantially from their pleni-glacial lows, they were still well below those of the present. The beginning of the Holocene was marked by a sharp increase in temperature and moisture after the cold, dry conditions of the Younger Dryas, a 1,500-year episode of climatic reversal at the end of the Pleistocene. However, temperatures were still several degrees below present-day values. They reached a post-glacial maximum around 6,000 years ago. The changes in temperature and rainfall were uneven, with fluctuations lasting many centuries (Hoek and Bos 2007). One sharp return to drier conditions has been detected $c.8200$ BP (Grove and Rackham 2001, 145; Weninger et al. 2006), and this appears to have had a marked effect on human settlement, especially in western Asia and the eastern Mediterranean (Moore 1982, 25).

Sea levels worldwide depend on the changing balance between water frozen in ice sheets and in the oceans. Eustatic adjustment caused by melting ice has been the main factor in sea-level rise since the Last Glacial Maximum. Sea levels along the coasts during the Holocene may also have been significantly affected by the response of land surfaces to the melting of ice sheets, i.e. to isostatic effects (van Andel 1989). The Mediterranean is a zone of active plate movements. Consequently, tectonic shifts had marked local impacts on sea levels (Lambeck 1995). Determining the nature of sea-level change around the Mediterranean is complex, but recent research has provided quite detailed sequences for these effects, at least for southern Europe and western Asia (Lambeck and Purcell 2005).

At the time of the Pleistocene–Holocene transition sea levels worldwide were about 55 m below those of the present day (Fairbanks 1989, figure 2), and have continued to rise ever since. This estimate has been confirmed for long stretches of the Mediterranean coastline (Lambeck and Bard 2000; Lambeck et al. 2004). Around 8,000 years ago, as farming spread through the central and western Mediterranean, sea levels were still 20 m below current levels. Around the Mediterranean during the early Holocene the shore often lay several kilometres out from the present coastline, especially in North Africa and the eastern Mediterranean, the Adriatic, southern France, and Spain (Forenbaher 2002; van Andel 1989, 736). Coastal sites occupied during the Mesolithic and earlier Neolithic would have been drowned as the level of the sea rose. Thus, most evidence for marine and coastal adaptations has disappeared. Shoreline resources are likely to have been an important element of the Mesolithic way of life so this loss is significant because it inhibits us from reaching a comprehensive understanding of human settlement and economy during this episode.

Towards the end of the Pleistocene much of the Mediterranean region was covered in grassland with scattered shrubs and trees. During the early Holocene this was replaced by open mixed, often deciduous, woodland, with scattered evergreens (Bottema 2003, 46–8; Grove and Rackham 2001, 156–61; Šoštarić 2005). The latter came to predominate over time. At higher elevations pines and firs became widespread. Thus, most Mesolithic and early Neolithic people inhabited a landscape that was lightly wooded with vegetation cover significantly different from the present day. It was not until the mid-Holocene that the typical modern vegetation of evergreen shrubs and small trees with open grasslands in drier areas became widespread (Grove and Rackham 2001, 166). There was, of course, much regional variation in this pattern of change.

Archaeological evidence for human settlement and economy during the early Holocene comes from a variety of sources. First, there are the habitation sites themselves, the inferences to be derived from their locations, and their patterns of distribution across the landscape. Then there are the artefacts recovered from them. The most numerous are those made of flint, with an admixture of modest numbers of stone and bone tools. Mesolithic flint assemblages around the Mediterranean, as elsewhere in Europe, tend to be dominated by small retouched pieces, of which various kinds of microliths are conspicuous. These manifest an especially efficient use of raw material to make composite tools. Pottery became ubiquitous after 8000 BP. Plant and animal remains recovered from archaeological sites are the main source of information about the economy. Here traditional reliance on morphological characteristics, kill-off patterns of animals, and percentages of relative abundance, is rapidly being supplemented by information from genetics. For chronology we depend entirely on radiocarbon dates, of which those obtained from short-lived species using accelerator mass spectrometry (AMS) are the most useful.

Open Mesolithic sites often consist of little more than a scatter of flints in the landscape. Given that these flints are usually small and few in number, such sites are particularly difficult to spot, even in intensive surveys. Archaeologists familiar with the locations preferred by Mesolithic hunter-gatherers in a particular region can use this knowledge to find sites (Komšo 2006, 60; Runnels 2009), but even so the density of such occurrences in the Mediterranean region seems always to have been low. Mesolithic occupation in caves and rock shelters can be clearly identified through excavation, but indications of such use are rarely visible on the surface. So, is the paucity of known Mesolithic sites a reflection of low initial population densities or their low visibility? Probably both.

In contrast, Neolithic sites are more visible, usually because they are larger and contain abundant artefacts, some of which may be seen on the ground surface. Such sites, however, rarely have structures above ground level. An exception would be the settlement mounds typical of northern Greece and Bulgaria.

Western Asia in the Early Holocene

Following the Late Glacial Maximum, hunter-gather populations in the more favoured parts of western Asia began to grow, and a few among them established the first substantial villages that were inhabited year-round. The onset of the Younger Dryas, c.13,000 BP, provided the catalyst for a fundamental change in economy. At Abu Hureyra in the middle

Euphrates Valley the inhabitants began to cultivate cereals and legumes (Moore et al. 2000, 479). The first attempts at caprine management followed, perhaps around 12,000 BP (Zeder 2008, 11598). Sheep and goats were first domesticated in south-eastern Anatolia and the Zagros mountains around 11,000 BP, and pigs and cattle a little later. This new agricultural economy, combining arable farming and animal herding, developed gradually over a large area of western Asia, though people continued to obtain some of their food from wild plants and game until quite late in the Neolithic.

The adoption of farming had a profound effect on settlement. Sedentary villages became the normal mode of habitation across a wide area of western Asia, from the Jordan Valley north and east around the Fertile Crescent, including the Middle Euphrates and Tigris valleys with their tributaries, and south-east along the lower valleys of the Zagros mountains (Figure 19.1). During this first phase of the early Neolithic, Pre-Pottery Neolithic A in the Jericho sequence (c.12,000 to 11,000 BP), these villages consisted of tightly-packed dwellings, a form of nucleated settlement that became characteristic, though with local variations, across much of the region. The houses were often circular with one or more rooms, a continuation of a building tradition that had begun in the Epi-Palaeolithic. Several villages that have been excavated recently exemplify this pattern, among them Mureybat (Cauvin 1977) and Jerf el Ahmar (Stordeur and Willcox 2009) in the Euphrates Valley, Nemrik on the upper Tigris (Kozlowski 2002), and M'lefaat on a tributary of the Greater Zab in northern Mesopotamia (Aurenche and Kozlowski 1999, 176). Some settlements, notably Jericho (4 ha), grew very large indeed, a direct result of the marked growth in population that followed the development of agriculture. Furthermore, at Jericho we see the construction of the first monumental architecture. The settlement was surrounded by a rock-cut ditch and a series of stone walls within which stood a stone tower with a central staircase (Kenyon 1981, 19, 26).

During the early Neolithic the inhabitants of these settled villages elaborated their ideas concerning the disposal of the dead. They buried some bodies within the settlements, either under the floors or in the yards outside. In some instances, they detached the skulls as, for example, at Jericho and Jerf el Ahmar (Kenyon 1981, plate 36; Stordeur et al. 2000, 37). This quite formal set of burial rites again has its roots in the preceding Epi-Palaeolithic, at Natufian sites such as Mugharet el Wad and Ain Mallaha (Garrod 1957, 220; Perrot and Ladiray 1988, 63), and even as far back as the early Epi-Palaeolithic site of Ohalo II, c.22,000 BP (Hershkovitz et al. 1995), inhabited during the last glaciation.

Several sites of this general time period have yielded quite rich assemblages of fine carved stone objects, attesting to rich symbolic preoccupations. At Hallan Çemi, c.12,000 BP, on the Sason River in south-east Anatolia, there were pestles with carved animal heads and notched stone batons; similar objects have been recovered from the slightly later site of Demirköy to the south (Rosenberg 1999, 30). Nemrik has also yielded rod-like objects, this time with bird heads (Kozlowski 2002, table 6, plates 138–41). More bird-headed rods have been found at Jerf el Ahmar with, in addition, a series of small oblong stones with engraved designs of animals and also abstract signs (Stordeur and Jammous 1997). These engraved flat stones appear to have been intended to convey messages, though their nature remains obscure.

In southern Anatolia on the fringes of the Fertile Crescent there is a cluster of sites that possess buildings of apparently ceremonial purpose. The two best known are Nevali Çori in the upper Euphrates Valley and Göbekli Tepe near Urfa (Hauptmann 1999). Each site had

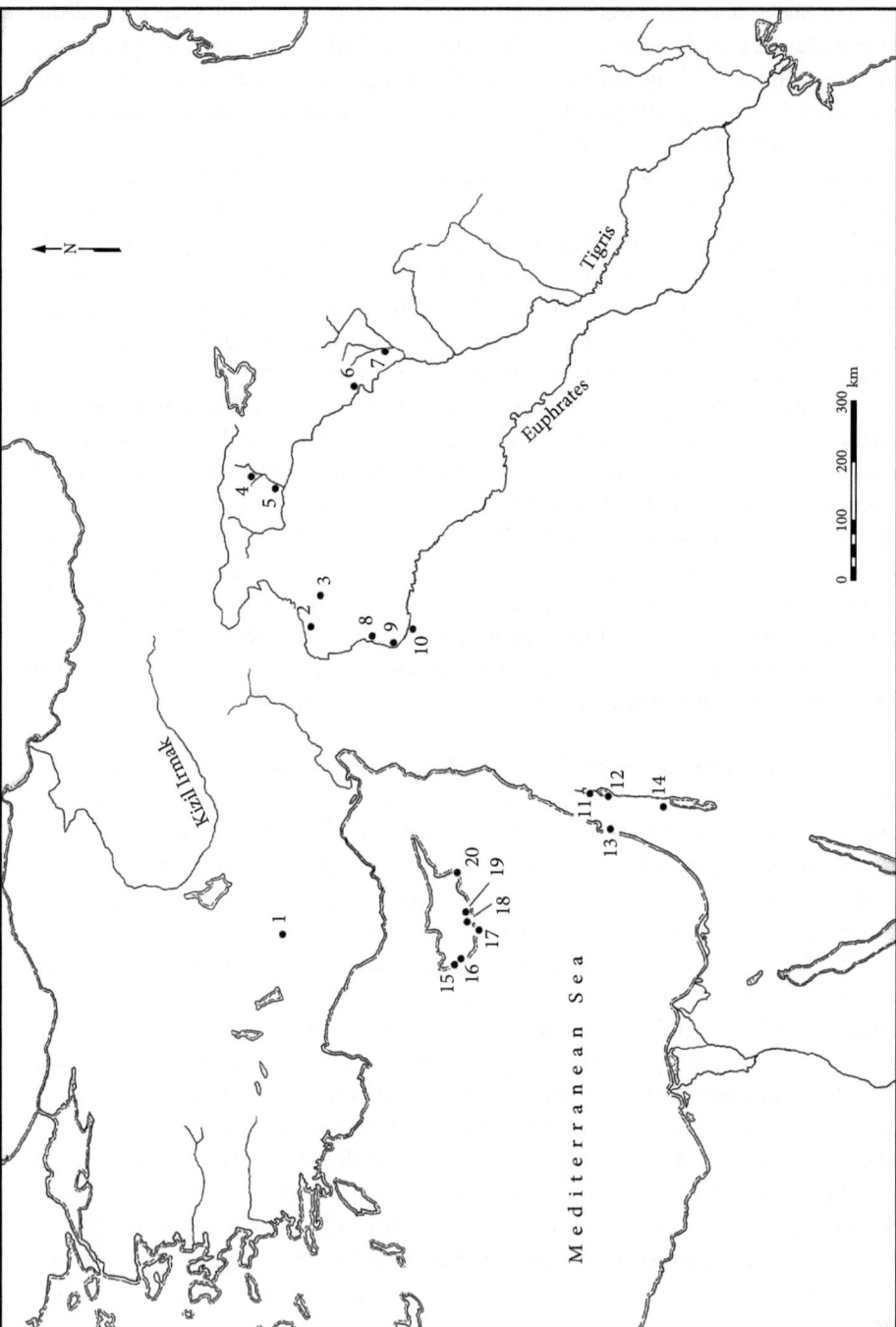

FIGURE 19.1 Selected Neolithic sites in Western Asia. 1 Çatal Hüyük; 2 Nevali Çori; 3 Göbekli Tepe; 4 Hallan Çemi; 5 Demirköy; 6 Nemrik; 7 M'lefaat; 8 Jerf el Ahmar; 9 Mureybat; 10 Abu Hureyra; 11 Ain Mallaha; 12 Ohalo II; 13 Mugharet el Wad; 14 Jericho; 15 Aspros; 16 Mylouthkia; 17 Aetokremnos; 18 Shillourokambos; 19 Kalavasos Tenta; 20 Nissi Beach.

buildings containing T-shaped pillars two to three metres high with carvings of animals and birds on their smoothed faces. Within the buildings were stone carvings of human heads and other creatures. The functions of these buildings remain unclear. What is certain is that the 'cult building' at Nevali Çori is unlike the houses and other structures uncovered there. Likewise, the large buildings with curved walls containing the carved pillars at Göbekli Tepe have yet to be found elsewhere. These structures may have served as gathering places for their communities as well as for ritual activities, among other possibilities. Whatever their purposes, they represent new forms of monumental building, as do the walls and tower of Jericho far to the south.

In the second stage of the early Neolithic in western Asia, c.11,000 to 8000 BP, Pre-Pottery Neolithic B at Jericho, the total number of settlements across the region markedly increased, a direct consequence of the rising productivity of farming. Some of the best known of these sites were very large indeed: Abu Hureyra extended over some 16 ha and Çatal Hüyük over 12.5 ha, while many others reached 10 ha in size. Most sites were much smaller than this, villages of a few thousand square metres up to perhaps a hectare. Yet the larger sites seem to have been simply that, expanded villages little different in form from their smaller counterparts. There is nothing here to indicate that there were marked differences in status among their inhabitants. Such sites do strongly suggest, however, that new forms of social organization had come into existence, with authority delegated to smaller groups of people who would have managed the affairs of the village (Moore et al. 2000, 520–1).

These villages were composed of densely packed, multi-roomed rectangular houses, a new form of architecture. In the lowlands most communities used mud brick for building, while stone was preferred in the hilly districts where it was abundant. The elaboration of burial rites continued, with evidence for multi-stage processing of corpses before final deposition, seen very clearly at Abu Hureyra (Moore et al. 2000, chapter 10).

By 8000 BP a mature mixed farming economy comprising an array of domestic cereals, legumes, and other crops, and all four of the main domestic animals, formed the basis of settled life across the better-watered lands of western Asia. In the steppe regions beyond, pastoralists herding flocks of sheep and goats were pursuing a mobile way of life that would have been recognizable as late as the last century. A combination of increasing pressure on the available arable land and an episode of aridity disrupted the agricultural economy over a period of several centuries. This was accompanied by movements of population within the Fertile Crescent, to the most fertile regions to the north, and west near the coast (Moore 1985, 52).

Beginning somewhat earlier, agriculture began to spread far wider, eastward into central and southern Asia, south-westward into the Nile Valley and North Africa, and westward into south-eastern Europe and around the Mediterranean. The key crops and animals that had already been domesticated in western Asia, wheat, barley, and other cereals, the pulses, sheep, goat, cattle, and pigs, became the basis of farming in these distant regions. The spread of farming to the Mediterranean was thus part of a much larger Eurasian phenomenon. We should ask, then, how it came about.

This process of economic expansion has not been well studied from where it began, in western Asia, but it is here that we should look for its initial impetus. Following the domestication of plants and animals and the expansion of village settlements, populations grew significantly. This is most evident in the development of many sites several hectares in extent whose populations may be counted in the thousands. The by-now numerous farmers had choices: they could intensify their agricultural system or they could maintain a less labour-intensive way of life by moving to new lands where population densities were lower. It seems that they did both (Bellwood 2005, 67; Harris 1996, 557, 563). We have already seen that there were considerable population movements within western Asia, but some took their well-established farming way of life farther afield. There may have been few of these migrants at first but, once settled in new lands, their numbers would have expanded rapidly. Small local bands of foragers would have been simply displaced or absorbed.

This view has been contested by some European archaeologists who have argued that local Mesolithic populations may have developed or, at least, adopted some elements of an agricultural economy themselves. These varying points of view have been explored in several recent volumes, notably those edited by Price (2000) and Ammerman and Biagi (2003). Those who claim that European Mesolithic groups themselves became farmers have not, however, explained why they should have abandoned hunting and gathering in favour of a way of life that demands so much hard work. Research over the last generation has confirmed that the plants and animals that formed the basis of the western Eurasian farming economy were first domesticated in South-West Asia. Recent genetic studies have indicated that several of these species may have been domesticated more than once, itself an important observation, but this research has also confirmed the primacy of South-West Asia as the location of the earliest domestications and mixed farming economy (wheat and barley: Morrell and Clegg 2007; Pourkheirandish and Komatsuda 2007; Salamini et al. 2002; sheep: Bruford and Townsend 2006; goats: Luikart et al. 2006; cattle: Bradley and Magee 2006; pigs: Albarella et al. 2006). Farming thus spread from this region through the Mediterranean.

Cyprus

The island of Cyprus may have been inhabited during the Palaeolithic given that it is large and readily visible in winter from the Turkish and Syrian coasts. But the earliest reasonably certain evidence for human activities from the site of Aetokremnos dates to around the Pleistocene–Holocene transition (Simmons 2004). It is here that we confront an issue that pervades Mesolithic studies in the Mediterranean: the question of visibility. Early Holocene sites of Mesolithic affinities have rarely been found anywhere in the eastern Mediterranean, and it is only recently with the use of more sophisticated survey methods that they have been identified on Cyprus and the coasts of the Aegean (Ammerman et al. 2008; Runnels et al. 2005). The site of Nissi Beach and others recently identified on Cyprus are located just above the present-day shoreline on formations of aeolianite and have been subject to much deflation. Such sites would originally have been situated on bluffs overlooking the coastal plain. It follows that there would have been other sites much closer to the ancient shoreline, but these would now lie under the sea. One such submerged site has been found at Aspros on the west coast of the island (Ammerman et al. 2008, 4). These sites appear to represent camps of small groups of hunters and gatherers that would have used these locations in a seasonal round. Their locations near the ancient coastline suggest that fishing, collecting shellfish, and fowling provided some of the sustenance of the inhabitants. Human occupation of such sites also confirms that people were travelling around the eastern Mediterranean by sea during the early Holocene.

Beginning just before 10,000 BP farmers arrived in Cyprus from the mainland. They settled at sites several kilometres inland from the ancient coastline, among them Shillourokambos, Kalavasos Tenta, and Mylouthkia (Guilaine 2003, 191; Peltenburg et al. 2001; Todd 1987). These substantial settlements were each occupied for much of the tenth millennium BP. The initial phases of occupation consisted of timber structures, followed by an episode characterized by substantial curvilinear stone buildings, some of which were clearly houses. Thus began a tradition of constructing circular buildings on Cyprus that remained a feature of settlements there until much later in prehistory. Deep wells have been excavated at Mylouthkia that contained abundant artefacts and organic remains. These wells and other deposits at Shillourokambos contained human remains that hint at special treatment of skulls (Peltenburg et al. 2001, 53–4), a funerary custom presumably brought in from the mainland where it had a long prior history.

These villages have yielded significant evidence for the cultivation of crops and herding of domestic animals. Among the domestic cereals from Mylouthkia were einkorn, emmer, and hulled barley, together with legumes and flax. Domestic sheep and goats were predominant in the faunal samples at Shillourokambos, with pigs, a few cattle and also dogs. All of these must have been brought to the island from the mainland, probably the nearby Syrian coast, where they had been domesticated. Among the other faunal remains were bones of fallow deer. It is assumed that these were imported as wild animals and then released to be pursued as game.

The flint assemblages at these sites closely resemble the blade industries characteristic of the second stage of the Neolithic on the mainland, the Pre-Pottery Neolithic B. The numerous pieces of obsidian recovered from Shillourokambos all derive from sources in Cappadocia. Thus, there must also have been close contact with the contemporary inhabitants of the southern coast of Anatolia.

There is as yet no evidence to suggest that these Neolithic farmers were anything other than immigrants. Certainly, their entire way of life has significant elements derived from contemporary communities on the mainland. It appears, therefore, that they effectively replaced the hunters and gatherers of earlier millennia on the island. This new economic and cultural configuration had a long and increasingly idiosyncratic history on Cyprus.

The Aegean and Greece

The mainland of Greece was inhabited during the Upper Palaeolithic, but there is no discernible continuity into the Mesolithic (Runnels 2001, 245). It was once thought that Greece and the Aegean islands were almost devoid of habitation during the Mesolithic. More sites have been discovered in recent decades and several of them have been excavated. Notwithstanding, the region still seems to have been sparsely inhabited and use of the excavated sites was intermittent. Mesolithic sites are mostly located near the present coastlines in north-west Greece, the shores of the Argolid, and on several of the Aegean islands (Runnels et al. 2005; Figure 19.1; Figure 19.2). Here, as in other coastal regions of the Mediterranean, more sites must lie beneath the sea. Inland sites are rare. Most known Mesolithic sites are

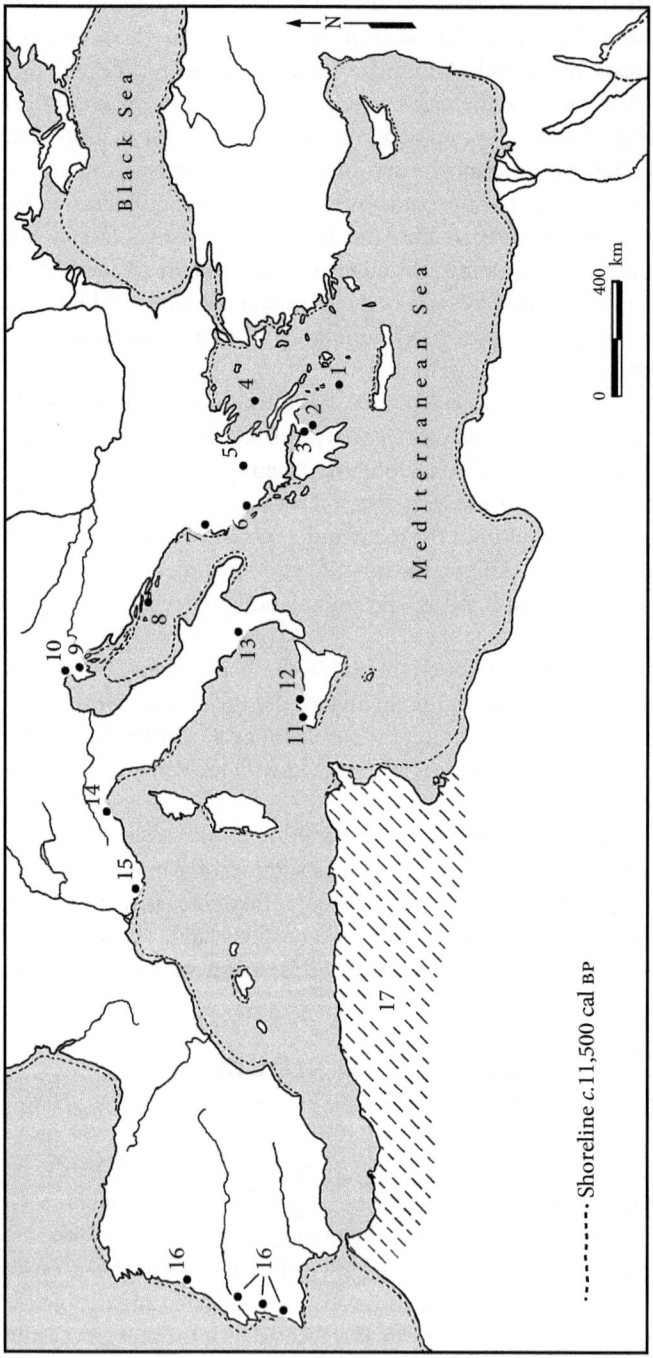

FIGURE 19.2 Selected Mesolithic sites in the Mediterranean. The shorelines c.11,500 cal BP and in the present day are delineated. 1 Melos; 2 Franchthi cave; 3 Cave 1, Klisoura Gorge; 4 Cave of Cyclope, Youra, Sporades; 5 Theopetra cave; 6 Konispol cave; 7 Kryegjata B; 8 Vela Spila; 9 Pupićina cave; 10 Grotta dell'Edera; 11 Grotta dell'Addaura; 12 Grotta dell'Uzzo; 13 Grotta del Santuario della Madonna; 14 Grotta delle Arene Candide; 15 Châteauneuf-les-Martigues; 16 Portuguese shell middens; 17 North African Mesolithic Capsian sites.

caves and rock shelters in which habitation deposits have been preserved. They often overlook river valleys, marshes, and more distant shorelines.

The absolute chronology for the Mesolithic has been determined with reasonable precision, though mostly from conventional radiocarbon rather than accelerator dates. It began early in the Holocene around 10,800 BP and continued until 8800 BP (Facorellis 2003), with local variations. This phase, then, lasted for about two thousand years before its abrupt end with the onset of the Neolithic.

The chipped stone assemblages from these sites are composed for the most part of small flake tools, with significant quantities of retouched pieces, scrapers, notches, and denticulates. Retouched bladelets and geometric microliths varied in abundance among sites and phases. Perlès has posed a strong functional link between the occurrence of these different kinds of tools, especially the microliths, and the nature of the local hunting and gathering economy at Franchthi cave (Perlès 2003, 82). She has suggested that geometric microliths may have been used to prepare equipment for tunny fishing. Her observation has clear implications for other sites in the region. Small quantities of obsidian have been found at a few sites, all of it from Melos. This provides further evidence for sea travel and also emphasizes how mobile these Mesolithic groups were.

Small quantities of bone and antler tools have been found at several sites. Among the most distinctive were the fish hooks and bipoints from the Cave of Cyclope on the island of Youra in the northern Aegean (Moundrea-Agrafioti 2003). The remainder of the artefact inventories from these sites sometimes included a few beads and other ornamental items, and small grinding stones. These artefacts could be swiftly manufactured and were highly portable. They reinforce the inference that the people who made them were very mobile and travelled light.

Franchthi cave has yielded significant evidence for the disposal of the dead. The remains of at least 28 individual burials have been recovered from the site and scatters of bones from several more (Cullen 1995, 274). Several of these burials came from the same spot where they had been interred in succession. Some individuals had been cremated. These individuals ranged from infants to mature adults. While the sample is small, it does indicate that individuals of all ages could receive formal burial within the habitation site and that certain places were preferred for such interments. A single burial of a young adult female from Theopetra cave in Thessaly confirms that similar burial customs were carried out elsewhere (Manolis and Stravopodi 2003). However, these modest samples suggest that most of the dead were disposed of beyond the habitation sites.

The plant and animal remains from Franchthi are relatively few in number, but they do provide some indication of the economy of this key site during the Mesolithic (Perlès 2003, 81). The inhabitants gathered wild lentils, barley, and oats as well as pistachio fruits, almonds, and wild pears. They also hunted red deer, wild boar, and hares and collected land snails. It appears that they followed a generalized pattern of foraging in a landscape that lacked abundant wild resources. This modest array of species suggests that the environs of the site were fairly open. During the Upper Mesolithic the inhabitants engaged in fishing, mainly for tunny but also for a few other marine fish and shellfish. This attests to some familiarity with boats, as does the presence of Melian obsidian.

This pattern of gathering, hunting, and, on sites near the shore, fishing, seems to have prevailed throughout the region. The few animal bones from Cave 1 in the Klisoura Gorge, for example, came from hares, wild boar, and fallow deer (Koumouzelis et al. 2003, 118).

There were also bones from rock partridge and great bustard. Abundant fish bones have been recovered from the island site of the Cave of Cyclope on Youra in the Sporades (Powell 2003). The most common species were sea bream and tunny with mackerel, but there were also many others. Among the animals were red deer, pigs, and some goats of enigmatic status. There were also marine and land birds.

The Arrival of Farming in South-East Europe

Neolithic farming sites are distributed quite widely around the Aegean basin and on the islands within it, while some sites are also known from Crete (Figure 19.3). There are concentrations in the lowlands of Thrace from the Bosphorus westwards (Özdoğan 1999), in Macedonia, a notable cluster in Thessaly, and others to the south in Boeotia and the Argolid (Perlès 2001). Most are located on arable land suitable for productive cultivation, and this helps to explain the paucity of sites in the more rugged terrain of western Greece and along the Ionian coast. The earliest Neolithic settlements date from about 9000 BP, with local variations (Perlès 2001, figure 5.5). The entire period lasted some 3,000 years.

These sites often form conspicuous mounds because the collapsed houses that make up their bulk were built of mud brick or wattle and daub (Perlès 2001, table 9.1). This represents a translation of a traditional western Asian mode of building, with some modifications, to new regions. Such mound settlements or tells are found widely distributed through the Balkans as well as the Aegean in the Neolithic. These villages were inhabited for many centuries, attesting to a stable pattern of settlement of long duration.

The houses were often square, single-roomed constructions, as at Nea Nikomedia, Otzaki, Argissa, and other sites. They were quite widely spaced, with open areas and pits in between. The artefacts found in and among them were abundant and varied. There were chipped stone blades of obsidian, flint, and jasper, and these raw materials were obtained from sources distant from the villages (Perlès 2001, 201). The tools were quite different from those of the preceding Mesolithic. In addition to these cutting tools, there were numerous axes, adzes, chisels, and grinding stones. Bone tools were abundant and carefully made (Perlès 2001, 239) and there are clear indications that baskets and mats were used.

Conspicuous among the new kinds of artefacts was pottery, at first simple in shape and manufacture, but later distinguished by an array of forms and exuberant painted decoration (Vitelli 1995). Other baked clay objects were made for the first time, among them stamps, spindle whorls, and missiles. Notable were human figurines of highly stylized form. These objects indicate that the villagers routinely engaged in a variety of crafts, some of which were new to the region.

The evidence for the disposal of the dead is both varied and incomplete (Perlès 2001, 280–2). Some adults were buried in pits between the houses while others were cremated in, apparently, quite complex rituals. There are a few instances of secondary burial. Children were sometimes interred in pits with the simplest of rites, but the rather scanty evidence for burials suggests that the dead were mostly disposed of away from the settlements, as was the custom in much of western Asia during the later Neolithic.

The economy of these Neolithic villages was based almost entirely on arable farming and husbandry (Perlès 2001, 154–70). The main crops were emmer, einkorn, barley, lentils,

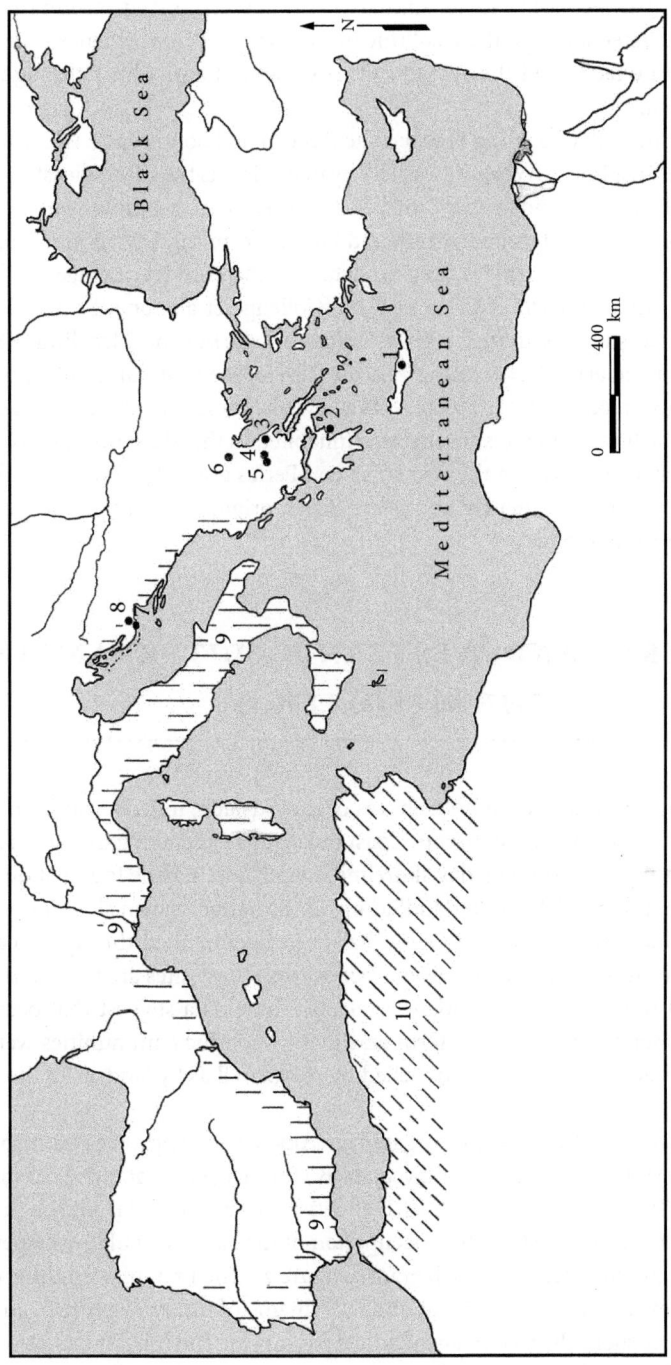

FIGURE 19.3 Selected Neolithic sites in the Mediterranean. 1 Knossos; 2 Franchthi cave; 3 cluster of sites in Thessaly; 4 Argissa; 5 Otzaki; 6 Nea Nikomedia; 7 Danilo; 8 Pokrovnik; 9 Impressed Ware sites in the central and western Mediterranean; 10 North African Neolithic sites of Capsian Tradition.

peas, and vetches, though other plants were also grown. Sheep, with some goats, were the most numerous domestic animals. Cattle were also abundant on some sites and pigs were commonly raised. This economy looks similar to the mature mixed farming economy characteristic of the later stages of the Neolithic in western Asia from whence it came. The similarities in climate facilitated the spread of this version of agriculture throughout the Mediterranean basin.

It used to be thought that farming reached the Aegean and south-eastern Europe from Anatolia across the Bosphorus. While it is still likely that this was the case, at least for Thrace and the nearer Balkans (Marinova 2007, 106; Özdoğan 1999, 211), it now seems probable that agriculture spread to Crete, the Aegean, and Greece from the Levant via Cyprus and the coast of southern Anatolia. This is because details of the crop assemblages and of certain artefacts are similar in each of these regions (Colledge et al. 2004, S47; Perlès 2001, 62–3). New evidence suggests that Crete was inhabited during the Mesolithic (Strasser et al. 2010, 186) but the arrival of farming and the development of village life, seen most clearly at Knossos (Sarpaki 2009, 231), represents a new phenomenon. This is also the case at Franchthi, one of the few mainland sites that was inhabited in the Mesolithic and Neolithic, though with a clear break between the two episodes (Perlès 2003, 84). The most plausible explanation is that farmers, ultimately of western Asian origin, were migrating westwards bringing agriculture with them.

The Central and Western Mediterranean in the Mesolithic

Mesolithic sites have been found on both shores of the Adriatic, in Italy, southern France, the Levantine coast of Spain, on the Atlantic coast of Portugal, and along the North African littoral. They occur from the present-day shoreline inland, and may be found at quite high altitudes in the mountains of the hinterland. Many of the better-known sites are caves and rock shelters in which Mesolithic occupation has been documented through excavation. There are also open sites in varying locations. Deposits on these sites are for the most part relatively thin and rarely contain abundant artefacts. These data suggest that occupation tended to be seasonal rather than long term and that Mesolithic communities were quite mobile (Pluciennik 2008, 340–3). They travelled by sea as well as by land, as in the eastern Mediterranean.

Several sites have recently been investigated in Albania, among them Konispol cave (Petruso et al. 1996) and an open site, Kryegjata B (Runnels et al. 2004), both near the present-day coast. The most significant site in Dalmatia is the cave of Vela Spila on the island of Korčula. At the time of the Mesolithic occupation of the cave, Korčula was a peninsula extending out into the Adriatic (Forenbaher 2002, figure 2). The 1.5 m of Mesolithic deposit yielded relatively few artefacts but quite abundant remains of tunny, swordfish, and other fish bones, as well as shellfish (Čečuk and Radić 2005, 61–2). The inhabitants also hunted wild boar, fallow deer, and hares. Mesolithic sites are scarce on the Dalmatian mainland. However, there is a concentration of open and cave sites in Istria and on the nearby offshore islands, of which several were discovered in recent, focused surveys (Komšo 2006,

60). During the Mesolithic, Istria would have been a hilly, well-dissected, hinterland overlooking an extensive open plain at the head of the Adriatic. The recently excavated site of Pupićina cave was probably inhabited seasonally during the early Mesolithic (Komšo 2006, 60–2; Miracle and Forenbaher 2006, 456). Mesolithic deposits in a cave high in the Velebit mountains that was scarcely habitable in winter also attest to seasonal movements (Komšo 2006, 70). The presence of marine shells at these inland sites confirms this observation. Further north there is a group of rock shelters and caves in the karstic mountains behind Trieste that was occupied in the Mesolithic. The best known of these is the Grotta dell'Edera which was inhabited during the earlier Mesolithic (Biagi and Spataro 1999–2000, 32–5). There are other Mesolithic sites in the Adige Valley extending into the Dolomites (Biagi and Spataro 1999–2000, 46).

In central and southern Italy both open and cave sites have been found, with evidence for fishing and shellfish collection on the coastal sites and hunting of small and medium-sized game inland (Barker 1981, 52; Mussi 2001, 304–32). A long sequence of occupation from the Palaeolithic into the Neolithic has been investigated at the Grotta del Santuario della Madonna on the Tyrrhenian coast. The best-known site on Sicily is the Grotta dell'Uzzo (Biagi and Spataro 1999–2000, 22, 29).

Another very long sequence of occupation, including a short early Mesolithic episode, has been exposed at the Grotta delle Arene Candide west of Genoa (Biagi and Spataro 1999–2000, 38; Maggi 1997). In southern France Mesolithic sites have been identified along the Mediterranean coast and inland, in Provence, the Rhône Valley, Languedoc, Roussillon, and the foothills of the Pyrenees (Binder 2000; Guilaine and Manen 2007). Many of these are caves and rock shelters in which the Mesolithic deposits have been investigated through excavation. Among the better known of these is Châteauneuf-les-Martigues (Escalon de Fonton 1976, 1376).

Mesolithic sites are apparently absent from the interior of the Iberian Peninsula (Zilhão 2003, 209). The known sites consist of caves and rock shelters with a few open camps in Catalonia, Valencia, and Andalucia. Notable are clusters of shell midden sites along the estuaries and coastline of south-west Portugal (Zilhão 2003, figure 11.1). Here there seems to have been a distinct shift towards the use of riverine and maritime resources early in the Holocene (Aura et al. 1998, 91).

In North Africa a century of research has identified Mesolithic sites eastward from the Straits of Gibraltar to the Gulf of Sirte (Tixier 1963, figure 1). These vary from caves and rock shelters to open sites, including the distinctive land snail middens of inland Algeria and Tunisia. The cultural remains found on these sites suggest some continuity with the previous late Palaeolithic Iberomaurusian phase (Linstädter 2008, 48), though with significant adjustments in the pattern of settlement during the transition to the Holocene. Developments in the Maghreb, while generally similar to those on the opposite shores of the Mediterranean, had some distinctive features, no doubt because the region was open to the Sahara to the south and south-east at a time of climatic amelioration.

Throughout the central and western Mediterranean the Mesolithic lasted for at least three thousand years. It developed in two phases marked by changes in the chipped stone assemblages. The terminal Palaeolithic, typified by the Azilian in south-west France and the Romanellian in Italy with many scrapers and backed blades, gave way at the beginning of the Holocene to industries of Sauveterrian affinities in which microliths were conspicuous, especially triangles (Binder 2000, 119; Escalon de Fonton 1976). In the Castelnovian of the later Mesolithic trapezes were a characteristic element (Mussi 2001, 288). There were usually small numbers of bone points and other tools and ornamental items. The sequence in the Maghreb parallels that of the northern Mediterranean coast, with earlier and later phases of the Capsian, again with microliths (Linstädter 2008, 47) that probably derive from the preceding Iberomaurusian (Bouzouggar et al. 2008, 5). There was, of course, much local variation in these assemblages from one region to another (Biagi 2003).

One of the more remarkable elements of Mesolithic culture in the central and western Mediterranean was art in a variety of media. While scarcely abundant, parietal cave art occurred from Levantine Spain to southern Italy (Pluciennik 2008, 349). It presumably derived from Upper Palaeolithic antecedents and so continued a lengthy prior tradition well into the Holocene. While many of the Spanish engravings and paintings are now attributed to the Neolithic (McClure et al. 2008, 332), some were probably created during the Mesolithic. At the Grotta dell'Addaura in Sicily there were numerous engravings of humans, some in acrobatic positions, as well as bovids, deer, and other animals, some of which may date from the Mesolithic or even later (Brea 1957, plates 4, 5; Mussi 2001, 340). To these striking images may be added numerous portable objects, among them carved and painted pebbles and bone artefacts, some with naturalistic carvings and others with abstract designs (Mussi 2001, 358–9). While difficult to interpret, and also to date, such engravings and objects attest to a continuation of an interest in representation with multiple meanings.

The evidence for disposal of the dead is widespread if far from abundant. At Vela Spila three young children were deliberately buried in stone-set graves dug into the occupation deposits (Čečuk and Radić 2005, 61). Similar burials of adults as well as children have been found on cave sites throughout the region, for example at Grotta dell'Uzzo, Arene Candide, the shell middens of Portugal, and elsewhere (Borgognini Tarli et al. 1993; Cardini 1980; Zilhão 2000, 161). These were either extended or crouched burials with few if any grave goods. At Grotta dell'Uzzo some of the bodies had been laid on a layer of red ochre. The Capsian land snail middens have yielded numerous burials that exhibit a distinctive local custom, that of upper and lower incisor evulsion, especially in women (Humphrey and Bocaege 2008, 4), that had a long prior history in the Maghreb. The total number of known burials across the western Mediterranean is still small given the length of time these sites were in use. It suggests that, as farther east, most of the dead were disposed of in other ways.

Few of the cave sites have yielded significant samples of plant and animal remains. Such evidence as there is from the Grotta dell'Uzzo and elsewhere indicates that a variety of wild legumes, tree fruits and nuts, including acorns, and wild grapes were collected in season (Costantini 1989, 199). The evidence from the animal bones is a little more substantial: the main species of medium-sized game were all hunted, including fallow and roe deer, wild pigs, wild cattle, equids, hares, and in more rugged, upland terrain, ibex and chamois (Aura et al. 1998, 100; Čečuk and Radić 2005, 61; Guilaine 1981, 28). Land snails seem to have been a favoured item in the diet, judging by the abundance of their shells on some sites (Lubell 2004). Bird bones found on a few sites confirm this broad-based pattern of gathering and hunting, adapted to the resources available in specific localities. The evidence from the eastern Adriatic, central Italy (Barker 1981, 141), and other mountainous regions offers strong indications of seasonal movement, with some Mesolithic hunters and gatherers spending part of the summer in the mountains and returning to the lowlands in the autumn, no doubt following the migratory movements of the main game animals, as well as seeking plant foods season by season as they became available.

There are clear indications from Vela Spila, the Grotta dell'Uzzo, and other sites that some communities devoted much time to deep-water fishing. The shell mounds along the Tagus and the coast of Portugal manifest another form of maritime economy (Stiner et al. 2003). Such sites offer a glimpse into what was probably a major source of sustenance, most evidence for which is now lost beneath rising sea levels.

On many cave and shelter sites in the central and western Mediterranean there is a clear hiatus in occupation between the last levels inhabited by Mesolithic foragers and those documenting Neolithic farmer-herders (Biagi and Spataro 1999–2000). This stratigraphic evidence is reinforced by the radiocarbon data which indicate that gaps in site usage from a few centuries to a millennium or more were common (Guilaine and Manen 2007, 26). Biagi (2003, 150) has mused on the possible reasons for this, an onset of disease perhaps or other setbacks, but for the moment there are no solid explanations. However, the implications are that local populations of Mesolithic foragers had been much depleted by the time farmers began to infiltrate the region.

The Transition to Farming from the Adriatic to the Atlantic

There was a delay of a millennium before farming spread to the Adriatic, Italy, and beyond, presumably from Greece (Ammerman 2010). This later episode of dispersal, documented from about 8000 BP, may have been stimulated by the 8200 BP climatic event, as we have seen (Weninger et al. 2006), the effects of which have been observed farther west in North Africa (Jackes and Lubell 2008). Within a few centuries farming communities were established along the coasts in the most favourable locations for arable agriculture from Dalmatia to the Straits of Gibraltar, the Atlantic coast of Portugal, and in North Africa. This rapid spread was clearly maritime, and it took some time for these farming communities to spread deeply into the hinterlands. Everywhere, the arrival of farming in the hands, we may suppose, of migrating farmers, was marked by the presence of the first pottery to be made in the region, Impressed or Cardial Ware, so named because the most characteristic surface decoration, at least in the early stages, was made using the edge of a cockle shell. Where appropriate recovery methods have been used, archaeologists have recovered the remains of domestic plants and animals from Impressed Ware sites. The settlement pattern clearly reflects this agricultural economy as villages were established on land suitable for cultivation.

This interpretation has been contested by many investigators until quite recently (Zeder 2008, 11599). Part of the reason for this is that archaeologists have tended to concentrate their attention on the numerous caves and rock shelters so characteristic of the broken Mediterranean landscape in search of evidence for long cultural sequences. Such sites would not normally contain evidence for intensive farming, and would be marginal for farmers who would have preferred prime agricultural land for settlement (Moore et al. 2007a, 16). It is only quite recently that archaeologists have begun to routinely apply methods of recovery that would yield significant samples of charred plant remains and animal bones suitable for detailed analysis.

The 'Early farming in Dalmatia' project has illuminated key aspects of the inception of farming in the Adriatic. Farmers rapidly spread up the eastern shore of the Adriatic, using the islands as convenient stepping stones (Forenbaher 1999). Their main settlements, however, were established in the fertile valleys of central Dalmatia between the coast and the Dinaric Alps. In this landscape there are scant traces of earlier Mesolithic foragers. The first villages of Impressed Ware affinities were established beginning around 8000 BP, of which Pokrovnik is a prime example (Moore et al. 2007b). The earliest AMS radiocarbon date from the site is 6999 ± 37 BP (OxA-17194, 7934–7737 cal BP) and it was inhabited for almost the entire eighth millennium BP. The village itself was around 3 ha in extent, with substantial stone terrace walls and houses built of wood and clay. From the beginning of settlement the economy was based on the cultivation of crops, domestic emmer, einkorn, barley, millet, lentils, flax, and grass pea, among other species, and the raising of flocks of domestic sheep with some goats, and herds of cattle, supplemented by a few pigs. Only the most modest amounts of wild foods were gathered and hunted. This economy closely resembles the agricultural system, by then nearly two millennia old, in the eastern Mediterranean, with origins, of course, even farther back in time in western Asia.

The next stage of development is best seen at the nearby site of Danilo, an even larger village in a nearby valley, inhabited from around 7300 BP. Here the inhabitants practised much the same farming system (Moore et al. 2007a). The most notable change, however, was in the pottery, which was made in new, more delicate, even exuberant, shapes and decorated with a much wider range of incised and painted designs, among them the well-known spirals. Maritime contacts seem to have quickened in this phase as obsidian imported from Lipari occurred in small but regular amounts at Danilo and Pokrovnik.

A similar sequence of an initial phase of farming settlement characterized by the presence of Impressed Ware pottery followed by local differentiation in material remains has been found widely around the western Mediterranean (Guilaine 1981; Guilaine and Manen 2007). Zilhão (2003, 215–19) has cogently argued that agriculture was brought to the Levantine coast of Iberia and Atlantic Portugal by migrating farmers. Interestingly, the local Mesolithic fisher-foragers seem to have coexisted with the incoming farmers for a while, probably because their locations of choice offered contrasting resources of little interest to incoming farmers. There is increasing evidence across the region that an array of domesticated plants and animals were raised by the earliest inhabitants of Impressed Ware settlements and their descendants (Buxó 2007; Peña-Chocarro 2007; Rottoli and Pessina 2007; Zeder 2008, 11600–1). All of these species, with the possible exception of pigs, had originally been domesticated in western Asia.

Farming seems to have reached North Africa by the same maritime route and also overland from western Asia (Linstädter 2008, 59). Here the earliest farming phase is termed the Neolithic of Capsian Tradition because it exhibits elements seen elsewhere in the central and western Mediterranean, i.e. the essentials of an agricultural economy and a variant of Impressed Ware, combined with a continuation of working chipped stone that owes much to Capsian antecedents (Linstädter 2008, 48–51). Some skulls found in burials had evidence of tooth evulsion (Humphrey and Bocaege 2008, 4), another element of continuity from the preceding phase. This all suggests that there was some mixing of traditions and, presumably, of populations with the arrival of farming.

Commentary

It would be too easy, as an earlier generation of archaeologists was given to suggest (Childe 1957, 14; Daniel and Evans 1967, 35), to say that the Mesolithic in the Mediterranean represented a decline in culture and economy from the supposed peak reached by the Upper Palaeolithic hunters of large game and painters of caves. What we observe instead is groups adapting to the very different world of the early Holocene with its more wooded environments which lacked the concentrations of food resources that would have permitted larger groups of people to congregate for part or all of the year. Their focus on the seasonal round, with its clear vertical dimension, and interest in exploiting wild food resources, whether terrestrial or maritime, represent a successful, and relatively enduring, way of life.

There were significant technological advances, notably in the use of chipped stone. Microliths can be used to manufacture a wide array of composite tools, with minimal use of raw material (Clarke 1978, 9). They thus represent one ultimate development of a technology that was as old as humanity. The continued development of a variety of artistic expressions over much of the Mediterranean during the Mesolithic indicates that the thinking of these people about their world continued to evolve.

Our understanding of this episode is partial, indeed, so limiting our understanding. For there was not only the impact of the post-glacial rise in sea level that has obscured much, but Holocene erosion and valley infilling may have buried many other sites (Grove and Rackham 2001, 305). Yet, the impression of a quite thinly populated landscape persists.

The first immigrant farmers may not have been all that numerous either, but they swiftly took over the land they occupied. Their villages grew in number and in size rapidly as their new way of life came to dominate the landscape. For it was farming, with its potential for population expansion and also drastic impact on soils and vegetation, that provided the economic foundation for all later cultural and social developments in the Mediterranean basin.

Note

All dates mentioned in this chapter are derived from calibrated radiocarbon determinations. They thus approximate actual calendar years.

References

Albarella, U., Dobney, K., and Rowley-Conwy, P. 2006. The domestication of the pig (*Sus scrofa*): new challenges and approaches. In M. A. Zeder, D. G. Bradley, E. Emshwiller, and B. D. Smith (eds), *Documenting domestication*, 209–27. Berkeley: University of California Press.

Ammerman, A. J. 2010. The paradox of early voyaging in the Mediterranean and the slowness of the Neolithic transition between Cyprus and Italy. In G. Vavouranakis (ed.), *Seascapes in Aegean prehistory*, 11–29. Athens: Monographs of the Danish Institute at Athens.

Ammerman, A. J. and Biagi, P. (eds) 2003. *The widening harvest*. Boston: Archaeological Institute of America.

Ammerman, A. J., Flourentzos, P., Gabrielli, R., Higham, T., McCartney, C., and Turnbull, T. 2008. Third report on early sites on Cyprus. *Report of the Department of Antiquities, Cyprus* 1–32.

Aura, J. E., Villaverde, V., Morales, M. G., Sainz, C. G., Zilhão, J., and Straus, L. G. 1998. The Pleistocene–Holocene transition in the Iberian Peninsula: continuity and change in human adaptations. *Quaternary International* 49/50, 87–103.

Aurenche, O. and Kozlowski, S. K. 1999. *La naissance du néolithique au proche orient ou le paradis perdu*. Paris: Éditions Errance.

Barker, G. 1981. *Landscape and society: prehistoric central Italy*. London: Academic Press.

Bellwood, P. 2005. *First farmers: the origins of agricultural societies*. Oxford: Blackwell.

Biagi, P. 2003. A review of the late Mesolithic in Italy and its implications for the Neolithic transition. In A. J. Ammerman and P. Biagi (eds), *The widening harvest*, 133–55. Boston: Archaeological Institute of America.

Biagi, P. and Spataro, M. 1999–2000. Plotting the evidence: some aspects of the radiocarbon chronology of the Mesolithic–Neolithic transition in the Mediterranean Basin. *Atti della Società per la Preistoria e Protostoria della Regione Friuli-Venezia Giulia* 12, 15–54.

Binder, D. 2000. Mesolithic and Neolithic interaction in southern France and northern Italy: new data and current hypotheses. In T. D. Price (ed.), *Europe's first farmers*, 117–43. Cambridge: Cambridge University Press.

Borgognini Tarli, S., Canci, E., Piperno, M., and Repetto, E. 1993. Dati archeologici e antropologici sulle sepolture mesolithiche della Grotta dell'Uzzo (Trapani). *Bullettino di Paletnologia Italiana* 84, 85–179.

Bottema, S. 2003. The vegetation history of the Greek Mesolithic. In N. Galanidou and C. Perlès (eds), *The Greek Mesolithic: problems and perspectives*, 33–49. London: British School at Athens.

Bouzouggar, A., Barton, R. N. E., Blockley, S., Bronk-Ramsey, C., Collcutt, S. N., Gale, R., Higham, T. F. G., Humphrey, L. T., Parfitt, S., Turner, E., and Ward, S. 2008. Reevaluating the age of the Iberomaurusian in Morocco. *African Archaeological Review* 25, 3–19.

Bradley, D. G. and Magee, D. A. 2006. Genetics and the origins of domestic cattle. In M. A. Zeder, D. G. Bradley, E. Emshwiller, and B. D. Smith (eds), *Documenting domestication*, 317–28. Berkeley: University of California Press.

Brea, L. B. 1957. *Sicily before the Greeks*. London: Thames and Hudson.

Bruford, M. W. and Townsend, S. J. 2006. Mitochondrial DNA diversity in modern sheep: implications for domestication. In M. A. Zeder, D. G. Bradley, E. Emshwiller, and B. D. Smith (eds.), *Documenting domestication*, 306–16. Berkeley: University of California Press.

Buxó, R. 2007. Crop evolution: new evidence from the Neolithic of west Mediterranean Europe. In S. Colledge and J. Conolly (eds), *The origins and spread of domestic plants in southwest Asia and Europe*, 155–71. Walnut Creek, CA: Left Coast Press.

Cardini, L. 1980. La Necropoli Mesolitica delle Arene Candide (Liguria). *Memorie dell'Istituto Italiano di Paleontologia Umana* 3, 3–91.

Cauvin, J. 1977. Les fouilles de Mureybet (1971–1974) et leur signification pour les origins de la sédentarisation au Proche-Orient. *Annual of the American Schools of Oriental Research* 44, 19–48.

Čečuk, B. and Radić, D. 2005. *Vela Spila*. Centar za kulturu 'Vela Luka'. Zagreb: Intergrafika.

Childe, V. G. 1957. *The dawn of European civilization*. London: Routledge & Kegan Paul.

Clarke, D. 1978. *Mesolithic Europe: the economic basis*. London: Duckworth.

Colledge, S., Conolly, J., and Shennan, S. 2004. Archaeobotanical evidence for the spread of farming in the eastern Mediterranean. *Current Anthropology* 45, 35–58.

Costantini, L. 1989. Plant exploitation at Grotta dell'Uzzo, Sicily: new evidence for the transition from Mesolithic to Neolithic subsistence in southern Europe. In D. R. Harris and G. C. Hillman (eds), *Foraging and farming: the evolution of plant exploitation*, 197–206. London: Unwin Hyman.

Cullen, T. 1995. Mesolithic mortuary ritual at Franchthi cave, Greece. *Antiquity* 69, 270–89.

Daniel, G. and Evans, J. D. 1967. The western Mediterranean. In I. E. S. Edwards, C. J. Gadd, N. G. L. Hammond, and E. Sollberger (eds), *The Cambridge Ancient History vol. 2, part 2*, 713–72. Cambridge: Cambridge University Press.

Escalon de Fonton, M. 1976. Les civilisations de l'Epipaléolithique et du Mésolithique en Provence littorale. In H. de Lumley (ed.), *La préhistoire française I*, 1367–78. Paris: Éditions de Centre national de la recherche scientifique.

Facorellis, Y. 2003. Radiocarbon dating the Greek Mesolithic. In N. Galanidou and C. Perlès (eds), *The Greek Mesolithic: problems and perspectives*, 51–67. London: British School at Athens.

Fairbanks, R. G. 1989. A 17,000-year glacio-eustatic sea level record: influence of glacial melting rates on the Younger Dryas event and deep-ocean circulation. *Nature* 342, 637–42.

Forenbaher, S. 1999. The earliest islanders of the eastern Adriatic. *Collegium Antropologicum* 23, 521–30.

Forenbaher, S. 2002. Prehistoric populations of the island of Hvar—an overview of the archaeological evidence. *Collegium Antropologicum* 26, 361–78.

Garrod, D. A. E. 1957. The Natufian culture: the life and economy of a Mesolithic people in the Near East. *Proceedings of the British Academy* 43, 211–27.

Grove, A. T. and Rackham, O. 2001. *The nature of Mediterranean Europe: an ecological history*. New Haven: Yale University Press.

Guilaine, J. 1981. *Premiers bergers et paysans del'Occident méditerranéen*. Paris: Mouton.

Guilaine, J. 2003. Aspects de la néolithisation en Méditerranée et en France. In A. J. Ammerman and P. Biagi (eds), *The widening harvest*, 189–206. Boston: Archaeological Institute of America.

Guilaine, J. and Manen, C. 2007. From Mesolithic to Early Neolithic in the western Mediterranean. In A. Whittle and V. Cummings (eds), *Going over: the Mesolithic–Neolithic Transition in north-west Europe*, 21–51. Oxford: Oxford University Press.

Harris, D. R. 1996. The origins and spread of agriculture and pastoralism in Eurasia: an overview. In D. R. Harris (ed.), *The origins and spread of agriculture and pastoralism in Eurasia*, 552–73. London: UCL Press.

Hauptmann, H. 1999. The Urfa region. In M. Özdoğan and N. Başgelen (eds), *Neolithic in Turkey*, 65–86. Istanbul: Arkeoloji ve Sanat Yayinlari.

Hershkovitz, I., Speirs, M. S., Frayer, D., Nadel, D., Wish-Baratz, S., and Arensburg, B. 1995. Ohalo II H2: a 19,000-year-old skeleton from a water-logged site at the Sea of Galilee, Israel. *American Journal of Physical Anthropology* 96, 215–34.

Hoek, W. Z. and Bos, J. A. A. 2007. Early Holocene climate oscillations—causes and consequences. *Quaternary Science Reviews* 26, 1901–6.

Humphrey, L. T. and Bocaege, E. 2008. Tooth evulsion in the Maghreb: chronological and geographical patterns. *African Archaeological Review* 7, 1–20.

Jackes, M. and Lubell, D. 2008. Early and Middle Holocene environments and Capsian cultural change: evidence from the Télédjène basin, eastern Algeria. *African Archaeological Review* 6, 1–20.

Kenyon, K. M. 1981. *Excavations at Jericho* 3. London: British School of Archaeology in Jerusalem.

Komšo, D. 2006. The Mesolithic in Croatia. *Opuscula Archaeologica* 30, 55–92.

Koumouzelis, M., Kozłowski, J. K., and Ginter, B. 2003. Mesolithic finds from Cave 1 in the Klisoura Gorge, Argolid. In N. Galanidou and C. Perlès (eds), *The Greek Mesolithic: problems and perspectives*, 113–30. London: British School at Athens.

Kozlowski, S. K. 2002. *Nemrik: an Aceramic Village in Northern Iraq*. Warsaw: Institute of Archaeology, Warsaw University.

Lambeck, K. 1995. Late Pleistocene and Holocene sea-level change in Greece and south-western Turkey: a separation of eustatic, isostatic and tectonic contributions. *Geophysical Journal International* 122, 1022–44.

Lambeck, K. and Bard, E. 2000. Sea-level change along the French Mediterranean coast for the past 30 000 years. *Earth and Planetary Science Letters* 175, 203–22.

Lambeck, K. and Purcell, A. 2005. Sea-level change in the Mediterranean Sea since the LGM: model predictions for tectonically stable areas. *Quaternary Science Reviews* 24, 1969–88.

Lambeck, K., Antonioli, F., Purcell, A., and Silenzi, S. 2004. Sea-level change along the Italian coast for the past 10,000 yr. *Quaternary Science Reviews* 23, 1567–98.

Linstädter, J. 2008. The Epipalaeolithic–Neolithic transition in the Mediterranean region of Northwest Africa. *Quartär* 55, 41–62.

Lubell, D. 2004. Prehistoric edible land snails in the circum-Mediterranean: the archaeological evidence. In J.-P. Brugal and J. Desse (eds), *Petits animaux et sociétés humaines: du complement alimentaire aux resources utilitaires*, 77–98. Antibes: Éditions APDCA.

Luikart, G., Fernández, H., Mashkour, M., England, P. R., and Teberlet, P. 2006. Origins and diffusion of domestic goats inferred from DNA markers: example analyses of mtDNA, Y chromosome, and microsatellites. In M. A. Zeder, D. G. Bradley, E. Emshwiller, and B. D. Smith (eds), *Documenting domestication*, 294–305. Berkeley: University of California Press.

McClure, S. B., Balaguer, L. M., and Auban, J. B. 2008. Neolithic rock art in context: landscape history and the transition to agriculture in Mediterranean Spain. *Journal of Anthropological Archaeology* 27, 326–37.

Maggi, R. 1997. *Arene Candide: a functional and environmental assessment of the Holocene sequence*. Rome: Istituto Italiano di Paleontologia Umana.

Manolis, S. K. and Stravopodi, H. J. 2003. An assessment of the human skeletal remains in the Mesolithic deposits of Theopetra cave: a case study. In N. Galanidou and C. Perlès (eds), *The Greek Mesolithic: problems and perspectives*, 207–16. London: British School at Athens.

Marinova, E. 2007. Archaeobotanical data from the early Neolithic of Bulgaria. In S. Colledge and J. Conolly (eds), *The origins and spread of domestic plants in southwest Asia and Europe*, 93–109. Walnut Creek, CA: Left Coast Press.

Miracle, P. and Forenbaher, S. (eds) 2006. *Prehistoric herders of Northern Istria: the archaeology of Pupićina cave*. Pula: Arheološki muzej Istre.

Moore, A. M. T. 1982. A four-stage sequence for the Levantine Neolithic, ca. 8500–3750 BC. *Bulletin of the American Schools of Oriental Research* 246, 1–34.

Moore, A. M. T. 1985. The development of Neolithic societies in the Near East. *Advances in World Archaeology* 4, 1–69.

Moore, A. M. T., Hillman, G. C., and Legge, A. J. 2000. *Village on the Euphrates*. New York: Oxford University Press.

Moore, A. M. T., Menđušić, M., Smith, J., and Podrug, E. 2007a. Project 'Early farming in Dalmatia': Danilo Bitinj 2004–2005. *Vjesnik Arheološkog muzeja u Zagrebu* 50, 15–24.

Moore, A. M. T., Menđušić, M., Smith, J., Zaninović, J., and Podrug, E. 2007b. Project 'Early farming in Dalmatia': Pokrovnik 2006. *Vjesnik Arheološkog muzeja u Zagrebu* 50, 25–34.

Morrell, P. L. and Clegg, M. T. 2007. Genetic evidence for a second domestication of barley (*Hordeum vulgare*) east of the Fertile Crescent. *Proceedings of the National Academy of Sciences USA* 104, 9, 3289–94.

Moundrea-Agrafioti, A. 2003. Mesolithic fish hooks from the Cave of Cyclope, Youra. In N. Galanidou and C. Perlès (eds), *The Greek Mesolithic: problems and perspectives*, 131–41. London: British School at Athens.

Mussi, M. 2001. *Earliest Italy*. New York: Kluwer Academic/Plenum Press.

Özdoğan, M. 1999. Northwestern Turkey: Neolithic cultures in between the Balkans and Anatolia. In M. Özdoğan and N. Başgelen (eds), *Neolithic in Turkey*, 203–24. Istanbul: Arkeoloji ve Sanat Yayinlari.

Peltenburg, E., Colledge, S., Croft, P., Jackson, A., McCartney, C., and Murray, M. A. 2001. Neolithic dispersals from the Levantine corridor: a Mediterranean perspective. *Levant* 33, 35–64.

Peña-Chocarro, L. 2007. Early agriculture in central and southern Spain. In S. Colledge and J. Conolly (eds), *The origins and spread of domestic plants in southwest Asia and Europe*, 173–87. Walnut Creek, CA: Left Coast Press.

Perlès, C. 2001. *The Early Neolithic in Greece*. Cambridge: Cambridge University Press.

Perlès, C. 2003. The Mesolithic at Franchthi: an overview of the data and problems. In N. Galanidou and C. Perlès (eds), *The Greek Mesolithic: problems and perspectives*, 79–87. London: British School at Athens.

Perrot, J. and Ladiray, D. 1988. Les sépultures. In J. Perrot (ed.), *Les hommes de Mallaha (Eynan) Israël*. Paris: Association Paléorient.

Petruso, K. M., Korkuti, M., Bejko, L., Bottema, S., Ellwood, B. B., Hansen, J. M., Harrold, F. B., and Russell, N. 1996. Konispol cave, Albania: a preliminary report on excavations and related studies, 1992–1994. *Iliria* 26, 183–224.

Pluciennik, M. 2008. The coastal Mesolithic of the European Mediterranean. In G. Bailey and P. Spikins (eds), *Mesolithic Europe*, 328–56. Cambridge: Cambridge University Press.

Pourkheirandish, M. and Komatsuda, T. 2007. The importance of barley genetics and domestication in a global perspective. *Annals of Botany* 100, 999–1008.

Powell, J. 2003. The fish bone assemblage from the Cave of Cyclope, Youra: evidence for continuity and change. In N. Galanidou and C. Perlès (eds), *The Greek Mesolithic: problems and perspectives*, 173–9. London: British School at Athens.

Price, T. D. (ed.) 2000. *Europe's first farmers*. Cambridge: Cambridge University Press.

Rosenberg, M. 1999. Hallan Çemi. In M. Özdoğan and N. Başgelen (eds), *Neolithic in Turkey*, 25–33. Istanbul: Arkeoloji ve Sanat Yayinlari.

Rottoli, M. and Pessina, A. 2007. Neolithic agriculture in Italy: an update of archaeobotanical data with particular emphasis on northern settlements. In S. Colledge and J. Conolly (eds), *The origins and spread of domestic plants in southwest Asia and Europe*, 141–53. Walnut Creek, CA: Left Coast Press.

Runnels, C. 2001. Review of Aegean prehistory IV: the Stone Age of Greece from the Palaeolithic to the advent of the Neolithic. In T. Cullen (ed.), *Aegean prehistory: a review*, 225–58. Boston: Archaeological Institute of America.

Runnels, C. 2009. Mesolithic sites and surveys in Greece: a case study from the southern Argolid. *Journal of Mediterranean Archaeology* 22, 57–73.

Runnels, C., Korkuti, M., Galaty, M. L., Timpson, M. E., Whittaker, J. C., Stocker, S. R., Davis, J. L., Bejko, L., and Muçaj, S. 2004. The Palaeolithic and Mesolithic of Albania: survey and excavation at the site of Kryegjata B (Fier district). *Journal of Mediterranean Archaeology* 17, 3–29.

Runnels, C., Panagopoulou, E., Murray, P., Tsartsidou, G., Allen, S., Mullen, K., and Tourloukis, E. 2005. A Mesolithic landscape in Greece: testing a site-location model in the Argolid at Kandia. *Journal of Mediterranean Archaeology* 18, 259–85.

Salamini, F., Özkan, H., Brandolini, A., Schäfer-Pregl, R., and Martin, W. 2002. Genetics and geography of wild cereal domestication in the Near East. *Nature Reviews/Genetics* 3, 429–41.

Sarpaki, A. 2009. Knossos, Crete: invaders, 'sea goers', or previously 'invisible', the Neolithic plant economy appears fully-fledged in 9,000 BP. In A. S. Fairbairn and E. Weiss (eds), *From foragers to farmers*, 220–34. Oxford: Oxbow.

Simmons, A. H. 2004. Bitter hippos of Cyprus: the island's first occupants and last endemic animals—setting the stage for colonization. In E. Peltenburg and A. Wasse (eds), *Neolithic revolution*, 1–14. Oxford: Oxbow.

Šoštarić, R. 2005. The development of postglacial vegetation in coastal Croatia. *Acta Botanica Croatica* 64, 383–90.

Stiner, M. C., Bicho, N. F., Lindly, J., and Ferring, R. 2003. Mesolithic to Neolithic transitions: new results from shell-middens in the western Algarve, Portugal. *Antiquity* 77, 75–86.

Stordeur, D., Brenet, M., Der Aprahamian, G., and Roux, J.-C. 2000. Les bâtiments communautaires de Jerf el Ahmar et Mureybet horizon PPNA (Syrie). *Paléorient* 26, 29–44.

Stordeur, D. and Jammous, B. 1997. D'énigmatiques plaquettes gravées néolithiques. *Archéologia* 332, 36–41.

Stordeur, D. and Willcox, G. 2009. Indices de culture et d'utilisation des céréales à Jerf el Ahmar. In Collectif (ed.), *De Méditerranée et d'ailleurs... Mélanges offerts à Jean Guilaine*, 693–710. Toulouse: Archives d'Écologie Préhistorique.

Strasser, T. F., Panagopoulou, E., Runnels, C. N., Murray, P. M., Thompson, N., Karkanas, P., McCoy, F. W., and Wegmann, K. W. 2010. Stone Age seafaring in the Mediterranean: evidence from the Plakias region for Lower Palaeolithic and Mesolithic habitation of Crete. *Hesperia* 79, 145–90.

Tixier, J. 1963. *Typologie de l'épipaléolithique du Maghreb*. Paris: Arts et Métiers Graphiques.

Todd, I. A. 1987. *Vasilikos Valley Project 6: excavations at Kalavassos-Tenta I*. Göteborg: Paul Åströms.

Van Andel, T. H. 1989. Late Quaternary sea-level changes and archaeology. *Antiquity* 63, 733–45.

Vitelli, K. D. 1995. Pots, potters, and the shaping of Greek Neolithic society. In W. K. Barnett and J. W. Hoopes (eds), *The emergence of pottery*, 55–63. Washington: Smithsonian Institution.

Weninger, B., Alram-Stern, E., Bauer, E., Clare, L., Danzeglocke, U., Jöris, O., Kubatzki, C., Rollefson, G., Todorova, H., and van Andel, T. 2006. Climate forcing due to the 8200 cal yr BP event observed at Early Neolithic sites in the eastern Mediterranean. *Quaternary Research* 66, 401–20.

Zeder, M. A. 2008. Domestication and early agriculture in the Mediterranean Basin: origins, diffusion, and impact. *Proceedings of the National Academy of Sciences USA* 105, 11597–604.

Zilhão, J. 2000. From the Mesolithic to the Neolithic in the Iberian peninsula. In T. D. Price (ed.), *Europe's first farmers*, 144–82. Cambridge: Cambridge University Press.

Zilhão, J. 2003. The Neolithic transition in Portugal and the role of demic diffusion in the spread of agriculture across West Mediterranean Europe. In A. J. Ammerman and P. Biagi (eds), *The widening harvest*, 207–23. Boston: Archaeological Institute of America.

CHAPTER 20

POST-GLACIAL TRANSFORMATIONS IN AFRICA

ANDREW B. SMITH

INTRODUCTION

THE continent of Africa has the distinction of being the place where modern humans came from some 50,000 years ago. Was the reason for their emigration that all the available ecological zones in North Africa were becoming too unstable, or was it that creative abilities allowed the colonization of unfamiliar regions? We do know that people had already occupied all the continent's ecological zones, and by the end of the Pleistocene regional technological variants demonstrated the ability to utilize all resources of the continent possibly by people speaking the different groups of languages known today: Khoisan, Niger-Congo, Nilo-Saharan, and even Afro-Asiatic.

TERMINAL PLEISTOCENE/EARLY HOLOCENE ENVIRONMENTS

Like the rest of the world, parts of Africa were affected by changing sea levels at the end of the Pleistocene as the northern-hemisphere glaciers melted. The coastal shelf around Africa does vary somewhat, but King (1967, 564) comments 'The most remarkable feature of the African shelf, taken as a whole, is its narrowness, associated with strong monoclines upon the coastlands. Exceptional indeed is a shelf more than 100 miles wide, while for long stretches the width is 10 miles or less.' This means that only in a few places around a long coastline did a wide coastal plain exist when the sea level was 130 m lower than today at the height of the glacial maximum. This was particularly the case at the southern tip of Africa, where the Agulhas Bank extended as much as 100 km beyond the present coastline. By 12,000 BP the rising waters had flooded the shelf, resulting in the coast being roughly in its present form.

In North Africa, wetter conditions existed, as seen in the high lake stands of Lake Chad after 13,000 BP (Servant et al. 1969). A relict flora of cypress and olive trees has, until very recently, survived in the central Sahara, a testimony to wetter conditions when the desert had shrunk considerably (Clark 2008).

This wetter period continued into the early Holocene. By 9000 BP, the Earth's axis resulted in northern-hemisphere solar radiation increasing by as much as 7 per cent during the summer (Kutzbach and Street-Perrot 1985). According to Street-Perrott and Perrott (1993, 348), 'The insolation maximum in northern summer at 9000 yr BP led to stronger monsoon rains right across northern Africa, extending along the East African Rift Valley down to about 9°S', and almost all lakes north of 15°30'S showed higher water levels than present at this time (Street-Perrott and Perrott 1993, 344).

In the forest regions of West Africa, Lake Bosumtwi in Ghana has produced one of the best records. Higher lake levels existed between 12,500 and 3750 BP, dropping to present levels after this time (Talbot et al. 1984). Discharge of the Niger River at its delta shows considerable increase, reflecting greater runoff from the interior, and there is evidence to suggest that the equatorial rainforest extended some 350 km north of its present distribution (Grove 1993). In the equatorial region, during the 'Kibangian' climatic phase, conditions were relatively wet during the period from 12,000 to 3500 BP (Maley 1993).

In his review of the literature on environmental conditions in southern Africa at the end of the Pleistocene, Mitchell (2002) shows that on the available evidence any changes are highly discontinuous across the subcontinent. In some areas it appears to have been cool around 10,000 BP, becoming warmer only by 8000 BP on the south coast. Wetter conditions are suggested at Elands Bay cave on the west coast (12,000–8000 BP), as a result of a weakening of the south Atlantic high associated with an insolation minimum during the southern summer. This could also have reduced coastal upwelling intensity off Namibia and produced more rain in the Namib (Street-Perrott and Perrott 1993, 348).

The fynbos region of the Cape Floral Kingdom showed the greatest variation between the Pleistocene and Holocene. A combination of warmer temperatures and rising sea levels reduced the grassland plains off the Aghulas Bank of the southernmost tip of Africa into more closed habitats. The large-mammal populations also changed from grazers (eland, buffalo) to browsers (small antelope), and at that time a number of species became extinct, including the giant cape horse (*Equus capensis*), giant buffalo (*Pelorovis*), giant hartebeest (*Megalotragus priscus*), and the southern springbok (*Antidorcas australis*).

North Africa

The Epi-Palaeolithic of North Africa and the Sahara had its analogues in the Levant at the end of the Pleistocene. There may have been interchanges between the two regions in this period, although these are difficult to document archaeologically. The similar timing of the Epi-Palaeolithic industries in both areas would suggest there was probably no barrier to movement. In the Sahara, these blade and burin industries were typified by the Ounanian, found in Niger at Adrar Bous (Clark 2008).

In the early Holocene the Epi-Palaeolithic was followed by a ceramic microlithic industry, known variously as the 'Khartoum Mesolithic' (Arkell 1949), 'Kiffian' (Smith 2008), 'Late

Acacus' (di Lernia 1999b), or 'Terminal Palaeolithic' (Wendorf and Schild 1980). The distinctive feature of these variants was their association with lakes and rivers, and the use of bone harpoons in fishing (Yellen 1998), referred to as the 'Aqualithic' (Sutton 1977; but see Holl 2005 for discussion). Pottery at that time in the Sahara and along the Nile is some of the earliest found, and has been suggested as an indication of wild-grain exploitation (Haaland 1999; Huysecom et al. 2009; Jórdeczka et al. 2011).

Because a small sample of large bovid bones, identified as cattle, was associated with this industry at Nabta Playa and Bir Kiseiba, in the desert west of the Nile, dated to 9300 BP, Wendorf et al. (1984) changed the name to 'Early Neolithic'. Their reasoning was that since the associated fauna was gazelles and hares, suggesting an arid environment, cattle were unlikely to survive without human intervention, so must have been domesticated (Wendorf and Schild 1994). In support of this argument is the more recent work on cattle genetics which indicates an 'African' line of cattle, distinct from Eurasian cattle (Hanotte et al. 2002), thus suggesting an independent African domestication event.

Not everyone agrees with this scenario. The problem is that the timing of this suggested domestication event is very close to the time when domesticated cattle were first to be found in the Levant (Peters et al. 1999). Domestic sheep bones only appeared in north Africa around 7800 BP. Unlike cattle that are known to have existed in the wild in North Africa, the wild progenitors of African domesticated sheep were all from Asia (Mugai 2002; Mugai and Hanotte 2013). This means that contact with the Levant (Smith 1988) or Sinai (Close 2001) would have been necessary for their introduction to Africa. The most parsimonious picture would then be that the idea of domestication as well as all species of domesticated animals in North Africa came from the Near East at the same time, but with the later addition of local African genetic material into the cattle line (Zeder 2008).

In the Early Holocene, when Nabta Playa was occupied, hunters in Libya at Uan Afuda were exploiting herds of the Barbary sheep (*Ammotragus lervia*) (di Lernia 1999a). As with other North African sites, e.g. Tamar Hat (Saxon et al. 1974), the faunal assemblage at Uan Afuda is almost all wild sheep. The site has the additional distinction of producing what looks like a stone wall behind which is a dung layer, interpreted as a corral for penning the sheep. On the rock walls of the cave are depictions of the sheep, which may indicate ritual use of these animals. There is no suggestion, however, that these animals were domesticated, and none of the genetic material of modern domestic sheep of Africa comes from *Ammotragus*. Thus we might infer a model of 'control' of the animals for a specific purpose, but no intentional modification of the genetic material.

These hunters were a robust population, sometimes referred to as 'mechtoids' (Petit-Maire and Dutour 1987), and more recently as 'Kiffian' (Sereno et al. 2008). They were subsequently replaced by later herding people of more gracile or 'Mediterranean' appearance.

After 7800 BP, a rainfall system occurred (Rindsberger et al. 1983) that permitted the expansion of grasslands, allowing domestic animals, both cattle and small stock, to spread across the Sahara. Three phases of pastoralism have been suggested by di Lernia (1999b). The early pastoral period (7800–6400 BP) indicates an intrusion of the new economy that existed side by side with the last of the Late Acacus hunters. The newcomers made different pottery to that of the hunters, and the herders appear to have moved between the mountains and the plains. There are no wild cattle bones on the hunter sites, and di Lernia thinks the animals were not native to the central Sahara.

Around 6400 BP was the onset of a dry spell that lasted for about four centuries, followed by a renewal of pastoral activity just before 6000 BP, called the middle pastoral period. Large pastoral sites were located around lakes that reached some of their highest levels at this time. Although transhumance is suggested, with dry season camps in the mountains, many of the lakeshore sites may well have been semi-permanent.

Destabilization of climatic conditions in the Sahara after 5000 BP probably made pastoral life somewhat precarious. This is clear from the decrease in cattle bones on sites, and although herding still survived until 3500 years ago in this late pastoral period, small-stock husbandry dominated the economy. Small villages started to appear then, along with much more elaborate funerary monuments, some of which clustered into cemeteries. This is also when the first evidence for domestic grains appears on archaeological sites (Amblard 1996).

The drying up of the Sahara after 5000 BP created new environmental conditions south of the desert as the Intertropical Convergence Zone retreated southwards. Previously, tsetse-fly belts fatal to livestock along what is called the Sahel today would have limited the expansion of cattle pastoralism. By 4000 BP sites in the Sahel were occupied by cattle herders. One of the areas where they were found was at the site of Karkarichinkat in the Tilemsi Valley, which runs southwards to the Niger River at Gao, and which would have had plenty of water to facilitate movement (Finucane et al. 2008; Smith 1979).

Ritual use of both cattle and small stock is well documented across the Sahara, from Egypt (Applegate et al. 2001), to Mali (Manning 2008). These rituals took the form of inhumations of whole animals, at least one of which probably had been slaughtered by having its throat slit (Paris 2000). Suggestions of archaeoastronomy have been mooted by Wendorf and Malville (2001) from perceived stone alignments at Nabta Playa.

Another important source of information about people in Africa is the large corpus of rock art to be found in both north and southern Africa. Saharan images probably go back at least to the terminal Pleistocene, with engravings of what are suggested to be extinct buffalo. Painted images of wild animals and people in south-west Libya, although difficult to date, as mentioned above may well pertain to the ceramic microlithic period, and others, showing domestic stock, drawn during the middle to late Holocene. Among the latter would appear to be images of black African herders, later replaced by people of Mediterranean ancestry, possibly when the Sahara was drying up (Smith 1993).

By the last century BC, towns already existed along the Niger (McIntosh 2005), and became the end points for the Saharan gold trade that supported the early empires of Ghana and Mali (Levtzion 1973). With the arrival of traders from North Africa, even before the Hillalian invasions of the eleventh century AD, Islam was introduced to the Sahel, and gradually incorporated into most of the societies there. Islam became the dominant religion of the complex societies of Bornu (Nigeria) and Songhay (Mali).

East Africa

Holocene archaeology has always taken a back seat to early hominin research in East Africa, and is consequently much more poorly understood. Ambrose (1998), in his attempt to place his important sequence at Enkapune Ya Moto in context, has suggested that during the Holocene altitudinal factors played a major role in determining where people lived, as conditions conducive to human habitation varied with height in the Rift Valley. Obsidian stone-tool using Eburran hunters, first seen some 12,000 years BP, moved up to Enkapune Ya Moto during a dry period (6000–3300 BP), contrasting with their occupation of the valley floor during wetter conditions of the early Holocene.

Domestic animals show up for the first time around 4500 BP (Marshall 2000). As this is concurrent with the drying up of the Sahara, it is possible that these animals accompanied herding people moving south, in a parallel to what was happening in the west African Sahel, as tsetse belts shifted. In spite of the known splendid grasslands of East Africa, the spread of domestic animals southwards seems to have been rather disjointed. Small stock have been identified from Enkapune Ya Moto, with what might be an aberrant date of 4800 BP, but cattle would seem to have been slower in expanding. Gifford-Gonzalez (2000) believes that this could have been the result of the need for newly immigrant pastoralists adjusting to epizootic disease patterns in East Africa that are potentially fatal to cattle. Modern herders in the region know how to avoid areas where these diseases may be rife.

Specialized pastoralism, adapted to two rainy periods in the year in East Africa, probably only started around 3000 BP (Marshall 1990). However, pottery variation across the region, as well as faunal analyses, suggest that herders lived alongside hunters and fishers, creating a complex mosaic of economic, cultural, and probably linguistic, strategies. This is called the east African Neolithic, and is recognized among three roughly contemporaneous groups: Savanna Pastoral Neolithic, Elmenteitan, and the aforementioned Eburran (Karega-Munene 2003). This is also when the first agricultural groups probably arrived. Their source has been greatly debated, tied closely to Bantu languages that are most likely to have originated in the Cameroon area of West Africa (see Eggert 2005 for historical discussion). The early pottery of these farmers is known as the Urewe tradition, of which two branches, Kwale and Nkope, have been identified. Haplogroup L3 is a common lineage in sub-Saharan Africa. The largest population size increase in L3 was between 4000 and 2000 years ago when L3 lineages spread out of central Africa into eastern and southern Africa (Soares et al. 2012).

Complex societies have long been recognized to have existed in Uganda, probably going back to the fourteenth century AD. Their origin is somewhat obscure, and although there are earthworks of considerable size, there is little in the way of occupation debris or elite goods, other than trade beads from the Indian Ocean at some sites (e.g. Ntusi), but none at others (e.g. Bigo). Robertshaw (2003) suggests that 'corporate political strategies' in the fifteenth century were responsible for the large earthworks that would have required considerable labour input. These sites may have been important ritual centres, whose power was taken up by the later Cwezi and formed the basis of control in the Bito dynasty and Nyoro state.

Contact with the east African coast goes back at least until Greek, Roman, and later Persian times. Excavation along the coast as far south as the Rufiji Delta in Tanzania has produced material from these periods (Chami 1999). The wider Indian Ocean trade as far as Indonesia probably extends from before the Islamic period. Certainly, the so-called 'Shirazi' culture of the coast indicates early contact with the Persian Gulf, although excavation of sites in Kenya suggests that the towns, such as Kilwa, were originally home-grown (Mitchell 2005). Swahili, the lingua franca of East Africa, is basically a Bantu language.

Southern Africa

Due to its long history of research, going back to the early twentieth century (Robertshaw 1990), southern Africa is the best-known area for prehistoric and historic archaeology in sub-Saharan Africa. In 1929, preferring not to use European terminology, Goodwin and van Riet Louw created the three main phases of African prehistory: Early Stone Age (ESA), Middle Stone Age (MSA), and Later Stone Age (LSA), which are still used generally today. The widespread microlithic LSA industry of Holocene hunters is called Wilton and probably derives from the previous Robberg and Albany (Oakhurst) industries (Deacon and Deacon 1999).

Faunal analyses indicate changes in hunting strategies, with large grazers being sought after during the MSA, and more solitary browsers and pigs in the LSA (Klein 1980). This may be due to the loss of open grassland on the south coast as the sea levels rose at the end of the Pleistocene, as well as more skilled hunting to tackle pigs.

The historic Bushmen hunters of southern Africa are no doubt descended from Wilton, but there are two distinct language groups of these modern hunters: !Ui-Taa and Ju, suggesting a long period of divergence. A third language group, Khoe, was previously thought to be part of the Khoisan family of languages, as all have clicks as consonants. This language, however, is so distinct that Güldemann (2008) says it should not be included.

Two thousand years ago there was a major break in the economic and social world of southern Africa. Domestic animals and pottery were introduced for the first time into an environment of hunter-gatherers. There is considerable debate on the origins and spread of domestic animals in the subcontinent, but no argument that they had to have arrived from the north. Some of the earliest dates for sheep come from the Western Cape Province in South Africa. The dates of around 2000 BP (Smith 2006) are as early as any for domestic stock further north in Botswana (Robbins et al. 2005), and argue for a rapid movement of the animals after their arrival in southern Africa.

Who brought the animals to the Cape is more contentious. Sadr (2003) believes the first sheep came via exchange systems among indigenous hunters, and thus constitute a 'Neolithic' of southern Africa. A more conventional view is that the Khoe-speakers brought the early animals (Smith 2006). Support for the latter view comes from linguistic analysis suggesting Khoe languages of southern Africa may have been connected to east African populations, such as Sandawe, and introduced as Khoe-Kwadi (Güldemann 2008) by groups who today may be represented by 'black' Khoe-speakers in northern Botswana and south-western Zimbabwe (Cashdan 1986). There is certainly an affinity between the languages spoken by these people and the historic Khoekhoen ('Hottentots'). In his analysis of human skeletal material north of the Zambezi, Morris (2002) was unable to find any individuals that would relate them to the Bushman hunters. If no Bushmen existed outside southern Africa, this gives support to the idea that Khoe was originally a language spoken by 'black' people from further north.

The rock art of southern Africa has become well known as a result of the work of David Lewis-Williams (1981), whose main work has been interpretation from using the ethnography of modern Kalahari hunters to suggest that it is mainly shamanistic and trance-related (but see Solomon 2000 and Blundell 2004 for discussion of this). The oldest date for this art is reputed to be 26,000 years ago from Apollo 11 cave in southern Namibia (Wendt 1976), although this has yet to be supported from other sites, and most of the naturalistic art, referred to as 'fine-line', was probably executed within the last 4000 years (Jerardino and Swanepoel 1999). It is generally accepted that this art was probably done by the direct ancestors of the Bushmen hunters of southern Africa. Other geometric rock-art styles may be the work of the Khoekhoen, as it conforms to the known historic distribution of these herders (Smith and Ouzman 2004).

By 1600 BP, farming economies had reached southern Africa, in the form of sorghum and millet production, alongside cattle. These domestic grains were probably introduced by Bantu-speaking people from further north. This period is generally referred to as the 'early Iron Age', since this is when the first iron-producers appear. Tracking connections with East Africa has been done using stylistic patterns on pottery, going back to Urewe, particularly the Nkope branch, but also another western tradition, called Kalundu from Angola, has been suggested (Huffman 2007). The early Iron Age was replaced by the later Iron Age at the beginning of the second millennium AD, when the ancestors of the modern farming groups of south-eastern Africa can be recognized.

The arrival of agricultural communities had the effect of often displacing indigenous hunters, especially on the more productive coastal forelands and interior. Hunters still managed to survive independently in the Drakensberg mountains and in the drier areas further west, especially of the Karoo. Elsewhere women from hunting societies were brought into polygynous farming communities as wives. This, however, was a one-way gene flow (hypergyny), as hunters seldom would have cattle needed to pay the bride-wealth required among Bantu-speaking farmers. An example of this is seen in the genomic analysis of Archbishop Desmond Tutu, of Xhosa-Tswana parentage, and whose genetic history shows that he is in part Bushman (Schuster et al. 2010).The wealth in cattle of the later Iron Age was the basis of centralized state formation beginning at Mapungubwe, and later at Great Zimbabwe. Relationships with the coast are evident in the number of exotic trade beads found at these sites coming from the Indian Ocean (Hall 1987; Mitchell 2005).

TROPICAL AFRICA

The least known of all the regions of Africa are the tropics. This has to do with the fact that fewer researchers work in tropical Africa, but it is also a function of a more difficult environment in which to find sites and to do fieldwork. Having said this, within the past few decades concentrated work has produced some good results, and while we often lack even basic data in some of the more forested areas, a general picture is emerging.

There has been more concentrated work done along the coast and immediate hinterland of West Africa, particularly in Ghana and Nigeria. Microlithic industries appear around 13,000 years ago, with ceramics and ground stone tools being added to the cultural inventory after 5000 BP. There has been some association made with the domestication of plants suggested from the ground stone component, but this is difficult to confirm due to the poor preservation of plant remains, and the fact that many tropical plants, such as yams, do not leave much in the way of residues. The question of 'domestication' of plants in this region is also fraught with the problems of dealing with those that are even today used in a semi-wild state, such as the oil producing tree, *Canarium schweinfurthii*, later replaced by the oil palm, *Elaeis guineensis*. The sudden rise in oil palm pollen around 3000 BP from Lake

Bosumtwi cores (Talbot et al. 1984) has been used as an indicator of arboriculture. In Ghana, the Kintampo industry is seen as a probable indigenous food-producing tradition capable of exploiting a variety of environments, with pearl millet in the more savannah regions of the north between 3500 and 3000 BP (Casey 2005), and possibly yams and domestic animals further south (Stahl 1986).

In the Democratic Republic of Congo two caves have yielded evidence of early hunters. At Matupi cave, two metres of deposit were excavated, with stone tools at the bottom beyond the limits of radiocarbon dating. From the palynological evidence it was only within the period 12,000–3000 BP that the cave was situated within forest. At Shum Laka rock shelter, a quartz microlithic industry goes back to the ninth millennium BP, with ceramics probably introduced by the fifth millennium (Eggert 1993).

A series of kingdoms developed in forest areas of West Africa: Mossi, Akan, Dahomey, Benin, and Oyo, starting in the eleventh century AD. Although in many ways initially isolated from the outside world, the northward export of commodities, such as gold to the Niger River and beyond, would have had the effect of supporting the powerbase. The trade focus, particularly with gold and slaves, changed towards the coast with the arrival of

Table 20.1 Timeline of important events in Africa

±50,000 BP	Major expansion of *Homo sapiens* out of Africa
12,000 BP	Sea levels around Africa rise to present levels. Extinctions of large herbivores in southern Africa
9300 BP	Earliest ceramic tradition in North Africa—debate on independent cattle domestication
7800 BP	Earliest sheep remains in North Africa—genetics show these came from Near East
5000 BP	Drying up of Sahara—pastoralists move south into West and East Africa by 4000 BP
4200 BP	Rise of Kush and Meroë
3000 BP	Specialized pastoralism in East Africa, expansion of Bantu-speaking, iron-using farming communities from West Africa
2000 BP	Earliest domestic animals enter southern Africa
1st century AD	Rise of Aksum
4th century AD	First farmers in southern Africa
11th century AD	Complex societies, such as Mapungubwe, begin in southern Africa
11th century AD	Kingdoms of West Africa, such as Mossi, Ashante, Benin, begin
AD 1444	First Europeans (Portuguese) arrive off Senegal River mouth
AD 1488	Bartolomeu Dias rounds the Cape of Good Hope
AD 1498	Vasco da Gama opens up Indian Ocean trade to Europeans

Europeans in the fifteenth century and the opening up of the Atlantic slave trade with Brazil, the Caribbean, and the southern American states.

AFTERWORD

From the above it should be obvious to the reader that although isolated in many ways, Africa was never cut off from the rest of the world (Table 20.1). Dynastic Egyptian society obtained many of its desirable goods from south of the Sahara, particularly the Land of Punt (Phillips 1997). Recent isotopic analysis of baboon mummies from Egypt in the British Museum collections by Nathaniel Dominy of University of California, Santa Cruz announced in the British press that the location of Punt was probably Eritrea and northern Ethiopia (*The Independent*, 26 April 2010). The Romans also controlled the trade in gold from the mines in Nubia. The Red Sea and Indian Ocean trade meant that goods moved to the Near and Far East, with even the Chinese visiting the east African coast in the fifteenth century AD, and glass trade beads from the Indian Ocean trade have been found in large numbers at Igbo Ukwu in Nigeria (Robertshaw et al. 2006). Africans may or may not have domesticated cattle, but certainly the donkey was independently domesticated in Africa (Beja-Pereira et al. 2004), and many plant species unknown outside Africa were brought under cultivation. Although wild grains were probably exploited at the end of the Pleistocene, from current data, grain agriculture lagged far behind the use of domestic animals (Marshall and Hildebrand 2002).

REFERENCES

Amblard, S. 1996. Agricultural evidence and its interpretation on the Dhars Tichitt and Oualata, south-eastern Mauretania. In G. Pwiti and R. Soper (eds), *Aspects of African archaeology*, 421–7. Harare: University of Zimbabwe Publications.

Ambrose, S.H. 1998. Chronology of the Later Stone Age and food production in East Africa. *Journal of Archaeological Science* 25, 377–92.

Applegate, A., Gauthier, A., and Duncan, S. 2001. The north tumuli of the Nabta Late Neolithic ceremonial complex. In F. Wendorf, R. Schild, and Associates (eds), *Holocene settlement of the Egyptian Sahara, vol. 1: the archaeology of Nabta Playa*, 468–88. New York: Kluwer Academic/Plenum Press.

Arkell, A.J. 1949. *Early Khartoum*. Oxford: Oxford University Press.

Beja-Pereira, A., England, P. R., Ferrand, N., Jordan, S., Bakhiet, A. O., Abdalla, M. A., Mashkour, M., Jordana, J., Taberlet, P., and Luikart, G. 2004. African origins of the domestic donkey. *Science* 304, 1781.

Blundell, G. 2004. *Nqabaya's Nomansland: San rock art and the somatic past*. Uppsala: Uppsala University Studies in Global Archaeology 2.

Casey, J. 2005. Holocene occupations of the forest and savanna. In A. B. Stahl (ed.), *African archaeology*, 225–48. Oxford: Blackwell.

Cashdan, E. 1986. Hunter-gatherers of the northern Kalahari. In R. Vossen and K. Keuthmann (eds), *Contemporary studies on Khoisan 1*, 145–80. Hamburg: Helmut Buske Verlag.

Chami, F. A. 1999. Roman beads from the Rufiji Delta: first incontrovertible archaeological link with the Periplus. *Current Anthropology* 40, 239–41.

Clark, J. D. 2008. Epipalaeolithic aggregates from Greboun Wadi and Adrar Bous. In J. D. Clark and D. Gifford-Gonzalez (eds), *Adrar Bous: archaeology of a central Saharan granitic ring complex in Niger*, 181–97. Tervuren: Royal Museum for Central Africa, Studies in Human Sciences 170.

Close, A. E. 2001. Sinai, Sahara, Sahel: the introduction of domestic caprines to Africa. *Africa Praehistorica* 14, 459–69.

Deacon, H. J. and Deacon, J. 1999. *Human beginnings in South Africa*. Cape Town: David Philip.

di Lernia, S. 1999a. *The Uan Afuda cave: hunter-gatherer societies of central Sahara*. Rome: Arid Zone Archaeology 1.

di Lernia, S. 1999b. Discussing pastoralism: the case of the Acacus and surroundings (Libyan Sahara). *Sahara* 11, 7–20.

Eggert, M. K. H. 1993. Central Africa and the archaeology of the equatorial forest: reflections on some major topics. In T. Shaw, P. Sinclair, B. Andah, and A. Okpoko (eds), *The archaeology of Africa: food, metals and towns*, 289–329. London: Routledge.

Eggert, M. K. H. 2005. The Bantu problem and African archaeology. In A. B. Stahl (ed.), *African archaeology*, 301–26. Oxford: Blackwell.

Finucane, B., Manning, K., and Touré, M. 2008. Late Stone Age subsistence in the Tilemsi Valley, Mali: stable isotope analysis of human and animal remains from the site of Karkarichinkat Nord (KN05) and Karkarichinkat Sud (KS05). *Journal of Anthropological Archaeology* 27, 82–92.

Gifford-Gonzalez, D. 2000. Animal disease challenges to the emergence of pastoralism in sub-Saharan Africa. *African Archaeological Review* 17, 95–139.

Goodwin, A. J. H. and van Riet Louw, C. 1929. The stone age cultures of South Africa. *Annals of the South African Museum* 27, 1–289.

Grove, A. T. 1993. Africa's climate in the Holocene. In T. Shaw, P. Sinclair, B. Andah, and A. Okpoko (eds), *The archaeology of Africa: food, metals and towns*, 32–42. London: Routledge.

Güldemann, T. 2008. A linguist's view: Khoe-Kwadi speakers as the earliest food-producers of southern Africa. *Southern African Humanities* 20, 93–132.

Haaland, R. 1999. The puzzle of the later emergence of domestic sorghum in the Nile Valley. In C. Gosden and J. Hather (eds), *The prehistory of food appetites for change*, 397–418. London: Routledge.

Hall, M. 1987. *The changing past: farmers, kings and traders in southern Africa, 200–1860*. Cape Town: David Philip.

Hanotte, O., Bradley, D. G., Ochieng, J. W. Verjee, Y., Hill, E. W., and Rege, J. E. O. 2002. African pastoralism: genetic imprints of origins and migrations. *Science* 296, 336–9.

Holl, A. F. C. 2005. Holocene 'aquatic' adaptations in North Tropical Africa. In A. B. Stahl (ed.), *African archaeology*, 174–86. London: Blackwell.

Huffman, T. N. 2007. *Handbook to the Iron Age: the archaeology of pre-colonial farming societies in southern Africa*. Scottsville: University of Kwa-Zulu-Natal Press.

Huysecom, E., Rasse, M., Lespez, L., Neumann, K., Fahmy, A., Ballouche, A., Ozainne, S., Maggetti, M., Tribolo, Ch., and Soriano, S. 2009. The emergence of pottery in Africa in the tenth millennium BC: new evidence from Mali. *Antiquity* 83, 905–17.

Jerardino, A. and Swanepoel, N. 1999. Painted slabs from Steenbokfontein cave: the oldest known parietal art in southern Africa. *Current Anthropology* 40, 542–8.

Jórdeczka, M., Królik, H., Masojć, M., and Schild, R. 2011. Early Holocene pottery in the Western Desert of Egypt: new data from Nabta Playa. *Antiquity* 85, 99–115.

Karega-Munene, 2003. The East African Neolithic: a historical perspective. In C. M. Kusimba and S. B. Kusimba (eds), *East African archaeology: foragers, potters, smiths, and traders*, 17–32. Philadelphia: University of Pennsylvania Museum of Archaeology and Anthropology.

King, L. C. 1967. *The morphology of the earth*. Edinburgh: Oliver & Boyd.

Klein, R. G. 1980. Environmental and ecological implications of large mammals from Upper Pleistocene and Holocene sites in southern Africa. *Annals of the South African Museum* 81, 223–83.

Kutzbach, J. E. and Street-Perrott, F. A. 1985. Milankovich forcing of fluctuations in the level of tropical lakes from 18 to 0 kyr BP. *Nature* 317, 130–4.

Levtzion, N. 1973. *Ancient Ghana and Mali*. London: Methuen.

Lewis-Williams, J. D. 1981. *Believing and seeing: symbolic meanings in southern San rock paintings*. Cambridge: Cambridge University Press.

McIntosh, R. J. 2005. *Ancient Middle Niger: urbanism and the self-organising landscape*. Cambridge: Cambridge University Press.

Maley, J. 1993. The climatic and vegetational history of the equatorial regions of Africa during the upper Quaternary. In T. Shaw, P. Sinclair, B. Andah, and A. Okpoko (eds), *The archaeology of Africa: food, metals and towns*, 43–52. London: Routledge.

Manning, K. M. 2008. Community organization in the mid-late 3rd millennium BC: a revised view from the Lower Tilemsi Valley, north eastern Mali. PhD thesis. University of Oxford.

Marshall, F. 1990. Origins of specialized pastoral production in East Africa. *American Anthropologist* 92, 873–94.

Marshall, F. 2000. The origins and spread of domestic animals in East Africa. In R. M. Blench and K. C. MacDonald (eds), *The origins and development of African livestock: archaeology, genetics, linguistics and ethnography*, 191–221. London: UCL Press.

Marshall, F. and Hildebrand, E. 2002. Cattle before crops: the beginnings of food production in Africa. *Journal of World Prehistory* 16, 99–143.

Mitchell, P. 2002. *The archaeology of southern Africa*. Cambridge: Cambridge University Press.

Mitchell, P. 2005. *African connections: archaeological perspectives on Africa and the wider world*. Walnut Creek, CA: AltaMira Press.

Morris, A. G. 2002. Isolation and the origin of the Khoisan: Late Pleistocene and Early Holocene human evolution at the southern end of Africa. *Human Evolution* 17, 231–40.

Mugai, A. W. T. 2002. Characterisation and conservation of indigenous animal genetic resources: genetic diversity and relationships of fat-tailed and thin-tailed sheep of Africa. PhD thesis, Department of Biochemistry, Jomo Kenyatta University of Agriculture and Technology, Kenya.

Mugai, A. W. T and Hanotte, O. 2013. The origin of African sheep: archaeological and genetic perspectives. *African Archaeological Review* 30, 39–50.

Paris, F. 2000. African livestock remains from Saharan mortuary contexts. In R. M. Blench and K. C. MacDonald (eds), *The origins and development of African livestock: archaeology, genetics, linguistics and ethnography*, 111–26. London: UCL Press.

Peters, J., Helmer, D., von den Driesch, A., and Saña Segui, M. 1999. Early animal husbandry in the northern Levant. *Paléorient* 25, 27–47.

Petit-Maire, N. and Dutour, O. 1987. Holocene populations of the western and southern Sahara: mechtoids and paleoclimates. In A. E. Close (ed.), *Prehistory of arid North Africa*, 259–85. Dallas: Southern Methodist University Press.

Phillips, J. 1997. Punt and Aksum: Egypt and the Horn of Africa. *Journal of African History* 38, 423–57.

Rindsberger, M., Magaritz, M., Carmi, I., and Gilad, D. 1983. The relation between air mass trajectories and the water isotope composition of rain in the Mediterranean Sea area. *Geophysical Research Letters* 10, 43–6.

Robbins, L. H., Campbell, A. C., Murphy, M. L., Brook, G. A., Srivastava, P., and Badenhorst, S. 2005. The advent of herding in southern Africa: early AMS dates from the Kalahari Desert. *Current Anthropology* 46, 671–7.

Robertshaw, P. T. 1990. *A history of African archaeology*. London: James Currey.

Robertshaw, P. T. 2003. The origins of the state in East Africa. In C. M. Kusimba and S. B. Kusimba (eds), *East African archaeology: foragers, potters, smiths, and traders*, 149–66. Philadelphia: University of Pennsylvania Museum of Archaeology and Anthropology.

Robertshaw, P. T., Wood, M., Popelka-Filcoff, R., and Glascock, M. 2006. Glass beads of southern Africa and Indian Ocean trading networks. Paper presented at Society of Africanist Archaeologist Meetings, Calgary, June.

Sadr, K. 2003. The Neolithic of southern Africa. *Journal of African History* 44, 195–209.

Saxon, E. C., Close, A. E., Cluzel, C., Morse, V., and Shackleton, N. J. 1974. Results of excavations at Tamar Hat. *Libyca* 22, 49–91.

Schuster, S. C., Miller, W., Ratam, A., Tomsho, L. P., Giardine, B., Kasson, L. R., Harris, R. S., Petersen, D. C., Zhao, F., Qi, J., Alkan, C., Kidd, J. M., Sun, Y., Drautz, D. I., Bouffard, P., Muzny, D. M., Reid, J. G., Nazareth, L. V., Wang, Q., Burhans, R., Riemer, C., Wittekinde, N. E., Moorjani, P., Tindall, E. A., Danko, C. G., Teo, W. S., Buboltz, A. M., Zhang, Z., Mal, Q., Oosthuysen, A., Steenkamp, A. W., Oostuisen, H., Venter, P., Gajewski, J., Zhang, Y., Pugh, B. F., Makova, K. D., Nekrutenko, A., Mardis, E. R., Patterson, N., Pringle, T. H., Chiaromonte, F., Mullikin, J. C., Eichler, E. E., Hardison, R. C., Gibbs, R. A., Harkins, T. T., and Hayes, V. M. 2010. Complete Khoisan and Bantu genomes from southern Africa. *Nature* 463, 943–7.

Sereno, P., Garcea, E. A. A., Jousse, H., Stojanowski, C. M., Saliège, J.-F., Maga, A., Ide, O. A., Knudson, K. J., Mercuri, A. M., Stafford, T. W., Kaye, T. G., Giraudi, C., N'siala, I. M., Cocca, E., Moots, H. M., Dutheil, D. B., and Stivers, J. P. 2008. Lakeside cemeteries in the Sahara: 5000 years of Holocene population and environmental change. *PLoS ONE* 3, e2995, 1–22.

Servant, M., Ergenzinger, P., and Coppens, Y. 1969. Datations absolues sur un delta lacustre quaternaire au sud du Tibesti (Angamma). *Comptes rendus sommaires de la Société géologique de France* 1, 313–14.

Smith, A. B. 1979. Biogeographical consideration of colonisation of the Lower Tilemsi Valley in the 2nd millennium BC. *Journal of Arid Environments* 2, 355–61.

Smith, A. B. 1988. The Near Eastern connection: Early to Mid-Holocene relations between N. Africa and Levant. In L. Krzyzaniak, and M. Kobusiewicz (eds), *Late prehistory of the Nile Basin and the Sahara*, 69–77. Poznan: Muzeum Archeologiczne.

Smith, A. B. 1993. New approaches to Saharan rock art. In G. Calegari (ed.), *L'arte e l'ambiente del Sahara preistorico: dati e interpretazioni*, 466–78. Milan: Memorie della Società Italiana di Scienze Naturali e del Museo Civico di Storia Naturale di Milano.

Smith, A. B. 2006. *Excavations at Kasteelberg and the origins of the Khoekhoen in the Western Cape, South Africa*. Oxford: BAR International Series 1537.

Smith, A. B. 2008. The Kiffian. In J. D. Clark and D. Gifford-Gonzalez (eds), *Adrar Bous: archaeology of a central Saharan granitic ring complex in Niger*, 199–220. Tervuren: Royal Museum for Central Africa, Studies in Human Sciences 170.

Smith, B. W. and Ouzman, S. 2004. Taking stock: identifying Khoekhoen herder rock art. *Current Anthropology* 45, 499–526.

Soares, P., Alshamali, F., Pereira, J. B., Fernandes, V., Silva, N. M., Alfonso, C., Costa, M. D., Musilova, E., Macaulay, V., Richards, M. B., Černy, V., and Pereira, L. 2012. The expansion of mtDNA Haplogroup L3 within and out of Africa. *Molecular Biology and Evolution* 29, 915–27.

Solomon, A. 2000. On different approaches to San rock art. *South African Archaeological Bulletin* 55, 77–8.

Stahl, A. B. 1986. Early food production in West Africa: rethinking the role of the Kintampo culture. *Current Anthropology* 27, 532–6.

Street-Perrott, F. A. and Perrot, R. A. 1993. Holocene vegetation, lake levels and climate of Africa. In H. E. Wright, Jr., J. E. Kutzbach, T. Webb III, W. F. Ruddiman, F. A. Street-Perrot, and P. J. Bartlein (eds), *Global climates since the Last Glacial Maximum*, 318–56. Minneapolis: University of Minnesota Press.

Sutton, J. E. G. 1977. The African Aqualithic. *Antiquity* 51, 25–34.

Talbot, M. R., Livingstone, D. A., Palmer, P. G., Maley, J., Melack, J. M., Delibrias, G. and Gulliksen, S. 1984. Preliminary results from sediment cores from Lake Bosumtwi, Ghana. *Palaeoecology of Africa* 16, 173–92.

Wendorf, F. and Malville, J. M. 2001. The megalithic alignments. In F. Wendorf, R. Schild, and Associates (eds), *Holocene settlement of the Egyptian Sahara, volume 1: the archaeology of Nabta Playa*, 489–502. New York: Kluwer Academic/Plenum Press.

Wendorf, F. and Schild, R. 1980. *The prehistory of the eastern Sahara*. New York: Academic Press.

Wendorf, F. and Schild, R. 1994. Are the early Holocene cattle in the eastern Sahara domestic or wild? *Evolutionary Anthropology* 3, 118–28.

Wendorf, F., Schild, R., and Close, A. E. 1984. *Cattle keepers of the eastern Sahara: the Neolithic of Bir Kiseiba*. Dallas: Southern Methodist University, Department of Anthropology.

Wendt, E. 1976. 'Art mobilier' from the Apollo 11 cave, South West Africa: Africa's oldest dated works of art. *South African Archaeological Bulletin* 31, 5–11.

Yellen, J. E. 1998. Barbed bone points: tradition and continuity in Saharan and sub-Saharan Africa. *African Archaeological Review* 15, 173–98.

Zeder, M. A. 2008. Domestication and early agriculture in the Mediterranean Basin: origins, diffusion, and impact. *Proceedings of the National Academy of Sciences USA* 105, 11597–604.

CHAPTER 21

POST-GLACIAL TRANSFORMATIONS IN SOUTH AND SOUTH-EAST ASIA

RYAN RABETT AND SACHA JONES

THIS chapter focuses on emergent patterns of human behaviour in South and South-East Asia between the end of the last glacial period and the appearance of agriculture. As such, 'post-glacial' is here defined as the period from the onset of the Bølling/Allerød-equivalent warming trend, c.14,600 cal BP, to the first millennia of the Holocene—accepted as commencing c.11,500 cal BP (Walker et al. 2009). Geographically (Figure 21.1), South Asia is defined here as including the countries of Pakistan, India, Sri Lanka, Nepal, Bhutan, and Bangladesh. South-East Asia is considered here to include all coastlines bordering and islands within the South China Sea, together with the eastern islands of Indonesia (within Wallacea). All calibrated radiocarbon dates (cal BP) were obtained using Fairbanks 0107 (Fairbanks et al. 2005); uncalibrated dates are given as 'uncal BP'.

PALAEOENVIRONMENTAL SETTING

Chronologically, most of the period under discussion falls within the deglacial phase of the Pleistocene referred to as the 'Last Termination' (here taken as c.19,000–11,500 cal BP). Globally, the end of the Last Glacial Maximum (LGM), c.19,000 cal BP, was followed by subdued warming until the end of Marine Isotope Stage 2 (MIS 2) at the transition to the Bølling/Allerød global equivalent interstadial (hereafter 'Bølling/Allerød'). This phase of comparative warmth lasted from c.14,700 to 12,800 cal BP, punctuated by brief cold snaps (Friedrich et al. 2001). Glacial conditions returned to higher latitudes c.12,800–11,500 cal BP (the Younger Dryas), with varied, sometimes muted, responses closer to the equator, before more sustained amelioration took hold, marking the start of the Holocene (see Blockley et al. 2006).

In South Asia, the post-glacial period was marked by major palaeoclimatic and palaeoenvironmental changes. The weakened south-west palaeo-monsoon and resulting widespread aridity of the LGM left a predominance of grassland habitats, with isolated areas of forest and swamp, and expanding desert in the north-west (Misra 2001). Marine core and ice core

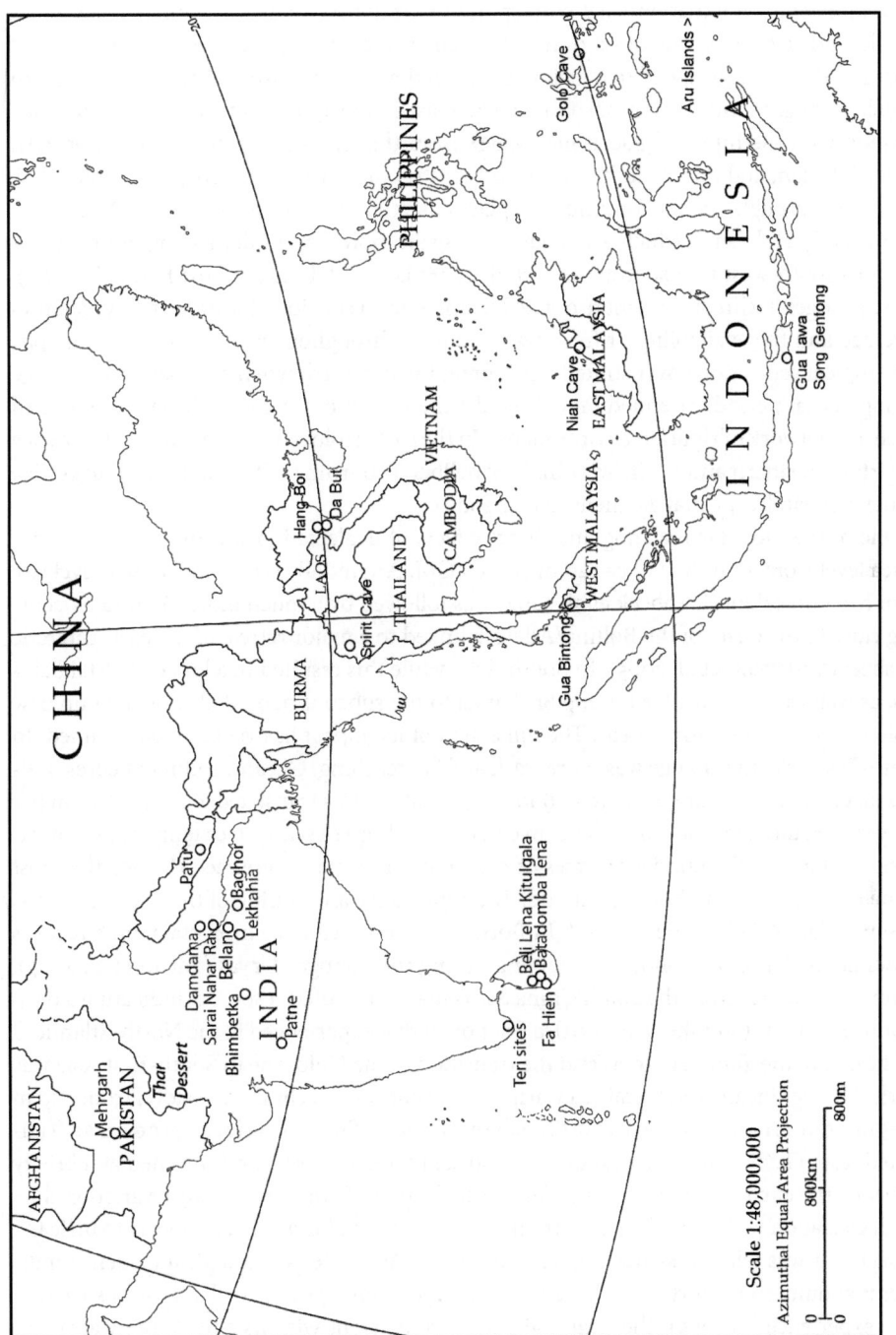

FIGURE 21.1 Locations of archaeological sites mentioned in the text.

records from south Asian and Himalayan contexts (e.g. Schulz et al. 1998; Thompson et al. 1997) have provided high-resolution evidence of regional palaeoclimatic changes, including rapid monsoonal fluctuations that correspond to the abrupt swings in climate recorded in high latitude ice cores. The onset of the Holocene saw a dramatic shift towards wetter and more humid conditions, tied to a major change in the Asian monsoonal system resulting in a much stronger south-west monsoon. The increase in precipitation to South Asia, in combination with the input of glacial meltwaters from the Himalayas into rivers of northern India, Pakistan, and Bangladesh, significantly restructured river systems (e.g. Prabhu et al. 2004). This brought wetter conditions to places like the Indus Valley and Thar Desert during the early Holocene, which are today once again more arid under a comparatively less vigorous south-west monsoon (Gupta et al. 2006; Jain and Tandon 2003; Kennedy 2000). These changes in climate and monsoonal dynamics had a considerable impact on vegetation coverage and the availability of fresh water sources throughout South Asia. For example, sub-tropical vegetation cover shifted ten degrees further north when compared to coverage during glacial periods (Kennedy 1999), whilst the retreat of northern glaciers fostered an extensive network of riparian environments. In the early Holocene, there is limited evidence in parts of northern and north-west India of deliberate burning of the landscape, suggestive of incipient landscape management (Fuller 2006).

One of the most far-reaching and direct effects of deglaciation was the worldwide rise in sea level from a minima of $c.$–120 m at the LGM. An initially sedate rate of sea-level rise from $c.$19,000 cal BP (Lambeck et al. 2002) was followed by a much more rapid rate occurring close to the onset of the Bølling/Allerød, linked to a major retreat of the east Antarctic ice sheet (Verleyehn et al. 2005). In South Asia, while this resulted in a loss of coastal habitats, as well as a land-bridge linking Sri Lanka to the subcontinent, it also opened up new ecological niches in littoral areas. The full extent of its impact has yet to be determined. In South-East Asia, the change was more stark and far-reaching. Oceanic sediment cores indicate that over a 300-year period ($c.$14,600–14,300 cal BP) this translated to a rise of 5.3 m per 100 years (Hanebuth et al. 2000), and an equally rapid rise in sea surface temperature of 1°C (Steinke et al. 2001). Inundation rates of $c.$1.3 m per 100 years were recorded for the most of the remainder of the Bølling/Allerød. The appearance and timing of the Younger Dryas in South-East Asia is more debated. In Borneo, isotopic evidence from stalagmite records shows no evidence of pronounced cooling during the Younger Dryas (Partin et al. 2007). Sediment evidence from the South China Sea echoes this muted response, indicating a drop of only 0.2–0.6°C (Steinke et al. 2001), a fraction of that experienced in the North Atlantic.

The end of the Younger Dryas and the transition to the Holocene in South-East Asia was marked by significant and sustained warming, causing a steep climb in sea level from −50 m to −5 m from $c.$11,000 to 8000 cal BP (Tanabe et al. 2006). From as early as $c.$7500 cal BP (calibrated from Geyh et al. 1979) and until $c.$4500 cal BP, regional sea levels reached and briefly exceeded the current value by $c.$2 m (Tanabe et al. 2006). While temperature variation during deglaciation was generally less extreme than in western Eurasia, this appears to belie the impact that was felt across regional environments. Available palynological evidence indicates that numerous short-term fluctuations in vegetation type and lowland forest structure were experienced through the deglacial period concurrent with its alternating warm and cool interludes (e.g. Sun and Li 1999). Overall, coastal inundation and environmental fluctuations presented post-glacial hunter-gatherers in South-East Asia with significant adaptive challenges.

Transformations in the Lifeways of Post-Glacial South Asian Hunter-Gatherers

In some areas of South Asia, particularly north-east and eastern India, Pakistan, Bangladesh, Nepal, and Bhutan, the early Holocene archaeological record remains poorly understood. This discrepancy may be explained by the limited research, or publication of research, in these areas, though deep burial of archaeological remains under thick alluvial deposits is also possible (Kennedy 2000). Few sites attributed to this period in South Asia have been excavated and radiometrically dated (e.g. Chakrabarti 1999), leading to uncertainty regarding the chronology of changes in hunter-gatherer lifeways. However, material remains of early Holocene foragers have been found in a variety of South Asian habitats, suggesting a comparatively large and well-distributed late Pleistocene population (Oppenheimer 2004). Sites have been identified in the upland jungles of Sri Lanka, littoral areas in the far south of India, the central plains of the Ganges, rock shelters of Central India, islands off the west coast of India, and fossil sand dunes in north-west India (Kennedy 1999). While a record of large sedentary sites in the early Holocene associated with microlithic technologies also exists, these are relatively rare. Some cave and rock shelter sites record perennial occupation; others indicate only seasonal habitation (Kennedy 2000). Evidence is beginning to emerge that the major climatic and palaeoenvironmental changes of the post-glacial had a significant effect on population distribution and concentrations. For example, the Thar Desert region was sparsely occupied during the Last Termination, yet occupation during the Holocene was prolific (Deotare et al. 2004). By contrast, archaeological evidence from other regions—e.g. the central Indian hills, the Belan Valley, and areas north of the River Ganges (Allchin and Allchin 1982)—shows broadly continuous occupation. Although knowledge of the archaeological and anthropological records of the terminal Pleistocene to early Holocene is clearly better for some regions of South Asia than others, a significant amount of information is currently available from a range of studies that allow us to assess the impact of the post-glacial on resident populations.

Technology

Unlike the situation seen in other parts of the Old World, the post-glacial did not instigate a cultural transition from Upper Palaeolithic to Mesolithic traditions in South Asia—and microlithic and Mesolithic are not synonymous here. While a large proportion of microlithic assemblages found in this region may have been manufactured by hunter-gatherers during the Holocene, contextual and chronometric data have now established that microlithic technologies had a long history in South Asia. The earliest microliths are dated to $c.38{,}500$ cal BP at Fa Hien cave (non-geometric microliths) in Sri Lanka (Deraniyagala 1992; Kennedy 1999; 2000), $c.34{,}000$ cal BP at Jwalapuram Locality 9 (Clarkson et al. 2009), and $c.29{,}000$ cal BP at Patne (geometric microliths: Sali 1989), both in India. Techno-facies of these microlithic industries continue across the Pleistocene–Holocene transition into the Historic Period (Chakrabarti 1999). Terminal Pleistocene sites that preserve microliths include Baghor 1 and 3 in the Middle Son Valley (Clark and Dreiman 1983; Kenoyer et al. 1983), and the 'teri sites' in the far south-east of India. However, these sites have yet to be accurately dated. Examples of early Holocene microlithic sites in India are dated to c.9300 cal BP at Baghor 2 in the Middle Son Valley (Mandal 1983), c.10,000 uncal BP at Bhimbetka, c.9400 cal BP at Lekhahia in the Vindhyan Hills, and c.11,600 cal BP at Sarai Nahar Rai, in the Ganges Valley (Kennedy 1999).

In addition to microliths, several other artefact types have been recovered from Holocene contexts. These include bone tools, fluted cores, scrapers, burins, and pressure-flaked bifacial points (Kennedy 2000; Misra 2001). An exception to the overall pattern of microlith production throughout South Asia during the Holocene can be found at Patu in the Himalayan foothills of eastern Nepal. Here, cobble tools and adzes were being manufactured during the early Holocene that shows greater cultural affinities with the Hoabinhian of South-East Asia. This has led to the suggestion of possible human migrations (or connections) from South-East Asia into eastern Nepal during the terminal Pleistocene and Holocene (Corvinus 2004).

Representational Art

While there is little evidence for major technological change through the post-glacial period of South Asia, examples of representational art appear to increase significantly. Early evidence of adornment and social identification, represented by the manufacture of ostrich eggshell beads, occurs in Upper Palaeolithic contexts at Bhimbetka, and dates to c.33,800 cal BP at Batadomba Lena in Sri Lanka, and c.30,000 cal BP at Patne. Although ochre has been found in various Pleistocene contexts, including the Acheulian, it remains unknown whether it was used for symbolic purposes (James and Petraglia 2005).

Paintings and engravings have been recorded on the walls of thousands of rock shelters and caves in India (Chakravarty and Bednarik 1998). The most studied of these are in central India. For example, paintings occur in about 55 per cent of 642 rock shelters in the area around Bhimbetka (Chakrabarti 1999). Art occurs in rock shelters where evidence of occupation is both present and absent (Misra 2001). Problems associated with dating rock art are well known, and in India, paintings continued to be made on rock-shelter walls up until the present day. Depictions supposedly created by early Holocene foragers include human figures, wild animals, sticks, slings, bows, arrows, stone-tipped spears, and scenes of fishing, hunting, honey and plant collecting, and social and religious life (Misra 2001). These painted rock shelters may have been central meeting places and possibly ceremonial areas (Chakrabarti 1999). Although accurate dating of these depictions remains to be perfected, their emergence at this time, if confirmed, suggests that significant social changes were beginning to occur in South Asia. This is further attested by increasing evidence for deliberate burial in the early Holocene.

Social Complexity

Human palaeontological evidence dating to the end of the Pleistocene in South Asia is very minimal, being restricted to that from the Sri Lankan cave sites. However, the record changes when burial areas are repeatedly used, creating almost 'cemetery-like' settings. This occurs earliest in Sri Lanka at Batadomba Lena (>19 individuals; c.18,000 cal BP) and Beli Lena Kitulgala (>12 individuals; c.14,000 cal BP: Kennedy 1999), and later in the mid-Ganga plains in association with geometric microliths (Lukacs 2007). From the latter, 14 individuals were recovered from Sarai Nahar Rai (*c.*11,600 cal BP), and 47 burials were uncovered at Damdama (*c.*10,000 cal BP). A further 21 individuals were discovered at Lekhahia ki Pahari (*c.*9400 cal BP: Kennedy 1999). The Holocene 'cemeteries' of the mid-Ganga plains appear within settlement areas, all located along the edges of desiccated oxbow lakes. Both single and sometimes double burials are represented and grave goods are occasionally present (e.g. microliths, shells, grinding stones, charred bone, antler ornaments, pieces of burnt clay, and haematite: Allchin and Allchin 1982). The burial of only certain individuals with grave goods suggests that, by this point, there was increased emphasis on social status and/or social complexity in hunter-gatherer communities in this region. Evidence of repeated intentional burial in the same area may also be an expression of greater territorial behaviour, and a way of maintaining tangible trans-generational kinship ties through the land (Chakrabarti 1999). Whilst there is evidence of more permanent settlements, or a relative increase in sedentism, at sites like those in the mid-Ganga plains, comparable settlement sites have not been found in early Holocene contexts elsewhere in South Asia (Allchin and Allchin 1982). Misra (2001) argues that increased food security with the onset of Holocene caused a reduction in nomadic behaviours and an increase in seasonally sedentary occupation. This is supported by the large size of some Holocene hunter-gatherer sites, the presence of 'cemeteries', and the thickness of habitation deposits in open-air sites and rock shelters.

One of the most important transformations already beginning to occur in South Asia during the late post-glacial period was the transition from hunting and foraging modes of subsistence towards those based on agriculture. The beginnings of agriculture in South Asia were probably linked to an increase in precipitation during the early and middle Holocene (Gupta et al. 2006), and a concomitant increase in population size. Mehrgarh, in the Indus Valley of Pakistan, is the earliest known agricultural settlement in South Asia, dated to *c.*8000 uncal BP or possibly *c.*9000 uncal BP, and has produced the earliest currently known evidence for indigenous processes of domestication as well as the introduction of subsistence species from the west (Fuller 2006). However, the adoption of agriculture occurred in different regions at different times, with some areas in the far south of India not adopting agriculture until the mid-Holocene, *c.*5000 uncal BP (Morisson 2007).

While there has been little systematic research into the post-glacial period specifically in South Asia, the available data suggest that major climatic and palaeoenvironmental changes were wrought on this landscape, yet there is little in the way of evidence to suggest that people were significantly altering the way they directly interacted with it through technological media. At the same time, there were trends towards more intensive land management practice and subsistence transformation, and substantial evidence for social change over this period, with an emerging emphasis on social and territorial identification.

Transformations in the Lifeways of Post-Glacial South-East Asian Hunter-Gatherers

The post-glacial record in South-East Asia appears to be better represented in some parts of the region than others (e.g. Mijares 2008; Zuraina 1998), though at the present time it is unclear whether this owes more to available research coverage than to genuine discrepancies in the distribution of the evidence. That said, the material that is available from this period reveals notable trends in subsistence strategies and technological innovation, while new genetic evidence suggests that a major wave of intra-regional human dispersal began during the course of the Bølling/Allerød.

Subsistence

Although there is a long tradition of recovering faunal remains from South-East Asian archaeological sites, with few exceptions, it is only in recent years that these typically diverse assemblages have been subjected to systematic zooarchaeological analysis (see e.g. Piper et al. forthcoming). Following excavation of Spirit cave (northern Thailand) Gorman (1970) presented a convincing picture of what was probably seasonal occupation of this site during the post-glacial period. There was clear targeting of a range of different local habitats and no apparent disjuncture in subsistence strategies across the Pleistocene–Holocene transition. Such continuity has since been noted elsewhere in the region. An intra-regional comparison of subsistence strategies in northern Borneo, the Song Hong River delta in northern Vietnam, and eastern Peninsular Malaysia through the Last Termination (Rabett 2012) suggests that certain taxa continue to account for high proportions of the diet irrespective of the changes in local conditions. For example, studies of fauna from the Niah caves (Sarawak: Piper et al. 2008, Rabett et al. 2006) indicate a long-term emphasis on hunting the bearded pig (*Sus barbatus*). At Hang Boi, a cave in northern Vietnam, the emphasis lies with the gathering of land snails (*Cyclophorus* spp.) and freshwater crabs (*Villopotamon* sp.: Rabett et al. 2009; 2011). These resources appear to represent dietary staples and site placement may be linked primarily to their reliable availability. There is further evidence from Hang Boi that existing karstic subsistence strategies were intensified before new resources, such as those from the coastal margin, were incorporated even when these latter resources were more locally available. The exploitation of coastal resources figures prominently in current palaeo-population dispersal models out of Africa (e.g. Lahr and Foley 1994) or post-glacial entry into the Americas (e.g. Dixon 2001). It is generally assumed that these rich environments would have been sought after by early hunter-gatherer communities and may have been pivotal in Pleistocene human colonization. The preliminary data from Hang Boi present both a caution to this assumption and a potential insight into the mechanism of adaptation to post-glacial environments.

With the rising sea levels of the post-glacial period, the palaeo-shoreline migrated landward and coastal habitats encroached on the massif where Hang Boi is located (see Hanebuth et al. 2006; Tanabe et al. 2006). Despite this, there is currently very little indication that people visiting the cave were exploiting marine resources, even during the final phase of occupation, 11,400 ± 108 cal BP (UBA-10166) to 10,631 ± 58 cal BP (UBA-10163). Significantly, this is despite the presence of a potentially worked fragment of cowrie shell from this phase, as well as deliberately perforated mangrove shells, indicating that some contact with the coast, either directly or through an exchange network, very likely existed (Rabet, 2012). From the excavated sequence, subsistence strategies employed at Hang Boi during its early occupation (from at least *c*.13,600 cal BP) were carried through, with augmentation, into later more intensive occupation at the site, but newly available coastal resources were not incorporated. There could be a number of reasons for this including differential transportation of food resources (depending on how far from the site they were procured), cultural preferences and constraints, or seasonality (Rabett et al. 2011). Evidence for the use of marine resources appears in this area from c.7400 cal BP at the site of Da But, where it forms part of an economy using also upland, freshwater swamp, river, and lake habitats (Viet 2005). Whichever of the aforementioned reasons (or combination of them) lies behind this evidence, the incorporation of marine resources into some settlement settings was out of step with their more general availability. It is one of the key problems with reconstructing early subsistence practices from South-East Asia that we continue to have only a limited understanding about group mobility and site function (Shoocongdej 1996). It is also becoming apparent that although many of the diverse subsistence practices that exist in South-East Asia today are affected by historical developments, this approach to tropical subsistence, involving switching between staple resources, may have deep roots (Rabett and Barker 2010). Conclusions drawn on the evidence from Hang Boi may be revealing something both of the adaptive strategies taken in response to climate change and inundation— namely the intensifying of existing systems—and of the complexities that there are for us still to unpick in order to fully understand them.

Another emerging feature of subsistence during the post-glacial period is a rise in the incidence of arboreal and semi-arboreal taxa (Bulbeck 2003; Morwood et al. 2008; Piper and Rabett 2009). Probably linked with post-glacial lowland forest development, in some cases, such as from the Lobang Hangus entrance to the Niah caves, there is a close association between the incidence of canopy species and the appearance of probable range technology—in the form of recovered bone point armatures (Piper and Rabett 2009). Alongside these threads of continuity in subsistence through the post-glacial period, there is also evidence for highly localized practices. Reanalysis of the Niah caves fauna (Barker et al. forthcoming) indicates differences not only in the frequency of particular semi-arboreal species, but also in the butchery *chaîne opératoire* applied to the same species at different entrances to Niah. The oft-cited similarity in species representation from South-East Asian sites dating to this period appears to belie a more complicated picture surrounding a continuity of practices, the adoption of coastal resources, and local site-specific variability. There is also now growing evidence that the post-glacial period witnessed a significant spell of regional population movement, a spread of a new technological focus, and the early translocation of species between islands.

Genetic Evidence of Intra-Regional Population Dispersal

Hill et al. (2007) indicated that the majority of modern South-East Asian mitochondrial DNA (mtDNA) lineages coalesced before the more well-known and well-documented mid-Holocene Neolithic dispersal in this region (e.g. see Bellwood 2007). Subsequent work by Soares et al. (2008) using complete mtDNA genomes from 1,704 samples from present-day communities across island South-East Asia has provided further detail to this post-glacial pulse of human migration, which may have had its origins in part of the region including north-east Sundaland and north-west Wallacea. They present further genetic evidence to suggest that this dispersal may have been preceded by a population bottleneck event. Plausibly linked to the rapid rise in sea level at the beginning of the Bølling/Allerød, this could have precipitated a period of population displacement and extirpation through overcrowding and competition for resources.

One line of evidence that supports the early movement of people is the translocation of species between islands in South-East Asia. More well known as a means of analysing later, Neolithic dispersal, research into such introductions is now revealing some instances of movement in the first half of the Holocene. For example, Anderson and O'Connor (2008) discuss the evidence for the translocation of the marsupial phalanger (*Phalanger orientalis*) from New Guinea to Timor *c.*9000 uncal BP, while new genetic studies into pig (*Sus* sp.) distribution in island South-East Asia (Dobney et al. 2008) have revealed that the Sulawesi warty pig (*Sus celebensis*) was likely moved from Sulawesi to Flores, where it appears a little before 6400 uncal BP. Though still in its infancy, the study of translocation, particularly through reconstructions of genetic affinity, supports the existence of long-term population movements in this region. The distribution of early bone technology here provides a second and more heavily researched (e.g. Olsen and Glover 2004; Pasveer 2006; Pasveer and Bellwood 2004; Rabett 2005; Rabett and Piper 2012) line of independent archaeological evidence that closely parallels the findings of the genetic research.

The Post-Glacial Appearance and Distribution of Bone Technologies

Technological trajectories in South-East Asia have tended to focus on the continuity of lithic industries in this region (e.g. Rabett 2011). However, bone implements have formed part of the technological toolkit of South-East Asian hunter-gatherers from at least *c.*45,000 cal BP, based on material from the Niah caves (Rabett 2012; Rabett et al. 2006). Until the end of the Pleistocene, though, at a regional scale instances were rare. Two initial regional 'centres' of this technology appear to have existed on current evidence from the earliest material (Rabett and Piper 2012). One encompasses the eastern Sunda Shelf and Wallacea, the other, an area of mainland South-East Asia with current points of incidence in the northern half of the Thai-Malay Peninsula and some sites in northern Vietnam. In both areas, the frequency of bone tools is low during much of the late Pleistocene, though in enough forms (such as split pig tusks, bone point and spatulate pieces) to suggest that it was not confined to a single sphere of activity.

Whereas evidence from the mainland suggests that bone technology continued to be used at a low level throughout the late glacial and until the Holocene, the situation seems to have been different in what would become island South-East Asia. Beginning during the Bølling/Allerød at the Lobang Hangus entrance to the Niah caves—14,484 ± 131 cal BP (OxA-13936) to 12,373 ± 95 cal BP (OxA-13939)—this minor tool component suddenly becomes much more prominent (Piper and Rabett 2009). Possible links between the rise of this technology and the exploitation of coastal resources (Rabett 2005) and additional comparatively early occurrences at Liang Nabulei Lisa and Liang Lemdubu in the Aru Islands (Pasveer 2006), and at Golo cave in the Northern Moluccas (Pasveer and Bellwood 2004) 7500–11,200 cal BP, accords well, but does not prove the existence of a link, with the genetic evidence of Soares et al. (2008). There are indications of similar bone tool assemblages appearing at other locations in the region on a broadly, though not exclusively, east–west axis; a pattern that is suggestive of population or information dispersal. Most occurrences date to after *c.*8000 cal BP, with those on the western Sunda Shelf, such as at Gua Bintong, generally appearing latest. At the same time, there is evidence that the east also continued to provide a source for further technological innovation during the early Holocene.

New excavations at the west mouth of the Niah caves have revealed a collection of worked stingray and catfish spines dating from the early Holocene—10,886 ± 148 cal BP (OxA-12391) to 8915 ± 103 cal BP (OxA-11864) (Barton et al. 2009). This material included two almost complete bi-points: one of bone, the other a stingray spine. On the latter, both sets of lateral barbs had been removed from the base with clear traces of oblique grinding—consistent with haft preparation—whereas the fine tip of the spine was intact. A yellow-red resinous crystalline substance was also found adhering to portions of six spine fragments and, in two of these instances, the remains of transversely aligned bundles of thin fibrous strands were found within the resin. Based on this surface modification Barton et al. (2009) conclude that these were almost certainly armatures to narrow-gauge single or multi-pronged projectiles (e.g. light throwing spears or arrows), possibly used for hunting arboreal prey or fishing activities. This collection is unique at Niah and currently comprises the earliest evidence for cartilaginous points in the region. Other archaeological evidence in support of early population dispersal comes from Bellwood (2007), who draws parallels between the lithic points that occur in the Gua Lawa assemblage from eastern Java and those that are characteristic of the Toalian from sites in Sulawesi, though this association is contested. There are also thought to be technological similarities between bone technology appearing at Song Gentong (East Java) and similar material from southern Sulawesi (Marliac and Simanjuntak 1996). Olsen and Glover (2004) also draw attention to another long-standing similarity, between the Toalian bone and stone technological suites and early tool traditions in Australia. The dispersal of human populations in South-East Asia across the Pleistocene–Holocene transition probably did not follow a simple west to east, mainland to island, spread.

Conclusion

In South Asia, the climatic changes that occurred during the Holocene led to an expansion of viable habitats for human occupation that were previously uninhabitable during the late glacial (e.g. the Thar Desert). These environmental changes would have affected migration behaviours and location of game, and humans would have adapted accordingly. Humans would have expanded their range and with the amelioration of conditions, their population size. There is evidence for the appearance of new subsistence practices with the onset of the Holocene, such as the use of fire by hunter-gatherers for vegetation management. However, one of the most important transformations to occur during this period was the appearance of the first agricultural societies in the north-west. It has been suggested that interactions between hunter-gatherers and neighbouring pastoral and agricultural populations would have been commonplace during much of the Holocene (e.g. Stock et al. 2007). Regionally, South Asia witnessed a diversification of hunter-gatherer behaviours during the post-glacial period. These included an increase in more sedentary and possibly territorial behaviours in some areas, such as the mid-Ganga plains, where hunter-gatherer populations repeatedly returned to the same location to bury their dead, sometimes accompanied by grave offerings. There was a burgeoning of artistic behaviours, with rock art created in thousands of shelters and caves, possibly marking increased social complexity, territoriality, and enhanced group identity.

The South-East Asian evidence suggests that the Bølling/Allerød may have witnessed a bottleneck event and a pulse of subsequent population dispersal. From both the genetic and archaeological evidence, this dispersal appears to have had its centre in eastern Sundaland and Wallacea rather than the South-East Asian mainland, though there are indications from these and other sources that a single axis of movement is unlikely. While coastal flooding resulted in a major refurbishment of the environment for tropical foragers, the inclusion of a maritime component to economies was not necessarily immediate. As the evidence from Hang Boi shows, even when such environments were available locally, and despite artefactual evidence of contact with the coast, pre-existing economic systems appear to have first persisted and seemingly intensified ahead of incorporation. The post-glacial period in this region was marked by juxtaposition between the affordance of established, localized socio-economic systems and the process of adaptation to a radically transforming geography.

Acknowledgements

The authors would like to thank the editors for inviting us to contribute to this important volume and the anonymous readers who reviewed the chapter; their constructive comments are greatly appreciated. RR wishes to thank colleagues from the Niah caves and Hang Boi projects, with a particular note of thanks to Phil Piper. Funding and backing for the Vietnamese project has come from the D. M. McDonald Fund, ASEASUK, Templeton Foundation, Xuan Truong Construction Company, and the Ninh Bình People's Committee.

References

Allchin, B. and Allchin, R. 1982. *The rise of civilization in India and Pakistan*. Cambridge: Cambridge University Press.

Anderson, A. and O'Connor, S. 2008. Indo-Pacific migration and colonization—introduction. *Asian Perspectives* 47, 2–11.

Barker, G., Gilbertson, D., and Reynolds T. (eds) Forthcoming. *Rainforest foraging and farming in island Southeast Asia: the archaeology and environmental history of the Niah Caves, Sarawak, Niah Cave Project, Vol. 1*. Cambridge: McDonald Institute for Archaeological Research.

Barton, H., Piper, P., Rabett, R., and Reeds, I. 2009. Composite hunting technologies from the Terminal Pleistocene and Early Holocene, Niah cave, Borneo. *Journal of Archaeological Science* 36, 1708–14.

Bellwood, P. 2007. *Prehistory of the Indo-Malay Archipelago* (3rd edition). Canberra: Australian National University E Press.

Blockley, S. P. E., Blockley, M., Donahue, E., Lane, S., Lowe, J., and Pollard, M. 2006. The chronology of abrupt climate change and Late Upper Palaeolithic human adaptation in Europe. *Journal of Quaternary Science* 21, 575–84.

Bulbeck, D. F. 2003. Hunter-gatherer occupation of the Malay Peninsula from the Ice Age to the Iron Age. In J. Mercador (ed.), *Under the canopy: the archaeology of tropical rainforests*, 119–60. New Brunswick: Rutgers University Press.

Chakrabarti, D. K. 1999. *India: an archaeological history*. New Delhi: Oxford University Press.

Chakravarty, K. K. and Bednarik, R. G. 1998. *Indian rock art and its global context*. Delhi: Motilal Banarsidass.

Clark, J. D. and Dreiman R. 1983. An occurrence with small blade technology in the Upper Member of the Baghor Formation at the Baghor III locality. In G. R. Sharma and J. D. Clark (eds), *Palaeoenvironments and prehistory in the Middle Son Valley*, 197–208. Allahabad: Abinash Prakashan.

Clarkson, C., Petraglia, M., Korisettar, R., Haslam, M., Boivin, N., Crowther, A., Ditchfield, P., Fuller, D., Miracle, P., Harris, C., Connell, K., James, H., and Koshy, J. 2009. The oldest and longest enduring microlithic sequence in India: 35000 years of modern human occupation and change at the Jwalapuram Locality 9 rockshelter. *Antiquity* 83, 326–48.

Corvinus, G. 2004. *Homo erectus* in East and Southeast Asia, and the questions of the age of the species and its association with stone artifacts, with special attention to handaxe-like tools. *Quaternary International* 117, 141–51.

Deotare, B. C., Kajale, M. D., Rajaguru, S. N., and Basavaiah, N. 2004. Late Quaternary geomorphology, palynology and magnetic susceptibility of playas in western margin of the Indian Thar Desert. *Journal of Indian Geophysical Union* 8, 15–25.

Deraniyagala, S. U. 1992. *The prehistory of Sri Lanka: an ecological perspective*. Colombo: Colombo Archaeological Department Memoir 8.

Dixon, E. J. 2001. Human colonization of the Americas: timing, technology and process. *Quaternary Science Reviews* 20, 277–99.

Dobney, K., Cucchi, T., and Larson, G. 2008. The pigs of Island South East Asia and the Pacific: new evidence for taxonomic status and human-mediated dispersal. *Asian Perspectives* 47, 59–74.

Fairbanks, R. G., Mortlocka, R. A., Tzu-Chien Chiua, Li Caoa, Kaplana, A., Guilderson, T. P., Fairbanks, T. W., Bloom, A. L., Grootes, P. M., and Nadeau, M. J. 2005. Radiocarbon calibration curve spanning 0 to 50,000 years BP based on paired 230Th/234U/238U and 14C dates on pristine corals. *Quaternary Science Reviews* 24, 1781–96.

Friedrich, M., Kromer, B., Kaiser, K., Spurk, M., Hughen, K., and Johnsen, S. 2001. High resolution climate signals in the Bølling-Allerød Interstadial (Greenland Interstadial 1) as reflected in European tree-ring chronologies compared to marine varves and ice-core records. *Quaternary Science Reviews* 20, 1223–32.

Fuller, D. Q. 2006. Agricultural origins and frontiers in South Asia: a working synthesis. *Journal of World Prehistory* 20, 1–86.

Geyh, M. A., Kudrass, H. R., and Streif, H. 1979. Sea-level changes during the late Pleistocene and Holocene in the Strait of Malacca. *Nature* 278, 441–3.

Gorman, C. F. 1970. Excavations at Spirit cave, Northern Thailand. *Asian Perspectives* 13, 79–107.

Gupta, A. K., Anderson, D. M., Pandey, D. N., and Singhvi, A. K. 2006. Adaptation and human migration, and evidence of agriculture coincident with changes in the Indian summer monsoon during the Holocene. *Current Science* 90, 1082–90.

Hanebuth, T., Stattegger, K., and Grootes, P. M. 2000. Rapid flooding of the Sunda Shelf: a late-glacial sea-level record. *Science* 288, 1033–5.

Hanebuth, T. J. J., Saito, Y., Tanabe, S., Quang Lan Vu, and Quang Toan Ngo. 2006. Sea levels during late marine isotope stage 3 (or older?) reported from the Red River delta (northern Vietnam) and adjacent regions. *Quaternary International* 145–6, 119–34.

Hill, C., Soares, P., Mormina, M., Macaulay, V., Clarke, D., Blumbach, P. B., Vizuete-Forster, M., Forster, P., Bulbeck, D., Oppenheimer, S., and Richards, M. 2007. A mitochondrial stratigraphy for island South East Asia. *American Journal of Human Genetics* 80, 29–43.

Jain, M. and Tandon, S. K. 2003 Fluvial response to Late Quaternary climate changes, western India. *Quaternary Science Reviews* 22, 2223–35.

James, H. V. A. and Petraglia, M. D. 2005 Modern human origins and the evolution of behaviour in the later Pleistocene record of South Asia. *Current Anthropology* 46, S3–S27.

Kennedy, K. A. R. 1999. Paleoanthropology of South Asia. *Evolutionary Anthropology* 8, 165–85.

Kennedy, K. A. R. 2000. *God-apes and fossil men: paleoanthropology in South Asia*. Ann Arbor: University of Michigan Press.

Kenoyer, J. M., Mandal D., Misra, V. D., and Pal, J. N. 1983. Preliminary report on excavations at the Late Palaeolithic occupation site at Baghor I locality. In G. R. Sharma and J. D. Clark (eds), *Palaeoenvironments and prehistory in the Middle Son Valley*, 117–42. Allahabad: Abinash Prakashan.

Lahr, M. and Foley, R. 1994. Multiple dispersals and modern human origins. *Evolutionary Anthropology* 3, 48–60.

Lambeck, K., Yokoyama, Y., and Purcell, T. 2002. Into and out of the Last Glacial Maximum: sea-level change during Oxygen Isotope Stages 3 and 2. *Quaternary Science Reviews* 21, 343–60.

Lukacs, J. R. 2007. Interpreting biological diversity in South Asian prehistory: early Holocene population affinities and subsistence adaptations. In M. D. Petraglia and B. Allchin (eds), *The evolution and history of human populations in South Asia*, 271–96. New York: Springer/Kluwer Academic Publishers.

Mandal D. 1983. A note of the radiocarbon dates from the Middle Son Valley. In G. R. Sharma and J. D. Clark (eds), *Palaeoenvironments and prehistory in the Middle Son Valley*, 285–9. Allahabad: Abinash Prakashan.

Marliac, A. and Simanjuntak, T. 1996. *Preliminary report on the site of Song Gentong Kabupaten Tulungagung, East Java (Indonesia)*. Communication to the 6th International Congress of European Association of Southeast Asian Archaeologists, International Institute for Asian Studies (IIAS), Leiden, 2–6 Sept.

Mijares, A. S. B. 2008. The late Pleistocene to early Holocene foragers of northern Luzon. *IPPA* 28, 99–107.

Misra, V. N. 2001. Prehistoric human colonization of India. *Journal of Biosciences* 26, 491–531.

Morisson, K. D. 2007. Foragers and forager-traders in South Asian worlds: some thoughts from the last 10,000 years. In M. D. Petraglia and B. Allchin (eds), *The evolution and history of human populations in South Asia*, 321–39. New York: Springer/Kluwer Academic Publishers.

Morwood, M. J., Sutikna, T., Saptomo, E. W., Westaway, K. E., Jatmiko, Awe Due, R., Moore, M. W., Dwi Yani Yuniawati, Hadi, P., Zhao, J.-X., Turney, C. S. M., Fifield, K., Allen, H., and Soejono, R. P. 2008. Climate, people and faunal succession on Java, Indonesia: evidence from Song Gupuh. *Journal of Archaeological Science* 35, 1776–89.

Olsen, S. L. and Glover, I. C. 2004. The bone industry of Ulu Leang 1 and Leang Burung 1 rockshelters, Sulawesi, Indonesia, in its regional context. *Modern Quaternary Research in Southeast Asia* 18, 273–99.

Oppenheimer, S. 2004. *Out of Eden: the peopling of the world*. London: Constable.

Partin, J. W., Cobb, K. M., Adkins, J. F., Clark, B., and Fernandez, D. P. 2007. Millennial-scale trends in west Pacific warm pool hydrology since the Last Glacial Maximum. *Nature* 449, 452–6.

Pasveer, J. M. 2006. Bone artefacts from Liang Lemdubu and Liang Nabulei Lisa, Aru Islands. In S. O'Connor, M. Spriggs, and P. Veth (eds), *The archaeology of the Aru Islands, Eastern Indonesia*, 235–54. Canberra: Terra Australis 22.

Pasveer, J. M. and Bellwood, P. 2004. Prehistoric bone artefacts from the Northern Moluccas. In S. Keates and J. M. Pasveer (eds), *Modern Quaternary Research in Indonesia*, 301–59. Lisse: A. A. Balkema.

Piper, P. and Rabett, R. 2009. Hunting in a tropical rainforest: evidence from the Late Pleistocene and Early Holocene at Lobang Hangus, Niah cave, Borneo. *International Journal of Osteoarchaeology* 19, 551–65.

Piper, P. J., Rabett, R. J., and Barker, G. Forthcoming. A zoologist with a taste for the past: the Earl of Cranbrook's contribution to zooarchaeological research in Southeast Asia. *Raffles Bulletin of Zoology*.

Piper, P. J., Rabett, R. J., and Kurui, E. 2008. Using community composition and structural variation in terminal Pleistocene vertebrate assemblages to identify human hunting behaviour at Niah caves, Borneo. *Bulletin of the Indo-Pacific Prehistory Association* 28, 88–98.

Prabhu, C. N., Shankar, R., Anupama, K., Taieb, M., Bonnefille, R., Vidal, L., and Prasad, S. 2004. A 200-ka pollen and oxygen-isotopic record from two sediment cores from the eastern Arabian Sea. *Palaeogeography, Palaeoclimatology, Palaeoecology* 214, 309–21.

Rabett, R. J. 2005. The early exploitation of Southeast Asian mangroves: bone technology from caves and open sites. *Asian Perspectives* 44, 154–79.

Rabett, R. J. 2011. Techno-modes, techno-facies and palaeo-cultures: change and continuity in the Pleistocene of South East, Central and North Asia. In B. Roberts and M. Vander Linden (eds), *Investigating archaeological cultures: material culture, variability and transmission*, 97–136 New York: Springer.

Rabett, R. J. 2012. *Human adaptation in the Asian Palaeolithic: hominin dispersal and behaviour during the Late Quaternary*. Cambridge: Cambridge University Press.

Rabett, R., Appleby, J., Blyth, A., Farr, L., Gallou, A., Giffiths, T., Hawkes, J., Marcus, D., Marlow, L., Morley, M., Nguyễn Cao Tân, Nguyễn Van Son, Penkman, K., Reynolds, T., Stimpson, S., and Szabó, K. 2011. Inland shell midden site-formation: investigation into a late Pleistocene to early Holocene midden from Tràng An, northern Vietnam. *Quaternary International* 239, 153–69.

Rabett, R. and Barker, G. 2010. Late Pleistocene and early Holocene forager mobility in Southeast Asia. In B. Bellina, J. Wisseman Christie, L. Bacus, and T. Oliver Pryce (eds), *50 years of archaeology in Southeast Asia: essays in honour of Ian Glover*, 66–77. Bangkok: River Books.

Rabett, R., Barker, G., Hunt, C. O., Naruse, T., Piper, P., Raddatz, E., Reynolds, T., Nguyễn Van Son, Stimpson, C., Szabó K., Nguyễn Cao Tân, and Wilson, J. 2009. The Tràng An project: late- to post-Pleistocene settlement of the lower Song Hong valley, North Vietnam. *Journal of the Royal Asiatic Society* 19, 83–109.

Rabett, R. J. and Piper, P. J. 2012. The emergence of bone technologies at the end of the Pleistocene in South East Asia: regional and evolutionary implications. *Cambridge Archaeological Journal* 22, 37–56.

Rabett, R., Piper, P., and Barker, G. 2006. Bones from hell: preliminary results of new work on the Harrisson faunal assemblage from the deepest part of the Niah cave, Sarawak. In E. A. Bacus, I. C. Glover, and V. C. Piggott (eds), *Uncovering Southeast Asia's past*, 46–59. Singapore: National University of Singapore Press.

Sali, S. A. 1989. *The Upper Palaeolithic and Mesolithic cultures of Maharashtra*. PhD thesis. Deccan College Post-Graduate and Research Institute, Pune.

Schulz, H., von Rad, U., and Erlenkeuser, H. 1998. Correlation between Arabian Sea and Greenland climate oscillations of the past 110,000 years. *Nature* 393, 54–7.

Shoocongdej, R. 1996. Forager mobility organization in seasonal tropical environments: a view from Lang Kamnan cave, Western Thailand. PhD thesis. Department of Anthropology, University of Michigan.

Soares, P., Trejaut, J. A., Jun-Hun Loo, Hill, C., Mormina, M., Chien-Liang Lee, Yao-Ming Chen, Hudjashov, G., Forster, P., Macaulay, V., Bulbeck, D., Oppenheimer, S., Lin, M., and Richards, M. B. 2008. Climate change and postglacial human dispersals in Southeast Asia. *Molecular Biology Evolution* 25, 1209–18.

Steinke, S., Kienast, M., Pflaumann, U., Weinelt, M., and Stattegger, K. 2001. A high-resolution sea-surface temperature record from the tropical South China Sea (16,500–3000 yr BP). *Quaternary Research* 55, 352–62.

Stock, J. T., Lahr, M. M., and Kulatilake, S. 2007. Cranial diversity in South Asia relative to modern human dispersals. In M. D. Petraglia and B. Allchin (eds), *The evolution and history of human populations in South Asia*, 245–68. New York: Springer/Kluwer Academic Publishers.

Sun, X. and Li, X. 1999. A pollen record of the last 37 ka in deep sea core 17940 from the northern slope of the South China Sea. *Marine Geology* 156, 227–44.

Tanabe, S., Saito, Y., Vu, Q. L., Hanebuth, T. J. J., Kitamura, A., and Ngo, Q. T. 2006. Holocene evolution of the Song Hong (Red River) delta system, northern Vietnam. *Sedimentary Geology* 187, 29–61.

Thompson, L. G., Yao, T., Davis, M. E., Henderson, K. A., Mosley-Thompson, E., Lin, P.-N., Beer, J., Synal, H.-A., Cole-Dai, J., and Bolzan, J. F. 1997. Tropical climate instability: the last glacial cycle from a Qinghai-Tibetan ice core. *Science* 276, 1821–5.

Verleyen, E., Hodgson, D. A., Milne, G. A., Sabbe, K., and Vyverman, W. 2005. Relative sea-level history from the Lambert Glacier region, East Antarctica, and its relation to deglaciation and Holocene glacier readvance. *Quaternary Research* 63, 45–52.

Viet, N. 2005. The Da But culture: evidence for cultural development in Vietnam during the middle Holocene. *Indo-Pacific Prehistory Association Bulletin* 25, 89–93.

Walker, M., Johnsen, S., Rasmussen, S. O., Popp, T., Steffensen, J.-P., Gibbard, P., Wim Hoek, Lowe, J., Andrews, J., Björck, S., Cwynar, L. C., Hughen, K., Kershaw, P., Kromer, B., Litt, T., Lowe, D. J., Nakagawa, T., Newnham, R., and Schwander, J. 2009. Formal definition and dating of the GSSP (Global Stratotype Section and Point) for the base of the Holocene using the Greenland NGRIP ice core, and selected auxiliary records. *Journal of Quaternary Science* 24, 3–17.

Zuraina, M. 1998. Radiocarbon dates and the cultural sequence in the Lenggong Valley and beyond. *Malaysia Museums Journal* 34, 241–9.

CHAPTER 22

POST-PLEISTOCENE TRANSFORMATIONS OF HUNTER-GATHERERS IN EAST ASIA
The Jomon and Chulmun

JUNKO HABU

East Asia is an exciting area for the study of post-Pleistocene cultural transformation. Prehistoric hunter-gatherer cultures in East Asia, namely the Jomon culture of the Japanese archipelago (hereafter Japan) and the Chulmun culture of the Korean Peninsula (hereafter Korea) are known for their artistic pottery and other elaborate artefacts, the production and use of which were closely intertwined with changes in Jomon and Chulmun societies (e.g. Cho and Ko 2009; Kaner 2009). Furthermore, Jomon and Chulmun data allow us to test conflicting theories about the mechanisms of long-term culture change. Topics to be examined include the impact of the global and local climate change vs. human activities, domestication vs. environmental management, specialized vs. broad-spectrum economies, sedentism vs. mobility, egalitarianism vs. social stratification, and continuity vs. discontinuity to the following agricultural phase. Finally, but not least importantly, bioarchaeological data from these regions help us to understand not only the population history of these regions but also changes in health conditions and lifeways of these people (e.g. Fujita et al. 2007; Fukase and Suwa 2008; Kimura 2006; Suzuki 1998; Temple 2007; 2008).

Overviews of the Jomon and Chulmun cultures are available in such references as Habu (2004; in press), Underhill and Habu (2006), Imamura (1996), Kobayashi (2004), Norton (2007), and Nelson (1993). Rather than repeat the contents of these publications, this chapter concentrates on issues that are key to understanding the importance of East Asian data in world hunter-gatherer archaeology and anthropology. Emphases are on the issues that are relevant to recent discussions in the field of historical ecology (Balée 2006; Thompson and Waggoner 2013). These issues include long-term sustainability, collapses and subsequent recoveries of human socio-economic systems, human impacts on the biosphere, and the examination of the processes operating among temporal scales of varying duration.

Chronology

Before moving on to the key issues listed above, a brief overview of the chronological framework will be useful. As discussed elsewhere (Habu 2004; 2008), temporal and regional variability within the Jomon and Chulmun cultures is extremely large. The only common cultural element for the entire span of these periods is the presence of pottery. Thus, it is more appropriate to think about Jomon cultures and Chulmun cultures rather than about the Jomon culture and the Chulmun culture. Both the Jomon and Chulmun periods are divided into several sub-periods on the basis of pottery chronology (Table 22.1). Each sub-period is further subdivided into multiple phases based on typological chronology of pottery.

The calendar dates for the sub-periods shown in Table 22.1 are still tentative. For the chronological placement of Jomon data, Japanese archaeologists moved slowly in systematically adopting radiocarbon dates (see Habu 2004, 37–42). Because Japanese archaeologists were relying heavily on the relative chronology based on their fine-grained typology of pottery, which goes back to the works by Yamanouchi (1932; 1937; 1939), most of them had assumed that radiocarbon dates were of little use in establishing a relative chronological framework until the 1990s.

New AMS 14C dates since the late 1990s have significantly contributed to our understanding of Jomon absolute dates (Kobayashi 2007; 2008; Kokuritsu Rekishi Minzoku Hakubutsu-kan 2003; Nihon Senshi Jidai no 14C Nendai Henshu Iinkai 2000; Nishimoto 2006). The correspondence between pottery chronology and calendar dates, however, has yet to be finalized. For the beginning of the Jomon period, radiocarbon dates for the carbonized adhesion on potsherds excavated from the Odai Yamamoto I site in Aomori Prefecture

Table 22.1 Approximate dates (calibrated BP) for the six Jomon and four Chulmun sub-periods (modified from Habu in press)

Sub-period	Jomon*	Chulmun**
Final	3300–2400 cal BP	N/A
Late	4300–3300 cal BP	4000–3300 cal BP
Middle	5500–4300 cal BP	5500–4000 cal BP
Early	7000–5500 cal BP	7000–5500 cal BP
Initial	11,000–7000 cal BP	N/A
Incipient	16,000–11,000 cal BP	11,500–7000 cal BP

* Based primarily on radiocarbon dates from the Kanto and Tohoku regions.
** Modified from Im (1997). For slightly different dates, see Norton (2007) and Lee (2006). The beginning of the Incipient Chulmun period is based on Cho and Ko's (2009) tentative estimate.

returned ages of approximately 13,800–12,700 uncal BP, or *c*.16,500–14,900 cal BP (see Habu 2004, 28–36). Because of the lack of dendrochronological data for calibration before 12,450 cal BP, these dates for the Odai Yamamoto pottery should be considered as tentative (see Kobayashi 2008).

Calendar dates for the end of the Jomon period show regional variability. Traditionally, scholars assumed that the end of the Jomon period in Kyushu, which was marked by the introduction of wet rice agriculture from continental Asia, was dated to *c*.2500 cal BP (see Habu 2004, 258; in press). More recently, a series of AMS dates obtained from Kyushu indicate that the end of the Jomon period, which was marked by the appearance of rice paddy fields, dates to as early as *c*.3000 cal BP in south-western Japan (Fujio et al. 2005; Harunari et al. 2003; Nishimoto 2006), but not all scholars have accepted this new chronological framework (Uno 2008). Using a small number of new AMS dates from the Tohoku region, Ken'ichi Kobayashi (2008) tentatively suggests the end of the final Jomon in north-eastern Japan as 2450–2350 cal BP.

Reliable radiocarbon dates for establishing Chulmun absolute chronology are still limited (see Lee 2011). Raised design pottery from the Osan-ni site (Han 1995; Nelson 1993) is dated to 7050 ±120 uncal BP (KSU-515) or *c*.8000 cal BP, which is commonly used as the oldest reliable date for Chulmun pottery. According to Cho and Ko (2009), the Kosan-ni site on Cheju Island is associated with 'archaic' plain ware, which dates to 10,000 uncal BP (*c*.11, 500 cal BP) or older if its stratigraphic context was intact. However, radiocarbon dates from the Kosan-ni site (Kuzmin 2006, 366) show wide variability, making further study necessary. Reliable radiocarbon dates to determine the end of the Chulmun culture are also rare. Ambiguity of the criteria for drawing the boundary between the Chulmun and the following Mumun periods is another factor that complicates the discussion of Chulmun absolute chronology.

Temporal and Regional Variability of the Jomon and Chulmun Cultures

As discussed above, marked regional and temporal variability has been observed among Jomon and Chulmun cultures. Changes through time were not necessarily gradual, nor directional from simple to complex. In some cases, the growth and decline of the population and changes in aspects of cultural complexity (see Habu 2004, 15–16) occurred within a relatively short time span. Cyclical changes are also observed. These data provide us with an excellent opportunity to understand the complex relationships among environmental, economic, and social factors, including (1) changes in, as well as human impacts on, the biosphere, including climate change and diseases, (2) subsistence/food diversity, (3) mobility of people, goods, and information, (4) technological innovations, and (5) rituals and social structure. Of the six Jomon sub-periods, the incipient Jomon period (*c*.16,000–11,000 cal BP) shares a number of cultural characteristics in common with the preceding Palaeolithic period. Since the incipient Jomon falls outside of the post-Pleistocene, the following discussion focuses primarily on the initial to final Jomon and the incipient to late Chulmun periods.

Two important lines of evidence to infer regional and temporal variability are site density and average site size data. For the four main islands of the Japanese archipelago (Hokkaido, Honshu, Shikoku, and Kyushu), the Jomon data of north-eastern Honshu (the Tohoku, Kanto, Chubu, Tokai, and Hokuriku regions; hereafter Zone I) reveal much higher site density and larger average site size than those of south-western Honshu (Kinki and Chugoku regions), Shikoku, and Kyushu (hereafter Zone II) (see Figure 22.1). In Zone I, site density, as well as average site size, increased steadily from the initial to the middle Jomon, reached its maximum during the middle Jomon period, and then declined through the late and final Jomon periods (see Koyama 1978; 1984). This zone is characterized by a larger amount of ornate pottery and ritual artefacts. In Zone II, where site density was much lower than in the former area, it increased steadily from the initial to the final Jomon (Koyama 1978; 1984). Many of these characteristics were noted as early as during the 1950s and 1960s and were clearly shown in Koyama's (1978; 1984) Jomon population estimates (see Habu 2001, 24–6; 2004, 46–50).

Detailed analysis of site density and site size for the Chulmun period has yet to be conducted. The lack of systematic analysis for site density and site size is due to two facts: the limited number of large-scale excavations of Chulmun sites, and the regional disparity in the availability of the excavation record. Nevertheless, the general patterns indicated in Lee (2001), Nelson (1993), and Norton (2007) seem to be more similar to those of the Jomon of south-western Honshu, Shikoku, and Kyushu than those of north-eastern Honshu. Thus, if we are to identify two distinct courses of post-Pleistocene cultural transformation, the regional boundary is not necessarily between the Korean Peninsula and the Japanese archipelago but may have been between north-eastern and south-western Japan.

In a previous paper (Habu in press), I divided the post-Pleistocene Jomon and Chulmun sequences into three distinct phases. The first phase, *c*.11,000–7000 cal BP, was characterized by the expansion of target resources and the beginning of subsistence specialization. The second phase, *c*.7000–4000 cal BP, showed evidence of subsistence intensification and the development of more sedentary lifeways. During the final phase, *c*.4000–2500 cal BP, the diverging pathways between Jomon Zone I and Jomon Zone II/Chulmun became pronounced. Put another way, the long time span of the Jomon and Chulmun cultures was punctuated by three major changes that occurred at around 11,000, 7000, and 4000 cal BP (see also Habu 2004, chapter 7).

It is also important to note that in Zone I of Japan the transition to the following Yayoi agricultural period occurred later than it occurred in Zone II of Japan and the Korean Peninsula, probably as late as 2450–2350 cal BP (see above). In the latter areas, influences from China (from the Neolithic and subsequent state societies) were more direct than in Zone I. Rice was possibly grown on the Korean Peninsula during the late Chulmun period, but more evidence is needed (Crawford 2006; Lee 2011). Rice paddy fields in northern Kyushu are dated to as early as *c*.3000 and 2800 cal BP (see above).

Hunter-gatherers of Hokkaido and Okinawa Jomon did not adopt rice cultivation at the end of the Jomon period. Unfortunately, no population estimate for these regions was available in Koyama's (1978; 1984) work. In Hokkaido, the Epi-Jomon culture, a distinct hunter-gatherer culture that followed the Jomon culture, lasted from the third century BC to the seventh century AD. The following Satsumon culture (eighth–twelfth century AD), which flourished in the south-western half of Hokkaido, was characterized by agricultural practice, but evidence reveals that residents used wild food resources continuously

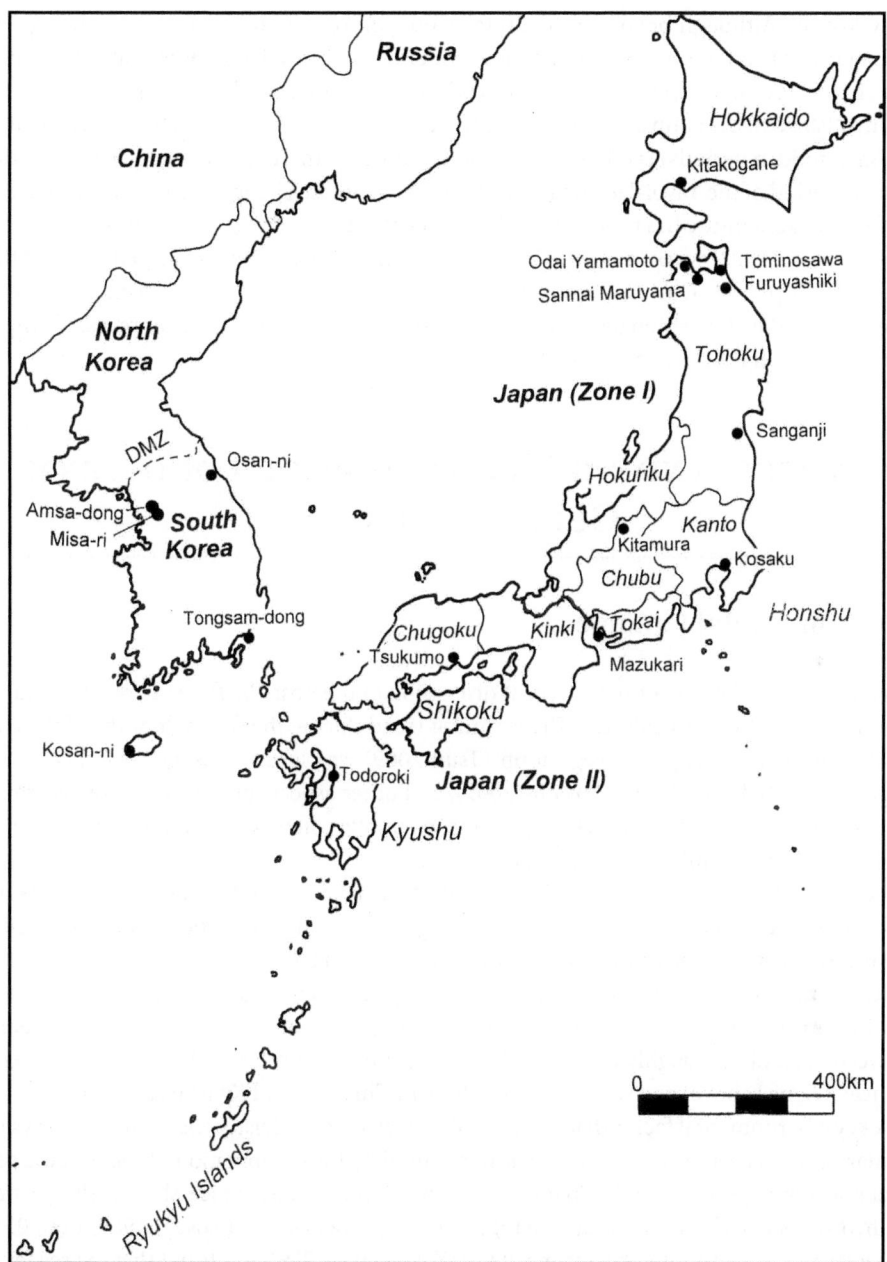

FIGURE 22.1 Map of sites in Japan and South Korea mentioned in the text, and regions of Japan.

as well. At about the same time, in north-eastern Hokkaido, Sakhalin, and the southern Kuril Islands, the Okhotsk culture (seventh–thirteenth century AD) flourished with its focus on sea mammal hunting and fishing. These two cultures formed the foundation for the proto-Ainu culture (c. twelfth–sixteenth century AD), which partly overlapped with the Okhotsk. Although people of the proto-Ainu culture were once assumed to have subsisted primarily on hunting-gathering, new evidence indicates that they actually played key roles in forming active medieval trade networks between Japan and China. In Okinawa (the Ryukyu Islands), the equivalent of the Jomon period (often referred to as the initial to middle Shellmidden periods) is followed by another hunter-gatherer period, which is called the Parallel period of the Yayoi-Heian (also referred to as the late Shellmidden period). No clear evidence of agriculture has been reported from the latter period (e.g. Shinzato 2010).

Takamiya's (2003) work indicates that the population remained small until the end of the Yayoi-Heian period. During the following medieval Gusuku period (*c.* twelfth–fifteenth century AD), state formation took place. Flotation at Gusuku period sites has revealed ample evidence of cultigens (Shinzato 2010).

Understanding Mechanisms of Long-Term Culture Change

Environmental Change

Environment is a key factor in the recent discussion of the post-Pleistocene transformation of Jomon and Chulmun cultures. The warming trend during the first half of the Holocene resulted in major changes in vegetation (Tsuji 2009), sea levels (Kosugi 1989; Lee 2011; Nagaoka and Nakano 2009; Yokoyama 2009), and other aspects of the biosphere, which in turn affected people's lifeways. This by no means implies, however, that the perspective of environmental determinism is widely accepted.

According to Tsuji (2009, 73), by 7000 uncal BP, the Japanese archipelago from Hokkaido to Kyushu was basically divided into four vegetation zones: (1) cold temperate coniferous forest zone in eastern Hokkaido, (2) temperate mixed forest in western Hokkaido, (3) temperate deciduous forest in north-eastern Japan, and (4) warm temperate deciduous and evergreen forest zone in south-western Honshu, Shikoku, and Kyushu. The boundary between (3) and (4) roughly corresponds to the cultural boundary between north-eastern Honshu (Zone I above) and south-western Honshu, Shikoku, and Kyushu (Zone II).

A key environmental factor that significantly affected post-Pleistocene human lifeways in insular East Asia was a sea level rise that was caused by the combination of the eustatic sea level rise (corresponding to the change in ocean volume because of ice-sheet melting) and the hydroisostatic change (isostatic change due to sea water load) (Kosugi 1989; Lee 2011; Nagaoka and Nakano 2009; Yokoyama 2009). Yokoyama (2009) points out that the sea level rise from the Last Glacial Maximum (LGM: *c.*19,000 cal BP) to 7000 cal BP was caused primarily by eustatic changes, whereas the marine regression and other minor sea level changes after 7000 cal BP were caused by hydroisostatic changes. The excavation of the initial Jomon Mazukari shellmidden (*c.*9000 cal BP; Aichi Prefecture), which is located 10 m below the sea level and was covered by marine silt and sand deposits, has revealed that during the early Holocene period the sea water often inundated coastal valleys even when the sea level was lower than the present-day sea level (see Habu et al. 2011). Takahashi (2009) suggests that many incipient to early Jomon sites on coastal plains might have been submerged under the sea as a result of the Holocene transgression, particularly in south-western Japan. The excavation of the Mazukari shellmidden and resulting early and middle Jomon data from north-western Kyushu provided by Nagaoka and Nakao (2009) indicate that micro-regional variability in hydroisostatic changes can be observed, which affected the distribution of sites with waterlogged nut-storage pits in the intertidal zone.

A controversial topic regarding the environmental changes in Holocene insular East Asia is the cooling climate that is said to have occurred at $c.4200$ cal BP. While many scholars suggest that the cooling climate was the direct cause of the rapid decline in Zone I in the number and size of settlements in the latter half of the middle Jomon period (e.g. Kawahata et al. 2009; Tsuji 2002; Yasuda 1989), Habu (2008) and Habu and Hall (2013) point out that cooling climate was not necessarily the main cause of these cultural changes. Ken'ichi Kobayashi's (2008) data also indicate that these cultural changes may have occurred as early as 4800 cal BP before the cooling climate hit the Japanese archipelago.

New environmental data, including pollen, phytoliths, and diatoms, could significantly enhance our understanding of human–environmental interaction in post-Pleistocene East Asia (e.g. Kawahata et al. 2009; Kitagawa and Yasuda 2004; 2008; Yi 2011). The problems of Jomon and Chulmun absolute chronology discussed above and the relative scarcity of high-resolution environmental data, however, make understanding the timing and causal relationships between environmental changes and archaeological data challenging.

Subsistence, Settlement, and Society

Subsistence data from the Jomon and Chulmun periods are extremely large. In the early history of Jomon and Chulmun archaeology, subsistence studies were under-represented because of the scarcity of zooarchaeological and palaeoethnobotanical specialists and because of the generally poor preservation of faunal and floral remains (see e.g. Habu 2004, 57–60). However, systematic flotation and water-screening of soil samples over the past several decades, including those from shellmiddens and waterlogged sites, have significantly enhanced our understanding of Jomon and Chulmun subsistence (e.g. Crawford 2011; Crawford and Lee 2003; Itou 2011; Lee 2011; Takamiya 2003; Tsuji 2002; 2009).

Food diversity, together with its correlate subsistence diversity (i.e. diversity in the methods of food acquisition), is a critical factor in the discussion of Jomon/Chulmun human–environmental interaction. Many archaeologists have suggested that the rich environment of Japan and Korea with a wide variety of food resources enabled the early development of 'complex' hunter-gatherer cultures in these regions (e.g. Kim 2006; Kobayashi 1977; Norton 2007). In terms of food diversity measured by richness (i.e. the number of different nominal classes of items observed in the sample), an expansion of target resource types from $c.11,000$ to 7000 cal BP is evident in the Jomon and Chulmun data. Faunal and floral studies revealed that the Jomon and Chulmun diet in this period incorporated plants, fish, and shellfish, including domesticated plants (Crawford 2011; Crawford and Lee 2003; Habu 2004, 248–50). On the south-west coast of Korea, an abundance of shellmidden sites, including the Tongsam-dong, seems to imply a heavy reliance on marine food (see the results of carbon and nitrogen stable isotope analysis below). Developments of new food-processing technologies, such as the removal of tannic acid from buckeyes (*Aesculus turbinate*) (Itou 2011) and adoption of several cultigens (see below), further increased food diversity measured by richness.

Many scholars suggest that this expansion of target resources resulted in a general shift from hunting terrestrial mammals to collecting plant and marine food. By the middle Holocene, limited types of food plant and/or marine resources such as nuts, tubers, and fish were intensively exploited and stored. In other words, early Holocene diversification in food richness eventually led to the process of subsistence intensification and specialization. In particular, the development of large early and middle Jomon (*c.*7000–4000 cal BP) settlements in north-eastern Japan is likely to have been supported by mass exploitation of plant food. In central Japan, abundant so-called chipped stone 'axes' (probably used as digging tools) are thought to be a reflection of an intensive exploitation of plant roots, such as the roots of yam, bracken, kuzu vine, and lilies. Reports of storage pits with nut remains and an abundance of chestnut pollens from several large Jomon settlements, including Sannai Maruyama in Aomori Prefecture, make several scholars think that chestnuts, acorns, and other nuts became Jomon staple food during and after the Middle Jomon period. Ultimately, analysis of starch grains may provide clues to determine the importance of plant roots and various nuts in overall Jomon diet, but the results are still preliminary (Shibutani 2008; 2010). Reports of acorn (*Quercus*) remains from several Chulmun sites in central-western Korea, including Amsa-dong and Misa-ri, are also indicative of the importance of nut collecting.

The heavy reliance on plant food may have required a form of environmental management or plant cultivation. Thus, one of the controversial topics is the importance of cultigens in Jomon and Chulmun subsistence and diet (Bleed and Matsui 2010; Crawford 2008; 2011). Several cultigens were utilized by Jomon and Chulmun people (e.g. Crawford 2006; 2011; Lee 2011; Kuro'o and Takase 2003; Yoshizaki 1995). Commonly reported taxa from early to final Jomon sites (see Habu 2004, 59) include egoma and/or shiso mint (*Perilla*), bottle gourd (*Lagenaria*), lacquer tree (*Toxicodendron*), barnyard millet (*Echinochloa utilis*), and beans (Leguminosae), including azuki and soy beans. In particular, charred remains of *Echinochloa utilis* have been reported from over 20 Jomon sites. Many of these are located in the northern part of Honshu and Hokkaido (Takase 2007; Yamada 2007), but many of these findings are small in number, and examples associated with reliable 14C dates are limited. Among these, barnyard millet from the Tominosawa in Aomori Prefecture was directly AMS dated, giving the dates of *c.*4800–4300 cal BP (Nishimoto et al. 2007).

Carbon and nitrogen stable isotope analysis of human skeletal remains has contributed significantly to our understanding of Jomon and Chulmun diet. For the Jomon period, regionally specific patterns have been detected. Minagawa and Akazawa's (1992) work indicates that Hokkaido Jomon people at the Kitakogane site (early Jomon) relied heavily on marine food, possibly marine mammals, whereas residents of the Sanganji shellmidden (middle–final Jomon) in the southern Tohoku region, the Kosaku shellmidden (late Jomon) in the Kanto region, and the Kitamura site (late Jomon) in the Chubu region relied more heavily on terrestrial resources. It is worth noting that the stable isotope data from the two shellmidden sites in Tohoku and Kanto, Sanganji and Kosaku, indicate low dependence on marine food. None of these studies indicate that C4 plants, including barnyard millet or grass, contributed significantly to the Jomon and Chulmun diet.

Isotope data also seem to indicate similarities between shellmidden sites in western Japan and southern Korea. Residents of two shellmidden sites in western Japan, Tsukumo (late

Jomon) in the Chugoku region and Todoroki (early Jomon) in Kyushu, were heavily reliant on marine food, probably fish (Minagawa 2001). Analysis of human and dog remains from Tongsam-dong shellmidden indicates that their diet was also dependent on marine food (Choy and Richard 2010).

Studies by Yoneda (2010) and Chisholm and Habu (2003) suggest that Jomon people in the northern Tohoku region and the Hokuriku region may have had higher intake of marine food than those in southern Tohoku, Kanto, and Chubu, but the sample size is still very small. Yoneda's (2010) work also shows great diversity among individuals excavated from nine shellmidden sites in the Kanto and Tokai regions: the data show linear distribution between terrestrial and marine food sources, suggesting that Kanto and Tokai Jomon people were relying on a varying degree of a combination of the two resources. Chisholm et al.'s (1992) results of carbon isotope studies also detected differences between individuals, including male–female differences.

In my previous work, I emphasized that the process of sedentarization went hand in hand with the diversification in the richness of target food resources and the following subsistence specialization (Habu 2004; in press). Although Jomon and Chulmun people are known as examples of 'sedentary' hunter-gatherers, most scholars agree that, with a few exceptions such as in southern Kyushu (e.g. Pearson 2006), signs of sedentism were not apparent until $c.$7000 cal BP. Using models of hunter-gatherer subsistence and settlement, I argued that early Jomon sedentism was not necessarily year-round sedentism but more likely seasonal sedentism, and the degree of sedentism changed within a short time span (Habu 2001; but see Kobayashi 2004). Ogawa's (2009) study of life histories of early Jomon pit dwellings in the Tokyo Bay area supports this view of flexibility in early Jomon residential mobility. I also proposed that, even for extremely large middle Jomon settlements such as Sannai Maruyama, the possibility of seasonal mobility and changing site functions should be considered (Habu 2004; 2008). Not all scholars agree with this perspective (e.g. Imamura 2006; Okada 2003). These differences are coming not only from different interpretations of the available settlement data, but also from different perspectives on the role of mobility in hunter-gatherer lifeways. Data to infer Jomon and Chulmun residential mobility in south-western Japan and Korea are still limited. Seguchi (2009) suggests that hunter-gatherers in the Lake Biwa area established fully-sedentary systems that relied on storage pits and dugout canoe transportation.

Changes in subsistence strategies and settlement systems were inextricably linked to changing Jomon and Chulmun social landscapes (Choe and Bale 2002; Habu 2004; Lee 2006; Kobayashi 2004; Pearson 2006). Developments of social networks are evidenced by the long-distance trade of exotic items (e.g. obsidian, jade, and asphalt; see Habu 2004, 221–33). Technological innovations can be seen in the production of various types of artefacts such as lacquerware and transportation technologies including dugout canoes (see Habu 2010). Belief systems are reflected in ritual artefacts and mortuary practice.

In order to understand the causes, conditions, and consequences of long-term culture change, it is critical to examine these lines of evidence with a fine-grained time-scale so that the sequence of these changes can be modelled and further tested. For example, data from the Sannai Maruyama site seems to indicate that subsistence specialization with a focus on plant food occurred first from the end of the early Jomon to the middle of the middle Jomon, which was followed by a decrease in settlement size and a decline of ritual practice represented by clay figurines (Habu 2008; Habu and Hall 2013). This may indicate that over-specialization among hunter-gatherers, which leads to the loss of subsistence and food diversity, can contribute to a rapid decline or a seeming 'collapse' in their socio-economic systems, followed by a shift to a new subsistence strategy among reduced populations. As a working hypothesis, this idea has the potential to be applied to multiple cases in not only prehistoric but also historic and contemporary situations. To further test the hypothesis, more AMS radiocarbon dates are needed to identify the precise timing of these incidents in relation to changing climate. Starch grain analysis of grinding stones and other artefacts, as well as residue analysis of pottery, may be the key to understanding the type(s) of plant food resources that played a critical role in these changes.

Concluding Remarks

From the above, it is clear that the rich Jomon and Chulmun data provide excellent opportunities to explore key issues in hunter-gatherer archaeology today. Results of these studies can be used for comparative studies with post-Pleistocene hunter-gatherers and early agriculturalists in other parts of the world, including hunter-gatherers on the Northwest Coast of North America, California, and Neolithic China. The diverging pathways between north-eastern Japan and south-western Japan/Korea after $c.4000$ cal BP make us reconsider the regional boundaries that we currently use to describe the post-Pleistocene hunter-gatherer cultures in these regions.

While the amount of data from Jomon and Chulmun sites continues to grow (see e.g. Crawford 2011; Kim 2006; Kosugi et al. 2007–10; Lee 2011), the total number of rescue excavations per year in Japan has been declining since the late 1990s due to a slower economy and a resulting decrease in large-scale land development projects (Habu 2004, 20). These circumstances not only provide scholars with an opportunity to reanalyse the large amount of data that have been accumulated over the past several decades, but a new generation of archaeologists who are conducting their research in a new socio-political environment will likely set new goals and approaches to the study of Jomon and Chulmun archaeological materials. Active information exchange between Jomon/Chulmun archaeologists and scholars working on post-Pleistocene hunter-gatherers and agriculturalists in other parts of the world will be critical.

References

Balée, W. 2006. The research program of historical ecology. *Annual Review of Anthropology* 35, 75–98.
Bleed, P. and Matsui, A. 2010. Why didn't agriculture develop in Japan? *Journal of Archaeological Method and Theory* 17, 356–70.
Chisholm, B. and Habu, J. 2003. Stable isotope analysis of prehistoric human bone from the Furuyashiki site, Kamikita Town, Aomori, Japan. In J. Habu, J. M. Savelle, S. Koyama, and H. Hongo (eds), *Hunter-gatherers of the North Pacific Rim*, 221–33. Suita: National Museum of Ethnology.

Chisholm, B., Koike, H., and Nakai, N. 1992. Dietary patterns of Japanese Jomon hunter-gatheers. In C. M. Aikens and S. N. Rhee (eds), *Pacific Northeast Asia in prehistory*, 69–73. Pullman: Washington State University Press.

Cho, D. and Ko, I. 2009. Hunter-gatherer ceramics of Neolithic Korea. In P. Jordan and M. Zvelebil (eds), *Ceramics before farming*, 149–66. Walnut Creek, CA: Left Coast Press.

Choe, C. P. and Bale, M. T. 2002. Current perspectives on settlement, subsistence and cultivation in prehistoric Korea. *Arctic Anthropology* 39, 95–121.

Choy, K. and Richards, M. P. 2010. Isotopic evidence for diet in the Middle Chulmun period. *Archaeological and Anthropological Science* 2, 1–10.

Crawford, G. W. 2006. East Asian plant domestication. In M. T. Stark (ed.), *Archaeology of Asia*, 77–95. Malden, MA: Blackwell.

Crawford, G. W. 2008. The Jomon in early agriculture discourse. *World Archaeology* 40, 445–65.

Crawford, G. W. 2011. Advances in understanding early agriculture in Japan. *Current Anthropology* 52 S331–45.

Crawford, G. W. and Lee, G.-A. 2003. Agricultural origins in the Korean Peninsula. *Antiquity* 77, 87–95.

Fujio, S., Imamura, M., and Nishimoto, T. 2005. Yayoi Jidai no kaishi nendai. *Sokendai Bunka Kgaku Kenkyu* [Sokendai Review of Cultural and Social Studies] 1, 73–96 (in Japanese).

Fujita, H., Asakura, K., and Ogura, M. 2007. Age- and sex-related dental caries prevalence in Japanese from the Jomon Period. *Journal of Oral Biosciences* 49, 198–204.

Fukase, H. and Suwa, G. 2008 Growth-related changes in prehistoric Jomon and modern Japanese mandibles with emphasis on cortical bone distribution. *American Journal of Physical Anthropology* 136, 441–54.

Habu, J. 2001. *Subsistence-settlement systems and intersite variability in the Moroiso phase of the Early Jomon period of Japan*. Ann Arbor: International Monographs in Prehistory.

Habu, J. 2004. *Ancient Jomon of Japan*. Cambridge: Cambridge University Press.

Habu, J. 2008. Growth and decline in complex hunter-gatherer societies. *Antiquity* 82, 571–84.

Habu, J. 2010. Seafaring and the development of cultural complexity in Northeast Asia. In A. Anderson, J. H. Barrett, and K. V. Boyle (eds), *Global origins and the development of seafaring*, 159–70. Cambridge: McDonald Institute for Archaeological Research.

Habu, J. In press. Early sedentism in East Asia. In C. Renfrew and P. Bahn (eds), *Cambridge world prehistory*. Cambridge: Cambridge University Press.

Habu, J. and Hall, M. E. In press. Climate change, human impacts on the landscape, and subsistence specialization. In V. Thompson and J. Waggoner (eds), *The historical ecology of small scale economies*, 65–78. Gainesville: University Press of Florida.

Habu, J., Matsui, A., Yamamoto, N., and Kanno, T. 2011. Shell midden archaeology in Japan. *Quaternary International* 239, 19–27.

Han, B. 1995. *Kankoku no kodai bunka*. Tokyo: Nihon Hoso Kyokai (in Japanese).

Harunari, H., Fujio, S., Imamura, M., and Sakamoto, M. 2003. Yayoi Jidai no kaishi nendai. *Nihon Kokogaku Kyokai dai 69 kai sokai kenkyu happyo yoshi* [Abstracts of presentations at the 69th Annual Meeting of the Japanese Archaeological Association], 65–8 (in Japanese).

Im, H. 1997. Sinsukki Sidae ui siki-kupun. In H. Im (ed.), *Hankuku-sa 2: Kusukki Munhwa was Sinsukki Munhwa*, 305–16. Seoul: Kuksa Pyonchan Wiwonwhae [National Institute of Korean History] (in Korean).

Imamura, K. 1996. *Prehistoric Japan*. Honolulu: University of Hawaii Press.

Imamura, K. 2006. Archaeological theory and Japanese methodology in Jomon research. *Anthropological Science* 114, 223–9.

Itou, Y. 2011. Aomori-ken Aomori-shi Sannai Maruyama (9) iseki ni okeru tochinoki riyo ni tsuite. *Aomori-kenritsu Kyoto-kan Kenkyu Kiyo* [Bulletin of Aomori Prefectural Museum] 35, 43–50 (in Japanese).

Kaner, S. 2009. Long-term innovation. In P. Jordan and M. Zvelebil (eds), *Ceramics before farming*, 93–119. Walnut Creek, CA: Left Coast Press.

Kawahata, H., Yamamoto, H., Ohkushi, K., Yokoyama, Y., Kimoto, K., Ohshima, H., and Matsuzaki, H. 2009. Changes of environments and human activity at the Sannai-Maruyama ruins in Japan during the mid-Holocene Hypsithermal climatic interval. *Quaternary Science Reviews* 28, 964–74.

Kim, J. 2006. Resource patch sharing among foragers. In C. Grier, J. Kim, and J. Uchiyama (eds), *Beyond affluent foragers*, 168–91. Oxford: Oxbow.

Kimura, T. 2006. Robustness of the whole Jomon femur shaft assessed by cross-sectional geometry. *Anthropological Science* 114, 13–22.

Kitagawa, J. and Yasuda, Y. 2004. The influence of climatic change on chestnut and horse chestnut preservation around Jomon sites in northeastern Japan with special reference to the Sannai Maruyama and Kamegaoka sites. *Quaternary International* 123–5, 89–103.

Kitagawa, J. and Yasuda, Y. 2008. Development and distribution of Castanea and Aesculus culture during the Jomon period in Japan. *Quaternary International* 184, 41–55.

Kobayashi, K. 2004. Book Review: J. Habu (2001), *Subsistence-settlement systems and intersite variability in the Moroiso phase of the Early Jomon period of Japan*. *Asian Perspectives* 43, 181–5.

Kobayashi, K. 2007. AMS tanso 14 nendai sokutei o riyo-shita Higashi-Nihon Jomon Jidai Zenhan-ki no jitsu-nendai no kenkyu. *Kadai bango 17520529: Heisei 17-18 nendo Kagaku Kenkyu-hi Hojo-kin Kiban Kenkyu (C) (1), Kenkyu Seika Hokoku-sho*. Sakura: Kokuritsu Rekishi Minzoku Hakubutsu-kan (in Japanese).

Kobayashi, K. 2008. Jomon jidai no rei nendai. In Y. Kosugi, Y. Taniguchi, Y. Nishida, K. Mizunoe, and K. Yano (eds), *Jomon jidai no Kokogaku* 2, 257–69. Tokyo: Dosei-sha (in Japanese).

Kobayashi, T. 1977. Jomon sekai no shakai to bunka. In T. Kobayashi, *Nihon Genshi Bijutsu Taikei*, 156–9. Tokyo: Kodansha (in Japanese).

Kobayashi, T. 2004. *Jomon reflections*. Oxford: Oxbow.

Kokuritsu Relishi Minzoku Hakubutsu-kan [National Museum of Japanese History] (ed.) 2003. *Tanso 14 nendai sokutei to Kokogaku*. Sakura: National Museum of Japanese History (in Japanese).

Kosugi, M. 1989. Kanshinsei ni okeru Tokyo-wan no kaigan-sen no hensen. *Chirigaku Hyoron* [Geographical Review of Japan] 62A, 359–74 (in Japanese).

Kosugi, Y., Taniguchi, Y., Nishida, Y., Mizunoe, K., and Yano, K. (eds) 2007–10. *Jomon Jidai no Kokogaku*, vols. 1–12. Tokyo: Dosei-sha (in Japanese).

Koyama, S. 1978. Jomon subsistence and population. *Senri Ethnological Studies* 2, 1–65.

Koyama, S. 1984. *Jomon Jidai*. Tokyo: Chuo Koron-sha (in Japanese).

Kuro'o, K. and Takase, K. 2003. Jomon, Yayoi Jidai no zakkoku saibai. In S. Kimura (ed.), *Mono kara miru Nihon-shi*, 29–56. Tokyo: Aoki-shoten (in Japanese).

Kuzmin, Y. V. 2006. Chronology of the earliest pottery in East Asia. *Antiquity* 80, 362–71.

Lee, G.-A. 2011. The transition from foraging to farming in prehistoric Korea. *Current Anthropology* 52, S307–29.

Lee, J.-J. 2001. From shellfish gathering to agriculture in prehistoric Korea: the Chulmun to Mumun transition. PhD thesis. University of Wisconsin–Madison.

Lee, J.-J. 2006. From fisher-hunter to farmer. In C. Grier, J. Kim, and J. Uchiyama (eds), *Beyond affluent foragers*, 54–79. Oxford: Oxbow.

Minagawa, M. 2001. Tanso, chisso doitai bunseki ni yori fukugen shita senshi Nihon-jin no shoku-seitai [Dietary pattern of prehistoric Japanese populations interred from stable carbon and nitrogen isotopes in bone protein]. *Kokuritsu Rekishi Minzoku Hakubutsu-kan Kenkyu Hokoku* [Bulletin of the National Museum of Japanese History] 86, 333–57. Sakura, Japan (in Japanese with English abstract).

Minagawa, M. and Akazawa, T. 1992. Dietary patterns of Japanese Jomon hunter-gatheers. In C. M. Aikens and S. N. Rhee (eds), *Pacific Northeast Asia in prehistory*, 59–67. Pullman: Washington State University Press.

Nagaoka, S. and Nakao, A. 2009. Hydro-isostasy to iseki-gun. In Y. Kosugi, Y. Taniguchi, Y. Nishida, K. Mizunoe, and K. Yano (eds), *Jomon jidai no kokogaku* 3, 25–34. Tokyo: Dosei-sha (in Japanese).

Nelson, S. M. 1993. *The archaeology of Korea*. Cambridge: Cambridge University Press.

Nihon Senshi Jidai no 14C Nendai Henshu Iinkai [Editorial Committee of the Special Volume: 14C dates from Japanese prehistoric periods] (ed.) 2000. *Nihon Senshi Jidai no ^{14}C nendai* [14C dates from Japanese prehistoric periods]. Tokyo: Nihon Daiyonki Gakkai [Japan Association for Quaternary Research] (in Japanese).

Nishimoto, T. 2006. *Shin Yayoi Jidai no hajimari*, vols. 1–2. Tokyo: Yuzankaku (in Japanese).

Nishimoto, T., Miura, K., Sumita, M., and Miyata, Y. 2007. Jomon 'hie' no nendai. *Dobutsu Kokogaku* 24, 85–8 (in Japanese).

Norton, C. J. 2007. Sedentism, territorial circumscription, and the increased use of plant domesticates across Neolithic-Bronze Age Korea. *Asian Perspectives* 46, 133–65.

Ogawa, T. 2009. Kaishinki no Oku-Tokyo-wan engan iseki-gun. In Y. Kosugi, Y. Taniguchi, Y. Nishida, K. Mizunoe, and K. Yano (eds), *Jomon Jidai no Kokogaku* 8, 165–75. Tokyo: Dosei-sha (in Japanese).

Okada, Y. 2003. Jomon culture of northeastern Japan and the Sannai Marauyama site. In J. Habu, J. M. Savelle, S. Koyama, and H. Hongo (eds), *Hunter-gatherers of the North Pacific Rim*, 173–86. Suita: National Museum of Ethnology, Japan.

Pearson, R. 2006. Jomon hot spot. *World Archaeology* 38, 239–58.

Seguchi, S. 2009. Kyojyu system no henka; Biwa-ko shuhen chiiki. In Y. Kosugi, Y. Taniguchi, Y. Nishida, K. Mizunoe, and K. Yano (eds), *Jomon Jidai no Kokogaku* 8, 211–20. Tokyo: Dosei-sha (in Japanese).

Shibutani, A. 2008. Zanzon denpun bunseki kara mita Sannai Maruyama iseki no shokubutsu-shoku. *Tokubetsu Shiseki Sannai Maruyama Iseki Nenpo* [Annual Bulletin of the Sannai Maruyama Site] 11, 47–55 (in Japanese).

Shibutani, A. 2010. Nihon retto ni okeru gensei denpun-ryu hyohon to nihon Kokogaku e no oyo. *Shokuseishi Kenkyu* 18, 13–27 (in Japanese).

Shinzato, A. 2010. Ryukyu retto no noko o meguru shomondai. *Kokogaku Journal* 597, 12–14 (in Japanese).

Suzuki, T. 1998. Indicators of stress in prehistoric Jomon skeletal remains in Japan. *Anthropological Science* 106 (Supplement), 127–37.

Takahashi, M. 2009. Heiya no keisei-shi to iseki-gun. In Y. Kosugi, Y. Taniguchi, Y. Nishida, K. Mizunoe, and K. Yano (eds), *Jomon jidai no Kokogaku* 3, 35–46. Tokyo: Dosei-sha (in Japanese).

Takamiya, H. 2003. Okinawa hunter-gatherers. In J. Habu, M. Savelle, S. Koyama, and H. Hongo (eds), *Hunter-gatherers of the North Pacific Rim*, 153–69. Suita: National Museum of Ethnology.

Takase, K. 2007. Honshu Tohoku-bu ni okeru Jomon/Yayoi-ki no shutsudo shushi. *Nihon Kokogaku Kyokai 2007 nendo Kumamoto Taikai kenkyu happyo shiryo-shu* [Proceedings of the 2007 Kumamoto Meetings of the Japanese Archaeological Association], 398–408 (in Japanese).

Temple, D. H. 2007. Dietary variation and stress among prehistoric Jomon foragers from Japan. *American Journal of Physical Anthropology* 133, 1035–46.

Temple, D. H. 2008. What can variation in stature reveal about environmental differences between prehistoric Jomon foragers? Understanding the impact of systemic stress on developmental stability. *American Journal of Human Biology* 20, 431–39.

Thompson, V. and Waggoner, J. (eds) 2013. *The historical ecology of small scale economies.* Gainesville: University Press of Florida.

Tsuji, S. 2002. Hito to shizen no kankyoshi. In Aomori Kenshi Hensan Koko Bukai (ed.), *Aomori Kenshi, Betsuhen 3: Sannai Maruyama Iseki*, 227–44. Aomori: Aomori Prefecture.

Tsuji, S. 2009. Jomon jidai no shokusei-shi. In Y. Kosugi, Y. Taniguchi, Y. Nishida, K. Mizunoe, and K. Yano (eds), *Jomon jidai no Kokogaku* 3, 67–77. Tokyo: Dosei-sha (in Japanese).

Underhill, A. P. and Habu, J. 2006. Early communities in East Asia. In M. Stark (ed.), *Archaeology of Asia*, 121–48. Malden, MA: Blackwell.

Uno, T. 2008. Kosa-nendai-ho ni yoru Yayoi nendai-kan keisei no keii. In H. Shitara, S. Fujio, and T. Matsuki (eds), *Yayoi Jidai no Kokogaku* 8, 199–207. Tokyo: Dosei-sha (in Japanese).

Yamada, G. 2007. Hokkaido ni okeru saibai shokubutsu shushi no shutsudo jokyo. In *Nihon Kokogaku Kyokai 2007 nendo Kumamoto Taikai Kenkyu Happyo Shiryo-shu* [Proceedings of the 2007 Kumamoto Meetings of the Japanese Archaeological Association], 409–19 (in Japanese).

Yamanouchi, S. 1932. Nihon enko no bunka. *Dolmen*, 1(4), 40–3, 1(5), 85–90, 1(6), 46–50 (in Japanese).

Yamanouchi, S. 1937. Jomon doki no saibetsu to taibetsu. *Senshi Kokogaku* 1, 28–32 (in Japanese).

Yamanouchi, S. 1939. *Nihon Senshi Doki Zufu*. Tokyo: Senshi Kokogakkai (in Japanese).

Yasuda, Y. 1989. Indus Bunmei no seisui to Jomon Bunka. *Bulletin of International Research Center for Japanese Studies* 1, 205–72 (in Japanese).

Yi, S. 2011. Holocene vegetation responses to East Asian Monsoonal changes in South Korea. In J. Blanco and H. Kheradmand (eds), *Climate change*, 157–78. http://www.intechopen.com/books/climate-change-geophysical-foundations-and-ecological-effects/holocene-vegetation-responses-to-east-asian-monsoonal-changes-in-south-korea (accessed 18 March 2013).

Yokoyama, Y. 2009. Kaisuijun hendo to kiko, kaishin/kaitai. In Y. Kosugi, Y. Taniguchi, Y. Nishida, K. Mizunoe, and K. Yano (eds), *Jomon jidai no Kokogaku* 3, 13–23. Tokyo: Dosei-sha (in Japanese).

Yoneda, M. 2010. Doitai shokusei bunseki kara mita Jomon bunka no tekio senryku. In Y. Kosugi, Y. Taniguchi, Y. Nishida, K. Mizunoe, and K. Yano (eds), *Jomon jidai no Kokogaku* 4, 207–22. Tokyo: Dosei-sha (in Japanese).

Yoshizaki, M. 1995. Nihon ni okeru Saibai shokubutsu no shutsugen. *Kikan Kokogaku* 50, 18–24 (in Japanese).

CHAPTER 23

POST-GLACIAL TRANSFORMATIONS
Danubian Europe

JIŘÍ SVOBODA

Geographic Characteristics

During the Holocene, the Danube River connected a variety of environments, starting with boreal zones in the north-western highlands and ending in zones of deciduous forest and steppes in the south-eastern lowlands. This major river of Europe passes to the north of the Alps (present-day Germany and Austria), subsequently enters the Carpathian Basin in the south-east (Slovakia, Hungary, and Serbia), crosses the plains, and subsequently funnels into a much narrower torrent of the Iron Gate at the Serbian/Romanian boundary. Several tributaries join the Danube on this passage: the Morava River which passes through the Moravian geomorphological corridor (Czech Republic) towards the North European Plain (present-day Poland), Váh, Tisza, Sáva, and others. The Bohemian massif (Czech Republic), as an adjacent geomorphological unit, encircles the Basin of Upper Elbe, a river that follows in an opposite north-western orientation towards the North Sea.

Due to its favourable location in the middle of the European continent and to its geomorphological characteristics enabling passage and communication by both hunters and animals, Danubian Europe played a central role during the Upper Palaeolithic. By the end of the Pleistocene and during the earlier Holocene, as the North European Plain and Baltic opened up to more systematic human occupation, the Danube region appears to have become more peripheral. Conversely, the Danube region was open to movements of people and ideas arriving from the south-east, namely Anatolia, which formed the expected source area for the introduction of agriculture and farming populations. The restricted area of the Iron Gate on the Lower Danube saw a complex and regionally specific transition from the Mesolithic to Neolithic around 6300 cal BC. Elsewhere in the Balkans and Hungary, the early Neolithic radiocarbon dates of the Starčevo-Körös culture extend back to about 6000 cal BC, whereas the middle and upper Danube territory was occupied by Linear pottery settlements about 500 years later.

Chronology and Environment

The late glacial (13,600–9500 cal BC, following Manegrud's boundaries, calibration after Walanus and Nalepka 2010) was marked by a milder climate with warmer and moister oscillations such as the Bölling and Alleröd. In the early part of the late glacial, loess ceased to accumulate and began to show initial pedogenesis or was replaced by shallow colluvial deposits. The formation of chernozem soils in arid loess areas began, and rendsina soils appeared for the first time in karst areas. As the landscape changed, lightly wooded taiga dominated by *Pinus sylvestris* and *Betula* expanded during warmer fluctuations, while thermophilous trees like oak extended in the Balkans and made their first appearance as isolated stands further to the north. Areas of marshes and shallow lakes appeared and meadows replaced steppe vegetation. Large areas were still open. Generally speaking, the landscape acquired a mosaic configuration and showed a much higher diversity in both habitat and species than the preceding pleni-glacial.

The pre-boreal (9500–8200 cal BC) was a period of climatic change, with mean annual temperatures about 3° lower than today, but the vegetation composition did not respond immediately. We observe a growing density and extent of the previous birch-pine stands and a simultaneous retreat of steppe vegetation.

The boreal (8200–7000 cal BC) saw a further temperature increase, with mean annual values 2–3° higher than today. *Quercus*, *Ulmus*, and *Corylus* invaded the birch-pine forests. Heliophilic and montane plants disappeared. By the end of the boreal, an episode of worsening wet climate has been recognized in various parts of Europe (Berger and Guilaine 2009).

The Atlantic (7000–3800 cal BC) is characterized by the continuity of warm and humid conditions. Thermophilous oak forest and mesophilous mixed lime/oak forest spread into the lowlands, with new trees such as *Tilia*, *Acer*, *Fraxinus*, *Ulmus*, and *Taxus* spreading over the whole territory. In the individual sub-regions, there was considerable variability within this general picture. This is especially visible if we compare palaeobotanical data from the Balkans and the Hungarian Plain (which show a larger extent of open areas alternating with deciduous forests; Kértész et al. 1994; Prinz 1987), with those from northern Bohemia (which was dominated by coniferous forests; e.g. Jankovská 1992).

Chronology and Archaeology

The archaeological chronology is based on the appearance of diagnostic points and microliths, such as curved-backed points and backed blades for the late Palaeolithic, triangles for the earlier Mesolithic, and trapezoids for the late Mesolithic.

The late Palaeolithic (11,700–8200 cal BC) is generally characterized by the expansion of microlithic artefacts compared to the previous Upper Palaeolithic. However, there is also considerable variability, partly due to local traditions. In the south-east, along the middle and lower Danube, we observe continuation of the Epigravettian traditions with short endscrapers and microliths. In the north-west, an Epimagdalenian tradition with rectangular backed microblades is found in karstic caves. Still in the north-west, there are assemblages with backed curved points such as the Federmessergruppe of northern Bohemia and the Tišnovian in Moravia. Sporadically, tanged points appear in the north. An 'exotic' typological feature, hitherto without parallel elsewhere, is the appearance of Helwan segments, typical of the Natufian, in south Moravia (Šakvice). From all of these sites, radiocarbon dates are very rare and do not provide a coherent picture.

The earlier Mesolithic (8200–7000 cal BC), with a dominance of microlithic triangles, segments, and Tardenoisian points as diagnostic tool types, was originally labelled Tardenoisian and more recently Beuronian, or the Beuron-Coincy culture. Radiocarbon dates are available from Jászberény and Smolín in the south-eastern plains, and from a number of north Bohemian rock shelters. The Lepenski Vir culture in the south-east represents a specific, new, and long-term regional tradition.

The later Mesolithic (7000–6000/5500 cal BC) is predominantly characterized by geometric trapezes. In the south-east, we observe a continuation of the Lepenski Vir tradition. Several sites on the Hungarian Plain and in south Moravia may fall into this interval, e.g. Jásztelek, Mikulčice (Kértész et al. 1994), even if these assemblages may not be culturally uniform. These sites would be contemporaneous with the earliest Neolithic of the Starčevo/Körös culture, expanding from the south-east, e.g. Gyálarét-Szilágyi at 6000 BC (Horváth and Hertelendi 1994). In terms of calibrated radiocarbon years, it seems that the first farmers were present in Hungary by 6000 cal BC and in Bohemia and Moravia after 5500 cal BC.

In northern Bohemia, a series of the later Mesolithic dates from Pod zubem, Bezděz, Dolský Mlýn, Kristova cave, and other rock shelters could theoretically represent trends towards further persistence of a foraging population in an agriculturally unfavourable rocky highland (Šída et al. 2011; Svoboda 2003). At Dolský Mlýn and Bezděz, Neolithic Stroked pottery was superimposed over the later Mesolithic, while the Linear pottery material between the two never occurred. At the Bezděz stratigraphic section, a sterile horizon of about 10–15 cm of greyish sand with dark brown bands in position has been recorded where the Linear pottery would be expected (Figure 23.3). In this rocky region it is possible to clearly document an occupation hiatus instead of a persistence of the hunting-gathering lifestyles into the Neolithic.

SETTLEMENT ARCHAEOLOGY: OPEN-AIR SITES, CAVES, AND ROCK SHELTERS

Post-glacial hunters' occupation, as reflected in the present-day archaeological record, demonstrates a change of settlement and subsistence strategies compared to the Upper Palaeolithic. Although a relatively large number of Mesolithic sites are recorded, and some from structured regional clusters, most of them are small in terms of size and artefact numbers. This is particularly evident in comparison with larger Mesolithic sites in the North European Plain and Baltic. The distribution of sites in the open air, in caves and rock shelters, and the inter-regional variations, can be used as starting points for discussing Mesolithic social organization and settlement strategies.

Open-Air Sites

The spectacular open-air sites, located on the shores of the Iron Gates above the Danube, form an extraordinary cluster in several aspects (Figure 23.1; Srejović 1969; 1972). Distribution of the other open-air sites demonstrates that an important portion of settlement is located on low elevation (100–200 m above sea level) sandy deposits along rivers and lake edges (Sklenář 2000; Valoch 1978). The formation of dunes, a favourite human habitat, was one of the important developments within the lowland regions during the late glacial and early Holocene. Dune sites are known in western Slovakia, e.g. at Mačanské vršky near Sereď and south Moravia, where a number of the sites coincide with lowland fortifications and cemeteries of early medieval age, e.g. at Mikulčice, Staré Město, Pohansko,

FIGURE 23.1 Lepenski Vir. Bases of elaborate trapezoidal houses and details of stone sculptures located inside. Courtesy Centre of Archaeological Research, Faculty of Humanities, Belgrade, and Dušan Mihailović.

Strachotín, and Dolní Věstonice. Unfortunately, the dune stratigraphy is not fine enough to supply good-quality contextual and archaeological data. Besides dunes, other important sites are Barca in east Slovakia, Jászberény in Hungary, and Kamegg in Lower Austria.

Mesolithic settlement patterns show a trend towards the occupation of extensive, previously unoccupied or sparsely occupied highland areas and plateaux, up to 500 m above sea level, with the Bohemian/Moravian highland and the hill regions of south Bohemia as typical examples of such landscapes. The cases of higher mountainous Mesolithic locations are sites on the periphery of the northern Carpathian mountains (Valde-Nowak 2010), south Bohemian sites in the Šumava mountains, with altitudes of 725 m (Vencl 2006), and especially the Alpine sites in the Austrian Tirol, reaching altitudes of 2,300 m (Stadler 1991), and continuing further to the Swiss and Italian parts of the Alps. These changes in settlement patterns may be correlated with ameliorations by the end of the Pleistocene and in the earlier Holocene, opening highlands and mountains for exploration and resource exploitation.

Karstic Caves and Rock Shelters

During earlier excavations in karstic caves, prior to the systematic application of sieving and flotation, it is highly probable that scattered Mesolithic artefacts of small size, stratified between easily visible Neolithic and Magdalenian layers, would have escaped attention. Thus we are probably currently dealing with only a fragment of the real settlement system in the karst. Biostratigraphic chronology provides a substitute for radiocarbon dates but, given the mosaic and patchy character of the early Holocene landscapes, chronological relationships are not always clear. It is especially difficult to draw a clear stratigraphic boundary between late Palaeolithic and Mesolithic occupation on the basis of the karstic record.

In Moravia, stratified late Palaeolithic and Mesolithic material was first recorded during systematic excavations at Kůlna cave in the Moravian karst, and at a smaller site with important stratigraphy in the Barová cave (Horáček et al. 2002; Valoch 1988). A few other smaller sites, always with a few artefacts, were recorded from Moravia, at altitudes of 350–520 m above sea level, at Soutěska rock shelter in the Pavlovské Hills (late Palaeolithic or early Mesolithic), Průchodice I cave in central Moravia, Velká Kobylanka rock shelter in northern Moravia, and Medvedia cave in eastern Slovakia. In the Bohemian karst, late Palaeolithic occupation has been documented in the small caves of Tří volů and Dolní, and Mesolithic occupation in the caves of Martina, Za křížem, and Na Skalici. The environment of these smaller caves comprised landscapes of forest and scrub and open rocky and steppe areas during the pre-boreal and boreal periods. Finally, a karstic fissure on the top of the Bacín Hill included human skeletal fragments, dated to the Mesolithic (Matoušek, 2002). With the exception of Kůlna, these late Palaeolithic and Mesolithic cave sites are just episodic hunting posts. Stone artefacts are scarce, and with almost no use-wear traces.

Pseudokarstic (Sandstone) Rock Shelters

Discovering and exploring Mesolithic settlement patterns in the sandstone regions of Bohemia is currently an important research topic (Figure 23.2; Svoboda 2003; Svoboda et al. 2007; Šída and Prostředník 2007). Compared to the predominantly episodic occupation

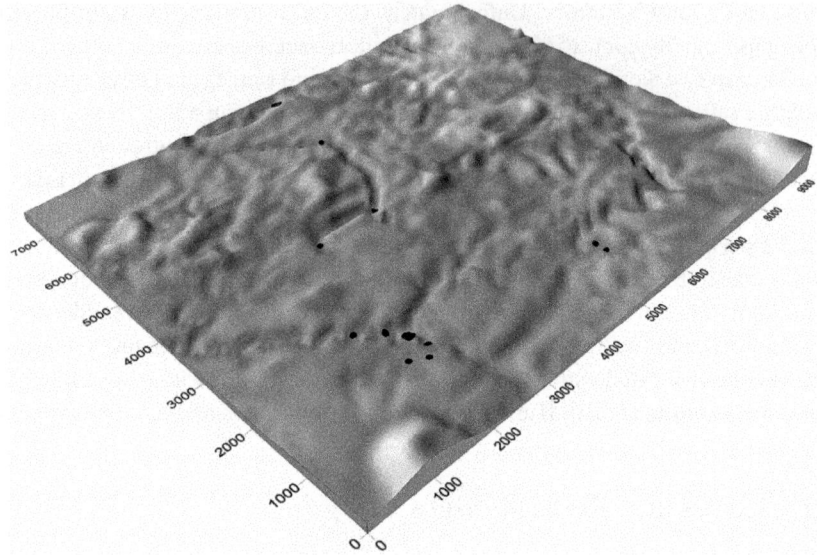

FIGURE 23.2 Example of a Mesolithic microregion: the Bohemian Switzerland National Park, showing the position of the Mesolithic rock shelters. Note the central agglomeration of sites in the south-west corner, at the confluence of the Kamenice and Bělá river canyons.

of karstic caves, some of the pseudo-karstic rock shelters include rich cultural layers, labour-intensive stone-built hearths, and lithic industries with evidence of use-wear traces. The quantity of artefacts varies from tens to thousands of pieces, but there is no correlation between the number of pieces and the complexity of features. The richest sites are in the extreme north (Údolí samoty, Okrouhlík, Arba, Švédův rock shelters) near the German border, suggesting possible relationships north of the modern border and onto the North European Plain. Some of the southern sites, on the other hand, offer better conditions for organic preservation, thus supplying better faunal evidence and some bone industries, and these seem to be related to the open-air sites of central Bohemia.

Resource Analysis and Subsistence

Lithic Resources

One of the dominant trends observed in European Mesolithic economies is an emphasis on local lithic raw materials for tool production, only partly supplemented by imports. This picture is in contrast to previous, labour-expensive Upper Palaeolithic economies, where we observe a clear dominance of imports from distances reaching hundreds of kilometres.

The most important imports are flint nodules of morainic origin from areas covered by the Pleistocene glaciations (the North European Plain generally). Local materials form a true mosaic following the individual sub-regions. In the south-east, the Carpathian Basin

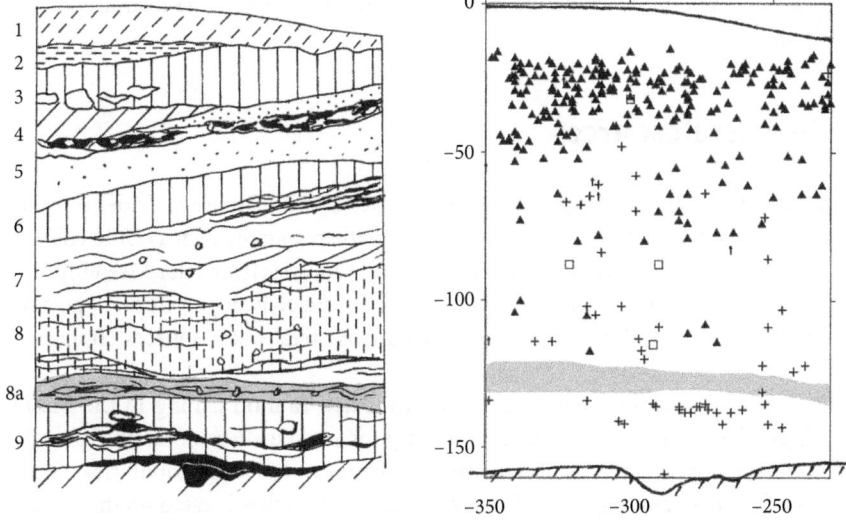

FIGURE 23.3 Bezděz rock shelter, North Bohemia. Stratigraphic section showing a sterile horizon 8a, sandwiched between the Late Mesolithic layer 9 and the Middle Neolithic Stroked pottery layer 8.

supplied quartzites, especially limnoquartzites, and menilites, while obsidian sources were available in the volcanic areas of the north-eastern part of the Basin and radiolarites in the Carpathians and Alps. Moravia supplied several types of cherts (Krumlovský Les-type, Olomučany-type, etc.), and Bohemia supplied various fine-grained quartzites (Bečov, Tušimice, and Skršín types), jasper, porcelanite, and serpentinites. Materials of south German (Bavarian) origin are also recorded in the western part of the region. The emphasis on the nearest available material may be explained by relatively small territories at a subregional level, whereas the ubiquitous presence of imports indicates contact at a larger geographical scale. In addition, coarse-grained sedimentary rocks and volcanites were used for a variety of other purposes (hammerstones, grinding stones, polishing stones, heat accumulators in hearths) and such materials were usually locally available.

The majority of lithic raw materials were available for exploitation on the surface, as outcrops of quartzite and chert, nodules from glacial moraines, and pebbles from fluvial deposits. An ochre mine at Lovas, Hungary, with typical mining pits and numerous bone implements and late glacial/early Holocene fauna (*Alces alces, Cervus elaphus, Rangifer tarandus, Capra* (ibex) *carpatorum, Sus scrofa, Equus sp., Grus grus*), recently provided a late glacial date of 11,740 ± 100 BP (ETH-15199), suggesting an Epigravettian classification (Dobosi 2006). In the North European Plain (Poland), evidence from the chocolate flint outcrops, such as Tomaszów, suggests an intensive exploitation, if not mining, and an adjacent burial at Janislawice has been ascribed to someone who worked in a mine (Cyrek 1995). From one of the pits excavated at the chert outcrops of the Krumlovian exploitation area, Oliva (2008) obtained a date of 9410 ± 50 BP (GrA-34410), which, if confirmed, could also indicate late Palaeolithic or early Mesolithic mining activity. At Stvolínky I, north Bohemia, large quartzite blocks are scattered around the site, and some of the stone artefacts were made from this material whereas the majority of artefacts were made from imported flint (Svoboda 2003).

Aquatic Diet Resources

In the south-east, at the Iron Age sites on the Lower Danube, there is evidence of fishing carp, sturgeon, catfish, and other fish, and other aquatic resources such as Unio collecting is evidenced at various sites of this region. Stable isotope analysis from later Mesolithic human bones at Vlasac and Schela Cladovei show elevated C- and N-isotope values suggesting that about 60–85 per cent of the protein was derived from freshwater sources (Bonsall 2008; Bonsall et al. 2000).

In the north-west, Jochim (1979) has also advocated salmon fishing in the Mesolithic on the Upper Rhine and we may argue similarly for rock shelters of north Bohemia, the positions of some of which control steep rocky canyons of the small tributaries of the Elbe river. In the faunal assemblage from Dolský Mlýn, a rock shelter located on the bank of the Kamenice River, fish vertebrae were recorded and some represent individuals up to 1 m long. Lembi Lougas (pers. comm.) recently determined them as salmon. This is the first evidence of salmon fishing so deep in the interior of the European continent.

Terrestrial Diet Resources

Valoch (1978) initially suggested the possibility of plant food exploitation on the basis of two grinding stones found at Smolín, although supporting palaeobotanical evidence was not available at the time. Analysis of the residue and use-wear data from the Pod zubem and Pod křídlem rock shelters (Hardy and Svoboda 2009) indicate that stone tools were used to exploit a wide range of resources. Plants processed at these sites include wood (specifically softwood/gymnosperm) and possibly roots, tubers, or nuts.

In the south-east, the prevalence of oak in the palaeobotanical record led Prinz (1987) to presume that acorns could have contributed to the diet. In the north-west, hazelnut shells and their fragments are repeatedly found in Mesolithic rock shelters of northern Bohemia (Šída and Prostředník 2007; Svoboda 2003). In addition, the presence of *Trapa natans* nuts was recorded in early Holocene layers in the littoral of the fossil lake Švarcemberk, South Bohemia, and it may be that humans supported its spread intentionally (Pokorný 2002; Zvelebil 1994). Finally, flotation of Mesolithic deposits in the Jezevčí rock shelter has revealed palaeobotanical macroremains, mainly seeds, of the following species: *Sambucus nigra, Picea abies, Rubus idaeus, Chenopodium album, Rubus* sp., *Pinus sylvestris, Corylus avellana, Poaceae*. These results suggest gathering of plants, as in the case of *Sambucus nigra*, or berries such as *Rubus*.

Traces of hair and feathers on lithic implements from the same sites indicate that both avian and mammalian resources were being exploited, most probably for food, which, of course, does not exclude other purposes. Evidence for frequent hafting at the site may relate to the construction of composite points or barbs, whereas the impact blows identified by Yaroshevich (pers. comm.) on some of the geometric projectiles complete the picture of hunting with projectiles. The osteological evidence also points to the exploitaiton of smaller fur animals.

Unfortunately, relatively little faunal evidence is available from open-air sites, probably because of factors affecting bone preservation. At the Iron Gate sites, there is complex faunal evidence composed of red deer, roe deer, wild pig, and aurochs, some carnivores (bear, wolf, badger) and birds (eagle; Bonsall 2008). At the Hungarian Plain sites of Jászberény and Jásztelek, Kértész et al. (1994) record the dominance of bovids (aurochs), supplemented by red deer, deer, horse, pig, and individual finds of turtle and birds' eggs. A similar faunal spectrum is available from Smolín in south Moravia (Valoch 1978), but dominated by horse (based on teeth), and accompanied by bovids, beaver, elk, wild pig, fox, and red deer. In some of the north Bohemian rock shelters (at Pod zubem) the larger species are outnumbered by smaller forest animals such as marten, wild cat, beaver, fox, wolf, and hare, and others yielded individual specimens of turtle, toad, and birds (Svoboda 2003).

In the inner parts of the Medvedia cave, east Slovakia, Bárta (1990) discovered skeletal remains of two bears (*Ursus arctos*) together with two bone projectiles. According to Bárta, at least one of the bears was killed by the projectile, which was found directly among the ribs. This provides a rare piece of direct evidence for bear kills in caves during the Holocene.

Technologies

Lithics

Generally, the cores at Mesolithic sites are mostly smaller than 3 cm, and some show remains of pebble cortex on the surface, which means that secondary sources in glacial and fluvial sediments were relied on more than primary outcrops. As in other parts of Europe, the technology of cores, microblades, and small flakes demonstrates an emphasis on microlithic implements used as inserts in composite tools. In addition, some Mesolithic industries are supplemented by larger hammerstones, stone plaques, and polishing stones, including typical grooved polishers, as at Smolín and Nizká Lešnice. Polishing stone as a technique has also been used to form surfaces of the spectacular sculptures of Lepenski Vir (Srejović 1972).

Wood

In a landscape more forested than in the Upper Palaeolithic, one may expect a large amount of woodworking. Recent findings of fragments of longitudinal wooden artefacts by Šída et al. (2007), in the littoral of the fossil lake Švarcemberk, confirm this hypothesis. One of the wooden artefacts provided a date of 9500 ± 50 BP (Poz-16752). Analysis by Hardy (Hardy and Svoboda 2009) shows that wood processing definitely occurred at Pod zubem rock shelter during the earlier and later Mesolithic, particularly of gymnosperms and in one case larch or spruce. There is evidence that conforms to hafting traces (striations, bright spots, resin) seen on experimental and archaeological material and hafting requires the preparation of a handle. Thus, the woodworking could relate to the preparation of a haft. In north-eastern Slovenia a wooden monoxyle boat has recently been dated by 14C to the Mesolithic period (Kavur pers. comm.).

Bone

Unfavourable conditions for organic preservation at most of the sites limits the possibilities of recovering any bone industry. Nonetheless, the Iron Gate sites provided a series of bone tools, especially the typical spatulas (Bonsall 2008). From the north Bohemian Mesolithic, we have a whole series of simple bone awls, supplemented by a chisel-shaped artefact from the Pod zubem rock shelter, and the cave of Martina in the Bohemian karst has yielded a pierced axe of deer antler. Two bilaterally grooved bone projectiles, with stone blades ready to be inserted, were found in the Medvedia cave near Ružín in association with bear skeletons (Bárta 1990). This, again, confirms Hardy's idea of hafting.

Architecture and Pyrotechnology

A good example of prehistoric architecture is the semi-subterranean trapezoidal houses with stone basements found at Lepenski Vir and other sites of the Iron Age area. The houses are arranged on terraces in several layers, with their broader edges facing the gorge. Trapezoidal huts often included stone-lined hearths and red plastered floors. As noted by Bonsall (2008), the shape of the houses may have been inspired by the trapezoidal mountain of Treskavac.

A number of other open-air sites along the Danube and Upper Elbe have features and pits of various shapes and dimensions, and some are interpreted as man-made structures, but a critical approach is certainly necessary (Newell 1981). At the site of Smolín in the Dyje and Svratka lowlands of south Moravia Valoch (1978) conducted a complex excavation of two Mesolithic features described as large oval-shaped pits, which produced a rich lithic industry with geometric triangles, faunal remains, and radiocarbon dates, and a site with a smaller circular pit and a lithic assemblage was later excavated nearby, at Dolní Věstonice V. In south Bohemia, circular and oval features were excavated on the shores of the Řežabinec Lake at Putim (Mazálek 1953) and later at several south Bohemian sites such as Strakonice, Dolní Poříčí, and Přední Zborovice (Vencl 2006). Other cases were recorded elsewhere in Bohemia, as at Tašovice and Hořín. It is interesting to note that authors who have found new evidence reject features previously excavated by others, even if the field situations are basically the same (Mazálek 1953; Vencl 2006).

In rock shelters, larger oval-shaped or circular pits were also excavated (Heřmánky, Pod zubem). Evidence from rock shelters provides an opportunity to analyse spatial relationships between natural features, such as the rock walls and sheltered areas, and man-made features such as hearths, post holes, and artefact densities. Recent excavation has revealed new evidence for hearth construction at certain rock shelters and for pyrotechnology in general, and the system of hearths, pan-shaped pits, and kettle-shaped pits inside the houses is similar to the one recorded at Upper Palaeolithic sites.

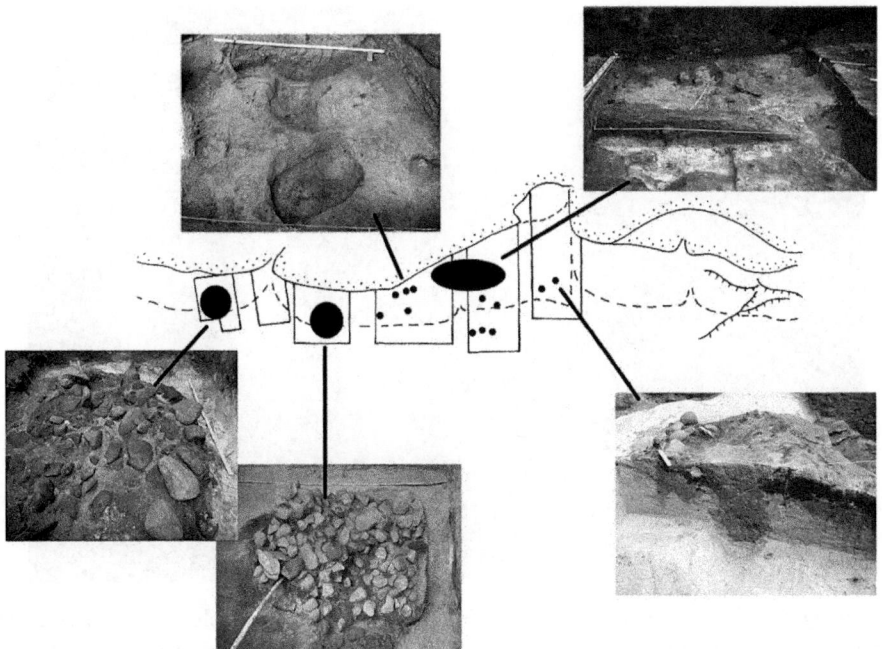

FIGURE 23.4 Okrouhlík rock shelter on the confluence of the Kamenice and Bělá rivers. Schematic plan showing the location of the features: central hearth, two stone-paved 'ovens', pits and boiling pits.

Whereas the 'normal' hearths, composed only of charcoal and reddened and burnt sand, are located in central parts of the sheltered areas, more elaborate hearths or 'ovens' with stone blocks or pebbles tend to be located at the peripheries. These hearths are elaborate, filled with blocks of sandstone (Pod zubem, Šídelník III rock shelters) and ferrous sandstone (Stará skála rock shelter), both available locally, or with basalt cobbles brought in from nearby river deposits (Dolský Mlýn, Okrouhlík rock shelters; Figure 23.4). The stones are interpreted as heat accumulators. In some cases, pan-shaped pits, filled with ash, were recovered below the stone blocks. A system of adjacent kettle-shaped pits were hollowed out around other hearths, and some pebbles showing the effect of heating, suggesting a use as a boiling pit. These hearths and related facilities have clearly been used both for warmth and for cooking food.

Art and Symbolism

The Magdalenian, with realistic art and sophisticated symbolism that reached as far as the middle Danube region during the late glacial, left no trace in the post-glacial. Further east, Ukraine and other areas provided a wealth of geometrically decorated objects and figurines of the Epigravettian, but there is lack of comparable symbolic evidence in Danubian Europe and most of it is questionable. There are simple rock paintings in geometric style in the 'sacred corridor' of the Domica cave, east Slovakia, believed to be Neolithic because of the

FIGURE 23.5 Fish cave, North Bohemia. Fragment of a schist pebble with engraved geometric patterns, possibly representing a fish bone and water (the zig-zag line) (Museum Česká Lípa, photo Martin Frouz).

context of the cave occupation. However, a charcoal spot on the rock wall of the subterranean Styx River recently provided a date of 11,310 ± 50 BP (GrA-32114; Šefčáková et al. 2009). A bone tool from the Lovas paint mine, Hungary, dated to 11,740 ± 100 BP bears a morphologically similar geometric pattern (Dobosi 2006). This line of research is continuing.

Of particular interest and originality is the accumulation of large stone sculptures at Lepenski Vir. The figures have large, egg-shaped heads with schematized faces, while the bodies, if present, are reduced and rounded, and covered by geometric and curvilinear patterns. The patterns evoke water and thus the sculptures are interpreted as riverine deities (Srejović 1972) or hybrid, therianthropic images (Borić 2007). However, their specific form and style recalls some stone sculptures from other places along the Mediterranean, be it in the Natufian (El Wad, Eynan) or in the southern French Neolithic (Capdenac le-Haut).

In the Mesolithic higher on the Danube there are several cases of small, simply engraved pebbles, without secure contextual evidence (Přibice, Putim, Fish cave; Figure 23.5), individual pierced teeth, and other items of decoration (Bezděz).

Cemeteries, Burials, and Scattered Human Remains

In Europe generally, Mesolithic cemeteries tend to be located in coastal locations (Bailey and Spikins 2008) and the absence of cemeteries along the Danube confirms these observations.

However, the accumulation of cemeteries around the important river passage of the Iron Gates is an exception in the interior of the continent. The cemetery at Vlasac with 85 graves (with more than 100 individuals) and complex ritual burials at Lepenski Vir are located on the right bank, while the cemetery of Schela Cladovei with more than 60 graves is on the left bank of the Danube. The standard position of the skeletons is extended on the back in a single grave, but there are variations and evidence of reburial and excarnation practices, as well as special deposition of the skulls. Evidence of arrow injuries appears on some of the skeletons.

Higher on the middle Danube, the only evidence for human remains comes from a small number of burials and some isolated finds or burials of somewhat uncertain age. The only complete burial was discovered in a large, $c.50$ m long, south-facing rock shelter, Zigeunerhöhle, near Elsbethen in the Salzburg Basin, Austria (Rettenbacher and Tichy 1994). Here the body of a two-to-three-year-old child was buried most probably in a crouched sitting position, facing south, inside a circular pit 0.4 m deep. A charcoal layer indicates that a fire was built over the burial after filling up the pit. The related fauna and lithic artefacts are of earlier Mesolithic date. A radiocarbon date obtained from the child's rib dates the burial to 8020 ± 125 BP. Still higher in the German part of the Upper Danube, two clusters of separated human skulls found in the small rock shelter at Grosse Ofnet and comparable finds in Hexenküche and Hohlenstein-Stadel complete the variable picture of Mesolithic mortuary practices in Danubian Europe, usually interpreted as a result of a skull cult, a violent act, or both.

Matoušek (2002) has documented another type of funerary behaviour at the top of the Bacín Hill, Bohemian karst, where remains of an adult male (20–30 years old) were found in a filling of a vertical karstic fissure. The radiocarbon date from the bones was 9490 ± 65 BP (OxA-9271). During investigations in the Bohemian sandstone rock shelters, isolated human teeth and small cranial fragments were discovered at the sites of Pod zubem, Vysoká Lešnice, Nízká Lešnice, Šídelník I, and Dvojitá brána. However, a direct radiocarbon date from one of the open-air child's burials from Obříství, originally published as Mesolithic, provided a Neolithic age (Svoboda et al. 2002).

Conclusion

Lepenski Vir and related sites in the Iron Gates, with spectacular architecture, art, and burials, clearly represent a Mesolithic highlight in Danubian Europe. Rarity of other large and complex sites elsewhere along the Danube may only partly be explained by the insufficient archaeological survey over the past decades. Rather, it reflects the real state of demographic and settlement patterns in the Mesolithic. It seems that the geographic centre of the continent lost the important role it held during the Gravettian and Magdalenian. The reason may be the climatic and environmental change at the Pleistocene/Holocene boundary and the social responses to these changes.

The sites of Lepenski Vir show a concentration of occupation and trends towards complexity of hunter-gatherer-fishers. Intensive exploitation of both aquatic and terrestrial resources has been suggested as one of the reasons behind this complexity, and the formation of cemeteries, for the first time in this part of Europe, is interpreted as one of the demographic consequences. More to the north, smaller Mesolithic sites expanded to a wide range of landscape types and altitudes, reaching from river floodplains to the highlands and high mountains. This suggests flexibility, adaptability of the population, and variability in resource exploitation strategies. In the rocky regions, the size of the settled rock shelters suggests occupations of maximally 10–15 people at the larger sites and of only a few people at the small sites. Although salmon fishing was recently documented in a rock shelter above the Kamenice River, one of the tributaries of the Elbe, this activity probably never reached the importance documented in the ethnological record. Human burials or fragmented human remains are extremely rare in northern parts of Danubian Europe and cemeteries are absent. On a European scale, the density of Mesolithic occupation along the Danube is scarcer than elsewhere in the continent, especially if compared with some of the marine regions. Paradoxically, large areas in the centre of the European continent turned to peripheries.

Acknowledgements

This research is part of the Czech Grant Agency project 'Before the Neolithic', GAP504/13/08169S.

References

Bailey, G. and Spikins, P. (eds) 2008. *Mesolithic Europe*. Cambridge: Cambridge University Press.
Bárta, J. 1990. Mezolitickí lovci v Medvedej jaskyni priRužíne. *Slovenská archeológia* 38, 5–30.
Berger, J.-F. and Guilaine, J. 2009. The 8200 cal BP abrupt environmental change and the Neolithic transition: a Mediterranean perspective. *Quaternary International* 200, 31–49.
Bonsall, C. 2008. The Mesolithic of the Iron Gates. In G. Bailey and P. Spikins (eds), *Mesolithic Europe*, 238–79. Cambridge: Cambridge University Press.
Bonsall, C., Cook, G., Lennon, R., Harkness, D., Scott, M., Bartosiewicz, L., and McSweeney, K. 2000. Stable isotopes, radiocarbon and Mesolithic–Neolithic transition in the Iron Gates. *Documenta Praehistorica* 27, 119–32.
Borić, D. 2007. Images of animality: hybrid bodies and mimesis in early prehistoric art. In C. Renfrew and I. Morley (eds), *Image and imagination*, 83–99. Cambridge: McDonald Institute for Archaeological Research.
Cyrek, K. 1995. On the distribution of chocolate flint in the Late Mesolithic of the Vistula basin. *Archaeologia Polona* 33, 99–109.
Dobosi, V. 2006. Lovas (Hungary) ochre mine reconsidered. In G. Körlin and G. Weisgerber (eds), *Stone Age—Mining Age*, 29–36. Bochum: Deutsche Bergbau-Museum.
Hardy, B. J. and Svoboda, J. A. 2009. Mesolithic stone tool function and site types in Northern Bohemia, Czech Republic. In M. Haslam G. Robertson, A. Crowther, S. Nugent, and L. Kirkwood (eds), *Archaeological science under a microscope: studies in residue and ancient DNA analysis in honour of Thomas H. Loy*, 159–74. Canberra: ANU Press.
Horáček, I., Ložek, V., Svoboda, J., and Šajnerová, A. 2002. Přírodní prostředí a osídlení krasu v pozdním paleolitu a mezolitu. In J. Svoboda (ed.), *Prehistorické jeskyně*, 313–43. Brno: The Dolní Věstonice Studies 7.

Horváth, F. and Hertelendi, E. 1994. Contribution to the C14 based absolute chronology of the Early and Middle Neolithic Tisza region. *Jósa András Múzeum Évkönyve* 36, 111–33.

Jankovská, V. 1992. Vegetationsverhältnisse und Naturumwelt des Beckens Jestřebská kotlina am Ende des Spätglazials und im Holozän (Doksy-Gebiet). *Folia Geobotanica et Phytotaxonomica* 27, 137–48.

Jochim, M. A. 1979. Catches and caches: ethnographic alternatives for prehistory. In C. Kramer (ed.), *Ethnoarchaeology*, 219–46. New York: Columbia University Press.

Kértész, R., Sümegi, P., Kozák, M., Braun, M., Félegyházi, E., and Hertelendi, E. 1994. Mesolithikum im nördlichen Teil der Grossen Ungarischen Tiefebene. *Józa András Múzeum Évkönyve* 36, 15–61.

Matoušek, V. 2002. Bacín. Místo pravěkého pohřebního kultu v Českém krasu. In J. Svoboda (ed.), *Prehistorické jeskyně*, 355–93. Brno: The Dolní Věstonice Studies 7.

Mazálek, M. 1953. Třetí rok výzkumů paleo-mesolitické oblasti u Ražic. *Archeologické rozhledy* 5, 577–89.

Newell, R. R. 1981. Mesolithic dwelling structures: fact and fantasy. In B. Gramsch (ed.), *Mesolithikum in Europa*, 235–84. Berlin: Veröffentlichungen des Museums für Ur- und Frühgeschichte Potsdam 14/15.

Oliva, M. 2008. Moravský Krumlov (okr. Znojmo). *Přehled výzkumů* 49, 239.

Pokorný, P. 2002. A high-resolution record of Late-Glacial and Early-Holocene climatic and environmental change in the Czech Republic. *Quaternary International* 91, 101–22.

Prinz, B. 1987. *Mesolithic adaptations on the Lower Danube: Vlasac and Iron Age gorge*. Oxford: BAR 330.

Rettenbacher, C. and Tichy, G. 1994. Ein frühmesolithisches Kindergrab aus der Zigeunerhöhle in Elsbethen bei Salzburg. *Mitteilungen der Gesellschaft für Salzburger Landeskunde* 134, 625–42.

Šefčáková, A., Svoboda, J. A., Farkaš, Z., van der Plicht, J., Gaál, L., and Balciar, I. 2009. Prehistoric rock art in the Slovak republic: first radiocarbon dates from charcoal drawings. *International Newsletter on Rock Art* 54, 1–7.

Šída, P., Pokorný, P., and Kuneš, P. 2007. Dřevěné artefakty raně holocenního stáří z litorálu zaniklého jezera Švarcemberk. *Přehled výzkumů* 48, 55–64.

Šída, P., and Prostředník, J. 2007. Pozdní paleolit a mezolit Českého ráje: perspektivy poznání regionu. *Archeologické rozhledy* 59, 443–60.

Šída, P., Prostředník, J., and Kuneš, P. 2011. New radiocarbon data for the north Bohemian Mesolithic. *Interdisciplinaria Archaeologica* 2, 151–7.

Sklenář, K. 2000. *Hořín III. Mesolithische und hallstattzeitliche Siedlung*. Praha: Národní Muzeum.

Srejović, D. 1969. *Lepenski Vir*. Beograd: Srpska književna zadruga.

Srejović, D. 1972. *Europe's first monumental sculpture: new discoveries at Lepenski Vir*. London: Thames and Hudson.

Stadler, H. 1991. Eine mesolithische Freilandstation auf dem Hirschbichl im Defereggental, Gem. St. Jakob, Osttirol. *Archäologie Österreichs* 2/1, 23–6.

Svoboda, J. (ed.) 2003. *Mezolit severních Čech—Mesolithic of Northern Bohemia*. Brno: The Dolní Věstonice Studies 9.

Svoboda, J., Hajnalová, M., Horáček, I., Novák, M., Přichystal, A., Šajnerová, A., and Yaroshevich, A. 2007. Mesolithic settlement and activities in rockshelters of the Kamenice river canyon, Czech Republic. *Eurasian Prehistory* 5, 95–127.

Svoboda, J., van der Plicht, J., and Kuželka, V. 2002. Upper Palaeolithic and Mesolithic human fossils from Moravia and Bohemia (Czech Republic): some new C14 dates. *Antiquity* 76, 957–62.

Valde-Nowak, P. 2010. The Mesolithic in the northernmost periphery of the Carpathian Basin. In J. K. Kozłowski and P. Raczky (eds), *Neolithisation of the Carpathian Basin: northernmost distribution of the Starčevo/Körös Culture*, 7–23. Kraków-Budapest: Polish Academy of Arts and Sciences; Institute of Archaeological Sciences of the Eötvös Loránd University.

Valoch, K. 1978. *Die endpaläolithische Siedlung in Smolín*. Praha: Academia.

Valoch, K. 1988. *Die Erforschung der Kůlna-Höhle 1961–1976*. Brno: Anthropos 24 (NS 16).

Vencl, S. (ed.) 2006. *Nejstarší osídlení jižních Čech: paleolit a mezolit*. Praha: Archeologický ústav AV ČR.

Walanus, A. and Nalepka, D. 2010. Calibration of Mangerud's boundaries. *Radiocarbon* 52, 1639–44.

Zvelebil, M. 1994. Plant use in the Mesolithic and its role in the transition to farming. *Proceedings of the Prehistoric Society* 60, 35–74.

CHAPTER 24

TRANSFORMATIONS? THE MESOLITHIC OF NORTH-WEST EUROPE

GRAEME WARREN

> Scholars no longer believe in a general model of the Mesolithic. Several researchers argue that there is now substantial evidence that Mesolithic societies displayed diversity in their constitution, structure and ways of interacting with the landscape.
>
> (Larsson 2009, xxviii)

THIS chapter examines the transformations in Mesolithic communities of north-west Europe, loosely defined as incorporating France, Holland, Belgium, southern Scandinavia, northern Germany, Britain, and Ireland (Figure 24.1). Post-glacial settlement by hunter-gatherers appears to have been associated with a variety of changes: from routines of movement and subsistence, through to changes in beliefs and political relationships. These have often been associated with the rise of 'complex hunter-gatherers', associated with sedentism, territorial rights, specialized economic routines, social hierarchy, developed exchange, and ritual. Archaeologically, these are exemplified by the Ertebølle of southern Sweden and Denmark. Beyond this, however, the Mesolithic of this region as a whole is variable and the character and nature of transformations within and between these communities is also richly variable.

The development of the concept of 'Mesolithic' communities in Europe demonstrates the intimate links that have always existed in archaeological thought between notions of change over time and conceptions of progress (see Clarke 1980; Rowley-Conwy 1986; 1996). Initial accounts of the Mesolithic struggled to reconcile the apparent poverty of these people with the rich archaeological record of the Upper Palaeolithic in Europe that preceded them. The Mesolithic was a challenge to dominant notions of progress over time. Whilst we have moved far from the notion that the Mesolithic was a period of regression 'between cave painters and crop planters' (Rowley-Conwy 1986) the notion of progress remains embedded in our constructions of the Mesolithic, especially in terms of the development of trends such as social complexity (see below). My main argument in this short chapter is that this notion of change over time has obscured our understanding of alternative transformations and that these require emphasis.

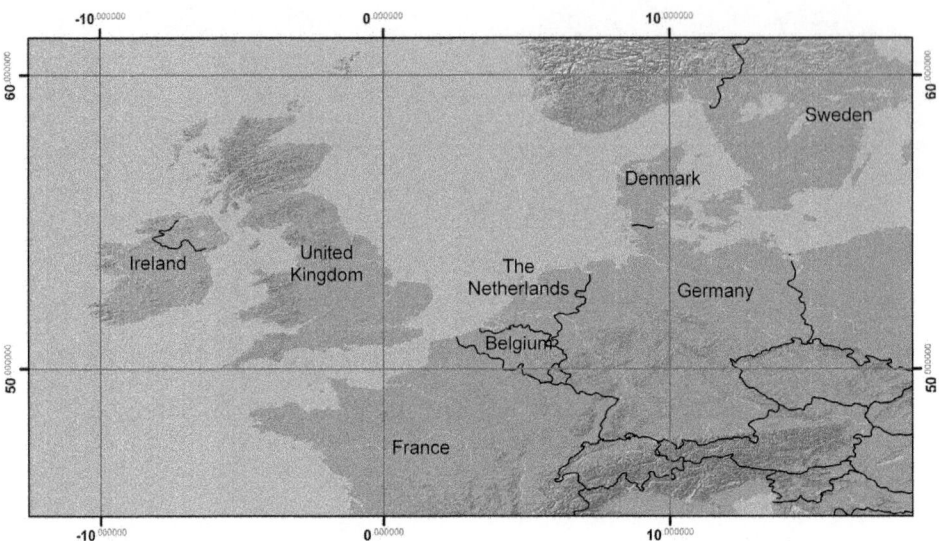

FIGURE 24.1 Location of key regions discussed in the text. (Map created using ArcGIS® software by Esri.)

Zvelebil argued that 'the Mesolithic is a social tradition, contingent upon the preceding cultures of the late Upper Palaeolithic, and situated historically from the end of the last glaciation within the post-glacial period... The Mesolithic represents a historical process involving hunter-gatherer communities' (Zvelebil 2009, xlviii). This broad framework underpins the discussion of transformations here (see below for discussion of this definition and a suggested refinement). The Mesolithic in north-west Europe sees particular historical communities, with particular traditions and ways of understanding the world, reacting to changes in their familiar landscapes and exploring new landscapes, encountering plants, animals, and people as they did so. One of the key historical processes that they engaged with, on a day-to-day basis, was the reaction of their landscapes to the climate changes characteristic of the Pleistocene/Holocene transition and this provides the starting point for our discussion.

Changing Landscapes

The impact of late- and post-glacial climate change on the physical landscape of north-west Europe was complex. Climate warming at the start of the Holocene was very rapid, but the response of the landscape occurred at varying speeds. Potential cyclicities of Holocene climate change (e.g. Bond et al. 1997; 2001) are debated, notwithstanding arguments that the Holocene sees a comparatively 'stable climate' in comparison to earlier periods. Solar, marine, and volcanic influences were significant at different times (Jansen et al. 2007). Differences in climate regimes, and not simply temperature, included variation in precipitation connected to changes in flood regimes in major river systems at a European level (e.g. Macklin et al. 2006), and the potential role of natural fire in maintaining vegetation

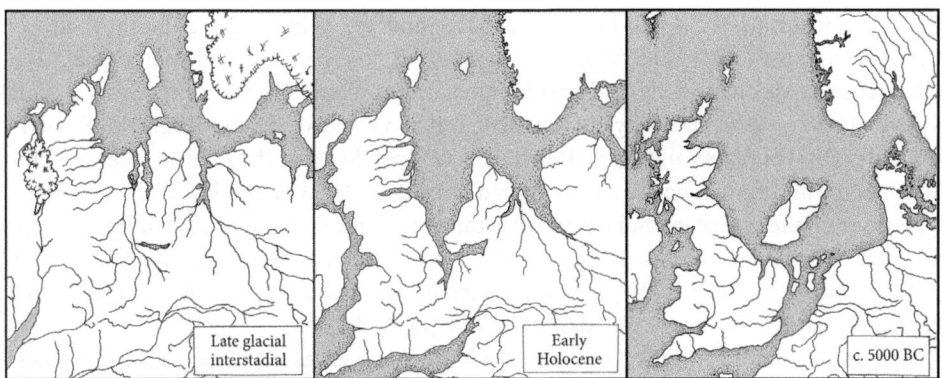

FIGURE 24.2 Changing sea levels since the late glacial had a profound influence on the north European landscape. Redrawn from Coles (1998).

regimes in northern Britain has seen substantial discussion (e.g. Tipping 1996). The scale of climate and environmental change during the early Holocene of north-west Europe was profound. Our models work better at the larger scale than the local, and in many cases they are underdetermined by local data. This is a key problem in relating scales of change in the past. Against this background, two key processes can be distinguished for ease of discussion: changes in sea level and in terrestrial fauna/flora.

Sea-level change resulted from the combination of ice-wastage feeding an absolute rise in global sea level (glacio-eustasy) and rebound of landmasses once ice was removed (glacio-isostasy), as well as the weight of water on landmasses (hydro-isostasy) and the forebulge in the Earth's crust created by loads. The resulting models are complex, especially in areas of ice accumulation where rebound is significant, but the processes can be generalized as involving sea-level rise inundating large areas of landscape, with some uplifting in and adjacent to areas where ice accumulated significantly, as for example in much of western Scotland and northern Ireland or parts of Denmark and southern Sweden, although not all areas preserve all coastlines. It is mainly in the small areas of uplift noted above that coastal sites from some parts of the Mesolithic are preserved above modern-day sea level, and these are very important for understanding the period. Comparing these places to those without preserved coastlines is a significant biasing factor in our accounts. The extent of landscape transformation is best illustrated by Doggerland, the extensive north-west European coastal plain that once linked Britain and the continent (Figure 24.2) and appeared to play a key role in late glacial/early Holocene settlement of these regions, its eventual loss leading to considerable transformations in people's lives (Gaffney et al. 2009; see below). Further east, the transformation of the freshwater Ancylus Lake into the saline Baltic Sea was another fundamental transformation of geographies.

Plants and animals recolonized north-west Europe at varied tempos resulting from the interplay of their dispersal speed, presence of refugia, and competitive interactions. The vegetation sequence is generalized as one of light scrub giving way to birch and hazel woodlands then full deciduous woodlands, although the nature of these woodlands was regionally variable. Some early Holocene woodlands have few modern comparisons, for example the birch woodland found at low-altitude and high temperatures in northern England in the early Holocene (Spikins 1999). Debate exists on the extent to which the early–mid-Holocene woodland incorporated open areas (Vera 2000; and see Whitehouse and Smith 2009). Changes in fauna saw the replacement, over varying time periods, of the large mammals (characteristic of open landscapes) with woodland dwellers. Thus reindeer, horse, giant deer/Irish elk were displaced by auroch, boar, red and roe deer. Major geographical barriers to dispersal of plants and animals included the Irish Sea and the English Channel, and both Ireland and Britain have more restricted floral and faunal assemblages than continental Europe. In the case of Ireland it is possible that most large fauna were absent; auroch were absent, red deer appear to have been introduced in the Neolithic (Woodman et al. 1997), and wild boar may have been deliberately introduced by Mesolithic settlers. They may also have been introduced to the major islands of the Baltic (Zvelebil 2008).

Reaction to deglaciation led to many other effects, such as the slow infilling of lakes, changing river regimes as sediment supplies from upstream and offshore transformed, and the initiation of peat growth in some areas (possibly locally facilitated by human activity: Simmons 1996). Many of these were slow processes, but local manifestations of readjustment could be dramatic. One of the most significant events of the early Holocene was a large tsunami associated with a major offshore landslip west of Norway at $c.8200$ cal BP: the Storegga event (Weninger et al. 2008). The Storegga event has been connected to a variety of archaeological evidence—not always convincingly—but its likely impact on a settlement system with a strong coastal aspect would have been profound. Weninger et al. concluded that 'the Storegga Slide tsunami would have had a catastrophic impact on the contemporary coastal Mesolithic population' (Weninger et al. 2008, 17). The '8200 cal BP cooling event', a regional cooling episode of considerable severity, has not yet been convincingly associated with particular changes in human settlement (but see Edwards et al. 2007 and Berger and Guilaine 2010). The final emptying of the ice-dammed Lake Aggasiz in North America, which may have provoked the '8200 cal BP' event, may have led to a rise in global sea level of $c.50$ cm at $c.6250$ cal BC (Weninger et al. 2008). The coincidence of the timing of these events in the late seventh millennium cal BC may have been significant and it is surprising that a concatenation of events of this scale has not produced more direct evidence for human response when the 8200 BP cooling event, shorn of any coastal impacts, does appear to correlate to significant changes in south-eastern Europe (Bonsall et al. 2002/3). This may relate to the comparatively poor chronological resolution of our models of human settlement.

Most of the time, the impacts of climate change were smaller scale and hard to identify, but were likely to be very important to past populations, especially as some, at least, took place on time scales recognizable across the generations or to individuals: a traditional settlement area, now flooded; an outcrop of high-quality stone, now lost; landscapes that one generation had walked on, now beneath the sea; stone tools, battered, rolled in beach deposits, but still recognizable as worked. These transformations were a key aspect of the textures of Mesolithic life in the region, if possibly expressed most dramatically on the coasts. That they remain analytically difficult to access does not mean we should ignore them.

The Big Picture

The Mesolithic in north-west Europe is defined by convenience and convention rather than hard boundaries. In much of the region the Pleistocene/Holocene boundary obscures continuity of human occupation, and drawing any kind of distinction between late/latest/ final Upper Palaeolithic hunter-gatherers and first Mesolithic (or even Epi-Palaeolithic) hunter-gatherers is meaningless (see below). The transition from the late glacial into the Holocene was characterized by a complex sequence of environmental changes associated with a sequence of warm and cold periods before the more sustained warming of the Holocene. The re-colonization of northern Europe sees a diverse range of archaeological cultures, and regional variations thereof, many seeming to have broad correlations with major environmental changes, although our understandings of cause and effect are rather limited. In overall terms, the late Upper Palaeolithic Magdalenian (with Hamburgian and Creswellian regional facies) is followed by *Federmessergruppen* associated with the warmer periods of the Allerød interstadial, and Ahrensburgian and related groups during the Younger Dryas stadial before the start of the Mesolithic, all with varied patterns of mobility and settlement (see, for example, Barton et al. 2003; Conneller 2007; De Bie and Vermeersch 1998; Street 1998; Street et al. 2002). Ahrensburgian groups appear to have made extensive use of the low plains of northern Europe, and relied heavily on reindeer, which appears to have been intensively exploited. These groups may have extended as far as northern Britain (e.g. Ballin and Saville 2003), but the cold conditions of the Younger Dryas are generally associated with very little evidence for settlement in the north of the region considered here.

The onset of the Holocene is generally associated with a transformation in final Upper Palaeolithic assemblages, especially in terms of increased microlithization. However, considerable technical and typological links exist, especially between the Ahrensburgian and early Mesolithic, but also with other traditions. In Benelux, for example, De Bie and Vermeersch (1998, 39) argue that Ahrensburgian groups expanded from the north into areas abandoned by Federmessergruppen and that 'with the onset of the Holocene, some Early Mesolithic tool assemblages are clearly derived from the Ahrensburgian, whereas knapping techniques at other sites seem to point to *Federmesser* influences', suggesting that even in its earliest manifestations Mesolithic cultures were not an outcome of a single tradition, but were formed by integrating different traditions or even, in this case, populations (for similar processes in northern Scandinavia, see Blankholm 2009). Genetic evidence (e.g. Oppenheimer 2006) may suggest two strands of Mesolithic expansions, from Iberia and the Balkans, further raising the possibility of discrete populations meeting, integrating, and transforming (see also Gamble et al. 2006). Recent years have seen some emphasis on interactions between communities at the end of the Mesolithic—with groups of hunter-gatherers and farmers (both possibly mobile at different scales and in different ways) forming new kinds of communalities in the context of frontier or border zones that allow for the renegotiation and transformation of identity (see Kostakis 2005). Gronenborn, for example, suggests of the fifth millennium cal BC in Germany that '(w)e know that out of migrant and local communities certain multi-traditional societies emerged which formed the basis for Neolithic social and political life' (Gronenborn 2009, 540). A longer perspective suggests that late Mesolithic communities adopting and integrating ideas from agricultural neighbours and reformulating and changing the nature of their communities is simply a continued manifestation of a trend that existed throughout the Mesolithic.

Again at the most general level, settlement expands back across north-western Europe in the Mesolithic, and most areas see Mesolithic settlement of some kind, including, it appears, the colonization of the Orkney and Shetland Islands, the latter lying at 60°N latitude, and which may have seen the deliberate introduction of ungulates (Edwards et al. 2009).

Evidence for settlement early within the Mesolithic is surprisingly absent from some areas, such as the island of Ireland where the first evidence lies in the centuries following 8000 cal BC (Bayliss and Woodman 2009; Woodman 2009), but colonization can only be considered in terms of the strategies and decisions of colonizing groups (Finlayson 1999) and there may have been little justification for colonization of some areas, whilst small-scale pioneering visits may have low archaeological visibility. Population growth has not been accessed in a meaningful way but is often assumed to have taken place at a gross level although there has been little or no serious discussion of the impact of oscillations in population over time (for discussion, see Spikins 2000). It should not be seen as a necessary driver of social change in the period without clear demonstration that it was happening at a particular time and place.

Subsistence strategies changed over time as landscapes changed. A diversification of settlement and resource base appears to have taken place with much local variation and a range of evidence for exploitation of a variety of plants, animals, and fish (both fresh- and sea water). It would be tempting to discuss a 'broad-spectrum' diet, but our models lack precision to really assess change over time to any meaningful degree. As noted above, some Mesolithic communities may have deliberately introduced boar to islands, and 'management' of wild animals has been discussed significantly in the literature: domestic dogs were present, occasionally treated with some formality in funerary contexts (Larsson 1990) and a captive bear from La Grande-Rivoire (Isère, France) suggests complex relationships linking humans and other animals (Chaix et al. 1997). Marine and lacustrine resources were important, to some communities at least. The role of deep-sea fishing has been questioned (Pickard and Bonsall 2004), but the extensive and intensive use of marine resources on a very large scale by some Mesolithic communities is well attested and exemplified by the Ertebølle (see below). Plants too, appear to have been very significant to some communities (for a review see Zvelebil 1994): at Staosnaig, in western Scotland, tens or possibly hundreds of thousands of hazelnuts were found in one feature, the product of some 5,000 trees (Mithen et al. 2001). Diets may have been very varied: even in comparatively small areas, such as the islands of Britain or Ireland, isotopic data suggest communities with very distinct diets, some appearing to rely mainly on terrestrial sources of protein, others on marine sources (e.g. Milner 2006): trends over time to an increasing marine influence at a European level are possible, but influenced strongly by biases (see below) and are the subject of fierce debate (see Milner et al. 2004 and responses, especially Richards and Schulting 2006).

The extent of 'regionalization' of Mesolithic groups varies over time. In the early Mesolithic some broad cultural groupings appear to exist and these can span large areas. The early Mesolithic (Maglemosian) is broadly similar in Britain, southern Scandinavia, and Germany: comparable artefact types, comparable site locations, depositional practices—even similar headdresses constructed of red deer antler. One must assume that these related groups of communities extended across the dry land of the North Sea Plain (e.g. Figure 24.2). David (2009) has demonstrated that traditions of bone and antler tool manufacture are also stable across broad areas in the earlier parts of the Mesolithic, itself suggesting a considerable strength of regional tradition at a broad scale. Later in the Mesolithic, in some regions at least, very small territories are apparently present. Marchand (2007, 27), for example, reviews multiple, separate inland and coastal archaeological groupings in late Mesolithic Brittany, and some models have attempted to track the movement of women in marriage between inland and coastal groups (Schulting and Richards 2001). Yven argues that this restriction of space in Brittany is a development from the middle Mesolithic onwards (Yven 2004). A genuine trend to smaller 'territories' over time appears to be present across much of the region. Yet the meaning of these archaeologically defined territories remains difficult to assess (Bergsvik 2003; Warren 2009) and it would be too simplistic to associate particular archaeologically defined groups with any kind of ethnic or biological population. Most groups appear to be extensively linked by exchange networks, which again operate at multiple differing scales. For everything that divides communities, other themes can be adduced that link them.

Across this broad region, one can sometimes identify periods of change, but there appear, consistently, to be exceptions or variations in how changes work through particular contexts. For example, at the largest of scales most of Europe switches to trapezoidal microlithic arrowheads at $c.6500$–6200 cal BC, the later dates coming from further north (Verhart 2008, 172), the change happening against a proliferation of local archaeological groupings. Britain and Ireland, the former probably newly separated from the continent, do not make this change, and might therefore appear cut off from broader trends. At some stage in the centuries following 7000 BC, however, changes in the nature of the Irish Mesolithic take place, from a structured and archaeologically visible early Mesolithic to a late Mesolithic situation characterized by limited evidence, sometimes interpreted in terms of an apparently more ephemeral, mobile settlement system, but in truth, poorly understood (for discussion and outline of interpretive models, see Woodman and Andersen 1990). These changes are also associated with transformations in the character of stone tools, creating a distinction between Ireland and Britain. The reasons for and nature of this change are poorly understood, but may be broadly paralleled in Germany following 7000 BC, where 'during the late Mesolithic the number of archaeologically visible sites decreases' (Gronenborn 1999, 137). In southern England and Wales a tradition of cave burial appears to end in the centuries immediately following 6000 BC indicating 'changes in attitudes to the dead' (Conneller 2006, 147); the tradition in England probably ending much earlier than it did in Wales and neither change matching wider transformations in the form of lithic assemblages from 'early' to 'late' Mesolithic in this region, often the basis for our chronological modelling (and that distinction itself increasingly broken down as more detailed work establishes more refined typological sequences).

The time-scales here are approximate, but hint of multiple changes across broad areas in the centuries following 7000 cal BC. Gronenborn suggests that this period was a time of 'crisis' for Mesolithic groups in central Europe (Gronenborn 1999, 137), and the impact of climate change and tsunamis at the end of this millennium was noted above, and may have formed part of the challenges facing communities. It would be tempting to think that the significance of changes at the end of the seventh millennium BC in north-west Europe was connected with this 'crisis', but we know all too little about the rhythms of change in Mesolithic Europe, as many of our chronologies are comparatively crude. Critically, it is difficult to assess whether this frequency of change is unusual in the period in this region— the long review of changes from the late glacial onwards may suggest that change of this kind was more-or-less routine. Speculatively, it is interesting to note that recent work in the Mediterranean suggests that:

> (t)he abrupt climate change of 8200 cal BP has had a clear taphonomic impact on the first Neolithic and the last Mesolithic sites in valley bottoms and in karst areas... These processes explain how difficult it is for prehistorians to find evidence for the transition between the Mesolithic and Neolithic.
>
> (Berger and Guilaine 2010, 45)

Some of the causal links between apparently synchronous events in different areas may need to be carefully evaluated.

In general, therefore, the Mesolithic can be seen as a number of transformations to existing ways of life including the combination of traditions from different sources. Changing landscapes presented a series of changes to settlement routines, especially, perhaps, the scale and character of routine mobility. There are hints of key periods of change, but our chronological resolution for connecting widely disparate changes is poor. Transformations were an ongoing aspect of Mesolithic life, even understood at this large scale.

The Ertebølle: Exemplars

The latest Mesolithic communities of southern Scandinavia (the Ertebølle) are a dramatic archaeological manifestation of Mesolithic lifestyles and provide evidence for both intensive and extensive subsistence strategies and complex internal and external social relationships. As noted above, they often form the dominant image of the Mesolithic of Europe (see below for discussion).

Marine resources targeted by Ertebølle communities include seal and small whales as well as an extensive range of fish and shellfish. Many sites are located in prime fishing locations and stationary fish traps were used and a variety of hooks, nets, and spears/leisters have been recovered to catch marine and freshwater fish. The Ertebølle utilized a 'delayed return' economic system (Woodburn 1980) whereby considerable investment in facilities is made; this included substantial log boats (Andersen 1985). Some forms of exploitation were very specialized: the inland site of Ringkloster appears to have been particularly targeted for pine marten fur (Andersen 1998; Richter 2005) and Aggersund for the exploitation of migratory swans (Andersen 1979). It has often been argued that such specialized practices were related to extensive trade networks, especially the role possibly played by fur in exchange with neighbouring farmers (for review, see Zvelebil 2008). Mammals were also extensively exploited, Blankholm arguing that land mammal exploitation was 'very substantial compared to that of marine resources' (Blankholm 2008, 117). Kubiak-Martens (1999) has demonstrated the wide range of plant foods also utilized alongside the archaeologically ubiquitous hazelnut. The economy in general appears to be broad spectrum, with some very specialized aspects.

Evidence for Ertebølle buildings is hard to come by: excavations at Tågerup, Scania include two circular huts (c.7.5 m diameter) and one 'long house', 15 m × 6 m with post holes and pavements (Karsten and Knarrström 2001). Such structures, however, are exceptional. Material culture includes some very fine and highly decorated objects, but is often fairly simple, described as being of a 'minimal nature' (Price and Gebauer 2005, 140). A small range of ceramics are present and appear to form part of a broader regional tradition of pointed-based vessels, and may relate to contact with ceramic-using hunter-gatherer groups to the east, as well as farming Neolithic communities to the south (Gronenborn 2009). Perforated shoe last adzes were imported from farming communities to the south and may have played a role in the maintenance of power and prestige relationships in Ertebølle communities (Klassen 2002). Metalwork was also imported, and some copper axes may indicate contact with Serbia (Klassen 2002). The nature of exports is less clear: seal fats, forest products, and furs are often discussed.

Burial evidence is varied in kind, but the archaeological imagination is dominated by cemeteries (see Nilsson Stutz 2003), especially Vedbæk-Bogebakken and Skateholm. These cemeteries hint at status variations between individuals, but there are few systematic patterns and the nature of hierarchy and gender relationships remains debated. Interpersonal violence is attested on many skeletal remains (for discussion see Thorpe 2003) and has sometimes been connected with evidence of territoriality in artefact distributions and morphology; some of the postulated territories are small (but see above for discussion of the difficulties of interpreting this data). The burials have allowed some examination of Ertebølle belief systems, sometimes drawing heavily on historical and environmentally founded analogies with (near) modern hunter-gatherers of northern Europe (e.g. Zvelebil 2003) and it has been argued that hunter-gatherer ideological systems of these kinds played a key role in structuring the adoption of agriculture in the Baltic (Zvelebil 2008).

The Ertebølle thus appear to manifest the culmination of many of the generalized trends of the European Mesolithic. In the face of increased aforestation and the increased length of coastlines caused by climate change, they operated an extensive and intensive economy, with a major emphasis on marine resources (most accounts stress this aspect of the economy rather than any other). Considerable investment was placed in substantial long-term facilities such as fish traps, and some communities appear to be sedentary, not mobile. Both are argued to lead to the increasingly exclusive association of communities with particular places. Territories were small, apparently representing the culmination of the reduction in territory size from the broad European plains of the late glacial and early Holocene. These territories may themselves be linked with the appearance of cemeteries, as ancestral markers, and the evidence for interpersonal violence. Ritual was complex, and wealth was present. Trade and exchange relationships existed with neighbouring communities, including farmers, and appeared to focus on non-utilitarian artefacts. As such the Ertebølle appear to be archaeological exemplars of 'complex hunter-gatherers' and, as the latest Mesolithic communities in their region, the climax of a historical process of change. Ultimately, for many commentators, the adoption of agricultural technologies by these hunter-gatherers is itself the outcome of these same processes.

OTHER STORIES

The detail by which we understand the Ertebølle, and the ease-of-fit of this model with generalized evolutionary schema, has allowed them to stand in for the Mesolithic as a whole in north-west Europe, with these particular processes of transformation often assumed to take place elsewhere. Many factors have encouraged this substitution including: a long history of research in south Scandinavia incorporating very high-quality excavations; an emphasis on excavating shell middens, with the consequent availability of faunal data; integration of archaeology and the natural sciences in the Scandinavian research traditions; an emphasis on underwater archaeology (e.g. Andersen 1985; 2009) that until recently was still comparatively unusual in north-west Europe; some spectacular finds not easily paralleled in other parts of north-west Europe; and a strong tradition of publishing in English. The Ertebølle are also the final Mesolithic culture in their region, and one that played an important role in the transition to agriculture in this area. Thus their particular manifestation of 'complexity' can be seen as a progressive historical trend. Archaeology is yet to shed the influence of social evolutionary thinking and this undoubtedly encourages the tendency to see the Ertebølle as the exemplars of the European Mesolithic. As Brinch Petersen and Meiklejohn argue:

> It looks as if this expression (complexity) instead of being an analytical term, a heuristic devise (sic), has become the ultimate goal, with all hunter-gatherers ending up with this designation... the tendency of today is quite clear, namely the later a Mesolithic group is to be dated, the more intensified tends to be its characterisation.
>
> (Brinch Petersen and Meiklejohn 2007, 187)

There are strong reasons to doubt that this process is universal or straightforward as a historical trajectory. Firstly, some of the assumed characteristics of 'complex' hunter-gatherers may not have been present in the Ertebølle: the identification of sedentism, for example, is much discussed, Blankholm concluding that '(t)he evidence for widespread sedentism or semi-sedentism is equivocal' (Blankholm 2008, 121). More importantly, the nature of coastal change in southern Scandinavia means that it is generally only later Mesolithic coasts that are available to us to examine coastal settlement. Therefore, 'we are prevented from evaluating the distinctiveness of the Ertebølle in relation to earlier periods of the Mesolithic' (Blankholm 2008, 120; see also Brinch Petersen and Meiklejohn 2007).

Furthermore, many of the attributes of 'complex' hunter-gatherers (long-distance exchange, hierarchy, sedentism, cemeteries, etc.) are not solely found late in the period, but move in and out of archaeological focus at different times in different places in Europe. Meiklejohn and colleagues, for example, have examined the appearance of cemeteries in the Mesolithic of Europe, arguing that contrary to the frequent statements that they appear in the latest parts of the Mesolithic 'they extend across the time breadth of the Mesolithic with apparent Upper Palaeolithic roots' (Meiklejohn et al. 2009, 639). Rowley-Conwy has argued that 'numerous examples reveal complexity coming and going frequently as a result of adaptive necessities' (Rowley-Conwy 2001, 64) and that evidence for intensification in the late Mesolithic of Britain, Ireland, and Denmark is lacking (Rowley-Conwy 2004). Rather than indicating the culmination of a particular trajectory, the transegalitarian/complex Ertebølle are best understood as one manifestation of one way in which hunter-gatherer societies may organize themselves, amongst many possibilities (see also Binford 2001; Kelly 1995).

As increasing quantities of work are undertaken by an increasingly dynamic community of Mesolithic archaeologists in Europe, alongside the wealth of materials recovered in the developer-led archaeological sector, a clearer sense of different hunter-gatherer lifestyles across time and space is becoming apparent. Louwe Kooijmans, for example, argues that:

> Until a few years ago and for want of something better; similar developments for the transition of hunter-gatherers to farmers to those supposed in Denmark were presumed for the Lower Rhine Basin late Mesolithic, i.e. a shift to a more sedentary society with a strong seasonal exploitation system, although archaeological evidence was almost non-existent and rather different from that in Scandinavia.
>
> (Louwe Kooijmans 2007, 292)

Detailed recent work in the Netherlands suggests both similarities—in the use of very long-term seasonal camps—and differences from the Ertebølle, the latter especially manifest in material culture, which is argued to provide links to the loess lands to the south and to northern France. Meanwhile, '(r)esearch in the southern Netherlands appears to point to the exact opposite (of the dominant Ertebølle model): more specialisation in the early Mesolithic, and smaller settlements in the late Mesolithic that also appear to have been used for shorter periods' (Verhart 2008, 181; note possible parallels to Ireland, above). The archaeological record of Britain and Ireland is, superficially at least, very different from that of southern Scandinavia, with little evidence of cemeteries, sedentism, or elaborate trade networks with farmers (see below) and Conneller and Warren (2006) have stressed that this material should be dealt with on its own terms and not as an impoverished reflection of the Ertebølle materials.

Understanding the Mesolithic of north-western Europe as encompassing a multitude of ways of living as hunter-gatherers each with their own trajectories of development in broadly related environments suggests that a finesse to Zvelebil's definition of the Mesolithic at a European scale as 'a historical process' is required (Zvelebil 2009, see above). Discussion of a singular process carries implications of a single outcome. A more useful definition would be of the Mesolithic as a multitude of historical processes, leading to different, if connected, end points. Such a definition is also more in keeping with current models of evolution. These are critical of the idea of progression over time and emphasize the ways in which evolution leads to variability, and in particular that evolution has itself led to 'the evolution of evolvability' (Sterelny and Griffiths 1999, 286)—the opening up of new possibilities for evolution.

Changing Archaeological Practices

Understanding alternatives to the Ertebølle model is complicated by the regional and evolving character of the evidence, which arises from the interplay of three factors: people's lives in the past, the preservation of evidence of those lives, and research histories; all of these heavily influenced by variations in the landscape. In this, of course, we must also consider the wholly transformative character of archaeological practice, where chance finds, or new analytical developments, can profoundly shift the study of a period. Liz Nilsson Stutz, for example, has argued that the discovery of Mesolithic cemeteries at Vedbæk-Bøgebakken and Skateholm played a key role in transforming the nature of archaeological understanding of Mesolithic communities in southern Scandinavia leading to a much richer perception of hunter-gatherer lives, and a focus on social relations:

> The effect on our view of the Mesolithic hunter-gatherer was immediate and thorough. This image was no longer other, no longer faceless.... our definition of the late Mesolithic society clearly began to shift from being 'simple' to being 'complex'... the discoveries also contributed to a re-evaluation of the late Mesolithic as a whole.
>
> (Nilsson Stutz 2003, 162–3)

Valdeyron (2008, 183, 200) suggests that the Péquart's excavations at Teviec and Höedic had a similar impact in France. The recent excavation of high-quality wetland archaeological sites in the Netherlands has led to a substantial increase in our knowledge of this region, but also to an expansion of dry-land archaeology, as Dutch researchers attempt to place sites with high-quality preservation into a broader archaeological context (see e.g. Rensink 2006). In this sense it is notable that the Mesolithic archaeology of Ireland, traditionally dominated by stone tools, has been enriched by finds of fish traps, baskets, lakeside platforms and related settlements, and burials within the last decade (e.g. Collins 2009; McQuade and O'Donnell 2007; Mossop 2009). These finds include significant examples of wetland archaeology and human remains, the two major transformative classes of archaeological evidence for the Mesolithic. The full impact of these finds on our broader models of Mesolithic life in Ireland has not yet been systematically explored.

Changing analytical techniques are also breaking down some of our familiar categories and thus causing their own transformations. Isotopic analyses of human bone for example present a challenge in providing information on an individual, which we must then find a way of relating to the time-scales of evidence incorporated into a midden, to choose another common source of dietary information: often these data seem incompatible, raising further questions about what, precisely, our different units of information relate to. The breaking down of our analytical units is also shown in new applications of high-resolution dating. The routine use of AMS dates on short-lived samples in conjunction with Bayesian modelling has been able to provide much greater precision in estimation of site age and longevity. Thus a possible short-lived phase of large (*c*.6 m diameter) huts appears to take place in northern Britain from *c*.8000–7600 BC on current evidence. It has also been possible to revisit old sites and challenge our interpretations: re-dating of Mount Sandel, in northern Ireland, demonstrates that rather than a sequence of huts, each associated with large and small pits, many of the large pits come after the use of huts on the site had ended, leading the excavator to make tentative links to contemporary pit features in Britain (Bayliss and Woodman 2009, 121) including pit alignments that may have served ritual functions (Murray et al. 2009). Increased resolution of this kind will transform our understandings of change over time in the Mesolithic. Zvelebil (2009) argues that at present we cannot write histories of the Mesolithic, but the increased application of Bayesian modelling to the Mesolithic–Neolithic transition in north-west Europe has begun to shift our attention to a generational time-scale, with profound implications for the kinds of histories that we are required to write of this period (Bayliss et al. 2007; Whittle and Bayliss 2007). It is wholly conceivable that, in certain circumstances, we will be able to write histories of the Mesolithic period.

Changing Scales

Running alongside changing analytical techniques have been significant changes in the nature of archaeological narratives of the Mesolithic period. The rise of an avowedly 'interpretive' Mesolithic archaeology since the late 1990s and early 2000s, has seen attention focus on particular contexts of human lives, often with an explicit emphasis on gender and other social identities and the relationship of communities with the landscapes that surround them. This 'shift from subsistence to substance, to a more explicit focus on the textures and tasks of daily life' (Finlay 2004, 68) suggests a further suite of transformations for us to consider.

An emphasis on the identification of children in the Mesolithic landscape, for example, has repopulated landscapes in Scotland and Denmark, and added to our understanding of site dynamics (e.g. Finlay 1997; Sternke and Sørensen 2009). The transformations in people's lives as they aged were probably the most immediate and profound transformations they experienced and yet we have often ignored them (but see Strassburg 2000). Similarly, startling evidence of ritualized burial practices of considerable complexity is often treated as a source of data for the nature of society, whilst the transformation of a living person into a dead relative, and the changes in social relations this implies, has seen less attention.

We must also assume that world views transformed, alongside changes in subsistence and settlement. This is, of course, difficult to access analytically. Finlay (2003a) has argued that the microlith itself may have served as an important metaphor for Mesolithic communities, with the multiplicity of components in a tool containing microliths potentially incorporating multiple people into a single object and acting as a reminder of the community. Changes in Ireland to a non-microlithic, non-composite stone tool technology are argued to be associated with changing metaphorical understandings of community, which may have been invested more in the construction of larger, semi-permanent features such as fish traps or weirs (Finlay 2003a; 2003b). Such accounts are stimulating, but still rare: all too often, we separate out the discussion of world view from consideration of changing patterns of settlement or subsistence. This is unfortunate, because the two were clearly linked. Crate, for example, discussing the impact of *recent* climate change on the Viliui Sakha of north-eastern Siberia argues that:

> These people can adopt some other mode of subsistence...Less is known about how the local effects of global climate change will play out in terms of a people's cultural predilections, the restacking and appropriating of their belief systems, and their cognitive orientation—their preconceptions of and assumptions about 'home', that cyclical arrangement of annual changes that supports the variety of plants, animals and ecosystems.
>
> (Crate 2008, 575)

It is in this context that the Intergovernmental Panel on Climate Change see the erosion of traditional Inuit knowledge as a threat to these communities' adaptive capacity, and that the Inuit Circumpolar Conference argued that climate change is an infringement of their human rights as it will lead to a loss of their culture and therefore their identity (Anisimov et al. 2007, 661). Too little is currently known about the long-term impacts of climate change on world view. The Mesolithic may provide a valuable point of reference.

Conclusion

I have argued that the Mesolithic of north-west Europe is characterized by ongoing transformations, many of which we only poorly understand the reasons for. The Mesolithic of this region witnessed profound transformations in people's lives. From our distant perspective, many of the day-to-day changes in people's lives remain obscure, and we have tended to focus more on the large scale and the general. Yet large-scale changes were manifest in people's day-to-day lives, and analyses that separate one from the other are incomplete.

Increasingly evidence demonstrates considerable variation in the Mesolithic of north-west Europe, and some of the dominant models of the period require finessing.

The multiple transformations in this period take place against a background of significant changes in the environment and in association with the complex histories of other groups, including, of course, those practising agriculture. Our descriptions of such transformations require us to emphasize variability and the developing potential for changes: the 'evolvability' of these cultures. In this sense, it is important to note that our understanding of the nature of hunter-gatherer diversity in the late glacial and early Holocene is very limited. As Jordan and Zvelebil have argued, the recent recognition of substantial ceramic use amongst many late- and post-glacial hunter-gatherers in northern Eurasia highlights strongly that 'the material and technological diversity of the late Palaeolithic and Mesolithic hunter-gatherers was probably far greater than we can even start to imagine' (Jordan and Zvelebil 2009, 76). In this sense, limiting the 'transformations' of the Mesolithic to one narrative is highly problematic. We know too little about the possible starting points, stopping points, and ends of such histories. The Mesolithic should not be perceived as part of a singular historical trajectory, nor as a process leading to complexity, but as a period of time when varied hunting and gathering communities actively constructed and negotiated their place in the world in a particular context. The Mesolithic was not a singular process, but the playing out of processes, with a variety of outcomes.

Acknowledgements

I would like to thank Vicki, Marek, and Peter for inviting this contribution and for their patience during its production. Nicky Milner and Thomas Kador provided valuable feedback on an earlier draft—I am grateful for their comments. Earlier versions of this chapter were presented at Aberdeen and Dublin, and I am grateful to the audience at both for discussion. Needless to say, all errors and misunderstandings are my responsibility alone.

References

Andersen, S. H. 1979. Aggersund: En Ertebølleboplads ved Limfjorden. *Kuml* 1978, 7–56.

Andersen, S. H. 1985. Tybrind Vig: a preliminary report on a submerged Ertebølle settlement on the west coast of Fyn. *Journal of Danish Archaeology* 4, 52–69.

Andersen, S. H. 1998. Ringkloster: Ertebølle trappers and wild boar hunters in eastern Jutland: a survey. *Journal of Danish Archaeology* 12, 13–59.

Andersen, S. H. 2009. *Ronæs Skov: Marinarkæologiske undersøgelser af en kystboplads fra Eterbølletid*. Moesgård: Moesgård Museum/Nationalmuseet.

Anisimov, O. A., Vaughan, D. G., Callaghan, T. V., Furgal, C., Marchant, H., Prowse, T. D., Vilhjálmsson, H., and Walsh, J. E. 2007. Polar regions (Arctic and Antarctic). In M. L. Parry, O. F. Canziani, J. P. Palutikof, P. J. van der Linden, and C. E. Hanson (eds), *Climate change 2007: impacts, adaptation and vulnerability. Contribution of working group II to the fourth assessment report of the Intergovernmental Panel on Climate Change*, 653–85. Cambridge: Cambridge University Press.

Ballin, T. and Saville, A. 2003. An Ahrensburgian-type tanged point from Sheildaig, Wester Ross, Scotland and its implications. *Oxford Journal of Archaeology* 22, 115–31.

Barton, R. N. E., Jacobi, R. M., Stapert, D., and Street, M. J. 2003. The Late Glacial reoccupation of the British Isles and the Creswellian. *Journal of Quaternary Science* 18, 631–43.

Bayliss, A., Bronk Ramsey, C., van der Plicht, J., and Whittle, A. 2007. Bradshaw and Bayes: towards a timetable for the Neolithic. *Cambridge Archaeological Journal* 17 (Supplement S1), 1–28.

Bayliss, A. and Woodman, P. C. 2009. A new Bayesian chronology for Mesolithic occupation at Mount Sandel, Northern Ireland. *Proceedings of the Prehistoric Society* 75, 101–23.

Berger, J.-F. and Guilaine, J. 2010. The 8200 cal BP abrupt environmental change and the Neolithic transition: a Mediterranean perspective. *Quaternary International* 200, 31–49.

Bergsvik, K. A. 2003. Mesolithic ethnicity—too hard to handle? In L. Larsson, H. Kindgen, K. Knutsson, D. Loeffler, and A. Åkerlund (eds), *Mesolithic on the move: papers presented at the sixth international conference on the Mesolithic in Europe, Stockholm 2000*, 290–301. Oxford: Oxbow.

Binford, L. R. 2001. *Constructing frames of reference: an analytical method for archaeological theory building using ethnographic data sets*. Berkeley: University of California Press.

Blankholm, H. P. 2008. Southern Scandinavia. In G. Bailey and P. Spikins (eds), *Mesolithic Europe*, 107–31. Cambridge: Cambridge University Press.

Blankholm, H. P. 2009. *Målsnes 1: an early Post-Glacial coastal site in Northern Norway*. Oxford: Oxbow.

Bond, G., Kromer, B., Beer, J., Muscheler, R., Evans, M. N., Showers, W., Hoffmann, S., Lotti-Bond, R., Hajdas, I., and Bonani, G. 2001. Persistent solar influence on North Atlantic climate during the Holocene. *Science* 294, 2130–6.

Bond, G., Showers, W., Cheseby, M., Lotti, R., Almasi, P., deMenocal, P., Priore, P., Cullen, H., Hajdas, I., and Bonani, G. 1997. A pervasive millennial-scale cycle in North Atlantic Holocene and Glacial climates. *Science* 278, 1257–66.

Bonsall, C., Macklin, M. G., Payton, R. W., and Boroneat, A. 2002/2003. Climate, floods and river gods: environmental change and the Meso-Neolithic transition in southeast Europe. *Before Farming* 4, 1–15.

Brinch Petersen, E., and Meiklejohn, C. 2007. Historical context of the term 'complexity' in the southern Scandinanvian Mesolithic. *Acta Archaeologica* 78, 181–92.

Chaix, L., Bridault, A., and Picavet, R. 1997. A tamed brown bear (Ursus arctosL.) of the Late Mesolithic from La Grande-Rivoire (Isère, France)? *Journal of Archaeological Science* 24, 1067–74.

Clarke, J. G. D. 1980. *Mesolithic prelude*. Edinburgh: Edinburgh University Press.

Coles, B. J. 1998. Doggerland: a speculative survey. *Proceedings of the Prehistoric Society* 64, 45–81.

Collins, T. 2009. Hermitage, Ireland: life and death on the western edge of Europe. In S. McCartan P. C., Woodman, R. Schulting, and G. M. Warren (eds), *Mesolithic horizons: papers presented at the seventh international conference on the Mesolithic in Europe, Belfast 2005*, 876–9. Oxford: Oxbow.

Conneller, C. 2006. Death. In C. Conneller, and G. M. Warren (eds), *Mesolithic Britain and Ireland: new approaches*, 39–164. Stroud: Tempus.

Conneller, C. 2007. Inhabiting new landscapes: settlement and mobility in Britain after the Last Glacial Maximum. *Oxford Journal of Archaeology* 26, 215–37.

Conneller, C. and Warren, G. M. 2006. Preface. In C. Conneller and G. M. Warren (eds), *Mesolithic Britain and Ireland: new approaches*, 7–10. Stroud: Tempus.

Crate, S. A. 2008. Gone the bull of winter? Grappling with the cultural implications of and anthropology's role(s) in global climate change. *Current Anthropology* 49, 569–97.

David, E. 2009. Show me how you make your hunting equipment and I will tell you where you come from: technical traditions, an efficient means of characterizing cultural identities.

In S. McCartan, P. C. Woodman, R. Schulting, and G. M. Warren (eds), *Mesolithic horizons: papers presented at the seventh international conference on the Mesolithic in Europe, Belfast 2005*, 362–7. Oxford: Oxbow.

De Bie, M. and Vermeersch, P. M. 1998. Pleistocene-Holocene transition in Benelux. *Quaternary International* 49/50, 29–43.

Edwards, K. J., Langdon, P. G., and Sugden, H. 2007. Separating climatic and possible human impacts in the early Holocene: biotic response around the time of the 8200 cal. yr BP event. *Journal of Quaternary Science* 22, 77–84.

Edwards, K. J., Schofield, J. E., Whittington, G., and Melton, N. D. 2009. Palynology 'on the edge' and the archaeological vindication of a Mesolithic presence? The case of Shetland. In N. Finlay, S. McCartan, N. Milner, and C. J. Wickham-Jones (eds), *From Bann Flakes to Bushmills: papers in honour of Professor Peter Woodman*, 113–23. Oxford: Oxbow.

Finlay, N. 1997. Kid knapping: the missing children in lithic analysis. In J. Moore and E. Scott (eds), *Invisible people and processes*, 203–12. London: Leicester University Press.

Finlay, N. 2003a. Microliths and multiple authorship. In L. Larsson, H. Kindgren, K. Knutsson, D. Leoffler, and A. Åkerlund (eds), *Mesolithic on the move: papers presented at the sixth international conference on the Mesolithic in Europe, Stockholm 2000*, 169–76. Oxford: Oxbow.

Finlay, N. 2003b. Cache and carry: defining moments in the Irish Later Mesolithic. In L. Bevan, and J. Moore (eds), *Peopling the Mesolithic*, 87–94. Oxford: BAR International Series 1157.

Finlay, N. 2004. E-scapes and E-motion: other ways of writing the Mesolithic. *Before Farming* 2004/1, 46–63.

Finlayson, B. 1999. Understanding the initial colonisation of Scotland. *Antiquity* 73, 879–83.

Gaffney, V. Fitch, S., and Smith, D. 2009. *Europe's lost world: the rediscovery of Doggerland*. York: Council for British Archaeology Research Report No. 160.

Gamble, C., Davies, W., Pettitt, P., Hazelwood, L., and Richards, M. 2006. The Late Glacial ancestry of Europeans: combining genetic and archaeological evidence. *Documenta Praehistorica* 33, 1–10.

Gronenborn, D. 1999. A variation on a basic theme: the transition to farming in Southern Central Europe. *Journal of World Prehistory* 13, 123–210.

Gronenborn, D. 2009 Transregional culture contacts and the Neolithization Process in North Central Europe. In P. Jordan and M. Zvelebil (eds), *Ceramics before farming: the dispersal of pottery among prehistoric Eurasian hunter-gatherers*, 527–50. Walnut Creek, CA: Left Coast Press.

Jansen, E., Overpeck, J., Briffa, K. R., Duplessy, J.-C., Joos, F., Masson-Delmotte, V., Olago, D., Otto-Bliesner, B., Peltier, W. R., Rahmstorf, S., Ramesh, R., Raynaud, D., Rind, D., Solomina, O., Villalba, R., and Zhang, D. 2007. Palaeoclimate. In S. Solomon, D. Qin, M. Manning, Z. Chen, M. Marquis, K. B. Averyt, M. Tignor, and H. L. Miller (eds), *Climate change 2007: the physical science basis. Contribution of working group I to the fourth assessment report of the Intergovernmental Panel on Climate Change*, 434–97. Cambridge: Cambridge University Press.

Jordan, P. and Zvelebil, M. 2009. *Ex Oriente Lux*: the prehistory of hunter-gatherer ceramic disperals. In P. Jordan and M. Zvelebil (eds), *Ceramics before farming: the dispersal of pottery among prehistoric Eurasian hunter-gatherers*, 33–89. Walnut Creek, CA: Left Coast Press.

Karsten, P. and Knarrström, B. 2001. Tågerup-fifteen hundred years of Mesolithic occupation in western Scania, Sweden: a preliminary view. *European Journal of Archaeology* 4, 165–74.

Kelly, R. L. 1995. *The foraging spectrum: diversity in hunter-gatherer lifeways*. London: Smithsonian Institution.

Klassen, L. 2002. The Ertebølle culture and Neolithic continental Europe: traces of contact and interaction In A. Fischer and K. Kristiansen (eds), *The Neolithisation of Denmark: 150 years of debate*, 305–17. Sheffield, J. R. Collis Publications.

Kostakis, K. 2005. Across the border: unstable dwellings and fluid landscapes in the earliest Neolithic of Greece. In D. Bailey, A. Whittle, and V. Cummings (eds), *(Un)settling the Neolithic*, 8–15. Oxford: Oxbow.

Kubiak-Martens, L. 1999. The plant food component of the diet at the late Mesolithic (Ertebølle) settlement at Tybrind Vig, Denmark. *Vegetation History and Archaeobotany* 8, 117–27.

Larsson, L. 1990. Dogs in fraction: symbols in action. In P. Vermeersch and P. Van Peer (eds), *Contributions to the Mesolithic in Europe*, 153–60. Leuven: Leuven University Press.

Larsson, L. 2009. The Mesolithic in Europe—some retrospective perspectives. In S. McCartan R. Schulting, G. M. Warren, and P. C. Woodman (eds), *Mesolithic horizons: papers presented at the seventh international conference on the Mesolithic in Europe, Belfast 2005*, xxvii–xxxii. Oxford: Oxbow.

Louwe Kooijmans, L. P. 2007. The gradual transition to farming in the Lower Rhine Basin. In A. Whittle and V. Cummings (eds), *Going over: the Mesolithic–Neolithic transition in north-west Europe*, 287–309. London: British Academy.

Macklin, M. G., Benito, G., Gregory, K. J., Johnstone, E., Lewin, J., Michczyńska, D. J., Soja, R., Starkel, L., and Thorndycraft, V. R. 2006. Past hydrological events reflected in the Holocene fluvial record of Europe. *Catena* 66, 145–54.

McQuade, M. and O'Donnell, L. 2007. Late Mesolithic fish traps from the Liffey estuary, Dublin, Ireland. *Antiquity* 81, 569–84.

Marchand, G. 2007. Mesolithic fragrances: Mesolithic–Neolithic interactions in Western France. In A. Whittle and V. Cummings (eds), *Going over: the Mesolithic–Neolithic transition in north-west Europe*, 225–42. London: British Academy.

Meiklejohn, C., Brinch Petersen, E., and Babb, J. 2009. From single graves to cemeteries: an initial look at chronology in Mesolithic burial practice. In S. McCartan, R. J. Schulting, G. M. Warren, and P. C. Woodman (eds), *Mesolithic horizons: papers presented at the seventh international conference on the Mesolithic in Europe, Belfast 2005*, 639–45. Oxford: Oxbow.

Milner, N. 2006. Subsistence. In C. Conneller and G. M. Warren (eds), *Mesolithic Britain and Ireland: new approaches*, 61–82. Stroud: Tempus.

Milner, N., Craig, O. E., Bailey, G. N., Pedersen, K., and Andersen, S. H. 2004. Something fishy in the Neolithic? A re-evaluation of stable isotope analysis of Mesolithic and Neolithic coastal populations. *Antiquity* 77, 9–22.

Mithen, S., Finlay, N., Carruthers, W., Carter, S., and Ashmore, P. 2001. Plant use in the Mesolithic: evidence from Staosnaig, Isle of Colonsay, Scotland. *Journal of Archaeological Science* 28, 223–34.

Mossop, M. 2009. Lakeside developments in County Meath, Ireland: a Late Mesolithic fishing platform and possible mooring at Clowanstown 1. In S. McCartan, P. C. Woodman, R. Schulting, and G. M. Warren (eds), *Mesolithic horizons: papers presented at the seventh international conference on the Mesolithic in Europe, Belfast 2005*, 895–9. Oxford: Oxbow.

Murray, H. K., Murray, J. C., and Fraser, S. M. 2009. *A tale of the unknown unknowns: a Mesolithic pit alignment and a Neolithic timber hall at Warren Field, Crathes, Aberdeenshire*. Oxford: Oxbow.

Nilsson Stutz, L. 2003. *Embodied rituals and ritualized bodies: tracing ritual practices in Late Mesolithic burials*. Stockholm, Almquist and Wiksell International: Acta Archaeologica Lundensia, Series in 8°, No. 46.

Oppenheimer, S. 2006. *The origins of the British: a genetic detective story*. London: Constable.

Pickard, C. and Bonsall, C. 2004. Deep-sea fishing in the European Mesolithic: fact or fantasy? *European Journal of Archaeology* 7, 273–90.

Price, D. T. and Gebauer, A. B. (eds) 2005. *Smakkerup Huse: a Late Mesolithic coastal site in northwest Zealand, Denmark*. Aarhus: Aarhus University Press.

Rensink, E. 2006. Stones or bones: on Mesolithic fieldwork in the Netherlands and the potential of buried and surface sites for the preservation of bone and antler remains. In C.-J. Kind (ed.), *After the ice: settlements, subsistence and social development in the Mesolithic of Central Europe. Proceedings of the international conference 9th to 12th of September 2003 Rottenburg/ Neckar, Baden-Württemberg, Germany*, 101–18. Stuttgart: Konrad Thesis Verlag.

Richards, M. and Schulting, R. J. 2006. Touch not the fish: the Mesolithic-Neolithic change of diet and its significance. *Antiquity* 80, 444–58.

Richter, J. 2005. Selective hunting of pine marten, Martes martes, in Late Mesolithic Denmark. *Journal of Archaeological Science* 32, 1223–31.

Rowley-Conwy, P. 1986. Between cave painters and crop planters: aspects of the temperate European Mesolithic. In M. Zvelebil (ed.), *Hunters in transition: Mesolithic societies of temperate Eurasia and their transition to farming*, 17–32. Cambridge: Cambridge University Press.

Rowley-Conwy, P. 1996. Why didn't Westropp's 'Mesolithic' catch on in 1872? *Antiquity* 70, 940–4.

Rowley-Conwy, P. 2001. Time, change and the archaeology of hunter-gatherers: how original is the 'original affluent society'? In C. Panter-Brick, R. H. Layton, and P. Rowley-Conwy (eds), *Hunter-gatherers: an interdisiplinary perspective*, 39–72. Cambridge: Cambridge University Press.

Rowley-Conwy, P. 2004. How the west was lost: a reconsideration of agricultural origins in Britain, Ireland, and Southern Scandinavia. *Current Anthropology* 45, S83–S113.

Schulting, R. J. and Richards, M. P. 2001. Dating women and becoming farmers: new palaeodietary and AMS dating evidence from the Breton Mesolithic cemeteries of Téviec and Hoëdic. *Journal of Anthropological Archaeology* 20, 314–44.

Simmons, I. G. 1996. *The environmental impact of Later Mesolithic cultures*. Edinburgh: Edinburgh University Press for the University of Durham.

Spikins, P. 1999. *Mesolithic Northern England: environment, population, settlement*. Oxford: British Archaeological Report British Series 283.

Spikins, P. 2000. Go forth and multiply? Gradual population growth reassessed—a case study from Mesolithic Northern England. *Archaeological Review from Cambridge* 17, 99–121.

Sterelny, K. and Griffiths, P. E. 1999. *Sex and death: an introduction to the philosophy of biology*. London: University of Chicago Press.

Sternke, F. and Sørensen, M. 2009. The identification of children's flint knapping products in Mesolithic Scandinavia. In S. McCartan, R. J. Schulting, G. M. Warren, and P. C. Woodman (eds), *Mesolithic horizons: papers presented at the seventh international conference on the Mesolithic in Eureop, Belfast 2005*, 722–9. Oxford: Oxbow.

Strassburg, J. 2000. *Shamanic shadows: one hundred generations of undead subversion in Southern Scandinavia, 7,000–4,000 BC*. Stockholm: Universitet Stockholms, Stockholm Studies in Archaeology 20.

Street, M. 1998. The archaeology of the Pleistocene–Holocene transition in the Northern Rhineland, Germany. *Quaternary International* 49/50, 45–67.

Street, M., Balles, M., Cziesla, E., Hartz, S., Heinen, M., Jöris, O., Koch, I., Pasda, C. T. T., and Vollbrecht, J. 2002. Final Palaeolithic and Mesolithic research in reunified Germany. *Journal of World Prehistory* 15, 365–453.

Thorpe, I. J. N. 2003. Death and violence: the later Mesolithic of Southern Scandinavia. In L. Bevan and J. Moore (eds), *Peopling the Mesolithic in a northern environment*, 53–58. Oxford: BAR International Series 1157.

Tipping, R. 1996. Microscopic charcoal records, inferred human activity and climate change in the Mesolithic of northernmost Scotland. In A. Pollard and A. Morrison (eds), *The early prehistory of Scotland*, 39–61. Edinburgh: Edinburgh University Press.

Valdeyron, N. 2008. The Mesolithic in France. In G. Bailey and P. Spikins (eds), *Mesolithic Europe*, 182–202. Cambridge: Cambridge University Press.

Vera, F. W. M. 2000. *Grazing ecology and forest history*. Wallingford: CABI Publishing.

Verhart, L. 2008. New developments in the study of the Mesolithic of the Low Countries. In G. Bailey and P. Spikins (eds), *Mesolithic Europe*, 158–81. Cambridge: Cambridge University Press.

Warren, G. M. 2009. Introduction: regional identities. In S. McCartan, R. Schulting, G. M. Warren, and P. C. Woodman (eds), *Mesolithic horizons: papers presented at the seventh international conference on the Mesolithic in Europe, Belfast 2005*, 333–5. Oxford: Oxbow.

Weninger, B., Schulting, R., Bradtmöller, M., Clare, L., Collard, M., Edinborough, K., Hilpert, J., Jöris, O., Niekus, M., Rohling, E. J., and Wagner, B. 2008. The catastrophic final flooding of Doggerland by the Storegga Slide tsunami. *Documenta Praehistorica* 35, 1–24.

Whitehouse, N. J. and Smith, D. 2009. How fragmented was the British Holocene wildwood? Perspectives on the 'Vera' grazing debate from the fossil beetle record. *Quaternary Science Reviews* 29, 539–53.

Whittle, A. and Bayliss, A. 2007. The times of their lives: from chronological precision to kinds of history and change. *Cambridge Archaeological Journal* 17, 21–8.

Woodburn, J. 1980. Hunters and gatherers today and reconstruction of the past. In A. Gellner (ed.), *Soviet and western anthropology*, 95–117. London: Duckworth.

Woodman, P. C. 2009. Challenging times: reviewing Irish Mesolithic chronologies. In P. Crombé, M. Van Strydonck, J. Sergant, M. Boudin, and M. Bats (eds), *Chronology and evolution within the Mesolithic of north-west Europe: proceedings of an international meeting, Brussels, May 30th–June 1st 2007*, 197–216. Newcastle: Cambridge Scholars Publishing.

Woodman, P. C. and Anderson, E. 1990. The Irish Later Mesolithic: a partial picture. In M. Vermeersch and P. Van Peer (eds), *Contributions to the Mesolithic in Europe*, 377–87. Leuven: Leuven University Press.

Woodman, P. C., McCarthy, M., and Monaghan, N. 1997. The Irish quaternary fauna project. *Quaternary Science Reviews* 16, 129–59.

Yven, E. 2004. The functioning of networks during the Mesolithic in western France: permanent traits and changes in the structure of territories. *Before Farming* 2004/2, 126–38.

Zvelebil, M. 1994. Plant use in the Mesolithic and its role in the transition to farming. *Proceedings of the Prehistoric Society* 60, 35–74.

Zvelebil, M. 2003. People behind the lithics: social life and social conditions of Mesolithic communities in Temperate Europe. In L. Bevan and J. Moore (eds), *Peopling the Mesolithic in a northern environment*, 1–27. Oxford: BAR International Series 1157.

Zvelebil, M. 2008. Innovating hunter-gatherers: the Mesolithic in the Baltic. In G. Bailey and P. Spikins, (eds), *Mesolithic Europe*, 18–59. Cambridge: Cambridge University Press.

Zvelebil, M. 2009. The Mesolithic and the 21st century. In S. McCartan, R. J. Schulting G. M. Warren, and P. C. Woodman (eds), *Mesolithic horizons: papers presented at the seventh international conference on the Mesolithic in Europe, Belfast 2005*, xlvii–lviii. Oxford: Oxbow.

CHAPTER 25

THE RESETTLEMENT OF NORTHERN EUROPE

FELIX RIEDE

Around 20,000 years ago, the Scandinavian ice sheet reached its maximum extent. Arctic desert regions devoid of vegetation were locked in permafrost and extended for several hundred kilometres to the south of the ice's edge, pushing plant and animal communities into refugia at lower latitudes, especially the Franco-Iberian region, Italy, and the Balkans (Hewitt 1999) as well as some cryptic refugia further north (Stewart and Lister 2001). Despite evidence for sporadic, perhaps exploratory excursions northwards dated close to the Last Glacial Maximum (LGM; Terberger and Street 2002) humans, too, had abandoned northern Europe at this time (Burdukiewicz 2001).

While information on past climate derived from traditional sources such as pollen has long shown that the period around the LGM was harsh in terms of both temperature and aridity, the new climatic proxy data derived from Greenland ice-coring projects clearly demonstrate that the amplitude as well as magnitude of the climatic changes that occurred at the end of the Pleistocene far exceeded any changes experienced by human populations in the Holocene, and that some of these changes occurred on time-scales shorter than one or two human generations—well within human experience (Figure 25.1).

The period following the LGM is known as the late glacial, which has been subdivided into a series of stadial (colder) and interstadial (warmer) phases. It is in this period that human populations expanded into previously depopulated landscapes. Western Europe was colonized by forager groups bringing with them a repertoire of tools that are most commonly referred to as Magdalenian, while eastern Europe saw the expansion of the makers of so-called Epi-Gravettian tool-kits. This recolonization process was contingent both on the ecological and geomorphological consolidation of previously glaciated landscapes, the successive northward movement of biotic communities of which these hunter-gatherers were members, as well as on a number of key inventions that facilitated the eventual development of recognizable arctic adaptations akin to those documented in the ethnographic record of northern peoples (see Hoffecker 2005a; 2005b). In addition, this process was structured by a number of environmental events and processes, such as the Laacher See volcanic eruption (c.12,920 BP; Schmincke et al. 1999), the inundation of the then dry North Sea landmass (Coles 1998; Gaffney et al. 2007; Weninger et al. 2008), and the step-wise formation of

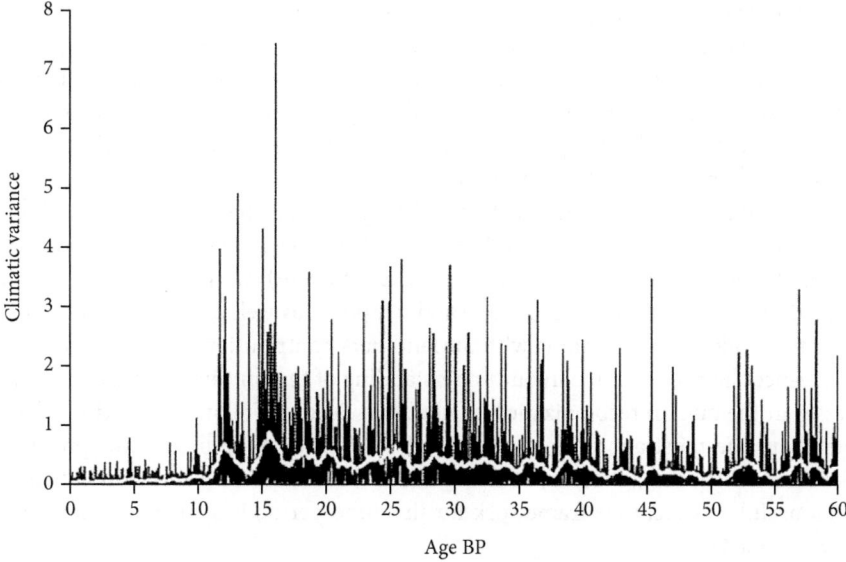

FIGURE 25.1 The 20-year interval measure of climatic variance (black) derived δO^{18} temperature proxy record of the GISP2 ice-core and its long-term trend (white line). This measure, calculated by taking the square of the difference between the δO^{18} values themselves and their 21-term binomial running mean, is an attempt to plot the intensity of climatic changes observable within an individual and generational time frame. Note how this variance increases in the last 16,000 years in spite of the overall warming trend following the end of the LGM. Modified from Burroughs (2005). For the most recent integrated ice-core chronology, see Rasmussen et al. (2008). Those peaks in excess of the mean plus one or even two standard deviations can formally be said to generate environmental stress, possibly beyond the damage threshold (Smith 2001).

the Baltic Sea (Björck 1995) that shaped the very landforms and thus the nature of human settlement in northern Europe. Following Maschner and Jordan (2008) these sudden and dramatic changes can be labelled as 'catastrophic' not in the sense that they were necessarily negative, but rather that they were rapid and of large geographic extent. Coupled with the very low population densities suggested for late glacial hunter-gatherers (Bocquet-Appel et al. 2005; Riede 2009b) these environmental upheavals would have posed a series of social, ecological, and demographic challenges for those groups moving into the empty and peripheral landscapes of northern Europe (Kelly 2003; Mandryk 1993). Rethinking this episode of pioneer human settlement in light of these considerations suggests a punctuated scenario, in which many archaeologically distinguishable technocomplexes or cultures are the direct or indirect result of such environmental or social catastrophes, as has been suggested for sequences of forager culture change in other parts of the world (e.g. Dumond 2004; McFadgen 2007; Prentiss and Chatters 2003).

The aim of this chapter is to review the pattern and process of the human resettlement of northern Europe and its attendant changes in the material culture, land-use, and economy of the participating forager groups. An understanding of the post-LGM recolonization of northern Europe must be underwritten by considerations of forager demography and the ecological, demographic, and social costs and benefits of reclaiming landscapes devoid of human settlement. While this process can, at a very general and geographically coarse level, be described as a rapid 'filling up' of the northern regions (e.g. Fort et al. 2004), analyses at smaller scales suggest a pronounced staggering of settlement phases contingent on, for instance, specific landscape types as well as the at times erratically oscillating late glacial climate (Conneller 2007; Riede 2007b).

Much previous research has focused on collating regional archaeological sequences (see chapters in Barton et al. 1991; Burdukiewicz and Kobusiewicz 1987; Larsson 1996; Soffer and Gamble 1990; Straus et al. 1996 and references therein), while more recent work has attempted to better understand the mode and tempo of, as well as the motivation for, this colonization endeavour. Beginning with the landmark contribution of Housley et al. (1997), large advances have been made in our understanding of the continental-scale patterns and processes in the human recolonization of northern Europe. Following a period of intense debate about the most appropriate use of radiocarbon dates to model this process (e.g. Blackwell and Buck 2003; Blockley et al. 2000; 2004; 2006; Housley et al. 2000; Pettitt et al. 2003), a useful and inclusive framework for this time-period has emerged (Gamble et al. 2004; 2005; 2006).

Gamble and colleagues have assembled a synthetic scaffold for the discussion of the human recolonization of northern Europe that incorporates recent insights from both environmental sciences (Lowe et al. 2008) and from population genetics (Forster 2004). Using radiocarbon dates as proxies for population density or activity, they recognize five phases:

1. Refugium (prior to 19,500 years ago).
2. Initial demic expansion (19,500 to 16,000 years ago).
3. Main demic expansion (16,000 to 14,000 years ago).
4. Population stasis (14,000 to 12,900 years ago).
5. Population contraction (12,900 to 11,500 years ago).

This framework will, with slight modifications in light of more recent work (Pettitt 2008; Riede 2008), serve as a scaffold for this chapter (Table 25.1). Phases 1 and 2 will only be described briefly here. We pick up the thread of these expansion pulses more firmly as hunter-gatherer groups begin to expand onto the Great North European Plain at around 16,000 BP.

Phases 1 and 2: The Magdalenian Prelude (<19,500 years ago to 16,000 years ago)

The contraction of human populations into LGM refugia is associated with three distinct technocomplexes—the Gravettian, the Solutrean, and the Badegoulian. The initially widespread and later fragmented Gravettian technocomplex probably formed the basis for the subsequent development of the western Solutrean and Badegoulian groups and the eastern Epi-Gravettian during the rapidly deteriorating conditions of the LGM. With a flourish of cave art, early ceramic technology, and the manufacture of organic tools, these

Table 25.1 The demographic framework for the resettlement of northern Europe, modified from Gamble et al. (2005). The phase divisions of the late glacial follow the suggestions of Björck et al. (1998) and Lowe et al. (2008). GS = Greenland Stadial, GI = Greenland Interstadial, IACP = Inner-Allerød Cold Phase, LGM= Last Glacial Maximum.

Event stratigraphy		GRIP ice-core years of onset (BP)	Chronozones	Population events
Holocene		11,500		
GS-1			Younger Dryas	5—Contraction
	GI-1a	12,650	Late Allerød	
			- LAACHER SEE ERUPTION -	
	GI-1b	12,900	IACP	4—Stasis or population decline
	GI-1c	13,150	Early Allerød	
	GI-1d	13,900	Older Dryas	3—Colonization, abandonment, and recolonization
	GI-1e	14,050	Bølling	
GS-2	GS-2a	16,900		2—Initial expansion in central Europe
	GS-2b	19,500		
	GS-2c	21,200		1—Refugia
GI-2		21,800		
			LGM	

groups represent a socially and technologically complex adaptation to Ice Age conditions (Roebroeks et al. 2000).

The subsequent Magdalenian technocomplex, named after the site of La Madeleine near Tursac in the Vézère valley (France) in turn furnished the demographic and material culture substrate from which the major western colonization pulses originated, bringing with them variations on the Magdalenian lithic tool-kit consisting of dihedral burins, endscrapers on blades (occasionally with fine, non-invasive lateral retouch), composite tools, and backed blades and points. The organic tool-kit includes *sagaies* lance tips (Bertrand 1999) and barbed points (Julien 1982; Weniger 1995) as well as other components of multi-part tools or weapons (e.g. semicircular rods). In addition, auxiliary tools used in the manufacture of arrow or spear shafts (e.g. perforated antler batons) as well as a host of personal ornaments and portable art are also preserved. In the open-air sites dominating the northern Europe record, however, such organic tools are rare, and their cultural affiliations are often not clear (e.g. Tromnau 1992). It is only in recent years that targeted dating programmes on late glacial organic tools have been able to shed light on the longevity of some Magdalenian traditions (Cziesla and Pettitt 2003), whilst also demonstrating that human occupation in some areas, for instance the Thuringian Basin (Grünberg 2006), was more curtailed than previously assumed.

The Magdalenian in the Franco-Cantabrian refugium went through a number of stages defined by parallel technological changes in lithic and organic technologies (de

Sonneville-Bordes 1963) with the earliest Magdalenian (sometimes referred to as the Badegoulian) bearing similarities to sites east of the Alps, such as Grubgraben (Austria; Montet-White and Haesaerts 1990). It is there, in the southern parts of eastern and central Europe, that the descendants of the cold-adapted Gravettians weathered the early stages of the LGM. Technological solutions to the challenges of arctic environments were developed and the subsequent recolonization of eastern Europe's river valleys began here (Dolukhanov et al. 2001; Hoffecker 2002). Attempts at modelling the spatial component of the human niche during the LGM (Banks et al. 2008) and the discovery and dating of sites located in the upland margins of central Europe (Terberger and Street 2002) attest to the spatially extensive but very low-intensity use of these landscapes (Gamble et al. 2005). Social alliance and marriage networks, reflected in shared symbolic currencies such as the classic 'venus figurines' known from both eastern and western Europe, provided the critical demographic scaffold for the adaptation to these exceptionally harsh conditions (Mussi et al. 2000). However, prior to the more sustained warming of GI-1, human occupation appears to have been strongly tethered to topographically complex landscapes and major river valleys, with cave sites targeted for habitation.

Phase 3: Expansion (16,000 to 14,000 Years Ago)

At, or just before, the onset of the GI-1e warm phase (the Bølling chronozone), hunter-gatherer folk of the middle/late Magdalenian traditions began to colonize more northerly latitudes. Central Europe (Jochim et al. 1999; Pasda 1998) and the North European Plain (Grimm and Weber 2008; Riede 2009c) as well as the British Isles (Barton et al. 2003; Conneller 2007) were first explored in this period. These new regions were, periodically at least, integrated into the Magdalenian world and these dispersals are associated with distinct changes in the material culture repertoires (Burdukiewicz 1986; 2001). The Creswellian, first defined by Garrod (1926), is the pioneer technocomplex in the north-westernmost regions of Europe, occurring particularly in Britain, but also in the Netherlands and north-western Germany (Barton et al. 2003; Gerken 2001; Thissen et al. 1996). Although separated by the lowlands now submerged under the North Sea, there would have been access to the flanking upland regions of southern and central England where human settlement is concentrated (Pettitt 2008), and where late glacial explorers integrated locales and landscapes visibly into their world though cave art (Ripoll et al. 2004). The precise role of the submerged landscapes of the North Sea during the late glacial remains difficult to assess, despite recent efforts at mapping out preserved sea floor features in search of prehistoric sites (Gaffney et al. 2007). While the low-lying land bridge between continental Europe and the British landmass would have, in the first instance, provided access to these northern uplands for the effectively terrestrial Magdalenian hunters, robust evidence for the sustained human use of the now submerged landscapes of the Dogger Bank—the so-called Doggerland—and the English Channel regions is in fact very limited, and generally dates to the Mesolithic or later (Andersen 2005; Coles 1998; Glimmerveen et al. 2006; Mol et al. 2006). In fact, low-lying and swampy, with little natural shelter and riddled with large rivers, these regions may not have been attractive or easy to traverse (Bjerck 1995).

The British late glacial assemblages reflect this duality of contact and isolation by, at times, showing clear links to continental European groups, and, at others, by displaying a degree of divergence that may be best explained by regional isolation. Creswellian assemblages display definite Magdalenian affinities, but are further distinguished by trapezoidal, angle-backed blades with a double truncation (Cheddar points) as well as backed forms with a single truncation (Creswell points). As in the continental middle Magdalenian, endscrapers on long blades, with the lateral edges often modified by fine retouch, are also encountered as are burins, often on prepared truncations, piercers, and *becs*, as well as blades, sometimes with scalar retouch, or truncated with heavily worn or 'rubbed' ends (for fire starting: Stapert and Johansen 1999), and splintered pieces. The blade and bladelet blanks for these tools are detached from single-platform cores probably worked with soft hammers and with prepared platforms in the *en éperon* style (Barton 1991; see also Barton et al. 2003; Jacobi 2004). Interestingly, the use of the landscape in this pioneering phase appears to have been restricted to locales and regions of upland character (Conneller 2007). As in earlier Magdalenian colonization episodes, landscape affordances and knowledge seem to have restricted human settlement to more or less familiar territories (Arts and Deeben 1987; Rockman 2003).

Until recently most information on the Creswellian came from old and, by modern standards, poorly conducted excavations. Its relationship to succeeding technocomplexes was not clear, but Pettitt (2008) has recently suggested on the basis of new results from the field that the Creswellian should best be seen as an initial, but ultimately unsuccessful, colonization pulse that is tightly circumscribed in its land-use and ends abruptly with the GI-1e. A plausible explanation for this demographic collapse may be sought in the isolation of these peripheral groups during this climatic downturn, which is mirrored in other regions further to the east on the North European Plain.

The pioneer settlement of that vast North European Plain is associated with the Hamburgian technocomplex first described by Rust (1937) on the basis of his excavations in the Ahrensburg Tunnel Valley north of Hamburg. Diagnostic tools are the Hamburgian shouldered points of initially 'classic' and later of the 'Havelte' type, *becs* with curved working ends (*Zinken*), and endscrapers, often with lateral retouch and a variety of burins. *En éperon* core preparation is also found, and the flint technology is generally extremely well executed (Madsen 1992).

While the colonization of Britain was facilitated by that region's complex topography that allowed people to target a fairly wide variety of resources, the Hamburgian occupation of the North European Plain was based on a specialized reindeer-hunting economy. Hamburgian settlement in the region seems linked to the initial immigration and a subsequent peak in reindeer presence in southern Scandinavia during GI-1e (Riede 2009c; Riede et al. 2010). Early Hamburgian settlement is restricted to landscapes that had not been glaciated during the LGM (Tromnau 1975; 2006). Only in its later Havelte phase do Hamburgian foragers include the newly de-glaciated landscapes of present-day Denmark and possibly southern Sweden as part of their territory (e.g. Andersson et al. 2004), whereas those areas of eastern Germany and Poland that had been fully glaciated were probably never settled during this pioneer phase (Terberger and Lübke 2004), and neither were regions to the east of the River Vistula (Bobrowski and Sobkowiak-Tabaka 2006).

Some have argued that these groups practised an early form of reindeer husbandry (Bahn 1984; Grøn 2005; Pohlhausen 1972), but there is little if any direct osteological evidence for such practices (Weinstock 2000). There is, however, considerable technological and ecological overlap between reindeer hunting and reindeer herding (e.g. Ingold 1986; Istomin and Dwyer 2010; Ventsel 2006), and the size and distribution of Hamburgian sites hint at a mobility strategy in which residential camps are relocated frequently, similar perhaps to that proposed for pioneer Palaeoindian settlers in North America (Surovell 2000). What little faunal evidence is available for this period points to a specialized reindeer economy, possibly of the herd-following type (Riede 2007b; see also Gordon 2003). It is likely that Hamburgian hunters used the bow and arrow, although the lack of readily available organic materials may have posed particular challenges for bow- and arrow-making (Riede 2010; Weber 2009).

The viability of specialized reindeer hunting has been much discussed, and it is generally acknowledged that although migrating reindeer effectively constitute a 'walking larder' (Clark 1967, 64) any attempts at herd-following in the absence of transport aids entail great costs due to the necessity of covering large distances, often in difficult terrain (Mandryk 1993). Fluctuations in the size of reindeer populations are pronounced and largely unpredictable due to their independence of predator–prey dynamics (Aanes et al. 2000; Solberg et al. 2001). Even in ethnographically documented societies living under much more benign Holocene conditions such fluctuations have led to severe economic hardship, starvation, and demographic collapse (Meldgaard 1983; Minc and Smith 1989; Stenton 1991). Interestingly, there is a close correlation between the radiocarbon dates for reindeer in southern Scandinavia (Aaris-Sørensen et al. 2007) and Hamburgian settlement (Grimm and Weber 2008). The Hamburgian appears shortly after the earliest evidence for reindeer in the area, but as reindeer populations declined sharply at the end of GI-1e, Hamburgian settlement appears to have ceased entirely. Taking into account the very low population densities of late glacial societies (Figure 25.2) and the challenges of operating at the periphery of human settlement it can be suggested that this way of life, and with it perhaps also these northern pioneers, disappeared as the climate once again deteriorated in GI-1d (Petersen 2009; Riede 2005; 2007b; 2009b; 2009c; 2011).

In sum, two major trajectories of change were introduced at this point, both with roots in the ancestral behavioural, technological, and economic repertoire of the earlier Magdalenian, and both relating to the rapidly changing environments of the late glacial:

1. In topographically complex and ecologically diverse regions, Magdalenian populations began to change their economy towards a more mixed and less specialized strategy (see Jochim et al. 1999).
2. Where the northward-shifting Ice Age habitat type was followed, the lack of ecological diversity was countered by specialization in particular resources, especially reindeer. Enhanced mobility served as the major mechanism mediating risk (see Halstead and O'Shea 1989).

Upland areas and areas long-since settled have yielded evidence of a more diverse economic strategy, incorporating seasonal horse hunting, small game, and, increasingly, aquatic resources (Costamagno and Laroulandie 2003), while the open landscapes of the North European Plain were settled by hunters who continued to practise specialized reindeer economies that included other resources only on a smaller scale and in a seasonal rhythm (Bratlund 1994; Kabacinski and Sobkowiak-Tabaka 2009). In addition to the pull factor of northward-migrating prey, late glacial foragers may have been drawn towards the harsh northern regions by attractive

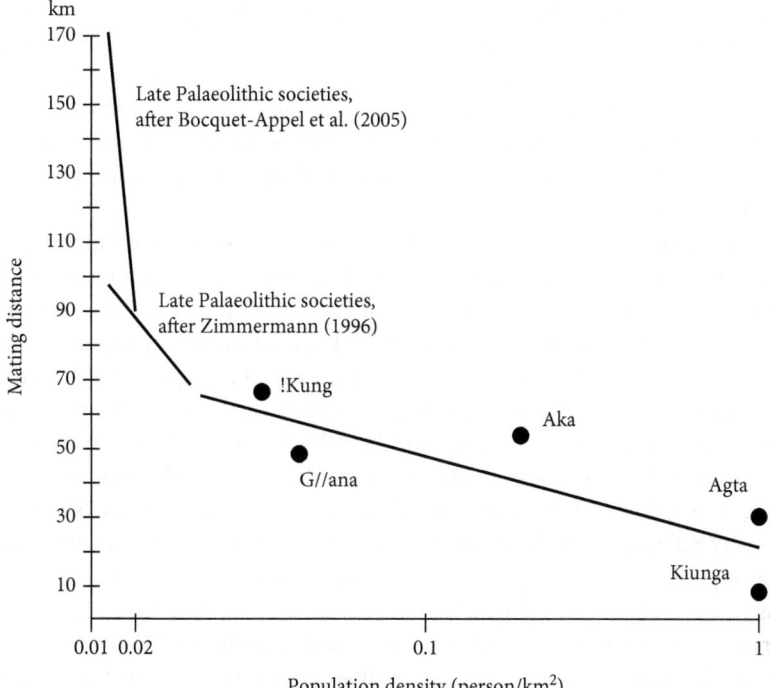

FIGURE 25.2 The mobility required to maintain viable bio-social networks amongst foragers (mating distance) has been investigated in ethnographic field studies (Boyce et al. 1967; Cavalli-Sforza and Hewlett 1982; Hewlett et al. 1982), and, using different estimates of late glacial population densities (e.g. Bocquet-Appel et al. 2005; Zimmermann 1996), can be extrapolated for the late glacial (see also Baales 2002).

resources such as arctic fur animals and other 'exotic' resources such as amber, which was used in the production of art objects and personal decoration (Álvarez-Fernandez 2009; Burdukiewicz 1999; Eriksen 2002). Indeed, this evidence for long-distance trade and exchange along natural corridors between widely dispersed Magdalenian groups at this time attests to the social and demographic imperative of maintaining regular contact (Gamble 1997; Whallon 2006). Wobst (1976) and more recently Gamble (1999) have argued convincingly that it was precisely these networks that underwrote the remarkable, nearly continental-scale material culture homogeneity of especially the middle Magdalenian.

Phase 4: Population Stasis (14,000 to 12,900 Years Ago)

Although characterized by population stasis in the scheme of Gamble and colleagues, the period between c.14,000 and 12,900 years ago witnessed a number of important demographic events, in particular the temporary contraction of populations along the settlement periphery—the groups that made Creswellian and Hamburgian tools—followed by a recolonization of some regions as early as GI-1d and certainly at the beginning of the GI-1c by late Magdalenian groups. The northern late Magdalenian is often referred to as the *Federmessergruppen* (Schwabedissen 1954), or by a variety of regional names: the *Tjongerian* in the Low Countries, *Penknife groups* in Britain, or simply by the generic terms *curve-* or *arch-backed point* (CBP/ABP) *complex*.

With the more sustained warming of GI-1d, woodland began to spread and northern ecosystems started to stabilize (Bennike et al. 2004). The source population for Allerød-period dispersal pulses is, as before, located in western Europe, although this time with a greater emphasis towards central Europe rather than the Franco-Cantabrian region. At the site of Le Closeau in the Paris Basin, for instance, a continuous stratigraphy covering most of the late glacial shows the development of the typical curve-backed *Federmesser* points and their continuation into the Holocene from earlier Magdalenian forms (Bodu 1998). Intriguingly, the peripheral populations appear to have made parallel use of the bow and arrow—tipped by those gracile curve-backed points—and the spear thrower—tipped by large tanged points usually referred to as Teyjat or Lyngby points (de Sonneville-Bordes 1969; 1988). Large tanged points are accordingly also found in the inventories of dispersing CBP groups, from England in the west (Barton 1992) far into eastern Europe (Sinitsyna 2002).

The organic tool-kit is further extended to include a plethora of harpoon forms, now primarily single-rowed with large barbs, as well as spear throwers, which are occasionally beautifully decorated, but again organic tools are rare in northern Europe. The first fishing implements are found (Cziesla 2001; Pasda 2001) along with a greater representation of fish bones in faunal assemblages (Le Gall 2003). While the economy and organic technology become more complex in this period, the stone-working technology trends towards shorter operational chains and simpler modes of execution (see De Bie 1999). Gamble et al. (2005) have noted that cave sites are increasingly abandoned in favour of open-air locales in this period. The richer sites dating to the early and middle part of the Allerød preserve traces of tent habitation structures, revealed by spatial analysis and refitting (Gelhausen et al. 2004). This shift in land-use preferences, coupled with changes in the distribution of animal and plant resources may have contributed to the abandonment of some previously occupied (cave-rich) areas such as the Thuringian Basin (Eriksen 2000), perhaps during the more hostile Intra-Allerød Cold Phase (IACP = GI-1b).

Labelling GI-1c and b as demographically stable hides a number of important shifts in the constitution and geographic distribution of the human meta-population at that time. However, the generally ameliorating climate of this period did allow populations to both consolidate their exploitation ranges and to again colonize peripheral regions that had become depopulated in GI-1d (Burdukiewicz 2001; Schild 1996).

Phase 5: Contraction

In contrast to Phase 4, the latter part of the Allerød and the GS-1 witnessed a substantial reduction in the extent of human settlement in northern Europe. Previously, this reduction has been attributed largely to the return of severe near-glacial conditions during GS-1.

However, recent work suggests that an initial population contraction began not with GS-1, but at c.12,920 BP following the catastrophic eruption of the Laacher See volcano, located in present-day western Germany (Riede 2007a; 2008).

It has long been known that volcanic material from the Laacher See is found at considerable distances from the eruption centre, and Schwabedissen (1954) already suggested that the widespread volcanic ash (tephra) layer from this eruption could be used as a chrono stratigraphic marker for the late Allerød. The Laacher See eruption (LSE) has been studied in considerable volcanological detail (Schmincke 2006; Schmincke et al. 1999) and its protective tephra blanket has contributed to the preservation of some of the richest late glacial campsites (Baales 2006). Laacher See tephra (LST) is found up to 1,100 km away from the eruptive centre with the main fallout lobes extending to the west, south, and north-east. An immediate area larger than 1,400 km^2 was covered in thick (>1 m) deposits, while an estimated total area of more than 700,000 km^2 was affected by fallout (Riede et al. 2011). A series of climatic fluctuations on an annual to decadal time-scale followed the eruption and may have depressed plant growth, at least in some areas (e.g. de Klerk et al. 2008; Litt et al. 2003).

While the general continent-wide climatic changes in the wake of the LSE may have affected contemporaneous forager populations in some way, it was the tephra deposition itself that precipitated—via a range of middle-range links (e.g. Riede and Bazely 2009; Riede and Wheeler 2009)—a number of population fluctuations and material culture transformations. Towards the north-east the landscapes covered in tephra fallout became virtually devoid of human settlement, leading to a breakdown of traditional trade, travel, and communication routes along the major river valleys (Floss 2000). The southern Scandinavian population found itself in a kind of 'splendid isolation': flint resources were plentiful in southern Scandinavia, and the environment during GI-1a was generally favourable. However, the result of their social isolation, coupled with the already peripheral position of these groups was that their tool-kit became 'simplified' (Barton 1992, 192), and their technology 'straightforward' (Madsen 1992, 134), 'poor' even (Becker 1971, 135). At this point, the so-called Bromme culture emerges, characterized not so much by the presence of large-tanged points (as these are ancestral in late glacial assemblages), but rather by the absence of curve-backed points. This absence may signify the disappearance of bow-and-arrow technology, as ballistic considerations suggest that—contrary to previous assertions (Fischer 1989)—such large-tanged points are better seen as tips for spear-thrower-propelled darts rather than arrowheads (Riede 2009a). The loss of complex technologies in connection with demographic isolation is known from the ethnographic record (Rivers 1926; Rowley 1985), and data on the exchange of 'exotic' raw materials and long-distance mobility for this period suggest a sharp decline in social/demographic connectedness during GS-1a (Whallon 2006). The catastrophic LSE therefore is causally implicated in the emergence of the Bromme culture in southern Scandinavia. It is less clear how foragers reacted to this volcanic fallout in regions such as south-western Germany and Switzerland (Nielsen 2009). Settlement clearly continued (Eriksen 1991), but population activity may have declined to a very low level (as judged by the number of sites: Newell and Constandse-Westerman 1999) and lithic technology experienced a decline in the quality of workmanship (Bandi 1968).

Some 200 years after the LSE, populations in northern Europe were again set into motion as temperatures plummeted with the onset of GS-1. Northern populations were pushed southwards and, coming into contact with the curve-backed point groups of the uplands, once again took up bow-and-arrow technology, albeit without changing the overall morphology of their armatures (Baales 1996). The Ahrensburgian and its eastern European counterpart the Sviderian (Kobusiewicz 2002) are characterized first and foremost by their diminutive tanged rather than backed points. It is likely that the British Isles remained depopulated for most of GS-1 (Jacobi et al. 2009), although there are enigmatic finds of Ahrensburgian points as far north and east as Scotland (Ballin and Saville 2003). These may indicate at least sporadic exploration from the east, or even the north, although a very late GS-1 or early Holocene date for these finds is most likely. Ahrensburgian reindeer hunters—for reindeer had reclaimed the North European Plain—roamed widely following their preferred prey (Petersen and Johansen 1996), but they did not encroach upon more southerly populations that continued the Late Magdalenian tradition (Cziesla 1992).

Into the Holocene

As the last Ice Age drew to its close, populations on the North European Plain were poised for yet another bout of expansion. As soon as temperatures began to rise at the very end of GS-1 Ahrensburgian and Swiderian groups travelled northwards. At first this may have been linked to the ecological succession driving reindeer herds northwards, but the settlement of the island-, sea-, and icescapes of the west coast of Sweden and south-western Norway attests to the rapid development of marine adaptations (Bang-Andersen 2003; Schmitt 1999) to take advantage of the extraordinarily productive coastal environs of Holocene Scandinavia following the drainage of the Baltic Ice Lake (Schmitt et al. 2006). It is likely that skin boats were in use for hunting and travel (Tromnau 1987) as was the dog (e.g. Baales 1992), which first appeared in the central European Magdalenian (Musil 2000) and Epi-Gravettian (Sablin and Khlopachev 2002). The tool-kit was re-expanded to include a wide array of organic tools—harpoons, bows, and arrows are known from the Ahrensburgian *locus classicus* (Rust 1958)—and the lithic material shows a bimodal trend both towards smaller as well as larger tools. This diverging trend may reflect a more hierarchical settlement organization, where light tools were carried on logistical, task-specific, and possibly largely pedestrian forays, while a more diverse array of activities carried out at the base camps increasingly required heavier tools, for wood-working, boat-, sledge-, or shelter-building. Despite the taphonomy-induced gaps in the record, the Ahrensburgian tool repertoire noticeably converges with ethnographic examples of arctic adaptations. By the same token, complex patterns of trade and exchange were re-established in northern Europe (e.g. Kindgren 2002), possibly with the development of economically symbiotic inland and coastal groups akin to the relationships found in northern societies of the recent past (Minc and Smith 1989).

North-eastern Europe, too, was incorporated into the settlement area and recent efforts at radiocarbon dating early Mesolithic finds from the Baltic region indicate a rapid movement of human populations into northern Fennoscandia (Bergman et al. 2004). Although north-eastern Europe appears to have been settled slightly later than corresponding western regions (possibly due to more pronounced continental climatic regimes), the eventual colonization proceeded rapidly and without major cultural upheavals. In contrast to the more punctuated development in the west, eastern Europe appears characterized by long sequences of cultural continuity and increasing regionalization lasting well into the late

Holocene (Zvelebil 2008). The descendants of the Ahrensburgian foragers, locally termed the Fosna (Bjerck 1986; Fuglestvedt 2007) and later Komsa traditions (Woodman 1992)—also known as the 'coastal Ahrensburgian' (Prøsch-Danielsen and Høgestøl 1995)—travelled along the Norwegian west coast, but others came, slightly later, via an eastern route with potential boundary and meeting areas in northernmost Norway and Finland (Grydeland 2005; Rankama and Kankaanpää 2008). Interestingly, these colonization routes correspond to those of other animals and plants (Hewitt 1999).

Although the demography of northern European populations by no means stabilized following the pioneer colonization (Price 1999), that process itself was complete by approximately 9000 BP. By this time, these northern foragers had developed a sophisticated technology and social systems adapted to survival in high latitudes. Dogs, sledges, skis, winter houses, summer tents, large and small boats, traps and snares, as well as a wide range of other specialized multi-component tools, instruments, and facilities were likely present. True marine adaptations in particular facilitated a permanent occupation of the northernmost arctic and subarctic parts of northern Europe (Bjerck 2009; Nygaard 1989), although it is only when rare instances of favourable organic preservation provide more complete glimpses of the sophisticated material culture of these peoples that more immediate comparisons with later prehistoric circumpolar groups are possible (see Hoffecker 2005b; Hood 1995).

Thanks to isostatic uplift, northern Scandinavia offers an additional line of evidence for the engagement of these pioneering groups with the environs and landscapes they inhabited: rock art. Although a precise dating of many examples of northern rock art remains difficult, some may be associated with the earliest phases of occupation (Bjerck 2008; Hejsedal 1994). The motifs (elk, reindeer, hunters on skis, boats, etc.) as well as their placement provide tantalizing insights into the social lives and cosmologies of these northern hunter-gatherers (Plumet 2006) and into the ways in which these foragers (socially as well as ecologically) enculturated pristine landscapes (Andersson and Cronberg 2007; Bergman and Zackrisson 2007; Fuglestvedt 2005; Riede 2005; 2007b).

Concluding Remarks

Stimulated in part by new population genetic methods of inferring past demography and population movements (see Forster 2004; Soares et al. 2010), the study of prehistoric movement, colonization, and migration has inched towards the archaeological centre stage once again. The human resettlement in northern Europe was certainly a demographically dynamic process that cannot be understood without reference to the complex patterns of, and reasons for, migration in hunter-gatherer societies (Table 25.2). Mobility and migration are fundamental tools of foragers for solving environmental and social crises, and the late glacial archaeological record attests strongly to the regular occurrence of the former and hints at the latter. The Laacher See event, for instance, led to widespread demographic and material culture changes, but what was the impact of the later, but equally dramatic, Storegga submarine landslide off the coast of Norway and the tsunami it generated (Weninger et al. 2008; see also Bondevik 2003; Dawson et al. 1990), or the numerous catastrophic lake drainages in inland Scandinavia following the rapid early Holocene wasting of the glaciers (Boaz

Table 25.2 The causes for migration found in the ethnography and ethnohistory of the Canadian Arctic, after Rowley (1985). Those causes marked with * are likely to have been important in the late glacial resettlement of northern Europe. Note that most of the 'social' reasons for migration can be brought on by environmental hardship, whilst subsistence and population failures—even those precipitated by environmental changes or events—ultimately have a social dimension (Mandryk 1993).

Cause
Environmental
• Natural disaster*
• Famine/illness*
Social
• Antisocial individual
• Fear of revenge
• Feuds
• Fear
• Expansion of territory*
• Search for rich(er) resources*
• Vision
• Desire to die in one's birthplace

1999)? Mindful of events such as these, future research must transcend current national borders and consider potential demographic and social cascade effects of population displacement, the destruction of traditional landscape affordances, and the collapse of trade and exchange networks due to demographic reconfigurations.

While we cannot readily equate particular tool types or technocomplexes with migrating populations, demographic models of culture change suggest that cumulative adaptive culture change (Shennan 2001) as well as the loss of cultural capital (Henrich 2004; Powell et al. 2009) are strongly contingent on the size, density, and connectedness of demes within a meta-population. The population densities of late glacial hunter-gatherer groups were low (Bocquet-Appel et al. 2005), making them vulnerable to stochastically induced loss of personnel, knowledge, and skills. As recognized by Gamble et al. (2005), the study of the resettlement of northern Europe in the late glacial is hampered by the lack of a coherent taxonomic system, within which archaeological units can usefully be employed in tracing past populations. If, however, demographic proxies such as radiocarbon dates are linked judiciously with material culture lineages, then the picture of the demography and migration history of the late glacial becomes much more turbulent, more punctuated, and more varied than has hitherto been assumed (Riede 2009c). The archaeological record of late glacial northern Europe overall quite clearly reflects the trends in the changing material culture repertoires and adaptations of more established continental populations, albeit in an incomplete manner. This incompleteness may be caused primarily by the periodic absence of human populations in the higher latitudes of Europe, and we should therefore not expect to be able to match the well-studied sequences of regions such as south-western France with those from northern Europe. Instead, future research should perhaps investigate the degree to which important connections and movements *along* the northern settlement periphery rather than between the periphery and the centre could have contributed to the observed material culture changes. What, for instance, is the precise (chronological and social) relationship between the Hamburgian, Creswellian, and curve-backed point populations on the British Isles? Recent discoveries have raised the possibility of both Havelte-phase Hamburgian (Ballin et al. 2010) as well as *Federmessergruppen* settlement in Scotland (Saville and Ballin 2010), whilst new finds in eastern Europe have pushed the boundaries of late glacial settlement also in that direction (Kabacinski and Kobusiewicz 2007). Major river networks have clearly structured communication and migration in the European Late Palaeolithic. Perhaps it will soon be possible to use the palaeotopography of Doggerland to make suggestions of salient routes of exchange and movement between the Magdalenian core and its northern periphery as well as along that periphery.

In a broader perspective, the late glacial human recolonization can be seen as an expansion of forager niche space along two fundamental dimensions, a geographic and a behavioural one. Following the lead of Odum (1971) and Odling-Smee et al. (2003) the former can be referred to as an organism's 'address', which changed rapidly following the LGM. Such geographic dynamics can be investigated using spatial analysis tools (Banks et al. 2008). The latter behavioural dimension, the organism's 'occupation' includes the introduction of dogs, of bow-and-arrow technology, of more efficient shelter, and of non-pedestrian means of transport, together forming a highly portable and adaptive niche package that allowed foragers to expand into the European Arctic (e.g. Forsberg and Knutsson 1998). However, the components of this package were only assembled gradually and were lagging behind the expansion of the geographic niche dimension, making earlier expansion attempts prone to failure. Prior to at least the very late GS-1 or more likely the Holocene, northern European prehistoric foragers should—in parallel with the environments they inhabited and the faunal and floral communities of which they were part (see Aaris-Sørensen 2009; Stewart and Lister 2001)—more appropriately be considered 'non-analogue', i.e. as markedly different from those hunter-gatherer groups known from the ethnographic record and as cultural evolutionary experiments, some which failed, some of which succeeded. Laland and Brown (2006, 98) note that 'even the most adaptable of creatures will experience limits to its tolerance space, outside of which it is unable to behave adaptively' and the environmental 'stress' (Brothwell 1998) generated by the rapidly and widely oscillating climate of the late glacial together with the numerous extreme geological events that occurred in this period may have pushed these opportunistic pioneer populations beyond their tolerance limits on more than one occasion. Clearly, these pioneers in western and eastern Europe were 'takers of opportunity' (Carlsson et al. 2005, 23), but if we are to seriously think about the human colonization of northern Europe as a demographic process we must be open to the possibility that the changes in lithic and organic technology documented in the late glacial and early Holocene record are not reflections of gradual changes in adaptation or identity of the same underlying population, but rather that these were carried by different populations. In meta-population approaches (e.g. Hänski and Gaggiotti 2004) regional extinction is common and a challenge for the years to come is to formulate models of prehistoric meta-population dynamics for northern Europe and to devise appropriate archaeological tools to put these models to the test. In this view, outlier sites such as Wiesbaden-Igstadt (Gravettian), Howburn and Kragola (Hamburgian), or Rundebakke (*Federmessergruppen*) may most appropriately be seen as reflections of opportunistic, short-term, and punctuated occupation episodes, which do not necessarily herald a viable human presence in these regions (see also Roebroeks 2006). Such models should also aim to incorporate the population genetic and ancient DNA data, which are becoming increasingly relevant to this debate (e.g. Karlsson et al. 2006; Lappalainen et al. 2008; Pereira et al. 2005).

Attempts to quantify and thereby clarify the demographic circumstances of particular colonization pulses will facilitate a more detailed comparative consideration of those aspects of the late glacial adaptive package that were critical for a socially and biologically sustained resettlement of northern Europe. Whilst the discovery and dating of the earliest sites in each region is of obvious and fundamental importance to addressing questions of pioneer settlement, we must also develop conceptual and methodological tools that can distinguish exploratory, transient, and perhaps unsuccessful settlement from a demographically viable presence of human populations in a region. While preliminary steps have been taken in that direction (Hazelwood and Steele 2003), future research into the human colonization of northern Europe may be best served by a multi-pronged approach combining the in-depth reanalysis of key assemblages (e.g. Jacobi 2004), with renewed efforts in the field (e.g. Pettitt 2008), and a review of (e.g. Grimm and Weber 2008), vigorous addition to, and meaningful analysis of our radiocarbon databases on a regional as well as a subcontinental level.

References

Aanes, R., Sæther, B.-E., and Øritsland, N. A. 2000. Fluctuations of an introduced population of Svalbard reindeer: the effects of density dependence and climatic variation. *Ecography* 23, 437–43.

Aaris-Sørensen, K. 2009. Diversity and dynamics of the mammalian fauna in Denmark throughout the last glacial–interglacial cycle, 115–0 kyr BP. *Fossils and Strata* 57, 1–59.

Aaris-Sørensen, K., Mühldorff, R., and Brinch Petersen, E. 2007. The Scandinavian reindeer (*Rangifer tarandus* L.) after the Last Glacial Maximum: time, seasonality and human exploitation. *Journal of Archaeological Science* 34, 914–23.

Álvarez-Fernandez, E. 2009. Magdalenian personal ornaments on the move: a review of the current evidence in Central Europe. *Zephyrus* 63, 45–59.

Andersen, S. H. 2005. En glittestok fra Dogger Banke i Nordsøen. *Kuml* 2005, 9–16.

Andersson, M. and Cronberg, C. 2007. Moving north: the first travellers to south Scandinavia. In B. Hårdh, K. Jennbert, and D. Olausson (eds), *On the road: studies in honour of Lars Larsson*, 145–50. Stockholm: Almqvist and Wicksell.

Andersson, M., Karsten, P., Knarrström, B., and Svensson, M. 2004. *Stone age Scania: significant places dug and read by contract archaeology*. Lund: Riksantikvarieämbetet.

Arts, N. and Deeben, J. 1987. On the northwestern border of Late Magdalenian territory: ecology and archaeology of early Late Glacial band societies in northwestern Europe. In

J. M. Burdukiewicz and M. Kobusiewicz (eds), *Late Glacial in Central Europe: culture and environment*, 25–66. Wrocław: Prace Komisji Archeologicznej.

Baales, M. 1992. Überreste von Hunden aus der Ahrensburger Kultur am Karstein, Nordeifel. *Archäologisches Korrespondenzblatt* 22, 461–71.

Baales, M. 1996. *Umwelt und Jagdökonomie der Ahrensburger Rentierjäger im Mittelgebirge*. Bonn: Verlag Rudolf Habelt.

Baales, M. 2002. *Der spätpaläolithische Fundplatz Kettig: Untersuchungen zur Siedlungsarchäologie der Federmesser-Gruppen am Mittelrhein*. Bonn: Verlag Rudolf Habelt.

Baales, M. 2006. Final Palaeolithic environment and archaeology in the central Rhineland (Rhineland-Palatinate, western Germany): conclusions of the last 15 years of research. *Anthropologie* 110, 418–44.

Bahn, P. 1984. Preneolithic control of animals in western Europe: the faunal evidence. In J. Clutton-Brock and G. Grigson (eds), *Animals and archaeology: 4. Husbandry in Europe*, 27–34. Oxford: Oxbow.

Ballin, T. B. and Saville, A. 2003. An Ahrensburgian-type tanged point from Shieldaig, Western Ross, Scotland and its implications. *Oxford Journal of Archaeology* 22, 115–31.

Ballin, T. B., Saville, A., Tipping, R., and Ward, T. 2010. An Upper Palaeolithic flint and chert assemblage from Howburn Farm, South Lanarkshire, Scotland: first results. *Oxford Journal of Archaeology* 29, 323–60.

Bandi, H.-G. 1968. Das Jungpaläolithikum. *Ur- und Frühgeschichtliche Archäologie der Schweiz* 1, 107–22.

Bang-Andersen, S. 2003. Southwest Norway at the Pleistocene/Holocene transition: landscape development, colonisation, site types, settlement patterns. *Norwegian Archaeological Review* 36, 5–25.

Banks, W. E., d'Errico, F., Townsend Petersen, A., Vanhaeren, M., Kageyama, M., Sepulchre, P., Ramstein, G., Jost, A., and Lunt, D. 2008. Human ecological niches and ranges during the LGM in Europe derived from an application of eco-cultural niche modeling. *Journal of Archaeological Science* 35, 481–91.

Barton, R. N. E. 1991. The *en éperon* technique in the British Late Upper Palaeolithic. *Lithics* 11, 31–3.

Barton, R. N. E. 1992. *Hengistbury Head, Dorset. Volume 2: The Late Upper Palaeolithic and Early Mesolithic sites*. Oxford: Oxford Committee for Archaeology.

Barton, R. N. E., Jacobi, R. M., Stapert, D., and Street, M. 2003. The Late-Glacial reoccupation of the British Isles and the Creswellian. *Journal of Quaternary Science* 18, 631–43.

Barton, R. N. E., Roberts, A. J., and Roe, D. (eds) 1991. *The Late Glacial in north-west Europe: human adaptation and environmental change at the end of the Pleistocene* London: CBA.

Becker, C. J. 1971. Late Palaeolithic finds from Denmark. *Proceedings of the Prehistoric Society* 37, 131–9.

Bennike, O., Sarmaja-Korjonen, K., and Seppänen, A. 2004. Reinvestigation of the classic Late-Glacial Bølling Sø sequence, Denmark: chronology, macrofossils, cladocera and chydorid ephippia. *Journal of Quaternary Science* 19, 465–78.

Bergman, I., Olofsson, A., Hornberg, G., Zackrisson, O., and Hellberg, E. 2004. Deglaciation and colonisation: pioneer settlements in northern Fennoscandia. *Journal of World Prehistory* 18, 155–77.

Bergman, I. and Zackrisson, O. 2007. Early Mesolithic hunter-gatherers and landscape acquisition by the Arctic Circle. *Journal of Northern Studies* 1–2, 123–42.

Bertrand, A. 1999. *Les armatures de sagaies magdaléniennes en matière dure animale dans les Pyrénées*. Oxford: Archaeopress.

Bjerck, H. B. 1986. The Fosna-Nøstved problem: a consideration of archaeological units and chronozones in the south Norwegian Mesolithic period. *Norwegian Archaeological Review* 19, 103–22.

Bjerck, H. B. 1995. The North Sea continent and the pioneer settlement of Norway. In A. Fischer (ed.), *Man and sea in the Mesolithic*, 131–44. Oxford: Oxbow.

Bjerck, H. B. 2008. Norwegian Mesolithic trends: a review. In G. Bailey and P. Spikins (eds), *Mesolithic Europe*, 60–106. Cambridge: Cambridge University Press.

Bjerck, H. B. 2009. Colonizing seascapes: comparative perspectives on the development of maritime relations in Scandinavia and Patagonia. *Arctic Anthropology* 46, 118–31.

Björck, S. 1995. A review of the history of the Baltic Sea, 13,0–8,0 ka BP. *Quaternary International* 27, 19–40.

Björck S., Walker, M. J. C., Cwynar, L. C., Johnsen, S., Knudsen, K.-L., Lowe, J. J., and Wohlfarth, B. 1998. An event stratigraphy for the last termination in the North Atlantic region based on the Greenland ice-core record: a proposal by the INTIMATE group. *Journal of Quaternary Science* 13, 283–92.

Blackwell, P. G. and Buck, C. E. 2003. The Late Glacial human reoccupation of north-western Europe: new approaches to space-time modelling. *Antiquity* 77, 232–40.

Blockley, S. P. E., Blockley, S. M., Donahue, R. E., Lane, C. S., Lowe, J. J., and Pollard, A. M. 2006. The chronology of abrupt climate change and Late Upper Palaeolithic human adaptation in Europe. *Journal of Quaternary Science* 21, 575–84.

Blockley, S. P. E., Donahue, R. E., and Pollard, A. M. 2000. Rapid human response to Late Glacial climate change: a reply to Housley et al. (2000). *Antiquity* 74, 427–8.

Blockley, S. P. E., Lowe, J. J., Walker, M. J. C., Asioli, A., Trincardi, F., Coope, G. R., and Donahue, R. E. 2004. Bayesian analysis of radiocarbon chronologies: examples from the European Late-Glacial. *Journal of Quaternary Science* 19, 159–75.

Boaz, J. 1999. The Mesolithic of central Scandinavia: status and perspectives. In J. Boaz (ed.), *The Mesolithic of central Scandinavia*, 11–25. Oslo: Universitetets Oldsaksamling.

Bobrowski, P. and Sobkowiak-Tabaka, I. 2006. How far east did the Hamburgian culture reach? *Archaeologia Baltica* 7, 11–20.

Bocquet-Appel, J.-P., Demars, P.-Y., Noiret, L., and Dobrowsky, D. 2005. Estimates of Upper Palaeolithic meta-population size in Europe from archaeological data. *Journal of Archaeological Science* 32, 1656–68.

Bodu, P. 1998. Magdalenians-early Azilians in the centre of the Paris Basin: a filiation? The example of Le Closeau (Rueil-Malmaison, France). In S. Milliken (ed.), *The organization of lithic technology in Late Glacial and Early Postglacial of Europe*, 131–47. Oxford: Oxbow.

Bondevik, S. 2003. Storegga tsunami sand in peat below the Tapes beach ridge at Harøy, western Norway, and its possible relation to an early Stone Age settlement. *Boreas* 32, 476–83.

Boyce, A. J., Küchemann, C. F., and Harrison, G. A. 1967. Neighbourhood knowledge and the distribution of marriage distances. *Annals of Human Genetics* 30, 335–8.

Bratlund, B. 1994. A survey of subsistence and settlement pattern of the Hamburgian culture in Schleswig-Holstein. *Jahrbuch des Römisch-Germanischen Zentralmuseums Mainz* 41, 59–93.

Brothwell, D. 1998. Stress as an aspect of environmental studies. *Environmental Archaeology* 2, 7–13.

Burdukiewicz, J. M. 1986. *Late Pleistocene shouldered point assemblages in western Europe*. Leiden: E. J. Brill.

Burdukiewicz, J. M. 1999. Late Palaeolithic amber in northern Europe. In B. Kosmowska-Ceranowicz and H. Paner (eds), *Investigations into amber*, 99–109. Gdansk: The Archaeological Museum in Gdansk.

Burdukiewicz, J. M. 2001. The last Ice Age and settlement break in the northern part of Central Europe. *Fontes Archaeologici Posnanienses* 39, 15–29.

Burdukiewicz, J. M. and Kobusiewicz, M. (eds) 1987. *Late Glacial in Central Europe: culture and environment.* Cracow: Prace Komisji Archeologicznej.

Burroughs, W. J. 2005. *Climate change in prehistory: the end of the reign of chaos.* Cambridge: Cambridge University Press.

Carlsson, T., Gruber, G., and Molin, F. 2005. The Mesolithic in Östergötland: an introduction. In G. Gruber (ed.), *Identities in transition: Mesolithic strategies in the Swedish province of Östergötland*, 8–23. Linköping: Riksantikvarieämbetet.

Cavalli-Sforza, L. L. and Hewlett, B. 1982. Exploration and mating range in African Pygmies. *Annals of Human Genetics* 46, 257–70.

Clark, J. G. D. 1967. *The Stone Age hunters.* New York: McGraw-Hill.

Coles, B. J. 1998. Doggerland: a speculative survey. *Proceedings of the Prehistoric Society* 64, 45–81.

Conneller, C. 2007. Inhabiting new landscapes: settlement and mobility in Britain after the Last Glacial Maximum. *Oxford Journal of Archaeology* 26, 215–37.

Costamagno, S. and Laroulandie, V. (eds) 2003. *Zooarchaeological insights into Magdalenian lifeways.* Oxford: Archaeopress.

Cziesla, E. 1992. Ahrensburger Jäger in Südwestdeutschland? *Archäologisches Korrespondenzblatt* 22, 13–26.

Cziesla, E. 2001. Neue Altfunde aus Pritzerbe (Brandenburg). Zugleich ein Beitrag zum Fischfang und zum steinzeitlichen Angelhaken. *Ethnographisch-Archäologische Zeitschrift* 42, 473–504.

Cziesla, E. and Pettitt, P. 2003. AMS-14C-datierungen von spätpaläolithischen und mesolithischen Funden aus dem Bützsee (Brandenburg). *Archäologisches Korrespondenzblatt* 33, 21–38.

Dawson, A. G., Smith, D. E., and Long, D. 1990. Evidence for a tsunami from a Mesolithic site in Inverness, Scotland. *Journal of Archaeological Science* 17, 509–12.

De Bie, M. 1999. Knapping techniques from the late Palaeolithic to the early Mesolithic in Flanders (Belgium): preliminary observations. In P. Bintz and A. Thévenin (eds), *L'europe des derniers chasseurs. Epipaléolithique et mésolithique*, 179–88. Grenoble: U.I.S.P.P.

de Klerk, P., Janke, W., Kühn, P., and Theuerkauf, M. 2008. Environmental impact of the Laacher See eruption at a large distance from the volcano: integrated palaeoecological studies from Norpommern (NE Germany). *Palaeogeography, Palaeoclimatology, Palaeoecology* 270, 196–214.

de Sonneville-Bordes, D. 1963. Upper Palaeolithic cultures in western Europe. *Science* 142, 347–55.

de Sonneville-Bordes, D. 1969. A propos des pointes pédonculées du nord de l'Europe: Pointe de Lingby et Pointe de Teyjat. *Quartär* 20, 183–8.

de Sonneville-Bordes, D. 1988. Les pointes à affinités nordiques dans le Paléolithique final au sud de la Loire. In M. Otte (ed.), *De la Loire à l'Oder: les civilisations du paléolithique final dans le nord-ouest européen*, 621–43. Oxford: Oxbow.

Dolukhanov, P., Sokoloff, D., and Shukurov, A. 2001. Radiocarbon chronology of Upper Palaeolithic sites in eastern Europe at improved resolution. *Journal of Archaeological Science* 28, 699–712.

Dumond, D. E. 2004. Volcanism and history on the northern Alaska peninsula. *Arctic Anthropology* 41, 112–25.

Eriksen, B. V. 1991. *Change and continuity in a prehistoric hunter-gatherer society: a study of cultural adaptation in Late Glacial-Early Postglacial southwestern Germany.* Tübingen: Archaeologica Venatoria.

Eriksen, B. V. 2000. Patterns of ethnogeographic variability in Late Pleistocene western Europe. In G. L. Peterkin and H. A. Price (eds), *Regional approaches to adaptation in Late Pleistocene western Europe*, 147–68. Oxford: Oxbow.

Eriksen, B. V. 2002. Fossil mollusks and exotic raw materials in Late Glacial and Early Postglacial find contexts: a complement to lithic studies. In L. E. Fisher and B. V. Eriksen (eds), *Lithic raw material economies in Late Glacial and Early Postglacial Europe*, 27–52. Oxford: Oxbow.

Fischer, A. 1989. Hunting with flint-tipped arrows: results and experiences from experiments. In C. Bonsall (ed.), *The Mesolithic in Europe*, 29–39. Edinburgh: John Donald.

Floss, H. 2000. Le couloir Rhin-Saône-Rhône: axe de communication au tardiglaciaire? In A. Richard, C. Cupillard, H. Richard, and A. Thevenin (eds), *Les derniers chasseurs-cueilleurs de l'Europe occidentale: actes du colloque international de Besançon 1998*, 313–21. Besançon: Presses Universitaires Franc-Comtoises.

Forsberg, L. and Knutsson, K. 1998. Converging conclusions from different archaeological perspectives: the early settlement of northern Sweden. In P. Bintz and A. Thévenin (eds), *L'Europe des derniers chasseurs. Epipaléolithique et mésolithique, Paris, comité des travaux historiques et scientifiques*, 313–19. Grenoble: UISPP – Commission XII.

Forster, P. 2004. Ice ages and the mitochondrial DNA chronology of human dispersals: a review. *Philosophical Transactions of the Royal Society B: Biological Sciences* 359, 255–64.

Fort, J., Pujol, T., and Cavalli-Sforza, L. L. 2004. Palaeolithic populations and waves of advance. *Cambridge Archaeological Journal* 14, 53–61.

Fuglestvedt, I. 2005. Contact and communication in northern Europe 10 200 – 9 000/8 500 BP: a phenomenological approach to the connection between technology, skill and landscape. In H. Knutsson (ed.), *Pioneer settlement and colonisation processes in the Barents region*, 79–96. Vuollerim: Vuollerim 6000.

Fuglestvedt, I. 2007. The Ahrensburgian Galta 3 site in SW Norway: dating, technology and cultural affinity. *Acta Archaeologica* 78, 87–110.

Gaffney, V., Thomson, K., and Fitch, S. (eds) 2007. *Mapping Doggerland: the Mesolithic landscapes of the southern North Sea*. Oxford: Archaeopress.

Gamble, C. 1997. Palaeolithic society and the release from proximity: a network approach to intimate relations. *World Archaeology* 29, 426–49.

Gamble, C. 1999. *The Palaeolithic societies of Europe*. Cambridge: Cambridge University Press.

Gamble, C., Davies, W., Pettitt, P., Hazelwood, L., and Richards, M. 2006. The Late Glacial ancestry of Europeans: combining genetic and archaeological evidence. *Documenta Praehistorica* 13, 1–10.

Gamble, C., Davies, W., Pettitt, P., and Richards, M. 2004. Climate change and evolving human diversity in Europe during the Last Glacial. *Philosophical Transactions of the Royal Society B: Biological Sciences* 359, 243–54.

Gamble, C., Davies, W., Pettitt, P., and Richards, M. 2005. The archaeological and genetic foundations of the European population during the Late Glacial: implications for 'agricultural thinking'. *Cambridge Archaeological Journal* 15, 193–223.

Garrod, D. 1926. *The Upper Palaeolithic age in Britain*. Oxford: Oxford University Press.

Gelhausen, F., Kegler, J., and Wenzel, S. 2004. Hütten oder Himmel? Latente Behausungsstrukturen im Spätpaläolithikum Mitteleuropas. *Jahrbuch des Römisch-Germanischen Zentralmuseum Mainz* 51, 1–22.

Gerken, K. 2001. *Studien zur jung- und spätpaläolithischen sowie mesolithischen Besiedlung im Gebiet zwischen Wümme und Oste*. Oldenburg: Isensee Verlag.

Glimmerveen, J., Mol, D., and van der Plicht, H. 2006. The Pleistocene reindeer of the North Sea: initial palaeontological data and archaeological remarks. *Quaternary International* 142–3, 242–6.

Gordon, B. C. 2003. The enigma of the far northeastern European Mesolithic: reindeer herd followers or semi-sedentary hunters? In L. Larsson, H. Kindgren, K. Knutsson, D. Loeffler, and A. Åkerlund (eds), *Mesolithic on the move: papers presented at the sixth international conference on the Mesolithic in Europe, Stockholm 2000*, 115–18. Oxford: Oxbow.

Grimm, S. B. and Weber, M.-J. 2008. The chronological framework of the Hamburgian in the light of old and new 14C dates. *Quartär* 55, 17–40.

Grøn, O. 2005. A Siberian perspective on the north European Hamburgian culture: a study in applied hunter-gatherer ethnoarchaeology. *Before Farming* 1, 35–64.

Grünberg, J. M. 2006. New AMS dates for Palaeolithic and Mesolithic camp sites and single finds in Saxony-Anhalt and Thuringia (Germany). *Proceedings of the Prehistoric Society* 72, 95–112.

Grydeland, S. E. 2005. The pioneers of Finnmark: from the earliest coastal settlements to the encounter with the inland people of northern Finland. In H. Knutsson (ed.), *Pioneer settlement and colonisation processes in the Barents region*, 43–78. Vuollerim: Vuollerim 6000.

Halstead, P. and O'Shea, J. 1989. Introduction: cultural responses to risk and uncertainty. In P. Halstead and J. O'Shea (eds), *Bad year economics: cultural responses to risk and uncertainty*, 1–7. Cambridge: Cambridge University Press.

Hänski, I. and Gaggiotti, O. E. 2004. *Ecology, genetics, and evolution of metapopulations*. London: Elsevier.

Hazelwood, L. and Steele, J. 2003. Colonizing new landscapes: archaeological detectability of the first phase. In M. Rockman and J. Steele (eds), *Colonisation of unfamiliar landscapes: the archaeology of adaptation*, 203–21. London: Routledge.

Hejsedal, A. 1994. The hunters' rock art in northern Norway: problems of chronology and interpretation. *Norwegian Archaeological Review* 27, 1–28.

Henrich, J. 2004. Demography and cultural evolution: how adaptive cultural processes can produce maladaptive losses—the Tasmanian case. *American Antiquity* 69, 197–214.

Hewitt, G. M. 1999. Post-glacial recolonisation of European biota. *Biological Journal of the Linnean Society* 68, 87–112.

Hewlett, B., van de Koppel, J. M. H., and Cavalli-Sforza, L. L. 1982. Exploration ranges of Aka Pygmies of the Central African Republic. *Man* NS 17, 418–30.

Hoffecker, J. F. 2002. *Desolate landscapes: ice age settlement in Eastern Europe*. New Brunswick: Rutgers University Press.

Hoffecker, J. F. 2005a. Innovation and technological knowledge in the Upper Paleolithic of northern Eurasia. *Evolutionary Anthropology* 14, 186–98.

Hoffecker, J. F. 2005b. *A prehistory of the north: human settlement of the higher latitudes*. New Brunswick: Rutgers University Press.

Hood, B. C. 1995. Circumpolar comparison revisited: hunter-gatherer complexity in the North Norwegian Stone Age and the Labrador Maritime Archaic. *Arctic Anthropology* 32, 75–105.

Housley, R. A., Gamble, C., and Pettitt, P. B. 2000. Reply to Blockley, Donahue and Pollard. *Antiquity* 74, 119.

Housley, R. A., Gamble, C., Street, M., and Pettitt, P. 1997. Radiocarbon evidence for the Late Glacial human recolonisation of northern Europe. *Proceedings of the Prehistoric Society* 63, 25–54.

Ingold, T. 1986. Reindeer economies and the origins of pastoralism. *Anthropology Today* 2, 5–10.

Istomin, K. and Dwyer, M. 2010. Dynamic mutual adaptation: human–animal interaction in reindeer herding pastoralism. *Human Ecology* 38, 613–23.

Jacobi, R. M. 2004. The Late Upper Palaeolithic lithic collections from Gough's Cave, Cheddar, Somerset, and human use of the cave. *Proceedings of the Prehistoric Society* 70, 1–92.

Jacobi, R. M., Higham, T. F. G., and Lord, T. C. 2009. Improving the chronology of the human occupation of Britain during the Late Glacial. In M. Street, R. N. E. Barton, and T. Terberger (eds), *Humans, environment and chronology of the Late Glacial of the North European Plain. Proceedings of workshop 14 (commission XXXII) of 15th U.I.S.P.P. Congress, Lisbon, September 2006*, 7–25. Mainz: Verlag des Römisch-Germanischen Zentralmuseums.

Jochim, M. A., Herhahn, C., and Starr, H. 1999. The Magdalenian colonisation of southern Germany. *American Anthropologist* 101, 129–42.

Julien, M. 1982. *Les harpons magdalénien*. Paris: Éditions du CNRS.

Kabacinski, J. and Kobusiewicz, M. 2007. Kragola near Kolo (central Poland): the easternmost settlement of the Hamburgian culture. In M. Kobusiewicz and J. Kabacinski (eds), *Studies in the Final Palaeolithic settlement of the Great European Plain*, 21–52. Poznan: Institute of Archaeology and Ethnology, Polish Academy of Sciences (Poznan Branch).

Kabacinski, J. and Sobkowiak-Tabaka, I. 2009. Big game versus small game hunting: subsistence strategies of the Hamburgian culture. In M. Street, R. N. E. Barton, and T. Terberger (eds), *Humans, environment and chronology of the Late Glacial of the North European Plain*, 67–75. Mainz: Verlag des Römisch-Germanischen Zentralmuseums.

Karlsson, A. O., Wallerström, T., Götherström, A., and Holmlund, G. 2006. Y-chromosome diversity in Sweden: a long-time perspective. *European Journal of Human Genetics* 14, 963–70.

Kelly, R. L. 2003. Colonisation of new land by hunter-gatherers: expectations and implications based on ethnographic data. In M. Rockman and J. Steele (eds), *Colonisation of unfamiliar landscapes: the archaeology of adaptation*, 44–58. London: Routledge.

Kindgren, H. 2002. Tosskärr. Stenkyrka 94 revisited. In B. V. Eriksen and B. Bratlund (eds), *Recent studies in the Final Palaeolithic of the European plain: proceedings of a U.I.S.P.P. symposium, Stockholm, 14.–17. October 1999*, 49–60. Højbjerg: Jutland Archaeological Society.

Kobusiewicz, M. 2002. Ahrensburgian and Sviderian: two different modes of adaptation? In B. V. Eriksen and B. Bratlund (eds), *Recent studies in the Final Palaeolithic of the European plain: proceedings of a U.I.S.P.P. symposium, Stockholm, 14.–17. October 1999*, 117–22. Højbjerg: Jutland Archaeological Society.

Laland, K. N. and Brown, G. R. 2006. Niche construction, human behavior, and the adaptive-lag hypothesis. *Evolutionary Anthropology* 15, 95–104.

Lappalainen, T., Laitinen, V., Salmela, E., Andersen, P., Huoponen, K., Savontaus, M. L., and Lahermo, P. 2008. Migration waves to the Baltic Sea region. *Annals of Human Genetics* 72, 337–48.

Larsson, L. (ed.) 1996. *The earliest settlement of Scandinavia and its relationship with neighbouring areas*. Stockholm: Almqvist and Wiksell.

Le Gall, O. 2003. Des Magdaléniens et...des poissons. In S. Costamagno and V. Laroulandie (eds), *Zooarchaeological insights into Magdalenian lifeways*, 119–28. Oxford: Archaeopress.

Litt, T., Schmincke, H.-U., and Kromer, B. 2003. Environmental response to climatic and volcanic events in Central Europe during the Weichselian Lateglacial. *Quaternary Science Reviews* 22, 7–32.

Lowe, J. J., Rasmussen, S. O., Björck, S., Hoek, W. Z., Steffensen, J. P., Walker, M. J. C., and Yu, Z. C. 2008. Synchronisation of palaeoenvironmental events in the North Atlantic region during the Last Termination: a revised protocol recommended by the INTIMATE group. *Quaternary Science Reviews* 27, 6–17.

McFadgen, B. 2007. *Hostile shores: catastrophic events in prehistoric New Zealand and their impact on Maori coastal communities*. Auckland: Auckland University Press.

Madsen, B. 1992. Hamburgkulturens flintteknologi i Jels (the Hamburgian flint technology at Jels). In J. Holm and F. Rieck (eds), *Istidsjægere ved Jelssøerne*, 93–131. Haderslev: Skrifter fra Museumsrådet for Sønderjyllands Amt.

Mandryk, C. A. S. 1993. Hunter-gatherer social costs and the nonviability of submarginal environments. *Journal of Anthropological Research* 49, 39–71.

Maschner, H. D. G. and Jordan, J. W. 2008. Catastrophic events and punctuated culture change: the southern Bering Sea and North Pacific in a dynamic global system. In D. Papagianni, R. H. Layton, and H. D. G. Maschner (eds), *Time and change: archaeological and anthropological perspectives on the long-term in hunter-gatherer societies*, 95–113. Oxford: Oxbow.

Meldgaard, M. 1983. Resource fluctuations and human subsistence: a zoo-archaeological and ethnographic investigation of a west Greenland caribou hunting camp. In J. Clutton-Brock and G. Grigson (eds), *Animals and archaeology: 1. Hunters and their prey*, 259–72. Oxford: Oxbow.

Minc, L. D. and Smith, K. P. 1989. The spirit of survival. In P. Halstead and J. O'Shea (eds), *Bad year economics: cultural responses to risk and uncertainty*, 8–39. Cambridge: Cambridge University Press.

Mol, D., Post, K., Reumer, J. W. F., van der Plicht, J., de Vos, J., van Geel, B., van Reenen, G., Pals, J. P., and Glimmerveen, J. 2006. The Eurogeul: first report of the palaeontological, palynological and archaeological investigations of this part of the North Sea. *Quaternary International* 142–3, 178–85.

Montet-White, A. and Haesaerts, P. (eds) 1990. *The Epigravettian site of Grubgraben, Lower Austria: the 1986 and 1987 excavations*. Liège: Université de Liège.

Musil, R. 2000. Evidence for the domestication of wolves in Central European Magdalenian sites. In S. J. Crockford (ed.), *Dogs through time: an archaeological perspective*, 21–8. Oxford: Archaeopress.

Mussi, M., Cinq-Mars, J., and Bolduc, P. 2000. Echoes from the mammoth steppe: the case of balzi rossi. In W. Roebroeks, M. Mussi, J. Svobod, and K. Fennenma (eds), *Hunters of the golden age. The Mid-Upper Palaeolithic of Eurasia 30,000–20,000 BP*, 105–24. Leiden: Leiden University Press.

Newell, R. R. and Constandse-Westerman, T. S. 1999. *Late glacial-early postglacial hunting strategies and land-use practices in the Swabian Alb and surrounding regions (southwestern B.R.D.)*. Assen: Van Gorcum.

Nielsen, E. H. 2009. *Paläolithikum und Mesolithikum in der Zentralschweiz. Mensch und Umwelt zwischen 17'000 und 5500 v. Chr.* Luzern: Kantonaler Lehrmittelverlag.

Nygaard, S. E. 1989. The Stone Age of northern Scandinavia. *Journal of World Prehistory* 3, 71–116.

Odling-Smee, F. J., Laland, K. N., and Feldman, M. W. 2003. *Niche construction: the neglected process in evolution*. Princeton: Princeton University Press.

Odum, E. P. 1971. *Fundamentals of ecology*. Philadelphia: W. B. Saunders Company.

Pasda, C. 1998. Der Beginn des Magdaléniens in Mitteleuropa. *Archäologisches Korrespondenzblatt* 28, 175–90.

Pasda, C. 2001. Das Knochengerät vom spätpaläolithischen Fundplatz Kleinlieskow in der Niederlausitz: ein Essay zum steinzeitlichen Angelhaken. In B. Gehlen, M. Heinen, and A. Tillmann (eds), *Zeit-Räume. Gedenkschrift für Wolfgang Taute*, 397–408. Bonn: Verlag Rudolf Habelt.

Pereira, L., Richards, M., Goios, A., Alonso, A., Albarran, C., Garcia, O., Behar, D. M., Golge, M., Hatina, J., Al-Gazali, L., Bradley, D. G., Macaulay, V., and Amorim, A. 2005. High-resolution mtDNA evidence for the Late-Glacial resettlement of Europe from an Iberian refugium. *Genome Research* 15, 19–24.

Petersen, E. B. 2009. The human settlement of southern Scandinavia 12500–8700 cal BC. In M. Street, R. N. E. Barton, and T. Terberger (eds), *Humans, environment and chronology of the Late Glacial of the North European Plain*, 89–129. Mainz: Verlag des Römisch-Germanischen Zentralmuseums.

Petersen, P. V. and Johansen, L. 1996. Tracking late glacial reindeer hunters in eastern Denmark. In L. Larsson (ed.), *The earliest settlement of Scandinavia and its relationship with neighbouring areas*, 75–88. Stockholm: Almqvist and Wiksell.

Pettitt, P. 2008. The British Upper Palaeolithic. In J. Pollard (ed.), *Prehistoric Britain*, 18–57. Oxford: Blackwell.

Pettitt, P., Gamble, C., Davies, W., and Richards, M. 2003. Palaeolithic radiocarbon chronology: quantifying our confidence beyond two half-lives. *Journal of Archaeological Science* 30, 1685–93.

Plumet, P. 2006. Le grand nord et la religion. *L'Anthropologie* 110, 383–400.

Pohlhausen, H. 1972. Standpunkte zur Diskussion über das Alter der Viehzucht. *Anthropos* 67, 176–95.

Powell, A., Shennan, S., and Thomas, M. G. 2009. Late Pleistocene demography and the appearance of modern human behavior. *Science* 324, 1298–1301.

Prentiss, W. C. and Chatters, J. C. 2003. Cultural diversification and decimation in the prehistoric record. *Current Anthropology* 44, 33–58.

Price, T. D. 1999. Human population in Europe during the mesolithic. In E. Cziesla, T. Kersting, and S. Pratsch (eds), *Den Bogen spannen...Festschrift für Bernhard Gramsch*, 185–95. Weissbach: Beier and Beran.

Prøsch-Danielsen, L. and Høgestøl, M. 1995. A coastal Ahrensburgian site found at Galta, Rennesøy, southwest Norway. In A. Fischer (ed.), *Man and sea in the Mesolithic*, 123–9. Oxford: Oxbow.

Rankama, T. and Kankaanpää, J. 2008. Eastern arrivals in post-glacial Lapland: the Sujala site 10000 cal BP. *Antiquity* 82, 884–99.

Rasmussen, S. O., Seierstad, I. K., Andersen, K. K., Bigler, M., Dahl-Jensen, D., and Johnsen, S. J. 2008. Synchronization of the NGRIP, GRIP, and GISP2 ice cores across MIS 2 and palaeoclimatic implications. *Quaternary Science Reviews* 27, 18–28.

Riede, F. 2005. To boldly go where no (hu-)man has gone before: some thoughts on the pioneer colonisations of pristine landscapes. *Archaeological Review from Cambridge* 20, 20–38.

Riede, F. 2007a. Der Ausbruch des Laacher See-Vulkans vor 12.920 Jahren und urgeschichtlicher Kulturwandel am Ende des Alleröd: eine neue Hypothese zum Ursprung der Bromme Kultur und des Perstunien. *Mitteilungen der Gesellschaft für Urgeschichte* 16, 25–54.

Riede, F. 2007b. 'Stretched thin, like butter on too much bread...': some thoughts about journeying in the unfamiliar landscapes of Late Palaeolithic southern Scandinavia. In V. Cummings and R. Johnson (eds), *Prehistoric journeys*, 8–20. Oxford: Oxbow.

Riede, F. 2008. The Laacher See eruption (12,920 BP) and material culture change at the end of the Allerød in northern Europe. *Journal of Archaeological Science* 35, 591–9.

Riede, F. 2009a. The loss and re-introduction of bow-and-arrow technology: a case study from the southern Scandinavian Late Palaeolithic. *Lithic Technology* 34, 27–45.

Riede, F. 2009b. Climate and demography in early prehistory: using calibrated 14C dates as population proxies. *Human Biology* 81, 309–37.

Riede, F. 2009c. Climate change, demography and social relations: an alternative view of the late palaeolithic pioneer colonisation of southern scandinavia. In S. McCartan, P. C. Woodman,

R. J. Schulting, and G. Warren (eds), *Mesolithic horizons. Papers presented at the seventh international conference on the Mesolithic in Europe, Belfast 2005. Volume 1*, 3–10. Oxford: Oxbow.

Riede, F. 2010. Hamburgian weapon delivery technology: a quantitative comparative approach. *Before Farming* [online version], article 1.

Riede, F., 2011. Adaptation and niche construction in human prehistory: a case study from the southern Scandinavian Late Glacial. *Philosophical Transactions of the Royal Society B: Biological Sciences* 366, 793–808.

Riede, F. and Bazely, O. 2009. Testing the 'Laacher See hypothesis': a health hazard perspective. *Journal of Archaeological Science* 36, 675–83.

Riede, F., Grimm, S. B., Weber, M.-J., and Fahlke, J. M. 2010. Neue Daten für alte Grabungen: ein Beitrag zur spätglazialen Archäologie und Faunengeschichte Norddeutschlands. *Archäologisches Korrespondenzblatt* 40, 297–316.

Riede, F., Newton, A. J., Bazely, O., and Lane, C. S. 2011. A Laacher See supplement to *Tephrabase*: investigating distal tephra fallout dynamics. *Quaternary International* 246, 134–44.

Riede, F. and Wheeler, J. M. 2009. Testing the 'Laacher See hypothesis': tephra as dental abrasive. *Journal of Archaeological Science* 36, 2384–91.

Ripoll, S., Muñoz, F., Bahn, P. G., and Pettitt, P. B. 2004. Palaeolithic cave engravings at Creswell Crags, England. *Proceedings of the Prehistoric Society* 70, 93–105.

Rivers, W. H. R. 1926. The disappearance of useful arts. In W. H. R. Rivers (ed.), *Psychology and ethnology*, 190–210. London: Kegan Paul, Trench, Trubner and Co.

Rockman, M. 2003. Knowledge and learning in the archaeology of colonisation. In M. Rockman and J. Steele (eds), *Colonisation of unfamiliar landscapes: the archaeology of adaptation*, 3–24. London: Routledge.

Roebroeks, W. 2006. The human colonisation of Europe: where are we? *Journal of Quaternary Science* 21, 425–35.

Roebroeks, W., Mussi, M., Svoboda, J., and Fennenma, K. (eds) 2000. *Hunters of the golden age: the Mid-Upper Palaeolithic of Eurasia 30,000–20,000 BP*. Leiden: University of Leiden.

Rowley, S. 1985. Population movements in the Canadian Arctic. *Études/Inuit/Studies* 9, 3–21.

Rust, A. 1937. *Das steinzeitliche Rentierjägerlager Meiendorf*. Neumünster: Karl Wachholtz Verlag.

Rust, A. 1958. *Die jungpaläolithischen Zeltanlagen von Ahrensburg*. Neumünster: Karl Wachholtz Verlag.

Sablin, M. V. and Khlopachev, G. A. 2002. The earliest Ice Age dogs: evidence from Eliseevichi 1. *Current Anthropology* 43, 795–9.

Saville, A. and Ballin, T. B. 2010. Upper Palaeolithic evidence from Kilmelfort Cave, Argyll: a re-evaluation of the lithic assemblage. *Proceedings of the Society of Antiquaries of Scotland* 139, 9–45.

Schild, R. 1996. The North European Plain and eastern Sub-Balticum between 12,700 and 8,000 BP. In L. G. Straus, B. V. Eriksen, J. M. Erlandson, and D. R. Yesner (eds), *Humans at the end of the Ice Age: the archaeology of the Pleistocene–Holocene transition*, 129–57. New York: Plenum Press.

Schmincke, H.-U. 2006. Environmental impacts of the late glacial eruption of the Laacher See volcano, 12.900 cal BP. In W. von Koenigswald and T. Litt (eds), *150 years of Neanderthal discoveries*, 149–53. Bonn: Terra Nostra.

Schmincke, H.-U., Park, C., and Harms, E. 1999. Evolution and environmental impacts of the eruption of Laacher See volcano (Germany) 12900 BP. *Quaternary International* 61, 61–72.

Schmitt, L. 1999. Comparative points and relative thoughts: the relationship between the Ahrensburgian and Hensbacka assemblages. *Oxford Journal of Archaeology* 18, 327–37.

Schmitt, L., Larsson, S., Schrum, C., Alekseeva, I., Tomczak, M., and Svedhage, K. 2006. 'Why they came'; the colonisation of the coast of western Sweden and its environmental context at the end of the last glaciation. *Oxford Journal of Archaeology* 25, 1–28.

Schwabedissen, H. 1954. *Die Federmessergruppen des nordwesteuropäischen Flachlandes. Zur Ausbreitung des Spät-Magdalénien*. Neumünster: Karl Wachholtz Verlag.

Shennan, S. J. 2001. Demography and cultural innovation: a model and its implications for the emergence of modern human culture. *Cambridge Archaeological Journal* 11, 5–16.

Sinitsyna, G. 2002. Lyngby points in Eastern Europe. *Archeologia Baltica* 5, 83–93.

Smith, K. 2001. *Environmental hazards: assessing risk and reducing disaster*. London: Routledge.

Soares, P., Achilli, A., Semino, O., Davies, W., Macaulay, V., Bandelt, H. Jr., Torroni, A., and Richards, M. B. 2010. The archaeogenetics of Europe. *Current Biology* 20, R174–R183.

Soffer, O. and Gamble, C. (eds) 1990. *The world at 18,000 BP, vol. 1: high latitudes*. London: Unwin Hyman.

Solberg, E. J., Jordhoy, P., Strand, O., Aanes, R., Loison, A., Saether, B. E., and Linnell, J. D. C. 2001. Effects of density-dependence and climate on the dynamics of a Svalbard reindeer population. *Ecography* 24, 441–51.

Stapert, D. and Johansen, L. 1999. Flint and pyrite: making fire in the Stone Age. *Antiquity* 73, 765–77.

Stenton, D. R. 1991. Caribou population dynamics and Thule culture adaptations on southern Baffin Island, N.W.T. *Arctic Anthropology* 28, 15–43.

Stewart, J. R. and Lister, A. M. 2001. Cryptic northern refugia and the origins of the modern biota. *Trends in Ecology and Evolution* 16, 608–13.

Straus, L. G., Eriksen, B. V., Erlandson, J. M., and Yesner, D. R. (eds) 1996. *Humans at the end of the Ice Age: the archaeology of the Pleistocene–Holocene transition*. New York: Plenum Press.

Surovell, T. A. 2000. Early Palaeoindian women, children, mobility, and fertility. *American Antiquity* 65, 493–508.

Terberger, T. and Lübke, H. 2004. Hamburger Kultur in Mecklenburg-Vorpommern? *Bodendenkmalpflege in Mecklenburg-Vorpommern* 52, 15–34.

Terberger, T. and Street, M. 2002. Hiatus or continuity? New results for the question of pleniglacial settlement in Central Europe. *Antiquity* 76, 691–8.

Thissen, J., Krull, H.-P., and Weiner, J. 1996. Eine Station des Creswellian im Rheinland? Der spätpaläolithische Oberflächenfundplatz Kleinenbroich. *Bonner Jahrbücher* 196, 373–96.

Tromnau, G. 1975. *Neue Ausgrabungen im Ahrensburger Tunneltal: ein Beitrag zur Erforschung des Jungpaläolithikums im nordwesteuropäischen Flachland*. Neumünster: Karl Wachholtz Verlag.

Tromnau, G. 1987. Late Palaeolithic reindeer-hunting and the use of boats. In J. M. Burdukiewicz and M. Kobusiewicz (eds), *Late Glacial in Central Europe: culture and environment*, 95–106. Wrocław: Prace Komisji Archeologicznej.

Tromnau, G. 1992. Anmerkungen zur Rengeweih-Harpune von Meiendorf. In B.-E. Krause and B. Mencke (eds), *Ur-Geschichte im Ruhrgebiet. Festschrift Arno Heinrich*, 79–83. Gelsenkirchen: Agora.

Tromnau, G. 2006. Comments concerning the gaps between Schleswig-Holstein and the Middle Oder in the expansion area of Hamburgian culture. *Archaeologia Baltica* 7, 8–10.

Ventsel, A. 2006. Hunter-herder continuum in Anabarski District, NW Sakha, Siberia, Russian Federation. *Nomadic Peoples* 10, 68–86.

Weber, M.-J. 2009. Fabrication and use of Hamburgian shouldered points: new data from Poggenwisch and Teltwisch 1 (Ahrensburg valley, Schleswig-Holstein, Germany). *P@lethnologie* 1, 98–132.

Weinstock, J. 2000. Osteometry as a source of refined demographic information: sex-ratios of reindeer, hunting strategies, and herd control in the Late Glacial site of Stellmoor, northern Germany. *Journal of Archaeological Science* 27, 1187–95.

Weniger, G.-C. 1995. *Die Widerhakenspitzen des Magdaléniens Westeuropas: ein Vergleich mit ethnohistorischen Jägergruppen Nordamerikas.* Mainz: Verlag Phillip von Zabern.

Weninger, B., Schulting, R., Bradtmöller, M., Clare, L., Collard, M., Edinborough, K., Hilpert, J., Jöris, O., Niekus, M., Rohling, E. J., and Wagner, B. 2008. The catastrophic final flooding of Doggerland by the Storegga slide tsunami. *Documenta Praehistorica* 35, 1–24.

Whallon, R. 2006. Social networks and information: non-'utilitarian' mobility among hunter-gatherers. *Journal of Anthropological Archaeology* 25, 259–70.

Wobst, M. 1976. Locational relationships in Paleolithic society. *Journal of Human Evolution* 5, 49–58.

Woodman, P. C. 1992. The Komsa culture: a re-examination of its position in the Stone Age of Finnmark. *Acta Archaeologica* 63, 57–76.

Zimmermann, A. 1996. Zur Bevölkerungsdichte in der Urgeschichte. In I. Campen, J. Hahn, and M. Uerpmann (eds), *Spuren der Jagd: die Jagd nach Spuren. Festschrift Müller-Beck,* 49–61. Tübingen: Archaeologia Venatoria.

Zvelebil, M. 2008. Innovating hunter-gatherers: the Mesolithic in the Baltic. In G. Bailey and P. Spikins (eds), *Mesolithic Europe,* 18–59. Cambridge: Cambridge University Press.

PART IV

PREHISTORIC HUNTER-GATHERER INNOVATIONS

PART IV

PREHISTORIC HUNTER-GATHERER INNOVATIONS

CHAPTER 26

PREHISTORIC HUNTER-GATHERER INNOVATIONS

PETER JORDAN AND VICKI CUMMINGS

INTRODUCTION

THIS part of the handbook focuses on the theme of long-term cultural innovation among prehistoric hunter-gatherers. This is an important topic because, for a variety of reasons, forager societies of the prehistoric past and more recent ethnographic periods have tended to have been regarded as possessing an inherent capacity for transformation and change. Innovations have been traced back to *external* influences and sources, and not linked to the *internal* dynamics of hunter-gatherer societies. Chapters in this part aim to redress this balance through a critical review of current archaeological evidence.

The roots of this thinking can be traced back to much older traditions of hunter-gatherer research. As discussed in detail in Part I, the emergence of the concept of hunter-gatherers as a distinctive *kind* of society had close links with notions of 'unilinear' or 'stadial' social evolution (see Barnard, Pluciennik, Part I, for more details). Economic and technological criteria were widely employed in the later nineteenth century to order the world's different populations into general schemes of ascending social progress. This perspective on cultural diversity was based on some deep assumptions: foraging was regarded as being an inherently less advanced way of life than agriculture, and hunter-gatherers tended to be cast as a conceptual 'base-line' for general development, while Western civilization was regarded as the pinnacle of human cultural, technological, and moral achievement. Coupled to this was the implicit belief that hunter-gatherers were relatively simplistic, lacking any *internal* capacity for innovation or cultural complexity. It was widely thought that further progress could only come from more advanced societies, but not from within hunting and gathering bands, who were widely perceived as being culturally moribund, and trapped within an earlier stage of outmoded cultural development.

Franz Boas's reaction to some of the increasingly racist formulations of social evolutionary thinking was to emphasize the inherent capacity for richness and complexity in *all* non-Western cultures, for example in kinship, ritual activities, and linguistics. In addition, he had already undertaken extensive ethnographic research and fieldwork among different hunter-gatherer communities (see the main introduction to this handbook by Jordan and Cummings), and was therefore sceptical on basic empirical grounds that the world's enormous cultural diversity could ever be condensed into such an abstract and highly uniform sequence of categories. His overarching conclusion was that each human culture should be approached and understood in its own *unique* terms (cultural relativism), because each was a product of very specific constellation of highly contingent cultural and historical factors (historical particularism).

These Boasian perspectives on cultural diversity went on to form a dominant strand in anthropological thought (and have close links to post-processual and interpretive archaeologies—see the main introduction), although neo-evolutionary ideas surfaced again in the mid-twentieth century in the work of V. Gordon Childe, Leslie White, and Julian Steward, with a renewed concern for understanding general patterning in human development and social organization. Childe was interested in using archaeological evidence to reconstruct how human cultures had gone through a series of revolutionary changes, such as the Neolithic transition to agriculture (Childe 1929). White (1959) was more interested in developing generalized schemes of evolution, and argued that human societies could be envisaged as forming elaborate thermo-dynamic systems. New kinds of technology enabled higher levels of energy to be captured from the environment, and this led to new stages of human development, for example, from hunting and gathering, which involved human muscle power, through to the initial use of domestic animals and plants, and later to the exploitation of fossil fuels such as coal and oil, which laid the foundations for industrialization, and finally to the nuclear age. In contrast, Steward's cultural ecology (1955) differed significantly in that it offered an alternative, 'multilinear' and more ecologically focused perspective on the evolution of human foraging cultures—the main concern here was to explore to what extent historically contingent adaptations to broadly similar local environments might generate common structures in hunter-gatherer social organization (see the main introduction to this handbook).

Given the enormous intellectual legacy of these earlier perspectives, this part of the handbook aims initially to stand back from these older research traditions. Social evolutionary thinking, in particular, tended to regard foragers as a rather uniform and timeless category of society, thereby stripping them of any inherent capacity for cultural advancement or technological creativity. Instead, the goal of this introduction is to take the 'long view' by critically reflecting on diverse archaeological evidence for processes of innovation *within* prehistoric foraging societies, exploring both the specific outcomes, and also some of the longer-term legacies generated by these changes. Adopting a more explicit focus on these *internal* innovation processes is especially important because it is now becoming clear that many major developments in human culture, technology, and social life occurred first among hunter-gatherers;, that is, long before the rise of agricultural economies and settled urban life. Such fundamental transformations include: the cumulative transformation of humans into a fully 'technological species'; the emergence of art; the rise of social complexity; and also the development of various other practices and technologies, ranging from the invention of pottery through to elaborations in mortuary behaviour, and the rise of coastal economies. Finally, it was hunting and gathering societies in different parts of the globe who took the first steps towards the active management, cultivation, and then full domestication of diverse suites of wild plants and animals. Over time, these initial steps led to the emergence of fully agro-pastoral farming economies, but paradoxically, also led to the eventual demise of hunting and gathering as humanity's main mode of subsistence.

For coherence, chapters in this part are organized along a broadly chronological sequence, reflecting the general temporal trends in the emergence and global dispersal of these key developments and innovations. More generally, each chapter investigates the prehistory of a specific innovation or cultural development, highlighting the enduring legacy of hunter-gatherers through to the present day. A final discussion returns to some of the themes raised at the start of this chapter—if prehistoric hunter-gatherers were relentless innovators, then how best can these dynamics be researched and understood? Can a concern with identifying *general* patterns in human cultural development be balanced alongside an interest in understanding the *particularistic* details of specific local sequences? How is the *agency* of prehistoric hunter-gatherer societies best studied, and how does localized social action contribute to long-term cultural transformation?

Key Innovations

The Transition to a Technological Species

In the first chapter in this part, Kuhn and Clark focus specifically on tracking major changes in stone tool technologies. Their broader concern, however, is tracing the rise of humans as a fundamentally *technological* species, reliant more than any other on material culture. Analyses of stone tool technologies are important because they form the first evidence of human technological abilities. Humans are not unique in using technology, but they do so to a degree unmatched by any other species—this is the same for forager bands as well as for urban dwellers. How and why humans became such a fundamentally technological species is one of the key questions in palaeoanthropology. One of the primary ways this question can be addressed is through the study of stone tool technologies.

Kuhn and Clark start by reviewing general long-term trends in the development of new kinds of stone tools and associated production techniques. One recurrent theme is the striking time lag between the first appearance and wider uptake and adoption of many new developments, a pattern also identified in other innovations such as cultural complexity, pottery, and the use of various domesticates (see Hommel; Hayden; Harris, in this section of the book). The general trend appears to indicate that new ideas tend to 'bump along' until subject to wider uptake, perhaps as their full advantages become fully realized, or whenever social and economic factors are more conducive to adoption among the wider population. All this directs attention to the crucial role of social learning and cultural transmission in generating many of these wider patterns in cultural development (see Garvey and Bettinger, this volume, Part I; Eerkens et al., this volume, Part VII).

Also notable is the rise of parallel developments in stone tool technologies across different regions of the globe, and the growing diversification in tool-kits and components, most often for processing the resources from prey, as well as just bringing down game. In many cases, there were different ways of making equivalent tool products, again highlighting the replication of distinct technological traditions through localized social learning networks. This also generates insights into contingent historical and demographic processes, rather than just simple or relatively automatic adaptive responses to local environments *per se*. Other technological trends include increased evidence for transport of tools, probably reflecting the desire to keep technology at close hand, and perhaps indicating the growth of a more general reliance on technology for daily survival. The increased use of hafted points and other multi-component artefacts underlines a growing complexity in technology and greater investment in manufacture. Sourcing and manipulation of the stone elements in these tools now formed only one part of a much longer operational sequence, which now widely involved the use of mastic substances, which also had to be collected, prepared, and applied.

In the Upper Palaeolithic, the spread of *Homo sapiens* into Eurasia, and the coeval dispersal and proliferation of blade technologies was certainly a major threshold in the use of new kinds of material culture, but this was only one element in a much wider trend towards growing technological elaboration. For example, it is true that there were some remarkable elaborations in the art of stone knapping and in composite tool manufacture at around this time. However, the biggest technological 'revolutions' in this period involved substantive changes in the working of 'new' kinds of materiality, such as hide, bone, antler, shell, and soft stone—there is substantial evidence for the production of elaborate tailored clothing and even the growing use of material culture as a media of communication in art and personal adornment. These changes marked a further shift towards humans becoming a fundamentally technological species, surrounded by an increasingly rich and diverse repertoire of material culture that was becoming central for subsistence, but also for other domains of social and cultural life.

More generally, the study of stone tool technologies highlights that the skills and cumulative stocks of knowledge required to make specific kinds of artefacts must have been acquired through teaching, imitation, and other forms of social learning, rather than forming a direct and simple reflection of innate cognitive capacities. Understanding variability and change in the production of stone tools—and other technologies appearing around the same time—therefore requires closer consideration of how this kind of cultural information was acquired and passed on. Archaeologists are just starting to explore the learning processes by which technological expertise was transmitted over generations, as well as the conditions that might favour persistence, elaboration, or even the eventual loss of this kind of knowledge within populations. More work on social learning and the dynamics of cultural transmission will undoubtedly generate new insights into some of these general patterns of technological transformation over the past 2.6 million years (and see Eerkens et al., Part VII, this volume).

Art for the Living

Lewis-Williams undertakes a thoughtful exploration of the main factors triggering the earliest appearance of art, which he argues was closely linked to the coeval emergence of religion. He defines 'art' as the deliberate manufacture of images. It is therefore *image-making* that makes his conceptualization of art distinct from a more general capacity for aesthetic appreciation (e.g. symmetrical hand axes) or symbolic expression (e.g. use of red ochre in ancient deposits). Most archaeologists now agree that art was integral to the business of living, but this is complicated by the fact that not all prehistoric societies made art. In order to try and understand the earliest origins of art, he therefore looks at what is currently the oldest evidence for image-making: the engraved pieces of ochre recovered from Blombos cave in South Africa, which date to 72,000 BP. Importantly, Lewis-Williams argues that the nature of this evidence also points to the coexistence of some form of religion at that time.

Some of the richest evidence for prehistoric art comes from Europe, although the evidence from Blombos cave in Africa indicates that production of art was probably a much more widespread phenomenon. However, evidence for very early art does tend to occur more frequently in Europe, and so Lewis-Williams centres his main analysis on this corpus of material. The Upper Palaeolithic art of this region consists of portable objects, cave paintings and engravings, painted and engraved geometric signs, and some engraved images of animals outside of caves. In Europe, the earliest appearance of art dates to the Aurignacian (45,000–35,000 years ago), and consists primarily of finely carved ivory figurines and pendants, along with the newly discovered parietal art at Chauvet cave in the Ardèche. It is clear that there was more to this art than just a utilitarian or purely decorative function: very specific animal species are repeatedly represented in the art recovered from broad geographic regions, and this seems to indicate that the appropriate subject matter of the art was established well before people starting making specific images. Making deeper interpretive sense of the art is extremely difficult, and this rich body of evidence has been approached by archaeologists in very different ways. Early studies drew heavily on ethnography, often citing Australian accounts of image-making among Aborigines. By the mid-twentieth century the theory of structuralism began to influence rock art interpretations. Of particular note was the work of Leroi-Gourhan, who suggested that a series of binary oppositions can be identified in the symbolism of the images, reflecting underlying cognitive distinctions between notions of male and female.

Lewis-Williams develops an alternative 'neurological' theory about the early production of art, and starts with the assumption that individuals in Upper Palaeolithic communities must have had broadly the same mental capacities as modern humans. He then suggests that it is important to differentiate between intelligence (as outlined by Mithen 1996), and the more general human capacity for consciousness, on which he places greater emphasis. This is due to the fact that there are intergrading states of normal human consciousness, ranging from being alert and focused, through to day-dreaming, and eventually to deep slumber. However, this spectrum of normal consciousness can be broadened further to include altered states of consciousness—these can extend from very mild symptoms through to some more extreme forms of experience. For example, when people are in these altered states of consciousness, they often experience mental visions (vivid hallucinations of various sorts).

It was the experiences of these altered mental states, Lewis-Williams argues, that were central to the first production of artistic images, and by the same token, to the origin of religion, which also drew upon this 'ecstatic' component of human consciousness. He suggests that the production of art was an attempt at 'fixing' the content of these personal visions into material forms, allowing the experiences and insights to be communicated to others who had not participated in the altered states of consciousness. Lewis-Williams is not arguing that the cognitive hard-wiring of people's brains forced them into the production of images; he is quite clear that the earliest production of images must have been socially situated—for example, many early examples of art appear to be concentrated in difficult-to-access locations such as deep caves, which may have allowed access to only a few ritual specialists, perhaps accompanied by new initiates. Understanding the motivations for the earliest production of images is extremely challenging, but Lewis-Williams's neurological approach does offer one way of investigating the origin of both art and early religion in these Palaeolithic hunter-gatherer societies.

The Rise of Social Complexity

The first two chapters in this part examine earlier phases in the transition of humans into a fundamentally 'technological species', with capacities to create—but also the need to rely on—a remarkable variety of material culture, ranging from more functional tools through to elaborate art. These earlier transformations appear to have played out within the behavioural settings of small-scale hunter-gatherer communities, who, in all likelihood, remained egalitarian societies lacking pronounced differences in social status, and with little in the way of archaeological evidence for the presence of private wealth or accumulation of prestige objects. In many ways, these early shifts constitute the antecedent cognitive and cultural foundations for a series of later cultural changes. Hayden identifies the onset of an entirely new phase in global human development—the establishment of cultural complexity. Long assumed by social evolutionary thinkers to be a defining achievement of agricultural societies, it is becoming increasingly clear to archaeologists that fundamental shifts in social relations were already well underway among earlier hunter-gatherer societies long before the onset of the transition to farming or the rise of urbanism. Hayden argues that it was probably the internal socio-political dynamics of earlier hunter-gatherer communities that went on to trigger these later socio-economic developments, a process explored in more detail later.

During the Upper Palaeolithic, there is increasing evidence for the emergence of new kinds of socio-economic relationships, but only in some hunter-gatherer communities. These early developments appear to gather pace and become much more widely established with the start of the Holocene. More generally, these transformations in social relations appear to be caught up with the coeval emergence of a series of other technological, economic, and cultural innovations, all of which are considered in more detail in the following chapters. As a bold attempt to critically synthesize the general patterning in diverse archaeological datasets, Hayden's chapter is therefore of central relevance to this whole part of the handbook, because it attempts to set out a general conceptual framework for making sense of these wider global trends. Importantly, it integrates a concern with understanding the underlying local socio-political processes, but also highlights the role of distinctive environmental contexts in which most of these cultural developments appear to become highly concentrated.

But what is—and what is not—cultural complexity? Hayden contrasts his approach to older Boasian traditions of research (see above and also the main introduction). As examined at the start of this chapter, Boas rejected nineteenth-century social evolutionist thinking on both moral and empirical grounds, and wanted to demonstrate that all non-Western populations—many of whom were hunter-gatherers—had the capacity to exemplify cultural attributes and behaviours that were as rich and elaborate as those of Western societies. In this sense, Boas was interested in highlighting the inherent cultural sophistication—i.e. 'complexity'—of all human cultures, for example, in dance, kinship, art, language, and other cognitive and social attributes. Hayden argues that this Boasian perspective on cultural diversity represents a staunch form of cultural relativism; that is, it assumes that each culture is unique, and cannot be placed within any general schema of development.

Hayden challenges these assumptions by drawing attention to the abundant archaeological evidence that now indicates general patterning in long-term cultural developments through time. These patterns, he argues, represent 'major evolutionary changes' in some of the most basic underpinnings of human cultural and social life, the most fundamental transformation being the emergence of a new kind of complexity. Cultural complexity in this sense is not about being inherently 'complicated' in art, kinship, or ritual practice, as was argued by Boas, but is something very different. For Hayden, the onset of cultural complexity is linked to the breakdown of an older, more resolutely egalitarian mode of social relations.

When discussing this kind of cultural complexity, archaeologists generally refer to the presence of hierarchical social, economic, and/or political structures, for example, the control of labour and resources beyond the immediate family. But how do these new kinds of relationship become established? Hayden argues that it is important to define and then differentiate the main features of 'egalitarian' societies and 'trans-egalitarian' societies. He suggests that (a) egalitarian societies lack private ownership, prestige goods, pronounced socio-economic differences, and economically based competition, but do emphasize sharing and equality. In contrast, (b) trans-egalitarian societies still lack formal social stratification but do exhibit growing evidence for private property, production of reliable economic surpluses, use of prestige objects, and the establishment of significant socio-economic differences. In fact, the obligatory sharing that characterizes true egalitarian societies (together with minimal private property or ownership of resources) is antithetical to the production of prestige items or accumulation wealth for personal use and display. In this way, the rise of social complexity must be linked first to the breakdown of these earlier egalitarian social relations, and also to the coeval emergence of trans-egalitarian social dynamics, which would, in turn, initiate the eventual shift towards more entrenched forms of socio-political stratification. Understanding exactly when, where, and why such trans-egalitarian societies first emerged is therefore key to Hayden's analysis, and also to understanding the onset of general changes in human social life.

So when does this particular form of complexity first emerge? Hayden notes that these developments cannot be linked to simple changes in human cognition—anatomically modern humans emerged around 90,000 years ago, but there is no substantive evidence for cultural complexity for another 50,000 years. Only around 40,000 years ago do the first coherent indications of cultural complexity enter into the archaeological record of the Upper Palaeolithic. These early developments appear to be concentrated into some very specific, highly productive environments, and are far from a universal phenomenon. A more widespread trend towards increasing social complexity can be noted for the Mesolithic, but this time the most intense developments are primarily focused on the exploitation of different sets of ecological resources. He argues that this is an 'amazing pattern in cultural evolution' and one that demands a full explanation—archaeologists should therefore attempt to make interpretive sense of these general patterns, and should not be content with a more descriptive and particularistic treatment of unique local settings, or a concern with the lived experience of the past (see the main introduction).

In the Upper Palaeolithic, most of these developments appear to be centred on the hunter-gatherer groups inhabiting rich glacial parkland environments characterized by abundant megafauna. Many such areas contain initial evidence for the first use of prestige objects, early cave art, hints at seasonal sedentism, and also indications of long-term storage. There are also preliminary suggestions of the opening up of inequalities in personal and family wealth, as indicated by lavish adult and adolescent burials. Later phases of the Upper Palaeolithic witness additional growth in the circulation of portable wealth and other prestige items. There are stronger hints of substantially higher population densities in certain resource-rich areas, with coeval ownership of the most productive extraction points. It becomes evident that these prehistoric societies were increasingly able to provision themselves with enormous economic surpluses, much of which must have been subject to seasonal storage and later redistribution. The period is also marked by the creation of fabulous cave art. All these lines of evidence point emphatically to the rise of completely new kinds of social and political complexity that had never before existed. Such developments stand in stark contrast to the kind of simple sharing out of scarce resources within egalitarian bands that appears to characterize the archaeology of earlier periods. Importantly, the trans-egalitarian hunter-gatherer societies who were at the vanguard of the shift towards increasing social complexity were concentrated in rich ecological 'heartlands'—such developments were likewise absent from egalitarian forager populations inhabiting more marginal areas, a phenomenon that persisted through to historic times.

Important regional changes to these general transformations were triggered by the climatic ameliorations that marked the terminal Pleistocene. The main locus of cultural development shifted away from the glacial parklands of Europe, and became increasingly focused on the exploitation of new kinds of resources in the early Holocene, driven on by the relentless socio-political demands for production of surpluses. The parallel development and uptake of new technologies (harpoons, leisters, fishhooks, nets and sinkers, basket traps and weirs) during the Mesolithic was linked in many areas to intensified exploitation of aquatic species, especially fish and shellfish, whose mass harvesting and storage opened up new reservoirs of food through systematic exploitation of species that had hitherto been used on a more opportunistic basis (see Wickham-Jones, this part). In the Near East, similar developments involved the emergence of new tool-kits for the mass harvesting of seeds. These wider developments, in turn, were linked to growing concentrations of population in resource-rich areas, and coeval developments in permanent settlements, as well as the rise of special locations for funerary and ancestral feasting rituals.

From Europe, the Near East, Siberia, China, Japan, and well beyond, many early Holocene hunter-gatherer societies bear all the classic archaeological hallmarks of emergent cultural complexity, but only those occupying the most ecologically productive environments. A string of other innovations, including very early uses of pottery, elaborations in mortuary practices, and perhaps also the first steps towards deliberate management and eventual domestication of wild plants and animals also appear to be caught up in the internal socio-political dynamics that characterize these early *trans*-egalitarian hunter-gatherer societies (see chapters by Harris; Hommel; Nilsson Stutz; Outram, in this part).

Pulling together a remarkable array of global data, Hayden concludes that increasingly competitive use of abundant ecological resources led directly to the rise of new forms of cultural complexity. At the same time, this new capacity for cultural complexity was highly contingent upon the characteristics of local environment, as well the ability of hunter-gatherer groups to invent and deploy technologies that could generate reliable surpluses in food supply. Absolutely central to this process of emerging complexity was the agency of specific individuals ('aggrandizers'), who sought increasingly to acquire and control these surpluses for their own political advantage and personal self-advancement, as well as the labour, technological facilities, and resource extraction points that underpinned the local economy. These relentless dynamics set the hunting and gathering world on edge, with a relentless political demand for the production of surplus generating ever more complex and competitive socio-economic systems. Importantly, this conclusion suggests that the rise of trans-egalitarian hunter-gatherer societies from the Upper Palaeolithic onwards marks one of the most fundamental watersheds in human socio-political relationships. In contrast, earlier social evolutionary thinking had predicted that shifts towards new kinds of social life would only emerge with the onset of agriculture. Interestingly, many other attributes that have traditionally been associated with the rise of farming societies—from increasing sedentism through to the invention of pottery—are now known to have emerged first among hunter-gatherers, and were very possibly linked to the shift from egalitarian to trans-egalitarian societies that Hayden traces.

FURTHER INNOVATION DYNAMICS AMONG PREHISTORIC HUNTER-GATHERERS

Building on some of the insights derived from Hayden's global overview of the rise of cultural complexity, the next set of chapters focuses on a range of more specific innovations that were appearing among many prehistoric hunter-gatherer populations at around the same time.

Hunter-Gatherers and the Emergence of Pottery

The emergence of pottery is investigated by Hommel. His starting point is the observation that in western Europe, the invention of pottery has generally been associated with the Neolithic transition to farming, and the spread of this 'package' of traits into new areas. However, Hommel cites growing evidence that pottery emerged first among Upper Palaeolithic hunter-gatherers, and that it has its own complex technological history that is entirely distinct from that of plant and animal domestications, and the rise of farming (Jordan and Zvelebil 2009; Rice 1999). Exactly how and why pottery first emerged within a foraging lifestyle—rather than a farming economy—therefore becomes an intriguing research question.

Hommel notes that the general use of clay has a much older history than the appearance of the first ceramic container technologies. Very early clay 'cultural' objects include models, figurines, and other items, all of which hint at a much more widespread and artistic use of wet clay in many Upper Palaeolithic societies. The increasing use of *deliberately* fired clay in the production of figurines also forms part of a wider trend towards increasing manipulation of different kinds of raw material, the cumulative development of knowledge, and the invention of new kinds of technology. However, the widespread fired-clay figurine tradition of the Upper Palaeolithic is unlikely to have led directly to the invention of ceramic container technologies. Instead, Hommel links the earliest origins of pottery to older 'soft' container technologies, noting the similarities between the 'additive' craft of weaving baskets and the building in of new strips of moist clay when coiling a pot. Even the production steps in the manufacture of early slab-build pots may have had broad conceptual similarities to the assembling of boxes or other kinds of soft containers from bark sheets or rawhide. This building and assembling of clay containers is therefore a very different technological exercise to the 'subtractive' craft of producing lithic artefacts by chipping, flaking, and polishing away surplus material to generate a finished artefact. Moreover, the frequent textile impressions commonly found in many early pottery traditions suggest that basketry, matting, or netting was also being used to support or mould the damp clay. In fact, the symbolic and cognitive associations between basketry and pottery may go much deeper. Many later hunter-gatherer pottery traditions, e.g. in the Japanese Jomon (see Habu 2004), appear to have deliberately incorporated stylized designs from organic container technologies such as basketry and wooden boxes, long after pottery-making had itself become well established as a distinct craft.

So where, when, how, and why did the earliest pottery emerge, and what relative advantages did pottery provide? The first pots may have emerged from the use of clay-lined baskets, as noted above, or even from clay-lined cooking pits; clearly, these societies were already familiar with the firing of clay to make cultural objects. As a result, the initial—and perhaps even accidental—integration of this knowledge with existing 'soft' container technologies may not have represented such a major conceptual breakthrough. Whatever its early origins, the appearance of pottery appears unlikely to have been linked to the development of new cognitive capacities, as human populations were already working with many other complex multi-component technologies long before the first evidence of pottery. Early uses of ceramic containers are probably best seen as evidence for the integration of older skills and insights into a new kind of cultural knowledge (Hayden 2009), albeit a set of technological practices that had to become properly 'embedded' within hunter-gatherer social life before it was able to persist over subsequent generations.

The world's earliest examples of ceramic containers are found in the Old World, especially in East Asia (Japan, China, and in the Russian Far East), where a widespread suite of hunter-gatherer early pottery traditions became well established in the Upper Palaeolithic. This appears to have been followed by a second independent emergence of pottery in sub-Saharan Africa, again among hunter-gatherers. By the early-to-middle Holocene, use of pottery had spread into new regions within a few millennia, generating a widespread 'horizon' of early pottery traditions that spanned Eurasia and also embraced many parts of Africa (Gibbs and Jordan 2013; Jordan and Zvelebil 2009). In its earlier phases, it is clear that these early pottery traditions were associated exclusively with hunter-gatherer societies, but in later periods, pottery became increasingly associated with new forms of plant and animal management. In other words, although initially a hunter-gatherer innovation, the later history of pottery becomes increasingly caught up with the rise and dispersal of agro-pastoral farming economies.

In the New World, the basic spatio-temporal patterns in the first emergence of pottery are highly complex: there appears to be an independent origin centre in South America, plus another in south-east North America. In later periods, pottery traditions are adopted by maritime hunter-gatherers in Alaska. Knowledge of the craft appears to have spread across the Bering Strait from Siberia, with the ultimate source of these northern traditions being the early pottery technologies of East Asia, discussed earlier.

Beyond the identification of these general spatio-temporal patterns, much more regional work will be required to clarify the specific relationships between the many different early-pottery traditions, as well as the timing and directionality of the later dispersal and uptake sequences. Importantly, however, Hommel also emphasizes that pottery must also have spread via local cultural choices, for example, the decision to invent, adopt, or adjust the new technology within particular social, cultural, and ecological settings. More generally then, it is clear that pottery was a 'socially constituted' technology, and that its wider uptake was not inevitable, but was highly contingent upon being attractive—and also acceptable—to the traditions and lifeways of local forager communities.

In considering the possible attractions of early pottery, Hommel highlights some of the basic roles that early pottery might have performed, perhaps triggering its initial invention, as well as its wider adoption into hunter-gatherer lifeways. These range from practical benefits for diet and health, through to use in ritual activity and in symbolic display. For prehistoric foragers, clay cooking pots must have had many basic attractions, including preparation of nutritious soups and also weaning foods (also see Jordan and Zvelebil 2009), but perhaps one of its key attractions was in processing seasonally abundant resources. In part, this may link the more widespread uptake of early pottery with the rise of the new 'aquatic' economies that were flourishing at the start of the Holocene (see Hayden; Wickham Jones, this part). More generally, Hommel concludes that despite the enormous regional variability in styles, most of the earlier hunter-gatherer pottery traditions tend to appear in contexts where they could, as a new technology, improve nutritional capture and minimize time invested in subsistence.

This broadly adaptive 'economic intensification' argument appears to successfully account for the wider take-up of pottery among early Holocene hunter-gatherers (Jordan and Zvelebil 2009). However, the early phases in the emergence of pottery in East Asia are more intriguing. Many sites in China, Japan, and the Russian Far East with very early evidence of pottery tend to indicate rather minimal use of a few vessels over many generations, not the kind of sudden 'explosive' take-off that might be predicted by the kind of more adaptive argument outlined above. At a more general level, this pattern might be linked to Kuhn and Clark's observation of how lithic innovations patterns emerge first on a very limited scale, tending to 'bump along' for extended periods, followed later by a much wider uptake across populations. This brings us back to the general theme of social learning and cultural transmission in the spread of new traits within and between populations (see above, and Eerkens et al., Part VII). In the case of pottery, these earliest phases of ceramic innovation may have closer links to the prestige technology arguments of Hayden (2009). Here, it is predicted that earliest use of pottery takes place among trans-egalitarian hunter-gatherers, and was linked to the production of desirable substances such as fats, oils, and intoxicants, which were then served within the competitive and politically charged settings of reciprocal feasting rites (see above, and Hayden, this part). To date, these ideas remain as working hypotheses, and more local work is required to explore them further.

More generally, much more empirical work will be required before archaeologists fully understand how and why this important new craft came to be embedded so widely within the lifeways of prehistoric foragers. It will be important to identify the range of foods cooked in these very early vessels (Craig et al. 2013), the specific design features and technical attributes of early pottery, and also the extent to which pots were moved around the landscape by people during the seasonal round, or the degree to which they were made and cached locally. Long assumed to be a Neolithic farmers' technology, it is now abundantly clear that the invention and earliest use of pottery was a purely hunter-gatherer innovation. Its emergence among prehistoric foragers also marks yet another phase in the cumulative shift towards humanity becoming a fundamentally 'technological species'.

Coastal Adaptations

In the next chapter, Wickham-Jones examines evidence for the rise of 'aquatic' economies among prehistoric hunter-gatherers. As discussed by Hayden, these water-edge adaptations appear to have provided the behavioural contexts in which many other innovations emerged or were elaborated, ranging from the first pottery through to intensifications in the long-term use of mortuary sites (see Nilsson Stutz, this part). Identifying exactly when coastal resources first became of such central important is, however, highly challenging due to the major rises in global sea levels in the later Pleistocene and during the early Holocene. The archaeology of many ancient coastlines, estuaries, and major river systems is now simply under water, and thereby inaccessible to research, adding major preservational bias to the study of early coastal adaptations.

These challenges aside, the emergence of coastal economies appears to follow a similar picture to that of pottery and other hunter-gatherer innovations—there is some initial evidence for very early and perhaps incidental use of aquatic resources in the Palaeolithic, followed by a much wider uptake, which becomes particularly marked in the Mesolithic societies of the earlier Holocene. For example, early coastal sites in the western Mediterranean date back to 200,000 BP; sites in South Africa, where birds, shellfish, and sea mammals were being exploited, date as far back as 100,000 BP. In Australia and Melanesia, similar kinds of evidence extend back to 35,000 years ago. The Palaeolithic colonization of remoter islands provides indirect evidence for the existence of ocean-going watercraft as well.

In contrast, evidence for the first fully adaptive reliance on coastlines appears only around 10,000 years ago (or at least the evidence becomes clearer at this point); that is, at the start of the Holocene. Extensive reliance on coastal resources has yet to be identified prior to this period, though more research will probably push this date backwards in time. Whatever the exact date for the first initiation of this trend towards increasing use of aquatic ecotones, it is clear that by the early Holocene, coastlines, estuaries, large inland lakes, and major river systems were starting to replace the rich parklands of the Upper Palaeolithic as the main epicentres for the development of new kinds of socio-cultural complexity. In the Mesolithic, these dynamics appear to have been underpinned by the dispersal of new technologies such as fishing gear and pottery, which facilitated the extraction and storage of increasingly reliable—and politically controllable—economic surplus from highly productive aquatic ecosystems (see Hayden, this part). In general then, Wickham-Jones notes that the increasing importance of coastal economies facilitated several other coeval developments, including major increases in the concentration of archaeologically 'visible' sites, both for routine dwelling, and also for a range of other more ritualized purposes, such as burial sites, which themselves became the focus of long-term elaborations in mortuary activities.

Cosmology and Hunter-Gatherer Mortuary Behaviour

The treatment of the dead (mortuary behaviour) provides archaeologists with important information about how prehistoric communities viewed their place in the world (cosmology). Nilsson Stutz traces the development and elaboration of this kind of cultural behaviour among prehistoric hunter-gatherers. Indeed, acknowledgement of the loss of individuals through death is expressed in specific behaviours in living apes, including chimpanzees, and so this kind of behaviour may have appeared very early within the hominin lineage. However, evidence for a more structured and symbolic treatment of the dead gradually increases in the Middle and especially in the Upper Palaeolithic. In general, Nilsson Stutz argues that these changing trends in mortuary behaviour express a gradual shift away from a more individualistic, emotional response to the death of close kin, towards a set of more culturally learned mortuary practices, which express and reproduce a wider set of cosmological ideas. As with many other innovations reviewed in this part of the handbook, there appears to be a qualitative shift in the Upper Palaeolithic towards a more elaborate set of practices associated with interment of the dead, which becomes much more pronounced in the Mesolithic. Moreover, interment of the dead becomes increasingly associated with particular places in the landscape, whose significance clearly endures over multiple generations. In turn, these developments may be linked to new kinds of territoriality, and the intensification of symbolic attachments to focal places in the landscape. These trends are also global, with clear evidence for elaboration of mortuary activities among Natufian hunter-gatherers of the Near East in the terminal Pleistocene, and further fluorescence in mortuary activities across Siberia (e.g. around Lake Baikal), the Russian Far East, Jomon Japan, in Mesolithic Europe, and beyond. These developments are often associated with a greater reliance on aquatic resources (see Wickham-Jones, this part), and may be associated with the ritual and political dynamics that these new kinds of economic strategy had generated (see Hayden, this part).

Nilsson Stutz also undertakes a deeper review of research into hunter-gatherer mortuary activity in the Baltic region of northern Europe. Here, concentration of burials in one place over time is not an entirely new phenomenon, but the Mesolithic marks an intensification of this trend, and appears to be caught up with increasing population densities, supported by intensive exploitation of aquatic resources. Illustrating this general trend are the world-famous hunter-gatherer burial complexes of Olenii Ostrov in Karelia, Zvejnieki in northern Latvia, Vedbaek and Skateholm in Sweden, and many others (e.g. see Zvelebil 2008 for a comprehensive inventory of Mesolithic cemeteries in northern Europe).

Earlier interpretations of these burial complexes tended to focus on two contrasting themes—for example, the identification of the 'horizontal' structuring of hunter-gatherer social relations, such as gender, age groups, and other social identities—but also an interest in understanding the 'vertical' structuring of society in terms of ascribed social status, ranking, and emergent social stratification. In fact, research into Baltic mortuary practices was instrumental in the 'discovery' of complex hunter-gatherers in the early 1980s (see the main introduction). Later, it became increasing apparent that the prehistoric reality may have been even more intriguing that these basic horizontal/vertical distinctions. O'Shea and Zvelebil (1984), for example, identified that at least seven different independent social variables appeared to have been structuring the materials recovered from graves within the Olenii Ostrov cemetery. Similar insights are now appearing from analysis of the extensive datasets from the Lake Baikal cemeteries (Weber et al. 2010). Both sets of regional insights underline the difficulty in 'mapping' relatively straightforward notions of social identity, or relative status, onto cemetery populations. As a result, Nilsson Stutz suggests that these hunter-gatherer 'cemeteries' are perhaps better understood as focal points for the performance of elaborate ritual practices associated with the reproduction of prehistoric cosmologies.

Nilsson Stutz argues that the form and content of these practices can best be approached as a kind of social-symbolic 'language'. This reflects—and also actively expresses—both general understandings of death and ideas about the appropriate treatment of particular deceased individuals. Together, these might require the community to engage in consumption of food and drink at the graveside, produce specific mortuary artefacts to be interred with the corpse, or perhaps undertake other ritualized acts and gestures, such as symbolically shooting the cadaver with arrows after it has been placed in the ground. Importantly, it is this kind of active collective participation in the negotiated performance of ritual practice that sustains more general cosmological ideas about the world, but also generates such variability between different mortuary events, as well as longer-term transformations between generations. Nilsson Stutz argues that when these kinds of theoretical perspectives are creatively combined with detailed archaeological datasets, then the specific form and content of prehistoric world views can be carefully reconstructed. For example, she cites Zvelebil's (2008) comprehensive analysis of hunter-gatherer world views in the Mesolithic of northern Europe, which integrated interpretations of mortuary data and rock art sites with ethnographic parallels from hunting cultures in Siberia. Clearly, a similar kind of interpretive approach could be expanded to other areas with a rich hunter-gatherer mortuary archaeology, such as Lake Baikal, the Russian Far East, and Jomon Japan—this is certainly a rich direction for future research.

Nilsson Stutz also highlights the importance of new work that examines the role of burial complexes as enduring places within a wider web of interlinked sites that together make up a cultural landscape, and questions whether it remains useful to continue applying the concept of 'cemeteries' to the hunter-gatherer archaeological record. This is linked to an equally important question about death and commemoration in Mesolithic societies—if only a very small fraction of the wider prehistoric population were actually interred in such places, how were other individuals treated after death, and how were these other practices linked to the performance and reproduction of prehistoric cosmologies? Members of the wider population may have been subject to other 'culturally appropriate' treatments such as boat burials, cremations, and exposure to the elements. Given the overarching emphasis on studying cemetery sites, the circulation and deposition of disarticulated human bones has long been overlooked, but may have been highly significant in expressing deeper notions of kinship, ancestry, and prehistoric personhood (also see Conneller 2006).

Together, these different strategies associated with adjusting to the physical loss of an individual from a living community, as well as in dealing with the inherent materiality of human death, must have constituted a diverse and highly contingent repertoire of mortuary practices that were central to Mesolithic cosmologies. Clearly, much more research will be required before the full significance of these wider practices can be fully apprehended by archaeologists, but the initial results from the Baltic appear highly promising, and underline that similar work could be done in other world regions. Finally, in stepping back from her detailed review of recent work on the Baltic Mesolithic, Nilsson Stutz concludes that there have been some general changes through time in the ways in which hunter-gatherers have treated their dead, but within these broader patterns, perhaps the most important threshold was the emergence of *persistent* places in the cultural landscape that went on to became the focus of repeated mortuary and commemorative activities over many generations.

Steps Beyond Hunting and Gathering: The Domestication of Plants and Animals

The final chapters in this part focus on the role of prehistoric hunter-gatherers in initiating two crucial innovations in subsistence—the increasing *management* and cumulative *domestication* of specific kinds of plants and animals. Together, these changes led to the eventual emergence of agro-pastoral farming economies, whose wider dispersal and relentless uptake triggered the eventual replacement of hunting and gathering as the primary form of human subsistence in almost all areas of the contemporary world.

In reviewing the domestication of plants, Harris argues that the process is both simple and also extremely complex. In a basic sense, hunter-gatherers intervened in the reproduction of wild plants that they procured for food and other uses, and began a process of domestication that led in many parts of the world to agricultural systems that were based on varied assemblages of crops. This profound economic transformation began around 12,000 years ago and resulted in a relentless loss of plant biodiversity, as an ever-expanding human population became increasingly reliant on a food supply drawn from fewer and fewer staples. In this way, prehistoric hunter-gatherers started a process of change that eventually went on to fundamentally reshape human relationships with the natural world.

Harris also notes a more general conceptual problem in studying this process—given the kinds of progressive social evolutionary thinking noted at the start of this chapter, hunter-gatherers, by definition, formed a distinct stage of human existence, and have generally been viewed as being pre-agricultural populations who subsisted on wild resources and made no use of domesticated plants. These assumptions tended to discourage research into the study of domestication as a long-term process of innovation. Understanding these earlier changes is important because they substantially pre-date the eventual dispersal of 'packages' of staple framing crops, as well as the initial domestication of individual plant species.

Much foundational research into plant domestication was done by botanists and geneticists, and after the 1950s and 1960s, by environmental archaeologists. By the end of the twentieth century there was a prodigious literature on crop domestications and the origins of plant-based agriculture. Much of this later work highlighted the myriad ways in which ethnographically documented hunter-gatherers actively managed and deliberately manipulated wild plant communities. Similar kinds of intervention by prehistoric hunter-gatherers appear to have resulted in the eventual domestication of wild species, which went on to become staple crops. Although there is now general consensus that prehistoric foragers were developing new kinds of relationships with different species of nuts, roots and tubers, seeds of grasses, and other herbaceous plants (forbs), there is also growing appreciation that this led to a wide range of highly contingent outcomes, ranging from diverse but sustainable strategies of wild plant management, through to intermediate subsistence systems, and only in some cases, to full domestication of staple crops and a deeper reliance on agriculture.

Harris emphasizes the importance of this relentless local variability and contingency in early human–plant relations—globally then, it is essential to grasp that there have been many different prehistoric transitions to agriculture, and that none of them were somehow automatic adjustments, or indeed inevitable outcomes, as social evolutionary thinking might have predicted. In total, there appear to have been about ten different regions in which the wild ancestors of modern staple crops were first domesticated, but even within these regions of early crop use, there are often smaller sub-regions that were the focus of more localized domestication processes; for example, millets were independently domesticated in northern China, and rice in southern China. In other areas, clusters of different crop species were domesticated in tandem. Over time, there also appears to have been a ready exchange in the use of almost all these early domesticates within and between different regions of the Old and New Worlds, adding further local complexity to the wider global process.

The move towards this greater general reliance on domesticated crops was certainly not a rapid shift: different 'packages' of crops formed very slowly, with new elements being added episodically, either via new phases of local domestication, or via the introduction of new crops from other areas. In general, this cumulative move towards greater reliance on domesticates tends to be reflected archaeologically in a protracted transition from broad-spectrum foraging, through intermediate subsistence systems, and only then to full reliance on agriculture (see Part V on the persistence of hunting and gathering). It remains a major challenge to track all this archaeobotanically, and much more work will be required before it is possible to understand even the most basic patterns in many regional sequences. Further research is also required to understand the human significance of these major subsistence transformations as they played out in different parts of the world (see Pluciennik and Zvelebil 2008). Beyond the contingency and complexity of these local trajectories of change, the cumulative global pattern is simple: increasing human dependence on an ever-narrower range of domesticated plants to satisfy basic dietary needs for carbohydrates, fats, oils, and other nutrients. This new kind of highly focused economic existence stood in stark contrast to the enormous diversity of plant foods exploited by broad-spectrum hunter-gatherer systems and other intermediate subsistence systems.

How did plant domestication actually come about? Harris highlights active manipulation and intervention by early hunter-gatherers in the life-cycles of plants, often to ensure availability and increase yield. Such strategies may have included burning, tilling, weeding, planting, sowing, irrigation, and drainage. In turn, this direct human intervention must have led—but only in *some* cases—to morphogenetic domestication of some species, particularly those that were inherently storable, as well as those that responded quickly to such manipulation through substantially greater yields, including grass and forbs seeds, roots, and tubers. Ultimately, only a very narrow range of wild species were ever domesticated, and Harris highlights that this process tended to occur in, and reinforce, the ecological and cultural settings that favoured sedentary rather than seasonally mobile settlement. Thus, it was some 12,000 years ago that our hunter-gatherer ancestors began the first steps along the pathways to plant domestication, generating 'an innovation of unparalleled magnitude in human history'.

In the final chapter in this part of the handbook, Outram completes exploration of the wider theme by investigating the domestication of animals, and reflects on the role of hunter-gatherer societies in initiating these processes. He notes that animal domestication is both older and also more recent than the domestication of many plant species. The domestication of dogs was clearly a very early hunter-gatherer innovation. In later periods, there may also have been a direct domestication of wild horses by hunter-gatherers in the steppes of Central Asia, which he explores in his central case study. Reindeer also appear to have been independently tamed and domesticated by hunter-gatherers living in several different parts of northern Eurasia, but this complex topic requires much more research.

More generally, Outram concludes that by far the majority of animal domestications *post-date* plant domestications. Why might this be the case? It may be lack of suitable animal species in many areas, but Outram argues that availability of fodder may also play a crucial role in the timing and onset of the process. Stocks of animal fodder are a common by-product of plant-based agriculture, and the manure produced by the animals that were sustained by this extra plant matter may have then been used to fertilize crops and improve yields. Concurrently, these animals also provided food and other secondary products, such as wool and milk, as well as traction. More generally, animal domestications were also symptomatic of a cultural shift, where greater interest was taken in sustaining the welfare of *living* animals, rather than in procuring carcasses of *dead* animals through hunting, especially if the secondary products of captive herds were highly valued. Thus, the initial emergence of plant agriculture may have resulted in widespread land clearance, generating new supplies of fodder that could have been used in some environments to facilitate year-round husbandry of tamed and then fully domesticated livestock. In contrast, such limiting factors may have been absent for control of steppe-adapted horses or the loose husbandry of northern reindeer, and are, of course, irrelevant to the domestication of dogs.

In conclusion, most animal domestications were undertaken by early agriculturalists, through there are some exceptions to this trend. Whatever the exact local sequence, the increasing integration of domesticated plants and animals into early agro-pastoral farming systems went on to have enormous implications for hunter-gatherers worldwide (see Part V).

Conclusion: Innovating Hunter-Gatherers, Local Histories, and Long-Term Outcomes

This introduction started with a brief overview of some of the main theoretical perspectives in hunter-gatherer research, ranging from the different strands of social and (general) neo-evolutionary thinking, the interest in multilinear evolution that was central to Julian Steward's cultural ecology, through to the historical particularism and cultural relativism of Franz Boas. The legacy of this older work remains central to the study of hunter-gatherers, and all of these theoretical perspectives continue to structure contemporary scholarship and debate. The more recent archaeological materials and interpretations reviewed above—and presented in more detail in the following chapters— also continue to highlight some of the major tensions between these different approaches. Viewed against this theoretical background, they identify remaining gaps in understanding, but also signal new areas for potential integration, where fresh research and synthesis might productively proceed.

The Legacy of Social Evolutionary Thinking

One of the key problems with early social evolutionary thinking—and to a similar extent, some of the later general evolutionary thinking of Childe (1929) and White (1959)—was that hunter-gatherers were regarded as a specific type of society. Generally then, hunter-gatherers were implicitly presented as lacking an internal capacity for innovation and change, until that is, they had ascended towards another economic or technological stage of development. Clearly, based on material reviewed here (and throughout the following chapters), these assumptions can be challenged—in fact, the relentless internal social, political, economic, and technological dynamism of prehistoric hunter-gatherers was a central driving force in some of the most important cultural transformations to affect global humanity. In this way, all chapters in this part of the handbook serve to emphasize the role of prehistoric hunter-gatherers as the 'great innovators'.

Importantly, the chapters also underline that fundamental changes in human existence were already well underway long before the rise of agro-pastoral farming and the emergence of the 'Neolithic Revolution'. Clearly, prehistoric hunter-gatherers were not culturally 'stagnant' or lacking in capacities for innovation and change—far from it. From the rise of entrenched social inequality, through to the invention of art, pottery, and other new technologies, as well as the establishment of farming economies, prehistoric forager societies were at the forefront of initiating these long-term cultural transformations.

Deeper analysis of the internal dynamics of hunter-gatherer lifeways, especially during the crucial terminal Pleistocene and early Holocene transition, could therefore be argued to represent one of the most fundamentally important periods of human prehistory. Developments in this crucial period certainly exerted a profound influence on later phases of global history, and the legacy of these changes continues to structure human existence through to this day.

Identifying General Patterns in Cultural Evolution

So where do these comprehensive archaeological insights into innovating hunter-gatherers leave social evolutionary thinking? Is it better to adopt a focus on understanding the particularistic features of specific local cultures, as Boas might have advised? Or can 'stadial' notions of human development be rehabilitated into contemporary scholarship? One of the key archaeological challenges to cultural relativism and historical particularism (and indeed to post-processual archaeology and its interpretive offspring more generally—see the main introduction) is that there are clearly some very striking general patterns in long-term, cumulative, cultural evolution, though these need not (and should not) necessarily be viewed in terms of 'progressive' changes in the older social evolutionary sense.

Evidence of these general patterns being played out in different parts of the globe can also be used to refute the Boasian assumption that all cultures are inherently unique. In a similar vein, when stripped of all their racist implications, the older general schema of prehistoric 'stadial' evolution were not empirically 'wrong' in their broad outline. For example, there are some common global trends in the main sequences of culture change: key lithic innovations pre-date the rise of pottery, pottery pre-dates farming, and most prehistoric foragers eventually went on to adopt some form of farming in more recent periods. In other words, despite the inherent flaws in early manifestations of social evolutionary thinking, it is clear that hunting and gathering—when viewed narrowly as a form of economic adaptation—were eventually overtaken by the cumulative historical transformations that had been unleashed earlier in prehistory.

Perhaps the main shortcoming in this kind of stadial view of cultural evolution was that foragers were generally denied a capacity for internal change—a flawed assumption that is confronted throughout this part of the handbook. Given this current re-evaluation of archaeological evidence, one of the most fundamentally important thresholds in human cultural development now appears to be the breakdown of an older egalitarian social order, and the rise of *trans*-egalitarian societies, though this rupture did not correlate with the onset of Neolithic farming economies: the key shift is within the hunter-gatherer mode of existence, and not at the threshold between foraging and farming. Humanity has clearly gone through some broad developmental stages, though older social evolutionary thinkers appear to have placed the boundaries at the 'wrong' juncture (though given the contemporary eighteenth- and nineteenth-century obsessions with the moral and economic obligations of farming, enclosure, and landscape improvement, this was perhaps understandable—see Barnard; Pluciennik, Part I). More importantly, this realization renders the renewed study of socio-political dynamics *within* earlier hunter-gatherer societies all the more important.

Studying Long-Term Process

Identifying the structure and content in such general patterns also opens up the potential for comparative analysis between specific historical contexts, with the higher goal of understanding the particular processes that generate such cultural regularities. For example, a cross-contextual approach to the study of this patterning indicates that early hunter-gatherer societies—from the Baltic, through to the Near East, Siberia, Japan, and well beyond—were all starting to exhibit similar sets of traits that reflected growing differentiation in personal wealth and status, increasing storage, and politicized control of resources, from the Upper Palaeolithic through to the early Holocene. Of course, the specific cultural details varied enormously between these regions, but this general pattern remains fast, and demands an explanation.

How best to develop this kind of enquiry? A second important point is that these general patterns were not evident in all areas of the prehistoric world. They are highly concentrated in certain, highly productive environments, such as glacial parklands during the Palaeolithic, and later, in rich aquatic ecosystems during the Mesolithic. One of the key insights from Steward's cultural ecology was that local adaptations are highly contingent, but that different environments can shape the general direction of different trajectories of development. This seems to be the case here—understanding the impacts of human–environment relations is important, and adds a further analytical dimension to much of the patterning that has been noted above, whether in the rise of social complexity, the emergence of pottery, or initial steps towards domestication, especially of plants. All develop in settings with very similar sets of environmental characteristics but, equally, tend to be absent in more marginal ecosystems.

Clearly, environmental factors appear to structure many of the broader patterns of cultural innovation, affording complex local intersections of opportunity and also constraint, especially during phases of major climate change. This is not about asserting simplistic environmental determinism, but something more subtle and pervasive. The economies and communities that became established in these kinds of highly productive ecosystems did appear to generate dense seasonal concentrations of people, intensive patterns of interaction, and new kinds of politicized activity, all of which become central themes in the rise of almost all the innovations explored throughout this part of the handbook.

Understanding Hunter-Gatherer 'Agency'

One of the key problems with cultural ecology was that it tended to focus on group-level patterns of adaptation; that is, it tended to view populations as being in equilibrium with their environments and local resources (see the main introduction). Often absent from this kind of study was the role of individuals in generating new patterns of behaviour. It is here that Hayden makes an important step by situating a sense of 'agency' between communities and their resources, thereby attempting to explain long-term change, and not just to describe basic patterns of adaptation. In his analysis, it is the highly visible strategizing of 'aggrandizer' individuals that appears to take cumulative developments into new directions, but these strategies only work in the context of rich ecosystems, where there are abundant resources. They are also historically contingent upon the groups possessing the required technologies to sustain surplus production over the longer term. Hayden's approach therefore represents a fusion of some of the key ideas in cultural ecology, along with a more resolute concern with the political economy of feasting and the impacts of aggrandizing behaviours in small-scale societies. Hayden terms this approach 'political ecology', and in his analysis of the emergence of trans-egalitarian societies, it is persuasive, though its links to other kinds of cultural innovation remain less clearly articulated.

Other authors also consider the role of 'agency' in generating long-term change, but adopt a slightly different, albeit complementary, focus. For Hommel, this involves understanding localized cultural choices in the uptake and modification of new technological traditions, though not necessarily by 'aggrandizers', but by individuals in the wider community. Nilsson Stutz adopts an even broader treatment of agency in generating both localized variability and also long-term change, and views Mesolithic mortuary practices as a set of contingent performances associated with ensuring the appropriate treatment of specific individuals and their material residues. These individual events must have been negotiated and highly improvised activities, at times perhaps dominated by the narrow concerns of some individual strategists in hosting ancestral feasts for political gain, but also motivated by more humble concerns generated by the need to grieve, and also to adjust to the loss and departure of a valued (or perhaps despised) member of the community. All of this creativity and cultural pragmatism builds on older traditions and stocks of knowledge, and thereby feeds into larger patterns of long-term transformation. History is therefore a cumulative process—many technological innovations also relied on older insights, skills, and understandings, the fusion of these generating new phases of development. The emergence of pottery through integration of older 'soft' container technologies and the knowledge of how to fire clay is a good example of this. It is also clear from many chapters that such a diverse suite of innovations (in stone tool types, pottery, plant and animal domestications) could only spread within specific kinds of historically contingent social networks. As a result, understanding human agency also involves the study of specific social learning processes, which go on to structure the long-term dynamics of cultural transmission, a general theme also considered by Eerkens et al. in the Part VII.

Perhaps most importantly in the study of hunter-gatherer agency, it is clear from the case studies that individuals and communities would not necessarily have fully understood or foreseen the long-term implications of the minor shifts in their local routines or the pursuit of specific personal or political goals. Probably the best illustration of this is the domestication of plants discussed by Harris—minimal daily or seasonal adjustments and interventions in the life-cycles of wild plant communities eventually went on to have outcomes of global importance, though none of the individuals involved in the early stages of this process could have known or anticipated this.

Understanding exactly how these types of highly localized and contingent adjustments lead to long-term culture change brings the discussion back to the importance of developing *particularistic*—though not necessarily culturally *relativistic*—insights into local contexts and sequences. At the same time, they also highlight the importance of maintaining a comparative perspective and an appreciation of long-term and global patterns in cultural evolution (see Cannon, Part I).

Further work on the prehistory of all these hunter-gatherer innovations should therefore engage creatively with the challenges of balancing analytical scale with questions of long-term cultural process, as well as maintain a concern with understanding the intersections between situated social action and wider environmental contexts. Older traditions of hunter-gatherer research continue to provide useful concepts to work with, but much new analysis remains to be done. In conclusion then, relentless innovation is one of the absolutely definitive features of prehistoric hunter-gatherer lifeways, but to fully understand these processes and their cumulative outcomes, it is important to situate these dynamics back within localized historical trajectories in order to fully understand their context of operation.

References

Childe, V. G. 1929. *The Danube in prehistory*. Oxford: Clarendon Press.
Conneller, C. 2006. Death. In C. Conneller and G. Warren (eds), *Mesolithic Britain and Ireland: new approaches*, 139–64. Stroud: Tempus.
Craig, O. E., Saul, H., Lucquin, A., Nishida, Y., Taché, K., Clarke, L., Thompson, A., Altoft, D., Uchiyama, J., Ajimoto, M., Gibbs, K., Isaksson, S., Heron, C. P., and Jordan, P. 2013. Earliest evidence for the use of pottery. *Nature* 496, 351–4.
Gibbs, K. and Jordan, P. 2013. Bridging the boreal forest: Siberian archaeology and the emergence of pottery among prehistoric hunter-gatherers of northern Eurasia. *Sibirica* 12, 1–38.
Habu, J. 2004. *Ancient Jomon of Japan*. Cambridge: Cambridge University Press.
Hayden, B. 2009. Foreword. In P. Jordan and M. Zvelebil (eds), *Ceramics before farming: the dispersal of pottery among prehistoric Eurasian hunter-gatherers*, 19–26. Walnut Creek, CA: Left Coast Press.
Jordan, P. and Zvelebil, M. 2009. Ex Oriente Lux: the prehistory of hunter-gatherer ceramic dispersals. In P. Jordan and M. Zvelebil (eds), *Ceramics before farming: the dispersal of pottery among prehistoric Eurasian hunter-gatherers*, 33–89. London: University College London Institute of Archaeology Publications.
Mithen, S. 1996. *The prehistory of the mind: a search for the origins of art*. London: Thames and Hudson.

O'Shea, J. and Zvelebil, M. 1984. Oleneostrovski Mogilnik: reconstructing the social and economic organisation of prehistoric foragers in northern Russia. *Journal of Anthropological Archaeology* 3, 1–40.

Pluciennik, M. and Zvelebil, M. 2008. The origins and spread of agriculture. In R. A.Bentley, H. D. Maschner, and C. Chippindale (eds), *Handbook of archaeological theory*, 467–86. Lanham, MD: Rowman & Littlefield.

Rice, P. 1999. On the origins of pottery. *Journal of Archaeological Method and Theory* 6, 1–54.

Steward, J. H. 1955. *Theory of culture change*. Urbana: University of Illinois Press.

Weber, A., Katzenburg, M., and Schurr, T. (eds) 2010. *Prehistoric hunter-gatherers of the Baikal Region, Siberia*. Philidelphia, PA: University of Pennslyvania Press.

White, L. 1959. *The evolution of culture*. New York: McGraw-Hill.

Zvelebil, M. 2008 Innovating hunter-gatherers: the Mesolithic in the Baltic. In G. Bailey and P. Spikins (eds), *The Mesolithic in Europe*, 18–59. Cambridge: Cambridge University Press.

CHAPTER 27

STONE TOOL TECHNOLOGY

STEVEN L. KUHN AND AMY E. CLARK

WHY STONE TOOLS?

THE simplest answer to this question is that we study stone tools because that is what we have to work with. All of the evidence we have for technological behaviour prior to 100,000 years ago or so, save a few rare artefacts of bone and even rarer preserved wooden tools, consists of battered and flaked stones. This fact is no cause for dismay, however. There is a great deal that is interesting and informative about stone tools, over and above their ubiquity. For more than 2.5 million years, stone artefacts have been an important part of the human behavioural phenotype. They provide unique information about the adaptive challenges faced by our forebears and about the developing role of technology in responding to those challenges. Humans are not the only animals that use or even make artefacts. However, as a species, we are dependent on technology to a degree unmatched by any other organism. This is true of hunter-gatherers as well as urban peoples, despite obvious discrepancies in the complexity and variety of technological knowledge and material products. How we became a fundamentally technological species is one of the key unresolved questions in palaeoanthropology.

Stone tools helped early human toolmakers cope with their environments, but the use of stone as a raw material also posed its own unique problems. Rocks suitable for flaking do not necessarily occur in the same places as other crucial resources such as food, water, and fuel. Studying the ways early humans dealt with these spatial incongruities provides unique insights about territoriality and landscape use, as well as clues about their cognitive capacities (e.g. Mithen 1996, 104–5).

Non-adaptive features of artefacts also carry information about past populations. Archaeologists have learned to read from stone artefacts subtle details of technological procedures and, more controversially, the conceptual models behind them. Some of these observations bear directly on issues of economics and cognition. Because part of this technological diversity is energetically neutral, not subject to strong adaptive constraints, it is also invaluable in establishing cultural phylogenies and potentially in understanding demographic processes among ancient populations.

Long-Term Trends

Table 27.1 presents chronological information for some important 'innovations' in stone tool technology. These include various methods for producing or shaping artefacts, as well as techniques related to hafting and projectiles. All of these have been considered important markers of different evolutionary phases or stages in human prehistory, including the appearance of *Homo sapiens* and so-called 'modern human behaviour'. Note that all dates for first appearance should be considered minimum estimates. Future discoveries will almost inevitably push maximum ages back in time.

One of the first things apparent from the table is that there is often a time lag between the earliest appearance of a particular behaviour and its widespread adoption. Thus, for example, there may be a gap of several hundred thousand years between the earliest known flaked stone tools and the point at which they became a regular feature of hominin behaviour, such that they are found in multiple localities and contexts (although problems of site preservation and taphonomy make this inference provisional). Likewise, the first hand axes may have been manufactured <1.5 million years ago (Asfaw et al. 1992), but they did not become the predominant technology in Africa until later. We are on firmer ground with Levallois, blade, and bladelet technologies. The earliest evidence for Levallois and blade production occurs at least 400,000 years ago in both Africa and Eurasia (Barkai et al. 2003; Porat et al. 2010; Tryon et al. 2005; Tuffreau 2004), but Levallois only became truly widespread after 250,000 years ago. Blade technology was only widely adopted on a global scale after 50,000 years ago. The systematic and specialized production of small bladelets and standardized geometric segments (Figure 27.1), presumably to be used as elements in composite tools, can now be dated back to as early as 90,000 years ago in Africa, and to around 40,000 years ago in Eurasia (Boëda and Bonilauri 2006; Maíllo Fernández et al. 2004; Marean et al. 2007). However, except for a brief florescence in the earliest Upper Palaeolithic, bladelet-based technologies did not really come into widespread use globally until well after 30,000 years ago (Elston and Kuhn 2002).

The received wisdom is that the development of technology is innovation driven, that great leaps forward are triggered by key inventions. In fact, this does not seem to be an accurate view of either recent history or the remote past (Henrich et al. 2008, 129–31). Novel forms of technology may remain in obscurity until the material and social contexts are right for their widespread adoption, at which point they may spread far and fast (e.g. Bar-Yosef and Kuhn 1999). Thus, the first appearance of certain kinds of technology may have fewer evolutionary implications than one might think. Like chance genetic mutations, they may have persisted at low frequencies or in small populations until their potential advantages were fully realized. Their widespread adoption in turn depends on a variety of social and economic factors (Powell et al. 2009; Schiffer 2004).

A second general trend apparent from Table 27.1 is that once hominin populations had dispersed across the globe, beginning about 1.8 million years ago, technological developments proceeded in parallel in different regions. Perhaps because of the much longer history of continuous hominin presence there, many developments have their earliest dates in Africa. However, it is very likely that artefacts such as hand axes were developed independently in East Asia (Dennell 2008), and that methods such as Levallois

Table 27.1 Estimated dates for appearance of significant production methods and artefact forms. Calibrated radiocarbon ages are used for compatibility with other methods. In column 'becomes common locally', multiple ages indicate that use of a particular technique or artefact form proliferated (and declined) more than once; question marks indicate where a particular form never became widespread.

Major innovation	Earliest date *	Location	Becomes locally common	References
Methods of production				
Flaked stone tools	2.6 my	Ethiopia	2.4 my ?	Semaw 2000; Plummer 2004
Bifacial hand axes	1.6 my	Ethiopia, South Africa	~1.0 my	Asfaw et al. 1992; Chazan et al. 2008
	1.2–1.4 my	Israel	<800 ky	Bar-Yosef and Goren-Inbar 1994
	~900 ky	Spain	<800 ky	Scott and Gibert 2009
	800 ky	China	???	Yamei et al. 2000
Prepared cores	>800 ka	Africa, SW Asia, India	<800 ka	Sharon 2009
Levallois method	450–550 ka	South Africa	<250 ky	Porat et al. 2009
	200–500 ka	Kenya	<250 ky	Tryon et al. 2005
	300–400 ka	Northern Europe	<250 ky	Tuffreau 2004
	~800 ka ?	Israel	<250 ky	Goren-Inbar et al. 2000
Blade production	450–550 ka	South Africa	60 ky	Porat et al. 2009
	200–380 ky	Israel	200 ky; <50 ky	Barkai et al. 2003
Hafting and projectiles				
Backed segments	60–70 ka	South, E. Africa	<30 ky	Jacobs et al. 2008a; 2008b
	<40 ky	Southern Europe	<30 ky	Koumouzelis et al. 2001; Higham et al. 2009
Bladelet production	~90 ky	South Africa	<30 ky	Marean et al. 2007
	<40 ky	Eurasia (mult. loc.)	40 ky; <30 ky	Boeda and Bonilauri 2006; Maillo Fernandez et al. 2004
Thinned bifacial points	70–90 ky	South Africa	???	Jacobs et al. 2008a; 2008b
	45–50 ky	N., C. Europe	20 ky; <10 ky	Hopkinson 2007

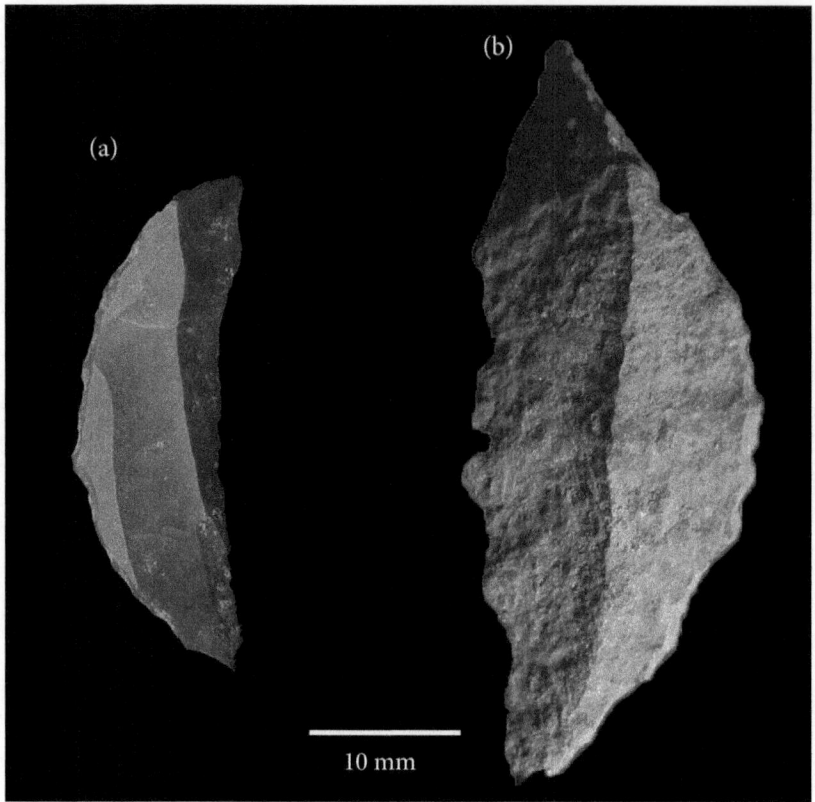

FIGURE 27.1 Geometric inserts for composite tools: (a) Klissoura cave, Greece, c.40,000 BP (photo by Dr Gidon Hartman; used by permission of Dr Margarita Koumouzelis); (b) Sibudu cave, S. Africa, c.70,000 BP (photo used by courtesy of Dr Lynn Wadley).

and blade production developed in parallel in different parts of Africa and Eurasia (see below).

The Earliest Artefacts

The first major innovation in stone tool making that we know of was the one that first made it visible to archaeologists. Sometime around 2.6 million years ago, human ancestors living the Ethiopian Rift Valley began to produce sharp-edged implements by striking flakes from pebble cores (Semaw 2000). Like living chimpanzees, earlier Pliocene hominins probably used simple hammers and anvils of stone as well as implements of other materials long before this time, but the evidence either is not preserved or goes unrecognized. For example, it is unlikely archaeologists would recognize as artefacts battered stones used by chimpanzees to open hard-shelled nuts. The earliest flakes and cores from east African sites, simple though they might be, are easily distinguished from naturally fractured stones. Moreover, hominins moved the artefacts away from the stream beds where they collected the raw materials, so that they stand out even more. Sites with stone tools are found in deposits dating to 2.4 million years ago or later in many other areas (Plummer 2004; Semaw 2000), suggesting that the technology was becoming widely adopted by this time.

The first recognized tools are quite basic: simply sharp-edged stone flakes and the cores from which they were struck. Over the next 1.0 million years or so there are some minor changes to this basic tool-kit. Cores show signs that they were worked more extensively and systematically. In the so-called Oldowan industry, artefacts known as choppers (which might be tools, cores, or both) occur in greater abundance, and the edges of some flakes are further shaped by retouch. New artefact forms such as spheroids—rounded, battered pebbles in various sizes—appear as well. But these changes are very gradual.

Simple as they are, these earliest artefacts tell us several things about the toolmakers. For the first time, hominins were doing something that required durable, sharp cutting edges. Cut-marked bones (e.g. de Heinzelin et al. 1999; Plummer 2004) show that collection of meat from large animal carcasses was one of the main applications for the first stone artefacts. This expansion of diet placed our forebears in a new ecological arena, in potential competition with large carnivores. The fact that hominins were fairly successful at detaching flakes (Roche et al. 1999; Semaw 2000), and even selected certain types of stone for making tools (Braun et al. 2009), demonstrates that they had some understanding of the working properties of these materials.

Although these developments were extraordinarily important, artefacts of stone probably played a minor role in the hominin adaptive repertoire. Plio-Pleistocene hominins did not invest much more than a few minutes in producing any single artefact. Moreover, although they sometimes carried artefacts to or away from sites, the hominins seldom moved their tools more than a few kilometres, probably within the limits of their day ranges. These observations suggest that hominins had a limited range of uses for their stone tools, and that they did not keep them around very long, preferring to make new tools when needs arose. Depending so much on the chance that stone could be found when tools were needed is not the mark of a tool-dependent hominin.

New Hominins, New Artefacts

Sometime around 1.6 million years ago, new forms of artefact begin to appear in African sites. These are bifacially worked hand axes (Figure 27.2) and cleavers, more extensively shaped than Oldowan choppers and with longer, more acute cutting edges, the signature tools of so-called Acheulian (or Mode 2) assemblages. Their appearance coincides with the earliest fossils of a new taxon, *Homo ergaster/Homo erectus*, with a larger brain and more fully developed mode of bipedal locomotion than earlier hominin forms (see review by Antón 2003, 128–9). The first hand axes are only marginally different from Oldowan tools. Fully realized bifacial shaping, which involves a series of staged actions and even different kinds of hammers, came gradually. Moreover, simpler, Oldowan-type assemblages continue to appear alongside assemblages with hand axes for hundreds of thousands of years (e.g. Clark et al. 1994). However, an even more important change comes sometime after 1.0 million years, with the appearance of *prepared core technologies* (the ages of the earliest sites remain uncertain). Here, hominins shaped large stone cores extensively enough to

FIGURE 27.2 Bifacial Acheulian hand axe (Göllü Dağ, Turkey) (photo by Berkay Dinçer).

predetermine the form of the final flake to be struck from them. The large flakes they produced were essentially ready-made hand axes and cleavers (Figure 27.3), with razor-sharp edges, usable with only minor modification (see Sharon 2009). Perhaps these large flake tools were more effective than bifacially shaped artefacts, although both varieties continued to be produced. What is clear is that they show an ability to think many steps ahead in a technological sequence, to work at forming a core from which a pre-shaped hand axe or cleaver could be detached with a single blow, rather than working gradually at paring down a pebble one flake at a time.

Hand axes and cleavers are fascinating tools. They strike us as being much more functional and fully realized artefacts than anything that came before. They look like tools that any of us could work with (if we were accustomed to using stone tools). What hominins used them for is another question. Experimental evidence suggests they could have functioned well in butchering large animals and other tasks, and limited evidence from archaeological contexts indicates that they were indeed multi-functional artefacts.

Along with more sophisticated tools, some east African Acheulian assemblages provide evidence that artefacts were transported over somewhat greater distances, 10 km or more in some instances. This indicates that hominins were ranging over larger areas, and perhaps that they were holding on to their artefacts for longer periods of time. Combined with the inference that bifacial implements were multi-functional, these observations suggest that hominins were growing more dependent on technology. Only a fairly dedicated tool-user would carry around a multi-purpose implement consisting of half a kilo or more of heavy stone for hours on end.

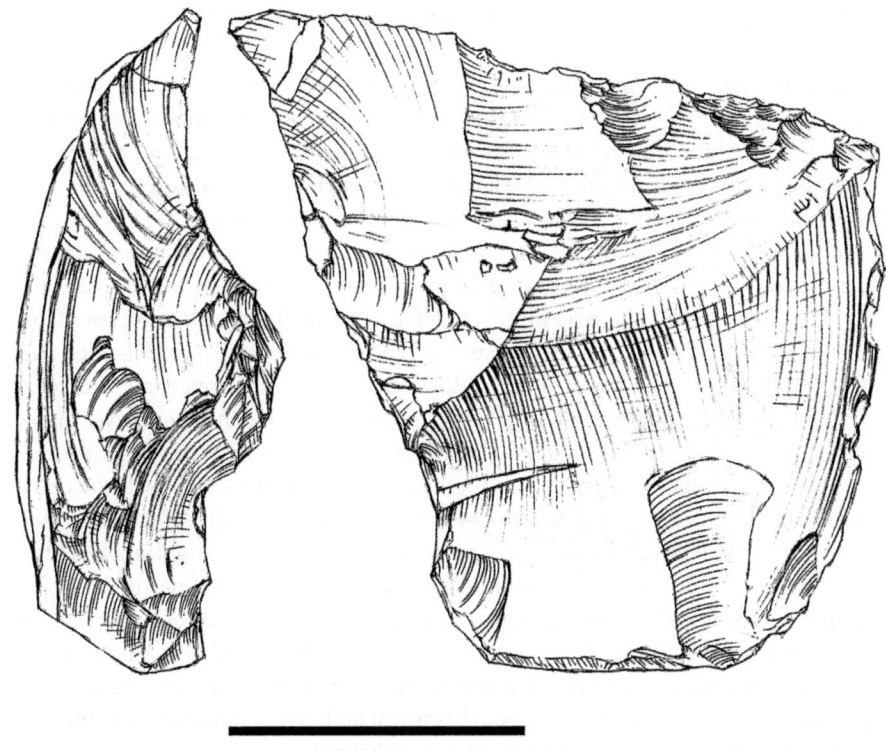

FIGURE 27.3 Acheulian cleaver flake from prepared core (Kaletepe Dersi 3, Turkey). After Slimak et al. 2008 (drawing by Michele Grenet).

By a million years ago, it is clear that hominin technologies had become more sophisticated and more important to survival. Yet there are still many missing elements. Given evidence for increasing carnivorousness at this time, the absence of obvious weapons is striking. Although they were skilled stone workers and effective carnivores, the first makers of hand axes do not seem to have produced stone tools specifically to help them bring down their prey. These facts are consistent with the hypothesis that early Acheulian hominins (*Homo ergaster*) relied on running down and exhausting prey, rather than killing it at a distance with thrown weapons (Bramble and Lieberman 2004).

Although hand axes seem like more effective tools than Oldowan choppers, they were not the tools that accompanied the first hominins who moved out of Africa into the rest of the world. The earliest stone tools from Europe and Asia, more than 1.7 million years ago, are simple flakes and cores, more like the African Oldowan. Clearly, hand axes were not instrumental in these earliest forays into other continents and other habitats (Gabunia et al. 2001). While they appear in Eurasia before 1 million years ago they only became widespread after about 800,000 years ago (Bar-Yosef and Goren-Inbar 1993; Scott and Gilbert 2009).

Middle and Upper Pleistocene Trends

The period between 700,000 and 40,000 years ago, which includes the second half of the Early Stone Age or Lower Palaeolithic and the entire Middle Stone Age or Middle Palaeolithic, is marked by a number of broad trends that speak to changes in the role of technology as well as cognitive developments. One of the most obvious is a greater emphasis on producing small tools, stone flakes with edges modified to achieve specific profiles and levels of sharpness. The production of more types of edges implies more functions for tools, a conclusion supported by studies of microscopic damage on the artefacts themselves. Accompanying the increase in the abundance of small flake tools is a proliferation in the array of techniques for producing flakes and blades (elongated, parallel-sided flakes). Levallois technology, the hallmark of the Middle Palaeolithic (in Europe) and Middle Stone Age (in Africa), takes the principle of predetermination to a much higher level than earlier technological systems (Boëda 1995) (Figure 27.4). Levallois becomes virtually ubiquitous in western Eurasia and Africa after 200,000 years, though its roots may be detected much earlier. But it is not all Levallois—researchers have identified a whole spectrum of different systems of flake production (Boëda et al. 1990). This technological diversity certainly reflects several influences. Some products are more suitable for particular activities or functions, and Palaeolithic toolmakers were aware of this. The kinds of stone available in local environments also constrained the range of methods that could be used. But a certain amount of technological variation simply represents alternative means of producing equivalent products. As such, it tells us more about historical or demographic processes than about the adaptive responses of Palaeolithic hominins (see below).

There are two other noteworthy developments over this period. One is the expanding scale of transport of stone tools. Although they often relied mainly on whatever stone was available locally, Middle Palaeolithic hominins in Europe (Neanderthals) regularly moved some artefacts as far as 50 km (Féblot-Augustins 1997), more rarely over distances of 100 km or more (e.g. Slimak and Giraud 2007). Middle Stone Age hominins in Africa (*Homo sapiens*) are known to have sometimes carried artefacts even further (e.g. McBrearty and Brooks 2000; Negash and Shackley 2006). Clearly, these populations took pains to keep artefacts on hand wherever they went. It is worth emphasizing that many of the implements were not directly used in the food quest, but were used to work wood, skins, or other materials. The

FIGURE 27.4 Modern experimental Levallois core and flake.

fact that hominins always kept stone tools ready to hand shows how important these other technological activities had become, and attest to an ever growing dependence on technology for survival.

A second development is the appearance of composite tools and the first hafted weapon tips. The earliest use of hafted stone points suitable for thrust or thrown spears may be associated with the African MSA (McBrearty and Brooks 2000), and points of all sorts are more common in the African record, but they are known from the early Middle Palaeolithic in western Eurasia as well. The presence of hafted points and cutting edges implies a greater complexity of artefacts and more investment in their manufacture. The stone element is only one part of the story. The wooden spear shaft or knife handle probably took longer to make than the stone point or blade. Other materials were needed to bind the stone securely to its wooden haft: evidence for mastics in the Middle Palaeolithic includes natural adhesives such as bitumen and, more remarkably, a kind of glue made from birch bark (Boëda et al. 1996; Grünberg 2002). Collecting or preparing these substances adds substantially to the cost of artefacts, and is further evidence that hominins were willing to invest a certain amount of time and energy in the production of effective implements.

Middle Stone Age and Middle Palaeolithic hominins (*Homo sapiens* and Neanderthals, respectively) were highly dependent on technology for survival, and of course it was not just stone tool technology—skin clothing and pyrotechnology were crucial to populations in the temperate zones. Looking specifically at the material record of the Neanderthals, however, there are some interesting anomalies. One is the lack of obvious technological responses to environmental variation, whether across space or though glacial/interglacial cycles. The archaeological and ethnographic records show clearly that the complexity, diversity, and contents of tool-kits of recent foragers varied in predictable ways across environmental gradients. It is difficult to identify analogous patterned variation in the Middle Palaeolithic, despite the vast range of environments in which it occurs (Bocquet-Appel and Tuffreau 2009; Kuhn and Stiner 2001). Currently, the African MSA record simply does not provide the density of information needed for detecting such patterns. This anomaly cannot simply be attributed to an innate inflexibility among the makers of Middle Palaeolithic technologies in Eurasia: like more recent humans, they were quite capable of adjusting their methods of stone working to the peculiarities of diverse raw materials, and of coping effectively with variation in the supply of usable stone. Perhaps we are just looking in the wrong place; perhaps the systematics used by archaeologists do not capture relevant variation. However, we cannot exclude the possibility that, important as it was for their survival, the role technology played in the lives of Middle Palaeolithic still differed from what we know of more recent humans.

One possible difference in the role of Middle Palaeolithic technologies concerns its functions beyond the practical realm. Middle Palaeolithic (and earlier) artefacts clearly helped their users to gain a physical advantage in the material world, to accomplish tasks they could not do with fingers and teeth alone. However, it is not obvious that the roles of these artefacts had expanded into social and symbolic realms. There is currently no compelling evidence that variation in technological procedures and artefact forms across Europe and Africa represents conscious signalling of identities rather than the result of random cultural drift in isolated populations. It is only later that *H. sapiens* begins to marshal a range of materials to express social identity, relations, and aspirations.

The Upper Palaeolithic

The dispersal of *Homo sapiens* into Eurasia is marked by the proliferation and expansion of Upper Palaeolithic technologies and the disappearance of Middle Palaeolithic ones (Bar-Yosef 2002a). In Africa, the evolutionary homeland of the species, the transition is more gradual, and begins earlier (McBrearty and Brooks 2000). Although the spread of the Upper Palaeolithic is often described as a technological revolution, the changes in lithic technology are only a small part of the story. The Upper Palaeolithic period is marked by the spread of blade technologies, a family of methods for producing elongated, parallel-sided flakes. Upper Palaeolithic blades are unusually refined and regular due in part to the use of special percussion techniques (Bar-Yosef and Kuhn 1999). Along with the widespread adoption of blade production come tool forms adapted to the shapes of blades, and a few novel techniques, such as pressure flaking, but most of these elements have much earlier precursors. In fact, most of the important technological developments associated with the appearance and dispersal of *Homo sapiens* are not seen in the stone tools, but relate to the use of materials such as hides, bone, antler, shell, and soft stone to produce new sorts of implements, more elaborate clothing, and even media of communication such as art and personal ornaments (Dennell 1984, 81–97; Gamble 1999; Kuhn and Stiner 2007; Mithen 1996, 170–5). Stone artefacts continued to be the main sources of durable edges and sharp points even into the early Metal Ages, and the Upper Palaeolithic and later periods saw some truly remarkable elaborations of the art of stone knapping and composite tool manufacture. Nonetheless, the most significant developments occurred in other technologies.

PRODUCTION AND LOSS OF DIVERSITY

It is satisfying to describe technological evolution as a single sequence marked by progressive improvements in the design of artefacts, increasing complexity in human cognition, or a growing dependence on technology for survival. Yet, while they may be valid in a broad sense, such linear narratives miss many other important trends pertaining to diversity in technological behaviour.

The Development of Global Diversity

It currently appears that hominins began expanding into Europe and Asia sometime around 1.8 million years ago. These pioneer populations encountered radically new kinds of environment and ecological challenges. At the same time, local populations inevitably became separated from one another by geographic barriers. One consequence was diversification, not only in the forms of artefacts and the techniques used to produce them, but in developmental trajectories as well. Due to geographic variance, east Asian, European, and African Palaeolithic technologies followed distinct evolutionary pathways. Many of the key technological developments marking different periods within the European and African Palaeolithic either do not appear, or appear at different times, in eastern Asia. So long as 'progress' was measured against the particular historical trajectories seen in Europe or the Levant, the east Asian record was seen as monotonous, even backward. However, the more that is learned about this vast area, the more it becomes clear that technologies simply evolved along independent lines.

For example, it was once thought that hand axes were absent in China, and that apparently primitive Oldowan-like artefacts persisted until the appearance of *Homo sapiens*. It is now well established that hand axe-like artefacts were sometimes made and used there as early as in Europe (Yamei et al. 2000). However, while they resemble Acheulian bifaces in shape (and functional attributes), the Chinese and Korean hand axes may be technologically distinct, produced by different flaking procedures. In other words, hominins in East Asia arrived at similar technological ends (large, pointed cutting tools) from different beginnings. Other phenomena very common in Africa and Eurasia, such as Levallois, seem never to have developed at all in eastern Asia (Lycett 2007). Hominins instead must have arrived at alternative solutions to the problems solved by these methods.

There are other examples of independent regional evolutionary trajectories. It is becoming clear that the Eurasian Middle Palaeolithic and African Middle Stone Age, once thought to be equivalent, actually trace rather different pathways of change between 250,000 and 50,000 years ago. These independent trajectories are certainly linked to the evolution of *Homo sapiens* in Africa, and to presumed cognitive and perhaps physical differences from the Eurasian Neanderthals, makers of the Middle Palaeolithic. Here again, measuring all technological development by a single yardstick—in this case so-called 'modern human behaviour'—misses out on an important fact: Middle Palaeolithic hominins in Europe and the Near East were not in a race with African MSA hominins to become behaviourally modern, but were instead evolving unique behavioural responses to conditions in temperate and sub-tropical regions.

Diversity and Demography

One of the most important developments in the study of stone artefacts over the past three decades is the elaboration and widespread use of the *chaîne opératoire* concept. This approach is based on the premises that technologies are best studied in their entirety, from the acquisition of raw materials to the discarding of used and worn-out implements, and that details of technological processes are rich in cultural information. The *chaîne opératoire* concept, and attendant methodologies, provides a diverse and nuanced view of technological behaviour, skills, and knowledge. It can be applied to almost any problem. However, researchers working in this tradition have focused a great deal of their attention on often subtle differences in manufacture procedures that have few consequences for the functional or economic properties of artefacts, but that reflect instead processes of learning and cultural transmission.

Just as diversity was produced as hominins expanded across the globe, diversity was also sometimes lost. The reduction of diversity, something not often discussed, has very important implications for demographic and macro-evolutionary processes. 'Pruning' of technological variety down to a few forms or techniques may be due to the rapid spread of a highly advantageous technological innovation: one example might be the spread of the bow and arrow in many regions during the later Pleistocene and Holocene. However, when there is no clear advantage to the surviving technologies, rapid loss of diversity is likely to reflect demographic events such as bottlenecks or replacement by allochthonous populations.

One example of such a loss of diversity occurred in South-West Asia towards the end of the Middle Pleistocene. Between 450,000 and 250,000 years ago, hominins living in the region encompassing modern-day Syria, Lebanon, Jordan, and Israel produced a variety of lithic assemblages, involving several distinct technological procedures to produce and shape artefacts. Several distinctive 'named' assemblage types (Acheulian, Yabrudian, Amudian, etc.) date to this time interval, and each of these encompasses significant variation in procedures and artefact forms (e.g. Bar-Yosef 2002b; Barkai et al. 2003). By 200,000 years ago the situation had changed markedly. All known sites from this time contain one of two similar assemblage types, called Hummalian or early Levantine Mousterian (Bar-Yosef 2002b), both marked by the production of many large blades and pointed flakes. The main difference is in the ways the blades were made: the early Levantine Mousterian is characterized by a heavy reliance on Levallois method, whereas the Hummalian involves more non-Levallois production. Eventually even the non-Levallois blade technology disappears, so that up until the appearance of the first Upper Palaeolithic industries around 45,000–50,000 years ago, every archaeological assemblage in the region is based on some variant of the Levallois method.

What can explain this remarkable reduction in diversity? It might be due to some inherent advantages of the new technological procedure: perhaps Levallois production was so much more effective or efficient than older ways of making stone tools that every population in the neighbourhood adopted it. Interestingly, however, that did not happen in western Europe, where Levallois coexisted with a range of very different methods for many millennia. This shift could also mark the dispersal of a new, more successful population that happened to be making stone tools in a different way (e.g. Foley and Lahr 1997), although Levallois has a longer history in the region (see Table 27.1). Alternatively, some catastrophic reduction in hominin populations could have created a cultural bottleneck, such that the region was repopulated by a small group of survivors who happened to be using a particular set of procedures to make flakes and blades. Although we currently cannot test these hypotheses, due in part to the scarcity of hominin fossils, it is important to emphasize that the rapid reduction of technological diversity may be more significant than the nature of the technologies themselves.

Another loss of diversity in Palaeolithic technologies is more clearly linked to a known demographic event, namely the dispersal of *Homo sapiens*. The technological features of late Middle Palaeolithic artefact assemblages in Europe, dating to between 45,000 and 35,000 years ago, vary widely. The last Neanderthal technologies may be quite similar within a single region, but globally there is much diversity. Yet by 33,000 years ago or so, this variability had largely disappeared. Except within areas that supported remnant Neanderthal populations, one finds a much more restricted range of lithic technologies associated with early Aurignacian assemblages. The appearance and spread of the Aurignacian, in all its variants, is thought to index the dispersal of *Homo sapiens* into Eurasia. The replacement of diverse assemblages created by late Neanderthals with a rather more uniform assemblage of material-culture traits and techniques can thus be attributed to a particular demographic cause.

However, if we examine this much discussed and debated 'transition' from Middle to Upper Palaeolithic more closely, interesting complexity appears. In much of Europe and western Asia, the Aurignacian is not actually the earliest variety of Upper Palaeolithic.

Instead, there are many local forms of 'earliest' Upper Palaeolithic, such as Uluzzian, Bohunician, Szeletian, and Châtelperronian (e.g. Kozlowski and Otte 2000; Zilhão and d'Errico 2003), nearly as varied as the late Middle Palaeolithic industries they follow. In other words, in addition to the turnover at the end of the Middle Palaeolithic, there is a significant loss of diversity *within* the early Upper Palaeolithic with the spread of the Aurignacian. These two phenomena are certainly linked to the same demographic events, but they reflect different sets of consequences. The loss of late Middle Palaeolithic diversity probably reflects large-scale disruption of long-established adaptations, due to a combination of rapid climate change and the appearance of new human populations (e.g. Banks et al. 2008; d'Errico and Sánchez-Goñi 2003). The diversity of the first Upper Palaeolithic assemblages is a function of the complexity of the processes of disruption. It probably encompasses adoption or invention of novel forms of behaviour of the part of local Neanderthals, adjustments of *Homo sapiens* groups to local conditions, and perhaps some cultural exchange and synthesis as well. A greater mystery is the subsequent truncation of this early Upper Palaeolithic diversity. It might be a result of the accelerated spread of a particularly successful set of technological adaptations along more extensive and stable social networks (Gamble 1999; Powell et al. 2009) or it could be due to the success of a particular sub-population carrying with it the Aurignacian technocomplex.

Assessments of diversity in early technological behaviour are a potentially rich source of insights into population conditions as well as processes of cultural transmission in the remote past. A strong case has been made that the rapid spread and persistence of cultural knowledge may be due as much to the stability and interconnectedness of human populations as to the cognitive capacities of humans and human ancestors (Powell et al. 2009). Instability of populations may have significant consequences as well. The fact that the two examples cited come from western Europe and the Levant simply reflects the large body of information from these areas. As the geographic scope of knowledge expands, as data accumulate from new excavations and from poorly known or isolated regions, our understanding of diversity in Palaeolithic technological behaviour and the processes behind it will only increase.

COGNITION AND TECHNOLOGY

As long as palaeoanthropologists have studied stone artefacts, they have viewed them as windows on the minds of the toolmakers. In the case of Palaeolithic technologies, the lithic record is one of the few documents of the evolving mental capacities of early humans. The first attempts to understand cognitive evolution from stone tools involved drawing direct parallels between the perceived complexity of artefacts and the cognitive sophistication of the toolmakers. Thus, some researchers read the apparent simplicity of Asian Palaeolithic artefacts in comparison with contemporary materials from Europe as a consequence of a lesser degree of mental development among Asian hominids (Movius 1948). The recognition that fully 'modern' cognitive abilities—elaborate social systems and oral traditions, and even sophisticated canons of graphic art—could be associated with very simple stone tools in recent societies put an end to this sort of simplistic interpretation. Contemporary researchers are exploring much more sophisticated approaches to reading the imprint of ancient minds on stone artefacts.

The longest established approaches to studying cognition from stone tools are based on the assumption that certain features of mind will be required to execute particular technological procedures (Mithen 1996, 117–21). The technological record is thus treated as a timeline of changes in hominin cognition, and researchers focus on the major developments. More than 20 years ago, Wynn (1989) argued that successful shaping and thinning of a bifacial Acheulian hand axe required a much better developed ability to coordinate actions in three-dimensional space than did making Oldowan tools. However, this view has been challenged (e.g. McPherron 2000). More recently, Wynn and Coolidge (2004) have asserted that Levallois technologies show an ability to coordinate sequential tasks and ramifying decision structures similar to many modern technological procedures, and that this demonstrates that Neanderthals possessed 'long-term working memory' on a par with living *Homo sapiens* (although they do hypothesize other cognitive differences). The marriage of several materials, in a particular order, to produce a finished composite tool such as a stone-tipped spear may also imply a significant cognitive advance, something analogous to a grammar of constructing artefacts (Ambrose 2001).

One recurring difficulty in reading mind from stone tools is that it requires an inference about the goals of ancient toolmakers. Yet many so-called 'finished' artefacts are nothing more than used up 'stubs' of tools, discarded when they were no longer of any use. Close attention to technological procedures, to sequences of actions habitually taken to produce tools, rather than final products, may help resolve this issue. Another important issue is whether cognitive processes identified in recent humans are good models for those present in earlier hominins; that is, whether earlier forms of intelligence were 'prototypes' of modern minds, or were evolutionarily distinct. Comparative studies across species, combined with neural imaging of brain activity during artefact manufacture (e.g. Stout et al. 2008), may help resolve this conundrum in the long run.

Other aspects of technological behaviour may provide a less direct reflection of ancient hominin minds. Laterality or handedness has long been a topic of interest to palaeoanthropologists. This lateralization of human physical and brain function has been linked to the localization of language in one hemisphere of the brain, so that the evolution of preferential right-handedness in hominins could be associated with the development of language. To date, attempts to infer preferential handedness among ancient toolmakers have been undermined by a range of methodological and technical shortcomings (Cashmore et al. 2008).

In viewing technology as the product of evolving human cognition, we should not lose sight of the fact that, in some small way at least, technology helped direct those same evolutionary processes. Social interaction or the challenges of negotiating complex natural landscapes of risks and rewards have more direct consequences for fitness, and may well have played a more important role in shaping the human mind as we know it (Alvard 2003). However, as artefact use became more important to the survival of hominins, the complexities of making and keeping a supply of tools must have imposed constraints on cognitive evolution as well. The demands of reconciling needs for food, fuel, water, and raw materials on landscapes in which they were seldom found together in the same place would have given a selective advantage to cognitive structures that help us map out temporal schedules and physical geographies.

Of course, although all people make and use tools, our abilities to make artefacts are acquired, not innate. Many a 'behaviourally modern' twenty-first century PhD has trouble matching a *Homo erectus* when it comes to making hand axes or cleavers. The range of skills and strategies manifested by hominins at any specific time would have been as much a product of the ways in which knowledge was acquired and passed on as a reflection of cognitive capacities. Palaeoanthropologists have only just begun to explore the learning processes by which technological expertise was transmitted across generations, and the conditions that favour persistence or loss of knowledge. Just as the approach known as 'Evo/Devo' (evolution and development) is revolutionizing the study of biological variation, understanding more about learning and cultural transmission will help us make better use of what we know of technological variation though time and across space over the past 2.6 million years.

REFERENCES

Alvard, M.S. 2003. The adaptive nature of culture. *Evolutionary Anthropology* 12, 136–49.
Ambrose, S. 2001. Palaeolithic technology and human evolution. *Science* 291, 1748–53.
Antón, S. 2003. The natural history of *Homo erectus*. *American Journal of Physical Anthropology* 122, 126–70.
Asfaw, B., Beyene, Y., Suwa, G., Walker, R., White, T., WoldeGabriel, G., and Yemane, T. 1992. The earliest Acheulian from Konso-Gardula. *Nature* 360, 732–5.
Banks, W. E., d'Errico, F., Peterson, A. T., Kageyama, M., Sima, A., and Sánchez-Goñi, M. F. 2008. Neanderthal extinction by competitive exclusion. *PLoS ONE* 3: e3972.
Barkai, R., Gopher, A., Lauritzen, S. E., and Frumkin, A. 2003. Uranium series dates from Qesem Cave, Israel, and the end of the Lower Palaeolithic. *Nature* 423, 977–9.
Bar-Yosef, O. 2002a. The Upper Palaeolithic revolution. *Annual Review of Anthropology* 31, 363–93.
Bar-Yosef, O. 2002b. The chronology of the Middle Palaeolithic of the Levant. In T. Akazawa, T. Aoki, and O. Bar-Yosef (eds), *Neandertals and modern humans in western Asia*, 39–56. New York: Springer.
Bar-Yosef, O. and Goren-Inbar, N. 1993. *The lithic assemblages of 'Ubeidiya, a Lower Palaeolithic site in the Jordan Valley*. Jerusalem: Hebrew University.
Bar-Yosef, O. and Kuhn, S. 1999. The big deal about blades: laminar technologies and human evolution. *American Anthropologist* 101, 322–38.
Bocquet-Appel, J.-P. and Tuffreau, A. 2009. Technological responses of Neanderthals to macro-climatic variations (240,000–40,000 BP). *Human Biology* 81, 287–307.
Boëda, E. 1995. Levallois: a volumetric construction, methods, a technique. In H. L. Dibble and O. Bar-Yosef (eds), *The definition and interpretation of Levallois Technology*, 41–69. Madison: Prehistory Press.
Boëda, E. and Bonilauri, S. 2006. The intermediate Palaeolithic: the first bladelet production 40,000 years ago. *Anthropologie* 44. 75–92.
Boëda, E., Connan, J., Dessort, D., Muhesen, S., Mercier, N., Valladas, H., and Tisnérat, N. 1996. Bitumen as a hafting material on Middle Palaeolithic artefacts. *Nature* 380, 336–8.
Boëda, E., Geneste, J.-M., and Meignen, L. 1990. Identification de *chaînes opératoires* lithiques du Paléolithique ancien et moyen. *Paléo* 2, 43–80.
Bramble, D. M. and Lieberman, D. E. 2004. Endurance running and the evolution of *Homo Nature* 432, 345–52.
Braun, D., Plummer, T., Ditchfield, P., Ferraro, J. V., Maina, D., Bishop, L.C., and Potts, R. 2009. Oldowan behaviour and raw material transport: perspectives from Kanjera Formation. *Journal of Archaeological Science* 36, 1605–14.

Brown, K., Marean, C. W., Jacobs, Z., Schoville, B. J., Oestmo, S., Fisher, E. C., Bernatchez, J., Karkanas, P., and Matthews, T. 2012. An early and enduring advanced technology originating 71,000 years ago in South Africa. *Nature* 491, 590–3.

Cashmore, L., Uomini, N., and Chapelain, A. 2008. The evolution of handedness in humans and great apes: a review and current issues. *Journal of Anthropological Science* 86, 1–30.

Chazan, M., Hagai, R., Matmon, A., Porat, N., Goldberg, P., Yates, R., Avery, M., Sumner, A., and Kolska Horwitz, L. 2008. Radiometric dating of the Earlier Stone Age sequence in Excavation I at Wonderwerk Cave, South Africa: preliminary results. *Journal of Human Evolution* 55, 1–11.

Clark, J. D., de Heinzelin, J., Schick, K. D., Hart, W. K., White, T. D., WoldeGabriel, G., Walter, R. C., Suwa, G., Asfaw, B., and Vrba, E. 1994. African *Homo erectus*: old radiometric ages and young Oldowan assemblages in the Middle Awash Valley, Ethiopia. *Science* 264, 1907–10.

de Heinzelin, J., Clark, J. D., White, T., Hart, W., Renne, P., WoldeGabriel, G., Beyene, Y., and Vrba, E. 1999. Environment and behaviour of 2.5-million-year-old Bouri hominids. *Science* 284, 625–9.

Dennell, R. 1984. *European economic prehistory: a new approach*. Cambridge and New York: Academic Press.

Dennell, R. 2008. *The Palaeolithic settlement of Asia*. Cambridge: Cambridge University Press.

d'Errico, F. and Sanchez Goñi, M. F. 2003. Neandertal extinction and the millennial scale climatic variability of OIS 3. *Quaternary Science Reviews* 22, 769–88.

Elston, R. G. and Kuhn, S. (eds) 2002. *Thinking small: global perspectives on microlithization*. Washington, DC: Archaeological Papers of the American Anthropological Association 12.

Féblot-Augustins, J. 1997. *La circulation des matières premières au Paléolithique*. Liège: ERAUL 75.

Foley, R. A. and Lahr, M. M. 1997. Mode 3 technologies and the evolution of modern humans. *Cambridge Archaeological Journal* 7, 3–36.

Gabunia, L., Antón, S., Lordkipanidze, D., Vekua, A., Justus, A., and Swisher, C. C. 2001. Dmanisi and dispersal. *Evolutionary Anthropology* 109, 158–70.

Gamble, C. 1999. *The Palaeolithic societies of Europe*. Cambridge: Cambridge University Press.

Goren-Inbar, N., Feibel, C., Verosub, K., Melamed, Y., Kislev, M., Tchernov, E., and Saragusti, I. 2000. Pleistocene milestones on the out-of-Africa corridor at Gesher Benot Ya'aqov, Israel. *Science* 289, 944–7.

Grünberg, J. M. 2002. Middle Palaeolithic birch-bark pitch. *Antiquity* 76, 15–16.

Henrich, J., Boyd, R., and Richerson, P. J. 2008. Five misunderstandings about cultural evolution. *Human Nature* 19, 119–37.

Higham, T., Brock, F., Peresani, M., Broglio, A., Wood, R., and Douka, K. 2009. Problems with radiocarbon dating the Middle to Upper Palaeolithic transition in Italy. *Quaternary Science Reviews* 28, 1257–67.

Hopkinson, T. 2007. *The Middle Palaeolithic leaf points of Europe: ecology, knowledge and scale*. Oxford: BAR International Series 1663.

Jacobs, Z., Roberts, R. G., Galbraith, R. F., Deacon, H. J., Grün, R., Mackay, A., Mitchell, P., Vogelsang, R., and Wadley, L. 2008a. Ages for the Middle Stone Age of Southern Africa: implications for human behaviour and dispersal. *Science* 322, 733–5.

Jacobs, Z., Wintle, A. G., Duller, G. A. T., Roberts, R. G., and Wadley, L. 2008b. New ages for the post-Howiesons Poort, late and final Middle Stone Age at Sibudu, South Africa. *Journal of Archaeological Science* 35, 1790–1807.

Koumouzelis, M., Kozlowski, J. K., Escutenaire, C., Sitlivy, V., Sobczyk, K., Valladas, H., Tisnerat-Laborde, N., Wojtal, P., Ginter, B., Kaczanowska, M., Kazior, B., and Zieba, A. 2001.

La fin du Paléolithique moyen et le début du Paléolithique supérieur en Gréce: la séquence de la Grotte 1 de Klissoura. *L'Anthropologie* 105, 469–504.

Kozlowski, J. and Otte, M. 2000. The formation of the Aurignacian in Europe. *Journal of Anthropological Research* 56, 513–34.

Kuhn, S. and Stiner, M. 2001. The antiquity of hunter-gatherers. In C. Panter-Brick, R. H. Layton, and P. Rowley-Conwy (eds), *Hunter-gatherers, an interdisciplinary perspective*, 99–142. Cambridge: Cambridge University Press.

Kuhn, S. and Stiner, M. 2007. Body ornamentation as information technology: towards an understanding of the significance of early beads. In P. Mellars, K. Boyle, O. Bar-Yosef, and C. Stringer (eds), *Rethinking the human revolution: new behavioural and biological perspectives on the origins and dispersal of modern humans*, 45–54. Cambridge: McDonald Institute for Archaeological Research.

Lycett, S. 2007. Why is there a lack of Mode 3 Levallois technologies in East Asia? A phylogenetic test of the Movius–Schick hypothesis. *Journal of Anthropological Archaeology* 26, 541–75.

McBrearty, S. and Brooks, A. 2000. The revolution that wasn't: a new interpretation of the origin of modern human behaviour. *Journal of Human Evolution* 39, 453–563.

McPherron, S. 2000. Handaxes as a measure of the mental capabilities of early hominids. *Journal of Archaeological Science* 27, 655–63.

McPherron, S., Alemseged, Z., Maean, C. W., Wynn, J. G., Reed, D., Geraads, D., Bobe, R., and H. A. Béarat. 2010. Evidence for stone-tool-assisted consumption of animal tissues before 3.39 million years ago at Dikka, Ethiopia. *Nature* 466, 857–60.

Maíllo Fernández, J. M., Cabrera-Valdès, V., and Bernaldo de Quirós, F. 2004. Le débitage lamellaire dans le Moustérien final de Cantabrie (Espagne): le cas de El Castillo et Cueva Morin. *L'Anthropologie* 108, 367–93.

Marean, C. W., Bar-Matthews, M., Bernatchez, J., Fisher, E., Goldberg, P., Herries, A. I. R., Jacobs, Z., Jerardino, A., Karkanas, P., Minichillo, T., Nilssen, P. J., Thompson, E., Watts, I., and Williams, H. 2007. Early human use of marine resources and pigment in South Africa during the Middle Pleistocene. *Nature* 449, 905–8.

Mithen, S. 1996. *The prehistory of the mind*. London: Thames and Hudson.

Movius, H. 1948. The Lower Palaeolithic cultures of southern and eastern Asia. *Transactions of the American Philosophical Society* 38, 329–426.

Negash, A. and Shackley, M. S. 2006. Geochemical provenance of obsidian artefacts from the MSA site of Porc Epic, Ethiopia. *Archaeometry* 48, 1–12.

Plummer, T. 2004. Flaked stones and old bones: biological and cultural evolution at the dawn of technology. *Yearbook of Physical Anthropology* 47, 118–64.

Porat, N., Chazan, M., Grün, R., Aubert, R., Eisenmann, V., and Kolska Horwitz, L. 2010. New radiometric ages for the Fauresmith industry from Kathu Pan, southern Africa: implications for the Earlier to Middle Stone Age transition. *Journal of Archaeological Science* 37, 269–83.

Powell, A., Shennan, S., and Thomas, M. G. 2009. Late Pleistocene demography and the appearance of modern human behaviour. *Science* 324, 1298–301.

Roche, H., Delagnes, A., Brugal, J.-P., Feibel, C., Kibunjia, M., Mourre, V., and Texier, P.-J. 1999. Early hominid stone tool production and technical skill 2.34 Myr ago in West Turkana, Kenya. *Science* 399, 57–60.

Schiffer, M. B. 2004. Studying technological change: a behavioural perspective. *World Archaeology* 36, 579–85.

Scott, G. R. and Gibert, L. 2009. The oldest hand-axes in Europe. *Nature* 461, 82–5.

Semaw, S. 2000. The world's oldest stone artefacts from Gona, Ethiopia: their implications for understanding stone technology and patterns of human evolution between 2.6–1.5 million years ago. *Journal of Archaeological Science* 27, 1197–214.

Sharon, G. 2009. Acheulian giant-core technology: a worldwide perspective. *Current Anthropology* 50, 335–67.

Slimak, L. and Giraud, Y. 2007. Circulations sur plusieurs centaines de kilomètres durant le Paléolithique moyen: contribution à la connaissance des sociétés néandertaliennes. *Comptes Rendus Palévol* 6, 359–68.

Slimak, L., Kuhn, S., Roche, H., Mouralis, D., Buitenhuis, H., Balkan-Atli, N., Binder, D., Kuzucuoğlu, C., and Guillou, H. 2008. Kaletepe Deresi 3 (Turkey): archaeological evidence for early human settlement in Central Anatolia. *Journal of Human Evolution* 54, 99–111.

Stout, D., Toth, N., Schick, K., and Chaminade, T. 2008. Neural correlates of Early Stone Age tool-making: technology, language and cognition in human evolution. *Philosophical Transactions of the Royal Society of London B*, 363, 1939–49.

Tryon, C. A., McBrearty, S., and Texier, P.-J. 2005. Levallois lithic technology from the Kapthurin Formation, Kenya: Acheulian origin and Middle Stone Age diversity. *African Archaeological Review* 22, 199–229.

Tuffreau, A. 2004. *L'Acheuléen de l'Homo erectus à l'homme de Néandertal*. Paris: La Maison des Roches.

Wynn, T. 1989. *The evolution of spatial competence*. Urbana, IL: University of Illinois Press.

Wynn, T. and Coolidge, F. L. 2004. The expert Neandertal mind. *Journal of Human Evolution* 46, 467–87.

Yamei, H., Potts, R., Yuan, B., Guo, Z., Deino, A., Wang, W., Clark, J. D., Xie, G., and Huang, W. 2000. Mid-Pleistocene Acheulean-like stone technology of the Bose Basin, south China. *Science* 287, 1622–6.

Zilhão, Z. and d'Errico, F. (eds) 2003. *The chronology of the Aurignacian and of the transitional technocomplexes: dating, stratigraphies, cultural implications*. Lisbon: Portuguese Institute of Archaeology.

CHAPTER 28

ART FOR THE LIVING

J. D. LEWIS-WILLIAMS

THE origin (or origins) of art in early hunter-gatherer societies has long been a controversial issue, not just in the answers that have been advanced but also in the framing of the question itself. First, the exact meaning of the key word 'art' is elusive. Does it denote something that can be applied to an object, such as a stone tool, to make it 'special' or is it something in itself, as it is in some Western commercial and aesthetic contexts? Or is it something else altogether? Secondly, it is difficult to define what could reasonably be said to be an 'origin' of a complex set of human behaviours such as the production and consumption of art. Was there an infinite regression of ever-simpler behaviours going back into the deep past without a cut-off point at which distinct art-making commenced? Thirdly, even if these questions could be answered satisfactorily, what sort of archaeological evidence should we consider relevant to them? Fourthly, were art and religion interrelated from the beginning of modern human behaviour? Finally, what is religion?

As yet, there are no definitive answers to any of these questions. There does, however, seem to be agreement that the earliest archaeological evidence for art does not point to activities that were divorced from, or 'above', the daily life of ordinary people. The idea that human beings could engage in the exalted pursuit of making art only after they had 'conquered the environment' and had 'leisure time' is now universally rejected. Researchers concur that the earliest art, however defined, was integral to the business of living. At the same time, we must acknowledge that art-making was not indispensable to the functioning of prehistoric societies: some made art and some did not. For example, in prehistoric times the San whose descendants still live in the sandy Kalahari Desert of southern Africa did not make art, while, farther to the south, other San, who embraced a suite of similar beliefs and rituals, made complex rock art (Lewis-Williams and Challis 2011; Lewis-Williams and Pearce 2004a). But were there other differences between the two San groups? Does a powerful art tradition bolster or contest social structures (Lewis-Williams and Pearce 2004a; 2004b)?

The questions that I have posed and this southern African example together imply the sort of definition of 'art' that I am using. I take 'art' to mean 'image-making', whether the images be two- or three-dimensional, representational or abstract. The last two words are themselves difficult to define. Nevertheless, they are frequently used as a base-line in the categorization of prehistoric images. Unfortunately, the distinction between them risks masking the forces behind image-making in general in any given society.

Some argue that a focus on image-making excludes potentially important evidence, such as symmetrical hand axes that modern Westerners consider beautiful or the presence of (presumably symbolic) ochre in ancient deposits. Despite its initial attractiveness, the idea that art is a gloss applied to otherwise ordinary objects to make them 'special' (beautiful or more richly symbolic) does not play a role in this chapter (see Dissanayake 1995; Lamarque 2005). The origin of image-making could not have been an inescapable component of an essentially aesthetic (special-making) tradition: image-making is something distinct from aesthetics and demands a distinct explanation. We must ask: how did the *concept* of an image come about? Then, why would anyone want to make an image of anything? Which of these two questions should come first? Perhaps the second encapsulates the answer to the first.

These key questions move away from reviews of ancient hunter-gatherer art that start with an apparently empirical inventory of *objets d'art* around the world (for useful surveys of ancient art see, for example, Bahn 1998; Clottes 2006; Conkey et al. 1997; Vialou 1991; Whitley 2001; White 2003). Detailed descriptions of these finds, rather sporadic outside western Europe, sometimes cause fundamental theoretical issues to be deferred or overlooked. Inevitably, our descriptions of ancient finds are, as is now widely accepted, set in an often tacit theoretical framework. Descriptions and, especially, classifications, are in themselves interpretations: they are not neutral foundations for subsequent interpretations. This stricture does not imply thoroughgoing relativism. Rather, it means that when we try to understand the roles that ancient items played in prehistoric societies we must guard, as best we may, against seeing them within a Western framework or in terms of social relations derived from a single ethnographically known community.

The Earliest 'Art'?

Researchers encounter definitional enigmas and the issue of what role art played in ancient societies when they consider the engraved pieces of ochre from the Blombos cave on the southern coast of South Africa. In the late 1990s they were discovered in levels dated to about 72,000 BP (Henshilwood 2009; Henshilwood et al. 2002). These now well-known finds are the oldest indisputable evidence we have for image-making. The engraved pieces of ochre were associated with shell beads and ground ochre. Taken together, this evidence has been interpreted as an index of 'modern human behaviour', a term that introduces other definitional problems, ones that we need not confront here.

The engraved Blombos ochre comprises two indisputable pieces and a number of others that are open to debate. Both uncontroversial pieces can easily be held in the palm of a hand; the larger surfaces have been ground to produce ochre powder. Remarkably, there is a cross-hatching motif engraved on a narrow edge of each. The better-preserved piece has a series of crosses (or composite cross-hatching) with a line running through the centre: containing lines above and below the crosses follow the edge of the engraved surface (Figure 28.1). The second piece has crosses but no other lines. The repetition of the core motif (a series of crosses), its position on the narrow edge, and its complexity are points that count against its being an idle doodle. It seems that we have here a repeatable, multi-component unit, or motif, rather like an ancient Egyptian cartouche.

FIGURE 28.1 Engraved ochre from Blombos cave, South Africa.

Did the repeated crosses within the containing lines of one example mean something, as do the individual elements within a cartouche? Did an isolated cross (no examples have yet been found) mean something that was extended by repetition and a containing line? Leaving aside the second of these two questions we may wonder, at what some researchers erroneously consider a simple level, if the series of crosses was representational in that it depicted, say, part of a net used for fishing or for carrying goods. This potential explanation raises deeper issues. It seems highly likely that ochre was, for the Blombos people, more than a utilitarian substance: the quantities of ground ochre found in the cave and its application to shell beads suggest some further than utilitarian significance. So, if the pattern of crosses did refer to nets, the relationship between the image and nets was not simple: for people to want to make images of them, nets themselves must have had more significance than we might at first guess.

Then we must note that the engraved motif was, in both instances, placed on the narrow edge of the flat pieces of ochre, not on the larger surfaces where it could, at least to Western researchers' way of thinking, be seen more easily. We may wonder if the motifs referred to something intangible and immanent in the pieces of ochre, possibly something that was released by the grinding of the surfaces and later, in powder form, used in staining shell beads, and, probably, body decoration. The hints are slender, but it does seem that these highly significant finds point to the sort of *conceptual thinking* out of which could grow beliefs in invisible, 'spiritual' concepts or powers. The reasons why it is reasonable to suppose that people at this early time may have entertained beliefs about non-material things is something that is considered below. For the present, we need notice only that the sort of thinking implied by the Blombos motifs opens up the *possibility* of some sort of religion at that early time.

Finally, in considering all prehistoric images, researchers should think in terms of production *and* consumption (Conkey 2001; Lewis-Williams 1995). What social role did the

Blombos motifs play? In some prehistoric contexts, it may be possible to provide tentative answers to questions about the social roles of images without stipulating the exact meaning (if they had only one) of the motifs in question.

As Blombos shows, early art was not confined to Europe. Nevertheless, because European art is more diverse, more abundant, and is (in many instances) found in its prehistoric context, it is there, accusations of Eurocentrism aside, that we must seek answers to our questions.

Upper Palaeolithic Art

West European Upper Palaeolithic art (40,000 to 10,000 BP) is diverse (Clottes 2001; Leroi-Gourhan 1968; Ministère de la Culture 1984; Renfrew and Morley 2009). In brief, it comprises pieces of portable art (carved figurines, engraved plaquettes, pendants, and spear throwers carved in the shape of animals; Figure 28.2), the well-known cave paintings and engravings of sometimes extinct animals and a few people (Figure 28.3), painted and engraved geometric signs (Figure 28.4), and engraved images of animals on rock surfaces outside caves (Figure 28.5). The apparently sudden appearance of such sophisticated art, without a long preceding period of simpler and cruder forms, led some writers to speak of a 'creative explosion' (e.g. Pfeiffer 1982). Others have taken the more likely view that image-making was part of a larger package of modern human behaviour that emerged sporadically over a long period (McBrearty and Brooks 2000).

Two- and three-dimensional images are notoriously difficult to date, but multiple radiocarbon and other techniques have shown that the earliest Upper Palaeolithic art dates from the Aurignacian (some 45,000 to 35,000 years ago). The art of this period includes a number of finely carved mammoth ivory figurines and pendants from Vogelherd, Geissenklösterle, Hohle Fels, and Hohlenstein-Stadel in southern Germany. Until the 1994 discovery of the Chauvet cave in the Ardèche department of France, these carvings were the oldest known pieces of Upper Palaeolithic art and were thought to be unique to that period. The discovery of the Chauvet parietal images (on the walls of caves) dating to approximately 35,000 BP made researchers realize that three- and two-dimensional images were both made at the beginning of the Upper Palaeolithic (Clottes 2003). For some years there were researchers who vociferously doubted the antiquity of the Chauvet images on stylistic grounds, but multiple dates from more than one laboratory now confirm their early provenance (Clottes 2009; Clottes and Geneste 2007, 17–18).

The carved portable art from southern Germany introduces interesting questions about context and function (Hahn 1993). Some of the pieces were manually polished or polished as a result of being carried in a leather pouch. In addition to the figurines, there are ivory pendants and perforated fox canines. It would be easy to conclude that most of these items were used merely for personal adornment, but their context calls for deeper consideration. The carved pieces were not mixed indiscriminately with stone tools. At Vogelherd the figurines were found well away from a stone flaking area outside the rock shelter and from an activity area within the shelter. At Hohlenstein-Stadel the pieces were far inside the shelter. At Geissenklösterle they were on the fringe of two artefact concentrations. Their separation

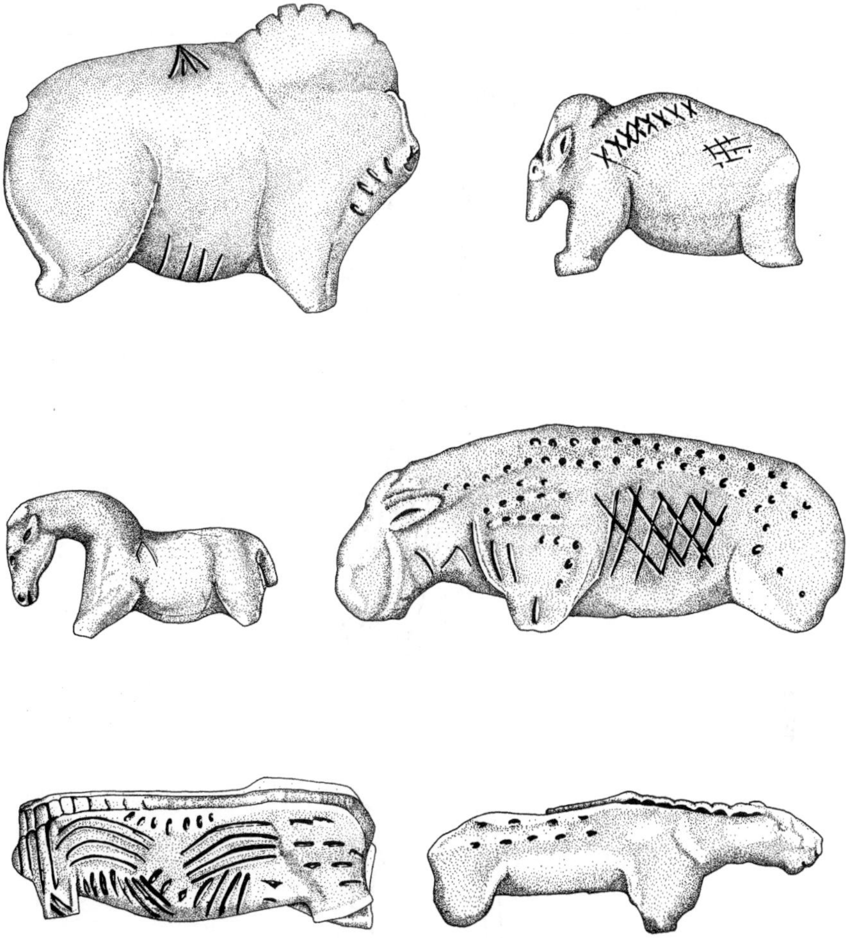

FIGURE 28.2 Aurignacian figurines from southern Germany.

FIGURE 28.3 Magdalenian image from Niaux, France.

FIGURE 28.4 Painted 'signs'.

from daily activities suggests that there was more to the carvings than utilitarian or merely decorative purposes.

Moreover, the animal species represented do not reflect the proportions of species (21 in all) found in the rock shelter deposits (Hahn 1993). The species represented by the carvings include three mammoths, four felines, two lion-men, two anthropomorphs, two bison, one bear, one bird, and two horses. The most recent find was a female figurine (Conard 2003; 2009). Other criteria than simply food were operating in the selection of species. Thomas

FIGURE 28.5 Magdalenian cave painting at Niaux, France.

Wynn and his colleagues conclude: '[I]f the Hohlenstein-Stadel [leonine] figurine is a reliable indicator of the abilities of Aurignacian people generally, then they relied on conceptual thinking that is indistinguishable from that of people in the modern world' (Wynn et al. 2009).

An even more significant point is that the set of species selected for representation is similar to that found throughout Upper Palaeolithic parietal art, though in later periods the proportions of the species depicted varied (Clottes 1996). For instance, the Aurignacian numerical emphasis on felines in southern Germany was confirmed by the discovery of the Chauvet cave, where there is a comparable emphasis on felines in the parietal images. Later, by the Magdalenian (22,000–17,000 BP), horses and bison dominated the subject matter, and felines were less numerous. But the core bestiary remained surprisingly constant.

The overall unity of the earliest Upper Palaeolithic art (the southern Germany carvings and the Chauvet images) suggests that the corpus of subject matter was established and widespread *before people started making images*. There was never a time when image-makers depicted whatever took their fancy. The crucial question now is: does this 'pre-image-making' selectivity tell us anything about *why* people began to make images?

Before answering this key question we need to look briefly at some of the explanations that have been proposed for Upper Palaeolithic art.

Early Explanations

The first explanation that researchers advanced was in some people's mistaken view the simplest: 'art for the sake of art'—prehistoric images were simply decorative or were made to satisfy an innate aesthetic impulse. The 'primitive' people who made them were deemed incapable of 'more advanced' symbolism and religion. Although a few writers later tried to revive this explanation in modified form (e.g. Halverson 1987), it has not lasted.

In the first place, the discovery of more and more subterranean images was challenging. The notion of *art pour l'art* did not explain why artists went deep underground to make images where few, if any, other people could see them. Once made, some seem never to have been revisited.

The next blow to the theory was delivered at the beginning of the twentieth century by the ethnography that was coming from, principally, Australia (Spencer and Gillen 1899). It appeared that people, like the Australians, who live in harsh environments, still had time to make images. Moreover, they had a religion, though one very different from the decorous Christianity with which the ethnographers were familiar: it was clear that so-called 'primitives' were capable of image-making and symbolic thought.

Today it is recognized that the making of art is a social activity rather than exclusively a matter of individual psychology, whatever individual talent may have to do with the finished product. The restricted 'vocabulary' of Upper Palaeolithic art is more consonant with social than idiosyncratic desires. In any event, it is impossible to depict an animal without giving resonance to its associations, and those associations are overwhelmingly socially situated. Rather than postulate an innate, species-specific drive to make artistic things, we should enquire about the social circumstances in which people made images of *selected* things. The notion of aesthetics probably developed only *after* people started to make images. We should enquire why people became image-makers, not about the origin of 'art'.

The next broad interpretation of Upper Palaeolithic art followed on from the newly available ethnography. Salomon Reinach (1903) drew on Australian ethnography to advocate totemism and related magical practices as motivations for the Franco-Cantabrian images. Simply put, people painted certain animals that stood for societal groups in the belief that their images would cause the animals to multiply or to fall prey to hunters. Totemism and hunting magic as explanations for Upper Palaeolithic art are less popular today (Sauvet et al. 2009).

Here fate played a role. In the 1870s, long before Reinach published his influential work, Wilhelm Bleek and Lucy Lloyd were recording the personal histories, beliefs, rituals, and explanations of rock paintings that they obtained from /Xam San people in southern Africa (Lewis-Williams and Pearce 2004a). San beliefs cannot be regarded as totemic. The 1870s ethnography shows that individuals in San communities induced altered states of consciousness to contact the spirit realm and experience out-of-body journeys to heal, make rain, foretell the future, etc. Tantalizingly, we may speculate on what direction Upper Palaeolithic art research would have taken had southern African rather than Australian ethnography been available to Reinach.

In adopting his ethnographic approach, Reinach encountered a problem that still exercises researchers' minds. Is it possible to use ethnography from small-scale societies around the world to understand west European Upper Palaeolithic art (Layton 2001)? Reinach himself advocated caution and stipulated that researchers should restrict themselves to hunter-gatherer ethnography. Unfortunately, some analogical arguments of this kind amount to little more than a game of ethnographic 'snap'. Others are more sophisticated and take into account what Alison Wylie calls 'relations of relevance' (Lewis-Williams 1991; Wylie 2002, 136–53, 161–7). Briefly, strong relations of relevance are said to exist when a causal or other inescapable relationship is evident between A and B in the source of an analogy. If A is found in the archaeological record, then B may be said to have occurred as well. In practice, strong relations of relevance are hard come by.

After the ethnographic work of Reinach and others (including Henri Breuil 1952), the next major advance came in the mid-1940s. The Marxist art historian Max Raphael moved away from ethnographic analogies and instead followed in the footsteps of the linguist Ferdinand de Saussure. One of Saussure's principal contributions was to distinguish between *langue* (the grammar, or structure, of a language) and *parole* (speech, or individual utterances). By studying a number of utterances it is possible to work out the grammar of a language.

While philology is diachronic in that it studies the history of words, structure is synchronic: it is studied as it exists at a single time. Raphael identified a closer relationship between diachronic and synchronic studies than is often allowed today. Rightly, he believed that 'the transverse section of historical existence...unfolds the qualities contained in the longitudinal section' (Raphael 1945, 2–3). If we can detect how a society functions at any given time, we may be able to identify forces that could lead to change without external stimuli. Some of the 'qualities' of which Raphael wrote were social relationships. For instance, he challenged the idea that Upper Palaeolithic hunter-gatherer communities were egalitarian. Instead, he argued that social relations between groups (as identified in a synchronic slice) led to change (diachronic trajectories). Summing up this position, he wrote that Upper Palaeolithic people 'were history-making peoples par excellence' (Raphael 1945, 3).

In some hunter-gatherer societies, such as the southern African San, class struggle ('class' being loosely defined) is masked by an ideology that also implicates image-making (Lewis-Williams and Pearce 2004a). For Raphael, images of animals fighting or depicted overlapping and facing in opposite directions signalled Upper Palaeolithic social struggles. In discussing this sort of conflict, Raphael interpreted the image of a female deer facing a bison in Altamira as 'a conflict between feminine tenderness and masculine bulk' (Raphael 1945, 51). The male/female opposition was, for him, fundamental to understanding Upper Palaeolithic art. (As we shall see, Raphael's view foreshadowed two later and better-known researchers.) But this kind of sexual binary opposition tended to estrange other researchers. Certainly, there is much in Raphael's analyses of painted panels with which few today would agree, but we should not lose sight of his two major contributions to the study of prehistoric art: social analysis and the notion that the distribution of images in a cave was in some way meaningful.

Also in the 1940s and into the 1950s, the highly influential French philosopher and anthropologist Claude Lévi-Strauss was transferring linguistic principles to anthropology and, especially, to the study of mythology. He was interested in the ways in which the human mind functioned. Like Raphael, he was a Marxist, though, as some commentators point out, in a somewhat ill-defined sense. Fundamentally, he believed that 'understanding consists in the reduction of one type of reality to another' and declared that 'true reality is never the most obvious of realities' (Lévi-Strauss cited in Leach 1974, 13). Upper Palaeolithic art researchers should heed these views.

Soon, Lévi-Strauss's application of linguistics to mythology inspired André Leroi-Gourhan and Annette Laming-Emperaire to seek the 'grammar' of Upper Palaeolithic art (Laming-Emperaire 1962; Leroi-Gourhan 1968). Of these two researchers it is Leroi-Gourhan who is today more remembered. He led the study of Upper Palaeolithic art into a new and more rigorous phase. To uncover the 'grammar' of the art he meticulously re-examined many of the Franco-Cantabrian caves, plotting on maps the positions of images. As a result of this empirical (though already interpretive) work and his Lévi-Straussian theoretical stance, the next comprehensive explanation for Upper Palaeolithic art derived from structuralism.

In simplified form, Leroi-Gourhan believed that the animals depicted could be divided into categories, the most prominent of which were horse (with which he grouped ibex, stag, reindeer, and hind) and bison (with which he grouped aurochs). Respectively, these categories of species stood for male and female moieties. To this binary opposition, Leroi-Gourhan added the so-called 'abstract signs'. He divided them into another binary opposition to parallel the one he devised for representational images. A male group comprised 'narrow' signs (single and double strokes, rows of dots, barbed signs); a female group comprised 'wide' signs (ovals, triangles, quadrilaterals, and claviforms). The forms that comprised these groups, Leroi-Gourhan argued, derived from, respectively, male and female genitalia. A third group of images comprised felines and other dangerous animals.

The distribution of these categories within the caves followed a 'grammar': so-called male species (principally horse) were painted near entrances and in the moderate depths of caves, while female species (bison) were painted in central areas along with some male species. Dangerous animals tended to be painted in the depths. Embracing all this was the cave, itself a female symbol. In sum, the groups of animals and signs and their distribution within caves constituted a 'mythogram', that is, a mental template, the *langue* of Upper Palaeolithic thought and art for the entire period.

Thus stated, Leroi-Gourhan's work may seem overly concerned with sex, almost Freudian. He himself was circumspect, believing that the male/female opposition was only one characterization of the mythogram. For him, the binary mythogram was a vehicle that could carry a wide range of meanings (Leroi-Gourhan 1982). Labelling his categories male and female was a strategic error from which his work never recovered.

Curiously, the influence of both Lévi-Strauss and Leroi-Gourhan was great, yet both seem to have had more critics than followers. Indeed, Leroi-Gourhan's work soon attracted criticism on empirical and theoretical grounds (e.g. Ucko and Rosenfeld 1967, 150–223). Variations in the topography of the caves and the distribution of images were found not to fit Leroi-Gourhan's 'mythogram'. Nevertheless, a point that has survived criticism is that depictions of felines and dangerous animals tend to occur in the depths of caves (Parkington 1969). Finally, as structuralism itself was abandoned, so too in Upper Palaeolithic art research many writers moved away from Leroi-Gourhan's sort of work to diachronic and empirical concerns. Some, however, did continue with modified and more restricted structuralist research (e.g. Bernaldo de Quiros 1999; Sauvet and Wlodarczyk 1995; Vialou 1987; 1991).

When sweeping changes in theoretical positions, such as this one, take place, there is a tendency to abandon valid elements along with those that are shown to be misleading. At this time, it was unfortunate that the idea of structured caves was lost. As we shall see, there was indeed some structure in the ways in which people exploited caves for the purpose of making images and performing accompanying rituals.

A Time of Reorientation

For Upper Palaeolithic art research, the twentieth century started on a high note. Reinach's identification of hunter-gatherer ethnography as a source of useful analogues seemed to open up a productive avenue for researchers. As it eventually became apparent that some of these analogies were weak, attention turned away from extraneous sources to the art itself. Leroi-Gourhan explicitly rejected explanatory analogies and argued that the art could be understood by internal analyses alone. When his approach fell, some researchers felt that they had burnt their fingers too often and began to adopt an obscurantist position. Any attempt to understand why Upper Palaeolithic people made images was treated with scorn. In some cases, writers invoked 'science' as a façade behind which to hide their capitulation.

At first glance, the vast temporal, social, and economic chasm between us and Upper Palaeolithic people does indeed seem unbridgeable. In a spirited contribution to the debate about the very possibility of any interpretation of any archaeological remains Reinhard Bernbeck wrote:

> Our profession lacks a dialogical impulse, and the past is under an unrelenting interpretive assault, made worse by myriad theories whose effect is the re-visiting of the same past people in different guises. If 'the past is a foreign country', we are those importunate tourists who expect that our every need will be catered to.
>
> (Bernbeck 2007, 219–21)

To this emotive attack, Bernbeck added a moral dimension: 'An ethically responsible archaeology implies self-censorship, the self-conscious suppression of the desire to interpret, to give coherent sense to a past that all too often defies meaning' (Bernbeck 2007, 210). In his view it is not just misguided but also unethical to try to understand what we rightly or wrongly regard as a 'foreign country'.

A positive result of disenchantment with the whole enterprise of interpretation was that a number of researchers contributed valuable work on the techniques that Upper Palaeolithic people employed in the making of their imagery (e.g. Beltrán 1999; Clottes 1993; 1995; d'Errico 2009; Fritz 1999; Lorblanchet 1991; 1992; Sharpe and van Gelder 2006;White 1993; and chapters in Clottes 2003). Some still believe that this is the only sort of research that can, or even should, be done on Upper Palaeolithic art (Conkey 2000).

Colin Renfrew has, however, advocated a more temperate position:

> Symbolic and structural archaeology was in many ways a magnificent beginning on a path which had and still has much to offer. But it contained the seeds of its own decline in the very antithesis which its proponents soon engineered when (rapidly recognizing the poverty of structuralism) they claimed to have devised a post-processual approach.... In reality,

archaeology needed both sources of inspiration. It remains the poorer for the failure of the two schools of thought to reach constructive accommodation.

(Renfrew 2007a, 224; see also 2007b)

Whether or not that constructive accommodation can be reached, there is another, if controversial, approach. It derives from the idea that the past is another country, but one that is inhabited, at least by the time of the Upper Palaeolithic, by people anatomically like ourselves. It developed in the 1980s and is still debated.

A Neurological Bridge

Today few doubt that Upper Palaeolithic people had, broadly, the same sort of brains as we have, though brains are socially situated and their evolution should be seen in social contexts (Malafouris and Renfrew 2008; Mellars and Gibson 1996; Mellars et al. 2007; and the articles they introduce). Principally, it is differences in intelligence between modern and archaic humans that are of paramount importance to most writers.

Steven Mithen (1996), for instance, turned to evolutionary psychology to explain the apparent creative explosion at the beginning of the Upper Palaeolithic. Evolutionary psychology proposes that intelligence is modular. There is said to be social intelligence, technical intelligence, natural history intelligence, and linguistic intelligence. In pre-fully modern humans these modules were separate, each dedicated to a specific task. In modern people, however, the modules are connected to give us *generalized intelligence*. As a result, metaphorical thought, created by links between modules, is possible. For instance, fully modern people can think of social relations in terms of natural history intelligence—thus was totemism born. The breaking down of the walls between the intelligence modules was effected largely by the generation of fully modern, complex language.

In daily life many creatures make marks on objects, but, Mithen argues, it was only when the barriers between intelligence modules broke down that they could give symbolic meaning to those marks. This argument brings us close to one of the earliest explanations for the origin of images: people made random marks and then, by chance, noticed that some of these marks looked like, say, horses (see Davis 1986 for a sophisticated version). In fact, the skill needed to recognize two-dimensional 'marks' as a representation of a three-dimensional thing has to be learned; it is not innate. One cannot notice a similarity between, say, damp marks on a wall and a human face unless one already has a concept of two-dimensional pictures (Lewis-Williams 2002, 180–5). In any event, even if the 'accidental discovery' explanation were valid, we should have to ask why Upper Palaeolithic image-makers did not depict a great many things right from the beginning rather than a restricted bestiary.

The construction of an alternative bridge to the Upper Palaeolithic commences with an important distinction. It is between intelligence and consciousness. Today, many researchers focus on the evolution of intelligence and ignore the equally important evolution of consciousness.

Modern human consciousness comprises a spectrum of intergrading states (Lewis-Williams 2002, 121–35). At one end of the spectrum we have alert attention to the environment, and, as environmental input diminishes, that grades into more introverted states in which problem-solving is accomplished by the mental manipulation of linguistic and other symbols. When an individual relaxes concentration, this state slides into day-dreaming and reverie. These waking states grade, via a hypnagogic phase, into dreaming and then on into deep sleep.

This spectrum of 'normal consciousness' may be subverted by numerous means, including intense concentration, meditation, sensory deprivation, severe pain, rhythmic sounds (such as drumming and chanting), sustained rhythmic dancing, fatigue, fasting, hyperventilation, visual stimulation (including flashing lights), the ingestion of psychotropic substances, and pathological conditions, such as schizophrenia, migraine, and temporal lobe epilepsy. The ingestion of psychotropic drugs is not essential for the creation of an altered state.

At the beginning of the 'intensified trajectory' people see iridescent geometric percepts that derive from the wiring of the brain. They are variously known as phosphenes, entoptic phenomena, and form constants. Their forms are independent of their cultural context. Next, subjects feel as if they are passing through a tunnel or vortex. Finally, along with persisting entoptic phenomena, subjects see full-blown hallucinations of animals, people, monsters, and compound images. At this point, all the senses hallucinate and people hear sounds or voices and may feel themselves turning into animals.

An important characteristic of both entoptic phenomena and visual hallucinations has been established by neuropsychological research: mental percepts are often projected onto surfaces, rather like a slide or film show (Klüver 1926; Siegel 1977). The fully modern people of the Upper Palaeolithic could not have avoided experiencing the normal spectrum of human consciousness, and, given the wide range of stimuli that induce the intensified spectrum, *some* of them would have experienced hallucinations projected onto rock surfaces. We may therefore reach an important conclusion. People did not 'invent' images: rather, the human nervous system presented some people with mental percepts projected onto surfaces, often but not always percepts that they themselves sought in their shifting altered states. In specific, socially determined circumstances, important visions were then 'fixed' on the surfaces with paint or engraving. This fixing could have been undertaken by people in a light altered state, or by people recalling their visions as they had been projected onto the uneven surfaces with 'anchor points', or by people experiencing 'flashback' percepts some while after the end of a full altered state. That is why some Upper Palaeolithic images seem to be 'alive' in that they appear to exit from or enter into the rock face or to blend with features of the surfaces. The very concept of an image probably emerged from developing human neurology. Those who experienced projected mental images and 'fixed' them could easily explain them to those who did not. They, in turn, could then make images without any neurological stimulus. It is now clear why the images of Upper Palaeolithic art seem to have derived from a pre-existent, determining set of important animals.

Here, wired into the human brain, is a possible explanation for the origin of religion (Lewis-Williams 2002; 2010; see also Boyer 2003; 2004). Hallucinations and dreams with deep emotional associations are, worldwide, part of religious experience. All religions have an ecstatic component that is experienced by some devotees. Because of the wiring and functioning of the human brain, strong relations of relevance exist between altered states and a definable range of mental experiences and percepts and their expression in rock art.

Given the role of the vortex, or tunnel, experience and the hallucinations ('fixed' or not) that follow, it comes as no surprise that, worldwide, many societies believe in an underworld inhabited by spirit beings, animals, and monsters. Because all communities have to come to terms with potentially confusing shifting consciousness, Upper Palaeolithic people, too, must have experienced it and divided it up in their own way. In doing so, they created their own understanding of shifting consciousness and, simultaneously, a tiered cosmos with 'spiritual' realms. Arguably, the human nervous system gave birth not only to art but also to belief in a supernatural realm and thus to religion.

Bearing this multi-component, neurologically grounded explanation in mind, we can see why Raphael and Leroi-Gourhan had a point when they argued that the embellished caves were planned. In many caves there are areas with concentrations of images and linking passages with no or few images. If individual caves are analysed with this in mind, patterns emerge, not those envisaged by Raphael and Leroi-Gourhan, but ones created by groups of people making images of certain kinds in specific places for specific purposes. Moreover, certain areas of the caves were probably reserved for special people. Early religion was thus expressed in social discriminations and, probably, ensuing discord (Lewis-Williams 2002, 228–67; 2010, 207–31). In this too Raphael was right.

The contention that, in brief, the caves were thought of as entrances into a subterranean spirit world and that *some* of the painted and engraved images of animals, human beings, and only certain geometric forms were believed to be 'fixed' visions has become known as the shamanistic interpretation, partly because of the strong relations of relevance that I have mentioned. The word 'shamanism' has, however, proved controversial and diversionary. Unfortunately, some writers have not distinguished between the definition given in comprehensive presentations of the argument (e.g. Lewis-Williams 2002, 132–5) and a narrow concept of shamanism derived exclusively from Central Asia. Further, this interpretation does not preclude a range of other activities. Upper Palaeolithic people probably recounted myths about the animals they depicted, and they may well have performed initiation ceremonies in parts of the caves (e.g. Montelle 2004). These and other ceremonies probably included music, chanting, and dancing (Delluc and Delluc 1990; Mithen 2005; Morley 2002; Scarre 1989; Scarre and Lawson 2006).

Much of the debate on this explanation comprises attacks on straw men (e.g. Hodgson 2006). For instance, critics often claim that altered states are too rare to have played any significant role. On the contrary, altered consciousness from mild to ecstatic states is a daily occurrence (Lewis-Williams 2010). There are numerous other misunderstandings. The explanation does not consider handprints specific to shamanism and does not argue that geometric images necessarily indicate the presence of shamanism; nor does it claim that both geometric and representational images necessarily co-occur in a shamanistic art. Nor does it suggest that there is any presently existing shamanistic society that is identical to Upper Palaeolithic societies—which themselves probably changed over time, though in ways that are open to question. Worst of all is the claim that the explanation reduces *all* rock art to a shamanistic explanation. In southern Africa, for instance, in addition to essentially shamanistic San art there are rock arts made by Bantu-speaking farmers that are part of initiation rites.

'Economic, Social, Political, Moral, Religious'

Today, debate about west European Upper Palaeolithic art is sometimes unfortunately strident. Perhaps because of the fame of the art and the feeling that the striking images seem to speak directly to viewers, some researchers believe that they can intuit meaning and function. Others, not realizing that we do not have to know everything in order to know something, resolutely remain in the 'we-shall-never-know' camp. Still, there seems to be a growing consensus that an explanation for Upper Palaeolithic art should, in some way, include human neurology. 'Art' itself is being addressed from a neurological perspective (Onions 2008; Pinker 2002, 404–9; Ramanchandran and Blakeslee 1998; Zeki 2008).

There is a danger here. All points of view should remember that neurology did not force image-making on people. The first and all subsequent image-making was socially situated: the principal key to the so-called origin of art lies in social contexts and interaction between individuals and their communities.

> The main task of a history of art is to show that these determined forms—forms not contents—must necessarily arise from definite economic, social, political, moral, religious, etc., roots, that these forms express them, represent them, manifest them; vice versa, that they react on these roots and play a part in their transformation.
>
> (Raphael 1945, 17)

REFERENCES

Bahn, P. G. 1998. *The Cambridge illustrated history of prehistoric art*. Cambridge: Cambridge University Press.

Beltrán, A. (ed.) 1999. *The cave of Altamira*. New York: Harry Abrams.

Bernaldo de Quiros, F. 1999. The cave of Altamira: its art, its artists and its times. In A. Beltran (ed.), *The cave of Altamira*, 25–57. New York: Harry Abrams.

Bernbeck, R. 2007. From the search for meaning to the recognition of ignorance. *Cambridge Archaeological Journal* 17, 207–10.

Boyer, P. 2003. Religious thought and behaviour as by-products of brain function. *Trends in Cognitive Science* 3, 119–204.

Boyer, P. 2004. Religion, evolution and cognition. *Current Anthropology* 43, 430–3.

Breuil, H. 1952. *Four hundred centuries of cave art*. New York and Montignac: Centre d'Etudes et de Documentation Préhistoriques.

Clottes, J. 1993. Paint analyses from several Magdalenian caves in the Ariège region of France. *Journal of Archaeological Science* 20, 223–35.

Clottes, J. 1995. *Les Cavernes de Niaux*. Paris: Le Seuil.

Clottes, J. 1996. Thematic changes in Upper Palaeolithic art: a view from the Grotte Chauvet. *Antiquity* 70, 276–88.

Clottes, J. 2001. Paleolithic Europe. In D. S. Whitley (ed.), *Handbook of rock art research*, 459–81. Lanham, MD: AltaMira Press.

Clottes, J. (ed.) 2003. *Return to Chauvet Cave: excavating the birthplace of art. The first full report*. London: Thames and Hudson.

Clottes, J. 2006. Spirituality and religion in Paleolithic times. In F. LeRon Schults (ed.), *The evolution of rationality: interdisciplinary essays in honor of J. Wentzel van Huyssteen*, 133–48. Grand Rapids, MI and Cambridge: Eerdmans Publishing.

Clottes, J. 2009. *Cave art*. London: Phaidon.

Clottes, J. and Genest, J.-M. Twelve years of research in Chauvet Cave: methodology and main results. In J. McDonald and P. Veth (eds). *A companion to rock art*, 583–604. Oxford: Wiley-Blackwell.

Conard, N. J. 2003. Palaeolithic ivory sculptures from southwestern Germany and the origins of figurative art. *Nature* 426, 830–2.

Conard, N. J. 2009. A female figurine from the basal Aurignacian of Hohle Fels cave in southwestern Germany. *Nature* 459, 248–52.

Conkey, M. 2000. A Spanish resistance? Social archaeology and the study of Paleolithic art in Spain. *Journal of Anthropological Research* 56, 77–93.

Conkey, M. 2001. Structural and semiotic approaches. In D. S. Whitley (ed.), *Handbook of rock art research*, 273–310. Lanham, MD: AltaMira Press.

Conkey, M., Soffer, O., Stratmann, D., and Jablonski, N. G. (eds) 1997. *Beyond art: Pleistocene image and symbol*. San Francisco: Memoirs of the California Academy of Sciences 23.

Davis, W. 1986. The origins of image making. *Current Anthropology* 27, 193–215.

Delluc, B. and Delluc, G. 1990. Le décor des objects utilitaires du Paléolithic Supérieur. In J. Clottes (ed.), *L'art des objects au Paléolithique*, vol. 2, 39–72. Paris: Ministère de la Culture.

Dissanayake, E. 1995. Chimera, spandrel, or adaptation: conceptualizing art in human adaptation. *Human Nature* 6, 99–117.

d'Errico, F. 2009. The archaeology of early religious practices: a plea for a hypothesis-testing approach. In C. Renfrew and I. Morley (eds), *Becoming human: innovation in prehistoric material and spiritual culture*, 104–22. Cambridge: Cambridge University Press.

Fritz, C. 1999. Towards the reconstruction of Magdalenian artistic techniques: the contribution of microscopic analysis of mobiliary art. *Cambridge Archaeological Journal* 9, 189–208.

Hahn, J. 1993. Aurignacian art in Central Europe. In H. Knecht, A. Pike-Tay and R. White (eds), *Before Lascaux: the complex record of the early Upper Palaeolithic*, 229–57. Boca Raton: CRC Press.

Halverson, J. 1987. Art for art's sake in the Paleolithic. *Current Anthropology* 28, 63–89.

Henshilwood, C. S. 2009. The origins of symbolism, spirituality, and shamans: exploring Middle Stone Age material culture in South Africa. In C. Renfrew and I. Morley (eds), *Becoming human: innovation in prehistoric material and spiritual culture*, 29–49. Cambridge: Cambridge University Press.

Henshilwood, C. S., d'Errico, F., Yates, R., Jacobs, Z., Tribolo, C. Duller, G. A. T., Mercier, N., Sealy, J. C., Valladas, H., Watts, I., and Wintle, A. G. 2002. Emergence of modern human behaviour: Middle Stone Age engravings from South Africa. *Science* 295, 1278–80.

Hodgson, D. 2006. Altered states of consciousness and palaeoart: an alternative neurovisual explanation. *Cambridge Archaeological Journal* 16, 27–37.

Klüver, H. 1926. Mescal visions and eidetic vision. *American Journal of Psychology* 37, 502–15.

Lamarque, P. 2005. Palaeolithic cave painting: a test case for transcultural aesthetics. In T. Heyd and J. Clegg (eds), *Aesthetics and rock art*, 21–35. Aldershot: Ashgate.

Laming-Emperaire, A. 1962. *La signification de l'art rupestre Paléolithique*. Paris: Picard.

Layton, R. 2001. Ethnographic study and symbolic analysis. In D. S. Whitley (ed.), *Handbook of rock art research*, 311–31. Lanham, MD: AltaMira Press.

Leach, E. 1974. *Lévi-Strauss*. London: Fontana.

Leroi-Gourhan, A. 1968. *The art of prehistoric man in western Europe*. London and New York: Thames and Hudson.

Leroi-Gourhan, A. 1982. *The dawn of European art: an introduction to Palaeolithic cave painting*. Cambridge: Cambridge University Press.

Lewis-Williams, J. D. 1991. Wrestling with analogy: a methodological dilemma in Upper Palaeolithic art research. *Proceedings of the Prehistoric Society* 57, 149–62.

Lewis-Williams, J. D. 1995. Modelling the production and consumption of rock art. *South African Archaeological Bulletin* 50, 143–54.

Lewis-Williams, J. D. 2002. *The mind in the cave: consciousness and the origins of art.* London and New York: Thames and Hudson.

Lewis-Williams, J. D. 2010. *Conceiving God: the cognitive origin and evolution of religion.* London and New York: Thames and Hudson.

Lewis-Williams, J. D. and Challis, S. 2011. *Deciphering ancient minds: the mystery of San Bushman rock art.* London: Thames and Hudson.

Lewis-Williams, J. D. and Pearce, D. G. 2004a. *San spirituality: roots, expressions and social consequence.* Walnut Creek, CA: AltaMira; Cape Town: Doubly Storey.

Lewis-Williams, J. D. and Pearce, D. G. 2004b. Southern African San rock paintings as social intervention: a study of rain-control images. *African Archaeological Review* 21, 199–228.

Lorblanchet, M. 1991. Spitting images: replicating the spotted horses of Pech Merle. *Archaeology* 44, 25–31.

Lorblanchet, M. 1992. Finger markings in Pech Merle and their place in prehistoric art. In M. Lorblanchet (ed.), *Rock art in the Old World*, 451–90. New Delhi: Indira Gandhi National Centre for the Arts.

McBrearty, S. and Brooks, A. S. 2000. The revolution that wasn't: a new interpretation of the origin of modern human behaviour. *Journal of Human Evolution* 39, 453–563.

Malafouris, L. and Renfrew, C. 2008. Special section: steps to a 'neuroarchaeology' of mind. Introduction. *Cambridge Archaeological Journal* 18, 381–5.

Mellars, P., Boyle, K., Bar-Yosef, O., and Stringer, C. (eds) 2007. *Rethinking the human revolution: new behavioural and biological perspectives on the origin and dispersal of modern humans.* Cambridge: McDonald Institute for Archaeological Research.

Mellars, P. and Gibson, K. (eds) 1996. *Modelling the early human mind.* Cambridge: McDonald Institute for Archaeological Research.

Ministère de la Culture. 1984. *L'art des caverns: atlas de grottes ornées Paléolithiques Françaises.* Paris: Ministère de la Culture.

Mithen, S. 1996. *The prehistory of the mind: a search for the origins of art.* London: Thames and Hudson.

Mithen, S. 2005. *The singing Neanderthals.* London: Weidenfeld & Nicolson.

Montelle, Y.-P. 2004. Paleoperformance: investigating the human use of caves in the Upper Paleolithic. In G. Berghaus (ed.), *New perspectives on prehistoric art*, 131–52. London: Praeger.

Morley, I. 2002. Evolution of the physiological and neurological capacities for music. *Cambridge Archaeological Journal* 12, 195–216.

Onions, J. 2008. *Neuroarthistory: from Aristotle and Pliny to Baxandall and Zeki.* New Haven: Yale University Press.

Parkington, J. 1969. Symbolism in cave art. *South African Archaeological Bulletin* 24, 3–13.

Pfeiffer, J. E. 1982. *The creative explosion: an inquiry into the origins of art and religion.* New York: Harper & Row.

Pinker, S. 2002. *The blank slate: the modern denial of human nature.* London: Allen Lane, Penguin.

Ramanchandran, V. S. and Blakeslee, S. 1998. *Phantoms in the brain: probing the mysteries of the human mind.* New York: HarperCollins.

Raphael, M. 1945. *Prehistoric cave paintings.* New York: Princeton University Press.

Reinach, S. 1903. L'art et la magie à propos des peintures et des gravures de l'âge du renne. *L'Anthropologie* 14, 257–66.

Renfrew, C. 2007a. Where did it all go wrong? *Cambridge Archaeological Journal* 17, 222–4.

Renfrew, C. 2007b. *Prehistory: the making of the human mind.* London: Weidenfeld & Nicolson.

Renfrew, C. and Morley, I. (eds) 2009. *Becoming human: innovation in prehistoric material and spiritual culture.* Cambridge: Cambridge University Press.

Sauvet, G., Layton, R., Lenssen-Erz, T., Taçon, P., and Wlodarczyk, A. 2009. Thinking with animals in Upper Palaeolithic rock art. *Cambridge Archaeological Journal* 19, 319–36.

Sauvet, G. and Wlodarczyk, A. 1995. Eléments d'une grammaire formelle de l'art pariétal paléolithique. *L'Anthropologie* 99, 193–211.

Scarre, C. 1989. Painting by resonance. *Nature* 338, 382.

Scarre, C. and Lawson, G. (eds) 2006. *Archaeoacoustics.* Cambridge: McDonald Institute for Archaeological Research.

Sharpe, K. and van Gelder, L. 2006. The study of finger flutings. *Cambridge Archaeological Journal* 16, 281–95.

Siegel, R. K. 1977. Hallucinations. *Scientific American* 237, 132–40.

Spencer, W. B. and Gillen, F. J. 1899. *The native tribes of central Australia.* London: Macmillan.

Ucko, P. J. and Rosenfeld, A. 1967. *Palaeolithic cave art.* London: Weidenfeld & Nicolson.

Vialou, D. 1987. *L'art des caverns: les sanctuaries de la préhistoire.* Paris: Le Rocher.

Vialou, D. 1991. *La préhistoire.* Paris: Gallimard.

White, R. 1993. Technological and social dimensions of 'Aurignacian-age' body ornaments across Europe. In H. Knecht, A. Pike-Tay, and R. White (eds), *Before Lascaux: the complex record of the early Upper Palaeolithic,* 277–99. Boca Raton: CRC Press.

White, R. 2003. *Prehistoric art: the symbolic journey of humankind.* New York: Harry Abrams.

Whitley, D. S. 2001. *Handbook of rock art research.* Lanham, MD: AltaMira Press.

Wylie, A. 2002. *Thinking from things: essays in the philosophy of archaeology.* Berkeley: University of California Press.

Wynn, T., Coolidge, F., and Bright, M. 2009. Hohlenstein-Stadel and the evolution of human conceptual thought. *Cambridge Archaeological Journal* 19, 73–83.

Zeki, S. 2008. *Splendours and miseries of the brain: love, creativity and the quest for human happiness.* London: Wiley-Blackwell.

CHAPTER 29

SOCIAL COMPLEXITY

BRIAN HAYDEN

For over 2.4 million years of culture history, there are absolutely no indications in the archaeological record of any significant social complexity. It is only within the last 40,000 years that some telltale material signs of social complexity appear (almost exclusively in Europe), and it is not until the emergence of Mesolithic technology that social complexity spreads to many other parts of the globe, cropping up in particularly productive environments. This is an amazing pattern in cultural evolution. The emergence of social complexity is all the more noteworthy in that it may be implicated in the cultural dynamics leading to the domestication of plants and animals, but it occurs thousands of years prior to the first episodes of domestication. In fact, most of the technological and social advances usually attributed to agricultural communities actually appear first among complex hunters and gatherers. These include: the first pottery, ground-edge axes, use of metals, sedentism, large communities, monumental architecture, socio-economic inequalities, slavery, craft specialization, ocean craft, cemeteries, and other related characteristics. Consequently, I would argue that the major watershed in cultural development was not the domestication of plants or animals, but the emergence of the more complex societies that first occurred among hunters and gatherers.

However, before delving into this topic it is important to define exactly what is meant, and what is not meant, by social complexity, at least from an archaeological perspective. In contrast to the usage in this chapter, ethnographers often refer to any non-stratified society as 'egalitarian'. Thus, they would include Mayan villages and villages with big men in New Guinea as egalitarian societies (e.g. Wiessner 2002). However, despite frequently professed egalitarian ethics in these communities, they harbour major inequalities in wealth and power that make it difficult to consider them as comparable to the sharing-based egalitarian societies such as the !Kung or the Hadza. Thus, archaeologists like myself tend to reserve the term 'egalitarian' for simple hunter-gatherers lacking private ownership, prestige goods, pronounced socio-economic differences, economically based competition, but emphasizing sharing and equality. We use the term 'trans-egalitarian' to refer to groups lacking stratification but having private property, surpluses, prestige objects, and significant socio-economic differences. In fact, the obligatory sharing that characterizes true egalitarian societies (together with minimal private property or ownership of resources) is antithetical to the production of prestige items or wealth for personal uses.

At the other extreme, and in contrast to people that depict all non-stratified societies as egalitarian, Franz Boas went to great pains to argue that hunting and gathering cultures were just as complex as the civilized societies of the twentieth century. Thus, he emphasized the complexity among hunters and gatherers of their kinship systems, dance patterns, artistic achievements, linguistic structures, and similar cognitive or social factors. In trying to elevate the value of non-Western cultures and argue that their populations were on a cognitive and mental evolutionary par with Western populations Boas's motivations were certainly laudible. However, in rejecting all cultural evolutionary notions, Boas excessively over-reacted to its shortcomings. Over the century since Boas and his students argued for a staunch version of cultural relativity (and there are still adherents of this position today), archaeologists have assembled abundant evidence for major evolutionary changes in some of the most fundamental underpinnings of culture and society. One of these involves what has come to be referred to as 'social complexity'.

By social complexity, archaeologists generally mean the development of hierarchical (and/or heterarchical) social, economic, and political structures that manifest themselves materially in a number of ways stemming from control over labour and produce beyond the immediate family (Arnold 1996). Complexity, or social complexity, as used most of the time by archaeologists, is really an epithet referring to social and economic (and to some degree political) complexity. Rather than the complexity of kinship terms, language, cosmologies, or various arts, it is the increasing control over labour and the ability to produce ever more labour-intensive crafted objects or edifices under the control of a few individuals or families that underlies archaeological concepts of initial and subsequent complexity. Even greater degrees of complexity are implied by settlement hierarchies which indicate community domination or control over others. There are some archaeologists who argue that rich specialized prestige items and edifices, such as the elaborately gold festooned burials at Varna, could have resulted from communal concerns manifested as craft specialization and substantial efforts for the communal good (e.g. Biehl and Marciniack 2000; compare also Saitta 1999; Saitta and Keene 1990). The extreme interpretations of these positions strain credulity and have not generally been adopted in archaeological interpretations. When we find burials such as the Sungir adolescents (discussed below), the thousands of hours and specialized craft work represented by their adornments are generally taken to represent an unusual amount of power concentrated in the hands of one or a few families in a community. Someone with an inordinate control over resources and/or labour needed to underwrite, plan, and oversee the production of such lavish garments and grave goods.

Why these developments only begin to occur in the last 40,000 years is a contentious topic. Was it simply a matter of the evolution of greater cognitive abilities of anatomically modern humans? If so, why are indicators of complexity generally lacking from the preceding 50,000 years in Africa where anatomically modern humans originated? Why were they absent in many other parts of the world like the Australian Western Desert, the American Great Basin, or the Canadian boreal forests? Were there special technological and/or environmental conditions that led to the earliest development of complexity? If so, what were they? I will pursue a 'palaeo-political ecology' perspective in wrestling with these questions.

The assumptions of my version of political ecology (versus the applications of the term to modern states) are: (1) that under conditions where it is possible to produce relatively reliable surpluses, (2) various individuals (aggrandizers) begin to develop strategies to use surplus foods to enhance their social, economic, and political self-interests. These ultimately result not only in significant reproductive and survival advantages for aggrandizers, but also in the concentration of power (or undue influence) and materials in their hands, which archaeologists think of as social complexity and social inequality. A corollary is that where resources were not abundant or reliable enough, or were too easily over-exploited, little if any socio-economic complexity developed. Ethnographic examples of these situations include the desert areas of Australia, Africa, and North America as well as many boreal forests. Woodburn (1988) has also suggested that egalitarianism in some African cases may result from 'encapsulation' and domination by surrounding, more complex societies, although this could not account for the egalitarian societies in Australia or the boreal forests of North America where there were no complex outsider societies.

Before delving into the details of how complexity was achieved, it is useful to examine the evidence for the emergence of initial social complexity among hunter-gatherers.

THE FIRST MATERIAL INDICATORS OF COMPLEXITY

Ethnographically, when we survey the complex hunters and gatherers that were extant and recorded in historical times, we find that they display a number of recurring features that seem structurally related to each other. The Indians of California, the Ainu, the native groups on the Northwest Coast and Northwest Plateau, the tribes of south-east Australia, the Aleuts, the Eskimos of Point Barrow, the Calusa of Florida, and others all shared some fundamentally similar characteristics. These included: high population densities, potentially large settlements, seasonal or full sedentism, apparent abilities to produce surpluses, long-term storage (possibly except the Calusa), pronounced socio-economic inequalities (often displayed in burials), feasting, the development of prestige objects and specialized art, and other evidence of aggrandizer strategies (e.g. rich child burials). None of these material indicators occurs to any significant degree in the archaeological record anywhere in the world prior to 40,000 years ago. Moreover, until the end of the Palaeolithic, they only appear in European contexts associated with the fabulously rich faunas of the glacial period savannas. There is no evidence in the Lower or Middle Palaeolithic of long-term storage, no monumental undertakings (with the possible exception of Régourdou), no personal prestige items, no grave goods or other indicators of inequality, and no sedentism (with a few dubious claims). Certainly, there must have been some inequalities in Palaeolithic societies based minimally on age, sex, and access to mates or ritual knowledge. However, these kinds of inequalities exist in the overwhelming majority of, if not all, cultures. They form a baseline of the common social fabric of traditional societies and do not constitute what archaeologists generally think of as complex societies with more than normal socio-economic inequality.

With the advent of the Upper Palaeolithic in Europe, this situation changes perceptibly. Moreover, these changes appear to occur as a specific constellation, or package, in certain areas indicating that at least in some locations complex hunters and gatherers had developed. The fact that prestige objects, rich graves, middens indicative of some sedentism, and storage occur densely concentrated in some regions of Europe like the Les Eyzies and the river valleys of the Russian Plain, but do not occur in other regions or only very sparsely, is an indication that resource variables played critical roles in the development of these socially complex societies. The same pattern can be observed on the Northwest Coast and Northwest Plateau (Figures 29.1 and 29.2). In fact, Donald and Mitchell (1975) have demonstrated that there was a strong relationship in early historic times between the local salmon productivity of streams and the degree of socio-political complexity of the resident groups that controlled those streams. A similar relationship is clearly evident on the Northwest Plateau where the most complex communities are associated with the fishing localities that could produce the greatest surpluses (Hayden and Schulting 1997). This same basic relationship characterizes a number of other geographical regions (Hayden 1995). Thus, it appears that there is an important relationship between resource productivity and surplus production on the one hand and socio-political complexity on the other hand.

On the basis of ethnographic and archaeological evidence, I have proposed that once surpluses could be produced on a fairly regular basis, ambitious individuals developed a range of strategies in which surpluses could be used to gain reproductive, survival, and other advantages. Many of these strategies left archaeologically visible remains, such as prestige items, burial inequalities, elevated value of children, and feasting refuse (see Hayden 1995). But more importantly, by tying reproduction and survival to surplus economic production, I suggest that these strategies altered the basic dynamics underlying culture, resulting in a positive feedback system that continually pushed productive capacities to their limits. Given competition between contenders over mates and military allies, there could never be enough pigs or cattle or food. Contenders were always trying to outdo each other to obtain the best benefits.

Beginning with the Aurignacian (c.33,000–25,000 BP), there is abundant evidence for prestige objects in the form of sculptured bone, ivory, and antler (e.g. at Hohlenstein), and individual wealth in the form of thousands of beads manufactured and left at Abri Castanet and Blanchard (in the Castel-Merle Valley), although few or no burials are known from this period to confirm this inference. Beaune (1995) estimates the overall population density of Aurignacian Europe at 0.1 people per square kilometre, and this must have been significantly higher in favoured areas like the Les Eyzies region. Some rock shelters in the Castel-Merle Valley were occupied so intensively during the Aurigancian that one might well infer that occupations were seasonally sedentary. Marshack (1972) and Jègues-Wolkiewicz (2005) have argued that occupations at this location lasted at least two full months based on the apparent recording of lunar cycles on the plaquette from Abri Blanchard. In addition, I have suggested that both the development of esoteric astronomical observations recorded on this plaquette and the use of deep caves such as Chauvet for creating prestige art in secret locations may reflect the development of secret societies, which are a common feature of many complex hunters and gatherers (Hayden 2003).

By the time that the Gravettian tradition becomes widespread in Europe (25,000–19,000 BP), there are more occurrences of portable and prestige art outside and within caves (including some of the parietal art and female figurines), there are good indicators of seasonal or even full sedentism especially along river valleys of the Russian Plain (Klein 1969, 222; Klima 1962, 201; Soffer 1985, 328, 411, 416), there is abundant evidence for long-term storage on the Russian Plain, and inequalities in personal or family wealth in burials reached an apogee. The remarkable burials at Sungir highlight the surprising degree of socio-economic inequalities in control over labour and wealth that developed in certain areas during this time period. There, a male adult and two adolescent boys were buried wearing an aggregate total of 9,000 ivory beads plus ivory lances,

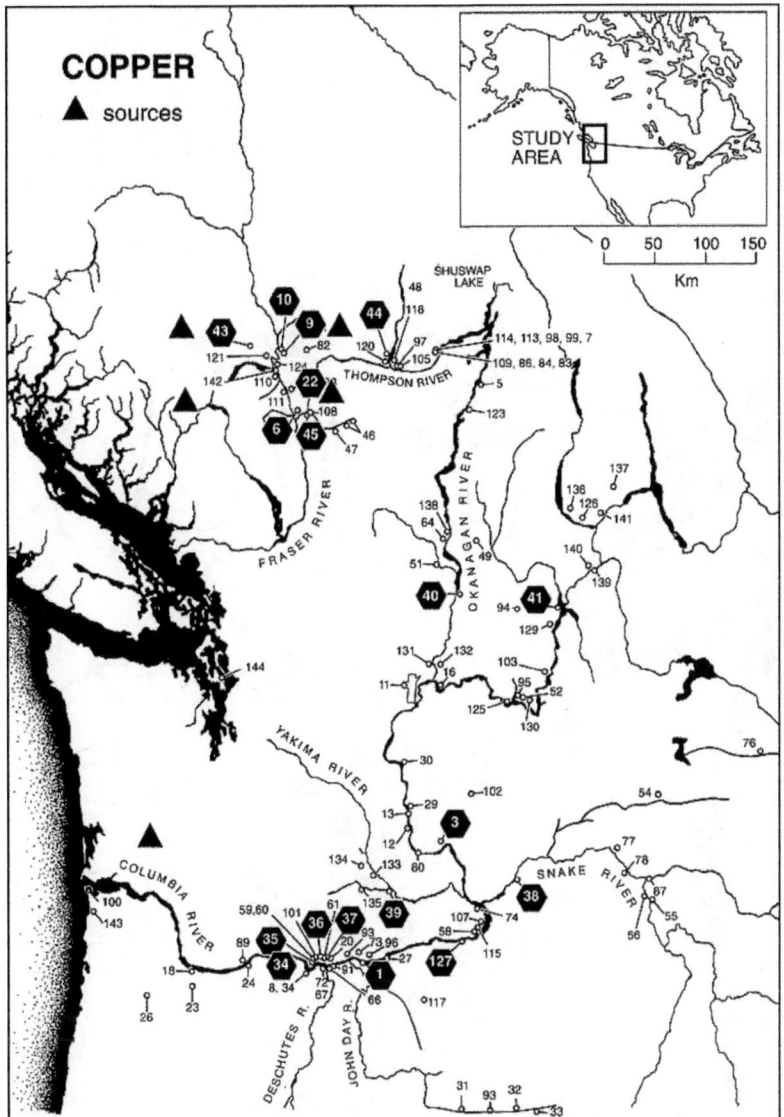

FIGURE 29.1 The presence/absence distribution of native copper on the Northwest Plateau of North America. Known sources are indicated by triangles. Note the strongly concentrated occurrences around the Deschutes and Columbia River confluence and around the Thompson and Fraser River confluence. These were the most productive salmon fisheries in these drainages and produced regular surpluses of salmon associated with socially complex communities. This illustrates the relationship between surpluses and complexity, as well as the geographical clustering of prestige items and complex societies (*Source*: Hayden and Schulting 1997, 59).

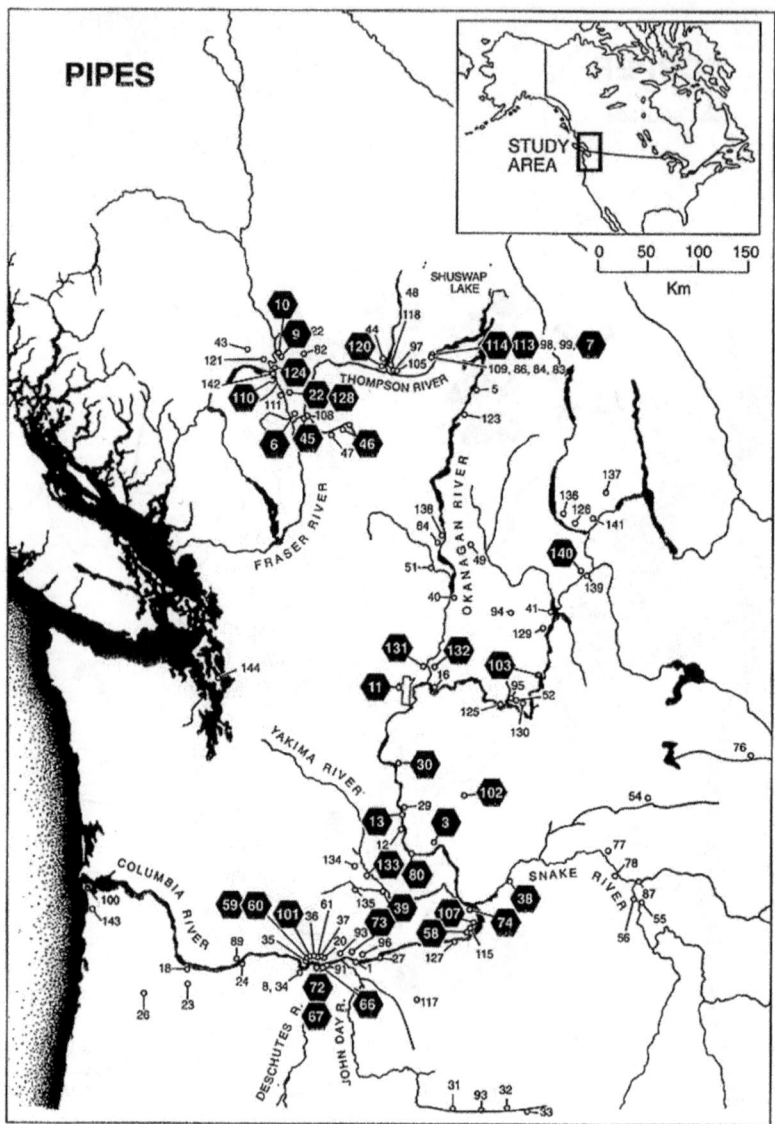

FIGURE 29.2 The presence/absence distribution of tubular stone pipes on the Northwest Plateau of North America. Note again the strong clustering of pipes around the confluences of the Deschutes and Snake Rivers with the Columbia River and around the confluence of the Thompson and Fraser Rivers (*Source*: Hayden and Schulting 1997, 71).

wheel-shaped cut-outs, and other prestige ornaments. The beads alone would have required about an hour each to carve, amounting to 9,000 hours of labour. This magnitude of wealth accumulation by one family is nothing short of astounding at this time and seems more commensurate with chiefdom-level concentrations of power and social complexity.

While many prehistorians continue to view the burial of children with wealth as evidence of ascribed status indicating chiefdom types of social stratification, such ascribed status also occurs in many trans-egalitarian societies as part of aggrandizer strategies to increase the value of their children for purposes of increasing marriage wealth exchanges. Thus, the rich adolescent burials at Sungir (and elsewhere) conceivably reflect either a complex trans-egalitarian society or a chiefdom-level society. The Gravettian, in general, is known for similar but less extreme burials with elaborate personal wealth (Pettit 2005, 161). There are also good candidates for restricted access to supernatural rituals as indicated by the small peripheral ritual structure at Dolni Vestonice and the elaborate, probably ritual, mammoth bone structure at Mezerich on the Russian Plain.

While there is no direct evidence for storage in the western European sites, the thick deposits that occur during this time at the major sites indicate that storage was a likely practice. Storage could have easily occurred on raised platforms that were archaeologically almost undetectable, as this was the common ethnographic practice in Siberia and north-west North America.

The Solutrean and Magdalenian, however, are the periods when the greatest abundance of portable and prestige manifestations were created and the highest population densities reached, even surpassing the population densities of later agricultural groups (Mellars 1994, 44, 64). Lascaux cave has frequently been described as the Sistine Chapel of the Palaeolithic, and I think the epithet is particularly apt in its innuendoes of exclusive use by a rich and powerful spiritual elite. Altamira, Font-de-Gaume, Les Trois Frères, and many other fabulously painted caves bear witness to caves that were decorated by highly trained (and probably commissioned) artists, and probably used for some kind of secreted prestige function. At other ritual sites such as El Juyo, monumental 1 tonne slabs of limestone were used in ritual constructions (Freeman and Echegaray 1981). Storage is implied by massive kills and filleting cutmarks as well as large hearths suitable for smoke-drying meat (Beaune 1995, 53, 81, 84, 132; Costamagno 2003, 81–4; Soffer 1985, 253–8, 459–62; 1989). The emphasis on blade production also makes sense in terms of cutting requirements in filleting meat for drying, since long, straight, sharp cutting edges are optimal for cutting large quantities of meat into thin slices. Semi or full sedentism is attested in the faunal record (Fontana 2000, 161–2), and feasting is implied by unusually dense animal remains inside caves such as Enlène and Gargas (Bégouën and Clottes 1981) as well as by the occurrence of spoons carved from antler and the intentional destruction of prestige items reminiscent of wealth destruction at Northwest Coast potlatches (Beaune 1995, 212). The treatment of human skeletal remains, especially the circulation of bones, follows similar patterns of much later Neolithic groups and may indicate ancestor worship practices that occur in the context of corporately owned resources. In fact, Randy White (1985) has argued that many large Upper Palaeolithic sites were located near fording locations along the Vézère River so as to be able to kill animals crossing at these points. These fording points are so closely spaced (every 2 km) and were probably so central to subsistence and political economies that they could have been corporately owned resource procurement locations just as lucrative fishing rocks were owned by corporate families in the Northwest Interior of North America (Kennedy and Bouchard 1992).

Craft specialization involving substantial training is evident in the artistic masterpieces of the later Upper Palaeolithic as well as in the remarkable thin large Solutrean laurel leaf bifaces that were produced but which were clearly never intended to be used for any practical purpose. The intensive occurrence of hide working implied by use-wear (at some sites like Cassegros accounting for 90 per cent of the activities—Vaughan 1985) and the generally high proportion of endscrapers at many sites, indicates that the production of buckskin was taking place at unprecedented levels in some areas. Together with sites demonstrating the specialized procurement, use, and/or storage of raptor bird wings or talons, or small fur-bearing animals (Beaune 1995, 92; Bouchud 1953, 556–60; Laroulandie 2003; Soffer 1985, 400), and the manufacturing of the many beads once attached to funeral garments, it is apparent that elaborately decorated clothes were being produced. In fact, the scale of buckskin production and the surpluses implied by regions with high population densities conjure up images of resident groups in the Les Eyzies region becoming rich off the export of dried meat, buckskin, and tailored prestige garments ornamented with fur, feathers, teeth, claws, and beads.

I suggest, in effect, that some corporate groups were based on the fur/leather trade. Up until the twentieth century, Siberian hunter and gatherers such as the Khanty built remarkably complex socio-political organizations (described as chiefdoms) based on just such a fur trade (Jordan 2003). Similarly, Northwest Plateau communities became rich and densely populated due to the production of surplus salmon, buckskin clothes, nephrite adzes, copper ornaments, and other prestige items for trade (Hayden and Schulting 1997). With such economic foundations, it should come as no surprise that prestige items should have proliferated in the most resource-rich regions of Europe, together with lavish burials, honouring of ancestors, ownership of resource locations, and claims that elite families had privileged access to the supernatural, whether via special spirit quests (as in north-west North America—Schulting 1995), special links with ancestors, or the creation of special secret societies open only to the wealthy. All of these developments represented far greater social and political complexity than had previously existed. These developments were typical of some of the most complex ethnographic trans-egalitarian hunter-gatherer societies and constituted a new direction of cultural development dramatically different from simpler, more egalitarian bands based on sharing scarce resources that characterized earlier periods and continued to exist in resource-poor areas up until historic times.

The Mesolithic

I use the term 'Mesolithic' in the broad generic sense proposed by V. Gordon Childe (1953), to indicate an intensified economic exploitation of the environment (in the western hemisphere, equivalent to the 'Archaic' cultural stage of development). This is similar to Childe's definition of the Neolithic in economic (domestication) terms rather than narrow technological terms. While the complex societies of the Upper Palaeolithic were based on unprecedented dense populations of ungulates in the glacial parklands of Europe, climatic amelioration and the encroachment of forests were the death knell for these cultures in their traditional heartlands. However, pressures to intensify production for exchange, wealth, and feasting may have spurred the development of new technologies capable of extracting more resources from environments—or perhaps even in attempts to maintain the kinds of privileged roles that had been created. Social and political demands for surpluses would certainly have constituted a strong motivational factor that had not previously existed for developing new technologies. In Europe, these new techniques focused largely on the exploitation of aquatic species, especially fish and shellfish. The effective mass harvesting and storage of these resources opened up vast new reservoirs of food encompassing many new species only opportunistically used previously. Although fish were certainly used in the Upper Palaeolithic and even earlier periods, carbon isotope analyses indicate that they were not harvested in any large quantities until the very end of the Magdalenian and the beginning of the Mesolithic periods (Hayden et al. 1987). Indeed, in the Upper Palaeolithic, the only fishing equipment in evidence are the harpoons during the Magdalenian, whereas with the Mesolithic, there are harpoons, leisters, fish hooks, net sinkers, and even basket traps. Settlement patterns of larger sites generally are associated with lucrative fishing locations, and it is here that social complexity continued to manifest itself in rich burials (e.g. O'Shea and Zvelebil 1984), prestige items, seasonal or full sedentism, and many other traits that have been noted. Schulting (1995) has quantified inequality in burials and house sizes using Lorenz curves and Gini coefficients (Figure 29.3). Interestingly, he points out that in some cases, inequality coefficients in the complex hunter-gatherer societies of the Northwest Interior were comparable to the degree of inequality in income distributions in the contemporary United States.

In the lucrative fishing region known as the Iron Gates on the Danube, the remarkable late Mesolithic site of Lepenski Vir produced abundant evidence of prestige goods, feasting, ancestral or totemic sculptures and burials, permanent architecture, large-sized settlement, and inequalities in burials (Radovanovic 1996). In fact, the entire site could conceivably be a special location for funerary and ancestral feasting rituals similar to some tribal funeral house constructions (Hayden 2003). There is certainly nothing quite like it anywhere else in Europe at this time, and the many burials under the structure floors, with human mandibles arranged around the carefully constructed slab-lined hearths, imply strong funerary components to the activities within the structures at the site.

Further afield, other Mesolithic innovations opened up additional resource possibilities. In eastern Europe and the Near East, mass harvesting and processing of grass seeds made available vast reservoirs of new resources in favoured locations. Seed grinding implements appear for the first time, with some precocious instances in the later Palaeolithic. Mortars and pestles may have also been suitable for producing acorn meal that could be detoxified and eaten. Fire-cracked rocks, too, probably attest to the extraction of bone greases, fish oils, and/or plant oils. While fire-cracked rocks begin to appear in the Upper Palaeolithic, they are rare, and do not become widespread until the Mesolithic.

All of these technological innovations, together with the storage technologies developed in the Upper Palaeolithic, were relatively simple to learn, and so spread throughout much of the world in only a few thousand years. Where they were adopted in localities rich in fish, game, grain, or nut resources, complex Mesolithic societies flourished. The most striking examples consist of the Natufians in the Near East, the Jomon of Japan, the Aleut and Northwest Coast/Interior cultures, and the California hunters and gatherers. In recent years, there has been considerable discussion about the possible practice of cultivation without domestication among most of these groups, including the creation of 'clam gardens' (Bar-Yosef 2002, 127; Bar-Yosef and Belfer-Cohen 1999, 409; Deur 2002; 2005; Peacock 1998; 2002; Unger-Hamilton 1989; 1991; Willcox 1998, 33; Williams 2006).

Where thick shellfish middens constitute new Mesolithic features, they can probably be accounted for by increased sedentism. Shellfish were certainly used in earlier time periods, but food remains appear to have been dispersed over a variety of locations in space and over time.

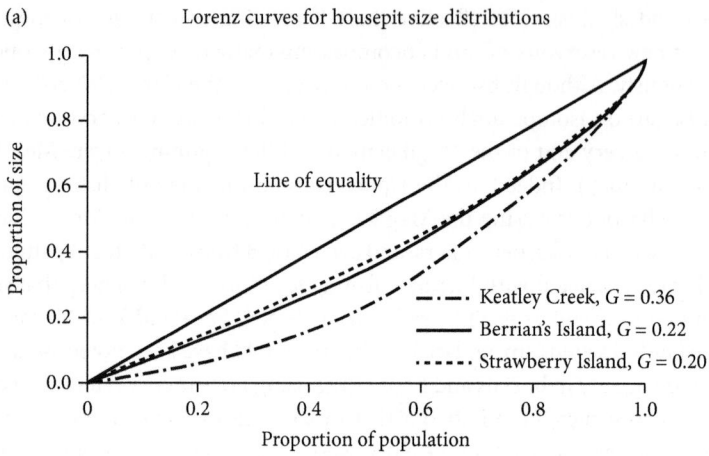

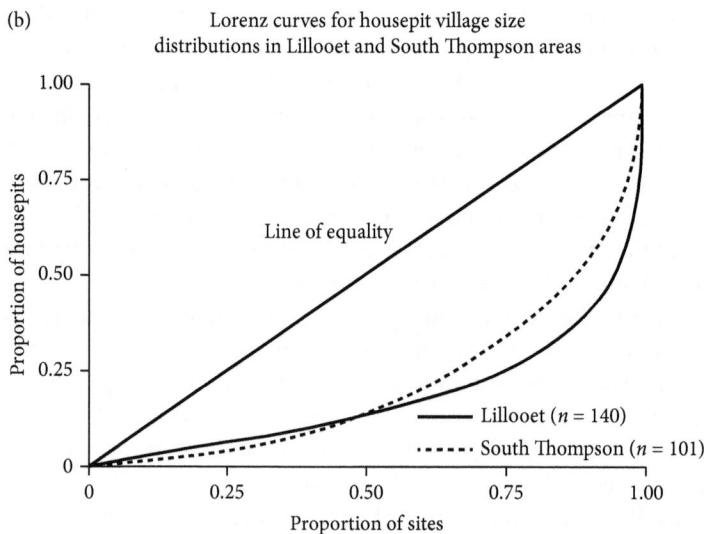

FIGURE 29.3 The graph at the top displays Lorenz curves and corresponding Gini coefficients indicating the degree of departure of an ideal egalitarian distribution of housepit sizes at Keatley Creek and two other sites. The bottom graph shows the degree to which the number of housepits per site in the region departs from a hypothetical line of equality (*Source*: Schulting 1995).

Natufians

The Natufian culture of the Levant (c.13,000–10,000 BP) displays all of the characteristics of trans-egalitarian social complexity. Settlements were much larger than earlier Upper Palaeolithic sites, with estimates of 100–300 occupants (Moore et al. 2000, 483, 489); there was seasonal if not full sedentism with permanent stone-walled structures; there were abundant game and plant foods (especially acorns, pistachios, wheat, rye, and barley). At key sites like Abu Hureyra, Natufian occupants had 'endless vistas', 'vast supplies' of riparian and other plant foods, as well as 'more than sufficient...meat in whatever amounts were needed' (Hillman 2000, 366, 370–1, 384; Moore et al. 2000, 480). The total of 250 food species included 20 staples and was so rich that full sedentism was apparently adopted (Moore et al. 2000, 491) even when wild cereals may have become increasingly distant during the Younger Dryas (Anderson 1991, 550).

Perrot (1966, 460, 482) excavated many storage pits at Mallaha, and Bar-Yosef (2002, 110, 112) postulates that baskets were probably extensively used for long-term storage of food. Prestige objects become abundant in the Natufian, especially dentalium and other shells. Small quantities of obsidian were imported from Anatolia (c.500 km away); the first use of jade occurs in Abu Hureyra; and the first use of copper occurs at Zawi Chemi. There are also prestige items such as: greenstone, malachite, and colourful beads, cinnabar, raptor claws and wings, and fox and leopard phalanges. Henry (1989, 197–202) has argued that Natufian bone artefacts became popular in the Natufian because they are highly visible, labour intensive to make, and easily decorated, characteristics that make sense in terms of prestige objects in general, but specifically for Plateau and Upper Palaeolithic bone or antler bone artefacts (Hayden 2004, 268). Heavy, decorated groundstone basalt 'mortars' and other ground stone items (bowls, dishes, pestles, and grooved pebbles) were imported by Natufians from 60–100 km away and probably also represent prestige items (Bar-Yosef 2002, 117). The use of lime plaster and flagstones in some buildings or burials also appear to represent prestige features that initially appear in ritual or funerary contexts.

Trans-egalitarian feasting is indicated not only by the basalt serving wares (decorated plates, 'mortars', and bowls), but also by the occurrence of unusually large hearths (up to 3 m in diameter), some containing fire-cracked rock, and some associated with dense accumulations of animal bone. Large quantities of animal bones are also associated with burial areas (Perrot 1961, 258; Solecki et al. 2004, 28, 105–6, 120), and central plazas where stacks of caprid skulls were erected (Rosenberg and Redding 2000).

The association of feasting remains with funerary deposits, including multiple burials and elaborate, plastered graves, indicates that the development of corporate groups and ancestor worship was probably pronounced in the richer Natufian settlements. Skull removal practices are generally interpreted as additional indicators that Natufians had adopted ancestor cults. Ancestor cults, in turn, are generally viewed as part of resource-controlling corporate kinship groups featuring inherited rights to resources such as stands of nut trees or cereals (Byrd and Monahan 1995, 279, 282; Henry 1989, 207–8, 211). That there are multiple examples of grouped Natufian burials from each site, indicates that corporate groups probably formed a heterarchical political organization. Certain burials were also invested with substantial wealth items such as headcaps covered with hundreds of dentalium shells. These occurrences imply significant socio-economic inequalities in some Natufian communities and most probably within corporate groups as well.

The occurrence of secondary burials in the Natufian has been attributed to communal ancestor worship (Kuijt 1996, 317) or to increased mobility (Bar-Yosef 2001, 17; 2002, 114; Byrd and Monahan 1995, 279). However, it is far more likely that Natufian secondary burials resulted from attempts to increase the status of the dead corporate members (and therefore also the living corporate members) by delaying funerary feasts up to five or more years until enough resources (especially dried fish and meat) could be accumulated to host a suitably impressive feast. This was typically the case on the Northwest Coast and Interior (Ostapkowicz 1992, 33; Romanoff 1992, 475) as well as among the Torajan horticultural groups (see Adams 2004). As Teit (1900, 336) observed among the Thompson Indians of British Columbia: 'The bones of a deceased relative were frequently taken up, bundled together, and re-covered with new material...As it was usual to give a large feast at such times, the custom was confined in a large measure to the wealthy.'

In general, funerary feasts were often the most overtly competitive displays of wealth in trans-egalitarian communities (see Hayden 2009).

Whether the earliest Neolithic communities that developed out of the Natufian should rightly be considered as fundamentally hunting and gathering societies or as agricultural societies is still open to discussion. Although the weight of tradition continues to view Pre-Pottery Neolithic A settlements as agricultural, to date no domesticated plants or animals have been found at such important sites as Jerf el Ahmar and Gobekli, while at other PPNA sites, the importance of domesticated plants is generally recognized as being almost insignificant in the overall subsistence economy. If some or all of these sites can be considered as fundamentally based on hunting and gathering, our conceptions of how complex hunter-gatherer societies could become will require some serious reconfiguring, especially with the monumental megalithic architecture displayed at Gobekli. But similar developments have been noted for late Archaic groups with minimal agriculture but monumental architecture on the coasts of South America and at Poverty Point and other late Archaic mound sites in North America. Similar developments may also characterize late hunter-gatherers in Japan at sites like Sanai Maruyama with its monumental wooden structures or Terano-higashi with its 100 m diameter circular mound (Habu 2004, 191-3), and even in China where evidence for complexity is more contentious.

The Far East

The Chinese early Holocene cultures are less well documented than the Jomon of Japan where increasing complexity is well documented (Habu 2004). In Japan, before the first appearance of a number of minor domesticates such as bottle gourds and mints in the Middle Jomon period, indicators of complexity emerged in the Initial and Early Jomon (c.9500-5000 BP). These included the presence of prestige items such as imported obsidian, stone beads, jade artefacts, amber, shell bracelets, antler pendants, earrings, dogs, stone circles and features, and the differential occurrence of prestige items in burials (Habu 2004, 157, 176-96).

The succeeding Middle Jomon (c.5000-4000 BP) is viewed as fundamentally a hunting and gathering-based economy, but indications of complexity become much more pronounced including large sedentary settlements with up to 500 residents and monumental architecture indicative of substantial control over labour. Remarkable examples come from Sanai Maruyama where massive towers such as the six 95 cm diameter posts were estimated to have supported a structure 17 m high. At Terano-higashi and other sites, circular mounds up to 100 m in diameter seem to have enclosed ritual areas (Habu 2004, 111-12, 192-6). Prestige items proliferate and increase in diversity, including the making of ground stone rods up to 1 m long, and elaborate ceramic figurines. Long-distance trade in exotic items also increases.

In addition to this well-known example of Jomon complexity, I will briefly summarize some of the less well-known indications of increasing complexity in China. For the majority of the Chinese Pleistocene, there are few indications of complexity and very little change at all from the chopper/chopping tool tradition established almost a million years ago or more. It is only around 18,000–12,000 BP at a few cave sites in the middle Yangzi Basin that a number of changes can initially be detected that are consistent with Mesolithic innovations and subsistence intensification elsewhere. At sites like Yuchanyan and Xianrendong, pottery appears together with hoe-shaped stone tools and notched axes interpreted as cultivation tools. There are also perforated shells considered to be sickles, bone drills, bone tools that may have been hoes or spades, grinding stones, edge-ground adzes, pierced stone disks (probably digging stick or net weights), bone arrowheads and harpoons, and perforated antler and shell implements also possibly used as sickles (Lu 2006; Yuan 2002; Zhang 2000). I suggest that ground-edge cutting tools likely emerged as a response to increased wood-cutting volumes and requirements (Hayden 1989). The discovery of an 8,000-year-old dugout canoe along the lower Yangzi (Jiang and Liu 2005) may indicate an early development of watercraft in the Chinese Mesolithic period. If so, this could explain the increased wood-cutting requirements of the Chinese Mesolithic, although forest clearance for some cultivation (before domestication) may also have been a factor. The development of effective watercraft during the Chinese Mesolithic may also help to explain the increases in sedentism, exploitation of aquatic resources, and technological changes that occurred during this period. The development of pottery can also plausibly be related to the extraction of fish or nut oils, arguably for feasting purposes (Hayden 2009).

Subsistence at these Mesolithic cave sites displays a remarkable range of plants and animals exploited, including many aquatic species. At Yuchanyan, for example, there were 28 mammal species represented (dominated by deer), 27 bird species (18 of which were waterbirds, especially ducks), 33 shellfish species, and 40 plant species, together with fish, land molluscs, and insects (Yuan 2002, 160, 163, 165). Thus, the subsistence remains and new subsistence tools in the Chinese Mesolithic appear consistent with an increased ability to extract abundant resources from certain environments especially where fish, water plants, and nuts like acorns occurred in abundance. In other parts of the world (like California, Mesoamerica, Japan, and the Near East), the ability to exploit these same types of resources in abundance constituted an important part of the subsistence foundation for the emergence of complex hunter-gatherers.

As might be expected, there are also indications of increasing sedentism in the Chinese Mesolithic as minimally evidenced by the use of pottery. There are also indications of increasing social complexity. While Lu (2006, 148) and others see little or no evidence for prestige items in Mesolithic China (except for a shell necklace from Donghulin in northern China), there are, in fact, some other important finds. The most well known of these are the grave goods that accompanied at least eight individuals in the Upper Cave at Zhoukoudian dated to 10,470–10,174 BP. These consisted of 125 perforated fox, badger, and deer teeth; stone beads; shells; bone needles; polished bird bones and other polished bone artefacts. One teenage girl wore a cap, hood, or headband ornamented with a row of small ochre-painted stone beads and a deer canine. Other ornaments appear to have been sewn or strung onto headbands, clothing, armlets, or necklaces (Huang 1986; Kamminga 1992, 392; Kamminga and Wright 1988, 741-2, 755-6). The sea shells must have been transported a minimum of 150 km and perhaps up to 1,000 km. A similar artefact assemblage with four perforated teeth, decorated drilled shells, and bone needles occurred at the Xiaogushan site (Huang 1986) and presumably dates to the same period or slightly earlier. Bone needles imply tailored skin clothes that were probably important prestige and wealth items in the past just as they were among ethnographic hunters and gatherers in North America (Hayden 1990, 32). The shells that formed the Donghoulin necklace (dated to 10,350–9540 BP) also originated from the east coast of China, at least 290 km away and possibly up to 1,200 km away (Hao 2001).

In northern Indochina, prestige items also begin to appear in the Vietnamese Mesolithic (Hoabinhian) sites. Grave goods include perforated and ground shell ornaments transported 100–200 km from sources, carnivore tooth pendants, carved and incised stone slabs, and a range of polished bone artefacts (Boriskovskii 1969–70, 225; Colani 1927, 44, 71, plate 12; 1931, 384, 388–9; Mansuy 1925, 23; Nguyen 1986, 11; 1994a; 1994b). Some Hoabinhian sites appear to have been cemeteries similar to the Upper Cave at Zhoukoudian and the Zengpiyan cave in southern China (dated to 8000–10,000 BP with 18 flexed burials, some with ochre). At this time, it appears that merely the act of burial was reserved for only a small proportion of the population, implying some important type of status distinction. However, the occurrence of cemetery areas carries with it additional implications of corporate kinship groups (descent groups) controlling some kind of important resources such as productive fishing or hunting sites, productive plant harvesting sites, or labour-intensive tools of production like nets or boats (Chapman 1981, 408). Thus, the beginnings of intentional burials and cemeteries in the Chinese Mesolithic are probably an indication of increasing levels of socio-economic complexity.

Additional support for these interpretations is provided from artefact remains outside of burial contexts, but largely overlooked by prehistorians. These consist of a number of likely prestige items including deer and carnivore canines that were suspended as ornaments plus a number of other faunal remains recovered at Yuchanyan cave (Yuan 2002, 159). The other faunal elements consisted of bones from six species of small carnivores and nine non-aquatic bird species. Although detailed species lists are not yet available, it seems likely that small carnivores were not being hunted for their meat values, but for their decorative fur values. Prestige decorative use was probably also the motivation for procuring at least some of the bird species. Fur and feathers are still used in various tribal costumes in South-East Asia, as elsewhere in the world, and talons from raptors may have been equally sought as symbols of power, as in many other complex hunter-gatherers.

In addition to burials, cemeteries, and prestige items, increasing social complexity is indicated by the probable advent of surplus-based feasting, especially in ritual contexts. While the archaeological remains from China are somewhat limited, and while it can be notoriously difficult to identify feasting from archaeological remains (witness the difficulties on the Northwest Coast where there is abundant ethnographic documentation of potlatches, but few archaeological indications), there are nevertheless some important indicators of feasting in Mesolithic China. For example, the faunal remains accompanying the burials at Zengpiyan included at least 67 pigs, 65 per cent of which were between one and two years old. There were no evident genetic changes from wild pigs, but this is the same proportion of immature pigs that Yuan and Flad (2002, 725) used to identify pig domestication in the 8,000-year-old assemblage at Cishan. Even if pigs were not being bred around Zengpiyan, it seems likely that they were being raised (perhaps from piglets captured in the wild) and husbanded for funerary or ancestral feasting, much the way that the Ainu captured bear cubs from the wild and raised them for one year in preparation for their bear ceremonies and feasting. Raising animals in this fashion requires significant surplus production to feed the animals as well as a pronounced degree of sedentism.

Another indication of feasting involves the occurrence of pottery in the Chinese Mesolithic as well as Siberian and Japanese sites from the same period. Although Pearson (2005) failed to see much support for the feasting role of early pottery, he narrowly focused on the possible serving role of early pottery in feasts, and he neglected the potential role of early pottery in preparing special feasting foods. There are several indications that early pottery was not, in fact, used for preparing food for everyday consumption. First, early pottery is rare, and must have been used very infrequently. At the site of Yuchanyan, several hundred small potsherds occur over the span of several thousand years. Altogether, these only represent two conical cooking vessels (Yuan 2002, 161). In addition to this, it appears that Yuchanyan cave itself was not a normal residential site, but its unusual prepared floors (Paul Goldberg, pers. comm.) indicate some kind of special site use, such as would be consistent with ritual activities and feasting.

Also, early pottery vessels seem to be strongly associated with prime fishing locations (Hayden 2009). However, one hardly needs ceramic vessels to cook fish. Thus, what are the possible uses of early pottery cooking vessels for preparing prestige feasting foods? It has been suggested that they may have been used for preparing rice in China. However, rice can be easily cooked in bamboo, and rice does not occur at this time period in other areas where early pottery is present such as Siberia or Japan. However, from ethnographic accounts of groups on the Northwest Coast of North America, it is apparent that fish oil was highly prized and very labour-intensive to produce. It also requires considerable boiling. Similarly, soups consisting of oily fish fins and heads or broken-up mammal bones would likely be relished cold-weather foods, but they were labour-intensive to prepare (Hayden, 2009). Pottery used by seasonal or fully sedentary groups could have made such oil extraction or soup preparation much easier.

In addition, nuts were traditionally processed in bulk with mortars and pestles by groups in North America in order to extract their nut oils. One hundred pounds of nuts yielded about one gallon of oil (Taché et al. 2008, 66). Again, boiling was an essential step that could have been greatly facilitated by the use of pottery among relatively sedentary groups. Nut trees might also be expected to be most abundant along streams where fish were exploited. Fuller et al. (2007) have suggested that the relatively sedentary communities in the middle Yangtzi drainage such as Pengtoushan relied heavily on nuts for subsistence c.9000 BP.

Finally, early pottery could have been used for brewing rice or other wild grains, a pottery-use tradition that goes back at least to 9000 BP in China as documented at Jiahu (Roach 2005).

Thus, there are a number of possible roles that Mesolithic pottery could have played in preparing feasting foods. Contrary to Pearson's conclusions, I think it is difficult to account for early pottery characteristics without reference to its role in preparing feasting foods.

So, in considering the emergence of complexity among hunter-gatherers in China, there are several important indications that this was well underway by the Mesolithic period as evidenced by subsistence and technological changes together with new burial, prestige, ritual, settlement, and feasting behaviours. All of these indicators imply significant potentials to produce surpluses upon which feasting and socio-economic complexity are predicated. However, as in the Near East, there is currently a debate as to whether even some of the earliest 'Neolithic' sites might not have also been essentially hunting and gathering societies. In spite of their evident sedentism, large sizes, developed prestige items, and pottery, Crawford (2006) and Fuller et al. (2007) have challenged the claims that Pengtoushan or Jiahu sites (c.9000–8000 BP) have any domesticated plants or animals. Fuller et al. (2007) argue for very late plant domestication, as late as 6000 BP.

While this issue remains to be resolved, if Fuller et al. turn out to be correct about the lack of domestication in sites like the Pengtoushan, Bashidang, and Jiahu, it would put these sites on a par with late Pleistocene hunter-gatherer sites in the Near East like Abu Hureyra, Zawi Chemi, Hallan Çemi, Ain Mallaha, and possibly Jerf el Ahmar and Gobekli Tepe—all sites that turned the hunting and gathering world upside down with their ever more complex and competitive socio-economic systems. I argue that the insatiable social and political demands for ever-increasing economic production generated by these new types of societies ultimately took the lid off a Pandora's box of food intensification techniques that led to the genetic modifications of other species.

Conclusion

In review, there is little or no evidence for any significant socio-economic complexity in the prehistoric record until the European Upper Palaeolithic and the subsequent rapid diffusion (or independent development) of Mesolithic techniques for extracting resource surpluses elsewhere in the world. Complexity appears inextricably linked to rich resource environments and to technologies capable of exploiting, processing, and storing seasonally abundant resources. The most plausible intervening factor that can explain the relationship between surplus production and complexity is the presence of ambitious individuals (aggrandizers) who developed strategies to use surplus production to increase their own power and self-interests, especially in terms of their ability to reproduce, to defend themselves from attack (both physical and political), to fend off starvation and misfortunes, and to enhance their life quality. Strategies that they developed, based on the use of surpluses, and which are archaeologically manifest, included: mate acquisition, investments in children for marriage exchanges, development of prestige items, private or corporate control of resources, feasting, and claims of exclusive access to supernatural forces. To the extent that these strategies were successful, aggrandizers obtained more mates; had more children; survived attacks, famines, and misfortunes; led better-quality lives; and were more ceremoniously buried. These benefits attracted followers and supporters who sought to share in the benefits, and these new socio-economic systems became relatively widespread during the Mesolithic. Because survival and fitness were based on the competitive production and use of surpluses, a positive feedback condition was created that constantly pushed production to its maximum limits and exerted continual pressure to develop new ways to increase production. This resulted in a proliferation of both new subsistence and new prestige technologies together with geometrically increasing populations and social complexity that have characterized human societies since the inception of complex hunting and gathering cultures in the Upper Palaeolithic and Mesolithic. Such unparalleled pressures to increase production constituted new forces in the evolution of culture and plausibly led to cultivation and later domestication of plants, and the rearing of animals for feasts.

References

Adams, R. 2004. An ethnoarchaeological study of feasting in Sulawesi, Indonesia. *Journal of Anthropological Archaeology* 26, 56–78.

Anderson, P. 1991. Harvesting of wild cereals during the Natufian as seen from the experimental cultivation and harvest of wild einkorn wheat and microwear analysis of stone tools. In O. Bar-Yosef and F. Valla (eds), *The Natufian culture in the Levant*, 521–56. Ann Arbor: International Monographs in Prehistory.

Arnold, J. 1996. The archaeology of complex hunter-gatherers. *Journal of Archaeological Method and Theory* 3, 77–126.

Bar-Yosef, O. 2001. From sedentary foragers to village hierarchies: the emergence of social institutions. In G. Runciman (ed.), *The origin of human social institutions*, 1–38. London: British Academy.

Bar-Yosef, O. 2002. Natufian: a complex society of foragers. In B. Fitzhugh and J. Habu (eds), *Beyond foraging and collecting*, 91–149. New York: Kluwer Academic/Plenum Press.

Bar-Yosef, O. and Belfer-Cohen, A. 1999. Encoding information: unique Natufian objects from Hayonim Cave. *Antiquity* 73, 402–10.

Beaune, S. de 1995. *Les hommes au temps de Lascaux*. Paris: Hachette.

Bégouën, R. and Clottes, J. 1981. Nouvelles fouilles dans la Salle des Morts de la Caverne d'Enlène, à Avantès (Ariège). *Congrès Préhistorique de France* 21, 33–57.

Biehl, P. and Marciniak, A. 2000. The construction of hierarchy: rethinking the Copper Age in southeastern Europe. In Michael Diehl (ed.), *Hierarchies in action: Cui bono?*, 181–209. Carbondale: Center for Archaeological Investigations, Southern Illinois University.

Boriskovskii, P. 1969–70. Vietnam in primeval times. *Soviet Anthropology and Archaeology* 8, 214–57.

Bouchud, J. 1953. Les paléolithiques utilisaient-ils les plumes?' *Bulletin de la Société Préhistorique Française* 50, 556–60.

Byrd, B. and Monahan, C. 1995. Death, mortuary ritual, and Natufian social structure. *Journal of Anthropological Archaeology* 14, 251–87.

Chapman, R. 1981. Archaeological theory and communal burial in prehistoric Europe. In I. Hodder (ed.), *Patterns of the past*, 387–412. Cambridge: Cambridge University Press.

Childe, V. G. 1953. The constitution of archaeology as a science. In E. Underwood (ed.), *Science, medicine, and history*, 3–15. Oxford: Oxford University Press.

Colani, M. 1927. L'âge de la pierre dans la Province de Hoa-Binh (Tonkin). *Mémoires, Service Géologique de l'Indochine* 14, 1–93.

Colani, M. 1931. Recherches sur le préhistorique Indochinois. *Bulletin, École Française de l'Extrême Orient* 30, 299–422.

Costamagno, S. 2003. L'exploitation des ongulés au Magdalénien dans le sud de la France. In S. Costamagno and V. Laroulandie (eds), *Mode de vie au Magdalénien*, 73–88. Oxford: BAR International Series 1144.

Crawford, G. 2006. East Asian plant domestication. In M. Stark (ed.), *Archaeology of Asia*, 77–95. Oxford: Blackwell.

Deur, D. 2002. Rethinking precolonial plant cultivation on the Northwest Coast of North America. *The Professional Geographer* 54, 140–57.

Deur, D. (ed.) 2005. *Keeping it living*. Seattle: University of Washington Press.

Donald, L. and Mitchell, D. 1975. Some correlates of local group rank among the southern Kwakiutl. *Ethnology* 14, 325–46.

Fontana, L. 2000. La chasse au renne au Paléolithique Supérieur dans le Sud-Ouest de la France. *Paléo* 12, 141–64.

Freeman, L. and Echegaray, G. 1981. El Juyu: a 14,000-year-old sanctuary from northern Spain. *History of Religions* 21, 1–19.

Fuller, D., Harvey, E., and Qin, L. 2007. Presumed domestication? Evidence for wild rice cultivation and domestication in the fifth millennium BC of the lower Yangtze Region. *Antiquity* 81, 316–31.

Habu, J. 2004. *Ancient Jomon of Japan*. Cambridge: Cambridge University Press.

Hao, S.-G. 2001. The Donghulin woman from western Beijing. *Antiquity* 75, 517–22.

Hayden, B. 1989. From chopper to celt: the evolution of resharpening techniques. In R. Torrence (ed.), *Time, energy and stone tools*, 7–16. Cambridge: Cambridge University Press.

Hayden, B. 1990. The right rub: hide working in high ranking households. In G. Graslund (ed.), *The interpretive possibilities of microwear studies*, 89–102. Uppsala: Societas Archaeologica Upsaliensis.

Hayden, B. 1995. Pathways to power. In T. Price and G. Feinman (eds), *Foundations of social inequality*, 15–85. New York: Plenum Press.

Hayden, B. 2003. *Shamans, sorcerers, and saints: a prehistory of religion*. Washington, DC: Smithsonian Institution.

Hayden, B. 2004. Sociopolitical organization in the Natufian, In C. Delage (ed.), *The last hunter-gatherer societies in the Near East*, 263–308. Oxford: BAR International Series.

Hayden, B. 2009. Funerals as feasts. *Cambridge Archaeological Journal* 19, 29–52.

Hayden, B. 2009. Foreward. In P. Jordan and M. Zvelebil (eds), *Origins of ceramics and hunter gatherers of northern Eurasia*, 19–26. London: UCL Press.

Hayden, B., Chisholm, B., and Schwarcz, H. 1987. Fishing and foraging: marine resources in the Upper Paleolithic of France. In O. Soffer (ed.), *The Pleistocene Old World*, 279–91. New York: Plenum Press.

Hayden, B. and Schulting, R. 1997. The plateau interaction sphere. *American Antiquity* 62, 51–85.

Henry, D. 1989. *From foraging to agriculture*. Philadelphia: University of Pennsylvania Press.

Hillman, G. 2000. The plant food economy of Abu Hureyra 1 and 2. In A. Moore, G. Hillman, and A. Legge (eds), *Village on the Euphrates*, 327–98. Oxford: Oxford University Press.

Huang, W.-W. 1986. Bone artifacts and ornaments from Xiaogushan site of Haicheng. *Acta Anthropologica Sinica* 5, 259–66.

Jègues-Wolkiewiez, C. 2005. Aux racines de l'astronomie, ou l'ordre caché d'une oeuvre paléolithique. *Antiquités Nationales* 37, 43–62.

Jiang, L. and Liu, L. 2005. The discovery of an 8000-year-old dugout canoe at Kuahuqiao in the lower Yangzi River, China. *Antiquity* 79(305), http://antiquity.ac.uk/ProjGall/liu/ (accessed 19 March 2013).

Jordan, P. 2003. *Material culture and sacred landscape: the anthropology of the Siberian Khanty*. Walnut Creek, CA: AltaMira Press.

Kamminga, J. 1992. New interpretations of the Upper Cave, Zhoukoudian. In T. Akazawa (ed.), *The evolution and dispersal of modern humans in Asia*, 379–400. Tokyo: Hokusen-sha Publishing.

Kamminga, J. and Wright, R. 1988. The Upper Cave at Zhoukoudian and the origins of the Mongoloids. *Journal of Human Evolution* 17, 739–67.

Kennedy, D. and Bouchard, R. 1992. Stl'atl'imx (Fraser River Lillooet) fishing. In B. Hayden (ed.), *A complex culture of the British Columbia Plateau*, 266–354. Vancouver: University of British Columbia Press.

Klein, R. 1969. *Man and culture in the Late Pleistocene*. San Francisco: Chandler.

Klima, B. 1962. The first ground-plan of an Upper Paleolithic loess settlement in middle Europe and its meaning. In R. Braidwood and G. Willey (eds), *Courses toward urban life*, 193–210. Chicago: Aldine.

Kuijt, I. 1996. Negotiating equality through ritual: a consideration of Late Natufian and Prepottery Neolithic A period mortuary practices. *Journal of Anthropological Archaeology* 15, 313–36.

Laroulandie, V. 2003. Exploitation des oiseaux au Magdalénien en France. In S. Costamagno and V. Laroulandie (eds), *Mode de vie au Magdalénien*, 129–38. Oxford: BAR International Series 1144.

Lu, T. 2006. The occurrence of cereal cultivation in China. *Asian Perspectives* 45, 129–58.

Mansuy, M. 1925. Contribution à la préhistoire de l'Indochine. *Mémoires Service Géologique de l'Indochine* 11, 1–23.

Marshack, A. 1972. *The roots of civilization*. New York: McGraw-Hill.

Mellars, P. 1994. The Upper Paleolithic revolution. In B. Cunliffe (ed.), *The Oxford illustrated prehistory of Europe*, 42–78. Oxford: Oxford University Press.

Moore, A., Hillman, G., and Legge, A. 2000. *Village on the Euphrates*. Oxford: Oxford University Press.

Nguyen, L. C. 1986. Two early Hoabinhian crania from Thanh Hoa Province, Vietnam. *Zeitschrift für Morphologie und Anthropologie* 77, 11–17.

Nguyen, L. C. 1994a. On human remains from the Hoabinh culture in Vietnam. *Vietnam Social Sciences* 5, 64–69.

Nguyen, L. C. 1994b. Researching on human remains from Hoabinh culture in Vietnam. Paper presented at the conference on the Hoabinhian, Hanoi.

O'Shea, J. and Zvelebil, M. 1984. Oleneostrovski Mogilnik: reconstructing the social and economic organization of prehistoric foragers in northern Russia. *Journal of Anthropological Archaeology* 3, 1–40.

Ostapkowicz, J. 1992. The visible ghosts: the human figure in Salish mortuary art. BA Hons thesis. Burnaby, BC, Simon Fraser University Archaeology Department.

Peacock, S. 1998. Putting down roots: the emergence of wild plant food production on the Canadian Plateau. PhD thesis. Victoria, BC, University of Victoria.

Peacock, S. 2002. Perusing the pits: the evidence for prehistoric geophyte processing on the Canadian Plateau. In S. Mason and J. Hather (eds), *The hunter-gatherer archaeobotany*, 45–63. London: Institute of Archaeology.

Pearson, R. 2005. The social context of early pottery in the Lingnan region of south China. *Antiquity* 79, 819–28.

Perrot, J. 1961. Eynan ('Ein Mallaha). *Israel Exploration Journal* 11, 257–8.

Perrot, J. 1966. Le gisement Natoufien de Mallaha (Eynan), Israel. *L'Anthropologie (Paris)* 70, 437–83.

Pettit, P. 2005. The rise of modern humans. In C. Scarre (ed.), *The human past*, 124–73. London: Routledge.

Radovanovic, I. 1996. *The Iron Gates Mesolithic*. Ann Arbor: International Monographs in Prehistory.

Roach, J. 2005. 9,000-year-old beer re-created from Chinese recipe. *National Geographic News*, http://news.nationalgeographic.com/news/2005/07/0718_050718_ancientbeer.html (accessed 19 March 2013).

Romanoff, S. 1992. The cultural ecology of hunting and potlatches among the Lillooet Indians. In B. Hayden (ed.), *A complex culture of the British Columbia Plateau*, 470–505. Vancouver: University of British Columbia Press.

Rosenberg, M. and Redding, R. 2000. Hallan Çemi and early village organization in eastern Anatolia. In I. Kuijt (ed.), *Life in Neolithic farming communities*, 39–61. New York: Kluwer Academic/Plenum Press.

Saitta, D. 1999. Prestige, agency, and change in middle-range societies. In J. Robb (ed.), *Material symbols: culture and economy in prehistory*, 135–49. Carbondale: Southern Illinois University Press.

Saitta, D. and Keene, A. 1990. Politics and surplus flow in communal societies. In S. Upham (ed.), *The evolution of political systems: socio-politics in small-scale sedentary societies*, 203–24. Cambridge: Cambridge University Press.

Schulting, R. 1995. *Mortuary variability and status differentiation on the Columbia and Fraser Plateau*. Burnaby, BC: Archaeology Press, Simon Fraser University.

Soffer, O. 1985. *The Upper Paleolithic of the central Russian Plain*. Orlando: Academic Press.

Soffer, O. 1989. Storage, sedentism and the Eurasian Paleolithic record, *Antiquity* 63, 719–32.

Solecki, R., Solecki, R., and Agelarakis, A. 2004. *The Proto-Neolithic cemetery in Shanidar Cave*. College Station: Texas A & M University Press.

Taché, K., White, D., and Seelen, S. 2008. Potential functions of Vinette I pottery. *Archaeology of Eastern North America* 36, 63–90.

Teit, J. 1900. *The Thompson Indians of British Columbia*. New York: American Museum of Natural History Memoirs 2, 163–392.

Unger-Hamilton, R. 1989. The Epi-Paleolithic southern Levant and the origins of cultivation. *Current Anthropology* 30, 88–103.

Unger-Hamilton, R. 1991. Natufian plant husbandry in the southern Levant and comparison with that of the Neolithic periods. In O. Bar-Yosef and F. Valla (eds), *The Natufian culture in the Levant*, 483–520. Ann Arbor: International Monographs in Prehistory.

Vaughan, P. 1985. *Use-wear analysis of flaked stone tools*. Tucson: University of Arizona Press.

White, R. 1985. *Upper Paleolithic land use in the Perigord*. Oxford: BAR International Series 253.

Wiessner, P. 2002. The vines of complexity: egalitarian structures and the institutionalization of inequality. *Current Anthropology* 43, 233–70.

Willcox, G. 1998. Archeobotanical evidence for the beginnings of agriculture in southwest Asia. In A. Damania (ed.), *The origins of agriculture and crop domestication*, 25–38. Aleppo, Syria: ICARDA.

Williams, J. 2006. *Clam gardens: Aboriginal mariculture on Canada's West Coast*. Vancouver: New Star Books.

Woodburn, J. 1988. African hunter-gatherer social organization: is it best understood as a product of encapsulation? In T. Ingold, D. Riches, and J. Woodburn (eds), *Hunters and gatherers: history, evolution and social change*, 31–64. Oxford: Berg.

Yuan, J. 2002. Rice and pottery 10,000 yrs. BP at Yuchanyan, Dao County, Hunan Province. In, Y. Yasuda (ed.), *Origins of pottery and agriculture*, 157–66. New Dehli: Roli Books.

Yuan, J. and Flad, R. 2002. Pig domestication in ancient China. *Antiquity* 76, 724–32.

Zhang, F. 2000. The Mesolithic in south China. *Documenta Praehistorica* 27, 225–31.

CHAPTER 30

CERAMIC TECHNOLOGY

PETER HOMMEL

AT the outset, it is necessary to make the distinction between *clay* (a natural argillaceous material that, when suitably processed, becomes plastic and can be shaped into almost any form), *ceramic* (which in this context is used to refer generally to clay forms, fashioned, dried, and deliberately heated at high temperature with the intention of producing a durable product), and *pottery* (which refers specifically to portable *ceramic* vessels). Though apparently minor, these distinctions are important and not merely for reasons of greater clarity in the following discussion. Although it has long been accepted that hunter-gatherer communities found various uses for argillaceous materials during the last Ice Age, including the production of the first ceramic artefacts (e.g. Absolon 1949; Childe 1936; de Villeneuve 1906; Osborn 1916), until recently the idea that hunter-gatherers could have been responsible for the independent invention and dispersal of ceramic *vessels* was given little serious consideration (Jordan and Zvelebil 2009; Zvelebil and Dolukhanov 1991). In Europe at least, it was widely assumed that the 'squalid...huddle[s] of marsh-ridden...forest-scavengers' (Wheeler 1956, 231–4), the simple hunters and gatherers of the Palaeolithic and Mesolithic periods, would have 'had little use for cumbersome and fragile pots [in their nomadic lives]' (Anderson 1984, 81). The vision of 'agriculture and the art of pottery-making...[as] a pair' (Dixon 1928, 156), the principal elements in a wider 'package' of 'revolutionary' traits that together defined the Neolithic Age, was for many years almost universally accepted within the European archaeological community (Childe 1936; Hawkes and Woolley 1963).

Over the last 50 years, the incorporation of analytical techniques borrowed from the natural sciences and theoretical approaches developed in anthropology has fuelled this gradual re-evaluation of the origins of pottery technology and a renewed investigation of its social context (Jordan and Zvelebil 2009; Rice 1999). Of these developments, two are particularly significant: firstly, the introduction of absolute dating techniques, which has helped to establish the surprising antiquity of the relationship between hunter-gatherers and ceramic technology; and secondly, the application of alternative theoretical frameworks, developed in anthropology, within which it has been possible to reconsider the place of ceramic vessel technology in hunter-gatherer societies (cf. Bettinger 1991; Dolukhanov et al. 2005; Hoopes and Barnett 1995; Jordan and Zvelebil 2009; Kelly 1995; Kuzmin 2006; Rice 1999).

It is important to remember that in many hunter-gatherer societies, both before and after the emergence of pottery, clay and ceramics have been used for many other purposes (cf. Clark and Gosser 1995; Gurcke 1987; Hays and Wienstein 2004; Karkanas et al. 2004; Kashina 2009; Kobayashi 2004). It is these other uses that mark the beginning of the relationship between hunter-gatherers and ceramic technology and it seems appropriate to give them some consideration at the outset.

Clay Hunters and Ceramic Gatherers: The Earliest Ceramics of the Pleistocene

Clayey soils and sediments are a reality of everyday life in many environments, and their plasticity is a matter of general experience, especially among people whose livelihood depended on the skilful interpretation of animal tracks (cf. Mithen 1988). The fact that the properties of clay were well known to prehistoric hunter-gatherers is enigmatically illustrated wherever exceptional conditions of preservation have allowed. Bison, horses, lions, and bears rendered in clay as large, free-standing models and *bas-reliefs* have been found in several of the Magdalenian painted caves of southern France, most famously at the Le Tuc d'Audoubert and Montespan (Bahn and Vertut 1997; Hawkes and Woolley 1963).

Though often referred to as *art*, there is more to these representations of animal life than aesthetic concerns (Mithen 1988). At Montespan, for example, one such model of a crouching bear seems to have been given an even more lifelike aspect by draping it with the actual skin of the animal with its own head 'instead of one also modelled in clay' (Breuil and Berger-Kirchner 1961, 50). While the clay body itself may show signs of having been 'wounded' by spears 'hurled...as part of a magic rite' (Breuil and Berger-Kirchner 1961, 50; though see Bahn 1991 and references therein for a more sceptical viewpoint). Deep in these caves, with flickering light giving life to the shadows, it is easy imagine how dramatic this inspired manipulation of the plasticity of clay might have been. These rare examples hint at the use of wet clay in hunter-gatherer societies, which was undoubtedly more widespread and more varied than its limited representation in the archaeological record might suggest (Breuil and Berger-Kirchner 1961; Rice 1999).

The available archaeological evidence suggests that the properties of clay when dry and burnt were also put directly into use. Hard, earthen slabs set around a Middle Palaeolithic (Mousterian) hearth at the Grotte du Prince (Italy) have been interpreted as heat-storing 'grills', perhaps used for cooking meat. At Klisoura Cave I (Greece), specially constructed shallow clay-lined basins from the Aurignacian inhabitation of the site, dated to around 35,000 BC (34,700 ± 1600 BP—Gd-7892; 31,400 ± 1000 BP—Gd-7893) were also used to store heat for cooking and have been connected with the toasting of wild seeds (Hayden 1993; Karkanas et al. 2004). Such practical uses for clay as a means of storing heat are also likely to have been common in prehistory, but are usually not fired at a temperature sufficient to undergo the transformation to ceramic and therefore suffer from the same preservation bias as raw clay itself. Although such examples demonstrate that the earliest uses of clay were as likely to be practical as magical, it is interesting to note that the first truly ceramic artefacts again seem to be found in close association with dramatic, transformative rituals.

At the site of Dolní Věstonice, two raised hearth structures of fired clay have been identified in direct association with the earliest-known portable ceramic artefacts, dated to around

28,000 BC (25,600 ± 170 BP—GRO-1286) (Gamble 1999; Soffer et al. 1993). One of these early 'kilns' was found within the remains of a small structure, known colloquially as the 'magician's hut', about 80 m upslope from the main encampment (Gamble 1999; Vandiver et al. 1989). Thousands of fragments of small zoomorphic and anthropomorphic figurines and other objects, modelled from clay-like loess and fractured by the heat of the fire, were recovered from the floor of this hut (Soffer et al. 1993; Vandiver et al. 1989; see also Verpoorte 2000 for a discussion of other 'Pavlovian' sites with similar material). Although precise intentions can never be known, it would seem that deliberate action, not careless craftsmanship, led to the destruction of most of these artefacts. If exposed to high temperature, damp clay will hiss, crack, or explode as the pressure of expanding steam forces its way out from within (Arnold 1985; Rice 1987). The manipulation of such knowledge suggested by this assemblage and its spatial separation from other structures has implicated these early ceramics in potent mystical rites or divinatory rituals, acts of symbolic destruction and pyrotechnic display (Gamble 1999; Jordan and Zvelebil 2009; Soffer et al. 1993). Fragments of more carefully finished

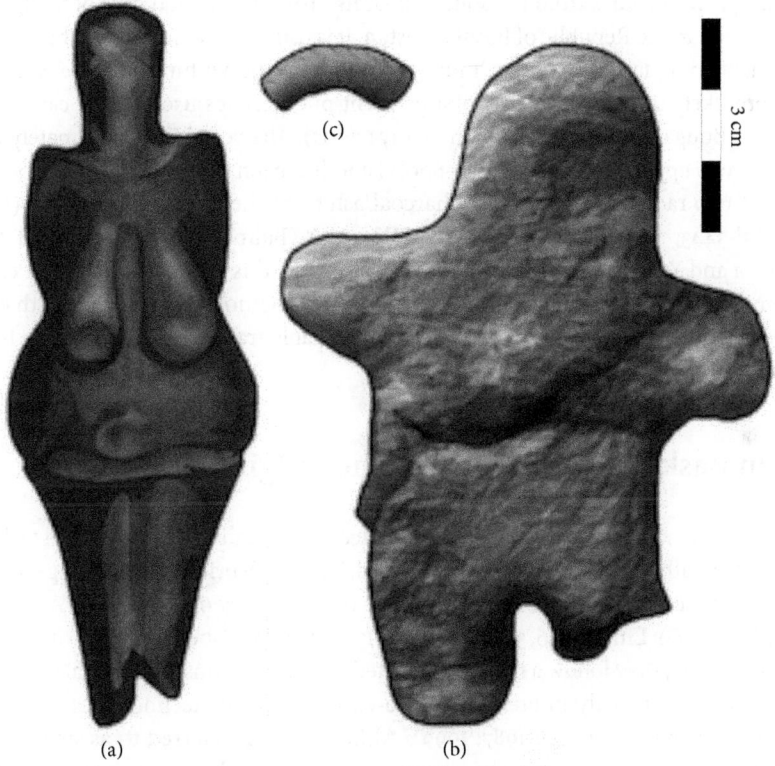

FIGURE 30.1 (a) The 'Black Venus' found at the site of Dolni Vestonice, in the Pavlov Hills of the Czech Republic; (b) Terracotta human figure found at the Maïninskaya site, near Maïna on the Yenisei River in Siberia (redrawn after Bougard 2003); and (c) Line drawing of ceramic fragment from Tamar Hat near the Mediterranean coast of Algeria, interpreted (by some) as a fragment of a zoomorphic figurine (redrawn from Saxon 1976).

figurines, including the famous Black Venus (Figure 30.1(a)) which have survived the millennia almost completely intact may imply that when objects were required to survive the firing process their creators were able to ensure that they did (Soffer et al. 1993; Vandiver et al. 1989; though see also Verpoorte 2000 for a different interpretation).

Similar ceramic objects and figurines, both zoomorphic and anthropomorphic, have been identified at several other sites in the Czech Republic, Austria, Slovakia, and further afield: the human-shaped 'gingerbread figure' found near Maïna, on the left bank of the Yenisei River (Western Siberia), dated around 18,000 BC (16,540 ± 170 BP—LE-2135; 16,176 ± 180 BP—nd) (Figure 30.1(b)); the so-called 'Barbary Sheep', a small, curved section of fired clay with incised decoration (Figure 30.1(c)), found at the cave of Tamar Hat (Algeria), associated with a single date of around 21,500 BC (19,800 ± 500 BP—nd) (Bougard 2003, 32; Budja 2006, 184–5; Saxon 1976; Vandiver and Vasil'ev 2002). Despite these early experiences with ceramic production, there are few indications to suggest that the figurine traditions of the Pleistocene ever led directly to the further development of pottery (Gamble 1999; Jordan and Zvelebil 2009; Soffer et al. 1993). Indeed, from across western Eurasia, only one single portable ceramic container has been confidently identified from Pleistocene deposits.

This unique find comes from the southern Urals, from the painted cave of Shulgan-Tash, or Kapova cave, in the Republic of Bashkortostan. It is usually described as the base of a small cup, or fat-burning lamp. However, mineral residues found within the vessel suggest that it was more likely to have been part of a pigment pot, perhaps used by the cave's painters (Bahn 1996; Bougard 2003; Zhushchikhovskaya 2005). The vessel is approximately 6 cm in diameter, it was apparently fired at 500–600°C and has been dated to around 16,000 BC on the basis of two radiocarbon dates on charcoal/ash from the same cultural layer (14,680 ± 150 BP—LE-3443; 13,930 ± 300/490 BP—GIN-4853) (Bahn 1996, 369; Bougard 2003, 7; Danukalova and Yakovlev 2006). If this dating is correct, this is one of the earliest examples of a ceramic vessel known in the world. It is, however, a technological ancestor with no identified descendants. The emergence of pottery as a durable tradition in society is to be found elsewhere.

Earthen Baskets and Clay Bags: The Origins of Pottery

Before we consider the evidence for the emergence and spread of ceramic vessel technology among hunter-gatherer societies across the world, it is worth briefly considering some of the theories that have been proposed to account for the discovery of pottery (cf. Amiran 1966, 242; Childe 1936, 89; Linné 1966, 36; Lubbock 1913, 492–3; McCabe 1912, 312). Although these theories are varied, they follow a theme supported by even the most superficial study of early pottery: that it was heavily influenced by pre-existing organic technologies (Brown 1989; Jordan and Zvelebil 2009; Rice 1987; 1999). Although often referred to as 'artificial stone' (Rice 1999, 3), pottery techniques share more in common with *additive* organic crafts than with *subtractive* lithic technologies (Kobayashi 2004). The cadenced movements of the potter's hands, turning the vessel slowly to guide a new coil into place, are very like the motions of the basketweaver's craft (Jordan and Zvelebil 2009). Even techniques like slab construction, which initially seem unique to the working of clay, share features with the production of vessels from rawhide or bark. Sometimes this connection was even more direct, when the impressions left by an organic mould on the surface of the clay in production gives the

FIGURE 30.2 Vessel from the site of Gasya in the Russian Far East (modified after Zhushchikhovskaya 2005 and Kuzmin 2002).

fired vessel a decidedly organic appearance. This kind of moulding technology, using baskets, sand-filled bags, and even sea-mammal bladders, has been found among many recent hunter-gatherer groups (cf. Glushkov 1996; Tsetlin 2006; Zhushchikhovskaya 2005) and appears to have been used for the production of the earliest pottery in the Russian Far East (Figure 30.2) (Zhushchikhovskaya 2005).

Although this kind of direct evidence for the relationship between ceramic vessels and other forms of container technology is interesting and may support the oft-cited use of clay to waterproof organic vessels as an origin for the craft (e.g. Childe 1936; Hoopes and Barnett 1995; Rice 1999), the stylized recreation of patterns, textures, or forms that are evocative of organic vessels are far more common (Childe 1936; Tsetlin 2006; Zhushchikhovskaya 2005; 2007). In different parts of the world potters drew inspiration from gourds, skin flasks, wickerwork, birch-bark containers, woven or netting bags and 'even [apparently] from human skulls [!]' (Childe 1936, 93; Rice 1999). This kind of skeuomorphism is common in human societies, creating continuity between old and new, helping to situate this unfamiliar material within an established technological syntax (Miller 1985; Miller 2007). It is not, however, restricted to the earliest phases of ceramic vessel use. In Japan, for example, more than nine thousand years after the first emergence of pottery, Middle Jomon vessels were not only being marked to give the impression of a woven or knotted product, but also ostentatiously decorated with applied and incised bands, often unmistakably representing a network of knotted ropes (Figure 30.3) (Aikens 1995; Tsutsumi 2002; Zhushchikhovskaya 2005, 2007). Nor does it constitute a

FIGURE 30.3 Middle Jomon pottery vessel from the site of Ookubu, Honshu (Japan) (redrawn after Zhushchikhovskaya 2007).

necessary phase in the evolution of ceramic technology. The pottery sequence at San Jacinto in northern Columbia, one of the very earliest pottery complexes in the New World, shows that potters exploited the plasticity of clay to its full effect from its first introduction to society (Figure 30.4), using relief modelling to produce dramatic, sculptural decoration that would be extremely difficult to achieve in any other medium (Oyuela-Caycedo 1995).

It is clear that in many cases the emergence of ceramics probably developed out of some earlier use of clay, such as the lining of organic baskets, as seems plausible in the Russian Far East, or the lining of cooking pits as has been suggested for San Jacinto (Oyuela-Caycedo 1995; Zhushchikhovskaya 2005). This does not explain why some of the earlier uses of clay in the European Palaeolithic and elsewhere did not lead to the same innovation. It is possible that cognitive evolution could explain why pottery did not emerge among earlier hominid species (Hayden 2009). However, to suggest that minds so obviously capable of subtle and dramatic manipulation of the physical, visual, and symbolic aspects of material did not possess the cognitive fluidity necessary to make a conceptual step, from experience of fired clay and the use of containers, to the specific idea of a usable *fired-clay container* seems rather implausible (Hayden 2009; Mithen 1996). Perhaps pottery vessels were intellectually conceivable, but remained ideologically, even morally, unthinkable in societies structured by the 'vigilant sharing' of food and power (Erdal et al. 1994; Vandiver et al. 1989). Perhaps

FIGURE 30.4 Fragment of decorated pottery from the site of San Jacinto I in northern Columbia (redrawn after Oyuela-Caycedo 1995).

the transubstantiation of earth into practical forms may have entailed an unacceptable shift in the perceived social relationship with the environment and its resources (cf. Childe 1936). Perhaps pottery was simply impractical in Upper Palaeolithic society. Ceramic vessels are certainly more fragile and less portable than their light and flexible organic counterparts, and their manufacture is subject to climatic constraints, which would not have affected the production of other kinds of container (Arnold 1985; Brown 1989; Rice 1999; Zhushchikhovskaya 2001). However, the barriers of high mobility and poor climate are not insurmountable and have probably been overstated (Reid 1989). Rather than focusing on the many reasons why pottery did not emerge until the end of the Pleistocene, it is perhaps more fruitful to consider contexts where it did.

The Emergence and Spread of Pottery in Hunter-Gatherer Society

What follows is a brief outline of the chronological distribution of hunter-gatherer pottery around the globe (summarized in Tables 30.1–30.6 and Figure 30.5). The drawback

Table 30.1 A selection of radiocarbon dates for Late Pleistocene sites with hunter-gatherer pottery in Japan, China, Korea, and eastern Russia. Maximum calibrated date range (2-σ) calculated using OxCal 4.1 with curve IntCal 09 (Bronk Ramsey 2009; Reimer et al. 2009).

	Site name	Region	Calibrated date range (BC) Published dates (BP) (Dating lab. code(s))	Source reference
China	Yuchanyan (Hamadong)	Yangtze Basin	16,546–14,834 14,795 ± 60–13,890 ± 50 (BA06867, BA05422)	Boaretto et al. 2009
	Xianrendong	Lower Yangtze Basin	19,309–11,787 17,420 ± 130–12,170 ± 140 (UCR-3561, BA95145)	Kuzmin 2006; Wu et al. 2012
	Hutouliang (Yujiagou)	Sanggan River Basin	14,719–13,149 13,080 ± 200* (GrA-10460)	Kuzmin 2006; Xia et al. 2001
	Nanzhuangtou	Baiyangdian Basin	10,729–8453 10,510 ± 140–9420 ± 95 (BK87088, BK86121)	Zhao and Wu 2000
Japan	Odai Yamamoto I	Northern Honshu	15,466–12,212 13,780 ± 170–12,680 ± 140 (NUTA-6510, NUTA-6506)	Habu 2004
	Kitahara	Eastern Honshu	14,505–13,201 13,060 ± 100–13,020 ± 80 (Beta-105401, Beta-105400)	Kudo 2004
	Fukui cave	Kyushu	14,833–11,630 12,700 ± 500–12,400 ± 350 (GaK-950, GaK-949)	Serizawa 1979
Korea	Kosanni (Gosanni)	Cheju Island	10,163–4453 10,180 ± 65–(6230 ± 320) (SNU02-096, AA-38105)	Kuzmin 2006
Russian Far East and Eastern Siberia	Khummi	Lower Amur Basin	14,828–9821 13,260 ± 100–10,345 ± 110 (AA-13391, AA-13392)	Kuzmin and Jull 1997
	Gasya	Lower Amur Basin	14,443–10,635 12,960 ± 120–10,875 ± 90 (LE-1781, AA-13393)	Derivianko et al. 2004
	Gromatukha	Middle Amur Basin	14,862–7583 13,310 ± 100–8660 ± 90 (AA-38102, AA-20940)	Derivianko et al. 2004; Kuzmin 2002
	Chernigovka	Maritime Region	10,610–6447 10,770 ± 75–7475 ± 65 (AA-20936, nd)	Kuzmin 2002; Zhushchikhovskaya 2005
	Ust' Karenga	Northern Transbaikal	12,288–10,197 12,180 ± 60–10,600 ± 100 (AA-60210, AA-21378)	Kuzmin and Vetrov 2007
	Ust' Kiakhta	Southern Transbaikal	11,660–11,208 11,505 ± 100 (SOAN-1552)	McKenzie 2009

* Though an associated thermoluminescense date on pottery returned a date c.9650 BC (Xia et al. 2001).

Table 30.2 A selection of radiocarbon dates from sites with early hunter-gatherer pottery across Siberia, European Russia, and Ukraine. Maximum calibrated date (2-σ) range calculated using OxCal 4.1 with curve IntCal 09 (Bronk Ramsey 2009; Reimer et al. 2009).

	Site name	Region	Calibrated date range (BC) Published dates (BP) (Dating lab. code(s))	Source reference
Eastern Siberia	Gorlei Les	Upper Angara Basin	7793–5305 8444 ± 144–6510 ± 100 (Ri-51, TO-4839)	McKenzie 2009
	Ust' Khaita	Upper Angara Basin	6426–5306 7245 ± 150–6625 ± 150 (SOAN 4431, SOAN 4647)	McKenzie 2009
	Ulan Khada	Ol'Khon Region	6588–4003 7560 ± 80–5495 ± 125 (LE-2277, SOAN 3336)	McKenzie 2009
Altai	Kornachak	Altai Mountains	6567–5881 7340 ± 175 (SOAN-2990)	Kuzmin and Orlova 2000
Western Siberia	Sumpanya	Upper Konda Basin	12,150–4842 11,970 ± 120–6100 ± 70 (LE-1812, LE-2540)	Kuzmin and Vetrov 2007
	Andreevskoe Ozero	Tyumen Oblast	8541–8256 9140 ± 60 (LE-2296)	Kuzmin and Vetrov 2007
	Sopka	Novosibirsk Oblast	7283–6641 8005 ± 100 (BGS-1805)	Kuzmin and Orlova 2000
	Tashkovo	Kurgan Oblast	6439–6213 7440 ± 60 (LE-1534)	Kuzmin and Orlova 2000
	Sartinya	Khantia-Mansia	5711–5227 6630 ± 80–6440 ± 80 (LE-1831, LE-4217)	Timofeev and Zaitseva 1996
European Russia	Chekalino	Sok River Basin	8204–6592 8680 ± 120–7940 ± 100 (GIN-7085, LE-4782)	Dolukhanov et al. 2005
	Ivanovskoe	Upper Volga Basin	6339–5344 7220 ± 90–6670 ± 140 (GIN-9359b, GIN-9630b)	Zaretskaya et al. 2005
	Pezmog	Komi Republic	5877–5558 6820 ± 70–6730 ± 50 (GIN-11915, GIN-12322)	Zaretskaya et al. 2005
	Chernaya Guba	Republic of Karelia	5623–3377 6530 ± 80–4840 ± 80 (TA-1315, TA-2023)	Dolukhanov et al. 2005
	Zales'ye	Tver Oblast	5613–5375 6530 ± 50 (LE-1144)	Dolukhanov et al. 2005
	Tsaga	Kola Peninsula	5018–3121 5760 ± 160–5020 ± 250 (LE-1087, LE-4292)	Dolukhanov et al. 2005, Timofeev and Zaitseva 1996

Table 30.3 A selection of radiocarbon dates from sites with early hunter-gatherer pottery across Fennoscandia and around the Baltic coast. Maximum calibrated date (2-σ) range calculated using OxCal 4.1 with curve IntCal 09 (Bronk Ramsey 2009; Reimer et al. 2009).

	Site name	Region/country	Calibrated date range (BC) Published dates (BP) (Dating lab. code(s))	Source reference
Northern Baltic and Barents Coast	Jokkavaara	Finland	5721–4463 6600 ± 110–5860 ± 110 (Hel-1580, Hel-1619)	Hallgren 2002
	Nordli	Northern Norway	5629–5215 6570 ± 60–6330 ± 50 (TUa-3028, TUa-3021)	Skandfer 2005
	Lossoas Hus	Northern Norway	5476–4491 6315 ± 90–5745 ± 45 (T-2468, TUa-3660)	Skandfer 2005
	Ylikiiminki	Finland	5320–4724 6170 ± 90–5995 ± 65 (Hel-4127, Hela-128)	Hallgren 2002
	Vargstensslätten	Åland Islands	5307–4688 6165 ±75–5990 ± 90 (Ua-17859, Ua-17857)	Hallgren 2002
Eastern Baltic	Katra	Lithuania	5623–4003 6550 ± 70–5360 ± 70 (Ki-7642, Ki-7646)	Hallgren 2002
	Zvisde	Latvia	5616–4947 6535 ± 60–6210 ± 80 (TA-862, TA-1593)	Derivianko et al. 2004; Kuzmin 2002
	Akali	Estonia	5470–4987 6255 ± 100 (TA-103)	Punning et al. 1968
	Riigiküla	Estonia	5209–3969 6023 ± 95–5268 ± 58 (Tln-1989, Tln-1992)	Kriiska 2001
South-Western Baltic	Schlamersdorf	Schleswig-Holstein	5478–4798 6385 ± 60–6105 ± 95 (OxA-4802, OxA-3326)	Hallgren 2002
	Salpetermosen	Denmark	5212–3975 6020 ± 100–5410 ± 120 (K-1233, K-1235)	Tauber 1968
	Lietzow-Buddelin	Isle of Rügen	4932–3714 5815 ± 100–5190 ± 120 (Bln-561, Bln-560)	Lübke and Terberger 2002
	Elinelund	Southern Sweden	4585–3665 5320 ± 210 (U-48)	Kohl and Quitta 1970

Table 30.4 A selection of radiocarbon dates from sites with early hunter-gatherer pottery across northern Africa. Maximum calibrated date (2-σ) range calculated using OxCal 4.1 with curve IntCal 09 (Bronk Ramsey 2009; Reimer et al. 2009).

	Site name	Region/ country	Calibrated date range (BC) Published dates (BP) (Dating lab. code(s))	Source reference
North-Eastern and Eastern Africa	Saggai	Sudan	10,258–9254 10,060 ±150 (Caneva 1983)	Close 1995
	Sarurab	Sudan	9121–8295 9370 ± 110–9340 ± 110 (HAR-3475, HAR-3476)	Close 1995
	Ti-n-Torha	Libya	8543–7572 9080 ± 70–8650 ± 70 (Ua-17859, Ua-17857)	Alessio et al. 1978
	Nabta	Egypt	8424–7741 8960 ± 110–8870 ± 80 (SMU-440, SMU-208)	Close 1995
	Amekni	Southern Algeria	8226–6690 8670 ± 150–8050 ± 80 (MC-212, UW-87)	Thommeret and Thommeret 1969
	Gabrong	Northern Chad	8165–7328 8560 ± 120 (Hv-3715)	Close 1995
	Lothagam Hill	Kenya	8330–6589 8420 ± 350 (N-1100)	Yamasaki et al. 1972
North-Western and West Africa	Tagalagal	Niger	9133–8286 9370 ± 130–9330 ± 130 (Roset 1987, Roset 1987)	Close 1995
	Adrara Bous	Niger	8542–7613 9130 ± 65–9030 ± 190 (Roset 1987, Roset 1987)	Close 1995
	Ravin de la Mouche	Mali	9441–8925 9785 ± 70–9510 ± 70 (ETH-28746, ETH-31279)	Huysecom et al. 2009
	Gobero	Mali	7585–6825 8470 ± 40–8060 ± 40 (P-584, P-535)	Sereno et al. 2008
	Aîn Naga	Northern Algeria	7025–5923 7500 ± 220 (U-48)	Delibrias et al. 1972
	Tintane Pécheur	Mauritania	5635–4561 6390 ±160–6020 ±150 (Ly-552, Lu-553)	Evin et al. 1975
	Khant de Saint-Louis	Senegal	4581–3948 5650 ± 40–5340 ± 120 (Ly-990, Ly-988)	Calvocoressi and David 1979
	Iwo Eleru	Nigeria	4651–4240 5570 ± 90 (Hv-1510)	Calvocoressi and David 1979
	Gao lagoon	Ghana	4258–2347 5219 ± 80–4180 ± 140 (N-2982, Gif-4241)	Calvocoressi and David 1979

Table 30.5 A selection of radiocarbon dates from sites with early hunter-gatherer pottery across South America and southern North America. Maximum calibrated date (2–σ) range calculated using OxCal 4.1 with curve IntCal 09 (Bronk Ramsey 2009; Reimer et al. 2009).

	Site name	Region/country	Calibrated date range (BC) Published dates (BP) (Dating lab. code(s))	Source reference
Eastern South America	Caverna da Pedra Pintada	Eastern Brazil	**7031–5479** 7580 ± 215–6625 ± 60 (GX17415, GX1742A-AMS)	Roosevelt 1995
	Tapeinha	Eastern Brazil	**6099–5365** 7090 ± 80–6590 ± 100 (OxA-1546, OxA-2431)	Roosevelt 1995
	Sambaqui de Urua	Eastern Brazil	**4714–4071** 5570 ± 125 (SI1034)	Roosevelt 1995
	Porta da Mina	Eastern Brazil	**4353–2886** 5115 ± 195–4380 ± 80 (GX2472, SI2544)	Roosevelt 1995
Northern South America	Barambina Mound	Guyana	**4981–2501** 5965 ± 50–4115 ± 50 (SI4333, SI4332)	Roosevelt 1995
	San Jacinto	Northern Columbia	**4983–3695** 5940 ± 60–5700 ± 430 (PITT-0155, Beta-20352)	Oyuela-Caycedo 1995
	Monsú	Northern Columbia	**4327–1311** 5300 ± 80–3230 ± 90 (UCLA-2149c, TK-625b)	Oyuela-Caycedo 1995
	Puerto Hormiga	Northern Columbia	**3971–2497** 5040 ± 70–4502 ± 250 (SI-153, I-1123)	Oyuela-Caycedo 1995
	Kakakaburi	Guyana	**3938–2578** 4890 ± 75–4215 ± 70 (SI7019, SI7020)	Roosevelt 1995
	La Gruta	Venezuela	**2905–1416** 4090 ± 105–3320 ± 100 (I-8970, I-10742)	Barse 2000

USA	Rabbit Mound	South Carolina	**3630–2904** 4570 ± 95–4525 ± 135 (GXO-345, GXO-343)	Hoopes 1994
	Grove's Orange Midden	Florida	**3497–2491** 4399 ± 123–4115 ± 75 (Beta-nd, Beta-nd)	Hoopes 1994
	Turner-Casey	Missouri	**3627–2923** 4550 ± 115	Hoopes 1994; Reid 1984
	Bilbo	Georgia	**3010–2347** 4125 ± 115 (O-1047)	Hoopes 1994
	Ford Shell Rings 1 & 2 (Skull Creek)	South Carolina	**2831–1635** 3890 ± 100–3585 ± 115 (I-3047, I-2850)	Buckley and Willis 1969; Hoopes 1994
	Stallings Island	Georgia	**2459–1667** 3780 ± 70–3510 ± 70 (Beta-138660, Beta-134458)	Sassaman et al. 2006
	Nebo Hill	Kansas	**2125–1696** 3555 ± 65 (UGA-1332)	Reid 1984
	Poverty Point	Louisiana	**1751–1056** 3160 ± 140–3040 ± 70 (Beta-122916, Beta-153804)	Kidder 2006; Hays and Weinstein 2004
	Tucker Site	North-west Florida	**1453–860** 2962 ± 120	Walthall 1990

Table 30.6 A selection of radiocarbon dates from sites with early hunter-gatherer pottery across the Arctic and subarctic of eastern Asia and western North America. Maximum calibrated date (2-σ) range calculated using OxCal 4.1 with curve IntCal 09 (Bronk Ramsey 2009; Reimer et al. 2009).

	Site name	Region	Calibrated date range (BC) Published dates (BP) (Dating lab. code(s))	Source reference
Yakutia	Bel'kachi	Aldan Basin	5042–3964 5970 ± 70–5270 ± 70 (LE-676, LE-656)	Dolukhanov et al. 1970; Kuzmin and Orlova 2000
	Sityakhi	Lower Lena Basin	4362–3661 5220 ± 170 (IM-530)	Kuzmin and Orlova 2000
North-Eastern Asia	Kukhtui	Sea of Okhotsk	3695–3110 4700 ± 100 (LE-995)	Kuzmin and Orlova 2000
	Terkuemkyun	Eastern Chukotka	3500–3104 4580 ± 40 (LE-2661)	Kuzmin and Orlova 2000
	Maltan	Upper Kolyma Basin	3497–2886 4450 ± 110 (KRIL-247)	Kuzmin and Orlova 2000
	Tyutyul	Western Chukotka	3329–2586 4290 ± 100 (MAG-1094)	Kuzmin and Orlova 2000
	Tokareva	Sea of Okhotsk	2032–1695 3540 ± 60 (MAG-554)	Kuzmin and Orlova 2000
	Opukha	NW Bering Sea Coast	969–411 2600 ± 100 (MAG-945)	Kuzmin and Orlova 2000; Orechov 1999
Alaska	Onion Portage	Northern Alaska	1741–366 3170 ± 120–2370 ± 50 (K-835, P-1066)	Lucier and VanStone 1992; Morlan and Betts 2005
	Cape Espenberg	West-Central Alaska	1288–379 2870 ± 75–2530 ± 130 (Beta-17972, Beta-33760)	Morlan and Betts 2005
	Choris	West-Central Alaska	1268–111 2646 ± 177–2190 ± 51 (P-203, P-611)	Morlan and Betts 2005

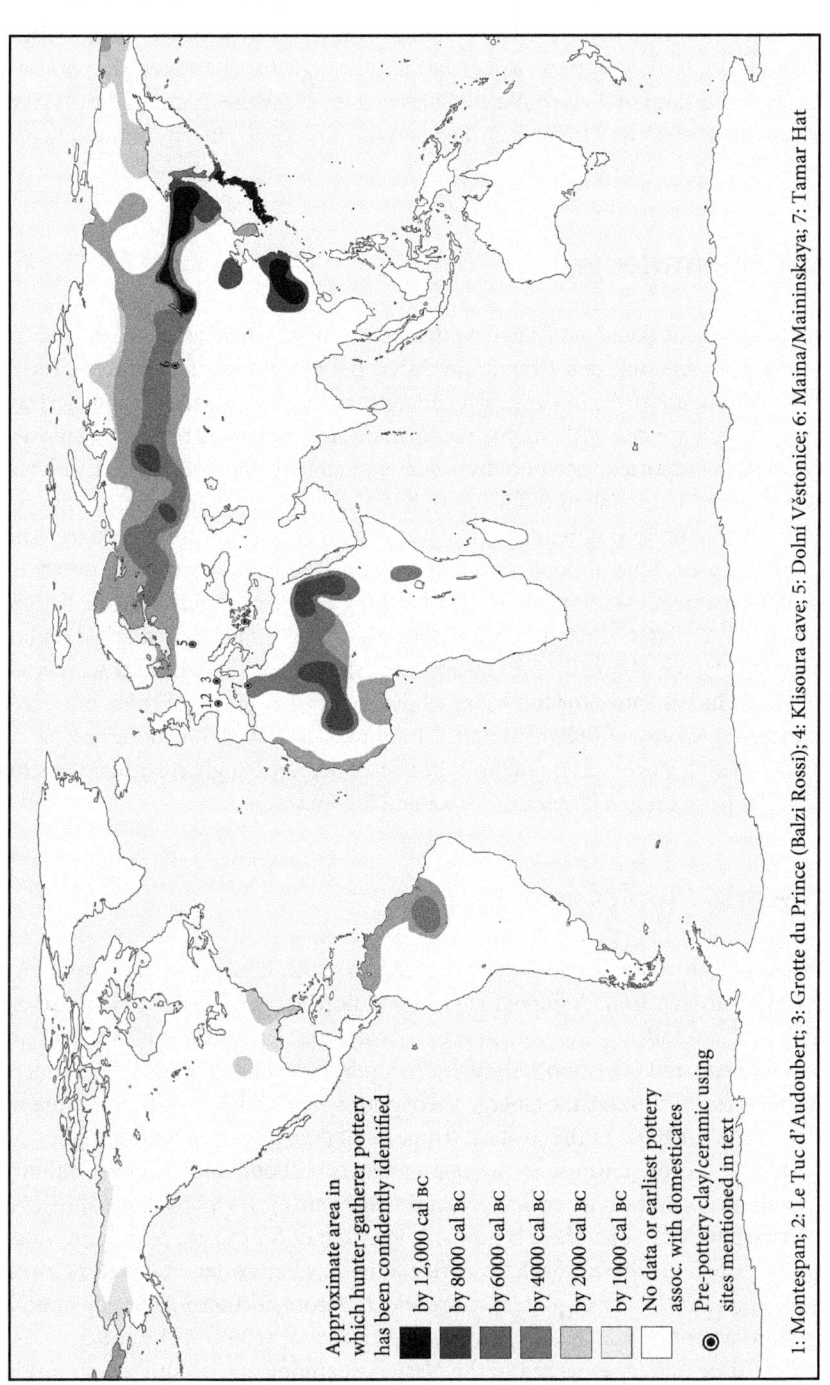

FIGURE 30.5 Sketch map showing the approximate distribution and chronology for the emergence of ceramics in hunter-gatherer societies across the world.

1: Montespan; 2: Le Tuc d'Audoubert; 3: Grotte du Prince (Balzi Rossi); 4: Klisoura cave; 5: Dolní Věstonice; 6: Maina/Maininskaya; 7: Tamar Hat to skimming the surface of the evidence in this way is to present an impression of continuous dispersal that cannot be realistically supported by the archaeological evidence. It should be remembered that the spread of ceramics is marked by a variety of non-linear, culturally relevant patterns that need to be clarified through further excavation and dating. Nevertheless, this kind of 'low-resolution' survey does allow the extent of the phenomenon of hunter-gatherer pottery to be identified and some general patterns in the data to be discussed.

Antiquity Acknowledged

Since the publication of dates associated with pottery sherds from the Fukui cave site (Japan) in 1965, East Asia has consistently produced the earliest reliable evidence for the use of ceramic vessels anywhere in the world (Boaretto et al. 2009; Kuzmin 2006; Serizawa 1979). Though initially treated with scepticism by many, these remarkably early dates were soon unequivocally supported, not only by a series of similar and even earlier radiocarbon results from sites across Japan (Table 30.1), but also by independent thermoluminescence dates on the ceramic fragments themselves (Flemming and Stoneham 1973; Kudo 2004, 257; Kuzmin 2006; Ono 2006; Serizawa 1979, 342). These first sherds and others like them mark the 'Incipient' phase of a remarkably long and varied relationship between hunters-gatherers and pottery, known more prosaically as the *Jomon* (cord-marked) culture (Aikens 1995; Aikens and Higuchi 1982; Yasuda 2002a). At first, this material was treated as exceptional and its relevance for the wider study of Eurasian prehistory remained 'very difficult to [assess]' (Aikens and Higuchi 1982; Chard 1974, 111). With the mounting pace of archaeological research since the late 1980s, it has become increasingly clear that the situation in Japan is far from unique (Tables 30.1–30.6 and Figure 30.5).

The Old World (Tables 30.1–30.4)

Late Pleistocene pottery assemblages dated between c.19,300 and 10,500 BC have been identified across eastern Asia: from *Xianrendong* in the Lower Yangtze Basin, to *Ust' Karenga* in the northern Transbaikal (An 1991; Boaretto et al. 2009; Kuzmin and Vetrov 2007; McKenzie 2009; Zhao and Wu 2000). Though often referred to as an 'East Asian model of Neolithisation' (Kuzmin 2002, 1), the emergence of pottery in the absence of agriculture was not restricted to the Far East. At the western fringe of Siberia, there are data to support the idea that pottery first came into use in the region between 12,000 and 8000 BC, although some of these dates are still under review (Kuzmin and Vetrov 2007; Usacheva 2001). Nor is it even restricted to Asia, since there is now strong evidence for the use of ceramic vessels in hunter-gatherer societies of sub-Saharan Africa sometime before 9400 BC, and a growing body of data to support the use of pottery more widely across northern Africa by 9000 BC (Close 1995; Garcea 2006; Haaland 1992; Huysecom et al. 2009; Sereno et al. 2008).

In fact, by the time pottery emerged in the Near East among agricultural communities, around 7500–6500 BC, pottery was already in use among communities of hunter-gatherers in many parts of the Old World.

Although the evidence of the earliest ceramic vessel use is still sparse, during the middle Holocene it seems to have become both far more common and more widespread. By 5500 BC ceramic vessels had been made and used in hunter-gatherer societies from Sakhalin to the coast of the Barents Sea and, in Africa, from Kenya to the Mediterranean. By 5000 BC, pottery had appeared along the Baltic coast, reaching the western edge of continental Eurasia and the Atlantic coast of Africa at around the same time that the first pottery-using agriculturalists appeared in north-western Europe (Calvocoressi and David 1979; Gebauer 1995; McKenzie 2009; McIntosh and McIntosh 1983; Timofeev 1998; Skandfer 2005).

It is important to realize that around the edges of this dispersal and in its wake, widespread changes in society and the environment seem to have increasingly favoured an economic shift towards the management of animal herds and the adoption of agriculture. This shift is often limited, with hunting, fishing, and gathering remaining the primary economic activities, but it is sufficient to blur the boundaries between hunter-gatherer and agro-pastoral communities. Since the focus of this chapter is partly to demonstrate that there is no necessary association between agriculture and pottery, areas in which economic demarcations are unclear, ill-defined, or disputed have not been discussed. These areas are geographically widespread and include large areas of Northern China and Mongolia, the Pontic-Caspian Steppe, north-western Europe, and northern Africa (Derevyanko and Dorj 1992; Gebauer 1995; Hassan 2002; Kotovo 2009; Telegin et al. 2003; Velichko et al. 2009). In most cases the temporal gap between the emergence of the ceramic vessels and the appearance of the first domesticated plants and animals has made it possible to chart, with reasonable clarity, the emergence and spread of pottery among the hunter-gatherer communities of the Old World. However, this gap is considerably narrower in the New World, and across much of the continent the emergence of pottery and horticultural products is essentially coeval (Damp and Vargas 1995).

The New World and the Far North (Tables 30.5 and 30.6)

As the first pottery began to be made and used along the western fringes of the Old World, groups of hunter-gatherers in the New World had already made the same discovery (Hoopes 1994). Across the Atlantic, the earliest evidence comes from the equatorial plains of the lower Amazon Basin in eastern Brazil and from a discrete cluster of sites in the Serranía de San Jacinto of northern coastal Columbia, dated to around 6000 BC and 5000 BC, respectively (Roosevelt 1995; Oyuela-Caycedo 1995). By 4000 BC pottery had become a common feature of hunter-gatherer communities along the north-eastern coast of South America (Barse 2000; Hoopes 1994; Roosevelt 1995). The earliest pottery in Central America, coastal Ecuador, Peru, and north-western Argentina, dating between 4000 and 1000 BC, seems to emerge and spread in the context of 'horticultural' societies, already involved in the active management of plant resources (Damp and Vargas 1995; Hoopes 1995; Rue 1989). It is not clear whether these two dispersals are related, and though hunting and gathering still played an important economic role (e.g. Smith 2001), these peoples and their pots are not considered further here.

In North America, the emergence and spread of pottery in and through communities of hunter-gatherers can only be clearly recognized in two discrete geographical areas at opposite ends of the continent: in the south-east and the far north-west. In other parts of the continent its precise distribution is difficult to trace, not only because it becomes blurred with the dispersal of 'pottery with agriculture' that followed it, but also because these porous and low-fired fibre-tempered ceramics are highly susceptible to the destructive action of frost and other erosive processes (Reid 1984). It is probable, therefore, that the currently identified distribution of pottery use in the North American archaeological record presents only a partial picture of its use in prehistoric society (Reid 1984; Sassaman 1995).

Pottery appeared in hunter-gatherer societies in the south-east around 3500 BC and was soon adopted at other sites along the Atlantic and Caribbean coastal lowlands to the east of the Mississippi and northwards to the Missouri. Whether this development of pottery here should be interpreted as technological diffusion from the south, or as another independent invention, is still unclear (Clark and Gosser 1995; Hoopes 1994; Sassaman 1995).

In the opposite corner of the continent, the picture is quite different. The emergence of pottery in Alaska and north-western Canada around 2500–1000 BC appears to be directly associated with a wider dispersal event among the hunter-gatherer communities of north-eastern Asia, occurring between 5000 and 2500 BC, which brought pottery to the northern and eastern extremes of the Old World and then across the Bering Strait into the New World (Hoffecker 2005; Kuzmin and Orlova 2000; McKenzie 2009; Stimmell and Stromberg 1986).

Discussion

Although the interpretation of the data is still a matter of contentious debate, it is evident that the idea of a single universal origin for pottery technology is implausible (Rice 1999; Jordan and Zvelebil 2009). It seems far more likely that communities of hunter-gatherers in the Asian Far East, North Africa, and South America were independently responsible for the invention of ceramic vessel technology. Some would take this further. For example, in East Asia it has been proposed that the emergence of pottery in China, Japan, the Russian Far East, and the Transbaikal could have occurred independently and almost simultaneously in each of these regions alongside climatic changes that followed Last Glacial Maximum (Khlobystin 1996; Kuzmin 2006). Similarly, eight 'plausible' centres of independent invention have been proposed for the emergence of pottery in the New World (Hoopes 1994, 42). The basic assumption that significant differences in the character of early pottery assemblages represent the operation of independent invention is logical, but it is not the only way to account for patterns in the data. Knowledge of pottery could have spread in many forms, whether through the physical exchange of pots, through encounters with potters, or even through myths or stories told around the fire. With the widespread experience of both plastic clay and fired earth, pottery as an idea or a finished product could be reinvented even in the absence of detailed technological information, permeating quickly across a wider range of social, political, economic, or ideological contexts than would be likely to result from direct cultural transmission. The resulting variation in the character of early pottery technology means that connections between communities 'cannot always be traced' in the archaeological record (Clark and Gosser 1995, 219). It may be more fruitful to consider the idea of repeated *dependent reinvention* (a conflation of the terms 'dependent invention' and 'rapid reinvention', found in Clark and Gosser 1995, 209–10) rather than isolated inspiration as a model for the early dispersal of pottery.

Whether transmitted as techniques or disseminated as ideas, pottery was not forced onto society (Clark and Gosser 1995). The different reasons for its adoption or rejection were woven into a web of human interactions within their natural, social, economic, and material environments (cf. Ingold 2000; Lemonnier 1993; Pfaffenberger 1992). The emergence and spread of ceramic technology was the result a series of active choices and judgements made on the basis of perceived economic, practical, ideological, and personal risk, benefit, and cost (Clark and Gosser 1995; Jordan and Zvelebil 2009). Such perceptions are, necessarily, socially constituted (see Pfaffenberger 1992) and should be expected to vary considerably both within and between different societies. Ultimately the best way to explore the reasons behind the adoption of pottery in prehistory is to explore its uses in society, both practical and symbolic.

From Household Crocks to Crocked Households: The Uses of Ceramic Vessels

Over the years many possible functions have been proposed for pottery vessels in hunter-gatherer society, from glue pots and oil lamps, to braziers and resonant drums. The majority of the attention has focused on their practical roles in the preparation, processing, and preservation of food and drink (Brown 1989; Hayden 1995; Jones 2007; Kobayashi 2004; Matson 1966; Reid 1989; Rice 1999; Sassaman 1995; Swanton 1979; Yasuda 2002b; Zhushchikhovskaya 2005).

Culinary Ceramics

As a waterproof and fireproof container, pottery is generally considered to have conferred the greatest practical advantage when used directly on the fire in the preparation of 'juicy foods' (Yasuda 2002b, 130). Although there are many ways of cooking food without portable containers, there are a number of significant advantages to cooking in liquids (Arnold 1985; Reid 1989). Perhaps most importantly, it is a comparatively thrifty technique, ensuring that juices otherwise lost to the fire are conserved, while enabling the use of 'leftovers, discards and scraps [from previous meals, allowing] many more people to be nourished from what might otherwise be insufficient food' (Crown and Wills 1995; Jordan and Zvelebil 2009; Rice 1999, 31–2). As a technique, it is also valuable in extracting the maximum nutrition from the foodstuffs at hand, facilitating the bulk processing of small and 'fiddly' food resources and expanding the range of both plant and animal resources that can be effectively exploited (Arnold 1985; Rice 1999). It would have provided a more hygienic method of cookery enabling the preparation of nutrient-rich broth that could have been used for weaning infants and sustaining the elderly or infirm (Hoopes and Barnett 1995; Jordan and Zvelebil 2009).

These benefits are often cited as reasons for the invention and adoption of ceramic vessel technologies. However, they are actually common to many 'moist' cookery techniques, which *rarely* require pottery to be used effectively (contra Garcea 2006, 214 and Yasuda 2002b, 129). There is a wealth of ethnographic evidence for the use of other containers for indirect (and even direct) moist cookery in the absence of pottery, though with the exception of clay-lined cooking pits, these would be rarely preserved in archaeological contexts (Reid 1989; Stahl and Oyuela-Caycedo 2007). Arguably, the most significant economic advantage of pottery was the saving in time (Brown 1989; Rice 1999); pottery could be left on the fire to bubble away, without the continuous, fuel-inefficient, and labour-intensive addition of hot stones needed to maintain the required temperature (Bettinger et al. 1994; Brown 1989; Hoopes and Barnett 1995). Where long-duration cooking was required, whether to denature toxic chemicals, gelatinize indigestible starches, or render fat, oil, and grease, the benefit in time would be magnified significantly (Arnold 1985; Brown 1989; Reid 1989; Rice 1999; Sassaman 1995). Even where pottery continued to be used for indirect heating with hot stones, as was the case for the early hunter-gatherer pottery of North America, it is argued that time and attention required during cookery would be still be reduced significantly (Rice 1999; Sassaman 1995; Schiffer and Skibo 1987). Cooking could be performed at the same time as other activities or delegated to less-active individuals, thereby further increasing the overall productivity of the group.

Compared with other vessel technologies, the production of pottery is generally thought to confer particularly significant advantages where vessels were needed for the processing of abundant, seasonal resources, which were only exploitable for a limited time and which required intensive processing to produce a storable resource (Brown 1989; Torrence 1983; 2001; Zvelebil 1986). Like all multi-stage crafts, pottery production could be fitted into 'spare' blocks of time between other activities, but when needed in quantity, ceramic vessels could also be made more 'cheaply' than other kinds of vessel, since communal bulk firings make possible an economy of scale in production that simply could not be achieved in other media (see Brown 1989, 217–19). In this context, the appearance of ceramics in hunter-gatherer societies across the world is frequently associated with other evidence for economic intensification, particularly the specialized exploitation of aquatic resources (Hayden 1990; 2009; Zvelebil 1986). The formation of shell mounds or middens (e.g. Brazil, the Western Baltic, the Atlantic coast of Africa and southern North America, and, to a lesser extent, southern China), the development of specialized fishing equipment, including nets, traps, or other mass-capture technologies for fish (e.g. Nile Valley, south-western Sahara, Baltic coast, and the Cisbaikal), or harpoons and floats for marine mammal hunting (e.g. Northern Baltic and the coastal low Arctic and subarctic), are all thought to be diagnostic of intensification and occur at around the same time as the emergence of pottery (Close 1995; German 2009; Haaland 1992; Hallgren 2009;McIntosh and McIntosh 1983; McKenzie 2009; Pearson 2005; Roosevelt 1995; Rowley-Conwy and Zvelebil 1989; Sassaman 1995; Sereno et al. 2008; Wu and Zhao 2000; Zhushchikhovskaya 2005).

Often paralleling such indications of the exploitation of animal resources is clear evidence for the intensive use of seasonally abundant plant foods: acorns, nuts, fruit, berries, seeds, and/or grains, whether in the form of actual bio-archaeological remains, or in the form of mortars, grinding slabs, and other more durable remains of prehistoric plant-processing (e.g. western Baltic, Japan, Nile Valley, southern China, northern Columbia, and the North American south-east) (Close 1995; Garcea 2006; Eerkens 2004; Eerkens et al. 2005; Jordan and Zvelebil 2009; Kobayashi 2004; Kubiak-Martens 1999; Sassaman 1995; Stahl and Oyuela-Caycedo 2007; Yasuda 2002b; Wu and Zhao 2000).

Even where faunal and other material indictors of specific types of resource exploitation are lacking, the earliest ceramic vessels are often associated with microlithic stone-tool assemblages that are considered to be an indicator of broad-based economic intensification (e.g.

Transbaikal, southern Japan, and northern China) (Elston and Kuhn 2002; Jeske 1989; Kuzmin and Vetrov 2007; McKenzie 2009; Serizawa 1979; Zvelebil 1986). Of particular relevance are the traditions of microblade production that form the basis of many late- and post-glacial 're-colonization' assemblages across large swathes of northern Eurasia (Goebel 2002). These kinds of adaptable and maintainable lithic technologies represent a response to relatively high residential mobility and resource stress, an interpretation that makes sense when set against the climatic fluctuations of the final Pleistocene (Bleed 2002; Elston and Brantingham 2002).

There is no single explanation for the emergence of pottery, and while ceramic containers could have helped to maximize the time available for foraging and improved the nutritional value of scant resources in times of hardship, in many cases it first makes an appearance against the backdrop of rich, stable 'aquatic' environments that would have provided an opportunity for the generation of significant seasonal surpluses (Brown 1989; Hayden 2009; Zvelebil 1986). It is therefore suggested by many researchers that pottery may have played a dual role, not only in the preparation and processing of seasonal bounty, but also in its safe, long-term storage for use in leaner times (Rice 1999; Testart 1982).

Storing Surplus

Despite its important role in storing agricultural surplus in later periods, the role of ceramic vessels in the long-term storage of food in early, pottery-using, hunter-gatherer societies is somewhat less clearly supported. Certainly, ceramic vessels offer a resistance to rodent and insect pests that organic vessels do not and, if sealed with beeswax, tar, or other compounds, they can provide excellent protection against the ingress of moisture (Crown and Wills 1995; Gosselain and Livingstone-Smith 1995; Rice 1999). However, unlike its projected use as a household stew pot, which poses few barriers to mobility (see Arnold 1985, 112; Reid 1989, 172), the use of ceramic vessels for the mass storage and transport of surplus seems less convincing.

Of course, ceramic vessels may have been made and cached for future recovery, either replete with stores or as part of on-site equipment used in resource processing (Beck 2009; Jordan and Zvelebil 2009). Either way, the 'front-loaded' nature (see Bettinger 2009) of the technology itself and many of the products it was used to process suggest that if it was stored, it was with the intention of subsequent recovery and use.

While this may be relevant in later phases of pottery use, it is important to remember that, so far, the number of vessels recovered from individual sites tends to be low, especially in the earliest phases of its use (Hayden 2009). Although this could potentially be explained in terms of off-site storage, site-function, mobility patterns, taphonomy, or excavation bias, it can be used to argue that ceramic technology produced at such an uneconomically small scale must have had some significance as a technology of prestige (Eerkens 2004; Gheorghiu 2009; Hayden 2009).

Presenting Prestige

The unique qualities of the material of early vessels, fashioned from earth and created through fire, may have given such items considerable value, extending beyond their functional performance. As objects of rare value, it is argued that the development of the potter's craft could have been bound together with the processes of social competition that drove the production, acquisition, and development of other desirable or exotic products, materials, and technologies (Hayden 1990; 1998; 2009). Interestingly, it is clear from the anthropological and archaeological literature that these processes also have strong links to indicators of economic intensification. In this context, economic surplus is not only stored against hardship but actively acquired and mobilized within the social sphere as part of networks of exchange, obligation, and competition, both within and between different social groups (Hayden 1998; 2009).

The idea that pottery might have been developed as a technology of prestige is currently rather popular, though it has been criticized for its 'methodological individualism' and inherent androcentrism (see Pearson 2005, 821). In this model, competitive individuals, seeking personal or familial aggrandizement, may have attempted to use the craft as a symbol of mastery and sought, through a variety of Machiavellian strategies, to accumulate and redistribute either the pots themselves or the valuable commodities they were used to produce (Hayden 1990).

One of the most frequently attested activities of 'aggrandizing' individuals or cliques is the organization and active exploitation of communal feasting events at which economic wealth could be displayed with social and political intent (cf. Boehm 1993; Gifford 2002; Hayden 1998; Helms 1993; Kelly 1995; Testart 1982). As a powerful symbol and a novel technology, pottery could have played a significant role at such occasions in the preparation of special or valuable foods or their presentation (see Hayden 2009); serving, perhaps literally, to draw distinctions between different communities, groups, or individuals.

Another plausible use for this initially rarefied technology could have been the production and distribution of intoxicants rather than foods (Hayden 2009). These substances may have been important for exclusive rites which were already common in many communities towards the end of the Palaeolithic, associated with periodic social aggregations of an otherwise disparate population (see Owens and Hayden 1997). The production of alcohol and many powerful hallucinogens alike would often require lengthy periods of controlled heating, for which pottery would have been well suited. The use of such fire-born 'baskets' might have added gravitas to these ecstatic rituals. Like the legendary asbestos tablecloth of Charlemagne, cast into the fire only to be removed unscathed, it is easy to imagine how impressive, even magical, this technology might have seemed, especially to the uninitiated (Leman 2006, 204).

Conclusion

Although the idea of pottery as a powerful symbol and prestigious technology is attractive, especially in the earliest phases of adoption, the available theories need to be used with care. Pottery was clearly important to the people who made it—socially, economically, ideologically, and even personally—but the level of significance it was given may have varied considerably through time. Ultimately, it is unlikely that any single model will ever suffice to cover the extraordinary variation in the ceramic material or the wide range of contexts in which pottery is first adopted into hunter-gatherer societies. While there seem to be recurrent relationships between ceramic technology and large-scale processes, such as economic intensification, social differentiation, decreasing residential mobility, demographic growth, and functional specialization in society, these relationships need to be explored rather than assumed a priori.

Though still in its nascent phase, the study of hunter-gatherer pottery is already challenging many long-held assumptions about the relationships between humans and the earth. We must continue to adapt our practical, analytical, and theoretical methodologies to address more relevant questions of these ceramics. It is likely that the models we use and our understanding of these materials *will* change dramatically in the future, but, however we understand the emergence of pottery among hunter-gatherer societies, their active role in the origin and spread of the first high-temperature technology can no longer be overlooked.

REFERENCES

Absolon, K. 1949. Moravia in prehistoric times. *American Journal of Archaeology* 53, 19–28.

Aikens, C. M. 1995. First in the world: the Jomon pottery of early Japan. In W. K. Barnett, and J. W. Hoopes (eds), *The emergence of pottery: technology and innovation in ancient societies*, 11–22. London: Smithsonian Institution.

Aikens, C. M. and Higuchi, T. 1982. *The prehistory of Japan*. London: Academic Press.

Alessio, M., Allegri, L., Bella, F., Improta, S., Belluomini, G., Calderone, G., Cortesi, C., Manfra, L., Petrone, V., and Fruscalzo, A. 1978. University of Rome Carbon-14 dates XV. *Radiocarbon* 20, 68–78.

Amiran, R. 1966. The beginnings of pottery making in the Near East. In F. R. Matson (ed.), *Ceramics and man*, 240–7. London: Methuen.

An, Z. 1991. Radiocarbon dating and the prehistoric archaeology of China. *World Archaeology* 23, 193–200.

Anderson, A. 1984. *Interpreting pottery*. London: Batsford.

Arnold, D. E. 1985. *Ceramic theory and cultural process*. Cambridge: Cambridge University Press.

Bahn, P. 1991. Where is the beef? The myth of hunting magic in Palaeolithic art. In P. Bahn and A. Rosenfeld (eds), *Rock art and prehistory*, 1–13. Oxford: Oxbow.

Bahn, P. 1996. Kapova. In B. M. Fagan (ed.), *The Oxford companion to archaeology* 368–9. Oxford: Oxford University Press.

Bahn, P. G. and Vertut, J. 1997. *Journey through the Ice Age*. London: Weidenfeld & Nicolson.

Barse, W. P. 2000. Ronquin, AMS dates, and the Middle Orinoco Sequence. *Interciencia* 25, 337–41.

Beck, M. E. 2009. Residential mobility and ceramic exchange: ethnography and archaeological implications. *Journal of Archaeological Method and Theory* 16, 320–56.

Bettinger, R. L. 1991. *Hunter-gatherers: archaeological and evolutionary theory*. New York: Plenum Press.

Bettinger, R. L. 2009. *Hunter-gatherer foraging: five simple models*. Clinton Corners, NY: Eliot Werner Publications.

Bettinger, R. L., Madsen, D. B., and Elston, R. G. 1994. Prehistoric settlement categories and settlement systems in the Alashan Desert of Inner Mongolia, PRC. *Journal of Anthropological Archaeology* 13, 74–101.

Bleed, P. 2002. Cheap, regular and reliable: implications of design variation in Late Pleistocene Japanese microblade technology. In R. G. Elston and S. L. Kuhn (eds), *Thinking small: global perspectives on microlithization*, 95–102. Arlington, VA: American Anthropological Association.

Boaretto, E., Wu, X., Yuan, J., Bar-Yosef, O., Chu, V., Pan, Y., Liu, K., Cohen, D., Jiao, T., Li, S., Gu, H., Goldberg, P., and Weiner, S. 2009. Radiocarbon dating of charcoal and bone collagen associated with early pottery at Yuchanyan cave, Hunan Province, China. www.pnas.org/content/early/2009/06/01/0900539106. Accessed 31 March 2013.

Boehm, C. 1993. Egalitarian society and reverse dominance hierarchy. *Current Anthropology* 34, 227–54.

Bougard, E. 2003. Ceramic in the Upper Palaeolithic. In A. Gibson (ed.), *Prehistoric pottery: people pattern and purpose*. Prehistoric ceramics research group: occasional publication, 29–34. Oxford: Archaeopress.

Breuil, H. and Berger-Kirchner, L. 1961. Franco-Cantabrian rock art. In H.-G. Bandi, H. Breuil, L. Berger-Kirchner, H. Lhote, E. Holm, and A. Lommel (eds), *The art of the stone age: forty thousand years of rock art*, 15–71. London: Methuen.

Bronk Ramsey, C. 2009. Bayesian analysis of radiocarbon dates. *Radiocarbon* 51, 337–60.

Brown, J. A. 1989. The beginnings of pottery as an economic process. In S. Van der Leeuw and R. Torrence (eds), *What's new? A closer look at the process of innovation*, 203–24. London: Unwin Hyman.

Buckley, J. D. and Willis, E. H. 1969. Isotopes' radiocarbon measurements VII. *Radiocarbon* 11, 53–105.

Budja, M. 2006. The transition to farming and the ceramic trajectories in Western Eurasia: from ceramic figurines to vessels. *Documenta Praehistorica* 33, 183–201.

Calvocoressi, D. and David, N. 1979. Survey of radiocarbon and thermoluminesence dates for West Africa. *Journal of African History* 20, 1–29.

Chard, C. 1974. *Northeast Asia in prehistory*. Madison, WI: University of Wisconsin Press.

Childe V. G. 1936. *Man makes himself*. London: Watts and Co.

Clark, J. E. and Gosser, D. 1995. Reinventing Mesoamerica's first pottery. In W. K. Barnett and J. W. Hoopes (eds), *The emergence of pottery: technology and innovation in ancient societies*, 209–219. London: Smithsonian Institution.

Close, A. E. 1995. Few and far between: early ceramics in North Africa. In W. K. Barnett and J. W. Hoopes (eds), *The emergence of pottery: technology and innovation in ancient societies*, 23–37. London: Smithsonian Institution.

Crown, P. L. and Wills, W. H. 1995. Economic intensification and the origins of ceramic containers in the American Southwest. In W. K. Barnett and J. W. Hoopes (eds), *The emergence of pottery: technology and innovation in ancient societies*, 241–54. Washington: Smithsonian Institution.

Damp, J. E. and Vargas S. L. P. 1995. The many contexts of Valdivia ceramics. In W. K. Barnett and J. W. Hoopes (eds), *The emergence of pottery: technology and innovation in ancient societies*, 157–68. London: Smithsonian Institution.

Danukalova, G. and Yakovlev, A. 2006. A review of biostratigraphical investigations of palaeolithic localities in the southern Urals region. *Quaternary International* 149, 37–43.

Delibrias, G., Guillier, M. T., and Labeyrie, J. 1972. Gif natural radiocarbon measurements VII. *Radiocarbon* 14, 280–320.

Derevyanko, A. P. and Dorj, D. 1992. Neolithic tribes in northern parts of Central Asia. In A. H. Dani and V. M. Masson (eds), *History of civilizations of central Asia*, vol. 1, 169–89. Paris: UNESCO.

Derivianko, A. P., Kuzmin, Y. V., Burr, G. S., Jull, A. J. T., and Kim, J. C. 2004. AMS 14C age of the earliest pottery from the Russian Far East: 1996–2002 results. *Nuclear Instruments and Methods in Physics Research B* 223–4, 735–9.

Dixon, R. B. 1928. *The building of cultures*. New York: Charles Scribner's Sons.

Dolukhanov, P., Shukurov, A., Gronenborn, D., Sokoloff, D., Timofeev, T., and Zaitseva, G. 2005. The chronology of Neolithic dispersal in Central and Eastern Europe. *Journal of Archaeological Science* 32, 1441–58.

Dolukhanov, P. M., Romanova, Ye. N., and Semyontsov, A. A. 1970. Radiocarbon dates of the Institute of Archaeology II: 1 January–31 July 1967. *Radiocarbon* 12, 130–55.

Eerkens, J. W. 2004. Privatization, small-seed intensification, and the origins of pottery in the western Great Basin. *American Antiquity* 69, 653–70.

Eerkens, J. W., Neff, H., and Glascock, M. D. 2005. Ceramic production among small-scale and mobile hunters and gatherers: a case study from the southwestern Great Basin. *Journal of Anthropological Archaeology* 21, 200–29.

Elston, R. G. and Brantingham, P. J. 2002. Microlithic technology in northern Asia: a risk minimizing strategy of the Late Palaeolithic and Early Holocene. In R. G. Elston and S. L. Kuhn (eds), *Thinking small: global perspectives on microlithization*, 103–16. Arlington, VA: American Anthropological Association.

Elston, R. G. and Kuhn, S. L. (eds) 2002. *Thinking small: global perspectives on microlithization*. Arlington, VA: American Anthropological Association.

Erdal, D., Whiten, A., Boehm, C., and Knauft, B. 1994. On human egalitarianism: an evolutionary product of Machiavellian status escalation? *Current Anthropology* 35, 175–83.

Evin, J., Marien, G., and Pachiaudi, C. 1975. Lyon natural radiocarbon measurements V. *Radiocarbon* 17, 4–34.

Fitzhugh, B. 2003. *The evolution of complex hunter-gatherers: archaeological evidence from the North Pacific*. New York: Kluwer Academic/Plenum Press.

Flemming, S. L. and Stoneham, D. 1973. The subtraction technique of thermoluminescent dating. *Archaeometry* 15, 229–38.

Gamble, C. 1999. *The Palaeolithic societies of Europe*. Cambridge: Cambridge University Press.

Garcea, E. A. A. 2006. Semi-permanent foragers in semi-arid environments of North Africa. *World Archaeology* 38, 197–219.

Gebauer, A. B. 1995. Pottery production and the introduction of agriculture in southern Scandinavia. In W. K. Barnett and J. W. Hoopes (eds), *The emergence of pottery: technology and innovation in ancient societies*, 99–112. London: Smithsonian Institution.

German, K. 2009. Early hunter gatherer ceramics in Karelia. In P. Jordan and M. Zvelebil (eds), *Ceramics before farming: the dispersal of pottery among prehistoric Eurasian hunter-gatherers*, 255–80. Walnut Creek, CA: Left Coast Press.

Gheorghiu, D. 2009. Early pottery: a concise overview. In D. Gheorghiu (ed.), *Early farmers, late foragers and ceramic traditions*, 1–21. Newcastle upon Tyne: Cambridge Scholars Publishing.

Gifford, A. Jr. 2002. The evolution of the social contract. *Constitutional Political Economy* 13, 361–79.

Glushkov, I. G. 1996. *Keramika kak arkheologichskii istochnik*. Novosibirsk: Nauka (in Russian).

Goebel, T. 2002. The 'microblade adaptation' and recolonization of Siberia during the Late Upper Palaeolithic. In R. G. Elston and S. L. Kuhn (eds), *Thinking small: global perspectives on microlithization*, 117–32. Arlington, VA: American Anthropological Association.

Gosselain, O. and Livingstone-Smith, A. 1995. The ceramics and society project: an ethnographic and experimental approach to technological choices. In A. Lindahl and O. Stilborg (eds), *The aim of laboratory analyses of ceramics in archaeology, April 7–9, 1995 in Lund, Sweden*, 147–60. Stockholm: Kungl. Vitterhets Historie och Antikvitets Akademien.

Gurcke, K. 1987. *Bricks and brickmaking: a handbook for historical archaeology*. Moscow, ID: University of Idaho Press.

Haaland, R. 1992. Fish, pots and grain: Early and Mid-Holocene adaptations in the Central Sudan. *African Archaeological Review* 10, 43–64.

Habu, J. 2004. *Ancient Jomon of Japan*. Cambridge: Cambridge University Press.

Hallgren, F. 2002. The introduction of ceramic technology around the Baltic Sea in the 6th millennium BC. In H. Knutsson (ed.), *Coast to coast–arrival; results and reflections, proceedings of the final coast to coast conference 1–5 October 2002 in Falköping, Sweden*, 123–42. Uppsala: Uppsala University.

Hallgren, F. 2009. 'Tiny islands in a far sea': on the seal hunters of Åland, and the north-western limit in the spread of early pottery. In P. Jordan and M. Zvelebil (eds), *Ceramics before farming: the dispersal of pottery among prehistoric Eurasian hunter-gatherers*, 375–94. Walnut Creek, CA: Left Coast Press.

Hassan, F. A. 2002. Holocene environmental change and the transition to agriculture in South-West Asia and North Africa. In Y. Yasuda (ed.), *The origins of pottery and agriculture*, 55–68. New Dehli: Lustre Press/Roli Books.

Hawkes, J. and Woolley, L. 1963. *Prehistory and the beginnings of civilization*. Vol. 1. New York: Harper & Row.

Hayden, B. 1990. Nimrods, piscators, pluckers and planters: the emergence of food production. *Journal of Anthropological Archaeology* 9, 31–69.

Hayden B. 1993. The cultural capacities of Neanderthals: a review and re- evaluation. *Journal of Human Evolution* 24, 113–46.

Hayden, B. 1995. The emergence of prestige technologies and pottery. In W. K. Barnett and J. W. Hoopes (eds), *The emergence of pottery: technology and innovation in ancient societies*, 257–66. London: Smithsonian Institution.

Hayden, B. 1998. Practical and prestige technologies: the evolution of material systems. *Journal of Archaeological Method and Theory* 5, 1–55.

Hayden, B. 2009. Foreword. In P. Jordan and M. Zvelebil (eds), *Ceramics before farming: the dispersal of pottery among prehistoric Eurasian hunter-gatherers*, 19–26. Walnut Creek, CA: Left Coast Press.

Hays, C. T. and Weinstein, R. A. 2004. Early pottery at poverty point: origins and functions. In R. Saunders and C. T. Hays (eds), *Early pottery: technology, function, style, and interaction in the lower Southeast*, 150–68. Tuscaloosa, AL: University of Alabama Press.

Helms, M. 1993. *Craft and the kingly ideal: art, trade, and power*. Austin, TX: University of Texas Press.

Hoffecker, J. F. 2005. *A prehistory of the north: human settlement of the higher latitudes*. London: Rutgers University Press.

Hoopes, J. W. 1994. Ford revisited: a critical review of the chronology and relationships of the earliest ceramic complexes in the new world, 6000–1500 BC. *Journal of World Prehistory* 8, 1–49.

Hoopes, J. W. 1995. Interaction in hunting and gathering societies as a context for the emergence of pottery in the Central American isthmus. In W. K. Barnett and J. W. Hoopes (eds), *The emergence of pottery: technology and innovation in ancient societies*, 185–98. London: Smithsonian Institution.

Hoopes, J. W. and Barnett, W. K. 1995. The shape of early pottery studies. In W. K. Barnett and J. W. Hoopes (eds), *The emergence of pottery: technology and innovation in ancient societies*, 1–7. Washington: Smithsonian Institution.

Huysecom, E., Rasse, M., Lespez, L., Neumann, K., Fahmy, A., Ballouche, A., Ozainne, S., Maggetti, M., Tribolo, Ch., and Soriano, S. 2009. The emergence of pottery in Africa during the tenth millennium cal BC: new evidence from Ounjougou (Mali). *Antiquity* 83, 905–17.

Ingold, T. 2000. *The perception of the environment: essays on livelihood, dwelling and skill.* London: Routledge.

Jeske, R. 1989. Economies in raw material use by prehistoric hunter-gatherers. In R. Torrence (ed.), *Time, energy and stone tools*, 34–45. Cambridge: Cambridge University Press.

Jones, S. 2007. Points, pottery, and hafting. *The Society for Georgia Archaeology* 134, 12–14.

Jordan, P. and Zvelebil, M. 2009. *Ex oriente lux*: the prehistory of hunter gatherer ceramic dispersals. In P. Jordan and M. Zvelebil (eds), *Ceramics before farming; the dispersal of pottery among prehistoric Eurasian hunter-gatherers*, 33–90. Walnut Creek, CA: Left Coast Press.

Karkanas, P., Koumouzelis, M., Kozlowski, J. K., Sitlivy, V., Sobczyk, K., Berna, F., and Weiner, S. 2004. The earliest evidence for clay hearths: Aurignacian features in Klisoura cave 1, Southern Greece. *Antiquity* 78, 513–25.

Kashina, E. 2009. Ceramic anthropomorphic sculptures of the east European forest zone. In P. Jordan and M. Zvelebil (eds), *Ceramics before farming; the dispersal of pottery among prehistoric Eurasian hunter-gatherers*, 281–98. Walnut Creek, CA: Left Coast Press.

Kelly, R. L. 1995. *The foraging spectrum: diversity in hunter gatherer lifeways.* London: Smithsonian Institution.

Khlobystin, L. P. 1996. Vostochnaya Sibir' I Dalnii Vostok. In S. V. Oshibinka (ed.), *Neolit Severnoi Evrazii*, 166–72. Moscow: Nauka.

Kidder, T. R. 2006. Climate change and the archaic to woodland transition (3000–2500 cal BP) in the Mississippi river basin. *American Antiquity* 71, 195–231.

Kipnis, R. 2002. Long-term land tenure systems in central Brazil: evolutionary ecology, risk management and, social geography. In B. Fitzhugh and J. Habu (eds), *Beyond foraging and collecting: evolutionary change in hunter-gatherer settlement systems*, 181–231. New York: Kluwer Academic/Plenum Press.

Kobayashi, T. 2004. *Jomon reflections: forager life and culture in the prehistoric Japanese Archipelago.* Oxford: Oxbow.

Kohl, G. and Quitta, H. 1970. Berlin radiocarbon measurements IV. *Radiocarbon* 12, 400–20.

Kotovo, N. 2009. The neolithization of northern Black Sea area in the context of climate changes. *Documenta Praehistorica* 34, 159–74.

Kriiska, A. 2001. Stone age settlement and economic processes in the Estonian coastal area and islands. Academic dissertation. Helsinki: University of Helsinki.

Kubiak-Martens L. 1999. The plant food component of the diet at the Late Mesolithic (Ertebølle) settlement at Tybrind Vig, Denmark. *Vegetation History and Archaeobotany* 8, 117–27.

Kudo, Y. 2004. Reconsidering the geochronological and archaeological framework on the Late Pleistocene–Early Holocene transition of the Japanese islands. In T. Terberger, and B. V. Eriksen (eds), *Hunters in a changing world: environment and archaeology of the Pleistocene-Holocene transition [ca. 11000–9000 BC] in northern Central Europe*, 253–68. Rahden/Westfalen: Verlag Marie Leidorf.

Kuzmin, Y. V. 2002. The earliest centres of pottery origin in the Russian Far East and Siberia: review of chronology for the oldest Neolithic cultures. *Documenta Praehistorica* 29, 37–46.

Kuzmin, Y. V. 2006. Chronology of the earliest pottery in the Far East: progress and pitfalls. *Antiquity* 80, 362–71.

Kuzmin, Y. V. and Jull, A. J. T. 1997. AMS radiocarbon dating of the Paleolithic–Neolithic transition in the Russian Far East. *Current Research in the Pleistocene* 14, 46–8.

Kuzmin, Y. V. and Orlova, L. A. 2000. The neolithisation of Siberia and the Russian Far East. *Antiquity* 74, 356–64.

Kuzmin, Y. V. and Vetrov, V. M. 2007. The earliest Neolithic complex in Siberia: the Ust-Karenga 12 site and its significance for the neolithisation process in Eurasia. *Documenta Praehistorica* 34, 9–20.

Leman, R. A. 2006. Epidemiology of asbestos-related diseases and the knowledge that lead to what is known today. In R. F. Dodson and S. P. Hammar (eds), *Asbestos: risk assessment, epidemiology and health effects*, 201–308. Boca Raton: CRC Press.

Lemonnier, P. 1993. Introduction. In P. Lemmonier (ed.), *Technological choices: transformation in material cultures since the Neolithic*, 126–56. London: Routledge.

Linné, S. 1966. The ethnologist and the American Indian potter. In F. R. Matson (ed.), *Ceramics and man*, 20–42. London: Methuen.

Lübke, H. and Terberger, T. 2002. New evidence on the Ertebølle culture on Rügen and neighbouring areas. *Greifswalder Geographische Arbeiten* 27, 47–53.

Lubbock, Sir J. 1913. *Prehistoric times as illustrated by ancient remains and the manners and customs of modern savages* (7th edition). London: Williams and Norgate.

Lucier, C. V. and VanStone, J. W. 1992. *Historic pottery of the Kotzebue Sound Iñupiat*. Fieldiana. Chicago: Field Museum of National History.

McCabe, J. 1912. *The story of evolution* (2nd edition). London: Hutchinson.

McIntosh, S. K. and McIntosh, R. J. 1983. Current directions in west African prehistory. *Annual Review of Anthropology* 12, 215–58.

McKenzie, H. 2009. Review of early hunter-gatherer pottery in Eastern Siberia. In P. Jordan and M. Zvelebil (eds), *Ceramics before farming: the dispersal of pottery among prehistoric Eurasian hunter-gatherers*, 167–208. Walnut Creek, CA: Left Coast Press.

Matson, F. (ed.) 1966. *Ceramics and man*. London: Methuen.

Miller, D. 1985. *Artefacts as categories: a study of ceramic variability in central India*. Cambridge: Cambridge University Press.

Miller, H. M.-L. 2007. *Archaeological approaches to technology*. Amsterdam: Elsevier/Academic Press.

Mithen, S. J. 1996. *The prehistory of the mind: a search for the origins of art, religion and science*. London: Thames and Hudson.

Mithen, S. J. 1988. Looking and learning: Upper Palaeolithic art and information gathering. *World Archaeology* 19, 297–327.

Morgan, L. H. 1877. *Ancient society: in the lines of human progress from savagery through barbarism to civilization*. Chicago: C. H. Kerr.

Morlan, R. E. and Betts, M. 2005. *Canadian archaeological radiocarbon database*. Gatineau: Canadian Museum of Civilization. Published online at http://www.canadianarchaeology.ca/. Accessed 26 March 2013.

Ono, A., Sato, H., Tsutsumi, T., and Kudo, Y. 2006. Radiocarbon dates and archaeology of the Late Pleistocene in the Japanese islands. *Radiocarbon* 44, 477–94.

Orechov, A. A. 1999. *An early culture of the northwest Bering Sea*, trans. R. L. Bland. Anchorage, AL: US Department of the Interior, National Park Service, Shared Beringian Heritage Programme.

Osborn, H. F. 1916. *Men of the old stone age: their environment, life, and art*. London: G. Bell and Sons.

Owens, D. and Hayden, B. 1997. Prehistoric rites of passage: a comparative study of transegalitarian hunter-gatherers. *Journal of Anthropological Archaeology* 16, 121–61.

Oyuela-Caycedo, A. 1995. Rocks versus clay: the evolution of pottery technology in the case of San Jacinto 1, Columbia. In W. K. Barnett and J. W. Hoopes (eds), *The emergence of pottery: technology and innovation in ancient societies*, 133–44. London: Smithsonian Institution.

Pearson, R. 2005. The social context of early pottery in the Lingnan region of south China. *Antiquity* 79, 819–28.
Pfaffenberger, B. 1992 Social anthropology of technology, *Annual Review of Anthropology* 21, 491–516.
Pluciennik, M. 2005. *Social evolution*. London: Duckworth.
Punning, J. M., Liiva, A., and Ilves, E. 1968. Tartu radiocarbon dates III. *Radiocarbon* 10, 379–83.
Reid, K. C. 1984. Fire and ice: new evidence for the production and preservation of Late Archaic fibre-tempered pottery in the middle-latitude lowlands. *American Antiquity* 49, 55–76.
Reid, K. C. 1989. A materials science perspective on hunter-gatherer pottery. In G. Bronitsky (ed.), *Pottery technology: ideas and approaches*, 167–82. London: Westview.
Reimer, P. J., Baillie, M. G. L., Bard, E., Bayliss, A., Beck, J. W., Blackwell, P. G., Bronk Ramsey, C., Buck, C. E., Burr, G. S., Edwards, R. L., Friedrich, M., Grootes, P. M., Guilderson, T. P., Hajdas, I., Heaton, T. J., Hogg, A. G., Hughen, K. A., Kaiser, K. F., Kromer, B., McCormac, F. G., Manning, S. W., Reimer, R. W., Richards, D. A., Southon, J. R., Talamo, S., Turney, C. S. M., van der Plicht, J., and Weyhenmeyer, C. E. 2009. IntCal09 and Marine09 radiocarbon age calibration curves, 0–50,000 years cal BP. *Radiocarbon* 51, 1111–50.
Rice, P. 1987. *Pottery analysis: a sourcebook*. London: University of Chicago Press.
Rice, P. 1999. On the origins of pottery. *Journal of Archaeological Method and Theory* 6, 1–54.
Roosevelt, A. C. 1995. Early pottery in the Amazon: twenty years of scholarly obscurity. In W. K. Barnett and J. W. Hoopes (eds), *The emergence of pottery: technology and innovation in ancient societies*, 115–32. London: Smithsonian Institution.
Rowley-Conwy, P. and Zvelebil, M. 1989. Saving it for later: storage by prehistoric hunter-gatherers in Europe. In P. Halstead and J. O'Shea (eds), *Bad year economics: cultural responses to risk and uncertainty*, 40–56. Cambridge: Cambridge University Press.
Rue, D. J. 1989. Archaic middle American agriculture and settlement: recent pollen data from Honduras. *Journal of Field Archaeology* 16, 177–84.
Sassaman, K. E. 1995. The social contradictions of traditional and innovative cooking technologies in the prehistoric American Southeast. In W. K. Barnett and J. W. Hoopes (eds), *The emergence of pottery: technology and innovation in ancient societies*, 223–40. London: Smithsonian Institution.
Sassaman, K. E., Blessing, M. E., and Randall, A. R. 2006. Stallings Island revisited: new evidence for occupational history, community pattern, and subsistence technology. *American Antiquity* 71, 539–66.
Saxon, E. C. 1976. Pre-Neolithic pottery: new evidence from North Africa. *Proceedings of the Prehistoric Society* 42, 327–9.
Schiffer, M. B. and Skibo, J. M. 1987. Theory and experiment in the study of technological change. *Current Anthropology* 28, 595–622.
Sereno, P. C., Garcea, E. A., Jousse, H., Stojanowski, C. M., Saliège, J. F., Maga, A., Ide, O. A., Knudson, K. J., Mercuri, A. M., Stafford, T. W. Jr., Kaye, T. G., Giraudi, C., N'siala, I. M., Cocca, E., Moots, H. M., Dutheil, D. B., and Stivers, J. P. 2008. Lakeside cemeteries in the Sahara: 5000 years of Holocene population and environmental change. *PLoS ONE* 3, e2995.
Serizawa, C. 1979. Cave sites in Japan. *World Archaeology* 10, 340–9.
Skandfer, M. 2005. Early northern comb ware in Finnmark: the concept of Säräisnieni 1 reconsidered. *Fennoscandia archaeologica* 23, 3–27.
Smith, B. D. 2001. Low-level food prduction. *Journal of Archaeological Research* 9, 1–43.
Soffer, O. 1985. Patterns of intensification as seen from the Upper Palaeolithic of the Central Russian Plain. In T. D. Price, and J. A. Brown (eds), *Prehistoric hunter-gatherers: the emergence of social complexity*, 235–70. London: Academic Press.

Soffer, O., Adovasio, J. M., and Hyland, D. C. 2000. The well-dressed 'venus': women's wear ca. 27,000 BP. *Archaeology, Ethnology, and Anthropology of Eurasia* 1, 37–47.

Soffer, O., Vandiver, P. B., Oliva, M., and Seitl, L. 1993. Case of the exploding figurines. *Archaeology* 46, 36–39.

Stahl, P. W. and Oyuela-Caycedo, A. 2007. Early prehistoric sedentism and seasonal animal exploitation in the Caribbean lowlands of Colombia. *Journal of Anthropological Archaeology* 26, 329–49.

Stimmell, C. and Stromberg, R. 1986. A reassessment of Thule Eskimo cooking technology. In W. D. Kingery (ed.), *Ceramics and civilization: technology and style*, vol. 2, 237–50. Columbus, OH: The American Ceramic Society.

Swanton, J. 1979. *The Indians of the southeastern United States*. Washington: Smithsonian Institution.

Tauber, H. 1968. Copenhagen radiocarbon dates IX. *Radiocarbon* 10, 295–327.

Telegin, D. Ya., Lillie, M., Potekhina, I. D., and Kovaliukh, M. M. 2003. Settlement and economy in Neolithic Ukraine: a new chronology. *Antiquity* 77, 456–70.

Testart, A. 1982. The significance of good storage among hunter-gatherers: residence patterns, population densities, and social inequalities. *Current Anthropology* 23, 523–37.

Thommeret, J. and Thommeret, Y. 1969. Monaco radiocarbon measurements III. *Radiocarbon* 11, 118–29.

Timofeev, V. I. 1998. The beginning of the Neolithic in the Eastern Baltic. In M. Zvelebil, R. Dennell, and L. Domanska (eds), *Harvesting the sea, farming the forest: the emergence of Neolithic in the Baltic*, 225–36. Sheffield: J. R. Collis Publications.

Timofeev, V. I. and Zaitseva, G. I. 1996. Problemi absolutnoi khronologii. In S. V. Oshibkina (ed.), *Neolit Severnoi Evrazii, Chast II: Neolit lesnoi zoni*, 330–48. Moscow: Nauka (in Russian).

Torrence, R. 1983. Time budgeting and hunter-gatherer technology. In G. N. Bailey (ed.), *Hunter-gatherer economy in prehistory*, 11–22. Cambridge: Cambridge University Press.

Torrence, R. 2001. Hunter-gatherer technology: macro- and microscale approaches. In C. Panter-Brick, R. H. Layton, and P. Rowley-Conwy (eds), *Hunter-gatherers: an interdisciplinary perspective*, 73–98. Cambridge: Cambridge University Press.

Tsetlin, Y. B. 2006. The origin of graphic modes of pottery decoration. In A. Gibson (ed.), *Prehistoric pottery: some recent research*, 1–10. Oxford: Archaeopress.

Tsutsumi, T. 2002. Origins of pottery and human strategies for adaptation during the termination of the last-glacial period in the Japanese archipelago. In Y. Yasuda (ed.), *The origins of pottery and agriculture*, 241–62. New Delhi: Lustre Press/Roli Books.

Usacheva, I. V. 2001. Stratigrafichesie positsii Neoliticheskikh tipov keramiki poseleniya 'VIII Punkt' na Andreevskoe Ozero i nekotorye obshchie voprosy Neolita Zaural'ya. In V. R. Tsibul'skij, A. N. Bagashev, and E. I. Valeeva (eds), *Problemy izucheniya Neolita Zapadnoj Sibiri*, 116–33. Tyumen': Institute Problem Osvoeniya Severa SO RAN (in Russian).

Vandiver, P., Soffer, O., Klims, B., and Svoboda, J. 1989. The origins of ceramic technology at Dolni Vestonice, Czechoslovakia. *Science* 246, 1002–8.

Vandiver, P. and Vasil'ev, S. A. 2002. A 16,000-year-old ceramic human-figurine from Maina, Russia. In P. Vandiver, M. Goodway, and J. L. Mass (eds), *Materials issues in art and archaeology VI: Materials Research Society Symposium Proceedings)*, 421–31. Warrendale, MA: Materials Research Society.

Velichko, A. A., Kurenkova, E. I., and Dolukhanov, P. M. 2009. Human socio-economic adaptation to environment in Late Palaeolithic, Mesolithic and Neolithic Eastern Europe. *Quaternary International* 203, 1–9.

Verpoorte, A. 2000. *Places of art, traces of fire: a contextual approach to anthropomorphic figurines in the Pavlovian*. PhD thesis. Faculteit der Archeologie Universiteit Leiden.

Villeneuve, L. 1906. *Les grottes de Grimaldi, Vol. II*. Monaco: Imprimerie de Monaco.

Walthall, J. A. 1990. *Prehistoric Indians of the southeast: archaeology of Alabama and the Middle South*. Tuscaloosa, AL: University of Alabama Press.

Wheeler, M. 1956. *Archaeology from the earth*. London: Penguin.

Wu, X., Zhang, C., Goldberg, P., Cohen, D., Pan, Y., Arpin, T., and Bar-Yosef, O. 2012. Early pottery at 20,000 years ago in Xianrendong cave, China. *Science* 336, 1696–1700.

Xia, Z., Chen, F., Chen, G., Zheng, G., Xie, F., and Mei, H. 2001. Environmental background of evolution from the Paleolithic to Neolithic Culture in Nihewan Basin, North China. *Science in China (Series D)* 44, 779–88.

Yamasaki, F., Hamada, C., and Hamada, Y. 1972. Riken natural radiocarbon measurements VII. *Radiocarbon* 14, 223–38.

Yasuda, Y. 2002a. The second east side story: origin of agriculture in West Asia. In Y. Yasuda (ed.), *The origins of pottery and agriculture*, 15–38. New Delhi: Lustre Press/Roli Books.

Yasuda, Y. 2002b. The origins of pottery and agriculture in East Asia. In Y. Yasuda (ed.), *The origins of pottery and agriculture*, 119–42. New Delhi: Lustre Press/Roli Books.

Zaretskaya, N. E., Zhilin, M. G., Karmanov, V. N., and Uspenskaya, O. N. 2005. Radiocarbon dating of wetland Meso-Neolithic archaeological sites within the Upper Volga and Middle Vychegda. *Geochronometria* 24, 117–31.

Zhao, C. and Wu, X. 2000. The dating of Chinese early pottery and a discussion of some related problems. *Documenta Praehistorica* 27, 233–9.

Zhushchikhovskaya, I. S. 2001. *Istoriya keramiki Vostochnoj Asii: ucheb. posobie*. Vladivostock: Vladivostock Gosudarstvennyj Universitet Ekonomiki i Servisi.

Zhushchikhovskaya, I. S. 2005. *Prehistoric pottery-making in the Russian Far East*. Oxford: Archaeopress.

Zhushchikhovskaya, I. S. 2007. Jomon cord-imitating decoration. *Documenta Praehistorica* 34, 21–9.

Zvelebil, M. 1986. Mesolithic societies and the transition to farming: problems of time, scale and organisation. In M. Zvelebil (ed.), *Hunters in transition: Mesolithic societies of temperate Europe and their transition to farming*, 167–88. Cambridge: Cambridge University Press.

Zvelebil, M. and Dolukhanov, P. 1991. The transition to farming in Eastern and Northern Europe. *Journal of World Prehistory* 5, 233–78.

CHAPTER 31

COASTAL ADAPTATIONS

C. R. WICKHAM-JONES

THE VALUE OF THE COAST

THOSE who live by the shore rarely go hungry. With the exception of the high Arctic or Antarctic, there is usually a wide range of edible foodstuffs to be found in the coastal zones around the world. Coastal regions also offer fresh water, shelter, fuel, routeways, and transport. No wonder that they were of particular value to the hunter-gather populations who, often mobile, sought to make use of the natural resources that were on offer. Crucially, in most places, the careful harvesting of coastal resources also reduces the possibility of seasonal famine. There is usually something to be found to eat so that dwelling by the shore can offer a measure of security from seasonal hunger that is rarely to be found further inland.

It is hardly surprising that people who lived by the sea made use of the resources that they found there, but archaeological opinion is unanimous that in order for a society to be termed 'maritime' it needs to be based upon more than simple opportunistic exploitation of foodstuffs. A truly maritime society is not just eating the occasional fish supper or limpet stew, but rather it favours the coastal zone for settlement, places a high reliance on coastal and marine resources, and carries out most of its activities within proximity of the sea. This is not to say that some, or all, members of that society do not venture inland at times, nor that terrestrial and inland resources are not exploited. For this reason, many of the earliest users of coastal resources are not considered truly specialized (see below).

Wright (2009) provides a comprehensive list of edible coastal resources in the UK, from obscure and long-forgotten seaweeds and littoral plants, to all the usual shellfish. The fish populations of any one region are usually well documented (e.g. Lythgoe and Lythgoe 1971), and freshwater fish should not be forgotten (Bagur 2009). There is also a wide range of sea mammals and birds to be harvested, as well as the land mammals that either come down to the shore seasonally, such as red deer, or live in close proximity year round (Kitchener et al. 2004).

Food is important, but human populations also have other needs. Shelter and water are often cited as two of the most basic. Hunter-gatherer structures are usually designed for a range of needs relating to a mobile lifestyle and rarely incorporate the levels of structural stability necessary to withstand the elements in all but the gentlest of climates (Faegri 1979). In general, therefore, settlement required a sheltered location, and in this respect the coastal zone could offer a twofold advantage. In many areas the very nature of the coast provided the wherewithal for occupation sites, in terms of caves, rock shelters, and rocky outcrops that could be made use of in a variety of ways (e.g. the range of sites recorded in west coast Scotland by Hardy and Wickham-Jones 2009). In addition, for those who prefer freestanding structures, the coastal topography frequently provides shelter from the wind. Rocky coastlines and island archipelagos may be most suited to the location of wind-free spots with provision for protection from shifting winds, but the high dunes to be found behind many sandy bays or depressions such as abandoned lagoon and river beds can become a haven in areas of less-dramatic landscape.

Fresh water is also a reliable coastal resource especially in higher latitudes where sweet water is a common element of any coastal spot. Other human needs include fuel and, for a shifting population, the possibility of transport. It is often forgotten that, just as a virgin forest contains an abundant supply of brushwood and deadwood, so an undeveloped coastline once offered abundant driftwood drawn from both near and far (finds of driftwood from North America have been documented archaeologically on the coasts of north-west Europe: Dickson 1992). Fuel was not scarce for those who lived by the shore and, in addition, there were supplies of seaweed that could be made use of as well as timber from coastal woodlands.

Transport is fundamental to a mobile population and coastal dwellers are at an advantage. It is for good reason that inland hills and mountain ranges have formed social boundaries for many human populations around the world (Kozlowski 2009). Many hunter-gatherer journeys are done on foot, but even this requires passage across the land. Contemporary and recent accounts of hunter-gatherers note that routeways are often not visible to modern eyes (Bridges 1947; Brody 1987; 2001), but given that they are used repeatedly it is clear that some form of marker and/or memory is in action. In many places coastlands and their associated waterways provide viewpoints, topographical features, and open ground that can assist travel. This would have been particularly significant in densely forested environments such as those to be found in many high-latitude areas. Travel is also, of course, improved by the use of vehicles, especially when goods have to be carried. One of the most efficient means of transport available from early on was the boat, which came in a variety of forms including dugout canoes, canoes of hide or bark, and coracles, each with their own particular advantages and disadvantages. The use of waterborne transport requires considerable local knowledge and skill, but it is obviously highly efficient along the coast, which in many areas offers both natural harbours for easy access and stretches of water together with currents and winds that facilitate movement. There may well also be rivers or sea lakes/lochs that open entry well into the hinterland. It is also worth noting that in most places coastal dwellers have relatively easy access to all of the materials required to make and maintain a variety of craft.

While there were clearly advantages to living by the sea, there were also disadvantages. Coastal life was not without its problems. Travel and transport may have been facilitated, but there were also strong currents, adverse weather conditions, and treacherous skerries to negotiate. Those who navigate coastal waters anywhere around the world have to be highly skilled. In some places the tidal range is so great that the very launching of boats can be problematic. Elsewhere, onshore winds and a long fetch can lead to the build-up of great rolling waves that limit access to the sea.

The sea may join, but it can also separate. Storms at different times of the year, or in different seasons, can build to levels that endanger not only those out at sea but also those on land. Storm damage may comprise not just wind and waves, but surging sea levels and airborne banks of sand. Coastal erosion could physically remove land and resources in some places, while long-term sea-level rise could alter the very face of the terrain and result in catastrophic loss of ground. This latter issue was particularly problematic for many dwellers of the early Holocene and the immediately preceding millennia. In north-west Europe, for example, the loss of Doggerland between roughly 11,000 and 8000 BP removed a landmass that had, seemingly, provided a major focus of settlement (Coles 1998; Flemming 2004; Gaffney et al. 2007; 2009). The dwellers of Doggerland and the north-west European coastlands must have been aware of their dwindling homelands, but they also had short-term disasters to cope with. Around 8200 BP they were struck by a massive tsunami, triggered by an undersea slide, the Storrega Slide, and there must have been catastrophic loss of life (Bondevik et al. 2003; Weninger et al. 2008).

Those who choose to dwell by the sea operate a fine balancing act.

The Limitations of the Evidence

Coastal dwelling may seem attractive, but it was a package that had to be learned and developed. Aquatic environments were certainly known and exploited by early populations (e.g. Erlandson and Fitzpatrick 2006; Erlandson and Moss 2001), and as Bailey and Milner (2002) point out, the archaeological evidence has certainly been affected by lower global sea levels particularly in the last 20,000 years. Nevertheless, a fundamental reliance on maritime resources has been a fairly recent development (see below). Where, and when, did this change occur? There are some basic challenges to our understanding of this.

To start, despite the concern of archaeology with process, it is inherently unable to spot change. Archaeology relies on the characterization of the evidence in order to recognize and classify the human processes by which the material record has built up. Those processes that are between classifications are hard to identify. For that reason, archaeological interpretation tends to focus on established lifeways, rather than on those that are in the process of formation. This is of obvious relevance to any consideration of the innovation of maritime adaption.

Secondly, in many parts of the world the evidence is itself lacking. Coastal adaption seems to have intensified, for various reasons discussed below, in the centuries that bound the end of the last Ice Age and the establishment of the early Holocene. This was a time of dynamic environmental change that included considerable changes to sea levels both on a global and a local scale due to the effects of differential crustal rebound. Many of the earliest Holocene coastlines were submerged (Bjerck 2009): Mesolithic Europe (Bailey 2008; Bjerck 2008a); north-west North America (Ackerman 1996); north-east North America (Bell and Renouf 2004); and southern South America (Orquera and Piana 1987). In some cases submergence was short-lived; elsewhere, coastlines and their associated archaeological evidence still lie underwater (Bailey and Flemming 2008).

The investigation of submerged landscapes, and the sites that may be preserved upon them, is progressing (Bailey and Flemming 2008; Erlandson and Fitzpatrick 2006;

Flemming 2004), but in many places it is still in its infancy (Bailey 2008). In order to find the sites that may preserve evidence of the changing lifestyles that led to a maritime adaption it is necessary to invest in this investigation. Recent fieldwork in the north of Scotland suggests that in order to understand fully both early settlement and submerged sites it is necessary to integrate a suite of techniques that provide a seamless archaeology from the terrestrial to the submerged landscape (Bates et al. 2013). Investigation of submerged sites without the terrestrial context, and vice versa, is inadequate.

Development of Technology

Inevitably, the coastal lifestyle results in the compilation of a suite of specialized material and behavioural culture. That of recent hunter-gatherers is relatively archaeologically visible. Further back in time the impact of unreliable preservation conditions and less materially robust artefacts has made the technology of coastal dwellers more elusive. Erlandson and Fitzpatrick (2006, 11–12) divide the technology into that associated with early developments such as foreshore scavenging, shellfish collection, generalized hunting and gathering, and simple fishing, and more complex techniques that appear later. In general the early techniques have left little evidence, though they suggest that they must have been practised by *Homo erectus* populations as they spread out across Africa and Eurasia. Techniques such as these, while successful ways in which to exploit the littoral zone, required no specialized equipment and have to be inferred from other evidence such as the location of the archaeological sites.

Inferred technology is still important as archaeology moves into more recent times, but the record is supplemented by the development of techniques that have left more abundant hard evidence. Harpoons and fish gorges of a variety of materials are a common feature of many coastal sites from the early Holocene onwards (e.g. Erlandson et al. 2005; Saville 2004), and a wide range of fishing equipment has now been recorded from Mesolithic Europe (Andersen 1995; Enghoff 1995; Kozlowski 2009; Pickard and Bonsall 2007). With time, fishing evolved to require more complex lines, hooks, and boats (though Pickard and Bonsall (2009) refute the idea that deep-water fishing in the offshore zone took place during the European Mesolithic). There is even the unfortunate pike from Kunda that apparently sank (in a freshwater lake) and took the fishing spear to the bottom with it (Indreko 1948; perhaps more unfortunate the hunter who went home hungry). Remains of nets may be few, but they do exist (e.g. Burov 1998) and net sinkers attest to their use as far back as 23,000 BP at Ohalo II on the shores of the Sea of Galilee (Nadel and Zaidner 2002). Fish weirs and traps are more common in later periods but little studied; Erlandson and Fitzpatrick (2006) suggest that targeted research might well uncover earlier examples. Whale bones, it should be noted, remain open to question, both among archaeologists and local people as the relative likelihood of strandings, as opposed to deliberate hunting, is still debated. In any consideration of the technology it is worth noting that we see the finished, working (or discarded) material, not the prototypes.

Boats remain elusive: examples of early Holocene craft do occur, but most evidence is inferential. The ability to cross water is attested well back into the early past among *Homo erectus* populations (Erlandson and Fitzpatrick 2006), and it has been suggested that the global expansion of *Homo sapiens* may well have been assisted by their development of more advanced craft, but in Europe they are not evidenced before the arrival of fully functional craft such as those indicated from Tybrind Vig (Andersen 1987), Star Carr (Clarke 1954), or Pesse (Rozoy 1978).

Familiarity with the coastal zone and an understanding of the sea are things that can only have arisen as populations settled into an area, but it is worth noting that both are highly transferable skills and humans are, if nothing else, well adapted to innovation and the subsequent communication of experience across the generations.

The First Coastal Users: Where and When

At what point did people first make full use of all that the coast had to offer? Erlandson has comprehensively summarized the archaeological information for coastal settlement and exploitation (2001). He, and others (e.g. Bjerck 2008a; 2008b), distinguish between the exploitation of freshwater and marine resources, as well as between coastal activity and activity in the full open sea. The early evidence is dependent on the location and density of sites as well as the survival of organic material indicative of food remains and applied technology. Some information, such as that for the use of boats, is lacking from the potentially earlier sites and has to be inferred from related information like terrain, as in sites on islands (Wickham-Jones 1990) or organic remains such as deep-sea fish (Parks and Barrett 2009).

There is archaeological evidence for the exploitation of coastal resources, often alongside terrestrial material, from early on. Not surprisingly, wherever settlement took place in the vicinity of the shore, people took advantage of the resources that were on offer. Thus, there is evidence from coastal sites such as Terra Amata and Lazaret in the western Mediterranean going back certainly 200,000 years and possibly as far as 300,000 years (Cleyet-Merle and Madelaine 1995; de Lumley 1969; Vila 1983), and this is backed by many other sites in the area, becoming more frequent as one moves forward in time (Erlandson 2001, table 1). At Klasies River Mouth and Boegoeberg II in South Africa the archaeological evidence suggested the exploitation of shellfish, sea mammals, and sea birds around 100,000 years ago (Klein 1999; Klein et al. 1999; Singer and Wymer 1982). In Australia and Melanesia there are remains of shell middens incorporating fish bones that date back some 35,000 years (Allen et al. 1989a; 1989b; Bowdler 1990; Morse 1988). The evidence in the Americas comes from both the far north and south and dates to 12,500–11,000 years ago (Dillehay 1997; Yesner 1996; 1998).

Many Palaeolithic groups may have practised an economy that was based on terrestrial resources, but it is clear that they did not completely eschew aquatic material. There is little evidence, however, for specialized maritime communities. Populations were small and widely spread, well adapted to making use of all that was available, and to the use of innovation when necessary. What happened to trigger the specialized use of aquatic material that is evidenced by the archaeology of later, typically, early Holocene groups?

The initial constraint on maritime settlement has to be the availability of the coast. Bailey and Bjerck have both commented on the floruit of maritime resources with the warming of high-latitude waters as conditions improved after the last de-glaciation (Bailey 2008; Bjerck 2008a). Prior to this, in many parts of the world, the coast was neither easily accessible nor quite as enticing. It is perhaps no coincidence that the innovation of full maritime adaption seems to come with the spread of human settlement in the early Holocene when both resource abundance and population pressures increased, but the picture is not as simple as that.

Access to the coast has not remained static through time. For the inhabitants of north-west Europe at the Last Glacial Maximum the coast offered an alien, difficult landscape. In many places the actual boundary between land and water had disappeared below the depth of ice. Where the waters were ice free, there were still calving bergs and cold conditions, not to mention the travails of actually reaching the sea, which in many cases lay beyond high land and mountains, well away from the familiar rolling plains and territories of the Palaeolithic hunter. The combined effects of glacial isostasy and eustasy meant that in some places the actual line of the coast was many kilometres further away from the European heartland than it is today (Dawson 1992; Gaffney et al. 2009), and in many cases it is now submerged.

This is not to say that the coast was unused or uninhabited at this time. Archaeological evidence may be lacking, but there are plenty of examples of communities in recent times that dwell amongst sea ice and frozen shorelines (e.g. Brody 1987). Nevertheless, it has to be noted that, so far, the archaeological evidence for hunter-gatherer settlement along the coast post-dates de-glaciation (sometimes by as much as a thousand years: Bjerck 2008a), and there is no indication of the early exploitation of ice-bound coastal landscapes. Of course this could be because of the fragility of the evidence: the archaeological material has had to survive millennia of permafrost and ice; original land surfaces rarely survive and in most places the ice-bound shores of the Late Glacial now lie underwater offshore and have rarely been examined in the detail necessary to pick up information on human settlement (Bailey 2008; Erlandson and Fitzpatrick 2006).

Prior to de-glaciation, Europe and much of the rest of the world was occupied by hunter-gatherer groups. In Europe, these groups are known today by a variety of names, reflecting technocomplexes of tool types. Best known perhaps are the Hamburgian and subsequent Ahrensburgian groups (Taute 1968), which operated across the North European Plain between 13,500 and 10,000 BC and have been characterized as highly mobile terrestrial hunters, largely reliant on big game such as reindeer. Despite their terrestrial homelands it is clear that these hunters did not ignore the aquatic resources available to them. Many settled or moved around lake systems and along rivers. Several writers have pointed out that they would have needed some sort of craft in order to cross the great rivers along their path (e.g. Bjerck 2008a; Erlandson 2001), and they may well have made more use of boats than the archaeological material suggests. Others have suggested that at least some of these peoples moved north as part of their seasonal round, to make use of the maritime resources along the south Swedish coasts, leaving behind the archaeological record now known as Hensbacka (Reide 2009; Schmitt 1995).

In Scandinavia ice-free coastal zones became available for human settlement around 13,000 BP (Andersen and Borns 1997; Andersen et al. 1995; Bjorck 1995). De-glaciation in Scotland was complex, but ice-free coasts seem to have been available at a similar time (Dawson, pers. comm.), though sea ice would have been an issue through the Younger Dryas (Dawson 2009) until about 10,000 BP (Clapperton 1997). In Ireland the pattern is similarly complex, though the impact of the Younger Dryas was less dramatic (Coxon 2008); the coast is generally accepted to have been properly ice free by 10,000 BP (Woodman 2008).

Elsewhere around the world, ice sheets seem to have reached their maximum in the period around 14,500–14,000 BP (Clapperton 1997; Dawson 1992), though the individual details of de-glaciation vary.

With the arrival of the early Holocene, maritime Europe opened up. Not only were ice-free coasts by and large the norm, but also generally ameliorating currents and climate served to increase the maritime resource base (Bjerck 2008a; 2008b; Kitchener et al. 2004; Walker and Lowe 1997; Zvelebil 2008). The coast became an attractive place to live and the archaeological evidence indicates the widespread use of marine and coastal resources from early on.

Maritime Mesolithic sites have been recorded around Europe, from the Mediterranean to northern Scandinavia. While many are making use of the available resources in a balanced yearly round, as summarized for the Mediterranean by Pluciennik (2008), in some areas a deeper level of specialization seems to have developed. While precise 'cultures' such as the Obanian (Bonsall 1996; 1997) are no longer considered to be separate entities, the north-western seaboards of Europe do seem to have become home to highly specialized groups of hunter-gatherers who favoured the resources of the coast over those of the hinterland. Pluciennik notes the apparent continuities from preceding occupation around the Mediterranean coastlands (2008), but it is interesting to note that in those areas where a more intense specialization developed, the evidence suggests the opposite. The evidence for earlier settlement in areas such as Scotland and Norway is patchy, and the ice-free coastlines were not, apparently, immediately made use of (Bjerck 2008a).

Case Studies

North-West Europe

The earliest evidence for stable maritime hunter-gatherer societies in north-west Europe comes from the coastal areas from western Sweden to the Arctic by hunter-gatherer complexes now known as Fosna (Bjerck 2009) in Norway and Hensbacka in Sweden (Kindgren 1995; Nordqvist 1999). This took place around 9000 cal BC. Settlement sites concentrated along the coast, and, though the resources of inland mountains were not ignored, there is evidence of a strong reliance on marine and coastal resources. Boats must have been a part of life, and considerable skill would have been necessary in both navigation and seamanship.

Further south, the Maglemose cultures of southern Denmark relied on both coastal resources, including fish, sea mammals, birds, and shellfish (Andersen 1995), and land mammals such as aurochs, elk, and red deer (Blankholm 2008). Coastal resources may not have been the mainstay of life, but the archaeological evidence indicates that a sophisticated technology for harvesting marine resources was already in use (Andersen 1995; Enghoff 1995; Pickard and Bonsall 2009). The actual Mesolithic coast in this region is now submerged in many places, but Kozlowski has pointed out that even in current terrestrial zones this was a region with considerable aquatic influence. There were abundant rivers and lakes. Aquatic and coastal resources were not ignored, but maritime resources were not apparently relied upon as essential until later: on Kongemose and Ertebølle sites such as Brovst (Andersen 1970), Tybrind Vig (Andersen 1985), or Segebro (Larsson 1982). The great shell middens, such as Ertebølle itself, speak of a people harvesting the sea, but date towards the final years of the Mesolithic (Johansson 1995). To the west, changes in the physical geography mean that a swathe of twenty-first century coastal lands lay, during the earlier Mesolithic, far from the sea. In countries such as Belgium and the Netherlands the earliest Mesolithic coastline is now submerged (Verhart 2008). The coastlands of today did not offer a fully maritime environment until the later Mesolithic, around 6500 cal BC (Weninger et al. 2008).

Further out, the existence of the plains of Doggerland, joining the island of Britain to mainland Europe, is now well known (Coles 1998; Gaffney et al. 2007). They are generally assumed to have been home to a Mesolithic population based on terrestrial hunting and gathering, though Gaffney et al. (2009) have highlighted the presence of a variety of aquatic environments in the region including lacustrine, riverine, and saltmarsh areas, and these were, no doubt, exploited. It is worth noting that the population here was, of necessity, adapting to the gradual reduction of their home-base as rising sea levels flooded across the Doggerland hills. This not only meant a diminishing landmass, but also the gradual replacement of terrestrial resources with littoral and then marine material. Whether or not the population of Doggerland were in touch with their coastal cousins elsewhere, they had no choice but to change. For them maritime adaption was not about innovation but about survival.

In Britain the exploitation of coastal resources along the western seaboards has been well documented (e.g. Bell 2007). The best-documented Mesolithic maritime economy lies yet further to the north along the coasts of western Scotland, where a series of rich shell midden deposits have been explored with dates around 5000–3500 cal BC. Recent work has pushed back the dated shell midden sites in Scotland to 7000 cal BC (Sand: Hardy and Wickham-Jones 2009) and 6600 cal BC (An Corran: Saville and Miket 1994). There are also non-shell midden sites from this period, many of which are coastal such as Kinloch in Rum (*c*.8000 cal BC: Wickham-Jones 1990), Links House, Orkney (*c*.7000 cal BC: Woodward et al., pers. com.), Newton in Islay (*c*.7000 cal BC: McCullagh 1989), and Camas Daraich in Skye (6500 cal BC: Wickham-Jones and Hardy 2004). All of these would have required the use of boats. The Scottish Mesolithic was thus essentially a maritime culture. There are sites inland, but the evidence suggests a strong preference for the coastal zone. To the west, on the fringes of Europe, the Mesolithic settlers of the island of Ireland were pioneers. Given that boats would have been necessary even to get them there (Edwards and Brooks 2008) these people are, perhaps, self-defined as a maritime culture. Not surprisingly, given the nature of the land, Ireland has coastal sites and inland sites, shell midden sites and other types of site. The site of Mount Sandel indicates that settlement was already established by 7700 cal BC (Bayliss and Woodman 2009). Mount Sandel lies not far from the coast, towards the mouth of the River Bann. It is not a maritime site, but the inhabitants of Mount Sandel were certainly making use of the aquatic environment. To the south, and on the west coast, lies Ferriter's Cove, a shell midden site, dating to *c*.4500 cal BC (Woodman et al. 1999) and other shell midden sites have been documented.

The North American Pacific Coast

In the north-west Pacific lower relative sea levels (*c*.−120 m) at the time of the Last Glacial Maximum resulted in the exposure of the landscape of Beringia. Ackerman (2003) has suggested that much of the Beringian coast at this time was cold and arid, it dropped quickly into deep waters and had little to offer in the way of resources. This is supported by Yesner (1997) but challenged by more recent work which suggests that the southern coasts of Beringia offered a varied topography with considerable resources for at least part of the year (Brigham-Grette et al. 2004; Erlandson et al. 2007). Evidence of human settlement is lacking so far even from shallower waters, but remains of animals such as brown bear and caribou indicate that conditions were suitable (Ackerman 2003; Heaton et al. 1996), and it may well be that the rises in relative sea level since then have served to obliterate the record. Settlement, if it did take place, seems likely to have been highly mobile and based on a mix of terrestrial and maritime resources.

Erlandson et al. (2008) suggest that there were three periods (around 17,500, 16,500, and 15,000 years ago) when warmer sea surface conditions may have facilitated human migration around existing coastlines and thus into the north-west coastal area (Sarnthein et al. 2006). De-glaciation had taken place by 15,000 years ago, and this was followed by a rapid rise in relative sea level in the years up to c.10,000 cal BC when the coastal lands of today were actually submerged; in some places present sea levels have only been reached in recent times (Ackerman 2003; Ackerman et al. 1985). Alongside this change in sea level came an increase in marine resources around present shores as currents ameliorated and conditions improved (Erlandson et al. 2008). Interestingly, this period of dynamic sea-level change (also the time when coastal conditions are suitable for archaeological preservation) coincides with the first archaeological evidence for settled groups of hunter-gatherers.

For many of the early communities of the area the sea provided both the wherewithal to survive and the means of transport (Blake 2010). Inland mobility was still complicated by mountain and glaciers. In south-east Alaska, sites such as Ground Hog Bay on the Chilkat Peninsula (Ackerman 1968; 1974; 1996; Ackerman et al. 1979), Chuck Lake on Heceta Island (Ackerman 2003), and Hidden Falls on Baranof Island (Davis 1989) dating to roughly 10,000 cal BC all provide evidence for early maritime activity both from shell middens and lithic scatters. The inhabitants of these sites must have been familiar with the use of boats and they made the most of the coastal and marine resources at their disposal. At Chuck Lake there is evidence for deep-water fishing. Actual evidence of the inhabitants in this area comes from sites like On-Your-Knees cave on Prince of Wales Island where isotope analysis of human remains dating to around 10,000 cal BC indicates the consumption of a diet rich in marine resources (Dixon 1999; 2001).

Further south, work has included prospection to document the underwater landscape around Haida Gwaii (Josenhans et al. 1997) and this is backed up by sites on land and in the intertidal zone with clear evidence of a developed maritime economy as far back as 11,000 cal BC (Erlandson et al. 2008). Ackerman (2003) links the present archaeological evidence for settlement in these areas with the dramatic rises in relative sea level, a period when the abundance of marine resources was growing over that of the land. While the impact of rising sea levels as an archaeological bias must be taken into account, it is also of interest that he suggests an increase in evidence for the development of specialized technologies associated with marine exploitation and the expansion of more complex societies as relative sea levels stabilized around 5,000 years ago.

Little evidence for early settlement survives from the zone between the Canadian border and north-west California, an absence that has been explained by Erlandson et al. (2008) as due to the vulnerability of the area to a combination of dynamic geomorphological processes including earthquakes, tsunamis, and coastal erosion (Erlandson et al. 1998; Punke and Davis 2006). To the south of this, past changes to relative sea level have also resulted in the loss of the coastal plain in early times, but work in the coastal zone and on islands has yielded many sites that date to the period between 13,000 and 10,000 years ago. Abundant shell middens and an associated specialized technology suggest the widespread use of marine and coastal resources particularly to the south of the San Francisco Bay area in the area around the Channel Islands (Erlandson et al. 2008). The earliest evidence from this area dates to some 12,000 years ago and comes from human bones at Arlington Springs on Santa Rosa Island (Johnson et al. 2002; Orr 1968), and from Daisy cave on San Miguel Island where the earliest use of a shell midden and rock shelter has been dated to 11,500 years ago (Rick et al. 2001; 2005). Erlandson et al. (2008, 2240) comment on the increasing evidence for a sizeable population exploiting both this coast and associated inland areas in the early Holocene.

Tierra del Fuego, South America

The island of Tierra del Fuego stretches some 400 km north to south and 500 km east to west and lies off the southernmost tip of South America between 54° and 56° S. It is bound to the continent by a maze of intercutting straits and islands, so much so that in places it is hard to distinguish where one begins and the previous one ends. The southernmost extension of the Andean Cordillera terminates along the western mainland where it forms a high mountain barrier that divides the rocky islands and coastlands of the south and west from the extensive low rolling steppe of north-eastern Tierra del Fuego. The east coast comprises long straight stretches of gravel ridge and has a tidal range of up to 11 m. There is little shelter here and it contrasts sharply with the deeply indented, rocky south-western coast.

The first settlement of Tierra del Fuego goes back to c.10,500 cal BC and relates to terrestrial hunter-gatherers (Orquera and Piana 2009; Piana et al. 2007). A likely second incursion of maritime nomads took place around 5500 BC (Orquera and Piana 1987; 1999a), centred along the channels and islands of the west and south. Both groups were nomadic and maintained a specialized foraging lifestyle, though there were marked differences. In the north and east the hunting of land mammals, especially guanaco, was particularly important, supplemented by fish, shellfish, and gathering. In the south and west the hunting of large marine mammals such as sea lions formed the basis of the economy, supplemented by the resources of the sea and coast: fish; shellfish; birds (including penguin); and the harvesting of the forest (Orquera and Piana 1999b; Piana 2005). Guanaco were only occasionally hunted here.

At the time of European contact and settlement in the nineteenth century, four distinct social and economic groups were recorded in Tierra del Fuego (Lothrop 1928). To the north and east lived terrestrial guanaco hunters, the Selk'nam. The Alacauf comprised a group of sea nomads living among the channels of the north-west whose territory extended into the Seno Otway region of mainland South America. The Yamana sea nomads lived along the Beagle channel and Wollaston islands. The Haush occupied the south-eastern tip of Tierra del Fuego and the Staten Islands. They lived by way of marine resources and terrestrial hunting. The archaeological evidence suggests that a similar division into separate groups existed from early on. While there was undoubtedly some contact, in general the groups seem to have maintained separate identities and territories. Archaeologically a rich material culture has survived from earliest times due to the nature of the sites. In the maritime south and west shell middens (representing the remains of dwelling sites and often comprising prominent mounds) abound along the channels used by the sea nomads (Orquera and Piana 2009). The range of flaked and coarse stone tools at sites like Túnel I and Imiwaia I is supplemented by assemblages of bone harpoons, points, and many other artefacts (Orquera and Piana 1999b; 2009). Analysis has documented various changes in material culture from earliest times to the recent past (Orquera and Piana 2009), but both the economic and social systems seem to have continued with little alteration (Piana et al. 2007). The Yamana developed a highly specialized and successful way of life that was geared to the exploitation of the sea and coast to such an extent that Orquera and Piana (2009, 69) comment that they 'used raw materials available only in the littoral zone and created techniques and tools that were not useful in other environments'. Yet Orquera and Piana also found no evidence that sites were located according to freshwater supplies or to shelter from the wind (2009, 64).

The Yamana spent little time on land; their maritime adaption was complete and has been attributed to a combination of factors (Bjerck 2009; Orquera and Piana 2009). Not least is the local topography; exploitation of the land presented far more problems than a life at sea (Orquera and Piana 1999b). Boats must have been developed from the beginning but, as is common in most maritime areas, archaeological boat remains are scarce—in the case of the Yamana, the later ethnographic records of craft suggest that they were not robust (Piana and Orquera 1998). Bjerck (2009) has noted the coincidence in timing between the appearance of the maritime innovations of the Yamana and the establishment of forest cover in the area. Given the importance of wood and bark as a raw material for so much of the material culture of the Yamana (Orquera and Piana 1999b) this may well be significant.

Whatever the reason behind their adaption, the Yamana lifestyle was highly successful (contrast the experiences of early Europeans in the area such as FitzRoy and Darwin: Darwin 1845; FitzRoy 1839). The reasons behind its collapse were complex but included European pressures on key resources such as the fur seals (Piana et al. 2007) and, most catastrophically, the deliberate 'civilizing' impacts of the European missionaries and settlers in the years of the early twentieth century.

Conclusion: The Multi-Faceted Coastline

For some hunter-gatherer groups the coast has been a significant milieu. This importance is clearly centred on food, but it also includes wider elements of life such as the availability of fresh water, transport and routeways, other resources, and shelter. Littoral groups around the world, and through time, have varied in the extent to which they made use of these resources. Some, such as the Yamana rarely left the vicinity of the sea, and indeed passed most of their day at sea. Others, such as the Mesolithic inhabitants of west coast Scotland or Norway, based their settlements along the coast, while making use of terrestrial resources, sometimes culled from far and high inland.

Coastal and aquatic resources were exploited far back into prehistory and across a wide range of environments. The adaption of full maritime specialization, comprising a fundamental reliance on a range of coastal and marine elements, has yet to be identified prior to the rough boundary set by the advent of the early Holocene some 10,000 years ago. The impact of global sea-level change on the archaeological record at this point has yet to be quantified, but it is unlikely to extend the development of maritime specialization back beyond a few centuries.

In Europe the seeds of innovation have been suggested for the marine-skerry landscapes of southern Scandinavia, where a mobile population well used to the exploitation of great lakes and rivers further south found the resources to make use of a landscape in which the distinction between water and land was often blurred. In this respect the role of woodland in the establishment of full maritime adaption should be considered. The development of the forested landscapes of the early Holocene not only provided the wherewithal to build and maintain a variety of craft in greater numbers and increasing size, they also helped to isolate the community from its hinterland. This, in conjunction with an inhospitable mountainous topography, was an important element in those areas where the strongest maritime adaption is seen such as Scotland, Norway, Tierra del Fuego, and the Pacific coasts of North America. This is not to say that life here was a struggle: people chose to settle in these areas and the evidence suggests a life rich in all aspects of human nature—ritual as well as functional (Warren 2005). Indeed, in Scotland and the surrounding areas it would appear that it was in these littoral zones that a new, more permanent, type of site, was able to develop. More permanent sites meant more permanent, or at least different, communities, though it is difficult to tell which came first—settled communities or deeper knowledge and exploitation of the coast. The sea also had an important role to play in ritual life. Kozlowski (2009) has drawn attention to the use of islands as special places, particularly as burial sites, and thus these sites serve as a reminder of the complexity of the human relationship with the sea.

References

Ackerman, R. E. 1968. *Archeology of the Glacier Bay Region, Southeast Alaska*. Washington State University: Department of Anthropology.
Ackerman, R. E. 1974. Post-Pleistocene cultural adaptations on the northern Northwest Coast. In S. Raymond and P. Schledermann (eds), *Proceedings, international conference on the prehistory and paleoecology of the western Arctic and Subarctic*, 1–20. Calgary: Archaeological Association, University of Calgary.
Ackerman, R. E. 1996. Early maritime culture complexes of the northern Northwest Coast. In R. E. Ackerman and D. B. Carlson (eds), *Early human occupation in British Columbia*, 123–32. Vancouver: University of British Columbia Press.
Ackerman, R. E. 2003. Early maritime adaptations along the Alaskan coastal platform. Paper presented at the 51st International Congress of Americanists, Santiago, Chile.
Ackerman, R. E., Hamilton, T. D., and Stuckenrath, R. 1979. Early cultural complexes on the northern Northwest Coast. *Canadian Journal of Archaeology* 3, 195–209.
Ackerman, R. E., Reid, K. C., Gallison, J. D., and Roe, M. E. 1985. *Archaeology of Heceta Island: a survey of 16 timber harvest units in the Tongass National Forest, Southeastern Alaska*. Washington State University: Center for Northwest Anthropology, Project Reports 3.
Allen, J., Gosden, C., Jones, R., and White, J. P. 1989a. Pleistocene dates for the human occupation of New Ireland, northern Melanesia. *Nature* 331, 707–9.
Allen, J., Gosden, C., and White, J. P. 1989b. Pleistocene New Ireland. *Antiquity* 63, 548–61.
Andersen, B. G. and Borns, H. 1997. *The Ice Age world*. Oslo: Scandinavian University Press.

Andersen, B. G., Mangerud, J., Sorenson, R., Reite, A., Sveian, H., Thoresen, M., and Bergstrom, B. 1995. Younger Dryas ice marginal deposits in Norway. *Quaternary International* 28, 147–69.

Andersen, S. 1970. Brovst, en kystboplads fra aeldre stenalder. *Kuml*, 67–90.

Andersen, S. 1985. Tybrind Vig: a preliminary report on a submerged Ertebolle settlement on the west coast of Fyn. *Journal of Danish Archaeology* 4, 52–69.

Andersen, S. 1987. Mesolithic dugouts and paddles from Tybrind Vig, Denmark. *Acta Archaeologica* 57, 87–106.

Andersen, S. 1995. Coastal adaption and marine exploitation in Late Mesolithic Denmark—with special emphasis on the Limfjord region. In A. Fischer (ed.), *Man and sea in the Mesolithic*, 41–66. Oxford: Oxbow.

Bagur, D. 2009. *Where the fish are: a science-based guide to stalking freshwater fish*. London: McGraw-Hill.

Bailey, G. 2008. Mesolithic Europe: overview and new problems. In G. Bailey and P. Spikins (eds), *Mesolithic Europe*, 357–72. Cambridge: Cambridge University Press.

Bailey, G. N. and Flemming, N. C. 2008. Archaeology of the continental shelf: marine resources, submerged landscapes and underwater archaeology, *Quaternary Science Reviews* 27, 2153–65.

Bailey, G. N. and Milner, N. 2002. Coastal hunter-gatherers and social evolution: marginal or central? *Before Farming* 3–4, 129–50.

Bates, M., Bates, C. R., Dawson, A., Dawson, S., Nayling, N., and Wickham-Jones, C. R. in prep. A multi-disciplinary approach to the archaeological investigation of a bedrock dominated shallow marine landscape: an example from the Bay of Firth, Orkney, UK. *Journal of Archaeological Science*.

Bayliss, A. and Woodman, P. C. 2009. A new Bayesian chronology for Mesolithic occupation at Mount Sandel, Northern Ireland. *Proceedings of the Prehistoric Society* 75, 101–24.

Bell, M. 2007. *Prehistoric coastal communities: the Mesolithic in western Britain*. York: Council for British Archaeology.

Bell, T. and Renouf, P. 2004. Prehistoric cultures, reconstructed coasts: maritime Archaic Indian site distribution in Newfoundland. *World Archaeology* 35, 350–70.

Bjerck, H. 2008a. Colonizing the so-called margins. The development of marine relations and the colonization of coastal north-west Europe. In J. J. Davenport, D. P. Sleeman, and P. C. Woodman (eds), *Mind the gap: postglacial colonization of Ireland*, 35–44. Dublin: Irish Naturalists Journal.

Bjerck, H. 2008b. Norwegian Mesolithic trends: a review. In G. Bailey and P. Spikins (eds), *Mesolithic Europe*, 60–106. Cambridge: Cambridge University Press.

Bjerck, H. 2009. Colonizing seascapes: comparative perspectives on the development of maritime relations in the Pleistocene/Holocene transition in north-west Europe. In S. B. McCartan, R. Schulting, G. Warren, and P. C. Woodman (eds), *Mesolithic horizons: papers presented at the seventh international conference on the Mesolithic in Europe, Belfast 2005*, 16–23. Oxford: Oxbow.

Bjorck, S. 1995. Late Weichselian to early Holocene development of the Baltic Sea—with implications for coastal settlements in the southern Baltic region. In A. Fischer (ed.), *Man and sea in the Mesolithic*, 23–34. Oxford: Oxbow.

Blake, M. 2010. Water travel and the definition of territories on the Northwest Coast: a coast Salish example. In A. Vila and J. Estévez (eds), *La excepción y la norma: las sociedaded indígenas de la Costa Noroeste de Norteamérica desde la arqueología*, 111–23. Madrid: Consejo Superior de Investigaciones Científicas.

Blankholm, H. P. 2008. Southern Scandinavia. In G. Bailey and P. Spikins (eds), *Mesolithic Europe*, 107–31. Cambridge: Cambridge University Press.

Bondevik, S., Mangerud, J., Dawson, S., Dawson, A., and Lohne, O. 2003. Record breaking height for 8000 year old tsunami in the North Atlantic. *EOS* 84, 289–300.

Bonsall, C. 1996. The 'Obanian Problem': coastal adaption in the Mesolithic of western Scotland. In T. Pollard and A. Morrison (eds), *The early prehistory of Scotland*, 183–97. Edinburgh: Edinburgh University Press.

Bonsall, C. 1997. Coastal adaptation in the Mesolithic of Argyll: rethinking the 'Obanian' problem. In G. Ritchie (ed.), *The archaeology of Argyll*, 25–37. Edinburgh: Edinburgh University Press.

Bowdler, S. 1990. The Silver Dollar site, Shark Bay: an interim report. *Australian Aboriginal Studies* 2, 60–3.

Bridges, E. L. 1947. *The uttermost parts of the earth*. London: Dutton.

Brigham-Grette, J., Lozhkin, A. V., Anderson, P. M., and Glushkova, O. Y. 2004. Paleoenvironmental conditions in western Beringia before and during the Last Glacial Maximum. In D. B. Madsen (ed.), *Entering America: Northeast Asia and Beringia before the Last Glacial Maximum*, 29–61. Salt Lake City: University of Utah Press.

Brody, H. 1987. *Living Arctic*. London: Faber and Faber.

Brody, H. 2001. *The other side of Eden*. London: Faber and Faber.

Burov, G. M. 1998. The use of vegetable materials in the Mesolithic of northeast Europe. In M. Zvelebil, L. Doman'ska, and R. Dennell (eds), *Harvesting the sea, farming the forest*, 53–64. Sheffield: Sheffield Academic Press.

Clapperton, C. M. 1997. Greenland ice cores and North Atlantic sediments: implications for the last glaciation in Scotland. In J. Gordon (ed.), *Reflections on the Ice Age in Scotland*, 45–59. Edinburgh: Scottish Natural Heritage.

Clarke, J. G. D. 1954. *Excavations at Star Carr*. Cambridge: Cambridge University Press.

Cleyet-Merle, J. and Madelaine, S. 1995. Inland evidence of human sea coast exploitation in Palaeolithic France. In A. Fischer (ed.), *Man and sea in the Mesolithic*, 303–8. Oxford: Oxbow.

Coles, B. J. 1998. Doggerland: a speculative survey. *Proceedings of the Prehistoric Society*, 64, 45–81.

Coxon, P. 2008. Landscapes and environments of the last glacial–interglacial transition: a time of amazingly rapid change in Ireland. In J. J. Davenport, D. P. Sleeman, and P. C. Woodman (eds), *Mind the gap: postglacial colonization of Ireland*, 45–62. Dublin: Irish Naturalists Journal.

Darwin, C. 1845. *The voyage of the Beagle*. London: Wordsworth.

Davis, S. D. 1989. *The Hidden Falls Site, Baranof Island, Alaska*. Anchorage: Alaska Anthropological Association.

Dawson, A. 1992. *Ice Age earth*. London: Routledge.

Dawson, A. 2009. *So fair and foul a day*. Edinburgh: Birlinn.

Dickson, J. H. 1992. North American driftwood, especially Picea (spruce), from archaeological sites in the Hebrides and Northern Isles of Scotland. *Review of Palaeobotany and Palynology* 73, 49–56.

Dillehay, T. D. 1997. *Monte Verde, a late Pleistocene settlement in Chile, Vol. 2: the archaeological context and interpretation*. Washington, DC: Smithsonian Institution.

Dixon, E. J. 1999. *Bones, boats, and bison*. Albuquerque: University of New Mexico Press.

Dixon, E. J. 2001. Human colonization of the Americas: timing, technology and process. *Quaternary Science Reviews* 20, 277–99.

Edwards, R. and Brooks, A. 2008. The island of Ireland: drowning the myth of an Irish land-bridge? In J. J. Davenport, D. P. Sleeman, and P. C. Woodman (eds), *Mind the gap: postglacial colonization of Ireland*, 19–34. Dublin: Irish Naturalists Journal.

Enghoff, I. B. 1995. Fishing in Denmark during the Mesolithic period. In A. Fischer (ed.), *Man and sea in the Mesolithic*, 67–74. Oxford: Oxbow.

Erlandson, J. M. 2001. The archaeology of aquatic adaptions: paradigms for a new millennium. *Journal of Archaeological Research* 9, 287–350.

Erlandson, J. M., Braje, T. J., Rick, T. C., and Peterson, J. 2005. Beads, bifaces and boats: an early maritime adaptation on the south coast of San Miguel Island, California. *American Anthropologist* 107, 678–83.

Erlandson, J. M. and Fitzpatrick, S. M. 2006. Oceans, islands, and coasts: current perspectives on the role of the sea in human prehistory. *Journal of Island and Coastal Archaeology* 1, 5–33.

Erlandson, J. M., Graham, M. H., Bourque, B. J., Corbett, D., Estes, J. A., and Steneck, R. S. 2007. The kelp highway hypothesis: marine ecology, the coastal migration theory, and the peopling of the Americas. *Journal of Island and Coastal Archaeology* 2, 161–74.

Erlandson, J. M. and Moss, M. L. 2001. Shellfish feeders, carrion eaters, and the archaeology of aquatic adaptations. *American Antiquity* 66, 413–32.

Erlandson, J. M., Moss, M. L., and Des Lauriers, M. 2008. Life on the edge, early maritime cultures of the Pacific north coast of North America. *Quaternary Science Reviews* 27, 2232–45.

Erlandson, J. M., Tveskov, M. A., and Byram, S. 1998. The development of maritime adaptations on the southern Northwest Coast of North America. *Arctic Anthropology* 35, 6–22.

Faegri, T. 1979. *Tents, architecture of the nomads*. London: John Murray.

FitzRoy, R. 1839. *Proceedings of the second expedition (1831–1836) under the command of captain Robert FitzRoy*. London: Henry Colburn.

Flemming, N. C. 2004. *Submarine prehistoric archaeology of the North Sea*. York: Council for British Archaeology.

Gaffney, V., Fitch, S., and Smith, D. 2009. *Europe's lost world: the rediscovery of Doggerland*. York: Council for British Archaeology.

Gaffney, V., Thomson, K., and Fitch, S. 2007. *Mapping Doggerland*. Oxford: Archaeopress.

Hardy, K. and Wickham-Jones, C. R. 2009. Mesolithic and later sites around the Inner Sound, Scotland: the work of the Scotland's First Settlers project 1998–2004. Scottish Archaeological Internet Reports 31.

Heaton, T. H., Talbot S. L., and Shields F. G. 1996. An Ice Age refugium for large mammals in the Alexander Archipelago, Southeastern Alaska. *Quaternary Research* 46, 186–92.

Indreko, R. 1948. *Die mittlere Steinzeit in Estland*. Stockholm: Almqvist and Wiksell.

Johansson, A. D. 1995. The Ertebolle culture in South Zealand, Denmark. In A. Fischer (ed.), *Man and sea in the Mesolithic*, 87–94. Oxford: Oxbow.

Johnson, J. R., Stafford Jr., T., Ajie, H., and Morris, D. P. 2002. Arlington Springs revisited. In D. Browne, K. Mitchell, and H. Chaney (eds), *Proceedings of the 5th California Islands Conference*, 541–5. Santa Barbara: Santa Barbara Museum of Natural History.

Josenhans, H., Fedje, D., Peinitz, R., and Southon, J. 1997. Early humans and rapidly changing Holocene sea levels in the Queen Charlotte Islands—Hecate Strait, British Columbia, Canada. *Science* 277, 71–4.

Kindgren, H. 1995. Hensbacka-Horgen-Hornborgasjon: Early Mesolithic coastal and inland settlements in western Sweden. In A. Fischer (ed.), *Man and sea in the Mesolithic*, 171–84. Oxford: Oxbow.

Kitchener, A. C., Bonsall, C., and Bartosiewicz, L. 2004. Missing mammals from Mesolithic middens: a comparison of the fossil and archaeological records from Scotland. In A. Saville (ed.), *Mesolithic Scotland and its neighbours*, 73–82. Edinburgh: Society of Antiquaries of Scotland.

Klein, R. G. 1999. *The human career: human biological and cultural origins*. Chicago: University of Chicago Press.

Klein, R. G., Cruz-Uribe, K., Halkett, D., Hart, T., and Parkington, J. E. 1999. Paleoenvironmental and human behavioral implications of the Boegoeberg 1 Late Pleistocene hyena den, northern Cape Province, South Africa. *Quaternary Research* 52, 393–403.

Kozlowski, S. K. 2009. *Thinking Mesolithic*. Oxford: Oxbow.

Larsson, L. 1982. *Segebro en tidigatlantisk boplats vid Sege As mynning*. Malmo: Malmo Museum.

Lothrop, S. K. 1928. *The Indians of Tierra del Fuego*. New York: Zagier and Urruty.

Lumley, H. de 1969. A Palaeolithic camp at Nice. *Scientific American* 220, 42–50.

Lythgoe, J. and Lythgoe, G. 1971. *Fishes of the sea: the coastal waters of the British Isles, Northern Europe and the Mediterranean*. London: Blandford.

McCullagh, R. 1989. Excavation at Newton, Islay. *Glasgow Archaeological Journal* 15, 23–51.

Morse, K. 1988. Mandu Mandu Creek rockshelter: Pleistocene human coastal occupation of North West Cape, Western Australia. *Archaeology in Oceania* 23, 81–8.

Nadel, D. and Zaidner, Y. 2002. Upper Pleistocene and mid-Holocene net sinkers from the Sea of Galilee, Israel. *Journal of the Israel Prehistoric Society* 32, 49–71.

Nordqvist, B. 1999. The chronology of the western Swedish Mesolithic and Late Palaeolithic: old answers in spite of new methods. In J. Boaz (ed.), *The Mesolithic of Central Scandinavia*, 235–54. Oslo: Universitets Oldsaksamling.

Orquera, L. A. and Piana, E. L. 1987. Human littoral adaption in the Beagle Channel region: the maximum possible age. *Quaternary of South America and Arctic Penninsula* 5, 133–62.

Orquera, L. A. and Piana, E. L. 1999a. *Arqueologia de la region del canal Beagle*. Buenos Aires: Sociedad Argentina de Antropologia.

Orquera, L. A. and Piana, E. L. 1999b. *La vida material y social de los Y'amana*. Buenos Aires: Eudeba-IFIC.

Orquera, L. A. and Piana, E. L. 2009. Sea nomads of the Beagle Channel in southernmost South America: over six thousand years of coastal adaption and stability. *Journal of Island and Coastal Archaeology* 4, 61–81.

Orr, P. C. 1968. *Prehistory of Santa Rosa Island*. Santa Barbara: Santa Barbara Museum of Natural History.

Parks, R. and Barrett, J. 2009. The zooarchaeology of Sand. In K. Hardy and C. R. Wickham-Jones (eds), *Mesolithic and later sites around the Inner Sound, Scotland: the work of the Scotland's First Settlers project 1998–2004*. Edinburgh: Scottish Archaeological Internet Reports 31.

Piana, E. 2005. Cetaceans and human beings at the uttermost part of America: a lasting relationship in Tierra del Fuego. In G. G. Monks (ed.), *The cultural importance of sea mammals*, 121–37. Oxford: Oxbow.

Piana, E. L., Alvarez, M. R., and Rúa, N. S. 2007. Sea nomads of the Beagle Channel and surrounding areas. In J. Rabassa and M. L. Borla (eds), *Antarctic Peninsula and Tierra del Fuego: 100 years of Swedish–Argentine scientific cooperation at the end of the world*, 195–214. London: Taylor & Francis.

Piana, E. L. and Orquera, L. A. 1998. Canoe fuegine: Etnografia storica e archeologia. L'esemplare del Museo L. Pigorini. *Bulletino di Paletnologia Italiana* 89 (Nuova serie: VII), 397–445.

Pickard, C. and Bonsall, C. 2007. Late Mesolithic coastal fishing practices: the evidence from Tybrind Vig, Denmark. In B. Hardh, K. Jennbert, and D. Olausson (eds), *On the road: studies in honour of Lars Larsson*, 176–83. Lund: Acta Archaeologica Lundensia 26.

Pickard, C. and Bonsall, C. 2009. Deep sea fishing in the European Mesolithic: fact or fantasy. *European Journal of Archaeology* 7, 273–90.

Pluciennik, M. 2008. The coastal Mesolithic of the European Mediterranean. In G. Bailey and P. Spikins (eds), *Mesolithic Europe*, 328–56. Cambridge: Cambridge University Press.

Punke, M. L. and Davis, L. G. 2006. Problems and prospects in the preservation of late Pleistocene cultural sites in southern Oregon coastal river valleys: implications for evaluating coastal migration routes. *Geoarchaeology* 21, 333–50.

Reide, F. 2009. Climate change, demography, and social relations: an alternative view of the Late Palaeolithic pioneer colonization of southern Scandinavia. In S. B. McCartan, R. Schulting, G. Warren, and P. C. Woodman (eds), *Mesolithic horizons: papers presented at the Seventh International Conference on the Mesolithic in Europe, Belfast 2005*, 3–10. Oxford: Oxbow.

Rick, T. C., Erlandson, J. M., and Vellanoweth, R. L. 2001. Paleocoastal marine fishing on the Pacific Coast of the Americas: perspectives from Daisy Cave, California. *American Antiquity* 66, 595–614.

Rick, T. C., Erlandson, J. M., Vellanoweth, R. L., and Braje, T. J. 2005. From Pleistocene mariners to complex hunter-gatherers: the archaeology of the California Channel Islands. *Journal of World Prehistory* 19, 169–228.

Rozoy, J.-G. 1978. *Les derniers chasseurs: L'Epipaléolithique en France et en Belgique*. Charleville: The Author.

Sarnthein, M., Kiefer, T., Grootes, P. M., Elderfield, H., and Erlenkeuser, H. 2006. Warmings in the far northwestern Pacific promoted pre-Clovis immigration to America during Heinrich Event 1. *Geology* 34, 141–4.

Saville, A. 2004. The material culture of Mesolithic Scotland. In A. Saville (ed.), *Mesolithic Scotland and its neighbours*, 185–220. Edinburgh: Society of Antiquaries of Scotland.

Saville, A. and Miket, R. 1994. An Corran, Staffin, Skye. *Discovery and Excavation in Scotland 1994*, 40–1.

Schmitt, L. 1995. The west Swedish Hensbacka: a maritime adaptation and a seasonal expression of the North-Central European Ahrensburgian? In A. Fischer (ed.), *Man and sea in the Mesolithic*, 161–70. Oxford: Oxbow.

Singer, R. and Wymer, J. 1982. *The Middle Stone Age at Klasies River Mouth in South Africa*. Chicago: University of Chicago Press.

Taute, W. 1968. *Der Stielspitzen-Gruppen in Nordlichen Mitteleuropa*. Koln-Graz: Fundamenta.

Verhart, L. 2008. New developments in the study of the Mesolithic of the Low Countries. In G. Bailey and P. Spikins (eds), *Mesolithic Europe*, 158–81. Cambridge: Cambridge University Press.

Vila, P. 1983. *Terra Amata and the Middle Pleistocene archaeological record of southern France*. Berkeley: University of California Press.

Walker, M. J. C. and Lowe, J. J. 1997. Vegetation and climate in Scotland, 13,000 to 7000 radiocarbon years ago. In J. E. Gordon (ed.), *Reflections on the Ice Age in Scotland*, 105–15. Edinburgh: Scottish Natural Heritage.

Warren, G. 2005. *Mesolithic lives in Scotland*. Stroud: Tempus.

Weninger, B., Schulting, R., Bradtmoller, M., Clare, L., Collard, M., Edinborough, K., Hilpert, J., Joris, O., Niekus, M., Rohling, E., and Wagner, B. 2008. The catastrophic final flooding of Doggerland by the Storrega Tsunami. *Documenta Praehistorica* 25, 1–13.

Wickham-Jones, C. R. 1990. *Rhum: Mesolithic and later sites at Kinloch: excavations 1984–86*. Edinburgh: Society of Antiquaries of Scotland.

Wickham-Jones, C. R. and Hardy, K. 2004. *Camas Daraich, a Mesolithic site at the Point of Sleat, Skye*. Edinburgh: Scottish Archaeological Internet Reports 12.

Woodman, P. C. 1985. *Excavations at Mount Sandel 1973–77*. Belfast: HMSO.
Woodman, P. C. 2008. Mind the gap or gaps? In J. J. Davenport, D. P. Sleeman, and P. C. Woodman (eds), *Mind the gap: postglacial colonization of Ireland*, 5–18. Dublin: Irish Naturalists Journal.
Woodman, P. C., Anderson, E., and Finlay, N. 1999. *Excavations at Ferriter's cove, 1983–95*. Dublin: Wordwell.
Wright, J. 2009. *The edible seashore*. London: Bloomsbury.
Yesner, D. R. 1996. Human adaptation at the Pleistocene–Holocene boundary (circa 13,000 to 8,000 BP) in eastern Beringia. In L. G. Straus, B. V. Eriksen, J. M. Erlandson, and D. R. Yesner (eds), *Humans at the end of the Ice Age: the archaeology of the Pleistocene–Holocene transition*, 253–76. New York: Plenum Press.
Yesner, D. R. 1997. From Beringia to Pacifica: early maritime adaptations in Alaska. Paper presented at the Annual Meeting of the American Association for the Advancement of Science, Seattle.
Yesner, D. R. 1998. Origins and development of maritime adaptations in the northwest Pacific region of North America: a zooarchaeological perspective. *Arctic Anthropology* 35, 204–22.
Zvelebil, M. 2008. Innovating hunter-gatherers: the Mesolithic in the Baltic. In G. Bailey and P. Spikins (eds), *Mesolithic Europe*, 18–59. Cambridge: Cambridge University Press.

CHAPTER 32

MORTUARY PRACTICES

LIV NILSSON STUTZ

DEATH is significant in any human society. As a social being disappears, roles, responsibilities, ownership, and relationships must be renegotiated. At the same time, a human cadaver emerges that requires action on behalf of the survivors. Mortuary practices, however variable they might be, always handle these two aspects of death—the social, metaphysical, and abstract as well as the practical and concrete. People respond to death with ritualized practices in an ultimate rite of passage that simultaneously passes the individual(s) from the world of the living to the world of the dead and produces a 'good' controllable death. The ways in which people treat their dead tell us a lot about their life and view of the world, their cosmology. When facing the crisis of death, people use ritualized practices to call on fundamental structures and ideas of who they are and why they are in the world. Death has to make sense, and the mortuary rituals are thus connected to the cosmology that structures and is structured by practices of the living. Cosmologies grow out of, and are reproduced through, the practical engagement with the world. It is through lived experience that people create their worlds as places, things, and practices, which are tied together in a symbolic web of associations. Mortuary practices are part of this, but so are more mundane routine activities such as hunting, foraging, tool making, eating, or simply movement through a domestic space. These practices constitute different experiences, which are tied together to a coherent, structured system, and it is likely that key cultural symbols and their relationships get reflected repeatedly from one set of practices to the next. Cosmology and beliefs about death and the dead are thus shaped and reinforced through practice, just like other socially defining cultural constructs such as gender. Through mortuary ritual, death is given a place within the cosmology, and simultaneously, social structure is reproduced (see Asad 1993; Bell 1992; De Boeck 1995; Parkin 1992).

In her book *Ritual theory, ritual practice*, Catherine Bell (1992) argues that it is through ritual practice that a structured world, a cosmology, is created. Following the logic of practice theory, the structures that give form to ritual may be said to structure and simultaneously be structured by actions. Every ritual becomes an event for the reconstruction of the social structure and the cosmology as a whole. It clarifies the relationships between humans and the world around them and between different individuals. It also gives form to central concerns about the place of humanity in the larger world, the place of life and death, the living and the dead. The structures thus generated are not completely rigid. It is possible to envision that mortuary rituals often would favour reproduction of existing relationships and practices, but because death, by definition, removes an active agent from a social configuration, the ritual also holds a dramatic potential for change. Every time the ritual is carried out, it is recreated, and in this process social change may emerge (see also Barth 1987).

Mortuary Practices as a Hunter-Gatherer Innovation

Mortuary practices appear to be fundamental in human life. Still, ethnographic accounts of hunter-gatherers have paid relatively little attention to the treatment of the dead and rather have focused on other rituals. So to what extent can we discuss mortuary practices as a hunter-gatherer innovation? One way to address this is to go back in time palaeoanthropologically and search for the emergence of these practices. Recently, Pettitt has argued that there may be indications that *Australopithecus afarensis* practised some kind of structured abandonment of the dead in a way that may be understood as mortuary behaviour (Pettitt 2010, 42–5). He points out that specific behaviours in connection to the loss of an individual can be found in living apes, including chimpanzees, and thus, it should not be ruled out for early hominids. While this behaviour may be understood as repetitive and even structured, it is not clear that it is *ritual*. We simply cannot know how these early hominids connected their practices to a more elaborate symbolic understanding of the world and a more general cosmology. In fact, it seems unlikely, given the lack of evidence for other complex symbolic communication at this period in human prehistory. Much later, in the Middle and Upper Palaeolithic, on the other hand, the archaeological record more clearly testifies to mortuary practices as culturally learned ritual responses to death in sites with Neanderthals, like Amud (Suzuki and Takai 1970), Tabun (Garrod and Bate 1937), Kebara (Bar Yosef et al. 1992), La Ferrassie (Peyrony 1934), Shanidar (Solecki 1972) and others, and in sites with anatomically modern humans, like Skhul (Garrod and Bate 1937), Qafzeh (Vandermeersch 1981), Dolni Vestonice (Svoboda 1988; 1991), and Predmosti (Svoboda 2008), to mention only a few. (For a more complete recent review of Palaeolithic burials see Pettitt 2010.) The formal disposal of the dead, often in places used repeatedly for this purpose, and with deposits of artefacts accompanying the dead, indicates that culturally reproduced mortuary practices were anchored in the cultures of these early hunter-gatherers.

The concentration of burials in designated places is something that emerges among hunter-gatherers as early as in the Middle Palaeolithic but the very large cemetery sites especially seem to mark a transition to a more *intense* use of place stressing continuity and perhaps territoriality. It is interesting to note that a similar development can be seen among prehistoric foragers in Siberia (Weber and Bettinger 2010), Japan (Habu 2004), and North America (in the Middle Archaic period, Emerson et al. 2009). In Siberia and Japan there are similarities to the European late Mesolithic–Neolithic transition, such as the adoption of pottery and the burial of dogs (Losey et al. 2011). In all of these regions, perhaps most importantly, we see a similar shift towards increased territoriality and aquatic resources. Epi-Palaeolithic hunter-gatherers in the Middle East show a similar—and even earlier, final Pleistocene—transition to intensification in mortuary practices, especially in the Natufian period (15,000–12,000 BP; Belfer-Cohen 1995; Bocquentin 2003; Boyd 1995; Byrd and Monahan 1995). Here, the transition to the repeated use of places as mortuary sites seems to be linked to a period of increased sedentism and an intensification of hunting and gathering, which involved over-exploitation of large game resources and increasing reliance on wild grains and lentils (Munro 2004; Stutz et al. 2009; Weiss et al. 2004).

Our understanding of the fossil and archaeological record thus seems to suggest a long-term gradual movement, from individual emotional, embodied responses to the deaths of close social relations towards culturally learned practices that are connected symbolically with a cosmology. It may be impossible to clearly pinpoint the emergence of the cultural practice as an innovation per se, and we may better understand it as a gradual process as part of human evolution; with the evolution of the capacity for culture in hominids, the inherent need to respond to the social loss, and the emergence of the cadaver became increasingly socially and symbolically structured. That being said, it is equally clear that Middle and Upper Palaeolithic mortuary practices, in all their diversity, emerge at a period in prehistory when all humans subsisted and lived as hunter-gatherers. Moreover, the most rich and varied information about hunter-gatherer mortuary practices may in fact be archaeological, rather than ethnographic. Through archaeology we can explore this evidence, not only to see the treatment of the dead per se, but also to analyse and interpret this treatment in order to get a glimpse of some of the structuring principles in past hunter-gatherer cosmologies.

The Mesolithic Hunter-Gatherer-Fishers Around the Baltic

One striking example of hunter-gatherer mortuary practices is provided by the Mesolithic around the Baltic Sea, sometimes viewed as an exception in Mesolithic Europe due its density of evidence for ritual landscapes and symbolic artefacts (Zvelebil 2008, 42). Northern Europe and the Baltic area offered a rich and varied environment for prehistoric hunter-gatherers. Due to isostatic changes and fluctuations, sea level was gradually changing along the coasts and throughout the archipelagos. The waters were rich in fish and seals, and people appear to have successfully exploited marine resources and skilfully travelled these waters (Pettersson and Wikell 2010). Throughout the inlands the Pleistocene tundra landscape gradually transformed into a dense Atlantic forest of oak, hazel, alder, and ash, populated by wild boar, red deer, roe deer, elk, beaver, and other mammal species, along with a range of bird species. The forest was broken up by marshes, rivers, and lakes supplementing what the forest could offer with fresh water resources, and providing waterways for communication and transportation. Beyond the economic landscape, the remains of settlements, ritual places, and burial grounds also testify to an enculturated landscape filled with meaning, history, and significance (Nilsson 2003). The places for the dead were part of this meaningful landscape.

The most striking mortuary remains that have come to dominate our archaeological understanding of the Mesolithic are the large formal disposal areas—or cemeteries—including Olenii Ostrov in Karelia (Gurina 1956), Zvejnieki in northern Latvia (Zagorskis 1987; see also

Zagorskis 2004), Moita de Sebastiao in the Muge estuary in Portugal (Ferembach 1974), the Breton sites of Téviec (Péquart and Péquart 1928) and Hoëdic (Péquart and Péquart 1954), the cemeteries in the Iron Gates gorge of the Danube (Radovanovic 1996), Vedbæk-Bøgebakken in Denmark (Albrethsen and Brinch Petersen 1977), and Skateholm in Sweden (Larsson 1988a). The sites are characterized by the concentration of large numbers of inhumed individuals, often but not always, in primary burials. We can debate whether the term cemetery is an appropriate one to use when discussing places in the landscape that have been used repeatedly for the disposal of dead bodies (see below). The number of individuals varies greatly in these so-called cemeteries (from 22 in Vedbæk-Bøgebakken to over 300 in Zvejnieki), and so does the spatial relation to other sites (including occupation sites), and it is reasonable to question whether these sites represent a single phenomenon. As we have seen, the concentration of burials in designated places is something that emerges among hunter-gatherers as early as in the Middle Palaeolithic and thus, it cannot be seen as an exclusively Mesolithic invention. However, as the phenomenon intensifies at the end of the Mesolithic in Europe, it is often seen as an indicator of increased social complexity preceding the transition to the Neolithic.

Social Relationships

While the large cemetery sites in Olenii Ostrov and Zvejnieki were known since the 1950s and 1960s respectively, it was the south Scandinavian sites Vedbæk-Bøgebakken (Albrethsen and Brinch Petersen 1977) and Skateholm (Larsson 1988a), excavated in the 1970s and 1980s respectively, that came to dominate the archaeological debate about Mesolithic mortuary practices. At Vedbæk-Bøgebakken in eastern Denmark an excavation in 1975 revealed 22 individuals buried in 17 graves. The dead were most commonly placed on their backs, most often alone but sometimes accompanied by one or more individuals. The dead were often interred with items such as flint tools, deer antlers, and perforated shells strung together like beads to decorate their bodies, often covered with ochre. The site, which also contained habitation layers, was only one of many Mesolithic sites distributed in the rich ecological niche of a prehistoric fjord landscape. A couple of years later (1980–5) the excavations at Skateholm on the south Swedish coast uncovered a complex of at least two cemeteries with 22 and 63 individuals respectively, along with associated occupation sites, all situated on small islands in a prehistoric lagoon. Here, the dead were buried in a variety of positions, but most often on the back with the limbs in extension. Crouched positions, sitting positions, and other more unusual positions—such as with the lower limbs crossed or on the stomach—are also represented. The dead were variably accompanied by ochre, diverse artefacts, deposits of food, and, in some cases, dogs. Another striking element present in the Skateholm cemeteries was the discovery of several individual interments including only dogs, who had received a burial similar to that of the humans.

The reasons for the prominent place of Vedbæk-Bøgebakken and Skateholm in archaeological discourse are probably many and complex, including language, contemporary politics, and so on, but the timing of the new discoveries, coinciding with a new theoretical focus on complex hunter-gatherers within processual archaeology, cannot be ignored. These sites testified to complex ritual practices and perhaps sedentism among affluent hunter-gatherers. The archaeological material lent itself extremely well to the ongoing debates within the field. Larsson has pointed out that the discoveries of the south Scandinavian sites were perceived as if a 'barrier to research of an almost mental nature had been broken through' (Larsson 1995, 95), and following these findings, the late Mesolithic was almost without reservation described as a period of complex social structures.

The social relationships between the people buried became the initial focus of the research, which also quickly came to include other Mesolithic cemeteries. These questions are central if we want to decode a Mesolithic cosmology, but while it seemed like a good place to start, it also soon became clear that it was more difficult than initially anticipated. The actual data are rich and varied, but still relatively limited, and evade all attempts at drawing uncontested conclusions. A lack of consensus is reflected in a debate that extended into the 1990s, and to some degree is still ongoing. The enquiries into the level of social complexity expressed in the cemetery practices came to focus on two dimensions of social relations. The first sought to elucidate different social roles through the distribution of burial goods focusing on horizontal differentiation, assigning different roles to different individuals according to age and gender (Albrethsen and Brinch Petersen 1977, 21; Kannegaard Nielsen and Brinch Petersen 1993, 79; Larsson 1989b, 215; Newell and Constandse 1988; 1994; Price 1985; 1991, 223; Tilley 1996, 40). A second focus was the search for evidence of vertical differentiation and differences in social status. While the evidence for horizontal differentiation has not been without calls for caution (see for example Meiklejohn et al. 2000; Nilsson Stutz 2003, 177ff; Schmidt 2001), the idea of differences expressed according to age and gender in Mesolithic society has not been as controversial as the discussion surrounding vertical differentiation. Some studies appear to indicate a ranked society (Newell and Constandse Westermann 1988; O'Shea and Zvelebil 1984); others, conversely, view the evidence as indicating egalitarian societies (Knutsson 1995) or follow the model of primitive communism (Tilley 1996). The most detailed study of social organization among Mesolithic hunters and gatherers is the work by O'Shea and Zvelebil on the Oleni Ostrov cemetery (O'Shea and Zvelebil 1984). In their study of the Karelian site they identified at least seven independent social variables (including age, sex, personal wealth, band membership, and specialized social positions such as shamans, office holders, and hunters), suggesting what appears to be a more complex social structure than had previously been recognized (but see the critique by Jacobs 1995).

There really is no consensus today about what the burials say about the social organization of late Mesolithic societies, but it became clear that it was no longer possible to sustain the idea that the hunter-gatherers of Mesolithic Europe were all composed of small-scale highly mobile bands. If anything, the critique that followed on from the debates regarding the studies of the cemeteries pushed complexity even further back in time. On the other hand there was no evidence to support the claim that the cemeteries reflected a Mesolithic society of inherited rank and status. Instead, not surprisingly, the burial practices seem to indicate a remarkable variability over time and across space.

Symbols and Cosmology

How people relate to each other is not confined to economic interaction; nor is it determined by normative social roles. In recent years questions concerning ritual, symbolism, and identity production on an individual level as well as on a collective level have emerged as central. The cemeteries have been approached as dense packets of ritual and symbolic practices. Larsson (1990) argued early on for the importance of considering the symbolic content of the burials. He argued that to understand the symbolic language of the mortuary practices, it is not enough to focus only on the burial itself, but on all of the practices relating to the ritual (Larsson 1990, 154). At Skateholm, where careful excavation revealed traces of a range of activities which may have been part of the ritual, the imagery is rich and varied, including fires on the graves, a structure that may have been used to prepare the body, tool production, eating around the grave, and even shooting into it at one occasion, along with evidence of bone removal (Larsson 1988b; 1990). Larsson (1990, 153) argues that the symbolic language may have been only partially understood by the people who took part in these activities, a position that articulates well with a practice-theory perspective on ritual (Bell 1992). It is through the active participation in the ritual and the active manipulation of symbols that the cosmology is recreated, rather than through reflection over the assigned meaning to these actions, which may be fluid or even personal.

The most ambitious attempt to reconstruct a Mesolithic cosmology including the use of symbols has been proposed by Zvelebil, who does not consider the burial record alone but takes a wide scope, examining rock art, artefacts, and historic and ethnographic evidence (Zvelebil 1993; 1996; 1998; 2008). Drawing explicitly on ethnographic analogies with hunter-gatherer communities in north-east Eurasia, Zvelebil has proposed a whole cosmology including 'environmental variables, seasonal food procurement regimes, and cosmological beliefs' (Zvelebil 2008) that would have been repeatedly 'interpreted and reinterpreted through the agency of individuals, communities, and outside groups linked by contact and exchange' (Zvelebil 2008, 43). The model includes provisions for the three-tiered world (a world view encompassing sky, earth, and underworld), the supernatural world, the fundamental principle of reciprocity, the conception of souls, and the central role of the shaman (Zvelebil 2008, 43). Some animals, such as elk, bear, and waterfowl, are given a special role as guardians of other animals or as messengers between the human world and the non-terrestrial world. The shaman, as a liminal and transgressing being is often linked to these specific animals as well. Zvelebil (2008) has pointed out the symbolic connections between this cosmology and the mortuary practices among the late Mesolithic hunter-gatherers around the Baltic, especially in the presence of zoomorphic artefacts such as bear- or elk-headed effigies, or representations of waterfowl or animal bones found in burial contexts, such as the swan's wing in grave eight in Vedbæk-Bøgebakken (Albrethsen and Brinch Petersen 1977). He also applies the concept of 'burial beyond the water' to describe the cultural ritual geography of some of the cemeteries. Shaman burials have been identified in Oleni Ostrov (O'Shea and Zvelebil 1984), Skateholm (Schmidt 2000; Strassburg 2000), Vedbæk (Meiklejohn et al. 2000; Zvelebil 2008, 50), Zvejnieki (Zagorska 2000; 2001; Zagorska and Lougas 2000), Janislawice in Poland and Dounkalnis in Lithuania (Zvelebil 2008, 50), and in Bad Durrenberg in Germany (Porr and Alt 2006). Recently, a Natufian burial in Israel has been interpreted as a shaman burial (Grosman et al. 2008). The idea of the shaman as a powerful, transgressing, and liminal figure with connections to the animal world and the supernatural realm, often through induced states of trance, fits into the model proposed by Zvelebil. The burials interpreted as shaman burials are characterized by being extraordinary in one way or another. The body may be placed in an unusual position, as with the shaft burials at Oleni Ostrov (O'Shea and Zvelebil 1984) or the sitting burials at Skateholm (Schmidt 2001), or the presence of unusual and rich headdresses and face coverings as in Zvejnieki (Zagorska 2000; 2001; Zagorska and Lougas 2000), or simply unusual, symbolic, and even exceptionally rich grave goods. Zvelebil has pointed out that headgear and masks form an essential part of the shaman's attire and the ethnographic record indicates that they would usually be buried in them (Zvelebil 2008, 51). In the case of the burial at Bad Durrenberg, the interpretation relies on a skull pathology indicating that the individual may have been prone to seizures, which may have been viewed as part of a trance-like state (Porr and Alt 2006).

Another trait that is often presented is the transgression of gender norms in the grave, either by a combination of grave goods that do not appear to correspond to the biological sex of the individual, or a combination of artefacts usually associated with both men and women and a sexually ambiguous skeletal morphology as in grave XV in Skateholm (Schmidt 2000). These ideas are fascinating, especially when viewed along with other evidence of shamanism expressed in the rock art (Zvelebil 2008, 48ff), but if we agree with Schmidt (2001) that sexual identity indeed may have been fluid among these hunter-gatherer groups, how then do we determine what breaks away from the norm? Another challenge to the model is the fact that the world of the hunter-gatherers around the Baltic shifted over centuries and millennia and eventually came to be rather different from that of the contemporary and historic groups used as analogies. Perhaps Zvelebil's model—based largely on ethnographic studies of reindeer-focused hunter-gatherers in steppic or taiga-like landscapes—would be an even better fit for the Mesolithic materials in the Baikal area.

In southern Scandinavia and on the eastern shores of the Baltic the open tundra landscape gave way to a dense climax forest inhabited by animals such as deer and wild boar, rather than by migrating herds of reindeer. It is not unreasonable to expect that some of the cosmology would reflect these changes, perhaps reflecting concerns with the density of the forest and the abundance of different animal species, and inscribing waterways and paths through dense forest with significance and history. It is also possible that some of these old symbols would continue to be used effectively or just slightly changed. Perhaps elk and bear were replaced by deer and wild boar as central partners in the relationship between hunter and prey. The strong seasonality of the waterfowl, and its transitional character (inhabiting water, earth, and sky), might still have been used practically within this new early Holocene world. The role of shaman, or shaman-like individuals, may also be understood as a phenomenon which remained relevant, but one which also changed through time.

Animals and Humans

The work proposed above is impressive in its scope and conclusions. The notion of the transitioning being, the fluid identity as part of this overall cosmology, may have been given other forms in the cemeteries and may not necessarily have been confined to humans. The dog burials in Skateholm invite us to reflect about the boundaries between the species. Larsson has pointed out that the dogs appear to have received varying treatment after death. Some were killed and placed in the grave with humans while others have been interred in individual graves with ochre and grave goods, included in the symbolic language of the human burial. Larsson (1990, 157) has suggested that they may have been interred as proxies of their master. It is also possible that personhood was not limited to humanity but extended to other species as well—as suggested by Fowler (2004). In fact, the noted variability may reflect the variation in the treatment of the humans on the site, where some have received rich grave goods, while others are buried in a way that could suggest a kind of dehumanization, as for example in the partially disarticulated human remains in one of the graves.

Other more discrete practices might reveal other forms of interspecies relations. The buried humans are often associated with animal remains in different forms. Among the more spectacular examples are the deer antlers found in several burials in Skateholm and Vedbæk. Animal parts are also used extensively as symbols in combination with the human body, either as beads or other forms of bodily adornment (e.g. boar tusks and strands of deer teeth possibly still adhering to the soft tissues of the gums at Skateholm, shells at Vedbæk, perforated and worked beads made from various animal species at Zvejnieki) or as unmodified objects placed with the dead human body at the time of burial. In her analysis of Star Carr, Conneller (2004) has proposed that faunal remains, and the objects made from them, may have retained some of their animality and acted as mediators, blurring the boundaries between the human and animal body. At Starr Carr she noted a privileged role for deer antlers (Conneller 2004), and it is possible that similar relationships are expressed in the burials, blurring the human and animal identity at death. This manipulation of animal bones associated to the living and the dead body may indicate a fluidity across species boundaries that was not limited to especially powerful individuals like shamans, but more generally part of the hunter-gatherer cosmology.

Larsson has explored the symbolic role of animal remains in a study of the beads made from animal teeth at Zvejnieki (L. Larsson 2006; 2009). He proposes that the teeth embodied a notion of domestication, having been shaped from their natural form into artefacts decorating the bodies of the living and dead. Being domesticated, they still retained some of their initial wild qualities, acting as mediators between the animal and human world (L. Larsson 2009, 177). A detailed study of the wear, which appears to have been highly variable, seems to indicate that the criteria for wearing certain beads were probably complex and may reflect transmission of objects from one generation to the next, with the acquisition of beads at specific events in the individual life history (L. Larsson 2009, 186). This practice would constantly link humans to animals throughout their lives, marking significant events in human biographies, and inscribing the animal remains with human and personal history. Mannermaa's work on bird remains from the same site reveals interesting symbolic strategies for the use of the wings of the jay for specific individuals, as strong and visible symbols, possibly associated with totemism (Mannermaa 2008).

Dealing with the Dead Body

While there appears to be evidence of a certain fluidity between humans and animals, human burials still seem to hold a special place in the Mesolithic world. The treatment of the dead human body and its interment seems significantly different from how other beings are treated after death. The handling of the human cadaver constitutes a recurrent and universal theme in mortuary practices. Through the treatment of the human cadaver the survivors control death with the aim of producing a death that is socially acceptable and holds a place within the general cosmology. The mortuary ritual redefines the cadaver, a process that allows for the mourners to separate from the dead, redefining the relationship between the body and soul, between the dead and the living (Nilsson Stutz 2003). What images of death were produced during these rituals? What did a 'good death' during the Mesolithic look like?

To find an answer to these questions I have conducted a series of analyses to reconstruct in detail the handling of the body at Skateholm (Nilsson 1998; Nilsson Stutz 2003), Vedbæk

(Nilsson Stutz 2003), and to a more limited extent at Zvejnieki (Nilsson Stutz 2006; Nilsson Stutz et al. 2008). The analyses revealed that at the southern Scandinavian sites the maintenance of the integrity of the body appears to have been a central concern, as all bodies, with a few exceptions, were buried intact in filled-in graves, with few disturbances occurring after the interment. The last image of the dead was lifelike, intact, and often assuming a lifelike position. When more than one individual was buried in the same feature, the deposited bodies were arranged to relate to each other by looking at each other or holding each other. In some cases the body appears to have been shielded from the surrounding sediment through wrappings or uplifted by being placed on a small platform in the feature (Nilsson Stutz 2003). This treatment of the dead bodies is radically different from how a hunter would treat the dead body of an animal. People are clearly different, set apart in life and death, albeit through practices that appear sometimes to include certain animals. This structuring practice goes to the heart of manifesting the place of humankind in the world. Mortuary practices become effective ways to reproduce both collective and individual identity. Humanity is not just a matter of the living but also reproduced in death. From this perspective we understand what an effective tool for social reproduction and control the rituals of death can be. To be excluded from this final treatment might mean being excluded from humanity.

However, variation existed. Several cremations have been found both at Skateholm and in the Vedbæk area, and in Skateholm an incomplete and partially disarticulated human was buried, probably contained in a sack or other container. We can ask what this variation means. In the case of the incomplete body, the burial might reflect a strategy to dehumanize the individual after death, but it is also possible to view it as a strategy to spare the onlookers from the horrors of a non-normative, bad death (Nilsson Stutz 2003, 348). While decomposition and decay were hidden in the production of death at these cemeteries, the processes were clearly not unknown. Some burials have clearly been destroyed in the Mesolithic period and in at least one case the analysis could reveal how the processes of decomposition were exploited in a premeditated way to extract isolated bones from a burial with minimal disturbance to the rest of the body (Nilsson Stutz 2003, 310ff). We shall return to these manipulations of the natural processes of decomposition, and of the dead human body itself, below.

The Cemetery Phenomenon

The cemeteries generate questions about the significance of the place for the dead in general. What does this cluster of the dead really mean, and what does it mean that this phenomenon appears to intensify towards the end of the Mesolithic? In accordance with the dominating processual paradigm, the cemeteries were initially viewed as an indicator of ancestral claim to territory (following the model of hypothesis eight proposed by Saxe 1970), thus indicating some form of pre-agricultural sedentism and perhaps reflecting population pressure on food resources. From this perspective the cemeteries were studied to understand their systemic connection to demographic and economic conditions (Chapman 1981; Clark and Neeley 1987; Price 1985, 355; 1991, 224; Price et al. 1995, 108; Zvelebil and Dolukhanov 1991, 263). These studies often articulate with an idea that the hunter-gatherers at the end of the Mesolithic were becoming increasingly complex, and the narrative fits within the greater story of transition from the Mesolithic to the Neolithic.

However, this impression of intensification may be somewhat misleading. It has been pointed out by Brinch Petersen and Meiklejohn that many other coastal sites with a high concentration of burials may have existed in the earlier phases of the Mesolithic, sites that today would be under water as a result of the rising of the sea levels (Brinch Petersen and Meiklejohn in press). They have also pointed out that the cemetery concept may not be the correct way to understand a place like Vedbæk-Bøgebakken, and they propose that the site must be seen as an occupation site including burials (Brinch Petersen and Meiklejohn in press; see also Kannegard Nielsen and Brinch Petersen 1993), probably part of a much more complex web of sites locally spread though the fjord landscape (see also Conneller 2013). These sites were simply places where people lived and buried their dead in a way that erased the distinction between the world of the living and the world of the dead, but the situation may well be different in the larger sites, like Zvejnieki, Oleni Ostrov, and perhaps even Skateholm.

The significance of a place can take other forms than as a marker of ownership and territoriality (Nilsson Stutz 2003, 189). More recently, this idea has been revisited from a perspective stressing not so much the notion of territoriality as the importance of place in a cultural landscape. Larsson has discussed the importance of placing the dead so close to the living, pointing out that the proximity may have acted as a constant reminder to the living—a special mutual proximity between living and dead including ancestors (Larsson 1990, 154; see also Nilsson Stutz 2005). In his work on shell middens, Thorpe has proposed the idea that the place for the dead can be seen as a focal point in a social landscape and that shell middens over time may have become monuments in the landscape (Thorpe 1996, 82; see also Pollard 2000). While monumentality *sensu stricto* is absent from the Mesolithic cemetery sites, the notion of a gradual accumulation of significance and memory bound to the site through ritualized practice remains important and applicable. Here, we can start to see how—in some privileged places like Oleni Ostrov, Skateholm, and Zvejnieki—the presence of the dead could create nodes in the landscape that were structured as transition places between the world of the living and the world of the dead (articulating with the transitory components of other aspects in the cosmology discussed above). Perhaps these places, over time, emerged as permanent places for the dead. The notion of persistent, liminal places in the landscape thus seems to emerge among these early Holocene hunter-gatherers as an innovation.

Where are the Others?

While the cemeteries are fascinating, they do not provide a full picture of how the remains of the dead were handled during the Mesolithic. Knutsson (1995) and Strassburg (2000) have both pointed out that if we take into consideration the number of individuals buried at 'cemeteries' like Skateholm and Vedbæk-Bøgebakken and the time period during which these sites were used, the individuals buried there represent only a small fragment of a natural population. What does the selection for burials in these places mean? Strassburg presented the thought-provoking idea that the cemeteries that we, consciously or not, tend to view as the norm, are actually the exception (Strassburg 2000). Only special people would be buried here, Strassburg suggests. He argues that it was the place for the rejected, the outcasts from society. Knutsson does not question the normative ideas surrounding these burials to the same extent, but uses the low absolute number of known burials to argue for a continued nomadic way of life, challenging the idea of these groups as sedentary or semi-sedentary.

This idea would also correspond to the high frequency of sites with a single or only a few burials. This model would definitively affect the way we view the Mesolithic landscape and the permanence with which we view these sites. Besides contributing to a potential re-evaluation of the sites themselves, these critiques also lead us to consider the following question: if the individuals buried at the cemeteries are but a fragment of the population, where is everybody else?

Of course, it is very likely that many additional cemetery sites are destroyed or not yet identified, an inescapable archaeological dilemma. The many sites with a single or just a few burials indicate that other forms of disposal existed. It is interesting to consider the possibility that there were other ways of disposing of the dead. Variation in the treatment of the dead has been identified at the sites themselves. In the Vedbæk area several cremations have been identified, and Skateholm contains three cremations and possibly a ritual structure for the post-mortem preparation of bodies (Larsson 1988b). Perhaps the preparations entailed more than just the arrangements of the inhumations that we know from the archaeological record. More widespread use of cremation with following dispersal of the remains is a possibility to consider here. It may seem that cremation and inhumation express radically different attitudes towards the dead body, but this difference may be overstated. While cremation radically transforms the body, it circumvents exposure to decomposition and putrefaction. But so does primary inhumation. We also know that the two practices coexist comfortably in our own culture. Other possible treatments of the body that would have left meagre traces in the archaeological record are exposure (as suggested by Gray Jones 2010) or water burials, for which there may be evidence in Møllegabet in Denmark (Grøn and Skaarup 1993). The variation of the treatment of the dead that can be seen at the cemetery sites thus seems to expand outside this realm and perhaps it characterizes in a more general way the human interaction with their dead throughout the period.

An increased attention to disarticulated human remains, sometimes found in what is not clearly a burial context (see for example Larsson et al. 1981), along with recent finds of structured depositions of human remains throughout the Mesolithic period, invites us to reassess our understanding of the place of the dead in the Mesolithic world. Amy Gray Jones's work on several sites with disarticulated human remains reveals that the image we have of the treatment of the dead as characterized by the primary burial in cemeteries may in fact be misleading. She has shown how extensive interaction with the dead body through disarticulation (Gray Jones 2008; 2010) and defleshing (Gray Jones 2010) seems to have been a part of the treatment of the dead, sometimes coexisting at the same sites with primary inhumation. Gray Jones (2008) has suggested that the variation could be due to difference in identity or perhaps snapshots of different phases of the same process of reduction. These studies challenge the view previously held by many authors, including myself, who have tended to focus on the inhumations as normative in the Mesolithic. When trying to understand these practices, the similarity with the hunters' treatment of animal bodies comes to mind. Does this indicate that this practice contributed to dehumanizing some of the dead, or should we view this as a practice that contributed to establish a connection with the animal world on a spiritual level? For the Baltic area in particular, it is also interesting to note that this practice of fragmentation, burning, and defleshing reoccurs in the Neolithic period within the coastal-bound hunter-gatherer-fisher Pitted Ware Culture, discussed recently by Åsa Larsson (Å. Larsson 2009).

Some of the evidence suggests that human bodies were fragmented in what appear to be premeditated and highly significant ways. Above, I mentioned the evidence at Skateholm for premeditated removal of human bones from the burial after the process of decomposition was far advanced. The inner tension within a system that on the one hand seems to hide decomposition, and on the other, uses the understanding and knowledge of it to produce human remains that return to the world of the living may indeed have been much stronger than the remains at the great cemeteries indicate. Recent discoveries at Kanaljorden in Motala (central Sweden) of a series of deposited human crania in water (Hallgren and Arnberg 2010) may in fact be indicative of much more complex and varying practices than has previously been recognized. Similar deposits of human remains have been found in Hindby Fen in southern Sweden as part of a long-lasting tradition of structured depositions starting in the late Mesolithic (Berggren 2010). Perhaps these deposits of human remains across the landscape contributed to inscribing it with significance and meaning, as suggested by Parkin (1992), creating nodes of meaning, different perhaps from that of the cemeteries and primary burials. Cauwe has also pointed out the fact that, even by the early phases of the Mesolithic, handling of human remains was complex and intense, reflected by the processing of bodies and fragmentation of human remains in sites such as Grotte de Margeaux and Abri de Autours in Belgium (Cauwe 1998; 2001). This tradition may in fact coexist along with the cemetery practices. Besides introducing a significant variation in the treatment of the dead in the Mesolithic, it also invites us to reflect over what we have tended to view as shifts in the attitudes to the dead between hunter-gatherers and farmers.

Conclusion—A World Created

Archaeological traces of the treatment of the dead provide a privileged window into past people's worlds. Through a fragmented archaeological record, the remains of the dead tell a story about life and death, about humanity and the place in the world that they constructed. But as soon as we think we have a grip on the story, it changes. The rich remains in northern Europe have, over decades, provided foundations for our understanding of Mesolithic life and lived experience. What seems to reveal itself is a landscape filled with significance, inscribed into a cosmology where humans and animals interact, perhaps sometimes changing places and roles. The production of death, the handling of the cadaver, the staging and transformation of the corpse and its incorporation into the ground created places of significance, memory, and myth of which we can only hear a whisper. But while the stories told are long forgotten, we can still connect to the experience of death, loss, and the need to make sense of death that we as humans share across millennia.

Acknowledgements

I want to extend my gratitude to Amy Gray Jones for generously sharing unpublished conference presentations of her important and fascinating work, and to Fredrik Hallgren for discussing the unpublished and highly interesting Kanaljorden finds with me. I am also grateful for the constructive comments made by an anonymous reviewer.

References

Albrethsen, S. E. and Brinch Petersen, E. 1977. Excavation of a Mesolithic cemetery at Vedbaek, Denmark. *Acta Archaeologica* 47, 9–54.

Asad, T. 1993. *Genealogies of religion: discipline and reasons of power in Christianity and Islam*. Baltimore: Johns Hopkins University Press.

Barth, F. 1987. *Cosmologies in the making: a generative approach to cultural variation in Inner New Guinea*. Cambridge: Cambridge University Press.

Bar-Yosef, O., Vandermeersch, B., Arensburg, B., Belfer-Cohen, A., and Goldberg, P. 1992. The excavations in Kebara Cave, Mt Carmel. *Current Anthropology* 33, 497–550.

Belfer-Cohen, A. 1995. Rethinking social stratification in the Natufian culture: the evidence from burials. In S. Campbell and A. Green (eds), *The archaeology of death in the ancient Near East*, 9–16. Oxford: Oxbow.

Bell, C. 1992. *Ritual theory, ritual practice*. Oxford: Oxford University Press.

Berggren, Å. 2010. *Med kärret som källa—om begreppen offer och ritual inom arkeologin*. Lund: Nordic Academic Press.

Bocquentin, F. 2003. Pratiques funéraires, paramètres biologiques et identités culturelles au Natoufien: une analyse archéo-anthropologique. PhD thesis. Université Bordeaux.

Boyd, B. 1995. Houses and hearths, pits and burials: Natufian mortuary practices at Mallaha (Eynan), Upper Jordan Valley. In S. Campbell and A. Green (eds), *The archaeology of death in the ancient Near East*, 17–23. Oxford: Oxbow.

Brinch Petersen, E. and Meiklejohn, C. in press. Paradigm lost? Intensification, sedentism and burial practice in southern Scandinavia: some questions and suggestions. In L. Janik, S. Kaner, and P. Rowley-Conwy (eds), *From Jomon to Star Carr: Holocene hunters and gatherers in temperate Eurasia*.

Byrd, B. F. and Monahan, C. M. 1995. Death, mortuary ritual, and Natufian social structure. *Journal of Anthropological Archaeology* 14, 251–87.

Cauwe, N. 1998. Sépultures collectives du Mésolithique au Néolithique. In J. Guilaine (ed.), *Sépultures d'Occident et génèse des mégalithismes, 9000–3500 avant notre ère*, 11–24. Paris: Éditions Errance.

Cauwe, N. 2001. Skeletons in motion, ancestors in action: early Mesolithic collective tombs in southern Belgium. *Cambridge Archaeological Journal* 11, 147–63.

Chapman, R. 1981. The emergence of formal disposal areas and the 'problem' megalithic tombs in prehistoric Europe. In R. Chapman, I. Kinnes, and K. Randsborg (eds), *The archaeology of death*, 71–81. Cambridge: Cambridge University Press.

Clark, G. A. and Neeley, M. 1987. Social differentiation in European Mesolithic burial data. In P. Rowley-Conwy, M. Zvelebil, and H. P. Blankholm (eds), *Mesolithic northwest Europe: recent trends*, 121–7. Sheffield: Department of Archaeology and Prehistory, University of Sheffield.

Conneller, C. 2004. Becoming deer: corporeal transformations at Star Carr. *Archaeological Dialogues* 11, 37–56.

Conneller, C. 2013. Power and society: Mesolithic Europe. In L. Nilsson Stutz and S. Tarlow (eds), *Handbook of the archaeology of death and burial*, 347–58. Oxford: Oxford University Press.

De Boeck, F. 1995. Bodies of remembrance: knowledge, experience and the growing of memory in Llunda ritual performance. In G. Thines and L. de Heusch (eds), *Rites et ritualisation*. Paris: Librairie Philosophique J. Vrin.

Emerson, T. E., McElrath, D. L., and Fortier, A. C. (eds) 2009. *Archaic societies: diversity and complexity across the Midcontinent*. Albany: State University of New York Press.

Ferembach, D. 1974. *Le gisement mesolithique de Moita de Sebastiao, Muge, Portugal*. Lisbon: Direcçáo-Geral dos Assuntos Culturais.

Fowler, C. 2004. *The archaeology of personhood: an anthropological approach*. London: Routledge.

Garrod, D. A. E. and Bate, D. M. A. 1937. *The Stone Age of Mount Carmel. Vol. 1. Excavations and the Wadi-el-Mughara*. Oxford: Clarendon Press.

Gray Jones, A. 2008. Mesolithic identities: (dis)articulated through mortuary practice. Paper presented at the 6th World Archaeological Congress, Dublin, Ireland, July.

Gray Jones, A. 2010. The 'loose human bone' phenomenon: complexity in Mesolithic mortuary practice in north-west Europe. Paper presented at the Mesolithic in Europe conference, Santander, Spain, September.

Grøn, O. and Skaarup, J. 1993. Møllegabet II: a submerged Mesolithic site and a boat burial from Ærø. *Journal of Danish Archaeology* 10, 38–50.

Grosman, L., Munro, N., and Belfer-Cohen, A. 2008. A 12,000-year-old Shaman burial from the southern Levant (Israel). *Proceedings of the National Academy of Sciences USA* 105, 17665–9.

Gurina, N. 1956. Oleneostrovski mogilnik. *Materialy i issledovaniya po archeologii SSSR* 47.

Habu, J. 2004. *Ancient Jomon of Japan*. Berkeley: University of California Press.

Hallgren, F. and Arnberg, A. 2010. Kanaljorden, en mesolitisk boplats. Published online: http://www.kmmd.se/Kanaljorden-Motala/

Jacobs, K. 1995. Returning to Oleniʼostrov: social, economic, and skeletal dimensions of a boreal forest Mesolithic cemetery. *Journal of Anthropological Archaeology* 14, 359–403.

Kannegaard Nielsen, E. and Brinch Petersen, E. 1993. Grave, mennesker og hunde. In S. Hvass and B. Storgaard (eds), *Da klinger i muld... 25 års arkeologi i Danmark*, 76–81. Aarhus: Aarhus Universitets Forlag.

Knutsson, H. 1995. *Slutvandrat? Aspekter på övergången från rörlig till bofast tillvaro*. Uppsala: Societatis Archaeologica Upsalensis, AUN 20.

Larsson, Å. 2009. *Breaking and making bodies and pots: material and ritual practices in the third Millennium BC*. Uppsala: AUN.

Larsson, L. (ed.) 1988a. *The Skateholm project I. Man and environment*. Lund: Regiae Societatis Humaniorum Litterarum Lundensis LXXIX.

Larsson, L. 1988b. Dödshus, djurkäkar och stenyxor. Några reflektioner kring senmesolitiskt gravskick. In K. Jennbert, E. Iregren, and L. Larsson (eds), *Gravskick och gravdata*, 63–72. Lund: University of Lund, Institute of Archaeology.

Larsson, L. 1989. Ethnicity and traditions in Mesolithic mortuary practices in southern Scandinavia. In S. Shennan (ed.), *Archaeological approaches to cultural identity*, 210–18. Southampton: One World Archaeology.

Larsson, L. 1990. Dogs in fraction—symbols in action. In P. Vermeersch and P. Van Peer (eds), *Contribution to the Mesolithic in Europe. Papers presented at the fourth international symposium 'The Mesolithic in Europe', Leuven 1990*, 153–60. Leuven: Leuven University Press.

Larsson, L. 1995. Man and sea in southern Scandinavia during the Late Mesolithic: the role of cemeteries in the view of society. In A. Fisher (ed.), *Man and sea in the Mesolithic: coastal settlement above and below present sea level. Proceedings of the international symposium, Kallundborg, Denmark 1993*, 95–104. Oxford: Oxbow.

Larsson, L. 2006. Tooth for a tooth for a grave: tooth ornaments from the graves at the cemetery of Zvejnieki. In L. Larsson and I. Zagorska (eds), *Back to the origin: new research in the Mesolithic-Neolithic Zvejnieki cemetery and environment, northern Latvia*, 253–87. Stockholm: Almqvist and Wiksell.

Larsson, L. 2009. Tänder tänder tankar. In F. Ekengren and L. Nilsson Stutz (eds), *I tillvarons gränsland. Tvärvetenskapliga perspektiv på kroppen mellan liv och död*, 174–96. Lund: Acta Archaeologica Lundensia.

Larsson, L., Meiklejohn, C., and Newell, R. R. 1981. Human skeletal material from the Mesolithic site of Ageröd I: HC, Scania, southern Sweden. *Fornvännen* 76, 161–8.

Losey, R. J., Bazaliiskii, V. I., Garvie-Lok, S., Germonpré, M., and Leonard, J. A. 2011. Canids as persons: early Neolithic dog and wolf burials, Cis-Baikal, Siberia, *Journal of Anthropological Archaeology* 30, 174–89.

Mannermaa, K. 2008. Birds and burials at Ajvide (Gotland, Sweden) and Zvejnieki (Latvia) about 8000–3900 BP. *Journal of Anthropological Archaeology* 27, 201–25.

Meiklejohn, C., Brinch Petersen, E., and Alexandersen, V. 2000. The anthropology and archaeology of Mesolithic gender in the western Baltic. In M. Donald and L. Hurcombe (eds), *Gender and material culture in archaeological perspective*, 222–37. New York: St. Martin's Press.

Munro, N. D. 2004. Zooarchaeological measures of hunting pressure and occupation intensity in the Natufian. *Current Anthropology* 45, 5–34.

Newell, R. R. and Constandse Westermann, T. S. 1988. The significance of Skateholm I and Skateholm II to the Mesolithic of western Europe. In L. Larsson (ed.), *The Skateholm Project I. Man and environment*, 164–74. Lund: Regiae Societatis Humaniorum Litterarum Lundensis LXXIX.

Newell, R. R. and Constandse Westermann, T. S. 1994. Balancing probabilities: integrating the archaeological and physical anthropological approaches to the identification of sex in western European Mesolithic societies. In M. Di Bacco, E. Pacciani, and S. Borgogniani Tarli (eds), *Statistical tools in human biology: proceedings of the 17th course of the International School of Mathematics*, 215–30. River Edge: World Scientific.

Nilsson, B. 2003. Sorbus aucuparia or extremely red rowanberries? Some naïve reflections on archaeology, palaeoecology, and the non-scientific dimensions of a scientific landscape. In L. Larsson, K. Kindgren, K. Knutsson, D. Loeffler, and A. Åkerlund (eds), *Mesolithic on the move*, 145–8. Oxford: Oxbow.

Nilsson, L. 1998. Dynamic cadavers: a field-anthropological analysis of the Skateholm II burials. *Lund Archaeological Review* 4, 5–17.

Nilsson Stutz, L. 2003. *Embodied rituals and ritualized bodies: tracing ritual practices in late Mesolithic burials*. Stockholm: Almqvist and Wiksell.

Nilsson Stutz, L. 2005. Minnet och glömskan av de döda i Skateholm. In S. Arvidsson, Å. Berggren, and A.-S. Hållands (eds), *Minne och Myt*, 81–98. Lund: Nordic Academic Press.

Nilsson Stutz, L. 2006. Unwrapping the dead: searching for evidence of wrappings in the mortuary practices at Zvejnieki. In L. Larsson and I. Zagorska (eds), *Back to the origin: new research in the Mesolithic-Neolithic Zvejnieki cemetery and environment, northern Latvia*. 217–33. Stockholm: Almqvist and Wiksell.

Nilsson Stutz, L., Larsson, L., and Zagorska, I. 2008. More burials at Zvejnieki: preliminary results from the 2007 excavation. *Mesolithic Miscellany* 19, 12–16.

O'Shea, J. and Zvelebil, M. 1984. Olenostrovski mogilnik: reconstructing the social and economic organization of prehistoric foragers in northern Russia. *Journal of Anthropological Archaeology* 3, 1–40.

Parkin, D. 1992. Ritual as spatial direction and bodily division. In D. de Coppet (ed.), *Understanding rituals*, 11–25. London: Routledge.

Péquart, M. and Péquart, S. 1928. Un gisement mésolithique en Bretagne. *L'Anthropologie* 38, 479–93.

Péquart, M. and Péquart, S. 1954. *Hoedic, deuxieme station-necropole du mesolithique cotier armoricain*. Anvers: Sikkel.

Pettersson, M. and Wikell, R. 2010. Coastal people ride seaworthy beautiful boats. In Å. M. Larsson and L. Papmehl-Dufay (eds.), *Uniting Sea II: Stone Age societies in the Baltic Sea region*. OPIA 51. Uppsala: Uppsala University Press.

Pettitt, P. 2010. *The Palaeolithic origins of human burial*. New York: Taylor & Francis.

Peyrony, D. 1934. La Ferrassie. Moustérien—Périgordien—Aurignacien. *Préhistoire* 3, 1–92.

Pollard, J. 2000. Ancestral places in the Mesolithic landscape. *Archaeological Review from Cambridge* 17, 123–38.

Porr, M. and Alt, K. W. 2006. The burial of Bad Durrenberg, central Germany: osteopathology and osteoarchaeology of a late Mesolithic shaman's grave. *International Journal of Osteoarchaeology* 16, 395–406.

Price, D. 1985. Affluent foragers of Mesolithic southern Scandinavia. In D. Price and J. A. Brown (eds), *Prehistoric hunters-gatherers: the emergence of cultural complexity*, 341–63. London: Academic Press.

Price, D. 1991. The Mesolithic of northern Europe. *Annual Review of Anthropology* 20, 211–33.

Price, D. and Brown, J. A. 1985. Aspects of hunter-gatherer complexity. In D. Price and J. A. Brown (eds.), *Prehistoric hunter-gatherers: the emergence of cultural complexity*. London: Academic Press.

Price, D., Gebauer, A. B., and Keeley, L. H. 1995. The spread of farming into Europe north of the Alps. In D. Price and A. B. Gebauer (eds), *Last hunters, first farmers: new perspectives on the prehistoric transition to agriculture*, 95–126. Santa Fe: School of American Research Advanced Seminar Press.

Radovanovic, I. 1996. *The Iron Gates Mesolithic*. Ann Arbor: International Monographs in Prehistory.

Saxe, A. A. 1970. Social dimensions of mortuary practices. PhD thesis. University of Michigan Microfilms.

Schmidt, R. 2000. Shamans and northern cosmology: the direct historical approach to Mesolithic sexuality. In R. Schmidt and B. Voss (eds), *Archaeologies of sexuality*, 220–35. London: Routledge.

Schmidt, R. 2001. Sex and gender variation in the Scandinavian Mesolithic. PhD thesis. University of California, Berkley.

Solecki, R. S. 1972. *Shanidar: the humanity of Neanderthal man*. London: Penguin.

Strassburg, J. 2000. *Shamanic shadows: one hundred generations of undead subversion in southern Scandinavia 7000–4000 BC*. Stockholm: Stockholm Studies in Archaeology.

Stutz, A. J., Munro, N. D., and Bar-Oz, G. 2009. Increasing the resolution of the broad spectrum revolution in the southern Levantine Epipaleolithic (19–12 ka). *Journal of Human Evolution* 56, 294–306.

Suzuki, H. and Takai, F. (eds) 1970. *The Amud man and his cave site*. Tokyo: Tokyo University Press.

Svoboda, J. 1988. A new male burial from Dolní Vestonice. *Journal of Human Evolution* 16, 827–30.

Svoboda, J. 1991. *Dolní Vestonice II Western Slope*. Liège: ERAUL 54.

Svoboda, J. 2008. The upper Palaeolithic burial area at Predmosti: ritual and taphonomy. *Journal of Human Evolution* 54, 15–33.
Thorpe, N. 1996. *The origins of agriculture in Europe*. London: Routledge.
Tilley, C. 1996. *An ethnography of the Neolithic: early prehistoric societies in southern Scandinavia*. Cambridge: Cambridge University Press.
Vandermeersch, B. 1981. *Les hommes fossiles de Qafzeh (Israël)*. Paris: CNRS.
Weber, A. W. and Bettinger, R. 2010. Middle Holocene hunter-gatherers of Cis-Baikal, Siberia: an overview for the new century. *Journal of Anthropological Archaeology* 29, 491–506.
Weiss, E., Wetterstrom, W., Nadel, D., and Bar-Yosef, O. 2004. The broad spectrum revisited: evidence from plant remains. *Proceedings of the National Academy of Sciences USA* 101, 9551–5.
Zagorska, I. 2000. The art from Zvejnieki burial ground, Latvia. In A. Butrimas (ed.), *Prehistoric art in the Baltic region*. Acta Academiae Artium Vilnensis 20, 79–92. Vilnius: Vilnius Academy of Fine Arts.
Zagorska, I. 2001. Amber graves of Zvejnieki burial ground, Latvia. In A. Butrimas (ed.), *Baltic amber*. Acta Academiae Artium Vilnensis 22, 109–24. Vilnius: Vilnius Academy of Fine Arts.
Zagorska, I. and Lougas, L. 2000. The tooth-pendant head-dresses of Zvejnieki cemetery. *Muinasaja Teadus* 8, 223–44.
Zagorskis, F. 1987. *Zvejnieki akamens laikmeta kapulauks*. Riga.
Zagorskis, F. 2004. *Zvejnieki: Stone Age cemetery*. Oxford: BAR International Series 1292.
Zvelebil, M. 1993. Concepts of time and 'presencing' the Mesolithic. *Archaeological Review from Cambridge* 12, 51–70.
Zvelebil, M. 1996. Farmers our ancestors and the identity of Europe. In P. Graves-Brown, S. Jones, and C. Gamble (eds), *Cultural identity and archaeology: the construction of European communities*, 145–66. London: Routledge.
Zvelebil, M. 1998. What's in a name: the Mesolithic, the Neolithic, and social change at the Mesolithic–Neolithic transition. In M. Edmonds and C. Richards (eds), *Understanding the Neolithic of north-western Europe*, 1–36. Glasgow: Cruithne Press.
Zvelebil, M. 2008. Innovating hunter-gatherers: the Mesolithic in the Baltic. In G. Bailey and P. Spikins (eds), *Mesolithic Europe*, 18–59. Cambridge: Cambridge University Press.
Zvelebil, M. and Dolukhanov, P. 1991. The transition to farming in eastern and northern Europe. *Journal of World Prehistory* 5, 233–78.

CHAPTER 33

PLANT DOMESTICATIONS

DAVID R. HARRIS

Introduction

In retrospect, it is self-evident that by domesticating plants hunter-gatherers began a process that was to reshape humankind's relationship to the natural world and lead ultimately to dependence on agriculture as the principal source of human sustenance. But the customary anthropological conception of hunter-gatherer societies as non- (and pre-) agricultural discouraged research on plant domestication. Anthropological interest tended to focus more on hunter-gatherer social organization than on subsistence activities, and even when such practices were recorded, hunting and fishing usually received more attention than the gathering and processing of plants. One influential exception was the work of Julian Steward in western North America in the 1930s. He stressed the importance of resource availability in determining the social organization of 'primitive bands' and was the first to document how hunter-gatherers living in the Great Basin regularly harvested, and even irrigated, grasses and other wild food plants (Steward 1930; 1936).

Here four main themes relating to plant domestication are examined: development of the field of study; types of evidence and techniques of analysis; concepts of wild-plant management, domestication, and intermediate subsistence; and transitions from plant domestications to agriculture. They are examined on a world scale and the emphasis throughout is on the domestication of food plants because they made possible the cumulative and eventually massive increase of the human population that has occurred through the past 12,000 years.

Retrospect on the Study of Plant Domestication

Although Steward's and other ecologically grounded field studies within the broader tradition of hunter-gatherer social anthropology, such as Lee's and his associates' work among the San people of southern Africa (Lee 1968; Lee and DeVore 1976), generated valuable records of subsistence practices, research specifically on plant domestication and the origins of agriculture was initiated mainly by botanists, geneticists, and after 1950 increasingly by archaeologists. The Swiss botanist Alphonse de Candolle published the first detailed account on a world scale of the origin of cultivated plants, having already discussed the subject in his earlier work on plant geography (de Candolle 1855; 1882), and in *The Variation of Animals and Plants under Domestication* Charles Darwin (1868, I, 309–10) speculated about how plants were first domesticated:

> The savage inhabitants of each land, having found out by many and hard trials what plants were useful...would after a time take the first step in cultivation by planting them near their usual abodes...and as the soil...would often be in some degree manured, improved varieties would sooner or later arise. Or a wild and unusually good variety of a native plant might attract the attention of a wise old savage; and he would transplant it, or sow its seed.

Darwin's speculations were later paralleled by Engelbrecht (1916), who proposed that crops originated as 'habitation weeds' growing on ground enriched by organic debris around the settlements of hunter-gatherers.

In the 1920s and 1930s such speculation was replaced by more rigorous and comprehensive study based on field observations and experiments in crop breeding. This change was pioneered by the Russian botanist Vavilov (1926; 1992), whose concept and delineations of centres of diversity and origin of cultivated plants profoundly affected how the questions of where agriculture originated and how it spread were approached later in the twentieth century (Harris 1990). The American economic botanist Ames (1939) and his student Anderson (1952) also made influential contributions to early studies of plant domestication. But it was not until the 1960s that a new phase of research started when a rising generation of botanical/genetic and environmental/archaeological specialists, working in their laboratories and with archaeologists in the field, developed new techniques of investigation. The focus now shifted from informed speculation, based on botanical, historical, and ethnographic evidence, to the acquisition of more specific data from plant remains found in early agricultural contexts. This change began in South-West Asia and Mexico, where archaeologists and botanists cooperated in field projects (Braidwood and Howe 1960; Helbaek 1960; MacNeish 1967; Smith 1967).

In the 1970s and 1980s the British botanist Hillman (1973; 1975; 1981; 1984) pioneered a new method in archaeobotany by constructing ethnographic models of crop processing and applying them to the interpretation of charred plant remains recovered from prehistoric sites in Turkey, Syria, and Britain. He also carried out innovative experiments on domestication rates in wheats and barley under primitive cultivation (Hillman and Davies 1990) and influenced and trained many aspiring archaeobotanists (Fairbairn and Weiss 2009). In the same period many plant geneticists made important contributions to the study of plant domestication, and some collaborated with archaeologists: for example, Mangelsdorf (1974), who worked with MacNeish and C. E. Smith on the origin of maize; Pickersgill, who undertook cytological and genetic studies of the domestication and diffusion of crops in the American tropics, particularly chilli peppers (Pickersgill 1989; Pickersgill and Heiser 1977); and Zohary (1969; 1989), who investigated the wild progenitors of the cereals and pulses that were the founder crops of South-West Asian agriculture, and, with Hopf, published in 1988 the first comprehensive account of the archaeobotanical evidence for the region (see Zohary et al. 2012).

By the end of the twentieth century the literature on plant domestication and the origins of agriculture had grown prodigiously as field projects in many regions of the world generated new data. Scholarly progress was marked by the appearance of numerous volumes that presented and compared current evidence on a world or continental scale (e.g. Cowan and Watson 1992; Damania et al. 1998; Ford 1985; Harlan et al. 1976; Harris 1996a; Harris and Hillman 1989; Piperno and Pearsall 1998; Price and Gebauer 1995; Reed 1977; Smith 1995; Ucko and Dimbleby 1969), and the process continued unabated into the twenty-first century (e.g. Barker 2006; Bellwood 2005; Colledge and Conolly 2007; Denham et al. 2007; Kennett and Winterhalder 2006; Price 2000; Price and Bar-Yosef 2011; Zeder et al. 2006). Much of the progress recorded in these volumes, and in myriad papers in scientific journals, has derived from the application of new methods to retrieve, identify, analyse, and date a wide range of 'macro' and 'micro' plant remains such as seeds, fruits, phytoliths, pollen, and starch grains. Molecular studies, principally of DNA, and analyses of stable isotopes of carbon and nitrogen have also become important sources of new evidence.

Types of Evidence and Techniques of Analysis

Initially, investigation of plant remains recovered from prehistoric sites was concerned almost exclusively with seeds and other macro remains observable by eye and by conventional microscopy. Such remains are still the main source of direct evidence, most of which consists of carbonized plant material charred on site in domestic fires, although macro remains preserved in other ways such as desiccation, mineralization, and waterlogging have also yielded evidence of ancient plant use, including finds of domesticated plants (e.g. desiccated potato and manioc tubers from coastal sites in central Peru; Ugent et al. 1982; 1986).

Archaeobotanical research on domestication has focused mainly on herbaceous seed crops, particularly cereals, and the ability to distinguish between morphologically wild and domestic taxa has been aided by the concept of domestication syndromes of diagnostic characters, some of which can potentially be identified in the macro remains. Adaptations that resulted from selection pressures associated with harvesting and sowing seeds of wild grasses were identified as part of a cereal domestication syndrome described in an influential paper by Harlan et al. in 1973. Some of the adaptations, such as increase in seed size, reduction in glumes, and the replacement of a brittle by a tough rachis creating a non-shattering ear, can often be identified in well-preserved archaeobotanical assemblages, and they have become the most frequently used criteria for distinguishing between the remains of wild grasses and domesticated cereals. Other changes that some grasses have undergone during domestication, which can also potentially be identified, include increases in the number of spikelets in the ear, as in the transition of wild two-row to domestic six-row barley.

In an elaboration of the concept of the domestication syndrome with reference to herbaceous seed crops, Fuller (2007) reviewed archaeobotanical data for a selection of Asian and African cereals and pulses (herbaceous legumes) in order to examine the rates at which such domestication traits as changes in seed size and loss of natural seed dispersal evolved under cultivation. This showed how pre-domestication cultivation practices that led to initial plant domestications produced varying outcomes in different groups of crops. The results suggested that when the cereals studied (barley, einkorn wheat, rice, and pearl millet) were first cultivated, selection for larger grains preceded (except in pearl millet) selection of non-shattering ears, perhaps by as much as a millennium, whereas among the pulses discussed (lentil, pea, soybean, adzuki, mung, and urd beans) selection for indehiscent pods that inhibited natural seed dispersal preceded increased seed size by two or more millennia. Fuller suggested that these contrasting evolutionary pathways of cereals and pulses under cultivation correlate with regional and chronological differences in the adoption of techniques of tillage and harvesting: sickles being applied late rather than early (as is commonly assumed) to the harvesting of the cereals, and selection of larger seeds in the pulses occurring only when tillage with ploughs, which led to deeper burial of seeds, was adopted long after initial domestication.

Fuller referred to early changes in grain size and shape in cereals and early loss of seed-dispersal mechanisms in pulses as 'semi-domestication', in contrast to 'domestication *sensu stricto*' when, later, non-shattering ears were selected in cereals and larger seeds in pulses. This terminological distinction emphasizes two important points: that all adaptations of the domestication syndrome did not occur together when hunter-gatherers first began to cultivate plants, and that the selection of domestication traits varied not only by taxa and region but also according to when, where, and how different tillage and harvesting techniques were employed.

Analysis of macro remains has also been the main method of studying other seeds or fruits that are sufficiently robust to be preserved for long periods of time in archaeological contexts. They derive mainly from perennial woody plants with hard seeds and/or pericarps, especially nut-bearing trees and shrubs. In contrast, macro remains seldom provide evidence of root crops, the soft tissues of which readily decay, especially in humid tropical environments, and only exceptionally survive in carbonized, desiccated, or waterlogged form. The underground storage organs (roots, tubers, corms, rhizomes, and bulbs) of many tropical and temperate herbs and shrubs were major sources of food for hunter-gatherers in all the inhabited continents. A large number were domesticated and became—and remain—staple crops consumed throughout the world. But, because their remains are only rarely preserved in identifiable form in archaeological contexts, archaeobotanical research on their domestication advanced much more slowly than it did for cereals, pulses, and other seed crops. This particularly held back understanding of early plant domestication and the origins of agriculture in the tropics, where root crops such as yams, taro, manioc, potato, and sweet potato, and their wild progenitors, are known to have been staple sources of carbohydrate for most hunter-gatherers and early cultivators (Harris 1977, 208–16; Piperno and Pearsall 1998, 110–28). This imbalance in the archaeobotanical evidence of seed and root crops led to a disproportionate research emphasis on the former, although, from the 1980s onwards, this distortion began to be corrected by the application of three techniques that allow remains of root (and other) crops to be more widely recovered and identified.

Parenchyma Analysis

This technique arose from the discovery that tissues and individual cells of the parenchymatous storage organs of root crops could survive charring, and, when examined by scanning-electron microscopy, were sufficiently diagnostic to enable fragments of parenchyma to be identified to genus or even species (Hather 1991; 1994; 2000). Hather succeeded in identifying remains of a species of yam, manioc, and sweet potato from prehistoric contexts in, respectively, Samoa, Belize, and the central Polynesian island of Mangaia (Hather 1994, 55–6; Hather and Hammond 1994; Hather and Kirch 1991), and although the technique has not been extensively used it has the potential to provide direct evidence of early root-crop cultivation in the tropics and elsewhere.

Phytolith Analysis

Use of this technique in archaeobotany was pioneered in the 1980s and, sometimes paralleled by pollen analysis, has generated direct evidence of both seed-crop and root-crop cultivation (e.g. Jones 1994; Maloney 1994; Pearsall 2000, 473–83; Pearsall and Piperno 1993; Piperno 2006a). Phytoliths are microscopic silicified particles of plant material that retain the shapes of individual cells and can often be identified to species or genus. They are frequently preserved in soils and sediments in tropical and temperate environments and can be recovered from archaeological deposits. Although phytolith analysis has been applied mainly to seed crops, notably maize (Piperno et al. 2009; Thompson 2006) and wheat and barley (Ball et al. 1999), progress has also been made in identifying phytoliths of several vegetatively reproduced tropical crops (e.g. bananas in Africa and Papua New Guinea and the South American tuber crops arrowroot and leren; Lentfer 2009; Mbida et al. 2006; Piperno and Pearsall 1998, 213–17). Phytolith analysis can provide valuable evidence of the early cultivation of both seed and root-and-tuber plants, but its capacity to demonstrate morphological changes associated with domestication is likely to be restricted to relatively few crops.

Starch-Grain Analysis

This technique is based on the occurrence of starch granules in many identifiable forms in the roots, shoots, stems, fruits, and leaves of green plants and on their capacity to survive in a wide variety of depositional environments (Torrence and Barton 2006). Their preservation in organic residues found on prehistoric stone tools stimulated archaeological interest in the technique (Loy 1994; Piperno and Holst 1998), and since then it has yielded evidence of early prehistoric use in the American tropics of such root and seed plants as manioc, yam, sweet potato, arrowroot, leren, maize, and common bean (Perry 2004; Piperno 2006b; Piperno et al. 2009). Also, in South-East Asia at Niah cave in Sarawak, finds of starch granules (and parenchyma) from yams and aroids (the plant family that includes taro and other root crops) have shown that rainforest hunter-gatherers were exploiting these plants in the Late Pleistocene and Early Holocene from at least 40,000 years ago (Barton and Paz 2007).

Increasing use of starch-grain, phytolith, and parenchyma analysis is generating valuable new data on ancient remains of root and seed crops, and such remains can be dated directly by the AMS (accelerator mass spectrometric) radiocarbon method, which can determine the ages of very small (<1 gram) samples of organic material. But more research on the diverse morphologies of phytoliths and starch grains is needed before identification to species level and discrimination between wild and domestic forms can be more widely achieved, and crop processing (Harvey and Fuller 2005) and other agrarian practices securely inferred.

Modern and Ancient DNA

Molecular studies, particularly of modern and ancient DNA, are transforming the science of crop-plant evolution and overturning earlier assumptions about the ancestry and areas of origin of many taxa (see e.g. Burger et al. 2008; Doebley et al. 2006; Zeder et al. 2006, 99–168). A significant outcome of this 'molecular revolution' is the replacement of the formerly widespread view that domestication could take place rapidly and that most crops had been domesticated only once (Blumler 1992; Hillman and Davies 1990; Zohary 1999) by a 'protracted' model (Allaby et al. 2008) that envisages much more gradual domestication, often involving a crop being domesticated more than once in different areas within the range of its wild progenitor(s). Such a multi-regional, multiple-domestication model has been shown to fit the archaeobotanical record of cereal domestication in South-West Asia better than the previous view (Brown et al. 2009), but it does not necessarily apply to most crops in other regions, many of which may have been domesticated only once in a single area.

Although studies of the DNA of present-day crops can successfully reveal their evolutionary pathways, the 'molecular clock'—which is based on the assumption that mutations occur randomly at rates that can be approximately estimated (and sometimes calibrated by reference to fossil records)—provides a secular time-scale in millions of years unsuited to the domestication process, which is measured in a few millennia. So, in order to tie the genetic data to the archaeological time-scale it is necessary to analyse fragments of ancient DNA that survive in plant remains preserved in archaeological contexts, the age of which can be determined by radiometric methods or, more rarely, from documentary records.

Pioneering studies of ancient DNA extracted from remains of rice, maize, wheat, and sorghum undertaken in the 1970s demonstrated the feasibility of the technique (Allaby et al. 1994; Deakin et al. 1998; Goloubinoff et al. 1993; Nakamura and Sato 1999), and the methods of analysis have since been improved and are being applied to a wider range of archaeological plant remains. Ancient DNA research has the capacity to provide direct, datable evidence of past plant use by hunter-gatherers, as well as early agriculturalists, but it is limited to archaeological contexts in which plant remains are sufficiently well preserved for fragments of DNA to have survived and be amplified for analysis.

Stable-Isotope Analysis

The last technique to be mentioned—analysis of stable isotopes of carbon and nitrogen in animal bones and plant remains—provides only indirect evidence of domestication. Since the late 1970s it has increasingly been used to investigate past human diets. It was first used mainly to distinguish the relative dietary contributions of marine and terrestrial foods, but it also enables the relative dietary importance of plants with different photosynthetic pathways to be detected. Carbon-isotope values in the tissues of C_4 plants are higher than those in C_3 plants and the former, which are mostly open-habitat tropical and warm-season grasses, are less widespread and abundant than the latter, which include trees, most shrubs and forbs, and temperate cool-season grasses (Pearsall 2000, 525; Sage 2004). Most cereal and legume crops are C4 plants and their contributions to past human diets can, in favourable circumstances of preservation, be assessed by determining C- and N-isotope values from collagen preserved in animal, including human, bones, and also directly from charred plant remains (Bogaard et al. 2007; DeNiro and Hastorf 1985; DeNiro and Schoeninger 1983; Finucane et al. 2008).

Although stable-isotope analysis cannot provide direct morphogenetic evidence of plant domestication, it can, by identifying preferential human consumption of particular plants, reveal situations in which close exploitation by tending, planting, and regular harvesting can be inferred. The potential value of this technique is exemplified by a study of human- and animal-bone data from a Neolithic site, Dadiwan, in north-west China where there is evidence that during the first phase of occupation broomcorn millet was preferentially harvested, stored, and consumed by the people and their hunting dogs, whereas during the second phase both broomcorn and foxtail millet were cultivated and contributed substantially to the diets of the people and their domestic dogs and pigs (Barton et al. 2009). The isotopic data suggest that millets were managed and perhaps cultivated during the first phase before millet-based agriculture was established in the second phase. The study shows how the technique can generate indirect evidence of close pre-domestication relationships between people and potential plant (and animal) domesticates. It also raises questions about the concept and definition of domestication.

Domestication, Wild-Plant Management, and Intermediate Subsistence

Semantic confusion has long characterized discussions of domestication and the emergence of agriculture (Harris 1989; 2007), and there is no need here to examine again the multiple meanings attributed to such terms as cultivation, food production, agriculture, and horticulture. But domestication does require clarification. Like agriculture and cultivation, it is a very broad concept that carries a wide range of biological and cultural connotations. It has been qualified and elaborated in many ways, but here I use it in its morphogenetic sense to mean a process of inadvertent and/or deliberate intervention by people in the reproduction of culturally selected plants that leads to their reproductive isolation from their wild progenitors and increases their dependence on sustained human care for their survival. To adopt morphogenetic change as a defining criterion does not preclude the use of other more general connotations of domestication, but it has the great merit of offering markers of domestication, such as increased seed size, loss of seed-dispersal mechanisms, DNA, and protein variations (Fuller 2007; Jones and Brown 2007), that can potentially be detected by archaeobotanical and genetic techniques. It also encourages awareness of the phenomenon of pre-domestication cultivation. However, when focusing attention on the cultivation of plants without evidence of morphogenetic change, we should not assume that such plants were necessarily 'on the road' to domestication and agriculture. It is probable that in many situations their cultivation was an integral part of non-agricultural patterns of subsistence that satisfactorily sustained groups of hunter-gatherers over many generations without developing progressively greater dependence on plants that subsequently became agricultural crops. The widespread past existence of such mixed modes of subsistence that combined hunting, fishing, and gathering with the management of particular plants has been postulated in several evolutionary models and denoted by such labels as 'specialized domestication' (Rindos 1984, 158–64), 'wild-plant food production' (Harris 1989, 17–20; 1996b, 444–6), and 'low-level food production' (Smith 2001a). When viewed from this evolutionary perspective such mixed subsistence systems can be seen to occupy an intermediate position between the hunting and gathering of wild plants without management of individual taxa, and agricultural systems of food production dependent on the cultivation of domesticated crops. But reference to these mixed systems as 'intermediate' does *not* imply that they collectively represent a general developmental stage that led progressively towards agriculture. In some regions they did indeed lead through increasing human intervention in the life-cycles of preferred plants to the domestication of suites of crops and the establishment of biotically distinctive agricultural systems (see below), but in other areas, such as California and much of Australia, intermediate subsistence systems sustained hunter-gatherer populations in the long term without leading to agriculture. The abundant ethno-historical evidence for the tending, planting, and harvesting of preferred plants within broad-spectrum hunter-gatherer systems shows that these practices were applied to a small proportion only of the taxa that contributed to the food supply, and that such management focused on three main categories of plant foods: tree nuts, roots and tubers, and the seeds of grasses and other herbaceous plants (forbs).

Tree Nuts

The kernels of many tropical and temperate tree nuts are edible and highly nutritious and they provided staple, storable food supplies for many hunter-gatherer societies. Nut production was enhanced by controlled burning and various techniques were developed to detoxify bitter kernels, but there is little evidence that nut-bearing trees were deliberately planted. This is unsurprising as most species only produce seeds after many years' growth. Such slow maturation makes planting less rewarding than managing stands of nut trees in the wild, which partly accounts for the fact that relatively few have been domesticated. Also, most herbaceous crops are self-pollinated and more readily become segregated from their wild progenitors and domesticated than cross-pollinated trees that are characterized by genetic mixing—which reduces the chances of desirable traits such as larger and sweeter fruits and less bitter nuts being selected if tree crops are raised from seed. This, combined with their slow maturation, made them unlikely candidates for domestication. Harvesting fruits and nuts in the wild was a more productive system of food procurement for hunter-gatherers than experimenting with tree-crop cultivation.

Although there is plentiful ethno-historical and some archaeological evidence of intensive nut use by hunter-gatherers, for example in California, eastern North America, Japan, and north-eastern Australia (Asch et al. 1972; Cosgrove et al. 2007; Harris 1987, 359–66; Munson et al. 1971; Takahashi and Hosoya 2002; Wohlgemuth 2004), there is no conclusive evidence that any of the nut trees anciently exploited in these regions were domesticated by the hunter-gatherers who harvested them. Such nut and fruit trees as were domesticated in prehistoric and early historical times, such as almond, hazel, pistachio, sweet chestnut, walnut, apple, apricot, cherry, peach, pear, pomegranate, plum, olive, fig, and date palm, were evidently first cultivated by agricultural communities, and their successful domestication depended on the replacement of sexual reproduction in the wild by techniques of vegetative propagation such as planting cuttings and suckers, and especially grafting (Zohary et al. 2012, 114–52).

Roots and Tubers

In contrast to nut trees, plants that produce edible roots, tubers, or other underground organs have long been staple sources of food (mainly carbohydrate) for many tropical and temperate hunter-gatherers as well as most agriculturalists. A great diversity of wild species have traditionally been managed to increase their productivity, by digging, weeding, burning, selective harvesting, and, especially, re-planting pieces of root, tuber, or stem to sustain annual growth in chosen patches (see for Californian examples Anderson 2005, 219–305, and for Australia Gott 1982 and Hallam 1989). This practice of *in situ* vegetative propagation facilitates the selection of clones with desirable characteristics, such as increased size and reduced bitterness or thorniness of the food-storage organ. These phenotypic changes can occur without altering the genotype, so the dividing line between wild and domesticated root and tuber plants is much less absolute than it is for cereals, pulses, and other seed crops subject to morphogenetic changes involving loss of seed-dispersal mechanisms such as non-shattering ears and indehiscent pods.

Grass and Forb Seeds

As a source of human food the seeds of grasses and forbs comprise an even more widely exploited and nutritionally valuable resource than roots and tubers. They are easily harvested, well suited to storage, and typically provide carbohydrate, protein, and oil, as well as vitamins, minerals, and fibre in varying proportions. They thus provide much better balanced nutrition than roots and tubers, and combinations of them were dietary staples in many hunter-gatherer as well as early agricultural subsistence systems. Wild stands of grass and forb seeds were regularly harvested in many parts of the world, for example in arid and semi-arid areas of Australia and North America, where, in the recent past, they were managed by burning, sowing, and sometimes irrigation, and large quantities of grain were stored (Allen 1974; Anderson 2005, 256–66; Cane 1989; Harris 1984; Steward 1941; Tindale 1977). Although seeds were staple foods over much of Australia and the western United States before the arrival of Europeans, there is no conclusive evidence that any of the harvested grasses and forbs were morphogenetically domesticated there. They were, however, in many other regions, where cereals such as barley, wheat, maize, rice, and sorghum, and various pulses, became staple crops in early agricultural systems. Such transitions—from partial dependence on managed plants in intermediate subsistence systems to dependence on domesticated crops in early agricultural systems—are considered in the next section.

Transitions to Agriculture

Recognition of regions where transitions to agriculture occurred independently must necessarily be somewhat arbitrary because it depends both on how evidence of crops in the prehistoric archaeological record is interpreted, and on the spatial scale at which regions are defined. At the world scale, present evidence points to some ten major regions in which crops that became food staples in early agricultural systems were independently domesticated: South-West Asia, China, South Asia, New Guinea, the African Sahel zone south of the Sahara, the west African forest-savannah zone, Mesoamerica, eastern North America, the South American lowland east of the Andes, and the central Andes. But when many of these regions are examined more closely, sub-regions of domestication can be recognized. Thus in South-West Asia, China, South Asia, Mesoamerica, and lowland South America there is evidence of areas within them where single or clusters of crops originated: for example, barley, one- and two-grain einkorn wheat, emmer wheat, and several pulses in different parts of South-West Asia; millets and rice respectively in north and south China; rice, millets, and pulses within the Indian subcontinent; maize, beans, and squash in Mesoamerica; and root, tree, and other crops in various parts of lowland South America (Fuller 2006; Fuller et al. 2007; Özkan et al. 2011; Piperno 2006a, 153–7; Smith 2001b; Willcox 2005).

These variations in the crop assemblages of early agricultural systems led to increased dependence on fewer (domesticated) plants to satisfy basic dietary needs for carbohydrate, protein, fats, oils, and other nutrients compared with the greater diversity of plant foods exploited in hunter-gatherer broad-spectrum and intermediate subsistence systems. How these basic needs were met varied from region to region. In South-West Asia, China, South Asia, and the African Sahel zone different combinations of cereals, pulses, tree crops, and herd animals provided the main food supply; cereals, pulses, and other forbs did so in Mesoamerica; tubers, pulses, other forbs, and camelids in the central Andes; tubers and tree crops in New Guinea, the west African forest–savannah zone, and northern lowland South America; and, before the introduction of maize, only a few species of native forbs in eastern North America.

Although there is evidence that plants were domesticated from native wild progenitors in all the major regions and sub-regions, it should not be assumed that the resulting crop combinations were formed rapidly and then tended to spread as unified 'packages'. The development of South-West Asian agro-pastoralism into a fully integrated system took some 3,000 years (Harris 2002), and although most of its component crops and herd animals later spread widely in western Eurasia, the crop–livestock complex and the associated techniques of cultivation and animal management underwent many changes as they adapted to novel ecological and cultural conditions (Colledge and Conolly 2007; Diamond 1997, 180–5; Fuller 2006; Harris 2010; McCorriston 2006; Price 2000; Zeder 2008). Other early agricultural systems developed even more slowly and episodically. For example, in eastern North America 4,000 years elapsed between the initial domestication of a few indigenous seed plants in an intermediate subsistence system that combined their cultivation with hunting, fishing, and gathering and the establishment of an agricultural economy after maize and later common bean, both domesticated in Mexico, were introduced and adopted (Smith 2006a; 2006b). Transitions from broad-spectrum hunting and gathering through intermediate systems to agriculture were even more protracted in some other regions, although evidence is largely lacking to document them adequately. In Mexico it took 6,000 or more years for the three staple field crops, pepo squash, maize, and common bean, to be separately domesticated and eventually routinely cultivated together to become the foundation of Mesoamerican agriculture (Kaplan and Lynch 1999; Piperno and Flannery 2001; Smith 2001b; 2005).

In all the other major regions the transitions from hunting and gathering to systems of crop cultivation occurred very gradually, with plants being episodically added to the evolving complexes by local domestication and the introduction of already domesticated crops from elsewhere. As yet there is insufficient archaeobotanical evidence to track these trajectories at all comprehensively, but some progress is being made. Sequences in which root crops attained special importance have been traced in New Guinea and tropical America. In the New Guinea highlands, at Kuk Swamp in the Waghi Valley, there is evidence of a gradual transition from broad-spectrum foraging 10,000 years ago to increasingly intensive agriculture based mainly on the cultivation of native yams, taro, sugar cane, and bananas, with sweet potato, introduced from tropical America, adopted later (Denham et al. 2003; Denham and Barton 2006); and at Aguadulce rock shelter in central Panama the exploitation between 7,000 and 5,000 years ago of manioc, yam, and leren tubers, and of maize dispersed from Mexico, has been inferred from starch grains and phytoliths in sedimentary strata and on grinding stones (Piperno 2000b; Piperno and Holst 1998).

Evidence of another long sequence of subsistence change is coming to light in northern Africa. In the Sahel zone south of the Sahara, indigenous cereals and pulses, principally sorghum, pearl and finger millet, cowpea, and two types of groundnut, have traditionally been cultivated and the seeds of many species of wild grass were until recently extensively harvested, while farther south in the west African forest–savannah zone native tuber and tree crops, principally yams and oil palm, have long been staples (Harlan 1989a; 1989b; Harris 1976). The antiquity of these agricultural systems is now beginning to be revealed as charred plant remains and potsherds with grain impressions and/or chaff temper are recovered from archaeological sites in both zones (D'Andrea et al. 2001; 2007; Fuller et al. 2007; Kahlberger and Neumann 2007; Manning et al. 2011; Stahl 1993, 263). Collectively these finds attest to the presence of several of the African crops by 4,000 years ago, and the fact that occasional remains of domesticated pearl millet and cowpea have been found at some sites with abundant remain of wild food plants suggests that the domesticates were initially minor components in intermediate subsistence systems and only became staple crops as an agricultural economy gradually became established.

The early agricultural systems that evolved in the Sahel and west African zones were based on native cereal, pulse, root, and tree crops, but in most of the other major regions exogenous crops domesticated elsewhere, which had the capacity to increase food production and enhance nutrition, were also introduced and adopted. The impact of maize on the establishment of agriculture in eastern North America has already been mentioned, and its earlier spread southwards from Mexico into lowland South America and the Andes had comparable effects on the evolution of agricultural systems there. Similarly, barley and wheat, which spread early to north-western South Asia and much later to northern China, added to the diversity and development of agriculture in those regions.

These examples of inter-regional crop transfers illustrate how, in many regions, the incorporation of exogenous crops originally domesticated by hunter-gatherers elsewhere contributed significantly to the transformation of intermediate systems into agricultural systems.

Conclusion

Ethnographic and historical evidence of hunter-gatherer subsistence behaviour indicates that in most environments food and other organic resources were procured from a wide range of plants, some of which served as staple foods, and that many groups also managed particular taxa to ensure their availability and increase their yield. Wild plants were managed by a variety of techniques: burning, tilling, weeding, planting, sowing, irrigation, and drainage. Such interventions in the plants' life-cycles led to the morphogenetic domestication of some species, particularly those that responded with higher productivity and/or were inherently storable, mainly roots and tubers, and grass and forb seeds. A small proportion only of the wild plants that contributed to hunter-gatherer subsistence were domesticated, and this tended to occur in, and reinforce, those ecological and cultural situations that favoured sedentary rather than seasonally mobile settlement. But not all sedentary hunter-gatherers domesticated plants that they managed. The settled Native American hunter-gatherer societies of California and the Pacific Northwest Coast manipulated many species of seed, root, and tuber yielding plants in diverse ways without morphogenetically domesticating them and developing agricultural economies (Anderson 2005; Deur and Turner 2005; Lepofsky and Lertzman 2008).[1]

It is now apparent that initial plant domestications resulted from a very protracted evolutionary process during which many species were managed by hunter-gatherers but relatively few were morphogenetically domesticated and incorporated into emerging crop assemblages, in which some became staple foods. These changes occurred slowly over many millennia from the Late Pleistocene through much of the Holocene. They took place in various tropical, sub-tropical, and temperate regions of the world where crops (and in some regions also livestock) formed environmentally adapted, productive, and nutritionally effective combinations. Some combinations, such as the South-West Asian agro-pastoral system and the Mesoamerican mix of maize, beans, squash, and chilli pepper, were exceptionally productive and provided well-balanced diets that largely freed farmers from dependence on wild foods. These systems could support increasing populations and they facilitated the spread of agriculture to new areas. Other crop assemblages, such as those that combined annual root-crop and perennial tree-crop cultivation, as in much of lowland South America and New Guinea, provided less well-balanced diets and cultivators continued to depend on hunting and fishing to obtain adequate supplies of protein. These assemblages were less capable of supporting increases in population and were inherently less expansive than annual seed-crop systems—a situation that changed in some regions when adaptable and productive crops were introduced from elsewhere, as maize was in South America and sweet potato in the New Guinea highlands.

Looking back across the vast sweep of time—beginning some 12,000 years ago—that separates our modern world from the earliest forays of our hunter-gatherer ancestors along pathways that led to agriculture, what is most ecologically apparent is a massive reduction in the diversity of plants on which humanity depends for food. From broad-spectrum hunter-gatherer diets through several millennia of resource management in intermediate subsistence systems during which plants began to be domesticated, to the establishment of agricultural systems, there has been a progressive narrowing of the range of foods that has fed the increasing world population. The slow transition from dependence on wild plants to dependence on a smaller number of domesticated crops, particularly the large-seeded cereals, pulses and root crops that became staple foods, has sustained the world's burgeoning population, but at the cost of a huge loss of plant biodiversity—in recent times among crops as well as wild plants. By intervening so long ago in the life-cycles of plants, hunter-gatherers initiated profoundly transformative changes in economy, society, and humankind's relationship to the natural world. It was an innovation of unparalleled magnitude in human history.

Note

1. Ethno-historical and archaeobotanical evidence of wild-plant plant management by Native American and Australian Aboriginal societies, and transitions to agriculture in the major world regions mentioned here, are discussed more fully in Harris (2012), on which this chapter is partly based.

References

Allaby, R. G., Fuller, D. Q., and Brown, T. A. 2008. The genetic expectations of a protracted model for the origins of domesticated crops. *Proceedings of the National Academy of Sciences, USA* 105, 13982–6.

Allaby, R. G., Jones, M. K., and Brown, T. A. 1994. DNA in charred wheat grains from the Iron Age hillfort at Danebury, England. *Antiquity* 68, 126–32.

Allen, H. 1974. The Bagundji of the Darling Basin: cereal gatherers in an uncertain environment. *World Archaeology* 5, 309–22.

Ames, O. 1939. *Economic annuals and human cultures*. Cambridge, MA: Botanical Museum of Harvard University.

Anderson, E. 1952. *Plants, man and life*. Boston: Little, Brown.

Anderson, M. K. 2005. *Tending the wild: Native American knowledge and management of California's natural resources*. Berkeley: University of California Press.

Asch, N. B., Ford, R. I., and Asch, D. L. 1972. *Paleoethnobotany of the Koster site: the Archaic horizon*. Springfield: Illinois State Museum.

Ball, T. B., Gardner, J. S., and Anderson, N. 1999. Identifying inflorescence phytoliths from selected species of wheat (*Triticum monococcum, T. dicoccum, T. dicoccoides* and *T. aestivum*) and barley (*Hordeum vulgare* and *H. spontaneum*) (Gramineae). *American Journal of Botany* 86, 1615–23.

Barker, G. 2006. *The agricultural revolution in prehistory: why did foragers become farmers?* Oxford: Oxford University Press.

Barton, H. and Paz, V. 2007. Subterranean diets in the tropical rain forests of Sarawak, Malaysia. In T. Denham, J. Iriarte, and L. Vrydaghs (eds), *Rethinking agriculture: archaeological and ethnoarchaeological perspectives*, 50–77. Walnut Creek, CA: Left Coast Press.

Barton, L., Newsome, S. D., Chen, F.-H., Wang, H., Guilderson, T. P., and Bettinger, R. L. 2009. Agricultural origins and isotopic identity of domestication in northern China. *Proceedings of the National Academy of Sciences, USA* 106, 5523–8.

Bellwood, P. 2005. *First farmers: the origins of agricultural societies*. Oxford: Blackwell.

Blumler, M. A. 1992. Independent inventionism and recent genetic evidence on plant domestication. *Economic Botany* 46, 98 111.

Bogaard, A., Heaton, T. H. E., Poulton, P., and Merbach, I. 2007. The impact of manuring on nitrogen isotope ratios in cereals: archaeological implications for reconstruction of diet and crop management practices. *Journal of Archaeological Science* 34, 335–43.

Braidwood, R. J. and Howe, B. 1960. *Prehistoric investigations in Iraqi Kurdistan*. Chicago: University of Chicago Press, Studies in Ancient Oriental Civilization 31.

Brown, T. A., Jones, M. K., Powell, W., and Allaby, R. A. 2009. The complex origins of domesticated crops in the Fertile Crescent. *Trends in Ecology and Evolution* 24, 103–9.

Burger, J. C., Chapman, M. A., and Burke, J. M. 2008. Molecular insights into the evolution of crop plants. *American Journal of Botany* 95, 113–22.

Cane, S. 1989. Australian Aboriginal seed grinding and its archaeological record: a case study from the western desert. In D. R. Harris and G. C. Hillman (eds), *Foraging and farming: the evolution of plant exploitation*, 99–119. London: Unwin Hyman.

Colledge, S. and Conolly, J. (eds) 2007. *The origins and spread of domestic plants in Southwest Asia and Europe*. Walnut Creek, CA: Left Coast Press.

Cosgrove, R., Field, J., and Ferrier, Å. 2007. The archaeology of Australia's tropical rainforests. *Palaeogeography, Palaeoclimatology, Palaeoecology* 251, 150–73.

Cowan, C. W. and Watson, P. J. (eds) 1992. *The origins of agriculture: an international perspective*. Washington: Smithsonian Institution.

Damania, A. B., Valkoun, J., Willcox, G., and Qualset, C. O. (eds) 1998. *The origins of agriculture and crop domestication*. Aleppo: ICARDA (International Center for Agricultural Research in Dry Areas).

D'Andrea, A. C., Kahlberger, S., Logan, A. L., and Watson, D. J. 2007. Early domesticated cowpea (*Vigna unguiculata*) from central Ghana. *Antiquity* 81, 686–98.

D'Andrea, A.C., Klee, M., and Casey, J. 2001. Archaeobotanical evidence for pearl millet (*Pennisetum glaucum*) in sub-Saharan Africa. *Antiquity* 75, 341–8.

Darwin, C. 1868. *The variation of animals and plants under domestication*, 2 vols. London: John Murray.

Deakin, W. J., Rowley-Conwy, P. J., and Shaw, C. H. 1998. Amplification and sequencing of DNA from preserved sorghum of up to 2800 years antiquity found at Qasr Ibrim. *Ancient Biomolecules* 2, 27–41.

de Candolle, A. 1855. *Géographie botanique raisonnée ou exposition des faits principaux et des lois concernant la distribution géographique des plantes de l'époque actuelle*, 2 vols. Paris: Victor Masson.

de Candolle, A. 1882. *Origine des plantes cultivées*. Paris: Germer Baillière [English translation 1884. *Origin of cultivated plants*. London: Kegan Paul, Trench].

Denham, T. and Barton, H. 2006. The emergence of agriculture in New Guinea: a model of continuity from pre-existing foraging practices. In D. J. Kennett and B. Winterhalder (eds), *Behavioral ecology and the transition to agriculture*, 237–64. Berkeley: University of California Press.

Denham, T., Haberle, S. G., Lentfer, C., Fullagar, R., Field, J., Therin, M., Porch, N., and Winsborough, B. 2003. Origins of agriculture at Kuk Swamp in the highlands of New Guinea. *Science* 301, 189–93.

Denham, T., Iriarte, J., and Vrydaghs, L. (eds) 2007. *Rethinking agriculture: archaeological and ethnoarchaeological perspectives*. Walnut Creek, CA: Left Coast Press.

DeNiro, M. J. and Hastorf, C. A. 1985. Alteration of $^{15}N/^{14}N$ and $^{13}C/^{12}C$ ratios of plant matter during the initial stages of diagenesis: studies utilizing archaeological specimens from Peru. *Geochimica et Cosmochimica Acta* 49, 97–115.

DeNiro, M. J. and Schoeninger, M. J. 1983. Stable carbon and nitrogen isotope ratios of bone collagen: variations within individuals, between sexes, and within populations raised on monotonous diets. *Journal of Archaeological Science* 10, 199–203.

Deur, D. and Turner, N. J. (eds) 2005. *Keeping it living: traditions of plant use and cultivation on the northwest coast of North America*. Seattle: University of Washington Press.

Diamond, J. 1997. *Guns, germs and steel: the fates of human societies*. London: Jonathan Cape.

Doebley, J. F., Gaut, B. S., and Smith, B. D. 2006. The molecular genetics of crop domestication. *Cell* 127, 1309–21.

Engelbrecht, T. H. 1916. Über die Entstehung einiger feldmässig angebauter Kulturpflanzen. *Geographischer Zeitschrift* 22, 328–34.

Fairbairn, A. and Weiss, E. (eds) 2009. *From foragers to farmers: papers in honour of Gordon C. Hillman*. Oxford: Oxbow.

Finucane, B., Manning, K., and Touré, M. 2008. Late Stone Age subsistence in the Tilemsi Valley, Mali: stable isotope analysis of human and animal remains from the site of Karkarichinkat Nord, Mali. *Journal of Anthropological Archaeology* 27, 82–92.

Ford, R. I. (ed.) 1985. *Prehistoric food production in North America*. Ann Arbor: University of Michigan, Museum of Anthropology, Anthropological Papers 75.

Fuller, D. Q. 2006. Agricultural origins and frontiers in South Asia: a working synthesis. *Journal of World Prehistory* 20, 1–86.

Fuller, D. Q. 2007. Contrasting patterns in crop domestication rates: recent archaeobotanical insights from the Old World. *Annals of Botany* 100, 903–24.

Fuller, D. Q., MacDonald, K., and Vernet, R. 2007. Early domesticated pearl millet in Dhar Nema (Mauritania): evidence of crop processing waste as ceramic temper. In R. Cappers (ed.), *Fields of change: progress in African archaeobotany*, 71–6. Groningen: Barkhuis and Groningen University Library.

Goloubinoff, P., Pääbo, S., and Wilson, A. 1993. Evolution of maize inferred from sequence diversity of an *adh2* gene segment from archaeological specimens. *Proceedings of the National Academy of Sciences USA* 90, 1997–2001.

Gott, B. 1982. Ecology of root use by the Aborigines of southern Australia. *Archaeology in Oceania* 17, 59–67.

Hallam, S. 1989. Plant usage and management in southwest Australian Aboriginal societies. In D. R. Harris and G. C. Hillman (eds), *Foraging and farming: the evolution of plant exploitation*, 136–51. London: Unwin Hyman.

Harlan, J. R. 1989a. Wild-grass seed harvesting in the Sahara and sub-Sahara of Africa. In D. R. Harris and G. C. Hillman (eds), *Foraging and farming: the evolution of plant exploitation*, 79–98. London: Unwin Hyman.

Harlan, J.R. 1989b. The tropical African cereals. In D.R. Harris and G.C. Hillman (eds), *Foraging and farming: the evolution of plant exploitation*, 335–43. London: Unwin Hyman.

Harlan, J. R., de Wet, J. M. J., and Price, E. G. 1973. Comparative evolution of cereals. *Evolution* 27, 311–25.

Harlan, J. R., de Wet, J. M. J., and Stemler, A. B. L. (eds) 1976. *Origins of African plant domestication*. The Hague: Mouton.

Harris, D. R. 1976. Traditional systems of plant food production and the origins of agriculture in West Africa. In J. R. Harlan, J. M. J. de Wet, and A. B. L. Stemler (eds), *Origins of African plant domestication*, 311–56. The Hague: Mouton.

Harris, D. R. 1977. Alternative pathways to agriculture. In C. A. Reed (ed.), *Origins of agriculture*, 179–243. The Hague: Mouton.

Harris, D. R. 1984. Ethnohistorical evidence for the exploitation of wild grasses and forbs: its scope and archaeological implications. In W. van Zeist and W. A. Casparie (eds), *Plants and ancient man*, 63–9. Rotterdam: Balkema.

Harris, D. R. 1987. Aboriginal subsistence in a tropical rain-forest environment: food procurement, cannibalism and population regulation in northeastern Australia. In M. Harris and E. B. Ross (eds), *Food and evolution: toward a theory of human food habits*, 357–85. Philadelphia: Temple University Press.

Harris, D. R. 1989. An evolutionary continuum of people–plant interaction. In D. R. Harris and G. C. Hillman (eds), *Foraging and farming: the evolution of plant exploitation*, 11–26. London: Unwin Hyman.

Harris, D. R. 1990. Vavilov's concept of centres of origin of cultivated plants: its genesis and its influence on the study of agricultural origins. *Biological Journal of the Linnean Society* 39, 7–16.

Harris, D. R. (ed.) 1996a. *The origins and spread of agriculture and pastoralism in Eurasia*. London: UCL Press and Washington: Smithsonian Institution.

Harris, D. R. 1996b. Domesticatory relationships of people, plants and animals. In R. Ellen and K. Fukui (eds), *Redefining nature: ecology, culture and domestication*, 437–63. Oxford: Berg.

Harris, D. R. 2002. Development of the agro-pastoral economy in the Fertile Crescent during the Pre-Pottery Neolithic period. In R. T. J. Cappers and S. Bottema (eds), *The dawn of farming in the Near East*, 67–83. Berlin: ex oriente.

Harris, D. R. 2007. Agriculture, cultivation and domestication: exploring the conceptual framework of early food production. In T. Denham, J. Iriarte, and L. Vrydaghs (eds), *Rethinking agriculture: archaeological and ethnoarchaeological perspectives*, 16–35. Walnut Creek, CA: Left Coast Press.

Harris, D. R. 2010. *Origins of agriculture in western Central Asia: an environmental–archaeological study*. Philadelphia: University of Pennsylvania Press.

Harris, D. R. 2012. Evolution of agroecosystems: biodiversity, origins, and differential development. In P. Gepts, R. L. Bettinger, S. B. Brush, A. B. Damania, T. R. Famula, P. E. McGuire, and C. O. Qualset (eds), *Biodiversity in agriculture: domestication, evolution, and sustainability*, 21–56.Cambridge: Cambridge University Press.

Harris, D. R. and Hillman, G. C. (eds) 1989. *Foraging and farming: the evolution of plant exploitation*. London: Unwin Hyman.

Harvey, E. and Fuller, D. Q. 2005. Investigating crop processing through phytolith analysis: the case of rice and millets. *Journal of Archaeological Science* 32, 739–52.

Hather, J. G. 1991. The identification of charred archaeological remains of vegetative parenchymatous tissues. *Journal of Archaeological Science* 18, 661–75.

Hather, J. G. 1994. The identification of charred root and tuber crops from archaeological sites in the Pacific. In J. G. Hather (ed.), *Tropical archaeobotany: applications and new developments*, 51–64. London: Routledge.

Hather, J. G. 2000. *Archaeological parenchyma*. London: Archetype.

Hather, J. G. and Hammond, N. 1994. Ancient Maya subsistence diversity: root and tuber remains from Cuello, Belize. *Antiquity* 68, 330–5.

Hather, J. G. and Kirch, P. V. 1991. Prehistoric sweet potato (*Ipomoea batatas*) from Mangaia Island, central Polynesia. *Antiquity* 65, 887–93.

Helbaek, H. 1960. The palaeoethnobotany of the Near East and Europe. In R. J. Braidwood and B. Howe (eds), *Prehistoric investigations in Iraqi Kurdistan*, 99–118. Chicago: University of Chicago Press, Studies in Ancient Oriental Civilization 31.

Hillman, G. C. 1973. Crop husbandry and food production: modern models for the interpretation of plant remains. *Anatolian Studies* 23, 241–4.

Hillman, G. C. 1975. Appendix A. The plant remains from Tell Abu Hureyra: a preliminary report. In A. M. T. Moore (ed.), The excavation of Tell Abu Hureyra in Syria: a preliminary report, 70–3. *Proceedings of the Prehistoric Society* 41, 50–77.

Hillman, G. C. 1981. Reconstructing crop husbandry practices from charred remains of crops. In R. Mercer (ed.), *Farming practice in British prehistory*, 123–62. Edinburgh: Edinburgh University Press.

Hillman, G. C. 1984. Interpretation of archaeological plant remains: the application of ethnographic models from Turkey. In W. van Zeist and W. A. Casparie (eds), *Plants and ancient man*, 1–41. Rotterdam: Balkema.

Hillman, G. C. and Davies, M. S. 1990. Domestication rates in wild wheats and barley under primitive cultivation. *Biological Journal of the Linnean Society* 39, 39–78.

Jones, J. G. 1994. Pollen evidence for early settlement and agriculture in northern Belize. *Palynology* 18, 205–11.

Jones, M. and Brown, T. 2007. Selection, cultivation and reproductive isolation: a reconsideration of the morphological and molecular signals of domestication. In T. Denham, J. Iriarte, and L. Vrydaghs (eds), *Rethinking agriculture: archaeological and ethnoarchaeological perspectives*, 36–49. Walnut Creek, CA: Left Coast Press.

Kahlberger, S. and Neumann, K. 2007. The development of plant cultivation in semi-arid West Africa. In T. Denham, J. Iriarte, and L. Vrydaghs (eds), *Rethinking agriculture: archaeological and ethnoarchaeological perspectives*, 320–46. Walnut Creek, CA: Left Coast Press.

Kaplan, L. and Lynch, T. F. 1999. *Phaseolus* (Fabaceae) in archaeology: AMS radiocarbon dates and their significance for pre-Columbian agriculture. *Economic Botany* 53, 261–72.

Kennett, D. J. and Winterhalder, B. (eds) 2006. *Behavioral ecology and the transition to agriculture*. Berkeley: University of California Press.

Lee, R. B. 1968. What hunters do for a living, or how to make-out on scarce resources. In R. B. Lee and I. DeVore (eds), *Man the hunter*, 30–48. Chicago: Aldine.

Lee, R. B. and DeVore, I. (eds) 1976. *Kalahari hunter-gatherers: studies of the !Kung San and their neighbors*. Cambridge, MA: Harvard University Press.

Lentfer, C. J. 2009. Tracing domestication and cultivation of bananas from phytoliths: an update from Papua New Guinea. *Ethnobotany Research and Applications* 7, 247–70.

Lepofsky, D. I. and Lertzman, K. 2008. Documenting ancient plant management in the Northwest of North America. *Botany* 86, 129–45.

Loy, T. H. 1994. Methods in the analysis of starch residues on prehistoric stone tools. In J. G. Hather (ed.), *Tropical archaeobotany: applications and new developments*, 86–114. London: Routledge.

McCorriston, J. 2006. Breaking the rain barrier and the tropical spread of Near Eastern agriculture into southern Arabia. In D. J. Kennett and B. Winterhalder (eds), *Behavioral ecology and the transition to agriculture*, 217–36. Berkeley: University of California Press.

MacNeish, R. S. 1967. A summary of subsistence. In D. S. Byers (ed.), *The prehistory of the Tehuacan Valley, Vol. 1, Environment and subsistence*, 290–309. Austin: University of Texas Press.

Maloney, B. K. 1994. The prospects and problems of using palynology to trace the origins of tropical agriculture: the case of Southeast Asia. In J. G. Hather (ed.), *Tropical archaeobotany: applications and new developments*, 139–71. London: Routledge.

Mangelsdorf, P. C. 1974. *Corn: its origin, evolution and improvement*. Cambridge, MA: Harvard University Press.

Manning, K., Pelling, R., Higham, T., Schwenninger, J.-L., and Fuller, D. Q. 2011. 4500-year old domesticated pearl millet (*Pennisetum glaucum*) from the Tilemnsi Valley, Mali: new insights into an alternative cereal domestication pathway. *Journal of Archaeological Science* 38, 312–22.

Mbida, C. H., de Langhe, E., Vrydaghs, L., Doutrelepont, H., Swennen, R. O., van Neer, W., and de Maret, P. 2006. Phytolith evidence for the early presence of domesticated banana (*Musa*) in Africa. In M. A. Zeder, D. G. Bradley, E. Emshwiller, and B. D. Smith (eds), *Documenting domestication: new genetic and archaeological paradigms*, 68–81. Berkeley: University of California Press.

Munson, P. J., Parmalee, P. W., and Yarnell, R. A. 1971. Subsistence ecology of Scovill, a Terminal Middle Woodland village. *American Antiquity* 36, 410–31.

Nakamura, I. and Sato, Y. 1999. Amplification of chloroplast DNA from a single ancient rice seed. *Rice Genetics* 2, 802–5.

Özkan, H., Willcox, G., Graner, A., Salamini, F., and Kilian, B. 2011. Geographic distribution and domestication of wild emmer wheat (*Triticum dicoccoides*). *Genetic Resources and Crop Evolution* 58, 11–53.

Pearsall, D. M. 2000. *Paleoethnobotany: a handbook of procedures* (2nd edition). San Diego: Academic Press.

Pearsall, D. M. and Piperno, D. R. (eds) 1993. *Current research in phytolith analysis: applications in archaeology and paleoecology*. Philadelphia: University of Pennsylvania Museum of Archaeology and Anthropology, MASCA Research Papers in Science and Archaeology 10.

Perry, L. 2004. Starch analyses reveal the relationship between tool type and function: an example from the Orinoco valley of Venezuela. *Journal of Archaeological Science* 31, 1069–81.

Pickersgill, B. 1989. Cytological and genetical evidence on the domestication and diffusion of crops within the Americas. In D. R. Harris and G. C. Hillman (eds), *Foraging and farming: the evolution of plant exploitation*, 426–39. London: Unwin Hyman.

Pickersgill, B. and Heiser, Jr., C. B. 1977. Origins and distribution of plants domesticated in the New World tropics. In C. A. Reed (ed.), *Origins of agriculture*, 808–35. The Hague: Mouton.

Piperno, D. R. 2006a. *Phytoliths: a comprehensive guide for archaeologists and paleoecologists*. Langham: AltaMira Press.

Piperno, D. R. 2006b. Identifying manioc (*Manihot esculenta* Crantz) and other crops in Pre-Columbian tropical America: a case study from Panama. In M. A. Zeder, D. G. Bradley, E. Emshwiller, and B. D. Smith (eds), *Documenting domestication: new genetic and archaeological paradigms*, 46–67. Berkeley: University of California Press.

Piperno, D. R. and Flannery, K. V. 2001. The earliest archaeological maize (*Zea mays* L.) from highland Mexico: new accelerator mass spectrometry dates and their implications. *Proceedings of the National Academy of Sciences USA* 98, 2101–3.

Piperno, D. R. and Holst, I. 1998. The presence of starch grains on prehistoric stone tools from the humid Neotropics: indications of early tuber use and agriculture in Panama. *Journal of Archaeological Science* 25, 765–76.

Piperno, D. R. and Pearsall, D. M. 1998. *The origins of agriculture in the lowland Neotropics*. San Diego: Academic Press.

Piperno, D. R., Ranere, A. J., Holst, I., Iriarte, J., and Dickau, R. 2009. Starch grain and phytolith evidence for early ninth millennium BP maize from the Central Rio Balsas River Valley, Mexico. *Proceedings of the National Academy of Sciences USA* 106, 5019–24.

Price, T. D. (ed.) 2000. *Europe's first farmers*. Cambridge: Cambridge University Press.

Price, T. D. and Bar-Yosef, O. (eds) 2011. The origins of agriculture: new data, new ideas. *Current Anthropology* 52, Wenner-Gren Symposium Supplement 4.

Price, T. D. and Gebauer, A. B. (eds) 1995. *Last hunters–first farmers: new perspectives on the prehistoric transition to agriculture*. Santa Fe: School of American Research Press.
Reed, C. A. (ed.) 1977. *Origins of agriculture*. The Hague: Mouton.
Rindos, D. 1984. *The origins of agriculture: an evolutionary perspective*. Orlando: Academic Press.
Sage, R. F. 2004. The evolution of C4 photosynthesis. *New Phytologist* 161, 341–70.
Smith, B. D. 1995, 2nd edition 1998. *The emergence of agriculture*. New York: Scientific American Library.
Smith, B. D. 2001a. Low-level food production. *Journal of Archaeological Research* 9, 1–43.
Smith, B. D. 2001b. Documenting plant domestication: the consilience of biological and archaeological approaches. *Proceedings of the National Academy of Sciences USA* 98, 1324–6.
Smith, B. D. 2005. Reassessing Coxcatlan cave and the early history of domesticated plants in Mesoamerica. *Proceedings of the National Academy of Sciences USA* 102, 9438–45.
Smith, B. D. 2006a. *Rivers of change: essays on early agriculture in eastern North America* (3rd edition). Tuscaloosa: University of Alabama Press.
Smith, B. D. 2006b. Eastern North America as an independent center of plant domestication. *Proceedings of the National Academy of Sciences USA* 103, 12223–8.
Smith, Jr., C. E. 1967. Plant remains. In D.S. Byers (ed.), *The prehistory of the Tehuacan Valley, Vol. 1. Environment and subsistence*, 220–55. Austin: University of Texas Press.
Stahl, A. B. 1993. Intensification in the West African Late Stone Age: a review from central Ghana. In T. Shaw, P. Sinclair, B. Andah, and A. Okpoko (eds), *The archaeology of Africa: food, metals and towns*, 261–73. London: Routledge.
Steward, J. H. 1930. Irrigation without agriculture. *Papers of the Michigan Academy of Sciences, Arts, and Letters* 12, 149–56.
Steward, J. H. 1936. The economic and social basis of primitive bands. In R. H. Lowie (ed.), *Essays in anthropology presented to A. L. Kroeber*, 331–50. Berkeley: University of California Press.
Steward, J. H. 1941. Culture element distributions: XIII Nevada Shoshoni. *University of California Anthropological Records* 4, 209–359.
Takahashi, R. and Hosoya, L. A. 2002. Nut exploitation in Jomon society. In S.L.R. Mason and J. G. Hather (eds), *Hunter-gatherer archaeobotany: perspectives from the northern temperate zone*, 146–55. London: Institute of Archaeology, University College London.
Thompson, R. G. 2006. Documenting the presence of maize in Central and South America through phytolith analysis of food residues. In M. A. Zeder, D. G. Bradley, E. Emshwiller, and B. D. Smith (eds), *Documenting domestication: new genetic and archaeological paradigms*, 82–95. Berkeley: University of California Press.
Tindale, N. B. 1977. Adaptive significance of the Panara or grass seed culture of Australia. In R. V. S. Wright (ed.), *Stone tools as cultural markers*, 345–9. Canberra: Australian Institute of Aboriginal Studies.
Torrence, R. and Barton, H. (eds) 2006. *Ancient starch research*. Walnut Creek, CA: Left Coast Press.
Ucko, P. J. and G. W. Dimbleby (eds) 1969. *The domestication and exploitation of plants and animals*. London: Duckworth.
Ugent, D., Pozorski, S., and Pozorski, T. 1982. Archaeological potato tuber remains from the Casma valley of Peru. *Economic Botany* 36, 182–92.
Ugent, D., Pozorski, S., and Pozorski, T. 1986. Archaeological manioc (*Manihot*) from coastal Peru. *Economic Botany* 40, 78–102.
Vavilov, N. I. 1926. *Studies on the origins of cultivated plants*. Leningrad: Institut Botanique Appliqué et d'Amélioration des Plantes.
Vavilov, N. I. 1992. *Origin and geography of cultivated plants*. Cambridge: Cambridge University Press (an English translation of Vavilov's collected papers).

Willcox, G. 2005. The distribution, natural habitats and availability of wild cereals in relation to their domestication in the Near East: multiple events, multiple centres. *Vegetation History and Archaeobotany* 14, 534–41.

Wohlgemuth, E. 2004. Archaeobotanical remains. In K. R. McGuire, M. G. Delacorte, and K. Carpenter (eds), *Archaeological excavations at Pie Creek and Tule Valley Shelters, Elko County, Nevada*, 96–104. Carson City: Nevada State Museum Anthropological Papers 25.

Zeder, M. A. 2008. Domestication and early agriculture in the Mediterranean Basin: origins, diffusion, and impact. *Proceedings of the National Academy of Sciences USA* 105, 11597–604.

Zeder, M. A., Bradley, D. G., Emshwiller, E., and Smith, B. D. (eds) 2006. *Documenting domestication: new genetic and archaeological paradigms*. Berkeley: University of California Press.

Zohary, D. 1969. The progenitors of wheat and barley in relation to domestication and agricultural dispersal in the Old World. In P. J. Ucko and G. W. Dimbleby (eds), *The domestication and exploitation of plants and animals*, 47–66. London: Duckworth.

Zohary, D. 1989. Domestication of the Southwest Asian Neolithic crop assemblage of cereals, pulses, and flax: the evidence from the living plants. In D. R. Harris and G. C. Hillman (eds), *Foraging and farming: the evolution of plant exploitation*, 358–73. London: Unwin Hyman.

Zohary, D. 1999. Monophyletic vs. polyphyletic origin of the crops on which agriculture was founded in the Near East. *Genetic Resources and Crop Evolution* 46, 133–42.

Zohary, D., Hopf, M., and Weiss, E. 2012. *Domestication of plants in the Old World: the origin and spread of domesticated plants in southwest Asia, Europe, and the Mediterranean Basin* (4th edition). Oxford: Oxford University Press.

CHAPTER 34

ANIMAL DOMESTICATIONS

ALAN K. OUTRAM

THE topic of animal domestication as a hunter-gatherer innovation is challenging for two principal reasons. Firstly, examining domestication from a hunter-gatherer point of view implies the study of the earliest stages in the process, which are the most difficult to see in the archaeological record. Many of the key indicators of domestication will only manifest themselves after the establishment of developed husbandry regimes. Secondly, with the exception of the dog, the majority of animal domestication events occur at a much later date than the emergence of plant agriculture in their respective geographic regions (Barker 2006; Clutton-Brock 1999; Reitz and Wing 2008, table 9.1). This chapter starts by examining what is meant by 'domestication' with respect to animals, then there is a discussion of the key ways of recognizing it in the archaeological record. The chapter then focuses on some case studies of animal domestication that relate specifically to hunter-gatherer innovation rather than the subsequent domestication of animals by early cereal agriculturalists.

DEFINING ANIMAL DOMESTICATION

To 'domesticate' means 'to accustom (an animal) to live under the care and near the habitations of man; to tame or bring under control...' (OED Online 2009), but there are both biological and cultural processes at play (Clutton-Brock 1999). The biological definition of domestication involves the reproductive isolation of domestic animals from wild stock (Clutton-Brock 1999) and controlled breeding conditions (Bökönyi 1989) that, deliberately or not, lead to the domesticates no longer being able to live or reproduce in the wild (Blumler and Byrne 1991). Such biological changes to animals are important to zoology and produce evidence that archaeologists can use to identify domestication, but the animals themselves are not the main focus of archaeological research.

From the human, cultural perspective, domestication involves significant social and economic change. In a practical sense, subsistence regimes change from extracting what one needs from the natural environment to a form of controlled production. Meadow (1984, 310) sees this as 'a shift from the dead to the living animal', with people investing time and effort in securing the future progeny of a herd rather than simply being interested in its immediate food value. This interest in the husbandry of the live animal becomes even more intense where the economy encompasses secondary products such as milk and wool. Beyond this basic economic interest in domesticated plants or animals, farming brings with it a whole new way of looking at and being in the world in symbolic and social terms, the *domus*, as Hodder (1990) puts it. As such, the narrow biological definition should not be the only one that archaeologists acknowledge. It is particularly important to note that biological changes take some time to manifest themselves (Ducos 1989) and they may significantly post-date marked economic and social changes. It is necessary to develop frameworks for identifying the first steps in the domestication process, employing multiple lines of evidence, involving more than just the faunal remains. When does interference and nurturing of the natural world become farming? When does the hunter-gatherer world view shift?

Some would argue that there is no simplistic dichotomy between wild and domestic (Vigne et al. 2005, 3) and it is meaningless to talk of it. There are few researchers who would still hold to a view of simple and unilinear progressive stages of cultural evolution. Layton et al. (1991) argue that hunting, gathering, herding, and cultivation are merely alternative strategies for subsistence that are selected adaptively according to circumstances and environment. These strategies can be used individually or in combinations, can involve symbiotic relationships between peoples, and reversion from one strategy to another is possible if adaptively beneficial. Redding (2005, 41) suggests that hunter-gatherers would have engaged in many 'failed experiments' regarding animal exploitation without having a goal of becoming farmers. Many such activities may not have been detected in the archaeological record, but some of the experiments did eventually lead to domestication.

Many peoples, considered to be hunter-gatherers, employ strategies that manipulate the natural state of resources, such as aboriginal Australians setting fires to increase productivity (Layton et al. 1991, 257). It has also been suggested that setting fires was a practice used in the European Mesolithic to create forest clearings and new growth to increase deer population and make hunting more productive (Mellars 1976). The use of tamed reindeer by the Saami, as draft or decoy animals within a hunting economy (Ingold 1980), is an excellent example of close control of selected animals that is not intended to change the mode of subsistence from hunting to pastoralism or farming.

Ingold (1980) argues that the transition from hunting to a pastoral economy is much more related to the social relations of production than it is to notions of domestication. He contends that 'pastoral property relations will become explicit and dominant at the point where the progeny of the domestic herds...become the principal subject matter of labour...where they come to function (ecologically) as productive resources rather than as agents of economic production' (Ingold 1980, 88). This is analogous to Meadow's (1984) view, above, as applied to domestication itself. Ingold (1980, 88), however, also makes the point that a domesticated animal could form a part of either a hunting or pastoral way of life.

To sum up, biological domestication, in terms of genetic isolation, results in useful lines of physical evidence, but it is not the most relevant concept to archaeological research. The key is identifying the point at which the human focus shifts to live animals and their progeny, and their mode of production has therefore changed. Attendant social and cultural changes must be considered alongside biological and environmental evidence in an integrated fashion.

Identifying Domestication

This section discusses the criteria that can be used to recognize the process of animal domestication in the archaeological record, including evaluation of whether those criteria speak to biological or cultural notions of domestication, and how quickly such traits are likely to manifest themselves. In order to be more comprehensive, examples are drawn from animal domestications by both hunter-gatherers and early cereal agriculturalists.

A number of key markers of domestication relate to changes in the skeleton caused by genetic separation, and thus provide evidence of 'biological domestication'. Some of these changes are likely to be the result of the 'founders' effect (Reitz and Wing 2008). The 'founders' are the originally tamed animals that bring with them only a limited selection of the total genetic variation found in the wild. Isolated domestic herds breed within this limited gene pool, with an increased likelihood that stock will develop particular traits. The herd may also be subject to selective breeding by humans to promote favoured phenotypes, but even without such deliberate intervention, the unintentional removal of certain natural selective pressures, such as competition between males for access to females, will result in variation from wild forms (Zeder 2006).

Among the most commonly employed indicators of domestication is a reduction in size (Zeder 2006; see Figure 34.1), although the reason why has been much debated. Suggestions that there was deliberate breeding for smaller stock to make herds more manageable are

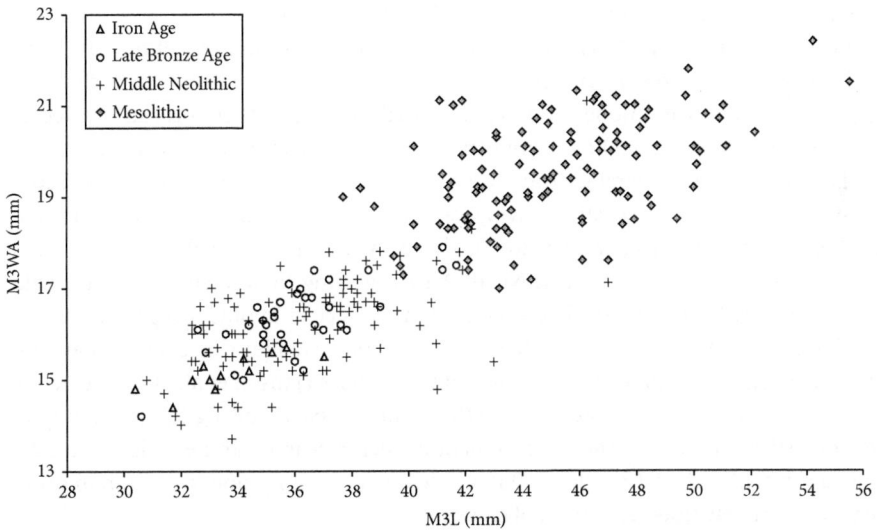

FIGURE 34.1 Biometry pig (*Sus*) third molars from prehistoric Denmark from the Mesolithic to Iron Age (M_3WA = width of anterior cusp, M_3L = maximum length). The wild Mesolithic specimens are clearly much larger, on average, than later domestic pigs of the Middle Neolithic onwards (courtesy of P. Rowley-Conwy, after Rowley-Conwy and Dobney 2007, fig. 7.6).

problematic as smaller stock are actually not necessarily more easily handled (Davis 1987). Non-genetic nutritional restrictions exerted by controlled husbandry are perhaps more likely to have had an effect (Meadow 1989). In island populations, reduced predation and competition removes selective pressures, allowing more reproductive success by smaller animals (Tchernov and Horwitz 1991) and early domestic isolation may be an analogous situation in these respects. Similarly, the removal of selective pressures relating to male competition might result in less sexual dimorphism and smaller males (Zeder 2006). Bias towards larger numbers of females in domestic herds may also give an impression of average size decrease (Zeder 2006). Furthermore, warmer climates can also reduce average animal sizes, because of selective pressures relating to body mass to skin surface area ratios and animals' ability to dissipate heat (Davis 1987). Considering the complexities of this particular indicator warns against reliance upon single lines of evidence. Even if the exact cause of size diminution is put aside, it should not be assumed that this indicator will immediately manifest itself upon initial domestication.

Another line of evidence that relates to genetic separation is morphological change. Many domestic animals display 'paedomorphic' (juvenile-like) physiological and behavioural traits (Zeder 2006). Domestic dogs and pigs both display shorter snouts and tooth rows and more pronounced foreheads than their wild forebears (Albarella et al. 2006; Reitz and Wing 2008). There are changes to the size and shape of the horns of sheep, goats, and cattle (Grigson 1978; Zeder 2006), which may be caused either by deliberate human selection, changes in selective pressures, or the founder's effect. In early domestic horses it appears that there is increased slenderness in the lower limbs (Outram et al. 2009) that might relate to differing selective pressures relating to locomotive capabilities. Again, one must ask how quickly after domestication such traits will display themselves, and this will vary according to the strength of selective pressures or deliberate breeding strategies.

With advances in DNA analysis, the genetic study of animal domestication has vastly increased, and there are three main approaches. Firstly, mitochondrial DNA or Y chromosome haplotypes taken from modern domestic animals in different regions can be used to model phylogenies (family trees) over time and space. Such data may show up clusters of closely related individuals separated from other clusters. If these are also very clearly separated in space, displaying alternative phylogeographic distributions, they may represent separate domestication events (Bradley 2006). This is the case for cattle, with one centre in India and another covering Europe and North Africa, relating to different progenitor wild species (Bradley and Magee 2006). Sheep and goats are less clear in phylogeographic terms, with a major dispersed cluster over the Near East and some smaller clusters that may represent separate domestication events (Bradley 2006). Horses (Jansen et al. 2002; Vilà et al. 2006) show a distinct lack of clustering in either time or space, raising the possibility of separate domestication events. The time element of such research can be added using the concept of a molecular clock (Bradley 2006), modelling rates of random mutation in order to understand the likely time separation of clusters.

There are difficulties with this approach as discontinuities are only interpreted as being related to domestication rather than environmental events that could lead to similar end results. The picture can also be made more complex by fast movement of animals, either due to their own migration or human trade (Bradley 2006). Interbreeding of wild and domestic stock may also produce new discontinuities (Olsen 2006a; 2006b) that represent something other than a pristine domestication event. One way to remove some of this equifinality is to integrate the study of ancient DNA (aDNA) (Bradley 2006), and this is the second major approach to archaeogenetics. By extracting, amplifying, and analysing aDNA from prehistoric animals, ambiguities in the interpretation of phylogenetic clusters are reduced by allowing characterization of wild ancestors and unambiguously dated remains from particular localities (Bradley 2006). A study combining ancient and modern DNA studies in cattle (Beja-Pereira et al. 2006) has shown that European cattle may not all have derived from Near Eastern domestic stock as there is evidence for local domestication, or at least interbreeding with wild aurochs, as well as introductions from North Africa. Whilst aDNA strengthens phylogenetic reconstruction, it is not problem free. aDNA does not preserve well in all conditions and heat is very damaging. The small amounts of recoverable aDNA usually need to be amplified through a process called PCR, and great care has to be taken to avoid contamination as that will get amplified too (Brown 2001). It is a method that requires great care and excellent facilities. The third approach is archaeogenomics, which uses modern and ancient DNA to study genomes and gene function (Bradley 2006). It is possible to identify genes responsible for particular traits. Some traits can be studied by zooarchaeologists from analysis of bone morphometrics, as discussed above, but it may be possible to track these changes genetically too. Importantly, this approach can be used to spot domestic traits that do not otherwise display themselves in surviving remains. Much of this work is still in its infancy, but a recent example has made use of genes that cause different coat colours in horses to come to conclusions about the timing and locality of early horse breeding in prehistory (Ludwig et al. 2009). This study showed that there was an expansion in coat colour range in Siberia from at least 3000 BC, indicating that region might have been the earliest to see extensive horse breeding.

Physical osteological evidence can also come from 'plastic' responses to domestication (Zeder 2006). These are not genetic changes to animals' morphology, but alterations made to individual animals as a result of conditions and activities related to their domestic status. Examples of this type of evidence are the characteristic wear of horses' teeth as a result of a bit being used (Bendrey 2007; Brown and Anthony 1998) (see Figure 34.2), vertebral pathologies associated with riding (Levine 1999), or foot pathologies in cattle caused by the strain of being used for traction (Johannsen 2005). Clearly such plastic responses will only develop if domestic animals are used or kept in a particular way.

Changes in the way that domestic animals were exploited are likely to produce different structures within herds. Most simply, there may be a shift in the emphasis on particular species or the arrival of new exotic species (Davis 1987). For instance, in the Near East, at sites like Tell Abu Hureyra, there was a sudden shift in emphasis from gazelle to sheep and goats (Legge and Rowley-Conwy 2000). However, within species, herd structures may also change to reflect particular methods of husbandry. Depending upon particular economic strategies that may aim at maximizing meat, milk, or wool production, or other uses like riding and traction, people may selectively cull within herds, resulting in characteristic ratios of sex and age of animals. There are well-established models for sheep and goats (Payne 1973) and cattle (Legge 2005). Such patterning will only display itself clearly if particular exploitation strategies have been adopted, and mixed uses of animals may be hard to interpret. Specialized herd use may also not develop at the same time as initial domestication.

There are many new, non-genetic biomolecular techniques that help us to understand animals' exploitation and domestication better, including lipid and protein residue analysis and stable isotope analysis of diets (Reitz and Wing 2008). The demonstration of the

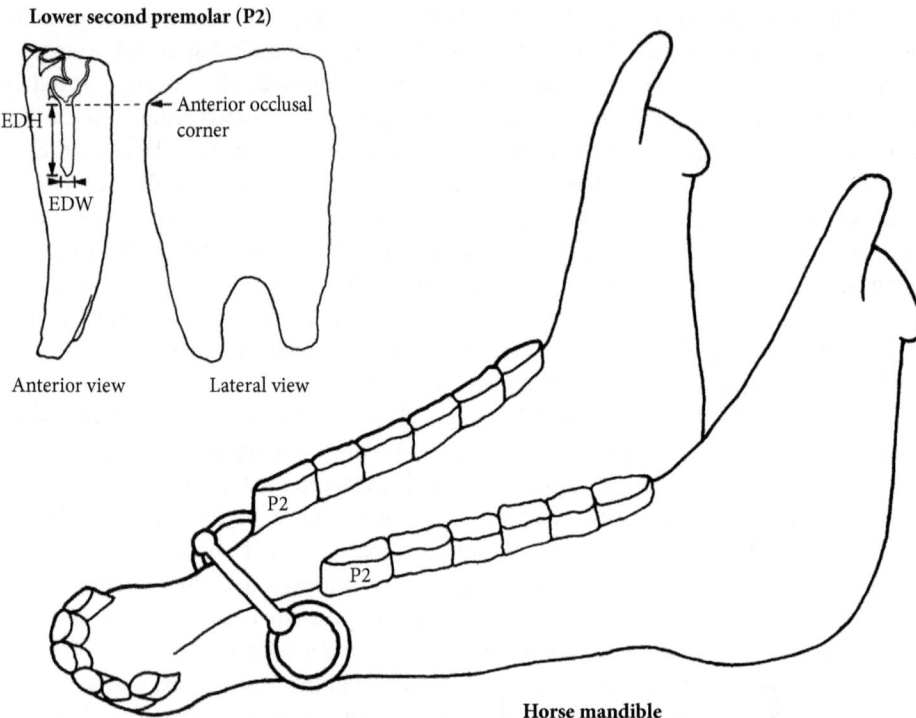

FIGURE 34.2 Diagram showing the position of the bit in a horse's mouth, and how it can cause wear on the second premolar (P2) and also irritate the bone of the jaw in front of the tooth row (diastema) causing further pathologies. The drawing of the P2 (top left) is of an archaeological specimen (Middle Iron Age), which had a bevel, and also a parallel-sided strip of enamel wear on the anterior face interpreted as biting damage (EDH = enamel/dentine wear height and EDW = wear width) (courtesy of R. Bendrey, after Bendrey 2007, figs 1 and 4).

presence of milk products from lipid (Dudd and Evershed 1999) and protein residues (Craig et al. 2000) in prehistoric pottery have clear potential in helping us to understand domestication. An advantage of lipid residues, from this point of view, is their greater ability to survive from the periods of early domestication events. Milk lipids have been recovered in abundance from seventh millennium BC ceramics from north-west Anatolia (Evershed et al. 2008) suggesting that milk exploitation started much closer to the earliest evidence of domestication than previously thought (see Figure 34.3).

Clearly, the transition to domestic stock rearing will impact upon a wide range of cultural practices including those not directly connected with animals. There may be significant changes to settlement structure, mobility, tool-kits, transport strategies, art, and ritual activities (Olsen 2006b). The best way forward is the combined use of biological proxies, integrated with a wide range of economic and cultural evidence. The most obvious proxies will not necessarily manifest themselves in the earliest stages of domestication, and it may be necessary to rely upon complex arguments that bring together many lines of contextual evidence.

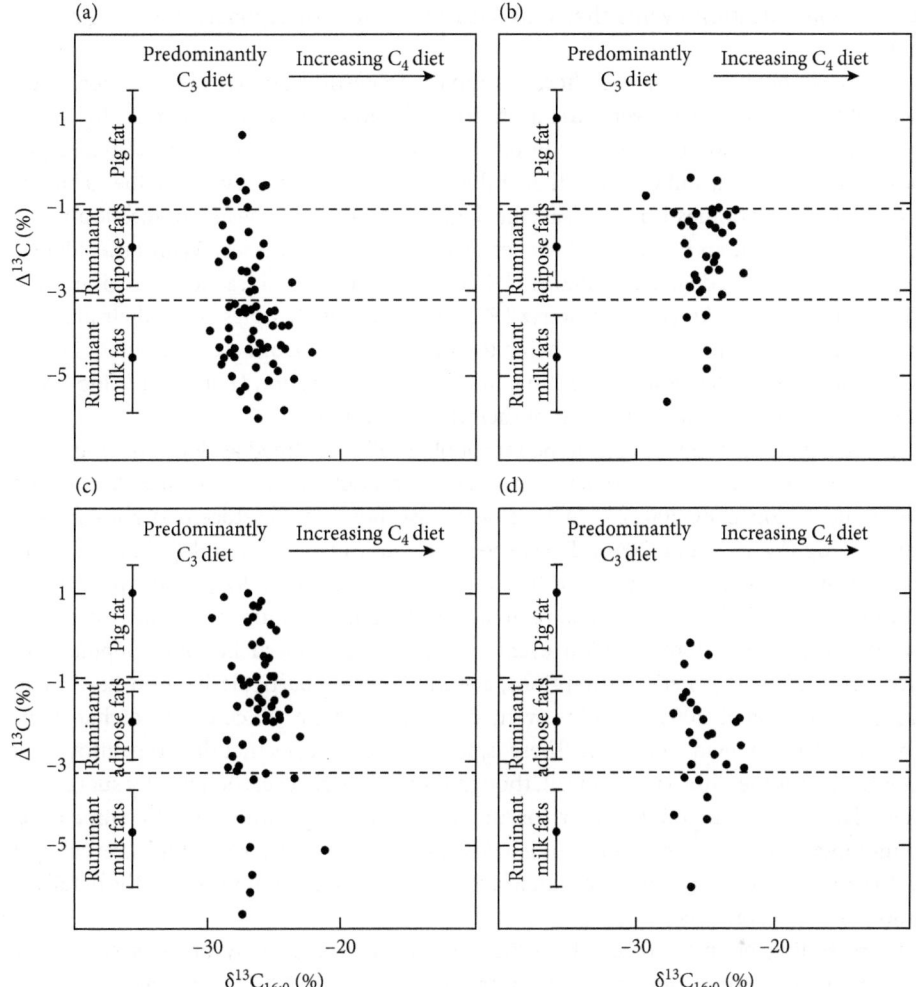

FIGURE 34.3 Plots of the $\Delta^{13}C$ (= $\delta^{13}C_{18:0} - \delta^{13}C_{16:0}$) values for archaeological animal fat residues in Neolithic pottery from: (a) NW Anatolia, (b) central Anatolia, (c) SE Europe/N Greece, and (d) Eastern Anatolia and the Levant. The plots show particularly strong evidence of milk use in NW Anatolia in pottery dating to the seventh millennium BC (courtesy of Richard Evershed, after Evershed et al. 2008).

ANIMAL DOMESTICATION AS A HUNTER-GATHERER INNOVATION

The majority of domestic animals, including goats, cattle, sheep, and pigs, were domesticated by populations who had already engaged for some time in plant agriculture (Harris 2013). These early plant farmers had already fundamentally changed their mode of production and world view, prior to extending domestic practices to fauna. Below

I review domestication events that were clearly, or, at least arguably, hunter-gatherer innovations.

The most obvious hunter-gatherer animal domestication is of the dog, and nineteenth-century scholars were already aware of the antiquity of this event. In *The origin of species*, Darwin (1910, 13; original edition 1859) stated 'barbarian man existed at an enormously remote period; and we know that at the present day there is hardly a tribe so barbarous, as not to have domesticated at least the dog'. As well as being the first domestic animal, dogs are also anomalous in the roles they perform within human society. Whilst there is evidence that prehistoric dogs were often exploited for both meat and traction in regions such as the plains of North America (Schwartz 1997), it is unlikely that these were their primary roles upon initial domestication, or thereafter, in most cases. Dogs are more ubiquitously seen as companions that assist in hunting, herding, and protection (Reitz and Wing 2008) and these uses are more likely motives for their domestication.

The earliest canid bone remains to be morphologically identified as domestic dog come from western Russia and date to between 13,000 and 17,000 BP in the Upper Palaeolithic (Sablin and Khlopachev 2002). Genetic studies also point to Pleistocene origins for the domestic dog (Wayne et al. 2006). Recent genetic studies have placed dog domestication very early indeed, at much more like 100,000 years ago (Vilá et al. 1997), which would place them in the Middle Palaeolithic before anatomically modern humans. If this were true, it would be the only domestication event involving pre-modern hominid populations. Based upon different genetic assumptions, a study focusing particularly upon East Asian dogs (Savolainen et al. 2002), puts the event at about 15,000 BP, which fits the archaeological and osteological evidence better. There is, however, consensus that the progenitor of all domestic dogs is the Eurasian grey wolf, though there are high levels of diversity suggesting either a large founding population or continued interbreeding with wolves for some time, and multiple domestication events are also possible (Wayne et al. 2006). Whilst revealing a Pleistocene origin of dogs from Eurasian wolves, genetics has not pinned down the details of the domestication process.

The reasoning behind wolves' domestication is not immediately obvious since they were originally hunting competitors (Schwartz 1997). Müller (2005) argues against purely functional uses of early domestic dogs and suggests that they started as emotional objects, becoming pets, with specific utilitarian functions being the result of later breeding. Wolves are very social animals that eat what humans eat and fit in well within a human social structure (Reitz and Wing 2008), so it is a distinct possibility that people affectionately rearing stray wolf pups could have led to domestication. Schwartz (1997) notes various ethnographic accounts of women suckling young animals and pet-keeping amongst native South American populations. Also, wolf packs expel adult wolves that continue to display the behaviour of pups, whilst these very animals are most likely to prosper and be accepted by humans (Schwartz 1997). Dogs do, after all, display paedomorphic traits.

Perhaps the roles of hunting and scavenging should not be totally rejected, however. Hunting cooperation need not have resembled the use of modern hunting dogs and it is easy to imagine wolves scavenging upon the large mammal kills of humans, and also being more effective than humans at tracking animals injured by the hunters. Without intention, wolves could have led humans to difficult-to-track kills. It is possible to envisage a kind of symbiosis that could have brought wolves and humans into regular contact, making association with juvenile wolves more likely. Food waste may well have attracted strays, and those less afraid and more able to fit into human society, and this could have been a successful survival strategy (Wang and Tedford 2008, 165).

Dogs were quite clearly domesticated by hunter-gatherers earlier than any other plant or animal, and they go on to be the most diverse of domestic animals, both in terms of physical form and their roles in society. It is less clear that it was a deliberate innovation, however. It was more likely a loose and organic process that led to much greater things, leaving a complex genetic and zooarchaeological record.

Horse domestication, on the other hand, was a relatively late event (Clutton-Brock 1999; Reitz and Wing 2008), well after the appearance of mixed farming in many regions of the world. As such, it seems a rather poor candidate for being a hunter-gatherer innovation, but recent work (Outram et al. 2009) raises this possibility. Genetic studies of modern domestic horses (*Equus caballus*) suggest there are several distinct phylogenetic clusters (Jansen 2002), meaning that there were either multiple domestication events, or a single event with domestic mares being impregnated by wild stallions, or deliberately captured wild mares being bred with domestic stallions, after some degree of separation in time and space (Olsen 2006a). Either way, the phylogenetic work does not clearly identify when and where horse domestication first took place, but a prime candidate is the Eurasian steppe during the Eneolithic period. Much attention has concentrated on the Botai Culture, northern Kazakhstan, in the mid fourth millennium BC, where faunal assemblages consist almost entirely of horse remains (Anthony 2007; Olsen 2006a).

Olsen (2006a; 2006b; Olsen et al. 2006) has made a wide-ranging archaeological case for horse herding, and at least some domestic horses, within the Botai Culture. She argues that the highly organized and semi-sedentary settlement structure contrasts greatly with the preceding period, which was characterized by ephemeral hunter-gatherer camps. Reduced mobility does not sit well with Botai people hunting mobile horse herds. Horse skeletal part abundances show none of the differential transport patterns associated with hunting and transporting large prey like horses (Outram and Rowley-Conwy 1998), and their tool-kit contains a relative paucity of projectile points and hunting equipment. Instead, one finds tools possibly used for the production of leather straps, more likely to be associated with animal husbandry (Olsen 2006a). Anthony (2007) supports this line of argument and refers to his work that showed possible bit wear, and harnessing, of Botai horses (Brown and Anthony 1998). However, that method of identifying bit wear has been criticized for possible equifinality (Levine 2004). Levine (2003) also argues that age structures at Botai do not show a pattern consistent with a specialized husbandry strategy, but it is illogical to conclude that this is evidence against domestication, since there is no reason why initial husbandry would be so specialized, as it could have encompassed mixed use of primary and secondary products, as well as keeping animals for riding.

Recently the picture has become clearer with three new lines of evidence that support there being domestic horses at Botai (Outram et al. 2009). Metrical analyses, involving indices of slenderness in horse metacarpals, have shown that Botai horses closely resemble domestic Bronze Age specimens from Kazakhstan, but differ significantly from Palaeolithic wild horses in nearby southern Russia (Outram et al. 2009). A novel technique for identifying bit wear (Bendrey 2007), that eliminates equifinality, reaffirms the presence of bit wear at Botai. Lastly, lipid residue analyses have directly demonstrated the presence of mares' milk (see Figure 34.4) in Botai ceramics (Outram et al. 2009), something that is fairly emphatic

FIGURE 34.4 A horse being milked in modern-day Kazkhstan. The milk is fermented into a mildly alcoholic drink called *koumiss*, which is sometimes also smoked to add further flavour (photograph by the author).

evidence of domestication. New conclusions based upon aDNA work investigating horse coat colour are consistent with the general timing and location of Botai (Ludwig et al. 2009).

The cultures immediately preeceding the Eneolithic Botai Culture in northern Kazakhstan were the Atbasar and Makhandzhar Cultures (Kislenko and Tatarintseva 1999). Whilst possessing ceramics, their economy was based upon hunting and gathering in the forest steppe, and probably also fishing (Kislenko and Tatarintseva 1999). It seems that there was a direct shift from hunting horses to herding them in this region, and that the horses were quickly exploited for secondary products such as milk and transport. All this occurred with no apparent exploitation of domestic crops. Further work is needed to be sure that this was a truly indigenous development, but, until further evidence comes to light, the earliest horse domestication remains a possible hunter-gatherer innovation.

Dogs and horses are the main two case studies in this chapter, because they illustrate different processes and evidence. Below is a brief discussion of other candidates.

Reindeer potentially share a number of characteristics with horses, being a hunted animal that can be tamed and exploited for meat, hides, milk, and traction (Ingold 1980) within a context lacking domestic plants. Whilst current reindeer herders are well understood (see Ingold 1980), the topic of reindeer domestication is in need of much further work and strong evidence of the earliest domestication is lacking (but see Baskin 2000; Mirov 1945; Weinstock 2000). Camelids (llama and alpaca) in the Andes of South America may have been domesticated by hunter-gatherers without a buffering period of domestic plant exploitation (Aldenderfer 2006; Mengoni Goñalons and Yacobaccio 2006). Some argue for early camelid herding in arid regions some time prior to plant domestication (e.g. Hesse 1982), whilst others see camelid domestication co-evolving in a mutual process with the domestication of chenopodium (e.g. Kuznar 1993). Whilst cattle domestication in the Near East followed a period of cereal agriculture, Marshall and Hildebrand (2002) present the case for North African cattle being domesticated independently by hunter-gatherers in the tenth millennium BP, 5,000 years before the domestication of African plants. The motivation could have been to develop higher predictability and mobility of food resources in the marginal lands of the Sahara, with its very localized and short-term droughts (Marshall and Hildebrand 2002). Whilst clearly domesticated from *Bos primigenius*, genetic analyses are potentially supportive of a separate domestication event in North Africa (Beja-Pereira et al. 2006).

The principal candidates for direct domestication by hunter-gatherers have been discussed above, but these are clearly the minority of cases, with the most significant centres of domestication (the Near East, East Asia, and Central America) involving a significant period of plant agriculture before animal husbandry develops. Why did animals come later in these cases? In Central and North America it may relate to the lack of amenable native species, but in the other areas the need for animal fodder may well play a role. In mixed farming regimes, fodder is a crucial by-product of plant agriculture, and manure is a return benefit from animals to plants. The introduction of agriculture may have resulted in the necessary land clearance and fodder required, in some environments, to enable year-round animal husbandry. In contrast, such limiting factors may have been absent in relation to the control of steppe-adapted horses or loose husbandry of reindeer, whilst being irrelevant to the dog domestication.

Simply understanding what we mean by 'domestication', when considering hunter-gatherer innovations, is something of a challenge. We need to distinguish between 'biological' and 'cultural' domestication of animals, but also be cognizant that humans can go through a domestication process too in terms of both world view and mode of production. Much work is yet to be done in understanding the timing and nature of animal domestications. Undoubtedly we need to approach the topic by employing multiple lines of evidence, whether direct, indirect, or contextual, and engage in interdisciplinary cooperation, to increase our chances of coming to a fulsome understanding of the issue.

References

Albarella, U., Dobney, K., and Rowley-Conwy, P. 2006. The domestication of the pig (*Sus scrofa*): new challenges and approaches. In M. A. Zeder, D. G. Bradley, E. Emschwiller, and B. D. Smith (eds), *Documenting domestication: new genetic and archaeological paradigms*, 209–27. Berkeley: University of California Press.

Aldenderfer, M. 2006. Costly signalling, the sexual division of labor, and animal domestication in the Andean Highlands. In D. J. Kennett and B. Winterhalder (eds), *Behavioural ecology and the transition to agriculture*, 167–96. Berkley: University of California Press.

Anthony, D. W. 2007. *The horse, the wheel and language*. Princeton: Princeton University Press.

Barker, G. 2006. *The agricultural revolution in prehistory: why did foragers become farmers?* Oxford: Oxford University Press.

Baskin, L. M. 2000. Reindeer husbandry/hunting in Russia in the past, present, and future. *Polar Research* 19, 23–9.

Beja-Pereira, A., Caramelli, D., Lalueza-Fox, C., Vernesi, C., Ferrand, N., Casoli, A., Goyache, F., Royo, L. J., Conti, S., Lari, M., Martini, A., Ouragh, L., Magid, A., Atash, A., Zsolnai, A., Boscato, P., Triantaphylidis, C., Ploumi, K., Sineo, L., Mallegni, F., Taberlet, P., Erhardt, G., Sampietro, L., Bertranpetit, J., Barbujani, G., Luikart, G., and Bertorelle, G. 2006. The origin of European cattle: evidence from modern and ancient DNA. *Proceedings of the National Academy of Sciences USA* 103, 8113–8.

Bendrey, R. 2007. New methods for the identification of evidence of bitting on horse remains from archaeological sites. *Journal of Archaeological Science* 34, 1036–50.

Blumler, M. A. and Byrne, R. 1991. The ecological genetics of domestication and the origins of agriculture. *Current Anthropology* 32, 23–35.

Bökönyi, S. 1989. Definitions of animal domestication. In J. Clutton-Brock (ed.), *The walking larder: patterns of domestication, pastoralism and predation*, 22–7. London: Unwin Hyman.

Bradley, D. G. 2006. Documenting domestication: reading animal genetic texts. In M. A. Zeder, D. G. Bradley, E. Emschwiller, and B. D. Smith (eds), *Documenting domestication: new genetic and archaeological paradigms*, 273–8. Berkeley: University of California Press.

Bradley, D. G. and Magee, D. A. 2006. Genetics and the origins of domestic cattle. In M. A. Zeder, D. G. Bradley, E. Emschwiller, and B. D. Smith (eds), *Documenting domestication: new genetic and archaeological paradigms*, 317–28. Berkeley: University of California Press.

Brown, D. and Anthony, D. 1998. Bit wear, horseback riding and the Botai site in Kazakhstan. *Journal of Archaeological Science* 25, 331–47.

Brown, T. A. 2001. Ancient DNA. In D. R. Brothwell and A. M. Pollard (eds), *Archaeological sciences*, 301–12. Chichester: Wiley.

Clutton-Brock, J. 1999. *A natural history of domestic mammals* (2nd edition). Cambridge: Cambridge University Press.

Craig, O., Mulville, J., Parker Pearson, M., Sokol, R., Gelsthorpe, K., Stacey, R., and Collins, M. 2000. Detecting milk proteins in ancient pots. *Nature* 408, 312.

Darwin, C. 1910. *The origin of the species by means of natural selection*. Corrected Popular Impression of 6th edition. London: John Murray.

Davis, S. J. M. 1987. *The archaeology of animals*. London: Batsford.

Ducos, P. 1989. Defining domestication, a clarification. In J. Clutton-Brock (ed.), *The walking larder: patterns of domestication, pastoralism and predation*, 28–30. London: Unwin Hyman.

Dudd, S. N. and Evershed, R. P. 1999. Direct demonstration of milk as an element of archaeological economies. *Science* 282, 1478–81.

Evershed, R. P., Payne, S., Sherratt, A. G., Copley, M. S., Coolidge, J., Urem-Kotsu, D., Kotsakis, K., Özdoğan, M., Özdoğan, A. E., Nieuwenhuyse, O., Akkermans, P. M. M. G., Bailey, D., Andeescu, R.,-R., Campbell, S., Farid, S., Hodder, I., Yalman, N., Özbaşaran, M., Biçakci, E., Garfinkel, Y., Levi, T., and Burton, M. M. 2008. Earliest date for milk use in the Near East and south-eastern Europe linked to cattle herding. *Nature* 455, 528–31.

Grigson, C. 1978. The craniological relationships of four species of Bos. *Journal of Archaeological Science* 5, 123–52.

Harris, D. R. 2013. *Plant domestications*. Oxford: Oxford University Press.

Hesse, B. 1982. Archaeological evidence for camelid exploitation in the Chilean Andes. *Saugetierkunde Mitteilungen* 30, 201–11.

Hodder, I. 1990. *The domestication of Europe*. Oxford: Blackwell.

Ingold, T. 1980. *Hunters, pastoralists and ranchers*. Cambridge: Cambridge University Press.

Jansen, T., Forster, P., Levine, M. A., Oelke, H., Hurles, M., Renfrew, C., Weber, J., and Olek, K. 2002. Mitichondrial DNA and the origins of the domestic horse. *Proceedings of the National Academy of Sciences USA* 99, 10905–10.

Johannsen, N. N. 2005. Palaeopathology and Neolithic cattle traction: methodological issues and archaeological perspectives. In J. Davis, M. Fabiš, I. Mainland, and R. Thomas (eds), *Diet and health in past animal populations*, 39–51. Oxford: Oxbow.

Kislenko, A., and Tatarintseva, N. 1999. The Eastern Ural Steppe at the end of the stone age. In M. Levine, Y. Rassamakin, A. Kislenko, and N. Tatarintseva (eds), *Late prehistoric exploitation of the Eurasian steppe*, 183–216. Cambridge: McDonald Institute for Archaeological Research.

Kuznar, L. A. 1993. Mutualism between chenopodium, herd animals, and herders in the South Central Andes. *Mountain Research and Development* 13, 257–65.

Layton, R., Foley, R., and Williams, E. 1991. The transition between hunting and gathering and specialized husbandry of resources: a socio-ecological approach. *Current Anthropology* 32, 255–63.

Legge, A. J. 2005. Milk use in prehistory: the osteological evidence. In J. Mulville and A. K. Outram (eds), *The zooarchaeology of fats, oils, milk and dairying*, 8–13. Oxford: Oxbow.

Legge, A. J. and Rowley-Conwy, P. A. 2000. The exploitation of animals. In A. M. T. Moore, G. C. Hillman, and A. J. Legge (eds), *Village on the Euphrates: from foraging to farming at Abu Hureyra*, 423–74. Oxford: Oxford University Press.

Levine, M. A. 1999. The origins of horse husbandry on the Eurasian steppe. In M. Levine, Y. Rassamakin, A. Kislenko, and N. Tatarintseva (eds), *Late prehistoric exploitation of the Eurasian Steppe*, 5–58. Cambridge: McDonald Institute for Archaeological Research.

Levine, M. A. 2003. Focusing on Central Asian archaeology: east meets west. In M. Levine, C. Renfrew, and K. Boyle (eds), *Prehistoric steppe adaptation and the horse*, 1–10. Cambridge: McDonald Institute for Archaeological Research.

Levine, M. A. 2004. Exploring the criteria for early horse domestication. In M. Jones (ed.), *Traces of ancestry: studies in honour of Colin Renfrew*, 115–26. Cambridge: McDonald Institute for Archaeological Research.

Ludwig, A., Pruvost, M., Reissmann, M., Benecke, N., Brockmann, G. A., Castaños, P., Cieslak, M., Lippold, S., Llorente, L., Malaspinas, A.-S., Slatkin, M., and Hofreiter, M. 2009. Coat color variation at the beginning of horse domestication. *Science* 324, 485.

Marshall, F. and Hildebrand, E. 2002. Cattle before crops: the beginnings of food production in Africa. *Journal of World Prehistory* 16, 19–143.

Meadow, R. H. 1984. Animal domestication in the Middle East: a view from the eastern margin. In J. Clutton-Brock and C. Grigson (eds), *Animals in archaeology. Volume 3. Early herders and their flocks*, 309–37. Oxford: British Archaeological Reports, International Series 202.

Meadow, R. H. 1989. Osteological evidence for the process of animal domestication. In J. Clutton-Brock (ed.), *The walking larder: pat terns of domestication, pastoralism and predation*, 80–90. London: Unwin Hyman.

Mellars, P. A. 1976. Fire ecology, animal populations and man: the study of ecological relationships in prehistory. *Proceedings of the Prehistoric Society* 42, 15–45.

Mengoni Goñalons, G. L. and Yacobaccio, H. D. 2006. The domestication of South American camalids: a view from South-Central Andes. In M. A. Zeder, D. G. Bradley, E. Emschwiller, and B. D. Smith (eds), *Documenting domestication: new genetic and archaeological paradigms*, 228–44. Berkeley: University of California Press.

Mirov, N. T. 1945. Notes on the domestication of reindeer. *American Anthropologist* 47, 393–408.

Müller, W. 2005. The domestication of the wolf—the inevitable first? In J.-D. Vigne, J. Peters, and D. Helmer (eds), *The first steps of animal domestication*, 34–40. Oxford: Oxbow.

Olsen, S. A. 2006a. Early horse domestication on the Eurasian Steppe. In M. A. Zeder, D. G. Bradley, E. Emschwiller, and B. D. Smith (eds), *Documenting domestication: new genetic and archaeological paradigms*, 245–69. Berkeley: University of California Press.

Olsen, S. A. 2006b. Early horse domestication: weighing the evidence. In S. L. Olsen, S. Grant, A. M. Choyke, and L. Bartosiewicz (eds), *Horses and humans: the evolution of human-equine relationships*, 81–113. Oxford: Archaeopress, British Archaeological reports, International Series 1560.

Olsen, S. A., Bradley, B., Maki, D., and Outram, A. 2006. Community organization among Copper Age sedentary horse pastoralists of Kazakhstan. In D. L. Peterson, L. M. Popova, and A. T. Smith (eds), *Beyond the steppe and the sown. Proceedings of the 2002 University of Chicago Conference on Eurasian Archaeology*, 89–111. Leiden: Brill.

Outram, A. K. and Rowley-Conwy, P. 1998. Meat and marrow utility indices for horse (*Equus*). *Journal of Archaeological Science* 25, 839–49.

Outram, A. K., Stear, N. A., Bendrey, R., Olsen, S., Kasparov, A., Zaibert, V., Thorpe, N., and Evershed, R. P. 2009. The earliest horse harnessing and milking. *Science* 323, 1332–5.

Payne, S. 1973. Kill off patterns in sheep and goats: the mandibles from Asvan Kale. *Anatolian Studies* 23, 281–303.

Redding, R. W. 2005. Breaking the mold: a consideration of variation in the evolution of animal domestication. In J.-D. Vigne, J. Peters, and D. Helmer (eds), *The first steps of animal domestication*, 41–8. Oxford: Oxbow.

Reitz, E. J. and Wing, E. S. 2008. *Zooarchaeology* (2nd edition). Cambridge: Cambridge University Press.

Rowley-Conwy, P. and Dobney, K. 2007. Wild boar and domestic pigs in Mesolithic and Neolithic southern Scandinavia. In U. Albarella, K. Dobney, A. Ervynck, and P. Rowley-Conwy (eds), *Pigs and humans: 10,000 years of interactions*, 131–55. Oxford: Oxford University Press.

Sablin, M. V. and Khlopachev, G. A. 2002. The earliest Ice Age dogs: evidence from Eliseevichi. *Current Anthropology* 43, 795–9.

Savolainen, P., Zhang, Y., Lou, J., Lundeberg, J., and Leitner, T. 2002. Genetic evidence for an East Asian origin of domestic dogs. *Science* 298, 1610–3.

Schwartz, M. 1997. *A history of dogs in the early Americas*. New Haven: Yale University Press.

Tchernov, E. and Horwitz, L. K. 1991. Body size diminution under domestication: unconscious selection in primeval domesticates. *Journal of Anthropological Archaeology* 10, 54–75.

Vigne, J.-D., Helmer, D., and Peters, J. 2005. New archaeozoological approaches to trace the first steps of animal domestication: general presentation, reflections and proposals. In J.-D. Vigne, J. Peters, and D. Helmer (eds), *The first steps of animal domestication*, 1–16. Oxford: Oxbow.

Vilà, C., Leonard, J. A., and Beja-Pereira, A. 2006. Genetic documentation of horse and donkey domestication. In M. A. Zeder, D. G. Bradley, E. Emschwiller, and B. D. Smith (eds), *Documenting domestication: new genetic and archaeological paradigms*, 342–53. Berkeley: University of California Press.

Vilà, C., Savolainen, P., Maldonado, J. E., Amorim, I. R., Rice, J. E., Honeycutt, R. L., Crandall, K. A., Lundeberg, J., and Wayne, R. K. 1997. Multiple and ancient origins of the domestic dog. *Science* 276, 1687–9.

Wang, X. and Tedford, R. H. 2008. *Dogs: their fossil relatives and evolutionary history*. New York: Columbia University Press.

Wayne, R. K., Leonard, J. A., and Vilà, C. 2006. Genetic analysis of dog domestication. In M. A. Zeder, D. G. Bradley, E. Emschwiller, and B. D. Smith (eds), *Documenting domestication: new genetic and archaeological paradigms*, 279–93. Berkeley: University of California Press.

Weinstock, J. 2000. Osteometry as a source of refined demographic information: sex-ratios of reindeer, hunting strategies, and herd control in the late glacial site of Stellmoor, northern Germany. *Journal of Archaeological Science* 27, 1187–95.

Zeder, M. A. 2006. Archaeological approaches to documenting animal domestication. In M. A. Zeder, D. G. Bradley, E. Emschwiller, and B. D. Smith (eds), *Documenting domestication: new genetic and archaeological paradigms*, 171–80. Berkeley: University of California Press.

PART V

THE PERSISTENCE OF HUNTING AND GATHERING AMONGST FARMERS IN PREHISTORY AND BEYOND

CHAPTER 35

HUNTING AND GATHERING IN A FARMERS' WORLD

VICKI CUMMINGS

INTRODUCTION: HUNTER-GATHERERS AND THE TRANSITION TO AGRICULTURE

THE rise of agriculture has widely been regarded as one of the most important shifts in human existence. Agro-pastoral farming economies can support higher population densities, and the capacity to feed greater concentrations of people in one place, and for long periods, was a crucial development that led to the rise of urban centres, states, and empires. The emergence of agricultural economies therefore underpins many important later developments in human history. However, the origins of farming, and the ways in which it spread, are highly complex, and have been the focus of some of the most long-standing debates in prehistoric archaeology.

Some of the earliest evidence for prehistoric plant domestications comes from western Asia in the closing phases of the Pleistocene, but other crops that went on to become staples were also domesticated independently in a number of other world regions during the early Holocene. Generally, a range of different early domesticates was used in close local combination, and these crop 'packages' were then adjusted slowly over time, either through further local domestications of wild species, or by adding in other domesticated crops from other regions (see Harris, this volume). In general, plants were domesticated before animals (Outram, this volume), but different local combinations of domesticated plants and animals went on to form the basis of a number of different early agricultural systems that emerged in separate parts of the world. After these early agro-pastoral economies became established, often as part of a slow process lasting many millennia, they then began to spread into surrounding regions, forming part of a much wider global transition to farming. Over time, this process constituted one of the most important economic transformations to affect global humanity, and this fact alone has ensured that it remained one of the most fundamentally important research themes in archaeology.

The role of hunting and gathering in the transition to agriculture has been regarded as both utterly central to its initiation but also somewhat tangential and indeed irrelevant to its later dispersal. For example, at a local level, hunter-gatherers *invented* farming—it is now clear that subtle modifications by foragers in their wild plant gathering and management practices, along with new kinds of selective hunting, taming, and herding strategies, were of fundamental importance as they must have created the contexts for the slow process of different plant and animal domestication events that played out in different parts of the world. In starting to incorporate increasing management of plants and animals into their subsistence strategies, many prehistoric hunter-gatherers began to create transitional or intermediate economies that included elements of early plant domestication, initial use of domestic animals, as well as additional forms of hunting and wild plant gathering. Over time they went on to develop a much fuller reliance on domesticates, leading to the first fully established farming economies.

Up until this juncture, the world had been inhabited solely by hunter-gatherers. Now hunter-gatherers were increasingly sharing the world with early farming communities. As the practice of farming began its relentless expansion into new areas throughout the Holocene, the role of hunter-gatherers in this wider transition tends to be obscured from view. This perspective is inherently problematic: hunter-gatherers were responsible for the domestication of plants and many animals and they may also have played a central role in the dispersal of this new kind of economy into other regions. Understanding the transition to agriculture, and the role of hunter-gatherers in this transition, has been the subject of some of the most important and enduring debates in prehistoric archaeology. This has especially been the case in Europe, but in other areas too. That farming eventually spread into most corners of the world is clear, probably by a variety of different processes and contingent scenarios. However, the exact role of hunter-gatherers in these regional transitions remains one of the most important themes in prehistoric archaeology.

More precisely, understanding the transition to farming requires an investigation of the form, content, and also the ideological significance of forager–farmer interactions and contact zones as they emerged and played out across different world regions during the Holocene. This is because these general debates tend to boil down to the same sets of questions: were hunter-gatherers swept aside or quickly assimilated by the expansion of early farming populations? Or was it merely knowledge of farming that spread among foragers, who then decided to take up agriculture? Was the transition to agriculture just about the rise of a new kind of economy, or did agricultural dispersals form part of a wider 'package' of innovations that included other kinds of material culture and technology? Was the spread of this new economy really of primary importance, or was it merely secondary to an earlier and more fundamentally important ideological shift that eventually made farming acceptable to hunter-gatherers? This chapter reviews treatment of these questions, and looks at how to move this debate forwards.

Aims of Part V

This part aims to critically examine how these general questions have been subject to regional debate, focusing on chapters which look at case studies from a wide range of regions across the world. Primary consideration is given to the emergence of early debates in Europe. Many of these debates about hunter-gatherers and the transition to farming first emerged in nineteenth-century Europe; their enduring legacy continues to structure debates through to the present day. They are also relevant to many other parts of the world, but in some cases have not been central. Of particular importance in Europe were early definitions of the Neolithic with explicit links to a farming economy, but also to other kinds of material culture, and indeed ideology: it is in Europe that forager–farmer interactions and the transition to agriculture have also become synonymous with the onset of the Neolithic. Having examined different definitions of the Neolithic, it is also important to examine how different mechanisms have been argued to be responsible for its spread. Was it a sudden economic and technological shift, or a more slow and drawn-out process—not so much the Neolithic but *Neolithization*? The goal of this part of the handbook, then, is to explore how these regional transitions have been approached and understood, highlighting the role of forager–farmer interactions, but viewing them specifically from a hunter-gatherer perspective.

Research Framework: The Neolithic Transition to Farming

Late nineteenth- and early twentieth-century traditions of research and thinking continue to structure current interpretations of forager–farmer interactions to a remarkable extent. In the nineteenth century the creation of the three-age system by Thomsen divided European prehistory into Stone, Bronze, and Iron Ages (Rowley-Conwy 2007). Apart from in Denmark (Kristiansen 2002, 20), most early archaeological considerations were focused on material culture, particularly stone tools for the Stone Age, and metalwork for the Bronze and Iron Ages. Early and mid-nineteenth-century excavations in Europe produced considerable archaeological material, so that by the latter part of the century Lubbock (1865) suggested that the Stone Age needed subdividing into the Old Stone Age (Palaeolithic) and New Stone Age (Neolithic). These two periods were distinctive in relation to both faunal remains found as well as stone tool types—extinct megafauna and chipped stone tools from the Palaeolithic, compared to cultivated plants and domestic animal species and polished stone tools and pottery from the Neolithic (Trigger 2006, 114). Later on, transitional stone tool technologies were recognized and a Middle Stone Age (the Mesolithic) added to the prehistoric sequence (and see Cummings, this volume).

Towards the end of the nineteenth century scholars started to pay less attention to the archaeological record, instead focusing their attention on ethnology. This followed the idea that the study of modern living peoples could inform our understanding of the past, to the extent that it is possible to comprehend every element of prehistoric life simply by studying modern living equivalents. So in order to gain insights into life in the Stone Age, scholars simply needed to study living peoples who were at an equivalent technological stage (Trigger 2006, 146). This approach tied in with a social evolutionary framework with a focus on the economy, since it was noted that hunter-gatherers tended to be technologically less advanced than farming groups. It was at this stage, then, that there was a shift in focus from material culture to economy, and that the Mesolithic became associated with hunter-gatherers and the Neolithic with agriculture. While this specific way of thinking saw little support beyond the nineteenth century, social evolutionary thinking had a long-lasting impact (also see Pluciennik, this volume).

In the first part of the twentieth century Gordon Childe wrote the first major synthesis of European prehistory using a culture-historical framework. Culture-history placed its emphasis not on understanding past peoples via ethnographic analogy but through their material remains. By studying sets of material culture found in the archaeological record it was possible to identify distinctive cultural groups (Childe 1925; 1929). Childe had a particular interest in the Neolithic period, and for him, the big change in prehistory came at the start of the Neolithic, which he described as a 'revolution'. While the culture-historical framework within which Childe was operating did not emphasize what people did (i.e. either hunt and gather or farm) but what they *had* (i.e. pots, polished stone tools, and so on: Barker 2006, 15), the Neolithic revolution nevertheless became synonymous with the advent of farming as it was part of the broader set of Neolithic traits.

Furthermore, Childe also emphasized the importance of pottery in the Neolithic revolution which he assumed was exclusively associated with farming populations (Childe 1942, 57). Thus, Childe had essentially mapped the social evolutionary categories of 'hunter-gatherer' and 'farmer' on the archaeological sequences of Europe, associating them specifically with two periods of prehistory, the Mesolithic and Neolithic. Childe's model did not just define prehistoric cultures, it also provided an explanatory framework for cultural change as well as a chronology (see below). For Childe, changes in cultures were caused by diffusion and migration (Green 1981, 52–3). Thus Childe explained how the Neolithic spread into Europe: agriculture and pottery spread via diffusion and migration from the Near East. This was to set the tone of debates for generations to come.

European Sequences and Debates

By the mid-twentieth century the transition from the Mesolithic and Neolithic was discussed in fairly simplistic terms: it involved the wholesale spread of people carrying a new *economic* regime, along with a distinctive set of new material culture, across the whole of Europe via migration and diffusion (only in Scandinavia were there hints of something more complex going on: Kristiansen 2002, 20). Thus agricultural peoples swept across Europe, and there was only limited discussion of the fate of the Mesolithic hunter-gatherer populations. Before radiocarbon dating attention was firmly focused on material culture not only as a cultural identifier but also to enable cross-dating with historical sequences. Indeed Childe used this method to date European prehistoric cultures, creating a short chronology for the European sequence (see Renfrew 1973, 39–47). The Neolithic was identified in the archaeological record as a cultural 'package'. Few regional sequences had been developed at this time (Whittle 2007, 617), although broad-scale differences had been noted.

The advent of radiocarbon dating revolutionized the chronology of the origins of agriculture. Initial dates from early farming sites in the Near East came back 1,500 years earlier than previously suggested, and once dates from Europe had been calibrated, these were also much earlier than previously believed. This essentially created a fault-line across Europe, severing previously assumed cultural connections (Renfrew 1973, 105). While scholars rebuilt chronological sequences as a result of suites of radiocarbon dates, New Archaeology, developed in the 1960s by Binford in America and subsequently adopted in parts of Europe, also had a significant impact. The ecological approaches pioneered by New Archaeology placed renewed emphasis on the Neolithic as an economic transformation. Thus, this emphasis on subsistence served only to strengthen the notion that the Neolithic primarily involved the spread of a new economy (Higgs and Jarman 1972).

The idea that the Neolithic (as an economic regime) was spread via population movement continued to structure research throughout the 1970s and culminated with the work of Ammerman and Cavalli-Sforza (1984). They suggested that Neolithic people moved across Europe in a 'wave of advance'. Through the careful analysis of both archaeological sites and radiocarbon dates they claimed that the Neolithic spread very slowly across continents, at a rate of roughly 1 km a year, and it involved the small-scale migratory movements of farmers rather than the wholesale movements of people. By the end of the 1970s, then, a new chronology was in place for the start of the Neolithic, the Neolithic was still predominantly understood as the spread of a new economy by migration of farmers, and thus, interest in the participation of foragers in this process was minimal.

Shifts in Interpretation

Several major new contributions emerged in Europe in 1980s, and these began to highlight the importance of understanding *forager*–farmer interactions in this process. These new perspectives were a result of the combination of a number of different traditions of research being utilized and explored at this time. Firstly, it was increasingly evident that hunting and gathering was a viable alternative to farming in many areas. This was demonstrable in many parts of the world where hunting and gathering continued to thrive alongside agricultural production (for example in both prehistoric and historic times in North America). Furthermore, hunter-gatherer societies did not just consist of small mobile bands with low population densities, scratching out a pitiful existence until swept aside by farmers, as many earlier models had assumed. Among archaeologists there was a growing appreciation of ethnographic evidence which demonstrated the existence of sophisticated hunter-gatherer societies from different parts of the globe (the 'complex' societies of the Northwest Coast of North America and the Ainu of Japan, for example). Importantly, these examples illustrated how the intensified use of particular natural resources led to elaborate cultural and social patterns.

Thus in Europe in the 1980s there were growing debates about the extent to which Mesolithic hunter-gatherers were both populous and complex. One of the first suggestions that foragers (essentially the indigenous population) may have been active agents in the way that agriculture was able to spread was written by Bender (1978), and this idea was applied to the European sequence in the 1980s. One influential discussion was Zvelebil and Rowley-Conwy's (1984; 1986) 'availability model', which offered a framework for understanding the change from hunter-gatherer to farmer which did not necessarily involve migration, but instead focused on the potential role of indigenous foragers in the process. Importantly, hunter-gatherer populations could adopt only selected elements of the Neolithic 'package' if they so wished, as well as at different rates. They suggested that there was an 'availability' phase (where domesticates were available to foragers but were not adopted in large quantities, domesticates making up less than 5 per cent of an assemblage), a 'substitution' phase (where domesticates made up 50 per cent of an assemblage), and finally a 'consolidation' phase, where people became fully dependent on agriculture. This highlighted the possibility that in some regions hunter-gatherers may have been *active agents* in what was potentially a slow and variable process of Neolithization.

Greater details of various regional sequences also began to emerge at this point. For example, in Scandinavia there was the suggestion that the phenomenon of indigenous hunter-gatherers switching to agriculture was a much longer and more drawn-out process which had the additional implication that a transition to agriculture—part or full—was not necessarily reliant on migration as the causal factor (Whittle 2007, 617). Instead there may have been much more complex forager–farmer dynamics than had been previously envisaged (Dennell 1984). It was therefore possible to identify in the archaeological record forager–farmer contact zones, as well areas where farming had been adopted but where hunting and gathering were still going on.

Thus, the transition to the Neolithic in Europe began to be viewed by archaeologists working at this time as a much more complex, regionally-variable, and drawn-out process, rather than the quick and uniform process created by migration that had previously been predicted. Furthermore, if some hunter-gatherers, for example those in the Baltic, could intensify foraging practices and become complex foragers providing a sustainable alternative to farming, there may well have been scenarios where well-established foragers confronted farming as it spread, either via direct migration or via the spread of objects and/ or ideas. This meant that at some point potentially both foragers and farmers would have encountered each other. This may have created quite complex forager–farmer dynamics at the Mesolithic–Neolithic transition. In order to make sense of these forager–farmer contact zones, ethnographic analogy was employed in several ways (see Zvelebil and Fewster 2001 for a summary). This drew on anthropological debates around forager–farmer interactions, with the emphasis on the effects this had on hunter-gatherers (e.g. Woodburn 1988). The growing field of indigenous archaeology (Spector 1993) further reinforced the tendency to highlight the agency of indigenous Mesolithic peoples in the prehistoric adoption of agriculture (Fewster 2001, 86–7). Thus, in Europe, farming may have spread at very different rates, and by fundamentally different processes, in different areas. For a time, at least, hunter-gatherers were exposed to new practices, people, things, and they could select which to adopt and in what order.

The Neolithic: An Ideological or Economic Shift?

Another major shift in debates about the Neolithic arose from a reaction against the ecological and economic focus of New Archaeology. Scholars such as Thomas (1988), for example, deliberately wanted to invert the emphasis on the economy during the transition and argued instead that the transition in north-west Europe was more to do with an ideological shift than an economic one. Thomas placed emphasis on tracing the arrival of new kinds of knowledge, particularly ritual knowledge, but also knowledge of agriculture and knowledge of making new types of material culture. None of this necessarily involved the movements of population, and it therefore became known as the 'indigenist' approach (Zvelebil 2000, 59). In a similar view, Ian Hodder argued that the spread of the Neolithic across Europe was a cognitive/ideological shift, driven primarily by the desire to a transform the wild into the cultural: essentially the cognitive domestication of the social and economic world (Hodder 1990). As the 1990s progressed, pan-European models, either economic or ideological, were increasingly being abandoned with scholars exploring regional sequences, backed up with detailed programmes of excavation (see, for example, Armit and Finlayson 1992; summary of work in the Low Countries: Louwe Koojimans 2007).

Moreover, other types of data were being explored in greater depth in order to inform this debate. Historical linguistics was investigated with the aim of tracing the dispersal of peoples via different language groups, specifically relating to the origin and spread of Indo-European (see, for example, Bellwood 2000; Renfrew 2000). Likewise, genetic evidence, specifically from mtDNA and Y chromosomes, has been used to map out the possible genetic spread of people from the Near East into Europe in the post-glacial period (with the assumption that this represented the spread of Neolithic people: Zvelebil 2000, 69–73). However, how these data are interpreted varies, with some authors suggesting major genetic replacement via population movement, while others interpret the evidence as supporting considerable continuity of population (Lahr et al. 2000, 81). Stable isotope and strontium isotope analysis have been used on skeletal remains from both the Mesolithic and Neolithic (see, for example, Bentley 2007; Eriksson 2003; Schulting and Richards 2002), again to understand the spread of populations, and the rise of potential forager–farmer contacts, but the production and interpretation of these data are contested (see Milner et al. 2004) and results can be interpreted to fit different models. Increasingly, then, interpretations of the start of the Neolithic in Europe now incorporate not only archaeology and ethnographic analogy but also genetic and linguistic data as well as the application of a range of scientific techniques. These add further depth, but also additional complexity to the debate. At this point, it is worth summarizing the main debates about the processes behind the transition to farming.

Current Debates About Processes and Patterns in the Transition to Farming

At present, there are two basic processes envisaged for agricultural dispersal in Europe, both of which are still being discussed, researched, and tested through a variety of different datasets. These processes have been neatly summarized by both Whittle (2007) and Zvelebil (2000) and at the most basic level involve either:

1. **Migration/demic diffusion (farming spreads, moved by people).** From Childe's original idea of folk migration from the Near East, through to discussions of demic diffusion, the spread of farming and/or associated material-culture sets occurring via different forms of population movement and colonization still remains an important process for explaining the spread of agriculture and the start of the Neolithic in Europe (also see Rowley-Conwy 2004).

Or:

2. **Indigenous involvement/cultural diffusion (diffusion of ideas/objects through contact).** Through frontier mobility, contact, and cultural diffusion, this approach

places more emphasis on the role of indigenous populations who were the prime decision-makers in the adoption of the Neolithic. This involved the selective adoption of domesticates and/or new material culture and/or a new ideology by local foragers. In relation to Europe, this scenario has been primarily applied to Britain, Ireland, and Scandinavia (Zvelebil 2000, 59).

Although many still favour either/or scenarios, at either regional or local scales, others now accept the general validity of both processes, but argue that they were relevant in different areas and at different times, all of which created complex continental patterns. These intermediate positions take two forms and can be summarized as:

3. **Integrationist (i.e. some migration, some diffusion).** Zvelebil (2000) in particular argued for an approach which allowed for both migration and indigenous adoption: he called this the 'integrationist' approach, where both general processes are valid but different processes work in different regional patterns creating a much more complex broader pattern—in other words, there is a general 'going over' to farming in Europe, but the pattern is one of regional variability in timing, pace, and inherent process. This means that the transition to agriculture was regionally variable, but importantly, he still retains the use of the central categories of foragers and farmers as useful and meaningful analytical categories and concepts. Thus farming may have spread by different processes at very different rates in different areas, and this would have generated potentially quite complex, historically contingent forager–farmer contact zones—but zones which were still discrete entities. This model has analytical utility and is well-defined and concise but it draws on older terms and concepts.
4. **Fusion.** Whittle (2007) took the integrationist approach one stage further in relation to the European sequence. He suggested that there is so much conceptual baggage attached to terms and concepts such as Mesolithic and Neolithic that these now impede further progress on understanding the transition. Scholars should start afresh and find new ways to describe and explain these processes (also see Robb and Miracle 2007). The sheer diversity of the phenomenon means it is not possible to reduce it down to a single transition or even locally variable processes which draw on the older ideas of diffusion or migration. Instead, there were a multitude of transition processes (also see Cummings and Harris 2011), essentially a 'fusion' (endless combinations of unique circumstances) and that each can only be understood in its own contingent historical and particularistic terms.

Thus, this short review of these rather entrenched debates forms a useful framework against which chapters in this part can be evaluated, and new directions identified. Firstly, given that so much debate about the transition to farming has been set in Europe it makes sense to start with a discussion of the chapters that summarize forager–farmer interactions in Europe, reviewing them in relation to this broader intellectual legacy. This is followed by chapters exploring forager–farmer interactions in a selection of other areas of the globe. These add useful and intellectually refreshing comparative insights because they move the debate beyond the unique European sequence and demonstrate that many other world regions are not restricted by the specific set of debates and explanatory processes. Indeed, they provide a useful set of comparative perspectives for scholars working in Europe as they highlight a range of possible processes for the adoption of agriculture across the globe, and query the emphasis placed on agriculture over a foraging way of life.

THE EUROPEAN CHAPTERS

The role of hunter-gatherers in the transition process in Europe is discussed region by region in the first four chapters in this part, all of which outline different regional scenarios of forager–farmer contacts along with the nature of forager–farmer interactions. All the chapters tie back into the debates reviewed above, but do so in different ways. Different strands of evidence are now being employed across the different regions of Europe which suggest a highly complicated and locally contingent transition process to farming, and also the continuity of hunting and gathering in different ways in different areas. In some areas, there is evidence for incoming peoples who relied virtually exclusively on agricultural products. In other areas, there were broad-spectrum foragers who kept a few cattle and took part in small-scale crop cultivation. It is these regional specifics which are now explored in more detail.

Gronenborn discusses the evidence for the Neolithization process in central and western Europe. As reviewed above, older discussions of this area suggested there were two dominant processes to explain to start of agriculture, firstly that the Neolithic (as an economic package) was a result of intrusive, incoming farmers (migration), or secondly, that there was substantial continuity from the Mesolithic through to the Neolithic (diffusion of ideas). Gronenborn suggests that these interpretations were far too simplistic, and instead this area saw a complex sequence of events which created a whole series of contact zones between different peoples, including between incomers and local populations, and between farmers and foragers. For example, the Neolithic of central Europe is called the LBK (Linear Pottery Culture) and the start of the LBK, Gronenborn argues, involved small pioneering groups moving into the area (demic diffusion). However, the arrival of LBK people into this area does not explain the entire sequence here: in the eastern part of the LBK area there is little evidence for an indigenous people living there, but to the west the LBK seems to have involved incomers mixing with indigenous people. Thus, on the western fringes of the LBK people making the La Hoguette style of pottery also practised a mixed economy involving both hunting and gathering as well as pastoralism. It is perhaps no surprise that the outcomes of these different processes also resulted in different Neolithics: the western LBK placed considerable emphasis on lineage which was expressed through house architecture, pottery, and lithics.

A different process altogether occurred in the North European Plain (present-day Low Countries, also discussed by Raemaekers below). In the fifth millennium BC LBK peoples were found to the south of this area, while indigenous foragers on the North European Plain continued to hunt and gather. This created a frontier contact zone with material culture in particular moving across the frontier. It is notable that some peoples on the North European Plain started to make their own pottery, but did not take up agriculture. However, again, Gronenborn stresses that the type of contact between farmers and foragers was not homogeneous, with distinctive regional variations in the kinds of exchanges that took place.

Gronenborn also shows how aDNA evidence can add new insights to the archaeological evidence. In the LBK region of central Europe aDNA cannot be used to differentiate between indigenous Mesolithic people and incoming Neolithic people. This is because there was an earlier movement of people, also with their origins in the Near East, in the Mesolithic. This would essentially mean that late Mesolithic foragers and early Neolithic farmers had the same genetic origins. This evidence, then, highlights potential problems with the straightforward notion of demic diffusion, particularly relating to new populations bringing a new kind of economy. It should also make us query the conceptualization of indigeneity. However, in the northern lowlands of Europe Mesolithic populations remained genetically distinct from LBK peoples with a Near Eastern origin, and it was only with the onset of farming that the two peoples mixed. In this case, Gronenborn concludes that aDNA supports the archaeological evidence for a distinct frontier contact zone between discrete populations, with the take-up of the Neolithic also involving population movement. It seems clear, then, that in central and western Europe there were a wide range of different processes under way as farming was introduced both by incoming peoples and by indigenous people. When these interpretations are viewed against the framework set out above, it is clear that it is a struggle to fit the data within simple either/or migration/diffusion scenarios—instead, there were no essential categories of foragers or farmers, just local historically contingent processes under way in the general transition to agriculture.

In the next chapter Raemaekers discusses in detail the evidence for forager–farmer interactions on the western part of the North European Plain (the Low Countries). Understanding the Mesolithic–Neolithic transition is dictated by large-scale environmental changes in this area. There were continuously rising sea levels in the Holocene which inundated the coastal zone. This means that, unlike southern Scandinavia, the archaeology from this zone is effectively lost. However, inland there are a range of very well-preserved Holocene deposits, which contain both botanical and zoological data. These have been the focus of attention in this area for understanding the process of Neolithization. As noted by Gronenborn, this area had indigenous hunting and gathering peoples who were in contact with the agricultural LBK groups to the south. There was clearly contact between the two, evidenced by the material culture record. However, the sequence here illustrates the fact that there was no sudden uptake of the Neolithic 'package'. Instead, there was piecemeal adoption of elements of this over an extended time period. Furthermore, it seems that the indigenous population of this area were the prime movers in this process. The first element of change in the older indigenous Mesolithic culture was the adoption of ceramic technology around 5000 BC (known as the Swifterband culture). While the technique of ceramic production was acquired from the LBK, the pottery made was striking different. Other than the adoption of pottery, people continued hunting and gathering as before; thus the adoption of pottery represents a change in cooking technology, not subsistence. This period can therefore be seen as an 'indigenist' adoption of pottery into an otherwise broad-based foraging society.

Five hundred years later, around 4500 BC, domesticated cattle, sheep/goats, and pigs were introduced into the area. Again, Raemaekers argues that this was the result of contact, not movements of people. It is interesting to note that while domesticated animals were introduced at this point, they were only of limited nutritional importance; people continued to rely heavily on a wide range of wild animals, birds, and fish. This highlights the point that the presence of domesticates does not necessarily mean people relied entirely on these. At 4200 BC cereals first appear in this area, but again there is substantial evidence for the continued use of collected wild plants. Basically, then, these were broad-spectrum foragers using pots with the use of a few cattle and small-scale crop cultivation. Raemaekers highlights that it is very difficult to classify people in this period as *either* hunter-gatherers *or* farmers, Mesolithic *or* Neolithic. It is clear that people exploited a wide range of wild plants and animals and that domesticates were simply incorporated into existing resource strategies, further widening the subsistence base. Thus, in this sequence, he argues, the traditional subsistence base was the backbone of a lifestyle in which a flexible use of resources, both wild and domestic, dominated. Again, it seems clear that Raemaekers is arguing that this created a new sort of Neolithic, unlike any other sequence in Europe. Again, this chapter illustrates the challenges of making local sense of these dynamics, and points to the inherent problems of the integrationist position as well as the greater validity of the fusion model, which demands new ways of writing about these processes.

In the next chapter Cummings and Harris argue that the transition to the Neolithic in Britain and Ireland is, at present, a highly contested and debated topic. One of the problems with this sequence is that the evidence from this area is limited as there is a general lack of archaeological sites that have produced evidence of both the very late Mesolithic and very earliest Neolithic. The late Mesolithic period is characterized by the presence of mobile hunter-gatherers, but unfortunately a lack of burial evidence and organic preservation (unlike in other adjacent European areas). In contrast, the early Neolithic period in general is characterized by the presence of domesticated animals and plants, pottery, evidence suggesting a more sedentary lifestyle, monumental construction, flint mining, and polished stone tools. As reviewed above, the two basic models are still used to explain the mechanisms behind this general sequence. First, there is strong support for indigenous involvement where the agents of change are the indigenous Mesolithic inhabitants who chose when to adopt different elements of the Neolithic. Second, there is the idea of farmer colonization (in keeping with the broader mass-migration model outlined above), the proponents of which argue that incomers from the continent moved into Britain and Ireland bringing with them the Neolithic package. These incomers then acculturated the native foraging populations.

Instead of arguing for either indigenous adoption or colonization, Cummings and Harris simply explore the different types of evidence. For example, there is good evidence for the widespread adoption of domesticated animals at the start of the Neolithic in Britain and Ireland, but the lithic evidence also suggests that hunting continued. Likewise with plants, there is good evidence for the continued use of wild plants and serious problems with understanding the take-up of domesticated cereals due to archaeological visibility and preservation. Cummings and Harris follow the suggestion of Whittle et al. (2011) that south-eastern England was the location of small-scale colonization from Europe in the century beginning 4100 BC. From this starting point they argue that these incomers mixed with native foragers, the resultant sequence being shaped entirely by this mixing of incomer and native. This is why the British and Irish Neolithic sequence is once again best described by the fusion model outlined above: it is unlike any other set of events Europe. They do highlight, however, that these are interpretations only, and that more evidence from the period 4300–3700 BC is required in order to understand the transition in more detail.

In the next chapter in this part, Damm and Forsberg examine the arrival and impact of elements of the Neolithic package in the northernmost part of Europe, Fennoscandia. This area is particularly interesting for considerations of the process of Neolithization as it is at the ecological limits of where agriculture is viable. Damm and Forsberg argue that for 4,000 years there was no clear-cut dichotomy between foragers and farmers, again in keeping with the fusion model outlined above. Nevertheless, while the sequence here is unique, it can inform broader debates on understanding the process of Neolithization and how scholars categorize people in relation to their economy only (and see Pluciennik, this volume).

Damm and Forsberg begin by discussing the first forager–farmer contacts in this area: as already noted above, Mesolithic peoples (the Ertebølle) in the south of Fennoscandia imported material culture from LBK groups to the south. Then, at around 4000 BC, there is evidence for the quick uptake by indigenous foragers in Denmark, southern Sweden, and southern Norway of agriculture, comprising both domesticated animals and crops. However, to the north, people continued to hunt, gather, and fish. In this early Neolithic period there was very limited interaction between the foragers in the north of Scandinavia and the newly agricultural populations to the south. However, this seems to relate back to older exchange networks (or lack of them) rather than being a product of the arrival of agriculture.

The middle Neolithic period marked a decline in agricultural activity in the northernmost areas which had initially taken up farming. These groups instead began to rely on hunting and gathering: interactions with farming groups are recorded by the movement of material culture between areas. Later on in the middle Neolithic (2800–2350 BC) more changes occurred, this time in the form of pioneer agro-pastoral settlements. Damm and Forsberg argue that a small number of farming groups set up along the coast in what was otherwise an area where foraging predominated. By the late Neolithic, farming communities expanded again, and interactions between foragers and farmers becomes much more conspicuous in the archaeological record. The end result of all of this is that in the later part of the third millennium, and throughout the second millennium, there was a mosaic of foragers and farmers in Fennoscandia.

In the first millennium BC Damm and Forberg illustrate further changes. Declining environmental conditions seem to have resulted in an increased reliance on marine resources, so that many coastal groups integrated fishing with herding and growing crops. Peoples relying solely on hunting and gathering in the interior relied increasingly on reindeer hunting, and their interactions with metal-producing societies also intensified. It is quite clear then that in this area of Northern Europe, there was no 'wave of advance' of incoming agriculturalists and simplistic shift from forager to farmer. Instead there was a multitude of interactions between people who primarily made a living foraging and those that primarily made a living farming. These lines were blurred even further as peoples switched between foraging and farming over time and space, essentially becoming composite economies that defy simple classification as either forager or farmer. Once again, this complex sequence highlights whether the integrationist approach is sufficient here, or whether this sequence could be described as in keeping with the fusion model.

Summary

What is clear from the chapters on the European transition to farming and Neolithization is that significant progress has been made in examining specific sequences and local processes over the last 20 to 30 years but these debates are still directly referencing older models of migration or indigenous adaptation. All this hints at an impasse: scholars are stuck using the terminology of older models and processes which no longer adequately describe or explain the unique sequences of each area in Europe. Instead the European chapters illustrate considerable local variability and dynamic and historically contingent processes all caught up in a much broader change of 'going over' from forager to farmer (cf. Whittle and Cummings 2007).

It is important to note here that the chapters on the European process of Neolithization are not the only ones in the handbook that struggle with categorizing people as *either* forager *or* farmer, one of the legacies of social evolutionary thinking (a point made by Pluciennik, this volume). Politis and Hernando (this volume) note that some hunter-gatherers in South America were once horticulturalists, but they took up foraging as a secondary re-adaption to new conditions. These people seem to have returned to hunting and gathering as a reaction to broader changes brought about during the colonial period. Jana Fortier (this volume) also discusses the varied ways in which people subsist in South-East Asia in more recent times, where there is plenty of evidence for people utilizing a range of different subsistence types (from agriculture right through to hunting and gathering, but most often, a highly fluid and dynamic mix of both), dependent on circumstances and also local choice and agency.

Thus, it is useful at this point to depart from European debates and examine how forager–farmer processes have been studied in other world regions. In other areas of the world it is clear that a simple forager–farmer dichotomy is also not often applicable, and that variability and flexibility are the norm. In these areas authors look at the persistence of hunting and gathering over considerable time periods.

Forager–Farmer Contacts in Other World Regions

Barton examines long-term forager–farmer interactions in South-East Asia. He begins by discussing the prehistoric spread of farming. As with similar models in Europe, it has previously been claimed that domesticated rice, domesticated pigs, pottery, and polished stone tools formed a package which spread into the region from 3500 BC. However, as this new subsistence economy spread south and east, domesticated rice may have been dropped in favour of tree and root-crop agriculture as rice was too difficult to grow in equatorial rainforests. There have also been suggestions of some indigenous innovations including plant cultivation where rice could not be grown. The role of rice and other plant adaptations is a key debate in this area as foragers would have needed a source of carbohydrates, which are otherwise in short supply in rainforest environments. Indeed, this whole debate frames the types of forager–farmer interactions in this region. There is no question that foraging persisted in this area, but foragers dependent on farmers would have had very different sets of interactions than those who were isolated or entirely self-sufficient. In contrast to the European sequence, then, in South-East Asia there is a preconceived assumption that foragers would need farmers: indeed, some argue, both could only survive by close mutual interdependence on one another.

The bulk of Barton's chapter, however, discusses the historical legacy of these early contacts in terms of later forager–farmer interactions. Barton describes a rich mosaic of foragers, farmers, and people practising both foraging and farming in South-East Asia, and how definitions of people in relation only to their economy are not sufficient to describe the variety of ways people make a living in this region. Peoples, therefore, cannot be classed as *either* foragers *or* farmers as there is a reliance on both wild and domesticated plants, wild and managed forests, and wild and domestic animals. Moreover, there is considerable flexibility and change, as people make the most of whatever is available locally. In this area, then, any attempts to map nineteenth-century social evolutionary categories of forager or farmer onto local cultural groupings (see above) are inadequate to describe a much more complex set of situations.

Barton also notes that there is an extensive ethnographic literature which charts trade and exchange between foragers and farmers. These are recorded for over two millennia in some areas as forest products have been, and remain, highly desirable to people across many parts of the world. There was a big increase in the exchange of forest products in the seventeenth century with the arrival of a Dutch trading company, along with more recent ethnographic records of indigenous groups. Forest products to be exchanged and exported were predominantly acquired by foraging groups. Material was acquired by foragers and exchanged with nearby farmers who then traded it on. This often created strong alliances between foragers and farmers, with economic and social benefits for both parties. Thus individual communities were not and are not autonomous self-sufficient units, but part of a broad and wide-ranging series of exchange networks. This is very much in keeping with the notion of 'contact' zones between foragers and farmers as outlined above, and demonstrates how such contact can be very stable and in place for thousands of years without either forager or farmer changing their subsistence economy as a result. Barton also discusses what happens when previously foraging groups take up sedentary farming. He notes that there is a great deal of variation even within individual communities. For example, some now-sedentary people do not farm every year, finding subsistence in other ways. It is also interesting to note that some settled farmers have abandoned farming and become professional collectors of forest products, filling a niche in the current economic situation. As far as it is possible to tell, forager–farmer interactions in South-East Asia are unlike the various situations outlined for Europe above, although the issues discussed by Barton could fruitfully be explored in relation to the European sequence. This sequence is therefore in keeping with the ideas outlined above which highlight historical contingency and a multitude of outcomes from the same basic start-point.

In the last chapter in this part of the handbook, Katherine Spielmann also demonstrates that there is no clear-cut dichotomy between foragers and famers by exploring complex interactions that existed between different groups in North America. Until the arrival of colonial peoples from Europe there were no large domesticated herd animals in North America, and no populations acquired their food exclusively from farming. However, many groups did grow domesticated plants, quite intensively in some areas (this included indigenous domesticates such as amaranth, chenopodium, and knotweed and imported species from Mesoamerica such as corn, beans, and squash). What is clear with the North American sequences is that it was common for people to move between agriculture and foraging and back again: flexibility was key. It is also clear that those people who spent most of their time growing crops traded extensively with foraging groups, ensuring that both forager and farmer had access to both carbohydrate and protein. Just as in South-East Asia, then, the trade and exchange of food was an essential part of life. To classify people as *either* foragers *or* farmers in this context would hide the complexities of how food was acquired from different sources and via different strategies.

Spielmann explores various interactions between foragers and farmers in three case studies. The first case study is that of the Algonquian and Iroquois Huron of the Great Lakes. Historically the Huron were farmers who grew corn and the Algonquians were foragers, with a particular emphasis on fishing. However, both groups took part in other activities, and sometimes the Algonquians would grow corn and the Huron would fish. This demonstrates the flexibility of making a living and how people can move easily between foraging and farming. Spielmann also considers middle Missouri forager–farmer interactions. Historically this involved Arikara, Mandan, and Hidatsa farming villages and Crow, Assiniboine, Cheyenne, and Sioux bison hunters. The two were involved in extensive trade relations. This example therefore shows that the mutual coexistence of foragers and farmers who exchanged foodstuffs was a viable economic choice. In her final case study she considers the well-documented Plains–Pueblo interactions. Historically, Pueblo groups grew corn and exchanged this for bison meat and hides acquired by Plains groups. However, there was considerable flexibility in this system. By the fifteenth century, however, the two became part of an interdependent system whereby each relied entirely on the other. Trade did not just involve foodstuffs, but the social networks that evolved were also crucial parts of society, making these groups economically and socially reliant on one another.

The chapter by Spielmann demonstrates unequivocally that many peoples were not *either* foragers *or* farmers, but adapted to individual circumstances, mixing foraging and farming, or at least having access to the products of both foraging and farming. This meant that many people in North America were a mix of cultivators, fishers, hunters, and gatherers, with considerable variability from year to year and from place to place. This quite clearly demonstrates that there is no simple and straightforward category of forager *or* farmer. Instead, people used a combination of wild and domestic resources as they saw fit, and which often varied from year to year. Foragers will incorporate domesticates into the suite of resources that they utilize. Farmers will rely on wild resources in addition to what they grow. This shows that the idea of people evolving from hunter-gatherer to farmer is inherently flawed, and not found ubiquitously in the archaeological record. The shifts from forager to farmer and back again in both Barton and Spielmann's chapters seem to relate not just to economic viability but also to both internal and external social relations. It is possible to postulate that the desire for individuals to gain material objects and/or prestige may also have played an important role (see Hayden, this volume). Again, Spielmann's chapter demonstrates considerable variability and diversity in how people made a living over time.

Discussion: Going Over, Moving Forwards

At one level, it is clear that in Europe, for example, and many other regions, there *was* a general process of 'going over' to an agricultural way of life—almost all the world's populations are now supported by the farming of a few staples. This is a general pattern that works at the broadest of scales and over long time periods as the vast majority of peoples across the world now get their food via agricultural methods. Some of the questions about this process refer back to the role of hunter-gatherers and to the nature of prehistoric forager–farmer interactions: after farming had become established and started to spread, were hunter-gatherers swept aside or assimilated by farmers? Was it only the knowledge of farming that spread among foragers? Finally, was the spread of farming only made possible by an earlier and indeed more fundamentally important *ideological* shift that eventually made farming acceptable to hunter-gatherers? These are the central questions in one of the longest-standing debates in prehistoric archaeology.

Some of most intense debate, for various historical and cultural reasons, has been centred squarely on Europe and its archaeological sequences. The legacy of nineteenth-century social evolutionary thinking and early twentieth-century culture-history means that many of the central perspectives, as well as the key terms of reference, refer back to these older phases of thinking and scholarship. For example, it is clear from the review of the chapters, especially those from Europe, that the social evolutionary thinking and the mapping of the economic categories of forager and farmer onto the archaeological record at the end of the nineteenth century still continues, to a remarkable extent, to structure interpretation and debate: scholars still choose to define groups of people in terms of distinctive units or cultural entities that are primarily defined by how they make a living. Likewise, the older explanatory ideas of migration and diffusion also remain influential. As data, knowledge, and suites of AMS dates have started to highlight regional variability on the pace, timing, and contribution of different processes, the result is increasingly nuanced models which illustrate the regional and temporal complexities of going from relying entirely on foraging to subsisting predominantly on farmed products. Despite this, economies are still discussed in relation to basic economic categories—either foraging *or* farming—spread via either migration *or* diffusion.

More generally, this critical review of the European chapters shows that scholars are struggling in their attempts to accommodate the new level of detail that they identify within their data to the rather rigid, older frames of reference that are a definitive feature of working in this intellectual archaeological tradition. In contrast, chapters from other world regions (and many of the ethnohistoric chapters in Part VI) appear to be much less constrained by the intellectual baggage associated with earlier Eurocentric scholarship. They appear to explore variability within regional sequences without referring to the older modes of thinking outlined above. If this is the case, there is an important message for scholars dealing with the European archaeological record: it is time to move discussions forward (cf. Robb and Miracle 2007; Whittle 2007). Thus, several key directions can be highlighted as being likely to structure the future kinds of work that are possible in this area.

1. **Regional variability in data coverage** (some regions are well-studied, others are not; even the former need more data). To move forward, scholars need more basic data on many world regions. While some regions of Europe now have excellent datasets, many could still benefit from higher resolution data. This will enable scholars to get a better sense of regional trajectories on the pace, timing, and uptake of different elements available to people at particular points in time.
2. **New frames of reference**. One approach would be to use Zvelebil's integrationist approach as a basic starting point. As reviewed in all these chapters, it is particularly important to find ways to move beyond essentialized descriptions of people (particularly in relation to the forager–farmer dichotomy). Instead the terms forager and farmer can be used as self-critical points of departure for thinking about new ways of understanding people and society. In contrast, the fusion model suggests that

scholars find entirely new ways to describe and explain these processes. Perhaps the best starting point for deciding which approach to take is to begin to think about precisely what it is we are interested in understanding. There has been plenty of work on economy in the past, but the most exciting avenues of current research explore identity. In areas with high resolution datasets there is a whole range of ways that we can interrogate the data to explore the issue of both individual and group identity and daily practice (i.e. what people do as well as how they create identity). Material culture can be investigated alongside isotopic evidence (Bentley 2012), the full range of bioarchaeological techniques (cf. Zvelebil and Pettitt 2012), and suites of radiocarbon dates (Whittle et al. 2012). Alongside theoretical approaches to this material, incorporating broader understandings of contextually specific personhood (see Finlay, this volume), connections with particular landscapes (David et al., this volume), and belief systems (Whitley, this volume), archaeologists should be able to get at the multiple dimensions of social life (see Whittle 2003). At the most detailed level, this will enable scholars to explore the life histories of individuals in particular areas, at particular times, and in different ways but also to situate these within general processes and transformations.

3. **Comparative contextual insights.** In areas where the biggest challenge is seeking out new ways of thinking about how these multiple intersections of subsistence, identity, and practice are caught up in what can crudely be defined as forager–farmer interactions, scholars might usefully start to develop an explicitly comparative approach to their materials by examining: (a) similarities and differences with analogous regional archaeological sequences in order to pull out unique, as well as universal, trends; (b) carefully selected ethnographic parallels with other areas, e.g. South-East Asia. Analogy, when used in this way, can generate new ways of thinking about active construction of identities and individual life histories and can assist in moving beyond the older debates and entrenched terminology. As such, analogies represent one way of transcending the constraints generated by using older terms and concepts (e.g. forager, farmer, and so on) and provide detail on how social and cultural life are created and experienced in specific cultural settings. For example, the chapters by Barton and Spielmann in this part both highlight the significance of structured mutual exchange networks as being a key component of why people subsist on specific resources within a wider region/network—similar concepts could productively be examined in detail in other parts of the globe. Barton and Spielmann also highlight the importance of access to carbohydrates, not just in terms of diet, but also as a way of enabling both storage and individual aggrandizement (see Hayden, this volume). There are clearly insights to be gained from ethnographic analogy as archaeological scholars seek to move debates forward about how best to explore the specifics of social life and identity in these transitional prehistoric economies.

Conclusion

Understanding the transition to farming, and the roles of foragers within that transition, is one of the oldest, most interesting and, as demonstrated by this chapter, also one of the most challenging topics in prehistoric archaeology. What this critical review of scholarship on this topic does reveal is that there are now more data and elaborate new analytical methods than nineteenth-century theorists could ever have imagined. So where are we in understanding it all? At one level of analysis, there clearly is a general process of 'going over' to agriculture at the broadest level, and all the data support this. Under closer scrutiny, and with increasingly more detailed local high-resolution datasets, however, the clear boundaries, categories, units, and even the main entities and actors that have traditionally been used in this long-standing debate now increasingly seem to be shifting, blurring, and taking on new significance. Perhaps the key challenge for future research is to move beyond mapping the general details, and to explore how best to make sense of this major human transformation at more local and more human levels. It also means that the old models, concepts, and approaches might not be best suited for this new task.

This raises an interesting predicament/question. Should archaeologists:

a. Retain older concepts, such as Mesolithic and Neolithic, forager and farmer, as they provide a bridge between older debates and new directions, but use them as points of departure for more critical considerations and new discussions on these processes?
b. Reject older terms and start again? The problem with this approach is how to best pursue this line of scholarship—what language should we use if there are no categories such as foragers or farmers, Mesolithic or Neolithic? This certainly poses a significant, but perhaps also an exciting challenge.

Whatever way individual scholars seek to advance their research and interpretation, it is clear that an interesting approach is to explore historically contingent regional sequences, as well as the significance of these broader changes for the individuals and communities caught up in them. For a topic that has seen so much discussion over the past century, it is clear that this will remain one of the most exciting, and controversial, processes in human history, but one that will continue to offer insights into the cultural significance of how we, as human beings, choose make a living, and into the nature of group and individual identity at this time. The primary challenge now seems to be to find new ways to explore and describe the multiple outcomes of particularistic histories in regions throughout the world.

Acknowledgements

I am extremely grateful to Peter Jordan for his help with earlier drafts of this chapter, and for his insights into this particular topic.

References

Ammerman, A. and Cavalli-Sforza, L. 1984. *The Neolithic transition and the genetics of populations in Europe*. Princeton: Princeton University Press.
Armit, I. and Finlayson, B. 1992. Hunter-gatherers transformed: the transition to agriculture in northern and western Europe. *Antiquity* 66, 664–76.
Barker, G. 2006. *The agricultural revolution in prehistory*. Oxford: Oxford University Press.

Bellwood, P. 2000. The time depth of major language families: an archaeologist's perspective. In C. Renfrew, A. McMahon, and L. Trask (eds), *Time depth in historical linguistics*, 109–40. Cambridge: McDonald Institute for Archaeological Research.

Bender, B. 1978. Gatherer-hunter to farmer: a social perspective. *World Archaeology* 10, 204–22.

Bentley, A. 2007. Mobility, specialisation and community diversity in the Linearbandkeramik: isotopic evidence from the skeletons. In A. Whittle and V. Cummings (eds), *Going over: the Mesolithic Neolithic transition in north-west Europe*, 117–40. London: British Academy.

Bentley, A. 2012. Mobility and the diversity of early Neolithic lives: isotopic evidence from skeletons. *Journal of Anthropological Archaeology* 32, 303–12.

Childe, V. G. 1925. *The dawn of European civilisation*. London: Kegan Paul.

Childe, V. G. 1929. *The Danube in prehistory*. Oxford: Oxford University Press.

Childe, V. G. 1942. *What happened in history*. Harmondsworth: Penguin.

Dennell, R. W. 1984. The hunter-gatherer/agricultural frontier in prehistoric temperate Europe. In S. Green and J. Perlman (eds), *The archaeology of frontiers and boundaries*, 113–39. London: Academic Press.

Eriksson, G. 2003. *Norm and difference: Stone Age dietary practice in the Baltic region*. Stockholm: Stockholm University.

Fewster, K. 2001. Petso's field: ethnoarchaeology and agency. In K. Fewster and M. Zvelebil (eds), *Ethnoarchaeology and hunter-gatherers: pictures at an exhibition*, 81–90. Oxford: BAR.

Green, S. 1981. *Prehistorian: a biography of V. Gordon Childe*. Bradford-on-Avon, Wiltshire: Moonraker Press.

Higgs, E. and Jarman, M. 1972. The origins of animal and plant husbandry. In E. Higgs (ed.), *Papers in economic prehistory*, 3–13. Cambridge: Cambridge University Press.

Hodder, I. 1990. *The domestication of Europe*. Oxford: Blackwell.

Kristiansen, K. 2002. The birth of ecological archaeology in Denmark: history and research environments. In A. Fischer and K. Kristiansen (eds), *The Neolithisation of Denmark: 150 years of debate*, 11–31. Sheffield: John Collis.

Lahr, M., Foley, R., and Pinhasi, R. 2000. Expected regional patterns of Mesolithic–Neolithic human population admixture in Europe based on archaeological evidence. In C. Renfrew and K. Boyle (eds), *Archaeogenetics: DNA and the population*, 81–8. Cambridge: McDonald Institute for Archaeological Research.

Louwe Koojimans, L. 2007. The gradual transition to farming in the Lower Rhine Basin. In A. Whittle and V. Cummings (eds), *Going over: the Mesolithic Neolithic transition in north-west Europe*, 287–309. London: British Academy.

Lubbock, J. 1865. *Pre-historic times*. London: Williams and Norgate.

Milner, N., Craig, O. E., Bailey, G. N., Pedersen K., and Andersen, S. H. 2004. Something fishy in the Neolithic? A re-evaluation of stable isotope analysis of Mesolithic and Neolithic coastal populations. *Antiquity* 78, 9–22.

Renfrew, C. 1973. *Before civilisation: the radiocarbon revolution and Prehistoric Europe*. London: Jonathan Cape.

Renfrew, C. 2000. 10,000 or 5000 years ago? Questions of time depth. In C. Renfrew, A. McMahon, and L. Trask (eds), *Time depth in historical linguistics*, 413–40. Cambridge: McDonald Institute for Archaeological Research.

Robb, J. and Miracle, P. 2007. Beyond migration versus acculturation: new models for the spread of agriculture. In A. Whittle and V. Cummings (eds), *Going over: the Mesolithic Neolithic transition in north-west Europe*, 99–116. London: British Academy.

Rowley-Conwy, P. 2004. How the west was lost: a reconsideration of the agricultural origins in Britain, Ireland and southern Scandinavia. *Current Anthropology* 45, 83–113.

Rowley-Conwy, P. 2007. *From genesis to prehistory: the archaeological three age system and its contested reception in Denmark, Britain and Ireland.* Oxford: Oxford University Press.

Schulting, R. and Richards, M. 2002. The wet, the wild and the domesticated: the Mesolithic–Neolithic transition on the west coast of Scotland. *European Journal of Archaeology* 5, 147–89.

Spector, J. 1993. *What this awl means.* St Paul: Minnesota Historical Society.

Thomas, J. 1988. Neolithic explanations revisited: the Mesolithic–Neolithic transition in Britain and south Scandinavia. *Proceedings of the Prehistoric Society* 54, 59–66.

Trigger, B. 2006. *A history of archaeological thought* (2nd edition). Cambridge: Cambridge University Press.

Whittle, A. 1996. *Europe in the Neolithic.* Cambridge: Cambridge University Press.

Whittle, A. 2003. *The archaeology of people: dimensions of Neolithic life.* London: Routledge.

Whittle, A. 2007. Going over: people and their times. In A. Whittle and V. Cummings (eds), *Going over: the Mesolithic Neolithic transition in north-west Europe,* 617–28. London: British Academy.

Whittle, A. and Cummings, V. (eds). 2007. *Going over: the Mesolithic Neolithic transition in north-west Europe.* London: British Academy.

Whittle, A., Healy, F., and Bayliss, A. 2012. *Gathering time.* Oxford: Oxbow.

Woodburn, J. 1988. African hunter-gatherer social organization: is it best understood as a product of encapsulation? In T. Ingold, D. Riches, and J. Woodburn (eds), *Hunters and gatherers: history, evolution and social change,* 31–64. Oxford: Berg.

Zvelebil, M. 2000. The social context of the agricultural transition in Europe. In C. Renfrew and K. Boyle (eds), *Archaeogenetics: DNA and the population,* 57–79. Cambridge: McDonald Institute for Archaeological Research.

Zvelebil, M. and Fewster, K. 2001. Pictures at an exhibition: ethnoarchaeology and hunter-gatherers. In K. Fewster and M. Zvelebil (eds), *Ethnoarchaeology and hunter-gatherers: pictures at an exhibition,* 143–57. Oxford: BAR.

Zvelebil, M. and Pettitt, P. 2012. Biosocial archaeology of the Early Neolithic: synthetic analyses of a human skeletal population from the LBK cemetery of Vedrovice, Czech Republic. *Journal of Anthropological Archaeology* 32(3), 313–29.

Zvelebil, M. and Rowley-Conwy, P. 1984. Transition to farming in northern Europe: a hunter-gatherer perspective. *Norwegian Archaeological Review* 17, 102–28.

Zvelebil, M. and Rowley-Conwy, P. 1986. Foragers and farmers in Atlantic Europe. In M. Zvelebil (ed.), *Hunters in transition,* 67–96. Cambridge: Cambridge University Press.

CHAPTER 36

THE PERSISTENCE OF HUNTING AND GATHERING
Neolithic Western Temperate and Central Europe

DETLEF GRONENBORN

CENTRAL and western temperate Europe stretches from the Vistula River to the Paris Basin and from the Alps to the northern European lowlands. The process of Neolithization in this region entails archaeological entities such as the classic Linearband Pottery culture (LBK—German: *Linienbandkeramische Kultur*), the lesser-known La Hoguette and Limburg pottery traditions in the west, and a third component, which has only recently been recognized. This latter component, comprising pottery but not farming, stretches from the south-eastern Russian steppe zones northward to the Baltic coast and into Scandinavia, then further west across the northern European lowlands up to the modern-day Netherlands and Belgium (Dolukhanov et al. 2005; Gronenborn 2003; 2009b). Following southern African approaches these broad entities may be conceived as streams and may be termed Occidental, Danubian, and Hyperborean, respectively (Figure 36.1c). Those streams follow ancient contact networks across western temperate Eurasia and may ultimately derive from routes taken during the human glacial recolonization (Gamble et al. 2006). Also, the three streams correspond at least coarsely to the modern-day dispersion of Y haplogroups which may be taken as the palimpsest of Holocene human interaction processes (Gronenborn 2011). They are equally visible in the distribution patterns of genetic matrilineal distances between the modern western Eurasian population and the LBK population mapped by Haak et al. (2010).

In any case, the distribution pathways taken by the three distinct streams of Neolithization are embedded in long-term interaction networks likely already established during the Palaeolithic. This brings up the immediate topic of the chapter: who, at the time in question between the seventh and fourth millennia cal BC, actually performed the archaeologically visible hunter-gatherer/farmer interactions—was it the same people only with different economies or was it, as traditionally conceived, immigrants and locals? This is still one of the most crucial questions of European Neolithic research, despite recent criticism of such an 'ethnic' approach (Robb and Miracle 2007).

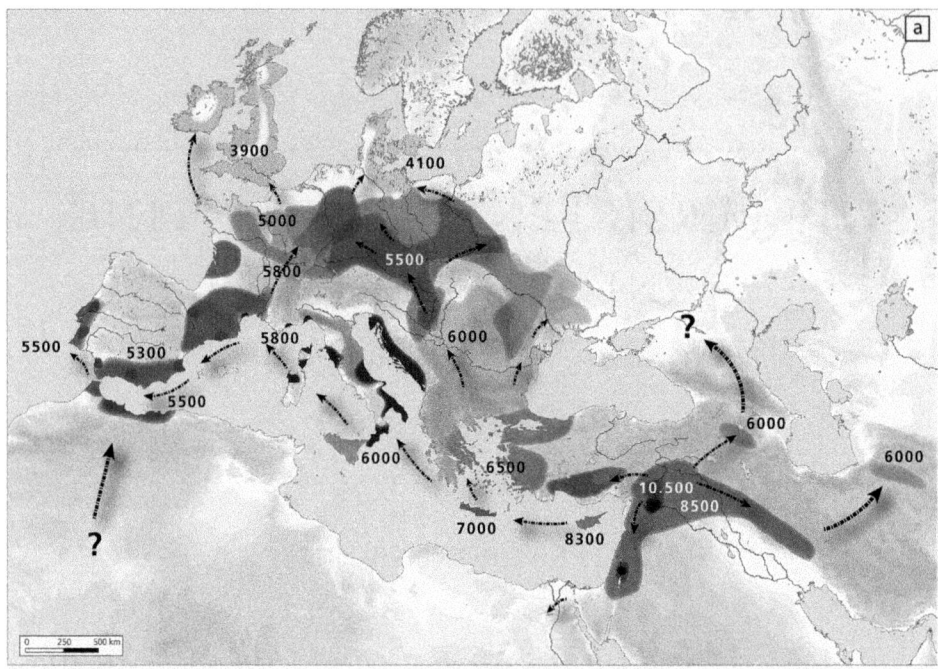

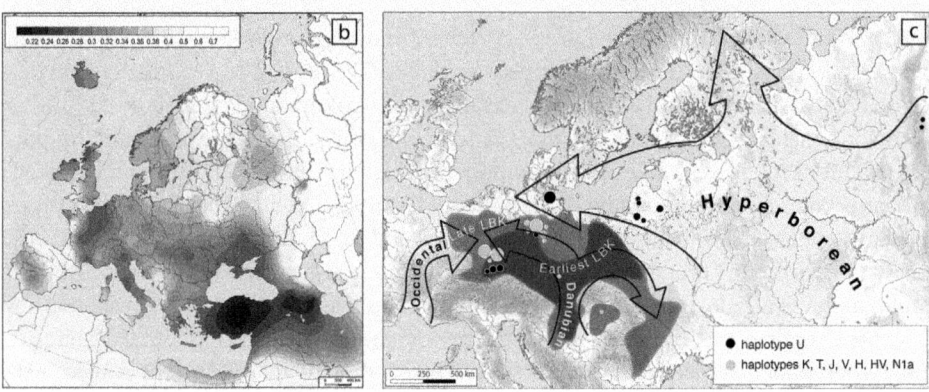

FIGURE 36.1 (a) The dispersal of farming across western Eurasia (modified after Gronenborn 2009a); (b) Genetic matrilineal distances between modern western Eurasian populations and LBK samples (modified after Haak et al. 2010); (c) The three streams of Neolithization with aDNA haplotypes superimposed (combined from Gronenborn 2009a and Bramanti et al. 2009).

Contact Period Archaeology in the Sixth and Fifth Millennia

Exchange and coexistence between hunter-gatherers and farmers has been a major topic in western and central European archaeology for many decades. While Childe (1927) saw no connections between immigrant LBK—or Danubian I—populations and local

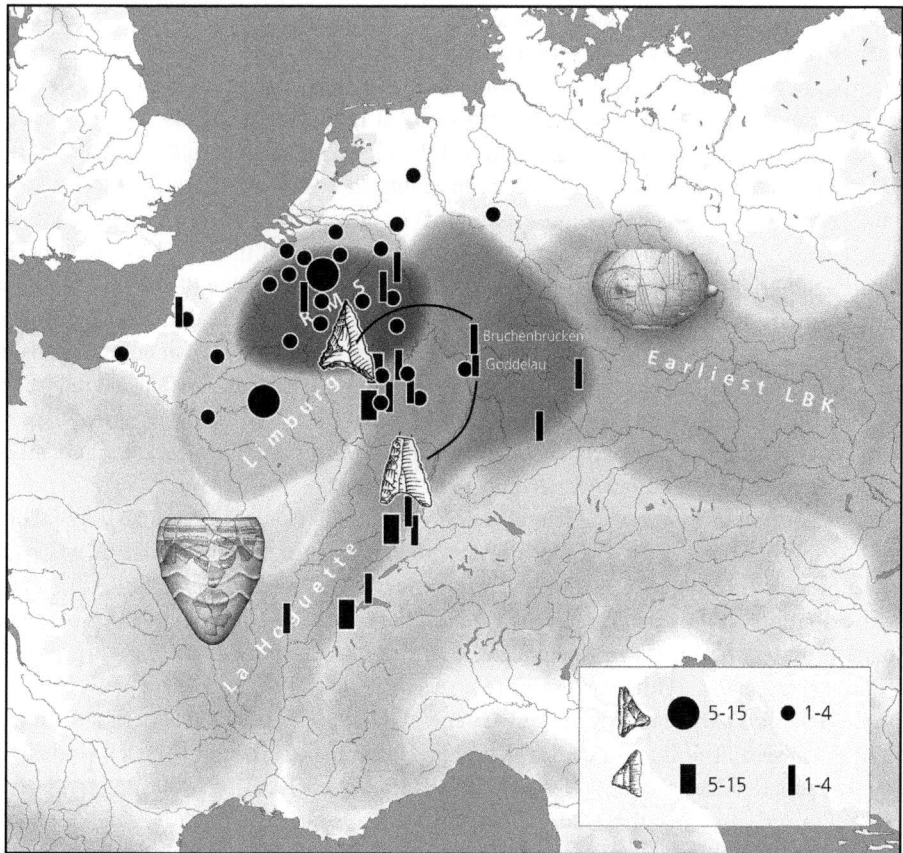

FIGURE 36.2 Lateralization of triangular points with extension of the pottery traditions of La Hoguette and Limburg and the Rhine-Maas-Schelde (RMS) complex (modified after Gronenborn 1999).

Mesolithic foragers whatsoever, Buttler (1938, 66) postulated a contemporaneity that would have ultimately led to the formation of the farming adaptations of the post-LBK horizon. Later Ankel (1964) discussed similarities between Mesolithic and Neolithic 'Danubian points' (Figure 36.2) as resulting from mutual contacts between farmers and contemporary hunter-gatherers. Somewhat contrary to this concept Rozoy (1967) saw such triangular points as an influence of LBK farmers on late Mesolithic societies in the west. This view has persisted in the Dutch and Flemish-Belgian research up to the present day where Danubian points are still seen as intrusive to late Mesolithic assemblages (Crombé 2010).

Other researchers see continuous traditions reflected in Mesolithic and Neolithic triangular points, not only on the individual stylistic-typological level but also on a supra-regional level of type-distributions. Rozoy (1967) already indicated that late Mesolithic triangular points had distinct distributions depending on their lateralization. This dataset was further completed by Löhr (1994) and Gronenborn (1990a). It was now suggested that Danubian points were actually a Mesolithic type that made their way into LBK assemblages. With the publication of the site of Bruchenbrücken in the Wetterau north of Frankfurt the Mesolithic component in the lithic industry of an earliest Linear Pottery site became still more obvious.

Now it was possible to distinguish between two mutually exclusive production sequences in which two distinct modes of blade production existed side by side. Moreover, raw material was brought to the site from the Maas Valley, some 180 km west of the earliest LBK settlements (Gronenborn 1997a; 2003). Also fragments of La Hoguette vessels, a pottery tradition quite distinct from LBK, were found in LBK pits (Lüning et al. 1989). After that the discussion about contacts between LBK immigrants and non-LBK hunter-gatherers arose again. However, it became clear quite quickly that La Hoguette ceramics were not produced by people adhering to a simple foraging economy but engaged in some form of a mixed hunting-gathering-pastoralism and possibly also crop-growing. One of the most convincing arguments came from the site of Stuttgart Bad-Cannstatt where domesticated sheep/goat were found in association with La Hoguette sherds. The subtle archaeobotanical analysis also showed that the group visiting the site must have been quite mobile as only short stays were documented for spring and autumn (Kalis et al. 2001). The lithic assemblage of Stuttgart-Bad Cannstatt is clearly late Meolithic in character and includes the fragment of an asymmetric triangular point (Strien and Tillmann 2001).

The recent publication on the lateralization of triangular points by Hauzeur and Löhr (2008) supports the general picture: symmetric and asymmetric triangular points have overlapping distributions but with different centres. In the case of the asymmetric points the distributions of those lateralized to the left correspond to the distribution area of the La Hoguette pottery tradition, those lateralized to the right correspond to the Limburg pottery tradition (Figure 36.2). However, there are no exclusive and distinct borders between these distributions and they may only be seen as general regional traditions that persist throughout the later Mesolithic into the earlier Neolithic (Hauzeur and Löhr 2008, 17). Nevertheless, they do indicate a certain local element in the farming societies of western and western central Europe. Such regional traditions may go back as far as the eighth millennium cal BC with the Rhine-Maas-Schelde group (Figure 36.2) with its marked use of Wommersom quartzite and the peculiar *feuille de gui* points (Gendel 1984; Street et al. 2001). The persistence of these broad traditions in north-western continental Europe throughout millennia and during the Neolithization process does signal that a considerable local element was embedded in the regional early Neolithic cultures (Jeunesse and van Willigen 2010). However, there were also new elements in the terminal late Mesolithic lithic assemblages of western Europe that only appeared several centuries before full-scale farming reached the region during the middle of the sixth millennium cal BC (Thévenin 1995; 1998). Only slightly later does pottery appear in western temperate Europe, in the south first as the Impressa tradition, then slightly later as the Cardial and Epi-Cardial traditions. The transition from the Mesolithic to the Neolithic seems to have taken place after 6000–5800 cal BC (Guilaine and Manen 2007; van Willigen 2006; van Willigen et al. 2009). Again slightly later, but it is unclear exactly when, La Hoguette appeared in western central Europe (Jeunesse and van Willigen 2010). Stylistically, La Hoguette may have been derived from the southern French Cardial and Epi-Cardial, but not directly as it does form a stylistically independent entity (Guilaine and Manen 1997). Economically, the La Hoguette tradition manufacturers seem to have followed a mixed economy with hunting and gathering but also sheep/goat husbandry, hence may be classified as hunter-gatherer-pastoralists (Chaix 1997). These highly mobile groups were encountered by LBK settlers in western central Europe during their westward expansion. LBK expansion itself was composed of closely tied lineages with an origin in Transdanubia from where, around 5600 cal BC, small pioneering groups must have migrated both westward but also northward, across the Carpathian mountain ridge into Little Poland and from there further east into Ukraine and Moldavia (Larina 1999; Wechler 2001).

Along the western 'frontier', contacts between immigrant LBK farmers and local populations have been well researched. Apart from the evidence mentioned above on the earliest phase at the site of Bruchenbrücken, recent work in Baden-Württemberg has further detailed the knowledge of the manifold mutual interactions. However, in order to fully comprehend these studies it is necessary to look back into the Mesolithic. Following earlier work by Taute (1973/74; 1988), Gronenborn (1997b), Kind (1997; 2003), Gehlen (1999; Gehlen and Schön 2003), and Nielsen (2009) have presented overviews on the development of the later Mesolithic in south-west Germany and Switzerland and were able to show that a major stylistic and technological break exists between the earlier Mesolithic ending between 7000 and 6700 cal BC, and the late Mesolithic with its characteristic trapezes and regular blades. In fact, from a lithic technology point of view, the break between the earlier and the late Mesolithic is much more evident than between the late Mesolithic and the earliest LBK (Gronenborn 1990b; 2003). Also, with the onset of the late Mesolithic, evidence for sporadic agricultural activities in the form of cerealia pollen and *Plantago lanceolata* pollen in various regions north of the Alps sets in (Beckmann 2004; Tinner et al. 2007). While the archaeobotanical evidence is still heavily debated (Behre 2007), archaeological evidence for far-reaching contacts between southern central Europe and south-eastern Europe is strengthening: earlier indications of contacts to the middle Danube through freshwater snails (Gronenborn 1999; Rähle 1978) is now supported by a clay token (*pintadera*) from the site of Arconciel 'La Souche' in the Swiss Jura, which dates between 6200 and 6000 cal BC and is associated with a late Mesolithic lithic assemblage (Mauvilly et al. 2008). Despite this evidence, groups still appear to have been highly mobile as no evidence for any larger, more continuously inhabited sites have yet been found (Kind 2003). Sites from the southern central European late Mesolithic are either short-stay camp sites—open air or rock shelters— and burials (Gehlen and Schön 2005). The most famous are certainly the skull depositions from the Ofnet cave (Schmidt 1913). Just like those from Hohlestein they point to a period of increased external and internal violence (Orschiedt 1998; 2005). While larger sites may still be buried deeply in the floodplains of major rivers (Gronenborn 1999) the evidence presently available from the late Mesolithic may be interpreted as indications for highly mobile groups with an ephemeral settlement system but wide-ranging exchange networks. These were maintained by societies with a high potential for inter-group and intra-group violence. Possibly this situation was fostered by climatically unfavourable conditions before, during, and after the so-called 8.2 ka and 6.2 ka events (Gronenborn 2007a).

In any case, nothing in the central and western European data indicates that Mesolithic societies may have been on a trajectory towards hunter-gatherer complexity. This situation continues into the sixth millennium up until the first LBK sites appear throughout southern central Europe. These settlers arrived in the western portion of their distribution area around 5500 cal BC and their origins in Transdanubia might date only slightly earlier (Bánffy 2009; Gronenborn 2003). While in the eastern realms of the earliest LBK distribution indications of interactions between farmers and local hunter-gatherers are minimal, the evidence from the western part and the northern border is more numerous (Gronenborn 1997a; 2010). The data on culture contact from Bruchenbrücken have been referred to already above. Detailed research at the site of Vaihingen by Strien (2005) showed that this village's inhabitants were divided into distinct groups living in distinct quarters throughout the entire duration of

Vaihingen from earlier to latest LBK. These sub-groups, possibly lineages, materialized their group identities through minute details in the pottery decorations, the so-called spandrel motifs (German: *Zwickelmuster*) but also microliths and differences in tool percentages. Specifically so-called rhombic trapezes (German: *Trapezspitzen*) are of importance as they constitute a local late Mesolithic tradition. They cluster with distinct ceramic markers and occur in a village quarter where sickle blades are rare. Strien (2005) concluded that the village of Vaihingen was inhabited by various different lineages that remained stable over many centuries, but had different cultural backgrounds: while some may have arrived from Transdanubia others may have had local origins. A similar scenario has been suggested by Lüning (2005) for the earliest LBK site of Schwanfeld where radiolarites of the Szengál type (Mateiciucová 2004) occur mostly in one row of chronologically successive houses (Figure 36.3). These might mark a specific lineage, originating from Hungary, while the other rows might be attributable to local lineages or those from different origins outside the Carpathian Basin. Certainly, there are local Mesolithic elements in the Schwanfeld lithic assemblage visible in rhombic trapezes but also in borers of the *mêches de fôret* type (Gronenborn 1997a; 2003). All in all, the evidence from Vaihingen and Schwanfeld shows that right from the beginning LBK societies were segmented and structured into lineages. Some of these lineages may have had their origins in the Carpathian Basin, others could well have their ancestry in the local hunter-gatherer or pastoralist population.

Strontium isotope analyses have in recent years complemented archaeological research on Mesolithic–Neolithic interactions. A number of studies have been concerned with the question of whether the mobility patterns visible may be attributed to the merging of two distinct groups with hunter-gatherers joining LBK communities. Bentley et al. (2002) suggested that during the earlier LBK the population buried at the Flomborn cemetery south of Mainz, Germany, was composed of two distinct groups, one of which may have been of regional Mesolithic ancestry. More recently, however, it became apparent that LBK communities were composed of members who, during their lifetime, changed their residence (Knipper 2009; Price et al. 2006). Some may indeed have come from outside of the traditional farming landscapes, mountainous areas, maybe at the time still used by terminal hunter-gatherers. A more likely pattern, though, may be related to a pastoral component within the LBK societies with herders spending part of their yearly cycle in the uplands together with their cattle (Bentley et al. 2008; Knipper 2009).

Interactions between local populations and immigrating LBK-tradition farmers are also suggested for western temperate Europe. Jeunesse (2000; Jeunesse and Winter 1998) had summarized previous data and was able to show that from the beginning of LBK settlements, exchanges between LBK communities presumably immigrating from more eastern regions across the Rhine and local La Hoguette-manufacturing groups are manifested in the material culture, notably in some pottery decoration styles. Particularly the so-called *décors en grille* of the late LBK is suggested to originally stem from La Hoguette decorations. Allard (2005) argues that while similarities between late Mesolithic asymmetric arrowheads and those stemming from LBK assemblages do exist, both traditions are otherwise quite distinct. The LBK lithic technology appears to derive from the eastern provinces in the Rhineland and Baden-Württemberg. LBK and its local expression (RRBP—*Rubané Récent du Bassin Parisien*) is intrusive in northern France. The wider implications of this intrusion are, however, strongly debated: while Jeunesse (1998–9) suggested a synchronic model with the RRBP being contemporary to the local Neolithic cultures of Villeneuve-Saint-Germain

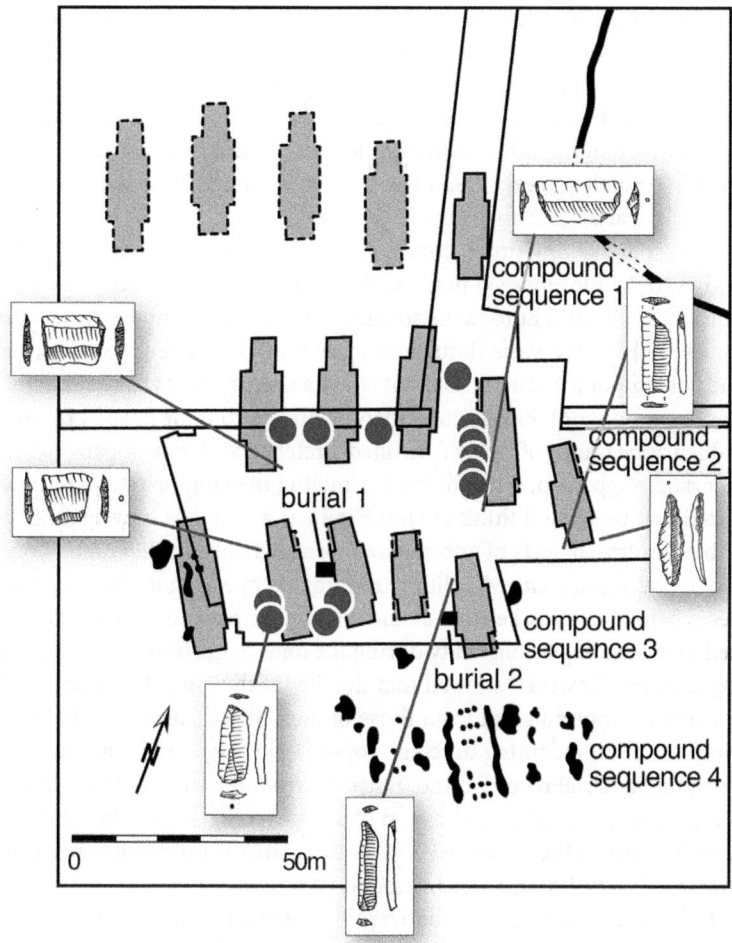

FIGURE 36.3 Schwanfeld, Ldkr. Würzburg, Bavaria. Plan of the site with findspots of radiolarites (dark circles) and microliths of Mesolithic tradition (after Lüning 2005 and Gronenborn 2003).

(VSG), Bliquy, and Augy-Sainte-Pallaye (ASP), others (Allard 2005; Constantin 1985) argued for a diachronic model in which Bliquy, VSP, and ASP succeeded the RRBP. This vivid debate is not without importance for the general question of acculturation of hunter-gatherer populations, as Bliquy, VSP, and ASP are seen as local Mesolithic adaptations of Danubian influences that become particularly visible in the adoption of the LBK longhouse architecture; pottery styles, instead, derive from the Mediterranean (Jeunesse and Van Willigen 2010). If LBK and ASP, VSG and Bliquy prove to be contemporary, interactions and contacts between immigrant groups and local individuals of Mesolithic ancestry should have been intense, yet with no complete admixture as geographically these entities do not overlap.

In this regard it is remarkable that on the map of genetic distances north-eastern France, southern France and Italy have strong genetic affiliations to the LBK population and their supposed Near Eastern location of origin. Apparently, and quite in concurrence with archaeology, these regions experienced a considerable influx of Near Eastern groups in the course of the Neolithization. LBK, La Hoguette, ASP, VSG, and Bliquy might be pottery traditions manufactured by a population that had considerable roots in Anatolia. These groups had taken different routes to temperate Europe, of which one went through the Balkans (the Danubian stream) while the other followed the Mediterranean coast and then the Rhône Valley towards the north and north-east (Occidental stream). These streams merged in the region between the Paris Basin and western Germany.

Out of these contacts and interactions of Danubian and Occidental-Mediterranean influences a new dynamic emerged in the wider Paris Basin which led towards the middle Neolithic. In western central Europe the so-called Hinkelstein Group evolves with contacts towards the late LBK in the Paris Basin. Hinkelstein marks a cultural disruption between previous and contemporary LBK although it is stylistically related (Hauzeur 2006; Jeunesse and Strien 2009; Spatz 1996). Burial rites differed notably from the flexed LBK inhumations with the sudden appearance of richly furnished stretched skeletons (Spatz 1999). As a new ceramic decoration appeared, with motifs resembling dancing or praying humans, it has been suggested that we should think of Hinkelstein as a religious movement (Spatz 2003). Also, many burials have objects of adornment fabricated out of wild animal bone or teeth, and trapezes of a seemingly late Mesolithic tradition reappearing in the lithic assemblages. Thus, earlier research saw Hinkelstein as the material remains of hunter-gatherers which had returned to archaeological visibility during the final stages of the LBK. Recent physical anthropological work, however, showed that the diet of the Hinkelstein population in the Rhine-Main area was not different from those of the LBK and also morphologically there are no indications of an incoming different population (Meyer and Alt 2005). Apparently the changes in the material record at the transition from the early to the middle Neolithic in western central Europe are no indication of a resurrection of previous hunter-gatherer traditions. An increase of the dependence on wild animals is only visible in eastern central Europe within the Lengyel complex (Jeunesse and Arbogast 1997).

With the fifth millennium, contacts between the farmer population of the southern central European loess belt and the northern lowlands intensified. Already during the sixth millennium contacts over distances of sometimes several hundred kilometres existed, with hunter-gatherers visiting LBK sites (Figure 36.4) (Gronenborn 2005; 2010). Also, LBK artefacts made their way into the north, notably Danubian shoe-last adzes and middle Neolithic perforated adzes. Throughout the fifth millennium the flow of materials from the south into the lowlands and beyond into the western Baltic continued with foreign artefacts, particularly those of copper; they may have had a prestigious role within the Ertebølle societies (Gronenborn 2009b; Klassen 2004). However, despite these exchanges, farming was not taken up in the north before the end of the fifth millennium (Hartz et al. 2007). Also, as said above, pottery in the north appears to have arrived by routes along the Baltic coastline and the northern lowlands and not—as previously thought—through interaction with Danubian groups towards the south (Gronenborn 2009b). In Pomerania contacts between farmers and the northern hunter-gatherers seem to have been minimal and are reduced archaeologically to a few prestige items (Terberger and Kabacinski 2010). But further east, in Kujavia, exchange with late Lengyel communities and hunter-gatherer groups of the eastern Baltic seems to be reflected in certain bone and pottery decoration styles, particularly for the late fifth-millennium Breść Kujawski Group (Czerniak 2007). It is only then, after 4200 cal BC, that the previously apparently impermeable border between these economically

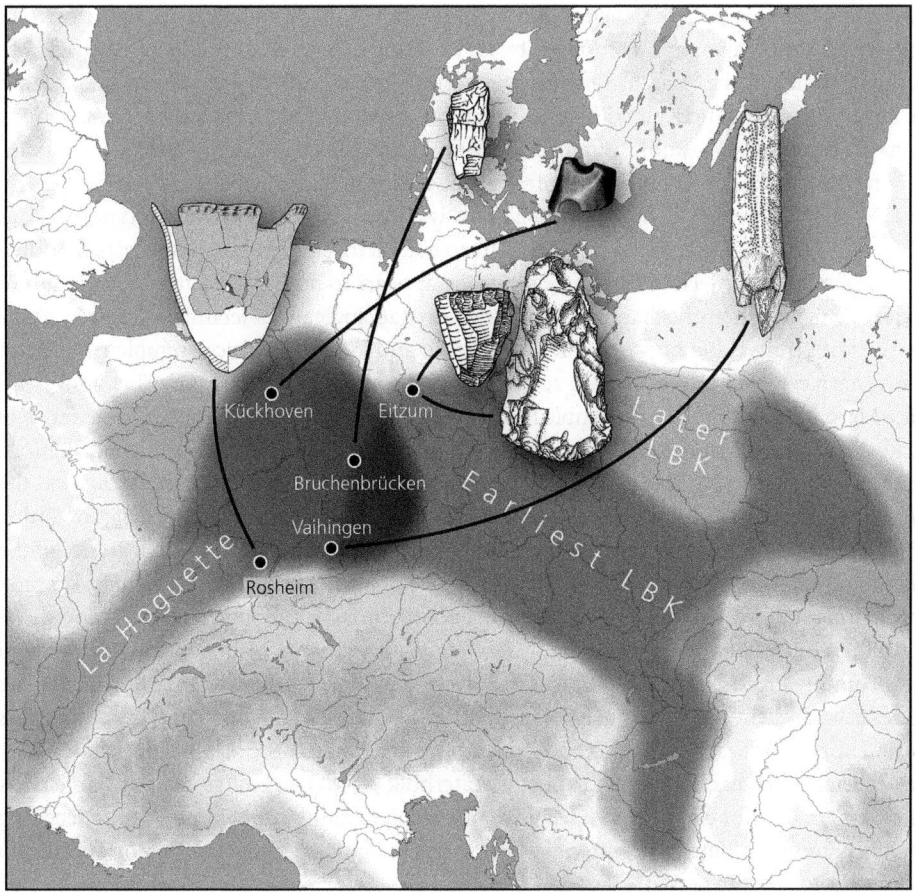

FIGURE 36.4 Imports of northern Late Mesolithic artefacts on southern European Early Neolithic sites (modified after Gronenborn 2010).

different societies began to dissolve and with the emergence of the Funnel Beaker culture after 4100 cal BC farming finally spread to the north. Possibly an eastward expansion of the western European Michelsberg Culture, which brought new agricultural techniques, had a triggering effect on these changes (Klassen 2004; Schier 2009).

THE PROCESS OF NEOLITHIZATION AND MIGRATION DYNAMICS

The earliest traces of farming appear in western and central Europe at least by the mid-seventh millennium. With this begins the 3,000-year lasting process of Neolithization (Gronenborn 2009a; Schier 2009). Throughout this transition period contacts between hunter-gatherers, hunter-pastoralists, and farmers occurred between the seventh, sixth, and fifth millennia. While debated over decades, in recent years it has become clear that the expansion of farming was fostered by an expansion of an incoming population, hence at least some of these archaeologically visible contacts and interactions should have occurred between genetically differently composed populations. This has been made quite clear by recent aDNA studies: the late Palaeolithic and Mesolithic populations of northern, north-eastern, and southern central Europe appear to have been composed of the U mtDNA haplotype while the LBK population was composed of other haplotypes such as H, T, and J (Bramanti et al. 2009). This still coarse picture nevertheless suggests that during the earlier to mid-Holocene central Europe appears to have been settled by immigrant groups. Exactly when this happens is unclear. Archaeologically, a technological and stylistic disruption is visible between early Mesolithic and late Mesolithic assemblages, at least for western central Europe (Gehlen 2009; Gronenborn 1990b; Nielsen 2009; Taute 1973/74). Late Mesolithic assemblages resemble those of the earliest LBK except for the appearance of sickle blades. At the same time, continuous and intensifying contacts towards south-eastern Europe appeared in the seventh millennium cal BC, culminating in the first cereals and the *pintadera* from Arconciel in the Swiss Jura. It may thus be argued that this population influx had already begun with the seventh millennium—if not earlier—with the appearance of the blade-and-trapeze lithic industries (Clark 1980). Possibly this and previous but also later migrations had been triggered by climate fluctuations (Gronenborn 2007b; 2009a). As from then onwards we have to account for contacts between an originally Palaeolithic and an incoming 'Proto-Neolithic' population. Given the indications of violence during the late Mesolithic discussed above, it may be justified to consider clashes and conflicts during this period, maybe between incoming and local groups—ultimately the original population may have been pushed back towards the north. Waterbolk (1968, 1101) suggested that 'large parts of continental Europe appear to have been uninhabited at the time immediately preceding the immigration of farmers'. This view, long thought outdated, may gain importance again under the light of the new aDNA data.

If an incoming population had already moved into central Europe during the seventh millennium, then contacts between LBK farmers and 'late Mesolithic' foragers occurred between two populations derived from the same origins. The LBK itself then may be regarded as a consecutive 'wave' of immigrants, whose source lay in the western Carpathian Basin (Bánffy 2004; Gronenborn 1999; Pavúk 2004). Even within the LBK we do have to account for considerable mobility and possibly repeated migrations from the Carpathian Basin (e. g. Schade-Lindig and Schade 2010). Beyond that, population movements may be expected from western Anatolia to the northern Balkans via the Bosporus but also via the Aegean. Another flux is to be expected across the south-west Russian steppe zone. These migrations are visible from the map produced by Haak et al. (2010) where the populations that genetically maternally resemble those of the LBK are also spread across southern Russia (Figure 36.1).

Equally in the west population movements throughout the later Mesolithic are to be expected. They are most easily visible through Mediterranean snails in Mesolithic contexts, a network that became intensified during the late Mesolithic (Gronenborn 1999). Population movements may also be inferred from the map of matrilineal distances (Figure 36.1b). It is thus questionable whether those archaeologically visible contacts between LBK and the late Mesolithic groups along the western border of the LBK occurred between incoming groups and those of ultimately Palaeolithic ancestry or rather populations that had arrived in Europe only towards the later Mesolithic and were equally of Near Eastern origins. These migrations may have begun as early as 7000 cal BC (Gronenborn 2009b).

The contacts and interactions between the LBK and the successive Danubian manifestations during the fifth millennium and the northern lowland Mesolithic groups, however, seem to have taken place between two distinct populations. While the northern lowlands and the regions further east in Eurasia were settled by a population in which haplogroup U appears to have been at least dominant, early central European Neolithic population members belonged to haplogroup K, T, J, V, H, HV, and N1a (Figure 36.1c) (Haak et al. 2005. The ubiquity of haplogroup U in the European north and north-east during the early to mid-Holocene and the genetically differently composed LBK communities indicate that the cultural and economic border which existed along the northern extension of the loess belt was one between populations that had been separated for a considerable time period, at least since the recolonization of the continent after the glacial maximum (Bramanti et al. 2009). While cross-cultural interaction is documented from the mid-sixth millennium onwards, assimilation seems to have been minimal. At the site of Derenburg in Saxonia-Anhalt only one individual belonged to clade U5: a mature female. She was one out of 42 individuals sampled from the LBK at the time of the study (Haak et al. 2010). Only in the course of the spread of farming to the north did these populations begin to mix. For the earlier fourth millennium the mixed Funnel Beaker-Mesolithic burial site of Ostorf dating to around 3200 cal BC (Bramanti et al. 2009; Lübke et al. 2007) was used by a genetically mixed community composed of individuals of the northern U5 mtDNA subclades but also southern clades such as K, T, and J. It is only then that the Neolithic immigrants from the Near East and the temperate European Mesolithic population mixed. Apparently during the previous millennia, exchanges had been largely reduced to mutual formalized communication but not to interbreeding, at least not incorporating hunter-gatherer females to any great scale. In accordance with this, based on ancient DNA-analyses Malmström et al. (2009) and Skoglund et al. (2012) recently showed that the southern Swedish late hunter-gatherer population of the Pitted Ware culture has only a distant genetic connection to the modern population and may have been partly replaced by farmers of the Funnel Beaker culture and possibly retreated to the eastern Baltic.

Models where the influx of hunter-gatherer females into farming societies (hypergyny) play a crucial role, as suggested by Zvelebil and Lillie (2000), must be rethought and nuanced for northern Europe. For southern central Europe the situation is less clear as the last hunter-gatherers may genetically have been the same immigrant population as the first farmers.

Lastly, the current state of research shows that both European but also ultimately Near Eastern populations contributed to the emergence of the Neolithic across western temperate and central Europe. Early Neolithic societies such as the LBK and possibly also La Hoguette were largely composed of people with an ultimately Near Eastern ancestry. It is, however, possible that the first migrations of these populations into Europe started at the beginning of the seventh millennium still during the period traditionally referred to as the late Mesolithic and characterized by a predominantly hunting-and-gathering economy. The temperate European Palaeolithic-Mesolithic population appears to have been then gradually pushed towards the north with little continuous interaction with the immigrants. Only very late on, during the fourth millennium, do populations mix to any greater extent at the northern fringes of the Neolithic.

References

Allard, P. 2005. *L'industrie lithique des populations rubanées du Nord-Est de la France et de la Belgique*. Rahden: Marie Leidorf.

Ankel, C. 1964. Eine linienbandkeramische Pfeilspitzen-Form. In *Studien aus Alteuropa Teil 1. Bonner Jahrbücher Beiheft 10*, 68–77. Bonn: Habelt.

Bánffy, E. 2004. *The 6th millennium BC boundary in Western Transdanubia and its role in the Central European Neolithic transition (The Szentgyörgyvölgy-Pityerdomb Settlement)*. Varia Archaeologica Hungarica XV. Budapest: Archaeological Institute of the Hungarian Academy of Science.

Bánffy, E. 2009. Variations on the Neolithic transition in Eastern and Western Hungary. In D. Hofmann and P. Bickle (eds), *Creating communities: new advances in Central European Neolithic research*, 44–62. Oxford: Oxbow Books.

Beckmann, M. 2004. *Pollenanalytische Untersuchung der Zeit der Jäger und Sammler und der ersten Bauern an zwei Lokalitäten des Zentralen Schweizer Mittellandes: Umwelt und erste Eingriffe des Menschen in die Vegetation vom Paläolithikum bis zum Jungeneolithikum*. Dissertationes Botanicae 390. Berlin: J. Cramer.

Behre, K.-E. 2007. Evidence for Mesolithic agriculture in and around central Europe? *Vegetation History and Archaeobotany* 16, 203–19.

Bentley, R. A., Price, T. D., Lüning, J., Gronenborn, D., Wahl, J., and Fullagar, P. D. 2002. Prehistoric migration in Europe: Strontium isotope analysis of early Neolithic skeletons. *Current Anthropology* 43, 799–804.

Bentley, R. A., Wahl, J., Price, T. D., and Atkinson, T. C. 2008. Isotopic signatures and hereditary traits: snapshots of a Neolithic community. *Antiquity* 82, 290–304.

Bramanti, B., Thomas, M. G., Haak, W., Unterlaender, M., Jores, P., Tambets, K., Antanaitis-Jacobs, I., Haidle, M. N., Jankauskas, R., Kind, C.-J., Lueth, F., Terberger, T., Hiller, J., Matsumura, S., Forster, P., and Burger, J. 2009. Genetic discontinuity between local hunter-gatherers and central Europe's first farmers. *Science* 326, 137–40.

Buttler, W. 1938. *Der donauländische und der westische Kulturkreis der jüngeren Steinzeit*. Handbuch der Urgeschichte Deutschlands 2. Berlin: Walter de Gruyter.

Chaix, L. 1997. La transition Méso-Néolithique: quelques donnés de l'archéozoologie dans les Alpes du Nord et le Jura. In C. Jeunesse (ed.), *Le Néolithique Danubien et ses marges entre Rhin et Seine. XXIIe Colloque Interrégional sur le Néolithique, Strasbourg 27–29 Octobre 1995*, 191–6. Zimmersheim: Cahiers de l'Association pour la Promotion de la Recherche Archéologique en Alsace. Supplément no. 3.

Childe, V. G. 1927. *The dawn of European civilization*. London: Routledge & Kegan Paul.

Clark, J. G. D. 1980. *Mesolithic prelude: the Palaeolithic–Neolithic transition in Old World prehistory*. Edinburgh: Edinburgh University Press.

Constantin, C. 1985. *Fin du Rubané, céramique du Limbourg et post-Rubané: le néolithique le plus ancien en Bassin Parisien et en Hainaut*. Oxford: British Archaeological Reports International Series 273.

Crombé, P. 2010. Contact and interaction between early farmers and late hunter-gatherers in Belgium during the 6th and 5th millennium cal BC. In D. Gronenborn and J. Petrasch (eds), *Die Neolithisierung Mitteleuropas: the spread of the Neolithic to Central Europe*, 551–68. Mainz: Verlag des Römisch-Germanischen Zentralmuseums.

Czerniak, L. 2007. The north-east frontier of the post-LBK cultures. In J. K. Kozlowski and P. Raczky (eds), *The Lengyel, Polgár and related cultures in the Middle/Late Neolithic in Central*

Europe, 233–48. Kraków: The Polish Academy of Arts and Sciences Kraków; Eötvös Loránd University, Institute of Archaeological Sciences Budapest.

Dolukhanov, P., Shukurov, A., Gronenborn, D., Sokoloff, D. Timofeev, V., and Zaitseva, G. 2005. The chronology of Neolithic dispersal in Central and Eastern Europe. *Journal of Archaeological Science* 32, 1441–58.

Gamble, C., Davies, W., Pettitt, P., Hazelwood, L., and Richards, M. 2006. The Late Glacial ancestry of Europeans: combining genetic and archaeological evidence. *Documenta Praehistorica* 33, 1–10.

Gehlen, B. 1999. Late Palaeolithic, Mesolithic and Early Neolithic in the Lower Alpione region between the rivers Iller and Lech (south-west Bavaria). In A. Thévenin (ed.) and P. Bintz (Dir.), *L'Europe des derniers chasseurs. L'Épipaléolithique et Mésolithique. Peuplement et paléoenvironnement de L'Épipaléolithique et du Mésolithique*, 489–97. Actes du 5e Colloque international UISPP, 18–23 septembre en Grenoble 1995.

Gendel, P. 1984. *Mesolithic social territories in northwestern Europe*. Oxford: British Archaeological Reports International Series 218.

Gehlen, B. and Schön, W. 2003. Das 'Spätmesolithikum' und das initiale Neolithikum in Griechenland—Implikationen für die Neolithisierung der alpinen und circumalpinen Gebiete. *Archäologische Informationen* 26, 255–73.

Gehlen, B. and Schön, W. 2005. Klima und Kulturwandel—Mögliche Folgen des '6200-Events' in Europa. In D. Gronenborn (ed.), *Klimaveränderung und Kulturwandel in neolithischen Gesellschaften Mitteleuropas, 6700–2200 v. Chr.*, 53–74. Mainz: Verlag des Römisch-Germanischen Zentralmuseums.

Gehlen, B. 2009. A microlith sequence from Friesack 4, Brandenburg, and the Mesolithic in Germany. In P. Crombé, M. Van Strydonk, J. Sergant, M. Boudin, and B. Marchteld (eds), *Chronology and evolution of the Mesolithic in northwest-Europe. Proceedings of an international Meeting, Brussels, May 30th–June 1st 2007*, 363–93. Cambridge: Cambridge Scholars Publishing.

Gronenborn, D. 1990a. Eine Pfeilspitze vom ältestbandkeramischen Fundplatz Friedberg-Bruchenbrücken in der Wetterau. *Germania* 68, 223–31.

Gronenborn, D. 1990b. Mesolithic-Neolithic interactions: the lithic industry of the earliest Bandkeramik Culture site at Friedberg-Bruchenbrücken (West Germany). In P. M. Vermeersch and P. van Peer (eds), *Contributions to the Mesolithic in Europe. Papers presented at the Fourth International Symposium 'The Mesolithic in Europe', Leuven 1990*, 173–82. Leuven: Leuven University Press.

Gronenborn, D. 1997a. *Silexartefakte der ältestbandkeramischen Kultur*. Bonn: Habelt.

Gronenborn, D. 1997b. Sarching 4 und der Übergang vom Früh- zum Spätmesolithikum im südlichen Mitteleuropa. *Archäologisches Korrespondenzblatt* 27, 387–402.

Gronenborn, D. 1999. A variation on a basic theme: the transition to farming in southern Central Europe. *Journal of World Prehistory* 13, 123–210.

Gronenborn, D. 2003. Lithic raw material distribution networks and the Neolithization of Central Europe. In L. Burnez-Lanotte (ed.), *Production and management of lithic materials in the European Linearbandkeramik/Gestion des matériaux lithiques dans le Rubané européen. Actes du XIVème Congrès UISPP, Université de Liège Belgique, 2–8 septembre 2001*, 45–50. Oxford: BAR International Series 1200.

Gronenborn, D. 2005. Eine Pfeilschneide aus Südskandinavien vom ältestbandkeramischen Fundplatz Friedberg-Bruchenbrücken in der Wetterau. *Archäologisches Korrespondenzblatt* 35, 159–68.

Gronenborn, D. 2007a. Climate change and socio-political crises: some cases from Neolithic Central Europe. In T. Pollard and I. Banks (eds), *War and sacrifice: studies in the archaeology of conflict*, 13–32. Leiden: Brill.

Gronenborn, D. 2007b. Beyond the models: 'Neolithisation' in Central Europe. In A. Whittle and V. Cummings (eds.), *Going over: the Mesolithic–Neolithic transition in north-west Europe*, 73–98. London: British Academy.

Gronenborn, D. 2009a. Climate fluctuations and trajectories to complexity in the Neolithic: towards a theory. In M. Budja (ed.), *Neolithic studies* 16, 97–110. Ljubljana: Documenta Praehistorica 36.

Gronenborn, D. 2009b. Transregional culture contacts and the Neolithization process in Northern Central Europe. In P. Jordan and M. Zvelebil (eds), *Ceramics before farming: the dispersal of pottery among prehistoric Eurasian hunter-gatherers*, 527–50. Walnut Creek, CA Left Coast Press.

Gronenborn, D. 2010. Fernkontakte aus dem nördlichen Europa während der Bandkeramischen Kultur. In P. Kalábková, B. Kovár, P. Pavúk, and J. Šuteková (eds.), *PANTA RHEI. Studies in Chronology and Cultural Development of South-Eastern and Central Europe in Earlier Prehistory. Presented to Juraj Pavúk on the Occasion of his 75th Birthday*, 561–74. Bratislava: Comenius University.

Guilaine, J. and Manen, C. 1997. Contacts sud-nord au Néolithique ancien: témoignages de la grotte Gazel en Languedoc. In Chr. Jeunesse (ed.), *Le Néolithique Danubien et ses marges entre Rhin et Seine. XXIIe Colloque Interrégional sur le Néolithique, Strasbourg 27-29 Octobre 1995*, 301–11. Zimmersheim: Cahiere de l'Association pour la Promotion de la Recherche Archéologique en Alsace. Supplément no. 3.

Gronenborn, D. 2011. Early pottery in Afroeurasia: origins and possible routes of dispersal. In S. Hartz, F. Lüth, and T. Terberger (eds), *The early pottery in the Baltic. Workshop Schleswig, October 2006*, 59–88. Berichte der Römisch-Germanischen Kommission 89.

Guilaine, J. and Manen, C. 2007. From Mesolithic to Early Neolithic in the western Mediterranean. In A. Whittle and V. Cummings (eds), *Going over: the Mesolithic–Neolithic transition in north-west Europe*, 21–52. London: British Academy.

Haak, W., Balanovsky, O., Sanchez, J. J., Koshel, S., Zaporozhchenko, V., Adler, C., J., Der Sarkissian, C. S. I., Brandt, G., Schwarz, C., Nicklisch, N., Dreseley, V., Fritsch, B., Balanovska, E., Villems, R., Meller, H., Alt, K. W., Cooper, A., the Genographic Consortium. 2010. Ancient DNA from European Early Neolithic farmers reveals their Near Eastern affinities. *PLoS Biol* 8(11): e1000536.

Haak, W., Forster, P., Bramanti, B., Matsumura, S., Brandt, G., Tänzer, M., Villems, R., Renfrew, C., Gronenborn, D., Alt, K. W., and Burger, J. 2005. Ancient DNA from the first European farmers in 7500-year-old Neolithic sites. *Science* 310, 1016–18.

Hartz, S., Lübke, H., and Terberger, T. 2007. From fish and seal to sheep and cattle: new research into the process of neolithization in northern Germany. In A. Whittle and V. Cummings (eds), *Going over: the Mesolithic–Neolithic transition in north-west Europe*, 567–94. London: British Academy.

Hauzeur, A. 2006. *Le Rubané au Luxembourg: contribution à l'étude du Rubané du Nord-Ouest européen*. Dossiers d'Archéologie du Musée National d'Histoire et d'Art X/Études et Recherches Archéologiques de l'Université de Liège 114. Luxembourg: Musée national d'histoire et d'art.

Hauzeur, A. and Löhr, H. 2008. Latéralisation des armatures rubanées: apports des données récentes de la Moselle dans le contexte du Rubané du Nord-Ouest. *P@lethnologie* 2008.1 [http://www.palethnologie.org].

Jeunesse, C. 1998–9. La synchronisation des séquence culturelles des bassins du Rhin, de la Meuse et de la Seine et la chronologie du Bassin Parisien au Néolithique ancien et moyen (5200–4500 av. J.-C.). *Bulletin de la Société Préhistorique Luxembourgeoise* 20–1, 337–92.

Jeunesse, C. 2000. Les composantes autochtone et danubienne en Europe Centrale et occidentale entre 5500 et 4000 av. J.-C.: contacts, transferts, acculturations. In A. Richard, C. Cupillard, and R. Hervé (eds), *Les derniers chasseur-cuilleurs d'Europe occidentale, Actes du colloque international de Besançon, Octobre 1998*, 361–78. Besançon: Presses Universitaires Franc-Comtoises 361 à 378, Annales Littéraires 699, Série 'Environnement, sociétés et archaéologie' 1.

Jeunesse, C. and Arbogast, R.-M. 1997. A propos du statut de la chasse au Néolithique moyen: la faune sauvage dans les déchets domestiques et dans les mobiliers funéraires. In C. Jeunesse (ed.), *Le Néolithique Danubien et ses marges entre Rhin et Seine. XXIIe Colloque Interrégional sur le Néolithique, Strasbourg 27–29 Octobre 1995*, 81–102. Zimmersheim: Cahiers de l'Association pour la Promotion de la Recherche Archéologique en Alsace.

Jeunesse, C. and Strien, H.-C. 2009. Bemerkungen zu den stichbandkeramischen Elementen in Hinkelstein. In A. Zeeb-Lanz (ed.), *Krisen—Kulturwandel—Kontinuitäten. Zum Ende der Bandkeramik in Mitteleuropa. Beiträge der internationalen Tagung in Herxheim bei Landau (Pfalz) vom 14.–17. 06. 2007*, 241–7. Rahden: Internationale Archäologie. Arbeitsgemeinschaft, Symposium, Tagung, Kongress 10.

Jeunesse, C. and Van Willigen, S. 2010. Westmediterranes Frühneolithikum und westliche Linearbandkeramik: Impulse, Interaktionen, Mischkulturen. In D. Gronenborn and J. Petrasch (eds), *Die Neolithisierung Mitteleuropas: the spread of the Neolithic to Central Europe*, 569–606. Mainz: Verlag des Römisch-Germanischen Zentralmuseums.

Jeunesse, C. and Winter, S. 1998. À propos de quelques décors 'non traditionnels' dans le Rubané. Réflexions sur les changements stylistiques dans la céramique du Néolithique ancien danubien. In X. Gutherz and R. Joussaume (eds), *Le Néolithique du centre-ouest de la France. Actes du XXIe colloque inter-régional sur le Néolithique, Poitiers, 14–16 Octobre 1994*, 345–57. Chauvigny: Association des Publications Chauvinoises, Mémoire no. 14.

Kalis, A. J., Meurers-Balke, J., van der Borg, K., von den Driesch, A., Rähle, W., Tegtmeier, U., and Thiemeyer, H. 2001. Der La-Hoguette-Fundhorizont in der Wilhelma von Stuttgart-Bad Cannstatt. Anthrakologische, archäopalynologische, bodenkundliche, malakozoologische, radiometrische und säugetierkundliche Untersuchungen. In B. Gehlen, M. Heinen, and A. Tillmann (eds), *Zeit-Räume. Gedenkschrift für Wolfgang Taute Band 2*, 649–72. Bonn: Deutsche Gesellschaft für Ur- und Frühgeschichte/Rudolf Habelt.

Kind, C.-J. 1997. Die mesolithische Freiland-Stratigraphie von Rottenburg 'Siebenlinden 3'. *Archäologisches Korrespondenzblatt* 27, 13–32.

Kind, C.-J. 2003. *Das Mesolithikum in der Talaue des Neckars. Die Fundstelle von Rottenburg Siebenlinden 1 und 3*. Forschungen und Berichte zur Vor- und Frühgeschichte in Baden-Württemberg 88. Stuttgart: Konrad Theiss.

Klassen, L. 2004. *Jade und Kupfer. Untersuchungen zum Neolithisierungsprozeß im westlichen Ostseeraum unter besonderer Berücksichtigung der Kulturentwicklung Europas 5500–3500 BC*. Jysk Arkæologisk Selskabs Skrifter 47. Aarhus: Aarhus University Press.

Knipper, C. 2009. Mobility in a sedentary society: insights from isotope analysis of LBK human and animal teeth. In D. Hofmann and P. Bickle (eds), *Creating communities: new advances in Central European Neolithic research*, 143–59. Oxford: Oxbow.

Larina, O. V. 1999. Kultura linenjo-lentochnoj keramiki pruto-denstrovskogo regiona (The Linear Pottery Culture of the area between rivers Prut and Dniester). *Stratum plus* 2, 10–140.

Löhr, H. 1994. Linksflügler und Rechtsflügler in Mittel- und Westeuropa. Der Fortbestand der Verbreitungsgebiete asymmetrischer Pfeilspitzenformen als Kontinuitätsbeleg zwischen Meso- und Neolithikum. *Trierer Zeitschrift* 57, 9–126.

Lübke, H., Lüth, F., and Terberger, T. 2007. Fishers or farmers? The archaeology of the Ostorf cemetary and related Neolithic finds in the light of new data. *Berichte der Römisch-Germanischen Kommission* 88, 307–38.

Lüning, J. 2005. Bandkeramische Hofplätze und die absolute Chronologie der Bandkeramik. In J. Lüning, C. Fridrich, and A. Zimmermann (eds), *Die Bandkeramik im 21. Jahrhundert. Symposium in der Abtei Brauweiler bei Köln vom 16.9.–19.9.2002*, 49–74. Rahden: Internationale Archäologie. Arbeitsgemeinschaft, Symposium, Tagung, Kongress 7. Marie Leidorf.

Lüning, J., Kloos, U., and Albert, S. 1989. Westliche Nachbarn der bandkeramischen Kultur: Die Keramikgruppen La Hoguette und Limburg. Mit Beiträgen von J. Eckert und Chr. Strien. *Germania* 67, 355–93.

Malmström, H., Gilbert, M. T. P., Thomas, M. G., Brandström, M., Storå, J., Molnar, P., Andersen, P. K., Bendixen, C., Holmlund, G., Götherström, A., and Willerslev, E. 2009. Ancient DNA reveals lack of continuity between Neolithic hunter-gatherers and contemporary Scandinavians. *Current Biology* 19/20, 1758–62.

Mateiciucová, I. 2004. Mesolithic traditions and the origins of the Linear Pottery Culture (LBK). In A. Lukes and M. Zvelebil (eds), *LBK dialogues: studies in the formation of the Linear Pottery Culture*, 91–108. Oxford: Archaeopress.

Mauvilly, M., Jeunesse, C., and Doppler, T. 2008. Ein Tonstempel aus der spätmesolithischen Fundstelle Arconciel/La Souche (Kanton Freiburg/Schweiz). *Quartär* 55, 151–7.

Meyer, C. and Alt, K. W. 2005. Kultur- und Bevölkerungswandel am Oberrhein? Ein osteometrischer Vergleich Früh- und Mittelneolithischer Populationen. In D. Gronenborn (ed.), *Klimaveränderung und Kulturwandel in neolithischen Gesellschaften Mitteleuropas, 6700–2200 v. Chr.*, 171–8. Mainz: RGZM—Tagungen 1. Römisch-Germanisches Zentralmuseum.

Nielsen, E. H. 2009. The Mesolithic background for the Neolithisation process. *Documenta Praehistorica* 36, 151–8.

Orschiedt, J. 1998. Ergebnisse einer neuen Untersuchung der spätmesolithischen Kopfbestattungen aus Süddeutschland. In N. J. Conard and C.-J. Kind (eds), *Aktuelle Forschungen zum Mesolithikum*, 147–60. Tübingen: Mo Vince.

Orschiedt, J. 2005. The head burials from Ofnet cave: an example of warlike conflict in the Mesolithic. In M. Parker Pearson, and I. J. N. Thorpe (eds), *Warfare, violence and slavery in prehistory*, 67–74. Oxford: BAR International Series 1374.

Pavúk, J. 2004. Early Linear Pottery Culture in Slovakia and the Neolithisation of Central Europe. In A. Lukes and M. Zvelebil (eds), *LBK dialogues: studies in the formation of the Linear Pottery Culture*, 71–82. Oxford: BAR International Series 1304.

Price, T. D., Wahl, J., and Bentley, R. A. 2006. Isotopic evidence for mobility and group organization among Neolithic farmers at Talheim, Germany, 5000 BC. *European Journal of Archaeology* 9, 259–84.

Rähle, W. 1978. Schmuckschnecken aus mesolithischen Kulturschichten Süddeutschlands und ihre Herkunft (Probstfeld, Falkensteinhöhle, Burghöhle Dietfurt, Zigeunerfels, Große Ofnet). In W. Taute (ed.), *Das Mesolithikum in Süddeutschland Teil 2: Naturwissenschaftliche Untersuchungen*, 163–8. Tübingen: Archaeologica Venatoria.

Robb, J. and Miracle, P. 2007. Beyond 'migration' versus 'acculturation': new models for the spread of agriculture. In A. Whittle and V. Cummings (eds), *Going over: the Mesolithic–Neolithic transition in north-west Europe*, 99–115. Oxford: British Academy.

Rozoy, J.-G. 1967. Typologie de l'épipaléolithique fanco-belge. *Bulletin de la Société Préhistorique Française* 64, 227–60.

Schade-Lindig, S. and Schade, C. 2010. Woher kommt Flomborn? Keramikimporte und Nachahmungen in der bandkeramischen Siedlung Bad Nauheim-Nieder-Mörlen Auf dem Hempler.' In D. Gronenborn and J. Petrasch (eds), *Die Neolithisierung Mitteleuropas: the Spread of the Neolithic to Central Europe*, 461–74. Mainz: Verlag des Römisch-Germanischen Zentralmuseums.

Schier, W. 2009. Extensiver Brandfeldbau und die Ausbreitung der neolithischen Wirtschaftsweise in Mitteleuropa und Südskandinavien am Ende des 5. Jahrtausends v. Chr. *Praehistorische Zeitschrift* 84, 15–43.

Schmidt, R. R. 1913. *Die altsteinzeitlichen Schädelgräber der Ofnet und der Bestattungsritus der Diluvialzeit*. Stuttgart: Schweizerbart.

Skoglund, P., Malmström, H., Raghavan, M., Storå, J., Hall, P., Willerslev, E., Gilbert, M. T. P., Götherström, A., and Jakobsson, M. 2012. Origins and genetic legacy of Neolithic farmers and hunter-gatherers in Europe. *Science* 336, 466–9.

Spatz, H. 1996. *Beiträge zum Kulturkomplex Hinkelstein-Großgartach-Rössen. Der keramische Fundstoff des Mittelneolithikums aus dem mittleren Neckarland und seine zeitliche Gliederung. Materialhefte zur Archäologie in Baden-Württemberg 37*. Stuttgart: Theiss.

Spatz, H. 1999. *Das mittelneolithische Gräberfeld von Trebur, Kreis Groß-Gerau*. Materialien zur Vor- und Frühgeschichte von Hessen 19. Wiesbaden: Landesamt für Denkmalpflege Hessen.

Spatz, H. 2003. Hinkelstein: Eine Sekte als Initiator des Mittelneolithikums. In J. Eckert, U. Eisenhauer, and A. Zimmermann (eds), *Archäologische Perspektiven. Analysen und Interpretationen im Wandel. Festschrift für Jens Lüning zum 65. Geburtstag*, 575–87. Rahden/Westfalen: Marie Leidorf.

Street, M., Baales, M., Cziesla, E., Hartz, S., Heinen, M., Jöris, O., Pasda, Cl., Terberger, Th., and Vollbrecht, J. 2001. Final Palaeolithic and Mesolithic research in reunified Germany. *Journal of World Prehistory* 15, 365–453.

Strien, H.-C. 2005. Familientraditionen in der bandkeramischen Siedlung bei Vaihingen/Enz. In J. Lüning, C. Fridrich, and A. Zimmermann (eds), *Die Bandkeramik im 21. Jahrhundert. Symposium in der Abtei Brauweiler bei Köln vom 16.9–19.9.2002*, 189–98. Rahden/Westfalen: Marie Leidorf.

Strien, H.-C. and Tillmann, A. 2001. Die La-Hoguette-Fundstelle Stuttgart-Bad Cannstatt: Archäologie. In B. Gehlen, M. Heinen, and A. Tillmann (eds), *Zeit-Räume. Gedenkschrift für Wolfgang Taute Band 2*, 673–81. Bonn: Deutsche Gesellschaft für Ur- und Frühgeschichte/Rudolf Habelt.

Taute, W. 1973/74. Neue Forschungen zur Chronologie von Spätpaläolithikum und Mesolithikum in Süddeutschland. *Archäologische Informationen* 2–3, 59–66.

Taute, W. 1988. Der Übergang vom Mesolithikum zum Neolithikum in Süddeutschland. *Natur und Mensch* 1988, 110–12.

Terberger, T. and Kabacinski, J. 2010. The neolithization of Pomerania: a critical review. In D. Gronenborn and J. Petrasch (eds), *Die Neolithisierung Mitteleuropas: the Spread of the Neolithic to Central Europe*, 375–406. Mainz: Verlag des Römisch-Germanischen Zentralmuseums.

Thévenin, A. 1995. Mésolithique Récent, Mésolithique Final, Néolithique Ancien dans le quart Nord-Est de la France: pour une reinterpretation des données. *Revue Archéologique Picardie* no. spécial 9, 3–15.

Thévenin, A. 1998. Le mésolithique du Centre-Est de la France: Chronologie, peuplement, processus évolutifs. *Revue archéologique de l'Est* 49, 87–133.

Tinner, W., Nielsen, E. H., and Lotter, A. F. 2007. Mesolithic agriculture in Switzerland? A critical review of the evidence. *Quaternary Science Reviews* 26, 1416–31.

van Willigen, S. 2006. *Die Neolithisierung im nordwestlichen Mittelmeerraum*. Iberia Archaeologica 7. Deutsches Archäologisches Institut Madrid. Mainz: Philipp von Zabern.

van Willigen, S., Hajdas, I., and Bonani, G. 2009. New radiocarbon dates for the Early Neolithic of the Western Mediterranean. *Radiocarbon* 51, 831–8.

Waterbolk, H. T. 1968. Food production in prehistoric Europe. *Science* 162, 129–37.

Wechler, K.-P. 2001. *Studien zum Neolithikum der osteuropäischen Steppe. Deutsches Archäologisches Institut*. Eurasien-Abteilung. Mainz: Philipp von Zabern.

Zvelebil, M. and Lillie, M. 2000. Transition to agriculture in eastern Europe. In D. T. Price (ed.), *Europe's first farmers*, 57–92. Cambridge: Cambridge University Press.

CHAPTER 37

THE PERSISTENCE OF HUNTING AND GATHERING AMONGST FARMERS IN PREHISTORY IN NEOLITHIC NORTH-WEST EUROPE

D. C. M. RAEMAEKERS

THIS chapter presents a relatively well-documented case study on the persistence of hunting and gathering in a nominally farming society. In geological terms, the study area is the western part of the North European Plain, which is the area between the rivers Scheldt (Antwerp) and Elbe (Hamburg). In topographical terms it focuses on the northernmost part of Belgium, the major part of the Netherlands and north-western Germany (Lower Saxony) (Figure 37.1). The time frame under study is 5500–2800 BC, that is just before the first contacts between hunter-gatherers in the area with the farming communities of the LBK until the late Neolithic of the Single Grave Culture.

Stray finds of artefacts in the study area from the central European tradition, especially adzes (Raemaekers et al. 2011, fig. 12; Verhart 2000, figs 1.14–1.17), indicate that the late Mesolithic hunter-gatherers had contacts with the farming communities of the central European loess areas. The intensity and implications of these contacts may be envisaged on the basis of various ethnographic publications (Raemaekers 1999, 133–6; Verhart 2000, 16–42), but in any case resulted in some knowledge about this new way of life. With this notion as a starting point, we can use high-resolution sites to map which Neolithic elements were incorporated at what stage. The first evidence of change is the start of a new ceramic tradition around 5000 BC. This is the start of the Swifterbant culture. Around 4500 BC small numbers of bones from domestic cattle, pigs, and sheep/goats are found, indicating the formal start of the Neolithic (cf. Zvelebil 1986: substitution phase). The date for the oldest cereal remains in the Swifterbant culture is several centuries later, around 4200 BC. Sites with a formal agrarian character (cf. Zvelebil 1986: consolidation phase) are found from 3800 BC onwards when the Swifterbant culture developed into the Hazendonk group (see Figure 37.2).

This chapter focuses on the developments in subsistence strategies of the hunter-gatherer communities that came into contact with farming communities from c.5300 BC onwards.

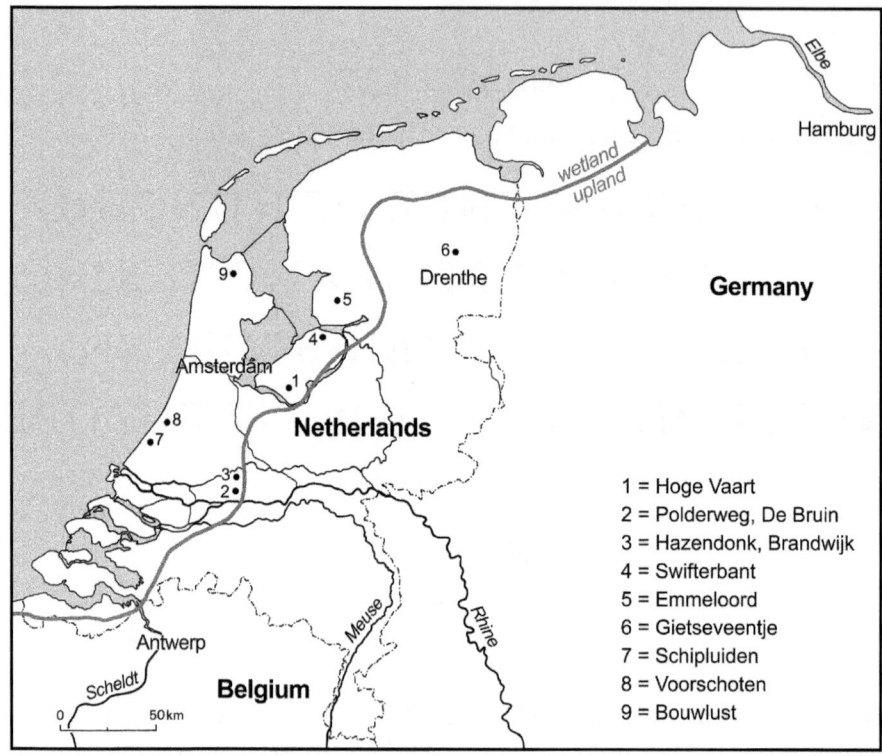

FIGURE 37.1 Map of the study area (map by S. E. Boersma, University of Groningen).

The specific landscape developments in our area allow a tight grip on the factor time (see below) and thus a detailed description of not only the incorporation of new subsistence strategies such as crop cultivation and animal husbandry, but also the persistence of the traditional subsistence strategies of hunting and gathering. As a rule, narratives on this time frame focus on these changes in subsistence (the Neolithization process). This contribution shifts focus to the substantial evidence of non-change: the persistence of hunting and gathering amongst the Neolithic farmers of the western part of the North European Plain (see also Peeters 2007, esp. 231–3).

Landscape Development

It is necessary to describe the post-glacial landscape developments because of their fundamental influence on both site characteristics and potential knowledge of the time period involved. At the end of the last glacial, the study area comprised a large sand-covered landscape cross-cut by several large river systems. From south to north these are Scheldt, Meuse, Rhine, Eem, IJssel, Vecht, and Elbe. In these river systems dunes developed when the river discharge decreased at the end of the last glacial period.

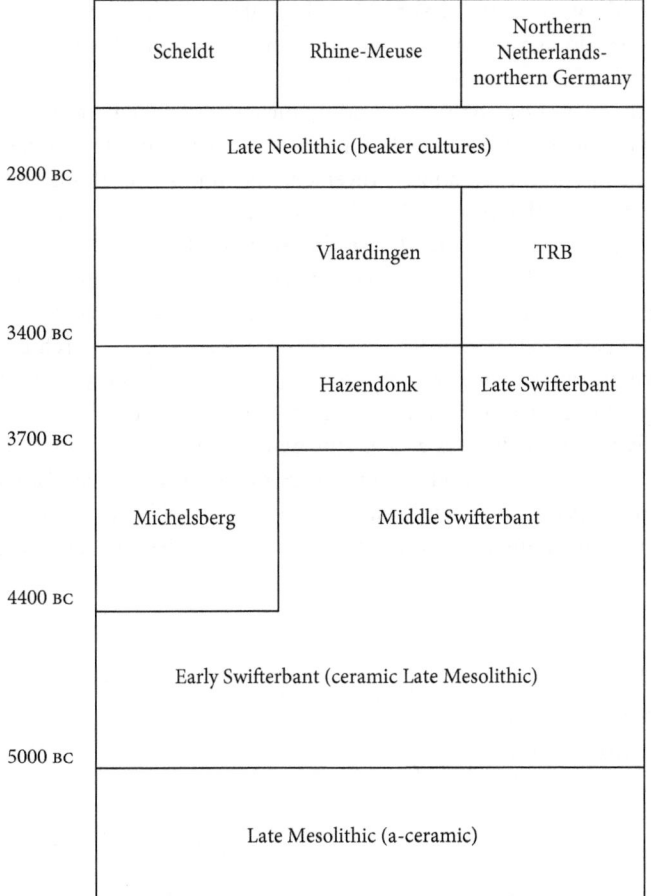

FIGURE 37.2 Spatial-temporal scheme for north-western Europe between Antwerp and Hamburg.

The post-glacial sea levels rose over 30 m in north-western Europe. This resulted not only in the drowning of the present North Sea area, but also in a rising groundwater table and growing peat marshes in the study area from c.7000 BC onwards. The continuous sea-level rise subsequently led to the deposition of marine clay on top of the peat deposits. As a result of the relatively flat late Pleistocene surface, these processes had a large influence in the horizontal plane: nowadays some 50 per cent of the Dutch land surface is covered with Holocene deposits (Figure 37.1). A specific situation relates to the coastal zone: the continuous sea-level rise and shift inland resulted in the reworking of dune sediments and prevented their preservation prior to c.4000 BC. Occupation of the coastal zone prior to this date will therefore be difficult if not impossible to attest. These observations lead to the conclusion that our record contrasts with that of contemporary Ertebølle occupation in southern Scandinavia. There coastal sites predominate and inland wetland sites are sparsely preserved.

These large-scale landscape developments determine our dataset. In the areas covered with Holocene deposits, preservation is generally good and botanical and zoological information provides detailed evidence of prehistoric subsistence. This good preservation is connected to good control of the age of archaeological sites: as a rule the Holocene sea-level rise resulted in enveloping archaeological sites in neat stratigraphic units. The deep sub-soil preservation is of course connected to a small chance of finding sites; due to the covering sediments these sites can only be found by means of detailed coring campaigns. Our knowledge is therefore based on a small number of high-quality sites. In the areas without Holocene sedimentation the situation is reversed. The number of sites is huge, but there is little control on the age of archaeological findings and preservation is very poor: as a rule Stone Age sites from these areas consist of surface scatters of flint.

In 1986 Zvelebil and Rowley-Conwy concluded that while the transition from hunting and gathering to farming in northern Europe was rather swift, the Swifterbant culture provided an anomaly (Zvelebil and Rowley-Conwy 1986, 76–8). Research in the 1990s did not fix this anomaly but re-dated the substitution phase from 4200–3400 BC to 4500–3800 BC. In 2003 I proposed that next to this Long Transition Model a Short Transition Model might be equally true (Raemaekers 2003). This new model is based on the notion that the formal agrarian sites of the Vlaardingen group are found in specific landscape settings, i.e. the large coastal dunes on the Dutch coast and on the levees of large rivers. Swifterbant sites are lacking from these sediments (Figure 37.3). Above I described the dynamics of Holocene

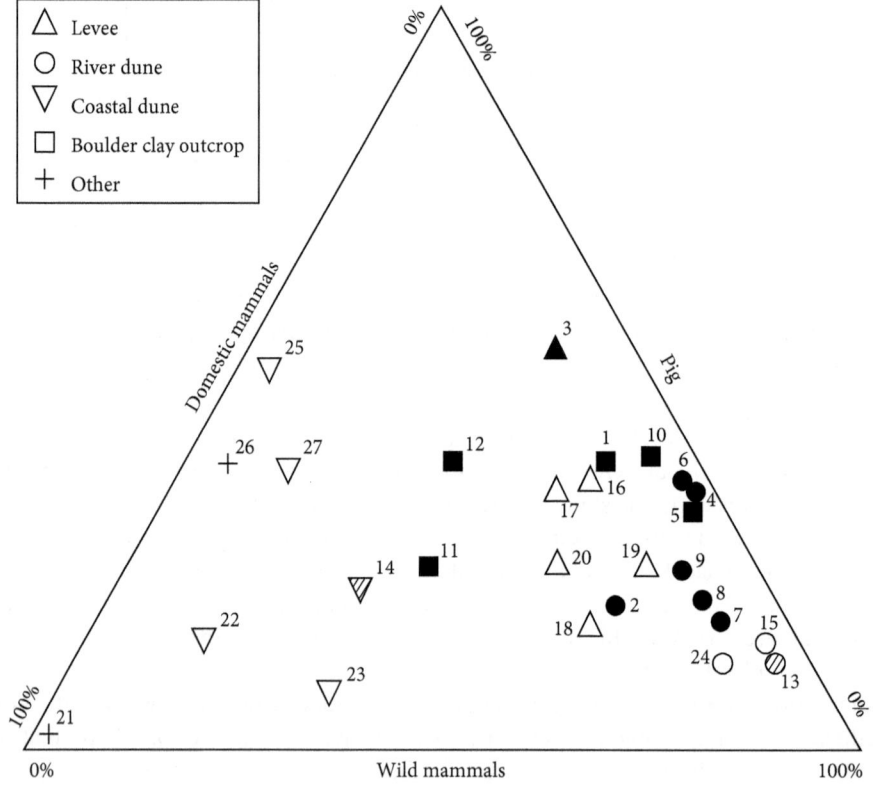

FIGURE 37.3 Triangular diagram depicting the proportion of bone assemblages reduced to the categories wild, domestic, and pig. The landscape setting is indicated as well (from Raemaekers 2003, fig. 2). Sites 1–12: Swifterbant culture; 13–14: Hazendonk group; 15–27: Vlaardingen group.

landscape developments and these are of extreme importance in order to understand the lack of Swifterbant sites in these specific settings. Hypothetical Swifterbant sites in the coastal area must have been eroded, thus hindering us in determining whether formal agrarian Swifterbant sites existed here. Swifterbant sites on levees of large rivers might be found in the future to help determine which of the models describes the transition to farming best. If the Long Transition Model holds true, the absence of fully agrarian Swifterbant sites and the rather similar site characteristics of most Swifterbant sites are indicative of a settlement system in which residential mobility is a key concept, and a settlement system with logistic mobility characterizes the Vlaardingen and TRB period (Raemaekers 1999, 115–23). In the Short Transition Model logistic mobility would also characterize the Swifterbant culture, and thus lead to reinterpretations of all known Swifterbant sites in terms of their place within the settlement system.

What's Cooking? The Introduction of Pottery and the Demise of Hearth Pits

The first change visible in the archaeological record of the late Mesolithic is the start of the Swifterbant pottery tradition around 5000 BC. Crombé (2009) questions this age on the basis of reservoir effect of 14C dates on food crusts. While this problem indeed is apparent, the presence of 14C dates on other materials underlines this early age (Louwe Kooijmans and Mol 2001). The oldest ceramics are found in two sites in the Rhine-Meuse river district (Polderweg and De Bruin; Raemaekers 2001a; 2001b) and Flevoland (Hoge Vaart: Haanen and Hogestijn 2001). Starting with the attested contacts between the hunter-gatherers and farmers, it may be concluded that the notion of pottery production was the result of these contacts. It is noteworthy to see that the early Swifterbant pottery is a distinctively new tradition. It is coarse ware: thick walled, coarsely tempered, and fired at relatively low temperatures. As such it is strikingly different from the fine wares of the contemporary LBK. Another important observation is the lack of decoration on this early Swifterbant pottery, with the exception of so-called Randkerbung which concerns a series of impressions on the rim. The lack of decoration might be interpreted as a lack of meaning: the function of these new containers might be of greater relevance than their potential role as signifiers. Similar remarks may be made for the earliest Ertebølle ceramics from southern Sweden (Stilborg and Holm 2009). In the middle phase of the Swifterbant culture (4600–3900 BC) decoration became common (Raemaekers 1999, 108–12).

A second observation concerning this early pottery is that it is found in the late Mesolithic: the animal and plant remains from these sites indicate a full hunter-gatherer menu. This observation is true for many Eurasian early pottery groups (see Jordan and Zvelebil 2009). Therefore the start of the use of pottery is not related to a change in diet, but to a change in cooking technology. Why this change occurred is still obscure, but analysis of the organic residues on these early pots might inform us on their content. Perhaps the pots were used as cooking pots, but more specific meals might be proposed as well, or even the production of non-food substances such as tar or poison.

The start of pottery production coincides with the transition from the use of hearth pits to surface hearths. This is best documented at Hoge Vaart where the lowermost late Mesolithic find layer has a large number of hearth pits, while the overlying younger late Mesolithic find layer only contains surface hearths. This transition is here dated around 5000 BC (Peeters and Hogestijn 2001). This shift can also be found in an extensive survey of available 14C dates on these feature categories in the northern Netherlands (Niekus 2006, 82). A tentative conclusion is that around 5000 BC a cooking revolution occurred in which a new food container found its place on a new type of hearth.

Hunting and Animal Husbandry

The first finds of bones from domestic animals come from De Bruin (phase 3; 0.1 per cent). The authors suggest that it concerns material that was relocated as a result of trampling (Oversteegen et al. 2001, 223). Their interpretation is followed here. It concerns bones from cattle, pigs, and sheep/goats. The 17 cattle bones from *Bos taurus* should be interpreted with caution; as all bones are from the postcranial skeleton, they do not indicate local butchering but are the result of transport from an unknown origin (Oversteegen et al. 2001, 228–30). Does it concern meat parts that derived from farming communities further away? A similar singular early find from Rosenhof (Schleswig-Holstein, northern Germany; Ertebølle culture, *c.*4800 BC) has recently been studied for ancient DNA (Scheu et al. 2007) and it was concluded that it was a bone from a wild cow and that the earliest domestic cattle in that area date to around 4000 BC. DNA analysis of the earliest cattle bones from De Bruin might result in similar conclusions. The interpretation of four pig bones is also problematic. Most bones cannot be distinguished between domestic and wild species on the basis of morphological criteria. Recent studies on ancient DNA suggest that domestication of European wild boar was independent of domestication in the Near East (Larson et al. 2007) and morphological attribution should therefore be considered with caution. Fortunately the bones from domestic cattle and pigs at De Bruin (phase 3) are accompanied by nine bones from sheep/goats, two from goats, and two from sheep. As both sheep and goats have no wild predecessors in the study area, there is no doubt that these domestic sheep/goats indicate that animal husbandry was practised around 4500 BC. Whether these animals were kept at the site is unclear as it again concerns postcranial bones. The finds are not indicative of local butchering, but might be the result of transport to the site.

De Bruin allows a comparison of late Mesolithic (phases 1 and 2) and Neolithic Swifterbant bone assemblages (phase 3) from one site, in an increasing wetland environment (Table 37.1). This suggests that domestic animals had a restricted nutritional contribution. Beaver is an increasingly important animal for both meat and furs (Oversteegen et al. 2001, 234), while wild pigs lose importance. These changes and the restricted importance of domestic animals suggest that the Neolithic occupants used De Bruin as station to hunt beavers, otters, and various deer, while the bones left behind by their late Mesolithic ancestors suggest a more general use. The limited importance of domestic animals is also found at younger Swifterbant sites, such as the type site of Swifterbant itself and Hazendonk, while again the high percentages for beaver and otter stand out. Are these proportions typical for Swifterbant settlement in general or are they characteristic of a wetland adaptation? In later phases of the Neolithic a

Table 37.1 Overview of Late Mesolithic and Neolithic bone assemblages (based on bone numbers). Based on Oversteegen et al. 2001 (De Bruin); Zeiler 1997 (Swifterbant S3, Hazendonk); Zeiler 2006a (Schipluiden); Groenman–van Waateringe et al. 1968 (Voorschoten); Van Heeringen and Theunissen 2001 (Bouwlust).

	Late Mesolithic			Swifterbant		Hazendonk			Vlaardingen		TRB
	De Bruin 1	De Bruin 2	De Bruin 3	Swifterbant S3	Hazendonk 1+2	Hazendonk 3	Schipluiden	Hazendonk	Voorschoten		Bouwlust
	5250–5080 BC	5030–4960 BC	4560–4510 BC	4300–4000 BC	4100–3750 BC	3700–3500 BC	3600–3400 BC	3200–2800 BC	3200–2800 BC		3000 BC
Domestic											
Dogs	4.3	1.5	4.6	1.3		2.0	11.6	4.7	1.9		4.6
Cattle			2.5	8.6	15.0	4.3	42.4	2.5	58.9		
Sheep			0.3			0.2					
Goats		0.1	0.2								
Sheep/goats		0.1	1.3	0.2	0.6	0.6		0.6	7.0		8.8
Pigs		0.1	0.5	0.9		0.4	12.1	0.2	12.1		
Domestic/wild											
Pigs	6.6	7.7	8.7	55.3	10.2	10.6		11.8			7.2
Cattle		0.1	1.1	0.0		1.4		1.0	2.3		12.8
Wild											
Beaver	30.7	45.5	48.2	13.2	35.9	52.9	1.7	27.8			
Aurochs	0.3	0.5	0.3	0.1			0.2		0.9		

(Continued)

Table 37.1 Continued

	Late Mesolithic			Swifterbant		Hazendonk		Vlaardingen		TRB
	De Bruin 1	De Bruin 2	De Bruin 3	Swifterbant S3	Hazendonk 1+2	Hazendonk 3	Schipluiden	Hazendonk	Voorschoten	Bouwlust
	5250–5080 BC	5030–4960 BC	4560–4510 BC	4300–4000 BC	4100–3750 BC	3700–3500 BC	3600–3400 BC	3200–2800 BC	3200–2800 BC	3000 BC
Elk	0.3	0.7	0.5	0.6				0.1		
Elk/red deer	2.3	4.0	3.1	0.6	1.2	1.4		1.4		10.5
Otters	12.6	25.4	19.3	13.7	30.5	8.8	2.1	9.4		0.2
Wild boar	28.9	3.7	0.8	1.2		1.6	20.5	1.1	1.2	
Red deer	5.7	6.1	5.9	3.2	6.0	14.5	8.7	13.3	9.7	50.9
Roe deer	0.3	1.0	0.7	0.0		0.8	0.0	22.3	5.6	2.5
Wild cats	6.3	1.1	1.1	0.0			0.3	0.4		
Others	1.7	2.8	0.8	1.2	0.6	0.4	0.4	3.5	0.5	2.6
Totals	349	1,777	610	3,729	167	490	7,734	1,214	431	650

Bone numbers and references to original publications.
Based on bone numbers.

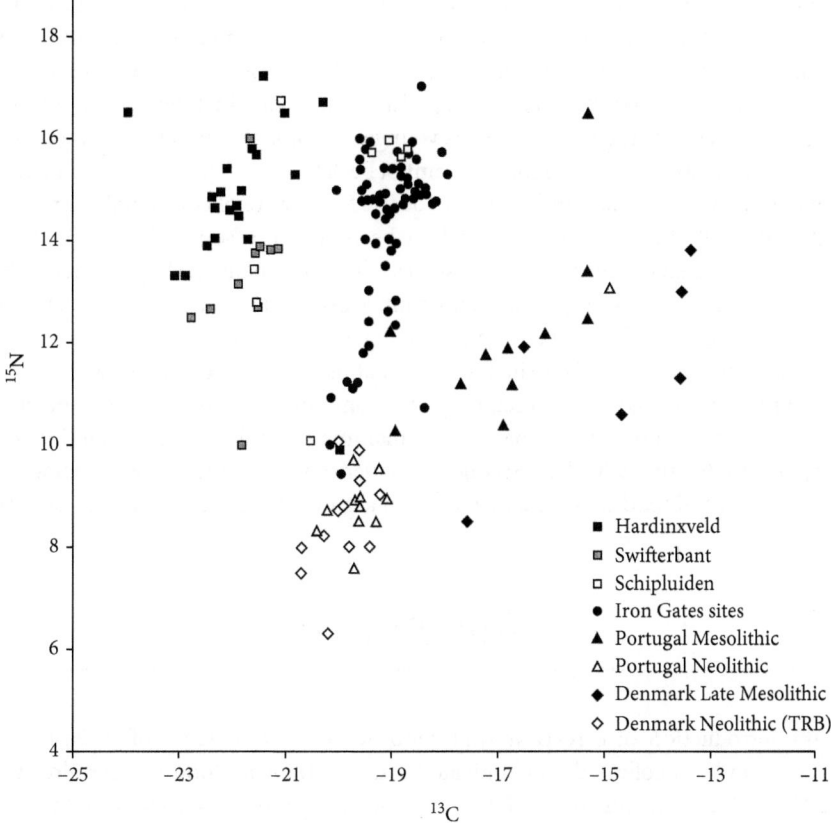

FIGURE 37.4 Stable isotope for human bones from Hardinxveld (De Bruin and Polderweg), Schipluiden, and Swifterbant compared to those from the Iron Gate sites Lepenski Vir, Vlasac, and Schela Cladovei, from Portugal and Denmark (after Smits and Van der Plicht 2009, fig. 14). The figure indicates differences in diets between hunter-gatherers (Mesolithic) and farmers (Neolithic) in four European regions. While the Danish and Portuguese regions show a strong distinction between Mesolithic and Neolithic sites, the Dutch sites are rather similar across the supposed divide in diet, suggesting the continuation of hunter-gatherer subsistence alongside the use of farming produce.

similar dataset is available with bone assemblages from the wetland areas (Hazendonk group, Vlaardingen group, one TRB site). Nevertheless the broader range of landscape settings from which sites are known is mirrored by a similar broad range in bone assemblages (but see above on Short Transition Model). At the latest, during the Hazendonk group, sites with a substantial proportion of bones from domestic animals are available. During the period at hand, fowling has been documented for all sites. The large variety of birds found suggests that they were captured not as a result of a species-focused hunt, but on a haphazard basis.

The continuing importance of traditional subsistence strategies far into the Neolithic is also found in the isotope analysis of human bones and food crusts on ceramics (Smits and Van der Plicht 2009). Recent research makes it clear that the Dutch data stand out from other European areas, such as Denmark. While the general notion is that the transition from Mesolithic to Neolithic is a shift in diet visible in isotopic parameters of human bones, the Dutch data appear more homogeneous across this divide: late Mesolithic and Neolithic populations had rather similar diets (Figure 37.4). This comparison includes late Mesolithic and Neolithic human remains up to 3500 BC, as younger remains are absent. Therefore, the continuation of Mesolithic isotopic signatures cannot be determined beyond this point. Like the human bones, the food crusts indicate that aquatic foods were of considerable importance. Indeed, at all Swifterbant sites fishing may have been the prime source for protein. Not only are many sites located in water-rich areas, such as the Swifterbant creek system itself (Figure 37.5), but remains from fishing gear are abundant. Most spectacular are the 11 fish wears and 44 fish traps from Emmeloord (Figure 37.6), dating to the periods 3500–3000 BC and 2400–1700 BC (Bulten et al. 2009). This site indicates that fishing remained an important activity even into the Bronze Age. Fish remains are also commonly found at Swifterbant sites, but it is impossible to compare the remains from mammals and fish to understand their relative importance for the daily diet. Secondary evidence such as the isotopic characteristics of human bones and food crusts are then the best argument for underlining the importance of fish.

Food Plants

With the introduction of cereals around 4200 BC there is evidence of the use of plant resources from both collected and cultivated sources. The wild food sources already used in late Mesolithic De Bruin are also found in various stages of the Neolithic and the variety does not appear to diminish (Table 37.2). The wild food plants listed mostly comprise berries and nuts, but are never found in such quantities that it is evident that they were used as staple foods. This is not to say that these sources were of limited importance. Whether the nutritional relevance of these wild food plants changed in this period is impossible to tell because a quantitative comparison to the yield of the cereal fields cannot be carried out. One instrument to gain some insight in the importance of cereal cultivation is pollen analysis. A detailed analysis by Bakker at Gietseveentje made it clear that the first disturbance of the natural vegetation dates to 4050 BC, just a bit younger than the earliest dates for cereals in the Swifterbant culture. This first small-scale disturbance was carried out to provide leaves for winter fodder, summer pasture, and small cereal fields (Bakker 2003: Neolithic Occupation Phase 1). From around 3450 BC the human interference with the natural vegetation increased. Grass and heather were used for fodder and there are increasing areas of exhausted, abandoned fields (Bakker 2003: Neolithic Occupation Phase). Bakker suggests that both animal husbandry and cereal cultivation increased in importance during the Neolithic. While the spectrum of wild food resources did not decrease, their nutritional significance probably did.

While einkorn and emmer wheat were the typical cereals for the early Neolithic of central Europe, the people of the Swifterbant culture relied on emmer wheat and naked barley. These types are of continued importance for the rest of the Neolithic. The occurrence of cereal finds (both grains, chaff, and field weeds) on the Swifterbant sites has been interpreted with great difficulty in the Netherlands. Until the finds from Swifterbant and Schipluiden discussed here, most archaeologists found it difficult to believe that cereal cultivation was

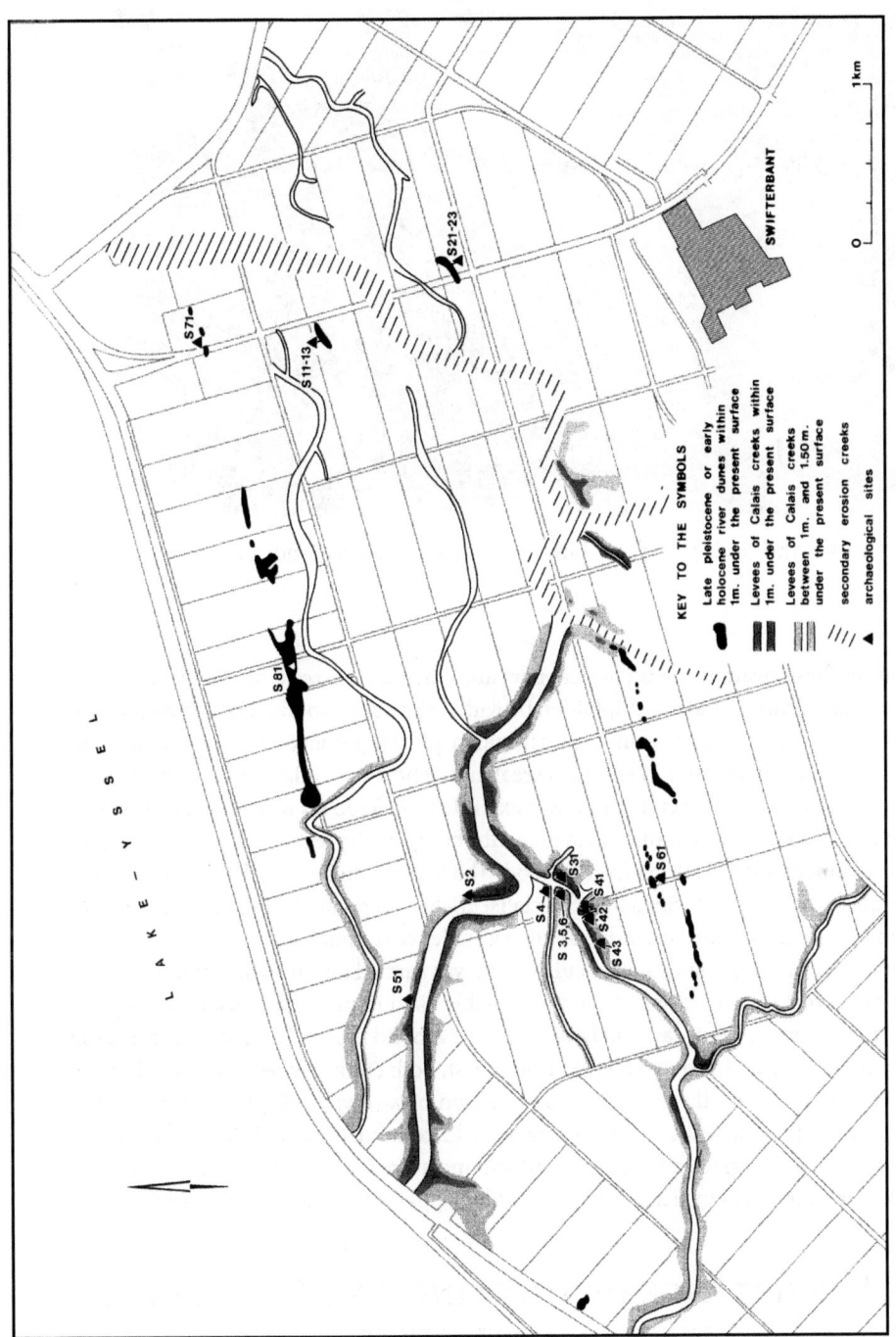

FIGURE 37.5 Map of Swifterbant area. Indicated are the Neolithic IJssel river system and the river dunes series delimiting the Late Glacial river valley. Archaeological sites are indicated with triangles (from Deckers 1979, fig. 1).

FIGURE 37.6 Fish trap from Emmeloord (photo Nieuwland, Lelystad).

carried out in these swampy areas (see Cappers and Raemaekers 2008 for the debate). The botanical research carried out at Schipluiden provided close correspondence between cereal remains and charred remains from high saltmarsh plants (Kubiak-Martens 2006a) and made clear that in this wetland landscape cereal cultivation was indeed practised. In 2007 the evidence of wetland cereal cultivation was extended to $c.4200$ BC when the University of Groningen excavated an agricultural field at Swifterbant S4. The features were preserved as a result of sedimentation resulting from a flood. The features suggested that the small field ($c.$100 m square) was worked with a hoe. Specialist analysis of botanical macro remains, pollen, diatoms, and thin sections provided auxiliary evidence (unpublished).

Noteworthy is that apparently cereal cultivation was carried out in such a manner that it did not aim for maximum yields but for a reasonable yield in most circumstances (a practice also known from present-day small-scale farmers around the world). This risk-reducing strategy may be deduced from two observations. First, both emmer wheat and naked barley are found on all sites from the period. A combination of two types of cereals increases the chance that at least one will provide a reasonable yield. Second, the field is located on a narrow levee resulting in variation in soil content and moisture within the field. This variation also resulted in differences in yield within the field (Cappers and Raemaekers 2008).

The Persistence of Hunting and Gathering

The sections above seem permeated by a focus on change. The traditional narrative on this period is that of Neolithization: when new elements were incorporated into the

Table 37.2 Overview of Late Mesolithic and Neolithic wild plant food resources. Based on Out 2009 (combined charred and waterlogged remains).

		Late Mesolithic De Bruin (all) 5250–4510 BC	Swifterbant Swifterbant S3 4300–4000 BC	Swifterbant Hazendonk 1+2 4100–3750 BC	Hazendonk Schipluiden 3600–3400 BC	Vlaardingen Hazendonk 3200–2800 BC
Cornus sanguinea	Dogwood	•		•	•	•
Corylus avellana	Hazel	•	•	•	•	•
Crataegus monogyna	Hawthorn	•	•	•	•	•
Malus sylvestris	Crab apple	•	•	•	•	
Prunus padus	European bird cherry	•		•		
Prunus spinosa	Sloe			•	•	•
Quercus sp.	Oak	•		•		•
Rosa sp.	Rose		•	•	•	
Rubus caesius	Dewberry	•		•	•	
Rubus fruticosus	Blackberry		•	•	•	
Sambucus nigra	Elder			•	•	•
Trapa natas	Water chestnut	•		•		•
Viburnum opulus	Cramp bark	•		•		•

hunter-gatherer lifestyle. In an alternative narrative the focus might be on those aspects of society that seem unchanged during the centuries under study. In fact, these aspects dominate our record. Site location, the importance of wild plant and animal foods, burial rituals, the absence of monumental architecture and large house plans are all aspects of this long period of the late Mesolithic and Neolithic.

The general impression is that of people making an opportunistic use of their natural environment, disregarding our categories of 'hunter-gatherers' and 'farmers'. A central concept in this perspective is that of risk strategy. In contrast to other areas in Europe, hunter-gatherers in our study area seem not to have focused on seasonally abundantly available resources such as salmon, birds, or acorns. Instead they exploited a wide variety of plant and animal sources. The low numbers of bones from domestic animals across the centuries under study indicate that these new food resources were incorporated into this risk strategy, widening their subsistence base even further. In fact, the analytical focus on bones from mammals might be misleading altogether: the isotope analyses indicate the importance of fish in the diet. Moreover, we should not suppose daily meat consumption comparable to that of present-day Western societies. Mammal meat must have been consumed sparsely because the large amounts of meat from deer or cattle certainly could not be eaten completely by small-scale local communities. In my opinion, the relatively large size of mammal bones and thus better chances of preservation resulted in an archaeological over-estimation of their nutritional importance. Instead, mammal bones should perhaps be interpreted with more attention to their significance in social events, such as feasting.

Similar remarks may be made about the importance of cereals. Although remains are recovered on all sites dating from around 4200 BC, their nutritional importance was certainly limited. There are two arguments for this conclusion. First, the archaeobotanical evidence is often restricted to cereal grains (chaff and weed flora are often lacking), while pollen research suggests a small-scale landnam until c. 3450 BC. Second, the wetland sites on which our understanding of this period is based seem unsuited for large-scale cultivation. It appears that cereals should be interpreted as an extension of the basically hunter-gatherer subsistence.

How to be a Hunter-Gatherer-Farmer: The Case Study of Schipluiden

To illustrate the various aspects mentioned above, a case study on Schipluiden is now presented. It concerns a wetland dune site that dates to around 3600–3400 cal BC, i.e. more than 1,500 years after the start of contacts between the hunter-gatherers of the western part of the North European Plain and band-ceramic farmers. The Schipluiden phase constitutes the oldest preserved remains in the coastal area and yielded several sites from a relatively small micro-region. These known sites result from favourable preservation in a sedimentation area and recent research in the highly dynamic economy of the Randstad: all sites were found in the last two decades. The site is located on a coastal dune. Spatial analysis of the material remains indicates that the dune surface was completely occupied, while the many postholes are interpreted to reflect four contemporary households. Intriguingly, only one of the four yards provided a group of burials. All four yards were occupied in the three phases defined on the basis of stratigraphy and developments in ceramic technology and decoration (Louwe Kooijmans 2006).

The good preservational circumstances and input of many specialists allowed a detailed insight into food subsistence. Microscopic botanical analysis of tuber fragments points to the exploitation of the ecological zones surrounding the dune. It concerns sea beetroots from the coastal area, tubers from the sea, club-rush from fresh/brackish areas, and bulbs of wild onion/leek from the local surroundings (Kubiak-Martens 2006a). The exploitation of wild food plants is also documented on the basis of the macro remains.

It concerns mostly sloe (*Prunus spinosa*), but in total ten different wild food plants were registered (see Table 37.2). Besides this abundant evidence of the continued importance of wild food resources, Schipluiden also presents strong evidence of local cereal cultivation. This evidence encompasses not only charred kernels and chaff of emmer (*Tricticum dicoccon*) and naked barley (*Hordeum vulgare* var. *nudum*), but also weed flora suggesting cultivation at the high margins of the saltmarsh or on low dunes nearby (Kubiak-Martens 2006b).

The animal evidence is equally varied and encompasses the remains of fish, birds, and mammals. Although it remains impossible to quantify the relative importance of these three resources, the large numbers of fish remains—deriving from a small number of selected samples—suggest that fishing was an important source of protein (see below). Throughout the occupation the migratory species eel, flounder, and sturgeon dominate, suggesting a focus on fishing in the estuary located to the south of the site (Brinkhuizen 2006). Bird remains are less numerous and considering their relatively larger size and therefore better chances of preserving and collecting, this might be interpreted as a lesser importance of fowling compared to fishing. Fowling appears to have focused on ducks, and the legs were cut off prior to their transport to the site (Zeiler 2006a). The mammal bones indicate that cattle herding was important: bones from cattle dominate in terms of numbers and weight. Domestic pigs were identified in substantial numbers as well, next to wild boar and various deer. Smaller numbers of fur animals were found as well. Judging by the cut marks, these were hunted for both their furs and their meat (Zeiler 2006b). The burial group provides some evidence on the daily diet. Nitrogen and carbon isotopes indicate that the proteins consumed by the Schipluiden inhabitants derived to a large extent from aquatic sources (Smits et al. 2010), especially from the marine food chain (Smits and Van der Plicht 2009). These signals stress the importance of fishing for the daily diet and the relative unimportance of mammal bone spectra, at least in our study area.

Schipluiden is an excellent example of a hunter-gatherer-farmer community that exploited a mosaic delta environment with a resource strategy based on a risk management strategy in which a wide variety of resources were used. This strategy is typical for our study area for a extensive period from *c.*4500 BC (small-scale incorporation of domestic animals in a hunter-gatherer lifestyle) to at least *c.*2800 BC (Single Grave culture).

Conclusions

How should we understand this long persistence of hunting and gathering in the Neolithic of north-western Europe? This conclusion focuses on two interrelated key aspects. To understand the long tradition more attention on the late Mesolithic is needed. Available zoological data suggest that a wide variety of animals was exploited and the subsistence base may best be described as a 'broad spectrum economy' (Louwe Kooijmans 1993). While in southern Scandinavia there are arguments to propose that during the final stage of the Mesolithic the hunter-gatherers of the Ertebølle culture had restricted mobility, for example the regional patterning of axe types (Vang Petersen 1984, fig. 15), comparable data are absent for our study area. The impossibility of determining that sedentary hunter-gatherer communities existed here (Raemaekers 1999, 188–9) may be related to a lack of data, but for the moment it is considered more plausible that the late Mesolithic hunter-gatherers of the Swifterbant culture had a different world view. The archaeological record suggests that in this world view tradition and flexibility interrelate: the traditional subsistence base is the backbone of a lifestyle in which a flexible use of resources dominates. In these hunter-gatherer-farming communities residential mobility and a risk management strategy of diversification were key concepts. From this perspective, first animal husbandry and second cereal cultivation were incorporated on a small scale creating a new sort of Neolithic (Raemaekers 1999, 190–2), based on an 'extended broad spectrum economy' (Louwe Kooijmans 1993). In this perspective the potential logistic nightmare of successful hunting (mobile) and cereal cultivation (sedentary) is a non-issue and more related to our modernistic view of societies consisting of nuclear families. With extended families as the basis of society there is an ample workforce for tending gardens, hunting, and keeping animals. The long time frame in which sites with hunter-gatherer-farming characteristics occur makes it clear that this new Neolithic apparently was a successful strategy in the mosaic wetlands of north-western Europe. It must be stressed that a lack of data from the sandy regions within our study area remains a hindrance in determining whether this also applies here.

The second and interrelated aspect discussed here is that it is questioned whether the categories of hunter-gatherers versus farmers are of relevance in our study area. While many publications on the Dutch Neolithic focus on Neolithization, the apparent long-term success of the combination of hunting, gathering, and farming is the first indication that the people of the Swifterbant culture and their successors may not have perceived the categories 'wild' and 'domestic' of any relevance. Aiming to shift focus from an 'etic' to an 'emic' approach, this perceived relevance might be studied in two specific settings. The first is the occurrence of cattle horn sheaths, the collagen-rich outer layer of horns. These were found in the peat areas of the province of Drenthe (Prummel and Van der Sanden 1995). Six dated horn sheaths are of relevance here, as they date to the period under study. The other dates indicate that the deposition continued into the medieval period. Two of the horn sheaths are of TRB age; it concerns depositions of horns from domestic cattle. Of more interest are the four horn sheaths from the period of the Swifterbant culture as they comprise two specimens from aurochs and two from domestic cattle. This is a first clue that in this specific context of deposition the categories wild and domestic are of no relevance. The fact that all six are from male individuals is suggestive that this aspect was perceived to be of greater meaning. Another way to analyse the importance of the categories wild and domestic is to compare the proportions of these two categories in bone assemblages and bone tool assemblages. The idea is that while a wide variety of bones is available for tool production, the selection of bones is an ideal setting to understand the perceived 'fitness' of the bones of domestic animals. If domestic animals had non-subsistence relevance it might be perceived that their bones were suited for tool production par excellence or, in contrast, taboo. Although there are a large number of bone tools, the number of tools of which the species could be determined is restricted to only 16 from three Swifterbant sites (Swifterbant, Hazendonk, Brandwijk). It appears that bones from wild and domestic animals are used fairly equally and neither category was favoured (Raemaekers 2005). The analysis of cattle horn sheaths and bone tools suggests that there is no archaeological clue that wild and domestic were categories of relevance to these people that we describe as Neolithic. The persistence of hunting and gathering amongst farming is a defining aspect of the new Neolithic in our study area and its long duration indicates that it is not an anomaly but an extremely successful strategy for the continuation of traditional society.

Acknowledgements

I would like to thank my colleague H. Peeters for his critical remarks on a draft version of this contribution. This chapter was realized thanks to a sabbatical leave granted by the Faculty of Arts of the University of Groningen.

References

Bakker, R. 2003. *The emergence of agriculture on the Drenthe Plateau. A palaeobotanical study supported by high-resolution 14C-dating*. Bonn: Archäologische Berichte 16.

Brinkhuizen, D. 2006. Fish. In L. P. Louwe Kooijmans and P. F. B. Jongste (eds), *Schipluiden: a Neolithic settlement on the Dutch North Sea Coast, c. 3500 cal BC*, 449–70. Leiden: Analecta Praehistorica Leidensia 37/38.

Bulten, E., Van der Heijden, F., and Hamburg, T. 2009. Prehistorische visweren en fuiken op kavel J97 bij Emmeloord. *Archeologie* 13, 47–62.

Cappers, R. T. J. and Raemaekers, D. C. M. 2008. Cereal cultivation at Swifterbant? Neolithic wetland farming on the North European Plain. *Current Anthropology* 49, 385–402.

Crombé, P. 2009. Early pottery in hunter-gatherer societies of western Europe. In P. Jordan and M. Zvelebil (eds), *Ceramics before farming: the dispersal of pottery among prehistoric Eurasian hunter-gatherers*, 477–98. Walnut Creek, CA: Left Coast Press.

Deckers, P. H. 1979. The flint material from Swifterbant, Earlier Neolithic of the Northern Netherlands. I. Sites S 2, S 4 and S 5. Final Reports on Swifterbant II, *Palaeohistoria* 21, 143–80.

Groenman-van Waateringe, W., Voorrips, A., and Van Wijngaarden-Bakker, L. H. 1968. Settlements of the Vlaardingen Culture at Voorschoten and Leidschendam (ecology). *Helinium* 8, 105–30.

Haanen, P. L. P. and Hogestijn, J. W. H. 2001. Aardewerk: morfologische en technologische aspecten. In J. W. H. Hogestijn and J. H. M. Peeters (eds), *De mesolithische en vroeg-neolithische vindplaats Hoge Vaart-A27 (Flevoland)*, part 17. Amersfoort: Rapportages Archeologische Monumentenzorg 79.

Jordan, P. and Zvelebil, M. 2009. *Ex Oriente Lux*: the prehistory of hunter-gatherer ceramic dispersals. In P. Jordan and M. Zvelebil (eds), *Ceramics before farming: the dispersal of pottery among prehistoric Eurasian hunter-gatherers*, 33–89. Walnut Creek, CA: Left Coast Press.

Kubiak-Martens, L. 2006a. Botanical remains and plant food subsistence. In L. P. Louwe Kooijmans and P. F. B. Jongste (eds), *Schipluiden: a Neolithic settlement on the Dutch North Sea Coast, c. 3500 cal BC*, 317–38. Leiden: Analecta Praehistorica Leidensia 37/38.

Kubiak-Martens, L. 2006b. Roots, tubers and processed plant food in the local diet. In L. P. Louwe Kooijmans and P. F. B. Jongste (eds), *Schipluiden: a Neolithic settlement on the Dutch North Sea Coast, c. 3500 cal BC*, 339–52. Leiden: Analecta Praehistorica Leidensia 37/38.

Larson, G., Albarella, U., Dobney, K., Rowley-Conwy, P., Schibler, J., Tresset, A., Vigne, J.-D., Edwards, C. J., Schlumbaum, A., Dinu, A., BăBăçsescu, A., Dolman, G., Tagliacozzo, A., Manaseryan, N., Miracle, P., Van Wijngaarden-Bakker, L., Masseti, M., Bradley, D. G., and Cooper, A. 2007. Ancient DNA, pig domestication, and the spread of the Neolithic into Europe. *Proceedings of the National Academy of Sciences USA* 104, 15276–81.

Louwe Kooijmans, L. P. 1993. Wetland exploitation and upland relations of prehistoric communities in the Netherlands. In J. Gardiner (ed.), *Flatlands and wetlands: current themes in East Anglian Archaeology*, 71–116. Oxford: East Anglian Archaeology 50.

Louwe Kooijmans, L. P. 2006. Schipluiden: a synthetic view. In L. P. Louwe Kooijmans and P. F. B. Jongste (eds), *Schipluiden: a Neolithic settlement on the Dutch North Sea Coast, c. 3500 cal BC*, 485–516. Leiden: Analecta Praehistorica Leidensia 37/38.

Louwe Kooijmans, L. P. and Mol, J. 2001. Stratigrafie, chronologie en fasering. In L. P. Louwe Kooijmans (ed.), *Archeologie in de Betuweroute: Hardinxveld-Giessendam Polderweg. Een mesolithisch jachtkamp in het rivierengebied (5500–5000 v. Chr.)*, 55–72 Amersfoort: Rapportages Archeologische Monumentenzorg 83.

Niekus, M. J. L. Th. 2006. A geographically referenced ^{14}C database for the Mesolithic and the early phase of the Swifterbant culture in the Northern Netherlands. *Palaeohistoria* 47/48, 41–99.

Out, W. A. 2009. *Sowing the seed? Human impact and plant subsistence in Dutch wetlands during the Late Mesolthic and Early and Middle Neolithic (5500–3400 cal BC)*. Leiden: Archaeological Series Leiden University 18.

Oversteegen, J. F. S., Van Wijngaarden-Bakker, L. H., Maliepaard, R., and Van Kolfschoten, Th. 2001. Zoogdieren, vogels en reptielen. In L. P. Louwe Kooijmans (ed.), *Hardinxveld-De Bruin: een kampplaats uit het Laat-Mesolithicum en het begin van de Swifterbant-cultuur (5500–4450 v. Chr.)*, 209–97. Amersfoort: Rapportages Archeologische Monumentenzorg 88.

Peeters, J. H. M. 2007. *Hoge Vaart-A27 in context: towards a model of Mesolithic-Neolithic land use dynamics as a framework for archaeological heritage management*. Amersfoort: Rijksdienst voor Archeologie, Cultuurlandschap en Monumenten.

Peeters, J. H. M. and Hogestijn, J. W. H. 2001. Op de grens van land en water: jagers-vissers-verzamelaars in een verdrinkend landschap. In J. W. H. Hogestijn and J. H. M. Peeters (eds), *De mesolithische en vroeg-neolithische vindplaats Hoge Vaart-A27 (Flevoland)*, part 20. Amersfoort: Rapportages Archeologische Monumentenzorg 79.

Prummel, W. and Van der Sanden, W. A. B. 1995. Runderhoorns uit de Drentse venen. In W. A. B. van der Sanden (ed.), *Van Rendierjager tot Ontginner, Nieuwe ontdekkingen in Drenthe (XL)*, 8–55. Assen: Nieuwe Drentse Volksalmanak 112.

Raemaekers, D. C. M. 1999. *The articulation of a 'new Neolithic': the meaning of the Swifterbant Culture for the process of Neolithisation in the western part of the North European Plain*. Leiden: Archaeological Series Leiden University 3.

Raemaekers, D. C. M. 2001a. Aardewerk en verbrande klei. In L. P. Louwe Kooijmans (ed.), *Hardinxveld-Polderweg: een woonplaats uit het Late mesolithicum in de Rijn/Maas-delta, 5500–5000 v. C.*, 105–17. Amersfoort: Rapportages Archeologische Monumentenzorg 83.

Raemaekers, D. C. M. 2001b. Aardewerk en verbrande klei. In L. P. Louwe Kooijmans (ed.), *Hardinxveld-De Bruin: een kampplaats uit het Late mesolithicum en de vroege Swifterbant-cultuur in de Rijn/Maas-delta, 5500–4450 v. C.*, 117–52. Amersfoort: Rapportages Archeologische Monumentenzorg 88.

Raemaekers, D. C. M. 2003. Cutting a long story short? The process of Neolithization in the Dutch delta re-examined. *Antiquity* 77, 780–9.

Raemaekers, D. C. M. 2005. Over benen werktuigen en deposities van runderhorens. De betekenis van de categorieën wild en gedomesticeerd voor de Swifterbant-cultuur. *Paleo-aktueel* 14/15, 74–7.

Raemaekers, D. C. M., Geuverink, J., Schepers, M., Tuin, B. P., Van de Lagemaat, E., and Van der Wal, M. 2011. *A biography in stone: typology, age, function and meaning of Early Neolithic perforated wedges in the Netherlands*. Groningen: Groningen Archaeological Studies 14.

Scheu, A., Hartz, S., Schmölcke, U., Tresset, A., Burger, J., and Bolloningo, R. 2007. Ancient DNA provides no evidence for independent domestication of cattle in Mesolithic Rosenhof, Northern Germany. *Journal of Archaeological Science* 35, 1257–64.

Smits, E., Millard, A. R., Nowell, G., and Pearson, D. G. 2010. Isotopic investigation of diet and residential mobility in the Neolithic of the Lower Rhine Basin. *European Journal of Archaeology* 13, 5–31.

Smits, E. and Van der Plicht, J. 2009. Mesolithic and Neolithic human remains in the Netherlands: physical anthropological and stable isotope investigations. *Journal of Archaeology in the Low Countries* 1, 55–85.

Stilborg, O. and Holm, L. 2009. Ceramics as a novelty in northern and southern Sweden. In P. Jordan and M. Zvelebil (eds)., *Ceramics before farming: the dispersal of pottery among prehistoric Eurasian hunter-gatherers*, 319–45. Walnut Creek, CA: Left Coast Press.

Van Heeringen, R. M. and Theunissen, E. M. 2001. *Kwaliteitsbepalend onderzoek ten behoeve van duurzaam behoud van neolithische terreinen in West-Friesland en de Kop van Noord-Holland*. Amersfoort: Nederlandse Archeologische Rapporten 21.

Vang Petersen, P. 1984. Chronological and regional variation in the Late Mesolithic of Eastern Denmark. *Journal of Danish Archaeology* 3, 7–18.

Verhart, L. B. M. 2000. *Times fade away: the Neolithization of the southern Netherlands in an anthropological and geographical perspective*. Leiden: Archaeological Series Leiden University 6.

Zeiler, J. T. 1997. *Hunting, fowling and stock-breeding at Neolithic sites in the Western and Central Netherlands*. Groningen: Archaeobone.

Zeiler, J. T. 2006a. Mammals. In L. P. Louwe Kooijmans and P. F. B. Jongste (eds), *Schipluiden: a Neolithic settlement on the Dutch North Sea Coast, c. 3500 cal BC*, 375–420. Leiden: Analecta Praehistorica Leidensia 37/38.

Zeiler, J. T. 2006b. Birds. In L. P. Louwe Kooijmans and P. F. B. Jongste (eds), *Schipluiden: a Neolithic settlement on the Dutch North Sea Coast, c. 3500 cal BC*, 421–42. Leiden: Analecta Praehistorica Leidensia 37/38.

Zvelebil, M. 1986. Mesolithic prelude and Neolithic revolution. In M. Zvelebil (ed.), *Hunters in transition: Mesolithic societies of temperate Eurasia and their transition to farming*, 5–16. Cambridge: Cambridge University Press.

Zvelebil, M. and Rowley-Conwy, P. 1986. Foragers and farmers in Atlantic Europe. In M. Zvelebil (ed.), *Hunters in transition: Mesolithic societies of temperate Eurasia and their transition to farming*, 67–93. Cambridge: Cambridge University Press.

CHAPTER 38

THE CONTINUITY OF HUNTING AND GATHERING IN THE NEOLITHIC AND BEYOND IN BRITAIN AND IRELAND

VICKI CUMMINGS AND OLIVER J. T. HARRIS

To what extent did hunting and gathering, practices that unquestionably dominated the British and Irish Mesolithic, continue into the first period of farming that followed, the Neolithic? Was this a moment of radical economic disjuncture? Did hunting and gathering come to an abrupt end? Or did these practices continue, remaining an important mode of subsistence into the Neolithic and beyond? There are many different arguments relating to this question, bound up with the way people envision the transition between the two periods. This in turn tends to be divided between advocates of colonization, with farming the sole outcome of the arrival of farmers from mainland Europe, and advocates of an indigenous model, with local hunter-gatherers actively choosing to change their subsistence strategies, but often continuing some of the old ways.

In this contribution we explore the sequence of continuity, change, and transition in these islands to explore these important issues. Of course the issue of the transition from the Mesolithic to the Neolithic has been one of the most hotly argued topics in European prehistory, and in no region is the debate more heated than in reference to Britain and Ireland. Here we hope to introduce readers to the key issues, while also referring to wider debates and models. This is an enormous topic, however, and inevitably not everything will be covered in as much depth as we would like. Finally, the chapter will highlight some new avenues for research, as well as suggesting that the polarized nature of the debate often obscures the complexity of history in the making. A position which recognizes the continuity of hunting and gathering without denying the dominance of farming promises more fruitful research in the future.

BACKGROUND TO THE MESOLITHIC

The Mesolithic in Britain and Ireland began at roughly 8000 BC with the onset of the Holocene. It is the last few hundred years of this period that are of particular interest to us here, given our focus on the role, and potential continuity, of hunting and gathering into the Neolithic. The Mesolithic terminates in the final centuries of the fifth millennium BC and, potentially in some parts of Britain and Ireland, the first couple of hundred years of the fourth millennium BC (Whittle et al. 2011 and see below). The final part of the Mesolithic in Britain is quite different to many areas on the continent. In contrast to the complex, pottery-using, and at least partially sedentary Ertebølle groups in southern Scandinavia, British and Irish Mesolithic groups seem to have remained predominantly mobile (see, for example, Darvill and Thomas 2002). Subsistence strategies in Britain revolved around coastal resources, where these were available (and some areas have good evidence for this in the form of shell middens), and the hunting of wild game, notably red deer. In Ireland, no such large wild ungulates were available (with the exception of wild boar), and so hunting strategies were quite different. Perhaps partially as a result of this we see different technologies in the stone tools used on each side of the Irish Sea, with small multi-tasking microliths favoured in Britain (particularly the south), which contrast with broader Bann flakes which characterize the later Mesolithic in Ireland. In both cases, however, the gathering of a large range of wild resources, including plants for food but also wood for fires, water, flint for knapping, antler, and so on (see Mears and Hillman 2007) would have been a key part of group survival. Scholars have argued that Britain and Ireland were isolated from mainland Europe in the late Mesolithic, but from Ireland there is at least one good example of domesticated animal bone in a Mesolithic context: domesticated cattle remains have been recovered from Ferriter's Cove in south-west Ireland (Woodman et al. 1999). As we will see, how you interpret this find depends upon your view of the transition to the Neolithic.

Unfortunately, where the British and Irish late Mesolithic sequence is really lacking is in burial evidence (see Conneller 2006). Only a handful of Mesolithic skeletal remains are known, which contrasts with the large late Mesolithic cemeteries in southern Scandinavia and Brittany. However, small quantities of human remains have been found at late Mesolithic shell middens. At Cnoc Coig on Oronsay, for example, a human hand was buried on top of a seal flipper (Meiklejohn et al. 2005). Excarnation may well have been practised elsewhere and this example does suggest an interesting relationship between people and animals (Conneller 2004). Drawing on analogies both with older Mesolithic sites such as Star Carr and with modern extant hunter-gatherers, it has been suggested that Mesolithic world views can be characterized as animist (Conneller 2004). This means that rather than seeing humans as radically opposed to the natural world they view all humans, animals, plants, things, and places as potentially alive, and potentially as persons (Conneller 2004; Cummings and Harris 2011; Viveiros de Castro 1998). This gives us an insight into the kinds of belief system that people had in the late Mesolithic, and the way in which they understood their place in the world. This may well have varied across both space and time.

One of the difficulties of understanding regional and chronological variation towards the end of the Mesolithic in Britain and Ireland is the poor dating resolution we have for this period, with very few well-stratified sites known. It is difficult to know how people's lives were changing in this period. In contrast, as we will see below, our understanding of the date of the start of the Neolithic, and its development over the first few centuries, are now far better understood. Rather than turn immediately to the transition period, however, we first want to set out some of the characteristics of the first few centuries of the Neolithic.

Background to the Neolithic

We discuss the dating for the start of the Neolithic in more detail below, but for now it is sufficient to note that it is now argued that it begins in Britain just before 4000 BC, and in Ireland around 3800 BC (Whittle et al. 2011). Throughout both countries there are a number of features that tie together the first few centuries of the Neolithic (what was once called the 'Neolithic package'). These include a substantial reliance on *domesticated animals* including cows, pigs, sheep, and goats. Cows in particular seem to have been very important to people's economies in many parts of Britain and Ireland. *Domesticated plants* were also in use from the very start of the Neolithic, although the relative reliance on these tends to be highly debated (e.g. Bishop et al. 2009; Bogaard and Jones 2007; Fairbairn 2000; Jones and Rowley-Conwy 2007). Indeed evidence of the diets of people buried at Hambledon Hill in Dorset, some time after the start of the Neolithic in that region, suggests that diets varied quite considerably between different groups (Richards 2000). *Pottery* also played an important role in changing people's eating habits, arriving in Britain and Ireland for the first time immediately at the start of the Neolithic. This was round-based and would have been used both in cooking and for storage, including of dairy products (Copley et al. 2005).

It has also been suggested that the Neolithic saw the beginning of *sedentism* in Britain and Ireland. For many years it was presumed that people were sedentary in the Neolithic as they had started farming, although there was a lack of good archaeological evidence for this. In the 1980s the lack of evidence led to the argument that people in the Neolithic were actually quite mobile (e.g. Thomas 1988; cf. Whittle 1997). However, a series of recent discoveries has challenged this interpretation. In Scotland, five large timber halls dating to the earlier Neolithic have been excavated (Brophy 2007), and supporters of a sedentary model have taken these as representative of a much wider trend, also indicated in England with at least one comparable example at Whitehorse Stone in Kent. In contrast, others have taken these sites to be the exception rather than the rule. In Ireland things are somewhat different. The extensive development that took place in the 1990s and 2000s has revealed evidence of upwards of 80 houses dating to the early Neolithic (Smyth 2006; 2010). Here it would seem that people lived a more sedentary life (though as we will see this may not have been from the very start of the Neolithic).

The *monuments* of the British and Irish Neolithic have also played a crucial role in popularizing this period. Almost exclusively, the first monuments built on both islands were funerary ones, including megalithic chambered tombs of various kinds, wooden mortuary structures, and earthen long barrows. These monuments created collective burial sites where communities could mark their presence in the land, establishing connections with each other, the past, landscape, and the ancestors. The prevalence of victims of violence within these monuments does suggest that they may also have played a crucial role in dealing with the aftermath of group conflict and dissension, in a world in which farmers were far more dependent on people beyond their immediate community than their Mesolithic forebears had been (Fowler 2010; Schulting and Fibiger 2012; Schulting and Wysocki 2005). Some deposits in these monuments include both humans and animals, especially cattle, but there seems little doubt that domesticated animals were not regarded as peers in the same way wild ones had been in the Mesolithic. While cows, for example, offered excellent food, and food for thought, they may not have been people in the way deer or seals may have been in previous periods: instead they were property to be given away, feasted on, and exchanged, and fuel for metaphors about descent, association, and community (Ray and Thomas 2003).

Other new things also appeared in the Neolithic, besides domesticates, monuments, and pottery. *Flint mines* were utilized for the first time, especially on the Sussex Downs, and people began to make, use, and exchange *axes of polished stone*. In this latter case, clear connections can be seen with the continent in the form of axes made from jadeite from the Alps that are deposited at early Neolithic sites like the Sweet Track near Glastonbury, built in either 3807 or 3806 BC (Coles and Coles 1986). Stone axes were also quarried from sources found on the shores of the Irish Sea, and exchanged within and between Britain and Ireland (Clough and Cummins 1988); however, the widespread trade in these did not really get going until the middle of the 37th century cal BC (Whittle et al. 2011).

Against this background of life in both the late Mesolithic and early Neolithic, the question is: what of hunting and gathering in this period? We will turn to the evidence shortly. Before we can tackle issues of continuity and change, however, we need to set out how the transition between these two periods has been conceptualized, and then think about how the evidence has been considered against this broader background.

Hunters and Gatherers to Farmers: The Debate

When people first started thinking about the transition from the Mesolithic to the Neolithic, it all seemed fairly straightforward. Key scholars such as Childe (1940) and Piggott (1954) thought that the Neolithic represented the start of farming, and that since this was something that spread across Europe, it would have started in Britain and Ireland with the arrival of farmers from mainland Europe. As part of a culture-historical approach to archaeology, they saw change as coming from the movement of external people into Britain and Ireland. These new arrivals brought with them the 'Neolithic package' of agriculture, domesticated animals, pottery, polished stone axes, and monuments. From early on, there were problems with aspects of this explanation. Where was the source of these incomers? Why did the British and Irish sequence not more closely match their continental counterparts? Furthermore, from the 1980s onwards scholars began to query the role of the native population: surely the native hunter-gatherers had a role to play in this transition (e.g. Thomas 1988)?

As a result of this, scholars in the 1990s advocated a much more dynamic role for the local Mesolithic populations, and suggested that they actively took up farming at a time and in a manner of their own choosing (e.g. Armit and Finlayson 1992). Yet such a perspective was heavily criticized, and in recent years in particular, there has been a resurgence of interest in the colonization model (e.g. Rowley-Conwy 2004; Sheridan 2010). While many scholars have advocated a position somewhere between these two extremes (e.g. Cummings and Harris 2011; Garrow and Sturt 2011; Whittle 2007), the debate in the literature is now dominated by these two competing and polarized positions (indigenous adaption versus colonization).

Indigenous Continuity?

The first position we examine suggests that there was considerable continuity from the Mesolithic through into the Neolithic, which involved a new way of thinking about the world, with less emphasis on an economic change (Thomas 1988; 2003; 2004; 2008; and see Armit and Finlayson 1992; Cummings and Whittle 2004; Milner et al. 2004; Tilley 1994; 1996; 2007; Whittle 1996). This approach can be described as the 'continuity model', and has been increasingly popular in post-processual approaches (Warren 2007). Here the agents of change are firmly cast as indigenous hunter-gatherers. Many archaeologists have argued that the lack of any notable similarity between continental and British and Irish Mesolithic material indicates that the islands were probably very isolated in the final centuries of the fifth millennium. However, drawing on numerous theoretical, anthropological, and archaeological studies, Thomas (2004) has put forward the counter-argument that we cannot trace interaction from material similarities in any kind of straightforward way (Hodder 1982; Robb 2001). Instead, Thomas (1999) suggests that the native hunter-gatherers were fully aware of the farmers living across the water but chose to maintain their existing lifestyles. It was only when the continental Neolithic began to change that it became attractive to Mesolithic people in Britain (Thomas 2004, 119). Furthermore, Thomas has suggested that domesticated plants, and to a certain extent their animal counterparts, were only used on certain special occasions. The Neolithic, then, was not a major economic change, but it did involve a change in identity. As such, Neolithic people in Britain were descended from Mesolithic forebears, and simply fitted the new forms of material culture and domesticated animals into their particular routines, most often maintaining a highly mobile lifestyle. It is important to note that Thomas does allow a role for some people coming across from the continent, in the form of potters (for example), but does not envision the whole-scale movement of communities that many advocates of the colonization hypothesis would suggest. For Thomas, a site like Ferriter's Cove, which, as we saw, has domesticated animals with a date normally deemed Mesolithic, is evidence of the existing contacts between Ireland and the continent, and the ability of hunter-gatherers to procure domestic animals, even if only to eat them rather than breed them and start a new way of life.

Colonization from Abroad?

There has been a backlash against this continuity model in recent years, with the suggestion that earlier models of quick economic change may actually be appropriate in the case of Britain and Ireland (Collard et al. 2010; Rowley-Conwy 2004; 2011; Sheridan 2004; 2007; 2010). This has been influenced by a number of new lines of evidence that have emerged. To list the main examples, these are: stable isotope analysis on skeletal material, which has suggested that the dominance of marine resources came to an abrupt end at the start of the Neolithic (Schulting 1998; Richards and Schulting 2006); the modelling of radiocarbon dates to argue for a swift population increase after 4000 cal BC (Collard et al. 2010); and the re-examination of the links and likeness in form between Neolithic assemblages from the continent and aspects of some of their British counterparts (Sheridan 2004; 2010). Finally, as noted above, the discovery of over 80 houses in Ireland (Smyth 2006; 2010) and a handful in Britain (e.g. Barclay et al. 2002; Murray et al. 2009) have been taken by some (e.g. Rowley-Conwy 2004) to be the footprint of colonizers arriving from abroad. It is suggested that the colonizing communities came from a range of places including Brittany, north-central France, and the Low Countries. Furthermore, they suggest that the Neolithic could not have become established without human expertise arriving alongside the domesticated plants and animals. The most sustained of these accounts has come from Alison Sheridan (2003; 2004; 2007; 2010) who has developed a detailed model of how the transition may have worked. Although her approach undoubtedly allows for the acculturation of the native populations as part of the process, it is always a secondary consideration to the main agents of change: the incomers.

Hunting and Gathering: The Evidence for Continuity and Change

How do we evaluate the continuity of hunting and gathering against this background? On the one hand, the indigenous model suggests that hunter-gatherers were the agents of change, and only adapted farming in a partial and piecemeal fashion. On the other hand, the colonization model suggests that there was the widespread arrival of farming communities from the continent who subsumed the native population into a new economic regime. In order to evaluate these two competing models we will now run through some of the key strands of evidence.

Animals, Diet, and Hunting

The first key element of the evidence to consider is the role of animals in the transition. While preservation is a serious problem, when recovered, Mesolithic animal bone assemblages comprise red and roe deer, wild boar, and aurochs. In contrast, Neolithic assemblages consist primarily of domesticated species, predominantly domesticated cattle in the early Neolithic (Schulting 2008). Only small amounts of wild animal bone are typically found in early Neolithic contexts, apart from in a couple of exceptional examples (the Coneybury Anomaly, Wiltshire, and Links of Notland, Orkney, for example, which have significant wild-animal bone assemblages; Richards 1990; Sharples 2000). This general pattern has been reinforced in recent years by stable isotope analysis of human bones, which indicates what kind of diet people were eating. Work has shown that many Mesolithic people ate a marine diet, but people from the early Neolithic onwards ate a terrestrial diet (Schulting and Richards 2002): this presumably was derived primarily from domesticated animals. While there has been an ongoing debate with regards to the validity of this method, and the ways in which the results are interpreted (see Milner et al. 2004; Richards and Schulting 2006), since these results are broadly comparable with the animal-bone evidence, it seems likely that this was the case.

However, there are some problems with this picture. Firstly, the animal-bone evidence is limited and from specific contexts only. In the early Neolithic this tends to be from monumental sites, such as chambered cairns and long barrows, or causewayed enclosures. Even the practice of pit-digging, where animal-bone assemblages are also recovered, could be seen as a ritualized act, so that these assemblages may be the remains of special feasts or ceremonies, and not necessarily representative of people's day-to-day diets. Likewise, those people whose remains have been subject to stable isotope analysis may also be exceptional, since they are the few who end up being buried in special circumstances (the vast majority of people in the early Neolithic did not end up being formally buried). It could be that these special people ate a special diet during their lives and prior to deposition in monumental contexts. It can also be argued that even if we do envisage the extensive use of domesticated animals from the start of the Neolithic onwards, this does not mean that people understood that these were 'domesticated' animals as opposed to 'wild' animals (cf. Hodder 1990). Instead, conceptually these animals may have been fitted into an understanding of the world that already existed (one that is animist: see Cummings and Harris 2011). If this was the case, then there may well have been considerable elements of continuity with the Mesolithic. It is therefore interesting to note that red deer were introduced into Ireland at the start of the Neolithic, along with domesticated animals (Milner 2010). This suggests a much more complex understanding of animals than simply as 'wild' and 'domestic'. If domesticated animals were conceptually fitted into a pre-existing, animist understanding of the world, it should also be noted that these animals did require new knowledge sets in order to look after them. Unlike wild animals, domesticated animals need specific care, which includes meeting dietary needs and husbandry. So while initially the arrival of these animals into Britain and Ireland may have seen them fitted into pre-existing conceptions of animals, over the long term, the care these animals required would have created new relationships between people and animals.

There is also the issue that lithic assemblages from the Neolithic period almost always contain a good number of arrowheads. Indeed, leaf-shaped arrowheads are indicative of early Neolithic occupation, and these are extremely common finds in the archaeological record. It seems likely that despite some arrowheads being found embedded in people (Smith and Brickley 2009), the vast majority were used for hunting animals. Therefore, it seems certain that people did carry on hunting in the Neolithic. The question is, to what extent did people hunt? The evidence, as briefly outlined above, is varied. Again, it seems to rest more on how you interpret the evidence than the evidence itself, which remains ambiguous in places and in relation to specifics.

Plant Food, Diet, and Gathering

The Neolithic also saw the first use of domesticated plants. If there are issues with understanding the role and impact of domesticated animals in Britain and Ireland, the situation is even more problematic with domesticated plants. There is only limited evidence of domesticated plant remains, because they usually survive only if the plant has been carbonized. However, carbonized plant remains are those that have been burnt, rendering them inedible, and so were probably carbonized by accident. As such, they frequently do not appear in the archaeological record (Fairbairn 2000). This does not mean that they are absent: sites such as the timber house at Balbridie in Scotland produced thousands of carbonized wheat grains (Brophy 2007). It is therefore interesting that one of the most frequently recovered plant materials from the Neolithic is hazelnut shells, which would have been gathered, and are also characteristic of Mesolithic plant assemblages. What is clear is that there are issues here with both preservation and archaeological visibility.

Pollen analysis offers another source of information on this issue, and for many years a significant decline in tree pollen, particularly elm, was noted around 3800 BC. In many places this was accompanied by a rise in cereal pollen. However, there is the possibility that the elm decline of 3800 BC was partially the result of elm disease, and not the clearing of the landscape for farming. Stable isotope analysis has also been used to suggest the input of cereals into people's diets. There is evidence for some people having a fairly substantial quantity of plant foods in their diet, presumed to be cereals, but this is variable over space and time (Richards 2000). It has also been suggested that investigating field boundaries may help us explore the role of cereals in the Neolithic. While some are known (the Ceide fields in Ireland, for example), again these are rare in the archaeological record. Furthermore, how useful they are for revealing the extent to which cereals were grown remains problematic, as they could just as easily have been used for keeping livestock, or to make statements about the division of the landscape.

There is now a strong argument that cereals were primarily cultivated on a fairly small scale in the Neolithic. It has been suggested that these were grown in garden plots that would have shifted around with people (Whittle 2003). In some cases, cereal may well have been reserved for use in ceremonies, or for brewing beer, as opposed to being used on a daily basis. While domesticated cereals are clearly new and introduced at the start of the Neolithic, the issue remains whether or not their cultivation represented a significant change for people. There is overwhelming evidence from the study of hunter-gatherers to indicate that the careful management of wild resources regularly took place. Furthermore, studies of the pollen sequences from Mesolithic contexts do show small-scale maintenance of clearances, presumably for encouraging game and/or growing particular plant species (Brown 1997). This actually suggests that cereal cultivation slotted into a pre-existing set of practices. It is notoriously difficult to find evidence for wild plant foods from both the Mesolithic and Neolithic, but we can only assume that people continued to gather into the Neolithic. If nothing else, the ubiquitous presence of hazelnuts from Neolithic levels shows that this was the case. This leads us to our final issue to consider with regards the continuity of hunting and gathering: the impact of new technologies, namely stone axes and pottery.

New Technologies: Axes and Pottery

Stone axes first appear in the Neolithic and originally they were thought to represent a new technology which was imported in order to cut down trees to make way for agricultural practices. We certainly do get imported axes right at the start of the Neolithic: jadeite axes originating in the Alps are found in Britain and Ireland, but these were not functional objects for felling trees (Pétrequin et al. 2012). These magnificent objects were unused and almost certainly objects of desire and prestige, which ultimately ended up being deposited in special places. Likewise, once people start quarrying stone sources in Britain and Ireland, many of the axes made from these sources ended up as prestige items that were never used. Some stone axe sources were actually first utilized in the late Mesolithic, and there are also some late Mesolithic axes known from both Ireland and Wales. This suggests an intensification of a practice which resonated with both late Mesolithic ways of doing things as well as new Neolithic ideas. At best, we would argue that polished stone axes are ambiguous in relation to informing us about the start of Neolithic.

On the other hand, pottery has long been considered as very important to farming populations. Firstly, it helps store agricultural produce; secondly, it is very useful in transforming food stuffs. One of the new components to a Neolithic diet was dairy, which would not have been regularly encountered in a Mesolithic diet. There is plenty of pottery from early Neolithic contexts, and lipid analysis shows that much once contained dairy products (Copley et al. 2005; also see Craig et al. 2005). Pottery enables the easy conversion of milk products into cheese, butter, and yogurt, all of which would have been more easily digestible for potentially lactose-intolerant people—that is, people who could not digest some of the sugars in milk. What is also interesting about the earliest Neolithic pottery in Britain and Ireland is that it is very well made. Carinated bowls are particularly fine wares, which demonstrate the makers had considerable knowledge of clay technology. This does not suggest communities experimenting with this technology, but suggests instead that there may well have been experienced potters arriving into Britain and Ireland with the knowledge of how to make fine pottery. While this may assist us in understanding the processes behind the start of the Neolithic, it does not necessarily inform our understanding of hunting and gathering practices across this period. As we have already seen, hunter-gatherers in nearby southern Scandinavia adopted pottery in the late Mesolithic, showing that it is not exclusive to Neolithic peoples (Tilley 1996).

Monuments

Finally, what of monuments? In some ways these represent a clear change from the preceding Mesolithic. While it has occasionally been argued that shell middens and other Mesolithic features (e.g. the 'totem poles' in the Stonehenge car park: Cleal et al. 1995) might represent a form of monumentality, the monuments constructed in the Neolithic are, without question, something very new. The funerary monuments constructed offer an image of a society which was capable of coming together, in numbers greater than that experienced on a day-to-day basis and constructing something together. These projects may not only have been related to violence, as we suggested above, but have been caught up in new understandings of temporality, seasonality, and sociality that were central to farmers' lives. However, it remains an open question as to whether or not these monuments really tell us anything about the transition between the Mesolithic and the Neolithic. In particular, it is likely that most Neolithic monuments were constructed a century or two after the start of agriculture had taken place, especially in southern Britain (Whittle et al. 2011). Thus the argument that they tell us about a radical break transition itself—and not the development of the Neolithic after this point—is suspect. To examine this point further we now turn to the final strand of evidence, that of the date of the transition itself.

Chronology

One of the most important lines of developing evidence for assessing the transition, and thus the continuity for hunting and gathering, is the reassessment of the chronology of the transition, recently undertaken by Whittle, Bayliss, and Healy (2011). A thorough examination of the dates, combined with Bayesian statistical modelling allows a much clearer picture of the period to emerge. To begin with, it now seems highly probable that Neolithic things appeared at different times in different places. Some of the earliest dates come from Neolithic material culture from the Thames estuary which dates to the 41st century cal BC (Whittle et al. 2011, 731). There then seems to be a spread outwards from this point, reaching the Cotswolds and Sussex by around 3950 cal BC. From here it spreads out over the rest of southern Britain, with the south-west and Wales potentially the last places to take up this lifestyle by around 3700 cal BC (Whittle et al. 2011, 738). The evidence for Scotland and Ireland is different. It seems unlikely the Neolithic begins in Ireland or Scotland before 3800 cal BC (Whittle et al. 2011). Despite pleading to the contrary (e.g. Sheridan 2010), there seems little evidence at the moment for a pre-fourth millennium Neolithic in either western Britain or Ireland.

This evidence strongly suggests a role for colonizers in the early part of the Neolithic in south-east England, with people coming from the continent farming and mining flint from very early on. However, they did not bring with them a complete Neolithic package. As noted above, monuments are later than the start of the Neolithic in many areas (Scotland may be an exception), and crucially houses do not represent the earliest evidence for the Neolithic in any area (Whittle et al. 2011). In all cases, houses, therefore, do not mark the arrival of the Neolithic, but rather a stage in its later development. What the evidence thus represents is a mixture of small-scale colonization followed by a process of movement by people and the uptake of new practices by local—formally Mesolithic—people. In turn, this suggests that the emergence of monuments takes place in this creolized world, a time of mixtures rather than homogeneous communities. Thus, while we can trace connections in the forms of early monuments to continental comparisons, many are located on sites previously occupied in the Mesolithic, or connected visually to landscape features of long-standing importance (Cummings and Whittle 2004). This process of a blended mixture of incomers and uptakers would have played out differently in various parts of Britain and Ireland and certainly requires further investigation. What it emphasizes is the importance of agency on all sides of the transition, both of incomers and locals. In acknowledging this role for both sides of the equation it is here we can begin to rethink the role of hunting and gathering during the Neolithic. It is within a world rich in local knowledge as well as new ideas that hunting could continue to play a small but significant role, and that gathering would have remained essential in daily life.

Conclusions: The Continuity of Hunting and Gathering into the Neolithic?

The Mesolithic–Neolithic transition has been the focus of considerable interest for many years. Much has been written on the topic and we have only been able to provide a very basic summary and overview of the key arguments in this chapter. It is important to emphasize that there is clearly considerable variety in the interpretation of the evidence, and it is this that accounts for the multitude of different, often opposing, accounts of the transition. It would be extremely desirable to have more evidence from the period 4300–3700 BC in order to understand the transition more fully. However, as we have outlined, new evidence, or new ways of engaging with the evidence, can provide more nuanced ways of understanding the transition, which was quite clearly not a single, straightforward transition from hunter-gatherer to farmer. In this chapter we have traced certain practices and suggested that there may well have been considerable elements of continuity between the Mesolithic and Neolithic. We have suggested that the Neolithic was a result of some incomers arriving into Britain and Ireland, and mixing with the indigenous hunter-gatherers. The result of this was something completely new: a Neolithic that did not resemble any of its European counterparts. This did not happen overnight, however, but was a long and drawn-out process which manifested itself differently in different parts of Britain and Ireland. What is clear, however, is that hunting and gathering practices continued into the Neolithic in some form or another.

REFERENCES

Armit, I. and Finlayson, B. 1992. Hunter-gatherers transformed: the transition to agriculture in northern and western Europe. *Antiquity* 66, 664–76.
Barclay, G., Brophy, K., and MacGregor, G. 2002. Claish, Stirling: an Early Neolithic structure in its context. *Proceedings of the Society of Antiquaries of Scotland* 132, 65–137.
Bishop, R. R., Church, M. J., and Rowley-Conwy, P. A. 2009. Cereals, fruits and nuts in the Scottish Neolithic. *Proceedings of the Society of Antiquaries of Scotland* 139, 47–103.
Bogaard, A. and Jones, G. 2007. Neolithic farming in Britain and central Europe: contrast or continuity? In A. Whittle and V. Cummings (eds), *Going over: the Mesolithic–Neolithic transition in north-west Europe*, 357–76. London: British Academy.
Brophy, K. 2007. From big houses to cult houses: early Neolithic timber halls in Scotland. *Proceedings of the Prehistoric Society* 73, 75–96.
Brown, T. 1997. Clearances and clearings: deforestation in Mesolithic/Neolithic Britain. *Oxford Journal of Archaeology* 16, 133–46.
Childe, V.G. 1940. *Prehistoric communities of the British Isles*. Edinburgh: Edinburgh University Press.
Cleal, R., Walker, K., and Montague, R. (eds) 1995. *Stonehenge in its landscape*. Swindon: English Heritage.
Clough, T. and Cummins, W. (eds) 1988. *Stone axe studies: volume two*. London: Council for British Archaeology.
Coles J. and Coles, B. 1986. *From Sweet Track to Glastonbury*. London: Thames and Hudson.
Collard, M., Edinborough, K., Shennan S., and Thomas, M. G. 2010. Radiocarbon evidence indicates that migrants introduced farming to Britain. *Journal of Archaeological Science* 37, 866–70.
Conneller, C. 2004. Becoming deer: corporeal transformations at Star Carr. *Archaeological Dialogues* 11, 37–56.
Copley, M. S., Berstan, R., Mukherjee, A. J., Dudd, S. N., Straker, V., Payne S., and Evershed, R. P. 2005. Dairying in antiquity, III. Evidence from absorbed lipid residues dating to the British Neolithic. *Archaeological Science* 32, 523–46.

Craig, O., Chapman, J., Heron, C., Willis, L., Bartosiewicz, L., Taylor, G., Whittle, A., and Collins, M. 2005. Did the first farmers of central and eastern Europe produce dairy foods? *Antiquity* 79, 882–94.

Cummings, V. and Harris, O. J. T. 2011. Animals, people and places: the continuity of hunting and gathering practices across the Mesolithic–Neolithic transition in Britain. *European Journal of Archaeology* 14, 361–82.

Cummings, V. and Whittle, A. 2004. *Places of special virtue: megaliths in the Neolithic landscapes of Wales*. Oxford: Oxbow.

Darvill, T. and Thomas, J. (eds) 2002. *Neolithic houses in north-west Europe and beyond*. Oxford: Oxbow.

Fairbairn, A. 2000. On the spread of crops across Neolithic Britain, with special reference to southern England. In A. Fairbairn (ed.), *Plants in Neolithic Britain and beyond*, 107–21. Oxford: Oxbow.

Fowler, C. 2010. Pattern and diversity in the Early Neolithic mortuary practice of Britain and Ireland: contextualising the treatment of the dead. *Documenta Praehistorica* 37, 1–22.

Garrow, D. and Sturt, F. 2011. Grey waters bright with Neolithic argonauts? Maritime connections and the Mesolithic–Neolithic transition within the 'western seaways' of Britain, c. 5000–3500 BC. *Antiquity* 85, 59–72.

Hodder, I. 1982. *Symbols in action: ethnoarchaeological studies of material culture*. Cambridge: Cambridge University Press.

Hodder, I. 1990. *The domestication of Europe*. Oxford: Blackwell.

Jones, G. and Rowley-Conwy, P. 2007. On the importance of cereal cultivation in the British Neolithic. In S. Colledge and J. Conolly (eds), *The origins and spread of domestic plants in southwest Asia and Europe*, 391–419. Walnut Creek, CA: Left Coast Press.

Mears, R. and Hillman, G. 2007. *Wild food*. London: Hodder & Stoughton.

Meiklejohn, C., Merrett, R., Nolan, W., Richards, M. P., and Mellars, P. A. 2005. Spatial relationships, dating and taphonomy of the human bone from the Mesolithic site of Cnoc Coig, Oronsay, Argyll, Scotland. *Proceedings of the Prehistoric Society* 71, 85–105.

Milner, N. 2010. Subsistence at 4000–3700 cal BC: landscapes of change and continuity. In B. Finlayson and G. Warren (eds), *Landscapes in transition*, 46–54. Oxford: Oxbow.

Milner, N., Craig, O. E., Bailey, G. N., Pedersen K., and Andersen, S. H. 2004. Something fishy in the Neolithic? A re-evaluation of stable isotope analysis of Mesolithic and Neolithic coastal populations. *Antiquity* 78, 9–22.

Murray, H. K., Murray J. C., and Fraser, S. M. 2009. *A tale of the unknown unknowns: a Mesolithic pit alignment and a Neolithic timber hall at Warren Field, Crathes, Aberdeenshire*. Oxford: Oxbow.

Pétrequin, P., Cassen, S., Errera, M., Klassen, L., Sheridan, A., and Pétrequin, A.-M. (eds) 2012. *JADE. Grandes haches alpines du Néolithique européean, V au IV millénaires av. J.-C.* Besançon: Franche-Comté University Press.

Piggott, S. 1954. *The Neolithic cultures of the British Isles*. Cambridge: Cambridge University Press.

Ray, K. and Thomas, J. 2003. In the kinship of cows: the social centrality of cattle in the earlier Neolithic of southern Britain. In M. Parker Pearson (ed.), *Food, culture and identity in the Neolithic and Early Bronze Age*, 37–44. Oxford: British Archaeological Reports.

Richards, J. 1990. *The Stonehenge environs project*. London: English Heritage.

Richards, M. P. 2000. Human consumption of plant foods in the British Neolithic: direct evidence from bone stable isotopes. In A. Fairbairn (ed.), *Plants in Neolithic Britain and beyond*, 123–35. Oxford: Oxbow.

Richards, M. P. and Schulting, R. J. 2006. Against the grain? A response to Milner et al. (2004). *Antiquity* 80, 444–56.

Robb, J. E. 2001. Island identities: ritual travel and the creation of difference in Neolithic Malta. *European Journal of Archaeology* 4, 175–202.

Rowley-Conwy, P. 2004. How the west was lost: a reconsideration of the agricultural origins in Britain, Ireland and southern Scandinavia. *Current Anthropology* 45, 83–113.

Rowley-Conwy, P. 2011. Westward Ho! The spread of agriculture from Central Europe to the Atlantic. *Current Anthropology* 52, S431–S451.

Schulting, R. 1998. Slighting the sea: stable isotope evidence for the transition to farming in northwestern Europe. *Documenta Praehistorica* 25, 203–18.

Schulting, R. 2008. Foodways and social ecologies from the early Mesolithic to the early Bronze Age. In J. Pollard (ed.), *Prehistoric Britain*, 90–120. Oxford: Blackwell.

Schulting, R. and Fibiger, L. (eds) 2012. *Sticks, stones and broken bones: Neolithic violence in a European perspective*. Oxford: Oxford University Press.

Schulting, R. and Richards, M. P. 2002. The wet, the wild and the domesticated: the Mesolithic–Neolithic transition on the west coast of Scotland. *European Journal of Archaeology* 5, 147–89.

Schulting, R. and Wysocki, M. 2005. 'In this chambered tumulus were found cleft skulls...': an assessment of the evidence for cranial trauma in the British Neolithic. *Proceedings of the Prehistoric Society* 71, 107–38.

Sharples, N. 2000. Antlers and Orcadian rituals: an ambiguous role for red deer in the Neolithic. In A. Ritchie (ed.), *Neolithic Orkney in its European context*, 107–16. Cambridge: McDonald Institute for Archaeological Research.

Sheridan, A. 2003. Ireland's earliest 'passage' tombs: a French connection? In G. Burenhult and S. Westergaard (eds), *Stones and bones: formal disposal of the dead in Atlantic Europe during the Mesolithic–Neolithic Interface 6000-3000 BC*, 9–26. Oxford: BAR.

Sheridan, A. 2004. Neolithic connections along and across the Irish Sea. In V. Cummings and C. Fowler (eds), *The Neolithic of the Irish Sea: materiality and traditions of practice*, 9–21. Oxford: Oxbow.

Sheridan, A. 2007. From Picardie to Pickering to Pencraig Hill? New information on the 'Carinated Bowl Neolithic' in northern Britain. In A. Whittle and V. Cummings (eds), *Going over: the Mesolithic–Neolithic transition in north-west Europe*, 441–92. London: British Academy.

Sheridan, A. 2010. The Neolithization of Britain and Ireland: the 'big picture'. In B. Finlayson and G. Warren (eds), *Landscapes in transition*, 89–105. Oxford: Oxbow.

Smith, M. and Brickley, M. 2009. *People of the long barrows: life, death and burial in the earlier Neolithic*. Stroud: The History Press.

Smyth, J. 2006. The role of the house in Neolithic Ireland. *European Journal of Archaeology* 9, 229–57.

Smyth, J. 2010. The house and group identity in the Irish Neolithic. *Proceedings of the Royal Irish Academy* 111C, 1–31.

Thomas, J. 1988. Neolithic explanations revisited: the Mesolithic–Neolithic transition in Britain and south Scandinavia. *Proceedings of the Prehistoric Society* 54, 59–66.

Thomas, J. 1999. *Understanding the Neolithic*. London: Routledge.

Thomas, J. 2003. Thoughts on the 'repacked' Neolithic revolution. *Antiquity* 77, 67–74.

Thomas, J. 2004. Current debates on the Mesolithic–Neolithic transition in Britain and Ireland. *Documenta Praehistorica* 31, 113–30.

Thomas, J. 2008. The Mesolithic–Neolithic transition in Britain. In J. Pollard (ed.), *Prehistoric Britain*, 58–89. Oxford: Blackwell.

Tilley, C. 1994. *A phenomenology of landscape: paths, places and monuments*. Oxford: Berg.
Tilley, C. 1996. *An ethnography of the Neolithic*. Cambridge: Cambridge University Press.
Tilley, C. 2007. The Neolithic sensory revolution: monumentality and the experience of landscape. In A. Whittle and V. Cummings (eds), *Going over: the Mesolithic–Neolithic transition in north-west Europe*: 329–45. London: British Academy.
Viveiros de Castro, E. 1998. Cosmological deixis and Amerindian perspectivism. *Journal of the Royal Anthropological Institute* 4, 469–88.
Warren, G. 2007. Mesolithic myths. In A. Whittle and V. Cummings (eds), *Going over: the Mesolithic–Neolithic transition in north-west Europe*, 311–28. London: British Academy.
Whittle, A. 1996. *Europe in the Neolithic: the creation of new worlds*. Cambridge: Cambridge University Press.
Whittle, A. 1997. Moving on and moving around: Neolithic settlement mobility. In P. Topping (ed.), *Neolithic landscapes*, 15–22. Oxford: Oxbow.
Whittle, A. 2003. *The archaeology of people*. London: Routledge.
Whittle, A. 2007. The temporality of transformation: dating the early development of the southern British Neolithic. In A. Whittle and V. Cummings (eds), *Going over: the Mesolithic–Neolithic transition in north-west Europe*, 377–98. London: British Academy.
Whittle, A., Healy, F., and Bayliss, A. 2011. *Gathering time: dating the early Neolithic enclosures of southern Britain and Ireland*. Oxford: Oxbow.
Woodman, P. C., Anderson, E., and Finlay, N. 1999. *Excavations at Ferriter's Cove 1983–95: last foragers, first farmers in the Dingle Peninsula*. Bray: Wordwell.

CHAPTER 39

FORAGER–FARMER CONTACTS IN NORTHERN FENNOSCANDIA

CHARLOTTE DAMM AND LARS FORSBERG

The prehistory of Fennoscandia is unique in many respects. It is one of the areas in the world where hunting-fishing persisted as a subsistence economy over vast areas at least until AD 1600, and in some regions even into the twentieth century. In addition it is the northernmost area with prehistoric agriculture and husbandry, thus providing a unique possibility to study long-term interaction between foragers and farmers.

Geographically Fennoscandia includes the Scandinavian peninsula and the adjoining areas of present-day Finland and north-west Russia, notably the Kola Peninsula and Karelia (Figure 39.1). Most of the area in question lies between 58° and 71° N. While this northern location obviously sets certain ecological limits for the northwards expansion of agriculture, history has shown that there are no definitive geographical or climatic limits. That northern hunter-gatherers chose not to engage in agriculture and traditional husbandry must therefore be perceived primarily as a part of the historical trajectory rather than determined by ecological circumstances.

In the following we will focus on the period c.4000–1 BC, that is from the introduction of agriculture in southern parts of Scandinavia, through the Bronze Age up to the beginning of the early Iron Age. This long-term perspective will allow us to illustrate the diversity in forager–farmer interaction chronologically and geographically. The data from Fennoscandia demonstrate that one model alone can explain neither the transition to farming, nor the form of interaction between foragers and farmers, even within this one region. Local strategic choices and other circumstances have led to different processes in different areas and periods.

We perceive the distinction between foragers and farmers as partly arbitrary. There is not necessarily, nor always, any clear-cut dichotomy between the two economies. Both invest in the landscape, both enter into constitutive relationships with the natural environment (landscape, plants, fauna, and other resources), and their economic organization may in both cases tend to have a conservative effect, hindering or delaying incompatible innovations or introductions. The following is, however, based on the traditional distinction between groups growing crops (e.g. barley and wheat) and keeping domesticated animals (e.g. sheep and cattle) and those living exclusively on fishing, hunting, and gathering.

FIGURE 39.1 Fennoscandia with geographical features, regions, and place names mentioned in the text.

Northern Fennoscandian Hunter-Gatherers: Background

The northern regions were settled early in the Holocene from several directions. There is much to suggest that the earliest inhabitants in the north came along the Atlantic coastline from south-western Norway to the Barents Sea and the Kola peninsula. Dates from Finnmark are as early as c.9500 cal BC (Grydeland 2005). The more easterly regions were settled partly from the south-east, as the land rose, with the earliest dates on the Karelian Isthmus around 8800 cal BC (Carpelan 2008). Other immigrants may have entered the area further north as suggested by the evidence from Sujala in northern Finland with dates at around 8300–8200 cal BC (Rankama and Kankaanpää 2008). Some groups on the Atlantic coast ventured across the Scandes mountains into northern Sweden some time during the boreal period, probably shortly after 8000 cal BC (Bergman et al. 2004; Forsberg 1996a;

Olofsson 2003). When, if, and how these various immigrant groups met and interacted is at present uncertain (Damm 2006). Nevertheless, the region would have been multicultural from the very beginning.

Resource exploitation would have varied across the region. Along the coasts fishing, sealing, and possibly whaling would have predominated, while there is evidence of hunting for elk, bear, reindeer, and beaver in the inland regions (presumably in addition to freshwater fishing) (Bjerck 2007; 2008; Forsberg 1996a; Halinen 2005; Rankama and Ukkonen 2001).

Settlement patterns and mobility vary in time and space. While the habitation prior to 4500–4000 BC in general appears to have been characterized by small groups and a high degree of mobility (Bjerck 1989; Forsberg 1996a; Halinen 2005), the period around 4000–2000 BC saw the development of larger semi-subterranean houses across the region, suggesting long-term occupation, although perhaps on a seasonal basis (Helskog 1984; Lundberg 1997; Norberg 2008; Ranta 2002).

As there is no flint in the bedrock in the region, other lithic materials dominate (quartz, quartzite, chert, rock crystal, jasper, slate, and greenstone). There is marked chronological variation as well, with polished slate tools being significant in the inventory in north-western parts of the region around 4500–1500 BC. Unfortunately, organic materials, both tools, macrofossils and osteological data, are rarely preserved.

First Forager–Farmer Contacts

The first evidence of agriculture in central Europe dates to about 5500 BC. However, the expansion of farming and husbandry into Scandinavia did not occur until roughly 1,500 years later, around 4000/3900 BC (Fischer 2002; Larsson 2007; Persson 1999; Price 2000; Zvelebil and Rowley-Conwy 1984). There is evidence of contact between the northern Mesolithic societies and the farmers within the Linear Pottery societies (LBK) through the better part of the period in the form of imports, as well as inspiration for certain local artefacts and customs (T-shaped antler axes and burials), with the largest number of imports (as well as variety of types) dated to the period 4300–4000 BC, i.e. immediately before or even contemporary with the transition to farming (Klassen 2004, 101). In spite of this there are no indications of the new economies in southern Scandinavia until 4000 BC, when both agriculture and husbandry spread across Denmark and southern Sweden up to Mälardalen in central Sweden and the Oslofjord region respectively, and possibly along the southern coast of Norway to the coastal areas of south-western Norway. There was practically no farming east of the Oslofjord area, but some husbandry along the southern coast is possibly indicated in the pollen records (Myhre and Øye 2002, 31). The cultural transition appears to have been accomplished very rapidly with corresponding dates from the entire region (Price 2000, 271), although the full implementation of the new economy was not completed until 3600–3500 BC (Fischer 2002; Price 2000, 299). While the new economic elements and associated material culture such as pottery and polished flint axes spread widely, several of the more prominent features of the Early Neolithic TRB (Funnel Beaker Culture) such as monumental tombs (long barrows and dolmens) were incorporated only to a minor degree in the northernmost farming communities, indicating some cultural and economic variation within the wider TRB phenomenon.

North of these areas hunting and fishing persisted. During the Early Neolithic (4000–3400 BC) there was a clearly delimited northern boundary for the TRB farming communities in eastern central Sweden, roughly along the River Dalälven (e.g. Hallgren 2008, 242-6, 277). Only limited amounts of material culture appear to have crossed this geographical boundary. Some TRB types such as polygonal axes and a few thin-butted flint axes are found further north. Similarly a small number of slate artefacts have been found south of Dalälven (Hallgren 2008, 236; Hallgren 2012; Taffinder 1998). This economic and cultural boundary is interpreted also as the border between social units that stretch back into the Mesolithic (Hallgren 2003; Knutsson et al. 1999, 114-17; Knutsson et al. 2003).

The existence of several Mesolithic social units has been argued by Knutsson et al. (2003) on the basis of the distribution of technological traits. While there are some indications of a very widespread Scandinavian technological network in the middle Mesolithic (c.7000–5200 BC), a border appears in the late Mesolithic stretching from eastern central Sweden across to south-western Norway (Knutsson et al. 2003, 420). The hunter-gatherers settled south of this were integrated in the Ertebølle social and technological network (for groups in Denmark and Scania from 5500 to 5200 BC, for groups in the remaining parts of southern and central Sweden and southern Norway from about 4500 BC). There are noticeable differences in, for instance, lithic technology, with macroblades common north of this border, while round-butted axes are found only south of it (Knutsson et al. 1999, 104, 114).

These technological and cultural differences are argued to represent borders between social units corresponding to possible dialect tribes, language families, and marriage networks (Hallgren 2003; Knutsson et al. 1999). While some suggest rather large social units (e.g. Denmark, south-eastern Norway and southern and middle Sweden as one unit, at least with regard to selected technologies (Knutsson et al. 1999, 116)), others argue for numerous regional groups within this area (Bergsvik 2006; Boaz 1998; Klassen 2004, 227-8. Similarly, some argue for long-term continuity in the units (Knutsson et al. 1999), while others see changes, for instance at the transition to the TRB (Klassen 2004, 361). Klassen further argues that communication was rapid within and between such units, due to frequent interaction, this assisting the transmissn of innovations and cultural and economic change.

The existence of such social units that were predominantly endogamous with regard to the transmission of technological skills and perhaps marriage partners (although for a different point of view see Fuglestvedt 1999), would explain why the new economy spread quickly within certain areas but not across to the next group. In other words, each social unit made a strategic choice as to whether or not to adopt the new cultural and economic concepts. In the early Neolithic there is much to suggest that both foragers and farmers maintained a distinctive repertoire, clearly distinguishing them from each other. It is more than likely that the relationship also included various derogatory terms based on mutual (or perhaps one-sided) exclusion and stigmatization (Damm 2010). This does not necessarily mean that there was little interaction across the cultural border, but it does suggest that contact was organized according to rather categorical identities.

As in central Sweden, there is little detectable contact between foragers and farmers in Early Neolithic Norway. Nearly all point-butted axes and polygonal axes are found in the Oslofjord area. As for the thin-butted axes they seem to be somewhat more widespread (Østmo 2007, 115). The data suggest that contacts and interaction between foragers and farmers took place along the coast rather than across mountain regions (Bergsvik 2006, 134), with the probable exception of contacts from the Oslofjord-area to Trøndelag (Alsaker 2005).

Although there was probably contact between farming communities in the Oslofjord area and adjacent hunter-gatherers, artefacts belonging to the farmers were for the most part not transported or exchanged any great distance away from their cultural source. In other words, the picture is very similar to the one encountered in Sweden.

Altogether this suggests a situation where foragers and farmers established and maintained fairly strict cultural distinctions. While some knowledge of the economic, social, and religious changes in southern parts of Scandinavia would have existed in the hunting communities in the immediate vicinity, it is uncertain how far north such information would have travelled. The fourth millennium BC saw an increase in emphasis and elaboration of inter-regional contacts and interaction between hunter-gatherer communities within northern Fennoscandia, as evidenced in import and exchange of copper, amber, red slate, and eastern flint. If the focus amongst the hunting communities was predominantly towards the north and east, then the events further south may have been a secondary backdrop at this point in time.

Intensified Interaction: Exotic Imports

In the early part of the Middle Neolithic (MN A c.3400–2800 BC) there is a marked decline in agricultural activity in the northernmost areas with farming and husbandry. In eastern central Sweden subsistence is once again dominated by hunting and fishing. Much the same has been suggested for Norway, although this is still under debate (Myhre 2002, 32; Østmo 2007, 115). This may be linked to the strong hunter-fisher networks that existed partly within northern Fennoscandia in the fourth and third millennium BC mentioned above, but which also had strong links with the Baltic and further east (Zvelebil 2008). Further south (Denmark and southern Sweden) agro-pastoral communities consolidated themselves with an increased emphasis on farming (predominantly wheat) and husbandry (pigs, sheep/goat and cattle). Burials took place in megalithic tombs, and settlement sizes increased. These southernmost Scandinavian regions were clearly integrated in the wider continental Neolithic network. Still, some Middle Neolithic TRB types (double-edged battle axes and thick-butted flint axes) found their way far north.

Most of the TRB finds (Early as well as Middle Neolithic) within hunter-gatherer areas are stray finds without secure context. An interesting aspect of the early forager–farmer interaction is that certain types of axes seem to have been favoured over others, and that preferences vary from region to region. Early Neolithic polygonal stone axes were favoured in the east, while the contemporary thin-butted flint axes are more widespread in the west (Hallgren 2012). In the Middle Neolithic only a few thick-butted flint axes found their way into central Scandinavia, while the rarer double-edged axes are relatively more common (Østmo 1999). The majority of the imported artefacts are complete. In other words, the flint axes do not seem to have been valued as raw material.

From about 2500 BC in the Middle Neolithic (MN B 2800–2350 BC) there was a marked increase in imported artefacts found in the far north, beyond Neolithic farming communities. These include thick-butted flint axes and battle axes of greenstone. This increase coincided with marked changes in the Neolithic communities of southern Scandinavia and the emergence of Beaker and Battle Axe groups. These agro-pastoral communities appear to have had a stronger reliance on cattle and pastoralism, barley rather than wheat was the preferred crop, and they are presumed to have had a less sedentary settlement pattern than the TRB farmers.

Stray finds of battle axes of south Scandinavian types seem to occur in five to six larger clusters from the lower reaches of the Dalälven River up to the northernmost part of the Bothnian Bay (Figure 39.2). It has been argued that these stray finds as well as those from earlier phases of the Neolithic are the results of exchange between local coast-based hunter-gatherers and the established agro-pastoralists in the Mälar area. This explanation of the distribution is to a large degree probable, but there are also a few indications of direct migration and pioneer settlement in the area. At the Bjurselet settlement in the northern part of the coast, it has been shown that a brief settlement of people with a lithic technology with marked south Scandinavian traits is connected with the caches of thick-butted flint axes there (Knutsson 1988). This short episode of direct settlement seems to have been followed by a reuse of the site by local hunter-gatherers, as evidenced by the use of the available flint according to local reduction methods. That there are several other short-lived sites with south Scandinavian assemblages situated within the clusters, points to a phase where the contacts have not only been based upon long-distance relationships, but on the presence of direct contacts in a local area. In accordance with post-colonial terminology these settlements might be termed settler colonies (Ashcroft et al. 2000, 193).

Looking at the distribution of these clusters, they tend to occur on the coast between the estuaries of the large rivers. The settler colonies, as evidenced by the sites and the caches of flint axes, tend to have been located in fertile valleys on the lower reaches of smaller forest rivers, away from the main rivers. This type of settlement frequently seems to have been somewhat retracted (5–15 km) from the coast. As these settler colonies evidently were not evenly spread along the coast, it is clear that there was no agro-pastoral 'wave of advance', rather the picture is one of scattered impact with 'bridgeheads' in four to five smaller regions.

There is no evidence of any such settler colonies on the Atlantic coast north of Trondheim. In the Trøndelag region there was a distinct concentration of both battle axes and flint axes from this period (Alsaker 2005, 74). Although there is as of yet no direct evidence of agro-pastoralism in pollen diagrams or as macrofossils, this may suggest the existence of an established farming community in the area. Another indication of this may be that nearly half of the battle axes in the area appear to be locally produced (they are incomplete, being discarded preforms lacking shaft hole, still unpolished, etc.) (Asprem 2005, 72).

Further north the imported artefacts appear to be integrated in the local setting. However, battle axes as well as flint axes do seem to cluster in particular areas, suggesting that some regions or groups had better contacts with or for some reason were more attractive to the farmers. In several cases the clusters coincide with locations that today are considered good agricultural areas. There is, however, no indication of any experimentation with agricultural practices at this point in time, and the locations may have been considered favourable for other reasons. Similarly when considering the distribution of stray finds from the Late Neolithic in northern Sweden, the Storsjö area stands out. The imports to this area are found where there are very few hunter-gatherer sites, but where the later Iron Age agricultural settlements cluster (Janson et al. 1962, 73).

As along the Bothnian coast, by far the majority of the axes found in Trøndelag and further north along the Atlantic coast are associated with agro-pastoral societies in southern Sweden rather than in Denmark, indicating that contacts were not necessarily dictated by

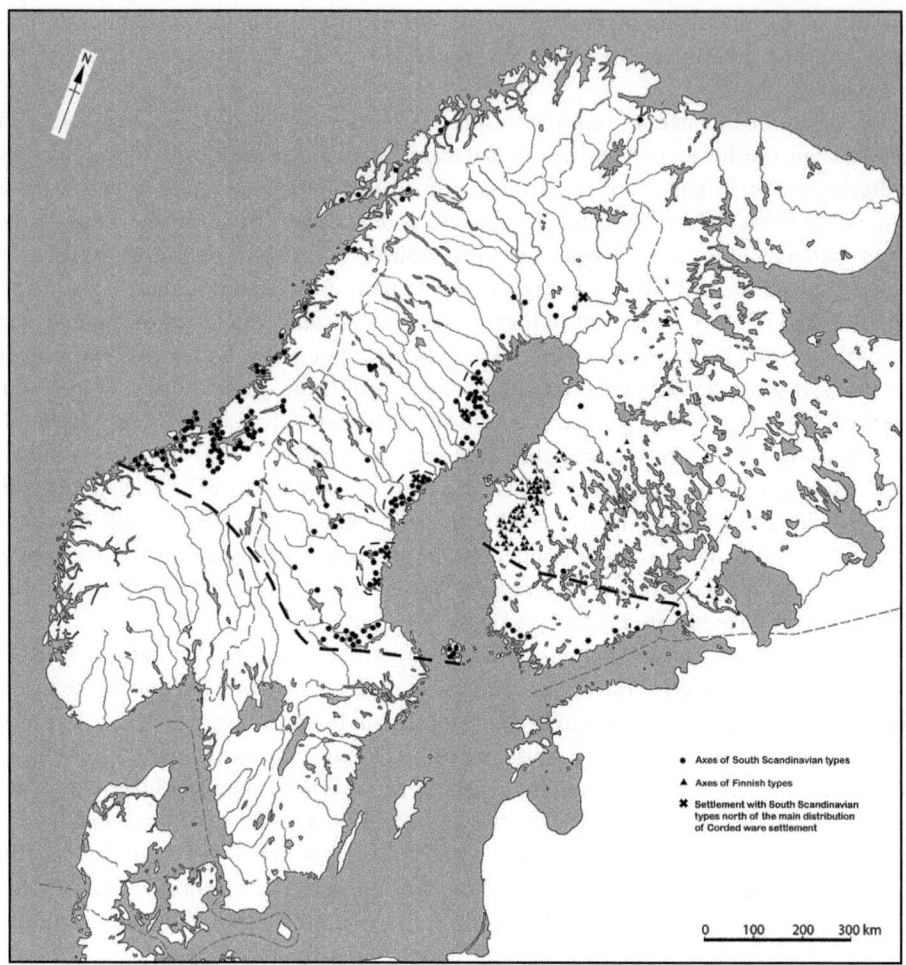

FIGURE 39.2 Distribution of battle axes of the TRB and Corded Ware cultures in northern areas. The thick dashed lines delimit the northern distribution of these axes from their main distribution in southern Scandinavia and south-western Finland. The thinner dashed lines mark clusters of such axes along the Bothnian coast. (Based on maps by Baudou 1989, figure 39.1; Broadbent 1982, 61; Asprem 2005, figures 14 and 24; Huurre 1998, 321 with some later additions).

shorter distance, but rather depended on specific patterns of interaction, which may again be dependent on historical circumstances and transportation routes.

Close Encounters

In the course of the later part of the Middle Neolithic (MN B 2800–2350 BC) and more extensively in the Late Neolithic (LN 2350–1900 BC), farming expanded northwards once again, and was quickly consolidated in the new regions (Figure 39.3). The relationship between foragers and farmers now appears to take a very different form with more conspicuous interaction.

During the Late Neolithic, agriculture and animal husbandry were well established along the Norwegian west coast up to the Trøndelag area and there have been finds of coastal settlements with long houses and traces of agricultural practices (Bakka and Kaland 1971; Bergsvik and Hufthammer 2009; Diinhoff 2006; Myhre and Øye 2002). During this period there was apparently a contact network along the coast all the way from northern Jutland up to the Trøndelag area. This is suggested by the distribution of elaborate flint daggers along the coast as well as a few local centres with dagger production (Apel 2001). While the distributions of artefacts from Neolithic societies were unevenly spread and clustered during the MN B, the Late Neolithic flint daggers are found much more widely along the coast and into the fjords on the Atlantic coast. Surprisingly we do not see a similar even spread north of the

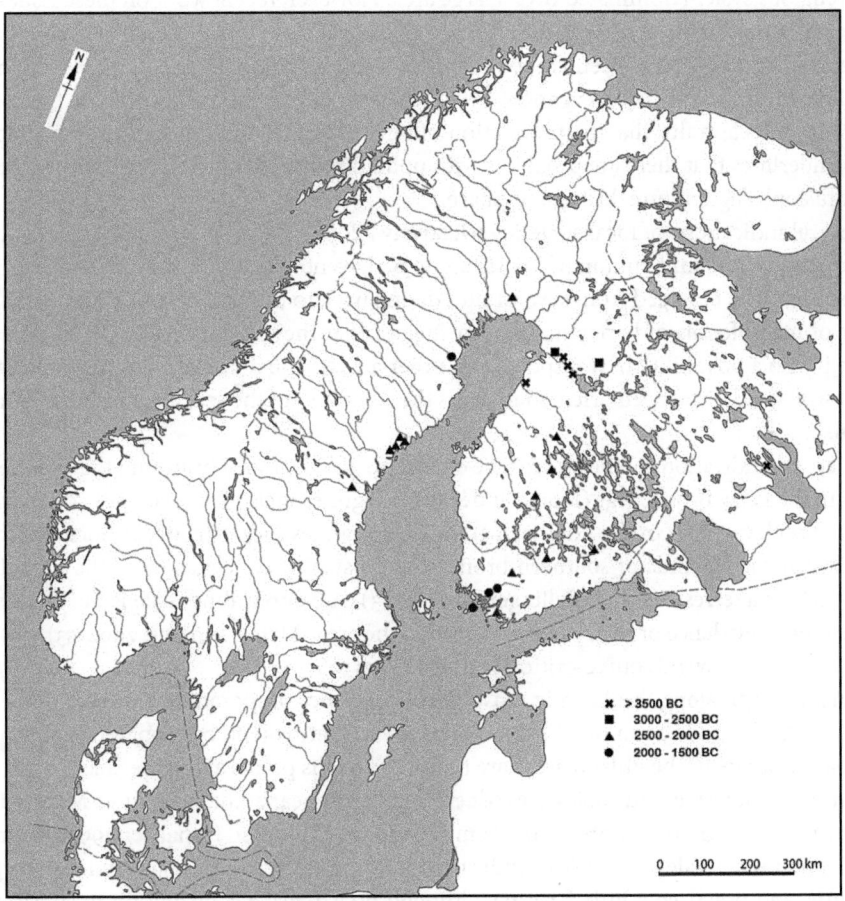

FIGURE 39.3 Map of the dating of cereal pollen. The Finnish data are derived from Mökkönen 2010, figure 39.1, and the Swedish data from Christiansson and Knutsson 1989; Engelmark 1997; Gustafsson and Spång 2007; Huttunen and Tolonen 1972.

Mälar region in central Sweden. Again there are different regional responses amongst the foragers in northern Scandinavia.

Societies along the west coast of the Bothnian Sea appear to have started to experiment with agriculture during the MNB phase. There is direct evidence of agriculture from a few pollen cores (Rudetjärn in Medelpad, Anundsjö in Ångermanland, and Bjurselet in Västerbotten) and sites with carbonized grains (Bjästamon and Lill-Mosjön in Ångermanland) (Christianson and Knutsson 1989; Engelmark 1997; Huttunen and Tolonen 1972; Lindholm and Runeson 2007; Runeson 2007). The early use of barley in this area makes sense, as this crop is more hardy when it comes to temperature and soil variations than wheat or barley. It is therefore more suited to farming in marginal areas than the other crop types.

The occurrence of coastal stone cairns and some bronzes of southern Scandinavian origin have frequently been taken as indications that the Bothnian coasts of Sweden and Finland in the second millennium BC became part of the Nordic Bronze Age culture (c.1900–500 BC) (Kristiansen 1987; Lavento 2005). The cairns are taken as a sign that the same ideological and religious system dominated over a large area. However, recent work on these issues has shown a more complicated picture (Forsberg 1999; Ikäheimo 2005; Okkonen 2003). Based on land uplift data, it has been argued that the cairn tradition may be at least as old in the north as in the south (Forsberg 1999; Okkonen 2003). Other characteristics of these sites show more local traits, like the production of bifacial points and usage of quartz scrapers. This underlines that there are problems with upholding the view of a large-scale migration or diffusion of agriculture during this phase.

Several indications of local societies selectively adopting agro-pastoral practices emerge during the second millennium BC (Forsberg 1999; Lavento 2005). Indications of sheep/goat husbandry have emerged from several sites dating back to the Early Bronze Age, and a few finds of macrofossils of barley might also suggest that they have been grown locally (but there is also a possibility of transport from other areas). The dominant economy along the coast would still have been oriented towards the resources of the sea, like marine mammals and fish.

There are indications of the emergence of an agro-pastoral society around the Trondheim fiord in the Early Bronze Age (Marstrander 1956; Sognnes 1993). This evidence comes in the form of rock carvings of the 'southern' tradition (Sognnes 1993), the occurrence of Bronze Age burial cairns, finds of southern bronzes, and osteological evidence of the pathological effects of a terrestrial diet (Fyllingen 2003, 32–3). A complicating issue is the absence of direct pollen evidence of barley in this period in the area (Myhre and Øye 2002, 53), but this might be due to several source-critical factors (Binns 1985).

Further north along the Atlantic coast there is evidence of sporadic clearance and heathland north of Trøndelag in the third millennium BC. Permanent, but apparently small and local anthropogenic heathland areas are found at various points along the coast in the second millennium cal BC. Reliable dates of cereal pollen appear at the same time. Macrofossils of cereals and domesticates are found from around 1500–1000 BC (Johansen 1990; Johansen and Vorren 1986; Valen 2007). This indicates that some communities had some sheep/goat or cattle, and practised a little farming, although no extensive contribution to subsistence need be inferred.

This northward spread of agricultural communities meant a new proximity between northern foragers and farmers in the late third and second millennia BC. It would appear that along the coasts of northern Scandinavia communities with different economic bases were interspersed with each other (Damm 2012). This resulted in an almost mosaic-like pattern of foragers and farmers (Forsberg 2012). There are several indications of direct interaction between foragers and farmers. Along both the Atlantic and the Bothnian coasts, local societies seemed to mix local material culture with items from the south Scandinavian agro-pastoral areas as well as from the eastern network.

During the Late Neolithic and the Early Bronze Age, flint daggers produced in southern Scandinavia are distributed along two major networks, one western and one eastern, as documented by Apel (2001, 307). Initially most of the daggers in the northernmost parts of Fennoscandia appear to have been transported along the west coast of Norway up to the Trøndelag area and then eastwards over the mountains to the Storsjö area. On the Atlantic coast daggers and other Late Neolithic imports are found continuously all the way up to the Arctic Circle and then more sporadically further north. After the initial phase of imported daggers from the Atlantic coast, daggers are almost absent north of the agricultural regions in Sweden. Again there are regional differences in preferences amongst the foragers.

Later bronzes of south Scandinavian types occurred among the local societies along the northern coasts (Bakka 1976; Ornell 1977; Skandfer 2009). The usage of burial cairns in these areas may also be related to the Nordic Bronze Age.

As noted above, many imports are located in areas that were well suited for early agriculture. In other parts of northern Fennoscandia such finds are located in the heartland of hunter-gatherers and are often found together with local artefacts. In other words, imports would appear to have been integrated partly in emerging agricultural societies as well as in forager groups.

While agro-pastoral practices were confined to the coastal areas, other fundamental changes occurred in the lifeways of the hunter-gatherer peoples in the interior of northern Fennoscandia from 2500 to 2000 BC and onwards. The changes included different raw materials for tools, different tool types, totally different settlement patterns with increased mobility, and changed economies (Forsberg 1989; Lavento 2005; Olsen 1994). It is safe to say of such profound changes brought about in both coastal and inland societies, that this must have been one of the most radical breaks in the societal development of northern Fennoscandia.

During the second millennium BC, societies of the interior seemed to employ logistical mobility to a much higher degree than in preceding periods. In northern Sweden these societies started to move into the mountain areas to the west, in addition to utilizing the forest plain. There seems to have been a widening of the resource base with an increased emphasis on reindeer hunting. The settlement pattern changed to one in which winter and spring settlement was located in the forest plain and base camps for reindeer hunting were moved up into the mountain foothills during the late summer and early autumn. The territorial map of these logistically based societies is radically different from the band territories of the Neolithic. It seems that a string of local societies based on river basins continued all the way from the southern part of Norrland up through the inland of northern Sweden to northern Norway (Bergman 1995; Forsberg 1985; Forsberg 2001; Holm 1991; Spång 1997). With minor changes, these societies upheld these ways of life throughout the second and first millennia. The intensification of the reindeer hunting should most probably be understood at least partly as a strategic response to new forms of interaction with the farming societies along the coast, producing large quantities of goods (hides, antler, furs) for exchange.

Other profound technological changes amongst the northern foraging communities involved the massive employment of the bifacial technique for producing arrowheads in vast quantities (related to the intensified reindeer hunting) (Forsberg 2010b; Holm 1991), the use of ceramic technology (Carpelan 2003; Forsberg 2001; Forsberg 2010a; Hulthén 1991; Jørgensen and Olsen 1988; Lavento 2001), and eventually the start of metallurgical activities (Forsberg 2010a; George 2001; Hulthén 1991; Olsen 1991). The latter two technologies both derived from interaction with societies towards the east, demonstrating again that when it came to learning networks and transmission of technological skills the northern foragers were more closely involved with these than with the farmers to the south, who had access to parallel technologies. The northern metalwork is to a large degree part of the Seima-Turbino tradition, suggesting indirect contacts with the metal-producing agro-pastoral societies of the forest plain in Russia. Textile pottery is an overarching category of quite different pottery styles spread all along the forests of north-eastern Europe that are characterized by textile or textile-like impressions on the outer surface of the vessel. As with most early metalwork, they point to contacts in an east–west direction along the boreal forest area.

FORAGER–FARMER DIVERSIFICATION DURING THE FIRST MILLENNIUM

During the first millennium BC there was a great diversity in the local societies along the coasts. In some areas, the incipient farming societies increased their dependence on the agro-pastoral resources (Baudou 1992, 113, 159; Engelmark 1997; Forsberg 1999; Ramqvist 2007). In other areas, the focus on marine resources seems even more pronounced than in the preceding period.

This increased focus on the utilization of marine resources by the local societies along the Bothnian coasts during the first millennium have been seen by some as a response to the cooler and wetter climate (Baudou 1992, 113–14). This increased marine focus has been observed in many places around the Bothnian coastal area (Forsberg 1999; Gustavsson 1987; Holmblad 2010; Ikaheimo 2005). In the northern part of this area large fields of cooking pits situated in the outer archipelago have been found (Forsberg 1999; Ikäheimo 2005; Okkonen 2003). They are the remains of a relatively large-scale production of seal train oil. Evidence of this can also be found at the southern limit of the Bothnian Sea, in the form of the abundant cairns of fire-cracked rocks in the Åland archipelago shown to be connected with train oil production (Gustavsson 1987). Some researchers suggest that this resource was used in the exchange for metal (Baudou 1992, 108). This could point to a new type of exchange network around the Bothnian coasts, based on specialization and surplus production.

The latter part of the first millennium saw the emergence of sedentary agricultural settlement on the coasts of the Bothnian Sea up to northern Ångermanland on the Swedish side and southern Ostrobothnia on the Finnish side (Baudou 1994; Liedgren 1992; Ramqvist 1983). Along the Norwegian coast, agricultural settlement occurred sporadically all the way to the north of Lofoten (Johansen 1990; Myhre and Øye 2002, 86). However, recent excavations unequivocally demonstrate an intensification in this area from about 400 BC (Arntzen and Sommerseth 2010).

Although the archaeological evidence from this phase is scanty, it is clear that most of the local societies employed economic strategies involving varying mixes of small-scale agriculture, animal husbandry, and, first and foremost, seal hunting and fishing.

The foragers in the inland of northern Sweden continued to pursue their mobile lifeways with annual settlement moves between the forest plain and the mountains to the west. A difference from the preceding period was that there seemed to be a marked split between the north and south parts of this huge area. In the northern part asbestos ware and bifacial points continued to be used as in the preceding millennium, suggesting a continuation of traditions from the second millennium BC. In these areas there is clear evidence that the contacts with eastern metal-producing societies continued and intensified. Axes and casting moulds of types that are common in the Ananino culture in the Volga-Kama area in central Russia are frequently found on sites in northern Finland, northern Sweden, and to a limited extent also in Finnmark in northern Norway (Forsberg 1996b; 2010b; Olsen 1984; Huurre 1986). In the later half of the millennium, iron production emerged, probably introduced from the Ananino culture, which was a centre of early iron production (Kosmenko and Manjuhin 1999; Mäkivuoti 1988; Olsen 1994). Asbestos ware of the Kjelmøy or Säräisniemi 2 type indicates a large contact network within the world of the northern hunter-gatherers (Carpelan 2003; Jørgensen and Olsen 1988).

In southern Norrland, the picture is more complicated. Here there are strong indications of interaction between the foragers and the Germanized agricultural societies to the south (Baudou 1989). The distributions of south Scandinavian bronzes from the late BA in the southern part of Norrland indicate this (Bolin 1999). Later, during the second half of the first millennium, so-called forest cemeteries located on large lakes emerged, exhibiting a mixture of south Scandinavian and local idiosyncratic traits. These were clearly associated with forager settlements (Ambrosiani et al. 1984; Bergstøl 2009; Sundström 1989). This suggests that a number of local societies in southern Norrland and eastern Norway chose a strategy that differed both from the agro-pastoralists to the south, west, and east and from the hunter-gatherers to the north of them, which resulted in hybrid material culture, a situation that became even more marked in the first millennium AD (Bergstøl 2009).

During this first millennium BC agro-pastoralism expanded and consolidated in northern Fennoscandia. It seems that a clear division between the foragers in the southern and northern parts of northern Scandinavia emerged. This is also underlined by the different direction and character of their contacts. The local societies along the coasts also seemed to differentiate, with the southern parts of the Bothnian coast and the societies along the Norwegian west coast converging more to the agro-pastoral mould of late Bronze Age and early Iron Age societies further south, and with coastal societies in Finnmark and the northern Bothnian area having a heavy marine focus (Broadbent 2010; Olsen 1994).

Conclusion

In northern Fennoscandia we have evidence of forager–farmer interaction over many millennia. In the course of this time agro-pastoralism gradually expanded northwards, but not in the form of a wave-of-advance colonization. After the initial introduction around 4000 BC there was a retraction of the northern limit of agriculture. Later expansion in the third and second millennia BC seems to take the form partly of settler colonies and partly of local adaptation of agro-pastoralist practices, creating a mosaic of farmers and foragers in the northern landscape. More widespread farming and consolidation in northern Fennoscandia took place only in the late first millennium BC.

Similarly the interaction between foragers and farmers did not follow any straightforward pattern. During the first agro-pastoral phase evidence of direct interaction in the form of exchange of items is very limited, and there is marked differentiation between foragers and farmers, manifesting exclusive identities. In the next phase (third millennium BC) interaction appears to increase. One new aspect during this period is the concentrations along the coasts interpreted either as settler colonies or as forager communities with more intensive contacts with farmers.

The intensification of interaction is perhaps most evident in the number of imports from agro-pastoral communities into foraging groups (mostly axes and daggers). Their purpose within the hunting societies is unlikely to have been purely functional (Østmo 2000). The most recent interpretations of these objects view them as playing social and/or ritual roles even in their northern contexts. They have also been interpreted as indications of conformity-seeking practices in order to maximize the benefit of the contacts (Olsen 1988). In other contexts increased imports have been considered to be a sign of inflation in the need for items in socio-political strategies and stratification (Fischer 2002, 382).

As farming societies gradually expanded northwards in the second millennium BC the interaction altered. Foragers and farmers were now more regularly in direct contact with each other. The intensified reindeer hunting in the interior must be understood in this context, with a growing number of communities that were not hunting for themselves, but still required hides for example. We do not know what goods and services were given in return (apart from prestige goods such as daggers and bronze).

During the first millennium BC a significant geographical diversification was established, with foraging communities in more southern regions interacting with late Bronze Age and early Iron Age societies in southern Scandinavia, and with the northernmost foragers consolidating relations with distant metallurgical societies towards the east. In this phase the specialization initiated in the second millennium BC appears to have played a significant role (hunting, seal oil production, farming products). Large-scale surplus production of selected goods eventually became an integral part of the interaction between foragers and farmers. While the exchange in the fourth and third millennia BC would appear to have been almost exclusively linked to socio-political relations, the economic aspects now become more pronounced with what must be presumed to be regular trade exchange.

While on the one hand there are undeniable similarities across northern Fennoscandia with regard to the forager–farmer interaction trajectory, it is also possible to document very distinctive regional variations. Different foraging groups selected to integrate different types of imported goods into their repertoire (e.g. thin-butted flint axes versus polygonal stone axes in the Early Neolithic, and the lack of flint daggers in southern Swedish Norrland in the Late Neolithic). In the first millennium BC the regional preferences led to distinct geographical orientations, towards the south and the east respectively. Quite obviously the local hunter-gatherer societies made different strategic choices. In some cases these may have been due to different conditions for interaction with respect to proximity to agro-pastoralists and transportation routes. In other cases local communities seem to have developed distinct social preferences and strategies, as in what axes were of interest or whether to engage in closer relationships with the agro-pastoralists or not.

The diachronic perspective of forager–farmer interactions in northern Fennoscandia, transcending modern national borders, has enabled an overview where variations in historical trajectories and regional social strategies become more apparent. The development from the first introduction of agro-pastoralist practices up to strategic specialization and trade exchange does not follow any direct evolutionary pattern. Most importantly, it is evident that the northern foragers made individual choices with regard to social and economic strategies for interaction.

Acknowledgements

This chapter is an output of the international research project 'Early Networking in Northern Fennoscandia' that was hosted by the Centre for Advanced Study at the Norwegian Academy of Science and Letters, Oslo, during the 2008–9 academic year. The chapter benefited from discussions with colleagues in the project, notably Dr Fredrik Hallgren, University of Uppsala, Sweden.

References

Alsaker, S. K. 2005. Fra jeger til bonde. In I. Bull (ed.), *Trøndelags historie*, bd 1, 59–81. Trondheim: Tapir akademisk forlag.

Ambrosiani, B., Iregren, E., and Lahtiperä, P. 1984. *Gravfält i fångstmarken*. Stockholm: Riksantikvarie-ämbetet och Statens historiska museer.

Apel, J. E. 2001. *Daggers, knowledge and power: the social aspects of flint-dagger technology in Scandinavia 2350–1500 cal BC*. Uppsala: Department of Archaeology and Ancient History, Uppsala University.

Ashcroft, B., Griffiths, G., and Tiffin, H. 2000. *Post-colonial studies: the key concepts*. London: Routledge.

Arntzen, J. E. and Sommerseth, I. 2010. *Den første gården i Nord-Norge. Jordbruksbosetting fra bronsealder til jernalder på Kveøy*. Tromsø: Tromura, Tromsø Museums rapportserie 39.

Asprem, F. 2005. *Jordbrukets røtter i Midt-Norge. En forskningsstatus*. Trondheim: NTNU.

Bakka, E. 1976. Arktisk og nordisk i bronsealderen i Nord-Skandinavien. *Miscellenea* 25. Trondheim.

Bakka, E. and Kaland, P. E. 1971. Early farming in Hordaland, Western Norway. *Norwegian Archaeological Review* 4, 1–35.

Baudou, E. 1989. Gränser och center-periferi-förhållanden i Norrlands bronsålder. In J. Poulsen (ed.), *Regionale forhold i Nordisk Bronzealder. 5. Nordiske Symposium for Bronzealderforskning på Sandbjerg Slot 1987*, 175–84. Aarhus: Jysk Arkæologisk Selskab Skrifter XXIV.

Baudou, E. 1992. *Norrlands forntid—ett historisk perspektiv*. Höganäs: Wiken.

Baudou, E. 1994. Den tidigare forskningen och den yngre järnålderns bebyggelse i Österbotten. In E. Baudou, R. Engelmark, L. Liedgren, U. Segerström, and J.-E. Wallin (eds), *Järnåldersbygd i Österbotten. En ekologisk-arkeologisk studie av bosättningskontinuitet och resursutnyttjande*, 18–27. Vasa: Acta Antiqua Ostrobothnia 2.

Bergman, I. 1995. *Från Döudden till Varghalsen. En studie av kontinuitet och förändring innom ett fångstsamhälle i övre Norrlands innland, 5200 f.Kr. – 400 e.Kr.* Umeå: Studia Archaeologica Universitatis Umensis 7.

Bergman, I., Olofsson, A., Hörnberg, G., Zackrisson, O., and Hellberg, E. 2004. Deglaciation and colonization: pioneer settlements in northern Fennoscandia. *Journal of World Prehistory* 18, 155–77.

Bergstøl, J. 2009. *Samer i Østerdalen? En studie av etnisitet i jernalderen og middelalderen i det nordøstre Hedmark.* Oslo: Acta Humaniora 325, Universitetet i Oslo.

Bergsvik, K. A. 2006. *Ethnic boundaries in Neolithic Norway.* Oxford: BAR International Series 1554.

Bergsvik, K. A. and Hufthammer, A. K. 2009. Stability and change among marine hunter-fishers in western Norway 7000–4500 BC: results from the excavations of two rockshelters. In P. Crombé (ed.), *Chronology and evolution in the Mesolithic of N(W) Europe*, 435–49. Cambridge: Cambridge Scholars Publishing.

Binns, K. S. 1985. De første tegn til jordbruk. In K. Pettersen and B. Wik (eds), *Helgeland Historie*. Bd. 1, 148–70. Mosjøen: Helgeland Historielag.

Bjerck, H. B. 1989. Mesolithic site types and settlement patterns at Vega, Northern Norway. *Acta Archaeologica* 60, 1–32.

Bjerck, H. B. 2007. Mesolithic coastal settlements and shell middens (?) in Norway. In N. Milner, O. E. Craig, and G. N. Bailey (eds), *Shell middens in Atlantic Europe*, 5–30. Oxford: Oxbow.

Bjerck, H. B. 2008. Norwegian Mesolithic trends: a review. In G. Bailey and P. Spikins (eds), *Mesolithic Europe*, 60–106. Cambridge: Cambridge University Press.

Boaz, J. 1998. *Hunter-gatherer site variability: changing patterns of site utilization in the interior of eastern Norway, between 8000 and 2500 BP.* Oslo: Universitets Oldsaksamling skifter.

Bolin, H. 1999. Crossroads of culture: aspects of the social and cultural setting in northern Sweden during the two last millennia BC. In H. Bolin (ed.), *Kulturlandskapets korsvägar. Mellersta Norrland under de två sista årtusendena f. K.r.*, 97–138. Stockholm: Stockholm Studies in Archaeology 19.

Broadbent, N. 1982. *Skelleftebygden historia.* Uppsala: Almquist & Wiksell.

Broadbent, N. D. 2010. *Lapps and LABYRINTHS: Saami prehistory, colonization and cultural resilience.* Washington, DC: Smithsonian Institution.

Carpelan, C. 2003. Varhaismetallikausi (1900 e.Kr. – 300 j.Kr.). In V.-P. Lehtola (ed.), *Inari/Aanaar. Inarin historia jääkaudesta nykypäivään*, 45–58. Oulu: Painotalo Suomenmaa.

Carpelan, C. 2008. On the history and recent studies of the 'Antrea Net Find'. In M. Lavento (ed.), *Karelian Isthmus: Stone Age studies in 1998–2003*, 88–127. Helsinki: Iskos.

Christianson, H. and Knutsson, K. 1989. *The Bjurselet Setlement III*, 2 vols. Uppsala: OPIA.

Damm, C. 2006. Interregional contacts across northern Fennoscandia 6000–4000 BC. In J. Arneborg and B. Grønnow (eds), *Dynamics of northern societies. Proceedings of the SILA/NABO Conference on Arctic and North Atlantic Archaeology*, 199–208. Copenhagen: PNM, Publications from the National Museum, Studies in Archaeology and History, Vol. 10.

Damm, C. 2010. Ethnicity and collective identities in the Fennoscandian Stone Age. In Å. Larsson and L. Papmehl-Dufay (eds), *Uniting sea II: Stone Age societies in the Baltic Sea region*, 11–30. Uppsala: OPIA 51, Department of Archaeology and Ancient History, Uppsala University.

Damm, C. 2012. Approaching a complex past: entangled collective identities. In N. Anfinset and M. Wrigglesworth (eds), *Local societies, identities and responses: the Bronze Age in Northern Europe*, 13–30. London: Equinox.

Diinhoff, S. 2006. En bronzealders bosætning ved Fremre Øygarden i Lærdal. In R. Barndon, S. Innselset, K. Klæboe Kristoffersen, and T. K. Lødøen (eds), *Samfunn, symboler og identitet— Festskrift til Gro Mandt på 70-årsdagen*, 67–86. Bergen: UBAS Nordisk 3.

Engelmark, R. 1997. Övergången bronsålder/järnålder i Mellannorrland. In K. Gullberg (ed.), *Arkeologi i Mittnorden. Ett symposium kring nya arkeologiska forskningsrön*, 45–52. Vasa: Studier i Österbottens förhistoria 4.

Fischer, A. 2002. Food for feasting? An evaluation of explanations of the Neolithisation of Denmark and Southern Sweden. In A. Fischer and K. Kristiansen (eds), *The Neolithisation of Denmark. 150 years of debate*, 343–93. Sheffield: J. R. Collis Publications.

Forsberg, L. 1985. *Site variability and settlement patterns: an analysis of the hunter-gatherer settlement system in the Lule River Valley, 1500 B.C.-B.C./A.D.* Umeå: University of Umeå, Department of Archaeology.

Forsberg, L. 1989. Economic and social change in the Interior of Northern Sweden 6000 BC–1000 AD. In T. Larsson and H. Lundmark (eds), *Approaches to Swedish prehistory*, 55–82. Oxford: BAR International Series 500.

Forsberg, L. 1996a. The earliest settlement of northern Sweden: problems and perspectives. In L. Larsson (ed.), *The earliest settlement of Scandinavia and its relationship with neighbouring areas*, 241–50. Lund: Acta Archaeologica Lundensia.

Forsberg, L. 1996b. Forskningslinjer inom tidig samisk förhistoria. *Arkeologi i Norr* 6/7, 165–86.

Forsberg, L. 1999. The Bronze Age site of Mårtenfäboda in Nysätra and the settlement context of the Cairns on the coast of North Sweden. In M. Huurre (ed.), *Dig it all: papers dedicated to Ari Siiriainen*, 251–85. Helsinki: The Finnish Antiquarian Society, The Archaeological Society of Finland.

Forsberg, L. 2001. Keramikken från Råingetlokalarna. Mångfold i tid och formspråk. In M. Bergvall and O. George (eds), *Tidspår. Forntidsvärld och gränslöst kulturarv*, 129–50. Härnösand, Länsmuseet Västernorrland.

Forsberg, L. 2010a. A consideration of the role of bifacial lithic technology in northern Scandinavia. In R. Barndon, I. Øye, and A. Engevik (eds), *The archaeology of regional technologies*, 127–48. Lewiston: Mellen Press.

Forsberg, L. 2010b. The spread of new technologies in Early Fennoscandia: a view without borders. In W. Østreng (ed.), *Transference. Interdisciplinary communications 2008/2009*. Internet publication: http://www.cas.uio.no/Publications/Seminar/0809Forsberg.pdf. Oslo: Centre for Advanced Study.

Forsberg, L. 2012. Asymmetric twins? Some reflections on coastal and inland societies in the Bothnian area during the Epi-Neolithic and Early Metal Ages. In N. Anfinset and M. Wrigglesworth (eds), *Local societies, identities and responses: the Bronze Age in Northern Europe*, 31–55. London: Equinox.

Fuglestvedt, I. 1999. Inter-regional contact in the late Mesolithic: the productive gift extended. In J. Boaz (ed.), *The Mesolithic of central Scandinavia*, 27–38. Oslo: Universitets Oldsaksamlings Skrifter.

Fyllingen, H. 2003. Society and violence in the Early Bronze Age: an analysis of human skeletons from Nord-Trøndelag, Norway. *Norwegian Archaeological Review* 36, 27–43.

George, O. 2001. Boplatsen vid Råinget. *Tidsspår* 2001, 105–28.

Grydeland, S. E. 2005. The pioneers of Finnmark: from the earliest coastal settlements to the encounter with the inland people of Northern Finland. In H. Knutsson (ed.), *Pioneer settlements and colonization process in the Barents region*, 43–78. Vuollerim: Vuollerim Papers on Hunter-Gatherer Archaeology, vol. 1.

Gustafsson, P. and Spång, L.-G. (eds) 2007. *Stenålderns Stationer. Arkeologi i Botniabanans Spår*. Stockholm: Riksantikvarieämbetet.

Gustavsson, K. 1987. Charred-stone cairns on Kökar. In G. Burenhult, A. Carlsson, Å. Hyenstrand, and T. Sjøvold (eds), *Theoretical approaches to artefacts, settlement and society, part ii*, 364–77. Oxford: BAR International Series 366(ii).

Halinen, P. 2005. *Prehistoric hunters of northernmost Lapland: settlement patterns and subsistence strategies*. Helsinki: Finnish Antiquarian Society (Iskos 14).

Hallgren, F. 2003. My place or yours? In L. Larsson, H. Kindgren, K. Knutsson, D. Loeffler, and A. Åkerlund (eds), *Mesolithic on the move. Papers presented at the Sixth International Conference on the Mesolithic in Europe, Stockholm 2000*, 592–9. Oxford: Oxbow.

Hallgren, F. 2008. *Identitet i praktikk. Lokal, regionala och överregionala sociala sammanhang innom nordlig trattbägerkultur*. Uppsala: Department of Archaeology and Ancient History, Uppsala University.

Hallgren, F. 2012. A permeable border: long distance contacts between hunters and farmers in the Early Neolithic of Scandinavia. In C. Damm and J. Saarikivi (eds), *Networks, interaction and emerging identities in Fennoscandia and beyond*, 139–154. Mémoires de la Société Finno-Ugrienne 265. Helsinki: The Finno-Ugrian Society.

Helskog, K. 1984. The younger Stone Age settlements in Varanger, North Norway. *Acta Borealia* 1, 39–69.

Holm, L. 1991. *The use of stone and hunting of reindeer: a study of stone tool manufacture and hunting of large mammals in the central Scandes c. 6000–1 BC*. Umeå: Archaeology and Environment 12. University of Umeå, Department of Archaeology.

Holmblad, P. 2010. *Coastal communities on the move: house and polity interaction in southern Ostrobothnia 1500 BC–AD 1*. Umeå: Archaeology and Environment XX, University of Umeå.

Hulthén, B. 1991. *On ceramic ware in northern Scandinavia during the Neolithic, Bronze and early Iron Age*. Umeå: University of Umeå.

Huttunen, P. and Tolonen, M. 1972. Pollen-analytical studies of prehistoric agriculture in northern Ångermanland. In P. Huttunen, I. Olsson, K. Tolonen, and M. Tolonen (eds), *Palaeo-ecological investigations in northern Sweden*, 9–34. Stockholm: Early Norrland 1.

Huurre, M. 1986. The eastern contacts of northern Fennoscandia in the Bronze Age. *Fennoscandia Archaeologica* 3, 51–8.

Huurre, M. 1998. *Kivikauden Suomi*. Keuruu: Otava Kirjapaino.

Ikäheimo, J. 2005. Re-assessing the Bronze Age of coastal northern Ostrobothnia: the lower Oulujoki river valley. In J. Goldhahn (ed.), *Mellan sten och järn*, 771–80. Gothenburg: GOTARC Serie C.

Janson, S., Biörnstad, M., and Hvarfner, H. 1962. *Jämtlands och Härjedalens historia. Arkeologisk inledning*. Stockholm: Norstedts.

Johansen, O. S. 1990. *Synspunkter på jernalderens jordbrukssamfunn i Nord-Norge*. Tromsø: Universitetet i Tromsø.

Johansen, O. S. and Vorren, K.-D. 1986. The prehistoric expansion of farming into 'Arctic' Norway: a chronology based on 14C dating. *Radiocarbon* 28, 739–47.

Jørgensen, R. and Olsen, B. 1988. *Asbestkeramiske grupper i Nord-Norge, 2100 f.kr.—100 e.Kr*. Tromsø: Tromura kulturhistorie 13.

Klassen, L. 2004. *Jade und Kupfer. Untersuchungen zum Neolithisierungsprozess im westlichen Ostseeraum under besonderer Berücksichtigung der Kulturentwicklung Europas 5500–3500 BC*. Aarhus: Moesgård Museum, Jutland Archaeological Society Vol. 47.

Knutsson, K. 1988. *Making and using stone tools: the analysis of the lithic assemblages from middle Neolithic sites with flint in Västerbotten, Northern Sweden*. Uppsala: AUN 11, Societas Archaeologica Upsaliensis.

Knutsson, K., Falkenström, P., and Lindberg, K.-F. 2003. Appropriation of the past: Neolithisation in the Northern Scandinavian perspective. In L. Larsson, H. Kindgren, K. Knutsson, D. Loeffler, and A. Åkerlund (eds), *Mesolithic on the move. Papers presented at the Sixth International Conference on the Mesolithic in Europe, Stockholm 2000*, 414–29. Oxford: Oxbow.

Knutsson, K., Lindgren, C., Hallgren, F., and Björch, N. 1999. The Mesolithic in eastern central Sweden. In J. Boaz (ed.), *The Mesolithic of central Scandinavia*, 87–123. Oslo: Universitetet Oldsaksamlings Skrifter, Ny Rekke no. 22.

Kosmenko, M. G. and Manjuhin, I. S. 1999. Ancient iron production in Karelia. *Fennoscandia Archaeologica* 16, 31–46.

Kristiansen, K. 1987. Centre and periphery in Bronze Age Scandinavia. In M. Rowlands, M. Larsen, and K. Kristiansen (eds), *Centre and periphery in the ancient world*, 66–9. Cambridge: Cambridge University Press.

Larsson, L. 2007. Mistrust traditions, consider innovations? The Mesolithic–Neolithic transition in southern Scandinavia. In A. Whittle and V. Cummings (eds), *Going over: the Mesolithic–Neolithic transition in north-west Europe*, 595–616. Oxford: Oxford University Press.

Lavento, M. 2001. *Textile ceramics in Finland and on the Karelian Isthmus*. Vammala: Vammalan kirjapaino Oy.

Lavento, M. 2005. Coastal and inland early metal period in Finland: territorial, cultural or economical zones? In J. Goldhahn (ed.), *Mellan sten och järn*, 755–70. Gothenburg: GOTARC Serie C.

Liedgren, L. 1992. *Hus och gård i Hälsingland. En studie av agrar bebyggelse och bebyggelseutveckling i norra Hälsingland Kr.f. – 600 e.Kr.* Umeå: Studia Archaeologica Universitatis Umensis 2.

Lindholm, P. and Runeson, H. 2007. Lillmosjön: en dagsresa bort? In P. Gustafsson and L.-G. Spång (eds), *Stenålderns stationer. Arkeologi i Botniabanans spår*, 147–60. Stockholm: Riksantikvarieämbetet.

Lundberg, Å. 1997. *Vinterbyar, ett bandsamhälles territorier i Norrlands innland 4500–2500 f.kr.* Umeå: Studia Archaeologica Universitatis Umensis 8.

Mäkivuoti, M. 1988. *Esi- ja varhaishistoriallinen raudanvalmistus Pohjois-Suomessa. Sivuainelaudatur-tutkielma. Suomalainen ja vertaileva arkeologia*. Turun: Turun yliopisto.

Marstrander, S. 1956. Hovedlinjer i Trøndelags forhistorie. *Viking* 20, 1–69.

Mökkönen, T. 2010 Kivikautinen maanviljely Suomessa. *Suomen Museo* 2009, 5–38.

Myhre, B. and Øye, I. 2002. *Jorda blir levevei: 4000 f.Kr.–1350 e.Kr.* Oslo: Samlaget.

Norberg, E. 2008. *Boplatsvallen som bostad i Norrbottens kustland 5000–2000 före vår tideräkning. En studie av kontinuitet och förändringar*. Umeå: Umeå Universitet.

Okkonen, J. 2003. *Graves of giants and cairns of dread: the archaeology of Ostrobothnian stone structures*. Oulu: Acta Universitatis Ouluensis.

Olofsson, A. 2003. Early colonization of northern Norrland: technology, chronology and culture. In A. Olofsson (ed.), *Pioneer settlement in the Mesolithic of Northern Sweden*. Umeå: Department of Archaeology and Sami Studies, Umeå University.

Olsen, B. 1984. *Stabilitet og endring. Produksjon og samfunn i Varanger 800 f.Kr.–1700 e.Kr.* Mag. art. diss. Tromsø: University of Tromsø.

Olsen, B. 1988. Interaction between hunter-gatherers and farmers: ethnographical and archaeological perspectives. Dyskusje I polemiki. *Archaeologia Polski* 33, 425–32.

Olsen, B. 1991. Kjelmøyfunnenes (virknings) historie og arkeologi. *Viking* 54, 65–87.

Olsen, B. 1994. *Bosetning og samfunn i Finnmarks forhistorie*. Oslo: Universitetsforlaget.

Ornell, P.-E. 1977. *Lokalt bronshantverk i nordskandinavisk bronsålder? C-uppsats i arkeologi*. Gothenburg: University of Gothenburg.

Østmo, E. 1999. Double-edged axes under the Northern Lights: the northernmost finds of the Funnel Beaker Culture in Norway. *Acta Archaeologica* 70, 107–12.

Østmo, E. 2000. Elleve trønderske steinøkser. Traktbegerkulturen nordafjells. *Primitive Tider* 3, 80–101.

Østmo, E. 2007. The northern periphery of the TRB: graves and ritual deposits in Norway. *Acta Archaeologica* 78, 111–42.

Persson, P. 1999. *Neolitikums början*. Gothenburg: Gotarc Series B no. 11.

Price, T. D. 2000. The introduction of farming in northern Europe. In T. D. Price (ed.), *Europe's first farmers*, 260–300. Cambridge: Cambridge University Press.

Ramqvist, P. 1983. *Gene: on the origin, function and development of a sedentary Iron Age settlement in Northern Sweden*. Umeå: Umeå University.

Ramqvist, P. 2007. Fem Norrland. Norrländska regioner och deras interaktion. *Arkeologi i Norr* 10, 153–80.

Rankama, T. and Kankaanpää, J. 2008. Eastern arrivals in post-glacial Lapland: the Sujala site 10,000 cal BP. *Antiquity* 82, 884–99.

Rankama, T. and Ukkonen, P. 2001. On the early history of the wild reindeer (Rangifer tarandus L.) in Finland. *Boreas* 30, 131–47.

Ranta, H. (ed.) 2002. *Huts and houses: Stone Age and Early Metal Age buildings in Finland*. Helsinki: National Board of Antiquities.

Runeson, H. 2007. Den goda ordningen. In P. Gustafsson and L.-G. Spång (eds), *Stenålderns stationer. Arkeologi i Botniabanans spår*, 309–25. Stockholm: Riksantikvarieämbetet.

Skandfer, M. 2009. History as if neolithisation mattered: the transition to Late Stone Age in northern Fennoscandia. In H. Glørstad and C. Prescott (eds), *Neolithisation as if history mattered*, 85–104. Lindome: Bricoleur Press.

Sognnes, K. 1993. The role of the rock art in the Bronze Age and early Iron Age in Trøndelag, Norway. *Acta Archaeologica* 63, 157–88.

Spång, L. G. 1997. *Fångstsamhälle i handelssystem. Åsele Lappmark neolitikum—bronsålder*. Umeå: Studia Archaeologica Universitatis Umensia.

Sundström, J. 1989. Järnåldersgravar i fångstlandet. In O. Hemmendorff (ed.), *Arkeologi i fjäll, skog och bygd 1. Stenålder—tidig järnålder*, 155–71. Östersund: Jämtlands läns museum.

Taffinder, J. 1998. *The allure of the exotic: the social use of non-local raw materials during the Stone Age in Sweden*. Uppsala: Uppsala University.

Valen, C. R. 2007. *Jordbruksimpulser i neolitikum og bronsealder i Nord-Norge? En revisjon av det arkeologiske gjenstandsmaterialet og de naturvitenskapelige undersøkelsene*. Tromsø: Hovedoppgave, Universitetet i Tromsø.

Zvelebil, M. 2008. Innovating hunter-gatherers: the Mesolithic in the Baltic. In G. Bailey and P. Spikins (eds), *Mesolithic Europe*, 18–59. Cambridge: Cambridge University Press.

Zvelebil, M. and Rowley-Conwy, P. 1984. The transition to farming in Northern Europe: a hunter-gatherer perspective. *Norwegian Archaeological Review* 17, 104–28.

CHAPTER 40

THE PERSISTENCE OF HUNTING AND GATHERING AMONGST FARMERS IN SOUTH-EAST ASIA IN PREHISTORY AND BEYOND

HUW BARTON

The Origins of Hunting and Gathering, and Farming

THIS chapter seeks to explore the nature of historic and ongoing forager–farmer interactions in South-East Asia, but specifically seeks to do so from the perspective of foraging communities. Within South-East Asia, there is an ongoing narrative of the persistence of hunting and gathering as a way of life, negotiating prehistoric and historic expansions of people, the introduction of exogenous domesticates, the later rapid terraforming under colonial systems of cash cropping and resource extraction, and of state-based development. While we have much less information about inter-group interactions in prehistory (though see Junker 2002), there are indications that systems of local and even inter-island trade may have been a significant factor in shaping prehistoric interactions in this region (Junker 2002; Kennedy 1977; Whitmore 1977, 141). While trade will be a central theme of this chapter, as here there remains a great deal of hisıtoric documentation, focus will be drawn to the ways in which hunter-gatherers have used trade to actively engage in a variety of social and political interactions with farming communities.

Occupation of island South-East Asia by modern humans dates to at least 50,000 years ago (Barker et al. 2007) and possibly as early as 70,000 years ago on the Malay Peninsula if the ash deposit at the site of Kota Tampan can be reliably assigned to the Toba eruption (Ambrose 1996). These foragers appear to have swiftly adapted to the exploitation of lowland rainforest environments, pursuing a wide range of game and plant foods, including several toxic plant species (Barker et al. 2011; Barton 2005; Barton and Paz 2007; Pasveer 2004; Paz 2005; Piper et al. 2008). They appear well adapted to equatorial rainforest environments, and had solved many problems of resource acquisition that were thought to have presented a barrier to permanent human occupation (e.g. see Bailey et al. 1989).

Archaeologist Peter Bellwood has long argued that the spread of farmers into South-East Asia is linked initially to the spread of domesticated rice and certain forms of red-slipped pottery, pigs, and polished stone tools from 3500 BC (Bellwood 2005, 128–41; Diamond and Bellwood 2003). In fact, Bellwood argues that prior to this date, nowhere in South-East Asia is there any evidence of food production (Bellwood 2005, 130). In moving south and east, the model further posits that rice is dropped as a cultivar, being too difficult to grow in the equatorial tropics, and farmers turn to the cultivation of tree and root crops (Diamond and Bellwood 2003, 601). Thus agriculture arrives as a coherent package or set of practices, introduced into a landscape of rainforest hunter-gatherers after 3500 BC, gradually spreading until around 1500 BC (Bellwood 2005, 134–9). As read, this then provides a relatively neat base-line for prehistoric forager–farmer interactions. However, there are critics of this model (e.g. Barton and Denham 2011; Denham 2011; Donohue and Denham 2010; Oppenheimer 2004) who suggest that the existing evidence also supports indigenous innovations including plant management, even cultivation, in the absence of domesticated rice (Barton 2012; Barton and Denham 2011). Resolving this debate is now a key issue in the region as many arguments about the nature of forager–farmer interactions revolve around foragers' need for rice to satisfy their demand for edible carbohydrates, which are otherwise in short supply in these rainforest environments (Bailey et al. 1989). From this also flow other inferences about the nature of forager–farmer contacts in which foragers are seen as dependent upon farmers, or rapidly become so, once farming communities appear in their neighbourhood (Diamond and Bellwood 2003).

If foragers are not dependent upon farmers for access to carbohydrate resources (rice and other cultivated plants) in the rainforest, then their motivations for engagement with farmers are dramatically altered. For example, Laura Junker (2002) explores the archaeological evidence of forager–farmer interactions in the Tanjay region of the Philippines. Junker provides detailed evidence of the structure of forager–farmer interactions including the flow of import commodities from farmers into forager landscapes; a process that is shown to have persisted for at least the last millennium (Junker 2002, 239). However, Junker cannot resolve the issue of independent forest foraging and concludes that interactions may have ranged from 'symbiotic' to 'mutualistic' to 'exploitative' (Junker 2002, 239). To a large degree this stems from the deep internal assumption that foragers 'need' farmers and may only persist interdependently with farmers in equatorial rainforests. As noted above, if foragers are indeed completely independent of farmers for their long-term survival in the equatorial rainforests of South-East Asia, then it is possible to view the nature of these ongoing relationships in a completely different way.

The Persistence of Hunting and Gathering

The history of foragers across South-East Asia demonstrates a rich mosaic of practices and of peoples that appear fluid and in flux rather than fixed and engaged in the worlds changing around them. These are not peoples rooted in the remote past, an echo of an earlier way of life, but proactive societies pursuing their own community and personal agendas. Many hunter-gatherer communities are now settled, or in the process of settling down, or have joined their lives with communities of swiddeners—with whom they share much in common. One of these commonalities appears to have been the opportunities for inter-group networking provided by trade and exchange in a wide variety of forest products, some of which, such as rattan, may have been actively managed, even cultivated, to ensure long-term use. This desire to trade, driven by a range of objectives, some of which are clearly social, others economic, and some motivated by prestige, may well be part of their long-term successes and of the resilience of hunting and gathering in this part of the world.

How we define hunter-gatherers in many areas is not at all straightforward. Established definitions of forager and farmer based largely on subsistence and partly on mobility seem to lose their currency under close scrutiny in this region. Nomadic hunter-gatherers and semi-sedentary and fully sedentary communities may all be engaged in the cultivation of wild and domesticated plants, while all communities make extensive use of wild, semi-managed, and heavily managed forest resources. Swidden farms appear to blend into, rather than stand apart from, the surrounding forest creating a managed ecosystem that reflects rather than replaces, natural forest dynamics (Geertz 1963, 25). While today, many farming groups are largely dependent upon the cultivation of monocultures, particularly of rice, even here the distinctions drawn between forager and farmer are, in some regions, subtler in practice than they might appear at first sight. Both farmers and hunter-gatherers rely heavily on the products of the forest that surrounds them; it is a place for gathering wild foods, collecting forest products for trade, for hunting, and a place that may be filled with spirits (Barker and Janowski 2011). It is the relationship between mobility, social organization, and cosmology that better defines hunting and gathering as a way of life in this region and which separates it from other modes of socio-economic existence (Fortier 2009).

While there exist similarities between Kelabit farmers and Penan hunter-gatherers in their lifeways (particularly in hunting and gathering), it is their perception of their worlds that really does seem to set them apart (Barker and Janowski 2011). The Kelabit conceptualize the cosmos as imbued with *lalud*, a term that translates as life force/power/potency/effectiveness (Janowski 2014). The Penan have an equivalent concept, *penyukat*, which derives from the word *sukat*, 'able to' (Janowski 2014). The way in which each group interacts with these life forces and the way they are seen to 'flow' through the world are quite different. The Kelabit are prepared to engage directly with these forces, and find ways to manipulate them. The Penan make much smaller efforts to do this and are more likely to 'go along with the flow' (Janowski 2014). A good example of this is in the cultivation of rice. For the Kelabit, rice initiates a particular way of 'being' in the world, it is regarded as 'proper' food or a 'real food' (Janowski 2014). The rice plant is highly ritualized, unlike any other plant, and its cultivation involves a great deal of interaction with the appropriate spirits to ensure its success (Hayden 2011). Rice also involves a great deal of human effort to grow; it is unlike other plants such as sago palm and yams, which grow on their own without human intervention (Barton 2012). Rice and its production have become tightly enmeshed in systems of status and prestige, and in efforts at directing the flow of spiritual power to ensure a successful crop. Success in rice for the Kelabit means successful interaction with the spirit world, and those successes were celebrated though the erection of stone monuments at *irau* feasts, and through other ways of physically marking the landscape, described as *etuu* (Janowski and Langub 2011). Swidden farming also involves felling and burning large timber, which may be filled with spirits (Janowski 2014), so these also must be overcome. By contrast the Penan do not mark the landscape in that way, they leave only *oban*, or 'footprints' (Janowski and Langub 2011) and do not fell big timber.

Did rice and rice cultivation usher in a new way of conceiving of the natural world (Barker and Janowski 2011, 9) and begin the process of setting farmers apart from hunter-gatherers, or was rice and its rituals adopted by peoples already predisposed to manipulate *lalud* and challenge the old ways? While we should not apply the patterns of the Kelabit and Penan to all hunter-gatherer/farmer interactions, their particular ways of seeing the world and how it works significantly shape their actions within the rainforest and the manner of interaction with each other. Across South-East Asia what we do see is incredible diversity in the actions of peoples and their responses to change. Hunter-gatherers and farmers appear willing to try new things and new ways of living, and this willingness has surely contributed to the resilience of hunter-gatherer lifeways into the twenty-first century.

Contemporary Foraging Peoples

Foraging communities in South-East Asia used to be divided into two main groupings on the basis of their physical appearance (Bellwood 1997; Benjamin 2002). However, these categories are unhelpful, have dubious origins, and maintain racial stereotypes largely of use for political ends with little real validity (Gomes 2007, 12). Linguistic studies (Benjamin 2002) and recent genetic studies (Peng et al. 2010; Soares et al. 2011) challenge these simple stereotypes by reinforcing long and complex histories of human movement throughout this region. Finding other ways to discuss ethnicity, though, is not easy. Gomes (2007) struggles to find a simple way forward in a discussion about the large number of ethnic minorities inhabiting the Malay Peninsula. People often describe themselves in opposition to other groups, particularly Malays, but in terms of their religious observances, not their dress or physical characteristics, where 'we do this, Malays do that' (Gomes 2007, 18). Frequently it is the cultural practices that are pointed out, such as the fact that Malays do not eat pork whereas they do.

A sense of relative 'freeness' of identity also seems to be a feature of this region. In a discussion of ethnic identity amongst the farming Bidayuh, Liana Chua (2007, 279) writes that 'rather than trying to "preserve" or "construct" a distinctive Bidayuh identity, I would argue that my informants are more interested in maintaining a certain freedom of movement which they associate with being Bidayuh—but which does not necessarily have to culminate in the formation of Bidayuh identity'. They are more comfortable with the idea of 'becoming' and of moving from one fixed state to another, which is viewed in stark contrast to Malay identity, which is 'fixed' and inflexible (Chua 2007, 264). This fluidity is also reflected in the use of language, where groups rapidly adopt words and syntax of neighbouring groups (Endicott 1997, 45). It also seems reflected in the manner in which some foragers have settled with swidden farmers, or experimented with various forms of cultivation, but returned to other ways of living, or focused on trade for a time, or been settled, semi-sedentary, or fully nomadic. Identity is complex and appears rather fluid, regardless of whether you are living as predominantly a hunter-gatherer or a swidden farmer.

Understanding the full range of ethnic diversity of forager groups in this region is further complicated by widespread use of collective exonyms both on the mainland and across the islands, conferred by non-members, often swidden farmers. Many of these terms refer to major geographic features such as mountains or rivers, or express their occupation of remote interior landscapes. Such collective terms may include: 'people who live at the source of a river'; 'people who live deep within the forest'; 'to wander in the forest'; and 'mountain people' (Hoffman 1984, 129; Sellato 1994, 16). Sometimes names may link people to particular places such as the Soah Penan (Penan of the Soah River) a practice that has created a wealth of exonyms for groups that relocated to new regions or new river systems where their new neighbours referred to them by new local toponyms. For example, a Penan group formerly from the Bunut River were known as the Penan Bunut, but after relocating to forests near Kayan settlements they became known as Penan Talun, or Penan of the secondary forest (Langub 2009).

Foragers of the Malay Peninsula are broadly referred to as the Orang Asli, 'Original People', and have been sub-grouped based on cultural, physical (Schebesta and Bladgen 1926; Skeat 1902), and genetic differences into:

- Menraq (foragers—the former term 'Negritos' is dropped for this chapter as the term is considered an inappropriate ethnic classification; derived from Spanish meaning 'little black'. The term 'Menraq', identified by Gomes (2007, 22), is preferred as this is an autonym used by these groups that means 'human' or 'people');
- Senoi/Semai (swidden farmers); and
- Malayu-Asli (farmer-traders) (Fix 2002, 202; Gomes 2004).

The Menraq have also been divided into various sub-groups, some of which are now settled and farm, including the Semang (another broad exonym that means 'debt slaves'; Datan 1998, 46; Schebesta 1929), Kensiu, Kintak, Lanoh (Williams-Hunt 1954), Jahai (Schebesta 1926), Medriq (Datan 1998, 46), and Batek (Endicott 1984). The Senoi and Malayu-Asli are swidden farmers, but include one forager group known as the Semaq Beri (Kuchikura 1987, 1). Other mainland groups include the Mlabri 'forest people' of northern Thailand (Endicott 1999; Ikeya and Nakai 2009; though see Oota et al. (2005) for an argument that the Mlabri are relatively recent hunter-gatherers having switched from swidden farming), and the little-known Saoch of Cambodia and Tac-cui (Nguoio-La-Vang) in Vietnam (LeBar et al. 1964). Forager groups from island South-East Asia include the Batak (Eder 1984), Aeta, and Agta from the Philippines (Griffon and Grffon 1985; Headland and Reid 1989; Peterson 1981), the Kubu (Persoon 1989; Sandbukt 1988), and other interior groups of Sumatra, and the Tonutil of the Moluccas (Ishige 1980, 338). Depending on the definition of hunter-gatherer/forager, we might also include some sedentary groups such as the Nuaulu of central Seram (Ellen 1998; 2011). Interior Borneo contains a diverse ethnic division of hunter-gatherers, now all broadly referred to as the Penan and/or Punan (Figure 40.1). Other identified foraging groups in Borneo included the Bukat, Bukit, Bukitan, Beketan, Lisum, Sru, Sihan, and Ukit, but many of these have since gone extinct or were absorbed into other groups (Sellato 1994).

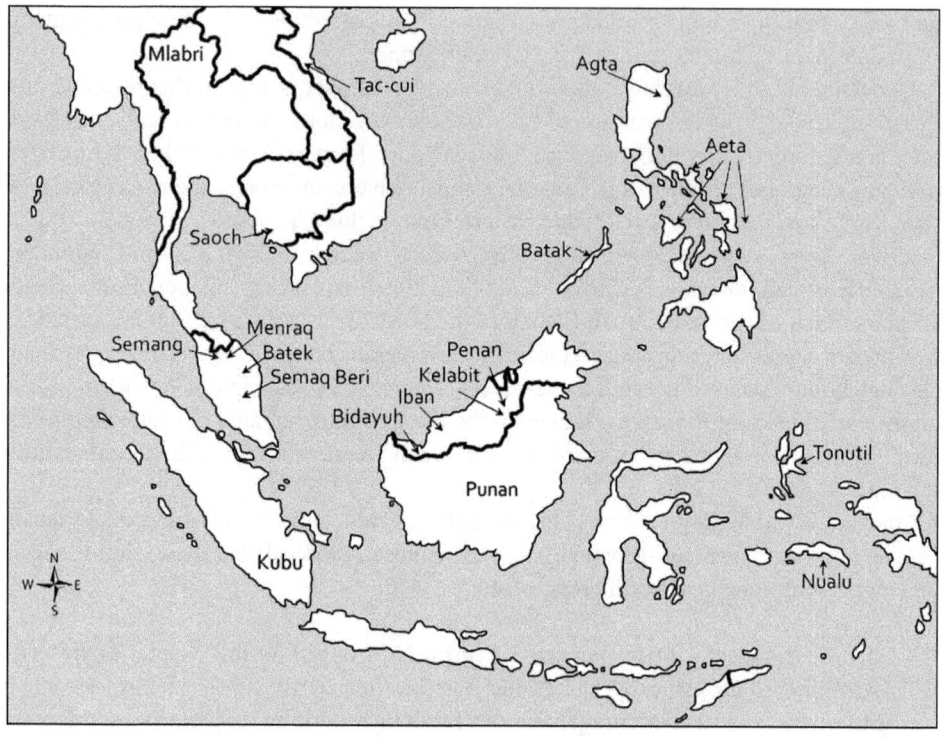

FIGURE 40.1 Hunter-gatherers in South-East Asia.

Histories of Trade and Exchange

The ethnographic literature on trade and exchange provides us with a relatively rich set of historic documents charting the nature of inter-group relationships between foragers and farmers in this region. Within the islands of South-East Asia in particular, the desire for forest products was strong and this remained so well into the twentieth century (Table 40.1). Overall revenue returns from export duties relating to forest products maintained strong revenue streams for the emerging governments of Brunei, North Borneo, and Sarawak (Cleary 1996, 320). For example, the trade in forest products accounted for nearly 90 per cent of the revenue of the Baram district until the 1900s (Lian 1988, 115). This was an extensive and sophisticated inter-regional trading system that required commitments from all parties at the local level. A wide range of indigenous groups were fundamental to its long-term successes, requiring effective and stable inter-group and inter-personal relationships between collectors and the river traders, who moved much of this material to the coast and ultimately into the hands of various polities and, later, government agents. Similar processes appear to have operated in other locations throughout the archipelago.

Recorded trade in forest products between China and Borneo dates back at least two millennia (Swadling 1996). Trade with China and southern ocean countries is mentioned in 140 BC (Tagliacozzo 2005, 27) and Indonesian trade missions were established in China by

Table 40.1 Examples of the forest products collected by hunter-gatherers from the Malay Peninsula and Borneo for trade

Timber/Plant	Resins/Exudates	Animal	Other
Aloes wood	Amber	Beeswax	Grass mats
Ebony	Benzoin[1] (Benjamin)	Bezoars[5]	Pandan matting
Gharu wood	Camphor[2]	Bird nests	Bamboo mats
Laka wood	Damar resin[3]	Bird plumes	Nipa mats
Sapan wood	Gutta-percha[4]	Civet glands[6]	Banana fibre mats
Sandalwood		Coral	
Bamboo		Cowries	
Betel nut		Giant clam shells	
Coconut		Honey	
Rattan (palm)		Hornbill casques	
		Ivory	
		Kingfisher feathers	
		Lac[7]	
		Monkeys Musk	
		Parrots	
		Pearls	
		Porcupine quills	
		Rhino horns	
		Tortoise shells	

[1] Benzoin (Benjamin) is the resin of the *Styrax benzoin* tree, used for incense (Reid 1993, 32).
[2] Camphor is formed in the crevices of the stems of *Dryobalanops aromatic* a. The tree is cut down, the stem split, and crystalline scales of pure camphor are shaken out onto mats (Hose and McDougall 1912, 152).
[3] Resins from a wide variety of tree species were sought after.
[4] Gutta-percha is solidified latex from a variety of trees of the family Sapotaceae. Trade in gutta-percha increased significantly after 1842 with European demand for the latex after it was found to have excellent properties as an electrical insulator by Michael Farraday. Gutta-percha was used to insulate the first submarine cables used for telephony in 1852 (Dunn 1975, 88).
[5] Bezoars are gallstones from a variety of animals including monkeys and porcupines. These were highly valued as medicinal by the Chinese (Hose and McDougall 1912, 155).
[6] Civet glands were highly sought after in Europe in medicines and as a base for perfume (Dannenfeldt 1985).
[7] Lac is a sticky deposit secreted on boughs and twigs by the female lac insect, *Tachardi lacca*. Lac yields a dye and a resin; the chief source of the Lac-dye, Seedlac, Shellac, and Stickylac (Rendle 1917).

430 AD (Wolters 1967, 151). Borneo is mentioned by Chinese envoys in the early sixth century (Hose and McDougall 1912, 10; Tagliocozzo 2005, 27). Brunei is also mentioned several times in annals of the Sung Dynasty who controlled oceanic trade in the region from 960 to 1279 AD (Hose and McDougall 1912, 13). Regular trade between Indonesia and China had developed between the third and fifth centuries AD (Wolters 1967, 36). Trade is also documented with India by the fourth century AD with recorded imports of Indonesian gharu wood, sandalwood, cloves, and camphor (Wolters 1967, 65, 68). The volume in trade is difficult to assess, but certainly by the fifth and sixth centuries, trading trips from China appear to be a regular affair.

During the seventeenth century, trade was radically impacted by the arrival of the Dutch trading company VOC (Verenigde Oost-Indische Compagnie). During this period the quantities of goods traded increased significantly. Imports consisted of cloth from India, silver from the Americas and Japan, and copper, cash, silk, ceramics, and goods from China in exchange for island spices, pepper, aromatic woods, resins, lacquer, tortoiseshell, pearls, and deerskins (Reid 1993, 23). The records from just one VOC port on the tip of Sulawesi give some indication of the volumes involved. Exports of rattans, which were always in demand, used in a wide variety of furniture and plaited objects, grew steadily from 63 pikuls (3,890 kg) in the 1720s to 3,267 pikuls (201,737 kg) by the 1780s. Birds' nests, highly desired by the Chinese for their medicinal qualities, increased to 12 pikuls (741 kg) by the 1780s. Beeswax, desired by the textile industry for dyeing, grew from 107 pikuls (6,607 kg) to 274 pikuls (16,920 kg) over the same period. Imports of iron bars rose from 49 pikuls (3,026 kg) during the 1720s up to 1,072 pikuls (66,196 kg) by the 1780s (Knapp and Heather 2004, 102–7). Overall it is estimated that between 1602 and 1796, the VOC had moved nearly 2.5 million tonnes of Asian trade goods. In just one small port located on Gessir, a small coral atoll at the eastern end of the Ceram group, the richness of goods on the move seems overwhelming.

> It is the rendezvous of the Paradise—and other bird-skin collectors from the mainland of New Guinea, from Salwatty, Mysore, and Halmaheira, and of the pearl-divers of Aru; hither the tripang, tortoise-shell, beeswax, nutmegs, dammar, and other rich produce from a multitude of islands is brought to be exchanged with the Malay and Chinese traders, of Macassar, Singapore and Ternate, for the scarlet, blue, and white cottons and calicos of the Dutch and English looms, for the yellow-handled hoop-iron knives, which form the universal small change of these regions, and for beads, glass-balls, knobs of amber, old keys, scraps of iron, and worthless but gaudy Brummagem.
>
> (Forbes 1885, 299)

Trading Natures

Trade in island South-East Asia between swidden farmers and mobile hunter-gatherers is often described in terms of 'interior' foragers engaged in various forms of exchange with 'lowland' farmers, usually situated on or near the coast (e.g. Dunn 1975; Hutterer 1977; Junker 1996). Interaction between 'lowland' farmers and 'interior' hunter-gatherers could occur between foragers and coastal farmers in direct contact with each other or between foragers and specialist traders (Rousseau 1990; Sellato 1994). Bernard Sellato (2005) argues that this system of interior and lowland trade may actually be relatively recent, dating only to the eighteenth and nineteenth centuries, as trading communities moved further inland as the lowland areas became exhausted. The coastal economies that ultimately received forest products would themselves exchange these for prestige goods, including trade-ware ceramics from China, Vietnam, and Thailand, earthenware, bronze cannons, gongs, iron tools, beads, earrings, bracelets, matches, glass beads, and other items locally rare (Hose and McDougall 1912; Wheatley 1964).

Nomadic groups of Borneo would seek to acquire prestige items such as gongs, brass objects, and Chinese jars that could be used by them as bride wealth to marry women from agricultural communities, to pay fines, or to gain prestige in the eyes of swidden farmers (Sellato 1994, 152). Amongst the Penan, leadership qualities include good rhetorical skills, knowledge of the group's history and traditions, but also highly desirable is someone who is a fluent speaker of the language of their farmer neighbours (Sellato 1994, 152). Relationships between hunter-gatherer traders and farmers are often characterized as largely 'one-sided' with farmers getting a significantly better end of the deal financially, politically, and socially (Junker 1996, 390; Rousseau 1990, 233). Just how one-sided this relationship actually was in practice is more difficult to discern as historical accounts may well privilege farmers and typically see emerging social complexity associated with agriculture as evidence enough of superiority.

Relations between nomadic groups and farmers varied across the region and are likely to have been intra-regionally specific (Junker 1996, 391) so simple generalizations are likely to obscure the true picture of regional diversity. For example, in Borneo, the Dusun used salt as the medium of exchange for small items (Williams 1965, 77) and exchanges of food between foragers and farmers were rare, whereas this appears more common in the Philippines (Rousseau 1990, 234; Williams 1965, 77), while food exchange between farming communities in Borneo appears to have been much more common, involving fruit, sago, and rice (Morris 1991; Nicholaisen 1986; Rousseau 1990; Rutter 1929 [2007]; Strickland 1985). Relations between hunter-gatherers and other nomadic groups and swidden farmers were not always cordial and hostilities did break out (Beavitt 1997; Puri 2005, 174; Sellato 1994, 50–1). Farmers offered their nomadic allies a degree of protection in times of war and also famine, and took action to prevent other groups from exploiting the territory of their foragers. In their turn, foragers served as border guards, warned of enemy attack, and provided farmers with severed heads and slaves (Sellato 1994, 51).

The Penan of Borneo could also be cautious about approaching outsiders in their territory. During a trip into the interior the guides leading Charles Hose set up a cleft stick with a large cake of tobacco in the gap, having noted foreign footprints about the camp. The stick was a silent message, opening communications and a willingness to trade with the as yet unsighted Penan (Hose and McDougall 1912, 188). These message sticks were part of a fairly sophisticated symbolic system used by the Penan, called 'Oro' (Figure 40.2) to communicate between individuals and groups, particularly when they wished to remain invisible to unwelcome visitors (Arnold 1958).

Alliances between nomads and farmers could be formed by 'blood-brotherhood' that created a fictive kinship between individuals (Beavitt 1997, 205) and also through marriage, though initially the movement of women was predominantly from hunter-gatherer groups to agricultural villages (Sellato 1994, 51). Farmers could be quite protective of neighbouring hunter-gatherer groups and refused to reveal their location to outsiders (Beavitt 1997, 205). Hunter gatherers were also known to maintain exclusive control of their own territory and might kill outsiders who tried to gather their jungle produce (Rousseau 1990, 273).

FIGURE 40.2 Oro using a woven circle of vine to indicate a brass gong. This oro denotes that a tree has been marked by an individual to preserve rights of access to its fruit. The gong symbol indicates that taking fruit without permission would incur a heavy penalty, in this case a brass gong, which would be extremely difficult for most Penan to acquire.

These resources were not widespread throughout the forest; the best-quality material could be restricted spatially (Sellato 2005). The desire for hunter-gatherers to retain control of resource access may stem from more than just the desire to trade. Patches of key resources, such as rattan (Figures 40.3 and 40.4), may have been 'owned' by individuals, and actively managed, in the same manner as sago palm, their staple food supply, to ensure longevity (Sellato 2005, 69).

Recently, Langub (2007) reviewed the concept of Native Customary Rights and ideas of resource tenure amongst the hunter-gatherer Penan. The Penan do maintain a clear concept of territorial domain and of rights of access to some resources, particularly those that come under the concept of *molong*—resources that are 'managed' or 'cared for' (Brosius 1993; Langub 2007; Puri 1997). Through the concept of *molong* an individual may lay a claim upon a particular stand of sago palms, a fruit tree, or a stand of rattan, in order to foster that resource for future use (Langub 2007). These rights may be inherited through the family

FIGURE 40.3 A bundle of rattan recently collected in the forest and ready for transport.

FIGURE 40.4 Splitting and shaving forest rattan in preparation for making woven baskets.

unit. Other members of the group may harvest these resources with permission of the person who *molong* it (Langub 2007).

> We go to get rattan at the Payao River. If it is finished there we move to get rattan elsewhere. A long time after, we can get it at the Payao River again—1 year, 2 years, 3 years, 4 years, it is large again... That is why when we get rattan, we don't cut the young plants, the offspring of the rattan, its children. We can't cut the offspring. We *molong* the offspring, so that we can get them later... We will get the rattan for mats, baskets, for us to get money.
>
> (Penan Geng recorded by Jayl Langub 2007)

Depending on the definition, this is either management or curation of a wild resource, or cultivation. Whether hunter-gatherers actively planted rattans is unknown, but their actions would certainly have created richer stands of the plant and enabled groups who controlled access a steady supply of a highly valued trade item.

Foragers provided forest products at the request of neighbouring farmers, but not to the exclusion of all else. Rousseau (1990) argues that the nomadic Punan (Penan) recognized that they were not necessarily the main economic beneficiaries of trade, but engaged in trade at the request of sedentary groups partly to derive some material benefit, but primarily to facilitate useful social outcomes. It was also the case that nomadic groups dissatisfied with current trade arrangements could search out new trading partners; neither group was permanently allied to the other (Sellato 1994, 59). In the traditional view provided by early writers such as Ivor H. Evans, relations between Malay traders and various hunter-gatherer groups were definitely one-sided, where he saw foragers 'swindled' and kept busy cutting rattans for their Malay 'protectors' (Evans 1937, 34). However, in most accounts there is actually very little evidence of hunter-gatherers being in complete thrall to local polities. Group mobility allowed people to choose to trade or not, and in many cases to determine the location of these exchanges (Lye-Tuck Po 2004, 77). Relations with traders could be broken off at any time and some enterprising individuals would simply go around the middleman and access markets directly.

> In the last decade demand for rattan for making furniture and fishtraps has caused four or five groups of Malay entrepreneurs to develop trade relations with the Batek. The traders come up the river in motorboats and camp near the Batek brining money, rice, salt, sugar, flour, swimming trunks, sarongs, flashlight batteries, etc. with which to pay for the rattan. Once an agreement on price and quantity is reached, the traders usually give an advance payment in the form of rice and other foods... when one contract is completed, the Batek will normally make another agreement with the same or a different trader, and the process is repeated. They never make contracts for more than they can collect in one to two months. Because there is competition among the traders and the Malays do not want to pull the rattan out of the forest themselves, the Batek can usually get reasonably good terms. If the terms offered are not good enough, the Batek either quit collecting rattan for a while or make up a load and raft it down themselves.
>
> (Endicott 1984, 35–6)

Contrary to some accounts, the terms of these exchanges were not obviously of economic detriment to forager groups. These forests were not devoid of resources, and peninsular foragers and swidden farmers had access to a wide range of roots, tubers, fruits, and nuts as well as abundant game (Endicott 1984; Gianno and Bayr 2009; Kuchikura 1987; Schebesta 1929). The same is true on the island of Borneo, though the staple carbohydrate there is flour from sago palms rather than from wild and cultivated roots and yams as it is on the mainland (Barton and Paz 2007). For part of the year, the Semaq Beri of Peninsular Malaysia would locate their camp within the forest about 1–1.5 km distance from Malay villages. During this time they would engage with the Malays in either paid labour or through a system of direct barter. The Semaq Beri might supply rattan, atap roofing, pandanus fronds, damar resin, tree barks, bamboo, medicinal herbs, mushrooms, and honey (Kuchikura 1987, 12). In exchange they would receive rice, salt, tobacco, and manufactured goods including cloth and bush knives (Kuchikura 1987, 12). The collection of rattan was seemingly quite profitable where a husband and wife could work one half day collecting and processing rattan for trade to receive approximately 1.8 kg of rice, enough to feed an average family group. When working in the fields weeding and clearing forest, payment was approximately the same for a full day's work, but they also had time to supplement their diet by collecting wild yams and hunting (Kuchikura 1987, 13). By comparison, the Eastern Penan would need to harvest wild sago palms for its starchy reserves two to three times per week, a process that normally demands a day or two of effort by the family unit (Brosius 1986, 177).

CONFLICT

Inter-group violence was well documented in Borneo, either as ongoing violent disputes between villages (King 1985, 53; Rousseau 1990), as part of aggressive territorial expansion (Beavitt 1997; Freeman 1955, 14), or headhunting (Gomes 2004 [1911]; Rousseau 1990). Headhunting amongst the Iban was a way of showing bravery and skills in warfare, but it was also a way to show respect for family members and gain prestige (Beavitt 1997, 211; Rousseau 1990, 264). Heads once taken were brought to the village and treated with ceremony and respect, offerings were made, and their spirits joined the Iban community (Beavitt 1997, 211).

Sometimes the instigators of inter-group violence were farmers and at other times hunter-gatherer groups. During a particularly aggressive period of expansion in the seventeenth century, Iban farmers moved into areas inhabited by the Bukitan hunter-gatherers in the lowlands of Sarawak. Some Bukitan were assimilated and became Iban through marriage, others migrated up the Rejang River (Beavitt 1997).

Benedict Sandin tells a story related to this conflict. The Ibans, led by Tindin, migrated from the Skrang to the upper Paku, a tributary of the Saribas. The region was populated by groups of Bukitan, some nomadic and some already semi-settled and growing some crops. The two sides fought but neither would give in. To settle the dispute over land a marriage was arranged between the son of Entingi (Bukitan) and the daughter of Tindin (Iban). The dowry included a padi bin filled with new heads, a large brass gong, a brass cannon, one blowpipe, and a hat worn by high-ranking Iban brides (Sandin 1967, 19–20). In another example, Langub (2009) relates a story where Penan were attacked by Iban resource collectors and several people were killed. The Iban were successfully defeated after killing Tedong, the Iban leader.

Penan would retaliate against headhunting, even if they had to wait years for their revenge, and could be much feared because of this (Rousseau 1990, 272). Bernard Sellato (1994, 76–86) describes in detail an aggressive history of raiding and counter-rading by the Kereho Busang living the southern part of the Müller mountains. Some of this is clearly related to control of forest resources for trade. In 1853 it was reported that the upper Kahayan was emptied of its inhabitants due to violent raids and enslavement (Schwaner 1853). After a series of raids the Kereho successfully drove the Ot Danum from the headwaters of the Busang River. This area was later recolonized by forager Seputan who had begun to farm. Over time the Kereho intermarried with the Seputan, settled, and also began to farm. As the region became less violent, other groups moved in to establish a trading centre and move goods downriver. The social and economic relationships of the Kereho and other groups were complex, and control of access to forest resources and trading partners was clearly high on the agenda of these groups of interior foragers.

Slavery

Sometimes hunter-gatherer groups were the targets of slave raids by hierarchical swiddeners who owned slaves and used them to maintain their own personal rank (King 1985, 53). War captives might also be taken into slavery by the victorious and kept or traded downriver (King 1985, 53; Low 1882, 72; Rousseau 1990, 242). 'The main Muruts are not only salt but slave dealers' (Spencer St. John 1862). While inter-group conflict does not seem uncommon, some of it certainly between hunter-gatherer groups and farmers, it was dwarfed by the expansion in slavery driven by the commercial interests of the VOC in the seventeenth century.

From 1660, warfare and endemic raiding expeditions by the VOC for slaves provided a steady supply. Makassar (Goa) in south-west Suluwesi was the main transit port for slaves from Borneo (Kalimantan), Sulawesi, Buton, and the north-eastern islands as well as to the east including Lombok, Sumbawa, Bima, Manggarai, and Solor (Vink 2003). Between 1653 and 1682 almost 10,000 slaves were shipped to Batavia of which 42 per cent came from south Sulawesi, 24 per cent from Bali, 12 per cent from Buton, and 7 per cent from the Tenggara islands and Maluku (Ambon and Banda) respectively (Vink 2003). As a result of these pernicious raids, many hunter-gatherer groups and swiddeners retreated from the coasts, moving upriver and becoming far more cautious in their dealings with traders. The practice in silent trade may have arisen at this time.

In this system groups left goods at a previously agreed location and they retired back into the forest awaiting a visit from their trading partner who left their goods and also retired. This process of offer and counter-offer made in complete isolation from each other would continue until both groups were satisfied with the result (Sellato 1994, 59). The following is a detailed description of silent trade amongst the Kubus of Sumatra:

> In the small trade carried on between them and the Malay traders of the Palembang and Jambi Residencies, the transactions are performed without one party seeing the other. The Malay trader, ascending to one of their places of rendezvous, beats a gong in a particular way to give notice of his arrival. On hearing the signal, the Kubus, bringing out what forest produce they may have collected, and depositing it on the ground at this place, hastily retire into close hiding, beating a gong as a signal that all is ready. The trader then slowly and cautiously approaches, lays down on the ground the cloth, knives, and other articles of barter that he has brought, to the amount which he considers an equivalent exchange, beats a gong and in like manner disappears. The Kubus proceed then to examine the barter offered; if they think the bargain satisfactory they remove the goods, beat their gong and go away; while the trader packs up the produce he finds left lying on the ground. If the bargain is not considered by them

sufficiently advantageous, they set on one side a portion of their produce, to reduce it to what they consider the value of the barter offered; and thus the affair see-saws till finally adjusted or abandoned.

(Forbes 1885, 235)

SETTLING DOWN AND LOOKING FOR MONEY

The Penan and other groups have been encouraged to settle and adopt village life since the late 1950s and early 1960s, but some groups continue to resist and maintain a nomadic or semi-nomadic lifestyle. Pressures from increased logging activities make it increasingly difficult to do this. The first major resettlement of Batak hunter-gatherers in Peninsular Malaysia took place in the Ulu Lebir area of Kelantan in 1956. The government provided free rations for the period of a year and encouraged the Batak to grow crops. Having agreed to settle, they consumed their weekly allocation of rice, and spent their time hunting and fishing and experimenting with cultivation. At the end of the trial period, when the rations were stopped, the Batak abandoned the camp and resumed a nomadic existence (Carey 1976, 118).

Trade still seems to define many interactions between hunter-gatherer groups, swidden farmers, and increasingly tourists and the occasional researcher. While staying at a Kelabit longhouse in Long Peluan, situated on the Peluan River just outside the highlands, Penan from the nearby village of Long Berurang would visit periodically to sell handmade items. On the occasions that I witnessed this, the Penan would quietly enter the longhouse and sit within the public gallery just inside the main door. The items they had for sale generally included basketry, bangles, and other craft items. After a while, interested Kelabit would sit down and begin talking as they looked through the goods on offer. Prices would be discussed and money exchanged. The Penan are well-known as excellent makers of woven basketry and sometimes Kelabit would request specific types of baskets or rattan mats, often made from rarer forms of rattan no longer found locally, that could be made to order.

Penan groups in Kalimantan that now live in Kenyah villages often feel compelled to maintain historical trading relationships with their Kenyah patrons in order to maintain access to useful resources and ways to obtain money (Puri 2005, 174). Living in villages places demands on Penan that require solutions that must be met with cash payments, such as paying fines, contributions to church, communal projects, festivals, and school clothing (Puri 2005, 174). The Penan often agree to accompany Kenyah on trips to acquire forest products for the Kenyah who control their sale and the distribution of any profits. As with other groups, this system encourages Penan to incur new relationships with non-resident traders where they can manage their own time and embed resource collection within other activities (Puri 2005, 174). One of the consequences of a more sedentary existence is the desire to acquire expensive items such as electronics, outboard engines, and clothes, which incur far larger debts than ever before (Chan 2007, 212). In some cases this has led to young men relocating further downriver engaged full-time in collecting expeditions to pay off their debts (Puri 2005, 175). The need for cash has also affected traditions of food sharing amongst some longhouse communities. Where people would have shared some foods, they now sell these for cash.

Gomes (2004) has looked in some depth at the issues associated with the system of traders advancing credit for forest products and the management of indebtedness that follows. It is not all bad news for those who acquire debts in this manner. Traders frequently advance cash or 'loans' to Semai for various forest products including rattan, resins, fruit, and insects. The prices of forest products would normally be set prior to collecting, and then the trader and the collector debate whether or not this is a good offer. For the trader it is to their advantage to have the producers in their debt, as this ensures future trading opportunities in a market where the traders themselves are in open competition with other potential buyers of Semai goods. For the collectors, they have a secure line of credit and access to money that is otherwise very difficult to acquire, and a secure demand for their products. Many of the materials collected deteriorate quickly, such as durian fruit, so people will be unwilling to collect unless there is clear demand backed by cash advances (Gomes 2004, 128–9). Collectors can sell some of the product to passers-by, but in such sales buyers will be selective about quality, whereas the trader will take the goods in bulk. Some collectors are unwilling to sell on the side, just in case they are caught out and they sour relations with their trading partner. Overall, the high demand for forest products and the range of trading options provide the Semai with a degree of autonomy and bargaining power. They are also in a position to misrepresent information regarding the availability and quality of goods sought after by the trader; in this way they can extract a better price for collecting than was originally on offer (Gomes 2004).

Penan from Long Berurang would work as labourers in Kelabit rice fields, often paid in rice, though increasingly they had their own swidden fields to take care of. Generally their fields were smaller than those of their Kelabit neighbours, and the Kelabit thought them too small and rather untidy. Whereas the Kelabit planted only rice with some crops, such as medicinals, around the edges of their fields, the Penan were fond of mixed planting. They often included maize, beans, cassava, and other plants with the rice. Initially they had learned some aspects of cultivation from missionaries, but they acquired the skill of cultivating rice by observing the activities of other groups. Households are not always self-sufficient in rice and often fall back on other staples such as cassava or sago from the forest. In the village of Long Berurang, rice, unlike other foods, is very much part of a cash economy. If people in the village run short of rice they may borrow rice from others, but this loan is repaid in cash rather than with rice or barter.

Shifting from a hunter-gatherer way of life to sedentary farming has engendered a mixed reception from various hunter-gatherer communities. Some Penan and other groups such as the Sihan, have been settled for decades and are proficient at cultivating rice, whereas others have shifted in and out of rice, or relied on other forms of mixed cultivation such as cassava, yams, sweet potato, banana, and maize (Nicholaisen 1976). Within individual communities there is a great deal of variation in how people respond to sedentary living and ways of making a living. Some households will not farm every year, preferring alternative strategies to earn income or find subsistence. Swidden fields may or may not be weeded, depending upon the choices people make to pursue other activities. Not everyone responds equally to pressures to attend church or go to school. Puri (2005, 178–9) comments that 'sedentism, and the accompanying changes in religious practice, education, and economic opportunity, have had an effect on Penan economic strategies by increasing the diversity of subsistence activities available to the Penan, while simultaneously reducing the range of territory covered, and constraining the time and labour available for these economic activities'.

As noted above, the desire to acquire money has also led some members of settled communities to leave farming entirely and essentially become professional collectors. This pattern would appear to mirror claims that many hunter-gatherer communities in the tropics are best described as forager-traders, either originating from swidden farmers or abandoning a fully nomadic existence to accommodate a patron–client relationship with farmers (Bailey et al. 1989; Endicott and Bellwood 1991). The full-time professional trader is considered to be a relatively new strategy, largely relating to the need for money in order to participate within an emerging cash economy (Puri 2005, 180). Prior to this the nature of collecting forest products was a more flexible arrangement that could be embedded in other activities. Groups could dictate the timing of these activities with more control than when they find themselves in a financial, rather than a promissory, debt.

We will always suffer from a tendency to over-generalize when looking at the big picture. When trying to come to terms with such large-scale processes such as forager–farmer interaction, at its heart are the short-term human-scale engagements that are really of most interest to us, especially when understanding the motivations for action. The following quote encapsulates the tensions felt between balancing different ways of life and the knowledge of future change and expectation associated with forced government relocation. As with many groups today, ways of accessing cash are of high importance, as this is the medium through which economic and many social exchanges are now mediated. Layu Lukap is a Penan woman from the Seping River, forcibly resettled by the Sarawak government before construction of the Baku Dam between 1998 and 1999 (Langub 2009).

> I came to Long Belangan because I fell in love. After several years, I not only fell in love with the man I am married to, Tingang, but also the place and its people. In terms of resources the Belangan area is as rich as that of the Seping River. The difference is that we have a large river, the Balui with plenty of fish. Here we can reach Belaga Town downriver in a matter of three hours to sell mats and baskets; the clinic at Long Linau is an hour's drive downriver by outboard motor. The primary school downriver and Long Pangai is a mere 20 minutes by longboat. I love this place more than I do my own in the Seping River. The Seping is isolated. It takes about three days to travel from the Seping to Belaga Town. It is far from any clinic and school. I feel sad about leaving this place; I fear the unknown future in Asap. I'll tell you why. Here in Belangan we have land to cultivate, the place is rich with sago, rattan, fruit, and game. Since I came here, we've never faced hunger. Penan women in Long Belangan are quite different from Penan women in other settlements in Belaga District. We not only sell mats and baskets, we also catch fish to sell at a cold storage at Long Pangai. We also collect ferns, bamboo shoots, and other jungle vegetables to sell to our Kayan and Lahanan neighbours, and also at the market in Belaga Town. We women also work for wages, debarking timbers for the local company. At the same time we have not abandoned our traditional role, nor have we lost the traditional skills taught to us by our parents. We are as good a weaver of rattan mats and baskets as other Penan women in the district. Here in Belangan we have the best of two worlds, the traditional and the modern.
>
> I fear the new life in Asap because everything there will cost money, food, water, and electricity. Here in Belangan food is free, all we need to do is cultivate it, or collect it from the forest. Water is free from the gravity-fed water supply system provided by the Medical Department. In Long Belangan we use paraffin lamp; it is cheap. Of great concern to us in Asap is space and scarcity of forest resources. In Belangan we are used to big space. Our nearest neighbours, the Lahanan downriver and the Kayan upriver are twenty minutes and a half an hour respectively by outboard motor from our village. We are told that Asap villages are located close to each other. With too many people squeezed in a small area, we will not be able to compete

with well-educated groups for jobs in Asap. Lack of access to forest resources means a loss of our earning capacity. The government admires our rattan mats and baskets, and advises us to teach our children the skill in weaving. How are we to teach the children the skill if there is no rattan nearby or access to it is beyond our reach?

As a woman, rattan has a special meaning to me. It is my way of contributing to the family income through weaving mats and baskets. Weaving intricate designs on a mat or basket gives me lots of satisfaction. We go out into the forest for a few days or a week with a group of families to collect rattan. It is hard work, but we enjoy being together. In a way it is an outing, an occasion to relax, to unwind. In Belangan we have different seasons for different tasks. We have a season to plant rice, a season to collect rattan and forest resources, a fruit season, a time we go to the forest as a group of families with our children to enjoy the fruit. This is the rhythm of life that has meaning to me and I believe to most Penan. If we can't compete with our neighbours for jobs in Asap, and there is no activity for us as we do in Belangan, what are we women going to do, stare at the sun till it comes down?

Another matter of great concern to us is the rising expectation of our children. When our children see Kayan families, Kenyah families with TV sets, their children provided with modern items such as hand phones, bicycles, or wear nice dress, our children too may want to acquire these. How are we to provide these when we don't have the money?

(Layu Lukap recorded by Jayl Langub 2009)

Conclusions

The persistence of hunting and gathering as a way of life in the region is marked not by a people who are timeless or the marginal remnants of a former less-productive way of life, but by the flexibility and mutable nature of foraging, and its direct engagement with other ways of living. Hunting and gathering has survived throughout significant changes of land use, colonial expansion, the spread of rice agriculture, and continued government pressures to abandon foraging altogether and settle down. The lives of swidden farmers and hunter-gatherers in Malaya, Borneo, and Indonesia have much in common. Both groups have long been engaged in collecting forest products for trade, sometimes with each other, and at other times with specialist river traders. The management of wild resources within the forest, sometimes for the express purpose of trade, is also a common practice, as is belief in forest spirits, though this is changing as groups convert to other religions.

The motivations of hunter-gatherers to engage with swiddeners is not always as clearly understood, largely because their voices have rarely been recorded. Often we view relationships from the perspective of swiddeners, or visiting government agents, not directly engaged with hunter-gatherer groups. The words of Layu Lukap express clearly both the optimism of life within and outside the forest, and the pessimism of being forced to leave a particular landscape into which their lives are bound. Logging, the expansion of oil palm plantations, difficulties in achieving recognition of their rights to land, and resettlement (Chan 2007, 220–3; Gomes 2007, 116–17; Klimut and Puri 2007; Langub 2007) continue to take their toll by removing access to resources, and removal of some resources completely, including patches of forest containing plants such as sago palm and rattans that may have been actively managed for generations.

For many if not all remaining groups of hunter-gatherers, loss of the forest, either through forced resettlement or industrial-scale resource extraction, means loss of livelihood and independence. As one Penan informant, Klimut, a Penan elder who has worked with researcher Rajindra Puri for several years, puts it: 'the fate of the Punan people is the forest. Everything is in the forest' (Klimut and Puri 2007, 119). Pressure to settle groups and engage in agriculture has generally increased rather than decreased dependency on the state (Gomes 2007, 123) as the capacity to raise income through the sale of forest products has been dramatically curtailed. Other unexpected issues have arisen such as the contradictions between traditional systems of sharing and reciprocity and the accumulative tendencies associated with commodity production and the need for money (Gomes 2007, 128).

In the face of enormous social and political change, hunting and gathering has persisted as a way of life, though perhaps today the nature of change is at such a scale that hunter-gatherer communities face some of their biggest challenges. While some communities may feel that they are 'permanently at the bottom' (Kaskija 2007) they are most definitely not passive agents watching the world change around them, but actively engaged and creatively seeking solutions to improve their circumstances. While we may not often hear their voices, or see the world through their eyes, their active engagement with the present is a lively lesson for thinking about the nature of hunter-gatherer inter-group relations in history and prehistory.

References

Ambrose, S. H. 1996. Late Pleistocene human population bottlenecks, volcanic winter, and differentiation of modern humans. *Journal of Human Evolution* 34, 623–51.

Arnold, G. 1958. Nomadic Penan of the Upper Rejang (Plieran), Sarawak. *Journal of the Malayan branch of the Royal Asiatic Society* 31, 40–81.

Bailey, R. C., Head, G., Jenike, G., Owen, M., Reichtman, B., and Zechenter, E. 1989. Hunting and gathering in tropical rainforest: is it possible? *American Anthropologist* 91, 59–82.

Barker, G., Barton, H., Bird, M., Daly, P., Datan, I., Dykes, A., Farr, L., Gilbertson, D., Harrisson, B., Hunt, C., Higham, T., Kealhofer, L., Krigbaum, J., Lewis, L., Mclaren, S. J., Paz, V., Pike, A., Piper, P., Pyatt, B., Rabett, R., Reynolds, T. E. G. Rose, J., Rushworth, G., Stephens, M., Stringer, C., Thompson, J., and Turney, C. 2007. The human revolution in lowland tropical Southeast Asia: the antiquity and behaviour of anatomically modern humans at Niah cave (Sarawak, Borneo). *Journal of Human Evolution* 52, 243–61.

Barker, G. and Janowski, M. 2011. Why cultivate? Anthropological and archaeological approaches to foraging-farming transitions in Southeast Asia. In G. Barker and M. Janowksi (eds), *Why cultivate? Anthropological and archaeological approaches to foraging–farming transitions in Southeast Asia*, 1–16. Cambridge: McDonald Institute for Archaeological Research.

Barton, H. 2005. The case for rainforest foragers: the starch record at Niah cave, Sarawak. *Asian Perspectives* 44, 56–72.

Barton, H. 2012. The reversed fortunes of sago and rice, Oryza sativa, in the rainforests of Sarawak, Borneo. *Quaternary International* 249, 96–104.

Barton, H. and Denham, T. 2011. Prehistoric vegeculture and social life in island southeast Asia and Melanesia. In G. Barker and M. Janowski (eds), *Why cultivate? Anthropological and archaeolgical approaches to foraging–farming transitions in southeast Asia*, 17–25. Cambridge: McDonald Institute for Archaeological Research.

Barton, H. and Paz, V. 2007. Subterranean diets in the tropical rain forests of Sarawak, Malaysia. In T. Denham, J. Iriarte, and L. Vrydaghs (eds), *Rethinking agriculture: archaeological and ethnoarchaeological perspectives*, 50–77. Walnut Creek, CA: Left Coast Press.

Beavitt, P. 1997. Fighters and foragers: warfare and the spread of agriculture in Borneo. In J. Carman (ed.), *Material harm: archaeological studies of war and violence*, 198–219. Glasgow: Cruithne Press.

Bellwood, P. 1997. *Prehistory of the Indo-Malaysian Archipelago* (revised edition). Honolulu: University of Hawai'i Press.

Bellwood, P. 2005. *First farmers*. Oxford: Blackwell.

Benjamin, G. 2002. On being tribal in the Malay world. In G. Benjamin and C. Chou (eds), *Tribal communities in the Malay world: historical, social and cultural perspectives*. Leiden: IIAS, Singapore: ISEAS.

Brosius, J. P. 1986. River, forest and mountain: the Penan Gang landscape. *Sarawak Museum Journal* 35, 173–84.

Brosius, J. P. 1993. Contrasting subsistence ecologies among Penan foragers, Sarawak (East Malaysia). In C. M. Hladik, A. Hladik, O. F. Linares, H. Pagezy, A. Semple, and M. Hadley (eds), *Tropical forests, people and food*, 515–22. London: Taylor & Francis.

Carey, I. 1976. *Orang Asli: the aboriginal tribes of peninsular Malaysia*. Oxford: Oxford University Press.

Chan, H. 2007. History and the Punan Vuhang: response to economic and resource tenure change. In P. G. Sercome and B. Sellato (eds), *Beyond the green myth: hunter-gatherers of Borneo in the twenty-first-century*, 192–226. Malaysia: Nias Press.

Chua, L. 2007. Fixity and flux: Bidahyuh (dis)engagements with the Malaysian ethnic system. *Ethnos* 72, 262–88.

Cleary, M. C. 1996. Indigenous trade and European economic intervention in north-west Borneo c. 1860–1930. *Modern Asian Studies* 30, 301–24.

Dannenfeldt, K. H. 1985. Europe discovers civet cats and civet. *Journal of the History of Biology* 18, 403–31.

Datan, I. 1998. Hunters and gatherers. In N. H. S. N. A. Rahman (ed.), *Early history: the Encyclopedia of Malaysia, vol. 4*, 46–7. Singapore: Archipelago Press.

Denham, T. 2011. Early agriculture and plant domestication in New Guinea and island southeast Asia. *Current Anthropology* 52, S379–95.

Diamond, J. and Bellwood, P. 2003. Farmers and their languages: the first expansions. *Science* 300, 597–603.

Donohue, M. and Denham, T. 2010. Farming and language in island southeast Asia. *Current Anthropology* 51, 223–56.

Dunn, F. L. 1975. *Rain-forest collectors and traders: a study of resource utilisation in modern and ancient Malaya*. Monographs of the Malaysian branch of the Royal Asiatic Society No. 5.

Eder, J. F. 1984. The impact of subsistence change on mobility and settlment pattern in a tropical forest foraging economy: some implications for archaeology. *American Anthropologist* 86, 837–53.

Ellen, R. 1988. Foraging, starch extraction and the sedentary lifestyle in the lowland rainforest of central Seram. In T. Ingold, D. Riches, and J. Woodburn (eds), *Hunters and gatherers, vol. 1: history, evolution and social change*, 117–34. Oxford: Berg.

Ellen, R. 2011. Sago as a buffer against subsistence stress and as a currency of inter-island trade networks in eastern Indonesia. In G. Barker and M. Janowksi (eds), *Why cultivate? Anthropological and archaeological approaches to foraging-farming transitions in Southeast Asia*, 75–94. Cambridge: McDonald Institute for Archaeological Research.

Endicott, K. M. 1984. The economy of the Batek of Malaysia. *Research in Economic Anthropology* 6, 29–52.

Endicott, K. M. 1997. Batek history, interethnic relations, and subgroup dynamics. In T. Ingold, D. Riches, and J. Woodburn (eds), *Hunters and gatherers, vol. 2: property, power and ideology*, 110–27. Oxford: Berg.

Endicott, K. M. 1999. Introduction: Southeast Asia. In R. B. Lee and R. Daly (eds), *The Cambridge encyclopedia of hunters and gatherers*, 275–83. Cambridge: Cambridge University Press.

Endicott, K. M. and Bellwood, P. 1991. The possibility of independent foraging in the rain forest of peninsular Malaysia. *Human Ecology* 19, 151–85.

Evans, I. H. 1937. *The Negritos of Malaya*. Cambridge: Cambridge University Press.

Fix, A. G. 2002. Foragers, farmers, and traders in the Malayan Peninsula: origins of cultural and biological diversity. In K. D. Morrisson and L. L. Junker (eds), *Forager-traders in South and South-East Asia: long-term histories*, 185–202. Cambridge: Cambridge University Press.

Forbes, H. O. 1885. *A naturalist's wanderings in the Eastern Archipelago*. London: Sampson Low, Marston, Searle and Rivington.

Fortier, J. 2009. The ethnography of South Asian foragers. *Annual Review of Anthropology* 38, 99–114.

Freeman, D. 1955. *Iban agriculture: a report on the shifting cultivation of hill rice by the Iban of Sarawak*. London: Her Majesty's Stationary Office.

Geertz, C. 1963. *Agricultural involution: the processes of ecological change in Indonesia*. Berkeley: University of California Press.

Gianno, R. and Bayr, K. J. 2009. Semelai agricultural patterns: toward an understanding of variation among indigenous cultures in southern peninsular Malaysia. *Journal of Southeast Asian Studies* 40, 153–89.

Gomes, A. 2004. *Looking for money: capitalism and modernity in an Orang Asli village*. Suban Jaya: Centre for Orang Asli Concerns, Trans Pacific Press.

Gomes, A. 2007. *Modernity and Malaysia: settling the Menraq forest nomads*. London: Routledge.

Gomes, E. H. 2004 [1911]. *Seventeen years among the Sea Dayaks of Borneo*. Natural History Publications (Borneo) Sdn. Bhd.

Griffon, P. B. and Griffon, M. B. (eds) 1985. *The Agta of northeastern Luzon: recent studies*. Cebu City: San Carlos Publications.

Hayden, B. 2011. Rice: the first Asian luxury food? In G. Barker and M. Janowksi (eds), *Why cultivate? Anthropological and archaeological approaches to foraging–farming transitions in Southeast Asia*, 75–94. Cambridge: McDonald Institute for Archaeological Research.

Headland, T. N. and Reid, A. 1989. Hunter-gatherers and their neighbours from prehistory to the present. *Current Anthropology* 30, 43–66.

Hoffman, C. L. 1984. Punan foragers in the trading networks of Southeast Asia. In C. Schrire (ed.), *Past and present hunter-gatherer studies*, 123–49. London: Academic Press.

Hose, C. and McDougall, W. 1912. *The pagan tribes of Borneo*. London: Frank Cass.

Hutterer, K. L. 1977. Prehistoric trade and the evolution of Philippine societies: a reconsideration. In K. L. Hutterer (ed.), *Economic exchange and social interaction in Southeast Asia: perspectives from prehistory, history, and ethnography*, 177–96. Michigan: Michigan Papers on South and Southeast Asia.

Ikeya, K. and Nakai, S. 2009. Historical and contemporary relations between Mlabri and Hmong in Northern Thailand. In K. Ikeya, H. Ogawa, and P. Mitchell (eds), *Interactions between hunter-gatherers and farmers: from prehistory to present*, 247–61. Senri Ethnological Studies 73.

Ishige N. 1980. The preparation and origin of Galela food. In N. Ishige (ed.), *The Galela of Halmahera: a preliminary survey*, 263–341. Osaka: Senri Ethnological Studie No. 7, National Museum of Ethnology.

Janowski, M. 1997. The Kelabit attitude to the Penan: forever children. *La ricerca folklorica* 34, 55–8.

Janowski, M. 2014. Life in the landscape? Relationships with spirits and the environment in the upper Baram river, Sarwak. In G. Sprenger and K. Arhem (eds), *Animism in Southeast Asia*. London: Routledge.

Janowski, M. and Langub, J. 2011. Footprints and marks in the forest: the Penan and the Kelabit of Borneo. In G. Barker and M. Janowski (eds), *Why cultivate? Anthropological and archaeolgoical approaches to foraging–farming transitions in Southeast Asia*, 121–32. Cambridge: McDonald Institute for Archaeological Research.

Junker, L. L. 1996. Hunter-gatherer landscapes and lowland trade in the prehispanic Philippines. *World Archaeology* 27, 389–410.

Junker, L. L. 2002. Economic specialisation and inter-ethnic trade between foragers and farmers in the prehispanic Philippines. In K. D. Morrisson and L. L. Junker (eds), *Forager-traders in South and South-East Asia: long-term histories*, 185–202. Cambridge: Cambridge University Press.

Kaskija, L. 2007. Stuck at the bottom: opportunity structures and Punan Malinau identity. In P. G. Sercome and B. Sellato (eds), *Beyond the green myth: hunter-gatherers of Borneo in the twenty-first-century*, 135–59. Malaysia: Nias Press.

Kennedy, J. 1977. From stage to development in prehistoric Thailand: an exploration of the origins of growth, exchange, and variability in Southeast Asia. In K. L. Hutterer (ed.), *Economic exchange and social interaction in Southeast Asia: perspectives from prehistory, history, and ethnography*, 23–38. Michigan: Michigan Papers on South and Southeast Asia.

King, V. T. 1985. *The Maloh of West Kalimantan*. Dordrecht: Foris Publications.

Klimut, K. A. and Puri, R. 2007. The Punan from the Tubu' River, East Kalimantan: a native voice on past, present, and future circumstances. In P. G. Sercome and B. Sellato (eds), *Beyond the green myth: hunter-gatherers of Borneo in the twenty-first-century*, 110–34. Malaysia: Nias Press.

Knapp, G. and Heather, S. 2004. *Monsoon traders: ships, skippers and commodities in eighteenth-century Makassar*. Leiden: KITLV Press.

Kuchikura, Y. 1987. *Subsistence ecology among Semaq Beri hunter-gatherers of Peninsular Malaysia*. Hokkaido: Hokkaido Behavioural Science Report.

Langub, J. 2007. Native customary rights land: indigenous perspectives. Paper presented at Malaysian forest dialogue: Challenges in implementing and financing sustainable forest management. Renaissance Hotel Kuala Lumpur, 22–23 October.

Langub, J. 2009. From the heart: voices of involuntary migrants. Paper presented at Migration, resettlement and diaspora: Borneo and beyond. Annual Meeting of the Australian Anthropological Society, Macquarie University, Sydney, Australia, 9–11 December.

LeBar, F. M., Hickey, G. C., and Musgrave, J. K. (eds) 1964. *Ethnic groups of mainland Southeast Asia*. New Haven: Human Relations Area Files Press.

Leh, C. M. U. 2001. *A guide to bird's nest caves and bird's nests of Sarawak*. Sarawak Museum. Kuching: Lee Ming Press Company.

Lian, F. J. 1988. The economics and ecology of the production of the tropical rainforest resources by tribal groups of Sarawak, Borneo. In J. Dargavel, K. Dixon, and N. Semple (eds), *Changing tropical forests: historical perspectives on today's challenges in Asia, Australasia and Oceania*, 113–26. Canberra: Centre for Resource and Environmental Studies.

Low, H. 1882. Journal of a trip up the Rejang. *Sarawak Gazette* 12, 52–4, 62–5, 72–3, 81–3, 93–6.
Lye-Tuck Po. 2004. *Changing pathways: forest degradation and the Batek of Pahang, Malaysia.* New York: Lexington Books.
Morris, S. 1991. *The Oya Melanau.* Kuching: Lee Ming Press Company.
Nicholaisen, I. 1986. Pride and progress: Kajang response to economic change. *Sarawak Museum Journal* 36, 75–116.
Nicholaisen, J. 1976. The Penan of the Seventh Division of Sarawak: past, present, and future. *Sarawak Museum Journal* 24, 35–62.
Oota, H., Pakendorf, B., Weiss, G., von Haeseler, A., Pookajorn, S., Settheetham-Ishida, W., Tiwawech, D., Ishida, T., and Stoneking, M. 2005. Recent origin and cultural reversion of a hunter–gatherer group. *PLoS Biol* 3, e71.
Oppenheimer, S. 2004. The 'express train from Taiwan to Polynesia': on the congruence of proxy lines of evidence. *World Archaeology* 36, 591–600.
Pasveer, J. 2004. *The Djief hunters: 26,000 years of lowland rainforest exploitation on the Bird's Head of Papua, Indonesia.* Leeuwarden: STIP Stencilwerk.
Paz, V. 2005. Rock shelters, caves, and archaeobotany in island southeast Asia. *Asian Perspectives* 44, 107–18.
Peng, M., Quang, H., Dang, K., Trieu, A., Wang, H., Yao, Y., Kong, Q., and Zhang, Y. 2010. Tracing the Austronesian footprint in mainland Southeast Asia: a perspective from mitochondrial DNA. *Molecular Biology and Evolution* 27, 2417–30.
Persoon, G. 1989. The Kubu and the outside world (South Sumatra, Indonesia): the modification of hunting and gathering. *Anthropos* 84, 507–19.
Peterson, W. 1981. Recent adaptive shifts among Palanan hunters of the Philippines. *Man* 16, 43–61.
Piper, P. J., Rabett, R. J., and Bin Kurui, E. 2008. Terminal Pleistocene vertebrate assemblages to identify human hunting behaviour at the Niah caves, Borneo. *Bulletin of the Indo-Pacific Prehistory Association* 28, 88–98.
Puri, R. 1997. Penan Benalui knowledge and use of tree palms. In K. W. Sorensen and B. Morris (eds), *People and plants of Kayan Mentarang*, 194–226. London: WWF-IP/UNESCO.
Puri, R. 2005. *Deadly dances in the Bornean rainforest: hunting knowledge of the Penan Benalui.* Leiden: KTLV Press.
Reid, A. 1993. *Southeast Asia in the age of commerce: expansion and crisis.* New Haven: Yale University Press.
Rendle, A. B. 1917. A list of economic plants native or suitable for cultivation in the British Empire. Royal Botanic Gardens, Kew. *Bulletin of Miscellaneous Information* Nos 7 and 8.
Rousseau, J. 1990. *Central Borneo: ethnic identity and social life in a stratified society.* Oxford: Clarendon Press.
Rutter, O. 2007 [1929]. *The pagans of North Borneo.* Kota Kinabalu: Opus Publications.
Sandbukt, O. 1988. Tributary tradition and relations of affinity and gender among Sumatran Kubu. In T. Ingold, D. Riches, and J. Woodburn (eds), *Hunters and gatherers, vol. 1: history, evolution and social change*, 107–16. Oxford: Berg.
Sandin, B. 1967. *The Sea Dyaks of Borneo.* London: Macmillan.
Schebesta, P. 1926. Kubu and Jakun as proto-Malays. *Wien* 56, 192–201.
Schebesta, P. 1929. *Among the forest dwarfs of Malaya.* London: Hutchinson.
Schebesta, P. and Bladgen, C. O. 1926. The jungle tribes of the Malay Peninsula. *Bulletin of the School of Oriental and African Studies* 4, 269–78.
Schwaner, C. A. L. M. 1853. *Borneo: Beschrijving van het stoomgebied van den Barito.* 2 vols. Amsterdam: P. N. van Kampen.

Sellato, B. 1994. *Nomads of the Borneo rainforest: the economics, politics, and ideology of settling down*. Honolulu: University of Hawai'i Press.

Sellato, B. 2005. Forests for food, forests for trade—between sustainability and extractivism: the economic pragmatism of traditional peoples and the trade history of northern East Kalimantan. In R. L. Wadley (ed.), *Histories of the Borneo environment*, 61–86. Leiden: KTLV Press.

Skeat, W. W. 1902. The wild tribes of the Malay Peninsula. *Journal of the Anthropological Institute of Great Britain and Ireland* 32, 124–41.

Soares, P., Rito, T., Trejaut, J., Mormina, M., Hill, C., Tinkler-Hundal, E., Braid, M., Clarke, D., Loo, J., Thomson, N., Denham, T., Donohue, M., Macaulay, V., Lin, M., Oppenheimer, S., and Richards, M. 2011. Ancient voyaging and polynesian origins. *American Journal of Human Genetics* 88, 239–47.

Spencer, St John 1862. *Life in the forests of the Far East*. London: Smith, Elder and Co.

Strickland, S. S. 1985. Long-term development of Kejaman subsistence: an ecological study. *Sarawak Museum Journal* 36, 117–71.

Swadling, P. 1996. *Plumes from paradise: trade cycles in outer Southeast Asia and their impact on New Guinea and nearby islands until 1920*. Boroko: Papua New Guinea National Museum.

Tagliacozzo, E. 2005. Onto the coasts and into the forests: ramifications of the China trade on the ecological history of northwest Borneo, 900–1900 CE. In R. L. Wadley (ed.), *Histories of the Borneo environment*, 25–59. Leiden: KTLV Press.

Vink, M. 2003. The world's oldest trade: Dutch slavery and slave trade in the Indian Ocean in the seventeenth century. *Journal of World History* 14, 131–77.

Wheatley, P. 1964. *Impressions of the Malay Peninsula in ancient times*. Singapore: Eastern Universities Press.

Whitmore, J. K. 1977. The opening of Southeast Asia, trading patterns through the centuries. In K. L. Hutterer (ed.), *Economic exchange and social interaction in Southeast Asia: perspectives from prehistory, history, and ethnography*, 139–50. Michigan: Michigan Papers on South and Southeast Asia.

Williams-Hunt, P. D. R. 1954. A Lanoh Negrito funeral near Lenggong, Perak. *Federation Museums Journal* 1–2, 64–74.

Williams, T. R. 1965. *The Dusun: a North Borneo society*. New York: Holt, Rienhart and Winston.

Wolters, O. W. 1967. *Early Indonesian commerce: a study of the origins of Srivijaya*. New York: Cornell University Press.

Zuarina M. and Tija, H. D. 1988. Kota Tampan, Perak: the geological and archaeological evidence for a late Pleistocene site. *Journal of the Malaysian Branch of the Royal Asiatic Society* 56, 123–34.

CHAPTER 41

THE EMERGENCE OF FORAGER–FARMER INTERACTION IN NORTH AMERICA

KATHERINE A. SPIELMANN

THE relationship between foragers and farmers is a complex topic in North American prehistory because there were no populations that relied solely on domesticated plants and animals for their subsistence. The lack of domestic herd animals meant that all prehistoric populations relied on wild resources for their meat supply. Moreover, it was not uncommon for some North American populations to rely on a flexible mix of cultivation, gathering, and hunting, and for others to move back and forth between a more agriculturally focused lifeway, and hunting and gathering. The only domestic animal common across the continent was the dog, which was not generally a staple source of meat. In the southwestern US, some late prehistoric populations domesticated the turkey, at least in part for food (Munro 1994).

This chapter begins by elaborating a bit on this forager–farmer flexibility, and then moves on to the primary topic, that of purely hunter-gatherer populations interacting with largely farming populations. Documenting the origins of prehistoric forager–farmer interaction is complicated by the archaeological invisibility of many of the trade items (dried meat, fish, hides, and corn), and the difficulty in distinguishing between foraging and farming sites in the archaeological record. Given this difficulty, the chapter also draws on ethnohistoric information from three North American forager–farmer interactive systems for which there are at least some archaeological data. Because the origins of Plains–Pueblo interaction are the best documented of all the prehistoric forager–farmer systems in North America, the chapter focuses in particular on that case. At the end there is a discussion of interesting parallels between the development of forager–farmer relations in North America and agro-pastoral relations in the Near East and a consideration of future research directions.

Hunting, Gathering, and Farming in North America

The diverse environments of North America were variably conducive to the production of both indigenous domesticates (e.g. amaranth, chenopodium, knotweed; see Smith 2006; Smith and Cowan 2003) and those imported from Mesoamerica (corn, beans, and squash). Population density and climatic conditions played a role over time in the relative emphasis on hunting and gathering vs cultivation. Thus, as others have noted with regard to the 'origins' of agriculture, it is generally not knowledge of farming per se that determines whether people farm or not, but the relative risk and productivity of farming vs hunting and gathering at particular times and places (e.g. see Barlow 2002). In some portions of North America, farming was never more reliable or productive than hunting and gathering. This is the case for the subarctic, Columbia Plateau, Northwest Coast, and both inland and coastal California, where cultivation was rarely practised prehistorically (Figure 41.1). Much of California, for example, is characterized by the close proximity of highly productive ecozones: marine, riverine, lake, and forest, which produce complementary floral and faunal subsistence resources. Hunter-gatherer populations were thus able to move among and exploit contiguous resource patches (Barrett 1952; Gayton 1948; King 1976; Kniffen 1939; Loeb 1926). In other regions, under certain climatic regimes, farming became a viable option for a period of time. Such was the case in portions of the Great Basin and Plains. In the Great Basin, people referred to archaeologically as the Fremont pursued a highly variable mixture of hunting, gathering, and cultivation from roughly AD 400 to 1150 (Barlow 2002; Coltrain and Leavitt 2002). Along the river valleys of the central and southern Plains, although there is some evidence for horticulture after about AD 400, it is not until the AD 1200s that evidence for farming became relatively common; hunted and gathered resources, however, remained significant components of the diet (Brosowske 2005).

In the south-eastern portion of the US south-west, archaeologists (Jelinek 1967; Speth 2004, 2005) have argued that the increasing productivity of bison hunting in the late prehistoric period (post AD 1250) led formerly farming populations to either become hunter-gatherers or to increase the hunted component of their subsistence base. In the north-eastern US Chilton (2005; see also Day and Trigger 1978) has documented that a flexible mix of cultivating, hunting, and gathering was integral to the long-term occupation of this region. Moreover, within farming populations, when crop production fell below a level that would support an entire village and stored food supplies were depleted, ethnographic sources indicate that some members of a farming village would be forced to leave, possibly becoming hunter-gatherers until conditions improved. This 'sloughing off' of a portion of the population is said to have been a strategy pursued among the Hopi Pueblo people of north-eastern Arizona, where lower-status lineages were expected to leave the village under famine conditions (Connolly 1956). On the Plains, when Arikara corn crops were inundated, most of the village population took up bison hunting full time until the next planting season (Blakeslee 1975, 256).

Clearly this complex historical relationship between hunting and gathering and farming complicates the question of interaction between foragers and farmers in North American prehistory. It also establishes the fact that both foragers and farmers are likely to have used

FIGURE 41.1 Locations of North American hunter-gatherer populations.

portions of the same landscape. Given that farmers hunted (and fished, where feasible) and gathered (nuts, fruits, medicinal plants), the relationship between foragers and farmers was not predicated on a stark complementarity between the products of farming and foraging. Nor was the landscape in which hunter-gatherers moved likely to have been considered 'the other' in the way that forests are described for more contemporary examples of forager–farmer relations (e.g. Bauchet and Guillaume 1982; Blackburn 1982; Williams 1974). It is thus helpful to use the North American ethnohistoric record of interactive relations between foragers and farmers as an entry point into an assessment of their prehistoric origins. Three regions in North America for which there is some degree of ethnohistoric information on forager–farmer interaction are the US north-east, Middle Missouri, and south-west/southern Plains. It is on these three cases that the remainder of the chapter focuses (see Figure 41.2).

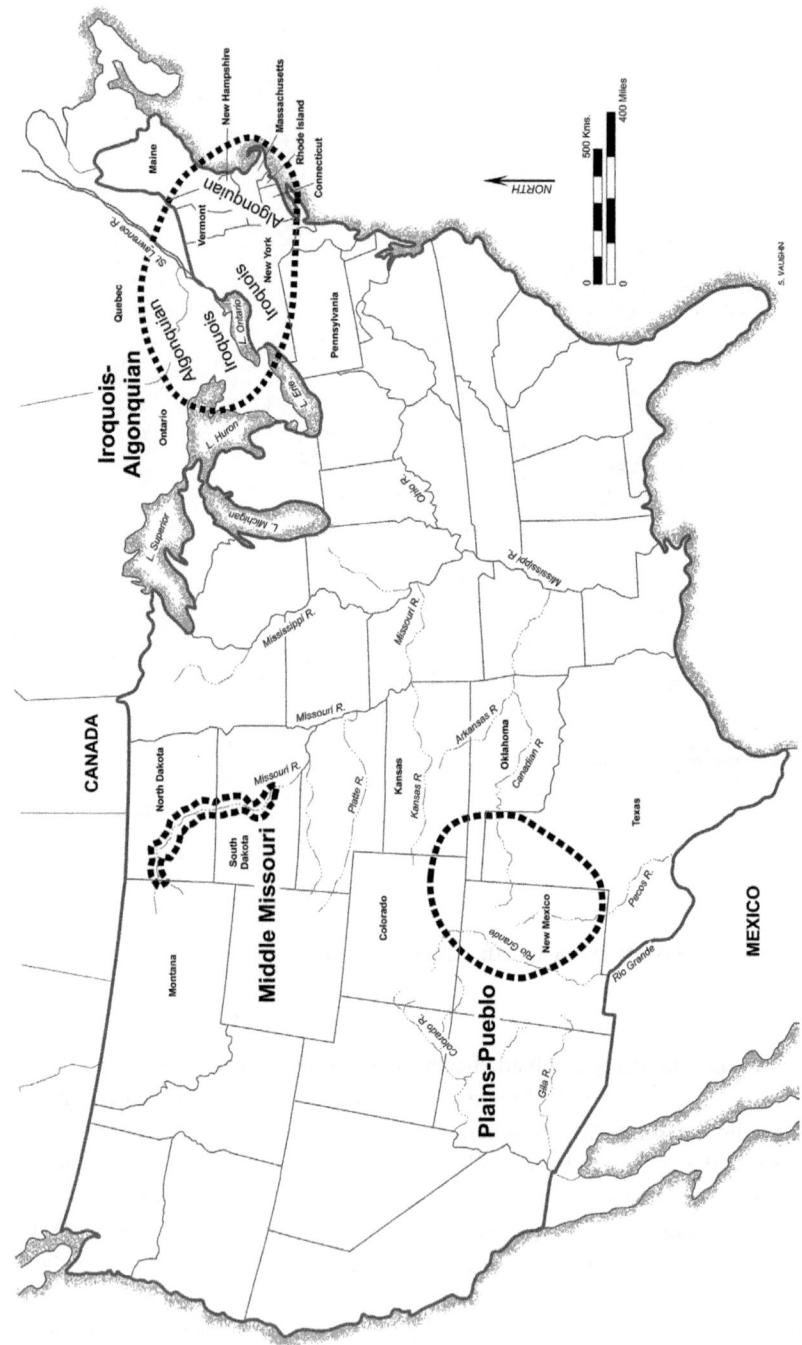

FIGURE 41.2 Locations of the three case studies discussed in the text, Iroquois-Algonquian, Middle Missouri, and Plains–Pueblo.

North American Forager–Farmer Interaction

Great Lakes: Algonquian/Iroquois Interaction

Ethnohistoric information on forager–farmer interaction in southern Ontario and the north-eastern US involves relations between the Iroquoian Huron in southern Ontario and Algonquian hunters to the north. The Huron farmers in Ontario occupied an upland area of arable land, and at the time of contact their diet consisted largely of corn and fish (Katzenberg et al. 1995; Schwarcz et al. 1985). Based on documentary data, hunting appears to have been relatively unimportant (Heidenreich 1978). Trigger (1963; 1976) attributes this to the prehistoric over-hunting of deer by the sizeable Huron population and notes that deer were eaten only on special occasions, such as feasts.

The location of the Huron on the edge of the Canadian Shield and at the lower end of an easy, along-shore canoe trail to the north was ideal for trade with Algonquian populations (Trigger 1963). Nipissing and other Algonquian groups sometimes wintered with the Huron (Day 1978; Day and Trigger 1978; Grant 1952, 305, 317) after fishing extensively and drying the fish for trade. At the Huron villages they traded deer skins, beaver pelts, and dried fish for nets and cornmeal. Trigger infers that the hunters needed corn to get through the winter. The Huron were also middlemen in the tobacco trade from the Iroquoian Neutral and Petun to the Algonquians, and the Huron also made cloaks from squirrel and raccoon skins that they received from the Neutral (another Iroquois population) to trade with Algonquian hunters. Similarly, the Montagnais of the north shore of the St Lawrence River visited and traded for cornmeal and tobacco with their Iroquois, Algonquian, and Abenaki neighbours (Rogers and Leacock 1981). Trade was conducted between formal trading partners, and Trigger stresses the importance of sociality to exchange (Trigger 1976, 64).

Scholars differ on the motivations they attribute to the Huron trade with Algonquian hunters. On the one hand, Heidenreich (1978) argued that it was generally to secure desirable goods for social standing and advancement. Trigger (1976) on the other hand suggests that due to over-hunting, the Huron depended on Algonquians for access to hides for clothing. Trigger suggests that the additional supplies of fish provided by the Algonquians would also have been important for the Huron, but does not explain why. It is unlikely that the Huron would have overfished the local waters (Trigger 1962; 1963). Thus, it is unclear how important the dried fish traded by the Algonquians were to Huron subsistence. The Algonquian supply may have given the Huron time to do things other than the labour-intensive tasks of processing and drying fish.

Just as the Huron did their own fishing, the Algonquian groups did some of their own farming. Ethnohistoric documents describe the Algonquian hunters as cultivating some fresh vegetables in the summer, and corn where there was good soil (Day 1978; Day and Trigger 1978). Given that Algonquian groups did not camp near Huron villages every winter, it is possible that this supplementary farming, when crops were successful, was sufficient for hunters to remain in their camps. Similarly, a fairly northern group of Iroquois (Laurentian) shared this sort of economic adaptation. Whether a population was agricultural or not depended, logically, on its geographic location; agriculture as a primary mode of subsistence in this region was confined to the warmer and more fertile country south of the Canadian Shield (Trigger 1963). The mixed cultivating, fishing, hunting and gathering lifeway described in the ethnohistoric documents on Algonquian and some Iroquois populations in Canada dovetails with the lifeway documented by Chilton (2005) for Algonquian populations in New England, who also interacted with Iroquois neighbours.

Prehistoric Iroquois–Algonquian Interaction

Given that the environment in which Canadian Algonquian populations lived was at the northernmost extent of agriculture in eastern North America, it was not conducive to successful corn farming. Thus, Algonquian trade relationships with the Huron appear to have been dietarily important, and likely prehistoric in origin. Moreover, the complexity of Huron trade suggested to Trigger (1976) that exchange relations with the northern hunters had existed in pre-contact times. The challenge comes with actually documenting this interaction in prehistory, and dealing with its beginnings and motivations. At this time, the archaeological research relating to Algonquian–Iroquois interaction is focused on sorting out how to identify it. Until that challenge is met, it is difficult to address the origins of interactive relations.

Whether dealing with Iroquois–Algonquian interaction in Ontario or in New England, archaeologists have tended to rely on ceramic data for evidence of contact. Early archaeologists posited that generalized trade between the agriculturalists of southern Ontario and the peoples of the Canadian Shield might be reflected in the distributions of incised pottery, presumed to be Iroquois pottery, in the latter regions (Pretola 2002; Wintemberg 1943; Wright 1981, 95).

In the early 1990s, Starna and Funk (1994) questioned archaeologists' ability to distinguish between Iroquois and Algonquian peoples based on material culture. They noted clines rather than abrupt breaks in the distribution of ceramic attributes across the northeast. Similarly, Michelaki (2007) has recently questioned simplistic assumptions about an Algonquian 'trait' (shell tempering) found in a small but significant numbers of Neutral Iroquois ceramics.

Research by Chilton (1998) and Pretola (2000; 2002) has called into question the use of pottery styles to differentiate between Iroquois and Algonquian populations in New England. While the New England Algonquian populations were cultivator-foragers and thus different in adaptation from the hunter-fisher Ontario Algonquians who were trade partners of the Iroquois, the New England research is directly pertinent to whether 'Iroquois' ceramics on Ontario Algonquian sites are indeed Iroquois. Are these ceramics trade wares, perhaps indicative of the interaction documented in the ethnohistoric period, or are they local products whose makers participated in the use of a pan-north-east design style? Both of these options are indicative of interaction, but differ in terms of their implications.

Chilton used technological attributes to differentiate between choices made by Late Woodland (AD 1300–1600) Iroquoian and Algonquian potters. She determined that the Algonquian ceramics were less resistant to thermal shock in a number of attributes, but more resistant to mechanical stress (breakage) than were Iroquois pots. The Algonquian pots were also smaller. She linked these attributes to the more mobile adaptation of the Algonquian cultivator-hunters and to less emphasis on corn (and thus the boiling of corn) in the diet, and she inferred that the Algonquian vessels were more important for the transport of food and water than they were for cooking. In addition, the high diversity in surface treatment on the Algonquian pots suggests a more fluid social context and context of production than in contemporaneous Iroquois villages.

Pretola (2000; 2002) has recently pursued the Iroquois/Algonquian question using both technological and design style attributes. The results of his research document pan-New England decorative traits that Iroquois and Algonquian populations combined in distinct ways on pots whose fabric and form are local.

To conclude this discussion of Algonquian–Iroquois interaction, it is apparent from the ethnohistoric documents that prior to European contact, these foragers and farmers had developed an interdependent system involving food, hides, and other material items such as nets and tobacco. At this time, however, archaeological data concerning the conditions under which this relationship developed are too limited to discern its initial timing and the factors that led to the exchange.

Middle Missouri

The Middle Missouri archaeological area is located on the Upper Missouri River in North and South Dakota. Historically it was the location of the Arikara, Mandan, and Hidatsa farming villages. Crow, Assiniboin, Cheyenne, and Sioux bison hunters regularly traded at these villages, and could spend the winter outside them trading bison meat and hides for corn (Denig 1961, 47). The confounding factor to using ethnohistoric information to understand the prehistoric antecedents of forager–farmer interaction on the Plains is that European visitors arrived relatively late in the Middle Missouri region, after significant migrations of the Sioux onto the Plains, after the horse and gun had substantially changed both subsistence practices and intertribal relations, and after European traders and their goods were important players in trade relations.

For example, one of the earliest Europeans to visit the Mandan, Pierre Gaultier de Varennes de La Verendrye (1968), a French trader and explorer, witnessed transactions in which European goods played a prominent role. In late November of 1738 Assiniboin hunters arrived at the Mandan villages to trade for corn and tobacco as well as bison robes, deer skins, and painted leather. The Mandan were apparently well known for their skills at dressing leather. In return the Mandan received guns, axes, kettles, gunpowder, and bullets, all European items, from the Assiniboin (La Verendrye 1968, 321–2). Earlier in his journal La Verendrye mentions a group of Assiniboin leaving the fort where he was stationed in January to trade with the Mandan for corn. La Verendrye noted later in his journal that many different tribes of hunters would arrive on horseback at Mandan villages in early June to trade dressed and painted skins in return for grain and beans, but this was not a trade he himself witnessed (La Verendrye 1968, 366–7).

Several decades later, Meriwether Lewis and William Clark wintered near the Mandan from October 1804 to April 1805. Assiniboin and Cree hunters came to trade with the Mandan in November that year as well, but Lewis and Clark noted that they traded primarily with European traders and only secondarily with the Mandan, and that in fact the Assiniboin controlled trade with the British, making the Mandan dependent on them for access to European goods (Lewis and Clark 1893, 193–5). That same month the Crow also visited the Mandan and Hidatsa, trading horses, mules, and leather goods for guns, ammunition, and metal tools. Given this information on the exchanges that took place and the regular hunting expeditions that the Mandan undertook from October through April (Lewis and Clark 1893, 177–262; see also Thomas and Ronnefeldt 1976; Will and Spinden 1906; Wilson 1924), Mandan reliance on Plains hunting populations for meat is not evident. Lewis and Clark mentioned (1893, 231) that the Mandan ate bison in the winter and relied on stored corn and beans in the summer.

Both La Verendrye (1968, 321) and Lewis and Clark (1893, 321) noted that harassment by the Sioux kept the Mandan from hunting as extensively as they would have liked. The Sioux instead traded hides with the Arikara to the south of the Mandan and Hidatsa in return for corn. The Arikara then supplied those hides to European traders (Lewis and Clark 1893, 164–5).

Curiously, there has been a tendency in North American ethnography and archaeology to assume that the historic Plains–Middle Missouri trading system was not that dissimilar from prehistory. John Ewers (1954; 1968) made this argument explicitly, though without any real data on interactions in the prehistoric period, and Raymond Wood (1972, 1980; see also Blakeslee 1975, 78) makes the case in prehistory, basing his argument on the appearance of dentalium and olivella shells from the west coast and marginella and conch shells from the Gulf Coast in Middle Missouri village sites. That some sort of trade network must have existed to move such objects across these long distances is not in doubt. Whether a subsistence-based interdependence based on the trade of corn and beans for meat and hides was in operation, however, is open to question.

The historic Plains bison hunters relied on the horse for easy access to both bison herds on the Plains and the Missouri river villages. The Missouri River villagers largely traded for European items rather than items of the hunt. Even Ewers notes that metal and metal objects were a primary trade item in the historic Plains–Missouri River trade. His supposition that European goods simply replaced prehistoric exchanges in native pottery and lithics does not make a great deal of sense. Missouri River villagers had local access to lithic materials, and prehistoric Plains nomadic hunters had little need or carrying capacity (without horses) for fragile ceramics. Denig (1961, 45) and Blakeslee (1975, 242–5) argue that challenges to corn production along the Missouri would have left villagers susceptible to crop failure. How a trade network linking them with hunters would have ameliorated this, however, is not clear. Blakeslee (1975, 256) in fact cites an Arikara example of crop failure that caused them to abandon their village and hunt bison until the next planting season. Denig also notes that in general the Arikara spent winters hunting on the plains and living in tipis 15–40 miles from their villages.

Prehistoric Middle Missouri Interaction

Beyond the small quantities of shell and other items (e.g. obsidian) found in Middle Missouri villages there is at present nothing much to work with in terms of the prehistoric origins of forager–farmer interaction in this portion of North America. As Ewers noted with respect to this system, the perishability of the subsistence items envisioned to underwrite the interaction renders inferences concerning such a system moot.

One topic that keeps the question of prehistoric forager–farmer relations alive, however, is the Crow–Hidatsa split that took place, based on linguistics, between the late 1400s and around 1600 (Hanson 1998; Matthews 1979). Differences between the Crow and Hidatsa in kinship, sodality, and medicine bundle systems suggest some length of time to this separation (Hanson 1979). When they were encountered by Europeans, the Crow were bison hunters on the northern Plains (Lowie 1935). At some point in the past, however, they had been Hidatsa, and likely were among the Hidatsa populations that migrated from eastern North Dakota to the middle Missouri region in the early 1200s.

A conflict over food distribution is said by both Crow and Hidatsa informants to have been at the heart of the split. Hanson (1979) conjectures that population pressure in general may have been the cause. He suggests that a farming-hunting lifeway already heavily dependent upon bison hunting might have 'pre-adapted' these farmer-hunters for a purely hunting lifeway, particularly given the social connections that likely would have remained among families after the split and that continued into the historic period (Lowie 1922; 1924; Meyer 1977; Thomas and Ronnefeldt 1976). In the 1970s, Plains archaeologists thought they had identified Crow encampments on the basis of unusual quantities of ceramics of Middle Missouri style. There are, however, significant debates over the dating and nature of those ceramics (e.g. remains of Mandan or Hidatsa hunting camps; see papers in *Archaeology in Montana* 1979; Hanson 1998). While the Crow–Hidatsa, forager–farmer relationship has yet to be elucidated, it parallels in interesting ways much better-documented farmer-to-hunter shifts in the southern Plains, and thus may be one case in a more common pattern than is generally realized in North America. It is to the Plains–Pueblo case that we now turn.

Plains–Pueblo Interaction

Spaniards first entered the south-west US on the Coronado expedition in AD 1539. That expedition was followed by several others in the later 1500s until 1598 when Don Juan de Oñate established a Spanish colony on the Rio Grande in the vicinity of the current Tewa Pueblo, San Juan.

Chroniclers of these expeditions recorded trading relationships between Plains bison hunters and Pueblo farmers in which the bison hunters would bring bison meat, fat, and hides to eastern border pueblos to barter for corn, cotton blankets, and ceramics (Hammond and Rey 1953, 400, 610, 838; 1966, 86, 283–4; Winship 1896, 274). These Plains hunters were said to have wintered outside the villages of their Pueblo trade partners (Winship 1896, 274). References to trade between Plains and Pueblo peoples continue into the seventeenth century (e.g. Ayer 1916; Hammond and Rey 1953, 660).

Prehistoric Plains–Pueblo Interaction

For a variety of reasons, the Plains–Pueblo interactive system is the best-known prehistoric forager–farmer system in North America, and is thus the best case on which to focus a discussion of the emergence of hunter–farmer interaction. These reasons include the ability to distinguish south-western larger prey species (deer and antelope) from those of the Plains (bison). Thus, unlike the north-east where both foragers and farmers hunted deer and caught fish, or the Middle Missouri where they both hunted bison, the differences in faunal species in the Plains/south-west system allow for some degree of tracking of one of the primary food resources involved in Plains–Pueblo exchange. Although we cannot track shelled and ground corn from the Pueblos onto the Plains, Judith Habicht-Mauche's study of the development of ceramic technology among Plains hunter-gatherers (discussed below) provides a proxy for identifying when corn became an important part of Plains forager diet.

Given the distance between the bison herds on the southern Plains and the eastern border Pueblo villages, most bison meat is likely to have been traded dried and without associated bone. Luckily, however, the drying of meat on rib segments for transport means that some bison bone is found in eastern border pueblos. Because bison bone presence in Pueblo middens varies significantly over time, we can use bison bone frequencies along with those of other Plains items to observe the development of Plains–Pueblo exchange over time.

Other factors that make this case study particularly helpful in research on the development of forager–farmer relations include marked differences between Plains and Pueblo populations in lithic technologies and lithic raw materials (e.g. south-western obsidian and Plains Alibates dolomite). The relatively precise cross-dating capacity provided by south-western Glaze Ware ceramics, which were traded to Plains hunters, has also allowed archaeologists to track hunter–farmer relations in a relatively detailed manner over a prehistory of several hundred years.

The Plains–Pueblo case provides an opportunity to explore two pathways to forager–farmer relations. One pathway (farmers and hunters) leads to the emergence of relations between long-term Plains hunters, such as the ancestral Athabascans, and long-term Pueblo farmers. The other (farmers to hunters) involves a shift from a farming-hunting lifeway to a specialized hunting lifeway by farmers living in some eastern border pueblos and in small villages along the Canadian and Beaver river valleys of the southern Plains.

Farmers and Hunters

Understanding the origins of relations between Pueblo farmers on the eastern border of the Pueblo world and hunter-gatherers on the southern Plains requires some background knowledge of the culture history of the two regions. Until the thirteenth century AD, much of the eastern Pueblo area was sparsely occupied. Dean et al. (1994, fig. 4.9) have estimated that perhaps 5,000 people lived in the entire northern Rio Grande area, from central New Mexico to the Colorado border. The majority of this population was concentrated west of the Rio Grande, while populations east of the Rio Grande were much smaller (Crown et al. 1996; Spielmann 1996). Beginning in the twelfth century and increasing in tempo in the 1200s, roughly 10,000–12,000 people migrated into the Rio Grande Valley from areas to the north and west (Wilshusen 2002). By the early fourteenth century the indigenous and immigrant populations were living in aggregated villages of a few hundred to a thousand people across the eastern Pueblo area.

At the time that the Rio Grande Pueblo farming population was growing in the thirteenth century, Plains farmers were also moving into the Canadian and Beaver River valleys of the southern Plains where they established villages and single homesteads (Plains Village tradition; e.g. the Panhandle Aspect; Brosowske 2005; Lintz 1986). There is no agreed-upon explanation for this timing. Brosowske (2005, 292–308) suggests that the production and trade of high-quality Alibates dolomite blanks in the Texas Panhandle may have drawn cultivator-hunter-gatherer groups to the area. The lack of any archaeological evidence of a relationship between the preceding foragers in this area of the Plains, and the Plains village archaeological record that abruptly appears in the mid-1200s suggests that farmers migrated into the area. These farmers subsisted on a variety of game animals; bison bone dominates the assemblage, but the villagers do not appear to have specialized solely on bison hunting. Corn has been recovered from these villages, but not in great quantities and the corn processing assemblage is limited (though wooden mortars and pestles may have been used to process the corn). Bone chemistry data suggest high consumption of C_4 foods, which would include bison as well as corn (Brosowske 2005, 96–8).

There is evidence in these thirteenth- and fourteenth-century villages of modest interaction between Plains and Pueblo farmers. Small quantities of Pueblo ceramics, Pueblo pipes, obsidian, turquoise, and shell are found at the larger Panhandle aspect villages (Brosowske 2005; Lintz 1991). Likewise, small quantities of bison bone and Alibates dolomite (from outcrops in the Texas Panhandle) are found in contemporaneous Pueblo middens (Potter 1995; Spielmann 1983; 1991). The infrequency of these materials in both areas suggests that they may represent gifts reflecting only periodic social contacts.

Beginning in the fifteenth century, however, quantities of Alibates lithic material, Plains-style stone tools made from Alibates, and bison bone increased substantially in eastern border Pueblo middens such as Gran Quivira and Pecos (Hayes et al. 1981; Kidder 1932; Potter 1995; Spielmann 1983; 1991). In addition other Plains items such as bison bone fleshers and shell ornaments made from Plains shell species are found at these eastern border Pueblos. This marked increase in the tempo of Plains–Pueblo interaction reflects a shift in southern Plains adaptations from farming to bison hunting, as well as the arrival of ancestral Athabascan hunter-gatherers onto the southern Plains. The following section discusses the shift from farming to hunting among populations in south-eastern New Mexico and the Texas Panhandle.

Farmers to Hunters

John Speth's long-term research along tributaries of the Pecos River in south-eastern New Mexico (Rocek and Speth 1986; Speth 2004, see especially 420–9; 2005) has documented an interesting process whereby farmer-hunter populations gradually began to emphasize bison hunting on the Plains over local hunting. This process began in the mid-1200s, and by the 1400s these populations appear to have abandoned their farming villages and become solely bison hunters (see also Jelinek 1967).

Excavations at a series of pueblos on tributaries of the Pecos River in the vicinity of Roswell, New Mexico document this gradual shift. The farmers who occupied the village of Fox Place in the early 1200s relied primarily on local fauna (antelope and rabbits), with bison bone present in relatively small quantities. Subsequently, the farmers at Henderson Pueblo (Speth 2004; 2005), a village of roughly 70–80 people (Speth 2004, 420), markedly increased their emphasis on bison hunting at some distance from their village, and their participation in trade with Pueblo populations to the west of the Pecos valley. Speth's research at Henderson has documented an early phase of occupation (*c.* AD 1250–75) and a later one (early 1300s). Bison age data indicate that roughly 50 per cent of the early-phase bison were acquired through communal spring kills, while 80 per cent of the late-phase bison were captured in this manner. An under-representation of ribs and vertebrae in the early period is interpreted to indicate trade in bison meat, given their prevalence at larger pueblo sites like Gran Quivira and Pecos discussed above. The late-phase bison assemblage contains even lower proportions of ribs and vertebrae, as well as a marked increase in decorated ceramics from Pueblo villages further to the west. Speth interprets these data to indicate an increasing reliance on bison hunting and bison trade over the course of the village's occupation. Bloom Mound, a pueblo occupied in the 1300s to the mid-1400s, contains even more Pueblo exchange items. After Bloom's occupation, people no longer occupied farming villages in this portion of the Pecos Valley (Speth 2005).

High corn ubiquity characterizes the flotation samples from both Henderson and Bloom. Corn was thus a significant component in the diet. Caries rates, bone chemistry data, and a somewhat crude groundstone technology, however, differ significantly from those at Pueblo villages further east (e.g. Speth 2004; 2005; Spielmann et al. 1990; Spielmann and Schoeninger 1992). Corn thus does not appear to have been the dietary staple in this area of the south-west that it was for Pueblo populations in the Rio Grande Valley.

On the southern Plains, Panhandle Aspect villagers appear to have undertaken the same transition as their contemporaries in south-eastern New Mexico (Lintz 1986; 1991), moving from mixed bison hunting and farming to purely bison hunting sometime in the late fifteenth century. This discussion relies heavily on Scott Brosowske's 2005 dissertation, which provides the most recent review and analysis of southern Plains hunting and farming.

Most of the Panhandle Aspect villages appear to have been abandoned by the mid-1400s (Brosowske 2005, 84), with no clear evidence of what their residents did after this time. Some researchers have suggested that they became the Teyas discussed in early Spanish documents, which distinguished them from the Querechos, hunter-gatherers who appear to have been ancestral Athabascans (Habicht-Mauche 1987; Hammond and Rey 1940, 292; Vehik and Baugh 1994). While the archaeological data for the southern Plains villagers becoming specialized bison hunters are more equivocal than those from south-eastern New Mexico, there remains the possibility that villagers in both areas ceased farming and became full-time hunters in the fifteenth century. Why was this the case?

In previous work (Spielmann 1991) I have interpreted the Plains–Pueblo system as, at least in part, a mutualistic system of exchange in which Pueblo farmers came to depend on Plains bison hunters for bison meat, fat, and hides, and Plains bison hunters came to depend on Pueblo farmers for corn. Over-hunting of antelope in the vicinity of Gran Quivira, for example, would have been a motivating factor in these farmers seeking to augment their access to meat through trade (Spielmann 1989; 1991; see also Potter 1995).

For mutualistic, interdependent systems to develop, the resources that each party brings to the exchange must be reliably available. Speth (2004, 424–6) argues that the timing of the transition to a hunter-farmer adaptation in south-eastern New Mexico coincides with Pueblo farmers aggregating into larger villages, thus making the possibility of annual surpluses more likely than when these farmers lived in smaller villages. That aggregation, however, did not take place until the fifteenth century (Spielmann 1996), the period during which hunter-farmers in the south-west and on the Plains ceased to occupy villages and seem to have become specialized bison hunters. Thus, in the Texas Panhandle and south-eastern New Mexico, leaving farming behind probably did depend upon sufficiently concentrated Pueblo farmers for reliable surpluses of corn. The less-intense exchange relations that developed in the thirteenth and fourteenth centuries, while these farmers were increasing their emphasis on hunting, would have established the social ties so crucial for mutually reliable access to one another's products. Reliability would have been particularly important for transitional farmer-hunter-gatherers as they increasingly came to depend upon Pueblo farmers for corn. In the 1300s the Pueblo villages to the west, the ones that Speth views as consumers of imported bison, were still relatively small, at perhaps 100–150 people per village (Chamberlin 2008), and extant faunal data do not indicate that over-hunting had occurred (Clark 2006; Potter 1995). Small quantities of bison bone in these fourteenth-century pueblos, however, may indicate the very beginnings of trade in bison.

Bison hides may have been as, if not more, important than meat and fat in Plains–Pueblo trade (Spielmann 1996). Spanish chroniclers (Hammond and Rey 1953; Kessell 1979; Winship 1896) noted sizeable numbers of bison hides in Pueblo villages from Pecos in the east to the Hopi Mesas in the west. Their observations concerned hides as male items of clothing. LeBlanc (1999; see also Speth 2004, 425) has argued that bison hides may have been particularly useful in making the tougher shields necessary for protection in warfare with the introduction of new bow technology (the recurved bow). Recent research in the Salinas area has documented intense warfare at the smaller pueblo villages of the fourteenth century (Chamberlin and Rautman 2009), which may support this argument.

That forager–farmer interdependence relied on durable social ties between particular south-western villages and particular bands of Plains hunters has been documented in an interesting ceramic analysis by Kathryn Leonard (2000). To investigate the nature of social relations between Plains and Pueblo populations, Leonard undertook a petrographic analysis of Pueblo Glaze Ware sherds from two groups of late prehistoric southern Plains hunter-gatherer sites, one on tributaries of the Red River and the other on the Brazos. Her findings indicate that hunter-gatherers occupying the Red River sites traded almost exclusively with Galisteo Basin pueblos, whereas those occupying the Brazos sites traded with people living in the Pecos, Salinas, or Galisteo Basin areas. Trade partnerships are likely to have developed between families, and social and perhaps ritual ties must have been strong between members of these populations, perhaps similar to the way in which more recent Jicarilla Apache families maintained inherited trade partnerships with Tewa families (Ford 1972) and intermarried with the people of Picuris (Brown 1973).

Judith Habicht-Mauche's analyses of protohistoric southern Plains ceramics substantiate the sociality of ties between Plains and Pueblo populations (Habicht-Mauche 1988; 1991; 2000). Through petrographic analysis, she demonstrated that although the plain ware ceramics found on late prehistoric southern Plains hunter-gatherer sites closely resemble Pueblo plain ware ceramics, they were not trade wares but instead were made on the Plains. The adoption of a Pueblo technology by Plains people suggests close contacts, perhaps intermarriage for instruction in ceramic manufacture (Habicht-Mauche 2000). Habicht-Mauche suggests that the adoption of Pueblo ceramic technology by southern Plains hunter-gatherers was specifically for processing corn, as corn became more important in their diet.

Discussion

The salient relationship in all of the ethnohistoric cases discussed above was the interest that forager populations had in the corn produced at the farming villages. Farmer interests included subsistence items as well—meat and fish—but hides were also an important commodity that farmers sought from their forager trade partners. Unfortunately, all of these goods are perishable, and proxies (bone, ceramics) must be used to evaluate their importance. Other goods, such as ornaments and ceramic vessels, were more likely gifts to trade partners than drivers of the exchange systems. While prehistoric examples of these durable items can document the development of exchange relations in prehistory, they do not help us understand the degree to which the flow of food or hides was important to the adaptation of either foragers or farmers.

The fact that one pathway to forager–farmer relations is through farmers becoming foragers makes other examples of the development of a 'specialized' meat-supplying sector of a subsistence economy relevant to the discussion here. I suggest, for example, that there is a parallel between some of the forager–farmer relations in North America and those of agro-pastoral relations in the Near East. Bates and Lees (1977; Lees and Bates 1974), for example, emphasized the critical relationship between surplus in the agricultural sector of the economy and the degree of specialization in the protein-producing pastoral sector. When agriculture is highly productive, the number of people able to be supported under specialized pastoralism increases, and the labour demands of intensive agriculture make it more efficient for the herding and farming sectors of the economy to be separated. In fact, pastoralists are, in some cases, the relatives of agriculturalists.

The Crow–Hidatsa ancestral relationship and the emergence of the Crow from a cultivator-hunter-gatherer past on the Missouri and in eastern North Dakota to a more hunting lifeway on the Plains seem to parallel this pattern. Likewise, while the farmers in the Texas Panhandle and south-eastern New Mexico were not related directly to their farming trading partners, their choice to move from farming to hunting and gathering is likely linked to the some of the same processes that historically caused people to become pastoralists—strong existing trade connections for access to grain, and a need for better access to animal products.

New Directions for Forager–Farmer Research

Given the difficulties of distinguishing between the foragers and farmers in interactive systems, we need some tools to think more creatively about what to look for and to evaluate competing explanations for motivations concerning the development of these interactive systems. Modelling of specific systems has a clear benefit. In my doctoral work (Spielmann 1982; 1991), for example, I modelled the costs and benefits of Pecos Pueblo residents hunting locally vs growing more corn to trade for meat. This exercise made it clear that, from the standpoint of meat and fat, only under conditions of resource depression would it make economic sense for Pecos farmers to trade with Plains hunters. Subsequent research in the Salinas pueblo region supported this hypothesis; exchange with Plains bison hunters intensified markedly following resource depression of local large game (Potter 1995; Spielmann 1989; 1991). A qualitative evaluation of the nature of carbohydrate and fat resources on the Plains made it clear that the carbohydrates in corn would in general be very beneficial to

Plains hunters (see also Speth and Spielmann 1983). In contrast, the results of Gregg's (1988) simulation of Mesolithic and Neolithic economies in Europe suggest that exchange with Mesolithic hunter-gatherers would not have provided better access to subsistence resources and thus interdependence was unlikely to have developed (Spielmann 1992).

The Huron–Algonquian case would benefit greatly from this sort of modelling, which would allow an assessment of the hunting and fishing returns to Huron farmers and Algonquian hunter-gatherers vs growing additional corn to trade for fish and hides. Developing some simple models of fish, deer, and corn productivity in light of reasonable estimates of prehistoric Iroquois and Algonquian population sizes and distributions would allow archaeologists to evaluate the degree to which dietary items drove this relationship, as suggested by Trigger, or whether, following Heidenreich, it was the more socially valued goods that were of interest.

A systemic understanding of changes over time in the productivity of farming and hunting across the interactive region of interest is also important in analysing the development of forager–farmer interaction. Modelling could allow the identification of thresholds of supply and demand on each side of a forager–farmer interactive system that might have led to interdependent exchange. This threshold would then serve as a hypothesis for evaluation with archaeological data. As discussed above, in the Plains–Pueblo case it appears that increasing bison herd density in the late prehistoric period on the southern Plains, which would have made that prey more productive to hunt, in combination with (1) increasing density of Pueblo farmers in the eastern border area of the Pueblo world, and (2) local game resource depression around Pueblo villages, which would have created a predictable, localized demand for bison products and production of sufficient corn in surplus (Speth 2004, 424–5; Spielmann 1991), moved Plains–Pueblo exchange from a relationship that appears minor (at least in the archaeological record) to one of interdependence in the mid-1400s.

More specific hypotheses derived from these models concerning where, when, and how forager–farmer interaction should develop in specific regions would then guide archaeological data collection. To be successful in this endeavour we also need to be able to identify hunters and farmers in the archaeological record. This will require a sophisticated understanding of how members of different ethnic and linguistic groups materially express their identity in interactive situations, and/or how material expressions of identity are a product of adaptations, as in the case of different kinds of ceramic fabric among hunters and farmers in the US north-east (Chilton 1998). Ethnographically, hunter-gatherers learn the language and conform, at least in part, to the social structure of their agricultural trade partners (Spielmann and Eder 1994). With this in mind, the fact that Algonquian and Iroquois potters shared the same repertoire of stylistic motifs but combined them in different ways (Pretola 2000) becomes particularly interesting.

When we can identify hunters and farmers in the archaeological record, then other material aspects of interaction can be investigated. For example, technological transfer may assist in evaluating the importance of exchanged foods, as Habicht-Mauche's (1988; 1991) study of Plains ceramics showed for the consumption of corn among Plains hunters. Settlement pattern shifts by hunter-gatherers towards areas inhabited by agriculturalists might allow the assessment of the degree to which farmers were incorporated into hunter-gatherer seasonal rounds. Bone chemistry analysis, where possible, may allow the assessment of the degree to which farmed grain was incorporated into largely hunter-gatherer diets (e.g. Coltrain and Leavitt 2002), and if hunter-gatherers were intensifying hunting to participate in trade, the organization of the hunt and/or species targeted may change from the pre-trade situation (Spielmann and Eder 1994), as suggested by Speth's data from the Henderson site. Clearly the systemic and evidential aspects of understanding the origins of forager–farmer relations in North America and elsewhere continue to make this both a compelling and challenging topic for further research.

References

Ayer, E. 1916. *The memorial of Fray Alonso de Benavides, 1630*. Chicago: R.R. Donnelley.
Barlow, K. R. 2002. Predicting maize agriculture among the Fremont: an economic comparison of farming and foraging in the American southwest. *American Antiquity* 67, 65–88.
Barrett, S. 1952. Material aspects of Pomo culture. *Bulletin of the Public Museum of the City of Milwaukee* 20, Pts I and II.
Bates, D. and Lees, S. 1977. The role of exchange in productive specialization. *American Anthropologist* 79, 824–41.
Bauchett, S. and Guillaume, H. 1982. Aka-farmer relations in the northwest Congo Basin. In E. Leacock and R. Lee (eds), *Politics and history in band societies*, 189–211. Cambridge: Cambridge University Press.
Blackburn, R. 1982. In the land of milk and honey: Okiek adaptations to their forests and neighbours. In E. Leacock and R. Lee (eds), *Politics and history in band societies*, 283–305. Cambridge: Cambridge University Press.
Blakeslee, D. 1975. The Plains interband trade system: an ethnohistoric and archaeological investigation. Doctoral dissertation, University of Wisconsin, Milwaukee.
Brosowske, S. D. 2005. The evolution of exchange in small-scale societies on the southern High Plains. Doctoral dissertation, University of Oklahoma, Norman, Oklahoma.
Brown, D. 1973. Structural change at Picuris Pueblo, New Mexico. PhD dissertation, University of Arizona, Tucson.
Chamberlin, M. 2008. Evaluating the cultural origins of complexity in the ancestral Pueblo world. PhD dissertation, Arizona State University, Tempe.
Chamberlin, M. and Rautman, A. 2009. Conflict and its aftermath in the Salinas Pueblo province. Paper presented at the Annual Society for American Archaeology meetings, Atlanta, Georgia.
Chilton, E. 1998. The cultural origins of technical choice: unraveling Algonquian and Iroquoian ceramic traditions in the northeast. In M. Stark (ed.), *The archaeology of social boundaries*, 132–60. Washington, DC: Smithsonian Institution.
Chilton, E. 2005. Farming and social complexity in the north-east. In T. Pauketat and D. Loren (eds), *North American archaeology*, 138–60. Oxford: Blackwell.
Clark, T. 2006. Production, exchange, and social identity: a study of Chupadero black-on-white pottery. PhD dissertation, Arizona State University, Tempe.
Coltrain, J. B. and Leavitt, S. 2002. Climate and diet in Fremont prehistory: economic variability and abandonment of maize agriculture in the Great Salt Lake basin. *American Antiquity* 67, 453–85.
Connolly, J. 1956. Clan-lineage relations in a Pueblo village phratry. Masters thesis, University of Chicago.
Crown, P., Orcutt, J., and Kohler, T. 1996. Pueblo cultures in transition: the northern Rio Grande. In M. Adler (ed.), *Pueblo cultures in transition*, 188–204. Tucson: University of Arizona Press.

Day, G. 1978. Nipissing. In B. Trigger (ed.), *Handbook of North American Indians, volume 15, northeast*, 787–91. Washington, DC: Smithsonian Institution.

Day, G. and Trigger, B. 1978. Algonquin. In B. Trigger (ed.), *Handbook of North American Indians, volume 15, northeast*, 792–7. Washington, DC: Smithsonian Institution.

Dean, J., Doelle, W., and Orcutt, J. 1994. Adaptive stress: environment and demography. In G. Gumerman (ed.), *Themes in Southwest prehistory*, 53–86. Santa Fe: School of American Research Press.

Denig, E. 1961. *Five Indian tribes of the upper Missouri*. Norman: University of Oklahoma Press.

Ewers, J. 1954. The Indian trade of the upper Missouri before Lewis and Clark: an interpretation. *Bulletin of the Missouri Historical Society* 10, 429–46.

Ewers, J. 1968. *Indian life on the upper Missouri*. Norman: University of Oklahoma Press.

Ford, R. 1972. Barter, gift, or violence: an analysis of Tewa intertribal exchange. In E. Wilmsen (ed.), *University of Michigan Museum of Anthropology Anthropological Papers* 46, 21–45. Ann Arbor: Museum of Anthropology, Ann Arbor.

Gayton, A. 1948. Yokuts and western mono ethnography. *Anthropological Records* 10 (1 and 2), 1–290.

Grant, W. (ed.) 1952. *Voyages of Samuel de Champlain 1604–1618*. New York: Barnes and Noble (originally published in 1907).

Gregg, S. A. 1988. *Foragers and farmers: population interaction and agricultural expansion in Neolithic Europe*. Chicago: University of Chicago Press.

Habicht-Mauche, J. 1987. Southwestern-style culinary ceramics on the southern Plains: a case study of technological innovation and cross-cultural interaction. *Plains Anthropologist* 32, 175–80.

Habicht-Mauche, J. 1988. An analysis of Southwestern-style utility ware ceramics from the Southern Plains in the context of protohistoric Plains-Pueblo interaction. PhD dissertation, Harvard University, Cambridge, MA.

Habicht-Mauche, J. 1991. Evidence for the manufacture of Southwestern-style culinary ceramics on the Southern Plains. In K. Spielmann (ed.), *Farmers, hunters, and colonists: interaction between the Southwest and the southern Plains*, 51–70. Tucson: University of Arizona Press.

Habicht-Mauche, J. 2000. Pottery, food, hides and women: labor, production, and exchange within the protohistoric Plains-Pueblo frontier economy. In M. Hegmon (ed.), *The archaeology of regional interaction in the prehistoric Southwest*, 209–31. Niwot: University Press of Colorado.

Hammond, G. and Rey, A. 1940. *Narratives of the Coronado expedition, 1540–1542*. Albuquerque: University of New Mexico Press.

Hammond, G. and Rey, A. 1953. *Don Juan de Oñate, colonizer of New Mexico*. Coronado Cuarto Centennial Publication, Vols 5 and 6. Albuquerque: University of New Mexico Press.

Hammond, G. and Rey, A. 1966. Gallegos' Relacion. In *The rediscovery of New Mexico, 1580–1594*. Albuquerque: University of New Mexico Press.

Hanson, J., 1979. Ethnohistoric problems in the Crow–Hidatsa separation. *Archaeology in Montana* 20, 73–86.

Hanson, J. 1998. The late high Plains hunters. In W. R. Wood (ed.), *Archaeology on the Great Plains*, 456–80. Lawrence: University of Kansas Press.

Hayes, A., Young, J., and Warren, A. H. 1981. Excavation of Mound 7. *Publications in Archeology* 16. Washington: National Park Service.

Heidendreich, C. 1978. Huron. In B. Trigger (ed.), *Handbook of North American Indians, volume 15, northeast*, 368–88. Washington, DC: Smithsonian Institution.

Jelinek, A., 1967. *A prehistoric sequence in the middle Pecos Valley, New Mexico*. Ann Arbor: University of Michigan Museum of Anthropology Anthropological Paper 31.

Katzenberg, M. A., Schwarcz, H., Knyf, M., and Melbye, F. J. 1995. Stable isotope evidence for maize horticulture and paleodiet in southern Ontario. *American Antiquity* 60, 335–50.

Kessell, J. 1979. *Kiva, cross, and crown*. Washington: National Park Service.

Kidder, A. V. 1932. The artifacts of Pecos. *Papers of the Southwestern Expedition* 6. New Haven: Yale University Press.

King, C. 1976. Chumash intervillage economic exchange. In L. J. Bean and T. C. Blackburn (eds), *Native Californians: a theoretical retrospective*, 289–318. Socorro: Ballena Press.

Kniffen, F. 1939. Pomo geography. *University of California Publications in American Archaeology and Ethnology* 36, 353–400.

La Verendrye, P. 1968. *Journals of la Verendrye*. New York: Greenwood Press.

LeBlanc, S. 1999. *Prehistoric warfare in the American Southwest*. Salt Lake City: University of Utah Press.

Lees, S. and Bates, D. 1974. The origins of specialized pastoralism: a systemic model. *American Antiquity* 39, 187–93.

Leonard, K. 2000. Directionality and exclusivity of Plains-Pueblo exchange during the protohistoric period (AD 1450–1700). Masters thesis, Arizona State University.

Lewis, M. and Clark, W. 1893. *The history of the Lewis and Clark Expedition*. New York: Dover Publications.

Lintz, C. 1986. *Architecture and community variability within the Antelope Creek Phase of the Texas Panhandle*. Norman: Oklahoma Archaeological Survey.

Lintz, C. 1991. Texas panhandle–Pueblo interactions from the thirteenth through sixteenth century. In K. Spielmann (ed.), *Farmers, hunters, and colonists: interaction between the Southwest and the southern Plains*, 89–106. Tucson: University of Arizona Press.

Loeb, E. 1926. Pomo folkways. *University of California Publications in American Archaeology and Ethnology* 19, 149–404.

Lowie, R. 1922. *The material culture of the Crow Indians*. New York: The Trustees.

Lowie, R. 1924. *Minor ceremonies of the Crow Indians*. New York: American Museum Press.

Lowie, R. 1935. *The Crow Indians*. New York: Farrar and Rinehart.

Matthews, G. 1979. Glottochronology and the separation of the Crow and Hidatsa. *Archaeology in Montana* 20, 113–25.

Meyer, R. 1977. *The village Indians of the upper Missouri: the Mandans, Hidatsas, and Arikaras*. Lincoln: University of Nebraska Press.

Michelaki, K. 2007. More than meets the eye: reconsidering variability in Iroquoian ceramics. *Canadian Journal of Archaeology* 31, 143–70.

Munro, N. 1994. An investigation of Anasazi turkey production in southwestern Colorado. Masters thesis, Simon Fraser University, Vancouver, British Columbia.

Potter, J. 1995. The effect of sedentism on the processing of hunted carcasses in the Southwest: a comparison of two Pueblo IV sites in central New Mexico. *Kiva* 60, 411–28.

Pretola, J. 2000. Northeastern ceramic diversity: an optical mineralogy approach. Amherst: Doctoral dissertation, University of Massachusetts.

Pretola, J. 2002. An optical mineralogy approach to northeastern ceramic diversity. In J. Kerber (ed.), *A lasting impression: coastal, lithic, and ceramic research in New England archaeology*. Westport, CT: Praeger.

Rocek, T. and Speth, J. 1986. *The Henderson site burials: glimpses of late prehistoric population in the Pecos valley*. Ann Arbor: University of Michigan, Museum of Anthropology.

Rogers, E. and Leacock, E. 1981. Montagnais-Naskapi. In J. Helm (ed.), *Handbook of North American Indians, volume 6, Subarctic*, 169–89. Washington, DC: Smithsonian Institution.

Schwarcz, H., Melbye, J., Katzenberg, M. A., and Knyf, M. 1985. Stable isotopes in human skeletons in southern Ontario: reconstructing paleodiet. *Journal of Archaeological Science* 12, 187–206.

Smith, B. 2006. Eastern North America as an independent center of plant domestication. *Proceedings of the National Academy of Sciences USA* 103, 1223–8.

Smith, B. and Cowan, C. W. 2003. Domesticated crop plants and the evolution of food production economies in eastern North America. In P. Minnis (ed.), *People and plants in ancient eastern North America*, 105–25. Washington, DC: Smithsonian Institution.

Speth, J. (ed.) 2004. *Life on the periphery: economic change in late prehistoric southeastern New Mexico*. Ann Arbor: University of Michigan Museum of Anthropology Memoir 37.

Speth, J. 2005. The beginnings of Plains–Pueblo interaction: an archaeological perspective from southeastern New Mexico. In M. Hegmon (ed.), *Engaged anthropology*, 129–47. Ann Arbor: University of Michigan Anthropological Papers of the Museum of Anthropology 94.

Speth, J. and Spielmann, K. 1983. Energy source, protein metabolism, and hunter gatherer subsistence strategies. *Journal of Anthropological Archaeology* 2, 1–31.

Spielmann, K. 1982. Inter societal food acquisition among egalitarian societies: an ecological study of Plains/Pueblo interaction in the American southwest. PhD dissertation, Department of Anthropology, University of Michigan, Ann Arbor.

Spielmann, K. 1983. Late prehistoric exchange between the Southwest and Southern Plains. *Plains Anthropologist* 28, 257–72.

Spielmann, K. 1989. Colonists, hunters and farmers: Plains–Pueblo interaction in the seventeenth century. In D. Thomas (ed.), *Columbian consequences, volume 1*, 101–13. Washington, DC: Smithsonian Institution.

Spielmann, K. 1991. *Interdependence in the prehistoric Southwest: an ecological analysis of Plains–Pueblo interaction*. New York: Garland Publishing.

Spielmann, K. 1992. Review of *Foragers and farmers* by S. A. Gregg. *Human Ecology* 20, 254–7.

Spielmann, K. 1996. Impressions of Pueblo III settlement trends among the Rio Abajo and eastern border Pueblos. In M. Adler (ed.), *Pueblo cultures in transition*, 177–87. Tucson: University of Arizona Press.

Spielmann, K. and Eder, J. 1994. Hunters and farmers: then and now. *Annual Review of Anthropology* 23, 303–23.

Spielmann, K. and Schoeninger, M. 1992. Multi-disciplinary studies of trade in meat at Gran Quivira Pueblo, New Mexico. Conference on Paleonutrition, Center for Archaeological Investigations, Southern Illinois University, Carbondale, 27–28 March.

Spielmann, K., Schoeninger, M., and Moore, K. 1990. Plains–Pueblo interdependence and human diet at Pecos Pueblo, New Mexico. *American Antiquity* 55, 745–65.

Starna, W. and Funk, R. 1994. The place of the in situ hypothesis in Iroquoian archaeology. *Northeast Anthropology* 47, 45–54.

Thomas, D. and Ronnefeldt, K. (eds) 1976. *People of the first man*. New York: Dutton.

Trigger, B. 1962. Trade and tribal warfare on the St. Lawrence in the sixteenth century. *Ethnohistory* 9, 240–56.

Trigger, B. 1963. Settlement as an aspect of Iroquoian adaptation at the time of contact. *American Anthropologist* 65, 86–101.

Trigger, B. 1976. *The children of Aataentsic I*. Montreal: Queen's University Press.

Vehik, S. and Baugh, T. 1994. Prehistoric Plains trade. In T. Baugh and J. Ericson (eds), *Prehistoric exchange systems in North America*, 249–74. New York: Plenum Press.

Will, G. and Spinden, H. 1906. *The Mandans: a study of their culture, archaeology, and language.* Cambridge, MA: The Museum.

Williams, B. 1974. *A model of band society.* Washington, DC: Memoirs of the Society for American Archaeology 29.

Wilshusen, R. 2002. Estimating population in the central Mesa Verde region. In M. D. Varien and R. H. Wilshusen (eds), *Seeking the center place: archaeology and ancient communities in the Mesa Verde region*, 101–20. Salt Lake City: University of Utah Press.

Wilson, G. 1924. *The horse and the dog in Hidatsa culture.* New York: American Museum Press.

Winship, G. 1896. The Coronado expedition, 1540–1542. In *Fourteenth Annual Report of the Bureau of Ethnology, 1892–1893*, Part 1, 329–613. Washington, DC: Smithsonian Institution. Reprint, Chicago: Rio Grande Press.

Wintemberg, W. 1943. Artifacts from ancient workshop sites near Tadoussac, Saguenay County, Quebec. *American Antiquity* 8, 313–40.

Wood, W. R. 1972. *Contrastive features of native North American trade systems.* Eugene: University of Oregon Anthropological Papers 4.

Wood, W. R. 1980. Plains trade in prehistoric and protohistoric intertribal relations. In W. R. Wood and M. Liberty (eds), *Anthropology on the Great Plains*, 98–109. Lincoln: University of Nebraska Press.

Wright, J. 1981. Prehistory of the Canadian Shield. In J. Helm (ed.), *Handbook of North American Indians, volume 6, Subarctic*, 86–96. Washington, DC: Smithsonian Institution Press.

PART VI

ETHNOHISTORY AND ANTHROPOLOGY OF 'MODERN' HUNTER-GATHERERS

CHAPTER 42

THE ETHNOHISTORY AND ANTHROPOLOGY OF 'MODERN' HUNTER-GATHERERS

PETER JORDAN

INTRODUCTION AND MAIN AIMS OF PART VI

THIS part links two major themes in the handbook. Specifically, it provides a bridge between the *archaeological* study of past hunter-gatherers through their surviving material remains (Parts II–V), and the increasingly professionalized *anthropological* study of contemporary foragers through direct observation, historical research, and ethnographic fieldwork.

Until a few centuries ago, there were at least some hunting and gathering populations still living in most world regions. Many of these foragers, for example, in Africa and across Eurasia, had already been in culture-contact for centuries, if not millennia; other groups, such as Australia's Aborigines and many Arctic peoples living in North America, interacted only with other hunter-gatherers, and had yet to experience more direct encounters with farmers, pastoralists, urban centres, and empires. However, by 1500 AD all these hunter-gatherers stood on the brink of a major new era of global transformation, and had yet to experience the full onslaught of European colonial expansion.

This historical process played out over the following centuries, causing major cultural dislocations and often painful local adjustments for many indigenous peoples. Impacts on local hunter-gatherer societies ranged from demographic collapses due to the introduction of new diseases, increasing government monitoring and control, forced resettlement and acculturation, through to full-scale persecution, and in several cases, to wholesale cultural annihilation.

It was also within this wider colonial and historical framework that the first detailed descriptions of hunting and gathering populations first began to emerge, followed by the more systematic documentations performed by government administrators, and only later by ethnographic studies conducted by professionalized anthropologists undertaking long-term fieldwork with the few remaining forager communities. The range of ethnographically documented foragers therefore reflects only a relatively small subset of a much wider range of earlier hunting and gathering populations, and many of these groups had already undergone fundamental transformations before detailed documentation had even commenced.

While the colonial encounter provided Euro-American intellectuals with the basic ethnographic subject matter for inventing the concept of 'hunter-gatherers', the term also expressed a uniquely Western interest in classifying the world's cultural diversity into ascending social evolutionary schema, which in turn reflected the wider Enlightenment concerns with the mission of moral and economic improvement that were prevalent at the time (see Barnard; Pluciennik, Part I).

Knowledge and understanding of the people who went on to become classified by Western intellectuals as hunter-gatherers are therefore products of highly specific historical circumstances. Reflecting this, some of the watershed debates about hunting and gathering societies tended to focus on rather narrowly defined selections of cultural groups and geographic regions, albeit leading to important early breakthroughs in anthropological insight and understanding. At certain times, some hunter-gatherer research initiatives pursued a comparative approach, and sought to identify *shared* features of foraging societies living in a range of different regions; at other junctures, the concern was to explore the *specificity* of local ethnographic and historical information about particular forager groups, whose attributes, ethnic identities, and cultural patterns were presented as being relatively unique features of specific world regions. As these debates about hunter-gatherers evolved and changed, so also did the thematic and geographic focus of enquiry. In many cases, several 'new' groups and regions that had initially been excluded from mainstream hunter-gatherer studies were later included, in some cases becoming a primary focus for fresh debates and alternative theoretical perspectives.

In focusing on understanding how these regional hunter-gatherer research traditions emerged and diversified, it is also important to understand that these do not necessarily map in a clear or predictable way onto national research traditions. Research into African hunter-gatherers, for example, has been highly international from the outset. In contrast, work within other national boundaries has been more isolated, and indeed idiosyncratic—Russian/Soviet work on its northern indigenous peoples is an obvious example, but there are others (see Barnard 2004).

In this way, modern geopolitics has also played an implicit role in structuring the history of hunter-gatherer research, with large areas like Siberia initially excluded from debates in the *Man the hunter* era in the 1960s, and then partially rehabilitated after the opening up of new academic contacts towards the end of the Cold War (Murdoch 1968; Schweitzer 2000). The contingent intersections between these regional and national research trajectories also generate highly complex 'landscapes' of scholarship and debate that can be daunting for both new and established researchers.

The primary goal of this part is, therefore, to focus on understanding some of the shifting content of the inherent historicity of divergent hunter-gatherer research traditions as they have played out in different parts of the globe. Individual chapters aim to critically examine some of these local traditions of scholarship across a broadly representative suite of regions.

Finally, it is also worth making it clear what this part does *not* aim to do. The concern here is not to present encyclopaedic or comprehensive descriptive treatment of different hunter-gatherer 'tribes' or 'bands', with summary accounts of material culture, social organization, and world view—this has been done many times before on both regional, continental, and even on global scales (e.g. Lee and Daly 2001). Readers seeking this kind of descriptive data should consult the extensive ethnographic literatures on individual hunter-gatherer groups in the chapters in this handbook and the references cited therein.

Modern Hunter-Gatherers: General Research Trends

As explored through this handbook, for complex historical and intellectual reasons, anthropological debates about global cultural diversity moved into different directions (Pluciennik, Part I). Within the framework of nineteenth-century social evolutionary thinking, it was commonly assumed that all foragers represented a similar kind of society, and that these 'modern' hunter-gatherers represented a rather straightforward analogue to 'ancient' peoples, for example, the hunting societies of the Palaeolithic and Mesolithic. Anthropologists and archaeologists went on to become interested in identifying the common features of both modern and ancient hunting and gathering societies living in different parts of the world, whether in terms of subsistence, social organization, ideology, or general mode of existence. This task was thought to be somewhat easier for anthropologists as they could directly observe these behaviours during fieldwork, but it was also assumed by archaeologists that these kinds of ethnographic insights could be applied relatively uncritically to the study of prehistoric foragers—past and present foragers constituted the same kinds of society, and occupied similar stages of general cultural progress.

Attempts at developing a more comprehensive and rigorous comparative analysis of the foraging mode of existence also became an important theme within the cultural ecology approach that emerged in the mid-twentieth century. These efforts reached a high point in the *Man the hunter* era of the late 1960s. In particular, they were reflected in initial formulations of 'nomadic style' and the depiction of hunter-gatherers as the 'original affluent society'. Here, the general goal for anthropologists working with modern foraging societies was to look beyond the 'noise' of local ethnographic detail, and to try and identify and explain the typical features of all hunter-gatherer societies, whether in terms of band-scale and egalitarian social organization, or through their adaptive responses to the demands of the local ecology. Approached from this highly comparative perspective, modern foragers were generally depicted as being rather timeless, isolated, and self-contained populations, whose salient features were primarily generated by the functional requirements of meeting specific kinds of environmental challenge.

Subsequent anthropological debates have primarily served to undermine these earlier attempts at identifying traits that can be used to define all hunter-gatherers as a single kind of society. Initial responses to the appreciation of inherent variability among hunter-gatherers included attempts to refine typologies and define smaller and more specific sub-sets, including the distinction between 'simple' versus 'complex' hunter-gatherers. More recently, anthropologists have accepted that hunting and gathering societies are perhaps best characterized by a relentless and highly localized flexibility—there is very little that can be said to be typical of all groups, whether in terms of subsistence, ideology, or social organization (Kelly 1995, 34–5). Some scholars have now gone so far as to reject the very term 'hunter-gatherers' as an outmoded concept that lacks intellectual utility (Pluciennik, Part I); others maintain that it remains a useful point of analytical departure into a more contextual analysis of forager variability (Kelly 1995, 35).

Equally important in these more recent debates has been the growing appreciation of the significance of long-term culture-contacts between foragers and 'differently organized others', including horticulturalists, pastoralists, states, and empires. Many central attributes of modern hunting and gathering groups may, in fact, be direct outcomes of these wider historical encounters, and not reflect timeless features of an older mode of human existence, as had earlier been assumed. If many central features of modern hunting and gathering societies are indeed responses to recent culture-contacts, then at least some of these local ethnographic patterns need to be understood within the context of specific historical trajectories.

A new 'interdependent' model now characterizes much current hunter-gatherer research. Modern foragers are now generally viewed as being local actors embedded within a wider regional matrix of contacts and exchanges that intimately link their lifeways to those of farmers and pastoralists, and also to broader trade and taxation networks, as well as to the constellations of empires and nation states that surround and often contain them as citizens. If mid-twentieth-century anthropologists were primarily interested in identifying the shared features of all hunter-gatherer societies through comparative analysis, more recent scholarship now seeks increasingly to understand the specific history, form, and content of these wider regional interactions, as well as the ways in which they intersect with more local patterns of forager subsistence and social life.

The current consensus is that modern forager lifeways are inherently flexible and historically contingent. Populations can switch quickly between different subsistence strategies in ways that defy older assumptions of simple linear progress from one economic stage to another, or from relatively simple to more complex forms of social organization. At the same time, there is growing appreciation of the cultural resilience of modern hunter-gatherers within a rapidly changing and relentlessly *globalizing* contemporary world. For many groups, the foraging lifestyle also entails strong moral, ethical, and ideological commitments to the land, and meeting these obligations is a central part of group identity and belief. Hunting, gathering, even moving through the forest and across the ancestral landscape, all form a fundamentally important expression of human existence and spirituality.

Another important development in more recent debate is the fact that modern hunting and gathering communities are no longer regarded as exotic 'others'; that is, as the last surviving exemplars of a rather timeless stage of human existence that had existed everywhere on earth prior to the prehistoric transition to farming and the rise of civilization. Instead, members of modern foraging societies have now regained their rightful status as global citizens. However, this shift in perspective does not bely the fundamental existential challenges that many of these communities now face—all recent or contemporary foraging societies endured long histories of colonial repression, and many still face political and cultural exclusion, economic marginalization, and the destruction of environments used for local livelihoods. Such contemporary situations require active political intervention in order to maintain foragers' property rights, access to ancestral lands and resources, and also to address the wider challenge of ensuring their cultural and linguistic survival. Anthropologists studying and working with these societies face the challenge of making their research more locally relevant. Increasingly, members of indigenous communities are also becoming professional anthropologists.

ORGANIZATION OF PART VI

In nineteenth-century western Europe and North America, the rise of social evolutionary thinking highlighted the importance of economic and social criteria for ordering populations into general schemes of progress. Coeval with this development, forager groups in *some* regions were assumed to represent relatively 'pure' exemplars of this timeless forager lifestyle—the hunter-gatherers of Africa, Australia, and the Americas figured particularly highly in these early discussions. Many have been central to hunter-gatherer studies ever since. In contrast, other regions appeared later in hunter-gatherer debates, while other groups and geographic areas have more isolated and idiosyncratic research histories. Reflecting these concerns, chapters in this part of the handbook are arranged in three groups:

- The first set of chapters examines some of the 'classic' forager societies that became central to the flagship debates of mid-twentieth-century hunter-gatherer studies. These include the paradigmatic hunter-gatherer groups of Australia, Africa, the Great Basin, California, and the Pacific Northwest Coast. Many figured highly in early formulations of 'nomadic style', iconic depictions of the 'original affluent society', as well as in early debates about hunter-gatherer 'complexity'. As research evolved and changed, African hunter-gatherer groups of the Kalahari Desert also became central to debates about the implications of culture-contact, and the importance of studying long-term forager histories.
- The second set of chapters focuses on regions that were initially excluded from earlier debates due to the existence of exactly these kinds of long-term culture-contacts with non-foraging societies. Research in South-East Asia (and other world regions) has tended to highlight the role of commercialized forager-traders as culturally resilient *bricoleurs* who play important roles within wider exchange networks, but who remain mutually dependent on farmers for the supplementary carbohydrate sources that enable them to live year-round in the tropical forest ecosystem. Other interesting and alternative insights into local foraging histories can be gained from South America. Here, many hunter-gatherers appear to have 'regressed' from horticulture back to foraging due to widespread colonial dislocations, a pattern that highlights the inherent historical contingency of the foraging lifestyle. Clearly, there are many possible 'pathways' to foraging, and these South American examples provide a fundamental challenge to social evolutionary schema, which assume an inevitable and irreversible cultural progression from hunting and gathering through to farming.
- The third and final set of chapters broadly examines hunter-gatherer histories across northern Eurasia, an extensive region that spans northern Europe (Fennoscandia), through Siberia, and across to North-East Asia. Here, the many different hunting, fishing, and gathering groups share a broadly similar set of historical trajectories, and while only the Saami and the Ainu are examined in more detail, the general insights have

relevance to hunter-gatherer research across the wider region. Particularly important here is the use of (ethno)historical data to study local strategies for cultural resilience within the complex dynamics generated by long-term culture-contact with incoming settler populations, states, and empires.

'Classic' Regions of Research

African Hunter-Gatherers

Hitchcock provides a detailed analysis of anthropological research into the hunter-gatherer societies of southern Africa. In the second half of the twentieth century this region emerged as the epicentre of debates about hunter-gatherer bands, their social and political organization, subsistence strategies, gender roles, and general work ethic. In the *Man the hunter* era of the late 1960s and early 1970s, the Ju/'hoansi were taken to exemplify one of humanity's oldest kinds of adaptation, a way of life captured by the concept of 'nomadic style' and serving to illustrate the notion of foragers being the 'original affluent society'. By the mid-1980s, these groups were again playing a central role, but this time within savage purist–revisionist debates about the degree to which these modern hunter-gatherers represented an older and rather timeless way or life, or the extent to which they were better understood as being members of a rural underclass that had been marginalized through long-term culture-contact and integration with the wider region's political economy. As this 'Kalahari Debate' slowly unfolded, increasing attention was paid to historical and also archaeological evidence to better understand some of these deeper patterns of regional interaction and long-term change. The intensity of ethnographic interest and debate has also been paralleled by long-term field research—today, the Ju/'hoansi are some of the best documented people on the planet, with much contemporary work also focusing on addressing developmental issues.

In a similar vein, Hewlett and Fancher provide a comprehensive critical analysis of the highly internationalized work conducted among hunter-gatherers in central Africa. This scholarship is also rather diverse, has likewise been broadly dominated by ecological and scientific approaches, but also includes a concern with understanding the deep cultural affinity that these groups have with the forest. More recently, there have been increases in development and conservation work, and growing interest in exploring culture-contact dynamics. The latter has included research into the 'carbohydrate question'; that is, the extent to which hunter-gatherers can actually survive in tropical forests without supplementary foodstuffs acquired through exchange networks that link them with farmers. If culture-contact is a fundamental prerequisite to foraging adaptations to tropical forests, how old can this way of life actually be? Hewlett and Fancher conclude their review with an outline of directions for future work. Basic ethnographic fieldwork is still required among some groups, and much more humanities-orientated research could be done to better understand how these forager cultures think and feel about sharing, egalitarianism, gender relations, family, religion, and the spiritual world, all of which would offset the predominance of ecological research themes noted above.

Australian Aborigines

A review of Australian hunter-gatherer research is provided by Keen. From the outset, this body of research has been marked by enormous intellectual diversity, but can be broadly characterized by an early and enduring focus on investigating Aborigine social organization, marriage patterns, and religion, rather than the role of ecology and adaptation. As an important source region for basic ethnographic datasets, descriptions of the Aborigines also fed into some of the foundational theories of kinship that were central to anthropology in the late nineteenth and early twentieth centuries as it gradually emerged as a professional academic discipline.

In the mid-1960s, attention was primarily focused on understanding the essential features of African forager societies, for example, in relation to definitions of 'nomadic style'. However, Australia also remained important, and ethnographic depictions of Aborigine groups were central to Sahlins's formulations of the 'original affluent society' (Sahlins 1968; 1972). Following *Man the hunter*, there was a marked growth of ecologically orientated field research among Australian groups, and interest in exploring gender roles also increased. Keen also notes that in Australia, anthropologists had engaged with policy-making initiatives from the outset, but this trend has grown exponentially in recent years, and now includes active participation by indigenous specialists who combine the roles of researcher and advocate, and who must make the difficult balance of integrating political activism and commentary alongside research and academic writing.

Hunter-Gatherers in Western North America

Robinson examines hunter-gatherer research in California and the Great Basin, regions characterized by strikingly different cultural and linguistic patterns. California's rich and varied environments were densely settled by hunter-gatherer groups, and at European contact, it formed one of the world's most culturally and linguistically diverse regions on the planet. In contrast, the arid deserts of the Great Basin were characterized by much sparser human settlement. Although there are some common roots and themes in the history of nineteenth-century and early twentieth-century scholarship in both these areas, early research interests in California generally focused on the study of cultural diversity, social complexity, and ceremonialism. In the Great Basin, scholars like Julian Steward were more concerned with making sense of the limiting effects of ecological factors on other aspects of hunter-gatherer social organization and behaviour. This work eventually led to the development of the Julian Steward's cultural ecology, which went on to be foundational to the emergence of hunter-gatherer studies as a specific field of enquiry in the mid-twentieth century.

Despite these divergent research trajectories, hunter-gatherer scholarship in both regions reflects the wider historical development of American anthropology, and so shares similar approaches, biases, methods, and theories, all of which evolved in the context of slowly changing relationships between European and First Nation groups. As with many other world regions, early colonialism and the subsequent nation-building project also generated an extensive ethnohistoric archive of information about indigenous communities, generally from a colonizer's perspective. Only in later periods did the colonial project include deliberate attempts by professional anthropologists to generate systematic knowledge of native peoples prior to contact. From this phase of primary ethnographic data collection, later efforts were directed towards synthesis and interpretation, with later revisionist accounts highlighting the legacy of colonialism, and the dynamics of culture-contact. Also notable is the eventual rise of indigenous activism, and the coeval engagement by anthropologists in these endeavours. Robinson also concludes that early anthropological research in this part of western North America has been important in producing a corpus of ethnographic and ethnohistoric data that is among the richest and most extensive records of hunter-gatherer cultures collected anywhere in world.

Pacific Northwest Coast

O'Neill retains a focus on western North America but focuses particularly on the Pacific Northwest Coast. In many ways, these local cultures have been a perennial source of frustration for scholars attempting to make more general comparative sense of hunter-gatherer societies. At other times, they have provided important ethnographic inspiration for exploring some of the most important features of hunter-gatherer variability. The reasons are simple: on the one hand, all Northwest Coast groups *are* hunter-gatherers (or more precisely, hunter-*fisher*-gatherers), but on the other hand, almost all their basic attributes and behaviours do not fit with the initial predictions of 'nomadic style' that emerged during the *Man the hunter* era in the 1960s. Instead of small, highly mobile, egalitarian bands possessing minimal property, the Northwest Coast was settled by highly stratified societies, with enduring and institutionalized status differences, who also practised slavery, lived in large, heavily decorated communal long-houses, engaged in endemic warfare, and practised competitive feasting in order to accumulate property and defend status.

The Northwest Coast has an enormous ethnographic literature, and so O'Neill focuses on reviewing two central debates. The first is how best to understand the competitive feasting dynamics that appear so central to socio-political life along the coast. These are epitomized by the large 'potlatch' events that have been well documented and widely analysed by anthropologists from a range of different perspectives. The second theme is the debate that emerged in the 1980s about hunter-gatherer complexity. Many ethnographically documented hunter-gatherer groups inhabit arid regions in Africa and Australia, the Arctic, and other relatively marginal environments, adding an inherent bias to the ethnographic record of variability among foragers. The Northwest Coast offers a relatively rare ethnographic example of a highly productive aquatic ecosystem inhabited entirely by hunter-fisher-gatherers. Importantly, these insights into relatively sedentary, highly stratified, and territorial societies have been widely used by archaeologists attempting to identify potentially similar patterns in prehistory, especially in regions with similar kinds of rich aquatic ecosystems, such as the Baltic region of northern Europe. Finally, O'Neill notes a gradual shift away from the study of the general cultural patterns along the coast using data primarily collected by ethnographers, towards more recent attempts at understanding the longer-term dynamics of the region's hunter-gatherer cultures through greater incorporation of archaeological research.

'New' Regions and Emerging Debates

Forager-Traders in South-East Asia

The numerous forager groups living across South-East Asia were largely absent from debates during the *Man the hunter* era. Much of this related to what Fortier regards as academic elitism associated with identifying and studying the last 'pure' hunter-gatherers, such as those in the Kalahari. In contrast, it was clear from the outset that foragers in South-East Asia were in intense contact with outsiders. In fact, one of the major challenges for hunter-gatherer researchers working in South-East Asia is attempting to understand the enormous cultural variability that characterizes both these local foraging groups and their links and contacts with outsiders—they inhabit a strikingly wide range of different environments, yet all are tightly embedded into local interaction networks. The remarkable diversity of foraging groups is matched by a similar degree of diversity in regional languages, culture, and also local political and economic settings, of which the foragers form an enduring part.

These general regional settings generate some common hunter-gatherer traits, but this remains challenging. At one level, foragers can be defined as people who collect rather than cultivate food, and who also valorize this food collecting as a laudable lifestyle. But even this simple definition is complicated by the fact that many of these forager groups gather food not to just consume it locally, but also to exchange it with outsiders for grown food. This is certainly not a new phenomenon, and ongoing genetic, linguistic, and archaeological work across the region indicates that these kinds of forager–farmer contacts are highly complex and probably of considerable antiquity, but this important topic needs much more research. Related debates have questioned whether foragers can actually maintain viable settlement in the region's tropical forests without access to supplementary carbohydrate sources, which only local horticulturalists can provide, generally in exchange for products gathered from the forests. As noted above for many African groups, if long-term occupation of tropical forests requires interaction with farmers, then foragers could only begin to move into and settle these ecosystems if they had reliable exchange networks linking them to farmers. This would suggest a situation of mutual interdependency from the outset. If so, can these groups really constitute genuine and 'authentic' foragers, and if yes, how best to classify and understand them?

As hunter-gatherer research expanded and diversified in the wake of the 1980s Kalahari Debate, the foragers of South-East Asia have become increasingly important examples of modern hunter-gatherers who provide a sustained critique to Eurocentric notions of 'pure' hunter-gatherers. They also serve to highlight the historical contingency of many foraging adaptations, as well as the importance of culture-contact and the widespread management of wild resources. Increasingly, these groups are seen as forager-*bricoleurs*, possessing the ability to create sustainable composite economies that they can adjust quickly with great flexibly and skill, a capacity that is important in regions increasingly characterized by resource-depleted environments. Often, these highly flexible strategies are not commercially motivated—trade is for subsistence, but not necessarily to maximize profit. Much more research is needed to understand better these relations between local cultures and diverse outsiders, and development and conservation work is also needed to ensure they retain access to protected areas of traditional resources. Broadly similar patterns to these identified in South-East Asia can also be noted in the study of hunter-gatherers from southern Asia (see Morrison and Junker 2002).

Alternative Pathways to Foraging in South America

Politis and Hernando also highlight the historical contingency of foraging patterns in their review of research into South America's numerous hunting and gathering communities, who over recent centuries inhabited a strikingly wide range of environments, exhibiting a remarkable degree of cultural and linguistic diversity. One overarching theme relevant to the study of all these groups is the fundamental disruption to older lifeways and cultural patterns caused by European colonialism. In some areas, earlier forager populations have now disappeared due to encroaching agricultural settlement and forced assimilation programmes. In other areas, some remoter groups remain in the most minimal contacts with outsiders, demonstrating that hunter-gatherer lifeways remain culturally and ecologically viable, even into the twenty-first century.

Perhaps the greatest paradox in South American hunter-gatherer research is that many modern hunter-gatherer groups appear to be relatively 'new' foragers. That is, the current practice of foraging does not form an older and relatively unchanged mode of existence that has persisted through from prehistory, but is a specific way of life that appeared quite recently, forming part of a widespread historical transformation away from the widespread horticultural economies that existed across the continent prior to European contact. Therefore, in many parts of South America, foraging forms a secondary *re*-adaptation to the new cultural, ecological, and political contexts generated by colonial dislocations. Understanding these local historical trajectories is important in hunter-gatherer research more generally, because they provide a fundamental empirical challenge to what are often assumed to represent 'logical' sequences of social evolutionary development.

Once cast as a cultural 'regression', this recent switch to foraging, along with the remote areas occupied by many groups, and their generally egalitarian social structures, are now widely regarded as evidence for deliberate political action, all of which was structured by the need for local responses to the painful colonial history of the continent. For those interested in the historically contingent dynamics of culture-contact, these unique 'pathways' to hunting and gathering make the study of the continent's diverse forager groups particularly insightful. Also interesting are the blurred lines between food procurement and food production strategies exhibited by some groups. Many practise highly sophisticated plant management strategies, often leading to the cumulative transformation of the forested ecosystem over many generations, confounding the assumption that foragers rely only on 'wild' resources and inhabit 'natural' environments.

HUNTER-GATHERERS AND THE ETHNOHISTORY OF NORTHERN EURASIA

The final two chapters focus on examining the historical experiences of hunting and gathering groups living at opposite ends of Eurasia—the Ainu of North-East Asia and the Forest

Saami of northern Europe. The ecological patterns, economic strategies, culture-contact dynamics, and historical transformations identified by these two chapters also reflect the wider indigenous histories of northern Siberia (Forsyth 1992). By 1500 AD, the various hunting, fishing, and gathering cultures living right across northern Eurasia had already been in different forms of culture-contact with more southerly states and empires for centuries if not millennia.

As these contacts intensified, these northern groups became caught up in a series of shared historical transformations, which involved balancing the emergence of increasingly commercialized hunting economies that were orientated towards fulfilling external tax and trade obligations, with also meeting the needs of local subsistence (Jordan 2010). Other important historical developments taking place during these centuries include the increasing reach of colonial settlement, commercialization of coastal and river fishing, and what appears to be the sudden and apparently simultaneous rise of large-scale reindeer pastoralism among indigenous groups living across the wider region (Krupnik 1993).

The Ainu

Hudson's chapter focuses on the Ainu, who originally inhabited Hokkaido, southern parts of Sakhalin Island, and the Kuril Islands. For various reasons, the Ainu have been the focus of intense international anthropological interest. As hunter-gatherer studies coalesced in the mid-twentieth century, ethnographic information about northern hemisphere hunter-gatherers was primarily drawn from New World sources. The Ainu of Japan were presented as a unique example of an Old World cold temperate foraging society that continued to engage in hunting, fishing, and gathering until relatively recently. For example, the *Man the hunter* (Lee and DeVore 1968) volume contained a chapter on the Ainu, which presented a rather timeless and ahistorical study of forager adaptations to the local ecology (Watanabe 1968). In contrast, examples of similar northern hunter-gatherer cultures from Siberia were bypassed by these debates due to perceived problems with culture-contact, Soviet collectivization, and the uptake of reindeer pastoralism (Murdoch 1968).

In reality, Ainu history is also very complex, as Hudson examines. For example, for many centuries the Ainu combined hunting, fishing, and gathering, with participation in maritime trade networks, and also undertook widespread plant cultivation. Ainu groups were particularly impacted by the incorporation of Hokkaido into the Japanese state in 1870, and by large-scale agricultural settlement of the island by migrants from the south. This coincided with bans on traditional Ainu subsistence and forced assimilation programmes. As a result of these sudden transformations, there was never time for developing a tradition of doing primary ethnographic work. Most ethnographic sources are based on a few elders' recollections of life in earlier times, and this has resulted in Ainu culture being presented in rather timeless, uniform, and descriptive ways. In fact, there was important regional variability in language and culture, and significant changes through time. These deeper historical patterns in Ainu culture are now seeing renewed attention from local archaeologists, historians, linguistics geneticists, and indeed representatives of contemporary Ainu organizations, and it remains unclear as to how the modern Ainu relate to older populations and archaeological cultures both within the Japanese archipelago and across the wider region. Hudson argues, in particular, that the extended and highly detailed ethnohistoric record associated with the Ainu represents a unique opportunity to study the effects of culture-contact on hunter-gatherers over extremely long time periods.

Ainu ethnographic materials have made other long-term contributions to hunter-gatherer studies, for example, emphasizing the central importance of ritual and world view in northern hunting economies. These more religious and spiritual dimensions of hunter-gatherer existence have often been overlooked in more ecologically orientated research, which focuses primarily on studying adaptation and subsistence strategies. Accounts of the elaborate Ainu bear festival have been particularly important, and although the bear is venerated across the circumpolar region, the festivals among the Ainu (and a few other groups in the Russian Far East) are rather unique in that they involve the capture and rearing of *live* animals before their eventual consumption as part of special rituals. These accounts also generate some useful insights into the range of possible motivations for the capture and rearing of wild animals by foragers for later use in competitive feasting events, a process touched upon by Hayden (in Part IV) in his discussion of socio-political dynamics typical of many trans-egalitarian hunter-gatherers.

The Forest Saami

Taavitsainen shifts the focus westwards, across the Eurasian continent, to analyse the more recent past of the Forest Saami. These groups of northern hunter-fisher-gatherers inhabited the boreal forest zone of Fennoscandia, and by 1500 AD, had already been in various forms of culture-contact with surrounding agricultural groups, chiefdoms, early states, and empires for several centuries. Understanding the final stages in the history of these 'last' European foragers has never really been linked to debates within the wider field of hunter-gatherer studies, but has tended to be subsumed into broader analysis of the region's numerous and interlocking ethnic and national histories. In much of this research, widespread use is made of the rich ethnohistoric archives associated with the Saami and other groups living in the region, most of which is derived from early tax and settlement records. As such, Taavitsainen's chapter is therefore not a critical review of hunter-gatherer scholarship in this region because there has never really been such a body of work. Instead, he presents a historically situated analysis of the profound challenges and possible cultural and ethnic survival strategies that confronted the Forest Saami in the context of the declining fur trade, encroachment by logging industries, settlement of their lands by incoming Finnish farmers, and the wider take-off of nomadic reindeer pastoralism among other groups further to the north. The European case study is important because it highlights the range of options that open up to northern hunter-fisher-gatherers within the challenges associated with later historical stages of culture contact.

Siberian Hunter-Gatherers

Both the Ainu and Saami chapters represent interesting examples of northern hunter-fisher-gatherers being drawn into long-term culture-contact with encroaching states and empires. The particular patterns identified by Hudson and Taavitsainen bear striking similarity to the historical fate of other hunter-fisher-gatherer groups living across adjacent areas of northern Russia and into Siberia as they became caught up in the expanding fur trade. However, hunter-gatherer research in Siberia has its own unique history of research, and for many decades was isolated from international debates, especially during the key *Man the hunter* era in the mid-twentieth century (Schweitzer 2000). For example, cultural ecology had little impact on the ethnographic research conducted in the Soviet Union on its northern peoples (Krupnik 1993), and Western scholars generally assumed that all Siberian foragers had either been collectivized, switched subsistence, or been assimilated, rendering attempts at further fieldwork rather redundant (Murdoch 1968).

The end of the Cold War opened up scope for more internationalized research into Siberia hunter-gatherers. There is an extensive Russian language ethnographic literature, highly detailed historical archives about northern populations extending back to the seventeenth century, and numerous opportunities for further fieldwork in the region. Renewed attention to these research opportunities would serve to integrate these diverse northern groups more effectively into international hunter-gatherer scholarship and debate, and important progress in this direction is now being made on several fronts (Anderson 2011; Jordan 2010; Schweitzer 2000; Sirina 2004).

Discussion and Conclusion

The chapters in this part highlight the enormous breadth and sheer scale of research effort that has been directed at understanding modern and recent hunting and gathering groups occupying a wide range of world regions. The chapters also provide a critical review of the most important debates and research directions that have structured this highly regionalized hunter-gatherer scholarship. Broadly similar global trends are reflected in basic data collection, and most of these areas have extensive historical archives generated by early phases of culture-contact and colonialism, followed only later by more detailed and professionalized anthropological field studies. Opportunities for further ethnographic fieldwork into communities still relying on foraging for the bulk of their subsistence needs are in long-term decline, and many groups are becoming increasingly assimilated into wider regional networks.

Several future research directions emerge. In many world regions, further ethnographic fieldwork remains possible and will be important to generate basic descriptions of some of the groups living in remoter areas of South America and in tropical Africa. Many study regions have also been largely dominated by ecologically orientated research, and more fieldwork could be done to broaden these themes and generate other insights, particularly into the social and ideological dimensions of modern forager lifeways. The importance of advocacy, community engagement, and making academic research more locally relevant also emerge as ongoing challenges for research into forager groups living in a rapidly changing world.

As emphasis has shifted away from attempts to identify the relatively timeless features and cross-cultural patterns associated with the last of the 'pure' hunter-gatherers, all modern foragers are now generally viewed within their wider regional and historical settings. Further analysis of the extensive ethnohistorical archives associated with many groups and regions represents an enormous research opportunity. Future research topics, especially in the Old World, might include understanding better the role of foragers in long-term culture-contact, especially in northern Europe, across Siberia, and indeed in Japan, where highly detailed archival sources on tax, trade, and other themes extend back over many centuries.

Archaeological, genetic, linguistic, and palaeoecological data are also making increasingly important contributions to the reconstructions of these long-term hunter-gatherer histories, and many interpretations are now starting to highlight the flexibility and dynamism of hunter-gatherer societies across both prehistoric and also more recent historic periods. These kinds of detailed, long-term insights are also important for 'descendant communities' as they seek to understand their own identities and cultural histories, as well as to meet challenges associated with contemporary socio-economic and environmental situations.

Broader archaeological engagements with these hunter-gatherer ethnographic insights are also changing. If in the past, ethnographic accounts of modern foragers were applied in a relatively straightforward and simplistic manner to the interpretation of prehistoric datasets, now archaeologists are much more critically aware of the highly contextual nature of all ethnographic information. Increasingly knowledgeable about the historical contingency of all ethnographic data, as well as the universal implications of culture-contact, archaeologists are now better equipped to appreciate the flexibility and cultural resilience of prehistoric hunter-gatherer societies. Understanding better the variability and range of cultural strategies potentially open to prehistoric hunter-gatherers as they came into contact with other groups can generate fresh perspectives on the dynamism of forager–farmer contact zones and other kinds of inter-cultural encounter. Certainly, the 'agency' of hunter-gatherers in major historical transformations such as the transition to farming is being fundamentally reassessed, partly through applications of ethnographic models. In Europe, the transition is now regarded as a much more contingent and regionally variable process than the kind of monolithic expansion of agricultural populations at the expense of foragers, as had hitherto been the case (see Part V).

To conclude, there remains an intense and enduring interest in the world's recently documented hunter-gatherer societies, both among anthropologists and especially archaeologists, but also increasingly among members of indigenous communities, policymakers, and the wider public. Understanding how ethnographic and historical information about hunter-gatherers has been generated and interpreted in different world regions is an important goal for this part of the handbook. Increasingly, variability among modern hunter-gatherer cultures is now viewed as the being the outcome of long-term processes, which involve the reproduction of deeper traditions alongside more recent adjustments and innovations associated with both specific ecological and historical contexts.

REFERENCES

Anderson, D. G. (ed.) 2011. *The 1926/27 Soviet Polar Census Expeditions*. Oxford: Berghahn.
Barnard, A. (ed.) 2004. *Hunter-gatherers in history, archaeology and anthropology*. Oxford: Berg.
Forsyth, J. 1992. *A history of the peoples of Siberia: Russia's North Asian colony 1581–1990*. Cambridge: Cambridge University Press.
Jordan, P. (ed.) 2010. *Landscape and culture in northern Eurasia*. Walnut Creek, CA: Left Coast Press.

Kelly, R. 1995. *The foraging spectrum: diversity in hunter-gatherer lifeways.* Washington, DC: Smithsonian Institution.

Krupnik, I. 1993. *Arctic adaptations: native whalers and reindeer herders of northern Eurasia.* Lebanon, NH: University Press of New England, Dartmouth College Press.

Lee, R. B. and Daly, R. 2001. *The Cambridge encyclopedia of hunters and gatherers.* Cambridge: Cambridge University Press.

Lee, R. and DeVore, I. (eds) 1968. *Man the hunter.* Chicago: Aldine.

Morrison, K. and Junker, L. (eds) 2002. *Forager-traders in south and southeast Asia: long-term histories.* Cambridge: Cambridge University Press.

Murdoch, G. P. 1968. The current status of the world's hunting and gathering peoples. In R. Lee and I. DeVore (eds), *Man the hunter,* 13–20. Chicago: Aldine.

Sahlins, M. 1968. Notes on the original affluent society. In R. Lee and I. DeVore (eds), *Man the hunter,* 85–9. Chicago: Aldine.

Sahlins, M. 1972. *Stone age economics.* Chicago: Aldine-Atherton.

Schweitzer, P. 2000. Silence and other misunderstandings: Russian anthropology, western hunter-gatherer debates, and Siberian peoples. In P. Schweitzer, M. Biesele, and R. K. Hitchcock (eds), *Hunters and gatherers in the modern world: conflict, resistance, and self-determination,* 29–51. New York: Berghahn Books.

Sirina, A. M. 2004. Soviet traditions in the study of Siberian hunter-gatherer society. In A. Barnard (ed.), *Hunter-gatherers in history, archaeology and anthropology,* 89–102. Oxford: Berg.

Watanabe, H. 1968. Subsistence and ecology of northern food gatherers with special reference to the Ainu. In R. Lee and I. DeVore (eds), *Man the hunter,* 69–77. Chicago: Aldine.

CHAPTER 43

HUNTER-GATHERER RESEARCH TRADITIONS IN SOUTHERN AFRICA

ROBERT K. HITCHCOCK

Six decades have passed since the Marshall family of Cambridge, Massachusetts began their research on Ju/'hoan San (formerly called the !Kung) in north-eastern Namibia (Marshall 1960; 1965; 1976; Thomas 2006). The Marshall family's work, along with that of the Harvard Kalahari Research Group (HKRG), which was also carried out among Ju/'hoansi but on the Botswana side of the Botswana–Namibia border in the 1960s and early 1970s, challenged extant anthropological views regarding hunter gatherers and helped to stimulate extensive field-based studies of foraging peoples (Kelly 2007, 14–28; Lee and DeVore 1968; 1976). These investigations reflected a significant shift in anthropological research towards intensive, long-term, interdisciplinary work among peoples involved in hunting and gathering for their livelihoods.

In many ways, the Ju/'hoansi are some of the best-documented peoples on the planet, having been the subject of exhaustive research, films, and development-oriented investigations for a period of more than half a century (Lee 1979; 2003; Lee et al. 1996; Marshall 2003; Wiessner 1982; 2004; Wilmsen 1989). The Ju/'hoansi have become, as Trefor Jenkins (1979, 278) notes, 'Southern Africa's model people'. It must be remembered, however, that the Ju/'hoansi are but one of sizeable number of different San groups in southern Africa, who are found today in six different countries (Angola, Botswana, Namibia, South Africa, Zambia, and Zimbabwe) and who were much more widespread in the past (Barnard 1992, 16–36; Lee 1976, 5–6; 1979, 31–5; Suzman 2001, 2–8; Tobias 1956, 176). There are dozens of other San groups, each of them with their own languages, cultures, histories, traditions, and belief systems. The diversity among San peoples is an important issue that a number of researchers have underscored in their work.

The San are highly diverse in terms of their past and present adaptations to the ecosystems in which they live, the ways in which they interact with neighbouring groups, and the degree to which they hunt and gather or depend on alternative sources of subsistence and income. The San represent one of two groups in southern Africa who claim indigenous identity, the other being the Khoekhoe; together, the groups are sometimes referred to as Khoisan (or KhoeSan) peoples (Schapera 1930; Barnard 1992). Table 43.1 presents data on the numbers of San and Khoekhoe peoples in southern Africa in 2010.

Table 43.1 Numbers of San and Khoekhoe in southern Africa, 2010

Country	Population size (July 2010 estimate)	Size of country (sq. km)	Numbers of San	Numbers of Khoekhoe
Angola	13 068 110	1 246 700	3500	-
Botswana	2 029 207	600 370	50 000	1000
Namibia	2 128 471	825 418	38 000	72 000
South Africa	49 109 107	1 221 912	7500	96 000
Zambia	12 056 823	752 614	1300	-
Zimbabwe	11 651 858	390 580	2500	-
TOTALS	90 043 776 people in six countries	5 037 594 sq. km	102 800 San	169 000 Khoekhoe

Note: Data obtained from the following: Working Group of Indigenous Minorities in Southern Africa (WIMSA), National KhoeSan Council (South Africa), Cape Cultural Heritage Development Council (South Africa); see also Chennels (2009); Chennels and Dutoit (2004); Crawhall (1999); De Wet (2010); Robbins (2007); Robins et al. (2001); Stavenhagen (2005). In South Africa, the groups covered include the /Khomani, !Xun, and Khwe San, the Nama (Khoekhoe), and the Korana, but not the Griquas.

While some of the best known and well-researched San groups are the Ju/'hoansi of north-eastern Namibia and north-western Botswana (Lee 1979; Marshall 1976; Wilmsen 1989) and the G/ui and G//ana of the central Kalahari region of Botswana (Silberbauer 1981; Tanaka 1980; Tanaka and Sugawara 1996), there are many other groups that have also received anthropological attention, including the Naro (Nharo) of the Ghanzi region of Botswana and extending into eastern Namibia (Barnard 1992, 134–55), the Kua of the eastern and south-eastern Kalahari (Vierich 1981; 2008), the !Xóõ of the south-western Kalahari, extending into eastern Namibia (Heinz 1994), the Tyua of north-eastern Botswana and western Zimbabwe (Hitchcock 1988a, 1995); the Hai//om of northern Namibia (Widlok 1991; Dieckmann 2007), the !Xun of northern Namibia, southern Angola, and the resettled !Xun and Khwe of South Africa (Chennels 2009; Chennels and DuToit 2004; Suzman 2001), and the Khwe of northern Botswana and the Caprivi region of Namibia (Orth 2003). Of these, the group that has had the most extensive interactions with non-San peoples, including Afrikaaner farmers, Tswana agro-pastoralists, and others was the Naro, much of whose land was taken over for commercial cattle farms (ranches) in the 1890s.

It is interesting to compare the mobility, land-use practices, subsistence, and interactions with other groups of the Ju/'hoansi and the G/ui and G//ana since they have very different kinds of habitats, the Ju/'hoansi having access to permanent waterholes, and the G/ui and G//ana having no permanent water and surface water only one to two months a year at most in the absence of boreholes. The Ju/'hoansi in the past aggregated in the dry season at pans with water, and dispersed during the dry season and the G/ui and G//ana aggregated in the wet season near places with melons and other water-bearing plant species and dispersed in the dry season in small family and sub-band units. The Kua, prior to the introduction of permanent water points in the form of boreholes, had a pattern similar to the G/ui and

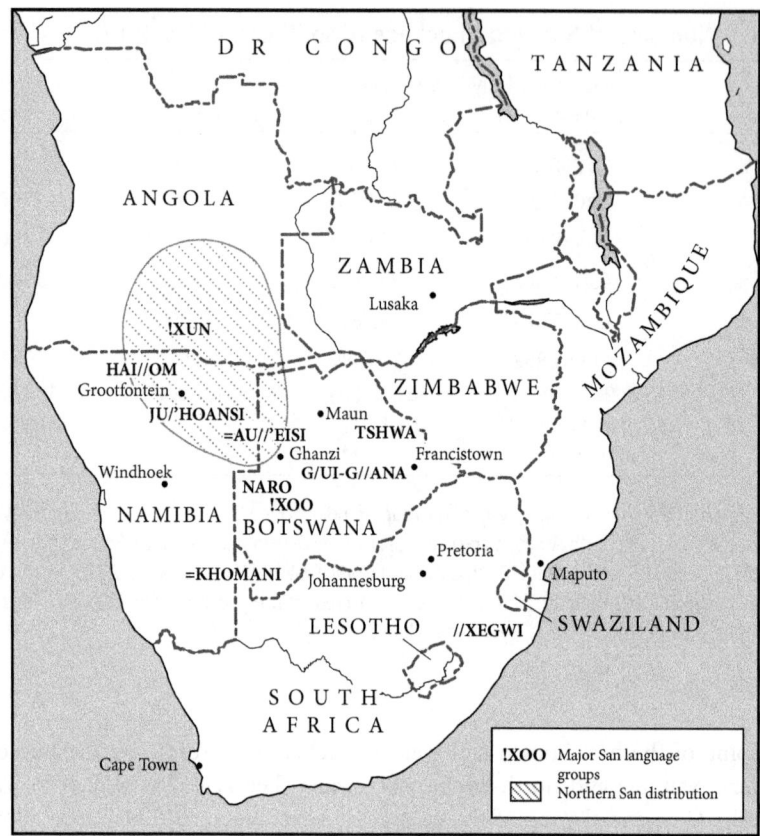

FIGURE 43.1 Map of southern Africa, showing the major San language groups.

the G//ana, but are now in an environment dominated by cattle posts and ranches owned largely by other people: Bamangwato, Herero, Kalanga, Bakgalagadi, Europeans (Hitchcock 1978; Vierich 1981). The Tyua of north-eastern Botswana were settled agropastoralists at the time of contact with European travellers and hunters in the nineteenth century, but they continued to engage in long-distance group hunts for large game in the late twentieth century (Hitchcock 1988a) (Figure 43.1).

The G/ui and G//ana of the central Kalahari, the /Khomani of South Africa (Chennels and DuToit 2004), and the Hai//om of the Etosha National Park region of Namibia have been largely displaced by the creation of protected areas, something that has also happened with the Tyua of the Hwange National Park region of western Zimbabwe (Dieckmann 2007; Hitchcock 1995; 2002). The !Xóõ of the southern Kalahari lost some of their land to the Kalahari Gemsbok Park, now the Kgalagadi Transfrontier Park, and have had settlements such as Bere established among them (Heinz 1994), but there are other !Xóõ who continue to hunt and gather for part of their subsistence and income in the Ghanzi and Kgalagadi districts of Botswana, as shown in the film *The Great Dance: A Hunter's Story* (Foster and Foster 2000). The Khwe (Kxoe) of Angola, northern Namibia, and north-western Botswana largely live in permanent settlements, some of them former military bases in northern Namibia

(Pakleppa and Kwononoka 2003; Robins et al 2001). Many Khwe interact extensively with their Bantu-speaking neighbours, in a sizeable number of cases working for them as herders, agricultural field hands, or domestic servants. For them, hunting and gathering is largely a buffering activity.

This chapter is an assessment of hunter-gatherer research traditions in southern Africa. There are a number of different trajectories of research on hunter-gatherers in this region, which, for purposes of this chapter, are broken down into the following categories: (a) the South African tradition; (b) the American tradition; (c) southern African government and non-governmental research traditions; and (d) the Japanese research tradition. An effort is made to identify research trends and conclusions and to review critically the various perspectives, approaches, and debates surrounding hunting and gathering societies in southern Africa.

THE SOUTH AFRICAN RESEARCH TRADITION

In the latter part of the fifteenth century, one of the individuals who visited what is now the west coast of South Africa with Portuguese explorer Vasco da Gama, observed people whose food was 'confined to the flesh of seals, whales, and gazelles, and the roots of herbs' (Barnard 2007, 11). Portuguese sailors and later Dutch sailors and settlers encountered people who were exploiting wild foods along the coasts and in the interior of southern Africa in the fifteenth to eighteenth centuries (Barnard 2007, 11–32; Elphick 1977; Penn 2006). Individuals and groups who were engaged in foraging were observed and documented by travellers, hunters, settlers, missionaries, administrators, and others who commented on their activities and speculated on their origins (Guenther 2005; Orpen 1874; Stow 1905). Some of the concerns of early observers related to the adaptations to their environments and the ways in which they interacted with other groups.

Early linguistic research focused on /Xam-ka !ei San who had been brought to Cape Town as prisoners from their homes in what is now the Karoo region of the Cape interior of South Africa. Beginning in the 1870s, Wilhelm Bleek, a German philologist, and his sister-in-law Lucy C. Lloyd, interviewed the prisoners and transcribed some 12,000 pages of texts that they then translated into English. This remarkable collection of materials, which is now in an accessible form, is a rich source of information on the /Xam and their lifestyles, beliefs, and traditions (Bank 2006; Barnard 2007, 24–7; Bleek and Lloyd 1911; Skotnes 1996; 2007). Wilhelm Bleek's daughter Dorothea carried out ethnographic and linguistic work among Naro San on the border between Namibia and Botswana in 1921 and 1922 (Bleek 1928). She also conducted studies of the San of central Angola and of the languages and phonology of San in general (see Bleek 1929).

In the early part of the twentieth century, the majority of work on the San by anthropologists was not based so much on fieldwork as it was upon an analysis of archival records and secondary sources. This is true, for example, of the important study of the Khoisan peoples by anthropologist Isaac Schapera of the University of Cape Town and subsequently of the London School of Economics. Schapera brought together an enormous amount of material on the Khoi and San (Schapera 1926; 1930; 1939). He was a gifted researcher whose work on issues ranging from customary law and social organization to land tenure and labour migration was extremely influential on policies of the Bechuanaland Protectorate. Schapera's work touched repeatedly on San issues, and he pointed out some of the problematic relationships between San and other groups.

An important contribution of Schapera to Khoisan studies was his compilation of data on the contemporary status of San in southern Africa (Schapera 1939). This study, which again was based on second-hand material and on statements made by district commissioners, was published in *Race Relations* in 1939. This work helped spark greater interest among San not only among academics but also administrators, and it fuelled arguments for the setting aside of blocks of land for San as a means of helping meet their needs for areas sufficient in size for them to be able to continue hunting and gathering and to allow them to maintain their cultural traditions and lifeways.

In the twentieth century, universities in South Africa began paying greater attention to San and Khoekhoe. In July 1936, for example, the University of the Witwatersrand in Johannesburg mounted an expedition to the southern Kalahari Desert region of northern South Africa (Rheinallt Jones and Doke 1937). Work was carried out on 70 /Khomani and Auen (/'Auni) by a physical anthropologist, a doctor, two linguists, two anatomists, an expert in music, and a psychologist. This investigation was probably the first interdisciplinary study of San peoples. Researchers examined biological, medical, cultural, linguistic, psychological, ethnobotanical, and technological dimensions of /Khomani and Auen societies and published the results in a widely read academic journal, *Bantu Studies*, now called *African Studies*.

Interest in San increased exponentially in 1936–7 when a group of southern Kalahari San was exhibited at the Empire Exhibition in Johannesburg, South Africa. The Minister of Native Affairs of South Africa was so impressed by the San that he said that they should be allowed to continue hunting freely in the Gemsbok National Park. As he put it, 'We must treat these Bushmen as fauna' (*The Cape Argus*, 25 August 1936). In 1936, a South African farmer, big-game hunter, and entrepreneur, A. C. (Donald) Bain, took a deputation of 55 San to the Houses of Parliament in Cape Town in order to protest about their mistreatment by Parks officials. The cause of the San was taken up by social scientists in late 1936, when a group of anthropologists from the University of the Witwatersrand in Johannesburg put forward a proposal to the High Commissioner that a substantial portion of the Kalahari be ceded over to San (Botswana National Archives—BNA—file S.469/l/l). This suggestion brought a quick reaction from the British Protectorate Administration. The Resident Commissioner at the time, C. F. Rey, said:

> In the first place I saw no reason whatsoever for preserving Bushmen. I can conceive no useful object to the world in spending money and energy in preserving a decadent and dying race, which is perfectly useless from any point of view, merely to enable a few theorists to carry out anthropological investigations and make money by writing misleading books which lead nowhere.
>
> (C. F. Rey, 6 November 1936, BNA file S.469/1/1).

Rey expressed the opinion that the main objective of anthropologists was to preserve the San as 'living fossils' for their own scientific and pecuniary purposes. He also suggested that development efforts among San would have little effect (BNA file S.469/l/l). It is interesting to note that anthropologists, missionaries, and colonial administrators all had called for greater protection of the human rights of San peoples and for development initiatives to assist them (Hitchcock 1987; 2004; Silberbauer 1981, 12–17).

In 1937, a group of academics at the University of Cape Town in South Africa formed a committee that was aimed at 'protection of the Bushmen through the provision of reserves' and at ensuring 'the preservation of the Bushmen as a separate race' (Schapera 1939, 68). A committee with similar goals was formed by the South African Association for the Advancement of Science in 1937 (Schapera 1939, 68). Schapera was on an inter-university committee that adopted a resolution on 27 November 1937 that called for an investigation into the conditions affecting the San in South Africa, South-West Africa, and the Bechuanaland Protectorate.

Relatively little work was done among San during the Second World War, although there were administrative reports from district commissioners in the Bechuanaland Protectorate and district administrators in Namibia that indicated that the numbers of San going to the mines in South Africa increased significantly during the early to mid-1940s. According to San informants this was done as a means of generating income and 'to help the war effort'. One unfortunate incident occurred at the height of the Second World War, when two Royal Air Force cadet flyers from Khumalo in what was then Southern Rhodesia disappeared on a training mission in northern Botswana, never to be found. A group of eight Tyua San were accused of having been responsible for their disappearance and were put on trial in the Bechuanaland High Court in Lobatse but were acquitted for lack of evidence (Hitchcock 1991; Botswana National Archives [BNA] file S.198/2).

Public interest in San populations and their situations increased in the 1950s as a result of a series of investigations by researchers from South Africa, Europe, and the United States (Silberbauer 1965, 1–2; Tobias 1975a; 1975b). Anthropological work on San was carried out in 1951 by the French Panhard-Capricorn Expedition, which included French and South African social and natural scientists, one of whom was Phillip Tobias of the Department of Anatomy at the University of the Witwatersrand (see Balsan 1955). As Balsan (1955, 83) noted, 'The Bushmen were our principal reason for visiting the Kalahari. Their race, said to be the oldest in Africa, is on the way to extinction.' The notion that the San were dying out was a common justification for research on hunting and gathering and other peoples, even though evidence suggested that the notion of San 'dying out' was incorrect.

Based on his work with the Panhard-Capricorn Expedition and population data obtained from colonial administrators and anthropologists, Tobias (1956, 183) pointed out that 'Most anthropologists will be surprised to learn that there are over 50 000 Bushmen alive today'. Tobias and his colleagues at the University of Witwatersrand went on to carry out a number of research expeditions in the Kalahari, some of them among the Naro of western Botswana (see Tobias 1956; 1957; 1975a; 1975b; 1978). Research foci included the anthropometry, anatomy, physiology, and adaptations of San peoples. One major conclusion of this work was the demonstration of a secular trend, an increase over time in height of San adults, possibly associated with the transformations in San lifestyles towards settled food-production and livelihoods made up in part of goods supplied by other groups and the state. Tobias (1978) and his colleagues also pointed out the important relationship between hunting and herding peoples in southern Africa, a topic that was to become the subject of intense debate in the 1980s, 1990s, and into the new millennium.

Research was carried out by H. J. Heinz, a German parasitologist turned anthropologist, among the !Xóõ San of the south-western Kalahari Desert region of Botswana in the 1960s (Heinz 1994). Linguistics work was conducted among the !Xóõ San by Tony Traill of the University of Witwatersrand (Traill 1985; 1994). Both of these research programmes laid the foundations for government-based and non-government-organization research and development work from the 1970s into the new millennium, some of it conducted by the Remote Area Development Program of the government of Botswana (Hitchcock 1988b).

One of the conclusions of the work on southern African San and Khoekhoe was that there were oscillations in adaptations, with some San becoming herders (and therefore becoming, in effect, Khoekhoe) and some Khoekhoe losing their livestock and falling back on foraging, and in effect, becoming San (Elphick 1977). It is for this reason that some San and Khoekhoe groups in southern Africa have argued that both San and Khoekhoe should be considered together as indigenous peoples and be accorded rights as minorities and indigenous peoples in the region (De Wet 2010, 16–31, 64–6).

THE AMERICAN HUNTER-GATHERER RESEARCH TRADITION

The San have long been the subject of exhibitions, museum displays, and film-making ventures, some of which have treated them in stereotypical ways (Gordon 1997; Gordon and Douglas 2000; Marshall 2003; Skotnes 1996). As historian Neil Parsons has noted, some of the interest in San came about because of their being exhibited on stage in the United States and Europe in the late nineteenth and early twentieth centuries (Parsons 2010).

Ethnographic work that was well-documented photographically was carried out by the Denver African Expedition (July 1925–April 1926), primarily in South-West Africa (now Namibia) (Gordon 1997). Some of this work focused on the Hai//om of the Etosha region in the northern and north-central parts of Namibia. Gordon (1997, 3) points out that in contrast to previous photographic records, which tended to present San as 'decadently impoverished' and emphasized their 'human exceptionality', the Denver Expedition was 'the first attempt on a large scale to present a systematically romanticized image of Bushmen'. Many of the photographs taken by the Denver Expedition, as Gordon (1997, 4) notes, 'allow the subjects to project personality'. Although the authenticity of some of the images can be questioned, Gordon sees the photographs as important in terms of helping to create a 'popular' anthropological image of those labelled 'Bushmen' (Gordon 1997, 9).

The Ju/'hoan San of the Nyae Nyae region of north-eastern Namibia were the focus the American Marshall family's work in the period between 1951 and 1958 (see Marshall 1960; 1965; 1976; 1999; Thomas 1980). The Marshall family included Laurence Marshall, his wife Lorna Marshall, their son John Marshall, and their daughter Elizabeth Marshall (now Elizabeth Marshall Thomas). While not trained anthropologists, the Marshalls made sophisticated observations on the lifeways of a people involved extensively in hunting and gathering. They covered a wide variety of subjects, from social organization to economics, and from belief systems to sharing and reciprocity (Marshall 1960; 1961; 1976; Marshall 2003; Thomas 2006). The Marshall family and their collaborators, who numbered over 20 specialists, managed to carry out an impressive series of visits to the Nyae Nyae region over an eight-year period (Marshall 1976, 1–11). By the late 1960s and 1970s, Lorna Marshall was considered the 'grande dame of hunter-gatherer anthropology' (Thomas 2006, 50).

As Lorna Marshall noted, a characteristic feature of hunter-gatherer societies like the Ju/'hoansi (the suffix -*si* in *Ju/'hoansi* denotes a plural) was sharing (Marshall 1961; 1976). Vegetable foods, which among some groups (e.g. those in deserts or savannas) tend to be more abundant than animals, and often far outweigh meat in the total diet, were not shared as rigorously as meat. Wild foods were shared by the woman who gathered them, mostly within her nuclear family, and the sharing was done more casually than was the case with meat. Though nuclear families are the units within which gathered or hunted foods are shared, one nuclear family alone generally was not enough to sustain food gathering full-time. But families organized into bands could do that job.

Bands, groups made up of families linked through kinship, marriage, friendship, and economic ties, usually provided sufficient numbers of adult men in cooperation and in rotation for hunting, and women enough to guarantee companionship and mutual help for both gathering trips and stay-at-home child care. Bands are small-scale communities consisting of several families and sometimes friends who reside together for at least part of the year. Some bands, especially those consisting of families that have been together a long time, had names, some of them drawn from the geographic features of the landscapes where they lived. These groupings varied in size but often numbered between 25 and 50 people, as was noted by participants in the 'Man the Hunter' conference held in Chicago in 1966 (Lee and DeVore 1968).

Lorna Marshall pointed out that bands formed alliances with neighbouring bands whose resources could be used in time of need. Ju/'hoan groups generally had flexible, overlapping, and interactive use of land and natural resources. There were times, however, when natural resource failures occurred, and groups had to move to other places where they could obtain food and other goods. Information on the spatial distribution, number, type, and state of these items (e.g. degree of ripeness of fruits) was shared among individuals, families, and larger groups. Information was also shared about potential threats such as the presence of predators or the direction that bush fires were heading. In addition, groups shared information about the location, size, composition, and activities of other groups on the landscape, some of whom could be either allies or competitors.

John Marshall had returned to the Nyae Nyae area in 1980 along with Claire Ritchie and for the next two and a half years they collected data and assisted the Ju/'hoansi in development efforts (Marshall and Ritchie 1984). The strategy that they employed was to encourage the Ju/'hoansi who had moved to a government-established settlement at Tsumkwe in the late 1950s, 1960s, and 1970s to move back to their ancestral territories (their *n!oresi*, sing. *n!ore*). The idea behind this decentralization effort was the notion that the Ju/'hoansi would prosper in their *n!oresi* if they were able to make a decent living through a combination of foraging, food production, and small-scale rural entrepreneurial activities, with a particular emphasis on food production (John Marshall, personal communication, 1987).

In 1983–4, the Ju/'hoansi were successful in lobbying against the establishment of a nature reserve in Bushmanland, a reserve which would have resulted in the Ju/'hoansi being dispossessed or, alternatively, having to serve as 'tourist objects' in what John Marshall described as a 'subsidized plastic Stone Age' (Marshall 1984, 14; also, *New York Times*, 9 October 1984; ITN news coverage with John Marshall speaking to Peter Sharpe).

The Ju/'hoansi of Nyae Nyae organized themselves in response to shifts in South-West African government policies, including those involving wildlife conservation and development, establishing a co-operative in 1986. In the latter part of the 1980s, as the country moved towards independence and democratic governance, the Ju/'hoansi sought to hold on to their land and to maintain their access to wildlife and other resources, in part through lobbying at the national level with the Namibian government and with international organizations (Biesele and Hitchcock 2011). The Ju/'hoansi of Nyae Nyae took part in a whole series of development initiatives with the assistance of anthropologists and non-government organizations as well as by the government of the new nation of Namibia after 21 March 1990.

Important reservations were expressed about the ways in which development was being carried out among Ju/'hoansi by anthropologists and development workers (see, for example, Garland 1999; Marshall 2003; Wiessner 2003). The development approaches being employed included placing significant emphasis on food provision which increased dependency and a focus on tourism and community-based natural resource management to the exclusion of those types of development such as domestic crop and livestock production which, it was argued, might have a better chance of strengthening livelihoods and enhancing subsistence security.

The Harvard Kalahari Research Group

The Marshalls were followed by Richard Lee and the Harvard Kalahari Research Group (HKRG) who worked in the Dobe-/Kae/Kae area of western Ngamiland (North-West District), Botswana, beginning in 1963 (Lee 1979; Lee and DeVore 1976; Lee et al. 1996). The research by Lee and his colleagues was distinctly interdisciplinary and was both ecologically and socially oriented. This work came at a time when ecological anthropology was transitioning towards a focus on interactions between variable ecosystems and humans, and on humans as dynamic parts of ecosystems.

In the 1960s, when much of the work of the Harvard Kalahari Research Project was carried out (1967–72), some of the Dobe Ju/'hoansi depended to a significant extent on hunting and gathering (Lee 1968; 1979; Lee and DeVore 1976). At this time some of the Ngamiland Ju/'hoansi were mobile, moving from place to place depending on the seasonal availability of resources and the distribution of other groups. During the dry season Ju/'hoansi resided near pans that contained water, whereas in the wet season they would distribute themselves more widely in order to take advantage of wild plants and animals (Lee 1979; 2003; Yellen 1977). Among the Ju/'hoansi, group sizes averaged around 25–50. These groups were made up of several families and people related through kinship, affinity, and friendship.

Decision-making was done on the basis of public consensus. The Ju/'hoansi were seen as egalitarian, reciprocity was valued highly, and goods and services were exchanged widely among Ju/'hoan and neighbouring groups. Some of these exchanges were delayed in nature and involved the reciprocal giving and receiving of gifts such as bracelets, ostrich eggshell necklaces, and beaded bags in a system known as *hxaro* which linked trading partners, a number of them consanguineous kin, together (Wiessner 1982). Useful observations on style and identity were also made by Wiessner (1983; 1984), some of them focusing on the variability in San arrow points.

Ju/'hoan and other San social systems have been described as egalitarian, with relatively equal access to resources and to positions of authority, although there is debate about the degree to which they are indeed egalitarian and what egalitarianism means (Cashdan 1980; Solway 2006a; 2006b; Wilmsen 1989). Among the Ju/'hoansi, women had high status, in part because of their important contributions to subsistence and to decision-making (Draper 1975; Shostak 1981). Children contributed relatively little to daily work until they reached their teens (Draper 1975). Work effort was relatively low, 12–19 hours per week (Lee 1968; 1979), though subsequent research suggested that labour inputs varied, depending in part on resource density and on the ways in which work effort was measured. The high return rates with relatively low work effort among the Ju/'hoansi contributed to the arguments about 'the original affluent society' (Sahlins 1968).

Investigations of the demography of the Ju/'hoansi revealed that they had very low birth rates, mortality rates were moderate, and nutrition was related, at least to some extent, to the demographic patterns (Howell 2010; Lee 1979; 2003). While it was argued, at least initially, that the Ju/'hoansi had relatively adequate diets, in part because of the availability of mongongo nuts, characterized as a 'superabundant' resource (Lee 1968; 1979), data on heights, weights, and consumption patterns of Ju/'hoansi over an annual and multi-year cycle revealed that there were periods of hunger and stress (Wilmsen 1982; 1989). Draper (1973) noted that the degree to which the Ju/'hoansi depended on mongongo nuts and meat varied, depending on the area in which they lived. The spiritual health and well-being of Ju/'hoansi and the ways in which healing was done through trance was examined by Katz (1982; Katz et al. 1997). There were changes, too, that occurred over time in the healing systems of the Ju/'hoansi, some of them the result of interactions with other groups, including Christian missionaries.

Long-term work on the Ju/'hoansi of both Botswana and Namibia was carried out by Polly Wiessner, originally of the University of Michigan, from 1973 onwards (see Wiessner 1981; 1982; 2003; 2009), and by Megan Biesele of the Harvard Kalahari Research Group and later the Kalahari Peoples Fund and the Nyae Nyae Development Foundation of Namibia from 1970 onwards. Some of Biesele's work examined folklore and belief systems (Biesele 1993), while her later work focused on education, language, land rights, and development issues (Biesele and Hitchcock 2011).

An area that should be touched on regarding research and development among the San is the degree to which the anthropological fieldwork and events on the ground have been documented using film, video, and tape records. This is seen especially in the cinematic work of John Marshall which was done over a 50-year period among the Ju/'hoansi of Nyae Nyae (Marshall 2003). Marshall raised important development and human-rights issues in his films, ones which San, development organizations, governments, and anthropologists are still attempting to come to terms with, including the balance among various approaches to development and the roles played by local people and people from the outside in decision-making.

Another set of data which was obtained over time is a tape archive of conversations, stories, meetings, and discussions of Ju/'hoansi over an extended period of time (1989–2009). These textual materials are in the process of being annotated, and they will be made available in digital form along with annotations for use by the Ju/'hoansi, including by Ju/'hoan students in recently established community schools (Biesele and Hitchcock 2011). This work is an example of some of the kinds of useful collaborations being undertaken by anthropologists, linguists, educators, and indigenous peoples in southern Africa.

The Kalahari Debate

In the 1980s, the conclusions drawn from the work on the Ju/'hoansi were the subject of considerable debate (see, for example, Barnard 2006; 2007, 97–111; Denbow and Wilmsen 1986; Gordon and Douglas 2000; Kent 1992; Kuper 1993; Lee and Guenther 1991; Schrire 1980; Solway and Lee 1990; Wilmsen 1983; 1989; 1993; 2003). The Kalahari Debate, as it has become known, had two very different perspectives on the Ju/'hoansi. One perspective was that the Ju/'hoansi were largely hunters and gatherers 'living under changed circumstances and maintaining an old but adaptable way of life' (Lee and Guenther 1993, 185). The other perspective was that the Ju/'hoansi were people who had been affected greatly by their interactions over time with other groups and by their incorporation into a global system of production, consumption, and distribution (Wilmsen 1989; 2003). This approach sees the Ju/'hoansi as having been a part of a complex, inclusive class structure as what Wilmsen (1983, 17) termed an underclass. Rather than being autonomous actors, then, the Ju/'hoansi were seen by those who identified themselves as revisionists as part of a much larger system of commodity capitalism.

This debate about the ways in which the Ju/'hoansi and other San were represented by anthropologists raged throughout the 1990s and into the new millennium. Some of this debate focused on the archaeological record of western Ngamiland, including the areas around Dobe and /Kae/Kae (/Xai/Xai) and the Tsodilo Hills (Shott 1993; Wilmsen 1989; Wilmsen and Denbow 1990; Yellen and Brooks 1988). Judging from the archaeological record, Iron Age agro-pastoral groups using ceramics and metal tools occupied the north-western Kalahari in the early to middle part of the first millennium AD (Denbow and Wilmsen 1986). One of the questions raised was how these groups affected the Ju/'hoansi, incorporating them, utilizing their services, and/or subordinating them.

A central question of the Kalahari debate was whether the foraging lifestyle of San seen by ethnographers in the 1960s and 1970s was (1) a long-standing adaptation, (2) a response to social, environmental, economic, and political changes that occurred relatively recently, or (3) a product of change over the past two millennia. In the latter part of the nineteenth century, in 1896–7, for example, widespread deaths of livestock and wild animals due to rinderpest resulted in San and other groups in the northern and other parts of the Kalahari having to resort to foraging or to dependency on other groups for their livelihoods (Wilmsen 1997). The Marshalls and the Harvard Kalahari Research Group were seen by the revisionists as having ignored the prehistory and history of the northern Kalahari region (Denbow and Wilmsen 1986; Wilmsen 1989; 2003; Wilmsen and Denbow 1990). Lee and his colleagues (Lee 2003; Lee and Guenther 1993; Solway and Lee 1990) noted that there was significant variation both across space and over time among San peoples, with some groups living in relative isolation and others living in close proximity to other groups and interacting with them in a variety of different ways. This was the case, for example, with the Tyua and Kua San of the eastern and north-eastern Kalahari investigated by the University of New Mexico Kalahari Project in the mid to late 1970s (Hitchcock 1978; 1987; 1988a) and the Kua and other San groups in the south-eastern Kalahari studied by Helga Vierich (1981). In these cases, there was a continuum in adaptations from mobile foraging to sedentary food production and from independence to subordination.

Other Hunter-Gatherer Research Traditions

The central Kalahari was the subject of research by government-appointed development officers, including George Silberbauer from 1951–8 (see Silberbauer 1965; 1981). The area was designated as a game reserve in 1961 in order to preserve the habitats and resources and to protect the livelihoods of G/ui, G//ana, and other groups who were heavily dependent on hunting and gathering. Beginning in 1967, after Botswana's independence from Great Britain, the central Kalahari became the focal point for intensive research by a whole series of Japanese social scientists, many of them from the African Studies Centre of Kyoto University (Sugawara 2004; Tanaka 1980; Tanaka and Sugawara 1996). Silberbauer's and Tanaka's work was ecologically oriented and demonstrated the complexities of G/ui and G//ana San adaptations to the largely waterless central Kalahari region (Silberbauer 1965; 1981; Tanaka 1980). In contrast to the Ju/'hoansi, who had some permanent waterholes in their area in both Namibia and Botswana, the G/ui and G//ana had to depend heavily on water substitutes (e.g. melons, roots) and to use unique methods of water collection such as sip-wells in order to obtain sufficient moisture to meet their needs during part of the year. Aggregation and dispersal patterns of the peoples of the central Kalahari were the opposite of those in the north-western Kalahari, with G/ui and G//ana coming together in larger groups in the wet season and breaking down into small, family units in the dry season. Mobility was relatively high, with moves of camps occurring as often as 10–15 times per year. In the late 1950s and 1960s, the people of the central Kalahari tended to range over large areas that averaged between roughly 900 and 4000 square kilometres (Silberbauer 1981, 193; Tanaka 1980, 81). These ranges were generally structured in such a way that they contained all or most of the resources necessary to sustain a group over the course of a year. Range sizes today are much more restricted.

The presence of livestock in the central Kalahari, combined with the fact that many of the residents of the central Kalahari were living in permanent settlements which the Botswana government was supplying with water, food, and services (e.g. schools and health assistance) and arguments by ecologists that the San and Bakgalagadi were over-exploiting resources in the reserve, led the government of Botswana to call for a commission of inquiry into the status of the Central Kalahari Game Reserve in 1985, the results of which were announced by the government in 1986, which called for relocation of the residents outside of the reserve. In 1997, the government of Botswana moved over 1,700 people out of the Central Kalahari Game Reserve to nearby settlements on the periphery of the reserve (Hitchcock 2002). In January 2002, the government relocated the rest of the people of the CKGR in settlements outside the reserve, shutting down the water points and destroying homes and other buildings.

One of these settlements, New Xade, in Ghanzi District close to the western boundary of the reserve, has been investigated by Japanese researchers, including Kazunobu Ikeya (2001) and Junko Maruyama (2003). These events led to the filing of a legal claim in the High Court of Botswana by the former residents of the central Kalahari in 2004. On 13 December 2006, after the longest and most expensive legal case in Botswana's history, the High Court ruled that the former residents of the reserve had the right to return to the central Kalahari (Solway 2009; Sapignoli 2012). In January 2011, the San and Bakgalagadi won an appeal of a Botswana High Court decision which had denied them the right to drill boreholes in the central Kalahari. At the time of writing, in early 2013, there are some 550–600 people living inside the central Kalahari, depending largely on foraging and occasional gifts of food from relatives and friends living outside of the reserve.

There are very few, if any, societies left in the world today that forage for 100 per cent of their subsistence. There are groups that might be defined as foragers because they get a substantial portion of their food from the bush, but the vast majority of groups get at least some of their food from other sources, including purchase, transfers from kin, friends, or other people, and government, international, and non-government organizations' food relief and poverty-alleviation programmes. This is true for at least some San in southern Africa, some of whom have opted to engage in community-based natural-resource-management programmes and in working for tourism and safari hunting companies in order to continue to have access to wildlife and other natural resources. The question remains: will hunting and gathering continue to be a viable means of making a living for at least a few groups in southern Africa, or will it become simply an object of anthropological and tourist curiosity, with individuals engaging in foraging primarily as a means of generating income and demonstrating what Elizabeth Marshall Thomas (2006) has so beautifully described as 'the old way'?

References

Balsan, F. 1955. *Capricorn Road*. New York: Philosophical Library.
Bank, A. 2006. *Bushmen in a Victorian world: the remarkable story of the Bleek-Lloyd collection of Bushman folklore*. Cape Town: Double Storey.
Barnard, A. 1992. *Hunters and herders of Southern Africa: a comparative ethnography of the Khoisan peoples*. Cambridge: Cambridge University Press.
Barnard, A. 2006. Kalahari revisionism, Vienna, and the 'indigenous peoples' debate. *Social Anthropology* 14, 1–16.
Barnard, A. 2007. *Anthropology and the Bushmen*. Oxford and New York: Berg.
Biesele, M. 1993. *'Women like meat': Ju/'hoan Bushman folklore and foraging ideology*. Johannesburg: Witwatersrand University Press and Bloomington.
Biesele, M. and Hitchcock, R. 2011. *The Ju/'hoan San of Nyae Nyae and Namibian independence: development, democracy, and indigenous voices in southern Africa*. New York: Berghahn Books.
Bleek, D. 1928. *The Naron: a Bushman tribe of the Kalahari*. Cambridge: Cambridge University Press.
Bleek, D. 1929. *Comparative vocabularies of Bushman languages*. Cambridge: Cambridge University Press.
Bleek, W. and Lloyd, L. 1911. *Specimens of Bushman folklore*. London: George Allen.
Cashdan, E. 1980. Egalitarianism among hunters and gatherers. *American Anthropologist* 82, 116–20.
Chennels, R. 2009. Vulnerability revisited: vulnerability and indigenous communities: are the San of South Africa a vulnerable people? *Cambridge Quarterly of Healthcare Ethics* 18, 147–54.

Chennels, R. and du Toit, A. 2004. The rights of indigenous peoples in South Africa. In R. Hitchcock and D. Vinding (eds), *Indigenous peoples' rights in southern Africa*, 98–113. Copenhagen: International Work Group for Indigenous Affairs.

Crawhall, N. 1999. *Needs assessment study: indigenous peoples in South Africa*. Report prepared for the International Labour Organization, Geneva, and the South African San Institute, Cape Town.

De Wet, P. 2010. *South Africa's unfinished business: the first nation indigenous Khoisan peoples*. Saarbruchen: Lap Lambert Publishing.

Denbow, J. and Wilmsen, E. 1986, Advent and the course of pastoralism in the Kalahari. *Science* 234, 1509–15.

Dieckmann, U. 2007. *Hai//om in the Etosha Region: a history of colonial settlement, ethnicity, and nature conservation*. Basel: Basler Afrika Bibliographien.

Draper, P. 1973. Crowding among hunter-gatherers: the !Kung Bushmen. *Science* 182, 301–3.

Draper, P. 1975. !Kung women: contrasts in sexual egalitarianism in the foraging and sedentary contexts. In R. Reiter (ed.), *Toward an anthropology of women*, 77–109. New York: Monthly Review Press.

Elphick, R. 1977. *Kraal and castle: Khoikhoi and the founding of white South Africa*. New Haven: Yale University Press.

Foster, C. and Foster, D. 2000. *The great dance: a hunter's story* (film).

Garland, E. 1999. Developing Bushmen: building civil(ized) society in the Kalahari and beyond. In J. Comaroff and J. Comaroff (eds), *Civil society and the political imagination in Africa: critical perspectives*, 72–130. Chicago: University of Chicago Press.

Gordon, R. 1997. *Picturing Bushmen: the Denver expedition of 1925*. Athens: Ohio University Press.

Gordon, R. and Douglas, S. 2000. *The Bushman myth: the making of a Namibian underclass* (2nd edition). Boulder: Westview Press.

Guenther, M. (ed.) 2005. *Kalahari and Namib Bushmen in German South West Africa: ethnographic reports by colonial soldiers and settlers*. Cologne: Rudiger Koppe Verlag.

Heinz, H. 1994. *Social organization of the !Ko Bushmen*. Cologne: Rudiger Koppe Verlag.

Hitchcock, R. 1978. *Kalahari cattle posts*. Gaborone: Ministry of Local Government and Lands.

Hitchcock, R. 1987. Anthropological research and remote area development among Botswana Basarwa. In R. Hitchcock, N. Parsons, and J. Taylor (eds), *Research for development in Botswana*, 285–331. Gaborone: Botswana Society.

Hitchcock, R. 1988a. Settlement, seasonality, and subsistence stress among the Tyua of Northern Botswana. In R. Huss-Ashmore (ed.), *Coping with seasonal constraints*, 64–85. Philadelphia: MASCA Research Papers in Science and Archaeology, University Museum, University of Pennsylvania.

Hitchcock, R. 1988b. *Monitoring, research and development in the remote areas of Botswana*. Gaborone: Government of Botswana and Oslo: Norwegian Agency for Development Co-operation.

Hitchcock, R. 1991. Kuakaka: an early case of ethnoarchaeology in the northern Kalahari. *Botswana Notes and Records* 23, 223–33.

Hitchcock, R. 1995. Centralization, resource depletion, and coercive conservation among the Tyua of the Northeastern Kalahari. *Human Ecology* 23, 169–98.

Hitchcock, R. 2002. 'We are the first people': land, natural resources, and identity in the central Kalahari, Botswana. *Journal of Southern African Studies* 28, 797–824.

Hitchcock, R. 2004. Human rights and anthropological activism among the San. In C. Nagengast and C. Velez Ibanez (eds), *Human rights, power, and difference: the scholar as activist*, 169–91. Norman: Society for Applied Anthropology.

Howell, N. 2010. *Life histories of the Dobe !Kung: food, fatness, and well-being over the life-span.* Berkeley: University of California Press.

Ikeya, K. 2001. Some changes among the San under the influence of relocation plan in Botswana. In D. G. Anderson and K. Ikeya (eds), *Parks, property, and power: managing hunting practice and identity within state policy regimes*, 183–98. Osaka: National Museum of Ethnology.

Jenkins, T. 1979. Southern Africa's model people. *South African Journal of Science* 75, 280–2.

Katz, R. 1982. *Boiling energy: community healing among the !Kung.* Cambridge, MA: Harvard University Press.

Katz, R., Biesele, M., and St. Denis, V. 1997. *Healing makes our hearts happy: spirituality and cultural transformation among the Kalahari Ju/'hoansi.* Rochester: Inner Traditions.

Kelly, R. 2007. *The foraging spectrum: diversity in hunter-gatherer lifeways.* New York: Eliot Werner Publications.

Kent, S. 1992. The current forager controversy: real versus ideal views of hunter gatherers. *Man* 27, 45–70.

Kuper, A. 1993. Post modernism, Cambridge, and the great Kalahari debate. *Social Anthropology* 1, 57–71.

Lee, R. 1968. What hunters do for a living, or, how to make out on scarce resources. In R. Lee and I. DeVore (eds), *Man the hunter*, 30–48. Chicago: Aldine.

Lee, R. 1976. Introduction. In R. Lee and I. DeVore (eds), *Kalahari hunter gatherers: studies of the !Kung San and their neighbors*, 3–26. Cambridge, MA: Harvard University Press.

Lee, R. 1979. *The !Kung San: men, women, and work in a foraging society.* Cambridge: Cambridge University Press.

Lee, R. 2003. *The Dobe Ju/'hoansi* (3rd edition). New York: Thompson/Wadsworth.

Lee, R., Biesele, M., and Hitchcock, R. 1996. Thirty years of ethnographic research among the Ju/'hoansi of Northwestern Botswana: 1963–1993. *Botswana Notes and Records* 28, 107–20.

Lee, R. and DeVore, I. (eds) 1968. *Man the hunter.* Chicago: Aldine.

Lee, R. and DeVore, I. (eds) 1976. *Kalahari hunter gatherers: studies of the !Kung San and their neighbours.* Cambridge, MA: Harvard University Press.

Lee, R. and Guenther, M. 1991. Oxen or onions? The search for trade (and truth) in the Kalahari. *Current Anthropology* 32, 592–601.

Lee, R. and Guenther, M. 1993. Problems in Kalahari historical ethnography and the tolerance of error. *History in Africa* 20, 185–235.

Marshall, J. 1984. Death blow to the Bushmen. *Cultural Survival Quarterly* 8, 13–16.

Marshall, J. 2003. *A Kalahari family* (5 videos). Watertown: Documentary Educational Resources (DER).

Marshall, J. and Ritchie, C. 1984. *Where are the Ju/Wasi of Nyae Nyae? Changes in a Bushman society: 1958–1981.* Cape Town: University of Cape Town.

Marshall, L. 1960. !Kung Bushman bands. *Africa* 30, 325–55.

Marshall, L. 1961. Sharing, talking, and giving: relief of social tensions among !Kung Bushmen. *Africa* 31, 231–49.

Marshall, L. 1965. The !Kung Bushmen of the Kalahari Desert. In J. Gibbs (ed.), *Peoples of Africa*, 241–78. New York: Holt, Rinehart, and Winston.

Marshall, L. 1976. *The !Kung of Nyae Nyae.* Cambridge, MA: Harvard University Press.

Marshall, L. 1999. *Nyae Nyae !Kung: beliefs and rites.* Cambridge, MA: Peabody Museum Monographs.

Maruyama, J. 2003. The impact of resettlement on livelihood and social relationships among the central Kalahari San. *African Study Monographs* 14, 223–45.

Orpen, J. M. 1874. Mythology of the Maluti Bushmen. *Cape Monthly Magazine* 9, 1–13.

Orth, I. 2003. Identity as dissociation: the Khwe's struggle for land in West Caprivi. In T. Hohmann (ed.), *San and the state, contesting land, development, identity, and representation*, 121–59. Cologne: Rudiger Koppe Verlag.

Pakleppa, R. and Kwononoka, A. 2003. *Where the last are first: San communities fighting for survival in southern Angola*. Windhoek and Trocaire: Working Group of Indigenous Minorities in Southern Africa (WIMSA), and OCADEC.

Parsons, N. 2010. *Clicko, the wild dancing Bushman*. Cape Town: Jacana Media.

Penn, N. 2006. *The forgotten frontier: colonist and Khoisan on the Cape's northern frontier in the eighteenth century*. Athens: Ohio University Press.

Rheinallt-Jones, J. and Doke, C. (eds) 1937. *Bushmen of the Southern Kalahari*. Johannesburg: University of the Witwatersrand Press.

Robbins, D. 2007. *On the Bridge of Goodbye: the story of South Africa's discarded San soldiers*. Johannesburg and Cape Town: Jonathan Ball.

Robins, S., Madzudzo, E., and Brenzinger, M. 2001. *An assessment of the status of the San in South Africa, Angola, Zambia, and Zimbabwe*. Windhoek: Legal Assistance Center.

Sahlins, M. 1968. *Stone Age economics*. Chicago: Aldine.

Sapignoli, M. 2012. Local power through globalised indigenous identities: the San, the state, and the international community. PhD thesis, University of Essex, Colchester, United Kingdom.

Schapera, I. 1926. A preliminary consideration of the relationship between the Bushmen and the Hottentots. *South African Journal of Science* 23, 833–66.

Schapera, I. 1930. *The Khoisan peoples of South Africa: Bushmen and Hottentots*. London: Routledge & Kegan Paul.

Schapera, I. 1939. A survey of the Bushman question. *Race Relations* 6, 68–83.

Schrire, C. 1980. An enquiry into the evolutionary status and apparent identity of San hunter gatherers. *Human Ecology* 8, 9–32.

Shostak, M. 1981. *Nisa: the life and words of a !Kung woman*. Cambridge, MA: Harvard University Press.

Shott, M. 1993. On recent trends in the anthropology of foragers: Kalahari revisionism and its archaeological implications. *Man* 27, 843–71.

Silberbauer, G. 1965. *Bushman survey report*. Gaberones: Bechuanaland Government.

Silberbauer, G. 1981. *Hunter and habitat in the central Kalahari Desert*. New York: Cambridge University Press.

Skotnes, P. (ed.) 1996. *Miscast: negotiating the presence of the Bushmen*. Cape Town: University of Cape Town Press.

Skotnes, P. 2007. *Claim to the country: the archive of Wilhelm Bleek and Lucy Lloyd*. Athens: Ohio University Press and Johannesburg: Jacana Press.

Solway, J. 2006a. Introduction: the politics of egalitarianism: essays in honor of Richard B. Lee. In J. Solway (ed.), *The politics of egalitarianism: theory and practice*, 1–17. New York and Oxford: Berghahn Books.

Solway, J. 2006b. The original affluent society: four decades on. In J. Solway (ed.), *The politics of egalitarianism: theory and practice*, 65–77. New York and Oxford: Berghahn Books.

Solway, J. 2009. Human rights and NGO 'wrongs': conflict diamonds, culture wars, and the 'Bushman question'. *Africa* 79, 329–43.

Solway, J. and Lee, R. 1990. Foragers, genuine or spurious? Situating the Kalahari San in history. *Current Anthropology* 31, 109–46.

Stavenhagen, R. 2005. *Human rights and indigenous issues. Report of the Special Rapporteur on the situation of human rights and fundamental freedoms of indigenous people, Rodolfo*

Stavenhagen. Addendum. Mission to South Africa. Economic and Social Council, Human Rights Council, Sixty-second Session. Item 15 of the Agenda, E/CN.4/2006/78/Add.2, 15 December 2005. Geneva.

Stow, G. W. 1905. *The native races of South Africa: a history of the intrusion of the Hottentots and Bantu onto the hunting grounds of the Bushmen, the Aborigines of the country*. London: Swan Sonnenschein and Co.

Sugawara, K. 2004. The modern history of Japanese studies on the San hunter-gatherers. In A. Barnard (ed.), *Hunter-gatherers in history, archaeology and anthropology*, 115–28. London: Berg.

Suzman, J. 2001. *An introduction to the regional assessment of the status of the San in southern Africa*. Windhoek: Legal Assistance Center.

Tanaka, J. 1980. *The San, hunter-gatherers of the Kalahari: a study in ecological anthropology*. Tokyo: Tokyo University Press.

Tanaka, J. and Sugawara, K. (eds) 1996. *Recent social, ecological, and linguistic research among the G/ui and G//ana San of the Central Kalahari*. Kyoto: Center for African Area Studies, Kyoto University.

Thomas, E. 1980. Over a span of thirty years, an American family records the disappearing culture of the Kalahari Bushmen. *Smithsonian* 11, 86–95.

Thomas, E. 2006. *The old way: a story of the first people*. New York: Farrar, Straus & Giroux.

Tobias, P. 1956. On the survival of the Bushmen, with an estimate of the problem facing anthropologists. *Africa* 26, 175–86.

Tobias, P. 1957. Bushmen of the Kalahari. *Man* 47, 33–40.

Tobias, P. 1975a. Profile of a hunter-gatherer people: the Bushmen of the Kalahari. *South African Journal of Science* 71, 69–73.

Tobias, P. 1975b. Fifteen years of study on the Kalahari Bushmen or San: a brief history of the Kalahari Research Committee. *South African Journal of Science* 71, 74–8.

Tobias, P. (ed.) 1978. *The Bushmen: San hunters and herders of southern Africa*. Cape Town: Human and Rousseau.

Traill, A. 1985. *Phonetic and phonological studies of !Xoo Bushmen*. Hamburg: Helmut Buske Verlag.

Traill, A. 1994. *A !Xoo dictionary*. Cologne: Rudiger Koppe Verlag.

Vierich, H. 1981. The Kua of the southeastern Kalahari: a study in the socio-ecology of dependency. PhD thesis, University of Toronto.

Vierich, H. 2008. Wilderness, wild foods, subsistence, and identity for hunter-gatherers: an ethnographic report. *Before Farming* 2008/1, 1–9.

Widlok, T. 1999. *Living on Mangetti: 'Bushman' autonomy and Namibian independence*. Oxford: Oxford University Press.

Wiessner, P. 1981. Estimating the impact of social ties on nutritional status among the !Kung San. *Social Science Information* 21, 641–78.

Wiessner, P. 1982. Risk, reciprocity and social influences on !Kung San economics. In E. Leacock and R. Lee (eds), *Politics and history in band societies*, 61–84. Cambridge: Cambridge University Press.

Wiessner, P. 1983. Style and information in Kalahari San projectile points. *American Antiquity* 48, 253–76.

Wiessner, P. 1984. Reconsidering the behavioral basis for style: a case study among the Kalahari San. *Journal of Anthropological Archaeology* 3, 190–234.

Wiessner, P. 2003. 'Owners of the future'? Calories, cash, casualties, and self-sufficiency in the Nyae Nyae area between 1996–2003. *Review of Visual Anthropology* 19, 149–59.

Wiessner, P. 2009. Experimental games and games of life among the Ju/'hoan Bushmen. *Current Anthropology* 16, 115–45.

Wilmsen, E. 1982. Studies in diet, nutrition, and fertility among a group of Kalahari Bushmen in Botswana. *Social Science Information* 21, 5–126.

Wilmsen, E. 1983. The ecology of illusion: anthropological foraging in the Kalahari. *Reviews in Anthropology* 10, 9–20.

Wilmsen, E. 1989. *Land filled with flies: a political economy of the Kalahari*. Chicago: University of Chicago Press.

Wilmsen, E. 1993. On the search for (truth) and authority: a reply to Lee and Guenther. *Current Anthropology* 34, 715–21.

Wilmsen, E. (ed.) 1997. *The Kalahari ethnographies (1896–1898) of Siegfried Passarge: nineteenth century Khoisan and Bantu-speaking peoples*. Cologne: Rudiger Koppe Verlag.

Wilmsen, E. 2003. Further lessons in Kalahari ethnography and history. *History in Africa* 30, 327–420.

Wilmsen, E. and Denbow, J. 1990. Paradigmatic history of San speaking peoples and current attempts at revision. *Current Anthropology* 31, 489–524.

Yellen, J. 1977. *Archaeological approaches to the present: models for reconstructing the past*. New York: Academic Press.

Yellen, J. and Brooks, A. 1988. The Stone Age archaeology of the !Kangwa and /Xai /Xai Valleys, Ngamiland. *Botswana Notes and Records* 20, 5–27.

CHAPTER 44

CENTRAL AFRICAN HUNTER-GATHERER RESEARCH TRADITIONS

BARRY S. HEWLETT AND JASON M. FANCHER

The largest remaining groups of mobile hunter-gatherers on earth live in central Africa. More than 350,000 foragers from at least 13 distinct ethnolinguistic groups occupy Congo Basin forests. Historically, these groups have been referred to as 'Pygmies' and no alternative term has emerged to replace that. Researchers actively debate whether or not to use the term 'Pygmy' in their publications. Some prefer the term because the public and non-specialist academics recognize it, or their publications get more attention if this term is used, while others feel it is derogatory. Political activist and development agencies do not hesitate to use the term. We take the position that reference to stature may not be derogatory, but it is denigrating the way it is used by farmers living in association with foragers. The term 'Pygmy' also tends to give the impression of a unified culture or ethnic group. In this chapter we use the names of specific ethnic groups when possible or refer to all groups as Congo Basin foragers or forest foragers. It is important to note that many Congo Basin foragers today farm, and that many of them are not short (e.g. Bongo and other groups in Gabon).

The chapter is divided into three parts. A brief overview of the ethnic groups and their genetic relationships is provided before we briefly examine the personal backgrounds and research trajectories of leading researchers from four national anthropological traditions. The Congo Basin has attracted particular kinds of researchers and these researchers have influenced how Congo Basin peoples are represented. Finally, major topical and theoretical issues in Congo Basin forager research are identified and critiqued, and we conclude with suggestions for future research.

WHO ARE THE CONGO BASIN FORAGERS?

Profound linguistic, cultural, and biological (genetic) diversity exists between ethnic groups (Hewlett in press). Figure 44.1 identifies the general location of the largest groups

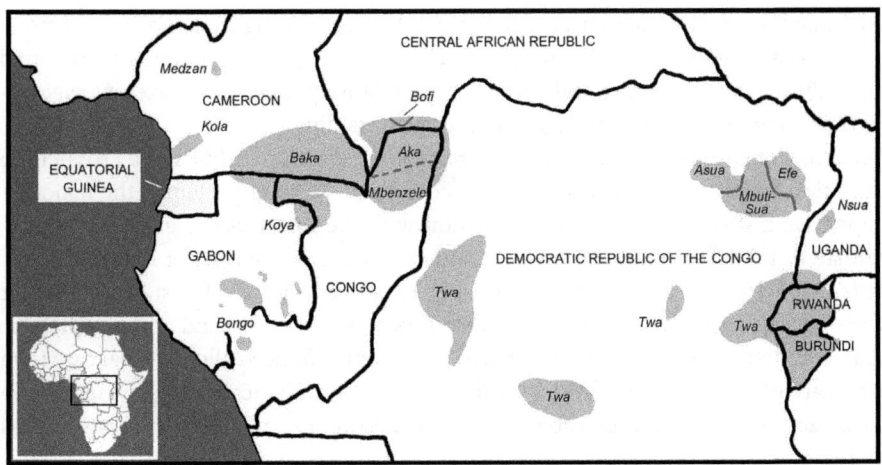

FIGURE 44.1 The general location of the largest groups of Congo Basin hunter-gatherers.

Table 44.1 Major ethnolinguistic groups of Congo Basin hunter-gatherers

Ethnic group	Approximate population	Linguistic family
Aka (Mbenzele dialectal sub-group)	35,000	Bantu
Asua	3,000	Sudanic
Efe	10,000	Sudanic
Baka (known as Bangombe in some areas)	40,000	Oubanguian
Bofi	3,000	Oubanguian
Bongo (also known as Akoa)	2,000	Bantu
Kola (also known as Gyeli)	3,500	Bantu
Mbuti-Sua	7,500	Bantu
Medzan (also known as Tikar)	250	Bantu
Nsua	1,000	Bantu
Twa (Ntomba region)	14,000	Bantu
Twa (Kasai region)	Unknown	Bantu
Twa (Rwanda and Burundi region)	10,000	Bantu

and Table 44.1 gives the names, approximate population size, and linguistic family of the larger or better-documented groups. Several other ethnic groups exist but they have not been documented. For instance, in the Central African Republic we are aware of Mbati foragers and Bolimba foragers, but their distributions, population sizes, histories, and cultures have not been described.

Research on Congo Basin foragers emphasizes understanding cultural diversity, but it is worth noting that some aspects of Congo Basin forager cultures are relatively similar. First, like mobile foragers in other parts of the world they lack strong leaders and food storage; gender and age egalitarianism, extensive sharing, and respect for autonomy are foundational cultural values; fertility and mortality are relatively high; camp sizes average 25–35 individuals; and seldom do they engage in warfare or raiding.

Second, Congo Basin forager cultures are profoundly diverse, but some cross-cultural similarities, which some may call a culture core, exist. Most importantly, the majority of groups have a strong identity and association with the forest. Some groups may live in savannah or mixed savannah-forest environments (e.g. Bofi foragers or Medzan), but the people's knowledge and identity are generally associated with the forest. Other elements of the culture core include: similar terms for several forest plants and animals (Bahuchet 1992a), distinctive polyphonic music (Fürniss 1993), pronounced allomaternal care (cooperative care of children by individuals other than their biological mothers; Hewlett 1991; Meehan 2005), and multidimensional (e.g. social, economic, religious) relationships with farmers.

Origin and Stature

This review does not cover biological anthropology and archaeology, but we want to briefly mention two recent areas of research that have generated considerable public and academic attention—what their origin is and why they are short. Recent phylogenetic studies (Batini et al. 2007; Patin et al. 2009; Quintana-Murci et al. 2008; Verdu et al. 2009) indicate that ancestral populations of Congo Basin foragers and farmers diverged about 60,000 years BP. This implies that the original divergence was not based on subsistence as both ancestral groups would have been foragers at this time because farming in central Africa did not emerge until 5000 BP. It is hypothesized that dramatic variability in African climate between 100,000 and 60,000 BP led to cultural innovations, population growth, and movements of peoples within and out of Africa. Genetic data also indicate that eastern (e.g. Mbuti and Efe) and western (e.g. Aka and Baka) Congo Basin foragers diverged about 20,000 BP, which suggests that the commonalities in culture described above are a result of shared history rather than convergent adaptation to the tropical forest. The timing of the separation is hypothetically linked to the Last Glacial Maximum, which led to a massive retreat of the Congo Basin forests as rainfall declined up to 50 per cent. Finally, the genetic data also indicate a relatively recent common origin of all western forager groups (about 2500 BP) and substantial gene flow between western Congo Basin foragers and farmers. Verdu et al. (2009) hypothesized that the western group's divergence was linked to the Bantu expansion, which occurred about the same time; i.e. Bantu farmers' relationships with foragers decreased mobility and increased the isolation of forager groups.

Another long-standing question within biological anthropology is 'Why are Pygmies short?' (Cavalli-Sforza 1986; Diamond 1991). Previous studies suggested short size was a thermoregulatory or other adaptation to the tropical forest or that nutritional shortages led to the short stature, but Walker et al. (2006) used life history theory to explain diversity in human stature, suggesting that short stature could be selected for in a context of high mortality. Migliano et al. (2007) tested the hypothesis among Pygmies, but their data and interpretation of life history theory were problematic (Becker et al. 2010).

Personal Trajectories and National Research Traditions

Before we examine research issues in Congo Basin forager research, we provide biographical sketches of the most prolific Congo Basin forager ethnographers. An understanding of their personal interests and academic backgrounds provides insights into research issues/questions and how Congo Basin foragers are represented. We focus on research in the last 50 years, i.e. since 1960.

British Traditions

Colin Turnbull (1961) (four monographs and first author on over 15 journal articles and book chapters on Congo Basin foragers) is probably the most recognized scholar of forest foragers because of his best-selling book, *The forest people*. Even though it is based on research with the Mbuti in the 1950s it is still a popular text in some introductory anthropology courses.

Turnbull was trained as a British social anthropologist at Oxford University. As an undergraduate he majored in politics and philosophy and spent considerable time with Indian students. After completing his undergraduate degree he received a scholarship to Banaras Hindu University in India to study religion with two famous Indian saints and eventually received an MA in Indian Religion and Philosophy. From India he travelled to Kenya where he started on a motorcycle journey across Africa with a friend. They were interested in African music and ended up in the Ituri forest in what was then the Belgian Congo at a hotel run by Patrick Putnam, a Harvard-trained anthropologist who had conducted ethnographic research with the Mbuti. Turnbull was impressed with Mbuti music and spent a month in the field. He was not supported at this time and took a job with filmmakers to help construct the boat used in the film *The African Queen*.

He returned to the UK, communicated with E. E. Evans-Pritchard about his interests in graduate school and decided to return to Oxford because its anthropology programme was not as science-oriented as other UK universities. For his BLitt (Bachelor of Letters, similar to MA in the US) he surveyed the ethnographic literature of the Mbuti and Efe. The review was critical of Father Paul Schebesta's 1920s research with the Efe because Schebesta wanted to test Father Schmidt's (1939) *Kulturkreise* (culture circle) ideas that Pygmies were the most primitive human circle, and he felt Schebesta's fieldwork was superficial because he did not live in Mbuti camps and he did not provide in-depth descriptions or understanding of the Efe. Schebesta said Efe had chiefs, had only instrumental music, and were dominated by villagers. Based upon his limited time in the field, he disagreed with all of these characterizations and returned to the Ituri twice in the 1950s to collect data for his PhD to refute them.

Turnbull was trained and influenced by Rodney Needham, Isaac Schapera, and Evans-Pritchard, classic British social anthropologists. Given this background, Turnbull had to pay attention to social structure, but as reflected in his Indian studies and becoming a Buddhist monk later in his life, he was especially interested in music, religion, and the inner lives of the people. His training in British social anthropology and a personal interest in religion contributed to his research focus on forager–farmer social relations, rituals that link foragers and farmers, and how Mbuti viewed the forest and their village neighbours. *The forest people* demonstrates his interest in and ability to convey the inner lives of the people and *Wayward servants* (Turnbull 1965) reflects his interests in religion and social structure. He became a naturalized American citizen in the 1960s when he took a position at the American Museum of Natural History (Grinker 2000).

Turnbull died in 1994 and for some reason he did not train a cohort of graduate students to work with forest foragers, but British social anthropologists studying with other well-known African forager scholars continue to make important contributions to Congo Basin forager ethnography. Jerome Lewis, a student of James Woodburn, provided rich ethnographic descriptions of the Mbenzele Aka (Lewis 2002), and Justin Kenrick, a student of Alan Barnard, provided insights into Mbuti relations with farmers, and foragers' views of conservation and other forms of international development (Kinrick 2001). These two anthropologists disagree with Turnbull's symbiotic characterizations of forager–farmer relations and are active in efforts to document how Congo Basin foragers are marginalized and how their lands can be protected (Kinrick and Lewis 2001).

French Traditions

France established colonies in the Congo Basin and it has a long and extensive history of research with forest foragers. Serge Bahuchet is the most prominent contemporary French anthropologist conducting research with forest foragers (three monographs and first author on over 30 journal articles and book chapters on Congo Basin foragers). Bahuchet wanted to be a zoologist. While in high school in the late 1960s he regularly went to the Natural History Museum in Paris and eventually met Raymond Pujol, an agricultural entomologist who was director of ethnozoology. In 1969 he travelled with Pujol and other students to the Central African Republic to collect zoological specimens. Pujol asked him to do ethnozoology of the Pygmies and he went to Kinga, Central African Republic to conduct the study. On his second field trip he met Jacqueline M. C. Thomas, a prominent linguist studying the Aka language; in 1975 she hired him to conduct a short ethnolinguistic study among the Aka. As part of Bahuchet's military service, Thomas was able to recruit Bahuchet for ethnolinguistic studies in the Central African Republic for two years. After two years in the field he attended the first (1978) Conference on Hunting and Gathering Societies (CHAGS) in Paris, France, organized by Maurice Godelier. Bahuchet took seminars on ecology and human sciences from Godelier, a Marxist and materialist anthropologist, and while attending the CHAGS conference was greatly influenced by Richard Lee who was working with the !Kung.

Bahuchet went on to receive his PhD (Docteur d'État) at École des Hautes Études en Sciences Sociales and took a position in the laboratory of Jacqueline M. C. Thomas who continues to work with Bahuchet on a ten-volume Aka Pygmy encyclopaedia. Currently, Bahuchet is Director of Human, Nature and Society studies at the place he started his career, the National Museum of Natural History.

Consequently, Bahuchet is best known for fine-grained ethnography of Aka ethnoecology (Bahuchet 1985) and his historical linguistic studies of the Baka and Aka (Bahuchet 1992a). He also used his ecological and ethnolinguistic perspectives in a variety of other topics: Aka settlement and spatial mobility (Bahuchet 1972; 1992b), ecological constraints on

Aka subsistence (Bahuchet 1978; 1988; Bahuchet et al. 1991) and the history of Aka–farmer relations (Bahuchet and Guillaume 1982). He has mentored and influenced several other Congo Basin forager researchers, including Motte's ethnobotanical research on Aka medicinal plants (Motte 1980; 1982; Motte-Florac et al. 1993), Dounias's research on Baka wild yams (1993; 1996; 2001), and Joiris's (2003) study of forager–farmer relations in Cameroon.

Japanese Traditions

This overview of the Japanese traditions is somewhat longer than British and French overviews because the number of Japanese researchers conducting research with foragers in this region in the last 30 years has been substantially greater than the number of British or French researchers. The Japanese research on Congo Basin foragers is generally ecologically focused, it is very inductive and descriptive, based on observations and some interviews, and is not organized around any one theoretical orientation.

Mitsuo Ichikawa is the most prominent Japanese Congo Basin forager researcher (one monograph and first author on over 25 journal articles and book chapters in English or French; several more in Japanese). In high school and his undergraduate college days he was an avid mountain climber and enjoyed fishing and gathering edible wild plants while hiking. After completing college he travelled to Bhutan, the Hunza Valley and several countries in South-East Asia.

He wanted to make a living where he could continue mountain climbing and travelling, and would not have to take rigorous methods courses. He decided to go into anthropology at Kyoto University and joined a research group directed by Junichiro Itani, a primatologist, to study human–nature relationships in hunter-gatherer groups. Itani, who was in the department of human evolution and helped to establish the Institute of African Studies at Kyoto University and the Japanese Society of Ecological Anthropology, was his mentor. Itani and Reizo Harako, a surgeon and anthropologist, conducted a brief survey of the foragers in the Ituri forest in the Democratic Republic of the Congo (Zaire at the time). Harako returned to conduct the first Japanese study of Mbuti subsistence patterns (Harako 1976). Tadashi Tanno replaced Harako to study subsistence patterns (Tanno 1976) in another part of the Ituri, and Ichikawa (1978) replaced Tanno a few years later.

Ichikawa's training at Kyoto took place in the Faculty of Science and emphasized a broad approach to ecology that adhered to Western theories or methods. Descriptive and inductive approaches were emphasized; 'Let the data speak' was the guiding motto at Kyoto. He hoped to 'become a researcher akin to a small time inventor who would never become part of the mainstream, but who would invent something that nobody had ever thought of' (Ichikawa 2004a, 3). Ichikawa was director of several research programmes at the Center for African Area Studies at Kyoto University and indicated that Kyoto's African studies programme was distinct from the one at Tokyo University because it emphasized fieldwork rather than armchair contemplation (his love of outdoors) and 'its own ecologically-oriented methodology' rather than theories and methods from the West (Ichikawa 2005). Ichikawa characterizes Japanese research as 'fearless' because it is not bound by theory and it can easily shift focus and topics.

Ichikawa is known for his rich and detailed descriptions of Mbuti subsistence and settlement (1978; 1982; 1983; 1987), the impact of a cash economy on Mbuti culture (1991), Mbuti ethno-ornithology (1998), and his Ituri forest ethnobotanical research (Terashima and Ichikawa 2003). By comparison to the French or British and consistent with his training by a primatologist, Ichikawa utilized more observational methods (e.g. participating in net hunts) and quantitative methods (e.g. measuring nets, counting how many game are caught per day). Ichikawa (2004b) considers his 'ecology in a broad sense' as holistic because he is interested in integrating cultural ecology, historical ecology, and political ecology into his research.

Terashima is also a prominent contributor to Congo Basin forager research (first author on over 12 journal articles or book chapters). He conducted extensive field research on Efe forest plant knowledge and social aspects of their economic exchange with neighbouring Lese farmers (Terashima 1986; Terashima et al. 1988). He also investigated why Efe girls sometimes choose to marry Lese farmers (Terashima 1987), and the many interactions between Efe and Lese that revolve around honey (Terashima 1998).

Because of political instability in the Democratic Republic of the Congo in the 1980s, Japanese researchers left the Ituri and initiated projects further to the west with Aka and Baka foragers. Takeuchi (1994; 1995) published ecological studies of hunting activities and dietary avoidance among the Aka of north-eastern Congo. Kitanishi's research among the Aka of the same area examined exchange between the Aka and cultivators (Kitanishi 1994), seasonal changes in subsistence (Kitanishi 1995), and food sharing (Kitanishi 1998). Kitanishi (1996) specifically analysed the acquisition and distribution of meat and honey by Aka males of different ages.

In recent years Japanese research among Baka of northern Congo and south-western Cameroon has increased. Studies have investigated Baka nutrition and dietary intake (Yamauchi et al. 2000), sedentary and migratory hunting camps (Hayashi 2008), conservation and hunting sustainability (Hattori 2005; Yasuoka 2006a), the many uses of Marantaceae plants (Hattori 2006), and the potential of wild yams as staple food resources in African tropical forests (Sato 2001; 2006; Yasuoka 2006b; 2009). Forest peoples preserve and maintain a vast knowledge of tropical species, and the scholars cited here share the priority of documenting this traditional knowledge and its behavioural expressions.

US Traditions

Unlike the other national traditions, two scholars have relatively similar academic productivity on Congo Basin foragers. Robert Bailey and Barry Hewlett have both published one monograph and over 20 journal articles or book chapters as first author. Bailey is better known for his theoretical contributions (e.g. wild yam hypothesis) and Hewlett is better known for his topical contributions (i.e. infant and child development).

Bailey wanted to be a primatologist. After completing an undergraduate degree in history at Harvard College he travelled to Colombia to be a resident biologist and conduct research with squirrel monkeys. In 1976, as he was ready to start his graduate training in biological anthropology at Harvard, Irven DeVore a primatologist and co-director (with Richard Lee) of the well-known Kalahari project, gave him the opportunity to go to Africa to observe various other primate ecology research sites. He visited several sites, but at the Dja Reserve in Cameroon he hired two Baka men to take him into the forest to observe monkeys. He was impressed with the Baka way of life and decided that studying monkeys to understand human behaviour was less effective than studying human behaviour directly. DeVore was delighted with Bailey's shift to humans because he wanted to work with forest foragers when he was a graduate student but Sherwood Washburn, his adviser, convinced him to work with baboons. Bailey took courses in biological anthropology and conducted a survey of Congo Basin foragers in 1978 and selected the Efe for study because he felt they were the most remote and unacculturated forest forager ethnic group. He started his research in the early 1980s with his wife and anthropology graduate student, Nadine Peacock. Bailey focused on men's subsistence and time allocation, as well as Efe and Lese growth, while Peacock conducted similar research with Efe women (Bailey 1991; Bailey and Peacock 1988; Peacock 1985). Bailey's graduate training took place at a time when neo-evolutionary theories (e.g. inclusive fitness theory, parental investment theory) were emerging, often coming from Harvard faculty (e.g. Robert Trivers).

In the mid-1990s Bailey and Peacock wanted to move away from basic research because they wanted to make more of a difference to the lives of African peoples, and they went to Emory University and received Masters in Public Health. They no longer conduct research with forest foragers, but conduct applied research in Africa (HIV/AIDS, maternal health). Both hold positions in the School of Public Health at the University of Illinois at Chicago.

Hewlett's career with Congo Basin foragers started before Bailey's (1973), but it was not as illustrious or conventional. As an undergraduate at California State University at Chico, Hewlett developed his own major and called it cultural transmission. After completing his BA he travelled overland to the Congo Basin several times in the early 1970s to work on an MA in anthropology at Chico. The first trip was a survey of Congo Basin forager groups while later trips were with the Aka. Hewlett selected the Aka because they were relatively unknown by comparison to the Ituri groups and he was unaware at the start of his research that Bahuchet was conducting research nearby. After several trips with the Aka Hewlett went to Stanford University in the late 1970s to talk to Luca Cavalli-Sforza, a well-known geneticist who had worked with Aka and other Congo Basin foragers. He introduced Hewlett to his cultural transmission theories, which were of interest because of Hewlett's undergraduate work. After completing the MA Hewlett worked for a Head Start programme (a child development programme for children in poverty) for five years. He returned to graduate school in the early 1980s to work on a PhD in cultural anthropology at the University of California, Santa Barbara, to study Aka father–child relations (1991) under Napoleon Chagnon. Chagnon introduced him to neo-evolutionary theories, but Hewlett did not use them in his doctoral research.

More than 15 researchers were associated with The Harvard Ituri Project (Bailey and DeVore 1989), and as director Bailey trained and influenced several researchers including Aunger's (1992) research on Mbuti and Efe food taboos and Jenike's (1985) research on Ituri subsistence seasonality. Hewlett's students have focused on the lives of Congo Basin children and include Fouts's work on Bofi forager weaning (Fouts et al. 2001) and parent–offspring conflict (Fouts et al. 2005), Meehan's work on Aka allomaternal care (Meehan 2005), and Boyette's research on Aka social learning in middle childhood (Boyette 2013).

These brief bio-sketches provide insights into the publications and the US research tradition with Congo Basin foragers. Hewlett is a cultural anthropologist interested in children and social learning, while Bailey is a biological anthropologist interested in subsistence patterns and social relationships, as well as growth and nutrition. Famous evolutionary theorists influenced both Hewlett and Bailey, so the theories and methods that guided their research were similar. Evolutionary and child development research projects were problem oriented and tested specific hypotheses. Research methods were systematic and quantitative; both Hewlett and Bailey utilized focal follow observations (extended observations of 'focal' individuals; Bailey followed men, Hewlett followed babies), the type of observations Ichikawa felt were inappropriate for humans. But Bailey and Hewlett also had pronounced differences. Hewlett viewed culture, or socially transmitted information, as having its own properties and an important force influencing human behaviour, whereas Bailey felt culture did not have special properties. Hewlett's background and training emphasized the importance of forager cultural models or ideas about research topics (e.g. their criteria of a good father) whereas Bailey's training in primatology and human biology led him to focus on what people did rather than what they said. In contrast to the other traditions, American studies frequently involve narrowly focused research questions and, in many cases, are explicitly guided by evolutionary theories such as behavioural ecology.

Another feature that distinguishes the American research tradition from others is its ongoing ethnoarchaeological research. Ethnoarchaeologists investigate relationships between human behaviour and its material consequences by observing both in the present. For example, Fisher (1993) documented forager–farmer exchange at Efe elephant processing sites in the Ituri Forest and the spatial organization of Efe campsites (Fisher 1987; Fisher and Strickland 1989; 1991). Ethnoarchaeological research of Aka and related Bofi foragers focused on net hunting and women's work effort (Lupo and Schmitt 2002), evolutionary explanations of meat sharing (Lupo and Schmitt 2004), small prey hunting technology and zooarchaeology (Lupo and Schmitt 2005), and taphonomic analyses of small animal bones (Fancher 2009; Landt 2007).

Finally, it is important to note that in trying to characterize particular national traditions, several domains of important research have been omitted. In particular, extensive ethnomusicology of forest foragers has been conducted in France (Arom 1991) and to a lesser extent in the US (Kisliuk 2000).

Comparing Traditions

The research traditions are similar in several respects. The French, Japanese, and US traditions are generally ecological and fall within the sciences rather than the humanities. Bahuchet had a background in zoology, Ichikawa was trained by a primatologist and surgeon in the Faculty of Science, Bailey was trained by a primatologist in biological anthropology, and Hewlett's work was influenced by a geneticist. By comparison, British researchers were trained in social anthropology and utilized humanities and social science approaches in their research.

While the Japanese, French, and US traditions were 'ecological', substantial differences existed in theory and methods. The French and Japanese viewed ecology from a natural history perspective and consequently emphasized detailed descriptions (if not encyclopaedic in the case of the French) of forest forager subsistence and settlement. US researchers viewed ecology from an evolutionary perspective so their research emphasized theory rather than ethnography. Japanese and French researchers shared a strong interest in natural history and ethnography, but their methods and approaches also differed. The French integrated their background in linguistics into natural history while the Japanese used the three ecological science perspectives described above. The three nationalities that comprise this ecological research tradition effectively complement one another, and have collectively revealed details of the relationships between people and the forest that Turnbull could never have foreseen.

Pronounced differences existed in field methods. British researchers used participant observation and interviews and very few or no systematic observations or quantification of behaviour, French ethnolinguists relied upon in-depth interviews with relatively few people, and Japanese researchers mixed observational data with some interview data. American researchers emphasized behavioural observations and varying amounts of interview data.

In summary, Americans tend to view French and Japanese research as too descriptive, atheoretical, and not very systematic/quantitative. The French and British tend to view American research as superficial because they pay little attention to language and interviews with local people. The Japanese tend to view the French research as too encyclopaedic and American research as too narrowly focused and not very creative. British researchers tend to feel the other three traditions are heavily biased towards ecological issues and methods and lack important social and historical contexts. The French have the greatest interest and number of publications on Congo Basin history, perhaps because of their long colonial and administrative history in the region, but Ichikawa says he was influenced by revisionism and the importance of history.

Why Did Scholars Conduct the Studies?

Several researchers were responding to perceived weaknesses in previous research. Turnbull thought Schebesta's research was superficial, and Ichikawa and other Japanese thought Turnbull's descriptions of the Mbuti were romantic and neglected to describe how they made a living in the forest. Other researchers, such as Bahuchet and Hewlett, were interested in describing the life of a relatively unknown hunter-gatherer group or wanted to cover a topic seldom discussed in the literature.

Early Japanese and contemporary American research took place, in part, because both felt that studies of hunter-gatherers, such as the Congo Basin foragers, might provide clues to understanding human nature and human evolution. This is not entirely surprising as Itani (who trained Ichikawa) and DeVore (who trained Bailey) were friends. While the Americans and Japanese shared this objective, field methods and approaches were very different. The Japanese rejected evolutionary theory, in part because it was associated with the West, they did not like American methods such as focal follows, and preferred more inductive, descriptive, and natural history approaches to research.

Research Questions

Several research questions have dominated Congo Basin forager research. Researchers from all or most of the four research traditions described above have tried to answer the questions from diverse theoretical and methodological approaches. In this section we examine four questions that have generated the most research.

Subsistence and Settlement

Can forest foragers live in the tropical forest without exchanging carbohydrates with farmers? Bailey et al. (1989, 60) proposed the controversial hypothesis that 'humans have never lived in tropical rainforest independently of domesticated plants and animals'. In light of the ubiquity of forager–farmer exchange observed throughout the region in modern times, it is reasonable to question whether a hunting and gathering subsistence system is possible in this context without access to domesticated foods (Bailey and Headland 1991; Headland and Bailey 1991). Headland (1987) argues that the natural availability of carbohydrate-rich resources, such as wild yams, is a critical limiting factor in rainforest subsistence. As a result, the issue of whether foragers lived independently in the rainforest prior to the arrival of Bantu farmers and their cultivated calories is referred to as the 'wild yam question'. Ethnoecological data centring on the environmental distribution of wild yams have been collected by French and Japanese anthropologists to explore contexts in which contemporary forest foraging is possible, and to extrapolate prehistoric possibilities (Bahuchet et al. 1991; Dounias 2001; Hladik and Dounias 1993; Sato 2001; Yasuoka 2006b; 2009). The most direct challenge to the cultivated calories hypothesis comes from archaeology. As more archaeological evidence is unearthed, it increasingly supports rainforest occupation by hunter-gatherers long before the arrival of farmers (Barham and Mitchell 2008), and possibly beyond 200,000 years ago (Mercader 2002; 2003). Nevertheless, as Bailey et al. (1989) hoped, the wild yam question has proved to be very successful at stimulating ecological and archaeological research in the Congo Basin.

Why do different subsistence technologies exist among Congo Basin foragers? Forest foragers rely on a range of cooperative and individual hunting techniques including nets, spears, bows, traps, and hand capture of small prey. Turnbull (1965) made a distinction between net hunters (Mbuti) and archers (Efe), but Harako was among the first to question *why* these different subsistence technologies coexisted within the Ituri Forest. He related it to language groups, suggesting that hunting nets were introduced by Bantu speakers and only those foragers who associated with Bantu-speaking villagers adopted the use of nets. Since Efe foragers maintained an exchange relationship with Sudanic-speaking Lese farmers, the Efe continued to use the same archery technology employed by the Lese (Harako 1976). This fundamental issue of forest forager diversity would be re-examined from many different perspectives in later years.

It was assumed that bow hunting was less efficient than net hunting, but studies have since demonstrated that the methods are comparable in terms of efficiency (Bailey and Aunger 1989). Numerous other factors have been investigated, although single-variable explanations are probably too simple to account for the observed variation. Many interrelated variables have been shown to influence hunting decisions: seasonal considerations, number of participants, targeted prey, method efficiency, risk sharing, proximity to farming populations, market involvement, and possibly the foraging goals of individual men, women, and children (Hewlett 1996; Lupo and Schmitt 2004).

Forager–Farmer Relations

What is the nature of forager–farmer relationships? How integrated or separate are the two ways of life? Are foragers serfs or slaves of neighbouring farmers? According to Turnbull (1965,

146) 'the relationship between the two neighbouring peoples, is of the greatest importance and has been subject to the greatest misunderstanding.' Few aspects of forest forager life have received as much scholarly attention as the interdependent relationship between forest farmers and foragers. Profound diversity exists in the nature and intensity of forager–farmer relationships and a range of variables have been identified to explain the diversity (Hewlett 1996, Takeuchi in press).

In terms of the level of interdependence of the two groups, Turnbull (1965) is known for emphasizing the dichotomy between village and forest worlds, giving the impression farmers do not know the forest and foragers are relatively independent from farmers. Hewlett et al. (2000) also gave the impression of different worlds by describing dramatically different foundational schema (ways of thinking that pervade many domains of life) of the two groups. By contrast, Bailey indicated the forest–village world dichotomy is misleading because Efe men are forest oriented while Efe women are village oriented; Efe men prefer to be in the forest as this is where they hunt and collect, while Efe women prefer to be in the village to obtain manioc in exchange for labour they provide village women. Grinker (1994) made the strongest case for the lack of separate worlds and advocated for a unity view of the relationship where foragers and farmers are considered one ethnic group because their relationships are so intertwined; they live together in houses in the rainforest. Several researchers described the multidimensional (social, ritual, economic) nature of forager–farmer relations (Bahuchet 1992a; Hewlett 1991).

In terms of political-economic power relations, representations of forager–farmer relationships range from being mutually beneficial symbiosis (Turnbull 1965) to pervasive inequality and farmer dominance (Joiris 2003; Rupp 2003). Schebesta (1933) described Efe foragers as serfs of Lese farmers, but Turnbull criticized his work because he relied upon village chiefs to summon Efe from the forest to be interviewed in the village; once Turnbull conducted interviews in the forest he found foragers to be relatively independent of farmers.

With the exception of the Twa in Rwanda and Burundi where a caste system exists, all ethnographically known forest foragers exchange foods with farmers to varying degrees, and none subsist by hunting and gathering alone. It is not clear whether this demonstrates forager dependence on farmers or simply an efficient alternative to full-time foraging. Based on his examination of Mbuti subsistence, Ichikawa (1983) concluded that a hunting and gathering life would be possible in the Ituri Forest from a caloric viewpoint, but very challenging without their exchange relationship with agriculturalists. Takeuchi (1995) found that Aka in northern Congo desired farmer carbohydrates more than farmers desired Aka forest products. Farmers knew the forest well and were able to obtain enough game meat on their own, while the Aka desired and were dependent upon farmers for manioc and other carbohydrates. Bailey et al. (1989), proponents of the wild yam hypothesis, felt the relationship benefits foragers. It is also worth noting that several ethnic groups of farmers live in the Congo Basin forest without relationships with foragers and that not all families in villages associated with foragers have relations with foragers. But little is known about the origin, development, and history of forager–farmer relations. Limited archaeology and recent genetic data suggest foragers lived in forested areas without farmers for a long time.

Finally, political-economic inequality in forager–farmer relations is a crucial issue in the Congo Basin today. Forest foragers are often denied access to health and education services in several Congo Basin countries because they are viewed as 'primitive.' The UN and other non-government agencies are involved with trying to alleviate the marginalization of

African Pygmies. Lewis (2001), Kinrick (2001), Joiris (2003), and Rupp (2003) document the various ways farmers exploit foragers, especially in the context of external extractive activities, such as logging, gold, and diamond industries. Relative interdependence and symbiosis in forager–farmer relations is more likely to occur in rural, low-population density settings with minimal impacts from a cash economy. As market economies (coffee, gold, diamonds, bushmeat trade) expand, farmers are more likely to exploit forest forager labour.

Conservation Issues

How can Congo Basin foragers be integrated into African tropical forest reserves and parks? In the last two decades, scholars from all four national traditions described above have increasingly transcended cataloguing ecological data and directed greater attention to the environmental challenges faced by modern forest foragers (Ichikawa 2006; Noss 2001). Relatedly, international wildlife conservation programmes aim to preserve the biodiversity of Africa's rainforests and support the lifeways of the forest's human inhabitants. Unfortunately, such well-meaning programmes often position forest foragers 'in the crossfire between forest exploitation on the one hand, and attempts to protect the natural environment on the other' (Ichikawa 2004b, 114). In one case study, Hattori (2005) explains several reasons that Baka foragers of Cameroon are indifferent to nature conservation projects. From the Baka point of view, such projects do not adequately consider the realities of foraging life; land-use zoning and hunting regulations are incompatible with their mobility. Further, Baka resist externally imposed environmental education, particularly when farmers play an intermediary role between conservationists and themselves, reinforcing the perception that the Baka are subordinate to neighbouring farmers. In contrast to this top-down approach, there is a growing consensus that conservation management plans are most effective when they actively engage local communities, including hunter-gatherers, as partners in seeking solutions (Bailey et al. 1992; Curran and Tshombe 2001).

Anthropological research can help rainforest populations address ecological challenges in many ways. One is to integrate aspects of conservation into general ethnographic research (e.g. Hattori 2005). Another is to accurately detail the sustainability of different hunting practices in specific contexts (Hart 2000; Noss 2000; Yasuoka 2006a), the impact of commercial bushmeat markets on local prey populations (Wilkie 2001; Wilkie and Carpenter 1999), and the effects of forest product commoditization on forager life (Kitanishi 2006). Ongoing research in these areas will help to reconcile the conservation of forest species with the needs of forest foragers (Ichikawa in press). But documentation of hunting techniques and prey densities alone is not enough. If foragers are to be active participants in conservation efforts and sustainable practices, anthropologists must better understand socio-cultural perceptions of the forest environment and the role that the forest people envision for themselves. Do they share the same environmental values as foreign conservationists? What is the cosmological significance of forest life, and how do foragers interpret international development, conservation, and sustainability? Anthropologists have begun to explore forager perspectives on these contemporary issues. Kinrick (2001; 2002) and Lewis (2001; 2005) have been particularly knowledgeable and vocal advocates for indigenous rights in conjunction with conservation efforts. Continued work along these lines is needed to lend relevant meaning to ecological data.

Critique and Future Research

Ecological and Evolutionary Bias

Since the publication of Turnbull's (1961) influential ethnography, *The forest people*, the 'forest' of his title has received almost as much attention from anthropologists as the 'people' and aspects of their cultures less directly related to environment. In other words, the literature on Congo Basin foragers is dominated by ecologically oriented studies. This ecological and evolutionary bias has a long history in the anthropology of forest foragers as exemplified in the German *Kulturkreise* (culture circles) school where Pygmies had a special evolutionary position as *Naturvolk* (people in close relationships with nature: Schmidt 1939). Congo Basin foragers consistently identify with the rainforest milieu, are fundamentally shaped by it, and express a strong preference for forest life (Hewlett 1996), but research in the region has focused on the economic domains of forest life while neglecting other dimensions, such as marriage and the family, social-emotional relations, and religion.

Ecological approaches have made significant contributions to our understanding of human–nature relations, but few studies exist that provide us with insights into how Congo Basin foragers think and feel about their lives. We know how many calories of meat they eat each day, how much time they spend hunting, and how much time they spend with infants, but we know little about how forest foragers think and feel about what is important to them—the forest, family relationships, religion, etc.

Gender and Nationality Biases

Anglo and Japanese males dominate Congo Basin research described in this chapter. This is primarily a consequence of the time period covered in this review; men were more likely to conduct research from the 1950s through to the 1980s so men had more time to accumulate publications. Since the 1990s, several women, including Hillary Fouts, Bonnie Hewlett (2005), Courtney Meehan, Veronique Joiris, Michelle Kisliuk, Ayako Hirisawa (2005), and Karen Lupo, have conducted long-term research on their own with forest foragers. Also, relatively few African anthropologists have conducted forest forager research. Jean-Félix Loung (1967) was one of the first African anthropologists to conduct research with forest foragers and Godefroy Ngima Mawoung (2006) is the most recent to publish. African anthropologists' research with forest foragers often takes place in the context of development, e.g. establishing parks or building an oil pipeline, so their work shows up in reports rather than academic publications.

Future Research

Given our knowledge of the literature and our particular biases (Hewlett as described above and Fancher as an ethnoarchaeologist), this section identifies areas of future research. First, qualitative and quantitative research is urgently needed on forest forager land tenure and utilization. Forest forager lands are being appropriated and exploited by conservation groups, lumber, gold, and diamond companies, farmers, and others migrating to the forest from urban areas or fleeing areas with warfare. A paucity of data exist on how forest foragers view land use, ownership, and the significance and meanings of their lands. Without this research, others will exploit forest foragers and their lands, and economic, political, and social marginalization will increase dramatically.

Second, several topics are seldom covered in existing studies. Oral histories, demography, and forest forager views on a wide range of issues are poorly represented in the literature. We have a few good studies of the impact of colonization on forest forager groups (Bahuchet and Guillaume 1982; Giles-Vernick 2002; Vansina 1990), but the majority of the research is based on archival work and we know relatively little about the oral histories of forest foragers.

It is surprising that we do not have one good demographic study of forest foragers given that several researchers have conducted ecological studies for several years at the same sites. Several studies identify the number of children and adults in the population, several try to estimate ages, and a few studies include relatively easy-to-collect demographic data, e.g. total fertility rates of post-reproductive women and mortality rates for infants or pre-reproductive adolescents. A complete and systematic demographic study that tries to establish good age estimates does not exist. Systematic hunter-gatherer demography is important in its own right, but it is also important for several evolutionary hypotheses, such as the life history hypothesis to explain forager short stature described above, and it is also important in development circles because demographic data are essential to understanding and responding to health risks in the populations (e.g. mortality data).

Ethnographic research is also needed on how foragers think and feel about a variety of topics, such as sharing, egalitarianism, gender relations, the family, and religion. Existing Japanese and American studies tend to emphasize observational methods and French ethnolinguistic research is descriptive and gives an indirect view of how forest foragers think and feel about the world. We know that forest foragers share extensively and are very egalitarian, but we know little about how they feel and perceive these topics and we know little about how they view such topics as family life, health, and the spiritual world.

Finally, basic ethnographic research is needed on several forest forager ethnic groups. Some anthropologists suggest that hunter-gatherer studies are a thing of the past because hunter-gatherers no longer exist. This is not the case in the Congo Basin. A few studies, but no complete ethnography, exist on some groups (e.g. Bongo, Kola), other groups are known to researchers but do not have any studies (e.g. Bolimba and Mbati foragers of the Central African Republic), and we are reasonably sure other groups exist, especially in other parts of the Democratic Republic of the Congo, Republic of the Congo, and Angola, but have not been identified or described. Studies have not come out of the Democratic Republic of the Congo and the Ituri since the early 1990s due to political instability, but it now appears possible to conduct research in these areas.

This chapter aims to provide an introduction to Congo Basin forager research traditions and how these traditions influence how hunter-gatherers in this region of the world are represented. French, American, British, and Japanese research traditions were examined and critiqued. Research has emphasized forest forager subsistence patterns and human–nature relations. Considerable research is needed in the region and several research opportunities exist to conduct studies with active hunter-gatherers.

References

Arom, S. 1991. *African polyphony and polyrhythm: musical structure and methodology.* Cambridge: Cambridge University Press.

Aunger, R. V. 1992. The nutritional consequences of rejecting food in the Ituri Forest of Zaire. *Human Ecology* 20, 263–91.

Bahuchet, S. 1972. Étude écologique d'un campement de pygmées BaBinga (Region de la Lobaye, République Centrafricaine). *Journal d'Agriculture Tropicale et de Botanique Appliquée* 19, 509–59.

Bahuchet, S. 1978. Contraintes écologique en forêt tropicale humide: l'example des pygmées Aka de la Lobaye (Centrafrique). *Journal d'Agriculture Tropicale et de Botanique Appliquée* 25, 257–85.

Bahuchet, S. 1985. *Les pygmées Aka et la forêt Centrafricaine.* Paris: SELAF.

Bahuchet, S. 1988. Food supply uncertainty among the Aka pygmies (Lobaye, Central African Republic). In I. de Garine and G. A. Harrison (eds), *Coping with uncertainty in food supply,* 119–49. Oxford: Oxford University Press.

Bahuchet, S. 1992a. *Dans la forêt d'Afrique Centrale: les pygmées Aka et Baka.* Paris: SELAF.

Bahuchet, S. 1992b. Spatial mobility and access to resources among the African pygmies. In M. Casimir and A. Rao (eds), *Mobility and territoriality: social and spatial boundaries among foragers, fishers, pastoralists and peripatetics,* 205–57. New York: Berg.

Bahuchet, S. and Guillaume, H. 1982. Aka–farmer relations in the northwest Congo Basin. In E. Leacock and R. B. Lee (eds), *Politics and history in band societies,* 189–211. Cambridge: Cambridge University Press.

Bahuchet, S., McKey, D., and de Garine, I. 1991. Wild yams revisited: is independence from agriculture possible for rainforest hunter-gatherers? *Human Ecology* 19, 213–43.

Bailey, R. C. 1991. *The behavioral ecology of Efe pygmy men in the Ituri Forest, Zaire.* Ann Arbor: University of Michigan Press.

Bailey, R. C. and Aunger, R. V. 1989. Net hunters vs. archers: variation in women's subsistence strategies in the Ituri Forest. *Human Ecology* 17, 273–97.

Bailey, R. C., Bahuchet, S., and Hewlett, B. S. 1992. *Development in the Central African rainforest: concern for forest peoples.* Washington, DC: The World Bank.

Bailey, R. C. and DeVore, I. 1989. Studies of Efe pygmies and Lese horticulturalists in the Ituri Forest, Zaire. *American Journal of Physical Anthropology* 78, 459–71.

Bailey, R. C., Head, G., Jenike, M., Owen, B., Rechtman, R., and Zechenter, E. 1989. Hunting and gathering in tropical rainforest: is it possible? *American Anthropologist* 91, 59–82.

Bailey, R. C. and Headland, T. N. 1991. The tropical rainforest: is it a productive environment for human foragers? *Human Ecology* 19, 261–85.

Bailey, R. C. and Peacock, N. R. 1988. Efe pygmies of northeast Zaire: subsistence strategies in the Ituri Forest. In I. de Garine and G. A. Harrison (eds), *Coping with uncertainty in food supply,* 88–117. Oxford: Oxford University Press.

Barham, L. S. and Mitchell, P. 2008. *The first Africans: African archaeology from the earliest toolmakers to most recent foragers.* Cambridge: Cambridge University Press.

Batini, C., Coia, V., Battaggia, C., Rocha, J., Pilkington, M. M., Spedini, G., Comas, D., Destro-Bisol, G., and Calafell, F. 2007. Phylogeography of the human mitochondrial L1c haplogroup: genetic signatures of the prehistory of central Africa. *Molecular Phylogenetics and Evolution* 43, 635–44.

Becker, N. S. A., Verdu, P., Hewlett, B., and Pavard, S. 2010. Can life history trade-offs explain the evolution of short stature in human pygmies? A response to Migliano and colleagues. *Human Biology* 82, 17–27.

Boyette, A. H. 2013. Social learning during middle childhood among Aka foragers and Ngandu farmers of the Central African Republic. PhD thesis, Washington State University.

Cavalli-Sforza, L. L. 1986. *African pygmies.* New York: Academic Press.

Curran, B. K. and Tshombe R. K. 2001. Integrating local communities into the management of protected areas: lessons from the DR Congo and Cameroon. In W. Weber, L. J. T. White, A. Vedder, and L. Naughton-Treves (eds), *African rainforest ecology and conservation: an interdisciplinary perspective,* 513–34. New Haven: Yale University Press.

Diamond, J. 1991. Why are pygmies small? *Nature* 354, 111–12.

Dounias, E. 1993. Perception and use of wild yams by the Baka hunter-gatherers in south Cameroon. In C. M. Hladik, A. Hladik, O. F. Linares, H. Pagezy, A. Semple, and M. Hadley (eds), *Tropical forests, people and food: biocultural interactions and applications to development,* 621–32. Paris: UNESCO.

Dounias, E. 1996. Sauvage ou cultivé? La paraculture des ignames sauvages par les pygmées Baka du Cameroun. In C. M. Hladik, A. Hladik, H. Pagezy, O. F. Linares, G. J. A. Koppert, and A. Froment (eds), *L'alimentation en forêt tropicale: interactions bioculturelles et perspectives de développement,* 939–60. Paris: UNESCO.

Dounias, E. 2001. The management of wild yam tubers by the Baka pygmies in southern Cameroon. *African Study Monographs,* Supplement 26, 135–56.

Fancher, J. M. 2009. An ethnoarchaeological analysis of small prey bones produced by forest foragers of the Central African Republic. PhD thesis, Washington State University.

Fisher, J. W. 1987. Shadows in the forest: ethnoarchaeology among the Efe pygmies. PhD thesis, University of California, Berkeley.

Fisher, J. W. 1993. Foragers and farmers: material expressions of interaction at elephant processing sites in the Ituri Forest, Zaire. In J. Hudson (ed.), *From bones to behavior: ethnoarchaeological and experimental contributions to the interpretation of faunal remains,* 247–62. Carbondale: Southern Illinois University at Carbondale Center for Archaeological Investigations Occasional Paper 21.

Fisher, J. W. and Strickland, H. C. 1989. Ethnoarchaeology among Efe pygmies, Zaire: spatial organization of campsites. *American Journal of Physical Anthropology* 78, 473–84.

Fisher, J. W. and Strickland, H. C. 1991. Dwellings and fireplaces: keys to Efe pygmy campsite structure. In C. S. Gamble and W. A. Boismier (eds), *Ethnoarchaeological approaches to mobile campsites: hunter-gatherer and pastoralist case studies,* 215–36. Ann Arbor: International Monographs in Prehistory Ethnoarchaeological Series 1.

Fouts, H. N., Hewlett, B. S., and Lamb, M. E. 2001. Weaning and the nature of early childhood interactions among Bofi foragers in central Africa. *Human Nature* 12, 27–46.

Fouts, H. N., Hewlett, B. S., and Lamb, M. E. 2005. Parent–offspring weaning conflicts among the Bofi farmers and foragers of central Africa. *Current Anthropology* 46, 29–50.

Fürniss, S. 1993. Rigeur et liberté: la polyphonie vocale des pygmées Aka (Centrafrique). In C. Meyer (ed.), *Polyphonies de tradition orale. Histoire et traditions vivantes,* 101–31. Paris: Creaphis.

Giles-Vernick, T. 2002. *Cutting the vines of the past: environmental histories of the central African rainforest.* Charlottesville: University Press of Virginia.

Grinker, R. R. 1994. *Houses in the rainforest: ethnicity and inequality among farmers and foragers in central Africa.* Berkeley: University of California Press.

Grinker, R. R. 2000. *In the arms of Africa: the life of Colin M. Turnbull.* New York: St. Martin's Press.

Harako, R. 1976. The Mbuti as hunters: a study of ecological anthropology of the Mbuti pygmies (I). *Kyoto University African Studies* 10, 37–99.

Hart, J. A. 2000. Impact and sustainability of indigenous hunting in the Ituri Forest, Congo-Zaire: a comparison of the unhunted and hunted duiker populations. In J. G. Robinson and E. L. Bennett (eds), *Hunting for sustainability in tropical forests*, 106–53. New York: Columbia University Press.

Hattori, S. 2005. Nature conservation and hunter-gatherers' life in Cameroonian rainforest. *African Study Monographs*, Supplement 29, 41–51.

Hattori, S. 2006. Utilization of Marantaceae plants by Baka hunter-gatherers in southeastern Cameroon. *African Study Monographs*, Supplement 33, 29–48.

Hayashi, K. 2008. Hunting activities in forest camps among the Baka hunter-gatherers of southeastern Cameroon. *African Study Monographs* 29, 73–92.

Headland, T. N. 1987. The wild yam question: how well could independent hunter-gatherers live in a tropical rainforest ecosystem? *Human Ecology* 15, 463–91.

Headland, T. N. and R. C. Bailey. 1991. Introduction: have hunter-gatherers ever lived in tropical rainforest independently of agriculture? *Human Ecology* 19, 115–22.

Hewlett, B. L. 2005. Vulnerable lives: the experience of death and loss among the Aka and Ngandu adolescents of the Central African Republic. In B. Hewlett and M. Lamb (eds), *Hunter-gatherer childhoods*, 322–42. New Brunswick: Aldine/Transaction.

Hewlett, B. S. 1991. *Intimate fathers: the nature and context of Aka pygmy paternal infant care.* Ann Arbor: University of Michigan Press.

Hewlett, B. S. 1996. Cultural diversity among African pygmies. In S. Kent (ed.), *Cultural diversity among twentieth century foragers: an African perspective*, 215–44. Cambridge: Cambridge University Press.

Hewlett, B. S. (ed) in press. *Congo basin hunter-gatherers: culture, history and biology of African Pygmies*. New Brunswick: Transaction.

Hewlett, B. S., Lamb M. E., Leyendecker, B., and Schölmerich, A. 2000. Internal working models, trust, and sharing among foragers. *Current Anthropology* 41, 287–97.

Hladik, A. and Dounias, E. 1993. Wild yams of the African forest as potential food resources. In C. Hladik (ed.), *Tropical forests, people, and food: biocultural interactions and applications to development*, 163–76. Paris: UNESCO.

Ichikawa, M. 1978. The residential groups of the Mbuti pygmies. *Senri Ethnological Studies* 1, 131–88.

Ichikawa, M. 1982. *The hunters of the forest: the Mbuti pygmies.* Kyoto: Jinbuin-Shoin.

Ichikawa, M. 1983. An examination of the hunting-dependent life of the Mbuti pygmies, eastern Zaire. *African Study Monographs* 4, 55–76.

Ichikawa, M. 1987. Food restrictions of the Mbuti pygmies, eastern Zaire. *African Study Monographs*, Supplement 6, 97–121.

Ichikawa, M. 1991. The impact of commoditisation on the Mbuti of eastern Zaire. In N. Peterson and T. Matsuyama (eds), *Cash, commoditisation and changing foragers*, 135–62. Senri Ethnological Studies 30. Osaka: National Museum of Ethnology.

Ichikawa, M. 1998. The birds as indicators of the invisible world: ethno-ornithology of the Mbuti hunter-gatherers. *African Study Monographs*, Supplement 25, 105–21.

Ichikawa, M. 2004a. Benefit of foresight: from evolutionary interest to global environmental problems. *Before Farming* 4, Article 7.

Ichikawa, M. 2004b. The Japanese tradition of central African hunter-gatherer studies: with comparative observation on the French and American traditions. In A. Barnard (ed.), *Hunter-gatherers in history, archaeology and anthropology*, 103–14. Oxford: Berg.

Ichikawa, M. 2005. The history and current situation of anthropological studies on Africa in Japan. *The African Anthropologist* (Journal of the Pan African Anthropological Association) 12, 158–71.

Ichikawa, M. 2006. Problems in the conservation of rainforests in Cameroon. *African Study Monographs*, Supplement 33, 3–20.

Ichikawa, M. in press. Forest conservation and indigenous peoples in the Congo Basin: new trends toward reconciliation between global issues and local interest. In B. Hewlett (ed), *Congo basin hunter-gatherers: culture, history and biology of African Pygmies*. New Brunswick: Transaction.

Jenike, M. R. 1985. Seasonal changes in Efe foraging behavior examined from the perspective of the diet breadth model. BA thesis, Harvard-Radcliffe College.

Joiris, D. 2003. The framework of central African hunter-gatherers and neighbouring societies. *African Study Monographs*, Supplement 28, 57–79.

Kinrick, J. 2001. Present predicaments of hunter gatherers and former hunter gatherers of the central African rainforests. In A. Barnard and J. Kinrick (eds), *Africa's indigenous people: 'first peoples' or 'marginalised minorities'?*, 39–60. Edinburgh: Centre of African Studies.

Kinrick, J. 2002. Anthropology and anthropocentrism: images of hunter-gatherers, westerners and the environment. In H. Stewart, A. Barnard, and K. Omura (eds), *Self- and other-images of hunter-gatherers*, 191–213. Osaka: National Museum of Ethnology.

Kinrick, J. and Lewis, J. 2001. Discrimination against the forest people ('pygmies') of central Africa. In S. Chama and M. Jensen (eds), *Racism against indigenous people*, 312–25. Copenhagen: IWGIA.

Kisliuk, M. 2000. *Seize the dance: BaAka musical life and the ethnography of performance*. Oxford: Oxford University Press.

Kitanishi, K. 1994. The exchange of forest products (Irvingia nuts) between the Aka hunter-gatherers and the cultivators in northeastern Congo. *Tropics* 4, 79–92.

Kitanishi, K. 1995. Seasonal changes in the subsistence activities and food intake of the Aka hunter-gatherers in northeastern Congo. *African Study Monographs* 16, 73–118.

Kitanishi, K. 1996. Variability in the subsistence activities and distribution of food among different aged males of the Aka hunter-gatherers in northeastern Congo. *African Study Monographs* 17, 35–57.

Kitanishi, K. 1998. Food sharing among the Aka hunter-gatherers in northeastern Congo. *African Study Monographs*, Supplement 25, 3–32.

Kitanishi, K. 2006. The impact of cash and commoditization on the Baka hunter-gatherer society in southeastern Cameroon. *African Study Monographs*, Supplement 33, 121–42.

Landt, M. J. 2007. Tooth marks and human consumption: mastication research among foragers of the Central African Republic. *Journal of Archaeological Science* 34, 1629–40.

Lewis, J. 2001. Forest people or village people. Whose voice will be heard? In A. Barnard and J. Kinrick (eds), *Africa's indigenous peoples: 'first peoples' or 'marginalized minorities'?*, 61–78. Edinburgh: Centre of African Studies.

Lewis, J. 2002. Forest hunter-gatherers and their world: a study of the Mbendjele Yaka pygmies of Congo-Brazzaville and their secular and religious activities and representations. PhD thesis, University of London.

Lewis, J. 2005. Whose forest is it anyway? Mbendjele Yaka pygmies, the Ndoki Forest, and the wider world. In W. Tadesse and T. Widlock (eds), *Property and equality: encapsulation, commercialisation, discrimination*, 56–78. Oxford: Berghahn.

Loung, J.-F. 1967. Le nom authentique du group pygmée de la région cotière Camerounaise. *Revue de Géographie du Cameroun* 7, 81–94.

Lupo, K. D. and Schmitt, D. N. 2002. Upper Paleolithic net-hunting, small prey exploitation, and women's work effort: a view from the ethnographic and ethnoarchaeological record of the Congo Basin. *Journal of Archaeological Method and Theory* 9, 147–79.

Lupo, K. D. and Schmitt, D. N. 2004. Meat sharing and the archaeological record: a test of the show-off hypothesis among central African Bofi foragers. In G. M. Crothers (ed.), *Hunters and gatherers in theory and archaeology*, 241–60. Carbondale: Center for Archaeological Investigations Southern Illinois University Carbondale Occasional Paper No. 31.

Lupo, K. D. and Schmitt, D. N. 2005. Small prey hunting technology and zooarchaeological measures of taxonomic diversity and abundance: ethnoarchaeological evidence from central African forest foragers. *Journal of Anthropological Archaeology* 24, 335–53.

Meehan, C. 2005. The effects of maternal locality on alloparental behavior and frequency of caregiving among the Aka foragers of the Central African Republic. *Human Nature* 16, 58–80.

Mercader, J. 2002. Forest people: the role of African rainforests in human evolution and dispersal. *Evolutionary Anthropology* 11, 117–24.

Mercader, J. 2003. Introduction: the Paleolithic settlement of rainforests. In J. Mercader (ed.), *Under the canopy: the archaeology of tropical rainforests*, 1–31. New Brunswick: Rutgers University Press.

Migliano, A. B., Vinicius, L., and Lahr, M. M. 2007. Life history trade-offs explain the evolution of human pygmies. *Proceedings of the National Academy of Sciences USA* 104, 20216–19.

Motte, E. 1980. A propos des thérapeutes pygmées Aka de la région de la Lobaye (Centrafrique). *Journal d'Agriculture Tropicale et de Botanique Appliquée* 27, 113–32.

Motte, E. 1982. *Les plantes chez les pygmées Aka et les Monzombo de la Lobaye (Centrafrique): contribution à une étude ethnobotanique comparative chez des chasseurs-cueillers et des pêcheurs-cultivateurs dans un même milieu végétal*. Paris: SELAF.

Motte-Florac, E., Bahuchet, S., and Thomas, J. M. C. 1993. The role of food in the therapeutics of the Aka pygmies of the Central African Republic. In C. M. Hladik, A. Hladik, O. F. Linares, H. Pagezy, A. Semple, and M. Hadley (eds), *Tropical forests, people and food: biocultural interactions and applications to development*, 549–60. Paris: UNESCO.

Ngima Mawoung, G. 2006. Perception of hunting, gathering and fishing techniques of the Bakola of the coastal region, southern Cameroon. *African Study Monographs*, Supplement 33, 49–69.

Noss, A. J. 2000. Cable snares and nets in the Central African Republic. In J. G. Robinson and E. L. Bennett (eds), *Hunting for sustainability in tropical forests*, 282–304. New York: Columbia University Press.

Noss, A. J. 2001. Conservation, development, and 'the forest people': the Aka of the Central African Republic. In W. Weber, L. J. T. White, A. Vedder, and L. Naughton-Treves (eds), *African rainforest ecology and conservation: an interdisciplinary perspective*, 313–33. New Haven: Yale University Press.

Patin, E., Laval, G., Barreiro, L. B., Salas, A., Semino, O., Santachiara-Benerecetti, S., Kidd, K. K., Kidd, J. R., Van der Veen, L., Hombert, J.-M., Gessain, A., Froment, A., Bahuchet, S., Heyer, E., and Quintana-Murci, L. 2009. Inferring the demographic history of African farmers and pygmy hunter-gatherers using a multilocus resequencing data set. *PLoS Genetics* 5, e1000448.

Peacock, N. R. 1985. Time allocation, work and fertility among the Efe pygmy women of northeast Zaire. PhD thesis, Harvard University.

Quintana-Murci, L., Quach, H., Harmant, C., Luca, F., Massonnet, B., Patin, E., Sica, L., Mouguiama-Daouda, P., Comas, D., Tzur, S., Balanovsky, O., Kidd, K. K., Kidd, J. R., Van der Veen, L., Hombert, J.-M., Gessain, A., Verdu, P., Froment, A., Bahuchet, S., Heyer, E., Dausset,

J., Salas, A., and Behar, D. M. 2008. Maternal traces of deep common ancestry and asymmetric gene flow between pygmy hunter-gatherers and Bantu-speaking farmers. *Proceedings of the National Academy of Sciences USA* 105, 1596–1601.

Rupp, S. 2003. Interethnic relations in southeastern Cameroon: challenging the 'hunter-gatherer'–'farmer' dichotomy. *African Study Monographs*, Supplement 28, 37–56.

Sato, H. 2001. The potential of edible wild yams and yam-like plants as a staple food resource in the African tropical rainforest. *African Study Monographs*, Supplement 26, 123–34.

Sato, H. 2006. A brief report on a large mountain-top community of Dioscorea praehensilis in the tropical rainforest of southeastern Cameroon. *African Study Monographs*, Supplement 33, 21–8.

Schebesta, P. 1933. *Among Congo pygmies*. London: Hutchinson.

Schmidt, W. 1939. *The culture historical method of ethnology*, trans. S. A. Sieber. New York: Fortuny's.

Takeuchi, K. 1994. Dietary avoidance among the Aka hunter-gatherers, northeastern Congo. *Journal of African Studies* 44, 1–28.

Takeuchi, K. 1995. Subsistence hunting in African tropical forest: hunting techniques and activities among the Aka hunter-gatherers, northeastern Congo. *Zooarchaeology* 4, 27–52.

Takeuchi, K. in press. Interethnic relations between forest foragers and farmers: dialectic symbiosis and diversity. In B. Hewlett (ed.), *Congo basin hunter-gatherers: culture, history and biology of African Pygmies*. New Brunswick: Transaction.

Tanno, T. 1976. The Mbuti net-hunters in the Ituri Forest, eastern Zaire: their hunting activities and band composition. *Kyoto University African Studies* 10, 101–35.

Terashima, H. 1986. Economic exchange and the symbiotic relationship between the Mbuti (Efe) pygmies and the neighboring farmers. *Sprache und Geschichte in Afrika* 7, 391–405.

Terashima, H. 1987. Why Efe girls marry farmers: socio-ecological backgrounds of inter-ethnic marriage in the Ituri Forest. *African Study Monographs* 6, 65–84.

Terashima, H. 1998. Honey and holidays: the interactions mediated by honey between Efe hunter-gatherers and Lese farmers in the Ituri Forest. *African Study Monographs*, Supplement 25, 123–34.

Terashima, H. and Ichikawa, M. 2003. A comparative ethnobotany of the Mbuti and Efe hunter-gatherers in the Ituri Forest, Democratic Republic of Congo. *African Study Monographs* 24, 1–168.

Terashima, H., Ichikawa, M., and Sawada, M. 1988. Wild plant utilization of the Balese and the Efe of the Ituri Forest, the Republic of Zaire. *African Study Monographs*, Supplement 8, 1–78.

Turnbull, C. M. 1961. *The forest people*. New York: Simon & Schuster.

Turnbull, C. M. 1965. *Wayward servants: the two worlds of the African pygmies*. New York: Natural History Press.

Vansina, J. 1990. *Paths in the rainforests: toward a history of political tradition in equatorial Africa*. Madison: University of Wisconsin Press.

Verdu, P., Austerlitz, A. E., Vitalis, R., Georges, M., Théry, S., Froment, A., Le Bomin, S., Gessain, A., Hombert, J.-M., Van der Veen, L., Quintana-Murci, L., Bahuchet, S., and Heyer, E. 2009. Origins and genetic diversity of pygmy hunter-gatherers from western central Africa. *Current Biology* 19, 1–7.

Walker, R., Gurven, M., and Hill, K. 2006. Growth rates and life histories in twenty-two small scale societies. *American Journal of Human Biology* 18, 295–311.

Wilkie, D. S. 2001. Bushmeat hunting in the Congo Basin: a brief overview. In M. I. Bakkar, G. A. B. d. Fonseca, R. A. Mittermeier, A. B. Rylands, and K. W. Painemilla (eds), *Hunting and bushmeat utilization in the African rainforest. Perspectives toward a blueprint for conservation*, 17–20. Washington: Conservation International.

Wilkie, D. S. and Carpenter, J. F. 1999. Bushmeat hunting in the Congo Basin: an assessment of impacts and options for mitigation. *Biodiversity and Conservation* 8, 927–55.

Yamauchi, T., Sato, H., and Kawamura, K. 2000. Nutritional status, activity pattern, and dietary intake among the Baka hunter-gatherers in the village camps in Cameroon. *African Study Monographs* 21, 67–82.

Yasuoka, H. 2006a. The sustainability of duiker (*Cephalophus* sp.) hunting for the Baka hunter-gatherers in southeastern Cameroon. *African Study Monographs*, Supplement 33, 95–110.

Yasuoka, H. 2006b. Long-term foraging expeditions (molongo) among the Baka hunter-gatherers in the northwestern Congo Basin, with special reference to the 'wild yam question'. *Human Ecology* 34, 275–96.

Yasuoka, H. 2009. The variety of forest vegetations in south-eastern Cameroon, with special reference to the availability of wild yams for the forest hunter-gatherers. *African Study Monographs* 30, 89–119.

CHAPTER 45

REGIONAL HUNTER-GATHERER RESEARCH TRADITIONS
Australia

IAN KEEN

AMATEUR OBSERVERS 1788–1880

APART from very early casual observations by explorers and colonists such as Grey and Eyre, the early decades of the British colonization of Australia saw a number of systematic ethnographic observations of Australian Aboriginal social life and culture (e.g. Nind 1831). During the third quarter of the nineteenth century when colonial domination was well advanced across a good part of the continent, interested amateurs such as Edward Curr, George Taplin, and R. Brough Smyth published compilations of accounts of Aboriginal customs and beliefs, collected from a variety of amateur observers living on the frontier (e.g. Curr 1886–7; Howitt 1904). Typically these observations took the form of responses to questionnaires, and covered colonies of the south and south-east of the continent. A. W. Howitt (1904) and Daisy Bates (1985) drew on their own fieldwork as well as, in Howitt's case, correspondence.

EARLY THEORETICALLY ORIENTED ETHNOGRAPHY

A. W. Howitt's reconstruction of several aspects of Kûrnai social life and custom (Howitt 1880; 1904), carried out when the colonization of Gippsland was complete and the Aboriginal population decimated, is the most comprehensive ethnography of a single people of the period, and a precursor to the ethnographies of Baldwin Spencer and F. J. Gillen (1927). What distinguishes Howitt's writing from earlier observers' accounts is that it is theory-driven (Mulvaney 1967). He was a correspondent of Lewis Henry Morgan, and adopted Morgan's evolutionist scheme especially in relation to kinship. Dawson's (1881) monograph about Aboriginal people of the western districts of Victoria has the air of fantasy, for he describes a hierarchical society of chiefs and their retinues, about which his contemporaries were highly sceptical. Other significant ethnographers of the period include the surveyor R. H. Mathews and Walter Roth.

Howitt was a geologist, magistrate, and Protector of Aborigines in Gippsland, while Mathews's profession was that of surveyor. K. Langloh Parker (1905) and Ethel Hassell (1936) were wives of sheep and cattle farmers, who became interested in the Aboriginal people living and working on their stations in north central New South Wales and south-west western Australia respectively. Both women's accounts were largely uninformed by anthropological theory, but provide valuable data on societies which would otherwise have remained largely unstudied (see Keen 2004). A number of missionaries left reminiscences or ethnographic works, published or unpublished (e.g. Love 1936). The most influential ethnography to appear at the end of the nineteenth century and beginning of the twentieth was by Baldwin Spencer, trained in biology, and F. J. Gillen, post master and Protector of Aborigines at Alice Springs in central Australia. Their monograph on the Arrernte ('Aranda') (Spencer and Gillen 1927), as well as a wider survey of Aboriginal people of central Australia, had a strong focus on ritual, with detailed descriptions and exegesis, and including photographs. Less well known (because there is no English translation) is Carl Strehlow's (1913–20) multi-volume work on the Arrernte. The studies of desert life have been largely forgotten.

STRUCTURAL-FUNCTIONALIST AND FUNCTIONALIST ETHNOGRAPHY

Durkheim's Synthesis

Howitt's research was of international significance through his links with Morgan, but the ethnographic research of such researchers as Howitt, Mathews, and Spencer and Gillen formed grist for the mill of Durkheim's (1965 [1915]) theory of the origin and nature of religion. His functionalist theory in general, and his theory of religion in particular, was to exert, in turn, a profound influence on the anthropology of Australian Aborigines, especially through the writing and teaching of A. R. Radcliffe-Brown. Durkheim's analyses were evolutionist in orientation, concerned as he was with the origins of religion. Radcliffe-Brown's version of structural-functionalism, however, largely rejected any concern with social evolution, espousing a focus on synchronic and holistic studies of communities.

In 1926 Radcliffe-Brown, who had carried out research in Australia from 1910 to 1912, took up the chair of anthropology established at the University of Sydney in the previous year. His research continued the tradition of extensive survey ethnography based on his own field research as well as publications by others. His focus was almost exclusively on kinship and social organization, and his most significant contributions to Aboriginal anthropology are his surveys of systems of kinship and marriage and associated forms of social organization, published between 1913 and mid-century (e.g. Radcliffe-Brown 1931). His work brought order to a wide array of reports of a variety of systems, and influenced research and analysis for many decades.

Radcliffe-Brown's students during his tenure of the chair at Sydney included the American W. Lloyd Warner, Ursula McConnel, whose research took her to Cape York Peninsula, C. W. M. Hart, who conducted research on Melville and Bathurst Islands, and Donald Thomson, whose fieldwork was in Cape York Peninsula and north-east Arnhem Land, and later in the Western Desert. The American Lauriston Sharp, who had trained under Ralph Linton in Wisconsin and Father Schmidt in Vienna, also worked in Cape York Peninsula. These were all 'remote' regions where the effects of colonization were to varying degrees less destructive than in the south-east and south-west, although Aboriginal people were encouraged or coerced into residence on missions (see Peterson 1991 on the institutionalization of anthropology in Australia).

In his preface to W. Lloyd Warner's (1937) monograph on Yolngu ('Murngin') society, arising out of fieldwork based at the Methodist mission at Milingimbi between 1926 and 1929, Lowie notes the demise of the evolutionist paradigm, and comments that anthropologists now studied Aboriginal society for its intrinsic interest, and not as representative of a stage of social and cultural evolution. Warner's study was the first full-length, comprehensive study of the social life of the people of a single region, and reflects the influence of Radcliffe-Brown, and of Durkheim's theory of religion, especially the distinction between the sacred and profane, which Warner (erroneously) mapped onto the division between the genders.

At the same time that Radcliffe-Brown took up the Sydney chair, the Rockefeller Foundation provided funding through the Australian National Research Council for the conduct of physical anthropological research among Aboriginal people (Gray 2007). The notable collaboration between Birdsell and Norman Tindale of the Museum of South Australia on the genetics of Australian 'tribes' and people of mixed descent followed. The Yale Trust funded research on sexual relations among Aboriginal people from 1927.

The Australian A. P. Elkin, who took over as professor of anthropology at Sydney University in 1934, continued the enterprise of survey ethnography in an ethnological approach that reflected his training at University College London under the diffusionists, Elliott Smith and Perry. Elkin was more strongly oriented towards the application of anthropology to policy than his predecessor, and was one of the architects of assimilationist policy (Wise 1985). Elkin's students before the Second World War included Phyllis Kaberry, who worked in the Kimberley and also studied under Bronislaw Malinowski at the London School of Economics, and Olive Pink, who worked in the Western Desert; at the beginning of the war his students included Ronald and Catherine Berndt (Western Desert, Arnhem Land), and W. E. H. Stanner, who began his fieldwork on the Daly River in the 1930s (Gray 2007).

Mid-Twentieth-Century Structural-Functionalist Ethnography

Institutionally, Aboriginal anthropology in Australia in the mid-century remained dominated by A. P. Elkin. The Research School of Pacific Studies at the Australian National University, founded in 1946, focused mainly on other regions, with some exceptions, such as Marie Reay, who carried out research in the south-east and the Gulf country, and W. E. H. Stanner.

The cohort of anthropologists carrying out research in the middle decades of the twentieth century included the Berndts, Stanner, Mervyn Meggitt, Reay, and L. R. Hiatt. Several of them studied in London as well as under Elkin at Sydney (R. M. Berndt, for example, at the London School of Economics), reinforcing the functionalist connections. The functionalist tradition also entered Australia through John Barnes, who succeeded Elkin in the Sydney chair (and later succeeded S. F. Nadel at the Australian National University), and who supervised L. R. Hiatt's PhD research (see Hiatt 1965). The American Arnold Pilling carried out research on Melville and Bathurst Islands, and co-wrote a monograph with C. W. M. Hart (Hart and Pilling 1960), succeeded by Jane Goodale. The Falkenbergs (who were from Norway) published on kinship and totemism in the Daly River region.

A focus on regions of Australia remote from white settlement characterizes the research of this cohort. There was a focus on reconstructionist accounts of traditional social structure, kinship and marriage, ritual, and myth; traditional 'local organization' was a matter for keen debate (e.g. Stanner 1963). This bias was in part due to the strong discouragement of criticism of the conditions under which Aboriginal people were living, and of state and territory policies towards Aborigines; research funding depended upon compliance (Gray 2007). Anthropologists such as Thomson and Piddington who spoke out against state government policy in the first half of the twentieth century tended to be excluded from access to Aboriginal communities and funding. An ethnological emphasis on the collection of texts characterized the Berndts' approach to ethnography (e.g. Berndt and Berndt 1945), reflecting their training under Elkin. Others, such as Meggitt and Hiatt, had a stronger sense of social systems. Notably lacking were systematic approaches to economy (see Anderson 1988). Some anthropologists also carried out research during this period among Aboriginal people of mixed descent in settled areas (see below).

T. G. H. Strehlow, the son of the missionary Carl Strehlow, carved a somewhat independent path in his research and writing, on Arrernte songs in particular (e.g. Strehlow 1974). Nancy Munn had been left to her own devices at the Australian National University during the time when S. F. Nadel held the chair, and her work did not conform to a structural-functionalist mould. She took a semiotic approach to Warlpiri and Pitjantjatjara sand drawing and body painting, and a phenomenological approach to cosmology (e.g. Munn 1973). Stanner contributed to the debate on the character of 'local organization', and his analysis of myth and ritual was strikingly original, bearing some similarities to Lévi-Straussian structuralism. He also contributed significantly to public debate on Aboriginal affairs.

Norman Tindale trained as an entomologist and had a long-term appointment as anthropologist at the South Australian Museum. His work, which lay outside the mainstream of Australianist anthropology, was notable for its focus on material culture and ecology (e.g. Tindale 1972), a perspective neglected by social anthropologists until the late 1960s, with the exception of Donald Thomson (1939). Tindale also travelled widely in Australia collecting genealogies with a view to developing a theory of 'miscegenation', collaborating with Birdsell in his investigation of the genetics of Aboriginal populations. Tindale (1974) also attempted to map the territories of 'tribes' across the whole continent, while others such as R. M. Berndt were questioning the utility of the concept of 'tribe'.

Research in Urban Areas, and Social Change

Around the middle of the twentieth century a number of anthropologists focused on Aboriginal people living in country towns and cities in the south-east and south-west (e.g. Elizabeth Fink, Jeremy Beckett, Malcolm Calley, Marie Reay, the Wilsons, and Diane Barwick), while others combined these studies with research in remote areas (e.g. Reay, Beckett, and the Berndts). Their focus was on social change, and the particular social structures that arose in these situations, such as social networks (Beckett), religion (Calley), and class relations (Reay and Sitlington) (see Keen 1988 for a literature review). No agreed approach to, or theory of, social change was brought to bear in this work; rather, social change became a special topic within social anthropology. Neo-Marxist anthropology promised a dialectical approach to social change, but the neo-Marxists were more interested in 'traditional' social life than in historical transformations (e.g. Bern 1979). The exception was the theory of internal colonialism (see below).

The Freudians

Psychoanalytic anthropology was quite independent of the structural-functionalist and ethnological mainstream. Geza Roheim's initial study drew on the published literature, as did the work of Durkheim and Lévi-Strauss, but this stimulated Roheim to carry out fieldwork in central Australia, leading to detailed psychoanalytical analyses of myth, ritual, and symbolism (Roheim 1945). John Morton (1993), a more recent exponent of psychoanalytic methodology, drew in turn on Roheim's as well as Strehlow's material in an analysis of Arrernte totemism.

Structuralism: Lévi-Strauss's Syntheses

Claude Lévi-Strauss's relationship with Australian ethnography was similar to Durkheim's, as he drew heavily on Australian materials in his syntheses on kinship and totemism (e.g. Lévi-Strauss 1969). His structuralist framework, in turn, influenced analyses by Australianist anthropologists, notably Kenneth Maddock (e.g. 1972) on myth and kinship. The structuralist approach has not endured in Australianist anthropology, although certain Lévi-Straussian categories remain salient, such as the contrast between generalized and restricted exchange.

The fortunes of Aboriginal kinship studies have fluctuated, however. The anthropology of the last quarter of the nineteenth century and the first two thirds of the twentieth century were rather dominated by a concern with kinship (Keen 1988). Ethnographic contributions as well as syntheses were made in the 1970s and 1980s by scholars such as David Turner (1980), Warren Shapiro (1979), and Kenneth Maddock. Interest declined markedly in the last quarter of the twentieth century, although there has recently been something of a resurgence, in the work of Laurent Dousset (2002) for example.

Ecology and the 'Man the Hunter' Programme

The economy of Aborigines living in remote areas had been largely neglected by researchers, not least because most were living on missions, cattle stations, and government settlements.

It was only later that geographers such as Elspeth Young began to carry out research on emerging economic relations. Donald Thomson had already reconstructed the 'seasonal round' in eastern Cape York Peninsula, while Norman Tindale described seasonal movement and ecology in the Western Desert, and Stanner (1963) sketched a programme for the study of ecologies across the continent. Sahlins's influential paper on 'the original affluent society' (1972) was based in part on brief studies of Aboriginal food getting.

The 'Man the Hunter' programme, centred on studies of indigenous people of the Kalahari Desert in southern Africa (Lee and DeVore 1968), stimulated similar research in Australia. Nicolas Peterson undertook the first intensive long-term fieldwork on the ecology of an Aboriginal 'band' in the late 1960s (Peterson 1971). Peterson's research linked up with the ethnoarchaeology of the period, and the use of ethnographic analogy in archaeology, for example by James O'Connell. Peterson's analysis also linked up with central concerns of the social anthropology of the day: he offered ecological explanations of what Strehlow referred to as 'totemic geography', and of the role of women in the structure of Aboriginal bands. During the same period (the 1960s) the archaeologist Richard Gould conducted detailed studies of subsistence behaviour in the Western Desert.

An Aboriginal ecology project centred on Cape York Peninsula during the 1970s and 1980s, fostered by the Australian Institute of Aboriginal Studies under the directorship of Peter Ucko, aimed to reconstruct pre-colonial ecologies (most Aboriginal people of the region were living on missions and government settlements). Research by Athol Chase, Peter Sutton, John von Sturmer, and others engendered a particular focus on systems of land tenure. Later research has included studies of particular Aboriginal subsistence practices and the ecology of coastal Yolngu communities (e.g. Chase and Sutton 1987).

Marxism and Neo-Marxism

Marxist and neo-Marxist anthropology comprised a distinctive stream in Australian Aboriginal anthropology in the 1970s and 1980s. The main earlier practitioners had been Frederick Rose and Peter Worsley, both of whom carried out research on Groote Eylandt among Wanindilyagwa people. Rose's work (e.g. 1968) focused on the age factor in marriage, offering an economistic explanation of age-related polygyny.

This Marxist orientation was revived in the 1970s under the influence of Althusserian 'structural-Marxism'. John Bern's (1979) neo-Marxist analysis of the 'Aboriginal social formation' provided a general model of traditional Aboriginal economy and society. Annette Hamilton's neo-Marxist orientation led her to conduct fieldwork on Aboriginal women's ritual and economy in the eastern Western Desert, and she made significant contributions to the study of Aboriginal gender relations (Hamilton 1980). Maurice Godelier's analysis of relations of production in the Western Desert (Godelier 1975), especially the role of subsection categories, was based on Aram Yengoyan's demographic ethnography.

These Marxian studies tended to be reconstructionist. Neo-Marxist theory of internal colonialism developed by M. Hartwig, however, was applied to relations between Aborigines and pastoralists that had arisen on the Australian frontier, and relations between Torres Strait Islanders and the state, especially in the context of pearl-fishing (Beckett 1987).

Other Approaches to Aboriginal Economy

There were other notable exceptions to the dearth of anthropological studies of Aboriginal economy. One was J. C. Anderson's study of the economy of Hopevale mission in eastern Cape York Peninsula, and his related account of the relationship between Aborigines and tin-miners on the frontier in that region (Anderson 1984). Jon Altman's (1987) analysis of the economy of a Kunwinjku 'outstation' in central Arnhem Land discusses the relationship between the traditional foraging sector and the market economy, while Diane Austin-Broos (2003; 2009) has more recently traced the emerging relationship between Western Arrernte people and the market economy.

The concept of 'demand sharing' (Peterson 1993), which modelled the logic of Aboriginal approaches to transactions and sharing, has been influential in the analysis of economic interaction in Aboriginal communities. Earlier anthropologists had pointed to 'reciprocity' as shaping transactions, a concept refined and elaborated by Sahlins, and they had documented customary obligations based on particular kinship relations (e.g. Berndt and Berndt 1964). Among the more influential approaches to the articulation of indigenous and market economies are the theories of internal colonialism (Hartwig 1978) and welfare colonialism (Beckett 1987), and the concept of hybrid economy (Altman 1987).

Studies by economists of the character of Aboriginal economies and their relationship to the development of capitalism in Australia have suffered from lack of information about the character of pre-colonial Aboriginal economies (e.g. Butlin 1993). Ian Keen (2004) attempts to redress the balance in his *Aboriginal Economy and Society*, a comparison of reconstructions of economy and society of seven regions of Australia 'at the threshold of colonization'.

THE RELATION BETWEEN RESEARCH AND POLICY

Anthropologists had contributed to policy-making from the very beginning. A. W. Howitt, for example, was a magistrate and Protector of Aborigines professionally, as well as an amateur anthropologist. Baldwin Spencer was called on to enquire into conditions among Aborigines in the Northern Territory in 1911. The case for establishing the Chair in Anthropology at the University of Sydney was argued partly in terms of the role of anthropology in colonial administration (Gray 2007). Perhaps the most active anthropologist in the field of social policy was A. P. Elkin, regarded as one of the architects of the policy of assimilation, framed in the years before the Second World War and put into practice following the war (Wise 1985).

In 1964 the Australian Institute of Aboriginal Studies was founded, with the brief of fostering and carrying out research on Aboriginal languages, cultures, and societies. W. E. H. Stanner was appointed to the Council of Aboriginal Affairs in 1967, an advisory body to the Commonwealth Government. In the early mid-1970s anthropologists played a significant role in the framing of the *Aboriginal Land Rights (Northern Territory) Act* of 1976. Both R. M. Berndt and W. E. H. Stanner had appeared as expert witnesses in the Gove Case (*Milirrpum v. Nabalco Pty Ltd. and the Commonwealth of Australia* 1971), in which Aboriginal people of Yirrkala sued a mining company and the Commonwealth Government over the excision of a portion of the Arnhem Land Aboriginal reserve for bauxite mining. Nancy Williams's study of Yolngu land tenure arose out of this process. The definition of 'traditional Aboriginal owner' in the *Aboriginal Land Rights (Northern Territory) Act* (1976) drew on the social anthropology of the time, especially the Berndts' (1964) account of land holding groups. Many anthropologists, linguists, and archaeologists were involved in the preparation and hearing of Aboriginal land claims under the Act from the late 1970s, as they have been in later native-title litigation.

More recently the Centre for Aboriginal Economic Policy Research at the Australian National University under the directorship of the economic anthropologist Jon Altman has been active in carrying out policy-related research. The role of non-Aboriginal anthropologists as advisers on policy and spokespersons on behalf of Aboriginal communities has diminished in recent decades, however, as Indigenous scholars such as Marcia Langton and Indigenous lawyers such as Noel Pearson have become prominent in Aboriginal affairs. This role was particularly evident during the debate over legislation following the Mabo case (1992), in which the High Court of Australia overturned the doctrine of *terra nullius* and recognized the applicability of the principle of native title at Common Law to Aborigines and Torres Strait Islanders. Nevertheless, anthropologists have mounted critiques of government policy in relation to Aboriginal people and Torres Strait Islanders (e.g. Povinelli 2002), and the many studies by Tim Rowse (e.g. 2002) have a strong policy orientation, some bringing an anthropological lens to bear on issues and analyses. Recent trends in Australian government policy have occasioned considerable anthropological debate (Sutton 2009).

Cultural and Linguistic Anthropology

Fred Myers's (1986) cultural anthropological perspective brought to bear an analysis cast in terms of key symbols of Pintubi culture. He linked these concerns to the relations of individual to society, conceptualized in terms of the opposition of autonomy and relatedness. This work articulated with the social anthropological tradition in Australia, however, offering a critique of social-structural approaches to group identity and relations to land, and bringing to bear a perspective from the point of view of the individual and of social processes. With the exception of Alan Rumsey's research and writing (e.g. Rumsey 1993), linguistic anthropology has not been strongly represented in Australian anthropology, although Sansom's monograph on a Darwin fringe camp (Sansom 1980) drew on the ethnography of speaking as well as Manchester School processual analysis.

Gender Studies and Feminist Anthropology

Warner (1937) had depicted Yolngu women as associated with the Durkheimian 'profane' in contrast with the supposedly 'sacred' status of men. Kaberry (1939) countered with a survey of Aboriginal societies of the east Kimberley, with a strong focus on the social lives of women, 'sacred and profane'. Writing by C. H. Berndt and Isobel White in the 1970s depicted the relations between men and woman as complementary, invoking the image of 'digging stick and spear' (e.g. Berndt 1970). Following her early research on socialization in north central Arnhem Land, Annette Hamilton turned to gender relations from a broadly neo-Marxian perspective (e.g. Hamilton 1980). This was in response to the overly uniform account by John Bern (1979) of 'the Aboriginal social formation'. In her ethnography of the women's camp in an Aboriginal township in north central Australia, cast overtly in feminist terms, Diane Bell (1983) argued that the boosting of male power by colonial authorities transformed indigenous gender relations (see Merlan 1988 for a review of anthropological approaches to gender in Aboriginal studies).

THE ANTHROPOLOGY OF ABORIGINAL RELIGION

Anthropologists working in Australia in the nineteenth century did not recognize Aboriginal beliefs and practices as 'religious', but described them under such headings as superstition, magic, and ceremony. Baldwin Spencer and F. J. Gillen coined the expression 'the Dreaming' to translate a key Western Desert concept, an expression that remains current and which has been incorporated (in its English form) into many Aboriginal languages. Durkheim *Elementary Forms of the Religious Life* (1965 [1915]) heralded a changing perspective. W. Lloyd Warner (1937), for example, drew both on Durkheim's categories of sacred and profane, and on his theory of the solidarity-enhancing effects of religion.

Rather few extended examinations of Aboriginal religion were written in the middle decades of the twentieth century, but there were many studies of particular rituals (e.g. Meggitt 1967) and movements (e.g. Berndt 1962), as well as overviews (e.g. Berndt 1974). The most intense examination and analysis of one group's religion, however, was by Stanner (1963), who took a quasi-structuralist approach to myth and ritual. More recent monographs include Keen (1994) on Yolngu religious knowledge, Dussart (2000) on Warlpiri women's ritual, and Poirier (2005) on cosmology and dreams in the Western Desert. Other studies of the significance of dreams include those by Barbara Glowczewski and Katie Glaskin.

The effects of social change on Aboriginal ritual and religion have been the topic of a considerable body of research. Religious 'movements' in response to white colonization burgeoned on the pastoral frontier, and formed the subject of research by German scholars such as Helmut Petri and Andreas Lommel, synthesized by Tony Swain (1993). Other studies include Berndt's (1962) account of an Arnhem Land movement and Kolig (1981) on the organization of ritual in the north of Western Australia's desert region. Aboriginal approaches to Christianity have been the subject of extensive research over the decades (e.g. Swain and Bird-Rose 1988), with pioneering research by Malcolm Calley (1964) on the Pentecostal Church of Bandjalang people of northern New South Wales, recently followed up by Akiko Ono (2007). There have been recent studies of Aboriginal interpretations of Christianity in outback towns (e.g. McDonald 2001) and remote Aboriginal townships (e.g. Schwartz 2010).

COMMUNITY STUDIES: 'FOURTH WORLD' COMMUNITIES

The Jigalong Mob by Robert Tonkinson (1974), a student of R. M. Berndt, broke the mould established by Warner, Meggitt, Hiatt, and others by tracing the lives of Aboriginal people of a Western Desert settlement in rapidly changing circumstances. Scholars carrying out research in Australia from the late 1970s also reacted against the 'reconstructionist' tenor of traditional Australian anthropological monographs, and sought to record patterns of life and relationships in contemporary Aboriginal missions, government stations, and townships. They drew on processual frameworks (Sansom 1980), neo-Marxist theory (Anderson 1984), a Weberian framework (Trigger 1992), practice theory (Martin 1993), and more recently phenomenology (Redmond 2001), among other approaches. David McKnight's works on Mornington Island focus on kinship and patterns of sorcery accusations, while Marika Moiseeff's research in a South Australian Aboriginal community draws on psychiatry. Recent work has included a cluster of studies of Aboriginal communities in Queensland (Glowczewski 2013), the north of Western Australia, and various parts of the Northern Territory, including remote communities and people living in or near towns (e.g. Austin-Broos 2009; Dussart 2000; Merlan 1998; Musharbash 2008; Povinelli 1993). Merlan's analysis of the 'intercultural domain' in and around the town of Katherine in the Northern Territory has been particularly influential.

The New Wave of Research in the South-East and South-West

During the 1980s a new wave of studies of Aboriginal communities in the rural and urban south-east and south-west took a fresh approach. Gillian Cowlishaw (1988) and Barry Morris (1989) drew on critical and post-structuralist perspectives to depict Aboriginal cultures as 'cultures of resistance' or 'oppositional cultures'. A number of scholars examined the specificities of Aboriginal cultures of these regions such as the structure of Aboriginal English (Diana Eades), patterns of fighting (Gaynor Macdonald, Marcia Langton), the language of racial stereotypes (Julie Finlayson), and family structure (Christina Birdsall) (see Keen 1988). Research in these regions continues (e.g. Cowlishaw 2009; Gibson 2011), much of it in connection with native-title claims (e.g. Sutton 1998).

The Anthropology of Aboriginal Music, Art, and Performance

A long tradition of ethnomusicological research on Aboriginal music in Australia is exemplified in the work of Alice Moyle, Richard Moyle, Alan Marett, and Aaron Korn. Although some anthropologists of an earlier generation, such as A. P. Elkin, wrote about Aboriginal songs, only recently has a specifically anthropological approach to Aboriginal music emerged (e.g. Magowan 2007; Toner 2001; and see Tamisari 1998 on performance).

The anthropology of art has been more fully represented. Structural-functionalist anthropologists such as A. P. Elkin and R. M. Berndt documented Aboriginal paintings in the 1960s, and during the same decade the amateur anthropologist Charles Mountford published works on Aboriginal art and ritual. Nancy Munn pioneered the rigorous semiotic and social analysis of Aboriginal art with her innovative studies of Warlpiri and Pitjantjatjara women's sand drawing, body painting, ritual, and cosmology (Munn 1973). This semiotic approach was elaborated by Howard Morphy in his monograph and articles on Yolngu art and ritual (e.g. Morphy 1991), and on Aboriginal art more widely. A lively programme of anthropological research on Aboriginal art has been continued by Christine Watson (2003) and Morphy's students, including research by Luke Taylor (1996). The study of Aboriginal rock art has been conducted by anthropologists (e.g. Layton 1992) and archaeologists such as Andrée Rosenfeld (1981). The effects of new media on Aboriginal lives have been the subject of recent research by scholars including Melinda Hinkson and Jennifer Deger.

Some Current Trends and an Overview

Aboriginal societies have undergone and are undergoing rapid change, as is Australian society more widely. So too the relationships between Aboriginal cultures and communities and non-Aboriginal Australians are changing, although many structural aspects of the relationships, such as indigenous disadvantage, endure. Aboriginal communities continue to be very diverse, although language loss and cultural change in remote communities proceed at a very fast rate. Trends in anthropological perspectives and research reflect those changes (Peterson 1991). Current perspectives in the anthropology of Australian Aborigines are diverse, however, ranging from the studies of hunting in remote communities (e.g. Bird et al. 2005), through phenomenological approaches to Aboriginal cosmology (Redmond 2001), to research on music and art in remote and urban communities, and conditions in urban communities. A return to an interest in the past links anthropology to historical linguistics and archaeology from the perspective of deep history (e.g. McConvell and Evans 1997). Internationally, research in Australia contributed to the study of hunting and gathering societies more widely (Myers 1988).

Debate continues on the immediacy with which anthropologists should respond to changes in government policy and practice, although direct engagement occurs in the form of research for the preparation of native-title claims. The last two decades have seen the emergence of Indigenous Australian archaeologists and anthropologists, the most notable among the latter being Marcia Langton (e.g. 2010), who has combined political activism and commentary with scholarly research and writing. The discipline is thus characterized by great diversity, from interest in the particulars of Aboriginal cultures, rural and urban, to the structural relationship between the indigenous minority and the state.

The teaching of Australian Aboriginal anthropology in Australian universities has been replaced to some degree by more general courses in departments of Indigenous studies. Australian Aboriginal anthropology is largely the concern of practioners in Australia, with some specialists located outside the continent. There are schools of Aboriginal studies in France (e.g. Laurent Dousset, Barbara Glowczewski, and Marika Moisseeff), Italy (e.g. Franca Tamisari), Japan (e.g. Sachiko Kubota, Sig Sugito), the Netherlands (e.g. A. P. Borsboom, Eric Venbrux), and Russia (e.g. Vladimir Kabo, Olga Artemova).

References

Altman, J. 1987. *Aboriginal hunter-gatherers today*. Canberra: AIAS.
Anderson, C. 1984. The political and economic basis of Kuku-Yalanji social history. PhD thesis, University of Queensland.
Anderson, C. 1988. Anthropology and Australian Aboriginal economy 1961–1986. In R. M. Berndt and R. Tonkinson (eds.), *Social anthropology and Australian Aboriginal studies*, 125–88. Canberra: AIAS.
Austin-Broos, D. 2003. Places, practices, and things: the articulation of Arrernte kinship with welfare and work, *American Ethnologist* 30, 118–35.
Austin-Broos, D. 2009. *Arrernte present, Arrernte past*. Chicago: University of Chicago Press.
Bates, D. 1985. *The native tribes of Western Australia*. Canberra: National Library of Australia.
Beckett, J. 1987. *Torres Strait Islanders*. Cambridge: Cambridge University Press.
Bell, D. 1983. *Daughters of the Dreaming*. Melbourne: McPhee-Gribble.
Bern, J. E. 1979. Ideology and domination: toward a reconstruction of Australian Aboriginal social formation, *Oceania* 50, 118–32.
Berndt, C. H. 1970. Digging sticks and spears, or, the two-sex model. In F. Gale (ed.), *Woman's role in Aboriginal society*, 39–48. Canberra: AIAS.
Berndt, R. M 1962. *An adjustment movement in Arnhem Land*. Paris: Mouton.
Berndt, R. M. 1974. *Australian Aboriginal religion*. Leiden: Brill.
Berndt, R. M. and Berndt, C. H. 1945. *A preliminary report of field work in the Ooldea Region, western South-Australia*. Sydney: Australian Medical Publishing.
Berndt, R. M. and Berndt, C. H. 1964. *The world of the first Australians*. Sydney: Ure Smith.
Bird, D. W., Bird, R. B., and Parker, C. H. 2005. Aboriginal burning regimes and hunting strategies in Australia's Western Desert. *Human Ecology* 33, 443–64.
Butlin, N. 1993. *Economics and the Dreamtime*. Cambridge: Cambridge University Press.
Calley, M. 1964. Pentecostalism among the Bandjalang. In M. Reay (ed.), *Aborigines now*, 48–58. Sydney: Angus and Robertson.
Chase, A. K. and Sutton, P. 1987. Australian Aborigines in a rich environment. In W. H. Edwards (ed.), *Traditional Aboriginal society: a reader*, 68–95. Melbourne: Macmillan.
Cowlishaw, G. 1988. *Black, white or brindle*. Melbourne: Cambridge University Press.
Cowlishaw, G. 2009. *The city's outback*. Sydney: UNSW Press.
Curr, E. M. 1886–7. *The Australian race*. Melbourne: John Ferres.
Dawson, J. 1881. *Australian Aborigines*. Melbourne: Robertson.
Dousset, L. 2002. Accounting for context and substance: the Australian Western Desert kinship system. *Anthropological Forum* 12, 193–204.
Durkheim, E. 1965 [1915]. *The elementary forms of the religious life*. New York: Free Press.
Dussart, F. 2000. *The politics of ritual in an Aboriginal settlement*. Washington, DC: Smithsonian Institution.
Gibson, L. 2011. 'Who you is?' Work and identity in Aboriginal New South Wales. In I. Keen (ed.), *Indigenous participation in Australian economies: historical and anthropological perspectives*, 127–39. Canberra: ANU E-press.
Glowczewski, B. 2010. Warriors for Peace: the political condition of the Aboriginal people as viewed from Palm Island. http://eprints.jcu.edu.au/7286/
Godelier, M. 1975. Modes of production, kinship, and demographic structures. In M. Bloch (ed.), *Marxist analyses and social anthropology*, 3–27. London: Malaby Press.
Gray, G. 2007. *A cautious silence*. Canberra: Aboriginal Studies Press.
Hamilton, A. 1980. Dual social systems: technology, labour and women's secret rites in the eastern Western Desert of Australia. *Oceania* 51, 4–19.

Hart, C. M. W. and Pilling, A. R. 1960. *The Tiwi of North Australia*. New York: Holt, Rinehart & Winston.

Hartwig, M. 1978. Capitalism and Aborigines: the theory of internal colonialism and its rivals. In E. L. Wheelwright and K. D. Buckley (eds), *Essays in the political economy of Australian capitalism 3*, 119–41. Sydney: Australia and New Zealand Book Company.

Hassell, E. 1936. Notes on the ethnology of the Wheelman tribe of south Western Australia. *Anthropos* 31, 679–711.

Hiatt, L. R. 1965. *Kinship and conflict*. Canberra: Australian National University Press.

Horne, G. A. and Aiston, G. 1924. *Savage life in central Australia*. London: Macmillan.

Howitt, A. W. 1880. The Kûrnai tribe: their customs in peace and war. In L. Fison and A. W. Howitt (eds), *Kamilaroi and Kûrnai*, 177–260. Melbourne: George Robertson.

Howitt, A. W. 1904. *Native tribes of south-east Australia*. London: Macmillan.

Kaberry, P. M. 1939. *Aboriginal women: sacred and profane*. London: Routledge.

Keen, I. 1988. Introduction. In I. Keen (ed.), *Being black: Aboriginal cultures in 'settled' Australia*, 1–26. Canberra: AIAS.

Keen, I. 1994. *Knowledge and secrecy in an Aboriginal religion*. Oxford: Clarendon Press.

Keen, I. 2004. *Aboriginal economy and society: Australia at the threshold of colonization*. Melbourne: Oxford University Press.

Kolig, E. 1981. *The silent revolution*. Philadelphia: ISHI.

Langton, M. 2010. The resource curse: new outback principalities and the paradox of plenty. *Griffith Review* 28, 47–63.

Layton, R. H. 1992. *Australian rock art: a new synthesis*. Cambridge: Cambridge University Press.

Lee, R. and DeVore, I. (eds) 1968. *Man the hunter*. Chicago: Aldine.

Lévi-Strauss, C. 1969. *The elementary structures of kinship*. London: Eyre & Spottiswoode.

Love, J. R. B. 1936. *Stone Age Bushmen of today*. Glasgow: Blackie and Sons.

McConvell, P. and Evans, N. 1997. *Archaeology and linguistics*. Melbourne: Oxford University Press.

McDonald, H. 2001. *Blood, bones and spirit*. Melbourne: Melbourne University Press.

Maddock, K. 1972. *The Australian Aborigines*. London: Allen Lane, Penguin Press.

Magowan, F. 2007. *Melodies of mourning*. Nedlands: University of Western Australia Press.

Martin, D. F. 1993. Autonomy and relatedness. PhD thesis, Australian National University.

Meggitt, M. 1967. *Gadjari among the Walbiri Aborigines of central Australia*. Sydney: University of Sydney Press.

Merlan, F. 1988. Gender in Aboriginal social life: a review. In R. M. Berndt and R. Tonkinson (eds), *Social anthropology and Australian Aboriginal studies*, 15–76. Canberra: AIAS.

Merlan, F. 1998. *Caging the rainbow*. Honolulu: University of Hawai'i Press.

Morphy, H. 1991. *Ancestral connections*. Chicago: University of Chicago Press.

Morris, B. 1989. *Domesticating resistance*. Oxford: Berg.

Morton, J. 1993. Psychoanalysis and Australian Aboriginal anthropology: the legacy of Géza Róheim. *Acta Ethnographica Hungarica* 38, 17–29.

Mulvaney, J. 1967. The Australian Aborigines, 1606–1929: opinion and fieldwork, part 2. In J. J. Eastwood and F. B. Smith (eds), *Historical studies: selected articles first series*. Melbourne: Melbourne University Press.

Munn, N. 1973. *Walbiri iconography*. Ithaca: Cornell University Press.

Musharbash, Y. 2008. *Yuendumu everyday*. Canberra: Aboriginal Studies Press.

Myers, F. 1986. *Pintupi country, Pintupi self*. Canberra: AIAS.

Myers, F. 1988. Critical trends in the study of hunter-gatherers. *Annual Review of Anthropology* 17, 262–81.

Nind, I. S. 1831. Description of the natives of King George's sound (Swan River Colony) and adjoining country. *Journal of the Royal Geographical Society of London* 1, 21–51.

Ono, A. 2007. Pentecostalism among the Bundjalung revisited: the rejection of culture by aboriginal Christians in northern New South Wales, Australia. PhD thesis, Australian National University.

Parker, K. L. 1905. *The Euahlayi tribe*. London: A. Constable.

Peterson, N. 1971. The structure of two Australian Aboriginal ecosystems. PhD thesis, University of Sydney.

Peterson, N. 1991. Studying man and man's nature: the history of the institutionalisation of Aboriginal anthropology. *Australian Aboriginal Studies* 2, 3–19.

Peterson, N. 1993. Demand sharing: reciprocity and the pressure for generosity among foragers. *American Anthropologist* 95, 860–74.

Poirier, S. 2005. *A world of relationships*. Toronto: University of Toronto Press.

Povinelli, E. 1993. *Labor's lot*. Chicago: University of Chicago Press.

Povinelli, E. 2002. *The cunning of recognition*. Durham: Duke University Press.

Radcliffe-Brown, A. 1931. *The social organization of Australian tribes*. Sydney: University of Sydney Press.

Redmond, T. 2001. Places that move. In A. Rumsey and J. F. Weiner (eds), *Emplaced myth*, 120–38. Honolulu: University of Hawai'i Press.

Roheim, G. 1945. *The eternal ones of the dream*. New York: International Universities Press.

Rose, F. G. G. 1968. Australian marriage, land-owning groups, and initiations. In R. B. Lee and I. DeVore (eds), *Man the hunter*, 200–8. Chicago: Aldine.

Rosenfeld, A. 1981. *Early man in north Queensland*. Canberra: Department of Prehistory and Anthropology, Australian National University.

Rowse, T. 2002. *Indigenous futures: choice and development for Aboriginal and Islander Australia*. Sydney: UNSW Press.

Rumsey, A. 1993. Language and territoriality in Aboriginal Australia. In M. Walsh and C. Yallop (eds), *Language and culture in Aboriginal Australia*, 191–206. Canberra: Aboriginal Studies Press.

Sahlins, M. 1972. *Stone Age economics*. Chicago: Aldine-Atherton.

Sansom, B. 1980. *The camp at Wallaby Cross*. Canberra: AIAS.

Schwartz, C. 2010. Carrying the cross, caring for kin. *Oceania* 80, 58–77.

Shapiro, W. 1979. *Miwuyt marriage*. Philadelphia: ISHI.

Spencer, B. and Gillen, F. J. 1927. *The Arunta*. London: Macmillan.

Stanner, W. E. H. 1963. *On Aboriginal religion*. Sydney: University of Sydney Press.

Strehlow C. 1913–20. *Die Aranda- und Loritza-Stamme in Zentral-Australien*. Frankfurt am Main: Joseph Baer.

Strehlow, T. G. H. 1974. *Aranda traditions*. Melbourne: Melbourne University Press.

Sutton, P. 1998. *Native title and the descent of rights*. Perth: Commonwealth of Australia, Native Title Tribunal.

Sutton, P. 2009. *The politics of suffering*. Melbourne: Melbourne University Press.

Swain, T. 1993. *A place for strangers*. Melbourne: Melbourne University Press.

Swain, T. and Bird-Rose, D. 1988. *Aboriginal Australians and Christian missions*. Bedford Park: The Australian Association for the Study of Religions.

Tamisari, F. 1998. Body, vision and movement: in the footprints of the ancestors. *Oceania* 68, 249–70.

Taylor, L. 1996. *Seeing the inside*. Oxford: Clarendon Press.

Thomson, D. F. 1939. The seasonal factor in human culture. *Proceedings of the Prehistoric Society* 5, 209–21.
Tindale, N. 1972. The Pitjandjara. In M. G. Bicchieri (ed.), *Hunters and gatherers today*, 217–68. New York: Holt, Rinehart & Winston.
Tindale, N. 1974. *Aboriginal tribes of Australia*. Canberra: Australian National University Press.
Toner, P. 2001. When the echoes are gone. PhD thesis, Australian National University.
Tonkinson, R. 1974. *The Jigalong Mob*. Menlo Park: Cummings.
Trigger, D. 1992. *Whitefella comin'*. Cambridge: Cambridge University Press.
Turner, D. 1980. *Aboriginal social organisation*. Atlantic Highlands: Humanities Press.
Warner, W. L. 1937. *A black civilization*. New York: Harper.
Watson, C. 2003. *Piercing the ground*. Fremantle: Freemantle Arts Centre Press.
Wise, T. 1985. *The self made anthropologist: a life of A. P. Elkin*. Sydney: George Allen & Unwin.

CHAPTER 46

FROM ETHNOHISTORY TO ETHNOGENESIS

A Historiography of Hunter-Gatherer Cultural Anthropology in California and the Great Basin

DAVID ROBINSON

At the time of European contact, the American Far West was home to an immense diversity of indigenous communities. The area encompassing what is now the state of California contained some of the most highly populated hunter-gatherer regions anywhere on earth (see Kroeber 1925). In contrast, the neighbouring Great Basin held some of the most dispersed hunter-gatherer populations in the world (see papers in D'Azevedo 1986). It is conservatively estimated that some 300,000 native people lived within the 164,000 square miles of what is now the state of California by the time the Spaniards set up their first missions along the Pacific coast starting in AD 1769. By comparison, estimates of Great Basin populations range from 22,000 to 45,000 in an area covering 400,000 square miles.

These two vast areas contrast sharply not only in terms of population density, but also in how anthropologists have interpreted different aspects of the hunter-gatherers who lived there. The trajectory of hunter-gatherer research in these two geographic regions have significant divergences; the intense complexity of native Californian languages coupled with dense populations have led to anthropological theories focused upon social complexity, status differentiation, ceremonialism, and 'proto' agricultural practices. The dispersed populations and apparent wide range of subsistence pursuits of the Great Basin has led to focusing on the limiting effects of ecological factors and its supposed corresponding limitations on ceremonialism and social makeup of desert groups due to the constant need for subsistence. However, the anthropology of both California and the Great Basin is similar in their shared history of the discipline itself as it developed from its colonial origins into the firmly entrenched four fields of anthropology. Thus research in both regions shares many of the biases, theories, and methodologies that have resulted in the changing anthropological understandings of Far Western hunter-gatherers.

Since colonial contact, the indigenous populations of each region have undergone dramatic transformations in the ongoing histories of nation building. The history of ethnohistorical accounts and subsequent anthropological research into the hunter-gatherers of the American Far West largely goes hand-in-hand with Spanish, Russian, Mexican, and American colonial endeavours. Because of the importance of the records made by these differing colonial groups concerning the indigenous peoples they wrote about, anthropology and ethnohistory are inseparable: ethnohistory is fundamental within hunter-gatherer studies. The importance of textual accounts recorded by colonial officials, soldiers, travellers, journalists, plus later amateur and trained anthropologists (as ethnographers) is absolutely paramount in the construction of knowledge about hunter-gatherer people in the American Far West. In this chapter, I focus on how anthropological understandings of the hunter-gatherers of these two regions, California and the Great Basin, have gone hand-in-hand with the changing relationships between Euro-Americans and native groups.

Ethnohistorical Origins

Much of what is known about the hunter-gathers of the American Far West comes from early ethnohistorical documents. The earliest accounts emerge from Spanish explorers who first sailed along the western coast of Pacific North America following the conquest of Mexico. Juan Cabrillo, a Portuguese explorer working on behalf of Spain, recorded the earliest documented encounter with indigenous groups of the American Far West along the southern California coast in AD 1542. Fragments of descriptions from Cabrillo's expedition described coastal Native Californians, including the maritime Chumash of the Santa Barbara Channel with their now famous redwood plank canoes called tomols. Coastal groups were characterized as confident in their contacts with Cabrillo and keen to trade. This confidence in the face of initial European contact was reflected in some early clashes: Cabrillo apparently died on San Miguel Island due to an accident associated with a Chumash assault. Like this account, subsequent explorer diaries are important pieces of information, giving glimpses of indigenous practices at the time, but also illustrating the colonial conditions within which ethnohistorical documents were made (see Brown 2001).

Throughout the next two centuries, various explorers' accounts, including those of Francis Drake who anchored on the north coast of Northern California in 1579, provide occasional accounts of indigenous culture. It is probable that pathogens were introduced into California populations in this 'proto-historical period' (Preston 1996). If so, populations may have been even larger than the estimates mentioned above. Beginning in AD 1769, the founding of the Spanish Franciscan Mission system along the California coastal strip was initiated by Portola's first overland expedition, with accounts of the journey such as Father Juan Crepi's providing valuable insights into Native society (see Gamble 2008). This also marks the start of sustained colonialism in the form of permanent European settlement and the beginning of the historical period; the founding of these missions dramatically impacted native communities along the Pacific coast but also had effects reverberating deep into the American Far West. Within the context of missions, presidios, pueblos, and the subsequent ranchero period, a rich, complex, highly variable but biased ethnohistorical record was created including detailed information from Mission records on marriage and kinship patterns (Johnson 1988) plus aspects of subsistence and social organization (see Hackel 2005). The Russian presence at Fort Ross north of San Francisco provided yet another colonial presence along with ethnohistorical perspectives on the frontier of European empire building (see Lightfoot et al. 1991).

It is during this same period that the first accounts of the interior regions of the Far West were recorded. The 1776 journal of Fray Escalante details information about the Numic-speaking groups of the Great Basin in present-day Utah and Arizona (Fowler 1980, 8). This expedition attempted to link Santa Fe to Monterey in California. Instead, the expedition looped through much of the Great Basin, describing the natural terrain and recording particular lakes and rivers as freshwater sources for potential future colonial prospects. Brief descriptions were made of local inhabitants, including the first account of Great Basin naming practices which remains a long-standing interest in anthropological literature. These first accounts mention that some group identity was based upon specific subsistence practices, such as the Timpangotizis of Utah Lake whose name meant 'fish eaters' (James 1974, 80). However, even at this early date, the US was initiating colonial encounters in the Far West. Lewis and Clark's famous expedition described numerous native groups across the American West, including the Northern Shoshoni in 1804–6 (Ray and Lurie 1954). During this period, Spanish and later Mexican incursions penetrated deeper into interior California from mission and coastal areas (Cook 1960) but to a much lesser degree to the desert regions of the Great Basin (Francaviglia 2005, 31–42).

For the most part, the Franciscan missionaries along the Pacific coast were little interested in documenting native life of the mission neophytes, but there are a number of significant documents that give important, if biased, information. The *interrogatories* were official questionnaires that provide much information. Boscana's writing on the Chinigchinich remains a remarkable account even though he wrote it 'to have before me the means of presenting to these poor Indians an account of the errors entertained by them during their state of heathenism' (Boscana 2005). Hunter-gatherer groups were not passive participants in Hispanic colonial processes. Ethnohistorical accounts are clear that the initial relationships were negotiations between Spanish and indigenous leaders: native translators acted as interlocutors, and native labour was the foundation of the Mission system, but the moving of coastal hunter-gatherers into the California missions caused a chain reaction of displacement and disruption (Milliken 1995). While the missionary enterprise drastically challenged hunter-gatherer society and belief systems, ecological colonialism profoundly changed the environment due to the repression of indigenous fire regimes and the effects of cattle on local plant populations and soil stability (see Lightfoot and Parrish 2009). Thus, disease and drastic ecological changes were the 'dual revolutions' that Hackel (2005) puts as the primary reasons for the dissembling of coastal communities. Introduced European diseases combined with introduced plants and animals created an ever expanding ripple effect moving from coastal areas towards inland and interior regions, transforming environments along with indigenous demographics, subsistence patterns, and socio-political relations (see Dartt-Newton and Erlandson 2006; see also Peelo 2009). Much of the documentation from this period reflects the challenges faced by indigenous groups and the choices they opted for in the changing circumstances. Unsurprisingly, few gave up hunting and gathering completely even as they became the labour force for the agricultural basis of the missions and despite being subject to Spanish law (Hackel 2005).

Just as Franciscan Missions were based upon work provided by native neophytes, with the establishment of Mexican rule, the subsequent rancho system utilized indigenous labour to sustain the tallow-and-hide trade (see Silliman 2004). The breakup of the Mission system caused further disruptions to hunter-gatherer groups and the ever increasing spread of the horse changed indigenous dynamics of the entire American West (Phillips 1993). Indian raiders stole coastal cattle and horses, creating new wealth and opportunity for interior groups (Broadbent 1974). Stocks were used as food, but also for trade as stolen horses from California and southern Spanish settlements were acquired by Great Basin groups (creating what is called the 'Equestrian Period' circa AD 1753 to 1830). Conflict increased, with Mexican punitive expeditions sent into Central California (see Cook 1962). Much of the ethnohistoric record concerning hunter-gatherers of this mission-to-post-mission transitional period is from documentation connected to conflicts and negotiations between the colonialists and interior native Californians.

With the coming of the Gold Rush in 1849, previously ignored regions along the California–Nevada border were suddenly and dramatically inundated with tens of thousands of Euro-Americans, Asian immigrants, and others from around the world. Immigrant diaries and trappers' accounts in the Great Basin provide some of the first, if patchy, accounts (Fowler 1980, 8–9). Growth was rapid, with mining camps, ferries, towns, and coastal ports growing at phenomenal rates. These changes catastrophically affected inland and interior areas that were previously at the hinterlands of Russian and Hispanic colonialism. The borderland of California and Nevada, with the rich gold and silver deposits of the Sierra Nevada mountains, was most immediately impacted by the flood of incomers. Newspaper accounts, diaries, and official documentation such as military diaries, treaties (typically unratified by congress), and later census records detail the mix of tragedy and survival of Californian and Great Basin groups (Heizer 1974; Hurtado 1988). Just as had happened on the coast, cattle drastically altered foothill environments impacting on native subsistence, while vigilante groups and officially commissioned and paid 'battalions' caused havoc for hunter-gatherers in the Sierra Nevada. Accounts illustrate the ever decreasing catchment range available which ran hand-in-hand with the destruction of storable foods such as acorn caches: this lead to stock raiding of Anglo-American camps and settlements, which continued the cycle of violence to the detriment of native populations (Seacrest 2003). As settlement increased, many native Californians were brought into the market economy via waged labour and coercion through state laws that essentially permitted forced servitude. While there were some discussions about moving California Indians entirely to the Great Basin, a number of unratified reserves or 'farms' were established across the state. Federally appointed commissioners signed treaties with local chiefs that effectively disenfranchised those hunter-gatherer groups from their traditional land-use practices (Phillips 1993; 2004). The treaties were not ratified by the US Congress, and by AD 1869 only three of the reservations remained. Towards the final quarter of the nineteenth century, the vast majority of indigenous populations in California had effectively lost control of their hunter-gatherer traditions: populations had dropped to as low as 20,000 and land ownership and therefore rights of access had effectively disappeared altogether. Hunter-gathering in any sustained manner was effectively over.

Bureau of American Ethnology

While early documents were recorded by urban writers such as Alexander Taylor (1860–3) and Hugo Reid (see Hoffman 1885), the beginnings of what can be loosely termed 'anthropology' began with Stephen Powers, a newspaper reporter who between 1871 and 1876 travelled thousands of miles recording native life in California (Powers 1977). Also during this period, the French Alphonse Pinart-Leon de Cessac expedition collected artefacts along with some linguistic information (Heizer 1978, 7).

However, most important at this time was the work of the Bureau of American Ethnology, based in Washington, DC. As Darnell (1998, 12) notes of the initial Bureau appointees, 'Prior to the establishment of academic anthropology, [ethnological] practitioners were self-taught and self-identified'. Western landscapes had been mapped by governmental expeditions such as the famous Wheeler expedition, and the goal of the BAE followed suit in its efforts to 'map' the anthropology of native peoples within the borders of the US. As stated by BAE founding director John Wesley Powell (himself a surveyor directing the Rocky Mountain Survey) in the inaugural annual report, the 'purpose of the Bureau of Ethnology [is] to organize anthropologic research in America' (1881, xxxiii) through a systematic ordering akin to methods of natural scientists. Powell was the first person to collate Great Basin ethnography, collecting information on subsistence, technology, social organization, mythology, religion, and linguistics (Fowler 1980, 9). In collaboration with George W. Ingalls, Powell produced the first survey of Great Basin demography and political organization at a time when indigenous Great Basin populations were confronted with Euro-American settler and agricultural colonization, railroad constructions, military repression, and enforced removal to reservations.

Early researchers were working within an explicit evolutionary paradigm, politically and economically bound to national policies of manifest destiny ultimately concerning indigenous peoples and the taking of land: Powell himself promoted that a key function of the BAE was to create a systematized knowledge of Native Americans to aid in the process of 'civilizing' them (see Hinsley 1981). Faced with widespread programmes of acculturation, Native responses were varied, from amelioration to armed resistance. It was in this context that James Mooney's (1896) famous BAE study of the Ghost Dance movement occurred. The Ghost Dance was a pan-western US response by native groups to the loss of land, removal to reservations, and the acculturating programmes of governmental agencies such as the Bureau of Indian Affairs. Great Basin groups were particularly involved in this 'messianic' movement, instigating two separate waves in the 1870s and 1890s. Shortly after the massacre at Wounded Knee on 29 December 1890, Mooney, acting as an ethnologist with the BAE, was sent to study the Ghost Dance movement as a contemporary and important Native phenomenon. His information initially came from research he conducted in 1891 of documents kept in the War Department and Bureau of Indian Affairs offices in Washington, DC (Moses 1979, 310). This illustrates the military and bureaucratic nature of many early accounts of hunter-gatherer groups. It does not mean that individuals may not have been very sympathetic to indigenous people and their culture, but the historical context of ethnohistorical information was deeply entangled with Anglo-American westward expansionism. Mooney was sympathetic to Natives, with little interest in evolutionary concepts (see Kehoe 1989). In

1892 Mooney interviewed the Nevada Paiute visionary named Wovoka (or Jack Wilson) at the Walker River Reservation, which led to Mooney's famous and influential 1896 Bureau of Ethnology publication on the Ghost Dance (see the discussion below on the Ghost Dance movements).

Kroeberian Anthropology and the Early Twentieth Century

In 1901 the Department and Museum of Anthropology was founded at the University of California at Berkeley, establishing a permanent base for anthropological work at the very moment when indigenous populations were thought to be on the verge of 'extinction'.

The foundations of anthropology in California and the Great Basin can be traced to Boas through two of his most influential students, Alfred L. Kroeber and Robert Lowie. In particular, for the next half-century, anthropological research in the American Far West would be fundamentally influenced by Kroeber and his students. By the time of Kroeber's death in 1960, he had over 500 publications in a career that spanned over 60 years. His 1925 publication *Handbook of the Indians of California* was a comprehensive and detailed ethnography of the entire state and remains an essential source for any research into indigenous California. Equally important, he directed a generation of anthropologists who headed out from Berkeley in an effort of 'salvage anthropology' to document Native cultures before they 'vanished'. Kroeber established much of what is still held to be the basic cultural interpretations of Native California: he coined the term 'tribelet' to describe the basic socio-political organization for California groups.

Kroeber's underlying principle was the culture area, based upon the principle of 'cultural elements' as the 'minimal definable elements of culture' (Kroeber 1936, 101): cultures could therefore be analysed through the atomization of 'culture traits' into their 'single element-parts' (see T. Kroeber 1970, 163). By empirically documenting cultural elements, a basis for defining cultures could be established, which affords cross-cultural comparison (see Lyman and O'Brien 2003). Applied to archaeological material, this principle was part of the impetus for Kroeber's creation of the Ethnological and Archaeological Survey, based out of Berkeley (T. Kroeber 1970, 143). Accordingly, the *California Publications in American Archaeology and Ethnology* was established as the vehicle to present 'factual summaries of [survey] work in progress' (Darnell 1998, 202). However, Kroeber looked to explain cultural similarity through processes of diffusion that might be analysed using element lists. Thus, anthropological research directed by Kroeber collated information from hundreds of informants in California and the Great Basin in an effort to present the cultural characteristics of aboriginal life as it was immediately preceding European contact. For instance, the dedicated work of Gayton produced one of the most important and detailed accounts of the Yokuts and Mono groups of the Sierra Nevada mountains and adjacent regions (Gayton 1930; 1945; 1948a; 1948b; 1976 amongst others).

There are many other examples of ethnographies from this period of research. Researchers engaged with memory anthropology, as it has come to be called, conducted interviews prompting the recollections of native elders to detail their knowledge of indigenous lifeways. The result of this is one of the richest corpuses of ethnographic publications of any region in the world.

Kroeber's work created detailed ethnographies of specific cultural groups, but he was equally engaged in drawing together grand theoretical models. Most famously, Kroeber (1919) conceived of culture as the *superorganic*, a universalizing theory of cultural change envisioned as analogous to the life-cycle of an organism; thus a culture went through the process of growth, climax, decline, and death (see Verndon 2010, 386). Kroeber saw the superorganic as a partly cyclical, though ascending, movement of civilization (Verndon 2010, 392).

While Kroeber's ethnographic works ultimately attempted to synthesize data to provide theoretical considerations of culture (see Kroeber 1939), there were non-Berkeley anthropologists gathering significant data from indigenous consultants. C. Hart Merriam (1955; 1967; 1970) was a botanist who independently interviewed many Californian Indians while Frank Latta (1977) documented Yokuts and neighbouring populations. However, the work of John Peabody Harrington would eventually become the most influential of the non-Berkeley anthropologists even though he rarely published during his own lifetime (see below). Harrington collected over a million pages of ethnographic and linguistic information plus numerous sound recordings from southern Californian and western Great Basin groups (Woodward and Macri 2005). The unpublished data would come to be of paramount value to ethnohistorians of the next generation.

STEWARD AND THE GREAT BASIN

While a graduate student at Berkeley under Kroeber, Julian Steward undertook ethnographic work with the Owens Valley and Mono Lake Paiute in the summers of 1927 and 1928. This work was the beginning of a series of influential studies that have been described as the first serious and 'systematic treatment of hunter and gatherers as a distinctive subject' ever undertaken in the world (Clemmer and Myers 1999, xi). In focusing on the dispersed population dynamics of the Great Basin, Steward put forward his highly influential notions of multi-lineal socio-political levels of hunter-gatherer evolution within an ecologically limiting framework (Steward 1938). Steward outlined his 'band' concept and the evolutionary classification system of patrilineal, composite, and matrilineal band types. Moving beyond conceiving of cultures as composed of traits, Steward advanced comparative approaches within behavioural and ecological parameters, coining the term 'cultural ecology', which has wide application to this day. His work influenced other researchers worldwide and was of major influence behind the seminal Man the Hunter conference (Myers 2004, 180). Concurrent with Steward, ideational and cognitive approaches based upon linguistic studies became known under the wider rubric of 'New Ethnography' which in part stressed emic mental perspectives rather than behaviour as developed by Steward (see Myers 2004, 181–2). This new ethnography included ethnobotany, ethnobiology, cosmology, and linguistic semantics by a variety of researchers culminating in the Great Basin volume of the *Handbook of North American Indians* published in 1986. Such work, especially linguistic work, led to increasing interest in Numic studies; in large part, defining this linguistic family changed the emphasis from Great Basin anthropology to one of Numic anthropology.

Increasingly, ethnographic research considered language as a defining structural characteristic of Great Basin hunter-gatherers. Even so, and as Kroeber's theoretical concepts of the superorganic gradually fell out of favour, the influence of research into hunter-gatherers in California became increasingly more insular. By contrast, Steward's work continued to influence anthropological discourse worldwide (see Clemmer and Myer 1999).

POST-ETHNOGRAPHIC FIELDWORK: COLLATING INFORMATION

In the 1978 *Handbook of North American Indians* on California, Heizer (1978, 15) announced that 'The old-style ethnographic work has ended because the aboriginal cultures are extinct.' While this statement ignored processes of ethnogenesis and survival of Native identities, Heizer was correct in predicting that descendant scholars 'will be mining and remilling the vast body of published direct-testimony ethnographies, ethnohistories, ethnohistorical accounts, unpublished archival material, and museum collections' (Heizer 1978, 14–15). Since that time, hundreds of publications have collated ethnohistorical and anthropological information on Great Basin and Californian hunter-gatherers. This has been particularly evident in California, where much more documentation exists. Much of this is descriptive, with the editing and presenting of unpublished material, typically with brief discussions. However, strong analytical works in the 1960s and 1970s by scholars such as Heizer (1978) and Cook (1976) began to look more closely at the consequences of colonial contact. Cook collated various sources to investigate population estimates, mortality rates, and colonial coastal interactions with inland native groups. In total, these papers stressed the destruction of the California Indians and presented a strong critique of the violence perpetrated upon native groups.

Starting in the 1970s, there were a plethora of anthropological publications investigating a range of social and theoretical issues derived from ethnographies. John Lowell Bean focused upon southern California, especially on the Cahuilla (Bean 1972), and was at the forefront of new theoretical modelling (see Bean and Blackburn 1976; and later, Bean 1992). Most importantly, a stream of work came out based upon the voluminous Harrington notes. Many of these publications focused on Southern Californian groups, with the Chumash of the Santa Barbara area being the most prominent. Bean and King (1974) edited a seminal study of the Chumash 'antap', a multi-village religious and political organization. However, the most influential works include Applegate (1978) plus Hudson, and Blackburn (for instance 1983; 1986; see also Hudson and Underhay 1978). Based upon Harrington's notes containing Chumash oral narratives, Blackburn's (1975) *December's Child* remains one of the finest applications of ethnographic analysis to indigenous culture by considering their mythology, legends, and stories. Importantly, Blackburn's analysis of the oral narratives put forward the underlying 'postulates' of the Chumash world view.

In many respects, Blackburn's book can be seen as a watershed in what is now one of the most intensely studied indigenous cultures in North America. Indeed, themes touched upon by Blackburn continue to be of central importance in Chumash studies, including the 'enormous importance of trade and money; the emphasis on vegetal foods, especially acorns and chia (in a group often considered more dependent on sea foods than these stories seem to show); the diversity of roles among leaders and priests; and the all-important role of *toloache* in dealing with the spirit world' (Anderson 1975, 242).

Research in ethnobotany likewise accelerated with the Harrington notes (see Blackburn and Anderson 1993; Timbrook 2007). A series of important publications by Blackburn and Hudson on the material culture of the Chumash were also largely derived from Harrington's notes. Equally, Blackburn's interest in political and social organization was followed on by John Johnson's work on Chumash cultural geography. While Johnson (1988) used Harrington's information, he turned to Franciscan Mission records to reconstruct Chumash political organization and marriage patterns (see also Johnson 2000). Johnson's research revealed unexpectedly that the Chumash practised matrilocal residence (i.e. the husband typically would move to his wife's community). However, village chiefs were found to have a different marital residence pattern: they were often polygamous and remained within their own village. These chiefly marriage relations often were cross-village alliances with other elite families, thus patrilocal, polygamous marriages helped to create and maintain economic and political relationships across Chumash geography.

These cases illustrate that the collating of information has produced fundamental interpretations of indigenous culture. While the collating of ethnographic and anthropological data continues to this day, I now move on to discuss more recent critiques of earlier anthropological work.

Memory Anthropology and Its Critique

The use of ethnographic texts to reconstruct pre-contact native Californian culture is increasingly considered as problematic. Critiques of these ethnographies point out that they were gathered in post-Mission times as a form 'salvage' anthropology in the mistaken attempt to record an 'aboriginal' way of life. Kroeber described his work as an attempt to 'reconstruct and present the scheme within which [Native Californians] in *ancient* and more recent times lived their lives' (1925, v; emphasis added). One of the major drawbacks of Kroeberian anthropology was its lack of participant observation as most anthropological work was done with interviews. As Lightfoot and Parrish (2009, 78) state:

> The memory culture methodology was predicated on the view that native cultures tended to be static and undynamic. Accordingly, this perspective allowed ethnographers to reconstruct the essence of prehistoric Indian worlds prior to European colonization by using the memories of tribal elders. But it was assumed that little culture change had taken place. Unfortunately, this methodology underestimates the magnitude of cultural transformations that took place among Indian cultures during the early years of European exploration and settlement.

Acknowledging the late colonial context within which ethnographic information was derived has led to a reappraisal of different facets of Native society. Lightfoot and Parrish (2009, 79–80) have detailed this critique, showing how Kroeber underestimated Native complexity, social hierarchy, regional trade, and craft specialization. Indeed, along with Anderson (2005) and others, they also argue persuasively that Native Californians engaged in much more extensive environmental management, particularly fire. Other revisionist approaches include Robinson's (2010) rethinking of ethnographic interpretations of rock art in South-Central California. Previous inferences of rock-art sites as being the exclusive domain of shamans to the exclusion of the larger populace were based upon a misapplication of projecting the ethnographic present into the deeper past.

While Steward's body of work has often been considered as one of the most influential for its theoretical contributions, it was not without its contemporary critiques. Omer Stewart doubted Steward's views of Great Basin simple social organization in his own ethnographic work and interpretation of the Northern Paiute (1966; 1970), arguing that some groups indeed had well-defined territories, a strong attachment to place, and that it was because of the historical introduction of the horse that groups attained the mobility that Steward attributed to prehistory (Ronaansen et al. 1999, 188–9).

These issues were important beyond the academy as they were key points of contention in the Indian Claims Commission Proceeding in the 1970s. Julian Steward was an expert witness for the Department of Justice; Omer Stewart was an expert witness for the petitioning Utes, Paiutes, and Shoshones. As Ronaansen et al. (1999, 199) state:

> The meanings the attorneys attached to the concepts of property and acculturation that Steward presented in his interpretation of the Shoshonean Indians were clearly motivated and framed in the legal context of affirming U.S. legal doctrine. The effect was to deny indigenous rights because property was construed in such a way as to exclude Shoshonean concepts of land use from the realm of validity.

Indeed, like many other anthropologists, Steward was brought into contact with official government agencies, including the Bureau of Indian Affairs. There, Steward was opposed to the 'Indian New Deal' which was proposed to limit processes of acculturation and return aspects of self-rule to native groups (Rusco 1999). As Rusco (1999) points out, Steward seemed to think that there was an 'inevitability of assimilation' for Great Basin groups. Retrospective critiques of Steward have put forward the notion that he fundamentally misunderstood Great Basin groups, which had a detrimental effect politically towards those very people. His view of them as non-territorial, decentralized both socially and politically, served to disenfranchise Native groups legally from their lands, effectively contributing directly to and continuing processes of colonialism (see Pinkoski 2008). In fact, Steward was not concerned with the historical processes of colonialization and change since European contact, but in reconstructing aboriginal society. More to the point, he was interested in developing grand theory to understand hunter-gatherers within an evolutionary category rather than the particulars of historical contingency (see Kehoe 1989). Ultimately, critics argue that this was a major flaw in both Steward's collected ethnographic data and his theoretical interpretation of that data. Steward was attempting to understand past Great Basin society by ignoring the historical developments that structured the lives of the people he was studying.

As Clemmer (2009a) points out, Steward's Great Basin model continues to permeate the 'anthropological imagination' with the Western Shoshone as examples 'of the primordial hunters and foragers who eked out a living in small family groups, constantly roaming in search of windfalls and cornucopias as well as the tiniest bits of edible food' (Clemmer 2009a, 865).

Clemmer has been at the forefront of recent rethinking of Steward and his theories of Great Basin society. In a case study of the Great Basin Tosawihi, Clemmer (2009b) proposes replacing the neo-evolutionary category 'band' with a more fluid idea of identity that he terms the 'ethnie'. In looking afresh at a suite of ethnohistorical documentation, Clemmer finds that 'The Tosawihi had, in fact, developed a degree of solidarity not on the basis of "bandness" but rather on the basis of a complex kinship system that operated in tandem with careful resource use based on encyclopaedic shared knowledge of a very large area' (Clemmer 2009b, 411). So Clemmer argues for adopting the term 'ethnie' as 'a collectivity of people possessing symbolic, cognitive, and normative elements, as well as behavioural practices, that bind them together as a population over generations.'

Others have followed suit. Dobyns and Euler (1998) have critiqued the ethnographic present concept that fails to recognize the changing and active circumstances within which Native people engage by analysing a Great Basin leader named Cherum. They track his changing identity, from a juvenile in a stressed culture in the 1850s; a chief; a 'Big Man'; a 'War Chief'; an Indian scout; an exile; a labour gang contractor; a millenarian movement leader; and a stubborn elder. Such detailed studies not only show the historical processes transforming individuals from hunter-gatherer traditions to an indigenous identity in changing modern conditions, but also illustrate the fluidity of identity in changing circumstances.

Rethinking the Ghost Dance

Originating from a single Paiute group on the Walker River Reservation in two subsequent generations, the two Ghost Dance movements of 1870 and 1890 influenced the religious practices across the indigenous American West. Studies of the Ghost Dance directly tackle that which Steward and the memory anthropologists attempted to distil: namely, the indigenous response to the colonial situation. Since Mooney's famous (and still highly respected) study of the Ghost Dance, it remains one of the most theorized hunter-gatherer social phenomena studied in colonial contexts.

Early studies such as Spier (1935) and Du Bois (1939) considered it under the concept of evolution and diffusion: precedents for aspects of the Ghost Dance were seen in a variety of different guises across North America, either being spread through prophets or through evolutionary changes. Du Bois (1939) tracked the emergence of the Earth Lodge Cult and Bole-Maru in California from the earlier 1870 Ghost Dance movement. Indeed, while firmly opposed to any form of evolutionary concept, Kehoe (1989) has discussed the ongoing influence of the Ghost Dance in social, political, and religious aspects of contemporary Native American society.

Other approaches to the Ghost Dance include concepts of cultural deprivation (Aberle 1962). This hypothesis was put forward to explain the differential acceptance of the Ghost Dance by different communities. In Wallace's (1956) influential paper on revitalization, he put forward the Ghost Dance as one example of 'a deliberate, organised, conscious effort by members of a society to construct a more satisfying culture' (Wallace 1956, 265). Thornton (1986) argues that the Ghost Dance was primarily a 'demographic revitalisation', a reaction to the loss of population. Calling forth the dead to return was meant to replenish a diminished population; its effect was to solidify group solidarity, thus maintaining group identity even though the prophecies were not realized.

Kehoe's (1989) study has most forcefully promoted revitalization, but in a less mechanistic and more humanistic approach. Kehoe suggests that terminology is less important than empathetically understanding the human process of change: 'What counts is that the culmination of the process remains cultural transformation... Without change, adaptation, reformulation, revitalization, transformation (call it what you will), a society—Indian, European, any society—cannot continue' (Kehoe 1989, 123–4).

In his detailed study of Wovoka, Hittman (1990) suggests that views of the Ghost Dance have been skewed by the subsequent manner of its adoption by the Lakota. This 'Plains bias' has had the tendency to homogenize the anthropological view of the Ghost Dance, both geographically and temporally. First, he argues for evidence that Wovoka did not always promote that the dead would return, rather that the dead 'lived' forever in heaven, and that the 'living' would joint them there one day (Hittman 1990, 208). Indeed, Hittman argues that deprivation seems to have had nothing to do with the origination of the Ghost Dance, rather that Wovoka 'might well have intended to fuse the Numu time-honoured status "weather doctor" with that of frontier Presbyterian "saddle bag preacher" exhorting kinsmen and other local Numus to hasten the end of the world by dancing' (Hittman 1990, 207–8). As a syncretic practice, Wovoka is here seen as expressing polyvalent processes, with the implication that the Ghost Dance in Mason Valley was quite different from that of the distant Lakota. Smoak recently states 'A more reasonable approach is to seek to understand the interplay between culture and history, pre-existing belief and deprivation, and internal order and external motivation' (Smoak 2006, 201). Smoak emphasizes prophetic aspects of indigenous religion, and the Ghost Dance as a means to express common 'Indian' identity in the face of colonialism while simultaneously a means of differentiating 'tribal' or local indigenous identity.

The Ghost Dance movements were therefore varied through time and space, a locally appropriated phenomenon based upon differing contexts across the American West. It is because of this that so many alternate interpretations can find validity.

'Indianness', 'Tribalism', and 'Neo-Traditionalism': Hunter-Gatherer Ethnogenesis

Through time, anthropology has moved from its associations with colonial appropriation towards one of indigenous advocacy and activism. The work of Heizer (1974) and Cook (1976) focused on the catastrophic effects of colonialism for Native Californians, but others have highlighted the survival of indigenous identity in processes of transformational ethnogenesis. In many respects, the Ghost Dance can be seen as a mechanism of such identity reformulation. Kehoe's (1989) work on the Ghost Dance is not an impassionate, clinical assessment but an active activism promoting the survival of the Ghost Dance into the late twentieth century: Hittman's (1990) study was in part sponsored directly by the Pauite, while Smoak's (2006) complex analysis of the Ghost Dance details the emergence of the very notion of 'Indianness' and the creation of the ethnic identifiers of Bannock and Shosheanean as a strategy to cope with the non-Native inability to comprehend indigenous culture. Thus, these studies explore the creation of Native American identity in the transformation of traditional hunter-gatherer communities into non-hunter-gatherers.

However, some studies have looked critically at the process of ethnogenesis in the light of the long-standing relationship between anthropology and Native groups. Sometimes termed 'retribaliation', Haley and Wilcoxon (1997; 2005) have brought up the contentious issue of validity in Chumash identity formation since the 1960s and the role that anthropology has played in constructing those identities. This process is explored in a case study that involves the full scope of previous research, including Powell, Kroeber, the Harrington notes, Blackburn's *December's Child*, and contemporary legal requirements behind attributing 'cultural significance' to Native American sites.

The role of anthropology in the process of modern Native ethnogenesis can be controversial. An example is seen in the creation of the very term 'Chumashan', a term originally coined by Powell (1881) as a linguistic designation before effectively becoming institutionalized by Kroeber's cultural definitions (1925). Focusing on the politics surrounding the proposed liquefied gas terminal development of Point Conception in the late 1970s, Haley and Wilcoxon (1997) detailed how potential misreading of anthropological literature played a role in creating a view that Point Conception was the pan-Chumash 'Western Gate', the place of departure for souls on the journey to the land of the dead. Indeed, they show that there were potentially many places that may have been where souls left for the afterlife for various Chumash speaking groups. Thus, it can be argued that those uncritical, or even erroneous, interpretations of ethnography were being utilized for contemporary political purposes: 'Errors that we have encountered in the portrayal of the ethnohistoric record on Point Conception reflect some anthropologists' promotion of a contemporary Chumash identity and also many environmentalists' and landowners' efforts to gain allies in the fight to preserve property, environmental resources, and archaeological sites' (Haley and Wilcoxon 1997, 769).

In an another paper, Haley and Wilcoxon (2005) examine some Chumash traditionalists and their genealogies, showing that they may in fact have Spanish rather than indigenous ancestry. They argue that the neo-Chumash identity arose through the transformation of Santa Barbara of families with Hispanic background, which at one level can be viewed as a fabrication, and on another as a revision of history. The genealogical records also allow them to trace mobility between ethnic categories, ultimately justifying their view of the constructivist rather than essentialist underpinnings of ethnicity.

In total, their papers show how indigenous identities are in a constant state of negotiation, with both anthropological literature, and contemporary practising anthropologists becoming embroiled in tensions between legal definitions of descent and cultural definitions of ethnicity. As they state, 'We find that anthropological practice and Chumash identity and tradition are so deeply entangled that there is little hope that anthropologists can avoid participating in the self-determination of Chumash people' (Haley and Wilcoxon 1997, 761). This example illustrates that long-term colonial ramifications of indigenous identity transformation, and its possible appropriation, are entangled within ongoing power struggles. As seen in the Indian Claims Commission Proceedings in the 1970s discussed above, the interpretation of the ethnohisotorical record thus is not simply an academic enterprise, but it plays a significant role within contemporary politics, in these cases concerning land property.

Conclusion

The history of research into the hunter-gatherers of California and the Great Basin has produced a rich corpus of ethnographic and ethnohistorical texts. In total, this record must be seen as one of the most extensive anthropological records gathered anywhere on earth. Even so, it is not an unproblematic record. The biases, methods, theoretical, and colonial contexts of that record challenge straightforward interpretations of hunter-gatherers. The entirety of the record can in fact be viewed as historical representations of anthropological/indigenous entanglements in the changing colonialism of the American Far West. Even so, the indigenous voice cannot be reduced to a mere product of colonialism. As Landberg (1965) said, 'though sometimes garbled, [the ethnohistorical record] does hark back to pre-European traditions, either to those only faintly remembered or to those that persisted in practice through the period of missionization' (Landberg 1965, 22).

There is another salient point to be made: hunter-gatherer practices that occur within colonial entanglements are no less 'hunter-gatherer' than those that occur in other situations. Therefore, the anthropological records of the American Far West are ideally suited for the study of hunter-gatherers in rapidly changing circumstances since the mid-sixteenth century.

Much revisionist work will continue to concentrate on the historical emergence of indigenous identities. Certainly, future work will continue to develop critical perspectives that challenge essentialist views of hunter-gatherers by deconstructing the categories, assumptions, and definitions implicit within the anthropological discourse of the past century.

References

Aberle, D. 1962. A note on relative deprivation theory as applied to millenarian and other cult movements. In S. Thrupp (ed.), *Millennial dreams in action: essays in comparative study*, 209–14. The Hague: Mouton.

Anderson, E. 1975. Review of Blackburn (ed.): *December's Child: A Book of Chumash Oral Narratives. Journal of California Anthropology* 2, 241–4.

Anderson, M. 2005. *Tending the wild: Native American knowledge and the management of California's natural resources.* Berkeley: University of California Press.

Applegate, R. 1978. *Atishwin: the dream helper in South-Central California.* Romona, CA: Ballena Press.

Bean, L. 1972. *Mukat's People: the Cahuilla Indians of Southern California.* Berkeley: University of California Press.

Bean, L. (ed.) 1992. *California Indian shamanism.* Menlo Park, CA: Ballena Press.

Bean, L. and Blackburn, T. (eds) 1976. *Native Californians: a theoretical perspective.* Romona, CA: Ballena Press.

Bean, L. and King, T. (eds) 1974. *'Antap: California Indian political and economic organization.* Romona, CA: Ballena Press.

Blackburn, T. 1975. *December's Child: a book of Chumash oral narratives.* Berkeley: University of California Press.

Blackburn, T. and Anderson, M. (eds). 1993. *Before the wilderness: Native Californians as environmental managers*. Menlo Park, CA: Ballena Press.

Boscana, G. 2005. *Chinigchinich: a historical account of the origin, customs and traditions of the Indians at the missionary establishment of S. Juan Capistrano, Alta Callifornia*. Banning: Malki Museum.

Broadbent, S. 1974. Conflict at Monterey: Indian horse raiding, 1820–1850. *Journal of California Anthropology* 1, 86–101.

Brown, A. 2001. *A description of unpublished roads: original journals of the first expedition into California, 1769–1770 by Juan Crespi*. San Diego: San Diego State University Press.

Clemmer, R. 2009a. Pristine aborigines or victims of progress? The Western Shoshones in the anthropological imagination. *Current Anthropology* 50, 849–81.

Clemmer, R. 2009b. Band, not-band, or ethnie: who were the White Knife People (Tosawihi)? Resolution of a 'mereological' dilemma. *Ethnohistory* 56, 395–421.

Clemmer, R. and Myers, L. 1999. Introduction. In R. Clemmer, L. Myers, and M. Rudden (eds), *Julian Steward and the Great Basin: the making of an anthropologist*, ix–xxii. Salt Lake City: University of Utah Press.

Cook, S. 1960. Colonial expeditions to the interior of California: Central Valley, 1800–1820. *University of California Anthropological Records* 16, 239–92.

Cook, S. 1962. Expeditions to the interior of California: Central Valley, 1820–1840. *University of California Anthropological Records* 20, 151–213.

Cook, S. 1976. *The conflict between the California Indian and white civilization*. Berkeley: University of California Press.

D'Azevedo, W. (ed.) 1986. *Handbook of North American Indians, volume 11: Great Basin*. Washington, DC: Smithsonian Institution.

Darnell, R. 1998. *And along came Boas: continuity and revolution in Americanist anthropology*. Amsterdam: John Benjamins.

Dartt-Newton, D. and Erlandson, J. 2006. Little choice for the Chumash: colonialism, cattle, and coercion in the mission period California. *American Indian Quarterly* 30, 416–30.

Dobyns, H. and Euler, R. 1998. The nine lives of Cherum, the Pai Tokumhet. *American Indian Quarterly* 22, 363–85.

Du Bois, C. 1939. *The 1870 Ghost Dance*. Berkeley: University of California Press.

Fowler, D. 1980. History of Great Basin anthropological research, 1776–1979. *Journal of California and Great Basin Anthropology* 2, 8–36.

Francaviglia, R. 2005. *Mapping and imagination in the Great Basin: a cartographic history*. Reno: University of Nevada Press.

Gamble, L. 2008. *The Chumash world at European contact: power, trade, and feasting among complex hunter-gatherers*. Berkeley: University of California Press.

Gayton, A. 1930. Yokuts-Mono chiefs and shamans. *University of California Publications in American Archaeology and Ethnography* 24, 361–420.

Gayton, A. 1945. Yokuts and Western Mono social organization. *American Anthropologist* 47, 409–26.

Gayton, A. 1948a. Yokuts and Western Mono ethnography: I: Tulare Lake, Southern Valley, and Central Foothill Yokuts. *Anthropological Records* 10, 1–142.

Gayton, A. 1948b. Yokuts and Western Mono Ethnography: II: Northern Foothill Yokuts and Western Mono. *Anthropological Records* 10, 143–302.

Gayton, A. 1976. Culture–environment integration: external references in Yokuts life. In L. Bean and T. Blackburn (eds), *Native Californians: a theoretical perspective*, 79–97. Romona, CA: Ballena Press.

Hackel, S. 2005. *Children of Coyote, missionaries of Saint Francis: Indian–Spanish relations in colonial California, 1769–1850.* Chapel Hill: University of North Carolina Press.

Haley, B. and Wilcoxon, L. 1997. Anthropology and the making of Chumash tradition. *Current Anthropology* 38, 761–94.

Haley, B. and Wilcoxon, L. 2005. How Spaniards became Chumash and other tales of ethnogenesis. *American Anthropologist* 107, 432–45.

Heizer, R. 1974. *The destruction of the California Indians.* Ramona, CA: Ballena Press.

Heizer, R. 1978. History of research. In R. Heizer (ed.), *Handbook of North American Indians, Vol. 8, California,* 8–10. Washington, DC: Smithsonian Institution.

Hinsley, C. M., Jr. 1981. *Savages and scientists: the Smithsonian Institution and the development of American anthropology 1846–1910.* Washington, DC: Smithsonian Institution.

Hittman, M. 1990. *Wovoka and the Ghost Dance.* Lincoln: University of Nebraska Press.

Hoffman, W. 1885. Hugo Reid's account of the Indians of Los Angeles County. *Bulletin of the Essex Institute* 17, 1–35.

Hudson, T. and Blackburn, T. 1983. *The material culture of the Chumash interaction sphere. Volume II: food preparation and shelter.* Los Altos, CA: Ballena Press.

Hudson, T. and Blackburn, T. 1986. *The material culture of the Chumash interaction sphere. Volume IV: ceremonial paraphernalia, games, and amusements.* Los Altos, CA: Ballena Press.

Hudson, T. and Underhay, E. 1978. *Crystals in the sky: an intellectual odyssey involving Chumash astronomy, cosmology, and rock art.* Santa Barbara: Ballena Press/Santa Barbara Museum of Natural History.

Hurtado, A. 1988. *Indian survival and the California frontier.* New Haven: Yale University Press.

James, H. L. 1974. The way of the fray: a pictorial diary of the Excalante expedition through North-Central New Mexico, 1776. In L. Woodward and J. Callender (eds), *Silver anniversary guidebook, Central-Northern New Mexcio,* 76–82. Ghost Ranch: 25th Field Conference New Mexico Geological Society.

Johnson, J. 1988. Chumash social organization: an ethnohistorical perspective. PhD thesis, Department of Anthropology, University of California, Santa Barbara.

Johnson, J. 2000. The uniqueness of California's ethnohistoric record. *Proceedings of the Society for California Archaeology* 13, 1–10.

Kehoe, A. 1989. *The Ghost Dance: ethnohistory and revitalization.* Forth Worth: Holt, Rinehart & Winston.

Kroeber, A. 1919. The superorganic. *American Anthropologist,* NS 19, 163–213.

Kroeber, A. 1925. *Handbook of the Indians of California.* Washington, DC: Bureau of American Ethnology Bulletin.

Kroeber, A. 1936. Culture element distributions III: area and climax. *University of California Publications in American Archaeology and Ethnology* 37, 101–16.

Kroeber, A. 1939. *Cultural and natural areas of Native America.* Berkeley: University of California Press.

Kroeber, T. 1970. *Alfred Kroeber: a personal configuration.* Berkeley: University of California Press.

Landberg, L. 1965. *The Chumash Indians of Southern California.* Highland Park: Southwest Museum Press.

Latta, F. 1977. *The Handbook of Yokuts Indians.* Santa Cruz: Bear State Books.

Lightfoot, K. and Parrish, O. 2009. *California Indians and their environment: an introduction.* Berkeley: University of California Press.

Lightfoot, K., Wake, T., and Schiff, A. 1991. *The archaeology and ethnohisotory of Fort Ross, California. Vol. I: Introduction.* Berkeley: Contributions to the University of California Archaeological Research Facility.

Lyman, R. and O'Brien, M. 2003. Cultural traits: units of analysis in early twentieth-century anthropology. *Journal of Anthropological Research* 59, 225–50.

Merriam, C. 1955. *Studies in California Indians.* Berkeley and Los Angeles: University of California Press.

Merriam, C. 1967. Ethnographic notes on California Indian Tribes III. Ethnological notes on Central California Indian tribes. *Reports of the University of California Archaeological Survey* 68, 267–393.

Merriam, C. 1970. Indian Rancheria names in four mission records. *Papers on California Ethnography. Contributions of the University of California Archaeological Research Facility* 9, 29–58.

Milliken, R. 1995. *A time of little choice: the disintegration of tribal culture in the San Francisco Bay Area 1768–1810.* Menlo Park, CA: Ballena Press.

Mooney, J. 1896. *The Ghost Dance religion and the Sioux outbreak of 1890.* Fourteenth Annual Report (Part 2) of the Bureau of Ethnology to the Smithsonian Institution, 1892–1893. Washington, DC: Government Printing Office.

Moses, L. G. 1979. Jack Wilson and the Indian Service: the response of the BIA to the Ghost Dance Prophet. *American Indian Quarterly* 5, 295–316.

Myers, L. 2004. Subtle shifts and radical transformations in hunter-gatherer research in American anthropology: Julian Steward's contributions and achievements. In A. Barnard (ed.), *Hunter-gatherers in history, archaeology and anthropology,* 175–86 Oxford: Berg.

Peelo, S. 2009. Baptism among the Salinan neophytes of Mission San Antonio De Padua: investigating the ecological hypothesis. *Ethnohistory* 55, 589–624.

Phillips, G. 1993. *Indians and intruders in Central California, 1769–1849.* Norman: University of Oklahoma Press.

Phillips, G. 2004. *Bringing them under subjection: California's Tejón Indian reservation and beyond, 1852–1864.* Lincoln: University of Nebraska Press.

Pinkoski, M. 2008. Julian Steward, American anthropology, and colonialism. *Histories of Anthropology Annual* 4, 72–204.

Powell, J. (ed.) 1881. Report of the Director, *First Annual Report of the Bureau of Ethnography, to the Secretary of the Smithsonian Institution, 1879–'80.* Washington, DC: Smithsonian Institution.

Powers, S. 1977. *Tribes of California.* Berkeley: University of California Press.

Preston, W. 1996. Serpent in Eden: dispersal of foreign diseases into pre-Mission California. *Journal of California and Great Basin Anthropology* 18, 1–37.

Ray, V. and Lurie, N. 1954. The contributions of Lewis and Clark to ethnography. *Journal of the Washington Academy of Sciences* 44, 358–70.

Robinson, D. 2010. Resolving archaeological and ethnographic tensions: a case study from South-Central California. In D. Garrow and T. Yarrow (eds), *Archaeological anthropology: understanding similarities, exploring differences,* 84–109. Oxford: Oxbow.

Ronaansen, S., Clemmer, R., and Rudden, M. 1999. Rethinking cultural ecology, mulitilinear evolution, and expert witnesses: Julian Steward and the Indian Claims Commission Proceedings. In R. Clemmer, L. Myers, and M. Rudden (eds), *Julian Steward and the Great Basin: the making of an anthropologist,* 170–202. Salt Lake City: University of Utah Press.

Rusco, E. 1999. Julian Steward, the Western Shoshones, and the Bureau of Indian Affairs: a failure to communicate. In R. Clemmer, L. Myers, and M. Rudden (eds), *Julian Steward and the Great Basin: the making of an anthropologist*, 85–127. Salt Lake City: University of Utah Press.

Seacrest, S. 2003. *When the Great Spirit died: the destruction of the California Indians 1850–1860*. Fresno: Craven Street Press.

Silliman, S. 2004. *Lost laborers in colonial California: Native Americans and the archaeology of Rancho Petaluma*. Tucson: University of Arizona Press.

Smoak, G. 2006. *Ghost Dances and identity: prophetic religion and American Indian ethnogenesis in the nineteenth century*. Berkeley: University of California Press.

Spier, L. 1935. The Prophet Dance of the Northwest and its derivatives: the source of the Ghost Dance. *General Series in Anthropology* 1, 2–74.

Steward, J. 1938. Basin-Plateau Aboriginal sociopolitical groups. *Bureau of American Ethnology Bulletin* 120, 1–346.

Stewart, O. 1966. Tribal distributions and boundaries in the Great Basin. In W. D'Azevedo, W. Davis, D. Fowler, and W. Suttles (eds), *The current status of anthropological research in the Great Basin, 1964*, 167–238. Reno: University of Nevada Press.

Stewart, O. 1970. The question of Bannock Territory. In E. Swanson Jr. (ed.), *Languages and cultures of Western North America: essays in honor of Sven S Liljeblad*, 201–31. Pocatello: Idaho State University Press.

Taylor, A. 1860-3. Notes: the Indianology of California. San Francisco: *The California Farmer and Journal of Useful Sciences* 13(3)–20(12).

Thornton, R. 1986. *We shall live again: the 1870 and 1890 Ghost Dance movements as demographic revitalization*. Cambridge: Cambridge University Press.

Timbrook, J. 2007. *Chumash ethnobotany: plant knowledge among the Chumash people of Southern California*. Berkeley: Heyday Books.

Verndon, M. 2010. 'The superorganic' or Kroeber's hidden agenda. *Philosophy of the Social Sciences* 40, 375–98.

Wallace, A. 1956. Revitalization movements. *American Anthropologist* 58, 264–81.

Woodward, L. and Macri, M. 2005. J. P. Harrington database project: an archival resource for anthropologists, archaeologists, and native communities. *Journal of California and Great Basin Anthropology* 25, 235–9.

CHAPTER 47

EXPLORING HUNTER-GATHERER-FISHER COMPLEXITY ON THE PACIFIC NORTHWEST COAST OF NORTH AMERICA

SEAN O'NEILL

THE growing body of anthropological and archaeological knowledge of the peoples of the Pacific Northwest Coast (NWC) remains an excellent arena for analysing the rise of social complexity and specific aspects of complexity such as rites involved in competitive feasting. Opportunities for direct observation of significant remnants of pre-contact Aboriginal cultures, and reconstructive 'memory' anthropology of these, are long gone. However, hunter-gatherer research has run through a number of different theoretical paradigms and models for analysis of what knowledge we have retained and are gaining through archaeology. It is crucial that current researchers maintain a balanced and even-handed critical assessment of all work done to date (Jordan 2008; Kelly 1995), at all possible scales of spatial and temporal magnitude (Ames 1991).

The study of hunter-gatherer (and in this case, -fisher) societies can contribute immeasurably to studies of the rise of socio-political complexity, by providing a 'bottom-up' model (as opposed to a 'state-down' approach, which is potentially more misleading: Arnold 1996b, 2). The wealth of the ethnographic record of the NWC is a boon to any workers interested in hunter-gatherers generally, the conditions for the rise (and fall) of socio-political complexity, or any other aspects of human prehistory (reviewed in Carlson 1990 and Suttles and Jonaitas 1990; also see Ames 1991; 1995; 2004; Arnold 1996b; 1996c; Hayden 1996a; Jordan 2008; Maschner 1991). The coast provides an ideal theoretical testing ground and source of ideas for these various studies:

> As researchers came increasingly to understand that they were dealing with hunter-gatherers in the past whose political, social, and economic organizations were unlike those of modern and ancient generalized hunter-gatherers, they turned more and more to the ethnographic

literature of the Northwest Coast to gain an understanding of what affluent foragers were like. Almost all interpretations of complexity among hunter-gatherers are dependent on that literature.

(Ames and Maschner 1999, 29)

As a starting point, this chapter discusses the potential analytical richness of this ethnology, illustrated with a case study describing later anthropological uses of the literature in interpreting one important strand of social complexity—competitive feasting, in the specific forms of the potlatch. We begin here, because in terms of historiography, this is where anthropological research concerning the NWC started. Only much later, in the past two generations, did more scientific, diachronic archaeological knowledge of coastal peoples' prehistories improve dramatically. This research supports explanations of the rise of social complexity on the NWC. Relatively speaking, this new strand of work on the coast is still in its infancy as a discipline, with many opportunities for uncovering new evidence and interpretation to come (reviewed in Carlson 1990; see also Ames and Maschner 1999; Arnold 1996a; Carlson 1983; Matson and Coupland 1995; Matson et al. 2008). Here, a second case study will look at more recent general attempts to hypothesize the rise of complexity on the coast from its archaeology. Along the way it will be seen that this anthropological and archaeological knowledge has been shaped by the vagaries and myriad biases of a specific history of research, but its sheer abundance provides fertile ground for new researchers.

The Culture Area

The Pacific Northwest Coast has been defined as a distinct 'culture area', meaning a geographic region with a regularized environment and a complex of uniform cultural characteristics with a related archaeological time sequence (Kroeber 1939; Wissler 1975). This general area has been circumscribed differently by scholars over the past century with major differing schemes proposed by Wissler, Kroeber, and Drucker (reviewed in Suttles 1990b, 10–11). Although for Drucker (1955; 1965) and Suttles (1990a) the area spans the coast from the Yakutat Bay on the Alaskan panhandle down to northern California, this chapter treats primarily with Carlson's (1983) more limited demarcation for an archaeological study area, from the Yakutat Bay to the Olympic Peninsula in Washington State. The area stretches from the coast inland up to one hundred miles, depending upon the terrain of the coastal range and access by rivers, the famous 'grease trails' developed to ease trade with inland areas, and the expansive Fraser River delta (Figure 47.1).

Traditionally, hunter-gatherer groups had been thought of as egalitarian in their ideologies and actions: in this schema, sharing behaviours superseded those of individual self-aggrandizement or kinship favour. However, since the 1960s there has been a necessary movement away from thinking of hunter-gatherers as simple egalitarian bands (Jordan 2008), beginning with simple binary oppositions that distinguish them: simple versus complex; immediate consumption versus delayed consumption; foragers versus collectors; and so on. More recently, fields plotting a wide range of multivariate states, cross-cutting categories such as technological complexity, economic complexity, social complexity, and symbolic complexity have been established (Zvelebil 1998, 7). This development has led to

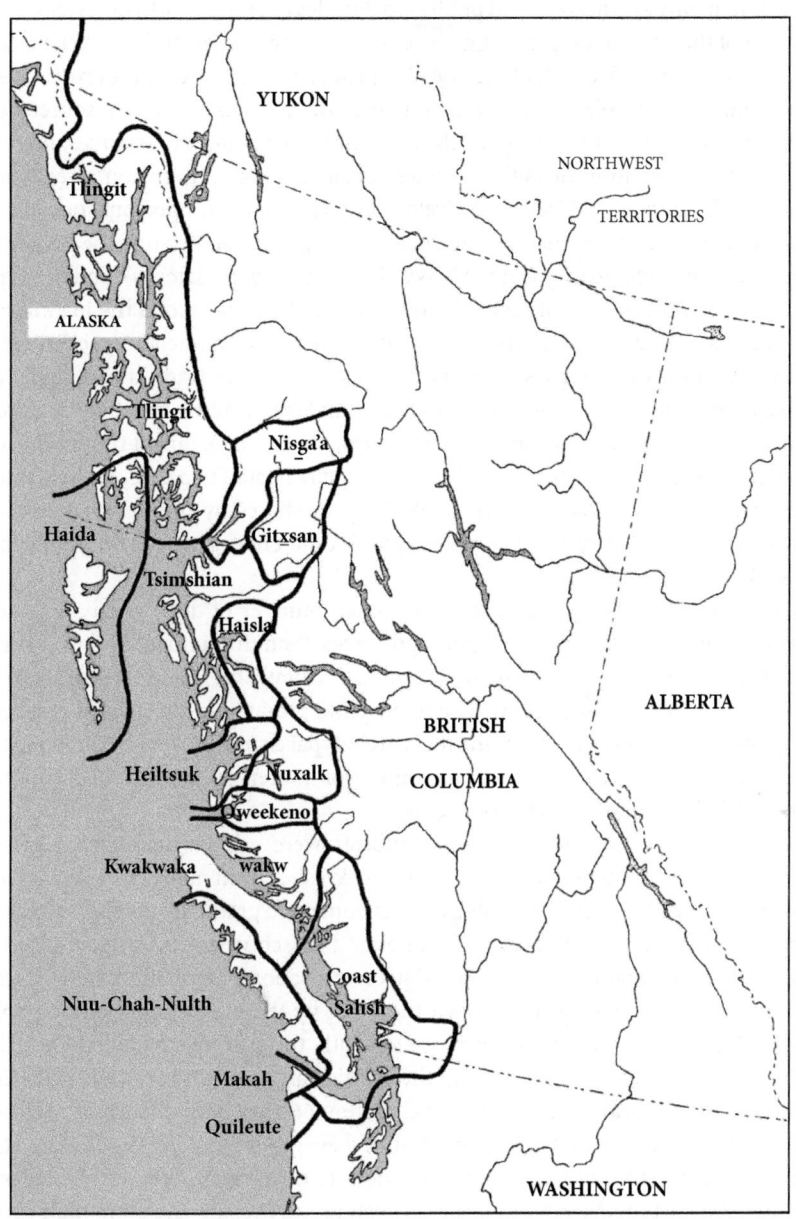

FIGURE 47.1 Pacific Northwest Coast culture area (after Shearar 2000).

one of the three major challenges in hunter-gatherer research set out by Burch (discussed in Jordan 2008, 459): with so much variability, what is the use of comparative categories, if every human group emerges as *sui generis*, a one-of-a-kind cultural system?

The myriad reports of the coastal peoples made during the golden age of ethnography c.1868–1937 (often only synthesized and published decades after fieldwork) describe cultures that bear most of the anthropological signatures of social complexity. In fact, Zvelebil (1998, 7) cites the Haida and the Kwakiutl of the NWC as primary examples of complexity. Overall, the 'salient features of complex hunter-gatherers include specialised use of resources, storage, investment in complex technology, delayed return, ownership of resources, increased sedentism, higher population densities, greater social ranking and erosion of egalitarian ideology…' (Zvelebil 1998, 8). Elsewhere, Zvelebil also adds to the list personal or clan ownership of resources, the emergence of 'big men' enjoying ascribed status, the ceremonial enhancement of social reciprocity (on the NWC, in the form of potlatches), and the expansion of trading networks (Zvelebil 1998, 7). To these could also be added the institution of slavery, the practice of warfare, the construction of monumental architecture requiring large organized supra-kin work groups, secondary product creation for trade, and a highly conventionalized symbolic art. Tracking comparative complexity trait by trait between groups is problematic, because no two groups will possess exactly the same mix of traits: 'The identification of complexity among hunter-gatherers is usually related to particular case studies, and covers a wide range of attributes, not all of which are shared by any single society: consequently we have relative degrees of complexity with different organisational implications' (Zvelebil 1998, 8).

However, if a careful score were kept of the actual number of designated attributes of complexity each hunter-gatherer study group possesses, then the cultures of the Northwest Coast would surely be among those carrying the most in total. This is one of the reasons why the continued study of these cultures will be so vital and productive for the next generation of hunter-gatherer scholars. They form the most archetypal example of delayed return/complex hunter-gatherers: 'The classic debating ground [for hunter-gatherer studies] appears to remain the Northwest Coast' (Jordan 2008, 460).

However, we cannot assume that these cultures were all 'survivals' from pristine, pre-contact societies, unpolluted by contact with the West. Indeed many of these characteristics have been shown through archaeology to have emerged gradually through prehistory, for at least five millennia back (Ames 1991; Ames and Maschner 1999; Carlson 1983; 1990; Maschner 1991; Matson and Coupland 1995; Matson et al. 2008). These traits were observed to be present in all the major groups down the coast by the pre-eminent ethnographers doing work in the region. Running from north to south, these groups included: the Tlingit (de Laguna 1991), the Haida (Swanton 1905), the Tsimishian (Garfield 1939), the Bella Coola (McIlwraith 1948), the Kwakiutlan (Boas and Codere 1966), the Nuu-chah-nulth (Drucker 1955; 1965), and the Salish (Barnett 1939). Across all of these groups, indeed, the observed traits of hunter-gatherer complexity were sedentism (despite no agrarian practices), ownership of corporeal and incorporeal properties, the competence to prepare and store high-protein foodstuffs for up to six months, stratified 'rank' societies (as defined by Fried 1967), with permanent elites bearing ascribed status, a commoner class and a slave class, intensely competitive feasting ceremonies that consolidated social loyalty and material debt within households and between them, other sophisticated technologies including monumental architecture (primarily in the form of the residential 'Big Houses' and large fishing weirs), wide regional trading networks, warfare by fleets of war canoes, craft specialization at both the individual and community levels, and highly developed conventions in 'non-functional', symbolic visual arts. Although there is a recognizable homogeneity in these characteristics down the coast, there was considerable variation between the groups. Moreover, even within groups it is not assumed that these traits naturally belonged in 'packages' together, as it is more productive to think of each trait discretely, in possible various relationships to other traits, before establishing historically contingent links (Arnold 1996b; Jordan and Mace 2006; Jordan and O'Neill 2010). Although these ethnographic traits present in all groups indicate a high level of social complexity (delayed-return complex hunter-gatherer-fishers; Arnold 1996b, 4–5), it is interesting to note here too that there were other traits (or absence of them) that are more associated with the category of intermediate societies that were not present, and which confound simplistic attempts at classification. For example, there was no incipient agriculture or irrigation, and generally no observed permanent supra-village political organization in the groups; nearly all power was wielded through the agency of household and village chiefs, and (less so) clan leaders.

The Golden Age of NWC Ethnography: A Snapshot of Complexity

Academic anthropologists arrived in the region in the second half of the nineteenth century, after over a century of intensive acculturation following contacts with the Spanish, the Russians, and the British. Unlike cultural comparativists such as Morgan, Franz Boas became interested in what made cultures *distinctive*, and not the same: historical particularism. He first visited the Pacific NWC in 1886, initially among the Bella Coola; most of his fieldwork after 1905 involved the Kwakwaka'wakw of northern Vancouver Island. Half of the 10,000 pages of research he published over the next half-century about the cultures of the coast were devoted to this ethnolinguistic group. Indeed, the compass of his scholarship was so wide (some have claimed diluted), that we cannot speak of a 'Boasian school', but we know that the Boasian programme launched the empiricist theoretical orientation and long careers of many subsequent workers on the coast and elsewhere, each carrying forward a specific strand of his work.

Never afraid to go against orthodoxies of his times, Boas rejected the reductionist methods of cultural comparison professed by social evolutionists such as Morgan, Taylor, and Brinton (Harris 1968). Most significantly, he came out firmly against the dogma of conventional Spencerian social evolutionism, on three counts. Firstly, he was a staunch opponent of biological/racial determinism, and insisted on universal rights and equality for all human beings, and in a prescient way railed against any form of essentialist thought, holding that 'A clear connection between race and personality has never been established' (Herskovits 1953, 7). Secondly, he rejected parallelism—the idea that civilizations everywhere had developed or were developing along the same unilinear continuum (albeit at different rates of change) from savagery, through barbarism, to civilization. Thirdly, he vehemently disagreed with the presumptuous, wholly self-serving Eurocentric imperial idea of 'progress' (Harris 1968). His proposed remedy to all of these problems and objections was, in each particular case, to attempt to understand cultures in their own terms and through their own internal dynamics. Boas emphasized the respectful study of cultural complexity and ritual life. He believed that any human society would be found to rival the sophistication of modern Europe, if observed and understood properly.

The World Boas Found

At the beginning of the ethnographic era the populations of indigenous peoples in the region had already been depleted by newly encountered diseases brought by the white colonists, and Western-style settlements had risen with forts, formed primarily by the Hudson's Bay Company. Many of the survivors had already relocated to new towns such as Fort Rupert, and were working in the new cash economy (Campbell et al. 2003; Codere 1950; Oliver 2010).

By the time Boas arrived, many Aboriginals lived somewhere in between the traditional world of their ancestors and the new Western capitalist order, often dividing their time between traditional subsistence practices and exploiting the new cash economy. It was acceptable for a man to fish for his family and then sell the surplus in town markets. The special gifting ceremonies, called potlatches, had been outlawed by the Canadian government and had been forced to go 'underground' two years before Boas began his initial research. This was the irrevocable, culturally hybridized world that Boas first encountered. Of course he was not the only anthropologist of his generation working on the Pacific NWC: other researchers under his direction of the Jesup North Pacific Expedition focused their fieldwork on other groups (e.g. Swanton among the Haida and later the Tlingit)—and in the wider region and beyond—in Alaska and Siberia. Subsequently there were a full five scholarly generations of Boas-influenced students who worked within a humanities-based orientation on the coast, with direct observation and reconstructive methods, or new interpretations of data.

There were other kinds of researchers, as well. Kalervo Oberg arrived in the early 1930s and used different methods of observation and analysis. Oberg (1973) can be seen as an exemplary 'non-Boasian' researcher, having trained as an economist in the eastern United States, and being more interested in the systematic dynamics of 'getting a living' within the three Tlingit communities he studied. Whereas the work of Boas and his students could be seen to be deliberately 'particularist', in keeping with Boas's theoretical aims, Oberg was not only interested in things that distinguished groups, but also what might be similar functional adaptive traits used in common. He also carefully focused on the social roles of individual agents and specialized groups in making functional contributions to the livelihood of their communities. Boas and his students had taken a greater interest in literary, dramatic, and visual/artistic cultural products, at the expense of economics and the understanding of social structure. Furthermore, there is an uneven coverage of these chosen materials between groups, as they appear to have emphasized wholly different strands of traditions within different communities. Beyond the work of Oberg, there were clear efforts made in the mid-twentieth century to redress the balance with more systematic comparative surveys of cultural traits (e.g. Drucker 1950; Jorgensen 1980), which compare structural and cultural complexity on a more like-for-like basis between different groups.

Beginning in the first half of the twentieth century, as opportunities for direct observation of even partially traditional Aboriginal cultures had disappeared, workers moved research forward in different ways. Some turned to the polemical reinterpretation of specific cultural traditions such as the potlatch (Benedict 1936; Codere 1950; Drucker and Heizer 1967; Jonaitas 1992).

The analysis and explanation of the potlatch itself has a long and complex history in anthropology, and provides an interesting indication of the wider and greatly differing theoretical approaches we can observe in work on the NWC in the half-century after Boas worked. These serve to underline how different 'what we know' can be, depending perhaps on current interpretive trends in hunter-gatherer studies, the wider concerns of archaeology and anthropology, the spirit of the age, and our own individual (and potentially myopic) personal and social interests.

Case Study One: Parsing the Potlatch

In rendering the potlatch, at first the missionaries' view held sway: the potlatch represented nothing more than bizarre, pathological, wasteful consumption—Herbert Spencer might say *savage*—and was often violent and dangerous. Even without the judgemental religious dimension, it seemed to confirm Veblen's notion of the absurdity of demonstrative, conspicuous consumption. But later, in her book *Patterns of Culture*, one of Boas's PhD students, Ruth Benedict, influenced by Boas's increasing interest in the relationship between individual personality and culture, attempted an idealist interpretation of the potlatch ritual (Benedict 1963, 125–60). The thrust of her overall argument was that each civilization and culture runs with a single main idea at its core, and in comparing cultures these governing ideas can be highly variable and seemingly arbitrary. The potlatch was practised in various forms across almost the entire NWC, and—according to Benedict—was based on the need for the tribal chiefs to compete with and ultimately *shame* their peers into inferior status positions—'fighting with property', as it was called. Property (such as large numbers of newly acquired Hudson's Bay Company blankets, and items from the highly valued copper complex) would be offered at potlatch feasts with the tacit understanding that the recipient would later return the gift (with ample interest) at another potlatch. This differed from the pattern observed in the gifting networks of the Kula Ring, as the reciprocation had to be direct. Meanwhile, such gifts as the blankets were never actually used, but were seen as a form of stored currency. Gifts could not be refused or left unpaid later without the loss of social status ('face') on the part of the intended recipient/debtor. Benedict goes on to describe the so-called 'Dionysian' practices involved in the potlatch, where valuable property is actually destroyed and at times the unflappable, unmoving guests' lives actually endangered during the event (for instance, by large houses being burnt down, or in the killing of slaves), in a show of conspicuous consumption and fearlessness on the part of the host. During the ceremony, there were often speeches made by seconds of the host—explaining that the host was so powerful, he could (and would) literally push his guests out of existence. Benedict characterized these impulses as 'megalomaniac paranoid'. (However, it is impossible for any impressionable youngster who grew up with the intentionally humorous hubris of Muhammad Ali to read some of the transcribed potlatch speeches without being amused by their possible intended theatricality—even tongue-in-cheek farce. Is it possible they were taken too seriously by Western observers such as Boas, who was never to master the nuances of the languages in tone and inflection? Harris (1968) supports this notion.)

There are a number of challenges inherent in understanding the potlatch. Firstly, there is the temporal issue—though often published much later, most of the ethnographies were researched between the early 1890s and the late 1930s—a relatively narrow window of time (see Drucker 1955, 211 and Suttles and Jonaitas 1990 for basic bibliographies). At this point in history, significant cultural responses to increasing intrusion over the previous century, precipitated after the opening of the Oregon Trail, were already happening. The introduction of guns had raised the stakes of warfare, thus the vital necessity to shore up status and alliances through potlatching. Much greater levels of wealth were now known through trade with whites, and disease had brought about a radical decline in population (Boyd 1990) that left many hereditary privileges, titles, and lands 'up for grabs'. Greater competition may have been spurred by a heightened sense of uncertainty and insecurity in the face of Western influence; competition itself is seen by some as the prime mover in the development of greater complexity (e.g. Hayden 1996a). The potlatches that Boas and his students wrote about probably represent a certain radical transitional stage of development that cannot be thought of as in any way stable through time. It is now impossible to think, as nineteenth-century historians did (then working with the erroneous idea that Native Americans had only arrived in North America a few centuries earlier), that these cultures were in any way static and unchanging. Nor should we think of these specific potlatches as a kind of high watermark in an evolutionary chain of ceremonies, in terms of 'progress' (a caution that applies to any aspect of the so-called Developed Northwest Coast Pattern; see Maschner 1991).

Secondly, the anthropological approach to 'understanding mentalities' makes for engaging—almost literary—reading, but leaves out social and ecological contexts almost entirely. We are given phenomenological accounts of live events, with very little data on social relationships and the natural environment—data points that would be very important to understand if we would know more about key factors that affect change through time, and that must be held to account in understanding complexity. We need a much bigger picture before building theories. Inferring patterns of historical development, Benedict herself suggests that the potlatch had 'evolved' from war practices:

> The fact that the slayer could claim the prerogatives of a victim in warfare undoubtedly reflects earlier historical conditions when the characteristic North-West Coast prestige conflict was carried on by warfare, and the contest with property was of lesser importance.
>
> (1963, 151–2)

The emphasis on psychological speculations keeps us focused on *descriptions* of momentary events, with no long-term explanatory power for tracking cultural change or continuity, or social complexity.

Interactionist theories presented another viewpoint. Marcel Mauss (1990) agreed on the importance of analysing the NWC potlatch, but not as the expression of a single, simplistic functional idea. He saw it as perhaps the ultimate manifestation of obligation-building gifting practices, which he believed intertwined many powerful social dimensions, both material and ideas-based: jurisprudence, religion and spiritualism, economic pragmatism, social structure and implicit mechanisms of solidarity, military allegiance—and even aesthetic enjoyment. For this reason, he claimed that the potlatch must be considered a 'total social fact' representing a suite of 'total services of an agonistic type' (Mauss 1990, 7). He adopted the template of the potlatch in the comparative analysis of the gifting practices of other societies. He was attempting to understand, through the inextricable network of rites, a general theory of how societies are bound together through interactive patterns of obligation. The underpinning mechanisms were the unquestionable obligation to give, to receive, and to reciprocate at appropriate scales. Since the gift as a spiritual entity was essentially a part of the giver, it must always be returned to him (with high interest). On the surface, this was all positioned as voluntary activity, but failure to deliver on any of these basic types of obligation resulted in a failure of perceived status, and a real loss of social power. Despite manifest intentions of goodwill or aggression, the real latent function of the institution of gifting was a constantly escalating alliance between groups.

Others such as Lévi-Strauss followed Mauss in regarding the potlatch as a total social fact, but went further in emphasizing its function in reinforcing overall social structure and complexity (Rosman and Rubel 1971). If status among elites could rise and fall from one generation to the next in dynastic relations, then the potlatch could be seen as the central mechanism of social mobility, moving all participants—hosts and guests—either up or down the scale. Rosman and Rubel (1971) carried this work further, examining each major ethnolinguistic group's potlatching practices, and carefully analysing the functional relationships between social structure and marriage residence rules, the specific obligations of host and guests (who assumed which role and why), and the precise relative meaning of the specific customs observed. They concluded that although the potlatch was practised down the entire coast, and appeared similar in many ways, its mechanisms and social functions were very different, depending on the structural dynamics of each specific group—for example, possessing specific traits such as level of egalitarianism, allowable social mobility (or not). In the north of the region, among the Haida, Tlingit, and the Tsimshian, social roles and status were more predetermined; the potlatch served to reinforce these patterns. However, in the south there was more acephalous (literally meaning 'without head, or established leader') fluidity of prestige and authority through meritocracy; there was more of a sense that titles and status could be earned, and primogeniture—which passed power to eldest sons—could be superseded. Here the potlatch functioned to demonstrate—through competitive hosting—who was the more worthy for promotion. Interestingly, there are also material-culture reflections of these same dynamics: in the north, large residential house plans were set and immutable, whilst in the more egalitarian south, the classic 'longhouses' could grow as needed by modular accretion, depending upon the changing needs of an extended family over many generations, and the protean status of individuals.

Towards the middle of the twentieth century, some critics moved completely away from idealism and sought purely materialist explanations for the functions of social institutions and customs on the Northwest Coast. A vociferous critic of Boas and his methods all through the 1940s, Leslie White attacked the psychological approach of the Boasian programme (Harris 1968).

Cultural ecology became the dominant theoretical programme for hunter-gatherer research; this coincided with an expansion in archaeological interests on the NWC. Here it was cultural responses to environmental constraints and opportunities that should be consulted first in understanding changes and continuity in lifeways. Patterns of ecological adaptation were sought, and a clear distinction made between traits and elements that were more determined versus freer cultural choices that were less so. The emphasis was taken away from the Boasian understanding of 'mentalities', to people as rational, pragmatic actors who will optimize their advantages in any given environment. Overall, this approach sought to put people back into their ecological contexts; it took into account pressures in a real physical world on the outside, rather than a phenomenological, mentalist view from the inside. With ecology in mind, Julian Steward (1955, 173–7) tracked the movement of potlatching practices from the Northwest Coast inland to the Carrier group, and from there further eastwards to groups over the continental divide. He found a direct relationship between the availability of surplus resources and the propensity to potlatch. As the groups became more generalized hunter-gatherers, driven to exploit more diverse and less abundant fields from which to procure resources, with less opportunity for easy procurement and storage of food and other resources, the elaborateness of potlatches diminished.

Due to the fragmentary evidence on elite ceremonies and events, we do not have a full picture of the actual cultural ecology of the nineteenth century on the Northwest Coast:

> The mundane facts of subsistence were not only less attractive to ethnographers than were myths, feasts, and rituals, but they were also less amenable to collection by single observations or texts provided by individual informants... The relation of food getting, population dynamics, work organization, and settlement pattern to these factors was considered as uncomplicated as it was uninteresting.
>
> (Netting 1986, 29)

However, all of this is not to say that one could not effectively reconstruct a plausible cultural ecology using the ethnographic descriptions and other sources, drawing on native oral traditions, human geography, archaeological data, and linguistics (Ames and Maschner 1999, 19).

Piddocke dismissed the explanations of the environmental possibilists—that the wasteful potlatches existed because of an over-abundance of food stocks, based on a kind of 'Garden of Eden' ecological model (Bettinger 1991, 54). Piddocke maintained food was never abundant in all places in the region, and at all times. In fact, he posited a diametrically opposed contextual model for explaining the social functions of the potlatch: they were better construed to be forms of the interdependent redistribution of social storage, or a kind of long-term social insurance. Kinship groups with surpluses could redistribute resources to those with shortages, dramatically marking the occasions where debts were incurred (therefore providing the pretext for prestige-seeking). Of course, each group would hope that they would receive help in the future, if needed. Over longer periods of time—perhaps decades or even generations—a social and environmental homeostasis could be achieved. Also, the potlatch could provide a constant 'equalizer' between the very wealthy tribes, who had rights to superior resource areas, and the tribes with poorer hereditary holdings—in a system upholding further social complexity. Addressing these imbalances in this way functioned to curb aggression and land-grabbing wars, if the wealthier chiefs did not *really* expect payment with high interest back from poorer neighbours. Merely the *idea* of indebtedness could bind tribes to each other. In addition, through these emotional and cathartic ceremonies, wider communities remained strong and well-bonded through temporary military alliances in the face of outside enemies.

Bettinger (1991) was highly critical of all of these ideas, because he questioned the notion that the potlatch carried with it any social benefit at all. He was critical of the processualist preoccupation with modelling organic stabilizing tendencies within societies that respond to changes from the outside by making reflexive changes on the inside, in an ongoing 'balancing act' that achieves a kind of homeostasis. If there were no real short- or long-term benefits of the potlatch—if by its very nature it was indeed dysfunctional and maladaptive, despite the conscious or unconscious intentions of the participants—then from the point of view of cultural ecology, we must return to the explanatory 'prime mover' as indeed being the quest for personal prestige, at all costs (see also Maschner 1991, discussed below). Bettinger does not close his case here. He simply states that no one has delved far enough into researching the total social and natural environmental systems surrounding the potlatch to prove that it provided long-term social and biological reproductive benefits for the actors involved (Bettinger 1991, 57). This was intended more as a research challenge than a scholarly assertion.

From the work of previous generations, we have moved from a mentalist understanding of culture, to social context and structure, and on to cultural ecology. In the past two decades, scholars such as Hayden (1996a) have generally rejected models from behavioural ecology, which is similar to cultural ecology, but brings selectionist theory in from evolutionary biology to explain diachronic selection of cultural attributes (Jordan 2008). Here cultural traits that enable inclusive fitness are reproduced more, commensurate with the higher reproductive rates of their bearers.

All of these issues concerning the potlatch underline vital differences in interpretation over the past one hundred years, and these differing approaches could apply to many other phenomena, such as social structure, the institution of slavery on the coast, and the development of technological traditions.

Towards Diachronic Explanations of Complexity

Through archaeology, we know that the region of the NWC has been inhabited for more than ten thousand years (Ames and Maschner 1999; Carlson 1983; Carlson 1990; Matson and Coupland 1995). Approximately five thousand years ago, due to dramatic sea-level changes and the shifting topography of the land after the last glacial recession (Duff 1963), a new superabundance of salmon and other anadromous fish stocks coming up the rivers of the region spurred population intensification and the nascent rise of sophisticated river-fishing technologies. Before the advent of Western industrialism, these stocks were *r-selected* food sources—meaning, it was impossible to over-harvest them (Hayden 1996a). At the same time, new social arrangements in the direction of greater complexity appear to have formed in a self-intensifying loop of development (Ames 1991; Carlson and Dalla Bona 1996, 218; Maschner 1991). With advances in riverine fishing technologies, greater amounts of fish could be procured, particularly during the salmon runs; eventually, ways were found to process and store the food safely for the long term. Cybulski has demonstrated the use of boxes for burial from nearly four millennia ago (Matson and Coupland 1995); because of

Table 47.1 Some causal factors in the rise of complexity towards the 'Developed Northwest Coast Pattern'

SALMON HORIZON: 5000 BP	
Rises in sea levels create new abundance of fising resources	• New riverine fishing strategies developed
	• Preparation techniques for immediate consumption
RED CEDAR HORIZON: 4000 BP	
More abundant stands of *Thuja plicata* enable expanded wood working	• Preparation techniques for delayed consumption
	• Crafting of airtight boxes for food storage
	• Monumental architecture with multi-family houses
	• Rise of social complexity
BONE USED IN TOOLMAKING: 1500 BP	
Move beyond stone technologies	• Enhanced fishing technologies for littoral
	• Greater prowess of ocean-going canoes
	• Wider trade systems/regional contact

the ability to stockpile foodstuffs for the long-term in similar boxes, social storage could engender property ownership and concomitant social stratification in a society, leading in the direction of power dynamics based on social inequality, for the simple reason that anyone who had the social power to maintain stored food resources had power over anyone who did not. The next important horizon was the greater proliferation of red cedar stands on the coast (*Thuja plicata*), between three and four thousand years ago, providing more raw materials for large-scale wood-carving projects and enabling monumental architecture. The multi-family rectangular houses that evolved from the smaller single-family pithouses of the intermontane Fraser Plateau and Basin Complex to the east of the coastal range would provide increasingly large and efficient storage facilities for a multitude of square boxes and rectangular chests, which would in turn increase the potential wealth and holdings of an elite property-holding family. Around fifteen hundred years ago, there was another technological horizon—the transition from the use of stone to the use of bone in many everyday tools, such as fishhooks (Carlson 1983), and the significant introduction of the bow and arrow for hunting and potentially for warfare. Maschner (1991) points to a difference in coastal settlement patterns after this horizon, evolving from smaller settlements in protected topography to larger settlements on straighter coastlines, drawing resources to the central place from a much larger area. Meanwhile, carved forms and iconography, well-known earmarks of the Developed Northwest Coast Pattern (Matson and Coupland 1995), became more elaborate. This pattern is characterized by monumental architecture, highly sophisticated wood carving and painting, adroit fishing and hunting strategies and techniques, complex social stratification involving elites, commoners, and slaves, cross-cut by clan affiliations, and a culture focused on the pursuit of high prestige and the acquisition and redistribution of valuable goods.

These are the rough contours of the long-term prehistory of the area, as summarized in Table 47.1. At least three centuries ago, the first Western contact came about through the scattered voyages of explorers: according to legend the Spanish explorer Juan de Fuca discovered the strait that today bears his name, to the south of Vancouver Island, in 1592; but this has not been confirmed (Suttles 1990c, 70). In the first half of the eighteenth century, the Russians arrived; Vitus Bering made the first recorded contact with the Tlingit in 1841. The historical era had begun.

CASE STUDY TWO: INTERPRETING COMPLEXITY FROM ARCHAEOLOGY

In attempting to reconstruct cultural change and continuity over the millennia, many archaeologists interpreting data from the coast have been explicitly concerned with understanding patterns of rising (or falling) complexity over time. These interests have reflected current debates in hunter-gatherer research worldwide in the past five decades, with its various vicissitudes and 'paradigm shifts' (Kelly 1995; Jordan 2008). However, many of the themes that emerged in the first half of the twentieth century recur here, but with sufficiently different focuses to reform knowledge. Overall, rather than just rendering cultural complexity as a complete package of traits, fixed in time, workers have chosen to emphasize certain traceable conditions or pre-conditions of complexity, usually without an attempt to define direct cause–effect relationships between the different forces. However, some occasionally venture hypotheses about 'prime movers' and 'ultimate causes' of increasing stratification and social inequality over time, comparing wholly different strands that developed at different rates through time and impacted each other at some point in prehistory (Ames 1991; 1995; 2004; Arnold 1996a; 1996b; 1996c; Hayden 1996a; Maschner 1991).

Hayden (1996a) contended that it is competitive behaviour that may frame the rise of complex societies and social inequality, but rejected models such as optimum foraging strategies developed in human behavioural ecology as too reductive to explain all decisions made regarding competitive behaviour. He posited that the move from a society based on immediate consumption of resources to one based on delayed consumption would be possible only in environments of great abundance where personal or group property ownership of hunter-forager-fishing sites, and (crucially) of stored food, was permissible to begin with, because they posed no threat. In areas with less abundance, only an egalitarian and sharing system would be tolerated socially. Further conditions would be increased available leisure time for craft specialization and therefore the wherewithal to create secondary products that signalled status. The *r-selected* resources, the ones that could not possibly be exhausted (such as salmon on the NWC, which were highly reproductive and impossible to over-harvest in the pre-colonial world), would certainly underwrite self-aggrandizement, but 'wealth' itself would have to take other, more symbolic forms to communicate the legitimating attributes of power, in the form of 'desirable items'. Here Hayden points out that the salmon never became significant totemic symbols, simply because of their pervasiveness—they were simply not rarified enough to emphasize symbolically. Competitive feasting in the form of the potlatch functioned to provide a stage for this communication, expressed through ceremonies and the presentation of the highly refined products of craft specialization. The attributes of power enabled individuals to gain control over the labour of others, especially non-kin. Hayden concluded that 'big men' did not rise due to functionalist explanations—nobody needed the desirable items, or baubles, to survive in that environment. Hayden theorized a causal chain that started with abundant resources, the development of technologies to exploit them and store food, control over the labour needed to do this, the rise of competition for this control, and other outcomes of this, such as directing the creation of desirable items signalling status, and organized warfare. Hayden calls this *political ecology*: a process whereby individual self-aggrandizers are allowed to create a line of ascribed 'big men'.

Other workers have emphasized different causal factors in the move towards complexity on the coast in their models. Critical of employing ethnographies in the direct historical approach (the use of a set of known recent ethnographic characteristics and working back from there to understand the deeper prehistory of a region), Maschner (1991) put greater emphasis on the archaeological understanding of developing technologies for apprehending the determinants of growing complexity. Contending that the so-called 'Garden of Eden' hypothesis—positing that environmental inputs of abundance were the prime mover in growing complexity on the coast, related to the 'original affluent society' lore within earlier hunter-gatherer studies initiated by Sahlins (Sahlins 1968; see also Kelly 1995)—was a conditional factor, it was not actually the prime mover; neither were population growth or subsistence intensification, per se. It was technological development that enabled the social and political arena to change first by giving some individuals and groups more control of the environment and other people: hence the rise of inequality. In this schema, once the technology was introduced—such as the introduction of the bow and arrow fifteen hundred years ago—then 'ranking developed on the northern Northwest Coast because individuals were in a position to exert political control and get away with it' (Maschner 1991, 932).

For Ames (1991) the key to understanding complexity on the coast was population intensification. The exploitation of abundant resources can be canalized in two ways: towards exploiting a wider diversity of resources, or developing a monoculture around the intensive exploitation of one vital resource: both trends can lead to population increases. The rise of the Big Houses led to further subsistence intensification, storage, and an increasingly domesticated environment in the area around villages. These could lead to occupational differentiation between villages and increased social stratification.

As part of a research programme of cultures throughout western North America and wider concerns about employing archaeology in understanding the ebb and flow of complexity of hunter-gatherer societies, Arnold (1996b; 1996c) was interested primarily in understanding how individuals or groups came to control the labour of non-kin groups. In the case of the NWC, Arnold (1996b, 64) argues that the 'big men' did not have circumscribed, institutionalized, enforceable power over the labour of other elites and commoners, but rather negotiated labour agreements by way of a complex series of ceremonies and feasts where loans and repayments were made and alliances consolidated, but that these conditional arrangements were not made in perpetuity. In terms of representing a possible developmental stage in the complexity continuum, this was power that must continually be negotiated and compensated for in some way, and not complied with due to a monopoly of legitimate violence—a state of affairs that may indeed set the stage for subsequent circumscribed authority or absolutist stages of control, but is not the same thing (although elites who owned slaves certainly did enjoy this monopoly over them, and this power could be exercised arbitrarily and without social censure—see Donald 1997).

Exciting new archaeological data will be uncovered in the coming decades, and these will undoubtedly fuel these debates further. In the meantime, we should not assume that the different traits that we understand as constituting 'complexity' developed at the same time. Whereas we do not have solid evidence for social stratification until approximately 1500 years BP (Ames 1991; Maschner 1991), it has been well documented that the classic NWC art style was well developed up to three millennia ago (Ames 1991).

Additional Streams of Scholarship

More recently, workers have also undertaken the research for more in-depth, comprehensive histories of specific ethnolinguistic groups, with a much greater emphasis on the explicit realities of the acculturation process and the use of diverse sources (Daly 2005; de Laguna 1972; Jonaitas 1992; Oliver 2010). Another strand synthesizes comparative studies of specific aspects of cultural traditions on a full regional basis (e.g. Stewart 1984 on cedar crafts and construction using museum and private collections, ethnographies, and experimental archaeology; Rosman and Rubel 1971 on the implications of the potlatch on overall social structure, making inferences with a systematic question-based analysis of all available ethnographies; and Donald 1997 on the institution of slavery on the Northwest Coast, using similar methods).

On a temporal basis, there has been a move towards understanding cultural change and continuity over time, in a diachronic orientation, as opposed to a synchronic one. On the spatial scale, microcommunity-based anthropology has grown alongside a plethora of archaeological approaches that give us great resolution at similar scales. Since we are well aware that even the earliest anthropological observations were made long after colonization, acculturation studies have become a vital strand of research. In enlightening ways, Oliver (2010) discusses the dynamism of multifaceted, hybrid First Nations/colonial cultures, and the importance of observing changing attitudes to landscape in understanding how these developed.

As stated, archaeological research is only beginning on the coast. Innovative wet-site archaeology, developed by people such as Croes (2005), has provided much new knowledge about pre-contact lifeways in the region by unearthing well-preserved artefacts and ecofacts which are usually unrecoverable in archaeological contexts. The Ozette site on the Northwest Coast of the Olympic Peninsula in Washington State (Samuels 1991) is constituted of a set of households buried by a mud slide 300 to 500 years ago. Due to the great quantity of artefacts and architectural elements that were preserved *in situ*, we can build up a picture of a much older community that shared many traits with ethnographically recorded communities in the nineteenth and twentieth centuries. The wet-site archaeology of the Hoko River site takes us as far back as 3000 years ago (Croes 2008), with such artefacts as well-preserved basketry. Continued analysis of these finds through newly developed statistical methods will make it possible to track change and continuity for longer periods of time, perhaps returning to the rich ethnographic material-culture data as a starting point and working backwards.

Evolutionary concepts have returned to studies of the NWC, but not at all related to the social evolutionist thinking proposed by Spencer. At least since 1996, some specialists have been calling for Neo-Darwinist approaches to the explanation of culture change and diversity in this area:

> First, no other currently accessible non-Darwinian theory allows one to deal with the cultural evolution of Northwest Coast art—and similar matters—and the evolution of the biological foundations of language, cognition, and culture within a single framework... of available Darwinian approaches, coevolution seems both the richest, and the most likely to be able to absorb and utilize anthropological insights available from other paradigms... I believe that coevolutionary theory will eventually allow us to theoretically link our everyday lives with broad-scale social and cultural changes.
>
> (Ames 1996, 128)

Neo-Darwinist approaches treat cultural systems as systems of inheritance, using various data on cultural assemblages such as material artefacts, languages, and rituals, and track these in some of the same ways as genetic inheritance (in some ways, but not all). The data used can be drawn from material-culture datasets (both archaeological and anthropological) and historical linguistics. The overall focus is on long-term change and continuity—what happens across the *longue durée*. Working in this vein, Jordan and Mace (2006) looked at a variety of cultural traditions on the coast recorded by ethnographers in the 1930s, including aspects of the potlatch. Using cladistical methods imported from evolutionary biology, they compared the relationship of cultural traditions passed down through social learning. They found that the cultural tradition with the closest relationship to the long-term evolution of language on the coast was the potlatch, suggesting a significant antiquity for this institution. Similarly, Jordan and O'Neill (2010) established a clear coevolutionary relationship between language distribution and traits manifested by the residential Big Houses: the different housing traditions mapped closely onto the different language traditions.

Conclusion

This chapter has reviewed various traditions of anthropological and archaeological scholarship concerning the Pacific NWC in the past century generally, and analyses of aspects of socio-political complexity specifically. It is proposed here that although the analyses appear to be within wholly different paradigms, they can be thought of as representing areas along a continuum of analysis from psychological inputs, through social dynamics and structure, to environmental conditions, and finally to the wide variations in approaches today, which carry forward many persisting themes in new ways to unlock a history of complexity. Indeed, this region will continue to play a prominent role in the analysis and understanding of the rise of hunter-gatherer social complexity.

References

Ames, K. M. 1991. The archaeology of the longue durée: temporal and spatial scale in the evolution of social complexity on the southern Northwest Coast. *Antiquity* 65, 935–45.

Ames, K. M. 1995. Chiefly power and household production on the Northwest Coast. In T. D. Price and G. M. Feinman (eds), *Foundations of social inequality*, 155–87. London: Plenum Press.

Ames, K. M. 1996. Archaeology, style and the theory of coevolution. In H. D. G. Maschner (ed.), *Darwinian archaeologies*, 109–31. London: Plenum Press.

Ames, K. M. 2004. Supposing hunter-gatherer variability. *American Antiquity* 69, 364–74.

Ames, K. M. and Maschner, H. D. G. 1999. *Peoples of the Northwest Coast: their archaeology and prehistory*. London: Thames and Hudson.

Arnold, J. E. (ed.) 1996a. *Emergent complexity: the evolution of intermediate societies*. Archaeological Series 9. Ann Arbor, MI: International Monographs in Prehistory.

Arnold, J. E. 1996b. Organizational transformations: power and labour among complex hunter-gatherers and other intermediate societies. In J. E. Arnold (ed.), *Emergent complexity: the evolution of intermediate societies*, 59–73. Archaeological Series. Ann Arbor, MI: International Monographs in Prehistory.

Arnold, J. E. 1996c. Understanding the evolution of intermediate societies. In J. E. Arnold (ed.), *Emergent complexity: the evolution of intermediate societies*, 1–12. Archaeological Series. Ann Arbor, MI: International Monographs in Prehistory.

Barnett, H. G. 1939. *The Coast Salish of British Columbia*. Portland: University of Oregon Monographs.

Benedict, R. 1963. *Patterns of culture*. London: Routledge & Kegan Paul.

Bettinger, R. L. 1991. *Hunter-gatherers: archaeological and evolutionary theory*. New York: Plenum Press.

Boas, F. and Codere, H. (eds) 1966. *Kwakiutl ethnography*. Chicago: University of Chicago Press.

Boyd, R. T. 1990. Demographic history, 1774–1874. In W. Suttles (ed.), *Handbook of North American Indians, Volume 7: Northwest Coast*, 135–48. Washington, DC: Smithsonian Institution.

Campbell, K., Menzies, C., and Peacock, B. 2003. *B.C. First Nations studies*. Vancouver: British Columbia Ministry of Education.

Carlson, R. L. (ed.) 1983. *Indian art traditions of the Northwest Coast*. Burnaby, BC: Archaeology Press of Simon Fraser University.

Carlson, R. L. 1990. History of research in archaeology. In W. Suttles (ed.), *Handbook of North American Indians, Volume 7: Northwest Coast*. Washington, DC: Smithsonian Institution.

Carlson, R. L. and Dalla Bona, L. (eds) 1996. *Early human occupation in British Columbia*. Vancouver: UBC Press.

Codere, H. 1950. *Fighting with property: a study of Kwakiutl potlatching and warfare 1792–1930*. London: University of Washington Press.

Croes, D. 2005 *The Hoko River archaeological site complex: the rockshelter (45CA21), 1,000–100 BP, Olympic Peninsula, Washington*. Pullman, WA: Washington State University Press.

Croes, D. 2008. Northwest Coast wet-site artefacts: a key to understanding resource procurement, storage, management, and exchange. In R. G. Matson, G. Coupland, and Q. Mackie (eds), *Emerging from the mist: studies in Northwest Coast culture history*, 51–75. Vancouver: UBC Press.

Daly, R. 2005. *Our box was full: an ethnography for the Delgamuukw plaintiffs*. Vancouver: UBC Press.

de Laguna, F. 1972. *Under Mount St. Elias: the history and culture of the Yakutat Tlingit*. 3 vols. Washington, DC: Smithsonian Institution.

de Laguna, F. (ed.) 1991. *The Tlingit Indians*. New York: American Museum of Natural History.

Donald, L. 1997. *Aboriginal slavery on the northwest coast of North America*. Berkeley: University of California Press.

Drucker, P. 1950. Cultural element distributions: XXVI, Northwest Coast. *Anthropological Records* 9, 157–294.

Drucker, P. 1955. *Indians of the Northwest Coast*. New York: American Museum of Natural History.

Drucker, P. 1965. *Cultures of the north Pacific coast*. New York: Chandler.

Drucker, P. and Heizer, R. F. 1967. *To make my name good: a re-examination of the Southern Kwakiutl potlatch*. Berkeley: University of California Press.

Duff, W. 1963. Sea levels and archaeology on the Northwest Coast. In D. N. Abbott (ed.), *The world is as sharp as a knife: an anthology in honour of Wilson Duff*, 122–6. Victoria, BC: British Columbia Provincial Museum.

Fried, M. H. 1967. *The evolution of political society*. New York: Random House.

Garfield, V. 1939. *Tsimshian class and society*. Seattle: University of Washington Publications in Anthropology.

Harris, M. 1968. *The rise of anthropological theory*. New York: HarperCollins.

Hayden, B. 1991. *A complex culture of the British Columbian plateau. Traditional Stl'àtl'imx resource use*. Vancouver: UBC Press.

Hayden, B. 1996a. Competition, labor and complex hunter-gatherers. In E. S. Burch and L. J. Ellanna (eds), *Key issues in hunter-gatherer research*, 223–39. Oxford: Berg.

Hayden, B. 1996b. *The pithouses of Keatley Creek*. Vancouver: UBC Press.

Herskovits, M. J. 1953. *Franz Boas: the science of man in the making*. London: Charles Scribner's Sons.

Jonaitas, A. (ed.) 1992. *Chiefly feasts: the enduring Kwakiutl potlatch*. New York: American Museum of Natural History.

Jordan, P. D. 2008. Hunters and gatherers. In R. A. Bentley, H. D. G. Maschner, and C. Chippendale (eds), *Handbook of archaeological theories*. Plymouth: Rowman & Littlefield.

Jordan, P. D. and Mace, T. 2006. Tracking culture-historical lineages: can 'descent with modification' be linked to 'association by descent'? In C. Lipo, M. J. O'Brien, M. Collard, and S. J. Shennan (eds), *Mapping our ancestors: phylogenetic approaches in anthropology and prehistory*. London: Aldine/Transaction.

Jordan, P. D. and O'Neill, S. 2010. Untangling cultural inheritance: language diversity and long-house architecture on the Pacific northwest coast. In J. Steele, E. Cochrane, and P. Jordan (eds), *Cultural and linguistic diversity: evolutionary approaches. Philosophical Transactions of the Royal Society B* 365: 3875–88

Jorgensen, J. G. 1980. *Western Indians: comparative environments, languages, and cultures of 172 western American Indian tribes*. San Francisco: W. H. Freeman and Company.

Kelly, R. L. 1995. *The foraging spectrum: diversity in hunter-gatherer lifeways*. Washington, DC: Smithsonian Institution.

Kroeber, A. L. 1939. *Cultural and natural areas of native North America*. Berkeley: University of California Press.

McIlwraith, T. F. 1948. *The Bella Coola Indians*. Toronto: University of Toronto Press.

Maschner, H. D. G. 1991. The emergence of cultural complexity. *Antiquity* 65, 924–34.

Maschner, H. D. G. (ed.) 1996. *Darwinian archaeologies*. London: Plenum Press.

Matson, R. G. and Coupland, G. 1995. *The prehistory of the Northwest Coast.* London: Academic Press.

Matson, R. G., Coupland, G., and Mackie, Q. (eds) 2008. *Emerging from the mist: studies in Northwest Coast culture history.* Vancouver: UBC Press.

Mauss, M. 1990. *The gift: the form and reason for exchange in archaic societies.* London: W. D. Halls.

Netting, R. M. 1986. *Cultural ecology* (2nd edition). Prospect Heights, IL: Waveland Press.

Oberg, K. 1973. *The social economy of the Tlingit Indians.* Seattle: University of Washington Press.

Oliver, J. 2010. *Landscapes and social transformations on the Northwest Coast: colonial encounter in the Fraser Valley.* Tucson: University of Arizona Press.

Rosman, A. and Rubel, P. G. 1971. *Feasting with mine enemy: rank and exchange among Northwest Coast societies.* New York: Columbia University Press.

Sahlins, M. 1968. Notes on the original affluent society. In R. B. Lee and I. Devore (eds), *Man the hunter*, 85–9. Chicago: Aldine.

Samuels, S. R. 1991. *Ozette archaeological project research reports. Volume 1: House structure and floor midden.* WSU Department of Anthropology Reports of Investigations 63. National Parks Service, Pacific Northwest Regional Office.

Shearar, C. 2000. *Understanding Northwest Coast art: a guide to crests, beings and symbols.* Vancouver: Douglas & McIntyre.

Steward, J. H. (ed.) 1955. *The concept of culture change: the methodology of multilinear evolution.* Urbana: University of Illinois Press.

Stewart, H. 1984. *Cedar, tree of life to the Northwest Coast Indians.* Vancouver: Douglas & McIntyre.

Suttles, W. (ed.) 1990a. *Handbook of North American Indians, Volume 7: Northwest Coast.* Washington, DC: Smithsonian Institution.

Suttles, W. 1990b. Introduction. In W. Suttles (ed.), *Handbook of North American Indians, Volume 7: Northwest Coast*, 1–15. Washington, DC: Smithsonian Institution.

Suttles, W. 1990c. History of research: early sources. In W. Suttles (ed.), *Handbook of North American Indians, Volume 7: Northwest Coast*, 70–2. Washington, DC: Smithsonian Institution.

Suttles, W. and Jonaitas, A. 1990. History of research in ethnology. In W. Suttles (ed.), *Handbook of North American Indians, Volume 7: Northwest Coast*, 73–87. Washington, DC: Smithsonian Institution.

Swanton, J. R. 1905. Contributions to the ethnology of the Haida. Publications of the Jesup North Pacific expedition. *Memoirs of the American Museum of Natural History New York.* Leiden: E. J. Brill.

Wissler, C. (ed.) 1975. *Societies of the Plains Indians.* Reprint of volume 11 of *Anthropological Papers of the American Museum of Natural History.* New York: AMS Press.

Zvelebil, M. 1998. What's in a name: the Mesolithic, the Neolithic, and social change in the Mesolithic–Neolithic transition. In M. Edmonds and C. Richards (eds), *Understanding the Neolithic of northwest Europe*, 1–36. Glasgow: Cruithne.

CHAPTER 48

REGIONAL HUNTER-GATHERER TRADITIONS IN SOUTH-EAST ASIA

JANA FORTIER

BRILLIANTLY adapting to their environments, hunter-gatherer communities have played an important role in the history of South-East Asia (Bellwood et al. 1995; Higham 1989; Morrison and Junker 2002; Sather 1995). Many of these foraging communities have served as cultural analogies, helping scholars conjecture prehistoric economic strategies and social relations. Astute resource managers, contemporary foragers of South-East Asia have demonstrated their indigenous technical knowledge to biologists and ecological anthropologists. Today's communities of people who rely on hunting, gathering, and/or seafood demonstrate remarkable resilience. As forest and ocean resources dwindle, many families have become 'forager-bricoleurs' who strategically choose when to forage and when to spend time doing other activities. Throughout the South-East Asia region, families may also procure forest or maritime resources for trade; accept tourism work; collect government stipends; harvest crops for neighbouring farmers, etc. Yet being hunter-gatherers and foraging for wild resources remains the core foundation of their cultural identity. Broadly, the alternative lifestyles of foragers—living in rainforests, along coastal strands, and as sea nomads—have enabled us to appreciate the range of human diversity.

Despite the important place of hunter-gatherers in anthropological theory-making, detailed ethnographic information about contemporary South-East Asian foraging societies can be difficult to locate and incorporate into the interesting chronicle of ongoing human cultural change. Among other difficulties, the South-East Asia region is culturally, historically, geographically, and politically diverse. For this chapter, the region is demarcated as the countries south of China, east of India, north of Australia, and west of Papua New Guinea. The countries discussed in this chapter include Indonesia, the Philippines, Brunei, Malaysia, Thailand, with occasional references to Vietnam, Cambodia, Laos, Myanmar, and Singapore (see Figure 48.1). Within this world area, South-East Asian foraging communities have been encapsulated within not only local polities, but spreading colonial states from South India, Portugal, Spain, the Netherlands, Great Britain, France, the United States, and Japan (while the standpoint of this chapter emerges from primarily English-language ethnographic scholarly books and articles, readers are encouraged to read further in the local languages of particular countries or ethnic groups). Although South-East Asian foraging

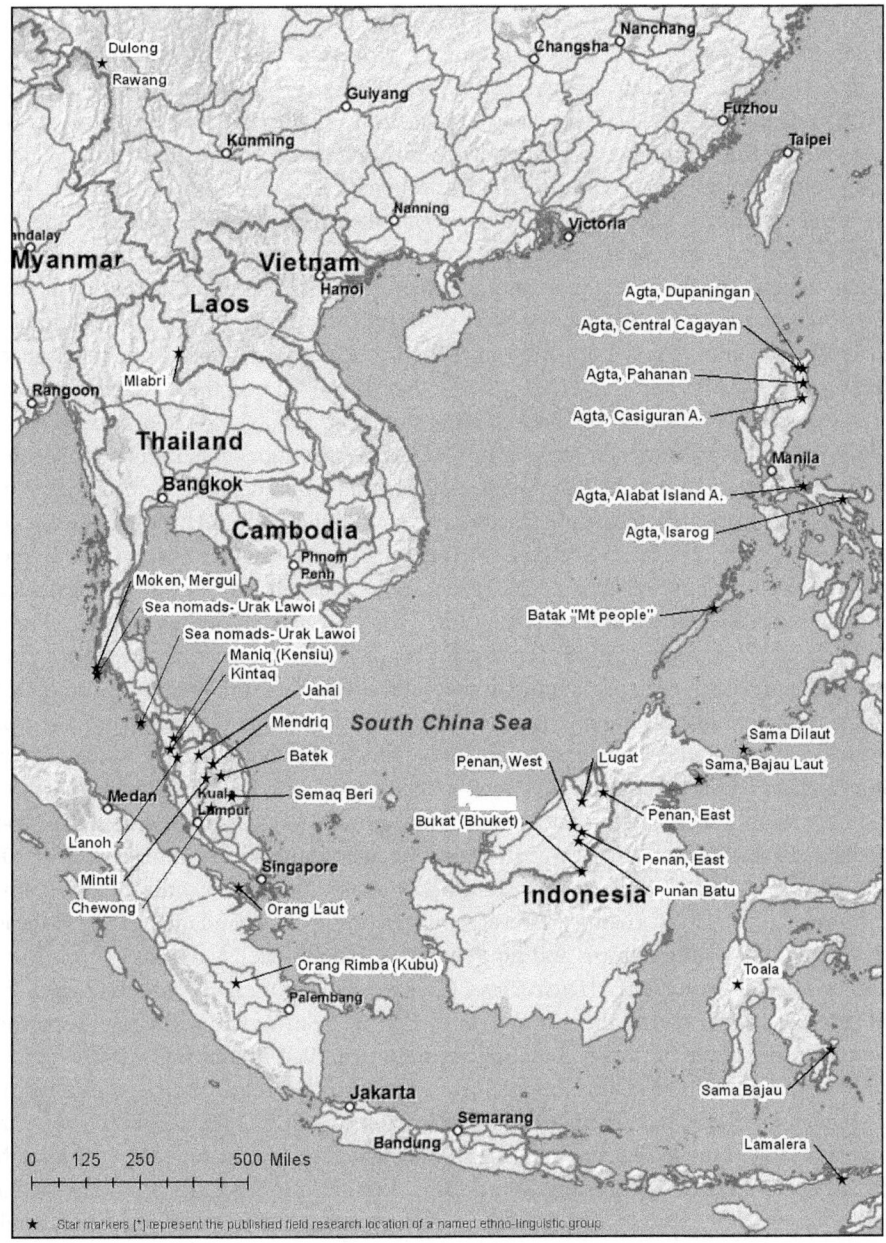

FIGURE 48.1 Location of referenced South-East Asian hunter-gatherer societies.

communities share certain distinct structural features, they also display notable regional variations, partly cultural differences stemming from the historical contingencies of colonial encounters concerning land encroachment, resource extraction, taxation, enslavement, patron-clientage, and other economic and political pressures (Bending 2006; Widlok and Tadesse 2005; Winzeler 1997).

The terms 'hunter-gatherer' and 'forager' have been used in a wide variety of situations, referring to people who subsist by collecting or procuring food, rather than cultivating food. Over long spans of time, foragers can be described as prehistoric foragers, recent foragers, or contemporary foragers. For the purposes of this chapter, contemporary foragers or hunter-gatherers are defined as communities of people who collect rather than cultivate foods and who also valorize food collecting as a laudable lifestyle. Recent foragers, on the other hand, are communities who now have few or no families that rely upon food collecting, but who were previously documented as food collectors and who continue to valorize their recent foraging lifestyle. The pride and valorization of food collecting is significant since it is often found among foragers but not among food cultivators. Communities of horticulturalists, farmers, and pastoralists may hunt and gather foods, such as wild game, yams, and sago, or collect non-timber forest products (NTFPs), but they do not valorize these activities. Instead they may mark such pursuits as hobbies, children's fun, poor people's food, old-fashioned, etc.

While the primary feature of foragers involves their identification, management, collection, and processing of undomesticated, non-cultivated, or wild foods, definitions do vary. Roscoe, for example, describes hunting and gathering as communities who derive their subsistence calories by procuring a certain percentage (>50 per cent) of wild resources, but he unlinks procurement from consumption (Roscoe 2002, 154). He astutely observes that hunter-gatherers may procure wild resources and then may trade some to neighbours for consumption of domestic crops. This would be especially true for coastal strand foragers who procure mainly fish or sea mammals since humans suffer from 'protein poisoning' if they consume more than 30–40 per cent protein in their daily nutrition. Maritime foragers may depend on procurement of seafoods, but they equally depend on the trade of these for starchy foods (Noli and Avery 1988). Another recent description of 'hunter-gatherer production systems' highlights 'those that subsist on undomesticated species of plants and animals, even if some domesticated species or their products are obtained through trade or ancillary cultivation' (Smith et al. 2010, 20).

The wild staple foods collected by South-East Asian foragers include tubers (yams, Dioscoreaceae), starches (palms, Arecaceae), nut proteins (pandanus, Pandananeae; ficus, *Bauhinia* sp.), green shoots and sap (bamboos, Bambuseae), leaves and corms (taro, *Colocasia esculenta*), and fruits (*Diplodiscus, Calamus, Pandanus, Zizyphus*, etc). Given the decimation of animal species throughout South-East Asia during the ethnographic period, the number and range of hunted prey species have dwindled dramatically. In the ethnographic record, protein has been obtained from prey species such as pig, deer, rhinoceros, and monkey (Puri 2005), with more broad-spectrum foraging of smaller prey species as numbers of larger prey have been reduced. Marine resources have included sea turtles, lobsters, sea cucumbers (Holothuroidea), and clams (Mudar and Anderson 2007) as well as dolphin, dugong, whales, etc. Contemporary South-East Asian foragers also increasingly rely upon cultivars, such as rice, manioc, breadfruit, and sugarcane. Sometimes these are grown in small garden plots by aboriginal families themselves; more often they are obtained through trade that contributes to the subsistence diet (Puri 2005).

Yet a rigid economic definition of hunter-gatherers misrepresents the nature of that mode of adaptation as it exists in South-East Asia. A second feature correlating with contemporary South-East Asian hunter-gatherers involves their notably egalitarian social structures. The archetypical features include egalitarian, heterarchical bands or patriclans, with families composed of monogamous couples, their children, and widowed grandparents or other unmarried family members. South-East Asian forager communities are small, diffuse, and easily partitioned, though variations occur, such as settlement pattern differences between East Penan and West Penan communities (Sellato 1994). Egalitarian South-East Asian foragers feature the diffusion of authority; mobile settlement patterns; sharing of resources and tools; immediate consumption of foods; limited control over others; a valuing of individual autonomy; and a valuing of food collection rather than food cultivation (Fortier 2009; Woodburn 1982).

All of the foraging communities in this chapter represent simple egalitarian societies. Exceptions, such as complex foraging societies, are found in archaeological studies. The prehistoric communities of Khok Phanom Di that resided near the Gulf of Thailand circa four thousand years ago are one example of a community of maritime hunters with distinct elite and commoner burials and artefact distributions (Higham and Thorsarat 1994). Unlike simple egalitarian foraging societies, complex foraging societies feature social stratification and inequality, elite political control, use of specialized monies, delayed consumption and storage, competition or warfare, and artisanal specialization (Kelly 1995, 294). One contemporary South-East Asian forager society, the Lamalera of Lembata Island, Indonesia, pursues whale hunting for subsistence and scholars have suggested these whale hunters are possibly examples of a complex foraging society (Smith et al. 2010, 25). For example, material differences appear based, not in material wealth, but on statistically insignificant differences in broader kinship networks, better health, or larger numbers of children rather than extrinsic material wealth (Pryor 2010; Smith et al. 2010). However, given their historical conditions as having been consigned to whale hunting by Portuguese colonial administrators, in addition to their material conditions and dual moiety kin system, Lamalera continue to fit the stereotype of simple egalitarian hunter-gatherers who flexibly have adapted their traditional maritime economic pursuits to fit the needs and desires of colonial interests in whale resources.

A third characteristic of South-East Asian foragers involves religions that are grounded in relational and animistic world views. Social identity is closely tied to a relational ontology in which supernatural persons are part of a more diffuse kinship network. Thus animals are often considered kin and the ontological boundaries between human and animal persons dissolve so that animals may be designated as brothers, sisters, and other kin. For example, the marsupial known as a cuscus (*Spilocuscus maculatus* and *Phalanger orientalis*) is regarded as an infant Alune boy among the Alune, horticulturist-foragers of Indonesia who traditionally procure sago palm (*Metroxylon sagu*), a particularly rich source of starch, supplemented with forest-cleared gardens of rice (*Oryza sativa*, Florey 2001; Latinis 2000; Latinis 1996).

Broadly, contemporary South-East Asian foragers are characterized as people who procure or collect wild foods and materials, observe noticeably egalitarian and democratic social relations, and respect other sentient and supernatural beings as part of their kin-based network. While they share a particular deep structure, foraging communities of South-East Asia display tremendous diversity of knowledge, culture, and beliefs.

What's in a Name? South-East Asian Forager Identities

A named community of South-East Asian foragers forms when people intermarry and share mutually intelligible ideas, language, and knowledge. Currently, there are about 40 contemporary foraging societies living in South-East Asian nations who share the cultural features of wild food procurement, valorization of the foraging lifestyle, egalitarianism, and animism. The mainland South-East Asian groups speak Austroasiatic or Tibetic languages while the island groups speak Austronesian languages. Cultural names for these groups vary, with many being called the equivalent of 'mountain men', 'original people', 'forest people', and other names given by outsiders. However, cultural groups themselves distinguish each other by dialect, language, and culture, and we will follow this convention, sometimes referring to 'ethnolinguistic' groups as those who share common culture, history, and language.

The South-East Asian hunter-gatherer groups range by latitude throughout territories spanning southern regions of China southwards to the southern islands of Indonesia. Maritime hunter-gatherers are discussed according to the country that controls the particular area of the sea in which the group generally forages (see Figure 48.1). Table 48.1 shows their most widely known common names together with their International Organization for Standardization (ISO 639) language codes in parentheses (Lewis 2012).

The mainland South-East Asian foraging societies mostly speak Austroasiatic languages, known as the Aslian family of languages, a division of the Mon Khmer branch of Austroasiatic languages (Benjamin 1976; Matisoff 2003). The contemporary foraging groups include the Batek, Chewong, Jahai, Kintaq, Lanoh, Maniq, Mendriq, Semaq Beri, and Temoq. (Some of the recent and part-time foraging communities such as Semai, Semnam, and Mah Meri are not included. Semnam, for example, were nomadic forest foragers until the mid-1900s when they were settled by the Malaysian government into a village (Dallos 2003; Burenhult and Wegener 2009). For a fuller discussion of the Orang Asli ('original peoples'), see Benjamin and Chou 2002; Dentan 1979; Dentan et al. 1997; Endicott 1979; Nicolas 2000; Nowak and

Table 48.1 The most widely known common names of hunter–gatherer groups together with their International Organization for Standardization (ISO 639) language codes in parentheses

Location	Name (language code)
China	Dulong (duu)
Myanmar	Taron (raw)
Myanmar-Thailand	Moken (mwt)
Thailand	Mlabri (mra)
Philippines	Alabat Agta (dul), Casiguran Agta (dgc), Central Cagayan Agta (agt), Dupaningan Agta (duo), Isarog Agta (agk), Pahanan Agta (apf), Paranan (prf), Batak (bya), Balangingi (sse), Sama Dilaut (sml, Dilaut dialect), Tasaday (mta)
Thailand-Malaysia	Kintaq (knq), Maniq (kns), Tonga (tnz), Urak Lawoi (urk)
Malaysia	Batek (btq), Chewong (cwg), Jahai (jhi), Lanoh (lnh), Mendriq (mnq), Mintil (mzt), Semaq Beri (szc), Temoq (tmo), Punan Ba (pna), Punan Batu (pnm), Lugat (ttw), Southern Sama (ssb), East Penan (pez), West Penan (pne)
Malaysia-Indonesia	Bukat (buk)
Indonesia	Sama Bajau (bdl), Lamalera (lmr), Toala (rob), Kubu (kvb), Orang Laut (lce)

Muntil 2004.) In social organization, Aslian families live in nuclear families composed of parents and children; they use a kinship classification system that resembles the Inuit system that distinguishes a person's +1 generation of parents from aunts and uncles (similar to English kin systems). However, other generations (+2, +3, −1, −2 generations) use a Hawaiian system that merges many relatives into a small number of kin categories (unlike English families which continue to distinguish 'grandfather' from 'great uncles' and other collateral relatives). All Aslian groups recognize cognatic, bilateral descent systems. In some of the ethnic groups, their members affiliate with a 'ramage', a non-exclusive cognatic descent group, often found in Hawaiian, ambilineal descent systems (Bishop 1996; Endicott and Endicott 2008). The family system used by the Aslian hunter-gatherers is most common in Malayo-Polynesian societies where husband and wife share most economic and childcare duties.

The Aslian-speaking ethnic groups reside in Peninsular Malaysia's fully humid equatorial climates with more than 2,000 mm rainfall per year. Numerous streams and rivers cut through the forests, providing key travel routes and fishing places. Malaysian contractors have increasingly logged the mostly lowland forests of the region for hardwoods to create more arable land. These intrusions have made hunting and gathering difficult, with contemporary Aslian-speaking foragers becoming encapsulated into Malaysia's growing global economic regimes. The foragers of the Malaysian peninsula increasingly procure forest products such as rattan and exchange the forest products with traders for commodities such as rice, tobacco, and shop goods.

Another Austroasiatic-speaking society, the Mlabri, live in border areas of Laos and Thailand. Unlike the humid tropics of Malaysia, the Mlabri's territories have a seasonal warm temperate climate, where they travel in forested hills ranging from 300 m to 1,500 m with rainfall of about 2,000 mm per year falling during summer monsoons with dryer winter seasons. Trying to eke a living from these evergreen forests, Mlabris have to resist the incursions of loggers and others seeking forest resources, who increasingly prevent Mlabris from collecting enough to meet subsistence. Altogether, the Aslian and Mlabri foraging societies of mainland South-East Asia number about 10,000 people, and perhaps 4,000 of them continue active subsistence foraging combined with trade. Others, such as the Dulong of China and their relatives, the Taron of Myanmar, have become either part-time foragers or recent foragers who now focus on subsistence farming or tenant labour for the major part of the year's subsistence activities (LaPolla 2003).

The island South-East Asian foraging societies all speak Austronesian languages with probable non-Austronesian substrate proto-languages (Reid 1994). Forest hunter-gatherer groups of Borneo, Malaysia, and Sarawak, Indonesia include the Eastern Penan and Western Penan (pronounced 'pa-naan' and meaning 'remote forest collectors') who continue to eke out a living of mixed foraging with other economic pursuits (Sellato 1994). More southerly groups of the island are known as Punan and mark ethnolinguistic distinctions by a toponym such as the name of their river territory, or another descriptive adjective. Some of the Penan and Punan cluster include the Penan Geng, Punan Malinau, Penan Tutoh, Penan Sulkang, Punan Batu, Bukat, as well as other groups distinguished by territory, dialect, or political band. (Brosius 1991; Hoffman 1986; Kaskija 2012; Lumholz 1920; Sellato 1994; Sercombe and Sellato 2007; Urquhart 1959). While originally dialect variations only, the difference between the exonymic epithets Penan and Punan came to signify 'Penan' as egalitarian forest foragers and 'Punan' as hierarchical and incorporating horticulture into their economic pursuits. More recently, however, the two terms are again being used to signify 'forest foragers'. The Penan number about 7,000 people; Punan foragers of Borneo number about 11,000 people; and altogether with recent foragers now practising horticulture, the Penan and Punan groups number about 20,000 in population. Most occupy territories upriver and closer to higher-altitude headwaters (agrarian communities occupy lands downriver, nearer to mouths of rivers). Punan ethnolinguistic groups consider a mountaintop and the headwater rivers flowing out of it to demarcate their territory. Most harvest the starchy pith of wild sago palms (*Eugeissona utilis*, *Arenga undulatifolia*, etc.), their carbohydrate staple. Individuals or families make claim to wild sago and other useful trees through a system of *molong*, meaning 'to preserve' the resource, incising distinctive territorial demarcations based on these resources. With decades of ensuing forest destruction, many Penan and Punan have been persuaded to settle in the last few decades, altering their traditional *molong* resource practices, yet they continue to forage for a wide range of plants and animals. The Penan Benalui, for example, hunt the bearded pig (*Sus barbatus*) primarily, but also pursue 45 other animal species and utilize over 300 species of plants (Puri 2005). Penan and Punan women reportedly hunted just as men did, except for differing techniques. Traditionally women have favoured dog-assisted spear hunting, while men favoured blowguns, but gun hunting has now also become common (Sellato 1994, 92 citing Lumholz 1920, 174).

In the Philippine islands, the foragers of northern Luzon Island and adjacent islands are known as 'Agta' ('person') together with a toponym. These include the Alabat Island Agta, Casiguran Agta, Central Cagayan Agta, Dicamay Agta, Dupaningan Agta, Isarog Agta, Pahanan Agta, and Paranan Agta who all continue to do either subsistence or part-time foraging. In addition, the foragers of Palawan Island in the Philippines are known as the Batak (meaning 'mountain people') and number perhaps 200 remaining subsistence foragers in a total ethnic population of about 2,000 people who have shifted away from subsistence foraging towards forest trade of rattan, honey, and tree resins. The Agta and Batak groups are blessed with a variable physical environment, stretching from Pacific coastlands to low mountains. In addition, monsoons bring over 1,300 mm rain in winter months but less than 150 mm precipitation in summer months, for a yearly total of more than 5,000 mm (Allen 1985, 47–8). With seasonal and environmental variation, the Agta and Batak communities forage in several ecotones, including coastal forests, lowland dipterocarp (*Sal* sp.) forests, montane oak forests, and higher altitudinal pine forests where they depend on prey species such as deer, monkeys, squirrels, bears, and pigs plus wild yams and other edibles (Allen 1985).

On the island of Sumatra, Indonesia, live the Kubu, who reportedly prefer the name Orang Rimba, meaning 'people of the forest'. Although most Kubu dialect groups practise horticulture and together number about 15,000 people, the nomadic Orang Rimba are foragers and number about 3,000 people who live on interfluvial riverbanks and other terrain near rivers (Sager 2008). The earliest observations noted no swiddening or other cultivation, but instead they practised broad-spectrum foraging and scavenging of fish, birds, and mammals using a range of hunting equipment, including traps, snares, knives, spears, dogs, and stone-flinging (Forbes 1885). Contemporary nomadic Orang Rimba families supplement these economic pursuits with the trade of beeswax, ivory, rattan, and tree resins to horticultural Kubu communities (Persoon 2000; Sandbukt 1988).

On the island of Sulawesi, Indonesia, live recent foragers known as the Toala, which also means 'forest people'. The Toala were first documented as full-time foragers in the eighteenth century, but today they mostly work as labourers on copra plantations (Sarasin and Sarasin 1905). At only two degrees south of the equator, the Kubu and Toala inhabit equatorial rainforest environs in which they compete with leopard, bear, crocodile, and other predators for diminishing numbers of prey species such as wild pig, monkey, deer, tapir, and other ungulates.

The final major category of South-East Asian foragers includes the 'sea nomads', maritime foragers who live throughout the small islands and shallow seas of south-eastern Asia. These nomadic communities live in coastal waters where they fish, hunt sea mammals and turtles, collect sea cucumber, molluscs, and other crustaceans in addition to coastal strand hunting and gathering on islands during monsoon storm seasons (Hinshiranan 1996). The focus upon maritime rather than land-based foraging distinguishes the sea nomads from other South-East Asian foragers; instead of forest products, the sea nomads procure marine resources in exchange for rice, cloth, and other commodities. Like the land-based foragers, the maritime foragers have experienced intense pressure to settle down and adopt farming or tourist-related work. As a result, younger generations are losing interest in traditional boat-making and indigenous knowledge about marine resources.

The maritime foragers, known as 'sea nomads', can be grouped by geographic region, stretching from Myanmar in the north to Sulawesi, Indonesia in the south and the Philippines to the east. From Malay languages, the name Orang (meaning 'people') is used, as when people call themselves Orang Laut, 'sea people'. Many are called Bajau, a Malay and Indonesian term referring to 'nomads' or 'sea persons' living off the coasts of East Kalimantan, Sulawesi, and elsewhere in East Indonesia. The term 'sama', from Malay, refers to a collective 'we [people]'. Frequently, these monikers are combined with geographic terms (e.g. Sama Bajau) to describe people of a given island or archipelago. All Sama are multilingual, but many have a mother tongue or home language with which they identify.

The most northerly dwelling of the sea nomads, the Moken, call themselves Manut Tau'au ('people of the sea') and live a large part of their lives in boats and on islands throughout the Mergui Archipelago in the Andaman Sea. Mokens fish and hunt seafoods (giant clams, sea turtles, parrotfish, octopi, and sea cucumbers, etc.), yet their plant knowledge is also extensive with over 100 culturally significant plant species utilized as food, medicine, construction material, and religious paraphernalia (Hinshiranan 1996). Their land-dwelling relatives are known as Moklen and reside on islands near Thailand and along the coasts of Myanmar and Thailand (Larish 1999). Together they number about 8,000 in population.

A second group of sea nomads are known as the Urak Lawoi ('sea people') and live on islands off the west coast of Thailand and Malaysia, numbering between 3,000 (Lewis 2012) and 6,000 people (Wongbusarakum 2007, 9). Similar to Moken, the Urak Lawoi forage for sea turtles, lobsters, sea cucumbers, and clams; in addition some practise horticulture, maintaining gardens with dry-land rice and tropical fruits. More recently, with a booming tourist industry in the area, Urak Lawoi's young men and women have neglected traditional culture practices, and opted to work in the tourist industry as sea-taxi drivers and guides.

Further south along the east coast of Sumatra and islands nearby live another maritime nomadic group known as the Orang Laut. Ethnically separate from other sea nomads, they speak a distinct language known as Loncong, and their population is estimated at 500 people (Lewis 2012). Like the other Sama peoples, the Orang Laut have experienced intense pressure by the Indonesian government to assimilate to national cultural and social standards (Chou 2003).

Spread along coastal strands and shallow seas from the Philippines to Indonesia, live Sama peoples who speak a series of nine closely related languages. Only some of these communities continue to practise sea-based subsistence fishing, but all are from ocean-based economies. Some of the dialect sub-groups of the Central Sama are well known for their sea-based foraging, such as the Sama Dilaut who engage in subsistence fishing and trade. Others, however, are not foragers; indeed the Balangingi are renowned for their piracy. Separate from commercial fishing groups, the subsistence Sama economy is traditionally based on a protein–starch exchange. Sama procure seafoods and commodities such as pearls, which they exchange for rice, yams, and other starches with coastal communities. While some of the Sama continue subsistence fishing, many have turned to commercial fishing, farming, pearl diving, etc.

Since the Sama population is large and diverse, dialects are an important marker of identity. For example, one southern Sama sub-group, known as the Sama Pala'au, carries out traditional spear fishing and other foraging pursuits as full-time boat people. Generally, however, other Sama peoples have been established for many generations in both subsistence and trade-based foraging, as salt-makers, seafood fishers, and entrepreneurs of precious commodities such as pearls, curry fish (*Stichopus variegatus*), and other types of valuable sea cucumbers (Holothuroidea). The Sama peoples generally procure some seafoods for subsistence and others specifically for exchange in a patron–clientage economic system. While not known for horticulture, contemporary Sama families may engage in labour and service work for governments as sea guards, guides, and ferrymen (Lowe 1999).

Although the various sea nomads are related by way of language, social customs, economic practices, religious beliefs, and occasional marriages, they have experienced long independent histories of adaptation to different coastal waters and coastal strand environments (Sather 1995; Sopher 1977). Their adaptations to different islands, archipelagos, and coastal strands have created divergent cultures, languages, and knowledge systems over the last millennium.

One group of South-East Asian hunting and gathering communities, the villagers of Lamalera, a fishing community on Lembata Island in eastern Indonesia, has been the subject of recent research (Alvard and Gillespie 2004; Barnes 1996; Nolin 2008; 2010; Smith et al. 2010). Rather than being sea nomads, these foragers live in a coastal village of about 1,200 people who specialize in hunting whales, stingray, manta ray, and dugong, sharing the large meat packages between patrilineal clans. Considered complex hunter-gatherers, Lamalera exchange dried salt, lime, and fish for rice, cotton, and vegetables from agrarian and horticultural communities.

In other cases, foraging communities have suffered ethnocide, becoming extinct, or being assimilated into the underclasses of neighbouring dominant societies. The Dulong of China, for example, continue to valorize the foraging lifestyle, but now farm dry-land rice and millet as their main economic activity (LaPolla 2003; Song and Shen 1999). Other moribund foraging communities were relocated by colonial regimes, and fell victim to slave raids, epidemic diseases, and encroachment of their native territories by expanding agrarian communities. In South-East Asia there have been strong forces of cultural change over the last two centuries, with the demise of cultural groups through assimilation and ethnocide.

While ethnocide has been documented among South-East Asian hunter-gatherers, ethnographers rarely document the emergence of a new ethnolinguistic cultural group, a process sometimes known as ethnogenesis. In one case, *puhuk*, or clans of Bornean hunter-gatherer nomads, have adopted the ethnic name Bhuket as a means of asserting a collective political identity (Thambiah 2007). In other cases, there have been tentative findings of foraging-based societies from horticultural-based societies. The Tasaday of the Philippines represent one such group who carry out hunting and gathering activities and trade forest products, yet appear to be an ethnolinguistic sub-group of a nearby horticultural society (Headland 1992). However, ethnographic studies have no long-term documentation to indicate the political and kinship interactions of the Tasaday. Historical linguistics has shed some light on these foraging people, finding that:

> This is the only case known in the Philippines where a formerly food-producing population is known to have acquired a hunter-gatherer subsistence secondarily, probably brought about by a small number of people escaping to the forest within the last two to three hundred years, [possibly] to avoid some catastrophic epidemic.
>
> (Reid 2007, 7)

In some cases, genetic studies indicate forager–horticulturalist ties. For example, the Mlabri exhibit genetic similarities with local horticultural Khmu peoples (Oota et al. 2005). However, linguistic studies indicate the Mlabri language emerged before the branching off of the Khmu language, suggesting that Mlabri branched off from proto-Khmuic speaking peoples (Rischel 2004). However, there is no resolution yet as to whether Mlabri and proto-Khmu peoples were hunter-gatherers or horticulturalists prior to their ethnolinguistic split over 600 years ago. Broadly, insights from archaeology, historical linguistics, and genetic studies must all be combined to shed light on the nature of South-East Asian foraging societies and past interactions with horticultural societies.

Finally, there are islands where few cultural studies have been carried out, limiting knowledge about the extent of foraging practices and foraging-based societies. In the still heavily forested island of Lembata, Indonesia, one of the local communities of Lewo Eleng (ISO 639-3: lwe) specialize in the collection and trade of candlenuts (*Aleurites moluccana*). Candlenuts are important for not only candle oil; like hazelnuts, they are a food high in fat and protein and have medicinal properties. They are also known as kukui nuts and have become popular as the beautiful black beads of Hawaiian-style *lei* necklaces in the United States. Like many part-time foraging societies of the region, the Lewo Eleng community was forcibly settled by the government in the last two generations and anthropologists have yet to document their culture or history.

Identity in Theory and Practice

How might the cultural practices of foraging societies contribute to understanding the nature of cultural change over time and regional space in South-East Asia? Responding to this question involves precisely defining the features of societies based on food collection. By definition, must foragers be 'pure', meaning they purely hunt, gather, and fish but do no food cultivation or trade? Do they have to be 'original' in some way, meaning they seem aboriginal, always to have been hunter-gatherers over the *longue durée*, while other societies experienced noticeable material changes? Do they have to be 'isolated', meaning they have had no contact with communities engaged in cultivating tubers, rice, fruit, and pigs? These and other questions reflect certain Western, or technologically complex societal underlying ideologies that have played a part in theoretical debates concerning South-East Asian foragers.

Historically, the field of anthropology is rooted in concerns with human origins. Studies of hunter-gatherers, as peoples without agriculture or complex technologies, were believed to provide a better analogy of prehistoric human cultural life, albeit accounting for their absorption into modern state societies. For example, Lewis Binford wrote about appropriate and inappropriate homologies between the contemporary and ancient societies of hunter-gatherers, while L. R. Hiatt reviewed the absorption of nineteenth-century scholars with Australian aborigines as exemplars of prehistoric cultures (Binford 2001; Hiatt 1996).

One of the notable late twentieth-century theories concerning South-East Asian foragers proposed that 'foragers have been dependent upon starchy foods and therefore live only in environments with sufficient amounts of endemic species of starchy tubers' (*Dioscorea* sp., Bailey and Headland 1991; Headland 1987). This hypothesis, nicknamed 'the wild yam question', started an anxious debate among South-East Asian foraging specialists concerning foragers and subsistence, and especially concerning whether 'genuine' foragers could subsist in hypothetically carbohydrate-poor rainforests. (Rainforests are found in several world areas and can be further sub-grouped as lowland, montane, tropical, sub-tropical, and temperate rainforests. Definitions of rainforests vary, but most describe minimums of 1,500–2,000 mm precipitation yearly: Dentan 1991; Endicott and Bellwood 1991.) The implication was that South-East Asian foragers, many of whom live in rainforest environs, were not aboriginal since they may not have been able to live in the rainforest environments of South-East Asia. Further, South-East Asian hunter-gatherers may not be 'genuine' or 'pure' if they could not have successfully carried out foraging independent of food cultivation. The foraging societies may have had to supplement their diets with proto-agricultural activities such as clearing and burning forest patches to grow yams, or caring for pigs to supplement meagre rations of protein from rainforests.

Worse yet, they may never have been 'isolated' or independent if they had to trade with farming communities for rice, yams, and other foods to supplement meagre gleanings of starch and protein in rainforests. Perhaps, it was suggested, the South-East Asian foraging communities were simply 'devolved' farmers who fled to forests to avoid political upheavals (Hoffman 1986). Following this line of reasoning in the wild yam debate, the 'interdependent' theory of foragers posited that foragers and farmers need the resources and expertise of each other in rainforest environments (Headland and Reid 1989). The theory of interdependence posited that hunter-gatherers have been interacting with, and mutually dependent upon, farmers for thousands of years (Headland and Reid 1989; Morrison and Junker 2002; Peterson 1978). For example, Headland and Reid assert that Casiguran Agta depend for only 2 per cent of their starch on wild plants and that the remainder comes from rice obtained from farmers and grown themselves (Headland and Reid 1989, 46). While extreme cases of interdependence exist, critics have pointed out that such theories fail to recognize the procurement of forest (and sea) resources for the foragers' own subsistence, with studies of other Agta foraging groups dependent more completely on food collection rather than cultivation (Allen 1985; Estioko-Griffin 1985; Griffin 1984).

Calling into question South-East Asian foragers' means of subsistence, and thus their identity as foragers, raised a clarion call to determine whether these foragers indeed were 'pure', 'independent', and 'aboriginal', at least those living in South-East Asian rainforests. On a deeper level, it also raised the question of whether contemporary hunter-gatherers represented appropriate models of analogy with prehistoric hunter-gatherer societies. The 'wild yam' question as posited, however, presented several problems, based on scientific and epistemological grounds. Notably, it was a scientific question that demanded negative evidence, evidence that foragers *did not* subsistence forage in rainforests, yet by social scientific standards, the lack of evidence cannot prove or disprove anything. Not finding wild yams in rainforests is not evidence of no foraging societies at any period in time. Further, cultural anthropologists address time periods of about 200 years; the 'wild yam question' addressed the *longue durée* spanning millennia, not hundreds of years.

The question of foraging in rainforest environments has since been addressed by scholars of archaeology, palaeoecology, palaeobotany, palynology, and palaeodemography (e.g. Barker et al. 2005; Barton 2005; Barton and Paz 2009; Kealhofer 2003; Kealhofer and Penny 1998). For example, at the Lang Rongrien rock shelter in southern Thailand, studies indicate the shelter was occupied since 43,000 years ago. Pre-Hoabinhian cultural levels yielded 45 stone tools and a concentration of turtle and tortoise faunal remains, indicating an emphasis on turtle foraging (Mudar and Anderson 2007). However, compared to the present subtropical rainforest environment, palaeoecology studies of the rock shelter environment circa 10,000–40,000 years ago indicated that there were dryer conditions more consistent with seasonal monsoon climates that supported oak and pine forests (Penny 2001). With increased seasonality, such conditions were optimal for the classic 'yam-based' foraging typical in seasonal monsoon forests, allowing human communities to carry out foraging in mainland South-East Asia that today are rainforests.

Although outside the scope of this chapter, genetic and molecular studies of human origins also have contributed to studies of prehistoric foragers many of which have drawn on genetic profiles from contemporary South-East Asian foraging communities (e.g. Bellwood 1993; Hill et al. 2006; Soares et al. 2008; Stoneking and Delfin 2010). Based on unique genetic signatures of mtDNA and Y-DNA, such studies are helpful for understanding human migrations into South-East Asian rainforests and island regions. For example, scholars find that given their unique genetic signatures, ancestors of the Batek and other Aslian-speaking 'negrito' groups of Malaysia migrated into the region about 50,000–60,000 years ago (Hill et al. 2006; Soares et al. 2008). Stoneking suggests that given their unique situation, these groups have probably maintained their hunting-gathering lifestyle since their ancestors arrived in East Asia (Stoneking and Delfin 2010, R190). The Aslian-speaking hunter-gatherers' language situation, however, indicates probable intense contact with horticultural Austroasiatic-speaking peoples since at least 4,000 years ago (Dunn et al. 2011). This reflects the condition that contemporary foragers have long histories of trade and contact with expanding agrarian polities. Thus information from both human genetics and linguistics can provide insight into long-term adaptability to rainforests, as well as other questions about human migration throughout South-East Asia and the peopling of South-East Asian regions in general.

Rejection of Contemporary South-East Asian Foragers as Pure, Pristine, or Isolated

Genetic markers change in populations over time, and likewise languages and ethnic identities change over time as well. Contemporary hunter-gatherers are descendants of Mesolithic peninsular South-East Asian cultures, but these Mesolithic peoples are probably ancestral to not only Batek but also other Malaysian cultural groups that have since adopted agriculture, died out, or emigrated to other South-East Asian regions.

In addition to the reification of foragers as pure, pristine, and isolated, such stereotypes have hurt the chances for cultural survival of lesser-known foraging communities. When South-East Asian foragers engaged in trade, intermarriage, or supplemented their diets with cultivated foods, they were dismissed as interdependent, devolved, culturally reversed, or worse as pariahs, thieves, beggars, and squatters on government lands. The academic disregard of peoples who pursued flexible or part-time foraging has resulted in less research of groups such as the Kubu, Mlabri, Penan, or Sama peoples. Further, less recognition as 'hunter-gatherers' has given aggressive developers of natural resources and logging companies reason to dismiss foragers' claims to their land, forests, and marine resources (Brosius 1997; Sandbukt 1988; Sodhi et al. 2006; Sponsel 2000). The scientific pursuit of 'pure' foragers at the expense of part-time foragers, recently settled foragers, maritime foragers, forager-horticulturalists, and forager-traders has enabled the further disenfranchisement of indigenous peoples who were already facing political domination by local commercial interests.

One outcome of the disenfranchisement of foragers who do not fit the classic stereotype of hunter-gatherers has been less research concerning their distinctive natural resource management activities. Since the categories 'hunter-gatherer' and 'forager' by definition do not encompass activities involving knowledge and management of animals and plants, this area has been under-researched. 'Management' in this case includes activities with wild flora and fauna such as moving plant seeds to new locations; chopping sago to encourage new growth; trimming branches and nodes from plants; burning coppices; returning soil to remaining tubers; returning part of a resource (plant, mollusc) to regenerate; clearing brush around plants; or slashing bark to increase insect and microbial activity. These visible ecological activities are often paired with strategies based on ideological frameworks, such as calling the animals to the hunter; being morally pure in thought and deed in order to capture animals; caring for tree 'relatives'; giving gifts to supernaturals or deities in exchange for successful hunting; singing bees to sleep or telling stories about grandfather bee; or avoiding words that will anger hunting spirits (Eder 1997; Puri 2005; Sager 2008; Seitz 2007). In environmental and ecological studies, such subtle management practices are considered highly technical knowledge and are only recently being fully appreciated. Most environmental studies scholars find it amazing that foragers simply know significantly more *names* of animal species than non-foragers (Cullen et al. 2007). Ethnographers have documented many interesting and useful examples of the complexities of foragers' ecological relations, but regrettably, managerial activities get overlooked when researchers privilege 'pristine' hunting and gathering over resource management.

In sum, anthropologists have given ethnographic evidence and testimony that contemporary foragers have indeed inhabited rainforests even when yams have been in short supply. They have documented that although *Dioscorea* are important, other starches such as sago and taro have been equally important (Roscoe 2002). One outcome of the discussions about the ability of hunter-gatherers to exist in tropical forests was the general agreement of a 'need for greater precision in the definition of future hypotheses about foraging in tropical forests' (Brosius 1991, 123). This led to more discussion concerning population patterns among the Agta (e.g. Early and Headland 1998) and a greater regard for ecological studies of foragers (e.g. Allen 1985; Benjamin 1985; Ellen 2007; Rolland 2008). Overall, the outcome of the debate enabled scholars to renew their efforts to avoid reifications about foraging societies; to avoid over-generalizations about South-East Asian foraging societies such as limiting their subsistence regimes to *Dioscorea*; and to place more emphasis on not simply hunting and gathering, but to understand contemporary foragers as bricoleurs who create composite economies.

South-East Asian Foragers as Bricoleurs

Historian and anthropologist Jack Goody opined that all socio-economic systems are complex and interesting, and that we should avoid viewing them from a European, capitalist perspective that discounts many as primitive, simple, and inferior (Goody 2006, 48). Highlighting South-East Asian foragers' diverse economic activities similarly refutes the notion that they have primitive economic systems. Claude Lévi-Strauss was acutely aware of this, arguing that in technologically simple societies, the bricoleur is adept at performing a large number of diverse tasks; they make do with what is at hand (Lévi-Strauss 1962, 11).

Contemporary foragers too can be considered bricoleurs; while they continue to enjoy their particular economic activities, procuring wild foods and materials, they also trade some of these materials, and probably have done so for thousands of years (Morrison and Junker 2002). Their economic exchange systems invoke interesting combinations of kin-based reciprocity, redistribution of resources, use of patrons, trade, marketing of goods and services, and use of both restricted and general forms of money (e.g. Chou 2003; Fortier 2012, 126; Holmsen 2006). This economic bricolage represents a composite, hybrid foraging social pattern that has emerged under particular historical circumstances particular to an environment of colonial encroachment in which foragers' communities are encapsulated into agrarian-based systems.

Increasingly, scholars have discussed the composite economic strategies of foragers, such as during the 2002 Conference on Hunting and Gathering Societies (CHAGS 9) session titled 'Foragers as bricoleurs'. In the last 20 years, scholars have explored foragers' breadth of economic activities, finding that variety improves well-being and food security (e.g. Dentan et al. 1997; Eder 1997; Ellen 2007; Endicott 1979; Sercombe and Sellato 2007). Activities such as 'hunting' for trade partners or 'gathering' government stipends, apparently do not hinder foragers' egalitarian social relations nor their indigenous, animistic, and relational religious beliefs. The basic components of contemporary South-East Asian foraging culture may be stretched and distorted at times, but it is still a 'foraging mode of subsistence' with recognizable patterns of sociality and belief distinct from the social hierarchies of agrarian communities and their theistic religious systems (Barnard 2002).

Part of what makes each community of South-East Asian foragers unique is their adaptation to changing social and physical environments. In the South-East Asian region, some of the notable changes over the last 200 years have included coastline changes, tsunamis, population increases, deforestation, brown clouds and atmospheric pollution, and decimating decreases in wild animal populations. For example, an increase in patchy forest areas has caused large animal species to reduce their movements across former territories, causing nomadic human foraging groups to also reduce their movements. Likewise, habitat destruction caused by logging, development, deforestation, dam building, and farming have changed foragers' adaptive strategies, causing many families to resort to a bricolage of economic activities (e.g. Bending 2006; Brosius 1997).

These and other changes have motivated many South-East Asian foragers to cement together economic activities to build up a secure food supply. For example, Penan traditionally rely on sago pudding and pork, using blowpipes as both a tool and a weapon when spear blades are mounted at one end, but with farm families nearby, many Penan foragers put down the blowpipe and take up the sickle, working agrarian neighbours' rice fields. This enables Penan communities to flexibly obtain crops in years of good harvests but procure sago and wild meat in others, giving them better food security than local farmers (Puri 2005, 160–1; Sercombe and Sellato 2007). As noted by a scholar of another Bornean group, the Bukat, being hunter-gatherers in Borneo today is not just related to engagement in the foraging mode of subsistence, but it has to do with the overall flexibility of hunting and gathering cultures (Thambiah 2007, 104). This bricoleur style of hunter-gatherer activity has been aptly described as a form of 'open' hunting and gathering by Tessa Minter while documenting the range of Agta economic activities in the Philippines (Minter 2010, 275). Today's hunter-gatherers live in modern times, working alternatively in farm and labour activities, but paradoxically they remain hunter-gatherers through their ideological commitment to egalitarianism, relational ontologies, and continuing procurement of wild resources.

Foraging-bricoleur patterns, however, are not often commercially motivated. When trade occurs, it involves trade for subsistence, not trade for profit since the accumulation of wealth would counter foraging social structures based on immediate sharing and consumption of goods. For example, Moken find it advantageous to procure parrotfish, boxfish, and other marketable seafood that they exchange for rice, but the basic sociality of egalitarian foraging remains strong among traditional Moken boating families:

> To have more of anything…is a crassness, an atavism, a behaviour incompatible with and destructive of their cultivated system and of their collective sense…The boats they live on, together with their simple seafood-gathering tools, are held in common by those who live and work together. As subsistence hunter-gatherers, not commercial fishers, they take from the sea just what they need for their daily livelihood. They do not catch to sell, have no use for nets, and take no joy in a large catch.
>
> (Sorenson 2004, 577)

Thus as foragers, Moken procure fish and seafood for their own subsistence and to trade for subsistence goods, but not to sell for profit as commercial fishermen.

Conclusions

Issues concerning foragers' access to natural resources, the nature and meaning of these resources, foragers' utility of resources, and political contestations over natural resources have become paramount considerations in South-East Asian foraging studies, with several notable contributions over the last decade. Lye (2005) has detailed the Batek ethos of environmental stewardship in which Batek families believe they should live in forests in order to protect trees and coexist with them. Langub (2008) has related how Penan consider their forests like a supermarket that provides all of their needs. Penan support government attempts to create national parks if they themselves are able to continue foraging in the parks and if logging activities are curtailed there. Samuel et al. (2010) have taken an applied approach to evaluate the potential of medicinal plants used by Aslian communities for Malaysian and Western health care. Nolin (2010) has studied the ecology of fishing and sea mammal hunting among Lamalera villagers and finds support for reciprocal altruism as a motivation for food sharing. Endicott and Endicott (2008) have looked at work and family relations of the Batek, bringing a nuanced discussion of gender relations that would be most welcome in studies of other South-East Asian foraging societies. Another comprehensive PhD thesis includes discussion of gender patterns (Sager 2008), and has enabled readers to appreciate the beauty and breadth of Orang Rimbas' religious beliefs and everyday activities. Indeed, a number of other PhD theses have emerged in the last decade (Burenhult 2002; Dallos 2003; Holmsen 2006; Kaskija 2012; Minter 2010; Nolin 2008; Robinson 2008), signalling a healthy trend towards continued interest in the scholarship of South-East Asian foraging societies.

In conclusion, we need more scholarship about contemporary South-East Asian foragers in order to document and appreciate their cultures and relations with outsiders. In terms of policy studies, they need research that documents and monitors their livelihoods based on procurement of wild plants and animals. Finally, more active scholarship concerning South-East Asian foragers' human and cultural rights may allow them freedom to access their traditional resources, and protect their health, languages, and territories in a manner similar to endangered species and endangered languages.

REFERENCES

Allen, M. S. 1985. The rain forest of northeast Luzon and Agta foragers. In B. P. Griffin and A. Estioko-Griffin (eds), *The Agta of northeastern Luzon: recent studies*, 45–68. Cebu City, Philippines: San Carlos Publications.

Alvard, M. S. and Gillespie, A. 2004. Good Lamalera whale hunters accrue reproductive benefits. *Research in Economic Anthropology* 23, 225–48.

Bailey, R. C. and Headland, T. N. 1991. The tropical rain forest: is it a productive environment for human foragers? *Human Ecology* 19, 261–85.

Barker, G., Reynolds, T., and Gilbertson, D. 2005. The human use of caves in peninsular and island southeast Asia: research themes. *Asian Perspectives* 44, 1–15.

Barnard, A. 2002. The foraging mode of thought. *Senri ethnological studies* 60, 5–24.

Barnes, R. H. 1996. *Sea hunters of Indonesia: fishers and weavers of Lamalera*. Oxford: Oxford University Press.

Barton, H. 2005. The case for rainforest foragers: the starch record at Niah cave, Sarawak. *Asian Perspectives* 44, 56–72.

Barton, H. and Paz, V. 2009. Subterranean diets in the tropical rainforest of Sarawak, Malaysia. In T. Denham, J. Iriarte, and L. Vrydaghs (eds), *Rethinking agriculture: archaeological and ethnoarchaeological perspectives*, 50–77. Walnut Creek, CA: Left Coast Press.

Bellwood, P. 1993. Cultural and biological differentiation in Peninsular Malaysia: the last 10,000 years. *Asian Perspectives* 32, 37–60.

Bellwood, P. S., Fox, J. J., and Tryon, D. T (eds) 1995. *The Austronesians: historical and comparative perspectives*. Canberra: Australian National University.

Bending, T. 2006. *Penan histories: contentious narratives in upriver Sarawak.* Leiden: KITLV Press.
Benjamin, G. 1976. Austroasiatic subgroupings and prehistory in the Malay Peninsula. *Oceanic Linguistics Special Publication* 10, 37–128.
Benjamin, G. 1985. In the long term: three themes in Malayan cultural ecology. In K. L. Hutterer, A. T. Rambo, and G. W. Lovelace (eds), *Cultural values and human ecology in Southeast Asia*, 219–78. University of Michigan: Center for South and Southeast Asian Studies.
Benjamin, G. and Chou, C. (eds) 2002. *Tribal communities in the Malay world: historical, cultural and social perspectives.* Singapore: Institute of Southeast Asian Studies.
Binford, L. 2001. *Constructing frames of reference: an analytical method for archaeological theory building using ethnographic and environmental data sets.* Berkeley: University of California Press.
Bishop, N. 1996. Who's who in Kensiw? Terms of reference and address in Kensiw. *Mon-Khmer Studies* 26, 245–53.
Brosius, J. P. 1991. Foraging in tropical rain forests: the case of the Penan of Sarawak, East Malaysia (Borneo). *Human Ecology* 19, 123–50.
Brosius, J. P. 1997. Endangered forest, endangered people: environmentalist representations of indigenous knowledge. *Human Ecology* 25, 47–69.
Burenhult, N. 2002. A grammar of Jahai. PhD thesis. Sweden: Lunds Universitet.
Burenhult, N. and Wegener, C. 2009. Preliminary notes on the phonology, orthography and vocabulary of Semnam (Austroasiatic, Malay Peninsula). *Journal of the Southeast Asian Linguistics Society* 1, 283–312.
Chou, C. 2003. *Indonesian sea nomads: money, magic and fear of the Orang Suku Laut.* New York: Routledge.
Cullen, L. C., Pretty, J., Smith, D. J., and Pilgrim, S. P. 2007. Links between local ecological knowledge and wealth in indigenous communities of Indonesia: implications for conservation of marine resources. *International Journal Interdisciplinary Social Science* 2, 289–99.
Dallos, C. 2003. Identity and opportunity: asymmetrical household integration among the Lanoh, newly sedentary hunter-gatherers and forest collectors of Peninsular Malaysia. PhD thesis. McGill University: Department of Anthropology.
Dentan, R. K. 1991. Potential food sources for foragers in Malaysian rainforest: sago, yams and lots of little things. *Bijdragen tot de Taal-, Land-en Volkenkunde* 147, 420.
Dentan, R. K., Endicott, K. M., Gomes, A. G., and Hooker, M. B. 1997. *Malaysia and the 'original people': a case study of the impact of development on indigenous peoples.* Boston: Allyn and Bacon.
Dunn, M., Burenhult, N., Kruspe, N., Tufvesson, S., and Becker, N. 2011. Aslian linguistic prehistory: a case study in computational phylogenetics. *Diachronica* 28, 291–323.
Early, J. D. and Headland, T. N. 1998. *Population dynamics of a Philippine rain forest people: the San Ildefonso Agta.* Gainesville, FL: University Press of Florida.
Eder, J. F. 1997. *Batak resource management: belief, knowledge, and practice.* Gland, Switzerland: IUCN (the World Conservation Union) and World Wildlife Fund (WWF).
Ellen, R. F. 2007. *Modern crises and traditional strategies: local ecological knowledge in island Southeast Asia.* Oxford: Berghahn.
Endicott, K. M. 1979. *Batek Negrito religion: the world-view and rituals of a hunting and gathering people of Peninsular Malaysia.* Oxford: Clarendon Press.
Endicott, K. M. and Bellwood, P. 1991. The possibility of independent foraging in the rain forest of Peninsular Malaysia. *Human Ecology* 19, 151–85.

Endicott, K. M. and Endicott, K. L. 2008. *The headman was a woman: the gender egalitarian Batek of Malaysia*. Long Grove: Waveland Press.
Estioko-Griffin, A. A. 1985. Women as hunters: the case of an Eastern Cagayan Agta group. In B. P. Griffin and A. Estioko-Griffin (eds), *The Agta of northeastern Luzon: recent studies*, 18–32. Cebu City, Philippines: University of San Carlos.
Florey, M. 2001. Threats to indigenous knowledge. In L. Maffi (ed.), *On biocultural diversity*, 325–42. Washington, DC: Smithsonian Institution.
Forbes, H. O. 1885. On the Kubus of Sumatra. *Journal of the Anthropological Institute of Great Britain and Ireland* 14, 121–7.
Fortier, J. 2009. The ethnography of south Asian foragers. *Annual Review of Anthropology* 38, 99.
Fortier, J. 2012. *Kings of the forest: the cultural resilience of Himalayan hunter-gatherers*. Kathmandu: Mandala Book Point.
Goody, J. 2006. *The theft of history*. Cambridge: Cambridge University Press.
Griffin, P. B. 1984. Forager resource and land use in the humid tropics: the Agta of northeastern Luzon, the Philippines. In C. Shrire (ed.), *Past and present in hunter-gatherer studies*, 95–121. Gainesville, FL: Academic Press.
Headland, T. N. 1987. The wild yam question: how well could independent hunter-gatherers live in a tropical rain forest ecosystem? *Human Ecology* 15, 463–91.
Headland, T. N. (ed.) 1992. The Tasaday controversy: assessing the evidence. *American Anthropological Association Scholarly Series* 28.
Headland, T. N. and Reid, L. A. 1989. Hunter-gatherers and their neighbours from prehistory to the present [and comments and replies]. *Current Anthropology* 30, 43–66.
Hiatt, L. 1996. *Arguments about Aborigines*. Cambridge: Cambridge University Press.
Higham, C. 1989. *The archaeology of mainland Southeast Asia: from 10,000 BC to the fall of Angkor*. Cambridge: Cambridge University Press.
Higham, C. F. W. and Thosarat, R. 1994. *Khok Phanom Di: prehistoric adaptation to the world's richest habitat*. Fort Worth: Harcourt Brace Jovanovich.
Hill, C., Soares, P., Mormina, M., Macaulay, V., Meehan, W., Blackburn, J., Clarke, D., Raja, J. M., Ismail, P., and Bulbeck, D. 2006. Phylogeography and ethnogenesis of aboriginal Southeast Asians. *Molecular biology and evolution* 23, 2480–91.
Hinshiranan, N. H. 1996. The analysis of Moken opportunistic foragers' intragroup and intergroup relations. PhD thesis. Honolulu: University of Hawaii.
Hoffman, C. 1986. *The Punan: hunters and gatherers of Borneo*. Ann Arbor: UMI Research Press.
Holmsen, K. 2006. Out of the forest and into the market: social and economic transformations in a Bornean foraging society. PhD thesis Tucson: University of Arizona.
Kaskija, L. 2012. Images of a forest people: Punan Malinau—identity, sociality, and encapsulation in Borneo. PhD thesis. Uppsala: Uppsala Universitet.
Kealhofer, L. 2003. Looking into the gap: land use and the tropical forests of southern Thailand. *Asian Perspectives* 42, 72–96.
Kealhofer, L. and Penny, D. 1998. A combined pollen and phytolith record for fourteen thousand years of vegetation change in northeastern Thailand. *Review of Palaeobotany and Palynology* 103, 83–93.
Kelly, R. L. 1995. *The foraging spectrum*. Washington, DC: Smithsonian Institution.
Langub, J. 2008. Penan and the Pulong Tau National Park: historical links and contemporary life. *Borneo Research Bulletin* 39, 128–65.
LaPolla, R. J. 2003. Dulong. In G. Thurgood and R. J. LaPolla (eds), *The Sino-Tibetan languages*, 674–82. London. Routledge.

Larish, M. D. 1999. *The position of Moken and Moklen within the Austronesian language family.* Manoa: University of Hawaii at Manoa.

Latinis, D. K. 2000. The development of subsistence system models for island Southeast Asia and Near Oceania: the nature and role of arboriculture and arboreal-based economies. *World Archaeology* 32, 41–67.

Latinis, K. 1996. Hunting the Cuscus in Western Seram: the role of the phalanger in subsistence economies in Central Maluku. *Cakalele* 7, 1732.

Lévi-Strauss, C. 1962. *The savage mind.* Chicago: University of Chicago Press.

Lewis, P. M. (ed.) 2012. *Ethnologue: languages of the world* (16th edition). Dallas, TX: SIL International. Online version: http://www.ethnologue.com. Accessed 28 March 2013.

Lowe, C. 1999. Cultures of nature: mobility, identity, and biodiversity conservation in the Togean Islands of Sulawesi, Indonesia. PhD thesis. New Haven: Yale University.

Lumholz, C. 1920. *Through Central Borneo: an account of two years' travel in the land of the head-hunters between 1913 and 1917.* London: T. F. Unwin.

Lye, T. P. 2005. The meanings of trees: forest and identity for the Batek of Pahang, Malaysia. *Asia Pacific Journal of Anthropology* 6, 249–61.

Matisoff, J. A. 2003. Aslian: Mon-Khmer of the Malay Peninsula. *Mon Khmer Studies* 33, 1–58.

Minter, T. 2010. The Agta of the Northern Sierra Madre: livelihood strategies and resilience among Philippine hunter-gatherers. PhD thesis. Leiden: Leiden University.

Morrison, K. D. and Junker, L. L. 2002. *Forager-traders in south and southeast Asia: long-term histories.* Cambridge: Cambridge University Press.

Mudar, K. and Anderson, D. D. 2007. New evidence for Southeast Asian pleistocene foraging economies: faunal remains from the early levels of Lang Rongrien Rockshelter, Krabi, Thailand. *Asian Perspectives* 46, 298–334.

Noli, D. and Avery, G. 1988. Protein poisoning and coastal subsistence. *Journal of Archaeological Science* 15, 395–401.

Nolin, D. A. 2008. Food-sharing networks in Lamalera, Indonesia: tests of adaptive hypotheses. PhD thesis. University of Washington.

Nolin, D. A. 2010. Food-sharing networks in Lamalera, Indonesia: reciprocity, kinship, and distance. *Human Nature* 21, 243–68.

Oota, H., Weiss, G., and Stoneking, M. 2005. Recent origin and cultural reversion of a hunter-gatherer group. *PLoS biology* 3, e71.

Penny, D. 2001. A 40,000 year palynological record from north-east Thailand. *Palaeogeography, Palaeoclimatology, Palaeoecology* 171, 97–128.

Persoon, A. 2000. The Kubu of Central Sumatra, Indonesia. In L. Sponsel (ed.), *Endangered peoples of Southeast and East Asia: struggles to survive and thrive,* 157–72. Westport, CT: Greenwood Press.

Peterson, J. T. 1978. Hunter-gatherer/farmer exchange. *American Anthropologist* 80, 335–51.

Pryor, F. L. 2010. Inheritance and inequality of wealth: a comment. *Current Anthropology* 51, 111–13.

Puri, R. K. 2005. *Deadly dances in the Bornean rainforest: hunting knowledge of the Penan Benalui.* Leiden: KITLV.

Reid, L. A. 1994. Unravelling the linguistic histories of Philippine Negritos. In T. E. Dutton and D. T. Tryon (eds), *Language contact and change in the Austronesian world,* 443–75. Berlin: Walter de Gruyter.

Reid, L. A. 2007. Historical linguistics and Philippine hunter-gatherers. In B. Billings and N. Goudswaard (eds), *Piakandatu ami Dr. Howard P. McKaughan,* 6–30. Manila: Linguistic Society of the Philippines and SIL Philippines.

Rischel, J. 2004. Pan-dialectal databases: Mlabri, an oral Mon-Khmer language. Chiangmai: Lexicography Conference. Online version: http://www.rencontredespaces.org/renespace/voyages/ASIESE/Ethnies/languesfiches/etudestech/mlabri/Rischel_MlabriDict.pdf

Robinson, L. C. 2008. Dupaningan Agta: grammar, vocabulary, and texts. PhD thesis Manoa: University of Hawaii.

Rolland, N. 2008. The initial hominid colonization of Asia: a survey of anthropic evidence from biogeographic and ecological perspectives. *Bulletin of the Indo-Pacific Prehistory Association* 22, 3–15.

Roscoe, P. 2002. The hunters and gatherers of New Guinea 1. *Current Anthropology* 43, 153–62.

Sager, S. 2008. The sky is our roof, the earth our floor: Orang Rimba customs and religion in the Bukit Duabelas region of Jambi, Sumatra. PhD thesis. Australian National University.

Samuel, A. J., Kalusalingam, A., Chellappan, D. K., Gopinath, R., Radhamani, S., Husain, H. A., Muruganandham, V., and Promwichit, P. 2010. Ethnomedical survey of plants used by the Orang Asli in Kampung Bawong, Perak, West Malaysia. *Journal of Ethnobiological Ethnomedicine* 6, 5–10.

Sandbukt, Ø. 1988. Resource constraints and relations of appropriation among tropical forest foragers: the case of the Sumatran Kubu. *Research in Economic Anthropology* 10, 117–56.

Sarasin, P. and Sarasin, F. 1905. *Die Toala Hohlen von Lamontjong (The Toala Caves of Lamontjong)*. Wiesbaden: Kreidel.

Sather, C. 1995. Sea nomads and rainforest hunter-gatherers: foraging adaptations in the Indo-Malaysian archipelago. In P. Bellwood, J. A. Fox, and D. Tryon (eds), *The Austronesians: historical and comparative perspectives*, 229–68. Canberra: Australian National University.

Seitz, S. 2007. Game, pets, and animal husbandry among Penan and Punan Groups. In P. G. Sercombe and B. Sellato (eds), *Beyond the green myth: hunter-gatherers of Borneo in the twenty-first century*, 177–91. Copenhagen: Nordic Institute of Asian Studies.

Sellato, B. 1994. *Nomads of the Borneo rainforest: the economics, politics, and ideology of settling down*. Honolulu: University of Hawai'i Press.

Sercombe, P. and Sellato, B. (eds) 2007. *Beyond the green myth: Borneo's hunter-gatherers in the twenty-first century*. Copenhagen: Nordic Institute of Asian Studies.

Smith, E. A., Hill, K., Marlowe, F. W., Nolin, D., Wiessner, P., Gurven, M., Bowles, S., Borgerhoff Mulder, M., Hertz, T., and Bell, A. 2010. Wealth transmission and inequality among hunter-gatherers. *Current Anthropology* 51, 19–34.

Soares, P., Trejaut, J. A., Loo, J. H., Hill, C., Mormina, M., Lee, C. L., Chen, Y. M., Hudjashov, G., Forster, P., Macaulay, V., Bulbeck, D., Oppenheimer, S., Lin, M., and Richards, M. B. 2008. Climate change and postglacial human dispersals in southeast Asia. *Molecular biology and evolution* 25, 1209–18.

Sodhi, N. S., Brooks, T. M., Koh, L. P., Acciaioli, G., Erb, M., Tan, A. K., Curran, L. M., Brosius, P., Lee, T. M., Patlis, J. M., Gumal, M., and Lee, R. J. 2006. Biodiversity and human livelihood crises in the Malay Archipelago. *Conservation Biology: The Journal of the Society for Conservation Biology* 20, 1811–13.

Song, E. and Shen, C. 1999. Dulong. In R. B. Lee and R. Daly (eds), *The Cambridge encyclopedia of hunters and gatherers*, 303–6. Cambridge: Cambridge University Press.

Sopher, D. E. 1977. *The sea nomads: a study of the maritime boat people of Southeast Asia*. Singapore: National Museum.

Sorenson, E. R. 2004. Sea nomads. In N. S. Bisht and T. S. Bankoti (eds), *Encyclopaedia of South East Asian ethnography*, 576–80. Delhi: Global Vision Publishing House.

Sponsel, L. E. 2000. *Endangered peoples of Southeast and East Asia: struggles to survive and thrive*. Westport, CT: Greenwood.

Stoneking, M. and Delfin, F. 2010. The human genetic history of East Asia: weaving a complex tapestry. *Current Biology* 20, R188–R193.

Thambiah, S. 2007. The emergence of the ethnic category Bhuket. In P. Sercombe and B. Sellato (eds), *Beyond the green myth: hunter-gatherers of Borneo in the twenty-first century*, 91–109. Copenhagen: Nordic Institute of Asian Studies.

Urquhart, I. A. N. 1959. Nomadic Punans and Penans.' In T. Harrisson (ed.), *The peoples of Sarawak*, 73–93. Kuching: Sarawak Museum.

Widlok, T. and Tadesse, W. G. 2005. *Property and equality: encapsulation, commercialisation, discrimination*. New York: Berghahn.

Winzeler, R. L. 1997. *Indigenous peoples and the state: politics, land, and ethnicity in the Malayan Peninsula and Borneo*. New Haven: Yale University Press.

Wongbusarakum, S. 2007. *Urak Lawoi' of the Adang Archipelago*. Bangkok: Themma Group.

Woodburn, J. 1982. Egalitarian societies. *Man* 17, 431–51.

CHAPTER 49

REGIONAL HUNTER-GATHERER RESEARCH TRADITIONS
South America

GUSTAVO G. POLITIS AND ALMUDENA HERNANDO

SOUTH America is a fascinating region not only for the study of modern hunter-gatherers, but also for theoretical reflection on the evolutionary scheme that anthropology and archaeology have used to define them. As the Selk'nam and Yámana of Tierra del Fuego, considered to be 'archetypically' 'primitive' hunter-gatherers (Borrero 1992; Gamble 1992; Martinic 1995; Vidal 1999, 114) (Figure 49.1), were almost virtually extinct by the 1930s, research attention has been focused on groups living in the tropical lowlands (Rival 1999a, 78–9). Since the beginning of the sixteenth century, when Europeans started to colonize the continent, the life of the South American hunter-gatherers suffered deep changes, which ultimately resulted in most of them becoming extinct or incorporated to other non-hunter-gatherer groups. However, this way of life still survives in the tropical lowlands, showing its strength and vitality.

There are several present-day groups in the lowlands of South America who maintain, or until recently maintained, a hunter-gatherer way of life. However, this fact does not necessarily imply that they do not also practise—or have practised—some type of small-scale horticulture (Wilbert and Simoneau 1992). It has been proposed that many such hunter-gatherers, especially the Tupí-Guaraní groups, are the product of a process of 'regression', having had in the past an economy with a greater reliance on horticulture, which they subsequently abandoned owing to the impact of Western colonization (Lathrap 1968; Lévi-Strauss 1968). Other authors include in this group most tropical South American foragers, who are considered to perhaps represent 'secondary readaptations' (Lee 1999, 825), that is, 'new adaptations, not primeval ones' (Roosevelt 1998, 206). Whether or not these hypotheses can be tested with the available data, the horticultural past of most of these groups does not diminish their potential for understanding the hunter-gatherer way of life. Most live, or lived until recently, as foragers, with minimal or no horticulture, a lack of marked hierarchies, a high degree of sharing, and a pattern of high residential mobility. They have maintained this dynamic for generations and are distinctively different in subsistence terms from their more settled, horticulturist

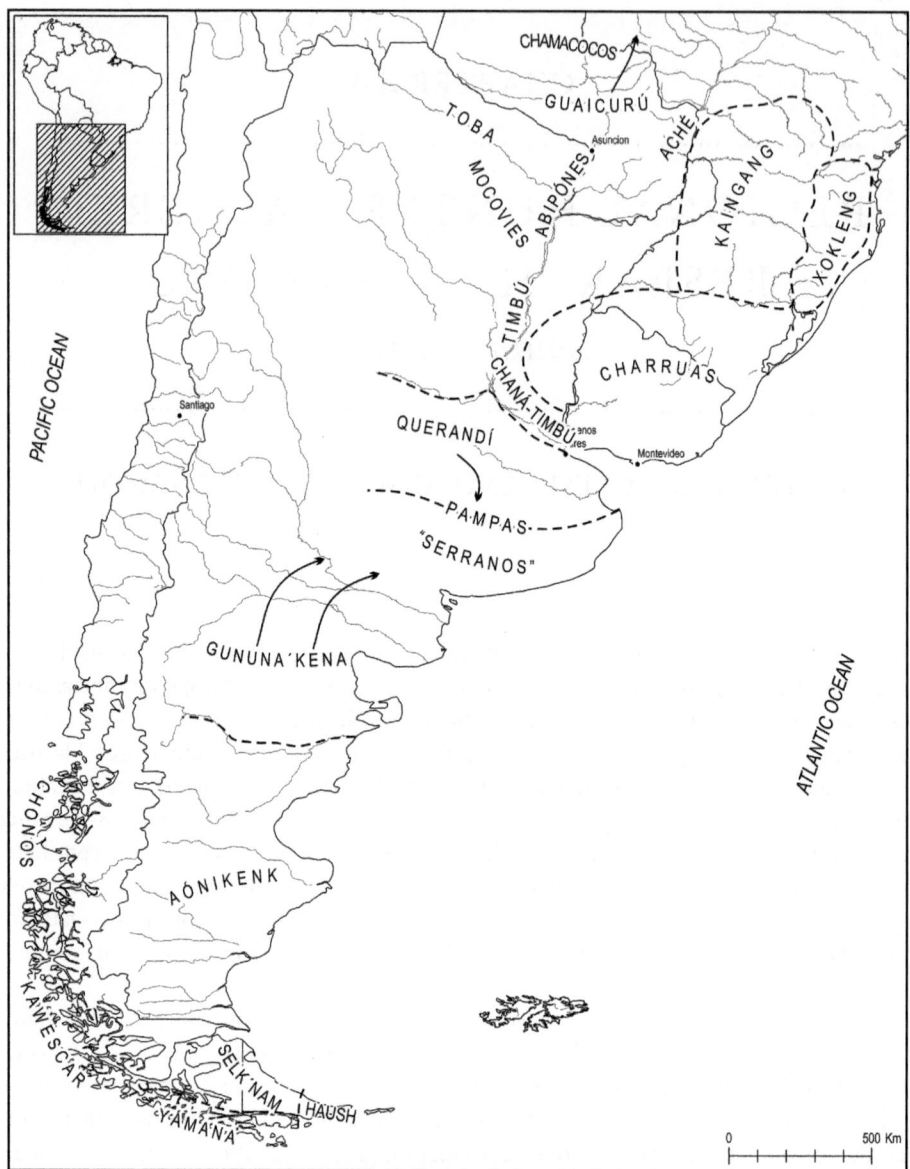

FIGURE 49.1 Map of southern South America showing the approximate location of the hunter-gatherers mentioned in the chapter.

and fisher neighbours. Moreover, the historical changes in their mode of life, before and after the sixteenth century, have a simple yet profound implication: among South American foragers the adoption of horticultural practices is reversible, and the incorporation of cultivated plants into their diet is not a linear process that once embarked upon cannot be abandoned. These examples demonstrate that under specific conditions tropical lowland indigenous groups can choose either to return to a forager way of life or to increase hunting and gathering to ensure their survival (Politis 2007; Rival 1999a, 81). This is a particularity of South American hunter-gatherers and would challenge the evolutionary models by showing that historical trajectories would greatly influence ecological adaptation.

The evolutionist prejudice has been questioned in recent years from several different perspectives. The 'hierarchical' status of evolutionary stages has been dissolved by new insights into the structural coherence of all cultures. In the hunter-gatherer case, several studies (Bird-David 1990; 1999; Descola 2005; Viveiros de Castro 1996) insist on an 'ecology of relations' as characteristic of how such groups perceive and relate to their worlds. This leads to the need to understand their culture from a different point of view than that which implies a clear distinction between the neat dichotomies 'which [constitute] the building blocks of the history of Western thought: nature-culture, nature-supernature, nature-art, nature-history, nature-mind' (Descola 1996, 98), and thus to escape evolutionism and ethnocentrism. This point has implications for other recent approaches to South American hunter-gatherers: the way some South American indigenous groups cultivate 'gardens', or use 'semi-wild' species, shows that no clear distinction can be established between hunter-gatherer 'food procurement' and 'food production' (Bird-David 1992; Ingold 1996; Rival 1999a, 80; 2006). Several authors working on distinct cases, such as Balée (1994) on the Awá-Guajá, Aché, Sirionó (Tupí-Guaraní groups) and the Kaingang (Jê), Posey (1983) on the Kayapó, Rival (2002) on the Huaorani, and Politis (2007) on the Nukak (Figure 49.2), reach the conclusion that these groups transform the forest as they live in it, either consciously as in the Kayapó case (Posey 1983) or unconsciously (see Balée 1994, 6). The interaction between plants and humans is as old as humankind and undoubtedly resulted in changes in the distribution of gathered species from the very beginning of such interactions (see the discussion in Hayden 1995). Hence, hunter-gatherers in one way or another always affect the natural distribution of some species, although the effect may be of low intensity. In the cases of the Nukak, the Kayapó, and the Huaorani, the identified processes imply complex actions—conscious or otherwise—that intersect several behavioural spheres (mobility, settlement, gathering, and discard patterns, etc.) and generate a concentration of resources that significantly favours human subsistence (Politis 2007).

It will be difficult to synthesize in this chapter the information that exists on South American hunter-gatherers. At present there are still several 'uncontacted' groups, or—as it is now more properly considered—groups in 'voluntary isolation', in the Amazon and the Gran Chaco (Parellada 2007), who, for obvious reasons, cannot be included in this brief review. In our need to be selective, we will necessarily leave out many prominent studies of hunter-gatherer societies. We hope, nevertheless, to reach a clear picture of the kind of dynamics that characterize these people, people who are still fighting to keep a way of life which belongs to the present.

The criteria used to classify South American hunter-gatherers are twofold: ethno/linguistic and geographical. Most Amazonian groups have been classified according to the former, but some, such as the Huaorani of eastern Ecuador or the Hotï of the Upper Orinoco Basin, whose language is not related to the main ethno/linguistic families, are better approached through their geographical location. The same applies to the peoples inhabiting the Pampas, Patagonia, Tierra del Fuego, and the Chaco. Our brief review will follow the criterion most used in each case, reproducing the common framework present in current academic literature.

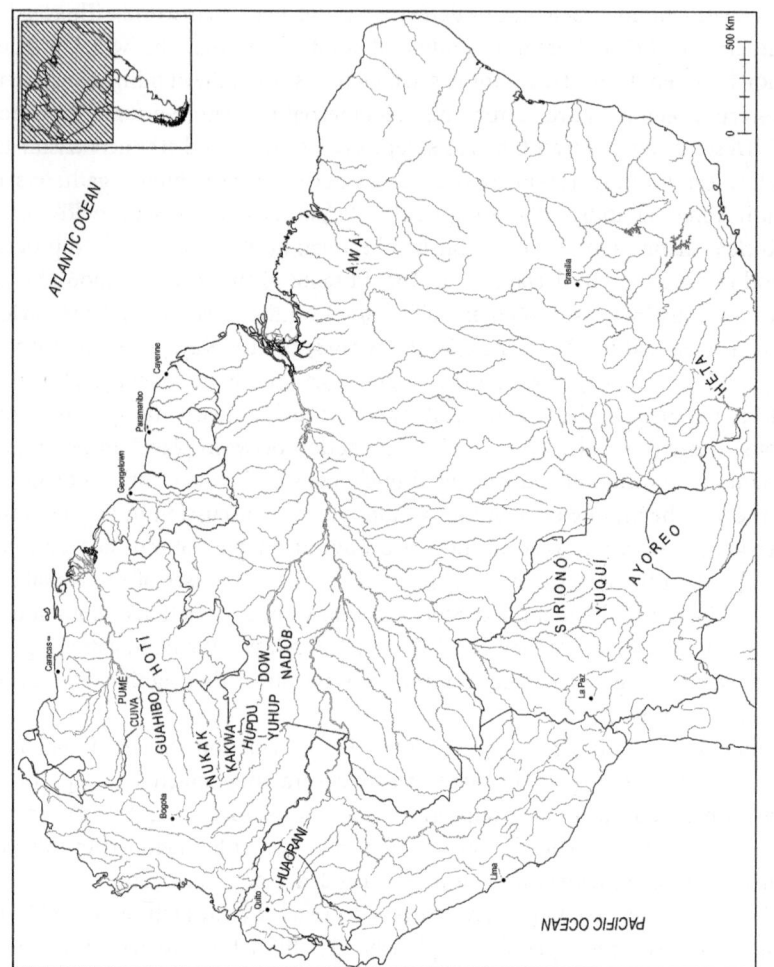

FIGURE 49.2 Map of northern South America showing the approximate location of the hunter-gatherers mentioned in the chapter.

The last introductory point to bear in mind is that this overview is based on different 'ethnographic presents'. From the early Querandíes of the eastern Pampas who became extinct during the first two centuries of the conquest to the still not-fully-contacted Awá of Brazil or Ayoreo of the Gran Chaco, there is a huge variation in terms of the moments of contact, decimation, and, when the case applies, extinction, as well as in the quality and quantity of the available written sources. Deep transformation, subordination, and extinctions of hunter-gatherers followed the paths of the colonial and neo-colonial expansion, usually stimulated by the value of the natural resources. These resources varied in time and regions, but mostly included land for European domesticated animals (such as in Patagonia and the Chaco), fertile soils for cereals and cattle (such as in the Pampas of Argentina, Uruguay, southern Brazil, and the Paraguayan Chaco), rubber and minerals in the Amazon Basin, ground for coca in the Llanos and in the rainforest of Colombia, and so forth. This chapter tries to capture this great diversity, whose main and most obvious consequence is that it reflects an uneven knowledge of South American hunter-gatherers.

Pampean and Patagonian Hunter-Gatherers

When the first Europeans arrived in the Pampas and Patagonia at the very beginning of the sixteenth century, they found a land of hunter-gatherers. With the exception of some Guarani 'colonies' and the Chana-Timbú complex (see Serrano 1950) in the Lower Paraná River and in the Lower Uruguay River, the whole Pampean grassland was occupied by the Querandí, also known as the 'Pampas' (Casamiquela 1969; but see Conlazo et al. 2006) in central-eastern Argentina and the Charrúas and the Guenoa-Minuanos in eastern Argentina, Uruguay, and south-eastern Brazil (Bracco 2004; López Mazz and Bracco 2010). The Querandíes were originally bola stone hunters of small- and medium-sized game (basically pampean deer) who quickly became horsemen and changed their way of life substantially: some merged with other groups (probably forming the peoples known as the 'Serranos' in the seventeenth to nineteenth centuries in the southern Pampas), while others, such as the Charrúas and the Guenoa-Minuanos (see discussion in Bracco 2004 and López Mazz and Bracco 2010), disappeared in subsequent centuries. By the beginning of the nineteenth century all of these ethnic groups were virtually extinct (with the exception of a few isolated populations in the southern Pampas).

In the lower Paraná and Uruguay rivers, several groups with an aquatically oriented way of life were found by the Spaniards upon their arrival. They were the canoe people known as Chaná-Timbú—a generic denomination that includes several groups or sub-groups such as the Chaná, Timbú, Chaná-Mbegua, and so on (Lothrop 1932; Serrano 1950)—with a mixed economy of hunting (swamp deer and coypo), gathering palm fruits and *algarrobo* (*Prosopis sp.*) fruits, and fishing. Some of these groups developed small-scale horticulture of maize, squash, and beans (Bonomo et al. 2011). At the very beginning of the conquest they were subjugated in 'encomiendas' or missionized, and by the beginning of the nineteenth century they disappeared as a distinct ethnic group.

The Aónikenk and Gununa'kena Patagonian hunter-gatherers, generically known as Tehuelches (Casamiquela 1969; Martinic 1995; Nacuzzi 1998) (Figure 49.3), were the

FIGURE 49.3 A Tehuelche camp (photo taken by Julio Koslowsky in 1895. Photo courtesy Archivo del Museo de La Plata).

last representatives of an early tradition of guanaco hunters, combining bola stone and bow-and-arrow hunting, who adopted horses slightly later than the Pampean Indians. During the eighteenth and nineteenth centuries the Mapuche (also known as Araucanos) from Chile exerted great influence upon them and changed the regional political scenario. The Tehuelches (partially 'araucanizados') remained in relative autonomy in a dynamic relationship of trade and transculturation (Pero 2002) until the end of the nineteenth century when several military campaigns launched by the Argentinian state led to their virtual annihilation. Nonetheless, small Tehuelche communities survive today in 'deep' Patagonia or are integrated in urban communities but still maintaining their ethnic identity. Most of the accounts of the Tehuelche are from nineteenth-century travellers (notably Claraz 1865–66 [1988]; Cox 1863; Musters 1871 [1979]), although more recent ethnographic research is also available (Aguerre 2000; 2008; Bórmida and Casamiquela 1958–9; Casamiquela 1969; Escalada 1949; 1953).

In Tierra del Fuego and in the southern and western Pacific Channels, two main hunter-gatherer ways of life survived until the twentieth century: the inland guanaco hunters of Tierra del Fuego, known as the Selk'nam (Borrero 2007; Chapman 1982), and the 'canoe' people of the channels (Orquera 2002). The latter included the Yámana of the Beagle Channel (Hyades and Deniker 1891; Orquera and Piana 1999), the Kaweskar—also known as Alakaluf—(Legoupil 1989; Rossi 2007), who lived in the western channels in Chile, and the Chonos in the Chonos and Guaitecas archipelagos. All maintained a traditional way of life until the very end of the nineteenth century, with the exception of the Chonos who vanished during the eighteenth century without significant testimonies (Orquera 2002, 145). Although decimated by the European and 'criollo' colonization, some managed to survive well into the twentieth century (Borrero 1994). These groups are principally known from historical accounts (Bridges [1880] 1947), but some remarkable systematic ethnographic studies were carried out among the Selk'nam, Yámana, and Kaweskar by the German priest Martin Gusinde (1931), among the Yámanas by Martial (1888) and Hyades (1885, see also Hyades and Deniker 1891), and by Ann Chapman (1982) among the Selk'nam.

THE GRAN CHACO

The vast forests and arid savannah plains of the Gran Chaco were occupied by a mosaic of ethnic groups when the Europeans arrived (Braunstein 1990–1; Braunstein and Miller 1999; Métraux 1946; Nordenskiold 1912; Renshaw 1996; Susnik 1971). Many groups maintained a foraging way of life with no or minimal horticulture, such as the Toba—or Qom (Mendoza 1999), the Mocovíes (Nesis 2005), the Abipones (Lucaioli 2005), the Chamacoco (Susnik 1969), the Ishir or Chamacocos mansos (Combès 2009, 107) and the Ayoreo (Bórmida 1973; Bórmida and Califano 1978; Zanardini 2003). Although the way of life of all has changed dramatically in recent centuries (see an excellent review in Combès 2009) some maintained a hunter-gatherer way of life until the twentieth century, and a few Ayoreo bands even remain in voluntary isolation in the Chaco forest of Paraguay and Bolivia (Fischermann 2007; Glauser 2007; Regehr 2008).

The Ayoreo are one of the most representative hunter-gatherer groups of the Gran Chaco. They belong to the Zamuco linguistic family (Combès 2009) and are divided into three major groups: the Garaigosode, the Guidaigosode, and the Totobiegosode (Regehr 2008). Originally, the Ayoreo occupied a great expanse of land, from the Central Chaco in Paraguay to the Chiquitania hills in Bolivia, but this territory has been reduced since colonial times. Until the mid-twentieth century they lived as nomadic hunter-gatherers with relative autonomy in large territories (Combès 2009). They were organized into 50 autonomous local groups, with independent leaders (Glauser 2007, 224). Between the end of the 1950s and the 1970s most of the Ayoreo were settled in missions, in both Bolivia and Paraguay. At least during the first half of the twentieth century, the isolated bands practised some small-scale horticulture during periods of peace or political quietness (Amarilla and Iquebi Posoraja 2011). At the beginning of the current century there were between 4,200 and 4,500 Ayoreo (Fischermann 2007; Regehr 2008), of whom only 50–100 remain in voluntary isolation in the remanent Chaco forest (Glauser 2007, 223).

Many hunter-gatherer groups in the Gran Chaco belonged to the Guaicurú linguistic family, first systematized by Kersten (1905 [1968]), which included the following ethnic groups: Abipones, Mocovíes, Tobas, Mbayás-caduveos, and Payaguás. Later classifications also included other groups such as the Pilagá, Gausarapos, and others (see the discussion in Nacuzzi et al. 2008, 40–4). Most of these groups incorporated horses, which augmented their mobility circuits and increased their territories by the eighteenth century (Nacuzzi et al. 2008). For this period the main source of information are the rich accounts produced by the Jesuits (Dobrizhoffer 1784 [1967]; Lozano 1733 [1941]; Paucke 1749–6/ [1943]; [1944]).

One of the most notable cases in this region is that of the so-called 'proper' Guaicurú (also known as Mbayá-Caduveo (Kersten [1905] 1968) or Guaicurú-Mabayá (Schindler 1985), who lived in the Paraguay River Basin (Santos-Granero 2009). Although at the time of contact they did not practise horticulture, it was mentioned that they had maize, manioc, and other cultivars that they obtained from tributary groups. With the early adoption of the horse, the Guaicurú increased their mobility and thus their hunting and gathering options (Métraux 1946), as well as their warring capacity and therefore the number of tributaries. In the early eighteenth century the Guaicurú-Mabayá were divided in three *cacicatos* (chieftainships) with more than 500 tributary families (Lozano 1733 in Santos-Granero 2009). By the end of the nineteenth century only one chieftainship survived, the Caduveo (although Vitar 1997 considered this an ethnic group distinct from the 'proper' Guaicurú), numbering about 200 people (Boggiani 1892 [1945], 242). Currently there are approximately 1,600 (ISA 2001). Notably, the Guaicurú were involved in a political macro-system in which, in spite of being hunter-gatherers (and contra evolutionist assumptions), they played a powerful role, subordinating horticultural neighbouring populations in a tributary system (Santos-Granero 2009).

Another well-known hunter-gatherer group of the same linguistic family is the Toba (or Qom), who lived in the Argentinean Chaco (Braunstein and Miller 1999; Mendoza 1999). They were foragers, although they also practised small-scale agriculture (Arenas 2003). Currently the Toba number about 2,000 people living in extremely poor conditions mostly in the provinces of Chaco and Formosa in Argentina.

THE ORINOCO BASIN

In the Orinoco Basin hunter-gatherers contacted Europeans in the early years of the conquest, but some groups, such as the Guahibo, maintained some kind of traditional way of life until the twentieth century. In the Maigualida Hills and in the neighbouring plains the Hotï were contacted in the mid-twentieth century (Cruxent 1961), and some bands still live in a high degree of isolation (Figure 49.4). The first systematic studies were as late as the 1970s (Coppens 1983). More complete studies (Storrie 1999; Zent 2006; Zent and Zent 2002) indicate that the Hotï are basically foragers, although around 30 per cent of their diet comes from cultivated plants. The total number of Hotï is about 1,000; approximately half live in two villages (a Catholic mission and a former New Tribes mission), while the other half maintains a semi-nomadic way of life. Detailed ethnobotanical studies (Zent and Zent 2002; 2004) show a sophisticated management of plant resources. Preliminary ethnoarchaelogical studies (Politis and Jaimes 2005) also indicate a complex and highly idiosyncratic management of animal bone discard.

The other well-known hunter gatherers of the Orinoco Basin are the Guahibo (Morey and Metzger 1974), especially the Cuiva (also known as Hiwi; Arcand 1972; Coppens 1975; Hurtado and Hill 1986; 1987) and Pumé (also known as Yaruro; Gragson 1989; Mitriani 1988) sub-groups. The Guahibos comprise the largest indigenous people of the western sector of the Orinoco Basin. They live in the tropical savannahs—regionally known as *llanos*— of Colombia and Venezuela. The population was estimated at between 10,000 and 15,000 in the 1970s, although today the number could be higher. Traditionally, the Guahibo were

FIGURE 49.4 A Hotï man entering his recently built hut. He is transporting most of the family belongings in his basket (photo Gustavo Politis 2002).

nomadic hunter-gatherers, or perhaps seasonal small-scale horticulturalists, who inhabited the interfluvial lands and the smaller rivers of the *llanos*. This somewhat peripherical position, far from the main routes of navigation such as the Meta and the Orinoco rivers permitted them to survive and apparently to increase numerically in the historical period (Morey and Metzger 1974, 21). Although the Guahibo have augmented horticultural practices in recent decades, they are still heavily dependent upon resources from the gallery forest-covered flood plains bordering the rivers. The Cuiva were contacted in the 1950s and settled on a cattle ranch in Venezuela. By the 1970s there were some 800 people (Arcand 1972), most of whom were settled in several permanent villages, although they spent much of the time hunting and gathering (Hurtado and Hill 1987). The Pumé, numbering 5,400, subsist on foraging and manioc horticulture. Detailed ethnoarchaeological research has been carried out among them since the early 1990s (Greaves 1997; 2006).

The Tupí-Guaraní Ethno/Linguistic Family

The Tupí-Guaraní family (which numbers at least 33,000 people speaking 21 languages) is dispersed over distant countries in South America (Brazil, Argentina, Bolivia, Paraguay, and French Guyana), showing a minimal differentiation at the linguistic level, a maximal dispersion in geographical terms, and a marked heterogeneity in social morphology (Viveiros de Castro 1992, 24). The Guaraní 'migratory complex' and the population dislocations caused by the European invasion have been alluded to as the causes of the first two phenomena. The adaptation to different ecological and cultural contexts has been used to explain the third (Viveiros de Castro 1992, 24). Some Guarani are nomadic hunters (the Awá, also known as Guajá, the Sirionó, Yuquí, Héta, and Aché), while others present more complex socio-economic organization systems. Their forms of residence, village morphologies, kinship terminologies, and ceremonial structures are equally diverse, to the point that Viveiros de Castro (1992, 26) refers to the 'eminently plastic capacity of the Tupi-Guarani matrix'. Attempts to explain this heterogeneity coincide in attributing these groups to a single and common origin: the complex Tupinambá society, which would have moved deep into the interior as a consequence of the European invasion in the first decades of the sixteenth century. The Tupinambá, extinguished in the eighteenth century (Jensen 1999, 125, note 2) were coastal Indians, living around the current area of Río de Janeiro and northward. They were so numerous that their language was known as the 'Brasilica' or 'Brasiliano' before the name 'Tupinambá' started to be used in the eighteenth century (Rodrigues 1986). The Tupí-Guaraní groups are a branch (or sub-group) of the Tupí family and its name preceded the attempt at linguistic classification carried out by Rodrigues (1958). We will refer here only to those Tupí-Guaraní groups who keep—or kept until recently—a hunter-gatherer way of life.

The best-known sub-groups are the Awá, also known as the Guajá, who number about 300 and are settled in three reservations protected by the government agency FUNAI (Fundação Nacional do Índio) in Maranhão, Brazil (Cormier 2003a; 2003b; Forline 1997; González Ruibal et al. 2011; Hernando et al. 2011); the Héta, now almost extinct (in the 1990s only eight people survived) who lived in the west of Paraná State in southern Brazil (Kózak et al. 1979; Laming-Emperaire et al. 1978); the Sirionó, around 600 people settled permanently at Llanos de Mojos, eastern Bolivia (Balée 1999; Califano 1999; Stearman 1987); the Yuquí, who numbered 73 in 1983, and inhabit an area of tropical forest near the eastern edge of the Andes mountains of Bolivia (Stearman 1989, 220–1); and the Aché, also known as the Guayakí, living in eastern Paraguay and distributed into four groups, the most numerous being the northern Aché (Cadogan 1965; Clastres 1972a; 1972b; Hill and Hawkes 1983; Hill and Hurtado 1995; 1999; Kaplan and Hill 1985). In 2008, the total number of Aché from seven communities was 1,592 people (Parellada and Beldi de Alcántara 2008, 21).

Besides their language, all of these groups have in common a history of massacres, epidemics, and, in general, violent contact with Spanish or Portuguese invaders or with later state societies (see for example Parellada and Beldi de Alcántara 2008 for a detailed account of the 'Aché genocide'). Some also have a long history of persecution and aggression on the part of their own indigenous neighbours, which could help to explain their nomadic lifestyle (see Hill and Hurtado 1999, 92). For example, the Aché were persecuted by Guaraní horticulturalists, and the Awá were persecuted by the Ka'apor horticulturalists (Balée 1994, 210). In contrast, the Yuquí, in spite of being defined as 'true foragers, having practiced no horticulture whatsoever until mission intervention', are characterized by the existence 'of an upper caste termed *saya* (and) hereditary slavery' (Stearman 1989, 221).

In most cases these groups' mobility has been significantly reduced from pre-contact life, as the majority currently live on reservations. These are either of missionary origin, as in the case of the Sirionó (Balée 1999, 105–6) or the Yuquí (Stearman 1989, 220–1), or government established, as in all Brazilian cases, where the reservations all depend on FUNAI (Coelho et al. 2009). The Aché reservations have resident Catholic or Protestant missionaries, except in one case where they were evicted by the Aché themselves (Hill and Hurtado 1999, 95). This reduction of mobility explains the in general forced introduction of agriculture (manioc, rice, or plantain in most cases), which tends, as a vicious circle, to reduce mobility. However, in some cases, such as the Awá and possibly the Sirionó and Yuquí (see Fischermann 2007), there are still bands or families who remain in isolation avoiding contact not only with Western society but also with their own, already contacted people.

The dramatic reduction of mobility of most Tupi-Guarani hunter-gatherers does not prevent hunting and gathering activities, which occur either as short daily foraging trips or in longer logistical expeditions that can last from days to weeks. Game (usually a variety of monkeys, peccary, tapir, agouti, deer, paca, and armadillo) is still the only source of meat and, besides enjoyment and prestige (Forline 1997; Stearman 1989, 221), provides a significant part of their diet, reaching 80 per cent in the case of the Aché (Hill and Hurtado 1999, 93). Although Holmberg (1969, xix) described the Sirionó as 'suffer[ing] from lack of food', Balée (1999, 107) attributes such difficulties to contact, as recent research suggests abundant resources in the area and other food, such as honey, were, and still remain, abundant (Lehm 2004, 148–71).

Technology is very similar in all cases. Bow and wood-tipped arrows are the most common hunting tools. Aché and Héta traditionally also hunted by hand and used 'a celt-type stone axe' to extract palm products, honey, and larvae (Hill and Hurtado 1999, 93; Kozák et al. 1979). Large fish are killed with harpoons and arrows in the case of the Awá (González Ruibal et al. 2011); and Holmberg (1969, 25) refers to the digging stick used for horticultural activities among the Sirionó at the time of his fieldwork (1940–1). Although the Héta quickly vanished after contact in the 1950s it was possible to record (and film) with some detail the main technological processes involved in making stone axes, bows, arrows, and so on (Kozák et al. 1979), and also present such processes from an ethnoarchaeological perspective (Laming-Emperaire et al. 1978; Miller Jr. 1979).

THE MACRO-JÊ (GÊ OR YÊ) ETHNO/LINGUISTIC FAMILY

The first synthesis including populations in the Macro-Jê branch was undertaken by Martius in 1867, who suggested the Jê denomination (Noelli 2005, 177). Throughout the twentieth century comparative linguistics among Jê groups was developed by several authors (Mason, Davis, or Loulkotka) and the Macro-Jê branch was defined (Noelli 2005, 178). Rodrigues (1999) classified the Jê languages into four groups: the north-eastern, north-western, central, and meridional southern Jê.

Although only some southern Jê (the Xokléng and Kaingáng) were foragers, hunting, gathering, and fishing were important seasonal activities in many others groups. This is the case among the Kayapó (Jê) (Posey 1982; 1983; Turner 1979; Verswijver 1992) and the Bororo (Macro-Jê) (Colbacchini and Albisetti 1942; Crocker 1985; Maybury-Lewis and Bamberger 1980). The Xokléng were hunter-gatherers who historically occupied the southern Brazilian Planalto and the Serra Geral e Do Mar, which are currently parts of the Paraná, Santa Catarina and Rio Grande do Sul states in Brazil. This area includes the Mata

Atlantica and the Araucaria Forest from where they obtained one of their main resources, the *pinheiro-do-Paraná* (*Araucaria agustifolia*) (Coelho dos Santos 1997; Henry 1964; Lavina 1994). Abundant historical accounts tell of the Xokléng resistance during the nineteenth century against the *caboclos* and the European immigrants (Germans and Italians) (see review in Lavina 1994, 23–9). Isolated groups managed to survive in the forest until the beginning of the twentieth century. After several years of attempts, the SPI (Serviço de Proteção aos Índios, the forerunner of the FUNAI) made Pacific contact and settled them in an Indian post in 1914. Currently most Xokléng are located in the Área Indigena de Ibirama, where 1,200 people live, the majority of whom identify themselves as Xokléng.

The Kaingáng live in south-eastern Brazil, west of the Xokléng territory in the Planalto, as far as the Misiones Province of Argentina (Basile Becker 1995; Métraux 1963, Mota et al. 2000; Noelli 1998). They represent one of the major indigenous populations in Brazil, with more than 20,000 people (Noelli 1998, 9), and comprise several sub-groups who, during colonial times, were hunter-gatherers (although some small-scale horticulture might have been practised, see Basile Becker 1995, 17). Like their Xokléng neighbours, medium- and small-sized game and the collection of *pinheiro-do-Paraná* were the main sources of subsistence. Major events in the history of the Kaingáng include the German and Italian colonization (beginning in 1824 and 1848, respectively), which produced a dramatic impact on their hunter-gatherer way of life and the substantial reduction of traditional territories (Basile Becker 1995).

The Makú Groups

The foragers of the north-west Amazon have been grouped under the generic name Makú (Koch-Grünberg 1906; Métraux 1948; Münzel 1969–72; Tastevin 1923). Linguistically they belong to the Makú-Puinave family (Reina 1992). However, a comparative study has proposed more recently the existence of a Tukano-Makú linguistic family. 'Maku' is not a self-denomination, as none of the indigenous groups call themselves by this name. It is considered a word of Arawak or Tukano origin that is used to designate some of the interfluvial hunter-gatherer groups of the north-west Amazon, and it generally has a pejorative connotation when used by other indigenous peoples (especially the Tukanos, for whom the term Makú means servant or slave, although see discussion in Santos-Granero 2009). For the Spanish-speaking *colonos* of Colombia, Makú is a synonym for 'wild Indian', and for the Portuguese-speaking Brazilian *caboclos*, Makú is synonymous with *indios do mato* (Indians of the forest). Therefore, a first point to bear in mind when undertaking an anthropological analysis of any of these groups is that the term 'Makú' is itself vague and imprecise. Each Makú group has their own historical trajectory and has suffered the impact of Western society in variable and significantly different ways at different times. However, all share a recent past as nomadic hunter-gatherers with a diet based on hunting monkey, peccaries, birds, and so on, gathering forest products (especially palm fruit and palm grubs), and fishing in small rivers and creeks. Blowpipes with poison darts and spears are common weapons.

The word Makú spread in the ethnographic literature following the work of Koch-Grünberg (1906), who recognized the existence of several groups between the

Negro, Tiquié-Vaupés, and Japurá rivers. He considered these groups to be ethnically distinct but sharing some traits in common. Subsequently, Rivet and Testevin (1920) examined Kock-Grünberg's work and arrived at the conclusion that all of the languages of the groups generically denominated Makú—the majority of which are mutually unintelligible—were dialects of a single mother tongue. As such, they proposed the existence of the Makú-Puinave linguistic family, which included not only the groups mentioned but also the Puinave. Métraux (1948, 864) caused a degree of confusion concerning the Makú, proposing the existence of 'three different tribes of Indians who are linguistically unrelated', which, as well as the classic Makú from the Rio Negro-Japurá, included two other distinct groups: the 'Macu of the Uraricoera Basin' (in Brazilian Guiana) and the 'Macu-Piaroa', a sub-group of the latter who live on the Lower Ventuari and Orinoco rivers. These last two are not now considered part of the groups generically known as Makú. During the second half of the twentieth century several authors referred to the Makú, drawing attention to their linguistic differences and distinct ways of life (Biocca 1965; Schultz 1959).

There are currently six recognized ethnic/linguistic Makú groups geographically distributed between Brazil and Colombia, principally on the eastern side of the Rio Negro between the Guaviare River and the Caquetá-Japurá rivers. These groups are the Hupdu, Yuhup, Dow or Kamaa, Nadöb or Kabori-Nadöb, Kawka or Bará, and Nukak (Figure 49.5). Some of these have been relatively well studied. Articles and monographs are available on the Hupdu (Athias 2003; Giacone 1955; Pozzobon 1983; 1992; Reid 1979), Yuhup (Pozzobon 1983; 1992; Reina 1986), Kakwa (Silverwood-Cope 1972; 1990), and Nukak (Cabrera et al. 1999; Politis 1996; 2007). There are fewer scientific references for the other two, the Kabori-Nadöb being the least well known (Münzel 1969–72; Schultz 1959).

FIGURE 49.5 Nukak wet-season camp (photo Gustavo Politis 1994).

The Hupdu are the most numerous and live in the interfluvial zone of the Tiquié, Uaupes, and Papurí rivers. Around 1989 their population was estimated at 1,144, divided into three dialectical groups (Pozzobon 1992). The Yuhup live along the tributaries south of the Tiquié Apaporis River and a tributary of the latter, the Trairá River. Their population has been estimated at 370 (Pozzobon 1992). The Nadöb inhabit the most south-easterly sector of Makú land, and their population has been estimated at between 300 and 400 (Pozzobon 1992). The Kamaa are probably the least numerous—numbered at only 70 people in the late 1980s (Pozzobon 1992)—and the most culturally transformed, as they live in the vicinity of the city of São Gabriel de Cachoeira.

The six known Makú groups had all incorporated some elements of horticultural practice by the time they were studied. Nonetheless, in the case of the Nukak (the most traditional) this still represented only a small proportion of their annual diet. In other cases, such as the Hupdu and Kakwa, horticulture contributes significantly to their subsistence, and its impact goes beyond diet with a notable influence on mobility patterns (Biocca 1965; Pozzobon 1992; Reid 1979; Silverwood-Cope 1972). The Kakwa, Hupdu, Yuhup, and the Nadöb are considered hunter-gatherers because until a few generations ago their subsistence was based almost exclusively on the hunting and gathering of wild products (Koch-Grünberg 1906, 879; Martius 1867, 247; McGovern 1927; Whiffen 1915). However, the Hupdu spend some six months a year at their residential base during which time 'carbohydrate [is the] base of the diet, more than 80 per cent of which is derived from manioc' (Reid 1979, 93). In the late 1950s manioc was the main food source for the Nadöb (Schultz 1959, 119), and in the 1960s labour related to the production of manioc occupied more time in men's daily lives than hunting and gathering combined (Münzel 1969–72). The Yuhup were also in a similar state when studied by Pozzobon (1983).

Western Amazonia

The main group in western Amazonia is the Huaorani (or Waorani), who speak an independent language, Huaorani, and live in the largest indigenous territory in Ecuador. Their territory includes the Yasuní National Park and the so-called 'Protectorate' created in 1969 by the Summer Institute of Linguistics to protect the Huaorani people (Rival 2002, xiv–xvi). The Huaorani are divided into (or related to) several groups, some of which, such as the Tagaeri and the Taromenane, seem to be intra-adversarial (as well as with other Huaorani) and still fight to defend their isolation and escape contact with modern society. As only the Huaorani have been systematically studied, we will focus on them here using the information provided by Rival (1999a; 1999b; 2002; 2006; 2007).

The Huaorani number approximately 1,400 and live as forest trekkers in the heart of Ecuadorian Amazonia. They are defined as nomadic, autarkuic, and highly endogamous as a way of defending themselves from the general threat represented by outsiders. Although they traditionally cultivate garden crops (manioc and plantain) rudimentarily and sporadically for ceremonial drinks, they are in fact more foragers than gardeners. Rival (2002, xiii) argues that their 'mobility is not primarily determined by economic or ecological factors but represents the historical development of a distinct mode of life that the notions of archaism and agricultural regression cannot explain satisfactorily'. Through their cycles of residential mobility and daily consumption of forest resources, they enrich the habitat through small but constant modifications, creating anthropogenic forests qualitatively different from those created through shifting cultivation. The longhouse, defined by uxorical residence and sororal marriage, is their basic social unit, organized around the collective sharing of food individually produced. Until the introduction of shotguns, dogs, and new garden crops, they hunted almost exclusively with blowpipe and spears. Gathered fruits are also an important part of their daily food intake, the peach palm being the main staple when in season.

Finally, it is important to note that in the western Amazon, especially the borders between eastern Peru and Ecuador and western Brazil, there are still a large number of indigenous people in voluntary isolation or ethnographically poorly known. Most are from the Pano linguistic family (Erikson 1996). In some areas such as the Javari Valley at least 26 concentrations of isolated Indians have been detected (Dos Santos and Nobre Mendez 2007), among whom there are probably several hunter-gatherer groups. In other regions, such as the Terra Indígena Massaco, on the northern bank of the Guaporé River (southern Rondonia State, Brazil) the presence of nomadic hunter-gatherers, probably related to the Sirionó, was reported until at least the mid-1980s. For obvious reasons, these groups cannot be summarized in this chapter.

Conclusions

Based on the information summarized above and despite the great diversity of South American hunter gatherers, some general trends can be drawn.

1. South American hunter-gatherers, with very few exceptions, are highly egalitarian ideologically and in practice, and lack strong social institutions. Sharing and cooperation are key elements in these societies. Gender equality in daily life seems to be common.
2. Resistance and struggle against Westerners have been constant since colonial times. Such strategies indicate the value of autonomy and independence for these societies. Even today, in the deep forest of the Amazon and the Gran Chaco there are people who fight with spears, bows, or blowpipes against invaders. 'Pure' hunter-gatherers still exist on the continent.
3. The tropical rainforest hunter-gatherers show a sophisticated management of the floral wild resources, developing various strategies to concentrate non-cultivated species. The Nukak, the Hotï, and the Huaorani provide good examples.
4. At the time of contact, hunter-gatherers were integrated into regional networks and macro political systems. In these contexts they occupied different positions and roles. For example, in the north-western Amazon the Makú lived in a complex relationship with their Tukano neighbours, which in many cases resulted in positions of subjection and servitude for the former. However, the Guaicurú-Mbayá coexisted with neighbouring peoples whom they subjugated as a tributary population. In other cases, such as in Tierra del Fuego and the Southern Channels, the Selk'nam, Yámana, Kawescar, and Haush seem to have lived in a symmetrical relationship. As such, the recent isolation of hunter-gatherers appears to have been the result of

Western colonization.

The hunter-gatherers of South America today live under a wide range of conditions of contact and assimilation with the Western world. While on one extreme there are still peoples in voluntary isolation in the Amazon rainforest, on the other, well-assimilated populations of former hunter-gatherers live as poor rural or city dwellers. One clear-cut example of the latter pole is Margarita Mbywangi, an Aché woman who in 2008 was the Minister of Indigenous Affairs in Paraguay (probably the only direct and full descendant of hunter-gatherers in South America who has reached such a high political position).

The supposed 'horticultural regression' of some hunter-gatherers (see above) also has significant implications. Such changes are not evolutionary events but rather are fundamentally political actions determined by the history of the colonization of the continent. So-called 'horticultural regression' actually shows that these groups made decisions throughout their history in which they privileged certain values, such as political autonomy and cultural integrity, at the expense of others, such as access to commodities or the supposed alimentary security that crops may provide (see Viveiros de Castro 1996, 194). Consequently, even in the case that some South American groups may be the result of an historical transformation from horticulturist societies, we should not judge this to be cultural 'regression', but rather evolution in a different direction than our own historical trajectory.

The richness and the diversity of South American hunter-gatherers as well as their resistance and struggles to maintain their traditional patterns (nowadays very active against logging and mineral extraction policies driven by the capitalist world system) demonstrate the vitality and trueness of this kind of economic, socio-political, and ideational way of life. Although hunting and gathering as a way of life has almost vanished from the South American scenario, some hunter-gatherers are still positioned in the interstices of globalization, resisting domination and maintaining their political autonomy.

References

Aguerre, A. M. 2000. *Las vidas de 'Pati' en la toldería tehuelche del río Pinturas y el después*. Buenos Aires: Facultad de Filosofía y Letras, UBA.

Aguerre, A. M. 2008. *Genealogía de familias tehuelches-araucanas de la Patagonia central y meridional argentina*. Buenos Aires: Editorial de la Facultad de Filosofía y Letras, UBA.

Amarilla, D. and Iquebi Posoraja, J. 2011. *Captura del Ayoreo José Iquebi*. Centro de Estudios Antropológicos de la Universidad Católica, Asunción.

Arcand, B. 1972. *The urgent situation of the Cuiva Indians of Colombia*. Copenhagen: IWGIA Documents.

Arenas, P. 2003. *Etnografía y alimentación entre los toba-ñachilamillek y los wichi-lhuku'tas del Chaco Central Argentina*. Buenos Aires: Edición del autor.

Athias, R. 2003. Territoriality and space among the Hupd'ä and Tukano of the River Uaupés Basin. *Estudios Latinoamericanos* 23, 1–26.

Balée, W. 1994. *Footprints of the forest. Ka'apor ethnobotany: the historical ecology of plant utilization by an Amazonian people*. New York: Columbia University Press.

Balée, W. 1999. 'The Sirionó of the Llanos de Mojos, Bolivia'. In R. B. Lee and R. Daly (eds), *The Cambridge encyclopedia of hunters and gatherers*, 105–6. Cambridge: Cambridge University Press.

Basile Becker, I. I. 1995. *O indio kaingang no Rio Grande do Sul*. São Leopoldo, Brasil: Editorial UNISINOS.

Biocca, E. 1965. *Viaggi Tra Gli Indi. Alto Rio Negro- Alto Orinoco. Appunti di un biologo*. Rome: Consiglio Nazionale Delle Ricerche.

Bird-David, N. 1990. The giving environment: another perspective on the economic system of gatherer-hunters. *Current Anthropology* 31, 183–96.

Bird-David, N. 1992. Beyond 'the hunting and gathering mode of subsistence': culture-sensitive observations on the Nayaka and other modern hunter-gatherers. *Man* 27, 19–44.

Bird-David, N. 1999. 'Animism' revisited: personhood, environment and relational epistemology. *Current Anthropology* 40, Supplement, S40–S91.

Boggiani, G. 1892 [1945]. *Os Caduveo*. São Paulo: Livraria Martins Editôra.

Bonomo, M., Politis G., and Gianotti García, C. 2011. Montículos, jerarquía social y horticultura en las sociedades indígenas del Delta del río Paraná (Argentina). *Latin American Antiquity* 22, 297–333.

Bórmida, M. 1973. Ergon y Mito: una Hermenéutica de la Cultura Material de los Ayoreo del Chaco Boreal. *Scripta Ethnologica* 1, 9–68.

Bórmida, M. and Califano, M. 1978. *Los indios Ayoreo del Chaco Boreal*. Buenos Aires: Fundación para la Educación, la Ciencia y la Cultura.

Bórmida, M. and Casamiquela, R. 1958-9. Etnografía Gününa-Këna. Testimonio del último de los Tehuelches Septentrionales. *Runa* 9, 153–93.

Borrero, L. 1992. Pristine archaeologists and the settlement of southern South America. *Antiquity* 66, 768–70.

Borrero, L. 1994. The extermination of the Selk'nam. In E. S. Burch and L. J. Ellanna (eds), *Key issues in hunter-gatherer research*, 247–61. Oxford: Berg.

Borrero, L. 2007. *Los Selk'nam (Onas)*. Buenos Aires: Editorial Galerna

Bracco, D. 2004. *Charrúas, guenoas y guaraníes. Interacción y destrucción: indígenas en el Río de la Plata*. Montevideo: Librería Linardi y Risso.

Braunstein, J. (ed.) 1990–1. *Hacia una nueva carta étnica del Gran Chaco*. Informe de avance PID-CONICET. Chaco: Centro del Hombre Antiguo Chaqueño.

Braunstein, J. and Miller, E. (eds) 1999. *Peoples of the Gran Chaco*. Westport, CT: Bergin and Garvey.

Bridges, E. 1880 [1947]. *The uttermost part of the earth*. London: Hodder & Stoughton.

Cabrera, G., Franky, C., and Mahecha, D. 1999. *Los Nukak. Nómadas de la Amazonía Colombiana*. Santafé de Bogotá: Editorial Universidad Nacional.

Cadogan, L. 1965. Algunos textos Guayaki del Ynaro. II parte. *Journal de la Société des Américanistes* 54, 93–115.

Califano, M. (ed.) 1999. *Los indios Sirionó de Bolivia Oriental*. Buenos Aires: Ciudad Argentina.

Casamiquela, R. 1969. *Un nuevo panorama etnológico del área pan-pampeana y patagónica adyacente. Pruebas Etnohistóricas de la filiación tehuelche septentrional de los Querandíes*. Santiago de Chile: Museo Nacional de Historia Natural.

Chapman, A. 1982. *Drama and power in a hunting society: the Selk'nam of Tierra del Fuego*. Cambridge: Cambridge University Press.

Claraz, J. 1865-6 [1988]. *Diario de viaje de exploración al Chubut*. Buenos Aires: Marymar.

Clastres, P. 1972a. *Chronique des indiens Guayaki: ce que savant les Aché, chasseurs nomads du Paraguay*. Paris: Plon.

Clastres, P. 1972b. The Guayaki. In M. Bicchieri (ed.), *Hunters and gatherers today*, 138–74. New York: Holt, Rinehart & Winston.

Coelho, E., Politis, G., Hernando, A., and González Ruibal, A. 2009. Os Awá-Guajá e o processo de sedentarização. In S. Figuereido Ferretti and J. R. Ramalho (orgs.), *Amazônia: desenvolvimento, meio ambiente e diversidade sociocultural*, 91–118. São Luis, MA: PROCAD-CAPES.

Coelho dos Santos, S. 1997. *Os Índios Xokleng. Memória Visual*. Florianópolis: Editora da UFSC, Editora da UNIVALI.

Colbacchini, A. and Albisetti, C. 1942. *Os Bororos Orientais Orarimogodogue do Planalto Oriental de Mato Grosso*. Brasiliana, Grande Formato, Serie 5a, vol. 4. São Paulo: Companhia Editora Nacional.

Combès, I. 2009. *Zamucos*. Colección Scripta Autóctona 1. Santa Cruz de la Sierra: Instituto Latinoamericano de Misionología.

Conlazo, D., Lucero, M. M., and Authié, T. 2006 *Los Querandíes*. Buenos Aires: Galerna.

Coppens, W. 1975. *Los Cuiva de San Esteban de Capanaparo*. Caracas: Fundación La Salle de Ciencias Naturales.

Coppens, W. 1983. Hoti. In W. Coppens (ed.), *Los Aborígenes de Venezuela*, vol 2, 243–301. Caracas: Fundación La Salle.

Cormier, L. 2003a. *Kinship with monkeys: the Guajá foragers of eastern Amazonia*. New York: Columbia University Press.

Cormier, L. 2003b. Animism, cannibalism, and pet-keeping among the the Guajá of Eastern Amazonia. *Tipiti: Journal for the Society of the Anthropology of Lowland South America* 1, 71–88.

Cox, G. 1863. *Viaje en las rejiones septentrionales de la Patagonia*. Santiago de Chile: Imprenta Nacional.

Crocker, J. Ch. 1985. *Vital souls: Bororo cosmology, natural symbolism and shamanism*. Tucson: University of Arizona Press.

Cruxent, J. M. 1961. *Los Shikana del río Kaima*. Caracas: Fundación La Salle.

Descola, P. 1996. Constructing nature: symbolic ecology and social practices. In P. Descola and R. Pálsson (eds), *Nature and society: anthropological perspectives*, 82–102. London: Routledge.

Descola, P. 2005. *Par delà nature et culture*. Paris: Gallimard.

Dobrizhoffer, M. 1784 [1967]. *Historia de los abipones*. Resistencia: Universidad del Nordeste.

Dos Santos, M. and Nobre Méndez, A. 2007. El trabajo de la FUNAI. In A. Parellada (ed.), *Pueblos indígenas en aislamiento voluntario y contacto inicial en la Amazonia y el Gran Chaco*, 208–19. Lima: TAREA.

Erikson, P. 1996. *La griffe del aïeux. Marquage du corps et démaquages ethniques chez les Matis d'Amazonie*. Louvain-Paris: Éditions Peeters.

Escalada, F. 1949. *El complejo 'tehuelche'. Estudios de etnografía patagónica*. Buenos Aires: Coni.

Escalada, F. 1953. Algunos problemas relativos al límite norte del complejo tehuelche.' *Publicaciones de la Comisión de Humanidades*, serie A, No. 1. Comodoro Rivadavia: Instituto Superior de Estudios Patagónicos.

Fischermann, B. 2007. Huida o entrega-vivir en aislamiento: el ejemplo de los Ayorei Totobiegosode. In A. Parellada (ed.), *Pueblos indígenas en aislamiento voluntario y contacto inicial en la Amazonia y el Gran Chaco*, 252–65. Lima: TAREA.

Forline, L. C. 1997. The persistence and cultural transformation of the Guajá Indians: foragers of Maranhão State, Brazil. PhD thesis. University of Florida.

Gamble, C. 1992. Archaeology, history, and the uttermost ends of the earth: Tasmania, Tierra del Fuego and the Cape. *Antiquity* 66, 712–20.

Giacone, A. P. E. 1955. *Pequena Gramática e Dicionário Português, Ubde-Neheren ou Macú*. Recife: Escola Saleciana de Artes Gráficas.

Glauser, B. 2007. Su presencia protege el corazón del Chaco Seco. In A. Parellada (ed.), *Pueblos indígenas en aislamiento voluntario y contacto inicial en la Amazonia y el Gran Chaco*, 220–33. Lima: TAREA.

González Ruibal, A., Hernando, A., and Politis, G. 2011. Ontology of the self and material culture: arrow-making among the Awá hunter-gatherers (Brazil). *Journal of Anthropological Archeology* 30, 1–16.

Gragson, T. 1989. Allocation of time to subsistence and settlement in a Ciri Khonome Pumé village of the Llanos of Apure, Venezuela. PhD thesis. Department of Anthropology, Pennsylvania State University.

Greaves, R. 1997. Hunting and multifunctional use of bows and arrows: ethnoarchaeology of technological organization among the Pumé hunters of Venezuela. In H. Knecht (ed.), *Projectile technology*, 287–320. New York: Plenum Press.

Greaves, R. 2006. Forager landscape use and residential organization. In F. Sellet, R. Greaves, and P.-L. Yu (eds), *Archaeology and ethnoarchaeology of mobility*, 127–52. Gainsville: Florida University Press.

Gusinde, M. 1931. *Die Feuerland-Indianer*. Band I: *Die Selk'nam*. Mödling bei Wien: Verlag der Internationalen Zeitschrift. Anthropos.

Hayden, B. 1995. A new overview of domestication. In T. Douglas Price and A. B. Gebauer (eds), *Last hunters first farmers: new perspectives on the prehistoric transition to agriculture*, 273–99. Santa Fe: School of American Research Press.

Henry, J. 1964. *Jungle people: a Kaingang tribe of the highlands of Brazil*. New York: Vintage Books.

Hernando, A., Politis, G., González Ruibal, A., and Coelho, E. 2011. Gender, power and mobility among the Awá-Guajá (Maranhão, Brazil). *Journal of Anthropological Research* 67, 189–211.

Hill, K. and Hawkes, K. 1983. Neotropical hunting among the Aché of eatern Paraguay. In R. Hames and W. Vickers (eds), *Adaptive responses of native Amazonians*, 139–88. New York: Academic Press.

Hill, K. and Hurtado, M. 1995. *Aché life history: the ecology and demography of a foraging people*. New York: Aldine de Gruyter.

Hill, K. and Hurtado, M. 1999. The Aché of Paraguay. In R. B. Lee and R. Daly (eds) *The Cambridge encyclopedia of hunters and gatherers*, 92–6. Cambridge: Cambridge University Press.

Holmberg, A. R. 1950 [1969]. *Nomads of the long bow: the Sirionó of Eastern Bolivia*. Prospect Heights: Waveland Press.

Hurtado, A. M. and Hill, K. R. 1986. The Cuiva hunter-gatherers of western Venezuela. *AnthroQuest* 36, 14–23.

Hurtado, A. M. and Hill, K. R. 1987. Early dry season subsistence ecology of Cuiva (Hiwi) foragers of Venezuela. *Human Ecology* 15, 163–87.

Hyades, P. 1885. La chasse et la pêche chez les Fuégins de l'archipiel du Cap Horn. *Revue d'Ethnographie* 4, 514–53.

Hyades, P. and Deniker, J. 1891. Anthropologie et Ethnographie. In *Mission Scientifique du Cap Horn*, tomo VII. París: Ministères de la Marine et de l'Instruction Publique, Gauthier Villars et Fils.

Ingold, T. 1996. Hunting and gathering as ways of perceiving the environment. In R. Ellen and K. Fukui (eds), *Redefining nature: ecology, culture and domestication*, 117–56. Oxford: Berg.

ISA. Instituto Socioambiental. 2001. *Povos indígenas no Brasil*, http://www.socioambiental.org/pib/index.html.

Jensen, C. 1999. Tupí-Guaraní. In R. M. W. Dixon and A. I. Aikhenvald (eds), *The Amazonian languages*, 125–63. Cambridge: Cambridge University Press.

Kaplan, H. and Hill, K. 1985. Food sharing among the Aché foragers: tests of explanatory hypotheses. *Current Anthropology* 26, 223–45.

Kersten, L. 1905 [1968]. *Las tribus indígenas del Gran Chaco hasta fines del siglo XVIII*. Resistencia: Universidad Nacional del Nordeste.

Koch-Grünberg, Th. 1906. Die Makú. *Anthropos* 1, 877–906.

Kozák, V., Baxter, D., Williamson, L., and Carneiro, R. 1979. *The Héta indians: fishing in a dry pond*. New York: Anthropological Papers of the American Museum of Natural History 55.

Laming-Emperaire, A., Menezes, M. J., and Andreatta, M. D. 1978. O trabalho da pedra entre os Xetá, Serra dos Dourados, Estado do Paraná.*Coleção do Museu Paulista, Série Ensaios* 2, 11–82.

Lathrap, D. 1968. The 'hunting' economies of the tropical forest zone of South America: an attempt at historical perspective. In R. B. Lee and I. DeVore (eds), *Man the hunter*, 23–9. Chicago: Aldine.

Lavina, R. 1994. *Os Xokleng de Santa Catarina: uma etnohistória e sugestoes para os arqueólogos*. São Leopoldo: Universidade do Vale do Rio dos Sinos, UNISINOS.

Lee, R. 1999. *Hunter-gatherer studies and the millennium: a look forward (and back). 8th International Conference on Hunting and Gathering Societies: foraging and post-foraging societies*. Japan: National Museum of Ethnology.

Legoupil, D. 1989. *Ethno-Archéologie dans les archípiels de Patagonie: les nomades marins de Punta Baja*. Paris: Éditions Recherche sur les Civilisations.

Lehm, Z. 2004. *Bolivia: estrategias, problemas y desafíos en gestión del territorio Sirionó*. Copenhagen: IWGIA.

Lévi-Strauss, C. 1968. The concept of 'primitiveness'. In R. B. Lee and I. DeVore (eds), *Man the hunter*, 349–52. Chicago: Aldine.

López Mazz, J. M. and Bracco, D. 2010. *Minuanos. Apuntes y notas para la historia y la arqueología del territorio Guenoa-Minuan (Indígenas de Uruguay, Argentina y Brasil)*. Montevideo: Librería Linardi y Risso.

Lothrop, S. 1932. Indians of the Paraná Delta River. *Annals of New York Academy of Science* 33, 77–232.

Lozano, P. 1733 [1941]. *Descripción corográfica del Gran Chaco Gualamba*. San Miguel de Tucumán: Instituto de Antropología.

Lucaioli, C. P. 2005. *Los grupos abipones hacia mediados del siglo XVIII*. Buenos Aires: Sociedad Argentina de Antropología.

McGovern, W. 1927. *Jungle paths and Inca ruins*. New York and London: Century.

Martial, L. 1888. *Historie du Voyage. Mission Scientifique du Cap Horn (1882–1883)*. Paris: Gauthier-Villars.

Martinic, M. 1995. *Los Aónikenk. Historia y Cultura*. Punta Arenas: Ediciones de la Universidad de Magallanes.

Martius, K. F. 1867. *Beiträge zur Ethnographie und Sprachekunde Amerikas, zumal Brasiliens* (2 vols). Leipzig: Friedlich.

Maybury-Lewis, D. and Bamberger, J. 1980. *Dialectical societies: Gê and Bororo of Central Brazil*. Cambridge, MA: Harvard University Press.

Mendoza, M. 1999. The Western Toba: family, life and subsistence of a former hunter-gatherer society. In E. Miller (ed.), *Peoples of the Gran Chaco*. 81–108. Westport, CT: Greenwood.

Métraux, A. 1946. Ethnography of the Chaco. In J. Steward (ed.), *Handbook of South American Indians*, vol. 1, 197–370. Washington, DC: Smithsonian Institution.

Métraux, A. 1948. The hunting and gathering people of the Rio Negro Basin. In J. H. Steward (ed.), *Handbook of South American Indians*. Vol. 3: *The Tropical Forest Tribe*, 861–8. Washington: Smithsonian Institution.

Métraux, A. 1963. The Caingang. In J. Steward (ed.), *Handbook of South American Indians*, vol. 1, 445-73. New York: Cooper Square Publishers.

Miller Jr., T. O. 1979. Stonework of the Xéta Indians of Brazil. In B. Hayden (ed.), *Lithic use-wear analysis: studies in archaeology*, 401-7. New York: Academic Press.

Mitriani, P. 1988. Los Pumé (Yaruro). In J. Lizot (ed.), *Los Aborígenes de Venezuela, Vol 3, Etnología Contemporánea II*, 147-213. Caracas: Fundación La Salle de Ciencias Naturales.

Morey, R. V. and Metzger, D. J. 1974. The Guahibo: people of the Savanna. *Acta Ethnologica et Linguistica* 31, Serie Americana 7.

Mota, L. T., Noelli, F. S., and Tommasino, K. (eds) 2000. *Urí e Wäxi: estudos inter-disciplinares dos Kaingang*. Londrina: Editora Vel.

Münzel, M. 1969-72. Notas preliminares sobre os Kaborí Makú entre o Rio Negro e o Japurá. *Revista de Antropología* 17-20, 137-82.

Musters, G. C. 1869-70 [1979]. *Vida entre los Patagones*. Buenos Aires: Solar-Hachette.

Nacuzzi, L. 1998. *Identidades impuestas. Tehuelches, aucas y pampas en el norte de la Patagonia*. Buenos Aires: Sociedad Argentina de Antropología.

Nacuzzi, L., Lucaioli, C., and Nesis, F. 2008. *Pueblos nómades en un estado colonial. Chaco, Pampa y Patagonia, siglo XVIII*. Buenos Aires: Editorial Antropofagia.

Nesis, F. 2005. *Transformaciones socioculturales entre los grupos mocoví. Siglo XVIII*. Buenos Aires: Sociedad Argentina de Antropología.

Noelli, F. S. (ed.) 1998. *Bibliografía Kaingang. Referencias sobre un povo Jê do sul do Brasil*. Londrina: Editora Vel.

Noelli, F. S. 2005. Rethinking stereotypes and the history of research on Jê populations in south Brazil: an interdisciplinary point of view. In P. P. Funari, A. Zarankin, and E. Stovel (eds), *Global archaeological theory: contextual voices and contemporary thoughts*, 167-90. New York: Kluwer Academic/Plenum Press.

Nordenskiold, E. 1912. La Vie des Indiés dans le Chaco. *Revue de Géographie*, Tomo VI. Fasicule III. Paris.

Orquera, L. A. 2002. The late-nineteenth-century crisis in the survival of the Magellan-Fueguian littoral natives. In C. Briones and J. L. Lanata (eds), *Archaeological and anthropological perspectives on the native peoples of Pampa, Patagonia, and Tierra del Fuego to the nineteenth century*, 145-58. Wesport, CT: Greenwood.

Orquera, L. A. and Piana, E. L. 1999. *Arqueología de la región del canal de Beagle (Tierra del Fuego, República Argentina)*. Buenos Aires: Sociedad Argentina de Antropología.

Parellada, A. (ed.) 2007. *Pueblos indígenas en aislamiento voluntario y contacto inicial en la Amazonia y el Gran Chaco*. Lima: TAREA.

Parellada, A. and Beldi de Alcántara, M. L. (eds) 2008. *Los Aché del Paraguay. Discusión de un genocidio*. Copenhagen: IWGIA.

Paucke, F. 1749-67 [1943]. *Hacia Allá y para Acá. Una estadía entre los indios Mocobíes, 1749-1767*. Vol. II. Tucumán: Universidad Nacional.

Paucke, F. 1749-67 [1944]. *Hacia Allá y para Acá. Una estadía entre los indios Mocobíes, 1749-1767*. Vol. III. Tucumán: Universidad Nacional.

Pero, A. 2002. The Tehuelche of Patagonia as chronicled by travelers and explorers in the nineteenth century. In C. Briones and J. L. Lanata (eds), *Archaeological and anthropological perspectives on the native peoples of Pampa, Patagonia, and Tierra del Fuego to the nineteenth century*, 103-19. Wesport, CT: Greenwood.

Politis, G. 1996. *Nukak*. Santafé de Bogotá: Instituto Amazónico de Investigaciones Científicas SINCHI.

Politis, G. 2007. *Nukak: ethnoarchaeology of an Amazonian people.* Walnut Creek, CA: Left Coast Press.

Politis, G. and Jaimes, A. 2005. Patrones de descarte entre los hotï del Amazonas, venezolano. In E. Williams (ed.), *Etnoarqueología: el contexto dinámico de la cultura material a través del tiempo,* 237–66. Michoacán: El Colegio de Michoacán.

Posey, D. A. 1982. *Agroforestry systems.* Amsterdam: Springer.

Posey, D. A. 1983. Indigenous ecological knowledge and development of the Amazon. In E. Moran (ed.), *The dilemma of Amazonian development,* 225–57. Boulder: Westview Press.

Pozzobon, J. 1983. Isolamento e endogamia: observações sobre a organização social dos indios Maku. Masters thesis. Universidade Federal do Rio Grande do Sul, Porto Alegre, Brazil.

Pozzobon, J. 1992. Parenté et démographie chez les indies Maku. PhD thesis. Université Paris VII, Paris.

Regehr, V. 2008. *El grupo Areguede-urasade en Chaidi Alto Paraguay -Chaco 2004.* Asunción: Oficina de Proyectos Editoriales.

Reid, H. 1979. *Some aspects of movement, growth, and change among the Hupdu Makú Indians of Brazil.* Cambridge: Cambridge University Press.

Reina, L. 1986. Análisis Fonológico, Lengua Juhupde-Makú, Amazonas. Masters thesis. Bogotá. Universidad de Los Andes.

Reina, L. 1992. Los Nukak: cacería, recolección y nomadismo en la Amazonia. In *Diversidad es Riqueza,* 62–4. Santafé de Bogotá: Instituto Colombiano de Antropología.

Renshaw, J. 1996. *Los indígenas del Chaco paraguayo. Economía y Sociedad.* Asunción: Intercontinental Editora.

Rival, L. 1999a. Introduction: South America. In R. B. Lee and R. Daly (eds), *The Cambridge encyclopedia of hunters and gatherers,* 77–85. Cambridge: Cambridge University Press.

Rival, L. 1999b. Huaorani. In R. B. Lee and R. Daly (eds), *The Cambridge encyclopedia of hunters and gatherers,* 101–4. Cambridge: Cambridge University Press.

Rival, L. 2002. *Trekking through history: the Huaorani of Eastern Ecuador.* New York: Columbia University Press.

Rival, L. 2006. Amazonian historical ecologies. In R. Ellen (ed.), *Ethnobiology and the science of humankind: a retrospective and a prospective.* Special issue of *Journal of the Royal Anthropological Institute,* 97–116.

Rival, L. 2007. Proies Meurtrières, Rameaux Bourgeonnants: Masculinité et Féminité en Terre Huaorani (Amazonie équatorienne). In C. N. Mathieu (ed.), *La Notion de Personne Femme et Homme en Sociétés Matrilinéaires et Uxori-matrilocales,* 125–54. Paris: Maison des Sciences de l'Homme.

Rivet, P. and Testevin, C. 1920. Affinités du Makú et du Puinave. *Journal de la Société des Américanistes* 12, 69–82.

Rodrigues, A. D. 1958. Classification of Tupí-Guaraní. *International Journal of American Linguistics* 24, 231–4.

Rodrigues, A. D. 1986. *Linguas brasileiras. Para o conhecimiento das linguas indigenas.* São Paulo: Edicões Loyola.

Rodrigues, A. D. 1999. Macro-Jê. In R. M. W. Dixon and A. Y. Aikhenvald (eds), *Amazonian languages,* 165–206. Cambridge: Cambridge University Press.

Roosevelt, A. 1998. Ancient and modern hunter-gatherers of lowland South America: an evolutionary problem. In W. Balée (ed.), *Principles of historical ecology,* 190–212. New York: Columbia University Press.

Rossi, J. J. 2007. *Los Alakaluf.* Buenos Aires: Galerna.

Santos-Granero, F. 2009. *Vital enemies: slavery, predation, and the Amerindian political economy of life.* Austin: University of Texas Press.

Schindler, H. 1985. Equestrian and not equestrian Indians of the Gran Chaco during the colonial period. *Indiana* 10, 451–64.

Schultz, H. 1959. Ligeiras notas sôbre os Makú do Paraná Boá-Boá. *Revista do Museu Paulista. Nova Série* 11, 109–32.

Serrano, A. 1950. *Los primitivos habitantes de Entre Ríos*. Paraná: Biblioteca Entrerriana, serie Histórica II, Ministerio de Educación.

Silverwood-Cope, P. 1972. A contribution to the ethnography of the Colombian Makú. Ph D thesis. Department of Social Anthropology, Cambridge University.

Silverwood-Cope, P. 1990. *Os Makú: Povo Caçador do Noroeste da Amazonia*. Brasilia: Coleçao Pensamiento Antropológico, Editorial Universidade de Brasilia.

Stearman, A. 1989. Yuquí foragers in the Bolivian Amazon: subsistence strategies, prestige, and leadership in an acculturating society. *Journal of Anthropological Research* 45, 219–44.

Stearman, A. M. 1987. *No longer nomads: the Sirionó revisited*. London: Hamilton Press.

Storrie, R. 1999. Being human: personhood, cosmology and subsistence for the Hotï of Venezuelan Guaina. PhD thesis. University of Manchester.

Susnik, B. 1969. *Chamacocos I. Cambio cultural*. Asunción: Publicación del Museo Etnográfico Andres Barbero.

Susnik, B. 1971. *El indio colonial del Paraguay. Vol. 3.1. El chaqueño*. Asunción: Publicación del Etnográfico Andrés Barbero.

Tastevin, P. C. 1923. Les Makú du Japurá. *Journal de la Société del Américanistes de Paris* 15, 99–108.

Turner, T. 1979. Kinship, household, and community structure among the Kayapó. In D. Maybury-Lewis (ed.), *The Gê and Bororo of Central Brazil*, 179–214. Cambridge, MA: Harvard University Press.

Verswijver, G. 1992. *The club-fighters of the Amazon: warfare among the Kaiapo Indians of Central Brasil*. Gent: Blandijnberg.

Vidal, H. J. 1999. The Yamana of Tierra del Fuego. In R. B. Lee and R. Daly (eds), *The Cambridge encyclopedia of hunters and gatherers*, 114–18. Cambridge: Cambridge University Press.

Vitar, B. 1997. *Guerra y misiones en la frontera Chaqueña del Tucumán (1700–67)*. Madrid: CSIC, Biblioteca de la historia de América.

Viveiros de Castro, E. 1992. *From the enemy's point of view: humanity and divinity in an Amazonian society*. Chicago: University of Chicago Press.

Viveiros de Castro, E. 1996. Os pronomes cosmológicos e o perspectivisimo ameríndio. *Maná* 2, 115–44.

Whiffen, T. 1915. *The north-west Amazons: notes of some months spent among cannibal tribes*. New York: Duffield and Company.

Wilbert, J. and Simoneau, K. 1992. *Folk literature of South American Indians*. Los Angeles: UCLA Latin American Center Publications. University of California.

Zanardini, J. 2003, *Cultura del pueblo Ayoreo*. Centro Social Indígena, Asunción.

Zent, E. L. 2006. Morar en la selva: humanidad, prescripciones y seres hipostáticos entre los Jotï, Guayana venezolana. Working Paper No. 19. Latin American Studies Center, University of Maryland, College Park.

Zent, E. L. and Zent, S. 2002. Impactos ambientales generadores de biodiversidad: conductas ecológicas de los Hotï de la Sierra Maigualida, Amazonas Venezolano'. *Interciencia* 27, 3–10.

Zent, E. L. and Zent, S. 2004. Los Jodï: sabios botánicos del Amazonas venezolano. *Antropológica* 97, 3–43.

CHAPTER 50

THE ETHNOHISTORY AND ANTHROPOLOGY OF 'MODERN' HUNTER-GATHERERS
North Japan (Ainu)

MARK J. HUDSON

THE main emphasis in this chapter is on one ethnic group (Ainu) rather than a broader region comprising a number of hunter-gatherer societies. This chapter takes AD 1200 as its starting point as this is the most important transition in recent centuries, reflecting the approximate time when economic growth in China began to stimulate widespread social changes in Japan that led to the beginning of the so-called 'Ainu cultural period' (*c.*1200–1870). This was also the time when Ainu expanded from Hokkaido into the neighbouring regions of Sakhalin and the Kuril Islands (Figure 50.1). AD 1500 does retain significance for Ainu history, however, in that European expansion forced Japan to reconsider its political relationship with the land of the Ainu, resulting in the gradual incorporation of Hokkaido into the Japanese state. After Europeans reached the Japanese Islands in 1542, they themselves quickly became fascinated by Ainu people, an interest that continued into the early anthropological research on Ainu in the nineteenth and early twentieth centuries.

Notwithstanding the apparently narrow focus of this chapter, it is enormously difficult to generalize about Ainu culture and lifeways. Geographically, our scope falls across territory ruled by two modern nations, Japan and Russia, yet during the period when Ainu were actually living as hunter-gatherers neither state had direct political control over Ainu lands. The main regions considered here are north-east Honshu, Hokkaido, southern Sakhalin, and the Kuril Islands; a more precise title for this chapter might thus be 'North Japan and Sakhalin Province'. Ainu people also traded and lived in the Amur Basin and Kamchatka. As noted by Segawa (2007), it is important to emphasize the *size* of this area of Ainu settlement. From the southern tip of Hokkaido to the centre of Sakhalin is about a thousand kilometres, a distance greater than that from London to Berlin, and from southern Hokkaido to the southern tip of Kamchatka is almost double that distance. Boats were important for communication across the wide area and Ainu had an active tradition of building oceangoing boats (Otsuka 1999).

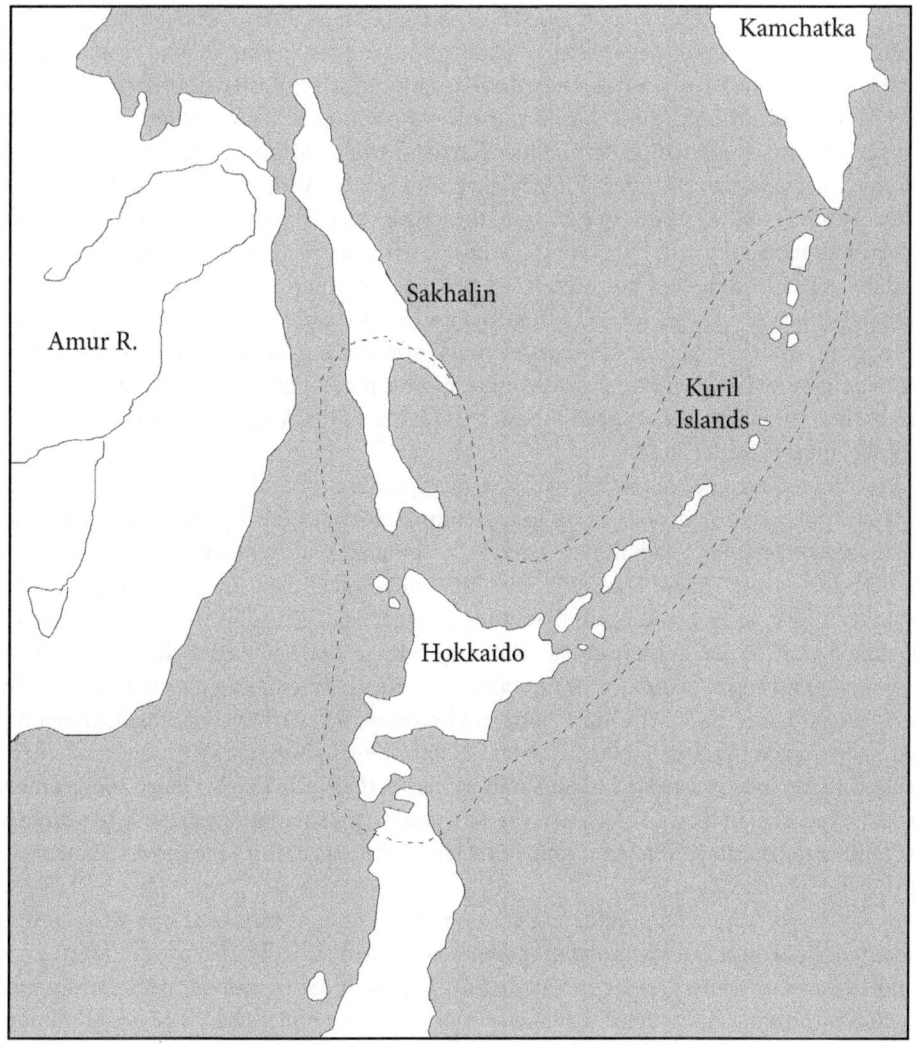

FIGURE 50.1 Area of historic Ainu settlement.

In 1804 the total Ainu population of Hokkaido, southern Sakhalin, and the Kurils as far as Kunashir was estimated at 23,797 people (Segawa 2007, 14). Ainu population levels crashed after colonization but have rebounded in recent years and the Japanese government recognized 23,782 Ainu in 2006 (Segawa 2007, 14). Since prejudice against Ainu people is still significant in Japan, many contemporary Ainu prefer to 'pass' as Japanese and the actual number of Ainu people is likely to be much higher. While very small numbers of people identify as Ainu in Sakhalin and Kamchatka, today almost all Ainu people live in Japan, primarily in Hokkaido and the Tokyo area (Watson in press).

In terms of chronology, the main focus here is the period from around AD 1200 to 1870, which is usually classified as the 'Ainu culture period' by historians and archaeologists. This period is characterized by a complex of cultural traits that are directly related to Ainu culture as known ethnohistorically (see Hudson 1999). There are two opposing approaches to this periodization and the problem of Ainu ethnogenesis. One argues that since a recognizably Ainu ethnicity did not develop until around AD 1200, it is technically incorrect to refer to Ainu culture before that date (e.g. Matsumoto 2006, 190). Supporters of this view do not deny the basic population continuities that gave rise to Ainu culture, but see the latter as something qualitatively different from what went before. Another approach classifies the 'Ainu culture period' as simply one phase in the long history of the Ainu people in Hokkaido and neighbouring regions. Segawa (2007, 14–16), for example, argues that the term 'Ainu culture period' is inappropriate since it implies that other periods of Hokkaido prehistory were not connected to the Ainu. These two approaches clearly involve politically sensitive issues about Ainu indigeneity. This chapter follows my earlier work in assuming basic population continuity between Jōmon and Ainu (Hudson 1999), but also accepts that there are major cultural differences between the various phases of Hokkaido prehistory that we are still struggling to understand.

The Ainu culture period ended with the incorporation of Hokkaido into the Japanese state and the beginning of large-scale agricultural colonization by Japanese settlers. In the nineteenth century, Sakhalin experienced a complex history of administrative control by both Russia and Japan. Southern Sakhalin, where most Ainu lived, was occupied by Japan from 1855 to 1875 and again from 1905 to 1945. Sakhalin Ainu were all relocated to Hokkaido after the Second World War. Russian explorers reached the northern Kurils from Kamchatka and began to impact the lifestyles of the Kuril Ainu in the eighteenth century. By the nineteenth century, north Kuril Ainu had become converted to Orthodox Christianity and had adopted the Russian language and culture (Stephan 1974, 28). These Russianized Ainu were forcibly transported to Shikotan in the southern Kurils after Japan took control of the archipelago in 1875. Living a wretched existence, the 'Shikotan Ainu clung tenaciously to their Russian heritage' (Stephan 1974, 108) before being again forced to move to Hokkaido during the Second World War.

In Hokkaido, Ainu hunter-gathering ended abruptly as legal bans were imposed on Ainu subsistence practices and assimilation policies attempted (usually unsuccessfully) to force Ainu to become farmers. Japanese law left no provision for traditional Ainu subsistence practices. The natural resources that had supported Ainu people, such as deer and salmon, were now exploited on an industrial scale by Japanese fisheries and canneries. While hunter-gatherer subsistence effectively came to an end in the late nineteenth century, hunting, gathering, and fishing continue to retain significance in debates over Ainu identity (e.g. Kayano 1999). Recent years have seen the revitalization of several areas of traditional Ainu food culture (Iwasaki-Goodman et al. 2009). Moreover, a distinctive Ainu world view has to some extent continued into the present. Many Ainu retain a world view that feels sharply different from the experiences of most ethnic Japanese (Aoyama 2012). Contemporary Ainu ideas about the world and nature may include some degree of 'readback' (Burch 1994) from Ainu ethnographies, but there has also been significant continuity through teachings transmitted by influential Ainu elders such as Shigeru Kayano (1926–2006).

This chapter focuses mainly on providing an overview of pre-modern Ainu as hunter-gatherers, with the proviso that major changes occurred over the long span of the Ainu period considered here (i.e. *c.* AD 1200–1870). Our understanding of the earlier part of this period relies primarily on archaeology and is still poorly understood. However, the past decade has seen significant advances in the field of Ainu archaeology and the overview of

Ainu origins found in Hudson (1999) is now outdated in certain respects. At the beginning of this chapter it is important to emphasize that, despite the long history of Ainu research in both Japan and the West, there are no real ethnographic accounts of Ainu hunter-gathering. In other words, there are no ethnographic reports written by anthropologists living in Ainu settlements for extended periods and observing Ainu hunter-gathering at first hand. The closest we get to such ethnographies are the reconstructions of Ainu subsistence produced by Watanabe (1973), Ohnuki-Tierney (1974a), and others from interviews with Ainu elders who were longer engaged in full-time hunter-gathering. Watanabe's *The Ainu ecosystem* (1973), based on interviews conducted between 1952 and 1959, is perhaps the most comprehensive ethnography of Ainu foraging available. There is also a large quantity of (mainly Japanese) historical records relating to the Ainu. Although these records are of enormous importance for an understanding of Ainu as hunter-gatherers, they were written for a range of mostly administrative purposes that do not always correspond to anthropological interests.

Population History

In 1548, a few years after Europeans had first reached Japan, a Japanese convert to Christianity named Yajirō travelled to Goa where he provided the Jesuit Nicolao Lancilotto with the first information about the Ainu. Lancilotto summarized this information as follows: 'In the Northeast [of Japan] is the island of Gsoo [Ezo, a former name for Hokkaido]; the inhabitants thereof are white, with long whiskers; they wear their hair on top of their heads; they are tall, and fight fearlessly, one against a hundred, like the Germans' (Kish 1939, 49). Lancilotto's letter marked the beginning of a long Western fascination with the Ainu, particularly with their physical appearance, which—being 'white, with long whiskers'— seemed to set them strongly apart from their neighbours in Japan and North-East Asia. The rise of academic anthropology in the nineteenth century introduced the concept of race as a way to think about this difference and Ainu became seen as a 'tiny island of alleged Caucasian people within a great Mongoloid sea' (Harrison 1954, 278).

By the 1970s, new research in biological anthropology, including genetic studies, had overturned the old 'Ainu as Caucasoid' theory and demonstrated that Ainu were in fact physically closest to Japanese and other east Asian populations (Hanihara 1970; 1979; Omoto 1972). By the late 1980s, there was a growing consensus that, whereas the mainland Japanese were primarily descended from agricultural immigrants who arrived in the Yayoi period (c.500 BC–AD 300), Ainu had experienced relatively little genetic admixture with Japanese populations prior to the modern era and were primarily descended from the prehistoric Jōmon people of the Japanese archipelago (Dodo and Ishida 1990; Hanihara 1991). Evidence supporting this so-called 'dual structure model' of Japanese origins is discussed in detail in Hudson (1999). Later research has largely supported this model, with the important exception that several recent studies have concluded that Ainu populations also experienced a significant genetic input from the people of the Okhotsk culture (Hanihara et al. 2008; Ishida et al. 2009; Sato et al. 2007). The Okhotsk was a foraging culture that spread from Sakhalin in the sixth century AD and occupied the eastern coast of Hokkaido until it was assimilated by the Ainu in the twelfth century (Hudson 2004; Ohyi 1975).

The study of Ainu skeletal remains still forms an active tradition in biological anthropology in Japan, but much of this research continues to focus on questions relating to Japanese population history. Other questions that might be approached using skeletal remains, such as how Ainu health was affected by Japanese colonization, have yet to be investigated in any systematic way. Many Ainu people, however, remain wary of research in biological anthropology because of the history of grave robbing and other unethical methods employed by earlier scholars (Lewallen 2007).

Until the forced assimilations of the late nineteenth century, Ainu spoke a language that was quite different from neighbouring languages such as Japanese or Nivkh. There were three main Ainu dialects found in Hokkaido, Sakhalin, and the Kuril Islands, as well as several regional variations in Hokkaido and Sakhalin (Tamura 2000, 2–4). There is no linguistic or archaeological evidence that the Ainu language arrived in northern Japan in historic times and the most parsimonious interpretation is that it is a very ancient language in the Japanese Islands, perhaps descended from a language of the Jōmon period. In the rest of Japan (including Okinawa), Jōmon languages seem to have been replaced by Japonic (Japanese and Ryukyuan) languages introduced by agricultural immigrants, but Ainu remained widely spoken until the early twentieth century (see Hudson 1999; 2002). Ainu had no writing system but possessed a vibrant tradition of oral literature of which the *yukar* epic poems are the best known (e.g. Philippi 1979).

Ainu contains a number of words borrowed from Japanese and linguists argue that the two languages must have been in close contact in the past, perhaps in northern Honshu where many Ainu place names can still be found (Janhunen 2002). Although, as noted above, Ainu populations seem to have experienced a significant genetic input from the people of the Okhotsk culture in medieval times, there is no evidence for language contact associated with this intermarriage. Despite these borrowings, Ainu does not seem to be genetically related to Japonic or to other language families in North-East Asia and is usually classified as a language isolate. Ainu is currently a moribund, endangered language with few native speakers, but there have been extensive efforts at language revitalization in Hokkaido in recent years.

Ainu History and Ethnogenesis

The evidence from biological anthropology and linguistics summarized above suggests that Ainu were primarily descended from Jōmon populations in northern Japan. Culturally, however, the picture is more much complex: from a Jōmon foundation, Ainu culture developed through a broad range of interactions with neighbouring societies. The Jōmon period in Hokkaido was followed by a phase that is usually termed Epi-Jōmon (*c*.100 BC–AD 700) even though it was characterized by quite significant differences from the Jōmon proper. The Epi-Jōmon would appear to represent a massive reorganization of Jōmon culture under the stimulus of the Iron Age cultures of mainland Japan. Some Epi-Jōmon groups moved south from Hokkaido into northern Honshu, perhaps in search of iron and the late Epi-Jōmon saw a significant replacement of stone by iron tools (Segawa 2007, 25). The Epi-Jōmon was contemporaneous with the agricultural Yayoi and Kofun cultures of mainland Japan, but there is no evidence of food production in the Epi-Jōmon tradition (Crawford 2011, 338).

The Epi-Jōmon was followed by the Satsumon period (c.AD 700–1200), an era that also saw even greater social and cultural transformations. Satsumon culture possessed raised floor granaries, mortars and pestles for husking grain, earthen *kamado* ovens built against the walls of houses, pottery strongly influenced by Japanese Haji wares, a range of cultigens including wheat, barley, and millets, iron sickles and hoe blades, spindle whorls, even chopsticks, all items that show clear influences from the agricultural societies of northern Honshu. Given the extent of these changes, Segawa (2007) argues that it is hard to see them all resulting from cultural diffusion and supports Matsumoto's (2006) theory that groups of north Honshu farmers migrated into parts of south-west Hokkaido at this time. As discussed below, however, most archaeologists, including Segawa, continue to see the Satsumon as primarily a hunter-gatherer society.

The complex relations between the Satsumon and the Japanese cultures of northern Honshu played a crucial role in the formation of Ainu culture, but connections with the Okhotsk people of north-eastern Hokkaido were also significant. The Okhotsk moved from Sakhalin along the Sea of Okhotsk coastline of Hokkaido from around the sixth century AD. The Okhotsk were maritime hunter-gatherers whose subsistence-settlement system kept them more or less separate from Satsumon populations until the ninth century when there was a dramatic expansion of Satsumon groups across Hokkaido and even into Sakhalin. In eastern Hokkaido an intermediate Tobinitai culture mixed elements of both Okhotsk and Satsumon before fusing into Ainu culture by the twelfth century (Ōnishi 2009).

The Satsumon was followed by the Ainu culture period which corresponds to the medieval and early modern eras in Japan. Japanese influence in Hokkaido and Sakhalin became especially prominent after 1600. Increasing numbers of Japanese lived in the Wajinchi area of Japanese settlement in south-west Hokkaido. Japanese merchants established fishing stations in Hokkaido and Sakhalin from the eighteenth century and forced Ainu to work in these camps. A detailed analysis of Ainu history in this period can be found in Walker (2001).

Subsistence

The Ainu and Hunter-Gatherer Definitions

Given the complex history of Ainu ethnogenesis summarized above, are we justified in classifying Ainu as hunter-gatherers? Although most scholars have indeed categorized Ainu as a foraging people, it has been widely noted that pre-modern Ainu subsistence is difficult to place within traditional definitions of hunter-gathering. As early as the 1940s, Japanese scholars such as Shin'ichirō Takakura admitted their inability to classify Ainu using the classical evolutionary schemes of Morgan and others (see Howell in press). Neither do Ainu conform to the 'neo-classical' *Man the hunter* model of hunter-gatherers (Lee and DeVore 1968). Ainu diverged from the *Man the hunter* model with respect to at least the following points: they were highly sedentary; they were socially quite complex with chiefs and slaves; they engaged in some plant cultivation; and they were widely engaged in trading relationships, including long-distance trade by boat.

Two main objections to Ainu as hunter-gatherers have focused on the role of agriculture and trade. Gary Crawford, a Canadian archaeologist who has been analysing cultivated plant remains from sites in Hokkaido for over 30 years, has been the most critical of traditional approaches to Ainu as hunter-gatherers in the English literature (e.g. Crawford 2008). Of course, many hunter-gatherers engage in some plant cultivation, but they usually rely on cultivated plants for less than 5 per cent of resources (Hunn and Williams 1982). The actual contribution of cultivation is unclear in both the Ainu and Satsumon periods. In the early modern period, Japanese authorities attempted to ban Ainu from farming in order to ensure a regular supply of hunted goods for trade (see below). Cultivation was more widespread in the Satsumon, at least in certain areas of south-west Hokkaido, but as Segawa (2007) has noted, even the sites on the Hokkaido University campus that have produced large quantities of cultivated plants were centred on salmon fishing streams and it is difficult to see these sites as primarily farming settlements.

Although trade was ignored by earlier scholars who saw Ainu settlements as self-contained (see Deriha in press), long-distance trading relationships were a central element in Ainu culture. Ainu trading activities were perhaps more extensive than many other documented hunter-gatherers. However, it is important to emphasize that wealth and prestige in Ainu society were generated through trade in products obtained by hunting, gathering, and fishing (Segawa 2007). Ainu no doubt engaged in plant cultivation in many areas, but farming offered few opportunities for prestige and for this reason I believe it is still appropriate to classify Ainu as hunter-gatherers.

Ainu Subsistence and Economy

By the time of the first detailed accounts of Ainu livelihoods in the nineteenth century, the influence of outside foodstuffs was already quite substantial and it is by no means easy to determine the precise pattern of the 'traditional' Ainu economy. In the early modern era, the Matsumae domain that controlled trade between Japan and the Ainu had a basic policy of attempting to limit Ainu cultivation in order to increase profits from trade in foraged goods (Takakura 1960). Fukasawa (1998, 12–14) argues that Ainu attempted to hide their cultivation from Matsumae agents. From nineteenth-century accounts we know that 'gardens' were common features of Ainu settlements. The missionary John Batchelor (1882, 215–16) wrote that Ainu 'cultivate gardens in which they grow all kind of vegetables, as turnips, potatoes, vegetable marrows, beans, pumpkins, and millet. Millet is the staple food. They also eat many kind of herbs and roots, which they get from the mountains'. Batchelor's comment that millet was the staple food of the Ainu may have been true at certain times and places by the early phases of Japanese colonization, but cannot be generalized to Ainu society as a whole. Only a few years earlier, for example, St John (1873, 250) had written in equally categorical terms that, 'Fish is their staple food'.

Whatever the extent to which Ainu actually cultivated plants themselves, it is important to emphasize that they were already consuming large quantities of imported rice by the early modern era. Matsumae policies aimed to prohibit Ainu from producing their own crops but not from consuming agricultural produce. Rice is mentioned as a trade good in Hokkaido as early as 1613 by Englishman John Saris (1941). Large quantities of rice were used in Ainu-Japanese trade during the early modern era (Tezuka 1998, 355). Ainu obtained rice as payment for a range of trade goods that they hunted or collected. This trading system underwent profound changes with the Meiji Restoration (1868) when Hokkaido Ainu were given land allotments and forced to grow their own crops (Howell 1997).

As discussed in detail by Watanabe (1973), deer and salmon were major Ainu food resources. A wide range of other resources were also exploited, including bears, reindeer, and musk deer (on Sakhalin), foxes, otters, hares, martens, seals, sea lions, whales, numerous types of fish, roots and green vegetables, and berries (Iwasaki-Goodman and Nomoto 1999; Kohara 1999; Ohnuki-Tierney 1974a; Watanabe 1973). Although Ainu subsistence is best characterized by its diversity, certain foods were regarded as being of particular importance. The starchy bulb *Cardiocrinum glehnii*, for example, was called the *haru ikkew* or 'backbone of food' (Haginaka 2000) and dog salmon was the *kamui chep* or 'divine fish' (Watanabe 1973, 72). Traded rice was boiled with other vegetables, and porridge was made with millet and other grains (Haginaka 2000). Soup or stew was the most common Ainu meal, with ingredients depending on season and availability. Rice wine (sake) became widely used in Ainu ceremonies by at least the early modern period (Walker 2001). Although large quantities of sake were traded from the Japanese, Ainu women were also involved in making this wine (Haginaka 2000). The various technologies involved in obtaining and processing these foodstuffs have been discussed by Ölschleger (1989; 1999).

As with other northern hunter-gatherers, the seasonal climate in which Ainu lived led to a wide range of different tasks for both men and women depending on the season. One Ainu word for 'summer' is *matnepa*, which means the 'year of women' because this was the season in which women worked hard to gather and preserve plant foods (Haginaka 2000). While ice fishing on lakes and rivers was one subsistence activity that was possible in winter, Ainu relied heavily on stored foods in this season. Dried salmon was an extremely important winter food and large quantities of this fish were processed in the autumn. On Sakhalin, Piłsudski (1998, 272) estimated that 'a family consisting of five members should store up to 3600 humpbacked salmons for one winter'. The seasonal round is described in detail for Hokkaido by Watanabe (1973) and for Sakhalin by Ohnuki-Tierney (1974a).

Trade

As noted above, trade was a crucial part of the Ainu economy. Ainu traded a wide range of goods including animal furs, dried fish for food or fertilizer, seaweed, eagle feathers for fletching arrows, live hawks, and bear gall bladders and other medicinal products. In return, Ainu obtained iron pots and tools, lacquer ware, silk brocades, glass beads, mirrors, rice, sake, yeast for brewing sake, and tobacco (Harrison 1954; Walker 2001). Ainu served as intermediaries in long-distance trade between the Ainu lands and Japan and the Amur region which was dominated by China (Sasaki 1999). Trade transformed Ainu subsistence and society, stimulating new opportunities for prestige and complexity, yet it also led to the growing dependence of Ainu on neighbouring state societies. Ainu trading autonomy was gradually undermined by Japanese merchants (Otsuka 1999; Walker 2001). From the eighteenth century, the establishment of Japanese fishing stations in several parts of Hokkaido and Sakhalin turned many Ainu into virtual slaves and decimated settlement in the regions concerned (Howell 1995; Hudson and Aoyama 2011).

Settlement and Social Organization

Settlement Patterns

Ainu lived in relatively sedentary villages called *kotan*. In Hokkaido, these villages were usually located near salmon spawning grounds. Most staple foods were obtained from areas within a one-day round-trip walking distance from the *kotan* (Watanabe 1999, 200). Bear hunting in the mountains and other logistic activities were associated with short-term camps. Ainu in Sakhalin appear to have been more residentially mobile, alternating between coastal summer and inland winter villages (Ohnuki-Tierney 1993, 8). This pattern had changed to one based on permanent coastal settlements by the beginning of the twentieth century when (Piłsudski 1998, 271) classified Sakhalin Ainu as 'settled fishermen'. The Kuril Ainu were the most residentially mobile of the three main regional groups (Ohnuki-Tierney 1993, 8; Ölschleger 1999, 217). In general, Ainu were at the more sedentary end of the hunter-gatherer settlement spectrum.

In Hokkaido, Ainu settlements owned communal hunting and fishing territories from which neighbouring groups were prohibited from entering, although records of frequent quarrels over these territories show that such rules were often broken (Takakura 1960, 15–16). Within local groups, food was widely shared, a custom that was frequently noted in Japanese documents (see Takakura 1960, 15).

Social Organization and Social Complexity

The general impression of Ainu social organization is one of considerable flexibility. Part of this flexibility represents change resulting from trading and other contacts with neighbouring societies. Ainu descent is usually classified as patrilineal and post-marital residence as patrilocal. This ideal pattern was realized in practice more often in Hokkaido than Sakhalin, perhaps because of the more sedentary settlement system of the former (Ohnuki-Tierney 1974b, 192). Ainu men with wealth were able to have two or more wives. On Sakhalin, the second wife would usually establish a separate household, sometimes in a different settlement (Ohnuki-Tierney 1974a, 79).

While many Ainu settlements remained physically quite fixed, household composition was more fluid and appears to have been strongly influenced by trade and the demands of seasonal labour for Japanese fishing stations (Endō 1987; 1994; 1997). Hammel (1988) also used nineteenth-century census data to argue that Ainu household composition in both Hokkaido and Sakhalin was complex and he similarly proposed that there is a strong possibility that inclusion in long-distance trading networks was a basic cause.

One of the most debated topics in hunter-gatherer research in recent years has been the question of social complexity. 'Complexity' can have several meanings in this context, but a non-egalitarian social organization is one of the main parameters. In the Western literature in particular, Ainu are often cited as an example of 'complex hunter-gatherers' (e.g. Kelly 1995, 302), but with the recent exception of Segawa (2007) there have been few studies of this proposed complexity. Western anthropologists often cite Watanabe's work as evidence for

Ainu complexity. Watanabe (1983) argued that occupational differentiation was the primary cause of Ainu social stratification. Occupational differentiation could serve as one way to obtain economic power through 'the ability to restrict access to key productive resources or consumptive goods' (Earle 1997, 7). In practice, however, actual control of production by Ainu chiefs seems to have been limited. Ainu chiefs instead had power over other areas of life.

Important evidence for Ainu complexity comes from Japanese documentary sources. Historians who examine such sources often argue for quite complex social organization amongst the pre-modern Ainu. In English, Brett Walker has made the strongest case in this respect, arguing that the pre-modern Ainu were organized into chiefdoms. The chiefs who controlled these chiefdoms 'appear to have been charismatic figures who sometimes extended their spheres of influence over neighbouring communities. They were often called "generals" (*taishō*) in Japanese manuscripts, a title that evokes a sense of authority based on military might and personal leadership qualities' (Walker 2001, 240). A discussion of Ainu warfare can be found in Hudson (in press.).

While the existence of chiefs who held power over several regional communities is indeed a commonly-used definition of a chiefdom (Carneiro 1981), such an arrangement was rare in Ainu society and seems to have been primarily limited to cases when Ainu groups cooperated at times of open conflict with Japanese settlers. At other times, Ainu chiefly power seems to have been limited to single villages (Takakura 1960, 18). Although membership in patrilineal lineages was an important aspect of power, the office of chief was regularly given to men who had particular practical abilities. Isabella Bird made the following comments about Ainu chiefs based on her visit to Hokkaido in 1878:

> If [the chief] has a 'smart' son, who he thinks will command the respect of the people, he appoints him; but if not, he chooses the most suitable man in the village...The office is not hereditary anywhere.
>
> ...
>
> An eldest son...does not necessarily inherit the house and curios [i.e. *ikor* or treasures]. The latter are not divided, but go with the house to the son whom the father regards as being the 'smartest'. Formal adoption is practised...I cannot get at the word which is translated 'smartness', but I understand it as meaning general capacity. The chief...is allowed three wives among the mountain Ainos, otherwise authority seems to be his only privilege.
>
> (Bird 1973, 281)

Takakura (1960, 18) makes the interesting argument that an originally hereditary system changed to one based on ability as a result of outside contact: 'as the Ainu village system became more complex and as contact and negotiation with the outside world became more frequent the simple attribute of respected descent was not sufficient to enable a man to rule and it became necessary that men with ability become chief'. Further research on this topic needs to consider the role of factions within Ainu society as it became increasingly subject to Japanese control.

Most scholars agree that Sakhalin Ainu society was less complex than in Hokkaido. On Sakhalin, however, Piłsudski (1998, 290) noted that Ainu *nishpa* ('nobles') 'stood out not only because of their parentage but also because of their wealthiness [sic]. Their houses were bigger and cleaner, they had plenty of useful implements and of food and an abundance of such valuable ancient objects as swords, silk materials, armours, beads, talismans, etc'.

Piłsudski goes on to explain that these *nishpa* could become impoverished but still retain some unspecified social advantages; alternatively, *nishpa* status could be acquired by the accumulation of treasures.

Slavery in Ainu society has been discussed by Takakura (1960), Watanabe (1983), and Fukasawa (1998). The Ainu term *utare* is usually glossed as 'slave' in early modern Japanese documents (Takakura 1960, 19). These *utare* engaged in manual labour and seem to have been important in the production economies of wealthy households. By at least the eighteenth century, *utare* were being bought and sold (Takakura 1960, 19).

To conclude, Ainu society of the seventeenth to nineteenth centuries as known from Japanese documentary sources displayed several features that are common to so-called 'complex hunter-gatherers'. Chiefs held considerable influence over the affairs of village settlements and, through trade and other activities, had opportunities to increase their wealth and reproductive success. Chiefs exploited an underclass of slaves and, in addition to extra wives, accumulated wealth in the form of larger houses, imported ceremonial robes, and traded 'prestige goods' such as swords and lacquer ware. Except for relatively brief periods of open conflict with Japanese settlers, however, Ainu chiefs were generally unsuccessful in extending their power beyond the boundaries of their home village. They were therefore unable to develop a sufficient economic basis to further extend their power. In terms of mortuary customs, moreover, Ainu complexity did not extend to the grave, most Ainu burials being simple inhumations, sometimes with grave goods such as swords or iron pots (Utagawa 2001, 452–67). Despite these provisos, however, if one adopts the definition of hunter-gatherer complexity suggested by Arnold (1996)—that '(1) some people must perform work for others under the direction of persons outside their kin group, and (2) some people, including leaders, are higher ranking at birth than others'—then we can indeed classify the Ainu as complex hunter-gatherers.

REGIONAL VARIATIONS

While 'the Ainu' are sometimes treated as a monolithic group in the hunter-gatherer literature, there were in fact quite major regional differences in Ainu society (Ohnuki-Tierney 1974b; 1976). The main divisions are between Hokkaido, southern Sakhalin, and the Kurils. Cultural differences between and within these regions reflect ecology and contact with neighbouring peoples (Ohnuki-Tierney 1974b, 191) as well as historical depth, the Sakhalin and Kuril Ainu having split from Hokkaido between the ninth and twelfth centuries. Analyses of Ainu skulls going back to Kodama (1940) have shown that Ainu were not biologically homogeneous, even in Hokkaido (Ito 1967; Kondo 1995).

Hokkaido is the best-known region of Ainu settlement and the one that has been subjected to the most research. Generally speaking, Hokkaido was ecologically more productive than Sakhalin and this led to a more affluent and sedentary Ainu lifestyle than on Sakhalin or the Kuril Islands (Ohnuki-Tierney 1974b). Major differences between the Hokkaido and Sakhalin Ainu adaptations include a greater dependence on plant cultivation in the former but a more developed use of domesticated dogs in the latter (Ohnuki-Tierney 1974b). Reindeer and musk deer, animals that were not found on Hokkaido, were widely hunted by Sakhalin Ainu, who also consumed more sea mammals than on Hokkaido. Compared with Hokkaido and Sakhalin, there has been less research on the Ainu of the Kuril Islands although important contributions have been made by Torii (1919) and others. The permanent Ainu population of the Kurils may have been quite low (Fitzhugh et al. 2004, 96). The Kuril Islands—especially those smaller islands beyond Urup—were in many respects a difficult place to live: terrestrial faunal richness was low (with only the fox and vole) and the weather was famously rough and unpredictable.

Ritual and World View

Ainu ethnography offers extensive evidence for the importance of ritual observances in Ainu life and this ethnographic material is now supported by a growing body of archaeological data. Ainu shamanism was more developed on Sakhalin than Hokkaido, perhaps because of the influence of neighbouring groups such as the Nivkh on Sakhalin. Sakhalin Ainu shamanism has been discussed in detail by Piłsudski (1998) and Ohnuki-Tierney (1973). Hokkaido Ainu rituals have been discussed in English in a number of works including Munro (1962) and Yamada (2002). Archaeologically, Utagawa's work on sending back rituals has been the most active area of research. As well as the classic bear ceremony, Utagawa's many publications have covered the sending back of tools, ornaments, and other animals including dogs and owls (Utagawa 1992; 1999; 2001; 2004). Utagawa (2001) has also published on the archaeology of burials and of legends associated with *chashi* forts. Another important contribution to the archaeology of Ainu ritual has been made by Fukasawa (1998, 79–92) who conducted a structural analysis of Ainu epic poetry or *yukar*.

The most well-known Ainu ritual, the *iyomante* or bear ceremony, is often regarded as a central defining element of Ainu culture (Akino 1999; Kindaichi 1949; Utagawa 1999; Watanabe 1966). Bear ceremonialism is widely distributed across the north, but the most distinctive Ainu form was the capture and raising of a bear cub prior to the ceremonial sending back to the world of the *kamuy* spirits. A large literature exists on the origins of the Ainu *iyomante*. While experts still debate the details and chronology, there seems little doubt that the classic Ainu *iyomante* was influenced by bear ceremonialism in both the Satsumon and Okhotsk cultures (Utagawa 1999).

Conclusions

The history of research on Ainu hunter-gathering has been as unusual as the Ainu themselves were complex and distinctive hunter-gatherers. Lacking first-hand ethnographies of Ainu foraging, scholars have been forced to rely on archaeology and historical records. However, research in both of these areas has expanded exponentially in recent years and works such as Segawa (2007) suggest that our understanding of Ainu as hunter-gatherers is only set to mature further in the future. What we lack in knowledge of the 'ethnographic present' is in part made up for by a rich and detailed record of long-term historical changes in Ainu foraging, a record that is perhaps unparalleled elsewhere in the world. The end of Ainu hunter-gathering under Japanese and Russian colonization was a process depressingly familiar to that in other colonial regimes, yet the rich heritage of Ainu foraging remains important in the modern world for thinking about how to maintain diverse and sustainable ways of living in the twenty-first century (Aoyama 2012; Nakamura 2008). Until the full territorial colonization of their homelands in the late nineteenth and early twentieth centuries, the Ainu were primarily a hunter-gatherer people and as such they represent a rare example of an Old World, cold temperate foraging society that continued hunter-gathering until recent times. The long, complex history of the Ainu as hunter-gatherers is of enormous importance for a general understanding of human foraging behaviour.

References

Akino, S. 1999. Spirit-sending ceremonies. In W. Fitzhugh and C. Dubreuil (eds), *Ainu: spirit of a northern people*, 248–55. Washington, DC: Arctic Studies Center, Smithsonian Institution.

Aoyama, M. 2012. Indigenous Ainu occupational identities and the natural environment in Hokkaido. In N. Pollard and D. Sakellariou (eds), *Politics of occupation-centred practice: reflections on occupational engagement across cultures*, 106–27. Oxford: Wiley-Blackwell.

Arnold, J. 1996. The archaeology of complex hunter-gatherers. *Journal of Archaeological Method and Theory* 3, 77–126.

Batchelor, J. 1882. Notes on the Ainu. *Transactions of the Asiatic Society of Japan* 10, 206–19.

Bird, I. 1973. *Unbeaten tracks in Japan: an account of travels in the interior including visits to the aborigines of Yezo and the shrine of Nikko*. Rutland, VT and Tokyo: Tuttle.

Burch, E. 1994. The future of hunter-gatherer research. In E. Burch and L. Ellanna (eds), *Key issues in hunter-gatherer research*, 441–55. Oxford: Berg.

Carneiro, R. 1981. The chiefdom: precursor of the state. In G. D. Jones and R. R. Kautz (eds), *The transition to statehood in the New World*, 37–79. Cambridge: Cambridge University Press.

Crawford, G. 2008. The Jomon in early agricultural discourse: issues arising from Matsui, Kanehara, and Pearson. *World Archaeology* 40, 445–65.

Crawford, G. 2011. Advances in understanding early agriculture in Japan. *Current Anthropology* 52, 331–45.

Deriha, K. In press. Trade and the paradigm shift in research on Ainu hunting practices. In M. J. Hudson, A.-E. Lewallen, and M. K. Watson (eds), *Beyond Ainu studies: changing academic and public perspectives*. Honolulu: University of Hawai'i Press.

Dodo, Y. and Ishida, H. 1990. Population history of Japan as viewed from cranial nonmetric variation. *Journal of the Anthropological Society of Nippon* 98, 269–87.

Earle, T. 1997. *How chiefs come to power: the political economy in prehistory*. Stanford: Stanford University Press.

Endō, M. 1987. Edo makki no Mitsuishi Ainu ni okeru ryūdōteki shūdan no keisei mekanizumu [Temporal residential groupings of the Ainu in the Mitsuishi district of Hokkaido, Japan, 1856–69]. *Chirigaku Hyōron* [Geographical Review of Japan] 60, 287–300.

Endō, M. 1994. Jinkō genshōki no Takashima Ainu ni okeru ie kōseiin no ryūdōsei mekanizumu: Tenpo 5 (1834)—Meiji 4 (1871) nen [The mobility of household members of the Ainu in the Takashima district of Hokkaido, Japan, 1834–1871]. *Chirigaku Hyōron* [Geographical Review of Japan] 67, 79–100.

Endō, M. 1997. *Ainu to shuryōsaishū shakai: shūdan no ryūdōsei ni kansuru chirigakuteki kenkyū.* [Ainu and hunter-gatherer society: A geographical study of group mobility]. Tokyo: Daimeidō.

Fitzhugh, B., Moore, S., Lockwood, C., and Boone, C. 2004. Archaeological paleobiogeography in the Russian Far East: the Kuril islands and Sakhalin in comparative perspective. *Asian Perspectives* 43, 92–122.

Fukasawa, Y. 1998. *Ainu archaeology as ethnohistory: iron technology among the Saru Ainu of Hokkaido, Japan, in the 17th century*. Oxford: BAR International Series 744.

Haginaka, M. 2000. Food: women's roles. In Foundation for Research and Promotion of Ainu Culture (eds), *Baba, Kodama korekushon ni miru kita no tami Ainu no sekai* [Ainu: Northern People and their World as seen in the Baba and Kodama Collections], 87. Nagoya: Nagoya City Museum.

Hammel, E. 1988. A glimpse into the demography of the Ainu. *American Anthropologist* 90, 25–41.

Hanihara, K. 1970. Mongoloid dental complex in the deciduous dentition with special reference to the dentition of the Ainu. *Journal of the Anthropological Society of Nippon* 78, 3–17.

Hanihara, K. 1979. Dental traits in Ainu, Australian Aborigines, and New World populations. In W. Laughlin and A. Harper (eds), *The first Americans: origins, affinities, and adaptations*, 125–34. New York: G. Fischer.

Hanihara, K. 1991. Dual structure model for the population history of the Japanese. *Japan Review* 2, 1–33.

Hanihara, T., Yoshida, K., and Ishida, H. 2008. Craniometric variation of the Ainu: an assessment of differential gene flow from Northeast Asia into northern Japan, Hokkaido. *American Journal of Physical Anthropology* 137, 283–93.

Harrison, J. 1954. The Saghalien trade: a contribution to Ainu studies. *Southwestern Journal of Anthropology* 10, 278–93.

Howell, D. 1995. *Capitalism from within: economy, society, and the state in a Japanese fishery*. Berkeley: University of California Press.

Howell, D. 1997. The Meiji state and the logic of Ainu 'protection'. In H. Hardacre (ed.), *New directions in the study of Meiji Japan*, 612–34. Leiden: E. J. Brill.

Howell, D. In press. Is 'Ainu history' 'Japanese history'? In M. Hudson, A.-E. Lewallen, and M. Watson (eds), *Beyond Ainu studies: changing academic and public perspectives*. Honolulu: University of Hawai'i Press.

Hudson, M. 1999. *Ruins of identity: ethnogenesis in the Japanese islands*. Honolulu: University of Hawai'i Press.

Hudson, M. 2002. Agriculture and language change in the Japanese islands. In P. Bellwood and C. Renfrew (eds), *Examining the farming/language dispersal hypothesis*, 311–18. Cambridge: McDonald Institute for Archaeological Research.

Hudson, M. 2004. The perverse realities of change: world system incorporation and the Okhotsk culture of Hokkaido. *Journal of Anthropological Archaeology* 23, 290–308.

Hudson, M. In press. Ainu and hunter-gatherer studies. In M. J. Hudson, A.-E. Lewallen, and M. K. Watson (eds), *Beyond Ainu studies: changing ccademic and public perspectives*. Honolulu: University of Hawai'i Press.

Hudson, M. and Aoyama, M. 2011. Occupational apartheid and national parks: the case of Shiretoko. In F. Kronenberg, N. Pollard, and D. Sakellariou (eds), *Occupational therapies without borders: towards an ecology of occupation-based practices*, 247–55. Edinburgh: Churchill Livingstone/Elsevier.

Hunn, E. and Williams, N. 1982. Introduction. In N. Williams and E. Hunn (eds), *Resource managers: North American and Australian hunter-gatherers*, 1–16. Canberra: Australian Institute of Aboriginal Studies.

Ishida, H., Hanihara, T., Kondo, O., and Fukumine, T. 2009. Craniometric divergence history of the Japanese populations. *Anthropological Science* 117, 147–56.

Ito, S. 1967. Local differences on Ainu skulls: metrical observations. *Bulletin of Institute for the Study of North Eurasian Cultures, Hokkaido University* 2, 191–238.

Iwasaki-Goodman, M., Ishii, S., and Kaizawa, T. 2009. Traditional food systems of Indigenous peoples: the Ainu in the Saru River region, Japan. In H. Kuhnlein, B. Erasmus, and D. Spigelski (eds), *Indigenous peoples food systems: the many dimensions of culture, diversity and environment for nutrition and health*, 139–57. Rome: Food and Agriculture Organization, United Nations.

Iwasaki-Goodman, M. and Nomoto, M. 1999. The Ainu on whales and whaling. In W. Fitzhugh and C. Dubreuil (eds), *Ainu: spirit of a northern people*, 222–6. Washington, DC: Arctic Studies Center, Smithsonian Institution.

Janhunen, J. 2002. On the chronology of the Ainu ethnic complex. In Hokkaido Museum of Northern Peoples (eds), *Proceedings of the 16th international Abashiri symposium: the Ainu and northern peoples with special reference to various phases of cultural exchange*, 19–22. Abashiri: Association for the Promotion of Northern Cultures.

Kayano, S. 1999. Ainu and the salmon. *Bulletin of the National Museum of Ethnology* 23(4), 815–20.

Kelly, R. 1995. *The foraging spectrum: diversity in hunter-gatherer lifeways*. Washington, DC: Smithsonian Institution.

Kindaichi, K. 1949. The concepts behind the Ainu bear festival (kumamatsuri). *Southwestern Journal of Anthropology* 5, 345–50.

Kish, G. 1939. Some aspects of the missionary cartography of Japan during the sixteenth century. *Imago Mundi* 6, 39–47.

Kodama, S. 1940. The craniology and osteology of the Ainu. In *Jinruigaku, senshigaku kōza* [A course on anthropology and prehistory], vol. 18, 1–79. Tokyo: Yūzankaku.

Kohara, T. 1999. Foods of choice. In W. Fitzhugh and C. Dubreuil (eds), *Ainu: spirit of a northern people*, 202–7. Washington, DC: Arctic Studies Center, Smithsonian Institution.

Kondo, O. 1995. An analysis of Ainu population structure, based on cranial morphology. *Anthropological Science* 103, 369–84.

Lee, R. and DeVore, I. (eds) 1968. *Man the hunter*. Chicago: Aldine.

Lewallen, A.-E. 2007. Bones of contention: negotiating anthropological ethics within fields of Ainu refusal. *Critical Asian Studies* 39, 509–40.

Matsumoto, T. 2006. *Emishi no kōkogaku* [The archaeology of the Emishi]. Tokyo: Dōseisha.

Munro, N. 1962. *Ainu creed and cult*. London: Routledge & Kegan Paul.

Nakamura, K. 2008. Jizoku ka hen'yō ka: Ainu minzoku o meguru kenkyū to kyōiku [Sustainability or change? Research and education about the Ainu people]. In T. Kimura (ed.), *Sen'nen jizokugaku no kōchiku* [Building a science of a thousand year sustainability], 112–27. Tokyo: Tōshindō.

Ohnuki-Tierney, E. 1973. The shamanism of the Ainu of the northwest coast of southern Sakhalin. *Ethnology* 12, 15–29.

Ohnuki-Tierney, E. 1974a. *The Ainu of the northwest coast of southern Sakhalin*. New York: Holt, Rinehart & Winston.

Ohnuki-Tierney, E. 1974b. Another look at the Ainu: a preliminary report. *Arctic Anthropology* 11 (Suppl.), 189–95.

Ohnuki-Tierney, E. 1976. Regional variations in Ainu culture. *American Ethnologist* 3, 297–329.

Ohnuki-Tierney, E. 1993. Ainu. In P. Hockings (ed.), *Encyclopedia of world cultures*, 7–10. Boston: G. K. Hall.

Ohyi, H. 1975. The Okhotsk culture, a maritime culture of the southern Okhotsk Sea region. In W. Fitzhugh (ed.), *Prehistoric maritime adaptations of the circumpolar zone*, 123–58. The Hague: Mouton.

Ölschleger, H. D. 1989. *Umwelt und Wirtschaft der Ainu: Bemerkungen zur Ökologie einer Wildbeutergesellschaft*. Berlin: Reimer.

Ölschleger, H. D. 1999. Technology, settlement, and hunting ritual. In W. Fitzhugh and C. Dubreuil (eds), *Ainu: spirit of a northern people*, 208–21. Washington, DC: Arctic Studies Center, Smithsonian Institution.

Omoto, K. 1972. Polymorphisms and genetic affinities of the Ainu in Hokkaido. *Human Biology in Oceania* 1, 279–88.

Ōnishi, H. 2009. *Tobinitai bunka kara no Ainu bunkashi* [Ainu culture history as seen from the Tobinitai culture]. Tokyo: Dōseisha.

Otsuka, K. 1999. Itaomachip: reviving a boat-building and trading tradition. In W. Fitzhugh and C. Dubreuil (eds), *Ainu: spirit of a northern people*, 374–6. Washington, DC: Arctic Studies Center, Smithsonian Institution.

Philippi, D. 1979. *Songs of gods, songs of humans: the epic tradition of the Ainu*. Princeton: Princeton University Press.

Piłsudski, B. 1998. *The collected works of Bronisław Piłsudski. Vol. 1: The aborigines of Sakhalin*. Berlin: Mouton de Gruyter.

St John, H. 1873. The Ainos: Aborigines of Yeso. *Journal of the Anthropological Institute of Great Britain and Ireland* 2, 248–54.

Saris, J. 1941. *The first voyage of the English to Japan*. Tokyo: The Toyo Bunko.

Sasaki, S. 1999. Trading brokers and partners with China, Russia, and Japan. In W. Fitzhugh and C. Dubreuil (eds), *Ainu: spirit of a northern people*, 86–91. Washington, DC: Arctic Studies Center, Smithsonian Institution.

Sato, T., Amano, T., Ono, H., Ishida, H., Kodera, H., Matsumura, H., Yoneda, M., and Masuda, R. 2007. Origins and genetic features of the Okhotsk people, revealed by ancient mitochondrial DNA analysis. *Journal of Human Genetics* 54, 409–13.

Segawa, T. 2007. *Ainu no rekishi: Umi to takara no nomado* [Ainu history: nomads of ocean and treasure]. Tokyo: Kōdansha (in Japanese).

Stephan, J. 1974. *The Kuril islands: Russo-Japanese frontiers in the Pacific*. Oxford: Clarendon Press.

Takakura, S. 1960. The Ainu of northern Japan: a study in conquest and acculturation, trans. J. Harrison. *Transactions of the American Philosophical Society* 50, 3–88.

Tamura, S. 2000. *The Ainu language*. Tokyo: Sanseido.

Tezuka, K. 1998. Long-distance trade networks and shipping in the Ezo region. *Arctic Anthropology* 35, 350–60.

Torii, R. 1919. *Études archeologiques et éthnologiques: les Ainou des Iles Kouriles*. Journal of the College of Science, Imperial University of Tokyo, Vol. 42.

Utagawa, H. 1992. The 'sending-back' rite in Ainu culture. *Japanese Journal of Religious Studies* 19, 255–70.

Utagawa, H. 1999. The archaeology of iyomante. In W. Fitzhugh and C. Dubreuil (eds), *Ainu: spirit of a northern people*, 256–60. Washington, DC: Arctic Studies Center, Smithsonian Institution.

Utagawa, H. 2001. *Ainu kōkogaku kenkyū: Yoron* [The study of Ainu archaeology: an introduction]. Sapporo: Hokkaidō Shuppan Kikaku Sentaa.

Utagawa, H. (ed.) 2004. *Kuma to fukurō no iomante: Ainu no minzoku kōkogaku* [Bear and owl iomante: Ainu ethnoarchaeology]. Tokyo: Dōseisha.

Walker, B. 2001. *The conquest of Ainu lands: ecology and culture in Japanese expansion, 1590–1800*. Berkeley: University of California Press.

Watanabe, H. 1966. Der sozialen Funktionen des Bärenfestes der Ainu und die ökologischen Faktoren in seiner Entwicklung. *Anthropos* 61, 708–26.

Watanabe, H. 1968. Subsistence and ecology of northern food gatherers with special reference to the Ainu. In R. Lee and I. DeVore (eds), *Man the hunter*, 69–77. Chicago: Aldine.

Watanabe, H. 1973. *The Ainu ecosystem: environment and group structure*. Seattle: University of Washington Press.

Watanabe, H. 1983. Occupational differentiation and social stratification: the case of northern Pacific maritime food-gatherers. *Current Anthropology* 24, 217–19.

Watanabe, H. 1999. The Ainu ecosystem. In W. Fitzhugh and C. Dubreuil (eds), *Ainu: spirit of a northern people*, 198–201. Washington, DC: Arctic Studies Center, Smithsonian Institution.

Watson, M. In press. *Japan's Ainu minority in Tokyo: Urban indigeneity and cultural politics*. London: Routledge.

Yamada, T. 2002. *The world view of the Ainu: nature and cosmos reading from language*. London: Kegan Paul International.

CHAPTER 51

HUNTER-GATHERER TRANSFORMATIONS IN NORTHERN EUROPE AFTER 1500 AD

JUSSI-PEKKA TAAVITSAINEN

In 1500 AD the last hunter-gatherer cultures of northern Europe inhabited the boreal forest zones of Fennoscandia (Fennoscandia is a geographic term signifying the north-western peninsula in northern Europe and eastern Europe made up by the Scandinavian Peninsula, Finland, Karelia, and the Kola Peninsula), and were undergoing major historical transformations as a result of the development of the deteriorating fur trade and the rise of large-scale reindeer pastoralism. At the same time, Fennoscandia was also the focus of colonization and settlement by incoming slash-and-burn agrarian populations, who were combining local hunting and fishing with their farming practices due to the fact that the northern environment and climate were marginal for agriculture. Hence, this integration of older and more recent subsistence strategies means that many features 'typical' of northern hunter-gatherers have persisted into the more recent traditions of local folk cultures. This chapter focuses primarily on the Sámi/Lapps, who were at the centre of these historical transformations.

Birger Steckzén (1964, 203–4) has estimated that in the thirteenth century the size of the Sámi population in the Pite, Lule, Torne, and Kemi districts (or *lappmarks*) of Lapland was roughly 1,760, while in 1553 the size had increased to 2,060. The total area of these *lappmarks* covers 205,000 km^2. This means that the density of population did not reach more than 0.9 persons per 100 km^2 in the thirteenth century, and only 1.0 person by 1553. Some of these Sámi populations kept to their traditional lifeways long enough for modern ethnographers and geographers to be able to document them in considerable detail.

The term *lappmark* incorporates the term 'Lapp' which is generally associated with the Sámi. In this chapter, the two terms are used synonymously denoting an economic group, or, to be more precise, the hunting-fishing populations living in eastern and northern Fennoscandia and comprising *diverse* local cultural groups. It seems to be a rather recent development that the term 'Lapp', as used in historical taxation documents, eventually became a derogatory label (on the term see Kulonen 2005, 184; Lehtola 2011).

Traditional Sámi Lifeways: *Siida*

The livelihood of the forest Sámi group called the Skolt Sámi which lived in Petsamo in Lapland was documented in great detail: their subsistence strategy was based on seasonal cycles (e.g. Nickul 1948; Tanner 1929; Tegengren 1952). For example, the Finnish ethnologist Kustaa Vilkuna visited Skolt Sámi communities living in northern Finland several times and documented their way of living with Karl Nickul. In late winter 1938, Vilkuna directed the film expedition of Kansatieteellinen Filmi Oy (Ethnological Film Ltd) to the winter village of Skolt Sámi in Suenjil (*Isien työt* III). Suenjil is the best-known case study, example, and basis of the discussion of the *siida* institution (Figure 51.1). The studies are also cited here as a starting point of our discussion.

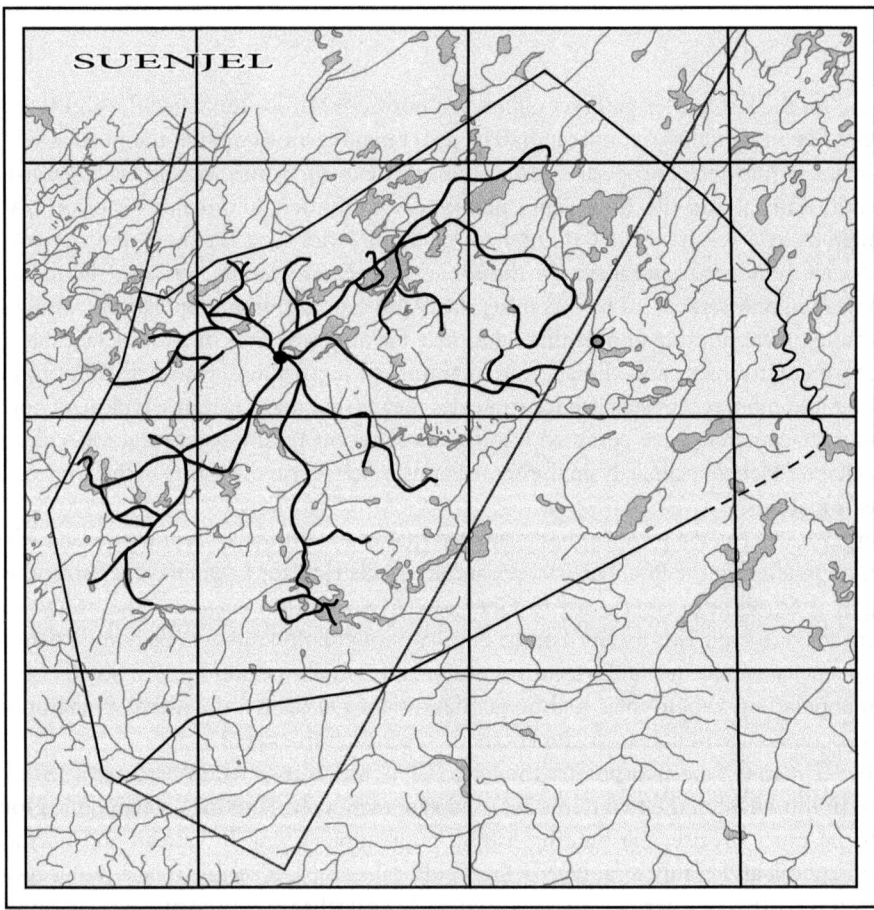

FIGURE 51.1 The annual routes of the seven families areas of Suenjil in the 1930s (Nickul 1959, 4, k. 4).

The population formed so-called Lapp villages or *siidas* (fi. *lapinkylä*). A *siida* was formed by a group of families that spent most of the year in summer camps, each in its own area that extended along watercourses around the winter village, into which all the people assembled for the mid-winter period. Traditionally, the Lapp village was a local community and functioned as a territorial, economic, and social entity (see, e.g. Joona 2005, 187-9; Hansen and Olsen 2006, passim).

The *siida* consisted of families whose representatives formed a body, *sobbar* or *norraz*, which divided the land between the constituent families. This means that the *siida* was the general owner of the territory, and that all the families had utilization rights to this land. The *siida* utilized the local lakes and forests which guaranteed their livelihood, and their main subsistence occupations involved fishing and hunting (wild reindeer, elks, beavers, bears, fur animals, and birds). Individual families moved around according to the spawning times of the fish and the movements of the game, and small settlements, camps, and stores were located along these routes. At the end of April, the families moved from their winter village to their spring sites, from there to the summer places, and from there to their autumn settlements. Fish catches were more or less used by individual families, but game was distributed equally to all members of the *siida* including the sick and the poor.

The main family resource areas seem to have been of primary importance, while the winter village—generally occupied for around four months—served a secondary but important role as a locus for the *sobbar* meetings and other social activities. The winter village locations were not fixed but moved occasionally to new sites when local firewood and lichen pastures had been exhausted. In contrast, the family areas were fixed, and their settlement sites tended not to move.

Vilkuna, when discussing the Lapp village and its function, raises the question as to why this basic traditional organizational form of the Lapp communities, the hunter-gatherers of the Fennoscandian taiga zone, vanished so easily (Vilkuna 1971). The answer appears to be linked to population growth and other historical processes affecting these northern hunter-gatherers. For example, historical data from Suenjil generate insights into these changes. The earliest taxation record of Suenjil *siida* survives from 1574 and lists 21 inhabitants, and by 1700, the number had increased to 48. Considering the area of the *siida*, approximately 6,800 km^2, these figures suggest a population density of 0.3–0.8 individuals per 100 km^2. By 1938, the population remaining in the Finnish side of the *siida*, covering 4,800 km^2, was 223, or five individuals per 100 km^2, representing a major increase.

Also, by this time the scale of reindeer husbandry had grown considerably and sheep farming was also becoming an important part of the community's economy (Nickul 1948). Of course, this growth in population may also have been a *consequence*—rather than a cause—of adopting new kinds of subsistence via growing with the external economic system. As early as 1906 Amund Helland suggested that the traditional Skolt's way of life consisted of a curious hybrid of hunting, fishing, and nomadic pastoralism, while still living in permanently settled communities (Hansen and Olsen 2006, 180).

It is also important to emphasize that there were notable regional differences in the historical transformations affecting the Sámi. For example, in the historical period, Sámi areas were being encroached upon by several different states: Denmark–Norway, Sweden, and Russia all imposed their own tax regimes, but also generated different kinds of trade opportunities, requiring local populations to adapt to these diverse new conditions. Lars Ivar Hansen and Bjørnar Olsen (2006) have examined the historical reactions of the Sámi to these developments, and emphasize how Sámi populations developed different economic and social responses in different geographical settings. In consequence, distinct strategies emerged, each conditioned by variations in the resource base, as well as the specific commercial and political relationship that linked local Sámi with neighbouring populations and the different states (see for example Hansen and Olsen 2006, figure 51). In light of these considerable local differences, it becomes difficult to identify a single 'original' or 'unified' village-based social community that was typical for all the Sámi, of the kind sought by Vilkuna, and described above. At the same time, there do seem to have been common patterns of change, largely because of the widely shared general characteristics of common social organization among the Sámi hunter-gatherer communities, akin to the broadly similar features that can be noted among many small-scale farming societies, as well as in reindeer pastoralist societies (Hansen and Olsen 2006, 172–3; see also Tegengren 1952, 16–19). As a result of these factors, questions about the transformation and persistence of hunter-gatherer cultures in Fennoscandia have to be understood as being a function of both diverse internal and also external socio-economic and political factors. In addition, responses were structured by local environments and also by the legacy of earlier historical processes.

The Iron Age and Medieval Background of the Utilization of Northern Wilderness Regions

Across northern Fennoscandia, local lifeways contributed to regional 'wilderness' economies that were built on active cooperation between the hunter-gatherers and incoming agriculturalists. A useful model for studying wilderness utilization, and the diverse inter-community contacts that resulted, is provided by *eränkäynti*. This term refers to economic exploitation of more distant wilderness areas, both inland and also in coastal regions, by people living in settled agricultural areas. These practices have been documented in written sources dating back to the medieval and early modern periods (e.g. Taavitsainen 1987; 1990; 1994), enabling the emergence of these unique economies to be reconstructed.

The growth of the fur trade during the Viking Age had given birth to a few widely spaced permanent agricultural settlements in the interior, more akin to wilderness 'stations' than large agricultural villages (e.g. Taavitsainen 1994; Taavitsainen et al. 2007). During this period, the forested areas of Finland seem to have become truly integrated within the wider trade networks spanning the Baltic realm. In this way, the earlier wilderness economy that had been focused on meeting local subsistence needs was transformed into a commercialized economy involving specialized hunting for furs (Voionmaa 1947). More generally, the expansion and intensification of the lucrative fur trade became the primary motivation for the development of new relationships between northern hunter-gatherers and the more recently arrived farmers.

As new populations moved into the wilderness, the first sites they established were temporarily inhabited hunting stations. Such sites were located along water routes and favourable for communication, and also for farming, which generated extra subsistence to support the commercialized fur-hunting activities. Over time, these stations most likely turned into growing centres of more permanent settlement, and this seems to have followed a pattern established in the older, permanently settled areas. For example, in south and west Finland, there is a clear correlation between stray finds, burial grounds, and clayey and silty soils, prerequisites for permanent agriculture in that period. In other words, burial grounds, the clearest indicators of permanent settlement, are found in the areas best suited for agriculture. This same pattern can be observed in the spatial distribution of the new 'forest-station' settlements, which were also located in similar kinds of settings that were suitable for agriculture. This probably indicates that the new settlers formed surplus population from the old, permanently settled areas. However, these new 'farms' were so sparsely distributed—small fertile areas remained separated by extensive areas of uninhabited wilderness—that they cannot be argued to represent a full-scale agricultural colonization of the wilderness (Taavitsainen 1990, 65–7, figure 25, 113).

During the Viking Age, and through to the fifteenth century, the border between the fully settled areas occupied by agricultural populations and the wilderness areas eventually stabilized. A similar kind of border also emerged and stabilized in northern Fennoscandia during the modern period (cf. Hansen and Olsen 2006, 169). These kinds of enduring border-zone situations were an expression of the inherent cooperation and symbiotic commercial and economic relationships that were emerging between peasants, who largely subsisted on agriculture, and the Lapps, who mainly remained as hunter-fisher-gatherers within the wilderness areas (e.g. Odner 1983).

As the global fur trade intensified, the Russian principalities began to compete for access to the same resources and trade articles. The fur trade was a cardinal factor in the foundation of the early Russian principalities, and in the subsequent Russian expansion into the vast regions of Eurasia, through to Alaska (Slezkine 1994), but the best furs were always obtained from the northernmost borders of the Russian empire. For instance, the wealth of the medieval Novgorod Republic was based on the exportation of northern furs to Bolghar, Kiev, and Byzantium, and later to the sphere of the Hanseatic trade in the North Sea and the Baltic Sea. In the fourteenth century, the grand duchy of Moscow challenged Novgorod, and by the mid-sixteenth century it had gained a firm upper hand in the region. In the early sixteenth century, the capture of Smolensk increased Moscow's trade with Lithuania and Leipzig. Moreover, the discovery of the Northern Sea Route, and the conquests of Astrakhan and Kazan in the mid-sixteenth century as well as the founding of Arkhangelsk in the late sixteenth century opened the central Asian markets for Moscow, which in turn was securing its own control of Siberia, an important source of new furs. The expansion of Moscow's economic interests across northern Eurasia occurred at the same time as the fashion of wearing furs spread across west Europe and the court of the Ottoman Turks (Slezkine 1994).

These continental-scale developments had important regional implications in Fennoscandia, and as competition for forest resources grew, new Finnish and Russian settlements were founded across the forest zone. These incoming populations also had to negotiate mutually beneficial exchange agreements with older local hunter-gatherers, the Sámi. The processes of change were similar across this zone, but are best illustrated with a Finnish case study.

Changing Sámi Strategies in Finland

As the fur trade intensified and then declined, new populations moved into the northern forests, and these pressures deeply affected the utilization of the taiga. Initially this triggered a transition from hunting and gathering to mobile slash-and-burn agriculture, and this eventually led to the cultivation of permanent fields and establishment of fixed settlements. In the tundra, these wider changes triggered the beginning of large-scale reindeer herding. Remaining Sámi hunter-fisher-gatherer groups eventually became trapped between the pressures exerted by these two trajectories of development: many were eventually assimilated by the newcomers; others merged with other Sámi groups, such as those practising sedentary fishing or large-scale reindeer pastoralism. These developments can be examined in more detail, with a focus on understanding the nature of *local* opportunities, choices, and motivations that characterized the diverse individuals and families of Sámi hunter-fisher-gatherers during the early historic period.

Strategy 1: Agriculture and Cultural Assimilation in the Forest Zone

In the late fifteenth century a new group of historic 'actors'—slash-and-burn cultivators—emerged on the scene from the east. These populations formed the Savo-Karelian culture, which was inherently a kind of 'frontier' culture, and thus accustomed to cooperate alongside other kinds of economies, languages, and ethnicities. This generated new ways of occupying the backwoods of the wilderness, both for the hunter-gatherers of interior Finland, as well as for the utilization of the wilderness by farmers of the permanently settled regions in the west. This also added a further level of historical complexity to the frontier, because the slash-and-burn farmers were also mobile, but over longer time periods: they did not stay long in their settlements, but shifted their homesteads to new areas as the fertility of their forest cultivation plots inevitably became exhausted after a few years of use. Over time, the territorial balance and the socio-economic, religious, as well as ethnic landscape of the wilderness began to be transformed.

But these changes were also due to the increasing efficiency of state administration and to adaptations to the new globalizing economy as well as the emerging political, ecclesiastical, and economic networks. The greatest singular change was the formal opening of the wilderness areas to new settlement by incomers. This Gustavus Vasa accomplished by taking wilderness territories owned by the western farmers into the crown's ownership. After that, some of the farmers moved into their lands in the wilderness, but mainly the wilderness areas were settled by new Savonian farmers practising slash-and-burn economy. Eventually, this had disastrous consequences on the older hunter-gatherer subsistence strategies of the Lapps/Sámi. Because it would have been against the *eränkäynti* traders' own interests to disturb the 'subcontracting' activities of the Sámi, wilderness traders also strongly opposed the founding of new farming settlements to their *erämarks* (Itkonen 1948, 32). Vilkuna (1971, 215) describes the impacts in the following ways:

> Families lived on their lands only by what the nature offered to be gathered and consumed according to the season. One had to constantly move from one area and dwelling to another,

always in the same order year by year, because the natural conditions remained the same and only certain areas provided enough food and other goods necessary for living. When a new settler took a good whitefish lake, on whose shores a Lapp family had fished for a couple of months every autumn, into his possession, it caused a great gap into the annual cycle of the Lapps. Usually, it was not replaceable with another lake, since another family already utilized that. The family which gathered its livelihood directly from wild nature needed a large territory, an entity for the annual cycle, to live. When the entity was broken at some point, the family was doomed to misery. Men became hired men of the settler, or the whole family turned into a group of beggars. Children learned, if they survived, a new language. They became Finns. The Lapps did not retreat but became Finns or they were destroyed.

The sixteenth century has been regarded as the climax of the Savonian expansion (see, for example, Kaukiainen 1980, 34). Helmer Tegengren (1952) describes how this process progressed in Kemi Lapland, when the economic basis of local Lapps was gradually destroyed by the encroachment of Savonian slash-and-burn farmers. In response, the crown tried to prevent excessive burning of the forests in order to protect forests, game, and the hunting of fur animals practised by the Lapps (for instance, the hunting of beavers was made a privilege of the Lapps). The new settlers, however, circumvented the restriction by deliberately marrying daughters of Lapps. As a result of this strategy, incomers and their descendants gradually gained the same hunting privileges as the Lapps (Tegengren 1952, 86–8). After this, assimilation remained the only choice for many marginalized Lapps, and by the eighteenth century, the whole region had become nominally 'Finnish', despite its complex multi-ethnic and multi-lingual history (Figure 51.2).

As a result of these processes, the overall importance of wilderness economy gradually decreased. The situation is well exemplified by analysis of hunting: in spite of the crown being particularly interested in hunted products, such as furs, which were part of the state's luxury trade, the importance of the fur trade diminished constantly. In 1559 the exportation of furs amounted to 22.3 per cent of total state export revenues, but by 1620 this had fallen away steeply to only 2.3 per cent. The decrease is highly significant, although other export products acquired from the wilderness areas, such as tar, did somewhat compensate for it. Another proof of the deterioration of the importance of the wilderness economy was the fate of ordinary farmers who had also specialized in the acquisition of furs for consumption only by the court. In return for these services, the farmers gained exemption from other taxes. The arrangement began during the time of Gustavus Vasa, but the last of such 'fur-hunter' farmers disappeared in the 1650s (Jokipii 1974, 336, 342, and literature mentioned therein).

On the Russian side of the state border, in Viena (Dvina) Karelia, the circumstances were very similar (Alenius et al. 2010; Pöllä 2001; 2003; Taavitsainen 2010). The even distribution of Sámi place names in the region suggests that they had once occupied the whole of the Viena region, although, as on the Swedish side of the border, the material traces of the Sámi are difficult to discover archaeologically, and all the written sources related to the region are relatively recent. Nevertheless, demographic sources indicate that around the 1600s Sámi settlements covered well over a half of Viena. The sparse Karelian settlements were established probably in the fourteenth century, though the first documentation of their existence in the area is from the sixteenth century. The oldest taxation documents providing information on the state of settlement in the eastern and southern parts of Viena were drawn up in 1591 and 1597. These and other sparse early seventeenth-century written sources do not provide, however, a sound basis for a reconstruction of the settlement and demographic developments. It is as late as the 1670s when the tax records allow more or

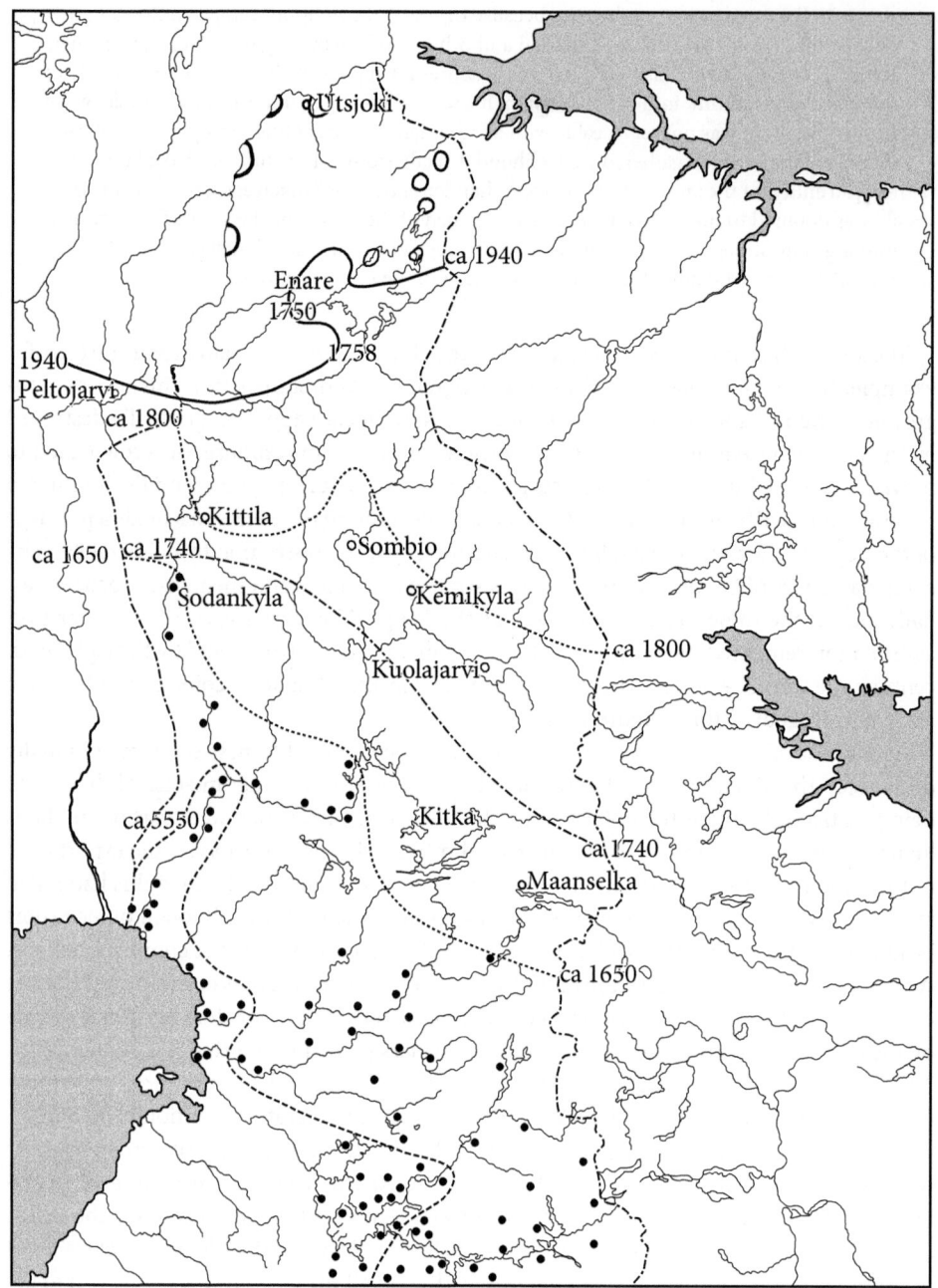

FIGURE 51.2 The spread of the Finnish settlement in Finnish Lapland (Tegengren 1952, 60).

less reliable understanding of the settlement in Viena. In the late 1670s, there were 53 peasant villages and four Lapp villages in the region with approximately 510 houses and 11 huts. The area of permanent settlement covered the whole of Viena except its north-western corner.

Administratively, the western strip of Viena or the eastern slope of Maaselkä belonged to populations of the Forest Sámi in spite of the extremely low density of their winter villages in the region. At the shores of Kuittijärvi Lake, Uhtua was settled by Sámi in 1588 and Vuonninen in 1620, but even Uhtua was settled by incoming Karelian populations by 1597. The oldest village of Ylä-Kuitti or Vuokkiniemi was founded around 1600 and Vuonninen in c.1620–35. Beside the new settlers, arriving from the provinces of Käkisalmi and Kainuu, only a few Sámi families remained in the area (Pöllä 2001). In the northern municipalities of Viena, the Sámi and Karelian populations lived side by side at the beginning of the sixteenth century, but the last members of the Sámi population had taken up cattle herding and slash-and-burn cultivation around 1850 and were eventually assimilated (Pöllä 2001; 2003).

The social and environmental dynamics sketched out here were replicated across the Eurasian taiga. Since slash-and-burn cultivation proved a highly profitable and successful means of Boreal forest ecosystem exploitation, it required extensive land areas to remain sustainable. Typically the population pressure was released by migration, first northwards, and during the late 1500s the crown was taking advantage of slash-and-burn peasants, sending them to other uncultivated forest areas in Scandinavia Finnskoga at the Swedish–Norwegian border (Lindtorp 1940; Tarkiainen 1990; Tvengsberg 1982), and northern central Russia, which was depopulated by war (Tver, presently the Kalinin area north of Moscow; Schwindt 1957). If we summarize the development of the expansion of slash-and-burn farming into the area, it could be seen as populations possessing a more highly adaptive cultural mechanism—combined fisher-hunter-farmers—which formed a highly competitive and disruptive new element in the older wilderness economy of the hunter-gatherers of the Fennoscandian interior. For example, the slash-and-burn farmers appear to have reduced the overall carrying capacity of the traditional *siida* system, and this first marginalized the Lapps, and then slowly forced them to adopt the new agricultural ways of life. Moreover, due to the fact that there was also a strong hunter-gatherer element in the intruding fisher-hunter-farmers' culture anyway, this threshold was not high, and many forest Sámi made the transition with only minor adjustments, so that local lifeways still retained many features of the older hunter-gatherer culture. Numerous place names of Lapp/Sámi origin and the surname *Lappalainen* (Lapp) emerging in historical documents during the sixteenth century tell their own story about the earlier masters of these forests and their eventual assimilation into local farming cultures (Vahtola 1999).

Strategy 2: Development of Large-Scale Reindeer Husbandry in the Tundra

In other regions of Fennsocandia, these general historical processes generated other outcomes, including the rise of large-scale reindeer husbandry in the mountains of the western parts of Fennoscandia. The basic geography and ecology of this region meant that cultivation and cattle herding were impossible; however, the natural environment—and other factors—provided all the essential prerequisites for the rise of reindeer pastoralism. This new kind of economy in fact represented an 'intensification' of older hunting practices via new steps of innovation. If exploitation of fish, birds, and wild game had dictated the seasonal round in earlier periods of hunting, fishing, and gathering, now it was the annual rhythm of the mountain reindeer that determined seasonal activities.

Initially, reindeer were used by hunters as a decoy for catching larger game. This was a common technique practised by many circumpolar hunters, and so cannot be traced back to specific origins in any particular geographic place (Ingold 1980). The domestication of reindeer, however, must have taken place on the Eurasian taiga and tundra, that is, within the natural range of wild reindeer, though it is not known exactly when the initial taming and intentional controlling of the reindeer populations first began. And although the origins and exact motivations for the early development of reindeer husbandry practices have been intensively debated, there is still no consensus as to whether reindeer pastoralism emerged from external contacts or as a result of internal 'failings' in the older hunter-gatherer economy (see, for example, Hansen and Olsen 2006, 198–209; see also Carpelan et al. 2005; Korhonen 2008; Kortesalmi 1969; Ruotsala 2002, 74–87). In Fennoscandia, the oldest written evidence on reindeer husbandry is a story told to King Alfred by a rich north Norwegian farmer Ottar in the early 890s. Ottar boasted to the king that he was the owner of 600 tame reindeers and six hunting decoys. The king incorporated the story as part of his translation of Orosius's *Historiae adversum paganos*.

Sámi communities eventually practised early forms of reindeer husbandry, but as hunter-fisher-gatherers, could also obtain their livelihood from a wide range of other strategies and resources, and so the local importance of domesticated reindeer varied greatly between families and communities. Only much later did the fully nomadic system of pastoralism emerge; at that point domestic reindeer became the primary basis of subsistence.

In Fennoscandia the main reason for the domestication of reindeer by hunter-fisher-gatherers may have been its milk, and this remained central in the domestic reindeer economy into historic times. Moreover, the concept of milking may have been adopted from other neighbouring populations. For example, the Sámi vocabulary for dairy farming was adopted from Proto-Scandinavian around AD 200–800, and it has been thought that this lends support to the idea that reindeer herding was a variation of the Norwegian husbandry of small domesticated animals. Ottar's story gives another clue as to why the domestication took place:

> The wealthy Norwegian peasant owned hundreds of reindeer, which he certainly had neither ability nor the desire to herd himself. In all probability, reindeer herding was an innovation that arose out of reciprocal arrangement between the Norwegian peasants and the Sámi hunters in which the areas of expertise of each side were combined and optimized.
>
> (Carpelan et al. 2005, 315)

For various reasons this cooperation had different stages, and similarly, for a range of reasons it waned, but Sámi herders working for outsiders preserved their know-how. The Nordic taxation records regarding Lapland from the late sixteenth century show how reindeer husbandry was practised to some extent over the whole region. Moreover, the Swedish tax books divide the Sámi population into Reindeer Sámi and Forest Sámi. The former were large-scale reindeer herders while the latter practised a semi-nomadic subsistence strategy and engaged in reindeer herding only on a small scale.

At the end of the sixteenth century, there emerged simultaneously several factors that encouraged the spread of large-scale reindeer herding across Fennoscandia: (a) the fur trade had provided the Sámi with a surplus and increased the population growth; this gradually strained the sustainability of hunting, and the fur-hunting economy was reaching a state of crisis; (b) moreover, the crown, which was becoming a more and more centralized force of social control, began to demand taxes in the form of food supplies instead of furs; it also requisitioned reindeer bulls as the unit of taxation, causing distortions to the structure of reindeer herds. As a response to both (a) and (b) some Sámi reacted by increasing the size of their herds and adopting a fully nomadic way of life which reached its full bloom by the end of the seventeenth century.

The rise of large-scale reindeer pastoralism had major—and perhaps even *revolutionary*—implications for Sámi settlement and mobility patterns, mainly because this new form of livelihood required the use of vast territories, as the seasonal rhythm of reindeer migrations now also dictated the movement of their human herders. Consequently, the traditional territorial range of the Lapp village, defined by the supply of food in the surrounding environment and hunting and gathering, was no longer sufficient for this kind of reindeer husbandry as they started to undertake long-range seasonal migrations from the interior, to the coastlines, and then back again.

Distinctive new populations of 'Reindeer Sámi' began to emerge, and expanded from their original areas of settlement into Finnmark, as well as the northern parts of Finnish Lapland, where the old Lapp villages were eventually transformed into reindeer-herders' settlements. Other changes were triggered: some 'Forest Sámi' living in adjacent areas reacted by adopting lifeways of the Reindeer Sámi, but some Reindeer Sámi also became Forest Sámi; others even began to specialize in fishing, becoming settled 'Fisher Sámi'. Around Lake Inari, many of these latter Fisher Sámi eventually became sedentary and established farmers. This seems to have been linked to population growth: as fishing families grew, their livelihood became increasingly tied to one location, and the temporary huts raised at a lakeshore were then replaced by a small log cabin. After this step, some cattle and sheep were then acquired, and subsistence was then supplemented by cultivation of a small potato field next to the cabin. Eventually, surrounding hay meadows became cultivated fields. At this stage the crown's administration interfered and demanded that inhabitants register their farms. When this happened, the Sámi families formally became permanent settlers and also the owners of a state-registered house and farm (Lähteenmäki 2004, 299–300).

It is important to emphasize that 'ethnicity', in its present-day meaning, was largely a secondary concern for Sámi caught up in this complex socio-cultural and economic process of cumulative adjustment and change. The inhabitants of Inari, Utsjoki, and Enontekiö defined themselves primarily according to their local areas, rather than to a larger pan-ethnic affiliation. Also, every ethnic group had its own social hierarchy, and even the Sámi had their own upper and lower classes. For instance, in the hierarchy of the Reindeer Sámi, the highest social positions represented the higher state authority, while in the next position were equivalents of county governors and parish ministers. Below them there were the bailiffs who collected the taxes, lower public servants, and, finally, the great reindeer owner-masters; below these were owner-herders and then the poorer hired herders. Even the quarrels over meadowlands and reindeers were not specifically ethnic, that is, reflecting some kind of inherent tension between Finns and the Sámi, but occurred frequently within ethnic groups as well as between them (Lähteenmäki 2004, 291–6; 2006, 194–7, and the literature therein).

Gradually, wealth began to accumulate among the richer reindeer nomads, and a new phenomenon of so-called 'reindeer capitalism' emerged. Like slash-and-burn cultivation, it bore the seeds of its own destruction—large-scale reindeer herding had inherent problems and also generated social tensions that reflected both competition between the new settlers and reindeer nomads and also problems related to the growing monopolization of reindeer ownership of larger and larger herds by fewer and fewer affluent individuals. As smaller-scale herders were crowded out of reindeer grazing lands the size of their herds fell, and those who could no longer support themselves by reindeer herding eventually turned into settlers (Ingold 1980, 78–81, 201–7; Lähteenmäki 2004, 97–8, and the literature mentioned therein).

Other historical developments also intervened, including the establishment of new national boundaries as nation states consolidated the formal division of northern Fennoscandia. For the first time, national borders were defined and marked in detail in the Strömstad Treaty of 1751, but this arrangement included guarantees of the free movement for the Sámi over the borders, so long as this was linked to hunting, reindeer herding, or trade. At the same time, the treaty obliged the populations to choose the formal citizenships of either Sweden or Norway. The historian Maria Lähteenmäki (2004; 2006) has analysed the impact of these new land boundaries in inter-community interaction in northern Fennoscandia during the nineteenth century. At this time, ethnic assimilation processes affecting the Sámi were also intensified due to the pressures exerted by the state administration, the arrival of new settlers, shifts in livelihoods, and the growing monopolization of reindeer ownership, which marginalized many poorer Sámi. The crown was also interested in supporting permanent settlements, in part due to opportunities for increasing tax revenues, but also by the need to find a viable livelihood for the growing national population.

The open borders did not remain for long. After Finland became part of the Russian empire in 1809, and Norway was incorporated into Sweden, the treaty was thoroughly revised. In 1852 the border between Finland and Norway was closed, putting an end to traditional mobility patterns and also routine border traffic. However, the Swedish Sámi retained the privilege of moving freely both in Finland and Norway. As a result, many of the nomadic Reindeer Sámi moved into Sweden, which allowed them access to the grazing lands of both Finland and Norway. However, the situation changed again in 1889, when the border between Sweden and Finland was also closed, triggering the movement of Reindeer Sámi southwards into Finland. As a consequence, reindeer herding in Finland expanded into areas that had previously been settled by the Forest Sámi (Figure 51.3).

In this complex new historical situation, families tended to make strategic choices, and often selected the livelihood that guaranteed the most secure welfare and relative prosperity (Korhonen 2008, 22–9; Ruotsala 2002, 82–3). This led to a major increase in the size of domestic reindeer herds, and also a growth in the number of Reindeer Sámi in Finnish Lapland. These trends were also intensified by the general modernization of economic life in North Finland, including the large-scale felling of forests by the new lumber industry. Reindeer were employed in this industry for short-distance transportation, and reindeer meat also provided a source of basic subsistence for loggers (Ruotsala 2002, 84). These additional factors reinforced the further growth of large-scale reindeer herding at the growing

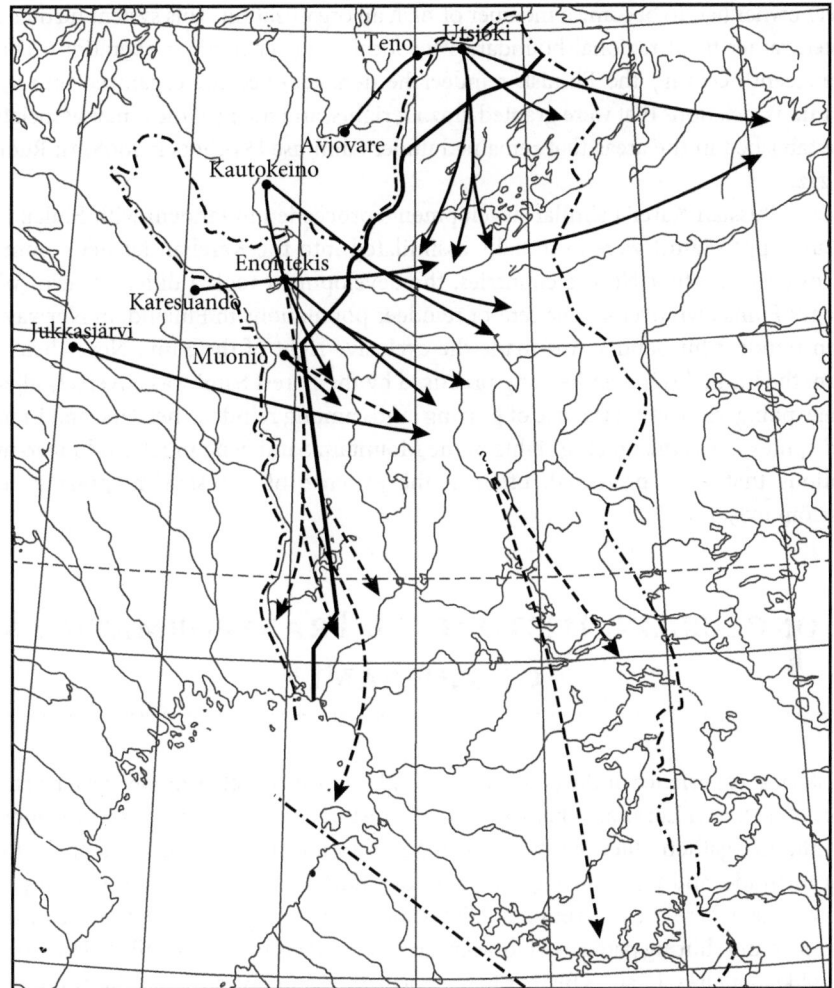

FIGURE 51.3 The migrations of reindeer nomads in the Finnish territory (Tegengren 1952, 157)

expense of the older Forest Sámi hunter-fisher-gatherer culture, which in the end eventually became moribund and then extinct.

Northern farmers were also highly adaptable within a nexus of growing forager–farmer and also farmer–herder culture-contacts. For example, reindeer herding also began to spread among the Finnish farmers, itself a population that had emerged out of the cultural and genetic fusion of the East Finns and the Forest Sámi from the sixteenth century onwards. However, as reindeer husbandry grew in scale at the end of the eighteenth century it eventually began to generate conflict between farmers, who needed to protect their crops from these grazing animals, as well as with the logging industry, which was damaging areas used for reindeer pasture. To solve these disputes a new jurisdictional body was established, so that claims for compensation could be assessed. Rights to graze on government-owned land could only be obtained if a reindeer-grazing association was founded, and each reindeer owner had to become a member of such an organization. This system further consolidated rather fixed regional boundaries for local reindeer herding operations. During the nineteenth century the Finnish reindeer herders also became organized into socio-economic associations that were granted grazing rights, and many of these new associations were established in the areas that remained under Sámi use (Korhonen 2008, 31; Ruotsala 2002, 222).

Over in Russian Karelia similar developments proceeded in tandem with Finland: the Karelian Lapps (Sámi) were eventually assimilated into the Karelian farmer communities. However, in other Nordic countries, the development took a different turn. While nowadays Finns own over 50 per cent of reindeer populations in Finland, in Norway and Sweden reindeer husbandry was made the exclusive right of the Sámi. Nevertheless, in Sweden, the limited reindeer herding practised by the Forest Sámi was adversely affected by a new policy restricting the use of grazing lands among reindeer-herders, and in many local disputes it was the grazing rights of the Mountain Sámi, who practised longer-range migrations that were protected, often at the expense of Forest Sámi grazing rights (Fjellström 1985, 17).

Conclusion: Historical Transformations of the Sámi

The historical experience of the Sámi is very similar to that of other hunter-fisher-gatherer peoples of northern Eurasia. What we see in the historical sources of AD 1500 are glimpses of older hunter-gatherer lifeways that are being transformed by the effects of a rapidly intensifying fur trade, and the growing settlement of wilderness areas. In the southern part of Fennoscandia, where the environment allows some forms of agriculture, there is evidence for complex and shifting patterns of forager–farmer contacts that eventually led to assimilation of old *lappmarks*. In areas further to the north, the Sámi response was the development of large-scale reindeer pastoralism. At the same time, national borders and associated tax regimes were emerging, forcing herders to adjust to yet further factors, such as the closing of the borders between Norway, Sweden, and Finland. This generated stark choices for remaining Sámi groups in the forest who became increasingly marginalized: they could either assimilate with reindeer pastoralists and adopt their lifeways; or they could become settled agriculturalists and assimilate with the Finns. Similar developments and choices emerged across the Russian areas of Fennoscandia, including the Kola Peninsula.

To conclude, this chapter has examined the historical fate of some of the last hunter-gatherer cultures of northern Europe, itself the westernmost extension of the enormous Eurasian continent. As these populations were brought into intensifying culture-contacts associated with the fur trade, as well as with expanding farming populations, they often experienced increasing marginalization and assimilation, but this was not always the case. In many other areas, the rise of full-scale reindeer pastoralism among older hunter-gatherer economies also resulted, providing opportunities for many aspects of their traditional culture to persist, albeit in a modified format. More generally then, this Sámi case study illustrates the long-term fate of hunter-gatherer cultures across much of interior northern Eurasia as they became increasingly brought into intensified culture-contacts, and yet remained living in areas somewhat marginal for full-scale farming. In fact, the parallels with Siberia's colonial history are particularly striking, but their full exploration remains beyond the scope of the current chapter (see Forsyth 1992; Jordan 2003; 2011).

AFTERTHOUGHT: CURRENT ETHNOPOLITICS AMONG INDIGENOUS HUNTER-GATHERER GROUPS

The story of these northern hunter-gatherers has not come to an end, at least not yet. The highly commercialized reindeer-herding industry—currently one of the most productive of all northern subsistence strategies, albeit with a background in ancestral hunter-gatherer practices—remains a thriving enterprise for Sámi populations across Fennoscandia. And thanks to the rise of a new large-scale ethnic consciousness, questions around the persistence of traditional forest Sámi hunter-gatherer cultures have also become a pressing political issue, especially in the old Finnish *lappmarks* (see, for example, Leukumavaara 2012 in *Helsingin Sanomat*, the biggest daily newspaper in Finland). In fact, current debates about ethnicity also revolve around *subsistence* strategies, as one of the main political issues focuses on the question of land rights, and the return of territories owned by the Finnish state back to the local 'indigenous' population.

In the Nordic states, with generous welfare support, indigenous peoples like the Sámi presently enjoy a relatively comfortable position, and they no longer suffer from the older challenges of socio-economic marginalization. (The situation in Russia is very different and more difficult. In 1996, the Association of Indigenous Peoples of the North, Siberia, and the Far East submitted a declaration on the discrimination against the native populations to the government of Russia. The document reflects well the low-point to which the natives had sunk during the Soviet regime, and how the Russian government still neglected all actions to support its 29 endangered ethnicities in the north (on the situation during the post-Soviet period, see e.g. Tuisku 1999; Ventsel 2005).) For example, the Nordic countries have all now developed national Sámi policies, and a politicized Sámi identity has also emerged. This ethnic political mobilization and struggle for decolonization is, of course, connected to the global changes in the position of indigenous peoples, and their growing visibility among the international community. In particular, indigenous political developments in Fennoscandia have attracted a lot of scholarly attention in recent years (e.g. Johansson 2008; Kraft 2010; Ojala 2009; Valkonen 2009).

One interesting development is the fact that across the extended Sámi region of Fennoscandia, which straddles several international boundaries, a new pan-ethnic process of nation-building is now well under way. According to the declaration of the 18th Sámi Congress held at Honningsvåg in 2004, the Sámi 'of these four states [Norway, Sweden, Finland, and Russia] are *one* people with a *shared* history, and also *common* culture, language, and traditions of civic life; moreover, state borders should not violate this sense of community'. More importantly, it states that it is the right of the Sámi people to exercise their culture and trade and to develop their community life *across* these international borders (see the declaration at [http://www.Sámicouncil.net/]).

One inherent flaw in this declaration is the implicit attempt to downplay the impacts and cultural changes that have resulted from colonialism, and its desire instead to return contemporary Sámi to a pre-colonial era of cultural 'purity' (Valkonen 2009, 13). More generally, it asserts the existence of a unified *ethnic* identity, which can then be mobilized as a vehicle for decolonization, and might be viewed as yet another kind of 'adaptive' strategy, albeit one for the political debates of the twenty-first century. The problem is that it generates unforeseen implications for the future of surviving hunter-gatherer cultures.

The notion of Sámi ethnic unity—'a nation broken by borders', to coin a phrase used as a chapter title by Valkonen (2009, 62)—is, however, an illusion. Historically, northern Fennoscandia has always been multi-lingual and multi-cultural, a region with many religions as well. Its cultural history has also been defined by multiple colonizations, migrations, and settlements, as well as the relentless churning of inter-community contacts; it has also been impacted in historical times by the political economy of new kingdoms and several emerging nation states. All this culture-historical dynamism has generated an enormously diverse range of Sámi individuals, groups, and populations, to the extent that many Sámi experience a sense of being different—even 'outsiders'—even *within* their own pan-ethnic 'national' entity. Perhaps misleadingly, attempts to portray traditional Sámi culture have also focused on iconic 'postcard' images of reindeer herding practices, to the extent that it can become difficult to be considered an 'authentic' Sámi without owning reindeer (Valkonen 2009, 249).

This is unfortunate, because only a fifth of all Sámi actually own reindeer, and so the dominant discourse aimed at decolonization in fact devalues all other non-authentic ways of 'being' a Sámi (Valkonen 2009, 15). Such discourse, for example, leads to the cultural marginalization of the Fisher Sámi of Lake Inari (Figure 51.4), the Sea Sámi of Finnmark, and the Skolt Sámi of Finland and the Kola Peninsula, as well as similar groups in Sweden. In fact, many of these other forms of 'Sámihood' tend to be based on hunting, fishing, and gathering practices, which ironically reflect an older and perhaps more 'original' subsistence strategy than reindeer herding, which emerged as a large-scale phenomenon only quite recently.

More generally, it seems that subsistence strategies and choice of language were selected strategically and opportunistically by particular individuals, families, and communities during many of the historic periods considered above—in no way is it possible to identify the modern conception of a 'fixed' or 'timeless' Sámi ethnic identity extending across the region. In fact, analysis of diverse historical sources strongly suggests that if an eighteenth-century Forest Sámi, who at the time was starting to use the Finnish language and also considering whether to take up farming or become a nomadic reindeer herder, had been asked about what was an appropriate 'ethnic identity', he or she would probably have considered the question rather absurd.

Resolving these challenges of integrating a sense of historical dynamism with the fixed notions of ethnic identity required by contemporary indigenous politics will therefore remain a challenge. For example, in recent years Finnish historians have clearly demonstrated that some government-owned tracts of land, which are now considered as forming part of Lapland, once belonged to Forest Sámi villages, although the direct descendants of these inhabitants were eventually assimilated and 'became' Finnish (see, for example, Enbuske 2008; Hiltunen 2007; Lähteenmäki 2004; 2006; see also Wallerström 2006). As a result, if these areas of land were eventually returned to Fennoscandia's 'indigenous peoples', as is currently planned, the land rights of the *assimilated descendants* of the original Forest

FIGURE 51.4 Changing roles: tutkija muuttuu tutkittavaksi. Amateur photographer and Inari Sámi fisherman Jouni Aikio taking of etelän professoreista in autumn 2012 (photo: J.-P. Taavitsainen).

Sámi, who once lived in the region's original villages, would be contravened. Consequently, the older, and now culturally assimilated Sámi origins of many nominally 'Finnish' populations have now been recognized, and this is generating a new mobilization of Sámi identity (or sense of Sámi ancestry), which provides a means for gaining a stake in discussions about land rights (on the controversy over the land ownership, see, for example, Valkonen 2009, 163–9). The controversy even continues to prevent the Finnish government from ratifying ILO Convention No. 169, which could potentially transfer vast areas of land from the Finnish state to the Sámi, but only to those Sámi who have been *accepted* as being properly Sámi by the Sámi Parliament.

References

Alenius, T., Saarnisto, M., Taavitsainen, J.-P., and Lunkka, J.-P. 2010. Pollen record of land use and medieval settlement history in Vuonninen, Northern Russian Karelia. *Geoarchaeology: An International Journal* 26, 1–22.

Carpelan, C., Linkola, M., and Heikkinen, H. 2005. Reindeer husbandry. In U.-M. Kulonen, I. Seurujärvi-Kari, and R. Pulkkinen (eds), *The Sámi: a cultural encyclopaedia*, 312–22. Helsinki: Suomalaisen Kirjallisuuden Seura.

Enbuske, M. 2008. *Vanhan Lapin valtamailla: Asutus ja maankäyttö historiallisen Kemin Lapin ja Enontekiön alueella 1500-luvulta 1900-luvun alkuun* (Bibliotheca Historica 113). Helsinki: Suomalaisen Kirjallisuuden Seura.

Fjellström, P. 1985. *Samernas samhälle i tradition och nutid*. Stockholm: Norstedt.
Forsyth, J. 1992. *A history of the peoples of Siberia: Russia's North Asian colony 1581–1990*. Cambridge: Cambridge University Press.
Hansen, L. I. and Olsen, B. 2006. *Samernas historia fram till 1750*. Stockholm: Liber.
Hiltunen, M. 2007. *Norjan ja Norlannin välissä: Enontekiö 1550–1808, asukkaat, elinkeinot ja maanhallinta* (Scripta historica 32). Oulu: Oulun Historiaseura.
Ingold, T. 1980. *Hunters, pastoralists, and ranchers: reindeer economies and their transformations*. Cambridge: Cambridge University Press.
Isien työt III (film) s.a. Suomen kulttuurirahasto.
Itkonen, T. I. 1948. *Suomen lappalaiset vuoteen 1945* I. Porvoo and Helsinki: WSOY.
Johansson, P. 2008. *Samerna: Ett ursprungsfolk eller en minoritet? En studie av svensk samepolitik 1986–2005*. Gothenburg: Institute for Global Studies, University of Gothenburg.
Jokipii, M. 1974. *Satakunnan historia 4: Satakunnan talouselämä uuden ajan alusta Isoonvihaan*. Pori: Satakunnan Maakuntaliitto.
Joona, J. 2005. Lapp villages and Lapp tax lands. In U.-M. Kulonen, I. Seurujärvi-Kari, and R. Pulkkinen (eds), *The Sámi: a cultural encyclopaedia*, 187–9. Helsinki: Suomalaisen Kirjallisuuden Seura.
Jordan, P. 2003. *Material culture and sacred landscape: the anthropology of the Siberian Khanty*. London: Rowman & Littlefield.
Jordan, P. (ed.). 2011. *Landscape and culture in Northern Eurasia*. Walnut Creek, CA: Left Coast Press.
Kaukiainen, Y. 1980. Suomen asuttaminen: Suurten sotien ja uuden asutusekspansion kaudet. In E. Jutikkala, Y. Kaukiainen, and S.-E. Åström (eds), *Suomen taloushistoria 1: Agraarinen Suomi*, 11–145. Helsinki: Tammi.
Korhonen, T. 2008. *Poroerotus: Historia, toiminta ja tekniset ratkaisut* (Suomalaisen Kirjallisuuden Seuran toimituksia 1165). Helsinki: Suomalaisen Kirjallisuuden Seura.
Kortesalmi, J. J. 1969. Suomalaisten huuhtaviljely: Kansatieteellinen tutkimus. *Scripta Historica* 2, 278–362.
Kraft, S. E. 2010. Sámi indigenous spirituality: religion and nation-building in Norwegian Sápmi. *Temenos* 45, 179–206.
Kulonen, U.-M. 2005. Lapp. In U.-M. Kulonen, I. Seurujärvi-Kari, and R. Pulkkinen (eds), *The Sámi: a cultural encyclopaedia*, 184 Helsinki: Suomalaisen Kirjallisuuden Seura.
Lähteenmäki, M. 2004. *Kalotin kansaa. Rajankäynnit ja vuoravaikutus Pohjoiskalotilla 1808–1889*. Helsinki: Suomalaisen Kirjallisuuden Seura.
Lähteenmäki, M. 2006. *The peoples of Lapland: boundary demarcations and interaction in the North Calotte from 1808 to 1889*. Annales Academiae Scientarium Fennicae Humaniora 338. Helsinki: Finnish Academy of Science and Letters.
Lehtola, V.-P. 2011. Miten lappalainen muuttui saamelaiseksi. *Hiidenkivi* 4, 27–30.
Leukumavaara, J. 2012. Minä olen saamelainen—ja minä myös. *Helsingin Sanomat* 1, C4–5.
Lindtorp, O. 1940. *Finnskogens folk* (Kansatieteellinen arkisto 4). Helsinki: Suomen Muinaismuistoyhdistys.
Nickul, K. 1948. *The Skolt Lapp community Suenjelsijd during the year 1938* (Acta Lapponica 5). Stockholm: Hugo Gebers.
Nickul, K. 1959. *Saamelaisten sopeutumisongelmia* (Lapin sivistysseuran julkaisuja 24). Helsinki.
Odner, K. 1983. *Finner og terfinner. Etniske prosesser i det nordlige Fenno-Skandinavia* (Oslo Occasional Papers in Social Anthropology 9). Oslo: Department of Anthropology, University of Oslo.

Ojala, C.-G. 2009. *Sámi prehistories: the politics of archaeology and identity in northernmost Europe* (Occasional Papers in Archaeology 47). Uppsala: Institute for Archaeology and Ancient History, University of Uppsala.

Pöllä, M. 2001. *Vienankarjalainen perhelaitos 1600–1900* (Suomalaisen Kirjallisuuden Seuran toimituksia 805). Helsinki: Suomalaisen Kirjallisuuden Seura.

Pöllä, M. 2003. Peasant and hunter households in Oulanka, northern Russia, in 1710–1910. *The History of the Family: An International Quarterly* 8, 162–81.

Ruotsala, H. 2002. *Muuttuvat palkiset: Elo, työ ja ympäristö Kittilän Kyrön paliskunnassa ja Kuolan Luujärven poronhoitokollektiiveissa vuosina 1930–1995* (Kansatieteellinen arkisto 49). Helsinki: Suomen Muinaismuistoyhdistys.

Schwindt, T. 1957. Matkamuistoja Tverin Karjalasta. *Kansatieteellinen Arkisto* 13, 7–56.

Slezkine, Y. 1994. *Arctic mirrors: Russia and the small peoples of the north.* Ithaca and London: Cornell University Press.

Steckzén, B. 1964. *Birkarlar och lappar: En studie i birkarlevasendets, lappbefolkningens och skinnhandelns historia* (Kungl. Vitterhets Historie och Antikvitets Akademiens Handlingar: Historiska serien 9). Stockholm: Almqvist and Wiksell.

Taavitsainen, J.-P. 1987. Wide-range hunting and swidden cultivation as prerequisites of Iron Age colonization in Finland. *Suomen Antropologi* 4, 213–33.

Taavitsainen, J.-P. 1990. *Ancient hillforts of Finland: problems of analysis, chronology and interpretation with special reference to the hillfort of Kuhmoinen* (Suomen Muinaismuistoyhdistyksen Aikakauskirja 94). Helsinki: Suomen Muinaismuistoyhdistys.

Taavitsainen, J.-P. 1994. Kaskeaminen ja metsästys erämailla: Metsä ja metsän viljaa. *Kalevalaseuran Vuosikirja* 73, 187–207.

Taavitsainen, J.-P. 2010. Nahodka lyz iz Uhtua—k istorii rannesrednevekovo rasselenija v Belomorskoj Karelii. In *Dialog kul'tur i narodov srednevekovoj Evropy. K 60-letniju so dnja rozdenija Evgenija Nikolaevica Nosova*, 410–15. Saint Petersburg.

Taavitsainen, J.-P., Vilkuna, J., and Forssell, H. 2007. *Suojoki at Keuruu: a mid-14th century site of wilderness culture in Central Finland* (Suomalaisen tiedeakatemian toimituksia: Humaniora 346). Helsinki: Finnish Academy of Science and Letters.

Tanner, V. 1929. *Antropogeografiska studier inom Petsamo-området: 1, Skolt-lapparna* (Fennia 49:4). Helsingfors: Societas Geographica Fenniae.

Tarkiainen, K. 1990. *Finnarnas historia i Sverige 1: Inflyttarna från Finland under det gemensamma rikets tid.* Helsinki: Suomen Historiallinen Seura.

Tegengren, H. 1952. En utdöd lappkultur i Kemi lappmark. *Acta academiae aboensis: Humaniora* 19, 1–287.

Tuisku, T. 1999. *Nenetsien ankarat elämisen ehdot tundralla ja kylässä: Poronhoidon sopeutumisstrategiat ja delokalisoitumisprosessi Nenetsiassa* (Acta Universitatis Lapponiensis 23). Rovaniemi: Lapin Yliopisto.

Tvengsberg, P. M. 1982. Gruen suomalaismetsien kaskiviljelystä. *Kalevalaseuran Vuosikirja* 62, 190–206.

Vahtola, J. 1999. Saamelaisten esiintyminen Suomessa varhaishistoriallisten lähteiden ja paikannimien valossa. In P. Fogelberg (ed.), *Pohjan poluilla. Suomalaisten juuret nykytutkimuksen mukaan* (Bidrag till kännedom av Finlands natur och folk 153), 109–15. Helsinki: Finska Vetenskaps-Societen.

Valkonen, S. 2009. *Poliittinen saamelaisuus.* Tampere: Vastapaino.

Ventsel, A. 2005. *Reindeer, rodina and reciprocity: kinship and property relations in a Siberian village* (Halle Studies in the Anthropology of Eurasia 7). Münster: LIT.

Vilkuna, K. 1971. Mikä oli lapinkylä sen funktio? Vanhaa ja uutta Lappia. *Kalevalaseuran Vuosikirja* 51, 201–38.

Voionmaa, V. 1947. *Hämäläinen eräkausi*. Porvoo: WSOY.

Wallerström, T. 2006. *Vilka var först? En nordskandinavisk konflikt som historisk-arkeologisk dilemma*. Stockholm: Riksantikvarieämbetet.

PART VII

FUTURE DIRECTIONS IN HUNTER-GATHERER RESEARCH

CHAPTER 52

NEW APPROACHES IN THE STUDY OF HUNTER-GATHERERS

PETER JORDAN AND VICKI CUMMINGS

INTRODUCTION AND AIMS

THE opening part of the handbook examined the different analytical perspectives that structured early understandings of foraging societies and later led to the increasingly diverse range of research efforts now focusing on hunter-gatherer societies. These overarching theoretical frameworks ranged from early forms of social evolutionary thinking, the rise of adaptive and ecological approaches, through to the historical and humanist perspectives that are now becoming increasingly important. Other chapters examined the central role played by ethnoarchaeology in the consolidation of hunter-gatherer studies as a fundamentally interdisciplinary endeavour, as well as the long-term research efforts that have been directed towards understanding gender roles in forager societies.

The core parts of the handbook (Parts II–VI) primarily consist of critical review essays covering the extensive thematic and regionally focused research literatures on the archaeology, ethnohistory, and modern anthropology of hunter-gatherer societies. More generally, all these chapters highlight the dynamic character of forager societies and their long-term histories, and together serve to underline the major contributions played by hunter-gatherers in the rise of many important cultural developments, as well as major economic transformations such as the transition to farming. Chapters covering more recent periods also highlight the cultural resilience of foragers operating in a range of historical culture-contact situations, and finally, demonstrate the ongoing viability and deep cultural significance of a foraging way of life in many parts of the contemporary world.

Chapters in this concluding part provide both detailed updates on some of the older and better-established ecological and evolutionary approaches, as well as a series of 'position statements' on some of the newer and more recently emerging themes in hunter-gatherer research. At one level, the range and sheer breadth of materials and ideas covered by these chapters serves further to track the relentless diversification of research away from the earlier unifying focus on seeking common, cross-cultural patterns, and studying hunting and gathering as a distinctive type of existence. However, at another level, intellectual diversification need not necessarily entail a one-way process of fragmentation, and several new research themes now appear to be emerging as the focus for renewed efforts at coordinated interdisciplinary research. The goal of this introductory chapter is to set these contemporary developments within a broader intellectual context, and to provide some general concluding reflection on where the field might be moving next.

General Developments in Hunter-Gatherer Research

Looking across all the chapters in this handbook, and also out over the wider hunter-gatherer research literature, several important developments can be identified:

1. *Exponential growth in basic information on hunter-gatherers:* forager societies past and present have been the focus of enormous research efforts over recent decades, generating detailed regional datasets pertaining to the archaeology, ethnohistory, and modern anthropology of hunter-gatherers. In many world regions, extended hunter-gatherer archaeological sequences continue well into the Holocene; in a few areas there is a relatively continuous record of hunter-gatherer societies stretching from prehistory through to historical and modern ethnographic periods. Some of these datasets and extended sequences have already been the focus of sustained analysis and interpretation; in other regions, the data exist but deeper synthesis is lacking. Traditionally the focus has been on *either* ethnographic fieldwork *or* archaeological excavation, but much more could also be done to expand the use of ethnohistoric sources in the study of hunter-gatherers. These generally detail earlier culture-contact dynamics between local foragers and expanding states, empires, and settler groups, both in the New World and also in many parts of the Old World, such as Japan, Russia, and Fennoscandia, where historical archives and taxation records detailing the lifeways of northern hunter-gatherers often extend back many centuries.
2. *Continued diversification in theoretical approaches:* this fragmentation within the core focus of hunter-gatherer studies has been a cumulative process—from the unifying concerns of early social evolutionary thinking through to the cross-cultural analysis of typical 'nomadic style' hunter-gatherer societies in the *Man the hunter* era, while more recent research on hunter-gatherers has addressed a baffling range of themes and topics, occasionally from opposing theoretical standpoints. The 1980s appear to be the primary 'tipping point' in this fragmentation process, with intensive debates about the role of history and culture-contact among modern hunter-gatherers (the Kalahari Debate), as well as the emergence of post-processual critiques and eventually the rise of interpretive research agendas in archaeology, which have led to a range of new questions being addressed. Tremendous diversity in themes and approaches now characterizes hunter-gatherer research, with clear intellectual continuity in some distinctive research streams, but also signs of convergence and

renewed integration among others. All specialists now readily agree that enormous variability characterizes forager lifeways and their long-term histories, but how best to describe, interpret, and explain this variability remains a topic of intense debate.

3. *Increasing engagement with indigenous communities:* many chapters in this handbook have touched on the narrowing gap between academic researchers, policy-makers, contemporary foragers, and other 'descendant communities' whose lifeways and cultural heritage are the focus of anthropological and archaeological research. Ethnographic field research amongst hunter-gatherer groups played an important role in increasing public awareness of the appalling treatment of indigenous peoples and the violation of their human rights by various nation states and interest groups, with environmental destruction and loss of traditional rights being some of the most pressing concerns. Historians have also shifted increasingly towards exploring the experiences of hunter-gatherers and other indigenous peoples in the colonization and settlement and nation-building projects in many parts of the world. Finally, archaeologists are also making efforts to ensure that their work is more inclusive and relevant to local communities. The older situation is now in a state of fundamental shift, with growing momentum towards greater engagement and mutual accommodation at all levels, and now generally involving anthropologists, historians, archaeologists, policy-makers, indigenous populations, and descendant communities.

In sum, what emerges from this brief overview is that hunter-gatherer societies, their belief systems, subsistence strategies, and long-term histories can now be investigated in unprecedented detail, and from a wide range of different theoretical perspectives. At the same time, there is growing obligation to ensure that these essentially academic research efforts are made more inclusive, morally responsible, and also more relevant to the members of the different communities that make up modern global society. The fact that these interlocking academic opportunities and ethical obligations have become central to the entire hunter-gatherer research project makes deeper critical understanding of the different theoretical frameworks all the more important. These approaches will structure both research efforts and can also guide community engagement efforts.

Organization of the Part VII

To maintain historical coherence and flow, the chapters in this final part of the handbook are organized into three broad groupings: (a) chapters tracing recent developments in some of the adaptive, ecological, and evolutionary approaches that were central to earlier hunter-gatherer research. These chapters illustrate the impact that modern evolutionary theory is having on hunter-gatherer research, and also illustrate how different these approaches are to earlier forms of evolutionary thinking—these important distinctions are examined in more detail below; (b) chapters that introduce a range of newer and more interpretive themes that are making more recent contributions to hunter-gatherer studies, each chapter generally taking the form of a 'position statement'. All these approaches fit in a relatively straightforward manner into Cannon's broadly interpretive research agenda (Part I), and in emphasizing symbolism, local cultural meanings, and subjective human experience are useful in providing a counter-balance to the overarching emphasis on ecology and adaptation that have long tended to dominate hunter-gatherer research (see Garvey and Bettinger, Part I); (c) the part ends with two chapters that revisit broad but potentially integrative research themes—the analysis of gender roles and subsistence studies. Both topics were central to the emergence of modern hunter-gatherer studies, but these final chapters provide an inspiring end to this part of the handbook by highlighting the extensive recent progress in both these fields, as well as the extent to which further exploration of these themes can serve as a catalyst for a new era of more integrative interdisciplinary research and synthesis.

Continuity and Change in 'Adaptive' and Evolutionary Approaches

Contributions by Kelly, Eerkens et al., and Černý and Pereira all work broadly within the scientific, adaptive, and evolutionary paradigm that helped establish modern hunter-gatherer studies in the mid-twentieth century, but, importantly, also highlight the extent to which these approaches have undergone major change, primarily involving the application of modern evolutionary theory to hunter-gatherer research. These developments are examined in some detail, especially the important distinctions between different forms of evolutionary thinking, which are often mistakenly lumped together.

Explaining Variability in Hunter-Gatherer Technology

Kelly's chapter on technology provides the most direct bridge between earlier hunter-gatherer research traditions and some of these more recent research avenues. According to nineteenth-century (progressive) social evolutionary thinkers, hunter-gatherers were largely defined by their *lack* of technology. Indeed, up until the 1960s, many anthropologists still regarded hunter-gatherers as being locked in the relentless demands of the daily food quest, which left little time for the development of more elaborate technologies. These older assumptions underwent a fundamental shift during the *Man the hunter* era. Through discussion of a range of evidence from forager populations around the world, it became clear that many hunter-gatherers have acquired extensive environmental knowledge which equips them with a deep confidence in their ability to procure food as and when they need it. Re-cast as the 'original affluent society' (Sahlins 1968; 1972), hunter-gatherers were now regarded as being able to make strategic choices, that is, they need to make daily, even minute-by-minute, decisions about how best to spend their time or where their efforts could be most productively focused. According to this new perspective, it was the operation of these cumulative decision-making processes that eventually generated wider patterns in subsistence, mobility, and social life (for example, as hunter-gatherers sought the most effective ways of positioning themselves in relation to available resources during the different seasons of the year).

It was not long before these perspectives were being directed at understanding better how hunter-gatherers made decisions about their technology, especially the range of equipment they needed to procure food. Clearly, important decisions were being made about trade-offs between accumulating tools, objects, and other possessions, and the extent to which they could be carried if later there was a decision to move on to a new area. More generally, researchers began to focus on the organizational dynamics of hunter-gatherer technologies, asking when, where, and why is technology worth the cost of manufacture, maintenance, and transport? Attention was also directed at specific details of tool-kit design, but also at identifying larger-scale global patterning in forager food-getting technologies and tool-kits, and the range of causal factors that might account for them.

Much of this early work on variability in hunter-gatherer tool-kits was framed within an adaptive and cross-cultural comparative framework that seeks first to identify, and then explain, general patterns in the way in which hunter-gatherers organized their technology in different environmental settings. A range of causal variables was eventually identified, and has been subjected to debate over the following decades, with risk being one of the major conditioning factors: hunter-gatherers in riskier environments, such as the Arctic, tend to exhibit more complex technologies, as the implications of coming back to camp empty-handed are much more severe here. Riskier environments like these also make technological innovation more worthwhile, as people in these settings also have the most to gain from effort invested in developing new technologies.

More broadly, Kelly illustrates the powerful insights that can be gained by applying a human behavioural ecology (HBE) perspective to the study of variability in hunter-gatherer technology. This applies a modern evolutionary perspective (see below) to the study of human behaviour in specific ecological contexts, and aims to quantify the different kinds of costs and benefits that arise from alternative strategies of action, most usually those associated with subsistence, as these have the most direct impact on human adaptation and long-term survival. There is a now a major research literature applying this kind of approach to general forager subsistence behaviour, but Kelly also draws on HBE to explore how technology plays an important and often transformational role in hunter-gatherer subsistence strategies. New technologies, such as mass-capture facilities, require major upfront investment but can dramatically transform capture rates and processing costs, leading to long-term shifts in adaptive strategies. In other settings, shifts, for example, from more specialized hunting to broader-based plant and shellfish economies can suddenly make the production and use of other technologies such as clay cooking containers and grinding tools much more worthwhile. Clearly, as well as studying ethnographic patterning in technology, insights derived from HBE can be a useful framework for trying to understand the mechanisms behind some of the major prehistoric changes in hunter-gatherer subsistence and technology, such as the widespread shift towards aquatic economies and later towards reliance on domesticated plants in the earlier Holocene, along with the coeval dispersal of new kinds of fishing kit, pottery cooking containers, and grinding equipment. All these developments must have involved major shifts in the costs and pay-offs associated with the uptake and use of new technologies in different kinds of subsistence strategy.

Kelly also argues that the role of technology needs to be studied within a wider behavioural context—there is, of course, much more to new technology than its immediate efficiency in acquiring foods at minimal cost or lowest risk; fresh technologies also need to be incorporated into a wider set of strategies, and within these, need to improve the efficiency of *overall* production before becoming useful. In looking at the broader role of technologies in society, Kelly concludes that their usage should also be regarded as being 'embedded' within social webs and local gender roles, which in turn give technology a deeper meaning and significance within local hunter-gatherer cultures, all forming general themes that are picked up on and explored in more detail by several of the later 'interpretive' chapters (see below).

Evolutionary Thinking and Hunter-Gatherer Research

Kelly's chapter employs an HBE approach to the study of hunter-gatherer technology and behaviour, part of a wider set of 'modern' evolutionary approaches now being deployed widely in hunter-gatherer research (also see Garvey and Bettinger, Part I). As noted above, it is worth situating these more recent developments within a broader intellectual context—evolutionary thinking has a long history in hunter-gatherer research, but it is important to note that there are important, and indeed *fundamental*, differences between late nineteenth-century social evolutionary thinking, which basically mapped different kinds of society into ascending stages of progress (see Barnard, Part I), and the mid-twentieth-century neo-evolutionary perspectives of Childe, White, and Steward. Childe, for example, was interested in using archaeological evidence in order to reconstruct how humanity had passed through major thresholds such as the 'Neolithic revolution'—the prehistoric transition to farming. White was interested in developing more abstract schemata that arranged different kinds of society according to the contrasting ways in which they used improvements in technology to capture ever higher levels of energy from the environment. Steward's cultural ecology focused most specifically on hunter-gatherer bands, and championed an alternative, more multilinear form of evolution, which examined the role of ecology and technology in guiding different forms of adaptation and social structure. It was Steward's cultural ecology that triggered renewed interest in hunter-gatherer adaptive strategies, and resulted in him being regarded as one of the founders of hunter-gatherer studies (see the main introduction to this handbook, and Garvey and Bettinger, Part I).

Over the following decades, evolutionary thinking in archaeology and anthropology has changed enormously yet again, and many of these 'modern' evolutionary approaches are now being applied to the wider study of human culture and behaviour, and also in many cases to the study of hunter-gatherer populations. Most of these more recent developments can ultimately be traced back to the Neo-Darwinian modern evolutionary synthesis in biology, which combined the process of natural selection with understanding of genetic heredity within a coherent modern theory of evolution. The application of HBE approaches to hunter-gatherer studies from the 1970s and 1980s was an early example of some of these modern evolutionary perspectives being applied to the study of forager subsistence behaviour, and has since generated a major research literature applying a kind of optimal foraging approach; similar applications characterized related work on hunter-gatherer technology (see above).

A more recent variant of modern evolutionary thinking is 'cultural transmission theory' (CTT) or 'dual inheritance theory' (DIT), which is seeing increasing application in archaeology and anthropology, and frames the materials presented in the next two chapters in this part (Eerkens et al.; Černý and Pereira). CTT/DIT focuses on the ways in which potentially useful cultural information can persist between generations due to the highly developed mechanisms for social learning that are possessed by humans. The approach starts with the observation that humans are unique among even closely related species in having to rely in daily life to such an enormous extent on information acquired from other individuals through teaching, imitation, and other forms of social learning—this is cultural transmission. For example, seal hunters in the Arctic can only exist there because they can draw on information—bodies of knowledge, technologies, and strategies—that have been built up over many generations and gradually refined and adjusted in the form of long-term cultural traditions. For example, novice hunters can acquire these older stocks of knowledge through parental teaching and imitation, but can also adapt and change them through later personal experience, or by copying other hunters they observe later in life. Humans rely more than any other species on acquiring these accumulated stocks of cultural knowledge, whether in basic subsistence activities, or in the acquisition of language, craft traditions, or in mastering other kinds of cultural practice. In fact, this deep reliance on cumulative culture, whether in language, technology, or other aspects of behaviour is what makes humans unique (Richerson and Boyd 2005).

Importantly, however, CTT/DIT also emphasizes that humans in fact have two distinct systems of information transmission, one cultural (through teaching, imitation, and other forms of social learning) and the other genetic (through biological reproduction). In some ways, these inheritance processes are broadly similar (children tend to learn a lot of basic cultural knowledge from their biological parents, so that genetic and cultural information is passed down via similar routes), but they also have some fundamental differences which make cultural transmission exhibit some unique dynamics (children can only acquire their genes from their biological parents but can learn new cultural information from a whole array of non-related individuals—this means that cultural information can potentially spread very quickly through a population within a single generation, following transmission routes that are unique to culture). As a result of these important similarities and differences, both genetic and cultural inheritance systems can be argued to exhibit Darwinian evolutionary processes of 'descent with modification', with each having its own unique dynamics due to the differences noted above. Evolution, when used in this modern Darwinian sense, refers to this process of replicating through time—but also cumulatively editing—stocks of information, either genetic or cultural.

CTT/DIT can therefore be useful at three possible levels: (1) it draws general analogies between the transmission of genetic and cultural information, which can provide new ways of thinking about the ways in which long-term cultural traditions persist but also change through time; (2) biologists have made enormous progress in devising powerful quantitative analytical models, methods, and theories for the analysis of genetic evolution; with the right kinds of data, some of these approaches could be applied to the study of cultural transmission; (3) as seen above, genetic and cultural information can be passed on in similar but also fundamentally different ways; with appropriate genetic and cultural information (e.g. on the genetic traits, languages, or material-culture traditions maintained by different populations), it is possible to examine the extent to which genetic, linguistic, and cultural histories have potentially mapped onto one another through time, generating deep insights into the tangled cultural and biological histories of different world populations.

The next two chapters in this part illustrate how modern evolutionary approaches are being applied to the study of hunter-gatherer technological traditions and also to the reconstruction of the genetic histories of different forager populations in Africa. In this way, all three chapters in this particular grouping illustrate the ways in which the broadly adaptive and evolutionary paradigm in hunter-gatherer research has changed fundamentally in recent decades. At the same time, the research has retained its general commitment to rigorous scientific and quantitative approaches, albeit around a renewed interest in studying social learning and cultural traditions, as well as the interconnected cultural, linguistic, and genetic histories of hunter-gatherer populations.

Hunter-Gatherers, Social Learning, and Cultural Transmission Theory

In their chapter, Eerkens et al. outline some possible archaeological applications of cultural transmission theory (CTT) to the study of hunter-gatherer material-culture traditions. They go to lengths to note that the use of cultural transmission theory is not specific to the study of hunter-gatherers, and that it can be applied to any kind of population that exhibits social learning and cultural inheritance. However, they argue that certain patterns and processes of cultural transmission may tend to predominate in many hunter-gatherer settings due to a range of factors, such as similarities in population size and density, information content and complexity, and common forms of forager social organization.

Their second important point is that archaeology is the only discipline that can directly study cultural transmission processes over long time periods. In this sense, hunter-gatherer sequences are also important because they form some of the longest cultural records on the planet, but require specific ways of studying how cultural traditions are replicated through analysis of the surviving material remains. Here, Eerkens et al. suggest that CTT can be particularly used to interpret and make predictions about these extended archaeological records. Indeed, they argue that the strength of studying cultural transmission in archaeology is the ability to make predictions about variation and diversity in material culture over large areas and extended periods of time. However, to accomplish these goals, scholars need large and geographically diverse suites of data.

They illustrate how cultural transmission can be studied in the archaeological record with two contrasting case studies. The first looks more at broad variation in artefacts across geographic space, and examines 5,000 hunter-gatherer projectile points from 40 sites across the Great Basin, in total spanning a seven-thousand-year time period. Their quantitative analysis lends preliminary support to the argument that there will be greater overall variation in projectile point traits when hunter-gatherers are organized into smaller group sizes than when they are living in larger groupings—this is because stylistic information is able to spread around other members of the group more easily when foragers are living in larger size groups, thereby serving to reduce overall variation in the assemblage.

Their second case study examines change in material culture through time, and they look at predictions about the uptake of new technologies. They hypothesize a general pattern in the spread of new technologies: rapid innovation and diversification characterize early stages as new technologies are first adopted; this is followed by a gradual winnowing out of this variation and a slowing in the general speed of innovation as specific types of artefact that best fit local requirements catch on and eventually become well-established within the population. They apply this model to the hunter-gatherers of southern Owens Valley in south-eastern California who began experimenting with ceramic technologies around 1200 years ago, and who adopted the technology more widely after 700 years ago. By modelling of vessel thickness and mica content of the clay pastes over time Eerkens et al. are able to explore the process of uptake of this new ceramic technology. Their analyses demonstrate the existence of changes over time, but crucially, that the rate of change was faster earlier in the adoption process than later, all of which confirms their hypothesis that new innovations are subjected to intensive experimentation and adjustment in early phases of adoption, but then settle down into more standardized formats once they have caught on.

More generally, this chapter illustrates how application of DIT/CTT to prehistoric hunter-gatherer material culture relies heavily on the availability of large, relatively high-resolution datasets, and that it deploys a model-based, hypothesis-testing approach with a heavy reliance on quantitative methods to rigorously test even relatively simple ideas and relationships. Similar approaches are required when applying CTT to the analysis of ethnographic or ethnohistoric datasets of hunter-gatherer material culture to test related questions about the ways in which these technological traditions evolve, and the extent to which they map onto local language history (Jordan and Shennan 2003; 2009; Jordan and O'Neill 2010). If research into hunter-gatherer *cultural* transmission has grown over recent years, so too have *genetic* studies of hunter-gatherer populations and their long-term histories.

Investigating the Genetic History of Hunter-Gatherer Populations

In addition to the development of new kinds of culture evolutionary theory, some of the most important and far-reaching developments have been linked to the development of molecular genetic methods in evolutionary biology. These approaches can also be used to shed new light on human origins, demographic histories, and general human genetic variability, as well as specific migrations and particular histories of contact between groups and geographic regions. The chapter on 'archaeogenetics' by Černý and Pereira considers just some of this growing body of research, which again is not limited to the study of hunter-gatherers per se, but opens out some exciting new prospects for the study of forager groups and their population histories.

Basically, there are two contrasting approaches in archaeogenetics: (a) *ancient* DNA (aDNA)—this involves extraction of information directly from preserved human materials such as bones and teeth, which are routinely recovered during excavations. Theoretically, this approach has enormous potential, but there are substantial problems with contamination of ancient samples due to modern handling. Authentication of results remains extremely difficult, though substantive progress is now being made; (b) *modern* DNA—the second approach involves recovering DNA directly from individuals in living populations in order to map the genetic variability of these populations—this information can then be used to reconstruct the deeper demographic history of the population, for example, identifying phases of expansion, contraction, as well as gene flows and admixtures.

This is a rapidly expanding research frontier, and Černý and Pereira focus their chapter on recent archaeogenetic research in Africa using DNA samples recovered from modern hunter-gatherer populations. Most of this work has been directed at understanding processes extending over very different spatial and temporal scales. Larger-scale studies have focused on exploring the evolution of modern humans within Africa, the subsequent sequence of migrations out into other parts of the world, as well as details of return migrations back into Africa. In this way, these larger-scale studies provide a background to the more localized study of demographic histories of forager populations still living within Africa; often the genetic patterning raises further questions about gender roles and inter-group marriage practices. Overall, archaeogenetic research generates additional lines of evidence that can be integrated into studies of hunter-gatherer diet, health, reproductive strategies, and demography; it can also be used to the reconstruct genetic histories of culture-contact between different populations, including interactions between different groups of foragers or between foragers and farmers.

Summary: Modern Evolutionary Approaches

These three chapters illustrate some of the main patterns of continuity and change in evolutionary and adaptive research over recent decades. Modern evolutionary methods and theory are now making a wide contribution to hunter-gatherer research, part of a raft of approaches that provide a means for studying the interlocking cultural and genetic histories of populations within a single framework. Some have gone so far as to argue that a culture-evolutionary framework will one day unite the general study of human biological and cultural diversity (Mesoudi et al. 2006; and see Ingold 2007), though this prediction may be rather premature.

New 'Interpretive' Directions in Hunter-Gatherer Research

The next set of chapters is united by a central concern with developing more particularistic insights into specific cultural contexts—all can usefully be grouped under Cannon's historical, humanist, and broadly 'interpretive' paradigm (see Part I). This general approach does not aim to define models or rigorously test hypotheses; instead, the chapters identify useful themes, concepts, or approaches that can be used as heuristic frameworks to carefully work through data, illuminate subjective cultural meanings, and generate interpretive insights into the significance and experience of local lifeways. Many of these approaches are somewhat new to hunter-gatherer research, which has generally concerned itself with studying adaptation and behaviour, rather than symbolism and social action, but most draw on much older and relatively mainstream approaches in anthropology. In contrast to the complex distinctions between different forms of evolutionary thinking (see above), all these chapters are united by a shared and relatively self-explanatory concern with developing rich and contingent interpretive insights into specific cultural contexts. As most of these approaches are relatively new, most chapters take the form of 'position statements' and tend to start out with a critique of older 'adaptive' perspectives that were central to earlier hunter-gatherer research, enabling them to develop an 'alternative' set of perspectives, which are illustrated with both archaeological and ethnographic case studies.

Hunter-Gatherer Mobility and Landscape

David et al. outline an alternative approach to the study of hunter-gatherer mobility, arguing that processual archaeologists tended to frame mobility studies within models built on assumptions that adaptive processes formed the primary drivers structuring forager behaviour (for example, the need to adjust mobility and settlement patterns in order to cope with seasonality and resource variability). In contrast, David et al. argue that the significance of the landscape is linked to the ways in which it is encountered through journeying and movement, highlighting the importance of human experience of places and pathways, which are in turn grounded within historical contexts. In this way, mobility should not only be understood as only a simple, functional, and rather predictable human response to particular environmental challenges, but should also be seen as being caught up with other more spiritual and personal motivations. One means of exploring these other aspects of mobility is through sustained reflection on perceptions of landscape among modern indigenous communities; a series of insights, analytical perspectives, and suggestions for further landscape work is illustrated by ethnographic insights from hunter-gatherers in Papua New Guinea. In general, then, this particular approach to the study of hunter-gatherer landscapes forms an extension of a much broader interpretive and historical approach to the study of landscape (see e.g. David and Thomas 2008).

Exploring Hunter-Gatherer Personhood

Finlay examines how the study of personhood is emerging as a new topic in hunter-gatherer research. This general theme has been inspired primarily by anthropological research in Melanesia (e.g. Strathern 1988), and basically examines the cultural significance attached to being a human person within different cultural and historical settings. Usually, it forms an entry point into exploring more localized and contextual forms of negotiated personal identity, as caught up in the lived experience of human existence. Recent work employing the personhood concept has included archaeological case studies, many of which have examined hunter-gatherer societies (e.g. Conneller 2004; Fowler 2004). However, Finlay also argues that the concept of personhood has enormous potential for furthering our general understandings of hunter-gatherers and their world views, both in the archaeological past and also the anthropological present. For example, personhood can only be fully understood in relation to many other aspects of culture, such as other gender identities, animals, material culture, and the landscape. In fact, the construction and significance of personhood is absolutely central to understanding the symbolic construction of local cultures because it articulates so closely with everything else in the world. Finally, Finlay argues that personhood also needs to be studied in relation to contextual life-histories, that is, expanded beyond rather fixed notions of personhood, and extended to embrace the study of how children become drawn into local cultural traditions and social identities, acquiring different kinds of personhood at each of these different life stages (and see Jarvenpa and Brumbach, this volume, and below).

New Approaches to Hunter-Gatherer Material Culture

Cobb discusses how archaeologists and anthropologists have approached and interpreted the study of material culture, broadly defined. She argues that processual approaches to technology (see, for example, the chapter by Kelly, Part VII, and discussions above) are embedded within a particular understanding of the world, one which follows a Cartesian division of matter and society, or at its most basic level, culture versus nature. Cobb follows other anthropologists (most notably Ingold 2000) in outlining an alternative approach that instead focuses on the capacity for material culture to convey meaning and to be caught up with the production and expression of local social identities, and she goes on to explore themes of enskillment, performative practice, identity, and personhood within broader landscape/taskscape settings. Cobb also argues for the need to better understand the embedded social choices that are caught up in the production, use, and deposition of artefacts, illustrating her insights with archaeological case studies from hunter-gatherer societies. Her general conclusion is that the creation and use of materials, objects, and artefacts are central to the process of cultural reproduction and are not simply a means for adapting to the environment—instead, they help create and rework people's identities and their sense of place in the world.

Exploring Variability in Hunter-Gatherer Ritual and Religion

Adaptation and ecology have been central themes in hunter-gatherer research. This led to major advances in understanding, but left other more social and symbolic dimensions of hunter-gatherer behaviour relatively under-researched. Whitley's chapter is therefore important, because it starts to redress a long-standing imbalance in the focus of research into foragers and their lifeways. In seeking to develop the broader theme of an archaeology of religion, Whitley suggests that ethnographic insights are important because they provide a useful framework for exploring variability in hunter-gatherer ritual, religious, and associated social life, ultimately generating ideas and insights with which the archaeological record of hunter-gatherer religion can more productively be approached. Whitley employs native Californian ethnography as the subject matter for his primary case study, and highlights the enormous variability in local ritual events and religious practices among the many different hunter-gatherer groups inhabiting this region. Clearly, belief permeates all aspects of local life, but some rituals find their primary expression in spectacular group events, although the structure and significance of these larger gatherings is also highly variable, but can be broadly categorized into a range of fundamentally different kinds of rituals and ceremonies.

Whitley then goes on to detail how evidence for prehistoric religion can also be identified in the archaeological record: rock art studies have traditionally been the one area of research which has seen considerable focus, but this focus now needs to be expanded to incorporate other kinds of evidence. However, addressing this task is challenging as there has been so little ethnoarchaeological field research into hunter-gatherer religion (see Lane, Part I), and so Whitley again highlights the importance of using ethnography to describe and establish a known range of variation with which to approach and 'calibrate' the prehistoric evidence. This integrated ethnographic–archaeological approach, then, offers exciting ways of exploring both contemporary and also prehistoric hunter-gatherer belief systems in different parts of the world, and adds a useful counterbalance to more established adaptive and ecologically oriented approaches.

Summary: Interpretive Perspectives on Hunter-Gatherers

Recent years have seen several new interpretive themes enter into the current range of hunter-gatherer research, though none of these concepts (personhood, materiality) or subjects (landscape, religion) is necessarily limited to the study of hunter-gatherers per se, and could equally apply to a range of other cultural or economic settings. Given the dominance of ecological and adaptive approaches, all look set to make increasingly important contributions to the study of hunter-gatherers, especially when combined with other broadly interpretive frameworks, and directed at relatively well-studied and high-resolution archaeological sequences.

Unlike modern evolutionary theory, which has a more explicit theoretical framework and associated set of methods, these new interpretive interests form a looser and more flexible grouping (but see Cannon, Part I, for an excellent general summary of this general perspective). What unites them is a shared concern with developing a more explicitly social and symbolic exploration of hunter-gatherer lifeways, as well as the ways in which these vary across different historical and cultural settings. In this way, their overarching goal is to enhance particularistic and often relativistic understanding of the subjective significance of local, lived experience in different historical contexts: no specific models are formulated or tested, no cross-cultural patterns are generally identified, and no higher-level generalizations are sought. Paradoxically, in seeking to extend this kind of a particularistic research agenda to the study of foragers, the focus on studying hunter-gatherers as a specific kind of society becomes, in the end, a rather incidental concern (see Pluciennik, Part I). More generally, then, these new and more explicitly interpretive themes highlight the healthy ongoing diversification of current hunter-gatherer research into a wide array of additional topics, directions, and approaches. However, in celebrating the uniqueness of particular cultural settings, they implicitly undermine the older unifying endeavour of studying hunter-gatherers as a specific kind of society that can be defined precisely by its distinctive subsistence base.

Integrative Research Themes: Gender, Identity, Subsistence, and Foodways

If the seven preceding chapters can be organized into two broadly divergent 'evolutionary' and 'interpretive' research streams, illustrating that major fault lines in basic theory, emphasis, and approach still run through the heart of current hunter-gatherer research, the two final chapters demonstrate the opposite trend, and illustrate how the inherently interdisciplinary nature of hunter-gatherer research often renders these evolutionary versus interpretive divisions rather artificial. In fact, these final case studies illustrate how a sustained focus on exploring central themes such as gender and identity, diet, subsistence, and foodways can actually serve to galvanize research efforts and provide a means to integrate recent developments in both method and theory around a renewed quest for gaining deeper insights into the dynamism and variability of specific hunting and gathering societies. Both chapters also make widespread use of archaeological, ethnographic, and also ethnoarchaeological research, all of which demonstrates that the field of hunter-gatherer studies has always been a fundamentally interdisciplinary endeavour that operates comfortably between archaeology, anthropology, and many other related disciplines. It is perhaps this highly-integrated and thematically-oriented kind of research programme that signals the best way forwards, and will perhaps continue to define hunter-gatherer studies as a distinct area of enquiry in the future. This targeted and thematic approach also enables a raft of new methods, ideas, perspectives, and theoretical frameworks to be combined in order to understand specific local contexts and particular cultural sequences.

Researching Hunter-Gatherer Gender and Identity

Jarvenpa and Brumbach critically evaluate recent research on gender dynamics in hunter-gatherer societies. In fact, gender is the oldest and most fundamental dimension of human experience and identity, and gender studies has been a central topic in hunter-gatherer research since the *Man the hunter* era (see Sterling, Part I). This chapter adopts a forward-looking perspective, and revisits some of the long-standing debates about the roles of men, women, and 'third' genders, highlighting some of the major research biases in the study of gender that still need to be addressed. More generally, their coordinated programme of comparative ethnoarchaeological research underlines the extreme flexibility of gender roles in almost all areas of activity, and also enables them to explore the ways in which gender is expressed and negotiated through subsistence work but also via access to sacred sites and cosmological power.

Against an enduring focus on the role of men in acts of hunting and killing, they emphasize the central role played by women in the processing, storage, and redistribution of these resources, which in fact places them at the epicentre of community cultural reproduction and social life, and, if anything, serves to marginalize male hunters. Evidence is also drawn from osteological analyses of prehistoric skeletons, underlining the fact that gender studies are interdisciplinary and can also draw on scientific methods, and study the health, work patterns, diet, and evolutionary biology of different genders, as well as deploying more interpretive approaches and concepts such as personhood, identity, landscape, ritual practice, all reviewed above—the key point is that gender and identity are *contextually variable*, and that understanding the full details and causality of that variability cannot be constrained by a subscription to a single body of theory or general approach. This chapter is packed with insight and areas for future research and critical synthesis, all of which highlight that exploring gender and identity from multiple perspectives and approaches is destined to remain both a central—and actively integrating theme—within future hunter-gatherer studies.

Exploring Hunter-Gatherer Diet, Subsistence, and Foodways

The chapter by Schulting provides a useful end point to the handbook, and steers discussion back full circle to the fundamentally important topics of diet, subsistence, and food. In fact, what hunter-gatherers eat and how they procure, prepare, and share food have all been central topics since *Man the hunter*. Going even further back into the nineteenth century and beyond, hunter-gatherers were defined by social evolutionary thinkers as a distinct kind of society primarily because of what they ate (wild foods) and how they acquired it (foraging).

Although taking an older and well-established research theme as its starting point, Schulting's chapter is important because it traces in a very precise and detailed manner just how far hunter-gatherer studies have evolved and changed in relation to this most central of all research themes—the hunting and gathering economy. Like Jarvenpa and Brumbach's chapter, this study also highlights that despite major theoretical and methodological diversification over recent years, overarching themes such as subsistence and diet can still serve to unite hunter-gatherer studies around a common research endeavour, one that now increasingly seeks to understand local variability and specific cultural context. This enables the research to draw easily on different disciplines and integrate approaches, methods, and theory from diverse sources in the pursuit of deeper and often more particularistic insights.

In this way, investigating diet and subsistence is central to understanding what makes hunter-gatherer populations all so very similar, but yet each so very distinct. But in the end, subsistence studies—like a focus on gender—lead off into an exploration of a wide range of other interlocking factors. Both new theoretical approaches and recent bioarchaeological developments in methods to study diet, health, and mobility of populations can play a role here, as well as organic-food-residue analysis to study the role of technologies like pottery in food processing and storage activities, as well as longer-term transformations in forager diets. Perhaps the most important general point to emerge from this detailed treatment is that archaeologists and anthropologists cannot understand the full significance of food in terms of calories alone. The creation and sharing of food are in fact central to cultural and biological reproduction in hunter-gatherer societies, and also feature highly in socio-political dynamics and negotiations of identity and expressions of world view. This promises to be an exciting research frontier and a renewed focus on understanding the full cultural significance of food will also serve to maintain the status of hunter-gatherer studies as a fundamentally interdisciplinary endeavour.

Conclusions

The different parts of this handbook have explored an enormously wide range of different geographic regions, time periods, and thematic research literatures. It is clear that hunter-gatherer studies have changed dramatically over recent decades, quickly outgrowing their initial concerns and early analytical frameworks such as social evolutionary thinking and, more recently, cultural ecology. While the concept of a 'hunter-gatherer' remains difficult to define, it still serves as a useful shorthand, and also as an important point of departure into a diverse and vibrant field of interdisciplinary research and scholarship.

Where next? In this final part alone, many new theoretical and methodological developments—ranging from archaeogenetics and cultural transmission theory through to interpretive perspectives on the cultural significance of personhood, mobility, landscape, and materiality—have been explored, and many have yet to be subject to a more sustained and perhaps more comparative kind of application beyond a few isolated regions or narrow time periods. There is clearly much future research and critical synthesis that still awaits. Other integrating themes such as the study of gender and subsistence also appear likely to play a useful role in bringing together the enormous progress that has been made in developing new methods and interpretive theory, especially if these efforts can be focused on addressing specific questions within particular regional sequences.

Understanding exactly how local hunter-gatherers have been caught up in specific regional trajectories of change, especially during the Holocene and through to the historic and ethnographic periods, is also emerging as a particularly integrating focus for interdisciplinary analysis, but one that requires large-scale coordinated and perhaps also explicitly comparative programmes of research. Likewise, in areas and sequences with the right kinds of archaeological, human osteological, historic, and ethnographic data, reconstructing the detailed biographic life histories of specific individuals and populations caught up within these trajectories of long-term change now appears to be increasingly feasible (Weber and Zvelebil 2012). In fact, this appears to be one of the most productive areas in which the most modern scientific methods (e.g. integrated stable isotope analyses of diet and mobility, aDNA research, and osteoarchaeological studies) can be combined with new theoretical and interpretive perspectives (e.g. on personhood, gender, identity, mortuary practice and its landscape settings). In addition, much more work could also be done within regional sequences in trying to link short-term phases of climate and environmental change that are now increasingly being recognized with the identification of hunter-gatherer cultural responses, spanning both cultural flexibility and community resilience through to regional abandonment and collapse. Finally, all of this research activity also needs to proceed within a wider context defined by greater proactive engagement with indigenous peoples and descendant communities.

This raises a final important point. If intellectual diversification is a sign of a vibrant research field then hunter-gatherer studies have clearly outgrown their early formulations. The increasing identification and targeted exploration of unifying research themes like gender, subsistence, and understanding the roles of specific individuals in long-term culture change, now generate unparalleled opportunities to study the flexibility and resilience of humanity's oldest adaptation, especially through archaeological research. But importantly, this research can—and should—now be conducted in ways that have greater relevance for current foragers, descendant communities, and for the wider global public.

References

Conneller, C. 2004. Becoming deer: corporeal transformations at Star Carr. *Archaeological Dialogues* 11, 37–56.

David, B. and Thomas, J. (eds) 2008. *Handbook of landscape archaeology*. Walnut Creek, CA: Left Coast Press.

Ingold, T. 2007. The trouble with 'evolutionary biology'. *Anthropology Today* 23, 13–17.

Jordan, P. and O'Neill, S. 2010. Untangling cultural inheritance: language diversity and long-house architecture on the Pacific Northwest Coast. *Philosophical Transactions of the Royal Society B: Biological Sciences* 365, 3875–88.

Jordan, P. and Shennan, S. 2003. Cultural transmission, language and basketry traditions amongst the California Indians. *Journal of Anthropological Archaeology* 22, 42–74.

Jordan P. and Shennan, S.J. 2009. Diversity in hunter-gatherer technological traditions: mapping trajectories of cultural 'descent with modification' in northeast California. *Journal of Anthropological Archaeology* 28, 342–65.

Mesoudi, A., Whiten, A., and Laland, K. N. 2006. Towards a unified science of cultural evolution. *Behavioural and Brain Sciences* 29, 329–83.

Richerson, P. J. and Boyd, R. 2005. *Not by genes alone: how culture transformed human evolution*. Chicago: University of Chicago Press.

Sahlins, M. 1968. Notes on the original affluent society. In R. Lee and I. DeVore (eds), *Man the hunter*, 85–9. Chicago: Aldine.

Sahlins, M. 1972. *Stone age economics*. Chicago: Aldine-Atherton.
Strathern, M. 1988. *The gender of the gift*. Berkeley: University of California Press.
Zvelebil M. and Weber, A.W. 2012. Human bioarchaeology: group identity and individual life histories—Introduction. *Journal of Anthropological Archaeology* 32, 275–9.

CHAPTER 53

FUTURE DIRECTIONS IN HUNTER-GATHERER RESEARCH
Technology

ROBERT L. KELLY

IN 1651, Thomas Hobbes famously speculated on what life was like in the time before 'society'. It was not pretty:

> no place for Industry...no Culture of the Earth; No navigation, nor use of the commodities that may be imported by Sea; no commodious Building; no Instruments of moving, and removing such things as require much force; no Knowledge of the face of the Earth; no account of Time; no Arts; no Letters; no Society; and which is worst of all, continuall feare, and danger of violent death; And the life of man, solitary, poor, nasty, brutish and short.

Although Hobbes did not even know of the existence of 'hunter-gatherers' his memorable passage came to typify European scholars' attitudes towards foragers. Hunter-gatherers were defined by what they lacked, most notably, things, *technology*.

Many hunter-gatherers do indeed survive with few material possessions. The food-getting technology of the aboriginal Tasmanians, for example, consisted of unmodified throwing stones and sticks; a straight, sharpened stick served as a spear; bark torches lit their way at night; bark ropes were used to climb trees, simple baskets to carry shellfish, and simple traps to catch birds. McGrew (1987; 1992), in fact, showed that Tasmanian technology was just slightly more diverse and complex than that of chimpanzees. This comparison was not meant to denigrate the Tasmanians. Instead, it showed just how little hunter-gatherers need to get by.

Until the 1960s scholars attributed foragers' paucity of technology to the severity of the food quest, which left foragers with no time for the intellectual development that was thought to be necessary for creating complex tools (to say nothing of the arts and sciences). But anthropology cast this explanation aside after the 1966 Man the Hunter conference (Lee and DeVore 1968), where anthropologists agreed that the foraging way of life was nowhere near as onerous as previously thought. Hunter-gatherers were well fed from the efforts of only a few hours of work a day, and were relatively free from material want. Forty years later, we know that the foraging lifeway is not as rosy as participants at Man the Hunter concluded (Kelly 2013), but neither is it 'nasty, brutish, and short'.

The most influential element of the Man the Hunter revision was Marshall Sahlins's (1968; 1972) characterization of foraging as the Original Affluent Society. Foragers trust their environment to provide, and their devil-may-care attitude towards the future was an expression of this confidence. And if foragers seemed cavalier towards material goods, this was only a response to a mobile lifestyle in which goods are an annoyance. In Sahlins's words, foragers have a Zen economy: wanting little, they have all they want.

Although Sahlins was not entirely right about foragers' desires (Kelly 2013), he was correct that nomadic peoples make a trade-off between having things and carrying them. Sahlins opened the floor to a more productive question that provides this chapter with its focus: when is technology worth the cost of acquiring, manufacturing, maintaining, and transporting it?

In archaeology this question led to a discussion of the 'organization of technology', the 'spatial and temporal juxtaposition of the manufacture of different tools within a cultural system, their use, re-use, and discard and their relation not only to tool function and raw-material type and distribution, but also to behavioral variables which mediate the spatial and temporal relations among activity, manufacturing, and raw-material loci' (Kelly 1988, 717; see also Bamforth 1991; Binford 1979; Nelson 1991). It also led to a focus on 'design theory', an understanding of 'the variables that meet the specific strategies or mixture of needs for which a tool is intended' (Nelson 1997, 376; Bleed 1986), which concerned tool properties of maintainability, versatility, reliability, and use effectiveness. Research in these areas points out that tool structure is not only a simple matter of function. In this chapter we focus not directly on tool design, but on large-scale patterns in forager technology, and on what might account for them.

What is Technology?

Technology can be 'soft' or 'hard'. Soft technology refers to the knowledge that foragers need to survive. Hard technology refers to the material things that foragers put between themselves and their environment to achieve a goal—be it acquiring food, staying warm, making social contacts, etc. Ethnographically known foragers have an awesome knowledge of their worlds, and so there is no relationship between the volume of soft technology and the amount, or complexity, of hard technology. The Seri of north-western Mexico, for example, survived with a simple technology, but they could name some 350–400 different indigenous plants, with most having known uses as food (for both humans and animals), building material, medicine, musical instruments, cleaning agents, etc. (Felger and Moser 1985). In this chapter, we are concerned with hard technology.

Hard technology can be divided into several different categories: food-getting, such as digging sticks, bows, and arrows; housing, which can include formal houses as well as shade structures and windbreaks; clothing; ritual gear, such as a shaman's 'medicine' pouches; 'prestige' items, such as ornaments; and even 'toys' (see Politis 2005).

To date, systematic anthropological analysis has focused on food-getting technology. To see the variation that exists in forager food-getting technology, let us briefly compare that of the Ju/'hoansi (aka !Kung, one of southern Africa's so-called Bushmen peoples) and of the Nuvugmiut (the Point Barrow Eskimo of Alaska).

Ju/'hoansi Technology

Africa's Bushmen live in the sub-tropical Kalahari Desert (Lee 1979). Seasons are primarily differentiated in terms of rainfall, and consequently in the availability of surface water. The Ju/'hoansi obtain some 85 per cent of their food from about 100 species of plants, including nuts, tubers, seeds, and fruits; hunted game makes up the rest. During the cool, dry winter (May–August), groups of up to 50 people congregate around water sources; in the hot, wet summer, these camps break into groups of two dozen people, who moved among seasonal water sources. While summers are hot, the winters can see some night-time freezing.

Bushmen technology, though constructed with skill and ingenuity, is relatively modest (Figure 53.1). The main piece of plant-gathering gear is a metre-long digging stick, sharpened at one end. This implement is made in an hour and lasts some six months (Lee 1979, table 9.10 provides manufacturing times and use-lives of Ju/'hoan technology). Also needed is the *kaross* (which serves as clothing and a blanket) and skin bags of various sizes. Ostrich eggshells are fashioned into canteens.

Hunting technology is slightly more complex. The bow, about a metre long, is fashioned from a particular wood species, and bent by repeated heating in sand warmed beneath a fire, and equipped with a bowstring of antelope sinew. Arrows have four parts: a main shaft of cane, into one hollow end of which is fitted a short polished bone; a tubular wooden joint fits onto the bone's other end, and a metal arrowhead (fashioned from fence wire) fits into the other end of the wooden joint. The bow is weak, with a pull of some 9 kg. But the arrows are made lethal with poison, fashioned from the pupal stage of one of a few beetle species. The men carry their arrows in a quiver fashioned from bark, with hide caps on either end. Some men carry a metal-tipped spear, a metal adze with the head mounted in a wooden handle with pitch, and a throwing stick. Men may also carry a springhare pole, four metres long and fashioned from several flexible saplings held together with pitch and sinew, with a curved metal hook attached at one end. Thrust deep into a burrow, the twisting hook catches onto the springhare's fur and the animal is pulled out. Men carry much of their gear, including perhaps a metal knife and firemaking equipment, in a woven sinew carrying net.

In camp, food is processed with nut-cracking stones and, in recent times, a wooden mortar and pestle, a variety of metal pots (or tortoise shells), bowls, and spoons. There are also personal ornaments, mostly beads, obtained in trade. Everything that a Ju/'hoan family owns can be packed in a kaross or net bag, slung onto their back, and carried from camp to camp.

Nuvugmiut Technology

We see a strikingly different technology among the Nuvugmiut, who live at Point Barrow on Alaska's northern coast (Murdoch 1892; Spencer 1984) in large semi-subterranean houses.

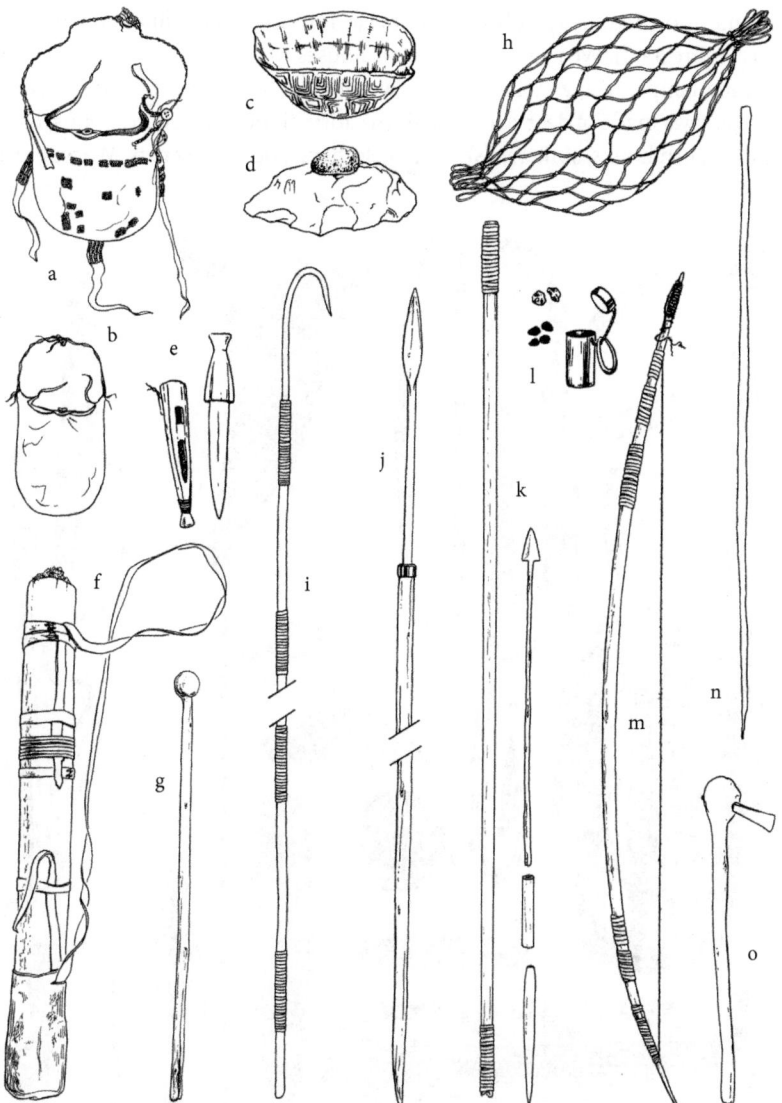

FIGURE 53.1 A selection of Ju/'hoansi technology: a, b carrying bags; c tortoise shell bowl; d nut-cracking stones; e knife and sheath; f quiver; g throwing stick; h men's carrying net; i springhare pole; j spear with metal point; k arrow (main shaft with two-part foreshaft and metal point); l firestarting kit; m bow; n digging stick; o axe, with hafted metal head (from Lee 1979, 125, 132, 140, 145, and 152).

They were primarily whale and seal hunters, living in large (250–300 person) settlements on the coast. Although families moved out during the short summer, inhabiting tents along the shore or travelling inland to trade with interior peoples, the winter settlements were more or less permanent.

The volume and complexity of Nuvugmiut gear is dramatically different from that of the Ju/'hoansi (Figure 53.2). We would find in their houses wooden pails; carved wooden bowls and soapstone lamps; heavy stone mauls; slate and metal knives, ulus (women's knives), adzes, chisels, saws made of deer scapulae, sheep horn dippers, wooden spoons, horn ladles, and a variety of fish hooks, sinkers, fishing line, leisters, and fishing nets. We would also find

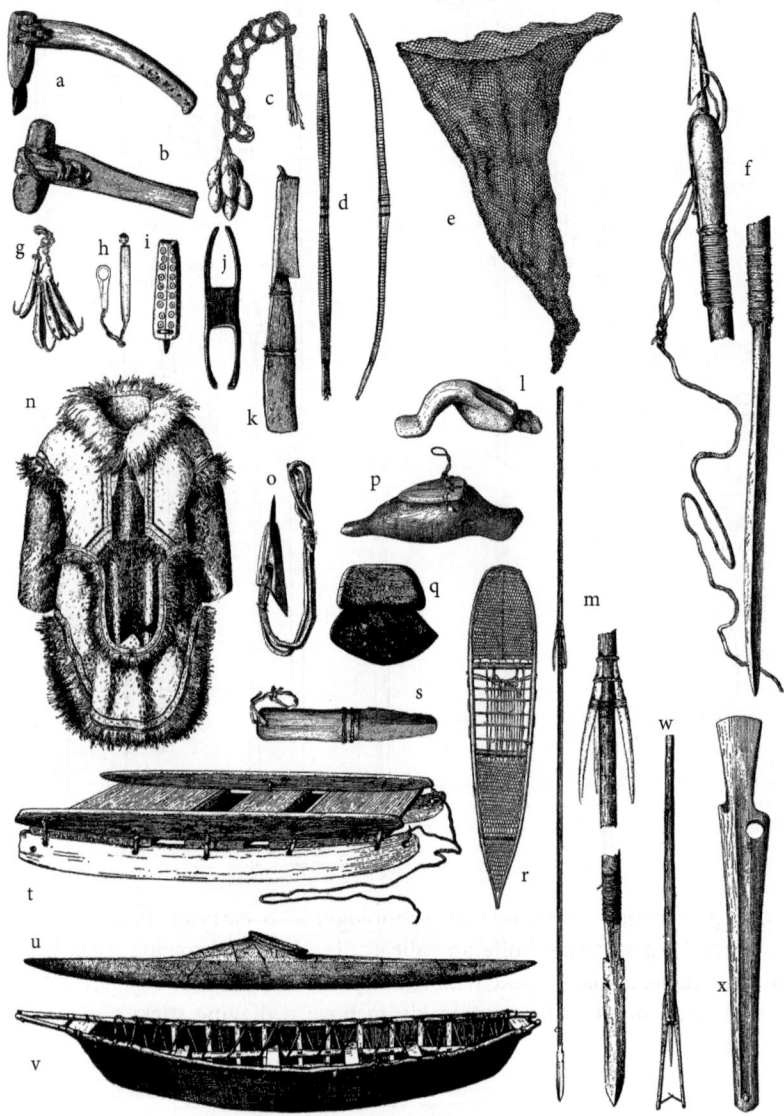

FIGURE 53.2 A selection of Nuvugmiut technology: a adze; b maul; c bird bola; d bow; e fishnet trap; f toggling seal harpoon; g fish hooks; h needle case; i metal-tipped awl; j netting needle; k netting mesh gauge; l hafted stone scraper; m bird dart; n women's coat; o walrus harpoon head; p wooden harpoon head case; q ulu; r snowshoe; s hafted slate knife; t sledge; u kayak; v umiak; w fish spear; x atlatl (spear thrower) (from Murdoch 1892: 95, 118, 151, 162, 170, 173, 198, 211, 217, 227, 232, 245, 249, 280, 285, 286, 297, 313, 314, 320, 329, 340, 345, and 355).

bow drills, ivory-tipped awls, whetstones, and wooden boxes, with cord for hinges, to hold harpoon heads and other tools. And there would be scrapers, with stone or metal tips that fit into wooden handles that were carved to fit a particular person's hand. The Nuvugmiut also had an abundance of clothing: boots and leggings of waterproof sealskin or deerskin, wooden snow goggles, belts, hooded caribou-hide coats fringed with fur, and deerskin mittens. While not directly linked to food-getting, warm, waterproof clothing was obviously essential to any outdoor activity.

There would be driftwood bows for hunting, probably shorter than a metre, and arrows, fletched, about 75 cm long. We might see four kinds of arrow in a quiver, each designed to kill a particular prey—bear, deer, large fowl, and small birds. These might have stone points as tips, barbed antler tips, or (in the case of arrows to kill small birds) bunts. Along with these are bird darts, thrown with an atlatl, with barbed antler or ivory tips and three forward-facing ivory barbs on the shaft; and there would be ivory-ball bolas, and a variety of snares to trap fur-bearing animals, and carved ivory meat cache markers.

There would also be seal harpoons. In the winter, seals were taken through their breathing holes. To detect a seal, the hunter inserted a small, lightweight, T-shaped rod into the snow that covered a breathing hole. A rise in the rod signalled the arrival of a seal, and time for the hunter to thrust his harpoon through the snow. The harpoon has a *toggling* head, designed to detach from the shaft and twist in the blubber beneath a seal's skin. The heads were attached to a long sinew cord that the hunter used to rein in the seal. There are also seal 'scratchers', designed to imitate the sound of a seal on the ice's surface and so to attract seals to a waiting hunter. Seals were also taken with nets strung below the ice.

Along with the seal harpoons, there would be those for walrus and whale. For these, however, a stitched sealskin bladder, its one opening plugged with a carved wooden stopper, is attached to the harpoon head with cord. With the bladder attached to the walrus or whale it cannot dive far, and after a chase it will tire and be dispatched by the hunter.

Unlike the Ju/'hoansi, the Nuvugmiut needed transportation, especially to hunt sea mammals. The Nuvugmiut had kayaks and umiaks (whaling boats), 20–30 feet long. Ingeniously made from numerous pieces of wood, fitted precisely and stitched together with baleen, they were covered in blind-stitched sealskins. For land travel, the Nuvugmiut used snowshoes as well as two kinds of sledge made from driftwood, pegged and lashed together, with runners of whale mandible. Obviously the Nuvugmiut had a lot of equipment, and many pieces were complex. Why is Nuvugmiut technology so different from that of the Ju/'hoansi?

What Conditions Food-Getting Technology?

Many ethnographic analyses of hunter-gatherer food-getting technology (e.g. Bamforth and Bleed 1997; Collard et al. 2005; Osborn 1999; Read 2008; Shott 1986; Torrence 1983; 1989; 2001; Vierra 1995) build upon data compiled by Wendell Oswalt (1973; 1976). He defined *subsistants* as tools used in the food quest. These he divided into *artefacts* and *naturefacts*, the latter being unmodified stones, wood, etc. Artefacts were divided into *implements* and *facilities*. A spear or bow is an implement; a trap, stationary fishing net or weir is a facility. Facilities can be *tended* and *untended*. A snare can operate without anyone tending to it, while a weir only works if someone is present to harvest the fish channelled through the weir's opening. Implements could be *instruments*, such as digging sticks used to act upon foods that are 'incapable of significant motion' (Oswalt 1973, 27), or *weapons*, such as spears or a bow and arrow.

Oswalt described facilities and implements in terms of *techno units*: 'an integrated, physically distinct, and unique structural configuration that contribute to the form of a finished artefact' (Oswalt 1976, 38). A Ju/'hoan digging stick, for example, has one techno unit: the stick itself. But a Nuvugmiut walrus harpoon has ten: (a) the slate (or metal) harpoon head, attached to a (b) bone or ivory toggling head, (c) the ivory foreshaft, (d) the line attaching the foreshaft to the main shaft, (e) the main shaft, (f) the line attaching the toggling head to a float, (g) the float, (h) binding on the spear to hold the foreshaft in place, (i) a finger rest on the spear, and (j) binding to hold the finger rest onto the shaft.

Oswalt also divided tools into *simple* and *complex*. Simple tools have parts that 'do not change their position relative to each other during use' (e.g. a weighted digging stick) while complex tools do (e.g. a toggling harpoon). By dividing a food-getting inventory's total number of techno units by the total number of subsistants, Oswalt also obtained a rough measure of the *elaborateness* of a particular group's technology. Theoretically, these two measures are independent (Read 2008), but in reality they are correlated: foragers with complex tools tend to have many such kinds of tools.

Recognizing that many foragers, such as the Tasmanians, can survive with a simple technology, we can ask: what causes technological complexity? Efforts to answer this question draw attention to three factors. First, certain types of food require more elaborate technologies. Digging up tubers requires little more than a stout, sharpened stick, but hunting is more successfully accomplished with technology (such as an atlatl or bow) that permits the hunter to strike with as little stalking as possible, and thus from as far as possible (though with less force than a thrusting spear—technology is all about trade-offs).

The second factor is risk, a difficult concept that encompasses three major dimensions. Two of the most salient are the probability of coming home empty-handed and the severity of that fact. In general, gathered foods are less risky than hunted foods in the first sense of the term. Either food, however, can be risky in the second sense depending on their importance to diet. A Ju/'hoan hunter can come home empty-handed, but will find tubers and mongongo nuts there collected by his wife. On the other hand, a Nuvugmiut hunter who fails to kill a seal may place his family in grave danger. In general, we expect technology to become more complex to reduce the likelihood of both elements of risk, but perhaps especially the second. A third element of risk is the cost to the forager of foraging. Environments differ in this regard, depending on temperature (extreme cold or heat), the length of daylight, and predators.

Several analyses point to risk as a major element conditioning forager technology (e.g. Bamforth and Bleed 1997; Bousman 1993; Collard et al. 2005; Torrence 1983; 2001). In general, technological innovation is most likely under conditions where risk is high because that is where people have the most to gain from effort invested in new technologies (Fitzhugh 2001).

The third factor is the one Sahlins identified: mobility. This is most clearly seen in the area of housing, for sedentary peoples invest more time in houses than nomadic ones (Binford 1990; Diehl 1992; Kelly 2006; Kelly et al. 2005). But, while mobile peoples are expected to carry fewer tools than sedentary ones, analyses of Oswalt's data disagree on whether

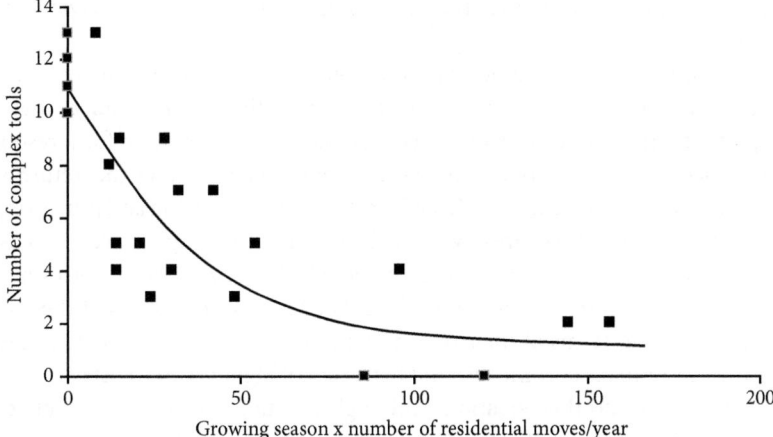

FIGURE 53.3 Relationship between the number of complex tools and Read's measure of risk: length of growing season times the number of residential moves per year (redrawn from Read 2008, figure 4; reproduced by permission of the Society for American Archaeology from *American Antiquity* 73(4), 2008).

mobility is a critical variable in determining the diversity or elaborateness of forager technology (e.g. Collard et al. 2005; Shott 1986).

Part of the reason for this is that while mobility and risk are theoretically independent variables, they are linked (for reasons discussed below). Accordingly, in his analysis of Oswalt's data, Read (2008) constructed an 'interaction' model that found a non-linear relationship between the number of complex tools and a variable measuring 'risk': the length of the growing season times the number of annual residential moves (Figure 53.3). Similarly, he finds a linear relationship between the elaborateness of a technology and risk. To sum up, highly mobile foragers who live in environments with long growing seasons have fewer complex tools and a less elaborate overall technology than sedentary foragers who live in environments with short growing seasons.

Obviously, sedentary foragers can invest time and effort in more kinds of tools and more complex tools because they do not have to concern themselves with the cost of transporting them. This makes a complex, elaborate technology possible, but it is not a cause. Instead, there is another reason, and to understand it we need to look at technology from the perspective of human behavioural ecology.

Behavioural Ecology and Technology

Behavioural ecology applies an evolutionary perspective to the study of human behaviour in ecological context. In the study of foraging societies, researchers have used it to study group size, mobility, food selection, sharing, parenting, mating, and other behaviours (Kelly 2013). Behavioural ecology relies on notions of 'fitness' since it assumes some relationship between behavioural choices and reproduction. But it does not argue that people are aware of a behaviour's reproductive consequences, or that behaviour is genetically linked.

One of the earliest models that behavioural ecologists used was the diet breadth model. This model predicts which foods foragers select out of all the possible choices that an environment presents. The model uses two variables: the cost of searching for a resource and the cost of processing it once found. The latter is often referred to as the 'return rate', the return per unit time in some currency (usually calories) of harvesting and processing a food resource. Low-ranked resources are low-ranked because of their high processing costs.

Diet breadth is narrow or broad depending on which array of food choices maximizes the overall rate of return from foraging (Kelly 2000; 2013). Applications of the model discovered that, ranked in terms of their return rates, food resources are added to the diet as high-return-rate resources become rare and hence entail higher search costs.

Technology enters into this equation. Although it is not impossible to hunt seals with one's bare hands, it is not very effective (to say the least). Boats reduce the search costs, and toggling harpoons reduce the harvesting cost. We can look at food-getting technology as providing the means to reduce both of these costs. For example, most early pottery was used to boil seeds, a generally low-return-rate food (e.g. Eerkens 2004). Along with grinding stones, pottery increases the food value of seeds and raises their return rate over that of unprocessed seeds. However, since the likelihood of breakage is high during camp moves, mobile foragers rarely make pottery, and when they do it is usually intended for short-term use and hence 'poorly' made (e.g. Bright et al. 2002; Simms and Russell 1997). However, less-nomadic foragers, and especially those who redundantly use particular places where pots could be cached, make 'better' pottery (Eerkens 2003). Effort was not invested in pottery (and grinding stones) until the depletion of high-ranked resources forced a broadening of the diet that demanded new technologies. But how does this perspective help us to understand the pattern discovered by Read?

Nomadic peoples are nomadic because residential movement is an easy way to cope with the possibility of local resource shortfall (Kelly 2013). As resource density reduces (a function of human exploitation, seasonal changes, etc.) the likelihood of coming home empty-handed increases. In responding, foragers weigh the cost relative to the benefit of moving camp. Although several variables enter into deciding to move, anything that constrains movement increases the risk associated with foraging. And in 'risky' environments, a reduction in mobility increases risk even more. Read's (2008) 'interactive' variable therefore combines two variables into one that measures how much risk a group lives under. Why does increasing risk result in more complex/elaborate tools? Does technology not entail its own costs—of procuring the raw material, of fashioning the tools, and of keeping them in good repair?

Risky environments are risky in large part because they contain few sources of food. If the primary source fails, there is little to fall back on—and so the forager cannot afford to fail. In such situations technologies must be specific to a food resource, and even, as is true for the Nuvugmiut, specific to a particular resource during a particular season of the year. In Bleed's (1986) terms, tools associated with the acquisition of 'risky' resources must be *reliable* by being overdesigned to capture a particular species under specific conditions. Alternatively, tools could be *maintainable* by being repairable through interchangeable parts and useful for a greater variety of food resources. Both efforts can result in complex and elaborate tools that enter the equation as upfront costs in raw-material procurement, construction, and maintenance.

As mobility is reduced, high-ranked resources become depleted locally. According to the diet breadth model, foragers will expand their diet breadth in response to depletion, adding resources that, while perhaps abundant, are more costly to procure and process. Holliday (1998), for example, found that trapping technology is more prevalent among sedentary than nomadic foragers. Traps generally take the form of deadfalls, spring-pole snares, or faux-floor pits, and are usually, but not always, aimed at small game. Traps reduce search costs by allowing hunters to be in more than one place at the same time, and they reduce processing costs by killing or containing the animal without direct input from the hunter. Holliday found that traps used by nomadic foragers are found where the game population mimics the situation created by sedentism—high search costs to pedestrian hunting and low post-encounter return rates.

There are two additional elements to the process of sedentism as well. Most ethnographically known sedentary foragers are coastal peoples who rely heavily on fish and/or sea mammals. In these circumstances, foragers operate under additional constraints because they must procure animals from one medium—the ocean—while operating from another—dry land or boats. Simple spears, for example, function less well than multi-pronged leisters in water partly because of the refractory properties of water. In many circumstances, fishing requires foragers to work 'blind' and thus demands nets, or hooks and lines. Foragers hunt large land mammals with a projectile and then track the prey while poison or bleeding weakens it. But sea mammals cannot be tracked in the water, and require a 'catch and grab' technology (Kelly 1996), such as toggling harpoons attached to floats or a boat, or the hunter to grab and 'hold' the animal (indeed, when the Point Barrow Eskimo first used guns they suffered high loss rates because wounded seals escaped below the ice where they died, but could not be retrieved; see Sonnenfeld 1960).

Secondly, sedentary foragers must store food (Kelly 2013), and if they are on the coast, which is likely, then they must harvest and store fish in large numbers. This requires mass-harvesting technologies such as weirs, nets, and drying racks to gather and process a large amount of a resource (e.g. salmon) in a short period of time. In short, sedentary coastal foragers 'elaborate' their technologies to reduce risk produced by low mobility and by the nature of marine resources.

Technologies that meet the demands of an expanded diet breadth can often elevate resource harvesting rates by mass-collecting technologies (such as fishing nets; Hayden and Gargett 1990), and yet they appear relatively late in prehistory (de Beaune 2004; Hayden and Nelson 1981). Why do they not appear sooner? The upfront costs of complex tools and elaborate technologies are often enormous. Large nets, for example, require hundreds of hours to manufacture (especially if we include the time to gather bark and roll it into cordage; see Lindström 1996). Once made, the technology cost is smaller, entailing maintenance only. But unless a technology is to be used regularly, then the upfront cost is a huge opportunity cost to a forager who could spend that time acquiring other, high-ranked resources (Bright et al. 2001; Elston 1990; Ugan et al. 2003). Noss (1997), for example, shows how communal net-hunting among African BaAka competes directly with other activities that use simpler technologies, such as individual snare-hunting.

It is crucial to realize, as Bettinger et al. (2006) point out, that the differences in return rates of major technologies are usually not small or incremental, but are more likely to be significant leaps ahead of a previous technology (e.g. a simple fishing spear versus a large dip net). This means that when technology changes, it changes (a) quickly, (b) pervasively across a population as its benefits become obvious, and (c) usually irreversibly, because it alters the perceived return rates of resources. Moreover, if new technologies increase return rates, and if increased return rates are translated into increased population growth rates, *and* if increased population density leads to a need to expand diet breadth further, then it follows that new food-getting technologies set off a positive feedback loop of new technologies and increasingly rapid change. This is certainly what the world has witnessed over the past 15,000 years as both marine resources and domesticated plants became crucial to human diet.

Technology, Gender, and Prestige

To this point we have only discussed food-getting technology, and we have discussed it primarily in terms of its function, getting food. But there is more to technology, even food-getting technology, than its obvious material function. Technology is embedded in a social web that gives technology meaning and that helps to direct choices (Pfaffenberger 1992). Mikea men, for example, carry spears with quite large metal tips, even though the largest animals they hunt are small hedgehogs—and the spears are not used on them. When I asked young men why they have such large spearheads, they replied, 'It's what men carry'. There has been far less research in this area than in the functional and adaptive aspects of food-getting technology.

It is probably safe to assume that people are always tweaking existing technologies and creating innovations. But how, and whether, a new technology becomes prevalent will depend in part on its effect on other areas of human life. For example, men and women target different resources while foraging, and Waguespack (2005) shows that as hunted foods become more important to diet, women do more activities that are not directly related to subsistence. This means that men and women operate under different technological demands, and that these change with changes in diet. And this means that the behaviour of men and women will be differently impacted by new technologies (and vice versa).

The introduction of the bow and arrow is one example. In most places in North America the bow and arrow is a late innovation, replacing the atlatl (spear thrower) after its successful use for millennia. The concept of a bow is not terribly difficult, and it does not require substantial antecedent technologies, so why should it appear so late?

Although many assume that the bow is a more 'efficient' hunting weapon, no solid data support this; in fact, hand-held spears may provide higher return rates (Shott 1993) although the bow may be more effective at shorter ranges than an atlatl (Churchill 1993). Many variables may come into play in determining whether the bow and arrow is used, such as vegetation, terrain, prey size, or the need to stalk game (e.g. Bartram 1997; Churchill 1993; Greaves 1997).

But another variable may be whether hunting is done primarily by groups or individuals. Spear throwers require the hunter to make himself known, to move, and hence to scare game. Thus they are suited to communal hunting where hunters' movements are intended to channel game into the path of waiting hunters. A bow can be used in a similar fashion, but it also allows a hunter to remain hidden, and make little movement to release a projectile. Bow hunting, therefore, is more conducive to individual hunting. So perhaps in order to understand the shift from spear-thrower to bow, we should also ask under what conditions individual hunting would be selected over group hunting. Individual hunting allows men to single themselves out and signal their value to others (perhaps women, especially) by focusing on high-risk/high-return large game (a behaviour referred to as 'costly signalling'). If the switch to the bow and arrow signals a reduction in large game, then women might be directly procuring more of the diet (e.g. seeds and tubers) and hence bow technology may reflect men trying to catch the attention of high-producing women as mates. If this is true, then bow technology should go hand-in-hand with technologies designed to increase the returns from plant collecting (e.g. pottery).

Hayden (1998) argues that technologies can be divided into 'practical' and 'prestige' technologies. So far, discussion in this chapter has focused on practical technologies. Prestige technologies can entail items of material culture whose purpose is to display wealth rather than accomplish some practical task (Hayden 1998, 11), and includes things such as copper axes, massive obsidian bifaces, or beads. But the search for prestige can also include technological innovations that were intended to mass-collect food to be used at a competitive feast. Satterthwait (1986; 1987), for example, shows that net-hunting in Australia was often used to provision social gatherings, and that the nets were considered sacred and their use controlled by senior ranking men. Hayden argues that many technologies that became central to subsistence originated as prestige technologies, including ceramics, open-ocean watercraft (see also Arnold 1995), and textiles.

Future Directions

No matter which approach one takes to understanding technology and technological change it is apparent that we need basic information on what it costs to produce a technology and what that technology provides in return (Kelly 2000), what Schiffer and Skibo (1987) called 'performance characteristics'. In doing so, we may find that many technologies do not simply increase efficiency, as is often assumed. Simms and Russell (1997), for example, show that sickles do not increase the efficiency of wild wheat harvest over that of hand harvesting. But the sickles do increase productivity by being more efficient at harvesting green wheat as well as wheat grown in hard soils (in both cases, the plants cannot be easily harvested by hand). On the other hand, Hurtado and Hill (1989) show that female Machiguenga can double or triple their foraging efficiency by using metal-tipped digging sticks instead of the traditional wooden ones. While this has no large benefit for the women, because they spend only an hour a day digging manioc, it could have a large impact where women spend more time digging and processing tubers, and where digging with wooden tools provides a low return rate (e.g. places with lots of rock or roots). Obviously, it is not simply a technology's efficiency that matters, but how that efficiency affects overall production. Unweaving this tangle is essential to knowing how and why technology changes, what effect it has on men versus women, and what new possibilities and constraints result.

These data could be gleaned from existing ethnographic data records, though I suspect we will be disappointed with the results. Instead, most new data will come from new ethnographic or experimental research. I suspect the latter will be more important, and obviously necessary for those technologies, such as chipped stone tool technologies, that are all but non-existent today (but see Allchin 1966; Binford 1986; Binford and O'Connell 1984; Churchill 1993; Flenniken and White 1985; Gallagher 1977; Gould 1980; Griffin 1997; Hampton 1999; Hayden 1979; 1987; Hayden and Nelson 1981; Miller 1979; Sillitoe 1982; Tindale 1985; Watson 1995; Weedman 2002). This research is essential because relying on indirect data or impressions will almost certainly lead us astray. For example, many archaeologists, including myself (Kelly 1988), once argued that bifaces are more efficient sources of hand-held flake tools than are amorphous cores. Thus, we argued that bifaces are more likely to be used by nomadic peoples, who, we expected, try to minimize the amount of stone carried. But with experimental assemblages Prasciunas (2007) found no significant difference in the efficiency of bifaces versus amorphous cores as sources of flake tools (see also Jennings et al. 2010). Some arguments now need rethinking because we did not initially collect the necessary technological data.

Many questions need answers. For example, how effective are weighted digging sticks compared to unweighted ones? Is the bow and arrow more efficient than the spear-thrower (Churchill 1993; Raymond 1986; Shott 1993)? What is the return from fishing with a hook and line versus nets (Lindström 1996)? How well do weighted versus unweighted digging sticks work in hard versus sandy soil, or how does bow technology fare in heavily forested versus desert conditions (Bartram 1997)? What conditions stone projectile point durability (Cheshier and Kelly 2006; Christenson 1997; Ellis 1997)? What is the return on quarrying activity (Jones and White 1988)? How much does heat treatment improve the 'return' on flint knapping (Bleed and Meier 1980; Cooper 2002)? Why use antler or bone points rather than ones of stone (Knecht 1997)? Is it more efficient to butcher with flake tools or bifaces (Tomka 2001)? How long does it take to manufacture a bow and arrow as opposed to an atlatl and dart? What is the cost and benefit of pottery, or clothing, or houses?

Humans adapt to their environments through both soft and hard technology. The latter leaves traces for archaeology, and is consequently the only means of tracking how humanity has used technology to reach the point it has. This means that some form of an evolutionary approach will always be a crucial part of the historical study of technology (Kuhn 2004). Especially challenging is understanding long-term patterns in human technological history, e.g. the significant spatial and temporal stasis in stone tools associated with the Early and Middle Palaeolithic as compared to the dramatic spatial diversity and temporal change of the Upper Palaeolithic (see Kuhn and Stiner 2001). In this chapter we employed the perspective of human behavioural ecology to explain an ethnographic pattern in food-getting technology. Stone tools are only a part, and more often than not only a small part, of the overall technology of foragers. The challenge that archaeologists face is to study the evolutionary nature of technological change through the small window of stone tools. The perspectives and data requirements outlined in this chapter will hopefully help to achieve that objective.

REFERENCES

Allchin, B. 1966. *The stone-tipped arrow*. London: Phoenix House.
Arnold, J. 1995. Transportation innovation and social complexity among maritime huntergatherer societies. *American Anthropologist* 97, 733–47.
Bamforth, D. B. 1991. Technological organization and hunter-gatherer land use. *American Antiquity* 56, 216–34.

Bamforth, D. B. and Bleed, P. 1997. Technology, flaked stone technology, and risk. In C. M. Barton and G. A. Clark (eds), *Rediscovering Darwin: evolutionary theory and archaeological explanation*, 109–40. Arlington, VA: American Anthropological Association.

Bartram, L. E. Jr. 1997. A comparison of Kua (Botswana) and Hadza (Tanzania) bow and arrow hunting. In H. Knecht (ed.), *Projectile technology*, 321–44. New York: Plenum Press.

Beaune, S. A. de 2004. The invention of technology: prehistory and cognition. *Current Anthropology* 45, 139–62.

Bettinger, R. L., Winterhalder, B., and McElreath, R. 2006. A simple model of technological intensification. *Journal of Archaeological Science* 33, 538–45.

Binford, L. R. 1979. Organization and formation processes: looking at curated technologies. *Journal of Anthropological Research* 35, 255–72.

Binford, L. R. 1986. An Alyawara day: making men's knives and beyond. *American Antiquity* 51, 547–62.

Binford, L. R. 1990. Mobility, housing, and environment: a comparative study. *Journal of Anthropological Research* 46, 119–52.

Binford, L. R. and O'Connell, J. F. 1984. An Alyawara day: the stone quarry. *Journal of Anthropological Research* 40, 406–32.

Bleed, P. 1986. The optimal design of hunting weapons: maintainability or reliability. *American Antiquity* 51, 737–47.

Bleed, P. and Meier, M. 1980. An objective test of the effects of heat treatment on flakeable stone. *American Antiquity* 45, 502–7.

Bousman, C. B. 1993. Hunter-gatherer adaptations, economic risk and tool design. *Lithic Technology* 18, 59–86.

Bright, J., Ugan, A., and Hunsaker, L. 2001. The effect of handling time on subsistence technology. *World Archaeology* 34, 164–81.

Cheshier, J. and Kelly, R. L. 2006. Projectile point shape and durability: the effects of thickness:length. *American Antiquity* 71, 353–63.

Christenson, A. L. 1997. Side-notched and unnotched arrowpoints: assessing functional differences. In H. Knecht (ed.), *Projectile technology*, 121–42. New York: Plenum Press.

Churchill, S. E. 1993. Weapon technology, prey size selection, and hunting methods in modern hunter-gatherers: implications for hunting in the Palaeolithic and Mesolithic. In G. L. Peterkin, H. M. Bricker, and P. Mellars (eds), *Hunting and animal exploitation in the later Palaeolithic and Mesolithic of Eurasia*, 11–24. Arlington: American Anthropological Association.

Collard, M., Kemery, M., and Banks, S. 2005. Causes of toolkit variation among huntergatherers: a test of four competing hypotheses. *Canadian Journal of Archaeology* 29, 1–19.

Cooper, C. 2002. A study of the morphological changes in tiger chert resulting from heat treatment. *Lithic Technology* 27, 153–60.

Diehl, M. 1992. Architecture as a material correlate of mobility strategies: some implications for archaeological interpretation. *Behavior Science Research* 26, 1–35.

Eerkens, J. W. 2003. Residential mobility and pottery use in the western Great Basin. *Current Anthropology* 44, 728–38.

Eerkens, J. W. 2004. Privatization, small-seed intensification, and the origins of pottery in the western Great Basin. *American Antiquity* 69, 653–70.

Ellis, C. 1997. Factors influencing the use of stone projectile tips: an ethnographic perspective. In H. Knecht (ed.), *Projectile technology*, 37–78. New York: Plenum Press.

Elston, R. G. 1990. A cost benefit model of lithic assemblage variability. In R. G. Elston and E. F. Budy (eds), *The archaeology of James Creek Shelter*, 153–63. Salt Lake City: University of Utah Press.

Felger, R. S. and Moser, M. B. 1985. *People of the desert and sea: ethnobotany of the Seri Indians*. Tucson: University of Arizona Press.

Fitzhugh, B. 2001. Risk and invention in human technological evolution. *Journal of Anthropological Archaeology* 20, 125–67.

Flenniken, J. J. and White, J. P. 1985. Australian flaked stone tools: a technological perspective. *Records of the Australian Museum* 36, 131–51.

Gallagher, J. P. 1977. Contemporary stone tools in Ethiopia: implications for archaeology. *Journal of Field Archaeology* 4, 407–14.

Gould, R. 1980. *Living archaeology*. Cambridge: Cambridge University Press.

Greaves, R. D. 1997. Hunting and multifunctional use of bows and arrows: ethnoarchaeology of technological organization among Pumé hunters of Venezuela. In H. Knecht (ed.), *Projectile technology*, 287–320. New York: Plenum Press.

Griffin, P. B. 1997. Technology and variation in arrow design among the Agta of northeastern Luzon. In H. Knecht (ed.), *Projectile technology*, 267–86. New York: Plenum Press.

Hampton, O. W. 1999. *Culture of stone: sacred and profane uses of stone among the Dani*. College Station: Texas A&M Press.

Hayden, B. 1979. *Paleolithic reflections: lithic technology of the Australian Western Desert*. Canberra: Australian Institute of Aboriginal Studies.

Hayden, B. (ed.) 1987. *Lithic studies among the contemporary highland Maya*. Tucson: University of Arizona Press.

Hayden, B. 1998. Practical and prestige technologies: the evolution of material systems. *Journal of Archaeological Method and Theory* 5, 1–55.

Hayden, B. and Gargett, R. 1990. Big man, big heart? A Mesoamerican view of the emergence of complex society. *Ancient Mesoamerica* 1, 3–20.

Hayden, B. and Nelson, M. 1981. The use of chipped lithic material in the contemporary Maya highlands. *American Antiquity* 46, 885–98.

Hobbes, T. 1968 [1951]. *Leviathan. Edited with an introduction by C. A. MacPherson*. Baltimore: Penguin.

Holliday, T. W. 1998. The ecological context of trapping among recent hunter-gatherers: implications for subsistence in terminal Pleistocene Europe. *Current Anthropology* 39, 711–20.

Hurtado, A. M. and Hill, K. 1989. Experimental studies of tool efficiency among Machiguenga women and implications for root-digging foragers. *Journal of Anthropological Research* 45, 207–17.

Jennings, T. A., Pevny, C. D., and Dickens, W. A. 2010. A biface and blade core efficiency experiment: implications for Early Paleoindian technological organization. *Journal of Archaeological Science* 37, 2155–64.

Jones, R. and White, N. 1988. Point blank: stone tool manufacture at the Ngilipitji Quarry, Arnhem Land, 1981. In B. Meehan and R. Jones (eds), *Archaeology with ethnography: an Australian perspective*, 51–87. Canberra: Australian National University.

Kelly, R. L. 1988. The three sides of a biface. *American Antiquity* 53, 717–34.

Kelly, R. L. 1996. Foraging and fishing. In M. G. Plew (ed.), *Prehistoric hunter-gatherer fishing strategies*, 208–14. Boise, ID: Boise State University Press.

Kelly, R. L. 2000. Elements of a behavioral ecological paradigm for the study of prehistoric hunter-gatherers. In M. B. Schiffer (ed.), *Social theory in archaeology*, 63–78. Salt Lake City: University of Utah Press.

Kelly, R. L. 2006. Mobility and houses in southwestern Madagascar: ethnoarchaeology among the Mikea and their neighbors. In F. R. Sellet, R. Greaves, and P. L. Yu (eds), *Archaeology and ethnoarchaeology of mobility*, 5–107. Gainsville, FL: University Press of Florida.

Kelly, R. L. 2013. *The lifeways of hunter-gatherers*. Cambridge: Cambridge University Press.

Kelly, R. L., Poyer, L., and Tucker, B. 2005. An ethnoarchaeological study of mobility, architectural investment, and food sharing among Madagascar's Mikea. *American Anthropologist* 107, 403–16.

Knecht, H. 1997. Projectile points of bone, antler and stone: experimental explorations of manufacture and use. In H. Knecht (ed.), *Projectile technology*, 191–212. New York: Plenum Press.

Kuhn, S. L. 2004. Evolutionary perspectives on technology and technological change. *World Archaeology* 36, 561–70.

Kuhn, S. L. and Stiner, M. C. 2001. The antiquity of hunter-gatherers. In C. Panter-Brick, R. H. Layton, and P. Rowley-Conwy (eds), *Hunter-gatherers: an interdisciplinary perspective*, 99–129. Cambridge: Cambridge University Press.

Lee, R. 1979. *The !Kung San: men, women and work in a foraging society*. Cambridge: Cambridge University Press.

Lee, R. B. and DeVore, I. 1968. *Man the hunter*. Chicago: Aldine.

Lindstrom, S. 1996. Great Basin fisherfolk: optimal diet breadth modeling the Truckee River aboriginal subsistence fishery. In M. G. Plew (ed.), *Prehistoric hunter-gatherer fishing strategies*, 114–79. Boise, ID: Boise State University Press.

McGrew, W. C. 1987. Tools to get food: the subsistants of Tasmanian aborigines and Tanzanian chimpanzees compared. *Journal of Anthropological Research* 43, 247–58.

McGrew, W. C. 1992. *Chimpanzee material culture: implications for human evolution*. Cambridge: Cambridge University Press.

Miller, T. O. Jr. 1979. Stonework of the Xeta Indians of Brazil. In B. Hayden (ed.), *Lithic use-wear analysis*, 401–7. New York: Academic Press.

Murdoch, J. 1988 [1892]. *Ethnological results of the Point Barrow expedition*. Ninth Annual Report of the Bureau of Ethnology, 1887–8. Washington, DC: Smithsonian Institution.

Nelson, M. 1991. The study of technological organization. In M. B. Schiffer (ed.), *Archaeological method and theory vol. 3*, 57–100. Tucson: University of Arizona.

Nelson, M. 1997. Projectile points: form, function and design. In H. Knecht (ed.), *Projectile technology*, 371–82. New York: Plenum Press.

Noss, A. J. 1997. The economic importance of communal net hunting among the BaAka of the Central African Republic. *Human Ecology* 25, 71–89.

Osborn, A. J. 1999. From global models to regional patterns: possible determinants of Folsom hunting weapon design diversity and complexity. In D. S. Amick (ed.), *Folsom lithic technology: explorations in structure and variation*, 188–213. Ann Arbor: International Monographs in Prehistory.

Oswalt, W. H. 1973. *Habitat and technology*. New York: Holt, Rinehart & Winston.

Oswalt, W. H. 1976. *An anthropological analysis of food-getting technology*. New York: Wiley.

Pfaffenberger, B. 1992. Social anthropology of technology. *Annual Review of Anthropology* 21, 491–516.

Politis, G. 2005. Children's activity in the production of the archaeological record of hunter-gatherers: an ethnoarchaeological approach. In P. Funari, A. Zarankin, and E. Stovel (eds), *Global archaeological theory: contextual voices and contemporary thoughts*, 121–43. New York: Kluwer Academic/Plenum Press.

Prasciunas, M. 2007. Bifacial cores and flake production efficiency: an experimental test of technological assumptions. *American Antiquity* 72, 334–48.

Raymond, A. 1986. Experiments in the function and performance of the weighted atlatl. *World Archaeology* 18, 153–77.

Read, D. 2008 An interaction model for resource implement complexity based on risk and number of annual moves. *American Antiquity* 73, 599–625.

Sahlins, M. 1968. Notes on the original affluent society. In R. B. Lee and I. DeVore (eds), *Man the hunter*, 85–9. Chicago: Aldine.

Sahlins, M. 1972. The original affluent society. In M. Sahlins (ed.), *Stone age economics*, 1–39. Chicago: Aldine.

Satterthwait, L. 1986. Aboriginal Australian net hunting. *Mankind* 16, 31–48.

Satterthwait, L. 1987. Socioeconomic implications of Australian aboriginal net hunting. *Man* 22, 613–36.

Schiffer, M. B. and Skibo, J. M. 1987. Theory and experiment in the study of technological change. *Current Anthropology* 28, 595–622.

Shott, M. 1986. Technological organization and settlement mobility: an ethnographic examination. *Journal of Anthropological Research* 42, 15–51.

Shott, M. 1993. Spears, darts, and arrows: late woodland hunting techniques in the upper Ohio Valley. *American Antiquity* 58, 425–43.

Sillitoe, P. 1982. The lithic technology of a Papua New Guinea highland people. *The Artefact* 7, 19–38.

Simms, S. R. and Russell, K. W. 1997. Bedouin hand-harvesting of barley: implications for early cultivation in southwest Asia. *Current Anthropology* 38, 696–702.

Sonnenfeld, J. 1960. Changes in an Eskimo hunting technology: an introduction to implement geography. *Annals of the Association of American Geographers* 50, 172–86.

Spencer, R. F. 1984. North Alaska coast Eskimo. In D. Damas (ed.), *Handbook of North American Indians volume 5: Arctic*, 320–37. Washington, DC: Smithsonian Institution.

Tindale, N. 1985. Australian Aboriginal techniques of pressure-flaking stone implements: some personal observations. In M. G. Plew, J. C. Woods, and M. Pavesic (eds), *Stone tool analysis: essays in honor of Don E. Crabtree*, 1–34. Albuquerque: University of New Mexico Press.

Tomka, S. 2001. The effect of processing requirements on reduction strategies and tool form: a new perspective. In W. A. Andrefsky (ed.), *Lithic debitage: context, form, meaning*, 207–24. Salt Lake City: University of Utah Press.

Torrence, R. 1983. Time budgeting and hunter-gatherer technology. In P. Halstead and J. O'Shea (eds), *Bad year economics: cultural responses to risk and uncertainty*, 11–22. Cambridge: Cambridge University Press.

Torrence, R. 1989. Retooling: towards a behavioral theory of stone tools. In R. Torrence (ed.), *Time, energy, and stone tools*, 57–66. Cambridge: Cambridge University Press.

Torrence, R. 2001. Hunter-gatherer technology: macro- and microscale approaches. In C. Panter-Brick, R. H. Layton, and P. Rowley-Conwy (eds), *Hunter-gatherers: an interdisciplinary perspective*, 73–98. Cambridge: Cambridge University Press.

Ugan, A., Bright, J., and Rogers, A. 2003. When is technology worth the trouble? *Journal of Archaeological Research* 30, 1315–29.

Vierra, B. J. 1995. *Subsistence and stone tool technology: an old world perspective.* Tempe: Arizona State University Press.

Waguespack, N. M. 2005. The organization of male and female labor in foraging societies: implications for early paleoindian archaeology. *American Anthropologist* 107, 666–76.

Watson, V. D. 1995. Simple and significant: stone tool production in highland New Guinea. *Lithic Technology* 20, 89–99.

Weedman, K. 2002. On the spur of the moment: effects of age and experience on hafted stone scraper morphology. *American Antiquity* 67, 731–44.

CHAPTER 54

CULTURAL TRANSMISSION THEORY AND HUNTER-GATHERER ARCHAEOLOGY

JELMER W. EERKENS, ROBERT L. BETTINGER, AND

PETER J. RICHERSON

IN this chapter, we highlight cultural transmission (CT) theory as a framework for understanding change over time and space in human material culture, with particular emphasis on how this approach can help archaeologists interpret the record. CT theory seeks to place the evolution of culture within a rigorous and scientifically defined context, and describes the broad range of mechanisms that humans (or non-humans, in some cases) use to acquire, modify, and retransmit cultural information. Such information can represent rules about eligible marriage partners, instructions for how to produce fishing nets, lyrics associated with a particular song, oral histories, gossip, or even misinformation or maladaptive information (e.g. the consumption of brains of dead relatives or the use of lead glazes on drinking cups). Many applications of CT attempt to define these mechanisms mathematically and to model their effects over time (e.g. Bentley 2005; Bentley and Shennan 2003; Boyd and Richerson 1985; Cavalli-Svorza and Feldman 1981; Henrich and Boyd 1998; Mesoudi and Lycett 2009).

By definition, CT applies to all humans over all time, hunter-gatherers, agriculturalists, and members of industrial societies alike. However, below we attempt to highlight more particular intersections between CT and hunter-gatherer lifeways. Although the processes of CT are similar, there are reasons to believe that certain modes of transmission will be dominant in hunter-gatherer settings. In this respect, we argue that CT has a predictable effect on structuring material culture and has a recognizable signature in the record of hunter-gatherers.

A common misconception about CT is that it only involves biological selection (e.g. individuals that do not survive are not able to pass on cultural information, resulting in selective or differential removal from the existing 'database' of cultural information; see also Dunnell 1981; Shennan 2006). While such processes are often included in CT modelling, we will argue that most of what is interesting about the predictions of CT stems from other processes, particularly human inventiveness and the biased, comparatively rapid, spread of useful (and sometimes distinctively non-useful) innovations, within and between populations. The accrual of such information and subsequent winnowing and modification is in many cases largely independent of the survival rates and fecundity of individuals. This is not to say that genes and biology are unimportant in CT processes. The human phenotype, including, for example, the structure of the brain, clearly affects how people acquire, sort, and store cultural information (e.g. accuracy and ability to recall information; e.g. Gabora 2004; Sperber 1996). Likewise, genetically controlled differences in manual dexterity affect the ability of individuals to materialize cultural information, and likewise, their ability to retransmit it (Eerkens 2000; Kerst and Howard 1984; Lachnit and Wolfgang 1990; Moyer et al. 1978). At the same time, culture, via gene–culture co-evolution, could well have influenced the genetic evolution of such things as manual and linguistic skills (Laland et al. 2010; Richerson and Boyd 2010), and there is much to learn regarding the interplay between genetic transmission (GT) and CT for specific human traits.

Although CT has been used to explain learned behaviour among some non-human species, such as birds (Bonner 1980; Slater and Ince 1979), fish (Brown and Laland 2003), dolphins (Krützen et al. 2005), and elephants (Poole et al. 2005), the human propensity for social learning has put anthropological and archaeological studies at the forefront of CT theory-building and testing. For example, chimpanzees are able social learners compared to most non-humans, but have a much lower natural (i.e. instinctive) propensity for imitation and social learning, as elegant comparative experiments have shown (e.g. Tomasello 1996; Whiten and Custance 1996). Because of the diachronic nature of most archaeological studies, the focus on material culture within archaeology, and the fact that material culture is an aspect of human behaviour that is transmitted entirely through cultural means, archaeology is uniquely situated and has an important role to play in understanding long-term (i.e. macro) CT processes.

CT Defined

CT should be thought of as a specific model within the more general class of inheritance systems, where information, be it genetic, language, or material culture, is passed between sources and destinations. The specific inheritance systems differ in their details, for example the form and context in which information is transmitted (e.g. as DNA or as verbal instructions), how information is received and stored (e.g. encoded within chromosomes, or remembered within the brain), the fidelity of such information transfer (e.g. copying error), and how individuals subsequently act upon information received (e.g. modification, transformation). These dynamics greatly influence the overall evolutionary trajectories of genes, material culture, language, and the like, but at their most fundamental level, all inheritance systems share some similarities in how they operate over time.

A nice feature of such inheritance systems is that they can be modelled using recursive equations or as Markov Chains, facilitating the analysis of change (or stasis) over time. Such equations have been well studied by mathematicians (e.g. Ewens 1979; Meyn and Tweedie 1993) and as a result, many Markov equations can be solved analytically (e.g. with mathematical equations with known solutions). Furthermore, with modern computers, extremely complex Markov processes can be analysed empirically, and equations that do not have defined analytical solutions can be examined and solved through computer simulation. From these efforts, anthropologists and others have been able to describe some of the regularities and patterns that should describe the transmission of cultural information, in other words, allowing researchers to *predict* the short- and long-term effects of CT. Thus, these two approaches, mathematical modelling and computer simulation, facilitate a scientific approach to CT studies, where hypotheses drawn from theory can be modelled and tested against actual data from the archaeological or anthropological record.

Commonly, mathematical modellers use the tools of population biology to study cultural evolution. The general form of such models is:

$$P_{t+1} = P_t + \sum_i^n forces$$

where P_t is some property of the population (say the frequency of a particular stone tool type) at time t, P_{t+1} is the property of the population at time $t + 1$, and $\sum_i^n forces$ represents the combined effects of the processes acting to change the population over time. For example, suppose we are interested in the change over time in a stylistic feature of stone points, for example ribbon pressure flaking (i.e. where flake scars are long, parallel, and run across the entire surface of a flaked tool). An aesthetic force might favour new variants as knappers become bored with the common design, while utilitarian forces might favour a variant with the least drag and best penetration. A theoretical investigation might focus generically on the way aesthetic and function biases interact to generate evolution by picking forms for the two processes and iterating the model algebraically or by computer simulation (Boyd and Richerson, 1985; Cavalli-Sforza and Feldman 1981). An experimental study might ask participants to iteratively design projectile points on a computer, simulate their performance, and allow performance information to be exchanged between participants, in a time-transgressive manner (e.g. Mesoudi and O'Brien 2008), or have participants listen to, and subsequently retransmit, a narrative, observing where information is modified, innovated, or deleted (e.g. Mesoudi and Whiten 2004). A field study would attempt to use the archaeological record to infer the forces in operation in a sequence of change within a particular social and physical setting (Eerkens and Bettinger 2008; Eerkens and Lipo 2005).

Genetic transmission has been well-studied and many, though certainly not all, of the details have been worked out. By comparison, there has been much less research on CT, though the literature is rapidly expanding (for recent works see McElreath et al. 2008; Mesoudi and Lycett 2009). As a result, much of the scientific study of inheritance systems has focused on GT instead of CT. One of the main reasons for this, we believe, relates to the fact that many social animals use simple forms of transmission. Humans are unique in the sheer quantity of information transmitted culturally. For example, it has been argued that humans have highly evolved cognitive and communication skills to quickly and efficiently acquire generic cultural knowledge, such as recognizing eye contact and the use of social referencing to interpret emotional displays (e.g. Csibra and Gergely 2009; Gergely et al. 2007). These mechanisms allow humans, but apparently no other animal, to evolve extremely complex cultural adaptations by successive innovations and transmission (Boyd and Richerson 1996; Tomasello 1999).

A second difficulty in studying CT is that the majority of species that do use CT to transmit information (e.g. humans, chimpanzees) are long lived, making empirical study, especially long-term evolutionary outcomes, difficult. Progress has been made in this regard using laboratory experiments of CT (e.g. Mesoudi 2007), but there is much still to be understood. By contrast, scholars studying GT can turn to short-lived species (e.g. peas, bacteria, fruit flies) to study such long-term effects, and such empirical studies have led to many refinements of GT theory.

Theory and empirical evidence suggest a number of means by which cultural information can be transmitted between individuals. CT processes vary in terms of the information content, the context of transmission, and the mode of transmission. Table 54.1 presents some of the possible variations (see Eerkens and Lipo 2007 for a more complete review and discussion of these ideas). These interacting factors affect the rate and accuracy of information transmission, which has important implications for evolutionary processes. Also, these processes act on both the originating (i.e. source) and recipient (i.e. destination) sides. Tehrani and Riede (2008) have recently referred to the process of teaching and learning together as 'pedagogy' and discuss the significance of such an approach to archaeologists (see also Caro and Hauser 1991; Thornton and Raihani 2008 for a discussion of these ideas among animals).

Transmission is also affected by the operation of various cognitive or psychological biases that affect from and to whom information is differentially transmitted, and how this information is packaged, stored, and subsequently modified (see Boyd and Richerson 1985; Henrich and McElreath 2003 for more extensive discussions). Table 54.2 presents some of the commonly discussed biases, though others are certainly possible. Much research in CT examines the evolution of the biasing mechanisms themselves (e.g. is copying a prestigious person hard-wired or learned behaviour?: e.g. Efferson et al. 2008), their universality among different cultures (e.g. Henrich et al. 2006), and their cumulative effects on culture over time. Cognitive biases, too, affect the rate and accuracy of information transmission. The biases listed in Table 54.2 affect primarily the recipients of cultural information. Less theorizing has been focused on cognitive biases that might affect the transmitters, though some archaeologists (e.g. Spencer 1993), have considered how aspiring leaders might use biased transmission systems to increase their power base and/or authority.

The exact nature and universality of such biasing mechanisms has been debated. In any case, the interaction of the different biasing mechanisms with different content (e.g. auditory vs. visual; complex vs. simple), learning contexts (e.g. ritual vs. apprenticeship vs. domestic), and modes create a myriad of different transmission pathways. This complexity makes application to the archaeological record, where we may not be able to reconstruct all

Table 54.1 Content, context, and mode of information transmission

Content	Context	Mode
Complexity of information (e.g. length, familiarity)	Environment of transmission (e.g. ritual, school, family)	Number of people (e.g. one-to-one, many-to-one, etc.)
Form (e.g. verbal, written, visual)	Cultural (e.g. foreign vs. domestic)	Direction (e.g. horizontal, vertical, oblique)
Degree of repetition		

Table 54.2 Cognitive biases in CT

Information acquisition	Information packaging	Information modification
Frequency-dependent (e.g. conformity, pro-novelty)	Independent biases (e.g. hitchhiking/info. bundling)	Copying error
Model-based (e.g. prestige, success, similarity)	Acquisition of traits one at a time from a range of models	Filtration through individual world view
		Purposeful innovation (e.g. directed vs. undirected)

of the different factors, challenging. However, as others have shown (and we hope to highlight below), there is interpretive ground to be gained by such applications.

CT AND ARCHAEOLOGY

Many of the basic ideas about the transmission of cultural information have been with anthropologists since the late 1800s. For example, Franz Boas (1896, 3–4, quoted in O'Brien and Lyman 2002, 229) suggested a general algorithm for understanding similarity in human cultures: the closer people lived to one another the more similar cultures should appear because similarity in culture was most likely due to dissemination of cultural information (as opposed to independent origin). Boas later suggested that most of the cultural inventory of a society was the cumulative result of 'diffusion' from neighbouring cultures (Hatch 1973).

Anthropologists such as Holmes (1886), Petrie (1899), and Kroeber (1916) were quick to pick up on these ideas, and to develop them further, to help explain similarity and/or difference in the archaeological record. For example, Kroeber (1940) considered how small errors during diffusion affected the distribution of culture-historical types over space and time. This view of culture included most of the important elements of a Darwinian evolutionary system, including the transmission of information (cultural in this case), mutation of that information (through copying errors), and retransmission of this information in the modified state. The only major Darwinian element lacking from this view is the notion of various global selective forces that winnow out some of these mutations. Today, such refinement of CT continues, and has focused on more rigorous and mathematical definitions of the specific processes involved. CT is being used by an increasing number of researchers in a diverse array of academic fields including anthropology, archaeology, biology, economics, and psychology, among others.

What is particularly relevant to archaeologists is not the ability to see and reconstruct every transmission event, but to deduce how transmission content, context, mode, and cognitive biases affect patterns in information and hence material culture, especially at a societal level (Eerkens and Lipo 2007; see also chapters in O'Brien 2008). Theory suggests that such patterning is likely to be evident especially in measures of information diversity or variance (e.g. Bettinger and Eerkens 1999; Eerkens and Bettinger 2001; Eerkens and Lipo 2005; 2007). In short, CT theory makes few predictions about modal or average tendency in assemblages of artefacts, but is more specifically concerned with measures of dispersion or variation. Testing CT theory then, requires population-level measures of dispersion or variation and archaeology is one of the few, perhaps the only, discipline that can generate the necessary data to do so, especially for long-term outcomes. For example, direct extrapolation of evolutionary processes measured in the short run by direct observation are often very different from long-run averages (Gingerich 1982). This is probably because evolution frequently meanders and reverses direction. Evolution observed over longer spans of time depicts long-term trends that average out much of the small-scale fractal variation that a direct observer of human transmission might see. Furthermore, many of the cultural traits transmitted by animals, such as birdsong, leave little material evidence behind, again, leaving archaeology as the main discipline that can contribute to the testing of predictions from CT over the long term. Humans, of course, have especially excelled at the use of material culture, which archaeologists readily recover and study, and nearly all of material culture among humans is transmitted via cultural information (e.g. it is not instinctive). For these reasons, archaeologists should take an active interest in developing and testing CT theory.

CT and Hunter-Gatherers

As mentioned in the opening paragraphs, CT has no *special* relevance to hunter-gatherers. There is nothing to suggest that economic mode of subsistence, in and of itself, has implications for how people transmit cultural information. However, because a number of other factors such as lower population density, less-complex material technologies, and simpler social organization *tend to* characterize hunter-gatherers, CT has important implications for how material culture might evolve among hunter-gatherers versus other groups. In the sections below, we define some models derived from CT theory, focusing on those that we think have special relevance to hunter-gatherers. We believe that some of these ideas could be expanded to include other aspects of hunter-gatherer ways of life such as niche construction (e.g. Laland and O'Brien 2010; Rockman 2009), but we do not pursue those issues here, focusing instead on material culture.

Effects of Population Size and Density

Cross-cultural research shows that hunter-gatherer groups tend to live at lower population densities and sizes than agricultural or industrial ones (Kelly 1995; Winterhalder et al. 1988). Also, CT modelling suggests that population size, especially the number of transmitters and receivers, affects the range of information that can be retained within a cultural system. For example, Henrich (2004) attributes the loss of a number of complex material technologies in ancient Tasmania to rising Holocene sea levels that cut Tasmania off from mainland Australia. This isolation dramatically cut the effective population size and the ability to retain and transmit complex technologies. Kline and Boyd (2010) detected a similar pattern in the Pacific Islands. Similarly, Richerson et al. (2009) argue that the appearance and subsequent disappearance of more complex lithic technologies during the Middle Stone Age of Southern Africa (e.g. Howiesons Poort) may be due to an uptick in effective population sizes that could not be sustained in the long run. Such notions are in line with others such as Diamond (1998), who argued that such an effect operates at all sizes of populations, not just small-scale ones, and recent modelling research by Shennan (2001) and Powell et al. (2009), which shows that population size and connectedness have a positive relationship with the maintenance of complex cultural information.

Thus, CT theory predicts that, due to their smaller population sizes, hunter-gatherers in general ought to be characterized by a more limited range of material technologies than agricultural and industrial ones (e.g. Powell et al. 2009; Richerson et al. 2009). This result is not especially surprising, but it might explain the long periods of apparent stasis witnessed in Lower and Middle Palaeolithic sites in the Old World. In those sequences, a narrow range of tools and technologies characterize tens to hundreds of thousands of years. Also, this line of reasoning may explain the explosion in the diversity of material culture observed during the Mesolithic and Neolithic periods as global climates warmed in the Holocene and populations appear to have grown (Shennan 2001). Likewise, the rapid evolution of very complex artefacts beginning with the industrial revolution involved both large numbers of communicating innovators and the expansion of formal education that made the transmission and storage of complex information much more efficient. Donald (1991) ranks the development of literacy and numeracy as one of the major human cognitive advances, although they are cultural not genetic innovations.

Effects of Information Content and Complexity

CT theory also predicts that the form in which information is transmitted (e.g. written, verbal, visual instructions) and the complexity of this information (the length and regularity of instructions; see Gell-Mann and Lloyd 2003) should affect fidelity and the preferred mode of transmission. For example, written instructions are likely to be transmitted with greater fidelity than verbal or visual ones, and given a particular transmission mode, complex information is subject to greater copying error (lower fidelity). Likewise, while simple technologies are subject to more tinkering and experimentation, the attributes of complex technologies are often transmitted together as part of information packages. This leads to greater linkage or correlation between the attributes or components of a complex technology.

Lacking writing, hunter-gatherers transmit information via verbal and visual means. Hence, one prediction of CT theory is that within a particular technology, there should be greater variation in the size and shape of tools than among societies where technological information is transmitted primarily by writing. Similarly, because hunter-gatherers tend to have simpler tools (as per the reasoning above), all other things being equal, we expect more tinkering and experimentation with these technologies, per capita, than more complex ones that characterize agricultural and industrial ones. The net result of these effects is that hunter-gatherer material technologies should have fewer technologies and artefact 'types', but a broader range of variation about a particular mean, and less covariation between attributes within a type. By contrast, material technologies among agricultural and industrial societies should be much more diverse overall (e.g. more types), but with less variation about means within a technology (or artefact type) and greater covariation between the attributes of those technologies.

Testing these hypotheses derived from CT theory will require the collection of large sets of data across diverse ecological and temporal scales, and examining diversity and variation in artefact types, and covariation among attributes within types. Limited datasets examined by Eerkens and Bettinger (2008; Bettinger and Eerkens 1999) for just hunter-gatherer groups of different population densities generally support these notions. However, additional comparisons using other datasets are clearly necessary.

Effects of Social Organization

Many, though certainly not all, hunting and gathering groups are characterized by simpler social organizations, generally lacking formalized and/or institutionalized positions of leadership (e.g. Fried 1967; Service 1962). In such settings, social and political organization tends to be much smaller in scale and localized. As a result, individuals tend to have greater interaction with the members of their immediate group and more limited contact with people living in more distant locations. In more complex societies, individuals from a wider range of social and political settings are often brought together (e.g. in markets or urban living), where they may acquire and transmit cultural information.

Individuals in smaller and simpler groups are apt to acquire information through social learning (e.g. copying) and individual learning (e.g. experimentation) in frequencies similar to their counterparts in more complex societies. However, the low degree of political organization in hunting and gathering groups will tend to limit the spatial extent over which material culture will spread (e.g. Powell et al. 2009; Richerson et al. 2009). For material culture that contains a high degree of stylistic information (as conceived by Dunnell 1978; see also Rogers and Ehrlich 2008), that is, where environmental or other 'global' conditions do not greatly influence performance characteristics (see Eerkens and Bettinger 2008), this should result in smaller and more localized distributions of attributes or artefact styles. In the archaeological record, this should appear as culture-historical 'units' with more restricted spatial distributions.

By contrast, in societies with large-scale political or social organization, and by extension larger-scale economic organization, cultural information has the potential to spread more quickly and over a larger area. Indeed, some political organizations may deliberately encourage or even force the adoption of a particular technology or production system across their sphere of influence or control. For artefacts imbued with stylistic information and/or produced under conditions of craft specialization (e.g. economic organization), this should be reflected in the archaeological record by culture-historical units with broader spatial distributions. Turning this back to predictions about variation and diversity of material culture, among hunter-gatherers we should expect to see lower diversity of artefact types as there is less transmission of ideas across larger social units, and greater variation per unit area for stylistic artefacts due to the more localized nature of transmission systems. Agricultural and industrial systems should be marked by the opposite patterns, greater diversity and less variation within a type. These predictions are the same as above.

Potential for Application

The application of culture transmission theory to the hunter-gatherer archaeological record does not require, but benefits immeasurably from, large, geographically diverse suites of data. For example, Eerkens and Bettinger (Bettinger and Eerkens 1997; Eerkens and Bettinger 2008) have made extensive use of statistics that summarize variation in a sample of more than 5,000 projectile points from nearly 40 individual site and survey collections representing all major sub-areas of the Great Basin, and more than seven thousand years of its prehistory, graciously made available by David Hurst Thomas. As detailed elsewhere (Bettinger and Eerkens 1997; Eerkens and Bettinger 2001), the coefficient of variation (CV, standard deviation divided by mean) is appropriate to the study of variation in such collections because it corrects for a near-universal scalar relationship between mean and standard deviation that prevents comparison between variables with different means using standard deviation alone. This mean–standard deviation relationship is particularly marked in Great Basin projectile points, the regression of the standard deviation on the mean being essentially identical for all major metrical variables (maximum length, axial length, maximum width, neck width, and thickness). Mean CV (CV averaged across all metrical variables) thus provides a fair representation of overall variation of a given point type in a given Great Basin collection. CV and related measures (see Eerkens and Bettinger 2001) are salient in archaeological studies of cultural transmission, which has fairly straightforward implications about artefact variation. As noted above, for example, cultural transmission will produce greater trait variation in smaller populations than larger ones.

Myriad other forces, many directly connected with environment, also affect cultural transmission and trait variation (e.g. Eerkens and Bettinger 2008). For example, three particularly well-defined Great Basin point types—Desert Side-notched, Large Side-notched, and Elko Eared—show a small but nevertheless consistent decrease in mean CV at higher latitudes ($r_{\text{Desert Side-notched}} = -.20$; $r_{\text{Large Side-notched}} = -.16$; $r_{\text{Elko Eared}} = -.10$). There are many potential explanations for this, the most likely being the greater dependence on hunting among Great Basin groups at higher latitudes ($r_{\text{latitude-hunting}} = 0.34$, $n_{\text{groups}} = 39$; Binford 2001). That projectile point mean CV decreases along with this suggests the hypothesis that as hunting becomes more important, hunters are increasingly inclined to standardize the projectile points they use, perhaps by more carefully copying the points knapped by good hunters, Desert Side-notched, Large Side-notched, and Elko Eared all showing this basic environmental relationship. Figure 54.1 shows these relationships for these three point styles, graphing the mean CV by latitude.

Environment, however, is unlikely to account for differences across these same three point types in the relationship between mean CV and sample size. In theory, mean CV should vary independently of sample size; it will vary more across small samples than large ones drawn from the same population, but the mean of many small samples and many large samples, both measuring mean CV, should be the same. This expectation holds for Large Side-notched and Elko Eared points, where the effect of sample size on mean CV is weak and conflicting, slightly increasing in Large Side-notched points ($r_{\text{Large Side-notched}} = 0.06$), slightly decreasing in Elko Eared points ($r_{\text{Elko Eared}} = -0.13$). In Desert Side-notched points, by contrast, mean CV is very strongly, and inversely, correlated with sample size

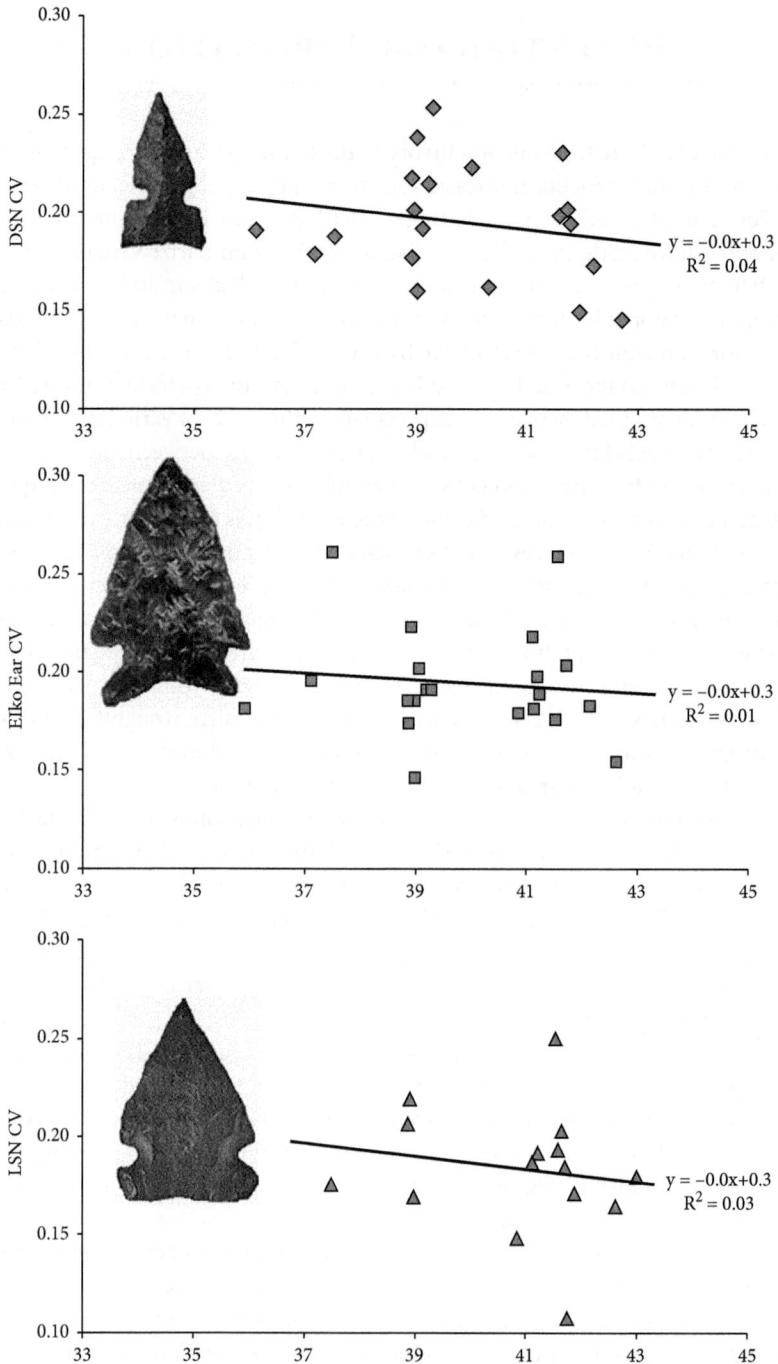

FIGURE 54.1 Variation in means, as measured by CV, with latitude in three projectile point types in the North American Great Basin. The graphs show a weak but consistent effect where points become less variable with increasing northerly latitude.

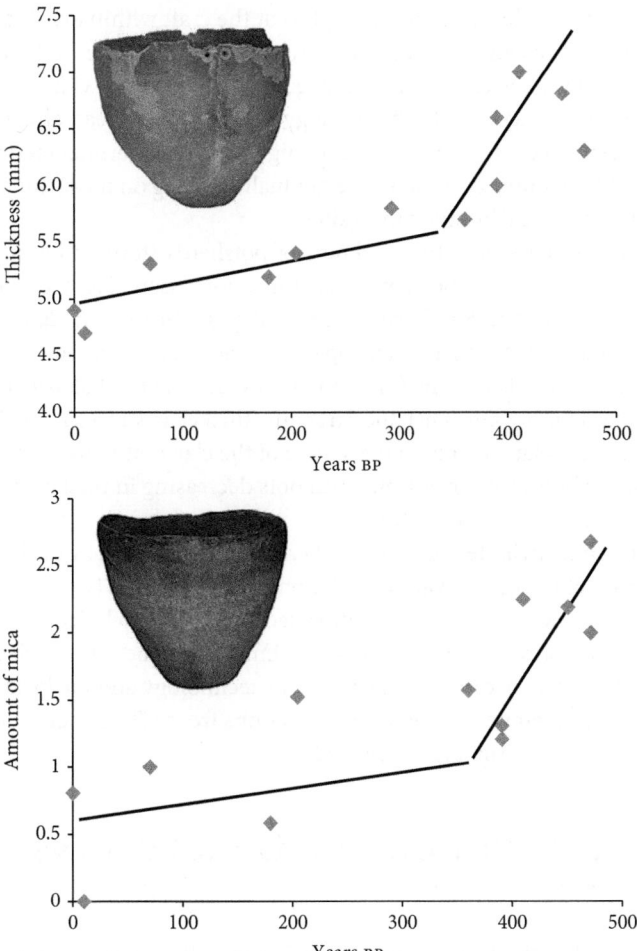

FIGURE 54.2 Variation over time in the thickness and amount of mica in pottery assemblages from radiocarbon-dated houses in southern Owens Valley. The figures show higher rates of experimentation and change before 350 BP, and less afterwards as the technology becomes commonplace.

($r_{\text{Desert Side-notched}}$ = −0.52). While sample size is jointly determined by a host of factors, including sampling intensity, that Desert Side-notched mean CV varies so strongly with sample size suggests that in this case sample size is closely tied to assemblage size, and potentially population size. While this is not a particularly strong test of the hypothesis that cultural transmission reduces trait variation in larger populations, it demonstrates the kind of data and statistics appropriate to testing the implications of cultural transmission theory in the archaeological record.

A second case study examines variation over time rather than space. Theory in both biology (e.g. Gould et al. 1977) and anthropology (e.g. Lyman et al. 2009) predicts that new forms typically exhibit a period of rapid innovation or diversification following their introduction, with gradual winnowing thereafter and a slowing of innovation. Following the adoption of a new technology, people attempt to fit the craft within existing social systems and learn to use local resources to fashion those goods. The hunter-gatherers of southern Owens Valley in south-eastern California began experimenting with ceramic technologies around 1,200 years ago and the technology became widespread about 700 years ago (Eerkens 2003; Eerkens et al. 1999). We expect high rates of experimentation following the introduction of this technology, with people gradually settling on the forms and production techniques that best fit local lifestyles thereafter.

Figure 54.2 shows changes in the thickness of potsherds (top) and a qualitative measure of the amount of mica (bottom) over time, for assemblages of potsherds from radiocarbon-dated houses in Southern Owens Valley, south-eastern California. Two pots are also shown, one in each panel, as examples of typical forms for this ceramic tradition. Thickness is believed to relate to the function of pots, especially a balance between heating efficiency (thinner is more efficient) and strength (thicker is stronger), while the amount of mica is believed to relate mainly to the source of the clay that potters used. As shown in the figure, both attributes vary over time, with pots decreasing in thickness and decreasing in the amount of mica that is present. However, the rate of change is faster earlier in time, before 350 BP, for both attributes, and slower thereafter, as indicated by the black trend lines. Greater experimentation, or innovation, with potting technologies is evident early when the craft was relatively new. This experimentation seems to have included changing the form of pots as well as the sources of clay. After 350 BP, innovation and rates of change slowed for these attributes as potters became familiar with the technology and the local sources of raw material (e.g. clay and temper). Again, the predictions from CT are borne out by archaeological data collected at the right temporal scale.

Discussion and Conclusions

At its most basic, CT is simply a means to explain how cultural information is transmitted between individuals. This is how CT theory was applied in the early part of the twentieth century. However, in the last several decades CT theory-building and modelling exercises now provide archaeologists with a rich explanatory framework to interpret and make predictions about the archaeological record, especially at different temporal and spatial scales.

In our view, the most powerful aspects of CT relate to predictions about variation and diversity in material culture, and changes over time and space therein. Although the majority of these predictions relate to other aspects of human societies, some of these predictions are of special relevance to hunter-gatherers. Thus, the population size and density of most hunter-gatherers, the types of tools they tend to produce, and the means by which they transmit culture (verbally and visually), are likely to structure the material culture left behind by such peoples. In particular, CT theory predicts a more limited range of tools (i.e. less diversity) for hunter-gatherers, but greater variation within a particular tool type, compared to subsistence strategies that support higher population densities.

One interesting aspect of these predictions regards the rate of evolutionary change within such material technologies. Rates of change in the diversity of technologies should be strongly and positively linked to population size. On the other hand, rates of change within a particular technology should not, but may be more strongly tied to the amount of time a technology has been used within a particular socio-economic setting. Thus, hunter-gatherer ceramic or bow-and-arrow technologies should change just as rapidly (and we specifically refer to change in within-type variation), if not more so owing to higher copying error, or drift-like effects, than agricultural or industrial ones. Of course, such changes may degrade the functionality of certain implements, which may cause them to be abandoned.

Owing to the nature of the data we collect, namely material culture as it appeared at different points in space and time, archaeology has much to contribute to CT studies. Testing hypotheses derived from theory with actual data is one aspect of this, but we hope that future research will also contribute to CT theory building. As we have shown, certain aspects of hunter-gatherer culture, especially long-term evolutionary change, can be informed and understood by CT. We hope that others will agree and continue to apply these ideas to other parts of the archaeological and ethnographic record.

References

Bentley, R. A. 2005. Academic copying, archaeology and the English language. *Antiquity* 80, 196–201.

Bentley, R. A. and Shennan, S. J. 2003. Cultural transmission and stochastic network growth. *American Antiquity* 68, 459–85.

Bettinger, R. L. and Eerkens, J. W. 1997. Evolutionary implications of metrical variation in Great Basin projectile points. In M. Barton and Clark, G. (eds) *Rediscovering Darwin: evolutionary theory and archaeological explanation*, 177–91. Washington DC: American Anthropological Association.

Bettinger, R. L. and Eerkens, J. W. 1999. Point typologies, social transmission and the introduction of bow and arrow technology in the Great Basin. *American Antiquity* 64, 231–42.

Binford, L. R. 2001. *Constructing frames of reference: an analytical method for archaeological theory building using ethnographic and environmental data sets*. Berkeley: University of California Press.

Boas, F. 1896. The limitations of the comparative method in anthropology. *Science* 4, 901–7.

Bonner, J. T. 1980. *The evolution of culture in animals*. Princeton: Princeton University Press.

Boyd, R. and Richerson, P. J. 1985. *Culture and the evolutionary process*. Chicago: University of Chicago Press.

Boyd, R. and Richerson, P. J. 1996. Why culture is common but cultural evolution is rare. *Proceedings of the British Academy* 88, 73–93.

Brown, C. and Laland, K. N. 2003. Social learning in fishes: a review. *Fish and Fisheries* 4, 280–8.

Caro, T. and Hauser, M. D. 1991. Is there teaching in nonhuman animals? *Quarterly Review of Biology* 67, 151–74.

Cavalli-Sforza, L. L. and Feldman, M. W. 1981. *Cultural transmission and evolution: a quantitative approach*. Princeton: Princeton University Press.

Csibra, G. and Gergely, G. 2009. Natural pedagogy. *Trends in Cognitive Sciences* 13, 148–53.

Diamond, J. 1998. *Guns, germs, and steel: the fates of human societies*. New York: W. W. Norton.

Donald, M. 1991. *Origins of the modern mind: three stages in the evolution of culture and cognition*. Cambridge, MA: Harvard University Press.

Dunnell, R. C. 1978. Style and function: a fundamental dichotomy. *American Antiquity* 43, 192–202.

Dunnell, R. C. 1981. Evolutionary theory and archaeology. In M. B. Schiffer (ed.), *Advances in archaeological method and theory: selections for students*, 35–99. New York: Academic Press.

Eerkens, J. W. 2000. Practice makes within 5% of perfect: the role of visual perception, motor skills, and human memory in artifact variation and standardization. *Current Anthropology* 41, 663–8.

Eerkens, J. W. 2003. Towards a chronology of brownware pottery in the Western Great Basin: a case study from Owens Valley. *North American Archaeologist* 24, 1–27.

Eerkens, J. W. and Bettinger, R. L. 2001. Techniques for assessing standardization in artifact assemblages: can we scale material variability? *American Antiquity* 66, 493–504.

Eerkens, J. W. and Bettinger, R. L. 2008. Cultural transmission and the analysis of stylistic and functional variation. In M. J. O'Brien (ed.), *Cultural transmission and archaeology: issues and case-studies*, 21–38. Washington DC: SAA Press.

Eerkens, J. W. and Lipo, C. P. 2005. Cultural transmission, copying errors, and the generation of variation in material culture and the archaeological record. *Journal of Anthropological Archaeology* 24, 316–34.

Eerkens, J. W. and Lipo, C. P. 2007. Cultural transmission theory and the archaeological record: providing context to understanding variation and temporal changes in material culture. *Journal of Archaeological Research* 15, 239–74.

Eerkens, J. W., Neff, H., and Glascock, M. D. 1999. Early pottery from Sun'gava and implications for the development of ceramics on Owens Valley. *Journal of California and Great Basin Anthropology* 21, 275–85.

Efferson, C., Lalive, R., Richerson, P. J., McElreath, R., and Lubell, M. 2008. Conformists and mavericks: the empirics of frequency-dependent cultural transmission. *Evolution and Human Behavior* 29, 56–64.

Ewens, W. J. 1979. *Mathematical population genetics*. Berlin: Springer Verlag.

Fried, M. H. 1967. *The evolution of political society: an essay in political anthropology*. New York: Random House.

Gabora, L. M. 2004. Ideas are not replicators but minds are. *Biology and Philosophy* 19, 127–43.

Gell-Mann, M. and Lloyd, S. 2003. *Effective complexity*. Santa Fe, NM: Santa Fe Institute Working Paper 03-12-068.

Gergely, G., Egyed, K., and Király, I. 2007. On pedagogy. *Developmental Science* 10, 139–46.

Gingerich, P. D. 1982. Time resolution in mammalian evolution: sampling, lineages and faunal turnover. *Proceedings of the Third North American Paleontological Convention, Montreal* 1, 205–10.

Gould, S. J., Raup, D. M., Sepkoski Jr., J. J., Schopf, T. J. M., and Simberloff, D. S. 1977. The shape of evolution: a comparison of real and random clades. *Paleobiology* 3, 23–40.

Hatch, E. 1973. *Theories of man and culture*. New York: Columbia University Press.

Henrich, J. 2004. Demography and cultural evolution: why adaptive cultural processes produced maladaptive losses in Tasmania. *American Antiquity* 69, 197–221.

Henrich, J. and Boyd, R. 1998. The evolution of conformist transmission and between-group differences. *Evolution and Human Behavior* 19, 215–42.

Henrich, J. and McElreath, R. 2003. The evolution of cultural evolution. *Evolutionary Anthropology* 12, 123–35.

Henrich, J., McElreath, R., Barr, A., Ensminger, J., Barrett, C., Bolyanatz, A., Cardenas, J. C., Gurven, M., Gwako, E., Henrich, N., Lesorogol, C., Marlowe, F., Tracer, D., and Ziker, J. 2006. Costly punishment across human societies. *Science* 312, 1767–70.

Holmes, W. H. 1886. *Ancient pottery of the Mississippi Valley*. Fourth Annual Report of the Bureau of Ethnology, 1882–1883, 361–436. Washington, DC: Smithsonian Institution.

Kelly, R. L. 1995. *The foraging spectrum: diversity in hunter-gatherer lifeways.* Washington, DC: Smithsonian Institution.

Kerst, S. M. and Howard Jr., J. H. 1984. Magnitude estimates of perceived and remembered length and area. *Bulletin of the Psychonomic Society* 22, 517–20.

Kline, M. A. and Boyd, R. 2010. Population size predicts technological complexity in Oceania. *Proceedings of the Royal Society B: Biological Sciences* 277, 2559–64.

Kroeber, A. L. 1916. *Zuni Potsherds. Anthropological Paper, No. 18, Part 1.* New York: American Museum of Natural History.

Kroeber, A. L. 1940. Statistical classification. *American Antiquity* 6, 29–44.

Krützen, M., Mann, J., Heithaus, M. R., Connor, R. C., Bejder, L., and Sherwin, W. B. 2005. Cultural transmission of tool use in bottlenose dolphins. *Proceedings of the National Academy of Sciences USA* 102, 8939–43.

Lachnit, H. and Wolfgang, P. 1990. Speed and accuracy effects of fingers and dexterity in 5-choice reaction tasks. *Ergonomics* 33, 1443–54.

Laland, K. N. and O'Brien, M. J. 2010. Niche construction theory and archaeology. *Journal of Archaeological Method and Theory* 17, 303–22.

Laland, K. N., Odling-Smee, J., and Myles, S. 2010. How culture shaped the human genome: bringing genetics and the human sciences together. *Nature Reviews Genetics* 11, 137–48.

Lyman, R. L., VanPool, T. L., and O'Brien, M. J. 2009. The diversity of North American projectile-point types, before and after the bow and arrow. *Journal of Anthropological Archaeology* 28, 1–13.

McElreath, R., Bell, A. V., Efferson, C., Lubell, M., Richerson, P. J., and Waring, T. 2008. Beyond existence and aiming outside the laboratory: estimating frequency-dependent and payoff-biased social learning strategies. *Philosophical Transactions of the Royal Society B: Biological Sciences* 363, 3515–28.

Mesoudi, A. 2007. Using the methods of experimental social psychology to study cultural evolution. *Journal of Social, Evolutionary, and Cultural Psychology* 1, 35–58.

Mesoudi, A. and Lycett S. J. 2009. Random copying, frequency-dependent copying and culture change. *Evolution and Human Behavior* 30, 41–8.

Mesoudi, A. and O'Brien, M. J. 2008. The cultural transmission of Great Basin projectile point technology I: an experimental simulation. *American Antiquity* 73, 3–28.

Mesoudi, A. and Whiten, A. 2004. The hierarchical transformation of event knowledge in human cultural transmission. *Journal of Cognition and Culture* 4, 1–24.

Meyn, S. P. and Tweedie, R. L. 1993. *Markov chains and stochastic stability.* London: Springer-Verlag.

Moyer, R. S., Bradley, D. R., Sorenson, M. H., Whiting, J. C., and Mansfield, D. P. 1978. Psychophysical functions for perceived and remembered size. *Science* 200, 330–2.

O'Brien, M. J. (ed.) 2008. *Cultural transmission and archaeology: issues and case-studies.* Washington, DC: Society for American Archaeology Press.

O'Brien, M. J. and Lyman, R. L. 2002. The epistemological nature of archaeological units. *Anthropological Theory* 2, 37–56.

Petrie, W. M. F. 1899. Sequences in prehistoric remains. *Journal of the Royal Anthropological Institute of Great Britain and Ireland* 29, 295–301.

Poole, J. H., Tyack, P. L., Stoeger-Horwath, A. S., and Watwood, S. 2005. Animal behaviour: elephants are capable of vocal learning. *Nature* 434, 455–6.

Powell, A., Shennan, S., and Thomas, M. G. 2009. Late Pleistocene demography and the appearance of modern human behavior. *Science* 324, 1298–301.

Richerson, P. J. and Boyd, R. 2010. Why possibly language evolved. *Biolinguistics* 4, 289–306.

Richerson, P. J., Boyd, R., and Bettinger, R. L. 2009. Cultural innovations and demographic change. *Human Biology* 81, 211–35.

Rockman, M. 2009. Landscape learning in relation to evolutionary theory. In A. Prentiss, I. Kuijt, and J. C. Chatters (eds), *Macroevolution in human prehistory*, 51–71 New York: Springer.

Rogers, D. S. and Ehrlich, P. R. 2008. Natural selection and cultural rates of change. *Proceedings of the National Academy of Sciences USA* 105, 3416–3420.

Service, E. R. 1962. *Primitive social organisation: an evolutionary perspective*. New York: Random House.

Shennan, S. J. 2001. Demography and cultural innovation: a model and its implications for the emergence of modern human culture. *Cambridge Archaeological Journal* 11, 5–16.

Shennan, S. J. 2006. From cultural history to cultural evolution: an archaeological perspective on social information transmission. In J. C. K. Wells, S. Strickland, and K. N. Laland (eds), *Social information transmission and human biology*, 173–90. London: CRC Press.

Slater, P. J. B. and Ince, S. A. 1979. Cultural evolution in chaffinch song. *Behavior* 71, 146–66.

Spencer, C. 1993. Human agency, biased transmission, and the cultural evolution of chiefly authority. *Journal of Anthropological Archaeology* 12, 41–74.

Sperber, D. 1996. *Explaining culture: a naturalistic approach*. Oxford: Blackwell.

Tehrani, J. J. and Riede, F. 2008. Towards an archaeology of pedagogy: learning, teaching and the generation of material culture traditions. *World Archaeology* 40, 316–31.

Thornton, A. and Raihani, N. J. 2008. The evolution of teaching. *Animal Behaviour* 75, 1823–36.

Tomasello, M. 1996. Do apes ape? In C. M. Heyes and B. G. Galef (eds), *Social learning in animals: the roots of culture*, 319–46. New York: Academic Press.

Tomasello, M. 1999. *The cultural origins of human cognition*. Cambridge, MA: Harvard University Press.

Whiten, A. and Custance, D. 1996. Studies in imitation in chimpanzees and children. In C. M. Heyes and B. G. Galef (eds), *Social learning in animals: the roots of culture*, 291–318. New York: Academic Press.

Winterhalder, B. W., Baillargeon, F., Cappelleto, R., Daniel, R., and Prescott, C. 1988. The population dynamics of hunter-gatherers and their prey. *Journal of Anthropological Archaeology* 7, 289–328.

CHAPTER 55

ARCHAEOGENETICS OF AFRICA AND OF THE AFRICAN HUNTER-GATHERERS

VIKTOR ČERNÝ AND LUÍSA PEREIRA

ARCHAEOGENETICS deals with the population history of humans and other species (Renfrew and Boyle 2000). A main source of information is the genetic variability of ancient DNA (aDNA) extracted directly from fossil material, mostly bones and teeth. This is, however, quite tricky as the authentication (proving that the DNA really comes from the fossil in question) is extremely difficult, particularly in the case of modern human remains due to the high risk of contamination during the handling of samples. Nevertheless, some advances in this field were recently achieved and promise more reliable results (Brotherton et al. 2007), but it is mainly the remains found in colder climatic regions that have provided usable data (Krause et al. 2010; Rasmussen et al. 2010).

The second source of archaeogenetic information widely used today is embedded in the contemporary genetic diversity. The genetic structure of the extant populations reflects its history, especially demographically important past events such as expansions, contractions, gene flow, and admixtures (Jobling et al. 2004). Population geneticists put a great effort into untangling these past population phenomena in our contemporary genetic structure, taking advantage of technological developments to extensively characterize genetic diversity at a worldwide scale. Concomitantly, improvements in statistical analysis and computer tools have been accomplished, enabling one to handle increasingly available genetic data (Bandelt et al. 1995; 1999; Drummond and Rambaut 2007; Drummond et al. 2005; Felsenstein 1993; Kumar et al. 1993; Schneider et al. 2000).

Uniparentally inherited genetic markers such as mitochondrial DNA (mtDNA) and most of the Y chromosome (the non-recombining part of the Y chromosome; NRY) have been particularly important for the archaeogenetic research. These specific parts of our genome do not recombine and their diversity is therefore accumulated exclusively by new mutations. As a consequence of the absence of recombination, mtDNA and NRY are transmitted in blocks, known as haplotypes. Present haplotypes differ in the number of mutations occurring along time, due to the divergence from a common ancestor. Haplotypes that are closely related, sharing mutations by ancestry, constitute a haplogroup. For the sake of simplicity, the haplogroup nomenclature follows a letter code (from A to Z), with newly discovered haplogroups receiving the next available alphabetical letter; sub-haplogroups receive a number (e.g. sub-haplogroups A1 and A2), followed by a letter, and so on (sub-groups of A1 are called A1a, A1b, etc).

Most mutations occurring in the human genome are neutral, not leading to effects on the phenotype of individuals, and as a consequence they accumulate over time at a constant rate, designated as the 'mutation rate'. It was found that the mutation rate in mtDNA is approximately 10 times higher than in nuclear DNA, leading that molecule to accumulate a higher genetic diversity within a shorter range of time (Excoffier and Yang 1999; Hasegawa et al. 1993). The date of a calibrated moment in evolution can be applied to calculate the time necessary for the accumulation of the observed diversity since divergence from the most recent common ancestor (TMRCA). In humans, the most frequently used episode for calibration is the moment of branching between the human and chimpanzee lineages (some 5–7 million years ago), but more recently, well-dated archaeological episodes within the human population history have been used in a Bayesian framework (Endicott et al. 2009).

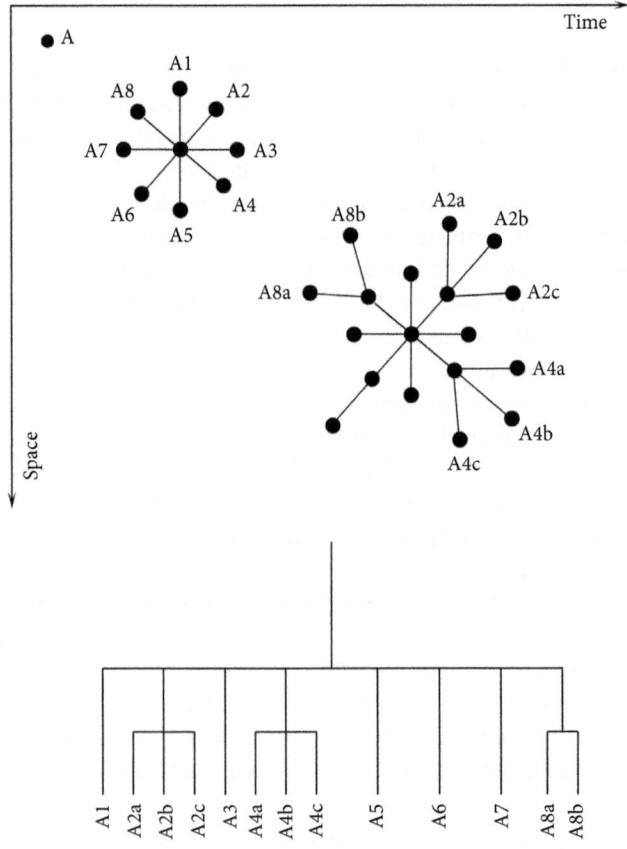

FIGURE 55.1 Schematic formation of a haplogroup; the constituent haplotypes emerge in certain time and space—A1, A5, A6 and A7 being older than A2a, A2b, A2c, A4a, A4b, A4c, A8a, and A8b.

Humans have lived, for most of their existence on earth, as hunter-gatherers highly dependent on their natural environment. Their populations thus experienced expansions followed by contractions according to changing climatic fluctuations in the past (Forster 2004). Logically, in times of more favourable conditions in some places of the world some fortunate haplotypes increased numerically and became new ancestors, but others died out. This is another important point when considering archaeogenetic thinking.

The current knowledge about both mtDNA and NRY human trees is extensive (see online updated phylogeny for mtDNA on http://www.phylotree.org/ and for NRY on http://www.isogg.org/tree/), with the main basal branches being already well defined but some refinements being contributed for the younger branches as new data become available. These trees are inferred by coalescence methods, finding common ancestors for current sequences, going from present to past. Those ancestors or haplogroup founders can be dated as explained above. Interestingly, a geographic distribution can be imposed on the human trees for the uniparental markers, with certain haplogroups being characteristic of African, others typical of the Asian, and others observed more frequently in European, Australian, Oceanian, or American populations. This observation in humans and in other species led to the emergence of a new research field named phylogeography (Avise 2000), which provides information about where and when ancestral and derived haplotypes originated. Figure 55.1 shows schematically how migration distributes haplotypes along time and space.

More recently, genome-wide screenings of single nucleotide polymorphisms (SNP) or resequencing of selectively neutral loci in autosomes are beginning to provide another insight into population genetic history (Gutenkunst et al. 2009; Li et al. 2008) and are complementing information obtained from the uniparental markers. These studies have been devoted to choosing between alternative scenarios of human evolution, and have been conducted in several human populations, including African hunter-gatherers.

African Archaeogenetics

Information about African archaeogenetics began to be gathered from mtDNA studies, and afterwards broadly confirmed by NRY and nuclear DNA results.

The African mtDNA haplotypes are classified as haplogroups L0 to L6 (Behar et al. 2008). The root of the sub-Saharan mtDNA L-phylogeny is situated at ~200 ka (thousands of years ago) (Behar et al. 2008; Gonder et al. 2007; Ingman et al. 2000; Torroni et al. 2006), coinciding chronologically with independent palaeoanthropological findings of the oldest fossils of anatomically modern humans (Haile-Selassie et al. 2004; McDougall et al. 2005; 2008).

The first branching of the human mtDNA tree occurs between haplogroup L0 and all the others (Figure 55.2a), with each branch having a large number of derived lineages distributed in sub-Saharan Africa (Černý et al. 2007; Pereira et al. 2001; Salas et al. 2002; Watson et al. 1997). Interestingly, the first split of the tree represented by the L0 leads to clades L0d and L0k, which are carried almost exclusively by the Khoisan hunter-gatherers of South Africa (Behar et al. 2008).

One of the most important demographic expansions within but also out of Africa can be demonstrated by the internal variation of the haplogroup called L3. In fact, L3 encompasses not only many sub-Saharan Africans but also all non-African mtDNA lineages such as

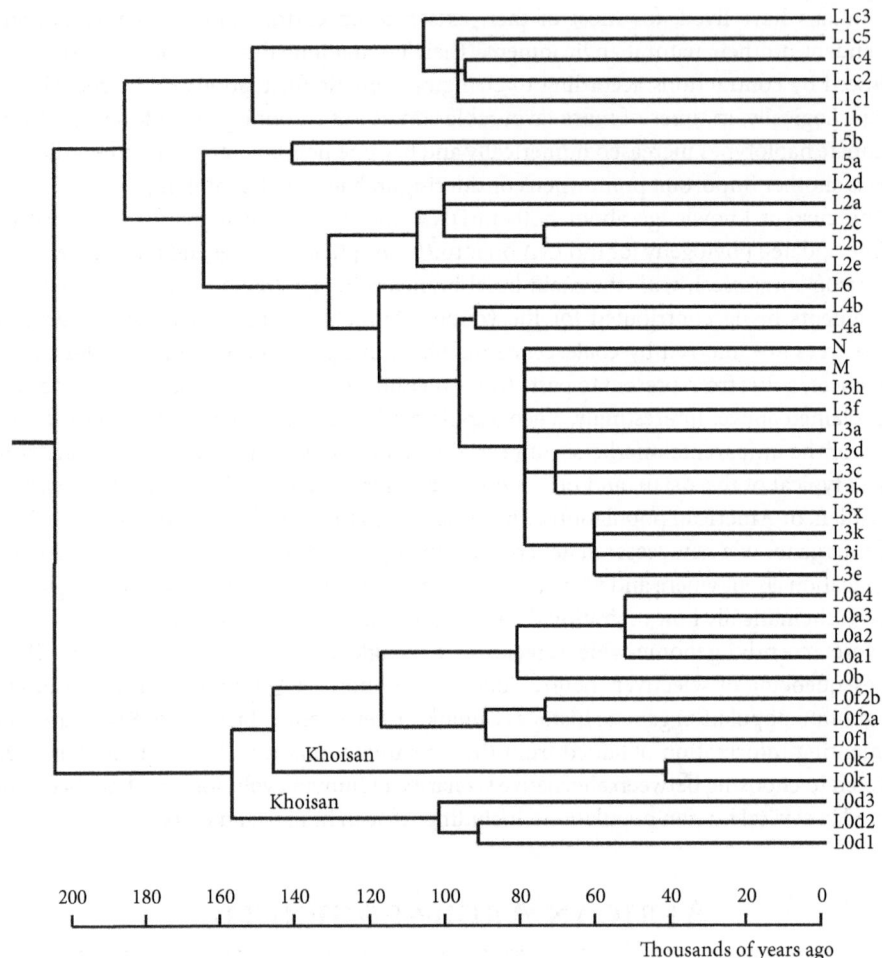

FIGURE 55.2 African mtDNA phylogeny showing the root ~200 ka, the divergence of the Khoisan pool ~100 ka, and first non-African diversification some ~70 ka.

M and N. The age estimate of L3 provides, therefore, an upper bound for the modern human dispersal out of Africa. By conducting a recent analysis of 369 complete L3 sequences collected across the African continent (Soares et al. 2012), we have placed this maximum at ~70 ka, ruling out a biologically successful exit of our mtDNA ancestors in MIS-5 (~130–74 ka) as suggested by recent archaeological Middle Palaeolithic findings in Arabia (Armitage et al. 2011; Rose et al. 2011). In spite of the very weakly represented Late Palaeolithic record in Arabia (Groucutt and Petraglia 2012), the Arabian and west Eurasian mtDNA data we recently analysed support the continual human presence in Arabia or in broader Near East from ~65 ka until today (Fernandes et al. 2012).

Some younger L haplotypes can also be found in neighbouring regions such as North Africa, where they spread in the Late Pleistocene in the case of L3k (Soares et al. 2012), or Southern Arabia, India, and the Americas, where they have been introduced more recently due to the slave trade (Černý et al. 2008; Eaaswarkhanth et al. 2010; Richards et al. 2003;

Salas et al. 2004). On the other hand, many 'back to Africa' migrations took place, enriching the African gene pool with haplogroups evolved beyond Africa such as U6 and M1 in the Late Pleistocene (Gonzalez et al. 2007; Olivieri et al. 2006), and later on in the Holocene some younger offshoots of the mtDNA tree such as U5 (Achilli et al. 2005), R0a (Černý et al. 2011a), HV1 (Musilová et al. 2011), H and V (Ennafaa et al. 2009; Pereira et al. 2010), and T2 (Kujanová et al. 2009). However, for the most part these migrations reached only northern and eastern Africa, while the bulk of the sub-Saharan gene pool stayed relatively undisturbed. The results of mtDNA data showing admixtures in North Africa were recently confirmed by the autosomal SNP data (Henn et al. 2012).

Identification of the NRY haplogroups was more complex due to the slower mutation rate of the Y chromosome, its predisposition to genetic drift, and longer segment to be analysed. The first haplogroups to emerge are denominated A and B, which are carried out mainly by the African hunter-gatherers (Karafet et al. 2008), and a detailed analyses of these clades (Cruciani et al. 2011) allowed to date the root of the NRY tree around ~142 ka (Figure 55.2b). Similarly to the mtDNA, the NRY African gene pool was further enriched by several non-African clades such as E and R (Arredi et al. 2010; Cruciani et al. 2010).

Hunter-Gatherers in Africa

Africa is the best place for the study of hunter-gatherers as it possesses the longest and the most continuous history of this pristine human subsistence pattern. If we consider only anatomically modern humans, the story of the contemporary African hunter-gatherer lifestyle starts ~200 ka (Willoughby 2007) and is in some way still continuing. However, the extant hunter-gatherers are reduced today to numerically very small groups; perhaps only about 25,000 people still maintain the hunter-gatherer lifestyle (Lee and Daly 1999). These people live in various natural settings from desert (the Khoisan), through the Savannah (the Hadza), to the tropical rainforests (Pygmies). It should be noted that apart from the above mentioned foragers, several other groups maintain occasionally hunting-gathering activities as evidenced for example from the Lake Chad Basin (Nicolaisen 2010).

Physical Features

Short stature is the common feature of the 'full-time' hunter-gatherers in Africa. Several adaptation hypotheses such as thermoregulation needs, easier locomotion, economy of energetic requirements, and endurance against starvation have been raised to explain it (Cavalli-Sforza 1986; Pennington 2001). Extremely small stature can be found especially in the Pygmies from central and western Africa. For example, the so called eastern Pygmies living in the Ituri forest of the Democratic Republic of the Congo measure in average ~140 cm and are ranged among the smallest people on earth (Cavalli-Sforza 1986). Their short stature is caused by the absence of a growth spurt in adolescence and it seems that it might have evolved merely as a by-product of selection for early onset of reproduction in order to counterbalance the high mortality of their population (Migliano et al. 2007).

However, the above-mentioned adaptive hypotheses are not mutually exclusive and must be considered together when trying to understand the small stature or so-called 'Pygmy phenotype' (Perry and Dominy 2009). Nevertheless, since the taller Pygmy individuals show more signs of admixture with non-Pygmies, the low stature of these African hunters is probably determined by genetic factors (Becker et al. 2011).

The South African Khoisan people can also be easily distinguished from their common neighbours. They have a small and gracile stature too, and the presence of eye folds, light yellow-brown skin colour, and 'peppercorn' hair are among the first traits that can be remarked on in almost all individuals. A more striking feature, usually seen in women (however, not observed in all individuals), is the steatopygia, the accumulation of fat over the buttocks and thighs, causing sometimes very strong lumbar lordosis (Krut and Singer 1963). It is considered to be an adaptation to food shortage, but this is not yet scientifically proven. Also, some genital features such as macronymphia, the elongation of the labia minora in females, and the horizontal position of the penis in males, have been stereotypically repeated in some anthropological textbooks (Hiernaux 1974). A linguistically interesting feature of the Khoisan people is the presence of phonemes called 'click' consonants.

Interestingly, all the above mentioned contemporary African hunter-gatherers differ from their agricultural neighbours by their gracile body with short stature. However, the Late Palaeolithic and Mesolithic hunter-gatherers, at least those from north-eastern and north-western Africa, where their skeletons have been unearthed (Dutour 1989; Greene and Armelagos 1972), were rather robust and it seems that only after the adoption of agriculture did their skull and body proportions reduce (Calcagno 1986; Carlson 1976; Carlson and Van Gerven 1977). It seems, therefore, that our knowledge of the ancient African hunter-gatherer population is still unsatisfactory. Nevertheless, a greater level of genetic variation and population structure can be expected in Middle and Late Pleistocene Africa as has been reported from the study of cranial remains (Gunz et al. 2009; Lahr 1996).

Only very small and scattered groups of hunter-gatherers still exist in East Africa, the Hadza of northern Tanzania. This group does not show the characteristic physical traits of the Khoisan or Pygmies, resembling more or less their Bantu neighbours (Hiernaux 1974). The only feature that the Hadza and the neighbouring agricultural Sandawe share with the Khoisan is the presence of 'click' consonants in their language.

Reproduction and Marital Exchanges

One of the most important biosocial features of the African hunter-gatherers is the role of women, and their supposed lower reproduction rate, which is potentially related to higher mobility. In practically all forager groups, men are hunters (and only occasionally gatherers) but women are only gatherers and usually more vegetable food is consumed than meat. Consequently, as an example of the most studied group of the Khoisan—the !Kung women provide about two thirds of all food consumed (Howell 1979; Lee 1979). It has been observed that when looking for daily food, together with the burden of 7–15 kg, a !Kung woman has to carry her children up to four years old and walk up to 20 km per day. It was shown that the inter-birth interval of the !Kung women is longer than in a still pronatalist and non-contracepting population of African farmers such as the Dogon from Mali (Strassmann and Warner 1998).

Logically, as a consequence of the longer inter-birth interval of hunter-gatherers, fertility should thus be much lower than in sedentary agricultural society. However, it was shown that the total fertility rate is rather variable among African foragers, and probably not much different from that of farmers (Blurton Jones et al. 1992). It has been further suggested that sexually transmitted diseases (such as gonorrhoea and chlamydia) introduced to some foragers groups via recent contacts with farmers can be a more important factor than mobility in reducing the growth rate of some contemporary hunter-gatherers. It has also been shown that hunter-gatherer demography is quite dynamic, displaying periods of rapid growth and decline, as observed in general in our species' history (Pennington 2001). Nevertheless, the worldwide comparison of the subsistence patterns and demography in human populations showed a higher mean total fertility rate in intensive agriculturalists (Sellen and Mace 1997).

The African hunter-gatherers provide an illuminating example of asymmetric mating exchanges. This has been especially well described in the Pygmies. The fact that Pygmy girls are relatively frequently married out into an agricultural family and that the opposite case is extremely rare was observed by the Czech anthropologist Pavel Schebesta, who studied the African Pygmies in the Ituri rainforest in the 1920s and 1930s (Schebesta and Lebzelter 1933). These asymmetric mating exchanges between Pygmy hunter-gatherers and Bantu farmers were later confirmed by the anthropologists working with the same populations several generations later (Bailey 1991; Cavalli-Sforza 1986).

Genetic Legacy

A few extant African population groups practising a hunter-gatherer subsistence have been surveyed in population genetics since the early application of classical genetic markers (Cavalli-Sforza et al. 1994). Nowadays, these populations continue to be investigated through mtDNA and NRY, which due to their particular characteristics mentioned above (no-recombination and lower effective population size), allow new insights into their population history. More recently some studies have also been devoted to investigating the nuclear DNA data of the African hunter-gatherers. There is now growing evidence that without the genetic diversity of these numerically small groups of foragers our understanding of the population history of Africa would be insufficient.

Population constancy. The demographic histories of the mtDNA and NRY gene pools of African hunter-gatherers (mainly Khoisan and Pygmies) and their Bantu neighbours were approached by applying standard genetic measures and by evaluating the fit to population size models. The statistical analysis of more than 4,000 mtDNA hypervariable segment I (HVS-I) sequences on worldwide populations (Excoffier and Schneider 1999) revealed current signs of Pleistocene expansions for most human populations, except for some groups of hunter-gatherers who passed through a strong founder effect. The population samples analysed in the Excoffier and Schneider study included the !Kung and Pygmies from Africa, as well as Australian Aborigines, the Mukhri from India, and four Saami groups from northern Europe.

The loss of the genetic signs of Pleistocene expansion in the extant hunter-gatherers is, according to some authors, due to the occurrence of recent bottlenecks associated with the agricultural expansion of farmers, who established social inequalities and blocked the current migration rate among hunter-gatherer sub-populations (Destro-Bisol et al. 2004b). We also showed that the hunter-gatherers do not display statistically significant values for the selective neutrality tests, a feature quite common for all farmer populations (Pereira et al. 2001) but, interestingly, not always for the pastoral nomads (Černý et al. 2011b). This also means that hunter-gatherers show population constancy in opposition to the expanded farmer populations.

The fit to models of constancy vs. expansion population dynamics was later tested on 6.6 kb of non-coding NRY region and on 780 bp of the mtDNA cytochrome c oxidase sub-unit III in some African farmers and hunter-gatherers (Pilkington et al. 2008). This study applied a greater number of statistical tests, which concordantly led to the observation that the patterns of mtDNA variation fit better a model of constant population size for hunter-gatherers and a model of population expansion for farmer populations. On the other hand, the NRY polymorphism pattern does not show evidence for growth for either population group. The authors concluded that these differences most probably reflect sex-biased demographic processes in the recent history of African populations, in particular, asymmetrical gene flow and/or reduced male effective population sizes, although Pleistocene changes of population sizes could have been a cause for the current observations as well.

Further evidence for recent sex-biased demographic processes was provided by the study of 50 NRY biallelic markers in 1,122 individuals from 40 African populations (Wood et al. 2005), comparing it with 1,918 HVS-I sequences in individuals from 39 African populations. For NRY there was a strong partial correlation between genetic and linguistic distances and no correlation between genetic and geographic distances; while for mtDNA both genetic–linguistic and genetic–geographic distances were weakly correlated. When the Bantu population samples are removed from the analyses, the correlation with linguistic variation disappears for the NRY and strengthens for mtDNA. The authors inferred that sex-biased admixture rates and/or language borrowing between expanding farmers and local hunter-gatherers played an important role in influencing the African genetic landscape.

The Khoisan. Cavalli-Sforza et al. (1994) compiled information from several protein and immunological polymorphisms in order to compare the Khoisan with other Africans. They found that the South African hunter-gatherers the San show the greatest genetic distance from all other African populations, while their neighbours the Khoi, who recently became cattle-herders, presented a much lower genetic distance from other Africans, probably due to a higher admixture between them and the farmers, from whom they acquired the agro-pastoral practices. According to these authors, the admixture between the Khoi and farmers occurred most probably in the Kalahari Desert ~1.5 ka. They also assayed an admixture evaluation between African and Eurasian ancestries in the Khoisan and Ethiopian populations, concluding that there was an early African–Asian admixture in the origin of the Khoisan, stronger for the San than for the Khoi. The Ethiopians also displayed a strong African–Asian admixture, but this seemed to be independent and to have occurred later on than the one observed in the Khoisan. This admixture with Asians could, according to the authors, explain the genetic difference observed between Khoisan and other Africans.

Cavalli-Sforza et al. (1994) also investigated the possible genetic relation between the Khoisan and East African populations sharing click sounds, such as the Hadza and Sandawe from Tanzania. The Hadza are hunter-gatherers, but the Sandawe have recently adopted agriculture introduced by the neighbouring Bantu-speaking peoples. Both the Hadza and Sandawe showed a high genetic distance from the San, being as similar to the Khoi as they are to any other Bantu group or to each other. Thus, this evidence did not support a common ancestry for the Khoisan and East African foragers sharing the click sounds.

The first mtDNA studies on Khoisan began to be published by the end of 1980s and in 1990s (Cann et al. 1987; Chen et al. 2000; Soodyall and Jenkins 1992; Soodyall et al. 1996; Vigilant et al. 1989; 1991). All these studies pointed to the deep phylogeny and strong isolation of both San (mainly the !Kung) and Khoi (or Khwe) populations. As mtDNA haplogroup classification and phylogenetic reconstruction have been further improving (Kivisild et al. 2006), it was possible to identify the typical Khoisan lineages, stemming directly from the root of the worldwide mtDNA tree (Ingman and Gyllensten 2001; Torroni et al. 2006). These lineages were designated as L1a (Chen et al. 2000; Watson et al. 1997), based on RFLP (restriction fragment length polymorphism) analyses, and afterwards renamed as L1d and L1k when based on sequencing of HVS-I (Pereira et al. 2001; Salas et al. 2002) and then as L0d and L0k, by incorporating further information from complete sequencing (Mishmar et al. 2003). These unique and specific Khoisan lineages have been recently investigated through complete mtDNA sequencing (Behar et al. 2008; Gonder et al. 2007; Tishkoff et al. 2007). By constructing a mtDNA phylogenetic tree with 624 complete sub-Saharan sequences, Behar et al. (2008) concluded that Khoisan matrilineal ancestry diverged from the rest of the human mtDNA pool some 90,000–150,000 years before present, remaining isolated as groups of small effective population size till ~40 ka, when the introgression of additional lineages into the Khoisan mtDNA pool occurred which accelerated much later during the Bantu expansion, some 2 ka.

The genetic isolation of the Khoisan, identifiable within the overall mtDNA African gene pool, was also reported in the comparison with the supposedly related East African populations speaking languages in which click sounds also appear, the Hadza and Sandawe (Knight et al. 2003; Tishkoff et al. 2007). No L0d lineages were observed in the Hadza and only a few in the Sandawe. In general, the Hadza and Sandawe were again genetically more similar to other neighbouring East African populations than to the Khoisan living in South Africa. Estimates for the times of divergence carried out by Tishkoff et al. (2007) were more than 35 ka between the Sandawe/Hadza and Khoisan, and more than 15 ka between the Sandawe and Hadza. Therefore, the divergence of all contemporary groups of analysed foragers was completed long before the arrival of Bantu farmers.

The mtDNA studies also led to the detection of gene flow between the Khoisan and Bantu. The Khoisan mtDNA lineages were shown to be present in South African Bantu populations, either in low frequencies of 5–7 per cent in Mozambique (Pereira et al. 2001; Salas et al. 2002) and 5 per cent in Dama (Soodyall and Jenkins 1993), or in such considerable frequencies as 25 per cent in Xhosa and 50 per cent in Zulu (Soodyall and Jenkins 1993). The opposite phenomenon, characteristic Bantu lineages (mainly L1a, L1e, L2a, L3b, and L3e) occurring in Khoisan populations, was also observed: 23 per cent in Vasikela !Kung (Chen et al. 2000); 24 per cent in Sekele !Kung (Soodyall and Jenkins 1993); and 61 per cent in Khwe (Chen et al. 2000).

The NRY studies confirmed the deep genetic ancestry of the Khoisan lineages (Semino et al. 2002; Underhill et al. 2001). The ancient haplogroup A defined by the mutations M91 and P97 in the recent update of the NRY phylogeny (Karafet et al. 2008) was described as being most frequent in the Khoisan but also in some Ethiopian and Sudanese populations. The other ancient haplogroup, designated as B (defined by mutations M60, M181, P85, and P90; Karafet et al. 2008), was also observed in the Khoisan gene pool, although it was found at the highest frequency among the Pygmies. The importance of central and north-west Africa as a possible origin of the human NRY tree has been recently suggested by more comprehensive sequencing of the above-mentioned basal lineages (Cruciani et al. 2011).

The sharing of ancient NRY haplogroups between the Khoisan and Ethiopians was initially interpreted as indicative of a common paternal history (Semino et al. 2002). Some differences detectable at the level of STR (short tandem repeats) haplotypes between the Khoisan and Ethiopian ancient lineages were further interpreted as the accumulation of differences since the divergence from the common gene pool (Semino et al. 2002). Later on, the improvement of NRY phylogenetic resolution allowed an estimation of the times of divergence between the groups—the divergence between Khoisan and Hadza of ~112 ka (Knight et al. 2003) and a separation of more than 35 ka between the Khoisan and Sandawe (Tishkoff et al. 2007). As is the case with mtDNA and autosomal microsatellites (Zhivotovsky et al. 2003), the isolation of the Khoisan, even from the populations sharing click sounds, seems thus to be quite ancient for NRY as well.

Above-mentioned features of the African hunter-gatherers such as deep common ancestry, high levels of genetic diversity, mutual differentiations among the sub-populations and various admixtures with farmers was further confirmed by genome-wide analyses (Henn et al. 2011; Pickrell et al. 2012). One of these studies (Henn et al. 2011), based on a half million of SNPs, reported further low linkage disequilibrium in many African foragers, pointing to their generally larger effective population sizes (N_e). A severe bottleneck was suggested only for the Hadza, resulting in their low recent effective population size (N_e ~2,590), which is comparatively much lower than for the Sandawe (N_e ~7,000) or the Khomani Khoisan (N_e ~11,670) for example.

A larger number of Khoisan samples analysed and representing three different language groups was recently studied through genotyping a similar number of SNPs (Pickrell et al. 2012). Here two genetically different Khoisan groups, whose population divergence was estimated ~30 ka, were identified. Interestingly, the proportions of the 'non-Khoisan' ancestry in the Khoisan sub-populations was highly variable, ranging from 6 per cent in the Northern Ju/'hoan up to 90 per cent in the Damara, and the estimates of admixture dates were not higher than 40 generations (i.e. 1,200 years), corresponding quite well with the archaeological evidence for the arrival of the Bantu farmers in the area (Pickrell et al. 2012).

Pygmies. Cavalli-Sforza et al. (1994), when analysing classical genetic markers, found that the eastern Pygmies or Mbuti are the most distant Pygmy group when compared with other Africans, followed by the western Pygmies or Aka (also Biaka and Babinga), and then by other so called 'pygmoids'. The genetic distance between the San and Pygmies was similar to the one between Pygmies and other sub-Saharan Africans, not supporting a closer relatedness between these hunter-gatherer groups.

The mtDNA gene pool of the Pygmies has been carefully investigated, leading to the identification of a haplogroup L1c, which is the most informative about their population (Destro-Bisol et al. 2004a). Investigation of the phylogeny of this haplogroup by analysing both mtDNA hypervariable segments I and II (HVS-I and HVS-II) of 455 L1c individuals resulted in an estimation of the divergence of maternal ancestors of the Bantu and western Pygmies around 60,000–30,000 years ago (Batini et al. 2007).

These conclusions were further improved by performing the HVS-I characterization of 1,404 samples from 20 Bantu and 9 Pygmy populations (Quintana-Murci et al. 2008). The authors confirmed the predominance of L1c in the western Pygmies (94.0 per cent vs. 35.7 per cent in Bantu), and further proceeded to the complete mtDNA sequencing of 27 L1c molecules. Eastern Pygmies were shown to be different from the western Pygmies as they had lineages such as L0a2, L2*, L2a2, and L5 rendering them similar to the neighbouring East African populations. This seems to suggest a diverse ancestry for both Pygmy groups.

The very frequent clade L1c1a with age estimate ~57 ka in western Pygmies (83.5 per cent) and Bantus (20.3 per cent) indicated a common maternal gene pool for both groups. The two populations seem to have diverged from an L1c ancestral population in the following way: the Bantus with their original L1c clades such as L1c1a, L1c1b, L1c1c, L1c2–6, and some others were enriched afterwards by the introgression of the L0a, L2, and L3, along with the Late Stone Age technologies leading to their massive expansion; the western Pygmies on the other hand retained L1c1a as the only surviving clade. The split of Pygmies from the ancestral population occurred no more than ~74 ka, when L1c1a began to diverge from L1c1. After a period of isolation a continuous asymmetric maternal gene flow started ~40 ka. It has taken place from the Pygmies' ancestors to the ancestors of farmers as inferred from the coalescence dates for shared L1c1a lineages (Quintana-Murci et al. 2008).

The typing of 28 autosomal STR loci in 604 unrelated individuals from 9 Pygmy and 12 non-Pygmy populations from south Cameroon and Gabon (Verdu et al. 2009) showed an ancient divergence between the ancestral western Pygmies and non-Pygmy populations, between 54–90 ka, concordant with the above-mentioned mtDNA data. However, a much more recent common origin (~2.8 ka) for individual groups of western Pygmies was also identified—in fact contemporary and congruent with the Neolithic expansion of farmers. Recent divergence of the particular groups of western Pygmies was explained by enhanced genetic drift and heterogeneous asymmetrical introgression from non-Pygmies into Pygmies (Verdu et al. 2009).

Another study (Patin et al. 2009) performed the sequencing of 24 non-coding DNA fragments (autosomal, mtDNA, Y-chromosome, and X-chromosome) in both western and eastern Pygmies and led to the following conclusions: the ancestors of Pygmies and farmers diverged ~60 ka but the western and eastern Pygmies share more recent common ancestry ~20 ka. Because their divergence still predates the arrival of the farmers it was suggested that their hunter-gathering subsistence in the equatorial rainforests together with their short stature may not be a convergent adaptation but the result of their recent common ancestry. Although the gene flow was quite low, some Pygmy groups (such as western Bakola or eastern Twa) seemed to be more admixed than others (Patin et al. 2009).

In total, 117 samples of the Khoisan, eastern and western Pygmies, together with Niger-Congo agriculturalists, were further analysed for the variation in the 40 non-coding autosomal loci each ~2 kb long (Veeramah et al. 2012). The study shows, in accordance with the results on other polymorphisms (Behar et al. 2008; Knight et al. 2003; Zhivotovsky et al. 2003), that the ancestral population of the Khoisan people diverged ~111 ka, that of Pygmies ~49 ka, and that of eastern and western Pygmies ~32 ka. The estimates of the effective population sizes confirmed a higher size for the Khoisans and western Pygmies and a lower one for the eastern Pygmies (Veeramah et al. 2012).

Conclusion

Archaeogenetic studies show not only that the contemporary human genetic makeup emerged mostly in Africa (Green et al. 2010; Yang et al. 2012), but also that almost two-thirds of our genetic history has taken place within this continent without any large-scale bottleneck (Sjödin et al. 2012). However, since the mutation rates of the nuclear polymorphisms are still not fully understood (Scally and Durbin 2012), the mtDNA molecule offers us today the most reliable tool for the dating of the demographic events our ancestors underwent in the past (Soares et al. 2009).

Probably only one successful migration associated with better climatic conditions in East Africa ~70 ka (Blome et al. 2012) led to the emergence of non-African basal mtDNA lineages. Later, at ~40 ka and after ~20 ka, when 'back to Africa' migrations occurred, later genetic lineages enriched the African mtDNA gene pool especially in the north and east of the continent but the vast sub-Saharan area remained more or less untouched.

From the archaeogenetic point of view, the African hunter-gatherers can be considered as unique population entities with a very high number of deeply rooted lineages by which our common genetic history can be much better understood. Incidentally, Khoisan specificity of the uniparental markers has also allowed the disentangling of the genetic ancestry of some African people still developing their identities such as the Karretjie in the south (Schlebusch et al. 2012).

The observations from uniparental markers are mostly confirmed by the study of autosomal data showing, moreover, the possible existence of a very ancient and widespread 'proto-Khoisan-Pygmy' population (Tishkoff et al. 2009). Interestingly, genetic signs of an ancient African admixture with still undefined hominins were described as been more clearly visible in the gene pool of the hunter-gatherers than in that of farmers (Hammer et al. 2011); these results need still to be ascertained in an independent study. No doubt further genetic studies are still needed as Africa is a huge continent with terrific genetic diversity and some regions and population groups are still poorly represented in our datasets.

The contemporary African hunter-gatherers are probably not good representatives of the lifestyle of their Palaeolithic ancestors. They certainly do not still live in isolation and they are not autarkic as several cultural exchanges were observed with neighbouring farmers and/or pastoralists (see for example Hitchcock or Hewlett and Fancher in this volume). However, we claim that the genetic legacy of the African hunter-gatherers shows us how precious these people are, at least for a deeper understanding of our own common genetic history and variation.

Acknowledgements

The project was supported by the Institute for Advanced Study in Paris and the Portuguese Fundação para a Ciência e a Tecnologia (Programa Operacional Ciência, Tecnologia e Inovação–Quadro Comunitario de Apoio III).

References

Achilli, A., Rengo, C., Battaglia, V., Pala, M., Olivieri, A., Fornarino, S., Magri, C., Scozzari, R., Babudri, N., Santachiara-Benerecetti, A. S., Bandelt, H.-J., Semino, O., and Torroni, A. 2005. Saami and Berbers: an unexpected mitochondrial DNA link. *American Journal of Human Genetics* 76, 883–6.

Armitage, S. J., Jasim, S. A., Marks, A. E., Parker, A. G., Usik, V. I., and Uerpmann, H. P. 2011. The southern route 'out of Africa': evidence for an early expansion of modern humans into Arabia. *Science* 331, 453–6.

Arredi, B., Poloni, E. S., Paracchini, S., Zerjal, T., Fathallah, D. M., Makrelouf, M., Pascali, V. L., Novelletto, A., and Tyler-Smith, C. 2004. A predominantly neolithic origin for Y-chromosomal DNA variation in North Africa. *American Journal of Human Genetics* 75, 338–45.

Avise, J. C. 2000. *Phylogeography: the history and formation of species.* Cambridge, MA: Harvard University Press.

Bailey, R. C. 1991. *The behavioral ecology of Efe pygmy men in the Ituri Forest, Zaire.* Ann Arbor: Museum of Anthropology, University of Michigan.

Bandelt, H.-J., Forster, P., and Rohl, A. 1999. Median-joining networks for inferring intraspecific phylogenies. *Molecular Biology and Evolution* 16(1), 37–48.

Bandelt, H.-J., Forster, P., Sykes, B. C., and Richards, M. B. 1995. Mitochondrial portraits of human populations using median networks. *Genetics* 141, 743–53.

Batini, C., Coia, V., Battaggia, C., Rocha, J., Pilkington, M. M., Spedini, G., Comas, D., Destro-Bisol, G., and Calafell, F. 2007. Phylogeography of the human mitochondrial L1c haplogroup: genetic signatures of the prehistory of Central Africa. *Molecular Phylogenetics and Evolution* 43, 635–44.

Becker, N. S., Verdu, P., Froment, A., Le Bomin, S., Pagezy, H., Bahuchet, S., and Heyer, E. 2011. Indirect evidence for the genetic determination of short stature in African Pygmies. *American Journal of Physical Anthropology* 145, 390–401.

Behar, D. M., Villems, R., Soodyall, H., Blue-Smith, J., Pereira, L., Metspalu, E., Scozzari, R., Makkan, H., Tzur, S., Comas, D., Bertranpetit, J., Quintana-Murci, L., Tyler-Smith, C., Wells, R. S., and Rosset, S.; Genographic Consortium. 2008. The dawn of human matrilineal diversity. *American Journal of Human Genetics* 82, 1130–40.

Blome, M. W., Cohen, A. S., Tryon, C. A., Brooks, A. S., and Russell, J. 2012. The environmental context for the origins of modern human diversity: a synthesis of regional variability in African climate 150,000–30,000 years ago. *Journal of Human Evolution* 62, 563–92.

Blurton Jones, N. G., Smith, L. C., O'Connell, J. F., Hawkes, K., and Kamuzora, C. L. 1992. Demography of the Hadza, an increasing and high density population of Savanna foragers. *American Journal of Physical Anthropology* 89, 159–81.

Brotherton, P., Endicott, P., Sanchez, J. J., Beaumont, M., Barnett, R., Austin, J., and Cooper, A. 2007. Novel high-resolution characterization of ancient DNA reveals C > U-type base modification events as the sole cause of post mortem miscoding lesions. *Nucleic Acids Research* 35, 5717–28.

Calcagno, J. M. 1986. Dental reduction in post-pleistocene Nubia. *American Journal of Physical Anthropology* 70, 349–63.

Cann, R. L., Stoneking, M., and Wilson, A. C. 1987. Mitochondrial DNA and human evolution. *Nature* 325, 31–6.

Carlson, D. S. 1976. Temporal variation in prehistoric Nubian crania. *American Journal of Physical Anthropology* 45, 467–84.

Carlson, D. S. and Van Gerven, D. P. 1977. Masticatory function and post-Pleistocene evolution in Nubia. *American Journal of Physical Anthropology* 46, 495–506.

Cavalli-Sforza, L. L. 1986. *African Pygmies*. Orlando: Academic Press.

Cavalli-Sforza, L. L., Menozzi, P., and Piazza, A. 1994. *The history and geography of human genes.* Princeton: Princeton University Press.

Cerný, V., Mulligan, C. J., Fernandes, V., Silva, N. M., Alshamali, F., Non, A., Harich, N., Cherni, L., El Gaaied, A. B., Al-Meeri, A., and Pereira, L. 2011a. Internal diversification of mitochondrial haplogroup R0a reveals post-Last Glacial Maximum demographic expansions in south Arabia. *Molecular Biology and Evolution* 28, 71–8.

Cerný, V., Mulligan, C. J., Rídl, J., Žaloudková, M., Edens, C. M., Hájek, M., and Pereira. L. 2008. Regional differences in the distribution of the sub-Saharan, West Eurasian, and South Asian mtDNA lineages in Yemen. *American Journal of Physical Anthropology* 136, 128–37.

Cerný, V., Pereira, L., Musilová, E., Kujanová, M., Vašíková, A., Blasi, P., Garofalo, L., Soares, P., Diallo, I., Brdicka, R., and Novelletto, A. 2011b. Genetic structure of pastoral and farmer populations in the African Sahel. *Molecular Biology and Evolution* 28, 2491–500.

Cerný, V., Salas, A., Hájek, M., Žaloudková, M., and Brdicka, R. 2007. A bidirectional corridor in the Sahel-Sudan belt and the distinctive features of the Chad Basin populations: a history revealed by the mitochondrial DNA genome. *Annals of Human Genetics* 71, 433–52.

Chen, Y. S., Olckers, A., Schurr, T. G., Kogelnik, A.M., Huoponen, K., and Wallace, D. C. 2000. mtDNA variation in the South African Kung and Khwe—and their genetic relationships to other African populations. *American Journal of Human Genetics* 66, 1362–83.

Cruciani, F., Trombetta, B., Massaia, A., Destro-Bisol, G., Sellitto, D., and Scozzari, R. 2011. A revised root for the human Y chromosomal phylogenetic tree: the origin of patrilineal diversity in Africa. *American Journal of Human Genetics* 88, 814–18.

Cruciani, F., Trombetta, B., Sellitto D., Massaia, A., Destro-Bisol, G., Watson, E., Beraud Colomb, E., Dugoujon, J. M., Moral, P., and Scozzari, R. 2010. Human Y chromosome haplogroup R-V88: a paternal genetic record of early mid Holocene trans-Saharan connections and the spread of Chadic languages. *European Journal of Human Genetics* 18, 800–7.

Destro-Bisol, G., Coia, V., Boschi, I., Verginelli, F., Caglia, A., Pascali, V., Spedini, G., and Calafell, F. 2004a. The analysis of variation of mtDNA hypervariable region 1 suggests that Eastern and Western Pygmies diverged before the Bantu expansion. *The American Naturalist* 163, 212–26.

Destro-Bisol, G., Donati, F., Coia, V., Boschi, I., Verginelli, F., Caglia, A., Tofanelli, S., Spedini, G., and Capelli, C. 2004b. Variation of female and male lineages in sub-Saharan populations: the importance of sociocultural factors. *Molecular Biology and Evolution* 21, 1673–82.

Drummond, A. J. and Rambaut, A. 2007. BEAST: Bayesian evolutionary analysis by sampling trees. *BMC Evolutionary Biology* 7, 214.

Drummond, A. J., Rambaut, A., Shapiro, B., and Pybus, O. G. 2005. Bayesian coalescent inference of past population dynamics from molecular sequences. *Molecular Biology and Evolution* 22, 1185–92.

Dutour, O. 1989. *Hommes fossiles du Sahara: peuplements holocènes du Mali septentrional.* Paris: Éditions du Centre national de la recherche.

Eaaswarkhanth, M., Haque, I., Ravesh, Z., Romero, I. G., Meganathan, P. R., Dubey, B., Khan, F. A., Chaubey, G., Kivisild, T., Tyler-Smith, C., Singh, L., and Thangaraj, K. 2010. Traces of sub-Saharan and Middle Eastern lineages in Indian Muslim populations. *European Journal of Human Genetics* 18, 354–33.

Endicott, P., Ho, S. Y., Metspalu, M., and Stringer, C. 2009. Evaluating the mitochondrial timescale of human evolution. *Trends in Ecology and Evolution* 24, 515–21.

Ennafaa, H., Cabrera, V. M., Abu-Amero, K. K., Gonzalez, A. M., Amor, M. B., Bouhaha, R., Dzimiri, N., Elgaaied, A. B., and Larruga, J. M. 2009. Mitochondrial DNA haplogroup H structure in North Africa. *BMC Genetics* 10, 8.

Excoffier, L. and Schneider, S. 1999. Why hunter-gatherer populations do not show signs of Pleistocene demographic expansions. *Proceedings of the National Academy of Sciences USA* 96, 10597–602.

Excoffier, L. and Yang, Z. 1999. Substitution rate variation among sites in mitochondrial hypervariable region I of humans and chimpanzees. *Molecular Biology and Evolution* 16, 1357–68.

Felsenstein, J. (ed.) 1993. *PHYLIP (Phylogeny Inference Package)*. Washington: Department of Genetics, University of Washington.

Fernandes, V., Alshamali, F., Alves, M., Costa, M. D., Pereira, J. B., Silva, N. M., Cherni, L., Harich, N., Cerný, V., Soares, P., Richards, M. B., and Pereira, L. 2012. The Arabian cradle: mitochondrial relicts of the first steps along the southern route out of Africa. *American Journal of Human Genetics* 90, 347–55.

Forster, P. 2004. Ice ages and the mitochondrial DNA chronology of human dispersals: a review. *Philosophical Transactions of the Royal Society of London B: Biological Sciences* 359, 255–64.

Gonder, M. K., Mortensen, H. M., Reed, F. A., de Sousa, A., and Tishkoff, S. A. 2007. Whole-mtDNA genome sequence analysis of ancient African lineages. *Molecular Biology and Evolution* 24, 757–68.

Gonzalez, A. M., Larruga, J. M., Abu-Amero, K. K., Shi, Y., Pestano, J., and Cabrera, V. M. 2007. Mitochondrial lineage M1 traces an early human backflow to Africa. *BMC Genomics* 8, 223.

Green, R. E., Krause, J., Briggs, A. W., Maricic, T., Stenzel, U., Kircher, M., Patterson, N., Li, H., Zhai, W., Fritz, M. H., Hansen, N. F., Durand, E. Y., Malaspinas, A. S., Jensen, J. D., Marques-Bonet, T., Alkan, C., Prufer, K., Meyer, M., Burbano, H. A., Good, J. M., Schultz, R., Aximu-Petri, A., Butthof, A., Hober, B., Hoffner, B., Siegemund, M., Weihmann, A., Nusbaum, C., Lander, E. S., Russ, C., Novod, N., Affourtit, J., Egholm, M., Verna, C., Rudan, P., Brajkovic, D., Kucan, Z., Gusic, I., Doronichev, V. B., Golovanova, L. V., Lalueza-Fox, C., de la Rasilla, M., Fortea, J., Rosas, A., Schmitz, R. W., Johnson, P. L., Eichler, E. E., Falush, D., Birney, E., Mullikin, J. C., Slatkin, M., Nielsen, R., Kelso, J., Lachmann, M., Reich, D., and Pääbo, S. 2010. A draft sequence of the Neandertal genome. *Science* 328, 710–22.

Greene, D. L. and Armelagos, G. J. 1972. *The Wadi Halfa Mesolithic population*. Amherst: Department of Anthropology, University of Massachusetts.

Groucutt, H. S. and Petraglia, M. D. 2012. The prehistory of the Arabian peninsula: deserts, dispersals, and demography. *Evolutionary Anthropology* 21, 113–25.

Gunz, P., Bookstein, F. L., Mitteroecker, P., Stadlmayr, A., Seidler, H., and Weber, G. W. 2009. Early modern human diversity suggests subdivided population structure and a complex out-of-Africa scenario. *Proceedings National Academy of Sciences USA* 106, 6094–8.

Gutenkunst, R. N., Hernandez, R. D., Williamson, S. H., and Bustamante, C. D. 2009. Inferring the joint demographic history of multiple populations from multidimensional SNP frequency data. *PLoS Genetics* 5, e1000695.

Haile-Selassie, Y., Asfaw, B., and White, T. D. 2004. Hominid cranial remains from upper Pleistocene deposits at Aduma, Middle Awash, Ethiopia. *American Journal of Physical Anthropology* 123, 1–10.

Hammer, M. F., Woerner, A. E., Mendez, F. L., Watkins, J. C., and Wall, J. D. 2011. Genetic evidence for archaic admixture in Africa. *Proceedings of the National Academy of Sciences USA* 108, 15123–8.

Hasegawa, M., Di Rienzo, A., Kocher, T. D., and Wilson, A. C. 1993. Toward a more accurate time scale for the human mitochondrial DNA tree. *Journal of Molecular Evolution* 37, 347–54.

Henn, B. M., Botigue, L. R., Gravel, S., Wang, W., Brisbin, A., Byrnes, J. K., Fadhlaoui-Zid, K., Zalloua, P. A., Moreno-Estrada, A., Bertranpetit, J., Bustamante, C. D., and Comas, D. 2012. Genomic ancestry of North Africans supports back-to-Africa migrations. *PLoS Genetics* 8, e1002397.

Henn, B. M., Gignoux, C. R., Jobin, M., Granka, J. M., Macpherson, J. M., Kidd, J. M., Rodriguez-Botigue, L., Ramachandran, S., Hon, L., Brisbin, A., Lin, A. A., Underhill, P. A., Comas, D., Kidd, K. K., Norman, P. J., Parham, P., Bustamante, C. D., Mountain, J. L., and Feldman, M. W. 2011. Hunter-gatherer genomic diversity suggests a southern African origin for modern humans. *Proceedings of the National Academy of Sciences USA* 108, 5154–62.

Hiernaux, J. 1974. *The people of Africa*. London: Weidenfeld & Nicolson.

Howell, N. 1979. *Demography of the Dobe !Kung*. New York: Academic Press.

Ingman, M. and Gyllensten, U. 2001. Analysis of the complete human mtDNA genome: methodology and inferences for human evolution. *Journal of Heredity* 92, 454–61.

Ingman, M., Kaessmann, H., Pääbo, S., and Gyllensten, U. 2000. Mitochondrial genome variation and the origin of modern humans. *Nature* 408, 708–13.

Jobling, M. A., Hurles, M., and Tyler-Smith, C. 2004. *Human evolutionary genetics: origins, peoples and disease*. New York: Garland Science.

Karafet, T. M., Mendez, F. L., Meilerman, M. B., Underhill, P. A., Zegura, S. L., and Hammer, M. F. 2008. New binary polymorphisms reshape and increase resolution of the human Y chromosomal haplogroup tree. *Genome Research* 18, 830–8.

Kivisild, T., Metspalu, M., Bandelt, H.-J., Richards, M., and Villems, R. 2006. The world mtDNA phylogeny. In H.-J. Bandelt, V. Macaulay, and M. Richards (eds), *Human mitochondrial DNA and the evolution of Homo Sapiens. Nucleic acids and molecular biology*, 149–79. Berlin: Springer.

Knight, A., Underhill, P. A., Mortensen, H. M., Zhivotovsky, L. A., Lin, A. A., Henn, B. M., Louis, D., Ruhlen, M., and Mountain, J. L. 2003. African Y chromosome and mtDNA divergence provides insight into the history of click languages. *Current Biology* 13, 464–73.

Krause, J., Briggs, A. W., Kircher, M., Maricic, T., Zwyns, N., Derevianko, A., and Pääbo, S. 2010. A complete mtDNA genome of an early modern human from Kostenki, Russia. *Current Biology* 20, 231–6.

Krut, L. H. and Singer, R. 1963. Steatopygia: the fatty acid composition of subcutaneous adipose tissue in the Hottentot. *American Journal of Physical Anthropology* 21, 181–7.

Kujanová, M., Pereira, L., Fernandes, V., Pereira, J. B., and Cerný, V. 2009. Near Eastern Neolithic genetic input in a small oasis of the Egyptian Western Desert. *American Journal of Physical Anthropology* 140, 336–46.

Kumar, S., Tamura, K., and Nei, M. (eds) 1993. *MEGA: molecular evolutionary genetics analysis, version 1.01*. University Park: Pennsylvania State University.

Lahr, M. M. 1996. *The evolution of modern human diversity: a study of cranial variation*. Cambridge: Cambridge University Press.

Lee, R. B. 1979. *The !Kung San: men, women, and work in a foraging society*. Cambridge: Cambridge University Press.

Lee, R. B. and Daly, R. H. 1999. *The Cambridge encyclopedia of hunters and gatherers*. Cambridge: Cambridge University Press.

Li, J. Z., Absher, D. M., Tang, H., Southwick, A. M., Casto, A. M., Ramachandran, S., Cann, H. M., Barsh, G. S., Feldman, M., Cavalli-Sforza, L. L., and Myers, R. M. 2008. Worldwide human relationships inferred from genome-wide patterns of variation. *Science* 319, 1100–4.

McDougall, I., Brown, F. H., and Fleagle, J. G. 2005. Stratigraphic placement and age of modern humans from Kibish, Ethiopia. *Nature* 433, 733–6.

McDougall, I., Brown, F. H., and Fleagle, J. G. 2008. Sapropels and the age of hominins Omo I and II, Kibish, Ethiopia. *Journal of Human Evolution* 55, 409–20.

Migliano, A. B., Vinicius, L., and Lahr, M. M. 2007. Life history trade-offs explain the evolution of human pygmies. *Proceedings of the National Academy of Sciences USA* 104, 20216–9.

Mishmar, D., Ruiz-Pesini, E., Golik, P., Macaulay, V., Clark, A. G., Hosseini, S., Brandon, M., Easley, K., Chen, E., Brown, M. D., Sukernik, R. I., Olckers, A., and Wallace, D. C. 2003. Natural selection shaped regional mtDNA variation in humans. *Proceedings of the National Academy of Sciences USA* 100, 171–6.

Musilová, E., Fernandes, V., Silva, N. M., Soares, P., Alshamali, F., Harich, N., Cherni, L., Gaaied, A. B., Al-Meeri, A., Pereira, L., and Cerný, V. 2011. Population history of the Red Sea: genetic exchanges between the Arabian Peninsula and East Africa signaled in the mitochondrial DNA HV1 haplogroup. *American Journal of Physical Anthropology* 145, 592–8.

Nicolaisen, I. 2010. *Elusive hunters: the Haddad of Kanem and the Bahr el Ghazal*. Copenhagen: Aarhus University Press.

Olivieri, A., Achilli, A., Pala, M., Battaglia, V., Fornarino, S., Al-Zahery, N., Scozzari, R., Cruciani, F., Behar, D. M., Dugoujon, J. M., Coudray, C., Santachiara-Benerecetti, A. S., Semino, O., Bandelt, H.-J., and Torroni, A. 2006. The mtDNA legacy of the Levantine early Upper Palaeolithic in Africa. *Science* 314, 1767–70.

Patin, E., Laval, G., Barreiro, L. B., Salas, A., Semino, O., Santachiara-Benerecetti, S., Kidd, K. K., Kidd, J. R., van der Veen, L., Hombert, J. M., Gessain, A., Froment, A., Bahuchet, S., Heyer, E., and Quintana-Murci, L. 2009. Inferring the demographic history of African farmers and pygmy hunter-gatherers using a multilocus resequencing data set. *PLoS Genetics* 5, e1000448.

Pennington, R. 2001. Hunter-gatherer demography. In C. Panter-Brick, R. Layton, and P. Rowley-Conwy (eds), *Hunter-gatherers: an interdisciplinary perspective*, 170–204. Cambridge: Cambridge University Press.

Pereira, L., Cerný, V., Cerezo, M., Silva, N. M., Hájek, M., Vašíková, A., Kujanová, M., Brdicka, R., and Salas, A. 2010. Linking the sub-Saharan and West Eurasian gene pools: maternal and paternal heritage of the Tuareg nomads from the African Sahel. *European Journal of Human Genetics* 18, 915–23.

Pereira, L., Macaulay, V., Torroni, A., Scozzari, R., Prata, M. J., and Amorim, A. 2001. Prehistoric and historic traces in the mtDNA of Mozambique: insights into the Bantu expansions and the slave trade. *Annals of Human Genetics* 65, 439–58.

Perry, G. H. and Dominy, N. J. 2009. Evolution of the human pygmy phenotype. *Trends in Ecological Evolution* 24, 218–25.

Pickrell, J. K., Patterson, N., Barbieri, C., Berthold, F., Gerlach, L., Guldemann, T., Kure, B., Mpoloka, S. W., Nakagawa, H., Naumann, C., Lipson, M., Loh, P. R., Lachance, J., Mountain, J., Bustamante, C. D., Berger, B., Tishkoff, S. A., Henn, B. M., Stoneking, M., Reich, D., and Pakendorf, B. 2012. The genetic prehistory of southern Africa. *Nature Communications* 3, article number 1143.

Pilkington, M. M., Wilder, J. A., Mendez, F. L., Cox, M. P., Woerner, A., Angui, T., Kingan, S., Mobasher, Z., Batini, C., Destro-Bisol, G., Soodyall, H., Strassmann, B. I., and Hammer, M. F. 2008. Contrasting signatures of population growth for mitochondrial DNA and Y chromosomes among human populations in Africa. *Molecular Biology and Evolution* 25, 517–25.

Quintana-Murci, L., Quach, H., Harmant, C., Luca, F., Massonnet, B., Patin, E., Sica, L., Mouguiama-Daouda, P., Comas, D., Tzur, S., Balanovsky, O., Kidd, K. K., Kidd, J. R., van der Veen, L., Hombert, J. M., Gessain, A., Verdu, P., Froment, A., Bahuchet, S., Heyer, E., Dausset, J.,

Salas, A., and Behar, D. M. 2008. Maternal traces of deep common ancestry and asymmetric gene flow between Pygmy hunter-gatherers and Bantu-speaking farmers. *Proceedings of the National Academy of Sciences USA* 105, 1596–601.

Rasmussen, M., Li, Y., Lindgreen, S., Pedersen, J. S., Albrechtsen, A., Moltke, I., Metspalu, M., Metspalu, E., Kivisild, T., Gupta, R., Bertalan, M., Nielsen, K., Gilbert, M. T., Wang, Y., Raghavan, M., Campos, P. F., Kamp, H. M., Wilson, A. S., Gledhill, A., Tridico, S., Bunce, M., Lorenzen, E. D., Binladen, J., Guo, X., Zhao, J., Zhang, X., Zhang, H., Li, Z., Chen, M., Orlando, L., Kristiansen, K., Bak, M., Tommerup, N., Bendixen, C., Pierre, T. L., Gronnow, B., Meldgaard, M., Andreasen, C., Fedorova, S. A., Osipova, L. P., Higham, T. F., Ramsey, C. B., Hansen, T. V., Nielsen, F. C., Crawford, M. H., Brunak, S., Sicheritz-Ponten, T., Villems, R., Nielsen, R., Krogh, A., Wang, J., and Willerslev, E. 2010. Ancient human genome sequence of an extinct Palaeo-Eskimo. *Nature* 463, 757–62.

Renfrew, C. and Boyle, C. (eds) 2000. *Archaeogenetics: DNA and the population prehistory of Europe*. Cambridge: McDonald Institute for Archaeological Research.

Richards, M., Rengo, C., Cruciani, F., Gratrix, F., Wilson, J. F., Scozzari, R., Macaulay, V., and Torroni, A. 2003. Extensive female-mediated gene flow from sub-Saharan Africa into Near Eastern Arab populations. *American Journal of Human Genetics* 72, 1058–64.

Rose, J. I., Usik, V. I., Marks, A. E., Hilbert, Y. H., Galletti, C. S., Parton, A., Geiling, J. M., Cerný, V., Morley, M. W., and Roberts, R. G. 2011. The Nubian complex of Dhofar, Oman: an African Middle Stone Age industry in southern Arabia. *PLoS One* 6, e28239.

Salas, A., Richards, M., De la Fe, T., Lareu, M.V., Sobrino, B., Sanchez-Diz, P., Macaulay, V., and Carracedo, A. 2002. The making of the African mtDNA landscape. *American Journal of Human Genetics* 71, 1082–111.

Salas, A., Richards, M., Lareu, M. V., Scozzari, R., Coppa, A., Torroni, A., Macaulay, V., and Carracedo, A. 2004. The African diaspora: mitochondrial DNA and the Atlantic slave trade. *American Journal of Human Genetics* 74, 454–65.

Scally, A. and Durbin, R. 2012. Revising the human mutation rate: implications for understanding human evolution. *Nature Reviews Genetics* 13, 745–73.

Schebesta, P. and Lebzelter, V. 1933. *Anthropologie středoafrických pygmejů v belgickém Kongu. Anthropology of the central African pygmies in the Belgian Congo*. Prague: Ceská akademie ved a umení.

Schlebusch, C. M., de Jongh, M., and Soodyall, H. 2012. Different contributions of ancient mitochondrial and Y-chromosomal lineages in 'Karretjie people' of the Great Karoo in South Africa. *Journal of Human Genetics* 56, 623–60.

Schneider, S., Roessli, D., and Excoffier, L. (eds) 2000. *Arlequin ver. 2.000: A software for population genetics data analysis*. Geneva: Genetics and Biometry Laboratory, University of Geneva.

Sellen, D. W. and Mace, R. 1997. Fertility and mode of subsistence: a phylogenetic analysis. *Current Anthropology* 38, 878–89.

Semino, O., Santachiara-Benerecetti, A. S., Falaschi, F., Cavalli-Sforza, L. L., and Underhill, P. A. 2002. Ethiopians and Khoisan share the deepest clades of the human Y-chromosome phylogeny. *American Journal of Human Genetics* 70, 265–8.

Sjödin, P., Sjöstrand, A. E., Jakobsson, M., and Blum, M. G. B. 2012. Resequencing data provide no evidence for a human bottleneck in Africa during the penultimate glacial period. *Molecular Biology and Evolution* 29, 1851–60.

Soares, P., Alshamali, F., Pereira, J. B., Fernandes, V., Silva, N. M., Alfonso, C., Costa, M. D., Musilová, E., Macaulay, V., Richards, M. B., Cerný, V., and Pereira, L. 2012. The expansion of mtDNA haplogroup L3 within and out of Africa. *Molecular Biology and Evolution* 29, 915–27.

Soares, P., Ermini, L., Thomson, N., Mormina, M., Rito, T., Rohl, A., Salas, A., Oppenheimer, S., Macaulay, V., and Richards, M. B. 2009. Correcting for purifying selection: an improved human mitochondrial molecular clock. *American Journal of Human Genetics* 84, 740–59.

Soodyall, H. and Jenkins, T. 1992. Mitochondrial DNA polymorphisms in Khoisan populations from southern Africa. *Annals of Human Genetics* 56, 315–24.

Soodyall, H. and Jenkins, T. 1993. Mitochondrial DNA polymorphisms in Negroid populations from Namibia: new light on the origins of the Dama, Herero and Ambo. *Annals of Human Genetics* 20, 477–85.

Soodyall, H., Vigilant, L., Hill, A. V., Stoneking, M., and Jenkins, T. 1996. mtDNA control-region sequence variation suggests multiple independent origins of an 'Asian-specific' 9-bp deletion in sub-Saharan Africans. *American Journal of Human Genetics* 58, 595–608.

Strassmann, B. I. and Warner, J. H. 1998. Predictors of fecundability and conception waits among the Dogon of Mali. *American Journal of Physical Anthropology* 105, 167–84.

Tishkoff, S. A., Gonder, M. K., Henn, B. M., Mortensen, H., Knight, A., Gignoux, C., Fernandopulle, N., Lema, G., Nyambo, T. B., Ramakrishnan, U., Reed F. A., and Mountain, J. L. 2007. History of click-speaking populations of Africa inferred from mtDNA and Y chromosome genetic variation. *Molecular Biology and Evolution* 24, 2180–95.

Tishkoff, S. A., Reed, F. A., Friedlaender, F. R., Ehret, C., Ranciaro, A., Froment, A., Hirbo, J. B., Awomoyi, A. A., Bodo, J. M., Doumbo, O., Ibrahim, M., Juma, A. T., Kotze, M. J., Lema, G., Moore, J. H., Mortensen, H., Nyambo, T. B., Omar, S. A., Powell, K., Pretorius, G. S., Smith, M. W., Thera, M. A., Wambebe, C., Weber, J. L., and Williams, S. M. 2009. The genetic structure and history of Africans and African Americans. *Science* 324, 1035–44.

Torroni, A., Achilli, A., Macaulay, V., Richards, M., and Bandelt, H.-J. 2006. Harvesting the fruit of the human mtDNA tree. *Trends in Genetics* 22, 339–45.

Underhill, P. A., Passarino, G., Lin, A. A., Shen, P., Mirazon Lahr, M., Foley, R. A., Oefner, P. J., and Cavalli-Sforza, L. L. 2001. The phylogeography of Y chromosome binary haplotypes and the origins of modern human populations. *Annals of Human Genetics* 65, 43–62.

Veeramah, K. R., Wegmann, D., Woerner, A., Mendez, F. L., Watkins, J. C., Destro-Bisol, G., Soodyall, H., Louie, L., and Hammer, M. F. 2012. An early divergence of KhoeSan ancestors from those of other modern humans is supported by an ABC-based analysis of autosomal resequencing data. *Molecular Biology and Evolution* 29, 617–30.

Verdu, P., Austerlitz, F., Estoup, A., Vitalis, R., Georges, M., Thery, S., Froment, A., Bomin, S., Gessain, A., Hombert, J. M., Van der Veen, L., Quintana-Murci, L., Bahuchet, S., and Heyer, E. 2009. Origins and genetic diversity of pygmy hunter-gatherers from western Central Africa. *Current Biology* 19, 312–38.

Vigilant, L., Pennington, R., Harpending, H., Kocher, T. D., and Wilson, A. C. 1989. Mitochondrial DNA sequences in single hairs from a southern African population. *Proceedings of the National Academy of Sciences USA* 86, 9350–4.

Vigilant, L., Stoneking, M., Harpending, H., Hawkes, K., and Wilson, A. C. 1991. African populations and the evolution of human mitochondrial DNA. *Science* 253, 1503–7.

Watson, E., Forster, P., Richards, M., and Bandelt, H.-J. 1997. Mitochondrial footprints of human expansions in Africa. *American Journal of Human Genetics* 61, 691–704.

Willoughby, P. R. 2007. *The evolution of modern humans in Africa: a comprehensive guide*. Lanham, MD: AltaMira Press.

Wood, E. T., Stover, D. A., Ehret, C., Destro-Bisol, G., Spedini, G., McLeod, H., Louie, L., Bamshad, M., Strassmann, B. I., Soodyall, H., and Hammer, M.F. 2005. Contrasting patterns of Y chromosome and mtDNA variation in Africa: evidence for sex-biased demographic processes. *European Journal of Human Genetics* 13, 867–76.

Yang, M. A., Malaspinas, A. S., Durand, E. Y., and Slatkin, M. 2012. Ancient structure in Africa unlikely to explain Neanderthal and non-African genetic similarity. *Molecular Biology and Evolution* 29, 2987–95.

Zhivotovsky, L. A., Rosenberg, N. A., and Feldman, M. W. 2003. Features of evolution and expansion of modern humans, inferred from genomewide microsatellite markers. *American Journal of Human Genetics* 72, 1171–86.

CHAPTER 56

LANDSCAPES OF MOBILITY
The Flow of Place

BRUNO DAVID, LARA LAMB, AND JACK KAIWARI

'I will tell you my origin story. I am from a person called Namiri who is the chief of Yoto'uki clan [Rumu tribe, Papua New Guinea] who was living in the jungle. His younger brother was Dabugai. I had a lot of boys like Namiri and Dabugai. Namiri and Dabugai and those boys always lived under the caves of Kuruma and Eiapo in the mountains, and sometimes they changed themselves into bats, and Namiri was the leader of those bats in the cave. And actually those bats were human beings. They were his brothers and his small children. My clan didn't go anywhere; they were not originated to move around. They didn't go anywhere. Our ancestral boys Namiri and Dabugai and all the other bat ancestors emerged from the caves at Kuruma and Eiapo, and they lived there in the time of our ancestors, to the time of our grannies and forefathers, until the time of our fathers and ourselves; and they still live there. We never moved anywhere. We didn't practise that kind of movement. We originated from that part of the area and we stayed there permanently.

On top of these two mountains at Kuruma and Eiapo we had some girls living there, and these girls were our girls also. They were not their wives but they were our girls. The girls were on top of the mountain, and sometimes these girls would change themselves into cucumbers now grown in the gardens. But originally my girls came from the cucumber fruit. And those cucumber vines were used by my ancestral clan men, Namiri and Dabugai and their boys to move around: they were using the girls to move around. Cucumber vines can creep from tree to tree, and the men were also using those same footings when the girls were moving, and when they were lost they could smell the cucumber and come back. They know that's their girls and their place of origin, so they used to follow back the smell of the cucumber. That was when they had a lot of people coming. When other people came to visit them they would change themselves into cucumbers and bats in the cave. But when they were by themselves they were their own community.

Today my land flows towards the Kikori River in the east and the Omati River in the west, but I have boundaries with the other clans somewhere in the middle of the jungle. What I have told you is part of the story about how my clan came to be where we are now.'

Jack Kaiwari, leader of Yoto'uki clan, Rumu tribe, Kopi village
(Gulf Province, Papua New Guinea), 12 April 2006

WE enter the archaeology of landscapes of hunter-gatherer mobility through the words of one hunting and gathering clan leader from Papua New Guinea as a means by which to broach both general achievements and deficiencies on the subject. Jack Kaiwari's tale speaks at once of the spatial fixity of his clan and the movements of his people, both of which locate his ancestors and present people in particular places, and in so doing allow us to reach beyond his own clan landscape to generalizing ways of addressing human location and movement. Here we address landscapes of 'mobility' via a series of heuristic themes that emerge from established hunter-gatherer mobility studies. We then reflect back on some of these themes through the words of Jack Kaiwari's origin story.

WHAT IS MOBILITY IN THE LANDSCAPE?

Human mobility refers to the movement of people across the landscape. It encompasses issues of origins (starting points in the landscape and through time), scheduling (the timing of movement), spatial structure (the 'where' of movement), technology (the means of movement), social conditions (social rules and regulatory forces of movement), social schedules and rhythms (e.g. times of aggregation, trade, solidarity), tempo (duration and frequency of movement), logic (the reasons for movement from fixed locations), proxemics (the spatiality of daily transactions), pathways and barriers (roadways and inhibitions to movement), forces of mobilization (e.g. weather patterns, social forces), population dynamics (how people interact across space and the effects of those interactions on populations), ontologies of movement and landscape perception (values and cultures of movement, including how the landscape is understood to operate), spatial scales of enquiry (the distances involved in particular moves), and temporal scales of enquiry (e.g. daily versus seasonal versus annual movements; long-term trends of mobility). Landscape refers to the place of human engagement at nested spatial scales, and mobility refers to, generally, the quality of being mobile across this landscape. The archaeology of landscapes of hunter-gatherer mobility thus refers to the archaeology of any of these factors as they relate to hunter-gatherers of the past and/or present.

Analytical Scale

The issue of analytical scale contributing to the outcome, and thus to the applicability of research results, has long been recognized in archaeology (Rossignol and Wandsnider 1992; Stein and Linse 1993). At a short analytical scale, as early as 1939, working among the Wik Mungkan of north-east Australia, the social anthropologist Donald Thomson reported on 'the seasonal factor in human culture', an important work that expounded a need to consider seasonal movements across the landscape, influential advice reflected in subsequent archaeological concerns with seasonality of occupation as determined by dendrochronological, seed, shell growth, deer-antler growth and shedding, and tooth eruption studies, to name but a few such studies in world archaeology (e.g. Geneste et al. 2008; Hiroko 1986). At the even shorter-term event scale, an interesting example of the archaeology of mobility across the landscape is the study of bullet cartridge distributions across the landscape to reconstruct patterns of movement at the Battle of Little Big Horn of 'Custer's Last Stand' (Fox 1997). At a longer-term analytical scale, evolutionary trends are usually not immediately concerned with seasonal cycles, but may, for instance, be more interested in biological developments in hominid locomotor biology such as bipedalism (Johanson and Edey 1981; Wolfpoff 1976, 596), the colonization of the earth by *Homo erectus* or *Homo sapiens* (as in Out-of-Africa 1 and Out-of-Africa 2, for example; e.g. Gamble 1993), the settlement of Europe by Neanderthals (Nandris 1976), the peopling of the Americas and the Pacific (Allen 1996; Kirk and Szathmary 1985), the evolution or history of modes of transport (Davidson and Noble 1992; Jones 1976), or the place of founder effects on descendant populations as a means of explaining patterns of variation (Binford 2001). The critical point here is that, as with other archaeological issues generally, the nature and scale of approach to landscape and mobility studies needs to match the nature and scale of investigative concern (Lourandos 1996).

One prominent approach to this question of congruence between investigative and intended scales (and between the scales of questioning and the application of results), with the potential to critically affect the unaware, has been presented by the French *Annales* school culminating in, and made famous by, Fernand Braudel (1949), whereby in the long term history is understood as fluid rather than the sum of fixed events, and where analytical scale is understood to affect both how we can access the past (i.e. only at some temporal scales are particular social processes accessible) and, therefore, how we construct the past (Bintliff 1991; Knapp 2009). Thus, the *Annales* school is characterized by a distinction between the *longue durée* (long-term trends), whereby slow and cumulative change results in major transformations to society and culture, and shorter-term temporal scales more applicable to life-world processes. Archaeological interests in shorter-term mobility *events*, such as seasonality studies or migratory journeys, require shorter-term scales of analysis more suited to those research questions. Because of the incongruity of the different analytical scales, most research questions are restricted to results that befit the particular scale of the original enquiry.

The issue of scale manifests itself in studies of mobility across the landscape when we determine what kinds of movements we want to talk about. Mobility may relate to the travels of a single individual or of a whole population; of visits, journeys of discovery or colonizing events; of one-way or reciprocal trade events or permanent migrations; of clan gatherings or the fulfilment of ceremonial obligations or pilgrimages; of accessing resource quarries or (re)distributing goods; of immediate effects or long-term impacts. There are as many options as there are case studies, and in each case the particular nature of the social and physical environment, and how it is culturally inhabited, is at stake.

THE EMERGENCE OF HUNTER-GATHERER MOBILITY STUDIES

Hunter-gatherer mobility studies have, given the varied issues raised by the topic, involved a broad range of applications, and preferred approaches have contingently changed through time along with disciplinary moves. Favoured late nineteenth- to mid-twentieth- century explanations for culture change in Australia, for example, focused debates on the arrival of immigrants with new objects or ideas (Birdsell 1967; Hale and Tindale 1930; Hossfeld 1966) and diffusion (McCarthy 1943; 1964). Such debates emerged as attempts to explain the onset of new stone tool types and the corresponding progressive sequence of artefact 'traditions' in various parts of the country (to some degree equivalent to the 'cultures' of national archaeologies from other parts of the world). Examples include Hale and Tindale's (1930) incoming waves of new migrants to explain changes in stone artefact types in the lower Murray River region of South Australia, and McCarthy's (1964, 239) diffusionist explanations for the onset of new stone tool types including 'the Bondi point, geometric microliths, elouera, gum hafting, the elaboration of the burin and later the introduction of the ground edge axe, and the working back of adzes into discarded slugs' in the Capertee Valley of New South Wales. Similar debates aiming to explain the cause of new artefact and site types took place in other parts of the world, with a predominance of explanatory models invoking human mobility (involving the movement of people, ideas and/or artefacts, as in migration and diffusion) rather than independent invention (for the United States, see Willey and Sabloff 1974; for Europe, Childe 1925). Thus Childe (1925), a renowned yet mild diffusionist, was famously wary of arguments for indigenous development, favouring migratory and diffusionary explanatory models (as Cunliffe (1973, 17) notes, partly in reaction against those such as Kossinna who argued for indigenous development).

In the shadow of a heightened awareness of ethnographic texts worldwide (which began to make a significant mark in the 1940s, but which peaked with the 'Man the Hunter' conference of 1966; Thomson 1939; Lee and Devore 1968), and with the onset of new analytical (including sourcing) techniques, a refinement in excavation methods and landscape mapping, and an increased awareness of the significance of the minutiae of excavated finds—as well illustrated by the British 'economic school' of archaeology (Higgs 1975) and excavations at the Mesolithic hunter-gatherer site of Star Carr in Yorkshire, England (Clark 1954)—archaeologists regularly began to study their excavated finds with an eye to details of mobility patterns such as seasonality movements (Mellars 1976), predictive modelling through methods such as site catchment analysis (Jarman 1976; Vita-Finzi and Higgs 1970), and transactions of foreign goods as an economic and political process (Renfrew and Dixon 1976) rather than to speak of new cultural traits through general notions of 'migration' versus 'diffusion'.

More recently, and in the wake of an archaeological history that now sees sourcing, biological including genetic studies (Matisoo-Smith 2008; Pate 2008; Serjeantson 1985), and the movement of goods and people as routine topics of investigation, discussion has turned to higher-order theoretical approaches to mobility, including adaptationist interpretations (Binford 1980), how social interaction leads to cultural transmission and diversity across the landscape (Jordan 2010a; 2010b; Jordan and Zvelebil 2009), proxemics and movements across micro-space in the undertaking of daily activities (e.g. Watson 1972, after Hall 1963), the effects of migration and mobility on subsequent movements (the 'Jones Effect'; Morauta 1981), engaged landscapes as territorial and interactive space (Costamagno 2001), exploration and the logistics of movement (including practicalities of return; Irwin 1992), phenomenological approaches (Tilley 1994), exile and the contesting of place (Bender and Winer 2001), the embeddedness of movement in culture as systems of *meaning* and social value (Paton 1994), spatial history (David 2008), sacred geographies (Ballard 1994), frontiers and identity creation (Bonnemaison et al. 1999), spatial prohibitions in the analysis of social space and time (to paraphrase Munn 2003, 92; McBryde 1984), and philosophical notions of 'dwelling' and 'inhabitation' (Ingold 2000; Thomas 2008).

In addition to general trends in larger archaeological theory, there are significant and varied nuances which together have led to the current state of the discipline. However, in an essay of this length we cannot do full justice to this rich tapestry and history of mobility studies. With this proviso in mind, we present below a selection of some of the major trends in the interest of eliciting directions and prospects for future intellectual movements in hunter-gatherer mobility studies.

TRADITIONAL APPROACHES TO THE ARCHAEOLOGY OF MOBILITY

Modern approaches to the archaeology of mobility among hunter-gatherers have largely emerged in compliance with or in reaction against the gambit of the New Archaeology. Three major dimensions of this founding agenda can be differentiated for the purposes of this chapter: an *adaptationist* explanatory logic; a *processualist* analytical framework, which understands necessary and sometimes sufficient relationships between types of behavioural phenomena; and *Middle Range Research* (MRR), which aims to uncover general associations between human behaviour and material patterns. While we would argue that the process should move from Middle Range Research to the formulation of process statements to broad explanatory paradigms, in practice the reverse has often taken place, beginning with an assumption of adaptationist processes leading to Middle Range Research devised to populate rather than test assumed adaptationist case studies. Here we outline separately fundamental aspects of mobility studies covered by the New Archaeology's predominant adapationist logic, processualist framework and their working face, Middle Range Research.

Adaptive Mobility

Traditional New Archaeology approaches to hunter-gatherer mobility have proceeded as a means of addressing settlement-subsistence logistics. As Binford (1982, 6) notes, 'I am interested in sites, the fixed places in the topography when man may periodically pause and carry out actions' that are 'long-term repetitive patterns in the positioning of adaptive systems in geographic space...arising from the interaction between economic zonation...and tactical mobility'. These logistical mobility strategies essentially amount to tactical positionings across the landscape + the time taken to exhaust the adaptive advantages of those locations. Such models vary in the way they approach the relationship between modelled and actual behaviours, and can range from general, indirectly or directly applied assumptions of adaptive causation to explicit optimizing models calculated mathematically with inputs from local environmental conditions (e.g. optimal foraging models). What they have in common is a general explanation of actual foraging behaviours that is also shared by animal ecologists and ethologists aiming to understand faunal behaviour through strategies of foraging efficiency, optimization or maximization (MacArthur 1972; Pyke 1984). Charnov's (1976)

Marginal Value Theorem, for example, predicts that duration of stay at a particular resource location will increase with distance from the next closest patch and with the relative richness of the patch. Optimal transit times between patches can be calculated as a cost-benefit computation between search and processing time on the one hand (representing cost), and consumption time on the other (representing benefit).

In behavioural ecology models such as these, hunter-gatherers can be expected to be less mobile between resource patches when high yielding local patches occur nearby and where the closest neighbouring resource patch is some distance away. In such models one thus finds a direct application of animal ecology to human behaviour to explain mobility strategies (Jochim 1981), evident, for example, in the common differentiation of 'search time' versus 'pursuit time' and 'capture time' whereby 'searchers' spend much of their time searching for food (e.g. as is the case with birds), and 'pursuers' spend much of their time pursuing and catching prey (e.g. lions). 'Such a distinction', writes Jochim (1981, 128), 'relates, in part, to the mobility of the resources: the foods of searchers are generally quite immobile, whereas those of pursuers are very mobile,' concluding that 'the distinction might be applied to the two economic strategies of hunters and gatherers: men who hunt highly mobile big game spend much time in the pursuit; women, on the other hand, devote most of their time to searching for plants, and once located, these foods require little time to capture'. A similar distinction was influentially modelled by Binford (1980) when he argued that hunter-gatherer settlement-subsistence systems can generally be separated into two types: 'collectors' who produce 'field camps', 'stations', and 'caches' and generally 'map onto' resources 'through residential moves and adjustments in groups size'; and 'logistically' organized 'foragers' who bring back resources to 'residential base camps' from 'resourcing locations' on a daily encounter basis (Binford 1980, 10; the 'collector/forager' distinction was recently reformulated by Binford and Johnson (2002) as a 'collector-forager continuum' to emphasize more the range of options and non-prescriptive nature of the categories). As Jochim (1976, 47) notes, citing household mobility among the Birhor of India (Williams 1974, 74) and numerous other hunter-gatherer studies (Balikci 1968; Lee 1969; Rogers 1962), in such approaches to hunter-gatherer mobility 'the duration and location of settlements are certainly influenced by many considerations, but the primary factors seem to be related to subsistence', and in particular the exhaustion of local food resources. (Although Jochim (1976, 69) also acknowledges other reasons for population movements, such as 'group fission for conflict resolution', these do not feature in any significant way in archaeological interpretations of this kind.) Mobility is thus largely confined to seasonal patterns of movement largely defined by fluctuating resource yields through the course of the year. Based on a review of ethnographic texts, and other things being equal, Jochim's (1976, 60) 'gravity model' of site location thus concludes that hunter-gatherer settlement sites will tend to be closer to less mobile resources, to more dense resources, and to less clustered resources, each of which would require less distant movements between people and resources. Within this framework of understanding, and 'subject to seasonal resource "pulls"', considerable variability in types of settlement systems are identified and account for the ethnographically documented variability in settlement systems, such as the coupling of base camps with short-term satellite extraction camps (Jochim 1976, 61). In such models, mobility is ultimately reduced to procurement logistics and cultural behaviour to 'strategies for survival' (Jochim 1981).

Within this same general school of thought, in some cases efficiency, optimizing or maximizing models of human behaviour have been generated as a means to identify biologically *idealized* adaptive strategies as a heuristic tool to compare and contrast with *actual* human practices (Ford et al. 2007; Jochim 1976; Koster 2008; Zeleznik and Bennett 1991; see Altmann 1998 for a similar approach to non-human primates). In such applications the degree of fit or difference between the idealized (modelled) adaptationist and actual behaviours are then said to better characterize the particular behavioural culture employed by the case in question. However, and paradoxically, this kind of modelling usually stems from theoretical frameworks that explicitly or implicitly see culture itself as a means by which animals (humans in particular) adapt to their environments, and thus by its own logic while the difference between the idealized and actual practices may be viewed as a measure of cultural particularity, that cultural difference stands both outside the idealized *adaptational* logic and within what is essentially a deviant but parallel *adaptational* logic by virtue of culture being preconceived as adaptationist in the first place. Similarly, human behavioural ecology 'studies variability in the adaptive design of human behaviour in specific ecological contexts' (Bird and Codding 2008, 398), and is thereby predisposed to understanding human behavioural variability as adaptive variability in the first place. Irrespective of the direct or indirect application of adaptationist reasonings to archaeological data, the net result of each of these interpretive frameworks to cultural practices and their archaeological correlates is that past and present behaviour, including patterns of mobility, are understood as (usually optimizing or maximizing) resourcing strategies ultimately functioning to meet subsistence needs. Human ecology—relations between people and their environments—is thus reduced to biological systems (individuals and groups) managing themselves in (or rather, being managed by) fluctuating (e.g. through climate change, environmental degradation) and spatially varied natural environments to meet biological sustenance needs through strategies of risk minimization or aversion in the management of uncertainty and food security, and subsistence optimization or maximization (Morgan 2009). Two ways of achieving this are to move consumers across the landscape, and resources to consumers, as noted above. Both options involve the adoption of mobility strategies to effect a rapprochement of consumers and resources, again an instance of human behaviour being reduced to subsistence (and thus sustenance) efficiency ultimately towards enhanced reproductive fitness. And because food procurement lies at the core of most hunter-gatherer adaptationist models, mobility itself is reduced to a series of idealized resourcing strategies.

In this logic the search for understanding mobility is not in itself so much a particularizing glance at social or cultural history as an exercise in understanding universal processes of mobility as part of the broader adaptational programme: how and when hunter-gatherers move is directly revealed by relating biological needs to locally available resources as natural products. The ensuing revelations are purported to be more evolutionary outcomes than historical contingencies, and even less are they considered social strategies following (at least in part) their own (and potentially self-destructive, i.e. non-adaptationist in an evolutionary sense) momentum.

Processualism

Processualism in archaeology relates to the systematic revelation and application of processes that direct cultural behaviour, usually set within a hypothetico-deductive logic. While processualism is often confounded with positivism, adaptationist approaches,

Middle Range Research, and the New Archaeology, in truth each of these can be addressed separately.

An example of processual logic often applied to hunter-gatherer archaeology is an apparent direct or linear relationship between decreasing levels of mobility, in the sense of increasing sedentism, and intensification of resource productivity and/or production (Gould 1985). Thus, a number of authors in Douglas Price and James Brown's (1985) *Prehistoric hunter-gatherers: the emergence of cultural complexity* relate nucleation, seeing 'increased sedentism and stability of settlement...as the hallmark of possible stratified communities of hunter-gatherers on the interior plateau of British Columbia'. Other authors in this same volume entertain similar ideas—long held by generations of archaeologists—of equating increasing hunter-gatherer complexity and a move from hunter-gatherer society to agricultural production, with increasing sedentism, the accumulation of uneasily moved material goods (such as pottery), a heightened potential for the storage of surplus products, the construction of immovable, high investment localized installations, the development of energy-harnessing infrastructure requiring permanent or semi-permanent use or maintenance, and centralized political and policing systems by which to defend decreasingly nomadic lifestyles and territory. 'Cultural complexity in one sense is a response to the problems resulting from decreased mobility,' write Brown and Price (1985, 437); 'Continual movement among foraging groups is responsible for the maintenance of certain archtypical features of primeval hunter-gatherer adaptations. Decreased mobility retards flexible response to stress and engages more institutional structures as essential solutions.'

However, there is by no means universal agreement as to cause and effect, or of necessary outcomes of increasing or decreasing mobility. Key variables much debated by archaeologists are the role of social relations (including conflict, territoriality, and social access to resources), kinship systems (such as the Australian eight-class system allowing or decreasing access to distant kin and goods thereby heightening or limiting response flexibility to resource depletions (Yengoyan 1968)), systems of alliance, trade relations, and competitive relations (such as of the famous Potlach-type: see, for example, papers in Flannery 1976; Price and Brown 1985).

Middle Range Research and Mobility

A central axiom of the New Archaeology is the search for general processes of human behaviour, affected through Middle Range Research (Binford 1981). Middle Range Research involves the accumulation of control data by which to investigate and identify 'organizational variables characteristic of past systems' (Binford 1987, 449), thereby allowing the construction of 'frames of reference' (Binford 2001). As Lewis Binford (2001) notes in the sub-title to his *magnum opus* of that name, the aim of Middle Range Research is 'an analytical method for archaeological theory building using ethnographic and environmental data sets'. Middle Range Research addressing processes of mobility has involved a range of concerns, most focusing on relationships between the degree of mobility, the structure and richness of natural food patches, and population size.

Based on systematic analyses of the world's ethnographic hunter-gatherer societies, Binford (2001) has thus argued a detailed set of generalizations and propositions that can be generally applied to hunter-gatherer mobility. Like much of his earlier work, these generalizations relate to organizational principles founded on an adaptationist logic. Thus, Generalization 7.20 states, 'The energy required to move from one foraging area to another is minimized by living in small groups, regardless of the level of food abundance', giving rise to Proposition 7.05 which states, 'Other things being equal, I anticipate that there is a minimum group size and an optimal small group size that should be characteristic of mobile hunters and gatherers regardless of other variable conditions'. Generalization 7.21 states, 'As the abundance of food in a habitat decreases, of necessity a group's mobility increases. Other things being equal, it is certain that greater net benefit is associated with small group sizes in food-poor settings', which leads to Proposition 7.06 whereby 'I expect the smallest groups and the most consistent relationships between mobility and group size to occur among peoples living in low-productivity habitats' (Binford 2001, 239–42).

A critical dimension of the applicability of such generalizations is that they are contingent on other things being equal, as Binford himself well recognized. One aspect of this condition long acknowledged by anthropologists and archaeologists concerns what is meant by 'hunter-gatherer' in the first place (for example, see Lévi-Strauss's (1968, 344–5) commentary from the 'Man the Hunter' conference). 'Some hunter-gatherers practise nomadism while others live in permanent residences...Now, nomadism itself may in some cases consist of wandering over several hundred square miles of territory; while among the Guayaki it consists merely in a daily inspection of a small bounded territory. From these and other types of variation—e.g. in social structure and in marriage rules—I conclude that it might be useful to widen the category of hunter-gatherer culture. Instead of defining it in terms of a number of specific groups that can be pointed out on a map, perhaps, the concept should be defined in terms of a certain way of life...Then we see that the object of our studies is not so much individual tribes as it is a certain type of behaviour', writes Lévi-Strauss (1968, 344). That is, rather than addressing 'hunter-gatherers' as a type, with their own laws of behaviour based on an adaptationist logic, we should address hunting and gathering as a practice. This would allow Binford's 'other things being equal' to be dealt with, for all things are never equal, varying by the very particular circumstances that generalizing assumptions cannot account for. Examples of critical factors which uneasily load the notion of 'hunter-gatherer', and problematic for the construction of 'frames of reference', include fishing, herding, plant management, and interactions with horticultural groups, all issues variably identified by Binford (2001), Testart (1982), Lévi-Strauss (1968), and others.

Successful attempts at modelling correlations between mobility patterns and the nature or structure of material behaviour have resulted from lithic studies which have been used to posit several central models of mobility in hunter-gatherer society. These have been inferred by examining the composition of artefactual assemblages and teaming this information with organizational factors such as distance from the source of stone and other procurement and transport costs.

Movement of people involves many permutations of what is often portrayed as a straightforward act. For instance, 'movement' can entail frequency, direction, distance, and motive (Close 2000). The stone tool record, as the often sole surviving archaeological record, is understandably regularly used to determine the nature of this complexity, with varying degrees of success (Kelly 1992, 55–6). Individual scales of movement are very difficult to trace archaeologically in all but the rarest of cases. Thus studies of mobility through the stone artefact record are restricted to what Brantingham (2006, 435) refers to as 'low level behavioural models'; models which refer to broad 'patterns of mobility' or 'mobility strategies' (Close 2000, 50). Such 'strategies' or 'patterns' can incorporate inferences made about site-occupation patterns and site types; for instance mobility patterns can distinguish 'long-term' from 'short-term' occupations or 'base camps' from 'special-activity sites' (including seasonally occupied sites: Close 2000, 51–2). In other words, the broad-brush concept of 'mobility' incorporates many different types of organizational factors, several of which will be discussed here.

Two of the principal variants of mobility which are discussed through the stone artefact assemblage are those of *frequency* and *distance* of travel. Both aspects have been inferred through variability of assemblages, principally the presence or absence of a curated (reworked/maintained) or retouched technology. Retouched stone tools such as bifaces or scrapers, coupled with the curation of these tools, usually implies a long and multifunctional use life, low raw-material consumption, low hafting costs, high production costs in terms of labour and expertise, and ease of portability (Bamforth 1991; Cowen 1999; Kelly 1988; Shott 1986; Wallace and Shea 2006). Conversely, expedient flake technologies have a short use life and less flexibility in terms of function, have few production costs in terms of labour, and are less portable (Wallace and Shea 2006). These factors have been utilized to infer that assemblages with a variety of curated and retouched tools are indicative of a people who have differential access to the source of raw material. By implication, they are mobile, and are thus invested in producing tools that can serve multiple purposes, are portable, and will last for longer periods of time than expedient flake technologies (see Odell 2001 for a review of these and other models).

This kind of modelling has been applied widely to hunter-gatherer mobility studies in a variety of geographic and temporal contexts. For instance, Hoovers (2001, cited in Wallace and Shea 2006, 1295) and Meignen et al. (2005) have argued for a decrease in mobility between the earlier and later phases of the Middle Palaeolithic period in the Levant based on an increased presence of expedient core technologies. Using similar principles, a converse model has been proposed by McCall (2007) for the Middle Stone Age of South Africa. Based on the presence of a bifacial point technology, McCall (2007) argues that people in this region ranged significantly from their sources of raw materials, which had become more widely distributed as a result of deteriorating environmental conditions (see also Dibble 1988; Kuhn 1995).

Stone tool technologies are also used to great effect to describe a number of disconformities between the Middle and the Upper Palaeolithic (often referred to as the 'Upper Palaeolithic Revolution'). For example, the technology of the Upper Palaeolithic can be characterized as a systematic production of prismatic blades (Kuhn and Bietti 2000; Mellars 1989). This shift from Levallois to Aurignacian technology represents a high degree of standardization and morphological variability (Mellars 1989) as well as greatly increased efficiency of raw material use, indicative of high procurement costs (see Bar-Yosef 2002). Coupled with an increase in exotic raw materials, there is also an inferred system of long-distance exchange networks operating during this time (Johnson and Earle 2000), indicating a certain kind of mobility.

The Pleistocene/Holocene transition is said to be marked by significant environmental changes and an increasing complexity within hunter-gatherer societies across much of the world. This is expressed by (among other things) a marked diversity and regionalization of subsistence strategies, an increased diversity in resource use, resource intensification, changing settlement patterns, craft specialization, and diversity of tool-kits. The sheer scope of this regionalization and diversity is such that a comprehensive discussion becomes impossible. There is, however, scope to present a case study dating to the mid-late Holocene, from the eastern Victoria River region, Northern Territory, Australia (Clarkson 2006).

Clarkson's study of three sites is indicative of two emerging trends in the analysis of stone tools in Australia: a move towards technological analyses of reduction for the characterization of tool typologies, and an increasing focus on regional sequences and modelling. Using an innovative technique aimed at quantifying reduction intensity (see Clarkson 2002a), Clarkson examines point manufacture throughout the mid-late Holocene and identifies changing reduction intensities from 3000 BP onwards. This takes the form of an increase in the frequency of bifacial points at 2000 BP and the emergence of new pressure flaking techniques (flaked lancets and Kimberley points) at 1000 BP. The points are standardized in design, suggestive of a specific role or function (as projectiles); they are maintainable and the use life is able to be prolonged through further invasive reduction. Clarkson (2006, 1–4, 105) posits that these factors act as a buffer against unpredictable access to resources, which is further indicative of changing land-use patterns, including a shift towards a logistical/radiating mobility pattern. Similar modelling has been successfully used elsewhere in Australia (Clarkson 2002b; Hiscock 1994; 1996; McNiven 1994; 2000), on the North American continent (Amick 1996; Bamforth 1991; Blades 2003; Bousman 1993; Kelly 1988; Kelly and Todd 1988; Kent 1992; Morrow 1997; Parry and Kelly 1987), in Asia (Madsen et al. 1996), and in Europe (Kuhn 1991).

Mobile intentions. In an influential study of historic mining camps in the south-west Yukon, Stevenson (1982) investigated site abandonment behaviour through the way objects were arranged spatially at the time of departure. Abandonment processes, he concluded, were not random, as departure with anticipated return generally caused people to leave sites clean and in good order, whereas intended permanent departure from a site left that site in a relatively unkempt state. It is arguable that these general principles apply to hunter-gatherers as well as historic miners, with departure from a location entailing anything from complete disregard for the ordering of space and material objects (in the case of unanticipated return) to their careful arrangement or packaging (anticipated return).

POST-PROCESSUAL APPROACHES TO THE ARCHAEOLOGY OF MOBILITY

Historicism

More than any other, archaeology's greatest defining strength is its ability to historicize the way we engage in the world: 'taskscapes' (Ingold 1993) need to be positioned in their historical settings, revealing ways of doing things that can be traced, and can themselves be understood as historical products. Each particular activity, cultural trait, and even adaptive strategy employed, including patterns of mobility as expressed in social interaction, mode of transport, short- to long-distance transaction, migration, reciprocity network, invasion, resource extraction, system of redistribution, seasonal cycle, pattern of access to place and people, transhumance, religious journey, and size and tempo of group movement can be historicized. As Tim Ingold (1993, 172) notes, 'the apprehension of the landscape in the dwelling perspective must begin from a recognition of its temporality. Only through such recognition, by temporalizing the landscape, can we move beyond the division that has afflicted most inquiries up to now, between the "scientific" study of an atemporalized nature, and the "humanistic" study of a dematerialized history. And no discipline is better placed to take this step than archaeology. I have not been concerned here with either the methods or the results of archaeological inquiry. However to the question, "what is archaeology the study *of*?", I believe there is no better answer than "the temporality of the landscape".' The archaeology of hunter-gatherer mobility is, essentially, about the temporality of movement in all its guises.

The Temporality of the Landscape: Ways of Walking

In his classic paper on the temporality of landscape, Tim Ingold (1993, 171) points out that the landscape 'is not a totality that you or anyone else can look at, it is rather the world in which we stand in taking up a point of view on our surroundings'. This is a temporal world in which actions are experienced in time and place, and in the passing of time in and across place: 'In the landscape, the distance between two places, A and B, is experienced as a journey made, a bodily movement from one place to the other, and the gradually changing vistas along the route' (Ingold 1993, 154). Our movements from one place to the next take place in a meaningful world where we 'hear the swish of scythes against the cornstalks and the calls of the birds as they swoop low over the field in search of prey. Far off in the distance, wafted on the light wind, can be heard the sounds of people conversing and playing on a green, behind which, on the other side of the stream, lies a cluster of cottages. What you hear is a taskscape' (Ingold 1993, 170). An archaeology of mobility that aims to write a history of people and cultures must thus go beyond adaptationist laws and subsistence needs, requiring rather an 'attentive involvement in the landscape' that goes to the heart of historical experiences and cultural specificities and that cannot be relegated to 'epiphenomena' (Ingold 1993, 171; see also Basso 1984). The archaeologist has a key role to play in this process, for it is through informed story-telling that 'stories help to open up the world' (Ingold 1993, 171). And as 'archaeologists study the meaning of the landscape...by probing ever more deeply into it' (Ingold 1993, 172), the archaeology of mobility allows us to study the relationships of places in human lives; the archaeology of mobility allows us to historicize the meaningfulness of the landscape for those who dwelt there in the past by historicizing the relationality of place. Moving across the landscape involves 'ways of walking', and archaeological sites come into being in the process of getting there and departing. Sites enchain action and actions enchain sites through the way each mediates movement and behaviour in an animated landscape. A site has ancestry, meaning, is built upon (and in this has movement), draws our attention, is in a state of interaction with various kinds of beings (animals, people, plants, spirits, ancestors, and so forth), and can have their own numinous powers. Like walking and thinking, sites have beginnings and ends, but 'every moment of beginning is itself in the midst of things and must, for that reason, be also a moment of ending in relation to whatever went before' (Ingold and Vergunst 2008, 1). A site is alive in the sense that it is in a continual process of transformation through the way it is engaged and connected with others. It is part of a mobile world in which people pass from one place to another, and this passing creates connectivities that are, in Chapman's (2000) term, an *enchainment* of time, place, people, meaning, and event. It is the archaeology of these enchainments that an archaeology of mobility allows (for an Upper Palaeolithic case study using faunal remains, stone artefacts, and 'objects of value', see Geneste et al. 2008).

One example of the temporality of the landscape and its temporal enchainment, with implications for a journeyed landscape, is offered by Lesley McFadyen (2008, 309–11) for the Beckhampton Road long-barrow site (Wiltshire, England):

> On a small chalky ridge of glacial drift deposits located in a gentle valley, long-standing grassland had been cut into and stakes erected. After the stakes had rotted, a large fire setting was created, over 4 metres in length and nearly 2 metres wide, which was then smothered by dumps of soil and turf. Time was marked in evident ways at this site. There was, for example, grassland that became established over a long period of time, and then came the cutting down of wood into stakes, which was followed by a period when things were allowed to decay. The setting of a fire and the burning of wood, then the addition of soil and turf and the quick smothering of the flames followed this period of inactivity. Then there was another delay or gap in the record of the past at this place.

These time gaps were not simply fortuitous but were a central part of the architectural process. The generation of a time gap was also a part of 'building' as an active process.

Time gaps in construction are points of departure that position mobility as integral to social activity. Seeds, micro- and macro-plant remains, seasonal faunal remains (both cultural and non-) including land snails, beetles, lizards, and sediments can each guide archaeological enquiry into the timing of past actions, helping establish how mobility has itself participated in past relations between people and the world in which they live. These temporal gaps of activity, together with the spatial connections evidenced by foreign archaeological objects (e.g. imported obsidians, shells, and so forth) and constructions evidencing group activities (i.e. agglomerations), identify mobility as a central component of historicized landscapes.

The Embeddedness of Mobility

One aspect of mobility studies that fundamentally differentiates post-processualist from adaptationist approaches is the former's reluctance to dislocate particular aspects of culture from their broader ontological contexts. Such contexts incorporate all aspects of culture as inter-referenced, without individual parts being from the onset differentiated as 'core' or 'determinant' versus 'marginal' or 'epiphenomena'. Rather, all aspects, including mobility in all its guises, are embedded in meaning—including what Ballard (1998) calls 'moral topography'—and this meaningfulness is the mark of the particular culture at stake; understanding life actions cannot proceed by reducing this meaningfulness to a single determining force (such as subsistence or survival). Thus, while adaptationist mobility studies are framed through principles or models of adaptive behaviour that allow *humans* (as biological beings) to cope with the resource richness or resource poverty of the spaces in which they find themselves, post-processualist approaches understand mobility as a means by which *people* (as social beings) go about their everyday lives, which includes but is not singularly reduced to food cycles and provisioning strategies, defence strategies or other survival imperatives.

As Linse (1993, 25) notes, 'Artefact density and sub-surface deposits, site size, and reoccupation are not entirely independent of each other', each helping structure, and to be structured by, patterns of mobility and sedentism. Mobility studies, rather, need to investigate the culture of movement in its historical context: technologies, social connections, social schedules, and social structures each need to be taken into account *for their particularities* when attempting to understand when, why, where, and how people travel from place to place. Far from being reduced to biological pawns of determining natural environments, people act with cultural values (sometimes breaking them), sometimes doing things that have low survival value, and repeatedly move in accordance with the way they understand the world to *be* (incorporating the religious, spiritual, and territorial embeddedness of the landscape and related social responsibilities). In these approaches to mobility the emphasis is on characterizing and historicizing particular modes and tempos of movement, itself part of the project of characterizing and historicizing cultural specificities.

A useful example of the ontological and cosmological embeddedness of mobility is offered by John Bradley (2008), working among the Yanyuwa of northern Australia. Here Bradley shows how landscapes themselves are imbued with a meaningfulness that can only be understood by reference to culturally specific orderings of the world. Thus for the Yanyuwa, places have spiritual significance, and the resources found in particular locations are themselves residual evidence of past sacred actions. Human mobility in this landscape takes place synergistically with sanctioned cultural understandings rather than through so-called 'rationalist' economic decisions that may be discordant with that specific cultural logic.

Elsewhere, Lemonnier (1993) notes that in the Highlands of Papua New Guinea particular forms of marriage arrangement such as sister exchange connect social groups and, in so doing, help structure ceremonial exchanges of pigs and other wealth. The fulfilment of such exchanges, including return gift-giving in delayed reciprocal arrangements, takes place between residential groups, requiring the movement of participants in the process. Through time the fulfilment of competitive and delayed reciprocity, ceremonial events, and ceremonial obligations take on an aggrandizing trend; patterns of mobility between groups can thus be expected to change along the way, a further indication of the embeddedness of mobility in broader social processes.

Territoriality and Social Structure

Hunter-gatherer groups, particularly during the Holocene, saw significant reconfigurations in social and demographic structures. Archaeologists have, through a range of analytical means, posited these changes in terms of smaller territories, more bounded areas, and, attendant to this, a restricted access to resources (see Price and Brown 1985, for example). Necessary conditions for this complexity include a high population, geographically or socially restricted movement, as well as plentiful and predictable resources (Cohen 1985; Hayden 1994; Price and Brown 1985, 10). With greater pressures on resources and a demographic emphasis on boundaries, access to resources became more tightly controlled or 'bounded' (Barker 2004, 20; David and Cole 1990, 789). An example of this idea of bounded access to resources comes from the Whitsunday Islands along the central Queensland coast,

Australia (Barker 1989; 1991; 2004; Lamb 2005a); specifically a stone quarry located on South Molle Island, some 2 kilometres from the mainland coast (Lamb 1996; 2005a).

The South Molle Island Quarry (SMIQ) was utilized by coastal-dwelling hunter-gatherers of the Whitsunday Islands from approximately 9000 BP to recent times (Barker 2004; Lamb 2005a). This extended use was documented through several lithic sequences in stratified rock-shelter sites across the region (Barker 2004; Barker and Lamb 2001). The very presence of these archaeological assemblages indicates a degree of open access to the raw material source, as people were travelling by sea for distances of up to 40 kilometres (round trip) to access the quarry. Analyses of these rock-shelter assemblages by Lamb (2005a) demonstrated that the discarded stone was a product of backed artefact manufacture—backed artefacts being the most prolific stone tool 'type' in the southern portion of the Australian continent. Throughout the Holocene in the Whitsunday region, there was a steady decline in stone artefact discard, indicating that people were no longer manufacturing artefacts in rock shelters to the same degree that they were during the early Holocene. Lamb (2005a, 213–17) thus posited that this decline represented a tighter control over access to the stone at the quarry, and that rather than people having more or less open access to the raw material, access became increasingly restricted by key figures from within the controlling social group. In this context, and in the face of declining discard within the occupied rock shelters, the quarry probably became the epicentre for the manufacture of backed artefacts by specialists who had principal control over the resource, as evidenced also by the presence of hundreds of backed artefacts in various stages of manufacture at the quarry itself (Lamb 2005a; 2005b).

Just who these key figures were is an issue that can be explored through gendered craft specialization. Elsewhere, the identification of task differentiation was utilized in an important study by Sassaman (1998). In highlighting that many of the subsistence changes that took place in the late Holocene (the addition of pottery, an increasing reliance on shellfish, plants, and starchy seeds) were attributable to women's activities, Sassaman (1998) makes the case for women requiring greater access to flaked stone technologies. Further to this, by examining the discarding of stone in domestic task areas that are typically seen as feminized, Sassaman argues that we can chart technological behaviour of women in the archaeological record. However, this issue remains contentious, and is still active in archaeological debates. While Gero (1991), for example, identifies a politicized interest in attributing stone tool use to men, ethnographically it appears as though *access to the stone source* is a male activity (Gould 1977; Hamilton 1980, cited in Gero 1991, 168; Jones and White 1988). Kearney (2008, 252–3) recreates the investigation for gender in the archaeological record as a search for complementary rather than opposing systems and suggests that the way forward is to continue to identify contemporary gender expressions for ethnoarchaeological investigation. It is clear that in the presence of gendered space, mobility itself becomes embedded in this culturally specific gendering.

That territory—the recognition of circumscribed land ownership—is critical to human movement across the landscape has long been recognized in anthropology (for a recent example see Politis 2006). The historicizing of territoriality through the archaeological distribution of material goods, including stone artefacts, portable objects of art, and rock art (David and Chant 1995) has, however, received less attention, although examples nevertheless remain numerous. Thus Castel et al. (2005) and Geneste et al. (2008) have applied a territoriality and social interaction approach to the archaeology of Solutrean mobility in south-west France by mapping regional faunal procurement patterns and the geographical distribution and circulation of valued objects. They argue that while procurement strategies relate in part to natural resource distributions including seasonal dynamics, human mobility and access to resources are not limited to those natural distributions but rather incorporate also social networks visible archaeologically through the spatial circulation of objects, thereby allowing archaeologists to demarcate territorially constricted and territorially enhanced patterns of mobility (see also Allard et al. 2001 for a similar approach to the provisioning of Upper Palaeolithic lithic resources through socio-territoriality).

Sacred Geographies

A major criticism of settlement-subsistence approaches to the archaeology of mobility is the silencing of what are often the most important reasons as to why people go to particular locations, or that structure human movement on the ground: the numinous endowment of the landscape. Lived landscapes are located in cosmological understandings: how we know the world to operate through spirit essences, sacred forces, and empowered ancestral legacies. It is as sacred geographies that places are located in culture, and the archaeology of hunter-gatherers would artificially evade a central guiding force to human organization and patterns of movement were this aspect of social life to be ignored and airbrushed away.

The issue of sacred geographies has been tackled by numerous archaeologists over the last two decades in particular (Ballard 1994; 1998; David et al. 1994; McNiven 2003). Here we restrict ourselves to a single example from Aboriginal Australia: the use of the sacred mountain of Ngarrabullgan by the local Djungan population.

Nagarrabullgan is an 18 km long and 6.5 km wide mesa in north-east Australia, and lies at the geographical and spiritual heart of Djungan country. Surrounded by 200–400 m cliffs and of difficult access along most of its periphery, during ethnographic times the mountain was (as it continues to be) also home to four 'devils' or potentially dangerous spirit-beings: Eekoo, Beerroo, Mooramully, and Barmboo. Eekoo and Mooramully in particular were responsible for sickness, residing on the mountain-top. As a result of these spirit-beings, few Djungan ventured onto the mountain in fear of the powerful spirits who could render them ill or bring death.

Archaeological explorations, including systematic excavation at all the known sites with excavatable deposits, revealed a paucity of occupation on the mountain during the last 600 years, but common presence during earlier times. As this period does not correspond with the timing of significant changes in resource availability on or near the mountain, and as sites immediately surrounding Ngarrabullgan do not exhibit this pattern of abandonment, David (2002) argued that these changes signified a change in systems of land use and signification, including the beginnings of the ethnographic period's Dreaming significance involving Eekoo and Mooramully in particular, the mountain's most dangerous spirits. The case of Ngarrabullgan represents a useful reminder of the place of cosmology in patterns of movement across the landscape, and the embeddedness of mobility in the spatialization of meaning.

Similar examples of the impact of spirit presences on patterns of movement can be seen elsewhere, as in, for example, the establishment of Rumu ossuaries and their access procedures in Papua New Guinea (David et al. 2008), whereby clan members travel to their clan ossuaries to accompany the recently dead to the gateway of the clan land of the dead. A further example of the role of sacred geographies in human movement is the pilgrimage (for example, to ancestral origin places), with its power to transfer material goods as well as people over vast distances.

The Flow of Place

As Stafford and Hajic (1992, 141) remind us, 'Particular land use strategies result in different patterns and rates of movement across a landscape.' Mobility is about going from place to place, and therefore the archaeology of mobility needs to consider the way places are connected into experienced and engaged landscapes; dwelling comes in the everyday flow of place through the passing of travelled time. Following local indigenous perspectives, Deborah Bird Rose (1992) writes of Australian Aboriginal connections to place through the notion of 'strings', whereby the movement of people across 'country'—itself a notion that is more than 'place', embedding sacred, ancestral, customary, and experiential relations to place towards a notion of 'home' and 'homeland', as in 'country of the heart' (e.g. Rose et al. 2002; see also Hercus et al. 2002)—entails a continuous re-enactment of the ancestral creative forces that gave and give the world its present shape. Strings 'are webs of connections', she writes, and 'Dreaming strings fix country and people, demarcating human and geographical identity' (Rose 1992, 52–3). The flow of place, the movement of people and resources across the landscape, connects present rights to live in places with ancestral actions that gifted descendant clans with landscapes that are also social and sacred topographies incorporating trade partnerships, ancestral creation tracks (e.g. in Aboriginal Australia, 'Dreamings'), kinship laws, ritual schedules, and rights to place flowing in a network of streams that articulate as sacred catchments historically carved in the social landscape as ancestral pre-stations (a case where the 'sacred' and 'profane' merge). By looking at the connectivity of place by historicizing movement and the way that locales and societies are networked, archaeology is well equipped to tackle that purportedly most difficult of historical tasks, the so-called intangible aspects of life: the archaeology of meaning and of the sacred.

CONCLUSIONS

Over many years anthropologists (e.g. Barthes 1970; Lévi-Strauss 1969; 1979) have taught us that myth lies in opposition to everyday earthly life while at the same time reflecting human action and being, a mirror image of life as we know it. In this sense Jack Kaiwari's mythical clan origin story acts as a useful means by which to reflect on our own models and investigative frameworks as intellectual myths: useful and necessary heuristic tools by which to understand the world, but always involving an outside onlooker who gives meaning to something else, and thus, in the mould of the hyper-real (Baudrillard 1994; Eco 1986), always constituting a perspective away from the existential reality we try to access. With these thoughts in mind, let us reflect on themes that emerge from established archaeological approaches to the archaeology of hunter-gatherer landscapes and mobility through the eyes of this other creation myth, allowing us to draw better-nuanced (and in this better-informed if not entirely new) perspectives on human movement. These reflections on perspectives relating to landscapes of mobility signal intellectual movements towards an archaeology of past *cultures of mobility* in engaged landscapes. This in turn signals future archaeologies of dwelling in what are essentially foreign landscapes: the archaeology of both mobility and landscape call for researchers to commence with a premise of 'the past is a foreign country' (Lowenthal 1985), it being the task of archaeology to shed light on those past and forever-changing cultural perspectives.

Emplacement: 'they didn't go anywhere': The act of moving across the landscape, or engaging in mobility, is given relevance and meaning by the positioning of people *who remain in place*. This concept of 'staying' and the lived experience of the people who stay, construct meanings of *origin* for those who leave. This is conducted through a process of inscription of sensual experience upon the landscape, which, it has been posited (Low and Lawrence-Zuniga 2003), transforms 'space' into 'place'; place being imagined by those who leave, and lived by those who stay. The archaeology of landscapes of mobility thus requires consideration of behaviourally and spatially fragmented but enchained (Chapman 2000) perspectives: consideration needs to be given to positions of initial emplacement, departures, transitions, arrivals, connections, means, and logics of movement as much as outcomes.

Emergence: 'we originated from that part of the area': Mobility can and does result from many varied root causes. The act of leaving a place can be experienced as a loss of territorial roots (Gupta and Ferguson 1992), an act of colonization, an expansion of economic productivity, or an act of exploration (Rockman and Steel 2003). Integral to the process of migration is the making of memory and the making of a collective identity that resonates as much of the place of origin as of the place into which people emerge (Leonard 1992, cited in Gupta and Ferguson 1992, 11). The role of remembering a locale from a distance (a 'homeland') reinforces the idea of territoriality 'just at the point it threatens to be erased' (Gupta and Ferguson 1992, 11); thus memories of lived experience in one place are inscribed upon the experience of another and come to both transform and create identity. This signals the relevance of interpersonal connections (at individual and social scales) and connectivities across space and through time.

Contextual mappings: 'I have boundaries with the other clans'; 'people came to visit them': Boundaries themselves can be posited as fluid and flexible (see also Goldman and Ballard 1998 for applications of 'fluid' thought in archaeology and anthropology). Among the people of the upper and middle reaches of the Kikori River, for example, boundaries are frequently comprised of a series of social relationships such as ancestral entrances which are '*implicated* in the landscape' rather than '*imposed* upon the landscape' (see Bender 1999, 39). Impermanent natural features such as creeks, trees, rivers, and flying fox populations can also formulate boundaries, and as such they can have a 'recognized transience and changeability' (Bender 1999). There is also a degree of fluidity to clan membership which characterizes 'customary law' in Papua New Guinea. In some instances, while a fixed village may represent the focal point for a group, the villages may be open in their recruitment, or indeed be in competition (Jorgensen 2007, 63), and if kinship is constructed cognately, or through affinal relationships of marriage, people can claim ties to multiple groups in several territorial estates. Through patrilineal descent, people are born into or become members of clans within those language groups by virtue of demonstrating an unbroken line of descent to founding ancestors, through male links. Movement from place to place is common, often in response to internal disputes. As in other landed, descent-based societies, people may gain membership to social groups through long-term residence or service to the group. For example, this would happen typically if a man moved to his mother's land, and then his descendants continued to work in the gardens that he established (James Weiner pers. comm. 2009).

Meanings: transformed and transforming landscape: 'my land flows towards the Kikori River in the east and the Omati River in the west'; 'those boys always lived under the caves of Kuruma and Eiapo in the mountains': The concept of 'landscape' has been utilized in anthropology and archaeology for decades to describe a physical entity which contains parameters for movement, territory, and economic resource placement. However, as Gosden and Head (1994, 113) point out, 'landscape encompasses both the conceptual and the physical', and this widening of the lens through which we view people and their place in the world is reflected in an increasingly varied approach to the concept (Bender 1993; 1999; David and Cole 1990; David and Thomas 2008; Head et al. 1994; Layton and Ucko 1999; Smith 1999). This is exemplified by Ingold (1993, 156) who describes landscape as 'a pattern of activities "collapsed" into an array of features' which remains visible after the people who created these patterns have disappeared.

Jack Kaiwari's mythical clan-origin story points to a layer of meaning that is indicative of a more non-Western, indigenous mapping. The mythical movements of, for example, 'those boys [who] changed themselves into bats' affect how people understand themselves within the landscape, including in relation to each other. This manner of understanding affects where they go, when they travel, who they interact with and how, what activities are undertaken upon their arrival, and how the actual act of moving is understood; whether as trade, pilgrimage, visitation, or migration. Thus the distribution of material goods, which constitutes the principal tool of archaeological interpretation, is shaped by mythical understandings of the landscape by the people who occupy it as a physical entity and create it as a conceptual entity. This relationship highlights the lived landscape as inherently entailing both the 'inside' and the 'outside' of myths (Hirsch 2006, 151; Wagner 2001) and exemplifies another layer of how the properties of 'landscape' can be understood.

Time and ancestral myth: 'they know that's their girls and their place of origin'; 'they lived there in the time of our ancestors': It has previously been argued (Ballard 2003) that archaeological explanation functions within frameworks that are fundamentally narrative-like in character. Further, that instead of detracting from our ability to function as a science, this allows us to widen the scope and richness of the areas we are able to explore (Ballard 2003, 135). *A propos* of this, societies' myths allow us to explore time—specifically perceptions of time and how time is received and given meaning/constituted within societies. Wagner (1986, cited in Hirsch 2006, 153) argues that it is not so much the *passage* of time that is rendered visible by myth (see Lévi-Strauss 1979) but the *presence* of time; thus the present is rendered apparent and obvious (Hirsch 2006, 153). Much as a migration experience is equally informed by the place of origin as it is by the place of emergence, so too is the broader present informed by the past. Therefore, it could be argued that ancestral myths such as the one told by Jack Kaiwari give meaning and visibility to the present, by constructing a meaning for/out of the past. Analysis of archaeological data, as the material record of this past, can benefit enormously from the exploration of mythology, because 'what is happening *inside* the myth is intrinsically related to what goes on *outside* the myth'

(Hirsch 2006, 158); thus visible form is given to the realms of 'present/past' and 'inside/outside myth'.

Gender and ancestral myth/movement: 'But originally my girls came from the cucumber fruit. And those cucumber vines were used by my ancestral clan men, Namiri and Dabugai and their boys to move around: they were using the girls to move around': The degree to which the mythical traditions of a society are either removed from, or integrated within social life (Silverman 1996, 32) can determine the extent to which human agents come to embody mythical elements. This can be an instructive issue with regard to social organization and differential access to power within a given polity; if, for example, agents embody mythical elements, then there is likely to be a certain homology between the human body, the social body, and the cosmology (Silverman 1996). While grounded in a Durkheimian functionality (Durkheim 1957), these interpretive tools can lend considerable power to the analysis of material remains, with a view to formulating models of social organization, kinship relations, sexual division of labour, and access to material resources. However, as Weiner (1988, 567) cautions, this is a viable approach only if we 'render the functionalist implications of our analysis supple, analogic, and historical, rather than reify them as superorganic principle' (see also Harrison 1985).

Landscapes of mobility—myth without endings: 'what I have told you is part of the story': The story of Jack Kaiwari and his clan is continually evolving out of the past, out of his origins, and in the present. His origin myth illuminates for us the importance of place as a 'basic unit of lived experience' (Casey 2008, 44) and allows us to reflect in new ways about landscapes of mobility with reference to place and origins in relation to both past and ongoing socio-spatial relations. It is instructive that in Jack Kaiwari's story, food and resource procurement does not feature as a central focal point. Instead, landscapes, mobility, residence, history, gender, kinship, and territoriality are centrally located in a world of mythical origins. By unpacking components of the myth, we can gain a more nuanced and differently understood version of the workings of Jack Kaiwari's clan history and its emplacement (incorporating ontologies of place). Through the examination of this origin story we have allowed a degree of mobility and fluidity to feature in how we think about others and how place itself features in their existence. It allows us to travel not only spatially and temporally, but also intellectually and ontologically, and in doing so to bring a fresh approach to the study of both landscapes of mobility and of the way we understand ourselves and others via the stories we tell.

References

Allard, M., Chalard, P., and Martin, H. 2001. Témoins de mobilité humaine aux Peyrugues (Orniac, Lot) durant le Paléolithique Supérieur: signification spatio-temporelle. In J. Jaubert and M. Barbaza (eds.), *Territoires, déplacements, mobilité, échanges durant la préhistoire: terres et hommes du sud*, 219–231. Paris: Comité des Travaux Historiques et Scientifiques.

Allen, J. 1996. The pre-Austronesian settlement of Island Melanesia: implications for Lapita archaeology. In W. H. Goodenough (ed.), *Prehistoric settlement of the Pacific*, 11–27. Philadelphia: American Philosophical Society.

Altmann, S. A. 1998. *Foraging for survival: yearling baboons in Africa*. Chicago: University of Chicago Press.

Amick, D. S. 1996. Regional patterns of Folsom mobility and land use in the American Southwest. *World Archaeology* 27, 411–26.

Balikci, A. 1968. The Netsilik Eskimos: adaptive processes. In R. B. Lee and I. DeVore (eds), *Man the hunter*, 78–82. Chicago: Aldine.

Ballard, C. 1994. The centre cannot hold: trade networks and sacred geography in the Papua New Guinea Highlands. *Archaeology in Oceania* 29, 130–48.

Ballard, C. 1998. The sun by night: Huli moral topography and myths of a time of darkness. In L. R. Goldman and C. Ballard (eds), *Fluid ontologies: myth, ritual and philosophy in the highlands of Papua New Guinea*, 67–85. Wesport, CT: Bergin and Garvey.

Ballard, C. 2003. Writing (pre)history: narrative and archaeological explanation in the New Guinea highlands. *Archaeology in Oceania* 38, 135–48.

Bamforth, D. B. 1991. Technological organization and hunter-gatherer land use: a Californian example. *American Antiquity* 56, 216–34.

Barker, B. 1989. Nara Inlet 1: a Holocene sequence from the Whitsunday Islands, central Queensland coast. *Queensland Archaeological Research* 6, 53–76.

Barker, B. 1991. Nara Inlet 1: coastal resource use and the Holocene marine transgression in the Whitsunday Islands, central Queensland. *Archaeology in Oceania* 26, 102–9.

Barker, B. 2004. *The Sea People: late Holocene maritime specialisation in the Whitsunday Islands, central Queensland*. Canberra: Pandanus Press.

Barker, B. and Lamb, L. 2001. Evidence for early Holocene change in the Whitsunday Islands: A new radiocarbon determination, Nara Inlet 1. *Australian Archaeology* 53, 42–3.

Barthes, R. 1970. *Mythologies*. Paris: Seuil.

Bar-Yosef, O. 2002. The Upper Palaeolithic revolution. *Annual Review of Anthropology* 31, 363–93.

Basso, K. 1984. 'Stalking with stories': names, places, and moral narratives among the Western Apache. In E. M. Bruner (ed.), *Text, play and story: the construction and reconstruction of self and society*, 19–55. Washington: American Ethnological Society.

Baudrillard, J. 1994. *Simulacra and simulation*. Ann Arbor: University of Michigan Press.

Bender, B. 1993. Introduction: landscape—meaning and action. In B. Bender (ed.), *Landscape: politics and perspectives*, 1–17. Oxford: Berg.

Bender, B. 1999. Subverting the Western gaze: mapping alternative worlds. In R. Layton and P. Ucko (eds) *The archaeology and anthropology of landscape*, 31–43. New York: Routledge.

Bender, B. and Winer, M. (eds) 2001. *Contested landscapes: movement, exile and place*. Oxford: Berg.

Binford, L. R. 1980. Willow smoke and dogs' tails: hunter-gatherer settlement systems and archaeological site formation. *American Antiquity* 45, 1–17.

Binford, L. R. 1981. *Bones: ancient men and modern myths*. New York: Academic Press.

Binford, L. R. 1982. The archaeology of place. *Journal of Anthropological Archaeology* 1, 5–31.

Binford, L. R. 1987. Researching ambiguity: frames of reference and site structure. In S. Kent (ed.), *Method and theory for activity area research: an ethnoarchaeological approach*, 449–512. New York: Columbia University Press.

Binford, L. R. 2001. *Constructing frames of reference: an analytical method for archaeological theory building using ethnographic and environmental data sets*. Berkeley: University of California Press.

Binford, L. R and Johnson, A. L. 2002. Foreword. In B. Fitzhugh and J. Habu (eds), *Beyond foraging and collecting: evolutionary change in hunter-gatherer settlement systems*, vii–xiii. New York: Kluwer Academic/Plenum Press.

Bintliff, J. (ed.) 1991. *The Annales school and archaeology*. London: Leicester University Press.

Bird, D. W. and Codding, B. 2008. Human behavioral ecology and the use of ancient landscapes. In B. David and J. Thomas (eds), *Handbook of landscape archaeology*, 396–408. Walnut Creek, CA: Left Coast Press.

Birdsell, J. B. 1967. Preliminary data on the tri-hybrid origin of the Australian Aborigines. *Archaeology and Physical Anthropology in Oceania* 2, 100–55.

Blades, B. S. 2003. End scraper reduction and hunter-gatherer mobility. *American Antiquity* 68, 141–56.

Bonnemaison, J., Cambrezy, L., and Quinty-Bourgeois, L. 1999. *Les territoires de l'identité: le territoire, lien ou frontière?* Paris: L'Harmattan.

Bousman, C. B. 1993. Hunter–gatherer adaptations, economic risk and tool design. *Lithic Technology* 18, 59–86.

Bradley, J. J. 2008. When a stone tool is a dingo: country and relatedness in Australian Aboriginal notions of landscape. In B. David and J. Thomas (eds), *Handbook of landscape archaeology*, 633–43. Walnut Creek, CA: Left Coast Press.

Brantingham, P. 2006. Measuring forager mobility. *Current Anthropology* 47, 435–59.

Braudel, F. 1990 [1949]. *La Méditerranée et le monde Méditerranéen à l'époque de Philippe II*. Paris: Armand Colin.

Brown, J. A. and Price, T. D. 1985. Complex hunter-gatherers: retrospect and prospect. In T. D. Price and J. A. Brown (eds), *Prehistoric hunter-gatherers: the emergence of cultural complexity*, 435–42. Orlando: Academic Press.

Casey, E. 2008. Place in landscape archaeology: a Western philosophical prelude. In B. David and J. Thomas (eds), *Handbook of landscape archaeology*, 44–50. Walnut Creek, CA: Left Coast Press.

Castel, J.-C., Chadelle, J.-P., and Geneste, J.-M. 2005. Nouvelle approche des territoires solutréens du sud-ouest de la France. In J. Jaubert and M. Barbaza (eds), *Territoires, déplacements, mobilité, échanges durant la préhistoire: terres et hommes du sud*, 279–94. Paris: Comité des Travaux Historiques et Scientifiques.

Chapman, J. 2000. *Fragmentation in archaeology: people, places and broken objects in the prehistory of south eastern Europe*. London: Routledge.

Charnov, E. L. 1976. Optimal foraging: the marginal value theorem. *Theoretical Population Biology* 9, 129–36.

Childe, V. G. 1925. *The dawn of European civilization*. London: Routledge & Kegan Paul.

Clark, J. G. D. 1954. *Excavations at Star Carr*. Cambridge: Cambridge University Press.

Clarkson, C. 2002a. Holocene scraper reduction, technological organization and landuse at Ingaladdi Rockshelter, Northern Australia. *Archaeology in Oceania* 37, 79–86.

Clarkson, C. 2002b. An invasiveness index. *Journal of Archaeological Science* 29, 65–75.

Clarkson, C. 2006. Explaining point variability in the eastern Victoria river region, Northern Territory. *Archaeology in Oceania* 41, 97–106.

Close, A. E. 2000. Reconstructing movement in prehistory. *Journal of Archaeological Method and Theory* 7, 49–77.

Cohen, M. 1985. Prehistoric hunter-gatherers: the meaning of social complexity. In D. Price and J. Brown (eds), *Prehistoric hunter-gatherers: the emergence of cultural complexity*, 99–119. Orlando: Academic Press.

Costamagno, S. 2001. Mobilité, territories de chasse et resources animals au Magdalénien final en contexte Pyrénéen: le niveau 7A de la Grotte-Abri du Moulin (Troubat, Hautes-Pyrénées). In J. Jaubert and M. Barbaza (eds), *Territoires, déplacements, mobilité, échanges durant la préhistoire: terres et hommes du sud*, 371–83. Paris: Comité des Travaux Historiques et Scientifiques.

Cunliffe, B. 1973. Introduction. In V. G. Childe, *The Dawn of European Civilization*, 15–28. St Albans: Paladin.

David, B. 2002. *Landscapes, rock-art and the Dreaming: an archaeology of preunderstanding.* London: Leicester University Press.

David, B. 2008. Rethinking cultural chronologies and past landscape engagement in the Kopi region, Gulf Province, Papua New Guinea. *The Holocene* 18, 463–79.

David, B. and Chant, D. 1995. *Rock art and regionalisation in North Queensland prehistory.* Memoirs of the Queensland Museum. South Brisbane: Queensland Museum.

David, B. and Cole, N. 1990. Rock art and inter-regional interaction in northeastern Australia. *Antiquity* 64, 788–806.

David, B., McNiven, I. J., Attenbrow, V., Flood, J., and Collins, J. 1994. Of Lightning Brothers and White Cockatoos: dating the antiquity of signifying systems in the Northern Territory, Australia. *Antiquity* 68, 241–51.

David, B., Pivoru, M., Pivoru, W., Green, M., Barker, B., Weiner, J. F., Simala, D., Kokents, T., Araho, L., and Dop, J. 2008. Living landscapes of the dead: archaeology of the afterworld among the Rumu of Papua New Guinea. In B. David and J. Thomas (eds), *Handbook of landscape archaeology*, 158–66. Walnut Creek, CA: Left Coast Press.

David, B. and Thomas, J. (eds) 2008. *Handbook of landscape archaeology*. Walnut Creek, CA: Left Coast Press.

Davidson, I. and Noble, W. 1992. Why the first colonisation of the Australian region is the earliest evidence of modern human behaviour. *Archaeology in Oceania* 27, 135–42.

Dibble, H. 1988. The interpretation of middle Paleolithic scraper reduction patterns. In L. R. Binford and J. Rigaud (eds), *La technique*, 49–58. Liège: Études et Recherches Archéologiques de l'Université de Liège.

Durkheim, E. 1957. *The elementary forms of religious life.* New York: Free Press.

Eco, U. 1986. *Travels in hyperreality.* Orlando: Harcourt Brace.

Flannery, K. V. (ed.) 1976. *The early Mesoamerican village.* New York: Academic Press.

Ford, R. G., Ainley, D. G., Brown, E. D., Suryan, R. M., and Irons, D. B. 2007. A spatially explicit optimal foraging model of black-legged kittiwake behavior based on prey density, travel distances, and colony size. *Ecological Modelling* 204, 335–48.

Fox, R. A. 1997. *Archaeology, history, and Custer's last battle: the Little Big Horn re-examined.* Norman: University of Oklahoma Press.

Gamble, C. 1993. *Timewalkers: the prehistory of global colonization.* Harmondsworth: Penguin.

Geneste, J.-M., Castel, J.-C., and Chadelle, J.-P. 2008. From physical to social landscapes: multidimensional approaches to the archaeology of social place in the European Upper Palaeolithic. In B. David and J. Thomas (eds), *Handbook of landscape archaeology*, 228–36. Walnut Creek, CA: Left Coast Press.

Gero, J. 1991. Genderlithics: women's roles in stone tool production. In J. Gero and M. Conkey (eds), *Engendering archaeology: women in prehistory*, 163–93. Oxford: Blackwell.

Goldman, L. R. and Ballard, C. (eds) 1998. *Fluid ontologies: myth, ritual and philosophy in the highlands of Papua New Guinea.* Wesport, CT: Bergin and Garvey.

Gosden, C. and Head, L. 1994. Landscape: a usefully ambiguous concept. *Archaeology in Oceania* 29, 113–16.

Gould, R. A. 1977. Ethno-archaeology; or, where do models come from. In R. Wright (ed.), *Stone tools as cultural markers: change, evolution and complexity*, 162–8. Canberra: AIATSIS.

Gould, R. A. 1985. 'Now let's invent agriculture...': a critical review of concepts of complexity among hunter-gatherers. In T. D. Price and J. A. Brown (eds), *Prehistoric hunter-gatherers: the emergence of cultural complexity*, 427–34. Orlando: Academic Press.

Gupta, A. and Ferguson, J. 1992. Beyond 'culture': space, identity, and the politics of difference. *Cultural Anthropology* 7, 6–23.

Hale, H. and Tindale, N. B. 1930. Notes on some human remains in the Lower Murray Valley, South Australia. *Records of the South Australian Museum* 4, 145–218.

Hall, E. T. 1963. A system for the notation of proxemic behavior. *American Anthropologist* 65, 1003–26.

Harrison, S. 1985. Concepts of the person in Avatip religious thought. *Man* 20, 115–30.

Hayden, B. 1994. Competition labor and complex hunter-gatherers. In E. Burch Jr. and L. Ellanna (eds), *Key issues in hunter-gather research*, 223–39. Oxford: Berg.

Head, L., Gosden, C., and White, J. P. (eds) 1994. *Social landscapes. Archaeology in Oceania* 29(3).

Hercus, L., Hodges, F., and Simpson, J. 2002. *The land is a map: placenames of indigenous origin in Australia*. Canberra: Pandanus.

Higgs, E. S. 1975. *Palaeoeconomy*. Cambridge: Cambridge University Press.

Hiroko, K. 1986. Jomon shell mounds and growth-line analysis of molluscan shells. In R. J. Pearson, G. L. Barnes, and K. L. Hutterer (eds), *Windows on the Japanese past: studies in archaeology and prehistory*, 267–78. Ann Arbor: University of Michigan Press.

Hirsch, E. 2006. Landscape, myth and time. *Journal of Material Culture* 11, 151–65.

Hiscock, P. 1994. Technological responses to risk in Holocene Australia. *Journal of World Prehistory* 8, 267–92.

Hiscock, P. 1996. Transformations of Upper Palaeolithic implements in the Dabba industry from Haua Fteah (Libya). *Antiquity* 70, 657–64.

Hossfeld, P. S. 1966. Antiquity of man in Australia. In B. Cotton (ed.), *Aboriginal man in south and central Australia*, 59–96. Adelaide: Government Printer.

Ingold, T. 1993. The temporality of the landscape. *World Archaeology* 25, 152–74.

Ingold, T. 2000. *The perception of the environment: essays in livelihood, dwelling and skill*. London: Routledge.

Ingold, T. and Vergunst, J. L. 2008. Introduction. In T. Ingold and J. L. Vergunst (eds), *Ways of walking: ethnography and practice on foot*, 1–19. Aldershot: Ashgate.

Irwin, G. 1992. *The prehistoric exploration and colonisation of the Pacific*. Cambridge: Cambridge University Press.

Jarman, M. 1976. Prehistoric economic development in sub-Alpine Italy. In G. de G. Sieveking, I. H. Longworth, and K. E. Wilson (eds), *Problems in economic and social archaeology*, 523–48. London: Westview Press.

Jochim, M. A. 1976. *Hunter-gatherer subsistence and settlement: a predictive model*. New York: Academic Press.

Jochim, M. A. 1981. *Strategies for survival: cultural behavior in an ecological context*. New York: Academic Press.

Johanson, D. and Edey, M. 1981. *Lucy: the beginnings of humankind*. New York: Simon & Schuster.

Johnson, A. and Earle, T. 2000. *The evolution of human societies: from foraging group to agrarian state*. Stanford: Stanford University Press.

Jones, R. 1976. Tasmania: aquatic machines and off-shore islands. In G. de G. Sieveking, I. H. Longworth, and K. E. Wilson (eds), *Problems in economic and social archaeology*, 265–75. London: Westview Press.

Jones, R. and White, N. 1988. Point blank: stone tool manufacture at the Ngilipitji quarry, Arnhem Land. In B. Meehan and R. Jones (eds), *Archaeology with ethnography: an Australian perspective*, 51–87. Canberra: Research School of Pacific and Asian Studies, Australian National University.

Jordan, P. 2010a. *Landscape and culture in Northern Eurasia.* London: UCL Press.
Jordan, P. 2010b. Understanding the spread of innovations in prehistoric social networks: new insights into the origins and dispersal of early pottery in Northern Eurasia. In W. Østreng (ed.), *Transference: interdisciplinary communications.* Centre for Advanced Stud, Oslo. (internet publication at http://www.cas.uio.no/Publications/Seminar/0809Jordan.pdf).
Jordan, P. and Zvelebil, M. 2009. *Ex oriente lux*: the prehistory of hunter-gatherer ceramic dispersals. In P. Jordan and M. Zvelebil (eds), *Ceramics before farming: the dispersal of pottery among prehistoric Eurasian hunter-gatherers,* 33–89. London: UCL Press.
Jorgensen, D. 2007. Clan-finding, clan-making and the politics of identity in a Papua New Guinea mining project. In J. Weiner and K. Glaskin (eds), *Customary land tenure and registration in Australia and Papua New Guinea: anthropological perspectives,* 57–72. Asia-Pacific Environment Monograph 3. Canberra: ANU E Press.
Kearney, A. 2008. Gender in landscape archaeology. In B. David and J. Thomas (eds), *Handbook of landscape archaeology,* 247–55. Walnut Creek, CA: Left Coast Press.
Kelly, R. L. 1988. The three sides of a biface. *American Antiquity* 53, 717–34.
Kelly, R. L. 1992. Mobility/sedentism: concepts, archaeological measures, and effects. *Annual Review of Anthropology* 21, 43–66.
Kelly, R. L. and Todd, L. 1988. Coming into the country: early Palaeoindian mobility. *American Antiquity* 53, 231–44.
Kent, S. 1992. Studying variability in the archaeological record: an ethnoarchaeological model for distinguishing mobility patterns. *American Antiquity* 57, 635–60.
Kirk, R. and Szathmary, E. (eds) 1985. *Out of Asia: peopling the Americas and the Pacific.* Canberra: The Journal of Pacific History.
Knapp, A. B. 2009. *Archaeology, Annales, and ethnohistory.* Cambridge: Cambridge University Press.
Koster, J. M. 2008. Hunting with dogs in Nicaragua: an optimal foraging approach. *Current Anthropology* 49, 935–44.
Kuhn, S. L. 1991. 'Unpacking' reduction: lithic raw material economy in the Mousterian of west-central Italy. *Journal of Anthropological Archaeology* 10, 76–106.
Kuhn, S. L. 1995. *Mousterian lithic technology: an ecological perspective.* Princeton: Princeton University Press.
Kuhn, S. L. and Bietti, A. 2000. The late middle and early upper Paleolithic in Italy. In O. Bar-Yosef and D. Pilbeam (eds), *The geography of Neandertals and modern humans in Europe and the Greater Mediterranean,* 49–76. Cambridge: Peabody Museum of Archaeology and Ethnology.
Lamb, L. 1996. A methodology for the analysis of backed artefact production on the South Molle Island Quarry, Whitsunday Islands. *Australian Archaeology '95: Proceedings of the 1995 Australian Archaeological Association Annual Conference.* Tempus 6. St. Lucia: Anthropology Museum, University of Queensland.
Lamb, L. 2005a. Rock of ages: use of the South Molle Island Quarry, Whitsunday Islands, and the implications for Holocene technological change in Australia. Canberra: PhD thesis, Australian National University.
Lamb, L. 2005b. Backed and forth: an exploration of variation in retouched implement production on the South Molle Island Quarry, central Queensland. In C. Clarkson and L. Lamb (eds), *Rocking the boat: studies in lithic reduction, use and classification,* 35–42. Oxford: British Archaeological Reports International Series.

Layton, R. and Ucko, P. 1999. Introduction: gazing on the landscape and encountering the environment. In R. Layton and P. Ucko (eds), *The archaeology and anthropology of landscape*, 1–20. New York: Routledge.

Lee, R. B. 1969. !*Kung Bushmen subsistence: an input-output analysis*. In A. P. Vayda (ed.), *Environment and cultural behavior*, 47–79. Garden City: Natural History Press.

Lee, R. B. and DeVore, I. (eds) 1968. *Man the hunter*. Chicago: Aldine.

Lemonnier, P. 1993. Pigs as ordinary wealth: technical logic, exchange and leadership in New Guinea. In P. Lemonnier (ed.), *Technological choices: transformation in material cultures since the Neolithic*, 126–56. London: Routledge.

Lévi-Strauss, C. 1968. Future agenda. In R. B. Lee and I. DeVore (eds.), *Man the hunter*, 344–5. Chicago: Aldine.

Lévi-Strauss, C. 1969. *The raw and the cooked: mythologiques 1*. Chicago: University of Chicago Press.

Lévi-Strauss, C. 1979. *Myth and meaning: cracking the code of culture*. New York: Schocken Books.

Linse, A. R. 1993. Geoarchaeological scale and archaeological interpretation: examples from the central Jornada Mogollon. In J. K. Stein and A. R. Linse (eds), *Effects of scale on archaeological and geoscientific perspectives*, 11–28. Boulder: Geological Society of America Special Paper 283.

Lourandos, H. 1996. Change in Australian prehistory: scale, trends and frameworks of interpretation. In S. Ulm, I. Lilley, and A. Ross (eds), *Australian archaeology '95: Proceedings of the 1995 Australian Archaeological Association Annual Conference*, 15–21. St Lucia: Anthropology Museum, University of Queensland.

Low, S. M. and Lawrence-Zuniga, D. 2003. Locating culture. In S. M. Low and D. Lawrence-Zuniga (eds), *The anthropology of space and place: locating culture*, 1–47. Maldon: Blackwell.

Lowenthal, D. 1985. *The past is a foreign country*. Cambridge: Cambridge University Press.

MacArthur, R. H. 1972. *Geographical ecology*. New York: Harper & Row.

McBryde, I. 1984. Kulin greenstone quarries: the social contexts of production and distribution for the Mt William site. *World Archaeology* 16, 267–85.

McCall, G. S. 2007. Behavioural ecological models of lithic technological change during the later Middle Stone Age of South Africa. *Journal of Archaeological Science* 34, 1738–51.

McCarthy, F. 1943. An analysis of the knapped implements from eight elouera industry stations on the south coast of New South Wales. *Records of the Australian Museum* 21, 127–53.

McCarthy, F. 1964. The archaeology of the Capertee Valley, New South Wales. *Records of the Australian Museum* 26, 197–246.

McFadyen, L. 2008. Building and architecture as landscape practice. In B. David and J. Thomas (eds), *Handbook of landscape archaeology*, 307–14. Walnut Creek, CA: Left Coast Press.

McNiven, I. J. 1994. Technological organization and settlement in southwest Tasmania after the glacial maximum. *Antiquity* 68, 75–82.

McNiven, I. J. 2000. Backed to the Pleistocene. *Archaeology in Oceania* 35, 48–52.

McNiven, I. J. 2003. Saltwater people: spiritscapes, maritime rituals and the archaeology of Australian indigenous seascapes. *World Archaeology* 35, 329–49.

Madsen, D. B., Elston, R., Bettinger, R., Cheng, X., and Kan, Z. 1996. Settlement patterns reflected in assemblages from the Pleistocene/Holocene transition of north central China. *Journal of Archaeological Science* 23, 217–31.

Matisoo-Smith, E. 2008. Using DNA in landscape archaeology. In B. David and J. Thomas (eds), *Handbook of landscape archaeology*, 521–29. Walnut Creek, CA: Left Coast Press.

Meignen, L., Bar-Yosef, O., Speth, J. D. and Stiner, M. C. 2005. Middle Paleolithic settlement patterns in the Levant. In E. Hovers and S. L. Kuhn (eds), *Transitions before the* transition: evolution and stability in the middle Paleolithic and middle Stone Age, 149–70. New York: Kluwer Academic/Plenum Press.

Mellars, P. 1976. Settlement patterns and industrial variability in the British Mesolithic. In G. de G. Sieveking, I. H. Longworth, and K. E. Wilson (eds), *Problems in economic and social archaeology*, 375–99. London: Westview Press.

Mellars, P. 1989. Technological changes across the middle-upper Palaeolithic transition: technological, social, and cognitive perspectives. In P. Mellars and C. Stringer (eds), *The human revolution: behavioural and biological perspectives on the origins of modern humans*, 338–65. Princeton: Princeton University Press.

Morauta, L. 1981. Mobility patterns in Papua New Guinea: social factors as explanatory variables. In G. W. Jones and H. V. Richter (eds), *Population mobility and development: Southeast Asia and the Pacific*, 205–28. Canberra: The Australian National University.

Morgan, C. 2009. Climate change, uncertainty and prehistoric hunter-gatherer mobility. *Journal of Anthropological Archaeology* 28, 382–96.

Morrow, J. E. 1997. End scraper morphology and use-life: an approach for studying Paleoindian lithic technology and mobility. *Lithic Technology* 22, 70–85.

Munn, N. D. 2003. Excluded spaces: the figure in the Australian Aboriginal landscape. In S. M. Low and D. Lawrence-Zuniga (eds), *The anthropology of space and place: locating culture*, 92–109. Malden: Blackwell.

Nandris, J. 1976. Some factors in the Early Neothermal settlement of south-east Europe. In G. de G. Sieveking, I. H. Longworth, and K. E. Wilson (eds), *Problems in economic and social archaeology*, 549–56. London: Westview Press.

Odell, G. H. 2001. Addressing prehistoric hunting practices through stone tool analysis. *American Anthropologist* NS 90, 335–56.

Parry, W. J. and Kelly, R. L. 1987. Expedient core technology and sedentism. In J. Johnson and C. Morrow (eds), *The organization of core technology*, 285–304. Boulder: Westview Press.

Pate, F. D. 2008. The use of human skeletal remains in landscape archaeology. In B. David and J. Thomas (eds), *Handbook of landscape archaeology*, 502–20. Walnut Creek, CA: Left Coast Press.

Paton, R. 1994. Speaking through stones: a study from northern Australia. *World Archaeology* 26, 172–84.

Politis, G. 2006. The different dimensions of mobility among the Nukak foragers of the Colombian Amazon. In F. Sellet, R. Greaves, and P.-L. Yu (eds.), *Archaeology and ethnoarchaeology of mobility*, 23–43. Gainesville: University Press of Florida.

Price, T. D. and Brown, J. A. (eds) 1985. *Prehistoric hunter-gatherers: the emergence of cultural complexity*. Orlando: Academic Press.

Pyke, G. H. 1984. Optimal foraging theory: a critical review. *Annual Review of Ecology and Systematics* 15, 523–75.

Renfrew, C. and Dixon, J. 1976. Obsidian in western Asia: a review. In G. de G. Sieveking, I. H. Longworth, and K. E. Wilson (eds), *Problems in economic and social archaeology*, 137–50. London: Westview Press.

Rockman, M. and Steele, J. 2003. *Colonisation of unfamiliar landscapes*. London: Routledge.

Rogers, E. S. 1962. *The Round Lake Ojibwa*. Toronto: Royal Ontario Museum.

Rose, D. B. 1992. *Dingo makes us human: life and land in an Australian Aboriginal culture*. Cambridge: Cambridge University Press.

Rose, D. B., D'Amico, S., Daiyi, N., Deveraux, K., Daiyi, M., Ford, L., and Bright, A. 2002. *Country of the heart: an indigenous Australian homeland*. Canberra: Aboriginal Studies Press.

Rossignol, J. and Wandsnider, L. (eds) 1992. *Space, time, and archaeological landscapes*. New York: Plenum Press.

Sassaman, K. 1998. Lithic technology and the hunter-gatherer sexual division of labour. In K. Hays-Gilpin and D. Whitley (eds), *Reader in gender archaeology*, 159–72. London: Routledge.

Serjeantson, S.W. 1985. Migration and admixture in the Pacific: insights provided by human leucocyte antigens. In R. Kirk and E. Szathmary (eds), *Out of Asia: peopling the Americas and the Pacific*, 133–45. Canberra: The Journal of Pacific History.

Shott, M. 1986. Technological organization and settlement mobility: an ethnographic examination. *Journal of Anthropological Research* 42, 15–51.

Silverman, E. K. 1996. The gender of the cosmos: totemism, society and embodiment in the Sepik River. *Oceania* 67, 30–49.

Smith, C. 1999. Ancestors, places and people: social landscapes in Aboriginal Australia. In R. Layton and P. Ucko (eds), *The archaeology and anthropology of landscape*, 189–205. New York: Routledge.

Stafford, C. R. and Hajic, E. R. 1992. Landscape scale: geoenvironmental approaches to prehistoric settlement strategies. In J. Rossignol and L. Wandsnider (eds), *Space, time, and archaeological landscapes*, 137–61. New York: Plenum Press.

Stein, J. K. and Linse, A. R. (eds) 1993. *Effects of scale on archaeological and geoscientific perspectives*. Boulder: Geological Society of America Special Paper 283.

Stevenson, M. G. 1982. Toward an understanding of site abandonment behavior: evidence from historic mining camps in the southwest Yukon. *Journal of Anthropological Archaeology* 1(3), 237–65.

Testart, A. 1982. *Les chasseurs-cueilleurs ou l'origine des inégalités*. Paris: Société d'Ethnographie (Université Paris X-Nanterre).

Thomas, J. 2008. Archaeology, landscape, dwelling. In B. David and J. Thomas (eds), *Handbook of landscape archaeology*, 300–6. Walnut Creek, CA: Left Coast Press.

Thomson, D. F. 1939. The seasonal factor in human culture. *Proceedings of the Prehistoric Society* 5, 209–21.

Tilley, C. 1994. *A phenomenology of landscape: places, paths and monuments*. Oxford: Berg.

Vita-Finzi, C. and Higgs, E. S. 1970. Prehistoric economy in the Mount Carmel area of Palestine: site catchment analysis. *Proceedings of the Prehistoric Society* 36, 1–37.

Wagner, R. 2001. Condensed mapping: myth and the folding of space/space and the folding of myth. In A. Rumsey and J. Weiner (eds), *Emplaced myth: space, narrative and knowledge in Aboriginal Australia and Papua New Guinea*, 71–8. Honolulu: University of Hawai'i Press.

Wallace, I. J. and Shea, J. 2006. Mobility patterns and core technologies in the Middle Paleolithic of the Levant. *Journal of Archaeological Science* 33, 1293–1309.

Watson, O. M. 1972. Symbolic and expressive uses of space: an introduction to proxemic behavior. In W. H. Alkire et al. (eds), *Current topics in anthropology: theory, methods and content 4: module 20*, 1–18. Reading: Addison-Wesley.

Weiner, J. 1988. Durkheim and the Papuan male cult: Whithead's views on social structure and ritual in New Guinea. *American Ethnologist* 15, 567–73.

Willey, G. R. and Sabloff, J. A. 1974. *A history of American archaeology*. New York: W. H. Freeman.

Williams, B. J. 1974. *A model of band society*. Washington: Memoirs of the Society for American Archaeology 29.

Yengoyan, A. A. 1968. Demographic and ecological influences on Aboriginal Australian marriage sections. In R. L. Lee and I. DeVore (eds), *Man the hunter*, 185–99. New York: Aldine.

Zeleznik, W. S. and Bennett, I. M. 1991. Assumption validity in human optimal foraging: the Barí hunters of Venezuela as a test case. *Human Ecology* 19, 499–508.

CHAPTER 57

PERSONHOOD AND SOCIAL RELATIONS

NYREE FINLAY

RECENT research on personhood offers fruitful ground for reconfiguring approaches to social relations in hunter-gatherer life-worlds. Current trends have a number of implications for hunter-gatherer studies, especially in light of the fluid understandings of personhood documented among known hunter-gatherers and the challenges for archaeology in exploring such aspects of identity, especially in our pre-modern ancestral past. This chapter begins by outlining some of the theoretical contours of personhood. This is followed by sections that highlight archaeological perspectives on animal relations and the wider implications of relational onotologies and non-human personhood. Another dimension to personhood studies is the place of the individual biography and configuring personhood using the framework of the life course opens many avenues for archaeological engagements. Finally, some discussion of the scales at which hunter-gatherer sociality operates is considered. The overall purpose is to highlight the primacy of relations and explore the direction of recent trends.

PERSPECTIVES ON PERSONHOOD

Personhood is defined as the quality or condition of being a person. Depending on the context, a person can be constituted in a number of ways (Carrithers et al. 1985). Personhood can be assumed at birth or assigned to the unborn foetus where ambivalent attitudes to personhood abound. In certain societies, full personhood is attained through time and lived experience, defined by age and stages in the life course. Alternatively, it can be the preserve of certain categories of individual or depend on gender, social status, sexuality, sub-group affiliation, and so on. Discrimination on the grounds of ethnicity, race, sex, and other institutionalized inequalities can create categories of non-persons or those for whom full personhood is negated or denied, as is the case with slavery.

Personhood encompasses the notion of the self and it concerns the internal processes of identity creation and the corporeal experience of being. Intercorporeality is significant—how bodies condition understandings of personhood—not only through changes tied to ageing and gender, for example, but via narratives of disability, impairment, and illness (Gammeltoft 2009). These mesh with other social sub-categories of identity such as corporate kin-group membership and other affiliations in complex ways. Time, also highlighted as the temporal basis for personhood, is unstable, reversible, or more persistent. Death need not be an ending but rather it can constitute a different threshold that signals the rebirth or transformation into some other (an ancestor, spirit, ghost, otherworldly being) or herald the return of a recently deceased person. Personhood has cosmological implications with respect to relationships between the living, dead, and supernatural others, and in particular for those who transcend spirit and other boundaries via shamanic means.

Melanesian ethnography, in particular, has been influential in offering alternative constructs of personhood that offer significant potential for reconfiguring archaeological approaches to identity. Salient is the notion of the dividual, where personhood lies in the distributed and partible person. Here, 'persons are frequently constructed as the plural and composite site of the relationships that produced them' (Strathern 1988, 13). Persons are perceived as complex multiple-authored entities that are shaped by their external relationships and internally composed of distinct and different bodily essences and elements. Personhood is therefore in a constant state of becoming and being and can be thought of as fractal in nature (Wagner 1991). More permeable forms of dividual personhood are also recognized elsewhere where there is greater emphasis on the flow of substances within and between bodies than the exchange of parts (Busby 1997). The privileged Western (Cartesian) notion of the autonomous individual is challenged in these discussions of the dividual, but as LiPuma (1998) has argued, persons emerge from the tension between dividual and individual aspects and reconciling these modalities is an aspect of all societies. In order to avoid essentializing personhood in any form we need to hold on to how relational notions of identity are culturally contingent, historically specific, and internally unstable and variable.

The category of hunter-gatherers is a historical product arising from colonial encounters, shaped by concerns with social evolutionism and defined by mode of production (Barnard 2004; Pluciennik 2001). The spectrum of societies grouped together under this banner encompasses highly mobile egalitarian foragers and complex, sedentary fishers and collectors with a penchant for accumulation and social stratification (Kelly 1995).

One of the main archaeological contributions to debates about hunter-gatherers' relations has been to challenge essentialist positions on forager life, raise questions about social inequality, and provide a unique long-term perspective. The hunter-gatherer individual has often formed a problematic category in archaeological thought; 'a shadowy creature lost in the long corridors of Palaeolithic time' (Gamble 1999, 419). An explicit focus on the individual agent within post-processual archaeologies sought to redress many of the inherent biases of scale within culture-history and processual approaches. Yet, until the last decade or so, an engagement with wider social theoretical issues was largely lost on the mainstay of hunter-gatherer archaeology, due to the dominance of evolutionary and ecological models such as optimal foraging theory (Winterhalder and Smith 1981). The autonomous individual was written into the equation but with actions limited largely within the domain of hunting and the simulation of decision making (Mithen 1990). The fault line between nature versus culture as the determinant of behaviour often falls at the Neolithic transition. The discordance between hunter-gatherers and others appears typified in the oft-quoted statement by Richard Bradley (1984, 11) that 'successful farmers have social relations with one another, while hunter-gatherers have ecological relations with hazelnuts'. Similarly, debates over emotion and intentionality appeared to consign Mesolithic people to the 'cybernetic wasteland' (Mithen 1991). All too often, discussion of hunter-gatherer social relations has overlooked individual experience at the expense of the group and concerns with the identification of breeding networks and exogamous bands (e.g. Constandse-Westermann and Newell 1988). Preoccupations with status differentiation and social complexity have also tended to deny the particular at the expense of generalized models (Price and Brown 1985; Price and Feinman 1995). For the Palaeolithic and the lives of pre-anatomically modern humans, adaptive and evolutionary explanatory models have tended to dominate the research agenda. Explicit social theoretical approaches have been slow to develop and issues of individuals and identity, sensitive to personhood, are still mostly explored in relation to the Upper Palaeolithic, although the tenor of research is shifting (see Gamble 1999; 2007; Gamble and Porr 2005 for discussion of these issues).

In archaeology, an explicit engagement with personhood emerged from post-processual theoretical concerns with the individual and agency (Dobres and Robb 2000; Gillespie 2001) in conjunction with explicitly feminist perspectives on gendered identities and embodiment (Clark and Wilkie 2007; Meskell and Joyce 2003). Melanesian and partible notions of personhood have been a particular source of inspiration more generally for European prehistory (Chapman and Gaydarska 2007; Fowler 2004; Jones 2005). These ideas have also been influential in Palaeolithic and Mesolithic studies (e.g. Gamble 2007; Janik 2000; papers in Gamble and Porr 2005). While researchers differ over nuanced definitions and expose inherent tensions, there is wide agreement that a focus on personhood prompts new engagements and different types of interpretation.

Action, Animals, and Non-Human Personhood

Hunter-gatherer ethnographies provide numerous examples of the myriad ways that people within these communities construct their relations with animals, diverse entities in their worlds, and each other. For many, personhood is not only the preserve of humankind but is open to animals, landscape features, other types of being, or inanimate objects. The need to label how humans construct their relations with animals and others has been foundational to anthropological practice since the writings of Tylor at the end of the nineteenth century. Within the spectrum of animistic and totemic beliefs there is much fluidity in the realities of how relations are defined and enacted (Descola 2009; Ingold 2000; Lévi-Strauss 1963; Viveiros de Castro 2004). In a relational epistemology as defined by Bird-David (1999), personhood emerges from perceptual and reflexive interrelations with the world. The complexities of commingled animal–human relations expose the often subtle distinctions that unfold with respect to personhood.

Among many peoples of the circumpolar and subarctic north, human and animal relations are mediated by different world views which incorporate shamanistic beliefs and practices. All relations between animals and humans are seen as social relations. The hunt is viewed as a reciprocal exchange between the human hunters and their animal prey. Animals offer themselves as a gift to the hunter and must be treated with proper respect to ensure the long-term continuation of these relations, which entails the human partners adhering to certain ritual obligations and modes of behaviour (Tanner 1979). In many cases such beliefs are seen as metaphors for understanding sociality rather than reflecting true representations of reality, a position which has also served to marginalize modern indigenous world views (Nasaday 2007).

In a classic study, Irving Hallowell explored social relations among the Ojibwa, living in the boreal woodlands of Canada. In Ojibwa ontology there exist nuanced sub-categories of personhood where animals, birds, other objects (such as stones, pipes, kettles), and natural phenomena (the sun, thunder) are considered persons in their own right. Here 'the concept of the person is not, in fact, synonymous with human being but transcends it' (Hallowell 1960, 21). For the Ojibwa all of these 'other-than-human persons' are unified conceptually because they have an inner enduring vital essence and an exterior form that can change. Similarly, in the Amerindian tradition the distinctions are also ones where humans and non-humans possess 'identical interiorities and different physicalities' or a shared identity of souls and a difference of bodies (Descola 2009, 151; Viveiros de Castro 2004). For the Ojibwa, as noted for others, such personhood is not an inherent property of all animals and things; rather it is a consequence of action and affordance (Ingold 2000). Among the Siberian Yukaghirs, non-human persons only emerge in certain contexts and via particular encounters as in the altered states of consciousness of shamanic intervention (Willerslev 2007). Animal and non-human personhood is often embedded within shamanistic and related cosmologies and constitutes a form of relations with much wider supernatural and spirit domains.

A couple of examples will serve to demonstrate the permeability of these ideas about animal relations and non-human agency within hunter-gatherer archaeology and the ways in which some of these relations may find material expression. Drawing on the perspectivism of Viveiros de Castro, Chantal Conneller (2004) has argued for a reinterpretation of the meaning of the perforated red-deer antler frontlets found at the Early Mesolithic site of Star Carr, Yorkshire. The skulls with antlers attached were originally interpreted as hunting aids by the excavator: masks to disguise the hunter from the deer and thereby conceal their human identity from others. Conneller, on the other hand, argues the effect is more revealing as people renegotiated corporeal boundaries by taking on this deer-effect. The hybridity of this not-human, not-deer entity created new ambiguous forms and types of bodily relationships. We need not think of this process solely as a performative device to temporarily transform identity and to simply mimic or acquire a type of animalness in the wearing of a deer costume. More than mimesis, the objects made from animal parts are reassembled into new forms with the capacity to affect in particular ways. The creation of barbed points fashioned from antler, some of which were probably removed from the frontlets themselves, would produce new connections through an assortment of acts taking place in the wider landscape. The extended biography of these pieces led ultimately to particular patterns of use and depositional practices. The production of assemblages of bodily effects from animal bodies with new meanings clearly has implications for conceiving agency and identity. These deer-effects and animality are transformed and extended through time, space, and social relations in a process akin to a distributed and permeable form of personhood.

Another example that challenges how we construct hunter-gatherer ontologies in the past is the evidence from mortuary contexts. The rich burial record from southern Scandinavia, the Baltic region, and other parts of Europe in the post-glacial period offers a wealth of material to explore how human–animal relationships are expressed and reflected in the treatment of the dead (e.g. Albrethsen and Brinch Petersen 1976; Jacobs 1995; Larsson 1989; 1990; Nilsson Stutz 2003). Humans are buried with animal parts: red-deer antlers, perforated tooth pendants, and other implements. Dogs are one category of animal that are treated differently in certain burials in the Mesolithic period dating to c.5250–4800 BC (Larsson 1989; 1990). At the Skateholm I and II sites in southern Sweden, ten dogs are buried separately, seven are interred with humans, some of the latter dogs being deliberately killed and dismembered. One dog at Skateholm II was buried with a red-deer antler along its spine, three flint blades at the hip—as is found in male burials at the site. Strewn with red ochre, a unique decorated antler hammer was laid on its chest. This dog in grave XXI is accorded one of the richest burials of all. Rick Schulting (1998, 214–15) cites a case of a 'chiefly' dog among the Bella Coola, where a hereditary title was passed to a dog in the absence of human heirs. The symbolism is suggestive of human equivalency, even if we can argue the subtleties of whether this Skateholm dog can be seen as a dog person, a person in dog form, or whether it reflects a human substitution. The highly variable treatment of dogs as well as humans at Skateholm necessitates an approach that acknowledges contingency in how forms of personhood are constructed. Dogs create an interesting case as a companion species, for they sit on the cusp between the worlds of both humans and animals; as such they are ambiguous mediators between the two in many cultural settings. A further illustration of close animal–human relations and probable ceremonialism in the early post-glacial comes in the form of the remains of a brown-bear jaw with signs of tethering at the La Grande-Rivoire cave site, France (Chaix et al. 1997). Bears hold special significance for a suite of Eurasian and North American groups as powerful symbolic and mediatory agents with the spirit realm, and it appears likely that this was also the case for certain earlier hunter-gatherers. Other significant species relations are evidenced in the European Mesolithic and Upper Palaeolithic in representational art, where figures such as the Aurignacian Hohlenstein-Stadel 'lion-man' statuette are also indicative of acts of shamanic transformation (Dowson and Porr 2001). Exploring the archaeological dimensions of shamanism provides another means of approaching personhood and its transformative and transitory properties, but studies need to be sensitive to the wider socio-political and spiritual contexts and acknowledge the diversity of practices (Price 2001; Schmidt 2000).

Boundaries between things, humans, and animals are fluid and open to multiple interpretations. In this sense personhood can be pervasive, and particular attention needs to be paid to mode, media, and materiality in order to fully nuance connections that are being cited in such practices, particularly within a given (archaeological) context. Material culture has always been central to the archaeological project, but it is the subject of a renewed focus of engagement via studies that explore materiality, the sentient properties of things, and the active role of objects. The biographical properties of material culture find metaphorical resonance with the human condition and the reciprocal ways people are created via things (Hoskins 1998). In this context the extension of personhood via the concept of the distributed person (Gell 1998; Strathern 1988), notions of enchainment (Chapman and Gaydarska 2007; Gamble 2007), as well as separate developments within actor-network theory (see Whitridge 2004a for an application to hunter-gatherers) continue to offer diverse ways of exploring the hybridity between humans, others, and wider processes of material entanglement. Future research will undoubtedly continue to elaborate on the role of non-human agency within hunter-gatherer life-worlds and dissolve and reconfigure the theoretical boundaries between humans, animals, and non-human others.

Personhood as Process

!Nisa is one of the best-known anthropological biographies and reveals much about the individual life of one woman and, by extension, modes of personhood among the !Kung (Shostak 1981). Situating the lived experience and considering the actual self of a differentiated individual is another dimension of personhood studies. The creation of archaeobiographies has a particular currency for historical periods where a range of material and documentary evidence can be assembled to construct a more layered view of personal experience and identity (Clark and Wilkie 2007). Such a project for prehistory is more challenging and is perhaps better thought of as material towards an 'archaeological silhouette'. This draws on the distinction made by Zeitlyn (2008) to convey the partial portrait that ensues in anthropological writing about an individual subject. Doing so acknowledges the inherent archaeological limitations of such an endeavour and recognizes that our grasp of personhood is always partial. Yet we are in a position, using osteological evidence, to record and chart the cumulative effects of various relationships on the body and infer wider social choices and routine practices. Integral to such an approach is the concept of the life course and the social marking of the physiological stages of the human life-cycle. This offers a framework to explore the way that personhood is mutable throughout life, as well as providing core themes for wider cross-cultural engagements. This has the advantage of teasing apart the specific historical conditions of identity creation and the contribution of other differentiating factors. The life-cycle concerns biological species as well as things and can be usefully applied to explore primate and hominin lives. The other strength of such an explicitly social biographical approach lies in its metaphorical extension to material culture. Therefore the threads from life course studies combine with personhood to weave together broader narratives that move scales between the individual and wider collectivities (e.g. Gilchrist 2000; Meskell 1999).

The impact of feminist scholarship has had a profound effect on the manner by which gender and age have been written into hunter-gatherer studies (see Jarvenpa and Brumbach, this volume). As a consequence, the child has emerged as a discrete subject of enquiry (see, for example, papers in Hewlett and Lamb 2005 on the anthropology of hunter-gatherer childhoods). Two main methodological pathways are followed when considering children in the past: firstly, the identification of their distinctive material culture or products; secondly, their actual physical remains in the burial record (Sofaer Derevenski 2000). The durable remains of flint-knapping and stonecraft usually provides the main entry point for presencing hunter-gatherer children archaeologically in the absence of organic preservation. A number of studies have identified children's products and the actions of novices in Europe and in the Americas (Baxter 2005; Finlay 1997). Processes of knowledge transmission and the situated context of skills acquisition provide a backdrop to monitoring the shifting status of the person as they acquire experience through these emergent practices. Approaches to technology have traditionally tended to consider the artisan in isolation, if at all (Dobres 2000), yet the processes of artefact creation and use bring together the skills and actions of different people and other entities. It often involves social negotiations, multiple recursive acts, and the actions of many. Personhood is actively created and finds definition through such practical tasks, leaving traces in production techniques that can be charted in the operational sequence or *chaîne opératoire*. Personhood is also shaped in the intimacy of the quotidian as objects are assembled from parts fashioned from a range of substances generated in encounters with others. Meaning is also layered by the associations of place, materials, and the specific conditions and contexts of creation.

The treatment of the individual in death offers particular perspectives on personhood, for mortuary practices give substance to narratives about social relations in the past. Notwithstanding the fact that the funerary context may be an idealized, transformed, or distorted representation of lived experience, it is the main medium that archaeologists use to define social persona. In one of the few specific studies that has combined age with constructs derived from Melanesian personhood, Liliana Janik (2000) has argued that the hunter-gatherer-fisher cemeteries of the Mesolithic of the south-east Baltic and Scandinavia display relational age-based distinctions. These are seen in the choice and arrangement of grave-goods, such as bone and tooth pendants and other implements. For her, the inclusion of such items with non-adults at Zvejnieki signifies their autonomous status, in contrast to Scandinavia, at sites like Skateholm and Vedbæk, where conditions are more relational as non-adults only receive such items when buried with adults. This particular study highlights the wealth of material available to move beyond gender to explore the primacy of age in social relations.

A focus on modern hunter-gatherer children as active agents also reveals their autonomous role in providing food for themselves and others. This can be seen in gathering strategies, shellfish collection practices, and the early ages of hunting competency and independence noted among the Martu (Bird and Bliege Bird 2000; 2005). Children often play a key role in food distribution and are central to the construction of community identity (Bird-David 2008). Ethnoarchaeological studies have also identified distinct uses of objects and types of constructions created through play, although they are seldom considered in archaeological interpretations (Politis 2005). The archaeological record also attests to the presence of hunter-gatherer children, from finger- and footprints in various media and in a range of contexts to preserved infant faecal matter and even teeth marks in discarded post-glacial resin chewing gum. Therefore the issues, as with anthropology, are not ones of the (in)visibility of children, but relate to what Bird-David (2005, 98) terms 'systemic blindness' to them (see also Lillie 2009). As well as it being a discrete category worthy of separate study, there is a wider symbolic importance to childhood, parenting, and notions of sharing, for 'persons are "grown" in a context of immediate sociality, through incorporating the substance, knowledge, and experience of others within a field of nurturance' (Ingold 1999, 408). In an ambitious project, Clive Gamble recasts the major transitions in human evolution via a model of identity based on material metaphors and articulated through changes in the childscape. Investigated at the locale and landscape levels, the childscape is 'where our identity is created and its metaphorical basis established through references to emotional, material, and symbolic resources' (Gamble 2007, 229). This development is significant, for it demonstrates the destabilizing effects that a focus on the child can bring—with the capacity to transform established paradigms and fields of study—and more centrally the value of life course studies to enhance understandings of personhood.

The body is a site of personhood and an embodied and corporeal focus has much to contribute. If a person is a microcosm of social relations, then each singular body retains the physical manifestation of some of these relations; not only encoded in DNA, but as other indelible traces. Patterns of bone growth and interruption visible as Harris lines and other stress indicators in dentition can contribute to new understandings of the community context of becoming and being a person. Personhood as a process is often marked by persistent social events and rites of passage that highlight physical changes in the body (Owens and Hayden 1997). A wealth of distinctions can be identified via bone stable isotope studies and results used to infer marriage alliances (Schulting and Richards 2001), as well as age, gender, and status differences in foodways (e.g. Eriksson et al. 2003; Lillie 2003; 2009; Lillie et al. 2003; Zvelebil 2000). Skeletal evidence of task-related activities also suggests daily expressions of difference (Constandse-Westermann and Newell 1989). Another advantage to adopting an embodied and corporeal focus is the perspective that it gives to understanding other aspects of identity. In relation to Neanderthals, the extent and character of physical injuries experienced from a young age suggest that impairment would probably play a defining role in their personhood (Pettitt 2000).

THE SKILL OF BEING (WITH OTHERS)

Much anthropological discourse on hunter-gatherer sociality highlights the relational basis of hunter-gatherer life and identity (e.g. Bird-David 1990; 1999; Ingold 1999; 2000). Acknowledging that there is no separation between social and ecological relations is significant, for it enables us to recognize the wider permeability of personhood. In this case, as Ingold (1999, 409) has asked, 'what need have we for a concept of the social at all?' If the 'social' still has any merit, then it must lie with unfolding the character and condition of particular types of relationships situated within these wider relational fields. Two aspects of sociality can be briefly highlighted that emerge from this reframing. Both concern scale: firstly, that of the individual; secondly, sociality within the wider landscape.

Hunter-gatherer personal autonomy is seen as the antithesis of Western notions of individualism, with its construction of the individual as a separate, autonomous agent (Ingold 1999). It is argued that for the individual hunter-gatherer autonomy derives from relatedness. It emerges from the practice of sharing and is reflected in universal kin relations, gift-giving, and reciprocity, subjects that have traditionally dominated discussions of hunter-gatherer sociality and band-living. Leadership by attraction and trust rather than coercion and debates about the nature of power in egalitarian societies highlight too the place of knowledge and inter-generational experience (Hayden 1995). Social tensions are mediated in a number of ways. Traditional models of fission and fusion for hunter-gatherers mask how actual people gain the necessary skills of living together well and maintaining social relations at a distance. Successful living is also an outcome of social endeavour. The success of social networks is a key element and the role of material culture is central for creating, maintaining, and mediating relationships of many kinds. Explorations of conviviality have wider currency in re-imagining how intimacy and immediacy create styles of relating that are conducive to effective living but where there are also threats and dangers requiring conflict resolution and negotiation (Overing and Passes 2000). Negative behaviour, disharmony, and violence feature in hunter-gatherer life past and present. If we accept that hunter-gatherers can generally be defined by relations of incorporation, then circumstances of separation, exclusion, and alienation are ones which should demand our particular attention. The conditions that lead to ambivalent attitudes and the creation of potential non-persons are equally worthy of examination.

A focus on personhood also gives insight into the metaphorical models that often underwrite hunter-gatherer sociality and how it connects with cosmology and world view. Such processes are bound with the character and affordances of the land- and seascapes people inhabit and the topographies and beings they encounter. It is bound with knowledge, experience, and memory and is as much concerned with the imaginary (Whitridge 2004b; Zvelebil 2003) as it is with the available resource base. From the Australian Aboriginal ancestral events of the Dreamtime to naming strategies among the Inuit, all create recursive relations with people, places, and persons from other times. Actions and identities are fused with place; all three are imbricated in person creation.

Conclusion: The Prospects for Personhood

Personhood is a challenging concept that has profound implications for understanding social relations. The reframing of the mind/body, subject/object, nature/culture dyads that are engendered by approaches that acknowledge the diverse qualities of personhood not only enables the extension of relations to other species, and a suite of diverse other entities and phenomena, but serves to obviate many of these ontological distinctions altogether. As well as decentring the individual, it destabilizes the human focus and offers rapprochement with the non-human others. Revising understandings of the boundaries of human/non-human interaction is fundamental to such a project. Here, the perspectives offered in theorizing agency, relational ontologies, and broader notions of the non-human not only unsettle traditional academic boundaries but offer new configurations. It is likely that alternative ways of understanding personhood will continue to emerge to encompass the theoretical challenges of such endeavours (see for example Ingold 2006; Wallis 2009). Concerns with personhood permeate many academic traditions and there need to be more entangled interdisciplinary dialogues, involving voices outside anthropology and archaeology, for it to truly inform new approaches for understanding hunter-gatherer sociality.

Personhood also concerns the lived experience. Distinctions between (in)dividuals, agents, and selves need to be unpicked and theoretically reconstituted. More nuanced configurations of personhood offer us a means of looking at the multiplicity inherent in identity creation and to acknowledge the partial and persistent properties behind the 'silhouette'. Age and the life course has particular salience for exploring personhood due to the fact that particularly ambivalent attitudes are heightened at various points—pregnancy, birth, infancy, during illness, as well as other key events in adult life (Vilaça 2002). Other goals lie with understanding how particular meanings of personhood are generated in the course of social life and how these are defined by relations of all types and shaped by other identities and embodied conditions. Many of these aspects remain underdeveloped or unexplored in studies of modern hunter-gatherers as well as for their prehistoric counterparts. To conclude, personhood provides a valuable focus for integrating various aspects of social identity in meaningful ways. Taking relational perspectives as a given within hunter-gatherer lifeworlds offers considerable fluidity and diversity in charting the way personhood is configured, but it has wider implications. If we are to gain intellectual purchase on personhood, which by its very nature is mutable and transient, then understanding the particular contexts and conditions of action and the form of relations is critical. Like its shape-shifting and metamorphic properties, it seems personhood as a project is likely to remain unfinished.

REFERENCES

Albrethsen, S. E. and Brinch Petersen, E. 1976. Excavation of a Mesolithic cemetery at Vedbæk, Denmark, *Acta Archaeologica* 47, 1–28.
Barnard, A. 2004. Hunting-and-gathering society: an eighteenth-century Scottish invention. In A. Barnard (ed.), *Hunter-gatherers in history, archaeology and anthropology*, 31–44. Oxford: Berg.
Baxter, J. 2005. *The archaeology of childhood: children, gender and material culture*. Walnut Creek, CA: AltaMira Press.
Bird, D. W. and Bliege Bird, R. 2000. The ethnoarchaeology of juvenile foragers. *Journal of Anthropological Archaeology* 19, 461–7.
Bird, D. W. and Bliege Bird, R. 2005. Martu children's hunting strategies in the Western Desert, Australia. In B. S. Hewlett and M. E. Lamb (eds), *Hunter-gatherer childhoods*, 129–46. New Brunswick: Aldine Transaction.
Bird-David, N. 1990. The giving environment: another perspective on the economic system of gatherer-hunters. *Current Anthropology* 31, 189–96.
Bird-David, N. 1999. 'Animism revisited': personhood, environment, and relational epistemology. *Current Anthropology* 40, 67–91.
Bird-David, N. 2005. Studying children in 'hunter-gatherer' societies: reflections from a Nayaka perspective. In B. S. Hewlett and M. E. Lamb (eds), *Hunter-gatherer childhoods*, 92–101. New Brunswick: Aldine Transaction.
Bird-David, N. 2008. Feeding Nayaka children and English readers: a bifocal ethnography of parental feeding in 'the giving environment'. *Anthropological Quarterly* 81, 523–50.
Bradley, R. 1984. *The social basis of prehistoric Britain: themes and variations in the archaeology of power*. London: Longman.
Busby, C. 1997. Permeable and partible persons: a comparative analysis of gender and body in South India and Melanesia. *Journal of the Royal Anthropological Institute* 3, 261–78.
Carrithers, M., Collins, S., and Lukes, S. (eds) 1985. *The category of the person: anthropology, philosophy, history*. Cambridge: Cambridge University Press.
Chaix, L., Bridault, A., and Picavet, A. 1997. A tamed brown bear (*Ursus arctos* L.) of the Late Mesolithic from La Grande-Rivoire (Isère, France)? *Journal of Archaeological Science* 24, 1067–74.
Chapman, J. and Gaydarska, B. 2007. *Parts and wholes: fragmentation in prehistoric contexts*. Oxford: Oxbow.
Clark, B. J. and Wilkie, L. A. 2007. The prism of self: gender and personhood. In S. Nelson (ed.), *Identity and subsistence: gender strategies for archaeology*, 1–32. Lanham, MD: Altamira Press.
Conneller, C. 2004. Becoming deer: corporeal Corporeal transformations at Star Carr. *Archaeological Dialogues* 11, 37–56.

Constandse-Westermann, T. S. and Newell, R. R. 1988. Patterns of extraterritorial ornaments dispersion: an approach to the measurement of Mesolithic exogamy. *Rivista di Antropologia* supplement 66, 75–126.

Constandse-Westermann, T. S. and Newell, R. R. 1989. Limb lateralisation and social stratification in Western Mesolithic societies. In I. Herskovitz (ed.), *People and culture in change*, 405–34. Oxford: British Archaeological Reports International Series 508.

Descola, P. 2009. Human natures. *Social Anthropology* 17, 145–57.

Dobres, M.-A. 2000. *Technology and social agency: outlining a practice framework for archaeology*. Oxford: Blackwell.

Dobres, M.-A. and Robb, J. (eds) 2000. *Agency in archaeology*. London: Routledge.

Dowson, T. A. and Porr, M. 2001. Special objects—special creatures: shamanistic imagery and the Aurignacian art of south-west Germany. In N. Price (ed.), *The archaeology of shamanism*, 166–77. London: Routledge.

Eriksson, G., Lóugas, L., and Zargorska, I. 2003. Stone age hunter-fisher-gatherers at Zvejnieki, Northern Latvia: radiocarbon, stable isotope and archaeozoology data. *Before Farming* 2, 1–21.

Finlay, N. 1997. Kid-knapping: the missing children in lithic analysis. In J. Moore and E. Scott (eds), *Invisible people and processes: writing gender and childhood into European archaeology*, 203–12. Leicester: Leicester University Press.

Fowler, C. 2004. *The archaeology of personhood: an anthropological approach*. London: Routledge.

Gamble, C. 1999. *The Palaeolithic societies of Europe*. Cambridge: Cambridge University Press.

Gamble, C. 2007. *Origins and revolutions. human identity in earliest prehistory*. Cambridge: Cambridge University Press.

Gamble, C. and Porr, M. (eds) 2005. *The hominid individual in context: archaeological investigations of Lower and Middle Palaeolithic landscapes, locales and artefacts*. London: Routledge.

Gammeltoft, T. M. 2008. Childhood disability and parental moral responsibility in northern Vietnam: towards ethnographies of intercorporeality. *Journal of the Royal Anthropological Institute* 14, 825–42.

Gell, A. 1998. *Art and agency: an anthropological theory*. Oxford: Clarendon Press.

Gilchrist, R. (ed.) 2000. Human lifecycles. *World Archaeology* 31, 325–8.

Gillespie, S. D. 2001. Personhood, agency, and mortuary ritual: a case study from the Ancient Maya. *Journal of Anthropological Archaeology* 20, 73–112.

Hallowell, I. 1960. Ojibwa ontology, behaviour and worldview. In S. Diamond (ed.), *Culture in history: essays in honor of Paul Radin*, 19–52. New York: Columbia University Press.

Hayden, B. 1995. Pathways to power: principles for creating socioeconomic inequalities. In T. D. Price and G. M. Feinman (eds), *Foundations of social inequality*, 15–86. London: Plenum Press.

Hewlett, B. S. and Lamb, M. E. (eds) 2005. *Hunter-gatherer childhoods*. New Brunswick: Aldine Transaction.

Hoskins, J. 1998. *Biographical objects: how things tell the stories of people's lives*. London: Routledge.

Ingold, T. 1999. On the social relations of the hunter-gatherer band. In R. B. Lee and R. Daly (eds), *The Cambridge encyclopaedia of hunters and gatherers*, 399–410. Cambridge: Cambridge University Press.

Ingold, T. 2000. *The perception of the environment: essays in livelihood, dwelling and skill*. London: Routledge.

Ingold, T. 2006. Rethinking the animate, re-animating thought. *Ethnos* 71, 9–20.

Jacobs, K. 1995. Returning to Olenii Ostrov: social, economic and skeletal dimensions of a boreal forest Mesolithic cemetery. *Journal of Anthropological Archaeology* 14, 359–403.

Janik, L. 2000. The construction of the individual among North European fisher-gatherer-hunters in the Early and Mid-Holocene. In J. Sofaer Derevenski (ed.), *Children and material culture*, 118–30. London: Routledge.

Jones, A. 2005. Lives in fragments? Personhood and the European Neolithic. *Journal of Social Archaeology* 5, 193–224.

Kelly, R. L. 1995. *The foraging spectrum: diversity in hunter-gatherer lifeways*. London: Smithsonian Institution.

Larsson, L. 1989. Big dog and poor man: mortuary practices in Mesolithic societies in southern Sweden. In T. B. Larsson and H. Lundmark (eds), *Approaches to Swedish prehistory*, 211–23. Oxford: British Archaeological Report International Series 500.

Larsson, L. 1990. Dogs in fraction—symbols in action. In P. M. Vermeersch and P. van Peer (eds), *Contributions to the Mesolithic of Europe*, 153–60. Leuven: Studia Praehistorica Belgica 5.

Lévi-Strauss, C. 1963. *Totemism*. Boston: Beacon Press.

Lillie, M. C. 2003. Taste the forbidden fruit: gender based dietary differences among prehistoric hunter-gatherers of Eastern Europe?, *Before Farming* 2, 1–16.

Lillie, M. C. 2009. Suffer the children: 'visualising' children in the archaeological record. In K. Bacvarov (ed.), *Babies reborn: infant/child burials in pre- and protohistory*, 33–43. Oxford: British Archaeological Report International Series 1832.

Lillie, M. C., Richards, M. P., and Jacobs, K. 2003. Stable isotope analysis of 21 individuals from the Epipalaeolithic cemetery of Vasilyevka II, Dnieper Rapids region, Ukraine. *Journal of Archaeological Science* 30, 743–52.

LiPuma, E. 1998. Modernity and forms of personhood in Melanesia. In M. Lambek and A. Strathern (eds), *Bodies and persons: comparative perspectives from Africa and Melanesia*, 53–79. Cambridge: Cambridge University Press.

Meskell, L. 1999. *Archaeologies of social life: age, sex, class et cetera in ancient Egypt*. Oxford: Wiley.

Meskell, L. and Joyce, R. 2003. *Embodied lives: figuring ancient Maya and Egyptian experience*. London: Routledge.

Mithen, S. 1990. *Thoughtful foragers: a study of prehistoric decision making*. Cambridge: Cambridge University Press.

Mithen, S. 1991. A cybernetic wasteland? Rationality, emotion and Mesolithic foraging. *Proceedings of the Prehistoric Society* 57, 9–14.

Nasaday, P. 2007. The gift in the animal: the ontology of hunting and human-animal sociality. *American Ethnologist* 34, 25–43.

Nilsson Stutz, L. 2003. *Embodied rituals and ritualised bodies: tracing ritual practices in Late Mesolithic burials*. Lund: Acta Archaeologica Lundensia.

Overing, J. and Passes, A. 2000. *The anthropology of love and anger: the aesthetics of conviviality in native Amazonia*. London: Routledge.

Owens, D. and Hayden, B. 1997. Prehistoric rites of passage: a comparative study of transegalitarian hunter-gatherers. *Journal of Anthropological Archaeology* 16, 121–61.

Pettitt, P. 2000. Neanderthal lifecycles: developmental and social phases in the lives of the last archaics. *World Archaeology* 31, 351–66.

Pluciennik, M. 2001. Archaeology, anthropology and subsistence, *Journal of the Royal Anthropological Institute* 7, 741–58.

Politis, G. 2005. Children's activity in the production of the archaeological record of hunter-gatherers: an ethnographical approach. In P. P. Funari, A. Zarankin, and E. Stovel (eds), *Global archaeological theory: contextual voices and contemporary thoughts*, 121–43. New York: Kluwer Academic/Plenum Press.

Price, N. 2001. *The archaeology of shamanism*. London: Routledge.

Price, T. D. and Brown, J. A. (eds) 1985. *Prehistoric hunter-gatherers: the emergence of cultural complexity*. London: Academic Press.

Price, T. D. and Feinman, G. M. 1995. *Foundations of social inequality*. London: Plenum Press.

Schmidt, R. A. 2000. Shamans and northern cosmology: the direct historical approach to Mesolithic sexuality. In R. A. Schmidt and B. L. Voss (eds), *Archaeologies of sexuality*, 220–35. London: Routledge.

Schulting, R. J. 1998. Creativity's coffin: innovation in the burial record of Mesolithic Europe. In S. Mithen (ed.), *Creativity in human evolution and prehistory*, 203–26. London: Routledge.

Schulting, R. J. and Richards, M. P. 2001. Dating women and becoming farmers: new palaeo-dietary and AMS dating evidence from the Breton Mesolithic cemeteries of Téviec and Hoëdic. *Journal of Anthropological Archaeology* 20, 314–44.

Shostak, M. 1990 [1981]. *Nisa: the life and words of a !Kung woman*. Harmondsworth: Penguin.

Sofaer Derevenski, J. (ed.) 2000. *Children and material culture*. London: Routledge.

Strathern, M. 1988. *The gender of the gift: problems with women and problems with society in Melanesia*. Berkeley: University of California Press.

Tanner, A. 1979. *Bringing home animals: religious ideology and mode of production of the Mistassini Cree hunters*. New York: St. Martin's Press.

Vilaça, A. 2002. Making kin out of others in Amazonia. *Journal of the Royal Anthropological Institute* 8, 347–65.

Viveiros de Castro, E. 2004. Exchanging perspectives: the transformation of objects into subjects in Amerindian ontologies. *Common Knowledge* 10, 463–84.

Wagner, R. 1991. The fractal person. In M. Strathern and M. Godelier (eds), *Big men and great men: personifications of power in Melanesia*, 159–73. Cambridge: Cambridge University Press.

Wallis, R. 2009. Re-enchanting rock art landscapes: animic ontologies, nonhuman agency and rhizomic personhood. *Time and Mind* 2, 47–70.

Whitridge, P. 2004a. Whales, harpoons, and other actors: actor-network theory and hunter-gatherer archaeology. In G. Crothers (ed.), *Hunter-gatherers in theory and archaeology*, 445–75. Carbondale: Centre for Archaeological Investigations, Southern Illinois University.

Whitridge, P. 2004b. Landscapes, houses, bodies, things: 'place' and the archaeology of Inuit imaginaries, *Journal of Archaeological Method and Theory* 11, 213–50.

Willerslev, R. 2007. *Soul hunters: hunting, animism, and personhood among the Siberian Yukaghirs*. Berkeley: University of California Press.

Winterhalder, B. and Smith, E. A. (eds) 1981. *Hunter-gatherer foraging strategies: ethnographic and archaeological analyses*. Chicago: University of Chicago Press.

Zeitlyn, D. 2008. Life-history writing and the anthropological silhouette. *Social Anthropology* 16, 154–71.

Zvelebil, M. 2000. The context of the agricultural transition in Europe. In C. Renfrew and K. Boyle (eds), *Archaeogenetics: DNA and the population prehistory of Europe*, 57–79. Cambridge: McDonald Institute for Archaeological Research.

Zvelebil, M. 2003. Enculturation of Mesolithic landscapes. In L. Larsson, H. Kingren, K. Knutsson, D. Loeffler, and A. Åkerlund (eds), *Mesolithic on the move. Papers presented at the sixth international conference on the Mesolithic in Europe, Stockholm 2000*, 65–73. Oxford: Oxbow.

CHAPTER 58

MATERIALS, BIOGRAPHIES, IDENTITIES, EXPERIENCES
New Approaches to Materials in Hunter-Gatherer Studies

HANNAH COBB

> Tool-using has often been cited as one of the major distinctions in behavior between what is quintessentially human as opposed to animal: in other words, as one of the fundamental traits in what sets culture apart from nature.
>
> (Torrence 1989a, 1)

As archaeologists it is an axiom of our profession that we study the things or the stuff of the past. Our daily work sees us continually encountering materials and the residues of materials. For many in hunter-gatherer studies those materials are largely stone tools, but whether it is tools and technology or the material remains of other aspects of hunter-gatherer lives, approaches to materials in hunter-gatherer studies have, until very recently, been typified by the kind of view in the above quote. For Torrence (1989a), like many others, culture and nature are distinct and separate categories through which we can conceptualize past hunter-gatherer interactions with the material world. Yet, beyond hunter-gatherer studies, how archaeologists have addressed past materials and interpreted their meanings has, like many other facets of the discipline, changed significantly as theoretical paradigms have also changed and developed.

Whilst questions of style, design, and function have until recently dominated our enquiries (see Conkey 2006 for a précis of various arguments), a growing critique has developed which has demonstrated that such concerns are typical of a way of understanding materials that is specific to the modern, post-Enlightenment West. This particular world view, within which culture is set against nature, is underwritten by the premise that materials are inactive and inert things upon which qualities may be placed (Thomas 2004). As Thomas has argued:

> Archaeology studies the past through the medium of material culture...Yet the very idea that material things are entities that we can stand apart from, and employ as evidence for the actions of people in the past, is, while not exclusively modern, at least a characteristic of a modern sensibility.
>
> (Thomas 2004, 202)

Beginning in the later 1970s, however, a series of counter-modern dialogues started to arise that have sought to question this division between culture and nature, mind and matter, and form and matter, in our understandings of past interactions between people and materials. Indeed when, in 1982, Ian Hodder suggested that all material culture is meaningfully constituted (Hodder 1982), this represented a radical new way of thinking about materials.

In the following decades, the trajectories in which these counter-modern critiques have taken the discipline now demand that we approach the encounter between people and materials in fundamentally different ways. In this chapter I explore these developments and trajectories, reviewing how, in recent years, they have begun to impact upon hunter-gatherer studies and examining how such new approaches to materials, material culture, and technology are vital for future developments of hunter-gatherer studies. The case studies that are discussed here are largely from Mesolithic studies the UK and Ireland, and this reflects the areas that my own research focuses on. However, it is important to emphasize that the various ideas here are equally valid and applicable to hunter-gatherer studies from other times and places.

Making Materials Matter

Materials and Modernity

Before addressing new approaches to materials in hunter-gatherer studies, however, it seems pertinent to examine how materials have come to matter, and how the discipline began to shift away from concerns with aspects such as functionality that dominated approaches to materials under the processual paradigm. Underpinning this shift, as I have briefly noted already, has been the idea that prior archaeological paradigms have conceptualized the past through a framework that is historically specific and particular to the modern West. Such modern approaches derive from a framework for understanding the world in which matter is understood as natural, as given, and as irreducible. This notion first arose within the work of Aristotle, but came to be firmly compounded through the development of the seventeenth-century philosophy and physics of proponents such as Locke, Newton, and Descartes (Thomas 2004). Indeed, the work of these three men developed both a conceptual framework and a supporting lexicon that for the first time enabled a detailed exploration of the stuff of matter (atoms), the physical properties that affected it (gravity, motion, inertia, and mass), and the qualities that enabled the experience of it (Thomas 2004, 206-7). The impacts of this upon our understanding of the world today, and specifically the ways in which we do archaeology, are fundamental. Thus past materials tend to remain inert and irreducible in the archaeological process. They are uncovered, classified, conserved, and displayed through procedure and process that more often than not renders them separate and divorced from the thinking, active minds of past and present people.

Such a perspective is problematic, not simply because of its cultural and temporal specificity, but also because this is simply not the way in which we encounter things in the world. Material things are not inert and separate from people, rather materials can have effects, they can contribute to statements about identity, they can accumulate detailed life stories and in turn provoke powerful memories. This is not because they are separate from humans, as a Cartesian world view may argue, but rather they are active because they are *in* life, caught in a complicated tangle of relations. As Ingold demonstrates, material things are 'the active constituents of a world-in-formation', and thus 'to describe the properties of materials is to tell the story of what happens to them as they flow, mix and mutate' (Ingold 2007, 14). This notion is perhaps most articulately expressed in Ingold's dwelling perspective, which draws heavily upon the work of Martin Heidegger to argue that:

> the forms people build, whether in imagination or on the ground, arise within the current of their involved activity, in the specific relational contexts of their practical engagement with their surroundings.
>
> (Ingold 2000, 186)

Thus, the dwelling perspective emphasizes that we are never a detached mind apprehending the world 'out there' as a passive object, but rather we are *in* the world, and our understanding of this emerges from our sensual, visceral, bodily immersion in the world. It is this view that has shaped many new approaches to materials in hunter-gatherer studies, and it is to this that I shall return shortly.

Firstly, however, it is important to be clear just how consistently and thoroughly the modern, Western, and Cartesian view of materials has, to date, pervaded hunter-gatherer studies. A very good example can be found in Thomas's critique of Lewis Binford's use of the analytical division between form and matter and mind and matter in formulating his Middle Range Theory. Here Thomas illustrates that the notion of the universality of matter that underpins Newtonian physics similarly acts as the crux of Binford's Middle Range Theory (Thomas 2004, 211). Consequently, for Binford, the static and inert archaeological record and the processes that enable its formation must first be studied and material facts established prior to any further interpretation of 'social' factors (Binford 1983). Thus 'it seems that he [Binford] has succeeded in forcing a division between the analytical frameworks appropriate for matter (nature) and society (culture)' (Thomas 2004, 212). Yet, as we have already seen, such a division is flawed because we can never apprehend or understand matter as pure, meaningless, and detached from the social. Indeed all of our encounters with materials are social, and they can be nothing else. Any mode of analysis of the archaeological record that separates matter and society or nature and culture in such a way can only ever produce an account of the past that is sanitized, reductionist, conceived within a historically particular milieu, and that simply cannot begin to explore in full the sociality of past material engagements.

This critique is highly significant for hunter-gatherer studies because Binford's work is often recognized as an authority in identifying factors that shape the organization of hunter-gatherer technology. In particular his most influential work has focused upon the Nunamuit hunter-gatherers of the Central Brooks Range of Alaska in an attempt to explore variability in Mousterian lithic assemblages (e.g. Binford 1973; 1978; 1979; 1983). This work has undeniably made important contributions to hunter-gatherer studies, but at the same time its disjointed and reductionist manner of examining material culture has also been influential. Many subsequent studies of hunter-gatherer materials, predominantly centred upon stone tools, have followed Binford's work in dividing natural and cultural factors shaping hunter-gatherer material choices, affording clear epistemological privilege to the examination of the former (e.g. Bleed 1986; 2001; Myers 1989; and papers in Torrence 1989b). In turn the resulting '[t]echnological discourse helps to objectify and limit technology to things and relations among things such that people often drop out of the picture altogether' (Dobres and Hoffman 1994, 230).

Moreover, the extent to which such notions have become so fundamentally rooted within the discipline are clear at a number of levels, from basic archaeological discourse to more formal recording and post-excavation techniques (Dobres and Hoffman 1994; Ingold 2000). Take, for example, a simple chipped stone report, the place in which past hunter-gatherer materials are most explicitly documented. Such reports typically list quantities of tool types, of waste material, of reduction strategies, and of use wear. Rarely is any interpretation offered as to the social roles of, and the human interactions with, these materials (although see some attempt to counter this in Mithen 2000). Beyond the level of site report, in articles addressing prehistoric technology, Dobres has illustrated that these too uphold the form/ matter dichotomy through the notion that we must first focus upon 'choice in raw material, fabrication techniques, artefact form, function, and so forth [aspects which] are argued to reside in the physical nature of the materials worked' (Dobres 2000, 37) before we turn to providing 'social' interpretations. This is typified by many approaches to stone tool studies where '[s]uch concepts as curated and expedient technologies, embedded procurement of raw materials, or forager and collector subsistence-settlement systems...at least provide a framework' (Torrence 1989b, vii) for how materials are considered. Ultimately, in their artificial division of form and matter and culture and nature, such approaches conjure images of prehistoric hunter-gatherers striving to mechanically exploit their environments to their optimum, engaging with the world only to continually develop specialist adaptations until this is achieved. Indeed so pervasive is this notion that even recent accounts that counter such Binfordian optimization approaches are still fundamentally reliant upon the suggestion that matter is natural and given, and cultural meaning is applied to it.

From Risk and Reason to Biography and Being

Despite the prevalence of the above approaches to materials in hunter-gatherer studies, since the late 1970s there has been a concerted move, both within hunter-gatherer studies and outside, to challenge the modern alienation of material things from people. Such approaches have suggested that materials mattered, not simply because they enabled optimal adaptation to, and exploitation of, an environment, but because they were able to transmit information. It was through the identification of style as the aspect of materials which could not simply be explained in functional terms, and the exploration of this, that such ideas were first addressed. One of the first people to explore this was Martin Wobst. As early as 1977 Wobst argued that style may be used to transmit information on aspects such as age, gender, ethnicity, and class (Wobst 1977). Yet whilst Wobst primarily argued that the variability he observed in material styles acted only to *reflect* social variability, subsequently Conkey (1978) went on to illustrate that material styles could themselves play a constitutive role in the formation of social identities. This work laid the foundations for a vigorous debate regarding the sociality of the interplay between materials, style, and identity (i.e. Sackett 1986; Wiessner 1983; 1984). For further overviews of this debate see Conkey 2006; Edmonds and Thomas 1987; Thomas 2004; Wobst 1999.

Subsequent interpretations of past material culture began to draw upon such foundations and developed throughout the 1980s in a range of ways; Hodder's (1982) argument that all material culture is meaningfully constituted was of course fundamental in shifting disciplinary attitudes towards the materials that we encounter. So too was the work of Kopytoff and Appadurai, in arguing that objects cannot be understood simply as fixed and static but as continually transforming in meaning through their accumulating biographies (Kopytoff 1986), and consequently that through arenas such as exchange we can see things as active and as having a social life (Appadurai 1986). In addition a range of groundbreaking ethnographies in the late 1980s provided a series of insightful illustrations regarding the extent to which material culture can be socially meaningful at a number of levels simultaneously (e.g. MacKenzie 1991; Moore 1986; Strathern 1988).

By the early 1990s the development of such ideas, accompanied by the translation into English of the work of Leroi-Gourhan on the *chaîne opératoire* (1964; 1965), led to a range of scholars (for example see Edmonds 1990; Karlin and Julien 1994; Lemonnier 1990; Pfaffenberger 1992; Schlanger 1990; 1994; and papers in the *Archaeological Review from Cambridge Volume* 9(1) 'Technology in the Humanities') who began to argue against the modern, Western, alienated frameworks that had come to characterize discussions of prehistoric technology and technical practices. For such protagonists *chaîne opératoire* perspectives raised the possibility for moving beyond the simple construction of operational sequences for individual tool types. Instead they illustrated the extent to which technological choices were socially embedded (e.g. see papers in Lemonnier 1993), and they illuminated the continual, embodied, sensual, and social practices generated in the production and use of different kinds of materials (Dobres 2000, 193; Dobres and Hoffman 1994; Edmonds 1990; Karlin and Julien 1994; Lemonnier 1990; Schlanger 1990; 1994).

Developing such arguments, Ingold has even gone as far as to argue that *'there is no such thing as technology in pre-modern societies'* (Ingold 2000, 314, original emphasis), a perspective only possible precisely because of the rejection of the modern view of technology and technique. Thus understanding technique not as the stamping of knowledge onto matter, but as recursive, skilled practice emerging from the embodied encounter between people and their world means that techniques cannot be applied *through* the use of tools, but rather they are *'embedded in*, and inseparable from, the experience of particular subjects in the shaping of particular things' (Ingold 2000, 315, emphasis added). This view requires a complete reformulation of how we understand technical knowledge, from the explicit to the tacit, from the application of knowledge *onto* materials to technical practice as a contextually situated, sensual, and embodied reciprocal revealing of the world:

> For acting in the world is the skilled practitioner's way of knowing it. It is in the direct contact with materials, whether or not mediated by tools—in the attentive touching, feeling, handling, looking and listening that is entailed in the very process of creative work—that technical knowledge is gained as well as applied. No separate corpus of rule and representations is required to organise perceptual data or to formulate instructions for action. Thus, skill is at once a form of knowledge and a form of practice, or—if you will—it is both practical knowledge and knowledgeable practice.
>
> (Ingold 2000, 316)

Following such developments in the conception of technology and the understanding of the biographical nature of objects, debate surrounding materials in the late 1990s, and since the beginning of the new millennium, has shifted once again and archaeologists have turned to examine the manner in which materials may have agency (e.g. see papers in Dobres and

Robb 2000 as well as others such as Gell 1998; Gosden 2005; Robb 2004). Whilst attempts to pin down the type of agency that objects exert (i.e. Gell 1998) may have attracted criticism (Ingold 2007; Robb 2004), ultimately our narratives of the past can be significantly enriched by acknowledging the complicated ways in which objects have effects (Gosden 2005; Ingold 2007; Robb 2004). The impacts of such debates have especially led to a development of a disciplinary concern with the production of personhood and the role that material culture plays in the constitution of identity (Fowler 2004). Moreover such debates have equally had significant impacts upon how we practise as archaeologists, raising the vital question of whether we can ever recognize a fixed and singular 'archaeological record' in the first place (Barrett 2001).

Challenging Materiality and Material Culture

Studies of materials have also taken an increasingly phenomenological turn since the turn of the new millennium. Ingold's (2000) dwelling perspective, for example, has become an often used heuristic framework for considering the nature of the relationship between people and materials. Moreover, Ingold's (1993) extension of the dwelling perspective in his discussion of the taskscape has also been incredibly influential. Such a perspective demonstrates that the implications of the activities in which we engage, of how we dwell, ripple out across time and space, continually affecting and being affected by our own being in the world. In turn such phenomenological arguments have in recent years led to two fundamentally important arguments. These are that we must dispense both with the notions of material culture (Thomas 2007) and materiality (Ingold 2007). Thus Thomas has argued that the term 'material culture' upholds the mind/matter dichotomy by suggesting that ideas, which exist in the realm of mind, are then made material in the form of material culture. Furthermore he has demonstrated that it also upholds the form/matter dichotomy, asserting the notion that inert and natural material must have cultural form applied to it in order to become 'material culture'. In contrast, Thomas suggests that we need to see the formation of objects as happening in the world, as they are disclosed against a background of 'skills, practices and tacit cultural understandings' (Thomas 2007, 21).

It is a similar phenomenological understanding of objects that also lies within Ingold's assertion that, like material culture, the term 'materiality' is also problematic. Ingold argues that a fixation with materiality has become an obstacle into any enquiry with materials, causing people to ignore actual materials in favour of abstracted discussions of theoretical qualities that may be applied to materials. For Ingold such qualities include 'agency, intentionality, functionality, sociality, spatiality, semiosis, spirituality and embodiment' (Ingold 2007, 2). Such discussions thus rest upon understandings of materiality as the artificial transformation of artefacts in contrast to untransformed, 'natural' materials found *in situ* in the landscape (Ingold 2007, 8). Furthermore, Ingold illustrates that a focus on materiality demands two further problematic aspects; firstly that we often focus on objects as the finished products of production, and secondly that the notion that materials can 'have' materiality suggests in turn that all materials share a common essence. Like Thomas, Ingold provides a counter to the notion of materiality by suggesting we must come to explore materials as continually emerging, as always gathering and regathering the world around them, so that they continually emerge from and disclose a complicated tangle of relations.

New Approaches to Materials in Hunter-Gatherer Studies

Materials and Identities

The various arguments reviewed above have all had significant impacts upon hunter-gatherer studies. Some of these debates, such as those about technology and agency, were originally framed around case studies of hunter-gatherer groups (e.g. Dobres 2000). However, since the beginning of the new millennium many of the questions about past and present relations with materials that have originated in wider social theory have rapidly and significantly begun to impact upon hunter-gatherer studies. One of the areas in which this has been most prevalent has been in exploring the relationship between materials and identity.

Of course questions of identity in hunter-gatherer studies are not new. Many of the debates around style in the 1980s focused on its role in the production of identity. Here ethnographic studies of hunter-gatherer groups, such as Wiessner's work with the Kalahari San (e.g. Wiessner 1983) in turn impacted on studies of past hunter-gatherers, such as Gendel's (1989) discussion of the relationship between Mesolithic hunter-gatherer group identity and microlith style. However, in recent years work has moved to consider aspects such as the production of personal identity through explicitly non-Western frameworks, and this has had a fundamental impact on new approaches to materials in hunter-gatherer studies. In this case approaches to personhood in both the anthropological (Busby 1997; LiPuma 1998; MacKenzie 1991; Moore 1986; Mosko 1992; Strathern 1988; Viveiros de Castro 1998) and more recently the archaeological (Fowler 2004) literature have been highly influential. Such approaches have demonstrated that rather than understanding individual identity as fixed and bounded by the skin, as is commonly assumed in the modern West, in many different societies (as well as our own), personal identity is something that is much more fluid and changeable, and *inextricably linked to the material world*.

Various ethnographies have demonstrated how, in many societies, identity is continually reformulated through the relationships in which people find themselves, both with other people and between people and things. In such examples identity can be understood as composite, dividual, and often multiply authored, '[p]eople are composed of social relations with others to the degree that they owe parts of themselves to others... The body itself also has different constituent elements, and changes in the balance of these may alter the disposition of the person' (Fowler 2004, 8). In this kind of dividual view of personhood material things may act to represent personal relations, or they may be regarded as the constituent parts of persons themselves. Either way they are not inert in such a process; materials may accumulate complicated biographies, incorporating parts of persons, places, and other things, and in turn this may affect the user significantly. For instance, amongst the Hagan of Melanesia, Strathern demonstrates that '[w]hat applies to human bodies applies equally to the "bodies" of food plants and to items such as valuables whose substantial capacity to attract wealth can be transmitted to others' (Strathern 1988, 208).

For the purposes of this chapter, this is of course an overly simplistic summary of such views of identity. The simplicity of such an account masks the complicated debates surrounding these issues. For example, whilst the literature undoubtedly demonstrates the presence of many very different perspectives on identity compared to those we traditionally hold in the modern West, in fact Western personhood is equally as complicated and to create a universalizing model of this masks the very many ways in which personal identity is constituted in Western society (LiPuma 1998). Moreover, it is important to emphasize that we should not simply supplant one universalizing set of assumptions surrounding identity in the West with another universalizing view of dividual identity in 'other' societies (Fowler 2004; LiPuma 1998). Nor should we simply and uncritically apply models of Melanesian, or any other, personhood onto the past (Jones 2005). Instead, what I want to stress here is that the many ethnographies which deal with personhood demonstrate that the creation of personal identity is complicated, multifaceted, and *fundamentally tied to material things*. The production of identity ultimately always emerges through relations, through connections, and through the visceral, embodied, *material* acts of daily life. It is this realization, which brings us back to Ingold's dwelling perspective, that has led to the development of a range of new approaches to material things in hunter-gatherer studies.

An excellent example can be found in Nyree Finlay's discussion of microliths and multiple authorship (Finlay 2003). Here Finlay has argued that traditional approaches to microliths are concerned largely with their functionality in modern, Western terms. This approach in turn alienates this ubiquitous form of Mesolithic hunter-gatherer technology from discussions of social relations, except in a problematic 'gendering' of microliths as used mainly by men due to their classification as predominantly hunting tools (Finlay 2003; 2006; and see the discussion below). In contrast, drawing upon Strathern's work in Melanesia, Finlay argues for a very different view of Mesolithic tool production involving a complex entanglement of relationships between people and things. Here she suggests that composite microlithic tools are likely to have been multiply authored, with several people making the multiple microliths required, and likely group efforts required to gather and prepare the wood, resin, and twine that would then enable the microliths to be hafted (Finlay 2003). In such an account, Finlay demonstrates that the production of tools would have demanded connections between persons and between different materials, individual bodily practices, and group actions. Furthermore, both the production and use of tools required intimate associations not simply between people, but between people and materials from diverse sources. The production and use of composite microlithic tools therefore required the fragmentation of persons, materials, and the essences of places, and the social transformation and renegotiation of all of these (Warren 2006), and as such may have been critical in engendering multiply authored identities (Finlay 2003).

Finlay's arguments provide a powerful way for reformulating not simply studies of microlithic technology, but Mesolithic technical engagements in general, and they have been highly influential in subsequent approaches to materials and identity. Warren has argued, for instance, that understanding tools as a nexus for social relations in the Mesolithic provides a dynamic and exciting means for examining elements such as the production and negotiation of identity (Warren 2006). Furthermore, as will be discussed below, a range of approaches have moved to explore the implications of such a composite and multiply authored view of technology for understanding the relationships between people and places amongst past hunter-gatherer societies (Cobb 2007a; 2007b; 2008; 2009; Conneller 2005; 2006; Kador 2007). In addition, such a view of microlithic technology also provides a nuanced new way to reconceive modern assumptions about gender identity that are associated with stone tool technology, and Finlay herself has developed this critique (Finlay 2006). She has illustrated that discussions of tool use and the division of labour largely stem from a series of now well-critiqued ethnographic analogies which argued that hunting activities were practised exclusively by men, whilst women predominantly gathered plant resources and were restricted to base camps by child-rearing tasks (for example Clark 1954). In contrast, Finlay has drawn upon the work of Judith Butler (1993), as well as ethnographic accounts such as Strathern's (1988), to examine the notion of gendered identities as continually being in production through bodily practices (Finlay 2006). Consequently, rather than fixed tool uses equating to gender identities that were equally fixed, instead she has suggested that the fluid meanings and uses of tools played critical parts in the creation of equally fluid gender identities, allowing gender to be continually enacted and performed (Finlay 2006). Finlay's argument is powerfully made through the example of the Mesolithic site of Mount Sandel in Northern Ireland, and it provides an important and long overdue challenge to the simplistic association of gender and tool type. Moreover, this critique can be further extended as it is clear that by the association of tool types with gender, a series of heteronormative assumptions are also sanctioned. Thus in many cases where areas of male and female activity are identified through tool type these are then further explained as structured *family* units (e.g. Grøn 1987; 1995; 2003), which in turn unquestioningly perpetuates modern Western sexual norms. However, by reformulating questions about the material conditions through which identities are performed, and by exploring a more nuanced relationship between materials and identities, such sexually normative narratives can also be challenged (Cobb 2008; Finlay 2006).

Whilst alternative conceptions of personhood have had an important impact upon our understandings of the relationship between hunter-gatherers and more commonly found materials, such as stone tools, it can be argued that they have also had a profound impact upon understandings of other types of materials as well. An excellent example of this is the early Mesolithic site of Star Carr in north east Yorkshire. Here the presence of 21 artificially smoothed and perforated antler frontlets has repeatedly drawn interpretations of ritualistic practices in which the frontlets acted as masks (Clark 1954; Conneller 2004). As Conneller has illustrated, however, such an interpretation involves a modern Western understanding of the individual as bounded and distinct from, and thus hidden, or masked by the frontlets. Instead, she has drawn upon a series of accounts of non-Western understandings of human/animal relationships and of animal bodies that are particularly influenced by Viveiros de Castro's arguments on perspectivism (Viveiros de Castro 1998). Such a view demonstrates the abilities of animals or parts of animals to have transformative effects on people so, for instance, hunters may use parts of and materials from a hunted animal in order to transform and become that animal, and to hunt more like it. With such a perspectivist view in mind Conneller has suggested that rather than disguise or hide human bodies, such masks actually revealed and transformed them, as part of wider performances that produced human and animal identities (Conneller 2004, 50). Additionally, the productivity of this approach is further illustrated through Conneller's extension of it to all of the different types of animal/human interactions that took place at the site. Through the working of hide, and the making and using of animals bones as tools, teeth as beads, and skin as clothes, Conneller suggests there existed an 'ambiguity about where human bodies end and animal bodies start. Parts of humans transform animals, who in turn alter and extend human bodies' (Conneller 2004, 47). In recent years Conneller (2011) has developed this argument in relation to the wider faunal remains at Star Carr and at other sites in the Vale of Pickering to create an increasingly nuanced and rich alternative conceptualization of the relationship both between people and animals, and also between people and material things in the Mesolithic of north Yorkshire.

Another similar reworking of the complicated relationship between humans and animals, this time in the final Mesolithic, has been proposed by Borić (2005) at the site of Lepenski Vir in the Danube Gorges of the north central Balkans. Once again, the starting point for this approach is a challenge to the view of materials as passive and static. Instead Borić has suggested that carved boulders with hybrid human and fish features acted to not simply represent but to reveal 'the corporeal metamorphosis of deceased humans into a hybrid being, reaching the stage of animality in death… through the existence of a special totemic relationship between fish (perhaps especially migratory sturgeon) and humans' (Borić 2005, 57).

Whilst it may be no surprise that new approaches to materials in hunter-gatherer societies, which have taken their inspiration from dividual and perspectivist conceptions of identity, have focused upon the most commonly archaeologically attested stone and faunal remains, such an approach has also been highly productive when explored in relation to other material aspects prevalent in Mesolithic daily life. In the southern Scandinavian Mesolithic, for example, Price has shown that normative economic and alienated approaches to non-stone tool technologies have led to the creation of analytical categories by tool type or raw material (e.g. 'fish trap', 'spear', 'paddle', 'timber', 'bark', 'bone': Price 2005; 2007). Instead he suggests that a more productive approach may be to explore the symbolic properties and associations of specific materials which 'may offer a suggestion as to how these people classified their world and show that technological choices were not based exclusively upon economic principles' (Price 2005, 99). Indeed, Price's work has identified that different woods were used for making different things (lime for canoes and elm for bows for example—see Figure 58.1), and in turn he has suggested that if different tasks, using specific types of wood, were undertaken then this 'allowed certain people to reiterate and reinterpret traditions from their personal histories and experiences and to manipulate social conventions in socially acceptable ways' (Price 2005, 103). Thus the relationships between humans and different tree species brought different identities into being through different contextual associations (Price 2005; 2007).

Whilst the sheer quantity of normally perishable items that have been found preserved across southern Scandinavia provides a Mesolithic dataset unrivalled elsewhere in north-west Europe, there is nonetheless an important point raised here: the lack of perishable material things elsewhere in Europe does not mean that such items would have been excluded from daily life, and occasional well-preserved sites such as the Oronsay middens (Mellars 1987) and Star Carr (Conneller 2004) in Britain attest to this. Such sites act as an important reminder of the value in remembering the use of these types of materials in Mesolithic daily life. Indeed whilst new approaches to materials have often examined identity, many have also argued that this is inextricable from people's relationships with their wider world, and it is to this that I turn next.

Materials, Landscape, and Taskscape

It is commonly accepted that hunter-gatherers, past and present, live predominantly mobile lives, whether in daily acts of hunting and foraging, or broader temporal cycles bound into

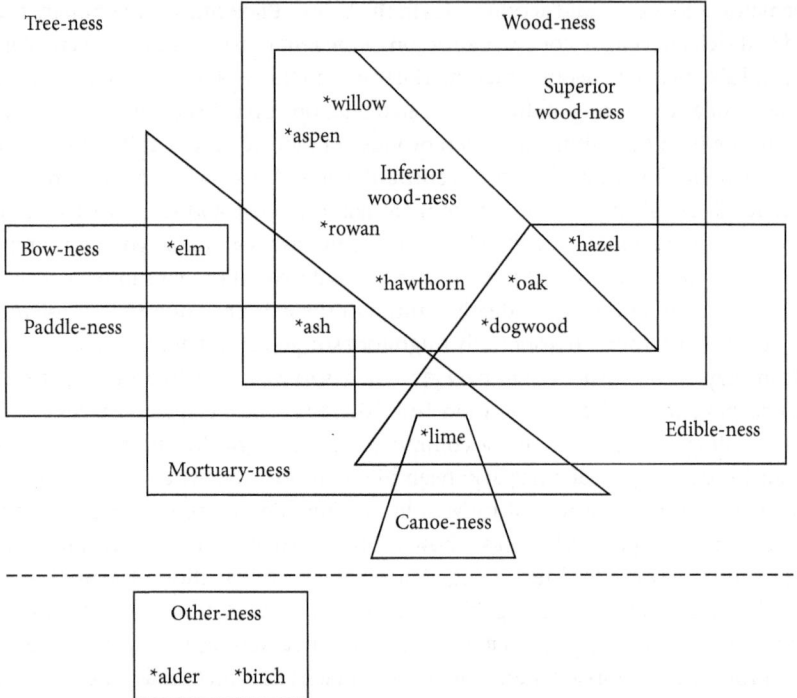

FIGURE 58.1 Price's schematic illustration to indicate characteristics of tree types as they cross cut and are associated with different objects in the Scandinavian Mesolithic (Price 2005, 100).

the seasonal round. As a result many new approaches to hunter-gatherer materials have been characterized by a fundamental argument; that as much as hunter-gatherers and their materials should not be examined in modern, alienated terms, the landscapes that people moved through and geographical contexts of such material interactions should similarly not be alienated from our narratives either. For instance, in a study of the earlier Mesolithic sites of the Vale of Pickering, Conneller (2005) argues that considering how activities were structured across the landscape enables the layering of different temporalities, in turn situating the *chaîne opératoire* in a broader context. Thus, if:

> we see lithic scatters as representing manufacturing and depositionary practices; interrelated sequences of action that were not bounded within a site, but extend across the landscape, we bring back in to view the diverse ways—and the different scales at which—people lived, worked and produced landscapes.
>
> (Conneller 2005, 54)

This follows the arguments central to Ingold's (1993) view of the taskscape, discussed above, and is highly productive in enabling a radical reformulation of approaches to materials in hunter-gatherer studies. Such an approach works simultaneously to explore the connections between people, places, and things, and the temporality of these connections, in a way that is able to go beyond modern, Western frameworks.

The efficacy of such a taskscape perspective for developing new approaches to hunter-gatherer materials is clear. By unravelling the view of materials as static or fixed to certain places, new approaches have been able to explore how materials may have gathered essences of places to them, and the biographies of such materials would have been rich and detailed as a result of their movement through both space and time. Warren's discussion of Scottish bevelled-ended tools (Warren 2006) and Kador's examination of the movement of materials across Ireland (Kador 2007) provide two accounts of the Mesolithic where such an idea has been employed to great effect. In both of these examples the notion that the movement, use, and reuse of bone bevelled-ended tools, and certain types of raw material led these objects to have complex biographies that both authors propose had significant resonances as they were employed in different contexts (Kador 2007; Warren 2006).

Considering material things in relation to place and taskscape also demands that we challenge the modern geopolitical and conceptual boundaries that have often structured hunter-gatherer studies. Take, for instance, the handful of examples from Scotland of the typologically distinct, and ubiquitously Irish and Manx late Mesolithic Bann Flake (summarized in Cobb 2008). These examples have traditionally been regarded in a relatively alienated manner; they are generally viewed as a-typical technical imports to Scotland in a time of geographical isolation around the Irish Sea. They also tend to be dismissed as not typologically 'true' Bann Flakes, instead reflecting local attempts at constructing such tool forms. However, by exploding the relationship between people, material things, and places beyond a static concern with typology and a fixation with modern geopolitical boundaries we can unravel the biographies of these tool forms. Doing so enables us to reach a more nuanced view of what they may represent and the effects these tools had. For instance there would have been a significant conceptual difference in the production and use of Bann Flakes compared to the composite microlithic tools used throughout Scotland in the late Mesolithic. If we adopt a view close to Finlay's (as discussed above) we could suggest that this very different tool form could have challenged deeply rooted social conventions about the means through which people and things were multiply authored. Where microlithic tools demanded the entwining of many different parts of people and the taskscape in their making and using, these occasional examples of Bann Flakes in Scotland might have involved a very different multiplicity in their authorship. Such tools may have embodied the knowledge of boat building, of making the crossing over the Irish Sea to reach the Isle of Man or Ireland, of successfully returning, of communicating with and learning different technological skills from people 'over there'. Or vice versa—embodying instead the knowledge of how to welcome and interact with and learn from others who had crossed the sea to Scotland. These collective knowledges and experiences, of trying out and experimenting with a new tool type, and of everything that this tool communicated, represented, and incorporated, may have led them to play an active and important role in the formation of very different conceptions of personal and group identity in the communities that used them. So much so that the symbolic importance of this tool type may have endured through time, leading to at least one known example in which a Mesolithic Bann Flake has been found with a cache of otherwise Neolithic tool forms on the Scottish Kintyre peninsula (Saville 1999).

Conclusion

This chapter presents a necessarily brief overview of new and developing approaches to materials in hunter-gatherer studies. As discussed above, the case studies presented reflect the focus of my own research, exploring mainly the Mesolithic in the UK and Ireland. Nonetheless, the theoretical approaches that are outlined here are clearly applicable to hunter-gatherer studies at a broader level, irrespective of temporality or geography.

Of course in focusing upon the development of new approaches to materials influenced by counter-modern arguments, this chapter inevitably sets up something of a polemic between these and the empirical lines of questioning arising from the philosophical traditions and concerns of modernity. Ultimately, however, the lines between these two schools of thought are not always so clear, and it is certainly dangerous to simply disregard any corpus of work on the basis of its philosophical approach. Indeed, in many cases the strength of new and counter-modern approaches lies in building upon or re-examining the already detailed corpus of work from the many traditional typological and other studies that already exist. Thus the legacy of empirical and modern, Western approaches towards hunter-gatherer studies should not simply be dismissed, but rather their value recognized as often providing the material foundations that have then enabled scholars to think through counter-modern perspectives in practice.

The application of such new approaches to materials in hunter-gatherer studies is still in its infancy. Yet at the time of writing it seems that these approaches are developing at a rapid pace. One monograph has been published (Conneller 2011) and a number of additional papers on the subject are currently in preparation and in press (e.g. Cobb 2013). And amongst current and recently completed doctoral students at British institutions various approaches to materials are burgeoning in a variety of directions. This includes innovative new work that develops Conneller's and Borić's accounts regarding animal affects (Conneller and Elliot 2009; Overton 2009), as well as research that is exploring the materiality of human bodies in life and in death by drawing upon the osteological record to explore the processes and practice of bodily engagement with the dead (Gray Jones 2011). Other exciting directions are reflected in studies looking towards environmental reconstruction to explore the materiality of people's surroundings. Here, in work by Taylor (2012), Dewing (2011), and Leary (2009) plants, trees, reeds, rivers, streams, and the sea are all considered as active materials in their own right. This is not in any environmentally deterministic sense, but rather in terms of the ways in which they too were entwined into the identities and world views of the hunter-gatherers who would have moved through and lived alongside them.

In conclusion, the new approaches to materials that are discussed here and that have characterized recent hunter-gatherer studies demand that we do more than consider materials in isolation. In contrast to the quote with which this chapter began, the value of such approaches lies in their rejection of frameworks in which culture and matter and mind and matter are seen as separate. Instead, the various new approaches to materials that exist in hunter-gatherer studies all call, in different ways, for us to focus not simply on the material alone, in an isolated, static, and alienated manner. Rather the productivity of such approaches lies in their ability to explore the currents of hunter-gatherer life, in which places, people, and things were all entwined. In turn this opens up diverse new ways of considering materials. In such narratives materials are never static or inert, but actively bound into the messy materiality of daily life.

REFERENCES

Anderson, J. 1898. Notes on the contents of a small cave or rock-shelter at Druimvargie, Oban; and of three shell-mounds in Oronsay. *Proceedings of the Society of Antiquaries of Scotland* 32, 298–313.

Appadurai, A. (ed.) 1986. *The social life of things*. Cambridge: Cambridge University Press.

Barrett, J. C. 2001. Agency, the duality of structure and the problem of the archaeological record. In I. Hodder (ed.), *Archaeological theory today*, 141–64. Cambridge: Polity Press.

Binford, L. R. 1973. Inter assemblage variability: the Mousterian and the 'functional argument'. In C. Renfrew (ed.), *The explanation of culture change: models in prehistory*, 227–54. London: Duckworth.

Binford, L. R. 1978. *Nunamuit ethnoarchaeology*. New York: Academic Press.

Binford, L. R. 1979. Organization and formation processes: looking at curated technologies. *Journal of Anthropological Research* 35, 255–73.

Binford, L. R. 1983. *In pursuit of the past: decoding the archaeological record*. London: Thames and Hudson.

Bleed, P. 1986. The optimal design of hunting weapons: maintainability or reliability. *American Antiquity* 51, 737–47.

Bleed, P. 2001. Trees or chains, links or branches: conceptual alternatives for consideration of stone tool production and other sequential activities. *Journal of Archaeological Method and Theory* 8, 101–27.

Borić, D. 2005. Body metamorphosis and animality: volatile bodies and boulder artworks from Lepenski Vir. *Cambridge Archaeological Journal* 15, 35–69.

Busby, C. 1997. Permeable and partible persons: a comparative analysis of gender and body in South India and Melanesia. *Journal of the Royal Anthropological Institute* 3, 261–78.

Butler, J. 1993. *Bodies that matter: on the discursive limits of 'sex'*. London: Routledge.

Clark, J. G. D. 1954. *Excavations at Star Carr*. Cambridge: Cambridge University Press.

Cobb, H. L. 2007a. Mutable materials and the production of persons: reconfiguring understandings of identity in the Mesolithic of the northern Irish Sea basin. *Journal of Iberian Archaeology* 9/10, 123–36.

Cobb, H. L. 2007b. Media for movement and making the world: exploring materials and identity in the Mesolithic of the northern Irish Sea basin. *Internet Archaeology*, 22 (Mesolithic Archaeology theme), http://intarch.ac.uk/journal/issue22/cobb_toc.html. Accessed 27 March 2013.

Cobb, H. L. 2008. Media for movement and making the world: an examination of the Mesolithic experience of the world and the Mesolithic to Neolithic transition in the Northern Irish Sea Basin. PhD thesis. Manchester: School of Arts, Histories and Cultures. Manchester, University of Manchester.

Cobb, H. L. 2009. Being-in-the-(Mesolithic) world: place, substance and person in the Mesolithic of western Scotland. In S. McCartan, R. Schulting, G. Warren, and P. Woodman (eds), *Papers presented at the 7th international conference in the Mesolithic in Europe (Belfast 2005)*, 368–72. Oxford. Oxbow.

Cobb, H. L. 2013. Disclosing the world during the Mesolithic/Neolithic transition in the Irish Sea Basin. In H. L. Cobb, M. Larsson, J. Thomas, and J. Debert (eds), *North-west Europe in transition*, 55–62. Oxford: Archaeopress.

Conkey, M. W. 1978. Style and information in cultural evolution: toward a predictive model for the Palaeolithic. In C. L. Redman, M. J. Berman, E. Curtin, W. T. Lanhorne, N. M. Versaggi, and J. C. Wander (eds), *Social archaeology*, 61–85. New York: Academic Press.

Conkey, M. W. 2006. Style, design and function. In C. Tilley, W. Keane, S. Kuchler, M. Rowlands, and P. Spyer (eds), *The handbook of material culture*, 355–72. London: Sage.

Conneller, C. (ed.) 2004. Becoming deer: corporeal transformations at Star Carr. *Archaeological Dialogues* 11, 37–56.

Conneller, C. 2005. Moving beyond sites: Mesolithic technology in the landscape. In N. Milner and P. Woodman (eds), *Mesolithic studies at the beginning of the 21st century*, 42–55. Oxford: Oxbow.

Conneller, C. 2006. The space and time of the chaîne opératoire: technological approaches to past landscapes. *Archaeological Review from Cambridge* 21, 38–49.

Conneller, C. 2011. *An archaeology of materials: technologies of transformation in early prehistoric Europe*. London: Routledge.

Conneller, C. and Elliot, B. 2009. Animal objects: tracing networks of people and red deer at Star Carr. Unpublished paper presented at the TAG (Theoretical Archaeology Group) conference, Durham, UK.

Dewing, E. 2011. Analysis of the Mesolithic of the southern North Sea basin through integrated palaeoenvironmental modelling and geospatial analysis. PhD thesis. Southampton: Department of Archaeology. Southampton, University of Southampton.

Dobres, M. 2000. *Technology and social agency: outlining a practice framework for archaeology*. Oxford: Blackwell.

Dobres, M. and Hoffman, C. R. 1994. Social agency and the dynamics of prehistoric technology. *Journal of Archaeological Method and Theory* 1, 211–58.

Dobres, M. and Robb, J. 2000. *Agency in archaeology*. London: Routledge.

Edmonds, M. 1990. Description, understanding and the chaîne opératoire. *Archaeological Review from Cambridge* 9, 55–70.

Edmonds, M. and Thomas, J. 1987. The archers: an everyday story of country folk. In A. G. Brown and M. Edmonds (eds), *Lithic analysis and later British prehistory*, 187–99. Oxford: British Archaeological Reports.

Finlay, N. 2003. Microliths and multiple authorship. In L. Larsson, H. Kindgren, K. Knutsson, D. Loeffler, and A. Akerlund (eds), *Mesolithic on the move. Papers presented at the 6th international conference in the Mesolithic in Europe, Stockholm, 2000*, 169–76. Oxford: Oxbow.

Finlay, N. 2006. Gender and personhood. In C. Conneller and G. Warren (eds), *Mesolithic Britain and Ireland: new approaches*, 35–60. Stroud: Tempus.

Fowler, C. 2004. *The archaeology of personhood: an anthropological approach*. London: Routledge.

Gell, A. 1998. *Art and agency: an anthropological theory*. Oxford: Clarendon Press.

Gendel, P. A. 1989. The analysis of lithic styles through distributional profiles of variation: examples from the western European Mesolithic. In C. Bonsall (ed.), *The Mesolithic in Europe*, 40–7. Edinburgh: Edinburgh University Press.

Gosden, C. 2005. What do objects want? *Journal of Archaeological Method and Theory* 12, 193–211.

Gray Jones, A. 2011. Dealing with the dead: manipulation of the body in the mortuary practices of Mesolithic north-west Europe. PhD thesis. Manchester: School of Arts, Histories and Cultures. Manchester, University of Manchester.

Grøn, O. 1987. General spatial behaviour in small dwellings: a preliminary study in ethnoarchaeology and social psychology. In C. Bonsall (ed.), *Proceedings of the 3rd international congress on the Mesolithic in Europe*, 99–105. Edinburgh: Edinburgh University Press.

Grøn, O. 1995. *The Maglemose culture: a reconstruction of the social organisation of a Mesolithic culture in Northern Europe*. Oxford: British Archaeology Reports.

Grøn, O. 2003. Mesolithic dwelling places in south Scandinavia: their definition and social interpretation. *Antiquity* 77, 685–708.

Hodder, I. 1982. *Symbols in action: ethnoarchaeological studies of material culture*. Cambridge: Cambridge University Press.

Ingold, T. 1993. The temporality of the landscape. *World Archaeology* 25, 152–74.

Ingold, T. 2000. *The perception of the environment: essays in livelihood, dwelling and skill*. London: Routledge.

Ingold, T. 2007. Materials against materiality. *Archaeological Dialogues* 14, 1–16.

Jones, A. 2005. Lives in fragments? Personhood and the European Neolithic. *Journal of Social Archaeology* 5, 193–224.

Kador, T. 2007. Stone age motion pictures: an objects' perspective from early prehistoric Ireland. In V. Cummings and B. Johnston (eds), *Prehistoric journeys*, 33–44. Oxford: Oxbow.

Karlin, C. and Julien, M. 1994. Prehistoric technology: a cognitive science? In C. Renfrew and E. Zubrow (eds), *The ancient mind: elements of cognitive archaeology*, 152–64. Cambridge: Cambridge University Press.

Kopytoff, I. 1986. The cultural biography of things: commodization as a process. In A. Appadurai (ed.), *The social life of things*, 64–91. Cambridge: Cambridge University Press.

Leary, J. 2009. Perceptions of and responses to the Holocene flooding of the North Sea lowlands. *Oxford Journal of Archaeology* 28, 227–37.

Lemonnier, P. 1990. Topsy turvy techniques: remarks on the social representation of techniques. *Archaeological Review from Cambridge* 9, 27–38.

Lemonnier, P. (ed.) 1993. *Technological choices: transformation in material cultures since the Neolithic*. London: Routledge.

Leroi-Gourhan, A. 1964. *La geste et la parole I: technique et langage*. Paris: Albin Michel.

Leroi-Gourhan, A. 1965. *La geste et la parole II: la mémoire et les rythmes*. Paris: Albin Michel.

LiPuma, E. 1998. Modernity and forms of personhood in Melanesia. In M. Lambek and A. Strathern (eds), *Bodies and persons: comparative studies from Africa and Melanesia*, 53–79. Cambridge: Cambridge University Press.

MacKenzie, M. A. 1991. *Androgynous objects: string bags and gender in central New Guinea*. Reading: Harwood Academic Publishers.

Mellars, P. A. 1987. *Excavations on Oronsay: prehistoric human ecology on a small island*. Edinburgh: Edinburgh University Press.

Mithen, S. J. (ed) 2000. *Hunter-gatherer landscape archaeology: the Southern Hebrides Mesolithic project 1988–1998*. Cambridge: McDonald Institute for Archaeological Research.

Moore, H. 1986. *Space, text and gender: an anthropological study of the Marakwet of Kenya*. Cambridge: Cambridge University Press.

Mosko, M. S. 1992. Motherless sons: 'divine kings' and 'partible persons' in Melanesia and Polynesia. *Man* 27, 697–718.

Myers, A. M. 1989. Lithics, risk and change in the Mesolithic. In I. Brooks and P. Phillips (eds), *Breaking the stony silence: papers from the Sheffield lithics conference 1988*, 131–60. Oxford: British Archaeological Reports.

Overton, N. 2009. Species and persons: ecological relations in the Mesolithic. Paper presented at the TAG (Theoretical Archaeology Group) conference, Durham, UK.

Pfaffenberger, B. 1992. Social anthropology of technology. *Annual Review of Anthropology* 21, 491–516.
Price, S. 2005. Can't see the trees for the wood: the social life of trees in the Mesolithic of Southern Scandinavia. In H. Cobb, F. Coward, L. Grimshaw, and S. Price (eds), *Investigating prehistoric hunter-gatherer identities in Palaeolithic and Mesolithic Europe*, 95–105. Oxford: British Archaeological Reports.
Price, S. 2007. The Mesolithic–Neolithic transition in Southern Scandinavia: to what extent does a change in material culture reflect a change in society? MPhil thesis. Archaeology, School of Arts, Histories and Cultures, University of Manchester.
Robb, J. 2004. The extended artefact and the monumental economy: a methodology for material agency. In E. DeMarrais, C. Gosden, and C. Renfrew (eds), *Rethinking materiality: the engagement of mind with the material world*, 131–9. Cambridge: McDonald Institute for Archaeological Research.
Sackett, J. 1986. Isochrestism and style: a clarification. *Journal of Anthropological Archaeology* 5, 266–77.
Saville, A. 1999. A cache of flint axeheads and other flint artefacts from Auchenoan, near Campbeltown, Kintyre, Scotland. *Proceedings of the Prehistoric Society* 65, 83–123.
Schlanger, N. 1990. Technique as human action: two perspectives. *Archaeological Review from Cambridge* 9, 18–26.
Schlanger, N. 1994. Mindful technology: unleashing the chaîne opératoire for an archaeology of the mind. In C. Renfrew and E. Zubrow (eds), *The ancient mind: elements of cognitive archaeology*, 143–51. Cambridge: Cambridge University Press.
Strathern, M. 1988. *The gender of the gift: problems with women and problems with society in Melanesia*. London: University of California Press.
Taylor, B. 2012. Perceptions of the environment in the British Mesolithic: case studies from the Vale of Pickering. PhD thesis. Manchester: School of Arts, Histories and Cultures. Manchester, University of Manchester.
Thomas, J. 2004. *Archaeology and modernity*. London: Routledge.
Thomas, J. 2007. The trouble with material culture. *Journal of Iberian Archaeology* 9/10, 11–24.
Torrence, R. (ed.) 1989a. Tools as optimal solutions. In R. Torrence (ed.), *Time, energy and stone tools*, 1–6. Cambridge: Cambridge University Press.
Torrence, R. 1989b. *Time, energy and stone tools*. Cambridge: Cambridge University Press.
Viveiros de Castro, E. 1998. Cosmological deixis and Amerindian perspectivism. *Journal of the Royal Anthropological Institute* 4, 469–88.
Warren, G. M. 2006. Technology. In C. Conneller and G. Warren (eds), *Mesolithic Britain and Ireland: new approaches*, 13–34. Stroud: Tempus.
Wiessner, P. 1983. Style and social information in Kalahari San projectile points. *American Antiquity* 48, 253–76.
Wiessner, P. 1984. Reconsidering the behavioural basis of style. *Journal of Anthropological Archaeology* 3, 190–234.
Wobst, H. M. 1977. Stylistic behaviour and information exchange. In C. Cleland (ed.), *For the director: research essays in honour of James B. Griffin*, 317–42. Ann Arbor: Research papers of the University of Michigan.
Wobst, H. M. 1999. Style in archaeology, or archaeologists in style. In E. Chilton (ed.), *Material meanings: critical approaches to the interpretation of material culture*, 118–32. Salt Lake City: University of Utah Press.

CHAPTER 59

HUNTER-GATHERER RELIGION AND RITUAL

DAVID S. WHITLEY

HUNTER-GATHERER religions and rituals have fascinated the Western world almost since the first contacts between European and small-scale non-farming societies and cultures. This interest has been fuelled partly by the perceived exoticism of the foragers' beliefs and practices, partly by administrative/religious concerns, and also for more purely intellectual reasons. Early encounters with and descriptions of Siberian shamans, for example, were widely broadcast in eighteenth-century Western Europe, where they influenced artists such as Mozart and Goethe (Flaherty 1992). Spanish missionaries in the Americas, starting with the Columbus expeditions, recorded detailed information on indigenous beliefs and practices, recognizing this knowledge as valuable in promoting conversions to Catholicism (e.g. Boscana [1822] 1978; Geiger and Meighan [1812–15] 1976; Pané [1494–6] 2006)—in the process inventing systematic ethnological research and ethnographic reporting. Academic concerns reflect numerous disciplines, including anthropology (e.g. Kroeber 1907), sociology (e.g. Durkheim [1912] 2001), the history of religion/religious studies (e.g. Eliade 1972), folklore and mythology (e.g. Gayton and Newman 1940), ethnobotany and pharmacology (e.g. Schultes 1977), psychiatry (Silverman 1967), and archaeology (e.g. Price 2001; Ross and Davidson 2006). Hunter-gatherer religions—at least as reinterpreted in contemporary Western terms—also figure prominently in the New Age/self-realization and alternative medicine and psychiatric movements (e.g. Senn 1989). The result is a very broad body of literature, ensuring that this topic will be researched and debated long into the future.

In order to develop a representative picture of hunter-gatherer religions and rituals, I use the nature and range of variation in Native Californian ethnographic examples as the foundation for this chapter. This is an appropriate source, partly because the ethnographic record is so rich (e.g. see syntheses in Kroeber 1925 and Heizer 1978), and in part because Native California[1] itself was so diverse. Occupied by hunter-gatherers until Euro-American contact in the late eighteenth century, Native California included approximately 80 mutually unintelligible languages, divided into an uncharted number of dialects (cf. Shipley 1978). Political organization ranged from bands with headmen, common among the very mobile groups in the eastern deserts, to simple chiefdoms, living in permanent villages with as many as 1,000 residents, along the coast (Whitley 2000). Subsistence likewise varied, with dietary staples including the acorn, pine nut, camas bulb, riverine salmon, and/or maritime resources generally, depending upon tribe[2] and environmental setting. Perhaps most importantly, Native California incorporates portions of a series of ethnographic 'culture areas' (Kroeber 1939): the Californian itself; the western Great Basin; the south-western Columbia Plateau; and a south-western extension of the Northwest Coast. Native California in this sense was a microcosm of the North American hunter-gatherer far west and, as we shall see, serves as a reasonable model for hunter-gatherers globally.

About Hunter-Gatherer Religions

It is useful to begin with a brief discussion of religion, partly because it is a familiar aspect of contemporary Western society. For this fact, many social scientists (including many atheists and agnostics) maintain a series of implicit ideas about religion that reflect a Western Judaeo-Christian bias that may be incorrect when traditional hunter-gatherer religions are considered. *Religion*, first, can be defined as a culturally shared set of beliefs and practices which involve *supernatural agents*—spirits or gods of some kind (Whitehouse 2004). All religions have a *cosmology*, which is a theory of the origin, structure, and nature of the universe (including the place of humans in it), but hunter-gatherers do not necessarily have a *theology*: a formally defined religious philosophy and theory. Despite this last circumstance, hunter-gatherer religions include a code of moral and ethical precepts and behaviours. Because these may be implicit, members of many hunter-gatherer societies may not recognize that they have a religion per se, as a distinct social institution, even though their religious beliefs and rituals are evident to an outsider (Whitley 2008). Hunter-gatherer religions, in this sense, are commonly defined by practice driven by tradition, and they are entirely interwoven with (if not inseparable from) all other aspects of social life. Hence, hunter-gatherer *rituals* or ceremonies—customarily or formally repeated acts or sequences of actions (Hayden 2003)—are invariably religious, or at least always invested with religious undertones. Some hunter-gatherer rituals constituted public ceremonies, often undertaken periodically, whereas others involved entirely private observances. Although ritual officials of some kind commonly conducted the first kind of rites, private observances often required no participation on the part of a religious specialist.

Five points require emphasis with respect to distinctions between hunter-gatherer versus Western Judaeo-Christian religious traditions. First, hunter-gatherer religions include animistic beliefs: they typically hold that the world is ensouled, or numinous. Supernatural agents may then appear as natural phenomena (such as specific rocks or lightning), as well as animal spirits or ghosts/ancestors. But all of these are personified in the sense that they always think and act like humans, regardless of name and outward form (Barrett 2004; Elkin 1964, 155; Forde 1931, 182). Further, because animals especially are perceived to be like humans spiritually—in Native America animals are widely conceptualized as 'non-human people'—special social and religious relationships are believed to exist between individuals and groups of humans, and certain animal species and animal spirits. These range from an individual's animal spirit helper or tutelary to a clan's or moiety's mythic ancestor or animal totem.

Second, stemming from the numinous nature of the world, hunter-gatherer religions commonly recognize sacred places on the landscape but, despite this fact, they often lack the rigid distinction between sacred versus profane space that Durkheim (2001) incorrectly characterized as a universal trait of all religions. Although certain locations are known to be sacred, based on tradition and previous experience, the ensouled nature of the world means that any location potentially can become so charged, due to subsequent events.

Rituals then can be associated with specific sacred places, especially locations of mythic events, but this is not a necessary requirement for all hunter-gatherer religious ceremonies, with many occurring in otherwise mundane settings (such as the middle a village). Sacred versus profane in these circumstances is a function of time rather than place (Whitley 2000), and this has a particularly important archaeological implication. Locational association in the archaeological record, normally interpreted as an indicator of functional association or equivalence (e.g. Gilreath and Hildebrandt 2008), may be meaningless with respect to ritual remains. Burials interred in house-pit floors—and thus within kitchen middens—are the most obvious example of this fact. Despite their presence in an otherwise profane context, burials in middens (common in many regions, such as California and the Great Basin) reflect temporally alternating uses of space, and not cannibalism due to their locational association with other dietary remains—as standard archaeological inference might otherwise imply.

Third, the relationship between myth and ritual varies, in some cases dramatically even between adjacent hunter-gatherer tribes. *Myth* itself may be defined as a corpus of accounts of supernatural agents and events occurring during a primordial, pre-human time. These beings are often the progenitors of the important species constituting the natural world, hence myths widely (but not invariably) involve a time 'when animals were people'. (*Folk tales*,[3] in contrast, may involve supernatural agents and events, but they invariably include 'real' even if historical or apocryphal humans.) Among some hunter-gatherer groups, religious ritual is closely linked to mythology—as in Judaeo-Christianity—with ceremonies often representing ritual re-enactments of mythic events, conducted at specific mythic locations. The Australian Aboriginal and Native Californian Yuman-speaking tribal religions are examples of this emphasis. But among other hunter-gatherers, including other Native Californian tribes, there is little if any connection between myth and ritual (Whitley 2000; 2008), and their ceremonies have no direct linkage with mythic events, locations, or actors.

Fourth, and somewhat paradoxically, hunter-gatherer religions are at once very conservative (Elkin 1964; Steward 1955; White 1963) and much more resistant to change than technology or subsistence (cf. Sahlins 1985). But they are also open (as opposed to closed) knowledge systems in the sense that they can be augmented or influenced by outside beliefs and events (cf. Horton 1982). Hunter-gatherer religions are syncretic rather than exclusionary, which has important implications for understanding changes to them. Instead of catastrophic change—the complete replacement of one religious system by another—hunter-gatherers typically maintain a core of beliefs and practices, with change consisting of the addition or subtraction of other elements over time (cf. Bloch 1986; 1992). Perhaps best illustrating this tendency is the fact that many contemporary descendants of hunter-gatherers practise their traditional religions along with aspects of a recently adopted Christianity (e.g. Bean and Vane 1978, 670; Elkin 1964; White 1963), and find no contradiction in this circumstance.

Fifth, indigenous knowledge concerning hunter-gatherer religions, like that in many traditional systems, was often carefully controlled. Knowledge was earned, through age advancement, initiation, and/or demonstrations of skill. Because it was secret or restricted, even within the confines of a given tribal group, certain specific beliefs and practices are referred to as *cults*: sub-sets of more general religious systems, such as secret or semi-secret societies. For the anthropologist and archaeologist, the secret nature of certain kinds of religious knowledge can make research difficult (Whitley 2007). In such cases a lack of ethnographic information does not always demonstrate the absence of a practice or belief, hence putative negative evidence about a given religion must be evaluated carefully rather than necessarily taken literally.

Hunter-Gatherer Religious Configurations

Most ethnographic hunter-gatherer religions can be conceptualized as falling on a continuum between two poles: shamanistic and world-renewal systems. Importantly, elements of both systems are present in the religions of many, if not all, hunter-gatherers, and the differences between any two specific cases often reflect distinctions of degree more than kind. Rituals practised in both systems likewise ranged from entirely (or largely) private and esoteric ceremonies to openly public ('exoteric') displays, with participants including ritual specialists and the uninitiated general public. Widely practised examples of the first include vision quests or cult initiations and, for the latter, mourning rites. Personal religious observances (often referred to as 'taboos') were also common. In Native California, these included practices such as menstrual seclusion for women, prohibitions against naming the dead, and various kinds of fasting and abstention associated with specific activities and events (such as hunting or childbirth).

Shamanistic Systems

Shamanistic religious systems are very widely associated with hunter-gatherers. Partly for this reason, many researchers have assumed that shamanism represents a kind of relict Palaeolithic religion (e.g. Furst 1977)—a point discussed below. Regardless of time-depth, shamanism was practised ethnographically by hunter-gatherers in North and South America, circumpolar Eurasia, and southern Africa. It was also common among horticulturalists (part-time farmers) in the Americas, especially in lowland South America, and reindeer pastoralists in Eurasia, while elements of shamanistic beliefs and practices are present in a variety of historical and modern complex and larger-scale societies.

Partly because of this widespread distribution and differing socio-cultural contexts—and the range of variation in specific beliefs and practices that this promotes—there is no universally accepted definition of 'shaman', and there is debate about whether the term should be restricted to north-eastern Asian groups or applied more generally. Based on a global synthesis, Eliade (1972) identified the shaman as a 'master of ecstatic trance', and argued that shamanism was widely present among hunter-gatherers—a view accepted by most anthropologists (e.g. LaBarre 1980). Earlier, Shirokogoroff (1935) suggested 'master of the spirits' as an alternative definition. More generally, shamans can be understood as (at least part-time) ritual specialists who are believed to have direct interactions with spirits, achieved by entering an altered state of consciousness (ASC); hence the two contrasting definitions reflect different emphases on shamanic practices.

The shamanic cosmos is commonly conceptualized as having three (or more) horizontal layers, vertically connected by a central cosmic axis, the *axis mundi* or world tree. Shamans were believed to access the supernatural spirit world by ascending this cosmic axis while in an altered state. In Native California, and perhaps elsewhere, the supernatural world was believed to be the perfect inverse of the natural world.

Fundamental to shamanism is the concept of supernatural power, thought to be the principal causal agent in the universe (Bean 1976). This power served as the primary explanatory paradigm for shamanistic thought systems, with success or failure in any endeavour, from hunting to gambling to warfare to love, seen as a function of the amount of power an individual controlled. Unlike our concept of 'grace' or 'manna', power was ambivalent in the sense that it could be used for beneficial or for adverse ends; most commonly, either healing the sick or performing sorcery that sickened or killed an enemy. While all individuals had some level of power, shamans were particularly strongly endowed with it, and many deaths were attributed to their actions.

The perceived nature of shamanic power was linked to a common shamanistic perspective. Meyerhoff (1976) described this as a *dialectical opposition*: the belief that the world is forever locked in a state of tension between good and evil, light and darkness, happiness and grief, etc. Unlike our Western concept of the dialectic, thesis in this shamanic world view is never dissolved by anti-thesis to yield synthesis—resulting among other things in our belief in the inevitable triumph of right over wrong. One reflection of the shamanic dialectical opposition, in contrast, was the ritual emphasis on maintaining the delicate cosmic balance.

Shamans were believed to obtain their power through an ASC—a vision during which they received this potency from specific spirits, especially animal spirit helpers. The vision might consist of a particularly vivid and emotionally charged but unsought dream, or it might result from a planned vision quest, conducted at a targeted location, perhaps because of the specific kind of power associated with that spot. Various kinds of hallucinogens (including especially native tobacco in the Americas; cf. Wilbert 1987) might be used to induce a vision. Alternatively, fasting, isolation and/or sensory deprivation can cause or at least contribute to achieving an ASC. Among the southern African San (or Bushmen), where about 50 per cent of the men and 25 per cent of the women are shamans (Katz 1976), individuals achieve an ASC through repetitive singing, clapping, and dancing in a group ritual known as the Trance Dance. More typically, shamans were restricted in number: in eastern California, only about 2–4 per cent of males were shamans (Whitley 2009). Native California shamanism, further, was in theory a ritual office open to anyone, regardless especially of gender. In practice, strong regional gender patterns existed: shamans were almost exclusively male in all parts of California except the north-west, where they were almost invariably female. As discussed below, these gender patterns were associated with larger distinctions in religious configurations.

Shamanic Rituals

Shamans served a series of ritual functions, resulting from their supernatural potency and access to spirits. These included conducting periodic ceremonies, as well as healing, sorcery, rain-making, finding lost objects, divination, and 'game charming' (e.g. see Park 1938). The last ritual activity included some examples of so-called hunting-magic per se (Keyser and Whitley 2000), but more generally can be understood as reflecting a larger shamanic responsibility: negotiating with the supernatural spirits to ensure well-being, including subsistence success. Among certain tribes a key spirit in this regard was the 'Master of the Game'. The shaman visited this spirit, during an ASC, in order to barter for the souls of the game animals that would be captured in a given year (cf. Reichel-Dolmatoff 1967). This reflected the wider beliefs that animals allowed themselves to be captured by hunters, and that their spirits would re-inhabit another body and return the following year if the animal had been properly killed (i.e. in accord with the proper hunting prescriptions and proscriptions).

Rituals in shamanistic systems, beyond personal observances, included both public and private ceremonies where the participation of the shaman varied. Shamanic rituals per se emphasized access to the supernatural world and the manipulation of its power. Private ceremonies conducted by shamans included their acquisition of power or vision quest, sorcery, rain-making, and prognostication (e.g. for the location of game or lost objects). The creation of rock art was often the culmination of these private rites. Public or semi-public shamanic rituals commonly included 'game charming', especially of antelope, healing, and, among certain tribes, various dances associated with specific secret societies.

The shaman's role as a healer is emphasized in much of the recent literature, and there is no question that it was an important activity and role. Throughout Native America, the term 'shaman' was often glossed in English as 'doctor', and supernatural power was called 'medicine', reflecting this function. But there is also evidence that this aspect of a shaman's activities has increased historically, and it may not have been quite so prominent during the pre-contact period (Whitley 2009), prior to the social and physical decimation of the tribes resulting from the Euro-American invasion and conquest. Indeed, many of the older ethnographies equally highlight the activities of the shaman as sorcerer, focusing on their essentially malevolent or dangerous reputations (e.g. Gayton 1930).

Shamanic curing rituals, nonetheless, were common globally and were typically directed towards one of two ends: either retrieving a 'lost' soul, in cases of 'soul theft', or sucking out a 'disease object' which was putatively infecting the sick. In both cases, sorcery was the presumed cause of the illness, and the emphasis was on spiritual and psychological rather than pharmaceutical/botanical healing (Laird 1976; 1984).

Native California Shamanism

Native California ethnography reflects these general patterns in ritual and belief, and illustrates the variability that they may nonetheless include. Shamanic cures were commonly conducted in the sick individual's hut or within an open area in a village. Other public shamanic rituals varied tribally. The Yokuts of south-central California—the single largest tribe in the state—practised a form of shamanism with little if any direct relationship between myth and ceremonies. Many public rituals instead involved shamanic dances and displays of power (cf. Gayton 1930; 1948; Kroeber 1907; 1925). Rattlesnake shamans—who had rattlesnakes as their primary spirit helpers and, for that reason, had a special relationship with these vipers—conducted a yearly rattlesnake dance, for example. The purpose of this ritual was ostensibly to ensure that tribal members were not bitten by snakes during the coming year. During the ceremony the shamans would handle and provoke captured rattlesnakes, inducing the snakes to strike them, in order to demonstrate their mastery of these creatures and their power. (In fact, most rattlesnake bites to humans are 'dry-bites', with no venom injected—though this is not always the case, and it is impossible to predict how an individual snake will react.) Bear shamans—again, with grizzly bears as their spirit helpers—would conduct a bear dance, during which they putatively transformed physically into bears. In the *heswas* ceremony, in contrast, groups of shamans from opposing moieties would conduct a ritual battle, wherein they would alternate shooting 'magical air-shot'—an invisible disease object which would strike down the intended victim, causing them to collapse in illness—at one another.

These displays of power were scheduled to coincide with the yearly Yokuts ceremonial round, which was always the same. It started, in the spring, with the jimson-weed ceremony (discussed below), then the rattlesnake dance, and (where appropriate) finally the first salmon ceremony. The autumn rituals began, in the late summer after the return from seed-gathering camps, with the mourning ceremony (including the *heswas*), which commemorated those who had died during the previous year. This was followed by first seed and acorn rites and then the bear dance (Gayton 1930, 379). In each case shamans served as ceremonial officials responsible for specific dances and power displays (Kroeber 1925). A temporary ceremonial enclosure/dance area might be constructed for certain of these rituals, especially the mourning ceremony, and residents of nearby villages would also be invited to attend—emphasizing that group rituals had important social and economic as well as religious implications (Blackburn 1974).

Although the location of these rituals—in plain view in the middle of villages—reflects their public nature, visibility alone played a limited role in the locational difference between certain group versus private ceremonies. This is due to the widespread existence of avoidance proscriptions, combined with the seasonally migratory nature of hunter-gatherers in general. A husband, for example, might live for the entirety of his married life in a small brush hut with his immediate family and mother-in-law, yet never be allowed to speak to his in-law directly. Similarly, Yokuts rock-art sites were typically located in the middle of villages, and were individually owned by specific shamans or shamanic lineages. They were known, generically, as 'shamans' caches', and they were the locations of shamans' vision quests (Gayton 1930; 1948). These last rituals were conducted privately, however, presumably during seasons when the village was otherwise unoccupied. And despite the fact that the rock art was in plain sight, the sites were 'avoided'—not looked at, never touched, and only approached with caution, reverence, and prayer (Whitley 2000).

The Yuman-speaking tribes (Mojave, Quechan, and Cocopa) living along the Colorado River provide a good contrast with the Yokuts shamanism, especially with respect to the relationship of myth and ritual. Yuman shamans conducted their vision quests at the mythic origin point, *Avikwame* (Spirit Mountain, or Newberry Peak, Nevada), inhabited by the creator spirit Mastamho. But they were believed to first obtain their power from a pre-natal dream. This was invariably a vision of Mastamho's creation of the world; they were born as shamans because it was believed that they had re-experienced the mythic creation of the world (Devereux 1969; Kroeber 1925).

Yuman rituals (much like Judaeo-Christian ceremonies) were based on mythic events and primarily involved lengthy recitations of mythic song cycles by the shamans. The curing ceremony, for example, consisted of a repetition of the origin story—a myth so closely associated with shamans that it was called 'the shaman's tale' (Kroeber 1925, 771). But unlike the ritual formalists practising in world-renewal systems (below), the repeated 'myth' varied from shaman to shaman, consisting in fact of nonsense syllables (Forde 1931, 127). The purpose of the recitation, as this was explained, was for the shaman to repeat the *pattern* or *essence* of the myth—not the actual narrative sequence of events, which everyone already knew (Devereux 1957, 1038–41; Kroeber 1957, 231).

A strong association existed between ritual locations and mythic places for the Yuman tribes, again in contrast to the Yokuts. This was most dramatically displayed in the *Xam Kwatcam* pilgrimage, which traced and commemorated Mastamho's journey up and down the Colorado River Valley, as he created the existing landscape and the cultural institutions and practices of the tribes. The locations of mythic events are marked along this river corridor with gigantic intaglios or geoglyphs, which were scraped into the desert pavement and portray the creator and other mythic actors—especially his 'evil' twin, Kaatar. Groups of pilgrims, led by a shaman, would visit these locations in sequence as they followed the path of the creation, stopping to pray, dance, and be cleansed as they—like the shaman in his putative pre-natal dream—re-experienced their mythic origin (Whitley 2000).

Initiations and Secret Societies

All Native Californian shamanistic religions had initiations of some kind, in some cases individual puberty rites; in others age-group sets subjected to isolation, secret instructions, and the ingestion of hallucinogens, resulting in membership of an esoteric cult. The least elaborated of these rites were individual puberty initiations. Among Numic-speaking (Shoshone and Paiute) tribes in the eastern California deserts these included a boy's first-kill and a girl's first-menses ceremonies, both oriented towards instructing the individual in the proper prescriptions and proscriptions involved in hunting (for the boys) and (for the girls) in menstrual practices and childbirth (Whitley 2006). Among the Modoc and Klamath in north-eastern California, in keeping with a widespread Columbia Plateau pattern followed in that region to the north, individual boys and girls were sent on private vision quests by their parents. The purpose was to enter an ASC, induced by fasting, physical exertion, and isolation, and receive a supernatural spirit helper. Rock art depicting the acquired spirit was created at the culmination of the initiation (Keyser and Whitley 2000). Among Yuman-speaking groups along the Colorado River, in contrast, groups of young boys were sent on a long run through the desert along a specific route—the 'Trail of Dreams'—in order to have a vision which they inscribed on rocks alongside the route. Subsequently their nasal-septums were pierced for a nose ornament. This occurred at the location where this ceremony was first conducted mythically, with the pierced septum thought necessary to acquire warrior status and eventually to enter the land of the dead (Whitley 2006).

The initiations in other Native California shamanistic religions were more directly linked to membership of secret societies or cults. Bean and Vane (1978) have usefully classified Native California belief systems in terms of three major cult systems: toloache, Kuksu, and world renewal (discussed subsequently). The emphasis on shamanistic beliefs and practices, including the significance of the shaman as a ritual official, along with the social and gender implications of these cults, varied substantially from tribe to tribe, as did many of the ceremonial specifics. Nonetheless, the initiations throughout Native California served as formal educational systems, and they were required for leadership or elite status.

Toloache cults were common in south-central and south-western California. They are so-named because of their emphasis on jimson weed—*Datura wrightii*, known widely in Native California by its hispanicized Aztec name, *toloache*. Jimson weed is a particularly potent, and difficult to control, hallucinogen: all parts of the plant contain hallucinogenic alkaloids, and even topical exposure—such as the application of a poultice of the leaves to the skin—can result in an ASC. It was usually administered, as a result, during group ceremonies where initiates could be carefully monitored and their safety ensured. The purpose of toloache ingestion was to have a vision, obtain a spirit helper, and some degree of supernatural power. Toloache cults were, in this sense, intrinsically shamanistic in substance.

Among the Yokuts, groups of young boys were brought together at puberty and instructed by a shaman (Gayton 1930; 1948). Included in their preparations and education was a group run that passed by a shaman's cache—a rock-art site—presumably so that initiates could view the shaman's supernatural visions to prepare them better for their own. Subsequently they were administered a toloache decoction, marking their entry into adulthood.

More social, political, and economic implications were associated with two other regional jimson-weed initiation cults: the *?Antap* among the Chumash residing along the coast north of Los Angeles, and the *Chingichngish* in south-westernmost California. The Chumash *?Antap* cult provided the political and economic leadership for that coastal society, with its members presiding over ceremonies intended to worship the Sun, a dangerous male deity, and the Earth and her three aspects, wind, rain, and fire (Blackburn 1974). Initiation into the society appears to have been necessary to ascend into certain trades, such as canoe building, which existed almost as craft guilds. In addition, world-renewal-like ceremonies were also conducted at the time of the acorn harvest and the winter solstice (Bean and Vane 1978). The leadership role of shamans in the *?Antap* cult is not entirely clear, but it is known that they performed curing rites and conducted the group solstice ceremonies, on a locally prominent mountaintop or peak, intended to maintain the cosmic balance (e.g. Outland 1956).

The *Chingichngish* cult was prevalent among the Luiseño, Gabrielino, and Ipai-Tipai (Boscana [1822] 1978; DuBois 1908; White 1963; cf. Strong 1929), and possibly may represent either a proto-historic/historic 'crisis cult' or revitalization movement, or appeared as a result of early Christian contact. Said to have been developed by the shamanic culture-hero Chingichngish, it included an explicit normative moral order enforced by a series of 'avenger' spirits, with its central features then paralleling Christian themes (White 1963). As DuBois (1908, 76) noted, Chingichngish religion 'had every requisite of a conquering faith. It had a distinct and difficult rule of life requiring obedience, fasting and self-sacrifice. It had the sanction of fear...It had an imposing and picturesque ritual. And above all it had the seal of inviolable secrecy.'

Boys' initiation into the cult was directed by a shaman's assistant and involved lengthy instruction, seclusion, and purification, in addition to ingesting toloache. An elaborate sand painting, depicting cosmological concepts, was created and explained at the culmination of the ceremony.

Kuksu cults were prevalent around the San Francisco Bay area, in the northern San Joaquin Valley, and in the foothills of the Sierra Nevada to the east, thus being practised by the Pomo, Miwok, Maidu, and adjacent tribes. It was characterized by substantial local variability. Bean and Vane (1978, 665) noted, 'What distinguished the [*Kuksu*] religion was its complexity and formalized organization rather than any given ritual feature of it.'

The *Kuksu* secret societies involved complex rites of passage and required significant formal instruction, with membership required for tribal leadership and political roles. Members of the cults—primarily male in most, but not all, cases—led cyclical rituals wearing elaborate costumes and were thought to represent ghosts, deities, or spirits. Typically there were at least three levels of membership—novice, initiate, and director—with a variety of positions associated with specific ceremonial roles, including the *Kuksu* impersonator who wore a particularly impressive and elaborate headdress. Among some tribes, there were as many as 10–12 ranks, achieved by performance and payment (Bean and Vane 1978, 667).

The primary goals of the cult ceremonies were to recreate sacred time and restore the community to its original, pristine condition (Kroeber 1923; Loeb 1932; 1933). Additional ritual purposes included youth initiation, curing, first-fruits recognition, and world renewal. Ghost societies often existed in addition to the other cults, but membership of them led only to a lower social ranking. Their primary ritual activity was to impersonate the spirits of the dead, serving the same purpose as the annual mourning ceremonies in the southern half of Native California (Bean and Vane 1978, 666).

The role of the shaman and shamanic beliefs and practices varied in importance and expression from tribe to tribe, and between different secret societies, although shamans were everywhere involved in some form or another. Perhaps more importantly, these cults demonstrate the inseparable links between ritual and social, economic and political organization in Native California (cf. Blackburn 1974).

World-Renewal Religions

The distinction between shamanic and world-renewal systems approximately parallels the differences sometimes drawn between shamanism versus totemism, increase rites, and/or priestly religions. Following long-standing Native California ethnographic practice (e.g. Kroeber 1907; 1971; Kroeber and Gifford 1949), I use 'world renewal' as the preferred generic term because 'totemism' is more restrictive and less adequate for describing the range of similar religions within the global hunter-gatherer ethnographic record; 'priestly' is too broad; and the term 'increase rites', common in the Australian Aboriginal literature, misrepresents the nature of its central ritual function (cf. Elkin 1964, 205).

World-renewal religions were practised in north-western California among the Yurok, Karok, Hupa, and Tolowa tribes (as well as in the Pacific Northwest and Alaska to the north). They included both esoteric and exoteric rites. The primary purpose of the secret, esoteric ceremonies was periodically to re-establish or renew the earth, ensure the continued availability of plants and animals (like Australian Aboriginal 'increase rites') and the health of individuals, and to prevent calamities. As Kroeber (1971, 466) noted:

> The core of the esoteric rite is the recitation of a narrative or dialogue formula repeating the words of these [creator] spirits in the past, accompanied somewhat variably by acts of mimetic magic symbolic of their actions at that time.

The creators were always nameless primordial spirits who had departed or transformed themselves prior to the human period. The male priest or ritual formulist, aided by one or more assistants, repeated their words and actions in a fixed order, at the precise locations where the original events had occurred—thus directly linking ritual and myth. Priestly lineages owned the secret ritual formulae and, reflecting the emphasis on individual wealth in these societies, the 'owners' of the formulae were paid to perform the ceremonies. The death and rebirth of the world were symbolically illustrated during these rites by the rebuilding of sacred structures (primarily sweat- and dance-houses) and the creation of sacred fires (Bean and Vane 1978).

Exoteric rites more strongly reflected the connection between status, wealth, and its exchange, through a complex series of ritual feasts associated with two major dance cycles: the White Deerskin and the Jumping dances. These were hosted by individuals who invited numerous people from neighbouring villages and tribes, resulting in ritual congregations as large as 1,000 people. Wealth and a network of rich and influential friends were required to host the events. The organizer paid for the feasts (with *dentalium* shell beads), provided the ceremonial regalia of the dancers, and owned (or borrowed) the wealth items that the dancers displayed. Principal among these were rare white albino deerskins, and very large ceremonial obsidian bifaces (Kroeber 1907; 1925; 1971).

Despite the formulist/priestly emphasis of the world-renewal religions, an element of shamanism was present where they were practised. This primarily involved curing. In an inversion of the pattern that was common throughout the rest of Native California, curing shamans in north-western California were typically female (Whitley 2000). This circumstance points to the fundamentally androcentric emphasis of Native California (and many but not all other hunter-gatherer) religions: the primary ritual specialists were everywhere typically male, with females usually fulfilling secondary positions.[4] Although shamans served the principal or sole ritual roles among some tribes, and in those situations were most often male, women were the shamans among the tribes where shamanism was of secondary religious importance.

Some External Comparisons

The Native California ethnographic record illustrates the remarkable range of religious variability among hunter-gatherers, even in a relatively small region, and it includes many, if not most, of the elements and characteristics of hunter-gatherer religions worldwide. Still, it does not reflect all of the known variability in hunter-gatherer religions worldwide, especially when specific aspects of ritual and belief are considered. What tends to vary is not so much the presence or absence of these elements and characteristics but the way that they are combined in specific cases, how they are emphasized, and how they are articulated with other aspects of society.

This point is illustrated by two outwardly different hunter-gatherer religions: the San (or Bushmen) of southern Africa (Katz 1976; Lewis-Williams 1981; 2002a; Lewis-Williams and

Pearce 2004), and the Australian Aborigines (Elkin 1964; 1977; Layton 1992). San religion is shamanistic. Approximately 50 per cent of the males are shamans, implying a high level of religious egalitarianism (as also argued for other aspects of San society; cf. Lee 1979; Marshall 1976). But often overlooked are, first, the fact that half of the males never become shamans, hence it is far from a universal role, even among the men. Second, the San themselves seem to recognize a distinction in kind between those individuals who are born with shamanic power, and those who must work to achieve it (see Katz 1976, 187), with the first group possibly maintaining more or perhaps a qualitatively different kind of supernatural potency. Regardless of specifics, those born with power seem to be acknowledged as the real San religious authorities and leaders, despite the relative commonness of shamans in general terms within the society as a whole. A parallel can be drawn in this case to the toloache cults of Native California. Although the shaman maintained a formal ritual role among these tribes, most but not all men were initiated into the cult organizations through a shamanistic experience. They were not shamans in name, but they had some degree of shamanistic power, and they had personally experienced the supernatural world. The primary differences between the Native Californian toloache cults and San shamanism then appear to consist of the greater levels of secrecy and training involved in the first, and the frequency of individual visionary experiences in the second. These are variations of degree more than differences in kind.

Australian Aboriginal religion, in contrast, is generally viewed as 'totemic' and therefore non-shamanistic, yet this belies the significance and place of so-called Aboriginal 'clever men'—i.e. shamans by a different name—as is well documented ethnographically (e.g. Elkin 1977). Shamanism is not a central emphasis of these religions, yet it is undeniably a component of them (Eliade 1972). Still, the outstanding characteristics of Aboriginal ritual and belief systems, seen comparatively, are their profound connection to (totemic) kinship, the strong correlation between myth and ritual, the fundamental importance of cults/secret societies and initiations, and the place of world renewal—the periodic 'increase rites' performed to ensure the continued existence of various species (Elkin 1964; Gould 1969; Layton 1992). Aboriginal religions are remarkable partly because of the complexity of Aboriginal kinship systems and, due to the close connection between ritual and social organization, the resulting complexity that this imparts on the specifics of religious practice. These again are matters of degree more than kind, when seen from the perspective of global comparisons. Aboriginal religions in this sense can also be understood as variations on patterns present among hunter-gatherers elsewhere in the world, including in Native California, where secret societies with elaborate initiations, close ties between myth and ritual, and central concern with world renewal also occur.

THE ARCHAEOLOGY OF HUNTER-GATHERER RELIGIONS

For much of the last half-century, and for a variety of reasons, archaeology ignored prehistoric religions. This situation has changed over the last decade, with the study of prehistoric hunter-gatherer religions representing one of the strongest focuses of this growing archaeological sub-discipline. Rock art has been the primary (but not exclusive) data source for the majority of this research. Topically, these studies have emphasized shamanism (e.g. Boyd 2003; Chippindale et al. 2000; Lewis-Williams 1981; Lewis-Williams and Pearce 2004; Turpin 1994), the social implications of ritual (e.g. Lewis-Williams 1982; Whitley 1994a), and the origin of hunter-gatherer religions (e.g. Clottes and Lewis-Williams 1996; David 2002; Lewis-Williams 1984; 2002b; Taçon et al. 1996; Whitley 2009; Whitley et al. 2007), among others. Methodologically, research has included a significant concern with the incorporation of ethnohistoric and ethnographic data in archaeological analyses (e.g. Layton 1992; 2001; Keyser et al. 2006), and analytical and interpretive approaches (e.g. Conkey 1989; 2001; Lewis-Williams and Loubser 1986; Ross and Davidson 2006; Whitley 2001), especially the use of neuropsychological (e.g. Lewis-Williams and Dowson 1988; Whitley 1994b) and communication models (e.g. Conkey 1985; Davidson 1989; McDonald 1994). Although the distinction is imperfect, research in shamanistic contexts tends to be more concerned with symbolism and meaning, whereas studies in regions with formulist/world-renewal systems more commonly emphasize the implications of religious expression in social interaction. Given the geographical patterning in the ethnographic distribution of these two opposite poles of the hunter-gatherer religious continuum, research in western North America and southern Africa, where shamanism is prevalent, has followed a different trajectory than in Australia, where totemic world-renewal religions are dominant. Research on European Upper Palaeolithic religion, dating between about 35,000 and 10,000 BP, in contrast lacks a relevant ethnographic starting point. Perhaps as a result, both analytical approaches have been applied to the early prehistoric religion of this region.

I consider just two of these many topics in the following discussion: firstly, archaeological (as opposed to ethnographic) analytical approaches pertinent to analysing shamanistic and formulist religious configurations; secondly, the origins of hunter-gatherer religions more generally.

Analytical Approaches

Two formal analytical models have been developed to determine whether a corpus of prehistoric rock art was created in a shamanistic or in a formulist ritual context. The first and most widely applied is the so-called Neuropsychological (N-P) Model for trance imagery (Lewis-Williams and Dowson 1988; Lewis-Williams 2001). Building on published clinical and ethnographic accounts and laboratory conclusions, Lewis-Williams synthesized a model of the characteristics of the mental images resulting from an ASC, consisting of three components. Visionary imagery, first, commonly includes the perception of a series of geometric light designs internally generated by an individual's optical and neural systems. Called 'entoptic patterns', these are simple images such as zigzags and parallel lines; seven of these are widely described by clinical subjects and ethnographic consultants. Second, visual perception during an ASC differs from 'normal' vision, resulting in a characteristic set of perceptual tendencies. These include features such as the rotation of an image off a standard visual plane (i.e. a ground or horizon-line), or the helter-skelter juxtaposition of one image atop another. Seven common 'principles of perception' were synthesized from the clinical and ethnographic literature. Third, the clinical descriptions indicated that ASCs commonly (though not invariably) progress through three stages. Initially an individual perceives entoptic designs—geometric patterns—alone. Next, these are construed as personally or culturally meaningful representational images (e.g. a set of nested curves is interpreted as the rack of a bighorn sheep). Finally, full-blown iconic hallucinations develop, sometimes with co-occurring entoptic imagery.

Subsequent to developing the N-P model with the independent clinical and anthropological data, Lewis-Williams and Dowson (1988) tested it by examining the rock art of two regions known, on ethnographic grounds, to have been created by shamans to depict their visionary imagery: the San rock paintings of South Africa, and the Coso rock engravings from California. Because the predictions specified by the model adequately accounted for the range of variation found in these two test cases, they concluded that the N-P model could be used to analyse true prehistoric cases, lacking any associated ethnographic record, to determine whether a given corpus of art probably depicted the mental imagery of an ASC. Because trance is a central component of shamanic religions (e.g. Eliade 1972; Siikala 1978), it follows inferentially that evidence for altered-states imagery implies a shamanistic origin for the art. They then used the model to determine whether European Upper Palaeolithic cave art was probably shamanistic. Importantly, however, the N-P model solely concerns the origin, not the symbolic meaning, of a corpus of art (Lewis-Williams and Dowson 1988). And although it is often used in conjunction with ethnographic data to develop multiple lines of evidence, in fact it is a formal model that is entirely independent of the ethnography.

A second useful analytical approach has been illustrated by Ross and Davidson (2006), based on an ethnographic model of ritual form first developed by Rappaport (1999).[5] The evidentiary emphasis in this case concerns repeated and stylized behaviour and, for that reason, the model is most appropriately applied in cases where investigators suspect, or wish to rule out, formal cults and/or formulist religious systems. The intent of the ritual-form model is to determine systematically whether a rock-art corpus originated in religious ceremony rather than due to secular activities, and to identify the associated ritual's structural form rather than its specific contents. The model has seven features: *invariance* resulting from an adherence to a sanctified set of rules; *repetition* of the ritual; periodicity or scheduling linked to *specialized times*; locational selectivity employing *specialized places*; *formal or stylized* as opposed to informal or spontaneous *behaviour*; *performance* by a ritual actor and *participation* by an audience; and persistence in the use of *canonical messages*—i.e. messages putatively encoded by the supernatural (Ross and Davidson 2006).

Ross and Davidson examined central Australian Desert rock art using a series of archaeologically visible characteristics that are a function of these seven features. Although some features were more difficult to operationalize or identify archaeologically than others, they nonetheless were able to distinguish ritual versus non-ritual art, to identify possible contemporaneous but different ritual forms, and to discover changes in ritual form over time.

It is important to emphasize that, as the ethnographic review illustrates, hunter-gatherer religions were not necessarily purely shamanistic and idiosyncratic, or entirely non-shamanistic/formulist/priestly. Instead a true continuum exists with many traits, characteristics, and elements combined and emphasized in a wide variety of ways. Seen in a global context, for example, shamanistic rituals range from private, highly individualistic ceremonies (such as a specific shaman's private vision quest, at a power spot that they owned and exclusively used) to cult initiations (e.g. the Native Californian toloache and Kuksu secret societies). The rituals in these last religious configurations, while ostensibly esoteric and secret, in some cases involved the creation of shamanic art portraying the characteristics predicted by the N-P model of the mental imagery of trance (e.g. see Whitley 2000). But they also were conducted periodically, were formally structured, included many (even if not all) of the members of a given tribal society, and were sometimes held at specific ceremonial locations. World-renewal religions, based on specific religious formulae recited by priests at mythic locations, were also similarly structured, but they lacked any concern with visionary imagery. The N-P and ritual form models, in this sense, are best understood as potentially complementary analytical approaches, reflecting the fact that the first emphasizes ritual content, and the second form or structure.

Origins of Hunter-Gatherer Religion

The origin and time-depth of hunter-gatherer religions, at both global and regional scales, have been important topics of recent archaeological research, with studies in southern Africa, western Europe, Australia, Siberia, and western North America. Rock art again has provided the primary data for these investigations.

Shamanism has long been assumed the earliest religion, thought to have first appeared with the development of behaviourally and cognitively modern humans. Exactly when behavioural and cognitive modernity first appeared is a heavily researched, and hotly debated, topic. I have recently argued that, while there are many behavioural traits that are *necessary* characteristics of 'modernity', two are *necessary and sufficient* from the perspective of archaeological identification: religious beliefs and practices, and representational art (Whitley 2009). The earliest currently known examples of representational art are from southern Africa (Apollo 11 cave, Namibia, dating to about 27,000 BP; Wendt 1976), and various sites in western Europe (from approximately 40,000 BP; see Clottes 2008). Consensus holds in both cases that these arts are the products of religion. A number of researchers, primarily based on analyses using the N-P Model for trance imagery, have inferred that this African and European art portrays the visionary imagery of trance, and is shamanistic (Clottes and Lewis-Williams 1996; Dowson and Porr 2001; Lewis-Williams 1984; Lewis-Williams and Dowson 1988; Lewis-Williams and Pearce 2004; Whitley 2009). These studies support the long-standing assumption that shamanism was in fact the original hunter-gatherer religion.

As the ethnographic review indicates, however, shamanistic rituals themselves are quite variable, and the ritual form(s) of these early religions are as yet unknown. Villeneuve (2008), in this regard, has provided a detailed analysis of the structural characteristics of the European Palaeolithic sites, from the perspective of ritual proxemics, or use of space. Her analysis suggests that, even within the framework of shamanistic beliefs and practices, different kinds of rituals may have been conducted at these Palaeolithic sites.

Siberian shamanism has been the focus of substantial attention partly because of its rich ethnographic record (e.g. Shirokogoroff 1935; Siikala 1978), and in part due to the emphasis it received in (Eliade's 1972) widely read global synthesis. Based on the numerous specific similarities between Siberian and North American ritual practices (e.g. Schlesier 1987), Americanist researchers have assumed that 'classic' Siberian shamanism was the source for New World shamanism, suggesting that it was a kind of Palaeolithic relict (e.g. Furst 1977; Kroeber 1923; LaBarre 1980). But archaeological research on the antiquity of Asian shamanism itself has resulted in a very different conclusion. Based on a variety of lines of evidence, there is consensus that shamanism only appeared in north-eastern Asia approximately 4000 years ago, at the end of the Neolithic or beginning of the Bronze Age (Devlet 2001; Jacobson 2001; Rozwadowski 2001; 2004; Rozwadowski and Kosko 2002). The prehistoric origins of Siberian religion more generally, and the nature of the earliest north-east Asian religion, are currently unknown.

This circumstance has implications for the origins of New World religions. A variety of lines of evidence indicate that the earliest Native American religions were shamanistic, and that they have about 12,000 or more years of time-depth (Whitley 2004; Whitley et al. 1999). The remarkable similarity between Siberian and Native American shamanism, in light of the disparity in their respective ages, promotes the speculation that 'classic' Siberian shamanism itself may represent the relatively recent diffusion of some religious beliefs and practices from North America (Whitley 2009), rather than having served as the original source of Native American religions, as has long been assumed.

A final topic related to the origins of shamanistic religions concerns the time-depth of the Native Californian *?Antap* cult, practised ethnographically by the Chumash. Rock-art studies, site surveys, and mortuary analyses suggest that this cult may have developed about 800–1000 years ago, accompanied by major changes in the location and nature of socio-political leadership (Martz 1984; Whitley et al. 2007). Among others, these include a shift in emphasis from shamanistic/religious leadership to increasingly secular socio-political control.

The antiquity of Australian Aboriginal totemic 'Dreamtime' religions has also been the focus of recent research. The conclusion of one study is that it may be as much as 6000 years old (Taçon et al. 1996); a contrasting investigation suggests that, at most, it is half that age (David 2002). In either case, given the very long prehistory of human occupation of the continent, these religions are relatively youthful, and much remains to be determined about prehistoric rituals on this continent (cf. Ross and Davidson 2006), including the possibility of earlier shamanistic beliefs (cf. Chippindale et al. 2000).

Conclusions

It is a well-known fact that hunter-gatherers had some of the most complex kinship systems ever recorded. The varieties of totemic social organization among the Australian Aborigines, and the inverse relationship between their technological/material cultural sophistication and kinship complexity, is a well-known example (cf. Elkin 1964). The conclusion is that the hunter-gatherer cognitive world was varied, quite complex, and that we should expect that their religious, ritual, and symbolic systems would be equally rich, nuanced, and variable. Ethnographic Native Californian religion demonstrates this point: practices varied from barely elaborated forms of shamanism, to formal shamanic cults and secret societies, to priestly world-renewal religions, with almost every variation in between. Similar variability is evident worldwide. The tendency to conceptualize hunter-gatherer religions as an opposition between either shamanism or totemism, as if all hunter-gatherer religions can be satisfactorily placed into one of these two categories, reduces a diverse empirical reality to near-unrecognizable simplicity. Future analyses will benefit from an explicit acknowledgement of the empirical complexity implied by 'hunter-gatherer religions'.

The archaeology of hunter-gatherer religions has been neglected, like the study of prehistoric religion more generally, for complex intellectual and historical reasons. This has started to change, largely through the efforts of rock-art research which, in portions of the world at least, has emphasized just this dimension of the past. But there are still areas of research that need development. As the above implies, further research necessarily must start with an understanding of religions in general terms, rather than the imposition of implicit assumptions about the nature of this phenomenon based on the Western Judaeo-Christian model. It will also require apprehension of the ethnography of traditional, non-Western religions. This is not because all prehistoric religions were necessarily equivalent to ethnographic cases, but because the ethnography provides a known range of variation that can be used to assay and calibrate prehistoric evidence. Equally importantly, archaeologists need an understanding of how religions can change. Although there are useful discussions of this topic in anthropology (e.g. Bloch 1986; 1992; Sahlins 1985), archaeologists too widely conceptualize change as always catastrophic rather than potentially gradual, or even reversible, over time. (Since Western Judaeo-Christian ritual and beliefs exhibit great time-depth, despite massive alterations in other aspects of society, we should recognize the potential for religious persistence in prehistoric cases, even in the light of other shifts in the archaeological record.)

Hunter-gatherers are, of course, an anomaly if not an enigma in our contemporary modern world. Are there still any 'full-time' or 'pure' hunter-gatherers—defined, as their appellation emphasizes, in terms of subsistence practices? Or are hunter-gatherers instead simply historical and prehistoric phenomena that are now only relevant to academic interests in evolution and history? Regardless of your opinion on this point, hunter-gatherer religions themselves persist, often alongside Western beliefs and practices (Bean and Vane 1978; Elkin 1964; White 1963). This is more than an esoteric fact, given the increasing importance of heritage management and environmental regulation in Western pluralistic societies, whose political and legal land-development processes award substantial influence if not control to indigenous stakeholders. Almost invariably, indigenous descendants' primary interests in these contexts concern religion, especially sacred sites, their protection and use. Hunter-gatherer subsistence and technology may have little if any direct relevance to contemporary Western societies, beyond intellectual interests (important though these may be). But hunter-gatherer religion, and its implications especially for land development and growth, is an important practical matter whose relevance is likely to grow. Understanding hunter-gatherer religion by all involved in these processes and procedures is critical in this regard.

Notes

1. 'Native California' as used here includes all of the indigenous groups residing, at Euro-American contact, in the modern political state of California. Because this includes portions of different culture areas, it is (historically at least) an artificial analytical distinction—although most members of California tribes now recognize themselves (after their own tribal affiliation) as 'Native Californians' rather than 'Northwest Coast' or 'Great Basin' Indians. Precedent for the use of the political state as a unit of anthropological study is provided especially by Alfred Kroeber (e.g. 1907; 1925) and, as indicated above, the cultural diversity of hunter-gatherers within the confines of contemporary California make it particularly appropriate for this current purpose.

2. I use the term 'tribe' in this chapter in its contemporary Native American sense—a cultural, linguistic, and social community with shared ancestry—rather than in its technical/anthropological usage (implying a specific kind of social organization).
3. Note that my definitions of myth and folk tale are not necessarily applicable beyond hunter-gatherer cultures. The melding of the primordial with the historical past is especially characteristic of world religions, or 'religions of the book'.
4. One ethnographic justification for the rarity of Native California female ritual leaders in shamanic religions involved the belief that menstrual blood was inimical to supernatural power; hence women were *de facto* excluded from obtaining shamanic power (at least until they reached menopause), even though in theory anyone could receive it. Contemporary (as opposed to ethnographic) tribal shamanism increasingly emphasizes healing over all other shamanic activities (such as sorcery), and much more readily accommodates female shamans, who are now common in tribal contexts.
5. Rappaport (1999) presented his model as a 'universal' structure for all religious rituals, but his definition of ritual was narrow, and his model ignores important aspects of the variability that characterizes hunter-gatherer shamanistic religions, seen globally. It remains a very useful though not universal analytical tool, however, especially as developed for archaeology by Ross and Davidson (2006).

References

Barrett, J. 2004. *Why would anyone believe in God?* Walnut Creek, CA: AltaMira Press.
Bean, L. J. 1976. Power and its application in native California. In L. J. Bean and T. C. Blackburn (eds), *Native Californians: a theoretical retrospective*, 407–20. Socorro: Ballena Press.
Bean, L. J. and Vane, S. 1978. Cults and their transformations. In R. F. Heizer (ed.), *Handbook of North American Indians, Volume 8: California*, 662–72. Washington: Smithsonian Institution.
Blackburn, T. C. 1974. Ceremonial integration and social interaction in aboriginal California. In L. J. Bean and T. F. King (eds), *?Antap: California Indian political and economic organisation*, 93–110. Ramona: Ballena Press.
Bloch, M. 1986. *From blessing to violence: history and ideology in the circumcision ritual of the Merina of Madagascar*. Cambridge: Cambridge University Press.
Bloch, M. 1992. *Prey into hunter: the politics of religious experience*. Cambridge: Cambridge University Press.
Boscana, G. 1978. *Chinigchinich: an historical account of the Indians of the Mission of San Juan Capistrano called the Acagchemem Tribe*, trans. A. Robinson, annotated by J. P. Harrington. Banning: Malki Museum.
Boyd, C. E. 2003. *Rock art of the Lower Pecos*. College Station: Texas A&M University Press.
Chippindale, C., Smith B., and Taçon, P. 2000. Visions of dynamic power: archaic rock paintings, altered states of consciousness and 'Clever Men' in Western Arnhem Land (NT), Australia. *Cambridge Archaeological Journal* 10, 63–101.
Clottes, J. 2008. *Cave art*. London: Phaidon Press.
Clottes, J. and Lewis-Williams, D. 1996. *Les chamanes de la préhistoire: transe et magie dans les grottes ornées*. Paris: Éditions du Seuil.
Conkey, M. W. 1985. Ritual, communication, social elaboration, and the variable trajectories of Paleolithic material culture. In T. D. Price and J. A. Brown (eds), *Prehistoric hunter-gatherers: the emergence of social and cultural complexity*, 299–323. New York: Academic Press.

Conkey, M. W. 1989. The structural analysis of Paleolithic art. In C. C. Lamberg-Karlovsky (ed.), *Archaeological thought in America*, 135–54. Cambridge: Cambridge University Press.

Conkey, M. W. 2001. Structural and semiotic approaches. In D. S. Whitley (ed.), *Handbook of rock art research*, 273–310. Walnut Creek, CA: AltaMira Press.

David, B. 2002. *Landscapes, rock art and the Dreaming: an archaeology of preunderstanding.* London: Leicester University Press.

Davidson, I. 1989. Freedom of information: aspects of art and society in western Europe during the last Ice Age. In H. Morphy (ed.), *Animals into art*, 44–56. London: Unwin Hyman.

Devereux, G. 1957. Dream learning and individual ritual differences in Mohave Shamanism. *American Anthropologist* 59, 1036–45.

Devereux, G. 1969. *Mohave ethnopsychiatry: the psychic disturbances of an Indian tribe.* Washington: Smithsonian Institution.

Devlet, E. 2001. Rock art and the material culture of Siberian and central Asian shamanism. In N. Price (ed.), *The archaeology of shamanism*, 43–55. London: Routledge.

Dowson, T. A. and Porr, M. 2001. Special objects—special creatures: shamanistic imagery and the Aurignacian art of south-west Germany. In N. Price (ed.), *The archaeology of shamanism*, 165–77. London: Routledge.

DuBois, C. G. 1908. The religion of the Luiseño Indians of Southern California. *University of California Publications in American Archaeology and Ethnology* 8, 69–186.

Durkheim, E. 2001. *Elementary forms of religious life.* Oxford: Oxford University Press.

Eliade, M. 1972. *Shamanism, archaic techniques of ecstasy.* Princeton: Princeton University Press.

Elkin, A. P. 1964. *The Australian Aborigines.* New York: Doubleday.

Elkin, A. P. 1977. *Aboriginal men of high degree.* New York: St. Martin's Press.

Flaherty, G. 1992. *Shamanism and the eighteenth century.* Princeton: Princeton University Press.

Forde, C. D. 1931. Ethnography of the Yuma Indians. *University of California Publications in American Archaeology and Ethnology* 28, 83–278.

Furst, P. T. 1977. The roots and continuities of shamanism. In A. T. Brodzy, R. Daneswich, and N. Johnson (eds), *Stones, bones and skin: ritual and shamanic art*, 1–28. Toronto: Society for Art Publications.

Gayton, A. H. 1930. Yokuts-Mono chiefs and shamans. *University of California Publications in American Archaeology and Ethnology* 24, 361–420.

Gayton, A. H. 1948. Yokuts and Western Mono Ethnography. *University of California Anthropological Records* 10, 1–290.

Gayton, A. H. and Newman, S. 1940. Yokuts and Western mono myths. *University of California Anthropological Records* 5, 1–110.

Geiger, M. and Meighan, C. W. (eds) 1976. *As the Padres saw them: California Indian life and customs as reported by the Franciscan missionaries, 1812–1815.* Santa Barbara: Santa Barbara Mission Library.

Gilreath, A. J. and Hildebrandt, W. R. 2008. Coso rock art within its archaeological context. *Journal of California and Great Basin Anthropology* 28, 1–22.

Gould, R. A. 1969. *Yiwara: foragers of the Australian desert.* New York: Charles Scribner's Sons.

Hayden, B. 2003. *Shamans, sorcerers and saints: a prehistory of religion.* Washington: Smithsonian Institution.

Heizer, R. F. (ed.) 1978. *Handbook of North American Indians, Volume 8: California.* Washington: Smithsonian Institution.

Horton, R. 1982. Tradition and modernity revisited. In M. Hollis and S. Lukes (eds), *Rationality and relativism*, 201–60. Cambridge, MA: MIT Press.

Jacobson, E. 2001. Shamans, shamanism, and anthropomorphizing imagery in prehistoric rock art of the Mongolian Altay. In H. P. Francfort and R. N. Hamayon (eds), *The concept of shamanism: uses and abuses*, 277–96. Budapest: Akadémiai Kiadó, Bibliotheca Shamanistica.

Katz, R. 1976. *Boiling energy: community healing among the Kalahari Kung*. Cambridge, MA: Harvard University Press.

Keyser, J. D., Poetschat, G., and Taylor, M. W. (eds) 2006. *Talking with the past: the ethnography of rock art*. Portland: Oregon Archaeological Society.

Keyser, J. D. and Whitley, D. S. 2000. A new ethnographic reference for Columbia Plateau rock art: documenting a century of vision quest practices. *International Newsletter of Rock Art* 25, 14–20.

Kroeber, A. L. 1907. The religion of the Indians of California. *University of California Publications in American Archaeology and Ethnology* 4, 319–56.

Kroeber, A. L. 1923. American culture and the Northwest Coast. *American Anthropologist* 25, 1–20.

Kroeber, A. L. 1925. *Handbook of the Indians of California*. Washington: Smithsonian Institution.

Kroeber, A. L. 1939. Cultural and natural areas in native North America. *University of California Publications in American Archaeology and Ethnology* 38, 1–242.

Kroeber, A. L. 1957. Mohave clairvoyance: ethnographic interpretations 1–6. *University of California Publications in American Archaeology and Ethnology* 47, 226–33.

Kroeber, A. L. 1971. The world renewal cult of northwest California. In R. F. Heizer and M. A. Whipple (eds), *The California Indians: a sourcebook*, 464–71. Berkeley: University of California Press.

Kroeber, A. L. and Gifford, E. W. 1949. World renewal: a cult system of native northwest California. *Anthropological Records* 13, 1–156.

LaBarre, W. 1980. *Culture in context*. Durham: Duke University.

Laird, C. 1976. *The Chemehuevis*. Banning: Malki Museum.

Laird, C. 1984. *Mirror and pattern: George Laird's world of Chemehuevi mythology*. Banning: Malki Museum.

Layton, R. 1992. *Australian rock art: a new synthesis*. Cambridge: Cambridge University Press.

Layton, R. 2001. Ethnographic study and symbolic analysis. In D. S. Whitley (ed.), *Handbook of rock art research*, 311–32. Walnut Creek, CA: AltaMira Press.

Lee, R. B. 1979. *The !Kung San: men, women and work in a foraging society*. Cambridge: Cambridge University Press.

Lewis-Williams, J. D. 1981. *Believing and seeing: symbolic meaning in southern San rock paintings*. London: Academic Press.

Lewis-Williams, J. D. 1982. The economic and social context of Southern African Rock Art. *Current Anthropology* 23, 429–49.

Lewis-Williams, J. D. 1984. Ideological continuities in prehistoric southern Africa. In C. Schrire (ed.), *Past and present in hunter-gatherer studies*, 225–52. New York: Academic Press.

Lewis-Williams, J. D. 2001. Brain-storming images: neuropsychology and rock art research. In D. S. Whitley (ed.), *Handbook of rock art research*, 332–57. Walnut Creek, CA: AltaMira Press.

Lewis-Williams, J. D. 2002a. *A cosmos in stone: interpreting religion and society through rock art*. Walnut Creek, CA: AltaMira Press.

Lewis-Williams, J. D. 2002b. *The mind in the cave: consciousness and the origins of art*. London: Thames and Hudson.

Lewis-Williams, J. D. and Dowson, T. A. 1988. The signs of all times: entoptic phenomena in Upper Palaeolithic art. *Current Anthropology* 29, 201–45.

Lewis-Williams, J. D. and Loubser. J. H. N. 1986. Deceptive appearances: a critique of Southern African Rock Art Studies. *Advances in World Archaeology* 5, 253–89.

Lewis-Williams, J. D. and Pearce, D. 2004. *San spirituality: roots, expression, and social consequence.* Walnut Creek, CA: AltaMira Press.

Loeb, E. 1932. The Western Kuksu cult. *University of California Publications in American Archaeology and Ethnology* 33, 1–137.

Loeb, E. 1933. The Eastern Kuksu cult. *University of California Publications in American Archaeology and Ethnology* 33, 139–232.

McDonald, J. 1994. Dreamtime superhighway: an analysis of Sydney Basin rock art and prehistoric information exchange. PhD thesis, Australian National University, Canberra.

Marshall, L. 1976. *The !Kung of Nyae Nyae.* Cambridge, MA: Harvard University Press.

Martz, P. C. 1984. Social dimensions of Chumash mortuary populations in the Santa Monica mountains region. PhD thesis, Department of Anthropology, University of California, Riverside.

Meyerhoff, B. 1976. Shamanic equilibrium: balance and mediation in known and unknown worlds. In W. D. Hand (ed.), *American folk medicine*, 99–108. Berkeley: University of California.

Outland, C. 1956. The story of Candelaria as told by her to George Henley and Dr. Bizzell of the Sespe in 1914. *Ventura County Historical Society Quarterly* 2, 2–8.

Pané, R. 2006. *The relación of Fray Ramón Pané.* Online at http://faculty.smu.edu/bakewell/BAKEWELL/texts/panerelacion.html

Park, W. Z. 1938. *Shamanism in western North America: a study in cultural relationships.* Evanston: Northwestern University Studies in the Social Sciences.

Price, N. S. (ed.) 2001. *The archaeology of shamanism.* London: Routledge.

Rappaport, R. A. 1999. *Ritual and religion in the making of humanity.* Cambridge: Cambridge University Press.

Reichel-Dolmatoff, G. 1967. Rock paintings of the Vaupes: an essay of interpretation. *Folklore Americas* 27, 107–13.

Ross, J. and Davidson, I. 2006. Rock art and ritual: an archaeological analysis of rock art in arid central Australia. *Journal of Archaeological Method and Theory* 13, 305–41.

Rozwadowski, A. 2001. Sun gods or shamans? Interpreting the 'solar-headed' petroglyphs of Central Asia. In N. Price (ed.), *The archaeology of shamanism*, 65–86. London: Routledge.

Rozwadowski, A. 2004. *Symbols through time: interpreting the rock art of Central Asia.* Poznan: Institute of Eastern Studies, Adam Mickiewicz University.

Rozwadowski, A. and Kosko, M. M. (eds) 2002. *Spirits and stones: shamanism and rock art in Central Asia and Siberia.* Poznan: Instytut Wschodoznawcze, Poznanskie Studia Wschodoznawcze.

Sahlins, M. 1985. *Islands of history.* Chicago: University of Chicago Press.

Schlesier, K. H. 1987. *The wolves of heaven: Cheyenne shamanism, ceremonies, and prehistoric origins.* Norman: University of Oklahoma.

Schultes, R. E. 1977. The botanical and chemical distribution of hallucinogens. In B. M. Du Toit (ed.), *Drugs, rituals and altered states of consciousness*, 25–55. Rotterdam: A. A. Balkema.

Senn, H. 1989. Jungian shamanism. *Journal of Psychoactive Drugs* 21, 113–21.

Shipley, W. F. 1978. Native languages of California. In R. F. Heizer (ed.), *Handbook of North American Indians, Volume 8: California*, 80–90. Washington: Smithsonian Institution.

Shirokogoroff, S. M. 1935. *Psychomental complex of the Tungus.* London: Kegan Paul, Trench and Trubner.

Siikala, A.-L. 1978. *The rite technique of the Siberian shaman*. Helsinki: Academia Scientiarum Fennica.

Silverman, J. 1967. Shamans and acute schizophrenia. *American Anthropologist* 69, 21–31.

Steward, J. H. 1955. *Theory of culture change: the methodology of multilinear evolution*. Chicago: University of Chicago Press.

Strong, W. D. 1929. *Aboriginal society in southern California*. Berkeley: University of California Publications in American Archaeology and Ethnology 26.

Taçon, P., Wilson, M., and Chippindale, C. 1996. Birth of the Rainbow Serpent in Arnhem Land rock art and oral history. *Archaeology in Oceania* 31, 103–24.

Turpin, S. (ed.) 1994. *Shamanism and rock art in North America*. San Antonio: Special Publication 1, Rock Art Foundation.

Villeneuve, S. N. 2008. Looking at caves from the bottom up: a visual and contextual analysis of four Paleolithic painted caves. MA thesis, Department of Anthropology, Victoria University.

Wendt, W. E. 1976. 'Art mobilier' from the Apollo 11 Cave, South West Africa: Africa's oldest dated works of art. *South African Archaeological Bulletin* 31, 5–11.

White, R. C. 1963. Luiseño social organization. *University of California Publications in American Archaeology and Ethnology* 48, 91–194.

Whitehouse, H. 2004. *Modes of religiosity: a cognitive theory of religious transmission*. Walnut Creek, CA: AltaMira Press.

Whitley, D. S. 1994a. By the hunter, for the gatherer: art, social relations and subsistence change in the prehistoric Great Basin. *World Archaeology* 25, 356–77.

Whitley, D. S. 1994b. Shamanism, natural modeling and the rock art of far western North America. In S. Turpin (ed.), *Shamanism and rock art in North America*, 1–43. San Antonio: Special Publication 1, Rock Art Foundation.

Whitley, D. S. 2000. *The art of the shaman: the rock art of California*. Salt Lake City: University of Utah Press.

Whitley, D. S. 2001. Science and the sacred: interpretive theory in US rock art research. In K. Helskog (ed.), *Theoretical perspectives in rock art research*, 130–57. Oslo: Novus Press.

Whitley, D. S. 2004. The archaeology of shamanism. In C. Pratt (ed.), *The encyclopedia of shamanism*, 15–21. Santa Barbara: ABC-Clio.

Whitley, D. S. 2006. Rock art and rites of passage in far western North America. In J. D. Keyser, G. Poetschat, and M. W. Taylor (eds), *Talking with the past: the ethnography of rock art*, 295–326. Portland: Oregon Archaeological Society.

Whitley, D. S. 2007. Indigenous knowledge and 21st century archaeological practice: an introduction. *SAA Archaeological Record* 7, 6–8.

Whitley, D. S. 2008. Religion. In H. Maschner, A. Baxter, and C. Chippindale (eds), *Handbook of archaeological theories*, 547–66. Lanham, MD: AltaMira Press.

Whitley, D. S. 2009. *Cave paintings and the human spirit: the origin of creativity and belief*. Amherst: Prometheus Books.

Whitley, D. S., Dorn, R. I., Simon, J. M., Rechtman, R., and Whitley, T. K. 1999. Sally's Rockshelter and the archaeology of the vision quest. *Cambridge Archaeological Journal* 9, 221–47.

Whitley, D. S., Simon, S. J., and Loubser, J. H. N. 2007. The Carrizo collapse: art and politics in the past. In R. L. Kaldenberg (ed.), *A festschrift honoring the contributions of California archaeologist Jay von Werlhof*, 199–208. Ridgecrest: Maturango Museum.

Wilbert, J. 1987. *Tobacco and shamanism in South America*. New Haven: Yale University Press.

CHAPTER 60

HUNTER-GATHERER GENDER AND IDENTITY

ROBERT JARVENPA AND HETTY JO BRUMBACH

PERHAPS the oldest and most fundamental aspect of identity in human experience is gender. To whatever extent sexual differences are biogenetically programmed, gender is socially constructed and negotiated. It is a highly malleable and adaptive feature of human social and cultural life. As Sassaman (1992, 71) argues, 'gender is the primary social variable of the labour process in forager or hunter-gatherer societies'. Gender dynamics among hunter-gatherers in recent times and in prehistory, therefore, are central to our understanding of the human condition at large. Since 90 per cent of our species' evolutionary history occurred in the context of hunting, fishing, and foraging economies, in the absence of domestication and food production, the kinds of relationships forged between women and men in those contexts are fundamental precedents in the development of human socio-cultural systems.

A comprehension of gender dynamics requires penetrating analyses of women in relation to men (the latter, until recently, the de facto focus of most research), an endeavour which brings us closer to achieving one of anthropology's most worthwhile goals: a comprehensive understanding of human social life and culture. Our field's long-lived scholarly focus on men has concealed half of human experience and, in turn, given rise to some peculiar interpretations of our species' historical development and recent biocultural adaptations.

Our own approach to these issues has been *ethnoarchaeological*, that is, examining gender dynamics in living communities as a means of generating models, analogies, and insights for interpreting the archaeological past. It is a research strategy which finds synergy between ethnography, ethnohistory, and archaeology and, arguably, offers a broad perspective for theorizing about gender. This perspective will inform much of the remaining chapter, which is arranged in two sections. The first will briefly review some key themes in recent research on gender, particularly with regard to prehistoric hunter-gatherers. Using the latter as a springboard, the second section will explore several profitable directions for future research on gender. Because much of our work has been conducted among hunter-gatherer communities in the subarctic and Arctic high latitudes of North America and Eurasia, liberal use is made of the literature for this region. However, larger implications about gender and gender analysis apply to hunter-gatherers worldwide.

Recent Themes and Directions

More than two decades ago, Conkey and Spector (1984) raised serious questions about the lack of interest in gender by archaeologists. This stands in contrast to developments in socio-cultural anthropology in recent years, where the importance of gender relations, sexual stratification, differences in female and male visions of society and culture, and gender bias and blindness in social research have been prominent themes (Dahlberg 1981; Leacock 1978; 1981; 1983; Morgen 1989; Ortner and Whitehead 1981; Quinn 1977; Reiter 1975; Rosaldo 1980; Rosaldo and Lamphere 1974; Sacks 1979; Sanday 1981). Increased ethnographic attention to women, in particular in hunter-gatherer societies, has been part of this critical perspective, including Goodale's (1971) study of Tiwi women in North Australia and Shostak's (1981) work with !Kung San in the Kalahari Desert. Archaeological research, however, has begun to address the dynamics of gender in past times and places (Arnold and Wicker 2001; Brumbach and Jarvenpa 2006; Claassen 1991; Claassen and Joyce 1997; Gero 1991; Gero and Conkey 1991; Kehoe 1990; Nelson 1990; 1997; 2006; Spector 1983; Spector and Whelan 1989; Watson and Kennedy 1991; Wicker and Arnold 1999; Wright 1996).

What kinds of evidence or *assumptions* have archaeologists marshalled in their discussions of gender? The distinction between evidence and assumption is not trivial. As Conkey and Spector (1984, 2) observe, the archaeological literature is 'permeated with assumptions, assertions, and purported statements of "fact" about gender', despite, until recently, a lack of interest in formal analysis of such matters. Because hunter-gatherers occupied the earliest and longest span of prehistory, the chasm between ethnographic-ethnohistoric patterns on the one hand and the archaeological record on the other is most daunting. This gap presents formidable challenges for analysis and uses of analogy. Accordingly, we seek an understanding of both overt and implicit interpretations of gender by archaeologists and the kinds and quality of information, if any, upon which they are based. Several significant generalizations about gender dynamics and the nature of work among prehistoric hunter-gatherers have emerged from the research and literature to date.

Labour Variability and Flexibility

Actualistic, field-based studies reveal that the division of labour was highly variable and more flexible than commonly assumed, both within and across populations. Thus, we reject the notion of a rigid or universally applicable 'man the hunter/woman the gatherer' protocol, even with respect to the narrower scope of food procurement (that is, ignoring food processing, storage, and distribution: Bird 1993; Brumbach and Jarvenpa 1997a; Claassen 1991; Endicott 1999; Frink 2002; Halperin 1980; Jarvenpa and Brumbach 1995; 2006a; 2006b; Kelly 1995, 262–5; Lee 1979; Moss 1993; Wadley 1998). Indeed, divisions of labour occasionally followed lines of age, ability, and experience, among other factors, rather than gender alone (Cooke 1998; Janes 1983; Kent 1998; Wadley 2000).

The variability and flexibility in work roles noted above is generally supported by skeletal evidence. Questions addressing disease, nutrition, physical injuries and trauma, and mortality, as well as gendered patterns of labour, can be profitably studied from human remains. A division of labour may be evidenced by gendered patterns of degenerative arthritis and/or robusticity of the skeleton. While arthritis and other palaeopathologies afflicted women and men differently within some populations, there is no consistent gender patterning in pathologies across populations which might suggest a universal or rigid separation of female and male workloads and behaviours (Cohen and Bennett 1993). Moreover, the intensification and gendered patterning of some diseases accompanying the transition to agriculture only serve to underscore the more variable and fluid situation for hunter-gatherers (Goodman et al. 1984; Hollimon 1991; 1992; Sealy et al. 1992; Smith et al. 1984; Wadley 1998; Walker and Erlandson 1986).

Although not consistent across populations, skeletal analysis has revealed some gender differences in patterns of diet and dietary stress. In Mesolithic Europe, for example, some female skeletal samples exhibit higher incidences of dental disease and nutritional deficiency compared to males, suggesting lower intakes of calcium and protein, perhaps due to less protein-rich diets combined with the stress of pregnancy and lactation (Meiklejohn and Zvelebil 1991, 134). In a related vein, Zvelebil (2000) suggests that inadequate fat intake also compromised the health of women, especially during pregnancy, a pattern that may have been reinforced by practices and beliefs that limited female access to fat-rich organs and parts of animal carcasses. However, chemical isotope studies of human bone samples in the western Baltic area do not support the notion of differential access to dietary items by gender (Meiklejohn et al. 2000).

In Mesolithic southern Scandinavia, tooth wear of adult women reflects working of hides by chewing while wear on the teeth of men indicates holding of materials. Although tooth wear increases with age for both sexes, it appears earlier among women (Alexandersen 1993; Blankholm 2008, 122). Finally, in some cases, such as Skateholm in southern Sweden, where mortuary remains indicate social stratification, higher ranking females have less limb lateralization than poorer females. Yet, higher ranking males exhibit stronger lateralization than poorer males. Such variability in work-related stress suggests that women achieved high status largely through means other than physical labour (Constandse-Westermann and Newell 1989; Zvelebil 2008, 40–1).

Some scholars envision a pervasive hunter-gatherer division of labour by invoking a 'meat for sex' hypothesis whereby one scarce commodity, meat hunted by men, is exchanged for another, the sexuality of women. In various guises, this argument has become popular in evolutionary biology, whereby men's hunting ability is interpreted as a competitive display process linked to their prestige and reproductive success (Hawkes and Bliege Bird 2002; Kaplan and Hill 1985; Smith 2004). However, labour is also a culturally constructed enterprise which cannot be easily reduced to matters of genetic fitness. Among the Cashinahua of the Peruvian Amazon, for example, Kensinger (1989, 20–4) notes that exchanges of meat by male hunters for female sexual favours have different qualities and meanings depending upon the social relationships involved. Meat for sex in extramarital affairs resembles supply-and-demand market exchange, but within the context of marriage it represents a domestic political process whereby wives ultimately may reward their husbands with sons, a significant asset in a patrilineal society. Kensinger (1989, 25) identifies a basic paradox in these arrangements:

> Although men can define themselves as indispensable as hunters and can attempt to control women through controlling their sexuality, men cannot reproduce themselves. Thus, they substitute the appearance of control for that over which they have no control.

Perhaps more problematic for the evolutionary biology position is the tendency to ignore real-world flexibility and variability in work routines in favour of a rigid 'man the hunter/ woman the gatherer' conceptualization of labour. A growing ethnographic literature documents the simple but undeniable reality that women also hunt. Indeed, they have hunted, trapped, and fished for a wide variety of animal resources, including deer and wild pig among the Agta (Estioko-Griffin and Griffin 1981), rabbits and other smaller mammals and reptiles among many Australian groups (Berndt 1981, 163–4, 176), and rabbits, muskrats, beaver, and occasionally larger game among the Chipewyan, Montagnais (Innu), and other subarctic peoples (Jarvenpa and Brumbach 1995; Leacock 1981, 36–41), to note some examples.

Household Organization and Activity Areas

Variability and flexibility in work roles is also supported by information drawn from activity area and household analyses. While female and male sitting areas, men's houses, women's kitchen wings, and other gendered spaces are occasionally decipherable in some archaeological contexts, there is also ample evidence for widespread commingling of men's and women's activities and work areas or, alternatively, organization of work and space along lines other than gender (Brumbach and Jarvenpa 1997b; Clark 1996; Jarvenpa and Brumbach 1999; LeMoine 2003; Reinhardt 2002; Shepard 2002; Whitridge 2002).

Tools and Tool-kits

Assignment of static gender categories (e.g. 'female' or 'male') to archaeological artefacts may bear a misleading relationship to the way such materials were employed in the real world. At best, the assignments reflect normative patterns culled from ethnohistory and ethnography, rather than conclusions drawn from empirical research. At worst, they are a kind of 'best-guess' gender stereotyping based on internalized assumptions from our own cultural background. Fine-grained ethnoarchaeological accounts of actual implements and facilities in living context, including scrupulous tracking of women's and men's behaviours vis-à-vis these use-histories and processing cycles, are needed to interpret how gender dynamics generate the static residues in the archaeological record. As Whitridge (2002) notes, to say that a lamp is 'female' and a harpoon 'male' may reflect meaningful symbolic or iconic associations in Inuit (Eskimo) culture. Yet these associations may obscure rather than illuminate the myriad ways such materials were actually manufactured, utilized, curated, recycled, and discarded by both women and men.

Arguably, archaeological approaches to the tools and technologies of prehistoric hunter-gatherers deserve major rethinking (Bird 1993; Gero 1991; Torrence 2001; Wadley 1998). The pervasive view of large stone projectile points and blades as quintessential male tools for slaying big dangerous animals is tied too closely to the Western iconic 'man conquers snarling beast' cover art gracing men's magazines. At the same time, the tendency to interpret 'hunting' as the fleeting moment of dispatch, or the kill, seriously distorts the complex behaviours and technologies in hunter-gatherer economies. Following Kehoe (1990), we recommend a renewed attention to 'lines' and other non-lithic technologies involving preparations, travel, logistics, and management of animal movements which, ultimately, made the moment of dispatch possible (Casey 1998; Lips 1947; Osgood 1940). As Kehoe (1990, 27) argues, early hunting techniques included a variety of traps, snares, enclosures, and other constructions, and tools to facilitate access to animals, thus moderating the difficulties and dangers inherent in the moment of dispatch. The full repertoire of procurement technologies and strategies, no doubt, required the complementary labour of women, men, and children.

Harvesting, Processing, and Asymmetries of Power?

If the pre-harvest procurement side of hunting has been seriously distorted, the post-kill processing dimension of hunting has been relatively ignored by archaeologists. Ethnoarchaeological research is useful for demonstrating how post-kill butchering, food processing, and storage arrangements for converting carcasses into useful food products, clothing, and implements made survival in adverse conditions possible for communities of hunter-gatherers (Jarvenpa and Brumbach 2006a; 2006b). Much of the processing aspect of hunting was managed by women. Indeed, the time investment of women's labour in such activity increases dramatically with the package size of hunted prey and is a compelling reason for decreased participation of women in the direct harvest phase of hunting large animals in some high-latitude societies. This does not deny that both women and men can be involved in various aspects of butchering, marrow and grease production, and meat storage, as seen in Binford's (1978, 94–100, 123–33, 152–67) detailed accounts of Nunamiut processing of caribou for both dry and frozen storage. Generally speaking, however, women have been especially prominent in converting animal carcasses into vital subsistence products and in developing technologies for storage and preservation. Facile arguments about women's 'marginalization' and/or men's 'high prestige' tend to wither in the face of such behavioural realities. Accordingly, we believe the archaeology of hunter-gatherers can only come of age with serious study of the material correlates of post-kill processing, storage, and distribution of food and the implications of these dynamics for gender relations.

The last point above cannot be overemphasized. Without compelling analysis of what women and men actually accomplished in their daily lives, questions about power, status, and prestige differences between the sexes cannot be addressed. Ideas about prestige hierarchies are particularly prone to contamination by gender stereotypes and biases from our own culture. Lest there be doubts on this score, one may recall how the *Man the Hunter* symposium 'gerrymandered' women out of hunting by semantic manipulation of definitions (Lee and DeVore 1968; Nelson 1997, 86). Similarly, archaeology has 'downsized' or 'redlined' women out of stone-tool manufacture by disassociating them from big formal lithic tools, purportedly the domain of male hunters only (Hayden 1992a, 42). This notion is seriously challenged by Weedman Arthur's (2010) study of Konso women, who make and use high-quality standardized stone tools. Finally, the contributions of women's work in producing cordage and strings, or 'lines', to be used in nets and snares, as noted above (Kehoe 1990), and the role these items play in pursuit strategies, are too often overlooked.

Carrying this point further, one might note the predominance of women in manufacturing hides and sophisticated tailored skin, gut, and fur wardrobes which allowed hunter-gatherer populations to live and work in cold environments. Likewise, pottery, for those hunter-gatherers who produced it, was primarily manufactured and utilized by women for a variety of food processing, cooking, and storage activities (Frink and Harry 2008, 107–10; Hodder 1982, 92–7; Sassaman 1993). It is likely, however, that entire communities, including men, became involved in the post-production life of pottery. As prestige technologies, ceramic vessels may have been integral to competitive feasting, ceremonial displays, and symbolic communication of emerging political elites in more complex hunter-gatherer societies (Budja 2009, 501–2; Hayden 1992b; 1995; Jordan and Zvelebil 2009, 61–5).

A critical issue here is that even though men can have negligible or limited roles in some activities of vital economic concern, these limitations are rarely recognized or used to revise entrenched ideas about the sexual division of labour. On the contrary, as we have seen, the profession has a history of interpreting hunter-gatherer society in terms of women's marginalization and exclusion (Brightman 1996).

We submit that these interpretations have little resemblance to hunter-gatherer gender relations in the past or in recent history. If we inverted the logic, one might well argue that men's 'show-off' or 'costly-signalling' kills of large game, a favoured model in behavioural ecology (Hill and Kaplan 1993; Jochim 1988; Smith 1999; Winterhalder 2001), are neither inherently prestigious nor displays of genetic fitness, but rather attempts to avoid exclusion or marginalization by women and children who represent the nurturing epicentre and future of society. Conceivably, we could build models of women's 'show-off' food processing or 'show-off' storage. However, there is little to be gained by replacing one set of questionable assumptions with another. Surely, *both women and men* actively negotiated their existence in hunter-gatherer societies, strategizing, coping, and making numerous decisions that facilitated their lives and livelihoods. Until the discipline ceases imposing Western gender ideology on its subject matter, there can be no compelling archaeology and anthropology of hunter-gatherers.

FUTURE DIRECTIONS FOR RESEARCH

Gendered Landscapes: Rethinking the Sexual Division of Labour

Despite recent findings on the variability and flexibility of women's and men's work among hunter-gatherers, this vital topic deserves more attention. Among other approaches, we recommend cross-cultural ethnoarchaeology as a means of exploring the subtleties and complexities of the sexual division of labour. Our own recent study of gender dynamics and subsistence systems (Jarvenpa and Brumbach 2006b; 2006c), for example, employed the same 'task differentiation' methodology (adapted from Spector 1983) to examine women's and men's behaviours and their repertoires of tools and facilities in four circumpolar societies: the *Kesyehot'ine* Chipewyan, boreal forest hunter-fishers of central subarctic Canada; the Trom'Agan Khanty, fisher-hunter-reindeer herders of western Siberia; the Kultima Sámi, intensive reindeer herding people of north-western Finland; and the Little Diomede Island Iñupiaq, maritime hunters of the Bering Strait, Alaska. A major goal of our controlled comparison is to explain the way that gender ideas and rules structure the acquisition, processing, storage, and discard of food resources and ultimately the formation of the archaeological record.

Along with our international colleagues and collaborators, Elena Glavatskaya (2006) among the Khanty, Jukka Pennanen (2006) among the Sámi, and Carol Zane Jolles (2006) among the Iñupiaq, we made extensive use of native testimony and interpretation to deliberately temper our external views and models with local understandings of the material consequences and meanings of economic behaviour (Hodder 1982). This information was integrated with our own direct observations, measurement and mapping of settlements and land use, and structured interviews regarding the social, spatial, temporal, and material dimensions of specific subsistence activities, whether these involved rabbit snaring, fishing, seal hunting, or reindeer herding.

Briefly stated, our comparison reveals varying types or degrees of differentiation in female and male subsistence roles in short-distance and long-distance food procurement, in food processing and storage, as well as gender-specific features and facilities, among other patterns. The analysis is not meant to reduce the complex interactions of subsistence, gender dynamics, and their material residues to a few rigid 'signatures' readily observable in the archaeological record as the 'Chipewyan type' or the 'Sámi type' or whatever. Rather, a major implication is that the archaeological landscape is not gender-neutral. The built environment, and its eventual manifestation as archaeological remains is a product of the interplay between alternatives in subsistence or resource management and degrees of differentiation in female and male economic roles and behaviours.

This interaction generates what might be termed 'gendered landscapes' of varying scale, complexity, and subtlety. It is notable, for example, that the Chipewyan have the highest proportion of 'women's gear' in their hunting and processing tool-kits, about 50 per cent, as compared with 27 per cent 'men's gear' and 23 per cent 'joint gear'. By contrast, the Sámi exhibit relative equivalence in the proportion of women's, men's, and joint tools. The Khanty offer yet another pattern with a comparatively high proportion of jointly-used gear, although even in this case women's tools are more prominent than men's. Such data in isolation may seem somewhat cryptic. However, they are more compelling when viewed in context with other classes of information, such as the kinds of storage structures and processing facilities utilized by women and men and their involvement in long-distance or short-distance procurement (Jarvenpa and Brumbach 2007; 2009).

Storage itself is a complex issue which cannot be fully grasped without considering women and gender as fundamental to the social relations of production. In the Arctic and subarctic, a variety of sophisticated above-ground caches, permafrost pits, subterranean chambers, drying racks, and techniques such as immersion in spring water or smoke-drying and thin-cutting have been developed as a means of protecting seasonal surges of food and stockpiling them through the warmer months and inevitable lean periods for future consumption with the goal of providing daily sustenance to all members of the community, and especially children. The capacity and sophistication of these storage systems are highly developed in response to logistically organized flows of resources to centralized camps and settlements on a periodic or cyclical basis.

It is notable that in all four societies food storage features and facilities are significant sites of female activity and domestic authority. Men may build the facilities and assist in depositing caches of food within them, but subsequent management, processing, and distribution of stored food supplies are controlled by women. Food storage features are, in short, de facto women's spaces within the communities.

Also relevant to this discussion is Frink's (2009) persuasive argument against essentialist views of women's and men's work roles. She demonstrates how subsistence expertise and productive power are variably learned and expressed by individuals within communities. In western coastal Alaska, those influential Yupik women who achieve master status as herring processors, for example, have invested a lifetime of apprenticeship and fine-grained understanding of complex skill sets. Stated another way, specialized knowledge and experience permit both women and men to make strategic choices about how to best allocate their labour as subsistence scenarios unfold.

Moreover, as we have argued, communities that rely on large animals must be able to deal quickly and efficiently with massive influxes of meat and other products before they spoil. That women predominate in many of these processing tasks is part of the adaptive division of labour characteristic of Arctic and subarctic societies faced with seasonal temperature extremes, profound fluctuations in key resources, and labour shortages exacerbated by demographic cycles and events in small populations. Timely processing and storage of large animal carcasses prolongs the availability of resources and ensures a steady, daily supply of food for members of a community.

We encourage others to experiment with comparative ethnoarchaeology as a means of casting light on dimensions of gender beyond subsistence. What some of these other issues might entail are considered in the following sections.

Accessing Cosmological and Sacred Power

The spiritual life of hunter-gatherers has often been characterized as an individualized, personal relationship with spirits or powerful animal-spirit beings. Aside from the enhanced abilities of curers and shamanic specialists, sacred or cosmological power has been assumed to be available to all or, at least, to all adults. While this generally may be the case, subtleties and nuances in how power is accessed, utilized, and displayed by women and men in varying social contexts deserve a more probing analysis.

Some possibilities in this regard may be suggested by recent ethnographic work in Chipewyan society, where a delicate material-spiritual symbiosis between humans and food animals is a fundamental means of interpreting causality. For example, there is a tendency to interpret major historical changes in animal distribution or abundance as withdrawals or withholdings due to flagrant 'disrespect' by hunters. One's ability to hunt, to cure illness, and engage in sorcery is affected by the state of one's (super)natural knowledge and power, or what the Chipewyan term *inkonze* or *inkoze* (Jarvenpa 1998; Smith 1973).

While all Chipewyan have knowledge and power, *inkonze*, women and men may exhibit different means of acquiring and utilizing it (Smith 1973, 8). For example, Smith (1982, 38) notes that historically women's *inkonze* was most often manifested in curing. In contemporary settings, Sharp (1981; 1988; 1991) argues that men obtain *inkoze* from spirit-animal beings in dreams and demonstrate the extent of their power in hunting success. The social divisiveness implicit in differential hunting prowess, in his view, is tempered within multi-family hunting groups by women, whose sharing activity binds the membership and occurs largely without direct reference to their men's *inkoze*. In this sense, *inkoze* is a key facet of gender regulation. However, there is always the potential for prolonged or disagreeable competition between men to compromise the social and economic integrity of the hunting unit, thereby requiring alternative forms of symbolic resolution.

It is worth noting that the interpretations of Sharp and Smith refer to northern Chipewyan groups (*Etthen eldili dene*) along the forest-tundra margin where women appear to be less active in the direct-harvest phases of hunting than among their southern Chipewyan (*Kesyehot'ine*) relatives in the full boreal forest. Southern Chipewyan men also acquire *inkonze* and hunting power through dreaming. They refer to the actual process of obtaining power from animals as *biu'aze* (Jarvenpa 1998, 155–6). While more research is needed in this area, preliminary information suggests that southern Chipewyan women's prowess in a variety of hunting, fishing, gathering, processing, and sharing contexts is, no less than men's, an overt manifestation of *inkonze*. Indeed, if *inkonze* is operating to regulate gender or draw symbolic boundaries between women and men, the process is assuredly more subtle among the southern Chipewyan. One implication here is the need to document and understand regional or inter-community variability in gender dynamics and spirituality within the same society.

Another way of approaching magico-religious dynamics and gender is through sacred or ritual landscapes. That is, how do people give transcendent meaning to their environment through the creation of sacred material objects, structures, spaces, and sites? Jordan's (2003) recent ethnoarchaeological work among the Mali Iugan Khanty, fisher-hunter-reindeer herding people in western Siberia, is a particularly compelling treatment of these issues. He deftly reveals the complex systems of social spirits (household, clan, and regional) which have a materialized presence upon the landscape most often in the form of anthropomorphic wooden idols which require veneration, care, and feeding to ensure the well-being of the Khanty.

Jordan's (2003, 140–5) analysis has important implications for understanding gender and spirituality. For example, he notes that Khanty women are often proscribed from certain ritual contexts and spaces accessible to men. At the 'holy areas' and specific 'holy sites' connected to the health, welfare, and hunting success of entire communities or localities of Khanty, the relevant spirits are generally male. Moreover, women's presence at such sites, containing the spirit shelters (sacred *labas*) and idols, is thought to be particularly offensive and threatening and, therefore, women are generally forbidden from entering the sites. Indeed, accessing such sites may require complex orchestrations whereby women remain behind on an opposite riverbank while men make a direct approach. There may be separation of women and men during ritual meals at or near such sites and other forms of gender segregation (Jordan 2003, 160–4). Similar proscriptions can occur at the household level where women must avoid the sacred *labas* housing a family's guardian spirits (Glavatskaya 2006, 106).

A key conclusion of Jordan's (2003, 208) study is that Khanty visits to their holy sites 'are important in the construction and maintenance of gender identities, many of which overlap and reinforce the realities of more routine praxis. For men this concerns strong links with hunting; for women a celebration of their fertility and role as mothers'. Relevant here is the behavioural rigidity associated with the holy sites. Unlike the yurt or domestic household which is the site of continuous and changeable activity, the holy sites are less frequented, more proscribed, less open to interpretation and creativity, and, in Jordan's words, 'more Khanty'.

Jordan's interpretation also provides a potential resolution to the seeming contradiction between rigid gender ideologies and everyday behavioural flexibility in women's and men's work roles and productive routines in hunter-gatherer societies. This is compatible with Glavatskaya's (2006, 154) findings that while Trom'Agan and Pim Khanty have a 'strong notion of gender roles and tasks in provisioning families, these ideas are quite flexible and permit the family to adjust itself to changing circumstances. During field research I had a chance to be convinced that women can assume their male relatives' roles for supplying their families with food or teaching their sons to shoot quite easily. The reverse is also true: if male members of a family could not hunt, they could perform some traditional "women's" tasks, including cooking and teaching young girls to sew'.

The realities noted by Glavatskaya exemplify a flexibility in the sexual division of labour that has allowed the Khanty to persist and adapt to environmental and political-economic change. This dynamic operates despite or, perhaps, in concert with those highly conservative elements of gender ideology defined by relationships with the sacred. Jordan views these latter relationships as defining Khanty identity in its most fundamental or profound sense. There is abundant theoretical and empirical space for further explication of these issues among the Khanty and other hunter-gatherers. We might ask, for example, under what historical circumstances the everyday practices of food getting and processing fade in importance as markers of group identity? Or as markers of gender identities? Indeed, how do we separate mundane practice from the sacred when food-getting among most hunter-gatherers involves transactions with powerful spirit-animal beings?

Finally, regarding gender ideology reflected in religious belief and ritual, how do we know if proscriptions on women represent accepted community-wide views rather than a male rendering of such ideology? The question is worth raising because women often do not accept male ideas about gender differences within their own cultures (Buckley 1982; Counts 1985). We are not disputing the specific portrayals of gender relations in the Khanty ethnographic literature. Rather, we are advocating caution in any analyses that characterize women in terms of proscription, marginalization, or exclusion.

As alluded to earlier in this chapter, for example, we take issue with Brightman's (1996) suggestion that the sexual division of labour operates primarily to exclude women from arenas of power and prestige dominated by men, such as 'hunting' (narrowly construed by Brightman as killing or dispatch), and that women may actively collude in reproducing gender asymmetries since such arrangements may be interpreted by women not as exclusion but as 'entitlement' and 'complementarity'. By emphasizing arenas from which women are 'excluded', we believe Brightman has perpetuated a distorted view of labour that has long obscured rather than illuminated research on hunter-gatherers. The distortion may well extend to religion, power, and other arenas of social life.

Future research on gender might benefit from a more critical evaluation of familiar tropes such as 'exclusion', and 'marginalization'. Simply stated, who is being excluded from what by whom? Under what conditions? And how do the putatively excluded view their own situation? Since most ethnographic accounts continue to be generated by lone researchers of one gender or the other, how can we assure that compelling female *and* male visions or interpretations are represented? Successfully addressing this dilemma will advance gender analysis immeasurably, whether the immediate focus is cosmology, food sharing, or other areas of cultural life.

Socializing Gender: Children in Hunter-Gatherer Society

Ackerman's (2002) probing questions about gender equality, or inequality, and its causes are relevant to the foregoing discussion, and they also bring children into view. Is gender equality or complementarity related to subsistence, or is it associated with concern for women as the producers of children? There is a widespread notion in anthropology that women's contributions to subsistence activity directly determine female power and status, even though large-scale cross-cultural studies provide little support for this idea (Levinson and Malone 1980, 275). At the same time, however, some comparative research distorts the nature of men's, and especially women's economic contributions by narrowly defining or viewing subsistence as a procurement process only (Barry and Schlegel 1982; Ember 1978).

The foregoing perspective is myopic (that is, it creates difficulties in 'seeing' women) because it ignores the indispensable contribution that women make in processing, storing, and managing food resources, for example, as discussed by Frink (2002; 2009), and as noted in our own research above. Such myopia also marginalizes women's reproductive role, reducing it to an idiosyncratic nuisance or limiting factor. Far from being a 'nuisance', the ability of women to bear children, and for women and men to rear children, is essential to the continuity of the culture. As Ackerman's work in Colville Indian society (North American Plateau) clearly attests, equality can derive from society's concern for the well-being of children and their mothers. In the Colville community, women are not accorded a lower status due to their childbearing, childrearing, and lactating functions, but rather, are honoured by men for these contributions.

Whitridge (2007) approaches children from another vantage point. He examines miniatures, such as soapstone pots and slate ulus, in late pre-contact Inuit archaeological sites in Labrador. Because these finely crafted objects fluoresce during a period of Inuit colonization in the fifteenth century, he suggests that the miniatures may have been part of a multi-layered 'material discourse' on women's work that served to reinforce gender roles and differences at a time of considerable social and economic flux. There is the possibility that the miniatures also may have served as toys and/or models of implements and material culture employed in adult work and life. Following Whitridge's lead (also see Park 2005), the role of toys, miniatures, and models of all kinds deserves more systematic attention in the formative years of gender construction among children in hunter-gatherer societies.

Barbara Crass's (2002) study of 305 infant and child burials from 50 sites across the Inuit range of the Arctic sheds light on the differential treatment afforded children after death. Although Crass effectively documents differences in many aspects of burial, she also notes that we must search for ways to interpret the meaning of these differences, including those associated with gender. Archaeological studies, such as those of Whitridge and Crass, might benefit from information on childhood revealed in life-history ethnographies (see section below).

Probing Personality and Politics: Sex and Temperament or Life History?

Related to the issue of socialization of children is the development of culturally prescribed adult female and male personalities or psychosocial roles. What are the prevailing affective postures, dispositions, and interpersonal behaviours for women and men in hunter-gatherer societies? Are they rigid, flexible, or interchangeable? How are gendered personalities reinforced or contradicted by practical work routines and routine social interactions? What are the implications of personality for relations between women and men and for influence and decision-making in varying socio-political contexts?

Such interests recall a nascent psychological anthropology when early scholars like Margaret Mead (1935) eschewed universal biological determinants of femininity and masculinity in favour of highly variable, culturally constructed female and male 'temperaments'. This was dramatically, if not sensationally, illustrated in her juxtaposition of three different schemata of female and male temperament for the Arapesh, Mundugumor, and Tchambuli of New Guinea. Of course, Mead was discussing horticulturalists rather than hunter-gatherers. And while aspects of her work have been vigorously challenged and defended by several generations of scholars (Fortune 1939; Freeman 1982; Holmes 1986), Mead's pioneering ideas regarding the malleability of gender were ahead of her time and anticipated themes which would re-emerge in feminist anthropology of the 1970s and later years.

Briggs's (1970) fine-grained account of family life among the Utkuhikhalingmiut of central Arctic Canada provides a remarkable insight into the emotional expression of adults, and how this is inculcated in children. Based on continuous immersion with eight families over a 22-month period, she vividly captures the distinctive demeanour of individual personalities in public and private settings while revealing broad features in the social psychology of Utku women and men. Some of these themes might be couched in anachronistic-sounding language. For example, Briggs (1970, 96–108) speaks of 'the warmth and luxury of male dominance' to refer to the relative passivity of women when their husbands and male relatives are away on trading ventures and their exuberance and activity when their men are back home. Nonetheless, her specific accounts of emotional states and female–male interactions are exceptionally detailed and contextualized within the daily activity of families' lives.

Briggs's work serves as a reminder that a compelling social psychology of gender is likely to be found in the dramaturgical realities of hunter-gatherer family life. At the same time, a more multi-dimensional view of personality might emerge by scrupulously tracking emotional and affective postures employed by both women and men in a variety of contexts, some relatively 'backstage' or domestic and others, perhaps, more 'frontstage' or public. These distinctions might appear contrived or irrelevant for smallscale hunter-gatherer communities. Even so, one can hypothesize rather different female and male emotional tenors or personae involved in nurturing or chastising a child, setting up an encampment, and leading a community curing or purification ceremony, among other scenarios.

An overlooked genre of anthropological inquiry, the life history or biography, has relevance for the present discussion. Women's and men's life histories can inject a more dynamic aspect into the process of childhood socialization and life-long personality formation. Beyond these concerns, such literature is compelling for the way it reveals individuals actively coping with a variety of life experiences and dilemmas and influencing the history of their communities. Shostak's (1981) *Nisa*, a life history narrative of a !Kung-San woman of South Africa, anticipated a wave of cultural biographical research among women in hunter-gatherer societies. Among these are Blackman's (1982; 1989) biographies of Haida and Iñupiaq, Cruikshank's (1990) work among Inland Tlingit and Tagish, and Jolles's (2002) life history of a Yupik woman. There is much untapped potential in this line of analysis. One possibility for shedding new light on gender relations might be the construction of dual life histories, or paired biographies, where wife–husband or sister–brother pairs are followed through their respective lives. By examining all the points of intersection and interaction between the parties over several generations, we may gain new insight into what it means to be female and male in Chipewyan, !Kung-San, or Tiwi society, for example.

Another potential benefit of life history is to put a human face on the sometimes murky discussions of influence, power, prestige, and status in hunter-gatherer society. Personal profiles of specific women and men using their skills, charisma, sacred power, interpersonal connections, and ties to colonial or post-colonial agents to realize goals and resolve problems under particular circumstances will go a long way towards tempering general models of egalitarianism or emergent asymmetry. How do women and men view their own standing and contributions to family and society? Are they 'asymmetrical equals' or are they profoundly different in ability to influence family and community decisions?

Revealing in this regard is Fewster's (2001) ethnoarchaeological study of Petso, a Basarwa (San) man who adopted farming amid his community of foragers in Botswana. Petso's innovative actions are contextualized in terms of Basarwa relationships with their agro-pastoralist neighbours, the Bamangwato, and with various Western development projects. Fewster makes a compelling argument for employing agency-based analogies for interpreting archaeological phenomena, such as the Mesolithic–Neolithic transition in Spain. In short, biography has the potential to identify specific incidents, situations, or scenarios where women's or men's actions may have far-reaching implications for the gender politics of their community.

Alternative Gender Roles

Stewart's (2002) fascinating analysis of the Netsilik *kipijuituq* raises questions about the prevalence of gender changing and/or third-gender phenomena among Inuit and hunter-gatherers generally. A larger implication of his study is the danger of imposing Western dualisms and categories of 'sex', 'sexuality', and 'gender' on other people. The *kipijuituq*, a young male raised partially as a female, defies conventional Western definitions of maleness and femaleness. Yet, as a sexually inactive or pre-sexual being, the *kipijuituq* does not easily mesh with our understandings of homosexuality or of berdache and berdache-like third-gender personae in various cultures. That is, the *kipijuituq* may adopt some, but not all, of the behaviours and mannerisms of Netsilik girls. A strict taboo against cutting the *kipijuituq*'s hair applies until the person is released from *kipijuituq* status upon killing a prescribed game animal, usually during adolescence. The full meaning of *kipijuitiuq* in the local cultural context requires an insider's appreciation of Inuit or Netsilik ethnobiology, world view, and ethos, including all of the symbolic apparatus which associates males and maleness with polar bears.

Moreover, matters such as gender identity may be determined by the interpretations and choices of others. Stewart (2002, 14–15) notes that Netsilik grandparents sometimes make decisions about who will become *kipijuituq* by interacting with and observing the reactions of their infant grandsons. While the *kipijuituq* role is confined to childhood and adolescence, alternate or androgynous third-gender personae in other cultures appear to be manifested in adulthood. These include the generous, spiritually gifted *berdache* or 'two-spirits' found among many Native North American peoples (Hollimon 1997; Roscoe 1994; Williams 1986).

Further study of alternate-gender and gender-transforming phenomena will be valuable in revealing new areas of creativity and malleability, thereby expanding the boundaries of what is and what has been socially possible in hunter-gatherer societies. Is there anything distinctive about such dynamics, and their intersection with cosmological and sacred power, that might be distinctive among hunter-gatherers as compared with horticultural and agricultural societies? Such insights might serve as a continuing challenge to narrowness and rigidity in interpreting women's and men's lives, particularly any lingering conflation of sex with gender.

Political and Colonial Transformations of Gendered Identities

Also, we need to keep in mind the potential for gender change or transformation, particularly given increasing involvement with non-local, post-colonial, international markets, agents, and ideologies. A rigorous treatment of the bureaucratic apparatus of the state and the myriad ways that hunter-gatherer groups have been displaced, relocated, and administered, and the consequences for women's and men's lives, is needed. Also needed is a systematic analysis of strategies of evasion, avoidance, and resistance to incorporation by the state (Clastres 1987). While these issues are beyond the scope of this chapter, a brief example will illustrate some of the issues involved.

As in many Canadian Indian communities, among the southern Chipewyan (*Kesyehot'ine*), a patriarchal facet of Canadian federal treaty law allowed a Treaty woman to lose her official registered status simply by marrying a non-Treaty man. Thus, a Chipewyan woman who had been since birth a member of the federally recognized English River Band (now English River First Nation) would immediately lose her status. Conversely, a non-Treaty woman could gain federal status simply by marrying a Treaty man. Yet, Treaty men kept their status regardless of marital history. This differential treatment of women and men by the state was implemented with the inception of Treaty No. 10 in 1906.

The legal inequality remained until the 1980s when Bill C-31 permitted any woman with prior Treaty status, who had become disenfranchised through marriage, to have her federal status restored. By that time, of course, several generations of Chipewyan women, and their heirs, had been denied access to treaty payments, reserve lands, housing, social welfare, and other resources offered by the federal government via the Department of Indian Affairs. The resulting ethno-status division and tension created within the southern Chipewyan community became a significant part of the political landscape which persists today (Jarvenpa 2004).

The Chipewyan case serves to remind us of how entire classes of people, in this instance women, can be disenfranchised by arbitrary legal measures. Whether women or men are disadvantaged by a particular statute or policy, differential treatment by gender can have unforeseen and long-lasting impacts on inheritance patterns, social structure, and local political systems. How states count and categorize hunter-gatherer populations, or make them legible or illegible for purposes of surveillance (Scott 1998), control, and appropriation of resources deserves more research.

Conclusion

Fine-grained, cross-cultural, field-based accounts of the realities of women's and men's lives are especially needed at this time to temper rhetorical assertions about gender. Ethnoarchaeology is well suited to this task. It approaches women and men as conscious actors, whose negotiations of opportunities and constraints in specific environments and cultural landscapes generate material residues which can be used to interpret hunter-gatherers' lives in the present and in ancient times. Where some of these interpretations might lead are suggested by the following themes:

(1) *The sexual division of labour:* Recent scholarship has revealed considerable malleability and interchangeability of women's and men's labour among some hunter-gatherers, on the one hand, but also the materialized presence of women's and men's work in 'gendered landscapes', on the other. Additional fine-grained analyses are needed of women's and men's *actual* work routines, their temporal and spatial integration into larger systems of provisioning and economy, and the interplay, if not contradiction, between these behavioural realities and local cultural ideas about gender.

(2) *Evolutionary biology of women:* Men's activities, especially in relation to hunting and reproductive success, have been productively studied in several hunter-gatherer societies (Smith 2004). Similar perspectives and methods could be applied to grasp more clearly the complexities and subtleties of women's lives and, therefore, of human populations *in toto* as evolutionary products. Perhaps because women's reproductive success tends to vary less than men's, it is assumed that men are the drivers of evolution. This is a faulty assumption. Women invest the most in reproduction and in ensuring the successful rearing of offspring. Additional studies of the challenges faced by women in hunter-gatherer societies, including such issues as maternal mortality, infertility, and domestic violence against both women and their children, would provide insight into the development of and selection for maternal strategies and behaviours and their implications for evolutionary change.

(3) *Relations with the sacred:* More research is needed on how hunter-gatherers engage with the spirits or spirit-animal beings that are fundamental to their livelihood, their place in the cosmos, and their cultural interpretations of causality. Is the nature of these transactions different for women and men or are any differences minor variations on a singe theme? Either way, we need a more sophisticated understanding of how modes of accessing spirit-beings translate into uses of sacred power and influences upon people (women upon men, men upon women, and so forth) in social life. Taboos upon menstruating women, and their potential defilement of men's hunting equipment, are widely reported in the literature on hunter-gatherers and may leave the impression of an almost universal suppression of women via magico-religious sanctions. Less widely reported, but with major implications for interpreting gender relations, is the fact that among some hunter-gatherers, such as the Iñupiat, it is the wife's generous, skilful comportment (or spiritual condition) which attracts the animals harvested by her husband (Bodenhorn 1990, 61–2). In a related vein, arrows are widely traded and given as gifts among the !Kung San. It is the owner of an arrow, whether man or woman, who becomes the owner of an animal killed with

that particular weapon and, thus, has rights over subsequent distribution of the meat (Lee 1979, 246–8; Marshall 1976, 296–9).

(4) *Childhood and youth culture:* A compelling, comprehensive treatment of hunter-gatherer child-rearing and childhood has yet to be written. Yet, the formative experiences of children are crucial in constructing the gender roles informing adult behaviour in later years. More systematic attention to the corpus of play activities, lore and games, miniatures and toys, and adult supervision and mentoring of girls and boys in the early phases of work will reveal cultural expectations about gender in adulthood.

(5) *Life histories and gendered personalities:* Building upon the previous point, penetrating biography can link the socialization of children with their development into complex multi-dimensional adults. Life histories are particularly useful for contextualizing individual choices and actions within the complexities of circumstance, time, and place. A promising avenue for future investigation involves the construction of paired biographies, such as husbands and wives, or brothers and sisters. By controlling for similarity in cultural and community background, such material will shed light on women's and men's coping strategies across years and generations, the extent of their power and influence, and how these patterns may be informed by culturally specific ideas about gender and personality.

(6) *Alternative gender identities:* Variability in gender formation within particular hunter-gatherer societies deserves further investigation. Third- and fourth-gender personae illustrate the creativity and flexibility of gender while underscoring what is conventionally female and male within a particular cultural milieu.

(7) *Colonial transformations:* How hunter-gatherers have interacted with farming peoples, or indeed have become farmers and agro-pastoralists, has received considerable attention by anthropologists (Kent 1989; Schrire 1980). With notable exceptions (Wilmsen 1989), the historical process by which external agents, markets, and state-level societies have dislocated, enumerated, classified, monitored, and managed hunter-gatherer groups has, perhaps, received less attention. Consciously or otherwise, the bureaucratic machinery of the nation state may impose gender ideologies of the dominant society upon its administered minorities and underclasses. The forms of 'gender surveillance' and 'gender management' facilitated by various statutes and policies for indigenous peoples, and how these have been resisted or accommodated by hunter-gatherer communities, is a potentially rich field of study.

REFERENCES

Ackerman, L. A. 2002. Gender equality in a contemporary Indian community. In L. Frink, R. S. Shepard, and G. A. Reinhardt (eds),*Many faces of gender: roles and relationships through time in indigenous northern communities*, 27–36. Boulder: Colorado University Press.

Alexandersen, V. 1993. Teeth. In S. Hvass and B. Storgaard (eds), *Digging into the past: 25 years of archaeology in Denmark*, 81. Aarhus: Aarhus University Press.

Arnold, B. and Wicker, N. L. (eds) 2001. *Gender and the archaeology of death*. Walnut Creek, CA: AltaMira Press.

Barry III, H. and Schlegel, A. 1982. Cross-cultural codes on contribution by women to subsistence. *Ethnology* 21, 165–88.

Berndt, C. H. 1981. 'Interpretations and facts' in Aboriginal Australia. In F. Dahlberg (ed.), *Woman the gatherer*, 153–203. New Haven: Yale University Press.

Binford, L. R. 1978. *Nunamiut ethnoarchaeology*. New York: Academic Press.

Bird, C. F. M. 1993. Woman the toolmaker: evidence for women's use and manufacture of flaked stone tools in Australia and New Guinea. In H. Du Cros and L. Smith (eds), *Women in archaeology: a feminist critique*, 22–30. Canberra: Australian National University.

Blackman, M. B. 1982. *During my time: Florence Edenshaw Davidson, a Haida woman*. Seattle: University of Washington Press.

Blackman, M. B. 1989. *Sadie Brower Neakok: an Inupiaq woman*. Seattle: University of Washington Press.

Blankholm, H. P. 2008. Southern Scandinavia. In G. Bailey and P. Spikins (eds), *Mesolithic Europe*, 107–31. Cambridge: Cambridge University Press.

Bodenhorn, B. 1990. 'I'm not the great hunter, my wife is': Iñupiat and anthropological models of gender. *Etudes/Inuit/Studies* 14, 55–74.

Briggs, J. L. 1970. *Never in anger: portrait of an Eskimo family*. Cambridge, MA: Harvard University Press.

Brightman, R. 1996. The sexual division of foraging labor: biology, taboo, and gender politics. *Comparative Studies in Society and History* 38, 687–729.

Brumbach, H. J. and Jarvenpa, R. 1997a. Woman the hunter: ethnoarchaeological lessons from Chipewyan life-cycle dynamics. In C. Claassen and R. A. Joyce (eds), *Women in prehistory: North America and Mesoamerica*, 17–32. Philadelphia: University of Pennsylvania Press.

Brumbach, H. J. and Jarvenpa, R. 1997b. Ethnoarchaeology of subsistence space and gender: a subarctic Dene case. *American Antiquity* 62, 414–36.

Brumbach, H. J. and Jarvenpa, R. 2006. Gender dynamics in hunter-gatherer society: archaeological methods and perspectives. In S. M. Nelson (ed.) *Handbook of gender in archaeology*, 503–35. Lanham, MD: AltaMira Press.

Buckley, T. 1982. Menstruation and the power of Yurok women. *American Ethnologist* 9, 47–90.

Budja, M. 2009. Ceramic trajectories: from figurines to vessels. In P. Jordan and M. Zvelebil (eds), *Ceramics before farming: the dispersal of pottery among prehistoric Eurasian hunter-gatherers*, 499–525. Walnut Creek, CA: Left Coast Press.

Casey, J. 1998. Just a formality: the presence of fancy projectile points in a basic tool assemblage. In S. Kent (ed.), *Gender in African prehistory*, 83–103. Walnut Creek, CA: AltaMira Press.

Claassen, C. P. 1991. Gender, shellfishing and the shell mound archaic. In J. M. Gero and M. W. Conkey (eds), *Engendering archaeology: women and prehistory*, 276–300. Oxford: Blackwell.

Claassen, C. and Joyce, R. A. (eds) 1997. *Women in prehistory: North America and Mesoamerica*. Philadelphia: University of Pennsylvania Press.

Clark, A. M. 1996. *Who lived in this house?* Hull, Quebec: Canadian Museum of Civilization.

Clastres, P. 1987. *Society against the state: essays in political anthropology*. New York: Zone.

Cohen, M. N. and Bennett, S. 1993. Skeletal evidence for sex roles and gender hierarchies in prehistory. In B. D. Miller (ed.), *Sex and gender hierarchies*, 273–96. Cambridge: Cambridge University Press.

Conkey, M. W. and Spector, J. D. 1984. Archaeology and the study of gender. In M. B. Schiffer (ed.), *Advances in archaeological method and theory*, Vol. 7, 1–38. New York: Academic Press.

Constandse-Westermann, T. S. and Newell, R. R. 1989. Limb lateralisation and social stratification in western Mesolithic societies. In I. Herkovitz (ed.), *People and culture change*, 405–34. Oxford: British Archaeological Reports International Series 508.

Cooke, H. 1998. Fieldwork, mothering and the prehistoric people of Blue Water Holes, Kosciuszko National Park. In M. Casey, D. Donlon, J. Hope, and S. Wellfare (eds), *Redefining archaeology: feminist perspectives*, 55–62. Canberra: The Australian National Museum.

Counts, D. 1985. Tamparonga: the big women of Kaliai (Papua New Guinea). In J. Brown and V. Kerns (eds), *In her prime: a new view of middle-aged women*, 49–64. South Hadley, MA: Bergin & Garvey.

Crass, B. A. 2002. Child and infant burials in the arctic. In L. Frink, R. S. Shepard, and G. A. Reinhardt (eds), *Many faces of gender: roles and relationships through time in indigenous northern communities*, 111–20. Boulder: Colorado University Press.

Cruikshank, J. (with A. Sydney, K. Smith, and A. Ned) 1990. *Life lived like a story: life stories of three Yukon native elders*. Lincoln: University of Nebraska Press.

Dahlberg, F. (ed.) 1981. *Woman the gatherer*. New Haven: Yale University Press.

Ember, C. R. 1978. Myths about hunter-gatherers. *Ethnology* 17, 439–48.

Endicott, K. I. 1999. Gender relations in hunter-gatherer society. In R. B. Lee and R. Daly (eds), *The Cambridge encyclopedia of hunters and gatherers*, 411–18. Cambridge: Cambridge University Press.

Estokio-Griffin, A. and Griffin, B. 1981. Woman the hunter: the Agta. In F. Dahlberg (ed.), *Woman the gatherer*, 121–51. New Haven: Yale University Press.

Fewster, K. J. 2001. Petso's field: ethnoarchaeology and agency. In K. J. Fewster and M. Zvelebil (eds), *Ethnoarchaeology and hunter-gatherers: pictures at an exhibition*, 81–9. Oxford: BAR International Series 955.

Fortune, R. F. 1939. Arapesh warfare. *American Anthropologist* 41, 22–41.

Freeman, D. 1982. *Margaret Mead and Samoa: the making and unmaking of an anthropological myth*. Ann Arbor: Books on Demand.

Frink, L. 2002. Fish tales: women and decision making in western Alaska. In L. Frink, R. S. Shepard, and G. A. Reinhardt (eds), *Many faces of gender: roles and relationships through time in indigenous northern communities*, 93–108. Boulder: Colorado University Press.

Frink, L. 2009. The identity division of labor in native Alaska. *American Anthropologist* 111, 21–9.

Frink, L. and Harry, K. G. 2008. The beauty of 'ugly' Eskimo cooking pots. *American Antiquity* 73, 103–20.

Gero, J. 1991. Genderlithics: women's roles in stone tool production. In J. M. Gero and M. W. Conkey (eds), *Engendering archaeology: women and prehistory*, 163–93. Oxford: Blackwell.

Gero, J. and Conkey, M. W. (eds) 1991. *Engendering archaeology: women and prehistory*. Oxford: Blackwell.

Glavatskaya, E. 2006. Khanty hunter-fisher-herders: a task differentiation analysis of Trom'Agan women's and men's subsistence activities. In R. Jarvenpa and H. J. Brumbach (eds), *Circumpolar lives and livelihood: a comparative ethnoarchaeology of gender and subsistence*, 115–57. Lincoln: University of Nebraska Press.

Goodale, J. C. 1971. *Tiwi wives: a study of the women of Melville Island, North Australia*. Seattle: University of Washington Press.

Goodman, A., Martin, D., Armelagos, G. J., and Clark, G. 1984. Health changes at Dickson Mounds, Illinois (AD 950–1300). In M. N. Cohen and G. J. Armelagos (eds), *Paleopathology at the origins of agriculture*, 271–306. New York: Academic Press.

Halperin, R. 1980. Ecology and mode of production: seasonal variation and the division of labor by sex among hunter-gatherers. *Journal of Anthropological Research* 36, 379–99.

Hawkes, K. and Bliege Bird, R. 2002. Showing off, handicap signaling, and the evolution of men's work. *Evolutionary Anthropology* 11, 58–67.

Hayden, B. 1992a. Observing prehistoric women. In C. Claassen (ed.), *Exploring gender through archaeology: selected papers from the 1991 Boone Conference*, 33–47. Madison: Prehistory Press.

Hayden, B. 1992b. Conclusions: ecology and complex hunter-gatherers. In B. Hayden (ed.), *A complex culture of the British Columbia plateau: traditional Stl'átl'imx resource use*, 525–63. Vancouver: UBC Press.

Hayden, B. 1995. The emergence of prestige technologies and pottery. In W. Barnett and J. Hoopes (eds), *The emergence of pottery*, 257–66. Washington, DC: Smithsonian Institution.

Hill, K. and Kaplan, H. 1993. On why male foragers hunt and share food. *Current Anthropology* 34, 701–6.

Hodder, I. 1982. *Symbols in action: ethnoarchaeological studies in material culture*. Cambridge: Cambridge University Press.

Hollimon, S. 1991. Health consequences of divisions of labor among the Chumash Indians of southern California. In D. Walde and N. D. Willows (eds), *The archaeology of gender: proceedings of the 22nd Annual Chacmool Conference*, 462–9. Calgary: University of Calgary.

Hollimon, S. 1992. Health consequences of sexual division of labor among prehistoric Native Americans: the Chumash of California and the Arikara of the North Plains. In C. Claassen (ed.), *Exploring gender through archaeology: selected papers from the 1991 Boone Conference*, 81–8. Madison: Prehistory Press.

Hollimon, S. 1997. The third gender in native California: two-spirit undertakers among the Chumash and their neighbors. In C. Claassen and R. A. Joyce (eds), *Women in prehistory: North America and Mesoamerica*, 173–88. Philadelphia: University of Pennsylvania Press.

Holmes, L. D. 1986. *Quest for the real Samoa: the Mead-Freeman controversy and beyond*. Westport, CT: Greenwood Press.

Janes, R. R. 1983. *Archaeological ethnography among Mackenzie Basin Dene, Canada*. Calgary: Arctic Institute of North America.

Jarvenpa, R. 1998. *Northern passage: ethnography and apprenticeship among the subarctic Dene*. Prospect Heights: Waveland Press.

Jarvenpa, R. 2004. Chipewyan. In C. R. Ember and M. Ember (eds), *Encyclopedia of sex and gender: men and women in the world's cultures*, 371–9. New York: Kluwer Academic/Plenum Press.

Jarvenpa, R. and Brumbach, H. J. 1995. Ethnoarchaeology and gender: Chipewyan women as hunters. *Research in Economic Anthropology* 16, 39–82.

Jarvenpa, R. and Brumbach, H. J. 1999. The gendered nature of living and storage space in the Canadian subarctic. In N. L. Wicker and B. Arnold (eds), *From the ground up: beyond gender theory in archaeology*, 107–23. Oxford: BAR International Series 812.

Jarvenpa, R. and Brumbach, H. J. 2006a. The sexual division of labor revisited: thoughts on ethnoarchaeology and gender. In W. Ashmore, M. Dobres, S. Nelson, and A. Rosen (eds), *Integrating the diversity of 21st century anthropology: the life and intellectual legacies of Susan Kent*, 97–107. Arlington: Archaeological Papers of the American Anthropological Association Number 16.

Jarvenpa, R. and Brumbach, H. J. 2006b. *Circumpolar lives and livelihood: a comparative ethnoarchaeology of gender and subsistence*. Lincoln: University of Nebraska Press.

Jarvenpa, R. and Brumbach, H. J. 2006c. Chipewyan hunters: a task differentiation analysis. In R. Jarvenpa and H. J. Brumbach (eds), *Circumpolar lives and livelihood: a comparative ethnoarchaeology of gender and subsistence*, 54–78. Lincoln: University of Nebraska Press.

Jarvenpa, R. and Brumbach, H. J. 2007. Ethnoarchaeological perspectives on gender and subsistence: circumpolar patterns and comparisons. In A. V. Kharinsky (ed.), *The ethnohistory and archaeology of northern Eurasia: theory, methods and practice*, 440–51. Irkutsk, Russia: Irkutsk State Technical University Press.

Jarvenpa, R. and Brumbach, H. J. 2009. Fun with Dick and Jane: ethnoarchaeology, circumpolar toolkits and gender 'inequality'? *Ethnoarchaeology: Journal of Archaeological, Ethnographic and Experimental Studies* 1, 57–77.

Jochim, M. A. 1988. Optimal foraging and the division of labor. *American Anthropologist* 90, 130–6.

Jolles, C. Z. 2002. Celebration of a life: remembering Linda Womkon Badten, Yupik Educator. In L. Frink, R. S. Shepard, and G. A. Reinhardt (eds), *Many faces of gender: roles and relationships through time in indigenous northern communities*, 37–57. Boulder: Colorado University Press.

Jolles, C. Z. 2006. Iñupiaq maritime hunters: summer subsistence work in Diomede. In R. Jarvenpa and H. J. Brumbach (eds), *Circumpolar lives and livelihood: a comparative ethnoarchaeology of gender and subsistence*, 263–86. Lincoln: University of Nebraska Press.

Jordan, P. 2003. *Material culture and sacred landscape: the anthropology of the Siberian Khanty*. Walnut Creek, CA: AltaMira Press.

Jordan, P. and Zvelebil, M. 2009. *Ex oriente lux*: the prehistory of hunter-gatherer ceramic dispersals. In P. Jordan and M. Zvelebil (eds), *Ceramics before farming: the dispersal of pottery among prehistoric Eurasian hunter-gatherers*, 33–89. Walnut Creek, CA: Left Coast Press.

Kaplan, H. and Hill, K. 1985. Hunting ability and reproductive success among male Ache foragers: preliminary results. *Current Anthropology* 26, 131–3.

Kehoe, A. B. 1990. Points and lines. In S. M. Nelson and A. B. Kehoe (eds), *Powers of observation: alternative views in archeology*, 23–37. Archeological Papers of the American Anthropological Association Number 2.

Kelly, R. L. 1995. *The foraging spectrum: diversity in hunter-gatherer lifeways*. Washington, DC: Smithsonian Institution.

Kensinger, K. M. 1989. Hunting and male domination in Cashinahua Society. In S. Kent (ed.), *Farmers as hunters: the implications of sedentism*, 18–26. Cambridge: Cambridge University Press.

Kent, S. (ed.) 1989. *Farmers as hunters: the implications of sedentism*. Cambridge: Cambridge University Press.

Kent, S. 1998. Invisible gender–invisible foragers: southern African hunter-gatherer spatial patterning and the archaeological record. In S. Kent (ed.), *Gender in African prehistory*, 39–67. Walnut Creek, CA: AltaMira Press.

Leacock, E. B. 1978. Women's status in egalitarian societies: implications for social evolution. *Current Anthropology* 19, 247–75.

Leacock, E. B. 1981. *Myths of male dominance*. New York: Monthly Review Press.

Leacock, E. B. 1983. Ideologies of male dominance and divide and rule politics: an anthropologist's view. In M. Lowe and R. Hubbard (eds), *Women's nature*, 111–21. New York: Pergamon Press.

Lee, R. B. 1979. *The !Kung San: men, women and work in a foraging society*. Cambridge: Cambridge University Press.

Lee, R. B. and DeVore, I. (eds) 1968. *Man the hunter*. Chicago: Aldine.

LeMoine, G. 2003. Woman of the house: gender, architecture, and ideology in Dorset prehistory. *Arctic Anthropology* 40, 121–38.

Levinson, D. and Malone, M. J. 1980. *Toward explaining human culture: a critical review of the findings of worldwide cross-cultural research*. New Haven: HRAF Press.

Lips, J. E. 1947. *The origin of things*. New York: A. A. Wyn.

Marshall, L. 1976. *The !Kung of Nyae Nyae*. Cambridge, MA: Harvard University Press.

Mead, M. 1935. *Sex and temperament in three primitive societies.* New York: William Morrow.

Meiklejohn, C. and Zvelebil, M. 1991. Health status of European populations at the agricultural transition and the implications for farming. In H. Bush and M. Zvelebil (eds), *Health status in past societies: biocultural interpretations of human skeletal remains in archaeological contexts,* 129–45. Oxford: BAR International Series 567.

Meiklejohn, C., Petersen, E. B., and Alexandersen, V. 2000. The anthropology and archaeology of Mesolithic gender in the western Baltic. In M. Donald and L. Hurcombe (eds), *Gender and material culture in archaeological perspective,* 222–37. London: Macmillan.

Morgen, S. (ed.) 1989. *Gender and anthropology.* Washington, DC: American Anthropological Association.

Moss, M. L. 1993. Shellfish, gender, and status on the Northwest Coast: reconciling archaeological, ethnographic, and ethnohistoric records on the Tlingit. *American Anthropologist* 95, 631–52.

Nelson, S. M. 1990. Diversity of the upper Paleolithic 'Venus' figurines and archaeological mythology. In S. M. Nelson and A. B. Kehoe (eds), *Powers of observation: alternative views in archaeology,* 11–22. Archaeological Papers of the American Anthropological Association, 2. Washington, DC: American Anthropological Association.

Nelson, S. M. 1997. *Gender in archaeology: analyzing power and prestige.* Walnut Creek, CA: AltaMira Press.

Nelson, S. M. (ed.) 2006. *Handbook of gender in archaeology.* Lanham, MD: AltaMira Press.

Ortner, S. and Whitehead, H. 1981. *Sexual meanings: the cultural construction of gender and sexuality.* Cambridge: Cambridge University Press.

Osgood, C. 1940. *Ingalik material culture.* New Haven: Yale University Publications in Anthropology 22.

Park, R. W. 2005. Growing up north: exploring the archaeology of childhood in the Thule and Dorset cultures of arctic Canada. In J. E. Baxter (ed.), *Children in action: perspectives on the archaeology of childhood,* 53–64. Arlington: Archeological Papers of the American Anthropological Association 15.

Pennanen, J. 2006. Sámi reindeer herders: a task differentiation analysis: In R. Jarvenpa and H. J. Brumbach (eds), *Circumpolar lives and livelihood: a comparative ethnoarchaeology of gender and subsistence,* 186–237. Lincoln: University of Nebraska Press.

Quinn, N. 1977. Anthropological studies on women's status. *Annual Review of Anthropology* 6, 181–225.

Reinhardt, G. A. 2002. Puzzling out gender-specific 'sides' to a prehistoric house in Barrow, Alaska. In L. Frink, R. S. Shepard, and G. A. Reinhardt (eds), *Many faces of gender: roles and relationships through time in indigenous northern communities,* 121–50. Boulder: Colorado University Press.

Reiter, R. R. 1975. *Toward an anthropology of women.* New York: Monthly Review Press.

Rosaldo, M. 1980. The use and abuse of anthropology: reflections on feminism and cross-cultural understanding. *Signs: Journal of Women in Culture and Society* 5, 389–417.

Rosaldo, M. and Lamphere, L. (eds) 1974. *Woman, culture and society.* Stanford: Stanford University Press.

Roscoe, W. 1994. How to become a berdache: toward a unified analysis of gender diversity. In G. Herdt (ed.), *Third sex. Third gender: beyond sexual dimorphism in culture and history,* 329–72. Cambridge, MA: MIT Press.

Sacks, K. 1979. *Sisters and wives: the past and future of sexual equality.* Westport, CT: Greenwood Press.

Sanday, P. 1981. *Female power and male dominance: on the origins of sexual inequality.* Cambridge: Cambridge University Press.

Sassaman, K. E. 1992. Gender and technology at the archaic-woodland transition. In C. Claassen (ed.), *Exploring gender through archaeology: selected papers from the 1991 Boone Conference*, 71–9. Madison: Prehistory Press.

Sassaman, K. E. 1993. *Early pottery in the southeast: tradition and innovation in cooking technology*. Tuscaloosa: University of Alabama Press.

Schrire, C. 1980. An inquiry into the evolutionary status and apparent identity of the San hunter-gatherers. *Human Ecology* 8, 1–32.

Scott, J. C. 1998. *Seeing like a state: how certain schemes to improve the human condition have failed*. New Haven: Yale University Press.

Sealy, J. C., Patrick, M. K., Morris, A. G., and Alder, D. 1992. Diet and dental caries among later stone age inhabitants of the Cape Province, South Africa. *American Journal of Physical Anthropology* 88, 123–34.

Sharp, H. S. 1981. The null case: the Chipewyan. In F. Dahlberg (ed.), *Woman the gatherer*, 221–44. New Haven: Yale University Press.

Sharp, H. S. 1988. *The transformation of bigfoot: maleness, power and belief among the Chipewyan*. Washington, DC: Smithsonian Institution.

Sharp, H. S. 1991. Dry meat and gender: the absence of Chipewyan ritual for the regulation of hunting and animal numbers. In T. Ingold, D. Riches, and J. Woodburn (eds), *Hunters and gatherers: property, power and ideology*, 183–91. New York: Berg.

Shepard, R. S. 2002. Changing residence patterns and intradomestic role changes: causes and effects in nineteenth century western Alaska. In L. Frink, R. S. Shepard, and G. A. Reinhardt (eds), *Many faces of gender: roles and relationships through time in indigenous northern communities*, 1–79. Boulder: Colorado University Press.

Shostak, M. 1981. *Nisa: the life and words of a !Kung woman*. Cambridge, MA: Harvard University Press.

Smith, A. B. 1999. Archaeology and the evolution of hunters and gatherers. In R. B. Lee and R. Daly (eds), *The Cambridge encyclopedia of hunters and gatherers*, 384–90. Cambridge: Cambridge University Press.

Smith, D. M. 1973. *Inkonze: magico-religious beliefs of contact-traditional Chipewyan trading at Fort Resolution, NWT, Canada*. Ottawa: National Museum of Man Mercury Series, Ethnology Division Paper No. 6.

Smith, D. M. 1982. *Moose-Deer Island House people: a history of the native people of Fort Resolution*. Ottawa: National Museum of Man Mercury Series, Canadian Ethnology Service Paper No. 81.

Smith, E. A. 2004. Why do good hunters have higher reproductive success? *Human Nature* 15, 343–64.

Smith, P., Bar-Yosef, O., and Sillen, A. 1984. Archaeological and skeletal evidence for dietary change during the late Pleistocene/early Holocene in the Levant. In M. N. Cohen and G. J. Armelagos (eds), *Paleopathology at the origins of agriculture*, 101–36. New York: Academic Press.

Spector, J. D. 1983. Male/female task differentiation among the Hidatsa: toward the development of an archaeological approach to the study of gender. In P. Albers and B. Medicine (eds), *The hidden half*, 77–99. Washington, DC: University Press of America.

Spector, J. D. and Whelan, M. K. 1989. Incorporating gender into archaeology courses. In S. Morgen (ed.), *Gender and anthropology*, 65–94. Washington, DC: American Anthropological Association.

Stewart, H. 2002. *Kipijuituq*in Netsilik society: changing patterns of gender and patterns of changing gender. In L. Frink, R. S. Shepard, and G. A. Reinhardt (eds), *Many faces of* *gender: roles and relationships through time in indigenous northern communities*, 3–25. Boulder: Colorado University Press.

Torrence, R. 2001. Hunter-gatherer technology: macro- and microscale approaches. In C. Panter-Brick, R. H. Layton, and P. Rowley-Conwy (eds), *Hunter-gatherers: an interdisciplinary perspective*, 73–98. Cambridge: Cambridge University Press.

Wadley, L. 1998. The invisible meat providers: women in the stone age of South Africa. In S. Kent (ed.), *Gender in African prehistory*, 69–81. Walnut Creek, CA: AltaMira Press.

Wadley, L. 2000. The use of space in a gender study of two South African stone age sites. In M. Donald and L. Hurcombe (eds), *Gender and material culture in archaeological perspective*, 153–68. Basingstoke: Macmillan.

Walker, P. L. and Erlandson, J. M. 1986. Dental evidence for prehistoric dietary change on the Northern Channel Islands, California. *American Antiquity* 51, 375–83.

Watson, P. J. and Kennedy, M. C. 1991. The development of horticulture in the eastern woodlands of North America: women's role. In J. M. Gero and M. W. Conkey (eds), *Engendering archaeology: women and prehistory*, 255–75. Oxford: Blackwell.

Weedman Arthur, K. 2010. Feminine knowledge and skill reconsidered: women and flaked stone tools. *American Anthropologist* 112, 228–43.

Whitridge, P. 2002. Gender, households, and the material construction of social difference: metal consumption at a classic Thule whaling village. In L. Frink, R. S. Shepard, and G. A. Reinhardt (eds), *Many faces of gender: roles and relationships through time in indigenous northern communities*, 165–92. Boulder: Colorado University Press.

Whitridge, P. 2007. Sexed things: material discourses on women's work in precontact Nunatsiavut. Paper presented at the 106th Annual Meeting of the American Anthropological Association. Washington, DC.

Wicker, N. L. and Arnold, B. (eds) 1999. *From the ground up: beyond gender theory in archaeology*. Oxford: BAR International Series 812.

Williams, W. L. 1986. *The spirit and the flesh: sexual diversity in American Indian culture*. Boston: Beacon Press.

Wilmsen, E. N. 1989. *Land filled with flies: a political economy of the Kalahari*. Chicago: University of Chicago Press.

Winterhalder, B. 2001. The behavioural ecology of hunter-gatherers. In C. Panter-Brick, R. H. Layton, and P. Rowley-Conwy (eds), *Hunter-gatherers: an interdisciplinary perspective*, 12–38. Cambridge: Cambridge University Press.

Wright, R. P. (ed.) 1996. *Gender and archaeology*. Philadelphia: University of Pennsylvania Press.

Zvelebil, M. 2000. Fat is a feminist issue: on ideology, diet and health in hunter-gatherer societies. In M. Donald and L. Hurcombe (eds), *Gender and material culture in archaeological perspective*, 209–21. Basingstoke: Macmillan.

Zvelebil, M. 2008. Innovating hunter-gatherers: the Mesolithic in the Baltic. In G. Bailey and P. Spikins (eds), *Mesolithic Europe*, 18–59. Cambridge: Cambridge University Press.

CHAPTER 61

HUNTER-GATHERER DIET, SUBSISTENCE, AND FOODWAYS

RICK SCHULTING

This chapter concerns the diet, subsistence, and foodways of hunter-gatherers, from both an anthropological and archaeological perspective, and on a worldwide basis. Comprehensive treatment of such a vast topic clearly lies beyond the present remit, and the discussion will necessarily be selective, highlighting some key topics and questions. An important point to keep in mind throughout what follows is that there is great variability in hunter-gatherer societies around the world; indeed, they are perhaps best defined by what they are *not*, i.e. farmers and herders. A basic division between 'generalized' and 'complex' hunter-gatherers has proved useful for some purposes, including characterizing subsistence practices (Kelly 1995; Price and Brown 1985; Testart 1982; Woodburn 1982). While some would argue that such typological divisions have outlived their usefulness, the fact that many writings on hunter-gatherers continue to implicitly emphasize the 'simple' end of the spectrum as somehow providing more 'genuine' insights would suggest that the existence of the full spectrum still needs to be acknowledged (cf. Kelly 1995). A question that has vexed many hunter-gatherer researchers is how to deal with such a range of societies under a single rubric, and, indeed, whether this is even possible.

In increasingly broad scope: *diet* refers simply to the foods that were eaten, always a sub-set of those potentially available; *subsistence* refers to the ways in which dietary items are acquired, including the technologies involved in both capture and preparation, and the organization of labour; finally, and most broadly, *foodways* refer to the entire set of activities, symbolism, and beliefs surrounding the acquisition, preparation, and serving of food. It is here that foods act to distinguish gender and age groups, to foster family and group identity, and, in some cases, to support an ethos of strict egalitarianism, while in others to legitimize socio-political inequality.

DIET AND SUBSISTENCE

At the most basic level, hunter-gatherers hunt (and fish) and gather what is available in their environment. They do not plant and tend crops, or at least not major food crops, and they do not keep domestic animals, other than the dog, or, via other sources, the horse, both of which were commonly used for purposes other than consumption. Hunter-gatherers have occupied most environments around the world for many thousands of years, and so it is not surprising that they demonstrate diverse diets and subsistence practices. Many were what Flannery (1969) has referred to as 'broad-spectrum' foragers, making use of a wide range of resources. Others were far more specialized, from the bison hunters of the North American Plains in the eighteenth and nineteenth centuries, to the large game hunters of Upper Palaeolithic Eurasia and the Holocene Arctic. The Epi-Palaeolithic Natufian's concentration on stands of wild grasses led—albeit in combination with other circumstances (Rowley-Conwy 2001)—to the earliest known domestication event in the world. Many groups in southern California, both ancient and historic, relied heavily on acorns (Basgall 1987), as did the Jomon of Japan on chestnuts (Imamura 1996; Matsui and Kanehara 2006); indeed, both would no doubt be classed as agriculturalists if these trees had been faster-growing plants amenable to domestication, and the morphological changes and dependency on humans that this concept entails (Rindos 1984). Driving this point home, ancient DNA (aDNA) in waterlogged chestnut remains from the Jomon site of Sannai Maruyama reportedly shows less diversity than would be expected in a wild population, raising the possibility of the planting or selective retention of trees (Sato et al. 2003; see also Mitchell 2005 re: oil palms in sub-Saharan Africa). The Jomon also present an interesting case of animal introduction. 'Wild' boar found on archaeological sites on Hokkaido are thought not to have been present naturally on the island; if this is correct, they must have been taken across from either northern Honshu or Sakhalin (as shown by aDNA analysis of archaeological boar remains) as young animals and then raised in captivity or intentionally released into the wild (Watanobe et al. 2004). The possibility of wild pig management has also been raised for the circum-Baltic Mesolithic (Zvelebil 1995).

The ways in which people exploited this wide range of resources varied enormously, and understanding this variation is one of the main goals of anthropologists and archaeologists. In some cases the nature of a species—its size, behaviour, and habitat—strongly influences capture methods used (small fish, for example, can only be exploited efficiently with the use of nets), while in others few such restraints apply, so that deer, for example, can be either stalked by a single hunter, or taken in massive game drives involving entire communities. The role of technology is a crucial one here, as the exploitation of many species requires highly specialized equipment (cf. Hayden 1990), for example sturdy sea-going craft and complex composite harpoons and floats to hunt large whales on the open ocean, as did the Nuu-chah-nulth and Makah of the Northwest Coast of North America and the Ainu of Hokkaido (Drucker 1951; Watanabe 1972). This raises an important point: the simple presence of a 'rich' habitat does not in and of itself mean that the foods in it are easily available for human consumption; there are often technological, as well as organizational, constraints. The ability to take large surpluses at certain times of the year, for example of salmon on the Northwest Coast of North America, is pointless without the concomitant capacity to preserve and store them, and it is often this that is the limiting factor, rather than simple availability (cf. Shnirelman 1992). There is also the issue of the purpose of such surpluses: for many generalized hunter-gatherers, there is simply no incentive to produce beyond immediate needs.

A relatively recent development has been the growing appreciation of the extent to which hunter-gatherers modified their environments and engaged in practices that, were the species involved more malleable, would doubtless have led to domestication (e.g. Bleed and Matsui 2010). This area of research has become theorized as 'niche construction', linked with broader evolutionary processes (Smith 2011). A prime example is the evidence for the intentional and controlled use of fire to encourage certain desired plants and animals, by artificially creating, extending, and maintaining their preferred habitat. Evidence for this practice is wide-ranging, and is particularly convincing when documented ethnographically, as it is for many Australian Aboriginal groups (Lourandos 1997), as well as for some regions of North America (Boyd 1986; Lewis and Bean 1973). Its detection in the past record is more difficult, relying on the interpretation of microscopic charcoal in sediments, which of course could also be the result of natural fires; nevertheless, a number of cases have been proposed and debated, including Mesolithic Britain (Moore 2000) and Jomon Japan (Imamura 1996, 106).

Perhaps less well known are cases of the transplantation and/or tending of wild plants by hunter-gatherers, in some cases certainly qualifying as horticulture. In some parts of the world, it is conceivable, and indeed likely, that this practice was the precursor to domestication. Broadcast sowing of wild seeds is reported for the Great Basin of North America, as is, more controversially, the pre-contact construction of large-scale irrigation ditches to create artificially flooded upland meadows, thereby recreating productive lowland water meadows (Downs 1966; Lawton et al. 1976). Native tobaccos, intended largely for ceremonial use, were widely grown throughout North America, and were often encouraged through pruning or transplanting. In some cases, however, such interference—literally an uprooting from their natural environment—was seen as impairing the efficacy of plants, especially medicinal plants (Fowler 1999). At least two root crops on the Northwest Coast of North America—springbank clover (*Trifolium wormskioldii*) and Pacific silverweed (*Potentillan anserine* spp. *pacifica*)—were specially tended by some groups in labour-intensive plots that were known as gardens, and were individually owned and inherited (Turner and Kuhnlein 1982). They were not used as a staple food, however, but rather were served at special feasts, starchy foods being much appreciated in what was a very high-protein diet (cf. Speth and Spielmann 1983). Archaeologically, evidence for the importance of other wild root crops in the region, most notably camas (*Camassia* spp.), takes the form of numerous roasting pits in upland locations. Complex cooking processes were required for some of these foods (Peacock 2008; Turner and Kuhnlein 1982), as indeed was also the case for tannic chestnuts and acorns (Basgall 1987; Imamura 1996; Kobayashi 2004).

A number of aquatic species were also susceptible to manipulation. Again, it is the fact that the reproductive cycles of many aquatic species have been, until very recently, beyond human control that prevented them from being 'domesticated'. From the Northwest Coast of North America, ethnographic accounts document the anchoring of hemlock boughs in tidal waters during herring spawning season; the abundant and nutritious eggs adhered to the boughs and were collected and consumed either fresh or dried (Emmons and de Laguna 1991). It is unlikely that traces of activities such as this would ever be recognized archaeologically. A practice that has recently come to light—at least to the academic community, since they were never forgotten by First Nations elders—is the extent to which artificially enhanced intertidal habitats, known as 'clam gardens', were created by some Northwest Coast groups (Williams 2006). Elsewhere, at Mount William and Toolondo in south-west Victoria, Australia, extensive networks of canals running several kilometres were dug to connect coastal and inland drainages, artificially extending and controlling the habitat for spawning eels (Lourandos 1997; Williams 1988). These then formed an important seasonal resource enabling large-scale social/ceremonial aggregations, which indeed appear to have been the main motivation for the considerable labour required to build and maintain the canals, recalling Hayden's (1990) proposal that the main impetus behind intensification was, at least initially, for feasting rather than day-to-day subsistence.

Foodways

Gender and Age

Diet and subsistence are closely linked with gender in hunter-gatherer studies, revolving first and foremost around the stereotypical view of men as hunters and women as gatherers (Dahlberg 1981; Lee and DeVore 1968). While on the one hand much ethnographic support exists for this position, on the other it can be questioned on a number of levels. One main objection to this gender-based division of labour appears to be not so much its existence, but the ways in which women's roles and economic contributions are supposedly devalued when based largely on gathered foods. This position itself has much to do with our own attitudes to meat and the generally high value placed on it, though it should be noted that many hunter-gatherer informants, including women, also value meat more highly than plant foods, and may speak of 'meat hunger' when it is in short supply (Wiessner 1996, 174–5; though see Berbesque and Marlowe 2009). But this sentiment need not be universal (in protein-rich societies, for example, carbohydrates may be more highly valued), nor does it follow that women's roles are necessarily devalued. Moreover, particularly in low latitudes with arid climates, plant foods may contribute the majority of a group's calories (Berbesque and Marlowe 2009; Gould 1969; Lee 1968; 1979).

Equally importantly, women's involvement may be essential to the success of the hunt, whether through such practical activities as creating the watertight seal-skin or warm caribou-skin clothing essential to the survival (let alone success) of the Arctic hunter (Kobayashi Isserman 1997), or through widespread beliefs concerning the link between women's behaviour and that of prey animals (e.g. Emmons and de Laguna 1991, 103). Nor should women's roles in butchery and the often complex and highly skilled preparation of foods be seen as somehow of secondary importance to the act of capture: as noted above, without proper storage, the fish surpluses of the Northwest Coast would be useless. Men's and women's roles should instead be seen as complementary (cf. Jarvenpa and Brumbach 2006). Finally, it should also be emphasized that many hunter-gatherer groups demonstrate considerable situational flexibility, even in otherwise strongly gendered activities such as large-game hunting, or in time-stressed activities such as the need to gather large quantities of plant foods quickly before they spoil or are consumed by other animals. In other words, men often gathered, and women often hunted (though usually not in the same ways as men: Endicott 1999). Archaeologically, of course, it becomes more difficult to identify which gender was responsible for which activities, and this is one of the areas where the resulting resort to cross-cultural ethnographic analogy has been criticized.

Despite the oft-mentioned male gender-bias in the writings and interests of early explorers and anthropologists, the role of plant foods is actually reasonably well-documented ethnographically for at least some hunter-gatherers (Dahlberg 1981; Lee 1968; 1979). Archaeologically, the situation is rather more variable. While wet-sieving and flotation of soil samples have become the norm for excavations on sites with food-producing economies, the practice is less consistent for hunter-gatherer sites, particularly in higher latitudes, where the economic focus is often assumed to have been on large game (which indeed it inevitably was in very high latitudes). Yet Zvelebil (1994) has documented the ubiquity of a restricted range of plant foods on northern European Mesolithic sites, most notably charred hazelnut shells, that do survive well and are easily recognizable even without sieving. In some cases the quantities involved are considerable, suggesting that hazelnuts were an important resource, collected and processed in large numbers, presumably for winter storage (Mithen et al. 2001). And this pales in comparison to the evidence for the processing and storage of various species of nuts, especially chestnuts, in the Jomon of Japan (Imamura 1996), or acorns both ethnographically and archaeologically in California (Basgall 1987).

Another controversial issue relates to gender-based differences in consumption, i.e. to food restrictions, or taboos. There is ethnographic evidence from a number of hunter-gatherer societies for (usually) periodic prohibitions against women eating certain foods, particularly meat. Among a number of Australian Aboriginal groups, for example, the consumption of foods rich in both protein and fat is restricted for pregnant and lactating women (Spielmann 1989). The interpretation of this, however, is far from straightforward, as such practices may conceivably be beneficial, for example by resulting in lower birth weights, that, while leading to higher infant mortality, may improve the mother's chances of survival, since larger infants present more difficult births, and both historic and archaeological evidence suggests that childbirth was a major cause of death (cf. Bereczkei et al. 2000). There is certainly great potential for archaeological investigations of differential diet and health for men and women through osteological and dental markers: most studies have shown little or no difference for hunter-gatherers, suggesting relative gender equality, at least in terms of broad nutritional requirements (e.g. Lieverse et al. 2007; Lillie 1997). As expected given the above discussion of gender-based labour divisions, some studies do show differences in skeletal activity markers that can be related, at least in part, to subsistence practices (Hawkey and Merbs 1995; Ruff 1999; Walker and Hollimon 1989; Weiss 2009).

More recently, biomolecular approaches have widened the possibilities for studying dietary differences both within and between populations. Stable carbon ($\delta^{13}C$) and nitrogen ($\delta^{15}N$) isotope values were found to differ between males and females at Ota in Middle Jomon Japan (Kusaka et al. 2010) and at Téviec and Hoëdic in Late Mesolithic Brittany (Schulting and Richards 2001); in both cases women show slightly but significantly less consumption of marine protein. The interpretation of such differences is not necessarily straightforward, however, as they could refer either to dietary differences/restrictions within the community, or to one sex marrying in from other communities with different diets, as has been proposed for Brittany (Schulting and Richards 2001). The complementary use of other isotopes, such as strontium, will in some cases be able to distinguish between these possibilities (Kusaka et al. 2009).

Age-based differences in diets are widely documented ethnographically, often involving rules (or guidelines) governing the distribution of meat along lines of kinship and seniority (Binford 1978; Gould 1967). As with gender, this is considerably more difficult to investigate archaeologically, but again the human skeleton offers some possibilities. Stable isotope analysis provides a promising line of enquiry, as do more traditional osteological methods. For instance, while adults in the Portuguese Mesolithic have surprisingly high caries rates for hunter-gatherers (*c.*12 per cent, as opposed to the often cited range of 0 to 5.3 per cent for hunter-gatherers (Turner 1979)), no juveniles (less than *c.*18 years) have yet been found with caries (Meiklejohn et al. 1988). This strongly suggests that only adults had access to the sugar-rich foods—presumably figs and honey—that were the most likely cause of caries for these groups, and, based on ethnographic accounts such as those of the Okiek in East Africa (Blackburn 1982), were undoubtedly highly valued for their sweetness (and hence their high caloric value).

To Share or Not to Share: Ownership and Territoriality

The strong expression of a sharing ethic is often considered as a defining characteristic of hunter-gatherers. Nowhere is this more evident than in the sharing of food. But while 'sharing' typically evokes a sense of generosity, this is not how the practice tends to be viewed by many hunter-gatherers themselves, where it is a given that meat in particular will be shared amongst all the members of the local group. Expressions of gratitude for such sharing are neither given nor expected, as this would entail an unacceptable sense of obligation. Rather, sharing is 'an expectation of the moral order' (Service 1966, 16; see also Bird-David 1990). Thus, the hunter does not acquire prestige from the distribution of meat, and indeed efforts may be made to ensure that this does not happen, for example by publicly belittling the amount and/or quality of the kill, or by undermining the entire concept of ownership by viewing it as belonging to the person who owned the killing arrow, which because of widespread sharing of arrows may not be the same person who actually shot the animal (Bird-David 1990). This 'demand sharing' is a prime example of a levelling mechanism, aimed at constraining any tendencies by status-seeking individuals (who will be present to some degree in any human society) to elevate themselves above their fellows (Cashdan 1980; Lee 1979; Peterson 1993; Wiessner 1996).

But the above characterization applies primarily to what Woodburn (1982; 1998; see also Binford 1982; 2001; Kelly 1995; Testart 1982) has termed 'immediate-return' hunter-gatherers, with minimal storage of foods. Such groups can be equated with generalized hunter-gatherers, for whom the sharing of game can be seen as a kind of social storage, ensuring that future kills by other members of the group will in turn be shared (even if it is not expressed in this way by informants). Yet even among these societies there is considerable variability, and in many groups hunters *do* gain prestige from the distribution of meat. One of the best-documented, though not uncontroversial, examples is that of the Aché of eastern Paraguay, where it has been argued that the best hunters are 'showing off', with the aim of attracting marriage partners by demonstrating their success as providers, or soliciting extramarital affairs by actually gifting meat (Wood 2006; Wood and Hill 2000). Such behaviour has potential evolutionary consequences (i.e. in terms of mating opportunities and the number of surviving offspring), and forms another strong thread in hunter-gatherer studies.

The question of ownership in generalized hunter-gatherers normally only arises, if at all, once resources are procured (e.g. once an animal is killed, or roots collected). Before this, living animals and ungathered plants are typically viewed as held in common within the loosely defined 'territory' of a particular local group, which itself often has a very fluid membership. Use-rights can usually be obtained from the 'owners' (those having the strongest attachment to a place, often through birth combined with intimate knowledge of the geographic, social, and mythic topographies) by those outside the local group simply by asking permission, which is rarely refused (Myers 1982). Subsistence resources are used in this way to maintain friendly relations with neighbouring groups, and can act as a safety net during times of hardship. It also makes better use of spatially and temporally dispersed resources, which may at times and in places be more abundant than the local group can exploit, especially in the absence of storage (which is not reducible to technical knowledge; there must be a perceived need for storage, and a use for stored foods, particularly when they may be subject to strong demands for sharing). However, access is not always free to all, and even this form of ownership, often termed stewardship, can form a pretext to create or renew hostilities between groups, when one takes without permission, or is denied access without sufficient reason being given (Cashdan 1983; Myers 1982; Williams and Hunn 1982).

A very clear contrast is seen on both accounts—sharing and ownership—between generalized foragers and what Woodburn (1982) terms 'delayed-return' hunter-gatherers, who rely to a significant degree on stored foods for at least part of the year, and may also invest in fixed facilities, such as stationary fish weirs and traps. Again, the Northwest Coast of North America provides the best-documented examples of the most extreme version of these societies. Far from being subject to levelling mechanisms, large-scale food distribution at events such as the potlatch was emphatically and explicitly concerned with the creation, maintenance, and enhancement of social, economic, and political status (Boas 1966; Codere 1950; Kan 1989). On the northern Northwest Coast, where social differentiation attained its strongest expression, potlatches were hosted by the heads of lineages, and were the primary means by which their leadership claims were legitimized, both in the eyes of their own lineage and clan, and those of the wider society. Large quantities of goods were distributed, and massive amounts of foods, many specially prepared, were consumed by the hundreds of people in attendance for a number of days or even weeks. Needless to say, hosting such an event required considerable organization and mobilization of labour (kin-based and slave), as well as access to the resources. Facilitating this, along the entire Northwest Coast, clan, lineage, and family heads were the owners of most, if not all, of the most productive resource patches within their well-defined territories, including first and foremost the salmon rivers and streams, but also berry and root patches, particular stretches of beach with especially good shellfishing, hunting grounds, and in some cases even firewood and freshwater sources (Boas 1966; Drucker 1951; Emmons and de Laguna 1991; Suttles 1987). Along much of the Northwest Coast, as well as parts of the adjacent Plateau and California culture areas, trespass by outsiders was almost invariably answered with lethal violence.

There is a very intimate link between resources and hunter-gatherers' understandings and perceptions of their landscapes, with important places forming nodes, and these and the pathways between them providing the basis for geographical knowledge (Brody 1988; see also Ingold 2000). On the Northwest Coast, procurement activities were embedded in the landscape, with place names forming a crucial link between geographic, social, and ritual knowledge, and supplying the basis of claims of ownership and use-rights (Thornton 1997; cf. Williams and Hunn 1982). 'Ownership', however strongly expressed, typically resided in these important places (often, though not exclusively, related to resources of one form or another) rather than in a parcel of land, though hunting territories provide something of an exception, being often claimed to some degree, but by their nature lacking the strongly localized aspect of immobile plant—including individual trees, for example those bearing honey-bee hives—and shellfish resources, and also seen in some of the best fishing sites, particularly along rivers. As noted above, such procurement sites were often enhanced through the construction of fixed facilities, such as stone fish traps, wooden platforms and fish weirs, and clam gardens.

While sharing and ownership are undoubtedly important topics, they are often difficult to investigate archaeologically. Because of their frequently high mobility, many (generalized) hunter-gatherers built relatively ephemeral dwellings, and so the kinds of inter-household comparisons that can be so fruitful in other contexts are rarely possible. There are, however, a number of important exceptions; unsurprisingly, because of their reduced mobility, these almost invariably relate to complex hunter-gatherers. Middle Jomon villages are exceptionally large by any standards, even given uncertainties over the exact number of pit-houses occupied simultaneously. One of the largest known sites, Sannai Maruyama, yielded some 650 pit-houses and numerous other structures and features, though this reflects occupation over millennia (Habu 2008). At Miharada, over 300 pit-houses were found arranged around a central space, an arrangement repeated at Kowashimizu, where 260 pit-houses surrounded a central space containing more than 1,000 storage pits (Imamura 1996, 94; Kobayashi 2004; Figure 61.1). An even more formal use of space is seen at the Middle Jomon village of Nishida, with a concentric arrangement comprising, in turn, a central cemetery, post-holes for raised-floor structures, pit-houses, and, finally, storage pits. Villages of this size were made possible by the skilled and knowledgeable exploitation of very productive forest (especially chestnut and oak trees) and, where available, riverine and marine environments. Interestingly, the placement of storage pits within a central space rather than within, or closely associated with, the pit-houses could be interpreted as suggesting more communal ownership of the stored resources (cf. Wiessner 1982), though, alternatively, it could relate to their display. Though the extent of socio-economic inequality in the Jomon period is still debated, at least some of the classic indicators do appear to be present, particularly in the Middle and Late/Final phases (Habu 2004; Pearson 2004).

The pit-house village of Keatley Creek in interior British Columbia, Canada, consists of over 100 dwellings (Figure 61.2). While not all would have been occupied simultaneously, the rarity of overlap and the evidence for repeated winter occupations over centuries indicate that this was a large community, with perhaps 1,000 people at its peak, making it considerably larger than the Lil'wat villages known in the region ethnographically (Hayden 1992; Teit 1906). There is notable variation in the size of the dwellings, with the largest (c.20 m diameter, as opposed to the more typical 10–15 m) exhibiting the greatest longevity, and also demonstrating excess storage capacity for the dried salmon that formed the winter staple, as it did on much of the adjacent Northwest Coast (the coast itself is some 200 km from Keatley Creek). Analysis of aDNA in salmon remains from a number of houses suggests that different households had access to different species, and hence fisheries, along the nearby Fraser River Canyon, with its enormous salmon runs (Speller et al. 2005; Figure 61.3). This suggests considerable antiquity for the pattern documented ethnographically, in which particular rocks that provided the best dip-netting fishing stations on the Fraser were individually owned and inherited (Romanoff 1992).

On the Northwest Coast of North America, household archaeology has only relatively recently become a major focus of research. After their abandonment and decay, cedar plank

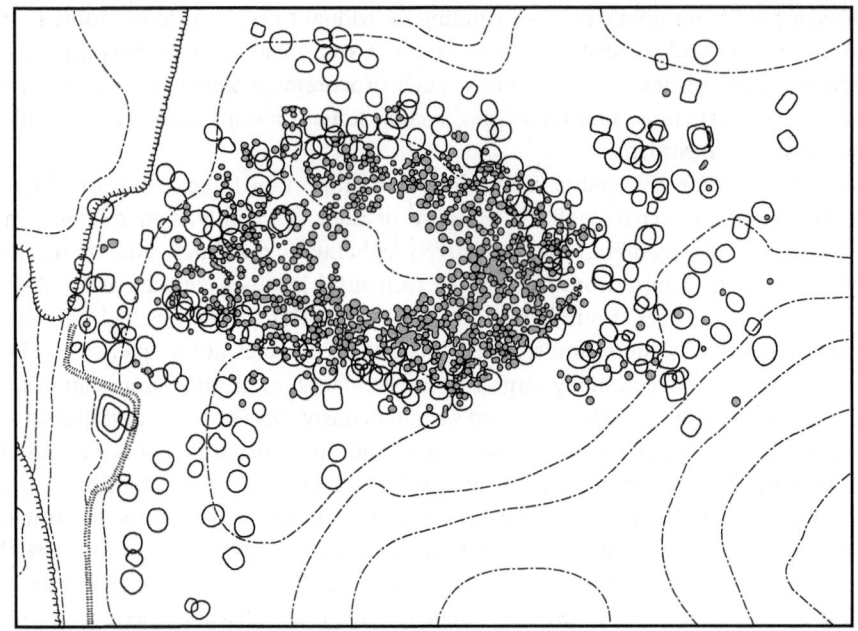

FIGURE 61.1 Middle Jomon site of Kowashimizu, Chiba Prefecture, Japan, with 260 pit-houses surrounding a central space containing more than 1,000 storage pits (after Imamura 1996, 97; drawn by Alison Wilkins).

FIGURE 61.2 View over the prehistoric pit-house village of Keatley Creek, interior British Columbia, Canada (photo courtesy of Brian Hayden and Roy Carlson).

FIGURE 61.3 Salmon drying racks (centre of photo) being prepared for the main autumn runs along a tributary of the Fraser River north of Lillooet, British Columbia, Canada, June 1994 (photo by author).

houses are visible as oblong depressions, resulting from the midden material accumulating around them during their use, which can often be demonstrated to be multi-generational (Grier 2006). These surface depressions were easily obscured by subsequent occupations, and so suitable sites of prehistoric date are not common. An exception is provided by the final component at McNichol Creek on the north coast of British Columbia, a moderate size late prehistoric winter village, with 15 houses arranged in two parallel rows facing the beach (Coupland 2006). One house in the front row was considerably larger than the others, potentially holding twice as many people (and so controlling twice the labour force, a crucial point in these corporate households). This dwelling also had a large central hearth, recalling the central importance of feasting on the Northwest Coast, and a distinctive faunal assemblage, with a higher proportion of mammalian remains. Moreover, this was the only house found to yield sea-mammal remains, noted as a prestige food in Tsimshian ethnographies (Coupland 2006).

On the southern Northwest Coast, part of the village of Ozette on Washington's Olympic Peninsula was buried under a catastrophic mudslide around AD 1700, some decades prior to direct Euro-American contact, sealing the contents of at least four plank houses. The remains associated with the final living floors suggest that the residents of different houses collected shellfish from different locations, which could relate to the access rights of households, and to the ownership of specific stretches of beach (Wessen 1994). The above three examples from north-western North America are noteworthy for their ability to combine archaeological and ethnographic data fruitfully, a clear benefit of working in areas exhibiting direct historical continuity.

Food for Status

Foods are particularly well-suited to marking out social and cultural distinctions (Wiessner and Schiefenhövel 1996). Examples relating to gender, kinship, and age have already been discussed, and these occur across the entire gamut of hunter-gatherer societies. More specific to complex hunter-gatherers, however, is the use of special foods and/or special ways of preparing them to distinguish social status. Unambiguous ethnographic examples include, not surprisingly, various Northwest Coast groups. For the Nuu-chah-nulth and Makah of western Vancouver Island and the Olympic Peninsula, only nobles were permitted to become harpooners, and the choicest part of the whale, the blubber-rich saddle, was reserved for them (Drucker 1951). The ways in which foods are served can present equally, if not more, powerful statements, including seating arrangements and the order in which people are served (both very important considerations at the potlatch), as well as the vessels in which food and drink are served. On the Northwest Coast, the largest wooden feast dishes were named and elaborately decorated with crest designs. One celebrated example among the Tlingit named *Thlukehotsick* measured over four metres in length, and was carved and painted with the owning clan's Woodworm crest, and inlaid with opercula shell (Emmons and de Laguna 1991, 160; Figure 61.4).

A recent study from the Final Jomon site of Inariyama, in east-central Japan, provides a particularly interesting example relating diet and social identity. Stable isotope results here demonstrate a very clear division between individuals with different tooth ablation patterns (Kusaka et al. 2008). All but one of the males with type 2C tooth ablation show substantially greater use of marine protein than do those with type 4I ablation (Figure 61.5), suggesting the presence of a surprising degree of economic specialization bound up with visible expressions of identity within this community. A subtler expression of the relationship between diet and identity is seen amongst the Bronze Age hunter-gatherers of Lake Baikal, Siberia. Here, three distinct clusters of graves within the large cemetery of Khuzhir-Nuge XIV differ significantly in their $\delta^{15}N$ values, suggesting varying dietary contributions of high trophic-level fish and seals (Katzenberg et al. 2009).

Most hunter-gatherers use organic vessels to prepare and serve food, and so, with rare exceptions involving outstanding preservation conditions, this material will be inaccessible to archaeology. There are, however, many prehistoric cultures that did use pottery, including a number of African groups, those of the circum-Baltic Mesolithic, and the Jomon of Japan, the latter being especially well-known for having some of the oldest pottery in the world—though finds in China have recently been placed as early or even earlier (Barham and Mitchell 2008; Chi 2002; Kaner 2009; see papers in Jordan and Zvelebil 2009). Of particular interest here is the great diversity of ceramic forms and elaborate plastic decoration seen in the Middle Jomon (Imamura 1996, figure 8.6), albeit alongside plainer wares that often dominate assemblages. The most highly decorated vessels were clearly intended first and foremost for display, yet many still show use for cooking, most probably in the context of feasting (Kaner 2009; Pearson 2007). The Ertebølle pottery of southern Scandinavia, by contrast, appears primarily functional, intended for cooking, as do the soapstone vessels of the Poverty Point culture in the American south-east (Gibson 2001). Where such vessels were used, they offer the opportunity—through traditional residue analysis and more recently through absorbed lipids and proteins (Heron et al. 2007)—to identify specific foods and combinations of foods, and to explore possible links between vessel type and use, and

FIGURE 61.4 The interior of the Whale House of the Gaanaxtedi Clan of Klukwan, Alaska, c.1895. The carved and painted screen in the background is called *Seew X'eenh*, the 'Rain Wall', and separates the dwelling space of the clan leader and his family from the rest of the house. The man to the rear left has his hand on the carved front of the *Thlukehotsick* feast dish (photo courtesy of the Alaska State Library, image no. ASL-P87–0010).

depositional context. Exceptional preservation conditions can yield unique insights: analysis of fatty acids and sterols in 'biscuits' recovered from the Jomon wetland site of Ondashi revealed a detailed list of ingredients including chestnut and walnut flour, meat and blood of wild boar and deer, and bird eggs (Imamura 1996, 99). Patterns that had been impressed into their surfaces are still visible (Figure 61.6).

Cosmologies and Foodways

Another characteristic that is often noted as defining hunter-gatherers is a particular way of engaging with and understanding the 'natural' world. A very pervasive world view is the one extending across much of northern Eurasia and North America, in which humans inhabit a world replete with other beings with similar qualities, including plants, inanimate objects, and natural phenomena. But it is animals in particular that are imbued with many of the qualities of persons, and indeed may become human when they remove their animal skins. Transformation plays an important role, whether of animal to human, or human to animal, and is often mediated by the shaman. Respectful behaviour towards the animals

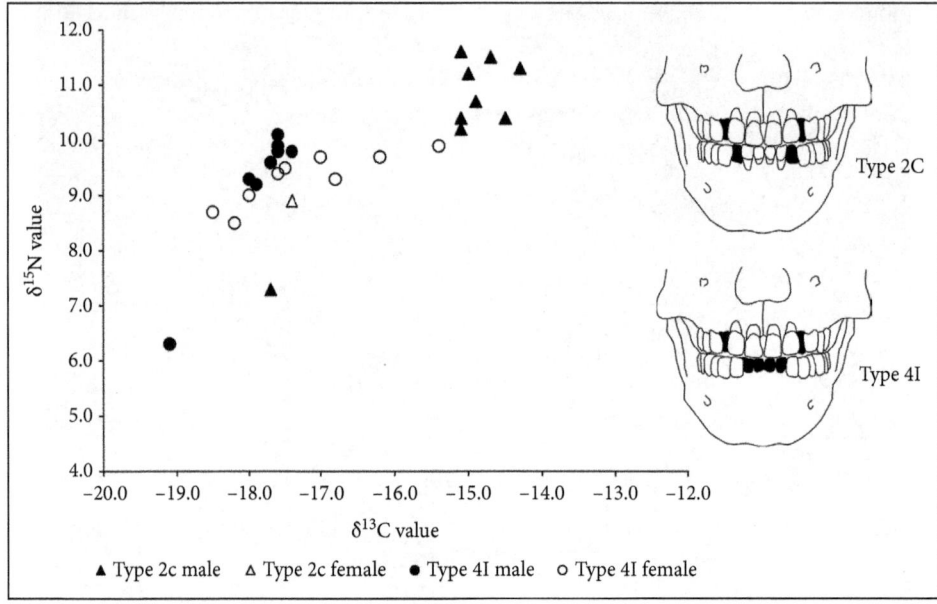

FIGURE 61.5 Bivariate plot of stable carbon and nitrogen isotope results on human bone collagen from the Late-Final Jomon site of Inariyama, Aichi Prefecture, Japan, with inset showing tooth ablation types (after Kusaka et al. 2008).

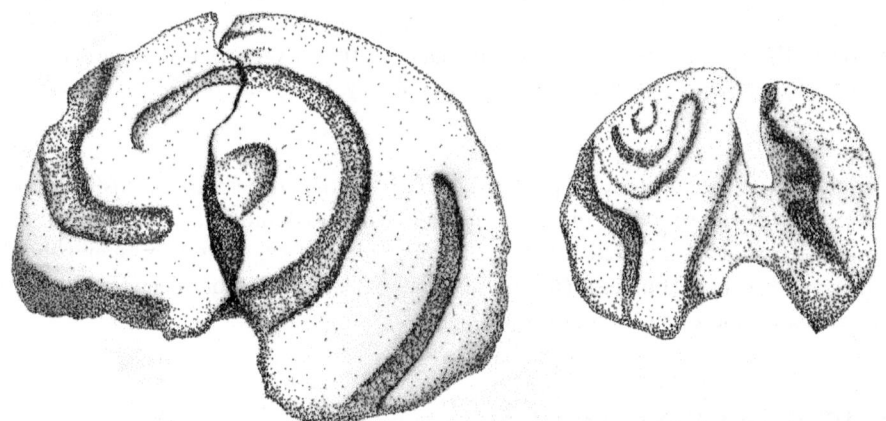

FIGURE 61.6 Jomon 'biscuits' with impressed designs, from Ondashi, Yamagata Prefecture, Japan (after Imamura 1996, figure 8.10; drawn by J. Ostapkowicz).

being hunted or plants being gathered is seen as crucial to success, which often relies on the goodwill of the master-spirit for that species. An individual's hunting skills, while they may be considerable, are typically seen as secondary at best to the maintenance of the proper relationship with the spirit world, and to the possession of spirit power (a concept that is not limited to the northern hemisphere: e.g. Lee 1979; Marshall 1976). Within such a world view, hunting, fishing, and gathering become far more than a matter of acquiring calories and protein: they define and reaffirm people's identities and places in the world (Brightman 1993; Jordan 2010; Willerslev 2004). A successful hunter or gatherer becomes imbued with superior moral and spiritual qualities (Suttles 1987).

The above need not imply the presence of elaborate ritual practices, or indeed any special material culture that would be recognized archaeologically. Sharp (1988, 188), commenting on the absence of overt hunting rituals for the Chipewyan of subarctic Canada, explains this as 'superfluous in a system where every encounter between a man and a prey animal has so many characteristics of a sacrificial event'. Of course, this creates a problem in the archaeological investigation of such beliefs, particularly as one very common practice is the placement of some or all of the bones of the animal away from settlements in special locations, whether in water, or suspended in trees (Ingold 2000; Jordan 2003). On occasion, however, ritual treatment involved burial: Jennbert (2003) documented some 40 Sámi bear graves in Norway and Sweden, the material outcome of ethnographic accounts emphasizing the ritual importance of bears and bear hunting. More speculatively, Mansrud (2009) has observed that elk dominates unburned bone assemblages in Mesolithic central Sweden, while beaver dominates burned bone assemblages. She also notes the surprising absence of bear bones, and draws on beliefs regarding animals as expressed in the ethnographies of northern hunter-gatherers to account for these varying treatments. While the specifics differ, a circumpolar 'bear cult' has long been recognized, with its apogee in the elaborate bear-sending ceremony (*iomante*) of the historic Ainu of Hokkaido and southern Sakhalin (Ohnuki-Tierney 1974; Utagawa 1992; Watanabe 1972; see Shternberg 1999 for a related ceremony among the Nivkh of northern Sakhalin).

THE FUTURE OF HUNTER-GATHERER FOODWAYS RESEARCH

There is still much about the practicalities of hunting and gathering foodways in archaeological contexts that remains poorly understood, let alone the associated social contexts, beliefs, and symbolism. While the ethnographic record may highlight the diversity of practices and beliefs, it has its own limitations, including restricted time-depth, and often disruptive post-contact situations. Yet it is the archaeological record to which we must increasingly turn for new data and insights. Hunting and gathering does survive in attenuated forms in some parts of the world, and continues to provide insights into processes of adaptability, survival, and reinvention, as well as the more negative processes of cultural dissolution and extinction. But such studies are ever more distanced from the pre-modern world, and cannot be expected to reliably inform on traditional cultures. What avenues, then, are open to us?

Recent advances in bioarchaeology—including a suite of stable isotopes, aDNA, and osteological analysis—are particularly exciting, in that they address individual life histories, and so provide an alternative to the long-term perspective that is often all that is accessible archaeologically (e.g. Weber et al. 2010). Biomolecular archaeology has made a strong contribution to the study of past diets, perhaps most notably through the application of stable isotope analysis. Measurements on bulk collagen are becoming routine, though a serious problem is the limited amount of human skeletal material available for analysis. This makes it all the more important to extract the maximum amount of information possible from the material that we do have. Measurement of different tissues—particularly teeth—can provide finer-grained temporal resolution, and potentially detect dietary changes from childhood through to adulthood. A more recent development, the isotopic analysis of single amino acids, can in some cases offer greater sensitivity regarding the foods consumed (Corr et al. 2009; Styring et al. 2010). Additional work also needs to be undertaken on the carbonate fraction of bone, informing on whole diet rather than emphasizing its protein component (Ambrose and Norr 1993). Some of the examples noted in the above discussion highlight the potential for isotopic analyses of diet to inform on gender and social organization. Aside from carbon and nitrogen, stable isotopes of lead, oxygen, and strontium are increasingly being used to address mobility (Bentley et al. 2007; Haverkort et al. 2008; Kusaka et al. 2009), which is often intimately linked with settlement and subsistence practices. Given the supposed high physical and social mobility of many hunter-gatherers, there is clearly scope here for further research.

Perhaps less obviously related to hunter-gatherer subsistence studies are the great advances being made in aDNA research. Nevertheless, the brief examples alluded to above (regarding chestnuts, wild boar, and salmon) make it clear that this field holds great potential for elucidating the complexity of human–animal and human–plant relationships in the past. More traditional osteological approaches continue to offer new insights, as seen for example in the investigation of musculo-skeletal stress markers and other evidence of activities carried out during an individual's lifetime.

Ongoing advances in the identification of organic residues show considerable promise for the investigation of past diets and foodways. Food residues on and within pottery, as discussed above, present an obvious example. Starch residues can survive both on tools and in dental calculus (Hardy et al. 2009), offering a means of identifying the exploitation and consumption of plant foods, certainly an area that would benefit from additional research. Further evidence on cooking methods can potentially be found through chemical and structural changes to bone, beyond the obvious signs of charring, though relatively little work has been carried out in this area (Koon et al. 2010).

Another important development that is in a position to make a real contribution to hunter-gatherer archaeology is the ongoing refinement of radiocarbon dating, including the more widespread use of carefully targeted, multiple samples of short-lived materials, and the application of Bayesian modelling (e.g. Bayliss and Woodman 2009). Given the time spans typically involved, and the often ephemeral nature of their archaeological record, there has been a tendency to view hunter-gatherers as relatively static, a 'people without history' (Wolf 1982). An improved chronology challenges this assumption, and allows a far more nuanced appreciation of short- and medium-term changes in hunter-gatherer subsistence practices and foodways. It is also clear that such changes need not be unidirectional, towards ever-increasing 'complexity' (Ames and Maschner 1999; Habu 2004; 2008; Weber et al. 2010). This in turn provides the potential to examine the underlying causes of such changes; to what extent, for example, were they in step with the kinds of rapid climatic shifts that are now being increasingly identified in the palaeoclimatic record (Alley et al. 1997)? This is not to return to a naïve environmental determinism, but at the same time it can hardly be doubted that people are affected by changes in their environments, which not only affect the material conditions of life (and in particular, the kinds, quantities, and distribution of resources), but also the ways in which the landscape is encountered, perceived, and understood (Ingold 2000).

The kinds of scientific analyses briefly outlined above and through the body of the chapter are, of course, only a means to an end, tools for investigating past hunter-gatherer societies in new ways. It is equally important to frame the questions we ask, and how we interpret the 'answers' we receive, within an informed theoretical framework. 'Mobility', for example, is a complex and multifaceted notion, operating at different social, spatial, and temporal scales. 'Diet', equally, is always about more than simple nutrition. It is in the interplay between new analytical techniques, the resulting new data, and theoretical concepts and models that the greatest potential for future investigations may be found.

Acknowledgements

Many thanks to Simon Kaner, Peter Mitchell, Joanna Ostapkowicz, Peter Rowley-Conwy, and an anonymous referee for their very helpful comments and suggestions.

References

Alley, R. B., Mayewski, P. A., Sowers, T., Stuiver, M., Taylor, K. C., and Clark, P. U. 1997. Holocene climate instability: a prominent, widespread event 8200 yr ago. *Geology* 25, 483–6.

Ambrose, S. H. and Norr, L. C. 1993. Isotopic composition of dietary protein and energy versus bone collagen and apatite: purified diet growth experiments. In J. Lambert and G. Grupe (eds), *Molecular Archaeology of Prehistoric Human Bone*, 1–37. Berlin: Springer.

Ames, K. M. and Maschner, H. D. G. 1999. *Peoples of the Northwest Coast: their archaeology and prehistory*. London: Thames and Hudson.

Barham, L. and Mitchell, P. 2008. *The first Africans: African archaeology from the earliest tool makers to most recent foragers*. Cambridge: Cambridge University Press.

Basgall, M. 1987. Resource intensification among hunter-gatherers: acorn economies in prehistoric California. *Research in Economic Anthropology* 9, 21–52.

Bayliss, A. and Woodman, P. C. 2009. A new Bayesian chronology for Mesolithic occupation at Mount Sandel, Northern Ireland. *Proceedings of the Prehistoric Society* 75, 101–24.

Bentley, A., Tayles, N., Higham, C., Macpherson, C., and Atkinson, T. C. 2007. Shifting gender relations at Khok Phanom Di, Thailand: isotopic evidence from the skeletons. *Current Anthropology* 48, 301–14.

Berbesque, J. C. and Marlowe, F. W. 2009. Sex differences in food preferences of Hadza hunter-gatherers. *Evolutionary Psychology* 7, 601–16.

Bereczkei, T., Hofer, A., and Ivan, Z. 2000. Low birth weight, maternal birth-spacing decisions, and future reproduction: a cost-benefit analysis. *Human Nature* 11, 183–205.

Binford, L. R. 1978. *Nunamiut ethnoarchaeology*. New York: Academic Press.

Binford, L. R. 1982. The archaeology of place. *Journal of Anthropological Archaeology* 1, 1–31.

Binford, L. R. 2001. *Constructing frames of reference*. Berkeley: University of California Press.

Bird-David, N. 1990. The giving environment: another perspective on the economic system of hunter-gatherers. *Current Anthropology* 31, 183–96.

Blackburn, R. H. 1982. In the land of milk and honey: Okiek adaptations to their forests and neighbours. In E. Leacock and R. Lee (eds), *Politics and history in band societies*, 283–305. Cambridge: Cambridge University Press.

Bleed, P. and Matsui, A. 2010. Why didn't agriculture develop in Japan? A consideration of Jomon ecological style, niche construction, and the origins of domestication. *Journal of Archaeological Method and Theory* 17, 356–70.

Boas, F. 1966. *Kwakiutl ethnography*. Chicago: University of Chicago Press.

Boyd, R. T. 1986. Strategies of Indian burning in the Willamette Valley. *Canadian Journal of Archaeology* 5, 65–86.

Brightman, R. 1993. *Grateful prey: Rock Cree human–animal relationships*. Berkeley: University of California Press.

Brody, H. 1988. *Maps and dreams: Indians and the British Columbia frontier*. Vancouver: Douglas and McIntyre.

Cashdan, E. 1980. Egalitarianism among hunters and gatherers. *American Anthropologist* 82, 116–20.

Cashdan, E. 1983. Territoriality among human foragers: ecological models and an application to four Bushman groups. *Current Anthropology* 24, 47–66.

Chi, Z. 2002. The discovery of early pottery in China. *Documenta Praehistorica* 29, 29–35.

Codere, H. 1950. *Fighting with property*. Seattle: University of Washington Press.

Corr, L., Richards, M., Grier, C., Mackie, A., Beattie, O., and Evershed, R. 2009. Probing dietary change of the Kwäda {ogonek}y Dän Ts'ìnchi {ogonek} individual, an ancient glacier body from British Columbia: II. Deconvoluting whole skin and bone collagen $\delta^{13}C$ values via carbon isotope analysis of individual amino acids. *Journal of Archaeological Science* 36, 12–18.

Coupland, G. 2006. A chief's house speaks: communicating power on the northern Northwest Coast. In E. A. Sobel, D. A. Trieu Gahr, and K. Ames (eds), *Household archaeology on the Northwest Coast*, 80–96. Ann Arbor: International Monographs in Prehistory.

Dahlberg, F. (ed.) 1981. *Woman the gatherer*. New Haven: Yale University Press.

Downs, J. F. 1966. The significance of environmental manipulation in Great Basin cultural development. In W. L. d'Azevedo (ed.), *The current status of anthropological research in the Great Basin: 1964*, 39–56. Reno: University of Nevada, Desert Research Institute.

Drucker, P. 1951. *The Northern and Central Nootkan tribes*. Washington, DC: Smithsonian Institution Bureau of American Ethnology Bulletin 144.

Emmons, G. T. and de Laguna, F. 1991. *The Tlingit Indians*. New York: American Museum of Natural History.

Endicott, K. L. 1999. Gender relations in hunter-gatherer societies. In R. B. Lee and R. Daly (eds), *The Cambridge encyclopedia of hunters and gatherers*, 411–18. Cambridge: Cambridge University Press.

Flannery, K. 1969. Origins and ecological effects of early domestication in Iran and Near East. In P. J. Ucko and G. W. Dimbleby (eds), *The domestication and exploitation of plants and animals*, 73–100. London: Duckworth.

Fowler, C. S. 1999. Ecological/cosmological knowledge and land management among hunter-gatherers. In R. B. Lee and R. Daly (eds), *The Cambridge encyclopedia of hunters and gatherers*, 419–25. Cambridge: Cambridge University Press.

Gibson, J. L. 2001. *The ancient mounds of Poverty Point*. Gainesville: University Press of Florida.

Gould, R. A. 1967. Notes on hunting, butchering, and sharing of game among the Ngatatjara and their neighbors in the west Australian desert. *Kroeber Anthropological Society Papers* 36, 41–66.

Gould, R. A. 1969. *Yiwara: foragers of the Australian Desert*. London: Collins.

Grier, C. 2006. Temporality in Northwest Coast households. In E. A. Sobel, D. A. Trieu Gahr, and K. Ames (eds), *Household archaeology on the Northwest Coast*, 97–119. Ann Arbor: International Monographs in Prehistory.

Habu, J. 2004. *Ancient Jomon of Japan*. Cambridge: Cambridge University Press.

Habu, J. 2008. Growth and decline in complex hunter-gatherer societies: a case study from the Jomon period Sannai Maruyama site, Japan. *Antiquity* 82, 571–84.

Hardy, K., Blakeney, T., Copeland, L., Kirkham, J., Wrangham, R., and Collins, M. 2009. Starch granules, dental calculus and new perspectives on ancient diet. *Journal of Archaeological Science* 36, 248–55.

Haverkort, C. M., Weber, A., Katzenberg, M. A., Goriunova, O. I., Simonetti, A., and Creaser, R. A. 2008. Hunter-gatherer mobility strategies and resource use based on strontium isotope ($^{87}Sr/^{86}Sr$) analysis: a case study from Middle Holocene Lake Baikal, Siberia. *Journal of Archaeological Science* 35, 1265–80.

Hawkey, D. E. and Merbs, C. F. 1995. Activity-induced musculoskeletal stress markers (MSM) and subsistence strategy changes among ancient Hudson Bay Eskimos. *International Journal of Osteoarchaeology* 5, 324–38.

Hayden, B. 1990. Nimrods, piscators, pluckers, and planters: the emergence of food production. *Journal of Anthropological Archaeology* 9, 31–69.

Hayden, B. (ed.) 1992. *A complex culture of the British Columbia Plateau: traditional Stl'átl'imx resource use*. Vancouver: UBC Press.

Heron, C., Craig, O. E., Forster, M., Stern, B., and Andersen, S. H. 2007. Residue analysis of ceramics from prehistoric shell middens in Denmark: initial investigations at Norsminde and Bjørnsholm. In N. Milner and G. Bailey (eds), *Shell middens and coastal resources along the Atlantic façade*, 78–85. Oxford: Oxbow Books.

Imamura, K. 1996. *Prehistoric Japan: new perspectives on insular East Asia*. London: UCL Press.

Ingold, T. (ed.) 2000. *The perception of the environment: essays in livelihood, dwelling and skill*. London: Routledge.

Jarvenpa, R. and Brumbach, H. J. (eds) 2006. *Circumpolar lives and livelihood: a comparative ethnoarchaeology of gender and subsistence*. Lincoln: University of Nebraska Press.

Jennbert, K. 2003. Animal graves: dogs, horse and bear. *Current Swedish Archaeology* 11, 139–52.

Jordan, P. 2003. *Material culture and sacred landscape: the anthropology of the Siberian Khanty*. New York: Rowman & Littlefield.

Jordan, P. (ed.) 2010. *Landscape and culture in northern Eurasia*. Walnut Creek, CA: Left Coast Press.

Jordan, P. and Zvelebil, M. (eds) 2009. *Ceramics before farming: the dispersal of pottery among prehistoric Eurasian hunter-gatherers*. London: University College London Institute of Archaeology Publications.

Kan, S. 1989. *Symbolic immortality: the Tlingit potlatch of the nineteenth century*. Washington, DC: Smithsonian Institution.

Kaner, S. 2009. Long-term innovation: appearance and spread of pottery in the Japanese archipelago. In P. Jordan and M. Zvelebil (eds), *Ceramics before farming: the dispersal of pottery among prehistoric Eurasian hunter-gatherers*, 93–119. London: University College London Institute of Archaeology Publications.

Katzenberg, M. A., Goriunova, O. I., and Weber, A. 2009. Paleodiet reconstruction of Early Bronze Age Siberians from the site of Khuzhir-Nuge XIV, Lake Baikal. *Journal of Archaeological Science* 36, 663–74.

Kelly, R. L. 1995. *The foraging spectrum: diversity in hunter-gatherer lifeways*. Washington, DC: Smithsonian Institution.

Kobayashi Isserman, B. 1997. *Sinews of survival: the living legacy of Inuit clothing*. Vancouver: University of British Columbia Press.

Kobayashi, T. 2004. *Jomon reflections: forager life and culture in the prehistoric Japanese archipelago*. Oxford: Oxbow.

Koon, H. E. C., O'Connor, T. P., and Collins, M. J. 2010. Sorting the butchered from the boiled. *Journal of Archaeological Science* 37, 62–9.

Kusaka, S., Ando, A., Nakano, T., Yumoto, T., Ishimaru, E., Yoneda, M., Hyodo, F., and Katayama, K. 2009. A strontium isotope analysis on the relationship between ritual tooth ablation and migration among the Jomon people in Japan. *Journal of Archaeological Science* 36, 2289–97.

Kusaka, S., Hyodo, F., Yumoto, T., and Nakatsukasa, M. 2010. Carbon and nitrogen stable isotope analysis on the diet of Jomon populations from two coastal regions of Japan. *Journal of Archaeological Science* 37, 1968–77.

Kusaka, S., Ikarashi, T., Hyodo, F., Yumoto, T., and Katayama, K. 2008. Variability in stable isotope ratios in two Late-Final Jomon communities in the Tokai coastal region and its relationship with sex and ritual tooth ablation. *Anthropological Science* 116, 171–81.

Lawton, H., Wilke, P. J., Decker, M., and Mason, W. M. 1976. Agriculture among the Paiute of Owens Valley. *Journal of California Anthropology* 3, 13–50.

Lee, R. B. 1968. What hunters do for a living, or, how to make out on scarce resources. In R. B. Lee and I. DeVore (eds), *Man the hunter*, 30–48. Chicago: Aldine.

Lee, R. B. 1979. *The !Kung San: men, women, and work in a foraging society*. Cambridge: Cambridge University Press.

Lee, R. B. and DeVore, I. (eds) 1968. *Man the hunter*. Chicago: Aldine.

Lewis, H. T. and Bean, L. J. (eds) 1973. *Patterns of Indian burning in California: ecology and ethnohistory*. Ramona: Ballena Press.

Lieverse, A. R., Link, D. W., Bazaliiskiy, V. I., Goriunova, O. I., and Weber, A. W. 2007. Dental health indicators of hunter-gatherer adaptation and cultural change in Siberia's Cis-Baikal. *American Journal of Physical Anthropology* 134, 323–39.

Lillie, M. C. 1997. Women and children in prehistory: resource sharing and social stratification at the Mesolithic–Neolithic transition in Ukraine. In J. Moore and E. Scott (eds), *Invisible people and processes: writing gender and childhood into European archaeology*, 213–28. Leicester: Leicester University Press.

Lourandos, H. 1997. *Continent of hunter-gatherers: new perspectives in Australian prehistory*. Cambridge: Cambridge University Press.

Mansrud, A. 2009. Animal bone studies and the perception of animals in Mesolithic society. In S. B. McCartan, R. J. Schulting, G. Warren, and P. C. Woodman (eds), *Mesolithic horizons*, 198–202. Oxford: Oxbow.

Marshall, L. 1976. *The !Kung of Nyae Nyae*. Cambridge, MA: Harvard University Press.

Matsui, A. and Kanehara, M. 2006. The question of prehistoric plant husbandry during the Jomon period in Japan. *World Archaeology* 38, 259–73.

Meiklejohn, C., Baldwin, J. H., and Schentag, C. T. 1988. Caries as a probable dietary marker in the western European Mesolithic. In B. V. Kennedy and G. M. LeMoine (eds), *Diet and subsistence: current archaeological perspectives. Proceedings of the 19th Chacmool conference*, 273–9. Calgary: Calgary University Press.

Mitchell, P. 2005. *African connections: archaeological perspectives on Africa and the wider world*. Walnut Creek, CA: AltaMira Press.

Mithen, S., Finlay, N., Carruthers, W., Carter, S., and Ashmore, P. 2001. Plant use in the Mesolithic: evidence from Staosnaig, Isle of Colonsay, Scotland. *Journal of Archaeological Science* 28, 223–34.

Moore, J. 2000. Forest fire and human interaction in the early Holocene woodlands of Britain. *Palaeogeography Palaeoclimatology Palaeoecology* 164, 125–38.

Myers, F. R. 1982. Always ask: resource use and land ownership among Pintupi Aborigines of the Australian Western Desert. In N. M. Williams and E. S. Hunn (eds), *Resource managers: North American and Australian hunter-gatherers*, 173–95. Boulder: Westview Press.

Ohnuki-Tierney, E. 1974. *The Ainu of the northwest coast of southern Sakhalin*. New York: Holt, Rinehart & Winston.

Peacock, S. L. 2008. From complex to simple: balsamroot, inulin, and the chemistry of traditional Interior Salish pit-cooking technology. *Botany* 86, 116–28.

Pearson, R. 2004. New perspectives on Jomon society. *Bulletin of the International Jomon Culture Conference* 1, 63–70.

Pearson, R. 2007. Debating Jomon social complexity. *Asian Perspectives* 46, 361–88.

Peterson, N. 1993. Demand sharing: reciprocity and the pressure for generosity among foragers. *American Anthropologist* 95, 860–74.

Price, T. D. and Brown, J. A. (eds) 1985. *Prehistoric hunter-gatherers: the emergence of cultural complexity*. Madison: Prehistory Press.

Rindos, D. 1984. *The origins of agriculture: an evolutionary perspective*. London: Academic Press.

Romanoff, S. 1992. Fraser Lillooet salmon fishing. In B. Hayden (ed.), *A complex culture of the British Columbia Plateau*, 222–65. Vancouver: University of British Columbia Press.

Rowley-Conwy, P. 2001. Time, change and the archaeology of hunter-gatherers: how original is the 'Original Affluent Society'? In C. Panter-Brick, R. H. Layton, and P. Rowley-Conwy (eds), *Hunter-gatherers: an interdisciplinary perspective*, 39–72. Cambridge: Cambridge University Press.

Ruff, C. B. 1999. Skeletal structure and behavioral patterns of prehistoric Great Basin populations. In B. E. Hemphill and C. S. Larsen (eds), *Prehistoric lifeways in the Great Basin wetlands*, 290–320. Salt Lake City: University of Utah Press.

Sato, Y.-I., Yamanaka, S., and Takahashi, M. 2003. Evidence for Jomon plant cultivation based on DNA analysis of chestnut remains. In J. Habu, J. M. Savelle, S. Koyama, and H. Hongo (eds), *Hunter-gatherers of the North Pacific rim*, 187–97. Osaka: National Museum of Ethnology, Senri Ethnological Studies 63.

Schulting, R. J. and Richards, M. P. 2001. Dating women and becoming farmers: new palaeodietary and AMS data from the Breton Mesolithic cemeteries of Téviec and Hoëdic. *Journal of Anthropological Archaeology* 20, 314–44.

Service, E. R. 1966. *The hunters*. Englewood Cliffs: Prentice-Hall.

Sharp, H. S. 1988. Dry meat and gender: the absence of Chipewyan ritual for the regulation of hunting and animal numbers. In T. Ingold, D. Riches, and J. Woodburn (eds), *Property, power and ideology in hunting and gathering societies*, 183–91. Oxford: Berg.

Shnirelman, V. A. 1992. Complex hunter-gatherers: exception or common phenomenon? *Dialectical Anthropology* 17, 183–96.

Shternberg, L. 1999. *The social organization of the Gilyak*. New York: American Museum of Natural History Anthropological Papers 82.

Smith, B. D. 2011. General patterns of niche construction and the management of 'wild' plant and animal resources by small-scale pre-industrial societies. *Philosophical Transactions of the Royal Society B: Biological Sciences* 366, 836–48.

Speller, C. F., Yang, D. Y., and Hayden, B. 2005. Ancient DNA investigation of prehistoric salmon resource utilization at Keatley Creek, British Columbia, Canada. *Journal of Archaeological Science* 32, 1378–89.

Speth, J. and Spielmann, K. 1983. Energy source, protein metabolism, and hunter-gatherer subsistence strategies. *Journal of Anthropological Archaeology* 2, 1–31.

Spielmann, K. A. 1989. A review: dietary restrictions on hunter-gatherer women and the implications for fertility and infant mortality. *Human Ecology* 17, 321–45.

Styring, A. K., Sealy, J. C., and Evershed, R. P. 2010. Resolving the bulk $\delta^{15}N$ values of ancient human and animal bone collagen via compound specific nitrogen isotope analysis of constituent amino acids. *Geochimica et Cosmochimica Acta* 74, 241–51.

Suttles, W. 1987. *Coast Salish essays*. Vancouver: Talonbooks.

Teit, J. A. 1906. The Lillooet Indians. *Memoirs of the American Museum of Natural History* 2, 195–292.

Testart, A. 1982. The significance of food storage among hunter-gatherers: residence patterns, population densities, and social inequalities. *Current Anthropology* 23, 523–37.

Thornton, T. F. 1997. Know your place: the organization of Tlingit geographical knowledge. *Ethnology* 36, 295–307.

Turner, C. G. 1979. Dental anthropology indications of agriculture among the Jomon people of central Japan. *American Journal of Physical Anthropology* 51, 619–35.

Turner, N. J. and Kuhnlein, H. V. 1982. Two important 'root' foods of the Northwest Coast Indians: springback clover (*Trifolium wormskioldii*) and Pacific silverweed (*Potentillan anserina spp. pacifica*). *Economic Botany* 36, 411–32.

Utagawa, H. 1992. The 'sending-back' rite in Ainu culture. *Japanese Journal of Religious Studies* 19, 255–70.

Walker, P. L. and Hollimon, S. E. 1989. Changes in osteoarthritis associated with the development of a maritime economy among southern Californian Indians. *International Journal of Anthropology* 4, 171–83.

Watanabe, H. 1972. *The Ainu ecosystem*. Seattle: University of Washington Press.

Watanobe, T., Ishiguro, N., Nakano, M., Matsui, A., Hongo, H., Yamazaki, K., and Takahashi, O. 2004. Prehistoric Sado Island populations of *Sus scrofa* distinguished from contemporary Japanese wild boar by ancient mitochondrial DNA. *Zoological Science* 21, 219–28.

Weber, A. W., Katzenberg, M. A., and Schurr, T. G. (eds) 2010. *Prehistoric hunter-gatherers of the Baikal region, Siberia*. Philadelphia: University of Pennsylvania Press.

Weiss, E. 2009. Sex differences in humeral bilateral asymmetry in two hunter-gatherer populations: California Amerinds and British Columbian Amerinds. *American Journal of Physical Anthropology* 140, 19–24.

Wessen, G. C. 1994. Subsistence patterns as reflected by invertebrate remains recovered at the Ozette site. In S. R. Samuels (ed.), *Ozette archaeological project research reports, volume II, fauna*, 93–196. Pullman: Washington State University.

Wiessner, P. 1982. Risk, reciprocity and social influences on !Kung San economics. In: E. Leacock and R. Lee (eds), *Politics and History in Band Societies*, 61–84. Cambridge: Cambridge University Press.

Wiessner, P. 1996. Levelling the hunter: constraints on the status quest in foraging societies. In P. Wiessner and W. Schiefenhövel (eds), *Food and the status quest: an interdisciplinary perspective*, 171–91. Providence: Berghahn.

Wiessner, P. and Schiefenhövel, W. (eds) 1996. *Food and the status quest: an interdisciplinary perspective*. Providence: Berghahn.

Willerslev, R. 2004. Not animal, not not-animal: hunting, imitation and empathetic knowledge among the Siberian Yukaghirs. *Journal of the Royal Anthropological Institute* 10, 629–52.

Williams, E. 1988. *Complex hunter-gatherers: a late Holocene example from temperate Australia*. Oxford: British Archaeological Reports International Series 423.

Williams, J. 2006. *Clam gardens: Aboriginal mariculture on Canada's west coast*. Vancouver: New Star Books.

Williams, N. M. and Hunn, E. S. (eds) 1982. *Resource managers: North American and Australian hunter-gatherers*. Boulder: Westview Press.

Wolf, E. R. 1982. *Europe and the people without history*. Berkeley: University of California Press.

Wood, B. M. 2006. Prestige or provisioning? A test of foraging goals among the Hadza. *Current Anthropology* 47, 383–7.

Wood, B. M. and Hill, K. 2000. A test of the 'showing off' hypothesis with Ache hunters. *Current Anthropology* 41, 124–5.

Woodburn, J. 1982. Egalitarian societies. *Man* 17, 431–51.

Woodburn, J. 1998. 'Sharing is not a form of exchange': an analysis of property-sharing in immediate-return hunter-gatherer societies. In C. M. Hann (ed.), *Property relations: renewing the anthropological tradition*, 48–63. Cambridge: Cambridge University Press.

Zvelebil, M. 1994. Plant use in the Mesolithic and its role in the transition to farming. *Proceedings of the Prehistoric Society* 60, 35–74.

Zvelebil, M. 1995. Hunting, gathering, or husbandry? Management of food resources by the Late Mesolithic communities of temperate Europe. In D. V. Campana (ed.), *Before farming: hunter-gatherer society and subsistence*, 79–104. Philadelphia: Museum of Applied Science Center for Archaeology, Research Papers in Science and Archaeology.

INDEX

Abbott, A. 78, 82
Aboriginal Land Rights (Northern Territory) Act (1976) 964, 965
Aborigines *see* Australian Aborigines
accelerator mass spectrometry (AMS) dating 458, 508, 509, 516, 733 *see also* radiocarbon dating
Aché (Guayakí) people 79, 1040–1
Acheulian culture 196, 310, 496
  Africa 229, 230, 611–13
  cognitive requirements 620
  hand axes and cleavers 183, 184, 611–13
  south Asia 332, 339
Acheulean-Mousterian culture 310
Ackerman, L. A. 1253
Ackerman, R. E. 701–2
acorns 1267, 1268, 1270
actor network theory 135, 1195
Adachi, N. 411
adaptive and ecological approaches 33, 36–7, 69–84, 92, 443
  ideas about adaptation before advent of ecological approaches (1600-1930) 70–2
  advent of ecological approaches 73–6
  Neo-Darwinian approaches 78–84
  New Archaeology 76–8
Adovasio, J. M. 168
Afontov culture 318
Africa
  Acheulian culture 229, 230, 611–13
  archaeogenetics 1101–2, 1145–7, 1146 Fig. 55.2, 1147–53, 1154
  'back to Africa' migrations 1147, 1154
  earliest evidence for Levallois and bladelet technologies 608, 614
  earliest stone artefacts 610–11
  early coastal exploitation, South Africa 596, 698
  egalitarianism 645

microlithic industry, Later Stone Age 484
Middle Palaeolithic-Upper Palaeolithic transition 616
Neolithic farming 483
'out of Africa' dispersal 310, 346, 358, 369, 440, 498, 1145–6, 1154
'proto-Khoisan-Pygmy' population 1154
rock art 108–9
Africa, contemporary hunter gatherers 1147
  genetic legacy 1149–53
  marital exchanges 1149
  physical features 1147–8
  population constancy 1149–50
  reproduction 1148–9
  see also central Africa; southern Africa
Africa, Middle Stone Age 484
  archaeological record 216, 233
  artefacts and cognitive processes and behaviour 230–2
  and modern human behaviour 229–30, 237
  stone tool technology 229–30, 614–15
  and symbolic expression 231
  toolkits 236, 237
  transition to agriculture 739
Africa, post-glacial period 446–7, 479–87
  animal domestication 483, 484
  east Africa 482–3
  north Africa 480–2
  southern Africa 447, 484–5
  terminal Pleistocene/early Holocene environments 479–80
  timeline 486 Fig. 20.1
  tropical Africa 485–7
agency 444, 1193
  belief, spirituality and ethnoarchaeology 132–4
  children 1197
  hunter-gatherer 604–5, 916, 1192

agency (*Cont.*)
  and Neolithicization 772
  non-human 1195–6
agriculture and farming
  Africa, arrival of 447, 472, 481–2, 483, 485
  Cyprus, arrival of 463
  Neolithic transition to farming 769–75
  role of hunter-gatherers in transition 767–8, 916
  slash-and-burn, Finland 1076–9
  south Asia, post-glacial 447, 497, 501
  south-east Europe, arrival of 466–8
  spread from the Adriatic to the Atlantic 471–2
  spread out of western Asia 461–2
  spread throughout the Mediterranean 473
  social complexity pre-dating 593, 602, 603, 643, 654
  south-east Europe, arrival 466–7
  transition to agriculture 586, 738–9, 767–8
  western Asia/near east, beginnings of 438, 445, 458–9
Agta people 14, 158–9, 1020, 1022, 1024, 1016, 1246
Ahrensburgian culture 541, 466–7, 699
Aiello, C. 184–5
Ainu people 165, 656–7, 771, 913–14, 1054–66, 1055 Fig. 50.1
  'bear cult' 1279
  bear ceremony (*iyomante*) 914, 1065
  'dual structure model' 1057
  history and ethnogenesis 1057–9
  and hunter-gatherer definitions 1059–60
  population levels 1054
  regional variations 1064–5
  ritual and worldview 1065
  settlement patterns 1062
  social organization and complexity 1062–4
  subsistence and economy 1060–1
  trade 1061
  whale hunting 1267
'Ainu culture period' 1054, 1055–6, 1059
Aka people 167, 940–1, 943, 947, 1152
Akazawa, T. 514
Akie people 166
Alacauf sea nomads 703
Al-Azmeh, A. 61
Aleut people 651

Alfred, King 1080
Algonquian/Iroquois interaction 781, 884
  Fig. 41.2, 885–6
  prehistoric 886–7
Allard, P. 792
altered states of consciousness (ASCs) 589, 632, 637–8, 1194
  and jimson weed 1229
  and rock art 1233–4
  and shamanism 1225
  and vision quests 1228
alterity/otherness and defining of hunter-gatherers 35, 56–65
  axes of 57–8
  barbarians and tribals 59–61
  and Chinese historiography 60–1
  and the cultivation of difference 64–5
  English portrayals 62–3
  Greeks and barbarians 58–9
  and Hindu thought 60
  invention of the concept 63–4
  normalcy and the Self 62
  precursors to hunter-gatherers 61–5
Altman, Jon 964, 965
Alu Kurumba people 164–5
Alune people 1013
amber 288, 563
Ambrose, S. H. 482–3
American Anthropological Association 156
Americas
  Barnes complex 414
  Clovis foragers and their contemporaries 412–14, 413 Fig. 17.2
  earliest hunter-gatherers 405–20
  early coastal exploitation 698
  early foragers, North America 414–17
  early foragers, South America 417–19
  gender roles in early foragers 416–17
  post glacial coastline submersion 696
  pre-11000 BP craneometric studies 411
  pre-11000 BP genetic studies 411–12
  pre-11000 BP linguistic evidence 412
  pre-11000 BP peopling models 406–11, 407 Fig. 17.1, 409 Fig. 17.2, 410 Fig. 17.3, 410 Fig. 17.4
  pre-11000 BP skeletal morphology 411
  transition to agriculture 738–9
  see also North America; South America

Ames, K. M. 992, 1004, 1006
Ames, O. 730
Amick, D. S. 415
Ammerman, A. J. 462, 771
Anadara granosa 387
analogical reasoning 33, 39, 40, 105–9
  arguments by anomaly 106–7
  boundary conditions 106
  'core universals' 108, 109
  cross-cultural analysis of data 106
  'historical analogy' 108
  and middle range theory 107–9, 138
  'tyranny of the ethnographic record' 106
Ananino culture 849
ancestor worship 649, 653
Andamanese people 165
  DNA studies 374
Anderson, A. 500
Anderson, D. G. 165–6
Anderson, E. 730
Anderson, J. C. 964
Anderson, M. 981
animal domestication 600–1, 749–59, 767
  defining 749–50
  DNA analysis 752–3
  earliest livestock 264
  'founders' effects 751, 752
  as a hunter-gatherer innovation 755–9
  identifying domestication 751–5, 751 Fig. 34.1, 754 Fig. 34.2, 755 Fig. 34.3
  morphological changes in animals 752
  Neolithic transition, Britain and Ireland 826, 827, 832
  osteological evidence 753
  post-glacial east Africa 483
  post-glacial southern Africa 484
  reduction in size 751–2
  as response to pressure to increase production 658
  see also specific animals
animal-human relations *see* human-animal relations
animism 444, 825, 1193, 1222
Ankel, C. 789
Annales school 1165
Antap cult 1229
Anthony, D. W. 757
antler frontlets, Star Carr 719, 1194, 1212

Appadurai, A. 1208
Applegate, R. 980
Arafura Plain, south-west Asia 369–70, 372
Arcand, B. 52
archaeastronomy, north Africa 482
archaeobiographies 1196
archaeogenetics 1101–2, 1143–54
  Africa 1145–7, 1146 Fig. 55.2, 1154
  African hunter-gatherers 1101–2, 1147–53, 1154
  ancient and modern DNA 1101, 1143
  concepts and terminology 1143–5
  L3 haplogroup 1145–6
Ardipithecus 179, 181
  form indicating function 180
Arikara people 781, 882, 887, 888
Aristotle 59, 64, 1205
Arnold, J. 1004, 1064
Arrernte Aborigines 961, 962
art 588–90, 625–39
  Blombos Cave pieces 588–9, 626–8, 627 Fig. 28.1
  central and western Mediterranean Mesolithic 470
  Danubian Europe 531–2, 532 Fig. 23.5
  disenchantment with interpretation 635–6
  early explanations 589, 632–5
  European Upper Palaeolithic 296, 297
  as 'image-making' 588, 625–6
  Magdalenian figurative art 293–5
  neurological approach 589–90, 636–8, 639
  social situatedness 633, 639
  south Asia, post-glacial 447, 496, 501–2
  Sulawesi sites 354
  Upper Palaeolithic 289–90, 589, 628–32, 629 Fig. 28.2, 629 Fig. 28.3, 630 Fig. 28.4, 631 Fig. 28.5
  see also rock art
Arthur, B. 376
asbestos ware 849
Assiniboine people 781, 887–8
Association of Indigenous Peoples of the North, Siberia and the Far East 1085
Aterian culture 230
Athabascan people 890, 891
Augy-Sainte-Pallaye culture (ASP) 793, 794
Aunger, R. V. 943

Aurignacian culture 279, 286–7, 312, 314, 1172
  art 589, 628, 629 Fig. 28.2, 631
  Classic Aurignacian 284, 285–6
  clay-lined basins 664
  Europe 336
  Levant 257
  'lion-man' statuettes 1195
  material indicators of complexity 646
  rock art 287
  Zagros mountains 255, 264
aurochs 753
Austin-Broos, D. 964
Australian Aborigines 109, 160, 161–2, 162–3, 368–90, 903, 909, 958–68, 1149
  amateur observers, 1788–1880 958
  anthropology of Aboriginal religion 966
  approaches to Aboriginal economy 964
  art and belief 377
  chronometric evidence for earliest human habitation 357–8
  cultural and linguistic anthropology 965
  demographic pattern of colonization 377–9, 379–84, 381–2 Fig. 16.4, 382 Fig. 16.5, 383 Tab. 16.2, 383 Tab. 16.3
  the Dreaming/Dreamtime 376–7, 966, 1179, 1199, 1236
  Durkheim's synthesis 959–60
  earliest people 348, 368–9, 441
  early coastal exploitation 596, 698
  early theoretically oriented ethnography 958–9
  ecology and the 'Man the Hunter' programme 909, 962–3
  eel habitat manipulation 1269
  egalitarianism 645
  evidence for early symbolic expression 360
  environmental conditions (last 45000 years) 369–73, 370 Fig. 16.1, 370 Tab. 16.1, 371 Fig. 16.2, 372 Fig. 16.3
  and extinctions 385
  'fourth world' communities 966–7
  Freudian research 962
  gender and food restrictions 1270
  gender studies and feminist anthropology 965–6
  genetic lineage evidence 373–4
  human impacts on megafauna 384–5, 386 Fig. 16.6
  impact of fire and 'firestick farming' 385–6
  language at contact 374–6
  languages 368
  Marxist and neo-Marxist approaches 962, 963
  material culture 376
  music, art and performance 967–8
  niche construction 1268
  plant food production 387
  regionalization of symbolic communication 388
  religion 632
  research relation with social policy 909, 964–5
  research in south-east/south-west 967
  responses to colonization 386–8
  ritual and social organization 376–77
  rock art 589, 632, 1234
  spear ownership 387
  structural-functional ethnography 960–1
  structuralism: Lévi-Strauss' synthesis 962
  Tasmanian food-getting technology 1110
  'totemism' 1232
  urban areas and social change 961–2
Australian Institute of Aboriginal Studies 963, 964
australopithecines 185
  gathering 155–6
Australopithecus 155–6, 178, 179
  form indicating function 180, 181
Australopithecus afarensis 181, 185
  mortuary behaviour 713
Australopithecus africanus 183
Avikwame 1227
Awa people 135
Ayorea people 1037
Azilian culture 279, 295–6, 469

Babylonian Paradise texts 58
Bacsonian culture 361
Badegoulian culture 292, 558
Bahuchet, S. 940–1, 943, 944, 945
Bailey, G. N. 696, 698
Bailey, R. 942–3, 943–4, 946, 947
Bain, A. C. (Donald) 922
Bajau 'sea nomads' 1017

Baka people 163, 167, 940, 942, 948
Bakker, R. 814
Baldwin Spencer, W. 958, 959, 964, 966
Balée, W. 1033, 1041
Bali, genetic studies 378
Ballard, C. 1175
Balsan, F. 923
Baltic Mesolithic 1276
  cemeteries 720–1
  mortuary practices 597, 714–23
  social relationships 715–16
  symbols and cosmology 716–18
Baltic Sea formation 557
Bamforth, D. B. 124
Ban Rai, Thailand 349
Bann Flakes 825, 1215
Bantu farmers 938, 946, 1149, 1151, 1152
  genetic studies 1152–3
Bantu languages 483
Baradostian culture 256, 264
'Barbary Sheep', Tamar Hat, Algeria 665 Fig. 30.1, 666
Barnard, A. 22, 63
Barnes complex in the Americas 414
Barnes, J. A. 960–1
Bárta, J. 529
Barton, H. 501
Basarwa San people 1255
Batak people 871, 1016
Batchelor, J. 1060
Batek people 1021, 1024, 1025
Bates, D. 894, 958
Batianova, E. P. 162
Battle Axe groups 842–3
Bayliss, A. 833
Beagle Chanel, Tierra del Fuego project 137
Beaker groups 842–3
Bean, J. L. 980, 1229, 1230
Bean, T. 980
bear burials, Sámi 1279
bear ceremony (*iyomante*), Ainu 914, 1065
'bear cult', Ainu 1279
bear hunting, Ainu 1062
bear shamans 1227
bears, human relations with 1195
Beaune, S. 646
beavers 810, 1279
Beck, C. 413

Beckhampton Road long barrow, Wiltshire 1175
Behar, D. M. 1151
behavioural ecology *see* human behavioural ecology
Bell, C. 712
Bell, D. 966
Bella Coola people 994, 995, 1195
Bellwood, P. 360, 501, 858
Bender, B. 65, 771
Benedict, R. 997, 998
Bentley, R. A. 792
berdacheor 'two spirits' 1256
Berger, J. 543
Beringia, North American Pacific 701–2
Bern, J. 963, 966
Bernbeck, R. 635
Berndt, C. H. 960, 961, 965, 966
Berndt, R. M. 960, 961, 964, 965, 967
Bettinger, R. L. 1001, 1119, 1134, 1135
Bhuket people 1019
Biagi, P. 462, 471
Bidayuh farmers 860
Biesele, M. 927
Binford, L. 7–8, 12–13, 18, 20, 37, 40, 76–7, 107, 111–12, 114–16, 123, 124, 125, 127, 200–1, 771, 1020, 1167, 1168, 1170–1, 1206, 1247 *see also* New Archaeology
Biological Species Concept (BSC) (Mayr) 238
biomolecular archaeology 1279–80
Bird, I. 1063
Bird-David, N. 15–16, 65, 167, 1193, 1197
bison hunting 888, 1267
  farmer/hunter-farmers' return to 882, 889, 891–3
bison meat and hide trading 781, 887, 889, 890, 893, 894, 895
Bjerck, H. 698, 704
'Black Venus' Dolní Věstonice, Czech Republic 290, 665 Fig. 30.1, 666
Blackburn, T. 980–1
Blackman, M. B. 1254
blade and bladelet technologies 588, 608, 616, 618, 649
  Caucasus, Upper Palaeolithic 265–6
  European Upper Palaeolithic 279, 283–6, 288, 291, 292, 295, 616

blade and bladelet technologies (*Cont.*)
  lag between first appearance and widespread adoption 608
  Levantine Upper Palaeolithic 257, 258
  northern Asia, Palaeolithic 311, 312–14, 313 Fig. 13.1, 317–18, 320–1, 322 Fig. 13.2, 323 Fig. 13.3, 324 Fig. 13.4
  northern Europe, post-glacial 561, 564, 565–6
  parallel development in Africa and Eurasia 608–10
  Zagros, Upper Palaeolithic 264–5
Blakeslee, D. 888
Blankholm, H. P. 544
Bleed, P. 123, 1118
Bleek, W. 632, 921
Bliquy culture 793, 794
Blombos Cave, South Africa 230, 231, 588–9, 626–8, 627 Fig. 28.1
Boas, F. 3, 5, 13, 15, 18, 34, 36, 47, 49, 71–2, 73, 585–6, 590, 601, 602, 644, 978, 995–6, 998, 1131
boats 567, 695, 697–8, 699, 700, 704
  Ainu 1054
  Chinese Mesolithic watercraft 654
  skin 566
Bodo cranium, Ethiopia 224, 235
body decoration *see* personal ornaments
Boemus, J. 63
Bofi people 943
Bole-Maru cult, California 983
Bølling-Allerød interstadial 440, 492, 494, 498, 499, 500, 502
bone and antler technology and artefacts 257, 265–6, 312, 314
  China 654
  European Upper Palaeolithic 283, 284, 286
  Mesolithic Mediterranean 465
  Natufian 653
  Neolithic 466
  Niah Cave, Borneo 352
  northern Asia 317, 318, 322 Fig. 13.2
  post-glacial Danubian Europe 530
  post-glacial south Asia 496
  post-glacial south-east Asia 447, 500–1
  south Asia 336
Bonsall, C. 697
'Boomerang Culture' 48

Bordes, F. 255
Bordes, J.-G. 264
Borić, D. 1213, 1215
Borneo 351–3, 358, 360, 378
  forager-farmer relationships 865
  inter-group violence 869
  see also Niah Caves
Boscana, G. 975
Botai culture, horse husbandry 757–8, 759 Fig. 34.4
Boule, M. 192
Bourdieu, P. 135
bows and arrows 1003, 1004
  bifacial arrowheads 848
  evidence of, Terminal Upper Palaeolithic 297
  introduction 1120–1
  possible evidence, Niah Caves, Borneo 352
  spread of 617
Boyd, R. 1132
Boyette, A. H. 943
Bradley, J. J. 1176
Bradley, R. 1192–3
brain size, and modern human origins 217–19
Brantingham, P. 1171–2
Braudel, F. 1165
bride-wealth, southern Africa 485
Briggs, A. W. 195
Briggs, J. L. 1254
Brightman, R. 1252
Brinch Peterson, E. 546, 721
Britain and Ireland, Neolithic transition 777, 824–34
  animal husbandry 826, 827
  animals, diet and hunting 829–30
  axes and pottery technologies 831–2
  cereal production 826, 831
  chronology 833
  colonization from abroad argument 777, 828–9
  dairy products 832
  diet Mesolithic/Neolithic 829–30
  indigenous development argument 777, 828
  Mesolithic background 825–6
  monuments 826–7, 830, 832, 833
  Neolithic background 826–7

plant food, diet and gathering 830–1
pottery 826
transition debate 777, 827–9
Bromme culture 565
Bronze Age (BA) 769, 838, 847, 849, 850
Brooks, A. S 229
Brosowke, S. D. 890–1, 892
Brown, E. R. 569
Brown, J. A. 1170
Brumbach, H. J. 123, 131, 132, 133, 151, 168
Bukat people 1024
Bukitan people 869
Bunn, H. T. 184
Burbank, V. K. 160
Bureau of American Ethnology 977–8
Bureau of Indian Affairs, US 977, 982
Burroughs, W. J. 557
Bushmen 163, 484, 485 *see also* San
butchery practices
  and cutmarks 127
  faunal assemblages and optimal
    foraging 127–8
  and faunal distributions 124–8
  forager/collector model 124–8
  inter-site and intra-site variations in faunal
    assemblages 125–6
  carcass processing, marrow extraction and
    sharing 126–7
  women's role 1247, 1269
Butler, J. 164, 1212
Buttler, W. 789

Cabrillo, J. 974
Cahuilla people 980
California and the Great Basin 36, 73, 74–5
  Bureau of American Ethnology 977–8
  Bureau of Indian Affairs 977
  cultural anthropology 909–10, 973–86
  Department and Museum of Anthropology,
    Berkeley 978
  'ethnie' term 983
  ethnohistorical origins 974–6
  Ethnological and Archaeological
    Survey 978
  Ghost Dance movement 977, 983–4
  Gold Rush (1849) 976
  Great Basin point types 1100, 1135–7, 1136
    Fig. 54.1

hunter-gatherer ethnogenesis 984–5
Indian Claims Commission Proceedings
  (1970s) 982
Kroeberian anthropology 978–9
linguistic studies 979–80
memory anthropology and its
  critique 981–3
Mexican rancho system 976
plant management 1268
Point Conception gas terminal 985
populations at European contact 973
post ethnographic fieldwork 980–1
reliance on acorns 1267, 1270
religion and ritual 1221–2, 1223, 1225,
  1228–30, 1231
shamanism, California 1226–8
Spanish Franciscan Mission System 974–6
Steward and the Great Basin 979–80
Calley, Malcolm 966
Camelid domestication 758–9
candlenuts 1019
Cane, S. 110
Cann, R. L. 214
Canny, N. 62
Capsian industry 470, 472
Cardial tradition pottery (Impressed
  Ware) 790
Carlson, R. L. 992
Carpelan, C. 1080
Carson, R. 76
Cartmill, M. 228
carvings
  southern Germany 628–31
  stone objects, Neolithic western
    Asia 459
  see also figurines
Cashinahua people 1245
Castel, J.-C. 1177–8
Castelnovian culture 469–70
Castiglione, Baldassare 62
Çatal Hüyük 445, 461
cattle, DNA analysis 810
cattle domestication 759
  Neolithic Britain and Ireland 825, 826,
    827, 829
  north Africa 446, 481
Cauwe, N. 723
Cavalli-Sforza, L. 771, 934, 1150–1, 1152

Caverna da Pinta Pintada, Brazil 409, 410 Fig. 17.4
cemeteries *see under* mortuary practices
central Africa (Congo basin) hunter-gatherer research 908, 936–50, 937 Fig. 44.1, 937 Tab. 44.1
  British traditions 939–40
  comparing traditions 944–5
  conservation issues 948
  divergence of people 938
  ecological and evolutionary bias 949
  ethnographic research needs 950
  forager-farmer relations 946–8
  French traditions 940–1
  future research 949–50
  gender and nationality biases 949
  Harvard Ituri Project 943
  Japanese traditions 941–2
  oral histories 950
  origins and human stature 938
  subsistence and settlement 946
  US tradition 942–4
  'wild yam' hypothesis 946, 947
Centre for Aboriginal Economic Policy Research 965
ceramic technology 438, 593–5, 663–85, 776
  association with farming 593, 663, 770
  basketry associations 594, 667–8
  Cardial/Epi-Cardial (Impressed Ware) 471, 472, 790
  China 654
  chronology, Jomon and Chulmun 508–9
  clay/ceramic/pottery distinctions 663
  container technology 593, 666–7
  culinary ceramics 681–3, 1276–7
  earliest ceramics 664–6, 665 Fig. 30.1
  emergence and spread of pottery 604, 669–78, 677 Fig. 30.5
  Ertebølle 809, 1276
  as evidence of Iroquois-Alconquin interaction 886–7
  feasting role 657
  Gasya site vessel, Russian Far East 667 Fig. 30.2
  Glazed Ware, North America 890
  and 'horticultural' societies 679, 680
  Impressa tradition 790
  La Hoguette pottery culture 775, 787, 789 Fig. 36.2, 790, 792, 794, 797
  Limburg pottery culture 787, 789 Fig. 36.2, 790
  Linear pottery 521, 523
  Linearband Pottery culture (LBK) 775, 776, 778, 787, 788–94, 796–7, 805, 809, 840
  Khartoum Mesolithic pottery 481
  'moist' cookery techniques 681–2
  Middle Jomon vessels, Japan 667–8, 668 Fig. 30.3
  Neolithic south east Europe 466
  New World and Far North, emergence and spread 594, 674–5 Tab. 30.5, 676 Tab. 30.6, 679–80
  Old World, emergence and spread 594, 670 Tab. 30.1, 671 Tab. 30.2, 672 Tab. 30.3, 673 Tab. 30.4, 678–9
  origins of pottery 666–9
  Owens Valley ceramic technologies, California 1100–1, 1137 Fig. 54.2, 1138
  post-glacial Africa 483, 484, 485, 486
  post-glacial Mediterranean and western Asia 458
  presenting prestige 683–4
  protohistoric American Plains 893, 895
  San Jacinto pottery sequence, Columbia 668, 669 Fig. 30.4
  and seasonally abundant plant foods 595, 682, 683
  for surplus storing 683
  women's prominence in manufacture and use 1248
cereal introduction (4200 BC), north-west Europe 814
ceremonial buildings, Neolithic western Asia 459–61
ceremonies in caves 638
Chagnon, N. 943
chaînes opératoires 129–30, 135, 256, 317, 444, 499, 617, 1197, 1208, 1214
Chaná-Timbú peoples 1035
Chapman, A. 1037
Chapman, J. 1175
Charnov, E. L. 1167–8
Charrúas people 1035
Châtelperron points 197, 198 Fig. 9.3

Chauchat, C. 419
Chauvet Cave art 287, 294, 589, 628, 631, 646
Cherum (Great Basin chief, US) 983
chestnuts 1267, 1268, 1270
Cheyenne people 781, 887
child burials 465, 470, 646–9, 1197, 1253
    Final Palaeolithic northern Asia 320, 321
    Neolithic 466
Childe, V. Gordon 34, 51, 586, 442, 601, 650, 770, 788–9, 827, 1098, 1166
childhood 167, 1258
children 158, 159, 161, 548–9
    as subjects of hunter-gatherer studies 1196, 1197
    gender socialization 1253, 1258
    genders 168
    see also child burials
childscapes 1107
Chilton E. 882, 886–7
chimpanzees 180, 183, 186, 195
    compared with archaic hominins 187–8
    tool use 610
China 60–1
    bone and antler technology 654
    ceramic technology 654
    Mesolithic feasting 656–7
    social complexity 655–8
    trade with south-east Asia 862–4
Chindina, L. A. 162
Chingichngish cult 1229–30
Chinigchinich people 975
Chipewyan people 122–3, 133, 161
    gender dynamics and subsistence 131, 132 Tab. 6.6, 1248–50, 1251
    human-prey animal relationship 1279
    inkonze 1250–1
    marriage and women's Treaty status 1256
Chisholm, B. 515
Chisholm, J. S. 160
Cho, D. 509
Chonos people 1036–7
Christianity, Russian Orthodox 1056
Chua, L. 860
Chulmun culture 448, 507–16
Chumash people 974, 980–1, 985
    Antap cult 1229
'clam gardens' 1268, 1273
Clark, D. 255

Clark, G. 6, 7, 11, 105–6, 442–3
Clark, W. 887–8
Clarke, D. L. 13
Clarkson, C. 1173
cleavers 196, 611–12, 613 Fig. 27.3
Clemmer, R. 982–3
Clendon, M. 375
clothing 265, 588, 615, 616
    elaborately decorated 650
    tailored skin 656
    women's manufacture 1247–8, 1269
Clovis culture 406, 411, 412–14, 413 Fig. 17.5, 418
coalescence theory, and modern human origins 235
coastal adaptation 596, 694–705
    development of technology 697–8
    disadvantages of the coast 695–6
    East Timor 355–6
    edible resources 694
    first users 698–700
    and fresh water 695
    limitations of the evidence 457, 696–7
    north-west Europe 700–1
    possible link with bone technology rise, south-east Asia 447, 500
    and shelter 694–5
    south-east Asia and Indonesia 352
    south-east Asia, post-glacial sites showing no evidence 447, 498–9, 502
    and transport 695
    value of the coast 694–5
coefficient of variation (CV), and cultural transmission 1135–7, 1136 Fig. 54.1
Cold War 904
Coleman, J. 58
collectors *see* forager vs. collector model
Collier, J. 156–7
colonialism 14, 35, 165, 1256, 1258
Colville Indian people 1253
Combe-Grenal rock shelter, France 199–200
'composite band' societies 51
composite (hafted) tools 616
    appearance 615
    cognitive requirements 620
    geometric inserts 610 Fig. 27.1
    Niah Cave, Borneo 352
    south-east Asia 361

cone point armatures 499
Conferences on Hunting and Gathering
    Studies (CHAGS) 9, 22–3, 41, 151, 153,
    156, 167, 1023
  effects of gender studies 157–67
conflict:
  Borneo 869
  ritualization of 158
  symbolised 633
  see also violence
Conkey, M. W. 157, 160, 1207, 1244
Conneller, C. 547, 719, 1112–13, 1194,
    1214, 1216
consciousness, evolution of 636–7 *see also*
    altered states of consciousness
contingent historical sequences 33
'Continuity' model 214–15, 228, 232
Cook, Captain James 374
Cook, S. 980, 984
Coolidge, F. L. 620
Cooper, Z. 110
copper 794
  distribution on Northwest Plateau of North
    America 647 Fig. 29.1
  first use 653
Corded Ware culture 844 Fig. 39.2
corporate kinship groups 649, 650, 653, 656
cosmology/ies 1222, 1277–9
  Baltic Mesolithic 716–18
  European upper Palaeolithic 290
  and foodways 513–15
  and gender 1250–2, 1257–8
  Kelabit farmers 859–60
  and mortuary practices 598, 712–13, 714
  Penan people 859–60
  and social relations 1199
Coso rock engravings, California 1234
Cowlishaw, G. 967
Crass, B. 1253
Crate, S. A. 549
Crawford, G. 658, 1060
Crepi, Father Juan 974
Creswellian culture 560, 561, 564, 568
Croes, D. 1005
Crombé, P. 809
Crow people 781, 887, 888
Crow-Hidatsa split 889, 894
Cruikshank, J. 1254

Cueva de los Aviones, Spain 201–2
cults and secret societies 646, 650,
    1228–30, 1236
cultural bottlenecks 618
cultural ecology 36–7, 73–5, 77, 586, 601, 603,
    604, 905, 915, 979, 999–1001, 1098
cultural evolution 72, 73, 74, 75, 82
  Boas' rejection of 590, 644
  identifying general patterns 602–3
  and social complexity 591, 643, 658
cultural relativism 586, 590, 601, 602, 644
cultural transmission (CT) 587, 588, 604, 617,
    619, 620, 698, 1098–1101, 1127
  and archaeology 1100, 1131–2
  coefficient of variation (CV) 1135–7, 1136
    Fig. 54.1
  cognitive/psychological biases 1130–1,
    1131 Tab. 54.2
  defined 1128–31, 1130 Tab. 54.1, 1131
    Tab. 54.2
  effects of information content and
    complexity 1133–4
  effects of population size and
    density 1132–3
  effects of social organization 1134
  and genetic transmission (GT) 1128
  Great Basin point types 1100, 1135–7, 1136
    Fig. 54.1
  Markov Chains, equations and
    processes 1128–9
  modes of 82
  Owens Valley ceramic technology,
    California 1100–1, 1137 Fig. 54.2,
    1138
  potential for application 1135–8
  process of 83
  testing the theory 1132, 1134
'culture areas' 72, 73
culture, intersection with environment 36–7,
    70, 71–2, 73–5, 603–4
  east Asia 512–13
culture change, understanding long-term, east
    Asia 512–16
culture-historical framework 770, 782
Cumberland culture 414
Cummings, V. 95, 444, 774, 777, 779, 825,
    828, 830, 83
Cunningham, J. J. 108

cuscus 1013
Cybulski, J. 1001–2

Dadiwan, China 735
Dahlberg, F. 155
Dalrymple, Sir John 46
Daly, P. 65
Daly, R. 22
Danubian Europe, post-glacial
    transformations 448–9, 521–34
  aquatic diet resources 528
  architecture and pyrotechnology 530–1,
    531 Fig. 23.4
  art and symbolism 531–2, 532 Fig. 23.5
  bone technology 530
  cemeteries, burials and scattered human
    remains 532–3
  chronology and archaeology 522–3
  chronology and environment 522
  geographic characteristics 521
  karstic caves and rock shelters 525
  lithic resources 526–8
  lithic technology 529
  open-air settlement sites 524–5, 524
    Fig. 23.1
  pseudokarstic (sandstone) rock
    shelters 525–6, 526 Fig. 23.2, 527
    Fig. 23.3
  terrestrial diet resources 528–9
  wood technology 529–30
Danubian Europe, Upper Palaeolithic 521
Darkinyung people 374
Darnell, R. 977
Dart, R. A. 179
Daruk language 374
Darwin, Charles 50, 70–1, 83, 704, 730, 756
Darwinian evolutionary theory 70–1, 442,
    1131 see also Neo-Darwinian approaches;
    New Synthesis evolutionary theory
David, E. 542
David, N. 137
Davidson, I. 1234
Dawson, J. 958–9
Day, M. H. 219
De Bie, M. 541
De Bruin culture 810, 811–12 Tab. 37.1, 814
de Candolle, A. 730
de Saussure, F. 633

Dean, J. 890
deer antlers *see* antler frontlets, Star Carr
Deger, Jennifer 968
delayed return economic system 119 Tab. 6.3,
    544, 994, 995, 1003, 1272
delayed vs. immediate return hunter gatherers
    (Woodburn) 11, 115, 992,
demography, prehistoric 160
Denig, E. 888
Denisova cave, Altai, Siberia 310, 311, 312,
    313 Fig. 13.1, 314, 317
Denisovans, DNA admixture with early
    human 215
dentalium shell artefacts 201, 260, 653,
    888, 1231
Denver African Expedition 924
Developed Northwest Coast Pattern 1003
DeVore, I. 8–10, 16, 65, 154, 942, 943, 945
Dewing, E. 1215
Di Lernia, S. 481
Diamond, J. 1133
diet, subsistence and foodways 1106–7,
    1266–81
  aDNA research 1267, 1273, 1280
  age-based differences 1270–1
  cooking technology changes (5000
    BC) 809–10
  cosmologies and foodways 1277–9
  diet breadth model 1118–19, 1120
  diet diversity, post-glacial east Asia 513–15
  'delayed return' strategy 544, 1272
  food for status 1276–7
  future of research 1279–81
  and gender 1106, 1245, 1248–50, 1269–70
  hunter-gatherer/farmer differences in
    diet 813 Fig. 37.4
  'immediate return' strategy 1271
  and landscape 1272–3
  Levantine Upper and Epipalaeolithic 254,
    260–4, 270
  Neolithic 829–31
  ownership and territoriality 1271–4
  post-glacial 528–9
  and radiocarbon dating 1280–1
  south-east Asia, post-glacial 498–9
  stable-isotope analysis 734–5, 1270–1,
    1276, 1279–80
  transition to Neolithic diet 814

diffusion vs. migration arguments 1166
Dikov, N. N. 319–20
Djungan Aboriginal group, Australia 1178
Dobres, M. 1207
Dobyns, H. 983
Dobzhansky, T. 192
Doggerland 440, 539, 539 Fig. 24.4, 560, 569, 696, 701
dogs:
    burials 320, 713, 718, 1195
    domestication 264, 542, 566, 567, 600, 749, 756–7, 881, 1064, 1267
    human relations with 1195
Dolní Věstonice, Czech Republic 664–6, 665 Fig. 30.1
Donald, L. 646, 1005
Donald, M. 1133
donkey domestication, Africa 487
Dounias, E. 941
Dousset, L. 961
Dowson, T. A. 1234
Drake, Sir Francis 974
Draper, P. 927
Dreaming, the/Dreamtime 376–7, 966, 1179, 1199, 1236
Drucker, P. 992
dry-and wet-season camps, Botswana 113–14, 113 Fig. 6.2
Du Bois, C. 983
dual inheritance theory (DIT) 20, 37, 81, 82–3, 84, 1098–1100
Dubois, C. G. 1229
Dufour bladelets 285, 286
Dulong people 1015, 1018
dune sites, Danubia 524–5
Dunnell, R. 81
Durkheim, E. 3, 959–60, 962, 966, 1182
Dussart, L. 966
dwellings
    Late Upper Palaeolithic Europe 292
    Neolithic south-east Europe 466
    Palaeolithic northern Asia 319–20, 323 Fig. 13.3
    'polinary' structures 319
    rectangular houses, Neolithic western Asia 461
Dzudzuana, Caucasus 265–6, 270

'early farming in Dalmatia' project 472
'early Iron Age', southern Africa 485
Early Stone Age 484, 614
Earth Lodge Cult 983
east Asia, independent technological evolution 608, 616–17
east Asia, post-glacial 448, 507–16, 511 Fig. 22.1
    chronology 508–9, 508 Tab. 22.1
    environmental change 512–13
    mechanism of long-term culture change 512–16
    settlement 515
    site density and size 510
    society 515
    subsistence 513–15
    temporal and regional variability 509–12
ecological approaches *see* adaptive and ecological approaches
'economic school' of archaeology 1166
ecosystems concept 77
Eder, J. F. 14
Eerkens, J. W. 83, 1134, 1135
Efe people 14, 939, 942, 943, 947
'egalitarian', definition 643, 591
egalitarianism, assumed in hunter-gatherers 992
'Egbert' 257
Egypt, dynastic 487
Ehrlich, Paul 76
El Jobo projectile points 413 Fig. 17.5, 418
El Niño-Southern Oscillation (ENSO) events 373
Eliade, M. 1224
Elkin, A. P. 960, 967
Emmerloord fish traps, Netherlands 814, 816 Fig. 37.6
en éperon style 560
Endicott, K. L. 1025
Endicott, K. M. 1025
Endicott, P. 235
Engelbrecht, T. H. 730
Enlightenment, the 35, 71, 84
Enloe, J. G. 126
'entoptic patterns' 637, 1233–4
environment:
    human-environment interactions 76–7

intersection with culture 70, 71–2, 73–5, 512–13, 603–4
relationship with technology 74–5, 586
environmental determinism 36–7, 74, 80, 443–4, 512, 603
'environmental possibilism' 36, 72, 1000
Epi-Cardial pottery 790
Epigravettian culture 266, 291, 292, 295, 522, 558
toolkits 556
Epi-Jōmon culture 510, 1058
Epimagdalenian culture 522
Epipaleolithic 256–64, 270, 442, 445, 459, 480
use of term 255
Erin, M. I. 22
Erlandson J. M. 697, 698, 702–3
Ertebølle culture 449–50, 451, 542, 544–5, 547, 700–1, 778, 794, 807, 819, 825, 841
burials 545
ceramics 809, 1276
Escalante, Fray 975
Estévez, J. 137
'ethnie' term 983
ethnoarchaeology 12–13, 18, 33, 39–41, 104–40, 168, 1197, 1255
and agency, belief and spirituality 132–4
alternative and emergent approaches 128–38
chaînes opératoires 129–30
Congo basin research 943
forager vs. collector model (Binford, 1980) 12=13, 115–23, 117 Fig. 6.2, 118 Fig. 6.3, 119–20, Tab. 6.3, 121 Tab. 6.4, 992
and gender dynamics 130–2, 132 Tab. 6.6, 168, 1243, 1247, 1248–50, 1257
and histories and intimacies of things 134–6
integrating historical and archaeological perspectives 136–8
material style and identity 128–9
research biases 110–12
research patterns 109–10, 110 Tab. 6.1
Ring Model (Yellen) 112–14, 114 Fig. 1
'toss' and 'drop' zones (Binford) 114 Fig. 6.1, 114–15

ethnographic analogy 12, 105–7, 633, 635, 772, 783, 905 see also analogical reasoning
'ethnographic riddles' 75
Ethnological and Archaeological Survey, US 978
ethnology 93, 441–2, 769–70
Euler, R. 983
Eurasia:
  earliest evidence for Levallois and bladelet technologies 608, 614
  earliest stone tools 613
  Middle Palaeolithic stone tool technology 614, 615
  modern human dispersal into 440
  transition to agriculture 738
  Upper Palaeolithic stone tool technology 616
Eurasian grey wolf, and domestic dogs 756
Europe:
  colonial expansion 903
  modern human dispersal into 441
  see also Danubian Europe; Baltic Mesolithic; northern Europe; northern Fennoscandia, north west Europe
Europe, Mesolithic 444, 448–51
  arrival of farming in south-east 466–8
  bone and antler technology 465
  coastline submersion 696
  fishing equipment 697
  future research areas 452–3
  gender difference in diet 1245
  maritime sites 700
  plant foods 1270
  social complexity 650–1
  spread of farming from south west Asia 462
Europe, Upper Palaeolithic 224, 279–97, 336
  archaeological record 233
  artefacts 231, 232
  chronology and environments 281–3
  climatic instability 282
  dispersals 282–3
  Early (EUP) (~35/32–29 000 BP) 280, 281, 285–7
  Early Period personal ornamentation 286–7
  Early Period rock art 287

Europe, Upper Palaeolithic (*Cont.*)
   Initial (IUP) (~50–35 000 BP) 280, 281, 282, 283–5
   Late Period (LUP) 280, 291–5
   Late Period burials 293
   Late Period Magdalenian figurative art 293–5
   Late Period portable art 294–5
   Late Period rock art 291–2, 293–4
   material indicators of complexity 590, 591–2, 645–50,
   Mid (MUP) Upper Palaeolithic 280, 281, 288–91
   Mid Period burials 290–1
   Mid Period refuges in 289
   Mid Period rock art 289–90
   Mid Period settlement and distribution 288–9
   Mid Period stone tools 288
   population sizes 282
   refuges 282–3
   technology 237
   Terminal Period adaptations 295–7
   Terminal Period climate 295
   Terminal Period burials 296
   Terminal Period portable art 296
Evans, I. H. 868
Eve hypothesis 198–9
'Evo/Devo' approach 620
evolution 69
   'multi-linear' 34, 51
   role of hunting vs. gathering 155, 155–6
   'uni-linear'/'stadial' 51, 585, 602
   'universal' 51
   see also Darwinian evolutionary theory; Neo-Darwinian approaches; New Synthesis evolutionary theory; social evolutionary approach
evolutionary psychology 636
Evolutionary Species Concept (Simpson) 238
Ewes, John 888
exaptations 79–80
excarnation practices 825
'expensive tissue hypothesis' 185–7
extinctions:
   Africa 480
   Australia 385
   Neanderthals 204–6

Fabre, V. 195
family bands 73
   social complexity, Jomon of Japan 654
farming *see* agriculture and farming
feasting 658, 818
   Chinese Mesolithic 656–7
   funerary 654
   and social complexity 645, 653, 654, 656–7, 994, 1004
Federmessergruppen culture 541, 564, 568
Federova, E. G. 163, 165
feminism 152, 154
   as inspiration for anthropological reserach 156–7
   corrective phase of anthropological critique 155–6
   critique of anthropology 157, 167
   rise of second-wave 153
feminist anthropology 1193, 1196
   Aboriginal societies 965–6
Fennoscandia *see* northern Fennoscandia; Sámi/Lapps
Ferguson, A. 46–7
Fewster, K. 132–3, 1255
figurines 466, 589, 628, 629 Fig. 28.2
   Final Palaeolithic northern Asia 321
   Palaeolithic northern Asia 322 Fig. 13.2
   Upper Palaeolithic Europe 290
   Venus 287, 290, 560
Finlay, N. 549, 1211, 1212, 1215
Finlayson, J. 160
fire, and 'niche construction' 501, 750, 1268
fire-cracked rocks 651
Fisher. J. W. 122, 943
fishing 465–6, 1119
   capture technology, Niah Cave, Borneo 352
   deep-water 471, 697, 702
   dried fish trade, Algonquian/Iroquois 885
   Emmerloord fish traps, Netherlands 814, 816 Fig. 37.6
   evolution of equipment 697
   northern Europe, post-glacial 564
   open-water, East Timor 355–6, 356 Fig. 15.4
   and production of surpluses, European Mesolithic 650–1
   see also salmon fishing

fishtail projection point (FPP) 'horizon' 413
    Fig. 17.5, 417–18
Fitzpatrick, S. M 697
Flad, R. 656
Flannery, K. 1267
Flores 348, 357, 360, 500
Florisbad cranium, South Africa 224
Folsom culture 414, 415–16, 418
food *see* diet, subsistence and foodways
forager vs. collector model (Binford,
    1980) 12=13, 115–23, 117 Fig. 6.2,
    118 Fig. 6.3, 119–20, Tab. 6.3, 121 Tab.
    6.4, 992
  butchery practices and faunal
    distributions 124–8
  'constrained mobility' 122
  criticisms and modifications 116–23
  food storage 122
  seasonal availability of resources 122–3
  sedentism 116–21
  'simple' and 'complex' systems 116, 121
    Tab. 6.4
  'tethered mobility' 122
forager-farmer interactions 38, 97–8,
    133, 768
  Africa 485, 946–8, 1149, 1150, 1151, 1154
  Botswana 1255
  comparative approach suggested 783
  complexity of 772
  early historic period,
    Finland 1076–9, 1083–4
  future directions 782–3
  eränkäynti, medieval Fennoscandia 1074–5
  importance of understanding 771
  influence of older models 769–70,
    778–9, 782
  North America 780–1, 881–96
  northern Fennoscandia 777–8, 838–51
  prehistoric 16–17
  south-east Asia 779–80, 857–75
  western and central Europe, sixth and fifth
    millennia 788–95
'foragers'/'collectors' distinction 115–16
Fosna culture 567
Fosna-Hensbacka culture 700
Fout, H. N. 943
Fouts, V. 949
Fowler, C. 718

Fox, R. G. 338
FOX-P2 gene mutations 233
Franchthi Cave, Greece 445, 465, 468
Franciscus de Victoria 63
free will 84
Freedman, P. 62
Freeman, M. 75
Fremont people 882
Frink, L. 131, 1250, 1253
Fruth, B. 184
Fuca, Juan de 1003
Fuhlrott, J. C. 191
Fukusawa, Y. 1064, 1065
Fuller, D. 657, 658, 731
functionalism 960–1
Funk, R. 886
Funnel Beaker (TRB) culture 795, 840, 841,
    842, 844 Fig. 39.2
  mixed Funnel-Beaker Mesolithic burial site,
    Ostorf 797
fur trade 650, 1074, 1077, 1081, 1084

G//ana people 919–20, 928
G/ui people 919–20, 928
Gaffney, V. 701
Gamble, C. 136, 282, 558, 559, 563, 564,
    568, 1197
'Garden of Eden'/Paradise 57–8
Gardner, P. M. 159
Garrod, D. 255, 560
Gasya site vessel, Russian Far East 667
    Fig. 30.2
gathering:
  importance in caloric terms 161, 1269
  role in evolution 155–6
  social factors 153
  Woman the Gatherer 154–6
Gauicurú linguistic family 1037
Gauicurú 'proper' people 1038
Gayton, A. 978
Geertz, C. 18
Gehlen, B. 791
Geis, Sally 155
Gendel, P. A. 1210
gender:
  and accessing cosmological and sacred
    power 1250–2, 1257–8
  and ancestral myth 1182

gender (*Cont.*)
  appearance of concept in hunter-gatherer studies 156–7
  biases, Congo Basin research 949
  and colonial transformations 1256, 1258
  concept absent in early hunter-gatherer studies 153–6
  concept absent from Man the Hunter 153–4
  cultural conduction 151
  and diet and subsistence 1269–70
  and ethnoarchaeology 130–1, 132 Tab. 6.6
  equality/inequality 156–7, 157–8, 163, 164–5, 1253
  evidence/assumption distinction 1244
  and food restrictions 1270
  future research directions 1248–56
  and grief 167
  and identity 1106, 1211–12, 1243–58
  as inseparable part of daily life 165
  integration into wider analysis 161
  Iñupiaq people, and subsistence 1248–50
  Khanty people 1248–50, 1251, 1252
  male/female opposition in Upper Palaeolithic art 589, 633, 634
  nature/culture debate 152
  norms, and Mesolithic mortuary practices 718
  not exclusively about women 152–3
  personality and politics 1253–5, 1258
  recent themes and directions 1244–8
  in relation to Mesolithic studies 444
  research needs 1257–8
  and 'sex' 152, 158, 164, 1256
  and shamanism 1225, 1231
  socializing 1253
  and technology 1120–1
gender-based division of labour 131–2, 158, 161, 165, 167
'gendered landscapes' 1249, 1257
harvesting, processing and asymmetries of power 1247–8
household organization and activity areas 1246
'meat for sex' hypothesis 1245
Neanderthal 199–200
rethinking 1248–50
skeletal evidence 1106, 1244–5

suggested origins 184
tools and toolkits 1246–7
variability and flexibility 132, 1244–6, 1252, 1253, 1269
gender identity/ies 158, 164
  alternative 1255–6, 1258
  fluidity, and materials 1211–12
gender relations 159, 160, 164–5
  Aboriginal 965–6
  and contact with Europeans 158
  imposition of Western gender ideology 1248
  and marriage 157–8
gender roles 162–3, 164, 165, 166
  Ainu 1061
  analysis 8
  and lithic technology 1177
  in early North American foraging communities 416–17
gender studies 33, 41, 151–68
  Aborigine societies 965–6
  influence on Conferences on Hunting and Gathering Societies (CHAGS) 151, 157–67
gene lineages/trees, and modern human origins 235–6
Geneste, J.-M. 1177–8
genetic transmission 1128, 1129, 1130
genetics *see* archaeogenetics
Geometric Kebaran culture 255, 258, 259, 261, 269
Gero, J. 416, 1177
Ghost Dance movement, North America 977
  rethinking 983–4
Giddens, A. 133
Gifford-Gonzalez, D. 483
Gillen, F. J. 958, 959, 966
'gingerbread figure', Maïna, Siberia 665 Fig. 30.1, 666
Glavatskaya, E. 1249, 1252
Glaze Ware ceramics, North America 890
Glover, I. C. 501
Gobekli Tepe, Anatolia 654, 658
Godelier, M. 52, 963
Gold Rush (1849) 976
gold trade:
  Roman control 487
  Saharan 482

tropical Africa 486–7
Gomes, A. 860, 872
González-Ruibal, A. 135–6
Goodale, J. C. 1244
Goodwin, A. J. H. 484
Goody, J. 1023
Gordon, R. J. 158, 924
Gorman, C. F. 498
Gosden, C. 1181
Goshen culture 414–15
Gould, R. A. 12, 106, 963
Gould, S. 80
grave goods 497, 501, 655, 656, 717, 718, 1197
 Baltic Mesolithic 714, 715
 Final Palaeolithic northern Asia 320
 Neanderthal 203
Gravettian culture 279, 288, 291, 295, 558, 560
 material indicators of complexity 646–9
Gray Jones, A. 722
Great Basin *see* California and Great Basin
Green, R. E. 205
Greenberg, J. H. 412
Gregg, S. A. 895
Griffin, P. B. 158–9
Grinker, R. R. 947
Gronenborn, D. 541, 543, 789, 791
Grotte Chauvet, France 287, 290
Grotte de Renne, France 200, 201, 202 Fig. 9.4, 203, 283
Guahibo people 1038–9
Guaicurú-Mbayá people 1045
Guenoa-Minuanos peoples 1035
Guilaine, J. 543
Gülderman, T. 484
Gusinde, M. 1037
Gustavus Vasa 1076, 1077
Guugu-Yimidhirr vocabulary 374

Haak, W. 787, 796
Habicht-Mauche, J. 890, 893, 895
Habu, J. 166, 513, 515
Hackel, S. 975
Hadzabe (Hadza) people 109, 111, 126, 127, 137, 643, 1147, 1148, 1210
 genetic studies 1150–1, 1152
Hagan people 1210

Haida people 993 Fig. 47.1, 994, 996, 999, 1254
Hajic, E. R. 1179
Halbfass, W. 60
Hale, H. 1166
Haley, B. 985
Hall, J. 58
Hall, M. E. 513
Hallowell, I. 1194
Hamburgian culture 561, 564, 568, 699
Hamilton, A. 158, 963, 965
Hamilton's Rule 76
Hammel, E. 1062
Han dynasty, China 61
handaxes 196, 611–12, 612 Fig. 27.2, 613
 east Asia 617
 lag between first appearance and widespread adoption 608
handedness (laterality) and development of language 620
Hang Boi, Vietnam 498–9, 502
Hansen, L. I. 1074
Hanson, J. 889
haplogroups 1143–4, 1144 Fig. 55.1, 1145
haplotypes 1143, 1145
Harako, R. 941, 946
Hardy, B. J. 529, 530
Harlan, J. R. 731
Harrington, J. P. 979, 980, 981
Harris, M. 998
Hart, C. W. M. 960, 961
Hartog, F. 59
Hartwig, M. 963
Harvard Ituri Project 943
Harvard Kalahiri Research group 926–7, 928
Hassell, E. 959
Hather, J. G. 733
Hattori, S. 948
Haush people 703
Hauzeur, A. 790
Hawkes, C. 6–7, 18
Hawkes, K. 79
Hayden, B. 1001, 1003–4, 1121, 1269
hazelnuts 831, 1270
Hazendonk group 805, 806 Fig. 37.1, 807 Fig. 37.2, 808 Fig. 37.3, 810, 811–12 Tab. 37.1, 813
Head, L. 1181

headhunting 869
Headland, T. N. 14, 946, 1020
Healy, F. 833
Heaney, L. R. 358
Heidegger, M. 1206
Heidenreich, C. 885, 895
Heinz, H. J. 923–4
Heizer, R. 980, 984
Hell Gap Site, Wyoming 414, 415 Fig. 17.6
Helland, Amund 1072
Hempel, C. 81
Henrich, J. 1132
Henry, D. 653
Hensbacka, Sweden 699
Herder, J. G. 47, 48
Herodotus 59
Herto cranium BOU-VP-16/1 226
Hesiod 58
heswas ceremony, North America 1227
Hewlett, B. L. 167, 949
Hewlett, B. S. 166–7, 938, 942, 943–4, 945, 947
Hiatt, B. 154–5
Hiatt, L. R. 154, 1020
Hidatsa people 781, 887, 888
Higgs, E. 77
Hildebrand, E. 759
Hill, C. 499
Hill, J. H. 412
Hill, K. 79, 1121
Hillman, G. C. 730
Hinkelstein-Group culture 794
Hinkson, M. 968
historical particularism (Boasian) 3, 4, 5, 6, 36, 71–2, 74, 586, 601, 602, 995
historical perspectives 38, 92, 93–4, 97–100
  value of studies 99
Hitchcock, R. 121
Hittman, M. 984
Hiwasaki, L. 164
Hoabinhian Period, south-east Asia 348, 349, 350, 361, 496, 656
Hobbes, Thomas 44, 1110
Hodder, I. R. 108, 750, 772–3, 1205
Hofman, J. L. 415
Hohlenstein-Stadel 'lion-man' statuettes 1195
Holiday, F. T. 416
Holliday, T. W. 1119
Holmberg, A. R. 1041

Holmes, W. H. 1131
hominins, early 177–88
  anatomy and dentition evidence of meat eating 184–7
  evidence for plant-based foods 181–2
  evidence for small animal protein 182–3
  expansion into Europe and Asia 616
  form indicates function 180–1
  invention of meat-eating 182–7
  large animal protein 183–7
  plant-based subsistence 180–2
  stone tool technology 610–11
Homo erectus 178, 179, 180, 183, 184–7, 194, 214, 224, 310, 315, 350, 611, 620, 697, 1165
Homo ergaster 184–7, 611, 613
Homo floresiensis 179, 348, 378
Homo heidelbergensis 193, 217, 219, 224, 225, 228, 332
Homo helmei 224, 238
Homo neanderthalensis see Neanderthals
Homo rhodesiensis 224
Homo sapiens see modern humans
Hooer, I. 1207–8
Hopf, M. 730
Hopi Pueblo peoples 882
horse bits 754 Fig. 34.2, 757
horses:
  bison hunters' reliance on 888
  domestication 600, 757–8, 758 Fig. 34.4, 1267
Hose, C. 865
Hotï people 1033, 1038, 1039 Fig. 49.4, 1045
Houseley, R. A. 558
Howitt, A. W. 958, 959, 964
Huaorani people 1033, 1044–5
Hudson Bay Company 996, 997
Hudson, M. J. 166
Hudson, T. 980, 981
human-animal relations 444, 1013, 1112–13, 1193–6, 1199, 1222, 1277–9
human behavioural ecology (HBE) 37, 78–80, 82, 84, 1001, 1097
  and mobility 1167–9
  and technology 1097–8, 1117–20
Humboldt, Alexander von 48
Hummalian culture 618
hunter-gatherer archaeology and anthropology 1–25

'balkanization' of subject 19
colonialism and imperialism impacts 14, 35, 165
current challenges 19–20
early research 2–4
emergence of modern studies 5–8
ethnoarchaeology, emergence of (within hunter-gatherer archaeology and anthropology) 12 *see also* ethnoarchaeology
ethnographic parallels 12
and historical frameworks 15–16
'nomadic style' formulations 9–10
post-processual and interpretive approaches 17–18
research outlook 20–1
revisionist approaches and culture-contact 13–15
variability debates 10–11
hunter-gatherer research, new approaches 1093–1108
diversification in theoretical approaches 1094–5
engagement with indigenous communities 1095
growth in basic information 1094
hunter-gatherers, defining 34–5, 43–52, 55–65
and alterity/otherness 35, 56–65
definitions as an invention 63–4
Enlightenment perspectives 44, 45–7, 55, 56
evolutionist theories 49–51
Man the Hunter conference 51–2
Romantic tradition 47–9
hunter-gatherers, as outdated concept 35, 38
hunting and gathering in a farmer's world 767–84
hunter-gatherers and the transition to agriculture 767–8
Neolithic transition to farming 769–75
hunting
privileged over gathering 161
as 'rite of passage' 267
seasonality, Upper Palaeolithic Caucasus 269–70
as shorthand for hunting, gathering and fishing 153, 154–5, 164
Upper and Epi-Palaeolithic Levant 262–4
Upper Palaeolithic Caucasus 266

by women 159–60, 161, 1246, 1251
see also human-animal relations; specific animals
Hupdu people 1044
Hurst, T. D. 1135
Hurtado, A. M. 1121
Hutton, J. 70
hxaro exchange system, San peoples 134, 926
Hyades, P. 1037

Iban people, and headhunting 869
Ichikawa, M. 941–2, 944, 945, 947
identity 444, 783
and the childscape 1107
construction of male 156
corporeal aspects 1191–2, 1198
forager, south-east Asia 1013–19, 1014 Tab. 48.1, 1019–21
gender and 1106, 1211–12, 1243–58
humans and animals 1212–13
and Mesolithic tool production 1211–12
as performance 164
and personhood 1191–2
Ikeya, K. 165–6, 929, 930
Imamura, K. 164
immediate return economic systems 119 Tab. 6.3, 1003, 1271
immediate vs. delayed return hunter gatherers (Woodburn) 11, 115, 992
Impressa pottery 790
Indian Claims Commission Proceeding (1970s) 982, 985
Indonesia *see* south-east Asia
Ingalls, G. W. 977
Ingbar, E. I. 415
Ingold, T. 750, 1174, 1181, 1198, 1206, 1208, 1209, 1211, 1214
Inoue, T. 164
intelligence, modular vs. generalized 636
interpretive and post-processual approaches 17–18, 20, 38–9, 443–4, 548–9, 602, 1102–5
Inuit Circumpolar Conference 549
Inuit people 49, 109, 1199, 1246
kipijuituq 1255–6
miniatures 1253
Iñupiaq people, gender dynamics and subsistence 1248–50

Irish Mesolithic 543, 549
  coastal adaptation 701
Iron Age 485, 769, 838, 843, 850, 1058
iron production 849
Iroquois people 50 *see also* Algonquian/
  Iroquois interaction
Isaac, G. 183-4, 187
Islam, introduction into the Sahel 482
Itani, J. 941, 945
Iyora people 374

jade, first use of 653
jadeite axes 831-2
Jain texts, and Paradise 57-8
Janik, L. 1197
Japan *see* Ainu people, Jomon culture
Jarvenpa, R. 123, 131, 132, 133, 151, 168
jasper 466
Jebel Qafzeh hominid fossils, Israel 225, 226
Jègues-Wollkiewicz, C. 646
Jenike, M. R. 943
Jenkins, T. 918
Jennbert, K. 1279
Jericho 459, 461
Jesup North Pacific Expedition 72, 996
Jeunesse, C. 792-3
jimson weed, and altered states of
  consciousness 1229
Jochim, M. A. 1168
Johnson, E. 416
Johnson, J. 981
Jolles, C. Z. 1254-5, 1249
Jomon (cord-marked) culture 448, 451, 507-
  16, 598, 651, 678, 1057, 1058, 1268
  'biscuits' 1276, 1278 Fig. 61.6
  diet and gender 1270
  diet and social identity 1276, 1278 Fig. 61.5
  Middle Jomon vessels 667-8, 668 Fig.
    30.3, 1276
  Middle Jomon villages 1273, 1274 Fig. 61.1
  possible plant management 1267
  reliance on chestnuts 1267, 1270, 1276
  social complexity 654
  wild boar management 1267
Jonaitas, A. 998
Jones, G. T. 413
Jones, N. B. 158
Jordan, J. W. 557

Jordan, P. 133-4, 135-6, 550, 1006, 1251-2
Ju/'hoãnsi (!Kung) 12, 109, 112-13, 122,
  126, 137, 153, 157-8, 643, 908, 918, 919,
  924-6, 926-7, 1196, 1254, 1257-8
  dry- and wet-season camps 113 Fig. 6.2
  genetic studies 1149, 1151
  hxaro system 116
  and the 'Kalahari debate' 14, 15, 17, 18,
    908, 911, 928
  study of women 1244
  technology 1112, 1113 Fig. 53.1, 1116
  technology compared with
    Nuvugmiut 1112-15, 1113 Fig. 53.1,
    1114 Fig. 53.2
  women's roles and reproduction rates 1148
Judge, J. J. 415
Jumping Dance, North America 1231
Junker, L. 858

Kaare, B. 166
Kaberry, P. M. 960, 965
Kabwe cranium, Zambia 224
Kador, T. 1215
Kaingáng people 1042
Kaiwari, Jack 1163, 1164, 1181, 1192
'Kalahari Debate' 14, 15, 17, 19, 908, 911, 928
Kamei, N. 167
Kames, Lord 46, 64
Kant, Immanuel 47
Kara-Bom tradition, northern Asia 314
Katz, R. 927
Kayano, S. 1056
Kearney, A. 1177
Keates, S. G. 353
Keatley Creek, British Columbia 98, 1273,
  1274 Fig. 61.2
Kebaran culture 255, 258, 259, 261, 269
Keen, I. 160, 164, 964, 966
Kehoe, A. 983, 984, 1246-7
Keith, A. 193
Kelabit farmers, south-east Asia 859-60,
  871, 872
Kelly, R. 78, 80, 82, 106, 116, 260
Kenrick, J. 940
Kensinger, K. M. 1245
Kent, S. 15, 121, 122
Kenyah people 871
Kenyanthropus 179

Kereho Busang people 869–70
Kersten, L. 1037
Khanty people 109–10, 133–4, 136, 650
　flexible gender roles 1252
　gender and spirituality 1251
　gender dynamics and subsistence 1248–50
Khartoum Mesolithic ('Early Neolithic'),
　north Africa 446, 480–1
Khmu peoples 1019
Khoe langages 484
Khoekhen/Khoekhoe ('Hottentots') 484, 485,
　918, 919 Tab. 43.1, 921, 922, 924
Khoisan people 109, 1147
　archaeogenetics 1145
　genetic studies 1150–2, 1153, 1154
　physical features 1148
　steatopygia 1148
'Khoisan' term 44
Khok Phanom Di communities, Gulf of
　Thailand 1013
Khwe (Kxoe) people 919, 920–1
Kim, A. A. 162
Kind, C.-J. 791
King, L. C. 479, 980
King, W. 192, 206
Kinrick, J. 948
Kintampo industry, Ghana 486
kipijuituq 1255–6
Kitanishi, K. 942
Klasies River, South Africa 226–7
Klassen, L. 841
Kleine Feldhofer Grotte, Germany 191
Kline, M. A. 1132
Knutsson, H. 721
Knutsson, K. 841
Ko, I. 509
Kobayashi, K. 513
Koch-Grünberg, Th. 1042–3
Kokorevo culture 318
Kolig, E. 160
Komsa culture 567
Konso women 1247
Kooijmans, L. P. 546
Kopytoff, I. 1208
Koslowski, S. K. 700
Kostenki-Avdeevo group 289
Kota Tampan, Malay Peninsula 346–8, 357
Kotias Klde, Caucusus 266, 267, 270

Koyama, S. 510
Kozlowski, S. K. 705
Kramer, C. 137
Kroeber, A. L. 3, 13, 36, 72, 73, 82, 978–9, 980,
　981, 985, 1131, 1230–1
Ksar Akil, Lebanon 256, 257, 262
Kua group sites 113–14
Kua people 121, 919–20, 928
Kubiak-Martens, L. 544
Kubu peoples 1016–17, 1022
Kuhn, S. 200
kuksu cults, California 1230
Kulturkreis theory 48, 949
!Kung *see* Ju/'hoãnsi
Kûrnai social life, Australia 958
Kusimba, S. 65
Kwakitlan people 994, 1004
Kwakiutl potlatch, North America 76

La Hoguette pottery culture 775, 787, 789 Fig.
　36.2, 790, 792, 794, 797
La Verendrye, Pierre Gaultier de Varennes
　de 887, 888
Laacher See volcanic eruptions 450, 556,
　565, 567
Lacilotto, N. 1057
Lagar Velho rock shelter, Portugal 205
Lähteenmäki, M. 1082
Lake Aggasiz event 540
Lake Baikal, Siberia 1276
Lake Mungo, Australia 227
Lake Turkana, Kenya 111
Lakota people 984
Laland, K. N. 569
Lamalera people 1013, 1025
Lamb, L. 1177
Lamb, M. E. 166–7
Laming-Emperaire, A. 634
Land of Punt 487
Landberg, L. 986
Lang Rongrien rock shelter, Thailand 1021
Langton, M. 965, 968
languages *see* individual languages and
　linguistic groups
Langub, J. 866–8, 869, 1024–5
Larsson, A. 722
Larsson, L. 715–16, 716–17, 718, 719, 721
Lascaux Cave, France 294, 649

Last Glacial Maximum (LGM) 258, 282, 288, 439–40, 512
  and the Americas 406, 701
  Australia 372–3, 377
  Congo Basin, Africa 938
  and the Late Upper Palaeolithic 291–2
  northern Asia 315
  northern Europe 556
  south-east Asia and Indonesia 346, 348, 349, 350, 352, 354, 356, 358, 360, 361, 492
  western Asia 263, 269, 445
'Last Termination' 492, 498
Late Ahmarian culture 257–8
late glacial climatic variance 556–7, 557 Fig. 25.1
Late Mousterian culture 265, 266, 269
Late Natufian culture 267
Late Palaeolithic African hunter-gatherers 1148
Latta, F. 979
Lattimore, O. 60
Layton, R. 750
LBK *see* Linearband Pottery culture
Leacock, E. 157, 158
Leakey, M. G. 183
Leang Burung 2, Sulawesi 354, 360
Leang Sakapo 1, Sulawesi 354, 360
Leary, J. 1216
LeBlanc, S. 893
Lee, J.-J. 510
Lee, R. B. 8–10, 16, 22, 65, 77, 154, 729–30, 926, 928, 940
Lees, S. 157–8, 894
Lee-Thorp, J. A. 182
Lemonnier, P. 129, 1176
Leonard, K. 893
Lepenski Vir culture 523, 524 Fig. 23.1, 449, 529, 530, 532, 533, 1213
  evidence of social complexity 651
  Iron Gates sites 715, 813 Fig. 37.4
Leroi-Gourhan, A. 129, 589, 634, 635, 638, 1208
Levallois technology 196, 256, 283, 310, 312, 313, 614 Fig. 27.4, 1172
  cognitive requirements 620
  lag between first appearance and widespread adoption 608
  parallel development in Africa and Eurasia 608–10
  Sulawesi 354
  take-over in south-west Asia 618
  ubiquity 614
Levallois-Mousterian culture 314
Levine, M. A. 757
Lévi-Strauss, C. 3, 52, 154, 633–4, 962, 999, 1023, 1171
Lewis and Clark Expedition, North America 975
Lewis, J. 940, 948
Lewis, M. 887–8
Lewis-Williams, D. 108–19, 158, 484, 1233, 1234
Lewo Eleng community, Indonesia 1019
Lewontin, R. E. 80
Liem's paradox 181
lifecourse studies/biographies 20–1, 1103, 1196, 1197, 1199, 1254–6, 1258
Lightfoot, K. 981
Lillie, M. 797
Limburg pottery culture 787, 789 Fig. 36.2, 790
Linear pottery 521, 523
Linearband Pottery culture (LBK) 775, 776, 778, 787, 788–94, 796–7, 805, 809, 840
  lineage structures 775, 792
  Near Eastern ancestry 793–4, 797
Linnaeus 56, 217
Linse, A. R. 1176
Lipo, C. 83
LiPuma, E. 1192
Little Big Horn, Battle of (1876) 1165
Lloyd, L. C. 632, 921
'logistical mobility' 115–16
Löhr, H. 789, 790
Lonergan, N. 179
long barrow burial sites 826, 830, 840, 1175
Lopez, C. 418
Loung, Jean-Félix 949
Lower Palaeolithic:
  northern Asia 310
  stone tool technology 310, 614
Lowie, R. 3, 36, 73, 978
Lu, T. 655
Lubbock, J. 4, 11, 49, 50, 51, 441, 769
'Lucy' 181

Lüning, J. 792
Lupo, K. D. 128
Lye, T. P. 1024
Lyell, C. 70

Mace, T. 1006
MacNeish, R. S. 730
Maddocak, K. 962
Magdalenian culture 279, 292–5, 531, 541, 559–60, 562–3, 651
  art 629 Fig. 28.3, 630 Fig. 28.4
  clay animals 664
  figurative art 293–5
  indicators of social complexity 649–50
  Late 296–7
  toolkits 556, 559
Maglemose culture 700
Makah people 1267, 1276
Maksimov, A. N. 52
Maku people 1045
Malaysian Orang Asli people 861
  mtDNA studies 374
Malinowski, B. 3, 6
Malkin, I. 58
Malmström, H. 797
Malthus, T. 70
Malville, J. M. 482
mammoths 441, 430
'man' as shorthand for all humans 153, 158, 159
Man the Hunter conference (1966) and volume 8–9, 17, 22, 35, 36, 37, 41, 157, 164, 260, 267, 443, 904, 905, 908, 909, 910, 913, 915, 925, 963, 979, 1110–11, 1166, 1247
  absence of gender concept 153–4
Mandan people 781, 887–8
Mangelsdorf, P. C. 730
Mannerma, K. 719
Mansi people 163, 165
Mansrud, A. 1279
Mapuche (Araucanos) people 1036
Marchand, G. 542
Marginal Value Theorem, and mobility 1168
Marine Isotope Stage 2 492
maritime societies, definition of 694
Markov Chains, equations and processes 1128–9

Marlowe, F. W. 106
marriage 154, 156–7, 159, 164
  and Chipewyan women's Treaty status 1256
Marshack, A. 646
Marshall, F. 184, 759
Marshall, J. 925, 927
Marshall, L. 153, 924–5
Marshall family 918, 924, 928
Martial, L. 1037
Martius, K. F. 1041
Maruyama, J. 929
Marwick, B. 349
Marx, Karl 50
Marxist anthropology 50, 963
Maschner, H. D. 557, 992, 1003, 1004
materials, new approaches 1103–4, 1204–17
  Bann Flake implications 1215
  challenging materiality and material culture 1209
  form/matter dichotomy 1209
  and identities 1210–13
  landscape and taskscape 1213–15
  mind/matter dichotomy 1209
  and modernity 1205
  from risk and reason to biography and being 1207–9
  technology, conception of 1208
  tree types and objects 1213, 1214 Fig. 58.1
Mathews, R. H. 959
Matoušek, V. 533
Mauss, M. 3, 129, 998–9
Mawoung, G. N. 949
Mayer, A. 191, 192
Mayr, E. 238
Mbuti people 158, 939, 940, 941–2, 943, 945, 947, 1152
Mbywangi, M. 1046
McBreary, S. 229
McCall, G. S. 1172
McCarthy, F. 1166
McConnel, U. 960
McCowan, T. D. 193
McFadyen, Lesley 1175
McGrew, W. C. 184, 1110
McKnight, D. 967
McNichol Creek, British Columbia 1275
Mead, M. 1254

Meadow, R. H. 749–50
Meadowcroft shelter, Pennsylvania 407–8
Mearns, L. 161–2, 164
Mediterranean, early coastal
    settlements 596, 698
Mediterranean and western Asia,
    post-glacial 442, 445–6, 456–73
  Aegean and Greece 445–6, 463–6
  arrival of farming in south-east
    Europe 466–7
  central and western Mediterranean in the
    Mesolithic 468–71
  climate 457
  Cyprus 462–3
  geography 456–7
  plant domestication 767
  sources of archaeological evidence 458
  transition to farming from the Adriatic to
    the Atlantic 471–2
  vegetation 458
  western Asia in the early
    Holocene 445, 458–62
Meehan, C. 943, 949
Meggitt, M. J. 154
Meignen, L. 1172
Meiklejohn, C. 546, 721
Melanesian constructs of personhood 1103,
    1192, 1193, 1197
Mellars, P. 330–1
Mellinkoff, R. 62
memory anthropology 981–3
Menraq foragers 861
Merlan, F. 967
Merriam, C. H. 979
Mesolithic 256, 267, 280, 437–8, 441,
    770, 769
  African hunter-gatherers 1148
  challenges of defining 441–2
  characterised as 'uneventful' 438
  coastal adaptations 596
  continuity and change 451
  diversity and variability 443, 451
  key areas of investigation 444
  landscape focus in studies 444
  long-tern cultural dynamism 438
  regional diversity 438, 452
  responses to environmental change 452
  Scandinavian 442
  social complexity 592, 650–8
  territorial groupings and
    regionalization 542–3
  transformations, north-west Europe
    449–50, 537–50, 538 Fig. 24.1
  see also Baltic Mesolithic; Europe,
    Mesolithic
metallurgy, northern Fennoscandia
    848, 849
Métraux, A. 1043
Meyerhoff, B. 1225
Mezinian culture 292
Michelaki, K. 886
Micoquian culture 196–7
microgravettes 266
microlithic industries:
  Capsian 470
  history, south Asia 495–6
  Khartoum Mesolithic 480–1
  Late Palaeolithic and Mesolithic south
    Asia 335–6
  Later Stone Age Africa 484
  Mesolithic Mediterranean 458, 465, 473
  post-glacial southern Africa 446
  post-glacial tropical Africa 485, 486
  Sauveterrian 469
  Upper Palaeolithic western Asia 258, 265
Middle and Upper Palaeolithic hominid
    fossils comparisons 219, 220 Tab. 10.1
Middle Missouri 781
  forager-farmer interaction 884 Fig. 41.2,
    887–8
  forager-farmer interaction,
    prehistoric 888–9
Middle Palaeolithic:
  hunters 112
  northern Asia 310, 311–12
  stone tool technology 614–15
Middle Palaeolithic-Upper Palaeolithic
    'transition' 618–19
Middle Range Theory 12, 17, 18, 77–8, 107–8,
    138, 1206
  and mobility 1170–3
Middle Stone Age see Africa, Middle
    Stone Age
Migliano, A. B. 938
Mikea people 1120
Mikoshiba culture 411

milk and milk products 601, 754, 832
  mare's milk 757–8, 758 Fig. 34.4
  reindeer milk 1080
Milner, N. 696
Minagwa, M. 514
Minter, T. 1024
Misra, V. N. 497
Mitchell, D. 646
Mitchell, P. 480
Mithen, S. 636
'mitochondrial Eve' hypothesis 192–3, 235
Mlabri people 110, 1015, 1019, 1022
mobility 1102–3, 1163–82
  adaptive approaches 1167–9
  analytical scale 1164–5
  behavioural ecology models 1167–9
  bounded access 1176–8
  change due to climate change, Thailand 349
  contextual mappings 1180
  craft specialization and task differentiation 1177
  and cultural complexity 1170
  embeddedness of mobility 1175–6
  emergence 1180
  emergence of mobility studies 1165–7
  emplacement 1180
  flow of place 1179
  forager vs. collector model (Binford, 1980) 12=13, 115–23, 117 Fig. 6.2, 118 Fig. 6.3, 119–20, Tab. 6.3, 121 Tab. 6.4, 992
  frequency and distance of travel and stone artefact assemblages 1172
  gender and ancestral myth 1182
  gendered task differentiation 1177
  historicist approaches 1173–4
  intentions 1173
  Marginal Value Theorem 1168
  meanings 1181
  and middle range research 1170–3
  myth without endings 1182
  and population density 563 Fig. 25.2
  processualist approaches 1169–70
  sacred geographies 1178–9
  South Molle Island Quarry (SMIQ) 1176–7
  'taskscapes' 1173–4
  and technology 1116–17, 119

  temporality of the landscape: ways of walking 1174–5
  territory 1177–8
  territoriality and social structure 1176–8
  time and ancestral myth 1181–2
'modern human behaviour' 608, 617, 620
  art and 626, 628
modern human origins in Africa 214–39, 234 Fig. 10.2
  archaeology of modern behaviour 228–32, 233, 237
  and behavioural modernity 216
  coalescence theory 235
  cranial morphology 217–28, 218 Fig. 10.1, 220 Tab. 10.1, 221 Tab. 10.2
  DNA studies 238
  fossil record and modern human morphology 217–28, 218 Fig. 10.1, 220 Tab. 10.1, 221 Tab. 10.2, 222–3 Tab. 10.3, 232–7
  gene lineages/trees 235–6
  Group 1–after 40,000 BP 226–8
  Group 2–200,000 to 40,000 BP 224–6, 238
  Group 3–Pre-200,000 BP 219–24
  Homo sapiens and modern humans 236–9
  molecular clock model 234–5
  mosaic morphology 219, 224, 225, 226, 227, 232–3
  mtDNA evidence 214, 215, 219, 233–4, 235–6
  'sapient paradox' 216
  species definitions/concept debate 237–9
modern humans (*Homo sapiens*) 265
  anthropological finds, Yenissei River 320
  as carriers of Upper Palaeolithic culture 315
  cognitive and physical difference from Neanderthals 617
  contact with Neanderthals 281–2, 619
  dependence on technology 615
  dispersal 265, 440–1
  dispersal and mtDNA 204
  dispersal and spread of Aurignacian technology 618–19
  dispersal into Eurasia 588, 616
  dispersal out of Africa, archaeogenetic evidence 1145–6
  evolution in Africa 617

modern humans (*Cont.*)
  Homo sapiens idaltu 238
  lineage splitting 204
  polycentric hypothesis 315
  replacement hypothesis 315
  south Asia 328–40, 329 Fig. 14.1
  south-east Asia and Indonesia 346–62
'modern' hunter-gatherers, ethnohistory and anthropology 903–16
  as analogue to ancient peoples 905
  comparative analysis 905
  'inter-dependent' model 906
  long-term culture-contact 906, 907
  research trends 905–7
Moiseeff, M. 967
Moken 'sea nomads' 1017, 1024
'molecular clock' model 234–5, 734
Mono people 978
Montespan cave, France 664
Montesquieu 44
monumental architecture 1003
  'Big Houses' 994
  Britain and Ireland, Neolithic 826–7, 830, 832, 833
  Gobekli 654
Mooney, J. 977–8
Morgan, L. H. 5, 34, 50, 74, 958
Morphy, H. 968
Morris, A. G. 484
Morris, B. 967
mortars and pestles 261, 651, 657
Morton, J. 962
mortuary practices 596–8, 604, 712–23
  Australopithecus afarensis 713
  Baltic Mesolithic 597, 714–23
  British and Irish Neolithic mortuary structures 826
  cave burial, Mesolithic Britain 543
  cosmologies and beliefs 598, 712–13, 714
  cremations 720, 722
  Cyprus Neolithic 463
  Danubian Europe, post-glacial 532–3
  emergence of cemeteries 713–14
  Europe, Upper Palaeolithic 290–1, 293, 296
  Ertebølle 545
  fragmentation, burning and defleshing 722–3
  gender norms 718
  and human-animal relationships 1195–6

  as a hunter-gatherer innovation 713–14
  Java 350
  Levantine Epi-Palaeolithic 259–60
  Mediterranean Mesolithic 465, 470
  Mesolithic cemeteries, Europe 443, 444
  northern Asia, Final Palaeolithic 320
  and prestige and status 646–9, 651, 653–4, 656
  and social relations 715–16, 1197
  south Asia, post-glacial 447, 496–7
  south east Europe, Neolithic 466
  tombs, megalithic 826
  tooth evulsion 470, 472
  western Asia, Neolithic 459, 461
  see also child burials; dog burials
Motte, E. 941
Mount Carmel cave sites, Israel 192, 193
Mousterian culture 196, 229, 256, 311, 314, 323, 369
  figurative art 202
  Levantine 618
  south Asia 332
Mousterian culture, Late 265, 266, 269
Mountford, C. 967–8
Mukhri people 1149
Müller, C. C. 61
Müller, W. 756
Munro, N. 961, 968, 1065
Murdock, G. P. 65
'mutation rate' 1144
Myers, F. 965
mythograms 634

Nabta Playa, Egypt 481, 482
Nagaoka, S. 513
Nakao, A. 513
Narmada hominin 332
Naro (Nharo) people 919, 923
Nassarius shells 231
Native Customary Rights 866–8
Natufian culture, Levant 259–60, 263–4, 270, 459, 651
  mortuary practices 713–14, 717
  social complexity 652–4
  use of wild cereals 1267
Natufian culture, Late 267
natural selection 37, 70, 78, 79, 82, 83
  group-level selection 37, 78, 75–6, 82
  see also selectionist archaeology (SA)

Neanderthal/Modern split 195
Neanderthals (*Homo neanderthalensis*) 178,
    179–80, 186–7, 224, 228, 232, 237, 279,
    283, 369
  biology 193–5, 194 Fig. 9.1
  body painting 202–3
  cognitive abilities 620
  cognitive and physical differences from
    modern humans 617
  contact with modern humans 281–2, 619
  cranial morphology 217
  diverse stone technology 618
  DNA admixture with modern
    humans 215, 374
  evolution and palaeoecology 191–206
  extinction 204–6
  gendered division of labour 199–200
  Iberian 199
  Levant 199
  material record anomalies 615
  'modern' behaviour 280
  and modern humans, assimilation
    scenarios 205
  mortuary rituals 713
  mtDNA 195
  mtDNA polymorphisms 204
  ornaments 201–2, 202 Fig. 9.4
  northernmost range 199
  physical injuries and personhood 1198
  in south Asia 332, 334
  social organization and symbolism 199–
    204, 202 Fig. 9.4
  technology and subsistence 195–9, 197 Fig.
    9.2, 198 Fig. 9.3
  thermoregulatory models 200–1
Near East 481
  dates of early farming 770
  forager-farmer relations 894
  new resource possibilities 651
  social complexity 592
Needham, Rodney 939
Neff, H. 81
Nelson, S. M. 510
Neo-Darwinian approaches 20, 37, 76–84,
    586, 1006, 1098 *see also* New Synthesis
    evolutionary theory
neofunctionalism 37, 75–6, 79
Neolithic (New Stone Age) 16–17, 18, 255,
    267, 269, 437, 438, 441, 442, 465, 769

  African 483
  association with agriculture 770
  as 'cultural package' 770
  dispersal, south-east Asia 499, 500
  as an economic transformation 771
  hunter gatherer/agricultural
    debate 654, 657–8
  Mediterranean sites 467 Fig. 19.3
  Pre-Pottery Neolithic A 459–61, 654
  Pre-Pottery Neolithic B 461–2
  south-east Europe 466–8
  visibility of sites 458
  'wave of advance' 771
  western and central Europe 787–91, 788
    Fig. 36.1
  western Asia 445, 459–62, 460 Fig. 19.1
'Neolithic Revolution' 602, 770
Neolithic transition to farming
  'availability model' 771–2
  current debates 773–5
  European sequences and debates 769
  fusion approaches 774, 782–3
  future research directions 782–3
  genetic studies 773, 793–4, 796, 797
  as ideological vs. economic shift 772–3
  'indigenist' approaches 772–3
  indigenous involvement/cultural
    diffusion 773–4
  integrationist approaches 774, 782
  migration/demic diffusion 773
  and nature/culture fault line 1192–3
  research framework 769–75
  shifts in interpretation 771–2
  stable isotope analysis 773
  strontium isotope analysis 773, 792
Neolithicization 769, 772
  and migration dynamics, western and
    central Europe 795–7
Netting, R. M. 1000
neuropsychologocal (N-P) model 1233–5
New Archaeology ('processualism') 7–8,
    11–13, 17, 18, 21, 37, 76–8, 81, 443, 771,
    772, 1167
  approaches to mobility 1169–70
  see also Binford, L. R.
New Guinea 348, 368, 369, 370, 371, 386
  early agriculture and cultivation 387
  languages 375
  mtDNA studies 374

New Guinea (*Cont.*)
  population and growth rates 380
  sex and temperament 1254
  transition to agriculture 738, 739
New Synthesis evolutionary theory 74, 75–6, 83–4 *see also* Neo-Darwinian approaches
Ngandi people 167
Ngarrabullgan sacred mountain, Australia 1178
Ngatatjara Aboriginals 127
Niah Caves, Borneo 351–2, 351 Fig. 15.2, 361, 498, 499, 500, 501
  starch-grain analysis 733
'niche construction' theory 1267–8
Nichols, J. 412
Nicholson, A. 110
Nickul, K. 1072
Nielsen, E. H. 791
Nilsson Stutz, L. 50, 547
!Nisa biography 1196, 1254
Nolin, D. A. 1025
Nordic Bronze Age culture 846, 847
North America
  berdacheor 'two spirits' 1256
  early foragers 414–17
  egalitarianism 645
  European traders and goods 887–8
  nut processing 657
  Spanish colonists, southwest US 889
  surplus-complexity relationship, Northwest Plateau 646, 647 Fig. 29.1, 648 Fig. 29.2, 650
  see also California and the Great Basin; Pacific Northwest Coast of America
North American forager-farmer interaction 780–1, 881–96
  Algonquian/Iroquois 884 Fig. 41.2, 885–7, 895
  hunting, gathering and farming 882–3, 883 Fig. 41.1
  Middle Missouri, 884 Fig. 41.2, 887–9
  new research directions 894–6
  Plains-Pueblo 881, 884 Fig. 41.2, 889–93
north European Plain 561, 562, 566, 699, 805
northern Asia, Palaeolithic, 310–25
  dwelling structures and settlement patterns 319–20
  Early Upper Palaeolithic sites and materials 312–15, 313 Fig. 13.1, 323–4
  Final Palaeolithic sites and materials 320–1
  Lower Palaeolithic 310
  Middle Palaeolithic 310
  Middle Palaeolithic sites and materials 311–12
  post-glacial colonization and transformations 315–17, 324–5
  technologies 317–18, 325
  Upper Palaeolithic 310–11
  Upper Palaeolithic origins 314–15, 322–3
Northern Dene (Athapaskan) people 109, 122–3
northern Europe, late glacial resettlement 450–1, 556–70
  demographic framework 558, 559 Tab. 25.1
  Holocene 566–7
  late glacial climatic variance 556–7, 557 Fig. 25.1
  Magdalenian techno-complex 559–60
  migration causes 568 Tab. 25.2
  Phases 1 and 2 558–60
  Phase 3 560–3, 563 Fig. 25.2
  Phase 4 563–4
  Phase 5 464–6
northern Fennoscandia, forager-farmer interaction (c.4000–1 BC) 777–8, 838–51, 839 Fig. 39.1
  battle axe distribution 843, 844 Fig. 39.2
  cereal pollen data 845 Fig. 39.3
  close encounters (2800–1900 BC) 788, 844–8, 850
  first 840–2, 850
  first millennium diversification 778, 848–9, 850
  hunter-gatherer background 839–40
  intensified, and exotic imports (c.3400–2800 BC) 842–4, 850
  settler colonies 843
north-west Europe:
  coastal adaptation 700–1, 705
  Palaeolithic constraints on maritime settlement 699
  sea-level rises 539, 696, 807, 808
  see also Ertebølle

north-west Europe, Mesolithic
　transformations 449–50, 537–50, 538
　　Fig. 24.1
　agricultural technologies 545, 546
　changing landscapes 538–40, 539 Fig. 24.2
　genetic evidence of repopulation 541
　overall picture 540–4
　regionalization and 'territorial'
　　groupings 542–3, 545
　subsistence strategies 542, 544
north-west Europe, Neolithic transition
　to farming (5500–2800 BC) 772,
　776–7, 805–21
　cereal cultivation 814–16, 818, 819
　feasting 818
　food plants 814–18, 817 Tab. 37.2
　hunting and animal husbandry 810–14,
　　811–12 Tab. 37.1, 813 Fig. 37.4
　introduction of pottery and demise of
　　hearth pits 809–10
　landscape development 806–9, 808
　　Fig. 37.3
　Long/Short Transition Models 808, 809
　persistence of hunting and
　　gathering 816–18
　Schiplunden case study 818–19
Norton, C. J. 510
Noss, A. J. 1119
Novgorod Republic 1075
Nueville, R. 255
Nukak people 1043 Fig. 49.5, 1044, 1045
Nunamiut people 12, 40, 109, 111–12,
　1206, 1247
　elders 127
　faunal assemblages 125–6
　'toss' and 'drop' zones 114–15
'Nutcracker Man' 181, 182
Nuu-chah-nutlh people 993 Fig. 47.1, 994,
　1267, 1276
Nuvugmiut technology 1112–15, 1114 Fig.
　53.2, 1116, 1118

Obanian culture 700
Oberg, K. 996
obsidian 321, 463, 465, 466, 482, 653, 654, 891
obsidian stone tools 482
ochre 291, 312, 336, 354, 360, 388, 496,
　715, 718

red ochre 231, 470, 1195
ochre engraving, Blombos Cave 588–9, 626–
　8, 627 Fig. 28.1
ochre mine, Lovas, Hungary 527
O'Connell, J. F. 112, 115
O'Connor, S. 355–6, 500
Odling-Smee, F. J. 569
Odum, E. P. 569
Ofnet Cave, Bavaria 98–9, 791
Ogawa, T. 515
Ohalo II, Israel 254, 259, 260–1, 263, 264,
　269, 270, 459, 697
Ohnuki-Tierney, E. 1061, 1065
Ojibwa people 1194
Okhotsk culture 511, 1057, 1058, 1059, 1065
Okiek people 126
Oldowan industry stone tools 183, 611
Olduvai Gorge, Tanzania 111
Oliver, J. 1005
Olivia, M. 527
Olsen, B. 1074
Olsen, S. A. 757
Olsen, S. L. 501
Omo Valley hominid fossils,
　Ethiopia 225, 226
Oñate, Don Juan de 889
O'Neill, S. 1006
Onge people 110, 165
Ono, A. 966
Oppenheimer, S. 373
optimal foraging theory 79, 127–8, 1192
　see also evolution; human behavioural
　　ecology
oral histories and traditions 95
Orang 'sea nomads' 1017
'Oro', Borneo 865, 866 Fig. 40.2
Orquera, L. A. 704
Ortvale Klde, Caucasus 265, 269
O'Shea, J. 597, 716
Ostorf burial site, Germany 797
ostrich eggshell (OES) artefacts 130, 231,
　312, 317
Oswalt, W. 1115–16, 1116–17
Otomac people 48
Ottar, farmer 1080
Ounanian culture 480
overspecialization and socio-economic
　'collapse' 448, 515–16

Owen, L. R. 168
Owens Valley ceramic technologies, California 1100–1, 1137 Fig. 54.2, 1138
Ozette, Olympic Peninsula 1275

Pääbo, S. 215–16
Pacific Northwest Coast (NWC) of America
  coastal adaptation 701–3
  'clam gardens' 1268, 1273
  culture area 992–5, 993 Fig. 47.1
  food and status 1276
  Golden Age of ethnography 995–7
  herring egg collection 1268
  interpreting complexity from archaeology 1003–5
  plant management 1268
  potlatches 910, 996, 997–1001, 1004, 1005, 1006, 1272, 1276
  recent streams of scholarship 1005–6
  salmon surpluses 1267
  sharing and ownership 1273–5
  social complexity 910, 991–1006
  towards diachronic explanations of complexity 1000–3, 1002 Fig. 47.2
  whale hunting equipment 1267
Page, J. 168
Paisley Five Mile Point Caves, US 408, 409 Fig. 172
Paiute people 978, 979, 983
  Northern 982
Palaeolithic (Old Stone Age) 437, 441, 442, 769, 1192
  coastal adaptations 596
  constraints on maritime settlement 698–9
  northern Asia 310–25
  terminal, central and western Mediterranean 469–70
  see also Upper Palaeolithic
Palaeolithic-Mesolithic transition 438
  Mediterranean 456
Paliyan people 159
Pama-Nyungan (PN) languages, Australia 374–5
Panhard-Capricorn Expedition 923
paranthropines 185
Paranthropus 178, 179
Paranthropus boisei 181, 182, 183
Paranthropus robustus 181, 182

Parker, K. L. 959
Parkin, D. 723
Parrish, O. 981
Parry, W. 78, 80, 82
Parsons, N. 924
patrilineal bands 51, 73
patrilineality 1062
patrilocal bands 6, 154
patrilocality 158, 160, 1062
Pavlovian culture 289, 290
Pavlovian/Willendorfian technocomplex 289, 290
Peacham, H. 62
Peacock, N. 943
Pearson, N. 965
Pearson, R. 657
Penan peoples 859–60, 861, 865, 866–8, 869, 871, 872–4, 1015–16, 1022, 1024–5
Pennanen, J. 1249
Perlès, C. 465
Perrot, J. 653
Perrott, R. A. 480
personal decoration 231, 257, 260, 376
  Europe, Upper Palaeolithic 285, 286–7
  northern Asia, Palaeolithic 312, 317
  south Asia, post-glacial 496
personhood
  action, animals and non-human 1193–6
  dividual 1192
  Melanesian constructs of 1103, 1192, 1193, 1197
  perspective on 1191–3
  as process 1196–8
  prospects for 1199–2000
  the skill of being 1198–9
  and social relations 1103, 1191–1200
Peterson, N. 963
Petraglia, M. 332
Petrie, W. M. 1131
Petso (Basarwa man) 1255
Pettitt, P. 560, 713
Pfefferle, A. D. 186
phylogeography 1145
Piana, E. L. 704
Pickard, C. 697
Pickersgill, B. 730
Piddocke, S. 75, 76, 1000

Piggott, S. 827
pig domestication, China 656–7
pigs, DNA analysis 810
Pilling, A. 961
Piłsudski, B. 1063–4, 1065
Pinart-Leon de Cessac, A. 977
Pink, O. 960
Pitjantjatjara Aborigines 961, 968
Pitted Ware Culture 722–3, 797
Plains-Pueblo interaction 781, 881, 884 Fig. 41.2, 889–93, 895
  prehistoric 889–93
plant cultivation
  Ainu 1060
  east Asia, post-glacial 514
  first signs, Levantine Epi-Palaeolithic 260
  pre-domestication 735–6
  as response to pressure to increase production 658
  south-east Asia, Late Pleistocene 361
  without domestication 651
plant domestication 599–600, 605, 729–41, 767
  Africa, post-glacial 482, 485–6, 487
  ancient and modern DNA 734
  domestication syndrome 731
  earliest known 1267
  grass and forb seeds 737
  intermediate subsistence 736
  and loss of plant biodiversity 599, 740–1
  and morphogenetic change 735
  New Guinea 354–5
  parenchyma analysis 732–3
  phytolith analysis 733
  'protracted' model 734
  retrospect on the study of 729–31
  roots and tubers 737
  'semi-domestication' vs. domestication *sensu stricto* 732
  south Asia 336
  stable-isotope analysis 734–5
  starch-grain analysis 733–4
  trait selection 731–2
  and transition to agriculture 738–9
  tree nut harvesting 736–7
  types of evidence 731–2
  variation in crop assemblages 738, 740
  western Asia 442

plant management (wild plants) 600, 736, 737, 740, 1268
Plio-Pleistocene hominins 40
  and the Hadzabe 111
Pluciennik, M. 700
Point Conception gas terminal 985
Poirier, S. 966
political ecology 604, 644–5, 1004
Politis, G. 1033
Pookajorn, S. 110
Pope, K. O. 377
Posey, D. A. 1033
post-glacial period (Holocene) 437–53
  Africa 446–7, 479–87
  archaeological research into 441–4
  Danubian Europe 448–9, 521–34
  definition 437
  east Asia 448, 507–16, 511 Fig. 22.1
  future research directions 452–3
  global environmental changes 439–41, 439 Fig. 18.1, 696–7
  hunter-gatherer adjustments 440–1
  northern Europe, resettlement 450–1, 556–70
  north-west Europe 449–50, 537–50, 538 Fig. 24.1
  south and south-east Asia 447, 492–502, 493 Fig. 21.1
  Mediterranean and western Asia 445–6, 456–73
post-modernist critiques 38, 92, 94–7
  and acculturation 95
  and social complexity 95
  and typological descriptions 95
post-processual archaeology *see* interpretive and post-processual approaches
potlatches 910, 996, 997–1001, 1004, 1005, 1006, 1272, 1276
pottery *see* ceramic technology
Poverty Point culture 98, 1276
Powell, A. 203, 1133
Powell, J. 50, 977, 985
Powers, S. 977
Prasciunas, M. 1122
prehistoric hunter-gather innovations 585–605
  further innovation dynamics 593–601
  and hunter-gatherer 'agency' 604–5

prehistoric hunter-gather innovations (*Cont.*)
   identifying patterns in cultural
      evolution 602–3
   key 587–93
   legacy of social evolutionary
      thinking 601–2
   studying long-term process 603–4
Pretola, J. 886, 887
Price, S. 1213
Price, T. D. 462, 1170
Primitive culture circle 48
Prinz, B. 528
processual archaeology *see* New
    Archaeology
progressive social evolutionary theory
    (PSET) 71, 72, 75
proto-Ainu culture 511–12
Protoaurignacian culture 205, 284, 285
psychoanalytic anthropology 962
psychological anthropology 1254
Pueblo Glaze Ware 893
Pujol, R. 940
Punan peoples 1015–16
Puri, R. 872
Putnam, P. 939
Pygmies 48, 109, 1147
   genetic studies 1152–3
   implications of 'Pygmy' term 936
   marital exchanges 1149
   stature 147–8
pyrotechnology 615

Qafzeh, Levant 261, 262, 369
   mortuary rituals 713
Quebrad Santa Julia, Chile 409, 410 Fig. 17.3
Querandí ('Pampas') people 1035
Quraishy, Z. B. 164–5

Radcliffe-Brown, A. R. 3, 5, 6, 959–60
radiocarbon dating
   and changes in subsistence
      practices 1280–1
   and the chronology of agriculture 770–1
   see also accelerator mass spectrometry
      (AMS) dating
Raphael, M. 633, 638
Rappaport. R. 75, 1234
Rasmussen, S. O. 557

rattan 863 Tab. 40.1, 866, 867 Fig. 40.3, 867
   Fig. 40.4, 868, 869, 1015
rattlesnake shamans 1227
Read, D. 1118, 1119
Redding, R. W. 750
Reid, H. 977
Reid, L. A. 14, 1020
Reinach, S. 632–3, 635
'reindeer capitalism' 1082
reindeer hunting 450, 561, 566, 778, 847, 850
   and economies 562
reindeer husbandry 758
   Sámi 750, 1076, 1079–84, 1083 Fig. 51.3,
      1085, 1086
'relations of relevance' 633, 637
religion and ritual 1104, 1221–38
   Aboriginal 966
   and altered states of
      consciousness 1225, 1228
   analytical approaches 1233–5
   animal inhumations, north Africa 482
   archaeology of 1232–3
   cosmology 1222
   cults 1224
   ethnographic model of ritual form 1234–5
   external comparisons 1231–2
   gender and spirituality 1250–2, 1257–8
   initiations and secret societies 1228–30
   link to art 588, 589, 625, 627
   myth and ritual relationship 1223, 1227
   origins of 637–8, 1235–6
   ritual-ceremonial practices, northern
      Asia 320, 321
   ritual practice and structure 712–13
   ritual theology 1222
   role of the sea 705
   sacred places 1223
   shamanism, Californian 1226–8
   shamanic rituals 1225–6
   shamanistic systems 1224–5
   south-east Asia 1013
   supernatural agents 1222
   vision quests 1228
   world-renewal religions 1230–1
Renfrew, C. 635–6
'Replacement' model 214, 215, 228, 232, 236
'residential mobility' 115–16
revisionist approaches 13–15, 38, 92, 93–4

revolution model, modern human origins 216, 233, 237
Rey, C. F. 922
Rhine-Maas-Schelde (RMS) 789 Fig. 36.2, 790
rice cultivation 448, 509, 510–11, 779, 858, 859–60
rice trading, Ainu-Japanese 1061–2
rice wine (sake) 1061
Richerson, P. J. 1132
Riede, F. 1130
Ring Model (Yellen) 112–14, 114 Fig. 1
'risky' environments 1097, 1118
Ritchie, C. 925
ritual *see* religion and ritual
Rival, L. 1044
Rivet, P. 1043
Roasman, A. 1005
Roberts, F. H. H. 415
Robertshaw, P. T. 483
Robertson, W. 47
Robinson, D. 982
rock art 93, 376, 1236
    Aboriginal 378, 388, 389, 589, 632, 1234
    Aboriginal, dating 379
    Aboriginal, as identity marker 379
    and altered states of consciousness 637–8, 1233–4
    California 982
    central and western Mediterranean Mesolithic 470
    Chauvet Cave art 287, 294, 589, 628, 631, 646
    Coso rock engravings 1234
    disenchantment with interpretation 635–6
    early explanations 632–5
    East Timor 357
    Europe, Upper Palaeolithic 287, 289–90, 291–2, 293–4
    as manifestation of prestige 649
    north Africa, post-glacial 482
    northern Scandinavia 567
    as primary source for religious research 1232–3
    San 625, 632, 1234
    and shamanism 108–9, 484, 638, 718, 1229, 1233–4
    south Asia, post-glacial 447, 496, 501–2

    south-east Asia 360
    southern Africa, post-glacial 484–5
    and vision quests 1228
    Yokut 1227
Rodrigues, A. D. 1040
Roheim, G. 962
Romanellian culture 469
Romans 487
Ronaansen, S. 982
Rosaldo, M. 156–7
Roscoe, P. 1012
Rose, D. B. 1179
Rose, F. G. G. 154, 963
Rose, L. M. 184
Rosenfeld, A. 968
Rosman, A. 999
Ross, J. 1234
Rousseau, J. 868
Rousseau, J.-J. 45–6, 47
Rowley-Conwy, P. 546, 771, 808
Rowse, T. 965
Rozoy, J.-G. 789
Rubané Récent du Bassin Parisien (RRBP) 792–3
Rubel, A. G. 1005
Rubel, P. G. 999
Rumsey, A. 965
Rumu people 1163, 1178–9
Rusco, E. 982
Russell, K. W. 1121
Russia
    Early Upper Palaeolithic 285–6
    see also Siberia
Rust, A. 561

Sackett, J. R. 129
Sadr, K. 484
Sahlins, M. 10, 116, 909, 963, 964, 1004, 1111
Sahul continent 355, 358, 368, 369–70, 371, 372, 374, 375, 377, 378
Salish people 993 Fig 47.1, 994
salmon fishing 646
    Ainu 1060, 1061
    Danubian Europe 528
    differential access to fisheries 1273
    drying racks, British Columbia 1275 Fig. 61.3

salmon fishing (*Cont.*)
    productivity, and social complexity 646, 1001, 1003–4
Sama 'sea nomads' 1017, 1018, 1022
Sámi/Lapps 750, 914, 1071–86, 1072 Fig. 51.1, 1149
    agriculture and cultural assimilation, Finnish forest zone 1076–9, 1078 Fig. 51.2
    bear graves 1279
    changing roles 1087 Fig. 51.4
    current ethnopolitics 1085–7
    effects of imposition of national borders 1082, 1084
    ethnic identity 1086–7
    gender dynamics and subsistence 1248–50
    historical transformations 1084–5
    Iron Age and medieval background 1074–5
    regional differences in historical transformations 1072–3
    reindeer husbandry 750, 1072, 1076, 1079–84, 1083 Fig, 51.3, 1085, 1086
    siidas system 1072–4, 1072 Fig. 51.1, 1079
Samuel, A. J. 1025
San Jacinto pottery sequence, Columbia 668, 669 Fig. 30.4
San peoples 12, 13, 44–5, 129, 130, 132–3, 134, 158, 625, 729–30, 918–30, 919 Tab. 43.1
    American research tradition 924–6
    development programmes 925–6
    genetic studies 1150, 1151
    Japanese research 929
    land and resettlement 920–1
    language groups 920 Fig. 43.1
    masked class struggle 633
    protection of human rights 922–3, 927
    resettlement 929–30
    rock art 625, 632, 1234
    shamanic practices 109, 1225, 1232
    South Africa research tradition 921–4
    and water resources 919–20
    see also specific San peoples
Sandawe genetic studies 1150–1, 1153
Sandbukt, Ø. 159
Sandin, B. 869
Sannai Muryama, Japan 166
Sansom, B. 965

Saris, J. 1061
Sartan Glaciation 315–16
Sassaman, K. 1177
Satsumon culture 510, 1059, 1060, 1065
Satterthwaite, L. 376, 1121
Sauveterrian culture 469
'savannah corridor' 358
Savo-Korelian culture 1076–7
Schaaffhausen, H. 191
Schapera, I. 921–2, 923, 939
Schebasta, P. 939, 945, 947
Schipluiden, Netherlands 806 Fig. 37.1, 814–16, 813 Fig. 37.4, 818–19
Schmidt, Father 960
Schmidt, R. 718
Schmidt, W. 48
Schmitt, D. 128
Schöningen wooden spears 196
Schrire, C. 158
Schulting, R. 651, 1195
Schwabedissen, H. 565
Schwanfeld, Carpathian Basin 792, 793 Fig. 36.3
Schwartz, J. H. 219, 238–9
Schwartz, M. 756
Scythians 59, 63
sea level rises 494
    Africa 479, 480
    east Asia 512–13
    Haida Gwaii 702
    investigation of submerged sites 696–7
    and loss of Doggerland 696, 701
    Mediterranean 457
    north-western Europe 539, 696, 807, 808
    and research difficulties 596
    south Asia 494, 499–500
'sea nomads' 1017–18
sea travel
    and colonization of Wallacea 353, 358
    and expansion of *Homo sapiens* 697–8
    Homo erectus 697
    Mediterranean 463, 465
seal hunting 840, 849
seal train oil 848
seasonal movement
    central and western Mediterranean Mesolithic 470

south-west Asia, Upper Palaeolithic 266–70, 268 Fig. 11.2, 269 Fig. 11.3
secret societies *see* cults and secret societies
sedentism
  east Asia, post-glacial 448, 515
  and the emergence of agriculture 336
  and the forager/collector model 116–21
  along the Ganges 336
  semi-sedentism, western Asia, Upper Palaeolithic 254, 258, 259, 269
  and shift from bifacial to generalized core technology 78, 80, 82, 83
  and social complexity 645, 646, 649, 651, 652–3, 654, 655, 994
  south Asia, post-glacial 497
  and target food diversification 515
  without plant domestication 740
Segawa, T. 1062, 1065
Seguchi, S. 515
Sel'kup people, Siberia 162
selectionist archaeology (SA) 37, 81–2, 84
Selk'nam people 703, 1031, 1036–7
Sellato, B. 864–5, 869–70
Semai people 872
Semaq Beri people 869
Semnan people 1014
sensory perceptions 95
Service, E. R. 6, 51, 154
sexual division of labour *see* gender-based division of labour
sexuality 158, 168
shamanism 93–4, 109, 444, 638, 1192, 1194, 1195, 1224–5, 1277
  Ainu 1065
  and altered states of consciousness 1225
  as earliest religion 1235
  and gender 1225, 1231
  ghost societies 1230
  Native Californian 1226–8
  and rock art 108–9, 484, 638, 718, 1129
  San 109, 1225, 1232
  shaman burials 717–18
  shaman roles 717–18
  shamanic rituals 1226
  Siberian 1221, 1235–6
  Yuman 1227–8
Sharp, H. S. 161, 1250, 1279
Sharp, L. 960

sheep/goat domestication 810
Shennan, S. 203, 1133
Sheridan, A. 829
Shidrag, S. 264
'Shirazi' culture 483
Shirokogoroff, S. M. 1224
Shnirelman, V. A. 164
Shoshone 73, 74
  Northern 975
  Western 982
Shostak, M. 1244, 1254
Shott, M. 93, 106
Siberia 162, 315, 650, 914–15
  exclusion from *Man the Hunter* 904, 913, 914
  shamanism 1221, 1235–6
  see also Khanty people
Silberbauer, George 928
Simms, S. R. 1121
simple/complex society debate 11 *see also* delayed vs. immediate return hunter gatherers; forager vs. collector model
Simpson, G. 238
Single Grave Culture 805
Sioux people 781, 887, 888
Skateholm Mesolithic cemetery, Sweden 597, 715, 717, 718, 719–20, 721, 722, 723, 1195, 1197, 1245
skeleton KNM-ER 1808 186
Skhul, Israel 225, 369
  mortuary rituals 713
Skoglund, P. 797
slave trade 486–7, 1146
slavery 1191
  in Ainu society 1064
  Pacific Northwest Coast 1004
  south-east Asia 870–1
Slocum, S. 155
Smith, Adam 34, 46, 55
Smith, C. E. 730
Smith, D. M. 1250
Smith, M. A. 381
Smoak, G. 984
Soares, P. 499, 500
social complexity 443, 590–3, 643–58, 771
  Ainu 1062–4
  aggrandizer strategies 592–3, 604, 644–5, 646, 649, 658, 1004

social complexity (*Cont.*)
    and concentration of power 644, 645
    and decreased mobility 1170
    diachronic explanations 1001–3
    east Asia 513
    ethnographical Golden Age
        snapshot 995–7
    Far East 654–8
    and feasting 645, 653, 654, 656–7, 658,
        994, 1004
    first material indicators 645–50
    interpreting from archaeology 1003–5
    Lepenski Vir 449
    meaning in archaeology 644
    Mesolithic 451, 592, 650–8
    Natufians 652–3
    Near East 592
    northern Russia and Siberia 321
    Pacific Northwest Coast 11, 910, 991–1006
    post-modernist critique 95
    and population density 592, 645, 646, 649,
        658, 1004
    and prestige items 592, 644, 645, 646, 649,
        650, 651, 653, 654, 655–6, 658
    and resource reliability and richness 591,
        592, 644, 645–6, 650–1, 653, 655, 658,
        1003, 1004
    and sedentism 645, 646, 649, 651, 652–3,
        654, 655, 994
    and social inequality 592, 645, 651, 652 Fig.
        29.3, 653, 1002, 1003, 1004
    south-east Asia 1013
    and storage 645, 649, 651, 653, 994,
        100–2, 1003
    and surplus production 592, 593, 645, 646,
        650, 657, 658
    Uganda 483
social evolutionary approach 2, 36, 585–6,
    590, 593, 599, 769–70, 779, 782, 905
    Boas' rejection 995–6
    legacy 601–2
    see also progressive social
        evolutionary theory
social inequality
    in 'egalitarian' societies 643
    house sizes 651, 652 Fig. 29.3
    and social complexity 592, 645, 646, 653,
        1002, 1003, 1004

social relations 633
    animal–human 1193–6
    bodily manifestations 1198
    and cosmology and worldview 1199
    and hunter-gatherer personhood 1103,
        1192–3, 1199–2000
    and individual autonomy 1198
    and Mesolithic mortuary
        practices 715–16, 1197
    primacy of age 1197
    and trade 781, 885, 893
Soffer, O. 168, 200
Sollas, W. 4, 11
Solutrean culture 279, 291, 406, 558
    material indicators of social
        complexity 649–50
    mobility 1177–8
Sonvian culture 350
South America 912, 1031–46, 1032 Fig. 49.1,
    1034 Fig. 49.2
    coastal adaptation, Tierra del Fuego 703–4
    early foragers 417–19
    evolutionary models and historical
        trajectories 1033
    Gauicurú linguistic family 1037
    Gran Chaco 1037–8
    linguistic Makú-Puinave family 1042, 1043
    Macro-Jê (Gê or Yê) linguistic
        family 1041–2
    Makú people 1042–4, 1043 Fig. 495
    Orinoco Basin 1038–9, 1039 Fig. 49.4
    Pampean and Patagonian
        hunter-gatherers 1035–7, 1036 Fig. 49.3
    Pano linguistic family 1045
    'regression' hunting and
        gathering 779, 1031
    'secondary readaptations' 1031, 1034
    Tupí-Guarani linguistic family 1031,
        1039–41
    'voluntary isolation' 1033, 1045
    western Amazon 1044–5
    Zamuco linguistic family 1037
south Asia, *Homo sapiens* societies 328–40,
    329 Fig. 14.1
    Acheulian culture 332, 339
    coastline dispersal routes 330
    dispersals out of Africa 329–32, 331 Fig.
        14.2, 440–1

emergence of agriculture 336–8, 738, 739
Himalayan passes dispersal routes 330
Late Palaeolithic and Mesolithic
   record 335–8, 337 Tab. 14.1, 338
   Fig. 14.4
microlithic industries, Late Palaeolithic and
   Mesolithic 335–6
Middle Palaeolithic environments 334–5
Middle Palaeolithic technology
   record 332–4, 333 Fig. 14.3
mtDNA evidence for colonization 329
populations growth, Late Palaeolithic/
   Mesolithic 335–6
'professional primitives' 338
south Asia, post-glacial transformations 447,
   492–7, 493 Fig. 21.1, 501–2
agriculture, post- glacial 447, 497, 501
palaeoenvironmental settings 492–4
representational art 447, 496, 501–2
social complexity 496–7
technology 495–6
south-east Asia, forager-farmer
   interactions 779–80, 857–75
cash economies and money 871–4
contemporary foraging peoples 860–1, 862
   Fig. 40.1
conflict 869–76
histories of trade and exchange 862–4, 863
   Tab. 40.1
origins of hunting and gathering and
   farming 857–8
persistence of hunting and
   gathering 858–60
recent hunting-gathering-agriculture
   mix 779
silent trade 870–1
slavery 870–1
trading natures 864–9, 866 Fig. 40.2, 867
   Fig. 40.3, 867 Fig. 40.4
south-east Asia and Indonesia, *Homo sapiens*
   societies 346–62
Borneo 351–3, 358, 360, 378
central Thailand 349–50
chronometric data 359 Fig. 15.5, 360
East Timor 355–7, 358, 360
entry of *Homo Sapiens* 340–1
Java 350–1
Late Pleistocene legacy 361–2

lithic technologies 360–1
Malay Peninsula 348–9, 358, 361
map of sites 347 Fig. 15.1
modern humans' colonization 357–60, 441
Moluccan islands 354–5, 358
mtDNA research 346
North Vietnam 350, 358, 361
Nusatenggara 354–5
Philippines and Talaud Islands 353
South West Sulawesi 353–4, 360
south-east Asia, post-glacial period 447,
   492–4, 493 Fig. 21.1, 497–501, 502
bone technology 500–1
genetic (mtDNA) evidence of intra-regional
   population dispersal 499–500
palaeoenvironmental settings 492–4
subsistence 498–9
south-east Asia, regional hunter-gatherer
   traditions 911, 1010–25, 1011 Fig. 48.1
environmental 'management' 1022
ethnocide 1018
ethnogenesis 1018–19
'forager-bricoleurs' 911, 1010, 1023–4
forager identities 1013–19, 1014 Tab. 48.1
genetic studies 1019, 1020
identity in theory and practice 1019–21
language groups 1014
rejection of pure, pristine or isolated
   stereotypes 1021–3
religions 1013
social organization 1015
staple foods collected 1012
wild yam hypothesis 1020, 1021
southern Africa, hunter-gatherer
   research 908, 918–30
American tradition 924–6
Harvard Kalahari Research Group
   (HKRG) 926–7
Japanese tradition 929
Kalahari debate 908, 928
South African tradition 921–4
southern Africa, post-glacial 484–5
agriculture 447, 485
microlithic industry 446, 484
South Molle Island Quarry,
   Queensland 1176–7
Spanish Franciscan Mission system,
   California 974–6

Spector, J. D. 157, 160, 1244
Spencer, Herbert 71, 997
Speth, J. 891–2, 896
Spielman, K. A. 14
Spier, L. 983
Spirit Cave 349–50, 498
Sponheimer, M. 182
Stafford, C. R. 1179
Stahl, A. B. 107, 108
Staniukovich, M. V. 163
Stanner, W. E. H. 960, 961, 964
Star Carr, North Yorkshire 6, 105–6, 442–3, 698, 719, 825, 1166, 1212–13
Starna, W. 886
Steckzén, Birger 1071
Stevenson, M. E. 1173
Steward, J.H. 5, 7–8, 17, 20, 34–5, 36–7, 51, 73–5, 80, 586, 601, 909, 979–80, 982, 1000, 1098
  Great Basin model 982
  see also adaptive and ecological approaches
Stewart, H. 1255
Stewart, O. 982
Stiner, M. 200
stone tool (lithic) technology 587–8, 607–21
  Africa, Middle Stone Age 229–30, 614–15
  cognition and 619–21
  Danubian Europe, post-glacial 529
  demography and loss of diversity 617–19
  development of global diversity 616–17
  earliest artefacts 610–11
  Levant, Early Upper Palaeolithic 256–7, 258
  lag between first appearance and widespread adoption 608
  long-term trends 608–10, 609 Tab. 27.1
  as a means of distinguishing between *Homo* species 346–8
  and mobility 1172–3
  Neanderthal 196–9
  Middle and Upper Pleistocene trends 614–15
  new hominins, new artefacts 611–13
  northern Asia, Palaeolithic 310, 311–12, 313 Fig. 13.1, 314, 317–18, 320–1, 322 Fig. 13.2, 323 Fig. 13.3, 324 Fig 13.4
  parallel developments 608–10
  prepared core technologies 611–12
  reasons for study 607
  shift from bifacial to generalized core 78, 80, 82, 83
  south Asia, Middle Palaeolithic 332–4, 333 Fig. 14.3
  south-east Asia and Indonesia 348, 349, 350, 351, 353, 354, 357, 360–1
  tool transportation 587–8, 611, 614–15
  western Asia, Upper Palaeolithic 264–5, 265–6
  see also blade and bladelet technologies; microlithic industries
Stoneking, M. 1021
Storegga Slide 540, 567, 696
Strassburg, J. 721
Strathern, M. 1210, 1211, 1212
Street-Perrott, F. A. 480
Strehlow, C. 959
Strehlow, T. G. H. 961
Strickland, H. C. 122, 943
Strien, H.-C. 791–2
Stringer, C. 219, 236
Strömstrad Treaty (1751) 1082
structuralism 589, 634, 961
style/function dichotomy 81
Sumerian Paradise texts 58
Sunda continent (Sundaland) 346, 348, 369, 371, 372, 499, 502
Sung Dynasty 864
Sungir burials 644, 646–9
Sus celebensis 500
Suttles, W. 10–11, 992, 998
Suzman, J. 13
Sviderian culture 566
Swahili 483
Swain, Tony 966
swidden farms 859, 861
Swifterbant culture 776, 805, 806 Fig. 37.1, 807 Fig. 37.2, 808, 808 Fig. 37.3, 809, 810, 811–12 Tab. 37.1, 813 Fig. 37.4, 814–16, 815 Fig. 37.5, 820
Symons, D. 79

Takahashi, M. 512–13
Takakura, S. 1059, 1064
Takamiya, H. 512
Takeuchi, K. 947
Tamils 159

Tanaka, J. 929
Tanner, N. 155-6
Tanno, T. 941
Taron people 1015
Tasaday people 1019
taskscape and landscape 1173-4, 1213-15
Tasmania 370-1, 372, 385, 387
Tattersall, I. 219, 238-9
Taute, W. 791
Taylor, A. 977
Taylor, B. 1215
Taylor, L. 968
technology 1096-8, 1110-22
    artefacts and naturefacts 1115
    and behavioural ecology 1097-8, 1117-20
    and the 'culture core' 73
    and demand for surpluses 650-1
    'design theory' 1111
    development of coastal 697-8
    diet breadth model 1118-19, 1120
    fishing compared with game hunting 1119
    future directions 1121-2
    gender and prestige 1120-1
    and human development 586
    implements and facilities 1115
    and mobility 1116-17, 1119
    as product of culture 80
    relationship with environment 74-5, 586
    and risk 1097, 1116, 1117 Fig. 53.3
    sedentary/nomadic comparisons 1118-19
    simple and complex 1116
    and social complexity 1004
    social aspects 1196-7
    'soft'/'hard' 1111
    techno units 1116
    traps 1119
    see also stone tool technology
Tegengren, H. 1077
Tehrani, J. J. 1130
Tehuelches people 1035-6, 1036 Fig. 49.3
Teit, J. 654
Templeton, A. R. 235
Terashima, H. 942
Terrell, J. E. 377
Testart, A. 1171
Testevin, C. 1043
textile pottery 848

textile production, Middle Upper Palaeolithic Europe 289
Tham Lod, Thailand 349
Thapar, R. 60
Thomas, E. M. 930
Thomas, J. 772, 828, 1204, 1206, 1209
Thomas, J. M. C. 940
Thomsen, C. J. 50, 769
Thomson, D. F. 123, 960, 961, 963, 1164
Thornton, R. 983
Thorpe, N. 721
three ages theory 49-50, 769
Thuja plicata (red cedar) 1002
Thylacinus cynocephalus (marsupial lion) 385, 386 Fig. 16.6
Thylacoleo carnifex (Tasmanian tiger) 385
Timpangotizi people 975
Tindale, N. 960, 961, 963, 1166
Tishkoff, S. A. 1151
Tiwi women 1244
Tlingit people 993 Fig. 47.1, 994, 996, 999, 1254
    Thlukehotsick feast dish 1276, 1277 Fig. 61.4
Toala peoples 1916-17
Toba (Qom) people 1038
Toba super-volcano eruption 335, 346, 357, 374, 857
Tobias, P. 923
toloache cults, North America 981, 1229
Tonkinson, R. 162-3, 966-7
Torrence, R. 124, 1204
Tosawihi people 982-3
'toss' and 'drop' zones (Binford) 114 Fig. 6.1, 114-16
totemism 632, 636, 962, 1193
trade:
    Ainu 1060, 1061
    china and south-east Asia 862-4
    forager-farmer, North America 781, 885, 887-8, 889-80, 892-3, 893-4
    forager-farmer, south-east Asia 862-4, 863 Tab. 40.1, 864-9, 866 Fig. 40.2, 867 Fig. 40.3, 867 Fig 40.4, 870-1
    fur and leather 650, 1074, 1077, 1081, 1084
    gold 482, 486-7
    Indian Ocean 483
    Jomon 654
    and social relations 781, 885, 893

trade networks
    medieval Japan and China 512
    Mesolithic 450, 544
    post-glacial east Asia 515
'Trail of Dreams' 1228
Traill, T. 923–4
Trance Dance, North America 1225
'trance hypothesis' 108–9
Trans New Guinea (TNG) languages 375
'trans-egalitarian' societies 321, 591, 643 see also social complexity
transitional (intermediate) economies 768
transport 695
    waterborne 695
Trigger, B. 885, 886, 895
Trinkhaus, E. 236–7
Tsimishian people 993 Fig. 47.1, 994, 999, 1275
Tsuji, S. 512
Tupí-Guarani groups 1031, 1039–41
Tupinambá people 1040
Turgot, A.-R.-J. 44
turkey domestication 881
Turnbull, C. M. 158, 939–40, 944, 946–7, 949
Tutu, Desmond 485
Twa people 947
Tylor, E. 74, 1193
Tyua San people 919, 920, 923, 928

Üçağizli cave, Turkey 256, 257, 262
Upper Palaeolithic 438, 608
    archaeological record and human 'behavioural revolution' 216
    art 628–32
    art, explanations 589–90, 632–9
    Europe 279–97
    loss of diversity in early 619
    and modern human behaviour 228–9
    non-stone technological developments 588, 616
    western Asia 252–70
Urak Lawoi 'sea nomads' 1017
Urewe culture 483, 485
Ust-Karakol tradition 314
Utagawa, H. 1065
Utkuhikhalimgmiut people 1254
Uttarakuru, Buddhist 57

Vaihingen, Germany 791–2
Valdeyron, N. 547
Valkonen, S. 1086
Valoch, K. 528, 530
van Holst Pellekaan, S. M. 374
van Riet Louw, C. 484
Van Tan, H. 350
Vane, S. 1229, 1230
Vasco da Gama 921
Vavilov, N. I. 730
Vedbæk-Bøgebakken Mesolithic cemetery, Denmark 597, 715, 717, 719–20, 721, 722, 1197
Venkateswar, S. 165
'Venus figurines' 287, 290, 560
Verdu, P. 938
Vermeersch, P. M. 541
Vilkuna, K. 1072, 1073, 1076–7
Villeneuve, S. N. 1235
Villeneuve-Saint-Germain (VSG) culture 792–3, 794
Vincent, A. S. 111
violence
    against women 162
    interpersonal 162
    Mesolithic 796
    see also conflict
Vita-Finzi, C. 77
Viveiros de Castro, E. 1040, 1112, 1194
Vlaadingen Group 807 Fig. 37.2, 808, 808 Fig. 37.3, 811–12 Tab. 37.1
VOC, Dutch trading company 864, 870

Wagner, R. 1181
Waguespack, N. M. 416, 1120
Walker, B. 1063
Walker, R. 938
Wallace, A. 983
Wallacea 346, 353, 355–7, 358, 360, 499, 500, 502
Wally's Beach, Alberta 414
Warder, A. 57
Warlpiri Aborigines 961, 968
Warner, W. L. 960, 965, 966
Warren, G. M. 1211, 1215
Washburn, S. 74
Watanabe, H. 1057, 1061, 1062–3
Waterbolk, H. T. 796

Watson, C. 968
Wattanapituksakul, S. 349
Weber, A. 22
Weedman, A. K. 1247
Weiner, J. 1182
Wendorf, F. 481, 482
Weninger, B. 540
western and central Europe, Neolithic
    787–97, 788 Fig. 36.1
  contact period archaeology in the fifth and
    sixth millenia 788–95, 789 Fig. 36.2, 795
    Fig. 36.4,
  genetic evidence 787
  Neolithicization process and migration
    dynamics 795–7
  Occidental, Danubian and Hyperborean
    streams 787, 788 Fig. 36.1c
western Asia, Upper Palaeolithic
    hunter-gatherers 252–70
  Caucasus 265–6
  climate 253–4
  cultural terminology 255–6
  geographic background 252–3
  Levant 256–8
  Levantine Epi-Palaeolithic cultural
    entities 258–60
  Levantine Upper and Epi-Palaeolithic
    diet 254, 260–4, 270
  settlement patterns 266–70
  Zagros 264–5
Westropp, Hodder 441
whale hunting 1267, 1276
Wheeler, P. 184–5
White Deerskin Dance, North America
    1231
White, I. 965
White, L. 5, 7, 17, 74, 586, 601, 999, 1098
White, R. 649
White, T. D. 226
Whitehouse, R. 152
Whitelaw, T. M. 114
Whitridge, P. 1246, 1253
Whittle, A. 773, 774, 777, 833
Wiessner, P. 116, 129, 134, 135, 137, 926,
    927, 1210
Wik Mungkan Aborigines 1164
Wilcoxon, L. 985
wild boar

  independent domestication, Europe and
    Near East 810
  introduction, Hokkaido 1267
wild rice 336
wild sago palms 1016
wild yam hypothesis 941, 942, 946, 947,
    1020, 1021
Wilkinson, E. 60
Williams, N. 964
Wilmsen, E. N. 415, 928
Wilton industry 484
Wingfield, C. 130
Winterhalder, B. 52
Wissler, C. 36, 48, 72
Wobst, M. H. 106, 563, 1207
women
  Aboriginal 160, 161–2, 163, 965–6
  and colonialism 165
  evolutionary biology 1257
  food restrictions 1270
  hunters 159–60, 161, 1246, 1251
  increasing attention in academia 151
  Mansi 163, 165
  and power 160, 161, 163, 165, 1247
  reproductive role 1253, 1257
  and reproduction rate in African
    hunter-gatherer society 1148–9
  role in food processing and storage 131,
    132, 132 Tab. 6.6, 166, 1247, 1249–50
  role in subsistence 1269–70
  role in protecting tradition 161–2, 165, 166
  technological behaviour 1177
  violence against 162
  Woman the Gatherer 154–6, 157
  see also gender and entries beginning
    with gender
Wood, B. 179
Wood, R. 888
Woodburn, J. 11, 50, 111, 645, 1271, 1272 see
    also immediate vs. delayed return
    hunter gatherers
wood-treatment tools 318
Woolf, S. 63
Wormington, H. M. 416
Worsley, P. 963
Wounded Knee massacre (1890) 977
Wovoka (Jack Wilson) 978, 984
Wright, J. 694

Wylie, A. 105–6, 107, 108, 632
Wynn, T. 620, 630–1
Wynne-Edwards, V. 75–6

Xam Kwatcam pilgrimage 1227
/Xam-ka !ei San 921
Xenophon 59
Xiongnu people 61
Xokléng people 1042
!Xóõ San 920, 923–4
!Xun people 919

Yajirō, Christian convert 1057
Yamada, T. 164, 165, 1065
Yamana sea nomads 703, 704, 1031, 1036
Yamanouchi, S. 508
Yanyuwa, northern Australia 1176
Yellen, J. E. 12, 112–14, 126
Yengoyan, A. 154
Yesner, D. R. 702
Yokoyama, Y. 512
Yokut people 978, 979, 1226–7
  initiation rites 1229

Yolngu people
  art and ritual 968
  women, 'profane' role 965
Yoneda, M. 515
Young, E. 963
Younger Dryas (YD) 256, 260, 263, 264, 266, 269, 296–7, 440, 457, 458, 492, 494, 541, 653, 699
Yuan, J. 656
Yuchanyan cave, China 655, 656, 657
Yukaghir people 1194
Yuman shamans 1227–8
Yup'ik women 131, 1250
Yven, E. 542

Zamuco linguistic family 1037
Zarzian culture 256, 265
Zeitlyn, D. 1196
Zihlman, A. 155–6
Zilhão, J. 472
Zohary, D. 730
Zvelebil, M. 450, 538, 547, 548, 550, 597, 598, 716, 717–18, 771, 773, 774, 782, 797, 808, 994, 1245, 1270